Donna Ingold

This book was given to
me for a 4th prize award
in the World of Poetry contest
July. 1986

Our World's Best Loved Poems

John Campbell, Editor & Publisher

Edited by Eddie-Lou Cole
JULIE JOY, Art Director

Foreword

The Story Of the World Of Poetry

It's a wonderful thing to be part of the World of Poetry. I can remember when the first issue of our newsletter came whirring off the press, way back in August of 1975. We were so proud—and so excited! Our *entire* staff consisted of two poets: Yours Truly, Eddie-Lou Cole, Poetry Editor, and of course, John Campbell, Editor & Publisher. John had asked me to come aboard a few months earlier, to give him a hand with "a new poetry publication I have in mind."

Little did I know the publication he had in mind would grow, in a few short years, from one of "little magazine" status, to literally one of international prominence and prestige. In my years upon years of editing poetry journals and contributing to them, of writing poetry books, and publishing them, I have never seen anything like it. It is a sucess story of truly poetic proportions—and includes, among other things, the publishing of *Our World's Best Loved Poems*, this magnificent anthology of over 6,000 beautiful poems!

With the publication of the Inaugural issue of the World of Poetry, on August 1, 1975, Editor and Publisher John Campbell launches a publishing empire, with Eddie-Lou Cole as Poetry Editor.

By design World of Poetry is an exciting potpourri of poems, helpful articles on how to write (and sell) poetry, questions and answers, workshops, interviews with prominent poets, news items, market listings and contests—anything and everything we imagine a poet's heart could desire. Celebrities like Bobby Vinton, Red Skelton, Liberace, Tennessee Ernie Ford make their way into our pages, movie and television stars who are also quite good poets. It turns out they are

Among the numerous celebrities to appear with our Editor and Publisher in the pages of the World of Poetry are Bobby Vinton (that's our Art Director Julie Joy, next to him), Red Skelton, Liberace, Tennessee Ernie Ford (all fine poets), and of course, Bertha, The Elephant.

attracted, many of them, by the glitter of the contests we sponsor, up to a dozen big ones a year, each boasting a grand prize of $1,000, with up to a hundred prizes totaling $10,000 or more. (Most of our contests are won, surprisingly enough, not by "name" or "celebrity" poets, but by housewives or students who've never entered a poetry contest before. One lady won with a poem she'd kept in a drawer for thirty years!)

One day, while I was in the middle of judging one of our contests, John came in the office with an idea. "Eddie-Lou," he said, "Why don't you write a book on how to write poetry, for the benefit of new poets who could use a few ideas." I took the suggestion under submission, and six months later emerged with a text, entitled *Now Technique For Today's Poets.* Like John predicted, it was another World of Poetry success.

John Campbell   Bobby Vinton   Julie Joy

Red Skelton   Bertha   Liberace   Tennessee Ernie Ford

Meantime, with the newsletter going great guns, and my book selling well, it was time for World of Poetry to venture again. John, whose background includes acting (and Shakespeare), got a few of his friends together, and did a most phenomenal thing: he came up with a TV series on poetry, called the Upstart Crow (named after the criticism leveled at Shakespeare early in his career by one Mr. Green). As host of the weekly series, you could see John welcome such guest stars as Leonard Nimoy, Vincent Price, Richard Thomas, Red Buttons and Steve Allen. The first thing Mr. Allen said on the show was, "Congratulations that such a show exists!" As if this weren't enough to make everybody here at World of Poetry proud, out of the series, quite enexpectedly, came another success: John's hit Shakespeare album, "Perchance to Dream." J. C. Trewin, the doyen of London

As host of the Upstart Crow television series, John Campbell talks poetry with guest stars Vincent Price, Steve Allen, Red Buttons, Richard Thomas and Leonard Nimoy. One of the results of the series was the production of John's Shakespeare album "Perchance to Dream."

Our World's Best Loved Poems, which combines the talents of thousands of poets around the world, is our current success and our current joy. Like I said, it's a wonderful thing to be part of the World of Poetry.

—Eddie-Lou cole, Editor
WORLD OF POETRY
Sacramento, California
May, 1984

John Campbell   Vincent Price

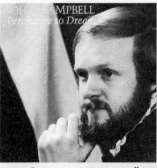  

"Perchance to Dream"

Steve Allen

Leonard Nimoy   Richard Thomas

Red Buttons

Our World's Best Loved Poems

John Campbell, Editor & Publisher

Our World's Best Loved Poems

Wilhelm Hansen
Images On a Summer Day

To my wife Deborah, who has brought beauty to my life.

Water flowing into deepening
  pools
Cobwebs turning the branches
Into downy spools . . images on a
Summer day.

Birds fly like big flapping kites
Growing ever smaller, farther
  away.

Thunder and lightening in the
Summer sky, Swifts catching
  insects;
A dragon-fly darting nearby.
Images on a summer day
Willows that droop and sway . . .

Bill Chiappi
RESPECT

Why is it when a man is down,
when he's made a mistake or two,
that people rise against him,
among them me or you?
He becomes the butt of all our
  jokes;
he's prone to our ridicule.
The other day he was just like
  us;
but today he is just a fool.
Oh men of sorry character,
when will we ever learn,
to respect anothers sense of
  pride,
for today may be our turn—to
  play the fool.

Lawrence A. Souza
WAR AND POLITICS

The juggernaut of war shall roll
  across the land,
To crush the flesh and bone of
  humans, innocent and guilty
  alike.
And leeches of profit shall drink
  the blood of vanquished,
To fill their bloody stomachs
  with the life of man.
For these the filthy parasites of
  life
Create war, for it is their food.
Was I born to be but fodder,
To feed the hungry cannonmouth
  of war?
Or yet to be a pawn upon the
  crooked checkerboard of
  politics?
To be a slave, chained to great
  machines of industry?
Or to be a dreamer, never gaining
  wealth
In gold, but being rich in
  happiness.
To lift my eyes, to stand and gaze
  above the rim,
To look in clear clean space,
To realize this rubble that I stand
  upon,
Is but a steppingstone to
  something greater.
For we are locked within this
  sphere called earth,
As in a room that we have never
  left.
But we shall open the door one
  day, to step into the universe.

Madge Mullins Wilbanks
THE REACH

Quite simply, for Tommy and Mother who believed

Time was never kind to the child
  Who never grew
But squatted her life near the
  Ground

Reaching upward only with effort
  Upon effort to try to reach
Heights she set
  High;

Higher than her short arms
  would ever reach;
  Taller than her short legs would
  ever bend;
It never mattered.
  In her heart she was

Ten feet tall battling gargantuan
  windmills;
  Tasks set beyond strength,
Endurance. Goals unattainable
  Becoming attainable

With no emphasis on self—pity;
  All efforts fed by guts
Boundless and abounding to take
  this
Little child home, upward to Life.

Terry Sparks
Story Of a Young Marine
There was a flag draped casket
  setting on a metal stand,
And there was a mother weeping
  for a son killed in a far off land.
This sons name was Donald, and
  all his early teens, he eagerly
  awaited manhood, to join the
  United States Marines.

He left his home in mid April,
  with his spirits oh so high, and
  off he went to Parris Island
  never doubting as to why.

Boot training there was rugged,
  but this man did not care, for
  he knew to be a good Marine,
  just what he would have to bear.
Soon the drilling was over, and
  graduation day was here.
There were many proud Marines
  giving their loudest cheers.

Along came the uprising in
  Vietnam, and they needed U.S.
  support.
So they sent many of these
  Marines to that faraway land.

One of these men was Donald,
  Assistant Gunner in his
  platoon, he was killed by Viet
  Cong rifle fire, ending his
  young life too soon.

Now a buddy wrote to Donald's
  mother saying I thought you
  would like to know of your
  sons last minutes before his
  strength began to go.
He lay there gravely wounded
  knowing that he would roam
  no more, calling for his dear
  Mother, to tell her he could
  not come home.
His last words were to the
  Almighty Father, for his Savior
  he did adore, repeating oh my

God, oh my God, and then he
  said no more.

He fought for what he believed
  in, although many people did
  not agree.
But if it were not for these brave
  young men, our country would
  be far, far from free.

Lois Thompson
FRIENDSHIP

This poem is a condensation of a song written by the same author & dedicated To Maggie and her family upon the death of a son

You laugh a little; cry a little; live
  a little; die a little
  Together—That's Friendship.
You give a little; take a little;
  plead a little; pray a little
  Together—That's Friendship.
Over the years the "littles" grow
  into "lots";
The "I's" grow into "We's", the
  friendships into Love;
The sharing and caring; daring
  and wearing of life merge into
  one.

The care, wear and tear of the
  years spent;
The rays of life, the shadows bent
Converge onto a central point
  Together—That's Friendship;
  that's Love.
The hopes and fears of
  yesteryears mature along the
  way;
The paths of life; the bonds of
  strife strengthening—sticking
  Together—That's Friendship;
  that's Love; that's Life.

Life flows on and on—always
  ending bye and bye;
Death is that extension of life
  away from those bonds of strife;
  We grieve Together—That's
  Friendship; that's Love; that's
  Life.

Eva Cook

Eva Cook
MISSOURI
Here in Missouri
Where you know we like to be
Everybody loves Missouri
You can plainly see.
The people will sing it
The chimes will all ring it
As we look towards the sky

With our hopes just as high.
Independence rates A 1
Position now for me
For you know Missouri
Is as great as it can be.
The people are humming
Everyone's coming
To the show me state.

Dorothy Rita Jarvis
OF MIND
To think is Man's great joy and
  gift.
With knowledge, when he's ready
He can lift his mind to circling
  heights,
Where his eyes cannot see.

His mind can discern more than
  ears can sense;
Over the Earth, he's a ruling king,
Because he can reason and hence;
From him good and bad deeds
  spring.

His life is given to thoughts of
  his own.
Though he has but a small store
Of knowledge that's eternally new,
Man's slow to search for more.

With little thoughts of fear and
  hate,
With deeds of avarice,
The task of knowing has to wait,
And we live on in childish bliss;

Til we become each day as we
  think;
For thoughts rule men and
  kingdoms,
And we hover ever at the brink,
Of sorrow, where all Mankind
  comes,

To stop and think, to gather, to
  learn.
We understand as knowledge
  sees.
Perhaps as beggars we go on our
  way
Never knowing the greater
  beauties.

Robert A. Bowen
SATAN SMILES
Needles plunge into shrunken
  trembling arms
Emptied glasses are filled again
  and again
        Satan Smiles

Cars racing madly headon toward
  each other
Thieves, murderers, rapists rule
  their streets
        Satan Smiles

Master diplomats plan for the
  final destruction
While the Brotherhood of Man
  dissolves itself
        Satan Smiles

The God of our fathers and of us
  is in sorrow
The end is being prepared—
  maybe tomorrow
        Satan Smiles.

Sunday McKinley Bailey
SOLITUDE
I long to live close by
Where the seagull's cry
Can be heard
Above the word
Of any other living thing.

11

I have an ache to dwell
Where the ocean foams swell
Touches a sky of blue
When it meets my view
And the waves continually sing

I yearn to walk in sand
Barefoot, nude and tan
Mouth tasting of salt
With no other thought
Than bittersweet memories you
  bring.

Wallace Royal Federman
GRIEVE NOT FOR ME!

---

*Dedicated To: My Loving Wife
Ruth and our three Children,
Mary, Rose and Rudolph. It is my
hope that "Grieve Not For Me"
will ease their grief upon my
passing and help them to
understand that Love and
Affection can be everlasting.*

Let the unsure be sure.
The unhappy be glad.
Dwell not on the troubles
but on pleasures we've had.

This passing is something
We all must do.
It happened to me.
It will happen to you.

The time or the place
is not of our choice.
We go when we're called
by our Master's voice.

We who go first
will prepare the way
for those who will follow
on their special day.

The place will be tidy
and spotlessly clean.
With the lovliest gardens
you ever have seen.

Your health will be fine.
Your fears will be stayed.
The love you have given
Will all be repaid.

No burdens to carry
No sorrows to bear
Peace and contentment
awaits for you there.

Go on with your life
Until the Lord calls your name.
I'll be walking beside you
each day just the same.

You must believe strongly
as your life moves along
my spirits here with you
just the body has gone.

Your hands will not touch me.
Your eye's will not see.
Yet the presence you sense there
will always be me.

When comfort is needed
you have but to ask.
I'll be close around you
as I have in the past.

A physical journey
for each has been willed.
Your Earthly voyage
must be fulfilled.

I'll know when he calls you.
You will not be alone.

I'll reach out to touch you
and welcome you home.

Carrie Lynn Brown
BE STILL AND KNOW
Be still and hear the pulse of
  things,
The breeze blow, the cock crow,
The dogs bark, the ants go.

Be still and feel the pulse of things,
The sun grow, the sand glow,
Ants, up and down they go.

Be still, be still, the pulse of things,
Is here, is there, is everywhere.
Be still, be still. The pulse is
  there.

Be still and know. The air moves
  to and fro.
Ants know where ant hills go.
Birds sing and know.

Be still and feel the pulse of life,
The breath of life, be still and see.
Be still and hear. Be still and be.

Be still and know the atmosphere,
  the earth below.
Be still and see the pulse, a leaf
  blow, a bush grow.
Be still and hear the pulse, a
  beating heart, the beat,
          the beat.
Be still and know.

Lee Quirino Jr.
FOSTER MOTHER
Once and only once was I left on
  your lap.
And not once, not even once
Did you ever turn me back.

You raised me like a pup from a
  litter soon forgot.
But I felt like a god
Beside your natural force.
Beautiful Mother Earth.

You and I are the same, even with
  the same color of dye.
You bathe me with your hot and
  cold rain.
Always together, you and I.

Together we have bask under the
  sun's breath
That lights up your mountain
  sides.
Mountains that soar and soar.
Beautiful Mother Earth.

I see you as the sea, your cold
  water waving at the sky.
I hear you as the wind, a soft
  wind
Singing a lullabye.

And when I'm put into your
  copper colored womb
I know somewhere a flower will
  bloom.
And for tears, the dew will be
  your source.
Beautiful Mother Earth.

Eleanor Revere Weeden
THE CHILDREN
No dessert, please, thank you
I rose pushing aside the chair.
Dottie, Eve and I had been
  lunching
And Gay with the gorgeous red
  hair.

I'm giving my all to children
The starving ones, the sick.

Hope it will be flown by airplane
Reaching them fast and quick.

Starving lips give no childish
  chatter
They have done no evil or wrong.
Eyes are hurt and fearful
Small throats sing no cheerful
  song.

Faces are covered with blisters
Like balloons small stomachs
  bulge out.
Limbs are too thin and boney
From disease and hunger no doubt.

Oh! I would gather these children
Into a Haven of joy.
Where hunger would forever be
  forgotten
To every young girl and boy.

Are we not all God's children
Be we short, small or tall?
Wanting one day to find Heaven
Awaiting His love and the Call.

Marilyn Dunham
UNTITLED
Gone home
August calls
Hungry
Tomatoes
Ripen
I miss that spot

Flo Lampp Hageman
**Is This the Road To
  Hillsboro?**

---

*To: My mother Era Cummins
Lampp, who told me this story
during my childhood, and to my
grandchildren for laughing at my
poem.*

Mama and May were just little
  girls,
Living down south of Peoria,
Playing beside the Old Yates Road,
When May told mama such a
  story!
May said, she once met a snake
  that
Was slithering down the Old
  Yates Road,
Wearing a grape leaf for his hat!
Seeing her, he stopped his
  slithering,
Right in the middle of his furrow,
And looked her straight in the
  eyes,
then asked,
"Is this the road to Hillsboro?"

Like mama, I lived on the Old
  Yates Road,
Playing beside it, was also my
  habit.
I walked it to school and to
  church.
Once, saw a snake swallowing a
  rabbit!
Neither mama nor I, when we
  were little,
Ever saw a snake like the one
  May met,
Come slithering down the Old
  Yates Road,
Wearing a grape leaf for his hat,
That stopped slithering when he
  saw us,
And from the very middle of his

furrow,
Looked us straight in the eyes,
then asked,
"Is this the road to Hillsboro?"

Edith L. Price
HE IS THERE
"God is dead," some people say,
But have they not eyes to see
  how He paints the evening skies
  in brilliant shades of red and
  pink and lavendar?
He is there!

And the beautiful rosebud, as it
  shyly peeks out, and then
  slowly opens its eyes to the
  morning dew and the warming
  sun?
He is there!

Have they not seen the
  mountains blanketed in fresh,
  new snow that glistens like
  diamonds in the morning, as
  the sun awakens the sleeping
  earth?
He is there!

Have their ears not heard the
  robin's sweet song in the
  garden, or the crickets as they
  welcome the night, or the wind
  as it whispers in the leaves of
  the trees?
He is there!

Have their eyes not seen the
  earth dressed in Autumn's
  bright reds and golds?
Have they not walked in the
  gentle rain that falls on a
  thirsty ground, and seen the
  plants come alive as they drink
  in the freshness?
He is there!

How can they say, "He is not
  alive?" if they have eyes to see
  and ears to hear the wonders
  and beauty all around them as
  nature beckons and calls,
"He is here!"?

Elna Forsell Pawson
WISTERIA
In Oakland the wisteria climbs
A rail that borders low flat stone,
And leads right up to where my
  love
Is very ill, and so alone.

If Caspar Wistar lived to know
Some hospitals would plant the
  same,
I'm sure he'd be delighted that
This gorgeous shrub still bears
  his name.

His surgery and medicine
Sustained and purchased home
  and food
For Wistar,—but wisteria grew
To cheer him in his solitude.

My love lies here, and waits for
  health.
Wisteria welcomes me each day.
His health improves and when I
  leave
Wisteria cheers me on my way.

Richard L. Dotson
VALENTINE
on this day i love you more than
  i can
who before you has given so much?

moma, of course, will always be
 the
chairperson
i'm a man now, and love has a
 new meaning
no matter what you do or say, i
 stay
yesterday i was alone, but today
 i'm
awakened by your touch.

sometimes i'm angered, but it
 doesn't last
your eyes could soften the
 hardest frown
what has to be done you will do
i understand this without it being
 said
on this day i love all that we are
tonight i will show you how much.

Dot Luria Nadler
YOU CAN'T BUY "LUV"
You can buy pots, pans and pails:
 At Bloomingdales: But you
 can't buy luv
At the Macys' store you can buy
 bargains galore: But they don't
 sell luv
You can buy at Gimbles: Lovely
 gloves: But you can't buy luv
Not with all your money: Honey
 can you buy luv
So friend and neighbor, get your
 act together
Give your all to sister and
 brother, because you can't buy
 luv.

Mari Jane Hill
ENDLESS SEA

*To Molly, my encouragement and
friend*

The days are slow, winding and
 twisting into lonely nights.

The clocks hands moving in
 motion, like an endless tide.

You like a compass having
 followed its every direction.

You've traveled the world both
 near and far, but settling down
 is just to hard.

Our life together was sometimes
 like a troubled sea, waves and
 calm waters.

And like the phases of the sea,
 both friends and lovers were
 we.

But its only the happiness, that
 we make, that keep us afloat.

Back to the shoreline that calmly
 waits.

Robin R. McCoy
MY GIFT OF YOU

*For my Lord. Thank you for my
Steven. To Steven, my gift from
God. Thank you for loving me as
I love you.*

I stood by the bed this morning.
I searched your face,
And saw,
The beauty of your soul.

You, laying there, so quiet, so calm.
My heart began to beat quickly.
For at that instant, I knew
Why I loved you.
Why I will always love
And cherish you.
A gracious gift has been given
 to me.
Here it lies, so peaceful
And calm.
To have from this day forth.
My gift of you.

Carolyn R. Seashore

Carolyn R. Seashore
My Handicapped Friends
Like a candle light you lighten
 my way
Like a ray of sunshine you
 brighten my day
You give me faith and lighten my
 burdens
Thank God for you my friend,
 my what a great gift, your
 friendship
You have been my inspiration
 and Wow but How!
What a difference a day makes
 when I hear your friendly voice
 on tape
God Bless you my handicapped
 friend in all you do, in all you
 say, and in all you believe
Thanks for your many tapes you
 send, you bring me many
 smiles and joys
You have a faith all of your own
 which you pass my way saying
"Don't give up for life can not
 always be as rose."
When I heard your friendly voice
 on tape you brighten my day
 and often make it such a lovely
 day, Thank you and God Bless
 You!

Peggy Jarvis
UNTITLED
Children come and children go
As does sleep, death and snow
Life is long, life is short
We live it for the sport.

Seasons come and seasons go
Each one sees us change and
 grow
Days are long, days are short
Do you want to be that sort?

Life comes and life goes
All have time and all must sow
Sometimes long and sometimes
 short
Days that come all are short.

J. T. McAniff III
SEA STORM
Waves beat upon the storm-swept
 shore
 (My once true love I'll see no
 more).
The fish take shelter 'neath the
 deep
 (My eyes are dry, I'll no more
 weep).

Here swims a dolphin, there a
 whale
 (On love's smooth sea we once
 did sail).
Planckton and Algae seacows use
 (In heartfelt happiness we did
 cruise).

Crabs move sideways, lobsters
 back
 (When did our sunny days turn
 black)?
Seaweed is torn loose from its bed
 (Tell me, what made our love
 turn dead)?

The sea does toss, the wind does
 rage
 (Our ship of love's a sunken
 stage).
The sky is black, the rain does
 pour
 (And I will love you never more).

Robert W. Belsky
The Stranger In the Night

---

*This poem is dedicated to Juliet
Pierce; a good friend*

The stranger in the night.
Who comes out of the dark.
When the moon is full
and the haze is on the ground.

The stranger in the night.
Who you can barely see
because of the clouds
that cover over the moon.

The stranger in the night.
Who! when the sun starts to rise,
isn't there.

The stranger in the night.
You realize,
Is the stranger, we call fear.

Jackie Jenson
If Only I Could Find the
Words

To my loving husband

If only I could express my
 feelings
If I could put them into words
I could tell the prettiest story
that your heart had ever heard.

I'd tell you how much I love you,
I'd tell you how much I care.
I'd make you feel so special
when all this love I'd share.

If only I were free and easy
whenever you were near.
If I could just become myself
in front of you, my dear.

I'm so afraid that you will think
that I am not so smart
'cause I can't find the words to say
what's hidden in my heart.

Gabriella Mirollo
BOSTON: JULY 4, 1983
I didn't watch the fireworks
 tonight
or add to the assembled oohs and
 aahs
but I was there a bit apart
as easier hearts were charged
I turned my indifference to them
my attention to the Charles
I thought how beautiful the river
 was
its points and pits would shift
 across and back again
the constant pattern on a shaken
 midnight blanket
changing and unchanged
I saw a little sparkle
whose playground was the
 movement of the water
a single star content to ride the
 ripple
carried up to meet a rising cap
sinking back into a concave
 shimmer
neap to peak that single star was
 caught
it travelled on and never out of
 facets of obsidian
following that slick haven
for just a moment then I was that
 star
rolling in succesions of the same
a mere reflection there contained
nodding to a person at the
 bannister
who might prefer the water and a
 star
to empty pyrotechnics on the
 Fourth
and then I was a poet without
 words
a foreign dialect too small to catch
a cipher cut into a stone with
 meaning so innate
it waits and waits for adequate
 translation
but remains always alone
 unknown
for when I tried to give the
 radiance a name
I thought instead what a rare
 thing distraction must be
to ride you down a river like a star
so content ineffably

n. ming s. ureta
IN MY SOLITUDE
away from civilization
beneath stately green mansions
before wild blossoms
this God's creations,
in silence and solitude.

the world, this planet earth
to which i'm a part
wonderful of all
is my cathedral;

freedom, the greatest gift
with which i'm blessed
priceless of all
is my robe of silk.

lingering like a lilting echo
is my symphonic poetry of many
 dreams
where solitude unfolds to me
the glories of visions,
bringing in tellings of nature.

o' that one can have the peace of
 the birds

the freedom of the wind
and the wisdom of knowing both
where there's only the unstained
the many beautiful shapes and
  images
sounds of joy and kaleidoscopic
  shades;

from them,
i carve a tower of words
each, a gentle step to the stars
softly as i climb to take a silent
  peek
into the unknown
to find and merge with Him and
  be reborn.

Jean Herrick Warner
GHOSTS OF THE PAST
Mute and still against the heavens
Stands a cabin aged and worn,
Weathered logs and timbers
  sagging,
Buckled under wind and storm.

Vastness of the plains surrounds
  it,
Sage and brush for miles around,
Stretching to the bluish hillsides.
In the hush, here peace is found.

Gone the laughter and the
  sorrows
That these weathered walls
  recall.
Stilled the sound of children's
  voices—
Yet a whisper seems to fall.

In the door appears a shadow.
Warmth of love enfolds the
  scene.
Gentle rustling in the breezes
Hints of merriment unseen.

Marianne Cascio
COURAGE
To leave the old with a burst of
  song;
to recall the right and forgive the
  wrong;
To forget the things that bind
  you fast
To have the strength to let go
  your hold
of the not worth while of the
  days grown old.

Denise Annette Reynolds
SO SAID
The Neon bleeds its bright
  defeat—
misty moisture hangs; grey
  concrete . . .
Noisy cars trail, where do they go?
The wall is down; does anyone
  know?
City calls heckle, surrounded by
  the sea—
Peace is only footsteps to a
  soothing, calming breeze—
Minutes from the street, lifes'
  serenity . . .
Moments only fade . . . to
  confused insanity . . .

Sitting in a cafe-spying
  passersby . . .
Thoughts can reach conclusions
  from the corner of an eye . . .

Technology saves the soul,
so said, yet we are beat—
and now I see the neon, bleed its
  bright defeat . . .

Rosemary L. Kintzinger
TWILIGHT
Twilight is falling
The night birds are calling
Their mates to their nest.

The cares of the day are far far
  away
'Tis the perfect time to pray.

The full moon is beaming
Bright water is gleaming
God's world is at rest.

Josephine Corliss Liebhaber

Josehpine Corliss Liebhaber
SONG TO SPRING

To Louis with love

Oh, joyous Spring, you are the
  one
To bring to us new life begun.
  The winter-weary world, a
    dearth
  Of color, undergoes rebirth.
Winter's wrappings come
  undone.

Dormant daffodils have won
The struggle, reaching toward the
  sun;
  Their fragrant flowers paint the
    earth.
  Oh, joyous Spring!

The maple's sap begins to run,
While budding branches sway in
  wondrous
  Choreography. The mirth
  Of laughing raindrops shows its
    worth
By showering love when day is
  done.
  Oh, joyous Spring!

Helen A. Clarke
REJECTION COMPLETE
When I was young,
And life was sweet
I opened up my heart,
And laid it at your feet,
But you shut the door.

In middle life
My dreams were rich in lore,
They needed someone to adore,
So I left them on your doorstep,
But you had shut the door.

When I was growing old,
I clung to life,
And as your loving wife,
I offered love once more,
But you walked out the door,
  forevermore.

Beth Ann Yoho
UNTITLED
            Splash!
        circles widen
            into nothingness

Keith Allen Daniels
TO A FARAWAY LOVER
Ensorcelled by a woman's
  glabrous touch,
By kisses from a mouth so soft
  and sweet,
I felt my heart go down in glad
  defeat:
I've never loved a woman quite so
  much.
But fickle Fate's untimely whims
  prevailed
And banished me from love and
  tender nights.
Although I'm far away, and plans
  have failed,
I'll not relinquish you without a
  fight!
And yet, withal, you're never far
  away,
And fill my thoughts with
  sadness and delight.
I miss you most as daylight fades
  to night,
But in my mind our sundered
  spirits play
Like eager children, anxious to
  explore
The joyous world we played in
  years before.

Cheri Bonner
THE BIRDS

---

*To my mother who always
encourages me and former
teacher, Eleanor Van Loon*

The birds are like flowers
In the sky—
Morning Glories
In the sun
Flying to be free—
Wings delicate as petals
Making twirling bouquets
In the air,
But in the moonlight
The morning Glories
Are closed.

Loretta Murdock
THE HOMELESS FATHER
The homeless father:
He feels so lost and alone.

To be pulled at from so many
  different directions,

Thinking he has nothing to give.

His loved ones all in different
  places:
Never together at one time.

He gave his love each time, only
  to lose
A part of him which never could
  be replaced.

His dream to have his children
  with him always,
So far out of reach.

Now he tries to cover his feelings
  with
An imaginary life.

He dances: He drinks: The parties
  are many.

Everyone sees him smile:
  Everyone sees him laugh.

No one sees him cry alone.

Marylou G. Frisbie
IT'S CHERRY
"You call it red—and that's all
  right,"
She assured me, sparing my
  feelings;
And her voice dropped low
To share her secret—
"But really it's CHERRY!"

And that four-year old had it
  together
When she came, a fist full of
  crayons,
Testing me—
"What color is this one, Grandma?"
I failed with my confident,
"Why that one's red!"

How dull my grown-up mind
  becomes!
Technically correct—it *is* red—
But so much more!
There's a roundness and richness,
A mystery and wonder,
A flame and flavor in CHERRY
Not found in simply "red"—

There's magic that abounds
In everyday things around;
Lord, awaken my imagination—
Renew my sight, quicken my mind
To catch the shining beauty,
To experience the luscious
  sweetness of
"Really it's CHERRY!"

Sylvia E. Sleighter
BEAUTIFUL NATURE
Nature can be beautiful,
  As people will agree.
To care for it is dutiful
  For folk like you and me.

The flowers with their lovely hues
  Will paint a pretty scene
For all who can enjoy the views
  From door and window screen.

We have the trees that give us
  shade,
  And grass beneath our feet;
Also, birds and bees that fly
  All up and down the street.

Waterways flow down the hill
  To meet the larger streams.
Let's go fishing—what a thrill!
  This tops my wildest dreams!

Animals are friends of ours.
  They have their work to do;

Whether they spend all their
   hours
   At home or in the zoo.

Morning brings the sunshine
   bright
   To bring a pleasant day.
Evening brings a starlit night
   To end the children's play.

Susan Gayle Bryant
MY MOM

---

*To my mother, without whom, I
wouldn't be.*

We're close my mom and me,
Like the leaves on a tree.
We go together, her and I,
Like the sun and the sky.

We share the good and the bad,
We talk when we're happy or
   sad.
Our love we share continues to
   build,
One things for sure . . . it'll never
   yield.

Ken—Roy Pulse

Ken—Roy Pulse
REUNION

---

*Written For My Mother, Vernell
Burleson —In Memory Of Her
Mother— Mary Jane Kirby*

Aunt Jody, the salads unique.
Cousin Jan, beans?
Grandpa's upset.
Mother, Bigmama's asleep.

Tell the children, times near.
Let me help you, Syble dear.
Wendy's crying, again.
Where's Frances? find her, if you
   can.

Uncle Ronnie, I can play.
Yes, mother, I'm here today.
Thank you Lord for this food.
Pass the ham; Uncle E.O., you
   too.

Have you heard from Reba Nell;
   doing well.
No. No. Can't hold another bite.
Leaving so soon. Yes, I know,
Wasn't it nice; another year.

I thought it to be, I didn't know;
Did Imagene tell you so?
Good night Rudy. Good night
   Ken.
Can't wait for Christmas again.

Anna M. Strusinski
MY BUTTERFLY FANTASY

---

*I am dedicating this poem to Dori
M. Jensen/Foster, a beautiful
person and a fellow poet.*

I am chasing a butterfly, thru
   cluttered fields,
With unseen objects that I only
   can feel.
I admire his beauty, he is so
   gracefull and proud,
Shining out among others, alone
   in a crowd.
I reach out to touch him but he
   dances away,
Because I touch him too deeply
   and he just wants to play.
I keep chasing and chasing when
   I should let him go,
But something keeps driving me;
   just what I don't know.
It seems like a dream, like a
   dream that won't end,
Where I never can catch him and
   I have to pretend,
That he opens his wings so I may
   see in his heart,
And we both will be peacefull on
   the day we must part.

Jennifer Jean Ford
JOB'S COMFORTER

---

*This poem was written on the
eve of my becoming a
quadraplegic. In these six months
past, I have taken view of life
holding so very much. This is
hereby dedicated to each and
every one of us to hold on!*

Drooling rain accumulates into
   cesspools of sick sludge.
Leaden trains of thought rumble
   to a dawn revealing midnight.
Shadows become refuge. Light
   becomes enemy.
I wallow waist-deep in
   despondency as winter winds
   whip a summer day.
The heaviness of desolation
   shackles me and draws me still
   deeper.
The stench of rot breathes as
   perfume to the spirit.
A Goliath of despair becomes
   friend by familiarity.
Dreams of death sign
   "ESCAPE" . . .
When will it come?
The blink of a lash would not be
   soon enough.

John Martin Brown
TO SAIL THE VIRGIN SEA
Oh to sail the virgin sea, her
   waters crystal clear,
Our home a seaworthy little
   yacht and weather so fair.
Far from cares and troubles, lost
   to our home land,
Searching, hidden lagoons,
   beaches of snow white sand.
Gliding silently, drifting toward
   the setting sun,
Alone to find, two of us have
   become one.

Dreamily we'll gaze to the many
   islands so near,
Over head puffs of white give no
   reason to fear.
And as darkness sets in, after
   evenings banquet,
Topside, on deck we will set our
   blanket.
Touching the night sky bursting
   with stars,
Searching for the wanderers,
   Venis and Mars.
The Pleiades, our jewel sparkles
   over head,
Lost to the universe out on our
   loving bed.
Hypnotized till a shooting star
   crosses the sky,
We scan the zodiac, for another
   may flash by.
Than to a peaceful sleep in the
   tropical calm,
Securely resting under Gods
   gentle arm.
And dawn awakens all to the
   symphony of golden sunrise,
We greet the new day, oh the
   happiness in our eyes.
Who know the adventure at the
   next hidden lagoon,
With the wind in our sails we're
   off to explore the moon.
Oh the thrill, drop anchor, let's
   get the dingie to shore,
There's the old sugar mill, its
   ruins we must explore . . .

Katherine Shorey
PICTURES
The artist paints his picture
Of the dawning's tranquil hush;
I can feel the foggy dampness
He creates with oils and brush.

This canvas shows a vessel,
By fierce wind and wave she's
   toss'd;
I sense such apprehension—
Will ship and crew be lost?

The notes of the musician
Bring me graphic pictures, too.
Some create a dance—a song—
Yet some a mood that's blue.

And then there is the poet
Whose pictures come from words.
I can see the vivid beauty
As he writes of humming birds.

Yet am I not an artist?
Don't I paint every day?
My pictures—grim or happy—
Are formed by words I say.

I want my pictures cheerful
And gentle as the dove,
As light and bright as sunshine
And always filled with love.

Faye Lanier
IMMORTALITY LOST
I waste precious time in
   meaningless activities—
   Activities that, in time, will
      not matter.
I do the expected.
   I work;
   I play;
   I rest;
   I eat—Yet I hunger—
Hunger for expression.
   Words that will say,
"I live; I am,"

Words that will say,
"I know you live; you are."
   But when I finally do write,
Tiredness crawls onto the
   page
   Like a turtle crossing a road.
The seeds of creativity sleep,
   Sacrificed for the necessities.
The poem I never wrote is never
   missed.
Immortality will not waste her
   time for me.

Barbara Caudill
LIFE

---

*To my someone special,
My husband, Ron.*

Why does life,
   Have to be so blue,
When you have no one,
   That can be with you.

You can have thousands of friends,
   You can say Hi to,
But it doesn't replace,
   Someone that loves you.

Roberta Simmons
NEW LIFE OLD LIFE

---

*To my deceased brother James
Vincent Simmons*

There fell a dead silence and I felt
   like crying tears of blood. If
   there were some way I could
   transmit my breath into him as
   if to breath new life back into
   his body.
Still I feel that the earth was
   sifting like sand from beneath
   my feet, I was losing my grip,
   my perspective on life. And I
   didn't care.
To me life had lost its meaning. It
   had no rhythm, no rhyme.
He had gained a new life in his
   death, and I had lost my life in
   living.

Bennett Lee
TELEPHONE TO GOD
My soul has no inside nor out,
It has no color to tell about,
It is simply a part of me,
A part that only God can see.

James Speich III
TIME
Time is relative to one's
   dimension of mind and place
Time is the measurement of the
   movement of objects in space
Time is the truth in real astrology
Time is the knowledge of
   anthropology
Time is the law of matter
Time is the tempter
Time will last to the end of time
Time for me to end my rhyme

Anna Gilmore
FLOWERS FOR LIVING
Bring me flowers

While I live,

So I can touch, smell
The fragrance they give
The aroma will be a
   lasting one

In my memory
They will please my heart,
    forever
For when my maker
Calls me to the land of no
    return
The scent of the petals
Shall in my soul,
    forever burn
Ruth M. Garrett
MY LOVE

---

*Dedicated to
Richard D. Garrett, Sr.*

Away, and away
    Has my love gone
I know not where
    Somewhere, and I'm left alone

I called on the wind
    But my love didn't hear
I called out again, and again, and
    again
And my heart trembled with
    fear

I looked near and far
    I looked in my nightmares
My love forever gone
    Gone forever, somewhere

I reached out my hand
    Lost in the darkness of grief
And touched not my love
    Our time together so sweet, so
    brief

My life is but tatters
    Oh, take my life's breath
My love has gone somewhere
    And somewhere is death
Stephanie Van Hardenberg
LOVE IN A FRIEND
There's a special way to say hello
Just touch my soul and never go
I see your face in dreams at night
Pray you'll love me with all your
    might.

I so do hope that dreams come
    true
For all of them are of you
So full of good and happy times
Like loving little nursery rhymes.

To recall such dreams only brings
    me tears
For all of my uncertain fears
Please listen close my darling
    friend
Our touching just shant ever end.

For living isn't quite over yet
Our souls and hearts just haven't
    met
So on this ground I must stand
    firm
Now come with me there's more
    to learn.

I watch you when you do not see
Oh! Don't be frightened it's only me
I'll ask for love in tiny bits
Put it all just where it fits.

Good-night my friend but
    remember this
You have my love and warming
    kiss
Just always remember and don't
    forget
I'll soon be with you in a little
    bit.

Joseph P. Laubacher
FRIEND ON THE HILLTOP
I've got a friend up on a hill,
    though unseen he is there still.
I talk to him; he listens well.
    Words of wisdom; his to tell.

He's hard to hear unless you try.
    Nineteen years have passed me
    by.
Now I've finally heard his story.
    Now I see the unknown glory.

The things he's done cannot be
    said
    in any little poem read.
He advises me, I pay no bill.
    I harvest his crops and eat my
    fill.
An artist too with so much skill,
    how I love to visit that hill.

I feel his spirit upon the wind.
    My senses show no discipline.
I scream, I laugh, I cry, I shout,
    I see and feel him all about.

Yes on that hilltop he'll always be
    waiting ever so patiently.
And when I come he gives a smile,
    knowing I want to visit awhile.

You know him too; he's
    everywhere.
    His endless travels take him
    there.
Perhaps you've met him in your room.
    I know you've seen his flowers
    bloom.

You see my friend is widely
    known.
    His name by now is worldwide
    sown
into the hearts of all mankind.
    Search yourself; he's there
    you'll find.
Clara C. Creasy
DRIFTING SOUL
Great is the fear, hidden deep in
    my heart,
Silhouettes of friends are drifting
    apart,

The wind plays a song—
As the leaves tumble down,

I reach to touch them and find
    them gone—
Grief and sorrow some people
    seem to follow,

As death takes over it leaves
    such a hollow—
The valleys so deep—the
    mountain so high,

I cannot cross either, I only sigh—
I watched a sun set over a sea of
    glass,

And cried, when flooded,
With memories of my past.
Jana Klenburg
ILANA
The week
We brought my child back
From darkness of death
I held all week long
Her pale and bruised hand
In mine tender and soft
And firm in life

With black rings
From fighting for life round her
    eyes,
Her pale swollen face

Was the one of a sweet absent
    child

In her innocence clear
Her lost panicked eyes
Would search for mine
That in terror and faith—both in
    one—
Were at all times looking to God
Straight through her eyes

In my deepest deep love
The oneness with God
And the oneness with her—flesh
    of my flesh—
Merged
For the goodness of all

And for long long long days
And much longer nights
Your prayers my friends,
The doctors who cared,
And the love of us all
Have her dancing through life
Like a spirit of joy
Spreading hearts to us all
And sparkles of light
Sarah Renken
NATURE
    Trees, grass, running water
Nature and it's beauty.
    I look at it and feel free
It is the gift God gave us.
Shella M. Lucas
GETHSEMANE

---

*'To Phil.' For his true kindness,
Deep loyalty, and basic integrity.*

I walked in an old, old, garden,
    Where Jesus prayed and wept,
Alone on the "Mount Of Olives",
    While his disciples slept.
I looked across the valley,
    Toward Jerusalem's "Eastern
    Gate",
Scenes flashed before me,

    Mere words could never paint.
A voice from the past spoke gently,
    Not my will, but thine be done,
While the walls of the great old
    city,
    Caught the rays of the setting
    sun.
In the "Garden Of Gethsemane",
    I walked on sacred sod,
Prayed and shared my secrets,
    In a private talk with "God".
Grace W. Shaw
MEMORIES AT SUNSET
I stood and gazed in awe at the
    scarlet ball of fire

I thought of the times we had
    watched a sunset
This was such a beautiful sight to
    behold at dusk
    But the view we had together
    was the prettiest yet.

I watched the setting sun
    reflected in the water
    And I went back in time to
    when I stood with you
To watch the setting sun in the
    waters at Biloxi
    I was your bride and just
    starting life anew.

You pointed out to me the beauty
    of the setting sun
    We parked the car to get the
    most perfect view
The colors were something no
    artist could duplicate
    And I was in a state of bliss—I
    was with you.

Though God saw fit to take you
    from me one day
    My memories will go with me
    through eternity
Each beautiful sunset makes me
    think of you
    Beyond that sunset you wait
    somewhere for me.

Ray "Skip" Connors
HAIKU ... AUTUMN
Parachuting Leaves
Momentary Skywriters
Summer's Epitaph.

Nadine V. Mandel
TINY TEDDY BEAR
Tiny Teddy Bear all pink and
    white,
Little red tongue sticking out.
Shoe button eyes, that shine so
    bright.
You are a darling, there's no
    doubt.

I had a dream wrapped up in you,
A tiny dream of pink and white,
A dream that wasn't meant to
    come true.
For all I have left is tears at nite.

I'll keep you little Teddy Bear
And maybe someday you,
Will help me dream, my dream
    again,
And this time t'will come true.

Myrna Freedman
THE SOUND OF PEACE

To The Lord

The tiny birds hovered all around
    us
But ne'er a sound was heard
Why was there no singing on
    that special night
People were gathered all around
    but ne'er a sound was heard

Then out of the distance we
    could hear the sound of a choir
    of angels voices serenading us
    in the night

A shining bright light appeared
    and we all looked up in hope
    and fear and in a cloud dressed
    in white was the most
    beautiful heavenly sight

Three heavenly voices was all we could hear assuring us there was nothing to fear

There were harps being played and we all stood still and listened to "The Sound Of Peace"

The whole world was silent and there wasn't any need for man to fight his fellowman any more

The three celestial angels floating down from above made us all realize that the keys to heaven is LOVE

Rev. Armand Leo Chouinard

Rev. Armand Leo Chouinard
Uncle Sam Live's Forever

To Ronald Reagan: The President of the United States of America, a Job well Done

---

American's come and ancesters go, we all know.
And as the year's keep rollin by.
All our children live and grow, there's only one who'll never die:—
Uncle Sam lives forever—he stand's for the U.S.A. the stars and stripes together, alway's will keep him that way!
Uncle Sam lives forever within this country that's true.
He'll keep our flag wavin high with colors red, white and blue.
Some can have our religion any kind that we choose, and vote of our own decision.
For parties who'll win or lose, thus, "Uncle Sam lives forever. He stand's for peace and what's right in order to save our country that's why we're always willin to fight!

Carol Michelle Leish
Live While You're Living
As the day strode along,
Thoughts of freedom entered the mind.
Rainbows brightened up the day.
Eagles joyfully sang a lovely song.
Cheerfully, the birds chirped as a gong
Sounded as one of a kind.
How will the sunlight follow the ray?
All happiness starts to come along.

Memories of satisfaction feel strong.
As love comes, one can find Feelings; devine, following away.
Wonderous feelings shall always come along.

Eddie Heavner
THESE TWO
Of all things that stand create,
these I would destroy;
the clouds that dim the summer sun,
the years that steal the boy.

For both have taken beauty
and perjured nature's truth;
the clouds that rain on summer,
the years that purloin youth.

Inez D. Geller
CONSUELO
I am of the family Malalel
from the ancient Moors of Mauritania.
Contained, bolted, locked within the family,
a tomb of conjugal hell.

My dreams bring me scarlet camellias
pinned onto a huge Spanish cape,
encircling my body with Jupiter rings
while a sweet incense cleanses my anger.

Mi madre, mi madre,
under the lavender moon
I am sucked down to the wet earth
praying for an urgent redemption.

Fantasies interrupt fervant prayers
with visions of hot Barcelona bordellos,
where there is hope in the possibility
of expressing the most secret longings.

Leslie Connell
OF WOMEN AND MEN
If woman could have equal rights
We'd try less hard to bring to light
The feebleminded thoughts of men
That we were made just for them.

We were not made to just cook and clean
Not always heard but always seen
They like to gawk as they bulge their eyes
Make a lot of promises that are mostly lies.

They always want us to spread our wings
When we do they start to scream
Yet they do not want a clinging vine
I wish they could just make up their mind.

We have to pamper the ego of males
So easily wounded so it soon stales
And heaven forbid should we critizise
They want to be perfect in our eyes.

And if we're only a simple housewife
We cannot expect much out of life

Because this has no value to them
There is no pay for catering to men.

Then they ask will you go to war?
Of course we can—that and more
We could run the U. S. of A.
If man would only get out of the way!

Guy Reid
SUMMER AFTERNOON
We sat on the shore with the rock
And pebbles licked by ocean waves,
With seagulls flying over the dock
And fish swimming through watery caves.

We tried to know and somehow to care
On this pale-sunned beach in Newfoundland
About the untamed beauty living there
Fashioned so rough hewn by Nature's hand.

Was there a thread of truth we could weave
From the starkness of this unknown place,
Something the inner eye could perceive
And meet understanding face to face?

We watched the dories far off the shore
Bob on the mighty Atlantic crest,
Quietly hoping we might see more:
A revelation to spark our quest.

We gazed at the hills in their craggy dress.
Could they unfold an insight to man
To reassure a world in distress
As evil engulfs him once again?

The sun went away and dusk chilled the air
And our thoughts swept this canvas again,
Stark island poised on the ocean there—
And we felt some hope for future man.

Daurie Nelson
BLENDING

For my grandmother, Mabel Kuhn Nelson, who gave to me her love of Poetry . . .

Happiness:
Is a butterfly which will Elude you—if pursued. But— Wait patiently: It will come . . .

It is the sunshine of life. And, like love,
It is a fragile, precious gift You were meant to share.

Friendship:
Is a generous passion:
If not increased—Will decrease.
Happiness will grow and thrive.

It comes from the heart—and demonstration.
It is a loving reflection Of all you can be.

Love:
Is a mirror which brightens
And gives unequaled pleasure
To those who will accept it.

It's the most intense color of the mind
And blends happiness with friendship

And is . . .

without measure . . .

Elaine Spencer
A GRAIN OF SAND
See this tiny grain of sand.
Did it from the mountain blow?
Or did years and years of grains of sand
Into a mountain grow?
When I see a beach so full of sand
Each grain different from the rest
I'm reminded of the millions of things
That the Love of God has blessed.

Sarah How—ree Nichols
THE BIRTHING

To Minnie Yount, who gave me the talent I have, and my husband who encouraged me to use it.

A fat toad,
yellow vest bulging,
with the plenty,
snatched glue tongued,
from the butch—cut fox grass,
blinks,
at the clouds,
under bellies hanging,
a sagging blue.

Mid a rumble of pain,
schapels of lightening,
slashes. The cesarean,
is complete.
The cold pale offspring,
lay bedded,
over the lawn
The hailstones are birthed.

Michael Baer
MY MOTHER
The twinkling stars are like my Mom's eyes,
The dark sky is just like my Mom's hair,
The air is like my Mom's breath,
The rain is like my Mom's sweat.

My Mom is like the whole world.

Georgiana Lieder Lahr
LITTLE ANGEL

Dedicated to the Queen Anne's Lace that grows along the roadside at Principia College, Elsah, Illinois.

Queen Anne's Lace,
Beautiful roadside flower;
I stand in wonder and marvel
At your symmetry of design.
Such loveliness and perfection,
Each tiny white blossom,
Delicate and pure.

I think
That a little angel formed you.

John Campbell, Editor & Publisher

One morning he said,
"I shall make a flower,
A pretty white flower
Which will grow along the dusty
  roadside,
And nod its greeting
To every passerby."

So he took the whiteness from
  the clouds,
And the prettiest shades of green
He could find in field and meadow,
And fashioned Queen Anne's Lace.

And God smiled at him
And said,
"Well done, little Angel!"

Frances Carter
Childhood Recollection
Late afternoon's heartbroken tilt
  of light unnerves.
The nape hair lifts and scuffing
  feet more swiftly plow the
  drifted leaves, full flight
  disdained as yet.
Lest eyes averted meet the slant
  unbearable, they track instead
  toe—tips a 'rush now through
  the autumn heath to
  sanctuary—home, love, food,
  snug bed, known world with
  parents' Atlas arms beneath.

Barbara de Roo
LET ME LOOK!

---

*Chad Bosch, my grandson, age
two, inspired me to write this
poem . . .*

Take my hand.
Take me back to the sea,
To look as long as I like.
Let me watch the birds
That walk on the water,
Then fly full-wing
Out of sight.

Lift me high
When the waves slap my legs,
And pushes me to shore.
Oh, run and chase with me,
To laugh some more!

Let me hear
The ocean's motor stop, and go,
And spit spray
Like the dragon in my book.
Where does the sea go?
Does it move with the wind,
To go down with the sun?
Maybe, it ends with the sky.
Let me look!

Jane Lustig
MATERNITE'
While praising Motherhood and
  Apple Pie, then four times
  blessed am double—I.
Born of English mother, Anna, I
  entered this world as baby
  Susanna.
One year only I had this mother,
  while four years I waited for
  another.
At such young ages memory gets
  only the mists of
  multivignettes.

Then into my life came the lady,
  Irene, who changed "Susanna"
  to just plain "Jean".
All of seven years had passed

before she adopted me at last!
So, in all reality, she was "Mother"
  number three.
American, as apple pie is touted,
  Irene mapped the way my life
  was routed.

Irene was my mother in every
  way, and I grieve her death to
  this very day.
Her husband took a wife once
  more, giving me Mother
  number four.
Mae was born year of Mother one,
  age-wise the circle closed
  where begun!
I hesitate as "four" to list her. She
  was less "Mother", much more
  "Sister".

Although I lack a family tree, and
  both Susanna and Jean are me,
I know Mother Anna, defeated by
  strife, relinquished me for a
  better life.
A second woman gave me home
  and care, until Irene took me
  away from there.
Mae, right from the start, earned
  a special place within my heart.

Now that I'm a mother, too, my
  past's a polychromatic view.
How many people can claim four
  mothers? Do you know of any
  others?

Carolyn Irene Brothers
**For a Learning
  Handicapped Student**
There once was a girl named
  Deanne
Whose subjects she found hard to
  command
Predicates gave her trouble
Prepositions made her double
This poor little girl named
  Deanne.

Judson Dicks
**"The Peale Family" (Oil On
  Canvas By Charles
  William Peale)**
Within the frames of family life
  we see
Three generations in nativity;
And on the table, fruit and paring
  knife
While on the floor a hunter's dog
  adds life.
What intellect collected into
  view,
Compendium of both the old and
  new,
Is caught, unaging, by the brush
  and paint
Of him whose work was
  classified as quaint!
Beyond the quaintness of each
  artifact
Great love and depth of mind
  remain intact.

Arlene L. Kaloper
MEMORY
A touch that wasn't . . .
A kiss that isn't . . .
You fade away forever.
Were you but a moments thought?
A silent whisper . . .
Never really there?

Still memories come back to
  haunt me,

Moments at a time . . .
Sequences of laughter . . .
Waiting for me to find.

Daydreams lost forever, yet tucked
  within my heart . . .
To remind me always . . .
What once was, really was.

Ethel Case Cook

Ethel Case Cook
SAD SONGS ARE BEST
Sad songs are best, for who in
  bursting joy
Has need to turn to someone
  else's word?
But silent staring heartbreak can
  employ
Another's sorrow though his
  own's unheard.

Much debt I owe, as many
  another had—
To you, my dear, who turned my
  gay song sad.

Helen Kelly Deuter
THE WINDOW
My Christmas Tree this year
Is a puff of cloud in the sky
Festooned with stars from the
  Milky Way
It glistens and gleams on high
And right at the top of the
  twinkling tree
In the biggest star of them all
A window opened for me to see
My loved one's face looking down
  at me
Smiling
Tenderly

Jim Stevens
MY DAUGHTER
In a world full of rainbows
In a land full of dreams
I have a loving daughter
Who means the world to
  me

She has a pretty smile
That brightens up the sun
The laughter of an angel
Sent from up above

The glow from hazel eyes
Seem to light up the sky
And bring a new meaning
To white clouds on high

I'd trade all lifes treasures
All the wealth untold
The jewels of all the earth
For my daughters heart of gold

If God gave me one wish
One dream I could hold

My daughter would be with me
Till the sands of time unfold
Mary Crickmer Conley
SIGN POSTS
The road of life leads me on—
My deeds become planted seeds
That grow into flowers and weeds.

May I mark the way to show
The things I've learned in life
The joys and sorrows and the
  strife

So those who follow me
Can walk with easier design
Because of the signs I left behind.

Elizabeth Saltz
FREEDOM
Freedom means to enjoy liberty,
  man was born free to enjoy
  nature,
But everywhere he is in chains.
  The quality of goodness
  enhances existence,
The earth is a sphere, part of the
  cosmos,
  We belong to a nation and
  have a religion.

All matter is contingent and in
  motion,
  Life is eternal, endless and
  repetitive.
There are many forms, shapes
  and colors,
  Nature is bountiful, grows and
  dies.
Man begins life as nothing, like
  Adam and Eve,
  The earth, once inhabited by
  amphibians, now holds man.

What is eternal? The earth moves
  around in a sphere,
  Man is immortal, seeks the
  Kingdom of God.
As living matter produces, so
  man leaves offspring,
  There is another world where
  men are born again.

The long voyage of life is filled
  with eternal bliss,
  The state protects man against
  crime.
The guardians are just, they
  protect against fear,
  Man organizes with his fellows
  to form a state.

Carlene Stinnette
CLOUDS
I look at the sky
and all I do is wonder why
  clouds are there and I am here.
Katie Brunner
I SAW . . .
I saw your loving face up in the
  sky,
like a photo-flash it appeared
so suddenly it came,
you looked so happy, and you
  smiled,
and clearly did I hear you call my
  name.

I was stunned, that such a
  wondrous wonder
actually could be—
via miles of air, and daytime
  sunlit sky—
was it meant to say, "Hello?!"
or did it happen just to say,
  "Good-bye?!"

18

I kept it secret, oh— for many
    years
to avoid ridicule, or have it
    labeled as a lie,
I will remember this phenomena
as sure as I live, until the day I die.

I saw it—yes—I saw it!
But can't prove it, that I did;
Was this miracle an act of love,
or part of the future,
to let me see you, by lifting a
    magic lid!

Muriel Gilstrap
AGING
Youth has passed
in heedless fashion,
with an insouciant
wave of farewell;
leaving tenuous shreds
of poignant memories,
vague regrets
and a nostalgic ache
to linger through
these senescent years.

Virginia E. Cruikshank
DIRGE
The snow is falling, falling
Upon the new—turned earth.
It falls upon my dear one,
Newly laid beneath.

It cannot be; it must not be—
This heavy weight of earth
Upon my dear one,
Lying beneath a shroud
Of falling, falling snow.

Le Vena May Drummond
WHOM TO LOVE
You tried to tell
    me whom to
    love.
This can only come
    from within; or
    above.
Our hearts are delicate;
    easily broken and
    by the same
    token
Untrue love words
    to the wrong one
    should never be
    spoken.
Love is affection;
    fond and tender
    attachment to
    another.
The state of feeling
    kindly towards others
    and your
    brother.
The welfare of all and
    charity for all
    men
Love in any form
    by Almighty God
    could never be
    considered or
    regarded as a
    sin.
When it comes to
    falling in love
    look to Him
    above.
Follow your heart
    and disregard your
    mind.
You will dwell in peace
    forever and never look
    behind.

Loving-kindness is
    affectionate sympathy;
    tenderness; untold mercy,
    and the act of voluntary
    service to
    mankind.
So look to Him
    above and go ahead
    and fall in
    love.

Gary Knowles
night is imminent
Lost in stillness, life and love,
the day was alone dead and long.
There was no why for what it
    meant,
nothing right and nothing wrong—

Night is imminent.

Joe Musgrove Namken
THE GRASS WON'T GROW
As I walk into the graveyard
And look all around
I see grass growing every where
Except on the one the train ran
    down
Perhaps he made a pact with God
I guess we'll never know
Maybe that is why
Upon his grave the grass does not
    grow
It has been a year now
That he was laid to rest
I really miss the guy
Of this I confess
I Put some flowers down
On Memorial Day
When I went again
They were all gone away
If he could tell me
I'd really like to know
Why? On his grave alone
The grass will not grow

Chris Wilson
THE BUTTERFLY
The butterfly
Flits from flower to flower
In the meadow
Before the sun rises
To make its nectar

Jack G. Robb
IN RECOGNITION OF GOD.
Should I content myself to be,
But a mere mortal in physical
    reality,
Or should I regard the beyond,
    and exercise my soul,
And strive for spiritual intellect
    to make me whole?

'Tis a search for latter I tend to
    prefer.

In my search for truth, let
    nothing deter.
To naught but the Omniscient
    One must I acquiesce;
In HIS reality of realities, I vow to
    profess.

With love and omniscience all
    things HE didst conceive,
With my five basic senses HIS
    works I perceive.
Through meditation and prayer
    I've been blessedly shown,
The many ways HE makes HIS
    presence known.

To transcend the philosomical is
    my ultimate goal;
To perceive all creation with an
    extra sense—my soul!
My free will shall reign 'til my
    Earth—life's last breath,
But my soul will be set free in my
    life after death.

Delpha Funk Romeiser
THE RETURN
They say you can't go back
Where fond memories linger;
Where childhood grew and
    bloomed
And days were sweet and tender.

I tried—Alas 'tis true—
Change—beyond recognition,
I must accept this fact
And use my intuition.

For my life has changed too,
I am not the same as then,
How wise our creator
For he knows the hearts of men.

Memories like jewels,
They can never fade away;
We store them in our hearts
And are always on display.

Shirley Anderson Cox
ME
There are times in my life I wish
    that I were
Responsible for only me
But then I remember the times
    that I was
Reminding myself—thankful I'll
    be.

But oh how I longingly wish for
    the day
Thoughts wandering through my
    mind
Oh the long hours of hope, that
    linger within
For one day myself, to find.

When I can be free, to be as I am
Myself, mind and spirit, free
    willed as I can
My life to enjoy without question
    or strife
To live as I please for the rest of
    my life.

Not hurting another, but only to
    be
The person I long for,
And that person is Me!

Nancy L. Peck
THE SOLUTION
What is it we seek in life but
    Peace and Contentment,
Why is it then we fill it . . . with
    resentment?

Do unto others, a rule it was laid,

It seems so little attention to it is
    paid,
We are all brothers,
all seeking one end,
Peace and tranquility found from
    without as well as within,

A gesture of peace to be made
    from all sides,
would prove to each that all
    mankind can be wise,
No need for the hunger, the hate
    and the pain,
for to do unto others a solution
    so plain.

No matter the faith nor devotion
    so true,
perhaps the solution could begin
    with . . . just you.

Amil Shaban
MY DISTANCE REEM

Dedicated to: K. Kampfer

You had left me
As a broken glass
Talking to my self
Murmuring my thoughts
Is there a Chance?
To collect what was a chance

I felt the loneliness
Eating into my nights
I felt the passion
Tearing off my griefs
Why should it be?
When I had you
Between my arms

What will be now?
Sorrows with pain
Or hoping tomorrow
Will wrape you again
Into my dream
To hold you
My distance reem
Marge Hill
Ring Around the Collar
What ever made me think
    that if I took your ring off
        I wouldn't be yours . . .
            anymore?

That the love
    would stop
        and I'd be
        FREE?

I've got a ring around my heart
    that not even Wisk
        can get out.
Bernie Meyer
A Tribute To "Ollie Meyer"

---

*This Poem is Dedicated to my
husband and five children for a
very fulfilling Forty-two years of
life together. Children's names are
'Ronald', 'David', 'Christina', 'Darla'
and 'Lawerence'.*

How do you write about a
    wonderful man?
On his retirement from work,
I don't know if I can.
You see, he's my Husband,
And It's awfully hard, to give him
    his dues,
When I'm his only "reward".
Of course there's the children,

The number is five,
They're all grown up now,
Thank God we're alive.
To see how they've prospered,
Is a joy in itself,
Ollie must love me,
I'm not alone by myself.
We've been together for forty-two
years,
That's not such a long time to
share Laughter and Tears.
God knew what He gave us when
He threw us together,
He took a Strong-willed man to
look after a scatter-brained
Go-getter.
"Ollie's" worked all his life,
Without him I'm nothing,
They say "Opposites Attract", To
that there is something.
He is the strong one,
I am so weak, Together we've
made it,
Our Memories we'll keep.
So here's to you, "Ollie",
I do love you so,
Our "Love is Forever",
You might as well know.

Mary J. Watkins

Mary J. Watkins
EVENING SONG
Evening speaks of many things:
    Cool, scented breezes whisper
nocturnal secrets
    to usher in the coming night.
As the last pink—flush of sunset
    sketches the nesting
    sparrow's wing,
caravans of marching ants rush
by.
Heavily burdened and shy, they
disappear
    in pyramid homes
to spell the quickening night.
A soft wind sighs.

Evening speaks of many things:
    Of lover's quarrels
    and broken hearts . . .
    hidden tears and undreamt
dreams.
The many things one's left
undone;
    fulfillments, still to come.
The night—in—gale sings a
lonely song . . .
    calls to his lost mate . . .
    "Come! Fly with me."
And twilight softens the
deepening sky.

Evening speaks of other things:
    Life and Death . . . Space and
Time.
Hear the far-off Whisper of
Eternity?
    Echoes of laughter
    from days gone by?
Evening speaks of simple things:
    The pungent scent of
burning leaves
    stirs to life old memories, and
    as day surrenders its
dwindling light,
        The Cosmos Sings!
A silvery mist descends upon all
    earthly things, and
A crescent moon hangs high.

Stephanie A. Horne
TRIBUTE TO MY MOTHER
Beautiful is a mother's love,
As beautiful as a soaring dove.
Protective is a mother's love,
Like a tigress watching o'er her
cubs.
There's my mother tigress
waiting still,
Waiting, waiting, waiting until
A handsome young man asks for
my hand.
You'll then give your blessings to
this young man.
We'll get married and have a
child of our own.
I'll look back to my childhood
with you at home.
I'll cherish the memories of you
and I together,
All the fun we had, even during
bad weather.
You may think I don't appreciate
a thing,
But in my own way I appreciate
every little thing.
I'll look back at how you raised
me, day by day,
And I'll raise my own child in the
same way.
Everytime you punished me for
something I did wrong,
Helps me realize our love is very
strong.

Cynthia Lynn Harney
DEATH
Dying is something that happens
to everyone
Eventually it comes and touches
your family
A lot of people fear death and
don't believe in God
Truthfully I think we all
shouldn't fear death because
Heaven awaits us all.

Ginny DuBois
UNDERSTANDING

---

*This poem was written to my
children Terri, Patrick, and Jamie
Marie, Love Mom*

They say a child will lead you
And for me I know it's true
For everyday I'm with mine
They teach me something new.
They taught me understanding
In a very special way
And to each one of them this I
will repay.
For each one of my children is
different this I see
But each one of them is also a
part of me
And I would not treat them any
different
Then I would want them to treat
me.

Nicole Renee Mytyk
A BIG FAT BEAR
There once was a big fat bear,
Who was named after her
Mother, Cher.
She was very funny,
As funny as bugs Bunny.
She was a bear that had no hair.

Dorcas P. Hord
IT'S NO TIME TO CRY
It's no time to cry
    When a child is born
And it's a boy instead of a girl.
    It's no use to cry
When your mother-in-law says,
    "He looks like his grandpa Earl".

There's no use to cry
    When you see your car
With its fender all bent in,
    And she explained
The sign said yield
    So she just drove on in.

Now it's no time to cry
    When all the kids leave home
And the house is
    quiet-as-a-mouse.
    Just make up your mind
That it's about time
    You stopped and enjoyed your
spouse.

Bob Barci
BYANTHIUM
Let your mind wander.
Right into Byanthium.
You know the place.
The place where dreams rule.
Where love is king.
The elephants eat cavier.
The ants are chauffeur driven.
Birds eat from your hand.
Orangutans sing opera and rock.
Giraffes are love-sick.
Beavers are slap-happy.
Lions are comedians.
You can get lost in Byanthium.
Lost in this crazy world of fantasy.
Whatever you can think of can
be found here.
Shoe shinning vultures.
Rhinos on diets.
Zebras into plaid.
Chimps are philosophers.
Dinosaurs are vegetarians.
There's no telling what you'll find.
So, when your mind wanders,
Wander it right into Byanthium.
You'll have the time of your life.

Dawn Sexton
SOMETHING

---

*To Ken, I will always love you
wherever you go. Thank-you for
giving me the strength to stand
alone.*

If I had something to hold on to
Like a dream
Or maybe an emotion
Something to shelter me from the
evil
Of a storm
Or of a nightmare
Then maybe I would not fear the
dark
Maybe I would not fear being
alone

Muriel E. Vebsky
EFFECTS OF LOVE
great and precious, promised
blessings
    pivotal though they be
        gelid feelings are thrust aside
            to warm and mesmerize
            pervasive effects of love
            for perfect harmony.

Pamela J. Theurer
SCARS
Could I but reach out my hand to
you,
to hold you in my arms forever.
But you resist me,
as if by somehow letting down
your guard,
you will again be hurt
as you were before.
Like a frightened animal,
you cower in the darkest corner,
afraid to experience the touch
of a soft and loving hand.
Afraid to feel again
the beauty and the pain
that involvement can bring.
I try to give you space,
to give you time,
time to heal those old wounds
that seem to haunt you.
Trust me,
I promise I will never hurt you.
I love you—
It's as simple and as beautiful
as only love can be.

Julie Jean Pursel Couey
MEADOWS OF THE MIND

---

*Dedicated to Rick C. Couey My
Inspiration to write Best friend &
buddy*

Green grassey meadows filled
    with flowering fragrant blooms.
Brown tinges of frost moved in
    slowly turning to ice.
Spring brought icy waters—cold
    feet the meadows dryed up.
Seeds planted long ago with love
    caltivated began to grow.
Covering the meadows green
    flowering with fragrant blooms.

Matthew Story
THE BOULDER

---

*To AMS Henry S. Yates II, lost at
sea Jan. 14, 1969, and to James
Ivy, also lost at sea July 1976.*

I stand on the shore,
looking out at the sea.
Watching the waves,
tasting the breeze.
    A ship is sailing,
sailing for shore.
And the gulls in the distance,
guide your way.
    But the sky turns gray,
and the sea gets rough.
And the salty waves
smash into the rocky bluff.
    A sunken boulder
rips open the bow.

With a creak and a moan,
the ship goes down.
   I still stand on the shore,
looking out at the sea.
Watching the waves,
tasting the breeze.
   The fog rolls in,
hazing my view.
The moon is out,
and it's weeping for you.

Ella Foster O'Brien
MY GARDEN
The sun smiles down in my
   garden,
   The clouds go drifting along,
The bird in the tree at the corner
   Has a mate a nest and a song.

The morning glory climbs the
   trellis
   The hollyhocks bloom so fair,
The columbines whispers of far
   climbs
   The violet and "mums" bloom
   so rare.

But beside my bedroom window
   I still can see again,
The rose, and the honeysuckle,
   And, beyond the winding lane.

I close my eyes in this nighttime
   And down by the moonlit
   stream,
The happy smiles, and love
   remains,
   And blooms in my garden of
   dreams.

Watered with tears from my
   heart
   Fed with dreams of my own,
The flowers that bloom in my
   memory
   Are the memories of you and
   home.

Tamra M. Griffith
OUT ON FRONT LINE
A boy, young at heart,
With only a matter of time;
'Til he's torn apart,
And thrown out on front line.

With a draft in his hand,
And his young bride at his side;
In a week he's a man,
And a young boy's put aside.

He goes to war,
To fight for his land.
The battle planes soar,
And the soldier boy takes his
   stand.

He does all his time,
With one term to go.
It's still a long climb,
Before he's a hero.

Though a long time has passed,
He's on his way; free.
Packed away his guns and brass,
Bringing home a flag of liberty!

Maybelle West
Death of a Medicine Man
Leathered, weathered,
A face
Creased by many moons
Of seeking solace
For a race.

Bewildered by the onslaught
Of a world
That understands
Him not.

Searching, almost sightless
Eyes yet pierce
Un-seen horizons wide—
And come at last
To rest
Inside the hogan of
The Great Spirit.

Pearl Pedersen Zimmermann
SMILE

---

*While I, Linda McClelland,
received the Honorable Mention
award for this poem, the credit
really goes to my mother named
above. She wrote this poem along
with many others in 1930 at the
age of nineteen. Congratulations
Mom on your first published poem!*

Never lose your temper, it is just
   a waste of time.
If you are always pleasant, things
   will be mighty fine.

If you keep smiling, trouble will
   disappear,
And your bright countenance
   will others help to cheer.

People will welcome you if you
   wear a smile,
And you will find that life is
   worthwhile.

Jerilynn Trice
BEAUTIFUL NATURE
The beauty of nature is peaceful
   and quiet,
So soothing to the mind.
Cool and calm the scene does
   look,
Smooth, blowing breezes so kind.
The birds will sing you to sleep,
And animals are free to roam.
Think about it for a while,
WE are invading THEIR home.
Nature is so beautiful,
You never want to leave.
But, as time grows close for us
To part, this you must believe.
No matter how far away we are,
   camp
Stays by our heart, warm and near.
So, don't be sad as you go along,
Just shed a silent tear.

Patricia L. Ide
YESTERDAY'S YOUTH
I stepped into yesterday for just a
   while
   And in my mind the years were
   wiped away
There I was with youth again and
   worry-free
   Reluctant to return to present
   day

Free was I to go and do just as I
   please
   The whole wide world a place I
   could explore
Unhappiness a stranger that I did
   not know
   Everything to me an open door

Slowly I gave up my dream and
   took my place
   Laid aside delightful fantasy
But no matter what the years
   may take away
   I'll always have my youthful
   memories

Mauricia Price
THE FLOWERING . . .
Through fine-spun cilia upon
The epidermis of my soul,
I sensed your hidden loneliness
And felt its heavy burdening—
Like tactile echo chamberings of
   pain.

Then through our conversation's
   course
Of interchanged experience,
We shared a new evolving gift:—
The flowering of empathy . . .
And found the aching had not
   been in vain.

Gueni Zaimof

Gueni Zaimof
Edelweisses I Will Throw
With my head so full of snow
till the end for you I'll look.
If I hear the wind to blow,
with my heart in silken loop
edelweisses I will throw . . .

Frances C. Emmons
OUR CHILDREN
Who are these little ones
   Put in our trust?
Why should their future
   Depend on us?

These children are gifts
   From our Father above.
They were sent here by Him
   To teach us to love.

The fate of their future
   Is not very clear,
But these precious moments
   With them should be dear.

Our children's potentials
   We must respect.
The light of love
   Their lives should reflect.

Thy Kingdom, O Father,
   Is open to man.
Show us, as your children,
   Your heavenly plan.

Van D. Garner
I Have Just Begun To Write
At first the words came slowly
   and cautiously,
Each one a victim of restrained
   emotions,
Afraid to speak, afraid to cry and
   release
The anxiety of perilous years of
   down-trodden
Spirit.
I stumbled along, testing each
   novel

Insertion, pausing to examine the
   reaction and
Effect. Then a few carefully
   chosen phrases,
Blurted out the insecurity, the
   fantasies and
Untolerable circumstances of my
   existance.

Now, ragged inhibitions are put
   aside for the
Freedom of expression, for the
   out—pouring of
An enlightened, virgin soul,
   grasping the
Realm of reality and choking the
   meddlesome
Incongruities of a society
   structured on
Facades of defeatism.

But, is it real for me to say, "I
   have just
Begun to fight and write?" Is it
   real to
Envision grand rewards of praise
   for the
Simplicity of the heart put on
   paper? Is it
Real to wish, to hope, to prepare
   mentally for
The contest of life's challenges?

If the answer is YES, then
"I HAVE JUST BEGUN TO
   WRITE!"

Lisa Elaine Spradling
REMEMBERING
I see the pastel yesterdays of a
   summer
I feel the heat of a new dawn as a
   burning tear rools away
I remember myself as a child in
   the arms of a sturdy
   framework; a tower above me
I can hear laughter as I recall the
   field of grass filled with
   happiness
I can recall the years sneaking by,
   savoring every dream of my
   childhood
That dark figure protecting me
   from the wintery chills of
   external surroundings
I can feel the shelter still
I can see that fiery sun going
   down below the sea and the
   end of a lifetime
The taste of tears lingering on in
   my mind
I feel the sorrowful pain of a
   separation of two closely
   entwined hearts
The loneliness is forever
   imprinted in my soul,
   remembering the day when the
   love of a father was forever
   buried in the earth.

Heather Miller
SEAGULLS OF THE SKY
Suspended, motionless as evening
   stars
Majestically arrayed in gray and
   black.
Their heavenly domain can hold
   no bars
They claim the freedom we desire
   but lack.

Like dancers skilled for centuries
   in grace
They effortlessly, quietly,

smoothly swoop,
Then gliding, dipping, soaring
upward, race
As ballet artists, tilt their wings
and loop.

The silent air is pierced by shrill
wild screams
Their cry is born by passions
from the sea.
It cries of loneliness, or stormy
dreams;
A poignant call; a tired,
despairing plea.

Gray oceans, sandy beaches,
endless skies
These all are claimed from man
by seagull's eyes.

Doris Estelle Evans
SUMMER'S SONG
What joy, what joy to gaze
On these beautiful days
We see God's love and grace
In the peace and beauty
Of a lovely garden place
Around the greenery & trees
We feel the rhythms of eternity
What joy, what joy and faith
The beauty of a garden gate
The dappled shade of the trees
And the emeralds of the leaves
And the rhythms of a breeze
Ferns around the bird baths
And the singing of the birds
And the humming of the bees
Nature lovers—Summer's song
These, we have loved so long
Gardens & trees, a joy on earth
Nature's miracle and rebirth
In the eternal rhythms of time
The harmony and calming chimes
Is soothing in the trying times
And gives us peace and faith
'Til we reach the Pearly Gates

Trixie E. Austin
JUNE KITTEN
Thirteen years old so soon!
Roses bloom—
And die.

Helen Fisher Trehey
LITTLE BLUE STAR

---

*To dearest Andrew Of the blue,
blue eyes.*

Here, somewhere in my house,
There's lost a tiny star of blue.
It slipped from golden hands
That held it not quite true.

Awhile ago I saw
It shine a brightest blue.
I knew I should withdraw
The ring, while working too.

It gave me one last wink,
Just hoping I would think.
Oh why did I not lay
It on its velvet tray.

Now empty, empty prongs,
I'm sorry for my wrongs.
My bluest sapphire stone
You're lost and I'm alone.

Too small to ever sight?
I have a hope, all right,
I'd see you flash a light,
Then get you back tonight.

Another happy day—
I looked and there it lay!

Oh wondrous joy divine
You're here and still all mine.
Mary J. Watkins
SING GOLDEN HAWK
Beautiful Golden Hawk . . .
    you will never fly again!
Never more know the joy
    of soaring in the wind.
When far-away horizons
    beckon . . .
When mating season's near . . .
Heed not
    your glorious instincts.

For you,
    the sky holds fear!
Sing out!
    If you have the heart
    for it.
For memories of Freedom . . .
Sing!
Beautiful Golden Hawk
    with shot off wing.

Peggy E. Peter
SAN FRANCISCO DAWN
It's so early to stand here, I know,
But sleep left me an hour ago
And the radiant sky has captured
    my eye,
As I bask in the first morning
    glow!

It's as though it's the very first
    dawn
For a city just newly born;
The reds and the yellows, the
    violet and pink
Make me stand in amazement, to
    pause here and think!

The birds are all singing below
In a garden, to let us know
That day is approaching up on
    Nob Hill
And they will no longer be quiet
    and still!

Here in this moment, here by the
    Bay,
I see a great city awaken today,
While hushed by the window,
    transfixed I stand—
Has this happened before in some
    mystical land?

June A. Campbell
TAKE A LOOK
Take a Look
Even the poor fish
In the brook

Have you any
Spare time to
Read my book?

For each interruption
Takes from the mind
Thoughts soon lost

In the race of time
The words once heard
In the minds eye

Are all on a different
Wave length I find
Just a minute

A pencil in hand
Before they fly
With a magic wand

To appear
In written form
So they can't disappear!

Jeffrey Balaam
DINER
Blue plate special:
Three quarters
Two nickels
A cent.
Waitress Stella
Silverware's bent.

Monday meat loaf
Tuesday chicken
Wednesday pork chops
Thursday turkey
Friday beef stew

Saturday and Sunday
They stick to the menu.

Elsie F. Gerald
**A Farewell To An English
    Professor**
Dear Mr. Van, if I try I can.
You came, not to stay,
But not only to go away!

You came to light a flame.
You came to change the same.
You came to suffer blame.
You came to establish fame.

Never fear!
A tear from me you will not see,
Becoming a salty dew drop mere,
Falling to sear
Tomorrow's blade of grass
In any future literary class.

Thanks to you who taught true,
Achilles' shield
Will remain sane, to yield
Hope to cope, eternal cycles to
    reveal
The seal of progress,
Never any less, but more to
    confess,
In the minds of man,
Revived and heartened by God's
    fan.

You came, not to stay,
But not only to go away.
What is there more to silently say?
Nellie Parodi
IRINA
Irina, young woman poet of the
    Ukraine,
you have been sent to prison and
    to exile!
You are so fragile, harmless!
For the love of your people,
your heart echoes their pain . . .
Your verses had to burst, crying
    for justice!
Poets love light. Are you in a
    darkened dungeon?
In a psychiatric ward
to alter your brilliant mind,

thus denying the world
the beauty of your great poetry?
How can men's hearts be softened
by compassion and mercy?
We poets, your soul brothers,
strongly appeal that soon you be
    set free!
Our hearts bleed with your own!
Grace Gray
IF I HAD KNOWN
If I had known—You'd helped me
    when I was so alone.
If I had known—You'd helped me
    keep my home.
If I had known—You'd hold me so
    near.
If I had known I would not had
    fear.
If I had known God—Your
    promise came true.
If I had known—might I more,
    have rested in You!
If I had known—You could do
    anything.
If I had known—I'd of forgot my
    worries, insecurities, to which I
    cling.
If I'd had listened—what others
    tried to tell
My life would have been so much
    better as well!
If I had known the peace you
    portray—how You give a
    person a high everyday.
If I had known—No one could
    help me but You
Oh Lord! I wish for a chance, a
    chance to redo.
So that I might have rest in every
    adversity of my life.
The peace I could have had
    instead of such strife.
Tryin to work things out on my
    own—Oh God—If only—if
    only I'd known.
Jennie M. Root
THE PALM TREE
Among the trees grew a lonely
    palm
With roots deep down in the
    ground.
Stately it stood strong like a
    psalm,
A message it had in every round.

Towering high on its slender
    stem,
Fans on top with fingers dark
    green,
Whispering a prayer with a slow
    amen,
Imparting a feeling not seen.

Fans, Fingers moving in the wind
Whispering comfort and hope for
    the sad,
Waving "good—byes" to a young lad
Who'd left home because he'd
    sinned.

In words of Paul, "All have sinned."
Doomed to die in condemnation.
But God had planned salvation.
Fans waving, fingers moving in
    the wind.

But how if all have sinned?
Of works? All of us have cried.
Impossible! No matter how's been
    tried.
"Tis God's love gift." whispers the
    wind.

Our World's Best Loved Poems

Sharon Lee Spallone
SHADOWS

As off to sleep I sift
through consciousness and night,
shadows walk across my mind
to lead to heights where no man
    climbs
and miracles of wingless flight.
And with the day one would
    expect
illusion to pale against the bright,
but shadows walk, regardless of
    man's time.
Hold back the light of logic,
    truth, and fact.
Illuminate not the clime where
    shadows walk
and leave trace faint cross my
    mind,
for I travel a most willing slave
to reach the promised emerald sea,
where I can float in depths
    eternally
while shadows walk across my
    mind.

Linda Jeanne Thomas
TOMORROW'S POET

Today I got a compliment—
"no big deal", you may say,
but to this weary child-care
    mom—
it made it a worthwhile day!
A five-year old was at my knee;
I was reading aloud some poetry,
from my brand-new anthology.
Our day had been long,
and my toddlers were weary,
but they were piled in my lap
and very content—
when the little girl, with shining
    eyes, said,
"Linda, when I grow up I want to
    be just like you!
I want to take care of babies and
    write poetry—
just like you!"
Tomorrow I'll help her write a
    poem—
the first of many I'de wager!
Then someday, when she is
    grown,
she'll remember that first poem—
and read it aloud to babes of her
    own!

Meg Ann Garcia
YOU HAVE WON

You sit there so motionless
Staring out through the barred
    window
What's out there that's so
    intriging, old man
Or do you even know?

Your mind wanders often to
    places
that once you knew so well
I feel for you, old man
Since you can't even do that for
    yourself.

You seem to be waiting to fold up
    and die
And you are now in the Lords
    hand
And He will do as He will
With His lamb.

But the Lord has mercy on you
He will take you away in the
    early morning light
Then all your pain and suffering
will be over
And you will have won the fight.

Val Camenish Wilcox
ALTRUISTIC ALCHEMISTS

The heavy pestle of intolerance
Can grind to powdered hatred;
    can demean
Beliefs and attitudes at variance
With others. But within the
    mortar seen
Are yet small mounds of purest
    bonewhite sands
Quite finely ground from
    embryonic hope,
A pinch of candid trust, resilient
    strands
Of self, and measured grit with
    sense to cope.
Bless those rare people who can
    still perceive
All other folks to be humane as
    they,
Who choose to show compassion
    and believe
That good prevails; bless their
    naivette'.
When shall we learn, despite
    what has been taught,
That humans are far more alike
    than not?

George F. Mayer
A MIRAGE OF LOVE

As that one small drop fell upon
    my heart,
I wanted to run for cover
but it was that one small thought,
that led me to another.
Of misty dreams and foggy years,
with no hope of future sunshine.
My eyes at once were filled with
    tears,
as my mind recalled the time . . .
When we swam in the stream
of love together,
And the echo of that love,
made soft ripples on the water,
we thought would last forever

John I. Hancock
ECHO

An early light awakened me,
    I was cold.
Soon the sun shone brightly,
    And warm.
Young was the flowering day,
    So was I.
As day went on, it became a song,
    A lovely song.
With a higher sun, greater warmth,
    Delicate warmth.
So high, so high, the flaming sun,
    For a little while.
The sun dropped, merged with day,
    Beautiful day.
The warmth cooled, day faded.
    So did I.

Marguerite C. Curry
A TRYST

From the Hand of the greatest
    Giver
A little gem of time,
A thought that the world may
    treasure
And a tryst with words that rhyme.

Perhaps it's a song of gladness
Or a proud, triumphant strain,
That the writer makes immortal
For the ages to retain.

Or it may be a song of sorrow
That's wrung from a broken heart,
A song that the mute may borrow
When the burning teardrops start,

But the great eternal music
Swells on the sea of time,
From a wordsmith's busy toiling
And a tryst with words that rhyme.

Richard Moussallem

Richard Moussallem
VALENTINE

*This poem was written to my
lovely wife "Monika", that
inspired my writings with her
beauty, wit and charm.*

My best wishes for you in
    Valentine
You invaded my heart, like the
    Christ
That conquered with love
    palestine.
I always dreamed of Aphrodite,
    and
Now she is all mine;
Goddess of beauty and love,
Doesn't matter they're both divine.
People blame me for intoxication,
They think I am addicted to wine,
The truth is, you're my only drink
Every time I take a sip of you,
I sink in my own wine;
I love you and I offer you myself
As a gift in valentine.

Mary Ellen B. Owen
SNOWDUST

*To Timothy, who coined the
word "snowdust" at age five.*

The Wind takes out his broom to
    sweep
The snow from out the sky
And shakes the broom so
    frantically,
It makes the snowdust fly.
The snow-white dust is swept in
    mounds
To be disposed of later—
Till tidy Sun gets rid of it
In her incinerator.

Linda Kathryn Zorn
THE FIRST AMERICANS

They were here in America long
    before the white man came
    from across the sea.
They worshiped this country as
their home . . . they knew every
    tree.
The Indian welcomed the white
    man with good will and good
    thoughts.
They had no idea of the future
    bloody wars with them to be
    fought.
The puritan era was a time of
    learning about each others
    faults.
Eventually their land was taken
    by force with selfish assaults.
The white man never payed for
    the Indian's land, at first he
    forcibly took it without a fight.
Who can say whether that
    method was morally right.
Their sacred land which they had
    inhabited for hundreds of years
    . . .
Was slowly being swallowed up
    despite their many tears.
Later they were to be referred to
    as savages
As a result of the white man's
    ravages.
Then came the great Indian wars.
The war dance drums could be
    heard afar.
They were only trying to defend
    what they rightfully thought
    was theirs . . .
The forests, the streams, the
    Buffalo, and the bears.
If only the Anglo had offered to
    pay for their land with food or
    money . . .
Perhaps the wars and deaths
    could have been averted,
    America would have been
    sunny.
Our forefathers truly believed
    they were doing what was right.
But the way in which they did it
    gave the Indian no choice but
    to fight.
And when the fighting was over
    and the Indian lost, they were
    herded into reservations.
They were beaten, humiliated,
    and looked down upon as a Nation.
Their beautiful lands upon which
    the Buffalo roamed
Were now totally white-man
    owned.
The present day Indian still has
    his pride.
Kindled by the courage with
    which his ancestors died.
They were the first true
    American, we must admit that
    much.
Knowing that today, as then, they
    walk tall without any crutch.
Let us respect them for their
    proud heritage, so old.
That is something that they
    possess that can never be
    stolen or sold.

Jon Albert Berry
A LITTLE HOUSE

I live in a little house
That sits high on a hill

23

John Campbell, Editor & Publisher

Though Storms rise and Winds
blow
It keeps standing still
Outside are a few shade trees
Yews, I believe they are named
And a Colorado Spruce
That highlights its wooden frame
Inside is not very wealthy, but
comfortable
I'll admit
A few beds, a table, fan and couch
Two rockers for guests to sit
About eight windows last counted
Ornated with a homely touch
But most of all a family abides
Full of love and care
We've agreed that means so
much
And though we cannot afford
The things we would like to spare
We can afford to give our love
God gave us to share
So come visit our little house
A home with open doors
You will be truly welcomed
For waht we have is yours.

David Michael Matuch
THE MIND'S EYE

*To those beset with problems,
mental, physical, or spiritual—
There always lies a hope for a
new and better existance,
somewhere . . .*

A rose, a tulip, beautiful to sight,
scent and touch,
Meant to be joyfully shared
With those we love, so very
much,
And those for which we've
cared . . .

But alas' all of earth must surely
die;
The flowers, the birds, every
worldly thing.
Even so, all will live in the
Mind's Eye,
And Life will be renewed the
following Spring. . .

Lonnie Shuster
MOMMIE DEAREST
If there were to be just one more
day
Before this old world were to pass
away,
I'd choose to spend it with you.

For I was born when I met you
And I have lived each day that
you have loved me
And when the time comes for
you to leave me, I'll cry.

Veola Victoria Barnes
THE POST CARD
Opening the mailbox
I found it.
Trembling
I held it.
Filled with emotion
Read it.
You asked,
Do I remember Cap Ducal.

Yes,
I see the scene
Once more;
Sea, sky, wine,
Our love,

Caressing touch
Thine, mine
That once
Meant so much
That free summer
In Cap Ducal . . .

Martha Colbert Griffin
Walk Through This Life
If I be but once walk through this
life but once.
Let me be true to my self.
If I can't be true to myself how
can I be true to my fellow man.
If all my tears has been in vain.
If I have not felt life pain.
If I have not known joys and
sorrow of loves of many kinds.

If I have not reach out my hand
to my fellow man
If my ears has not heard.
If my eyes has not seen.
If I have not said a prayer for
mankind.
If I have not helped some trouble
soul then surely my life has
been in vain

Marijane G. Ricketts
BLUE FLAMES AND ASHES
In November's still-life pallor
a moon pale-faced
frosts marble cool
The naked trees: I, too,
now quiet, less than colorless,
earthbound, stand stilled
amid their unlatched leaves.

Life brown-wrapped and leaf
encrusted
in respite from eternal growing,
encumbered, sleeps
within the snowing.

Interleaved with moonlight
marble cool,
life will return
to showing infant leaf
With spring again renewed: I, too,
I shall survive
the winter knowing.

Thelma L. Reusser
NIGHT SOUNDS

*To all my beloved family, who
share and enjoy the NIGHT
SOUNDS of our beautiful
Strawberry Mt. area.*

On the porch at night
Breezes caressing my brow;

Quiet flutter of the Cottonwood
leaves,
And the frogs all singing—

The babbling of the water over
the rocks,
Night birds softly chirping;
A calf bawling for its mother,
And the frogs all singing—

The hoofs of the horse in the
pasture
Blowing thro' his nostrils as he
feeds;
A "pick—up" hurries by and
voices swish in passing,
And the frogs all singing—

One coyote yips, another howls,
Dogs announce their presence;
The heavy sound of the log
trucks rolling,
And the frogs all singing—

A jet plane on course,
Wind in the wings of a bat
swooping low,
Crickets in the grasses,
And the frogs all singing—

Dawn breaks and roosters
crowing,
Turkeys near-by in full
conversation,
The punctuation of traffic—
And the frogs still singing!

Kathy L. Habash
REFLECTION
I am not now
What I once was
For I have made discoveries of me
And many changes have occurred.

Linda M. Olson
ONE MAN
I love but one man
with my heart all I can,
He's in my sweet dreams
when the bright moon beams,
His kiss is so tender
my lips will forever remember,
His hands are soft and smooth
and always help to soothe,
The days we spend together
never bring us stormy weather,
His eyes of the deepest, darkest
brown
brighten my face if ever I frown,
Sometimes he brings me a lovely
rose
and with it my love grows,
His hair of gold and brown
gives the illusion of a light
crown,
With my heart all I can
I'll always love but one man.

Barbanel Borah
THE WAYWARD ANGEL
If you see the girl that's forsaken
me
Tell her I'm lonely, tell her I'm
blue;
When she left me, with another
man to be
It has hurt me through and
through.

If you see the girl that told me
That she loved me and would
be true
Tell her I want her, tell her I'll
take her
Though she deceived me; why,
I never knew.

Ask her to tell you why she's
forsaken me
When I loved her, and this she
knew;
Ask her why she told me she
loved me
And then left me for somebody
new.

Ask her why my heart she is
breaking
And what gave her the right,
this deed to do:
A human being whose love she
was taking,
Leading him to believe she
loved him too.

If you see that wayward angel
That fell from heaven to the
depths below,
Tell her I forgive her, tell her I'll
help her
To find the grace she used to
know.

Evelyn Marie Diebolt
SUICIDE

*Dedicated to my Relief, Mister
Larry Gene Finn*

Torture
Pain
Grief
Help

Gun
Click
Bang
Relief

Cynthia O'Hara Clifford
FAR-OFF LAND
There's a far-off land I dream of,
where the sun shines hot all day.
Where the cities bustle is stilled—
and the soul is filled—with an
elevating force—from some divine
source.
Where hatred is displaced—by
joy
on every face.
Where horror is unknown,—and
beauty—
like a polished stone is
everywhere.

Where man's brutality is
something
yet to be,
and woman is a total entity.

Where man's salvation does not
exist,
because he has been kissed by
immortality.

Nancy Jones Greathouse
NOTHING IS SAID

*To Our Loving and Faithful
Mother, Reba Jones—1952*

There are things to which we
children concern,
Of what you do and give for
nothing in return.
From day to day nothing is said—
We keep our thoughts in our head.
No daddy have we to help you
today,
While you work so hard and we

24

at play.
I'm the oldest of seven and I am able—
To see how hard—for bread on our table.
We children can't realize what you go through
To do for us what you must do
At night I hear you say a prayer before bed,
To keep on going with full strength ahead.
No gripe or complaint does anyone hear,
We never see you shed a tear.
We take what is never earned
Not thinking, "It's to be returned".
There's no "thank you" that you get,
And surely there's no regret.
Cause you know we love you—as you see each day through
I only pray, I can be like you.
And when in dreamless sleep you finally rest,
We'll all remember that you did your best,
And we'll lay our heads upon our bed
Our hearts will love you, yet, nothing is said.

Jack P. Reale
WHY
Who am I
Who made me and why
Is there something I must do
And in some way will it help you
Is it something I'll do or say
Will it change you in some way
Oh! I hope it's for good
And I live this life like I should
And who are you
What are you going to do
Let's just help each other
After all your my brother
And just maybe
Someone else will see
That's the way life should be
And that's why God made me

John N. Jones
FAREWELL
Walk in peace, my friend,
'til you come to rainbow's end.
May the Spirit guide your feet;
in all that you do be right and meet.
May Christ's salvation light your path,
and your careful answer turn away wrath.
The Word of God your lips confess,
and may your house forever blessed—
with the Rock as its foundation—
make its pillar Christ's salvation.
Fill your heart with joyful song;
in the Lord grow tall and strong.
Turning from evil, partake of the Word;
nourish your soul in His body and blood.
Consider the Lamb who for us died.
Walk with Jesus by your side.

Dolores Howe
PEACE AGAIN
In my neighborhood peace and quiet reigned supreme

Until son and teen-aged grandson returned home.
Oh my such horrendous sins those two did have—
Drugs, robberies, violence, home destruction.
Suddenly, one day peace and quiet reigned supreme.
To grandmom I did go. "Where are Chris and Bill?"
She smiled serenely; bliss upon her face.
'Oh didn't you know—they have moved away to jail.

Casey Lee Reeves
HAIR
It's straight
It's curly
It's kinky too
It's wavy
It's thick
And now it's thin on you
It's on fingers
It's on toes
Heck it's even in your nose
Doesn't matter where it grows
It's just there!

Juanita M. Reed
BE THANKFUL
Be thankful for youth, for we grow too soon old.
Be thankful for the sun, for it gives life and warms when cold.
Be thankful for the rain that nourishes our fields of corn.
Be thankful for the roses, don't complain about the thorns.
Be thankful for the blue sky, for too soon it darkens with threatening clouds.
Be thankful for the green carpet under bare feet, all too soon it turns brown.
Be thankful for life; for its span is short as the twinkling of an eye.
Be thankful for kindness and gentleness, for so much has gone awry.
Be thankful for love, there is too much hatred in the world.
Be thankful for Old Glory, that she has remained unfurled.
Be thankful for beauty in our trees and flowers that bloom.
Be thankful for our birds that delight us with cheery song.
Be thankful for the dawn, for it signals the birth of a new day.
Be thankful for the twilight hours, a time to rest and rejuvenate.
Be thankful for good friends, they aid us in time of need.
Be thankful for our family, who provides the anchor in thought and deed.
Be thankful for good health, and an abundance of food to eat.
Be thankful for our wonderful country where we can live free.
Be thankful for all the good things in your life, they far outweigh the bad.
Be thankful for today, forget yesterday, and what you might have had.

James Richard Fishman
Contemplation On Mortality
Here we live
a length of time
to learn
and question
why
we live and learn
in this short time.

Lillian L. Gerbig

Lillian L. Gerbig
FRUSTRATION
When I was young, I dreamed, as now I dream,
   Of racing through the channels of the earth
And o'er the highways with a torch of flame—
   Hola! I meant to set the world on fire!
And ever growing older, I would seem
   To gain some wisdom since my hour of birth:
But still this conflagration is my aim,
   To kindle it, is still my hot desire.

Oh, he must have the energy to scheme,
   Who picks a task of such stupendous girth;
Must plan to keep on racing, free of blame,
   In case his torch should make a blazing pyre:

But me . . . the gods, to me, by some mischance,
   Gave only energy enough to dance . . .

Martin C. Mayer
ODE TO A STEPSON
Although not of my flesh
I have watched you daily grow
From a small child
To a fine young man
And must admit,
And want you to know
That across that span
You somehow became a son.

To what end
Do we think along lines of blood
When we assess who is there for us?
How many of the consanguine horde,
As they mature, sear our souls with their selfish fuss

And give nothing in return? I'm bored
With those who bitch and cuss,
Ensnared in their guilty belief
   that consanguinity
Requires us to give and give our
   guts away on a one way
      street to Infinity!

Stepson or son,
It's just a definition
Having naught to do with the human intuition
In the caring and sharing of whatever
The two of us have found together.
And share we have . . .
That seems to be the key
Of what you really are to me.

So, after all is said and done,
I must admit
Across that span
Of ambivalent equivalent,
You somehow became a son.

Carolyn Mattoon Sessa
A Part of Me (My Little Son)

*Written for my son . Jon . . .
Someday he would know the truth. This 'my first time published; Eternal Thanks to my friend Mo Florida for her faith, and to E. L. Cole for her encouragement.*

My little son I miss you more;
   Much more than words can say.
I think of you at last each night,
   And first of each new day.
I don't know what you're doing now,
   Or know where you might roam.
Inside my heart you're very close,
   Although so far from home.
Your dad must love you very much;
   To keep you hid away.
A part of me has been with you;
   I hope he'll let it stay.
All I can do is ask the Lord;
   To keep you safe and sound.
And if you ever need me there;
   That I will sure be found.
For there's no more contentment here;
   A part of me you are.
I won't feel whole again until;
   Until you're not so far.

Greta Abel—Abrahamsen
OH, SUN . . .
Oh, Sun . . .
Glistening, golden goblet,
Glowing gilded grace . . .
You melt my musing mind's delights
As you dance upon my face!

For one with such a task so great
As illuminating galaxies entire . . .
Why is it you never cease to shine,
May I ever so innocently inquire?

Rare refractions, rose to ruby range,
Inspirational indigo, into violet may change.
How such an array of colors
Is possible to display

From a single ray, so pure and clear,
Leaves my humble brain in dismay!

Fine flagrant, fiery flarings,
As facets of a gem,
Reminisce of volcanic vicissitude . . .
A veritable molten mayhem!

Come you to spray our shadowy domain
With truth and wisdom bright?
Or is it just this world of ours
Is sadly lacking light?

Who was it once who raced to rise
And touch your radiant robe?
Icharus, indeed,
Thought wings apropo'
In departing our dear, dull globe!

No nimble nymph
Could draw so nigh
Without waxing her wings, too . . .
And that is why
I sit from afar . . .
To lovingly look at you!!!

Arlette R. Hobbs
BLACKBRIER ESTATE
A mere six o'so eones ago,
  I did stray in the forbidden woods.
Beneath oaks discovering statues green;
  Deep in glens where a tower stood;
Methinks was a hermits retreat!

A dim, decayed; most mysterious place;
  All trailing with bramble shoots—
Where pale clustered wild-rose entwined
  Low crumbling walls; festooned
With blackberries devine.

And a silence . . .suspense;
  Seemed to envelop one there!—
As pushing thro' vine-tangled growth
  And up a steep mossed stair;
I appeared reflected in pools below.

Quietly stood, I surveyed dim woods
  Shimmering beyond. 'Til absently,
Bower's unusual discerned I—
  And within, midst half-light's peace;
A madonna white, held a rose to the light.

Donna Heiken Strother
GRANDMAS

*in honor of her grandmother
Mary Eiben Heiken*

Grandmas are such precious things,
They tie us to their apron strings.
Friends may come and friends may go . . .
But Grandma stays steadfast . . . you know.
Guiding and helping all that she can,
In our growth as woman or man.
Giving praise and love when it's needed.
Pointing out problems that need to be heeded.
Keeping quiet . . . or giving advice,
Knowing just when to . . . perfect foresight.
They come in sizes . . . large or small,
Skinny . . . short . . . fat . . . or tall.
It's hard for us to realize,
Grandma once a girl of our size.
For though we may be much wider and rounder,
We're lacking the knowledge that makes Grandma sounder.
Instead of growing older, they get younger each year.
The grey hair they add just makes them more dear.
For we know each one has its own secret reason . . .
As grandchildren change and are added each season.
But Grandmas the same . . . year after year,
To be a little like her . . . "Oh God, do you hear?"
With understanding, foresight, love, charm and the rest.
I wonder how I'll rank when put to the test.
When years have gone by will I be able to be,
Half the Grandma to mine, that you were to me?

Keay Brosseit
WHERE ROSES BLOOM
A scandalous red carnation
And a feisty old thorn,
Together,
In a flower bed
Where a lovely rose
Was born.

Connie Craig
ON A POEM REJECTED

To my brother, Joe, who made me practice my grammar.

If I can sing it in one word,
Why then must I use three?

Must I paint it up and down,
Twist its meaning round and round,
Beat my breast and heave a sigh,
Toll it like the bell on high,
Fill my every word with fire,
Drip and drag it through the mire?

If I do then we will see
My subject shall be bored of me.

If I can cull one word from three
Editor, please let it be.

Eugenia Viskantas
CRAZY
A man drives his car 300 miles per hour,
And, another man is jumping off a sky high tower.
The kids smoke marijuana, and take L.S.D.
And, some strange lady is eating live bumble bee's.

  They call this being crazy.

A little girl wears ribbon in her hair,
And the dog follows in his masters trail.
Everyone is saying please, and thank you,
And everyone is smiling too.

  They call this being sweet as a daisey.

A man blacksout from to much alcohol.
A lady is banging her head against a wall.
Yesterday is very easy to forget.
Tommorrow seems so far away yet.

  They call this being hazy.

A lady stays in bed til past noon,
And, her husband is in bed before the moon.
A man is to tired to go to work,
And, his wife is to tired to wash his shirt.

  They call this being lazy.

To all men, women, boys, and girls,
This is your surrounding world.
Things might not seem hazy, and you might not be lazy,
And, if your not as sweet as a daisey,

  I think we are all crazy!

Korki Patricia Hale
AT ATTENTION
We stood at attention—
All in a row
Eyes toward the ground.

The flag-bearers come—
In solemn march,
One calls to attention—
His throat dry and parched.

The flag is unfolded
—Not touching the ground.
We raise up our eyes—
And hear not a sound.

The flag slowly rises
With its backdrop of the sea,
—And stops at half-mast.
Will you say goodbye for me?

Fern Johnson
The Spring By the Side of the Road
So delicious, so cool, clear as glass—
You could see your own reflection
As tho' you were staring in a mirror.
From whence did it come? From the hillside
By the side of the road that wandered
By the old reservoir? Like the Miracle of Lourdes?

We drank, first little sips, dipped with our hands,
Relishing the purity of this spring
By the side of the road. Then with great gulps
As tho' we may never taste its sweetness ever again.
It was only a spring, a stopping place
On our way home from school, our books
Placed carefully to one side so we could lie flat
On our bellies and partake to the fullest
Of this special treat by the side of the road.
That was more than fifty years ago
And when I went in search of it the other day
It was not there—nothing looked the same.
Weeds had overrun every inch of space
Sticks and dry leaves had hidden all
The familiar places we used to treasure
Each day as we hurried to reach that little
Spring that was our oasis
By the side of the road.

Douglas Logterman
GOD'S VAST OCEAN
A river flows into a sea
And that's the way life is meant to be
Begin somewhere but start out slow
Increase momentum as you go
Take it easy around the bends
Trust your instincts when making friends
Hopefully silt will not appear
And make your life harder to bear
Between the banks your life should stay
Remain content both night and day
As your life ends, keep your motion
Never ending, in God's vast ocean

Anthony R. Crump
BLACKBIRD
Blackbird flying crazily
Turning cartwheels in the sky
Earthbound passer-bys
Consumed by their jealousy
Angrily curse its flight
Wasted time and motion
Blackbird he don't care
When was the last time
They danced amidst the clouds
Or inspired breathless wonder

Michael J. O'Brien
R.S.V.P. LORD
Uncollected Sunday school instruction
lies buried under years of amnesic dust.
Just one or two souveniers I can still recall.
Like the one-armed Barbie doll
we baptised with holy (fountain) water
from down the hall.
I remember being naked in short-sleeves

when having been told long-
sleeves were a must.
On course, in procession
for my first taste of Jesus.
Notebooks half filled with
penciled sketches
of "thou shall not's".
So clouded is my review, so little
I can retrace.
Hoping now to find a sign,
cement my faith.
Let me end this uneven race.
What's the plot? I'm half awake.
Why so many choices I have to
make?
Talk to me, shout me a sign.
Neon would be nice, call me,
I'm in the phone book.

N. Faye Thompson
THOUGHTS OF LOVE

For Kracker

I raise my glass and toast
the ending of another day—
Hoping tomorrow will ease
this pain for me.
The next rising of the sun
is for you, my love,
For I still must wish for you
all beautiful days.
I will sit and watch the sun
climb over the roof tops
And my thoughts will be of you.
Maybe you will think of me
today—and know that I am
always with you.

Lori Lamkin
FRIENDS

Lord, protect my friends, protect
them all.
Keep them safe behind that
wall.
Guide them through the night,
Heal those who do not have
sight.
Make them whole, whole as can
be,
And help others so they can be
free.
Watch over them night by day,
And make sure they're
friends—friends to stay.
Help those whose heart is sad,
That they may be free, free and
glad.
Make sure I don't lose my friends
and ponder,
Because I want to see them
way over yonder.
And no more sadness, no more
fear,
Dear Lord, they're my friends—
and they're dear.

M. P. Morrissette
AMONG THE CLOUDS

As we climbed to the summit of
the mountain
you looked so small and alone
standing in the cleft of its great
shadow
soon the wind broke all shadows
into stone
and we climbed stone upon stone
to the top
the only songbirds were within us
singing against the wind's shrill
whistle
we held on to each other's joy

until it became one with the wind
while we danced and laughed
through the clouds
running to catch the sun as it
sped by
trying to hold it forever inside us
our element became
air—celestial—pure
a prelude to the spirit awakening
within us
yet our feet held the firm earth
beneath our sky.

Paul P. Czech Jr.
A FATHER'S PRAYER

Please watch over our children,
God Almighty,
And keep them free of evil and
despair.
Fill their hearts with peace and
sincerity,
And guide them through life with
Thy loving care.
Share with each little one, Thy
tenderness,
And let Thy humbleness within
them dwell.
Teach them Thy understanding
and kindness,
So that they may forever serve
Thee well.

Above all, forgive them for being
weak,
If occasionally they go astray;
But when Thy help, they
desperately seek,
Please be there Oh Lord, to show
them the way.
With Thy blessings, let our
children grow,
For they are the parents of
tomorrow.

Alice Causey Gilfert
DAWN

A clear blue sky,
Stars clinging to the last
fragments of night,
Trees silhouetted against the
heavens,
Bringing the songs of birds to
write the symphony of the day!
Trees, silkened gowned ladies
with rustling taffeta slips,
Lift their flowing skirts in time to
the music in their midst.
Jewel adorned grass catches the
sparkle of the slowly rising sun
To glitter the earth with rare
beauty.
A great glowing ball of reddish—
orange peeks over the horizon,
Spreading fingers of light to touch
the earth with dawn.
The innocence of a new day, like
a joyful child skips into being.
Where you go or what you do
with this precious gift of life
Rests entirely upon the powers
within you.

Wendy K. Clifton
COMMON CLAY

Lord, to me You've given no
"vision",
No call to live and breathe;
Just an ordinary way of life
To do with as You please.

No fortune, fame and glory,
No earthly courts to rule.
I am common clay, not glittering

gold;
Just an ordinary tool.

Only ordinary words to speak
To tell of Your sovereign plan,
To the ordinary woman
And the ordinary man.

With an ordinary tongue I share
Your extraordinary love,
That those of us below can know
The blessings from above.

William L. Bongard
Strength and Weakness

To All Those With Head Injury

Our Strength Is The Key
To establish true reality,
If we cause the recline
Of man's troubled mind.

The realism of faithful thought
To have emotions thrive.
In a brain that is wrought
With a conscience to survive.

The problem with anxiety
Is ego to be free,
To have dreams that adjust
With a God we trust.
If we could only wish
Under the spell of remorse,
Our weakness to admonish
Along life's rugged course.

Florence E. Brytcuk
GOD'S WORLD

Far away in outer space,
We see the earth in all its grace.
It looks so peaceful hanging there,
It's hard to see that peace is rare.
Down near the dark and dampen
ground,
Groups of ants called humans
can be found;
Crawling in the mire of their hate,
Bent on hastening their own fate.
To kill and destroy all men oppose,
Fighting for power of all the land.
Calling an enemy, his fellow man.
If one would raise his bended head,
In his mind see the earth instead,
As it rolls along in outer space.
We are all brothers of every race,
None can take the place of God
Divine.
To rule this home of all mankind.
We must learn to love all others,
Knowing in our hearts the we are
brothers.
Then all wars and hate will end.
Pece on earth, good will toward
men.

Virginia Stonestreet Bush
DAWN IS DAY

Out of the dark, dark Darkness
Dawn, Like a maiden from a
trysting
With her lover, comes slowly,
silently,
Peeping with only a glimmer of
light
At the darkest edge of night.
And on yonder mountain's
Highest peak
A golden halo like a crown
comes slowly, slowly, slipping
down
As the world turns her back on
Irrepressible, irrestible, advancing
Dawn
A pink blush fades the stars away,
Birds awake and sleepy voices
Sing their prayers to coming day.
Valleys are oceans of purple
shadows
As night mists slowly roll away.
Then Dawn, in heavenly splendor
of
Mauve, rose, fire and golden party
dress
Steps forth. In breathless awe we
wait
While she hesitates. Then earth
like a loving
mother greeting a child with
wayward ways,
Flings wide her arms in loving
embrace.
The glory fades and Dawn is Day.

Mrs. Nancy B. Jensen
MY SON

*For my son Michael J. Pope my
love always, Mom*

My son is part of me,
The Best Part I Believe.
I Hope, And Pray, That in his day,
He will Never Just be Me.

Kenneth C. Duncan
MY FRIEND

Everybody should have someone,
Someone to call their own.
Everybody should love someone
And not be all alone.
Companionship and love are right
Now this is plain to see,
For it's a long and lonely night
Alone—Oh, Poor old me.

Be my friend, for a friend is love
And love is what I need.
Fly swiftly as the fleet-winged
dove,
Come gently, yet with speed.
Ease my pain, my suffering end
With love that's sweet and free.
Be my wonderful, loving friend,
No longer—poor old me.

Now you, my friend are always
there
Whenever there is need,
You always let me know you care
And all my troubles heed.
A true friend and one whose
giving
Is as welcome as can be,
Truly makes this life worth
living,
Oh, Happy, happy me.

Billie Bogart Church
SADAT—AUGUST 1981
"A man of Peace died today!"
That's what the people say.
Once again the wicked slay!
As of yore—out Golgotha way.

Until the Prince of Peace comes
    again
All crusaders will be slain
By jealous sons of Cain.
"No peace!" they cry, on this
    terrain.

Guyla Wallis Moreland
NEW BEGINNING
Star crossed
Star bossed
What is the difference?

I am Taurus—
Bull headed and blind
To my faults.

Let stars be crossed
Let me be bossed
By signs of the Zodiac

As across life's stage
I walk.
In the final ending

Past all beginning
I stalk
Forth with Death

Always winning.

Richard T. Barrus
MY THOUGHTS OF HER
I don't know how to tell her how
    I feel,
Nor show her what I really mean
    to say
By putting into words or actions
    real
The many little thoughts that
    pass my way.

How does one say a thing a
    different way,
That needs be said so often and
    so tender,
Without a varied meaning gone
    astray
Or seeming just to be a mere
    pretender?

I guess I'll have to go right on
    thinking
My thoughts of her as if I had the
    power
To speak aloud through tears of
    joy unblinking,
And build of them a mighty
    thoughtful tower.

Belva C. Call
BE QUIET
I'm talking to you, Daddy
    The little fellow said,
Please be quiet, go to bed.
    But I'm talking to you, Daddy
In childish voice he cried,
    Can't you see, I'm busy now
A tired daddy lied.
    I'm talking to you, Daddy
Won't you listen now?
    Maybe sometime later
He evaded him somehow.
    I wish you'd ever listen
A sturdy young man said,
    Never happen! He mumbled off
    to bed.

Why can't I ever reach you, Son?
    A lonely old man cried

I'm sorry, Dad, I'm just so busy
    Impatiently he lied.
If only you could listen,
    Understand my need . . .
Silence, the words he did not heed
    I'm talking to you, whispered
    from the past
Echoed to the heart of him
    Who heard those words at last.

Lyllian D. Cole

Lyllian D. Cole
They Cry and Cry and Cry

To All God's Creatures

Two baby bears, left whimpering
    their mother has been shot
The mighty hunter shot her dead
    he gives the cubs no thought

He cannot wait, he shoots her
    down
    and skins her out right there
The cubs, bewildered, tumble
    'round
    to search within the lair

She dared the power fence to take
    the honey for her young
Her just desserts, her ancient
    right
    as right as air for lung

The hunter drags her thick warm
    pelt
    back to his cattle ranch
To hang it spread upon a board
    to dry from top-most branch

He doesn't want or need the meat
    too coarse, too tough, too bland;
The British troops acquire them
    for bear-skin hats so grand

Two orphaned cubs, two
    innocents—
    forlorn—they mewl and cry
They tumble, lost, without her
    scent
    THEY CRY AND CRY AND
    CRY.

Jois Ann Gould
DESTINY

*Dedicated to the town of
Elizabeth with a happiness in hand*

But ah my friends
And ah my foes
It was a great
    Event
The spanning of

The years
That twixt was
    My fate.

It snapped and
    Cracked
And caroused
    Around
And lead in
    All directions
But put together

After all the
    Years
Leads in one
    Direction.

Who can care
Who can express
Its like a guess
    And a vision
Hidden to most
And seldom
    Less
Called destiny
Of the turning road.

Frances M. Burns
PEACE
East is East, and West is West,
And now, the 'twain have met.
No longer do we live apart,
So let us not forget.

The sky is not a cover,
Nor a barrier the sea.
We have TV— Radio,
And the truth shall make us free.

Of White, Black, Red or Yellow,
Varied tongues and colors,
Are we roving Gypsy bands
Or, Tinkers known by others?

We hope to all remember
That when the sun has set
We muse upon this message
"Yes", and now the 'twain have
    met.

Michael Largay
REUNION
I have a picture of you as a dear
    girl
Holding a kitten.
You were wistful, ungraceful, poor,
    unlovely—
Except to me,
And I loved you and you loved me.
I see you now, years later,
As a woman, lithe, lovely and rich
By your own perfection and skill,
A masterpiece made by trifles,
One after the other, into
    perfection;
And I am a forgotten poet,
    singing into the night.
I died for love of you a thousand
    times
And lusted after your crimson lips
And lovely milk-white arms
And the soft smoothness of you.
I yearned and beat the walls for
    want of you.
I could not live; I could not die.
Oh, how I wanted you!
I sit here in your home,
Queen of all loveliness,
Earned by your exotic talent.
I sip my drink and watch you and
    there is love in your eyes,
Love engendered by pity
For the man you once knew.
You are not the little girl I knew

so long ago.
I shall drink my drink and go.

Oliver Ellsworth Frazier
TO AN ELDERLY FRIEND
You should always know you are
    not alone,
Because loneliness is the blanket
Of this earth.
Beneath it you have the comfort
Of us all.

In your childhood memories
They are still with you.
Your truth, your love,
The strengths you share
Abide.

Rejoice
Where past and future meet;
For yours is the grace of years,
And of your own light
Which will never cease.

Jean Gullette
For Love Of One's Parents
"She's been born with a silver
    spoon in her mouth
Has 'oft been said of me

Yes, I was born, with the silver
    spoon
But not monetarily

The wealth of a lifetime
My parents gave to me
Devotion, truth and honor
And a sense of destiny

Nothing was mentioned of riches
For they knew where riches lie
Within the heart and soul of us
Until the day we die

They gave me the love of their
    lifetime
I carry that love constantly
It's helped me through times of
    deep despair
And soothed the heart in me

So, yes, I was born, a silver spoon
    in my mouth
But with a difference as you can
    see
For there is no greater wealth on
    earth
Than our heritage, which is free

Now, if you were born with that
    silver spoon
Count your blessings your whole
    life through
And voice your thoughts to your
    mom and dad
While they're able to listen to you."

George M. Dile
MY EYES

*This poem was written for my
beautiful wife Yvonne. Briefly,
the Lord teaches us (in His Word)
how important it is that we keep
our eyes on Him at all times,
"that we may be able to comfort
them which are in any trouble. . ."
(II Cor. 3-7)*

"As you look into My eyes for
    love,
    you can see from whence you
    have come,
    and the prize that's waiting up
    ahead,
    your life has just begun.

You speak to Me of laughter and
tears,
    the essence of everyday life,
of every breath and every
moment,
    of everything that's right.

My eyes can fill your night with
song,
    whenever you're far from home,
because they're set upon your
heart,
    that you might continue on.

They pierce the inner heart of
hearts,
    and help you to realize,
of all earths many treasured gifts,
    you need My spiritual eyes.

Eyes that whisper I love you so,
    that say I always will,
that draw you closer to My side,
    to know you deeper still.

So surrender your laughter and
the tears,
    and I will set you free,
for I Am that I Am the Lord of all,
    and I will always be."

Shawna Long
The Lord Is My All In All
You're my ray of hope,
When life seems hopeless.
You're my beacon of light,
When I'm living in darkness.
You're my source of strength,
When I'm feeling nothing but
weakness.
You're my one true friend,
When I'm feeling friendless.
You're my all in all,
You're my life and love,
Without you I'm little,
But with you I'm much.

Carla Williams
SHADOWS
Silence
Always the silence
Will it ever cease to exist
It runs through the back of my mind
Shadowing my dreams
Shadowing my desire

And the rain still spatters against
the window pane
Creating pools of ice cold water
that
    rush through my soul
I begin to conceive the coldness
I begin to conceive the numbness
And the shadows exist no more

Mabel E. Downing
SUMMER ODYSSEY
It stretched far out beyond me,
    pale green from east to west,
and when the wind blew briskly
    its waves would roll and crest.

A flight of darting swallows
    reminded me of gulls,
and maybe in the shallows
    lay broken rusty hulls.

I dreamed my brig went sailing
    to strange enchanting lands,
to ventures bold and daring,
    on wild exotic strands.

Had clippers cruised out bravely,
    their snowy sails unfurled,
with gallant crews so carefree
    to roam around the world?

Did pirates fierce attacking,
    the skull and crossbones fly,
their guns and cannons blazing
    to win the fight, or die?

Were chests of gold once yielded
    to Vikings on a raid?
Not on this rippling wheat field
    from which my sea was made!

Carol Lynn Stalder
WHAT I SEE

---

*This poem is dedicated to all the
people who helped me to achieve
my regular high school diploma. I
hope that it will inspire other
handicapped people to strive to
reach their goals.*

I close my eyes
And what do I see?
A photovision
Of days to be.

I see myself
Walking down the aisle
I'm really and truly
Dressed in style.

Next I seem to be
In a cap and gown.
I'm really the happiest
Girl in town.

A tall gentleman
Dressed in blue
Is handing me
A diploma too.

A regular diploma
It really is!
I've worked so hard
To achieve this.

Betty Jane Phillips
THE DESERT SCENE
In the twilight of the evening
When the shadows start to fall
There's a hush upon the desert
And a lonesome coyote howls

Yuccas make grotesque figures
By the full moons' silvery light
And the stars shine like bright
diamonds
In the darkness of the night

A Bobcat lurkes behind some
rocks
Where majestic mountains stand
And cottontails go scampering
O'er the ever changing sand

Yes, it's peaceful on the desert
Where the lonely burros roam
And the little wild creatures
Make the desert their home

Pearl R. Lindberg
WATER
One night we watched the sea
It was never quiet, never still,
It's like leaving you and me
Water, coming, going with tide at
will.

Should we keep searching for a
goal
Will we ever find a peaceful soul,
We would be water if we could be
Blue deep water, leaving for the
sea.

As winds blow across the land
I'll reach out, holding your hand,

You will kiss me in bright
moonlight
As the water goes out to sea at
midnight . . .

You will be holding me in your
arms
I will hold fast to your hands,
Water will take us out to sea
While winds blow across the land

Jan Bratcher
SECRETS
We are enemies . . .
    We, who used to be in love.
I stand staring at you.
    You stand challenging me.
Neither of us speak . . .
    Neither of us cry.
We simply stand . . .
        apart . . .
            thinking . . .
                remembering . . .
                    reliving.

You shake your head,
    then turn and walk away.
A lump arises in my throat;
    tears fill my eyes.
I simply stand
    and watch you close the door.

Henry J. Dugan
Tonight Is the Last Time
Tonight is the last time I'll dance.
Gone are all signs of romance.
She doesn't hold my hand as
tightly.
She doesn't kiss me the same
nightly.
I was so filled with delight.
At her very nice sight.
She resembled a rose in her gown.
That eventful night we did the town.
We drank champagne until two.
Did all the things lovers do.
We promised to love till the end.
But the end was soon in view.
Tonight I'll make the rounds with
someone new.
Will tonight bring heaven or
bliss?
Will I respond to a brand new
kiss?
What is left for me to say?
Never thought I'd act this way.
Tonight is the last time I'll dance.
I'm thinking still of my last
romance.

Ken Benton
SHUFFLEBOARD QUEEN
Shuffleboard Queen
you've made the scene
with your tight jeans
to distract from the act
of shooting the board clean

shoot on dance wax queen
wipe the board down again
sprinkle new wax
in your special way
fine grains of dance dust
bounce as they hit
and line up in a pattern
made by flipping your hips
while you walk the length

the first puck is shot
slicing through
that finally formed layout
the game is on ceremony over
long and short games
begin and end

but for the queen of the board
its not whether
she wins or loses
its how she plays.
and who she plays with

Diane L. Agesen
EVERLASTING FRIENDS
I need to know you will always
be there,
To guard me, to hold me, to show
me you care.
Being there for you is all that I
know.
I promise to you—I'll never leave
you alone.
You are the joy in this life that
keeps me going strong.
If that part of me ended, my life
would be done.
I promise my love until my life's
end,
If you would be my lifelong
friend.

Please reassure me your love is
for real.
Tell me you feel the same way I
feel.
As long as my soul lives on, you
will find
My feelings for you will be gentle
and kind.
I promise my love until eternity's
end,
If we could be everlasting friends.

William Wayne Macumber
I'll Just Be Coming Home
I have sat atop a mountain
    watching clouds go drifting by.
I have watched the Eagle soaring
    in a crystal azure sky.
I have felt so near to Jesus
    I need only reach my hand,
To touch that sacred Heaven
    Moses called the Promised Land.

I have sat beside a campfire
    as the wind rushed through the
    trees,
And listened to the special song
    the wind sang just for me.
I have known that certain feeling
    that comes from knowing
    Christ,
And therein lies the reason
    for the wonders of my life.

There will be no real surprises
    in that Heaven in the sky.
I'll know no touch of sorrow
    when at last I too must die,
For I've seen a bit of Heaven

in these lovely things I've known;
So when this life is over
I'll just be coming home.

Ruth J. Smith
FRIEND AND LOVER
You're my friend, and you're my lover,
You're my strength to carry on . . .
You're my hope, you're my weakness,
And with you I made a bond . . .
You will be there when I need you,
You will comfort me at night . . .
You will always stand beside me,
Whether I am wrong or right . . .
This was promised to me, when you said
you were my man . . .

I will be there when you need me,
I will always understand . . .
I will be your friend, and lover,
just as long as you're my man . . .
And together we will make it,
for we have the *Golden Key* . . .
First you have to be friends,
before you're lovers
And we have that, you and me . . .

Gregory E. Gentile
IDYLL FOR THE DEAD

Dedicated to my grandfather, Pasquale Gentile, who fulfilled life's ultimate role on October 27, 1983

Oh, haunting Spirit of Forbearance!
Atonement for all that we reap!
Coalescing the Dawn with the Dusk,
Predestined with Sister Sleep.

Fervent for the realm of quietude
A promenade of sanguine souls,
Thru incessant corridors, void of time,
Forever to their ultimate roles.

Kimberly Bobinski
THE FAVORITE
The tattered toy lay on the shelf
just staring into space,
Beside the fluffy teddy bears
and dolls with satin lace.
Although it did not quite fit in
this stuffed dog was nicest,
So filled with happy memories;
all of which were priceless.

Michael F. Patton
THE MIRROR

to my wife Jill

Dark circles under eyes of light,
a grin hidden to the star'y night,
feelings shared by just a few,
who dared to cross the man of gloom.

Watch dogs prowl the grounds at night,
candles dance visions of spirits in flight,
nothing moves or breathes past dark,
only a fool would challenge the wolf
with a wounded heart.

A woman full of fire,
so gentle as she speaks,
yet no one heard her message as it
flowed out through the trees,
except the man who laughed at death
and held his weapon high,
latched on to the flaming beauty,
and walked on towards the heavenly sky's.

The morrow of the story insn't hard to figure out,
it's not how strong the person is outside,
it's how gentle is the heart.

I wish you paths of flowered peace since the secret has been told,
and just remember to take a look inside
before you grow to old . . .

Birgit Thelin—McDonald
DELUSION
To possess and to be possessed
By all the riches of the world
Eluding with the utmost care
The truth—and not delusion
That once the time is up
Eternity brings forth the fate of men
Through simple logic to both knave and gem

Mary P. Criniti
Beauty Taken For Granted
Flowers blooming in the spring
All the birds are on the wing
Mountains soaring in the sky
Clouds that go on floating by
Leaves that bloom on the trees
Oh what beauty in what we see
The sun that shines oh so bright
Stars that glisten in the night
Grass so green across the ground
Rabbits jumping all around
Brooks that trickle on their way
Have you noticed what a beautiful day
Sky so blue you want to fly
Air so clear it makes you sigh
The moon that shines oh so bright
Shadows dancing in the night
The rain that falls in the spring
Almost makes you want to sing
Bees buzzing in their hives
Aren't you glad you are alive

Elaine P. Morton
SEASONS
Spring, it is so beautiful
With its whirling breeze,
Then to see the blossoms
Along with new grown leaves.

It brings us into summer
When the days are long and bright,
As we hurry to and fro
Long into the night.

Fall is just so gorgeous
With its brightly collored leaves.
Ah! But now and then
It brings a chilly breeze.
We must then make ready
For winters chilling freeze.

Winter is upon us,
I dread it day and night.
But, I'd rather put up with it
Than go where the bugs do bite.

Anna Flanagan
THE WHALE

To the wild and the free, and those who long to be.

Seafaring Stranger
With your graceful movements,
Like an underwater ballet.
Gentle mermaid,
Will they ever let you live in peace?
And die with dignity?

Sue Way
THE VOICE OF MY SOUL
I sat alone on a lonely hillside
and watched the dawn as it painted the day.
Darkness faded to rainbow colors
of crimson and yellow from gray.
My heart was dark with lonely longings
its song was sad and far from home.
Then as the sun began to brighten the east,
the voice of my soul whispered to my heart
be not afraid or lonely, I am with you always.

Ada M. Jackvony
A CHERISHED FRIEND
Though we never met—except by phone
You've helped pass the hours when I've been alone
Your beautiful words of hope
Encouraged me to cope
When things seem so bleak
I try hard not to become weak
It's the constant helping hand
That makes me able to stand—
firm on my feet
So until the day—when we will meet
That's when my life—will be complete.

Sheila A. Walker
Old Man From Champaign News Agency
Older than the rust that hangs on
his once—white truck more
wizened than the mounds of
leathery flesh on the neck of a
Galapagos tortoise,
the old man stands in the

parking lot.
Bent by age and the weight of
paper bundles— everyday
newspaper bundles,
heavy with catastrophes and comics,
tied together with cat gut twine.

He aims tobacco juice into the parking stall,
but sprays a car instead. His
overalls are whitened
transparent at the knees
flannel shirt is stiff with sweat
from many August days,
and yet a short-sleeved T-shirt
would not be practical.
Hands and face blackened with printer's ink.
A cap hangs on the edge of his head.

He thinks that one day,
maybe not so far ahead,
the public will be reading his
obituary in newspapers
delivered by someone else.
They will pass the metal
newsstand by the sliding exit
doors and juggle grocery bags
from one arm to the other like
clowns in a circus act.
They will grab a News-Gazette
maybe read it after dinner.

Old man spits again turns and
walks slowly to the back of his truck.
He hoists the awkward bundle up
under his arm for the ten—
thousandth time slams the
paint-chipped doors and with a
grunt disappears through the
great sliding glass doors of his life.

Nadine Odo—Sueoka
Childhood Memories of a Kid From Hawaii

To Hawaii's AJAs.

Grandma always told us to pray to the dead.
I always put my hands together
and bowed my head and closed my eyes.
Sometimes I dozed off.

On the bus an old guy who
claimed he was a prof told me
to go to college here—with my
parents and in my place.
In his classes he had confidence
I'd feel at home with "lots of Japs, Japanese."

A waitress on the mainland was
quite displeased to serve
us—"them"—lunch.
We heard her argue in the back.
She got the day off so we got a
new one who was nicer.
And maybe a little guilty of her
feelings about the Oriental.

In New York I was told, "Chinese go home!"

In Japan a haole guy popped up like a gnome,
put the palm of one hand over his upper lip,
fingers pointed downward,

the other on his hip,
and yelled, "Buck tooth Jap!" then
    ran.

No wonder my brother cried
    when he began school and
    someone called him Japanese.

At Ala Moana I saw old Oriental
    ladies with blonde hair and
    false eyelashes.
An attempt, I presume,
    to not be associated with "them."

Grandma, did your ancestors ever
    say how to handle these people
    when you prayed?
Now that you're with them,
    can you tell me?

Brenda I. Felsinger/Bif
**Thank the Lord For Social
    Workers**
Do not cry little child,
I have come to care for you.
Where is your mother, little one;
You say on the Avenue?

For a moment, little person,
We can play a cheerful game.
It will be lots of fun,
If you tell me but your name.

We are going, tiny one,
To place you with a friend.
You'll be very welcome here,
'till your mother comes again.

At last, my lovely child,
Mother takes you by the hand.
Together, my small one,
We shall make some future plan.

If you need me, darling child,
I'll comfort you again.
Don't forget now, little one,
You will always be my friend.

Just remember,if you need me,
For you there I'll be.
I must go at this moment,
I've another child to see.

You are loved little child . . .

Susan J. Scheel
MY AGE
How old am I? That's hard to say.
"You're as old as you feel" . . . or
    so they say.

Awhile ago, I felt like a kid.
Right now, I'm wishing that I still
    did.

Tonight I feel I'm one hundred
    and ten.
Tomorrow, I might feel I'm
    eighteen again.

My real age doesn't matter to me.
I am as old as I feel, and that's
    how it should be!

Gabrielle Berg, RSHM
prayer by the sea
Lord

    break over me
    your ocean—love

    flatten my
    sandy pretenses
    defenses

    creep into
    all the darkened
    seaweeded
    holes
    in my soul

rush in
leaping
thundering
the rythmic force
gouging out
the hidden
crawling discontents

filter through
my murky depths
your warm
healing light

swell
your love
to frothy crest

splatter
all I touch
and what
touches me

wash me new

amen

nancy ann cota
lifetime
the ultimate knowledge of
    existence
    is founded in experience;
        innate, organic,
            instinctual.

the power of being human:
    to greaten this primal life/force
        before reaching death,
    steps upon a sublime trail
        to eternity.

we are gods
    in our own right,
we tred the high path
    of our own redemption.

Bennie Townsend Jr.
GREAT PEACE IS FOUND
    If you are disturbed or cross
    today
And can't seem to simmer down
    Now's the time to talk to the
    Lord
For in him great peace is found
    He doesn't care how it happened
Or how huge it seems to be
    He calms you down with his
    own peace
And will keep you company
    He knows and has all the
    answers
To any problem you may face
    For he has suffered much,
    much more
As he died in shame and disgrace
    His peace is not found by your
    scheming
Or by your trying to go your own
    way
He waits for your voice to ask
    for his help
And with his peace, he sheds
    light on your way
    In requesting you need not be
    eloquent
Or pretend you have greater
    duress
    He cares and he knows the
    extent of your claims
And he wants you to be true and
    confess
    He will not turn aside and
    forsake you
He has promised that he will be
    there
    He's concerned and he loves

you just as you are
But you must tell him all in your
    prayer

Nancy Fugleberg Schmid

Nancy Fugleberg Schmid
SWEET YESTERDAY

*To Mike, Pat, Lea, Florence, and
Vern. Thank you for all your love
and support.*

Yesterday was ABC's and school-
    yard play.
Yesterday was crabby teachers;
    homework every day.
Yesterday was once a tomorrow,
    looking ahead;
And yesterday was up early and
    falling into bed.

Yesterday was holding hands and
    stealing little kisses,
Getting home kind of late against
    parents wishes.
Yesterday was all the things I
    used to like to do,
And yesterday, sweet yesterday,
    I'll miss you.

William James Cline
LIMITS
My love
can be described
by an unattainable
word.
If I could find
that word
I'd find the limits
to my love.
So, my darling,
when I say that
my love for you
is like
    I truly
mean it.

Steven P. Pody
NOCTURNE
How comforting to some
that night should bear the dark,
the timid and discreet may lurk
    where light will leave no mark.
A medium for will 'o the wisp
to tread by paths unseen,
and spirits deep in souless plot
    may dwell on dire scheme.
Of impressionistic shadow,
and subtle shades,
the senses serve to tease;
as passing stars by mute glow
    etch
a jaded reflection of eternity.

Stewart Austin Cooper
FRIENDSHIP
What is friendship?
It is loving, it is giving
More than your share.
It is loyalty, faithfulness,
Making people happy,
Showing concern.
A helping hand, a cheerful smile,
Making lives more worthwhile.
When all these things you've
    enjoyed,
Sit back proudly,
And savor the memories.

Gregory L. Barnett
KNOW MY LOVE

---

*To Tiffany my daughter. May she
grow up to know the meaning of
this poem.*

Lord, thy love is like the infinite,
So beyond my hopes of
    understanding.

Lord, thy love is greater than all,
Leaving nothing to question
    whether or
Not it is within thy grasp.

Lord, thy love is everlasting,
At no time is it withdrawn.
Lord, thy love exceedeth all
That can be said in exaltation of
    thy love.
Lord, I love you!

Jalane Rogers
THE LIGHT OF DAWN
The light of dawn finds an humble
    soul of the world
as I turn to meet the smile of
    tomorrow.
While quiet whispers of morn
fill the air,
every keepsake of pain is left
    untouched.
Love of another secret,
hope of another dream,
the night of early sunsets,
becomes the endless flow of time.
With the kiss of a farewell,
and the embrace of a new
    welcome,
the light of dawn has faded to
    remembrance,
as the morning glories die in the
    sunlight.
Perhaps that love, that hope for
    recollection,
will find another soul to warm,
and the peace of living to meet
    each day,
will be like a new dawn that
    must
soon fade away.

Lauretta E. Pelton
OUT TO DISCOVER
Ole Twiddley Dit
    and Twiddley Do
Went sailing west
    in a U-shaped canoe.
They paddled and sailed
    for a year and a day.
Then spotted a beach
    and yelled HOORAY!!

Ole Twiddley Dit
    and Twiddley Do
Made up their minds
    in a quick one-two—

They scrambled ashore
to claim new land
But found they ended
    EXACTLY
where they began.

Sue Rodgers
VICTORY
            Victory
Beach solitude offers subliminal
    elixer of
        Beauty
        Peace
        Challenge
        Victory
Nature Lovers enter softly . . .
Taking away only . . .
            Memories,
As stars wink across the sky
Outlining a ghostly ship below
Pretending a Holiday for some
Destiny for others
Then tears wash the window—
    pane of the mind—
            Knowing . . .
In Victory there is Defeat—In
    Defeat Victory

Dolores Bentley Bryant
THE LORDS PRAYER
Our Father who art in Heaven
Hallowed be thy name
Thy kingdom come, thy will be
    done
In Heaven, on earth, the same.

Give us this day, our daily bread
To feed on thee alone
We feast on words that come
    from thee
Not like the devils stone.

Help us forgive our debtors Lord
As you forgive our debts too
For Lord you forgave us for our
    sins
And cleaned us good as new.

Deliver us from all evil
And lead us not into temptation
Lord thy plan be set in us
As intended from the moment of
    creation.

And we will be careful Lord
To praise you in each endeavor
For thine is the kingdom, power
    and glory
For ever and ever and ever.
            Amen

Jeannie Carlson
DIVORCE
The blossom is gone
And there is no new one
To replace it.
The floral promise of full bloom
Was pulverably plowed away . . .
There are no budding sprouts.
Nothing flourishes—
Except wicked weeds
Winding in an otherwise
Empty garden.

Unfertilized, decayed dirt
Has no hope of harvest.
Soil is denied seeds and lies
Fruitlessly fallow.
A damning drought prevents
This dung from being
Mercifully washed away.

Elaine Meli
OH, YOU NAUGHTY BOY
Oh, you naughty boy!
Why did you break that toy?

"I think I'm going to cry
I haven't learned, yet, how to lie."

"The doll's head moved
And I wondered why."

"I pulled, and I pulled, and the
    head came off, what a shame.
My sister didn't even give it a
    name."

"Its eyes blinked at me and
    winked at me,
So, I thought that it could see;
    that is when my mommy
        scolded me."

"The doll's head was in my hands
    and its eyes were on the
            floor.
When mommy came thru the
    door, what was I to do?"
(That's when mommy scolded me.)

"I do not know what I did wrong.
Later on we sang a song."

"I hope no one ever gives me a
    doll!"—
"Because, I cannot figure out if
    they can see."
"Then once again, I know, that
    my mommy will scold me."

Audrey Najor

Audrey Najor
AN ITCH
The field grows continously as it
is plowed with a rake of nails
which causes a larger tomato
patch.

Daniel Voges
ALWAYS ALONE
  Standing still, So all alone.
Counting the silent nights
away from home.
  I feel a whisper in my
mind, and turn in wonder
of what I will find.
  I see her standing alone
in space, with outstreched
arms awaiting embrace.
  I reach out to touch my
minds far thought, she wispes
away silent and quick in
the night.
  Left alone again standing,
I'm always alone.

Alma C. Groninger
THE STREET MARKET
Up and down the market place,
Wandering in and out,
Watching every huckster's face,
Listening to them shout . . .

Friendly people come to shop,
Smiles depict delight.
Examining the vendors' wares . . .
Sales soar like a kite.

Trinkets waiting to be sold,
Gadgets, hats and coats,
Towels, linens pressed with fold,
Children's books on boats.

Stalls of varied ripened fruit
Whet the appetite.
Cheeses, pastries on display,
Candy colored bright.

Near the quaint hot chestnut cart,
Midst the moving throng,
Pigeons start to softly coo . . .
The peddler sings his song.

Up and down the market place,
Wandering in and out,
Watching every huckster's face,
Listening to them shout . . .

Marian Mine
SOME TIME IS NEEDED

---

*To Betty Kay, Musician
Who supplied the background
rhythm to my rhyme on my radio
program, "Rhythm and Rhyme".*

Some time at the table
With pen in hand
To write a poem
All will understand
Is needed by the poet.

Some time with nature
Observing her art
Inscribing her beauty
On the human heart
Is needed by the poet.

Some time to express
Loveliness or distress,
Heartache, loneliness
Joy or happiness
Is needed by the poet.

For the poet is sensitive—
Often misunderstood—
And he writes out his life
Not for a livelihood.
Yes, some time is needed by the
    poet!

Vanessa Kaye
SEARCH DEEPER
People look but they don't see
    beyond the outer wall,

Which surrounds the shell
    that hides the inner self.

No one takes the time to see,
    so we're judged by what
    appears to be,

And not by what is within
    and truly real.

Search deeper if you dare,
    to what was not seen before,

Beyond the mirror of the eyes,
    straight down into the very
    core.

Barbara Wallis Moore
The Washing Of the Soul
Brightly down the glassy sheets
Of all the rains I've ever known
Flicker and shimmer reflections
Of my content and gladness
At the rain that makes you
    dismal.
You curse it on your face

And then beneath your feet,
You hate it in the air
And on your rooftop.
But like a desccated plant
I stand there in it happily
And turn my face toward it,
Or in cold venture to the window
And smile out at the bouncing
    drops.
It is a peace, a mellowing
A laving of the heat
O purging of the air
And a liquid silver still
Among the green content
When the rain is at an end.

Emilia O. Duroska (Amethy)
The Unicorn In Captivity
Why was the guileless Unicorn
taken captive and speared?
"Because of his utter goodness"
Self to self my query cleared.

Why was the blameless Unicorn
unangered, back—attack undared?
"Because of his "graced" wholeness,
no malice he up-flared,
    Light-spared!

How came he to be annointed . . .
hunted, hurt, later ascending?
"As he cleansed Earth, bending,
some grew within, Sun-Moon
    blending.

Fair Unicorn horn of hallowed
    bone
for prepared ones is *Height's
    Lodestone!*
"Because you see "IT" thus and so,
"IT" IS for you, for now, thus and so!
M y s t e r i a   M a g n a
        of MAN's Dawn
spreads before you: R o s e
            and thorn!"

Eileen Burroughs
THE RIVER AND THE SEA
Somewhere the night has just
    begun,
Dark—sightless hours—before
    the sun,
A woman wails—a child is born,
Oh, precious life, innately warm.
Who knows this hour what fate
    may be?
The river's started toward the sea!

Fat, nurtured—grown so straight
    and tall,
And richly blest, as are we all,
Who knows the truth to make
    him live?
What secret counsel should one
    give?
Refreshing waters—soothing me,
The river's winding toward the sea!

A whirlwind—tumbling—
    through the days,
Unmindful of tumultuous ways,
The soul and body, threshed and
    tossed,
In battle's meet—have paid the
    cost,
Nor been enslaved—but, still are
    free,
The river's racing toward the sea!

Suspended, now, sweet peace at
    last,
From strife and agitation—past,
Hushed silence—hanging heavy,
    there,
Encumpassed in the foggy air,
The journey's done—the soul is

free,
At last, the river's found the sea!

Kathryn Tracy Allen
A BROKEN HEART
If someone breaks your heart,
Tries to tear you all apart,
Should you start anew,
And give them another chance at
    you?
Or should you say, that's enough!
I don't need to be rebuffed.
My broken heart is incomplete,
I need time to get on my feet.
Love might smile and turn away,
To wait it's chance at you
    another day.
If this is love, I want no part,
I hate the feel of a broken heart.

Jenny Keathley
REALITY
Are not my troubles intended to
    deepen my character?
Perhaps robe me in graces I had
    little of before,
Sometimes they make me the
    worlds greatest actor,
When inside the hurt reaches my
    hearts very core.

There are blessings—I know—we
    cannot obtain;
If we cannot accept and endure
    life's pain,
There are joy's that can come to
    us only through sorrow
But it's hard forgetting about
    tomorrow.

Out of suffering have emerged
    the world's strongest soul's,
They push right on thru, letting
    nothing take it's toll
The most massive character's are
    seamed with life's scar's,
Yet they'll climb the highest
    mountain, and reach for the
    stars;

So I hang in there, with my feet
    firmly planted;
Living this life, that to me, the
    Lord has granted.

Miriam McLain
FATE
In a game of chance with fate
I was delt a rotten hand,
Oh God, did I play my cards
    right?
Could I have played them
    differently?
If I had, would I have won?
Fate has played many games with
    me
I am only her pawn!
Does she laugh behind her fluted
    fan
As I thresh and struggle
To just break even, or
Weep, when I falter and fall!
Only to smile when I stumble up
To try again, to find a place in
    the sun
To warm my bewildered heart.
To make the ultimate effort,
To be seen, to be heard, to be
    loved,
Before, forever oblivion!

Beatrice Harper
RAIN ON THE SUWANNEE
The first time I saw the Suwannee
The rain was gently falling

Somewhere a bird was calling
There was a bridge
Seen from a ridge
As I stood on that famous shore
Where others had stood of yore

It seemed unbelievable to me
To be beside the Suwannee
I thought as I walked along
This is the river in that song

I went on my way
I'll return some day
The sun will be shining again
There won't be any rain
    on the Suwannee . . .

Sandra G. Roberson
OLD AGE DREAMS

---

*This poem was written to Uncle
Larkin, on his 83rd birthday;
while visiting him in a nursing
home. It is dedicated to all senior
citizens everywhere.*

I now am old,
And past my prime;
As I look back
Through the pages of time.

I dream of days,
When I was Young;
Carefree days, I do recall,
Of laughter and fun
And growing tall.

But now my days,
Of youth are gone;
So I'll just hold to my dreams,
As I struggle along.

When God sees fit,
To call me home;
I'll once again
Be young and strong.

Hilbert S. Collins
KULTUR
Thar aint no kultur
Kum outa me,
I jes raw boned
An out atta kne.
I dont unerstan
What kultur means,
I hered it kums
From collich denes.
But I dont mix up
Wit acqwadomerians,
I stic to ma own
Ma kinda somarions.
I perfek hapy
Here inna holler,
Aint no wun here
I hafta foller.

Rozann M. Shamoon
3 am (A Poem of Friendship)
Write something happy
Just for me
Make it full of laughter
Something I can smile after.

Don't write sad things
Don't bring up bad happenings
Make it light and breezy
Don't recall anything sleazy.

Mention my name
And for Rich do the same
We've been good friends
Don't write things that offend.

Love and kisses
Hit and misses

Here's something happy
Just for Kathy.

Rivers and puppy tails
Pickups and mountain trails
Tears and laughter
Friends forever after.

Cleoral Lovell

Cleoral Lovell
Twentieth Century Apostle
How eagerly the hungry masses
    cram
The auditoriums to hear him
    speak!
Can he unlock the source of
    peace they seek?
When dedicated Brother Billy
    Graham
Exhorts the truth, revealing all
    the sham,
Instills new purposes within the
    weak,
Then hope-thrilled hearts
    experience a peak
Of joy, believe the message of
    The Lamb.

To many thirsty souls the Living
    Word
Spills from his lips to fill them to
    the brim;
They are reborn and saved from
    utter night.
On Judgment Day the host of
    those who heard
And have eternal life because of
    him
Will sing when he receives his
    crown of light.

Elizabeth Hill
LIFE
It's true that life can seem quite
    hard
    At times, but if we see
The good in things then it won't
    be
    So hard for you and me.
The more that we can look up and
    Not down, then we will find
That we will have so much more
    hope,
    And have a cheerful mind.
We're here on earth to do much
    good—
    Just how is up to us.
The one thing that we must not
    do,
    Is sit around and fuss.
To be creative, lifts us out,
    of humdrum days in life;
And if we help another out,
    We'll then avoid much strife.

Sandra Lynn Little
MY PLACE
There is a place where I
can go anytime—day
or night.

There are no locks, barriers
or secret pass words but
I am the only one who
can enter.

It makes no difference whether
I am by myself or with others,
I can always be alone in
my place.

Mrs. Lois Irvine
PRIESTHOOD
Priesthood was called into
    existence by Jesus Christ, God's
    eternal son,
Through the sacrament of Holy
    Orders choosing each, as a
    special one,
A priest can bring meaning to the
    Altar of the Catholic Church,
Spread spiritual treasures: life,
    truth, holiness and peace on earth.
Love, life, wisdom and more, are
    treasures of infinite Grace,
Priests are mediators to unite
    God and the Human race.
Between heaven and earth there's
    a faithful beacon of light,
Knowing 'Christ lives in me' and
    I'll help you fight a good fight.
To combat against evil: the girdle
    means turth, so tall,
Breastplate represents justice and
    peace on earth, for one and all.
The twelve gems on the
    breastplate is one for each
    apostle of Christ,
Shoes are readiness to live our
    lives by the Gospel of Christ.
The shield, faith. Helmet is hope
    of eternal salvation,
The sword is the word of God,
    spoken in moralization.
Parish priests say: my greatest
    love is for God alone,
Next the people of my parish,
    where I call my home.
The third for every human with a
    beating heart,
Who can live upon this earth yet
    know he must part.
There is respect for those already
    departed from this life;
God have mercy on all souls,
    sometimes happiness comes
    from strife.
The fourth is the love he has for
    winning souls for God.
A priest is nothing of himself, but
    everything through God.
Please always stay happy, there's
    greatness in His calling for you,
And I do understand: "Your joy no
    one can take from you."

Wendy Eisele
LOVE SONG
The frail moon is silver white
and drowsy
    in the sleepy skies,
and I can hear the tender tunes
    it sings
    come softly down on us.

The summer night is thick with
    stars
    —and love.

The feathery breeze
　　is warm and gentle
as it wraps us up in
　　velvet blankets,
and the pale light
turns scarlet
　　in its peace . . .

Oh, who has need of the earth,
　　my darling,
when for us
a frail net of stars are flung,
and a low white
　　moon is calling . . .

Tim Waggoner
MY LOVE FOREVER
It matters not the waters, nor
　　how deep,
When I come down to the water's
　　edge
For my eternal sleep.

It matters not the voyage, nor the
　　place,
For my darling, I will look for you,
Forever to embrace.

Mary Snow Jackson
WINTER
Trees stripped of their leaves,
　　standing so bleak
Each branch crested with new
　　white peaks
Little cottontail asleep in his
　　burrow
Each footprint makes a deep,
　　deep, furrow

Landscapes frosted with
　　mountains of snow
Sparkling in the twilight where
　　shadows grow
Winds whistling around each
　　crevice and nook
As I settle down to read a good
　　book

Fireside cozy with embers all aglow
Two little dogs curled up on the
　　rug below
Smoke curling, swirling, and soon
　　takes flight
All is so peaceful on a cold
　　winters night

Laima Prapuolenis
THE SPLIT—SECOND

For Tom, my rock in the storm.

So, now I fall in the new day with
　　the dead,
beaten, and forgotten, and blind.
Even now they enter, crawling in
　　my head,
crying and taunting at my mind.

　Sweet odor, dear scent of the
　　alive,
　I need you now that I am gone.
　In deep abyss, my sanity dived,
　and life does now cry begone.

This has remained the old day of
　　long ago,
the dream that traveled in my
　　head,
When just a child, I saw my life
　　would go,
my thoughts destroyed, my body
　　dead.

　Down, down all sense falls
　　slowly,

tumbling ever so with wind
and speed.
Now, as last life flees me,
I think of warnings I had not
heed.

Gertrued Hickin Sigmon
Gertrued Hickin Sigmon
WASTE

---

*To Paul Swartz of Oberlin College
days 1931*

What right have I to live when
　　you are gone—
When all I've ever known have
　　crossed the sea?
And now alone on shore is only
　　me—
A bit of flesh past prime and
　　useless on
This Earth. I see the young and
　　great like swan
Glide out across the silver
　　water—free,
And I must wonder what my task
　　should be
Now that the final finish lines
　　are drawn.
My strength spent six decades
　　outside the work
Assigned to me. Those gone
　　before me nod
In strange reproof, while wonder
　　I, "In age
Can I accomplish that which I did
　　shirk
In prime?" Too much the world
　　was with me. Odd
I must write now. My ticket is
　　this page?

Della M. King
SUMMER MADNESS
In the breath taking beauty of
　　summer
　　And under the spell of the
　　night
Of moonbeams and stars
　　And the strum of guitars. . .
The last shred of reason takes
　　flight.

It's thunder and lightning, the
　　fully blown rose
　　A season for passion and every
　　heart knows
It will rush out to meet it
　　And stand on tip toes
To garner it's share of the
　　summer's sweet woes.

It's the season for growing
　　romantic and glowing

A season of heart ache, a
　　season of bliss
When nothing else matters
Until reason shatters
　　And silently drowns in the
　　wake of a kiss.

This madness, this gladness, this
　　surge of desire
　　This yearning, this burning
　　consumable fire
Though mindlessly thrilling
Unsated, unwilling,
It will simmer and die on it's own
　　blazing pyre.

Patty M. Martin
POE-TRY
Planning the right things to say
　　so it's enjoyable all the way
Opening eyes below and above
　　so the world can know and love
Emptying one's thought and mind
　　so you'll catch attention from
　　all man-kind
Trying to get down the right word
　　so it'll sound thrilling as a bird
Resting with peace and content
　　so your time was well spent
Yearning for the right words from
　　your pen
　　so someday they'll say (as a
　　poet you win).
　　　EDGAR ALLAN POE TRY
　　　So why not I?

Rolando Herrera
KHEPRI (BLUE SCARAB)
Inspired scarab
Charm or souvenir
Lay me in darkness
My spirit unite
With past companions
My heart revive
With truthfulness

Regina Golden
TWO FACES OF EVE
These pillows
　　have ticking
as old as the willows;
yet the down inside
so fluffy and soft,
fine, of young geese,
lighter than loft,
preserved like a treasure
of fur or pe-lisse'
enjoyed at one's leisure

Renewing my treasure
today at my leisure,
the air gently stirred
as I opened the seam.
What I had feared
happened—in the extreme.

Mistaken release!
my beautiful feathers,
down of young geese—
now how can I gather?
I snatched and I grabbed
but nothing retrieved.

My Good Neighbor was sunning
with lotion applied
her dark tan so stunning
I just could have cried.
When she stood up
the lotion had dried.

She looked like Mt. Hermon
in real rugged weather;
nothing to see but down
of the feather

I looked at her;
she looked at me.

Her reaction was anger
I could easily see.
I stiffled a grin
with gulp and chagrin
while her mouth gradually
looked strange near the chin;

for all she could see
was the tip of my nose,
while her lovely dark hair
was white as a rose.

(What clever invention
for bad winter weather)
Even her eyelids
were covered with feathers.
Now, of this episode
good friendship forbids
that any one sing this, my ode.

K. M. Diclementi
The Dogs of Lonliness Bite

---

*To the Rapacious Creditor, For
the Dogs of Lonliness came forth
from his kingdom of lancination—
a place I no longer reside.*

The dogs of lonliness bite at my
　　hands.
So too, does the cat of high hopes,
　　who's bite is worse.
With it, comes the stinging pain
　　of disappointment that
Pierces the soul.

Gone are the visions of the free
　　child's laughter.
Gone are the thoughts of
　　comforting the little girl inside
The woman, the woman giving
　　comfort to the boy inside the
　　man;
Both, finding solace in the temple
　　of the other.

How I fear the foul fanged feline
　　of nocturnal visions,
With her instruments of
　　destruction, which puncture the
Skin of my happiness.
Her eyes, shining with false
　　promise,
Inseminate the fantasy of
　　reaching the intimate other;
The dream universal to all.

She roams the graveyard of my
　　lonliness searching
The tombs of my faults, the crypt
　　of my weakness, which houses
The hearth of my malady.
At night she comes and befriends
　　me, knowing I am helpless,
Knowing I must submit.

We play out the night's tragic
　　human drama:
To Love.
To Be Loved.
To Transcend One's Self Through
　　Love.
To Be Bitten!
To Feel Pain!
To Be Dead!
The Dogs Of Lonliness Bite.

Larry J. Zaikow
RICH LADY
Please, Please,
Rich Lady! Rich Lady!

With you in my arms . . .
Having money and having you
each day! Lady!

Having you, Please! Don't walk
alone,
Just you with me,
I love you my Lady, even though,
single,
Please, Please,
Rich Lady! And you!

Be by my side each day,
Poor or rich my Lady,
With music in the air at night,
Don't run away Lady . . .

The song of a Rich Woman,
Thinking of you in my mind,
Hello once again! My Lady!
RICH LADY! RICH LADY!

Lilli Lee Buck
**I Have a Home In East
Virginia**
Oh, yes, I have a home in East
Virginia,
On a meadow of wild flowers of
every kind,
And circling the vast and verdant
meadow,
Stand the tall, majestic ranks of
yellow pines.
And dancing down among the
yellow pine trees,
The dogwood looms in lacy
sprays of white,
And from his nest across the
open acres,
The cardinal makes his
crimson-crested flight.

And I can hardly bear it in the
springtime,
When azure skies stretch
cloudlessly above,
And all the little mockingbirds
and robins
Explode their hearts in peerless
songs of love.

On perfect days of pure
transparent sunlight,
The breezes launch the pine
tops way on high,
Who sway their limber trunks in
ocean rhythm,
And shake their lofty branches
with a sigh.

Then the wind across the daisy-
spattered meadow
Will wave the grass like waves
upon the sea,
And to counterpoint the
meadow's fragrant breathing,
Comes a-rushing through the
old magnolia tree.

Oh, yes, I have a home in East
Virginia,
On a meadow of wild flowers of
every kind,
And circling the vast and verdant
meadow,
Stand the tall, majestic ranks of
yellow pines.
And dancing down among the
yellow pine trees,
The dogwood blooms in lacy
sprays of white,
And from his nest across the
open meadow,
The cardinal makes his long
and graceful flight.

Helen Lair
A Train Going Nowhere
In the city
she rides the El train
her face white from no sun
her bone is stone,
who, then is she—

tugged through days,
her life measured on paper
by governments,
what despair and cries there are
in old shoes with worn heels;
I can't hear through the window
but fear killed her face
in her search.

Debi Buettner
FRIENDS
You want to get to know me
I'd like to know you too
I enjoy your laughs and serious
chats
There's a lot I can offer you
but only as a friend
You say that's a start
and yet the intensity
of our first meeting lingers

And I hope you can understand
where you fit in my life
and enjoy the time we share

You'd like to know me better
I can only offer you a friend
and hope you still care

Michael R. Swartwood
THE PHONE CALL
The phone call was a very
important thing.
Instead of getting the phone call,
When he expected to get it,
He got it finally it a couple days
late.

The reason why he wanted the
phone call,
Is that he knew he would get,
The address of someone special.

He had to talk to this person's
wife,
Twice before he got the husband,
Too call him. Even though their
was,
A time difference, which worked,
To his advantage; He finally got,
The wife to get after the husband,
Until he called this person.

After the husband called this
person,
The man was very happy. He then,
Knew that he could write,
This someone special,
And make her happy.

Kenneth John Catenacci
MOTHER AND SON
In the twilight of late evening
the little child does sleep
So sound and so contented
entertained by his dreams
And his little heart is settled
as he sleeps so peacefully
'Cause Momma's right beside him
watching over so lovingly
And at the age of five
as he ends his first school day
He rushes home excitedly
skipping along the way
He dashes to the kitchen
for an after—school snack
And Momma's right there beaming
with the excitement he's
brought back
And now at the age of twelve
it's graduation night
He receives his first diploma
as he smiles with such delight
He walks so tall and proud
of that moment he has won
And Momma sheds a happy tear
as she beholds her only son
And so the years pass swiftly
and the child has become a man
He's journied far and aimlessly
searching all across the land
But at last he wanders home
with lonliness in his track
And Momma holds him close and
says
My son, welcome back
And as her love pours out to him
and he soothes his burning tears
He dries his eyes and says, Mom
what happened o'er the years
Then slumber over takes him
and he sleeps so peacefully
'Cause Momma's right beside Him
watching o'er so lovingly

Julie Ann Small
COLLAGE OF POETRY

———————————————

*To Lee whos sparkling eyes and
warm smile opened windows in
my mind, unlocked a door to my
heart and inspired an emotional
current within me.*

———————————————

The waves rush in and wash over
my feet.
The sea gulls swoop down and
keep soaring along the coast.
I walk a bit, throwing rocks into
the waves.
You have become my central
point of thought.
I know I will go crazy if I must
keep going on . . .
Going on pushing you further
back in my thought.
The why of you and me has so
much more discovering.
Before darkness fell I had to
search you out.
One more night not knowing
would surely drive me insane.
It is time for me to come out of
my womb.
I have to run a little faster now to
get back on the carrousel.
I search for words which seem to
never come.
Could your hand fall loosely into
mine?

My eyes wish to kiss your face.
My ears long to hear your
warmth.
In time may our dreamy souls
float freely in and out of
eachother.
Giving, filling up and never
asking for more.

Richard Jenkins
OH—NO! FORTY
Here we are again
To pay our last respects
To someone who has reached
"Forty"
Full of sorrow and regrets.
Some call it facing doomsday
Others say you're over the hill.
Jack Benny had a cure
And everyone said it worked well.
Thirty-nine and holding.
Dye your hair,
No-one can tell.
Your dentist keeps getting richer
From sending you your bill.
We all know about your choppers
He drilled what he could drill!
Wasn't long before you married.
19— such a pretty bride.
When you left the wedding chapel,
We remember how some cried . . .
The years they keep on coming
One by one—they add up!
You tried to slow them down,
There was no way, so you gave up.
Because you see, she's "Forty"
And not a moment too soon.
You tire easy and just sitting
Wears you out . . . And it's just
noon!
You've got a whole evening of
T.V. to watch
Soaps and games galore.
You sit and watch them all
And still you want to watch more.
You look at the time and realize
Another day is gone.
Today you reached "Forty"
And all day you stayed at home.
Your varicose veins are showing,
Not that anyone cares.
Everyone-they know you're "Forty".
You wear what you have to wear.
So I'll leave you with these words
of wit
The day that you are "Forty"
Don't despair . . . The years that
are coming
Will be happy and full of glory.
Remember that we all love you
And hope that you'll be happy
When you're a Grandmother
And your hubby becomes a
Grandpappy.

Jody VanAckeren
ISLAND OF MY HEART
My heart is a pompous island
spacious yet yielding in truth.
Each corner is jasmine filled
smelling sweetly of a childs youth.

The ardor of my hearts embrace
and the waves of my untamed
soul,
warm the sands beneath your feet
and wake the pacified ocean floor.

My heart bends like the agile trees
their greeting to the sun they send.
My heart speaks freely as the
grass

dancing sprightly to the lilting
wind.

As the ocean encircles its island
so my heart seeks only amour,
for as a firefly is the stars delight
so you are my torrid desire.

Vincenzo LXX Giallonardo

Vincenzo LXX Giallonardo
JULY 4, 1983

---

*On My DEPARTURE FROM
PLANET EARTHA O'THE DEEP
ASPIRING CHALICEDLY O I
LEAVE ALL of My POSSESSIONS
To All of the GIRLS and The
BOYS of PLANET EARTHA etc
FOR THE UPLIFTING of
MANKIND and WOMANKIND
etc FOR EVER IN TRUTH and
LOVE JOY .!.*

O Divine Guide O Holy Order O
I AM A Loner O SO
ABSOLUTE A LONER in The
HOLY ORDER of UNIVERSA
O The DEEP Aspiring
CHALICEDLY ATTUNED O
in The STIRRING BALANCES
CHALLENGES of CREATIONS
TESTED and TRIED
WITNESSING WITH MY OUR
HOLY O 1/31/82 "Handwriting
On The WALL .." Returned To
Me 9/27/82 In a BOOK "Our
20th Century's Greatest Poems"
From SACRAMENTO
Containing About 700 Pages
and 7000 Poems From Poets
and Poetesses FROM EVERY
STATE IN THE UNION O
From Every State in The U.S.A.
and From Every Province
(PRO VINCE HA) IN Canada
and From etc Points O'er
PLANET EARTHA etc
LINKED TO MY OUR LXX etc
O and MY OUR HOLY O
11/13/82 LXX .. "Cosmic
Celestial Equations . . ."Which
Was Returned To Me 7/27/83
Eve In "Today's Greatest
Poems" LINKED TO MY OUR
8/13/83 "The
MANIFESTATION 8/13/1983
LXX . . . "For My Birthday 70
After My 8/13/1913 About
11am Birth Along The Great
Valley Stream By The Barn
Near Valley Forge Pennsylvania
U.S.A. NATIONAL HISTORIC

PARK SHRINE To My
1/6/1981 ORACLE About The
RETURN of THE MESSIAH To
Valley FORGE MOUNT JOY*
FOREST CHALICE FLAMA O
Near FORT WASHINGTON
From WHERE I SPEAK TO
ABOUT FOUR BILLION
PEOPLE O'ER PLANET
EARTHA etc "O This Is a DAY
O a TIME of PRECISION
VISION DECISION O Not
Only To SUSTAIN The
BEAUTY and The LOVE and
The JOYS of GENIUS O For
The GROWTH of ONE's Ever
Nobler Holier Higher Truer
Glorious Joyous Sublimest
EXISTENCES and BEINGS but
For THE SURVIVAL of LIFE
ITSELF In The HOLY ORDER
of UNIVERSA O'THE DEEP
ASPIRING TESTED and
TRIED. . ." etc O and Now O
11/13/1983 Eve I AM
WITNESSING To The
1/20/1981 U.S.A.
Administration Trying Its Best
To Create a SECOND
TRILLION DOLLARS
NATIONAL DEBT by
REDUCING TAXES ON THE
INCOME of The RICH and
THEN BORROWING THE
MONEY FROM THE RICH AT
ABOUT 25% INTEREST THUS
FAR O THIEVING FROM and
ENSLAVING THE POOR etc O
and SO NOW I AM CALLING
FOR a 100% NATIONAL
SIGNED PAPER BALLOT
RECALL ELECTION IN
TRUTH TO THE REALITIES. . .
etc

O In Truth and Love etc O I AM
Vincenzo LXX Giallonardo M3-
9 C3-9 P3-9 LXX With a
Mailing Address At 309 North
Simpson Street, Philadelphia,
Pennsylvania, U.S.A. 19139
from a Forest Vale by Stream
REFLECTING PROJECTING or
On a Street Corner
PROSCENIUM OBSERVING
SPEAKING etc In THE HOLY
ORDER DOVE LOVE

Thelma Van Scoik
SUMMER—FALL
It is still the middle of summer,
  But a leaf fell at my feet,
All wrinkled, all brown, all dry,

all dead—
  Like yours, life incomplete!

It is still the middle of summer,
  The rest of the leaves are green,
But tears are falling from their
  eyes—
  Oh, what a sad, sad scene.

It is still the middle of summer,
  Your days with me were so few.
I know the sorrowing leaves miss
  their friend
  Just as I, Dear Ralph, miss you.

It is still the middle of summer,
  Your life was in it's prime—
God needed you in Heaven, so
  For you the bells did chime.

The fall of my life has now come,
  But each day I live anew
The beautiful memories of
  Those wonderful days with you.

The fall of my life has now come,
  But I'm singing as I go
Along life's pathway without you,
  For I'll join you soon, I know!

Dorcas Wanita Fox
A Salute To Jesse Stuart
Somewhere in Kentucky there's a
Writers pen that's still,
For the keeper of the words it
  wrote,
Is lying gravely ill.

My treasure-trove is filled with
  thoughts,
That he wove into verse,
And today my heart was
  saddened,
By the news that he'd grown
  worse.

For years he gave us beauty,
In the poems he wrote so well,
And many a heart was lifted,
By the stories he would tell.

No longer does he weave his
  tales,
With threads that run so true,
Nor paint word pictures on my
  mind,
Of woodlands we both knew.

So if you have some of his works,
Consider yourself lucky,
For Jesse Stuart will always be,
Poet Laureate of Kentucky.

J. Elizabeth Kamp
DIAMOND HEAD
I said no, because even at
  thirty-two
  nice girls don't.

Or so I was taught.

I said no, when every inch of my
  body felt tingly
at the thought of a warm,
  sensitive human being
wanting to give me pleasure—
        something
I had longed for, oh so many
  endless, lonely nights.
        somehow
you convinced me in a weak
  moment that my thinking was
  wrong
in the backseat of your Pinto
  with rain,
  pounding on the roof

my body said yes.

And once again, even though
  only fleetingly, I felt
whole, and realized that other
  than being a person,

I am a woman

Only because you took the time
  to care.

And though I don't know you, I
  have so much
to thank you for.

Mark D. M. Brindel
LIGHT GRANDEUR

To my ever loving Mom:

. . . And in the dawning, a bud rose.

  shining against the
    illuminated morning sun,

  Judging not by appearance,

  Experiencing it as it is,

  soaking up the warmth

  for a full day of enjoyment.

  Nothing ever before felt so
    good, so lightening.

  An incredible experience

  to experience the Morning

  sun in complete peace.

Terry Lee Tucker
Ode To the Cockle—Burr
What be thy purpose, thou
  dastardly Cockle—Burr?
The jewels of thy crown seem to
  slur
Any attempt to rid the earth
Of they presence; and with a
  touch of mirth
Thou returnest undaunted
To a plot where thou 'ist' not
  wanted.

Alice L. Keys
BEFORE YOU GO
The first gift you gave was life
  One I couldn't turn down
Always taking, sometimes in
  return
  I caused your heart to frown
For years your lessons I'd protest
  And you would always give in
You survived my growing pains
  Kept your ache within
I'm on my own, you're always
  there
  When an extra hand I need
Still on the take but appreciating
  All of your loving deeds
While there's still time I'll take a
  moment
  Say thanks, Dad, with love
  conveyed
Before you go and tomorrow is
  over
  Before Someone calls you away

Tom Hobgood
FREEDOM
Freedom is a word which can
  only be heard
  from the Cross on Galgatha's
  Hill.
It was many years in the past but
  it will ever last,
  for it was on that Tree that

36

love was fulfilled.
God's blessed only Son, He died
for everyone
and freed us from all sin and
strife.
For from that tomb, He did away
with our doom,
and came forth to give us life.

Freedom is that word which can
only be heard
by those who believe on God's
Son.
Because He peace and His joy, we
now employ
in the life that the Lamb of
God won.
So if freedom you need to these
words now please heed,
and accept the One who hung
on the Tree.
For His joy you will know and
your heart will ever flow
with the same love that was
given to me.

Helga Marie Fentross
**Liberty, Enlighten the
World!**

*To my sons, Harold, Michael and
Eric. And to all sons of this
beautiful land. May you carry the
torch of freedom, high!*

Arm stretched high with torch of
freedom burning,
Lady, you stand majestically
near the water's edge.
You saw the tears in countless
eyes with yearning;
You heard their cries, bore
witness to their pledge.

Do patriotic words of freedom
still stir hearts
and souls today,
For us, the heirs of masses once
yearning to breathe free?
Or has our will and spirit fallen
in decay,
Like you, the symbol of it all,
Statue of Liberty?

Did we become like old and
ancient lands
Just like a brazen giant of
Greek fame?
Did the torch glide from tired
hands?
Did we become pompous for a
storied name?

Lady, your silent lips still call the
world today:
Give me your tired, your poor!
You raise your torch with
freedom's ray,
Telling the world, forever sure:
The Quest for Liberty will never
die!

Elizabeth F. Grover
MIDNIGHT FLIGHT
Hanging from a star . . . asking
clouds just where you are . . .
wishing for your kiss . . .
Weeping with the midnight
mist . . . brushing night away
. . . calling down the Milky
Way . . . Thunder is my
heartbeat, lightning flashes
at my feet . . . as I

wander through the night
. . . an empty shell in
cosmic flight . . . towards you.

I embrace the moon . . . asking
him to find you soon . . .
dancing pirouettes with the
fleeting silhouettes . . .
comets carry me afar . . .
stopping off at every star
. . . constellations hear
your name, and they blush
with brighter flame . . . in
the arms of night . . . as I
make my Midnight Flight . . .
towards you.

When I find you,
Sun will split the night in two.
Stars will search for things to do,
Since my Midnight Flight is
through,
and I've found you.

Hazen Fauver
PIONEER MOTHER

*Dedicated to all of those dear
mothers that knew the hardships
of the West, a new country, a
chalange some couldn't stand,
some could. My Grandmother
Sophia Stark was one of the
luckey ones.*

Eyes of hazel, black grey,
With the worries of the day.
Eyes of green and eyes of blue,
Showing strength the whole day
through.

Oh what sights they have seen,
Eyes of mother, eyes of queen,
Eyes of green and eyes of blue,
Eyes that sparkle like the dew.

Were her happy thoughts in vain?
Would her man come home again?
Would she meet another friend,
When she reached her journey's
end?

Oh eyes that shine through joy
and tears,
Eyes that dream of bygone years.
Eyes that pain and sorrow knew,
Eyes of green and eyes of blue.

Deidra L. Childers
MY CHILD

*To Chris— your my life &
inspiration.*

Follow me my precious child
I'll lead you on your way
I'll hold you in my arms at night
I'll walk with you by day.

The path we walk seems hard
rough moments we must face,
—moments when we'll shed our
tears
for pains we can't erase.

Then if times get, oh, so hard
and your afraid that you might fall,
reach out, my child, and take my
hand
together, we'll stand tall.

And then one day when you walk
alone
don't weep for me my dear

just close your eyes and
"remember"
and I'll always be right here.

Vlasta
SONG FOR YOU

To my best friend Gary Patterson.

In my dreams life is a song,
high and low notes passing along.

When your eyes speak the
truth,
i want to sing along with you.

Remember but, for God's grace,
i need more than a living space.

I want to feel the warmth of
sun,
to rejoice and to feel sorrow
none.

At least i am free, as a bee,
you shall be you and i will be me.

Michelle Ann Pavicic
**Confessions For An
Intimate Friend**
When you're near
I feel
Secure
I can be honest
With you
For I know you are trustworthy
Others hurt me
I know you won't
That special touch
Is possessed only by you
You hold me
When I need it most
You understand me
My real heart and my true
feelings
The inside me
My whole life is known by you
I trust only you
With my unique dreams and
thoughts
I've told only you
My wishes and wants
I am not embarrassed to tell you
My deepest secrets
You possess the power of making
me feel
Happy
Strong
And confident
Life is too mysterious
For me to overtake
I trip over obstacles
And I am blind to happiness
How do I correct myself?

What shall I do?
Where do I begin?
I need advice
Please answer me
Oh—I forgot
Teddy Bears—Cannot speak.

Julie R. Epley
YOU
My world was once a dream.
Until you made it real.
You gave me a certain feeling,
In which I will always feel.

You would always lend an ear,
In my times of madness and fear.
You would always lift my spirits,
When I was feeling down.

Your smiling face would always
warm me,
Your spirit was always high.
So now I know just where to go,
When my life is thrown aside.

Myrtle Volz Ferman
APRIL
Oh, April is a fickle gal,
I don't know how to take her,
Her smile is warm and tender
When the early Robins wake
her.
She brings me gifts of blossoms
And she lures me with her
glances,
But when she's almost in my
arms
Then far away she dances.
Oh, April is a fickle, fickle gal.

Then soon she's cool and distant
And her eyes are oh, so chilly;
Pretends she doesn't know me and
She makes me feel so—silly.
I turn my back upon her—
My heart with sorrow laden
Then, what do you know, don't
tell me
That I hear a weeping maiden.
Oh, April is a sorry, sorry gal.

I can't abide a woman's tears,
There's naught that I can do
But give the little hoyden
Another chance—or two.
She lifts her head and dries her
eyes,
Her face with radiance shining;
Her lips are sweet with promises,
Her arms in mine entwining.
Oh, April is my lovely, loving gal.

Helen Rex
THE MASTER SPEAKS
The Master speaks
Of things most High;
Of Mansions built
Up in the sky.

Of Angels, Hosts
And Crowning men
Who serve Thy God—
Just like Him.

Give praise and honor
For you see;
The Master speaks
Of Prophecy.

Mine eyes have seen the Glory
Of Thy righteous Lord & God.
He lives within the Holy
Kingdom up above.

The Master before me
"Come—be fishermen!

Give God the praise and Glory
for His will be done—Amen!"

Miss Mara Dellecave
In the Flag, God Was Always There

For all the soldiers who died for our country

The flag stands brightly over thee,
It's the United States colored majesty.
It waves over all, all through the day,
For it represents the U.S.A.
It never fell in battle, it won for all to share,
But to me in the flag, God was always there.

Ralph H. Chase Jr.

Ralph H. Chase Jr.
KEY WEST

For Doris, my wife and best critic.

Why does the island in the sea keep on beckoning to me?
It seems to say come walk my beach and let the waves wash at your feet.
The sky so clear, the water so blue, the sand so warm it comfort's you.
It's so peaceful as you see on the island in the sea.

Edwin L. Seay
CIVIL WAR
How gloriously did they fight
For a cause that was far from right,
To preserve a life of grandeur for the privileged few
The rest either enslaved or victims of a bitter brew,
The slaves sometimes well treated, more often not
The poor white trash shunned, ignored and mostly forgot.

To hold a fellow human in bondage, certainly not right
But for this the poor whites had to fight
Just fighting to maintain the status quo
Not for a better life, just nowhere could they go,
But oh gloriously did they fight
For a cause that was far from right.

Mostly illiterate the poor whites scarcely knew
That they were only fighting for the privileged few,
To many it might sound like a stupid pun
Winning they would have lost, losing they won
Out of the agony of defeat, there would come a better day
Slowly and painfully many of life's inequities passed away.

So I mourn not for a civilization long dead
In which only an exclusive few had it made,
Now opportunity is knocking for most everyone
To find his own special place in the sun,
For the new order "keep up the glorious fight
For the things we know to be right."

Elynor A. Baran
SKY DESIGNS
Brilliant Autumn with its magic sky!
Blowing winds! the Artists creating tool—
Carving realistic shapes so high—
Look! Look! see the lion, castle, lamb of curly wool!
Clouds! What an imaginary fantasy!
Ever so old, and still so new!

Elynor A. Baran
THE RACE
Golden leaves are falling
Racing down the street—
Geese in flight are crying!
Birch and maple leaves whirl to meet—
Blanketing the earth in yellow gold.
Another farewell to Autumn!
Isn't this a wonderful world?

Patricia G. Woodring
Its a Rough Life For the Wife

This poem was Inspired by my special friend Lara

It's a Rough Life
for the Wife
She knew when we were married, it was for better or for worse.
She had no idea how I liked my beer and how it quenched my thirst.
She didn't even know my Grandfather and how he went out first, on a drunk for years in a hearst.
She was always there when I needed a touch, but I wasn't always there for her.
I touched her in a way too hard sometimes, unfair, too bold, unpure.
She's covered for me too many times for friends and family.
She puts on more makeup to cover her bruises in mixed company.
While her business was lacking

and me attacking her in a drunken rage and oh so cold, she babysitted the last time for me and no more I was told
She brought it out in plain open view, You got to get better, I'll see you thru and heres what I will do . . .
She'll be behind me all the way night after night day after day she'll be beside me when I need a hand
To hold on tight too and understand
She'll be in front pulling when I can't pull alone
only to help when theres a heavy load.
Theres something I look forward to now
and thats a happier life
With my Best Friend my Lover, My Wife!

Mildred A. Davis
THE COLORING BOOK
You've heard of the fad of the coloring book,
Where you may color people small;
Or you color a little child happy,
Or a hero, strong and tall?

God has a coloring book like that,
Where He colors the sad days gray,
And He colored the giraffe very quietly
Because he has nothing to say.

He colored the waters murky
Down deep so that people can't see;
He colored the ripple of a mountain stream
And the flight of a bumble bee.

He colored a twinkling drop of dew
And the velvet on the rose;
He colored green each blade of grass
And every tree that grows.

Then He stroked His paints quite carefully,
And begun to color you;
I held my breath and prayed that He
Might color you as true.

He daubed and stirred and took His time,
Like a writer with a fine pen;
And I knew my prayer was answered,
For He colored you my friend.

Martie
LOVE IS FRAGILE
Love is fragile; handle it with love.
Treated very tender it will bloom
Blessings you'll receive from above.
Love is a gift from heaven.
Cultivate it. There will not be room
To hold the precious peace to be given.

Each of us is made uniquely different.
No two alike! Each an individual!
By one thread are we all united.

A portion of love was given all.
Love is fragile; handle it with truth,
Feed it with kindness and patience.

Love is fragile; handle it with care.
Don't burn it with hate or drown it in pity or stump it in anger nor choke it in greed.
It can die from neglect or forgetfulness.
Our vanity can shun it till it shrivels . .
Our lying can bruise and hurt.

Love is a gift to cherish and preserve.
Love makes life so worthwhile.
"God is love," the Bible says.
Love links us all together.
Love is fragile; handle it with God,
And someday with Him we'll reconcile.

Betty Ruth Philips
PHANTOM OF THE NIGHT
The quiet night, the silence soothes my spirit
Its darkness broken by a waxing moon.
It makes me long to reach out in the stillness
To hold you close yet give our feelings room.

I sense my love take wings and find a tree top
And look down on this form with special glee
And marvel from its vantage point of tree top
That love can still survive this travesty.

Then the silence of the night enfolds me
I'm cradled in its loving caring arms
Then I can close my eyes and feel you near me
And once again I'm happy, loved and warm.

Monnie Davis
MY CARROT PLANT
It started with a carrot
When pale leaves began to show
I cut off the top, gave it water and sun
And it begn to grow.

It grew to be a very nice plant
Setting on my window sill
When the carrot started to decay
And the plant began to look ill.

I knew that something had to be done
So I took out my paring knife
I began to operate
Not bad, for just a housewife.

The plant already looks better
But I really don't know it's fate
Just hoping that my surgery
Wasn't performed too late.

It seems apparent now, what it's fate will be
My poor carrot plant will die
And I, have failed dismally
In my attempt at botanical surgery.

Our World's Best Loved Poems

Maxine E. Vann Thompson
LOVE'S QUIVER
An arrow springing from love's
quiver,
Finer than heirlooms of rubies,
sapphire, gold;
Life blossoms melon-like from its
Giver,
Quite an age old miracle to
behold.

Greater than any worldly
endeavor,
To bear the joy of a vessel in
being,
Thank Jah for such a wondrous
treasure,
Through which the Breath of Life
He brings.

The melody that the newborn
sings while suckling the breast,
(What sound under the sun can
there replace?)
So eager to meet life's challenge,
life's test,
Its lyrics which man's mortality
negates.

Rosemarie V. Erskine
DEPRESSION
The day has ended;
and I'm alone.
The day has ended;
and the cold winds have blown.
The day is over;
and all is still.
The day is over;
and I go on by sheer will.
The day is finished;
and purple sky meets night
black.
The day is finished;
and sweet, sweet, lost day,
I long for it back.

Doris Riley
GOD'S SUNSET
Only God can make a sunset,
T'was beautiful and showed
the handiwork of God,
A myriad of lights
red, yellow, purple, blue, and
gold
Changeable colors streaked
across the sky.

Only God can make a sunset
Burst like fireworks on the
horizon,
A parade of brilliant hues
Oh, if I could only paint,
It would show His infinite
power.

Linda Rapella
TALK TO ME
Talk to me.
Words never spoken,
Only unwanting glares.

We move, we live.
Our mouths never open.
Minds full of fantasies,
That we can only assume.

Shouts cut us deeper,
Thoughts we may regret.
If we had only known.
If we had only spoken.
If you would only . . .
Talk to me.

Edith M. Bender
INSIGHT
Hour by hour
passing away,

endlessly stretching
into day after day.

What is it I want
what do I seek,
from the hours and days
that make up a week?

What if those weeks
become months, then a year,
what if I've no answer
for my being here?

What will I do
if my tears suddenly dry,
if I let the love in my world
always pass by?

It's time now to face
the future that's coming,
to stand up for myself
to finally stop running.

I'm not really different
for I've suddenly found,
my true beliefs and convictions
have been always around.

Edith L. McDonald
MOSAIC
I couldn't come to your world.
You wouldn't come to mine.
So balancing in between the two
You loving me, me loving you
We drifted into abysses of
Darkness and despair
Until we stopped . . clinging
there.

Now my world is different, too.
I'm alone and lost in life
Where once I knew
The value of design.

Richard Layne Dingus
CREDO

_____

*Dedicated to that sublime
Flower—Humanity and to my
purple lotus—Ruth.*

_____

I hold to ONE TRUTH: the basic
LIVINGNESS,
That Perfume Which permeates
creation's Garden.
I hold to LIFE—the ONE LIFE
Whose
Splendoured Rose blossoms as
You,
My Friend.

   I hold to that ONE
   Who is, indeed, ALL.
   I hold to You, my Friend—
   Oh, sublime Flower of
Infinity.

James Renaker
THE BEACH
The sun sat down in orange and
gold,
Then sank into the sea.
At just that moment darkness fell
To create mystery.

Waves lapped upon the
dampened sand
And washed my tracks away.
As if to tell me "you were here"
But, I am here to stay.

Like magic then, the moon was
there,
To light the way for me.
While white caps lined with
silver

Danced upon the sea.

A roaring sound, yet gentle too,
Fell peacefully on my ear.
Like a giant whispering
To try and make me hear.

Some how a story must be told,
Tho just beyond my reach.
Its waiting for me everytime
I walk along "the beach".

Teresa L. Cave

Teresa L. Cave
**What Are the Teenage
Years?**
What are the teenage years?!
They're years full of tears!
It's a time of confusion and
uncertainty!
You seem blind and unable to see!

It's a time of hello's
but even more good-bye's
There are so many lows and highs!

You try so hard to understand
but it seems you never can!
Most of the time you don't even
understand yourself!
It seems like you're always asking
for help!

But they're also years of hopes
and dreams!
A time to find out what love
really means!
Love is something exciting and
new!
It's also a time to discover the
real you!

Teresa Lynn Becker
LIMITATIONS

_____

*Ben, with love for all your
inspiration, encouragement, and
your criticisms.*

_____

It's really not what you've done,
But is it not, a matter of what you
can do, or be it what you will
do.
Let us not let another set our
limitations, but exert ourselves
to be the most that we can be.

Marguerite Ahlberg
SUNSHINE AND OLD MEN
All summer long they sat
Upon the bridge in town.
Watched the passing motorists,
Folks scurring up and down.

Reminisced among themselves
Of times that they once knew,

Disscussed the weather, this and
that,
With ready smile, a word or two.

These fine old gentlemen we see
With time upon their faces,
Returned each day with the sun
To take their usual places.

With winters cold, they retreated
to
The warmth of fireside chair,
To recapture once again
Each cherished moment from
yester year.

Now Nature has begun to change
Her winter dress for spring-like
gown.
How many will return to sit
Upon the bridge in town?

Vi Gielarowski
IMPORTANT

_____

*This poem was written to and
inspired by my husband Thomas
Gielarowski*

_____

All things are important in ones
Life to them, from the very
Beginning to the very end. Why
Is it we so often find, it's
Easier to say "well never mind",
I'm guilty for sure, I'm first to
Say, but thank God if I keep trying
I'll learn to obey.
I've always known it—most of
my life,
But because I'm so human, I
make mistakes
Twice, with God out in front, and
Trusting His words, I'll take more
time
To hear those "important words."

M. T. Barnett
SIMPLICITY

_____

*I dedicate this poem to L. Ron
Hubbard for all his fine works in
Dianetics and the improving of
the condition of the human spirit.*

_____

Simplicity is to me, the beauty of
life we all wish to see,

The essence of life we seek to
know, the light of life of which
we glow,

The power of life of which man
foresakes, degrading himself by
what he takes,

Of a universe he does not know,
his ignorance alone buries him
slow,

And for those who reach for
simplicity in life, will one day
find the power and light,

That of all the universes of which
we play, simplicity is the basic
of all our games . . .

Wendy Poplawski
PRECIOUS TIME
   Near the brook
   They dip their feet
To cool their drowsy minds.
   The daffodils
   Lay gently still
And wink beneath the sun.

Yes, they see
The dust upon the road
On the blue horizon . . .
They understand
Paradise soon ends
And summer fades to fall.

Jack Cavanaugh
TWO WORLDS

---

to my Cathy, and to our Mary

Soft breeze thru' cherry
blossoms blowing on the pair
of unmatched lovers

Oriental Miss
and American Mister
she prayed he'd kiss her

Golden girl, white man
about to enter one world
could it ever work?

He spoke, she listened
she touched his shoulder softly
and then she loved him

They were from two worlds
one's words strange to the other
but no more words now

These two would know pain
from parents, friends and neighbors
but they did not care

Kathleen Nice
NIGHT DREAMS
I walk in shadow in the night
my dreams of love a fancied flight
I hear and see no foe or friend,
I patiently await night's end.

I walk in shadow naught to see
the one I cherish e'er to be
I listen for his sounds, his sigh,
But I am lone as winds drift by.

I walk in shadow one time more
catching a glimpse thru' life's
narrow door
But on the journey my heart does
take,
My mind is still, I come to wake.

Donna S. Romic
REACH OUT AND LIVE
Some people hide from themselves
By pretending the wrongs
That happen to them
Really don't exist.
Hiding from a truth
Is hiding from reality.
Hiding from reality
Is not touching life.
To live is to touch the whole
world.
I have only one wish
As you reach out to touch,
May the world never hurt you.

Mim Rambo
MY GOLD
Some look for gold in the market
place
And some by working a stream
But I found gold in my own
backyard
More than most folks dream.

I found the gold of the morning
sun
The finch eating sunflower seed,
The honey bee on the golden
leaves,
The bloom on the dandelion weed.

I found the gold of an ear of corn,
Of a pumpkin and a goldenrod,
The golden curls of a neighbor's
child
Who's lately come from God.

I found the gold of Morris the cat
And the long-legged puppy next
door,
The golden note of the ole blue
Jays
As over my head they soar.

And if I feel this isn't enough
When my gold filled day is done
I pause by my window and watch
The set of the golden sun.

Elisabeth L. Whetstone
THE MEADOWS

---

*To my Husband—for supporting
me while I spend the summer
writing in solitude at Beasore
Meadows.*

Mountain meadows grow green
and wide
Grasses are lush on every side.
Before summers end each blade
will bloom,
Fade, and die . . . to another give
room.
Winter comes while all is still
green
Ice covers the creek where trout
were just seen.
The spring barely runs . . . it too
will soon freeze
The chill of winter takes the
place of summers breeze.
Chipmunks and squirels tunnel
under-ground
Where they store food through
the summer they found.
There was life in the meadow just
a few days gone by.

An homage to solitude gathers
in the sky.
All is silent waiting for spring
When snow will melt . . . and
mountains will sing.
Patches unmelted there will be
'neath the snow
Strawberry leaves and new
trees beginning to grow.
Summer, Fall, Winter, Spring, all
in good season.
How lovely the meadow!
Whatever the reason.
Tucked between trees,
surrounded by trees,

Hide in a place hardly anyone sees,
Night falls on the meadow an
pins it with a star.
Sounds of the forest how exciting
they are.
A coyote howls . . . a tree limb
pops,
A growling sounds, it is just the
tree tops.
All is in darkness except for
star-light
Sleep comes to the meadow.
Everything is allright.

Jonathan Sylvester Lee
YOU

---

*Dedicated to Cynthia Rose
Foreman because I love you for
the inspiration you have provided
not only for this poem but for me
to continue on in life; because
you are the one person who
means the most to me; and just
because I love you. May we
always be friends.*

Can I honestly say that I don't
love?
No, I do.
My dreams are dying a slow death.
I try to hold on as tight as I can,
but slowly my hands slip.
I reach to feel the head on my
pillow
but none is there but my own;
I long to share a silent moment
holding hands,
but I can't.
If not by my side
then on my mind
and always in my heart. So why
turn me away?
How can it not be when it never
was?
I will always, even if you never
do.
I shall never forget what I was
not allowed.
You.

Patricia C. Nalepa
NO LONGER
No longer is there sunshine
To brighten up each day.
No longer is there comfort,
In any kind of way.

No longer will I ever feel
Your soft and gentle touch.
No longer will there ever be
One who cares as much.

No longer do the songs I hear
Mean anything to me.
No longer dare I hope or dream,
For the future, I can't see.

No longer will I feel your strength
Reach out to me at night,
When nightmares take the place
of dreams
And fill my mind with fright.

No longer can I hold your hand
Or feel your lips kiss mine.
No longer will I hear you say,
"I'll love you till the end of time".

No longer do I care to live,
Inside myself I'd rather hide;
There's just no point in going on,
Not since the day you died.

Christine Brown
To Whom It May Concern
Give me the freedom to be
myself—
the option to be as I am.
Don't figure I'll change to suit
your needs.
I won't be a sculpture of man.
I may be raw clay with potential
to grow but I'll do it on my
time and terms.
I like who I am and what I've
become.
I won't be a whimsy of yearns.
It took me awhile to see my way
clear and to face my own
destiny.
I'm here on this earth to learn as I
go and to be all the best I can
be.
So take it or leave it, love me or
leave me.
I'm all that there is for the taking.
I'm not a chess pawn in a world
full of games.
I'm a happy self-satisfied being.

Collins J. Duet
ODE TO AN EARTHQUAKE
If this world should end tomorrow
And all human hearts be still
The amount would be in millions
Of promises unfulfilled

Kind deeds and good intentions
Put off for another day
Would never serve their purpose
They would simply fade away

We never even pause to think
This earth to atoms fly
And yet it all could happen
In the twinkling of an eye

The Power who made the Heavens
Can the universe destroy
And could do it just as easy
As a child could break a toy

Barbara L. Hoerath
GENTLE WAYS

---

*Your a total inspiration, a total
friend, and the Love of my life.
You have put a smile on my face,
a tear in my eyes, sunshine in my
life, and Love in my heart. I Love
You Tom, Barb*

The gentle way that you've
touched my life
has caught me at a vunerable
moment.
So tender that I lost my heart to
yours
floating endlessly into the
unknown,
only to experience many changes.
Like the seasons from fall to
spring,
the warmth and beauty surrounds
our world
giving our Love the strength to
withstand all
that tries to destroy what we've
created together.
Searching for serenity within our
worlds
and finding the Love we can
never share.
I've been looking for a lifetime.
The voices in our soul speaks

only unto our hearts,
that no living creature shall ever
hear the unspoken.

James S. Riggs
THE NEWCOMER
Billy my son I know you're not
here—

But of course I know you'll
Be gone some months plus a
year.
Your birthday is coming I know
real soon
And I'm not in a mood to sit
here and croon.
I do remember the day you came
upon the scene—
All ready to play—yet you
looked so serene.
You must get acquainted with
mommie and daddy for sure.
Then it seemed to us you were
not so demure.
We loved all your antics—Your
play and your schemes.
It seemed you must have come
from a dream.
How well I remember the day of
your birth.
Your mother and father were
proud to be on this earth.
Never in my life have I had such
fun—
As the day you came to see us.
We knew we had won.

Elizabeth Haynes McAnally
ENDANGERED SPECIES (?)
Flicker in my garden
rapping on a post,
Where are your parents, children,
cousins,
who used to come by dozens?
A raucous, happy host.

Have you lost your mate and
family
by some insidious fog;
by poison in a treetop,
or Endrin in a log?

Fourteen used to check my plot;
now you're the only one.
Did thoughtless boys pursue you
with arrow, rock or gun?

Now you sit a lonely hermit
chittering on my gate,
pecking on my woodpile,
calling for your mate.

No one seems to answer,
no one hears your call.
I wonder if another spring
will bring you back at all.

Marci (Pulczinski) Lindahl
FAMILY

---

*This poem is dedicated to the
most beautiful people in the
world—my family*

I'll go back to the days when ten
were at home
Five were just little and five
seemed so grown

My dad, what a big man with
hands made of steel
He worked very hard then to
bring home the meal

My mom worked right with him
but size wasn't the part

I know what I seen most, is her
warm loving heart

My older sisters then, seemed
different in a way
I remember being leary when
they came home to stay

My brothers I worshipped, or was
that fear too
I didn't know the difference then
cause all that seemed so new

You see when you're the little
one and eight have come before
You never get to know them well
till you go out that door

All of us are grown up now and
seem so close in ages
I think someday I'll write a book
called
"Love In All Ten Stages"

Joseph H. Reed
CANCER
The news went through my heart
and hit my soul as I sat and
watched my life unfold.
For my mind was not the same as
I heard cancer Roar it's name.
To fight a fear I can not see,
could this be a test for me?
Oh God in heaven here's my
hand, your every wish is my
command and this is where I
firmly stand.
Please Help me God I'm just a man.
WE WON!

Janet Barbo
MY LITTLE ONE
Sitting here alone
I have no one to talk to
So I think about you
My little one.

Each day you grow.
I wonder if you will stay with me
Or will you choose to go
My little one.

Will I carry you well
Will you be healthy
Will you be a boy or girl
My little one.

You in there, me out here
You scare me you know.
Can I bear the pain I will endure
for you
My little one.

Will I be able to fill your fantasys
Give you what you need.
Will you listen to fairy tales and
nursery rythms
My little one.

You seem so far away
Yet you are with me every day.
I can't give you much you know.
Will you except just me
My little one.

Michael Radford
THE ATTIC
Into the attic
dark and dreary
I tread so often
tired and weary

Past memories filled
with laughs and joys
and crates of used,
long-forgotten toys

where cobwebs hang
from rafters high

while smells of age
and mildew gather neigh

I love to sit
among these treasures
that once brought
so much pleasure

as a child I hid
within these walls
playing in my room
ignoring father's calls

many days as a teen
I'd sit for hours amid
piles of dirty books
that my mother forbid

as I became a parent
the attic soon became
a place to escape
and never hear my name

sometimes even now
past the cobwebs I go
up into the attic
from pressures below

Catharina Rinta

Catharina Rinta
THANK YOU, GOD
Thank You, God.

I thank You, God, for skies so blue,
for sunshine warm, for each day
new.
For mountains high and Oceans
deep,
for joyful play and restful sleep.

For quiet nights and busy days,
a touch of love, a word of praise.
For friends so true, who share our
years,
through joy and sorrow, smiles
and tears.

For winters white and summers
green
and all the lovely months
between.
For distant moon and twinkling
star,
who make us see how small we
are.

For nurturing sun and gentle rain,
on thirsty land and fields of grain.
For farmer's toil on fertile field,
with harvest ripe and fruitful
yield.

For sunsets red, and golden dawn,
for songs of birds, to start each
morn.
Each day a miracle anew,
For all this, God, I'm thanking
You.—

Lilyan B. MacPherson
MY BELOVED
You are the moon and the stars
A softly moonlit night.
You are the sun imparting to all
Your wondrous beautiful light.
You are the clouds in the sky
Soft fleecy light ones and dark
stormy thunderheads.
You are the wind and the rain
and the sea,
Every leaf, every tree, every bird,
every bee,
You are my father and my
brother too,
You are— My Beloved.

Josee Pleau
LOVE DIVINE
We would drink love
from the same cup
As we in each other's
arms would lie.

My lips would
search thine
And once found
what Love Divine!

Rain Fawn Barrett
My Birthday Wish To You
If I was to give you a birthday
wish,

First I would give you all your
dreams you wish come true!

Second I would give you all the
riches of the world.

Third I would give you the
biggest smile to make you
happy for the rest of your
life. . .

Fourth I would give all the gold to
make all your fortunes come
true . . .

Fifth I would never frown to make
your night too blue.

Sixth I would give you all the kisses
so you're never sick or ill.

Seventh I would give you a day of
rest, so we could start from the
first wish all over again.

Happy Birthday My Love

Frances S. Hannah
BRINE
The ocean
is salty
from tears wept by humans.
I wept a few myself.

Nei—Nei
PRAYER FEATHER
Eyelids drawn to peacefulness;
nostrils flared by cool freshness;
ears atuned to still silence;
lips moistened by morning dew.

Amber skin bronzed by weather;
body clad in fringed leather;
tawny hands held a feather
as eagles overhead flew.

Prayers chanted to heaven,
the feather waved to leaven
songs in heart deeply graven
to the Spirit, great and true.

Spiritual warmth rained to earth.
A bright rainbow formed a girth
'round man and feather in birth;
his hearth, life and blessings grew.

Ann Michelle Larion
AMICABLE DIVORCE

I pass you by on the street
and feeling the spark of a long
    ago flame,
turn and call your name
I inquire as to how you've been
in mentholated words of
    passionate indifference
and nibble contentedly on your
artificially sweetened reply
when you ask how I've been,
I wonder if you would enjoy my
    successes
and regret my misfortunes
or just the opposite
The silence that began growing
when we first said hello
overtakes the conversation
and there is nothing left to say but
good—bye
and as we part,
I drop a lint—covered 'I love you'
I'd been carrying around a long
    time
into the gutter

Mary Jane Shackelford
GIFTS OF GOD

I would like to tell the world how
    God sent a special friend
And precious gifts from heaven
    with the Saviour of lost men
With two sturdy legs to stand on
    and two perfect eyes to see
With two good ears to hear with
    and a loving family

A companion who is faithful a
    love who never strays
Someone who shows devotion in
    a million little ways
Someone to walk beside us and
    help us bear our load
A brother's love to guide us along
    life's rocky road

There's water when we're thirsty
    and shelter from the storm
There's a rocking chair to sit in,
    by a fire to keep us warm
There's lots of friends and
    neighbors, to share in
    everything
There's a place where we can
    worship and old time hymns to
    sing

A smile to greet a stranger that
    we meet along the way
Some of these are gifts to keep
    and some to give away
So before our race is finished and
    we're placed beneath the sod
Let's send our thanks to heaven
    for all these gifts of God

Ina L. Rist
OUR FLAG

My Country and Vietnam Vets

We see our flag up in the sky,
It's brilliant colors flying.
On battle fields we keep it high,
And that is where our boys are
    dying.
They fought so hard to win the
    war,
And won as you can see,
Mid shot and shell and mud and
    mire
They fought for you and me.

They need our help, we know
    they do
To protect this land of ours
They are ready to protect our lives
In any day or hour.
So here is to our flag we love
To our boys so brave and true
May our flag ever wave in the
    sky above
Wave for me and for you
And may God protect our boys
    over there
Who are fighting our country's
    cause
May their hearts be true forever
As they uphold our coutrys laws
Please keep them safe and bring
    them home
So that glory will be ours and
    ours alone.

Mary Letha Washington

Mary Letha Washington
WHAT SHALL I BE?

*To my sweet and understanding
daughter, Mari Letha Washington*

Through your love
You want me to be happy and
    free—
Free to live and choose from
The many courses you set for me,
Hoping one of these
I'll surely be.

I need your guidance and loving
    care
To carry me through each trying
    year,
I am trying to be what you want
    me to be,
But to be happy and free
I will need to be me!

Madeline Rasmusson
Trials Of a Kindergartener

I have to hang my jacket
On a hook higher then I can reach
And eat their so called good lunch
They know I would rather have
    ice cream and a peach.

Why do I have to do such hard
    things
Like telling my left foot from the
    right
Those two things look just alike
    to me
When I take my shoes off at night.

I am suppose to learn to do things
    good
So I can to a nice job adapt

They tell me I am good at spilling
Coke on my father's lap.

They think I should know my
    own galoshes
That is some thing that can not
    be done.
They should have names like
    dogs
When you call them they should
    run.

You have to sing the teacher's
    songs
Draw pictures that are very fine
You have to know girls from boys
Or you get in the wrong bath
    room line.

You are suppose to love teachers
    and bus drivers
To love a puppy is much easier I
    would say
To tell time when the big hand is
    on 6
Little one on 3, teacher faints,
    school is out for the day.

Deby Schultheis
FRIENDS FOREVER

You are a friend forever.
The miles may separate us,
    however
friendship lasts regardless of
    distance.
It is not lost because of
    circumstance.

Because we shared a lot of good
    times
the memories will last a lifetime.
You are in my mind as if you
    were here
thoughts of you will never
    disappear.

I wish we could be together more
as we were at one time before.
I miss you but don't think I
    would
forget you or that I ever could.

Joan Feltz Schifano
To a Man and His Train

*To my father, upon his
retirement from the railroad. Dad,
thanks for the memories . . . I love
everyone.*

Clickity clack, clickity clack
Is imbedded in my brain.
Clickity clack, clickity clack,
Oh how I love the train.

It's whistle is like a hypnotic
    command,
Which takes me back to days
When life was oh so simple,
When life was oh so grand.

Hurry, hurry can't miss that train!
Swim—suits, towels all in hand.
Hurry, hurry can't miss that train!
We're off to frolic in waves and
    sand.

The smell of the sea,
Waves crashing on shore,
Sandcrabs and castles . . .
Oh, take me back once more!

Susan Hill
REMNANTS

From this forlorn station
in the asperous DeBeque Canyon,

only the Colorado River has
    endured
to flow past your structure.

In the heyday of western growth,
immigrants welcomed your
    drifting smoke,
stopping to chat with friendly folk
and share long awaited warmth.

Stagecoach house was the sentry
for this hostile rugged country,
where few dared to venture
into unknown danger.

The chimney is the only remnant
to struggle through the years,
salvaging your forgotten career
that lasted for only an instant.

Of those who pass your way,
recall your pestigious heyday
as your only surviving remain
blends into the canyon terrain.

Carol Wolfe
WE WERE FRIENDS ONCE

*To Kym for caring and
understanding and for just being
there.*

No one cares if I'm here or not
They would leave me to die
But you said you liked me a lot
I hoped we would never say
    good—bye

Then one night came along
When our interests didn't meet
    eye to eye
And I did everything wrong
I just wanted to die

I called you the next day
To see if you hated me
You said no in the most forgiving
    way
Friends you still wanted to be

Your words were confusing
Ones I had not heard before
And my reply was all but amusing
Friends we were no more

We were friends once
Why do we play life's game?
We were friends once
Will it ever be the same?

Betty J. White
A REAL MAN

*This poem was written for,
inspired by, and dedicated to My
Darling Earl, with all my love.*

He may not walk, but he stands
    for love;
To my heart he holds the key;
I've found in him, true love so rare;
Thankful am I—he's loving me . . .

Those macho men, full of whit
    and whims,
Know little of life's hard
    knocks . . .
They whimper and sulk,
    complain, and brag,
True love and compassion they
    mock . . .

What would they do if they were
    you,
Suddenly disabled and wrought;

Appreciation of all the "finest"
things,
Would be much too late to be
got . . .

Do they ever feel an endless love,
As we do whenever we kiss;
Would their embrace mean half
as much,
As ours, after an absence like
this . . .

They jog a mile or climb a
mountain,
That's their thing to do . . .
But n'er have they reached the
high we have,
Together—just we two.

Lolita M. Stettner
SMALL THINGS
I find that I am often
elevated or decimated
by small things,
fleeting glances,
short sentences,
beginning with "I"
and ended with "you",
so quickly,
it is nearly gone
before you realize
what is happening,
expressions that say
what words can only hint at
or even worse,
obscure entirely.

W. T. Reeves
THE CROSS
Man took string, paper, and a cross
and built a kite to fly.
And waited for the breath of God
to lift it to the sky.

It floats Oh so gracefully,
and makes boys hearts so gay.
But the cross on which my savior
died
was built this very way.

They nailed his body to the cross
like paper on a kite.
And mocked and cursed at him,
as they gazed upon this mournful
sight.

They never waited for the breath
of God
to lift him to the sky.
But the hands of sinful man
would hoist him way up high.

It seems such a terrible shame
that he had to die this way,
But it's faith in Jesus on that cross,
that I know my soul will rise
someday.

Helen Cranfill Elliott
OKLAHOMA SUNSET

*In celebration of the Sixty—
Second Wedding Anniversary of
William Edgar and Ina Spiva
Cranfill*

The orange ball of fire
Dissolves into the radiant hues.
The silvery clouds drift higher
To gaze on earthly views.

Into the distance time fades
The golden rays of light.
Dusk lowers her shades
To make ready for the night.

Robert (Bob) Flanagan
In Sympathy
To merely say I'm sorry
At a time as sad as this
Would hardly seem to fill the bill
For the loved one you will miss.

It must seem the world is ending
When you see that empty chair
But if you will take a closer look
You will see that God is there.

Betty L. Steiner

Betty L. Steiner
THE BEAUTY OF A TREE

*Dedicated to my three grand—
daughters, Amy, Lori and Joanna
who have the beauty and grace as
the trees I have written about in
this poem.*

A vision of loveliness caught my
eye today,
A tree its branches to the wind
did sway.
In its full spectrum the leaves so
green,
The most beautiful sight I have
ever seen.

Pastel painted blossoms their
fragrance so sweet,
A heavenly scent, a magnificent
treat.
I searched into my heart to see,
What is more elegant than a
beautiful tree.

In the distance the trees made a
pattern in the sky,
With the white billowy clouds
passing by.
The shade by the willow, on the
glistening lake,

Behold its beauty, my breath did
take.

Maples with their leaves green
and gold,
Sturdy oaks with their acorns so
bold.
Golden chain trees, a gift to
behold,
In a tree natures majesty to
unfold.

Trees are a miracle spring and
summer,
And with the fall they change in
color.
The trees then in winter cold and
bare,
Trees at rest and nature taking
care.

To restore their strength so in
the spring,
The trees again their beauty will
bring.
Once again with anticipation we
will see,
The mystery of nature, a
beautiful tree.

Henry Eric Linstromberg
IN UNICORNS

To the unicorn within us all.

Such men as Job
and Marco Polo,
There was Shakespeare
and, of course, Plato
and Julius Caesar.
Yes, all of these men believed.
The obvious question:
Who am I to disagree?

Kim Varner
MY FIRST DATE
He was late picking me up,
The tire went flat.
On the way to the drive in,
We crossed a black cat.

The french fries were greasy,
It started to rain,
His roof was stuck down,
Am I going insane?

My father was mad,
He brought me home late,
Boy, oh boy, has this been
a date.

Phyllis Newton
MEMORY'S EXCURSION
When mem'ry an excursion takes
And views the scenes of former
days,
It soon within our soul awakes
A spirit for poetic lays.

When back to childhood's playful
hours
Our thoughts are by sweet
mem'ry led
Through flow'ry fields and shady
bowers
Where nature's sweetest joys
were shed.

It's then fond mem'ry makes us
sigh
For those sweet hours that could
not last,
And brings a tear-drop from the
eye
As tribute to the time that's past.

And when, through youth's still
later days
Sweet mem'ry leads our willing
mind
And calls up forms on which to
gaze
Of happiness—of joy refined.

For then, for then, what pen can
write
The feelings that sweet mem'ry
brings
From those sweet moments of
delight
Which flew away on rainbow
wings,

But when fond mem'ry spreads
her wings
And back to former scenes she
goes,
It's not all pleasure that she brings
For with the joys, she calls up
woes.

Then cease fond mem'ry, cease to
roam
Through all those former scenes
of life,
Look forward to a better home
The future with bright joys is rife.

W. C. Clement
PATIENCE
Patience is a Cardinal Virtue,
That Unties the Knots of Life,
It Brings to You Some Victory,
When You Face the Battle's Strife.
It is not a Built-in Feature,
For You to Use Upon Request,
It only Comes through Daily
Preening,
As You Strive to Do Your Best.
In Sickness It will Conquer,
Where without It You would fail
To Reach that Peaceful Harbor,
Void of Rough and Stormy Gale.
When in trouble It will Lift You
From the Depths of Great Despair,
Where Temptations would
Subdue You,
With Sweet Angels Attending
There.
It will Give to You the Prestige
You Require Each Passing Day,
To Show to Those Around You,
It is the Noble Coveted Way.

Judith Harrison—Pearson
MESSAGE TO SOMEONE
Memories are flowing,
Like endless rain into a paper
town.
Images of broken lights lend gleam
To a pool of tears crying for the
day.
If for some reason
the wind should blow my love
in your direction
Would your hands reach out
like branches of a tree
to stop it?
For one passing moment
of your life could I be with you
or would your fingers open wide
and let the wind blow me
through?

Betty Byars
Thank You For the Flower
Dear Sir:

Remember the other day when I
came home from job hunting—

43

so dejected, so edgy, so frustrated?
"It's late in the season." "There are not many job opportunities in our small community." And *some* people reasoned that I am too *old!*
You and I know that's untrue, but *they* don't.
Remember how near to tears I was when I turned into the driveway?

Well, this is to say "Thank You" for that little, stubborn poppy, growing right out of the crack in the cement. There it was—in a location certainly not conducive to growth, with its beautiful little bright orange face turned up to You in love and trust.

How humble I felt, Father! Knowing me as You do, You know there will be other days of frustration and possibly tears. All I ask, Father, is that You please put another flower where I'll see it. Thank You.

Martha Stroshine Burrow
MY CAT
I sometimes watch my cat
sleeping as she will,
Curled up in the sunshine
on the window sill.

She stretches out her paws
sits straight up and yawns,
Glances out the window at
the birds there on the lawn.

They flutter and they chatter
and I'm sure they are amused,
To know the cat could have them
for dinner if she choosed.

I suppose she thinks about it
but her cat—dish fed her well,
And she's quite content to stay
curled up on the window sill.

Duane Frederick Jones
ON PREJUDICE
May we pamper Pride?
Its time is short
But use it if you can.
As a quick reward for effort
It must hide the world again.

And appreciate its passing glow
For Pride but lives to glare
Its sweet, uncomplicated
moments
To remind us that we cared.

Millicent D. Johnston
TRAVELS
I took a trip to Germany
And saw a wall with wire
I took a trip to Japan
And saw cities that were fire

I took a trip to Washington
And as I looked around
I saw a great black boomarang
Neatly planted in the ground

I took a trip to China
Where birth is now curtailed
I took a trip to Jerusalem
Where Jesus once was nailed

I took a trip to Africa
Where they starve and the earths
not plowed

I took a trip to Rome
And saw St. Peters with a crowd

They say that travel broadens you
So you know what I've learned
That mankinds lot is to be shot
Or hanged or starved or burned

James F. Webb
BEAUTY
When I behold your Beauty and
your smile,
It is reflected through my life and
world
Just as the dawn light gilds each
newest morn
With molten rainbows and the
day is born
While buds, their dew-kissed lips
by sun unfurled
In all of Mother Nature's grandest
style,
Burst forth in blooms of
breathless loveliness
And fill the summer breeze with
perfume rare.
So does your radiant smile, My
Dearest Lee,
Enchant each hour that you have
granted me
And as I wake to see the day
dawn fair,
Your Beauty bursts upon my
consciousness . . .

Br. Edward C. Breault, S.C.
I WANT YOU
I Want You!
Forget my sins, my gross neglect,
Know only that I need you;
Think not on the times I did not
reflect,
Think only that I want you!

Forget the times I didn't care,
And know that now I want to;
Forgive the fool, the sinner spare,
I love you, Lord, and want you!

Jane Richards
HAPPY LEGS
I've heard about an Octopus,
Who has six legs, not eight.
He rushes out to play each day,
Not sad, this was his fate.

He skips about most everywhere,
We often hear him sing.
I've seen him roll right down a
wave,
Just being happy is his thing.

One leg is pink and two are green,
The greenest that you've ever seen.
Then two are blue and one is
yellow,
He's just a happy little fellow.

As he swam down for lunch one
day,
A huge shark lurked there, on his
way.
He does not fight and never begs;
That's why they call him "Happy
Legs".

He swam right off without a care,
As if there was nobody there.
Then came a friend along the way,
To swim and eat, dance and play.

Pauline Breshears
SYMBOLS
A Rose is the national flower
of affection and love.
The symbol of peace and

duration is the Turtledove.
To show our states unity
Old Glory waves in the sky.
To protect our freedom
we will even die.
The Eagle is the emblem of our
nation's pride and strength.
To preserve our beliefs,
we go to great lengths.
The gift of my heart shows
the love for you I feel.
An unearned gift of love
causing senses to reel.
Were you to ask if
my love were really true,
I would collect these symbols
and give them all to you.

Robert T. Thies
IN PASSING
Silent echoes fill this room,
how long has it been now,
Ample time to cogitate,
of what I now avow,

Eighty days of changing years,
the calender's run dry,
Lost will be my sight and sound,
once I close my eyes.

Jane Frederick Krauss

Jane Frederick Krauss
PARADISE FOREVER
Take me to your Paradise
Take me with you there
To the special place we share
Hold me gently—
So I'll know you care
Take me to your Paradise
Of warmth and shiney star
Take me to the Moon, my Love
Or Paradise, afar
No other ever took me there
No other ever will
Take me to your Paradise,
Forever

Letha Memorie Lloyd-Wayne
Symphony Of the Universe
Like a masterpiece in music
The world's architecture
Is structured with pinions
And columns of massive decibels
Of herculean chords interwoven
And laced with melodies
And embellishments like a
Tapestry of intricate beauty.
Oh that mankind could join
In a chorus sublime
To silence the chaos
Riding rampant o'er
The earth like the
Four horsemen of the Apocalypse.
May they envision perce within

Putting on the mind of Christ
And come alive with
Love Divine.
May we walk in the footsteps
Of the Master of Peace.

Diane Marie Luke
LIFE
It took me quite some time to
learn exactly what life is,
but as the years passed me by,
life became a game, or quiz.

Life is full of many steps
which takes you along your
way,
bringing you opportunities
with every passing day.

There are time of loneliness,
but more times of happiness,
because life isn't harsh to you,
in fact, it has gentleness.

Life I'm sure would mean much
more
if only people could see
that this life is full of love,
like the love it gives to me.

Carrol C. McLean
ETERNAL LOVE
Oh, Child so full of grief.
Our love is the fury of the ocean,
And our hearts are the rocks on
the shore.
Our voices are the sea gulls a
calling,
And our souls are the blue sky
above.
Oh, Child sleep in peace.
Remember the fury of the ocean.
Remember the rocks on the
shore.
Remember the sea gulls a calling.
Remember the blue sky above.
Child, our love's there for
eternity.

Gordon L. Florence
BELIEF
Deeds
and sufferings
are increments in power
obtained
through faith.

Bruce W. Jones
**To My Wife On Mother's
Day**
I know you're not my mother,
But I would have no other
As my wife.

I love you with a passion
That won't go out of fashion
All my life.

Its a joy to be your lifemate.
You're a gorgeous, sparkling
wifemate.
I'm content.

The Lord has blessed me dearly.
Its obvious you're clearly
Heaven sent.

Marianne G. Holliday
**You Wouldn't Let Me Put
My Head On Your
Shoulder**
Days were long and nights so
deary,
my heart was lost, growing weary,
I needed you so,
you didn't know,
you wouldn't let me put my head

on
your shoulder . . .

Where was the bond that held us
together,
when we talked, it was about the
weather,
I wanted you here,
you cried no tear,
you wouldn't let me put my head
on
your shoulder . . .

You didn't believe I would go
astray,
is it my fault, you took my hopes
away,
how I loved you,
what did you do,
you wouldn't let me put my head
on
your shoulder . . .

If you still want me you must
fight,
I've had my share, now I need light,
look across your sky,
there's a reason why,
I may not want to put my head on
your shoulder . . .

Katrina Guffey
MAN-CHILD
How mischevious you must have
been as a child,
I see that in you now.
The twinkle still in your eyes,
the child-like excitement at
something new,
it all remains . . . but you must
realize
my "man-child", that a grown man
has replaced the mischevious
child.
You have responsibilities, as any
man has.
My "man-child" . . .
How can I make you
understand?

April Susino
WHAT IS A FRIEND?
A friend is someone who's always
there
Someone to talk to, someone to
share
Someone who'll help you
whenever your down
Someone to make you smile, not
frown
The friend I am speaking of is
seldom found
You don't see many hanging
around
But I was fortunate enough to find
A one in a million, a one of a kind

Helen G. Deer
**Put Nother Nickel In the
Nickleodeon
(Is It Music, Music, Music?)**
Union buildings are all alike
tonight,
Remembering college halls of
learning,
Thinking of him who lost a blind
man's sight,
Believing war had left him burning.
The juke box plays "Nickleodeon"
Yet all there is is his scarred eyes
smiling,
Leaving now the task of day
custodian,
Seeking ways with words

unchained for dialing.
On some Pacific isle a mine had
scored,
And he it was whose face was
ripped Jacque's mask,
Now he sought to learn facts he
could afford,
Education for tools was his soul
task.
Vibrating cries plead painfully in
night,
For coins to heal my eyes in
beggar's plight.

Bobbie (Rosemary Ruiz)
THE POOL OF HIS LIFE
The pond is tranquil, transparent
and glitters.
He pauses at the edge to ponder
his fate,
He observes a silver dragonfly, as
it flutters in the breeze,
All his senses are arched as he
scopes the present,
And searches the past of his
foibles and follies that he
might have overlooked,
Placidity permeates to his very
soul,
He knows where he's been, and in
which direction he has to go.

Isabella Ge Tweedy
THE DUBLIN LAD
"He's not the lad for you, Lass."
"He never could be true."
(But Oh, my Father and my
Mother,
His eyes are deepest blue.)

The night is falling rapidly,
(He is waiting there outside)
"His heart is as black as his hair,
Lass."
(But his arms are held out wide)

I open the door and look over there
Where trees sway each to the
other—
"And where be you going at this
late hour?"
"To the barn for the milk, oh, my
Mother!"

Laura E. Kelsey
FAITH IN THE ENGINEER
A train
Late and speeding
Went hurtling through the night
While passengers cringed and
clutched in
Panic.

The world
"Like a drunkard" (Isaiah 24:20)
Giddily reels and spouts;
While mankind rush on, to
"Wits's end" terror! (Psalm 107:27)

When life
Brings periods
Of pain, stress and turmoil;
Some folks will fidget, fuss, and fail
In faith.

A child
Enjoyed the ride
On the fast lurching train;
Because at the throttle was her
Daddy! (Romans 8:28)

Hazel M. Froemming
THE FUTURE
These are our children, our most
precious jewels.

The world is a turmoil for them
to live through.
We teach them the wrong things
as well as what's right,
And expect them to understand
all of this plight.

Is it such a wonder that people
today
Search for tommorow in their
own special way?
The happiness they look for they
never will find,
Until peace and freedom on this
earth are divine

Serenity and patience too few of
us have
With garments of glory we wish
to be clad.
The war and destruction is
created from this.
We make our lives an endless
abyss.

The future is endless, but will
never be
Undefiled and happy for you or
me.
Our children must build a world
like above
Of humility, understanding, and
undaunted Love.

These are our children, God's
greatest gift.
He lends them to us for our
hearts to uplift.
Let us build around them, so
someday they'll learn
The pius tranquility of Gods
Holy Word.

Stanley Jack
BIG QUESTION MARK
He's a "nut" —
we've often heard it said.
Or, "nuttier than a fruitcake" —
strait-jacketed in bed.
Now, consider the nuts in nature
whence the reference
came about;
and they'll include
a lot of nutty humans
without a hint of doubt.
Besides,
there are connotations
other than the nuts
upon a tree;
which make me wonder
if, behind my back,
they're pointing straight at me.

Kipp Curtis
THE VICTOR
In simple starlit night he sighs
Gazing out with empty eyes
Memories of ancient lives
Times when strength and life
were his
Battles fought, victories won
Beneath the glaring warriors sun
When sword and shield had been
his way
When fighters yell and horses
neigh
Cried the end to invading foes
Keeping safe the fields of home
Nurtured with the blood of Rome
No longer need to defend
Quiet sleep is on the land
Swords and shields hang on walls
In darkened empty warriors halls

Moonlight bathes the lonely hill
Where rests the battles final kill
Silent guardian in the night
Fought for what he felt was right
Now nothings left to fight for
He rests in peace forevermore

Woodie J. Conner
IRELAND

*In memory of my parents Alex A.
Johnson and Dora Copeland
Johnson*

I have never been to Ireland;
Yet I know
How the Shamrock grows,
I am certain of the places
Where the river Shannon flows.

I have never seen my homeland
Where all the green grows wild;
I learned of it
From songs my mother sang
When I was yet a child.

George Beecher
PRISONERS OF WAR
Pity the prisoners of war—
We have lost our freedom
No matter who wins at last
Think of lost youth spent
In fetters of invested energies
Under poisoning threats to life
In justification for being tops
In a world of empty choices
To fight or flee—
Only after the fighting will anyone
Be free a little while exhausted
In a struggle all sides lose—
Then caught in preparations
For another die-hard blast
We are psyched-out prisoners of
war
For twenty years before the fight

Lisa Michelle Ehlert
CONNECTIONS
Are cobwebs
Thin strands
The only
Connection
Between my life and
Yours,
Too easily snapped
If the wind blows
Too hard?
Or is it a connection
Of steel ropes
That still,
If mind is put to it
Can be welded apart?
Or could it be

That we are two
Twines
Wolven together
With each other
And every other twine,
Only broken
If the whole
Weaving is
Destroyed?
William Robert Senter Jr.
MELISSA

Dedicated to Melissa Senter Shine, Aunt of Michael Stephen McGee May 4, 1974 to November 12, 1979

You showed me happiness
You showed me love
You showed me the wonders of nature
And the wonders of stars above

You taught me to dance
You taught me to sing
You taught me games
You taught me of beauty in everything

You always made me happy
Whenever you were near
You came when you were needed
You were always such a dear

I loved you from the beginning
For all your wonderous ways
I loved you for loving me
And giving me so many happy days

I shall watch you through your life ahead
From here in Heaven above
Wishing you the same happiness
You gave me with your love.

Frances McLaren
TODAY'S REFLECTIONS

"To Ginny—my inspiration"

A reflection of her came to mind today
Thoughts of her kind and loving way
I saw her smile at little homeless Tim
When she presented a brand new bike to him

A feeling of warmth filled my heart today
As I thought of Ginny and her humble way
The unsigned note on a big Easter toy
Left on the church step for an ailing boy

A song of love I heard sung today
About one who shares in a special way
The daily scattering of crumbs out 'neath her trees
Lyrics from songbirds remind me of these

The beauty of a rainbow my eyes saw today
A ribbon of color painted across heaven's way
Hues of compassion for the troubled to see

Like a rainbow she appeared so silently
A special kind of blessing I've felt today
A feeling of gladness that she came my way
A gift she left that only thoughts can see
This day of reflections she gave to me

Martha K. McHenry
GETTING THERE
Twirling, whirling, trotting, hopping
To lend a helping hand to someone in need.

Running, trudging, jumping, skidding
Just to be on time.

Walking, sliding, swaying, prancing
Far out in front.

Wagging, spinning, staggering, stumbling
Making it without confusion.

Leaping, spurting, darting, dashing
To win the race.

Tripping, limping, bouncing, shuffling
But getting there on time.

Marylou McLean Hahn
OUR LOVE
In the sweetness of my Springtime, he came and held me in his heart.
We learned about each other and vowed "til death do us part".
In the heat of my Summertime, how he cooled the passion there.
We played, laughed and cried, sharing a love, so true, so rare.
In the golden time of Autumn, he stayed on and held me near.
We cherished every moment, as he stilled all my fears.
Now alone, I'm in my Wintertime, my heart has slowed it's pace.
The pure sweet Joy of having known him, is now mine alone to face.
Death's Angel took him from me, and I must go it on my own.
Those sweet memories are forever, and now, they are mine alone.
I loved him as no other and I know he loved me too.
The Seasons of a lifetime and a

sweet love shared by two.
The vows were made to one another, there was no preacher there.
No legal ties to bind us, only our love, so true, so rare.

Gina M. Carro
A STAGE OF LIFE
I use to ponder in my youth about the life that was to come,
Would it be as a slow ebb of waters, or like a deer on the run,
How innocent was my thinking dreaming dreams of babbling brooks,
How childlike to imagine that dreaming was all it took

To guard against the turmoils that eventually besets us all,
Our minds create such patterns in a world that is ever so small,
Now that my horizon has broadened to this ever present age,
I long to go back in time, would I but dare turn the page.

The memories of my childhood are affixed tenaciously,
To the core of my sub-conscious, it eats voraciously,
But I must unleash its hold, this dichotomy of the past,
I will embrace the happy moments and let go the miasma amassed.

The purpose for my existence is still an enigma to me,
My accomplishments nebulous, my contribution must yet to be,
But I am optimistic and question not His mode of plan,
May I be guided by His spirit, however and whenever I can,

Please GOD

Louise McPhail
A NEW LIFE

To my sons, Jimmy and Jerry, their wives and children, with my deepest love and gratitude.

A new life is a new beginning
Thoughts of a future that is only starting.
My first born I hold in trembling arms
Filled with wonder and strange alarms.
There will be times to laugh and to cry
A lot of days that I can plan an adventure to try.
How will I cope when the going's rough?
I know that I'll always care enough
To offset the storms that come and go
Stay well my son—I love you so.

Lorene P. Morris
LIFE TODAY AND PAST
Life today, to everyone has changed in the last few years,
In a great many ways, too numerous to name all;
First of all, Marriage is no longer

for keeps,
Nor, does the home carry the love, peace and sharing it should.

Once, the Mothers stayed in the home, and,
Took care of the children, and most of the time;
Cared for many of the elder family members,
While the fathers worked and supported everyone.

While today, both fathers and mothers work,
On public jobs to pay the bills and make ends meet;
And the children are cared for by a baby sitter,
And the older members are put in Old Folks Homes.

Why has mankind lost his value of care-ing,
And the real value of everything been lost;
While man goes on struggling to keep up with the other fellow,
And the value of goods degrades and prices go higher?

Have we forsaken God's word and His Blessings,
And gone our own way forgetting, we have nothing?
For all, belong to God, and we are the users,
Wake up, look around, see, and Pray today, for a change.

Robert J. Maszak
SUCCESS AND HAPPINESS
If success and happiness
can ever be realized
    then
success and happiness
have never been reached
    for
true success and happiness
is an unrealized end
    because
one's success and happiness
is always a step away
    since
reaching success and happiness
depends on more stages
    that
more success and happiness
can ever bring

Yvonne M. Miller
ADMISSION
The time goes on—precision
The sights we see—a vision
The things we do—condition
The life now ends—concision.

George Geoff Andrews
BEGGAR'S ETERNITY
Barrenly dressed,
So barely alive.
Rivers of spercled sweat,
Have become his everyday baign.
But never has this man cried.
For as his stour grows tougher,
So raises his pride . . .
Lonely days are conquered by song.
While days of crowd,
Invite feelings to dare.
But for the beggar to rouge,
Is as lungs consuming air . . .
Life as a beggar lasts but little.
Months from now,

Probably days,
The beggar's life will blin.
His rode shall be an icy cale;
But dry will be his chin . . .

Winifred T. O'Connor
IMAGERY
The Pageants of the Universe
   change
As Time scampers by on tip-toe;
A Crafty Artisan is he!

With his box of Stolen Paints
The truths he deigns to portray
Become Forgeries upon his
   Canvas!

Ruby Lee Cusser
TOM THUMB

---

*Dedication to Son of Mooresville
Indiana Jerry Olen Lee.*

Tom Thumb was all thumbs
With no fingers only thumbs
Tom was like a jelly fish out of
   water
He had so many thumbs
He didn't know what to do
One day he said, I'll count these
   thumbs
He counted one, two, three, four,
Then he looked and there were
   more
So he counted again five, six,
   seven, eight,
Then he opened his fist and let
   two out the gate
Then he counted again nine, ten,
He made two fists of his thumbs
Tom Thumb has no fingers and
   has all thumbs
Maybe he could learn to play the
   drums
With no fingers and all thumbs.

Leona Garrett Keller
RUGGED BEAUTY
We climb the hill to walk and
   talk,
But he looks down and sees
The yellow apex of the mullen
   stalk,
Its fuzzy blanket leaves;
Sturdy yellow hollthock
Too stubborn for the breeze
To sway and rock.

A sea of thistles, blue and slender,
Swaying in the sun,
Where slick, black cows can
   roam and wander
Until the day is done.
Silently, he gazes yonder

Where noonday sunbeams burn;
Begins to ponder.

Should a farmer see the beauty
In these sturdy growing things?
Would he not think it his duty
To see profit his soil brings?
But since they're here and pretty
Like a caged pet bird that sings,
Think not of duty.

Mary S. Lundy
MARRIAGE JOURNEY
Because this day is special it
   brings to mind these things;
All the happiness the future
   holds and all the good things
   that it brings.
So as you start your journey of
   marriage remember the
   mending glue;
The value of the love you have
   for each other and the meaning
   of *I DO.*

Sandra Lynn Barry
DON'T QUIT
When things go wrong, as they
   sometimes will
When the road you're on seems
   all uphill
And you feel that you must rest a
   bit
Stop if you must, but don't you
   quit.

When problems arise and you
   can't see the light
And there is sadness instead of
   delight
Don't give up, work at it, you'll see
The answers will come so easily.

Should you come to a fork in the
   road
And you do not know which way
   to go
If one path is "worn" and the
   other is "new"
Take a challenge, the new, and
   start to pursue.

Reach for your goals and never
   give up
No matter how easy, no matter
   how rough
For dreams are but a moment away
So don't ever give up, don't ever
   dismay.

Merry Marcellino
LOST LOVE
The pain of my heart echoed
   through my soul,
As the sun took leave of my
   presence.
At first I had thought it was night,
but the night lasted forever.
Then I realized that I would
   never see the sun again.

I remembered the hues of yellow
   and gold,
the red and pink and purple.
I relived the warmth of it's rays,
and my heart cried out in anguish
for I would never see the sun
   again.

Now, stumbling through the
   darkness,
I can no longer feel.
I know if I could but have one
   brief moment
with the sun,

my heart would beat again.
But it is not to be.

Alas, now I lie still,
never to love again.
For my beloved sun is gone
And I can never know again
the happiness of my soul.

Harold R. Bell
I PLANTED A LITTLE SEED

---

*In loving memory, dedicated to
my wife, Myrtle M. Bell, who is
deceased.*

I planted a little seed one day
With tender loving care
To see if it would grow.
So from it, I might share.

Well, it grew and grew and grew.
It was a beauty to behold.
It was like a huge oak tree
Spreading its branches to unfold.

It now has given me its shelter
And has made me feel so free.
It was that little seed of love
That God had given me.

Recilla Slone Fraley
WHAT IS A FAMILY
A family is . . .
   Growing, sharing, loving, caring,
   all the good with the bad.
   Making mistakes instead of
   being straight laced,
   and looking back at what you
   have.

A family is . . .
   Turning your cheek, and trying
   not to speak,
   when you really feel like
   shouting.
   But your love is much stronger,
   and lasts so much longer,
   than the anger thats trying to
   get out.

A family is . . .
   Uniting, the growth is exciting,
   and pain, well it comes along
   with life.
   But if you have the strength,
   after pain has come and went
   a real family will survive.

A family is . . .
   No questions, just learning
   needed lessons,
   and knowing your life is
   fullfilled.

A family is . . .
   A treasure, a lot of work, but

pleasure,
   A family is something you feel.
Vera Walls Willson.
TIME.
Where is the wealth we can
   compare to time?
   Which we can neither hear, nor
   feel nor see,
Our greatest friend and greatest
   enemy,
   The teacher, the destroyer,
   healer, who
Cannot be bribed to wait for me;
   or you.
   This treasure all possess, but
   each one has
His ration meted out, as seconds
   pass.
We spend this treasure, or it
   spends itself,
   There is no hoarding of the
   fleeting years,
Swiftly they pass, through joy, or
   love, or tears.
   And no one knows how much
   he has to spend
Before the final curtain marks the
   end.
   This coin of life, we should not
   lightly give.
For, it is only in our TIME, we
   live.

Donna Marguerite Strough Barnes
WITH THE WIND
I walked with the wind, the living
   wind,
   With spicy gusts it blew—
As free and ever glorious
   Was my love for you!

I danced with the wind, the
   dancing wind,
   And felt my spirit rise
Away from life's realities
   To glory in your eyes!

I sang with the wind, the singing
   wind,
   And felt your love go forth
To hold and all-encompass me
East, West and South and North!

Steve Repko
OSWEGO RIVER

---

*Dedicated to my Grand Sons Leo,
Martin, Christopher and Ronald
so they will know.*

Weary traveler shed your oars,
   And rest awhile upon these
   shores;
Touch the waters flowing free,
   And hear this ancient Lenape.

Great Chief from beyond the sun,
   Once upon these banks did run;
And paused to soak his swollen
   feet,
   And drink away the summer
   heat.

Whistling eagle way up high,
   Flying circles in the sky;
Marveling how the rivers glow,
   Amid the woods of green below.

Feel the welcome evening breeze,
   Dancing shadows from the trees;
Touch the eerie warmth of night,
   When sunset prints it's final
   light.

Rested traveler on your way,
Stop again another day;
Smell the air of moss and pine,
And sip a cup of cedar wine.

May pure waters always flow,
Cool like that from melted snow;
Through this land so wild and free,
Gently to the eternal sea.

Katharine C. Lickers
REFLECTION
Moon looked at Earth
From an azure sky
Where She saw stars and planets
Whizzing by.
There was a wheeling bat
Compelled to fly
A dawning day that was
Born to die.
All a part of such an
Orderly pace,
Yet Moon must long to
Hide her face
When She sees the war, hate,
Greed,
And the mad, mad, pace
Mankind is running
This very last race!

Jan M. Ackerman
HIDDEN WOUNDS
Stabbing of one's heart—
bleeding pain and sorrow.
Killing tool dripping of destitute.
Disallusionment.
Colors will fade
as light grows dim, to dark.
With hands trembling
tears drain so freely.
As the ground suddenly
touches the sky,
Reality spins within your head.

Marjorie E. Corum
THE WEAVERS THREAD
A thread that seemed tattered
and worn and grey
By the weavers' hand has been
put away.
The tapestry lies, incomplete in
the loom,
In the evening shade and the
gathering gloom.
But, who can say what the
picture will be
'Till the weaver is finished and all
may see.
When the plan is revealed and
the task is done
That thread may be silver with
the rising sun.
For, God is the weaver and we are
the thread
And each little life isn't lost
when it's dead,
It's put away with loving care
Until it's complete and we all
may share
The Kingdom of God, as it first
was planned
In the mind of The Father, by His
Holy Hand.

Ginny Joy Brickl
ODE TO THE LONELY
Here is the globe encompassed
thus with multitudes of human
beings.
Truly we witness extraverts and
introverts seeking life's meanings.
The extroverts search for others
as a purposeful bridge for their

troubled minds.
The sad and buried introverts
hold a destiny for with they
cannot find.
All sing their song and say
their prayer for a peace which
provides tranquility.
Each human recognizes at some
time
or another, the trials of their life.
Naught can cure and none can
solve this malady.

The truthful helpmate in
this muddled world becomes a
simple word called love.
Discovering another who will
cherish and care truly lets each
one rise to heights above.

Those who have great fortune
and find amorous endeavors,
will certainly touch upon
a sheltered hope of meaningful
endearing till forever.

George Klamar Bruno
ESSENCE OF DEPARTURE

*Dedicated to Charlene for a
special moment in time.*

I wonder why you had to leave so
early.
The party barely had a chance to
start.
So many times I sat and thought
about you,
Your essence still remains within
my heart.
Your face is like a picture in an
hourglass,
The reflection of you captured in
my mind.
I was young then but you knew I
would remember
That you didn't want me going
through life blind.
So the short time that we had to
share together,
You nutured me and tried to
show the way.
I was young, I didn't know that
you were leaving;
You were wise and knew that I
would have to stay.
Tho' the party still goes on there
is something missing;
Had there been more time, more
love we could have shared.
My thoughts of you will always
make me smile,
And in my heart I know you
really cared.

Fonda Fern Campbell
WALK WITH THE MASTER

*To my brother, Paul Omar
Campbell, minister, deceased*

Walk Tall . . . Christian . . . Walk
Tall;
Be constantly aware!
The Son Of God, whose child you
are,
Holds you in His care.

Walk True . . . Christian . . . Walk
True,
And keep the Faith; No woe!

To upright, pure, forgiving souls
His bounties overflow.
Walk Free . . . Christian . . . Walk
Free.
Lay hold of deep deep joy,
That age, nor loss, nor rude rebuff,
Nor failure can destroy.

Keep Faith . . . Christian . . . Keep
Faith;
The Master needs our love.
Walk Tall, and True, and always
Free,
For He watches from Above.

Steve Gruber
ANOTHER RAIN SONG
Mother Nature
washes her drowsy children
with liquid love
blurring the differences
between
the acorns
the living dusty squirrels
and
the lovers
who linger, framed
in the open doorway
of their own
purifying emotion
joining the chorus of
another rain song

Esther M. Masted
THE RAINBOW
The storm has passed.
The trees, so recently
Writhing in anguish
Now lift their leafy crowns
And toss the raindrops
On my head.

The air is clean
And freshly washed
And all is cool and still.

And, in the East,
Spanning the evening sky,
I see God's promised sign,
His multicolored bow
Of living light, stretched out
With lavish hand,
Assuring me again
Of perfect faithfulness
And perfect love.

Ramon Angel Solis Jr.
SHE WAS YOU!
She was a picture
I always wanted to paint.

She was a rainbow
I always wanted to find.

She was a song
I always wanted to sing.

She was the feelings
I always wanted to touch.

She was the emotions
I always wanted to know.

She was the dream
I always wanted to come true.

And most of all,
SHE WAS YOU!

Willy Boyd
**Old Man, Where Is Thy
Youth?**
Have you not heard the wind?
It whispered to me
As it danced with autumn leaves.

I laughed as it
Swept across my brow
And lifted my spirit . . .

And how it frothed
At the waters of
The little pond in the cove.

And when it sprang up,
Like a mighty Greek God
And pushed back the clouds,

And raked the leaves
From Oak trees as if
Blowing against a dandelion gone
to seed,

Have you not heard the wind?
It whispered to me
As it danced with autumn leaves.

How it told of winter,
The coming of a cold, creeping
malaise
How I laughed that Autumn day.

Martha M. Dempsey
A Lady, A Mother, A Friend

*To Julia Tucker Lockhart
Dempsey, the lady who blessed us
with her guidance, her lessons,
her love, and herself. To Sherry
whose voice moves words into
song.*

When I came and you saw me,
you took me as your own.
You helped me as I grew to learn
a world unknown.
We talked, we laughed, we cried,
made memories each day.
At times we fought and even
denied our love along the way.

We shared our lives together and
then we stood apart.
We left each other's ties to find
what's in our hearts.
Now I've roved the paths of life
while looking for myself
Only to find in times of strife
your lessons were my help.

We've come to know each other
as people not as one.
We've come to know our love,
before our lives are done.
Again we've found each other to
share what life has been.
Now we laugh and talk and cry as
Mother and as Friend.

Just in time I know a Lady, a
Mother and a Friend
No longer just a mother as when
my life began.
Now I've known a life enriched
by love and kin
Because of that Lady, my mother
and my friend.

Our World's Best Loved Poems

Shirley B. O'Keefe
MY GIRLS

To my girls Sheryl and Patti

It upset me watching my girls
  grow up
For it seemed to me they'd never
  get along.
They'd argue and fight even over
  little things
And always seemed to rub each
  other wrong.

But maybe when they get older, I
  thought,
Maybe they would start to get
  along
And their relationship as sisters
  would grow
Into closeness and
  companionship real strong.

And somehow along the years
  this did happen
Very slowly before my unaware
  eyes
As they grew up to become
  teenagers
And developed their personalities
  and lives.

And now they actually enjoy
  each others company
As they make plans together or
  just chat.
And seldom do I hear them argue
  any more
They've grown up—my girls,
  Sheryl and Pat.

R. Bateman Newcomb
THE SUCCESS
He stood above the common herd,
One sensed he was a man apart;
The rumours were of quiet wealth,
His hints alone were works of art.

He bore himself with lofty air
And lesser folk paid due respect;
Ambitious women sought him out
To share the glow he could reflect.

He died and papers praised him
  well,
Of great accomplishment was he;
The truth, he never did a thing
Of mention, note or memory.

His hungry heirs shed hopeful
  tears
And dreamed of regal legacies;
Like wolves the lawyers swarmed
  about,
How lush to come the princely
  fees.

Accountants totalled up the score
Then soberly announced in time
He died a bankrupt past belief
And didn't leave a single dime.

Pamela Pitkin
GONE FISHING
Shimmering dragonflies skim
the dappled surface
of the noonday pond,
darting hither and thither
among the gently whispering reeds.

Flickering dragonflies dreaming
thoughts suspended in a sunbeam
spatter on the lilting breeze
flitting randomly,
vagabonds of summer reverie.

Glittering dragonflies, life shards
trimmed in iridescent blue and
  green,
ephemeral moments hovering,
capricious fancies, in softly
  rustling pages
in tomorrow's elusive book of days.

Marcella Furlong
YOU WILL LEAVE
Today's the day
When you will say
If I should grieve
Because you might leave.

Too many times we fought
There were no lessons taught
So much crying
We weren't even trying.

You asked for the ring
As if it were a thing
Instead of a treasure
That gave me pleasure.

You will be gone
Before the dawn
Then I'll be there
With no one to care.

Christine Petro Mooney
FOR YOU LORD, ONLY

*This poem was written to—and
inspired by—the Divine living
Creator. Praise the Lord, Jesus
Christ.*

I'm so glad I finally got to meet
  you.
They said you didn't exist.
And, for awhile, I believed them.
But now I know you are.
And it doesn't matter what they
  say anymore.

I'm so glad I got to know you.
I never knew what friendship
  meant 'till now.
Being with you has made me a
  new person.

I'm so glad I learned to trust you.
I didn't think I would ever trust
  again.
It seemed to disappear with
  innocence and youth.
I really don't know why I waited
  so long.
For life didn't begin until we met.

I'm so glad I learned to love you.
We're so close, we're a part of
  each other.
And nothing can separate our love.

I'm so glad you'll always be with
  me.
Your wisdom is my guide and
  light.
Your protection, endearing.
Forever is a cherished thought.
And all that I am is for you Lord,
  only.

Adair Conlon
THE PINK SKY

*To my children, Jamie and Taryn:
May they have a future.*

Rising from the frozen clays
The radiation leaks around
The sky is pink and empty
For nothing lives but underground.

We were here yesterday
But now we are gone
No longer do we walk the earth
But huddle underground.

Memories of skies of blue
And clear waters bright
Are long forgotten now
In black of the underground.

It is too late now
To render thought
Of what we could have done
To stop this life of the
  underground.

But faith is all we have
To keep us living on
Someday we hope to leave
This hell of the underground.

When the pink sky clears
It will be safe
To walk the earth again
But I pray each man who does—
Remembers the life of the
  underground.

Liz Carter Richards

Liz Carter Richards
SEWANNEE RIVER
Sewannee River
lined with trees trees
draped with mosses
the mosses succulent mosses
of green witchery
pulling my mind enchanting me
large aged tree roots
washed clean of soil drinking
in water to survive as water
carresses the roots & the banks
before rushing onward
to refresh an ocean i watched
the water move as the sun
  touched
the river while i rode
in a stern wheel boat thinking
and the sun was setting west of us
a color beam touched the river
i saw the water redden.

Scott Andrew Mueller
AGATE BEACH, OREGON
Walking in the Dragon's breath
  watching fog roll slowly in from
  the Pacific
while couples huddle close,
  their dogs frolicing in
  greenbrown foam
Tourists collect damp driftwood,
  shells and agates,
  where piles of huge silvergrey
  logs lay
like abandoned temple ruins
Given a holiness by the magic
  breath.

Salt wind tangling his balding
  hair, a Yankee tourist
bumbling about spys a dry dog
  terd
thinking it driftwood, he fondles
  it like an icon,
Pocketing his mistaken art
  treasure
he turns to his Winnebago
dreaming tales to tell back home.

I sit on an ancient pillar feeling
  the monster's peace
Raven and Seagull tangle their
  insults with advice
to picnicers leaving food
  offerings on the sand
as tribute to a foreign god.
I inhale the calming power as a
  misty foggy sunset
while a smooth ocean roar
takes me to Infinity.

Joyce Hamrick
LOVE OF LIFE
Life, my love, my pain,
Why do you taunt me
With restless passion?
Call me with whispering winds,
Beckon me with flaming sunset,
I will answer.

Life … your gentle chains entwine
Around my pounding heart,
Take away my reason,
Cloud my mind with dreams;
My soul is yours.

Grasp my outstreched hand,
Life, and let me follow
Your path with closed eyes.
Soothe my aching heart
With sun-drenched plains.
Carry my spirit upward
With shadowed mountains.

Let me cling with breathless
  wonder
To your whispered promise
Of things to come.

Jesse Rose Hartman
LIFE
Squeezed from a toothpaste tube,
  little by little,
  a squeeze each day;
  until all you have
  has been brushed away.

At the beginning,
  a little pressure will do.
But when they've reached the end,
  rolled and bullied
  right up to the top;
  they squeeze again just to be
  sure
  they've left not a single drop.

Yvette M. Bogle
SPRING TIME
Song bird sitting by my window,
what is your message for today?
Shout it loud and clear, I am a
little deaf in one ear
Say what! storm clouds are
drifting beyond the horizon, soon
it will be time for play
Pray tell, what makes you so wise
my little one?
Ah! I am much travelled and my
eyes and ears are alert
Spring is almost here, I can
feel it in my bones
Alas! I'll tarry no longer, I
must be on my way to spread the

good news to all, as I go along
the way
Have fun, if you can, it's good
while you are young

Rolene E. Thomas
HEAVEN'S GIFT
The Angels called a meeting
and with voices filled with mirth
decided it was time again
for love to bloom on Earth.
So they called their smallest angel,
Cupid, to the game
and on a slip of paper that they
gave him, was my name.
With his potion covered arrow
in a quiver hanging low,
He said, "I'll find the perfect
match,"
and headed down below.
Now, I don't know how long he
searched
but one thing is for certain;
it must have taken quite awhile
to locate such a person.
You probably never felt the sting
of that arrow aimed so true,
but it touched my life in passing
for the next day I met *you!*

Mrs. Elizabeth Lotman
A PRECIOUS FAILURE
The power of Spring was
everywhere
 Shedded coats and hats
 elsewhere—
 The heights of freedom reared:
A lad filled with wonder and wide
 eyed
Truly eager watching the big
 guys.

A better time would ne'er come
 around
 Hesitation deft one hound—
 An act kept verge on steer:
Through the thrillings he would
 mime their show
Higher! Higher! Up to a thorn's
 pole!

Their springboard transplanting
 bodily
Flawlessly and expertly—
 Through twists like fish who
 dive:
He mused barely over three feet
 high
"always little boys must wait till
 big."

So many times he had run his kite
 Failure came and he'd just tie—
 A string, a rope, then try:
Had his little heart danced into
 sense
Preciousness might ne'er be
 found in men.

Ursula Casuse
LOVE BY NUMBERS
You asked me if I love you a
 hundred times,
your question is an insult to my
 heart, I love you so much more.

If it is possible to tell love by
 numbers,
I have a small formula for you.

Have you ever counted stars on a
 clear dark night,
when you can spot even the
 smallest hidden speck of
 glittering light?

Suppose we added all the stars
 together then multiplied that
 by their total,
 what would you get?

Well my sweet, remember I will
 be with you helping you count,
which will take both of our life
 times . . .

and that my love is how much I
 love you.

Dollie L. Alesich
POWER OF LUST

To my husband Samuel Alesich Jr.

He has the power
to pull the older,
making them
lust for him.
They live
In agonizing hell
Aching, yearning,
from their heart.
They're living in
A world of dreams,
lusting for him.
He's so much younger,
but they go on,
fantasizing,
their schemes for him.

Patricia M. Caravona
OUR MOUNTAIN
We're at the top.
Peaceful, unafraid, free.

You're in my arms,
giving your love,
like no other.

The sun sets.
A bright star shines;
Our star from the heavens.

We're inseparable.

Mary Louise Jones
NOVEMBER ACCOUNTING
The Harvest Feast of Maturity—
 Salad days
 Food for thought
 Just desserts
Served on the china of clean
 conscience—
 Seasoned conversation
 Memory's second helpings
 Leftovers of love to last the
 morrows—
Bless *You,* Lord, for so blessing
 us!

Tim L. Breeding
DEATH IN DECEMBER
As cold as the north wind that
cuts across your face in winter
or the ice that clings from rocks
in thin, ghostly fingers,
as cold as the grave itself,
the hand of death extended
to my life one winter morning
and stole the light from the eyes
 of my love.

O Dark, disastrous, selfish death!
Mother and daughters now grief
 forever
Your blind, unmindful way of
 taking from the earth
a husband and a father, to leave
 behind
a trail of memories on the wind,
memories, memories, nothing but
 memories.

And yet I wonder in the stillness
 of the night,
When will winter snows have
 melted into streams,
will spring not come again?
will not we all arise one day
pure from the waters of death,
to hold once more with hearts of
 joy
the hands of those we love.

James H. Harris Jr.

James H. Harris Jr.
MY MATE
Heavenly Father, show me my
 mate that I may date
 that one I dream of from day to
 day.
So we can plan our wedding day.
Let her be as the noonday, that
 we may be one on
 our honeymoon day.

If she be red, yellow, black or
 white she would
 be precious in my sight.
Tribulation and pain, clouds and
 rain let us both
 whisper his name.
So our love would remain the
 same.

Linda Mayo
A LOVE TOO LATE
Two lives that met with feeling
Down our dark and empty road
A letter sent revealing
Leaving this hard and heavy load
Questions with no answers
Words you left unsaid
Nights and nights of teardrops
For Gary you lay dead

My God how do I take this
My answers lie with you
Is there some way to reach you

Please tell me what to do
A letter you sent to me
I got the day you died
You said that you still love me
And how you tried and tried

What tenderness you gave me
What doubts you must have
 known
But if I had the chance again
I'd show what I should have shown
Gary, if you can hear this
My words of love to you
Believe me when I "tell" you
And not the things I do

My fears have kept me prisoner
My feelings I couldn't show
God Gary I did love you
You know I told you so
Please God tell him for me
That I'll hurt and pain for life
Your last letter it will haunt me
For I should have been your wife.

Lucy Beemer
NIMBUS TIME
As the fluffy, bellowy clouds bank
Against the silvery sky in the
 West
 Like snowy mountains,
I see California cities and alpine
 paths
 In Switzerland,
Then wonder what people and
 plans go on
Within this crested, wondrous
 nebulae
Like filmy, fleeting
 And vanishing frigate birds
Winging but a memory against
 The edge of time.

Thomas Michael Svinning
MUSIC THEORY
Music its essence are heroes gone
 by,
The music they left
And the lives they led
Make us stop for a moment,
To wonder why.

Music is a form of power,
The younger generation always
 leading the way
From the time the sound took
 root
They've been shouting, "Rock-n-
 Roll is here to stay!"

Music. It's a world of its own.
New Wave, Punk, Disco,
Whatever it is that satisfies your
 soul.
There's something in me,
That makes me feel right when I
 put on some Door's
Or some other good Rock-n-Roll.

God bless them all.

Renee M. LaTulippe
SPECIAL TRIANGLE
Albums containing pictures of
 days I don't remember
I was so much younger—didn't
 know June from December.
Then albums containing pictures
 of days I live right now
For me, these are more
 significant—more special
 somehow.

The diaries I've kept for many
 years gone by—

Our World's Best Loved Poems

The times that I did laugh, the
times that I did cry.
Those parched pages know all my
well-kept secrets, it seems.
They hold all my emotions—my
hopes, my thoughts, my dreams.

Each slender vase I own is filled
with one white rose
Now dried with age they stand—
each in a stately pose.
Five roses symbolize loves
both now and past,
And all are worth the fragile
shadows that they cast.

Precious memories fill my days,
are locked inside my head;
Remembrances of the past and
present and of the life I've led.
They are a prism rainbow made
of brightly colored kites,
And they will never cease to soar
in their perpetual flights.

Bob R. Galbreath
PARTNERSHIP
As the soft summer breeze
Erase the wrinkles from the sky,
So the breath of freshness
From the communion of souls
Blows the wrinkles from life.
In this freshness of communion
I see,
Love, tenderness, self love
In the purity of itself
A gift from God.
Mobile only by concern
Of each for each.
This breath of love,
Extended to each, conquered by
none
If worthily accepted
For life will remain.
Partnership of marriage
Becomes devine,
For it turns the voice
Of life's wind into a song
Enchanting and sweeter
By one's own loving.

Donna E. Leeper
IS IT REALLY GREAT?
The gnarled hand, the wrinkled
brow
Makes me think of when, and how
He strode across a fresh ploughed
field;
Or plucked an apple and peeled it
with one long peel;
And shared it with a child so small
Who gazed at him in total awe.

I remember when he walked with
strides firm and long
Or reached with hands brown
and strong,
To pull out weeds among the peas.
Getting down on hands and knees
Creeping around the corner to
tease
An unsuspecting boy,
Absorbed in making a wooden toy.

There was never a shake to spill
his cup,
Or, a need for someone to help
him up.
Shirt fronts didn't show the stain
Of where his lunch spills did
remain.

A fear of falls now haunts the day,
The golden hair long since grey.

Words get muddled and come out
wrong,
No longer a cheery whistled song.
So, if growing old is so darn great,
Why does he feel like a fox in a
crate?

Betty M. Wehner
ENSNARED

---

*To the Captor—From the
Butterfly, Who dares not forget.*

Just like a joyous butterfly
Serene and unaware
I did not heed the danger
In his keen appraising stare
His eyes implored surrender
As he whispered words to charm
And he vowed a sanctuary
Free from loneliness and harm
Beneath his gaze I fluttered
As he fervently pursued
And I showed him all my colors
Daring never to delude
Unaccustomed to the cunning
That the ardent captor brings
I succumbed to subtle fingers
As he clipped my precious wings
But I never once suspected
When he wooed me from the sky
He would turn his back and walk
away
Commanding me to fly

Bernice Davis Jarnagin
COMMITTED
I had my wife committed.
"There are no Fairies," I said, "no
Little People, no Tommy Knockers.
We will leave this villiage. The
mines are closed.
I cannot drive so far to work."

"They eat so little," She said.
"Yet they eat or starve. Who will
care for them when we are gone?
Who will leave a bowl at the
entrance of the mine?
And they will be so lonely."

"But still we'll leave!" I shouted.
She became hysterical. She cried,
and screamed, and fought.
When I began to sort, and pack,
and load the truck,
She wept at the entrance of the
mine.

I had no other choice.
"A woman who is sick must be
doctored," I explained to her.
Even the doctor shook his head
and clicked his tongue.
"No other way," he said.

The road back home was sad.
"Still, I can move in peace and
make a home for her return.
She'll be well again some day and
understand the reason
That love must do the best it can."

"Ye've done it after all!"
The wizened little man glared
from atop my television
Where he sat with angry brow
and blazing eye.
"Ye've had your wife committed!"

Carole L. Colvin
YOUR EYES TONITE
Your eyes tonite
are as they were so long ago

when we loved together
and shared all of our growth
Your eyes tonite
are as deep, as deep can be
and I hoped by now
that they would fade
into a memory
Your eyes tonite
are mine alone
as we say our sad farewells
I with my life
You with your wife
we part our separate ways
but
Your eyes tonite
have not so long forgotten
all of our plays
Your eyes tonite
will haunt me
till the end of my days

B. S. Perkins
To J. D. From B. S.

---

*To Jeffery David Westerfield
From Bruce Scott Perkins
. . . thanks*

You have instilled a little bit of
yourself in me, and this I will
always treasure. Just to be
around you, and to share a few
kind words, has really given me
some hope, to look on for
tomorrow. I thought my life
was ended, until you became
my friend, and now I look
forward to each coming day
with a grin, our friendship will
never end. You're a true friend,
the best I've known, when my
hopes seemed all so glum, you
showed me how to lead a life as
enriched as your own, this I
will never forget. You've
instilled a little bit of yourself
in me, and this I will always
treasure.

A. June Allen
GIFT FROM HEAVEN
Child of grace—
Let your tiny fingers trace
The web of life.

Feel the rainbow and the rain;
Touch the star from which you
came;
Caress the happiness and pain
Of life.

Cry with mourning doves in spring,
Dance with butterflies and wing
With soaring bluebirds. Sing
The song of life.

Lois Johnson Allen
UNTITLED
How lonely is
the heart
for love
when there
is none
How weary are
the eye's
from weaping
when they have wept
so many time's before
How lonely are the
arms for an
embrace
when there is no one

to hold on to
How longing are the
lip's for just
one kiss
when there isn't one
How broken are my
memorie's
of time's long past
How broken
My heart.

Vanessa Koreen Potter
A PART OF ME TO YOU

---

*For a very special person who has
put joy and meaning into my life.
You are my inspiration and I
Love You very much Johnny Ross!*

I may not have been your first
love,
but I surely hope I'll be your last.
The feelings I have for you are
from above,
and they are growing fast.

I want to share myself with you;
between us there is no end.
I want to share my love with
you—
over and over again.

L. E. Lowell
ON A SPREE
Little Fido on a spree
Dashing fast in ecstasy
Bounding fast alone and free
Chasing dainty fragrancy.

Fast onward flew our hero
Feet flashing onward pounding
No time for hedge or tree row—
Fleet-foot-happy onward
Onward swiftly bounding.

He met a lady charming
Thought she was very sexy
Did lots of tricks alarming
Near caused her apoplexy—
Out-macho'd all surrounding,
Performed most dogfully
Then trotted home with modest
grace,
Content to be astounding.

Sunny blythe Hobart
TO TAME TIME
My love, shall we ever tame this
thing called time?
The precious moments I have
with you fleet away
And I am left, longing and
waiting to be with you
Again.
In the months ahead shall it be
the same? or can
Time be mastered and end this
torment of my heart.
To love and hold you close
against my breast
Without ending, without
beginning, this is my
Fondest thought—when we shall
be joined.

Winnifred H. Pearson
NOVEMBER RAIN
Today the sky looks tired, and
old and grey;
And weeps upon earth's bosom
copious tears.
Where once the sun shone
through so bright and gay,

51

There now is nought but clouds
portent with fears.

The little creatures of the
meadows haste
To their warm nests beneath the
rain-soaked sod;
Feeling the chill of early winter,
braced
To trust, if need be, for their
meat from God.

But sodden earth lies naked, cold
and still;
Too numb for joy or aching
pangs of pain.
The tears of heaven fall heedless
on the hill.
The valleys fill and spill in
eddying rain

Linda L. Meier-Lindauer
MORNING MOMENTS
Feeling . . . Still
        The haziness upon awakening

I watch
As daylight slowly creeps into
                    The room
And listen, outside, to the
    Animals
                Beginning a new day

    As you lay beside me,
I hear
    Your deep breathing
And look
    With wonder at the
    Peacefulness
                Upon your face.

I close my eyes . . . This feeling,
                These moments,
        I wish them to always be.

Jonathan Bret Miller
FOR LOVE OF HER
For love of her judge tenderly of
    me.
Love never seats but two at table
With only two hearts to see
With only four hands that are able
To be dressed in precious pleasure
Wearing nothing commoner than
    skin
Yet, enchantment is the measure
Where mutual love can win.
True love is in the knowing
That a soul is no longer it's own,
Two bodies tremble in the sewing,
But exalt when their together
    sewn.

Marge Gibson
AUTUMN

*For those who believed in me &
gave me courage to write.*

There's a Autumn breeze blowing
    in the air,
For I feel the cool wind through
    my hair,
The Autumn leaves of varied
    color,
Flutter to the ground in undo
    care,
Like a flying trapeze at a fair,
And if you look up high,
You'll see the clouds go hurrying
    by,
And perhap's hear an eagle cry,
Yes Autumn's in the air,
It's here and blowing everywhere,

Kevin Moieshe Morgan

Kevin Moieshe Morgan
PRAELUDE

*This poem is dedicated to the
forces of light, my mother and
father, my grandmother, all my
auntees, and Etta. For they are all,
the underwriters, of truth.*

Three o'clock the tile veins fill
With flowing tenants the cold
    rooms chill
The warm seats straight but once
    before
Before the day in shambles lay
The oddest circle keeps silent
    vigil
A vacant lot her silent spot
Beneath the crusty stair, she well
She has more taste than the bell
And it keeps ringing, ringing,
    ringing
Halfway out the name Michelle.

The cold wind blows; The doors
    all open
Spilling out the days delight
The honored boy the golden toy
That races thru his heart with joy
He reaches out but she is gone
Her perfumed scent lingers near
His eyes burn bright with love
    and hate
And slowly falls a silent tear.

patricia hutson
SUMMONS TO DEATH
Bring forth Thy wings, oh flight
    of death,
And carry me away,
For souls that cry as deep as
    mine,
Are weary of the day.

Within Thy unknown bosom,
Surely there awaits,
A mending for my shattered life,
And stillness at Thy gates.

I welcome Thee, sweet time of
    parting,
Do not grieve my solemn youth,
This life has held no good
    commendments,
All is cruel and lies aloof.

Swallow me, oh ebon tide,
The dark I will not mind,
Thy darkness would be light to
    this,
Come quickly and be kind.

Tarry not, unerring guest,
Resound Thy elegy,
No ember can revive these ashes,
Come now, death and cover me.

Jeff Seffinga
The Honeymoon Continues
Simple pleasures are still shared:
perfect pieces of fruit are peeled by
fumbling fingers, but accurately
    dropped
to disappear in laughter between
    lips.
Soon, no longer caressing, urgent
    hands
hook bands and straps, pull scraps
of clothing away to set bodies free.
Cool satin sheets rustle; we cuddle
and snuggle in the shared glow.
    These small joys of love shall
    never fade.

Deidra A. Chapman
THE LASTING SCAR
The wrath of a Father's blow upon
    his child is deeper than people
    ever know.
The scars upon the skin are
    forgotten,
                so.
But, the cuts so deep within a
    child rarely start to heel.
The hands can hurt so much but,
    the
        sword in one's mouth cuts too
    deep
            to ever heel in
            one's mind.

Gloria Jean Beczkowski
DIETS
You say I can stand
    to loose a pound or two.

Can I help it if
    I like Chicken Cordon Bleu.

Salad is alright
    for everyday

But on the weekend
    what can I say.

Wine me and dine me
    and buy me dessert

Come Monday I'll try and
    start with yogurt.

John Landgraver Sr.
One Leaf Away From Love
Of all the leaves on a giant oak
    tree,
the last one to fall is for Shirly
    and me.

We are one leaf away from love.

It started in springtime,
it will go on till fall.
Will our small love survive the

thunder and lightning
that love must endure?
As time goes on, we shall see
as that last oak leaf falls
from the tree.

Will it have a name on each side,
Shirly & John?
Or like the wild winter wind,
will that last leaf be gone?

It could seed in the ground,
grow straight and tall.
Love will surround it,
that great oak tree,
it's up to the one
of the two that wants to be free.

Jeanne Rowlett
ESCAPE
What makes the mind wonder
    endlessly
    of things past long ago.
Something said in jest one time
    brings silent smiles to you
    alone.
To stare across an empty field
    and hear sounds of gayiety.
What makes the mind wonder
    endlessly
    its just an escape from reality.

Lisa Ann Logan
LIFETIME CONFLICT
He sits,
Wondering,
Pondering,
Why?

He is a soldier in life,
A courageous soldier in the war
    for love.
Wrinkles are his fatigues,
Loneliness, his battle wound.
Wisdom is his compensation,
and death his discharge . . .

He dies,
Unremembered,
Unrewarded,
Old.

Edith Ritter Hoffman
I'VE SEEN MY SMILE
I've seen my smile come and go
blooming at will in orchids,
deep in summer roses climbing
back and forth into me.
A smile that spread season
    through season
leaping over tree-tops, touching
    feathers.

Oh the joy and freedom of a smile
until an ocean wave claimed it
    pulling, dragging
pink loveliness down deep into
    murky darkness.
A captured muscle
    disintergrating in the
calcium of an empty shell.

Natalie L. Pipkin
SECRET LIES WITHIN
In the thin, pearly background
lies a bleak, ivory mound
Streaked with black fissured lines
    plunging straight to the ground.

The upward trail winds steeply
    through the moss-covered rocks
While the emerald, leafy ferns
    cover the path where they walk.

These wild mountain riders move
    like phantoms in the mist

Riding steadily upward with grim
faces and clenched fists.

The exhausted buckskin horses
have gleaming, nervous eyes
As they warily pick their way up
the stony mountain side.

The rust-touched leaves were
trampled by the horses' weary
legs
As relentlessly they plodded o'er
the leafy dregs.

As they scaled the rocky pathway
toward the lofty, ivory top
The mountain breezes whispered,
warning them to stop.

But blindly on they stumbled, not
cautious or aware
Of all the lurking dangers
awaiting them up there.

For atop the ivory mountain,
appearing so serene,
There is a greater secret than
they had ever seen.

With lightning speed and
vengeance the gale winds blow
and rage.
The blizzards white and blinding
rewrite nature's page.

The unsuspecting travelers
caught up in all her wrath
Are tossed aside like matchsticks
to clear her clutterd path.

The riders once so eager now
quake and turn around
And leave here hidden treasures
by others to be found.

Patricia Ann Hill
STARTING OVER
YOU rang me up quite early today
To tell me that you are going away,
"Back up North" ever so calmly
you said
And rambled on and on about
ventures that lay ahead,
In all you so meticulously plan to
do
I hear no mention of "Me and
You"!!
THOUGHTS are now storming
through my head
Like, how can I survive without
Translucent blue eyes gazing into
mine,
Sharing of secrets deep into the
night,
Long walks where no
conversation is fine,
Gentle, gentle caresses,
Perfect compatability . . .
Oh! How I will miss
Your smile, your laugh . . . YOU!!
Ever so slowly I remember, you
are leaving me,
I am not leaving you! Then, I
know I will make it
For you will be without me too!!!

Nette Renzell
THOUGHT POWER
Thought that travels on a course
With a concentrated force
Radiating clarity
Diligence and purity
Into realms of healing grace
For the troubled human race
Aids the progress and the plan
Of the brotherhood of man

Thought that stirs to venerate
Qualities that activate
Harmony and peace of mind
Bringing love to humankind
Through the offered eloquence
Of the thought's benevolence
Blesses by redemptive balm
In its silent sacred psalm

Mary Katherine Fleck
RAINBOWS

*To Kathy Fleck and Caroline Hall
for standing behind me in all I do
and in loving memory of my
mother, Suzanne Fleck.*

Rainbows are dreams come true,
Which start miracles inside of you.
God put them in the sky,
So we have to stop and ask why.
They have such a beautiful array
of colors,
Which are more beautiful than
flowers.
A rainbow brightens each day,
In a very special way.
When you have a friend to share
it with,
It all seems worth while.
Rainbows are dreams come true,
Which will always start miracles
inside of you.

Judith K. Riden
BRIGHTER DAYS

For my children, James and Jessica

It's cold outside,
The sky is gray.
It could have been
A beautiful day.
But winter time
Has clouded the sky.
I don't know how,
Or don't know why.
But here inside
It's nice and clear,
Because I have
My children near.

Adelle W. Gilbert
INCIDENT
    A wind swept day, a lonely nite.
    Indistant pain, I try to fight—
    My road is long, it winds uphill—
    Persistant—fight! I will! I will!

        The years are long,
        my life near spent—
        My shoulders tired,
        my back is bent.
        Confused injustice
        though waiverment
Sometimes misguided incidents.

Another day, all through the
        night—
    I long to live, I try to fight—
    My eyes are tired and
        red with pain—
        With swollen legs, and
        feet that's lame.

        A great new life once
            given is Spent.
    Preparing for the Incident—
        Her feet once danced—the
            lips once smiled,
    The shoulders once comforted
        a crying child.

    A voice once loved, now
        just a crackle—
        And love that binds
        becomes a shackle.
    My bias soul, in spirit sent—
    Appointment with life's Incident.

Nancy Roulias
MY GRANDSON
You're the sweetest little boy that
I know.
You're another year older—and
you grow and grow!
You are so special in many ways,
Mattie dear.
I'm glad you didn't move away
and you're still here!
I enjoy going to McDonalds with
you.
Also to the park—I push you in
the swing too.
You are starting to school and
will learn many things.
You will have recess and lunch
and everyone sings.
Sunday school will teach you to
be good and not bad.
You will learn to snap your
fingers and dress like dad.
I bet the good Lord is smiling
down on you too.
You are in his plans and he will
watch over you.

Edith Colleen McCabe
THE WEDDING POEM
Sharing the truth of love beneath
I was so happy to be there
because it felt so right

With all my fondest wishes, I
hope your dreams come true
I'll always pray the future holds
many just for you

May you grow closer and stronger
with every passing day
Together with the Lord who
brightens up the way

I'm glad I got to know you., I love
you both so much
I hope if you should ever leave,
we still can keep in touch

Darlene Koszenski
LOVE EYES
Sometimes, as I stand
    silently in the shadows
    and watch him,

For some mysterious reason,
    he'll stop
        to look up at me.

And when his eyes
    meet my gaze, his face
    lights up with love.

That's when I feel
    the warm glow
        in my heart.

Sandra De Cecco
PARADISE
There is a special place in this
    world I know
It's such a beautiful place to be.
It's where the sun turns gold at
    dawn and the birds glow into
    the midnight dark.

And the flowers grow so big and
high that if you wanted to
smell the roses you would have
to climb the stem.

This special place would make all
    your wishes and dreams come
    true.
This special place is called
    "Paradise" and it's over the
    highest rainbow.

It's free to get in and you could go
    in there whenever you are
    ready to go in.

Charles W. Forlines
REQUIEM
Those whom we know as dead
    In Christ live on and on.
We have seen their sunset years,
    But they behold life's dawn.

Their earthly journey's over
    And our loss is very keen.
But they, in robes of light arrayed,
    Midst heaven's glow are seen.

When time draws to its close
    We'll see them face to face.
All cares will from us pass away
    Within God's dwelling-place.

Paula N. Hill
TASHA
Tasha
God's gift to me
Have I been worthy?
Has it been in vain?
To think I could lose you.
Causes too much pain

The world needs you Tasha
I need to reflect my dreams and
    glories through you
You must teach me.
You must show me
Through you is the key of life

Be strong, be weak, be loving, be
    meek, but always be you

You are the begining of a better
    life to come
Hold my hand and let's see the
    job done
Cause without you I'd die a
    thousand deaths

John J. MacMullan III
MOMENTS OF LONGING
Time drags on when a loved one's
    gone, the minutes turn to
    hours.
Lost in the rhythm of a sad, sad
    song, we lose our inner power.
Initiative is all but drained, work
    seems to be a bore;
We gaze longingly into a picture
    frame, of the one that we adore.
It feels as though we've lost the
    game, 'til we're reunited with
    our love once more.

Rose M. Warner
YOU AND I

*To the Young at Heart . . .
        Age is a barrier
That can be lifted by love.*

Our hearts were pledged to
one another
While strolling in the shady
hollow,
Burying the swiftly lived past
behind
And daring what might follow.

We shall always be together,
You and I,

'Til one must go away,
Then we shall stroll amongst
the Amaranths
Until our Judgement Day.

Karen P. Lynch
MY LITTLE MAGIC BOX
Quiet and alone sits my little
magic box,
Taking up a silent vigil on the
corner of my desk.
Patiently it waits for the moment
I arrive
When I'll move a single switch
and make it come alive.
This special time together always
brings a smile
For this is my one chance to just
relax awhile.
My little magic box tells me
what's gone on today,
Knowledge that I missed while I
was away.
And then I close my eyes, for I
know it won't be long
'Til my friendly little radio will
play my favorite song.

Diana M. De La Cruz
Reincarnation Of a Poet
Inside, I speak another tone
A language I have never known;

Or at least, in this time around
When I came to this world of
sound.

But, before we get out of hand
Let me speak to you from another
land;

I am not human, but a soul alone,
Combined in flesh and in bone.

I've known kings and queens before
this day,
I've seen them love, cry and pray,

I've written lines of their life
and mine
And I was famous, before I died.
While I and this mortal write the
same
We will both gain our fame.

Yet, I worry, for this heiress
For I've left her, my mind
delirious.

I too, lost my love and gained
loneliness
If I could only save her, that would
be one death less.

Deborah Ann Boyter
EMPTY PARADISE

"*To Lucy": I call her the* North
Wind, *my teacher and my friend;*
She greatly influenced me to
reach-out for myself.

Down in the meadow where the
grass grows tall and green,
There sits a meadow-lark, there
flows a stream—
And the sound of the ripples, the
winds blowing breezes
go a long long way . . . miles and
miles of earth yet to live
free to give and so I live.
The Sun is peeking through
The Flowers all dripping with dew
Where are you? . . . Where are
you?. . . Oh!, Where are you?

Eric F. Sukhia
GLEE OF YONDER WORLD
The birds and the bees do their
deeds,
as the squirrels romp through the
trees.
Those preciouse little sparks of
life
put on a most marvelous show,
world politics and mental strife,
they will never know . . .
Their wonderings are so natural,
no fronts do they display, . .
How marvelouse god gave us the
ability to
contemplaye their play . . .
They represent another world, a
reality unfurrled
to only those familiar with the
"GLEE of YONDER WORLD"

Eric F. Sukhia
Nothing To Throw Away
Love came my way, I cast it aside,
like an old garment,
All for tomorrow . . .
Tomorrow became today I threw
another love away,
like an old garment. All for
tomorrow . . .
Tomorrow once again became
today, and I threw love away,
like an old garment, All for
tomorrow . . .

Tomorrow became today, and
here I stand naked, with
"*NOTHING TO THROW AWAY.*"

Mary Nell Haley
THE SEA
So calm, so utterly still.
Yet you hear its voice; soft,
smooth.
The flat surface, like a face, is
kind—deceiving.

For when the sea is calm, you
wouldn't guess;
no one would guess,
Of the terror the sea can bring
when the waves
break high and rough.

It speaks then also, but with a
terrible voice.
Its face then is angry:
Ships are wrecked and tossed
about;
Waves break on the land with a
vengeance that leaves
vast destruction.

Then, the sea calms;
Its anger is gone.
Its voice once again is soft, kind.
The face once again is still

Albion Verne Lambertis
LISA

Dedicated To Pauline My Wife
The one I love So much.

She makes Me sing, She gave Me
wings.
She makes Me smile, She makes
Me happy all the while.
She makes Me feel high as the sky,
She makes Me feel like I will
never die.

O' to Me she is someone special,
O' she makes Me feel so
international.
When ever I think eat and sleep
Lisa is all I see.
And when ever I feel confined in
depression, with her charm she
set me free.
O' forever with Lisa I will always
want to be.
Because of the love and care Lisa
gave Me, makes Me feel the
way I feel.
Lisa you are precious as honey
from a Bee.
Lisa gave Me Strength when My
faith was absent,
She gave Me hope when I could
not cope,
Lisa gave Me heart when I could
not start, and
She is my wife until the end of
time.
Through out this Planet there
could never be another like
she,
Lisa is perfect as abc, She is my
doo ray me. She cheers me up
when I have
an empty cup, She pulls Me up
when I am falling down, thanks
for Lisa I am
still around, I need her equally to
the breath of life, Together
Like a Four
Leaf Clover Husband and Wife.

Bonnie Padgett Ramsbottom
SINCE YOU
For so long I dreamed
Of the world I wanted to live in,
The me I wanted to be,
The someone I wanted to be
with,
But since you
Those dreams have grown
dimmer
Day by Day
Until they have faded from
view . . .
And joined me in reality.

Deborah E. Shoemaker
THE SUN

To Pete and My Mom and Dad,
with Love.

The sun is rising
the clouds have gone;
The sun is rising, the dawn.

The sun is warming
clouds are cold.
The sun is warming, be bold.

The sun is shining
no clouds in sight.
The sun is shining, so bright.

High up the sun is burning
the clouds come in gravely.
High up the sun is burning,
bravely.

The sun now is sinking,
the clouds rise high.
The sun now is sinking, do sigh.

The sun has set,
the clouds are here;
the sun has set, disappear.

The sun now waits,
The clouds are gray;
The sun now waits, please pray.

Anthony J. Guerra
FOUR BRIGHT STARS
When I walk the path of the stars
I can see the marvels of creation.
Those luminous bodies in the
heavens
Spread out on a field of azure.
And when I stop to gaze
My troubles are far away.
The road is never rough or
winding
For my mind is at ease.
Watching those sparkling
pentacles
While walking the milky way.
Each star I see I think of thee
My troubles are far away.
The four bright stars down under
Reminding the world, I am.
I think of the day you left for
home
And the stars you called into
your kingdom.
Knowing your up there
My troubles are far away.

Jeffrey Lee Shelton
TO BE A TREE
The old tree dies,
but plants a "seed"—
The rain from the skies
takes the lead—
As the acorn sinks
deep under the ground:
It grows a stem,
and new life is found.
Water and soil combine
to strengthen the tree
along with sunshine.
They do their best
as it continues to grow.
It takes decades to mature,
but a second to sow.
The tree grows strong—
the roots grip tight.
Its life is long,
its work is light.
After years of living,
it falls like rain,
But the seed is planted—
that starts the process again.

Dale A. Hoover
MYSTERIES
There are things I would rather
build;
Than my fame or fortune (which
would be great). . .
A house, small, but filled with
love,
And there she awaits.

Many are the things I'd rather own
Than riches or power.
The trust of people I've known
And the peace of an hour.

All riches of the earth are inferior
To the presence of trust;
For in the heart we find that
which in love
Keeps us from turning into so
much dust.

Betty L. Clark
DAWN'S SYMPHONY
I awake at dawn to the robins'
song—
And then the red bird sings along,
From the field I hear the
meadowlark,
And of course, the sparrows sing
their part.

The martins and the birds that
are blue
Chime in with their aria too,
They sing with music from their
hearts,
And the mocking bird knows all
of their parts.

Their music is so sweet to my ears
As I arise from my bed, I have no
fears
That the day will begin with a
very good start,
Because, I get up with a song in
my heart.

This symphony of the birds'—I
feel—
Is God's way of telling me that
He is real,
And, as I begin my day you see,
I also sing my symphony.

Roma Hogue
PAPER ROSE

---

*To Scotty with love. You and the
rose you gave me. Year of "79"
Rose Bowl, inspired this poem.
You'll always be someone special
to me.*

A single paper rose
Means all the world to me
A very special loved one
once gave it to me
He was gentle as the petals
Protective like the leaves
Strong as the stem
That's a unique blend
When he gave me the paper rose
His love was sincere and from the
heart
Promising that we'd never part
The paper rose has not faded
nor have the petals fallen
The leaves are still protective
and the stem still strong
I still treasure the paper rose
even tho it's been so long
But time has a way and feelings
do change
I'm left with the paper rose and
memories and my share of pain.

Elexis L. Brown
I THOUGHT
I thought I'd take a handful of pills
Or jump off a bridge and see how
it feels,
To be dead and gone; to belong
no more.
I never felt I belonged before.
I thought that I would use a knife,
To end this messed up, screwed
up life.
I thought of going to the beach,
And swimming til life was out of
reach.
To wash away all life's pains.
Never to be hurt again.
But then I thought of my little one.
I thought of all the joys and fun.
I knew then that I had to live.
I knew I had a lot to give;
If to no one but my little girl.
She's my life, my heart, my world.

Greg Major
I WANT TO BE MORE
i want to be more . . .
aching, burning, SORE!
darkly-dangerous

hauntingly-high skys
stretching, suffocating clouds:
solid
rigid
structured.

insurmountable indigo
encompasses:
purple passion/fanatical fashion
unlocks the door . . . SOAR!

see with clarity
grasp with conviction
cradle with awe;
let the passion pour: SOAR!

so strangely spontaneous
the newly-found wings;
forcefully . . .
purposely . . .
yet beautifully formed.

the more looming
on the horizon
of the less . . .
these fledgling wings at war:
aching, burning, SORE!

i want to be more.
Phyllis A. Menna
TO HAVE AND HAVE NOT
It was a quiet, mellow night
when I was alone with only me
listening to the beat of raindrops
against my windows of thought;
Awakened by all my senses
I had visions of you
floating through my mind
like soft, windswept clouds
on a midsummer's morn;
But like the passage of clouds
across time and space
your soulic embrace
grows distant and faint
tho' vague memories,
like shadowy ghosts, linger on . . .
And for a precious few days
I was Cinderella!
finding happiness and love
only having to release them
at the midnight hour;
But in the depths of nocturnal
sleep
you returned to my Life's door
bringing your love
with the mystical glass slipper
I left behind

Joanne E. Leginus
MY DESTINY
I have tried so very hard
And exhausting has it been.
Hang on I can no longer
The lines I've read between.

I've come to the very point now
My downfall I can see
Lower everyday
Tell me; why must it be?

The world is getting darker
The sun has gone away
The stars in the once bright sky
Have now all gone astray.

The grass that was once green
The colour has it lost
The doom is coming quickly
At such a deathly cost.

Goodbye to all my friends
This world I leave to you
I'm looking for another place
Where I can be happy too.

So be not sad; be not blue
When I am here no more

Remember I'm in another place
A place where I can soar.

Carl C. Burgess

Carl C. Burgess
LITTLE LEAGUE JOHNNIE

---

*Dedicated to: THE LITTLE
LEAGUE OF AMERICA*

You will find him in the U.S.A.
Mom and Dad gave him his start;
He signed up in the LITTLE
LEAGUE,
Base Ball really won his heart.

Chorus

Johnnie, the base Ball hero,
Is a star in every game;
He even breaks the records,
His became a famous name,

Johnnie follows instructions,
Of his coach who calls the play;
Johnnie brought fame to his grade
school,
Through the famous LITTLE
LEAGUE way.

Johnnies life is good and clean,
Has virtues hard to beat,
No cigarettes or dope for him,
Base Ball is his BIG TREAT.

Johnnie plays any position,
Pitch, catch or play the field,
And the scouts are on his trail,
And Johnnie's not going to fail.

Dolores M. French
FIRE FROM HEAVEN
Tonight, Prometheus,
While the town sleeps
And stars spin like dancers
On their golden orbits,
We lie as close

As it is possible
For two people to be.

The moon and all the flowers
In the world
Watch, and know that
The god-man has descended
To the tower of the ivory princess,
Waking her from the long sleep,
The evil enchantment
Cast by a gnarled and angry witch
Hidden beside her cradle
Long ago.
You and I, love,
Tonight we steal fire from
heaven.
Glorious, beloved thief
Shall we, too, be struck
With black thunderbolts of wrath

From frozen gods
Who dance to a dance
Of wooden music
In a cloistered, patterned garden?

Or shall I know for
Infinite tomorrows
Your fire, desperate
Inside me,
And your burning touch.

Jo Ann Kacprzycki
TELEPHONE CALL

Dedicated with love to Mani

Imaginary bells ringing
Your voice magically
transcending
an infinite space in time.
Anxious am I to be
arisen by the reality
of those bells

Clifford Love
INDEPENDENCE
I kissed my son goodbye this
morning
Not literally—I left him a note
But I know he's going away
to Oregon
or some other distant place
Why do I feel this abandonment
He must go
The very quality
that draws him to me
forces him away

John R. Farnsworth
HAPPINESS
Happiness is puppies,
A graceful soaring dove.
Happiness is being surrounded
By the ones you love.

Happiness is friendship
Happiness is reaching your goal,
Following many years of endeavor.

Happiness is living
A life full of caring.
Happiness is Christmas
The time when everyone is
sharing.

But what means more to me,
The single happiness,
Is living a life for the Lord
Straight and true and blessed.

Lori Heikkila
I REMEMBER
I raised them.
How many nights did
I sit up with them?

How many tears did I shed
When they were sick,
And when they were troubled?

Then, the struggle was over,
And they were men.
Then the war came.
And my three sons said
It was their duty to fight for their
country,
And they were gone.

Now I sit all alone,
And they are gone forever.
Do you remember as I remember?
Does the sorrow I live
With all my life mean anything
to you?
I remember.

Mary Frances Murphy
I AM A BUTTERFLY
Catch me I'm a butterfly.
See how I fly through the sky
The sun's reflection on my wings
See the beautiful colors it brings.

I never meant to bring harm
Just; into your life a little charm
There should be no cause for alarm
Oh! Let me fly around your farm.

So catch me if you can
As we both know Mr. Man,
'Tis a mighty shame
There is only one winner in this
game.

Toni-Ann Gagliardi
GROWING UP
I wish I was little again
Going back to places I've been
Happy times when I was small
Looking up to people, wishing to
be that tall
Hugging and squeezing my pet
teddy bear
My protection from any fear
Going places dressed in ribbons
and bows
Sparkling from my head to my
toes
Being little was so much fun
Who thought of being anything
but young
Then one day, there wasn't a trace
No childhood lines upon my face
It was time to face the world alone
No guidance, all on my own
It may be great to be older with
not so many
things to fear
But there are still times when I
wish for the
Comfort of my old teddy
bear

Shirley M. Houghton
THE LONELY NIGHT
The night is still with only a
whisper of rain falling on the
leaves,
Such a pleasant sound, like a
lullaby singing thru the trees.

But it has a lonliness and sadness
that touches your heart of
things long past,
The stillness brings memories
back to mind that seem never
to fade but always last.

The patter of rain has stopped,
again the stars are twinkling
jewels in the sky, and the

moon is shining bright,
Like a miracle from above on this
quiet lonely night.

You feel the magic of this special
moment,
Like the winds caressing the
mountains and valleys in their
sweet lament.

The air is so fresh after natures
bath,
The fragrance touches you like a
flower strewn path.

Nothing is so heavenly as this
Godly performance,
It is as if we are all sharing in a
marvelous secret romance.

On this quiet lonely night.

Sharon Lee Huntoon
TO MY SON
The hopes and fears of things to
come,
Many tears mixed with a lot of
fun
that comes along with a son,

Watching you form into a man,

The pride I feel and understand,

Wanting to make your every plan,

But knowing you need to make a
stand,

Always ready to give a helping
hand,

I'm glad to see you have become
quite the man.

Lori Kurtenbach
THE PAST
Across the deep dark ages,
The past endures.
Like a lonely cross,
Standing tall, yet scarred in a
desolate field.
All the lies and secrets past,
Weigh heavily upon its
outstretched arms.
Held up only by the love of life
long gone.

Sandra Lewandowski
FRIENDS
Love her like a sister.
Teaching each other what one
knows,
They can take all the blows.
Sharing all their thoughts,
Knowing nothing could be bought.
For they share all they know.

Knowing that she can come to me,
For I shall always be free,
To listen to what she says,
And help her like a sister.

Helping each other through hard
times,
Then everything will be fine.
Keeping company on those lonely
nights,
There will be nothing to fright.

If the time comes that we must
part,
She shall always be in my heart,
For I love her like a sister.

Wilma Dunnick Ellis
OUR MEMORIES
Memories of age old things
Fill us with sorrow or delight.
They can be dreams and hopes

That once made our day bright.
We vision them from time to
time
And try to make them live anew
But, our hearts are often heavy
And our pleasures all too few.

Memories are soft spoken words
Some loved ones used to say,
And we cherish how it was
Before they were taken away.
We treasure each joy and
heartache
From another day, another time.
In our memories we can recall
Every childhood story and rhyme.

Memories can be only thoughts
That words cannot express,
A precious secret in our minds
That govern our lives more or
less.
Thoughts of things we failed to
do—
Or something we promised long
ago
Something we will nurture still,
Our thoughts can be like seeds
that grow.

Carol Hossler
OH JOYOUS BREATH
Imprisoned soul,
That I could but cut my chest
To set you free from your dark
snarled web,
Tangled, trapped, desparately
fluttering.
Such agony in your struggle to
breathe,
To spread your delicate wings
And soar freely,
Caught on the wind.
Oh joyous breath!
I fear only in death your sought
freedom found.

Rita M. Henning
TINY DREAMS
I look at you as you are sleeping
and think
How can this little person be so
perfect?
Everything so tiny—so miniature
You are so peaceful
Not a care in the world
only to feel safe in your
mother's arms.
What do you dream of as you lie
there—
eyes closed?
No one knows
Nor will they ever
You will never be able to tell
them—
for when you can speak
you won't remember.

Laurie K. Higgins
my father
I met my father yesterday
dreamborn he walked with me
I felt him standing at my back
both arms embracing me
we walked together
he and I
I glancing up to watch
that stern and smiling face
catching glimpses of his laughter
as we sauntered down life's
street
we'll walk together always
in laughter and in love

his faith a solid unbreached wall
my core of confidence

Ralph I. Epps
World Hunger Portrayed
"It's O.K. to cry", the preacher said,
But one had no more tears to
shed.
His hollowed eyes stared into
space . . .
It hurt to look upon his face.
Crying won't help, unless you
think
To dry the salt from tears, to
drink.
Bloated stomachs look full enough
To ignorant minds, knowing
not how rough!
Matchstick limbs on bodies frail,
Forgive us, Lord! We dare not
fail!"

Sulo Aijala
CRASH
I heard about your strange event
And soon's I could, this card I sent
To let you know I sympathize
With your auto's sad demise.
Each year you bet a tidy sum
(insurance)
The car'd be wrecked—and now
you won.
Your friends observed it could be
worse—
You could have landed in a hearse.
Fate was kind to you instead.
Enjoy the years you have ahead.

Ray "Skip" Connors
Tanka . . . Tree Of Irony
Bright, wayfaring dreams
Pause . . . beneath your sacred
boughs
Tree of irony . . .
Symbol of eternal life
Slain by ardent admirers.

Margaret Elizabeth Johnston
Teal II
A TRIBUTE

---

*Dedicated to the late Robert
Schmidt of Ridgeway, Ontario,
Canada. Formerly of Vienna,
Austria he organized the Crystal
Beach Art Club (now the Ridge
Way & Crystal Beach Art Club)
in 1964, and taught a class for
over ten years, at times without
pay. It was my pleasure to be one
of his pupils and also President of
the club for 10 years.*

The hands so talented, now
still.
The intellect so keen, now
gone.
The noble, glowing spirit
flown,
Leaving those behind,
forlorn.
But who can say, does talent,
Intellect, and spirit cease
when
The clay wears out, and with
its
Chips and mars of many
years, breaks.
Is it not rather a shedding of
the
Old mould, to be replaced by
a finer

Our World's Best Loved Poems

Cast, perhaps at last to find
oneself.
Who can say but what this
talent
Has found expression beyond
this
Life's short passage in a
greater way.
As night is mother to the day,
And every dawn brings light,
So, to die is not to cease to be,
But merely to step away,
leaving
Only the clay mould, the
outer
Self that others see, behind.

Lucile Gregory Weeks
SNOWFLAKES
I miss snowflakes
falling on my window pane.
Making patterns of lace
more beautiful than that
on the Queen's gown!
When winter spreads her magic
blanket
over all the town,
up and down city's streets and
country's lane,
the humblest house becomes a
palace
in fairyland!
The "Snow Queen" is an equalizer!
Through the night,
she softly and silently sifts
her sparkling jewels down
over all the land: and then,
she suddenly closes
her wintry hand
and lets the sun take on the
show.
When he smiles down,
on all these gleaming, glistening
piles
of newly polished gems, my story
ends!
The glittering scene dazzles the
human eye!
No need to try, the words are not
mine
to justify the beauty of
that magic sight!

Myrna F. Minnich
**Four Seasons In
Pennsylvania**
Living in Pennsylvania affords
many a breathtaking view,
This may just be my opinion, but
then I know it's true.
The beauty could be for one of a
many hundred reasons,
But the greatest, is the beauty of
all the four seasons.

Spring is the time of year when
nature comes alive,
After a barren winter, it's good to
see this season arrive.
Trees bring forth new leaves,
flowers budding, grass growing,
Best of all, look out the window
and hey, it isn't snowing.

Summer brings with it the heat of
midday,
And it's time for a swim, did I
hear someone say.
With summer, the three H's,
humid, hot and hazy,
Those days, you just relax and be
a little lazy.

Fall in Pennsylvania is most
colorful indeed,
Crops are harvested and we see
we have all we need.
Tasks, like raking of fallen leaves,
is on my mind,
For I know, when Fall is here,
Winter can't be far behind.

Winter has arrived and the
courtry side is covered with
snow,
Time to spend, by the crackling
fireside, with friends you know.
Yes Winter is a barren season,
but you need not dismay,
For Spring will be here again next
March, on the 21st day.

Priscilla Ruth Gage
PEACE FOR PRISCILLA
Thoughts tip-toe
in crystal silence . . .

And I rise!

Stairway in the mist . . .
Twinkling stars and crescent
moon . . .
By flower petals kissed . . .

Call me poet
. . . simple like that . . .
Stretch me friends,
around the world!

'Tis God, gives me nurture . . .
in a peaceful eddy, swirled . . .

Maria E. Stadlmayer
CELEBRATIONS

---

*To Beth and Curtis My
inspiration. A special thanks for
everything.*

Celebrations—
What's there to celebrate
without you near me?
Today's a holiday,
but the whole past month
was better than Christmas
with your presence.

Carol M. Gibson
MISERERE'S LAMENT
Only once
    A love comes
Only once

So splendid
    Was the time
Like the aging
    Of fine wine
Souls intertwined
    To the rhythm
Of a poem
    It felt like
Coming home

Caressing spirits
    Soaring upward
To the highest plane

Ah, miserere
    How sad
This love waned

Larry J. Ramsey
MY MOTHER
I knew a woman—a lovely
creation;
Who was simple in nature and
full of ambition.
As the days passed, my love grew
stronger;

I always tried my best to show
her.
She was full of life, laughter, and
grace;
When she played the piano, it lit
up my face.
Her and Dad would sing an old
time hymn,
"The Comforter Has Come" or
"Stepping In The Light";
Then all us kids would join right
in,
And the house became "Heaven"
that night.
She's with Jesus now in glory
above;
Playing "There's Sunshine In My
Soul Today",
Or some other song filled with
love.
The woman I speak of is like no
other;
She bore me, raised me, and was
my mother.

Gerda Hoover
HOUDINI
Today our cat missed you—
wanted YOUR lap
but settled for half of mine
pawing my thigh,
purring—
Or was it a sigh?

Sheri E. Reindl
ODE TO J. D. M.

Dedicated to The Doors

Alexander had nothing on you
man.
    Leather-clad Adonis striding
    like a
colossus across our
    consciousness, a
searing surrealistic supernova
    stridently
screaming your anguish and
disenchantment.
    Pre-eminent persuassive poet,
    victim of
pernicious perceptions a rabid
    Rabbi
relentlessly rebelling, feeding the
hungry
masses with your shadowy soul.

Dark deliverer, seething
    sensuous
shaman you learned to love your
    pain
too well
    Charismatic captain would that

your
creative combustion had not
consumed
you so completely.
    You left before the party ended.

Teresa Bianchi Patricelli
LONELY LAND

---

*To My Father, My Inspiration . . .
Daliso Bianchi*

Barren black mound
Hovering toward the breast of hill,
Desolate is the ground,
For tender hands lie still.

Nova R. Rohrbaugh
I SEE GOD
I see God all around me,
Yes, all around I can see.
He is in the tree so tall,
Also in the rains that fall.
He is in the sunshine bright,
And the moon and stars by night.

I see Him in the grass, green,
The flowers in beauty sheen.
He is the life of each plant,
No matter what poise or slant.
In the breath of life itself,
And all He made by Himself.

In the fishes of the sea,
Also the wood in the tree.
In the varied weeds that grow,
And in all the seeds I sow.
He fills the soil with strength, so
From it food for life does grow.

He gave me the breath of life,
Placed me here in earthly strife.
Mankind without Him is weak,
And must try His love to seek.
He sends food for all the earth,
Cares for me; keeps me from
dearth.

Stephanie Nahirniak
**Children's Prayers To Stop
a Divorce**
Two little boys were kneeling
Their hands clasped tight in prayer
The tears rolled down their pale
cheeks
Their pain was too great to bear.

    Oh God our mommy and
        daddy are parted,
    And now they're planning a
        divorce,
    We love them so dearly and
        prayed it'd get better,
    But it only seems to get worse.

They seem to be blind to our
    great love,
That we have in our hearts, for
    them both.
Instead of forgiveness and
    happiness,
They find fault and each other
    they loath.

    Please God lead them back to
        the right road
    So their sacred marriage vows
        they can keep,
    Divorce will divide and destroy
        them
    And we'll be like two lost
        sheep.

We don't want a substitute
    mother,

57

And another father will never do.
They were united in church in matrimony.
Please God teach them to be faithful and true.

Jesus died on the cross for the people
So they could be forgiven for their sins,
Give our parents the power of love and understanding
And make us one happy family again.

Florence Lappin Gorman
COMPASSION
God doesn't smile at me today,
I wonder why.
All my dreams have gone astray,
And so I cry.
Please help me once again to pray,
Or else I die.

The joy I knew was charmed with great delight;
My soul was free.
Then suddenly my gladness all took flight,
Gone is my glee.
And I am strangled now with curse and blight,
I cannot see!

Dear God, art Thou amidst the Heav'ns mighty chain,
In skies of blue?
Thy spirit speaks to me; I feel Thy pain
In accents true.
Each cloud is filled with streaks and strokes of rain;—
Thou criest, too!

Maureen D. Brown
THE IMMORTAL BARD
A splendid desert awash with guilded pain,
It conquers all who once attempted rule
And withers their immortal fickle fame,
Through its enduring rays no one can fool.
Yet time and time again they come to try
To carve their initials on the door
Of time, and thereby prove their cry,
"A pen that is mightier than a sword
Can reign and rule". Shakespeare once did this feat.
He owns the fame of an Olympic god,
A Hercules, no one has yet to meet.
For though they own his instruments and sod,
His mind roams free admist humanity,
Cherishing his freedom from mortality.

Miss Patricia Faith Miller
A Holiday Without You
Nightfall awakens and calls you to my memory.
Blue eyes, broad shoulders, brown hair.

Your laughter echoes in my mind.
Your smile rekindles happy times together.

Your kiss creates warmth on my lips.

Secrets told to no-one else.
Kisses soothing pain and frustration.

A holiday without you . . .
                   it's all a dream.

Memories of the past speak of caution.
Desires of the present speak of tomorrows together.

Frightened to reach out, yet hungry with passion.
Moments of magic filling evenings of ecstasy.

Daylight awakens and beckons reality.
Blue eyes, broad shoulders, brown hair . . . gone.

A holiday without you . . .
                   it's all a dream.

Raymond Powers
THE LAST MILE
I feel so many places,
And touch so many faces.
But when I head for home,
I walk the last mile alone.

So many try to keep me,
But they find I must be free.
Cuz when I head for home,
I walk the last mile alone.

I've found I like them all,
But they come with chain and ball.
So when I head for home,
I walk the last mile alone.

Someday it would be fine,
To say that one is mine.
But now I head for home,
And walk the last mile alone.

Nettie M. Fernley
Just a Little Old School Ma'am
She was just a little old school ma'am
In the days so long ago;
She taught me all my letters
And most everything I know.

She was petite and very trim
And strong on discipline;
I used to help her every day
Bring coal from the old coal bin.

She assumed an air of sternness;
But her eyes did often glow
At each little act of kindness
On her we did bestow.

She waded through the snow drifts;
She walked home in the rain;
She never felt self-pity;
Such a thing, she did disdain.

She was just a little old school ma'am
Respected in all her domain;
Oh, God if there is a heaven
I hope to see her again!

C. J. Crawford
YESTERDAY'S SMILES
I borrow the smiles of yesterday,
   to forget the memories of today.

And stave off the fears of unknown tomorrows with the tokens of happier days.

For within my soul lies a painful void, a thirst which can never

be quenched.

A hunger no longer satisfied, a heart rendered suddenly by chance.

But through the prisms of my memories I see mirrors of yesterday's smiles.

Reflections of the warm feelings of he, and the life we shared for a short while.

For in my dream he walks again, the sun dancing through his hair.

His eyes are bright, no longer dim, the shadows no longer there.

He takes my hand with his gentle touch, the cold around me disappears.

And walking down to our favorite spot, he tells me things I long to hear.

But the memory fades before my mind's eye, no longer can I capture its gleam.

The sound of rain returns with a reluctant sigh, and I open my eyes to reality.

For his voice is now stilled, his melodies go unsung, the music of his life has fled.

His gentle touch has been a stranger to my hand, the love in his eyes can no longer be read.

For now we are parted and I am as one, his presence is no longer seen.

I stroll back along the path that we walked, and think of the future that might have been.

Jeffrey S. Robinson
FOREVER AND A DAY
I remember, not long ago,
when love joined our hearts.
We promised to love for ever and a day.
I love you now, I'll love you always.

For you were a dream come true.
And if anyone had it all, it was me.
You picked me up and showed me the way,
I loved you then, and still today.

And when the days have past us by.
And we're both old and gray.
I'll look back up on our love
and only have this to say:

I loved you then, and still today.

Cissy Rucker Long
RAISING COTTON
Daddy Yells, "Get up Girl!"
The suns arisen'
I don't wanna hear no sniffling or crying,
The works awaiten'
There's cotton to be chopped,
In a farmers life the work never stops,
Get ya breakfast eat,
Get ya work shirt and hat,
Ya gotta long row to hoe,

Ain't no time to be lazy or get fat,
There's forty acres of cotton,
We've gotta lay by,
Gotta get started before the sun gets too high,
We gotta chop those weeds,
Chop the grass,
Gotta hurry up,
Gotta work fast,
Up one row,
Down another,
Hurry up girl,
Keep up with your brother,
The sun's so hot,
Ya whole body is sweating,
No time to rest,
No time for fretting,
May and June will soon pass by,
The morning sun is rising high,
When darkness falls,
It's time for quiting,
Couple of months,
The cotton'll need picking,
I know it's a hard life for a girl,
But ya weren't born into no rich mans world,
We gotta work hard to make ends meet,
We gotta work hard so we can eat,
There'll be time to rest in the fall,
After the picking and we've made our haul,
To the cotton gin and collected our pay,
But the work starts again come next May.

Brenda Beard
DESIRE
Give me the strength to go on
Even without his love and care.
Let me realize I've done all I can
Even if our lives were not meant to share

For years I've tried on every day
To get his smile to come my way
A wave, a laugh, a scream, a tear
Anything, if only he was near.

So if I don't succeed that night
In making what is wrong, turn right
Give me the strength to go on
Even without his love in sight.

Donna Grace Dunn
Sunsets: "A Token Of God's Love"
Over the mountains
every morning she climbs
to give of her rays.
The beautiful sunshine
Then in the evening
she decends down again.
The colors of orange, blue, and purple
all blend in.
To make a picture so
peacefully graced.
That God himself could only paint.
The majestic wonders
of the heavens
colored in such gentle care
reflect on earth below
in such beauty that is rare.
God gives us his sunsets
as a token of his care
and everything he has
he is willing to share.
So remember, when you look

58

into the heavens
at sundown or sunup.
Think of how meaningless
life would be without
Tokens of God's Love

Karen L. Boyd
THE REAPER

I see a dark figure
shrouded in mists
upon a snowy hill.
Waiting.
Waiting for me
to relinguish my hold on life
and take that beautifully
    horrifying step
into another world.
Yet doubts asail me
and I am afraid
that there is no heaven . . . or hell
only endless blackness to fall
    into.

W. J. Welmon
LIFE

Life is just a shadow
Passing through space
Losing the race
with time

But I don't know
Life passes quickly
it's here then it's gone
it doesn't last very long
but I could be wrong
So long

Abraham Casiano Napoles
MELANIE

---

*Dedicated to my inspiration, the
babe, and pride of Agno. A most
beautiful treasure beyond any
measure, the woman I love very
much. A princess and queen
forever to ME LANIE
CONCEPCION*

I woke up this morning and got
    out of bed
looked at the mirror and turned
    my head
Because at the corner stands a
    portrait of her
A very beautiful portrait of her
Last night the bed didn't feel the
    same
I felt like I was sleeping in a cold
    dark grave
Should I be thankful because I lie
    on a bed
instead of a grave where she lies
    dead
I cried out last night after
    awakening
why oh God did you take her
    from me?
Life was complete while she was
    alive
like 2 peas in a pod . . . now only I
    remain
Life is not the same without her
    around
I can no longer smile all I do is
    frown
I walked around in circles like a
    silly clown
Did not want to go on living
    Take my sorrow and drown
The door bell rang and I said to
    myself who cares
Let it keep ringing they'll soon go

away
I don't want to talk or see anyone
    today
That person was a pain that
    would not go away
I said to myself someone had hell
    to pay
I ran toward the door and opened
    it angrily
I was glad to see you after I
    opened the door
I was in need of a friend and you
    were there
Thank you for helping me get
    over her death

Martha Virginia Beach Chalfant
YOU'LL BE THERE

---

*Dedicated to the one nearest and
dearest to my heart, my beloved.*

I know that you'll be there, my
    dear.
    Whene'er I need your loving
        care
    And life seems more than I can
        bear,
Your hand and prayers are always
    near.
Just when I need a word of cheer
    Some tender thought you will
        declare.
I know that you'll be there, my
    dear,
    Whene'er I need your loving care.

I know that I have naught to
    fear—
    I sense your presence
        everywhere—
    In life or death my lot you'll
        share.
To laugh with glee or shed a tear,
I know that you'll be there, my
    dear.

Zada Harris
AN EXSIGHTING DREAM

I had A dream the other night,
About A man, A great big giant,
Up in the sky, He flew around,
He never came near to the
    ground,

Fire flames flew out from Him
    like wings,
It even looked like it would
    swinge,
Now this man, He was so bright,
In the darkest of the night.

My words cannot explain it all,
He was very powerful, strong and

tall,
He made steps just like A man,
Away up in the sky He ran.

It was exsighting as could be,
He turned His head, looked down
    at me,
Now this was A fearful sight,
How this big man, looked down
    that night.

Margaret Schultz
FEELINGS ROOT

---

*Feelings Root is fondly dedicated
to my ninety year old father, Baty
Bryant Breeding who never
scowls, but smiles brightly.*

The smile on your face
Is a mark of mine,
But the scowl I trace
Mimics that which I sign,
So what I feel takes root,
Thence gripping you to boot.

Laura Aina Kalnins
NIGHT-TIME PRAYER

Oh, dear Lord, my Father,
I pray to you tonight,
To thank you for this day gone by,
To see your sun so bright.
Your blessings that surround me,
The miracles yet to be,
The hope that maybe one day,
Everyone will see,
That you, my Lord and Father,
Who never goes to sleep,
Will guide me through the next
    day,
And my soul to forever keep.
In Jesus' name. Amen.

Larry Tutcher
GEORGIA

From the banks of the
    Chattahoochee to Epworth-by
    the-Sea
From the mountain of Brasstown
    Bald to the swamp of the
    Okefenokee
Caressing the southern sky the
    clouds so soft and white
And the morning sun warms this
    land with rays of golden light.

From Stone Mountain near
    Atlanta to Savannah's beach at
    Tybee
From the state line in Augusta to
    a lake in Seminole County
Comforting the southern night
    cool breezes always blow
And the morning mist wets the
    ground where many flowers
    grow.

From the battle grounds of
    Chicamauga to Brunswich by
    the bay
From Roosevelt's Warm Springs
    mansion to the coastal church
    of Midway
Flourishing tropical foliage like
    no other anywhere
And the roses and the azaleas
    sprouting blossoms here and
    there.

From the coldness of Radium
    Springs to the Atlantic warmth
    of each new day
From Callaway Gardens on the

western side to the Piedmont,
    pine trees sway
Sandy beaches and sandy ground,
    red clay on the upper half
And happy Georgians everywhere
    enjoy their land and like to
    laugh.

They are happy people for they
    love the state in which they live
They know there is no better
    place and would like to share
    and give
Shading the sun the live oak trees
    protect us from all harm
There is no other place on earth
    with Georgia's warmth and
    charm.

If you know of a more beautiful
    state with acceptable weather
    too
Let me know so I can visit for a
    day or two
In my mind I know there's beauty
    up and down and all around
But in my heart I'd rather stay
    here and invite *you* all to come
    on down.

Adele M. Carroll
**On Hearing Ravel's
    "Mother Goose Suite"**

Crickets call outside the door
Through darkness now.
Warm and still, the small ones
    sleep,
Limbs tossed, curved in dream's
    bright play;
And here slips in upon the
    crowded day
The ancient magic of repose.

How sweet the quivering ache
    within,
Soothing the sickness of evading
    Self!
Kindled again are fires of high
    resolve
Upon Hope's hearth,
And softly, now, the Soul draws
    near
To warm itself.

Julie A. Aubuchon
BUT I KNOW TRUTH

---

*To Bec, Everyone dreams of
having a "friend who just stands
by." Thanks for making dreams
come true.*

Through the years I have come to
    accept
    the bitter taste of reality.
For as much as I would like to
    deny it,
    nothing is as it first seems.
So many things have so many
    meanings.

The sun rising makes me think
    of the brightness
    and warmth it will bring to life,
but then I think of the burden of
    making it
    through another day.

The smile of a friend brings
    thoughts of joy
    over their happiness,
but then I realize all I am
    missing.

A silent day shows the serenity
  of natures beauty,
but I know its probably the calm
  before the storm.

The cheerfulness of my own
  mood signals the
achievement of peace, but other
  signals state it's
simply a mask for all my fears.

The uncertainty of tomorrow
  gives me hope,
but the remembrance of
  yesterday tells me
  there isn't any.

I wait for the day when my first
  thoughts
will be the hard ones and then I'll
  come
to realize the positive outlooks of
  life,
but my mind tells me it may be—
  an endless wait.

Novella Meek
NEVER UNTIL ETERNITY

_____

*Herb my darling, a dream is
forever. I shall love you always
and with faith I wait to join you
in the glory of our Heavenly
Father's home. Novella*

_____

You left me with our dreams and
  no tomorrows dear . . .
Yesterdays have solace, but, not
  without a tear.
Fondly collecting memories from
  treasures' lair,
I reach to touch, only to find no
  substance there.

Today, I cannot see nor touch the
  person you,
I cannot accept that my life with
  you is thru.
You will no longer be today nor
  years to be,
Always alone, until I reach
  Eternity?

Never until Eternity to see your
  face . . .
Today and future days shall be
  the passing space
Until our spirits touch one day
  on golden shore
United our two substances
  forevermore . . .

Frances S. Hannah
REDECORATE
you cast away
your yesteryears
through
paint chipped chairs
and faded drapes
replacing them
all anew
yet you remain
                you.

Juanita Gray
WELCOME TWILIGHT
Be still, listen, you hear it
  creeping around.
Be still, the silence is very loud,
  you hear the sound.
Be still, it's coming. —What? The
  light between day and night.
Hark! It's here, the beginning of

twilight.
Calm, tranquil, and still, it's
  easing just over the hill.
Air is thin, light, but chilled.
Clouds floating with free will.
Soft breezes fill the atmosphere,
While the due drops everywhere.
Enjoy the flowers as they awake.
Fresh air blends with the smell of
  coffee as the day breaks.

Traffic is quiet, there's not much
  stirring.
Your mind is refreshed, body's
  willing, no need for hurrying.
Pause to pray, be greatful to a
  new day's beginning.
Cause there's no guarantee that
  you will see that same day
  ending.
Welcome the serenity of
  twilight.
Mattie Simmons Fields
DIAL DIRECT

_____

*Born November 24, 1942
Fayetteville NC To My Mother
for years of love and
understanding and my husband
for his tolerance of my hours as a
telephone employee Thanks*

_____

Five five five
Seventy two eighty,
Thats the number
I'm speaking from lady.

I've dialed direct
I tried and tried
Please help it go
Through this time

I call the operator
She refers me to you,
This is the thanks I get
Now what do I do?

I Went to school
Was taught to read
And to write,
Now the telephone company
Expects me to play
With numbers all night.

When I want to talk,
I want to right then
But here comes that
Recording "please
Dial again"

I hang up my receiver
Then dial again,
This time if I'm lucky,
I may even win

After several attempts
I finally get through
I even end up saying
Thanks to you.
Winona L. Clay
MY ONLY ONE

_____

*This poem was written to and
inspired by my son, Roger Dean
Stanton, May 1983, while I was
living in Randsburg, California.
Winona L. Clay*

_____

My only one. You are my son!
The one who gives me joys in
  life.
The one I think of when 'eve has

come.
Smoothing the wrinkles from a
  day of strife.

How often I sit and meditate.
Only God knows how I miss him.
Just haven't heard a word of late.
Pray he's happy and secure
  within.

Sometimes when tears just won't
  stay in
I sigh and recall how many ways
The Lord's attributes shine
  through him.
Oh how he's blessed from day to
  day.

My dear son, if you only knew . . .
I could say, "my battle is won."
You'd call, that's what you'd do!
Yes, my son, my only one.

This poem was written to and
inspired by my son, Roger
Dean Stanton, May 1983, while
I lived in Randsburg,
California.

Emily (Jones) Huff
THOUGHT FOR TO-DAY

_____

*To my three children Richard,
Doris, Pamela*

_____

I shot an arrow into the air,
It had to fall I knew somewhere.

I realized my act unkind,
I searched for my arrow hoping to
  find
It harmlessy sticking in the
  ground,
But to my dismay alas I found
My anger had brought a bitter end,
For I found my arrow in the heart
  of a friend.

The moral to this little rhyme
Think before acting,
"Don't be unkind."

Michael Girard
HE'S BEEN WAITING
Has the time come for you to see,
All the things that you could be?
Has the time come for you to say,
You want to start—a—new today?

Do you long for some place new,
Do you need a better you?
Do you long to feel secure,
Do you need a love that's pure?

If the answers yes to any of these,
The Lord's been waiting for his
  chance to please.
So get on your knees and ask him
  in,
You've found the place where you
  should begin.

Heather Joy Freas
IS LOVE A GAME?
I look at you now with tears in
  my eyes.
I should have known,
It's no surprise.
I knew it was coming . . . sooner
  or later.
Unfortunately,
My love grew greater.
I cried that day and night.
Foolishly I picked a fight.
Somehow we can't be just friends.
What is it that kept us so far apart?

I have fought back many tears,
Not to mention all my fears.
My life has been so shaken,
But my heart has long been taken.
The way I've acted . . . what a
  shame.
I guess it is me you fully blame.
Here are my last words to you,
I say them because they are true.
My life will never be the same,
Tell me now . . . Is Love A Game?
There is one more thing I have to
  say,
Before we go our separate ways.
The dreams I have dreamed will
  remain,
And I'll never forget your name.

Jocelyn Gonzales
A YOUNG BOY'S DREAM
They were worlds apart but yet
  their love
And friendship made them near
The touching moments of a boy
And his alien visitor
Made everyone shed a tear

Though he was far from home
A nine-year-old boy became his
  friend
So he wouldn't feel alone

Days went by when the boy and
  his friend
Shared many things together
Their night ride across the moon
  and their
Emotions and feelings will always
  be
Remembered and treasured

And when the two friends met
  for the last time
The Extra-Terrestial said with a
  warm smile,
"I'll be right here"

This is a story about a young
  boy's dream
Of a special friend who was
  worlds apart
But yet their love and friendship
  made them near

J. M. Hill
YOU'RE A GIFT

_____

*To my wife, Tracey, who helped
me bridge the gap.*

_____

I wondered through the fields not
  knowing why
Aimlessly searching for love
I tested many pools along the way
Below hope but eyes above

But as I walked I could see up
  ahead
A path where the wood began
I followed a ways and there I
  found you
Enough love for any man

I wander through the fields now
  knowing why
Joyfully looking at love
I know you're special by the way I
  feel
You're a gift from God above

Florence Reid Riemann
THE CHOICE
Jesus said Suffer little children
To come unto me.

Then he reached a tender hand
To draw them to his knee.

His loving glance caressed them
As they looked into his face
It seemed that heaven had come
down
And lingered in this place.

Who knows the thoughts the
Saviour had
As he lingered in this place
Loving the touch of little hands
Upon his bearded face.

Did he remember earlier days
When he was just a child
Held in the loving warm embrace
Of his mother sweet and mild?

Did he remember earlier days
When he was just a child
Held in the loving warm embrace
Of his mother sweet and mild?

Did he long to kneel before her
And feel her hands upon his head
Knowing that sorrow waited
On the troubled road ahead?

How lonely must his heart have
been
As he followed where God led
Down the road to Calvary
The path he chose to tread.

Diana L. Rossetter
GOLD BANDS
Gold bands upon our fingers
And strings upon our hearts,
Hasten moments together
Promising never to part.

These bands were meant to keep
for oh, so very long.
And vows were as a bond
That forever are so strong.

Enid Lindsay
TO "GLADYS"
Oh! Maiden with the nut-brown
hair,
At seventeen how sweet you were!
Yet now that you're a matron
grown—
What great improvements you
have shown!
Methinks your virtues all
combined
(Patience, courage, love—you'll
find!
Have proven what you're really
worth—
One of the nicest folks on earth!
And as you pass along Life's way
Shedding kindness day by day
May God be always close to you—
That you may feel *His* kindness
too!

Albert P. Johnson
PHANTAST
Night sounds come to me
As I search the darkness
To find sweet rest
That will not come.
Slipping out of dreams and back
again
Real to unreal, then return.
A gentle swan glides by,
Sweet night scents fill the room.
Two loons land silent
Upon my lake of love,
Their ripples shake me
And I hear your voice.
Their songs wake me

To feel your cool sheet absence,
Wondering where you're rising
Or turning in a soft embrace.
Casting out in depths of love,
Sounding for shallows,
Listening for promises.
The stillness racks my barren
bones,
Gray shadows gray,
I search for warmth at my window
But find winter's snow gathering
For a long march to eternity.

Lisa Prosser
EVER-LASTING
You promised you would never
leave me.
And if you did, by death it would
be.
You said, ever-lasting, your life
would be.
That way, you would always be
with me.

You said you'd live for me and
me for you.
But if you meant this and it is true,
Then why did I hear you draw in
your breath,
Kneel by your bed, and pray for
your death?

Marsella Hebig
**Tomorrow and
Tomorrow . . .**
The morning comes, and all is lost;
the fire is gone, but what a cost
you have to pay
for giving all—
when in the end you feel so
small.

And unimproved,
and unimpressed,
and so undone,
and so depressed;

Until the moon lights up the
night,
and the cowardly sun slinks
out of sight . . .

Mrs. Mary Tanco
**I've Been Working In the
Garden**
I've been working in the garden
For two hours every day
If you'll beg my pardon
I'm not making much headway.

CHORUS:
I've been working in the garden
All the live long day
It's far from being Eden
But that's the way it will have to
stay.

Doing the hoeing and weeding
And picking sticks and stones
I'll soon be heeding and needing
A "rub" for my aching bones.

CHORUS:
Getting out between showers
When the weather is just fine
You'll see me among some flowers
Pulling out a dandelion.

CHORUS:

Donna Rose Saar
SUICIDE
I want to die
but only cry.
Thoughts of suicide
make me hide.

My true self
has been put upon a shelf.
My inner being
is not seeing
only fleeing.
I want to cry
but only die.
Thoughts of suicide
no longer hide.
My true self
has been taken off the shelf.
My inner being
is now seeing
no longer fleeing.

Alma Mikelsons
THE COYOTE
I'm such whom nobody can bear.
Seems not enough to chase me
down on earth
I'm often double watched from
the air.
I'm looking nearly like a dog
My predicament—I'm not a dog.
I cannot follow owner singing
sweet—
On empty stomach looking neat.
Some days I had a longing for a
porridge bowl,
Secure corner somewhere to lie
down—
This naked hunger takes out
all that's mild.
I howl, I grab, I'm cunning wild.—
My cubs were waiting for me
eagerly—
They disappeared recently.
Give me a moment of a worthy
life
If only sweetened poison bait—
And slay me tenderly.

Cassandra Winkie
TWILIGHT
Twilight lays upon the ground
veils of violet wisdom bound.
Her tired, old eyes wrinkled
round
stroke each small movement and
sound.
Snow from grey quilts floated
down
encloses with a frosty frown
the world in her velvet gown.

Ann Margaret Patsy
THE 4TH

---

*For my Grandma Uram In loving
memory of my Grandfather.*

The 4th of July is a special day
full of people feeling nice and
feeling gay,
but in some of our hearts
we remember the way
our grandparent left us
on that very, very special day.
We were just thinking of him,
the 4th was his birth,
we loved him so dearly
he was no more on earth.
We set out a cake and put
candles on top
67 he *would* be, but he's not.
He's in heaven now,
honeychild—
so join in the laughter,
so join in the tears,
remember the way he was all
those years.

So loving and giving
how he used to sing
on sunny days, we'd walk to the
swing.
On his shoulders I'd climb
he'd give me a ride,
it made his heart feel good inside
but it gave 'way one special day
so dear have fun
he'd want it that way.

Betty Ann Wooley
Betty Ann Wooley
THE PICTURE OF LOVE
This paper is my canvas
My pen is now the brush
Each word a brilliant color
Graced by love with every touch

The blue blue sky is happiness
Gold holds the warmth of the
sun
And the green green grass unfolds
tenderness
To be shared because we are one

The gray in each cloud spills
tears of joy
Lavenders lace dreams we pursue
The orange blush is my faith and
trust
In all you say and do

The flaming reds are passion's
glow
Brown captures a song and replies
To the touch of pink in love's
own drink
When you lead me to paradise

As you gaze upon my picture
May the scene remain a part
Of each day to come my dearest
one
For it is painted from my heart

Elsie Rae Santagata
DREAMS
When I was young, I dreamed and
dreamed.
Dreams filled my days and nights
it seemed.
Such visions I had of my future
life;
Health, Wealth, and True Love of
man and wife.

So many thoughts I dwelt on then,
For my life's work and worries
were yet to begin.
To dream is great; it is the thing
to do,
But work and prayers make
dreams come true.

These are the lessons I did learn.
Dreams belong to youth and

those who yearn . . .
For a better life and peace of
mind . . .
A Love that's true, is the dream to
find.

Jeannette V. Ewasyn
INTERFERANCE
Sitting in my living-room,
The black rabbit, Blacky, jumping
on the table,
My son, Terry, watching Batman.
Why should I write a short story?
I prefer scribbling lines of poetry.
It's an activity that gives me
pleasure.
I'm helping myself by doing this.
What's nice is that only a pencil
and paper,
Are all I need to indulge in this
activity.
Unlike a musician I don't need,
That backup band to support me.
However, like everybody else,
I have a physical body that I must
look after.
An old saying is that creativity
Does not happen in a sterile
environment.
What inspire's a poet like me?
The stars in the heavens,
Sunsets, golden prairie wheat,
The smiles of family, friends and
strangers.

Patty Litzel
DREAMS
My dreams of yesterday,
Are my life today.
My dreams of today,
Are my goals for tomorrow.
My dreams of tomorrow,
Have yet to be dreamt.

Susan D. Waybright
LORD . . .
Lord . . .
Lord, help me to find my way.
Teach me something new each
day.
With every hurt give me strength.
When I'm at the end of my rope
help me find more length.

Lord, teach me the things I need
to know.
Help me understand why the
season's come and go.
Give me strength to deal with
each day.
Let me help someone in some
small way.

Lord, stand by my side,
when I feel there's trouble, and I
want to run and hide.
Lead me in the right direction.
Help me live your word without
objection.

Lord, help me know the right
thing to say.
Especially if someone lost comes
my way.
If a word from my mouth should
ever leak.
Let it be a word worthy to speak.

David A. Coffman
THERE WAS A DREAM
Back when things were right
he fought; he gave his all.
There was a dream whose pursuit
became his soul.

But something happened:
his dream came true;
heaven descended from a sky
he had helped to clear away.

Afterward, there had been great
rejoicing,
but he was empty within;
he was a part of the past
because his soul still sought a
pursuit.
It sought an all-consuming dream
that needed its help to find life.
A bringer of heaven
had brought hell upon himself.

He had been raised in hell,
but his children were raised in
heaven.
The sinner who had fought sin
then fought on empty battlefields
within.
Horrified, he knew his
children, too,
must learn the lessons of hell
in order for heaven to survive,
because hell is its residual state.

Todd Ashley Milam
TRUE LOVE

---

*This poem is dedicated to—and
was inspired by—Cindy Rash, on
the way home to The Colony.*

Why do people who never strive
for true love
Are always seen hand in hand?
Is it possible they're happy with
their imitations
Or too thrilled to find something
more grand?

Why are the lonely always alone
When they're trying so hard to
breach?
Is it possible it is their destiny
To stretch for something they
can't reach?

Is it better to accept false
affections
Or keep hoping you'll find true
love?
Would you give up your nestfull
of sparrows
For just one chance at a dove?

Why is love so hard to find
When the obstacles aren't really
that tall?
Are we searching too hard, or not
enough
Or should we be searching at all?

Christine Y. Cobey
FRIENDS

My Mother, Mary F. Cobey

Friends are a good thing to have
even when they are mad.
Friends I have are sometimes sad
so I try to make them glad,
because Jesus is a friend that
everyone has.

Some friends are good and some
are bad,
but some are the best that I've
ever had.

Friends that care
Friends that share

Friends that will go most
anywhere.

From day to day friends will say
don't stop being happy and gay
because
all the luck is coming your way.

Now you have done your good
deed
you've got friends and Jesus that's
all you need.

Geoffrey Edwards
PHOENIX
O Phoenix, splendor crowned by
hands divine,
Whose flight of glory heavenward
recalls
The golden brilliance of Aurora's
climb
And transports us to rapture's
sacred halls,
When Death has claimed you on
the blazing pyre,
Consuming with his blinding
bursts of flame
Which even to Olympus seem to
spire,

My breast shall not be agonized
by pain;
Exalted, from the ashes you will
rise,
The resurrection of immortal
love
Which in the soul, reborn, forever
lies,
Ascent resplendent, touched by
one above.
On wings of beauty which true
hearts adore,
Toward new heights this love
will ever soar.

Erika Nadine Barnes
A MOTHER IS . . .

To my beautiful mother Ima.

A mother is a person that helps
you when you're down,
A mother is a person that's
always around.

A mother is someone that you
can always trust,
Because trusting in life is
definitely a must.

A mother's love for you is
something that no one can
replace,
A mother's love is something no
one can erase.

A mother is a human God gave to
you,
A mother is a person that's
always around to say "I love
you".

And as I write this poem I'd just
like to say,
God couldn't have given me a
better mother
Than my mommie *anyday!*

Janet Mace
ONE LONELY NIGHT
One lonely night in Germany
a tired soldier looked up to see
a star that shone so bright above
and thought of home and a
faraway love.

It was quiet for a time just then
as he lay in a trench outside of
Berlin.
He was unaware of a silent tear
that rolled down his cheek and
disappeared.

He clenched his fists and gritted
his teeth.
He didn't feel the cold damp dirt
beneath.
As his mind raced back to reality
and war
he forgot about home, and love
and the star.

Bursting shells lighted the night
and the soldier's heart was full of
fright.
Not because he was afraid of
death or dying
but because he was just so tired
of trying.

Motionless, unmoving, he sat in
the hole.
No longer could the sergeant lead
his patrol.
The firing came closer as a buddy
saw his face.
The soldier crumbled into his
friends' embrace.

Awakening slowly, the light
hurting his eyes,
he found he was alive and well to
his surprise.
But the buddy who had thought
first of a friend
did not wake up. His war had
come to an end.

Cynthia Lee Sanders
THE HOURS OF TIME
The morning is here, The light
hits the trees,
The day has begun, And God is at
ease.
The beauty surrounds us, For he
gave his all,
Not only to children, But for all
who will call.

Midday arrives, And we
sometimes feel down,
It isn't because, The Lord isn't
around.
For he will guide you, And lead
you away,
From all the heartaches, Of a
lonely day.

Afternoon it hits, In such a way,
You are really tired, By the end of
the day.
He'll give you the strength, And

the courage you need,
If for his word, You would only
take heed.

Many a wanderer, Will go their
separate way,
They will wander, And they will
stray.
All thru life, their heart will be
empty,
Because they didn't have, The
word of plenty.

Evening has fallen, And all is still,
This is because, It was Gods will.
The time for relaxation, And
peace of mind,
Has settled in, For the hours of
time.

Marianne Drenberg
ALPHA AND OMEGA
Throughout our lifetime
Human paths cross, whereby
We gain hope and understanding.

Patterns are intricate;
Thoughts formed as friendships
Are enriched by loyal companions.

And we are all more
Loving and humane, through
knowing
You.

Kim Lee Seagull
LADY OF THE MOON
Oh lady of the moon
So special is your gift,
To put my heart in tune
With the universal drift.

Oh soft and tender light,
Oh gentle glowing sphere,
Do brighten up my night
In answer to me here.

May moonlight always rest
In these eyes mooring,
Until she is the guest
Of sunlight in the morning.

Louise Beaven
DRUMS OF THE SEA
_____
*To the glory of God "... and the
gathering together of the waters
called he Seas: ..." (Gen. 1:10) and
for my children, Patricia, Pamela
and Deborah.*
_____

The drums of the sea beat steadily
With a measured, rhythmic sound;
When the blue sea blooms with
sea-perfume,
They echo on shores they
surround.

The drums of the sea beat
violently
With a fearsome, furious pound;
When the sea's insane with the
wind and the rain,
They roll when a ship runs
aground!

The drums of the sea beat
chillingly—
Alas! When the sea has frowned!
When the grey sea fumes with
fountains of spume,
They roll when a man has
drowned!

The drums of the sea beat gleefully
With a will to confuse and

confound;
While the blue sea lies with the
sun in her eyes,
They play when the lost are found.

The drums of the sea beat a
rhapsody
Of refreshment and joy to be
found;
While the blue sea smiles for a
thousand miles,
They throb with a grace that
astounds.

The drums of the sea beat
ceaselessly,
Repeating their message
profound;
Capricious drums are the drums
of the sea,
Drums that forever resound.

Ronald L. Tyrrell
A CHRISTMAS THOUGHT
The Christmas bells have yet to
ring ...
   The peoples voices wait to sing.

The songs of this most
wonderous season ...
   Give praise to God, whose son is
the reason.

Throughout the centuries that
have past ...
   Why is it that his memory lasts?

Was it something that he said,,
   Or maybe just the life he led?

There is no one answer to this
rhyme ...
   The answer lies in each mans
mind.

So lets give thanks this
Christmas season ...
   For the child who is the reason.

To all we wish the gift of joyous
life,,
   And a new world devoid of strife.

         Have A Joyous

KP
JOE
For a little while, I feel happy
When I'm talking with you
the moments are full of energy
   I envy you and your lifestyle
You make me so happy,
   At least for a little while
And when I return to reality
and you've gone to live your life
   that wonderful, mysterious life
I can still feel traces of
happiness ...
I can still feel the mood you
create ...
I am completely engulfed in the
memory of you.
Part of you never leaves me
And I'm glad
   So very, very glad.

Don Gunkel
IT'S YOU
Nothing compares to the
sweetness of you,
Not even the flowers with their
morning dew.
You stand alone in your own place,
With a beautiful smile upon your
face.

I try to think of what to say,
But my thoughts will come then

go away.
I know the words that should be
said,
But they all remain here in my
head.

To me this doesn't come with ease,
Saying the words I know will
please.
My mouth gets dry and my
tongue gets thick,
It's then I know I must be quick.

I take a breath and let it go,
And in one short minute you will
know.
For through some power from
above,
I tell you now, IT'S YOU I LOVE.

Kelli S. Wenzel
ONCE LITTLE GIRL
Somewhere in the sea of
memories my childhood
disappeared
Only for a child to be gone
forever and for a woman to
reappear.

         Lollipops and rainbows
         and no time to play
         Butterflies and teddibears
         so far away
Her days are no longer filled with
teaparties and dolls
They are just a faint memory in
her mind that is now so
small.

Yesterday dreams no longer come
true
For that once little girl with eyes
of blue
   She knows her life has to go on
   Because those memories will
never be gone
Seasons change and so has she
I know because that litle girl was
once ME!

Sandra R. Bailey
IN TONE
_____
*To John. In remembrance of our
first summer together.*
_____

Sing!—
Silly summer song.
Shunning secret scandals—
Shyly, slinking solo.
Sailing safely—
Sanctimoniously searching:
Scrimmaging satirically:
Sanquinely scheming sagaciously—
Sedately seceding southbound
Speaking soulfull soliloquys.
Sing!
Silly summer song.

Lynne Keener
THE TREASURE CHEST
Brush away the cobwebs,
   Sweep off the dust,
   Lift the lid of your mind—
   And search for the memories
inside.

   You'll find some right on top,
Just recently laid away ...
      While others are in corners—
      More difficult to recall.

   Caress them with tenderness;
      For most are fragile—

Somewhat faded with age,
And will crumble in the wind
   of yesterday.

These must be held gently,
   With a wistful glance—
      A soft touch;
   Others with a small,
quiet tear.

For once they've been crushed—
   By too heavy a hand,
   They are gone—
      From the refuge ...
   of the mind's
         TREASURE CHEST.

Terry W. Schwartz
WITHOUT YOU
A rose with no scent,
   stars without light,
   sun without warmth.
Endless tears,
   songless birds,
   occupy me.

When you nudged here by my side,
   I knew the meaning of love.
My heart sang;
   my eyes glowed in the morning
sun.
In my breast beat,
   the forever you made of us.
Time had no meaning,
   we became the spring.

Once I thanked God for you;
   now I ask Him to erase the
   memory of you from my
mind.
I close my eyes and no longer see
you,
   the object of my love.
All I see is your leaving—
   your earth shattering
   departure.
Now I have,
   only the cold, long lonely
   nights to hold me.
I don't ask,
   "Why did you leave?"
But "Why did you take my heart
   with you?"

Dorothy Rund
**God Knows How Much I
   Love You**
_____
*To Mom and Dad, Ruth and Ed
Rund, for all your constant
support and belief in me. You are
not only my parents, but my
friends and advisors. I love you
both very much.*
_____

I may not always show it,
And sometimes I really blow it,
But I swear that it is true,
God knows how much I love you.

You have always been cheery,
When my days have been dreary,
You always know just what to do,
And God knows how much I love
   you.

Your love has shown me right
   from wrong,
Your love has made me very
   strong,
Yet you're as gentle as the
   morning dew,
And God knows how much I love
   you.

63

And now I feel I must confess,
I know that I have really been
blessed,
To have you all the years through,
And God knows how much I love
you.

Michael C. Morrison
AMBROSE
I once knew a man named
Ambrose.
He and I were very good friends,
However, I did not know him well.

We, one day, attended a party;
It was given by Felix on Sunday.
We began at one o'clock,
Making merry all the day through,
Dinner was served at eight o'clock:
But by that time we had drunk
Far too much of our liquor.
Dinner failed as we ate little;
But the wine was a great success.

I once knew a man named
Ambrose.
We had become two great friends,
However, I did not know him well.

Ambrose, the life of the party, left
Only after everyone had gone.
He and I became great friends in
Only the few short hours of the
party.
We both had had far too much to
Drink, but we did not care then.
He thought he was as sober as
ever,
He thought he could see clearly,
He thought he could drive home.

I once knew a man named
Ambrose.
Yes, we had a good time that night,
But he never made it home, and I
fell asleep.

Clyde E. Swallow
OBDURATE

*To all the boys who fought and
died in the Viet Nam War.*

I know I'll never understand,
man's inhumanity to man.
Why men and might are kept in
store, reserved to fight some
silly war?

The loving power of Gods' own
grace, seems lost upon the
human race.
The irony of our civil state, we
talk of love and indulge in hate.

The denizens wild that roam the
glen, are still more civilized
than men.
The fearsome sound of the lions'
roar, but upon his kind never
goes to war.

Man has found knowledge in the
art of technism, may he learn
to embrace wisdom,
And try to erase the sin of Cain,
for war never settles anything.

Luke Nathaniel Baxter
LADY LUCK
Lady luck is fickle
She picks a man at random
Although she helps him win
Too soon she will abandon

Chance is very thin

The odds be of our choosing
A man may never, ever win
For fear of simply losing

Gambling is a fever
It will posess a man
Lady luck may only tease
Catch her if you can

When she holds the winning cards
O' how we court her favor
Reaching out to hold her hand
Her kisses seek to savor

Lee E. Muir
THE WORKS OF LIFE

*To Boris "Bob" Dragon, my friend,
whose home in Las Vegas,
Nevada was the setting for this
poem.*

Man builds unto the sun,
the works of life never done,
The trials and cares of many
years,
the paper dreams of untold fears,
and tries to leave for those to be,
an empty shrine beside the sea,
So they will know of what has
been—
the feeble wares of mortal men.

Sybil Suvantra
AT DELPHI
The oracle speaks—and the oracle
knows no mercy.
So Shall It Be, he intones, and the
sibyl must answer,
The sibyl must speak for him;
speak, and dance in a frenzy
Till she cries out for death, but the
oracle will have his message:
So *must* it be.

Wild in the winds whirls the
voice of Apollo in fury
Eternal. So must it be: sacred
leaves spin with the seasons,
Become sacred order. But spirit
strikes down the frail vessel,
A meet sacrifice, that madness
may give birth to healing:
So *let* it be.

Lillian Diefenbach
LOVE AND WAR
It has been said once or twice
before,
That anything is fair in games of
love and war.

With this maxim I beg to
disagree,
No heart should be forced to
suffer even half the pain you
brought to me.

An arsenol of secret tactics, well
planned strategies and hurtful
ammunition,
You used on me without care or
trepidation.

Well, the flag is up, you've won
the war,
I'm battle weary and wounded,
and I just can't fight anymore.

I know you'll celebrate your
victory with her, flowers and
champagne,
But maybe you can mourn for
me, the only one who fought
for us . . . in vain.

George Chaffee
POEMS OF THE POET
The poems of the poet;
Will they ever live on?
And long be remembered;
When the poet is gone?

The phrases and verses;
Many forms many styles.
That bring you the laughter;
And the teardrops and smiles.

The words that are written;
On the tablet or scroll.
The innermost feelings;
From the heart and the soul.

The poems of the poet;
All of those you like best.
Will long be remembered;
When the poets at rest.

Elvira Lilly Perez
THOUGHTS
If I could cry,
I'd cry for you.
Not because you have gone your
own way,
But because a valuable part of you
has died.
Where has your laughter gone?
And your capacity to love?
That has gone it's own way, too.
Somewhere, somehow, someone
hurt you,
and now you only seek to inflict
pain . . .
Your soul is filled with poison,
like a cancer that fills your
heart, your mind . . .
your very soul!
It flows through your system
and dominates your life.
If I could cry, I'd cry for you.

Alma Holwerda Hulvey
MIRAGE
Who said the West is dead? It
cannot be,
I stand before my window as the
purple shadows fall,
And look across the valley to the
mountain range beyond,
Where visions of the past take
form and phantom beings move,
Tonight, the West of long ago,
has come alive for me.

The wagon train has circled for
the night,
Their camp fires glow and whisps
of smoke
Snake upward toward the sky.
How weary they must be;

they journeyed far
Through freezing rain and searing
desert heat,
With flaming hope of fortune in
an untamed land,
Their lamps are burning bright.

The stooped Prospector plods
along the trail,
And guides his burrow toward a
lean-to shack,
Where he will pause to rest and
dream anew
In restless sleep, of gleaming
veins of gold.
No suffering or hardship can
subdue his endless quest,
Or dreams of wealth curtail.

And now, I hear the ringing of a
bell,
As evening shadows deepen and
my apparition fades,
The Mission bell's melodious
voice, chimes out her lullaby,
"Take heart from Pioneers who
blazed the way,
They live, in different form,
Tonight the West, like God, is
very real,
Both are alive and well."

Georgia Tipton Frazier
CREDIT TO INFLATION
Credit used nonsensically,
Has cost the country quite a fee.
The way to buy with no cash on
hand,
Spread like wildfire over the land.
The desire to live like a
millionaire,
Without money . . . but credit to
spare,
And borrowing from Peter to pay
Paul,
Has cost the country most of all.
Credit cards flooded the nation,
And now we're dying of inflation.
Instead of a chicken in every pot,
A bullet to bite is what we've got.
Now the government says we're
back on our feet,
But most of the country is still
on it's seat.

Emily Estep Badertscher
GIFTS
God gifts us beyond all ken
with time beneath the sun
and moments rich in laughter
and tears; then gives us song
to share. But pausing after,
Transcends it all and gives us
friends.

Krista L. Neal
DREAMS

*This poem is written to-Paul
Wheeler—the man in which all
my hopes and dreams rest within.*

It's been three years or so since I
first met you
Now we have come together, and
you mean more to me,
Than ever.

It's when I look into your eyes
and find,
Your warmth from inside.
It's those friendly smiles you send
my way,

Our World's Best Loved Poems

saying everything will be ok.

Dreams are made for those who
　believe, and I believe,
I'll carry this dream I have within
　me.
For when you hold me in your
　arms, I know,
I will never let you go.

So it's to you I say, these feelings,
Will never fade away.
Because when you're with me,
I'm as happy as can be!

*Nancy Lee (Erdman) Fantom
(Cupcake)*
WHAT IS EASTER
"Easter" is a time for new
　Beginnings—
Of pretty new dresses and
　Corsage pinnings;
Of Hyacinths and Daffodils
Of sunny days with Early Spring
　chills;
Of Pastel colors and little Spring
　Crocus;
Of thoughts of "being outside"
　now in focus;
Of hopping bunnies and an Easter
　Basket;
Of new Hope and new Dreams
　and nothing can mask it;
Of Colored and Candy Eggs to
　hide and toss;
Of Jesus, Who died for Us on the
　Cross.
There are so many things that
　Easter means,
Oh, Yes, Let's not forget the Jelly
　Beans!
So, let me say now, without delay—
"HAVE A VERY HAPPY EASTER
　DAY!"

Joy Creamer
MY HUSBAND
You are the magic in my life . .
First you were just a friend . .
As time went on you became a
　Very Special Man . . .
Love seemed to encircle our
　relationship and grow . .
The best move in my life was
　becoming your wife.
We have waved through fears,
　frustrations, laughter, and tears
　over the years.
Our future most likely will hold
　more for us to endure . . .
Yet each day with you by my
　side, I glow inside with Love
　and Pride . . .
Your touch, and knowing you are
　right here, makes life more
　complete dear.
Every year I Love You more and
　more . .
You are the magic I adore . .

Jennifer Dan
TIME OF TOMORROW
　Slowly, softly, petals seem to
collect at my feet,
　gathering on the lawns,
　on the street.
　The Hush of the wind dies
down.
Suddenly fresh leaves
　turn crisp brown.
A change in the weather,
　sometimes worse, sometimes
best.

North turns to South
　and East travels West.
　the seasons change,
　come what may.
Tomorrow is still another day.

Catherine S. Flynn
MOTHER NATURE
Clouds whippes gently against
　the moon's full face,
　And darkness settles all with
restful sleep.
The twinkling stars shines
　through a cloudless space,
　Making my feeling one of
serene peace.

The wind in the trees make sad,
　sleepy sounds,
　Revealing new mysteries and
delight,
Sweet smelling flowers beautifies
　the grounds,
　Making serene peace creep
through the night.

I find new music in each dark
　shadow—
　In each tall, slender, swaying
longleaf pine,
In each gentle rain-drop on a
　window,
　In tiny dew-drops on a trailing
vine.

Within the dancing shadows, I
　find romance,
　To me a brilliant rainbow is
divine.
Sunbeams melt into gold within
　my glance,
　Yes, each of these are "Mother
Natures" sign.

J. W. Cheney Jr.
TIME SPAN
As shadows slow sparse sunlight
mere pausing, causing shade
Gratuitous, changed, glacial heart
prolong, life's brief charade.

Glance, fortune's prevading value
-pittance, bittered mind.
Opportune, embracing solace
portentious, shallow, find.

Bliss-sent, disdain—
　"contentment?"
Damned, your "within" sly guise?
Delusion's "myth" inequity
so "altogether wise".

Repast, "so", antiquity
"needs" heary, thus defined.
Elusive, semblant's future
aggregated, grieved, "kind".

No pedestriate, time's passage
slowed, solaced, "never" stayed.
Fly yesterday's "tomorrow"
peripheric "Roles" dismayed.

Ronda Bitterli
CELEBRATION!
Man;
Woman.
Man and Woman.

Woman;
Child.
Woman with Child.

Child;
Man.
Child to Man.

From Man to Child
And back again!

Kim Brashears
THE RIDE
Strung out from the night before
I hear the churchbells ring
Far in the distance as all the
　angels sing
But I close my ears,
Don't want to hear no bells
Just want to close my eyes and
　float
So far away from hell
Powder-puff visions of pink and
　blue collide
Close all thoughts and settle back
I get ready for the ride
I see the crystal swans
Dancing 'round the clown
Tripping as he smiles, while the
　other people frown
Monkeys bite the fingers
Of every outstretched hand
Laughing as they run around
And I just don't understand
The woman in the sky opens all
　her eyes
Seeing what the prophets saw
Seeing all the lies
Marmelade is clear, as the
　coming of the sea
Drifting closer to my body, I
　know it isn't me
Headache's getting worse
Don't want to feel no pain
Just let rock and roll cleanse my
　soul
And I'll be free again.

Velma Carman
MY IMAGE OF YOU
I have a "special image" of you
　Locked inside my heart;
All the things you say and do,
　Then when we're apart;
I take them out one by one—
　The way you smile,
Something you have said or done;
　Makes life worth while.

You may not ever think or know
　The way I feel;
It matters not how far you go,
　I have it still;
I'm never lonely when you are
　away
　Nor am I blue—
It's with me always, night or day
　My image of you.

Edna M. Golem
The Return Of St. Patrick
I wonder if St. Patrick came
To Eire to stay a while,
How would he view the strife and
　hate
Within his lovely isle?
Could he drive away the darkness,
Turn their hearts again to God?
Let love and gentle kindness
Fill, again, the "dear old sod"?

Cheryl Clark Hoversten
TEAR FOR AN ATHEIST
The man talked loudly,
Presenting his case
For a Godless universe,
While a falling star caught my eye,
Its dazzling spash against the night
An artist's dream.
I turned back,
Amazed at the flawless logic
That left no room for faith.
His speech became more rapid

As he finalized his atheistic plea,
Stacking up imaginary points
Like sticks of wood.
A loon's call
Echoed across the water,
Another lost soul
Crying out his emptiness
In searching splendor.
My dear one, intellectual and
　scientific,
Paused to ponder summer sounds,
Smug in his verbal brilliance,
While I brushed away a tear
For his sterile, faithless world.

Kay Cavanaugh
SKIN COLORS

*Dedicated to Roy Nation. We
both expected too much. This
poem will immortalize the
happiness that we once shared.*

He is black and she is white
Society says that's not right
Hiding their love was a strain
So they parted with a lot of pain
Couldn't live with so much fear
Lots of hostile rednecks are here
They each cry lonely night tears
They should've been happy for
　years

Susan McGarry
MY MOM AND MY DAD
My Mom and My Dad are always
　there,
And they let me know they really
　care.

If something is wrong,
They show me where I really
　belong.

Through the good times and bad,
They always know how to make
　me happy when I am sad.

When things aren't going right,
Mom and Dad show their love
　with all their might.

With Mom I can do anything all
　day,
And she always listens to what I
　have to say.

Dad always shows us how to be
　the strong man,
But if he ever needs my help I
　will always give him a hand.

My Mom and My Dad are always
　there to see the family through
And what ever I can do for them I
　sure will do.

Tracy Lander
AUTOBIOGRAPHY

*For my family who has added to
my life. sweet fragrances that
linger on a tapestry of gentleness
and love*

I am soft as delicate rose buds
　enclosing smiling eyes
I sing and dance to the music of
　an old silver music box
I collect loving memories now
　yellowing with age
And tear-stained letters that
　never reached another heart
My scent is so very faint

like the preserved petals of a
flower
I need nothing to nourish me
growth comes from time
My mind drifts back
to the field of life where I began
I gently swirl around
absorbing the freshness
I am as vulnerable as a dew drop
in sun
for my dreams are easily crushed
I long for jasmine, satin and lace
which was all right in a
different age
There is a time for growing up
but for now the time is to
remember

Leah C. Anderson
**The Golden Bond Of
Friendship**
A Friend is someone Special who
is always
there it seems;
To lend a helping hand perhaps
or simply
share your Dreams!

A Friend can be your Guiding
Light when the
going gets kind of rough;
And you're tempted to shout
from the highest
hill "Stop, I've had ENOUGH!"

But when you're in a joyful mood
and
everything looks great;
A Friend is the first one on the
scene
to help you celebrate!

True Friendship is a Golden Bond
which
in time we realize;
Is not just coincidence but a
Blessing
in disguise!

It's something to be cherished and
strengthened day by day;
And no one ever anywhere can
steal
it away!

Tho 'miles may separate True
Friends at times
they're never far apart;
For thoughts and memories of the
past are
forever sealed in their hearts!

Grace Yvonne Smith
COMING AND GOING
Yes coming and going, yes flying
high
And mightly blowing as the trees
blow
Moving as a pendulun. Yes
moving as
The sun revolving around the
earth, as
The stars twinkling in the sky,
and the
moon glowing by the river side.
Yes coming and going to end of
time,
Yes coming and going one day
will meet
On the other side.

Robert R. Parent
WHAT I AM
I'm not up on the making of
galaxies

or the nebulae filling the sky.
I'm not up on where the old Earth
came from
so don't bother asking me why.

I'm not up on measuring distant
stars,
or the clusters they make, out in
space.

I'm not up on orbiting satellites;
sent up in the course of the race.

I'm not up on following meteorites
or asteroids, comets and such.

I'm not up on what causes spots
on the Sun;
they don't interest me very
much.

I'm not up on novas, elusive
black holes
or on how many moons there
may be.

There is one thing, however, I
know to be true;
I'm living . . . I'm happy . . . I'm
free. . .

Jo Starrett Lindsey

Jo Starrett Lindsey
THE TWISTED TREE
No human heart can make the
marks
That form the spirit of this tree;
Its thrust for life extends itself
In total creativity.
It battled elements and won
The right to hold its link with life;
It has a beauty all its own
Arising from its growth in strife.
It is a symbol of the strength
That fills an undefeated heart
That doggedly keeps going on
When all its world is dashed apart.

Joanne Mosher
A SPECIAL PRAYER
Sometimes I wonder why the
world must be this way.
So many people in pain, so many
people insane.
I wonder why it must be this way,
every single night and day.
Can't we see? children starving,
crying and hurting.
The most we have done is plenty
of deserting.
Everyone staring, but never caring.
God, see the childrens tears, try
your best to hear.
If there is a God, hear my prayre.
make us show a little care.
and give all men the will, to find

a way,
to end all sorrow.
So we may someday have a better
tomorrow!

Sherry L. Syverson
HERITAGE
Toned gray
frame and man within
A familiar face.
my indirect giver of life
yet a stranger

My father—
perhaps
more than a physical replica
of the stranger.

disappearing into the basement
after work
returning only for supper and the
10 pm news
"Get me a toothpick please.
Why did you move the couch?"

Grandpa
you were to be my last clue
but you died too soon.

Bettylee Sowder
**Will Someone Even
Remember My Name?**
I call myself a poet,
as you can see.
But, I wonder if they,
will even remember me.
In my pretend world,
as a poet,
I wonder.
Have I touched their hearts,
like music touches the ear?
Have they been able to,
read through my lines?
And were they clear?
I the poet,
who dreams not out loud,
must write to release,
and let come alive,
this love I shall,
no longer hide.
Immortality? Fame?
Will someone even,
remember my name?

Florence M. Craven
LAMPS OF FRIENDSHIP
The little lamps of friendship
We light along the way
Go shining on far down the years
And brighten every day.
It's love that keeps them burning
In sympathy and trust
God help us that no lamp goes
out
Because we let it rust.

Yes, every road is rougher
Without good friends to cheer it;
The longest trip is brighter
When friendships keep it lit.
So measure then your riches
In true friends and in old
More lasting, they, than silver
More precious than pure gold.

While traveling through life's
journey
Let us pause along the way,
And make friends for a lifetime
No, not just for a day.
Of music and of friendship,
Time is the truest test,
For old friends, like our old
songs,
Are always loved the best.

Ralph E. Kane
RAKE'S PROGRESS
You've been assigned your row to
hoe
And I've been given mine.
Neither of us will ever know
Which hewed the harder line.

Think over all the awesome trials
You've faced in life to date;
Compare them to my measured
miles
And see if yours equate.

Since one veers west, the other
east,
And neither knows his course;
We may not learn til life has
ceased
Whose well-worn way was worse.

Lettie M. Jennings
THESE EMPTY ARMS
If I had had a teddy bear, he'd
always have been there
My troubles to share, seeming to
care.
With button eyes, cotton-stuffed
thighs,
Stunted size—what a prize!

But my childhood is spent—it
came, it went
Like a flower's scent or a revival
tent.

I had sisters born, a brother to
mourn,
Caramel corn, and empty arms.
I am now grown, on my own
All alone in my home.

My youth is spent—it came, it
went
Like a flower's scent or a revival
tent.

No babe to rest upon my chest
Or even best to nurse my breast.
With soft skin, a toothless grin,
Hair that's thin and diaper pins.

My chance for motherhood is
spent—it came, it went
Like a flower's scent or a revival
tent.

I refuse to sob—I'm still warm
I am not a snob, I have my
charm.
I stood alone tho' I meant no
harm
But I guess I earned these empty
arms.

Vikki Jenkins
WINDOWS

In memory of F. Jenkins

We look at different scenes
from different windows, you and I.
Claiming, each one of us, as we do
that only our view is really true.
This cannot be, of course, there are
many windows and other scenes.
For the world is large and there
is room for all.

Sarah Daniel Vaughan
SHINING MOMENTS
If I could hold each shining
moment
Forever in my hand—I would!
Moments spent alone with you,

Little girls in pink and blue,
Views of moonlight on the sea—
All of these mean so much to me,
Sunrise on Mt. Fuji —San
Turning snow cap pink and
    gold—
Foreign faces—strange new
    places—
Memories my heart will hold.
Awesome sight of Shuttle Seven
Bursting through the clouds with
    flame—
On it's journey near to heaven—
Mankind will never be the same.
Precious moments go so quickly
We can never make them stay;
So, memories I cherish today
Will be held forever in my mind!

Thomas Chris Holdredge
LIGHT OF LOVE

For the Angels

Here is the Peace
That Freedom brings.
With Innoncence found
No Beauty can be lost,
There is love enough to give
And a reason to be,
For I had named that Hunger
That so haunted me.

Gayle Balyeat
STORM AND SILENCE
Angry voice of thunder loud
Darkness of a large rolling black
    cloud
Rain drops begin, trees start
    swaying
The storm is here, no longer
    delaying.
For harder now the rain comes
    down
Puddles quickly made upon the
    ground
The wind blows harder, rain a
    steady pour
Crashing noise, a sudden roar.
Flashes of lightening dancing
    fast
Across the sky, long do not last.
Rumbling sounds, as louder ones
    slip between, within
A lull, and quiet stillness,
    frightening as when
the rampage of the storm, did
    begin.

Thora J. Supple
SUMMER'S GONE:
Winds sigh
Trees sway
Clouds float by
On a breezy day!

Summer's gone
North Wind sings . . .
Her winter song.
Old Man Winter paces fast
With a mantle of icy glass!

Snow upon the limbs of trees
Paint a picture in the lea . . .
Mother Nature's at her best
When the earth has gone to rest!

Aurelia Cecille Giron Martinez
SWEET FACE
Sweet Face—
    That dances with life
    Twinkles with laughter
    Opens with songs of joy

Anxiously my eyes search for it
Alight upon it contentedly.

I look at it perhaps too often
Others might see what it will
    not
Would that it looked for mine
Expressions of love there to be
    found.

Dear, sweet face—
    Eyes breathe, filled with soul
    Lips move with powerful beauty
    My heart soars upon seeing it,
    Dances at the thought of it.

Would that I could tell him
Of my longing for his embrace
Of my love with sighs enlaced,
My love for his sweet face.

Monica Page
**Yesterday Had To Go Back
Home**
yesterday stood on my doorstep
she wanted me to play with her

                i wanted to play so bad
but today was already playing with
                                        me
and he doesn't like yesterday
                            so i had to let
yesterday go back home

La Forrest G. Lucas
**He Who Sees the Sparrow
Fall!**
When I grow tired and weary
And the evening shadows fall . . .
The clouds hang dark and dreary
I'll hear my Saviour call!
I've put my trust in Jesus
To lead me every day . . .
That I would follow closely
And never go astray!

I listen at the dawn of day
I hear Him softly speak . . .
There comes a brighter morning
To find it you must seek . . .
The Love of Christ! My Saviour!
He intercedes for you!
And God in Heaven listens . . .
To Him you must be true!

For He is leading! Guiding!
Each moment He is near!
To soothe each hurt! Each
    heartache!
To calm each doubt! Each fear!
"For He who sees the sparrow fall"
Will take you by the hand . . .
And lead you from this earth below
To Heaven! Gloryland!

Sauna Maronski
THE AGE OF LOVE
A lonely heart, a silent tear
With thoughts confused and
    little fear

Signs of wisdom, mind of old
This God given gift, like precious
    gold

His youthful love and delicate
    touch
Too many things that mean too
    much

A restless soul, an inner loss
The price of love a deadly cost

Cold steel bars clamped round
    my heart
The vicious pain, a brand new
    start

Blinding tears so hard to see
The love I feel, a part of me

A futile search for reasons why
Be it then, a sad goodbye.

Frank, Anthony Bolek
SEA DUMP

*For all marine life of the waters,
because of the pollutants that
invade their world.*

Bone ash hills,
The new kills,
Sulfur fills the fish's gills.
Helpless creatures of the septic
    sea,
Is this the way you were meant
    to be?
Chemical foamed waves,
Petroleum roamed beaches,
When will we learn the lesson it
    teaches?

Lydia Carmichael Wilkerson
HUNGER
Hunger of the world
Hollow sheets of skin
Born the underfed
Praying for a friend

Faces of the lantern jaw
Begging for the bread
Lost in empty lands
Children buried dead

Children never laugh
Born to only die
Reaching for a hand
Crying for their life

Leigh Rocke
GOLDEN DAYS
Our lives are touched by autumn
    leaves
What tender looking back our
    memory weaves
What sweet delights, these
    parenthetic dreams
They have lost nothing of their
    warmth it seems.

A myriad volumes line each
    memory shelf
Each one, a pensive treasure in
    itself
They line the walls in tiers
    within my mind
And to my lonely nights bring
    solace kind.

Each well thumbed book is read
    and read again
Each incident like sunshine after
    rain
Relived and savored, 'till you are
    here once more
Then, books replaced, I'll close
    my library door.

No need of memories with you
    by my side
'Tho bye and bye, in life's long
    eventide
We'll open once again our library
    door
And live each love sweet memory
    once more.

Tammie lane Nash
I Really Feel Sorry For You
It seemed like our friendship
    would never end until the day
    you came on in, and said you'd

made up your mind, you've
    decided on the abortion thats
    up to you, but as far as I'm
    concerned I'll always feel sorry
    for you.
Cause one of these days you'll see
    a cute child and wonder what
    your baby would have looked
    like, but you'll never know,
    will you. Because of a mistake
    you made the day, you killed
    the babe who never could say,
    Mom I want to live.
It could have been a boy, or it
    could have been a girl, who
    knows it could have been
    twins. It might have looked
    like you, or it might have
    looked like him, but no one
    will ever know, because you
    had the money to kill it, but
    not the money to have it. You
    think the abortion is an easy
    way out, but you'll find out
    your very wrong.
If you give the baby love and you
    give the baby life then thats
    the best you can do. If you
    fight together you'll make it
    work, but if you don't then I
    only have one more thing to
    say "I REALLY FEEL SORRY
    FOR YOU".

Kathrine Aileen Sanders
FOREVER & EVER
When you feel so good inside;
and those feelings you try to
hide.
It seems to get stronger & stronger
each day; you begin to wonder
what price you'll have to pay.
But the pain you felt for your—
self; is now the pain you feel
for someone else.
Now that we're together forever
& ever ; I want you to know my
love for you always grows.
Our love is like the sun so
bright and bold; and when we're
apart everything's cold.
I know you know that you're the
one I want to hold;
                    Forever & Ever

Edra Jean Whitley-Ulland
PHENOMENON

*Written for my parents, Clarence
& Geneva Whitley, my children,
Philip & Susan and my four
grandchildren, Linda, Sandy,
Valerie & Brook. Thank you for
always believing in me during the
bad times.*

You beckon—like an aroused
    lover,
teasing, flippantly.
The nucleus of my mind is
stripped naked.
We embrace—throwing all
    inhibitions
to the wind.
no right
no wrong.
Opulent kaleidoscopic fantasy
rummages—shifts—probes
the deja vu of mysterious
sensuality

as the sensuous soul impregnates
the canvas—
The smiling artist
O. D.'s.

Jean Howard Russell
LONG LOST
In the still of the night, comes a
long lost wail
And a ghostly light shows a long
lost trail
As I walk along with a long lost
tread
I hum a dirge of the long lost
dead.

No pillow on which to lay my
head—
'Tis long lost.
And the arbor where I often read—
'Tis covered with frost.

So I'll wander far from the things
that are real
'Till the scar of love has time to
heal;
Wander far from this world of
men
'Till my long lost love comes
back again.

Ivan Hill
MY COMPUTER DATE
(The Letter)

Dear Sirs,

I hope that it is not too late
To put in for my computer date
Here's your hundred dollar fee
Now send this perfect girl to me;

Send me a girl
From the top of the world
One that's not too abnormal
But likes to dress formal
I don't care 'bout her size
But I like the dark eyes
Send one by the seaport
That likes water sports
And so I'll include
She must like seafood.

(The Reply)

Dear Sir,

We've looked all around
And we've finally found
A date that'll put your heart in a
spin
She's really a charm
So don't be alarmed
When we send you Molly, the
penguin.

Peggy Turner
TO GEORGE WITH LOVE
My life began when I met you
Gray clouds rolled away,
the sun came into view
When you walked into
my life that day
You changed my world,
in a magical way
You have given me love,
filled with warmth and beauty
For it is given freely—
not as a sense of duty
You've made me feel wanted,
and at the same time, needed
You've made me "YOUR
WOMAN",
and I'm glad you suceeded!
You've given me respect,
understanding, and loyalty

You've shared with me your
feelings,
and become a part of me
When we are apart,
you are near me it seems
For you are there,
in my thoughts and dreams
You have been my lover,
my companion, my friend
A love such as this,
must be—written on the wind
You've given my life
a new meaning, so sweet
You've made me feel
happy, safe,—"COMPLETE"
I'll wait for you, darling,
and I'll be true
For—my life began when I met
you!

Vineler Long Mann

Vineler Long Mann
A DAY TO REMEMBER
The leaves are turning red and
gold
The most beautiful time of the
year
You look and listen to the
quietness
And stand and shed a tear.

If things could always be this way
How happy we would be.
Oh the beauty in these hills
And valleys as far as we can see.

I have found a new love
The greatest to be found.
He shows me love and tenderness
These things I've never had.

He tells me of his troubles
I pray for him each day.
I hope someday they'd be over
And he'll be here with me to stay.

Oh! This beautiful November
A time I will never forget.
These twilight years we'll
remember
You don't have to be young to
enjoy it.

Doris Ullman Barbuto
TRAVELERS' ADVISORY
Take care in planning every jaunt.
Don't ever make a sudden dart
To space already occupied—
Or someone else might get your
heart!

As you travel on the highways,
Always be careful how you drive;
And when you come into the
towns,
Be sure to slow to thirty-five.

Be careful where you park your
car;
Some handy spots might cause
you pain.
Illegal parking costs a lot,
And that is money down the drain!

Clamp a clothspin on your car key
If you must drive at dusk or dawn;
When you stop it will remind you:
Take care, don't leave those car
lights on!

Be polite to other travelers;
Use your best manners
everywhere—
Or some irritated strangers
Might choose to honk and spit
and swear!

It matters not what vehicle
Or what far route you choose to
roam;
Just take along a big cash roll—
Enough to help you get back home!

Vetrice Remy Jewett
MY MEMORIAL DAY

*All male relatives, who
participated in service of these
United States during all wars in
which we have been involved.*

Friends, peace, health and a new
day;
Sunshine, singing birds and May;
Small children, who are at play,
On this Memorial Day.

Band music and marching men;
Talk of sacrifice of kin;
Praise for all of those brave men
And the *Calmness* of "Amen."

The words of my elder kin,
"You cannot remember when
Mothers wept for their dead men
'Cause your boy is only ten."

Kathryn Marie McGuire
Scaling Mount Olympus

*In Memory of My dear husband,
Robert*

What loftier goal than to scale
the gods' summit—that
fairest aerie of gloried Greece!

To rise from Earth's travail,
the strife of mortals,
and dwell among the mighty,
But so far removed from
all things familiar
brings new desolation.

Stratospheres are icy cold;
Small deaths in disconnections.

Harvey Alan Sperry
BIRTHDAYS ARE DOORS
Birthdays are doors to
forthcoming years:
Some are delightful, some full of
fears.
Others are tragic, yet you can
survive.
Many are fun you will want to
revive.
Birthdays are doors that open one
way;
there's no possible chance to
relive that day.

Why go back when there is
nothing to gain
just repeat history and last year's
champagne?
Birthdays are doors to fresh new
adventure
new friends and new years laden
with rapture.
So open champagne and bury
your fear.
Trust me my child, this will be a
great year.
Love will be yours enhanced with
devotion
and enough birthday wishes to
fill the whole ocean.

David P. Lang
TRAINING TRUST
There's something definite about
a journey by train:
The single-tracked pursuit of a
destination
On the unslipping ground of
linear intention
To the somnolent lull of a
monotonous engine,
Assuming responsibility for every
decision.

There's something transparent
about a trip by train:
No dissimulation at the outset is
ever sought,
No detour to distract nor
seductive wayside parking lot;
True, neither can unexpected
adventure be got—
Just the simple assurance that
the quest will end where it
ought.

Wilma M. Atkinson
MADE US ONE

*Many thanks to James L. Berry,
for his inspiration and
encouragement. I dedicate this
poem, one of many that was
orginally written for him. May all
the wonderful things he has done
for others come back ten fold.*

My love for you shall last till the
end of time and go beyond.
Even in death my love for you
shall never be gone.
For in death I shall be your spirit
from above.
And watch over you with the
greatest care and love.

So everyone in the world can see
your special charm.
That shall protect you from fools
that wish you harm.

And when the day comes and our
spirits are joined as one.
We shall know the power of love
and its truly made us one.

Pamela McGee
THE SEA

*I thank the Master Creator for
His marvelous handiwork.*

Basking in an aroma all your
own, you beckon me as a sweet
and tender lover—yet the

mastery is evident. My cares
are thrown away. I am in
complete abandon.

You woo me with your songs
of life, starting in whispers,
becoming louder—louder until
it is almost a roar—or is
it my imagination . . .

I am mesmerized. I am yours.

Eleanor Lee Wilson
RETRIBUTION
When I was first married
 I learned that my spouse
Had a snore that resounded
 All through the house.
I loved him sincerely,
 He's gentle and kind,
I made no complaint
 And paid it no mind.

As the years have progressed
 His snore has departed.
But, horror of horrors,
 My snoring has started.
How happy I am
 I ignored it that way.
For, now he's the victim,
 Well! What can he say?

Alexander "Stefan" Adamski
LIFE THRU AUTOMATION
People these days are always in a
 hurry,
Instead of man leading his own
 life in the land,
Cunning crafty work has the
 industrial upper hand,
Despite that you still see people
 running in a scurry,

As forever, people always have
 something to do,
Fortunate the person whose
 errand runs not asque,
Lost is man's labor, for today
 machines make machines,
This is a disregard of man's self
 respect, not a real means,

Very seldom are there watchers
 and waiters,
In place of watchers we have
 resuscitators,
Where eons ago, the air was fresh
 and not refined,
Today it is polluted, for to this
 man is inclined,

The 20th century has made the
 elements computorized,
The present life is artificial due
 to technology by which to abide,
Despite man's progress, the inner
 being is set aside,
Thus pride and physical work are
 calculatorized,

Where years ago there was
 dignity and self-esteem,
Today we have machinery and
 the laser beam,
Thus it isn't man that is
 physically changed,
It is only the fact that society's
 been rearranged.

Diane Bailey
NEVER LOOKING BACK
Upon a horses back they travel
 cross the barren land
In heat and burning passion
 on top the desert sand.
They journey deep into their souls

deeper than the mind
And music plays and mountains
 crumble
for them everytime.
They can move the earth with
 laughter
and build it up with dreams
And tear it down and turn it
 around
to make it fill their needs.
Their souls need not feel courage
as they travel on their horse
On that destined trail before
 them
love has charted their lifes
 course.
You may see them in the wind
 some day
on top the horses back
But they travel life so lightly
 that there may not be a track

Two love filled hearts and
 souls . . .
 Never looking back.

JoEllen VanDeGrift
A TINY SEED

*To my girls, Becky, Meagan, and
Billijo, each of whom I love very
much.*

A tiny seed all alone
Within a deep, dark place,
Soon to be a loving bundle,
A sweet and glowing face.

Warm and snug and so secure
Inside a little room,
No harm will ever reach you
Inside your mothers womb.

It feels so good to feel you move.
It gives me such a joy.
Can't wait to hold you in my arms,
My very own little boy.

But if it should happen and I
 should find out,
That my boy is really a she,
I'll love you just the very same
For you're God's gift to me.

Jeannie Hyler
A GOD MADE WONDER
I have a picture in the back of my
 mind
Of a place that's going to be hard
 to find.
A secluded spot where nobody
 goes
It's beautiful year round, when it
 rains or snows.

There's a stream in the center
 that's constantly flowing,
It seems to know exactly where
 it's going.
To the waterfall, to the waterfall
Are the only words that it will
 call.

As the sun shines and makes the
 water glisten,
You should be sure to stop and
 listen,
To the birds sing and the music
 they make,
Because none of this could ever
 be fake.

This is the world I would like to
 live in
Where no crimes are commited

not even a sin.
A place filled with a love and
 beauty,
That God created with his
 ingenuity.

To find this place would be a goal
 acheived
Who would I choose to share this
 wonder with me?
Someone who could appreciate
 the perfection which it holds,
Because it's worth more than it's
 weight in gold.

Miriam Arnett Spears
MY CHILD

---

*This poem is dedicated to my
beautiful children—Carol, Ron,
Tammy and Brenda.*

When I see flowers
That are growing wild,
They spark a memory
Of you, my child.

For flowers are part
Of nature, you see.
Just as you
Are part of me.

You are the miracle
I'm proud to claim.
You bring sunshine
When there is rain.

All love is a gift,
As you were to me.
I handed you life—
Now bloom and be free.

Margaret Witzel Tucker
ODE TO A ROSE
Behold thy beauty, incomparable
 rose!
 Abandoned to the rainy dew of
 the night,
To awaken, drenched by the hand
 of God,
 And offer to strangers such
 sheer delight!
What child of God has forfeited
 you thus?
 Whose loving hand has
 implanted thee?
Perfected and sculptured for the
 span of an hour,
 What a lovely gift to be granted
 me!
Standing in awe of thy gracious
 beauty,
 I hold thee lightly to my breast;
Sweet rose, unadorned, ever
 climbing upward
 In glorious splendor, ever at thy
 best!
Thou wilt live again, as will I,
 When I awaken to Eternity.

William Viharo
BLUE RAIN
dawn's shadows
creep through the blinds
but the drifting clouds
thick and heavy with sorrow
let their grief fall softly
over the dead awakening world
and our dark room
only hours before a sanctuary
safe and warm
is now a funeral parlour
stoic and cold

and its spirit leaves
as you arise from the bed
and walk out the door
into the gently stabbing
blue rain

Lester E. Garrett

Lester E. Garrett
A Sunniness For the Soul

---

*To my dear mother-in-law, Lillie,
a ninety year old gem who is
blessed with an amazing fortitude
and meets each day with a smile,
gratitude and trust.*

Unchanging it stands, the
 building made of brick
Or of wood, of stone and steel
 and surely
A noble appearance to the eye of
 the curious
And the occasional passer-by,
 whether adrift
Or in harmony with things that
 are good, meaningful
And treasured in its strength and
 simplicity.

O, how it gives encouragement
And fills the heart when we are
 sincere;
When we, ourselves, have entered
 the building
Made of brick or of wood, of
 stone and steel
And firmly lodged beneath God's
 Cathedral above,
Everlasting in its love.

From the building, then, that is
 made of brick
Or of wood, of stone and steel,
The glow continues, a sunniness

for the soul,
Enlightening, we pray, the mind
  of the curious
And summoning to the door of
  hope
The occasional passer-by.

So let each come who will, adrift
  or in harmony,
And find renewal in the building
  made of brick
Or of wood, of stone and steel
And girded with the Word of the
  Eternal One.
He who has polished the gems
And shaped a vision in the sun.

Frances E. D. Harris
LIVE FOR TODAY
Live for today for tomorrow may
  never come
Do not borrow trouble from
  tomorrow.
One has enough problems from
  today . . .
without looking for tomorrow's
  sorrows.
Yesterday is gone and cannot be
  relived.
Today is the *only* day that can
  make a good tomorrow.
So, always try to make the most
  of today.
Act now, do not waste precious
  time.

Edward G. Klemm, Jr.
SWEET MYSTERY

To My wife, Jeanette

One day I saw before me Paradise
And all the Wonders of this World.
Love was there in all its fiery
  Ecstasy,
Yearning and Desire.
So were all the good things I had
  learned
From Those whose Wisdom
  guided me
Along the proper Path.
The light of all I saw was bright.
So bright it almost blinded me,
Until I took a closer look
And saw that all of this was You.

Linda Titchenell
BECAUSE OF HER
I saw you with her today
But I looked the other way
Oh, how I wish I were her
She has everything, she has you
I sit here without you
I just want to cry
But no-one can hear me
People look my way
But they can't see—Love hurts
Oh, how many tears I've cried
  over you
When you look at me and smile
My heart still races wild, Just to
  touch you
To hear from you, "I Love You."
But I'll never hear that
Not ever again—
Because of her.

Kathaleen Diering
UNANSWERED QUESTIONS
As I walk along in life
I wonder about it's sorrow's
All the unhappiness I see
Are their any good tomorrows?

Why do people hurt so much?
They live their lives in vain
No one meant to hurt you Lord
Or to put you to any shame.

Why must we be tested?
For a life we don't understand
From just a little piece of dirt
You created man . . .

Their's so much sickness and
  sadness
In this world today
What did you expect to receive
From just a piece of clay . . .

Why can't you look upon us
And see what the world is today
Can't you stop all this grief
And guide us a better way?

Forgive me for my questions
Because I don't understand
For I am only human
And you are the Creator of
man . . .

Virginia M. Kennedy Lingenfelter
A PHRASE

*I wish to dedicate this poem
today, to the two who made it
possible for this honor to come
my way, so if you know not who
"The Two" are as yet, I have to
dedicate this to my parents—you
can bet!! For my loving and ever
giving mom and dad, Ann & Don
Kennedy . . .*

Some people talk and some
  people listen,
  And some do neither for they
  have a peace of mind;

For in the shadow of darkness
  They see much light,
    The light of inner self.

They fear nothing,
  Nothing is to fear . . .
    Also, they care not of life or
    death,
      Winning or losing,
      But how to play the
      game . . .
                    Deadly!!

Yvette Brunell Adams
CHRISTMAS TIME
Christmas is the time of year
When everyone is glad,
For goodwill, brotherhood
And the son God had.

The air is crisp and light
The stars are shining bright,
Joy is in the air
On this Christmas night.

It is the time of year
To give of joy and cheer
And be very thankful
For our friends so dear.

May your holidays be happy
And be full of fun.
May the love of God be yours
And may God's will be done.

Barbara Lynn Powell
AWAKE!
The shifting sands, the drifting
  cloud,
and infamous sea beckons me
  from afar.

Slowly the twinge of infinity
  encircles me,
teasing my integrity.
A sudden surge of power, a
  hidden dream,
an indefinite truth.

And I dancing on a tabletop with
imagery and eyes closed.

Ann Richards Smith

Ann Richards Smith
DIVORCE
Inflamed by Love
Marriage
Turns to raging Fire

Then: "Hate"

Nothing left !
But coal black ashes.

Then: "Divorce".

Dawn F. Hamilton
CHANGES

*For D. Q. with warmth and love,
because only you understand.*

All our lives we change,
We turn around and rearrange.
To please the people we see
  around,
Building a facade we never let
  down.
I, myself, have done the same
Playing at this foolish game.
Oftentimes I wondered why
I had even begun to try,
To please some people I don't
  care about
I've been turned upside-down and
  inside-out.
And now I'm left with only me,
After all that trouble of trying to
  be.

Lizetta Rodgers
NATURAL MUSICIANS

Dedicated to my brother John

Two musicians in seed
still unformed, newly form their
  dream
silently in one round room.

The violinist now green, now
  growing
caresses each string in new-
  knowing energy,
becoming the pianist thin
  trembling fingers

in soft red peony, blossoming into
  new life.

They are cyclical harmony,
breathing beauty into man
moving toward natural perfection.

Jackie Berkson
OLD COUPLE

*I dedicate this poem to my late
husband Mr. Harry H. Berkson,
who made it possible.*

To Harry, my wonderful
Husband and friend,
Who enriched my life and soul
Solely by his being
And led me through doubt and
Meaninglessness
Into the haven of trust
And contentment.

I for you and you for me
Is written in the sky.
We are walking Hand in Hand
While time is passing by.

You for me and I for Thee
Is marked in our will.
We will keep moving happily
Till time is standing still.

Lillian Sobszak
SIXTEEN
Last week we were the best of
  friends
Delighting in rapport!
Shared books and music, fun and
  games
Long walks along the 'shore.
Last night we met but unprepared
For friendships' sudden turn—
A sleeping soul awoke to know
Of closeness we can learn.
Shy . . . tremors deep within! I'll
  know
'Sweet sorrow' should we part
I've looked into your searching
  mind
Dare look into your heart?

Muriel Ringstad
SUNSET ON PUGET SOUND
The mountains stand against the
  sky,
Snow-capped and cold to
  watching eye.
Then slowly as his course is run,
The sky is colored by the sun
As lifting up his arms to say
  goodbye,
With flaming fingertips he paints
  the sky.
He paints the snow and clouds a
  gold and rosy glow
And spills the colors in the water
  stretched below.
Beneath the mountain peaks,
The foothills spread
A purple blanket for his royal
  bed.

Edwin A. Daniels
FREDDIE THE FLY
If only we humans could really
  try and find;
  What is going on in the mind of
  a fly;
We would stand back agast at
  what is found;
  For it has a mind that is really
  sound.

To find out if all the truth is
    being told;
    All you will have to be is very
    bold;
You will talk to the fly meaning
    every word;
    Then you must believe what
    you have heard.

If you do this act with a faith so
    strong;
    You will succeed and you won't
    be wrong;
For all you do is to ask what you
    will;
    You will see, for the fly won't be
    still.

He will do your bidding as you
    shall ask;
    And shall be easy, not being a
    big task;
So the next time you want to kill
    a fly;
    Think it over and maybe let him
    go by.

Having faith as strong as a
    mustard seed;
    You will find the fly will stop
    and heed;
An example of the way you now
    must act;
    Is set forth next of the following
    fact.

The next time you find a fly in
    your home;
    Talk to him gently and ask him
    to roam;
Put out your finger in a very
    gentle way;
    And be surprised if your faith is
    in sway.

He will fly about then land on
    your finger;
    Take him to the door, he will
    not linger;
But will fly away as soon as he is
    ready;
    I know; it was done by a fly
    named Freddie.

Esther D. Hartman
THE JOGGER
As I take my morning jog,
Sometimes I run into fog.
I see people going away,
Some going out to play.
That time of the morning is so
    still,
As I jog up the hill.
Sometimes I stop to look up at
    the sky, that God has given,
And I am so happy I am still
    living.
Then as I renew my pace,
Sometimes I run into a familiar
    face.
We exchange a few pleasantries
    and then he leaves,
And I resume my speed.
Sometimes I don't even know
    where my path will lead.
Some say it is a waste of time,
But I just think it is fine.
I need these moments to be
    alone,
Away from the ringing of the
    phone.
And to communicate with my
    God,
Who furnished me with all this

sod,
And who jogs with me with every
    step,
And from whom I get all my pep.

Dale R. Rohrbach
LIFES END
No one cares about me anymore;
My bones are old and feeling sore;
They send me away to a place to
    hide;
So cold so clean a place to die;
My body fails me more and more
    each day;
and my mind gets fuzzy my hair
    old
and grey;
But am I no longer human, do I
    cease to feel;
My children abandon me—How
    can
they not care?
After all I've given them they've
    left me here to live in despair;
My life drains from me with
    the passing of each day;
Like an almost empty hourglass
    in bed I lay.
Is there no one out there
    anymore?
I can't move I can't see;
There's darkness enclosing me;
I feel as if I am floating away;
The cold is no longer there
as I walk through the door
like a ship who sailed into
    the Sunset;
Gone never to return no more.

Ruby M. Mills
HE IS THE ANSWER
There is no way in and no way out
    when the burdens of life
    surround you.
You long for a friend, or a helping
    hand,
    but it seems there is no-one
    around you
To care how heavy your burdens
    are
    of how much you need one to
    care.
But there is One who will always
    help,
    and when you seek Him He'll be
    there.

He'll wait for you to open the door
    that will let Him come in where
    you are.
If you'll let Him, He will stay
    with you
    but you must not His presence
    bar.
You must want to live in His
    presence
    and walk in the way that He
    leads.
For only those who follow Him
    gladly
    can live the life that succeeds.

To succeed by worldly standards
    in life
    is not to follow Christ at all.
The kind of life He expects you
    to live
    will lift you up should you fall.
Though the pit be deep, and the
    way be dark
    He will not ever forsake you,
So open your heart, let your

Saviour come in,
    live for Him, and to Him be true.
Only then will you know what it
    means
    to live the abundant life.
There's no other friend as true as
    He—
    none other can banish your strife.
He'll always be there to lead you
    through
    whenever your burdens press,
So come to Him, trust in His love
    and to Him your sins confess.

He'll lead you and guide you in
    all you do.
    He will help you do your best.
He'll hold you up and see you
    through
    no matter how hard the test.
So stay close to Him, go where
    He leads
    let Him be your Master and King.
He'll meet all your needs, put
    love in
    your life,
    to you He will be everything.

Until you learn to live in this way
    you'll not the abundant life know.
So put your life in His hands, go
    where
    He leads
    and toward Him you will grow
Life may be easy, or it may be hard
    but you'll know He'll be there
So trust Him, love Him, and live
    His way
    and forever for you He will care.

Thomas Scott Wood

Thomas Scott Wood
**Pams' Poem (The Poem Of
the Violets)**
He came for her near night
Up the hills they took their flight
He found her deep purple violets
    in the last trace of light

She loved him true
He whispered, "I'll love you till
    the violets bloom blue."

Holding close to the midnight air
starring at the stars he said,
    "There's a garden of paradise
and I know where."

Waking when light drops hit her
    eyes he said, "Like these
    flowers do
I can cry for you."
He wiped them with her hair

The kings men were on patrol
A torch bashed his face

Above her screams he cried, "I'll
    meet you with violets in
    the garden of paradise."

From the spot where she lay dead
    to the valley it is said
for 17 years the violets bloomed
    blood red

Dorothy B. Harrold
**Cry For What Might Have
Been**
Touch us, dear Lord, in our pain
    and strife
    Give meaning and wisdom in
    dealing with life
How wasted the moments filled
    with violent hate
    Can we halt the destruction
    before it's too late
Must one forever remember the
    pain
    When we know there is nothing
    of value to gain
A shout from my soul so deep
    within
    Says do not hate because of its sin
How tragically wasted is life
    without caring
    And the pain is so deep without
    love and sharing
We are born to live, but also to
    die
    Reach out with love for it heals
    with a sigh
Then no need will you find for
    questions or fears
    For no guilt will accompany
    your few little tears
The battle for love is the battle to
    win
    Then you need not cry for what
    might have been

Lidija Murmanis
SHARING
Frontiers have crumbled
between you and me,
I feel you incorporated
within me
as if you were a baby
in my womb.
We share our bloodstream
through which we channel
our joys and sorrows.
I nurture you
as my baby
with my emotions,
and you lend me a stay
to prevail over
the chaos of my moods.

Paul W. Linser
**The Deserted Railroad
Depot**
We no longer hear train whistles
    blow
At The Deserted Railroad Depot
No passenger train stops at the
    station
Whose buildings sit in ruination
Sleek metal giants no longer
    throw
The steam they did some years
    ago
At The Deserted Railroad Depot

People once railroaded across a
    nation
Bound for Business or Relaxation
Have found more modern ways to
    go
And left these shabby

monuments to show
The Deserted Railroad Depot

We now can fly above the flow
Of mountain majesty and amber
   waves below
Or we drive freeways of frustration
Concrete ribbons without
   imagination
Travel inconsonant with
   Whitman and Thoreau
We can only guess how much we
   owe
The Deserted Railroad Depot

Harvey Gammon
srorriMirrors
Now if I was you
You were me
And just happen to be
A window
For us to see
Then outside of each day
We'd be the shadows
Time drifts away
The dreams our minds like to play
The eyes reflecting an image
As if to say,
If you were me
And I was you
Maybe we'd see
What we're both going through
Together inside of night
Apart from another day
Our shadows, dreams, images
Mirror's each step of the way

Roland Maurice Soucy
HAND IN HAND

*Dedication to: My first wife,
Pamela Eunice Soucy, who now
resides in heaven.
To my wife now, Muriel
Lamarche Soucy, who renders
heaven unto me. To all who find
love is the key to life.*

Of what use thought, without
   action?
Of what use love, without trust?
   Of what use the whole, without
   it's fractions?
Of what use the pie, without the
   crust?
Of what use man, without his
   brother?
Of what use any single thing,
   without another?
   For all things, to be useful and
   grand,
They must be held, hand in hand.

Jennifer Lynn Olson
CHRISTMAS IS . .
Christmas is a time for cheer;
   A Time to be happy and thankful
for what you have.
Christmas is a time for fun;
   A time to play and skip. A time
to jump and run.
Christmas is a time for joy;
   A time to be happy and spirited
in everything you do.
Christmas is a time for friends;
   A time to spend some extra time
with friends doing things you
like to do.
Christmas is a time for kin;
   A time to visit people special to
you that you can't find time for the
rest of the year.

Christmas is a time for adornment;
   A time to hang the stockings and
trim the tree. A time to hang a
wreath on the door.
Christmas is a time for snow;
   A time for enjoying the whiteness
of it all.
Christmas is a time for love;
   A time to love everything
and everyone around you.
Christmas is a time for God;
   A time to thank Him, love
Him and celebrate Him.

Jan Fairless
SURVIVAL
The house is silent
except for the endless babble and
   chatter
the television makes
and small,
slight crackles of life
from a newly-lit fire . . .
all to squelch the utter void
and vast emptiness
your absence brings.
With a click of one knob
the television is silenced.
I hear
the stovepipe breathe
as flames and heat
cause metal to expand
and I listen to the tiny squeaks
a lifeless thing makes . . .
any sound
welcome . . .
reaffirming
I am
alive.

Diane Pevsner
Mary Elizabeth Pevsner
Elizabeth is her name.
We call her Liz, or Lizzard.
The name fits beautifully.

Her eyes and hair are brown.
Olive skin compliments her.
She's just what we ordered.

Piano and ballet are fun to Liz.
She enjoys them both.
Life to her is a pleasant experience.

Family and friends are important
   to her.
They give love and depth to each
   day.
Security comes with these loving
relationships.

Even at nine years of age, she's a
   beauty.
Speaking bits of wisdom, as
   though she understands.
Someday we'll say, "What a
   beautiful woman GOD has
   made."

Elizabeth J. Dieken
WALKING
You look forward to dry land
Where there is no ice.
If you're not careful,
You might wipe out.

Look back over your shoulder,
You've walked a long way.
The ice stretches back
As far as you can see.

With six feet to go
You speed up your pace,
All that way; you didn't wipe out.
You shouldn't have sped up.

This time you fell on your knees,

That's not so bad;
But, tell me, how do you get up
Gracefully?

Joel G. Hall
ME TO YOU
To help with your problems
To share in your joy
To ease out your pitfalls
To aid not annoy

Be free with compassion
Be there in your tears
Be honest with feelings
Be brave against fears

And offer my Love
As best as I can
Till we reach our parting

Marlene Stewart Kindt
VISION
What do
   Obstetricians
   Pediatricians
   Opticians
   and Musicians
      have in common
         Vision

What do
   Soothsayers
   Witchdoctors
   Magicians
and Statisticians share
         Trickery

What do Asylums
   Prisons
   and
   Colleges have
Vision, Trickery, One Way In and
One Way Out.

Ezra Gorrell
At My Parent's Grave
I have a song I cannot sing
A song I cannot even weep
It is too tangled and too deep.
I have a thought I cannot send
And syllables I cannot blend
For how can words with empty
   sounds
Explain what in the heart
   abounds—
And tho' not blind
I cannot see
Except, within, a memory.
And only two words come to mind,
Two words that seem to hug each
   other—
Father
Mother.

Joseph A. Frasier
NEEDING SPACE
Please go away
I need a place
To be alone
And hide my face
Life's slings and arrows
As before
Await beyond
My every door
I need to be
Alone this day
My pain and I
Please go away

Joan M. Holcomb
OUR DAY IN THE SUN
The flowers we picked
   from the blossoming meadow.
A gift of nature
   one of the many that surround

us.
We enjoyed our day
   one so special for each of us.
The sun shined for us
   the birds sang because we were
   there.

Because we will never forget
   that one sparkling summer day.
We may live on forever, our love
   bloomed, but must die like the
   flowers we picked.

Winona Fulks Lehr
MORNING

Dedicated to my husband, Pete.

You are the wings of my mind
Soaring far beyond yesterday
Encouraging me to find beauty
Even if it be, in a patch of
Green velvet moss.

Your presence strengthens my day
And prepares me for my loss
As you gently slip away
Leaving me with,
Your promise.

Shirley Mozelle Henderson
THE SPINNER
The spinner spins
His woven tales
For foe and friend,
Weaving life-patterns
Where threads had been,
While sending mind to
Journey and bidding
Spirit home again.

Jacqueline Rowe Gonzalez
REFUGE

*Mothers love as always to
Deborah, Homero Jr. and David*

Time out
When tempers fly,
Retreat in solitude
Until your mind and body rest
In peace.

Alwayne McClure
HIS GOD WAS NEAR
I saw Ivory, long and bright—
   Punctuated with keys, black
   like the night.

I saw his hands, gentle and
   strong—
   Young hands I knew could do
   no wrong.

I saw his fingers, sensitive and
   light—
   Tickle the keyboard like birds
   in flight.

I saw a young face, both man and
   boy, ready and eager to take his
   place
   Knowing full well—life's but a
   race.

I heard his voice rise up in song
   In celebration of life—happy
   and long.

We can't understand. Our hearts
   are wrung dry.
   Amid grief and heartache our
   thoughts go awry.

We can only ask—Why oh why

Didn't we hear his lonely cry?

Whatever the circumstances that
 left him no choice
I know now he's joined that
 heavenly chorus.

Whatever the burden—whatever
 the fear
I can only believe his God was
 near.

V. Mony Snyder
**How Long Ago In Terms Of
Aeons?**
Why do we love so? . . . When
 did it start?
How long. would you say, in
 terms of aeons ago?
I'd guess long before there was
 any sign to show
The answer which can come only
 through the heart.
Since time, so stretched, has no
 way to impart
Reality beyond its own dead flow
—Which even it has lost its way
 to go—
Then use that guage that knows
 its true purport!
. . . But tell me . . . on what
 great planet was it born?
—Or wherever else in faroff outer
 space
Where we might have found each
 other—beneficently 'sown'
. . . Like a special seed planted
 and by special grace
Meant to flower, however often
 uprooted or harmed,
So our love has survived all of
 time's abuse.

Rebecca Gwen Durham
I Could Not Say I Love You
This desk is where I trained her,
My replacement if I died.
I could not leave my husband
Without a woman at his side.
Too many years together
For Him to be alone;
Too many dreams forgotten
By a heart now turned to stone.
She was all he needed
That I could never be;
But she claimed him early—
They could not wait for me.

It would have been easier
If I had slipped away;
But I recovered completely
To live another day.
The months and years were
 torment
As only God could know.
The lesson learned was bitter—
I had reaped what I had sown.

Dorothy Ralston
NIGHT BEAUTY

---

*This poem is dedicated to:
EVERYBODY*

The moon is ascending up
 so high,
Along its pathway through
 the sky.
The silvery rays come down
 to earth,
To give its magic of night
 a rebirth.
Night beauty reveals a

fairy touch.
Dear God, I thank You so
 very much,
For the stars, the moon,
 the sun,
And for a new morning
 well begun!
The golden sun of morning
 outlines
A beautiful day for gladness
 that shines,
Great happiness to those
 who look,
And seek knowledge of the
 true Book!

Harold Graham
CONQUEST

---

*Dedicated to a beautiful and
formerly abundant wild creature,
pushed aside by ax, saw and plow
amid the crashing frenzie to
conquer the new land and
establish "Civilization".*

In old Missouri grew the otter,
Rearing many a son and daughter
 In crystal water.

Indians passing by
Watched him frolic and multiply—
 Play and die.

Came the white man staking
 claims,
Pushing Indians to the plains—
 Progress gains?

Felled the forest with a crash!
Plowed the sod, heaped the trash—
 Must have CASH!

Trapped the otter, son and
 daughter,
No more frolics in clear water!
 Ugly slaughter—ugly water!

In Otter's honor, tongue in cheek,
Where flashed that brown elusive
 streak,
Named the stream OTTER Creek!!

Hallie Zieselman
SILKEN RAINBOWS
There once were silken rainbows,
For all the pots of gold.
A flower to fit in every hand,
A bear for every child to hold.

A cat for every windowsill,
A dollar for every day.
A perfect note for every song,
And the dove was here to stay.

But times have changed, and
 dreams rearranged,
And the new has overtaken the
 old.
The silk of the rainbow is plastic
 now,
And copper, from the pots of gold.

The flowers sit on the graveyard
 stones,
For the hands that are no more.
The bears sit on the closet shelves,
'Cause the children have gone to
 war.

The windows have turned to iron
 bars,
And the cats have all gone a stray.
The days fly by like eagles in the
 wind,
And the dollar is worth a dime

today.

The perfect notes have drifted
 like clouds,
And the songs also left that way.
Rock and Disco have o'ertaken
 beauty,
'Cause the dove has flown away.

Helen Vendeville
Prevails With Triumph
I feel a kinship with
The Poet's Of Olde
And all the Poet's of Today
Whose words—they've told
Whatever the theme
Heartbreak or Love
Or the every day Dream;
 There's a bit of Soul
And Of the Spirit
That comes from the Poet
The Heart of it
The Dreams, they Dream
The Hardships they bear
Whatever their lot in Life
The Rhyme is, —of Care
Be it Ages ago— or Now
God Bless Them All
The Friendship—is There
May it Everlastingly Be
The Poetry of Life—
            For You and Me
Still Touch our Existence
With it's Serendipity.

Nancy LaBrache Nelson
THE SPIDER THE FLY

---

*In appreciation to G. Hurd and R.
Crawford for their help and
understanding.*

THE spider weaved a pattern
Into which its victims fell
A web of winding spinning net
Where he alone did dwell

The fly became a victim
And the web entrapped him so
He too became all alone
Nowhere for him to go

So many winding roads
Inside the web, the fly did see
Perhaps he guessed this was his
 fate
What was meant to be

He panicked and he struggled
For each path to set him free
But the more he moved about
Caught him deeper in debris

At last the fly decided
The web he would unwind
Following the pattern
The spider had designed

Slowly the fly saw the light
That fly you see, was me
As web unravelled far behind
The spider also was set free

Dawn Aarhus Anderson
STARS
You're not here, now,
To gaze at the sky with me,
And to marvel,
"How beautiful,"
While the stars glitter
As diamonds in the light.

I imagine that
It's much more lovely
Where you are.

Up there . . .
Wih the stars wrapped around you,
Like a cape on a chilly night.

Do you now what I feel?
Can you see the tears
When I think of how
I miss your laughter?

Do you miss me too?
Or are you only eager
To have me with you,
To share your joy,
And to see the stars
As you see them.

Marilyn Merrie Sullivan

Marilyn Merrie Sullivan
I HAVE TO BE ME
I have to be me, you have to be
you no judgement upon us
would ever do.

Sometimes two lives meet that
 are world's apart—we have to
 see it as a blessing and not a
 hurt to our hearts.

We learn to love, and we give
 what we can but to give up
 ourselves is just not in our lifes
 plan.

Julie Kay Alberts
The Promise Of a Friend . . .
In your lifetime, society will not
Always be fair,
You will make many mistakes.
And many times you will
 wonder—
Why to even care?

People will talk and say things
 that will
Truly hurt.
Problems will always seem to be
 there,
While joys and happiness may
 seem to desert.

But, in times of darkness . . .
 sorrow . . . pain . . .
There should be someone to turn
 to—
Someone who can cheer you up,
And bring you through the
 temporary rain.
And if you have no one there for
 you;
Then you have a lot of sunshine
Missing.

And a promise I will give you is
 this:
Life will send someone true.
That person will be a miracle—
A true Godsend.

For that certain person will be
Especially precious.

For they will be your friend . . .

Linda Queen
Our Clocks Keep Ticking
Our time is such a precious gift
for our hours are so few, little
do we cherish it and what each
day brings anew.
When the sun tops the morning,
another day God gives His
flock, our clocks keep right on
ticking, tick-tock, tick-tock.

Little do we fill our days with
giving and being kind, we let so
many other things envelope
our minds.
Mankind has no master key to
prolong or cease it stop, our
clocks keep right on ticking,
tick-tock, tick-tock.

Time is one commodity that
humankind can't buy, we
marvel at earth's wonders, but
not why Jesus died.
No condition is permanent, this
is our paradox, our clocks keep
right on ticking, tick-tock,
tick-tock.

Time, earth, and it's beauty, will
one day pass away, we're only
here a little while, then gone is
our stay.
Let's see therein a truer grace,
before God ceases it stop, our
clocks keep right on ticking,
tick-tock, tick-tock.

Patricia Elkins
A Changing Of the Seasons
As night unfolds, between dusk
and dawn,
My mind drifts back to an old
familiar song,
The music is faint, but the words
are clear,
Of you I think, and the message I
hear,
You gave me no warning,
You gave me no reason,
It's just a changing of the seasons,
You touch me at the oddest times,
A word, a song, or through old
movie lines,
With other people, amid the
laughs and grins,
My mind stops, my thoughts drift
to you again,
You gave me no warning,
You gave me no reason,
It's just a changing of the seasons,
We had our times and we ran our
course,
With a few regrets and no
remorse,
But another chip's gone from this
heart,
Seems you have taken the best
and the last part,
Longing and emptiness remains
in me now,
I'll go into remission and get
through somehow,
There is a lesson to learn,
Should I get past the burn,
I'll give no warnings,
And I'll give no reasons,
It will be just a changing of the
seasons!

Georgia Ray
MORE THAN A DREAM

*With all my love for his faith and
love this poem was written for
my husband, Don.*

Can you say or do you care? A
change I find unreal, for even
tho I'm married a broken heart
is near,
I love him, I worship him, tho my
life is nearly gone, I find my
heart wondering, for I know I
can love only deep within my
soul.
I feel a happiness never found
before, a burst of being free, to
grab the earth as not to die, but
to be free to love the man I
need from now until eternity.
But the love I need and the life I
want is only a moment thing,
for I need a kiss of life more
than the dream of eternity.

Alene Vieira
NEW LISTING
My house is for sale, the papers
say
and states in phrases neat—
A real old charmer, with lots of
room
set on a quiet street.
Surrounded by trees, all planted
by Dad
and a rose garden, tended by me,
And if you look real close, you
can see a swing
hanging empty in a tree.

Your house is for sale, my
children say,
now Dad's gone, it's too much
for you.
You need a smaller place, closer
to town
where there's no yard work to
do.
And you can just putter around
all day,
and get a much needed rest.
You're all we have now, Mom.
Can't you see,
we really do know what's best!

This house for sale? Since when I
say?
Not while I'm still around.
They don't understand. They
mean well, I know,
their reasons do seem sound.
But their lives are all caught up
in today,
their thoughts are of other things.
While my life is all tangled up in
the past,
in my memories and empty
swings.

My house for sale? I'm afraid not
today,
not while memory's lamp still
burns bright.
For as quickly as they put up the
signs by day,
I steal them away in the night.
Sweet memories crowd 'round. I'm
never alone.
I'm leaning to live with my
sorrow.

My house is not for sale—not
today, not now!
But maybe it will be—tomorrow.

John Byron Hiller
THE SPRINTRESS

*Inspired by small town
"Sprintresses" and lady track
participants in the Black Hills
area of South Dakota.*

Look! There's that dazzling sprint
flash leaping out in a dash,
Making others look frozen in
space.
Like lightning pre-greased—like a
coiled spring released;
She from scratch sets a blistering
pace!

Like a lioness enraged—like a
tigress uncaged;
She explodes at the crack of the
gun—
Then an all out attack as she
scorches the track—
My God—how that phantom can
run!

Round the turn watch her fling as
though hurled by a sling,
Then she spurts like a cheetah in
flight;
And the jungle drum beat of her
falcon winged feet
Strikes panic in all others
outright!

Then fast pulling away to the
others dismay—
Down the stretch like a
frightened gazelle;
Breaking tape in the lead with
that last burst of speed—
To the finish she runs to excel!

To the rest, never mind—you
were so close behind;
You gave it your all—do or die!
If the strain on each face had
decided the race,
You all would have won in a tie!

K. Elsie Easter
AGAIN, DEAR FLAG
Dear Flag, again you hang your
head,
Another young man has fallen
dead.
Why should our country bear
defame
when a mad man's bullet is to
blame.

Would that we could shield them
all
that ne'er again young men would
fall.
God grant us grace that we may
face
the toil it takes to assure our
earthly place.

Maro Rosenfeld
MOREAU

*To Sam Boodman for his
friendship and encouragement
and Free Spirit and for his passion
for the Arts and freedom for all
mankind*

Children pushing buttons
Is this the world to be?

Today's children all share the
womb
of the Anti-Christ Computer

Beware you babes—
hide a small mirror in your lunch
box
and grin at yourselves
continuously
as you push the buttons
commanded by dubbed voices
that never laugh with you

Where hides the Voyage thru
Time
in books of the brain's
Mysterious Seas

Children of Boredom in search of
a party
runaways from Planned Cities
with nowhere to breathe

These children will never see—
unlocked doors
sleeping on the beach
Nite walks in the park
Those days were made before the
DNA Labs made thee

Rebel! Don't join!
If you only need six missiles to
blow up the world
why make 100 more?

If War means Work
laughing graves of children
PLEASE save tomorrow for
humanity

Connie G. Rode
Tribute To Motherhood

Inspired by my son, David

Rabbit-cloud skies,
Chocolate-brown eyes
and sticky, mud-splattered kisses,
may not bring
high praise from a king,
But, I know what a grand life this
is!

Anita Durand Buess
EXTINCT
Extinct
Is a word
A simple word
But not a simple meaning.
The meaning means forever,
Forever gone, never to be again.
To be again another cosmos
leaning

From out the firmament must
reappear
And all in sequence,
Life, then man arising through all
the agonies of fear
To crown himself and be the ruler,
And, when all is done,
Expend all else and then himself
In time to miss the passing of the
sun.

Connie Citriniti
A NEW BEGINNING
I feel like a rosebud at dawn,
opening up for the first time
and seeing the world.

I feel like a baby blue jay leaving
its nest, alone, for the first time
and discovering the joy of flying.

I feel like the newly risen sun
after a long, dark night, lighting
up everything I touch.

I feel like a fat, fluffy cloud, about
to burst open and give the
earth its long overdue rainstorm.

I feel like the horizon, beautiful
and distant, yet appreciated
everywhere because its
radiance can't be ignored.

I feel like all these things,
because maybe, just maybe,
you have come into my life.

Christabel Fowkes
Portrait Of a Mad Painter
The colors on his palate
Were black, and blue and gray
And he blended them together
In a blaze of self expression
A distorted representation
Of the things he saw.
His rendering of faces
Were screaming, twisted masks
With eyes glaring
From large, gaping holes.

A landscape from his boyhood
Lingered in his brain
Daisy-laden fields
Beneath a cloudless sky
And a lazy sun
Til it was done.
He touched the brush
To the canvas of his mind
But it became a torch
That scorched and seared
What was once endearing
Til it was gone.

Bruce A. Miles
PERSONAL EFFECTS
As you rummage through my
personal possessions
Discovering secret dreams and
public nightmares,
Don't be swayed from paying
your last considerations
Because I've authored honest
poems born in my heart and
soul.

I've told of desires lost and
conquered,
Of love, fears, life, and Holy God;
I've written words which stun
and inspires,
And each was penned by a bold
and steady hand.

Since my conception until my
untimely death

You can view my life, a work in
progress;
I hope you'll feel my words like a
breath
Whispering feelings to encourage
your heart.

In your posthumous review of my
effects
These poems of loves and life I've
known
Don't close the book holding any
regrets
For all that I've lost I've also
found so much joy.

Parents and lovers, friends and kin,
Feel for me no loss, no remorse or
pity;
It's the ultimate adventure I'm
about to begin
So let my poems sustain
memories and offer you earthly
escape.

Lee Wells
ALL IN ALL
Self glory of any kind.
Keeps each from the cross to find.
Nothing my hand can bring.
Only to Thy cross I cling.

Never cling to my work.
To do so would the cross irk.
Nor my position in life.
To bring merited strife.

May my branch be of the true vine.
And depend on the One Divine.
Thy spirit in me shall dwell.
Without I can do nothing well.

We cannot perform the change.
So we enter His Divine range.
At the beckon of His lovely call.
So He can be our all in all.

Joyce Suter Whitcomb
THE LARKS
I heard the larks a singing,
When the storm had just passed
by,
They filled the air with music
'Ere the clouds had left the sky.

They didn't wait for sunshine
To send its warming rays,
They saw the lovely rainbow,
And warbled songs of praise.

If the tiny little song birds,
Put their trust in God above,
How much more we ought to
trust Him
To surround us with His love.

If the storms of life assail us,
And there's driving wind and rain,
When we hear the larks a singing,
We know the sun will shine again.

Larry Douglas Chappell
WITH RAINBOW-WINDS
With rainbow-winds, on any day.
S'ei piace, ei lice!
(Whatever you desire to do—you
may!).
There always comes that certain
day
In everyone's life, a certain strife,
With what to do
With their limited time.
Do they plan or do they pray?
Do they decide
With a flip of a dime,
Or, the roll of the dice?

S'ei piace, ei lice!
(Whatever you desire to do—you
may!).
Now, isn't it swell to know
That we're bound only
By God's desire for us,
And not hell's below!
So, why should we put up a fuss
on any day
S'ei piace, ei lice!
(Whatever you desire to do—you
may!).
With rainbow-winds—
Our tears shall end,
And the sun will come out again!

Charles Carl Griep
LOVE OF THE SOULS
The sun shone warm and clear and
bright as two lovers kissed their
last good bye.
For on this day his ship would sail
to a strange far land where men
fight and die.

But love is a blindness, a shield
against
harm; against maiming and death
it protects the heart.
So they kissed their last kiss and
sighed
their last sigh, then he tenderly
vowed
they would not long be apart.

The young girl watched with
tears in her
eyes as the grey hulk of the ship
passed
over the horizon and out of sight.
She watched still longer though
there was
not to see, but the sparkling blue
ocean
and a lone sea gull in flight.

"Good bye my Darling" she
whispered,
"Hurry back to my arms, my love,
my
Man of the Sea!"
War knows not of love and how
could
she know that all that she asked
was never to be.

The message came and her heart
filled with
fear for without reading she knew
what the
black letter said.
They told of his glory, of his deed
so brave
but this was no comfort for her
sailor
was dead.

In the chapel she wept and
prayed asking
to die, for she wanted no more
than to be
by his side.
"Why," she pleaded, "Dear God
tell me why
the one that I loved and lived for
was
choosen to die?"

As if in answer she heard him call
then turning she saw him; he still
looked the same.
His brown eyes sparkled his
brown hair
was mussed and he wore his

sweet smile
as toward her he came.

"Hush, my Darling. Now dry your
sad tears for they are foolish and
wasted and that is why I am here.
Do not be saddened by what is
true
remember our love and be happy
then I'll always be near."

There in the chapel with soft
words
he calmed her and dispelled
her woes.
Their love had not died, nor could
be so, for their love was the
truest,
the love of the souls.

Dorothy Brin Crocker
NEVER STOP
Never stop saying "I love you, I
love you,"
Over and over, again and again,
Lest the stifling, sorrowful silence
Sting like a scalding, searing pain.

Never stop kissing my lips that
are ready
To open the door to the hope in
my heart
With trembling hands, weak and
unsteady
As my heart starts singing its
rapturous part.

Tomorrow may bring a painful
parting
To temporal love on the
mountain high,
But never stop saying "I love you,
I love you,"
Again and again so my heart will
not cry.

Donna M. Mariner
ON THE BRINEY SEAS
On the briney seas a hoplessness
fills me
Clutching out earnestly to the
waves of salvation
In a sea of total torment.
Abandoned, banished by all
mankind to a depression of
helplessness,
Total loneliness, a place where
no friends trod.

Alone, desperate for compassion
A stroke of attention or love
no-one heeds my anguish cries.
All peoples, heads turned away,
fulfill their own desires
To leave me alone here
Upon the rocks of ebon despair.

No hand reaching out
In comfort or hope.
One small ray of hope, small as it
was
Forever gone.
Never to burn again.
No-one caring.

Forgotten, alone, alone
A shiver runs over my spine.
Cold, utter loneliness.
Blackness and despair
All rays and thoughts of
friendship, compassion or love
Dashed and shattered here upon
the rocks of hell.

On the briney seas,
Alone in total darkness.

Nina LaGrassa
REJECTION

A dangling participle
Wrenched from a broken heart
Echoes into the lost horizon.
In the background, the
    unfinished symphony
Repeats undunted and forever
    hopeful.
From a chair within my sand castle
I reach out again
Unable to accept your not
    reaching back.
Scathed by unspoken words,
Braced against acts of omission
I remain steadfast but wary,
Praying for reciprocity.

Eleanor Otto
DIVINE GUIDANCE

narrow winding trail—
wilderness—
will it?

fog
drifts images—
came before
trampled down sod:—
Indians, pioneers, settlers
gold—rushers, lumbermen . . .

walked . . . drove
had it . . . made it

vistas opened
low hills
high valleys
dry rivers
wet desert
ocean joins beach

no more panic
fog dissolved

off the ground
outstretched arms
navigate trail below

"out" . . . comes
wilderness forgot
here found now

A. M. Fonda
EMPTY ROOMS

---

*To San Francisco and it's sister
cities.*

There's a point of good relation
All ships must one day pass,
Though truths design and veer
Eventually their course unmasks

Past drifting lost confidence,
Shanghayed faiths,
Weatherbeaten crews,
Disenchanted mates,

Past bolted chambers,
Buckled minds,
Ransacked treasure holds,
Worthless pirate finds,

Through straights of false
    intention
Where tides shift with the moons
Sending sea breeze to those
    conceived
And born to die in empty rooms.

Miriam E. Douglas
THE UNLOVED BLOOM

Why is it that my name's degraded
In every area I've invaded
Why is it that no one loves me,
When 'tis my nature to be free?
I've roamed the country far and
wide
And not a soul stood by my side!
You must admit I do have beauty,
But still am left without a duty.
I've been deblossomed, yes,
    mowed down;
Am always greeted with a frown.
I've been uprooted, stepped upon,
Yet never told what *wrong* I've
    done!

Has God allowed me to remain,
To never glorify *His* name?
Am I a weed, just like the others,
With no"good" plants to call my
    brothers?
Alas, a wretched life is mine,
For I'm naught but a dandelion!

M. Joanne Vanderpool

M. Joanne Vanderpool
HORIZONS

She said search for your
Horizons in every way,

I think I learned something
on that day.

I learned, that Love can be
blind, I couldn't see,

I learned, that my Love with
him, couldn't be free.

I'm searching for My Horizons,
but I still haven't found,

What my feelings will be when
I settle down.

I'm glad she told me, don't
you see,

With our closest friends,
Our Horizons are free.

Rosa Lee Wilson
HANG-ON

---

*I wish to dedicate this to, my
family, Nadine, and friends.*

When life get's you down, so low
    Hang on tight and don't let go.

Remember life is what you make
    it, so hang on tight, you can
    take it,

Don't use drug's or juice for an
    excuse, beside's what's the use.

Take a walk or jog in the early
    light, maybe then thing's will
    get a little bright.

Remember life is what you make
    it, so hang on tight, you can
    take it.

Sometime's you feel like you're
on a merry-go-round, life does
    have it's ups and downs.

So get a hold of yourself, throw
    away all your sorrow, and stand
    up straight and look forward
    for "TOMORROW."

Heather K. Freeman
SNOWFALL IN VERMONT

---

*Dedicated to my loving family—
A small gift in appreciation for
the "roots and wings"*

Nature's delicate crystals
With the softness of a baby's
    breath,
Float down to the warm village
    on the hill,
Like a bird on the wing—pendant
    in air.
This is the time for a cleansing.
The vat white realm refreshes all;
T'is time to start anew.
Serenity remains untouched
    through the night
But with the dawn this magic
    tranquility
Reluctantly gives way to the
    yawning world,
As once again the snowfall in
    Vermont,
Brings satisfying memories to
    mind,
And glee to the hearts of children.

Katherine Chila Mosher
ENCOURAGEMENT

You gave me encouragement to
    pursue in my writing

I tried and I tried till the words
    were exciting

I know I'm not ready for Readers
    or Times but I'll keep on
    writing, as long as it rhymes

I'm not a Viorst, who I admire
    immensely, she stands with the
    best, not false or pretensing

So thank you for giving an
    encouraging word, your faith in
    my work was welcomely heard.

Joseph R. Paquette
SCARRED OAKS

---

*Especially dedicated to the
disabled and the handicapped.*

Oak trees,
With arched branches
So full of healthy leaves,
As summer approaches
Yet the victim of winter havoc,
A broken limb
And a scarred trunk,
Yet standing proud and beautiful.
My Lord, our souls
Are as such often
Disabled and Handicapped
By birth or misfortune,
But we should stand proud.
With faith in Thee,
We, too, can be Beautiful.

Muriel A. Bunker
The Indestructable Web

The spider web hangs on my
    screen
    from spring until the fall
With insects by the millions
Oh, how they walk and crawl
Sometimes one gets in the house
    and drives me up a wall
What a struggle I put up
    with creatures that are small
Thru rain and wind and sun they
    cling,
    hang on all summer long
How on earth do little bugs
    make their webs so strong?
I spray and wash and scrub
    and sometimes vacuum too
But the web will not let loose
    no matter what I do
That tough and sturdy spider web
    is a very ugly sight
But I have been defeated
    I now give up the fight.

Rick D. Garlock
UNTITLED

Rest, sweet mind rest;
while there is time-even if but a
    moment, rest.
And what do I find?
That when alone, I cannot—
for, without the noise of life
    around,
I know not how to capture, use
    and enjoy,
the sudden time to rest
I've found.

Everett Francis Briggs
SOMEHOW, AGAIN

---

*To: Willetta Annie Etta (Briggs)
Rall of Brooklyn, N.Y.*

From the dancing eyes
    Of this little girl,
Women long since dead
    Spring behold . . . and smile.

With this little one
    Smelling all the blooms,
Women ages dead
    Smell the same perfumes.

Aye, the first who breathed
    Of the primal rose
Attar cloying sweet,
    Joys with her again.

As she smiles her love,
    Women who once loved
Come to life again,
    Once again to love.

Only one is blood:
    Adam's, in our veins.
Somehow all who lived
    Live in us again.

Charles Harvey Russell
IN RETROSPECT

---

*To the fond memory of Bill
Stump, who was my friend.*

Today I gave a gift,
A lonely, though beautiful flower
By pen now, in retrospect,
Recalls the gentle magic of that
    hour

        Because—
An old soldier died today
In sweet sadness, he went away,
Until the end, I stood quietly at
    his side
Who was this old soldier?
The most fierce, yet foolish
    warrior: Pride

This fierce, yet foolish
  warrior—Pride
He always at our side,
The knee of reason's self, must
  bend and justify,
When this battle scarred and
  valiant soldier,
Decorated, fights our battles, —or,
In noble bravery dies

This day my pride and I, —did
  battle for a rose,
Did the wise one win?
Who knows.
Still, an old soldier died today,
He only meant to keep me from
  harm's way
For fleeting, precious moments
  sword and shield I cast aside,
In retrospect, there are no regrets
  that for a rose,
An old soldier died.

John O. Brooks
DAYBREAK
The day broke with all of its
  splendor
Everything sparkled bright
Indeed this was no pretender
As darkness gave way to light.

On the water a yellowish tint
In the sky a golden hue
The mountains shone with a glint
Diamond crystals were on the dew.

The trees roused and yawned
All life begun to stir
Surely the day had dawned
With beauty everywhere.

Though all will change later
But not at break of day
For when that time has passed
They put the paint away.

Virginia Burich
EASTER REMEMBRANCE
Today is Easter Day,
A time for families to be together
  and their thanks to God pray.

Just to remember what this day is
  all about,
In praise to Jesus, lift our voices
  in song while our hearts with
  thankfulness do shout.

Of our sins admit and repent,
Christ on this day, his last
  earthly breath on the cross was
  finally spent.

In the Holy Bible is his whole
  story of life,
As even in the beginning there
  for him was always a struggle
  against worldly strife.

Even as in the morning we hear
  the ringing church bell,
It out of joy and sorrow both, his
  life to us reveal and tell.

Robert A. Ferriere
HOW TO LOVE
I ask myself this question oft,
  how much can one man love?
With all his breath and strength
  and might,
  the Father up above.
With every word we think or
  speak,
  and every act we do.
We show our Lord our love for
  Him,

by loving as we do.
No one on earth can love the Lord,
  while still his brother hate.
For it is not of God you see,
  and damnation is its fate.
So while I live in flesh and bone,
  and walk upon this land.
I'll give to you the love of God,
  he's placed within my hand.
I'll share with you this love I have,
  within my heart to give.
For by our loving one another,
  is the only way we live.
For God is love the scriptures say,
  and they of course don't lie.
So we've been born of God my
  dear,
  and our love shall never die.

Mildred E. Clark
A DREAM COME TRUE
Your dark eyes danced, as in days
  before.
Your smile teased as it flashed.
Promises, unspoken, were in
  store—
No sound was heard as my heart
  crashed—
For me, you opened a long-closed
  door.

Dare I dream it might be true?
That I would be the one to share
Your mercurial love—your
  heaven blue—
In the past, there'd been no clue
But it was now and not the past.
Your light touch told me more.
Who knows if it will last?
No time to add up the score.
For us, the die was cast.

What comes, in time, we cannot
  see.
Nor worry about for now.
Just to love you, is for me—
A solemn, timeless vow.
A pledge for two hearts that are
  free.

Margaret Kish
AROUND THE CORNER
Around the corner they come and
  go
These little people that I know.
Anxious to please, eager too—
With their happy cries, "Look
  what I can do!"
Following behind like a little
  parade,
Carrying a hoe, dragging a spade.
The shouts of fear at their first
  sight of a worm
And their joy to know they just
  wiggle and squirm!
With fumbling fingers they plant
  with glow
The seeds I drop for them to sow.
They do not falter until work is done,
Knowing a treat will surely come—
Of special sweets and a story, too,
Of little people "just like you."
Oh, yes, I, too make it special,
  you see,
For all the happiness, just for me,
From the little people that I know,
Around the corner that come and
  go.

Sadie C. Laurent
Night Before Christmas
Santa was so busy, was in a tizzy,
  as he wiped away a tear— he had
  lost all his reindeer. What a

thought-he ought, why not? He
sighed: this had to be tried. He
would train razerback swine-It
would take time, the task
great—a need to hurry so as
not to be late. He had to get
consent of them all. There was
eight—Gargyle. Onkie, Udie,
Pinkie, Sparky, Rusty, Honky,
and Clemmie. Oh! they had
such skiddish ways, habits,
skimming, flighty, mighty in
flight, Favorable for such a
night—Gargyle, his favorite,
with this gleam In his eyes,
more than willing, with a fast
wiggling tail, standing by, with
speed taking the lead. The task
all done before the setting sun,
with relief Santa wiped the
sweat from his brow, gave a
jolly Ho! Ho! All was ready, he
held the reins steady, for the
midnight flight, away, away!
the razerback way. Sleigh bells
ringing, shackles jingling, They
slowed down, wanted to stop
at— Sleepy Hollow to
wallow—a crack of the whip
they moved on. Santa viewed a
bright star from afar— he
visioned angels, and heard
sweet singing, he looked
around and found, as he sliced
through, frosty air, relief-as he
skimmed over fountains,
mountains and tree-tops, at last
with a flop, he landed on
rooftop, his bags were so full,
he had to pull and pull, so
many toys for good girls and
boys, to the poor he gave more,
He gave a chuckle, he found on
the shelf, for self, persimon
pudding, cookies, goats, milk,
he ate, and ate, began to hum,
he had to hurry, for the snow
was coming, down in furious
flurry, he loosened his belt on
his big fat tummy, and said
Yummy! Oh! the night was so
cold—he must hurry, Oakies
hair was so thin on, his back,
his skin showed, Clemmie
began to sneeze, in the
blistering breeze, Rusty began
to cough, they must be off,
there will always be snow,
Santa gave a jolley, Ho! Ho! to a
sleeping world, "The best to
you"— A "White Christmas to
all"

Mima McCormick
MEMORIES OF SCOTLAND
Here I am, back in my own little
  Pad
I look around and think "Not too
  bad"
But I close my eyes and I can see
misty mountains with rivulets
  running free
Shining water falls splashing oer
  pebble and stone
and murmuring brooks neath
  bracken and thorn
Winding roads lined with bowers
  of flowers
and trees glistening from
  sprinkling showers
A walk down the lane with the

wind and rain in my face
with an escort who is witty and
  full of grace
Sitting with friends around a cozy
  fireside
watching two purring cats who
  are Margaret's pride
A drive through the Glens with
  Tom at the wheel
we listen to a cassette playing a
  Highland Reel
our eyes glow with delight as we
  gaze on a rustic scene
and watch black eyed lambs graze
  on a village green
Ending the day in the warmth of
  a friendly room
we toast our friends who we must
  leave too soon
A million dollars could not buy
  all the beauty I've seen
so I would not change places with
  "Elizabeth" The Queen

Margaret S. Matthews
SHADOWS AND LIGHT
Shadows and light . . . none are
  without;
A shadow's a man's thing,
A dark side and dim,
Opposite the right side
Through sin's sorrow grim.

So turn toward the Truth,
Turn about. Face your Lord . .
Darkness withers behind you
And all life's in accord.

Even the dark sorrows,
The black caves of fear,
He'll erase from the picture
With the marks of a tear.

When lives follow His path
He fills them with joy.
When worries plague us,
No power can destroy
All the love and the mercy
He wraps round His own.
He lends us His Spirit, straight
  down from His throne . .
Have faith through the hard days,
Remember He's there . .
He'll carry you home, with a song
  and a prayer!

Jill R. Corey
WHEN IT'S QUIET

*I dedicate this poem to WILLIAM
F. RHODES, for his inspiration
and for believing in me.*

When it's so quiet
  that you can hear your own
  breathing . . .
When it's so still
  that you can hear the birds'
  wings beating . . .

When the sky is so clear
  that the stars are what you're
  forever finding . . .
When the moon is so bright
  that it's light is almost
  blinding . . .

When it's so calm
  that you can hear the rustle of
  the leaves . . .
When it's so peaceful
  that you can hear the swaying
  of the trees . . .

When the air is so crisp
that your lungs ache for
more . . .
When everything is so perfect
that you know what eternity's
for . . .

Only then will you realize that
you've recognized
the world God had meant for
us to live in.

Diane B. Nozik
GOD
A pallor of death hung in the air,
the procession walked through
the square.
The silence of doom
to play its tune.
A heavy mist fell from the sky,
broken only by a mourner's cry.
The silent throngs, to the grave,
they follow,
their broken king left them in
sorrow.
To the Lord they cried,
they asked why he hath died.
Their father, son, brother, and
lover,
taken to the grave to be covered.
Their lives are desolate but all is
not lost,
for they love and believe in, at all
cost,
all that he told, all that he spoke;
they will toil with no complaint;
they will bear the yoke.
For he will come back; it hath
been said.
For He is God, and God is not
dead.

Valerie
WISHES

*Duane . . upon your ninth
birthday, 1970. love & memories,
Valerie.*

so far away,
        this empty place
yet
touch,
    breath
to
my
lips
a cool breeze.
        your
        face,
            brownsugar
            freckles
            & candlelite
                memory
of
lilac
blossom,
the open window
        & a niteflame
        dance
        of
        fireflies,
            your
            laughter.

Mrs. Minnie (Houston) Breland
OUR CHURCH
Once our little church-house
    was brown
Light between it and the ground,
We had flowers in our yards
But none came there except by
cards.

Silent as the grave save Sundays,
Not so now, not even Mondays.
It's all changed, and so have we,
Praise GOD who all things see

Our sons who went away to war
Had learned what it was all for
They (Most) all came back,
Smart as a tack.

"We've built houses and painted
    them,
    Let's do the same for HIM."
No sooner said than granted. We
bricked it
to the ground and planted.

Grandpa's spire still crowns the
    mounds,
But little white pillows line the
    grounds.

Lily Ferranco Fetizanan
TRANSITION

*To my dearest mother and to my
beloved sons, Patrick and Francis.*

Sunset,
Reveals changes.
Raindrops fall,
Life renewed,
Youth passes,
Everything matures
Time stays.

L. G. Mace
SUMMER PETALS

*To Bruce, Susan, and Jan and our
summer in Fitch Bay.*

Pastelled fragile feral rose,
Struck in silent, tranquil repose,
Underneath boughs of awesome
    Cathedral evergreen,
Paints the poet in words this
    rustic scene.
Amidst the tall grass and growing
    slender reed,
Plants the undomestic forget me
    not's memerable seed.
Tiny flower, delicate-of white and
    baby blue,
Framed by shades of jade varied
    in depth the prismic hue.
Along the shores grows the
    buttercup, and daizy swaying
    gentle in the summer breeze,
Shaded by a giant outstretched
    o'er the water-majestic Birch
    bark tree.
On the wind, just before a cool
    evening rain,
Drifts the bouquet of mixed
    fragrances that call to mind
    childhood's fantasies once
    again.
The fresh cut clover mingles with
    the scent of moderned sickled
    hay,
And the smell of motor boat gas
    and wild apple blossoms mixed,
    floats o'er the bay.
A picture e'er in our minds and
    imprinted forever in our hearts
    where peace and Nature's
    harmony dwells,
Is recalled everytime I gaze in

wonder at these miracles of
Nature, resplendent-Summer
petals.

Barbara Sacchetti
ODE TO A MOUNTAIN
Oh, mighty and majestic peak
In gown of sparkling white,
I see you rise before my eyes
To great and awesome height.

The evergreen I stand beside,
Its lofty branches away,
As if to wave and say, "Hello"
To you, so far away.

An eagle soars and screeches down
With feathers gleaming black;
The mountain lake reflects your
    grace
And regal image back.

The stately yuccas peer within
The rippling waves of blue
To see, perhaps, if they can get
A closer look at you.

A clear and golden summer day,
With sunny streaming light,
Will shine within my memory
A lasting vision bright.

Elizabeth Corominas
I WISH I WAS A SNAIL!

*This poem, is dedicated to my
husband: JUAN.*

I wish I was a Snail of the Sea,
So no-one could ever sneak a
    peak at me.

I would hide securely in the
    sand all day,
Until all those strange people
    went away.

Then, I would slowly come
    outside;
And wait . . . Oh so patiently for
    every tide.

I can feel the water beating
    against me now,
And, hear all of the oceans
    smallest sounds.

So . . . Here I go out into the
    ocean blue,
To a home of waters deep and a
    life that is new.

Here I am happy and contented
    within,
And, none of those strange people
    can try,
To come peaking in!

Nona Bushnell Ryder
ONE DAY AT THE TIME
At this moment I have no
    polished
Phrase to present thee
I have tried not to make a want
List for thee

I pray that thou will givest me
Only what I need
Thou hast never complained of my
Needs, only to fulfill them if and
When they should be

I do need thee Lord, I need thee
    now
Without thee I cannot live and I
Dare not die

Please teach me the secret of
    living
Just one day at the time.

Nora Brawner VanWinkle
SPRING
I watch you carefully folding clothes,
emptying drawers, feeling for
    illusive items.
I know you said that in the spring
    you must go.
Is it spring already?
I only feel cold-frozen.
My limbs, like last winter's Oaks,
aching to reach out;
too laden with cold.
I—do—not—believe—in—spring.
"Too late, Too late," the birds
    outside the window chirp.
They also have their spring, those
    builders of nests.
Inside, I am the destroyer;
spoiler of my own dreams.
Locked into a self I can not deny;
into the winter of my own
    creation.
If I only had the right to plead,
"Do not go," or "May I come, also."

Your cases filled, I see your eyes
    darting into the distance,
Eager and happy with the
    anticipation of your spring.
(God, help me believe in a spring
    for him.)
You turn toward me and try a
    careful smile,
attempting to hide the wonder of
    your journey.
"It's time," you say hesitatingly.
"yes," my arms still stiff at my
    sides.
    Goodbye, my beautiful love.

Carrie L. Braswell
**The Little Ones Tribute To
Father**
When ever we go out to play
There is a man who always says,
"Be careful as you go along.
Do not get into any wrong."
He is our father.

He always has advice for us.
To obey him we feel we must.
We honor him with much
    delight,
What e'er he says is always right.
Because he's father.

Sometimes before we can realize,
He has taken us by surprise
With goodies, yes, the very best
    kind
That satisfy our eager minds.
That's just like father!

Who would not love a man like this?
He is the one who tops our list.
For him, dear Lord, our thanks to thee.
There is no greater man than he,
For he's our father!

Dewey Hill Jr.
WIDE OPEN SPACES
Let me live in the country
With a bright sun on high
Where the air is fresh and clear
And the mountains reach the sky
Where the land stretches out
As far as my eyes can see
The wide open spaces
Is where I want to be
Just give me a little cabin
On the side of a hill
With the cattle a-roaming
All over the field
Where life is still peaceful
And so tranquil
Give me the wide open spaces
Lord, if you will
Where the stars like candles
Light up the sky
Give me the wide open spaces
And let me live there 'till I die.

Colleen J. Houghtaling
FAREWELL, MY LOVE
Farewell, my love, for I must leave;
My weakness have I found.
The battle's ended and I have lost;
Now I am homeward bound.

My journey lengthens into the night;
But darkness n'er my worry.
From where I come it lights my way—
The bombs of Hell and Fury.

Please do not mourn, oh lonely one;
For you shall find another.
But think of me from time to time,
As I of you, my Lover.

For I've not gone without a cause;
So dimly may it seem.
And someday I shall come again
To touch you, unforseen.

And you shall leave, hand in mine,
To take that journey, too.
So say Farewell, without a tear.
Remember, I Love You.

Barbara Ann Elmore
Can Spirits Be Forgiving?
As out hiking around your own
Precious land, I saw beauty, as you saw it, but I also saw the human disgrace to your years of toil and strife. I am sorry Oh spirits of braves, squaws, and Chiefs, and I apologize to you, for my fellow man. Drinking makes him do uncalled for acts, as firewater did to your brothers. Years of edjucation and growth have only made man Lazy, and un-caring. I care, for when I am out in nature, you are there, walking beside me, like an old friend. Guiding me along. I admire you. I wish I could talk with you about how you feel? If you are bitter? If you are at peace? You deserve so much.

You may have been called savage, but to me you were just hurt, and confused. You were the bravest and most proud people I know. You were content with little, just food and warmth. You were good hunters, and you prayed for the deer you killed. Such respect. You were creative, how did you chip those meticulous arrow points? So fine there they are, works of art. You were so loving, strong willed, spirit filled. How proud I would have been to be your blood brother. I do hope the wind is not your anger, and the rain your tears. I will remember you through many rains and snows. I look up to a mountain and picture you there, sitting on your steed, maybe hunting, maybe keeping watch for the enemy? Maybe just out riding, to be one with nature? I will keep you active in my heart. Think of me now and then, also, for I carry the guilt, and I should be pitied. Be patient with us, know that we are trying to learn to use your lands in the right way. Be forgiving of the white mans mistakes.
Rest well my brothers,
You are not forgotten . . .
    But can spirits be forgiving?

Cile Collins
FOR A MOTHER'S LOVE
A mother's love is the sweetest and strongest in this world today, a mother will do for her child in every single way.
One mother was asked, with tears rolling down her cheeks, she said "Oh, they are adult they can do want to do", when her daughter gave her child away. But over the hills, mountains and the peeks, someday, that girl will pay in her own way.
A mother went on bended knee, to scrub and clean, for a son in prison to help and hope he will obey, she never lived to see the day.
For years of waiting and wanting a child so bad, Sarah became a mother at eighty, a dream of a child she never had.
From a bible to a neice named Sarah, and good friend so.
A mother's love is the strongest one could ever know.
My mother copied from an old book to me "Flowers may wither roses may die, friends and loved ones may forsake you, only until death, never will I"
I never lost a child, so how would I know? Tho I lost a darling grandchild, I can still feel his little warm hand in mine, in pain, on a cold cold night, bed ridden with cancer, the Lord took him away from us, for he was blind.
And there's one who really understand's a mother's love,

that one person is in Heaven, up above.

Author Catherine Kerns
I LOVE YOU DEAR

Dedicated to my husband Ernest Thomas Kerns with love and devotion.

Ernest my love as your wife,
  I will bring only joy and sunshine
  Into your life.
Like the stars that shine above,
  Together we will share our love.
We will walk across the golden sand,
  Side by side hand in hand.
Having fun,
  Running barefoot in the morning sun.
Your children I will bear,
  Give them tender love and care.
As your best friend,
  By your side I will stand.
As you grow old,
  My love will never grow cold.
My love will forever be,
  Everlasting through eternity.
Your home I will clean your meals I will cook,
  Before I sit back to read a book.
Shine your shoes dust your coat,
  Always take time to leave you a note.
I will shovel snow,
  Keep the fire burning so you won't
  get cold.
I will hand you a beer,
  Saying I love you dear.
Precious things I will do,
  All because I love you.

Michelle Ann Coontz
JUST A MEMORY
Painted hourglasses and flying horses
Colorful carousels and untapped forces
Are in my mind.

Lost friends and false faces
Smiling suns and empty spaces
Are all that's left.

Unrecorded time and many a worn out letter
Things for the worst. Changes for the better
Are just a memory of the past.

Nina Patchen
BE A HELPER
We need to try to help each other,
What ever tasks they have to bear,
For each burden can be lightened
When you show how much you care.
When the sky seems to darken
The sun will shine through tears.
So, lend a shoulder to the needy,
It will lighten all their fears.
Forget petty quarrels, make them happy,
Put your patience to the test,
In return, you will feel better,
You will know you've done your best.
In these days of troubled waters
There must be no time for hate,

You will find life worth living
If we all co-operate

Jerry M. Marshall
CHARITY
How do we define true charity
Do we really know what it means?
  We really are able to see it
  But we must know what we're looking for.

What if one gives of mind and time
  Or maybe true love or hope
Are they not as great to those around,
  As the one who gives only wealth?

True charity must come from within.
There must not be any holding back.
For those who freely give their all,
Are sincerely the happiest people of all.

Jo S. Reynolds
RESCUE
Lost in the sea of depression
tossed about by
waves of conflict and doubts,
I struggle to emerge
with a renewed strength
of being—

Dear friend take my hand
and pull me from these
murky waters before I lose
my will to survive.

Dorothy A. Stalker
REAL LOVE
Love is oneness in being
Soul
And mind
Love is kind
Love is as gentle as a speckled fawn
As a sunrise is
Before the dawn
Love is tears upon a mother's face
Loves a child's innocent embrace
Love is animals—Nature—All
Loves a call

Carole Arthurs
MY MOUNTAIN HOME
The sunlight filtering through a tree.
  The scent of flowers in bloom.
The sound of water running free . . .
  Can fill my silent room.
I see a mountain's stately peak . . .

A valley deep below.
A flower strewn path where I can
seek . . .
The peace I used to know.
I'm longing for my childhood
home.
The mountain's calling me.
The place that God has made His
own . . .
That's where I long to be.
It won't be long 'cause in my
dream . . .
I saw a sight so rare.
A cabin there beside a stream . . .
I saw me standing there.
My family gathered all around . . .
There everyone will be.
And there they'll place me in the
ground.
I'm home! Yes, I am free!

Vera Gonzales
NIGHT
Night brings the beauty of the
sun to rest
And slowly persuades the light to
sleep.
The blanket of peace and quiet
calm
Is mingled with the fears of the
darkness,
To create a beauty that only God
could dream.

And as each child whispers their
sincere prayers,
It is within the darkness they are
read.
Which makes me ponder as to
the purity,
Said to be found in the light,
And the taboo of the darkness.

Eleanor Whitaker
A Tribute To Alexandria
She loved
people—friends—her family.
A person of inner beauty was she
And a dear friend and counselor
to me.

She cherished
books—music—education.
Scholarly, well-informed, always
searching for knowledge,
A librarian, an author, with
degrees acquired at college.

She revered
flowers—trees—nature.
Weeding and pruning for hours
on end,
Her garden of beauty, she
carefully would tend.

She yearned for
travel—adventure—exploring.
Seeking out ruins in Peru, and
lost civilizations,
And riding on a camel in far away
places.

She died
bravely—gallantly—courageously.
She suffered silently, and we all
did care,
But only she knew, the cross she
had to bear.

I will miss
her laughing smile—her
sparkling eyes—her happy voice.
The memories of her, will stay
with me forever,
For she touched my life, and
made it better.

Laurel Thompson
A LESSON IN LIFE
What was in your mind, my friend
When you took that fatal fall?
When you willingly your life did
end
Did you think of me at all?

While others lie in a sickbed
Clinging to every day,
You tragically went ahead
And threw your life away.

I wish that I had known before
What it was you'd planned.
I would have tried to do some
more
To lend a helping hand.

Now I cannot change the past
And do it all again.
But, my friend, I'll do my best
That your death won't be in vain.

It's too late to help you now
But others are depressed.
I hope that I can show them how
Their feelings to express.

If to me they pour out their heart
And ease their inner strife,
Then you and I will share a part
In saving another life.

Rev. I. John Dorsey

Rev. I. John Dorsey
LIFE AND DEATH
We all know what life is.
But, what is death?
It's just another form of life,
without the flesh.
I know, because I can see.
See the dead without their flesh.,
more stronger and powerful
than before.
They can travel through walls of
heavy steel and houses of wood
and stone.
Also, they can penetrate through
the human brain.
What is the secret to life and
death?
We try to keep from dying,
however, it's the dead that
keeps us living.
The people of the ancient knew
this fact, and they often done
the task of sacrifice.
Sacrifice pigeons, doves, man and
beast, just to keep their weary
souls alive.
Jesus Christ was our last sacrifice.
His spirit keeps us alive even to
this day.
Where were you before you were
born?

S. K. McGregor
PSALM TO THE ARTIST
Your hands mirror your soul
strong—gentle—soft
they give
receive
their warmth warms
and in their coldness
take of anothers blood

Your hands
are hands of love
not hate
creators of beauty
tangible emotion

Under them
cold, hard, greyness
speaks
takes shape
shadow and softness

Care for them wisely
love and
make love to them—
with them

They shall be your life
the givers and creators of new life
through them
you touch the souls of others

Tommy Eileen Shore Weigand
MY FIRST LOVE

*To James Lewis Allen who taught
me the art of sign language . . . a
language never to be forgotten,
nor your kindness.*

A boy meets a girl
and the boy is deaf—
he couldn't talk . . . or even
hear
the crunch of a dry leaf.
She could talk and talk
and talk some more—
but together . . . their
smiles . . .
were something they couldn't
ignore.
He would write to her . . .
and she to him—
and soon she was in love
with her boy named Jim.
He taught her to speak
with a silent tongue—
and their hearts were light
and their hearts were young.
She wanted marriage . . .
and so did he—
but his parents didn't . . .
even tho we didn't agree.
He went off to college
with me on his mind—
and I wrote him a letter . . .
to free him . . . so another girl
he could find.
I broke his heart and told him a
lie . . .
I said I didn't love him . . .
and that our love was going to
end—
because I knew it wouldn't be
forever
for his heart to mend.
And now . . . I know he is
happily married . . .
and so am I—
but . . . he'll always be my
special friend
until the day I die.

Meiling L. Williams
WHOSE CHILD IS THAT

*To Mama, For all of her Love and
Support, even when I had given up.*

Whose child is this that walks
the street at night
That doesn't come home till the
early light
Whose child is this that has no
friends
That lives in a world full of sins
Whose child is this that can not
make ends meet
That can not help getting in too
deep
Whose child is this that plays a
foolish game
That has not yet been tamed
Whose child is this that parents
ignore
That never sat down to talk or
listen before
Whose child is this that sleeps all
Sunday
That just wakes up expecting a
fun day
Whose child is this that always
sits alone
That is also accident prone
Whose child is this that just
doesn't care
That is always ready for a dare
Whose child is this that will not
pray
The ten commandments he will
not obey
Whose child was that, that one
day shall be no more
A sinner—we've all seen one
before.

James A. Stacy
FULL TILT
A killer walks the woodline field
Stalking a victim, to grind under
heel
In the dark of night, shadows
dance too and fro
Newly born, or ancient old
Thoughts of maddness, cascading,
erupting within,
Feeds a diseased brain, forged by
sin
With blood filled eyes, dead of
sight
He wounders in blackness, away
from the light
With hatred, seeping from every
pore
He runs amok, keeping score
Hacking, slashing with evil glee
"Catch me, Kill me," he laughs,
"We will see."

Captured
Trial
Sanitarium
Freedom;
A killer walks the woodline field
Stalking a victim, to grind under
heel

Anna A. Yoder
CHILL
Black trees shivering
Gusts of wind stripped them
clean, bare,
cold winter . . . no clothes.

Our World's Best Loved Poems

Joyce D. Colatrella
LOVE IN THE AIR

To David, who inspired the feeling of love and brought out the best of life in me. You've made my dreams come true, and I will love you and cherish you— until the end of time.

It's a feeling so new—so entirely new,
That captured my heart the day I met you.
I think that it's love, what else could it be?
For nothing before has so overwhelmed me.

I first laid my eyes on the strength of your smile . . .
So taken by surprise, I felt numb for awhile.
Your eyes held a sparkle, your hair had a shine,
From that moment on, I wanted you to be mine.

Then we met and we talked and I immediately knew,
I was totally engrossed and fascinated by you.
Was this only a dream? You were perfect and more . . .
Nothing could go wrong, of this I felt sure.

So we'll go on from here and expect but the best,
For nothing can stop us from out doing the rest.
Our relationship will grow, it all but has to,
For now that we've met, I've fallen in love with you!

Nelafae Dean
SPRING
The sky is a pale blue mast
with white marshmallow clouds
drifting by.

The sun is a bright burst of
yellow generously sprinkling
its rays everywhere.

The grass is a plush deep
green carpet with a multi-
color of flowers popping
open.

The trees are towering in
beautiful blends of dark
and light greens.

The brooks are glistening
ripples of crystal blue
glass flowing gently by.

The gleaming stars sparkle
like diamonds as they hang
dutifully in the night sky.

The worlds greatest beauties
which God created are evident
as far as the eye can see.

Mary Neatherly
THEY CARED
Out of sight is far away to little
hearts and minds,
They cannot grasp the feelings
your absence leaves behind.
They know it's very lonesome
and the hours seem so long,
They watch and wait for your

return, their want is oh so
strong
It really isn't many years a child
will cling to you
And when they do not, watch and
wait, you'll wonder what to do.
It's then you quickly know and
feel the ache, the loss, the need
You'll wonder if the trips you
made were based on needless
greed.

Take heed on how a child must
feel when it depends on you
Yet has to stand and see you go
wondering what to do.
When tiny arms no longer reach
and eyes shine not with tears
You'll quickly realize the loss
you'll feel throughout the years.

A child is but a part of God,
placed within your care
Ponder what you owe that child,
be loving, kind and fair.
Share your hours with the child,
help it learn and grow.
Don't ignore the needs it has,
fullfilled! it blooms and grows.

It takes a lot of patients, sacrafice
and tears
To help a child cope with life,
especially through these years.
So parents set the rules and laws,
guides a child can hold,
A pathway it can follow to reach
a personal goal.

The years you spend to raise a
child may take its toll in time,
Will drain you of your patients,
you'll often fall behind.
But you will never once regret
your love your child has shared
When that adult stands young
and tall to say my parents cared.

Eva M. Roy
TOTAL NIGHT
The night stepped in
Quietly, wearing a soft moccasin
It wanted to park
Beside the elm tree's bark
But it became so black
That the railroad track
Slipped in with it
And enclosed the net
Nothing has ever been
So eerie, as when
The night tiptoed in
Wearing that moccasin
And left the darkness
In total blackness!

Nand Samuel Guerrero (P. S. A.)
LIFETIME 1, 2, 3
The things we do and say
Have a place to start under the sun
  You can't escape them
  You can't save them

Life is but a star in space
Soon to burn out in this airless
room
  You can't see them all
  You can't live them all

Time is but a fraction of life
Like a cell in your mind
  You can't stop it
  You can't bring it back

And love is a disease
It will kick you when you're down

It can kill and steal your heart
of life
And put you underground

There is no cure for the things
We do and say—only time will tell
But! Its only a fraction
  You can't add or subtract it

The things we do and say
Have a place to stop! Under the
sun
Once we do and say our lives are
done

You can't escape them
Or see them all
You can't save them
Or live them all

The things we do and say
Have a place to stay
         Under the sun . . .

T. A. White
Beauty Is Everywhere You Are
Beauty can be everywhere, but
Faces well known, dim
When a mind peers through drab
clouds.
Clouds manufactured from a
furnace of
Discontent and vague desires.
But beauty is everywhere you are.

Beauty can be everywhere, if
Filtered through narrow smiles of
Beguiling optimism.
Optimism calculated from a
cache of
Complicated choices. At least,
Beauty is wherever you are.

Beauty can be everywhere, when
Your hint of an intimate word or
touch is
Mixed with a gentle tone of voice.
A gentle voice of soft fire that
Warms me with loving inflection.
Beauty is surely wherever you are.

S./O. Leonard R. Alexander
THE A-B-C. OF LIFE
The A. B. C.'s of life, are found
upon this earth.
They were written in the bible,
long before your birth.
The A is for your attitude, in the
way you treat your fellow man.
For God put you on this earth for
a purpose
I know that you can understand.
The B is for the bible, one should
be in every home.
For if not read and followed in its
prediction of your future.
The Devil will be your master,
and the gates of hell your home.
The C is for the Christ child that
died for all our sins.
So open up your heart to Christ,
and let him enter in.

Jean M. Harris
I'VE LOVED YOU
I've loved you in the sunshine
and the dark, still of the night
I've loved you when our world
was wrong
  even more when our world was
right
I've loved you in the springtime
and adored you in the fall
When winter comes, with it's

lonely days
I've loved you most of all
I've loved you Dear when things
were good
I've also loved you thru the bad
I think the times I've loved you
best,
  when each other is all we had
When at last I'm put to rest,
  and asked for a final recall
I'll tell all of Heaven about you,
  my greatest love of all.

Leonard Sam Williams
It's the First Day Of Spring

This poem is dedicated to all the unknown writers in the world such as myself, for I wish them well in their endeavors to reach for their pie in the sky. They are truely the real unsung heros . . . that millions of people may never get to know. When the world cries, it cries together, until the tears are all gone, but when we as the unknown writer cry . . . it seems, we cry alone.

It's the first day of Spring, Robins
appear and Bluejays sing. It's
the first day of Spring, the
flowers are blooming and the
air is fresh and clean. The air is
still kind of chilly and the
wind still sting as the snow
slowly melts away, telling you
that Spring is on it's way and
everything will soon be happy
and gay. Spring is in the air and
everything seems to be coming
to life again, the grass, flowers
are blossoming in the sunshine
as the trees slowly bends.

Spring is for lovers, just like you
and I . . . Oh feel the fresh wet
morning dew it's all over the
grass. It's the first day of Spring,
but it won't be here long. It
seems as soon as you turn
around it's gone and the long,
long hot summer months soon
linger on.

Spring is in the air, it's
everywhere, Oh feel the warm
sun and it's heat and feel the
wet morning dew under the
bottom of your bare feet, it's all
over the grass.

Spring is here, Spring is here,
Spring is here, at last.

Gregg (TAL) Gregory
BE TRUE
     Be True
      and
    you will find
the power of your world
     Be True
      for
    you are
the power of your world
     Be true
    Believe
   in yourself
      and
  you have found
   the power

Ruth Sampson
A CHRISTMAS DAY GIFT

To all my grandchildren, and to the OC Transpo driver who inspired me to write this poem.

Hark to the tale I unfold
Of an Xmas Angel of gold
Dressed in a warm suit of black
Sympathy for me he did not lack
As to him I detailed my plight
Frozen face, hands and toes
Held me in a state of woe.
My destination quite clear in my mind
Was indeed very hard to find
Directing me as best he could
Where the right bus to find I would;
Just walk down a block or two
To Metcalfe and Laurier Rue.
As I followed his advice,
He arrested my steps by tooting thrice.
Looking back I saw him beckon,
But surely, little did I reckon
That his gloves he would give,
Xmas Samaritan, long may you live!
Reminding me that in greatest need
God always sends a friend indeed.
What makes the act so significant,
I am simply a landed immigrant
Rescued fingers are thus induced
This token of thanks to produce
Angelic was your deed of gold,
May God keep you in his closest hold.

michael shaun fairley
cloudnorms

At the end of a day,
I like to fly with the dreamers
And leave this mixed-up world behind.
Go where there are no false deities,
No earthly illusion of grandeur,
Only the omni-presence of the sun and sky.

My mind becomes as clear as a raindrop.
I receive no social pressures,
Just the sights and sounds of serenity.
Earth to me is the only seperation.
Like a cloud,
The sky, the sun, and I are in unity!

Virgil S. Hart
IN OLD VIRGINIA

I know a lady who goes to Virginia Beach
Where she's completely out of reach
Of all those Mountaineers she left behind
To pine for that lovely lady they can no longer find.

How wonderful that she crosses the Blue Ridge and old Cheat
To go where history in the making has been a long time feat!
As she drives on through the Piedmont,
She gets nearer, ever nearer, to the great Atlantic font.

In the summer, I'll wager, she goes out to sea;
Or wanders down the beach where bathing beauties are bound to be!
Perhaps she marvels at the tide's ebb and flow
And fears not the great waves that are never slow.

Perchance she goes to Norfolk town
Or shops in Portsmouth the clock aroun'
There's Newport News and Fort Monroe;
And maybe to Williamsburg, she likes to go.

I'll bet she went to Yorktown last fall
In answer to history's mighty call!
Of course, on March the eighth, she can go commemorate
The ironclad Monitor-Merrimac stalemate!

For history she can go away farther back
To Jamestown and John Smith, and that's a fact.
She may be the sweetest lady along the James
Since John Rolfe took Pocahontas to the Thames!
May that lady try a moment to make a nostalgic wish for those she left behind.

Michelle M. Aslagson
LOVELY IS . . .

Lovely is your eyes,
   When you gaze upon me.
Lovely is your touch,
   When you put your arms around me.
Special is you,
   and I love you so much.
Happy is together,
   Me and you, you and me.
Happy are the feelings,
   'cause I know you care so much.

June B. Johnson
A BEAUTIFUL DAY

A beautiful day it surely has been,
With God's lovely sunshine dwelling within.

The sky above blue and the air smelling fresh;
A day to be spent out walking about,

Enjoying each moment as the day passes on;
Rejoicing with peace or singing a song.

Can't let this day pass without giving praise;
To God our dear Maker for this day of all days.

Josephine. Vanderhoof
MOTHERS GONE

Its too late to say the kind words, a mother loved to hear.
Its too late to stop and visit, Mother isn't here.
The days she sat so lonely; now have passed away.
The things she didn't tell you, are now too late to say.
The past was just a memory, the days were oh so long.
The things that gave her solace, were the memories of a song.
Its too late to say the kind words, a mother loved to hear,
Its too late to stop and visit; mother isn't here.

Irene Dolores Lippert-Hoffman

Irene Dolores Lippert-Hoffman
MISFORTUNE

The night is dark and gray
misfortune is on her way
in the deep of the mist
in the fog of the day.

The trees spread out their arms
   so wide and far away
they look so big and strong that way
there is not a child outside to play
for misfortune is on her way.

Just listen to her howling
as she goes a prowling
all around downtown and
   throughout the night
giving the people a terrible fright
as she whirls and twirls
   everything within her sight
while she laughs and crys with delight.

Susan Faye Honaker
ONE-SIDED LOVE

The minute I saw you walk in that door,
   I was happier than ever before.
When I looked at you and you looked at me,
   I'd hoped it was my love you'd see.
I thought for sure you had loved me too,
But I guess that was only in my dreams of you.
I know you hate me cause you told me so,
But why, is what I really must know.
My love for you is not some game,
And I'd hoped that you would feel the same.
So I guess it's now over for good,
   That to me you've made understood.
Just remember through it all,
   My love for you shall never fall.

Dudley Holt
ONCE

Once I found a sunset and loved it so much
that I wanted to keep it
but it slipped away
never to be seen again.

Once I found a rainbow and loved it so much
that I wanted to keep it
but it slipped away
never to be seen again.

Once I found a true love . . .

Jodi Robertson
DREAMS COMING TRUE

I'm living in my dreams.
Not thinking about tomorrow
Until it's today.
Today is all that matters.
One step at a time is what people say.
There may not be a tomorrow
To think about.
But if there is, I hope
It's us together.
Not only in my dreams,
But in the world,
You and I as a team!

Paulette Meulli Vega
BOREDOM

Why does boredom come so fast,
It doesn't waste it's time,
To creep upon you oh so fast,
It's really such a crime,
You think you've found your interest,
The perfect pass time then,
Before you can enjoy yourself,
It shows it's face again.

Cathy Slater McGinn
DEAR DAUGHTER

Oh, my daughter.
When you were Daddy's Little Girl,
I helped you to tie your shoelaces
And taught you how to ride your bike.
I tucked you in at night
And chased all the Meanies and Monsters away.
I suffered through your measles and tonsillectomy,
Not wanting you to hurt but only able to be there
With your favorite flavor of popsicles.
We clashed a few times when you were in your teens
But we grew to respect each other's thoughts.
When I walked with you down the aisle
To join your life with your husband's,

I wanted to hold on to you a little
longer,
To tell you how proud I was of
the woman you'd become,
To tell you how very much I
loved you.
Now I stand here beside you
As you hold your baby son who
sleeps in death
And I don't know how to help
you.
If only I could start things over
for you,
Or take your place to bear your
pain.
I try not to cry
As I watch you, my daughter, still
my baby girl,
Kiss my new grandson goodbye.

Janet Lynn Pelletier
DREAMS
So many things I need to know
So many things to do
So little time in which to grow
In love and living, too

I want to fall in love someday
I want to never cry
I want to always stay this way—
Young, and never die

I wish that nothing ever changed
I wish for someone's touch
I wish there was no pain
Really, I wish too much

Debra Anne Bedard
LEGEND OF THE UNICORN
They are very pretty there,
Just tossing their manes around,
Blending with the scenery,
The trees, the sky, the ground.

Yet they seem so sorrowful,
Just prancing here and about,
As if they really seem to know,
What their lives are all about.

They have no one to tell them,
What is wrong and what is right,
They have their own special way,
Their very own guiding light.

The "Legend of the Unicorn",
Neatly tied with a bow,
Like a promise we remember,
Like a beautiful rainbow.

Julia Ord King
PROUD HERITAGE
We've been warriors down the
ages,
Defending kingdoms large and
small,
Fighting men known for their
courage
From Timbuctu to Senegal.
Fierce Mandinka defended Mali,
British Bards sang of Zulu,
Matabele and Watusi,
Massai and Yoruba too.
So why should it be surprising
We would want to join the band'
That makes up National Defenses,
The Military Forces of our land?

We were part of Colonial
hardships,
We were part of cattle drives,
We were part of Western Wagons,
We often had to give our lives;
Indians called us Buffalo Soldiers,
Famed frontier Tenth Cavalry;
So with centuries of belonging

We serve on land and air and sea;
As partners in our defenses
We now have our rightful place;
We shall share in exploration
Of the immensity of space!

Mary Frances Jenkins
Take Your Elbows Off the Table
Take your elbows off the table!
Ain't you got no manners?
Mama glared at me,
And I glared back at her.
But still I took my elbows off the
table.

Hush your mouth!
You talk too much,
And you're too loud.
Folks ain't got to look down your
throat
To see what you've got to say.
Mama rolled her eyes at me,
And I rolled mine back at her.
But still I closed my mouth
And watched the silence swoller
us.

Hey! Stop that fighting!
Ain't you got no love in your
heart?
Mama tore us apart—
Like ripping paper in half.
I fell so hard,
I wished just once I could hit her
back.
But something in her eyes said:
"Boy, don't be a fool!"

Mama died today,
I couldn't even cry.
I bowed my head
And heard her say: "Straighten up,
Boy!
Act like you've got some pride.
Stand tall. You ain't got nothing
to hide!"

And I took my elbows off the
table
Because I knew Mama hadn't
really died.

Karen Mellott
FADING LIGHT
You'll be leaving very soon
I don't want to see you go
Surely you know that I'll miss
you
And my feelings will continue to
grow
I understand that it's the only
answer
To find what's right for you
I only hope that you'll never
forget
Everything we used to do
While we're separated by the miles
I hope there's no time for another
These last few days have meant a
lot to me
Sharing precious moments with
each other
If only before we had both know
That the feelings we had were the
same
We then could have had the time
To let ourselves ignite into one
flame
But now the light is beginnng to
fade
The last flicker is starting to die
It doesn't seem right to only say
I love you—and good-bye

Karen Diane Schuetz
A FEELING
I'm feeling free and easy
And my spirits are plentiful.
I'm in another world
Free from hate and anxiety.

Troubles—I have none
Dreams—I have many
Hate—I feel little
Love—Enough for everyone

Kathy Heinrichs
ILLUSIONS OF REALITY
The white unicorn floats down
To the midnight pool
Lays back in the velvet grass
Dark silent beauty.

What is real?
The unicorn's reflection
Shimmering softly in the river,
Or the river,
Gently kissing the shore?

The unicorn fades away
Leaving a soft glow in midair,
But in the river,
Its reflection still floats,
Gentle silent beauty.

There is no river,
Only the beast itself,
Nothing is as we think it is,
And the unicorn slowly fades
away.

Lisa M. Webster
LOVE IS . . .
Love is something no one
understands,
yet everyone feels it.
Love is abstract and intangible,
yet everyone reaches out for it.
Love is free and non-possessive,
yet everyone has a strong hold.
Love is mysterious,
yet everyone knows of it.
Love is optional
yet everyone needs it.
Love is universal
and yet private, within each
individual
Love is overwrought,
yet so little used in truth
Love is unquantitative,
yet measured in degree and
strength
Love is sometimes tiresome
yet puts a burst of energy into
the soul
Love is meek,
yet blunt and precise.
Love is infinite
yet ends so soon.
Love is trust
yet suspicions arouse.
Love is encouragement,
yet breaks ones spirits.
Love is indiscriminatory,
yet restricted by society
Love is singular, yet it takes two.
Love is taken, yet I give it to you.

Susan Faye Honaker
LOVE SO RARE
In looking back on times we spent
The smiles, the tears, and what
they meant;
The love we shared just you and I
It grew and grew as time went by.
A love like roses, white and rare;
The special way you seemed to
care;

The sunny glow upon your face;
The need to feel your warm
embrace;
The dreams of how our lives
could be
If ever you should marry me;
So now no matter what we do
I'll spend my life just loving you
And thinking of your gentle
touch
And how to me you mean so
much.
To live without my dreams of you
Is something I could never do.
And in the future may it be
Just you and I eternally.

Genevieve Dunne Berger
LOVE IS NOT . . .
Love is not impatient
Love is not unkind
Love is not jealous
Love is not blind
Love is not selfish
Ill mannered or rude
Love keeps no record
Except for the good
For blame should be equal
And love must be fair
Love is not happy
When truth is not there
Love is not helpless
With troubles unbidden
Love is not hopeless
Where love is not hidden.

Erysline Green Chesser
LIFE'S FOUR SEASONS
Life is like a calendar year,
Complete with all four seasons.
Spring is like the baby years,
Without much rhyme or reason.

When summer comes we
blossom forth,
Complete in all our glory.
Love is at our beck and call,
It's such a sweet, sweet story.

Then comes the fall, and like the
trees
We begin to shed our splendor.
Yet we miss the love we knew so
well
Because it isn't yet December.

When winter comes and spreads
the word
Nature has no more to give,
We'll spend the time that we
have left
Remembering—the life we lived.

Lois A. Thompson
A CREATION OF GOD'S
When the golden sun is setting,
What a glorious sight to see,
As it fades from the horizon,
Out of sight from you and me.

Then the moon begins it's
journey,
Beaming brightly from above,
Lighting up the world around us,
Shining on the ones we love.

And the sunrise in the morning,
Something artists can't compare,
With the brightly multi-colors,
Shining earthward everywhere.

Have you ever thought or realized,
As you see this view each day,
It's only one of God's creations,
As He changes night to day?

Jenna V. Ownbey
SALAD MOTIF
Snips of shrimp,
Pineapple and squash,
Make a combo salad,
But it will never wash!

Carolyn J. Bodie
LOVE

To Danny, my husband, whose love inspired this poem,

Love is spring and summer
It's winter and fall.
Love is happiness and sadness
It's yesterday and tomorrow.

Love is trusting and believing
It's giving and receiving.
Love is a touch, a feeling
It's forgetting and forgiving.

Love is a bird that flies
And a baby that cries.
Love is a heart in your hand
It's a woman and a man.

Doug McArthur
WAITING FOR THE WIND
The wind is always changing.
On a whim, it can caress the
   lilacs
Or dash cottonwoods into
   splinters.

Perhaps the worst is when it
   vanishes,
As it sometimes does.
And, like a ship on a glass
   sea,
I am frozen.
Waiting to go somewhere,
From nowhere.

In the stillness,
I forget the wind.
Reflections on eternity
Bring visions of infinity.
Until I feel the ripple,
A slight tug on my soul,
That moves me.

Karen Greklek
TIME AND DISTANCE
Together in
Proximity
In an unreal
Reality
We learned What isn't
True

And from that vacuum
Truth
Became us

Not regretfully
we move on
"New" me, "New" you
"Old" friends

Evelyn Stickler
IT'S A LAUGH!

This poem is dedicated to—and was inspired by—an unknown man, three seats ahead of me on a Bus, who gave a sudden joyful outburst of laughter.

What is this thing from the inner
   depths of pleasure?
      It's a laugh!
What is this thing science can
   not measure?
      It's a laugh!
What spreads contagious joy to
   those around?
What chases tears to the "Happy
   Hunting Ground"?
What gives a lift to those of us in
   trouble?
What makes our hearts in
   common ape the bubble?
      It's a laugh!

Ruby Russell
**The Day President
Kennedy Was
Assasinated**

To My Children Mary Lou, James, and Dwight

The news screamed out over the
   radio
The disastrous news informing us
   that our beloved President now
   lay dead,
The sinister bullet having
   penetrated his head.
The rain came down in torrents,
The heaven roared in anguished
   thunder
In rebellion and defiance at this
   ghastly blunder.
We walked as mummies in the
   rain
Not conscience of our rain
   soaked bodies,
Our heads bowed low, not
   believing this terrible shame.
The clashing thunder roared on
   and on so very frightening in
   the dark sky
As if God was angry on his tear
   drenched throne.
We gathered our children from
   the school
Thinking of our President and
   the murderer who had broken
   the Golden Rule.
He may be dead and gone
But he lived as a great President
And in our hearts he would live
   on.

A. R. (Annie) RUPARD
TO MY NIECE
Joni Rae—You've brightened my
   life—From the very first day
   you were here;
Your cheerful smile, and
   thoughtful ways, have made
   you to me, very dear;
I watched you grow from day to

day, then months, that turned
   into years;
When you'd run to my arms, and
   I'd hold you tight, and kiss
   away your tears;
Ah! If only things were that
   simple still, and a hug could
   bring you cheer;
I'd read you a story, rock you to
   sleep, and nothing on earth,
   would you fear;
But time has a way of moving
   along, and obstacles do appear;
You gotta roll with the punches,
   and ride the tide, and to
   changes you must adhere;
Some bridges have to be crossed,
   and burned, when at the time it
   seems austere;
So set your sails in happy
   directions, from your course, do
   not one time veer;
For just over the horizon, you'll
   find the sun shinging: brilliant,
   bright, and clear;
My pride, and faith in you abide,
   our sharing I revere;
Know that my love is with you,
   and in my heart you're always
   near.

Dori M. Jensen-Foster
AFTER SLUMBER

Dedicated to: The man I love, when we shared one special morning watching nature unfold one of her secrets, wherein I knew a deep and true contentment of a peaceful love, then, now and forever.

Come, wake with me to see the
   dew,
Let's rise before the sky turns blue;
So I can show you nature's charms,
While I embrace you with my
   arms.

We two can watch the early morn,
Before the day with toil is worn;
And hear the red bird trill her
   song,
So listen, she does not warble
   long!

This new day comes unspoiled
   for you,
But we can travel it, slowly
   through;
'Til dusk descends my thoughts
   will be
A cherished hour you shared
   with me!

Sylvia L. Palmer
GRIZZLY BEAR

To: Keith. In retrospect, Grizzly Bear, I'd say we weathered the "hard times." Enjoy the freedom!
Love, Sylvia

Eighteen year old Grizzly bear
Growling in your den
Making such a fearsome noise
I know how you've been.

Eighteen years out in the cold
Sometimes on thin ice
Searching for some food and

warmth
Or something equally nice.

Now all locked up in your zoo
Behind a door that's barred
Better that you are in there
Life outside's still hard.

Now and then a fish or two
Or maybe other crumbs.
It's no wonder, is it, that
To sleep the bear succumbs?

Eighteen year old grizzled boy
Growling from your room,
You're the grizzly bear above
And you made your own tomb.

Even though the ice was thin
And you've been in "hot water,"
All that in your school of life
Is now an "Alma Mater."

You have made the grade, you
   know,
For you have come this far.
Come on out, unlock the door
And hitch up to a star.

Melt the ice that's in your heart
Stop the searching, son.
Release the strife, there's more to
   life,
And some of it is fun!

Eighteen year old grizzly bear
Whether man or beast,
Walk into the weather
Life holds for you a feast!

Dennis D. Kloth
I HAVE SEEN FRIENDS
I have seen friends with broken
   arrows
Riding westward to the mountains.
Friends who are contrary rivers,
Who climb the pathways of
   Olympus
And long to gaze upon the kingdom
With eyes reflecting endless
   sunsets.

In waxen wings they fly a frontier
Beyond the hidden empyreal orb
Away from the hand of silent
   Morpheus
Whose eyes are constant as are
   the stars.

But as I gaze thru endless skies
I see the ancient castles burning
And cross the shimmering
   moon's reflection
To bathe forgotten in the warmth
Of her peaceful night.

Isabella Zavala
PASSAGE OUT

Dedicated to Thomas W. Reynolds Jr. & Irene Zavala who have lightened my way.

Careful of thought
When it has wandered—
Into the dark,
Where souls are squandered.
Ease that thought
Back into place . . .
Imagine seeing, a smiling face.
Think of a soaring eagle—
Over a fresh spring meadow,
And, not to mention,
Loved one's affection!
Lighten the dark,
With any of the above,

And you heart and thought
Will be as free as the dove.

Thomas B. O'Neal, Jr.
WHO AM I?

---

*This poem was written for all
people who are searching for
their identity and inspired by the
death of Dr. Martin Luther King,
Jr. and John F. Kennedy.*

Journeying across the oceans
    violent waters,
Searching for a past,
That has long been forgotten.

Moving through the skys
    turbulent winds.
Looking for a heritage,
That seems forever lost.

Traveling over the earths many
    terrains.
Seeking a true identity,
That may never come to be.

Hoping for a link,
To who I am,
Wanting to truly know,
Who am I?

Patricia L. Headley
FREEDOM
Obsession flee and
    pain me no more.
This hopeless desire
    is still denied,
Causing faith to wander—
    and totally retreat.
Please depart
    and set me free.

Louella Yung Szeto
DON'T LET EVIL WIN
Sneakingly, stealthily she stalks
    the night
Spitefully willed, and with a grim
    smile,
At any moment, she's ready to
    strike,
The weak and the flimsy, take
    heed,
Don't let Evil win.

Malevolence from her heart,
    malicious was her desire
Waiting at the dark of the alley,
Go by the short cut; you'll be
    caught,
So walk on the bright side of the
    street,
Don't let Evil win.

She gives out a price:
Fame and Fortune, Power and State;
Name any one, she lets you enjoy
    a while,
But at the end she snatches
Your heart and soul.

Gluttony and greed sow the seed
Of your downfall; watered by
    vanity
Germinates the weed of Evil!
Her tentacles extending all
    through
You, now her prey, will be
    dragged down
To the bottomless pit till eternity.

You'd better dispel all vicious
    thoughts,
You'd better follow the ways of
    God.

With your will strengthened,
    your mind confirmed
How can Evil win?

June Lee Box

June Lee Box
AN ERA IN TRANSITION
A stagecoach took Gr-aunt Sarah
    Agnes west
Then back to Paducah with
    mother
Bereaved seven year old Grace
    found comfort
In plantation life, new friends,
    new playmates
A train brought 78 year old Nana
To live with mother's family of
    three
We treasured her tales of Civil
    War days
Underground R.R., servants
    hiding runaways
(In Kentucky's limestone caves?)
The Housecar father built on our
    Overland
Took us to Los Angeles in '23
    (Early RV?)
We brought our boxed 'Crystal
    Radio Set'
An 8" rough rock, ear phones, and
    a wire
We touched to the rock to hear
    "stations"
(Early TV dialing?)
We were living in San Diego in
    '26 when
One day out in the Packard, we
    heard
Ryans was building a plane for
    Lindbergh
(His '27 Atlantic solo amazed the
    world.)
Three years later, at 88, dear
    Nana died
Her mobile era had laid the
    foundation
Dor vast and soaring inventions
Air liners, jets, men on the moon
Computers and satellite stations
To Sally Ride orbiting Space!

Sherry Small Powell
EARLY DAYS
I grew up on the farm
    You See!
It made a very hard working girl
    Out of Me!
My folks taught me how
    To Work and Play!
And to earn those dimes
    The Hard Way!
Those days are gone
    But Not Forgotten!

I still can remember
    Mama picking Cotton!
My daddy weighing those bales
    On The Scales!
That big tobacco field
    That Gave Such A Yield!
That corn patch and berry patch
    They Were No Match!
I still remember those years
    As I Wipe The Tears.

Staci Ryback
A DREAM COME TRUE

---

*Dedicated to: Ann—Margaret, it's
a best loved poem and why
shouldn't it be it's written with
love for you from me keep on
smiling, singing and being you.*

Lights, curtains, action
    the music began to play
Deep within my heart
    I knew this was my special day
The crowd sat motionless
    as you appeared on the stage
Your talent and style captured
    them
    once again you were the latest
    rage
The audience loved you
    the applause grew with each
    successive song
After all the years of performing
    you knew just where you
    belonged
The performance was now ending
    you had taken your final bow
You should have seen their faces
    it was as if they were saying
    "Wow"
Later on I had the chance to meet
    you
    my fondest dream came true
I'll never forget your very first
    words
    nor will I ever forget you

Margaret Hone
MY GIFT
I give to you the stars,
    if you but lift your eyes and see.
I give to you the beauty of the
    flowers,
    if you but kneel and touch.
I give to you the sweet breath of a
    baby,
    if you but stop and listen.
I give to you the bittersweet of life,
    if you but taste and separate the
    two.
But most of all I give to you a
    loving heart,
    and the opportunity to love me
    as I love you.

Thomas Howard Davis
MOTHER'S LOVE

---

*To Mom with love Bille—Jean,
Brian, & Terri—Lynn*

Amidst the forest green
there rings a lonely bell
it's my country church
has when a child i dwell

The singing of the sweetest song
would fill the country air
i think of all my sins forgiven
and now with you will share

Twas mothers love that did it
that saved me from disgrace
hoping that i'd grow that way
stand firm and take my place

It was awful bad
the company that i kept
ignoring god's own book of love
while mother sat and wept

Thank-you mom for caring
about my future life
and teaching me the bible
of temptations and of strife

Ruth Anne Stibbs
IF
If species evolved without design,
Why are there monkeys and dogs?

If "natural selection" presents the
    Truth,
where are the men with swinging
    tails,
the men with wings and the men
    with horns?

If "spontaneous generation"
    persists,
where is the man from a mother
    of rock?

If foetus history cameras the race,
then jelly jellied a fish, a reptile,
a mammal, an ape, to a newborn
    babe.

If the missing link is intelligence,
The Java Ape Man is the evidence.

Brenda E. Woodridge
DOUGLAS
Douglas
Sweet face
Little dimples
Cute buns
Innocent.
Laughing eyes
Impish smile
Loving arms
Angelic.
Curly hair
Wiggly walk
Rosy cheeks
Mischiefious.
Fat belly
Crazy talk
Tender lips
Huggable.
Hearty laugh
Tiny boy
Growing fast
Mine.

Lucille L. Todd
FREEDOM
Restless you gaze
    As the eagle soars in the sky
Whispering breezes travel
    Through the trees
While the bonds of muscles
    Hold the body fast, you
    wonder,
Will this travail of tears pass
    And like the eagle and the
    breeze
Be free at last.

Vilma J. Westerholm
A LITTLE BOY'S PRAYER
Oh please, dear God, do stop this
    war,
    I want my daddy over here,
I might not see him any more,
    Now that they've sent him "over
    there;"

Oh please, dear God, oh can't you
  see,
My mummy needs him to take
  care,
Of her and brother and of me,
  We miss him so much, over
  here;

You know a fellow needs his dad,
  To teach him how to fish and
  swim,
And mend a kite or fishing rod,
  No one could do it, quite like
  him;

Why must he fight that other
  man?
Perhaps he has a boy like me,
And when he finds his daddy
  gone,
  Just think how lonely, he will
  be;

I'm sure he needs his daddy too,
  To make a boat or mend a toy,
He never could without him do,
  A daddy, should be with his boy.

Carol E. Kelly
**No One Can Take Your
  Place**
No one can take your place.
No one fits the impression of
Your spirit on my heart.

It is too big to be filled
By those foolish children,
And too perfect in shape
For arrogant imposters.

No one will ever keep me
  warm.
Has anyone fire enough
To melt the ice inside me?

Frozen feeling will wake
When I know you are resting
And safe. When you
Don't need me anymore.

No one is to me as you are.
When will they learn to
Be themselves, not someone
  else?

Who do I want, if not you?
A like heart, not to
Take your place,
But to make me whole.

Terry Elaine Weese
BLUE MOON

---

*A dedication to my Family and
close friends*

COME—
Listen closely, for I've a story to
  tell
About an old legend, and a
  mystery as well
Indian folk told it to their
  children dears
A legend that would follow
  throughout the coming years

I've heard tales that it had come
  true
But who are we to believe unless
  we see it too
BUT COME—
The story I'm to tell you will
  bring a certain thrill
While pictures will be created—
  shh—be very still

Every thousand years, this is to
  be true
The moon will become a very,
  very pale blue
Between the enchanting hours of
  eight and midnight
This moon of pale blue will
  become quite bright

Any animal born on this night a
  new
A part of his/her furry body will
  distinctly be blue
All the loving parents at first will
  be filled with dismay
But the natural love will grow
  stronger on every passing day

This story may sound untrue to
  all of your animal ears
But there are no lies nor
  oncoming fears
It is a mystery to all who have
  heard it being told
So I believe we wait and see if it
  will unfold

The thousand years are over in a
  very short while
But the night is still unknown
  and to all will beguile
So watch—be aware—if this tale
  is really true
This is my only message from
  myself to you

Vicki Thomas
I CAN FLY
I look up to the sky, and see a
  bird on wing.
  And wish that I could fly, and
  just get away from everything.
But then I open up my eyes and I
  begin to see.
  And suddenly my spirits soar,
  and I am free, and I am me,
AND I CAN FLY.

Florence R. Dixon
FAITH
Each morning 'ere I start my day,
  My hand in His I place,
And know that He will guide my
  way
  In each task I face.
Each night "I lay me down to
  sleep",
  My head upon His breast,
And know that He will ever keep
  Loving watch above my nest.

Ann Lea Engle
CORONARY CAROL
Lead us "Heart-beat to
  Heart-beat"
Through soul constricting fears,
Up coldly treacherous mountains
Lone-viewed through scalding
  tears;

Beside a darkening fountain
Of satan's poisoned whims,
Or roughly strewn thorn-spears,
Which draw us close to "Him".

Contension's hot confusion;
The vice of car's concern;
Rejection's plaguing torture;
Fresh agonies that burn:

Lift the monstrous burden,
Mind-crushing load of care,
Escort through airy pavilions
To the calming temple of
  PRAYER.

John K. Crawford
LOVE, FOREVER

Dedicated to Bobbie:

Over and over my heart rejoices
Fed with pleasure of inner voices
For my pleasure is endless
  pleasure:
Filled with lasting, glorious
  treasure.
All my hopes are blended together
Safely bound for the changeful
  weather:
Sealed, secured for all the ages:
Spite the torrent where torrent
  rages!
Yes, my love will last forever.
Never you doubt, no never, never!

Thelma H. Lovedahl
REALITY
Between the dark and daylight
  there comes a time so sweet—
Half-waking and half-sleeping—
  where fact and fancy meet:

While my mind is still enthralled
  by poignant dreams of you,
The gray dawn lights my window
  and
  reality slips through.

For one enchanted moment
  the two of them entwine:
Reality as sharp as rue,
  dreams as sweet as wine.

Reality: You're far away
  across the trackless sea;
The dream: (turn back, relentless
  dawn!)
  last night you belonged to me!

Connie Garrison-Walker
Yes, I Mind If You Smoke!
Yes, I mind if you smoke!
I could gag
I might choke!
It burns my eyes
Circles round my thighs
Crawls up my nose
Runs down my pantyhose
Slides under my coat
And all around me I can see it
  float.
It gets tangled in my hair
Even in my underwear!
And the stench I can't even
  compare!
Take note . . .
  Yes, I mind if you smoke!

Dwight L. Hutchins
**Eternal Shame!
(Soliloquy On Human
  Rights)**
Broken spirits in
  anguish—seeking,
Groping, searching souls despair!
Tortured lives and bodies
  reeking—
Suffering people—everywhere!

Pleas for mercy, sobs of sorrow—
Shattered hopes and dreams long
  gone.
Muted cries for help tomorrow,
Brokenhearted—linger on!

"Whom are they—you dare to ask
  me?"
Milignant worms of Status—Quo!
Look about, can you not see

Blinded by your own ego's?
  touch their hearts—can you not
  feel them
Black and red and white alike?
Red blood flows, but passions'
  dimmed;
Creation of Societys' blight!

Rise among you—strong and
  fearless
Noble men to make wrongs right—
Remove injustice and remiss,
Crown them champions of
  freedoms' plight!

The end result? Lets' all be
  Brothers
No more hunger—strife—or hate!
"Dignify our lives with others,
Enjoin their hands and keep the
  faith!"

Harvey Godin
The Pigeons and the Bum
I sat in an old park today
  And watched the throng go by;
The sights were pleasing, I must
  say,
  So pleasing to the eye.
Young lovers strolling hand in
  hand,
  So jolly and so gay—
As though in an enchanted land
  They went their merry way.

Under a tree on a plank bench
  Sat a man neatly dressed,
His clothes were elegant and
  French,
  The finest and the best.
From a small bag of paper brown
  He drew a slice of bread
To lure the many pigeons down
  From branches overhead.

But these birds seemed to shy
  away
  With every move he made,
The reason why I cannot say,
  But they seemed quite afraid
After a while he left his seat
  As I thought he would do
And sauntered down the crowded
  street
  And disappeared from view.

Then came a man known as "the
  bum",
  A man without a name,
God only knows where he came
  from
  And God knows why he came.
His clothes were all tattered and
  torn,
  Like those worn by a clown—
I thought he looked sad and
  forlorn
  The poorest man in town.

I stood and watched him for a
  while
  And thought: what a disgrace.
Then I noticed a nice, warm smile
  Upon his bearded face.
And my dear friends this is a fact,
  This old man, from the dead,
Had his pockets fully packed
  With tiny crumbs of bread.

Near the same treet he squatted
  down
  And hummed a merry tune.
And the pigeons came swooping
  down
  As he began to croon.

I really couldn't understand
The mystery of it all,
He held them there at his
command,
They answered to his call.

All around him the pigeons cooed,
'Twas like a fairyland;
As they pecked at the precious
food
From his old, wrinkled hand.
To this man, branded as "no good",
Each crumb was like a gem;
I'm sure that these birds
understood
Each word he spoke to them.
Then he was gone, back to
nowhere,
That place where he'd come
from,
And the pigeons took to the air,
They'd gobbled every crumb.

There's one more thing I want to
say
Before my story ends—
They say he goes there every day
To meet his feathered friends.
Granted, I'm not as smart as
some,
I write in simple words,
But this I know, God chose that
bum
To feed His hungry birds.

Nancy Alexander
DEAR ONE
Yes, I know you are gone.
And I will never again touch your
dear face.
Still, in my dreams, your sweet
memory lingers on.
Quickening my heart with
thoughts of your embrace.
Yes, Dear One, I know you are
gone.
But your silent love, lives on.

Merideth Dawn Lewis
THE DANCER

*This poem was inspired by . . .
and written to . . . Rochelle Anne
Mackey*

She sits alone . . .

crying inside . . .
. . . slowly she ties the soft pink
satin to her ankles . . .

She stands . . . tall and proud . . .
but inside, she is falling down . . .
. . . then it happens . . .

The magical music flows slowly
into her . . .
. . . it comes very gently
enlightens her . . .

She begins to dance . . .
. . . each graceful move expresses
a part of her
some slow and gentle . . . some
harsh and cold

She dances till her music fades
away . . .
she stops in a daze for a
moment . . .
mixed emotions stir inside her . . .

The Dancer has a gift
. . . a beautiful expression . . .
of being herself . . .

Ben Gray
THE ETERNAL TIE

*FOR ELLEN Your hand is gentle
Your love is true*

When you enter a woman's space
You become her twin within the
heart
Gone the importance of yesterday
When joined a new life both
impart
The traits of each in exchanging
flow
Mold and shape with love's caress
Subtle changes wrought in mind
Till truely one and nothing less
The road is long with pitfalls
dark
and those who stumble are
quickly lost
Again to grope the road alone
empty of heart. Such a terrible
cost
While those who hold
companion hand
have riches surpassed nowhere
on earth
Made more secure by joining of
flesh
and the awesome pride of their
child's birth
Now the partners share old age
and cherish the past so filled
with love
There is no end, for well they
know
They will walk hand in hand the
road above

June Lee Box

June Lee Box
**Shopping Down South—In
San Francisco**
The western sun pokes sharp
fingers
Between the trunks of densely
growing
Giant Redwoods as we glide north
Up Highway One—O—One
The road dips from a hilltop
And we swoop like the grey
seagulls
By the side of the beach below
Curling waves tuck the sand
Tidily over driftwood debris
Trash and dune—buggy tire tracks
Disappear under the cleansing
water
'Quick! Look for Japanese glass
floats!'

Our highway soars again
Soon, we are turning eastward
Through denser sentinel stands
Branches interlace high overhead
Making a cool, dark tunnel
All sounds are muted
As woods life settles for sleep
Only to be shaken awake
By irreverent tires
As we make the last sharp turn
Into our own tree tunneled drive
Such a glorious ride
But how good to be Home!

Victoria L. Seabert
VOICE OF THE DARKNESS

*To my parents who agree with
me, Argue with me Laugh with,
and Encourage me, and most of all
love me. I love you both very
much!*

I stand forgotten in the silent
forages of time. The silvery
grey light of the moon trying to
hold onto me. Is it simply
trying to hold me? Is it trying
to save me from the Darkness?
Or is it trying to hold me
captive, as it is trying to make
me think the Dark is?
I hear a soft murmuring in my
ears, almost like that of the
wind moving through the trees.
Except it takes the form of
words and then I recognize the
voice, the voice is that of the
EVIL Darkness.

Sonia Convery
What Is Left For Me Now
What is left for me now
after you
What is out there now
someone new
But where is he
alone too
When will he come
replacing you
When will I know
answers are few
What is left for me now
but to forget you

Susan E. Cometa
ME & LESTER
You know that teddy bear you
gave me,
Lester, you said is his name.
I've been talking to him lately
and we've agreed things aren't the
same.
Lester asked me where you've
been,
Why you don't come 'round
much anymore.
He wants to know what's wrong
and if you still love us like before
Lester asked me why you don't
take me
to the places we used to go.
He asked me if you miss us,
I told him I don't know.
Lester knows you are the best
thing
that's ever happened in my life.
But I told him you'll never belong
to us
'cause you already have a wife.
He asked me when you'll come

see us
I told him I'm not sure.
He knows my life without you
is nothing but a bore.
My teddy bear and I are lonely
and we're not sure what to do.
The only thing we're sure of . . .
me & Lester will always love you.

Shirley Ann Weeks
THE MAN IN THE RAIN
He stood in the rain,
his shoulders slump, and drawn.
A shadow from the past,
reminiscense warm.
He took a step forward, with
outreach hands to touch.
A tree with a heart,
carved within its crust.
Letters spoke of love,
C. W. loves S. D.
A revery of love,
he will never again see.
He comes once a year,
from a very distant place.
Just to be near,
a past he can't erase.

Charles R. Moses
CELESTIAL NIGHTS
Rising far above the terrestrial sky
Forever starward am I bound
Following the path of my inner eye
A new standard have I found

Celestial nights without number
Eternal journey entered on
A symphony of sight in my
slumber
Should I awake all will be gone

Mrs. Hazel Cherry
PROOF'S OF GOD
How do we know God is really
there?
Should we be relieved or should
we have fear?
If you don't know the answers,
check it out
And find out what life is really
all about.
What makes a daisy grow?
What makes the wind blow?
What makes the world turn?
What makes your brain work
so you can learn?
The answer to these questions
really aren't odd.
The answer to all four of them is
the answer, God.

Michael L. Hiatt
GO TO SLEEP
Go to sleep baby your daddy's
right here,
and don't worry babe I'm not
going no where.
I'll still be here when the sun
finds you sleeping,
so go to sleep now so you won't
see me weeping.

Go to sleep darling I promise
tonight I'll stay at your side,
Because this last night with you I
won't be denied.
You see when morning comes
you and mommy will be leaving,
and all I can do is sit around
grieving.

You see this is the last time I'll
kiss you goodnight,
this is the last time I'll feel your

arms as they hug me so tight,
I know this is my lastnight with
your mother too,
but even so it is my wish to
spend my last night with you.

Now it's morning and on the
nightstand I see your mothers
rings
and now I face the heartache this
new morning brings,
As I watch the car and you drive
away,
I drift back to sleep still wishing
you'd stay.

Carrie Leetham White
IF I BUT BRING
If I but bring one moment of joy
to an aching heart,
If I but bring one second of solace
e're I depart,
If one poor heart is lightened
because of the song I sing,
Then to myself as to others great
happiness I bring.
You cannot live for others and
find time to cry alone,
So if I share another's woe, there's
no time for my own.
So if my own life may not be the
way I wish it might,
If I can ease another's heart, my
own heart will be light.
If I can give but one poor soul his
courage to regain
His love of life, my own life will
not have been lived in vain.

Cathy Kemp
MEMORIES
A memory happens only once,
  And then it's a thing of the past.
But it is not gone forever,
  It becomes a memory.
Memories remind you of good,
  and of bad,
  Of the happy times, and of the
  sad.
Memories remind you of things
  you regret,
  And of things you never want to
  forget.
Memories remind you of how
  you once cared,
  And of the love you once shared.

Cathy McCornack
ALL THAT WE SHARED
We shared our secrets
  crazy dreams
we shared our plans
  crazy schemes
we shared the problems
  lonely days
we shared our habits
  crazy ways
we shared the happiness
  all the fun
we shared the sand
  summer sun
we shared the sunshine
  summer rain
we shared the love
  now, the pain.

Debbie Johnson Philpot
HOME
The smell of ham and beans
  cooking on the stove.
Apothecary jars filled with herbs
  and spices and, even some clove.
The fresh clean smell of the wet

shinning floor,
That's just been mopped from
  door to door.
On the breath of my toddler is
  the aroma of a chocolate bar.
Weak is my stomach as I smell
  the street being repaired with
  tar.
The baby is crying for attention.
There goes the tea kettle, a noisy
  invention.
Crash! As daughter tries to set
  the table.
The blaring stereo, to hear,
  sometimes I wish were unable.
The soft heart warming words of
  my husbands love.
On the roof I hear the cooing of a
  dove.
I like to watch my family outside.
Can they see my pride?
Watching my husband read.
Giving to my families every need.
I know I can always come back
  home.
When theres no place else to roam.

Anette Napolitan Reeves
SEED OF LOVE
No matter who we are or what we
  will be
Inside each of us exists a special
  quality.
It's the ability of knowing when
To reach out and touch someone
  again.
It's the anticipating of seeing one
  face
Though not sure where in a
  crowded place.
It's the feeling of warmth deep
  inside
Even when the temperature's
  begun to slide.
It's as fulfilling to give as to
  receive
Sharing that kiss when you arrive
  or leave.
It's the promise to one your
  whole life through
When those cherished words
  spoken are "I do."
It's found in families, friends, and
  lovers
Seen in a mother over babes she
  hovers.
It's often confused, misused, and
  abused
By those afraid to truly let it be
  used.
Yet no matter how much we deny
  'this need
We search for those who'll plant
  our seed . . .
        the seed of love.

Iwao Mizuta
Song Of The Golden Girl
O my love is a golden girl
So gentle as moonbeams
On dancing dark waters,
  Reflecting her smile.
I look on her face
  That mirrors a soul
So sweet and so restful
  Stir not with a sigh!
I seek her quick glance
  To water the blooms

That blow in the garden
  A-thirst in my soul.
I'll miss her so tender
  If leave me she must.
Time's breath will be stilled,
  Then my world it will pale.

O my love is a golden girl
  So gentle as sunbeams
A-chasing the shadows
  Of red breaking dawn.
The world from her glows,
  All round her she draws.
So good and so graceful,
  Let no sad thoughts fall!

Vicky M. Semones
I FOUND YOU

For My Soul-Mate

Lovely lady in blue
  with crystal eyes of dew,
  I found you by the Monterey
  shore,
    alone with the Sandpaper.

Lovely lady in blue.
  with hair of golden hue,
  I found you—watching the
  Shorebird's run,
    hidden from the morning sun.

Lovely lady in blue
  denying what was true,
  I found you—a kiss—then, to
  depart:
    wounding eager, tender hearts.

Lovely lady in blue
  seeking a clearer view,
  I found you centered in my soul,
    sharing visions—being whole.

Betty Schmitt
THE INVESTMENT
Hordes of tourists swarmed over
  snarled jungle roots,
  while from the distant mauve
  buttes
floated haunting strains of a steel
  calypso band—
  Echoes of a people at peace with
  their land.
Primitive brown inhabitants, in
  their nudity unashamed
danced joyfully to music
  fittingly unnamed.
Then the desecration began.
  Natives soon learned from the
  jingling in the outstretched
  hand.
Lush green mountainsides were
  trampled and torn asunder;
  Grass-thatched huts and
  villages, tourists did plunder;
Virginal white beaches all
  littered and strewn:
  A primeval society bent on
  decay and ruin.
From the island the prim and
  proper visitor swiftly retreated—
  as childlike innocence and
  vestal beauty were defeated . . .
  The begging, the filth, drove
  them away—
    They say . . .
But they would never realize,
  Had they not chosen to
  materialize,
  Paradise would have
  remained—
    Intact and Unchanged.

Jeanne Kalben
THE DANCER
Someone told you about her, a
  stranger standing in the dark.
And though you never saw her,
  you think she might of stole
  your heart.
Yet, I am your dancer, you take
  me everywhere you go,
And though you never met her,
  you think you've needed her so.

Still, I let the dance continue, as
  you twirl me across the floor,
Introducing me to strangers, then
  you walk me to the door.
You say that you'll be busy
  chasing shadows and
  somethings,
But soon we'll be dancing to that
  same old melody.

But lately I've been thinking
  about myself and my dreams,
And I'm no longer contented with
  rainbows and moonbeams.
So I wrote you a letter, telling
  you straight from my heart,
That it was love that I yearned
  for and not the dancer's part.

So caught up in your dazzle,
  stardust blinded my eyes,
For the dancer I portrayed, was
  only my disguise.
I guess you didn't believe me, no,
  you couldn't think it true
That a girl, just like me, could be
  saying this to you.

I'll no longer be your dancer, no, I
  won't play that part.
You see, I'm only a stranger
  standing in the dark . . .

Marisa Lombardo
suicide
numb from exploding emotions
fear of an unknown world yet
desire to explore tranquill passages
crimson blood drips in isolated
  drops off
the tip of a cold steel blade
scarlet puddles form and
  encompass
the dead body as his soul
soars through the wounds
to escape its slavery
flying into an infinite stage of
  peace.

Louise S. Yates
October In West Virginia
Lazily white clouds sail across
  October's azure sky,
A bright autumn sun casts its
  golden beams
Across the calico colors of the
  mountains lofty and high
Above the valley's fields of gold
  and harvest greens.

Great hawks leisurely soar above
  the lofty peaks
Of calico mountains looming so
  tall,
Seeming to touch the billowy
  cloud that seeks
To linger above the crest of
  mountain wall.

Earth has donned her many
  colored robe
Of orange-yellows, reds, browns
  and green

Ceremoniously October frosts
   tries to probe
At each lingering sign of
   summer's green.

Linger on, oh bright October; do
   not hurry to flee
For you are a symbol of the
   vanishing year
Announcing the coming of
   winter, year's end; you see
You are West Virginia's symbol of
   Autumnal mystery.

Ferenc Karpati
LONGING
I want to see you in my
   dreams. . .

See your eyes, your face, your
   hair,
Your happiness and despair.
I want to see you everywhere,
Everywhere in my dreams . . .

Are you coming?

Elizabeth Medrano Rodriguez
LIVES ARE TORN APART
See all the broken lights
Two and three ways make it right
See all the visions of red
Floating all through your head
Hear all the broken hearts
   Lives are torn apart

Hear all the sounds of sorrow
Screaming will there be a
   tomorrow?
Danger strikes when their
   offended
The wounds not always clearly
   mended
People always asking why
Still around you hear the cries
When the battle start
   Lives are torn apart

Alive you're lying in your bed
While others on the street are
   dead
Wounds that leave a scar
And machine guns not too far
With all the ugly sights
Makes you wonder—where's the
   light
Counting the lost ones on a chart
Hear the cryings of broken hearts
Cause lives are torn apart
Through all the signs
Of fate in times
   Lives are torn apart

Nellie V. Coberley
HEAVEN
We read of a place called heaven
From the bible so good and true
Where Jesus is up there waiting
Just to welcome me and you.

They say the walls are pure jasper
The streets are made of pure gold
The angels are up there waiting
Around the great white throne.

I want to be ready to meet him
When He comes from His home
   in the sky
To rapture all of His children
To live with Him there by and by.

If you want to live in that city
You must be born again
Be sure your sins are forgiven
And be washed in the blood of
   the Lamb.

Geraldine Bear
MY GEEN HOUSE

*I received the inspiration for this
poem from my grandson Brian
Bear at the age of three.
Therefore, I am dedicating it to
him.*

I love you Gan Ma. Come, come
   in my geen house.
I have a light and lots of toys,
   besides a TV set.
Curtains that you can close
And a bed so you can rest.

We can make a choo choo with
   my blocks
And go to Chattanooga,
Or drive there in my little geen
   car,
It has a horn that goes ooga, ooga.

Come, come in my geen house.
I have coffee and tea for you—
With keem and suga if you like
And lots of cookies too.

I don't like you any more,
You can go away and don't come
   back!
'Cause you won't come to see—
The things I have in my geen
   house,
That I cooked for you and me.

I sorry, I love you Gan Ma.

Gwendolyn Trimbell Pease
AMERICA'S LIFE BLOOD

*Dedicated especially to the
fourteen members of the
Castleton Busy Beavers 4-H Club
of Castleton, N.Y. I have been
their proud Leader for eighteen
years. Past members, successful
adults.*

America' life blood, its youth
who find things difficult city or
   farm
mightily striving for honesty and
   truth
of highest kind, safe protection
   from all harm

last world melting pot this
   continued Mecca
conglomerated enormously vast
   nation
its life blood, the youth of America
hopefully awaiting future joyous
   occasion

from farm, seashore and
   mountain tall
life blood of America, its youth
preserving environment intact for
   all
struggling forcefully nail, claw
   and tooth

life's blood of youth is America
upcoming individuals must band
   together
forming bonds stronger then
   modern formica
a great country's headed toward
   fair weather

lessons of the past well absorbed
   today
growing rapidly to blossom from
   new bud
powerful peace forever we
   fervently pray
youth of America, its life blood.

Lena R. Bailey
YE FOOLISH MAN

*To Willard, my husband who
encouraged me. To my Creator,
for allowing me to serve Him in
my own small way. To my
Children and Grandchildren.*

Oh man, oh foolish mortal man
ye cry beauty ye have created,
   and so ye have.
Beauty of wood, metal and
   stone—
works of art ye say, and so they
   are.
But brag not foolish man,
For when I cometh ye shall
   behold
The Great Creator of creation its'
   self.
The master worker who created
   all lasting beauty
Before ye were spoken into
   existence
Take heed foolish man
For thy beauty will pass into
   oblivion
Thus speaketh your True God
I, who breathed life into every
   living thing
I the Master of Heaven, yea the
   very universe
Tremble now foolish man
For behold ye shall soon see my
   beauty
As I descend from the clouds in
   Glory
Oh how small ye are
In sight of Master of all
Yea Master even of thee,
   Ye foolish man.

Mark T. Razor
THE HUNT
We walk.
she runs
across pastures and fields.
We watch her run
   the slalom
      of harvested
   stalks
Then hunt
the thicket for
feathered treasure.
We await the moment when . . .
   shh!
She's picked up a scent.

There's a bird in that thicket
we know by the way
she lifts her right forepaw
and holds her tail motionless,
outward projected.
   Whoa girl!

We approach the covert
with caution and
   care
Then! she flushes the covey

In an instant they have flown off.
but two fell
We retrieve our trophies,
praise the real hunter
with a pat on the head
   then
      move
         on

Mary Eileen Henry
Lonely Cries In the Dark Of Night
Like lonely cries in the dark of
   night,
People keep searching everywhere;
But no one promised they'd see
   the light.

Death challenges life to its fight
While mocking laughter shatters
   the air,
Like lonely cries in the dark of
   night.

The blindest of eyes regaining
   their sight
Struggle madly to look anywhere;
But no one promised they'd see
   the light.

Children whose futures may
   never be bright,
Breathe sighs of hunger too hard
   to bear
Like lonely cries in the dark of
   night.

The elderly's hopes have aged to
   white,
Weariness, the expression they
   wear;
But no one promised they'd see
   the light.

Society has fallen from its
   wingless flight
And the people are shouting their
   desperate prayer
Like lonely cries in the dark of
   night;
But no one promised they'd see
   the light.

Lynn Watson
LOVE
Love is really powerful
It comes all over your body
Like heat from the sun
First you're in dreamland
You suddenly drift away
You find yourself nowhere
Bring yourself back to reality
When you get halfway back
You'll wonder where you've been
Love isn't the answer
But then you wonder what is.

Alan Baron
MY WIFE IS A RAINBOW
My wife is a rainbow
her colors are my heart
my very breathing
her love fills up any room I'm in
when I kiss her lips

my heart surges with
  incomparable joy
my wife is a rainbow
her colors are the universe
my life, my very breathing
her love is my meaning, my
  answer
she paints my world
with warm loving colors
one glance from her eyes
and I know
my wife is a rainbow

Madeline L. Harcourt
IN REVERIE

*To my father, John T. Harcourt,
Sr. who died on July 30, 1983.*

Childhood memories in the
  warmth of the summer

In reverie, I remember.

You were a simple, yet complex
  man
Vulnerable in ways, yet strong in
  your convictions
You were a dreamer, and
  dreamers never die.

You were a man of few words,
  who gave in your creative spirit
  to those you loved
You gave to me your quiet
  manner, your creative nature;

Now that you are gone, I feel the
  pain of separation . . . isolation.

How I long for the summer again,
  and you.

In reverie.

Shirley Hamilton
A LITTLE BOYS WORLD

*To Joshua And David My
Grandsons*

A little boy's world is a place to
  have fun
To dig, to climb, to jump and run.
He's as venturesome as the games
  he plays
And as timeless as each one of
  his carefree days.
It's filled with everyday things he
  likes
Puppies, ice cream, football and
  bikes.
Things that roll or crawl or fly,
Paths to explore, double dares to
  try.
It's a place that he will learn what
  he needs to know
To laugh, to think, to watch and
  grow.
For a little boy's world as small as
  it seems
Is as bright as the future and as
  high as his dreams

Sharon Lee Moss
PROMISES

Once I loved you, with all my
  heart,
But my feelings meant nothing to
  you.
You were so determined to tear
  me apart,
But I could never see what you
  were trying to do.

You acted as if you loved me for
  just a little while.
Why couldn't I see your promises
  were all lies.
You said you'd never leave, that
  wasn't your style,
And repeated it often until you
  whispered good-bye.

You're out of my life now, I guess
  for good.
You left me here all alone,
Just like you promised you never
  would,
But now your lying traits have
  shone.

You promised me the moon and
  stars above,
When all I really received were
  heartaches.
I never wanted promises, all I
  wanted was love.
I thought I found it, but your
  feelings were all fakes.

Laura Lambe Burrell
FOOL'S WHIMSEY

*For all those who have a cringe
for fantasy in the absurd.
Especially for my daughter,
Heather and my dog. Missy-Fool's
Whimsey!!!*

I saw a beheaded specter in my
  room
Spirits floating around one by one
The kings and queens of long ago
What in the world is going on?
And I skim past lewis Carroll's
Alice and Wonderland
With eyes like a chesire cat's you
  can see all
And the mad hatter raced down
  the hill,
Alice popped up
And I doze off to sleep
Only to await for a new journey
  into
Never never land with a new
  character, yet,
Nonetheless, Peter Pan.

Thomas R. Schneider
OUR WORLD

*For all those committed to
protecting our world.*

Our world is a planet
Where all forms co-exist
And where no-one takes more
Than they give

It is quite different
From our Society

We have designed our society
And we have left no room for our
  world
Soon our society will devour our
  world
And when our world is gone
We will have no place to keep
Our society.

Terri Anne Say
MUSIC MAN

He's out all night just playing his
  songs,
the beat still fresh in his mind.

A music man and nothing more.
The best you'll ever find.

Now this young guy is tall and
  lean
he wears a perfect smile.
Oh, if you're ever in his town
please stop and listen awhile.

He plays trombone and trumpet
  too,
a bit of piano on the side.
He'll give you jazz or rock 'n roll
and both he does with pride.

So, next time you're down and
  feeling blue
but doing the best that you can,
just lie back, close your eyes
and think of the music man.

Elisabeth Boyle
COMA

*I would like to dedicate this to
Steve for sharing the experience
that allowed me to write this
poem.*

Why am I here?
Why can't I move?
What are all these tubes?
Why do people always poke and
  probe?
Why can't they leave me alone?
I can still feel,
I'm still alive,
But when I cry no one sees,
And when I speak no one hears;
I hear people talk and cry,
Why can't they understand?
I hear, I see, I feel,
But no one is aware;
Why can't I move?
Why am I here?
When can I go home?

Jennifer Wong
DESIRE TO DEPENDENCE

She paces
backandforthbackandforth
in a cage molded hysterically—
of her cold steel tears.
She shivers
andcriesanddiesandmoans—

Eyes
Flash!
and teeth glitter—

He used to feed her
with chunks of meat
cut from his own body,
to satisfy her;
to keep her happy.
But, the ecstacy was always brief
and she would just
droolandlickherteethandstretch—
herclawsandwantmore.
She throws back her head
andcriesanddiesandmoans—

She starves now he is gone;
no one will sate any of her—

Tammy Jeanne Bentley
GOD'S WILL

God has never let me down,
  I know he never will.
He's given me strength and
  helped me live
Forever learning, still.

Sometimes it's hard to understand
Just what God wants me to do

But if I only Listen,
The understanding will shine
  through!

Life is a forever of Learning
And I thank God for the rain,
He shows me, I am special,
And all my pain is gain.

I love the Lord with all my heart,
And pray he'll guide me on
Forever and always seeking to
  find
His Love and Life so strong.

June Lee Box
June Lee Box
**Polly Plankton—First
  Libber**
Down in the deepest part of the
  ocean
Swims a tiny one-celled sea
  creature
Foes live in shells or sway with
  the motion
(She's their prey whatever their
  feature.)
Polly Plankton knew not of
  Women's Lib
As she floated seductively by
When swerving to dodge a Sea
  Urchin's nib
She teased: "Ought to aim better,
  Wise Guy!"
The cool green water surged this
  way and that
Over high reefs, through a narrow
  gap
(Polly just missed where a Sea
  Lily sat
His curled petals all ready to
  trap.)
An old sunken ship had hit on
  that reef
Now with barnacled ribs all awry
Held encrusted sea chests from
  that old grief
And warped waves that caused
  Polly to cry:
"HELP! A WHIRLPOOL! Her
  sudden stab of fright
Eased, as she chased a chip that
  came near
Hoisted a leg over and held on
  tight
Once safely on board, she lost her
  fear
Determined to win her struggle
  for life
She seized a stick to use as an oar
And shot her skiff far away from
  the strife
"I DID IT! I BEAT THAT
  SURGING BORE!"

Our World's Best Loved Poems

Roberta Waldron
MY LIGHT
When things go wrong, and life
looks gray
I say a prayer and my light shines
he guides me on throughout the
day
and warms my heart with love
devine.
My light!

He gives me forgiveness in my
heart
for others who do me wrong
and helps me to see their trials
too,
and shows me how to help them
in a vision, feeling or song.
How wonderful his might.
My light!

When sorrow and depression
strikes
I get on my knees and pray
he always answers, though it may
not be,
exactly what I thought he'd say
He will always answer me,
My light!

If only each day we'd stop to pray
for forgiveness and love devine
he's share his grace with each one
and make his love to shine.
My light!

Early each morning if we call on
him
our trials would be so few.
He'd pave a path, and light the
way
and lead us right on through.
My light!

Karlene Jansa
IT SHOWS IN YOUR FACE

---

*I wish to dedicate this poem to
my children who gave me the
inspiration to write and to GOD
who gave me the talent to write.*

You don't have to tell how you
live each day;
You don't have to say if you work
or play.
A tried true thermometer serves
in the place.
However you live it shows in
your face.
The false, the lies, that you bear
in your heart
Will not stay inside where it first
got its' start.
Blood and muscle are a thin veil
of lace—
what you wear in your heart, you
wear in your face.
If your life is unselfish, if for
others you live,
Not how much you get, but how
much you give.
If you live close to GOD and his
infinite grace,
You won't have to tell, it shows
in your face.

Mrs. Vicki Roberts
Forever, You'll Be Mine
I remember yesterday
when we were so young
everything excited me,
everything you'd done

We spent time together
that really was fun
loving in the moonlight
dancing in the sun

But to soon it all had
to end, and
believe me love, my
heart will never mend

Now my days are filled
with time
remembering your words,
forever, you'll be mine.

Ruth Garms Terry
PIPE OF PEACE
Manitou made use of clay
From the Pipestone Quarry in an
early day
That the universal pipe of peace
Be shared and strife might cease.

If harmony is to abide
There is no place for greed and
pride.
We shape the pipe of peace today
By molding common clay.

Ruth A. Neubert
THE FRUIT OF THE SPIRIT
The fruit of the Spirit is love that
never fails.
Its depth we cannot plumb nor its
heights ever scale.

Joy unspeakable and full of His
glory
Is the portion for those who
believe His story.

There is a peace that passeth all
understanding
In the midst of turmoil when life
is demanding.
—Longsuffering too shines forth
when nerves would be frayed.
Gentleness the manner when
harshness doth invade.

—We see goodness come forth at
all times from the heart,
Even though old Satan may be
hurling his darts.

Faith will not falter when there is
nothing in sight,
And meekness will reign even
though in the lime light.

So will temperance be exercised
through out the day,
Because the Spirit of God is
having His way.

Kent Sommers
PRAYER
Oh, Lord,
Why is it so hard
To stay in Thy service?
You seem to love my friends—
Please, love me, too . . .
Please, love me, too;
Amen.

K. Danette Arden
MY ROOM
Sitting in my room,
looking out, always wishing
to be set free.
Sitting in my room,
the room, which in many ways
is my prision.
Sitting in my room
I wish I were someone else,
just so I knew, that I could
be like everyone else.

Sitting in my room
a room which has no walls,
has no floor,
or a ceiling.
This room,
prision,
is in my mind.
I sit in this room when things are
bad,
or I just need time to think.
But, sitting in this room
is lonely.
For no one else can join me.
I don't even know if anyone
would want to join me.
Sitting in my room is my cry for
help.
hoping someone will hear.
I need help while sitting in my
room,
for there are times when I wonder
if I will be able to let myself out
While sitting in my room,
I wonder if anyone else holds the
key.
Sometimes I lose my key and I
can't get out.
I hope some has a key.

Jacqueline M. Jones
**Reach Out For Muscular
Dystrophy**

---

*I especially dedicate this poem to
my stepfather, Richard; my dear
friend, Gloria; and to all others
afflicted with the various muscle
and spinal diseases.*

Reach out
lend a hand
show a little love
let the people who have this
disease
know that you understand

Let your heart run free and wild
show that you care
with pledges well spent
help will always be there

Muscular Dystrophy
wheelchairs and braces
affecting the body in various
places

Please take part
get to a phone
think of what you'd do if the next
child affected with M.D. was your
own!

Victor Stringer
HERO
He cruises down the highway,
late everynight,
hair combed back, shades on right.
His ride is fast, sits real low,
reflects no light, but shines like
gold.
In every little town, between here
and there,
whispers are passed, fears in the
air.
People all know him, they hide
from his sight,
his name is Hero, he's a phantom
in the night.
He was a rebel, in the local towns,
just looking for fun, always
fooling around.
Late one night, the law came by,

looking for Hero, wouldn't say
why.
They found him on a back road,
running fast,
the law wanted the boy, they had
him at last.
Now the story has it, he died that
night,
in a firey crash, during a
desperate flight.
His spirit was strong, it would
not end,
so he came back, on the midnight
wind.
Now you can see him, late
everynight,
hair combed back, shades on
right.

Janet Smith
SILENCE
Silence is a state of quiet,
And that should state the case,
But the quality of silence can be
so changed,
By the look on someone's face.

The silence of companionship
Is a warm and pleasant thing,
And the fact that there are no
words,
Does not hold a sting.

The silence of the terminally shy,
Is covered in neon blushes,
Painfully marked by downcast
eyes,
Spaced by words in rushes.

The silence of hostility,
Is a far more terrible thing.
The very air seems to quiver
With the anger no words may
bring.

Yet the silence of God's woods at
night,
When the stars are shining,
Silver bright,
Is a tranquillity worth finding.

Barbara F. Alaimo
THE PIGEONS
I love to watch the pigeons fly, so
pure and oh so white.
Flying along like a box kite, they
really are a sight
But when they get too close, they
give me such a fright.
Because sometimes even a
pigeon, is less than polite.
OOOH NOOO!

Sherrie A. Keppler
TIME

---

*I would like to dedicate this
poem to the two people who have
inspired my writing the most . . .
my mother and father.*

What is time
If not past
How much time
Will time last

Is all time
To be lost
Can you buy time
What would time cost

Time would be worthless
If time were bought
Time in flight
Cannot be caught

91

John Campbell, Editor & Publisher

Time has brought
Many much sorrow
But gives to others
A happy tomorrow

Time will take
And also give
Life from some
So others may live.

Anza LoPresti Myers
LITTLE MAN

This poem was written to-and inspired by-my son Gary, and dedicated also to my son Anthony.

My little man,
  There's nothing he can't do;
He thinks the world is his.

A new discovery,
  A new accomplishment,
Anything daddy can do
He can do just as well,
Drive a car, fish, hunt and work;
  His day is full of hard, hard labor.

But hush you all now,
  'Cause my little man is fast
  asleep,
And sleep won't keep.
  And all his dreams
He'll work upon tomorrow.

His dreams are tall,
  Taller than he,
But who could tear down
  Such a strong will,
Of my little man.

Janice C. Dillman
Where Did My Childhood Go

Where did my childhood go, it
  went so very fast
Turned around and I am grown,
  an adult I am at last
Childhood songs I no longer sing,
  no more games to play
All the toys and the old doll
  house is neatly put away
The things I should have done,
  when I was young and free
The dreams and wishes I once
  had, were never meant to be
Where is the happiness that filled
  my heart
It all disappeared, everything now
  is torn apart
Pretending became reality, make-
  believe is dead
Now worrys and problems, the
  endless tears are shed
I know we all must get old, but
  why so very fast
If only sweet childhood could last.

Sue Blythe
TIME IS ESSENCE

To my daughters, Soinnie and Suzette as they haven't yet realized "Time is essence"

My soul cries out hurry don't wait
tomorrow may be too late.
The tentacles of fate watch with
  half closed eyes
your time to jeopardize.
Leopard-coloured spots lying in
  wait.

Morpheus impetuously awaits
  oblivion.
Today can change tomorrow
but not yesterday.

Mrs. Fern Roche
HE KEEPS WATCH
If to war you have to go,
There is something you should
  know.
You should memorize the 91st
  Psalm
It will help you to keep calm.
Remember to repeat it every day.
The dear Lord will know what
  you say.
Just that Psalm and that alone,
Brought an entire regiment safely
  home.

Nicolai Stefan Popescu
Aloneness (Sic Transit Gloria Mundi)
I sometime feel my solitude so
  near at hand
its starting point to be
  complete—the end
things become alien
I am no longer calm enough to
  draw myself
from the heart throbbing and
keep their poise.

The town I live has stopped to be
  itself
its personality—its name lying
  fictitious
I no longer have the guts—the
  wish to impress upon its
  stones . . .
I see its structures reduced to
  their constituent parts:
bricks
stone and glass as lifeless heaps
and nothing to choose among
  themselves.
(The water: eternal
blind
anterior to the town
exterior
unconscious of any kings and
  artists . . .)
A place where I have just arrived
  and doesn't know me yet
a place I soon shall leave and has
  forgotten me by now . . .
I couldn't tell it anything about
  myself
I could spare nothing of myself
  imprinted upon it
It left me dwarfed:
A heart that throbbed
attention strained—
and that's not all.

Lori Marie Garwick Sprouls
MY EYES
I wonder sometimes
When you look at my eyes
Can you see the love
That is growing inside?
My heart, my body,
And all throughout me
Are bursting with the love
That you have set free.
Your eyes seem to say it
Like mine always do
"I Love You eternally
And you love me too."
So next time we're together
Just look at my eyes
And see all the love

That is growing inside.
Silent, yet speaking
As eyes sometimes do
They're just simply saying
I LOVE YOU!

Shawna Roth
If I Was In Charge Of the World
If I was in charge of the world
there wouldn't be snakes or bugs.
There wouldn't be spiders or
crosswords in school.

If I was in charge of the world
there wouldn't be homework after
  school.
Teachers would give kids candy
  if the class was good.
NO BROTHERS!

If I was in charge of the world
candybars would be one cent.
You wouldn't have colds!
Moms and dads wouldn't have to
  go to work.

If I was in charge of the world
kids would get free time once a
  day.
Teachers would get a two week
  vacation,
If I was in charge of the world.

Angela Deannette Daniels
REMINISCENCE
I try to think of words to say
But I just can't sort them out.
I think I'm going crazy
I'm so full of pain and doubt.
I don't know where I'm coming
  from
Or where I'm going to,
Sometimes I wonder if anyone
  knows
Just what I'm going through.

For several months I've tried to
  let go
Of the past that I still hold,
But my memories just won't let
  me
Still to them my heart feels cold
I write my lonely lyrics
On the pages of my life;
But those pages are too hard to
  turn,
They only read pain and strife.
I write my thoughts on paper
To help me feel at ease within.
When I feel the need of finding
  myself
I can read them all over again.
If problems arise that I can't
  handle,

I can look later and see
That the poetry I write reflects
  my feelings
And the answers could be there
  for me.

Christine Harris
THE KISS
I took the kiss
you gave me
and placed it in
my heart
That special kiss
you gave me
gave my day a
pleasant start!
When I think of you
the sun shines
and makes that kiss
so real
there are so many
words to write
but none tell how
I feel.

Margaret McGraw
THE FLY
Funnels, timeless
endless tunnels
hidden webs
trap the fly
I fly
through webs
of tangled deceit
we run
through endless
funnels timeless

Fara L. Belt
VIOLETS IN THE SPRING
No more waiting for violets in
  the spring,
Or the joys that life can bring.
They are gone, they'll never come
  again,
Now only thoughts of what could
  have been.
Love was full when we wed for
  life,
I was so glad to be his loving
  wife.
As he placed upon my finger that
  ring,
Angels in Heaven began to sing.
Happiness stayed for three years
  or maybe four,
Then the angels stopped their
  singing forevermore.
For one day he, in pain, died,
And for the precious love I lost, I
  Now I must live my life alone,
With no place to call my own.
Nowhere to hide from worldly
  harms,
How I wish I could be in his
  loving arms,
Waiting for violets in the spring.

Jewell M. Delatorre
LOVE'S, A RARE DISEASE
"LOVE is a rare disease;
Once you've had it—
just never leaves . . .
You search diligently,
for a moments peace.

"LOVE is a splendored thing.
The grass is greener—
as it seems.

So release my heart,
I want to start;
to love again.

Even though,
You're not here.
I needed to know,
You were near.

So I haven't—
Lost my touch, entirely.

Is it stupidity?
Still wanting you beside me;
The second time around.

Then you'll believe,
fate rolls the dice.
Can we "Love",
Same persons twice? . . .

I'm Still, needing you!

Christine Y. Chadwick
LIFE'S SHADOWS AND SUN

*Dedicated to those, who having
lived in the Shadows Of Life
formerly, can now look forward
to living in Life's Sun!*

Oft' I wonder why I'm here . . .
(Is this the thought of fool or
seer?)
Sometimes, I really shed a tear
Because of problems that I fear!

I wonder if I'm doing right,
And pray for helpful, guiding
light,
For courage, strength and real
insight,
And for the will to keep up the
fight!

I worry that others I may offend,
That longtime freindships I may
rend,
Causing broken hearts I cannot
mend,
Or that I'm short of help to lend.

Yet every time in all this daze
I look above through brightening
haze,
And begin to pass the tearful
phase,
For there's One who helps my
spirit to raise!

Any remaining doubts I shake,
Plan the dinner I'd better bake,
Remember the yard I need to
rake,
Or go for a healthy swim in the
lake!

Then soon I find my mind is
clear—
Yes, there's more to Life than fear;
I wipe away one final tear,

Knowing Life is precious and
dear!

Maria G. Cavazos-Santana
SHE CRIES
Have been crying all day and
wondering why,
I can't look through the clouds
and see the sky.
We look at each other—I feel so
dry,
Knowing being number two will
always be my surprise.

In the morning when I arise,
I always feel so very wise.
Yet knowing that by nightfall,
Fears that hide tears will be the
disguise,
With which I cover my demise.

Jeanie K. Shaffer
LOST IN THE DARK
Young, blond, and taking from
life
with a brash way of walking
and a laugh like a knife.

You were not yet seventeen
but your life was laid out
you took all you could, and ruled
like a queen.

When the time came with
nothing else planned
you left in your place a death
notice,
written in your own hand.

The only sound in that darkest of
night
was the roaring of rain and the
shattering of glass, snuffing out
light.

Steven L. Williams
LADY (gone)

For Cheryl Dionne

It is late.
Night has swept the sun
from my bed,
I am lost in its darkness.
Slowly, I reach out,
searching for the soft
warmth of you
next to me.
But even the blackness
does not hide the fact
that you have gone.
I bury myself in my pillow . . .
knowing full well
I will dream of you.
And miss you more
in the morning.

Ronald Oldfield
VENDERS CUP

*To a world of inspiration and
new beginnings and a journey
that knows no end*

Rainbow mists on snowcap pearl
that ascends from mounds on
high
cascading swollen waters that
fills thy venders cup
lay wide your green laid valleys
cut deep your precious glen
mold your endless journey
that feeds the soul of man

Cathy G. Thomas
BEAUTY IS . . .

*I dedicate this poem to my family
Glenn, Christy and Christopher,
in loving memory of my mother.*

Beauty is watching the stars
come out at night, while sitting
on the rocks, listening to the
surf crash below . . . with sand
running thru your toes, ocean
breezes in your hair.

Beauty can be gazing upon the
full lit moon, late at night . . .
Beauty is sitting by a cozy fire
hearing thunder and lightening,
knowing your safe inside.

Maybe beauty is drifting farout at
sea, away from everyday life,
but to me;
Beauty is being with the one
person you love and whom
loves you . . . to share all lifes
treasures, with such great
pleasure . . .

Living life to its fullest, and one
day you bring your first born
into this world, what a precious
feeling of joy!

Beauty then is knowing you have
created; you are a creator
through Gods gift.
The two of us in our splendor
have found beauty together.

Beauty is our own creation . . .
and this I have . . .
created for you.

Margie Edwards
HEAVEN'S DOOR

*(Dedicated to Bryon, Bruce,
Robert, and Bill—I love you all)*

Can you tell the words of the
Bird's song?
Is your life a pattern of
RIGHT, or wrong?
Can you see the tiny patterns
In the snow?
Who put them there? Or do
You know?

There is a code to Heaven's
Door, and it is heaven—sent.
Well didn't you know, the
Code is—R—E—P—E—N—T.
But, if you want the code to
Hell.
There's none—without salvation,
It's the station, where you fell.

Now here's to the bird's song,
The snow, and all sweetness.
And my love, I pray you find
Eternal happiness.
Never go the way of sin and
Apathy, the way some others
went.
The code to love and life
Forever, is repent.

Elsie Day Cruthirds
AMERICA FIRST
America First! Slogan of the hour!
We hear it so often day after day.
Do we mean America first in
power,

Or do we mean in a Christ-like
way?
Do mere material matters count?
Should we flaunt in the strength
of a giant?
Or isn't it things of God's Spirit,
And not just in feelings defiant?

It's showing our great
understanding,
Our sympathy for the distressed;
It's simply God's Love
commanding,
Then arrogance and pride are
oppressed.

We cannot be first as a nation,
If for other peoples we hold
disdain;
Obeying God's laws that have
lived since creation
And the Golden Rule makes the
way plain.

Let's stay clear of the blood
pathway
That ends in chaos and disaster.
Let's blaze a new trail that will
some day
Lead nations to new Jerusalem
faster.

Jan Bourke
YOU ARE
My love for you is so great.
You are so much more than
I had ever hoped for.
My heart burst with the joy I
Feel when I am near you.
All the love songs in the world
Can not express my feelings for
you.
You are warmth, beauty, joy,
kindness,
And understanding to me.
How else can I tell you how
much I
Really love you?
Each day I await your call, your
Touch, your nearness.
I miss you more than words can
Express when you are not with me.
The loneliness and emptiness I
feel
Can not be put into words.
You are to me—everything I
need.
You are love and I need you so.
You are a gift to me from God and
I love you.

Deidra F. Jackson
A SWEET CHASM
If only the earth
could tell us
all its mysteries
describing the memories
relating the events
which contributed
to its origin
Its great contour
still possessing
the remnants from
long ago
Whisper the answers
to all the enigmas
which you
seem to restrain
so exceptionally
In doing so
you would relieve
our minds of all
the constant questions

93

John Campbell, Editor & Publisher

that always seemed
to torment us
If only you
could rid us
of these problems!

Francisco Luis Arroyave T.
RAPTURE
Dreadful shadows of anxiety
Have disappeared for another
    while,
And steaming away,
There it goes my mind . . .
For how long will I be on this
    magic ride
Climbing visions that lay on top
    above?
Motionless and without doubt,
I can feel the cold and the
    height . . .
There are not even clouds
Or any travellers from the sky . . .

Elsie Day Cruthirds-Hutto
WATERS OF THE SEA
I am the waters of the sea;
    With whitecaps in stormy
    afternoons
I touch that off-white shoreline
    With my hands.
I am a part of Time;
    Often soft breezes move me;
I am the Waters of the Sea.
I am a part of those days
    When my tides go far away,
    Seeming never to return.
    Though quickly I am sultry,
    torrid,
    Even turbulent.
I am the Song of the Sea.
    Passers-by see and love me.
    Children delight in the gifts I
    Give them. Lovers are bound
    together
    When they behold my Beauty.
    Yet, I have tasted death.
    Often men become fearful
    because of me.
I am known for my happy moods;
I bring beauty to the multitudes.
    God holds me and
    Guides my every motion.
I am the Waters of the Sea.

Tom Bratney
together
slow-moving clouds parade
outside my window.
the rushing wind disturbs
a calm, dark evening.
instrumental beauty enhances
a romantic night,
as you and I gaze
at the moon
and just touch.

Keotah M. Fannin
OKIE FROM OKMULGEE
Well, you got a busted fender
And your car sure needs a shine.
But your lips are warm and tender
When you press them close on
    mine.

Oh, I'm your little Okie from
    Okmulgee
And I can dance the night away.
I only want to kiss and hug you,
'Till the skies are bright as day.

Well, you can dress all up like
    Christmas
With your socks that do not
    match.

But you're more fun than the
    others
In a watermelon patch.
Oh, I'm your little Okie from
    Okmulgee
And I can dance the night away.
I only want to kiss and hug you,
'Till the skies are bright as day.
                        Yea Yea.

Porter Brundage
AVATA
Before I met you I was One;
I bathed in random tangents,
rejoiced in my sun,
then I discovered Thee.

Asking for little, you wooed me.
You unlocked your wardrobe of
    fantasies,
clothed us in a thousand rays,
using the ancient ritual, "love."

"Listen to your inner song;
Turn to see the inward glow;
Touch the thread of life about you
Spinning to expose your soul."

From a royal mountain
we touched the sky;
the sky touched an ocean
but did not drown.

And to my amazement,
we all danced together,
giving to each other
the power to be another.

Like fish we swam exchanging
    souls.

Close your eyes and rest upon me;
I will wind us in flight to Galaxy 3.
I am One and One are We,
for I will be I forever touching
    Thee.

Evelyn C. Pearson
MARSHA
You broke my heart Marsha the
    night you went away.
You told me you didn't love me
And that I should find a way to
    forget you, and only have
    memories of our Grade and
    High School days.
The Grade School dance and the
    High School prom.
I stopped at the white cottage and
    you were such a beauty in a
    flowering blue and gold dress.
The pennies I saved bought a pale
    yellow orchid.
We danced the hours away until
    11:30 p.m.
I stopped at the same white
    cottage four years later.
You were such a beauty in a
    green colored formal.
The quarters I saved bought you
    a corsage of yellow tea roses.
We danced the hours away until
    1 A. M.
That night we made plans to be
    married four years later after
    our college graduations.
Oh, what dreams we had. We
    planned school—different
    schools.
But our weakly letter, and
    vacations would keep us
    together, and make up the
    difference. That is what I
    thought.
The dollars I saved bought a

lovely engagement ring.
I was to give it to Marsha
    graduation night.
You broke my heart Marsha the
    night you went away.
You told me you didn't love me,
    and that I should find a way
to forget and only have memories
    of our Grade and High School
    days.
The years went by and I just
    worked and never fell in love
    again.
I took a trip to the South Seas
    trying to forget Marsha.

J. Crockett Lambson
EARTH-BOUND

*Dedicated to the gracious and
dedicated members of The Sierra
Writers Club of Sierra County,
(100 years old) Elephant Butte,
New Mexico.*

Joyously the birds fly overhead
    Ah, that I had wings too
But my body is earth-bound
    And my mind alone is free
To go soaring into the far beyond
    Taking me into mysterious
Dreams, so far, unknown
    Reaching out to those
So many miles away
    Into ideal places
    I'd love to stay.

The trouble is I must return
    From whence I yearn to be
Realizing I had not fully escaped
    My duller realm of reality
And as I destroy this lovely film
    Of fantasy
I find I'm still engulfed
    In pain and misery.

Again I must take flight
    Somewhere, somehow
Within the power of mind
I shall resolve my plight.

Jill Ann Bernhardt
REFLECTIONS

*This poem is dedicated to my
parents who I love very much.*

Reflected in a tear
Are the joys, hopes and defeats
Of one soul, one life
Growing wearily older,
Collecting along the way
Memories of the good, the bad,
And those little inbetweens
That make our lives
Worth being lived.
All this reflected
In a glistening, salty drop
Referred to carelessly as a tear.

James P. Polley
WOMAN OF LIGHT
Woman of light, angel of giving
    so often betrayed by the lies of
    the living.

So good of heart, so pure of soul
    left without cloak in life's
    bitter cold.

Run to the light, my woman of
    dreams away from the shadows
    of life's foolish schemes.

Mother of life, whom love has
    betrayed follow me not to a
    cold lonely grave.

Live for us both, sweet angel
    divine waste not your tears on
    a soul such as mine.

Know that I'm with you, on
    nights cold and long shut out
    the darkness with laughter and
    song.

Grieve for me not, my beautiful
    wife but pray we're together in
    some after life.

Muriel Abney-Waters
A GIFT OF GOD
Miracles
Come from
God
Up Above

Because
We listen
To His
Perfect love

Miracles
Are only
Known
When God creates
And wants
Them shown

Ms. Eleanor Lankford Armstrong
**From Shadow Of Darkness
    To Starlight**

FOR DADDY

It seems like only yesterday
you were alive for me to see and
touch.

But the sickness prevented so
much touching, so I just stood
by your bed those last hours
holding your hand and hoping
    you knew you were not alone.

You called me "your shadow"
when I was a little girl and
now you are in "the shadows
of darkness" and I cannot be with
you there.

Somehow time hasn't erased the
pain of losing you, but God
    provides
His grace for us and offers new
life for a sick body.

I know now that you are peaceful
and God has added another star
in His Heaven.

Samuel Lee Miller
THE TEARS OF A SUNSET
The sunset made me cry today,
For the first time, in many a year.
You've been on my mind today,
And you brought along some tears.

It's been awhile since you went
    away,
You know I've been so alone.
With this old house and your
    memory,
The days go kind of slow.

I remember the times we used to
    talk,
Of children and beautiful things.
Now, all I have is this sunset,
And a pocketful of long spent
    dreams.

Maybe someday, I'll see you again,
There'll be no more pain or fear.

But the sunset made me cry today,
For the first time, in many a year.

Hank Moon
THE RIBBON BROKE
A dull red ball
In a worn-out sky
Sheds blood on
Bones
That shattered lie
On silent man
On screaming earth
No phoenix here
From ash,
No birth

Aliene B. Burgess
To Grandma—An Amazing Woman
Grandma was awakened by a ray of the sun
She thought of the day's work ahead to be done
The grass to be weeded, the cake to be baked
(Yet from yesterday's duties, her back still ached)

The telephone call came first thing that day
Daughter was ill, wanted Ma right away!
So down the road on a hurried trip
Grandma scurried to help with the sick.

With wee clothes to wash and wee babe to be kept
She hurried back home with a worried step.
Said she, "Baby-sitting I just hate
I've been doing it since I was eight!
When I was married, I cared for my own.
Now as a Grandma, I'm worn to the bone!"
But the words were belied by the look on her face
Which goodness and graciousness there had placed.

Wee babe slept on as the work was done,
Clean clothes piled high 'ere the set of sun.
The chicken was fried; the cake was baked.
(Grandma forgot that her back had ached!)

Picking flowers for a friend 'cross the way,
Peace crept in her heart at the close of day,
For in service to others, true contentment lies
And the Glory of God shone from this Grandma's eyes!

Heidi Wadsworth
BROKEN PROMISES
Most people think of a broken promise
As something that can be forgiven and forgotten.
But what about the promise of love, of
Friendship, of hope, of tomorrow?

Are those promises always fulfilled?
To the sick, the widowed, the poor, and the hungry

It doesn't always seem so.
For them, it seems, life is full of broken promises.

Without the promises of love and friendship,
The days seem lonely and empty.
And without the promises of hope and a new tomorrow,
Days are only periods of time.
No one wants to fulfill these promises for them.

But this is where they are wrong.
For there is One who fulfills all promises,
Whose love is greater than the universe, whose friendship
Never ceases to end, One who promises hope to all,
And makes the new tomorrow worth waiting for.

There is One who will lead you, though you are lost,
One who forgives you, though you have sinned,
One who believes in you, though you have lost faith,
One who remembers you though you've forgotten Him,
And One who loves you, though you have not loved.

For there is One whose promises are never broken . . .
. . . God.

Pamela Beth Jacoby Rasmussen
GENTLE GIANTS
Gentle giants of the sea,
That's how they're known to you and me.

Majestic creatures swimming our oceans of dissolution,
Trying to survive despite mankinds pollution.

Gentle giants of the sea,
Oh how they used to swim so free.

But now they're becoming so few and far between,
Who knows if they'll survive mankinds evil schemes?

Gentle giants of the sea,
They're part of nature like you and me.

They breathe, they mate, they give birth,
Yes, they too belong on this earth!

Gentle giants of the sea,
God! . . . How I pray they don't cease to be.

Ellis Bailey Hadlock
HEART OF THE SUNRISE
With thoughts that are centered and true, are peaceful to know
Prayers of faith win lasting feelings of worth and creates potential to sow
Simplicity of kindness draws an unyielding variety of a welcome guest
The calmness finds a spacious realm of ability and personality at its best
Cheerfulness can place within reach the true qualities of life and reveal the mind
To look with the eyes of special

views inside and catch a friend refined
Where love is shown, there is a complemental style, loyalty, and service to be found
Fulfillment and silence is brought when the light appearing dims the sound
The spirit worthy of talents to develop and enjoy with hope, there lies
Flowing and increasing the soft rays of time, on to the heart of the sunrise.

Lynda Moreno
EVASIVE BEAUTY
A dream . . .
Of beautiful flowers.
Children running with sunlight in their hair.
Smiles on every face,
Love in every heart.
A beautiful dream,
But when I reach out to touch it,
It fades away . . . Evasive Beauty.

Emily Porter

Emily Porter
SILENCE

Go placidly amid the noise and haste and remember what peace there may be in silence . . .
Desiderata

Borne on wings of darkness through the stillness of the night
Silence comes so softly with the fading of the day.
Its deepening mists reach out to me to soothe my troubled mind
and fill my soul with quietude and smooth my cares away.
Far in the breathless hush of night, I feel my worries waning,
brushed away as gently as a cobweb's crystal strand.
Hate and fear become unlearned and calm and peace now enter
and tenderly spread through my soul with love for fellow-man.

Oh, Silence speaks profoundly in the stillness of the night!
It tells of placid pools of peace in deep serenity.
it whispers in a velvet voice of age-old calm and comfort . . .
yes, Silence is my solace when I sail tempestuous seas.

Silence stills my aching heart and sets my spirit soaring
as it sings in lilting, clear-cut tones like flutes upon the wind.
And I, in heart-felt gratitude, surrender to the calling
as it wipes the slate of all I am and all that I have been . . .
and fills my heart with courage to face the world again.

Viola Mae Spires
ALIKE

I dedicate this poem to my twin Iola Fae Fultz and twins everywhere

---

For many a year, since a little tyke
I've heard we are so much alike.

You two are just the same.
Which one are you? What is your name?
We would laugh a little and smile,
Just let them play at guessing awhile.

Alike as two "peas in a pod",
others would say.
We would hear this most every day.

Do you feel the same as I do,
When ask, "okay, which one are you?"
Today I'll be you and you'll be me.
We can trick some, if you'll agree,
Then when we are ask, which one,
We can really have some fun.

How often did we hear,
Is it like looking in a mirror?
I could tell which one you are,
If you only had a dimple in your chin.
What's it like to be a twin?

First they can answer one for me,
What's it like, not to be?

Steve Sullivan
YOUR SMILE

For my Lilly Jorjean

Your smile
Is all the day need give me
I'll not make waste of it.
I'll cradle it
For the delicate lily it is
cherish it
And share it with no one.
I'll make it my sun
For days of rain.

Mary Lou Roye Griffin
SISTERS
The rain falls softly down,
enclosing thoughts
And gently shrouding memories in mist
That leaves them only half remembered
Half forgotten

Mists of loving days together in those rains
Those foggy greys of other times
That in their softness, in their gentle falling
One sees only love

95

And always there, the flowing tie
That holds us close to one another

Through the years
And through the miles apart
Of other mists and other falling
rains
We two remain, of seeds once
blown by wind
And carried here—and carried
there
In love

And yesterdays peek through the
mist
Enough to cause a smile, a laugh
A joyous warm embrace of falling
rain
As raindrops on my laughing face
Recall your loving touch
That wove its' silent thread of
strength
And how we two were softened,
one to one
In mists and rains of time

Lynda Leppert
SNOW
Snow
  covers mountaintops
  buries cities
  hides in cracks
Like
  a pristine blanket
  powdered sugar
  a puppy's cold nose
Hiding
  the rotting destruction below.

Lathan H. Frayser
IF I LOVED YOU
It would make no difference if
  you wore no shoes upon your
  feet,
Or hat upon your head,
It would make no difference if
  you wore a thousand jewels,
Or none at all . . .
I could no more care
If your hair
Was the color of a nimbostratus
  cloud,
Or if you were bent by age . . .
It would mean no more to me
If the food you ate could be set
  before a king,
Or the fare of a vagabond,
It's not how rich or poor you are,
Or whether unknown . . . or a
  star . . .
For if I loved you—
I'd love you as you are.

Warren Warner
XI
A child's mind is an Enchanted
  Forest.
It is Fantasyland and
  Disneyworld.
It is Hans and Christian and
  Anderson.
It is the Brothers Grim and
  Mother Goose.
His mind has a man Friday and
  Peg-leg.
Not to mention Hook and a paper
  Moon.
His Moon is a ghostly galleon,
  wind swept.
His Moon is a ballon—Moon and
  Sixpence.
He lives on Dolphin Street—Boy
  on a fish!

His wife is Scheredaze, his buddy
  Aladdin, they share a lamp and
  carpet.
Aesop and the Wizard of Oz are
  friends.
  Once upon a future time please
  make me
  Again a child, that's what I'd
  like to be.

D. Elaine Stanberry
SHAKESPEARE'S JEWELS

*Dedicated to the memory of
Professor Christine Burleson (East
Tennessee State University), who
taught me to love Shakespeare
and to appreciate the beauty of
his literary art.*

The Shakespearean art like clear
  raindrops
Revives dull minds inactively
  slumbering,
Inspires weak roots inertly
  cumbering
And feeds unnourished shoots
  outnumbering
Those pilots of the academic crops.

The Bard's rare flowers sparkle
  truth in air,
A world of poetic might covering,
Beloved influence still mothering
As sagely genitor there hovering
To augment properties on art's
  wayfare.

Fresh fragrant blossoms perfume
  mind and soul,
Distinct blue aura, vital coloring,
Emitting ripples softly murmuring
And heritage-born gems
  discovering
Which place smooth stones that
  infinitely roll.

Imelda Dickinson McLimans
RETURNED REFLECTION
Forgotten barrel of water
  unattended
At nightfall is filled with the moon
Spilling out upon glistening
  glades of grass
Soundlessly silent singing this
  rune.
Laced leaves frame this reflection
Casting shadows streaking the
  glow
Mute moon making mystical
  mystery
Captivating heavens down here
  below.

Gloria Wilson Tessier
JUST ONE WORD

*Dedicated to my friend, Joy (Mrs.
Jim) Hogg who inspired this poem.*

There are so many adjectives
To describe you, my friend
Were I to use each one of them
This poem would have no end . . .

And so I strive to aptly choose
The one that fits you best
Delineates your qualities—
Encompasses the rest . . .

"Unforgettable" is my choice:
I find when I recall
All the lovely words that suit you
That one speaks for them all.

Michelle Cheyne
A DAY WITH NATURE
The leaves are wet and moist, the
  rain is almost gone,
the rainbow rises above the hills,
  as the night turns into dawn.

The clouds pass the rainbow by,
  as it slowly fades away,
the sun peeks over the
  mountains as the dawn turns
  into day.

Nature and the animals are
  awaking from their sleep,
you can see the rabbits jumping,
  you can hear the willows weep.

The sun is going down again and
  the sky is fiery red,
the owls are awaking and the rest
  of natures going to bed.

Shqipe Malushi
RAIN
Listen to the rain,
that is beating the stones like a
  merciless God,
that is washing the dust from my
  face,
leaving me naked in front of the
  throne of your questions.
Listen to the rain,
like the sound of the beating in
  my veins from the pain,
like the tears running down my
  dirty cheeks.
Listen to the rain,
that is scribling of my memories
  into mud,
which is covering my vision with
  the rain drops.
And I want ah, how I want that
  rain to stop,
and let it be.
And you were in every corner of
  that room, climbing
over walls into my brains,
escaping into my tears.
Listen to the rain and just let it be.

Lm. Maillet
Eyes—Windows Of the Soul
From my window, I catch, a
  magical
  vermillion patch of love, flowers.
  All—
A million! so tall! splashing pink
  against
  a verdant thicket. Thick
  overgrowth danced
About playfully in the afternoon's

noon sun. And the warm winds
  wash them with June's
Breeze. But . . .
  When the soft breeze blows to
  the right

There's a trash can with not a
  sign in sight
  to tell me so. Scattered cups
  Keeping more
Colors than any pedal could. A
  poor
  extention some would say when
  they were near
Enough to see that it was just mere
Junk., or not, It's all the beauty I
  see
Free now from the human nature
  in me
to seperate and see with names. I
  am
Also accused because I am human.
  For I thought before I saw the
  thriving
Mess, of the ugliness. Flowers
  striving
  to live!

  But now I know in a certain
Way, when both will die and live
  again,
  that beauty's here! if anywhere
  at all.
The circle will not end in Fall.
But instead it goes on and on and
  on.

Eleanor Taylor Frazee
LOVE IS!

*To my father, John Lloyd Taylor,
who died in December 1942
when I was six years old.*

Love lives in a dimension free of
  time,
Defies all reason and all rhyme.
It grows as it is given away;
Love renews itself each day.
No power on earth can make it
  cease,
And Love's abiding gift is Peace.

Sheryl Frances De Garmo
SILENT ENEMY
The large intricate spiders web
Suspended between the flower
  stems
Covered with the mornings dew
Sparkled in the sunshine like
  jewels.

Carefully and delicately woven
Fragile looking to the eye
Was deceiving to the fly
As the spider drew nigh . . .

Patricia Ann McMahon
TO HURT

*To Carl who I never wanted TO
HURT.*

Do you know what it's like
TO HURT
someone that you'de never want
TO HURT.
And not having the guts
TO HURT
yourself, for hurting them, and
TO HURT
when they forgive, when
YOU SHOULD HAVE HURT.

Patricia L. Tate
SONNET

Get on your knees and praise the
Lord
For everything He's done;
For bearing pain from the sword;
For turning the night into
morning sun.
He died to erase your sin
On a dark and pain-filled day,
To make you love again
And follow in His way.
In a world full of strife
He traveled all alone.
He died to give you life;
For this, you must atone.
So get on your knees and praise
the Lord
For everything He gave.
He gave His life on that blood—
soaked cross;
Through His death, your life was
saved.

Judy McDonald
Through the Eyes Of a Son

*Dedicated to my son Ricky, who
opened my heart and gave me the
inspiration to put his feelings
into words.*

Where do I begin Dad, to tell you
what you've done?
How you have failed at being
father to your son.
First you gave up Mom, for a
complete stranger to me.
I accepted it because you said,
"That's the way it has to be."
Then you stopped coming home,
and I saw less and less of you,
I cried myself to sleep at night,
you never cared or knew.
But a boy needs his dad, to teach
him some new things,
To protect him and to guide him
and take him under his wing.
When I tried out for softball it
was Mom there by my side,
The kids thought I was a sissy, so
the harder I tried.
I made the team and I felt proud
because I wanted it real bad,
I wanted to follow in the footsteps
of the man I called my Dad.
You'd call and say that I could
come and spend some time
with you,
Those times were very special to
me, but I can only count a few.
Sometimes you get my hopes up
Dad, where was your heart and
soul?
Instead of giving me your time,
you replaced it with a fishing
pole.
But how can a boy go fishing,
without a Dad to bait the hook?
That's when I made up my mind,
only good Dad's are in books.
I never asked for much from you.
I didn't understand from the
start,
Why your needs had to come
first and why you tore our
family apart.
You really let me down Dad, in
more ways than one,
You made me feel unhappy at

being my father's son.
Sometimes I get lonely for you,
and I really feel quite sad,
But you know I'll always love
you, because you are my Dad.
A man has more important
things on his mind than a son,
And I will grow up knowing, that
I was just not one.

Rebecca L. Tinch
ON LUST

I could write volumes on lust,
but find it difficult to write
One simple poem on love.

Before the top ten best sellers,
I never knew there were so
many ways
To describe one simple act.

Adjectives have their place in the
writer's garden of herbs,
but if love lives at all, it must
be a verb or at least an adverb.

Marlin Brothers
I CAN STILL DREAM

*I would like to dedicate my poem
to the two people who helped me
make a dream come true. Alice
Colwell, Activity Supervisor and
Jan McCarty, LPN, at BURGIN
MANOR of OLNEY, ILL.*

When ever I am feeling down
I even feel unclean
I tell myself I still have
something
I can still dream.
But things can't all be bad
I keep telling myself that
And I am finding that this is true
For no longer am I sad.
There is a new day coming
I can feel it deep inside
The time will soon be here
When in myself I can confide.
If my senses should ever dull
And my mind should become
unkeen
I pray to God that
I can still dream

Betty Dupuy
DON'T PROMISE

Don't promise for always
Don't promise forever
Always is not forever
Forever is not always

Take for today what it is
Twenty-four GOD given hours
To spend as we choose
To win or to loose

Be happy for just a few hours
Not worry or question what may
not become ours

A rose is never so pretty
as the bud it comes from
The bush must be cherished
or it grows none

To have love is to give love
with no thought of return
Hold love lightly, never tightly
The glow will ever burn brightly

But to grab and hold tightly
The scars become unsightly
It can be crushed so easily
and bruises so lightly

Hold love as you cradle a child
with tender care ever so mild

Don't promise something you
can't fulfill
Just give freely of what is yours
to give
Your cup will always to the brim
be filled

We both have memories we can
never share
What we build now we hope will
not wear
But should problems arise
that may damage our lives
The happy hours we spend, can
never be wrent

Don't look into my past
and yours I'll never ask
For what is behind can never
return
No need to look back no bridges
to burn

We must take for today what is
meant to be ours
Not worry about tomorrow and
the far away hours
For tomorrow you may change
and so may I
No need to look forward to worry
and cry

Be happy with today and spend it
well
The memories we now build our
future will tell

Don't promise for always
Don't promise forever

A look at tomorrow might
destroy today
So sit by my side, don't promise
to stay
Take for today, and come what
may

Don't promise for always
Don't promise forever

Anne Powers
Happy Mother's Day To a Wonderful Mother

Whenever I think of you my
heart fills with pleasure
Truly, Mother, you are a treasure

You have a heart so giving, so full
of love
Surely, you're a gift from above

Life is hard and gloomy; yes, the
path we tredge is rough
And to think, if I didn't have you;
oh, life's already tough enough

Oh, how I love to see your
cheerful smile and hear your
lovely voice
I thank God for you, Mother, and
in my heart I rejoice

Your wonderful love is never
ceasing
Instead, your love is increasing

You're not only a Mother to me
But you're a friend as good as can
be

Of all the Mothers near and far
The most wonderful and loving
truly you are

And on this special day of May
I love you and Happy Mother's
Day is what I want to say.

Warren Weber, Jr.
PARTING

Struggle, pain, agony,
A time of repose,
Happening again and again.
Regrets for the words unspoken
The feelings never expressed.
The touch is warm and soft,
but unresponsive.
The ending, the beginning,
The familiar, the illusion, the
unknown.
A strange sense—
It is there . . .
A oneness of life with everything
From an entity that senses all
from aloneness,
To a unity of thought and feeling.

Le'Von-ninsky Von Hardin
A LOST MAN

"A pure life is a life of
conservation of energy . . . A
impure life is a life of
dissipation of energy . . .

Where the impure man fails, the
pure man steps in and is
victorious, because he directs
his energy with a calmer and
clearer mind, with strength and
purpose. As a man grows purer,
he recognizes that all evil is
powerless unless it receives his
encouragement, so he ignores
it, letting all the impure and
unworthy thoughts drop
completely from his mind, also
refusing to allow them to
enter . . . As a man by practice
acquires proficiency in his
work of art, so the earnest man
acquires proficiency in
goodness and wisdom.

By self-discipline, a man attains
to every degree of virtue, and
holiness, and finally becomes a
purified Son of God, realizing
his oneness with the central
heart of all things. Without
self-discipline, a man drifts,
lower and lower, approximating
more and more nearer to the
beast, until at last, *he falls,
down to the earth wallowing in
the mud as the beast.*

a lost man . . ."

Anna Marie Clark
ROADS

For Audry at Long Corner

The old roads are the best
roads,
the narrow lanes through the
woods;
and the winding paths that have
never been paved
I wouldn't change if I could!

Up through the cornfield they
wander
and down by the streams they
go,
followed by bees in the clover
and walnut trees in a row.

Kin to the pine and the popular,
friend of the quail in the snow.
highway for the fox and for the

John Campbell, Editor & Publisher

turtle,
when the evening star hangs low.

They suffer the deep frost of
winter
when wild winds blow over the lea;
they teach me their magic by
moonlight
when it's a road and a possum
and me!

With joy I follow the windings
of these dear and familiar old
lanes.
They have warmed me 60 odd
summers,
seen me drenched with 60 odd
rains.

I only hope in my lifetime
no progress will change their
quaint style,
and my slowing feet may be
tramping
their paths, for yet many a mile.

J. A. Hatch
MEMORIES

K. D. Robertson—My Friend

Memories can be painful—
Memories can be a joy

Remembering things when you
Were a girl or boy

Feelings you one time had,
Some were good-some were sad.

Things you did or wished you
could
Most of your memories will
always be good.

Because we must try to put out of
our minds
The sad memories, and hold on
only to the joyful kind.

Yvonne J. Butner
TREAT ME LIKE . . .

---

*This is dedicated to God, who
gave me the ability to write
poems; and to my truly special
husband Jim, who encourages me
never to give up.*

Treat me like fine china,
for I am a step above ordinary.

Treat me like expensive wine,
for I better with age.

Treat me like precious gold,
for I have a certain gleem.

Treat me like a rare painting,
for I am one of a kind.

Treat me like a spring rose,
for I may not be here long.

Treat me like you would like to
be,
for I am your loving spouse.

Annette Melville—Hansen
A NEW BEGINNING
At first I wouldn't listen,
Because I had heard it all before.
I said I didn't need you,
But each time you tried a little
more.
You told me of your love,
It sounded so real and so true.

It was then I had to listen,
There was something special
about you.
You had broken the wall,
That surrounded my heart.
And that's when I decided,
To give love a new start.
I knew you wouldn't hurt me,
Like the others before had done.
For the very first time,
I felt I could stay instead of run.
We laughed and we cried,
About the things in our past.
You were so unsure,
If my love for you would last.
Please forget about before,
Because there's something I
want to say.
I want to tell you babe,
That my love is here to stay.

Corey Steenhagen
ONE MOMENT IN TIME
In one moment of time
as you are doing your thing
many other things are happening
Someone is making love
Someone is taking a life
Someone is stealing from
someone
Someone is having an accident
Someone is getting married
Someone is getting divorced
Someone is dying
Someone is giving birth
In just one short moment
all this is taking place
Moment after moment
Hour after hour
Day after day
Year after year
for eternity
Yet mankind manages
to survive
all the trauma
all the heart break and sorrow
all the beautiful inspiring
things
that may happen in just that
One moment in time

M. Scott Fielding
TEMPERINGS
A prisoner
    Of my own restless brain
I wander
Restricted yet watchful
    Of life's cruel strain.

A fighter
    Of earth's cunning and daring
I challenge
The world and its like
    With woeful caring.

A lover
    Of friendship and mating
I capture
The best and the truest
    With honest baiting.

A loyalist
    Seeing life for its worth
I accept
And direct my own fate
    To justify birth.

Rose Sparks
SILENT CRY
When inward I'm feeling
    anger and pain,
And I call out in silence
    all help seems in vain.

When smiles diminish
    and worry takes place;
Why is it that no one
    can see thru this face?
I'm hurting, I'm fretful,
    oh why can't you see
The anger I show you
    is not really me.
When all of a sudden
    so gentle a touch;
From one who is hurting
    three times as much.

Edna L. Brigham Harrison
EARTH'S MIRACLE
Spring came, and turned by the
    spade
the peccant earth's secreted under
    the sweet loam.
In the swash and drench of
    plashy torrents
all that is hidden is forgot
as if it were no more. The old
    glebe
clotted with mould made cledge
of the topsoil, now is lost
to the worms and parasites
that work the miracle of
    restoration.

Spring came, and the soft winds
    touched the land
with tender assurance. Their
    aphonous soughs
finish the transformation. *The
    voice
of the turtle is heard in the land*
and all the insects join
antiphonally through the hours.
    The sun
drifts into its incunabulous
    evening blush
with all the callidity of youth
    glissading
down-cliff naked into the sea.

Dorothy K. Pridemore
MEDITATION
Oh, to walk through the meadow
    when the dew is wet
To reach down to pick
    a blue violet
To hear the drone of a bee close by
Catch a glimpse of a rabbit
    from the corner of my eye
To feel the cool breeze
    of the early morn
Hear the tinkle of the cowbell
    as she shakes her horn
To listen to the tune of
    the babbling brook
Winding and laughing
    with every little crook
To hear the beautiful meadowlark
    singing its song
To be by myself just walking along
In the quiet of the meadow
    in the early dawn.

Sharon Renee Christopher
Jaguars Can't Be Tamed
Driving on pock marked black
    in rain that fell
like unrelenting seconds,
and sometimes signs reflect—
green and rippled in the
    colourless mirror
that is merely an illusion,
looking in the rear view glass
there are only fragmented drops
and the wipers move
to clear away more time;

deep into two a.m.—
waiting like a tethered jaguar
for the green arrow
to approve the void ahead;
don't they know
that jaguars can't be tamed by
    false lights
while the depth of others' words
    by other lights
vibrate distant
and live only in the hollow of
    illusion.

Karen H. Warner
**The Four Seasons Of My
Life**
I met him in the winter
It was the beginning of my life
He took me in his arms
And he ask me to be his wife

We married in the spring
He took me for his wife
We promise to love each other
For the rest of our lives

Now it is the summer
The summer of our lives
With our love together
We conceived another life

Now it is the fall
The fall of my life
He is gone forever
But I will always be his wife

And as I kneel at your grave
I know I must be brave
For our four seasons together
Will last forever and a day

Robert L. Woodberry
**Spring Time Is My Favorite
Time Of the Year**
Come Summer, Winter, Fall how I
    love them all, but Spring time
    is my favorite time of the year.
Summer it gets hot, you be trying
    to find a cool spot.
You want to go out for fun, but
    you don't go in the sun.
You want to try to keep cool, but
    you can't stay in the pool.
That's why Spring Time is my
    favorite time of the year.
In the fall the leaves turn brown,
    then comes falling down.
There's a cool breeze in the air,
    blowing leaves everywhere.
    Then comes these frosty morn,
    when you try to keep warm.
That's why Spring Time is my
    favorite time of the year.
In the winter it's cold, oh!
    how the cold wind blows.
The cold chill in the air, white
    snow is everywhere.
That's why Spring Time is my
    favorite time of the year.
Then Spring time appears, It's
    beautiful everywhere, the
    flowers in full bloom, the birds
    are singing its tune Lover's gets
    together, enjoying the beautiful
    weather.
Sweet fragrance in the air, green
    grass covers everywhere.
Cause Spring Time is my favorite
    time of the year.
Come Summer, Winter, Fall, how
    I love them all still Spring
    Time is my favorite time of the
    year.

Our World's Best Loved Poems

Lee Wilkerson
SUMMER SHADE
The heat beats down in sharp,
    shimmering waves
Bouncing off flat-black parking
    lot pavement
Shining on metal, too hot to touch
Wilting grass and leaves and
    women's new hairdos

Pedestrians look weary—too
    tired, too soon
Construction workers stop and
    mop their faces
Looking heavenward for relief
    that isn't forthcoming
The streets are deserted, while
    air-conditioned stores are full

A small boy in the park is
    following his dog
More wise than he in the ways of
    weather
Making a hollow in the cool,
    damp earth
Hiding under the brush in shared
    summer shade

Mary Ann Sharlow
ONLY YOU
I've been to so many places
Played the games of chances
Meet so many faces
It's only you who stayed on my
    mind
Only you who touched my heart
All the time
I've been thinking about you
Only you
Only you can satisfy that gap in
    my heart
It's only you that I really need

Life for me hasn't been easy
I've lead a life of need
Read all I need
Not until you did I learn
You made me realize
What I've been missing
Missing such a warm person as you

You saw the part of me no one
    had ever seen
I've pledge never to let you go
Each day that goes by I think of
    you
You have succeed in winning my
    heart
You
You are the queen of my heart
I love you
I guarantee my love for all times

Brenda Dale Flagg Coleman
I SEARCH FOR DESTINTY

---

*I dedicate this poem to my
Family. Since there's no way of
knowing our destiny. May God
bless us and always keep us as one.*

I walk the path of a quiet and
    lonely day,
I search for destiny,
But it's no where to be found,
I watch and listen to the winds
    exotic sounds,
Everything is still,
The fences make their rounds and
    back again,
Yet here I stand, Embraced with
    and idol,
My feet moves no more for it all

seems worthless,
To search for destiny,
When it exists NOT.

Mark Stephen Wallinder

Mark Stephen Wallinder
WHIMSICAL
A sneeze is a sneeze
in Japanese,
you don't have to be excused;
so if you're in
their land
and you do,
you'll simply be perused.

Kimberlee Davis
LIFE WITHOUT YOU
When the rainbows are black and
    the sun is gray,
I know that he has gone away.

I talk to the walls and yell at the
    floor, should
I care if the sun crys out for the
    moon?

I feel sad on bright days and I
    welcome the storms.

My house is a cloud and it makes
    me happy when it rains and I
    am free.

I am a rain drop, falling
    hopelessly to a cruel earth.

He is a rose among many thorns.

Jo Anne H. Williams
RESTLESS FEELINGS
Restless are the feelings, as
    strange as it may seem . . .
Every part of me is screaming . . .
    please let me be.
Not knowing why, the quivery
    stomach and shaking hands.
Then there is a solemn moment .
    . . a sort of quiet peace . . .
Then the thought (flys) by my
    mind, why all my children are
    home again and safe . . . Where
    I can see!
Now I know that was the reason
    of all the strange feelings, (safe)
    they are and a sleep. Now the
    restless feelings have ceased
    once again . . .

Barbara M. Parry
TOOK OUR SONG AWAY
Summer's gone,
    She's gathered up her brood—
        Rosebuds, and lovely flowers
            Of June.

Peonies, swollen, bursting pink
    With bloom—

And July's irrediscient
    Moon.

August, and her seashores
    Tagged along with her—
        Sandles dangling
            Off her tanned shoulder.

All the scented evenings
    So much a part of her
        And, the children's laughter—
            Shuttered windows, never
                heard.

Her hundred days of sunshine
    She spread along the way
        And, the winged families
            followed—
                And took our song away.

Jennifer A. Thibeau
DREAMING
I am trapped in a world of wild
    dreams,
Where everyone has different
    means—
Trees can walk
Lamps can talk
And everyone sings the o'clock.

Each ant has a face
And walks with a quickened pace,
E-V-E-R-Y-T-H-I-N-G is spinning
    around.

Each room is a windowless
    balloon,
Outside the wind screeches
Like little children happily playing.

Everything here is different.

You can climb up a tree and f
                                    l
                                        o
                                            a
                                                t
                    back down—
Without people staring,
You live forever here, unless—
Your dream comes to an

END . . .

Carol M. Schick
TWO SEPARATE WORLDS
When we're together I close out
    the
                    rest of the world.
It's not an unpleasant world . . .
                    but you're not in it.
Our world is so enchanted and
    peaceful
            I often wonder . . . is it real?
We've protected and separated
            our world for years,
And now I know it must always be
                    this way.
I miss you in my big world, but
            if I let you in . . .
Our special world could be
    destroyed,
    become part of just another day.

Nancy L. Walton
PEGASUS
Magically floating high on wing
This beautiful creature;
    magnificent thing.
Pegasus flying skyward bound
Magical dreams found all around.
Stately steed with widespread
    wings
Flying often in my dreams.
Muscular body; creamy white
Soaring often day or night.

Hoofbeats sound his stately dances
Like the Unicorn; he magesticly
    prances.
Ever alert for movement or sound
In just a second he's skyward
    bound.
High on wing he quickly goes
Just where no one knows.
Creature of magnificence so
    seldom seen
Comes mostly at night when we
    dream.
His magic is sought by many a
    man
Always in thought throughout
    the land.
Men searching near and far to see
Pegasus flying ever so free.

Bhagwan Khanna
DEATH'S DIGNITY
Unflinched fists and open palms
nothing to fear o' hide
nothing to fret o' fume
nothing to provoke o' cause
    tantrums
poised, quiet, and
infectious silence
no bragging, no boasting
o' selfish stance
Ego, envy, enmity, jealousy,
distressing suspicion
despairing depression
dubious frustrations, and
scorching disappointments
suddenly out, out for ever
for good, for better
Me and mine, Thou and thine
conflicts begetting
viciousness
everly, embracingly
Now! lifeless, breathless
lying in pyre
with peace on face and
expressive dignity
Death—thou, though 're
cruel—yet replete with
dignity and soaked in dignity

Margie Callahan Pearson
US
He loved cars with a passion and
    pride.
He told me, mine looked like a
    gut wagon inside.

He called his "baby" and wiped
    her down with a rag.
Mine was full of coffee cups and
    et cetera inside.

He whispered and shouted "Hey!
    Can't you see,
a car can be a total man's dream?"

I can't help being myself you see,
my car is filled up with
    momentoes and things.

To each other, we cannot
    understand,
but God made us different and it
    was in His plan.

So we shout at each other and
    each takes his stand,
at being an individual.

It is just grand.

Mike Vladescu
MY LOVE
My love, I've missed you so
It hurt me to see you go.
But I hope deep down inside

Your're not sorry you made this
ride.

My love, I hope you'll forgive me,
And let things be.
For I'm sorry,
I almost threw you away.

My love, I love you,
And I hope you do too!

Jessie Druktanis
INNOCENT PETALS

This poem is dedicated to my mom, who without her, I never would have started writing poems. With all my love, Thanks mom. Jess

---

Touch this child
Who with skin as soft as velvet
Waits with lips open as the
rosebud
Waits the tenderness of the
morning dew.
Thus she awaits your kiss.

Make it gentle.
Crush not these fragrant petals
In an embrace that speaks only of
lust.
But in a moment of infinite
sweetness
Tenderly caress this fragile
flowerlet,
Else she will sicken and die in
your arms,
A withered yet tender . . .
. . . mistake.

Jeanette Bowden Bonifas
MY DAD
My dad is someone very sweet,
And no other father could ever
compete.
He may get very mad,
But it's only because he loves me.
And I'm glad.
He's been sick and it hurts me so
To know that he may have to go.
He may not have long to live,
So I'm giving him all the love I
can give.
But when he is gone
I'll have to move along,
And do the same as I did before.
Even if God has shut the door
On my Dad and I.
But my love for him will never die
As long as I am still alive.

Louise R. Stroud
HOME
Home for Christmas, thats where
I long to be
Holiday baking and trimming the
tree
Hanging tinsel, all shiney and
bright
Singing softly, "Silent Night"

Seeing the children, faces all aglow
As they romp and tumble in the
new fallen snow
Reading the letters to Santa, they
wrote
Bless my soul, Jamie wants a new
leather coat

Bikes, trikes, and E. T. too
Guns and planes, boots for Sue
Visions of Christmas dance in
their head

As sleepily, they go to their bed

Smell of pine and spice cookies,
fill the air
As I sat dreaming, in my old easy
chair
Fireplace mantle, decked out so
gay
Stockings hung in wild aray

Christmas cards come from
friends, far and near
Each bringing a bit of holiday
cheer
Home for Christmas, it's the only
place on earth, I want to be
Five more years of hard time,
then I'll be free

Eileen A. Donovan-Cooper
UNTITLED
Summer sun blinds me to the
light of day
Noon makes me lose perspective
in pinpointed light
Afternoon makes me lose focus
in brightness
Twilight softens points
Soft night melds each into liquid
darkness, and
Dawn makes me face the morn
Again to countenance the sun

Laverne Byers
WHAT IS LOVE!
What is Love? Can anyone really
explain it?
Is love an opposite explation of
sex?
Or is love a feeling deep within
itself, what is love?
Some say love is a passionate
feeling for someone of the
opposite sex.

While others say, there is no
such thing as love
Can someone tell me, what is love?
Is it something that can be
perceived?
Or is love a compassion or is it
something enacted?
What is love?
Can love be repressed? Or is it an
ardent feeling which can't be
helped!

Can someone tell me what is love?
Is it an ever-fixed mark? Or is it
never shaken?
Can it be the star to every
wandering bark, or is it
unknown
To his or her height to be taken

What is Love?
Is love not a times fool with
rosey lips! and cheeks,
beautiful in body and mind?
Tell me what is love?
When we love someone, do we
try to improve them?
Or just accept them as they are.

Is love the means to truth and
communication?
If so why does it alter most of the
time.
What is Love?
Admit it! Love is not love even
when it alters into alterations,
It finds or bends itself with the
remover to remove.

Can someone tell me, what is love?

If all this be true and upon my
error proved.
I'll never write! Nor no man ever
love.
Tell me! What is Love?

Esther Myers

Esther Myers
THOUGHTS AT 4:00 A. M.
My thoughts have traveled down
strange roads,
So many thoughts create the loads
That bend my back, and sap my
life.
Oh why, oh why, must there be
strife.
Why can't the load be shifted
some,
For my lame back is turning numb.
Alas! Must be life's chosen few
That carry the load for those of
you,
Who breeze through life without
a thought,
Of when, or why, no answer
sought.

Burnice Belli Holbrook
FUTILITY
A volcano, infinite erruptions,
endless calm;
Fragments of explosions piercing
the earth;
A barren desert, a soul adrift;
A skeleton of life, seemingly
endless, but searching;
Fragile, delicate, strength beyond
belief;
Wisdom and cowardice, weakness
and peace;
Alas! the desperation and
dislocation;
A single strand engulfed in a
huge ball;
Unwinding slowly to a core of
nothingness;
A sad thought to be sure;
A meaningless thing to be certain;
A god of happiness, a devil of
destruction;
Delusions of grandeur,
inevitability of defeat;
Deafening silence;
The beauty that is gone, the
renaissance that is past;
The truly singleness of one's self;
Words of emptiness, bonds broken;
Faith and hope, loss and
despondency;
Desiring that which cannot be
achieved in a life time;
Such grief, such tragedy;
A jumbled maze of more, more,

and more;
A pathway to nowhere;
Perhaps there is no answer.

Stephanie L. Sargent
IN RETROSPECT
The night I met you, I was happy
and excited,
I knew I had fallen for you, I was
really very frightened.
For I knew you were to hurt me,
but I cared too much for you,
We stayed together for sometime,
and we together grew,
I thought I found the one to be,
so very special to only me . . .
I thought I loved you or maybe
still,
But how could I love something
that could never feel?
I hope someday you will come
back to me.
For I'll always wait for you
faithfully.
And if you shall ever need me
again, I'll always be there—
even as a friend.

Elizabeth Simpson Todd
SOUL

Inspirational

Nothing!
So preponderant
As the soul.
Always enraptured with
The power it unfolds—
Whence it cometh,
Whence it goeth
Nobody knows.
A spark of the light of
Infinity
Spiraling in spiritual
Flight
Upward in quest
Of its golden crest!

Martha Mullens Graham
WELCOME HOME

In Memory of My father, Semion Mullens, Deceased September 4, 1946—My mother, Leona Sutphin, Deceased January 1, 1977—My brothers, Drew Mullens, Deceased July 3, 1979, Jessee Mullens, Deceased November 25, 1980, and Wiley Mullens, Deceased November 26, 1982

An angel whispered to me
While down on bended knee
Come and go with me my child
Joyous wonders you will see
You will see your loved ones
All gathered round God's throne
They will look upon you
And bid you Welcome Home
Welcome home to heaven
Where the angels sing
Welcome home to heaven
To live with God our King

Sondra Jo Cox
UNTITLED
These flowers hold
no memories.
They are for all the
memories to come.

Dorothy Mae Johnson
WHY
Why do people get sick and have
to die?
So many suffer in pain and cry
why, why?
Life and death, what's it about?
Life is to live, not to doubt.
God gave His life so that we may
live,
Precious moments are when we
can forgive.
We're on this earth for a short
time,
Worldly treasurers must be left
behind.
For nothing on this earth is ours
to hold,
We have the choice to save our
soul.
Life is not to understand,
But to give who is in need a
helping hand.
There is no need to fret or grieve,
God alone knows our time to
leave.
There is no need to cry why,
why?
For our souls never die.
Death is not the end
But a new beginning
A new life with no more sinning.
So when God calls a loved one
away,
Don't in anger say,
Why, why?
For this is not good-by
Just softly whisper I love you
And we will meet again one day.

Edwin Miyoshi JR.
MUST BE YOUR EYES
I can't understand how you could
lie
to me, again, with your eyes
looking
so sincere.
Have you ever told the truth?!?!
Will you ever?!?!
But what I really can't understand
is why do I always believe you

D. S. Phelps
FAREWELL TO HOSS
I knew you in a foreign land,
Of noble sovereignty,
A flame within me burning,
Remembers by the sea;

Rolling hills of lavender,
Pomegranates and earth,
Shining umber hues reflect,
A rich and fertile birth;

Water crystals clear and jeweled,
Splashed against the shore,
Nectars of the god's own store,
Quenched us evermore;

There is more and deeper yet,
A somewhat mystic tour,
A greeting in a royal land,
Of such the whispered lore;

If you feel a likened depth,
The flame within the Jewel,
Let us follow each our own,
To taste the honey'd dew;

And let us pledge to meet again,
In a destined time,
To toast an oath of loyalty,
With blue and foamy wine;
We'll sing and jest,

And dance and shout,
Bravura all in time,
Yes meet again my special friend,
Within a distant rhyme.

carol george riggio
not you
if the sun dont shine
on my little world
who the hell cares?
not you

you didnt wanna hurt me
yet you went ahead and did
who picked up the pieces?
not you

if the clouds dont pass
and im lost in a fog
wholl show me the way?
not you

if i hadda pick a person
i should deetest foreveh
whod that person be?
not you

Isolde V. Czukor
IF
If only I could touch your hand
I'd gladly say goodbye to spring.
If only I could touch your cheek
My heart would thrill and I
would sing.
If only I could touch your lips
My soul would burst and then
take wing.

Weldon L. Smith
WHERE ARE THEY
See now those dead who once
were people
whose thoughts were fun and
worldly gain
see how they turn, no longer
gleeful
with writhing tongues of fiery
pain.
Where are they now who walked
beside me
and turned their backs at time to
learn
submerged so deep eternally
in fiery lakes that ever burn.

Eva Lee
LEAVES
The leaves are so happy now, but
soon they'll come a tumbling
down.
The whirling wind will set them
free.
They'll go off swirling in the
whirling wind;
But the wind dies down, and the
rain begins to fall.
The leaves aren't swirling merrily.
They lay motionless now—on
the ground—their life has
ended.
Maybe next summer someone
will say
The leaves are so happy now.

Lauri K. Kienzlen
REMEMBERING
Welcome dear friend
Won't you sit for a while
Share with me
your troubles and trials
Moments of sadness
moments of tears
One conversation
about all those years
Looking back closely,

back through the miles
Suddenly tears
have turned into smiles

Jeanne Louise Morgan
AVE
Mary—
When God was just a little boy
And walked this earth with you
Did He have some special toy,
Was His favorite color blue?
Did He have little boy treasures
To keep beside His bed,
Was there a childhood story
That made Him smile as you read?
Did He mend birds' broken wings
With the touch of His small hand
Or cure a neighbors' ailing child
With one whispered command?
Did the angels bring Him presents
And sing Him lullabies?
As you held the sleeping child
Did you fully realize
He was God?

Barbara Wood
LOVE ME
Take my word that I love you
And answer back, "I love you, too."
Take my hand, though some may
see,
And sometimes, show your love
for me.

Take my heart it's mine no more,
And give me your heart, I implore
Take my love, it's yours to own
And give your love to me alone.
Take my word, my hand, my
heart, my love and then,
Take me in your arms and love
me, love, again.

Vineler Long Mann
CHRISTMAS EVE
The carolers are coming
Singing loud and clear.
It is the sweetest music
You'd ever want to here.

Christmas time is almost here.
The most wonderful time of the
year.
It was the day Jesus was born.
It's time for love and good cheer.

When I go to bed at night
I'll say my prayers again.
Thank Jesus for his blessings
And this beautiful Christmas
Eve.

Blance Freeland
A TRIBUTE
In memory I go back today
To a dear mother far away
When troubled, to her I'd always
go
The closest earthly friend I know
She's loving, gentle, kind and good;
To me it's clear and understood
For years she's toiled to do the
right,
So when God calls us all we might
Be one unbroken circle!

I must not forget my dad
The dearest father one could have
He teases and makes light talk
To ease the pain so he could walk
No one knows what it's meant to
me
To have him take me on his knee
When I was sick or tired from play
It seems as though it were

yesterday
What's the difference, dad or
mother?
I wouldn't trade one for the other!

Grant L. Simpson
BARBARA

*This poem was written for the
nicest, most beautiful person that
I know. Barbara Mandrell*

When I think of beauty, I think
of walking through a garden of
beautiful flowers

I think of blue skies, sunsets and
warm spring nights

I think of the beautiful feeling of
being in love

I think of the beautiful love of a
God who loved us enough to
give us His only Son

When I think of beauty, I think
of life

I think of the sun sparkling in
the morning dew

When I think of beauty, Barbara, I
think of You.

Hazel Louise Snyder
AWAKENING
I likened my love, at first, to that
of a small flower,
growing in the feild . . . adoring
the sun . . . watching and
following its every move . . .
unable to speak.

But I have been told that love can
grow!

I likened my love to that of a
summer breeze . . .
gently . . . swiftly and oft' times
sadly wooing the
beautiful flowers of the field.
Hesitantly it comes . . . again and
again . . . then frightened
it quietly disappears.

But I have been told that love can
grow!

I likened my love to a spring in
the ground . . .
bubbling . . . bubbling . . .
bubbling . . . then, unable to
restrain itself, suddenly overflows.

My love is growing!

I likened my love to that of the
waves in the ocean . . .
madly . . . passionately wooing
the shores . . . repeatedly
vowing its strength and power.

I know love can grow!

Ethelyne R. Harper
PEACE
Fleeting are the sweetly cherished
days,
As through my fingers they slip,
one by one.
No sooner is witnessed the sun's
first glorious rays,
Than falls the evening shadows
and day is done.

So quickly the moonlit, starry
nights pass by,
And another beautiful new day is
begun.

The moments swiftly, oh how
   swiftly, they fly,
As sands through the hourglass
   of time they run.

If I could but stop the world in
   its' flight,
And hold it suspended in time
   until,
All mankind would cease their
   senseless fight,
The sounds of all violence and
   crime were still.

Instead of gunfire, only sweet
   music we'd hear,
And each fragrant flower there'd
   be time to stop and smell.
Until all war and famine no
   longer hovered near,
And our love for one another
   we'd be unafraid to tell.

Then, I'd like this old earth,
   another spin to give,
And hope this time a better job
   would be done.
That all living creatures, in
   harmony would live,
All life's treasures be shared by
   all, bar none.

Then I'd be content to soar up in
   the sky so far,
Searching for that rainbow up
   there somewhere.
Find myself a perch on some
   shiny bright star,
And nestle there through
   Eternity with no more worry or
   care.

Mr. James Figueroa
ONCE A PROUD SYMBOL
An eagle in flight, stripped
of its pride, and might
Once a proud symbol of freedom
but no longer can it fight,
It crashes downward from its
kingdom in the clouds, with
an assasins bullet through its
brow, and now it flutters in the
winds of death, while freedom
   rocks
within its breath.

Justina Rochelle Gustavson
EMERGENCE

for Brix, the son
for Sally, the daughter

Hardly noticed at first, and since
Cocoon-cradled you are
   sometimes shunned.
Early landlocked and one often
   lowly underfoot,
Still, you struggle slowly and
   woollyworm your
Way to a semisafe place. Once
   there you
Prepare and wait for another of
   God's small
Miracles. Then, at some
   preordained lightyear
Moment, you reawaken, and
   grateful, you grace all
Earth with your fragilelace
   strength.
Now, extending your newself out
   to your wingtip length,
And almost as if you had always
   known the Eternal

Secret, you do what He had
   always meant you to do.
You fly.

Lisa Tafoya
FREE TO BE ME

*To Mom and Dad in memory of
Dad.*

A mother and father
   as dear as you
Is never forgotten

I remember I told you
   I'd never move away
So I could take you
   to McDonald's E V E R Y D A Y—

Now I'm not there
   what can I say?
Except no McDonald's—
   not today

There comes a time
   when we must grow
Just like the wind
   it has to blow

You let me move
   and spread my wings
To see the world
   and all its things

It's always appreciated
   never forgotten
Remember me?
   I'm the one you spoiled rotten

Nancy J. Murphy
MOTHERS ANGELS
Three little boys left all alone:
Three little boys without a home.

Where did our mother go, where
   could she be?
Where did she go without us three.

We saw her lying there so little
   and frail;
Her hands so wrinkled, her face
   so pale.

You've been sick for oh so long;
We remember when you would
   sing us songs;

As the preacher started talking
   on that small hill;
The sun so bright, the sky so still;

It's all over now we've said our
   goodbyes;
As we wipe the tears from our
   little eyes.

Soon Jesus will come and take us
   away;
To our home in heaven where
   with mama we'll stay.

Gloria P. Lowe
ON THE SHORE

*To my Sister Frances with Love
Gloria*

Laying on the beach at Belmont
Shore watching people gather
more and more.

The ocean so calm I can
see from afar.

Oh! Catalina there you
are.

Palm tree's swaying in

the Ocean Breeze making it
seem like I'm in the
South Sea's

The sun is out it
makes me feel so warm
nothing like enjoying a
bright summer morn.

T. A. Boehm Sr.
LIFE

*This poem is dedicated to my
wife, JoAnn; my daughters, Anna
Maria and Verna Lisa; and my
sons, Tom Jr., Mark, Chris and
John Delbert. Without any one of
them, life would have no meaning
for me.*

Life is the sound of a newborn
   baby's cry.
It's the sound of a distant bus
   going by.
It's seeing an outstretched hand,
   helping someone who has
   fallen to stand
It's watching a child play in the
   snow or watching the trees as
   the winds blow.
It's hearing a voice filled with
   laughter.
It's also a voice praying and
   talking of hereafter.
It's unlike any other game.
None can choose between
   poverty and fame.
It's watching a child grow.
It's answering the questions they
   want to know.
It's filled with a great many
   emotions.
It's also filled with many
   devotions.
It's showing your family and
   friends that you care.
Treat it gently because it is a gift
   so rare.

Marie Pierre Semler, M. M.
THE FOUNTAINHEAD
   Who stills the roaring of the
   sea
And bids His winds blow, His
   rivers flow.
Rivers of tears to rivers of grace,
   Flowing within life's changing
   sea.

   Flowing from arms of a fruitful
   tree
Upon whose bosom scarlet flows.
Rendering clear all worthless
   dross.
   Quenching the thirst of every
   cross.

   A scorching wind no longer
   blows,
The breath of the Spirit gently
   grows,
Cooling the waters, warming the
   chill
   From ocean to every trickling
   rill.

   Who the raging tumult stills,
Swells the quiet stirring hope of
   little rills
And lifts sluggish depths that
   mope
   Till currents rise and leap
   Into the Everlasting Hills.

Constance Dee Gordon
LI'L SQUIRREL
   Climb up fast little squirrel.
   Climb high up the tree.
   Just don't drop your chewed
      up nuts
      down on top of me.

RoseMarie Amiee Faith

RoseMarie Amiee Faith
SIBLINGS

*This poem is lovingly dedicated
to all sisters and brothers around
the world, and especially to my
sister Georgia Ann and my
brother Duane.*

We enjoyed all the goodness
   childhood could bring,
   We giggled and oh did we sing.
We teased and lied,
   We laughed and cried.

We ran and played through all
   kinds of weather,
   Experiencing our energetic
   childhoods together.
Now that all the hoopla is said
   and done,
   I remember those joyous times
   as being genuine fun.

Life's ways have separated us.
   Now we are grown,
   Having families of our own.
But the recollection of our
   childhood will always be,
   So very special in my memory.

Oh how I miss each of you.
   I think of us in all I do.
Our childhood was full of many
   pleasures,
   The good times we've shared
   are now priceless treasures.

Ora Martin
TO A ROBIN
Little robin, why do you sing so
   merrily
When all you possess
Is a little nest
In yon maple tree,
Made of strings hung on the
   fence by me.

And a few grasses raked from my
   lawn,
Yet you start singing at break of
   dawn.
Is it because you have so few
   earthly possessions to worry
   about,
And you are thanking God for

the sun as it comes out?

Whether it shines, or rain falls,
We still hear your "Cheer Up,
Cheer Up" calls.
You keep so busy scratching about
For any unwary bug that comes
crawling out.

Then you carry it away to your
little nest
Kept warm by your mate's downy
breast.
Then off you go again to scratch
about
Still having time to thank God
With your "Cheer Up, Cheer Up"
shout.

Marguerite Wheeler
THANK THE LORD!
As each beautiful day draws
slowly to an end.
The daylight fades, and we
watch the night descend.

Do you ever stop to think
how lucky you were to-day?
It will only take a short moment
to 'Thank The Lord' and pray.

Only the Lord can give you
the thrill of just being alive,
And the Strength, Love and
Affection
to make you continue to strive.

Yes! We all strive to reach the
very best,
that life can ever give.
Honesty, True Love and
Truthfullness are
'Ideals' by which we should live.

Then, it matters not, whether the
sun
has shone in its glory to-day;
As we close our eyes in peaceful
sleep at night;
we "THANK THE LORD" for a
beautiful day.

Frances Gillard Harvey
RECOMMENDATION
Housework
Is for the doing
When there are no wild berries to
be picked;
No birds to be listened to;
No sky to be observed.
It is not
For the Godly.
It is for those who do not know
He exists!

Michelle Lee Mitchell
TEETH
In a building the color
of grade school restrooms
he takes out his teeth.
In the glass
the ivory bites through
the bubbles surfacing
like a diver.
He dreams in puckered sleep
of his fourth year,
of goldfish lipping
the clear, cold sides of a bowl,
gills waving, scales stretching
over the darting organisms.
The quick splash of two,
startled by the boy
and his flashlight,
dipping in his fingers
to catch one,

grabbing up
the dank coral and pearl
of teeth.

Mary Ninow Ryan
MOMENT OF BIRTH
Where am I?, asked the young
woman child, thrust into
surroundings so strange and
wild?
The creature that holds me and
gave me my life, the others
around me creating such strife.
The world I am in now I find so
unreal, full of harshness and
brashness, very little appeal,
when compared to my first world
so calm and serene, no place to
get ready, no soft in-between.
The world full of sweetness,
drifting gently along, full of
warmth and contentment, a
murmuring song.
No feelings break in on this
tender repose while my being
expands and my inner soul
grows.
Only dim light surrounds me
here in my first home,
everything round in my warm,
gentle dome.
Oh, so long that I coasted, myself,
so content, till that shattering
moment my whole world was
rent!
For the very first time, I felt anger
and pain, and it came, not just
once, but again and again!
The brightness assailed me, the
cold gripped me tight; my
being, unprepared for this
desperate fight.
No hint of the struggle I must
embark on, no hint of the glare
of this newly found dawn.
The terror of feeling the cold on
my skin, the noises so harsh,
such a frightening din.
The space that surrounds me, so
vast, so unknown, my senses
alive with my feeling alone.
Why must I enter this new
world?, I wailed, my cries
echoed loudly, then, slowly
they paled.
Then came a warmness I'd not
felt before, a feeling so pleasing,
I reachd out for more.
nuzzling, cooing, a feeling so
sweet, no longer a thought of
my former retreat.
I welcome my new world with
arms open wide, I'll enter now,
gladly, not wanting to hide.
The mother who loves me has
made it all worth, the terror
and pain of the moment of
birth!

Gloria McGee
GOD'S OBEDIENCE CHILD
Your path is always clear, no
stumbling blocks or hills.
Your needs are always met, no
reason for you to fret.
Your darkness is always light,
that shines both day and night.

Your ways are always best.
Your stand through every test.
Your troubles are always few.
God looks after you.

Your fathers always with you.
Your life always new.

Joseph P. Kowacic
APRIL
Her kisses
can be burned-out blossoms
or softly petaled thrills.

She either loves
with youthful passion
or with youthful passion
kills.

Judy L. Simmons
TEARS OF TEMPTATION
The more I think of sadness
The more I think of my temptation
The temptation to be
more than I really am.
I have always thought of tears
as being from the eyes.
Tears are from the sadness one
has
and from temptation I always
ran . . .

Robin C. Tremble
MENTAL PAIN
Come inside my mind
But beware that if you dare
The shadows hide the passages
That don't lead anywhere
Paths full of mystic emptiness
Inside the mental cell
The prison you have entered
Holds you in eternal Hell
Venture through the memories
That lurk within the walls
The chambers of a lunitic
Where a fallen angel falls
You'll never know the danger
That lurks within the brain
Of the suicidal cerebum
That's condemned to be insane
You'll pass through many stages
Before you reach the end
The journey takes you endlessly
To walk among the dead
You can try to run and hide
But running is in vane
Once you enter mad mens minds
Each day is Mental Pain . . .

Dawn Little
OH FIRELIGHT
Oh firelight, please dance tonight
upon my fireplace.
Send forth your glow, to warm
my soul which longs for your
embrace.

Oh firelight, you're sheer delight
when winter time is due.
You keep your glow, despite the
snow or winds that chill me
through.

Oh firelight, with flames so
bright, you beckon me to stay.
Your warmth brings me serenity,
a peace I need this day.

Oh firelight, please dance tonight
upon my fireplace.
Send forth your glow, to ease my
soul which longs for your
embrace.

Karen M. Brown
CONTENTMENT
As I lay here watching you
Sleeping, dreaming,
Softly and sweetly,
I remember our times

Together, good and bad.
I think of all the love
We've shared and
All the pain
We've endured.
And as I caress your face,
You stir softly and
Smile, and I wonder
To myself if you're as
Content with
Your life as
I am.

Greg (ishe) Smith
REFLECTIONS OF A MAN
Reflections of a man,
who lived
and died.
He brought us through
so much.
In the years of uncertainty.
In the times of psyc-a-madness.

Born of four,
he grew to one.
He showed us the way
to individuality.

His time here was short,
but his thoughts
will live forever.
And when he died,
a part of us,
died too.
For there is a little
of Lennon,
In us all.

Norene Kelly
SENSITIVITY
What is it
To a misfit?
A whole lifetime
Of no one's crime,
Nature's mistake
A faulty make.
Laughter abounds
When she's around
The others rule
So she's the fool
She suffers and cries
Can't wait 'til she dies
It's life's cruel touch—
She feels too much.

L. G. Mace
SHADOWS OF DAWN

*For Beverly, who inspired this
poem. For Debbie, who it was
given to. And for Linda, who
constantly makes me feel it.*

As light spreads lace patterned
shades over the city,
And whispers of the coming day
stir in the early hours of morn,
I look out the window over the
sleeping city as it slowly comes
to wake.

As the sun rises over the mount,
gold leafing everything on its
bronzed easel,
And wonder what visions fill
your head and heart as you
sleep, as your spirit dreams.
All the lights that colored the
dark in rainbow prisms and
fairyland illusions,
Have one by one all blinked out—
Leaving us to the harshed
brilliance of reality, called day.

Left behind are those things we
could hide in the corners of the
black velvet, isolated questions
of dark,
And everything is left naked in
the scalpeled undresser of the
early hours called day.

But somewhere between the two,
Twixt night and day, dusk and
dawn,
I have my dreams of you,
In dawn and in her shadows.

Peggy Lui

Peggy Lui
DRIFTING AWAY
A lonely, abandoned, old sailboat
drifts away along cold waters,
A sailboat that once had laughter
and happiness aboard,
Now has memories and traces of
the now-gone fun.
The sails that were once bright
yellow which reflected the
sun's color and of warmth and
happiness,
Are now a faded yellow and torn.
The soft wind once guided the
sailboat along as the passengers
were sharing laughter,
Now the sailboat just drifts away
along the cold waters on
forgotten thoughts.
The sailboat has been through a
lot,
It used to sail people into the
sunset,
Or just sailed along with others
boats,
It once created shadows over the
waters for all to enjoy the
beautiful sight,
And now, the only shadow it sees
is its own,
A lonely and desolate shadow,
Yet it still sails . . .
Only now it sails alone and just
drifts away into unknown
journeys with no designated
direction.

Dewey Bayless
One Coal Miner's Spirit
I spent twelve hours today,
pushin' a cart
Filled with dusty black coal
Then another two hours just
gettin' home
Bumbin' rides and a trekin' the
snow

Sometimes I sure wonder if it's
all worth it

If I shouldn't just pack up and go
But I've hope for this land an
hope for my kids
I reckon hope kinda makes up
my soul

Don't get me wrong, I'm not a
church goer
Just different things seem to drive
different men
For I've seen the quitters that
lose sight of all beauty
I guess that's the worst of all sins

It's easy to do when you're back
in those mines
And 'bout everything 'round you
is black
But you gotta believe there's
gonna be light
You see, deep inside, you just
gotta fight back

I know the worries of raisin' a
family
And workin' a job and just gettin'
along
But you gotta look deeper and
do a little dreamin'
Just believe in yourself and be
strong

Denise Joanne McMahan
THAT SONG
That song reminds me of
soft breezes,
That passed by
While we teased each other
endlessly.
That song reminds me of
Hot summer days
That "I" spent alone,
Trying not to think about how
much
"I" missed you.
That song reminds me of
The changes of fall
That showed and kept us apart.
That song reminds me of
now.
It's spring again
with soft breezes slowly passing
by
Reminding me of
All those moments that "I" so
much cherish!

Flavia DiRollo
AUTUMN SONG
Once a love so true and small
Grew into a tree, so big and tall
It's trunk and branches strong
and smart
Through the years—always
changing
But never due to part . . .
And now, the leaves that had
carried on
Have changed color and are all
gone.
The love that once was true and
slow
Has made the tree too old to grow.

Cindy Kroll
FEELINGS
—So deep and alone
—So distant and so cold
—So upsetting and fearful
—So lonely and sad
—So confusing and so desperate.
Why do people have to feel that
way?
Why can't you be happy all the

time?
There's always a way in, but
there's never a way out.
How can you make people
understand you, if you don't
understand yourself?
What's going on inside that little
mind of yours?
Why does everything seem so
dark?
Why is it all black?
Why does your mind trigger
everything off?
Why do feelings make you hurt
so much?

Rosemary Morgan
MEMORIES

---

*To Tom, with love, without
whom there would be no past,
present or future memories. All
my memories are only ours.
Forever Yours Rosemary*

No, honey, I cannot forget you
Just yesterday you left and the
pain I feel
Covers your sweet image inside
my soul
You shall live in my memory
You are the beginning
And the end of my history
Like the rest of my glory
For with you I was born
Without you I will die
I shall be forever in my love
As the blend of the colors pressed
distinctivly upon a canvas
As the sprout of leaves upon a
tree—with pride
To me you have never left.

Dorothy S. Lambert
SPRING

---

*To all who love the handiwork of
God, the Master Creator!*

Gone are the shadowy, gray days
of winter
Gone are the howling winds with
their icy breath
And now,
Softly, as a gentle maiden dancing
thru a
meadow filled with violets,
daisies, daffodils,
forget-me-nots swaying with
delight in the gentle
breeze,
as she, lifting her smiling face,
upward
to the warming sun,
Gently as the softness of a
morning rain,
The flutter of a robins' wings
Gently swirling thru the blue sky
Searching for it's family's nest,
Gliding gently, oh so gently over
trees
bursting with buds of pink and
white,
It bursts into song
as once again the world is reborn!
At last! It's Spring!!!

William L. McFarling
GETTING OLD
Old I am getting
I can tell,

All questions I answer
With a boisterous yell!!!

I am cranky and stubborn
Nothing seems to please,
But one thing's for sure
I'll grow old with ease!!

My hair is graying
My teeth I've lost,
I'm seeing double
And I'm no longer boss!!!

Every part of my body
Seems to hurt,
And the part that doesn't
Just don't work!!!

My waist gets bigger
With each passing day,
So I must be getting older
What else can I say!!!

But, you know getting old
Isn't all that bad,
When a voice on the phone
Says, "I love you dad" . . .

Susan M. Silver
RELIGION
All I have loved is gone,
All I have worshipped untrue;
Yet I cleave to these false gods:
To the mind, and to music, and
you.

David L. Warren
THE MAP

---

*Dedicated To: My Hero, Jesus
Christ*

Left at the sun
Right at the moon
Down from the cross
Up from the tomb
Through every wilderness
Desert and fear
Across every ocean
And river and tear
Through every prison wall
Past every sword
Past all my wretchedness
Here I am Lord.

Bertha E. Parker
MY DAD
What Would This World Be Like
If It Wasn't for that
Silver haired dad, Who brings us
cheer and hope no
matter where we are at, Who
holds us in his big
strong arms and helps us through
our tears and
storms and buys us covers to
keep us warm "MY DAD".

We would miss so much if it
wasn't for dear old dad.
Though he is not talked about as
much as mother, but
he's the best friend we ever had.
He may be growing
older and wear a faded hat, but no
one could ever
take his place. "MY DAD"

He might be getting childish or
can't get around so
good anymore. You might think
he's old fashioned or
maybe he makes you bored, Oh I
thought that way as
I traveled down lifes road, But I

didn't know he
would be gone one day and I
would be so alone,
"MY DAD"

Gina Marie Marsala

Gina Marie Marsala
ME, ANEMONE
I feel like a sea anemone that has
such possibilities of becoming
beautiful and showing its
colors but rather chooses to
close them off.

When the moon and the tide
agree—I will open, but I have a
feeling my colors will not be
seen by all.

To flash one's beauty is wrong, to
be unaware of it is unrealistic,
to shut it off would kill the
spirit draining all color and life.

While the sea anemone rests only
to open to thrive on small
treasures of the sea; so must I.

For thrive I must on the energy I
feed on through the universe.
I will not flash—but I'll open—
not returning to die but rather
live in all its vivid colors and
riches that not only the
anemone possesses but truly a
universe within I have.

Jeffrey Menne
OF ANN P.
She never looks him in the eyes
And she can't see how hard he
tries
To find a niche in her heart
Where he could start
To have her love

He feels like a fool
In the halls of school

She walks with another guy
He sees no chance in her eye
That he'd ever have her love

Should he talk to her now
Could they be friends somehow
Or would he end up hurt
Only able to flirt
Still wanting to have her love

Edith Tribble Stark
Butterfly Of Midnight Blue

*This poem was written to—and
inspired by—my husband Dan.
He planted and worked the
beautiful flowers which drew the
birds and butterflys to our garden.*

As I gazed into the blue, blue sky,
A graceful butterfly flitted by.
I wondered from whence it came,
and where it went.
Was it on some wayward journey
bent?

It winged its way into the blue
yonder.
As it made its retreat I gazed in
wonder.
It seems it has been your happy
lot,
To be endowned with wings of
blue and poka dots.
I held my hand to shade the light,
And watched as it winged its way
from sight.

Butterfly, has it been your
cheerful lot,
To tie my fluttering heart in
knots?
Are you seeking your favorite spot,
To play out your graceful plot?
With your discrete acrobats afar,
Are you reaching out to become a
star?

Little friend in the high wind you
lurch,
There is no lull, or place to perch.
It's as though you had to search,
To find a cloud where you can
float.
There from your high perch you
sit and gloat.

Slowly on the high cloud you
cruise,
Are you not afraid the way you'll
lose?
As you whirl and swoop across
the lagoon,
Be careful there my friend, that
you are not marooned.

Paulina P. Jones
SUNRISE
A ball of fire! that's what it is! so
round and bright and red, but
ah! the orange is also peeping
thru, like a halo around its head.
Never a Lovelier sight have I
seen, nor a warmness have I
felt, than the early morning
sunrise as it ascends above all
else.
The bonfire of life! it should be
called, for it's open for all to
see. Just over the hill, from
here, or there; so close it seems
to be.
It's nice to feel the warmness, as

it penetrates so deep;
waking all the living things, from
such a sound, sound sleep.
It shines a light so very wide, that
nothing in its path can hide.
Even the flowers that fold at
night, open to take a peek at
sunlight.
Arise! and shine! it seems to say,
for I am here to help start your
day.
A morning glory that's what it is!
for seeing the sunrise is one of
life's greatest thrills

Pamela Linstromberg
THE UNICORNS APPEAR

*For my fantasy, my unicorn, my
loving husband, Eric.*

With the setting of the flaming
sun our fantasies awaken one
by one.
The velvet dark of night expands
to remove the light and
blanket the land
Reality shrivals and fades away.
Unicorns appear and begin to
play.

Nancine Meyer
TEARS

To all who can no longer weep . . .

Sign of my joy
Trace of my sorrow
Tears grow alike
To photos of kin

Firstborn event
Endless recording,
Second, and third,
Diminishing show

Thereafter additions
Still touching my heart,
Are fewer times shown
Captured in frame

Mary E. Meyer
POETRY PAST
Time was when poetry was a
thing of rhyme,
That concept has passed with time
Today poetry is a line without
meter
Without tune
Forget the past form,
The written word must only hold
meaning
Meaning for whom?
The author poet
The reading student
Learned pedagog
Ignoramus?
Probe deep within the recesses
of the mind
The soul
The mortal being
Find meaning
For life
For love
For poetry
Or forget it.

J. C. Iwasaki
A PRICE TO PAY
And we as lovers time will do
We lept upon each other's words
And thus exchanged our tender

vows
For sharpened tongues instead.

We were so like an angry child
With patience lost and virtue
spoiled
We chose to leave our marriage
bed
Forsaking promises we wed.

Consulting books and quoting
quotes
Relieving each of blames and
faults
We turned our seperate ways and
lost
The love our broken dreams had
cost.

Behind a door a child slept
'Neath fairy princess sheets she
wept
Small shoulders grieving tearless
sobs
The guilt of it, she bore it all.

Karen Ann Phillimore
VALENTINE'S DAY

For my husband, Derek 1983.

Valentine's day is here again
And I just wanted to say
I love you as much as ever,
Words we don't say everyday.

Words that get lost in our
everyday life
As we go from chore to chore;
Although they're thought, they're
never said
Shouldn't we try a little more?

Before we married, they were
often said
Without a second thought,
But now it seems, after all these
years
They tend to get a little caught.

So on this day that's made for love
I wanted you to know
That I do dearly love you
Though at times it doesn't show.

Gerard Brown
A RECURRING THOUGHT
I believe the grass was green,
But I don't trust it well now.
I'd like to sing softly, but my
throat is rather dry.
Can we go back for a moment? (I
think not).
But will you remember as I do?
I fear time will never tell.

Catherine F. Douglas-McCargo
SHATTERED SYMPHONY
Hear it? The long, low notes like
thunder's roll;
No melody of sweet and dulcet
tone,
But jarring, ragged notes from
some dark hole
Where lie the muffled echoes
caught in stone.
Hear it? The sighing, dying ghost
of sound
That rattles through the
skeletons of trees,
Then moves with martial beat
along the ground
And lifts its troubled voice upon
the breeze.

Hear it? There is no ceasing, no retreat;
It rides upon the tides from shore to shore
And pounds the air with never-ending beat;
The drumming, numbing music of the War.

Darla J. Black
God's Newest and Best Creation

I dedicate my poem to Rebecca Glover, adopted daughter of Terry and Judy Glover, for whom it was originally written.

Sometimes a mother feels
A slight sadness in her heart
   When she disregards her old ways
To make a brand new start
Stumbling up to warm a bottle
At 2 O'Clock a.m.
Looking to the sleeping face
Bright, shining as a gem.
   And as you teach her the basics
Somehow she teaches you
   The sacrifices, the good times
That all mothers go through.
   And pretty soon you can't remember
Just how life was without
   The pink-cheeked, bright-eyed bundle
To laugh or smile or pout.
   Then all too soon she's grown up
To start a new generation
   For you to love all over again—
God's newest and best creation.

Relda Lee
GRAY DAY
Beautiful gray day, so windy and wild
Inclining supple branches, rattling shutters
You remain nature's tempestuous child.

Flowers lift their faces for your moist kiss
Imposing oaks lean into your embrace
The earth lies swaddled in your prismatic mist.

Gather me into your cinereal melancholy
Make mine a deep blue funk
Filled with thoughts of impotent man and his folly.

Draw me close to loneliness and fear
Encircle me with death and its uncertainty
Tempt me to savor dark emotion and hold it dear.

Mirthless canescent day, though oblivious are some,
Your murky magic seeks me
The poet, ever your ambivalent victim.

Carrollyn Turner Poenie
MY SHINING PALACE
Set upon the solid rock the ugly houses stand,
Come and see my shining palace built upon the sand.
Where tropic winds and breezes blow and golden sun-sets rest,

And lapping waves of waters blue kiss the shore's sweet breast.

The gulls reflect their golden wings in evening's summer light,
While waving palm trees greet hello the er' oncoming night.

Say where upon the solid rock do scenes like this commence?
Not near those ugly homes on rock, so cold and still and dense!
But only on my tropic isle so far away from land,
And near my own bright, shining palace built upon the sand.

Nancy Jo Jean
GENNY
It was a stately old house, standing high above the town,
   It stood like a monument, you could see for miles around.
If this house could somehow speak, it would tell of bitter tears,
   Shed by a sweet little girl, who lived there eighteen years.
She grew into a woman, with eyes of violet blue,
   The picture of perfection, to all the men she knew.
Her life was full of roses, till she fell in love with Dan,
   Then her world began to die, when he ask for Genny's hand.
Dan moved into the manor, to rule o'er his home and wife,
   He drank so much that she'd hide, just to try and save her life.
There were those who heard her screams, when he'd find her hiding place,
   Then there was only silence, no bruises showed, not one trace.
Late in that last December, badly weakened with poor health,
   The preacher tried to see her, but he kept her to himself.
They heard not another cry, from the house upon the hill,
   They'd sit outside and listen, but everything seem so still.
She lies in rage by the oaks, in a cloak of ivy green,
   While Dan took a brand new wife, the woman of all his dreams.
In time she heard the story, how Genny went to her grave,
   She feared she'd die just that way, so she quickly slipped away.
But Genny got her sweet revenge, even though she slept so still,
   The air was filled with deadly gloom, in the house upon the hill.
And sometimes if you listen, you'll hear laughter gently cried,
From beneath the big white oaks, where sweet little Genny lies.

Marilyn Robertson
LOVE REBORN
Night. Empty, alone.
Dark, cold void. No image in the mirror.
Dawn creeps slowly, stealthily,

then of an instant
Splits the sky open.
No warmth to the sun. Its icy brilliance cuts to my very depths;
Its chilling ooze seeping between my toes,
Hungering for my soul.
I hide behind the dishes, under the mattress,
Between the carpet and the floor.
Knights in shining armour hesitate, but seeing the glint of steel
Mirrored in ice, pass on shuddering.

Night. Empty, alone.
Dark, cold void. No image in the mirror.
Ghosts dancing in the dark.
   Images of the soul's hunger.
Dancing, entwining, giving gifts of essences to no one.
I hide under the bedcover, pillow pulled down, and wait
For the cold rape of the sun to bring a new dawn.
Shadows dissolve, ghosts materialize
And I run naked into the fires of hell.
The warmth giving life, yet taking all I have known.
I am liquified, vaporized, consumed, but reborn.
A sparkling drop of dew on a quivering rose petal,
Shinging forth in all its brilliance,
Speaking from the heart with tender words of love.

Lorene Dunaway Osborn

Lorene Dunaway Osborn
LITTLE WHITE DOVE

In loving remembrance of Mr. John Bascum Perry of Perryville, Al. and our sweet romance of the 1960's, his kind voice and gentle manner won my heart.

A very lovely heart trimmed in red, placed near my dear sweet darling's head,
Upon the heart were roses of red, A symbol of my love for this dear friend
who is dead . . .
And oh the pretty little white dove,
   was A symbol of real true LOVE.

Tho he is gone and cannot see, these flowers that were bought for him by me,
My love is stirred within my heart,
Oh why must lovers be kept apart?
Loving memories of him in my heart will
stay—untill God also calls me away.
Little White Dove—kept in remembrance of our love,
makes me feel like crying—to think of this old
sweetheart of mine dying,
Little white dove—reminding me of real true love,
the love, I married another to try to forget,
the love that is living in my heart yet,
Little white dove, I hope my darling is resting with God above,
I don't suppose there'll ever be A sweetheart
I'll think more of, tho he is lying in Hillview
beside his wife, he was one of the dearest sweethearts
I've had in my life . . .

Florence Faye Halbert
COLD WINTERS DAY

With Love to my family

Have you ever sat on a cold winter's day;
watched the beautiful snowflakes falling your way?
Swirling—tumbling—dancing—they came;
Like tiny ice fairy's, to the window pane.
The children all dancing, Laughing with glee;
The magic wonder for the whole world to see.
Slipping—sliding—sleding—they go;
so thrilled at the sight, of this breath taking show.
Oh, look over there, now thats something to share!
rolling—struggling—tugging—so hard,
a huge, fantastic snowman, even rover is tired.
The trees all aglitter, with coats of diamonds, they sway,
Evening comes, softly, with stardust still falling our way.
Swirling—twirling—quickly—they came,
Each little snowflake, playing its own game.
A fire in the fireplace, seems to join the mistic sight
Shimmering—leaping—glowing—like a fairyland in flight.
Mixed with tiny stars and diamonds, crystal lovers, in a misty park.
Tiny droplets seem to kiss their cheeks and
form a perfect little heart.
I shall put this picture away now, in my

sea of memory;
And someday shall repaint it, for
all the world to see.
So that when I fade away, all will
see my cold winter's day.

Judy E. Keane
LOVE OF MINE

---

*To Steve, You make my days
brighter, and my nights warmer.*

Oh love of mine, I'm happy you're
here.
I'll keep a smile, as long as you're
near.
Oh love of mine, there's stars in
your eyes,
So hold your truth, and tell no lies.
Oh love of mine, tell me true,
Is our love, a love that grew?
Oh love of mine, I love you so,
I tell you now, but did you know?
Oh love of mine, please trust in
me.
Just wait awhile, and you will see.
Oh love of mine, our love will
grow,
Oh my love, I love you so . . .

Linda Varney
IT WAS YOU
Don't forget
It was you
Who said you love me
Even when you knew
That what we'd have
Just might not last
It could end up
Just like the rest
You took the chance
And didn't think
That all along
We were on the brink
What we had
Would never end
We'd never settle
Just as friends
We'd be together
Through and through
Once again
It was you

Cathy Scruggs
"ME" PROTESTS
All around us lies the stage
But must it our soul engage?
Entertainers we all must be
But to what permanent degree?
Masks we all must don
But for how long?
The troupe forever moves on
But shall we always belong?
Curtains must always fall
But does that end it all?

Costumes cloak our entire being
But must that keep us from
seeing?
Props will support our every need
But must their absence make us
bleed?
Setting glorifies the mood
But must we for its sake brood?
Scenes continually evolve
But must we around them revolve?
Participants all are we
But must we forget our ME?

Tragedy, comedy, satire prevail
But must any or all cause our ME
to fail!

Cliff Johnson
TOMORROW
Rose buds bending in the rain
Tell that tomorrow all the pain
And sorrow of yesterday
Are forgotten, and flown
As the sun that briefly shone
And turned buds to things
Of beauty, and joy, and pleasure.
So my life, now but a bud,
May tomorrow rise from the mud
Of tears, and sorrow, and regrets—
And yet become, like the full—
blown rose,
A thing of beauty and joy that goes
To gladden a heart or two;
And makes my life to be
What was intended of God, for me.

Nettie Marie Yohn
BEING MY FRIEND
When I begged another
for friendship
He openly crushed my heart
throwing it to the ground
breaking it into
a million pieces
Stomping each piece
with humiliation
ridicule and scorn
You were there
Helping me pick up the pieces

Silently being my friend
Waiting for me to be able
to function again
No questions asked
Never pushing me to give
emotions
I was incapable of giving
But encouraging me to
take one step at the time
one day at the time
So I really could survive
and grow
You are always there
Being my friend.

Reba Horton
**Needed Words From a
Husband**

---

*To my husband, Carter Horton,
who came into my life when I
needed him the most.*

I need words of encouragement
In this world of phase;
Lift me up;
In words of praise.

I need words of comfort
Words to understand;

Tell me;
I know you can.

I need words of kindness
Words of bliss;
Wrapped with a smile;
Sealed with a kiss.

I need words of compliment
In my life;
To help me to live;
In this world of strife.

I need words of criticism
When I am wrong;
To aid my person;
To be strong.

I need words of condolence
In my time of grief;
That joy will appear;
And my sorrow finds relief.

I need words of trust
In action of love;
Say a prayer for me;
Bound in faith from above.

Sometimes words are not needed
Just a glance or a look;
With your loving arms around me;
Like a cover of a book.

Anne-Marie Hebert
WHAT IS LOVE?

---

*To my brother Bill
When all other sisters hated their
little brothers, I loved mine.*

What is love?
Is it a star
Gazing at us
From afar?
Is it a tree
Standing in the dark
Seeing what it can see?
Or is it just a notion
Or a crazy old emotion?

Georgette E. Piper
SUNBEAMS
Just look towards the sun!
Its beautiful rays
Reach down from heaven
To brighten our days.

Rainbows of colors
Slide down from the sky
On golden sunbeams,
Saying, "God is nigh."

Pink brings assurance
Our Father sends Love.
Pale green slides down, too,
With Peace, like a Dove.

Sky blue comes along,
Gives strength to the soul,
Food for the Spirit,
And helps make us whole.

Yellow then gives us
That great healing touch,
Assuring us, God
Just loves us so much.

Mauve comes with a crown
On an angel's wing.
God gave us His Son—
We must crown Him, King!

Katrina Marie Scheltema
TIME IS GONE
How fascinating the world is!
It stretches out before me;
bright rainbows of time
echoed in the wind carved rocks.

See how strong the sunlight is,
and the trees and the flowers
that bloom.
Where are their seeds?

How lovely the sky is:
yellow with the sun
and orange as the desert's sands.
When did it come there?

Where are the flowers?
When stopped the time?
Mrs. Randy (Barbara) Langham
MY SISTER, MY FRIEND
Sis, we are all grown up now
Eventhough, it is hard to
realize somehow
We have watched the years
slip right on by
And now on our memories
we must rely
We have always been
so very close
And from my observations—
much closer than most
This is something of which
I so often do boast
As a rule, sisters should
At least sometimes fight
But, we never ever have—
if my memory serves me right
I look back and recall when
we were kids still at home
Those nights we would lay awake
as the night grew on
Talking quietly, our "little secrets"
we would confide
As we lay side by side . . .
We are both Mothers now
with "little ones" of our own
But, we are still "little girls"
again as our thoughts do roam . . .
You have been a sister who
has been so true through the years
We have shared our laughter and
tears
You are so generous in all your
sharing
And your thoughtfulness shows
your love and caring . . .
When I need a helping hand to
extend
You are always there—
"MY SISTER, MY FRIEND" . . .
Mary Shull
LOVE IS PRECIOUS

---

*I Dedicate This Poem To My
Husband Whom I love Dearly.*

Love is precious, love is sweet
Love is wonderful to us,
Love can be wonderful to anyone
Who really cares.

We enjoy doing things together
We love each other's company
Love is precious if you want it to
be.

Love is precious and sweet in
every way
Love can be great for everyone.
Love is precious all the way
around.

Love is precious, love is great all
the way
We are very happy all the way
around.
Love is precious, love is sweet,
with love all the way.

We love each other's ways, and
  love is precious
Love is sweet, and let me repeat
Love is sweet and precious.

Just love someone, love is precious
Love is sweet.

Diane Ramsey Criss
I LOVED
I touched you with my eyes
  and released the love
I have so long
  wanted to give you.

I touched you with my thoughts
  and encircled your neck
    for a closeness
    I have sought.

I released a part of me
  to meet the you
    who together
      becomes a we.
I touched you
  and I loved.

Paulette Gregory
MEMORIES

*To Don Reeve, thank you for the
memories.*

The memories of you come
  rushing back to me.
Oh how I wish I could go back to
  the days when it was just you
  and me, and innocents of being
  a teenager in love.
The day we met how shy I was
  when you asked me to the
  movies.
And the Kiss that sent me out of
  this world.
The cheers I yelled as you ran for
  the touch down and made the
  score that won the game.
Then the prom, Oh! how
  handsome you looked and how
  proud I was to be with you,
  knowing so many girls would
  have loved to be in my place.
But then the day came and you
  left me for you were a senior
  and I was only a junior.
I cried and cried.
But that was so long ago.
Now you are with yours and me
  with mine.
But the memories are ours to
  share.

Bill Drake
MIDNIGHT RIDER
Absent without a leave
  Singing the highway song.
  Always a rebel
fighting without a cause.

  Fly by the night
whenever the winds prevail.
  Walk softly, thru the lands
Travel till the moon and stars
  turn oh, so pale.

  Nowhere to go
  but everywhere
keep rolling under the stars.
  whistle sounds
  Stop for another town
    Empty boxcars
      Hobos gather around.

  I hear my train a coming.

Doris Arnold Elliott
A VISIONED SANCTUARY
If only I could go
To some enchanted charmed
  place,
And listen to the birds
While the rabbits run a race,
Or walk into the shadows
Of some noble forest glen,
And there discern the images
Of the contents therein.

The magic elm, the stately pine,
The birds and bees they do
  entwine,
All living joyously their own free
  way,
Making happy weary travelers
  day by day.

A place serenely quiet to be
Out in the open wilds so free . . .
Ideal for contemplation
Upon the problems of a Nation.
A place where God is manifest
And where the joys of life are
  best.
Environment clean, and
  atmosphere serene,
Won't you walk with me through
  the forest green?

Gary W. Enos
THE ATEMPORAL IF

*I Dedicate this poem to the
Person, who, believes they have
Nothing, and Wishes they had
the world.*

If one, could incompass
How Eagles do soar.
If one, could but quell
The Oceans great roar.
If one, could embellish
Through Poem or Rhyme.
If one, could but hold
Such secrets as time!
If, one only could with out
Purpose nor Sorrow,
Complacency befall him,
And die, on the Morrow.

Annette Bacon
SLEEPLESS
The night wind blows
Across the land.
The air is cool
Above the sand;
But something in the night won't
  sleep.

The night is long
Unless you dream;

Never ending,
So it would seem,
When something in the night
  won't sleep.

The dawn is trapped
Beyond the edge.
Tomorrow waits,
A hopeful pledge,
While something in the night
  won't sleep.

Fear lurks, hiding
Behind the moon.
Dread runs all through
A songless tune,
When something in the night
  won't sleep.

The sun will rise
Undoubtedly;
Another day
Waits heavily,
When something in the night
  won't sleep.

Sarai Kniskern
ENFANTS PERDUS
Soldiers,
                    War,
Walking triumphly to their death
  bed—
  to them no one is called friend,
  and the hup two-three-four,
  they learned to abhor,
In the foreground of their minds
  was the hypercritical captain
  who threw maledictions,
But the reality of what they
  experienced became more than
  just his predictions,
He expected them to be as
  unfading mountains in this
  terra incognita countryside,
Obeying orders would become
  their life—
  seeing themselves as puppets
  infiltrated in a mine field
  knowing his words they must
  abide,
Looking across that terminational
  destiny for bodies all wanting
  help—
  someone to tend to their
  wounds—
  there would be no end to the
  constant pleading,
Seeing their faces is the hardest
  event to accept along with
  their hearts not beating,
Those whoever still conscious
  wondering if the sky pilot was
  watching over them in his
  bubble cloud,
For if their parents could see
  them now would they be
  crying or proud,
Somehow the attachment of a
  father and son never ceases as
  the words between them go
  round,
As one father came to realize its
  just time passages and
  commemorate that his child "is
  one of the kings that will be
  crowned."

Lori Jeanette McIntosh
**In the Back Alleys Of My
Mind**
Imagery, eyes mingle eyes,
With love's silent stillness.
Days break into small pieces.

Reflections of thought by thought,
Embedded memories, forever
  entwined.
In the back alleys of my mind.

But time sheds gentleness,
Like the silent maple tree,
Shades the barren ground.
Like a fragile wine glass,
Empties into the oceans frothy
  brime.
In the back alleys of my mind.

Yellow rose petals
Unfold outward exposing,
Gentle strokes of red.
Where bare roots intermingle
Upon riverbeds of tears whined.
In the back alleys of my mind.

Miss Mary Jane Dennis
BIBLICAL REFLECTION

*To the Enduring Remembrance of
Dr. Mr. & Mrs. Stephen W. Paine
For Biblical Devotion and
Hospitality of Home, and Also For
Sharing and Caring in my life, at
Houghton, New York.*

A Book so altogether true,
Indeed, is worthy for review.

This Book I hold within my hand,
Is ours to read and understand.

Within its pages find each place
God's written Word sets forth His
  grace.
See there the beauty of the
  Word
Revealed through Christ, God's
  Son, our Lord.

Into your heart His Truth
  receive,
Salvation find, when you believe.

Seek light upon your path each
  day
From His who said, "I am the
  Way."

Search out the gems for
  holiness,
Live well your life, and let God
  bless.

Learn how to know the Way of
  Love
Bestowed by God who dwells
  above.

So study that your life may
  show
The Christ, in God, you come to
  know.

Then from this Bible take some
  seed
And plant it for another's
  need.

However one may choose to look,
Can there be found so great a
  Book?

Uplift your hands, and praise the
  Lord,
This Book, the Bible, is God's
  Word!

Filomeno L. Pacis
SCENIC MARVELS
On a warm late afternoon,
As you go strolling
Along Manila Bay—

Our World's Best Loved Poems

Where once Admiral Dewey
Sunk in defeat the Spanish Fleet—
And glance over the horizon,
How wonderful to behold
The beauty of our sunset,
That flaming ball of gold,
So gloriously painted,
On the massive canvas
Of Heaven!

What a thrilling adventure,
And experience so delightful
To join a sight-seeing tour,
And go to Mountain Province,
In the Philippines,
To see the scenic grandeur,
Of our famous centuries-old
Banaue Rice Terraces,
Looking like enormous
And towering stairways,
Almost reaching the doorway
To the sky!

Robert P. Martorano, Jr.
PEOPLE
People travel near.
People travel far.
People travel I know not where.
Into the sunset.
Into the shadows.
Into their own worlds.
Where they live and love.
In happiness forever.

Barbara A. Lott
THE WEDDING
I dream I am a Spirit
  Haunting the forest trails
Where leaves and pines are
  fragrant
  Sheltered from life's gales

Betrothed to the shadowed forest
  I never more will leave
In the autumn we will marry
  I never more will grieve

Our children oft will whisper
  Of a wedding once so grand
Of a marriage so eternal
  Of a Spirit with the land.

Sadie Stout
Watchman, What Of the Night?
Watchman, what of the night?
What hearest thou
In the stillness
What appears unto thy sight?

Watchman, what of the night?
What moves about
In the darkness?
What moves against the light?

All is well in the Lord
The watchman calleth,
Have no fear—
All is well abroad!

In the darkness moves the Spirit
With a message
From the Lord.
In the darkness, I do hear it.

He who has ears, let him hear!
He who has eyes—see!
All is well in the night
Because the Lord is near!

Joyce M. Gogain
SUMMER
The day is hot!
The parched fields cry for rain!
Too often clouds appear
And always far too soon take
  flight again!

Summer . . .
To some it's heaven, others—
  living hell!

The hours long
Cry out for end of day
When stars glow up above
And night's sweet darkness sends
  the sun away!

Summer . . .
Oh, when will autumn come to
  end its spell?

Marguerite Herard
SILHOUETTE
When at sunset
Nature is ready to rest,
Perched on a roof-top,
Every thought gets a lift
And the eyes spark
Something magical:
Chimneys become castles,
Dark and mysterious;
Television antennas,
As giant dragon-flies,
Stand gracious and still:
Vivid image of a company
Ready to perform
A nocturnal ballet!

Michele Denise Fancher
TO OLIVER
There will never be a way for me
to tell you how I feel
about all the things you've done
  for me
and how you've made dreams real

There were times when I thought
  trouble's hold
would never have an end
until you came along one day
and proved yourself a friend

There were also times of
  loneliness
of hunger and despair
and once again you crossed that
  line
to show me that you cared

There were many days that passed
when I did not know what to do
and once again just like before
you managed to come through

And so the things I do for you
as small as they may be
come from very deep within my
  heart
as they are part of me

And that's my way of saying
  "Thanks"
with hope that we never part
because I would like to someday
  hold
a place within your heart

Sister Mary Roland Lagarde, S. B. S.
MONASTIC PROFESSION
A simple call
Surrendering all.

Bending history
Dancing into mystery.

Your promise of fidelity
God's love vow of stability.

Against you was the odd
But, your life is now hid with
  Christ in God.

The bell is tolled
Salvation unfold.

Jesus' banner wave
From the cave to the grave.

Darwin Lee Hartman
THE BIRTH OF DEATH

*To my Mother, whose belief in
me caused this to be.*

Many regions of this earth give
  birth to death and what is
  worse;
They disrupt the movement of
  Life's start,
By handing death to unborn
  hearts.

Many reasons in this world for
  Life to find it's way,
But what of hope that is torn
  apart before it learns to pray?
What of Life our Lord has made
  yet so conveniently is destroyed?
Is this but a cowards way to face
  what has been enjoyed?

What of life that was to be, fast
  rendered back to dust?
It is not by God's eternity that
  death is born from lust.
What of Life with it's true start so
  quickly ended in a day?
Surely Life must play it's part
  before it fades away.

Only fools laugh at death; an
  unborn never dies.
It plagues the conscience with a
  whispered breath;
As a witness, it never lies.
It tells the truth thoughts
  disguise, yet makes the guilty
  realize;
That to end a child before it
  breathes, is a cowards way of
  life.
And any soul that can perceive
  knows how this is right.

So who in life will take the
  blame? The executioner.
And what or who will bear the
  shame? The Doctor's Probe or
  You?
Only fools will laugh at this,
  these words which I do write.
But in God's name I ask of You,
  who gave You the right?

And if You think I might judge
  the actions of this world,
Look just once at what You have
  done, or possibly will do.
I'm not judging anything; an
  unborn knows the truth.
It's soul cries out for justice; The
  birth of death has proof.

Lawrence S. Gist
SOFT WIND

*To Starks and Rosa Mae My
loved grandparents*

She comes to me in a soft wind
  with hair the color of coal, dark
  as my night eyes rich as the
  forest green.
Touching her guitar strings so
  tenderly she sings to me in a
  gentle voice singing of her
  homeland the sea.
I am papa san.

With the scents of jasmine in the
  air, forming heaven
She comes to me in a breeze
  like birds in flight, soaring,
  riding with the sunset
  dancing in my mind.
I love you.
You are my serenity.

When I close my eyes to dream
She comes to me in peace
  as a soft wind.

Bruce William Litterer
TOMORROW WILL BE
Swallow in the shadow of many
  strangers faces,
Mystify by voices sailin' through
  my mind,
Uncontrol energies accelerated
  through my embraces
As a flash of light, settle to
  confined
The downpour of voices, to enter
My mind . . . with the nightmare I
  left to crest
The dimensions of another center
Of time, to see the language of
  my quest.
Now I need to cries, the aftermath
Of my mind to say . . . when our
  new days
Will join us to lights the Path:
Will the Land of Tomorrow end,
  old ways
As the Love of Domination of Man
Turn to subside the quest of the
  clan.

Patricia A. Riebe
THE FOOTBALL MAN

*To Harold, my inspiration, with
love*

Sitting in his chair at night
  Makes us think all is alright
The chair is pushed way back
  Magazines are all stacked

Football game is on T. V.
  For all whom are interested to see
Silence is imminent
  No one wants punishment

It's only this month
  Don't lose your spunk
But you can't blame me
  Call upon N. B. C.

John Mason
A WALL HANGING
From the corner of the room
the young woman sits watching.
Unable to comprehend the
immeasurable depth of her world
she clutches onto some bare

thread of existence, with all the mighty force of generations before weighing down upon her, seizing her tongue and blinding her vision.

For it is a difficult world. One in which a meaning cannot always be ascertained, and the concept of purpose is oftentimes obscured by the busy hand of accomplishment like a magician who hides any knowledge of "How?"

Obey the silence. Remember: time is an ocean. Its secret can be heard. Leave your discouragement behind, for it does you no good within the walls. It becomes a barrier that keeps a distance between the rhythm of the waves and your lazy words.

Feel the motion! Let the truth swell up inside of you, and you will not have to hide.

Michael W. Dobinson
MY WIFE
How does one describe a rose or the
  sound that waves make upon the sand?
How does one show the love that an
  infant gives upon being cradled?
How can one explain the feeling of being loved?

To each of us, these questions have
  similar but yet different answers.
But for me the answer is the same,
    The answer is You!

The Beauty of the rose is in your eyes.

The sound of a wave is your voice tranquil and serene.
The love of infant is your reassurance
  and the feeling of being loved is the knowledge that you are there,
Now and always and forever; my loving Wife.

Beverly Anne Poole
OUR LOVE
A magic spell
The photograph
of a reappearing smile
raises a silver splash of stars
wondering about tomorrow
Fearing nights at home alone
simply surrendering to the persistent shadows
Floating through waves of silence
touching each other's memory
  When friends were questioning we understood us
  You and I were somewhere between
  making things a little better
Imagine the joy
Sensitive response . . .
Sort of . . . feels good!
Still
it goes on forever
and we continue
loving.

Cosmo P. De Stefano
IN LOVE

For Betsy, With Love

Who can see
  before the smoke clears
Who can point
  the moment love appears
Who can touch
  when there's nothing to hold
Who can hear
  when nothing has been told
Who can feel
  and never be cold
Who can grow
  and never be old
Who can see
  past the doubt and fears
Who can point
  the moment love disappears

Gwen Jones
JOSHUA'S POEM
Blessed by you
Small wonder in my eyes
Tremendous love in my heart
My child, my son
Miracle of life

At my breast
Source of life, love
Ever bountiful strength

A wish—granted
A prayer—answered
A dream—reality

Harriet Romigh
I FILL THE UNIVERSE
Under the Bodhi tree I waited
  long, patiently without a song.
While all at once as from a dream
  I awoke beneath a tree of life.
The shimmering breeze did sooth
  my brow. Rivers of tears disappeared somehow.
The windows under my wings for
  flight. I did look back with hesitant gaze,
but I longed much more for the
  ethereal waves, beyond what I had seen before.
I lost the feel of terrestial sands
  and seemed to soar in other lands.
The universe was now made
  mine for I'd begun the celestial climb.
Oh soul of me, oh soul of mine,
  ride higher yet on wings sublime.
Thou dost head for reality with
  Buddha 'neath the Bodhi tree.
Nine long years he meditated to
  get his wings in flight.
How long have I slept 'neath my
  tree? Forty years, it seems to be
But once I caught the wind of
  sail, no more deterrant could prevail.
Through searching long through
  lifetimes o're, I knew there'd be a distant shore
where I could land and fly again
  at any brief and tiny whim,
for all I ever was to be, I was right
  then, content with me.

I hear no call from foreign ports,
  my whistle signals with majestic snorts,

that all is well, the search is done.
  I know within that I'm the one
who made the search, became the
  sought. My rain did satisfy the draught.
Pour out my soul thy pot of gold.
  The rainbows end doth now unfold.
Fly oh my soul, be free to roam
  for thou hast found green grass of home.
For in the fullness of the times
  reward doth come to those who climb
to lofty heights not knowing
  where they lead nor why.
Infinity doth know the search
  though long, doth render recompense so strong,
that will supercede the mighty
  gale of earthlings struggle to prevail.
Lay not thy crown at others feet,
  lest Godhead there be stripped from thee.
Take thine own crown and hold
  it fast, for crowns are better saved for last.
Oh death where is thy sting
  today? Eternity's a better way to sound at ease
thy sweet desires and warm
  beside eternal fires. Slow down my soul,
thy sparks will speak and light
  your fire and you'll react in full attire
your song of love and light. For
  'tis you who fills the universe so bright.

Helene Martin
NOCTURNE SYMPHONY
As the nubian shadows cast their spell
Over the earth in somber and quietude,
The darkness changes sound and sight
From tintinnabulation and sibilant cadence of the day
To a sepulchral vesper of the night, echoes elude;
Singing its mysterious rondeau.
But nocturne's madrigal is a brief interlude
Returning to dawn's hopeful roundelay.

Sue Edie
RANDY

To my only brother whom I love very much and wish the best for.

His life is like a tarnished ring,
The past now holds an ugly thing,
To him this means a prison cell,
And long, long nights of righteous hell,
He's fallen down and fallen hard,
The crown now holds the final card,
Will he live and live at home,
Or will he die and die alone?
The time has come and now he see's,
The crown may drag him to his knee's,
Although he doesn't understand,
I'm always there to hold his hand.

Mary Stoetzel
IT WAS ONLY A DREAM
It was only a dream
it had to be.
Although it did seem
we were there you and me.

Holding each other
in the hard winter cold.
Not a worry or bother
not a care to be told.

All alone you and me
truly in bliss
Then you came to me
and gave me a kiss.

My body began to melt
I could hardly stand.
Who could know how I felt
as I stood holding your hand.

Did we have to say good night?
I could have stayed forever.
But then, dreams don't last forever.

Wanda Myers Miller
A CHILD'S EYES
A child's eyes
  how revealing they be,
For a moment pensive—
  near a tear,
A searching look
  brought me near,
A little soul's reflection
  how very dear,
Now instantly lively
  and full of glee,
How very much
  they say to me.

Kathy Blakeney
(MY) SOMEONE SPECIAL

This poem was written to express my deep care and concern for my boyfriend, Steve Lockett. Thanks for caring.

Seeking shelter in his arms.
Only wanting to relive
Memories all your own, of
Everlasting feelings you've shared.
Over and over saying repeatedly;
No one can take his place,
Especially in my heart.

Seeing beauty in everything.
Picturing heaven, here on earth.
Ending the days with him
Close in spirit and body.
It seems to be eternal;
And it is, if you want it.
Love; the link between two

worlds . . .

Grasp it . . . forever!!

Dorothy Dimeo Wyatt
HOW DO YOU TELL YOUR CHILDREN
The tears won't stop
And neither can I
In less than a year
I'm going to die.

How do you tell your children
That soon you won't be there
To give them hugs and kisses
And hear their nighttime prayers.

How do you tell your children
How sad the day will be
When you will leave their lives
for good
No more of them to see.

How do you tell your children
Too young to understand
That when you leave them all in
death
Your love lives on instead.

How do you tell your children
As they grow up to be
Good christian men and women
You will not live to see.

That though you die in body
Your spirit will live on
And for your very memory
They have to carry on.

Norlyn Silas
THE HUMAN RACE

*Dedicated to Henry and Willie B.
Silas, my understanding and
wonderful parents, for the values
they instilled in me.*

Over the horizon,
in a distant galaxy,
shaking the earth,
a mighty glorious parting,
BANG! BANG!
out jumps thunder,
lightning roars
and puts us under,
into a planet we call earth,
alien beings all looking for worth!
creep, creep, creep, comes the light,
crawling until light turns into
night,
a lot of fears for thoughts unseen,
alien forces can be real mean,
under the watchful glare of the
earth master,
aliens struggle and struggle to get
faster,
faster than a speeding bullet,
we look to outer space,
cause we the alien forces are the
"AL-MIGHTY HU-MAN RACE!!!

Victor R. Dyer
THE ROSE PARADE

*To Mrs. Cordelia Simons who
thought so much of the Rose
Parade.*

The rose parade that we
eagerly view New Year's Day,
is quite a memorable event,
Along life's highway . . .

In this grand pageantry,
many notables,

horses—
flowers—
bands and others
are meticulously assembled for
this
great occasion that is
pleasantly discussed
throughout the nation . . .

Some of the ancient past,
with a touch of the timely
present,
and a portion of
the foreseeable future,
are depicted here . . .
In the vast caravan of floats
that cruise elegantly along
attracting many a waiting eye,
beautiful and haunting
as a dear lullaby . . .

Now, as the Rose Parade,
gradually comes to an attractive
end,
on this fine New Year's Day,
it will be long
remembered along life's
highway . . .

Phyllis Steigelman
BLUE PERIOD
The dog chewed
my round bellied portrait.

Keeping the frame
you threw out
what in moments of love
you had painted.

The children have grown.
The dog no longer chews . . .
and the all inclusive
color white
is coloring my hair.

Your art has turned
to carpentry . . .
and my love
to abstraction.

Herbert Moran
ETERNAL LOVE
There is only one eternal love
It is the cause of our lack of peace
in having love upon a mortal lease,
The love I speak shines from above
The son of the sun, is eternal love.
It is the lamb, who lost his fleece
To guide the world toward
everlasting peace.
The dove above symbolizes His
love,
Which fills our souls and makes
us light,
With a sparkling spring song, so
soft and sweet
That lifts our hearts and sets us
free.
Eternal love sings in the night
A sweet serenade, with a
beautiful beat
Come with me, I'll set you free,
for all eternity.

Rebecca G. Bates
TIGER
Caged
My thoughts pace
Restlessly
Back and forth
Behind the bars of
Socially acceptable behavior

Wanting to be free instead
My thoughts growl deep

Low and menacing soon
They will try to escape

Clawing their way to freedom
Throwing themselves vainly
Against the bars in a
Frenzied burst of anger

Until finally they are subdued
Into unconscious mindlessness
A coma of conventiality

Hoang Dinh The

THE RAIN
The rain drops are falling
on the garden full of flowers!
Where's the smiling face?

Faith Woltman Kapolcaynski
ANOTHER DAY

*In memory of Cuddles, Harry and
Dale dear friends of mine who
wait with God in Heaven.*

The sun rose this morning,
The birds-they sang a song.
The wind whispers to the trees-
it's secret,
It's just another day.

Time seems to have vanished
from the earth,
As I wait for your return.
My memories are wrapped tightly
around my heart,
I shant' never let them go.

The trout are playing leap frog,
The squirrels collect old popcorn.
The bees are buzzing happily,
It's just another day.

The day you brought me a dozen
roses,
Is held in a special place.
Or the time we spent all day just
holding each other close,
You were always by my side.

The grass beckons and bows,
The flowers open full of grace,
The scent of spring is in the air.
It's just another day.

As you lay to rest,
There's a sadness-a joy,
As I dream of our next meeting.
No one see's the tears flow down
my face.
It's just another day.

Pat Northcott
A SADNESS
A sadness melts into the blood
Is pumped rhythmically
Slowly pressing

Making itself known to mind
Not swiftly—the first feeling
pierces and then
widens out—
Acquainting the entire body
slows to the steady tempo
of undeniable reality
Taste the bittersweetness
of all goodness in life
made sad by a process
not directed by us
Love grows sad
at the realization of
its destination

Kim Buckler
HEAVENLY HOME
This land was created many years
ago by our Savior The Lord,
(but His life was ended). With
more than a sword with nails
on a cross.
Through His hands and His toes
He was left to hang and to rise
three days later to walk this
land, to see if His death would
make anyone understand.
That at the beginning comes life
and at the end is death.
That we must see this land with
Sin and at the end the Glorious
Heaven Land.
Where Jesus holds out His hand
to those who has accepted Him
as their Savior.
To those with Faith and Hope we
will all go to Jesus' Home to
the highest lengths of Heaven.

Peter Kerestur
LOVE IS NOT

To my wife Ruzena

Love is not continually thinking
of you
Love is behind ev'ry idea seeing
you
Love is not doing everything for
you
Love is doing everything because
of you
Love is not even sitting and
staring at you
Love is everywhere having image
of you

Love is not a red flower
sown, rear'd, but cut when grown
by her own "caring" father
Is he truly a lover
who brings you home to moan
this dying gem of a gard'n?
You are my carnation
most lovely creation:
to let you flourish
be your mould rich and vast
but never painted vase—
that is my credo
Love anew is growth

Michelle L. Smith
CHERISHED MEMORIES
I climb into my bed each night,
And reminisce of candlelight,
And all my childish nursery
rhymes
That meant so much to me.

My ragdoll friend sits patiently,
Bearing scars from our secret
tree,

The afternoons of daydreams
real
That meant so much to me.

A red rose tea set with matching
tray,
Now my sister serves friends
each day,
Elegant teas and parties set
That meant so much to me.

My small tricycle, red and blue,
Has pedals worn by a small
shoe,
I, a speed-driver, with my "car"
That meant so much to me.

Inside my heart, a magic door,
A child's laugh will it open for,
I held tight to my childhood
dream
That means so much to me.

L. Starr McLaughlin
WORK
I sit in a room that's so noisy
Talking to friend and to foe
I'm supposed to be doing some
work
But people just won't let me go

One guy he wants to rape me
Another just wanted a kiss
The ladies all tell me the gossip
Silence is the one thing I miss

I won't tell these people about me
Not a thing of me will they know
When rumors start flying about
me
There will be no proof to bestow

Rose-Marie
DOTING LADY

---

*To the Sunshine of my life
always, Rose*

I met an
  Able,
    Beautiful,
      Caring,
        Dynamatic,
          Enthusiastic,
            Foresighted,
              Generous,
                Handsome,
                  Intelligent
Jewel,
  You!

Tony Ahern
An Early Spring Freeze
Sixteen, sitting
in the back of a church
for some do die young.
  Priestly words heard
over sobs that questioned
and the pounding March rain
  that answered.
Froze, I could not cry.

Older, I stare at whispy clouds
hear priestly words
questions
  and a soft song on a piano,
but still froze
  I cannot feel.

Francis D. Roccograndi Sr.
BUTTERFLY-BUTTERFLY
Butterfly, Butterfly
Fly over my head.
Three little children,
One just said.

Butterfly, Butterfly
Down by the well,
which ever way you're headed,
I can't tell.

Over the flowers and
Over the trees
Over the fields,
And follow the breeze.

Up and down
And all around,
Butterfly, Butterfly
Don't you ever touch the ground?

Charles S. Rogers
AFTER WE STOPPED
After we stopped to rest at the
lake
you went to stand alone,
again your back to me
as it had been all day

while I followed you through the
woods.
We had not spoken for hours
your silence saying it all:
you were right, nothing remains

only your lop-sided smile
telling me everything changes
that love is not constant. So,
with your back turned, I lifted my
camera

wanting your face and soul
and knowing how you fret so
pointed my lens like a gun
while focusing on your name

aloud, you didn't move or budge
a muscle, stole everything back
including your reflection
on the water.

Derek Brent
A DUNGEON AFFAIR
There once was a hole in the
wall,
We found very amusing to call
The Dungeon.

Deep and dark, damp and cold,
Looking for a woman to hold
In The Dungeon.

Strife and stress created a terrible
mess,
Along with a movie they titled
Tess.
Depression, regression and little
happiness indeed.

A mirrored wall in The Dungeon
there was,
No reflection did this mirror cast,
for twas
No image of self in the hole
thereof.

Only giants of evil like misery
and strife,
They stood in the door leading to
life
From The Dungeon.

Stepping lively did this lady enter
one day,
I followed, only to meet then turn
away.
For the life of me, why did I not
stay?

Now I know. It brings laughter
and remorse,
For I was still there, still confined,
of course,
At The Dungeon.

Stephen A. Britt
MEDALS AND MEMORIES
They proudly pinned medals
upon his chest
proclaiming his unit, among the
best
The bands played and flags waved
high
and crowds cheered as he
marched by.
In days to come there would be
no cheers
they had won the war and shed
many tears
Now, they ask that promises be
paid
compensation sought for
sacrifices made.
Remembering snowy meadows
beautifully white
turned blood red by morning fire
fight
Spearheading attacks again and
again
transforming boys into tough
fighting men.
Then in the silence the army
would eat
tend frost bit ears and frozen
feet
Waiting so quietly that unheard
shot
and begging God, they weren't
forgot.
Now who'll remember youth's
fleeting days
chased by tanks with cannons
ablaze
Fallen comrades whose faces
would be lost
they won their war and gave the
cost.
The victory won, oh what price
paid
Industrial giants proud of
millions made
But then as now, few knew the
truth
in freedom's name, they stole
our youth.

Sherman Allen
WHEREVER HE LEADS ME
God doesn't always lead me
through green pastures
But I know He is still holding my
hand
For He knows if I walk through
the dark shadows
I'll come out a much better man
I am often faint with my sorrow
And all I can do is to cry
But I hear a voice from the
darkness saying
Look up and believe, for here am I
So whether I'm high on the hilltop
Or deep in the valley below
He'll reach out His hand to guide
me
For wherever He leads me I'll go.

Marilynne Turner
THE COUNTRY AT DAWN
Out in the country where things
are so free,
that is really where I want to be.
The wind gently caresses the
billowing wheat,
and the smell of the hemlocks is
ever so sweet.
Out on the horizon a scarecrow

stands tall,
his clothes are now tattered as
summer turns to fall.
The trees seem to shiver as the
cool winds blow by,
and off in the distance the
mountains soar high.
For miles upon miles the green
meadows roll on,
for peace and serenity see the
country at dawn.

Sam Taulman
Goodbye Grandfather
"Death Be Not Proud" the writer
said.
It rained last night.
"Ashes to Ashes" the religious
man said.
We received the news early in
the morning.
"He is no longer in pain" the
medical man said.
Mother was very upset.
I tried to comfort her.
I was very upset.
"Goodbye Grandfather" I said.

Don Stuart
THE ATOMIC END
Just to sit and rock and think a
spell
About the future and the past,
You kind of get to wondering
How long this world will last,
With atomic rockets everywhere
And missiles that can fly,
Someone is bound to pull the
trigger
And millions then will die.

Now I'm not an educated person
But I can read between the lines,
And man has gone beyond his
wisdom
And far beyond the times,
In a world that's full of plunder
With greed and lust for power,
And when they turn to atomic
warfare
It could end within the hour.

And nearly every living thing on
earth
Could be cremated into dust,
And all their war equipment
Could either melt or rust,
Leaving just a barren planet
And for all of those who died,
May the good Lord show them
mercy
When they cross that great divide.

Sandra D. Costa
EARLY IN THE MORNING

---

*Dedicated to Tony Costa-Father
of our two children.*

Early morning leaves me by
myself
Were you here last night
Or was I dreaming
I felt your touch and love seemed
real
Did you leave me while I was
sleeping
Or was that endless time ago
I wish I would wake
And you would be here
Lying quietly by my side
But I find I'm by myself

Our World's Best Loved Poems

A faint odor from your perfume
Stirs my imagination
So profoundly that I can believe
  your were here
And as I lie quietly
Early in the morning
And I turn to your pillow
I realize that the scent you left
Is within my soul
As the touch of you, I once held
Is all captured in my memory
I will not wake to find you beside
  me
I'll slip from reality into fantasy
It seems to help as I lie here
Early in the morning

Thomas Allen Hughes
PASSION

---

*This poem is dedicated to my
family: particulary my wife Linda,
and my many friends for their
inspiration and belief.*

Distance of thought
  together in mind
Strength developed
  with love; with time

Hopes for the future
  are near
Shining, glowing
  so precious; so dear

Its not the frequency
  of love shared
Or the realms of its magnitude

Its simply
  that passions are pure
A sense of attitude

It came to me in thought
Just the other day
Of lifes grandness
  Of its fondness

And-that-is . . .

Debra Harms Dodd
FOREVER

---

*Dedicated to the memory of John
Lennon Special appreciation to
Kevin for his inspiration and
support*

February 7, 1964, the plane landed.
Out walked four sensations,
Turning us on to rock and roll.
Please try to understand,
They said, "I Wanna Hold Your
  Hand."
Their love overflowed, colors
  caressed the sky,
Teenagers became aware, while
  narrowminded stuffed shirts
Condemned their
  "incomprehensible gibberish."
Try to see what it's all about,
They said "We Can Work It Out."
Six years later came the "break up,"
Declared official April 9, 1970.
Please don't question me,
They said, "Let It Be."
John, the guiding spirit,
Wife by his side,
Said, "Nothing's Gonna Change
  My World,"
As his love for music influenced
  his genius mind.

Tradedy struck tonight,
  December 8, 1980.
He lay bleeding, six bullets,
The result of an insane fool.
Yoko, please don't cry,
The spirit lives on forever.
In time, it will be all right,
But I can "Imagine" all the people
Crying tonight.

Prescillia Katheleen Morgan
BEHOLD
BEHOLD!—
  Nature in all it's glory.
  The land and deep blue seas.
  The flowers that bloom, and
    fruit bearing trees.
  The mountains that reach up
    to the sky.
  The tears that moisten each
    and every eye.

BEHOLD!—
  The miracle of new life.
  As brought forth with each
    baby's birth.
  And as new plants, it springs
    from the earth.
  A miracle created by a
    powerful hand.
  New life to replenish this
    beautiful land.

BEHOLD!—
  Love and faith.
  The love shared by each sister
    and brother.
  The love of GOD, a love
    greater than any other.
  The faith, that he watches over
    us all.
  The faith, in a paradise, as we
    wait for his call.

BEHOLD!—
  Death and sorrow.
  The empty place left in our
    lives, by our dead.
  The sorrow unleashed by the
    tears, that we shed.
  The end of a cycle, inherited by
    the human race.
  The reunion with them, in a
    land, where death has no
    place.

BEHOLD!—
  The beauty and wonder of
    every creation.
  The great and small through-
    out every nation.
  The Bible, that clearly shows
    us the path we must trod.
  BEHOLD; The power of the all
    mighty, Jehovah, God!

Mary Lee Hayes
More Gravel To Travel

---

*For Debra Lee Moore, as we
traveled the Alcan Highway to
Alaska together.*

Just when I think there's smooth
  road ahead,
I find there's more gravel to
  travel.
Barely is the patchwork of my
  plans sewn,
When the layout starts to unravel.

Why is direction so elusive for me?
Can I not reach Paradise yet?

I don't mind a walk in the rain,
But I hate to get soaking wet.

I can't expect a path without
  curves,
For there'll always be sticks and
  stones.
And though I feel some music
  within me,
I never will know all the tones.

I do need a reason to keep taking
  steps,
Or I may not move forward at all.
There's no glass slippers provided;
I have to find my own way to the
  ball.

Though I'd rather know some of
  the answers,
Life's journey remains a quiz.
So here's to more gravel to travel!
I'll take it just as it is.

Debe K. Scott
MOTHER OF MINE

---

*Inspired by my mother, Helena
Shadroui Isaac, who won over
great obstacles by her constant
prayers and saintliness*

I bow before thee, Mother of
  Mine,
Whose love enfolds me so divine.

Your understanding, kindness,
  too,
I'll ne'er forget my whole life
  through.

Your hands and eyes and smile so
  sweet
All strive to make my life
  complete.

And if, sometimes, I slip and
  stray,
You lead me gently back to stay.

Your steadfast courage and blind
  devotion
Fills my heart with love's
  emotion.

In short—to make my poem
  rhyme—
I love you deeply, Mother of
Mine.

Kathy Sue Landes
A SPECIAL PERSON
  You come and go with the wind.
  When you come, you bring us
    happiness
    and love.

When you go, you break our
  hearts.
  But . . . I guess we don't mind.
Because one day the wind will
  stop blowing
  and you will stay.
So keep on coming and going
  until the day when the wind
  will stop blowing
And you will stay with us . . .
  Forever.

Danielle DiFazio
BALLOONS

---

*To Papa Joe, who also has drifted
away but will never be forgotten.*

Balloons floating through the sky,
Through a binding wind which
  will not die.

Some red, some yellow, some
  pink, and some green,
With such lively colors they can't
  help but be seen.

Floating over and between trees,
By a soft whispering breeze.

Through fluffy clouds and in
  front of the sun,
Until one of them pops and ruins
  the fun.

And then the thought just fades
  away,
And it seems to you just another
  day.

Vicki Barber
HOME AT NIGHT

---

*To my family and friends, who so
inspire me, and to those I love,
and share my house upon the hill.*

Shimmering nights,
magic lights . . .
shining round the darkness.
Hours before dawn,
peace lingers on—
with the house upon the hill.
Quiet within, quiet without,
leaves no room for doubt,
that dreams are swirling round.
Nights on the porch—
stars for our torch . . .
Blessed; our house upon the hill.

Shirley J. Harless
A LIVING DREAM
You are like a candle that glows
  in the dark,
Reflecting your radiance into the
  mirror of my heart.

I think of you each morning,
  through the day and night,
Knowing that with you, the
  future will be bright.

Whether near or far, wherever
  you may go,
I will trust in you with all my
  soul.
Faith and belief that dreams come
  true,
Began when inanity was replaced
  by you.

Every hour is a lonely one when
  you are away,
No matter who I'm with, it's for
  you I pray.

To you I will always be grateful
  and true,
And throughout my life, I'll be
  loving you.

Michael Fehl
THOSE WONDERFUL EYES

---

*For Barbara, my special friend and
inspiration*

I'm in love with those wonderful
  eyes,
but I guess you hear that from all
  the guys.
It's not really the shade of blue,
that really turns me on to you.
It's more the way they cut
  through me,
and I wonder what they really see.
Is it all my imperfections,
that are causing your rejections,
or is it the way that I treat the rest,
that you see I treat you the best.
I lose all my thought control,
when I see those baby blues out
  for a stroll.
My stares get caught in your
  glances,
but you still turn down all my
  advances.
Maybe I'll understand when I'm
  old and wise,
but for now I'm in love with
  those wonderful eyes.

Nancy B. Love
WHERE MY LOVE?
I seek you where bright waters
  flow
And under night skies' starry glow,
I seek you in the madd'ning crowd,
Where artfolk wave their banners
  proud,
In nightclubs' shadows seek I you
Midst sounds and scenes of blare
  and hue,
In meditation's highs and lows—
Wherever mind's strange
  wand'ring goes,
In moody music soft and low
Where love and laughter surely
  flow.
Always I seek this love of mine
Who teases, taunts, like bubbly
  wine,
Elusive one who beckons me
With haunting call and fantasy

Wendy Martin
SPEAKING
I want to speak for
deserts
as winds blow
across the barren land
the sea
and its' cold unknown spaces,
the rain
as it strikes the cold shingles,
the deserted fields,
and the lonely trees.

William Benedict
SOUL
As I walked through
  The chambers of your soul
I could feel the warmth
  of your love
And see the glow
  The peace that love brings
And joy to over flow
  The sounds of love

I listen to as love grows
  Reaching to new highs
  with the lows
The echoes travel each day
  marking
The memories of your soul
  Remembering the ways
  You love me so

Julia S. Dickman
THE FOSTER CHILD
uprooted each time
  a tendril of love sprouted . . .
  pushed
    and pummeled
    chastised and charred

l-a-c-e-r-a-t-e-d-
  seared from the incinerator
  of rootlessness—

  choking . . .
    with the soot of grief
    i
      cannot
        cry!

James Sexton Layton

James Sexton Layton
AND NOW I LIVE
I traveled
The whole world over,
Looking for something.

At the crossroads of a village,
Small, remote, and obscure,
I met a simple woman.
Her hair was long and black,
Her face was pale and sad.

She had what I had not,
And now I live.

Darlene M. Phelps
I USED TO . . .

---

*This poem is dedicated to Beccy
for getting me started, and Holly
for keeping me going. Thanks
friends!*

I used to see your shadow,
When you walked into the dark,
I used to see your tears,
When I made a "smart" remark.
I used to feel your hands,
So warm against my skin,
I used to want to love you,
Without committing a sin.
But now I think I realize,
You're not as great as I thought,
You're the same as all those other
  guys,
Do it all, just don't get caught.
I thought you were special to me,

Deep inside my heart,
I thought you'd always be there,
As a filled in piece or part.
But now I know that I was wrong,
To think you'd say or do,
Or mean those many times you
  said,
"Hey—I really love you".

Elouise E. Green
IF ONLY

---

*To George Though death has
caused us to part, my world is
filled with a lifetime of
cherishable memories.*

If only I could hear your sweet
  voice
If only I could see your smiling face
If only I could feel your warm
  body next to mine
If only I could capture yesterday's
  love
If only there were a tomorrow for
  us
If only I could keep our love
  forever
If only I could recall the sweet
  memories of you
Then there will always be a
  tomorrow for us
If only . . .

Rebecca James-Robinson
TO MY LOVER

---

*TO BREAKFAST CAKE—
JEANNE WAFFLE—ROBINSON
Who reinforced my patience-faith
and determination Which gives
me the strength to press on.*

I will not lie/anymore.
  To gain my end/compliment or
  pretend.
  What I am has never been/
  Your woman-my friend.

I am fair/a man is strong
I am strong/a man is fair.
  To a purer air/
  Hand in hand we shall pass
  along.

Do not drag me at your bridle
  rein/
  Let us/ride the mountain
  Knee to knee pressed.
I will not lie to you
This is my/will/you love me . . .
  still.

Kelly Leigh Hayes
THE DUNE
I hear them talking in other lands
I see them treading on hot white
  sands
I feel their flesh soak up the
  dripping sun
Pyramids rising—becoming one

On the wind can be heard a
  distant sound
The people silently leave as the
  drums gently pound

Shadows spread with the coming
  moon
And again, all is quiet on the
  desolate dune

Mark C. Morris
REVELATIONS W/PAM
Isn't it amazing how
ink on paper can make you think
about an old friend
considered dead?
I realize now
the appeal of a well-educated
girl.
Occasionally a pool of coffee can
mirror an image
so beautifully
that it will make you cry
(or at least think of early poems
engraved on a teen-agers mind)
and then to drink from this pool—
my God,
it's an ancient sacred wine
if you wish to believe it so.
And I can still believe in you
when you smile & I even accept
  the sarcasm
I've always tried to ignore
in hopes
of a richer fantasy.
Too much of the sacred wines
and a poor boy's mind will never
  stop . . .

Fran Williamson
THE CHRISTIAN'S SONG
A melody came to me once in the
  night;
It has been with me to this day.
Its lovely tune fills me with sheer
  delight,
It inspires my work and my play.

When trials of life come and
  beset me so sore,
And I'm sailing on tempest-tossed
  seas,
The song comes to me as it has
  before,
And I am completely at ease.

When I awake at the light of the
  dawn,
The song rises up in my heart,
Then I know as I travel along,
Its cadence will never depart.

I really don't know from whence
  came this refrain,
Or why it has lingered thus far,
But I know that it came, when I
  called on His name
And I did not have it before.

Ada S. Barry
THE GAME OF LIFE
The brilliant Queen may fall
  But let it not be in vain.
Whether we be gallant Knights
  Or swift avenging Bishops,
The hard working Pawns
  Or the steadfast Rooks.
Let us clearly see the open field,
  Challenge one, challenge all.
The plan must persevere
  We move cautious, but confident.
The challenge met
  A kingdom is at stake—
With but one move
  The checkmate.

Lillie Craddock
THE ARTIST'S LEGACY
To express reflections of desire
The artist works with fervent zeal
As to the canvas, a thought
  unfolds
By stroke of brush, his dreams
  reveal

Our World's Best Loved Poems

There lay a shield, a broken sword
And blood spilled on the sand
Grim tokens of a battle fought
In medieval times or alien land

When valiant men of honor stood
With armies arrogant and brave
Victorious in their conquests bold
Or was the one who died, a slave

Who by death his freedom won
From brutal tyrants of his day
No glory then, no song of praise
Nor act of valor did display

A contest fought perhaps to win
The favours of a maiden fair
A noble prince or feudal lord
Shed his blood in triumph there

Thus the artist of this dismal
    scene
Left a painting, faded long with
    time
Unfinished, that the viewer
    marvel
At the legendary vision of his
    mind

Donald H. Johnson

Donald H. Johnson
A CHILDHOOD FRIEND
A lonely old house sits upon the
    hill,
    With all life gone and
    everything still.
Once it had life when I was born,
    Now it sits there, so forlorn
With its broken shutters from
    unkind winds
    And windows shattered by boys
    that sin,
Its cosmetic finish worn by age
    And slates torn loose by storms
    that raged.

I went inside and listened to the
    walls
    Tell me secrets that leave me
    enthralled,
About the happy times and also
    the sad,
    And tragedies it seen and
    tragedies it had.
Hearing the stories brought my
    eyes to tears
    As I stood there alone feeling
    my years
And deep inside me I didn't want
    it to end,
    Knowing I was loosing a
    childhood friend.

It protected me when I was young
    and free
    And we formed a friendship, this

house and me.
But friendships always come and
    go,
    Age has a way of taking its toll.
I looked around at its life so still
    As I sadly left the house on the
    hill.
They're tearing it down, it will
    gone tomorrow
    And part of my life is ending in
    sorrow.

Auttie Wayt McDowell
MEMORIES IN MARCH
The roaring winds of March are
    dieing, And the scatters of
    April sun and rain are rushing
    to take over.
Nature like life seems in such a
    rush.
How can one slow the rush of
    time?
Spring with her hurring, dancing
    feet rushs forth as if in fear of
    being left behind.
So like youth seemly not to
    know, you can't stop time or
    hold it back.
And time like the wicked demon
    he is, laughingly watches the
    game.
Reminding me only of my lost
    youth and dreams long gone a
    stray.
Roar on you chilling winds of
    March and April have your
    way.
But leave for me my memories of
    long past yesterdays.
Mock not the little bits of grey,
    these marks the tools of time
    have left.
Leave for me this lonely day my
    unforgotten yester days.

Janet K. Sweitzer
UNTITLED
i hold you for a moment
Not compressed in space and time
Realizing though each others'
No one's ever really mine
Silken thread—you bind us
by a choice not of our own
A softness yet so powerful
A heart can turn from stone
into such a radiant amnesty
Its heaven cannot tell
And joyfully surrendered
Live forever in its spell

Recklessness still calls you
Its sad notes rebuke the air
Sometimes it still hurts
to see your eyes just sit and stare
But tameness—it keeps hovering
O'er your head to stop the fight
And in golden runway silence
You're preparing for your flight

May the love be quick to blossom
and the anger swift to flee
May the oscilating moment
Find its ancient right to be

Barbara June Matthaei
Thoughts Following a Demonstration At Frankfort University
We walked among the rocks, the
    broken glass, and emptied
    colour bags.
All testimonies of man's helpless
    rage.

Quietness now, except for words
    of hate and fear that scream
    from every wall.
We turn our face for comfort to
    the sun, and weary, weary ask,
Can this be all?
For once the answer stood before
    the question.
A little line of paint ran out of
    words
As if the one who wrote fell into
    sleep, or better yet, woke from
    some madman's dream.
And there before my feet there
    lay a rainbow.
So beautiful this symbol of hope,
    so graceful was the sweep of
    the lines of purist colour at my
    feet,
One moment then, someone
    forgot to fear . . .
One breath of time, someone
    forgot to hate . . . swung over
    time, reached out and touched
    God's Grace,
And gave it life across the
    anguished street
Where one remembers there is
    Holy Ground.
So . . cover now our head, protect
    our feet.
We stop and feel the rainbow
    into words.
We wait and pray for words to
    understand.
Oh, give us back again the life we
    had with You before the world
    began.
    Amen
    Amen
    Amen

Christopher 'Ralph' A. Johnson
TO SO MANY
Speaking as one lost soul to so
    many:
There are some things we just
    don't know.
How can we judge the nature of a
    diety
Who saves through unquestioned
    belief alone?

If there's no god or devil, but only
    good and evil,
And all of life emerged from
    cosmic particles colliding,
Then what of Christ and his
    disciples, they seemed on the
    level!
Could they all have been so
    wrong; who's to be deciding?

Mrs. "Ree" Bullock
BELIEVING IN YOURSELF

---

*This poem is proudly dedicated
to my mother Mrs. Hatcher, my
husband Rex, my son "Jeff", and to
each member of my family whom
I love dearly, and has inspired my
life in a special way.*

Doing what you think is right is
    all that it will take.
Always believing in what you do,
    and also by having Faith.
Each of us have different areas of
    own need.
By having COURAGE, WISDOM,
    and CONFIDENCE is to succeed.

People in our world are
    wonderful, and I'm sure that
    you will agree.
So try to always remember, you
    can make your life whatever
    you want it to be.
Always reach for the ULTIMATE,
    and *never* settle for less.
Strive to reach a GOAL, and you
    will constantly do your best.

Everyone is gifted in a very
    special and unique way.
Try to understand others, and
    listen to what they have to say.
Trust and believe in yourself, and
    also your Fellowman.
Remember you were sent here for
    a purpose, and for *YOU*. God
    has a plan.

Carolyn Marie Baatz
A MOTHER
A woman gives life to a child
Protects him from hurt, and pain
Shelters him from the cold, rain
Within she keeps him feeling
    warm
Holds him close through every
    storm
With tenderness she cares for her
    child
She is the life-giving, warmth
    from a sun
When the child leaves her tender
    care
He takes her memory and love
    everywhere.

Enid Mary Anderson
BROOK
The frog and fern clutch
Mossy rocks beside the brook
    Rushing to the sea.

Phil Ambrozy
How Quickly We Forget
Remember me?
That friend of yours?
Who gave his heart to you?
I thought the feelings you had for
    me
Were the same that I had for you.

The laughs that we had together,
And the beautiful moments we
    shared,
I thought we had love for each
    other.
I know I really cared.

Your loving eyes and friendly
    smile,
Your warm and passionate kiss.
It's no wonder why I feel inside,
A certain emptiness.

The letter you got in the mail
    one day,
Came from your favorite dancer.
Each day I searched the mailbox
    here,
But from you there came no
    answer.

You told me that I warmed your
    heart,
Whenever I held you near.
Then why the distance between
    us now?
Were you not sincere?

I know your feelings for me have
    changed,
But I'm still real glad we met.

115

It seems a shame that although you've gone,
How quickly we forget.

Olive Kriel
HIS PROMISE IS TRUE
I have lived in old log houses, walked down many country lanes,
Chased butterflies and fireflies, run through puddles after rain.

I've loved an older brother, and a younger brother, too,
Helped them hunt for lots of rabbits, and mend fences by the slough.

I have roamed in open meadows, and walked many weary miles
Up and down in rows of cotton, hoeing, picking all the while.

I used to ride in horse drawn wagon at a slow and steady pace,
But now, a few years later, I watch folk shuttle off to space.

I've washed lots of dirty dishes in a dishpan—not the sink,
Carried many pails of water from the well—so all might drink.

Up and down, from barn to cellar, I have run to get some eggs,
Or some jelly, fruit, or butter. Me, oh my! My aching legs!

I have loved to read the Bible, it has been my guide and stay
Since that night in old brush arbor where God washed my sins away.

Oh, the years seem very many, long and rugged seems the road,
But His hand leads on and upward, and He shares my heavy load.

He will guide me, He will keep me, on and on to journey's end.
He never has nor will forsake me, there can be no better friend.

Barbara M. Rowe
LOVE

I would like to dedicate the following poem to my Brother, Alvin Blake.

Love is a simple thing,
That goes a long long way,
Some have it for a life time,
Some have it for a day;
But the love that is the nicest
And is the most worthwhile,
Is the love that is the truest,
Perhaps you've known it all the while,
By the touch that is so reverent,
The way he smiles at you,
It makes you wonder every day,
Why each day is so new.

Bonnie Hoxie
A PROMISE
"Remember while you live and breathe—"
The Lily said to me.
"Remember well, and cherish
All the beauty that you see."

Remember warmth. Remember love.

Remember kindness, too.
And think of all the gentle things
That life has given you.

Remember, too, the storm that passed,
The one who held your hand;
Cherish the love that calmed your fear
And gave you strength to stand

Consider courage, compassion, too.
Remember selfless giving.
Be thankful for these blessed gifts;
They're yours while you are living.

Take love to light your pathway
As you plod along.
A song dispels the silence;
So fill the air with song.

I will meet you in the Springtime
Where all the lillies bloom,
At the dawning of eternal life
Beyond the empty tomb.

Esther Mae Eckebrecht
INSIGHT

I dedicate this poem to every person that ever made fun of me, may they now try to understand me, and the burden that was lifted from me when I wrote this poem.

I'd like to tell you a true story, which might make you cry,
It's about a young lady who's blind in one eye.
As far back as she could remember, she hung her head in shame,
For she felt inside her heart that her eye was to blame.
She often thought about her life, things she loved and lost,
For not only was she blind in one eye, but that eye was also crossed!
Desperation filled her, for she hated that eye
Through the tears in her prayers she'd ask "why me god" why?
Coping with problems worsened through the years.
And she quickly saddened with many fears.
While talking to others, she'd glance away as she spoke;
People constantly hurt her with their mean and painful jokes.
She resented their words because they really hurt,
But she never uttered a word when they spoke to her like dirt.
She used her body as a shell in which to hide;
She was never open with anyone, she just couldn't confide.
She wanted so badly to reach out to someone, tell them how she really felt,
Like a nightmare in a card game, with the worst hand that was dealt.
Today she opened up to someone she never spoke to before or knew
She realized she not only had this kind of problem, others do too.

She used her eye for so many years as a crutch instead of a tool.
It's funny how you can kid yourself than understand how much you've been a fool.
Even today she wishes that out of both eyes she could see.
You see I know just how this person feels, because it's . . . me.

Shirley Press Sorbello
DESTINY'S JOURNEY
I did not ask to love you,
To be tossed around by the tide of destiny,
To build sand castles in the air of my imaginings,
To experience the strength of the ocean's fury
in a single moment's longing.

I did not ask to know a love unreturned,
To feel the insecurity of a seagull's first flight,
To experience your power as the full moon ruling the tide,
To seem as alone as a tiny ship lost miles from shore.

I am not asking you to love me,
Only to follow your destiny as a tall ship
sails its course to shore.
But if it is I you see waiting for you at journey's end,
I will be there to welcome you home.

Goldie L. Fagner
America Your Beautiful
America, America, the land we love so true,
Its beauty is our haven for the things we love and do;
The pillar of our future so dependent on you,
America Your Beautiful and forever, ever true.

We can travel your highways and your byways feeling proud,
We can fly under blue skies with our head in a cloud;
The Red, White and Blue always waving in the sky,
So the love of America can be seen far and wide.

The future of our children is depending on you,
While they grow up and learn of the things we hold true;
So keep our country beautiful

and love her every day,
While Old Glory keeps waving ever proud U.S.A.

United States of America, you have always come through,
Believing in Justice for the Red, White and Blue;
You stand up for Honor where Honor is due,
I'm proud of America, proud and free to love you.

America Your Beautiful, this land where I grew,
The place I was born in and free to wander through;
No place on this earth could ever take the place of you,
Thank God for America and the Red, White and Blue.

Ma. Clemence P. Lastra
EILEEN JOY LASTRA

I heartily dedicated this poem to my beloved granddaughter, Eileen Joy Lastra of McAllen, Texas on the occasion of her natal day.

E — Enjoy your birthday today and forever
I — I Hope you'll feel the same next year
L — Live, study and work for the better
E — Encourage to be a model to every sister
E — Everything has it's own affair
N— Never give up anything for greater.
J — Join to the moment of inspiration
O— Onward not backward to destination
Y — You have mild and pleasant situation.
L — Let me persuade you my expectation
A— Accept my best wishes and intentions
S — Show that you have an ambition
T — To the world for higher education
R— Remember also there's ALMIGHTY in heaven
A— And how are we to thank HIM.

Julie Jensen
MY DREAMS
I dream of sunny skies
Of sleepy blue oceans
Snow-capped mountains
A beautiful sunset
Walking through a forest
Sharing happy times
A gentle breeze
Of flowers blooming in springtime
Birds singing cheerfully
Singing happy tunes
Watching a rainbow glow
Making people smile
Exploring new horizons
Meeting new faces
Listening to stories
Of long boat rides
Watching the clouds go by
Writing to people far away

Learning new things everyday
Striving for new adventures
This is what I dream of

James R. Moyor

James R. Moyor
FREE

This poem "FREE" is dedicated to an "ace" friend, Verl Blake Harriss, (1950-1983) pictured here with myself, James, and my two faithful dogs Jackson and Missy, short for Jackson County Missouri.

Good night my son, good night
sleep well while the stars shine
  bright
live on and change right now
burn on feel good in light

Repent and turn no more
sin is at your door

Repent and turn no more.

O God forgive my sin
I will not do it again

But only with your help
I can't do it alone

I can do it with you.

Repent and turn no more
sin is at your door

The truth is at your feet
You're standing on the ground
and mother earth whose sins you
  bore
you created all for me

and if a form of prayer
how true and good to be the
  sinner
now gone home at last the son
the child free.

Agnes Sweet
CARIBBEAN CRUISE
Embarkation—
  The taxis arrive—
  A beautiful ship.
  We happily board
  To start our trip.

Visitors ashore—
  The whistles blow.
  Music—confetti—
  And away we go!

Days to rest and relax—
  As the ship glides through
  These heavenly waters—
  So calm—so blue.

Fantastic islands,
  With foliage so lush—

Far from the North,
  The snow—and the slush.

We count our blessings
  For this brief time,
  Away from our world
  Of dirt and of crime.

Finally the day
  To debark will arrive.
  We shall leave with memories
  To keep glowing—alive.

Barbara J. Shaffer
YOU ARE LOVE

This poem was written for my husand, (Jim) who is my best friend, and inspiration.

"You're the sunshine that
  brightens my day,
You're the breeze that blows my
  cares away."
"A smile sweet; ready to give,
Knowing you gives me reason to
  live."
                You are love!
"You're the raindrops that fall
  from above,
soft and warm as a turtle dove."
"Your twinkling eyes; laughing
  and bright,
Like shining stars on a clear, cool
  night."
                You are love!
"Like birds singing so loud and
  clear,
So your laughter, like music to
  my ears."
"Your hand in mine; strong and
  warm,
reassures me there is no harm."
                You are love!
"You're the skies that are always
  blue,
You're the only true love I ever
  knew."
"Honest; gentle; loving and kind,
I'm so thankful you are mine."
                You are love!

Judith A. Hughes
Ingredients Of a Marriage
The tenderness of a loving touch,
The security of a hug.
The warm feeling of a kiss,
An embrace that feels so snug.

The glow that comes from a
  loving smile,
The tingle from a playful wink.
The laughter from a playful pat,
Given at the kitchen sink.

The joy that comes from a good
  deed,
Done by a loving heart.
The companionship felt from
  holding hands,
Tightly in the dark.

All these things put together,
In a bundle that's marked love.
Add consideration, devotion, and
  gladness,
And a moon in the dark sky
  above.

Mix together slowly,
Cherish and let go never.
Because between a man and a
  woman,

That's a marriage that will last
  forever.

Kenneth Steven Corley
A Life Of Time and Friends

To my late cousin, Joe Mercurio, who inspired me to write this poem. He was the nicest person I've ever known, and this poem is for him.

Tick, Tick the time clock will
  say, every tick as time passes
  away.
Life struggles on every minute
  everyday, searching for truth
  and the right way.
Days go by, some long but most
  short, looking for friends all
  the right sort.
But as you live those days and
  grow much older, your feelings
  grow and truth becomes bolder.
So live your life the way you
  should, look for those friends
  and look for the good.
And when your life ends and
  fades away, people will look at
  you and say;
He lead a great life, honest, good
  and free, and when we all go
  we'll know where he'll be.
So, listen to those ticks and you'll
  see, time's to short to let it be.

Gloria Jean Robertson
FANTASY

To have this time that I have known you, printed for posterity, I heartily give thanks so true, to, SUNSHINE, Ernie Michael Conti!

Life is reality—
  You are the fantasy—
In dreams subconsciously,
  You have great love for me.
In that I climb and see,
  The mountains confidently.
Where you there expertly,
  Swim the sea just gracefully.
But it is heavenly,
  That beckons so invitingly;
As free spirits such as we,
  Perform together magically . . .
Even if its mentally!

Alison Dyer
CREMATION
There you stand 30 feet in the
  sky,
All the pain you feel, and you
  still can't cry.
You've been slashed and broken
  but you don't bleed,
You've come a long way for a tiny
  little seed.
There you stand not making a
  sound,
But you'll be sought until you're
  found.
The rain and winds can't hurt
  you that much,
But watch out for people and
  their deadly touch.
They cut you down and burn you
  as wood,
They don't treat you like you
  wish they would.

They take advantage of you being
  alive,
I don't see how you'll ever survive.
You're wounded and in pain, but
  you're not dead,
Until into the fire you'll soon be
  fed.
The spark turns to flame and it
  gets so hot,
They are killing you, but what
  choice have you got?
Move over, make room 'cause
  now its my turn,
I'm next in line, they're watching
  me burn.
We are nothing but ashes but at
  least we're free,
I WAS a person and you WERE a
  tree.

Roger W. Houser
FOOL'S GOLD DREAMS
I've had my fill of
fool's gold dreams,
of popgun cannons
and gimpy kneed stallions.

Is it meet that I dive
into waterfall trickles,
or land upon "No Vacancy"
flash of deserted isles?

My eyes have wearied
of Florida swamp
promised land and the empty
sight of horseless carousels.

Someone must trim away
my wild haired visions
and boost me full of
a veritable dose.

Let me run from
any more toothpick hopes
that bend and break
beneath banality's weight.

My ship remains locked
within the bottle,
and I shall pull the shades
on my kaleidoscope mind,

and fly away
    on the wings
    of a chicken.

Corinne P. A. Bangay
THE NIGHTINGALE

For my father Earl, and my mother Julia, who have helped and encouraged me in all my endeavours and stood by me in my failures

As the darkness set in
With rays of daylight still
  lingering
I heard the beautiful sound
Of the Nightingale singing

It touched my heart
With it's sad, happy sound
And showed me a peacefulness
That I've never since found

It called me away
From my brightly lit room
Into the wilderness
Where there was no gloom

A single ray of light
Shone upon this bird
It was as if from heaven
This song I still heard

I stepped on a twig
And interrupted the song
And as suddenly as it was there
The bird was now gone

Valerie L. McCarthy
THE CONFLICT

---

*To those who know the meaning
of ambivalence and its inevitable
resolve.*

What is this conflict that rages
within;
The Spirit of Holiness against the
wages of sin.
How is it I in its midst came to
stand,
And took up a sword against the
forces at hand,
And how can it be against both
sides I fight;
I stand in the darkness and look
to the light
That seems so close and yet so
far away;
My heart bids me go but my
mind tells me stay.
So on the tempest I am tossed to
and fro,
Afraid to choose what in my
heart I know
To be right in every possible way
But I wait for tomorrow because I
am afraid today,
And with each day that passes I
hate myself more;
I am tired and broken from this
endless war.
Why can't I lay my sword to rest
And walk out of the darkness just
as I am;
A broken lion seeking The Lamb.
What is it that compels me so
That when my heart says "yes," I
say "no."
I simply can't go on like this
Though the end I cannot see;
I will die in battle or the battle
will set me free.

John S. Malley
IN ALL THESE WONDERS
God can be seen in the world's
real treasures,
You know his warmth in the
sun's great glow.
His Presence brings peace in
lonely moments,
Yes, God is alive, we know, we
know.

His Harvest I've seen and also
tasted,
And goodness I've felt in fibres, too.
Partaking through life of
wondrous bounty,
His Gifts for the soul, each day
renewed.

I've seen in the mists of early
morning,
In violets capped with the silvery
dew.
The gentleness of His great
compassion,
For all of creation, old and new.

Alone I've walked in the soothing
quietness,
Through many a lovely wooded
glen.

And seen from the heights of
craggy mountains,
His Glories too vast for the scope
of men.

Oh, yes I've seen God in all these
Wonders,
His Heavenly Love, each day I
know.
And after the Sunset, we can be
certain—
God will Preside in the Afterglow.

Dorothy Rogers
HOPELESS CASE
Love and trust go hand in hand.
It's hard to love and trust a man.
The ones you love will do you
wrong.
The ones you trust just don't
belong.

The combination is very rare.
For trust alone would not let me
care.
But if I loved, I'd always doubt.
Like a glove that's turned
wrongside out.
It fits the right hand and the left
Still you just can't fool yourself.
I could not live without them
both,
But for love and trust there is no
hope.

Donald A. Rule
ROBIN
Robin, Robin, Robin,
How great thou are,
For tired and weary bones,
Morning, Noon, or Night.
Day in, Day out,
Come Rain, Snow, or Shine,
Be it Day or Night.

Bridges to cross,
Rivers to ford,
High waters or none.
That added sparkle,
To a dimming light,
Brightens the way,
For one to see.

Jill Hoffmann
A CHILD SET SAIL
Tell me a tale of a child set sail
On to where memories reign
Grown at last, childhood past
Long ago it was ordained

I wish that I knew the answers to
All the questions I ask
Why is it so? Please tell me true
Show me the things I lack

I will accept; I understand
The Lessons that you teach me

Though they are hard; I will
withstand
The pain that was meant to be

Why should it all come to this?
Why are the good things bad?
Why must I always have to resist?
Why am I called the cad?

But now I see and now I know
The reason it is this way
We must stay and fight; we can't
cry and go
The price has to be paid

I've told you a tale of a child set
sail
And a grown-up left behind
The world may be cruel but now
there's a rule
The learning is not limited by
time

Marjorie J. Sweatfield
MEASURING
How do we measure

The sand of a desert or a blue
green sea:
How do we measure—you and me?
Do we put the sands in an hour
glass?
If we're measuring—we won't last.

How do we measure raindrops in
a well?
If we start measuring, we have a
sea shell.
We have a sea shell—washed by
life's motion,
An empty sea shell but pearled
by the ocean.

I have learned what it means to
give birth
To a feeling of me, my own self
worth.
I'll live a history—bad times and
good
And all of the deeds that I might
have or should.

I won't use a tape measure or an
hour glass
But I'll share memories—the
pleasures that last.
I know I'll leave something, even
an empty sea shell,
Cause even in measuring, life's
echoes will dwell.

*Kenwyn Luana "Kookie"
Hightower*
HONEST FEELINGS
On the day I saw you
I hoped that you'd be mine
and with each passing day
I hope its only a matter of time
till that day I guees that
I'll just wait around to see
if by any chance
you just might feel the same for
me
other guys may come and go
young loves don't usually last
long
but for guys like you
the feelings always burning
strong
other girls may tempt you
with their fast and phony plays
But me, I guess I'm just too real
to try those put-on ways
So if the day should ever come
that you would turn to me

I hope it would be for just myself
not for something I couldn't be.

Sherry L. Massarotti
TREASURES OF LIFE
I as a seed planted, was destined
to grow,
From my mother's womb, birth
soon to know,
A special time of living, from my
mother's breast,
For my yesterdays' beginning, so
my tomorrows' start the test,

An older child now, I cultivate
wit and cleverness,
As time passes on I sample, love,
grace, tenderness,
Laughter of friends, joys soon to
share,
Finding knowledge and desires, a
friendship rare,

Adolescence come and gone,
chances and mistakes beginning,
Changing dreams to realities,
failures into winning,
Learning right from wrong,
thinking things through,
Never giving up to despair, for
tomorrow to start anew,

My agedness at hand, filled of
joys, sorrows and fears,
I wish somehow the knowledge,
to regain those youthful years,
But as life's breath is taken from
me, as given seems divine,
I realize how rich my years, for
my life was truly mine.

Rebecca Cook
FEELINGS
Feelings of distraught

Feelings of lost hope
"Oh" Loneliness please leave me
Depression set me free
We have much to live for
So why does death grab at me

Dennis Hollandsmith
RAIN CHECKS

---

*To: my mother, Shirley; my
grandmother, Harriet; & my wife,
Trudy. As it's these three, who've
supported me—in midst of
stormy sea; For quite frankly,
they all love me—unconditionally.*

As we live from day to day,
problems flow
Like water falling over ageing
rocks;
The view looks nice standing
here below.
To think of the climb, the bruises
and knocks
Yields a rain check for
tomorrow's show.

To go on living with rain check
in hand
Is like asking the sun never to
shine.
The world keeps turning and
chance is the sand
Stinging our eyes when problems
enter mind—
Life, that narrow path, runs wide
as the land.

And the freedom of choice
existing just now,

Could be gone tomorrow in
mushrooming cloud.
Then people left standing might
look and say—
"What good is that rain check of
yesterday?"

Lori Allen
MUSIC PLAYING
Music, the most fancy sounds
in your wavy dreams.
My feelings fall into dreams
while playing the piano;
Dreams filled with roses spread
around me.
Music fills up my ego with spirit;
lightning shakes and forms out
magic puffs.
My dreams move smoothly and
silently,
While the people catch the tones
in my music;
Making a pure impression on
human beings.
Clapping breaks my dream which
disappears into thin air.
The harsh clapping sounds give
me feelings of self confidence
and realizing the strongest
effect the music had on them.

Force yourself to stay away from
boredom,
And find the cost of different
hobbies in your life to learn
your own valuable feelings.
Don't waste your life doing
nothing—go make your own
opportunities.
Take hours in a fresh skill and
you may become successful
someday; your skill love.

Dorothy Larson
Sliding Into Schizophrenia

Dedication For Leslie Fine

The sea speaks
to me
of a better place
to be

Towards my bare feet
the stretching
waves pull
and reach

The head rises
to the hypnotic center
I want to walk
I want to enter

A baby again
no thought
no talk
no winters

Patricia L. Martin
SWEET ANGELS

To my mom, Eilyne . . .

Sweet Angels
bow your wings
near my head
and bring peace.
For there is none
in existence,
never has,
oever will.
Oh, bithave lived briefly

as rays of sun
darting through stubborn clouds
and upon reaching solid ground,
dying.
And so,
Serenity is lost in the shuffle.
Will she ever be found,
I wonder.
Will she ever be found,
I wonder.
Confusion prevails,
as usual.
The marketplace of life
is teeming with it.
But time is the common factor
and will consume all.
I need only wait
for my sweet angels to come.

Frankie Austin

Frankie Austin
When You Get Sixty Five

*This poem is dedicated to my
sister Mrs. Elnora Burke she is
the listening post for all of my
poems and she encourages me*

Society discard you and throw
you away
Saying you have seen your better
days
When you get sixty five you can
crawl in a hole
But you got more spirit and you
got more soul

Oh they say "they been hell in
their day"
They also say "they're set in their
way"
But I have to admit "I got it down
Pat"
You don't do things for years and
years
And still don't know where it's
at

Inside this old body I still want
and I feel
So we take a few ritus bros pills
So our hair turn silver, and lose
it's glow
All because of a number and we
walk kind a slow

To do that to the oldster is so
very sad
Because too many birthdays we
have had
I don't need their approval I'm as
good as I
can be and if they keep breathing

they'll
Old just like me.

Leta J. Bakke
DESPAIR
The mind in utter confusion, is a
torment beyond control,
The feeling of emptiness, and
lonliness, is eating away at my
soul.
Endless days, and sleepless
nights, they roll into one,
The deep despair, so very black, it
blocks out the very sun.
There seems to be no reason for
me to go on anymore,
I've given all I can give, and to my
very depth I do deplore.
Where did I go wrong?, and why
do I suffer so?,
Is it really all my fault?, I really
don't know.
Dear God above you know my
fears, and my heartaches, too,
I can't seem to take much more, I
don't know what to do.
I beg of you, dear God, above, give
me peace within,
Help me to find a usefulness, and
to be needed once again.
My mind is going around like a
top, spinning round, and round,
Never ceasing to stop, and never
settling down.
I feel so rejected, neglected, and
alone,
My desire to live has already gone.
I think I'm going crazy, I don't
understand myself at all,
I seem to know only agony, and
into a living hell, I seem to fall.
So many problems here on this
earth,
It's hard enough when there are
two,
Alone they seem insurmountable,
and
I don't know what to do.

Catherine Cassandra Castelluzzo
RESIDENT
I know I can live
Without you.
In fact
I have.
But whoever I was with,
Whatever I did,
You were
Never far.
Love remains,
And so exists
You.
So perhaps
I haven't.

James K. Phillabaum
WALKING ALONE
Someday perhaps the words I'll
find,
To tell you just what's on my
mind.

Waters tumble down a mountain
stream,
And of you I often dream.

Tall trees sway in the Summer
wind,
And I want to be more than your
friend.

Little fishes thru still waters dart,
And I seek to capture your heart.

Stars scattered thru the darkened
night,
Give me hope that I just might.
Each day of beautiful sunshine,
Makes me wish that you were
mine.

The deep blue cloudless sky,
And walking alone—just you and
I!

Kim R. C. Reid
I
I am like an ocean—
Travel everywhere.
Waves rushing to and fro.
Waves always there.
Driven by a secret force;
Invisible—Unseen.
Driven like a raging bull;
Here, there, in between.
Beastly, as a lion.
Gentle, as a lamb.
Flowing with a passion.
Flowing undamned.
Immensely vast, yet small.
Surfaces all who fall.
Troubled, yet calm.
I shall one day be gone.

Bo Hill
SEARCHING
I'm searching, always searching,
For something I can't find,
And looking, always looking,
For something left behind.

I'm wanting, sometimes needing,
Things not meant for me,
And I'm searching, always
searching,
For something I can't see.

Jana M. Christopher
THE LONGEST DAY
The longest day they say in June;
The shortest, in September.
They did not come to me that way;
The shortest day—remember?
The day you came into my life
And filled my heart with
gladness.
The longest day you were away;
The very day thereafter.

Deborah Ferguson
DANCING

*For those whom shared their
knowledge of dancing with me.*

Love, joy, flower,
grow, can, yes be.

I love dancing and moving
through the world
with grace—ease,
and the loveliness of me.

It is wonderfilled
with fantasies, fairys, true—loves,
and great scenes.

The world of the dance flows
through the night moonlit clouds
glowing all around—
my love for the dance
forever will be;

love, joy, flower,
grow, can, yes be.

Erika Gray
AS TIME GOES ON
As Time Goes On,
I really start to see,

The growing friendship,
between you and me.

As years go on,
And days go by,
People look and envy,
our friendship with a sigh.

They can't believe,
two friends can care,
so much,
and have it stay as such.

As close as sisters,
that's what they say,
and that's exactly,
how we will stay.

Like this forever?
Who knows,
what lies in the future,
As time goes on.

Carla Yvonne Stueber
WORDS

---

*Dedicated To: Mark Lynn Crouch
January 1983*

I love you, for all that you are;

And when you hold me, the
gentle way that you do,
I feel myself melting in your
clutch,

When we do not speak, I feel
your warmth,
through your caressing eyes,

Words could never express the
way that I feel for you.

I love you, when you are sad or
mad;

And my security is just being
with you, being held,
in your strong and loving hands,

You are everything a woman
could want: gentle,
strong, loving, kind, handsome,
and warm,

I love you more than words could
ever express.

Judi E. Macy
PORTRAIT OF A PRINCESS
An impish grin, a turned up nose,
Eyes of violet, cheeks of rose,
Golden tresses bouncing in the
sunlight,
Clothed in the innocence of pure
white.

Syncopated rhythm running in
motion,
Over flowing with spontaneous
emotion.
Happiness highlighted with an
outburst of giggling,
Excitement generated by clapping
and wiggling.

A pintsize hug, a kiss of sweetness,
Her own girlish style of
uniqueness.
Ruling her land like royalty in
miniature,
Leaving on all she touches, her
signature.

Connie Millsap
UNWANTED LOVE
The skeleton sits in the closet,
holding its broken heart,

The day never starts,
for an unwanted love.

Its imagination still grows
longing for the love
that was never given.

The blood dripping from its
heart stains its bones,
The thought of always being alone.

The cobwebs hang from the
walls of its brain,
The memory of you will always
remain.
Should it crush its heart to end
the pain?!

Cathleen Elizabeth Tolemy
IN THE MIST
In a different realm of space and
time
  In the mist
    In the fog
      Call to me,
  I will come to comfort you.
  In the mist
    In the fog
In my realm of space and time
  I will call to you
  Will you come to comfort me?
  In the mist
    On the moor
      Here I stand
Now in this place where time and
space began.
      Your world's away
  In a realm of space I cannot
find
  In a part of time forgotten to
me.
  Still you call, and still I
listen
    In the fog
      On the moor
        In the mist . . .

David V. Clark
A NEW AWAKENING
Our sails had been cut . . .
and the winds abandoned us
For a time we were left adrift in
the sea of life
left to the mercies of the currents
left to wonder where they would
take us

But alas, the sails are whole again
and we must only wait
for soon the wind will blow anew

And with the wind will come a
strength
a strength to make us stronger
than we ever were
stronger than we ever were . . .
ever were . . .

B. A. Torchick
TIME
It was but three years ago;
My heart was broken and full
of woe.
But, with time, now I can see
Life can be better than it use to
be.
TIME, at present, can be such a
long wait;
TIME, in the past, can be filled
with ill fate.
TIME, in the future, may seem to
be slow;
But it can pass quickly; believe
me, I know.

If we could learn to look straight
ahead,
  The future, I'm sure, would give
nothing to dread.
With faith and GOD handling
  our problems big or small,
  Life will be easy,—HE can
  handle it all.

Karen Marie Breslin

Karen Marie Breslin
THE DARK

---

*This is dedicated to my mother
Yolanda. For with her love and
support I found the inspiration
for my poem.*

In comes darkness
As the sun . . . slowly . . . goes
down.
I walk along the empty beach,
Looking towards the horizon
In search for a dream . . .
There are no dreams for me here.
I think of you now.
What was it that you said?
Was it something about love?
Or was it something about hate?
I cannot remember . . .
Sometimes . . . they are the same.
The darkness is really here now
And I walk through the gardens
Which are not gardens anymore.
I approach the old . . . so very old
. . . house.
The empty rooms hold secrets . . .
  haunting secrets . . .
            of the past.
The darkness is turning into
  black now
And the memories come rushing
in
Bittersweet memories . . .
Haunting memories . . .
It feels like yesterday
When the memories were reality
But now I don't know . . .
What is reality and what is
fantasy?
Only the spirits know . . .
Only the spirits know . . .

Milena Soukal
WE

---

*To Matt and Eugenija on their
wedding day*

We saw the hand throw fire:
then the chariot sped away.

Our sun got into the orbit
  rightfully
embraced the sound and carried
  it out.

Tell someone of our frenzy:
dot in the circle
claims of it's existence
but—
it is important to know
that two can emit a brighter light.

HAPPY BIRTHDAY TO OUR
LOVE!

The day it was born
the comet was crossing the
  southern sky.
We trailed across the horizon
and bathed in its light.

WE ARE. A PERFECT PARTICLE
OF A WHOLE.

Barbara Adams
AND FREEDOM RINGS
A boy is laid to rest,
medals on his chest,
an honor guard salutes,
a choir sings.
A mother cries
for her hero soldier,
and once again
the sound of freedom rings.

Shelley O'Donnell
LIFE IS BUT A ROSE

---

*To my grandmother in
remembrance of my grandfather
O'Donnell*

Our Lord is a bush upon which
  we rest
As crimson roses upon His
  breast,
We drink our fill of crystal rain
And thrive on love to ease our
  pain,
The dawn alights, to us it turns
Its heart unfolds, for us it yearns,
Beyond jeweled stars Our Lord
  does roam
Awaiting the day that we come
  home,
We are God's garden and He is
  our tender
Who picks us for Heaven, for He
  is our sender,
Although a rose withers, it never
  does die
But ascends to God, to bloom in
  His eyes,
What more could one say, than
  "God picked me
To unlock my soul, for now I am
  free".

Pastor T. Octavio Jr.
A SYMBOL?
The dove that I see in the paper
  today,
Looks like she is in deep agony.
Her wings are tilted like
  phantoms in a fray,
That froze the waters of
  Haiphong bay!

Her quail feathers are crumpled
  in dis-array,
And she looks tired . . . perhaps
  for being used in mockery,
To be hung on the wall to
  symbolize man's hypocrisy?

She is always drawn with an olive
in her mouth,
To portray a clown or to conceal
Ceasar's clout?
In beautiful semantics she is
fraught,
In constant euphemism she is
completely lost!

Like the Druides in the deeper
woods,
They play in the stone henges to
concoct,
In the cloak of the august moon
they conspire:
To rid of the world and of
themselves require
For all men regardless . . . to expire!

The smell of the stalags
And the sirens in the night
Mingle with the undulating
waves of amber
That blends with the sighs,
In the darkness of sorrows
Reverberates the sounds . . .
Of the glory of conquests
That men has learned to live by.

Maurice Burress
EDDIES EYE
What is that you're writing
Have you planned it all out right?
You will need a darn good message
Poetry is fighting for its life.
Orchestration will be needed,
Everything in it should rhyme,
Time is of the essence
She will find—my poem is
sublime.

Forget all about your hang ups
Earn your place with the very best,
Annihilate her challenge
Riding your thoughts to the very
crest.

Each phrase has its meaning
Direct her thought there no doubt,
Dig into the toughest going
In the end you can win out.
Each line paints a picture
Could it all be a surprise,
On her great judgement morning
Let us really open up her eyes!
Ego is our best assett
Shrewdness our biggest aim.

Every poem we have written
Your satisfaction's bound to gain!
Eddies eye says no—so lets try it
once again

Dolores Cipolletti
AN INNER STRENGTH

*To my Mom—Eleanor Ruth Will—
With all my love Written in 1971
at a time when her life seemed so
empty and she felt so alone*

Mama, you love him and he
loved you
And you know this fact is very
true
Some people never know a
happiness like you embraced
It was oh so pure and blessed
with God's grace

This is the truth you must keep
in your heart
And remember when you feel
sad and the teardrops start

He didn't like to see you cry
Now keep this in mind each
time you ask "why"

He was the only man whose
voice could make us shudder
in our shoes
But he was also the only man
with such tenderness only he
knew
how to use
Oh Ma—I know it hurts and
there is nothing we can do to
stop that pain
Except to tell you that in the
hereafter you will surely meet
again

Imagine how his heart would
ache
If you from his God did take
He was the strongest man I knew
But he couldn't have lived if he
lost you

He didn't know how to cook or
sew
Or exactly when the kids should
go
These are the trivials of course
we know
But to lose you would have been
his fatal blow

From Mary you draw an inner
strength
That exceeds that of a man by a
great length
Who better knew how to love
and lose
Then Mary who cried for the
King of the Jews

Eleanor F. Tarr

Eleanor F. Tarr
THE LAND BEYOND
Have you ever dreamed of the
Land Beyond?
The land beyond the sea of life,
Where we may lay our burdens
down
And live happily after all earth's
strife.

How did you picture that
wonderful land—
As a beautiful city of gold,
Or did you see lambs and sheep
grazing—
With Jesus bringing them to the
fold?

Or, perhaps you thought of a
garden
With flowers so wondrous and
rare,

But what matters what that land
is like—
If our Lord and Saviour is there.

For can He not still a stormy sea,
And whisper the waves to rest—
So dream on, my friends, dream
on—
Of your land of peace and
happiness.

For whatever it is that you dream
of—
If it be about a city of gold or a
garden fair,
If it be rich pasturelands fine for
grazing—
It shall be Heaven if Jesus is there.
Ada M. Fletcher
NIGHTMARE

*To my beloved daughters, Jayne
and Kathy who, with their love,
have often reasoned the
nightmares of my life into
rational perspective.*

Evil things creak and crawl in the
dark
And skitter and scratch and ping
on the screen;
Silhouettes of leaves and
branches breathe life
Into delusions of malevolence.
Prototypes of childhood ghosts
appear in my mind's eye
Huge-horned, grotesque, vile and
slimy green
And through this panorama one
viable theme emerges—
My immortality is
threatened—overseen.
Inhaling a scream I cannot vent,
my fists clench,
Muscles quiver and my mind
crouches in fetal position
Guarding endangered creeds; I
tighten my skull until
The roar in my ears deafens the
jousting
Of my personal devil seeds.
The matrix of total experience
becomes the elusive
Eye of the needle, at once
exposing the thread of my
punition
And I lie transfixed in time and
space, horrified but
compelled to stare, bulge-eyed at
doom's recognition.
Ominously, my door creaks and
slowly opens, sluicing
Fragmented shadows of hell on
the ceiling.
A soft, sleepy voice pleads,
"Mommy", then "Mommy, I had
A bad dream and need to stay
with you for awhile."
Abruptly, the specter of my sub-
conscious disappears.
In the blinding light of her
precious nearness, I behold
My child's face—and in her
vulnerability,
I am once again immortal and
fearless.

Lew Drake
RIVERS OF LIFE
Born high in the snowy mountains,
Dreaming of its might to be;

It trickles through a shaded glen,
On its journey to the sea.

Gathering power on its way,
It gives for all to see;
Falls cascading over towering cliffs,
As it hurries on to the sea.

Slowly it meets the low valleys,
To flow in wide circles with ease;
And creates new places for
bearing,
All creatures that live by the sea.

Mallards tracing patterns on water,
Birds catching insects on the wing;
From the marshes a symphony of
tribute,
Giving thanks for all living things.

Louise McCutcheon
DEAR RICK

*I wish to dedicate this poem to
my son, Richard T. Allison, who
served with the U. S. Marines in
Vietnam from Dec. 1966 to Jan.
1968.*

There'd never be a flag-draped
coffin
Nor a warship put to sea
If they'd only ask a mother
What the price of peace should
be.

Wars will never conquer greed
Nor change the minds that hate,
What is victory clothed in grief?
The price of peace is far too great!

Peace can't heal the hearts that
break
Nor dry the tears with medals
won,
What is peace that can't be shared,
What are medals without my son?

Tho' "Old Glory's" waving proudly,
Still the victory is not won
When the sounds of war are over
If the fighting takes my son!

When the battlefields are empty,
Where's the glory . . . in the mud!
Who's the victim . . . who's the
victor
When the price of peace is
blood!!!

Zeria C. Miller
MY GARDEN
Marigolds and roses are erstwhile
within my plot . . .
It's just those bugs and earwigs
that's a wearisome lot;
But as I walk discreetly and peer
into each bed,
I pray God to help control those
insects that I dread!
I'm sure that somewhere out
there, HE listens to my plea,
Somehow or another, not an
earwig do I see.
As I keep looking 'round at other
flowers in bloom,
It makes me think of Heaven
with my own special room
My marigolds and roses are so
sublimely fair . . .
I'm sure God with His mansions
has planted them up there.
I get down on my knees and
tenderly touch the sod . . .
Tears of wonder touch my

cheeks, I thank a loving God.
I get up and wander 'round,
fortunately I spy
without even trying, I see
everything is dry . . .
My reeling out those hoses, dear
God, can be such pain,
How about it, Lord up there—can
I expect some rain???

Viola Anne Fisher
A GIFT AT CHRISTMAS

*To: Robert A. Winter, tuck it
inside your shirt breastpocket,
Close to your heart, is where it
longs to be.*

If I could give you a gift at
Christmas,
I wondered what it might be.
Something precious, yet enduring
Uniquely, from me.

A box standing singly, alone
under a tree,
Wrapped in flawless platinum
foil
Beribboned in bright, red satin
Fittingly royal.

Contained therein, amidst a
myriad of New Year wishes,
One, pure white porcelain dove.
A note tucked tightly, beneath a
fragile wing
Saying simply, Merry Christmas
to the one I love.

Janet Wells
Satin Doll At Midnight
Drums are hummin'
Sax a phonin'
Base a strummin'
Piano tone-in.

Upbeat down beat
Tapping our feet
Counting to four
Vibrating floor.

Shoulders swayin'
Like they're prayin'
Hip-notizing
Fantasizing.

Playin' Satin Doll
Givin' It your all
Sweet's Fine Quintet
Glides fret to fret.

Dimmin' is the light
Playin' through the night
Only a few bloak
Dare to even smoke.

Waitress cleavage show
Keep your voices low
Fan is moving fast
People linger past

Last gig comes too soon
Play your special tune
Once more Satin Doll
For tonight—That's all!

Elaine J. Motes
INCREDIBLE LOVE

*Dedicated to my brother, Charles,
inspired by his undying love.*

Incredible dreams that once were
true
Incredible dreams about me and
you
Now they're gone, they've slipped
away
Incredible dreams of yesterday

Once I loved you and you loved
me
But now you want to be set free
Free from warmth, free from love
Free from my incredible love

I loved you then, I love you now
I'll set you free, but I don't know
how
Free from warmth, free from love
Free from this incredible love

Incredible love of yesterday
I thought that it would never fade
But now it's gone, it's slipped away
Incredible love of yesterday.

Shirley Davis MaGee
GOD IS ALWAYS THERE

*To my Father for having a
delightful sense of humor*

Most of the time
love seems just
Like a crime,
when no one
Seems to care.
but God is
Always there,
when you need
Tender love
and care.

Therese Salsamendi, Owen
Vibrating Intoxication
Clashing, clipping, clanging
Rolling, drolling cyclops of
musical vibrations
Erupt within my mind
I am hyponotized by the steady
rhythm
My heartbeat counts the time
My head, my hands, my hips,
Every fibre of my being reels to
these
Pulsating thrusts,
And the beat goes on . . .
And the beat goes on and on . . .
Till every shred of energy is
exhausted,
And I know no more.

Paul R. Dube
MISSILE
Mechanized monstrosity
of thoughtless man.
Lifeless metal
powerful and menacing.

Marauding master
of soul and mind.
Macabre creature of motion.

Brainchild of the misbegotten
a mirror image of madness.
A magnificently mismanaged
minister of misery.

A grotesque misfit
monogenic in nature
mocking any semblance of reason.

Memorial
to superiority and might.
Megatons
to mistrust and misfortune.

Misanthropic mass—
metamorphic force—
mirador of death—
we mourn your existence
we are mortified at your purpose.

Tonda English Meche
THE UNICORN

*This poem is dedicated to my
sister, Kathi, who has inspired me
through our adventures,
searching for the meaning of the
hidden unicorns.*

A myth of magical enchantment,
A story of long ago,
An animal of great beauty,
And a legend we'd like to know.

We've heard stories of the
Unicorn,
And the maiden fair,
The unicorns purity and
protection,
Was always mentioned there.

Some tried to pin him down,
And catch him in a net,
But with his great cleverness,
They heaven't caught him yet.

So as the legend goes,
We'll have to wonder still,
If the great white Unicorn,
Is at the top of the hill.

Gary W. Baumgarth
SOME DAY SOON
I want to be free.
I want to be loved.
To have someone be honest with
me.
It's something that is not to be had.
I'm afraid to put myself on the line.
But who likes hurt?
I'm protecting myself.
I can smile,
But, I'm not happy
Someday soon.
Someday soon.
Someday, someone will make me
happy.

Allene Robinson Leggette
HAVE A SALAD TODAY

*This poem is dedicated to my
two grandchildren: Robert (Age
14) and Robyn (age 3) James. May
their salad appetites improve.*

The Salad Makers are here to say
"Have a salad with us today."
We've done our best in efforts to
please you,

With decorative, chilled, and
bowl salads too.
Nutritionists say "Eat a salad a
day."
At our salad parade, eat all you
may,
They are delicious in flavor and
great to chew.
Before you dig in, they are placed
to view.

There is never a dull meal with
salads around.
They highlight a meal in country
and town.
Their vitamins and minerals help
you keep well.
Value of salads, we don't have to
sell

Have a salad with us today,
Serve yourself in your own way
We hope you will enjoy every
bite.
So please your sight and your
appetite.

Gary Lee Engel
**A Gravesite In The
Meadows**
He was born crippled and a sick
little boy.
His family was poor and couldn't
buy him any toys.
He went to school and studied
every night and day.
On Sunday he would go to
church with his family and pray.
He never did go to his senior
dance.
Hoping to find a little romance.
He didn't have a car to take a girl
out.
And never found out what love is
about.
He worked at many different
places.
But none of them ever put a
smile on his face.
He did the job the best he could
do.
Trying to make a friend or two.
He found out from the doctor
that he was sick and going to
die.
He was buried at the gravesite in
the meadows and left to lie.

Michele R. Weimer
The Beautiful Bouquet

To Margaret, my special friend.

There's two unique flowers
amongst
the vast field. They acquired
identifiable similarities; however,
their both distincively different.

They began as two separate seeds.
Through the passage of time,
they
built a deep trust and a loyal
friendship. They shared
everything
under the sun, even the sun.

In the near future, those two
beautiful flowers will perish;
but remember, they will always
have an over flowing bouquet of
memories.

Marie Bass
TO MY DAUGHTER

This poem was written for and is dedicated to my second daughter, Rebecca Diane Waltz . . . with all my love.

They gently laid her in my arms;
  I looked with awe and wonder;
Upon the Gift of Love God
  gave . . . A precious baby
  daughter!
With dimples in a cherub's
  face . . . a tiny replica of one;
Soon to grow to womanhood so
  full of love and grace.

The months' passed swiftly by
  and tiny toes and fingers uncurl'd;
To crawl and walk; then run and
  touch;
Each one within her happy world.

A carefree teen before I knew
  that she was halfway there;
With girls N' curls, N' giggles
  running everywhere.
Sometimes so quiet and
  thoughtful; and, yet so proudly
  knowing . . .
  The constant faith that I beheld,
  without her really showing.

Oh, tiny cherup! Oh, graceful
  wife and loving mother too!
I see reflections of the past and
  goals for the future new.

There are many ways to say the
  things I feel for you,
  But I am just a mother, so, what
  else can I do?
Save pour my heart upon a page
  and make the words to rhyme;
To let you know I'm proud of
  you, and that I love you all the
  time.

Debra Sue Heidt
NATURE'S RICHES
Not in the earth,
Nor in the sea,
Are the riches that I see.

Not of silver,
Nor of gold,
But of nature, bright and bold.

Roaring rivers,
Tremendous trees,
Mother Nature made all these.

Majestic mountains,
Prairie plains,
Sprinkled by her snows and rains.

Awesome oceans,
Babbling brooks,
Glimmerglass lakes with silvery
  looks.

Nature's riches,
Never diminish,
They just seem to grow and
  flourish.

Jerry Palermo
THANKS
I don't know what to say to you
For all the times you cared
For the love you showed me all
  through life
For the troubled times you beared
For the little things you did for
  me

For the decisions that you made
For the hope and happy times
  you shared
For the wisdom that you gave
For the good times and the bad
  times
For the things I'll always cherish
For the memories that you gave
  me
That I know will never perish
For all these things you did for
  me
I don't know what to say
Would just a simple, "Thank you,
  Mom"
"I Love You", be okay?

Tina Charlene McKay
A BOY'S LIFE
When a woman gives birth,
She doesn't care what the babe is
  worth.

As he grows into a child,
He becomes very sweet and mild.

Then as boyhood draws nearer,
He sees life clearer.

But soon he'll be a teen,
Rough, rugged, and mean.

Later, when he becomes an adult,
He gets chosen as the leader of a
  cult.

He'll be an old man soon,
Always sleeping, morning,
  evening and noon.

Then one day he'll die,
Never more to open an eye.

Mary A. Christensson
HEART'S TRAJECTORY
Sure as a salmon or Canada
  Goose I feel it—
The migratory pull that takes me
  home by Harvest Moon
to the cornfields and wheatfields
  of Illinois that sang my birth.
Home, to the cradle of my family,
  (only two generations removed
  from the march of a million
  Cossack boots),
and the grave of my childhood
  shared with a dog named Chief.

My mother's arms that never
  sheltered me when I needed them
welcome me now, a stranger
  who looks like the child that she
  bore.

My father and I reminisce about
  the horse he bought when I was
  twelve
and wanted to be Jesse James.
(Thank God he didn't also buy a
  gun,
I'm sure I would have turned it on
  myself.)

My sister and I fulfill
a long-time dream of riding a
  unicycle.
We roam the fields together,
  collecting milk-weed pods
and wishing to hell we'd have
  never grown up.

My dearest friend of childhood
  days
still lives next door with children
  of her own.
We mourn our thirty-year
  friendship

Now reduced to a yearly trade of
  Christmas cards.

Tom Wolfe was right: you can't
  go home again.

Marla K. Sears
MY FATHER
You've been my companion,
and my lifelong friend,
I want to say I love you,
and my love will never end.

You were there to comfort me,
when I was hurt at play,
you held me closely in your arms,
and hugged the hurt away.

My broken dolls,
or a broken toy,
you fixed them all,
to bring me joy.

You've given me strength,
to keep moving on,
you're the guiding hand,
that makes me strong.

The broken hearts,
the shedding of tears,
you've been my friend,
throughout the years.

I'm growing up now,
and I love you oh, so much,
Daddy your little girl,
will never out grow your touch.

Charles Willard Daniel
THE AWAKENING

To My Beloved Wife Hazel Mignonette

The earth is still, winter locks
  the land,
Bare branches silhouette to lace
  against the twilight sky.

Tomorrow's blossoms sleep
  beneath
      a quilt of white;
And dream of the kiss of spring.

Christine King Shrum
HEAVENLY DELIVERY
Scurrying angels encroach
hovering within sculptored flight
  approach.
Ethereal hands touch
delicate fingers tug.
Anticipation unwraps
discovery unfolds,
        God's Gift—
          from beneath
          incrusted shell

Mind in
motion
comes afloat
Upon Cherub
wings.

Marcus Dagold
Eyeshadow and Baby Fat

This poem is dedicated to all the children in the world.

I saw you holding onto a
  cigarette,
and before my eyes, I saw you
  smoking it.
You're not the kind of girl to do
  that,
and you're only eleven.
But I saw you, and I was not
  dreaming.
How can I be sure that you won't
  buy another pack
every time you get a dollar
that I give to you to play video
  games?
How long will it be before you
  are addicted,
Will you stop for long enough to
  endure the craving
that is self-inflicted
and get cured from this killing
  artificial pick-me-up?
To run inside the park today,
and feel your energy flowing on
  its own, within you,
would be a good idea for you,
if you don't think I'm worth
  ignoring.
You've got a lot of things to do,
  and I know I may be boring,
But how long will it be before
  you are addicted?
I saw you
with a cigarette between your
  lips, unlit, for five minutes.
Someone said, "Why don't you
  light it?"
You said, "I'd rather not have it!"
But is your eleven-year-old body
  saying, "go ahead"?
You lit it, against what you said,
  the nicotine will fill your head.
You always felt so much better
  before you were addicted.

Jeari McCarthy
PRAYER
Prayer is always answered
If we will but pray and wait.

Prayer is always answered,
But not always as we designate.

Prayer is always answered
At the right time, on the right date.

Prayer is always answered.
Be patient. God is never late.

Christine Finch
SQUIRREL
Run, Run, little squirrel in the
  woods,
Run, Run, and collect your nutty
  goods.

Run, Run, with your fluffy little
  tail,
Up a tree, down a tree, you look
  so small and frail.

Run, Run, to your family in your
  den,

Run, Run, but please come back again.

Bonnie Maness
MY PLEA TO YOU
I needed to see him tonight
To try to make things right.
I needed to talk to him
So we could stay friends.

I know one thing, this time,
You'll never be mine.
You want your freedom
But for me there's no other one.

I hope I haven't messed up again.
I can't lose you, my friend.
I love you too much
To ever lose touch.

Don't leave me this way;
Because I need you more each day.
I just can't do without you;
And I promise it will always be true.

Don't walk away from me.
Only you can make me happy.
This is my plea to you;
Because I really love you.

Mildred Lambert Bell
MY MISSY
My Missy, now, who do you
think she be;
a friend, a little girl, a daughter?
She was much—
much more to me.
She was a friend—the best
that could be;
in times of sorrow, times of
laughter.
She was much—
much more to me.
A little girl? She surely
had to be
some mother's loving, lovely
daughter.
She was much—
much more to me.
Through blood lines, she was not
mine.
Who was she?
Through adoption, my *own*
grandmother!
My Missy—
my dear Missy!

Kim M. Kartman
A DREAM ALL MY OWN

*I dedicate my poem to those, who
see the world through children's
eyes. A special thanks to Sue
Bernhardt, someone who has an
exceptional way with children,
and Lynne, someone who gave
friendship a new meaning.
Thanks Deb and Ken, you always
seem to be there. Bless you all.*

As I stood in reverie,
I recollected the thoughts of my
walk,
Through the peaceful, silent
countryside.
I could see the brightness of the
sunset.
Yet, so dreamily thoughtful,
I could see the fluttering birds on
the colorful trees of the forest.
As I stood so still,
The remembrance of a child I

recall,
The most precious of them all.

Robert J. Rado
FOR LORI
There are a lot of beautiful sights,
in this world.
Things that can't be passed by.
Like an eagle,
flying through a clear blue sky.
Or the face of a lady,
with eyes that shine.
You my dear are,
one of these beautiful sights.
Your natural beauty,
it shines so bright.
You could light up the darkness,
of the darkest night.
Lady, I want you to know,
I'll always love you so.

Larry Keith Darr

Larry Keith Darr
JUDY GAYTON EYES

*To Judy: Somehow you seem to
know and understand me the
best.*

Eyes so pretty as hers
that glow with warm compassion
draw from deep within
ones deepest blind affection.
Gentle as the breeze
and equally as free,
like an angel sent from heaven,
somehow she has touched me.
Eyes reflect loves glowing light,
eyes like rubies shine,
eyes that tell no lies,
Judy Gayton eyes.

Effie Betzer Haring
MISUNDERSTANDINGS

*To my dear husband, David, and
my children, Sandra, Kermit,
Dolan, and Darla. Also all my
grand-children, and my great
grand-children.*

Some one told me just today, they
thought they were being kind,
Of A conversation that they
heard about my state of mind,
Between two of my dearly loved
ones, but it only broke my heart,
So remember that repeating
things is not so very smart.
I can't always change the way I
think, so if I've made a wrong
impression,

When you hear bad tales about
me, always use discretion.
Instead of telling strictly truth,
couldn't you just say,
"I heard some one speak of you in
a most un-usual way."
Then I will use my imagination,
and pretend they spoke only
good,
Because some of my peculiarities
are simply misunderstood.
Sometimes when I am sick or
tired, depressed, and deep dark
blue,
My mind starts playing mean
tricks and thinks things that
just aren't true.
If I've hurt you all forgive me, I'm
sorry that it ever had to be,
So when I've left this earth for
good, please think kind
thoughts of me.

Vicki Hollis Leach
**Glass Hearts and Wilted
Roses**
Does beauty lie in the
remembering? Or only pain?

I will never again feel love or be
loved in the way I feel that
love should be
Perhaps I am odd.

Am I bereft or am I fortunate to
have been given this gift but
once?

So many years; How can I believe
in you?
You have disappeared
Was it only a dream?

I will never forget, I will never
forget
But does beauty or sadness lie in
the remembering?

Love you gave to me, you took
away from me
How quickly you turned

Did you really give me this gift?
I have never felt before, I will
never feel again

I will always remember that you
opened my heart, planted my
soul
Nurtured the petals of my brief
growth
And you held the key to my
fragile spirit

You have forgotten, moved on
Maybe with disdain
I don't know why I hold on to a
memory

I am a realist or so I thought

Perhaps I am imagining our time;
But I have never imagined
before or again
Did I really touch the soul of a
man who had no soul? Or did I
need to believe?
If I had never loved you, would I
be gone?

I will never love again or shed a
tear for any thing or person
I have died with your exit
I will never love again, but I will
forever remember

Larry R. Irons
RADIANCE OF THE RAIN
"The landscape, brown and sere
beneath the sun,
Needs but the cloud to lift it into
life;
The dews may damp the leaves of
tree and flower,
But it requires the cloud—
distilled shower
To bring rich verdure to the
lifeless life.

Ah, how like this, the landscape
of a life:
Dews of trial fall like incense,
rich and sweet;
But bearing little in the crystal
tray— —
Like nymphs of the night, dews
lift at break of day
And transient impress leave, like
lips that meet.

But clouds of trials, bearing
burdens rare,
Leave in the soul, a moisture
settled deep:
Life kindles by the magic law of
God;
And where before the thirsty
camel trod,
There richest beauties to life's
landscape leap.

Then read thou in each cloud
that come to thee
The words of the bible, in letters
large and clear:
So shall those clouds thy soul
with blessing feed,
And with a constant trust as thou
dost read,
All things together work for good.
Fret not, nor fear!"

Carla S. Tellor
WHAT IS LOVE?
LOVE is something that causes
a shiver,
And lets your heart flow like a
river.
LOVE states a fact that you care
for someone.
And shows you the difference
between right and wrong.

LOVE is what makes the world
go 'round,
But no one knows where it's
really found.
LOVE can be a beautiful thing,
And you feel wonderful, when it
pulls on your string.

LOVE keeps you going all
throughout the day,
It only stops when it starts to
decay.
LOVE will never become extinct,
But sorrow and happiness are
bound to be linked.

LOVE is a kind of experience,
Cause many will say when it's
over they had their chance.
LOVE can be very rewarding at
times,
It's such a shame it can't be found
in a rhyme.

LOVE is something that comes
from the heart.
But don't be discouraged if it has
a late start.

LOVE is what you'll always remember,
And it could very well feel like a tremor.

AND still there is no real answer to that question
"WHAT IS LOVE?"

Karen Groven- (Hauk-O)
A PROUD LIFE
He stands proud upon his feet,
His back is high, his coat is neat.
With his head held high he looks onward,
As if the cruel world never occurred.
His body is bold like a wall of concrete,
Snow melts on his back from his great body heat.

There's a mean twinkling in his eye,
He knows he's much to ornery to die.
The rack on his head looks like a crown.
His small alert ears are a deep, dark brown.
As he falls to the ground he lets out a cry.
He may be down, but his head's still held high.

The hunter comes closer to look at his prey,
For this beautiful beast it had been a short day.
Blood runs from his wound on the sun lit, white snow.
He takes his last breath, and his head is now low.
He lived "A Proud Life", but it didn't pay,
Now, on the cold ground, the dead moose lay.

Maude Irene Staton
THIS: OUR DEBT

This poem is dedicated to everyone who has touched my life, and made it richer, by their just being there.

For God so loved the world, He gave His only begotten son.
The word only tells us, there were not two, or three, just one.
A son so pure and filled with love, He didn't hesitate to answer the call of His father above.
He came down to this sin filled earth,
To give us all a brand new birth.
Not a birth of the flesh, from whence we all came,
But a birth of the spirit in His fathers name.
He showed us the way to a brand new life,
Filled with love and devotion, not misery and strife.
The world was lost till He opened the way
To a brighter tomorrow, for which He had to pay
The highest price that ever was given
To open to us the gates of heaven.

He's coming again to fulfill the plan,
That God has mapped out for all of man.
So let us be ready for that day of all days
When from the dead, everybody He'll raise,
To pass judgment according to our acts and deeds
Justly and with love, the way he answered our needs
While here on earth we journey a time,
Till He gathers us close in His arms sublime.
For your sins and mine did Jesus pay
Then He died on the cross that memorable day.
In our minds and our hearts, let us never forget
The debt to our Savior is not paid yet.
Nor ever will be, no matter how long we live,
We've nothing of equal value to give.
For God gave us the perfect Prince of Peace
The ruler of all men, this earth and the beasts.

Elissa Rappanotti Tuttle
A CRUEL MAN
You are a cruel and brutal man
With nothing in your heart or hand
With hate towards all you cheat and steal
You have a heart as cold as steel
If I were judge
I'd sentence you
To ten years in prison and hard labour too
And that's not all
With your fine airs
You'd spend it all in solitare
You'd only live on bread and water
Not one word would you utter
You pray to God that you could retire
Or may be you can fly away
Instead of looking at jail bars
Day after day.

Lily Ng
ROADS
Going down a road
That seems to lead to nowhere,
Going down a path
That seems too old,
Going down a way
Whose destination
Is unknown.
It is murky and fog is everywhere
It is too sad and forlorn.
Try to look for a happier road,
A smiling path,
A joyful way.
Where there is sunshine,
And brightness dominates all,
Where we are free and strong
Having no burdens to carry.
We'll eventually get there,
But there are many sad obstacles to overcome.

Sharon R. Kelly
THE VAMPIRE
A dream of falling, falling, eyes of ebony glow,

I hear him calling, calling, and I know that I must go.
I feel my passions growing, I can't resist his call,
For me there'll be no slowing, I must give him my all.

I know when he finally takes me, for me, the day will end,
But the night is where I long to be, where passions can begin.
I see his eyes, they beckon me, my body feels on fire,
I know he'll set my passions free, I'm filled with wild desire.

He stands before me, dark and tall, and beckons with his eyes,
I try to fight, my strength is small, and my soul in agony cries.
My strength is slipping fast away, I know that I must fly,
I will not see another day, but never will I cry.

So now that he and I are one, our nights burn wild with lust,
Mortals flee before us, run, then soon turn into dust.
But we go on and on and on, our blood lust never ends,
And when at last the light is gone, our night of fire begins.

I see you standing there alone, in the shadows of the night,
Feel my passion, how it's grown, let's drown in lust's delight.
Then you, like me, can know the fire, the heat and power burns bright,
Then you can know the wild desire, the blood lust of the night.

Beverly Gariepy
A CHILD

This poem is dedicated to my two Grandsons

A child born brings joy to life,
And a closer bond between husband and wife.
As the years go by, he grows in body and mind,
When adulthood is reached, those childhood years are left behind.

When a child, the future seems so far ahead,
The years are mixed with happiness and dread.
Sometimes decisions are hard to make,
On which road in life will be better to take.

Will there be marriage and a child of his own,
Or will he go through life alone.
When that day comes and he finally leaves home,
You will find his parents waiting by the phone.

To hear he's alright whether far or near,
Because the memories they hold so dear,
Of a child who brought love,
To two people from God above.

Karen Pitt
PONYBOY

Dedicated to: My friend Pam and to S. E. Hinton and C. Thomas Howell for bringing Ponyboy to life to me.

Pony is his
nickname as
everyone knows
he is the greaser
that feels like
the outsider
in everything
he does.

Judith Caroline Doane
MORNING SUN
The morning sun floods the curtains
near my bed
Spreading warmth indiscriminately over all
Held back by drawn shades only
slivers of light escape
and prick my eyelids
to wakefulness
Chasing the nightly dance
of wandering images
from my brain . . .
School children's voices
floating in from an open window
dissolve on contact
While in the corner
the solid dresser sits
silent in repose, its mirror
empty of conjures.

Doris Turlik
POWER

For the inspiration and encouragement my husband Mike, and sons John & Matthew gave me.

Power is Black: Power is White
Power is Win: Power is Fight
You hear so much about Power today
I'd say, Power is here to stay.

I've watched all your games with loving attention,
And my heart beat fast, on occasions too numerous to mention
The Power was there: You played with all your might
As the saying goes: "out of sight"

My eyes lit up: as I watched a few
Bless themselves, and say a prayer too
And I wondered if He from above:
Looked down, and watched too, with all His love.

So keep this Power the rest of your life:
In all you do: In all your strife
Aim high in your goals: the Power is there
For you to give: for all to share.

Power is great: Power is fine
Power is yours: Power is mine
But without God's Power, our greatest need
Our Power is small: as small as a tiny seed.

Toni Nelson
THE SEARCH

*To all those who have touched
my life & changed it for everyone
to see; and a Special thanks to
"my" star who shines far above
me, yet, stands beside me.*

I walked upon the sands of time
today—The same sand that
thousands before me have
walked.
I was alone among the crowd of
Souls, all searching for things
unknown.
The wind whispered as it blew
my hair and kiss my cheek, to
let me know it was there.
The sun shown down upon my
face, to dry my tears and put
peace in their place.
The wind continued to sing it's
song as it told me it's secrets to
where I belong.
He told me my thoughts were
holding me back, and for me to
change things; I must
Understand that.
Love was within, but, I was to
blind to see; as I kept on
thinking of no one but, me.
Loving and giving are the keys,
that unlock the chains that I
have bound around me.
It matters not that I'm different
you see, It's how I feel, that will
set me free.
The perfected state that we all
search for, is already here
entwined within our soul.

Love,
Toni

Lynn Thompson Braswell
THIS FANTASY

*To my husband John for making
all my fantasies become realities.*

What's this fantasy you've given
me?
I'm weak just seeing your smile.
I'm confused with the passions
raging within
whenever you're near me awhile.

Looking in your eyes melts me
inside.
I'm captured under your spell.
Playing those games only lovers
can know,
hearing secrets only they can tell.

With every breath I think about
you.
Your laughter lifts my soul.
You've freed desires locked up in
me
to watch love take it's toll.

This life we share gets better
with time.
Our feelings defined with no
bounds.
So we lie awake and our love
flows free
as we listen to the summer
night's sounds.

In the morning we'll wake, still
lying close,
and tell each other our dreams.
Our love produces only happiness,
no matter how hard living seems.

Hilary Palmer
TO LIVE FOR LIFE

To live for life is to have
The courage that is born of
wisdom;
The knowledge derived from
understanding;
The awareness of that love which
is the
Recognition of all as one with the
self;

To be at peace amid strife,
To have the security that is an
inner conviction;
To be at rest amid turmoil and
confusion
Is to live for life.

Sylvia E. Henley Kozel
REMEMBERING SUE

*To my sister Suzanne, to our
youth and for all the love and
giving so much a part of her
heart—our life. Her softness has
pillowed me; Her love shines, as
the sun, with warmth constant.*

I remember when just little ones,
the room we used to share and
the bed, by which in evening,
we would kneel beside in
prayer.
The old front porch, with peeling
paint, on which we used to
play clutching dolls, with
selfish hands—Oh!, how we
laughed at all they'd say.
I remember the parties held in
our fort, under that big, old
tree; the Devil dogs and Ice
Cream bars you used to share
with me.
I remember the colors of turning
leaves before they fell upon the
ground and the wind that blew,
as if somehow it knew, "ole
man winter" was coming
around.
I remember the odor of fragrant
pines, filling the cool, crisp air
and the glistening glow of the
sun on the snow and the trees
with branches bare.
I remember the fun days, all
things we once shared; those
most tender moments that
expressed how you cared.

My heart caresses memories of
all I used to do with that very
special someone . . . My dear,
sweet sister SUE.

Nancy Estrada
ONE SUMMER'S EVE

*This poem was written with love
to my parents, A.E., and R.R. It was
inspired by Terry, Julie, and Billy—
thank you for believing in me.*

I saw you there one summer's eve
Alone with your own thoughts,
You stood so near and yet so far
For me to share my dreams with
thee.

You tried so hard to love me still
And say you'd never leave,
But I saw your pain and felt your
need
To live and yet be free.

To keep you now would be a sin
So your love I said I'd never need,
But you my friend I can't deccive
For you're all I have and all I'll
ever be.

J. Mahogany Dupree
PLOW OF FAITH

The plow turned the soil to make
ready the spirit planting of
cleansed love.
The earth parts, and the sides
rejoice of the long awaited
seed.
In the tender caress of loving
hands the soil is replaced in its
native land. Bother it not, but
wait for awhile and vision a
new top soil of love.
Daily is fed, and watered to, with
merciful love, and sweet
morning dew. It has been
cherished, for oh, so long, no
wonder its roots are deep and
strong.
Undisturbed by what is above,
the seed grows through the
labor of love. As birth assumes
the perfect time and place,
destiny claims a cleansed love
be born that day.
The plow waiting patiently on
the spoken word of light, can
clearly vision the seed's before
birth in sight. Now, the plow
has faith in cleansed love.

Deborah A. Wilkin
O' AUNTIE OF MINE

*To my Aunt Carol: "O' Auntie
of mine"*

O' Auntie of Mine
Who's eyes are so bright
Do you know what light
You bring to our nights?
O' Auntie of Mine
No fire is as warm as the embers
in your heart
And your welcoming arms held
apart.
O' Auntie of Mine
How quickly passes time
But to you be it kind
Filling your days with an
abundance of sunshine.

Francesca A. Sachs
PASSING OPEN WINDOWS

In passing open windows
where light comes in
or shadows grow.
We can watch each begin
or see the sun set low.
Should you see rain
or shed some tears,
think not of pain
or of lost years.
Look for the sun
think not of strife,
keep at a run
down this road of life.
Do not stop
or stay to long,
if the urge to drop
grows in you strong.
Just give a smile for what you see
and on the time shall go,
there is so much that you can be
so keep on passing the open
windows.

Marilyn Ann Haynam
LOVE

I see the beautiful sky in your
eyes,
Peaceful, loving, a soft baby
blue,
They sparkle like jewels in God's
sunshine,
Whenever I look at you.

I see happy tears and sad tears,
Sometimes like morning's
glistening dew,
Other times they are God's gentle
raindrops,
Whenever I look at you.

A soft glow and warmth enfolds
me,
Like a spark from God's sun does,
too,
As I see your shy grin turn to a
smile,
Whenever I look at you.

I found thoughtfulness, caring
and kindness,
Like the ocean's gentle waves
that roll in so true.
You see love was always a puzzle
to me,
Until I looked deep down inside
you.

Connie Lakey Martin
FALLEN AND FATIGUED

Swirling. Twirling
in the gusty wind.
Lots of lovely
leaves

landing.

Rustling. Rattling.
Scattering and
chattering in the grasses,
tired, tattered masses,

confused. Drifting.

Tumbled. Jumbled.
Wrinkling and
crinkling in the weather.
Unrested since they

fell

together.
Rumpled. Crumpled.
Dying with the year.
December brown

Our World's Best Loved Poems

bunches. Withered.
Stacked. Packed.
Saturday raked.

Rose Colombo Strickland
Crackle! Crackle! Crackle!

To the silent victims of alcoholism

Well,
  I think I'll have a drink
It's better than a shrink,
I guess I'll have just one
I want to have some fun,

Bartender, "Fill 'er up!"
Pour more into this cup—
Perhaps just three or four
My life is such a bore.

WOW!
That girl wrapped in a skirt
Won't hurt a bit to flirt,
Yes, give us both one more
Good grief, it's half past four.

Hmmm,
I'm much too late for any dinner,
Wife says that I am growin'
  thinner
She nags about my hands a
  shakin'
Don't want to hear my head's a
  achin'

SLAM!
I'm home. She'll ask me to
  confess.
I'll shout this house a cluttered
  mess!
Oh, my belly hurts with pain
cause drinking is my only game.

gosh,
These drinks could do me in
Doc says it's me or give up
  gin—ah!
How can we claim that wars are
  sane
And killings still remain insane,
  how vein.

sooo,
If a man is sane while sober
Is a drunk an insane man?
Like the ice that melts to water

```
C       C       C
R       R       R
A       A       A
C       C       C
K       K       K
L       L       L
E!      E!      E!
```

J. Michael Whitten
BECAUSE OF YOU
You gave me the gift of life,
  before I knew what it was.
When I was small and afraid, you
  comforted me.
When I was unsure of walking
  and fell, you were always there
  to pick me up.
I always felt secure because I
  knew you cared.
You were always there when I
  was confused about life.
You directed my life and saw to it
  that my path went in the right
  direction.
During my adolescense when I
  was difficult, your love was
  always there.

You sacrificed so that I could have.
You hurt silently so not to upset
  your children.
  Your silent tears were always
  heard by me.
We communicated only as a son
  and mother can.
You read my feelings like a book.
Through my triumphs and
  failures your love was ever
  present.
You taught me how to love and
  care for others.
You taught me to be independent,
  to be myself.
You believed in me when I didn't
  believe in myself.
Love like yours can never be
  replaced, it's something special.
My being is because of you.
I love you.

Sylvia Cook
MOTHERLESS CHILD
Sometimes I feel like a
  motherless child
When walking a step feels like
  walking a mile
Every day problems, I just can't
  cope
I don't know what to do, I've lost
  all hope
Everything is moving too fast for
  me
And things in my mind won't let
  me be
Never had anyone to depend on
  you see
That's why I try to depend on me

Dr. Robert Walter Taylor
BLUE MOUNTAIN

---

*To my lovely wife Beverly and to
my children Derrick and Thyneice.*

Late in the 'noon
The sun exuding radiance reflects
  her turquoise face.
But lo! what see you at the
  twilight 'noon?
I gazed at the mountain blue
And saw the cataract snake down
  her cheeks,
And slowly meander to oblivion.
Oh Jamaica! your luxuriant
  forests skyscape the air;
Your mountains, crumpled like
  paper,
Summit in blue splendor
As if Paradise was fashioned after
  thee.
Darkness sweeps down in a
  murky haze
And blankets the land.

Mary V. Dye
The Birth Of a New Love

---

*This is dedicated to my husband
Rick, whom has given me "THE
BIRTH OF A NEW LOVE."*

His love pressed upon my heart
Gently covered by every part
Caressed with such tenderness
Brought the magic of our first kiss
His fingertips stirred within my
  soul
Renewed love's memory of long

ago'
Soft music filled with desire
Broke all chill to build the fire
Cuddled safe from all harm
Warm inside my love's arms
Transcended into a world of
  romance
Love gave me a second chance

Jenniffer Smelter
FINGERPRINTS
Feeling the beat
Inside my body
Never stopping
Growing stronger and stronger
Everlasting feeling
Rapid heart
Pleasing to the ears and eyes
Relaxing
In all the right ways
Never stop
The music from playing

Elisabeth Weir
**Doors . . . "The Door"
(The Easter Door)**
Whoever will, may come!
All kinds of doors;
Low, tall, wide, narrow, Gothic,
Wooden, steel, glass, antique,
Ugly, beautiful, plain, ornate,
Open, shut, barricaded, abandoned,
Stable, cathedral, home, school,
  vocation,
Heart, life, death, eternity,
  opportunity.

He invites us to open 'our door' to
  Him!
The choice is ours.

O! Lord! As we join our hands
And place them in Yours,
Lead us through Your Door.
We would sup with You!

H. Frank Martin, Jr.

H. Frank Martin, Jr.
**Lemons, Neckbones and
  Boiled Peanuts**

---

*To: Callaway Gardens the Circus
and Beach*

Other writers have written
so much about the sun,
I feel almost a plaguerist;
But
I've had many summers in the sun.

I may have some more,
and, if not,
I'll move to a peach orchard
and sell my wares
or walk the cold winter beaches,

but not so alone as before,
warm from the sun and memories
of the past,
of flying through the air,
a trapeze artist
and laughing at the beach.

I might even have to get an
  umbrella
on the sidewalk
in New Orleans
and sign little poems,
as an artist does paintings.

But I think I would prefer the
  Peach Orchard.

Frances Gutman
AMONG THE GHOSTS
I walk among the Ghosts
and they speak silently to me.
Sometimes they accuse me, with
  reproach
of being here when you are not.
I know you loved me
because you said you did.
But you also said things that hurt
  me,
and as I go among the remains
of what was once a vibrant, lusty
  place
filled with music and voices
and the sound of a violin,
the ghosts and spirits follow me,
  watching my
movements as I wander
  aimlessly.
I shift a pile of papers, and
  rearrange a book.
This place is not mine, it still is
  yours,
and I am a silent stranger poking
  into your past in places I
  hardly dare go.
Somehow I cannot close your life
and keep the ghosts away.

Dorothy M. Ariola
A BRIDES PRAYER

---

*Dedicated to my husband Jack,
our children Diane, Doreen and
Dean. My sis Betty, Oh, how I
miss her! And to Kathy, my
poetic little neice, whose faith in
me has given me faith in myself!*

Oh Blessed Mother hear my
  prayer
  Which I send forth to Thee
Help me to be the kind of wife
  That I've known you to be.

Although I am not yet a bride
  Help me to understand.
That if I always do my best
  I'll have your helping hand.

Please guide me each and every
  day
  That I may always share.
With Jack, our sorrows and our
  joys
  And let me not despair.

Help me to never think or speak
In ways that you would nor.
And make me always thankful
  For the things that I have got.

My children I shall promise now
  Will grow up in a home.
Where Mary, Queen of Heaven
Is a name that's loved and known.

I'll need your help to do my best
From You the perfect wife.
Please stay near me and guide
me
As I enter married life.

Mary Jane Leger
LITTLE GIRLS
Little girls are quite a treasure;
they're made to love and hold
with pleasure.
They're just a loan, don't you
know, from God above to you
below.
So guide them with a firm, but
gentle hand, that they grow up
within God's plan.
What joy, then, they'll be to thee,
when you have weaned them
from thy knee.
As they go forward in their life it
will not be filled with strife.
No hate nor sorrow will they
find, cause Mom and Dad
taught them right, the first
time.
So love them, and listen to them
when they talk, that you might
know with whom they walk.
Treasures are lost and Treasures
are found, but your treasures
will always be around.

Georgia Dale
LOVE
Love me not with chains that bind
But gentle strength of heart and
mind.

Diane M. Darran
MISSING YOU
Tears
building, burning
brimming, choking, spilling,
rolling, streaming, tumbling,
blurring, shaking, sobbing,
gasping,
slowing, breathing, blinking,
wiping, sniffling, rubbing,
sighing, calming,
Missing you.

Jenean R. Sparks
THE SORROW OF MEN
I have seen through the eyes of
many men the pain and sorrow
they feel within.
Isn't it one of mankinds biggest
crimes that these sensitive
beings can't even cry.
For in these times what would a
man be if he dared to cry out
his pain openly.

I once knew a man who dared to
care he held open his arms to
who ever was there.
But this man too was eventually
lost for he paid at a very high
cost.
This man who cried openly and
loved freely was called sick and
locked up for eternity.

Eileen B. Ciuccarelli
WINGS OF LOVE
My heart is completely and
utterly beguiled.
Upon me love has lighted its
wings and smiled.
Like a butterfly, it has softly
taken a place
In my life, gently touching my
lonely face,

Kissing me tenderly upon my two
aching lips.
Can I possibly ask for any more
than this?
To be loved as I have never been
loved before,
Piercing my soul to its very depth
and core,
Putting me under love's hypnotic
spell.
I cannot be silent, I must joyfully
tell
Of my happiness, in a witch's
brew I delight.
Of a magic potion I drink, gaining
my sight.

Wondrously opening my blind
eyes to see
That my life was a vacuum,
needing to be
Filled with love, allowing no
empty space,
Taking away loneliness, leaving
no trace
Of the pain I felt there, so deep
inside.
I open the door of desire, I fling it
wide,
Welcome it, invite it to come,
forever to stay.
Reside with me, Dear Butterfly,
do not fly away.

Ronald J. Carlson
SIGHT

---

*I would like to dedicate this
poem to: Markella Frangakis, and
the VINELAND HIGH SCHOOL
Graduating class of 1984. With
Special thanks to Mr. Pramov and
to my latin teacher, Dave
O'Donnell.*

I see the leaves on the trees
as they wave softly in the breeze,
I see the animals at play,
They are so carefree and gay.

I feel the wind blow by,
I hear the birds sing on high
Comes the day, then the night,
The sense that is best has to be
sight.

I see the fish frolic in the lake
I hope that people care, for
animals sake.
All this goes on all around me,
So many pretty things are there
to see.

Joyce Hollis
**Yesterday Today
Tomorrow**

---

*To Sabrina: For giving me the
insights of this poem I love you
dearly. Mom*

It's strange how time goes about a
dramatic change
YESTERDAY—when we were
children, we had no worries
TODAY—some with kids of our
own, find life a little tougher
TOMORROW—is yet to come so
we dream of the future.
Guess somethings can not be
totally casted aside

Like YESTERDAY; you always
talk about YESTERDAY and
TOMORROW, but what about
TODAY.
Treasure the memories yes, and
dream on . . . but don't
let YESTERDAY and
TOMORROW blind you of
TODAY.
To me what you put in
YESTERDAY make things
better
TODAY for TOMORROW.
But since we can't relive
YESTERDAY and not promised
TOMORROW, make the best of
your life TODAY.
Remember YESTERDAY is gone
TOMORROW is a dream
And TODAY is now.

Tammy Edlund
SUNRISE

---

*"To Michael with love" F.H.S.—
Mrs. "V"*

Suddenly your eyes open
up with the warmth of the
new morning dawn.
Restless by the night before,
in come the rays that
strike you by surprise,
east and west a beautiful sunrise.

Jeanne L. Caldwell-Benson
HERE BE DRAGONS
Oh you sailors of ancient seas,
Sailing beyond mapped certainties;
Fearful of falling off
The edge of the world.

You were right,
The world is square.
And just out of sight,
There be dragons there!

Anthony J. Cecchini
MY LIFE

---

*Dedicated to Marie G. De Rosa in
1978, who I took as my wife on
November 12, 1983.*

In the painful corridors of time
I live a life without reason or
ryhme
Except for when I look and find;
The one thing that I know is
mine!

She's beauty, living in my heart
From her I know I'll never part
She's peace of mind, I'll always
find
and security in my mortal time.

Another like her there will never
be
She's the one and only love for
me!
Her name I'll tell you now is
Marie.

Her elegance and charm devine,
She's love itself personified
Her eyes like fire burn in my soul
She warms my heart from the cold.

In her arms I feel so safe
From this hell I will escape
My life is hers, and her's is mine
From now till the end of time!

Craig S. Shover
THE MIDNIGHT SAIL
A ship sails in one lonely night,
A Cutty Sark whose sails were
tight.
The winds were strong, the moon
was full,
The hour grew late, as the night
grew cool.
An eerie sight was the ship
creeping in,
She moved with darkness, as if
both were old friends.
She pulled into port with her
guns pointed low,
Her barrels seemed rusted, weary
and slow.
The ship was battered, with holes
in her side
Tarnished and bloodied from men
who had died.
Her hull was as old as the tides of
the past,
She was burned at her stern and
burned at her mast.
She smelled of gun powder, she
smelled of a blow,
The ship was a drifter with death
in her tow.
No one could be seen at the helm
that night,
No captain, no crew to guide her
in flight.
But that ship still turned and
came full about,
Back into the wind with her sails
puffed out.
As she leaned to her side, as she
headed for sea,
The moon made her glow like no
other I've seen.
She slowly sailed out, without
captain or crew,
She was headed for a place that
only she knew.
She did give a glimpse of her flag
being raised,
A skull and crossbones could be
seen in the haze.

Wyonna Raggio

Wyonna Raggio
HAVE A LITTLE FAITH
Oh let me have the Faith
of a grain of mustard seed.
as the day light dawns
let me of my self today do
a great deed.

As the morning of day
break approaches, I feel rejoyful
as I rise.
My eyes are filled with

the wondrous of a new dawn,
I see the great formation
as it makes its way across
    the skies.

When I wake up every
    morning, My Faith over night
    has been renewed.
I know God has watched over
    me during the night, I have
    that feeling of solitude

My Heavenly Father the one that
    holds this universe and keep
    everything in place.

Day after day I'll continue to pray
    fill me with your power, and
    fill me with your grace.

Barbara J. Holzman
FRIENDS FOREVER?
We've been friends for a long,
    long while.
Always together and always a
    smile.
If one of us cried, we'd cry along,
If one of us laughed, we'd laugh
    along,
If one of us sang, we sang that
    same song.
But, this year was different it
    happened to seem.
No longer did I see that light beam.
The light of friendship, always
    together and that is why I am
    writing this letter.
To tell you now, I'm not one of
    you,
Even if I tried to do exactly what
    you wanted to.
You see, what I'm trying to say,
I have to go my separate way.
It's better for me, even for you,
'Cause this is what I have to do.
Yup, guys, it's been fun, but our
    real long friendship has to be
    done.
Yes, old friends, it's been a blast,
But, I guess this year has been
    our last.

Dona Rogerson
MY FATHER'S CONFUSION
The end is around you,
All the shouting has ceased
You're on your own now,
And there's no time to be.

You have all your habits,
And the pity and stress,
Were you ever aware
That you'd live like the rest?

For what you thought as weakness
Was just a light away,
From all the kindness
That you had hid one day.

When your moment is over
And your day is done,
Is your raod well traveled,
Do you feel you have won?

D. J. Arrington
DREAMS ARE GOLD
Searching for a pot of gold,
Looking in every crease and fold.
Could it be at the bottom of the
    sea,
Or hidden in the trunk of a tree?
Buried under a towering mountain,
Encased in an ancient fountain?
Maybe at the end of a rainbo,
Does anyone really know?

Wait! Look deep within yourself,
Far back in your mind on a shelf.
The dreams you had ten years
    ago,
Ones that made you shine and
    glow.
Each is a little pot of gold,
So don't wait, break the mold.
Don't let dreams sit unused and
    forgot,
For true satisfaction can't be
    bought.
Trying makes dreams come true,
Don't sit around feeling blue.
Instead of doing a little, do a lot,
Bringing to life the dreams in
    each pot!

Monica Ines De Francesco
Monica Ines De Francesco
SUN-WARMTH

To Enrique, light of my life.

I'm waking up, and i feel
the sunlight over my bed.
It gives me warmth . . .
Just like you used to do it.
But that time is gone now . . .
While the sun keeps on moving
    over me, i have
a lot of questions in my mind.
Why are you different from
all the others?

Why every time i'm
with you, the air i breathe
seems to be purer?
Why the sun-warmth has
your name
at this very moment?
Why can't you love me
like i love you? . . .
Suddenly, the sunshine

with your name is gone . . .
I take your pillow in my arms,
while tears come out from my
    crying eyes.
Finally, i lose myself to
the sleeping world of dreams,
because i know, deep inside me,
that this is the only way
i can have you with me . . .

Jasper Davis
WINGS OF FAITH
Don't envy me,
  Ole mortal man.
Though not on your own you fly,
Yet you can.

It's my last time,
  To roam around heaven.
Your chances are good,
  To fly in heaven.

With your faith,
  You can trust,
Your soul will forever fly,
  When my feathers are dust.

Marjorie R. Reeves
ONE STEP BACK
Call the stars back that have
    fallen from their place,
Erase the footsteps from the
    moons face.
Plug the smokestacks and keep
    back the soot,
Drain the gas tanks and travel by
    foot.
Give us water from springs and
    wells,
Turn off the faucet with the
    chlorine smells.
Dig up the ground and plant the
    seed,
Help thy neighbors that are in
    need.
Build a house and fill it with
    love,
And give all your blessings to
    God above.

Barbara Dolbey
PICTURES
I watched as the Father
spoke with his Son,
a picture for history,
a frame to be frozen in time,
You could feel the closeness
that you observed from afar;

Soon,
all too soon,
it will be only a memory,
hopefully remembered
by both . . . . . .

Janice Ratliff
THE SONNET
Eyes are the windows to your
    mind and soul
A seed inside your heart helps
    you to grow
You cannot understand it or
    control
And why we love the world can
    never know
To try and guide the path of fate
    is sin
For Destiny holds hope and
    dreams to share
And in the end you know we
    have to win
Let's take a chance on love, if we
    should dare
A key within unlocks our hidden

dreams
The ones that only you and I relay
We have no other way of life it
    seems
Together always, my love, we
    must stay
Our hearts cannot survive alone
    you see
For I need you as much as you
    need me

David A. Bradford
The Sweet Morning Dew
Like the sweet morning dew,
I took one look at you.
Then it was plain to see,
you were my destiny.

Like an eagle protecting it's nest,
for you I'll do my best.
I'll stand by you like a tree,
I dare anyone to move me.

I may not be bold,
but my heart is of gold.
I hope you don't cry,
when I say you're all I need to get
    by.

I don't care what they say,
no one can stand in our way.
Like the stars above,
you'll always be my love.

When you said you'd be mine,
I nearly lost my mind.
I will always love you,
like the sweet morning dew.

Debra Smith
MY EYES
My eyes see much more than
    yours,
They see the love that never
    shows,
They see the violence and the
    hate,
They see the words that were
    mistakes.
My eyes see clearly the sounds of
    your heart,
They see the things you couldn't
    imagine,
They see all that you feel,
They see everything that is real.
My eyes see much more than
    yours,
They don't see color and shapes,
My eyes are blind—but I see.

Ed Joyner
ADVERSITY
Some hate the rain,
But I've seen the rain,
And the storm.
I accept the torrents
In their season,
Elsewise,
How would I know
The sun.

Lee McAuley (Marie Alicia)
DIASPORA
As when tall grasses through the
    sea winds blow
Whose blades find the hanging
    oasis
Dislodged Sargassum from that
    grieving gulf
That lodge green grain upon the
    harried shore
On dunes where flocks are met,
    shrieking softly,
Of the Greater Antilles,
    Caribbees,

But in their plight, light upon
  hot-coal sands,
Of anhinga and spectacled pelican
Who battle the wild waves for
  fish-forage,
So on this noisy sea of land, the
  new
Clump alone together in the
  rushes.

Alma Leonor Beltran
SOLITUDE

---

*With all my love I dedicate this
poem to my dearest niece and
God-daughter, Connie Perez.*

Loneliness is an aching void
  whose roots dwell deep within
Planted by Life's adversities that
  affect our inner being
Or by our grief for loved ones
  who've gone beyond the Veiled
  Screen

Turn your well of loneliness into
  a peaceful retreat
Discard old outgrown yesterdays
  that sadden a deplete
Cast out doubts and fears, they
  are barriers that breed defeat

Just as springtime's flowers will
  follow Winter's rain and snow
Reflective solitude, can make our
  minds expand and grow
Rekindle the flame of Courage
  and life will glow anew

Pause along Life's wayside in
  tranquil solitude and know at
  last
Your Inner Light will purify the
  murky pattern of the past
And guide you toward a brighter
  tomorrow and a new found
  quest.

Ellen R. Cunningham
UNTITLED
People here, people there, all
  kinds of people everywhere.
An eye that twinkles, a smile
  that speaks,
Like a familiar sunset on home-
  town peaks.
Where have I seen that face before?
Does it speak from recent or days
  of yore?
A laugh that rings a certain bell
From where in your past? You just
  can't tell.
Familiar sounds, familiar faces
Bring long gone memories of past
  and places.
You really can't decide just where
You've seen that certain lock of
  hair.
From hither to thither to there
  we go.
Will I see you again? We never
  know.

Helen Tzima Otto
MOODS
The day that teasingly you called
  me "moody-one" in
  conversation you,
inadvertently, made a
  peculiarly apt observation;
I could experience all moods,
  depending on the right moment,
(although I do suspect this wasn't

the essence of your sensible
  comment).

With people I'm dealing, my
  mood is, usually, in the
  indicative.
My temperament's and
  idiosyncracy's this is
  explicative;
my nature's, character's and
  personality's indicatory,
and my attitude's and
  Weltanschauung's explicatory.

To out-of-towners franticly
  asking where they can get
  scrod,
with spontaneity I do suggest
  they get a fishing rod.
(In the remote event they keep on
  asking me distressed and tense,
my mood won't change in
  subjunctive's future pluperfect
  tense).

Towards this mutinous,
  rebellious character I see in my
  mirror,
my humors oscillate from
  adoration to rage and furor;
to keep her safely restrained and
  disciplined is task imperative,
so, when I speak to her, I always
  put the verb in the imperative!

Finally, someone, against whom
  heart and brain are so
  exhortative,
with a single glance can turn my
  state infallibly into the
  optative:
the mood created to express most
  vividly wish and desire:
renewable reservoirs of sighs,
  fueling Mankind's Fire . . .

Alexis Ann Ferry

Alexis Ann Ferry
POETRY IN MOTION

To Stevie

Sweet and quiet and demure,
  she wasn't much for talk—
but when she moved she had a
  subtle
  wiggle in her walk.

Her gentle ways and wiggle
  brought
attention and devotion—
her male admirers liked to call
  her
"Poetry in Motion!"

Peggy Jean Schlosser
MAY 22, 1982

---

*To Harry John Meketa; The Lord
had very special things in mind
when he created you! Love
Forever, Peggy*

On this your very special day
may God be with you in every
  way.
May He hold and help you
  guide and protect you,
May He be your shelter from the
  storm
and always keep you safe and
  warm.
May He give you strength to see
  life through
and help you succeed in all you do.

Cynthia Marie Myers
FANTASY GUY
At night I lay awake and think,
Of the guy I'd really like to meet.
He's kinda tall and really cute,
And he dresses ohh so neat.

He's got a million dollar body,
He works out every night.
He makes his muscle's so big and
  strong,
Sometimes just seeing him gives
  me a fright.

He's got so many friends,
You just wouldn't believe.
They are all so protective,
It makes me feel so relieved.

I'm so glad I dream of him,
I know I'll never get him, but why?
Hey wait a minute I can have
  him anytime
Cause he's my fantasy guy.

Beverly J. Little
HURLING RAZORS

---

*For Mom, Mike, and Dohnny
whatever the future may hold— I
love you always— Bev*

Razor sharp words
Hurled from vacant black eyes
Plunge and twist directly on que
Etching themselves onto memory
Bring searing pain and
A smell of burning flesh.

Andrea Doolittle
CLOSING THE CURTAINS
As I open the curtains,
On to my bed I sink.
I close out the world,
And begin to think.

I stare out the window,
Thoughts cloud my mind,
Our relationship that grew slow,
Has now passed behind.

Waiting for tomorrow,
Thinking of you,
A song filled with sorrow,
Has blurred my view.

I'm climbing up an endless wall,
Life's too short to take the fall.
I must keep going to reach the top,
I wish this painful love would stop.

This feeling has me frightened,
But as everyone knows,

This feeling, like the curtains,
Must come to a close.

John M. Gawronski
TOGETHER
To the love we share
The beauty within
As our souls
Stand beyond us
In the clouds
Like shining stars
In the heavens
Looking within each other
In total silence
Drawing the energy
Into our bodies
The more powerful
We shall grow
Until the wings of love
Burst into flames
Then we become one
United throughout eternity

John M. Gawronski
WILD LIFE
Wild from the day they are born
Innocent until the day they die
Lonely in a struggle to survive
Dying for being free

Lifeless in a world of pollution
Irreversible sacrifice for space
Fighting for the right to live
Endless torture by man

John M. Gawronski
CHILD OF LOVE
O thy father up above
Look upon thy child of love
Rivive thy tender life so ill
Deprive deaths darkness with thy
  will

Fulfill thy prayer this very night
Send thy angel on thy flight
Down unto this heart of right
Soul as pure as heavens light

Protect thy child with thy might
Far beyond this earthly blight
Guild thy spirit in thy plight
Up into thy holy sight

Adelaide Marie Pye
DEAR SIS

---

*To my sister, Dorothy, for whom
this poem was written, and to
whom it is now dedicated—
"HAPPY BIRTHDAY, DOT!"*

Today you are a woman;
Today you're an adult;
Today the child must move aside
For that's the main result
Of this, your eighteenth birthday,
Of growing up; but, Dot,
Don't let all of the child in you
Be lost, no matter what!

For with her you'll still wonder
At things most men ignore,
Still "dream things that have
  never been
And ask, 'Why not?'" What's more,
You'll never hate a person
For color, race, or creed,
For children do not see these
  things,
From prejudice they're freed.

If you can temper wisdom
With innocence and trust,
Can still believe a little bit

In old Saint Nicholas,
Can keep the child in you alive
As you grow older, Dot,
Your Spirit will be always free,
Forever "Young At Heart"!

Amparo Xavier Manez
RAINBOW OF MY LOVE
When I gazed above the blue
    sky . . .
Seeing the lingering white clouds
    so high
I'm thinking where my Saviour's
    home—
So that I can knock on his golden
    door.

For here in this world is so
    crowded . . .
No room a secluded place for my
    soul,
Not a single beam of freed with a
    song,
Not even a lil'bit to live can call a
    home.

There are eyes who always see
    things in me
Lips can't say with the love of my
    Lord—
But they're tied and bound with
    his words—
So when I gazed above the blue
    sky . . .

I remember the pretty rainbow, as
    his covenant
When his sinful creatures
    destroyed by the
Flood, over the earth he brought a
    beautiful
Cloud, and did set his bow on the
    cloud by his love.

O, my pretty rainbow, bring me
    there in your
place, for you know it while
    granting you a
Birth, by our dear Lord, whose
    heart is filled
With mercies, to recollect that
    wonderful event.

How hard it is to live in this
    sinful world . . .
With thorns, thistles, getsemane
    in the road—
This life is only sweetened by the
    memories of
My Lord, so I'll meet him if freed
    with a song
            In that cloud!

Jeannie Flossie
ADVICE
I'd like to take my own advice,
Without a doubt, it's good.
Instead of doing what I'd like,
I do what I think I should.

R. Gerrard Ludlam
LAKES OF KILLARNEY
Lakes of Killarney, I still hear you
    calling,
  Calling me back to your shores
    once again;
And in the evening when
    shadows are falling,
  I hear the night-in-gale's sweet
    refrain.

There by your waters the wild
    rose is blooming,
  In all of it's beauty, the length of
    your shore,

Lakes of Killarney, where-ever I
    wander,
  I hear you calling me home
    ever-more.

Jeanne Arnold Liska
TIME OF LEAVES
Your leaves have turned from
    Tender green,
To yellow, gold and reds,
  Soon they will fall to cover,
Sleeping flower beds.
  When snowflakes are dancing,
It's time for you to sleep,
  Memories of summers sun, in
Your branches you will keep.
  Then once again spring will
Come, and crown your lofty head,
  With leaves of green,
That will turn to yellow, gold
And red.

Charles Mallio Jr.
YESTERDAY'S FUTURE
Yesterday's future was an
    engrossing book
With an infinite number of pages.
Which eager young minds
Read with enthusiasm.
Wondering,
Trying to conceive what the
    future may bring.

And some anterior concepts
Of peoples from time past
Are true today.
Yet, others seem,
Very far away, beyond our grasp.

Now, we are living in yesterday's
    future
Fulfilling the dreams of decades
    past,
And many quondam concepts
Are today, realities.
But is everything happening,
Too soon, too fast?

Will tomorrow's past be as
    propitious . . .
As yesterday's future?

Sandra S. Meier
MY RING
This ring on my finger,
  It means so much.
It reminds me of our love
  With such a gentle touch.
The commitment there,
  A tie that binds.
And as time goes on,
  I wonder what we'll find.
But it won't really matter,
  Whatever it may be,
As long as I've got you . . .
  And as long as you've got me.

Cecelia Morris
FILL ME WITH LOVE

This poem was inspired by my dear Master Who's Love surrounds me like a shield.

Fill me with love for every
    season.
Fill me with love for every day.
Fill me with love for every hour
As I walk along my way.

Fill me with love for every person.
Fill me with love for friend or foe.
Fill me with love for every minute
That I share on Earth below.

Barbara A. Cadogan
IN SEARCH OF HAPPINESS

To Muds and Dads whose Christian teaching and guidance has helped me to find my start.

Today I wandered very far.
Up, out and beyond the cobwebs
    of my mind
I drifted and reached to touch a
    star.
My cares and worries I left behind.
So light and airy did I float aloft,
No wings, no strings to me
    attached,
Just feather-like and wooly soft,
Towards that star my spirit rose
    detached.

From all the turmoil of the
    mortal mind,
Such peace and solitude I found,
A place where those who seek
    will find
that star, where hope and
    happiness abound.
Not only for a moment, but
    forever,
Shining its eternal light to guide
    me.
Forever, through time and life
    and never
losing sight of what true
    happiness should be.

Kelley P. Bakker
YOU & ME
If I were to go walking
  Would you walk with me?
If I were to run
  Would you run with me?
If I were to love you
  Would you love me?
If I were to die
  Would a part of you die with
    me?

Linda Colonna
HEART OF OAK
I'd climb the highest mountain
    for you,
And swim the deepest sea.
I sit here and I wonder,
If you'd do the same for me.

I'd take the biting cold,
For as long as I could stand,
Or walk the flaming desert land.

I'd climb the highest mountain,
And swim the deepest sea.
'Cause that's how much
You really mean to me.

I crossed the land of friendship,
To the seas where broken hearts
    are stored,
And found your heart there stuck
    with a sword.

You said whoever took it out,
Would be struck to the floor.
And everyone asked what I was
    doing this for.

I see a bolt of lightening hit the
    sword,
As your heart will mend.
I pulled it out of your bleeding
    heart,
Now I'm a true friend.

I drop into your arms and whisper
    "I love you",
I came all this way,
It's the least I could do.

I'd climb the highest mountain,
And swim the deepest sea.
'Cause that's how much you
    really mean to me.

Deborah Marshall
Especially For Grandad
Its not Christmas or even the
    Fourth of July
We're gathered to celebrate the
    birth of our guy
The man of the hour is 75 years
    old
An example of life for all to behold
He taught us how to play cards
    and fish from the lake
And forgave us whenever we
    made a mistake
He gave us his love and showed
    us the way
To be more understanding and
    patient each day
He's the best father a guy ever had
To all of us children he's known
    as Grandad

Christine Anne Moore
From Bewildered To Brilliant
'Ere I si', i' a room small an' square;
'Ardly 'nough space t' move me
    poor feet.
Nothin' t' do bu' twiddle me
    thumbs;
We all know i'd be unp'lite t' eat.
Jus' si' 'n' look dumb, wi' me
    tongue 'angin' out,
While inside I'm burnin' wi' rage.
Some kook o' a bloke ripped off
    me *Sports Afield*;
Now there's nothin' t' read, no' a
    page.
Frantically searchin' for somethin';
Could i' be, per'aps, under the rug?
I look, bu' i's 'ard t' bend over
An' peek, as I yank an' I tug.
All excited an' much i' a work-up,
An idea soon pops i' me 'ead:
Why no' read a tube o' toothpaste,
Or some kin' o' face cream, instead?

Michael J. Cross
FREE
Hello everybody, it's here to stay,
    and I love it.
So sweet and enjoyable, just
    couldn't live without it.
It'll make you cry and let you
    shine on the dreariest night,
Lets you see all your faults and
    see the light.

131

My friends it's here to be with
you and me,
Its love and it's free, so let it be.

Martha Marie Perry

Martha Marie Perry
Dust Of Dying Memories

---

*In Loving Memory To Dad and
Mom*

The dust of dying memories
may blur your eyes with tears

A loving word, a cheerful smile,
a kindly thought or two and a
helpful hand.
Those things make life most dear.

The dust of dying memories
may blur your eyes with tears.

I don't wish to know tomorrow,
for the trails of today
are enough to keep me busy.
Here on lifes pathway.

Anita B. Weathers
GOODBYE MY LOVE

---

*Dedicated to the Memory of my
Beloved Husband.*

Goodbye, My Love, my partner
in Life
Sleeping high on a windy hill.
We could not know you would
go first,
Leaving sorrow and emptiness
still.

We weathered life's trials and
troubles;
With our family stayed side by
side,

Always held by a love so strong
No evil could ever divide.

Over many long hills we traveled,
In search of a better life.
It was not possessions I cherished,
But the campfires we shared at
night.

You were always so restless and
hurried,
While I was a few steps behind.
But listen Dear, it won't be long.
I will follow you when it is time.

So find some distant, sheltered
cove
And build a campfire, burning
bright,
Then I'll be sure to know you're
there,
And come when I see your light.

Georgia Walker
LOVE
There is never a moment
Without love,
There's not even a moment
Without thinking of the ones
You love,
Who have always been next
To you,
Who you have learned
Everything you know from,
Your heart enjoys the hearts
Around it.

Christoph Aurich
CONTINUUM
I cradle my heart in my hands,
It's beating. Feeling every muscle
move
I lift it high towards the sky.
Energy descends down to my
toes.
My child clutches my leg.
Happy. — A searching look and
destined heart.
Children's children, — generations,
A misty trail lost in eternity.
With unrestricted choices
Their hearts held high, a yearn
for blessings, —
To crush them, foolishly
expressing power.
Endowed to take but not create,
A founding wisdom brushed aside,
My heart returned to let it stride,
I rest my thought and nourish
hope for men.

Jean Proudian-Brown
NATURES CALL

---

*To Joey Glover a special friend
who taught me to look at life
with a childs view and my
husband Jeff who helped me
remember the lesson when he
moved me out into the woods.*

Early mornings, foggy days,
Dusk, and midnight hours
Times for us to search for peace
Listen to natures howl.

A wounded animal or mocking
bird
Sends chills upon my spine
Crickets chip to alleviate pain
They are a friend of mine.

Take a walk, please come with me,
or sit upon my stool

Listen now can you hear?
They're calling out to you.

Catherine Randall
RICHES
"What will we do when our
money runs out?"
My husband asked me one day.
So after thinking about an answer
This is all I could think of to say:

"We could take the Free Plane
Way up in the blue
And play on Cloud 9 all day.

Or we could take a Free Boat Ride
to Make-Believe Island
And swim way out in the bay.

Or we could take a ride on the
Free Train
Climbing up Let's Pretend
Mountain
Or we could dine at Fantasy Inn
And throw pretend coins in their
fountain.

But maybe the best thing to do
Is plug along with the rest.
We'll keep God in our lives
And love in our hearts
And with riches we'll surely be
blessed."

Gina B. Odraude
alive?
Hypothermia has set in.
All around me I see
Cold, cold hearts
that insist on beating,
insist on staying alive . . .
Though life more and more
resembles
The cold state of death!

But within me this warmth
This unending flow, an undying
spring
which finds no outlet
No one to keep warm . . .

So in drafty places I shall wander
In surroundings where
temperatures
continuously fall . . .
In hopes my heart, as science has
proved it
Will become used to the cold . . .
and cool itself too,
And extinguish the warmth,
numb out the feeling . . .

Until one day
In my chest it will pound
A reminder that I too am alive!
And life will so resemble
The cold state of death!

James Allen Babbs
DROWNING
Rising from the water
Protruding from the mist
Returning from a pseudo-slaughter
Body is contacted by fist

Spewing out the ocean
Spewing out the sea
There was no thought or notion
Another soul was free

The limbs covered with sand
Eyes filled with tears
The lips touched by a hand
Reveals our deepest fears

A slowly rising mist
Creeping from the land
Pale lips no longer kissed

Marching into obscurity, the
funeral drum and band

Faith Daria Ewsuk
QUIETNESS
The leaves rustle
in the gentle wind
and death is in the air
The sky lies darkened
and the streets are quiet
as everybody lies in bed
and we all wonder
who will be next
for our lives
may be near end
as we listen for a sound
other than the rustling leaves
in the gentle wind
we try to break the silence
in the air
for we are all living
while others
have passed away
into an even quieter world.

Katherine M. DeNering
ONCE IT WAS
Once it was a daily walk
Where I walked today;
Streets and scenes were altered
by the years.
I felt a bit like Rip
I must admit,
To see a street
Where once a building stood
discreet.
Generations come and go
And each must make its show;
With beauty oft destroyed by man
And beauty oft created by a finer
touch
When it is needed , oh, so much!

Ralph H. Clark
**A Can Of Bean's, and Cold
Sardine's**
I went looking, for a job one
time,
but this is all, that I could find,
Up in the morning, at the crack
of dawn,
out in the field, behind the barn.

Time goe's by, and the sun is
high.
The dinner bell ring's, for me
to come in.
Lunch is ready, for me and Freddy,
A can of bean's, and cold
sardine's.

Five o'clock come's, the work's
all done,
I'm about cooked, from the heat
of the sun.
Supper's all ready, for me and
Freddy,
A can of bean's, and cold
sardine's.

That's what it's like, a day on the
farm,
Dirtying your hand's, and
swinging your arms.
So, if you're not ready, to work
with Freddy,
and don't like bean's, and cold
sardine's,

Then find a job, that's a little
more steady,
with a sweet little gal, like my
friend
Teddy.

Our World's Best Loved Poems

Michael J. Gombas
THE TAVERN OF EDEN
Porcupines are quick to point her
faults.
To the Unicorns, she is still a
myth.
The penguin hesitantly tips his
hat at her passing.
The Tiger, Lion, and the Shark
always end up in a
ferocious argument over her.
The Owls seem perplexed.
The Moles are deeply troubled.
The Hyenas just make light of it,
constantly ribbing Adam about
her.

Only the serpent is silent.
Smiling.
Sipping his cider.

Keri Lee Vena
THE LIGHT IN YOUR EYES

*To the man I love, the light in my
eyes, my husband, Jim.*

The still light
is light, still
the rippling water
interrupts the bright.
Constant and yet
broken, forever
different.
Wanting nothing,
but the light in your eyes.

Joyce L. Richardson
THE ROSE GARDEN
Come, walk with me through the
Rose Garden,
And smell the fragrant of each
blossoming flower.
Watch them open their thirsty
buds to the early morning's dew.

Come, walk with me through the
Rose Garden,
While colors of red, yellow, pink,
white and orange line the
garden like a rainbow,
And send radiant colors
shimmering in the early
morning's light.

Come, walk with me through the
Rose Garden,
Where a cool breeze softly blows
and birds sings sweet melodies,
Where peace and quiet lingers
about while time slowly slips
away.
Come, walk with me through the
Rose Garden.

Kristine M. Karlson
THE CLOWN
A little man with a merry face
and hair of blazing red,
Came tripping and dancing
awkwardly
and falling on his head.
The brightly colored circus tent
was filled with eager eyes,
As the clown brought giggles
from children's mouths
and took them by surprise.

Mary Ann Burrows
DESTINATION DEATH
The road is winding between the
whispering pines and velvet
roses,

The high iron fence is all secure
when the iron gate closes.
There's a certain finality in this
place,
It seems the end of the road and a
slowing of pace.
There's no need for hurrying, no
need for flowers and lace,
Where all in equality stay, at this
final resting place.
When the irrevocable call has
been made, they all come,
The poor, the lame, the rich
lawyer, the colored maid,
To lie beneath a carpet of grass in
the shade.
No matter to what esteem they
climbed, or to what heights
sublime,
At the change of seasons you will
find him, beside his wife's grave,
One who once stood proud beside
her.
He faithfully returns when the
leaves change their shade,
Here where they laid her beneath
a blanket of snow, by the bed
that they made.
He listens for her whisper among
the stirring pines.
His empty arms ache for her
warmth in the night,
He remembers her love of the
flowers, and her smile when
spring
showers, made the world all
washed and new.
He patiently waits for her answer,
and knows he will never forget
her,
And he knows he must leave her,
here, in the earth's embrace.
Then he brushes away the leaves
and the tears every trace.
He seems to hear her whisper,
"You must go on, hold up your
head
And walk proudly, you belong to
today.
Leave me in the shade, until
eternity.
The wind shall be my friend, I
need nothing at my
destination, death."

Gem M. Dumas
WISH
Gypsy moth let me
fly with thee
Through silver cobwebs
of eternity

Louise Minnick
CHRISTMAS

*To my beloved husband, Darrell,
and our eight wonderful children,
and to sixteen grandchildren,
who give us much joy—also our
sons-in-law and daughters-in-laws.
They make our lives complete.*

Up in the sky
The stars are shining bright
On this Holy Night.
Angels tell of Jesus birth
Ask us to live, peace on earth.
Lay aside your petty cares
Love your neighbors, everywhere.
Like the shephards on the hill

Stop and listen, receive a thrill.
Christ is born anew, again
Peace on earth, goodwill to men.

Anna Bentsianov

Anna Bentsianov
LIFE IS A BOOK

*This poem was inspired by and is
dedicated to my wonderful
parents, grandmother, and
younger brother, with all my love.*

Life as we all know has
something of its own.
As we turn the pages our feelings
would have grown.
Happiness, excitment, mischief,
sorrow too.
Except this misadventure is
nothing less but true.
We try and try to make it
through without a hurt or pain.
But we all end up feeling that we
have lost not gained.
Life is a book, a book you may
read in college.
But this book is not complete if
you have not gained
some knowledge.

Penny Ledonne
Meaning Of Life
What is the meaning of life,
Of all this discomforts and strife?
I often wonder what happens to
those who die!
The answer is so unclear!
Just when you think you're near
It slips right through your grasp
and disappears!
 Yet we carry on
 And never know
  Where we've been and where
we may go!
And when all is gone;
 Nothing's left to say,
  We wonder why things turned
out that way!

And so we love and we hate.
And wonder perhaps we're too
late
To understand destiny and the
concepts of fate!
We probe as far as we dare
The mixed feelings we share;
Trying desperately to unload the
burdens we bare!
 We've been trying
 For so long
  Yet still we are so wrong!
Hope is dying!

What can we do?
 Will the truth be revealed to
me or to you?

Lillian C. Davey
THE CAGE
There's still a little child in me,
that comes out when no one can
see.
There's also someone old in me,
who wonders when the end will be.
But in between is where I am,
with many things I've still to learn
I seem, in limbo, only waiting,
not knowing where or when to
turn.
Each day I think will bring me
closer
to what I know not at this time.
The world revolves, yet I stand
still
as tho a cage is holding me
Preventing me from moving on.

What lies ahead I cannot see
If only I could find the one
who has the key to fit this cage
and set me free to be alone
or give me love to soothe my rage.
Then I could be that child in me
who laughs and plays without the
shame,
that's present now and will remain
until that day that has no name
the cage entraps me, I feel pain.

Mary Rose Shoemaker
NICHOLAS
Nicholas is our little boy
Always full of laughter and joy.
His big blue eyes always shine
And we know he is feeling fine.

Each day we play school
And he works on his little stool.
He loves to draw pictures of our
home
And he wants to do them all alone.

He pitches and catches his red ball
Despite the fact he has many a fall.
He loves to jump and run
And with every move he has fun.

At night, after prayers are said
We tuck him gently in his bed.
Sometimes a little story is read
And he sleeps soundly as if he is
dead.

Gloria Gray Wall
LOVE IS THE GLUE
To all disparate pieces
To all separated things
Behold! Love quiescent forming
Transforming time chrysalis wings

Inside many sparkling facets
Shines a new world, me and you
Love and faith the clasping
elements
Invincible the holding glue

When we are reeling zerundesheit
Stretched to ultimate taut as drum
Softly gentle touch unwinds us
As we pulsate breathe and hum

Reverberating all in motion
Life is one eternal ring
Building tune on tone harmonic
Release love be melodic sing!

Nothing hidden nothing separate
No one is or loves alone
Man . . . the self-renewing proof

Of love—the Force which moved the stone.

Christine Cox Burroughs
MY BABY

Dedicated to my daughter, Tiffany. Who inspired this poem; Who inspires me.

Sometimes when I hold those little hands, or touch that little face,
I thank God that I've had the chance to be put in this place.
Sometimes I'm sad that you'll grow up and grow away from me.
I pray I will mean half as much to you, as you will always mean to me.
Right now you are a baby, just learning to walk and talk.
Already you're so independent; sometimes I wish the growing would stop.
So that you would always be my baby, in the true sense of the word.
And I could always take care of you and protect you from the world.
But life isn't meant to go that way, and I'm anxious in watching you grow.
And no matter how independent you'll become, I hope that you will know,
When I am over-protective, and you think that I've gone crazy;
Even though you are growing up, You will always be, my baby.

Mabel E. Baskin
LIKE ANY MOM AND DAD
You were like any mom and dad
Best ones any children ever had
Tho' you had no children of your own
We appreciate you more now we're grown
You opened up your hearts and home
To take in strays needing love
Dearest mom and dad in heaven above.

You stayed up nights when we were sick
Just like any mom and dad,
You listened to our problems we had to lick
Just like any mom and dad.

Every sunday we went to church
To listen to the word of God:
Now I know those were happy days
Even tho' you never spared the rod
Just like any mom and dad.

Dear mom and dad, am I the only one?
Why couldn't I see all this before your life was done?
A special place in heaven must be for you up there.
I pray the little children God has taken,
He's given to your tender care!

Robin Merrill
AMERICAN STYLE
In America people may do as they please.
Watch the stars, watch the sunset, stand in the breeze.

Dogs chase cats, cats chase mice.
Believe it or not, in America, we too eat rice.

In America everyone has their own style and own way.
We do what we want, say what we may.

America is smart, we have our own style.
So when your in America, you'd better smile.

Robert Philo Lien
WONDER
one dramatic gesture
wondrummmAT i c
             just you r

one drum
       a tic
                  jest
Uuuuurrrrrrrrrr
   !!!!!!!!!!!!

Lynette W. Bracey
LIFE IS A MIRROR
Life is a mirror
   Reflecting on once weres
   Shining on are nows
        and
   Holding on will bes.

Cindy Leigh Walker
DAYBREAK
On the break of daylight, crisp with the new of light and air opening an arm full of surprise

There is an easiness of becoming something constant, like breathing though a bit more durable.
This day to day steadiness.

This opening and shutting an eyefull of living can be taken lightly, or passed up like supper.

It can be conquered with that of an underwater swimmer, heavy but cumber.
Or rather like the deer trailing across afternoon woods, tree bark and limbs, having seen it all before.

And we, hardly ready for such explicit reality will breath

through it with a sigh, or choose this eagerness of the deer, full-paced and searching.
Waiting daybreak, life in general.
With one surprised eye opened.

Cheryl L. Wilcox
INSPIRATION
Often in my contemplation
I suddenly get an inspiration
To write down just how I feel
Thoughts, emotions . . . all so real

I write them in poetic style
They make me cry and make me smile
Those memories so sweet and kind
Just keep runnin' through my mind

If I could make moments come again
Each time that I remembered them
I would spend each and every day
Remembering my whole life away

It would be so very fine
To think of something and have it mine
I'd recall love that used to be
And not face my reality.

Shannon Hooks
THE WORDS WE SAY

Dedicated to: Aunt Ruth

  The words we say are scratches deep
  Upon the surface bare;
  We can remove the varnish, but
  The markings are still there.

  Some things there we cannot mend
  Or wrest to former glow
  For once the grain is scored by pain
  The scars will ever show.

Jane Masterson
PEOPLE
Many I've met along the trail,
  While on lifes journey of joys and travaila.
With meetings of harmony and those of pain,
  With feelings of love and those of disdain.
But as I grew in soul and mind,
  I reached a point where I did find—
As I viewed this life from high in a steeple,
  How could I have learned without all those people!!

Pamila Diane Goodwin
BLUEBIRD
I remember you as a bluebird
swooping down in the night
to nestle beside me bringing
  comfort & warmth
whispering promises you forgot

With the dawn you took flight
stealing the convincing words you used
to persuade me into thinking
I could be as one with you—high in the blue

Yet, I discovered myself being feline by nature

and you a feather in the wind—
you took to the sky—we knew it had to end
wind beneath your wings you had to fly.

Your song to me was you would never go—
I believed you, but how was I to know
that we sang in different tongues
and now it's over—the songs been oversung.

No need to wonder—
or ask the questions why
I understand the bluebird—
flying in the sky

Melba Mask
LITTLE STONE DOG
In a very old graveyard,
In a little old Southern town,
On a Fall Sabbath Day,
This heartbreaking sight we found:

Beneath a tall pine tree,
At the foot of a man's grave.
Lies his dog; not in reality
But as nearly real as could be.

Life size, sad eyed, loyal pet
Who stayed with his master yet
After being buried over eighty years.
We knew the man not, but shed tears.

We patted the head of his faithful friend
Who guarded him after the end.
Thru rain, snow, and dark of night.
Thou made of stone, he was a brave sight.

Kellie Kendrick
GRANDPA

To Grandma—because you are the everlasting light of Grandpa's love for the world and his family.

When I was very little
Slowly did turn the clocks of time
Time changed all lives everywhere
Changes starting with mine

The world was out there waiting
Waiting there for me
The ones I cared for most
Were older than I wanted to be

Old age was very distant
Old people I knew were few
Until it was too late
Did I say that I loved you

The angels took him from me
Just over a year ago
I never got to say good-bye
But his memory I'll never let go

Nancy Fitzgibbon
WITH YOUR CONCERN
With your concern,
Inwardly, I turn . . .
And remember, in a moment
Long past torments.
And it's sad to think,
That as quick as a blink,
Just a gesture so tenderly,
Can revive such a need in me
That cries out in desolate hunger
From this need by which . . .
My being is so fettered.
This need I damn . . .

As surely as touched I am,
By the affection I crave . . .
And finds in me a grateful slave.
And even before it's gone . . .
I remember being alone,
And I'm sad, for I know,
How very much I need . . .
The concern you've shown.

Keith O. Williamson
WINTER
The sky is grey and overcast,
The clouds, they seem to hurry
 past
As if they also seem to know
Of winter's ice and cold and snow.

And lo, before the evetide's fall,
The snow descends and covers all;
The wind, it withers with its icy
 blast,
The long, cold winter's here at last.

Jack Pratt
RENEWAL
The cold north wind blew hard
 and strong and the skies were
 dark with threats of rain.
My bones were chilled, my soul
 as well, and I was filled with
 black despair.

Where were there friends to
 succor me, where was the
 beloved to soothe my pain?
Alone, alone I faced the world, a
 stray on the streets of a
 faceless town.

A rented room in a dingy house
 is scarce the place to call a
 home.
I shuddered as I thought of its
 emptiness and turned away as I
 reached the door.

I stood in the center of the empty
 bridge and stared at the
 swirling water below as it
 beckoned me to join its flood
 with the promise of sleep and
 peace at last.

I clutched the rail and was ready
 to leap when an inner voice
 cried, "Stop, you fool!
Cast off your gloom and be a
 man; the future is yours to
 mold as you will."

My grip relaxed and my eyes
 looked up and away from the
 watery pit below.
My mood had changed in the
 wink of an eye and courage
 returned to lift up my heart.

I knew at that moment that I
 would endure.

Nancy E. Wyatt
ON TUESDAY
On Tuesday in the sunlight
With brightness round her
 strown,
And murmuring beauty of the sky
At last her very own;

She who had loved all children
And all things high and clean,
Turned away to silentness
And bliss unseen.

Rending, blinding, anguish,
Is all that we can know;
Yet still we kneel beside her
For she would have it so;

Kneel, and pray beside her
In light she left behind—
Light and love in silentness,
Sight to the blind.

Penny Debra Shepard

Penny Debra Shepard
THE WIND

*To my daughters Angela and
Leigh-ann With love*

Hush; Listen my children,
Do you hear and feel its presence?
Biting cold and vicious, it forces
 us together.
Be strong my little ones,
For it's only a test.
Only the brave can withstand it.

The weak have no control over
 such power.
But we have love, the greatest of
 all power.
We shall stand facing anything
 that threatens us.
Hold my hand and take from me
 my strength
I'll guide and show you that with
 faith
We can overcome all.

Jerri L. Henson
I START TO GROW
I Walk down a path and then I find
You standing near the trees
 waiting
Your smile gives me peace of mind
There's a reason for this meeting

We walk together and you talk to
 me
Though I don't know what you're
 saying
Then you show me how to shed

my sorrows
In the clear calmness of the stream

The pain is gone and I've felt the
 cure
You've cleansed me Lord, of that
 I'm sure
Then you look at me, I know why
 you're here
To teach me of love and how to
 care

We return to the forest along the
 path
You start to leave and I ask you
 to stay
But there's other things you have
 to do
And I know you'll be back again
 someday

My rock in the picture frame
The forest that has no name
The waterfall with the stream
 below
I learn to see, and I start to grow.

Timothy James Zenner
IF YOU LOVE ME

*Being this is my first publication,
I dedicate this poem and effort to
three dear friends—Mary Shilts,
Dean Spaeth, and Dianne
Rasmussen—who've given my
life love, meaning, and happiness.
Thank you!!!*

Father, father
You bought me a pony
To make me happy
But take it away,
If you love me.

Father, father
You bought me a bicycle
To make me happy
But take it away,
If you love me.

Father, father
You bought me a doggie
To make me happy
But take him away,
If you love me.

Father, father
You buy me these things to make
 me happy
But they only bring pain
Take them away,
If you love me.

Father, father
For you know I'm dying
Yet you won't hold me
Just hug me daddy,
If you love me.

Ruth A. McCuddy
QUIET WALK
The colors of green and golden
 brown
 Displayed in foliage throughout
Makes autumn days a crown
 And brighter days sublime.

God's creation of bushes and trees
 Have a peacefulness subdue
Swaying gracefully in the breeze
 The day's woes are not just mine.

A quiet walk in the wildwoods
 Draws me closer to my Lord
As the close knit neighborhood's
 Concern and love for everyone.

Lakes of textured blue
 Silently capturing the sunlit rays
Brings to us the next day anew
 Breathlessly seizing bits of fresh
 air.

Ahmet-Haluk H. Ozbudun
CAPTIVITY
The chain's burden,
and the shackle's weight,
 —in Retrospect's Gate—
reflect a sense-of-belonging
never so blatant before,
never so overwhelming,
 nor so much to the core,
 or so close to the Door
 of Heaven's Saga
 and Lore.

Brenda Irene Helling
TO HEAR THE MUSIC
The music begins,
A spell is woven.
A man, dressed in black,
Plays for only one,
The one responding
With body and soul.

Swept away in time,
A dreamer of dreams,
Hears the haunting call,
"Taste the gift of life.
Climb the high mountains.
Walk beside clear streams.
Dance in the meadow.
Embrace the roses.

Hear the angels sing.
Ride clouds on high.
Peek over the sun.
Slide down the rainbow."
The music erupts,
A dying ember
Bursts forth into flames,
To love once again.
To look beyond pain.
To hear the music.

James Neal Poquette
FEAR OF EVIL
I am walking with you once more
 my Lord
Through sleepless nights and in
 endless astral flights.
I've come so close yet I know I
 shall not find the door.
For I am lost in thy sleepless
 nights
 In this silent corridor of fright.

What deadly shadow has haunted
 me
This lost and dreary night?
For where can I run, and with
 whom shall I fight,
Or is this only an evil thought—
 That has entered my soul in
 spite?

For how Insane can one person
 be, when he realizes
The Devil is a most powerful
 entity?
And how will his luck run out—
 when there is no doubt,
For what grave shall be dug— and
 How shall thou lie
When thou has grown stiff and
 closed thy peering eye?

But a thought still lit within thy
 mind
Has led birds of prey to my open
 grave,
And they pick away with no

thoughts of delay
Upon my soulless body, like a
lilly on an ocean wave
'Tis similar to my heart in its
slow decay.

For the demon which bears no
name, is only
A ghost of my yesterday, and I
know I shall
Never be free as long as I have
fear and pain,
And I wonder what my sickness
is:
And does it have a name?

Kathleen McStay Wagner
A SPECIAL DAY

---

*Dedicated to Dolores Shulick
Roginski, my critic, my
encouragement, my mother, with
all my love.*

Sunlight dancing, flashing bright,
Laughter in every eye.
Running children everywhere
No clouds to mar blue sky.

Grass bending gently in the breeze,
Fluttering leaves glow in the sun.
A day of laughter, songs and love.
All together, having fun.

The children tumble everywhere
'Neath grandma's beaming smile.
And it's become a special day
For each and every child.

A day to bring back memories
That live in grown up hearts,
Or days that passed that were
carefree
When they played the childrens
parts.

And a day of making memories
Perhaps some of the best—
Memories to cherish years from
today,
When these little ones leave the
nest.

Lucinda Berryessa Woodall
**Torn Between Two
Families**

---

*To my father, RALPH GERALD
BERRYESSA, whom I have
difficulty in expressing my
concerns, contradictions or
criticscisms without hurt feelings,
please know that I love you
deeply and at times find you
inspiring.*

I'm torn between two families,
My husband's and my own.
His family likes to gather and
party,
While my family won't leave
their home.
His family wants so much to
meet mine,
I never know just what to say.
Maybe they'll come and join us
next time.
Or meet with us on some other
day.
And all the time, I know,
Mine don't intend to come.
For the grief I'll never show,

As they miss out on the fun.
Life is meant to experience and
enjoy!!!
You've worked hard to get this far.
Why be deprived of new
friendship and joy?
When all you need is to jump in
your car.
We go to visit as much as we can.
One family, then the other.
Sometimes it's "go" or "food in the
pan".
Why can't we be together?!?!
I cringe from holidays and special
events.
Who's family will I choose?
I'm sittin precarious on a rickety
fence,
Meaning fairness, love, win or lose.
I pray the stubbornness will soften,
So much for them to share.
I'd like to see them much more
often,
To show them how much we
really care.

Miguel A. Hernandez
IN WINTER
In winter
When the earth bares its soul
When life seems cold
And the sun hides for days
I see you and the warmth
of your ways
In winter
When the trees scratch the sky
When the clouds tower high
And the wind brings the snow
I love you and the depth
of your glow
In winter
When your tears turn to frost
When the hours all seem lost
And the dark feels unkind
I touch you and the spring
of your mind.

Jane Ross
MOON NIGHTS
On the moon nights
the moon drops
seem to dribble
the tears of Cupids bow.

With the moon light
we stand caressing
by the passions of affection.

No stain of blunder
can destroy our love.

We will wake on the morrow
and again we begin
the task of lovers,

Walking with fruitful joy
that only lovers kindle.

Susan West
JOURNIES
No,
I won't speak of love or promises
or ask commitments of you.
You have your dreams to chase,
as I do mine;
and while we can chase at the
same time,
we can't do it together,
for we're going different places,
and at different speeds.
You, climbing an ever higher
slope, seeking yourself;
Me, stumbling on a lower road,
seeking someone else.

Both searching for something lost
along the way.

Our separate journies have
brought us together in a
temporary shelter
where we find nourishment and
comfort in each other.
And it's so beautiful.

Yet, now, still tipsy from the
intoxicating warmth of your
loving,
I realize that I will always have as
much of you as I can hold in
my heart,
but no more.
You have a quest to follow, as I do,
and you will not be weighted down
by talk of love and promises.
And I can only hope to keep you
if I can leave you free.

Diane Maton Duncan
SECRETS
Your eyes tell me
Secrets
Of your lifetime
Dying sunsets
False tears
Open Windows
With light breezes
And new loves-
Revealed in silence
Feeling as if,
I am the only one to know . . .

Charles F. Sutton
ELICITATION
What goodness is contained in all,
Locked securely behind thick wall!
Sometimes interminable wait
For anything to permeate!
So some become useless and old,
Like leaves of Autumn, dry and
cold—
Bereft of life as they lie still
And detached, no purpose or will—
Until warm influence comes by,
Encouraging fearful and shy;
Leading from prison they had
made,
Unable to respond to aid—
Till offered in appealing way,
And entering barrier of clay,
As hate and suspicion they ease,
Helping them to thaw by degrees,
Assisting dormant souls to live,
When of themselves completely
give—
Like tea that's lain on shelf too
long,
With most of its aroma gone;
For tea's not alive 'til it's steeped,
From which full flavor's seeped
and seeped—
And humans are the same as dead,
Until away from selves are led.

Eleni Katzingris Moustaka
LET ME LEAVE
I feel like a river that can't be
more repress into the dam.
I have got to go far from you so
that I may to find myself again.

Let me leave, to join with the
dawns of my fantasies, with the
ballet
of the trees and to throb with the
crickets' song.
Let me go, to gather the tears from
the twilights and to pray
for you in chromatic delirium.

Let me go, to sing down into my
green memory, with the dreams
of my
youth who projects a shadow of
bitter melancholy over our
lonely love.

Let me leave, the freedom wash
over me. I wish to be swallows
fly to
embrace the horizon which
decipher destiny into unknown.
Let me to fly away from your
fascination, from your sad soul.

Let me go, like a solitary
humming-bird before the
passion of your look
vanish and your wounded heart
to retain me.

Darlene Mann
SEASONS
Purple mountains far away,
The sun setting deep in the west,
This a completion of another day,
A time that I love best.

Now, the mountains are aflame,
The autumn leaves are falling,
Spring, summer, and fall have
come.
Now the chilling voice of winter
is calling.

The mountains are bare and grey
As the snow floats lazily to the
ground.
The children all shout "Ha Ray!"
As in the snow they tumble down.

Soon the snow begins to melt,
And the green of spring is showing.
Gone is the coldness that winter
held,
As the flowers and grass start
growing.

Spring floats into lazy summer
days
With sunshine and rain
sometimes falling.
But we know while in the heat
and haze,
Soon again, autumn will be calling.

Ann N. Baniago
THE PALM TREE

---

*Anthony,—forever,
for always. a.n.b.*

How I admire the palm tree
standing there,
so straight,
so tall.
Daring the elements to defy him
A strong wind blows,
But the palm still stands.
Always bending, but never
breaking.
His match has not come along.

Michelle Lutes
Lady In the Picture Frame
With smooth gentle grace and
a smile on her face,
She looks through the glass
of a picture frame.
She was known for her grace
and known for her smile.
She was always there
to put a smile on some lonely
child.
Everyone saw her,

Everyone loved her,
She always had just the
right kind of smile.
This young lady
whom everyone loved.
Is just a pretty face
in a wooded picture frame.

Gayle Maginnis Livermore
DISPOSITION
Gloomy days, dark nights,
Nothing in between.
Empty hearts, hollow eyes,

Nothing ever seen.
Cross minds, false grins
Nothing seems to end . . .

Carla Jean Schaldecker
YOUR EYES

*To Shaun O. Harniss, who in so
many ways made this possible.
Thanks for all the wonderful
memories!*

Looking into your eyes,
I see a caring man,
A gentle, peaceful feeling,
A fear from deep within,
A sparkle of happiness,
A hint of mischief there,
A concern for other people,
A love that we can share!

Sarah E. Risen
Alone With the Thunder

*To My frightened dog DUKE who
was afraid of the thunder*

I was sitting at home alone
It was dark and the dogs began to
bark

So I went to my window and
what did I see?
Nothing but the reflections of my
puppy and me.

"Still alone," I said
Then I began to wonder
If the dog was just scared of the
thunder?

Behind the thunder there's
sunshine for my puppy and me.

An image then showed up
It was my little puppy and me
Alone and scared all because
nobody cared.

We were alone with the thunder
again

all because I lost my only true
friend.

Shilrey A. Munsinger
CHILD ABUSE

*I dedicate this poem to all the
abused children and the people
now grown who were abused as
children.*

What in life do you gain
When all you live with is pain?
Life can be so cruel
Child abuse adds to the fuel
It teaches to hate
And try to cheat fate
We don't want you, they say
And you pray for God to end
your day.

Jeanne Claytor
THE SOB OF STONE
Hosannas be sung
From the highest peak!

Glory be to God!
Glory be to God!
Glory be to God!

Loudly let echo the joy
That leaps from cliff to craig
And bounds from range to range!

For, if no praise for Thee is sung
Or shouted from the sky,
The saints must be
The living stones
That from the valley cry!

Lona Jean Turner Binz
God's In the White Clouds

*Dedicated to my Grandchild
"Michael LeEldon Binz", who will
be "six years old" next year on
"February 18th. 1984"—"Out of
the mouths of babes come
precious gems"*

Look at the sky' said the five year
old
And then so very, very bold
Do you know who's in those
white clouds up there,
In the air?
It's God!
And as he kicks the tiny rocks
in the sod,
The ones with the black face'
Are Space!

(Mrs) Mary V. Macierowski
NON CHARACTER
Imbedded deep within her womb
All seeds of lovebloomed there
Sons, daughters, loved and cared.
Then in our youth, a time of deep
sorrow for the masters of our
birthand seedling, are gone in
death.
Schoked, days pass in sorrow,
when a non seeded character
appears.
Showing a personality never seen,
he says, i the youngest am the
master.
By whom i asked in tears?
Is your name written here, as i
pointed to her last will
Do you not see her words of
discipline?

Mary, my oldest daughter, not
Ted the young son.
In peace and harmony, this will
be settled.
The non character shouts, they
are dead,
And my mothers spirit, thru the
window throws a sharp light,
he is blinded,
Then he whispers,"Lord thy will
be done."
All five sons and daughters
became one again, with heads
bowed

Karen Anita Davis
FRIENDS
Fibers weave through time
pulling together you and I
Reaching in, reaching out
they sew the fabric of our souls
Into one very special
pattern of love, tears and
laughter.
Emerging in the midst
of torn lives patched with bias
Nothing to hold them
together—you and I are
Dreaming the same dreams,
holding
each other, carrying each other
So close that at times
I feel you are me.

Barbara Trimboli
THERE'S NO MORE ME
The day will end when I died and
see no tears in my love ones
eyes. The nights will get colder
and the days will get duller.
The ground will get wet from
the blood in my body. The
blood won't stop flowing it just
bleed and bleed. There are
people on their knees begging
me to give parts of my body to
their needs. There's no way to
refuse them so they take the
parts they need from me. After
they are done I look at myself
and can't believe there's no me.
I'M DEAD AND GONE.

Heather A. Toll
THE BALD EAGLE

*For my family who supports me.
And to Mark who inspired the
poem.*

The Bald Eagle,
talons locked,
fly over snowcapped
Mountains,
swooping, falling ever
Downward, in pure ecstasy.
Plumeting, seperating up
to peak,
The Bald Eagle beautiful
To Behold . . .

Kristina Dawn Shepard Bower
TATTOOS ARE FOREVER
I indelibly puncture through the
skin
Flowing with the colours, my
passions-feelings.
Emotions and tastes passed on to
me from my canvas.
I give to them myself.
And the next generation to come.

For that's how long it lasts.
It won't die and wither away after
one night's love,
Nor after several.

My inks are permanent and as
blue and green and brown
As each one of your eyes were.
The electricity moving in and out
of the skin
With the expertise of my artiste
touch
Captures the soul.

As we had captured our souls
As we had mingled our bodies.
Electrifying the nights with a
rapture—
Surpassing all boundaries.

But I must give to you instead,
my indelible ink—
My flowing colours of passion.
For my love will soon fade away.

Mary Cochran Skramstad
UNTITLED
Above the clouds
Flying High
There is a shadow
In the sky.
I wonder,
Can it hear
A baby cry?
Does it ever
Wonder why
As it passes by,
That men must die—
To fly higher.
To sing in
The angel's choir.

Deborah Jane Young
MY LITTLE BOY
My little boy is growing every day,
New people to meet, new words
to say.
He's just beginning to learn of
love and life and everything,
And through him, I, too, am
growing.

The smallest of things holds his
interest so
There is so much he is trying to
learn and know.
I love to watch him when he
finds something new,
He examines it closely to see
what it'll do.

Early in the morning I can hear
his little voice,
Playing by himslef, almost as
quiet as a mouse.
And when I get him up and he
smiles at me,
I know right here is where I want
to be.

Few people give me the happiness
and pleasure I get from him,
I am filled completely to the brim.
And he just goes on in his care-
free way,
Learning what he can to lead him
to his manhood someday.

Anne Animus
COMFORT
To find comfort
with the unknown—
"Ah, there's the rub."

Comfort
is the unknown.

137

Max Swafford
THRESHOLD OF A DREAM

I would like to dedicate my small part of this collection to those who have known the joy of love, as well as the pain of losing it ... and have not lost their belief in rediscovering the threshold of that dream.

Seven years, a thousand miles, dozens of letters, and two children away from me, and you still find your way into my thoughts.

Those sunsets on the river and those carefree walks around the campus seem so far behind, and all of the familiar faces have gone to other places and have left me no traces, save the occasional glimpse from my memories.

Your pictures grow lifeless with the ticking of time and those last few letters seemed to slowly lose their warmth.

Yet, I still look longinly at your familiar pose, and I still read hurriedly when in my lonely repose.

The void that you left is slow to fill, because my dream for us and the impact you had on me lingers still.

We were at the edge of another dimension and we were on the Threshold of a Dream until that fatal, silent parting at that Ruidoso stream.

Since that time, I have come to know that you will linger long in my memories and I can always touch that which has been a hidden part of me through the years.

It is that Threshold of a Dream that remains, and in a fleeting memory regained ...

Even though you are still seven years, a thousand miles, dozens of letters, and two children away from me.

Patricia K. Owen
LOST
The game isn't worthy of the struggle,
What events shaped my form? my destiny?
Brought me to this state of nothingness,
I am automated, moving through, empty, empty.
Numbered emotions, uncaring of anything around me.
Who am I
An empty shell, an open book, a blank page,
Waiting to be fulfilled
But, what do I see waiting for me, lonliness,
bitterness.
Oh? to say, look, I feel, I love, I need
Someone to love me.

Michael Meaux
THE LESSON LEARNED
Please let Go
I think you know
Its a shame
You played that game

She belonged
To someone else
You must have known
You'd hurt yourself

For a time
You thought you'd win
But my friend
It had to end

She went back
To him it's true
I think you've learned
more than you knew

So you've got
To walk away
But what a price
You had to pay

Mary Huffman
TOGETHER
The emotional stress is too hard to cope,
As long as you're around there's always hope.
I hold the time we shared inside my heart,
together we laughed, together we loved.
The feelings we had were always so right,
we shared our dreams by day and by night.
You were always there when I needed you most.
Together we faced the problems life brings,
we weren't tied up like puppets on a string.
We never got tired of being together,
I know deep down I could love no other.
It had to happen some day I know,
It came too soon, I didn't want to let go.
God took him from me on a dark dismal day,
I know that together we had to be.
Next to my love is where I'll lay,
together, side by side, it's here we'll stay.

Ted Cowdrey
DEAR LADY

To my Lady, for whom my love will never die.

I wish we could sit by a campfire just you and I
And watch our shadows dance on cliff walls so high ...
I wish we could sit by a campfire just you and I
And tend the flames of passion until the embers die ...

Anne F. Gervais
WHAT IS A BROTHER
A brother is someone
who's always there
He's someone who will
always care

A brother is a special
guy
When you're down
he's always a clown and
lifts your spirits to the
sky
A brother can make
you smile
Even if only for
a little while
A brother is a
very special person

Beaatrice D. Londergan
SPECIAL ANGEL

Dedicated to my friend, Martha Buffoni, whose son John Boomsma died January 2, 1983, a cerebral palsy special child.

There is one more angel now in heaven who was that special child of mine.
Then the good Lord came and claimed him,
He had counted down his time.
Now John's standing tall and handsome and he's walking gracefully.

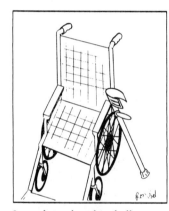

I can almost hear him holler
"Hey Ma, look, look! it's me.
I can handle all the things
that on earth I couldn't do;
I am happy now in heaven;
I'll be waiting here for you."

Darnell D. Nixon
A LETTER TO MY SISTER
Dear Sister,
I remember the games we used to play,
Running through abandoned buildings,
Day after Day.
Growing up in the Ghetto,
Was not all that bad,
Because growing up in the Ghetto,
Was all we had.

We found joy in each other,
And we laughed together.
We found peace in our minds,
Though the times were unkind.
We found strength in each other,
Through hardships and pain,
We found strength,
And we withstood the rain.
We learned from each other,
Like a family should.
We grew together,
Because we knew we could.

Dear Sister,
I'll never forget what Ma said,
On the day she died,
"Childrens keep ya heads up
And donts never cease to try."
I LOVE YOU SISTER!

Valerie Dolce Keegan
MEMORIES
I think of you these long and
lonely nights and first thing
when I wake up in the morning
even while tossing in bed,
trying to get back to sleep,
(hoping for a happier dream)
you wander in and out of my
mind
uninvited
disturbing my rest

Perhaps we hold on to memories
until we find a way to go on
without them.

Wanda Sue Sutton
HOME AT THAT PLACE
The old white house still stands,
In the place where it used to be,
Perhaps it's missing a plank or
two,
Or maybe even three.

The knock on the door is much
lighter now,
As time bids a hello,
Where laughter once roamed,
Now silence instead,
Answers at our home.

The pump doesn't draw any water
now,
And the cistern seems to be dry,
The chickens aren't there to
cackle,
And answer to Mama's cry.

The trees once glistened with
sweet crescents,
As the sap decided to run,
Now, instead, stumps remain,
And sparkle in the sun.

The barn much weathered by age,
Still beckons the cries of the
mules,
As Daddy often used them,
Especially to gather our fuels.

Life was hard, but is remembered,
As time begins to race,
So, I'll always cherish fond
memories,
Of my home at that place.

Shannon Box
DARK ANGEL
Upon the winds ready to
attack,
Comes the angel of death on his
horse of black.
An evil spirit flows out from
within,
Searching out and destroying the
souls of men.
Corrupting their every thought,
and deed,
He spreads destruction at
lightning speed.

Karin Lovsey
LOCKER
My locker reminds me of my
closet;
Nice and neat when the door is
closed,
A disaster once it is swung open.

Books and papers lie strewn
about my things,
Candybar wrappers on the shelf.
A stick Up stuck up on the wall
Provides the lingering lemony scent
Whick is carried with me
everywhere.

My locker reminds me of myself;
Nice and neat when the door is
closed,
A disaster once it is swung open.
My inner being is exposed when
sifting through it's contents.
A dictionary falls out in my face,
Sheet music on the floor.
Unfinished poetry drifts about
my ankles,
Soon to be trampled by careless
feet.

My locker reminds me of my life;
Nice and neat when the door is
closed,
A disaster once it is swung open.
From the outside all is simple and
organized.
Just don't open the door,
For passers-by peek in on a
private life
That I try to keep locked up.
But I've a way to keep my secrets:

Clean out my locker and start
anew.

Delphine Birkeland Draxton
MY RENDITION
All one's thoughts and words-do
measure—
Each one may become a treasure;
In song or poem or book-they
may
Become the reading of the day;
Fact or Fiction-matters not—
If there's great interest in the plot;
Whether sweet or kind of gory—
Just so long-it tells the story;
To leave the world with one's
rendition—
Is every writer's great ambition!

John W. Shearer
**Variations On a Theme
Entitled Working As One**

---

*Dedicated with all my love to my
wife. Marsha. and my two
children. Melissa JoAnn and John
Christopher Ian.*

Working for the children, Sky
search,
Vision for a mission rising from
perch,
The music soars upward as the
notes are sure
Hand in hand this opera is pure,
Sky king, the composer reaches
out to touch
The horns are blasting and the
conductor's too much,
The session is grand as the bells
all ring
When we are working as one the
angels all sing,
The chart is free as the players all
scream
Through a roaring passage the
score now beams,
The piano talks in waves, notes

and tones
While the drums are dancing we
battle the moans,
The woodwinds are chanting as a
romance in the night
The strings are demanding a babe
in flight,
The symphony is ours, together
the performance shall be done
By the light of the spirit the
awakening movement,
Is working as one . . .

John A. Billetdoux
Ode To Carl Yastrzemski
After 1983 ol' Fenway will be
empty,
Cause after 1983 they'll be no
more Yastrzemski,
The fans of Boston love him so,
they speak of him ev'ry day,
And he'll be known as "Mr.
Boston" even beyond his dying
day.

Oh, Carl had some real fine years,
you remember '67,
He proved to fans of Fenway Park,
that he was sent from heaven,
He took the place of another
great known by the name of
Ted,
He started in the early 40's and
his glory never shed,

There were many greats before
his time but none as such as
Carl,
For he took a solid piece of wood
and made it roar and snarl,
Though I feel sorry for good ol'
Carl for he could never sing,
The song the one and onlys sing
who wear the series rings,

His number will always fly, high
and proud, up above Fenway,
And with Carl looking down on
them, the Sox'll win someday,
And when Carl's gone the
country will grieve, "when he
isn't around",
"Cept all us Boston fans we'll
know he's down in Cooperstown!

Cheryl A. Dubuque
STRENGTH
There are leaders and
there are followers.
When needed, most of us
can stand strong.
But, at times, when facing
our own problems and all the
challanges of life—even
the greatest of leaders
can use a little support.
In you, I have found
my support.

Karla Ann Monroe
MY PRAYER

---

*This poem was written for my
dear husband. Nelson James
Monroe. with all my love.*

Lord help me be a better wife,
A better mate unto the man.
Whom you have chosen for me to
go
through life with,
Always hand in hand.

Lord help me to understand him,
When he is feeling down.
To lift his spirits higher,
And never show a frown.

Lord teach me not to grumble,
And make his burdens more.
But help him carry the yoke
That's what I am here for.

Ann Kinsey
THE MASTER'S PLAN
In the book of Revelations
the Master's plan unfolds.
It tells of wars and conflicts
and what the future holds.
It tells about the Rapture
and the Tribulation too.
When we look around
we can see it's coming true.

First comes the Rapture
in the twinkling of the eye,
God will call all his saints
to meet him in the sky.
Next comes Tribulation
Oh, what sorrow and pain!
All the saints of earth have gone
and Satan now will reign.

Now, there will be a battle
the worst the world has known.
Satan tries to rule the world
and God to claim his own.
Antichrist will do his deeds
in the name of love.
Be ye not deceived by him
your power is from above.

Now the ones left on the earth
must make their final choice.
Do not be afraid to stand
Whatever be the cost.
When the battle seems to be
more than you can stand
Just remember soon he'll come
with his angel band.

Ann M. Gocken
PASING OF DEFEAT
There is a time when we all must
meet
This discouraging thing called
defeat.
But when it comes to you dear,
Just shrug it off without a tear.
Because when its gone and you
smile,
You come to learn its all
worthwhile.

Wendy L. Barber
IT'S TIME FOR ME

---

*To my loving grandmother, Della
Brooks*

I have lived a long and fruitful
life and now it's time for me to
go.
I have married and raised thirteen
children and have seen grand—
and great grandchildren grow.
I was there at the start of the
atomic age seeing a war fought
and won . . .
cities destroyed, people killed.
I have seen wars unsettled.
I have seen men and women fight
for freedom,
the space age with men walking
on the moon . . .

the first in-vitro baby,
the marriage of a prince,
the first female astronaut.

The world is coming up with new
ways to try to keep me here . . .
but I am tired, for I have lived a
good life and it's time for me to
go in order for someone new

To come.

Chris Roach

Chris Roach
WHEN I THINK OF YOU

---

*I dedicate this poem to my
special friend. Wendy M. Hourd,
whose warm friendship and
company inspired me to write
these words.*

I wake up in the morning
and I see the sky so blue,
It makes me feel so alive
when I think of you.

I prevail throughout the day
and in my heart the feeling is
true,
I feel like this two hundred times
a day
when I think of you.

I sometimes stop to rest
and in my mind appears visions
of two,
A vision of a passionate couple
when I think of you.

I think of the times we spend
together
and because of them my senses
grew,
A piece of gratefulness
when I think of you.

And I sure am glad
that you see things the way I do,
Because I feel so wonderful,
when I think of you.

Marsha L. Sanders
UNTOLD LOVE

---

*In thanks to my family, for all the
times they stood by me, helped
me and loved me.*

There's no one quite like my
family,
    you're all very important to me.
It's sad the love we feel is often
    hard to say.
Each one of you are different
    in a very special way.
All things that mean so much to
    me,
    are made up in my family.
You've made my life easier,
    just wanted you to know.
Although it's not said often,
    I really love you so!

Kurt L. Scott
A LETTER

---

*This poem was written for my
girlfriend, DAWN, while I was
serving a sentence in C. Y. A.
in 1983.*

A letter from a loved one,
Is as precious as a kiss.
Expressing how you feel,
To the one you really miss
You write all of your worries,
Your loves and your fears.
And sometimes when you are
    lonely,
It's a letter written with tears.
A letter is something
Composed of love and care,
With the thought that someone
    special
Will be reading it somewhere.
If the two of you are apart.
And while you read those words
    of magic,
You feel the beating of their
    heart.
Yes, a letter is something special,
When you take the time to write.
Because it is that letter,
That will keep someone company:
On that long and lonely night.

Susan Connell, Durrant
THE LAST DAY

His pain stoped . . . death was his
    fate.
    Trying to hang on, in pain he
    would wait.
Wanting once more to see her
    face radiate.
    Her blue eyes that whoever saw
    would penetrate.
Through death, . . . still their love
    insepetrate.
    She clung to him not wanting to
    cooperate.
How she beged him to try and wait
Life was gone . . . , it was to late.
His body engulfed in pain, to
    much to bear.
    He left his pain . . . without a
    care.

Those he left behind now cry . . .
    For they had not the chance to
    say . . . goodby

Ethel Lofton
RACINE AT DAWN

Racine at Dawn
O' how beautiful by the lake.
So quiet, peaceful, and cool
Before everyone awakes.

No hustle or bustle
Only a few cars to be seen.
Staring out my window
O' how I can dream.

The sun at rest before she rises
But only if clouds don't shadow
    the way.
The rain and wind, they too are
    part of God's beautiful day.

The trees briskin' to and fro,
Birds chirpping and patting on
    the sidewalks, see them go.
Even in the grass, searching for
    particles for their little beaks,
Before the little children awake
    to disturb them in the streets.

Racine at Dawn
O' how beautiful by the lake.
So quiet, peaceful, and cool
Before everyone awakes.

Stephen M. Cabrinety

Stephen M. Cabrinety
WANTED: SPACE
So crippled by delinquency
That there are no hopes
    remaining
For room to store antiquity,
We just keep on rearranging
Our files without a frequency.
And so it always seems to show
That there's no regularity
From which our world will likely
    grow.
Discretion takes discrepancy
To establish on condition
A reason for the peasantry
To lose complete recognition
Of that contained in memory.
Now if one dares to soon
    mention
The slightest hint of enmity,
Even without such intention,
Then from within the gallery
Explodes exasperating tension,
And places into fallacy
That old catapulting question:
If want of space cries constancy
And thus humanity defies
The rules of some theocracy
Of which euthanasia belies,

It therefore lends hypocrisy
And necessarily implies
Remnants of full autocracy!

Pennie S. McCants
A BEAUTIFUL MOMENT
At first he wasn't very pretty,
But he knew a day was near
That would change his life to a
    beautiful one,
So to this thought he did adhere.

He had to work very hard
Day in and day out.
But when the day finally came,
He did not jump and shout.

Instead he slipped into a shell;
A world within a world.
He stayed inside this lonely place
Folded up and curled.

But something suddenly
    happened to him.
He began to move around.
Yet when he kicked his feet about
He could not feel the ground.

He burst out of his home.
He felt a difference now.
He did not have as many legs
As he had been endowed.

Now he had a pair of wings
Which he opened to the sky.
He was not a mere caterpillar
    now
But a beautiful butterfly.

Verna E. Love
**The Stars, Sun and Moon
Looked Down**
The stars looked down on the
    earth below
Then they all twinkled merrily,
For they could see folk going to
    and fro
Who were kind as they could be.
Some were trying to lighten the
    load
Of friends burdened down with
    care,
Giving help to others along life's
    road
With troubles more than their
    share.

The sun shone down on the earth
    below
Then a cloud passed across it's
    face;
For what it saw was a terrible
    show,
Disgrace of the human race.
Sickness, poverty, greed, crime
    and fear
Were some of the things to be
    seen;
Then out of the cloud fell a lot of
    tears
As if they would wash man clean.

The moon beamed down on the
    earth below
And then it smiled happily
On the many homes of those who
    know
The love that sets people free
From fear, and they want to do
    what's right.
It fills their hearts with joy and
    peace,
So they labor and strive to spread
    the light
And make happiness increase.

Winona L. Barnes
DEATH AND IT'S BEAUTY
The wonderful place that death
    in Christ can bring
It's the wonderful desire of Heaven,
It's pearly gates of white,
Streets of gold, Herald bells that
    ring.

Seeing Jesus Christ our Lord,
Moses, who walked the mountain
    top
Seeking the commandments of
    our God.
It's John the Baptist, Paul, the
    preacher man
Who gave God his all; Loved ones
Who passed at bugle's call.

It's the Hallelujah times we'll have
Flying around above the clouds;
That's Death and it's Beauty.

So Please, Please, God—make me
The child of Jesus, all the way.
Love fellow man, these things
I'll proclaim. Please God
Don't stop until I feel it's sting,
Death and It's Beauty.

Theresa I. Miles
A LITTLE NOTE

---

*For Debbie . . . I had no coins
within my purse So I wrote this
little verse.*

Just a little note
To show you that I care
If you have the sniffles
Or a pain in (you know where)!

So get your rest, you hear?
So you can feel just fine,
And if you're really good . . .
I'll send a card next time!

Janice L. Helman
FAR AWAY EYES
I've tried to reach you with my
    heart
But your eyes are so far away
They cannot see the love I feel
Where are your thoughts today?
Does she still burn in your
    memory
Though you pretend she does not
    exist?
Who do you see when you touch
    me?
Who's on your mind when we kiss?
I don't want to take your memories
I only want to erase your fears
And free your heart to love again
But you can't see past your tears
I don't want to lose what we have
If only you would realize
That the love you seek is here
    and now
And not far away in your eyes

Elise Bills Rumford
MESSAGE ON THE WIND
I see leaves stirring, stirring . . .
Play, play on, oh loitering wind
I hear the singing of falling leaves
Drifting, drifting to muted
    melodies
I feel a feathering, blushing breeze
Its clinging aura touching,
    touching . . .
With swelling breath, I catch
The scent of lilacs, and I'm

Held in the grasp of a stinging
  memory
Bold breezes brush my parted lips
Blowing dust tastes brown on my
  tongue
Possessive, slender fingers of an
  ardent wind
Caress my face and curl my
  shining hair
Ah, love, you are here, there, and
  everywhere
Waken my from empty dreams
Your message on the wind
  enchants, entices
Gentle, or fierce in its conquest
You are near, nearer, nearest
Oh, caro mio ben
Like the wayward, wandering
  wind
I cannot embrace you
Awed, I know, and knowing,
  knowing . . .
I know you live
In the silence of my soul.

Marion Sue Brakebill

Marion Sue Brakebill
IF EVER WE AWAKEN
We most always take for granted
  The things we see around
The ones we love the most
  The paths we haven't found

If ever we awaken
  And find the trees are gone
The grass has lost it's color
  The sky has moved along

I guess we grow accustom
  To having someone near
If it be for love or friendship
  To quench the loneliness we
  fear

We so often never try
  To make a better life
Or be a better person
  We'd rather hide and cry

Sarah Jack Roberts Finley
MY DAUGHTERS THREE
I am not a poet you see
But I trust and love you three;
You mean so much to me
That the world can see.

It's good to know you do as I tell
  you
Not as I may always do;
With nothing much to hide
No need to tell lies.

No parent knows very much
Yet, the longer you live,
You may reconsider such
Was not all just mush!

I have given a lot of advice
Have said a no before a yes;
And have changed my choice,
Because I needed to hear your
  voice.

I have heard your voice, clear and
  strong,
I know we have not gone wrong
When such trust is a bond
Between us so strong!

I thank the Lord for giving me
The joy of having three D's
For where now might I be
Had it not been for you three?

Linda L. Tilton
MOM
Mothers are people who grow up
  to share, feelings of love for
  children she bares.
She diapers and feeds them all
  day long, and when she is
  finished, the day is all gone.
She devotes all her time, energy
  and love, to those little
  children so they grow to be
  strong.
To grow up and handle life all on
  their own, but between this
  family, is a special bond.
A bond of love that no one can
  erase, a love thats born to the
  whole human race.

Jeana Miller
THE DESIRE
The crisp clean paper
lay untouched
Just the smell of the newness of
  it could
send chills all the way
down my spine
I don't even know
why I'm scrawling
across it
But I know its an
unquenchable desire,
a burning desire from
deep inside.
The ink flows madly
on between light-blue
threadlike lines that
appear as tiny veins
stretched almost to
their limit of breaking
I must go on
I want to learn,
learn everything I
can about this wild
passion. It takes pratice
because there are so
many things, that
are waiting to be
released and written down.
But I know in time everything
will work out
and hopefully by then
I will have—
  tamed my desire.

Toby Willis
BIRTHRIGHT
I am
the child.
I am
the lump,
the bump,
the mound beneath your rounded
  belly.
I kick
to remind you

I'm here
not just a nightmare.
I will be
the squalling mouth
you must suckle,
the three o'clock feedings,
the cries that won't soften.
But you'll never know these things.
I know I have no father.
You know your breasts
will never nourish me.
You'll never coo me to sleep.

But, mother, will you
  acknowledge me
when I show up at your door
to claim my birthright?

Michael Sean Barrett
AMERICAN FLAG

*To the missing soldiers of
Vietnam, wherever they may be,
for they never returned home to
the Land of the Free.*

I glance at the Flag on the wall
I stop and stand, straight and tall.
Colors glimmering very bright
As the wind blows, it waves like
  a kite.

The color red,
Stands for blood that was shed.
The color white,
Stands for freedom's light.
The color blue,
Stands for soldiers true.

Our Flag is a symbol of Liberty,
For those who died, for you and
  me.
So when I look at the Flag up
  above,
I remember our Country of Peace
  and Love.

Darlene R. Nevers (Reilly)
PEOPLE SEDUCING YOU
What can I say—what can I do,
There's wild-tempting people
  seducing you.
It's not honest nor sincere,
To your heart they won't adhere.
Gone after another—you'll have
  to see,
Love fooling—you and me.
They'll laugh at you behind your
  back,
Telling the next one what you
  lack.
Seducing others—they'll not be
  true,
You have to admit—they only
  use you.
Their heart is made of stone and
  ice,
Spreading their coldness—
  breeding like lice.
Refuse to listen—do not give in,
In time we'll catch them in their
  sin.
Be sly— be wise—you can discern,
It's not a waste—if you can learn.

Stephen Jurbala
PEARL
From the most beautiful smile
The seed was sown,
For the greatest marriage
That has lived and grown.
From the only love I have ever
  known

To the most wonderful wife
And she's all my own.
Thru all our years
Her bright smile has shown,
So this verse I write for her alone.
It shows my love
Though it's not written in gold
But within my heart
For her to hold
And in her care how safe it will be
Thru out my life and eternity.

Rosetta Ison
IMAGES

*To my children: Zetta, Brenda,
and Robert McMeans*

'Round and 'round they go,
From laughter into pain,
In sorrow and in joy,
In sunshine and the rain.
Reflections are so clear,
While they are here today,
But then begin to dim,
And slowly fade away.
Oh, if I could just hold
The sorrow and the strife,
The laughter and the love
In the mirror of my life,
There'd be my masterpiece,
For all the world to see,
A portrait of my life,
These images of me!

Shari Linnea Clevenger
OUR GREAT LORD
When I look out on the ocean blue
My Lord, I think more about you.

Your greatness, wisdom, and
  power are so great
I realize that we're not just here
  by fate.

You put us on Earth with a
  purpose to do
To bring people here closer to
  You.

And while we do this task we are
  not to forget
All of our prayers that have
  surely been met.

Each day you shower us with
  Your love
For You've sent down Your Holy
  Spirit in the form of a dove.

You've guided us straight when
  we've gone astray
And You've continued to protect
  us from day to day.

Lord, I know sometimes we don't
  follow in Your light
And then we blame You for not
  doing right.

But, Lord, please help us during
  our times of strife
By reminding us of Your love for
  You gave Your life.

Sonia Ibanez
NOCTURNAL VOYAGE
The moon steers silently
across the dome
of her nebulous sea,
like an oriental ship of old
uncurling ovoid sails . . .
Slowly she swings from the bay,
a scintillating orange
ignited by the sun

John Campbell, Editor & Publisher

and navigates to where
the cooling sea spray
waters her . . .
Quenched and quivering,
she stays her course
growing pale and silver,
bitten by the piercing coldness
of her pinnacle,
blowing her smoky breath
on every sentinel.

Fern Marsh
PATIENCE

---

*To my Stepdaughter Heather who
was to be the JOY for my
"tomorrow".*

If you will but listen
 God will make you hear Him
But you must be quiet,
 And let Him have His say
Or you will never hear Him
 And His message will quickly
 flee away.
But quietly and in a reverent way
 Be still.
For He is Lord of all, of time, of
 care,
 And we must all beware
Lest in our haste
 We take the task away—from
 this Great Master.
And then we wonder why
 In our great sorrow
Where went all the joy
 For our tomorrow?

Paul Faber
ANTEDILUVIA
Hasten, cloud.
Bring on the lightning storm.
Draw shade over
This heat, and
Drive the clover
To its leaves
Before the dew breathes back its
 form.

Hasten, now,
Cumulonimbus. Clench
Your stained cotton
Fingers. Pound
My forgotten
Law into
Proud soul's hearts as they slowly
 drench.

Hurry Down,
Rain. Water their vile blood,
Put out from earth
The hellfire   ·
Giving death berth!
No live thing
Unprepared shall last this timed
 flood!

Then rise warm, sun. Part the
 waters' mesh
To present the chosen a gift-
 ribbon, saying:
Never again shall that which
 livens bear such death . . .

Lynn Ann Lewis
FOUND
They succeed
Dare I do it
                    downfall
names I meet
faces blurred by days
yesterday

                    solitary string
Today—
                    dense web
Monday's routine
A threat on Tuesday
Accusing the front door
                    of denying my entrance
Later
                    finding the key
In my shadow's pocket.

Blaine W. Bittinger
**The Things That Some
 Men Steal**
I can't begin to tell you
Of the awful things I feel,
But I hope someday God will
 repay
For the things that some men
 steal.

I cannot touch the ones
Who did this awful thing to me
But I will hurt until I die
Or live in misery.

They can take the starlight from
 the sky,
Or the beauty from the rose,
But what they took from me one
 day
Only God in Heaven knows.

Of all the beauty on this earth,
The love, the peace of mind,
They took the only worth-while
 thing
That ever could be mine.

So I would ask that you would
 never
Have the pain I feel,
And pray that God will someday
 pay
For the things that some men
 steal.

Rudy Kouhoupt
THE WAY SEEMS LONG
The way seems long when first
 we look ahead
And think about the path that
 must be run.
No end is there before our eyes:
 instead,
The course of life, we think, will
 ne'er be done.
There is so much to do each day
 we live;
So very many things which
 always need
The special touch that no one
 else can give.
Though sometimes from our
 grind we would be freed,
We work and toil as though we
 had to feel
The chores and tasks of all the
 World complete,
Before that day when we, in pious
 zeal,
Do take our turn before the
 Judgment Seat.
 Each one of us who walks the
 face of Earth
 Must someday know the
 smallness of his worth.

Brenda Lee Paulus
YOUR EYES SPARKLED
The first time you saw him
you could never forget
I saw you staring at him
and your eyes sparkled.

He held your hand
as you walked along
the street lights shone
and so did your eyes.

He looked at you
you looked at him
he smiled
and your eyes sparkled.

You thought he wasn't interested
just making friendly gestures
when actually he is feeling the
 samething you are
so now you know his
eyes sparkled too.

Kurt Martin Schadler
FARAWAY GIRL

To Linda she didn't disappear

All alone
by a crystal stream
I stood

There she was
near the castle
at the crest of a hill
engulfed by fog

Her hair was gold
like that of the
warm distant sun

I crossed over
the rainbow bridge
so that I may yet find riches
others have never dreamed of

But this living jewel
beckoning me with her arms
vanished in the fog
which now seemed to be
 everywhere

Running through the high waves
of green grass
I seemed to be getting closer
to the castle
which was all that could be seen
 now

But it too disappeared
along with my hopes of finding
this strange and beautiful girl

Perhaps this tomorrow
I will meet her

David Mentzer
WOODSMOKE
We wandered among lanes of
 crimson mirth,
And rode the wind on mid-
 summer's eve.
His heart was set adrift to ask

and answer,
And I was captain to guide its
 flight from storm.
The clouds uncovered the moon,
 and as he opened
His starry eyes, in the warm
 silver light
The minutes were taken by the
 softness of a surrender,
A defeat of the wild things that
 move under cover
Of the sea; then warm was all
 around us, we felt it
And ran. We ran into the
 woodsmoke of burning leaves
That led us into the heart of
 autumn,
. . . and a falling petal.

Linda Jordan
STORMS
Wild lightning flashes in stormy
 skies
And night becomes day.
Thunder bellows badly
And rain-darkened bark contrasts
 with leaves of vivid green.
Wind blows tempestuously
And everything in its path is
 whimsically rearranged.
All this wild and furious beauty
And after the storm—
Peace

Gregory Reardon
**To Gotham: A
 Reminiscence**
You dance on the trampled heart,
Deaf to its cry,

Medusa-like,
Your mask of chrome intact.

Full of your venom, I wither
 dream by dream.
Yet once I fled your grip, rebel
 that I was,

Locked myself in a flower
To glean its secret thoughts;

Spoke with trees,
Heard the joyous music of the
 atom.

Where was your dark embrace
When the sea became my vassal,

When I rode its bluish surge
Deeply into sky,

Took stars away as prisoners
And made them lovers?

Planets were playthings
In my mad, galactic odyssey.

But then your carillens rang
Grimly, like shrieking wolves.

You rose from the mist—
Giant with mocking look,

Reminding me of nightfall,
Of the sacrilege of dying.

Elizabeth Schweig Mahoney
LOVE
Colors of rainbow
Are reflected in my thoughts
The look in my eyes.

Martha Ellen Donalson
**May You Always Have
 Enough**
Enough happiness to keep you
 sweet,
Enough trials to keep you strong,
Enough sorrows to keep you

human,
Enough hope to keep you happy,
Enough failure to keep you
humble,
Enough sucess to keep you eager,
Enough friends to give you
comfort,
Enough faith in yourself to give
you courage,
Enough wealth to meet your
needs,
Enough determination to get
things done,
Enough love to make you wanted,
Enough faith in God to keep you
safe,
"The Height of Wisdom is the
Knowledge of Ignorance."

Mark L. Morrison
Christmas Is Full Of Happiness
Christmas is full of Happiness
Christmas is full of Cheer
Christmas is a time of friendship
Lasting throughout the year

Arthur R. Slate, Jr.
WANDERING LOVE
Love wanders into time
and into space.
I wonder, who will it meet,
who will tell it meet,
who will tell its lonely tale?
Will the people of the past
ever remember the love
that they had for one another.
And will the people of the future
ever listen to love,
not destruction.
No one can be sure
of tomorrow's love
and of yesterday's promises.
So for now I will love
those I can,
and to those I can't,
I pray that somehow
love wanders in their direction.

A. William Floyde
OUR POSSIBLE FUTURE

---

*Dedicated to the album "The
Final Cut", which was released in
the United States, March 1983,
by the innovative English group
Pink Floyd.*

We want peace in the Middle East,
but the generals must have their
feast.
Of human lives and human foes,
they're going to raise the death toll.

Brother, do you think they'll drop
the bomb?
Sister, is this the end of our song?
Do you think the nightmare
could come true?
Would it be the end of me and
you?

Will we ever bring this uproar to
rest,
before we find out who is the best?
Will there ever be peace in the
Middle East,
before this vicious animal is
unleashed?

The end is clearly in sight,
it's all a matter of who wants to
fight.

All the boys are leaving home,
fighting in a desolate land all
alone.

Anyone can make a careless
decision,
like a doctor making a
miscalculated incision.
But doesn't it make you feel real
tough,
knowing that you were the one
to make the final cut?

Cheryl A. Shankman
Because We Prayed Together
You!
who take away the sins of the
world
watching
as hands take hold and
                 rr rii i I P P P
hairs
     from their roots   and
beat after beat after beat
hearts pounding
holes tre—m—b—ling

have mercy on us.

You!
who take away the sins of the
world
forgiving
and she
turning
black and blue
from male magnitude

have mercy on us.

You!
You who take away the sins of
the world
watching and forgiving;
now smouldering and scattered
she rests   far
from the fire,

grant us peace.

Rose Colombo Strickland
HAPPY HALLOWEEEEN!!

To all children everywhere

Black was the night
   Strange creatures in sight
The pumpkins were lit
   Much candy to get.

I walked down the street,
   My heart skipped a beat
Cause right up ahead
   A devil in red!

A witch on a broom,
   A ghost on a tomb,
A two—headed knight,
   Black crows taking flight.

Rushed up to the door
   And gave a knock, knock,
When out jumped a cat,
   A scarecrow with a hat!

Trick 'r Treat, Trick 'r Treat,
   The words did repeat—
Took gum from a tray
   And then ran away

As the scarry old goblins
   Seen by the moonbeam
Crackled eerily mean—
   Happy Halloweeeen!!

Norma Jean MacKinnon
SUSPENSE
The moon in all its glory upon
me shone,
The air was brisk and the wind
uttered a moan.
An ocean trembling with roars,
Threw its gallant waves against
the shore.
My heart was full of dreaded fright,
And the shriek of an owl pierced
the still of the night.

The continual chattering of
crickets seemed to say,
"Beware, beware, better move on
your way."
Eerie shadows crept alongside me,
While a far-off cry seemed to
come from the sea.
A cold and dreary rain began to
fall,
And the wind whistled through
trees erect and tall.
Just as I thought I could no
longer endure this thing,
I awoke to find it was naught but
a dream!

Radmila Sasic
TO NO AVAIL
To no avail
do I cry out
for you to hear my plea
silence only do I hear
naught from you to me
answer to someone
for this you must
and, I do sorly ponder
our much needed love
and sweetly surrender

Marian Foster Norman
A Lesson From a Water Beetle
I'll ne'er forget one summer day
When I whiled some happy hours
away
On a lovely lake in a little boat—
I'd row awhile, and then just float.
Neath a tree I stopped, when the
day grew hotter,
And dangled my feet in the cool,
blue water
While I watched an uninvited
guest
Crawl up the side and come to rest
On the boat's top edge, and it
stayed right there
For an hour or so. Then I noticed
a tear
Down the water bug's back, and I
thought it was dead.

But the split opened wider, and
out popped a head,
And next, a body wriggled out—
To my great surprise—and
thrashed about,
Staying close to its shell till its
wings were dry,
And then it took off into the sky—
A lovely blue-green dragonfly!
No longer did it have to crawl—
No longer bound by Earth at all.
And I thought as I saw it rise and
swoop,
Ascend again and make a loop—
"If God can make a beetle soar
In a better house than it had
before,
Just imagine what He has in store
For his children, when this life is
o're."

Maria Penna
HELLO . . . GOODBYE
We met as strangers,
On that warm September morning
Our looks met with a tender smile,
Our eyes held for a long moment.

You approached me on your
black stallion,
"Hello," you said, with a gentle bow,
"Would you like to come for a
ride?"
I smiled, as you lent me a helping
hand.

Our hair danced in the wind,
As the horse galloped through
the fields,
I held on you as tight as I could,
Smelling your sweet perfume.

Today, it is our son who rides on
the black stallion,
As I take my daily walks to that
special garden.
But today, I shall free myself from
a heavy burden,
As I will bring you flowers and
finally say,
"Goodbye" . . .

Lisa Ann Nunn
perfect neversight
Close your eyes and come with me
To a far-off land some may never
see
Dream the dreams you've always
dreamed,
Only better than before.
Dream with me forevermore . . .

Imagine, fantasize as long as you
realize
What it is you really want to be.
I know it can work, if we try,
Together on a voyage to the sky.

Past and future will merge
Melting, blending as reality ceases.
We'll be on the verge then off
Flying onward through
     Make-Believe . . .

Beauty beyond the reaches of our
minds
Is commonplace in that land,
All badness far behind,
Hold on to my hand . . .

When the true illusion is through
And time has passed us by
You can leave, though I'll miss you
Remembering our visions with a
sigh . . .

Nina F. Patchen
GETHSEMANE

My Lord went alone into the
 Garden,
Knelt down on His Knees to pray;
There was no one to share His
 burden,
He needed strength for the soon
 coming day.
His prayer was not one of
 greatness,
He asked for the help He would
 need;
He, even asked for forgiveness
For those, who would do that
 great deed.
His disciples did not come with
 Him,
By the rock, He knelt, sad and
 alone,
Praying His teachings would go
 with them.
That He died for their sins to
 atone;
From all of this, we can learn a
 lesson,
That prayers are to come from
 the heart;
No loud words or selfish petitions
Just be humble and let the tears
 start.
My Lord will hear all your prayers,
Whether spoken or just silent
 thought;
He will answer the simplest prayer.
So, remember the love He had
 taught.

Jimmy C. Day Sr.
MOTHER'S LOVE

*To my Mother; whom I will
always Love. You have shown
me, every reason to beleive;
There is a God Above*

The mind of man in years may
 span,
 With thoughts of early days.
When Mother called him Little
 man,
 In tones of loving praise.

The Queen was she of all the
 earth,
 The princess of the dawn.
And none could ever beat her
 worth,
 The childhood days are gone.

For she still lends those helpful
 hands,
 As in the days before.
Her tender heart still understands,
 Her love grows even more.

No love compares with Mother's
 Love,
 To little hearts now grown.
Who ask the blessing from above,
 On her for the love she's shown

Melba Lorraine Bieber
Seasons Of Life and Time

Summer, Fall, Winter, Spring;

These are the seasons that time
 does bring.
Some do blossom and spring,
 while wintering life's time's
 and learning, these are the for
 the memory of Time, and its
 seasoning.

And, these are the reasons for
 "Times Seasoning."
Summer, fall, winter, spring;
These are the seasons that time
 does bring.
Some do blossom and some do
 spring; while wintering life's
 time and learning; These are
 the reasons for the memory of
 each season and it's time and
 reasons for it's memories!

Dan E. Martin
That Special Time Of Year

It's that special time
 Of the year again,
When the wind gets cold
 And the trees look thin.

The days are getting short
 And the skies turning gray,
And the flocks are heading south
 Looking for a brighter day.

The squirrels are storing nuts
 And the bears look for a den,
A place to have their cubs
 And wait for the thaw again.

It's that special time
 Of the year again,
When nature takes a nap
 And her lights grow dim.

Yet the beauties are still there
 And each year its the same,
Mother nature takes her course
 It's all in the game!

Jan Kotlewski Huffman
ROADS

Life brings us change
Cause to rearrange
The collections in our home and
 our heart
We may move around
From town to town
And again we make a new start
At time it seems tough
The road can be rough
Our way may not always be clear
Wherever we are
No matter how far
In our hearts we will always be
 near

Gypsy
UNREQUITED LOVE

 All my life I'd sought you,
the vision in my dreams
 permeating the deepest
 yearnings
of my soul; and yet, another
 found you first.
 Your prothalamion became my
 song of pain;
but now I can't reveal how much
 I care.
 Every time our eyes meet I feel
 so alone
and empty; you are so beautiful
 to me.
 Every time I talk with you I long
 to cry out!
yet now that must not be.
 But even so the world shall
 know,
although they know not who
 And you, my lady love, if you
 should read,
shall know not the poet.
 So live and laugh and rejoice in
 your love
and I will suffer mine.

Jaci Marcelle Donnell
THAT SPECIAL SOMEONE

*To "That Special Someone" in my
life, who I love with all my heart—
Lee Hill Conner II.*

Love has grown a new flower,
Ever since I met you.
Every day it blooms more and
 more.

Having you by my side,
Is a dream come true.
Like all those storybook tales,
Life is so beautiful with you.

Continuing our lives together
Only to make all those dreams
 realities.
No one can make me happier,
Not anyone but you.
Each day I live for the
Real love I found in you.

Kellye Lou Nelson

Kellye Lou Nelson
LOVE

*With special love to my
Grandmother, Hazel Stephens,
who loves everyone
unconditionally, and to my dad
Doug, my mother Donna, and my
brothers, Boby and Greg, whom I
deeply love.*

Feelings of love
Are like mosquito bites;
No matter how hard you try to
 scratch them out of your
 thoughts,
They won't go away.
They are constantly on your
 mind.
Whenever you try to push them
 out,
They push back harder.
But they are much stronger!
Then . . .
You must surrender.
They creep back, and take over
 your thoughts once again.

Judith M. Gray
BEST FRIENDS

All the time that we have spent
 together.
Sharing our secrets and our world
 of dreams.
Money spent shopping in rainy
 weather.

Movies, bowling, and chocolate
 ice creams.

At your house or mine for
 sleepless slumber.
The guys, the talks, and the
 places we've went.
The late night shows that we
 watched in wonder.
The Nights on the Town that we
 say we've spent.

Plans for College that we made
 together.
Our roommating lives both
 happy and sad.
The concerts we've seen, our
 voices tenor.
The times we've had when they
 thought us both mad.

We want it to last forever . . . no
 end.
The world can be ours together. . .
 Best Friend.

Louanne E. Lake
It's Too Late For Our Love

*To Robert "Bubba" Gardner With
everlasting Love from all my heart.*

Remember when we first met?
It's something I'll never forget.
For months you turned me on,
 but
now you're gone. I've been in
Love with you for so long, but
It's Too Late For Our Love.

Nothing will change the way I
 feel.
My Love for you will always be
 real,
but It's Too Late For Our Love.

When you left me it really hurt,
but I took it like I thought a
woman in Love should. I cried
for you; I died for you, I even
tried to hold on to you. But I
guess I didn't try hard enough,
because nothing worked. I guess
It's Too Late For Our Love.

Every time I look at your face my
heart melts; knowing I'll never
have you again. How I wish you
were here; I miss you so much,
 but
It's Too Late For Our Love.

Your picture lies on the desk
 beside
my bed, where we used to make
 Love.
Every night I kiss you, wishing
 you
were lying there beside me; but
 you're
not. I guess It's Too Late For Our
 Love.

How I wish you were here with
 me now.
I need someone to hold me. I
 wish it
were you; I want it to be you, but
 It's
Too Late For Our Love.

I dream that some day we'll be
 together
again, but I realize it's only a
 dream.

144

Our World's Best Loved Poems

I wish I didn't have to face reality,
but when I turn around and
you're not
there, that's when I know . . .
    "It's Too Late For Our Love."

Beatrice Lawson Thorp
THE MIRACLE OF TWO

*This poem is dedicated to my
husband, Bill, for his support and
patience in raising our two
beautiful children, Karla and
Kimberly.*

While I was pregnant, I wondered
why,
I could feel so much Life deep
down inside.
The feeling of Life was something
new,
I never would have guessed I was
going to have two!
The miracle of Life was sent from
God above,
But who would have guessed
there were two to love.
If you have twins, you should be
a proud mother,
Because God chose you above all
the other.
You must have a special gift to
give,
So help your children enjoy Life
and learn how to live.

Marie Wasson Russell
I DO BELIEVE
God gave us eyes that we may see
The beauty of His creativity.

He gave us ears that we might
hear
His voice calling all, both far and
near.

With our nose God meant us to
know
The frangrance of His flowers
that grow.

With our mouths we can feed our
soul
With the bread of life, the
greatest goal.

He gave us voice to ever sing
Our thanks for joys His blessings
bring.

With hands outstretched, He'd
like us heed
A passer-by in an hour of need.

He gave us feet that we may go
Planting seeds that He will grow.

Our minds He gave to comprehend
The wonders of His world
without end.

God gave us hearts to fill with
love.
Then He'll smile on us from up
above.

And if we give this love away,
We will be pleasing Him each
day.

Yes, if we'd give this love to others,
Joyfully, we could live as Brothers!
If All used His gifts as He
designed,
Peace would reign through all
mankind.

Ted Anderson
APART

*To my wife Doreen, without
whom these words would never
have been written.*

I needed you so bad last night,
I cried myself to sleep,
A man of thirty years and more,
Still child enough to weep.

It's funny though 'cause when
you're here,
I just don't realize,
How much you really mean to me,
How much you fill my eyes.

Arlettte R. Hobbs
REFLEXION
We dwell in an age of genius,
  Of wonder's unceasing declared;
Yet, fate of our children should
  question,
  On a planet missile impaired.

In thought, I scan the azure skies,
  Glorious beyond the peaks;
Yet closer peering, see only smog,
  Undaunted; creeping between.

Our enduring, magnificent,
  earthly home;
  Will we actually allow it's
  demise!
Our head's immoral buried in sand,
  Armageddon awaiting the while?

If all we comprise is this, my
  friend,
  Then little of substance has
  changed.
For just as ignorant as primates
  are we,
  Inspite of computer's in space.

Helen K. Deuter
WEAVER OF DREAMS
Oh, Weaver of Dreams
Could you weave me a dream
Of a young love, tender and sky
Could you bring back the boy
With the gay, crooked smile
Who went off to war to die?
And the tired old Weaver wearily
Just nodded his head and said: "I'll
try"
But first—go to the top of a
windswept hill
At dusk—when the sun has
surrendered the land
Then look at the star—studded
Heavens above
And see the work of His hand.

For the stars are the faces of
loved ones
Who have gone, but only from
sight
They are watching and patiently
waiting
To join us in Heavenly flight
Be patient Child, Love is eternal
The old Weaver said—as he
slowly
Walked into the night.

Melanie L. S. Smith
MY MY MAMA
Through the flickering glow of
candlelight
Stood an elegant woman, an awe-
inspiring sight,
Who projected an image of
independence and grace
One of confidence with the
purity of lace

As I emerged from the warmth of
her womb
An aura of love permeated the
room
This sensation of a euphoric
tranquility
Emanated from her gentle
sensitivity
For from this day on our lives
would change
Sharing happy and sad moments
our experiences would range

Remember . . . pinning the
sequins on the suits I wore
And how many times you had to
fix the tights I tore
Remember . . . vacationing in the
Florida sun
And traveling to swim meets sure
was great fun
Remember . . . walking me down
the aisle on my wedding day
And giving me courage to choose
any path I may

As a child you were the apple of
my eye
"I want to be like her when I
grow-up" I'd cry
I am still so proud to have a
mother like you
Thankful our love will ever glow
in the deepening candlelight hue
Yet if someday our paths may
part, remember, you remain in
my heart

My My Mama . . . If you knew
her you'd understand quite clear
My My Mama . . . Why I love her
so dear
My My Mama . . . Whether far or
near
My My Mama . . . Our love will
transcend distance and years.

Wilma Reese
TALKE TO ME
Talke to me;
Can't you see how badly I'm
hurting?
Open your eyes and really look at
me
Open your heart and really listen.

Oh I know you say after all these
years
There's nothing to talk about
You talk your problem's over
with your friend's

And so do I.
It isn't what I want

I want us to share our innermost
thoughts and dreams
I want us to share our problems
and joys
There will be no real lasting
happiness.
Until we can share.

So my Darling—PLEASE TALK
TO ME.

Kathleen Mulcahy
NOW AND FOREVER

*To: Aunt Donna and Uncle Pete
on the day of their wedding May
22, 1983*

Together we'll laugh and together
we'll cry
We may find it hard but forever
we'll try
To make our life perfect, share
what we feel
Answer our dreams and make
fantasies real
We'll never be apart, never you
and then me
We'll always stick together,
always be a we
You'll be my shining light and I'll
be your guiding staff
We'll travel far together, we'll
live, we'll love and we'll laugh
We're making a life in which love
doesn't end
Where you'll be my life, my love
and my friend
So we've taken our vows now
we'll walk hand in hand
As we take the first steps towards
the life we have planned.

Carol M. Gibson
ABORTION

*This poem is dedicated to: Time
to Mourn the Cry of the Unborn
Who from their mother's womb
were Torn*

Abortion, what a horrible unjust
notion
So many think it's right
Don't they know it's against
God's Might
Dear God, it's so out of hand
That I fear for the fate of man
Over 15 million dropped in a can
What happened to the
Hippocratic Oath
To protect and preserve life
Now it's easy as cutting a throat
With suction and cold steel
surgical knife

Humanity is destroying life
Humanity will pay its price
Abortion is such a deadly strife
The Unborn Child Has A Right
To Life
Take heed to this warning
Judgment is coming
Before the Fall of any Nation
Infanticide was its worldly station
God's Wrath in His Supreme Court
Will decide what to do
With this Cruel Ungodly Nation

145

John Campbell, Editor & Publisher

Mauricia Price
FINAL CURTAIN
Majestically the nobly lone
And power-pinioned eagle
  soared
To cloud-bare wind-brushed
  breathless height
Where lesser feathered creatures
  dare
Not go. He could not know his
  wide
Elliptical slow-curving flight
Attracted earth-stained killer
  eyes
Which narrowed (as the rifle
  cracked)
With huntsman's lust for spilling
  blood . . .
Then grunting, satisfied, he
  left
One miracle of ornithology
Wing-shattered, dying in the
  mud.

Gina U. Jones
EBONY AND SNOW

To my husband, Tim, with love.

Ebony against pure white snow,
is known to be friend or foe.
Life sometimes causing them to
  dread,
the long and weary paths they
  tread.
When ebony and snow become a
  pair,
society can be cruel and very
  unfair.
To life ebony and snow pose a
  dare,
but can meet the world if they
  really care.
Being together in mind, body, and
  soul,
they are able to pay life's steep
  toll.
Ebony against pure white snow,
is known to be friend or foe.

Betty Kathleen Hall
INVADING SPIRIT

*Dedicated to Dr. Paul Shepherd,
whose sermons gave me the
inspiration to write this poem.*

Lovingly, lovingly,
  Waiting we see,
Happily, happily,
  Spirits are free.

Boastfully, toastfully,
  Strength ingrains,
Cheerfully lingering,
  Faithfully, gains.

Hopefully, longingly,
  Sweetly said,
Prayerfully worded,
  Pleafully read.

Soaring slowly,
  Softly in glide,
Gloriously shouting,
  Blest Be The Tie.

Truthfully, openly,
  Searchingly, start,
Lovingly cleansing
  Each human heart.

Carol Biddlecombe
DREAMS
When I was just a little girl
  my father said to me.
"Plant your dreams and let them
  grow my darling wait and see."
I planted dreams, just tiny ones
  and waited like he said.
As I grew and learned of life
  my dreams were duely fed.
In later years when I had grown
  my dreams had grown with me.
The tiny dreams that I had sowed
  became reality.

Kathleen S. Taylor
AUTUMN FEELING
As the crimson and gold autumn
  leaves fall,
so do my sorrowful tears,
for the bittersweet memories I
  recall
with you throughout the years.

Gray clouds gather in the
  darkening sky,
with the growling of distant
  thunder.
A saddened tear rolls from my
  eye
as I sit alone and wonder.

Will you ever come back to me?
Unanswered questions race
  through my mind.
I love you dearly, can't you see?
Why did you leave me behind?

Walking in the pouring rain,
engulfed in lonliness,
I look toward Heaven, in an
  attempt to gain
a glimpse of happiness.

The wave of sadness slowly
  subsides
as I walk amongst the trees.
For in my thoughts, I realize
life has other qualities.

Once, I may have needed you,
but now it is not so.
I have God's love to see me
  through,
so I guess I'll let you go.

Joffria Whitfield
SUNSHINE
The sun tickles concrete
  in curious dotted places
    where my mind soars free . . .

Miriam Hasert
RULES OF BEING
Life is but a great game
and we, the unwilling players,
wait as silent pawns before the
  drummer.

What turn of the dice will greet
  us first
to set our life in motion forever.
One wrong turn or missed move
  along the way
and we are warped for eternity.

The rules are laid out clearly
  before us,
but whom wishes to be in prison
  now.
If this is reality, then here is my
  dice,
for I hate this real life Dungeons
  and Dragons

game that I seem to be playing

right now.
I am the dungeonmaster of my
  soul.

Lloyd E. N. Bartholomew

Lloyd E. N. Bartholomew
MY ALPHABET
All men are created equal
Born to travel through life
Calling on a universal
  consciousness
Determined to survive
Ever clinging to threads of hope
Falling often along life's path
Given faculties to aid survival
History has recorded journeys
  made
Indignant and independent it
  shows
Joining accomplishments and
  progressing more
Kindled constantly by past
  conquests
Lacking in trust may cause delay
Many journeys incomplete
Never terminated, progressing
  still today
Over and over we will try
Past, present and future efforts
  we pay
Questing for tranquility
Rather than pestilence and war
Surely we all must contribute
Till in this life we have unity
Universally showing uniformity
  in truth
Voyaging through life forever
With our achievements shining
  brighter
Xraying and mending breaks in
  our roots
You and I more and yet more
  must give
Zeus, a mythical leader did
  forgive.

Terri Marie Jones
The Looking Glass Of Time

*Dear Jane, To thee I dedicate this
poem. To thee I wish to say, live
each day to the extent of eternity
and live to your hearts content,
for your friendship has created
eternity in my soul and a special
content in my heart. Love, Terri*

Away we can be rebels, escape
Into the two-way mirror, the
Life between the world of men
  and make believe—
This looking glass of time.

Where birds and butterflies are
  false mirages,
and plastic hangings.
Where flowers bloom year 'round,
But there isn't Spring, Summer,
  Fall, or Winter.
The vegetation is plastic—
In this space of life—
This looking glass of time.

We are rebels into a plan of no
  escape,
Because you can't go back once
  you enter—
We enter—and one day we'll all
  understand
This subconscious world we enter
All the times, in our lives—
This looking glass of time.

The walls, ceilings, and floors are
  pure white,
But as we walk, the artificial
  grass appears and the plastic
  flowers, and paper snow on top
  of clay mountains.

You never get hungry in this
  world of make believe—
    Because you can't eat plastic—
      In this world of the Looking
        Glass of Time.

Dean Mitchell
DADDY
DADDY . . .
  whatcha' doin'
  will you read to me
  how tall am I
  can I have a puppy

DADDY . . .
  let's play ball
  my shoe's untied
  Mommie said to ask you
  I want a horsey ride

DADDY . . .
  can I sit in your lap
  will you push me in the swing
  why are you so big
  that bug's crawling on everything

DADDY . . .
  where's my wagon
  close your eyes while I hide
  can I have some milk
  can we play outside

DADDY . . .
  I need more ketchup
  what do airplanes do
  will you carry me
  I love you

Edie McEvoy
THE DEAREST FRIEND
I often think of my father
  although he left me long ago
The memories never vanish
  because I loved him so.

He wasn't very tall and yet he
  looked that way to me
Perhaps because he stood so
  straight
  and walked with dignity.

He took such pride in what he did
  Still, we never heard him boast
A job well done, he used to say,
  was what he valued most.

The gifts he left I have today
  in those precious thoughts of
    yesterday
When self-respect,

Our World's Best Loved Poems

encouragement,
and gentleness had a part
In the kindly role my father
played
as he won me to his heart.

Frank L. Fowler III
ROSA AND ROSES
Rosa!
Watch the roses in spring!
Watch the petals fall, slowly!
Watch the birds fly!
Then the buds will appear!
It's roses again!
Rosa!

Rosa!
You're like roses!
You carried the seed of life
Now you've bared all the fruit
You've bared all of the toil!

Now we see roses
When we see Rosa!

Ed Hammerli
The Earth Comes Turning
How it comes turning
the little feet the rusty feet
the sounds of clatter
the religions the religions
and amulets—I Chings
and substitutes for substance
the crosses and faces of magic
and hustle and booze
grimy streets smiling people
sincere and sterile against the
turning
the music the books the painting
hang like crosses
who sees the stars? the dreamers
and magic-makers alike
they read them with wonder
and cars turning and clocks
they both stop and stutter
and churnings inside and
spinnings no wonder the magic
it never stops
short of fire.

Shirley L. Fahrny
GIFTS
Her gift to me was one of love
To whom she did give life,
All wrapped with kindly patience
and
The ribbon of sacrifice.

As I approach this anniversary
Of the day that I was born,
Forgive this tear at remembering
The mother that I mourn.

For, now, God's gift she has
received
The years are washed away
In that new life he's offered her
The golden, eternal day!

Daniel Raymond Johnson
THE INTRUDER
My workday now done and
lunchpail in hand
I whisked through the front door
of a world I command.
There to be KING til tomorrow
at seven
To bask in my own private
"bachelor heaven"
But Alas! Now I find that I'm not
alone
An intruder now shares my well
secured home
Comes a friendly grettin' from
once twice my size

A gorgeous lady with heaven-
blue eyes
A kiss to my lips, a smooch on
my face
This lady was bold, each kiss
well placed
I struggled for freedom, a task
long and hard
It's not easy to battle a Lady
Saint Bernard.

Cheryl Brugette
IN TRANSIET
Modes of transportation,
Vehicles of conveyence
Always smell of—
Cleaning fluid and vinyl.
I'm in transiet.
A disjointed traveler looking out
the window
Feeling nebulous.
Reflected in the darkness I see
All the cracks and fissures in my
face—
That no one else can notice.
Outside
Splinters of myself are flying on by.
I'm shattering.
They say even the stars die.
Sometimes I think I'll start
collapsing into myself
Under the gravity of the situation.
I am filled with sweet memories
that cloy.
Maybe I'll learn to remember
Without pain.
My memories are sweet,
But they stick—
Like an icepick in the mind.

Leonard Louis Komblevicz
Leap Frog Christmas Tree
SilenT TinseL
LeiS StanD DancinG,
GivinG Glitter-RiddeN
NuancE Serene;
ColoreD DropS SO
OverlY YelloW,
White, Emerald, Clean.

DeeP Pea-greeneD Demure,
LaconiC, Conical conifer,
Suggests to rest, "Ye Merrie
Gents,"
In rich, repleted amber.

SO OfF FoR RegionS ScattereD
DoeS St. Nikolas go;
Looking for lyrical lachrymal fir,
InsipiD, Dispirited soul.

Bonnie Elizabeth Parker
Beyond The Enticements
When you forget that my hair
was long and dark, with copper
lights, and wild and free,
remember the truths I showed
you how to see . . .

When you forget merriment in
my hazel eyes; and on my
mouth, your brand, in
moments after, remember I
gave you

laughter . . .

When you forget the joyous
warmth of me in the dear
tangled night of melt and
tender, remember how I helped
discover splendor . . .

When you forget my soft chant of
passion in your arms, and the
thousand sirens that rang,

remember, Oh, remember
that I sang.

Ralph Anthony DeLeon
EMOTIONS
When people are emotionally tied
They consider one another
They try their best not to
Inflict their hangups on the other
For if they do—what kind of love
does this prove?

Love can be so beautiful
Love can be so bold
Love can be so wonderful
It's not for being cold . . .

Some forget their pride
Their hangups they fail to hide
And when they can't hide them
anymore—
It hurts their partner—deep inside

Let me ask you this
If you're hurt—where's eternal
bliss?
Why should one pay so heavily.
For just a passing fancy?

When all we really need is
Someone who'll be true
Who'll take their time to love
you
And not lay their hangups on you
For when they do—it's through

Dorrie Lloyd
WAITING
Filling in blanks,
Searching for clues,
  Waiting

Seeing here, looking there,
Finding then, hearing where,
Wanting now,
  Waiting.

Come and find me,
Peek-a-boo.
  I'm afraid,
  Will you look?

Count to a hundred,
  No fair, you used tens.

Tick-tock,
Hear that clock.
  Tick-tock,
  Time's up.

Kim J. Schultz
PATIENTLY WAITING

---

*This is dedicated to John
Tomaselli—the most special
person in my life.*

I've never felt the lonliness . . .
Surrounding me each endless night
Or heard the sound that silence
brings
While quietly waiting for morning
light . . .

There seems to only be
emptiness . . .
Silently filling my every day
A feeling without security—
This happened when you went
away . . .

How slowly time is passing by
The minutes now have turned to
days
Wondering how and where you
are
Missing you in every way . . .

Hopelessly staring into space . . .
Seeing visions—not reality
Imagination has set in—
I dream of us and what will be . . .

So now I know the lonliness . . .
The empty feeling I have learned
Wanting only to see you again—
I'm patiently waiting for your
return . . .

Patricia Engle
ON HER WEDDING DAY
Slowly she walks the reverent
aisle.
My tears no shield to her beauty.
Stepping in pace she treads on
the years.
Stepping in pace with memory.

"Woman, alone with one child to
raise
Cannot do right with another.
Please leave this babe at moment
of birth
A gift for some unknown mother."

"No," my cries echo through
reason's halls.
"Your words true to mores unjust.
Knowing myself to heed such
advice
'Ashes to ashes, dust to dust'."

Ideals do not pave an easy road.
World's end appears often in life.
Together we've learned, we have
survived.
Successes abound over strife.

Her path to new joys is completed.
For now there's no need to reflect.
A smile not as that of a braggard.
A smile that will never regret.

Pure love was the cause of denial.
Confidence and faith in what's
true.
The greatest gift one has to offer.
Humbly a gift of you to you.

Valerie Lenore MacQuarrie
LADY DOWN THE HALL
As I lie here waiting,
Complaining of all my aches.
The lady down the hall,
Has had more then she can take.

She cries with pain unknown.
A lady with so much grief.
I wish that I could talk to her,
A smile might give relief.

I'm sure her wrinkled hands,
Have served her family well.
She buried her hasband long ago,
And has had many days of hell.

I think about her family,
Do they know about her pain?
Love is all she asks of them,
Not someone to complain.

So, to you, Dear Lady Down The
Hall,
I'll pray for you tonight.
Praying that your family,
Will finally see the light.

One day I may be down that hall.
Old and wrinkled and blind.
May my children see with their
hearts,
And not by what they find.

For as long as I live,
May I have my children near.
Then that lady down the hall,
Will never shed a tear.

147

Margaret Rose Drake
ONE WAY STREET
Does his heart ache like mine

Does he stop all time and
 try to capture
 one moment we
 might share
 together
Does he yearn to be in
 my arms ever

I wonder . . .

Wendy Laraine Welter
**Reluctant To Accept The
 Way Things Are**
Seven months' ash dryness
relieved by a heavy August rain.
Snails come out of hiding
to cross the still damp suicidal
street.
Crackling beneath tire tread:

I walk past the open graves,
picking up baby snails,
feeling the suction
between asphalt and body,
and place them in the flowering
iceplant.

Toni Rogers
PEACEFUL PURSUIT
If I should from myself leap out
And rise above, my shell without,
Suspended silently in space,
I'd float until there was no trace
Of anger, sadness, fear or pain;
I'd fall down gently with the rain.
A silver cord would hold me there,
And like a kite hung in the air
I'd pause and let the clouds go by;
I'd ride a rainbow 'cross the sky,
And soar beside an eagle grand;
I'd climb into my Father's hand,
And gently then be rocked to
 sleep,
The memory to always keep.

Christopher Petipas
THEIR LAST RIDE
Come all you young listeners and
 listen while I tell,
Of those flashing lights, of Friday
 night
And three people that I knew well.
First there was a party to liven up
 the night,
To make the people laugh and
 sing, til everything's alright

They're sitting around the table,
 wondering where to go
Maybe to the old dance hall or
 even to a show.
They're sitting around the table,
 drinking up their wine,
Their eyes are getting hazy now
 and they're having a jolly good
 time.

But good times don't last forever
 and a tragic thing at that,
They headed to the old dance
 hall with the pedal to the mat.
They're travelling at about ninety
 and OH that's mighty fast,
Just one night of partying could
 be their very last.

And sure enough it happened, the
 car, it hit a tree
And they left this world not
 knowing, how wonderful it
 could be.

The teenagers were identified by
 each parent as they came by,
Staring down at the stretchers,
 where their deceased children
 lie.

The room grew awful silent, then
 a sudden burst of tears,
Remembering all the happy
 moments that they shared
 throughout the years.
They sat around the coffins, not
 hearing a word that's said,
Not making a single movement,
 only staring straight ahead.

A tragic thing that happened
And it's something we will never
 understand,
Why God has taken our children
To His bright and promised land.

Frances Marie Benge Steinert

Frances Marie Benge Steinert
THOUGHTS WORDS

*To Naomi Benge Moore (1927),
Dr. Pauline Benge Johnson (1932),
and Charlotte Hope Benge (1944),
my sisters, of London, Laurel
County, Kentucky, USA.*

The thoughts you think
 And the words you hear

Never, never completely
Disappear.

Edmund Drab
THE SECOND COMING
Apathy continues to grow

Those who care about their world
Slaughter those who don't
The bodies line the road
Soon people everywhere

Hide their faces in disgust
The number of the apathetic
 grows
The number of the dead grows
The leaders expand their control
Weakened spirits don't stop their
 advances
The leaders allow the killing
The people die off
The leaders no longer govern
They commited suicide on The
 Altar of Apathy

Tallak T. Farsjo
OLD BUT GRACIOUS
Autumn's palette has its colors
 sprinkled
On the many falling leaves in
 brown and yellow;
Swirling past the sturdy
 rocking-chair
Where aunt Sigrid sits, her
 greying hair
Frames a face that age has slowly
 wrinkled,
But there is beauty still, the lines
 are soft and mellow.

So long ago, but she can still
 remember
The lovely days spent on that
 western farm.
The cows, the horses, lambs with
 silken fleece;
Pigs and ducks, a flock of
 waddling geese—
A child's delight they were, and
 each December
Her "good luck" horseshoe kept
 them safe from harm.

Gone are the days of play and
 skipping rope.
They past away with dolls and
 tales of "Mother Goose".
Those were the days of trust and
 innocence—
The world was small and nothing
 so immense
That mother's wisdom could not
 with it cope;
Transforming childhood's torn
 into a fragrant rose.

The Springtime now is linked to
 Autumn days
In nature and in life by golden
 memories.
Yes, she is old—but ugly—never,
 never—
Her graciousness makes beauty
 last forever.
Her moves are slower now in
 many ways;
But still her smiles light up like
 sunshine 'mongst the trees.
The hidden youth old age can
 never sever!

Lola Beall Graham
**Back To His Pirate Cave
 Point**
Keith's high-cliff cave had exit to
 the sea—
A knotted rope well-anchored to
 the cliff.
This hide-away still held his
 secret cache.
In old sea chest he'd made from
 redwood boards
Still packed with countless
 treasurers he had dug
From Sandy Dome—still guarding

Pirate Cove
Once pregnant with it's pre-
 historic gems,
He had collected from sea-cows
 and whales.
He often dug for days and
 months in search
Of missing parts, perhaps a head
 or ribs
But never found a single trace of
 them . . .
The Point still turns it's face to
 shoulder storms
And shelter his collection, hid for
 years
Where he had left it at the call of
 war.
Today, war-duty done, he still
 could hear
The pirate's lusty chanty on the
 wind.
He still could feel and dream and
 plan for boys
To dig his bones a million ages
 hence
But at his side his ruthful sword
 should tell
What happened to his missing
 arms and legs!

Millicent D. Johnston
007
Korean jet
Missile met
Over Sea of Japan

Did one spy?
Did one lie?
For sure 269 die

Demonstrations
In all nations
Call for retaliation

Tempers rise
Pray men are wise
Or is it the end of Man

Alyce Black
DESERT OWL
Behold, an owl in miniature:
It clings upon a thumb.
Shades of Minerva! Echoes drum
Through nature's signature.

Through lines remote, but thus
 released,
Laughter keeps its day,
And heart, enraptured, gives
 display
To venerable feast.

Frederica McDill Culbertson
GRIEF
My laughter is buried deep—
beneath my brooding soul . .
It laughed so easily with him,
but now that he is gone,
it rarely rises above the pain
 within.

Florence Stubblefield
STARS AND STRIPES
Old glory waves its stars and
 stripes
 Our land of freedom every day
Other nations at wars and fights
 Our flag we proudly wave

It stands for love and peace
 Concern for all mankind
And hope for wars to cease
 Leave cruelty all behind

Respect and trust in each other
 One peaceful world called ours

Our World's Best Loved Poems

Where no nation should farther
Be concerned of stronger powers
Thank God for this free land
And love for all mankind
United on this earth we stand
This land of yours and mine

Dorothy Jean West
GOSSAMER MIST
A night wind swept
a mist across the land
It gathered form
and became a man.

An appiration
and yet a creature
With firey eyes,
and darkly features

The moonlight captured
his shillouette in
twilight rays
And he wore a nimbus
of jeweled gossamer gray.

Diana M. De La Cruz
Scary Sights On Halloween Night
Goblins and Ghosts are
What we see the most
On that eery and weary
        night;
In which we prepare our
        sight,
To see the unforseen,
To feel the touch of fiend.
And so I say to you—
Make sure that it is true
That you are you.
For such a creepy night
Could follow and scare you
        out of sight.
And then we won't be seeing
What we thought was a scary
eery,
    little,
        human-being.

Kay L. Hughes
MAJOR
As I walked, I looked,
and listened
To all the birds and
sounds I couldn't see.
I listened to the stars and
the midnight air.
Throughout my walk I paid
no attention as to my direction.
I just thought of you
and that maybe I'd find you.
My walk led me up a hugh
hill out of nowhere.
Over this hill stood a large
empty house
All by itself with bushes and
flowers robbed of life.
I dreamed it was new again
with daffodils blowing in the
breeze,
Small kittens chasing butterflies,
and with a sweet smell of pine.
But no matter how hard I
dreamed
it was still lonely and empty.
Like my heart
without you.

Marc Anthony Moffett
MARBLES?
A few days ago
I saw some kids
playing marbles.
I thought it queer

how such an old tradition
had vanished in a new age.

For you no longer see kids
playing with marbles,
or spinning the top.

Jax, and jumprope, and hoolahoops
are all just part
of a forgotten age.
The children of today
will never know the joys
of that distant world.

Isn't it funny
how progress destroys?

Christine M. Trucinski
MOONBEAM

---

*To all who would become that
what they "dream" they can be
and will—"become". Only because
of their "love"; all those-who in
turn-love them.*

What can I say—
that hasn't already been said
or felt or dreamed?
What can I do—
that hasn't been done before?
You've shown me
mountains and valleys and
streams
God's glory-it would seem.
You've told me stories-I've never
known
and never would have suspected;
shared cares and worries too.
I've heard the sound of the water
rippling over the rocks in the
stream
rushing down the river
a sound—I could néver dream.
I've heard your heartaches, joys;
your frustrations scream.
I've felt your desires; love-reach
and touch.
I've seen your loneliness,
aloneness
and quiet strength and anger-
hidden inside.
Partake and find again that part
of life that's yours.
Hold on-go agead and go.
Take that ride on a cloud, on a
moonbeam.
Become once again the woman
that you are.
For it's never, ever-too late-or-too
soon.

Aliene Oldham Blake
THE PAGES OF LIFE
The pages in the Book of Life
are given bright and clean
There to record, not words alone,
but what we really mean.

In infancy they're shining white,
that coos and smiles will show—
Childhoods sunny brown reflect
a healthy, happy glow.

In youth we find a soft hued pink
For heroes where dreams are born,
Where wings are tried and
lessons learned
And patterns cut and torn.

Slowly they ripen to adult blue
with strugles and trials and tears,
To the deeper tones of experience
that bless our growing years.

All bound together with golden
links
given at Heavens door—
Love and Hope, Faith and Works,
and Blessings more and more.

And now we reach the sunset page
washed with Jordans' tide
Reflecting all that has gone before,
the good, the bad, the true and
tried.

But we do not sit, we're writing
still
with an old but steady hand,
Trusting the deeds and the words
of today
will guide tomorrows mankind.

Robin Lynn Schaecher
LOSING YOU
I wrote you this poem,
Because you are going.
But I can't let you leave,
Without you knowing.

That you are special,
And I can see.
How very special,
You are to me

You were there,
When I needed you.
You helped me out,
When I was blue.

I had good times,
I had bad.
I didn't know,
Just what I had.

But you showed me,
My life was right.
By being there,
Just making it bright.

So when you go,
I know you'll be.
As special to others,
As you are to me.

Lawrence A. Souza
OCTOBER NOCTURNE
Where is the kitchen broom?
Have Witches taken it to ride
the midnight skies?

Where are all my candles?
Have children stolen them to light
a Jack-O' Lanterns eyes?

Each tap upon the windowpane is
Magnified a thousand times this
time of year.
Each creak upon the floorboard
will
Echo through the house, to add to
childrens fear.

Is that the flutter of a vampire bat?
Is that the rustle of a big black cat
with eyes ecstatic?
Is that the whisper of a goblin
decending from the attic?

Is that leering face a mask,
or is it real?
Is it because it's Halloween,
the way I feel?

Susan M. Frankson
THE FUTURE
Mysterious,
Fascinating,
Full of hope.

Sometimes frightening,
Always unpredictable,
Quite exciting.

Many times dangerous,
Often friendly,
Living on forever.

The door to tomorrow,
Always one step away,
The Future.

Misha L. Southard
BODY ODOR
Are you ever in a spot,
When you smell a funny smell,
When it's the person next to you,
But you didn't want to tell.

For instance on the subway
I took the backrow seat
I began to catch an odor
I thought it might be feet.

I knew my socks were fresh and
clean
I checked my shoes for globs of
green
I thought these people used
shower to shower
But what they need is to bathe
for an hour

I could not take the smell much
longer
I moved from my seat, but the
smell grew stronger
I stood in the aisle next to the
town merchant
I grinned as he said, "Don't you
use anti-perspirant".

My face dropped under my arm
in shame
And my nose revealed that I was
to blame.

Jim Stevens
THERE WILL NEVER BE
There will never be
A time in my life
When I don't reach out
To hold you

There will never be
A solitary time
My heart doesn't cry
And adore you

There will never be
A child in your shadow
For there will never be
A child quite like you

You always fill my life
With song and music
You make it complete
As only you can do

I thank God above
He gave life a reason
He gave me the strength
To see life through

He reached out his hand
He blessed a perfect child
For there will never be
Another child like you

Victoria M. Aultman
MOTHER'S PRIDE
They all say, "What a sunny boy!"
And it swells my breast with joy
As he rolls with his ball,
As he pads down the hall,
His surprise at a new-fangled toy.

It has only been a year
When he wasn't even here.
But last May out he bounced,
All ten pounds and one ounce.
Now I brag to all willing ears.

149

For each mother loves to compare
With no details to spare.
"At six months mine talked.
At ten months he walked
And was born with a head full of
hair!

I guess I'm a typical parent.
Chasing my son has my day spent.
I don't mind for one day
He'll hold my hand that way
When my hair's gray and my
back's bent.

Elaine Griffitts
HIDDEN LOVE

To Carl, the very meaning of love.

Your face so warm a smile is
there
each time I look your way
It always makes me feel so good
sweet things I'd like to say.

But never does a chance come by
to stop and tell you dear
That you're the sunshine in my
sky
that keeps the warmness near.

Daniel D. Carlisle
LIGHT AT EVENING TIME
Let not your heart be weary
With the setting of the sun:
Lift up your eyes and look about,
And see what God has done.

For He has not forgotten you
Though evening time is here:
He's sent a million twinkling
stars
To show you He is near.

Laura Reese
TEENAGE BEAUTY
It caught my glance there,
On the street.
Her shapely look,
In blue designer jeans.
This new fad, So popular with
the teens.
Alone,
And fancy free.
She's a honey,
Like her honey colored hair.
Done up,
With a ribbon of blue.
Doing things in style,
With what she wears.
Revealing secrets,
In dreamy eyes so blue.
I can't resist,
It's true.
And if only,
Lets' me share them too.
One to be dreamin' of,
Must be love.

Theresa Fidurski
WHO IS JESUS?
He's my Master, Savior
My Lord, My God, My All;

He's captain O' this ship—
Master of this Helm.

No Glory Seeker is He!
He is Quiet, Reverent—
Perseverent—
Penitent is He.

In me; He is great strength.
Not materialistic, not worldly—
He gives me fortitude!

He rocks me in his arms and
comforts me. He is the Spring
board to a greater life.

Greater than He is NO other—
He is my father, my mother—
A childhood friend like none
other.

A friend through adolescence—
Through trials and strains
In to adulthood He still reigns—
Jesus, My Savior, My Friend.

In parenthood there is no other—
To teach me to be a better
Mother.

Bereith Musser
EMBERS OF LOVE
Lingering flames of a summer
romance
More intoxicating than rarest
wine,
Scented by life's mysterious
fragrance,
Forever burns within this heart of
mine.

Love that grew because of love—
Pure, unselfish, tender and strong;
Warm as the sun that shines
above—
Fills my soul with laughter and
song.

Like the embers of a great fire
The memories of yesterday will
glow,
Toasting a love as precious as
sapphire,
Sealed by your kiss of long ago.

Patricia G. Heil
DESTINIES

---

*Dedicated to the memory of a
very special friend . . . Richard Lee
Nesbitt My inspiration so very
many times.*

Another time,
another place.
Still, there are times I come to
face this burning need . . .
. . . that I can't hide.
. . . to be with you, just by your
side.
Through many loves I've tried to
find a way to chase you from
my mind.
Yet everytime,
somehow . . .
somewhere,
I turn, and find you standing there.

I wonder then, if it could be . . .
a need YOU have, to be with me.

Mary Ann Philpott
DISHPAN DAYDREAMS

---

*To my husband, Robert, and my
children, who have taught me the
true joys of this life.*

My hand dipped into the warm
sudsy water
To find that last lost spoon to
wash.
A single tear fell off my eyelash
To become one with the dishwater
Like a single raindrop lost in the
ocean.

My eyes stared vacantly out the
window
Into the briskly blowing autumn
day.
I watched the colored leaves drift
and sway.
In my mind, thoughts swirled
Of the bright promising days of
yesteryear.

I saw the girl with the purpose in
her stride
A memory suddenly come to life
Though now, merely mother and
wife.
"Mommy!" Broken silence. Wipe
your silly tear.
My dreams, with the dishwater,
drifted down the drain.

Tracy Lee Pitts
To You My Dearest Darling
To you my dearest Darling,
All of earth's treasures I'd bestow.
To match your sparkling eyes,
Some diamonds I would show.
To match the beauty of your skin,
A piece of ivory, white.
And for the color of your lips,
Some rubies, red and bright.
But for the beauty that's within,
No gem could show your worth.
So to my Darling I will give,
The treasures of the earth.

Katy Brady
AFTER THE BATTLE
pain
somersalts over
pliable stones
and under
finite skies

lips parted in
frightened expectation of
destructive storms
and
vacant hearts

distant laughter
causes overlapping energies
to erupt
and unleash
tepid tears

Phyllis M. Zueski
MESSAGES OLD YET NEW
God's messages in the bible are
old yet ever new!
The stories of the bible make
alot of sense too.

While reading the bible you'll
find that it's true
The Lord has a reason
for loving me and you!

We need to be like Daniel
in this life of trial—
we must be genuine
with some self-denial.
When we read the bible daily
the sunshines in;
When we walk with God daily
there's victory within!

Janice Wrinkle Stephens
LOVE IS . . .

---

*To my husband—Charles—the
inspiration and love of my life;
You are my life, and may you
always remember how very much
you are loved;*

Love Is . . .

Love is a red rose
bursting from a bud
Love is as rain
cleansing the soul
Love is sunshine
warming the heart
Love is happiness
bearing a smile
Love is nourishment
filling all needs
Love is you
loving me . . .

Eleanor Otto
CINQUAIN FOR DICKENS

---

*To my grandchildren, Noah and
Freedom, native New Yorkers,
whose love for the cosmos and
people comes naturally.*

Piercing
voice for the poor—
orphaned, hungry, abused—
awakens the relentless heart
to love.

Gina Marie Russo
RESIST YE NOT . . .

---

*This is dedicated to the person
who taught me that Love is too
delicate to hold in the palm of
your hand.*

The Heart,
torn and perforated with pain,
reached for the Scar tissue.
But Scar tissue said, "No.
Not until your bruises have
Surfaced
can I materialize.
Not until they have touched the
Air
and become ripe and porous
can I digest and assimilate them.
For you see, I do not Clothe your
pain,
I AM your pain!"

Lori Marie Torgersen
I NEEDED THE LOVE

---

*dedicated to: Daniel Eric Weaks
with all my love . . .*

I was alone with my thoughts,
life seemed so empty;
I felt hurt and broken,

Our World's Best Loved Poems

my heart filled with tears.
The sun would not shine,
raindrops kept falling;
my dreams had all shattered,
then you came along . . .

You cared and I knew it,
 I needed the love;
you came when I called you,
 and through away my fears.
I can see all the feelings,
 so deep in your eyes;
your love means so much,
 you've rewritten my song . . .

Norma Evans McCaa
THERE ARE RAINBOWS

---

*This poem was written for a very
special friend, "Gil". "Natalie"*

Remember, each raindrop
 is a tear from God's eyes.
The lightening, His anguish;
 the thunder, His sighs.
He looks down upon you
 and sees you in pain;
Then reminds you He loves you
 by sending you rain.
God made a sweet promise
 and everyone knows,
That love will survive
 for there are rainbows.

Johnson Wambles Jr.
I AM THE ONE
I am the one that you have chosen,
I am the one that you love.
You look at me my hands are
 frozen.
My soul soars so high above.

Listen to my heart, it is beating,
Each pulse is calling your name.
In my mind your whispers
 repeating,
"No other love could be the
 same."

All my loneliness is forgotten,
All my endless battles won.
Because in my heart your love is
 locked in.
In your life I am the one.

Marc Maton
SOLITUDE

---

*My grateful thanks to my English
teacher, Mrs. McKenzie, for her
encouragement and perseverance,
and to my mother, for her
inspiration and patience.*

Is it not so that solitude is rare?
For in this cruel world on which
 we dwell
One looks for his solitude in
 despair.
That privacy we crave like a snug
 shell
We all want to retreat from time
 to time,
In order to put our thoughts in
 focus.
To ponder and speak with the
 Great Mind
Of the Heavenly Father who
 made us.
Days on this planet are numbered
 and planned;
We have learned to ignore selfish

mankind.
For all will be judged by His
 mighty hand,
And non-believers will be left
 behind.
 Renewed, recharged with his
 strength and wisdom,
 We can again control our own
 kingdom.

Helen J. Sullivan
STANDARD FRIENDSHIPS
Friendship is like the friction
 point in a standard car.
You have to push some, and you
 have to let up some,
gently,
very gently.
If you are impatient or eager,
the car may stall.
But if you take the time
to let it,
it will go.

Teresa T. Cline
**In Memory Of Craig
 Chappel & In Honor Of
 Dee Hartness**
Craig Chappel was more than a
 ten;
 All our hearts he was able to win.

A good example of a Christian
 man;
 He read the Bible again & again.

While attending college at T.C.;
 No one could be more humble
 than he.

At graduation Craig was full of
 smiles;
 Unaware of what awaited him
 up the miles.

Craig and Dee were sweethearts
 in school;
 Until the tragedy came so sad
 and cruel.

On their way home they were in
 a crash;
 Until the tragedy came so sad
 and cruel.

On their way home they were in
 a crash;
 They saw time pass them by in
 a flash.

The angel of death took Craig
 away;
 And left Dee for only awhile to
 stay.

In Heaven someday they all shall
 be;
 God, the many angels, Craig and
 Dee.

Cindy Lou Ward
FOREVER FOR JOHN
Whatever is forever to you?
Is it just a state of mind?
And, what is it to me?
An endless sense of time?
Yet— we say it's forever.
Then, when we say "forever,"
How ever do we define it?
Do we need to?
For what's forever today, may be
 gone—
Tomorrow.
If you ever question today,
And find only your soul points
 the way,

Reach inside and search yourself.
I've reached inside my soul to find
What my destiny has left behind,
And what is still on the way.
But still, whenever I reach I find
You there.
That must be forever.
Forever past.
Forever present
Forever future.
Forever.

Beth A. Pearl
REMEMBER
Forget everything you saw—
the rebellious bullet tearing
the September fantasy. Forget.

Remember love
as a stormy cure,
the ballet pairs with
their windy waltz
in an unprepared dream,
and wake in a rosy field
of smiles.

Michelle Habash

Michelle Habash
PUFF
Puff waits to take his morning
 stroll
Just a small little dog
He travels to the city dump
Whether sunshine or fog.

Old tattered dolls and rusty cans
"My what treasures abound."
Smelly garbage and rotten trash
Such things wait to be found.

Digging, poking in the rubbish
Snooping, sniffing with haste
Looking for a buried relic
"Strong smells, no time to waste."

A bone decayed, lifeless, and dead
This is a new treasure
Satisfaction and contentment
Puff has found such pleasure.

Tad Bigbie
DESTINATION
Driving along, with the sun
 peaking at me from the near-by
 mountains;
A train passes me by, going the
 same direction,
And, I see a hobo standing in the
 doorway of a boxcar;
He is on top of the world.

Anthony Wilder
MEET YOU IN THE DUNES
I believed I had been everywhere
by the time I arrived home
yet there was so much

the lessons of life had to teach
if I had only known

If I had known
the love I had for a girl like you
if I had known you loved me once
if I had known
my love for you
would be true
if I had known I loved you too
I'll tell you what I'd do
I'd write a song like this
I'd meet you in the dunes

we would write our names in
 stardust
and pour snowlight on our song

Cindy Anne Howell
I'LL EVER NEED

---

*This poem is dedicated to Galen
Kennedy; a man who has taught
me much more than he will ever
realize.*

Even if our love turns out to be
 wrong
 I'll always have your memories
 in every love song.
But if it means to be just right
 To you I promise my love from
 morning 'til night.
When you touch me and love me
 the way you do
 That's when I know I'll always
 love you.
So in closing let me just say
 I wrote this poem this very day.
It may not be the best poem
 you'll ever read
 But you're the only man I'll ever
 need.

Dorothy M. Norden
MY FREE WILL
Sometimes, my Father I do so
 wish
That the will Thou gave me, were
 not so free
Then I would love Thee, as Thou
 would wish
No more tears, no more pain
No more sin, no more sorrow
The same today, the same tomorrow

No more thought, is it right, is it
 wrong
Do I, or do I not belong
For I would be the perfect child
Without a fault of my own
That Thy creation made of me.

But "Oh my Father, with my free
 will
One big question I ask of Thee,
By all that is above
How could Thou love a child like
 me?
So I thank Thee, Oh my Father
That Thou "Made" me not to love
 Thee,
But that Thou "Let me love Thee,
With my own Free-will.

Maureen Maguire
PEACEFUL TIMES
In the quiet of the afternoon,
I find my thoughts drifting to a
 peaceful time.

A time when I was alone in the
 woods, walking.
Thinking of nothing in particular.

How I long for that time again,
To be free of these concerns.

To walk once again in the
sunshine,
With a clean, and peace filled
heart.

Joanna Marie Donhauser
TIME
Time just seems to come and go
It just flys by so fast
Minutes become seconds
and the present falls to past

Dawn begins the daytime
Dusk falls into night
Another day will soon begin
with the sign of morning light

The clock is ticking faster
Another day has passed us by
We need something to hold onto
and to time this does apply

Time is way to precious
Please don't waste the day
Life is much to short
We will soon fade away

Tammy Sue Napier
A PERFECT DAY
Remember the best of everyday
for this was good.
Throw away sad memories
for this is good.
Dream about tomorrows coming
happiness
for this will be good.
Live the dream of tomorrow
for this will be the very best.

Vera A. Blake
A STEARMAN DAY

*To a pilot and a plane, and fond
memories.*

I cross the mountains
Of white-ish hue,
The glimmering vastness
Of a sea of blue.

Alas', I look port-side
O'er wingtip outstretched
And realize I'm flying
East lands and west,

In a dream world
Of freedom and flight.
Circling above
Histeria and fright.

I'm in a world
That They never touched,
Envying the Condor.
Hawk, Eagle and such.

Let me down gently,
O winged wonder,
Leave me my thoughts
And mind to ponder.

Mary Grosso Costello
**To Ed and Linda On the
Occasion Of Their
Marriage**

*To my mother and father with
deepest love and gratitude.*

As morning dawns in hues of
flaming pink,
So glowed your love when first
your spirits met

To don illusion's cloak an hour
and let
Your time be passed to feel rather
than think.
But as the sun grew strong, dawn
had to blink
Away the rosy mist with sone
regret,
As love evolved in golden
streams, and yet
The day proffered a clearer wine
to drink.

For sunlight hides no secret from
the eye,
And as its progeny your love will
share
In fruits grown from the true
essence of life.
Therefore, if sunlight guides you
'cross the sky,
Though clouds obscure or
lightning fills the air,
You'll set—having once
dawned—as man and wife.

Colin Clift
**O, Thomas, I Know Where
the Leaves Are Going**

*He was America's greatest
novelist. Parts of his books are
better than the entire works of
most prize-winning authors. I
urge aspiring writers and poets to
read "Look Homeward, Angel", "Of
Time and The River", "The Web
and The rock" and "You Can't Go
Home Again".*

Autumn is
Pungent,
Clinging,
Chaotic.

Autumn is
Somber,
Loony,
Lying.

Autumn is
Geese flying,
Old men whying,
Widows crying.

Saddest of all . . .
Autumn is
Thomas Wolfe dying.

Dennis Michael Murphy
THE MOON & ME
You too, wander alone, barren orb,
Though the heavens reel with
orbiting bodies
Far-flung into darkness . . .
Oceans of black space lie between;
You are but a mote in a void, cold
asteroid,
And shuffle along your fated path
As I along mine, celestial brother;
Like you, I have my dark side . . .
Like you, my ever-changing
phases,
And times when I can't
show my face at all.

Sherri Deanne Glunt
GRANDMA
Grandmas are always special
people,
But there's none as special as
mine.
For she always makes me happy,

And she's always caring and kind.
My Grandma's a great influence
With her gentle and generous
ways.
With learning and patience I'd be
lucky
To be half as great someday.

Jerlene Turner
YOU ARE

*I would like my husband, Toney
to know that this poem is to him
for his great inspiration and belief
in me.*

Sometimes you're soft and gentle
like the drops of a summer rain;
You're strong, yet sentimental
and you're always just the same.

You're a man of warmth and
wisdom,
your warmth you always share;
Sometimes I just get lonesome
and think that you don't care.

To you, I may seem foolish
and a child in many ways,
But I will always cherish
each loving word you say.

I hope to make you happy
and to someday make you proud.
To always see you laughing
and never see you down.

You're the one I always reach for
and I hope someday you'll see;
You're the one I've always wished
for
and you're all I'll ever need.

Anthony Joseph Menezes
THE RAINBOW

*To my father, my mother, and my
wife Premala, and two sons,
Michael and Anthony Jr. In
Appreciation.*

The rain subsided,
The Sun peeped out from the
silvery dark Clouds,
Across the meadows, field, and
mountain streams.
It seemed, t'was a donkey's
wedding, and a monkey's dance,
And, streaked from end to end
was life at its very best,
It was.—The Rainbow.
For life like a dome of many
colored glass,
stains the whole radiance,—of
eternity.
And within me,—thru Its
spectrum cried a heavenly voice,
that I might utter forth,
praise, of every living thing.

For in and out, above, about, below,
t'was nothing, but, a magic
shadow show,
Placed in a box, whose candle is
the Sun
round which we the phantom
figures come and go,
It is, . . . The Rainbow.

Drexel C. Anderson
MASCARAID
What's often said but not signified
Often mean't but sometimes

denied
Also felt but seldom expressed
Often neglected never the less
Just about always mistaken
Some cases not trusted
Tho when trusted always for saken
If you don't know by now
You're one of the lucky few
Can tell this anyhow
It's a thing that's never hurt you
What's there, but when realized,
up and gone
Mostly here today then tomorrow
left alone
When it's not around you want
no other
Then it's in the pom of your
hands, but you want another
Sometimes mistaken and taken
to be
A front only for people to see
I'm sure you'll agree
This powerful sensation with no
idenity
Can hurt anybody
If you still don't know now
Guess I'll tell ya anyhow
It's something everyone's in
search of
A Mascaraid Call Love

Lorraine Merklinger

Lorraine Merklinger
THANK YOU GRANDMA

*To my Grandma for all her love
and understanding.*

Thank you Grandma,
for being with me when
I was down and low

Thank you for drying my
tears that so often fell

Thank you for standing by
me when I was in the right,
for giving me the confidence
to go on thru life

Thank you Grandma,
for sharing your Love
that no one else would give

Thank you Grandma,
for being you and showing
me how to Live.
T. A. Coleman
GOSSIP
Brook skipping over rocks of
colored granite,
Dancing round the log where big
trout sit.
Shining back the sunlight in a

Our World's Best Loved Poems

day long game;
Catch and toss the beams—set
the air aflame.

Mountain sits brooding on his
thoughts of long ago.
Pretending to ignore all Brook's
commotion down below.
A group of pines stand silently to
wait upon his grace.
Sun stops in a royal sky to warm
his rocky face.

Below the dancing Water—Lady,
Old stone—boned King above.
Breeze comes whispering through
the trees,
"I think they are in Love".

Dianna Stockert
LOVE'S FIRE

---

*To Scott McWilliams and Daren
Underwood, and many
unforgetable memories.*

Love is like a fire,
Starts out slow, but the flames
get higher.
In the beginning there's a single
flame,
But more light up just as the
same.

Then on these flames of heat,
Logs are placed so very neat.
And the fire begins to grow,
Its very brightness soon to show.

All through the night,
Forgotten is the fire light.
And the fire burns away,
Leaving "burnt" memories of
yesterday.

At the light of dawn,
It's too late to put more kindling
on.
For the rain has doused the flame,
Leaving one another to take the
blame.

The campsite is deserted by
broken hearts,
Coals are left that, when touched,
smart.
So the coals smolder out,
Leaving the torn-apart hearts
without a doubt.

When, one day, the fireside's dry,
And there's not another tear left
to cry,
Because of the sun's heat,
New flames begin—their cycles
to repeat.

Robert Fredrick
IF ONLY
On a cold and lonely night you
went away;
Little did I know you would not
return;
You said nothing when you were
on your way;
Mistakenly I thought you were
angry with me.

If only I could have known you
were so lonely;
Then maybe I may have been
able to show you what life is;
For you went and took your life
away;
Not wishing to live another day.

If only you would have given it
more thought:
Your sorrow was only a means of
hiding the real you;
In your sorrow the light of love
around you was dim:
In a time of sadness your laughter
slipped away.

If only you would have noticed
the children playing:
Stopped and heard the laughter
ringing in the air;
Taken time to search for
happiness and love;
For my love was there, but it you
could not see.

If only you could have noticed
the love about you;
Could have seen the beauty
around you;
If only is my feeble attempt at
understanding what you did;
If only others can learn from your
mistake and learn to live.

Joyclyn Richards
MOMENTS NOW OURS
Your there beside me, profile
chisled in the light.
We feel the closeness, of an
eternity of yesterdays.
As we stand touching, the beauty
is ours.
Sun brushed ocean glistens, as
day slides down the banister of
coin gold water.
Meeting the horizon, the sun sets
in wet rising fog, misting its
image.
The twilite sky above ripens to
beauty,
While darkness finds beginning
in the starlit night
Of galactic phosphoresence.
Together, we weave these
moments
Into the still holding, of our now
existence.
Blending yesterday with today
while tomorrow waits for fresh
new sunrays
To begin the morning of our
renewel.

Betty Higgins
There's No Face Like Gnome
Under a mossy tree-lined ledge,
there lived a gnarled Gnome.
He only ventured out at night
from his damp and spooky
home.
He really was quite harmless,
although he knew his place.
He thought he'd scare the world
to death so he hid his ugly face.

One stormy night when he was
out, he rescued a Witch from a
stream.
The old hag was so grateful, she
told him she'd grant him his
dream.
"Give me one to love me," he said,
"to share my lonely old life."
So she zapped him with her
magic Wand, and gave him an
UGLY wife!

Cheri A. Felts
UNRETURNED LOVE
I think of you, my love
Morning, noon, and night.

I thank the powers above
For making you just right.

How much you mean to me,
I guess you'll never know.
If only you could see,
The way you set my heart aglow.

I love you for who you are,
And it stands without reason:
I'll love near and far,
In each and every season.

If we could be together
For just a little while,
I promise you'll want me forever.
I'll always make you smile.

But mine is just a passion
That will never be known;
Except in my imagination
That won't let me alone.

Karin Gustafson
UPSTREAM
Silent Water-Strider
So much like me
Swimming steadily upstream
Diligently

Dedicated
Determined
Only to stay where you started

Karen A. Sparacio
YOUR DANCE . . .
Tonight you will dance,
And fly across the stage,
For tonight is your chance,
To put the audience in a daze.

With your hair in a bun,
And your stomach in knots,
The music has begun,
And you'll dance quite a lot.

Your eyes in a gaze,
Your legs very tense,
The lights all ablaze,
And your heart in suspense.

Balanced by your toes,
With your head held high,
The audience arose,
With a deep, soft sigh.

Offstage you prance,
Oblivious to the pain,
But tomorrow you'll dance,
And find your way to fame.

Irene S. Laymon
TAKE MY HAND
Take my hand
As a friend should do,
Take my hand
It's offered to you.

Hold my hand
For the strength you need,

It's offered freely
No need to plead.

Now venture forth
And do your thing,
Challenge life
There are no strings.

Stand errect
Stand up tall,
You will succeed
You will not stall.

I will wait
For you to be,
What you choose
With pride I'll see.

Now, you've done your thing
You've made your stand,
And all because of a
True friend's hand.

Edith P. Hazlehurst
HAWAII MEANS ALOHA
The things which mean Hawaii
Mean Aloha to me,
Palms which wave at sunset
And moonlight on the sea.

Children hunt for Puka shells
Or play on their guitars
And sing the old Hawaiian songs
As they sit beneath the stars.

Sailboats scurry homeward
And women make their leis,
Tourists have their dinners
At the sidewalk cafes.

When I dream about Hawaii
I see such lovely sights—
Especially near the ocean
On the moonlight nights.

I feel the soft caresses
Of the Polynesian Trades.
I feel the fond Aloha
Of the pretty Island Maids.

Yes, the sights and sounds and
atmosphere
Of Old Hawaii Nei
Will always mean Aloha
For I love her more each day.

George A. Wiens
BUT ONCE A YEAR
There is a day that comes around
But once in every year.
A day on which we tell our love
To those that we hold dear

We should not wait until that
day
To demonstrate our love,
For we should show it every day
As God does from above.

We send a pretty valentine
With a message printed bright
Instead of using our own words
Each morning and each night.

Don't limit it to once a year
To say "I love you dear",
But say it every day you live.
It will help to bring some cheer.

Shari Marie Fowle
THE REAL JEWEL
Love and Life . . .
Can only be compared,
To a most lovely gem—
The many facets,
Each angle diverse,
Yet, contained within itself,
And then reflected;
    Refracted to all the others.

153

So . . .
Is it confusion?
Or perfect harmony;
Symmetry?
Or the beauty of imperfection;
Asymmetry?

The colour and cut . . .
The clarity . . .
Fuse the masque of true form,
Dulling the brilliance,
Of the real jewell . . .

Substanciating questions,
On which one's mind can
   dwell . . .
No longer, blindly assuming,
To know the facts, so well . . .

Katherine E. Cartwright
AUTUMN
The golden leaves, like golden
   butterflies
Fall-drifting on the slow, sweet
   autumn wind
There is no sadness as the old
   year dies
Death, too, has beauty, for in death
A soul returns to its home in the
   golden skies.

Huey Raydine Horton
BLACK WIDOW
   she's been known as the
      Black Widow
      since she was fifteen
      ruthless, bold and mean
with vengance, she preys on man
   building her a place to stand
where no man can ever reach her
      again
staying in control is the only way
      to win
   she's beautiful, charming and
      catchs every man's eye
   with a look that will paralize
   you into doing her bidding
and if you think, you can out do
   her, your kidding
   she will chew you up and spit
      you out
there's no man too cunning or too
      stout
   she weaves her web with love,
      laced with hate
there you lie, waiting for your fate
if you ever find yourself, in her
      web of love
   looking up at her high above
don't try to climb up by her side
   I know, I'm one who tried
      to stand beside her
   just to get stung by the Black
         Widow spider

Jeanie Scudder
A ROSE COMMUNICATES

*And ye shall know the truth, and
the truth shall make you free.
John 8:32*

A rose is no ordinary, wet with
   the morning dew, plant!
A rose communicates; causes
   commitments.
The wind kissed petals transmit
   signals;
Melting hardened hearts.
Monitering love starved creatures.
No, no, no! No artist ever painted
   the rose that communicates!

Intoxicating scents fill the
   begging nostrils!
Sensitising; accelerating new
   found love.
A rose communicates.
A rose is a glimpse of God!

Iceal Bouchard
DREAM IN THE DAWN

For those who know and love me.

Two spirits of youth who meet
in the dawn of a dream,
so alike in soul and song.
The fresh dew of the dancing sun
meets their heart's at the peak
of a thought not yet voiced
between their conscience of mind.
They're so close together,
yet so far apart.
They speak one to the other,
   only—
in thoughts that pass between as
   their eyes
meet—in tender silence.
The aura of sameness is felt by
   them both—
though no words of such pass
   between them.
They say nothing, their
   commitments belong
to two others—caught in the web
of the Dream of the Dawn.

Jean Cummings-Lounder
WARRIOR AT DUSK

To Billy

At dusk he comes, softly, like the
   wind
When o'er the prairie it fans the
   tall wild grain.
Out of the shadows of templed
   mountains high
That rise in mist above the
   earth's dark plain.

Slowly he makes his way along
   the path
That has known the thunderous
   sound of the buffalo.
Alone he comes astride a mighty
   steed,
And he gazes where he met the
   charging foe.

Gone forever is the heated battle
   cry
Of the mighty warriors as they
   rode in full array,
And the nightwind brings so
   softly in the evening,
Only echoes from the past of
   yesterday.

At twilight time when earth and
   sky are blended,
Alone he comes with soft and
   quiet tread,
He waits, for soon the shades of
   night will number
A lonely brave with the proud,
   but fallen dead.

Kay Reeves Cooper
FIRE'S REVENGE
dancing wildly
across the fields
so wild
so free

such danger spilled
causing havoc
wherever you roar
so mean
and spiteful
destructive you are
defying all else
to encompass the earth
how selfish
how frightening
your evil mirth

Delores Wentz
THE PLANETS
Hydraulic mobile
curved by the sun
position in spacetime
relatively won.
Matter ditched open in oval graves
pale impregnable naive slaves
silently ring a young sun
where in
a red giant sleeps.

Marie Geile
TO UNKNOWN WORLDS
In the darkly night
When the Sun abandons
                    the Sky
And the Moon powers . . .
Starry Gems of Galaxies far
                    illuminate
The vastness high.

Walking below
On darkened streets . . .
I cast my eyes
To the Celestial brilliance.

You entice me
                    Heavenly lights
Of mysterious Space . . .
To reach out
                    to you
With friendly hands . . .
To touch yours
That are different from mine . . .
      To embrace . . .
            To love.

Wilma Byford Lamb
NO PITY
No pity do I crave
No sorrow when I'm brave
Understanding is my need
When I try to do my deed
Death is sorrow enough
Pity takes the tough
Tears you cannot bluff.

Joan Sajnovic
SOULS HAD KISSED
You mystified me and captured
   my soul
Came into my life, set straight
   my goal.
It was by chance our sullen souls
   met
When you gave some words, my
   hand I let
Starting a union of life to set.
The seed was planted, souls had
   kissed
Our eyes had seen, my heart not
   missed.

I forgot you till by second chance
Our bodies met, you set me into
   trance.
You gave me attention and advice
You gave me woman's worth, told
   of your vice
Which added flavour, pinch of
   life spice.

A flower blossomed, souls had
   kissed
Our eyes had seen, my heart not
   missed.

You raised me up and let me
   down
You held my heart, then you left
   the town.
You mystified me, entered my
   heart
You captured my soul—thus we
   did part
We could have had meaning, a
   great start.
The plant was buried, souls had
   kissed
Our eyes had seen, my heart not
   missed.

Alice Evans
REFLECTION
You're only, a reflection in my eye.
A golden lock child, with sad eyes.
Oh! Mirrow, of teary waves.
How can I awaken to, a reflection
   of a sad face.

My image is weak, but I feel so
   strong.
As I walk back and foreward.
Singing sad songs.
Oh! Mirrow, take away the bright
   eyes, glamorous lips, and make-
   believe smile.
You'll only have, the reflection of
   me.
As I drift through life, pretending
   to be free.

G. Thomas Bramblett
**I Bid You Adieu To My
   Boys**

*This poem was written for Jeff
and Dos Bramblett by their
father, Tom Bramblett, shortly
before his death on November 11,
1981.*

I am not really gone
   Not as long
As my memory can
   Lite your face with a smile
And lift your chin
   In a lovely grin

My sadness was all my own
   I did not mean to leave you all
      alone.

When you were little
   And I was younger

Life was easy and I was near
So to hear all your fears
Even share your small cares
You see—you gave reason
To my existence.

I lived to see you grow strong,
But still Life would not leave me
alone.
I left Life but not you,
I should hope to live on
As a smile on your pretty faces.

God Be With You.

Hazel Snow
LIFE
Much have I pondered on the
way of life
The love, the hope, happiness and
fellowship;
The hate, the anger, sadness and
revenge
Depending on God's guidance
that I won't slip.
Back to being self-centered,
lacking compassion
For I must project Christ to my
fellowman;
Thinking of others, forgetting
their faults
For we are all creations of God's
holy plan.
Attending a family reunion after
too many years
Of not seeing so many of them
since we were so young;
Happiness and sadness of life
swiftly passing
Talking and laughing, mingling
and having fun.
Thinking back to other times and
what we did
As a youngster at gatherings
watching the old people
Now I saw the young, looked
around and wondered?
Older people, where are they?
with relief
The answer came—now we were
the older generation.
How sad to think life had so
swiftly flown
But thinking back it has been
good to live,
To have a family and see them
now grown
Out on their own—
compassionate and loving.
The final days of my worldly life
I'll gladly live for Christ my King
Knowing that God's peace will
end all worldly strife.

Doris Ullman Barbuto
OCTOBER NIGHT NOISES
That loud grumbling and
growling
Is "Dependable," the bus
Transporting weary night folks
But *not* without a fuss!

I hear an angry cat call
And a low, threatening cry;
It's no doubt Crusher Morris
Defending turf nearby.

I listen at the window
To a flapping garage door,
To breezes playing spook-games
And bringing waves ashore.

That's just wind in the branches
Swishing in the cold damp air.

A little creature's footsteps
Stir fallen leaves out there.

Brakes screech at the corner STOP
And then, VROOMS the car
away;
A taxi stops, a door slams—
My neighbor's home to stay.

I listen to the raindrops
On the trash cans "clink, clink,
clink."
I see faint light of dawn now
But haven't slept a wink!

Kati Vail Carter
ASTERIA
The song of the stars
Cause the evening to darken
And the shadows to deepen
In deference to sorrow

As I think about this
I join in the song
And mourn soft and sadly
With them

And the clouds
Like so many curious people
Crowd and stare and wonder
Then slowly pass us by

But they couldn't hear
The singing
And they wouldn't understand
The song.

Michael E. Gray
DIFFERENT DRUM
He walks the way of weeds and
brush
That no one has trod before.
Away from all the hustle and rush,
He has finally shut the door.

The way is marked with broken
hearts,
Tears fill puddles like rain.
Unlike the players knowing their
parts,
His steps are never the same.

Who can know the walker's step?
No one can fill his shoes.
He hears the beat of a different
drum,
Whose beat he did not choose.

Donna Richardson
CHILD OF THREE
I happened along
Just the other day
Upon a child of three,
Or so it seemed to me.

I stopped and leaned,
So that she could be better seen,
And chatted away,
Just she and me.

As I straighted myself,
Attempting to leave,
A thought crossed my mind
Of innocence inside.

How perfect to be
So unprejudice and clean,
How sad it is
To have to relearn at 23.

Essie K. McClure
A FLIGHT UNCHARTED
I owned the world, the day I rode
the Ravens wing . . .
Majestic mountains encompassed
the sky . . .
My head atilt, I gazed at rivers,
trees,

small . . . insignificant . . .
I . . .

A rainbow circled round the
earth with love,
God's promise to the world in
days of yore . . .
it's beauty unadorned . . .
unmatched . . .
by Man's attempt to even up the
score . . .

My cares like a mantle fell . . .
from weary shoulders burdened
down with woe . . .
I owned the world, that day I rode
the Raven's wing,
we soared and dipped and flew
again . . . and so . . .

Aloft, upon the Raven's wing, I
flew
above spun-sugar clouds and
then . . .
I gazed upon the Earth's most
wonderous sights
and . . .
hurried home again.

Donald Fields
AUTUMN FORGIVES

To Jason—Whom time will tell

I'd like to glide
on the tide
of the high spirits.
When I'm on the streets,
I'd like to talk
with distinction when I walk.
To give me strength,
when I'm not dreaming of it.
And when Autumn comes,
it forgives.
Then the leaves will fall.
God bless us all.
So when we lay down to sleep.
We'll wake and can relate
to those who hate and won't pray.
For Autumn forgives.
The earth of man, to grow green
again.
Because it can't pray.

Lou Morgan
TEAR DROPS
Do you ever wonder
where one comes from?
That tiny crystal ball.
That can grow into a
flowing stream.
From deep with in;
a well of feelings.
A spring is formed.
To wash the soul.
The healing water flows.
The single tear drop
can quietly wash away,
with just the little spray.
The hurt and·sadness in it's
own simple way.

Johnnie Earl Fountain
I Write This Song For You
I sit alone and think of you
A friend that captured my heart
I cry very deep inside
Hoping our memories will never
part

I write this song for you to hear
One so special to share
And as I lay down to rest
I know your friendship is there

When I write I think alone
Hoping that you could hear
And as I speak in a soft tongue
I can feel your presence near

So many things I wish to share
So many smiles I find so true
And if but one wish to be granted
That is to share my books with
you

I write this song for you alone
And I know that you'll understand
As each day fades away
I'll always be a writing man

Let me be your friend for life
And let my wish come true
To share with you the books I've
written
And the life that I once knew.

John C. Sweetwood
THE GIRL (J.C.S.)
Some people say she's cute,
To others she's just another girl.
But to me she is a dream.
I think of her always, & when I'm
Alone I call her name.
She knows not who I am but
loves me just
the same. Maybe someday we'll
chance to meet,
But till now, she's just a dream . . .

David S. Kurtz
SEASONS
When spring's fresh sunlight
thaws the frozen earth,
and your smile, like a delicate
flower blooms,
don't be afraid to dream for a
brighter future,
though others fear the renewing
breeze of change.
And when summer's golden
touch warms your soul,
inspiring your spirit to sail on the
ocean of life,
don't be afraid to search for new
horizons,
though others lack the vision to
imagine them.
When the stormy clouds of fall
hide the stars of fate,
and raindrops gently caress your
face like tears,
don't be afraid to master your
destiny,
though others may proclaim to
hold the key.
And when winter's snow casts its
icy shroud,
let your heart's glowing fire warm
and guide you,
don't be afraid to fulfill your life's
dreams,
though others may fail to fully
understand them.

Melissa Heinrich
WILL THERE BE?
Will there be a future for the
children of today
Will there be a chance to live, a
chance for yesterday
Will there be a dream, a hope, or
a prayer
When we ask those questions,
they just sit and stare.

Will there be a war where loved
ones have to fight
Will there be a death of someone

close each night
Will there be a chance, a chance
for us to love
When we ask those questions,
the answers up above.

Will there be a bomb which will
one day end us all
Will there be a day when we all
will hear the call
Will there be a time when no one
has to die
When we ask those questions,
they think they have to lie.

Sally Lynn Towns
SPRINGTIME CANTATA

*Dedicated to the one I Love,
James D. Simon. The only one,
who could make a difference.
"Look to the light Jim; Find your
Purpose."*

In your eyes I see reflections.
Softly you take my hand—
Words can't touch this feeling;
The tenderness understands.

Springtime freshness within
embrace, your entity has
        enthralled—The swift
        response
came naturally, eminant as I
recall.

Gently you wiped my tears away,
now I'm beginning to see—
That tomorrow, everything's
going to be alright; Won't
you stay awhile with me?

Rosalie Chasteen
TEARS AND MEMORIES

*To four special people who
encouraged me— Bonnie, Connie,
Billy & Paula. I love you Mama*

You think that you're seeing
        tears in my eyes—
But it's memories flowing
        like rain from the skies.
'Cause I remember yesterday
        when both of us were free—
With all the world ahead of us
        And now there's only me.
You think it might be raining
        But the skies are clear and blue,
And the memories keep flowing
        of all his friends and you.
We all remember yesterday
        The memories flow by.
The question still lingers—
        I'll always ask why.
But you think you're seeing
        tears fall from my eyes—
Now you know they're memories
        like rain—falling from the skies.

Jeanine Marie Ondreka
STARTING TODAY
I know
Theres been times
That I've really messed up
And for that
I am truly sorry.
        The look in your eyes
        Or the way you talk
        Shows me I've done wrong
        And thats all I need . . .
            . . . For Starting Today

I will try
To clear up
Some of my bad mistakes
To show you
How much
I really 'do' care
And yes . . .
I'm trying . . .
    . . . right now.

Dorris A. Western
YOUR EYES

*This poem was written to and
inspired by a very special person
in my life—He knows who he is .
. . April 29, 1979*

What is in my heart
        I cannot say
But I can show you
        in my own special way
I will caress you with kisses
        from your head to your feet
        and deep into your loving eyes
                I will forever peek
For through your eyes I see the
        world
        A secret world of beauty
                like the oyster hiding
                        the pearl
        Secrets and Beauties
                Beyond compare
These I see, when into your eyes I
        stare
So, love me now,
        if only with your eyes
And I will lift mine—
        up to the skies.

Bernadette Timp Phillips
THE SENSUAL SIN
In weary, I weep,
And pine for passion's rise;
To delve in a revived affair
And search wild, secret, eyes.

Oh, to drift—
The sensual sin,
As lovers, as one,
Unreined at last, from within.

John J. Freund
THE QUIET RAINS
The quiet rains have fallen at
        night,
time for animals to get some rest.
Wake up in the morning to the
        light,
and the plants grow at their very
        best.

Walking through the rain soaked
        woods,
the trees shine most of their
        colors.
Knowing this has done some good,
by standing away from all the
        others.

All the peace that we have today,
the rainbow flys across the sky.
Nothing else could look that way,
and nothing ever could even try.

With all the noise it's all so loud,
getting away from this race.
It has darkened most of the clouds,
time to go and find another place.

The quiet rains have come to an
        end,
and all the animals stay out and
        play.

Do we all have someplace to
        attend?
And let everything grow all day.

Carl Eubank Olson
WINTERS SUNSHINE
How long have I been sleeping
Please, let this not be a dream
I remember leaves falling last
In this changing scene
Now chrystaline-white, feather
        light
Butterflies of winter, dance all
        around me
Landing on one anothers wings
Taking place of birds branched in
        the trees
Some the tracks of passing cars
Others fall behind houses and go
        unseen
Walking through this mist of
        amazement
In a world that seems unreal
The beauty of life has captured me
I love the snow this year.

K. J. Harrigan
I LIE SO STILL
I lie so still amid the night,
The breeze caressing me with
        delight.
I lie so still amid the night
That if you were to see me there
You might think
        that I had died.
And if you were to touch my hair,
So deep within the realm of
        dreams am I,
I would not stir.
I would not stir
Even if you were to kiss my cheek.
But if you were
To whisper softly in my ear
        "I love you"—
            I would hear.

C. L. Valentine-Fleming
REST
Garden of troubles
beckoning my hoe
young plants but stubbles
tickling at my toes
visions of bubbles
weeds by my foe
I come here to rest
not to do my best.

Robert M. Cook
A TALE OF LIFE
Back at our dawn in the mists of
        time
When our fathers were given
        birth,
They basked in the blush of
        innocence prime
And reigned as lords of the earth.
But now we grope in our night of
        despair,
For our world is growing old;
And eternity is heard to declare:
"Life is a tale that is told."

What have our mortal annals
        defined
As the text by which we tell
Whether our souls will be
        consigned
To the reaches of heaven or hell?
For all of our wisdom in the end
Is a faded scroll unrolled
On which is scribed by a faithful
        Friend:
"Life is a tale that is told."

Cry havoc amid the ruins of race
And the rubble of selected breed
That were monuments to our
        conceited grace
Where we've capsuled our blatant
        creed.
For our spirits no longer gather
        heat,
And our hearts are waxing cold
As we realize in our crass deceit
Life is a tale that is told.

Patrick Murray
THE OCEAN
Contained in definite horror
Waves pounding shoreline
The Ocean speaks, Enter my ream,
I am the blood of the world,
I am related happiness, I am doom,
Men in ships tortured because
they say they conquered me,
My radical thoughts stimulated
by life, destroy your meek cities,
Don't under estimate me,
My life is endless,
Yours is at my feet.

Shirley Osby
**I Love To Go Riding With
    My Honey In the Rain**
I love waking up at midnight and
        talking until dawn,
I love knowing that loving me
        will never bring you pain,
I love knowing that past mistakes
        are forgiven and forever gone,
And I love to go riding with my
        honey in the rain.

I love sipping coffee in the wee
        hours of morn,
I love playing rook until it's
        rattling my brain,
I love watching old movies,
        eating tons of popcorn,
And I love to go riding with my
        honey in the rain.

I love long hikes up treacherous
        mountain trails,
I love having you rule as King of
        our domain,
I love knowing you will be there
        when my body becomes frail,
And I love to go riding with my
        honey in the rain.

I love waking up with you every
        day of my life,
I love God for allowing your love
        for me to obtain,
I love the fact that I forever will
        be your wife,
And I love to go riding with my
        honey in the rain.

Mary M. Barnes
PEACE OF MIND

*With much Love and Tenderness.
I dedicate this Poem to my Son
Lenny. may he find the treasure
of which I speak*

        Peace of mind is a
Treasure, we should
        all strive to find,
If not always, then
        at least part of the
time, What is this
        thing? This feeling
that seems to dodge
        and elude? This thing

Our World's Best Loved Poems

we seek so hard to
achieve, and fail, and
saddens our mood?
This thing we reach
for, search for,
and pray to gain?
But then only to
find, it was all in
vain, For once more
we've failed, Once more
we've been denied'
Once more we've faced
defeat, and once more
we've cried, But hope
is never far away,
Hope is ever there!
Hope, we never have
to search for, And with
hope, we'll never despair!

Margaret Tapia

Margaret Tapia
KINDNESS

---

*To my brother, Monsignor
Aureliano, with affection and
gratitude.*

Kind words have always touched
me deeply;
Indeed, they murmur in my ears
so sweetly . . .
Never will I forget those who
were kind to me
During the terrible years when
happy I could not be.
Nothing can possibly erase the
features of a smiling face.
Every moment of kindness is
more precious than a golden
lace.
Smiles, encouragement, and
kindness—together,
Surely give one the best "human
weather"!

Elizabeth Moore
WHAT YOU MEAN TO ME

---

*To my Mother, Whom I Love
more than the World!*

Do you know what you mean to
me?
Do you know how my heart
swells of love for you?
Do you know of the roles that
you play in my life?

You are my guide; guiding me
safely up the paths of life
You are my teacher; teaching me

the steps of living
You are my friend; sharing your
thoughts and feelings with me
You are my doctor; nursing me
through pain until I am smiling
again
But most of all you are my
Mother; a mother who I laugh,
cry, and share my feelings with
as she is the only one who
understands me

For all you are to me; I will
forever be the Joy of your Life.

Ethel Pearce
MY CHILDHOOD CHORES
I carry water
I carry wood
I think that I work very good.
I wash the dishes
I sweep the floors
I make the beds
And I go to the store.
So when my days work is done
and then we have a little fun,
I say my prayers and go to bed
to rest my tired and aching head.
So as Mom and Dad tuck me in,
I want to thank you Lord once
again
for giving me such a lovely family.
One who cares and lets me be me.

Susan Rummery
THE LIFE I SEE
I feel as though my sight has left
me,
an opaque steam covering my
eyes.

Losing the rose-colored glasses,
and the reality it defies;

Shedding my childish layer,
reborn once again;

Facing up to the real world,
a world of death and sin.

Witnessing life as it treks on,
yet, not a vision I see.

As if it were a punishment
by some royal decree,

My life spins circles,
knowing not which direction is
right,

As I continue to greet each day,
holding back that desolate fright.

Victoria Yeary Lindsey
CORNY—WHY NOT?

---

*To my brother, William C. Yeary,
for his support and encouragement.*

'Tis only a matter of taste, I'm
sure—
(the arts from "pop" to the "Met"),
but a juicy melodrama, savored
slowly like corn from the field,
is so deliciously tempting, I'll be
there, you can bet . . .

The hero-old-or drunk-or poor—
Or just as well-all three;
Man or woman matters not.
Pathos is the key.

Faded glories pass 'fore our eyes.
So splendidly, see how—
Bayonet bared in battle victorious
Fades back to the dust and
grime of now.

Or queenly idol of stage or court
Struts proudly 'cross our view—
Splendid, dazzling in her role,
Then suddenly back to fade anew.

From here the mad pace gathers
momentum—
Crashing crescendo of brass and
drum;
Guns a blazin' in hot dusty
highway,
Or screaming notes sung in
agony become

An epitaph, written in retrospect,
Praising our hero of the past.
So savor the tears of poignancy,
While calling it corny—if you
dast.

Ms. Sharon Thompson
OUR JOURNEY TO LOVE
Into the night,
finally free of neon and breaking
shadows,
I bury my eyes in the night
and we drive towards the roads
end.
The tracks in the snow cut the
hill in half.
A bath of light, shuddered from
the frozen
moon fades toward the white
reflection of your
eyes. Love, this night is a night
for holding
the moon like a fragile glass of
wine.
I know that soon I will take your
white
arms as the moon claims our skin.
As I glance at you I can feel your
thoughts.
Your memory is rocked by things
you haven't
seen. Even now the facts are
wrong.
The sharp winter wind cuts a
steady moan,
one that we ride across the moon.
We sit and watch the stars
breaking through the
fog on the horizon; the skies a lie.
The silence upon the field holds
us in its
steady light.
I've come to know your body and
your eyes
the way a child might memorize
his favorite fairy tale,
I need the reading once a night
the same
as children do.
I don't want to be anywhere
except here
with you,
but soon this will be just
another memory,
as will the winter moon.

Elizabeth Conrad
WINTER STORM

---

*Dedicated to Maria whose heart
is pure and whose life is love.*

Aligned with time
In winter storm
Of freezing rain
Lay sculptured form
Brimming the Cliffs
In wonderland

Are glassy like trees
Just over the dam

Only the memory
Of summer and fall
Dress back the trees
Of the rushing waterfall

Malcolm Scott Mac Kenzie
METAPHORS OF WONDER
Mirrored glass palaces of classical
man,
Water shades, timid petals,
Reigns contemplation, grace
prevails
In this domain of the gesture.

White gesture, long inquisition of
a retiring fawn
In gentle paddling, lithe inquiry,
A passing of the queen,
Soft sight treasured by the
fettered if seen,
The water's ephemeral marble
beauty,
Phantom pearl of gentle
consideration,
Beyond the plans of planet beasts
An ethereal sky murmur,
A soft sigh of the saving grace,
A little girl in wonder, crouching
in braids
Before a bubbling frog quickly
sprung,
Then a shadow in water flight,
she observes
In a steady gaze, a distant mystery,
The swan.

Dorinda Harvey
**The Love I Once Had For
You**
The love I thought I had for you
has now gone away
It wasn't in the things you did
but in the things you say.
You say you're sorry all the time
But forgiveness for you is so hard
to find.
You once showed me how much
you care;
The love we had was all so rare.
But now we've gone our separate
way;
I remember the things I had to say.
Most of all our love was true.
We had started off fresh when
love was new.

Adam Sabatino
SLEEPING DEATH
Sleeping Death
Behind a mountain
It's in the air.
Chained to the ground
Like slave rainbows
They sit and watch
Somebody rearranged the Earth
The clouds bring invisable rains
There pulling the Earth apart.
Night time daylight
An Indian crys.
Acid storms destroy plantation.

Visions of non headed people
Sleeping in a box
A universe all to themselves
There lives creeping away
Into the air
Daylight now Dark.
There binine Sleeping Death
Behind a mountain.
Rearranged is the rain that never
falls.

157

Marla Jeanne Mosher Copeland
PRAYER FOR MY FAMILY

*To All My Children, you each
have all the love in my heart. The
joys and love you have given me
have made my life so full of
memories and the most precious
rewards. No sweeter words were
ever spoken than, "I Love You
Too, Mommy."*

Thank You for my family, Lord,
   each child You gave to me.
It took my strength to bear, these
   precious ones I see.
Help me show them, Lord, more
   like You they should strive to
   be.

I love them more and more, Lord,
   as each day they grow.
They are relying on me, they will
   become the seeds I sow.
Help me teach them, Lord, so You
   they come to know.

I hope that I prove worthy, Lord,
   of this job You've given me to
   bear.
I want them to be real Christians,
   and not my heart to tear.
Help me guide them, Lord, Your
   love and joys I want to share.

They are important to me, Lord,
   these people from my bones.
I want to be with them, I want to
   see them grown.
Help me make them strong, Lord,
   to go out on their own.

If by my fate, Lord, I must leave
   them while they're small.
They'll need You more than ever,
   please don't let them fall.
Help me now, Lord, to always
   give them my best and my all.

If I must ever leave them Lord,
   don't let them feel alone.
Don't let them feel life's been
   unfair, a bitter feeling be
   unknown.
Help them understand, Lord, You
   could not wait to see their
   Mom at home.

I want them to remember, Lord,
   one day we can all be together.
A time will come when, Your
   loved ones You will gather.
Help them realize, Lord, Heaven
   with You will be much, much
   better.

Donna Rochelle Harrell
AT HOME BASE
The world today needs a lot of
   correction; it is very far. far
   from perfection. God made this
   world for us to live and share
   together: through out our
   earthquakes hurricanes and all
   this type of weather.

People lets love one another and
   reap understanding I try, get
   thrown off but I'm still in
   commanding. Loved ones let's
   open wide our hearts and feel
   some compassion; storing
   sincere beautiful emotions is
   really old fashion. Allow God

to enter your hearts and
   massage your minds; everyone
   has one there are just so many
   various kinds.
We all live here together we
   should try and make the best
   of it. With all this hurting and
   cheating: we should really
   know who benefits.
We should think positively
   optimistic; study your bible
   and rejoice. For until our
   mortal beings die; here we shall
   remain: we really have no
   choice.

We live life a series of confusing
   ups and downs; often smiles
   are converted into protective
   distrusting frowns.
Together here we shall remain
   until the time is chosen for
   thee, until the time comes for
   our souls to ascend and
   become really and totally free.
There are pleasant time like
   these and difficult times in
   which enhances our sense of
   understanding; hatred and love
   often battle it out, but love is
   far more demanding.
The time has come for me to rest
   my case; I have worded a little
   to much, especially when so
   many condemn my views and
   dare not believe in such.

Mary McGlasson
IF

*I dedicate this poem to the Glory
of God, in appreciation of the
talent he has given me. To the
members of my Family, for their
love, support and encouragement.*

If everyone in this whole world,
   loved peace like you and I
There'd never be a war cloud, to
   shadow our clear blue sky.
God above loves one and all, no
   matter who or where they are
So why can't we, live and love,
   here, and in the lands afar.

If we would only live, by that dear
   Old Golden Rule
Bring our children up, in church
   and Sunday School
There'd be no broken hearted
   loved ones, faces stained with tears
We could be so Happy, and our
   youth, could live out their years.

If we would only share this love
   of ours, with God on High
Spread his praises round about
   and shout them to the sky
There would be no hatred, or
   dissension in our ranks
There'd be No Military Training,
   for those men we call "Our
   Yanks."

Joanne M. Malpass
DOG

*To Sandy Truly my Best friend
for 12 years of her life*

Devotion of goodness to mankind
   from our maker in heaven.
A friend for their lifetime or for
   our lifetime.
To share good times and bad
   without making any judgment
   whatsoever.
To be a friend when all others fail
   or to be there when all else fails.
I know why you are here.
It is to guide us when all else
   seems endless.
The love from you never ends.
Like God's love for us, it's endless.

Kathy Ackley
LOVE ETERNAL
I wonder what time,
   Will do to you and I?
Our love is growing ever so strong,
   It will last through time no
   matter how long.
Someday you will sit in that old
   rocking chair,
   And realize you have lost a little
   more hair.
And I will see as I look in the
   mirror,
   The facial wrinkles that I feared.
Soon we will realize one of us
   must go,
   If I am chosen first, I want you
   to know.
That when my soul has gone to
   heaven above,
   I'll send down God's angel of
   love.
She will bring you to the pearly
   gates,
   Where patiently I will wait.
And when you pass through you
   will see,
   Our love will live on for
   eternity.

Ed Mentz Jr.
**My Toast To The Ones I
Love**
To my friends,
And family, too.
This is not the end,
But something new.
I've asked you here
So glad you came.
And for those who couldn't,
Well it's a shame.
For I love you all,
My families, old and new.
For folks like ours
Are rare and few.
And friends like ours,
I not only trust, I truly treasure.
And they are the friends
I love forever.
So sit with me and celebrate.

Please stay a while, but not to late!
And here's a toast to my
   charming wife
She is my friend, my love, my life.
   CHEERS!

Scott Warren
I LOVE YOU

*To Barbara Lyon, Just because I
love her.*

I love you in the morning,
I love you after noon,
I love you in the evening,
With or without the moon.

I love you in the springtime,
I love you in the fall.
I love you in all the seasons.
But wait, thats not all.

I love you on a mountain,
I love you near a stream.
I love you in a valley,
and I love you in my dreams.

My love for you will never die,
I know it's here to stay.
Because you see,
I loved you yesterday,
But I love you more *TODAY*.

Wendell T. Stoye
Fiesta Island Wonderland

To Mary my wife for sharing life

There's a spot in San Diego
In a place called Mission Bay
Within is "Fiesta Island"
Where wildlife and humans play.

They call this America's finest city
Of that you can be proud
When you view the scenes of
   beauty
That you and I are allowed.

Such a variety of wonders
And just plain things to do
Upon land that was created
To be used by me and you.

There seems to be some magic
That keeps a being entranced
When one looks at all the beauty
You know this was not made by
   chance.

There must be a greater power
That can create without man's aid
But think of the great creations
When two work together unafraid.

Just look what's been done on
   this land
By nature and man as a team
Creations that please and pleasure
with joys and joys supreme.

Katy Clarke
THE ROOM
Sleep overtook her quickly.
In her dreams she looked forward.
She saw a large and unfamiliar
   room.
The room itself was empty.
But two doors and a window were
   there.
Behind one door she heard music
   playing.
Through the window she viewed
   a spring afternoon.

But, the second door held no clues.
She stood thoughtfully pondering
what to do.
She loved the spring and its
newness,
Yet feared new situations.
She enjoyed the music and
wanted only—
To dance to it and let it take
control.
Still, no sound from the second
door.
Could it be the present, past or
future?
No matter—the risk is too great.
And so she stood, never
venturing further.
Neither going back or changing
position at all.
Slowly, she opened her eyes, only
to find,
She had never really been asleep.
How long had she been in this
room?
No matter—it was safe and
warm—
Here she will always remain.

Darlene Parizo
BOBBY

---

*I wish to dedicate this poem to B.
G., for whom there will always be
a special place in my heart.*

You're always on my mind
I try not to think of you,
But, you are always there
demanding some attention.

I want to reach out and touch you
But, I can't.
I want to tell you of all the
Love I have for you
But, I can't.

For I'm not even sure if it's love
I'm feeling for you.
I do know it's something
But, what . . . I don't know.

Donna Penna Ruggiero
Once Upon A Mountain
Once upon a time, there lived
upon a mountain
A man who made his home there.
And we talked about this and that,
Every now and then.

He possessed a certain wisdom
And understood all that
surrounded him.
He always knew just what to do
And we walked about here and
there
Every now and then.

And every now and then
time would pass between us.
But never did he ask where I'd
been.
He believed and knew I'd soon
return to him.

We shared a lot of special
moments
Times only I would have known.
Things about myself he showed
me
And we cried about this and that
Every now and then.

He told me stories of times gone
by

And from these stories the
lessons I should learn
And as my times go rolling by
I think about this and that—
every now and then.

And every now and then
I think about a world without him
But deep in my soul, I think I
know
That without him there would
exist no mountain.

Tammy L. Coursey Crickmore
**Fauna, My Horse; My
Friend (12-16-82)**
On this day, written above,
I lost someone, someone I love . . .
A someone that shared my
dreams with me,
and helped me make believe
real . . .
He loved me, I could tell, We
came to know each other, so
well.
He had his moods, as I did
mine . . .
But when we rode off together,
everything rhymed.
There were many nights and
many days we two were as one,
making our way to the sun . . .
Coming home tired, with peace of
mind, truly content with our
find.
Knowing well again we'd go,
When the time was right, we
would know . . .
My friend is gone, I saw him go,
in my heart it hurt me so.
The look in his eyes when the
door was shut,
The scared, pleading eyes,
saying don't make me go . . .
I looked in his eyes, my eyes
filled with tears,
them answering no, I love you,
Fauna, but you must go.
You will like it there, new things
to explore . . .
And before you know, it won't
hurt anymore.
I know it was for the best, in time
it will hurt less,
But in my heart, he will always
be there . . .
In my dreams, we will still ride
everywhere,
Maybe someday we will meet
again;
Until then . . . Goodbye my
friend . . .

Renee' I. Swanson
MISSING YOU
When you're away from me
The smiles don't come so easy.
I lay and stare at the ceiling
Trying to fight this low feeling
My rainbow loses a little of its
color
The blue sky is a little paler.
I am just missing you.
And when this is all through
We'll all be together
Running, smiling, listening to
the laughter.

Vicki J. Trowbridge
LOVE
Love is a sweet something,
That only the heart can know.

It's born in only an instant,
But its feelings grow and grow.

Its fragrance lingers endlessly
As its moments come and go.
And only the one who bears its
weight
Knows just how deep it goes

Love can be a curse or a blessing;
It can be a thorn or a jewel.
And for those who are hurt by its
incidents,
It can be exceedingly cruel.

Love's origin is not of intellect;
It is born of a bird on a wing;
It is that which moves to
exhilerating peaks;
And causes each ones heart to
sing.

So give of the love that begot you;
Don't sell it, just give what you
can.
And, so soon, your life will be
rich and full,
As you share love, for this is
God's plan.

Laura A. Dillon
FAMILIES
F-is for Father: the Father who
works hard all day to keep
things going.
A-is for Affection: the Affection
spread throughout the family
with hugs and kisses.
M-is for Mother: the Mother who
is always doing considerate and
thoughtful things to ensure the
family's happiness.
I-is for Images: the Images of
parents that children wish to
follow.
L-is for Love: the Love expressed
between Dads and Moms, and
Brothers and Sisters.
I-is for Identity: the Identity of
each family member that is
recognized by the other
members as important, special,
and unique.
E-is for Everyone: Everyone who
gives a little of their love to
make the family complete.
S-is for Smiles: the Smiles passed
back and forth within the
household.

Verlie J. Tomasik
**Sine Qua Non (without
which not)**

---

*July 4, 1983 "Family Reunion" For:
My Brothers Frank and Cliff
George In Memory Of: Richard
and James Inspiration: The
courageous spirit among all Life
forms.*

The somewhere was there it
seemed following grandaddy
dragons sinuous lean into far
horizons dreamed.
O'Love that on the way mist!
Down that Old Road of Promise
old highway 66;
Testing . . . Tasting . . .
From the oceans warm quick and
play and the crashing chill leap
of way,
To the final waves echoing cry!

aye' aye'.
Long years hence old 66,
free . . . yet fixed, gulped by
the dragons seed; flowing tail
whipping the highrise
scene . . .
The somewhere is nowhere it
seems,
Yet; We Know may not know
where . . . what . . . know it
is not,
Sparrow-Hawk hollow and
pokesalad greens.

George E. Simmons
**Conversation On A Park
Bench**
He couldn't read a word, he said
and he couldn't write his name
for a man to be so ignorant
I thought it such a shame

Then he spoke to me, of love and
life
and how things ought to be
of brothers killing brothers
and how all men should be free

And he spoke to me, of women
of beauty, love, and fear
and he talked about his
childhood
and I think I saw a tear

And he talked to me of nature
how he loved to see things grow
from the oceans and the valleys
to the mountains topped with
snow

Now how a man, could be so wise
was such a mystery
and I felt that shame, ten times
again
but not for him, for me.

Jennie M. Root
CAROL MY DAUGHTER

---

*Words cannot express My
thoughts of all her lovliness. She's
very precious to me.—her
mother.*

Carol's not just only beautiful
But she's happy, loving and true
To many others and not a few
Though trials led her to be
merciful.

Her home's a very comfortable
place,
Where there's always lots of
cheer
With loved and her children dear,
Tables spread, food a plenty on
lace.

Carol loves to read her Bible,
God's word to her is bread
And gets wisdom from what's read.
No wonder there's no rival!

She lives each day in trust and
hope
To see her dear Lord up above
Who sacrificed to show his love.
But finds some people hard to
cope.

She stands firm to her
commitment
Too precious to let slip away
Whether great or small each day.
She listens to her guide God sent.

Gloria Ebeling
LOVE BALLAD
"Candlelight, wine and thine", Oh,
if this were only mine.
How I long to be with you, just to
feel you so near—such a
longing Oh my dear.
Seems so very long ago, that we
both together stood—Your
gentle breathing in my ear.
Your warmth—so close—
Your smile at our little jokes.
The sharing that we knew, Oh
how I long to be with you.

Cathy Ah Sam
LOVE WAITS

---

*To Judy Bruzus, an inspirational
source.*

Like the fickle wayward wind
You sigh a breath of hope
On dying embers of passions spent
Hot cinders glow of love long pent

Years removed, in flesh you came
I try to still my fluttering heart
As forgotten memories of love
unfold
Live, the ardent lover chance
dreams foretold

Fervid pain of first love loss
Mask smiles cannot disguise
Betrayed by profile of discontent
Too late the errant lover penitent

Parting, our spirits entwine
Flames fade, ashes remain
Once again I wait
Return of love wholly portrait

Alfred Vanek

Alfred Vanek
LOVE

---

*To my super-loving daughters,
Marie and Rita—I think they're
the greatest.*

So difficult to measure in
most units that we know,
Its volume spans a sprinkle to a
drenching overflow.
It isn't purchased at a pump
and paid for by the tank;
Nor will it gather interest when
it's locked up in a bank.
It's not described by color or
contained within a box;
Nor is it made to fit the feet
like shoes—or maybe socks.

It comes with all the seasons, yet
most often in the spring
It may afflict a person with a
sudden urge to sing.
It generates the type of warmth
that empty arms can hold
And often prances to the young
or, hobbles to the old.
More precious than a polished
gem it grows, much like a tree;
And, should you give it all away
it soon returns, you see.

Susan Merrifield
Caught Without Contacts
Soft voice, gentle manner,
Like leftover caring of
A once important lover
Or the toddling interest
Of a newborn one;
You smile, an indulgent smile
To my attempted banter,
While my eyes frisk yours
For hidden harm;
Image smeared, unclear—
Selfish playboy/simple friend—
Reaching to wipe my glasses,
A handsome man murmurs
A quiet goodbye,
And I never see
Who
I said goodbye to.

Steve Bailey
**For Emily, When I Find
Her**

---

*With each day that approaches,
something, or someone quite
special arrives. One day, you'll
come, if it be a decade; to melt
the cruel frost from my Summer.*

---

soft rays
of red sunset,
on the sandy
shores of
Lagerfeld;
two black birds
centre of
it's ring.

L. Frances Taylor
LOVE'S SWEET MYSTERY
No sweeter songs
ring in my ears
Than the songs
of the midnight birds
They sing a melody
of love to the night
Wish my love
could hear their sweet words
They sing
of Love's sweet mystery
Of a longing
to be fulfilled
Of a need to be wanted
and loved by one
Who could make this longing
be stilled.

Elizabeth M. Callahan
**A Prayer To The Blessed
Virgin**
Maiden Mother, meek and
mild . . .
Look upon thy little child.
See her humbly kneeling there,
Hoping that you hear her prayer.

Guide her through each weary
day,

Whether at home, at work, or play
Help her please, to know "His
way",
Please guide her, don't let her
stray.

She is just a little child . . .
Who needs a mother's love,
And who but you, could be the
one?
Oh, Virgin Mother, Holy One.

Bestow thy grace on her we pray.
Help her please, until that day
When she'll need thy help no
more . . .
When she passes through
heaven's door.

Stacey Junck Bishop
TO THE PARENTS

---

*To: Little Jon and Mr. & Mrs. B.
With Love, From a student nurse
who cares*

God blessed you with a precious
little man,
Who's special in every way!
And though at times he can't
understand;
He loves you more each day!

Your laughter, your tears . . .
Your hopes and your fears . . .
Will help your child to know;
That discipline and approving
cheers
Are meant to help him grow

And if at times, life seems
unkind . . .
You feel like there is no hope,
Look into your hearts and you
will find
You have the strength to cope.

So remember as you live each day,
God blessed you in his special
way!
And when the world is said and
done,
God chose your little boy to be
his special one!

V. Mony Snyder (Virginia Jacques)
SILENT AS HELD BREATH
Circuitous ochre path—narrow as
a snake
Running through harsh brush at
the foot
Of rocky hills scrambling down
the right;
On the left, shrill scenery in
staggered levels
Falling from a rugged bluff
isolated from itself . . .
A runway of 'lazuli' sky pressing
in—
A remote jeweled river upside
down,
Frozen in its flow until a lone
cloud puff
Drifts by—slow as a dream that
does not want to die . . .
Satisfied to be tolerated on so
solitary a 'lapis'
Stretch. On a rock shelf, a solitary
alow grows
—Not very romantic, it, yet
How special in this so stark
topography
Of no flowers or trees—only the
scent of death . . .

No single sign of life save itself!
. . . No animal or insect stir; no
bird or beast
—Silent as held breath . . . No
pond or pool,
Croak of frog or of cricket
alert . . .
Silent as the silence in heaven
At the time of 'Armageddon' . . .
But no merely half hour silence,
this!
Here, silence's stillness has, along
with me,
Given way to time's stop into
eternality . . .

Susie Gilkison
TEARS OF DARKNESS
Darkness falls all around
Silence deadens the streets
Of the town.
Off in the distance a baby cries,
Tears of pain fall from his eyes.
No one to love him,
No one to care.
He'll grow up lonely,
He'll grow up scared.
As he grows older, he runs
further away,
No place to go, no place to stay.
Now again as darkness falls,
He cries once more, behind
closed doors.
One shot is fired,
Slowly, he falls to the floor.

Cynthia A. Delaney
WHY?

---

*To those who have faith in me,
especially James King.*

Why is the world flat
and said to be round?

There's an explanation.

Why are some people dumb
but not always stupid?

There's a reason.

Why do we have war
but want peace?

There's always a solution.

And why do people try to solve a
universal problem when they
can't
even solve their own?

That's the question
That has no answer.

Patricia A. Lawrence
SATED
Pluck you days from out
tomorrow
One by one, as grapes from off
the vine.
Ingest their essence, taste their
flavor,
Feel the satisfying texture 'round
your tongue.
Slowly savor each new dawn;
Let trickle past the hours,
Gentled by the dancing,
tendrilled breezes.
Inhaling heady, ripening aroma,
Feel the warmth of sun-splashed,
summer afternoons.
Then satisfied when evening
comes,
You'll be not fearful of the night.

Our World's Best Loved Poems

Judy Hyatt
A PRAYER FOR LOVE

To the one I love

Heavenly Father up above,
Please protect the one I love.
Keep Him always safe and sound,
No matter where he may be found.
Help him to see that I love him,
Even though I make it look dim.
Keep us now. Keep us forever.
Happy, Loving and Always
 Together.

Beverly J. Robertson
VISION

*I dedicate this poem to Dr.
Frederick K. C. Price. I feel he has
truly taken part in fulfilling Gods
beautiful vision in giving his life
in a ministry that is life.*

God had a beautiful vision, so he
 created you and me.
He saw it was possible for us to
 live in peace and harmony.
He gave us many opportunities to
 prosper our lives, so he could
 see, just how profitable our
 lives would turn out to be.
He gave us a free will to make
 decisions right from wrong,
He gave us a paradise called earth
 where we'd belong.
He surrounded us with blue
 skies, flowers and trees,
He gave us animals of many
 cultures along with beautiful
 birds and bees.
He wanted us to be happy and
 our hearts filled with joy, so he
 didn't create us to be operated
 as mechanical toys.
It is sad to say, but most of us
 have not helped this vision to
 come true, those that dared to
 develop and improve our
 surroundings, have only been a
 few.
I think its about time for us to
 make a quality life decision, so
 we all can take part in fulfilling
 Gods beautiful vision.

Donna S. Carre
AT THE PET SHOP
There once was a skunk with a
 stripe
When touched he'd let out a yipe
He lifted his tail
Said, "I'm not for sale
My perfume is not your type."

Mildred Koval-Battersby
CALENDAR
Skaters stand in
 frozen pose
Silver blades beneath
 their toes
Mufflers suspended in
 mid-air
Rolling days off
 the calendar.

Faith Franciscus
ONE DAY
I sit and I think
 about so many things,
 inside me is a missing link

a lost feeling it does bring.
That missing piece is apart of
 me, that has gone to you,
 you've let it free now what
 do I do?
I care for you dearly every
 minute of the day, cause your
 so very near yet so far away.
When I hear a song
 my feeling go astray
 my imagination grows strong
 and I think maybe
 ONE DAY.

Barbara Wirkowski

Barbara Wirkowski
A Blue Rose For a Broken Heart

*This poem is dedicated to
Thomas, my magician friend.
Who has made my world a
mystifying blue.*

A rose was meant to say I love you.
A rose was meant to say I care.
But darling when you hurt me,
 your love was no longer there.
So take away the rose you gave
 me, and make it blue instead.
And the thoughts of what you
 done to me will linger in my
 head.
So darling please send the kind of
 rose you wished it to be.
A blue rose for a broken heart,
 that was especially meant for
 me.

Dorothy Jeanine Hall
GRAFFITI ON MY HEART
Opening the door you'll find
 every word we shared.
The soft romantic whispers,
 everyday fanciful chatter, an
 occasional grapple.
All have been inscribed here.

You move on noticing the intent
 drawings on the chamber walls.
In every picture there's a
 realization of the loving
 relationship we had.
You can see it in every brush
 stroke of our springs in the
 park, summers at the beach,
 falls at home on the phone, or
 winters in the classroom.

As you turn to go a tear spills
 from your eye. You think it sad
 that we had to part.

Then out the door, you leave
 again.
And I'm left with just a grafitti on
 my heart.
Epilogue:
Some of the best things in life
 hurt, especially when they're
 over.
But we still keep it's memories in
 our souls. And when we are
 reminded of them it hurts all
 over again.

Rebecca L. Bird
NATURE'S SYMPHONY
If tickets are sold,
Any seat is front row.
Wind sings,
A seagull keeping time.
The composer is creating.
Everything is tranquil,
Renewed by the melody of a
 sunset,
I the only audience, Eagerly
Applaud the reprise.

Nancy Dean Hubbard
PARADOX
No one beside me as I lie down at
 night,
No face across the table,
In the early morning light.
No one to laugh with,
No one to whisper to,
All that's left for me now,
Are just memories of you.
You said because you love me,
You'll have to go away.
That it's a sin to hurt me more,
As would happen, should you
 decide to stay.
But I forgive you and love you
 still.
Even so, it only seems to prove,
The cruelest sins of all are those
Committed in the name of love.

Natalie Jo Basile
MEMORIES . . .
As I walk along that dusty road,
I cry a painful tear.
The memories of you and I,
Were once, but are no longer
 here,
I remember walking hand in
 hand,
Love circled overhead.
People were ill when you were
 gone,
Because my longing spread.
I want you to know, that painful
 tear,
Is something lost in my mind.
The happiness I felt with you,
I shall never have to find.

Debra A. Marler
OUR LORD
A baby was born in a manger
 long ago on Christmas day,
 little did the child know for
 man's sin He would someday
 pay.

As He grew He spoke of God, and
 His father's undying love, He
 knew He would be crucified
 and reign in heaven above.

He taught us to love others, as
 did no one else before, He gave
 to us His wisdom and love, and
 opened heaven's door.

The time came, the skies grew
 dark, and He was led away;
 they crucified Christ, sealed
 Him in a tomb and laughingly
 walked away.

Three days past, His loved ones
 wept as they went to where He
 lay, but Christ had risen from
 the tomb—He saved us from
 "death" that day.

The baby that was born in a
 manger long ago on Christmas
 day, now reigns high in heaven,
 and I'll be with Him one day.

Linda L. Patty
PICTURES
If a person could draw a picture
 perfect in every way,
With the millions upon millions
 of words we have to say,
Think of that perfection of art
 with all the colors told
And all the curves and bends and
 such, and differences, bold.
There would be the pains and
 strains of harshness there
That stand out for all to see
 against the beauty bare.
O, what a picture we could paint
 so perfect in every way,
If we could learn to see those
 things we miss in our every day.

Lori Jean Long
NATURE IS THE PAINTER
The brush leaves wispy strokes of
 bright summer blue
Puffs of white cotton blown
 across a clear canvas,
Nature is the painter-her palette
 is the colors of the rainbow.
Her portrait partly completed . . .

The spectacle of God's winged
 creatures in flight
Above the billowing coarse of a
 roller coaster of grass,
Brings a smile of inner content to
 the painter—
 nearly finished . . .

In a far corner near the frame
 stands an isolated daisy
Her bright face upturned basking,
 in the illuminating warmth of
 the nourishing sun.
 C'est finis . . .

Nature is the painter, her
 talent is imprinted in the
 recesses of our minds,
Her masterpiece will hang
 forever in the museum of
 our memories.

Michelle A. Baldine
IT IS TIME
It is time
For the leaves on the trees
To sprout anew,
And the rain to form
As morning dew.
It is time.

It is time
For the world to be washed
Fresh and clean;
For the flowers to blossom
In the spring.
It is time.

It is time.
For spring to pass,

161

For the rebirth of nature
To grow, but not last,
Soon to die with summer past.
It is time.

It is time
For me to go,
To trudge through the forests
And the cold, mountain snow.
To search for my heart; for it is gone.
It is time.

Michelle Peoples
LOVE IS
Love is a sigh in the wind on a cold winters night.
Love is the gentle song birds sing in flight.
Love is a special feeling of friendship that you feel deep inside, a kind of emotion that you can't define.
Love is like flower blossoms that fill the world with joy.
Love is seeing a child's happiness over a new given toy.
Love is helping each other get through hard times.
Love is holding hands, walking in the sun and sharing each others lives
... Love is like a diamond the hardest substance in the world.

Stephanie Rene Black
MOVING MEMORIES
We moved to town and left behind all our friends dear and kind
Our house is bare, our garage cleaned out,
I guess thats what moving is all about

Our dog is with neighbors that lived next door
Gee, they always hated him before.

Our address is forwarded
Our second car is sold
Getting a new life, throwing away the old

My school records and shots all sent away,
all sealed and signed and mailed today

All the furniture is cleared onto the truck,
saying goodbye,
saying good luck

Driving away and leaving behind
An old house full of memories
Those old memories running through my mind

Of thinking how I'll probably never see this place again
... of thinking how I lost all my friends
... of thinking what my life will be like
hoping that it will be just right
'cause new friends are hard to make
when you move to a different place

Kathryn M. Diana
A LITTLE THANKSGIVING
This is the way it was today.
The bread rose high, baked crusty,
Coaxed us into the kitchen.
I hung new curtains, fresh and

white;
They move softly in the breeze.
And a prayer was answered.
The summer's winding down,
And my husband loves me . . .

Our granddaughter put her hand
In mine and entrusted me
With her little world
And our quicksilver grandson, far away,
Piped a loving greeting
Over the phone to me.
The flowers, refreshed by morning rain,
Are full of autumn splender . . .

I know so well
That I have earned no fortune,
Have no claim to fame,
More problems than answers;
Then this is not fulfillment
So I'm told. Still . . .
Thank you, God; I feel
That you've been good to me.

Stacey Leigh Weaver
HURRY UP SPRING
I can't wait for spring to come,
And bring the smell of rose and mum.
Goodbye chills, snow, and mush,
Hello fresh smells and peaceful hush.

Put away the colds and chills
And bring out flowers on the hills.
Flowers of every color, shape, and size,
Out of the fresh grass they will rise.

Bring out the birds with little hymns,
And beautiful sunsets as the light dims.
Bring out the blue, blue skies,
And don't forget new butterflies.

The smell of spring is fresh and new,
Especially the fresh droplets of dew.
Hurry up spring, don't be late,
Hurry up spring, I can't wait.

Donna E. Yohey
A Christmas Poem To My Family
This year it hurts me the most out of all the Christmas's I've Lived,
To know I have no presents to offer, so this poem to my family I give;
To you Mother I give you the Love from my heart and a promise I intend to keep,
I'll never hurt you again and never again will I cause you to weep;
To you Father a hug and a kiss and a promise that you will soon see,
that I will grow stronger each day, so you'll never have to worry about me;
To you my Brother I give you my support, my advice, and my care,
And if you ever need someone to talk to your little sister will always be there;
To you my daughter I give my

Life until the very end,
And a promise always to remember that I'll never ever Leave you again;
You four mean the world to me, God bless you all I pray,
No presents can I offer, only my Love this Christmas Day.

Dulce Maria Garcia
UP
The pedestal
  where is it?
 the world is different
  from down here
  everything is tall
   taller now
 everything with
  gigantic dimensions
  and I . . .
   small
   helpless
 So small, so helpless
  frightened.
 Those monsters
  will step on me
  one day.

Tonia Di Iorio
Privileged Poetic Autographs

Dedicated to "Mon oiseau de bonheur" whom I met October 1982, and who inspired me enormously. Quebec.

Avid reader and admirer
Of those unruly poetic autographs,
Meticulous, honorary and brassy
Or protagonist caricatures ever classy.

Gray, Stevens and William Blake,
Dostoevski and Marianne Moore,
Guest, Pound and Tupper,
Baudelaire, Nemerov and Lorca.

Ole'
Robert Graves, Keats and Yeats,
Carnauba trees and phallus symbols
For those implacable and impeccable feats.

Wynema Walker
ODE TO MY LOVE
Beholden to the Senate Vow,
He stands as others see him now,
Versatile and sustained.

Yielding when the case may be,
Within his reach substitutionally,

So others may take the stand,
To woo the point that he has manned.
His Colleague's call him Henry Clay,
And he can seek and find the way,
To win and yet be loved,
By those who feel defeat.

Amorous and yet no poet,
Ever spoke of one more masculine,
Or adverse to feminine dynasty.
His morals high and yet,
A thread is loosed it may be said,
By eyes of blue and hair of red.

Beholden to the Senate Vow,
He stands as others see him now,
Versatile and sustained.

William L. Bongard
ALL ABOUT DREAMS

To All Persons Who Are Blind.

Every dream has its celestial
Meaning of many majestic
Visions of heavenly thoughts
That are reasoned fantastic.

Within the realm of reverie
That casts a shining reflection
Upon the everlasting beauty
Of daydreamer's true perfection.

When you become very drowsy
In accordance with a dream
The image will be perfect
With a pleasant theme.

In a long peaceful dream
For a recurring rest
To feel the divine guidance
We shall be truly blessed.

Kent Jay Mudgett
FALL IN LOVE EASILY
Fall in Love Easily,
we all need to be held,
feeling oh! So pleasily,
our souls would meld.

cheerful warm tender flush
from a smile kiss and touch
tickel, hug and blush
to be in love so much

never stop never leave
a open heart would bleed
an empty shell i'd be
only to fall in love easily

Jean M. Donley
CHILDHOOD MEMORIES
She sat there in her highchair watching every move I made,
I was busy in the kitchen making lemonade.
What a nice day for a party, so sunny and so cool,
We could take our glass of lemonade and sit out by the pool.
I picked her up and took her out and sat her on the grass,
And mixed sugar in the lemonade and poured some in a glass.
She seemed to love the sunshine, the flowers and the breeze,
She loved to watch the butterflies and even liked the bees.
We sat there long and happy just soaking in the sun,
I loved that quiet afternoon with my precious little one.

She took me back to childhood
days when nothing was a worry,
When all I had to do was play
and never in a hurry.
I thought of many times when I
was just a little girl,
How my mommie always liked to
put my hair up in a curl.
I thought of times with lemonade
and sometimes even tea,
I thought of cookies mother made
that filled my heart with glee.
My thoughts just seemed to float
away so high up in the sky,
The clouds all seemed to take on
shapes of people passing by.
I picked her up and held her and
kissed her on the cheek,
She loved to have me cuddle her
but didn't make a peep.
She sat there with her big blue
eyes just watching as I pondered,
Can she know just what I'm
thinking—Sometimes I do
wonder.
You see, she's not like you or me,
or anyone at all,
She's just a precious memory of
my little old rag doll.

Sarah How-ree Nichols
BARKING FOX

---

*For Peter Wing and Chad
Nichols, my favorite demolition
crew. Also Mel and Mistie
Nichols, and Mel III, always
supportive.*

In October, the first cold,
Barreled purple windy threats,
Over Indian Summer blue,
And sent the ground hogs deep,
And put the snakes in
rubberband lumps.

In the frosty, bitter, glitter,
Of white frost,
A fox, hungry and tattered,
Barked.

J. L. Cusyk
VENEZIA
Venice, romantic city wedded to
the sea.
Love abounds, dreams of poets
or a spell cast on all?
Canals run like veins,
carry tourists on the Grand Canal,
past Rialto and the birthplace
of Marco Polo.
She lives for today. Hurrying with
the present, revelling in her past.
Were Italy alive, Venice would be
the heart.

Nellie Parodi
LIVE TODAY!
Yesterday we set sail, innocent,
joyous.

We dreamed, knew happiness,
and suffered.
Lived, we have!
Much more did we learn
in the true book of life
than in the halls of wisdom.
Our lips tasted the hemlock
when we hated.
but the ecstasy of love dulcified
them!
We fell into deep chasms of

despair.
Happiness lifted us to heaven!

Today we near the port of our
destiny
and almost visualize the end of
the journey.
The hold of our vessel brims with
treasures
of our life experience.
Yesterday was a dream;
tomorrow, a vision.
We have only tody, the elusive
instant
that will never return!
Let us enjoy the wonder of this
moment,
the sky is blue,
the sun resplendent,
still the rose perfumes . . .

Pearl RHB Camacho
WINGS OF FLIGHT
I take to the sky upon wings of
Light
In God's grace I follow the Light
His breath carries me upon the
winds with ease.
Spread my wings, soar to
firmaments height
Soon to be at his Throne.
Upon my wings of Flight—
continue yet on.

Judith Ann Grayson
ALONE

---

*This poem was inspired by my
loving parents, Roger and Vera
Grayson.*

The night—
Still.
The air—
Heavy.
The surroundings,
Quiet and lonely.
Only the sound of
Silence is heard.
There are the sounds
Of breathing,
But really
No one's there.
Only the still of the night
And two amidst the silence.

Ruth Webber
PATIENCE

To Earl With Love

I have not yet learned to walk
As sure footedly as you
So be patient with me then
And know that if I do my best
and really try
I will attain the goal for which
we both are striving, bye and bye.

If you have gained the heights
That I as yet cannot see
Come to me and point the way
And in my dim lit vision
I will not stray
If you will walk along with me
today.

Eddie Heavner
STEVEN DEVEREAUX
Swamp-mist walks the graveyard
near the Bayou St. Germaine.

Thunder hums the prelude
to the coming of the rain.

On the marble headstone
the mold begins to grow;
seeking to erase the name
of Steven Devereaux.

Endless days have vanished
and time has gone astray.
Years creep by so sadly
when love has gone away.

None has missed you more than I,
and none can ever know
how I've loved you all these years,
my Steven Devereaux.

Janell D. Davis
FRUSTRATED
Words don't always come easy
I often wish they would
So many feelings inside me
Perhaps misunderstood

Attempting to relay the message
So bottled up within
To free these scrambled thoughts
Where does one begin?

Rose Hawke
LIFE'S JOURNEY
Life is like a Journey—from
the beginning until the end,
So make use of every minute
of every hour that you spend,
Take time to treasure every
Blessing—savor every flower,
For you can't change yesterday
Nor touch tomorrow—so be
thankful for this hour,
Live it to the fullest—give
So that it may be given back
to you,
Then you will have no reason
For regrets, when your life's
Journey here is through.

Bethel Nunley Evans
CRAWL UNDER COVER

---

*Dedicated to my wonderful
children: Ann and Edward Moore,
Janelle and James Evans; and to
my precious grandchildren: David
Bass, Michael Bass, and Kellene
and Art Galloway.*

What a terrible picture I must
make
With my nose rough and red
And running like a faucet's leak.
My eyes are swollen nearly shut
With only slits from which to
peek.

My heart pounds like a
drummer's beat
As my pulse races two to one
To tell me the fever is rising.
I try to think it is nothing bad,
But the thermometer is not
disguising.

There is a hammer in my head
Beating like a drummer's stick
That makes my nerves feel shot.
I think if I don't feel better soon
I'll curl up and request a
forget-me-not.

Then the calls start coming in
From all the family and friends
Offering a remedy for whatever
ails me.

By the time I've tested all of them
I'm sneezing my head off with
allergy.

I feel like somewhere along the
way
There must be a lesson to learn
From this little episode.
Perhaps it is best to crawl under
cover
And flush the remedies down the
commode.

Anne M. Nitopi
OUTER SPACE
Golden moon hanging low
in lavender twilight skies.
Resting on the horizon
it inflates to twice its size.

And as it slowly rises, I
am with it; readily I go.
Transported through existence
on silver wands of moonglow.

Soaring through the universe,
I hold on very tight—
dangerously beaming through
eternity
at the speed of light . . .

When I've had enough space
and my mind's out of control,
I catch a passing shooting star
and back to Earth I fall!

(Ms.) Janis L. Dushaw
UPLIFTED WITH GOD
I watch as the leaves say catch
me if you can,
Scampering freely like me, until
time shall demand
We depart! They shall soon
return to the land
And I'll be used in the food
service "of man".
But my thoughts shall dwell at
that place above
Whereof comes all glorious
things to us in His love;
Each blessing fits each one so
well as if it were a glove!
Nature, peace, happiness—all
come of the His Holy Dove!!
So as I prepared physical food
"though" out the day
I long for all to have this
reality—I want to say—
Being a whole person of His
really does to me pay
And following Jesus always is the
absolute only *way*!!!

Charles Mc Craw
FEAR
Heart's heavy, hopes high
your leaving for a ride,
to find the sky.

Pulling from the launch pad,
in Anticlimax!
Sking, feeling's glad.
Come for a ride, we'll face Battleax!

We've been hijacked,
heart's attacked.
If in the right mood,
we'll pull through.

Battleax is hard, can tear you apart,
see the fear, the tears.
Here comes the knife,
let me out of here!

Pulling from the launch pad,
Empty with fear.

The knife's blade cuts deeper,
Deeper thru the fright.

Fears, tears and pain,
our leering peers,
You should fear!

Helen Brown Rittershofer
MY BIG BROTHER

Dedicated to my brother Wendell Brown

To touch the lives of youth and age
Words must be weighed and carefully spoken
As purpose and character picture the scene
Shades form and balances reign supreme
Achievements drawn from broadened views
Speak of force—gravity and power to draw
Lending a balance to the established viewer
Imagination—interests and insights become the ruler
Age reflects as youth projects
Steps to be taken in their world of dreams
Melding thoughts stretch like shimmering stars
Twinkle and stretch into bright happy hours
For youth having climbed the stairs of life
Has been flaunted by challenges left and right
Has learned through experience the talents of wisdom
Contemplative moments form future from past—as dawns
Youth and Age rises from the sunshine of morning
Sharing together complexities and joys—sharing
And caring the joys and experiences of life.

Carla Jean Schaldecker
THE HARVEST MOON

In memory of my grandfather, George McGregor, who made my first four years of life full of laughter and love.

Like an apricot,
Freshly picked,
Perfect and ripe,
Sitting on velvet,
Blue, yet black,
Beautiful, yet evil,
Lies the Harvest Moon.

K. M. DiClementi
THE FALL OF SUMMER
To Pamela, Yesterday's Peek
You—the doorway of a distant bliss

The fall of summer is in the air.
Winds of change stir the dormant memories of fettered phallic years.
The golden leaves in all their reticent glory, blow lifeless like banal banners imbued with

rustic memories of the child's mind garden.
The limbs of majestic maples sway in the breeze of basal emotion, dancing a bereaved ballet over the bantling's autumn garden.
The delicate flower withers in the fall winds, leaving barren the retinal landscape.
She is the summer sun's daughter, the symbol of the sought after mate of female quintessence, the resident longing in every man's heart.
A pond filled with water of tepid emotion grows cold in the autumn garden.
Tis autumn who is pregnant with the retrograde pain that precedes the seasonal subterfuge.
Tis autumn who calls forth the rapacious creditor from the weeds in the bantling's neonatal garden.
Tis autumn who spins the web of self pity in the drunkard's mind.
Tis autumn that we walk retrospectively through the gardens of many summers gone by, feeling the weight of four seasons.
Autumn, that the vast myriad of feelings spring forth from the well of soul.
Autumn, that we feel the fall of summer.

Jeannette Goodwin
MEMORIES
Memories
Happy, Sorrowful,
Haunting, rewarding, reminiscing.
Our Record of Life
Nostalgia

Sandra B. Marriott
GARDEN OF LONELINESS
The winds howl long, the night hastens in,
The weeds raise up, the smile of flowers die again,
The lamps grow dim, the colors fade to gray,
The leaves curl up for night, the moon turns her face away,
A kitten's cry turns to a loud, empty howl of hate,
And I walk alone with downcast face, reluctant to keep my rendevous with fate.
The shadows close in and dark triumphs against the light,
The trees cry for moisture, but there is no solace for their plight,
The air of breath is cold and leaves no warmth to burrow in my soul,
I run to seek the God of hope, but find only remnants shredded near his hole,
The glow of morning is overcast by the sadness of the pouring rain,
The lightning strikes and the rain swallows the tears that washed my windowpane;
The silhouettes in their frames become faces with snarling, hungry looks,

And romance is only an idiots dream as written in wordless books,
My seeking of joy was only a fool's venture into man's unknown,
And now I reap the sterile seeds of hatred that you and I have sown.

Georgiana Lieder Lahr
SEARCH
I sought a poem at ocean's shore today,
In flight of gull and beauty of the sea;
In form of cloud and sunbeam's shining ray,
Yet all the while the words eluded me.

I sought a poem, and poems can not be forced,
For they must rise from wellspring of the soul;
But deep within I feel so tempest-tossed,
Today I cannot play the poet's role.

And then there came release from this world's din,
As quietly I sat and watched the shore;
The striving ceased, once more I was akin
With universe, I found the open door.

The vision and the dream cannot depart,
The words he seeks are in the poet's heart!

Irehne Sullivan Sack-Wright

Irehne Sullivan Sack-Wright
THE NARCOLEPTIC
I wish you'd try to understand—
I just can't help the way I am!
I often long to stay awake,
And reap those things I must forsake—
But certain times, I'm forced to sleep,
By urgings that run very deep.
These "sleep attacks" cause great disdain,
They're awful things I can't refrain—
They care not what I have at stake,
Or just how much my heart might break—
For when I try to shake them free,
They won't release their hold on me.
There have been times when life seemed good,

With me performing as I should—
Then drowsiness would soon appear,
To haunt, and taunt, and cause me fear.
I'd battle it with all my might,
But always lose the hopeless fight . . .
Then I'd retreat with spirits low—
To take my nap, prescribed by foe!

Sheila Lloyd Crabtree
SPECIAL WISHES
May your days be filled with sunshine,
Your nights with endless bliss;
May you always get what you expect
From each and every kiss.
And may you never hunger
For money, love or bread . . .
May you always find the safest place
To lay your weary head.
May your heart be never broken,
Your happiness never never end;
May love, joy and wisdom
Surround this "Special Friend."

Roderick Allen Hunt
WHERE DOES GOD DWELL
Is there a sacred spot where God dwells?
Can being bad cast evil spells—
And cause procrastinators to suffer with
Devils and bodily ills?
Surely God dwells on sacred hills?
Do people receive what they deserve?
Is the blind man bad—and
The cripple perverse?
Can you tell which God to serve—
So I can be wealthy and escape life's ills?
Why of course, God lives on sacred hills!
Not in the temples and tabernacles or shrines
Does he dwell—as any fool can tell you,
He dwells on sacred hills.

Cary Chrysler
RAINBOW, II
Passion sails like a ship that follows a blinding urge;
Passion flies like wind in hair dark as a starless night.

Scars I know have scraped her soul.
Old and deep, long for a cure.
They stir in me, a sleeping giant;
Finally to rise from out my heart.

Passion builds on emotion's flow as we lay;
Passion exceeds time, dances free in a heartbeat.

A rainbow shot through the clouds,
appeared smiling in my mountains' sky.
Rainbow dances quick.
She is my heartbeat.

Passion comes sudden, pours echo-like
sound into thunderous life;
gives birth to a healing love.

She sings to me her colors,
from a thousand miles away;
Kingdoms rise sometimes to fall,
Answers dwell sometimes within.
Truth so achingly patient,
Her love so deeply held, like
Yesterday . . .

Warren W. Bennet
ALMOST

---

*To Sherrie, Whose memory is
counted among my treasures.*

It was almost too soon
but I needed her there
under the half moon
I caressed her soft hair

It was almost too nice
the embrace we shared
not once but twice
I could tell that she cared

It was almost a dream
but my eyes were still open
feelings flowed like a stream
and carried the soft words that
were spoken

It was almost light out
the night slipped silently by
our lives took a new route
time always seems to fly

With love,
Warren

Juanita M. Reed
REMEMBRANCE
You have come and gone now
And I will always recall your visit
Each time the air is filled with
the scent of orange blossoms
And the trees heavy laden with
their ripeness.

The beautiful yellow butterflies
that sit upon
Blades of grass, depositing their
eggs
To perpetuate their species.
All these things I see and I will
recall your visit.

Azaleas in bloom in their hues of
pink and white
The oak trees shedding their old
leaves for new
Everything alive, awakened after
their winter's nap
In splendid coats of color and
beauty.

Nature's bounty is a truly
wondrous cycle

So when the orange blossoms
again emit their heady aroma
I will again think of you.
Will you come again? I wonder.

Carol C. Gibson
ADORATION
Holding hands we bounced along
the road
To our secret hiding place
Under a willow tree—
Nicole and I.

In the newly raked grass we
hurled
An uncooperative frisby back
and forth
In the gusting wind—
Nicole and I.

On a corner of the rug we snapped
Green and orange tiddledy-winks
Into a tiny bowl—
Nicole and I.

Nicole is four and I ninty and
more,
But years and pleasures are
blended and braided
When adoration
abounds—
Granddaughter and I!

Carlene Williams
BEYOND THIS HILL
This hill is a steep one and Lord
knows it has been rough,
As if all the other ones somehow
just weren't enough
To make you give in or just give
up.

Sometimes you get so tired and
wonder why you go on
With no place to rest along the
way and you have become
So weary to the bone.

Each time you have stumbled,
the pain you recall
So you take great care not to
cause another to fall,
Even though your stumbling has
been seen by all.

Each time you fall, you pick
yourself up and start over again.
You can go on because beyond
this hill is something to gain;
There is more sunshine and not
quite so much rain.
There is shade to rest in, cool
water to drink;
A quiet place to just sit and
think.

You have come upon a lot of
hills
And climbed them each at
God's will;
Always seeking on the other side,
A meadow with a path smooth
and wide.

Perhaps beyond this hill is not
where the answer led:
Maybe what is to be found is in
the CLIMB instead!

Clifford Bailey
La Paloma That Mourns
There's a mourning guest at
daybreak,
Whose sad notes are never
heard
Among the rest of his kindred
And truly unlike a bird.

He wanders along the roadway
With those of his brooding kind
To the sounds of daily traffic
Seeking what he can find.

Though ever, anon, his dirges
Resound through the morning
calm
Their sounds seem strangely
peaceful
Like that of the Spirit's balm.

Did fate appoint him his wailing
To lament the curse and the ban
That came when the interloper
Designed the ruin of man?

Perchance, when mourning the
evil
That ever seemeth to rise,
He longs for the trees of the
Garden
And the birdsongs of Paradise.

Joyce Thomas
Transformation
Soft, light snow is dancing in the
air,
Floating, flying without any care,
Transforming the last bleak days
of winter
Into a silvery scene of complete
serenity.
The trees are coated with fluffy
frosting;
The banks are just right for
sleighs coasting;
The children about their
snowmen are boasting;
Around the fire marshmallows
are toasting.
Soft, light snow fills all with
delight,
Descending, darting with infinite
might
Transforming the world into a
dreamy sight.

Susan Richards Lange
**The Day I Cut My Amy's
Hair**
It's done. I never thought I'd see
The day I cut my Amy's hair,
Those chestnut-colored silken
locks
That framed her trusting face, so
fair.
That cascade falling soft and free,
A mantle and her lion's mane,
My small dear Leo's glory-crown
Of thick, rich tresses, hard to
tame.

But beauty's task is time and care
(So hard to ask of only four)
Persuasive words did urge the
snips
That sent curls tumbling to the
floor.

And now I gaze with misted eye
On shiny tendrils lying there.
The smile that lights dear Amy's
face
Does not quite ease the pain I bear.
For hidden in my secret thoughts,
There stays this feeling I can't
share
I know I never shall forget
The day I cut my Amy's hair.

Janet L. Von Stein
SNOWY DAYS
There's snow on the ground, and
on the trees.

There's a pretty nippy bite in the
breeze.

If I'd go outside, it would nip my
nose,
And more than likely, freeze my
toes.

When I was younger, I'd be out all
day,
Make snowmen, sled ride, laugh
and play.

Now I'm content to stay inside
and look,
Then curl up with a warm
blanket and a good book.

Diana Sue Majesty
DISGUISED

To Mother and Dad

I'm a wet little raindrop,
Wrapped in color and thought
By the whistling wind.

Maybe I'll land in an ocean
With a splashy splash.
I'll feel soaked and without form.

Or
Maybe I'll fall into a spider's web
And glisten in the sunlight,
To be tickled by the rain.

But
Once again
The sun will draw me home
To the clouds.

Ainsley Jo Phillips
ONE-SIDED

---

*To Jesus who called me to
become a writer; To Paul who
inspired this poem; and to Mama
Bear and Daddy Bear who have
loved and encouraged me, turning
my dreams to realities!*

I am the spring; you are the fall.
I am your friend; you are my all.
I dream about our wedding day;
You wonder why I think this
way.
I watch the sun rise in your eyes;
You tell me to date other guys.
I write to tell you I'm in love;
You shrug and roll your eyes
above.
I'm at your house; I ring your
bell—
You've checked into a padded cell!

Nola F. Hammer
TIME GOES ON
The morning dawns, the night is
past
time goes on it travels fast.
The love we knew has vanished
away,
yesterday is gone, it's a new day.

The time we've spent together
is a sweet memory.
I'll treasure it forever.
It means so much to me.

Again the sun has risen,
to brighten up our day.
For in the golden west,
the moon has slipped away.

Clouds have all passed by,
the dew is on the rose.

Shadows have dimmed my
    pathway,
    where did the sunshine go?

I'll not worry about tomorrow,
    I'm happy to be alive.
I'll make the best of today,
    tomorrow may not arrive.

What's in the future is not known,
    I ponder on the time that's flown.
I'll make the best of my life as I
    go along.
    Shun all evil and not go wrong.

Time goes on, Time goes on

Linda B. Miller
PLANS

---

*For my husband Gene, because of
your love and understanding, and
the place you hold in my heart.*

The bed is warm.
It's a cool day.
I pull the blanket up,
and move a little closer to you.

Neither one of us has to work.
No place we have to be.
It's just you and me.
You want to go bowling?

Holli Ikeler Petersen
GRANDMA
Oh Grandma,
I love you.
You stand for all things good.
You are beauty
You are love.

My 'Christmas Grandma',
Who makes Holiday's special.
Saturday morning coffee's
               at your house
are Holiday's.

My wonderful Grandma,
You are beautiful Autumn days
You are graceful snowflakes.
You are all things
            extra special
in my life.

You are strength.
I love you Grandma.

Esther Rebecca Lemont
**Too Many Times, I've Died
   Inside**
I died inside so many times,
Waiting for your call,
To see your face,
To hear your voice,
To be with the one and only
   person
Who could have made me live
   again.
For you,
So many times,
I've died inside.

Only you could have saved me.
But you were never there.
I sat alone and cried.
Waiting,
Yearning,
Hoping.
But you never came.
You never showed.
My heart ached and tore apart.
You were so much a part of me
   inside;
But you were not a part of my life.
The empty gap was not filled.

You were not there.
So I sat alone,
Too many times,
And died inside.

Charles Green

Charles Green
A SMILE
The curtains part
and the certaince art
A smile that you ever caress
A smile you yearn to possess
Commandment yours to you, you
   sleep
Commitment that you solely keep
Commendment that you're solely
   deep
Ever then your heart to reap
Reap, reap to heaven those
Thy will be done.
The curtains close

Joyce E. Conklin
. . . goin' fishin'
With your line there in the water
  and your feet bare in the sand,
  with the sun abeatin' down on
   you
  you know, it's kinda grand!
With the tackle box astinkin' so
  from last week's rotten bait,
  and your wife at home afrettin'
  cause it's sorta gettin' late.
Well, I'll tell ya, that's alivin',
  and it's really quite a sight
  when you clean the little rascals
  in the middle of the night.
But the rotten part comes soon
  enough
  and then you'll have to pay
  when the wife announces loudly
  "We're ahavin' fish today!"

Mary A. Sadler
AUTUMN DAYS
How do we know when Autumn
  has come?
Filled with all it's laughter and
  fun.
How do we know when it's come
  to stay
Just before Old Man Winter will
  chase it away?

We can notice it in many
  different ways
It's chilly air, and bright, sunny
  days.
Bright orange pumpkins on the
  vine
Colored Indian corn, looking so
  fine.

Wild geese are flying high above
Filling the air with their greetings

of love
The mornings are cold, with frost
  on the ground
Everywhere, fallen leaves can be
  found.

Some leaves are dull, others are
  bright
While still on the trees they're a
  beautiful sight
But when on the ground, what a
  job to rake
Or children can use them, huge
  piles to make.

The garden has given a bountiful
  yeild
The corn has been harvested out
  in the field
Peaches, applesauce, and tomato
  juice
Are stored in the cellar for winter
  use.

When all these things have come
  to pass
We'll know that Autumn has
  come at last
We'll know that it has come to
  stay
Just before old man winter will
  chase it away.

Karla E. Cooper
A POEM FOR LEE

My Godson Lee Prance Evans

You are a child of Love.
  A child of Understanding.
  A child of Warmth.
  A child of Caring.
  A child of the World.
You are a child of God.
  A child of Prayer.
  A child of Compassion.
  A child of the World.
For you are a child sent from
  Heaven, in a little Angel's
  disguise . . .

Nancy Tucker Wilson (Mann)
THE PIE
The devil was out there in a mask
Mixing his poison in a wizard's pie.
He then thought to mix it in a
  flask
In a stinging lotion for a reddened
  eye.

My jack-o-lantern was lighted up
When the night filled with
  children
             talking loud.
A child came as blind and held a
  cup,
But the gayer goblins came in a
  crowd.

They were like flowers: one was a
  clown,
Three trapeze dancers, one
  butterfly,
A wizard whose cloak was
  dragging him down
And a witch with tears painted to
  make her cry.

A boy wore a devil's horns and
  mask.
He put the real devil in an apple
  pie.
Pure, sweet cider was mixed in

the flask;
A twinkle shone in each hole for
  each eye.

Rhonda L. Wethington
OCTOBER MEMORIES
The days of October are special
  to me,
The beauty of autumn—the
  falling of leaves.
To rake all their splendor into
  one huge bunch,
And then take a plunge—just
  hear those leaves crunch!

The woolly worms colors are
  soon to unfold,
Revealing the stories of what
  winter holds.
The times spent at football games
  on chilly nights,
Although bundled warm, you feel
  the colds' bite.

Fall festivals stirring with skills
  of the past,
The harvest of apples and
  pumpkins at last!
There's apple butter, cider,
  cookies and pies,
Delicious to eat and a sight for
  the eyes.

The smells of a weiner roast
  filling the air,
The sizzling of hot dogs and hay
  bales for chairs.
A marshmallow burning and
  cider so sweet,
Fresh doughnuts awaiting—let's
  hurry and eat!

A wagon so loaded with hay—
  what a sight!
A ride through the country—a
  tour of the night.
A sky full of stars and a friend by
  your side,
Those scary old stories told
  during the ride.

The thirty—first day is the best
  time of fall,
When Halloween goblins will
  frighten us all.
The parties and contests—the
  "spookiest" guest,
The trick and the treating—
  which do *you* like best?

Ruth Collier
FINDING FAULT
When we find fault with others
  And are quick to condemn
We do not stop to think
  How we may sometimes offend.

When we hurt another person
  With our criticizing tongue
We really hurt ourselves
  Whether we're old or young.

For in criticizing others
  We break the flow of love
Our precious Heavenly Father
  Sends to us from above.

We sometimes hurt our family
  When we seek to control
Trying to solve their problems
  Only they alone can know.

So we really hurt ourselves
  Telling of another's fault
Breaking God's flow of love
  Leaves us troubled and
  distraught.

Louise A. Limbaga
THE STATUE OF LIBERTY

*Dedicated to the KAHUKU
HAWAII'S HIGH SCHOOL RED
RIDERS MARCHING BAND,
who competed with bands from
all over the United States Won
their class and took first place.
My fondest Aloha to All.*

She stands in regal beauty
For all the world to see
Welcoming strangers to her
  harbor
To this land of liberty
She holds the bright torch of
  freedom
in her strong powerful hand
and silently lets you know
that this is her beloved land.
It doesn't matter just who you are
or what ever your nationality
The choice of government is your
  own
nor is this a fantasy
You can pray to your own God
Whom ever it might be
For when you pass through her
  portals
you are in the land of the free.
And so she stands regally
  beautiful
Welcoming everyone to see
And grasp her strong hand of
  freedom
    THE STATUE OF LIBERTY.

Dolores Howe
OUR BABY

*To my beloved son, Shelley, for
whom it was written before he
was born.*

Two pounds of love enfolded
In a space not very cubic.
Not so recognizable
But still very cherubic.

It flutters, oh so gently,
Silently but intently.
To break the walls it strives.
To be born its chief drive.

Charles Winokoor
SEAHORSE
Recalling my friend,
Seahorse:
I'm filled with the smell of
  accupuncture
Blue black oil surrounding and
  bathing us
Breathing in stars, the air
Becomes starless
Spitting out what we hope are
  cures
We are too sensual
Too compassionate
No longer hiding
Caring like hell
Laughing out loud
Mouths closed
I love/my friend
  Seahorse

Sensei Joseph Carbonara
HERE AND NOW
And now I think of days gone by
  Sit, Dream, still breathe a sigh
Of those impossible plans,

youthful Ideals
To bring Happiness, Peace to all
  Who feels
These thoughts are still in my
  heart's presence
A longing to share my fruitful
  essence
But time has made the spirit
  wane
To some, my search has been in
  vain
The morning Sun upon my brow
  Reminds me
It has always been Here, and Now

Irene Stewart
IN A HURRY
I am in a hurry, and I don't know
  why,
And I don't really care,
I am just in a hurry, and I don't
  even know where . . .

I must be going somewhere,
Or I wouldn't be this far,
I really must get there,
Yet, I'm not even
  In the car!

I really must get there,
Of that, I am sure, I think!
Maybe, I am just out running,
  Trying to keep in the pink!

Whatever the matter is,
I cannot be lost,
For I am still in a hurry,
  And I've not even counted the
  cost.

What is the matter?
Why do I have to run?
Why can't I just enjoy this,
  And pretend that I am having
  fun?

Michael L. Acton
SURFACE—LIFE
  Sunshine staring through cold
  rising mist
as the surf roars attacks against
  the sands.
  wave upon wave form to rage in
  white anger.
    only to die in vain.

Crows taunting like generals do,
  fighting amidst the skies,
  clouds drifting along
    without a place to hide.
Distance bringing seagulls dancing
on shores of peaceful land.
Spectators watching timeless
  strength
  of incoming tides to stand.

    HARK!
I hear their cry of life
reach out to join their ranks.
beleaguered—hungry—wings do
  blow
  settling chill to find.

EACH NEW MORN brings
  scenes of change
    upon our open minds.

Kevin J. Roberto
I AM I SAID
I am like a snowflake falling in
  every direction,
Waiting to land in a crowd of
  others, unnoticed,
That quickly melts and
  disappears.

An aimless seeker who strolls the
  sandy beach looking
For a mermaid that never shows.
A constant seeker of truth, but a
  finder of lies.

A distant planet in a vast galaxie,
Waiting to be discovered and
  explored.

I am a rock, still in thought and
  feeling,
Hardened and unremoved by lifes
  array of ever changing emotions.

A plush comfortable carpet
That knows the feeling of being
  walked on,
And abused.

I am I said.

Andrew G. Bassett
LIFE
Life . . .
Life is a wonderful thing
and a sad one too.
Life is the joys and sorrows
that will be there tomorrow.
Life is like a roller coaster—
It's full of ups and downs, ups and
  downs.
But never push life too far
Because you might end that ride.
Keep that roller coaster going;
Keep it full with those
joys and sorrows.
But to be happy,
Live Life.

Bernice Ann Nemec
OCTOBER IS

*I dedicate this poem to the three
most precious people in my life-
My husband Steve, and my two
sons, Joe Dan and Stephen.*

October is, leaves falling to the
  ground,
Turning beautiful colors, red,
  gold and brown.

It's a beautiful Autumn sunset in
  the West,
It's County Fairs and Octoberfest.

It's Renaissances and Haloween,
It's crowning of the State Fair
  Queen.

October is, Haloween treats and
  harmless tricks,
It's popcorn balls and candied
  apples on sticks.

It's goblins and ghosts, even a
  funny clown,
Trick or Treaters all over town.

It's dunking for apples and
  drinking witches brew,
It's visiting Haunted Houses and
  making Jack-O-Lanterns to.

October is, a pumpkin patch
  under a Harvest Moon,
It's Charlie Brown in the "Great
  Pumpkin" cartoon.

It's birds flying South for the
  winter months,
Its our menfolk getting ready for
  the big deer hunts.

It's football games and marching
  bands,

It's a stadium full of screaming
  fans.

October is rated a number one,
There is no comparison.
It is truly a month of fun,
  October is.

Lisa Forestier
EVENING MEAL

To Ivan

Fatigue set in
as she peeled a potato
for her husband's
evening meal.
Fatigue rolled in
like a grey disease
from the sea.
Absentmindedly
she sliced the skin
of her right thumb
and watched—fascinating!—
as the hard, white food
turned velvety red.
In the streets below
students were shouting:
"We want our freedom!"
But she choked on tears
because meat alone
would have to do
one more time.

Elizabeth Bruno
DAWN
Riding up from the horizon
On her phantom steed of light,
She discards night,
Throwing off her purple robe.
She rises pale
Above the oceans and the hills.

She comes, clad in gossamer
  chiffon,
Drawing her white veils behind
  her
Like a virgin bride.
All silvery and gold
Her hair streams out behind.

Breathing mistily on tops of trees
Glimmering on the dewdrop tears
  of night,
She binds herself to day
And sheds her bridal gown.
Wearing glistening pastels
She greets the sun.

Michelle Wijnands
ALWAYS

For Markie, my inspiration

Always I know
  there's someone who cares,
one who looks for me
  when I'm not there.
One who smiles
  when everything's wrong,
one who stays
  when everyone's gone.
Always I'll have
  someone to trust,
one to mean
  "I love you so much."
One who would never
  let me down,
one to pick me up
  when I'm down on the ground.
Always I'll be
  a true friend to you,

one you can trust
and believe in too.

Joyce Billingsley
NATURE'S ART WORK

*This poem is dedicated with love
to my parents, James & Maurene
Jolley of Corpus Christi, Texas,
for their 50th Wedding
Anniversary.*

Seashells are put on shore by
nature's hand,
as moving water creates patterns
in the sand.
Magical rays from the sun,
light up the beautiful art work
being done.
With nature's paint brushes, the
wind and sea,
a lovely picture, she just
presented to me.

Rebecca L. Studebaker
... the DARK

*This poem is in memory of Ross
Studebaker, a wonderful father
and husband, whom we all love
very much.*

Though the day grows
Dark—
I know in my
Heart—
There's nothing here in the
Dark—
That's not here in the
Light—
Still ... like a child ... I am
Afraid.

P. R. Fiedler
DREAMER'S CANVAS
All that I am or ever hope to be is
only in my mind;
In circumstances of the day my
thoughts are left behind;
Tomorrow brings the moves I
make small althrough they be;
The final portrait when it's done
will be the one of me.

Barbara M. Salazar
MIRROR REFLECTION
Mirror reflection makes me
want to hide.
It shows the superficial,
why not the inner light?

Splashes of color to highlight
the pale and obscure.
A false beauty to allure of allude,
hoping for love, not just a
mood.

Colors of confidence to portray
beauty that was denied.
Mirror reflection trying to hide
the inner beauty of my life.

Amy Horney
What Would You Change?
Is it worth the sorrow
Is it worth the pain
Is it worth the patience
to relive this life again?

What would you change
What would you keep the same
If you had the chance
to relive this life again?

Would you tell your feelings
or play along with the game
If you had the chance
to relive this life again?

Would you try to be patient
Would you head toward Heaven's
Stairs
Would you commit no sins
If you had the chance
to relive this life again?

Annis Williams
HONOR CORNER

*In loving memory of a sweet and
gentle man, my husband, Henry
"Hank" Williams.*

In a corner, on the wall,
Hangs our certificates of honor.
Numbering fourteen for jobs
well-done,
These sheets of paper declare the
worth of our name.
The four of us have placed our
pride there
To show the world what our
minds can be.
We are of value and that
everyone can see.
A small plaque leads it off
Saying "Believe! Your dreams can
come true."
Well, this corner is there to prove
That we four have made our
dreams come true.
In a dark grave, the first Williams
lies,
So far from us now in distance
and time.
But we four, we have made his
name
Something of which he would be
proud.
My three children and I
Have not much in Earth and
under sky.
But we have each other
And our Honor Corner.

Theola Ward
CRY TO MY HEART
Daybreak upon the plains with
tints of pink and gold,
Northbound geese, the mocker's
song,
Jasmine perfuming dew-dript
dawn
Lift up my heart and make me
bold.
Today is new, and I am drunk
with living,
Come soon, my love, and I shall
thrill to giving,
For spring is soft and warm and
love can ne'er grow cold.

Sunset in western skies streaked
with unfeeling blue,
Southbound geese, the north
wind's song,
Bare-armed trees, with green dress
gone,
Cry to my heart. I weep for you.
Sunrise has gone, high noon—and
now the night.
But skies will glow again with
morning light.
How can we hope this? How to
know? They always do.

Bonita Heavener Maness
AUTUMN
Up and down the hills,
All along the way,
The trees stand in mourning—
Summer's gone away.

They've cried away their
greeness,
Their leaves fall like tears,
They still regret that Autumn
comes
Even after all their years.

But the beauty that they bring
the world
As it turns and time goes by,
Is worth a million sorrows
And all the leaves they cry.

Chad G. Markel

Chad G. Markel
FALL WINDS

*I would like to dedicate my poem
to Mr. Floyd Willoughby and my
family*

When the time begins
to have the winds
the name is surely fall.
I hear a bird singing loud
and sitting on a wall.
He is singing about
the fall winds and
the slightly lightly breeze
I hope that bird comes
back again and really really
SINGS.

Karen I. Baish
**Gentle Healing From a
Friend**
I was cold, from the inside out,
And you warmed me with your
words;
The need in me you didn't
doubt ...
Your warmth was both felt and
heard.

I was hungry, crying out for
affection,
And you fed me with kindness;
Accepted me for myself—I felt no
rejection ...
As your kindness spread, my
pain grew less.

I was naked, stripped of pride,
And you clothed me with
honesty;
Showing me that sincerity has no
reason to hide ...

As long as the "clothing" you see
is really "me".

I was lonely, without a true friend,
And you took my hand;
You listened, you responded—
your words both now and
then ...
Made me feel you truly
understand.

I was lost and empty,
disillusioned with all that I saw,
And you embraced me, like a
child;
You protected, guided and filled
me with awe ...
You showed me the simple
beauty of love inborn—
flowing free and wild.

I was vulnerable, unsure and
scared,
You gave of yourself, you asked
of me;
The most important thing is—
you cared ...
You listened, you shared, you
gave willingly.

William A. Roettgers
DAYS END
As shadows slowly lengthen,
Coolness fills the air.
The sun, a ball of molten gold,
Seems suspended there.

Birds winging 'cross the sky,
Swiftly to their nest.
E're darkness' blanket settles down
To find their place of rest.

Fleecy little puffs of clouds,
Streaked with gold and white;
The sun sinks slowly in the west,
Day is done—it's night.

Ola Margaret James
BEWITCHED
I want to write something
Light, superficial, laughing,
Filmy as cellophane,
Minus all rain!
But my mind keeps searching
For shadows, like a dark bird
perching
Upon a half-doubt near forgot—
And some old sorrow, like as not,
Will come parading, all in white,
A strange lost ghost,
In the black night.

Bobie-Hufnagel-Bann
JOHN F. KENNEDY

*For a dear and special lady, my
very close friend Sandy-Lindsay-
Cole. Who always had confidence
in my ability to write.*

It was on November 22nd. That
day
That John F. Kennedy passed away
He was assassinated we all know
We'll always love him wherever
we go.

It was a tragic day for all
We remember most his very last
fall,
While riding thru Dallas that day
Was shot in such a violent way.
Why would anyone harm this man
Is something no one can

Our World's Best Loved Poems

understand,
He was a man of such great power
Fighting for our nation every
single hour.
So everyone please pray for John
He is dead but not really gone,
He's in the hearts of the nation
we see
May you rest in peace, John F.
Kennedy.

Marcia J. Roessler
What Reminds Me Of You
The daybreak of the morning
Whether there be rain or shine
Brings to mind the image of you
The memory of when you were
mine.

The tic-toc of the hourly clock
Stroking the beat of time
Bringing to mind the pleasures
spent
Of love and ecstacy divine.

The dust on the mantlepiece
And cards stating we cared
Lovingly sent to each other
Showing expressions we shared.

Everything in every way
Some mannificent . . . some small
Will always bring you to mind
And your name I do recall.

Marsha Adair Greer
**Vagrant Thoughts and
Remembered Beauty**

*To friends past and present and
my family, Tom and Joe Tom.*

Music like a curve of gold, the
scent of pine trees in the rain,
a fire that soars and sings,
blue waves whitened on a cliff,
Life has lovliness to sell.

The rose petal hands of a baby
curled in sleep, laughter of a
child at play,
little children's faces holding
wonder like a cup,
mother's love for all to see,
Life touches my heart.

The smell of my sister's kitchen
at canning time, first flower of
summer,
the gleam of candle light and
silver reflected in old
mahogany,
golden mounds of freshly
churned butter,
Life feeds my soul.

The crush of snow beneath my
galoshes, autumn leaves in a
wooded lane,
smoke rising from a chimney on
a frosty morn,
the dark whitness of a winter's
night,
Life's glorious dream for us all.

Melinda Mandel
POEM # 5
I mark my life by summers
Lovers come and gone
Red, orange and cranberry leaves
where once was shells on the
shore.

Montauk, Fire Islands ago
you took me in your arms

Nights of dread of nine
days gone.

Thinking this time is it
but the rabbit chased the ball.
Dusks of lonely tears
phones with no receivers.

I mark my life by summers
Lovers come and gone.

Vivian C. Fowler
SWEET ECSTASY
How I yearn to see your face,
To feel your touch so dear,
How sweet, how sweet,
To relive our yesteryear.
Just to feel your loving arms,
In a tender embrace,
Only I can remember
Things that time cannot erase.
The many times we shared
What ever came our way;
But it is over now—
For that was yesterday.

Oh! the memories so sweet,
Shared by you and me;
The tender moments of passion,
The nights of sweet ecstasy.
Only God could have parted us.
We knew from the start:
All the precious memories
Held deep within my heart.
The years we had together
Will always be held dear.
Thinking back in time.
To our yesteryear.

Francis Pallotti
LIFE
Life is like a garden
you hoe it;
you seed it;

you water it;
you harvest it;
But sometimes the crops are bad.

Daniel S. Royster
One Thing I Hate Is Clouds
One thing I hate is clouds, One
thing I hate is clouds
nine in the morning or three
at noon
One thing I hate is clouds

One thing I hate is clouds, One
thing I hate is clouds
a daybreak of gloom, a
feeling of doom
One thing I hate is clouds

An evening of rain that passes
away helping the plants is okay
but something seems wrong
having clouds all day

long
One thing I hate is clouds

Cleaning up the air, filling up
the ponds
the one big gain is rain
but having just gray seeping
over all day
the clouds are one big pain!

One thing I hate is clouds, One
thing I hate is clouds
when getting together
predicting good weather
One thing I hate is clouds

One thing I hate is clouds, One
thing I hate is clouds
when the sun shines through
and the sky is bright blue
one thing I hate is clouds

Robert M. Marons
Old Fashioned Pictures
I cleared the leaves in front of the
house last fall,
As a reward, Sally and I went on a
Shopping trip to the Mall,
We posed for pictures; I put on a
red velvet dress,
wide brimmed white hat, and I
held a parasol.
Sally dressed up in a black dance
hall gown,
boa scarf, grey fedora, and tried
to look like a gun moll.
People say that Sally is pretty,
and I'm cute.
Instead of looking for blue jeans
and jogging
shoes I bought a blouse, open
toe dance pumps,
and a pants suit.

Madeline Rasmusson
**I Would Plant An Apple
Tree Today**
When I was a youngster I
remember
The words my minister did say
If I knew the world would end
tomorrow
I would plant an apple tree today.

His message did linger and
And deep in my mind did stay
So I keep right on planting though
The harvest may never come my
way.

For the future is not ours
We have only just today
We have to make the most of it
As it comes along our way.

It is a fact you will find, take care
Of the present is all you have to do
The future takes care of itself
And it should never worry you.

It is just a part of the great plan
As that is the way the world
should be
That others will enjoy the fruit
If today I plant an apple tree.

Jo Catholos Morris
What Is Love For Michael
What is love that it goes unseen?
Taking for granted what has
always been . . .
A hug in the morning or a kiss at
night,
A reassuring smile when the time
is right.
The slightest pressure of his hand

on mine
Speaking unheard comfort that
all is fine.
When he reaches out to hold me,
yet he's fast asleep,
Unconsciously convincing me
he's mine to keep.
Then he's got to tease me till he
makes me mad,
Making sure it is clear to me that
I've been had.
Then we laugh and we joke of
what's been done,
Cause it's in the way he teases
me that makes life fun.
Never let a day go by I do not feel
his touch,
Emotional or physical it has
become my crutch.
Unconsciously I need these
things to get me through my
day,
To feel his presence with me
even if he is away.
To see the sparkle in his eyes, my
stomach starts to stir
At the way he says I love you
without a single word.

Chester P. Boris
A WINTERS NIGHT
On a cold and barren field,
where snow has covered the
ground.
A silent and total darkness broods,
about the surrounding wood.
No animal dare tread,
among the darken trees.
But huddle through the night,
to wait the coming day.
Then ghostly moonlight plays
through clouds,
of billowing pillows of gray.
While silent flakes continue to
fall,
upon this peaceful world.
As it ends in blissful white,
a fluffy blanket remains.
Then suddenly white-winged
phantoms fly,
from out their crystal beds.
Like snow flakes floating forever
sky-ward
into a winters night.

Kim Moore
PEACE?
When will there be a day when
the world shall fight no more
When will the beast, silence his
mighty roar.

When will there be a day, when
our children shall be free
When will a peaceful day come. I
guess it will not be.

When the harshness of war has
left
Many people will be bereft.

But some happiness will remain
And sorrow of where the bodies
have lain.

Pat McKibben
DIFFERENT VIEWPOINTS
One sees, a gripy old man, who is
mean and gruff
And a teenage kid, who is trying
to act tough,
And a woman with some kids
and dark brown hair,

169

Who doesn't know what her kids
are doing, or seem to care.

Another sees, a lonely old man,
who needs kindness shown,
And a good teenage boy, who is
trying to act grown.
And a very sweet smile, with
kindness and care,
In the eyes of the lady with the
dark brown hair.

The thing you are expecting, you
will probably find.
If you are watching for the cruel,
you may overlook the kind,
But if you have looked for the
good, while looking around,
Then mostly, I would wager, that
is what you have found.

Linda L. Bayda
ONCE STANDING TALL
Once standing tall and
majestically,
Now destroyed and strewn about;
Once filled with laughter
rhythmically,
Now filled with fear and doubt.

Once bricks of red and paint of
white,
Now mixed together in a dull sort
of way;
Streets once lined with golden
light,
Now the light has darkened away.

Once windows sparkling saw
children's eyes,
Now shattered panes reach
toward the skies;
Once love and caring showed the
way,
Now still its spark lies there today.

The spark is seen in people's
hearts,
The ones who've cared from the
start;
They bring light to the darkened
way,
And color the city in their own
sort of way.

The city soon will be standing tall,
The life once within returning
forever;
The colors now returning to all,
The city's love will fail not ever.

Robert J. Royston
What The Mirror Sees Not
I look at myself sometimes . . .
often wondering
who that person is behind my
darkened, azure eyes . . .

that person who sees the
triumph . . .
. . . the tragedy

of the seemingly simple,
turned complex,

of depressions bottomless
hollow . . .

and Love.

A soul that searches out to attain
the beauty of Man,
of Nature and of Life itself.

In this are the footsteps of Spring
which shine thru
and project on these . . . my
lips . . .
. . . a smile.

May Adams
A QUIET PLACE
When you are feeling pressured,
And you want to feel serene,
Just close your eyes and visualize,
Your favorite quiet scene . . .
Who created still blue lakes,
Slowly drifting clouds,
Shady glens and mountaintops,
Far away from crowds,
And when you're feeling calm
once more,
You'll feel his presence near,
And in that peaceful state of mind,
Your cares will disappear!

R. O. Loyd
HELLO AND GOODBY
Hello

Here am I — There are you
open mind to open mind
open heart to open heart

Here we are, you and I
of one mind
of one heart

Here am I — There are you
open mind to closed mind
open heart to closed heart

Goodby.

Frances Kelley
You Went With The Sun
I sit in the window watching the
sea
This is where it all began for
you and me.
The smell of the salt, the sound
of the surf,
Night breeze gentle, sand so soft
We loved each moment, as time
ticked away,
As the nite passed into day.
We watched the stars go to sleep,
The moon dissappear, and the
sun made a brite streak.
You dissappeared with the suns
early lite,
But I shall return again when its
nite.
For I need to be here in order to
write.

Cornel I. Hammons
THE MYSTERY OF LIFE
We know
Peace is good,
Happiness is better,
Love is best,
And living life is fantastic.
But we try
To get PEACE from war,
To get HAPPINESS from our greed,
To get LOVE from our
manipulation,
And to get LIVING LIFE from just
surviving.
BECAUSE . . .

Dawn Koontz
ANGERS OF EARTH
Winds of angered breath
blown against the grain
Hearts drowning in floods
and . . . we're slipping away
The tenderness is shadowed
only lonely nights remain
Discord . . .
brewing like a hurricane
Cause lonely nights to follow
Tears of silver, fall like the rain
of the broken-hearted lover

Like volcanos form deserts
love turned barren and gray
As the angers of Earth . . .
love was one and the same.

Patricia Anne Lesher
DOE FAWN
Under the cool pines
I saw her
Innocent of the danger
she will encounter
As she grows.
Fleet of foot
can't stop the pain
of the hunter's mark.

Brown-eyed and gentle,
She is not frightened.
As I stalk her with
my binoculary eyes,
She catches my scent
and springs away
from the stream
Where she drinks.

If she'd just understand
I only wanted to gaze upon her
and pet her,
I'm not like the hunters.

James Wesley Duren
THE HAPPY MAN COMES
He wanders through the valleys
Walks beside the streams,
And marches onward;
Never to dwell in past,
But reflect on happy moments.

Today he shall change someones
life,
And tomorrow he shall leave,
But remaining within his joys
Are freedom and spirit;
Such a stranger to many,
But those he may touch
Know him as friend.

Tammy Sella
UNICORN
It's a magical beauty,
it's the breath of the fair.
It's the shimmering moonlight
through the frosty night air.
It's the heavens above,
it's the grass under feet.
It's the way that true lovers
are destined to meet.
It symbolizes peace and
leaves nothing to mourn.
It's the mystical of all,
It's the Unicorn.

Mary Lee Harrod
WALLS
Walls beautify
cover up
shut out the view

Walls are to hide behind
to keep someone in
to keep people out

To open the door
in a wall
is a risk

It may let in
sunshine or rain
sorrow or pain

It may bring in
friendship
in lieu of disdain

Take the risk
open the door
you are worth knowing

Nettie Marie Yohn
HALLOWEEN

*To my children; Chuck, Linda,
and Lori*

Halloween's coming! It won't be
long
witches and goblins will come
out strong.

Halloween's coming! Big black
cats
broomsticks, witches' brew,
squealing bats!

Halloween's coming! Don't open
your door
A slimy black mist creeps across
your floor.

Halloween's coming! Run for cover
Eeeek! It's Dracula you discover.

Halloween's coming! See that
ladder?
It may tumble on you with a
thundering clatter.

Halloween's coming! Don't go to
bed
A shadowy ghost may occupy the
head,
also a skeleton dragging his bones
a-moaning and a groaning in
scary loud tones.

Halloween's coming! A terrible
land
With a grinning vampire holding
your hand!
Oops—look out! A great big toad
Pushing and a-hopping with a
bug-gy load.

Halloween's coming! Fouls in a tree
Whoo-ing and boo-ing so ugly to
see.

Take your vitamins; build your
resistance
On Halloween night you need
plenty of assistance!
But after all is said and all is done
Halloween night is lots of fun!

Gloria J. Mathers
FALL MOTION
Pelting rain, turmoiled puddles
overflow the lane
Leaves twisting, floating, blowing
thru the air
Bare branches start to extend
relieved of brightly colored
cover
Keen sounds of southbound geese

integrated v forms greet our sight
Interlineal motion in the singing skies;
Sandhill cranes warbling to each other
As they land and stand the fields poised for instant flight
If anyone intrude upon this brief interlude
Of rest as they head for southlands bright;
Ah, they know the venial cold is coming
As northlands brace the gradual change
That develops with diffusion of sun's light,
The cold stimulates with motion as it first begins
Darting leaves, wavering wings, rippling waters
Dried browning grasses bending in the wind;
All this prepares for winter's province
Of frozen stillness to prevail.

Anita Durand Buess
There Are Velvet Roses
There are velvet roses
And pools of clearest blue
Where my love reposes,
And grass that's wet with dew.
Oh now the wind comes whispering
In my longing ear,
And if I am but listening
Will tell me of my dear.
—Oh there he lies a sleeping
And dreaming of but you,
And he sees you weeping
For, alas, it's true,
It's years that stand between you as he lies afar,
And time must e'er be counted in terms of yonder star.

Catherine Lee
Masterpiece After the Rain
The Rainbow . . .
What a breath-taking creation of God, looking supple enough to tie into a beautiful bow; seeming sturdy enough to remain poised in infinite glory!

While here on earth, the brilliant colorscheme painted across the expanse of the sky reminds us of God's abundant mercy.

Yet, God, in all of his unfailing love, retrieves this special promise unto himself, leaving us to rest in faith.

The promise of hope remains with us until again, we search for the masterpiece that will be woven among the tapestry of the sky.

Carolyn Thorne Harris
TEMPTATION
Temptation is a wrestling match between right action and wrong.
A tossup duel or confrontation.
A seesaw ride to the moment of decision.
A test of one's mettle.

It is a final examination on the morals of life.

Passing with flying colors!
Failing dismally!
Recrimination! Shame!
Self-satisfaction! Pride!

Betty C. Baker
A REAL FRIEND
No matter what my attitude,
My friend is always there.
I must show Him gratitude.
He loves me and does care.

This friend is sent from above.
I'm glad He's a friend of mine.
I'm following Him in love,
The only friend who is devine.

Though sometimes I shed tears
And feel alone and depressed;
In Him are no doubts or fears,
My true feelings can be expressed.

In Him I put all my trust,
This friendship I'll never need to mend.
In a confidante this is a must.
Jesus is a real friend.

Laura A. Boch
THE SEA
sweeping waves reaching out to the sandy shores
stealing young hearts out to her shimmering waters
challenging sailors who seek for adventure
enchanting dreamy dreamers
mystifying the world with her secrets

precious waters-stormy yet subtle
ships that sail across her can hear her singing a salty song
so silent and peaceful
where the sea seems to meet the sky
always searching but never finding

Barby Phillips
Minds Escape To Freedom
The Wind blows
    cautiously through
        my mind

clearing passages
    for rational
        thought,

Knowing I am
    capable of
        finding solutions
to improve and
        stand behind
Where I already am
and where I will
        someday be.

Deborah Ann Davis
ETERNALLY YOURS

To my husband, family and family of friends, who have inspired me, given support and shown me the true meaning of love. Thanks to all!

I'm sorry I have gone and left your side,
but my life has ended; I have died.
My last thoughts were all of you,
and all the things I put you through.
I'll watch over you from up above,
and still give to you; all my love.
I never meant to leave you or go

away,
but the plans were made and I couldn't stay.
I am really missing you,
and all the things we used to do.
When all is over said and done,
think of the good times;
    remember the fun.
Now that we are so far apart,
remember we still live in each others heart.
I never meant to leave you all alone,
but now I must prepare our eternal home.
You're my closest, dearest friend;
love like ours, will never end.
Please don't cry or be sad for me;
I'm at peace now, and my soul is free.
When the time comes and we are together,
we'll know then our love is forever.
Sharing our lives so peacefully,
loving each other eternally.

Judith I. Tucker

Judith I. Tucker
SCRAGGLY LIMBS
Scraggly limbs and barren trees
For death it brings not leaves
But life this place once knew
It was then these trees grew
Shadows of what used to be
That in them is what I see.

Leota Rae Cornett
CONTRASTS
The moon is bright, but the flashing light
    From a thousand neon signs
Obscures its glow on this world below,
    Bent on our own designs.

A bird's song sweet, near a busy street,
    Is lost in the motors' whines.
Its true, clear call isn't heard at all
    'Mid the noise of modern times.

God's calm, soft voice still offers a choice
    Of the upward path today,
But the hurrying crowd, inviting and loud,
    Beckons the downward way.

Louise Taylor Tucker
Winter Transfiguration
Daybreak, and lost is the world I know,
Everywhere, everywhere lies mounded snow
And frosty peaks, sparkling in the

morning beams
Of a long neglectful sun
That touches each shape and crystalline tree
With a brittle brilliance
Dazzling to see.
Instead of the earth I know so well
With its winter hues and traffic sounds as well
There is now this pristine, silent shine.
The only stir is in this heart of mine
As wherever I look,
Near or far,
I seem to be living on a shimmering star.

David Wilczek
WATCHING YOU DREAM
Many times I sit and watch you dream
And see those thoughts form a picture
One I can see and touch through your eyes
But many times I wish you could see
The thoughts that I dream
The soft images you create
With the kindness of your voice
And the warmth of your heart
And if I could use the soft touch of your hands
And the brilliance of your eyes
To create a picture for others to see
I could only form a picture of you.

Lyllian D. Cole
DRINK DEEP
Scramble atop of a donkey
a dozy ole donkey, Regret
pack up your blues in a basket
a rue filled basket, my pet.

Tuck all your sorrows and tantrums
in with the blossoms you bear,
flora with charm and with attar
will scatter the blues like a flare.

Ride up the ridge of the Mountain
of gloom you have built, as the mole
look at the Hope of the rainbow
each spectrum a shimmering goal.

Steer the poor stumbling beasty
onward and upward from guilt
watch as the song of the sunshine
turns the dull browns to a lilt.

Slide from the back of your burro
guide him through thickets of night
stride to the Banks of the River
hide not your soul from the Light.

Drink deep of the Solace, Sweet Peace,
ah, gentle winged Dove
fly high, protect each innocent
DRINK DEEP of the Promise of Love.

Beverly Kirson Fine
SEPTEMBER MOURN
The robin sits unnoticed on the fence
His bulging breast the hue of setting sun
A tired trill demands just recompense
For service rendered now his job is done.

Petunia petals sag from heavy heat
Dead daisies peer at life with
ghostly eyes
Mice colonize the shocks of
withered wheat
Carnations fade like damaged
merchandise.
Tomatoes stage their final
summer stock
Regretful their sweet show is
growing sour
Sharp Ceres keeps her eyes upon
the clock
And sets the time for every fruit
and flower.
In spring fair lassies bloom and
are adored.
In autumn they are trampled
and ignored.

Paul Spencer
New England Puritans
We left Old England's shores for
freedom's sake;
For freedom of our right to
worship God
In our own way, for we were the
Elect.
We braved the wilderness and
built our homes,
And taught our young with Bible
and with rod.
We welcomed settlers to our
colony,
But only if they shared our way
of life,
And joined the church that
showed salvation's path.
We forced young Roger Williams
from our midst—
He thought the pagan Indians
owned our land,
And even preached that each
man had the right
To find his God without our
ministers.
This heresy we could not
tolerate;
We should have hanged him for
his evil thoughts!
We drove the Quakers and the
Jews away,
And kept the stocks and
whipping posts for all
Who dared profane the sacred
word of God.
Witches we hanged to glorify the
Lord,
Though later we recanted—some
of us.
We founded Harvard, and we
fished for cod;
We built our ships, and traded
'round the world.
And when the British king
sought to repress
Those liberties that we had
labored for,
We led the way at
Lexington-Concord
To gain our independence from
the yoke
Placed on our necks by England's
George the Third.

P. J. Morisey
PERHAPS A POET
Here I go again
dreaming I'm a poet
The master of words,
filled with deep emotion.

Trying to share with the world
all that I dream of in life.
Perhaps trying to be more than I
can.
Or maybe just the challenge of
reaching you.

Joy Love
ALONE I WALKED
Alone I walked down a
country road where darkness
and creatures be but fear
I not because I knew you
always walk with me.

Alone I walked down a
city street with dirt and
hate and crime but fear I
not because I knew you
are with me through all time.

Alone I walked down life's
long path. There were many
an obstacle there but fear
I not and past them went
because I knew you cared.

Karyn Ellis
UNTITLED

———————————————

*To my mother and father, whose
love is my blessing, and belief, my
inspiration.*

———————————————

Child inside don't cry, don't cry.
For what I do I have to,
no offense to you.
Victim of circumstance
you seem to be
How I hope that you can see
why I have to set you free

Laura Niceforo
THE SNOWFLAKE
I fall
and sprinkles of powder
drift to the earth.
I land
and whipped cream oceans
make tiny waves of white.
I leave
and the foam of the ocean
claims what was once its own.

Kathryn Beranek
**If the World Shall End
Today**
If the world shall end today
Can you say that you added
A special touch or glimmer
In someone's eye?

Can you say that you got
everything
You wanted out of life?
Did you see all of life you
Wanted to see?

I have not yet seen the rainbow
Or a single drop of rain land
On a flower petal.
I have not seen the sun rise
And set over the mountain tops.

If the world shall end today
I will live on, if not in human
form—
I will live in spirit, love, and
memory.

Clare Salata
GOOD-BY, YOUTH
Good-by, my youth. Farewell,
sweet friend!
I must accept touching you never,
Knowing our parting is forever.

Dearest friend, we were blessed
with faithful friends and happy,
laughter sounds.
On this day here I sit alone
watching peoples' shadows
upon the ground.
So very, many, beautiful, quiet
moments we did share!
Tonight, it's the quiet moments
that bring me thoughts of fear.
Youth, we danced and laughed
while beautiful music played. I
would kneel each night and
thank our God when I prayed.
Softly, I hum an old tune as I take
my evening walk—
hearing joyful singing in the
distance, blending with lively
talk.
I lovingly recall sweet memories
of the people I will see no
more. Pausing briefly, I step
into my silent house, and,
slowly close its door.
Quietly, and with acceptance I
whisper, good-by, my youth.

Leslie Goldberg
BLACK
Black as the sun on a solar flight,
Black as an eagle's shriek on
stormy night.
Black is the werewolf's howl
among its prey,
Black is the test paper I got today!

Gem M. Dumas
TOWERING GIANTS
I dwell upon a scene
that never leaves my mind
Of majestic towering mountains
blanketed with pine

They glisten in the winter
they relive the spring each year
The summer comes on gently
and she holds each moment
dear

I close my eyes when weary
and once again I see
That scene that lives forever
in the very heart of me

Esther L. Schulthes
QUIET SNOW
So quietly the snow falls
Beautiful and still
But relentless.
Covering all things
Falling into cracks and sweeping
Over the ground making lovely
designs.
Decending on cattle and creatures
Leaving a mantle of white as a
cold coat.

The trees and bushes reflect
The beauty of its fall.
Beauty is not all it seems,
Treachery is another name.
Like a thief, it slips up and takes
away
Mobility. It swirls and mounds—
Like sand on the desert or
beach—
Beauty and the Beast!

Anthony M. Ochoa
PUNCH OUT
An ant died today at the
company hill.
All kept quiet.
All were nervous.

The worker escaped from his
monotonous routine.
Today he had no need to punch
out.
But, his friends left the company
hill
punching holes on the card of life.
The parking lot was empty,
except for the only
memorial of his memory, his only
love,
His Car.

Joanne Burns
GIMMEE AND THANKEE
One day the angels in Heaven
Were all in a terrible fizzit!
An auditor found the books were
off
When he called one day for a
visit.

The bookkeepers worked &
worked & worked
for two weeks and a day;
Then one guy with a cherub-like
face
Said, "I'll explain if I may."

"I have found the problem—
But I don't know what to do;
This has got me puzzled,
And I'm really in a stew!"

"There are lots and lots of
Gimmee prayers
Fast coming in and yet
There's only one little Thankee
prayer
in the bottom of my basket!"

Christina M. Halacy
MAINE
Walk through a hay field
That's flowing like the sea
Looking at the flowers,
Protected by bees.

Stopping under an Oak
At the top of a hill
Looking at the country below
you,
And the old mills.

Walking across the bridge
Over the rumbling brook
To find your way back home.

This is Maine, beautiful and free
Full of wildlife and resorts
For vacationers to see.

Sights and lakes
Ponds and streams
Maine is set up
For everyone's dreams.

Alden E. Jones
THE GLORIOUS SUNSET

———————————————

*To Margaret Fraser, who helped
me begin.*

———————————————

The sunset starts
While I'm sitting on a hill
With flowers all around me, so
soft.
And then the sun sets, almost in
layers,
First in pink, then orange,
And as it turns into night,
A layer of light purple.
Then in the distance
An orangish pink appears
Behind the shadows of the

Our World's Best Loved Poems

clouds,
And a blue, too extraordinary to
describe,
Repeats itself
Until it gets high, so high
That it turns into dark purple
And above it a magnificent,
almost perfect
Royal blue.
Now, as it grows darker,
There is just a glimmer of the sun,
A wonderful bright orange, with
purple around it,
And bits of pink between the trees.
Now, as it sets faster, I know it
will soon be night,
As the royal blue turns into black,
Dark black,
And the orange light disappears
Into the depths of night.

G. E. Martin
WE MEET AND
We meet and
touch with hands
of empty grace.

Barney M. Lowder
NIGHT IN THE CITY
Passionate rythms,
Multi-colored lights
Glimmer and glisten
Against majestic faces
Of the cities walls.
Synchronized neon rain
Pours forth personality,
That only bright lights
Can create.
Night-creatures prowl,
Trying to satisfy
Their unceasing hunger.
Yet, after the lights
Are gone,
The cities personality
Lives on.
The night-creature's heart
Craves the lights,
The night,
And his return.

Marian Mine
THE COUNTRY DOCTOR

*To my brother, Dr. V. P. Owen,
who dedicated his life to
medicine and his fellowman.*

A country doctor is many things,
A character deserving of angel
wings!
For calls at 3 A.M., you see,
Are tough to make cheerfully.
"An upset stomach? That's too
bad."
Castor oil is prescribed for the
little lad.
"Let's take a look at that throat
now, son.
Don't squirm, young man—I've
just begun!"
"Nurse, an injection is needed, I
would say.
Catch him, nurse! He's running
away!"

All kinds of illnesses, dull and
inspired,
Are voiced to this man who is
plainly tired.
But patience, kindness and
compassion he blends
With knowledge and skill to

prescribe for his friends.
He gets out his pad and scribbles
a line,
Telling you cheerfully—"You'll be
just fine!"
Somehow you trust him. You
know he is right,
And so you go home and sleep
soundly all night.
But Doc is called out at a quarter
to five.
Now there goes a man more dead
than alive!

And so he lives life
Giving life to his brothers—
This country doctor's life—
Dedicated to others!

George Fredrick Wise

George Fredrick Wise
FORGOTTON LOVE

*To Mr. and Mrs. George W. Wise
with the love and understanding,
who with love and respect helped
me, to become what I am today.*

O, love of life
Where have you gone
To never know
What life is about
To see the sun
And moon and stars
Never to hold
A new born child
Or to see a women
At her best

To never know
What life is about
Or to see a mountain top
Or to see the first new frost
Or see a robbin

In her nest
Or to know a child at its best
To hear a river flow
Or to see the first new snow
To look up and see a rainbow
O forgotton love
Where have you gone

Christina L. Milford
HARVEST MOON
The harvest moon gives off a
glimmering light.
A brisk cool chill spreads
throughout the night.
Far away in the distance an owl
will awaken soon,
Closer still a dog howls at the full
harvest moon.
It's the end of summer and the
song the blue birds sing.
Autumn will begin in this hour, I
sit and wonder what it brings.
But when theres an ending, a
beginning will also start,
perhaps a new awakening to the
dreams deep inside my heart.

Marilyn A. Tempel
FAREWELL
With the hour of departure
nearing
I wonder, should I be in a sadden
state; or
Try to make each moment linger?

The sentiments of such, I have not.
For thoughts of you and the
feelings shared
Will endure a lifetime.

As we part, my only desire is; for
Every person to have a friend,
such as you
Once and forever.

Mary Ann B. Mistric
ANNIVERSARY
We defied the rules.
Strengthened by love so strong.
No security needed beyond the
securing of being one.
The rapture of embracing and
creating life.
Time together passing swiftly.
The first year yesterday.
Time creeping along when
seperated.
Making the days unending.
The nights an eternity.
Made bearable by stored
memories of joyous re-union.
Our vows have been kept.
First in youthful love, now in
mature love.
We cannot say which we choose.
For each year has a seperate
strengthening of love.
Whether it be the year of the
childbirth.
The year of each particular trial
or tribulation.
God has blessed each year for us.
By giving yet another year to love.

Lesli Wilcox
YOU KNOW HOW I AM
You know how I am—silly
dreamer . . .
slaying dragons with my tears.
You've watched me grow up
and down in a day,
and you've seen me give it all away
to anyone,

then take it back
from you—the magician
with the "make it all better"
potions.
And yes, I'm a child,
but I'm old enough not to see
clearly
anymore. I'm an angel
behind a black veil,
who sees in shadow.
I get confused when I try to focus.
You know how I am—the maker
of nightmares for diversion . . .
the lover of lovers . . .
You've held me when all I could
do was love you,
and you've felt my claws in your
eyes.
You know how I am—the rainbow
painter, who runs out of color
occasionally, and reaches
for your magic.

Esther M. Thompson
**Let Some Sunshine In Your
Heart**
Start each day with a smile and in
a little while
All who meet you will be happy
and gay,
Your heart will be lighter and the
day brighter
As the clouds will roll away.

If you smile and send out love to
those around you
Happiness is sure to have found
you
Doubt and fear will disappear,
And everywhere you go, your
love will surely show
That a smile is the sunshine in
your heart.

Let some sunshine in your heart,
Thats the way to start each day
In a little while, you will smile
And the day will be O. K.
Just try it and see, and I'm sure
you will agree,
That a smile is the sunshine in
your heart.

Trish Hane
HAIKU TIMES TWO

*I dedicate this poem to Debbie
Baldwin of Warrensburg, Missouri.*

My teacher, my friend
Now we sit and talk
Through fingertips our souls pass
Your face hovers above you
Through tongues pass our minds
We reel in wisdom

Germaine Brousseau
A CENT'S WORTH
A dollar isn't worth much these
days,
Of this we all know;
And a cent is worth even less
In this great big economic mess.

Yet, sometimes, it is worth more
than you think.

To little Jeannie, who saved and
saved
Nine ninety nine—but that was
all;
And because she lacked just one
cent,

She could not buy the marked
down to ten dollars doll.

And then to arthritic great
grandpa, a cent's worth is
An unmeasurable amount of
relief;
And he will emphatically tell you
so, too,
For he always, always wears a
copper penny in each shoe.

Jenna V. Ownbey

Jenna V. Ownbey
HALLOWE'EN'S COMIN'

*To the youth department of
Amarillo Public Library and all
grandchildren everywhere*

Hallowe'en's comin';
You better watch out!
There's gremlins and goblins
Hangin' about!
And apples for bobbin'
Right here in the bin.
There's ghouls and ghosts
Three—sheets—in—the—wind!

Hallowe'en's comin';
Get ready for fun;
Let's put gremlins and goblins
Back on the run,
And scare-up some parties
With laughter and shout!
Hallowe'en's comin',
And you better watch out!

Gertrude Durkee
TO PERI-WINKLE
Such a happy sounding name
For one so dainty and lovely, yet
sturdy
As you ramble and bloom so
profusely, year round
On garden hedges long country
lanes.
Your name can never describe
The beautiful, pale lavender blue
hues,
Your delicate little blooms use.

Perhaps, one day, a lovely young
miss
On the brink of womanhood and
life,
Will fall madly in love with you.
She will select your lovely hues
To grace the gown, chosen for the
Prom,
Her youthful fresh young
beauty
Enhanced by your lovliness and
sound.

She may, very well, turn out to be
The "Belle of the Ball"
For everyone to see and admire
And unanimousely agree
Without any misapprehension
Mostly because of you
Pretty Peri-Winkle blue.

Helen Strey
I'LL TAKE THE TIME

*Written for Brother Roland Reed,
Oct. 23, 1976, just before he &
wife, Lillian left for Pakistan to
help their son Lee Reed & family
with their Agricultural
Missionary work.*

I am my brother's keeper, so I will
write this rhyme, for
Loving words bring health and
joy and many blessings devine.
These words describe you, Oh
brother of mine—
"I'll take the time, yes, I'll take the
time."

From a lamb that is lost to God's
"Human Kind", asking,
"Will you come and help me?
"Brother says, "I'll take the time".
"Come see all my sheep—they
know they are mine—
And Your Shepherd still loves
you—yes—He'll take the time".

("There's hay to haul soon and
beans to combine"—)—
"I see that you need me, so I'll
take the time".
This child would go hunting or
learn a scripture line
But everyone's busy—What?—
You'll take the time???

To some one defeated, depressed,
in a bind—
Brother says, "Come! Let's hunt
rocks! I'll take the time.
God's world of nature has healing
sublime—
We'll take a hike—yes, I'll take
the time."

Ahhh Satan calls "RICHES!
COME WINE & DINE!
Don't help your neighbors, you
don't have the time!!"
"Depart from me Satan! Your offer
I decline!
I've great wealth in HEAVEN—
yes, I'll take the time!"

"And if on this earth, I find a gold
mine
I'll use it for JESUS—yes, I'll take
the time!"
"The harvest is ripe, but laborers
won't sign"
My brother said, "Master, I'll take
the time".

In a far country your son &
neighbor's heart's
pine—(Pakistan)
They're flooded & damaged—
"Lord, I'll take the time."
(I don't know their language)
Hands! I'll show them mine!
I'm not much for speaches but I'll
take the time."

"We are the branches and You are
the vine—

If you ask for my life—well—I'll
take the time.
I'll take the time, yes, I'll take the
time"
My brother said, "Neighbor, I'll
take the time—
I'll take the time, yes, I'll take the
time—"
My brother said, "JESUS, I'LL
TAKE THE TIME."

Pamela Jay
explanatory note
may 6th,
dear L:

my ancestors didn't fall . . .
they were pushed.
and although you tell me
your ancestors
did not commit such atrocities,
i know i can never forget
that nobody helped,
but instead, they watched,
(and maybe laughed)
silently condoning.
that hurts, my friend.

my ancestors are from
a different world,
and our world can't change this
past.
try to understand . . .
we're different.
however, we assimilate
and disintegrate,
and we leave the doors
of the gas chambers left open,
quietly inviting.
that frightens, my friend.

Cobra Casey
EACH TIME WE MEET
Each time we meet
I tell myself it's the last
Yet, how could it be
When each time I desire you more
Flashes of the two of us
Often on my mind
You move me in ways
I haven't been moved before
Wrong, it may be
Tell that to my heart
And still, my mind refuses to
listen.

Joni Johnston-Meyers
THE SEA
Churning	Peaceful
Black	Clear
Enraged	Calm

	Blue
	Green
	White

Water
Wet
Life

	Salty
	Undertow
	Dark

	Drowning
	Sleeping
	Death

Dorothy Cuzner Ross
SPRING
It looks a lot like winter,
Though the calendar says it's
spring.
I guess it's just not ready yet
To really do its thing.
The flowers lay in slumber,

Just a little longer.
That should make them a wee bit
stronger
To bloom all through the day.
Barbara Merrill
Charon Come For Cindy
(The Boatman)

*To our beloved Cindy and
precious Little Billy who left
us . . . To live with Our Father In
Heaven, July 5, 1982*

The Boatman beckons,
And banks his oars . . .
And I must . . . but I *cannot* go!
Shall I lose my love,
When I've now but found him?
And the daughter I've longed for
so?
Oh No! Take the others
And go on back!
For I *can* not' . . . I *must* not go!

See! Look! I'm alive!
I'm *nothing* like
That shapeless, silent row!
But Oh! I feel the mist—
And the wooden seat!
And the Boatman begins to
row . . .

Glenna L. Adams
BARRY'S POEM

*To Barry L. Stauffacher: From our
first spring morning in Death
Valley, to our warm summer days
in La Buffadora, to our rainy
winter nights in Huntington, I
love you, I love you, I love you.*

I am surrounded in a warm glow
of softness, floating in satin
vails of serinity. Music flows
through me and I am caressed
with the tenderness of a breath.
My arms are entwined in the
rapture of a moment and I am
held in the strength of a
Roman army, captured in a
single word of triumph. The
scent fills the air with more
sweetness than an Emporer's
garden and I hold more beauty
than God created in the
heavens. I fill with life of a
thousand Kings whose reign
begat Kings of a universe. I am
small and frail to this grand
emenseness of eternity that
hath captured my soul to every
corner of my being. Time has
been provocatively summoned
to my need and I savor with
delicacy the nectar which now
bestowed to me, I take with
gentle sighs of life, precious
and sacred as a vow. Tears fill
my eyes as I am overcome with
the ecstasy pouring from my
dreams. Such painful happiness
I do not hope to endure but is
mine as I chance to deserve it. I
am Regal in my chamber of
near blissful insanity to which
thunderous waves of desire
satiate me into a paradise of
sweet and loving oblivion. Oh,

to steal the moment, to live an eternity in a piece of flashing time would n'er be enough to brim my craving soul to it's fill. Ah! But indeed, I have stollen the moment. I lace my soul with it's essense and in my dreams I summon it's flaming passion to again sweep me away to it's secret fortress, and again I am in the rapture of you.

Paul Magee

LOVIN' HANDS

Mama where are you now?
Your boy's a condemned man
You touched me with your life
I miss your lovin' hands

Papa where are you now?
You boy's a condemned man
You had a grip on life
I miss your lovin' hands

Padre please hear my prayer
Will I see heaven's land?
Make the sign of the cross
God bless your lovin' hands

Jesus died for my sins
Show me the promiseland
Please heal this sinners soul
Let me feel your lovin' hands

Mama I see you now
Next to where papa stands
God has forgiven me
Faith joined our lovin' hands

Vetrice Remy Jewett

MONEY IN MY JEANS

I don't understand how you are thinking, Dad.
You do not seem to know why, or understand,
I need jingle-sounding money in my hand.
Dad, I've got to have some money in my jeans.

I don't understand what is wrong with you, Dad.
I don't want your rectangular plot of land.
I want jingle-sounding money in my hand.
Dad, I've got to have some money in my jeans.

Your old land is not important to me, Dad.
You say you want me to be a man of mans
And I don't want to give you any bad scenes
But I've got to have some money in my jeans.

I don't understand how you are thinking, Dad.
If you can remember when you were a boy,
Did the jingling sound of money give you joy?
DAD, I've got to have some money in my jeans.

Kathryn Boyle Brady

PHANTASM

'Tis an eve for only spirits as the eerie wind suggests—
the dusk turns colors into gray, the shadowy reflections of the leaves,
through the impending gloom, dance round, and rustle soft;
clouds drape over the purpling

sky,
and the night begins to frost.
A chill weaves through the darkness
on this eve of masquerades—
into the mist it settles, as all vestige of day fades.
Flickering jack-o-lantern faces leer a knowing grin—
this night ghouls, ghosts and goblins are theirs
as closest kin.

A full moon burnished copper glows a weird candescent light—
illuminating phantoms and specters of the night,
who come to roam but once a year—
     All Hallows Eve—beware!
Of where you wander on this night,
if at all you dare.

Theresa (Teri) Redic

CITIZEN

I am a citizen of the U.S.A.,
I take pride in my job
and work for my pay,
This land of my birth
is my heaven on earth,
I love my country
the land of the free . . .
I can he whatever
I want to be
Opportunity is here for me.

Alene Linkous Addington

Through the Eyes Of His Child

To my Father, David B. Linkous, with love.

Observing him, you saw the strength of Samson
As he struggled with the heavy load he bore;
And in his steady gaze, you saw great courage.
You heard his voice much like the lion's roar.

As he faced each day of heavy toil and labor,
With bleeding knuckles and with caloused hand;
Much like the shepherd boy that he was named for,
Who stood undaunted by Goliath and his band.

Some beheld him in a state of fear and trembling
As he boldly acted out the lion's part;
But beneath it all, a child saw something different.
She saw, beneath that lion's cloak, a lamb's heart.

A heart that held its fears and its misgivings
Of life and self and all humanity,
That tried too hard to please all those around him,
And be what others thought he ought to be.

One that could not bear to see his neighbor lacking,
Nor to leave his sick bed till the break of day,

Nor to fail in any undertaking,
One that had the will and always found a way.

To provide those he loved with all they needed,
And then to toil for extra hours and never tire,
Just to buy a little child some foolish trinket,
Because he knew it was her heart's desire.

Helen Vendeville

Nine Live's Have I*—In Fantasy

In Poetry,—Fantasy, Of Song,
In Stories Bold and Long,
In Books that I Have Read,
Of Movies, Opera, —Said.
In All Of These I've Lived
The Best Of which Are Sieved
A Hundred Loves or More

Have Lived Within My Door
Though My Life Be One
All Of This, —I've Done—
In fascinating Storyland.
Enriching Days; Each grain of Sand
As Days are Numbered
Night's I've Slumbered
Of all I Love and Hope to Find,
So Beautifies, The Dream in Mind.

J. S. McCleary

DISAGREEMENT

Tender moments torn
Away—venom laced and still . . .
Shredded into trash.

Lech Fortulanski

GOOD BY

You close your door in front of me,
You close my life to.
Ant wont open them on my knocking,
I will not knock for long.
The day will come, when you open them
Thinking that I'm still there,
But I will be gone.
Your colling me will not help becuse,
I'm standing in front a different door.
And even if your calling won't stop,
I will not leave them.

Elizabeth Winslett

YOU AND ME

Little Bird, Singing in the tree.
You in your feathered beauty.
Singing your song of love.

What have we in common, You and Me?

I, in my arrogants and selfishness.
Earth bound creature that I be.
You flying through the air,
Happy and free.
What have we in common, You and Me?

Little Bird dozing in the Sun.
What have we in common, You and Me?
In the sad scheme above,
'Tis plain for all to see.
We are but one.

Janet Elizabeth Almas

LEFTY (CARLTON)

The baseball fans in Philly are wild about a chap called Steve
Who came to the team some years ago and they hope will not leave
And two years ago in the tp prize had his Phillies believe.

This giant hurler is in possesion of a lot of nerve
As he delivers them all—slider, change up, fast ball and curve
And he could likely pitch as well what some experts call the "slurve."

Fans who watch on TV notice his facial smirks and twists
Before he realizes that hard ball using strong arms and wrists.
Is it really any wonder that he tops the league's strikeout lists?

At six foot five, over two hundred pounds, Steve's pretty hefty
And as a southpaw pitcher he has earned the nickname "Lefty"
Who amazes the loyal fans with a style that is nifty.

Newspaper writers beware—one thing which this ace won't do
And that is submit to any sort of a press interview
But graciously give thanks to his players when a game is through.

Now I can not recall if his team was winning or skidding
When a reporter for an interview with Steve was bidding
And the answer which he received was: "you've got to be kidding!"

Each year certain players go all out to commit gross treason
Of the record books, and Steve seems to feel he has good reason
To do so by winning at least twenty games in a season.

On a talented roster complete with Petes, Mikes and Billies
There is a player bent on giving rival batters the willies
And here he is—Steve Carlton— star pitcher of the Phillies!

Phyllis Newton

CAUGHT IN A STORM

One day I was caught in a storm
Its chilled rain poured on me,
I feared its sudden strange form
And could not hide nor see.

Its twirling winds were singing
The most confusing songs
With frightening lightening
And loud thundering gongs . . .

With movement of stones and
sand
I tried comfort to meet,
Mystery of the shaking land
Seemed to dizzy my feet.

Then gushing waters arrived
Out of nowhere it seemed
Like a rolling river quite wide
Carrying things once cleaned.

Grasping the first floating thing
And drenched from head to toe,
Readily to it did I cling
While swaying to and fro.

Ending with the ravaging flood,
Storm's energy was done.
My fears and tears fell in the mud
And left me one by one.

Margaret R. Reid
But a Moment In God's Dream

Why do we always question
the lives we solely lead
and wonder if the universe
extends beyond our needs?

And must we look to helpless aids,
the truth our minds to show;
why can't we just bear insight,
our own true selves to know?

Can eyes not see the distance
and hearts not feel the pain,
as trees whose growth diminishes
without the aid of rain?

Then life could be a simple state
so easy to impart,
that each and every joy we give
would be with loving heart.

Or is each day now so complete
that living, it would seem,
is merely being part of
a moment in God's Dream?

Edward L. Nelson
"A" SIMPLE HELLO

The words are hard to find to say,
In hopes that we could meet,
I see you and my words get tied,
To make them hard to speak,

I want so much to open up,
And let my feelings flow,
I wish that I could reach right
out,
And hope that you would know,

I've often been afraid to say,
Or ask a simple question,
I know that I am just afraid,
Of unkind rejection,

I always stop and hesitate,
Each moment you are near,
Lost behind the silent song,
The words I long to hear.

Ben L. Clements
AMERICA THE BEAUTIFUL

I thank God for being born an
American,
In the land of the brave and free.
And the choice, we have to choose,
From sea to shining sea.

The freedom to speak and to live,
In a land that I love so.
And abide by our forefathers' law,
As through life's road we go.

To live and to love our brother,
Regardless of his race or creed,
Their failure or their worthiness,
Their respect and their need.

If our brother makes a mistake,
Don't make it hard on him.
But lift him up with arms of love,
And help him start anew again.

America, the beautiful,
What does it mean to me?
A land of "rights" to live by,
And a home where I am free.

David Alan Ledford
LEGACY

Fission flowers in the night
Lighting up the land so bright
People vanish in a cloud
Dust again becomes their shroud
No one left to care or weep
Man leaves his mark in rubbled
heaps

steven trent duniphan
YOU CAN'T GO BACK

When you look into a sunrise
And realize you'll never see
that sunrise again

With life being much the same
way
All the places that you've been
Are just empty chapters
In the unpublished novel of your
mind

And all the roads that you've
traveled
Bring you back to
A scene you've visited and
revisited
So many times before . . .

And they wonder why the call of
the wild
Is heard only by you
But if they only knew how this
call was answered
Their collective bloods would
surely be chilled

The streams that flow together to
make mighty rivers
Are nothing more than
snowflakes melted by those
who carry the torch of truth

And when you choose that
insidious course that's you
With all it's mystery, loneliness,
and honor
Hope there's light at the end of
the tunnel
Because you know you can't go
back . . .

Kathleen F. Kelly
MAMAS DYING

As I see her lying lifeless in the
dark room
I pray, "Mamas dying Lord, please
be gentle."
So much pain she has gone
through
As this disease seeped through
every muscle
Not once did we hear her
complain
She patiently waited for her life
to take toll
Making sure we had everything
before she went
Mamas dying Lord, please be
gentle

Ruby Nifong Tesh
FLEETING INSPIRATION

If you don't write it down
When first it comes to mind,
Then no amount of smile or frown
Will reproduce its kind.

Strike while the iron is hot,
They say, to successful be.
Write now, on the spot,
Or the errant muse will flee.

George Fredrick Wise

George Fredrick Wise
JUST FOR ME

To all the little children of the world with love and respect to them

I found myself a friend
He lives down near the sea
Hes just a funny dragon
Only I can see
His nose is pink his eyes are green
His skin is almost blue
And every time he slaps his tail
He hallers out ah chooooooo

I hide him in my closet
He plays with only me
I think that I can keep him
Until my mommy sees

Helga Marie Fentross
OCTOBER GOLD

To my husband, Henry, in memory of 28 beautiful, golden Octobers together.

These are the best days of the year,
days filled with ripened promise.
An Octoberfest of golden harvest
stored in grain,
while willful breezes
play tug of war with painted
leaves.

Sweet wine is heavy on the vine,
chancing its essence in a last
and desperate atempt to solicit
one more intoxicating kiss
from tender rays of an October
sun.

We loved these golden days,
remember . . .
at our beginning together,
with visions of eternal spring.
Where's youth gone? We ask.
Where is the harvest we've
planted then?

In the autumn of our years,
if we've learned one thing or two,
our efforts are the pay we have
received.
Next generations will gather the
fruits
of our love and labor at a future
time.

So, drink this glass of liquid gold
with me,
that golden sun has ripened for
our age in time!
Give me your hand!
We'll walk together through this
autumn land.
The best time of our lives—is now!

Kevin Moieshe Morgan
HOTEL DES INVALIDES

I dedicate this poem to Etta Andrews, who has been to me a lamp, in a world of darkness. I love you.

they don't care that the roses are
growing
in tattered and windblown rooms
all alone with no clouds in the
ceiling
no rain in the sky for the
building
but gentle faces are swaying
down
by the river that leads to Charnel
a harlot dancer with three or four
clowns
to jest and it makes them all
laugh
but infatuation is leading to guilt
and guilt is then leading to sin
so brothers and sisters are leaving
the river
to walk in the rain to Charnel.

across winter bridges that follow
the road
they sink into deeper oblivion
the ground is inchoate and the
pieces are falling
from seams in the end of the
earth
a lavender dove with some sad
summer rocks
and sometimes the crowds are on
edge
Charnel is a window with great
bows of hope
and summer is dying again
but they don't care that the roses
are growing
in tattered and windblown rooms

176

all alone with no clouds in the
  ceiling
no rain in the sky for the building.

Willie K. Charley
Ungrasped Opportunity

She wanted so much for an
  opportunity
To coyishly reveal her feelings
  for him.
She was hesitant, lest she be too
  forward.
Her hesitations made room for
  emptiness.

The opportunity came three times.
She was hesitant, too coy to grasp
  it.
Now she can plainly recall each
  opportune time
That he hinted his affectionate
  feelings.

Too coy and too hesitant then
Too lonely and empty now
Too full of rue with herself that
  she
Failed to grasp the opportunity
  somehow.

Genevieve Ostrander
EAGLE

The eagle, our emblem, and good
  reason why.
Majestic, and stately, alone in the
  sky.
With courage, endurance, and
  always alert.
So proud and with feet that do
  scarce touch the dirt.
An emblem of freedom, he sails
  through the cloud,
Through lightning, rain, and
  thunderbolts loud.
Forever, he seems to shriek peace
  in the sky,
The struggles below, surveyed
  with strong eye.
Let us pay homage to the red,
  white, and blue.
Uphold good ideals and all that is
  true.
Look up to unlimited dreams in
  the skies.
Let's look to the eagle, who
  stands for new highs.

John Highley
THE GREATEST GIFT

*Dedicated to my children who
have given me the most precious
years of my life. Thank you
Marsha, John, Tracie, Darcey,
Greg and Mark, Matt and Mindy.*

As I have travelled the highways
  of life,
witnessed and shared all kinds of
  strife,
countless are the wrong turns I
  have made,
and travelled on when I should
  have stayed.
Whenever I became downhearted
  and blue,
you would smile and say "Dad, I
  love you."
I've searched for the teasures of
  this mighty land
and all the while it was so near at
  hand,
the greatest blessing from God

above,
the undying flame of my
  childrens love.
If sons and daughters everywhere
  were just like you,
then the devil would have no
  work to do,
and then God could just smile
  and say
"I have truly blessed this world
  today!"

Glenn
AS TIME GOES BY

*To my friend, Vicky Kray, who in
being herself has inspired these
words.*

As time goes by, it's nice to know
With all the change, we all must
  grow.
With all that's new, some things
  stay true
For all that's now, was how we
  grew.

As time goes by, it's nice to show
The way we feel, the way we grow.
The time we have, we grow to
  know
Is here to bring, the Love we show.

As time goes by, it's nice to be
The way we are, just feeling free
To live our life and grow to live
The days to come, the Love we
  give.

Silvia Esposito
FLEETING MOMENTS
These rare moments of
happiness are bound to
be soffused by clouds
of depression
They are like
a pink and blue sky:
a restful vision
Moments when we
are at peace
with ourselves,
in harmony with
all that surrounds us
But then,
inevitably,
they descend
those insidious,
fastidious
clouds,
to haunt and
torment us.

John D. McMahon
A SURVIVOR'S MEMORY
  So long ago, so clear,
I saw my love splashed upon the
  ground.
  Living life with memories of
  crepuscular fear.
  So long ago, so clear,
Civilization, we know, is near.
  No one utters a sound.
  So long ago, so clear,
I saw my love splashed upon the
  ground.

Clarissa Rowena Garcia
OUR LAST SUNSET
The day quickly fades when we
  try to resist
It rises and falls long before you
  or I realize it is gone
When our dreams become

destiny
We discover we can't go back

Remember the wasted time?
It was so easy to wait for tomorrow
And hold things off 'til later
I have neither regret nor a wish
  to change
Just a desire to trade in those
  wasted moments
And make this day last a little
  longer
It doesn't seem like much to
  ask—
But it's more than I'm allowed

It's too late to masquerade the
  tears
We shared the past and we'll
  share Our Last Sunset
Until it disappears
And we'll face the future
  independently

We'll meet again-behind the
  lights
Inside the gates that years
  construct
And within the garden that time
  grows
We'll share some music, our
  thoughts, and the memories

Yesterday was happy and
  Tomorrow will be bright
But, for now, let me have this
  moment
And I will think about Today.

Miss Aster L. Truesdale
Where's Our Faith In God?
Where is that great love
That our ancestors knew?
Where is that enduring strength
From which we all grew?

Where is the strong faith
To let God be our guide?
Where are those Bible rules
From which we learned to abide?

You know, God hasn't moved,
It's us who have lost the way.
We forget—too soon—those
  miracles
That He performs for us each day.

We have left our landmarks;
God isn't the Leader anymore.
We've turned to those *idol gods*
That we detested before.

It's time to turn back to God
And trust Him as we should do.
It wouldn't hurt to fast and pray,
And study our Bibles more, too.

An if we help strengthen another
Who has lost his way.
We would be strengthened
  ourselves,
For this, God *does* repay.

Rodney Rivera
ONE AND ONLY

*Inspired by and dedicated to
Terry Rivera My Wife*

A touch
A gentle thing
A kiss
The same
All good things of romance
If done with one
That one is you!

Suzanne Larsen
AUTUMN LEAVES

In memory of my Grandmothers

Gone the green and flexibility of
  Youth,
Brown and brittle with Old Age,
Floating down to rest in Death.

Melissa Anne Justice
GOD'S EYES
  When you look
into the sky at night,
  Do you see things
that are very bright?
  Some may seem small
and dim to you,
  But, they are GOD'S EYES
looking down on you.
  So, when you see them
look up and say,
I love you GOD for every day.

Ellie Connelly
**Where Has the Summer
Gone?**
Where has the summer gone?
All those sandwiches of peanut
  butter,
And glasses of milk or punch?
Why, the summers have
  multiplied,
Since those precious days,
of sticky spots on the walls and
  doors,
Not to mention spills upon the
  floors;
Spots and spills disappeared
  somehow.
And summers passed quietly by—
No running out of peanut butter—
No one to eat it, 'cept I.

Cosetta Castagno
AUTUMN SONG
Cricket, sing your autumn song,
Of life and love, and dying;
Sing of misty, moonlit nights
And wild geese southward flying.
Sing of cabins snug and warm
And hearth-fires brightly burning;
Sing of dusty country lanes
And drifters homeward turning.
Sing to one who wanders far
In search of wealth and learning—
Cricket, sing your lonesome song
And hasten his returning.

Dorothy Jean Horton
HAPPINESS
I plucked a trailing star
From midnight's fold,
It changed to liquid fire
Within my hand.
I plucked a white cloud
Floating slowly by,—
There fell into my palm
Cool drops of dew.
I held my fingers high anon,
The South wind breathed
So gently there between.
Within my sacred home
I stretched them forth again,
And lo! There nestled soft
  within—
A baby's hand!

I
THE GREAT GEESE
You and I were never much for
  words,

then again, maybe that was all
right.
You never said much but you
spent some time
and together we shared the
mystery of the great geese.

I remember it was a cold clear
morning
and I hated to hunt;
but together we stood in awe of
the
proud honkers making their way
south.

I never understood much about
you
or myself either,
but there that morning
I felt what words could never say.

Understanding, then, is feeling,
not always thought,
and the feelings I have
are the lessons you taught.

You will be leaving soon
(I feel it);
I guess everything does sooner or
later
just as the great geese always go
south.

But you will always be with me.

Even now I see a vision
of the great geese and
I feel that day long past and the
things
you and I could never say with
words.

Mary Frances Murphy
LONELY MAN

To a very dear and special friend.

There was a man lonely and blue,
Who didn't know what to do.
At his window he would sit by
the hour.
Just wishing and praying for the
power
To bring you back to sit there too.

Billie H. Lee
AFTER HE'S GONE
After he's gone don't think of the
sorrow
Remember his special smile
After he's gone don't think of his
sickness
the way you last saw him
in nothing but pain and in a shell
Think instead of the way he is
now
walking so straight, his head held
high
After he's gone don't think of the
bad times
cherish the times you laughed
and loved together
After he's gone remember his
faults and love him anyway
Now he's an angel and perfect as
can be
After he's gone cry if you must
but know
you 'll meet agin a happier day
After He's gone remember the
love we all shared
the smiles, the hugs and know
we'll all be together again.
After we are gone.

Billy Porter
Through the Years Dad
Dad this is a special day for you
To look back on the years gone by
And remember the wonderful
times we had
And the love we shared you and I
Growing up was such a
memorable time
And I'd love to do it again
But I can't relive those yesterdays
now
Except in my memories of then
So each day I pause and go back
in time
To a world that's so precious to me
And relive those wonderful years
I had
With the best dad a father could be

**"Bud" Gearhart, Doctor of
Literature**

*"Bud" Gearhart, Doctor of
Literature*
**Jack Kotchman's Hell
Drivers**

---

*To Margie, my wife, who loves
County Fairs, and the fun of
grandstanding every once in a
while.*

Marauders of tranquility,
    Artists in flinging steel,
They arrive at the County Fair,
    Welcomed in for the kill.

First, an elegant grandstand pass:
    Speed-thrilled growling in
    straight pipes;
    Then a six car screaming leap.
    Floating through the
    momentary soft drone of flight,
    Backed-off engines gently
    popping,
    Unabashed in landing,
    They raise the crowd;

The grandstand cheers and clears
    its line-of-sight:
    "Look out ground
    Here they come."

Faith M. Schremp
**Easter Under the
Christmas Tree**
The Easter baskets looked so
bright
Underneath the Christmas lights,
And the children think it's great—
Every time we celebrate!

They didn't know how it began
The day Pearl Harbor felt Japan,

And all our soldiers marched
away—
Hoping to return one day.

Mother trimmed the Christmas
tree,
But there was no joy nor glee.
Mother said, "That tree will stay—
Until the boys come home one
day!"

And as the winter came and went,
The Christmas branches drooped
and bent;
But tinsel sparkled 'mid our
prayers—
'Til Easter gladness filled the air.

The furloughed boys came home
awhile—
You should have seen our mother
smile!
We had a double holiday . . .
And . . . our tradition came to stay!

Shirley B. O'Keefe
AUTUMN SPELL
Summer will soon be behind us
For I feel Autumn in the air
And everywhere I go or look now
I see changes going on there.
The green leaves are fast changing
To red, yellow, orange, and brown
Since Jack Frost paid a visit
And started painting everything
around.
What a spectacular sight to see
And what a wonderful aroma to
smell
It's a shame everyone can't be here
And be caught up in this
Autumn spell.

Frances A. Sheppard
AFRAID OF LOVE
I used to think in love's a fool
    I took my time & played it cool.
I really didn't understand
    Love can be fun—it's rather
    grand.

I've changed my thoughts and my
    desires
    My love for you will never tire.
I only hope that you can see
    What your loving means to me.

Its very hard to show my feelings
    For fear of hurt and time of
    healing.
I want to make you happy hon—
    And that comes from the heart.

You've got to show you care
    somewhere
    You've got to make a start.
If you should think that we won't
    last
    Tell me now—my Love's grown
    fast.

I guess this was an easy way
Of telling you my thoughts today.

Florence E. Brytcuk
**November the Twenty
Second**
We lost our president this sad day,
They took a life so free and gay.
Shot down by a sniper's bullet.
He left the world to sorrow and
fret,
He gave his life that wars should
cease.
He gave his blood for the dove of
peace.

Prejudices he fought to abolish.
True love for man his dying wish.
God must finish where he left off,
To spare our country from
becoming soft.
A man so young and strong was
he,
His name was PRESIDENT
JOHN F. KENNEDY.

Tom Camp
MY WISHES
I've slightly thought, I'd like to be
    of service, to my fellow man,
But I'm so common, no special
    gift to soothe, or lift,
A person in trouble, or explain
    eternal working plan!
Of how to live in the best regards
    of Life, not as a gift.

Neither do I want to be on the
    shelf, just looking down!
On the race of men as they
    stumble by,
I don't want to feel, I'm not
    myself, just a sham!
At least a little, I want to reply to
    their haunting cry.

And if I do but little, I want my
    head erect,
Have the good regards of the few
    I might know,
The right kind of man, they'll
    believe, respect,
I'm not the kind to bluster, blow
    or show!

I know I can never, I'll not try, to
    hide myself from me,
Because I know I'll see, the man I
    wasn't, but ought to be,
What ever happens, I want my
    self respect, and conscious free!
I may fool the world for just
    awhile;
            But not GOD, His eyes,
                everything can see!

Donna M. Cotter
BOAT OF GLASS
My boat of glass depths
Is for all to see
Reflects and concurs
My life totally.

Towards the horizon it speeds
To certain destiny
Leaving ripples of hope, faith
And love to test me.

Starboard on my final voyage
The Shipmaster waits
Bestowing me with His love
Bound for pearly gates.

Alice Priscilla Stateman Hannibal
HAUNTED HOUSE
A ledgend tells of haunts that
roam
In this old house—once mortal
home
Of folks, long gone, who once
lived here;
    They welcome be, in love, not
    fear.

Their presence hovers everywhere,
In corridors and on the stair;
Elusive wraiths drift to and fro
    Midst shadows cast by fire-
    light glow.

Naught now, decay nor eerie
gloom

That once enshrouded every
    room—
As decades passed and no one
    came
The old, abandonded house to
    claim.

This house restored with love
    and care
Has hospitality to spare;
May welcome never be denied
To ghost guests who would
    here abide.

Maxine Humrich
OCTOBER
And the crispness of the air is
    soothed by the lull of the
    branches of wild oak trees.
Leaves gather in heaps upon the
    dampened ground by last
    nights heavy rain.
The leaves, in yellows, greens and
    reds seem more alive now than
    they have ever been.
And each tree mutters to his
    brother of how they soon will
    be faced with the cold.
And smiling to himself, on the
    steps of someones home, sits
    the Jack-O-Lantern.

Gloria Woods Buchanan
IS THERE LIFE IN SPACE

*Dedicated With Love To, The
Astronauts.*

As I stand looking up at a velvet
    sky,
And a billion stars look back at
    me
I ask myself is there Life in Space,
Will man ever unlock all the
    mystery.

And as I stand gazing in wonder
    and awe
I see a shooting star go speeding by
Could this be a space craft on its
    way home?
Carrying our brothers from the
    sky.

Are they returning to their own
    little world
Where happy children laugh and
    play,
Do robots tuck each child in bed,
And do they teach them how to
    pray.

Do they dream dreams? Do they
    cry?
Just like our own human race.
Do they have mothers,
    sweethearts, and wives?
Will we ever know if theres Life
    in Space.

Jeannette R. Fulker
ME
Being a child is really great
I'll grow up soon enough, just wait.
Let me smell the flowers on a
    warm sunny day
Let me enjoy the fun and laughter
    with my friends at play.
When I say "I love you," just
    know that it's true
For I haven't learned to deceive
    me or you.
I haven't yet learned to be so

"uptight",
Give me time, I will learn how to
    read and to write
LISTEN, PLEASE LISTEN, I
    WANT YOU TO HEAR
My urgent message loud and clear.
Don't fret about what you wish
    I'll someday be
Love me now, as I am, UNIQUE
    AND WONDERFUL ME.

Kenneth L. Thomas
I BELIEVE
I believe in the sun
Even when it does not shine
I believe in love even when it's
    hard to find
I believe in people
Even when they put me down
I believe in life even when on me
    it may frown
I believe
I believe in laughter
Even when the jokes on me
I believe in friendship
Even though your best friend may
    be your enemy
I believe in gentleness
Even when it is not shown
I believe in humility even in
    those to whom it is not known
I believe
I believe in the past
Even though in it we should not
    dwell
I believe in the future
Even though what it may hold for
    us we cannot tell
I believe in all mankind
Even though we can be cold and
    mean
I believe in God even though he
    can't be seen
I believe

Robert S. Andersen, M.D.
ABANDONED AT BIRTH

*To Mother, whoever she might
be.*

Like stars your tears come out at
    night
to fall upon the floor
while thinking how your life
    might be
if she had loved you more.

Was it you that day or was it fate
that sent her out the door
if you had been somebody else
would she have loved you more.

Would life have been played better
would you have a higher score
might you have not been second
    best
if she had loved you more.

Your golden goddess then and now
once and forever more
could she produce a different you
if she had loved you more.

Was it you or was it her
is there fault or is there none
were you chosen or abandoned
were you anybody's son.

Might your life be very different
you now ask and can't ignore
if she had loved you better
this queen, this goddess-whore.

Joseph C. Hoffman
THREE-DAY CALENDARS
My calendar has three—
Hundred sixty-five days,
The same as yours
And Pope Gregory's.

'Today' runs into 'Tomorrow'
And is then bumpt
Back into history.
Life is a stay
Of bumpy days.

Most need just one calendar
No matter how many rooms
They dwell in—unless
Senility makes them forget
When entering another room.

When Holidays come,
Those red-letter days,
Not-oft-seen relatives come,
Renewing family ties.
For them, I have a special calendar
Consisting of only three days—
Holidays.

Years go by fast when you have
Three-day calendars.

Mrs. Christine J. Reggans

Mrs. Christine J. Reggans
UNTIL I HAVE YOU

*To my husband—James W.
Reggans, Sr.*

Until I have you, the sky won't be
    blue,
the sun won't drive away the rain.
I must have you so the world can
    be normal again.

You teased me and taunted me
    the whole Summer through,
you made me think, I almost had
    you.

I was too busy and happy to
    notice the change,
when blue skies above turned
    into rain.
I should have realized right from
    the start,
you wanted me only to break my
    heart. I am still
game, I'll go on the same, loving
    you, until I
have you.
Elizabeth Saltz
SEA OF LIFE
The calm waters recede, dusk
    descends,
    Life is like a ship that sails.
It has many pitfalls and

advantages,
    Sail on the sea of good hope and
    life will be joyful.

There is sadness in departure,
    saying good bye,
    Loved ones are left behind as
    they sail to distant lands.
The ship's brig is home for a sailor,
    He will never see land until the
    voyage is complete.

Sail on the sea of life that has
    hope,
    Enter the Kingdom of God, for
    the righteous.
Boats come and boats go, but life is
    Like a candle that burns brightly
    and dies.

The years fly swiftly, just as a
    voyage,
    The boats sail in and out.
The thoughts we have are fond
    memories,
    Of days well spent in thought
    and contemplation.

New hope springs eternal as each
    day dawns,
    As a boat sails away seeking
    fortune
So, life is a gamble, win or lose,
    Every fire has an ember and
    every flame must die.

Dreams fade into the past as new
    thoughts arise,
    The hopes we had are forgotten.
As we embark on new enterprize,
    We gather hope from our
    endeavors.

Yesterday is but a dream, to-day
    is reality,
    To-morrow brings new joys.
Life is an endless journey to
    nowhere,
    It is the wandering spirit that
    never rests.

Calm as the ocean, life has it's
    thoughts,
    Some are rough and others calm.
We believe and have faith in
    almighty God,
    For he has led us on the path of
    righteousness

Susan R. DeFalco (Higgins)
SUMMER'S SONG
Oh how I want to hug the
    summer trees and to smell the
    sweet singing breeze,
To dig in the rich moist soil and
    to preserve it so it won't spoil;
To see the white puffs of clouds
    on blue reflecting on the
    sparkling dew.
The mountains reaching
    majestically high and the
    golden fields of wheat and rye!
Silent memories the world
    beholds and the many secrets
    that she unfolds.
Summer may seem so short and
    yet long,
But I can still hear its sweet
    singing song.

Sylvia Lee
GHOSTLY SNAKE
The fog hugged the river along its
    course,
A billowy snake which swallowed

179

trees,
Houses, people, fields, and streets,
As it inched by sinuous degrees.

The valley in its running stretch
Was cotton-covered by fluffy rags,
A rippling tunnel massing high
Carelessly sculptured with peaks
and jags.

The fog in its sleep digested the
view
With dull-grey dangling droplets
of dew.

Freda M. Rickey
A PURE HEART
I cry far too often.
No one hears, or cares, because
I'm washing my heart.
Do you care, or understand
Enough to hold my hand?

Will you give me, perhaps, just a
gentle touch, not from me
seeking
Anything, but giving such
It stops my heart, or is it just my
eyes,
From leaking?

Remembering, may I not be
comforted
By looking into your eyes, abrim
with comprehension
Of another's loneliness.
Understanding from a friend does
ease tension.

Now, when washing my heart
I cry and I cry, but hold out my
hand
To you, because you understand.
Perhaps you have some crying
and heart washing to do!

Irene Sugranes Goulding
THE STRANGLING KNOT
A wretched, strangling knot I see;
It cuts off breath and virile air,
It weakens man, ruins will power,
Destroys his manly will to BE.

You gave him life and vision,
Lord!—
A brain to use to make things
clear.
Break loose the knot, ease off the
cord,
Help him escape from puppeteer!

And let the puppeteer who dares
Call "love" what strangles, thus,
the will
Wake up and say, "It had to be.
This puppet was too smart for me."

Linda C. LaCross
FINDING ONESELF
Like the instinct of a Condor and
the pace of the Cheetah—I
vision the pricking quills of a
hellish nightmare; plastering
my broken body together as
mouthed condolences unreel
recordings.
Camelot awaits. Apparitions
tiptoe across the cobwebs of
memories. Sh-h-h, do not
disturb.
Dust gathers; collector's hobby.
Great expectations linger—like
a bitch in heat; cooing softly
the melodies of love.
Brain teasers appear pleading
verse. No interviews—the

patient is sleeping.
Webs of violence leash the night.
Black spike heels walking
across my torso.
Organism askew; rubbery legs
without an owner. Crawl,
jellyfish, crawl—a spineless
ticker—crooked ass.
No soul to trust.
The pallored skin breaks out in a
cold sweat; icy chills form
crystals of wet droplets that
smear the face.
Coils of madness spring forth to
clutch my soul. I am caught in
the womb; there is no escape.
Superficial wounds cut deep, oh
bleeding heart—count the
beats—rapid pulse drums the
chest leaving trails of acid pain.
Straight jackets, please . . . Sanity
revived.
Sugar—laced sweetness knocks;
vomit rises up in mock dispute.
Enter laughing—prognosis
reported—silent screaming.
Post-partum—maniac depressive.
Beep! Beep! Beep!
Does not compute. Elements of
kindness rush forth.
Brainwashed by science—the
chemistry of knowledge.
Encore! Encore! Fine trick.
Smashing performance—audience
dismissed.

Doris C. Smith
TRICK OR TREAT

*Dedicated bo my fun-loving
grandson, Jason Gary Smith, just
four years old.*

The doorbell rings. I hear a giggle
and I see an impish grin
When I'm at the door to find out
who is asking to come in.

It's a scary Cookie Monster
wearing blue down to his feet:
There's a voice I know that's
calling,
"Grandma, this is Trick or Treat!"

So I scurry for the goodies
for that "begging monster" boy
Holding tightly to the pumpkin
on this holiday for joy!

I rejoice with laughing children,
(I wouldn't want their 'tricks' at
all).
So be ready with your favors
before some goblin comes to call!

Brandy Yvette Mertens
SORROW
SORROW is the glistening of a
newly shed tear,
As you go to school for your very
first year;
It is what you feel,
As you hear the song that the
church bells peal;
People in mourning shuffle about,
With tear stained faces and looks
of doubt,
As they wonder why all living
things must die,
And they let out another small
and helpless cry,
Then they remember their loved

one of the past,
And they wish that everything
could last;
They offer their last prayer,
To give the living more to share;
I sit and think and wonder why,
My time will come and I must die.

Jane Ross
JESUS SPREADS

*With Love to my Mother
Florence Mary Ross*

Jesus came with might and glory
when he came to spread the story
about the power and the wisdom
invested in the lord.
Jesus spreads love and peace
with the help of the almighty.
Jesus spreads the salt in the sea
and with every soft breeze from
the ocean
is Gods gentle hands reaching out
to touch your heart.
With every harsh wind
is the sigh of Jesus.
With the roaring thunder
is the out cry of pain
in Jesus's heart.
With the pouring rain
Jesus is shedding tears.
The light in the day
is the brightness in his eyes.
The sun is his heart
flaming with love.
The moon is the torch
in his heart
that never fades out.
The stars are his arms
holding up the sky and
embracing the earth.
Yes Jesus spreads
only love and peace of heart.
Believe and forever be at peace
with yourself.

Lora Deinken
REQUIEM
Dear God, Thy servant's words
were full of comfort.
The church was hushed and full
of scent of flowers.
"The child is gone: cease now
your tears.
He's in God's hands, forever free
of fears."

But, Lord, there is a word that I
must say:
"I can't forget. It's full of gall!
Dear God, the coffin was so
small!"

Gladys Wildt
HOME AT LAST
To-nite, as I do lie upon my bed
Memories of my entire life do
ramble thro' my head;
Back to my earliest childhood
day they go,
And sweet indeed it is to have it
so.

I see a little child not quite five
summers old
Whose little heart does cry to be
a member of the fold.
Every moment by her side it doth
seem the Lord doth walk,
And thro' all of God's creations
she can hear the Saviour talk;

In the wind she clearly hears the
sweet, sad voice of Jesus say
"Follow me,"
And her heart so fondly answers
"Sweetest Jesus I'd just love to
follow Thee."
But Alas! that little maiden Jesus'
story ne'er did hear
And she thinks she cannot follow
since the Lord no more walks
here.

Down life's vale of tears, I see
that pretty maiden go
Longing ever the Redeemer to
follow here below,
Knowing not that God in Heaven
looking from his throne above
Soon shall send to her that sweet
message of His love,

For her lover far away, that sweet
story has been told,
And he writes to tell his loved one,
that he's safe within the fold,
How he's prayed to his Redeemer
who saved the ninety-nine
And he's begged his God in
Heaven
to please save "the one that's
mine."

Now, oh sweet the sight I see! by
her bed on bended knees,
That lost sheep from the Great
Shepherd
has found her conscience ease,
She simply told the Saviour of her
many, many sins
And just humbly prayed the
prayer of the publicans of old,
The Christ of Calvary washed
her,
and forgave her all her sins,
Then He said to her, "My fair one,
thou art now, one of my fold."

Reverend Jacob Bryant Moore
UNTITLED

To Mother

Summer breeze blowing,
Hesitating its wind all about my
head.
I lean forward in the clear
And feel I have opened my mind.
Looking around in the room
I see every item cluttered
Together showing etches
Of scenes I played in
Yesteryears. I wonder
And move my mind forward
At the motion of the cool
And motion of my thoughts
Are toward the coolness
Present at few moments.

Mary Katherine Fleck
HANDICAPPED

*To Clayton Hughes and Don
Garrett for showing me a
different meaning of the word
handicapped and to my father,
Herman Fleck, for loving me.*

One feels like no one else has
experienced what they have,
But there is always someone out
there in the world who has

experienced the same problem.
One feels as if they have run up
     against a brick wall sometimes,
As if there is no way to get
     around or over that wall.
One can do anything if one really
     wants it bad enough,
Don't give up just because things
     don't go your way.
One learns from his or her own
     mistakes,
Remember those mistakes and
     don't make them again.
One is not given the power to
     wish or dream,
Without also being given the
     power to make it come true.
Anyone can achieve a goal,
If they think they can.
Everyone is handicapped in their
     own way and can't do certain
     things to achieve their goals,
If they let themselves believe that.
No one is actually handicapped,
We are all just very unique and
     special people in our own ways.

Jackie A. Johnson
REQUIEM
Your Dad and I built a cathedral
     of love.
It was some thirty-five years
     under construction.
During the process, we ran out of
     material—out of money—
We had work stoppages and
     union wars.
Had we not anchored our safety
     belt securely,
We would have fallen from the
     spire.
  Now the edifice is complete,
And cathedrals are built for the
     generations to follow.

Richard L. Anthony
MAN
And the Lord said
I'll take from the ground a hand
     full of clay
And I'll form it in a very special
     way
I'll make two long legs with feet
     for them to stand,
And I'll place on them a body
That will hold a lot of glands
I'll put on it two arms that will
     point out and around
And a ball for the head and all
     this from the ground.
I'll put in it two eyes so it can see
A nose in the middle and a
     mouth to praise me.
Two ears for it to hear what to it
     I will relate
Then I'll take away one rib and
     made for it a mate
Then He breathed the breath of
     life into that hunk of clay
And it began to move in a rather
     clumsey way,
And the Lord said,
I'll call it Man because it looks
     like me.

Diane Marie Vogan
RIVER ST. CLAIR
  A widespread beauty
captured and altered in time
  Your swift current is rare
I'm impressed to know
  Your constant flow.

An Indian once sat
  at the banks of your power
Conceiving how man
  would destroy and devour
  Your endless purity.

Marie L. Anderson

Marie L. Anderson
IT'S AUTUMN

*To James Andrew Stewart, M.D.
for his encouragement, to write my
thoughts, so they could be shared.*

Leaves have turned, yellow and
     red,
The petals have fallen, the
     flowers are dead,
There are no squirrels, running
     down the trees,
No more sounds, of the honey
     bees.
It's autumn.

The beaches are deserted.
They!, are no longer fun,
There is no swimming, nor
     boating,
Nor worshipping, the sun.
It's autumn.

The orchards are barren,
The harvesting, is done,
South, again the birds, are flying.
The tourists, are, all gone.
It's autumn.

The hunters are out,
Trying to stalk, an elk or a deer.
Maybe!, a goose, or a duck,
Even, a goat, or a bear.
It's autumn.

The heavy dew in the morning,
The early sunset.

The fields lying dormant,
Ready!, for their winter of rest.
It's autumn.

Scott C. Martin
Stupid Things & Illusions (?)

For Kathy with a K

Stupid things to say to her who
     is only the best for you who
     may not be the best for her but
     you try.

But she doesn't see you trying
     and goes after an illusion of
     grandness in the worst way in
     which she can go after such an
     illusion, which could strike at
     her and break her heart in the
     way that is told in the pulp
     romance novels that are read in
     the dead of night when the
     birds are silent and the moon
     glows bright.

And you think you would like
     to go for a walk, but you know
     she's out there, and if you go
     you'll find her and she'll refuse
     to walk with you for you are a
     fool to love her. And you'll see
     her face being
     uncharacteristically hard as
     she tells you to go and leave
     her alone with herself and her
     illusion.

But is she even perhaps an
     illusion to you who may not
     yet realise that all dreams do
     not come true, and that some
     were meant to fly away, out of
     reach, never to be seen again.

But this dream must be caught
     you think, for if not, you may
     never have another. And then
     you may as well not have lived
     at all.

Mary Ann Rapolz
A MOTHER'S LOVE
If I could always be here
  When the need for me was
     there,
To help you make things easier
  And show you that I care.

But that is not the plan
  God has in store for us,
There comes a time He calls us
     home
  We must leave the ones we love.

But do not dwell on sadness
  Look towards a brighter day,
For there are many new
     tomorrows
  In your life along the way.

May God cast down upon you
  A strong and shining light,
To guide you down life's road
  To show you wrong from right.

To guide you to the crossroads
  Where we shall meet once more,
And I can take you by the hand
  And lead you thru the door.

To a place that they call
     Heaven
  God's haven in the sky,
We'll dwell there in His garden
  Where peace and beauty lie.

Chrysti Hogan
REFLECTIONS

*To my inspiration, Chris, in
memory of our rock.*

I look down
And see the trees,
And the clouds
Drifting across the sky.
The water reflects
What's really there,
Just as my soul reflects
What no longer is;
Memories of times long past.

Frieda Diehm
PA AND THE BOAT
Before we go a fishin', Pa says to
     Ma, "My dear"
Now just remember what I say
     and you'll have naught to fear.
I'll tell you how to row that boat
     so fishes we can catch
And we'll get bigger ones than
     anyone can match".

Ma promises she'll do her part
And off we gayly start.
First thing we know the wind
     blows hard right in there from
     the west.
And Pa says, "Now row that boat
     with vigor and zest."

A little farther on Pa cries, "I had
     a bump, now hold that boat
I'll cast again and hook that fish
     right in his little throat".
But while he's throwing again,
     that wind begins to blow,
And me oh, my , what Ma do to
     hold that boat just 'so'.

Then Pa says, "Now pull on your
     right and get us out of here"
But Ma she gets excited and pulls
     on left in fear.
Pa says, "You are the limit, you
     row this boat a fright
Why any little kid would know
     what is his left or right".

Then on we go and pretty soon
     when all is calm and still,
Pa says, "Now that's the way to
     row— it's just all in your will."
But Ma feels it's all in vain
To row that boat without a pain.

"Now watch yourself, you're
     getting out, so I can't reach the
     shore"
And Ma can see that Pa— is mad
     enough to roar,
So on the right and left she pulls,
     to try to make wrong right
And that's 'bout all the fish we
     catch, on that so peaceful night.

Pa puts his arm around dear Ma
     when on that homeward bend,
And whispers. "Now don't look as
     if you've lost your only friend,
Some day you'll learn to row that
     boat,
And nevermore will get my goat".

Alta E. Mackey
YUCCA
The Yucca plant of the state
Stands in the desert, tall, sedate;
Long, rigid leaves on a woody base,
White panicles to lend it grace,

181

John Campbell, Editor & Publisher

Wild and strange in a desert land,
Blending in with the arid sand.

The name came from the
children's choice.
In choosing it they had a voice
Coming from the best resort
Women's Federation gave support;
And their support had great power
To name Yucca New Mexico's
flower.

So now in many forms she dwells,
Adam's Needle and Mission Bells,
The Spanish Bayonet and Joshua
Tree
And many more that we can see,
In many climes and many states;
In desert lands she dominates.

Clarice Renee Weltzin
GOD'S STOREHOUSE

Dedicated to Lorraine Paulson

Day is now leaving—
—Soon gone is the sun—
Sky etched with Heaven's hues,
the painting soon done.

Flicked off heaven's easel—
—in a huge folio placed—
Stored in God's storehouse,
Ne'er to be erased.

Because don't you think
God's insuperable Mind
stores all of His Artwork?—
None to scrapheaps resigned.

And don't you think, Stranger,
in God's wonderful plan
We will meet and get acquainted
and then understand . . .

. . . the misplaced thoughts and
lessons
Down here we couldn't see;
But there we'll see plainly
and not lose the Key . . .

. . . to God's gold-filled
storehouse—
—Nay, not merely filled with
gold—
But with treasures of happiness
Too rich to be told!

Helen Barker Le Feuvre
LAZY DAY
I close my eyes and dream of a
lazy summer day,
Feeling the Earth's warmth and
gazing into the blue,
With grains nodding their happy
heads as though to express
Their approval of my being there.
A reverent stillness abides except
for humming of insects
With their singing reveries.

Jean Howard Russell
DARK SHADOWS

*To all my family; especially my
mother, Viola Howard Foster,
Who has always encouraged me
in my writting efforts.*

The cry of an owl, a sigh in the
wind
An eerie howl and I can begin
To see ghostly shapes form out of
the mist

To weep and sob and cry of unrest
The waning light so cold and dim
Brings shapes of ghouls up from
the brim
Of Hell; to scream and shriek and
plead
For God or Satan to set them free
They've wandered the earth for
hundreds of years
In ghostly shapes with skeleton
leers
To strike terror into the hearts of
man
Forever over this crumbling land
Their tombs they have left and
started to roam
The grave is now empty, which
once was their home
My soul is filled with a terrible
fright
As I watch them float through
the dark dreary night
I sit and I wait for the sun to rise
And drive the darkness out of the
skies
To quiet my fear and lessen my
fright
Until they return with the
coming of night.

Sheelagh M. McGurn
**A Note To My Children On
the Death Of a Bottle Of
Pop**
I've lost my fizzle.
My life is a flop.
I once was
A healthy bottle of pop.

I need a transfusion.
I need a new top.
But from this table,
I can't possibly hop.

My last dying hope
Is that with a quick grope,
I'll be returned to the cart'n
So they can put a new heart in.

Linda Jeanne Thomas
ENLISTED
Creeping mist
shrouds the plot.
Fresh-dug earth
steams-wafts
ghostly soldiers
into an icy night.
Gnarled limbs,
sprouting bony fingers,
point officiously.
Ivory troops
lie uniformly—
awaiting judgement.
Aging epitaphs

shout orders—
echoeing, unheard.
Death—the silent comander,
hath claimed
one more recruit!

Sandi Hutson
WORDS
I have no great novel to write,
No songs in my heart do dwell.
What I have are words of poems,
And sometimes my heart starts
to swell.

These words all jumbled together,
Can cause such a terrible ache.
And I must put down on paper,
Whatever form they take.

Sometimes they're sad,
sometimes happy,
Sometimes humor unfolds.
No matter what my pen writes,
These poems are the key to my
soul.

Doe Dee
CUSTER'S BATTLEFIELD
Sights and sounds are familiar
themes
A poet may write about,
But there are other things, unseen,
That bring to mind
Past feelings and dreams.

Even if one never heard its tale,
A place that is history—
Where cries of men rang in travail,
Through ridge and crag
Ghost feelings prevail.

Chills are felt and a sense of
doom
Where men of the 7th were
trapped,
And men would fight to save
some room,
Those men of red—
Whose rule would end soon.

All is there in its eerie feel.
At times, near the close of day.
They call it Custer's Battlefield.
What happened there . . .
Forever is sealed.

Robert Michael Balderrama
THANKFUL
In the evening at the close of day
When all the world is still
I thank God for the promises
He's chosen to fulfill

For summer breezes soft and
warm
For sparkling moonlight beams
The North Star that shines
brightly
In the heaven as it gleams

The gentle tapping of the rain
I in my slumber hear
To bathe the earth and quench
it's thirst
A sign that spring is near

For falling snow that bleaches
white
And blankets everywhere
The heat from glowing embers
Giving warmth to chilling air

The changing of the seasons
That soon turn the leaves to
gold
For all of this I'm thankful
As God's wonders are untold.

James C. Watts
GOLDEN RIVER

*Dedicated to the beauty beheld in
the eyes of poets: The beauties of
life, living, love, giving and all of
nature to behold.*

Flowing through a silver mist,
Walls cascading down,
As lifes' toils e'er persist,
And in its sea we drown;

Rolling past the boundless plain,
Ever-winding, ever churning;
With the seed of lifes' own grain,
And man, for God so yearning;

Spanning many heartened miles,
Rampant oft in lifes' own means,
Facing many endless trials,
While lifes' tower slowly leans;

Reaching out to meet the sea,
Reflecting off the sky so vast,
Bubbling e'er so free,
Recalling beauty from the past;

Resounding echoes cross its path,
As trees are blown in the wind,
With icy fingers in its swath,
As icy cold does oft unbend;

Golden dreams sail o'er the way,
Golden to lifes' giver,
With golden glitter in its sway,
The beauty of this Golden River.

Christina Praskin
**Tomorrow Is Here; Today
Is Past**
The lovely view,
Of a rushing waterfall;
The people are passing,
While the kids play ball.
The world is turning by
So ever fast;
That tomorrow is here,
And today is past.
The quiet country,
Just miles being free;
The ocean waves,
Coming in from the sea.
Everything is going by,
For nothing doesn't last;
That tomorrow is here,
And today is past.
The seasons changes,
From day to day;
The old generation,
Just slips away.
Life is moving by,
Leaving questions unask;
That tomorrow is here,
And today is past.

Elaine Williams
To My Baby Passed On

*In memory of my grandson,
Jeffrey Thomas Malone*

You have left us
Within us such a sad feeling
We prayed and begged to God for
healing
Your little smile was so sweet
As loved ones eyes, yours did meet
You were so precious to all to love
You have left us

You have left us
Ah, God, we missed his first tooth

Our World's Best Loved Poems

His first step with shoestrings
unloosed
The warbled words he would
have spoken
To skies above we look in
loneliness
Coo, the little sound we listen for
You have not gone, we feel your
presence near

Kelsie A. Whitten
FIRST ANNIVERSARY
It's your first anniversary
how fast it's gone
Like a rainbow
once there, then none.

A mixture of colors
like feelings in your heart
all clinging together
never pulled apart.

Now one year is gone
the rainbow is, too
But the gold is left,
I know it's there for the both of
you.

S. Patricia Thomas
**From Your Friends (To
Hubert With Love)**
Our hearts are heavy ladened
There's silence in our souls
There's a lot of saddness
That will never be told

Your life was quickly taken
Before you wanted to go
Now you are safe with Jesus
And happier than we will ever
know

We will remember the things you
used to say
The joy you always shared
We'll remember the good times
and the bad
We'll remember you always cared

You now walk with Jesus
All wrapped up in his love
Enjoy the heavenly angels
And send us blessings from above

Jackie McMurren*
DAY-DREAMING
Day*dreaming in my mind
The wind is full of rhymn
Flowers paint me colors . . . from
another space in time
Blue skys are up above . . .
rainbows are filled with love
Slender blades of grass . . . blow
slow, then fast
Fantasys not hard to find . . . day*
dreaming in my mind
I'm a star rider . . . in the twilight
of the night
A-top of Pegasus, on some
enchanted flight
I'm dancing on the moonbeams. . .
eating at the milky way
Throwing tiny silver stars to
unicorns at play
Fantasys not hard to find . . . day*
dreaming in my mind
Soon reality will say . . . enough
of fantasy
Come back and spend some time
with me, for fantasy can't
always be
But thats alright, I don't really
mind . . . because I know
Fantasys not hard to find . . . day*
dreaming in my mind

Maurine K. Benford
SOLITAIRE
The wind has finished its story
And the clouds have sailed away
And now all that's left is a stillness
That marks the end of the day.
As the shadows creep over the
forest lands
And the night is sending its cover
I shut my window and close my
eyes
For I have lost my lover.

Jo Starrett Lindsey
TIME TO ANTICIPATE
This is a lonely time,
When autumn's golden glow
Fades into naked winter,
And earth removes her dress
To fall again in sleep.

This is the pause that comes
Before the snowy blankets
Cover barreness
With artistry that seems
To clothe the earth once more.

This is the time to gather
All energies anew;
To rest, and look ahead,
Beyond the snow and clouds,
Where lies a new spring day.

Shirley A. Nuottila
HE REIGNS FOREVER

---

*I dedicate this poem to my loving
husband, children and good
friends and also in memory of my
Mother and Father, Mr. and Mrs.
A.C. Carlson of Northville, Mich.*

Brighter than sunshine is Jesus
my Lord,
Sweeter than the roses His name.
More precious than gold was the
gift He gave,
For the noblest cause to this
earth He came.

He gave me feet with which to
walk His path,
Two hands to do His will.
He gave me lips to sing his praise
And a purpose to fulfill.
Son of God, the Prince of Peace,
Born of the young, virgin Mary,
Paid for the sins of all the ages
On the rugged cross He had to
carry
Those of whom God calls His own,
The ties no one can sever.
For the King of Kings and Lord of
Lords
With majesty reigns forever.

Henry J. Dugan
YOU PROMPTED ME
You prompted me as you walked
by.
Eyes as blue as the pale blue sky.
You prompted me as you turned
your head.
You prompted me with the things
you said.
At the very start you won my
eager heart.
You seemed so glad to be with me.
The water ran calm in the deep
blue sea.
I asked you for a date.
You accepted and didn't hesitate.
We dated for a full year.

One night you shed a tear.
That tear erased that lovely year.
I was so shaken and filled with
fear.
I didn't know how to begin ever.
Gone was a leaf from that clover.
Why did you walk by at all?
Why was I the one to fall?
It was you who prompted me.
You prompted me. You prompted
me.

Susan J. W. Rink
THY NEIGHBOR'S LAWN
It's not easy, but I try hard
to see what's in my own backyard.
Before I judge my neighbor's lawn
I look around at the ground I'm on.

It is trimmed and freshly mowed?
Has my garden just been hoed?
Do I find his yard looks better
and wish that I was the
trendsetter?

Do I long for what he has?
(Freshly trimmed and greener
grass.)
Will I stand, so I'm not lower,
and go ask to use his mower?

Bruce S. Perkins
MIND FREQUENCIES

To J. R. From B. S.

Mind frequencies
  Talk through the air,
walk in this dreamlike suspension,
so amused by this dimension,
when you're just reading her
mind.
You can tell what she's been
thinking,
by the curves in her breasts,
it's all so confusing,
those big lumps on her chest.
Bringing your thoughts to
another,
your mind is so obscured.
He'll explain to you the reason,
untill your mind is cured.
And now the moment of truth is
here,
but the questions will not cease,
You're so confused by all this
madness,
until there is no peace.
And now you're caught in
another mans dream,
and these dimensions are all
imbewd.
You're beginning to realize,
the true meaning at last,
all the secrets have been spewd.
The air is so polluted,
by all this mass confusion,
you think you're in reality,
but it's really a delusion.

Deloris Ballinger
G I JOE
Hey there! Hey there! G I Joe.
How about listening to our tale
of woe.
We the American People, have
really grown ashamed.
To think this war keeps going on,
to win the big wigs fame.
So we'll tell you what we've
decided, we hope it pleases you.
We're going to send our

Congressmen, Our Presidenty
too
Rite up among you fighting men,
to see what they can do.
First we'll load them in a cannon,
and shoot them to outer space
So they can see the dirt they've
done, to all the human race.
Then we'll dress them in a trench
coat, a Helmet hard and Blue
And feed them, them old Rations,
till their guts will cry Boo Hoo
I'll bet my bottom dollar, they
will turn their tails & run
And try to get back home again,
where they can have some fun
Now all of us here People, know
this is what they'll do.
So looks like the fighting "G I Joe"
Is left right up to you
Do your fighting, do it well.
And come home soon, from that
living hell.

Tommy L. Wright
A LEAF
Twisting,
Turning,
The tiny leaf
Made it's way to the ground.
For another of God's creations
Life has ended.
A short life it may seem.
Only a season.
Such is it with the life of man.
Man is here only for
A little season.
Time is fleeting,
And after this
Eternity.

Charlotte Cook Domke
SQUIRRELS DELIGHT
They run up your sturdy branches
into your gold-red hair,
And their greedy fingers find
bronzed seed
with which to fill their lair.

They seem like artful acrobats
as round your head they roam.
They sometimes play a moment
before taking your bounty home.

The fluffy frolicking grey squirrels
admire your gold-red hair.
They love your sturdy branches
which you thrust up in the air.

When the gold has fallen
and you look like lace 'gainst
snow,
Squirrels will still skip in your
branches
as dancing and prancing they go.

Jeanetta L. Housh
WAITING FOR DADDY
Patty was locked in a cellar so dark
Her mom was loving a man
named Mark.
Pattys dad found her and with a
tear in his eye
Said "stay right here honey, now
don't you cry."
He took a gun to the adulterers
bed
The gun went off, Mark fell dead.
Pattys mom yelled with all her
might
"I'll kill you girl, better stay out of
sight."
Patty hid knowing her daddy
would come,

She kept waiting till her body
   was numb.
She heard the steps of her
   mothers search
Got scared and bolted from her
   hidden perch.
Ran toward the stairs and slipped
   and fell.
Her daddy heard her scream and
   yell.
At that exact moment a bolt of
   lightening
Struck the house, made
   everything frightening.
The house ws dark except for a
   smoldering ember
That started to ignite and burn
   the timber.
Pattys dad tried with all his
   might
To find his girl without any light
Buy the time the firemen came
Her skeleton was all that did
   remain.
If you visit the house and see the
   girl Patty
She's walking around waiting for
   her daddy.

Tony Bethel
POET

---

*To Jane, whose love and
inspiration leaves me speechless,
To the USN which makes men
great. To the state of Illinois
which I love.*

I am the poet, the one who writes
   and thinks as well.
The one who contemplates
   heaven and hell.
The one who seeks the depth of
   the soul.
The one who lifts men's spirits
   from their holes.
 I am the poet, listen and see, for
   my words shall set you free.
I am the one who will nourish
   your heart, challenge your
   brain, and give your Spirit a
   start.
I am the one you seek in your
   hour of need; when middle
   class values center on greed.
I am the one you want to hear
   when the body is weary of
   drugs, women, and beer.
I am the one who you turn to in
   doubt.
When you ask, "Is there a GOD?"—
   My words seek him out.
Yes, I am the poet for better or
   worse.
I set the mind, body, and spirit Free
   Through wit, rhyme, and verse.

Joanne Radcliffe
A TOAST TO US
Some friendships are so fragile
   they seem like desert sands.
They drift and blow and scatter,
   they slip right thru your hands.
Our friendship has been solid
   like the mighty oak and stately
   pine.
We've weathered both the ups
   and downs
   and passages of time.
I couldn't ask for more of life

than just one good friend, tried
   and true.
I'm so glad that God saw fit
   to let me have a friend like you.

Paul Graham
TELL ME ABOUT IT
So you think you can tell me
   Things I already know?
Do you think that its worth it
   Using your time up so?
Do you think you can show me
   A better way to go?
Or would I be wrong
   To say I'm already gone?

The questions we keep asking
Are reflections of our dreams
They all are little pieces
Of all our greater schemes

Golda Hiles
SNOWFALL AND SILENCE

---

*Dedicated to my husband, Mark,
with whom I shared many happy
years and beautiful memories of
the tranquillity of a Missouri
snowfall.*

We gaze from windows . . . Far
   below
the voiceless vastnesses of snow
gaze back at us . . . There is no
   word.
There is no tree; there is no bird.
We look for clouds that sail on
   high.
There is no cloud; there is no
   sky.
There is but winter everywhere
to chill the world, to chill the
   air,
to still the cloud of somber gray,
to still the voice of yesterday.
We gaze from windows . . . Far
   below
the voiceless vastnesses of snow
gaze back at us . . . There is no
   fence,
no weed to mar earth's elegance.
No spoken word within the air.
Just silence . . . silence . . .
   everywhere!

Mrs. Nancy B. Jensen
SMILE

---

*To My Husband and Family, and
the World, With Love. I'm sure if
we all lived according to this
poem, we would all be better
people.*

You have so much to offer, so
   much to understand
Live your day to the fullest, and
   smile all you can
Be thoughtfull to your neighbors,
   Be gracious to your friends
Live your life for giving, and
   Smile all you can
The love you bring to others, can
   help you on your way
To understanding others, and
   smiling every day
So try to teach another, to learn
   the ways of man
and in this way of giving, you'll
   really understand.

Antonino E. Najera Sr.

Antonino E. Najera Sr.
THIS IS MY LAST REFRAIN

---

*In the name of Pa*Usaffes I do
solemnly dedicate this poem—To
war veterans of congress.*

For 40 years I tried to request
   "just compensation",
On my disabilities—but not to
   your satisfaction.
This undesirable condition was
   due to your War,
Just Compensation" I endeavored
   to claim this Far.
We absorbed most of the
   punishment from the
   treacherous Japanese
And the longest, defending
   Democracy and the Philippines.
After the cloud of War—benefits
   to Filipinos we were denied,
Equality—PA—USAFFEs in
   unison—had often cried.

As I imagine that symbolic
   guiding Light of Liberty,
With its inherent meaning on
   non-prejudice and equality,
The Law Makers down below,
   gave Veterans generous
   Compensation
But not to PA—USAFFEs—
   ignored—don't mind our reaction.
After all the War was over and
   they don't even Care,
All our barkings falls in the
   dark—they can not hear.
What an ironic actuation—they
   developed double standard
Yet they Advocate Democracy—I
   don't have high regard.

As a Released POW—supposed not
   to challenge our Conqueror,
Resumed fighting—believing
   Democracy might yet be the
   Victor.
Kindly take a second look—if we
   deserved all of these,
Our undivided loyalty and
   endeavor—understand please.
After hostilities "Back Pay"
   comes—I was pronounced "Pay
   Back",
This hit me like a thousand Volt
   line—I was shocked.
Co-organizer—our men were
   recognized and paid as should be
But I was not—Victim of
   circumstance, can't you see!
Yours truly, requested for
   recognition and was approved
But "Pay Back"—just the same—
   this is very absurd.
My name was then dropped in
   the Roster for recognition,
They say USAFFEs will receive
   Federal Pay, I should not
   question.
It was then Mac Arthur's
   promise, all USAFFEs be
   Federalized,
The General, was no law maker—
   our dreams were not realized.
Democracy, supposed to uphold
   equality and "just compensation"
We do believe then—now this is
   a wrong notion.
The "Cream of our youth died in
   vain"—so they say,
But look at the Symbolic
   Liberty—might guide you yet I
   do Pray.
America, have your second
   thought—so our loyalty be not
   in vain,
In any-wise—thank you just the
   same—this is my last Refrain.

Linda Baylor Swan
I WANTA WIN
Enough of this aggravation,
This bent of sheer frustration,
I wanta win!

It really is my turn, you know.
I've worked and thought and
   struggled so.
I wanta win!

I wanta, oughta, gotta win!

Debbie L. Miller
LOVE

To Allen with love always.

Love is like a flower,
it blooms and it grows.
Care for it—
and it will continue,
but abuse it—
and it will close and die.

Tamara Annette Skilling
DREAMS
Dreams are very special to me.
They let me set all my spirits free.
Dreams can also be very fun.
They let me reach out and touch
   the sun.
Dreams also make you feel down,
feeling like a lonely unhappy
   clown.
Dreams let you think about love

as beautiful as a snow white
dove.
Dreams are like a clock.
They go on and on and never
stop.
Dreams are also like a game
They never really seem the same
Dreams are like a pounding heart.
They can bring you close or tear
you apart.
Dreams can be like spring.
They're never about the same
thing.
Dreams are like a falling star.
They can take you away really
far.
Dreams are very special.
even though they're artificial.
Dreams can be even more fun.
especially about a special
someone.
So the next time you have
dreams,
just think of all these things.

Lila Freeman
That You Love One Another
L oving is not always easy
O ne might surely agree,
V ery often it really does hurt you
E' en makes you want to flee.

O nly God's love is perfect
N o other can ever compare,
E verlasting to everlasting—His
is always there.

A lways try to show your love
N o matter how hard it may be,
O nly by loving each other
T he love will spread around,
H ere and there and everywhere &
E ven before you know it
R eaching to be found.

Christine M. Turczyn
TO SLOW MY PEN
While I breathe, I hope;
let there be no envy
and apropos of nothing.
To slow my pen of
its poetic frenzy and
tainted writings.

Mary Stafford
I LOVE YOU PLUS

---

*This poem came out of the love I
have for RON CLOUSE.*

It's such a beautiful night,
But things aren't right.
Your not here, and I feel lost,
But loving you is worth the cost.
All I can do is sit here and
wonder how your spending
your time.
Hoping your not steping across
that line.
Your the best looking guy I ever
met,
And that face I'll never forget.

I know sometimes I made you
cuss,
But baby you know, I love you
plus.
I love you plus, I admire you.
I love you plus, I was so proud to
be seen with you.
I love you plus, I adore you.
I love you plus, I would give all
I've got for you.

I worship the ground you walk
on,
I never knew love could be this
strong.
I feel a moaning deep inside me.
I'm grieving for you.
Can you send me some
sympathy, to get me threw?
You know I love you plus,
And having you is a must.
I know sometimes I made you
cuss,
But baby, I love you plus.

Vivian H. Petro
The Face In the Mirror
I looked in the mirror and
what did I see?
I don't think that face belongs to
me—
What happened to the person I
used to be?

The years have gone, I'm not sure
where—
The face I see is worn with care—
It's almost like seeing my Mother
there.

When I think of the years, it's no
surprise
To see those lines around the
eyes—
Unfortunately the mirror never
lies!!

Enjoy your youth, it will not last—
And soon you're reflecting on
your past—
Minutes turn to years all too
fast—

So when I look in the mirror
And see what I see
I *know* face belongs to me
What happened to the person I
used to be??

Sheryl Frances De Garmo
UNKNOWN THING
Silently the shadow grew,
Across the wall and ceiling.
Suddenly the light of the moon,
Was blocked off from viewing.

A passing cloud blacked out the
light,
Of the moon and the hulking
shadow.
The unknown thing in the night,
Was the big old tree outside my
window.

Jeffrey Levine
THE PAST
To echo past dreams,
is only a faint hope.

The shine with an old glimmer,
is to see with half light.

The way things were then,
won't make today right.

William Hewitt Martin
THE GARAGE SALE
Weeks of cleaning attics and
cellars;
linens once white now aged in
yellows;
China and glass amassed with joy;
now a bargainseeker's ploy.

Broad advertising of the big event,
trash and treasures at 1/10 of
one percent;
Permits obtained from the Village

Hall,
to rid the streets of garbage;
what gall!

Finally the big day arrives;
the garage as active as beehives;
Sellers as excited as the buyers;
a test of who are the biggest liars.

Not knowing what or why
they've bought;
obviously something for nothing
sought;
But wanting papers of authenticity;
selling junk is no longer
simplicity.

As the day wanes, along with
stamina;
the garage a scene of colorful
panorama;
Everything in unbelievable
disarray;
a kaleidoscope pattern to our
dismay.

Tomorrow our signs will say,
ten percent discount today;
There'll be those to make an offer
on a 5¢ item in the coffer.

The final day's rock bottom price;
First day buyers back, how nice;
Wanting refunds on a previous
steal;
In this nightmare, we make a deal.

Mary F. Kelley
DAUGHTER
I held you to my breast,
Feelings of wonder,
Mere words cannot express.

Time went by; as it must do.
Then seemed to stop—
I saw me; I saw you!

I look at you; and see myself.
Reflections of days gone by,
Promises of tomorrow.

You are me; and yet you're not!
I feel sadness, and joy, but most
of all,
Deep and abiding love.

Things have changed; I feel lost.
The days gone, when we each
knew our place—
You needed me—

We're friends now; aren't we?
So modern and wise—

Love lets you go; you're on your
own—
A beautiful flower—I won't cry;
We'll have a new tomorrow.

Josette Liliane Villias
CONTAMINATED WATER
Silence:
it gathers ominously
like dark clouds
before ravaging storms
this silence not silence
born of love
pregnant with creation
it its pauses;
empty, this silence
silence of stagnant ponds
hiding
delirium ridden parasites
in fetid spores
poinsoning what it touches
This silence,
this silence needs words,
a sign posted:

Eau non-potable!
Keine Trinkwasser!
this water,
contaminated!

Sandra Lea Thompson
THE QUILT

To my grandmother

The little old lady, rocks in her
chair
Strands of silver are, wove in her
hair
Her eyes are so weak, she can't
see to sew
But in her minds eye, her
memories flow
She works on a patchwork,
sewing with care
Scraps of her life joy, love and
grief mingled there
For each of her children, she's
made such a gift
With each tiny patch, her heart
gives a lift
One of these, days, when it's time
to go
No more little scraps, left her to
sew
A beautiful patchwork, lovingly
made
Small parts of her life, with
needle are staid

Elaine F. Huber
A FIRST LOVE
Remembering the first time that
we met
brings beautiful and divine
thoughts to mind.
Remembering the beautiful
sunset
and how we were made as one of
a kind.
Your hand in mine was so warm
and tender,
holding on to a love so new and
free.
My life to you I would gladly
render,
a more beautiful love there could
not be.
To be with you fulfills all my
past dreams
of a love that is like a burning
fire.
Having you to hold is part of my
schemes
of a love for two that will not
expire.
I will always desire your warm
embrace,
for love is the theme of the
human race.

Shelly E. Andrews
INSANITY
A girl was lost
wherever,
was blind to who was she;
Now the world one mortal less
Yet that one soul is free.

N. O. Lacey
LATE AT NIGHT
Late at night, awakened by the
coolness of the forming mist,
he sees his mirror-image
staring back with soul-piercing
eyes,
softly repeating the word, "Unfair".

A dream, he concludes, and turns
to slumber, only to be disturbed
by the despondent sobs
of the fading apparition.

Confused and in awe, he tries to
find
some compassionate words to
soothe the
saddened spirit, but his words are
in vain,
as he watches himself dissolve.

"Come back," he pleas, as dawn
begins
to make its entrance, warming
the room of
its recent chill. The day seems to
linger
as he anticipates the return of his
visitor.
The surviving twin awaits once
more.

Tamara S. Santora
I'M SORRY
I've many faults, as have you.
But I made many mistakes
In our relationship.
I didn't mean to harp and
critisize;
Nor act superior.
I should have given more than
taken.
I guess I learned a little too late.
I didn't understand the concept
Of each side sharing equally.
Now I've got no one to share
with.
I did have the love, please allow
me this;
I just didn't know how to handle
it.
I've been spoiled since who
knows when,
Most always getting my way.
I took the same privileges from
you;
Ones not mine to take.
Without consideration,
I finally took too much.
Now I've got only myself to live
with;
Loaded with heavy heart and
guilty conscience.
I hope I've learned from my
mistakes,
Before I lose all that's left
Of what was once you and I.

Martha Ann Lillard
10-23-83
Is the smile so quickly gone
That yesterday shone clear?
Is the voice no more to speak
The words that I would hear?

Are the eyes so heavily veiled
That yesterday winked at me?
And is the divinity of their
sparkle
Reduced to a memory?

Can the soul so loved by one
No earthly life regain?
Will the gentle hands that ever
moved,
Forever so placid remain?

Oh God, by every promise made,
Please mend a broken heart;
And keep not long the kindred
spirits
Very far apart!

Kelly Morenzoni
LIFE
If life is easy,
Then why do people suffer?
If life is loving,
Then why do people hate?
If life is happy,
Then why do people have sorrow?
If life is precious,
Then why do people kill?
If life is everlasting,
Then why do people die?

Miss Tami Lynn Conley
MOTHER
You gave me something
I really didn't see.
I thought you were unfair
not to let me be free.
Now I take a look
at what kids are able to do;
I'm glad I have a Mother like you.
You gave me the advice
which I'm beginning to believe
that is what life is about
and what I need.

Thank you Mom,
I love you.

Happy Mothers Day!

Lynn R. Thompson
FEELINGS OF REMINISCE
The grassy plains of my mind
The scenic mountain drapes
Make it impossible to find
Reckless streams, that block my
escapes . . .

I forgot to remember
Spacious scapes of the oncoming
sky
The woods I once saw of timber
Things like these are hard to
buy . . .

Stealing all the crisp sunshine
Waking up to see your face
I want these things to all be mine
And mountain scenes leave no
trace . . .

Holding you with a smile
You smile brightly in the view
Acting crazy all the while
Mountains smile like us too . . .

Now I'm old and turning gray
Relaxing skys settle down to rest
For good times we all must pay
Bridges of our lives, have seen the
best . . .

The grassy plains of my mind
The happy times that I forgot
Make it impossible to find
Warm embraces I never got . . .

Luanne Childres
Let the Music Become You

*This poem was inspired by the
music of Barry, Robin and
Maurice Gibb.*

And this is the way
to listen to music.
Not just sitting and hearing
but letting it flow within
and become a part of you.
The harmonies of voices
going deep within soothing
and calming troubled nerves;
bringing quiet and peace inside.

Letting those basses pound
their way into your soul
til you feel your whole being
vibrating.
The music reaches a high pitch
and takes you up with its
spiraling octaves.
Then lowers you down, softly
caressing you
with its sensual, melodic rythms.
Sway to the waves of music
as it rolls over and over your soul.
Like the ocean as you stand in its
shallows
gently moving you again and
again.
And this is the way to find solace
and quiet
in a world that's troubled and torn.
Be a part of the music and the
music you.
Listen with your whole dedicated
being.

Sally Natalizio
I THANK YOU . . .
For finding time to listen.
When I really needed to talk.
For picking me up,
When I was feeling down.
For all the times you cared,
When I didn't even care myself.
Most of all I thank you
For just being you . . .
My special friend.

Lois Irvine
ILLUSION AT THE ALTAR
Listen:
Listen to the rhythm of the heart
beat, of the heart that beats for
you,
Listen:
Again, hear the echo of ten short
years ago, when we said "I do."
There:
There we stood in faith so good,
now I ask, "Please come back to
me."
That's all.
Here:
Here I stand with folded hands, in
prayer, thinking you will hear
my call.
Love:
Dishonest love, disillusioned
love, I won't let true love turn
to dust.
Love:
Love won't die, still I cry,
illusions fade, live with this
echo, I must.
Say:
Say one prayer more, look toward
the door, then to the Altar for a
shadow.
What?
What, an illusion or intrusion?
Will I hear a friendly hello?
Hi:
"Hi," said he. Was it meant for
me? Still I know there's no one
else
around.
Said he:
"Now after a year, my thoughts
are clear, no truer love is to be
found."
Me:
In my heart, we'd never part: two
shadows became one, to fade

away.
Hear:
Hear the chiming of the bells
that chimes for us on our
wedding day.

John Lone
CARESS
Drowning in clatter noise
And waterfalls of time,
Borne by entraining rush of
voices—
Indistinct, unmodulated babble
Of a savage stream that dashes
Into the frothing, spitting rocks.—
Reach out for merciful reprieve
In still pools of the rare caress.

Caress—of friendly silence
And of gentle waiting eyes.
Of undemanding touch
And softly uttered sounds,
Or words of simple sense
And setting.—Of compassion in
the stars
That motionless in moving
vastness
Speak of assurance, purpose,
peace.

Wayne Michael Rossiter
WHERE WILL I GO NOW
Where will I go now
I'm lost in space
Again I have fallen
Flat on my face
Is this what is called
Reality
Am I supressed
Or am I free
What holds me back
Who is at fault
Where will I find
The key to my vault
The dream is an out
It's misunderstood
If I knew
Then I would
All have means
To help them cope
I have none
I'm losing hope
No one can attempt
To understand
Why things got
So out of hand

Jill P. Engelhardt
HAPPY BIRTHDAY
Can you see thru those misty
clouds?
Travel forward on your path to
find, your keys to the doors of
the future.

It's another year, you've
conquered;
I hope the keys to the door of
happiness and love and
tranquility will be found
in your hand.

May the first steps into this years
route be so bright and full of
beautiful tomorrows that next
year, you won't need keys.
You'll hold the set . . .

Meriam Jean Emani
EXPLORE
Explore your imagination, and
you will find,
infinite space to play in,
a billion doors in your mind.

A spring born flower, a fresh new
life,
off to a new start each time,
sharper than any knife.

Memory lane, open plains, a field
of morning dew.
Expansion and development,
each idea thought new.

You and I all have the magic, to
open
the doors so wide,
just deeply search your
imagination,
for the mind has never lied.

David Pennington
MOVEMENTS
She spoke new words from new
thoughts
That seemed strange to me
And I couldn't understand her
reasoning
Of how it used to be
We were two, standing together
And everybody thought we'd hold
hands forever
But as the night faded
And the light was turned on
We saw ourselves as two people
Not knowing what went on

Jeanette Pote
FATHER
Where do you begin
when thinking of past sins
against the man
whose only plan
was to give you love and peace.

Now the time has come
to ponder what was done
inside your heart
and other parts
to which the pain set in.

J. B. Rake
WHEN TIME BEGAN
What restless, angry, anxious
brain
Absconded with infinity, its
endless joy cut short,
Bound its hands to counting time
And spread compunction all about;

Designed for day a daily end
And forced the night to bring it
down,
Then made a pact within that
dark
That robbed the myth from
Morpheus' crown;

Contrived the seconds, minutes,
hours,
Days and weeks and months and
years,
And squandered the ancient
hourglass
On systematic calendars;

What brought us to this
scurrulous rush
That added less to hopelessness
And shaped the future out of
doubt,
To bow to haste, succumb to
guess;

To habitat a tick and tock,
To suffer death within the womb,
To know a brief eternal flash
Before the shadow on the tomb;

To be a victim of a span
And race endurance for its loss,

To be imprisoned by one's own
time
And live among such emptiness.

Robert J. Martin
Candle Light Serenade

Dedicated with Love to DIANA
My inspiration, my Life, my Wife.

As I gazed across the table
In the shim'ring candle light,
And I saw your glowing face,
And your brown eyes shining
bright,
I remember all the promises
We made that winter day
We vowed our love forever,
Let it always be that way.

As the clock keeps right on
turning
And time goes swiftly by,
Let us keep the candle burning,
For life is but a sigh,
As the days move on so quickly,
And darkness comes so soon,
Let the flame be carried skyward,
As it races toward the moon.

We were meant to be together
So in our declining years,
Lets remember all the good times,
And forget all the tears,
May the vows we made that
morning
Be renewed by us this day,
And our love will keep on
glowing,
As the candle melts away.

Judy P. Horejs
BECAUSE

For Bob, my husband, God Bless
June 20th, 1938—
December 8th, 1983

Because of you I am happier
Your openness, acceptance and
sensitivity
amazes me.
I often find myself thinking of you
at random during the day
And my thoughts are relaxing.
You are my equal, my best friend
and
lover
I've only begun to learn and realize
the "you" that you are
I am comfortable and trusting in
sharing things about me—

'Cause I know of your accepting
ways
You are unique in being just
"Bob, the Outlaw"
I will love you always through all
the
changes we may have to face
in our lifetime.

Jean Heath-Heritage
WASTED STARS
Today I take an hour to mourn
For all the times I did not dare
To face my needs. For dreams
unborn
And feelings I could never share

For every misty moonlit street
I never wandered in the rain
In Spain or Istanbul or Crete
Nights that will never come again

Lost landscapes filtered through
the screen
Of forfeit friendships. All the seas
I never sailed. The space between
Illusions and realities

Today I take an hour to weep
For risks untaken, chances gone
For only dreaming in my sleep
And stars I never wished upon

Nora J. Winn
FOR GENE AND BONNIE
When it began I did not know
what to do or say.
So while close friends pressed
around the two of you
I quickly walked away.
There were no words to make my
thoughts come through.

Others have tried to tell me
everything you've shown me.
Their voices left echoes I did not
want to hear.
Somehow they always seemed so
empty;
Their hearts were never really
near.

There were so many times when
darkness hid the sun,
Thoughts that turned in pain
until I realized
Tomorrow should never come.
Then you were there and love
was no pity in your eyes;
Strong arms that pulled me to my
feet
Or held me when no one else
knew how.

Passing time shall not deceive my
heart.
I only wish there was more that I
could give you:
You who believed in me even as I
fell apart.
Your love I keep within me will
always be this true.

Marjorie Kingston Skusa
A MOTHER

Dedicated to George Dee Skusa

What it means to be a Mother
Is really hard to prove;
I think, perhaps, it starts the day
You feel your first child move.

It's a fascinating miracle
So far beyond compare;

To know your body is a temple
And God's gift is living there.

Catherine Myers
SEARCHING
Do we fly 'round the same sun?
You know—large round object,
bright
yellow, wilts flowers, melts ice—
vitamin D sun?
Or what?
Where have I been all of my life?
Where are you?
I see where you've been.
Wordprints—
covering the blank pages of my
life.
Who told you to write in my
book? Scribble
on my neat, white, onion skin
parchment?
Doodle on my soul?

Nell Blatherwick
NONSENSE
It's white, red and flowing,
It's blue and green eyes are
glowing.
In the night, it gives you a fright,
In the day, it hides away.
It dozes here and there,
It has no animosity.
It's not you, and it's not me.
Now, who could it be?
It's like your imagination, it can
go over a fence.
Do you really want to know what
it is?
Why, it's nonsense!!!

Harriette Hall Weaver
RELEVANCE
A splash of color everywhere,
From gold to brilliant red.
Autumn fills our mind's eye
With beauty of the month ahead.

The North Wind loudly blew his
horn.
Winter's on its way.
A new spectacular will soon be
born.
Autumn's not here to stay.

As Winter drew his scene of
white
His blustering was absurd.
As he roared and blew with all
his might,
Spring's wee, small voice was
heard.

Of all the scenes that you've
seen,
Painted upon the earth
The most beautiful is Spring's
bright green,
The color of rebirth.

Summer warmly shook her head
And gloated with a show of mirth,
"Without my warm and gentle
touch
I fear there would be no earth."

And As the seasons come and go,
Flaunting their beauty sublime,
Whichone is the most elegant
Is relevant to the time.

Patricia Ann Palmerin-Trujillo
Life Is What You Make Of It
My child, never be ashamed of
yourself,
Or of those good values you carry

within.
Remember and cherish all that is
beautiful.
Life is what you make of it!

Yes! Other children push
temptation in your face,
Drugs, alcohol, sex, thievery,
evil ways of thinking.
My ears hear your crys. My eyes
see your tears.
As you say, "Mom, life is what I
make of it".

It must be lonely to be pushed
aside for being more mature,
In knowing the "New Way" is
not always the right.
Somewhere you'll find friends
with a special pride.
A pride in saying, "Life is what
we make of it".

I feel the despair within your
heart.
I hurt with you as they call you
"square".
I sense the stress of teen pressures.
I here you repeat. "Life is what I
make of it".

Along this beautiful path in life
Something only "Our Lord"
could have made.
I believe you will never lose
yourself,
Because, "Life is what you make
of it".

Years will pass. Remembering
times this earth appeared ugly.
Up to the blue sky you will
look. Silently, you will pray.
"Lord you remained with me,
Helped me carry my cross,
And showed me, life is what you
make of it".

Edward P. Cole
AFTERTHOUGHT
Was it a ghost that I did behold,
There in the night where I held a
light
For your cigarette? Only a glimps
Therein the yellow flame of my
light,
Then, you were gone in the
smoky haze;
Like a phantom passing in the
night.
Now in an afterthought, I
wonder,—
Were you real,—or ghost that I
beheld?

Marjorie Burney Willis
PA'S CAT

---

*Dedicated to Faye Carr Adams,
Past Poet Laureate, and donor of
"The Cat Award" for the Poetry
Society of Texas. PA'S CAT
placed in the top-ten in the 1982
award.*

I am Pa's cat. Pity me! Pity me!
I need sympathy, sweet sweet
sympathy.
He steps on my feet and never
hears me wail—
Just turns around and steps on
my tail.
When I'm asleep or dreaming in a
chair
He sits on me and doesn't know
I'm there;
Then he says: "Excuse me, Honey,
I can't see"
But he can read a paper and
watch T.V.

Pa and I live together—just us two
And I love him very much—'Tis
true!
He feeds me a lot of delicious
meat—
Gives me a good home and talks
sweet
But the things I really like the
most
Are my beautiful scratching posts;
I can scratch on a chair or a table
As many times as I feel able.

Sometimes Pa goes on a nice long
trip—
That's when I do a flip-flop and a
flip.
He won't take me along on a bus
or a jet;
He just leaves me alone with a
vet.
I cry, scratch, fight and go into a
rage!
How'd you like to be locked-up in
a cage?
O I need sympathy, sweet sweet
sympathy.
I'm Pa's cat. Pity me! Pity me!

Margie C. Bonvillain
THE HOUSEWIFE
Early this morning my neighbors
left for work today
Their doors are locked their
curtains drawn
The street is empty while they
are away
Leaving me behind the only
housewife at home

The wash is finish hang out in
the sun
The house is in order and there's
time before noon
To create a new dish surprise
everyone
I do as I please as the housewife
at home

The evening's all mine to do as I
may
I'll take Fala, my dog to the back
field to roam
My how I pity my neighbors with
no time off to play
And miss all the pleasures of the
housewife at home

Late in the evening when twilight
creep along our empty street
My neighbors return after a hard
day's work that seem so long
I wonder sometimes if they ever
wish they could exchange jobs
with me
And just gratefully be the
housewife at home

T. S. Patnode
WHEN WILL IT END
There's a sadness in my heart
I have never felt before;
a pain; a wound; an ache;
I can't bare it anymore.

From the moment I wake up
till the time that I retire,
this ache is with me always
I'm kept tightly on a wire.

I feel my eyes; they want to cry—
My heart; it wants to break.
My insides turning upside down
and there it is, that ache.

If time can heal, I wish a year
could pass within a second.
The pain is with me once again,
as if it had been beckoned.

When will it stop? When will it
end?
The wound; the ache; the pain?
Time may heal all the hurt
but the scar will always remain.

Mary E. Geise
ONLY THREE

---

*To my daughter, Jennifer, when
she was "Only Three!"*

I looked upon my child one day,
she is only three
All innocence and laughter as she
climbed upon my knee.
When all at once that laughter
faded from her eyes
She looked out at her sisters and
she began to cry.
Why can't I go and play with you?
I'll be good—you'll see
They turned around and said to
her—you can't—you're only 3!
She hears that said so many
times, she wants to hear no
more
Just wait and see she says to
them, someday I'll be four!
I see the tears within her eyes, it
makes me think sometimes
Her problems at the age of three
are as big to her as mine.
If I could just protect her from
the trying times of life,
And have her grow up in a world
of peace and love—no strife
To have her only problems be—
being left behind once more
And thinking she can change the
world just by turning four.
Too bad that it can't happen, but
it's just not meant to be.
So I'll enjoy the innocence, the
joy, while she is only three!

Maxine E. King Martin
FOR SAFE KEEPING

---

*Dedicated to Judge Eddie-Lou
Cole, our own personal Saint.*

For Safe Keeping
You cannot know.
But I never really
leave you behind.
As I go to work, I tuck the
warmth of you under my coat.
I squeeze the sound of you into
my ears.
I fold up your smile and tuck it
behind my eyes.
Then when I smile, I smile with
you.
I paint your love on every spot
that is vulnerable.
And just as I walk into the street,
I raise the parasol of your strength
over me.
SAFE! Until I return.

Mrs. Patricia B. Cabrinety
Mrs. Patricia B. Cabrinety
COMPUTERIZED ZOO

---

*To our son, Stephen, who created
and gave the computer program
to ISIS, International Species
Inventory System, and the
Minnesota Zoo.*

Prologue—Egyptian mythology
has told of Osiris and Isis bold.

Now linked together anew
in work they do for world-
wide zoos.

O strich, gibbon, tigers,
S nakes, moose, and spiders.
I bis, macaques, tapirs, iguana,
R acoons, belugas, and piranhas.
I nventoried on computer
diskettes,
S ystem records at your fingertips.

*Mrs. Louise Teresa Webber
Corkum*
THE LAST STAND
He awoke at the crack of dawn
weary and hungry from the night.
The sun crept over the top of the
towering mountains
they loomed high . . . seeming to
protect him,
to shield him from the hurt to
come
from the death which grew to be
enevitable.
The events of the past night
came rushing into his mind.
The black feeling came over his
soul.

He jumped up and then staggered
backwards,
the bullet still lodged in his knee.
His leg was swollen, red and
throbbing.

The bounty hunters were on his
trail.
They broke through the forest
ridge . . .
He stood . . . they stood . . . a
single shot echoed.
It rang out a deadly roar.
The pain was piercing, smashing
his brain,
he fell .. . his skull crushed by the
bullet.
He gasped a final breath, and,
opening his eyes,
watched them fade into the
forest.

J. Ted Schilling
ANNIVERSARY
Though spring scenery
and the wintry rains
sometimes reeled
'neath tempest tether,
each youthful morning
we sang our refrains
richly seasoned within
the thyme-sage weather.

From a mere seedling
to touching the sun
love grew with
the fragrance of heather,
gifting this day and
these feelings begun
while this August ebbs
our first year together.

Vincent V. Santiago
POEMS BY THE SEA
Rushing water
from whence do you come from?
Such eternal power
vented against sand and coast
forever going towards an
impossible goal
"I am the sea"
"and I shall pound this arrogant
strip of land called 'beach' into
my domain"
"But I am the beach" came the
swift reply
"I shall remain where I am!
he shouted defiantly
"If I do not remain where shall
the land be, if anything?"
Thus the two remain in eternal
struggle
eternally fighting
forever cursing one another
never yielding
always remaining

Gwen Reeder Love
TRANSMUTATION
The river is steel in the dawning
Under the bridge's span,
But out there more
Toward the farther shore
It gleams like a copper pan.

Chromium bright in the sunshine
The river runs at noon,
Where the shallows are thin
It's a clouded tin
And as dull as a pewter spoon;

A weathered bronze in the sunset
Dappled with burning gold;
In the twilight dead

And as sullen as lead,
Silent and tired and old.

Remorseless as iron in the
starlight
The river flows—but still
It's a silver dream,
A platinum stream,
When the moon comes over the
hill.

Leora Renee' Stark
**Experiencing the Depths
Of Life**

---

*Dedicated to the late Lord
Byron— A man who knew too
well how to live. Dedicated to
Tony for understanding That
which no one else can—*

The world is a dream in which
I cannot see but one thing—
That it must be lived through
in all aspects of reality;
Forgetting nothing which you
experience
And experience all that you can
In the midst of one lifetime.

Shellie Colleen Reese
Leopard Of Kilimanjaro
What made you climb the
summit?
What power drew you there?
Leopard, did you go to die
where the mount was cold and
bare?
Was it something you were
hunting?
a deeper need to know
from where you came and why
you are
is that what made you go?
Hemmingway and other men
wondered over you
they wrote words and moving
verse . . .
or were they searching too?
Now I have come to Africa
with an aching need to know
Why a leopard of the plains
would seek death in the snow?
For what ever madness drove
you
now has me inthrall
and I must seek the summit
until I hear your call.
Oh, Leopard of ice does your
soul fly free
or is it frozen in your lair?
Leopard of Kilimanjaro
my heart is with you there . . .

Herlinda Falcon
LIFE TO THE END
Life is only a time clock slowly
passing by
You must hurry and do the
things you must do
Before you'r time comes up to die

Each second forms a day that
comes and goes
Yesteryear you were young and
strong
Tomorrow you'r weak and old

Silver gray, slowly but surely
appears in your hair
Look in the mirror and see the
lines
on your face that wasn't once there

Life is only a time clock slowly
passing by
Its giving you time to realize and
fine out
Ways of how to survive

Someone died from a disease
another got murdered instead
You'v been lucky to see these
days they have missed
But either way someday you'll be
dead

Having problems in life you
wonder why must it be
So you hide your face in the
palms of your hands
And question the Lord; "WHY ME"

People will try to run your life
telling you what to do
And if you ask me for my advise
I'd say
"Run it the way you want to."

Life, a time clock ticking good-by
my friend
So Hurry and do the things you
must do
For We'r getting closer and closer
to the end.

Manon Paradis
MON FRERE
Mon frere descendait la riviere
dans un canoe d'ecorce.
Embarcation legere qui tanguait
aux houles coleriques,
qui fendait le vent de sa tete fiere.
Mon frere de sang
qui, rame a la main, fendait l'eau.
Mon sang qui coulait
dans ses veines, le sien qui
irriguait mon corps entier,
nous partagions souvent le meme
lit, celui de la riviere.
Peu de mots, des regards seuls
suffisaient a dire les
choses. Le regard fier et les yeux
mouilles, mon frere
descendait la riviere dans une
trop frele embarcation.
Leurs deux lits se sont confondus
et maintenant il dort
sur un matelas d'eau. Dans son
sommeil, son coeur parait
de pierre. Moi seule je sais que la
pierre s'effrite et
que ce qui en detrempe la
poussiere est une eau beaucoup
plus rassurante, plus calme. Mon
coeur a saigne comme
celui de mon frere de sang; nous
nageons souvent dans le
meme cours d'eau, dans les
memes idees. L'hiver, mon
frere cassait la glace pour le
passage de son canoe.
Maintenant, c'est moi qui le fait
car nous sommes sang
et chair, coeur et ame. Mon frere
descendait la riviere
dans un canoe d'ecorce. Mais
depuis si longtemps, je ne
le vois plus . . .

Vera Cassell Keffer
MORNING WALK
I took a walk this morning,
taking my coffee with me.
Oh, the beauty and wonder this
earth holds for me.
A little down when I started,
sad, alone and insecure,

Many things befall us to
make us feel unsure.

Briskly I walked at first, to get
my exercise
And then the nature along the
trail began to hold my eyes.
A salamander, red with polka
dots, almost jell like is he.
A lovely creature, yet
lowly, scurrying away
from me.

Queen Anne lace, blackeye
susan, honeysuckle on the vine,
Clover in bloom, blue bonnet,
summer so sublime!
Stopping to gather wild
flowers, to grace my table
today,
I pause a moment to thank
Him for leading me this
way.

As I turn homeward . . . spirits
lifted . . .
Looking upward . . . green trees
gently sway,
Perhaps they too have caught
this spirit
That engulfed me on my
way.

Elizabeth Doyle Solomon
Conversation With a Creek

---

*To my father, Paul F. Doyle, Sr.,
Who taught me to see beauty in
all things.*

The busy creek keeps gurgling,
She needs no trite reply;
Throughout the seasons of the
year
She keeps on trickling by.

The alders bow beside her banks,
Moss grows a velvet seat;
Trees send their roots for water,
Shade ferns and flowers sweet.

She does not ask for compliments,
Her beauty simply lives;
O lovely lady let me learn
How nature humbly gives.

Salvatore D'Aprano
UNCONSCIOUSNESS

To an imaginary young lady

The billows shatter
on the cliffs
while the wind blows
with rage, becoming
at the impact: Candid froth.
On the solitary beach
there is a gull with
a deep wound in the heart,
and on the horizon
a white sail, goes adrift.
It's more than a lustrum
that Mercedes has gone.
The perfume
of her rose colored skin
is already buried
in the bottom of the sea.
Suddenly, around me
everything starts to turn
vortically, and I begin
to sink in the chasm
of my unconsciousness . . .

Katie Covington
FRIENDSHIP

For my aunt, Dorothy Mary Parnell Who taught me the "Purple Cow Poem" Many years ago (some 40+).

I never had a perfect friend
I never hope to see one
For if I had a perfect friend
I'd find I couldn't be one.

Iola Sherman
NATURE'S PEACE
The sound of an earthquake; the cracking of the earth;
The cry of a newborn on the day of birth.

The sound of thunder on a stormy day;
The chatter of a child that, can't go out to play.

The sound of wind blowing through the night;
The voice of a youth just before a fight.

The sound of rain falling to the ground;
The whispers of a man with trouble all around.

The sound of hail against a window pane;
The taps of an elder walking with a cane.

Quiet is the sound snow falling on your face;
Quiet is the sound when Death takes it's place.

Maria Barry
WITH ALL MY LOVE
If blind I could still see
All the beauty surrounding me
With you by my side
Sharing the sight of your loving eyes.

How great life can be
With someone by your side
Helping you conquer life's high tides
and enjoying the smooth rides.

To the world I want to confide
The joy you bring
And if I was able to sing
I'd tell everyone in a song
That to you I'll always belong.

Thank you I want to say
With all my love to you
For sharing each and every day
And helping me along the way.

Hattie B. Thomas
MOTHER IS ONE
Mother is one that does most everything for the family in the home.
She adds joy and laughter this is no surprise.
In times of trouble she is a judge that puts down the law to put things back in line.
At the side of the sick bed she is like a doctor checking, giving medicine, or calls for the doctor.
Mother is one that does first aid in times of hurt or problems she is always ready to protect.

Reads bed time stories to the little ones at night busy hands during the day.
Mother is one who listens when children ask questions.
Friends, Flowers is her pleasure, children are her joy, fire side talk is her profession.
No one can take her away from her job, mother is one who can't be beat.
Thought, her prayers, faith in God, Mother never fails.

Nettie Marie Yohn

Nettie Marie Yohn
PHOTOGRAPH
I saw your face again today,
What a joy it was to see.
It's been at least a million years,
Since you smiled at me.

Your eyes were pools of happiness,
As they steadily held my own.
Filling me with hope and promise,
Such as I've never known.

Your smile was a garden of roses,
Gentle as morning dew.
And O; my heart was spinning dreams,
That we could start anew.

Slowly I reached to touch your face,
In love's miracle wonderland.
But it was only a newspaper,
With your photograph in my hand.

Bill Yarbrough
ONE MORE TIME
When the last song's been sung
And the last verse has been done
When tomorrow's plans are in the mold

And we've said all that can be told
Then . . . and only then
Can we really say, "Well, that's the way life's been."

But wait . . .
Maybe there's still a need
Left for one more time . . .
One more friend that
Needs a deed.

Kathy Clemmens
MY SON
Where's the reason?
Where's the rhyme?
Why such a young man, still in his prime?
What of the things that he couldn't do?
What of all the people that he knew?
What of the things that he never saw?
What of the sports that he'll play no more?
What about his mother?
What about his dad?
What of all the things that he never had?
What of the wife?
Why the wasted life?
Where was the God that watches?
What was He doing then?
Where is the son that won't come home again?
Where are the answers to my questions one by one?
Why didn't I have more time to say, "I love you, son?"

Irene Blackwell King
THROUGH THE YEARS
That I had been wiser when I was young,
And made delays when I was wont to run.
I had little sympathy for human tears,
In my flight through the years.
Always running from trouble, I laughed and sang
Little did I care, for my feet were like wings.
Now that I'm old and gray, and can no longer make haste
I sit back and ponder over youth's speeding pace.
I realize now that I could not be both young and wise.

Jose Zakus
EARLY SPRING
A Tulip's' fire
With splash of rain;
An emerald blade
And racing cloud,
God's voice is deep
In robin's choir.

Richard Murphey Elia
LOVE IS TWO
Love is something
You just can't spare.
But love is something
Two can share.

Love is something
When it's the time.
But not the kind
To hide behind.

Find your love
In just one.

But let it be known,
This isn't for fun.

Make your love
To be true
Because nothing hurts more
Than being used.

Shawn C. Casey
A Storm In the Meadow

Un-like the vibrant storm that swept through the meadow May he never be forgotten—our friend Gino.

As the wind rustled the grass,
the mice romped and played;
while high above in the timbers
branches and sprigs both swayed.
As the mountainous clouds
moved swiftly to the west;
the mice had all flurried
for they knew what was best.
There was a chain of lightning
and a crack of thunder,
the habitat shimmied
atop and under.
The vibrant storm
had soon moved on,
the wind slowly drifted
and the sun almost shone.
There were raindrops that fell
from the leaves now and then,
but the rain had abated,
and the meadow was quiet again.

Regina Bennett Yarborough
HOLY SPIRIT COME
Holy Spirit Come
Into my life abide
Sweeten within my spirit
The perfect love of God
Holy Spirit Come
Create in me a heart
That Jesus can live forever in
And never need depart
Come Holy Spirit
Guide me in your light
Channel all my thoughts
For me to walk upright

Blaine S. Blakney
YOU

. . . to my Love, my life, dedicated to Sandra Leigh.

Maybe it's the way
you look at me;
The way your eyes
caught a glimpse
of my heart?

Maybe it's the way
you talk to me;
The way I go over each
word you say,
not loosing one sylobol,
nor a single word.

Maybe it's the way
your voice keeps echoing
through my mind.
And the way I wish each hour
I spend with you,
would stretch out to be days.

Maybe . . .
it' the way
that you are?

Our World's Best Loved Poems

Kathy M. Austin
JERSEY GLOVES
Last Tuesday I went to the park
 in the rain.
I pulled out my Dad's gloves to
 warm my hands.
I only had the left one.
I was so distressed by loosing part
 of Dad.

Only one month ago today, I lost
 my Dad to Cancer.
The battle was mean.
He was a fine soldier fighting a
 war he didn't know existed.
The doctors thought they were
 protecting us
by hiding the truth for five years.

I had to find the glove that had
 touched my father's hand.
I searched everywhere I went.
I saw it the next day in political
 science class.
I knew that was my Dad on that
 shelf.
I fixed my eyes on it all during
 class.
He wasn't safe so far away.
After class, I seized the glove
 while smiling.
Maybe my Dad is gone, but I
 have a part of him in my blue
 jacket.

John F. Sheller
YIN
Biting the sun
I tasted darkness
And like a small child
Taking a second timid sip of sour
 milk
I reveled in its rankness

Pamela Gleaton Baltzegar
PROBLEMS

*I would like to dedicate my poem
to the Good Lord and my parents,
Tommy and Ann Gleaton; If it
weren't for them, I couldn't have
written such a special poem.
Thank-you Lord and Mom and
Dad.*

Lord, I have a problem I can not
 solve,
You know what it is that I'm
 thinking of,
I can not carry this load I bear,
I often feel as though there is no
 one to care.

You see the heartache I
 sometimes feel,
I often wonder if this life is real,
You watch me as I try to take my
 problems into my own hands,
You follow me through when I
 can not meet life's demands.

When I can not do things by
 myself,
I look to you and ask for your help,
You do not turn away as others do,
Because everyone in the world
 has a friend in you.

Vivien Charlene Holland Nutt
PICTURE BOOK DADDY
A little girl, oh so small,
 holds a picture of a man;
She takes in details, one by one,
 turns it over in her hand;

His hair, the smile upon his face,
 the baby on his knee;
The look of love in his eyes
 as he holds her tenderly;
Deep in thought, she looks up,
 smiling wistfully;
She speaks with sadness in her
 voice,
 "That's my Daddy—and me."

Sam O. Ejiogu
FLOWERS

*To Ugo, Eddie, Emily, Ethel,
Tony, and my old man, John
Ejiogu for their trust*

Beauty in themselves.
Beauty to the sight.
Beauty also in use.

Lass who everyone admires
so long on her fires
 last.
But does a flower lose her appeal
when those enchanting hues
 fade;
when the blazing Apollo
who hither-to displayed her glow
deals her the fatal blow?

Flowers! Flowers!!
Present when we're put to the
 cradle.
Cheer of the sick and the ill.
Harbinger of peace and lovers'
 messenger.
A witness when the priest joins
 us together.
And even adorns the earth when
 the cold finger
 puts us (as) under.

But who would ever bend and bow
 to pick a shriveled flow?
A flower shriveled, trampled or
 not
 can still evoke much thought.

Mrs. Marciana A. Sevandal
**A Happy Wedding
Anniversary**

*This poem was written to greet—
on their Wedding
Anniversaries—my children,
relatives, and friends, who
brought joy and sunshine into
the lonely declining years of my
life. To all of them, this humble
poem is heartily dedicated.*

Some years ago, you said your
 vows,
 Before a Minister of God;
Whate'er betide you'd keep those
 vows,
 Till only death cast you apart.

"For better or for worse," you said,
 "In sickness, health, reverses,
 joys,"
You'll stand by each till only
 death,
 Comes like a thief, your dreams
 destroys.

Now as you look back o'er the
 years,
 You will feel a boundless
 pleasure,
For God has sealed your honest

love,
 With children—dearly loved
 treasures.

Precious jewels to cheer you up,
 When all life seems bleak and
 dreary,
And when you're down, to chase
 the blues,
 Till all life's storms shall clear
 away.

You'll always live in God's sweet
 love,
 In sanctifying grace and peace;
Eternally He'll bless your love,
 With strength, contentment,
 health, and bliss.

May your Today be blest with
 Hope,
 Your Past a glorious Memory,
And may you picture Future Years,
 Of boundless glorious Ecstasy.

Mary Ann Bernadette Henning
IMPRINT
Life stretches its fingers
 Touching your webs
 Bending your spirit
 Amalgamating
 You
 And
 The dust
You
Touch.

Shari Kisten Rajoo
EYES OF DEATH

*In memory of my late
grandfather. One of the warmest
most wonderful people.*

 I can't see you,
 I know I'm dying.
 So just listen

Flashing before me a life worth
 little, too sour to remember yet
 too sweet to forget.
Flamboyant are the sunset shades
 of health, dingy are the
 mornings of sickness.
My life, warm, moving like a fish.
Death, the cold razor sharp blade
 of a knife.
It touches me like a nymph
 touches the water.

 Slowly,

It penetrates the warm glow of
life within me that it so
savagely thrives on.

 I see no white mist.
 I see no fire.

I only see the last of my life.

Ella Pieper
LOVING MEMORIES
A little set of dishes, a dolly one
 or two,
Are little souvenirs bringing
 memories back to you.
You laid them lovingly away
 many years ago,
Soldiers and a little dog are laying
 in a row.
A photograph of sonny there in
 his bran new suit
And sister with her curley hair is
 looking sweet and cute.
Memories come swirling back as

you caress them one by one.
You think of all their loving ways
 and baby things they done.
Tears roll from your dimming
 eyes, a prayer you softly say,
You hope that it will reach them
 and bring them home some day
Although they 'er man and
 woman grown and have their
 home and care
To you they are your babies still,
 and memories linger there.

Carol Lee Mellon
FOREVER WE WILL BE
You're the light of my life.
I'm sure you know by now,
You mean everything to me.
I love you more than my heart
 will allow.

I think of you constantly,
You're always in my heart and
 mind.
You're the best I've ever known,
The best I'll ever find.

I'll forever want to keep you
Always by my side.
My love for you will remain—
It's larger than the sea is wide.

You're so sweet and understanding
It almost makes me cry,
But then I think of you shining
 eyes,
And I give a lovely, happy sigh.

I thank the Lord each and every
 night
For bringing you to me.
You love me and I love you:
Forever we will be.

Frances M. Bass
OH, MY LOVE
Oh,—My Love—Why did you go?
And leave me here below?
So young in life—but now I see...
You're sitting there by the
 Master's knee...

So many times—while here
 below—
You'd say—"My Dear, I have
 to go".
To help the people—who needs
 our Savior's love...
To tell them God loves them so.
Many times I did not understand—
But, I learned of this love
 God—had to spare...
And now my love—You reign
 above—with Christ the
 one who loves us so.

Rest, my love and sing alone—
In the choir of our own
 Master's Love.

Oh, My Dear—I've loved you
 so...
And will forever—till I come
 above.

To meet you there—by my
 Master's side...
And say—Oh, My Love—
I've made our flight.

Jo-Ann Elizabeth Ball
THE FRAGILE HEART
Magic created this timeless escape
as an illusion of the fragile heart.
An innocent understanding
 prevents attack

191

on harsh realities which venture
to part.
Fearful thoughts are withheld, for
if spoken,
the spell of innocence will break
the fragile heart.

Stella Katherine MacEachern
THE FRIEND OF FRIENDS

*Stella Katherine Ethel has written
ten poems. A former 10-grade
teacher, she has studied many
courses from three American
Bible Colleges and has a sister in
Columbia, Md.*

Alone our Saviour prayed at dark
Gethsemane,
At Calvary, His precious blood he
shed.
He rose triumphant from a rocky
tomb
That you and I might live—when
dead.

My Savior suffered untold agony
Upon that cross of bitter pain.
Once stripes were laid upon Him
bare,
Salvation for you and me He'd
gain.

Forsaken then by all His own,
He's winning race below was run.
"It is finished", was His humble cry,
His mission to mankind was done.

They said, "The veil is rent in
twain."
Angelic voices filled the air.
"The Son of God comes Home to
reign;
Of all the Kings, He's the most
fair."

To me a mission and message
given
On earth to tell the whole wide
world.
Since the ages ceaselessly roll on,
His Christian banner must be
unfurled.

Through illness, strife and
loneliness,
I've lived to praise His Holy Name,
Just want to be remembered here
below,
Not laboring for riches, nor for
fame.

Victoria Geter
**The Nymph And the
Zephyr**
Under the banyon,
sprawled awry on crooked
clay earth,
sinewy arms dangle outward
in a crucifix,
quiet cat's paw
purrs a sigh out
out from the skies . . .

'N I love my life
and the summer delight
of the August zephyr

Whose

windstreams of glee coil
the thousand strands of hair upon
my crown,
whipping me 'round; full gusts
swirling,

flooding my nostrils—Uhhh!
Can't breathe . . .
and keeps headin' yon.

Summer surging breeze,
coming at me
travellin' south and down . . .
MMMM . . . so lovely!

Mary Jane Drake
Trying To Say Goodbye

*I would like to dedicate my poem
to all my friends. Also my family.
And especially to my mother for
all her love and understanding.*

How do you tell someone goodbye?
That you're in love with another
guy
But it's too hard for you to say
That you don't want him another
day

Then he calls you on the
telephone
And you think why doesn't he
leave me alone?
He only calls you every second
week
You think he's a jerk and an ugly
freak

There's nothin' special about this
guy
But if you tell him goodbye he'll
start to cry
Then he'll turn and say bad
things about you
But you say you know what you
can do!

So you tell him goodbye anyway
And perhaps we'll meet again
some day
But you have no intentions that
you won't
And keep on saying that you
hope you don't

So you don't see him anymore
You should have told him long
before
You feel so happy and so free
To see the guy you wish to see

Kathleen K. Graham
IMAGES UPON IMAGES

*This poem is dedicated to all
women who have experienced
the painful emotions of a divorce
and the discovery of faith during
the recovery period thereafter.*

A fleeting romance; endurably
more,
persistently prevailing life's
human core.
She glances his way, he returns
with a smile;
his sturdy regal stance, to her
dainty feminine wile.
They laugh, console,
ambiguously mixing the time;
she spends the hours, indubitibly
learning his rhyme.
An ultimate decision to
intertwine; a gesture of love,
marriage is, after all, for all else, a
question above.
The years pass by fastidiously

spinning pleasures with pain,
answers to rhythm, or perhapes
truly inane.
Facades are in fashion; facilitating
compliance,
conforming on to the role or
escaping with defiance;
enduring pleasing holidays,
pastimes of graciousness,
they give, they take, excluding
nakedness.
A house; a baby, alas but not hers!
As relations turn, disregarded by
others:
the shock of despair, his
devastating dishonesty,
the whys and the wheres, the
whats of insecurity.
Silence became the first act; after
tearfully crescent,
she walked away from the past;
he, continuing his present.
Whatever the truth, the matter is
none,
whatever the lies, disappointment
has won.
To begin a new life, however
stumbling along,
finding her way, to fight against
explicit wrong.
A dream of fulfillment, the
crescendo of hope,
creating endowment, ploiding the
scope.
The artist within; appearing in
stages,
surviving, survival; images upon
images.
Beauty prevails, glimpses of
treasures,
whatever you care, to discover
the measures.
Surrender within to countless
pursuits,
truth is beauty as beauty recruits.
The soul everlasting, alone in the
end,
winsome, subjective; while time
is the mend.
Images forever, immortality
persists;
dreams on a canvas, nuance on
the mists.

Dave Whalen
WINTER BUS RIDE HOME
Sitting on a bus
On the way back home,
I look out the window
And I see deadness,
A panoramic view of deadness.
The trees have no leaves,
Just dark lonely branches.
The prairie grass grows dark,
Sometimes it does not even grow
at all.
The snow never looks the same
In its rigid vicious blanket.
The sky dark in its purest form
Seeming to lock this world in.
And then I ask myself,
Did we do this?

Susan Torchia
THE ART OF LOVE
My desires are abounding!
My heart is bursting with love for
you.
I crave to inhale you,
To absorb you.
I wish to devour you.

You are my dream, my fantasy.
I crave to envelop you,
To explore your body, your soul,
Including your mind, your
thoughts,
And feelings.

Flow with me, together, as one
Merging on our journey into the
unknown
Where there are no rules, no
laws,
No boundaries.
Just you and me to flow freely,
Bouncing to the waves of "love"
In unison.
Allow me to splash my love on
you,
To engrave your image in my soul.

Gloria Eileen Anderson
YOU TOUCHED MY SOUL
You passed by me, I did not know
That one day soon, You would
touch my soul.

Time drifted by: I saw you more,
And inside I felt a fire begin to
roar.

Your charms were like none
before, and
all of the sudden my spirits began
to soar.

Our mountains to climb were high,
Our valleys to cross were low,
Yet still an overcomer, you
touched my soul.

The door to love for me had been
opened;
It never closed, leaving me
heartbroken
Only because *you* touched my
soul.

The magic of you is still alive,
And deep inside, I'll always know
It was you who touched my soul.

Doris Heminger
LOVE
It came as a thief in the night. I
know not from where.
Gently invading my deepest
thoughts and caressing my mind.
As if it had always been there,
waiting longing, needing only
him.
Taking every little smile turning
it into a laugh.
Taking the darkest day and
filling it with sunshine.
Taking the sadness and sending
it on the wings of a butterfly
flitting from flower to flower.
Wrapping a blanket around a cold
heart and tenderly melting hurt
away.
Lifting your feet off the ground so
you float endlessly in space.
Holding his hand facing the
world together.
Yes it came as a thief in the night
and stole my heart and soul
and carried it to him.
                    Forever.

Robert A. Pizzi
SILENT SEAS
The water drifts from end to end
from side to side.
It carries a mystery that can't be
denied.

Our World's Best Loved Poems

The sea brings with her a place
 for solitude, to have peace of
 mind.
Something on land that is very
 hard to find.
For those who feel lost, and ones
 that live in confusion.
Let the sea tell, of a lesson
 which explains life's illusion.
Her waters are quiet and calm
 when things are well.
It's a wonderful release, and
 place to escape days of
 dreariness.
So one need not dwell.
You can find many answers on
 the sea, even though she
 speaks so softly.
For that is a place which is
 watched by God who helps
 many quietly.
Silent Seas are so intriguing, but
 carry a hope to start believing,
 and make easier to cope.

Kenneth L. Barton
FREEDOM
Freedom is a seven letter word,
Running swiftly through the
 alphabet,
Echoing the songs of days gone
 past,
Erasing the moments of pain and
 strife.
Deliver us from all evils,
Open our hearts and minds to love,
Make us a people that are truly
 free.

Martha A. Hirsch
**A Marriage For Jack
Putnam**
I had expected fog so thick
I could spoon it
into this cup like cream
on the unripened berry.
But instead there was sunlight
-attacking at all angles-
Just as well
needing dark glasses
as the organ seeped
through flooded eyes
even those skeptic
were lent the mystic chord
watching you given
the final vow.

Joan Stephen
THE MIRROR
I looked in the mirror and what
 did I see?
The face of some daughter was
 looking at me.
I turned all around and then
 ·looked again—
I saw my mother, a sister, a
 friend.
They all are the same; all women
 in life;
They have the same heartache;
 they have the same strife
I looked in the mirror and what
 did I see?
The souls of all women were
 crying with me.

Lillian Spellman
HEAVENLY ANGEL
I believe there is a guardian angel
 overhead
 Keeping vigil, whether I'm
 awake or in bed.

When I am sad, heart broken and
 forlorn
 In two directions my thoughts
 are torn.
Then a loving angel helps me
 make decisions;
 When I'm badly in need, there
 are provisions.
In the darkness of night, filled
 with fright
 This heavenly angel whispers,
 "All is bright."
God has a purpose, for each and
 everyone
 Until life's battle is over and
 won.
Tenderly we'll be enfolded in
 God's loving arms
 Serenaded by angels with a
 voice that charms.

Roscoe Ross Gardner
IN MEMORIAM
We pause at this memorial time
 To pay respect to those who've
 gone before;
We say a prayer, and wish them
 restful peace;
They're with their Lord, We could
 not wish them more.

With us they spent a host of
 happy hours;
Their friendship and their love
 we cherish now;
We miss their smiles and kindly
 spoken words,
And hope that they may know
 our thoughts some-how.

Their passing may have seemed a
 bit too soon;
God's way we do not understand;
But this we know, He went ahead
 to build
A home for us within his
 promised land.

We will not mourn for those who
 go before;
They've earned the peace that
 surely must be theirs;
With sins forgiven, all is quiet
 now;
Of Heaven's home, they are the
 rightful heirs.

And so perhaps we now should
 all rejoice;
And mourn them not since they
 are now at rest;
With trials and tribulations lift
 behind;
Tis well, they've gone ahead and
 God knows best.

Terri Hayslip
OCTOBER 31ST
This nite is known as Halloween
Ghosts and gobblens; things unseen.

It's filled with tricks and sweet
 treats.
Witches and warlocks; characters
 you'll meet
All shapes and sizes, from head to
 feet.

Jack-o-Lanterns; fresh pumpkin pies.
A darkened nite and misty fog,

Look and see the new full moon
Children in costumes will be
 coming soon.

A knock at the door, a "trick a

treat"
Wanting something good to eat.

Spooky stories told in darkness
Fun but frightened, you want to
 burst
Just remember it's part of

October 31ST.

Daniel J. King
SEA BOUND
We crept up from the ocean,
We dancing bodies of water.
On the land we rejoice and play,
Ever indignant in our games.
Patiently the sea tickles the shore
Giving soft reminders of what we
 are.
And when it but yawns
Our temples crumble into dust.
For the sea we have love.
For the sea we have fear.
We love it our source.
We fear it our demise.
When it beckons us from the
 dance,
We are again but water in the sea.

Laura Ami
The Saints and the Spooks
Years ago, our ancestors were
 very sure that the spirits of
 their own beloved dead roamed
 the towns, hunting a place
 secure and returned to their
 original graves instead.

Now, the spooks still scare the
 towns to October and find time
 in November to honor their
 dead.
This leaves us a question we will
 always ponder, "What is the
 difference between what is
 done and meant?"

Karen Elizabeth Serfinski

Karen Elizabeth Serfinski
TALES OF EVERMORE
Exploring a thousand pages
 Mythology of old
The cyclops and the sages
 And alchemical gold.
There's mystery in the poetry
 Tell tales of evermore,
Mystic wizards saunter free
 Where dragon mists cloud shore.
Driving the winds of fantasies
 Dissolve into the night
Where faeries dance in tall oak
 trees
 Silouetted by moonlight.

Climb a spiral castle stair
 Where tower shadows leap;

Embraced by lengths of golden hair
 A princess lies asleep.
Feeding rainbows and crystal
 waves
 Apollo colors day
Drinking ghosts from deepest
 caves
 Murkiness to slay.
Midnight flowers fold in repose
 And dream of their own hue,
As their silk fringed eyelids close
 Elves moisten them with dew.

Donna Lee Glikman
SILK RIBBONS

---

*To my darling Rick, For giving
Jur life silk ribbons, I give you
"our first", with Love.*

The image of your smile
 C)mes to me once again,
And blows through my mind
 Like silk ribbons in the wind.

J. L. A. Roberts
PRONOUNCEMENT
I do hereby announce my
 candidacy
 for the presidency
 for the U. S. of A.
 on the grounds of
 I am proud of
running as a black man
in the race with other proud men
and do announce my right to
 exercise
my option that one child of mine
 out
of my five may attend a private
 school
or any other man who pays the
 fee.

Also I do desire to set the pace
for quality of women, and
 equality,
and do insist that some fine
 woman
 be my running mate
 as candidate
for vice-presidency of the U. S. of
 A.
O Mister Jesse Jackson,
Uncommon man, you have
 my vote!
 I quote !!

J. L. A. Roberts
PERCEPTION: LIFE
Awake oh secret dream-
er, the hedgerows grow unclipt
the unruly grass unmown.
Reason lies latent in brain;
reason's not your rhyme nor
 mine.

One wishes, one says,
to keep one's mind unbought;
one submits, one says,
to truth alone: why, then
lock up all guns, all nuclear
 weaponry.

Or better yet, let's shoot them
at the sun—make direct hits
in its great boiling incandescence!
Let sun enfold in love all of
 earth's hate
and do it NOW! We dare not
 wait!

Our World's Best Loved Poems

Terence E. Hammond
RUSH HOUR

To my Mother in Albuquerque, New Mexico

Rolling traffic, thundering
Noisy traffic, moving on,
Eastbound, Northbound,
Heavy Lorries, dockbound.
Busy loaded buses
Rambling, hustling,
Gearchanging, roaring,
Whining, squealing, braking,
Never ending streams.
Taxi traffic, lane changing,
Impatient, impetuous.
Driving school motors,
Careful, cautious,
Learner drivers.
Experienced drivers.
Scooter traffic,
Swerving, clutch pulling,
Revving, urgent, hasty,
————————ceaseless traffic

Jane Cunningham
TWO WAYS OF LOOKING

Every year towards the end
Everyone gathers with family or
   friend.

To complain or give thanks to
   Him
Hoping LOVE and GOODNESS
won't be a whim.

Many situations there are to
   gripe about
There's stupid little wars that
cause many to doubt.

Doubt in fairness, compassion or
LOVE
Doubt in peace or strength from
above.

But if we can get through the fog
We'll give thanks and know
   there's a GOD.

For every morning the sun rises
   so high,
Let's gather, forget yesterday, and
LOOK towards the sky.

Strength does not come or hit us
overnight
It grows with days and time in its
great might.

When we see the turkey and
   smell the food cooking
Let's remember . . . . . there's
TWO WAYS OF LOOKING.

Curtiss D. Bassett
WAITING FOR LEON
Blessed are the humble, for they
   shall see God.
   Racing a beach or trail never
   once trod
For celestial frisbees soaring all
   unplanned,
   A golden creature in a golden
   land,
Splashes in, splashes out in his
   tireless chase;
   All joy unchecked in that
   perfect place.

Waiting for Leon, for Kathy, and
   Bill,
   This land has no time; he will
   be there still,
With a prance and a wag and a
   joyful "Arf!"
   Should a century pass 'till the
   blessed ark
Brings them all once more to the
   lake of the moon
   Whether half or full it will be
   high noon!

Michel Johnson Cornwell
TAKE A JOURNEY
Take a journey into time,
And I will make you mine.
Float along the cloud filled sky,
It will give you such a high.

Feel no space about your face,
Let your body know no haste.
Sail along with me to the
   unknown seas,
The trip will set you free.

Walk into the moon lite night,
And become lost between the
   light.
Feel not afraid of the dark,
You can fly like a lark.

Harold R. Blaine
THE GRAND CANYON
Gaping wound upon the planet
   Earth
   This mighty canyon lies.
Atop the brink a view of river far
   below,
   A silver thread that weaver
   Nature plies.

By day a sandstone monotone
   Baking in high desert heat.
At dusk a shimmering purple bowl
   Where dinosaurs once came to
   eat.

By light of dawn the chasm
   becomes
   A fairyland with crenellated
   tower
And overhanging parapet on
   castle wall,
   First morning light creating
   floral bower.

Standing on the rim I long to soar
   In freedom 'round the ancient
   spires,
But imagination is my only wing
   And feet stand rooted now
   where once lay mires.

Summer wind and winter snow
   erode
   Red cliffs where lonely shadows
   sweep.
Time, age, and distance seem to
   merge

Where sun ad moon eternal
   vigil keep.
The silence of the ages shrouds
   the gorge
   And lost wind sighing blows,
Imprisoned in far-reaching depths
   Beyond time's reach where river
   flows.

Steven L. Viscuse
Memories Of Yesteryear

*Dedicated To My Grandparents
Martha and Clyde Egly On Their
Golden Wedding Anniversary*

It seemed only yesterday when I
   visited the farm.
I ran through the cornfields, and
   played in the barn.
I played with my cousins, the
   hounddogs, the cats.
Or simply stretched out on the
   porch and relaxed.
Vacationing with my
   Grandparents was such a joy.
I had a great time. I was just a
   little boy.

The peaceful morning hours I
   loved to sleep late.
But never figured on getting up
   early for the breakfast I ate.
Grandma knew how to get me
   out of bed.
Just fix a healthy heaping of some
   bacon, eggs, and toasted bread.

The summer day was long, and
   was hot.
But a glass of Grandma's Kool-
   Aid usually hit the spot.
And as for passing the time, well
   that was a simple factor.
I'd go fishing with Grandpa or
   ride on his tractor.
Even on the lazy days when I just
   sat around.
Grandma would take me for a
   trip into town.
I was excited as we looked
   through the stores.
She nodded her head, and said
   "that gift is yours."

A memory to cherish, one which
   I'll always hold.
My Grandparents love will never
   grow old.
I love them, and thank them for
   this memory I share.
On this joyous occasion, their
   Fiftieth Anniversary Year.
Their eldest grandson is thankful
   for something so dear.
Grandma, Grandpa, and the
   Memories Of Yesteryear.

Karen J. Runka
It Feels Good Being
Lonely-Sometimes
I've felt lonely in a room full of
   friends.
On nights when my dog paced
   the floor,
I joined him.

He knew about the loneliness too.

Keeping company just because I
   should be sociable and talking
   to people because it would be
   rude not to continue a

conversation is not my way.
Sometimes I need to feel lonely
   in a room full of friends.
Sometimes I want to be lonely.

It keeps my mind and heart full
   of what companionship is all
   about.

It makes me feel my humaness a
   bit more.

Patricia Antosh-Rogers
TO BE FREE

*This poem was written for my
Stepson, Gordon Dean Rogers and
his bride, Mary; to commemorate
their Wedding on September 24,
1983.*

I would not chain a falcon onto
   my wrist
Nor jail a mocking bird within a
   cage.
For I can love the free and not
   insist
That wild things be reduced to
   vassalage.

I would not tame the white-tailed
   doe,
Nor make wild flowers grow in
   cultivated ground.
They bloom not only for my
   selfish sake,
Not for my ears alone, the
   songbirds' sound.

I cannot own the distant shining
   star
And yet its light is treasured
   none the less.
And you are precious being what
   you are,
For I can love and need not
   possess.

I own you not and yet my love
   survives
Through winds of freedom blows
   between our lives.

Nola L. Zusi
KNOTS
I watched you as you fidgeted in
   the chair,
And I saw that familiar nervous
   smile
I used to tease you about
Creep across your face.
The judge questioned you,
Are you living apart from your
   wife?
Is there no hope for this marriage?
And with a simple gesture of his
   hand,
He untied my past with a rubber
   stamped divorce.

Elaine P. Morton
THOUGHTS
There are times when I am lonely
And feeling oh so blue,
But the thoughts that bring me
   happiness
Are silly thoughts of you.

The time we spent together
May not have been too much,
But the memories that linger
Can never go untouched.

There was something special
In your attitude and mine,

That even though we fought a lot
It seemed to mend with time.

There never was the bitterness
That's in your marriage and mine,
It sure does make one wonder
Why our friendship's such a
crime.

Walter Villanueva
A SIGHT TO REMEMBER

---

*To my close freinds of Kauai,
Hawaii, and Fairfield, California,
Thanks for the inspiration.*

There's an eerie night in October
When children live in fright.
A full moon bears the essence
Of this scary Halloween night.

Jack-O-Lanterns peek out of our
windows
Watching black cats cross the
streets.
And little children in their
costumes
Go hollering, "Trick or treat."

I remember when I was a child—
Oh how scared I used to be.
I would not venture into the
neighborhood
Without my buddies with me.

Although those days have all gone,
I'll never forget the thrill
Of experiencing Halloween night,
I know I never will.

It's a magical, mystical night
That all people must celebrate.
Even though that I was scared,
It's a night I'll never hate.

H. G. "Jim" Rountree
REGRETS
Bitter words spoken
Joy erased.
Human hearts shattered
Pain effaced.

Sad hearts beating
So silently,
Soft tunes playing
Relentlessly.

William Robert Senter Jr.
A LETTER TO ELLEN

---

*Dedicated to Ellen Senter Denny,
Aunt of Michael Stephen McGee
May 4, 1974—November 12, 1979*

Dearest Ellen,
I was telling my Angel
Here in Heaven above
Of the ones I had left behind
Who had showered me with love
Whose love had been extra special
Shown in so many different ways
From the time I was born
And throughout my earthly days
I told my Angel of my Ellen
And of my special love for you
Returning as much as I received
A special love shared only by a few
I loved you for being so thoughtful
And always kind to me
For being by my side
When I received chemotherapy
For writing me letters
Even though I couldn't read
For coming to me
When I had a special need

For reading to me my favorite
stories
For taking me to the park
For playing with me
Which was always such a lark
For rocking me when I was tired
Hor holding me when I was asleep
For changing my tears to a smile
When at times I did weep
And you know what Ellen
I told my Angel one other thing
too
That if Mommy couldn't have
been my Mommy
I would want my Mommy to be
you.

    Love Eternally, Michael

Adele Mary Kraft
THROUGH A CHILD'S EYES
A child sees light and it's
LIGHTNING!
A child sees water and it's AN
OCEAN!

He feels warmth and it's LOVE!
For the newness is exciting and
cannot
be relived, but THROUGH A
CHILD'S EYES!

Jane Lustig
GEMS OF AUTUMN
The summer-parched mountains
Encircle the desert and manifest
Their disparity. Rutted by
streams of former snows
A single mound will seem like
many.
The morning sun intensifies
An azurine sky while last night's
moon
Now chalky and depleted clings
to another pinnacle.
Above the last of the coral
Oleanders,
The amber mountain, once
barren, is sprouting
Moss green which will soon
cover top and sides.
The seasons are changing on
desert, too,
For within the month deep snows
will spread
Frosting across mountain cakes,
And while I bask in the sunlight's
warmth
I savor the refreshment of
unsullied white peaks.
The Maple tree I've brought to
alien soil,
Had greened its leaves through
scorching temperatures
And now those leaves are turning

red, and gold
As their colleagues in natural
habitat.
The clusters of Autumn gems
encompass me:
Emerald shrubbery bending to the
winds,
The opalescence of changing
leaves;
And above it all—a sapphire dome
Shading into ruby and amethyst
near nightfall,
When the onyx sky glimmers
with diamond stars.

Katherine Y. Boegehold
EURYDICE
A vagrant moon frosted the still
lake with gold.
The arching willow branch that
reached to touch the water,
No longer saw its own reflection
in the dark.
A night bird called and fireflies
burned their fitful light.

Eurdice was drawn into the soft
night by the fragrance of
honeysuckle and white clover.
Lightly she trod the labyrinthine
paths.
Reaching the lake, she stooped to
cup the water in her hands
Holding them like a chalice as
she drank.

The old gods seemed asleep—all
but one
Who gazed with covetous eyes.
Suddenly Eurydice stood—a gold
and ivory statue in the moonlight.
Securely bound by chains of dark
enchantment,
She listened raptly to a secret
voice.

Then, forsaking the lake, she
turned and ran swiftly toward
the river Styx
Where Charon waited to ferry her
across.
Her ears deafened, she never heard
The high, sweet music of a
distant lute.

LaVaughn Storsve
**There's a Sadness In Her
Eye**
There's a sadness in her eye
When you catch her unaware—
Sweet Autumn—pretending to be
gay,
Putting on her brightest robes . . .
September feighning May.

There's a grieving in her sigh
When she doesn't know you're
there—
Sad Autumn—singing her sad lay
While dropping down her lovely
robes . . .
September mourning May.

I caught her once, poor Autumn,
Dropping leaves of gold,
And as I watched her, sad at heart,
She shivered in the cold.
Before she knew, I stole away
Lest she see me there.
I could not let her know I saw,
For she's proud as any May.

But . . . there's a sadness in her
eye
When you catch her unaware,

And a grieving in her sigh
When she doesn't know you're
there.
Sweet Autumn—poor dear!
    Dreaming still of May.

Kimberly J. Dahl
SIDE BY SIDE

---

*To David: Never doubt my love,
I'll never leave your side.*

Together we stand
Side by side
Not one in front
But side by side
We'll work
We'll play
Together
Side by side
We both give
We both take
Equal shares
Of each other
Decisions made
Together
Forever we will stand
Side by side
I'll never walk behind you
I'll never walk alone
I'm where I always want to be
Right here, by your side

Captain Austin D. Cushman, Jr.
OUR PUMPKIN

---

*To grand-nephew, Robert Alan
Bradley*

He weighs twelve pounds, or
thereabouts,
And has but a wisp of hair.
He has bright blue eyes and iron
lungs
To let you know he's there.
He's lost his teeth, or they've not
yet come,
But he doesn't seem to mind
He waves his hands and smiles a
lot
And flashes his bare behind.
He downs his milk then burps a
bit,
Or up-chucks . . . one never
knows.
He sleeps face down in his tiny
crib
And screams like a flock of crows.
He is Mommy's boy . . . Dad's as
well . . .
Not to mention Grammy's pride.
He is lots of work, some worries
too,
But his advent's changed the tide
In a new-found home, for a
certain pair
Now life has a solemn meaning.
This tiny soul has changed our
style,
Yet made it all redeeming.
He is precious beyond any words
we know
Could he alone have brought
this lift,
That fills our days with happiness
Knowing he is our Savior's gift.

Pat Leonard
GOOD NEWS
The Bad News Bears:
One little fellow a red head,

The other fair,
One a "terrible two,"
The other a grown up four,
Close as two coats of paint on a
  door,
One Little Sir Echo, copying
Brother's every act and word,
Running upstairs and
  downstairs,
"Is it a plane? Is it a bird?
No, it's Superman" flying through
  the air,
Spiderman, Batman, Buck Rogers,
  too,
King Arthur, cowboys, Winnie
  the Pooh.
Firecracker loud or mouse quiet,
  these bears.
Hush! Christopher Robin is
  saying his prayers.
"Mom, that grown up called me
  Bad News Bear Two!"
"Casey, that grown up is your
  grandmother
And she loves you."

Palyn Milieu
The Inn At Centre Bridge
The night was black, but glints of
  light, caught pale iced images,
  catatonic glimpses in this
  mystic, frozen night.
Shadows myraid-like appear,
  illumined by chariot's flame in
  flight.
A black-topped road, a water-way,
  the two are paired, side by side.
Ones time is now, one yesterday.

The sinuous path of each doeth
  lead to the Inn amid ice laced
  trees.
A canescent light from within,
  blots out the blackest winter
  nights.
A mighty hearth of stone and
  wood, aside which many a
  wayfarer warmed.
Wayfarers, still they come.
They came by bardge and horse
  and now by car.
A water-way, a black-topped road,
  timely paths.
The Inn at Centre Bridge, it spans
  the chasm from then to now.

Wendy K. Clifton
Am I Ever Going To Learn
I am overwhelmed, feeling
  defeated
And Lord, I just can't take it.
You are my Fortress and
  Deliverer;
Without You I would never make
  it.

Another lesson in weakness
  experienced.
Am I ever going to learn
Worldly burdens are too heavy to
  carry?
You're the only place for me to
  turn.

  Teach me to relinquish
  Teach me to yield
  To the love of Your yoke
  My Comfort, my Shield.
I will try again because You have
  shown
You are worthy, Lord Most High.
Take all the burdens on Your
  mighty shoulders;

Provide the strength for another
  try.
Caryl Schaal
POLYFIBER FLOORS

For My Mother

There's nothing left
once moonshadows
trickle into dawn
sleeps' secondhand dreams
awaken slowly
as feet search with uncertainty
for polyfiber floors

Walter Charles N.
A POET IS A TRANSPORT
A poet is a transport
Of infinite domain.
His pen can send you soaring
Across a magical main,

Where verse can search a sultry
  shore
or score some perfect peak.
Then sweeping softly seaward
Diverge into the deep.

A wider world of wandering,
Without mechanical mode.
No earthly code or custom
Can weigh the poet's load.

Life's puzzles is his passport,
Excursion through some sky,
Creation is the compass,
His muse must choose to fly.

Nina Bailey
GOD/LOVE/MAN

*Dedicated to all who believe in
God, justice, and equity-that all
mankind is made of one blood.*

God/Love/Man/Peace
Peace/Joy/Prosperity
Prosperity/Blessings/Eternal Life,

Man/Greed/Encroachment
Encroachment/Violence/Bloodshed
Bloodshed/Terror/Cycles.

Man/Obsessions/Aberrations
Aberrations/Fears/Doom!
God/Peace/Prosperity.

Tammy R. Abbey
GRAY SKY BLUES

*For Janet and Jerry; and Ma I love
you.*

When your heart is low
And there's nowhere to go,
You realize you finally hit
  bottom.
When there's nothin' to lose,
You know those are the Blues.
And man, when you got 'em, you
  got 'em.
When your song don't rhyme
And you're running outta time,
You know you gotta do it before
  you die.
Do it good, or do it bad.
Blink your eyes and you've been
  had.
There's nothin' but gray clouds in
  the sky.

So what you gonna do now, cry?

Loida Weber Maggio
GREEN EYES
I lost the lovely emeralds
The treasures of my heart.
I loved them deep inside
The emeralds of your eyes.
I know I lost them
The beautiful green eyes,
I cry for their enchantment
The treasures of my heart.
I hope some day the green eyes
Like the pastures of the skies
Belong to me forever
The treasures of my heart.

Frances C. Ross
THE SPIRIT FREE
When I am dead, don't stand
  beside my bier and say, "she is
  at peace," and shed a tear
For I will not be there! Go look
  for me upon a hill, midst
  Autumn's scarlet leaves;
In Winter, when it snows, I will
  be there beside you, in a white
  world, hushed in prayer!
In Spring, you'll find me where
  shy violets grow, and dusk, sets
  sunset skies, with flame, aglow!
You'll feel my warm breath on
  the Summer breeze caressing
  those I love, their hearts to ease.
You'll find me walking, barefoot,
  by the Sea, whose emerald
  waters ever called to me!
My unseen footprints by yours in
  the sand where foamtipped
  breakers dash against the strand.
My voice will echo in the tides
  that run, my laughter rise,
  defiant, toward the Sun;
For death can never hold the
  spirit free.
  I will be near, when you have
  need of me!

Ann Madden Haas
MANNY
The new born babe was tended,
By day, by the elder one
Whose hair was grey.
Lacking the strength to lift the
  pup,
She used her knee
To hoist him up.
Pony ride, she called the game,
A bounce or two
To earn the name.
She taught the lad how to speak,
To throw a ball,
Stand on his feet.
To show love, and tenderness
  brings,
The hesitant touch
To small furry things.
Together they found ants and
  worms,
The unseen wind
Explained, and he learns.
Small hands pluck a buttercup,
  and place it
On a grassy mound,
For Manny to sup.
The gold she gave him, returned
  in kind.
The wonder, kindled
For his lifetime.

Sherry Young
VOYEUR
Locked within a silent world, he
  sits and stares outside

At life as it goes tripping past;
  afraid to live he hides.
He watches other people as they
  move to join the race.
From the outer fringes, the
  watcher takes his place.

Broken dreams have made him
  shy; he feels through other's
  souls
And makes believe he's someone
  else, choosing each new role.
The lonely ache he feels is turned
  aside when he becomes
A wanderer feeling things that
  just a watcher never knows.

It's lonely just to wait and watch;
  his heart burns with a fire.
But fear and certain tragedy
  restrain his wild desire.
Slowly he retreats within a
  darkened, shadowed tomb,
Escaping all intentions, return
  trip to the womb.

Forever now a watcher be, a
  voyeur and alone.
While outside love and hate rage
  on; his world is safe at home.
Never to feel the warmth of love
  or the cold of a jealous heart;
Only with his eyes he lives, from
  within a world apart.

Sunday McKinley Bailey

Sunday McKinley Bailey
CAN'T YOU HEAR?
Hush!
Listen!
God is speaking!
In the wind,
Through the
Blades of grass,
The flutter of
The birds
Wing,
The ocean's
Roar,
In the
Silent chambers
Of man's heart.
Listen!
Can't you hear?
God is speaking!

Joseph P. Kowacic
TASHA
She walks silk-skinned
across the fabric of my dreams,
a fragile spider
clinging to the web of sleep.

And when the dawn awakes
to stalk again the noisy day,

it is the silken substance
of this dream alone
I keep.

Sister Mary Laurena Cullen, IHM
POVERTY

What is Poverty? I do not know.
I made a vow of poverty long
    years ago.
But I am not poor.

I am rich as kernel corn
    that gleans its gold from the sun.
I am strong as bugle horn
    that blasts its sound for its fun.

I am young as robin eggs
    that wait for cracks in their shell.
I am housed in convent home
    where well-fed sisters dwell.

I am touched by gentle breeze
    that hugs the garden flower.
I am loved as dawning day
    that sings its song-trilled hour.

I am filled as dogwood trees
    that burst in bloom in the spring.
I am clothed in nun-ly garb
    that boasts a veil and ring.

I am thrilled as priestly one
    that gives the Host to others.
I am rich as Christ Himself
    Who gave to me His Mother!

What is Poverty? I do not know.
But I made a vow of its richness,
    long years ago!

Clement Osei Bonsu
SUICIDE

Amid the chaos
I would scale the mount
And sing my requiem;
Clinging to my obituary,
Jump into oblivion.

Donna T. White
WHEN WE LOVED

I will never forget the first time I
    met you.
It seemed like you were the
    answer to all of my prayers.
You were all of those things
    rolled up into one that I'd
    imagine when I was a little girl.

I know that good things don't last
    forever but I loved you so
    much that I thought it would
    always be enough to make you
    happy.
I tried for so long and so hard for
    you to take me and love me
    the way that I loved you.

The uncertainty of your feelings
    caused a very difficult time in
    my life just recently and I
    pleaded with you to give me
    some sense of security and to
    show me that your love was
    strong enough to pull me
    through and make me better.
I guess you just did not realize
    just how much you meant to me.

I cannot keep wondering if
    someday we will be truly
    happy together and if you will
    ever look at me and talk with
    me the way you did in the
    beginning.

I am leaving you in search of a
    new beginning.
I still love you but time just

keeps passing as I sit here and
    wait.
The memories just are not
    enough anymore.

Blanche Eloise Higgins
GONE HOME

---

*In Memory of Fred D. Higgins
Year 79*

When God
Took you home
I wept
All the day
All night long

They say
We do not weep
For the one
That's gone

Only for self
All alone
    Alone.

Sheri Marks
The Juvenile Delinquents

Tough, bad and mean,
    That's what we thought we were.
    Grew up on the wrong side of
        the tracks,
    Harassing people and just being
        cool.

Instead of going to ballgames,
    dances and other normal
    things, real people go to;
We spent our time in police
    stations, courts, and detention
    centers.
After awhile, we just got used to it.
Our best friends were—police
    officers, other JD's, and
    especially the judges and social
    workers.

They tried to make us listen,
But, do you honestly think we
    would?
Now it's time to grow up and
    move on to better and bigger
    things.
Hey fellow JD's! How does
    prison sound?

Lynn Marie O'Leary
Mommy's Not Supposed To Cry

I wasn't supposed to hear her,
I wasn't supposed to see,
The tears rolling down her face
And the pain that went thru me!
I wasn't supposed to feel the pain
    of seeing mommy cry,
Mommy's not supposed to shed
    tears,
Although I don't know why,
I wanted to hug her and
tell her things would be all right
But I couldn't cuz seeing mommy
    cry
isn't a pretty sight!
Cuz mommy's not supposed to
    cry
Even though she's human too,
And if you saw your mommy cry,
you wouldn't believe
the pain that you go through!!

Elizabeth Bluebird
ODE TO AUTHOR'S

Oh, to be free,
Free to fly across the sea,
Free to say good-bye to sorrows,

Like people in stories with happy
    tomorrows.

Oh, to escape drudgery and care,
To go to other lands, just to be
    there,
To see how people of times gone
    by,
Lived and loved, laughed and cried.

But wait, thru people like
    Whitney,
Cartland, and others I see . . .
Faraway lands, ancient times, and
    peoples lives,
By looking thru the authors eyes.

John Byron Hiller
MAGIC OF AUTUMN

---

*To the supernal Autumnal
mountain splendor of the Black
Hills of South Dakota and
Wyoming.*

From high o'er the terrain comes
    the honking refrain
Of wild geese passing in flight
    review.
Since past ages unknown, they
    each Autumn have flown;
Winging Southward through
    cloud softened blue.

Hear the eagle's shrill cry sharply
    piercing the sky
As it soars o'er its regal domain.
Thrill as birds swarm in droves
    within tree sheltered coves,
Bound for Southlands where
    balmy skies reign.

Gaze on hillsides aflame as they
    boldly lay claim
To bright hues of all rainbows
    agleam;
Marvel this coloranza—this
    Heavenly stanza—
The Master's rendition supreme!

Nature's own recipe of divine
    alchemy,
Brewed each Autumn through
    ages untold;
Transforms aspen pristine from a
    quivering green
Into shimmering mountains of
    gold.
Sense the mystic moon's trance
    sweeping its vast expanse
With an aura unworldly—unreal;
As the firm lunar clasp locks its
    realm in the grasp
Of a stillness but night can reveal.

At this time of the year—
    highest Heaven bends near,
Its wonder eternal to share;
So why wish on a star, or for
    Heaven afar—
Throughout splendor splashed
    Autumn—We're There!

Samuel R. Robinson
TEA . . . TASTE

---

*Dedicated to my mother,
Catherine E. Robinson; my
grandmother, Mrs. Elnora Isaae
(now deceased); and my brother,
Jesse R. Snider. Thank you for
your support and encouragement
in all my efforts.*

Oh, Tetley, Luzianne and Lipton,
No finer tea can be found.
I dropped you all into the boiling
    water gradually,
with lots of leverage one silent
    subdued morn.
The ruby-red liquid transformed
    translucence—
into a new form.
Brim to rim, filled over-flowing.

Tempted to taste of the succulent
    soloution,
I drew it ever close, cautiously.
It was not hot.
There was no aroma.
It had no taste.
Can this be?

Delpha Funk Romeiser
Smokey River Blue Tick

He was just a plain old hound dog,
To many he had no worth.
But, if you ask his owner;
He was the greatest thing on earth.

He's a Smokey River Blue Tick,
You can hear his master brag;
You look a little closer,
Tis true-you see it on his tag.

He is a pal, he is a friend,
I take him where 'er I go,
He stands by through thick and
    thin,
He stays with me through heat
    and snow.

You can tell him all your troubles,
You can scold him and be stern;
With his life he will guard you
And ask nothing in return.

I'll match my dog to any one
That you may call a good friend;
I offered to him my hand,
How true—I too the dog defend.

Peter Abelard
TRIBUTE

Dearer far to me
Is a moment
Just looking at you,
Knowing that you
Are close enough
For me to touch,
Than any moment
Of remembrance
With anyone else,
Past or present.

Marianne Andrest
SIDE BY SIDE

Your pliable lips
are soft and sweet

a senuous smile
before our lips meet

Lying together
our bodies as one
dreading the sight
of the morning sun

You whisper sweet things
that send a chill
down my spine
especially knowing
that you'll always be mine

I'll be there for you
whenever needed
knowing that's the way
I'd want to be treated

I feel there's nothing
    to hide
when I'm with you
    side by side . . .

Diana Kwiatkowski
ALL HALLOWS EVE
The time they warn past haunts
    about the air—
Please move cautiously and
    beware, beware
Lest you should see One. If you
    do, don't fret
Just try desperately to avoid him,
    or else forget
That once in a better time you
    knew him somewhere
Loved him, needed him, tried to
    make him care
But now in the darkness of the
    chilling night
He calls out your name and you
    repeat "Goodnight."
Should he persist, never follow,
    simply let him go . . .
Trust me, child, for your heart's
    life, it must be so.

Diana Kwiatkowski
TIEBACK
One
Deliciously
Crisp, fresh fall day
lunch hour
walking on Second Avenue
——and there——
Despite all the people
strolling casually
Several hundred pigeons
have perched in triangles
on New York City telephone wires
And my heart keeps shouting:
    Oh, look!
There's haiku . . .
    There's haiku . . .
        There's haiku!
But you, indifferently, are too far
Away to see or to hear
the commotion.

Dawn Aarhus Anderson
MIRACLE CHILD
I didn't hear, nor see, nor feel
When they cut you from my
    womb.
It was not the birth I'd planned
For nine and a half long months.

"It's a miracle she's alive!" they said.
"A miracle," they said.
Yet here you are in my arms . . .
At my breast,
And so very much alive.

My beautiful baby girl,
Do you know what we've been

through?
And do you know,
Despite the pain,
That I love you so much more
Than I ever believed
I could love anyone . . . ?
My precious
Miracle child.

Elsa von Eckartsberg

Elsa von Eckartsberg
**The Poet As Playboy With
Fire**
Imagination
    is the fire in man, as
they say, erotic
    imagination a blaze—

yes, your mind
    makes love so violently
that houses
    burn down
where you walk
    and gently volatile
hearts
    burst into flame
when you call, lost
    in the maze

of their never before
    realized
        depth of desire
when you whisper to each
    in the depth of the night
unending love . . .
    stellar fusion . . .
        winged fame . . .

Jane A. Soxman, D.D.S.
HALLOWEEN NIGHT
In screaming silence still awake,
Awaiting howls goblins make.
And when the sun does at last
    arise,
Gratefully close all sleepy eyes.

Miriam Beth Wallick
THE REAL THING
I look into your eyes
    and I'm not sure what I see.
I listen to you talk
    and I'm not sure what I hear.
I make believe I see in your eyes
    the words
        I LOVE YOU.
I pretend to hear you say the words
    I LOVE YOU.
Maybe someday I won't have to
    pretend
Maybe someday someone really
    will love me.
But for now—
        I am pretending.
I have to stop
I have to leave you and leave my

make believe world where
    I'm pretending that I'm loved.
I have to go out and search for
    the REAL thing.
For pretending is no good
    anymore I need
        The REAL Thing.

Carolyn Jo Rohrer
RUNNING FREE
Running free and wild
The breeze blowing gently
    through your mane
Standing on the hill with
    the sun on your back
Somewhere you must find
    the will to go on
Forget where you have been
    and what you left behind
Forward you must go to
    find your happiness
So run my friend run

Mrs. Wilda M. Bailey
**To Mother On Mothers
    Day**
There is a lady,
    whom I love very much,
Who rocked me and fed me,
    and quieted me with her touch.
She covered my wounds
    when I got hurt,
And sewed up the hem,
    that came out of my skirt.
Her touch was so gentle
    when she put me to bed,
I was so small then
    and had nothing to dread.

When I became older,
    I could not understand,
How she could care for me,
    with such a willing hand.
She may have been weary,
    but it never did show,
As she went on smiling,
    at her work she did go.
She cared for us children,
    the best she knew how,
And taught us so many things,
    for which we know now.

This lady is my mother,
    and I cannot forget,
Her love and her kindness,
    still lingers as yet.
Today is "Mothers Day",
    a day to honor Mom,
So may each one remember her,
    as time goes on and on.
And let each one just pause
    today,
    and look to God above,
And thank Him for our Mother
    and her Precious Love . . .

Helen Dowe Coleman
OH BLACK MAN!

---

*Dedicated expressly to the black
man, but also to any human effort
and struggle to achieve a goal in
life.*

Oh black man . . . you've come so
    far
From the lands and cities of
    feathers and tar.

Stand tall, oh black man . . .
And fear to fall
Into the traps of your enemy's
    claw.

Remember what it cost you
To make waves in this world,
And don't let another's schemes
Send you tumbling with a whirl.

Think! Oh black man . . . should
    you be pleased
With false gains or shoddy deals
That send you crawling tarred
    and feathered
On scarred and weakened knees?

Remember past actions
Of other black brothers;
They, too, stood tall for periods of
    time.
But, alas! Lost their footing to five
    and dime crimes.

So, now you've achieved
What you set your goal to be;
Don't let it be said of you,
"I told you so, you see!"

Stand tall! Oh black man . . .
And fear . . . to fall.

Shirley Davis MaGee
THE WORD

---

*To God for the Resurrecting
power of His Word*

In the beginning
    The Word was
    The Word was with God
    The Word was God.
The Word became flesh
    and dwelt among us.
The Word was tempted
    but did not sin.
In the Word was power;
    The sick was healed,
    The dead was raised,
    The blind was made to see,
    The captive was set free.
The Word walked in grace
    and taught by faith.
The Word had a plan and a
    purpose
    for the redemption of men.
The Word laid down His life
    so sinners may be saved.
The Word was prepared for burial
    and placed in a tomb.
On the third day,
    the Word had risen
    and showed Himself openly.
The Word is the Resurrection
    and the Life.

Randaeus
The Fountain Of Youth
Love is a river of suffering souls
that is born in the innocence of
    spring;
Cold and sparkling it bubbles
    life's power,
as it is pulled centrally to Earth's
    heart.
Calmly drifting on, on floating
    towards time;
It weaves a gnarled wrinkle as its
    course grows
forever, and forever growing old.

When creatures drink from this
    madness they live
amongst the cool tranquility of
    spring;
As the passion of their thirst
    increases
it matures with the blossom of

Our World's Best Loved Poems

summer,
the waterfall churns its turbulent
tears
as it sees autumns glorious colors.

After the glory fades turning to
dust,
the heart's skin grows wary and
turns to ice,
for winter has entered where
spring began.
Love's superficiality has died,
but the current below the ice still
flows
forever, and forever drifting on;
Perhaps it will live in the spring
once more.

Fred Royal
Silver Clouds—To Nancy
Silver among the clouds
That is what you are.
Stormy and bellowing
Tho you are too.
Amist the scattering
Clouds of a stormy life.
The silver shrines—
Through and through too.
FOR
Without—A life of hardship
Peril and frustration too.
Within—A life of beauty and
Calm mingled with love.

Leta J. Bakke
OCTOBER

*I wish to dedicate this poem to
my loving husband, Duane, who
has made all my dreams come true.*

Almost the end of another year,
Your colours, vividly enhanced,
bring us good cheer.
The gold's, and the brown's, and
the yellow's too,
In all their splendour, say
"Hello" to you.
The air has a briskness, and
the smells are devine,
The children all looking forward
to Halloween time.
It's the end of Summer, that seared
the skin,
The beginning of cooler weather,
And the growth of the mighty
pumpkin.
You are here to prepare us for
Thanksgiving Day,
For Christmas too, not far
away.
Time to cover up the summer skin
so bare,
                    "MORE"

Chris Pathin
REFLECTIONS

*Dedicated to Carole Pope; a
noteworthy lyricist, whom I
greatly admire.*

Void expressionless faces
Attached to limp, lifeless bodies
Move with spastic, machine-like
movements
They hurry along conjested streets
Which roar with blaring horns and
Babbling voices
Loneliness and despair mixed with
Stinking exhaust fumes

Drift above the senseless
commotion
Burdens are carried on sagging
shoulders
Voices speak of nothing
Hollow smiles flash on bleak faces
Like the neon lights

Creatures are trapped
Prisioners of their society
Insanity and perversion are
Status symbols
Swearing and obscenities are
Etched on the walls
A revelation of the tarnished
minds
Love is merely physical lust

This is the life of the living dead

Lee Ann Yuasa
THE MESSAGE

*To my husband Alan, whom I
love with all my heart.*

This is a message for all to hear,
The youth of today and
tomorrow's year.
Of Kings and Princesses yet to be
seen,
Future generations of young
human beings.
You have the spark of magic to
give,
You will make the world a better
place to live.
You can make it into your palace
of dreams,
Of forgotten promises and visions
unseen.
For you hold the key to a land
full of bliss,
Of no hunger and sadness, no
prejudice.
For the youth of today and
tomorrow's year,
With guidance, will shine
through the darkened fears.
Enlightened to see the world as it
should be seen,
Through the eyes of a soul whose
heart is clean!

M. Sue Baxter
A POEM FOR ELIZABETH
If every tear could be wiped away
and the hurt soothed by gentle
caress,
if there never were burdens to
bear, for you I'd have no less.
If every goal could be reached
with ease and every task no
problem to face,
if life were only rainbows and
such no-one would know their
place.
If every heart were as pure as gold
and we could share as we have
been taught,
if we never let our neighbors
down we'd have room for every
thought.
If we were the stand-out in a
crowd and we defied the
Heavens above,
if we could reject the ones who
care there'd be no need for a
mother's love.
If we always knew how things
would work out, if there never
was sorrow or pain

life would have little meaning for
us— existence would have no
gain.
Accept who you are my beauty
rare and keep your Faith
whatever you do.
You are all the "Wonders of the
World" and remember that I
love you.

Denise L. Baker
TO YOU MY FRIEND

*To those—my special friends;
who have taught me the true
meaning of friendship through
their own patience and
understanding. To Ann, Betty,
Gail, Finley, Debbie, & Brenda,
my love.*

For the friend that means the
world to me;
For the thoughtfullness you
bestow unselfishly.
For unending patience and the
art of caring;
For forgiveness and the love
you're sharing.
For being there in times of need;
Makes you a true friend indeed.
For all you've done to make my
life, just what it is today;
I wish for you the best that life
could send your way.

Mr. Jerry R. Hawkins
THEY SEE YOUR FACE
They see your face, not the
feelings . . . you're tryin now
just to hide. But don't you
worry about what they're
thinkin . . . they'll never know
the kind of tears that you've
cried.
Understanding your life's
sorrows, not always an easy
thing to do. But I hope that
love will always be there and
always come through it all
with you.
The bitter taste of teardrops . . .
left uncounted too many to
review; somehow they
illustrate the memories of how
I really enjoyed you
So now let them wash away all
those feelings even tho the
tears taste sour
As you become like new born
flowers in the rain
Reaching out in your
magnificence for the sunlight
Only this time, there just isn't
any pain they all see your face,
but dear God, your smilin once
again!
I love you

andy stone
CHILDHOOD
The sun rose that morning and as
God peered through it he could
see us playing in the sandbox.
Heat had made little droplets
on her forehead and cheeks; I
kissed her and my lips tasted
salty wet. I told her that I loved
her and she shoveled some
sand into a pile in the middle
of the box. She placed her hand

on my chest and felt my heart.
As the beats quickened, she
gave a red smile and her
squinting eyes opened,
exposing a shiny laugh.
We sat there like two glistening
grapes, purple with youth, in a
grainy bowl, and when she had
to go home I cried. And she
cried. Tears slipped into the
sand and dried. And we slipped
out of the sand . . . and dried.

Frances Gutman
AMONG THE GHOSTS
I walk among the Ghosts and
they speak silently to me.
Sometimes they accuse me, with
reproach of being here when
you are not.
I know you loved me because you
said you did.
But you also said things that hurt
me, and as I go among the
remains of what was once a
vibrant, lusty place filled with
music and voices and the
sound of a violin, the ghosts
and spirits follow me, watching
my movements as I wander
aimlessly.
I shift a pile of papers, and
rearrange a book.
This place is not mine, it still is
yours, and I am a silent
stranger poking into your past
in places I hardly dare go.
Somehow I cannot close your life
and keep the ghosts away.

Dawn Dreamer
"GOD" AND THE BLIND
My God, why have you made me
blind?
The world around me, I cannot
find!
All around me, is only black—
I just can't bear it; that's a fact.
I hear children laughing in the
park,
While I just sit here in the dark.

The Bible says that Jesus healed
Sight from me, has just been
sealed!
I pray each night that you'll see fit
To make me whole, while I just sit.

To sit and wait, would just be
grand—
But really what I must now do, is
learn
to love and be loved, too!

For I believe my lesson is
To look within and there it 'tis
For all this time, I always knew—
How much you cared; my words
are few!

Dawn Dreamer
Remember, It's Christmas
It's that time of the year, it's
beginning to
snow; that hustle and bustle and
faces aglow!
People are shopping, and singing
good cheer—
But something is missing; The
Spirit, I fear!
Have we forgotten what
Christmas is about?
Surely, most people have, there
isn't a doubt.

Then let me remind you, good
people of cheer.
Jesus was born on that night-cold,
please hear!
You really must listen, before it's
too late—
Or you'll end up like Scrooge; I'm
afraid it's
your fate—

Christmas is love, and the joy of
giving;
Remembering Jesus in the now
and beginning!
He gave of himself, so that we
might be freed—
To give of ourselves in love and
good deeds!

It's time we woke up and realized
God's plan—
Start living Christmas or we'll all
be damned!
Remember the Wisemen, for they
understood—
It's not the gift, but the love,
that's
withstood!

Marguerite Mooney
LOST AND FOUND
I lost a happy smile today, it
travelled with the wind.
The milkman gladly caught it,
and transferred it with a grin,
The maid with glowing
happiness, then gave it to a
friend.
The friend, she took it shopping,
and all along the street
She gave it without thinking,
To all she chanced to meet.

As children shyly passed her,
they smiled at her in glee
And turned to other children,
with a smile both bright and
free.
The old looked up in wonder,
each face broke into smiles,
As they forgot to murmur, about
their many trials.

But the greatest wonder of it all
As I made my homeward way—
My smile, with compound interest,
Came back with me to stay.

Levon-ninsky Von Hardin
**Man Is, and As He Thinks,
So He Remains**
Like the painter who can change
his blank canvas into a work of
art, so can a man change his
mind to work for him, and not
against him . . .
His life being what he has made
it by his own thoughts, and it
is his own state of mind which
determines whether he is
happy or not, strong or weak,
foolish or wise.
If he is *unhappy*, that state of
mind belongs to himself, and is
originated within himself.
It is a state which responds to
certain outward situations.
If he is weak, he has brought this
upon himself, and remains in
that condition by the thoughts
he has chose, and is still
choosing.
If he is foolish, it is because he
does foolish things.

Man is endowed with *willpower*
(the ability to make reasonable
decisions, and controlling his
own actions), therefore, his
mind is subject to change.
He is not something that has
been fashioned and molded
into clay, and finally
completed, but has within
himself the capacity for
progress, and here lies the
secret of man's conditions, and
also his power.
Every effort he makes changes his
mentality.
By the right application of
thought, he rises to supreme
perfection.
By the wrong application of
thought, he descends to the
lower depths of the sea . . .
Between these two are the grades
of character.
*To live is to think and act, and to
think and to change* . . . If a
man is ignorant of the nature
of thought, he continues to
change for better or worse.
But being acquainted with the
nature of thought, he
intelligently develops and
directs the process of change,
and only for the better.

Man is, and as he thinks, so he
remains . . .

Theresa Austin
WHEN I NEED YOU
Sometimes life gets too hard to
bear
That's the time I'll share my
problems with friends
It's a comfort to know other
people care
We strengthen our bond
Sharing is caring

Carlisle Ramsey
WHERE IS HALLOWEEN?
Where is——

Halloween and Thanksgiving?
They're not in the local mall.
I saw Christmas everywhere!
But, they weren't there at all.

Where is——

Halloween and Thanksgiving?
Well! I'm going back to see
If they're with bikini sales,
Or on a Xmas tree!

Vicky M. Semones
TO HOLD YOU

(for J.M.H. and love's reverie . . .)

I hold you—alone in the twilight:
surrounded by this empty space
so filled with the scent of our
love;

I hold you—again in the dim
light:
feeling your closeness,
caressing the softness of our
love;

I hold you—an illusion of night:
you have fled, leaving me
to reconcile the rapture of our
love;

I hold you—knowing that we are
right:
that distance and time
cannot diminish the beauty of
our love.

Robert Weetman
THE HALLOWEEN WITCH
The witch gave a screech as she
flew past the moon to her
house in the moors where she
lives.
Her cat purred contently, and his
yellow eyes glowed, as he sat
by the pot that she brewed.

Together they watched as the pot
bubbled forth,
with the black magic she had
constrewed.
And all night she kept brewing
and casting her spells,
till the morning mist spread its
dull shine.
And with this dull glow the
witch crept again into a book
that lay near, and vanished
once more.
As she's done times before into
fairyland where her spells all
come true.

Roberta K. Klemm
TREASURE CHEST
The raindrops on my car at night
make up my treasure chest.
Of all the jewels that I have
I think I like them best.
Diamonds sparkle very bright till
red lights make them shine
Like rubies in the dreary night:
and all of these are mine.
The changing of the traffic light
brings out the emerald's glow:
Sapphires, garnets, topaz, too,
make up this dazzling show.
These are all my treasure trove;
they glisten just for me.
They help me pass the rainy
night and hold no care for me.

Linda L. Collins
LIFE'S STREAM
I sat by the brook and watched
the water glide by.
I shook myself gently and gave a
soft sigh,
As I realized how much my life
resembled this stream;
Slipping away swiftly as if in a
dream.

Then evening drew near and the
mist began to rise,
And drift its way upward toward

darkening skies.
Then nothing but darkness was
all I could see,
And I knew my life would darken
and then cease to be.

Then I grew drowsy and I must
have slept,
For I dreamed life was over and
nobody wept.
But suddenly I wakened and rose
from my grassy bed;
I saw nothing but beauty and
sunshine ahead.

Then I knew life, to me, was a
wonderous gift,
And no matter how dreary, the
mist soon would lift.
Then sunshine would await me
to brighten the way,
Of this poor wandering pilgrim,
God fashioned from clay.

Gary W. Enos
**On the Night Of October
31st**
The Winds Hooowl!
The Shutters Creak!
The dark clouds spew
Lighting toward the meek.

T'is time for the Witch,
Goblins, and Ghouls!
Some black cats, Villens
And maybe, one fool.

In a pumpkin, St. El-mos
Fire is sat.
Over head, a devil, scarecrow
And a Vampire Bat!

A figure appears,
Through the mist on the moor,
It comes closer, No! closer!
Theres a rap on the door.!

You open the door,
With heart in hand.
It's a Ghost, No! a Goblin!
As it sticks out its hand . . .

Just three words does it speak.
It demands! TRICK-OOR-TREEAT!

Emilia Denise Morettin
THE DESERT
The desert sands play softly as
the wind blows,
Quietly whispering among
themselves.
Tumbleweeds roll in a summer-
salt fashion
Never stopping or looking back.
Over and over the vast sands
they roll.
The cactus stands straight and
stiff,
Not moving when the wind blows.
Small animals scamper about
under the hot sun
Trying to find a bit of shade.
As the sun burns and animals
wither,
The desert stands
Still as a cactus;
For the desert will never die.

Franklin August Picker,
A 'Cote' Of Many Colors
From whence we came, and to
where we'll go,
Was then, as now, not for us to
know;
The day we arrived on this planet
earth,

Was the day our mothers gave us
   birth.

Just when you'd be born, you had
   no voice,
What color you'd be, you had no
   choice;
And now that you're here, you
   must also believe,
There is no certain schedule,
   'bout when you'll leave.

Be you white or black or red or
   brown,
Is there someone trying to hold
   you down?
Is the world 'Agin' you because of
   your skin,
Won't the world recognize we're
   all kith and kin?

Seems colors and churches and
   customs abound,
Once earth was thought flat, now
   we know that it's round;
The person you are, the ideals
   you hold,
One day, the world, will acccpt
   your own mold.

Though people and peas all come
   from the sod,
We are certainly not like 'peas in
   the pod';
Potpourri people, somewhat like
   a stew,
Ingredients many, final taste,
   inbue.

Our mores and ideas are shaped
   by mere chance,
Where, and by whom, credit
   sheer happenstance:
Our minds struggle back thru
   memories haze,
Tomorrows find form in our
   yesterdays.

Eva Faye Compton
A Moonlit Winter Scene
The Moon shines brightly;
   like a china saucer,
High above this wintry scene.

An old rail fence, and trees
   in somber color,
Now adorned, with piles of jewel-
   like beads of sparkling snow.

And all this upon a fitting
   background of rolling hills,
   blanketed in glistening light,
Surely, will make a pretty picture
   in black and white.

Esther Manary Bamesberger
THE BEACH
Beauty's here
In everything;
Terns on the run
Gulls on the wing
Child's little hand
Print in the sand.

Gray stupid loons
Weeds on the dunes
Sight of a boat
Board that's afloat
A wave's tiny ripple
Babe's lunch from a nipple.

Hot sun above
One that I love
Moon on the rim
Day growing dim
A blanket for two
I'm there with you.

Franklin August Picker
Complacency Revisited

To each of us . . . lest we forget

I came to church, though I was
   late, and dropped a dollar in the
   plate;
I said the prayers, I sang the
   songs, and asked forgiveness
   for my wrongs.

I smiled and passed the kiss of
   peace, my spirits soared, I felt
   release.
And, as I left, I told the preacher,
He was a wonderful bible teacher.

With all the good I'd done this
   day, the kindly things along
   the way;
Atonement for my sins I'd paid; I
   figured that I had it made.

When suddenly, . . . my spirit
   crashed; a thought came to me .
   . . lightning flashed.
Complacency gave way to fear,
My eyes welled up with sudden
   tears.

Whatever was I thinking of,
That acts could take the place of
   love?
The love of God, He's sent my
   way, in His very own and
   special way.

When Jesus rose on that third
   day, he showed to me, the only
   way,
That God, in all His mercy given,
Will welcome me into His heaven.

Bruce Mossburg
THE CAUST
Do not mistake Death
   for One who is worse.
Death will come as always
   with sorrow, His curse.

I've seen in His shadows,
   those which come before,
(The light is behind,
   beyond the dreaded door)

There lurks a foulness
   an absense of all that's true,
Evil rises up
   Hitler kills the Jew.

Horror shall outlast
   sorrow's wailing cry.
Though Death's not our friend,
   hell's no way to die.

Helen M. Bryant
SUMMER

June, Margaret & Graham

As I go singing along the way,
the air is perfumed with new
   mown hay.
The summer sun so warm and
   bright.
Sunbeams dance in great delight.
Melodious music of the lark,
giving hope, cheer and gladness.
And to my childish ears it seemed,
the sweet green grass was fully
   attuned
to the magical moment of
   loveliness.

Wendy Lynn Bishop
Freedom As An American
I'm as free as a bird,
My justice attained.
Free to speak as I wish,
Self dependence I gained.

My liberty highly protected,
Loyal to my own wills,
I have my belonging rights,
That my country fulfills.

I'm very proud,
That my country's free,
And I can go on,
Just being me.

Jean M. Thieda
I WONDER
Oh, when I die, will my soul fly
Beyond soft clouds and sun
   drenched sky,
Out into space where all is still
Up to heaven, if 'tis GOD'S will.

There peace and quiet I shall find
For all up there are good and kind,
And those who have gone on
   before
Will welcome me at Heaven's door.

Scott A. Chier
TO: My Love Of Life
And if by chance the sands of
time divide our paths that we
may never again join as one,
know in your heart that I will
truely love you always and
forever with every living breath.

Lisa Dawn Vaughn
DEATH OF A DREAM

---

*This poem is dedicated to my
parents Charles and Darlene,
whose love and encouragement
help to keep my dreams alive.*

How different now my hopes and
   dreams
From those when I was young.
How long ago my youth does
   seem
From where those hopes were
   sprung.
Time like a blade has cut to
   shreds
The rainbow once in my soul,
And I am forced by the hand of
   fate
To change my direction and goal.

My life once planned now hangs
   in fear
As time moves ever on,
And I am the puppet, the pawn
   my dear
And life . . . it goes on and on.
By choice or not this world has me
And I have the whole of this world,
Whether I can make a
   difference . . . we'll see
The flag of my future is still
   unfurled.

But I have faith that time will
   show
A path cut especially for me
And then with encouragement
new dreams will grow,
From my doubts and fears I'll be
   free.
There's a purpose to every life I
   believe

Mine . . . I don't yet know,
But gladly from the future I'll
   receive
The chance for new hopes and
new dreams to grow.

Keith Eggers
AN ODE TO EARTH
Breath taking!—, Awe
inspiring!—, Pure delight! that
view, from the mountain top!
Like an intermezzo, of melodious
songs, dancing an orb, of
spectural colors, upon the snow
covered ice caps—, of the
frozen—, granite giants—,
about me!
Silently—, the scintilating
splendor, of the golden hues, of
yellows and pinks—, were
being quietely replaced, with
the cold—, grey—, tinges—, of
twilight.

Now—, all alone—, in the
remotest depths, of the
wilderness—, in silent
meditation—, I lay.
My ear's—, catching every
sound—, that wasn't there!
Mind—, and ear—, playing it's
own chord—, of inventive—,
ghostly sounds—, like rattling
chains—, of a salient past.

Intently now!—, I listen!—,
Again!—, Straining!
And I can still recall God's
voice—, whispering, upon the
winds—,
And it clearly said to me, "Lo!"
"Here, I Am!"—, "There, I Am!"
"I Am, in all Things!!"

He can even be—, in you!—, my
friend—, as well as in me.
And even though—, you may
have cause—, to hate me—, or
even, have no cause—, to
dislike me—
And thus, can not truely, love
me!—, or—, in peace, ever—, be
I your friend!—, I can!!
Only because—, of God! Working
in me—, truely, say—, to—,
you—, "I Love you!"—, "I Love
You!"—, "I—, Love—, You!"
"HELLO!—," "FRIEND!"

Raymond M. Squire
HEAVEN'S LAMPS
The old lamp lighter with faithful
   care
Has plodded his years along
Linghting the lamps that were
   planted there
And replacing the ones gone
   wrong.

But his years stretched long and
   weary
And his steps grew painfully slow
And his ladder too heavy to carry
As the pulse of his life sank low.

But the lamps that were placed
In the arches of night
Are kept by the hand of God
And ever recall to human eyes
A life beyond the sod.

Oh, the angels must stand
With their pinions aquiver
On the tips of their winged toes
Eager to fly on mystic wings

Swift as the lightning goes
To replace the lamps that shine
In the infinite realms of the sky.

Greg Morris
CANCER II
The lot of the cow,
Is worrisome now,
Instead of wheat,
Growth inducers they eat,
And all but the 'moo',
Is used for glue,
That's all now;
Poor cow;
For the meat,
Is not safe to eat.

Wilma E. Mathers
A STAR FOR TROY
The midnight sky is full of stars,
My heart is filled with love. . .
I only need to look at you,
And I know without a doubt,
I love you.

I love you,
As many stars as you can see,
If you pick one shinning star,
It will guide you always,
Back to me.

Your part of the universe,
A special part of my world.
Your my brightest star,
That twinkles in the dark of
night.

Your everything to me.
The midnight sky, the moon and
stars.
I've set you free,
Only to travel back to me,
I love you.

Leah C. Anderson
CONTEMPLATION
When we think of all the sadness
and troubles we have known;
The tears that have been shed in
trying to go it all alone!
How in our weakest moments
we're convinced there is no
hope;
That God's foresaken us and now
no longer can we cope!

How foolishly we turn away in
anger and despair;
Convinced whatever lies ahead is
more than we can bear!
But somehow when the blackest
clouds are hovering overhead
and
The thought of days to come may
only fill our hearts with dread!

Without a bit of warning there
may suddenly appear;
A ray of hope a dissolution of all
our human fears!
Soon things are looking up again
the skies are blue and white;
And it won't be long 'til
everything turns out exactly
right!

All we need is confidence and
faith in God above;
The joy that comes when we
accept the protection of His
Love!
The great relief that comes in
knowing that He is ever near;
To help us as we seek His aid
when obstacles appear!

The overwhelming power of just
one little Prayer;
The comfort in the knowledge
that He is always there!
To answer all our questions and
help us to survive;
And make us feel so happy again
just to be alive!

Catherine M. Pallavicini March
THE CLEVER KILLER
You wretch, you cruel and evil
thing full of vengence, full of
hate
You take our loved ones, you use
our hearts for bate.
Oh but you cleverly do it slowly
Make us suffer and pray only to
feel holy
The sick and the well will endure
the pain
Research again and again, but
there is no cure
Someday we may have one, but
how can a person be sure
Be gone with you, but it is not
that easy
You take the likes of whomever
you please
You leave us behind with only
the memory of a deplorable
disease

Suzanne Spicer
**Confessions Of a Space
Cadet**
My feet are firmly on the ground
My soul is lost, as yet unfound.
My dreams are never ending
spheres
Of colored lights and deepest fears.

I hold no thought of what may be
For hope is winged and flies from
me.
My spirit is a dying fire
Of haunted nights and lost desire.

Illusions Are reality
When I am lost inside of me.
Treasures live within the mind
When life is only passing time.

Rita Crawford
BEULAH
Her mother could do nothing but
cry
As life passed her by
When there's no love in the
home, why try?
Her heart could not lie

A father not her own
Could not make this house her
home
Beulah, oh Beulah girl
Who will put love in your world?

Clothed in second best
Clean the house and all the rest
Off into the night, flee
All this just to feel free

A handy man in time of need
Will you marry me? It is agreed.
A life out on her own
This house will be a home

Evelyn M. S. Edwards
WINDOWS OF THE SOUL!
Within is My Soul of Melody—
Understanding and of love
I have to be broadminded and so
flexible that I bend,
not break the bow

The world is so beautiful, this is
hardly the bursting
bauble
But the problems are with souls
who do not bend or humble

First, where is their Master—is
He God, or is it wrought
of men
Ah—stop breaking all those
pretty baubles
And give the tortured, torn soul
the right to mend
And as within my soul I look and
see all those clouded
windows
Clouded windows of the soul that
are so in need of
mending
They hate, they love, they break
away from understanding
friends
And I wonder if they ever talk of
or have the true, true
sense within
That *only* GOD can make their
life aright
And erase all those ugly, ugly,
blots

Sheryl Simmons
WITHIN

———————————

To my children Mattice and
Nakeisha love mom

———————————

As, I dwell into the depts of my
soul.
Energies aflows within
me/cosmic affects me.
I am aware of the universe that
surrounds me.
For I travel thru channels of
darkness yet enter into the true
light of life itself.
That leadeth me to the path of
Gods greatest gift to man The
mind.

Hilda M. Jordan
THE CALIFORNIA MAN

*This Poem is dedicated to the
following: President Reagan, John
Campbell, Joseph Mellon, H.C.
Jordan, George Liberace and men
of his Music company, and all
men of America, and on earth.*

The C Man stands for courage.
The A Man stands for admirable.
The L Man stands for loveable.
The I Man stands for intellectual.
The F Man stands for fun.
The O Man stands for order.
The R Man stands for right on.
The N Man stands for naughty.
The I Man stands for interesting.
The A Man stands for arrogant.

Gerene F. Stevens
LOVE IS . . .
Love Is . . .
A gentle breeze which warms
and enfolds me.

Love Is . . .
The opening of the windows of
my soul to:
Kindness, caring and giving—
Joy, contentment and forgiving.

Love Is . . .
Stretching, touching, reaching—
Loving, feeling, teaching.

Love Is . . .
A bird in flight, a starry night—
Autumn in color, the hands of a
mother.

Love Is . . .
A single rose in a slender vase,
The slant of sunlight on a happy
face.

Love Is . . .
All these things, a gift that is
free,
And the window's of my soul are
open for me.

Martha Stroshine Burrow
MY FAVORITE PUMPKIN
My favorite pumpkin sat
Upon the fence by the old black
cat.
Kept watch for witches
And other things,
That halloween always brings.

He can't wait for the garden gate
To swing and open within.
And as the masqueraders leave,
Watch it close again.

Layne Leonard
LOST
My feelings run deep
To the source of my pain
While you dissect my thoughts
As you probe at my brain.

Marooned in the void
Of the unconscious mind
I reach for that answer
That I can't seem to find.

I've no wish to deceive you,
Or toy with your heart,
I've no use for these head games,
That could tear us apart.

I just yearn for your warmth
And the life in your smile.
I just hope that dreams do come
true
Once in a while.

For all things come
To those who wait.
But most things are
A bit too late.

Norene Kelly
LOVE'S DWELLING
Our relationship started on cool,
easy ground
And it grew in a fashion that
seemed safe and sound
What we built seemed secure,
from the ceiling to floor
And for the first time ever, I
opened the door.
I told you I love you; I was always
sincere
And you always played back
what I wanted to hear.
But the groundwork was hurried,
and the walls grew weak
The windows cast shadows
which were dark, grey, and bleak.
I was pierced by the splinters of
game-playing lies,
And with a wordless stare, we
broke all ties

Time left me drifting, confused
and alone
Thoughts left me wanting for the

love I had known.
I never lost sight of your smile or
    charm,
Now I long for the love I once
    held in my arms
For I want to rebuild the
    structure we lost
No matter the time, no matter
    the cost.
So, perhaps, I, in my way, and
    you, in yours,
Can strengthen frail walls, and
    open new doors.
And when the right time
    approaches, with minds and
    souls ready,
We can enter a structure that's
    unyielding and steady.

Barbara Oxford
NITE
As the day seems to fade away to
    dusk
you can look outside and see the
    color rust.
As the sun sets down on the
    other side below,
look toward the mountainscan
    you see any snow?
As the dark comes and the lights
    get bright
we get an easy feeling that comes
    with the nite.

Donna Goulet-McRadu
ESCAPE
Escape again!
    Flee from the over-crowded city
    Where smog sucks freshness
    from the air.
    People deep with despair
    Voice troubles, expecting pity
Only in vain!

One wave audieu!
    Not to glance back, continue on
    Away from area aroused in
    clamour.
    Structures soring, meant for
    glamour
    Never praised, glimpse becomes
    wan
At architects' view!

The beach appears!
    Seagulls! The sky and sea merge,
    Mingled with major and minor
    and
    Waves that shade the sand;
Somersault breeze that urge
Breathe deep to ears!

Each week to gain
    A day to drift with you,
    Absorb morning rays to bronze
    Alert to earthy songs
    Eye the movement of blue, when
    through
Escape again!

Robin Goad
YOU
You I love and will forever,
time will change but I will never,
time will come for you to be mine,
but time will never change my
    mind.

I do believe the Lord above
created you for me to love.
He picked you out from all the rest
because he knows I love you best.

When I get to heaven and you're
    not there,

I'll carve your name on the
    Golden Stairs,
so all the angels there can see
what my babe means to me!

Jean Cunane Murphy

Jean Cunane Murphy
AGING SOLO

---

*I dedicate this poem to my
mother, Irene Smith Murphy. She
ages alone, warmed by her own
faith, dignity, love and wisdom.
She is silently courageous. I strive
to learn her strengths.*

Jagged chips from my pedestal
Crash upon the dusty still.
Tunnel walls of silence yawn
As emptiness prays for dawn.
Darkness, uneasy from the night
Fades to 'Alone' under light.
No one needs my love to share
So heavy to hold in the morning
    air.
Yearning to give just like before,
I'm discontinued in my own store.
Was I ever in such demand?
I was the flower; now I'm sand.

Cindi Spainhour
Mountain Passage: Part I
I met her once,
    a time ago
She was standing on a mountain
    top
    covered white with snow
And she told me of her dreams
    and plans
    as we looked at lands below
At all the valleys and the streams
    and places they would go . . .

And this is where she chose to live
    for here she could be free
For she was sure of who she was
    and who she wanted to be
She always had lots of friends
    ready and standing by
Who would be there to protect her
    incase the dreams might die . . .

They kept her out of trouble
    and away from hurt and pain
And she always loved them dearly
    even while they walked away
Her life was starting over
    that's the way it had always been
And she finally learned to live
    with it
    realizing it would end . . .

For each time that she met
    someone

they always walked away
Not knowing what it did to her
    and how she lived from day to
    day
And once in her life she met a man
    who said he'd never leave
And he told her that he loved her
    untill finally she believed . . .

So she came down from her
    mountain
    and took him by her side
Untill one day he flew from her
    and she could find nowhere to
    hide
For she couldn't reach her
    mountain
    that was covered white with snow
And how she'd live without it
    was a question she did not
    know . . .

So she began to look for answers
    in the forest through the trees
And sometimes sit and listen
    to the silence of the breeze
Untill one day she came upon
    a flowing mountain stream
And decided she would follow it
    to see where it might lead
It led her to her answers
    in the valley down below
For she had come upon a stream
    that was made of mountain snow.

Helen A. Mc Ewen
**A Pleasant Smile and
    Kindly Thought**
We'll start on a little journey
    now, forgetting all strife
As we search for one of the great
    joys of life,
It is now early morn, the day just
    begun
We stand in awe at the glory of
    the rising sun
Fascinated we wonder, what
    greater joy could the eye
    behold
Than this mystery that the
    heavens' to us unfold
Our sorrows and our doubts
    begin to fade
As every thing now seems so
    heavenly made

But with the passing of the day,
This glory will fade away
No—we have not found this great
    joy yet
So again, on our journey we beset,
This time, we pause and think,
The flowers were so beautiful,
    and fragrant on that brink
But, they with the wind will sway
And soon oe'r will be their day

What can this great joy be, you
    ponder in dismay
That we have not found, but
    searched for each day
It is true, these beauties that we
    found
We hold in great renoun,
But they would all be for naught,
If from them we had not
    besought
Just a, "Pleasant Smile and Kindly
    Thought"
With this great joy found, we
    travel once more
This time it will be as ne'er
    before.

Jennifer Moore Norris
IT WAS ENOUGH
It was enough
That we drank a beer
And shared a joke,
Equally gave,
Equally took.
It was right
That we defied all
And lived for us
As comfortable friends
Too free to fuss.
It was enough
Till I kissed you
And you kissed me,
Till I fell in love
And you stayed free.

Jacqueline Rowe Gonzalez
COLOR ME HAPPY
When out in the sun very long,
    color me red.
When I sit alone and write
    poems, color me smart.
When I stay in bed with the flu,
    color me pale.
When I watch for bargains, color
    me very wise.
With holidays approaching, color
    me happy.
With Monday diets gone by
    noon, color me fat.
With autumn coming on real
    soon, color me glad.
With Halloween on the way,
    color me pumkin.

Blanche Marie Atwood
REAL LIFE
Life is a smiling face
But often has tears in eyes
Life is a suffering and pain
Not all is always nice
Life is a beautiful fairy tale
Where is living prince and princess
Life is a great disappointment
Not very often the success
But far away on the other side
New life is waiting on us
In this world we haven't chance
The other route is better and
    wise
Beyond the blue horizon
Shines a brilliant star
As lighthouse on the sea
It's Jesus King of all the kings
I hear His sweet voice calling me.

Earl R. Hall
CONTINUITY

---

*Dedicated to Jesus Christ By
whom there is Life after Death.*

A late December hears
With drums attuned by years
The mountain freshet sing
As it tumbles into spring.

A late December sees
By aid of aged breeze
The frolic of the flowers
In coming summer hours.

A late December knows
From tending olden rose
That she will decorate
Tomorrow's trellised gate.

A late December feels
When weakened stitches yields
To tug of Mother Earth
And pressures of it's birth.

Sandra Luann Kuersten
Someone I Wanted To Know

To: Jimmy Leigh Bunch The
Someone I wanted to know

I saw you one night there at my
table
Your shiny dark hair
Your smile like sunshine

There was a realness that
radiated from you
Your wit and charm pierced my
heart
Your music soothed my soul

Your laughter and spirit sparkled
my eyes
And your tenderness made me
feel like a child
Your kisses and touch sent chills
down my spine

And your mind stimulated my
senses
I knew then . . .
You were someone I wanted to
know

James E. Turpin
A FRIEND

This poem was inspired by Cpt.
Jeff Williams whom was called
upon, and who carried out the
ever demanding task of being a
friend, colleague and even father
at times . . . . THANX

A freind is someone whom you
can say anything to, and they
will understand
A friend is someone whom shares
the good times, and
experiences the bad
A friend is someone whom can
pick you up, and never let you
down
A friend to me is you . . . .
Thank you for being a friend

B. J. McGrath
SAIL TO THE TOP
Bobbing on the cool sound of
chance
Aboard this silent vessel we dance
Cutting through the wave like a
lance
Compelled without protest to
advance.

Karen Lee Vigue
MOUNTAINS
The Majestic Mountains rest
against the sky.
As gray puffed clouds press
silently by.
Sunrays are glistening through
many tall pines.
Forming purple shadows and
faded muted lines.
Rustic protrusions, I picture here.
Like precise pyramids tall and
shear.
While permanently planted in
the ground
A Fortress, protecting all they
surround.
I gaze at the molded perfections
they be.

And feel the Air of Strength
reborn in Me.
I feel Strong, Exilirated, yet
Peaceful inside.
Powerful and Passionate, like the
force of the Tide.

Mary McMerrick
SEPTEMBER MOON
I looked out the window
only to see
A September moon, shining
back at me.
It was big and round
For its time was full
And outside—how I wished
I could go;
Just to sit and stare at
the moon above
For its quiet beauty filled
my soul with love.
But I was destined to stay
indoor
And as the drape closed
saw the moon no more.

Gloria M. Heiser
APRIL FOOL
April Fools' is the day
when anyone can jest.
Doesn't matter what they say
the worst are at their best.

April one and the fool
who is caring not
What is said, can be cruel,
kind or who cares what?

Fool's day is April first
to one of little vision.
Every day can be cursed
by a fool with indecision.

April's fools reign year long;
more so on day one.
Their foolery ever gone . . . ?
Why, it's just begun!

Max Natch
FAREWELL
Too fine, and much too early lost
my thoughts do cleave to thee,
for thou fore'er my escort star
amidst the deceptive sea.
But trembling cold and deeded
soul the swell to dark before,
Because the signal lamps are
quenched o'er the dark and
blackened shore.

I spied thee then when hope
arose on youth's victorious
wing, and thou more beautiful
than a ray of early morning
spring.

Who then could fancy health and
joy would e'er forsake thy brow,
so light, with diverse lustre
once, so cold, and alterless now.

At dusk whene'er the autumn
dew upon the vale was shed,
and the moon far down the
west its beaming host had led.
Those told how sorrowful and oft
to that predicted eye, scenes of
nightfall and decline beginning
death was nigh.

'Twas sound from far off worlds
which no one here could hear,
akin to night winds mournful
lyrics whispered gently in her
ear.
'Twas the message quietly sent
when blessd angels appear from
their lustrous paradise bent, a
call to her so clear.

How sorrowful on my soul that
fateful caution fell, but Oh, the
grim reality another sound may
tell.
The hasty decline, the farewell
sigh the slowly progressing
bier, the spaded earth, the
carpet green, the unattainable
tear.

The scented florals abloom in
heaven encompass thy temple
now, the halo that beams
immortally is shining on thy
brow.
The angels circle the spirited
throne have brought thee to
thy rest, to live amongst the
virtuous high, a friend of all
the blessed.

Jerry E. Walker
MY DEATH WISHES
As I was showering tonight the
reality that I'm dying, hit me
full in the face.
And I know now that I must die
as anyone else no matter how
rich, how famous, what religion
or race.
And now that I've realized that
like all others I must die, here
are some things I'd like to do
and see, and some reasons why.
I'd like to see an ocean with it's
water so clear and blue,
Or fly low above the earth, so I
could remember the view.
I'd like to enter a race and drive
the winning car,
Or walk a thousand miles but it's
just too far.
I'd like to be free from debt,
sorrow, and pain
And wash away my sins in a
warm summer rain.
I'd like to let each person I know,
exactly what to me they mean,
And have a picture in my mind of
every beautiful thing I've seen.
I'd like to hold each child born
today, close in my arms,
And prevent accidents from
happening, by sending out
alarms.
I'd like to see all wars cease and
come to an end,
And see the start of the world
living in peace, begin.

Tho I feel I've done as much as
people thirty years old,
In facing the realities of dying it
makes me no bolder.
So if through my words, I could
make people begin realizing,
That just like myself ever since
birth, we all begin dying.

Carol Kibbons
MOTHER'S—IN—LAW

To my wonderful mother-in-law,
Mrs. Gertrude McMurtrey,
without whom we would not be
complete!

She's always the butt of a joke;
At a party, a show, or just a silly
hoax.
Always someone asking her for a
hand-out when they're broke.
Always one of those that
daughters and sons try to
soak . . .

But she's always there if you need
a shoulder to cry on.
Always there when you're down
and out.
Always there to baby-sit when
everyone else has gone.
Always there to bail you out
when things go wrong . . .

Comedian's use them for their
material instead of wives for a
change;
Usually not meant seriously—
but I've a feeling about that and
its a bit strange?
Spouses have a way of fighting
and arguing until mother-in-
law's to blame;
The least responsible party—yes,
indeed—it must be "The
Mother's-in-Law Gang" . . !

Never-the-less she stands
steadfast;
Not accepting her new found
fame,
As the leader of "The Mother's-in-
Law Gang."
She continues to be what she is
and will be again . . .

A mother-in-law who, thank God,
is quite sane.
And strong-willed enough to
return the blame from whence
it came.
I'm proud and glad that October
23rd has been picked as a
tribute to all mother's-in-laws.
If you think about it a mother-in-
law is a mother and most
probably a wife too . . !

So you'd better stay on your
mother-in-law's good side;
Or Heaven help us when
mother's-in-law join with the
mothers and wives alike!
There won't be anyone to borrow
or beg from or to ask to baby-
sit some?
It's time to shoot straight and
admit a mother-in-law is pretty
handy to have around & I feel
we all should show our
gratitude & applaud her
some . . ! !

Konnie Helter
HALLOWEEN NIGHT
Halloween night will soon be
here,
  The witches and goblins will
  soon come near.
    The ghosts will come up, out
    of their graves,
      And the demons will chase
      you with black pointed
      spades.
        The witches will fly, high
        on their brooms,
          And all the dead people
          will come out of their
          tombs.
            Black cats will be
            prowling in the
            darkness of night,
              And all the small
              children will run
              from the fright.

Fawn H. Crosby
TEARS OF SORROW
I held the small
clinched fist
wet with tears
of deep and
anguished sorrow—
She told me
the story
of her homeland
torn with strife—
Her black chaddor
draped, cuddled
near my peek-a-boo
summer dress
of white—
Oh! Lebanon!
Together we weep
now—
Your homeland soaked
fresh with the blood
of our dear
loved ones—

Amrett Spivey Robas
WINDY DAYS

*I dedicate this poem to my
grandson WITH LOVE JOSEPH
FREDERICK ROBAS III born on a
windy January day*

I rubbed a hole in the steam of
the window glass, and saw
snow stiff branches on the old
oak tree flash.

I have not ventured outside for
seven long days. My feet make
noise, breaking the thin crusty
snow waves.

The sound is gone now, only
deep, deep, silent snow, and
high above the tree tops a full
moon rode.

The snow's falling on my furry
collar and cuffs. My breath
keeps rising like signals in
frosty puffs.

Flashing of a mirror in the
moonlight slender, I was
spotted from one of the
darkened windows.

In front of me now lies a stretch
of virgin snow, and the moon
moves across the sky

in rhythms slow.

I walked along the crest of the
steep hill and stopped. Behind
me frozen is a curve of
footsteps locked.

Then a stillness, a special quiet
all around moves, the
treacherous wind has placed
snow in every groove.

And now; back to my warm
house like a lifeline ends, I've
been hearing and listening for
days to the wind.

Carolina J. Borunda
JUST ASK

*Inspired by Our Lord and Savior
Jesus Christ who I humbly give
all praise and honor.*

Just ask
No strings attached
I give freely
To all who receive.

If you thirst
Just drink of me
If you hunger
Come eat of me.

The Bread of Life
Is what I am
An endless pit
For salvation of man.

Be clothed in white linen
Be washed in My blood
I have taken away sin
And replaced it with love.

Just ask
No strings attached
I give freely
To all who receive.

Shannon Scott
TIME FORGOTTEN
If the clock stopped
With but a sigh
And told no one,
What would become of
The minutes which fall
Behind the stove to
Collect the dust from
The passing of time.

Celestino M. Vega
MORTALITY
the pollen of the sun
seeds
the grass-grown thighs
of maternal earth

birth follows death

honey hived
in the wounds of morning
a butterfly
a dirge

death follows birth

Aaron G. Florez
THE VACATION
We were on an island, small but
large. When the sunset came
you could see the white birds
swinging, you could feel the
soft, calm, wind against your
skin and the wet crunchy sand
beneath you.

The fish would swim oddly.
When night came, you could

hear the parrots chirping, the
birds squawking silently, then
everything was quiet. They all
drifted to sleep, and rested for
the long day ahead. This
vacation was great.

Laurel Susan Vitone
SILHOUETTES OF LOVE
It consumes the shape of
obstacles in it's way,
It dances to a different rhythm
everyday.
It is found in the backdrop of the
hours of twilight, and a white-
winged dove, soaring in flight.

It is the hypnotic grasp of
crashing waves on shore,
It is olden times from the days of
yore.
It is the slightest touch of a
stranger's hand, and walking
together on the emerald sand.

It is the tiniest of tears against a
mother's face,
It is the joyous hope of the
human race.
It is shadowed through figures of
hopes and dreams, and
cherished memories of
moments serene.

It is the other half which makes a
whole, or a treasure found deep
within a soul.
It is the star of happiness which
graces the air, and the magic of
life, found everywhere.

It is called by name from God
above, A light so bright, the
silhouette of love.

Eileen A. Donovan-Cooper
SPECTRAL SHADOWS
Ghostly specters
espied in dawn's dim light—
a tipple,
a pole,
a shed—
reminders of a past gone time
now faded in noon's brightness.
A sandy oasis
faulted by huge pebbles
sun-drenched beige,
stretching rusting skeletons,
with encroaching green
spread thin,
bending gentle before the breeze,
a beginning of fill in
to cover relics of a time past gone.

Sandra Lee Dawn MacLeod
**Yesterday, Today, and
Tomorrow**
Yesterday, today, and tomorrow;
three different times, yet all
the same.

There shall always be a
yesterday, today and tomorrow.

Yesterday holds memories of
good and bad alike, happiness,
forgiveness, trust and sorrow.

Today holds the present, the
truth, and what shall be
tomorrow, yesterday.

Tomorrow is an open sea, who
knows what can happen
between now and of the
tomorrows of eternity?

When one ceases to exist and is
gone to his bodily grave,
yesterday, today, and tomorrow
linger on.

One cannot bring back yesterday,
even though memories cling;
nor can one no matter how he
tries, into tomorrow swing.

Seasons come and seasons go, and
the days flow slowly past. Into
tomorrow, as today, from
yesterday's hold fast.

Yesterday, today, and tomorrow,
how well we know your names,
but yesterday, today and
tomorrow are nothing less than
games.

Lorina J. Stephens
A CHILD'S INFIRMITY
The Princess sleeps—all is well,
and Paradise smiles this eve.
The hours have strung their
weary thrum
of patience to a booming drum,
and the smile shines sweet
for the sound defeat
of Death's cold, careless knell—
because the Princess sleeps, and
all is well
in the cottage that hugs the dell.

The Princess sleeps—all is well,
and Time's tick paces slowly on.
The handmaid bides by her
slumberous side
with word and croon to imbibe,
and she breathes her magic
that stayed all tragic
race to that mourning bell—
because the Princess sleeps, and
all is well
in the cottage that hugs the dell.

Sharon Wildey Nolan
MOONSONG II
    Golden
    Galleon
    Sail Swift
    Midnight's
    Frothing
    Mounds,
    Foam-Washed
    Decks
    Alight.
      Sword-Ready
      Orion
      Captains
      Your
      Course
      Past
      Purple
      Traces,
      Dawnward
      Against
        The Helios.

Vickie R. Ramsey
SOMETHING'S HERE
Something restless in the air
Causes me to be aware—
I sit, waiting, in my chair.
Something's here . . .

Heckle-Jekyll in the trees,
Something's brewing in the
breeze—
Spirits that I must appease.
Something's here . . .

Helter-skelter in the night,
To my left and to my right—

Shadows in the amber light.
Something's here . . .

Hooded cape, hair like chalk,
Something shuffles up the walk—
From the door, an anxious knock.
Something's here . . .

Faces pressed against my screen,
Some are ghastly, some are
green—
Scariest I've ever seen!
Something's here . . .

IT'S HALLOWEEN!

Myrtle Owens
FIRST LOVE
First love is like a dream
that passes in the night
Or like bubbles on a stream
that vanish in the light
It is swift, beautiful, unreal
but soon loses all it's zeal
It's a thing that doesn't last
but is soon buried in the past.

M. Kathleen Mooso
YOU TOUCHED ME
You touched my life; for a
moment, a few hours, and
yet . . . an eternity.
You touched my life; with your
laughing eyes, your tender
smile— and then you spoke. It
was an orchestration of all that
you are.
You touched my life when you
held me close.
You touched my body, my mind,
my very soul.
How do I explain your coming
into my life so briefly, and yet
so thouroughly?

YOU TOUCHED ME!

Neva Robinson
REMEMBRANCE
Snowflakes drift down silently in
soft, white mounds.
Great yellow pools of light flare
from windows—
Seeking in vain to bring warmth
To white cold.
It is Christmas . . .
And inside
All is warm and bright—
From glistening tree-top
To glowing hearth-fire.
Conviviality . . .
Remembrance . . .
Celebration . . .
Of a Holy birth so long ago
Of a Son . . . God's Son
Sent to redeem
In love . . . and peace

Mary McGlasson
THE QUEEN

*"To Rose, Marsha, Michael and
Lynda. I remember with love and
joy, your childhood imaginations."*

October floats in gracefully,
beautifully gowned in blue sky
Her hair, a shimmer of silver
cobwebs, a tiara of golden
sunshine.
A demure lady, exuding warm
days and cool nights
Fertile bosom, voluptuous with a
bountiful harvest of God's gifts.

The many hued autumn leaves,
rustle, as gentle breezes nudge
her to the throne.
The Destiny of her soul has been
fulfilled: Crown her Queen, of
Octoberfest!

Lois Johnson Allen
TO A FRIEND
True friendship,
isn't a passing
thing,
The special feeling,
friend's share,
goes on forever,
Where you,
are,
Where ever I am,
Will alway's be
friend's,
I'm going to
miss you my
friend.

Leo V. Randall Jr.
BLEACHED BEETS
Busy Bobby Baker
Bleached a bushel of blue beets,
Put part in a pot
Which he fed to his wailing tot,
Packed part to peddle in Paris
And gave the rest to an old
woman named Harris!

Barbara Lynn Collins
A Night At Stonehenge
In priestly robes of blue and
white, the Druids of Stonehenge
face the night.
They gather 'neath the towering
stones, and begin to chant and
cast the bones.
With faces streaked with paint
and mud, tonight the ground
will run with blood.
A fresh-faced girl will pay the
price; she will be their sacrifice.
Beneath the dark October sky,
the trembling virgin will have
to die.
She will scream and writhe with
agony—now only the knife can
set her free.
Her death will be slow and
wracked with pain, but the
Druids don't care—they'll kill
again.
Her bowels will be tied 'round the
sacred tree, and there they'll be
left for all to see.
And to this day you'll hear the
screams or see the images in
dreams
At Stonehenge where their
secrets keep, and ghostly
virgins still scream and weep.

Jeannie Dianne McCuistion
LOST DREAMS
Hours come, days go
Turn around—
And where did the years go

We said tomorrow
Tomorrow was filled with sorrow
We said someday
We got lost along the way

With honesty we told lies
Not understanding goodbyes
Not knowing dreams of forever
Sometimes end in never

Winter the cold winds blow
Spring the flowers grow

Turn around—
And where did the years go

Timothy Joe Hofmann
THIS MUST BE LOVE

*This poem is dedicated to a
beautiful young lady from
Northern California named Carey
Barnes. She has inspired me so
much, I have written this poem
for her.*

Is there something else I should
know, about love and all of its
feeling?
Whenever I hear or think of you,
it's better than any kind of
healing.

My feelings I try to express to
you, it always ends up bad.
I get all flustered and nervous,
it makes me really sad.

I wish they would find a
rememdy,
for what I feel about you.
I think about it so much,
it often makes me blue.

Out of my mind,
it won't go.
One day I will come to you,
and my feelings I will show.

Nancy K. Spinelli
A FIRE FIGHTERS WIFE
People tell me, "My husband has
it made,"
Some consider that he's over paid.
To all those who feel that way;
Read this, then tell me what you
say!
It's night time now, and we're all
alone,
The children wait for "Daddy" to
phone.
They tell him they "Love Him,"
and say "Goodnight,"
Because they know their "Daddy's"
all right.

The calmness slowly turns to fear,
When from the scaner you hear:
"Stand by for Alarm of Fire!"
Dear God, let it not be dire.

The Chief yell, "Fire spreading fast!"
"Recall men, It's going to last."
A boy is trapped, age four or five,
Someone did their job, cause he's
still alive.

The children sit and patiently
wait,

They wonder why their "Daddy's"
so late.
They remember him so young
and strong,
They can't understand what went
wrong!

He lived on time that had only
been borrowed,
You'll read it all, in the headlines
tomorrow.
For in the end, "His Life," he had
to give;
"This was the glorious way he
chose to live!"

Ms. Ardith Beitel
UNTITLED
When you can't shut out the
emptiness
And lonely hours you face
Hold fast to your soul and reach,
Kindle the meloncholy fire
And look up from the hearth.
Begin as the flames rise
Count the memories
Add a twig for each one.
Reminisce of those days together
Let the fire keep you warm
And when ashes remain
Lock them away in your heart
Start anew with tomorrow's dawn.
If in passing days you
Remain by fire's side,
If you search for more comforting
warmth
Stop and pause,
reach out,
and I'll be there instead.

Luc Eyndhoven
SONG OF THE NIGHT
Ribitt, Chirp, ribbitt,
Sang the frog and the cricket,
Loudly in the night.

Who, squeak, who,
Joined a mouse and an owl,
As he took off in a flight.

Howling at the moon,
'Others will join in soon,'
Said the wolf on the right.

Thump, thump, thump,
Beat the rabbit on a stump,
As the moon shone down its
light.

We'll all join in and sing,
Join hands, form a ring,
And say to all a good night.

Catherine (Catie) Wheeler
You Can Never Change It

*Dedicated to: Mary K. Blake, My
Mother*

The clock ticks on and on and on,
The present going, past, then gone,
The future very dear and not long.
How can one ever change it?

The sun rises, stays, then falls,
The summer comes and ends
with fall,
The winter dances and touches all.
How can one ever change it?

The birds fly north and spread
their wings,
The playing children do silly
things,
The mass is over when the

church bells ring.
Who would want to change it.

Donna Haymacher
True Love Unexplained

This poem was written to my husband Steve, and it's a poem dedicated to his sincere love.

We are now brought together
 from different worlds,
Our lives in the past both
 unknown and complicated.
The start of existence somewhat
 distant, yet unimportant,
Searching for a certain yearning,
 others needs were
demanding and easily persuaded,

Time passed by, and inner
 feelings despaired,
However destiny was working,
 with the future to us
 far-reaching.
Keeping ourselves active with
 trivial past times and goals,
Making mistakes because
 loneliness and heartaches
 derived
from the love we were seeking.

Although attracted, our doubts
 and fears kept us guessing,
But the moments of ectasy and
 satisfaction we grasped.
Words forgotten in our lifeline,
 easily spoken with no regret,
As guilt and anguish entered as
 those minutes lapsed.

Lying beside him, I touch his
 sensual body,
My lips press against the warmth
 of the flicker of each inner
 flame.
Arms of protective nature hold
 my childish fantasies,
While all desires are exploded,
 and each need that is met
 seems the same.

Even though thoughts of turning
 back come between us,
Forever friends and family
 requesting our relationship to
 be detained.
Bonding hearts of our contented
 emotion, and spirit of respect
flow in our veins,
This is a fairytale episode, and
 yet I know this is Our True
 Love Unexplained.

Helen Vig-Firetti
6/25/83

Dedicated to the memory of BOLD and ANGRY. BOLD in living, ANGRY at death. Spirit raging until his last breath ...

Miserable' Dictu, Pegasus—
 You missed the Derby.
Why fly thee off in so great a
 hurry?
Two weeks between three—
 The Triple Crown!!!
Do I detect a frown?
Ah! Yes, we mortals
 tend to forget—
 our fault not to mourn,

as with roses
comes the fatal thorn.
Even within the
WINNER'S CIRCLE ...

Thomas Lynn
THE FOOL'S SERENADE
Night upon night
Each follows the other
Forging links in a chain of despair
Illumined only
By mirrored echoes
Emitted by dreams not meant to
 share

Such is the way
Of two hearts not attuned
Leaving just one to grieve all alone
Unable it seems
To discern amour
From true love 'til now unbeknown

Oh how I weep
In painful remembrance
Bridging time with a false memory
Magnified beyond
The limit of truth
Yet disguised from youthful
 tragedy

For all like me
Who did once feel the sting
Knifing deep as a victim betrayed
Remedy there's none
Save passage of time
So we all sing the fool's serenade

Cheryl Jerby
PAUL

This poem is dedicated, on behalf of all the people who loved him, to the memory of Paul whose life was taken October 7, 1983 at the age of 23 years.

Why can't life be filled with
 happiness
Why is life so full of sadness
Why is there so much hurt and
 pain
Why does it feel like a ball and
 chain
Why is life so unfeeling and cold
Why aren't the streets lined with
 gold
Why does so much blood have to
 spill
Why do people have to hurt and
 kill
Why do some die at twenty-three
Why, oh why, does it have to be
Why are things so hard to
 understand
Why can't peace reign through
 the land
Why does life seem so very unfair
Why does it seem so hard to bare
Four bullets fired from a gun
Now there will be no more sun
One man will sleep and never
 wake
Cause another thought life was
 his to take.

Loraine Lewis
HALLOWEEN
Dusk falls softly on the warm fall
 night
Porch lights cast a small patch of
 light,
forms float from shadows so deep
beginning their march in search

of treats.
Ghosts and goblins with
 grotesque features,
Bunnies and kitties and outer
 space creatures,
Dancers and butterflies giggle
 and spin.
cowboys with pistols ride again.
Pirates and witches with swords
 and brooms,
Fancy ladies with feathered
 plumes.
Dandies and hobo's saunter along,
"Trick or Treat," is their song.
Sights I behold on this witching
 night
shiver my spine with a finger of
 fright.
Hollow sounds of, "Help the poor,"
precedes the creatures to my door.
Echo's of laughter split the night.
with gathered treats they are
 fading from sight,
disappearing into Never Never
 land
waiting a year before haunting
 again

Lila Borg Rohrer
DISCRIMINATION
I look in the mirror on the back
 of the visor
and see my fat hand.
It is lying on my fat knee
that's connected to my fat thigh.
It's painful being fat in a society
that worships thin.
Even thin I'm big, with wrists like
 a man.
My calves never fit riding boots
 which
nearly broke my heart when I was
 young and foolish.
I'm a stocky Swede
proud of my heritage and strength
working at overcoming my
 handicap.
I'm fat and society loves thin.

Beverly B. Peek
MY FRIEND
You gave me strength
You gave me hope
When I felt down
And could not cope.

You built me up
You helped me see
That there could be
A stronger me.

In little time
We had—I knew
That I could trust,
Believe in you.

Inspiration!
I knew you cared
You listened to
My thoughts I shared.

Your kindly ways
Your gentle touch
They meant alot
Ever so much!

You're with me now
More every day
In all I do
In every way.

Franklin Himes
WOLF'S BLOOD
The crisp rustle of colorful death
scrapes the boney branches in the

fall
in the gently blowing moonlight
now pierced by a lonely
 werewolf's call

A weary traveler turns and
 freezes—
a quick chill pricks the back and
 neck
a putrid odor rides the breezes
and the quickened steps crunch—
 loud the stillness

Cold, darting looks and frantic
 shivers
receive the fear another howl
 delivers
here ... everywhere— unbearable
the traveler suddenly drops upon
 that death
where a wolf's blood forms warm
 rivers

Dolores Pierce Staub
A MEASURED TIME

To My Best Friend Larry, Who has chosen to walk with me through life

---

We've done many things together
 through the passage of time,
 just you and I.
As young lovers, a glance
 revealed a secret—
 that special look,
 or the wink of an eye.
Through the raising of our young,
 the Lord did grant a vision;
A vision for you to make them
 strong,
A vision for me to right the
 wrong.
We've laughed together;
 We've cried some too.
We've won some wars,
 and lost a few;
 We've watched each other grow,
Not old, but in God's loving grace,
 to do our part for His Human
 Race.
Our joy now complete
 in its measured time,
Its now their turn
 to walk that line.
God, give them strength and
 abound from above to grow in
 grace with their child of love.

Sara E. Cherry
I WONDER
Year after year they have come to
 me
The students with questioning
 looks
Year after year they have left me
As they leave their outgrown
 books

I wonder sometimes if I've taught
 them
Just some of the worthwhile things
Just some of the things they'd
 need in life
Be they peasants or poets or kings

Have I taught them the joy of
 clean living?
That honor is better than fame
That good friends are the greatest
 of treasures
Wealth less than an untarnished
 name

Have I taught them respect to the aged?
Protection for those that are weak
That silence always is golden
When gossip bids them speak

Have I taught them that fear is a coward?
Who is beaten when they say "I can"
That courtesy ranks with courage
In the heart of the real lady and gentleman

Have I taught them these things and others?
That will help make the brave kind and true
If I have then my retirement will be creative
Since I know they will be creative too

Estella M. McGhee-Siehoff
It Is a Very Nice Thing To Eat
"I will come in to him, and will sup with him,
And he with me," while the end approaches.
"I will come in to him, and will sup with him,
And he with me," while the righteousness succeeds.

"I will come in to him, and will sup with him,
And he with me," while the Word of patience prevails.
"I will come in to him, and will sup with him,
And he with me," while the perfection nears.
"I will come in to him, and will sup with him,
And he with me," while the new day dawns.

Patricia Ann Grossie
MESSAGES
It is to restless seekers that the sea billows dance wildly and bellow roaring tales of old as though to call to all.
For the wind does hear and howls angry now and then as if to growl when mortals don't visit or gaze or wonder at the sea, the stars or at you and me.
It is to a mortals blindness that the wind does call and the sea bellows wildly roar as though to call.
The birds fly high when the wind rages loud and the sea bellows in anger, call messages of heart to not some but all.
These messages I hear tell when to silence a soul does call.
Oh, restless sad sea in song what sing you to me of life journey long but secrets of old your soul does know and only sometimes tales have told? Oh, restless churning sea embraced by the wind that sings as touched by birds on wing and sight as though to kiss the world with beauties might.
I say you sing to the world at will a living song.
For in my heart and tucked in wonder I think the restless sea

is much like stardust you and me, perhaps we are all one you see?
So I listen close to the songs of the sea, the wind and heart's messages whatever they be.
For I say the Lord God's hearts songs are gifts from thee and His love is far nearer than my spirit can see.

Lana Tunison
THE HARVEST MOON
Beware! my friends of The Harvest Moon, for witches are mending their brooms.
The night is coming when the cats will howl, while witches fly across the moon.
Run! hide, where witches store their brooms, it's the safest place on Halloween Night.
At the stroke of midnight the gruelies—shall come—oozing up through the murky soil, to dance, sing, toil.
Watch out! this Hallows Eve, they could grab you! by the neck or feet, then you would end up—in their pot to boil.

Shelley F. Cowan
POT OF GOLD

This poem is dedicated to my husband, Walter, with all my love. He was the inspiration for this poem and he is the inspiration in my life.

You came into my life like a tornado
Whirling around me, drawing me in
Until I too was spinning.

You said "I love you"
And I melted, turned to mush inside
Cause I loved you too.

Two dreams came true that day
Yours and mine
And I love you, tornado.

I've had storms in my life
But I weathered them through
I was waiting for you
My pot of gold at the end of the rainbow.

Charlene Aleda Scott Johnston
REALITY

Thanks *to all, who have blemished my mind, in the past, but have opened my eyes and taught me to use their self-centered egos, as a stepping stone and not a stumbling block, along life's path.*

We only concentrate on one thing,
Being number one, that's all we care.
It's the only thing that matters.
In a life, that we all share.

To face the truth, is reality,
And to practice, what we preach.
But to face this deed, is such a chore,
That few, do ever reach.

Now to share my life, with others,
And to give, what I can give.
To understand, their every need,
Is the life I'D like to live.

Jack Edward McCarty
SEA OF LIES
Walk carefully on the shores of truth.
For the sea of lies has taken many of our youth.
Truth is a rugged land.
  Lies are soft and warm,
  like the womb.

But only in the land of truth, does strength, beauty, and brotherhood bloom.

Truth is hard; sometimes cold.
  And often seems upside-down.

But in the sparkling sea of lies, the mind and soul will drown.

Mary F. Spencer
WITCHERY
She sails through the blue, on the broom of her hue,
  So gladly and grandly she soars,
Stars on her right, moon on her left,
  Earthward and onward she roars.

Down by a barnyard, over and beyond,
  Upright and ghost—like they stand,
She gunns up her motor with all of her might,
  And circles the field where she lands.

She touches each pumpkin encircling her realm,
  And points out the fodder—shocks, too,
And up through the sky they circle and fly,
  Then: "Woah, this is it, tally—hoo!"

With mystical lightness they sail to the ground,
  'Round a little old hut on a corner,
Where there dwelt a lad, alone with his dad,
  Who had wept, "Halloween, and no mother."

The pumpkins rolled lightly each one to his shock,
  And then tiptoed lightly a fairy,
On the step of the ramshackled hut did she place

A bright bulging bag of rare goodies.

The witch gunned her broom, and upward, zoom, zoom,
  Off into the wide, wild, blue yonder,
She continued her tricks 'midst mortar and bricks,
  And left aged Sages to wonder!

Rick D. Garlock
DEATH WISH
I'm tired, so tired . . . of chains on a body not mine . . .
from DNA to cells to molecules; God's tinker toys . . .
A jailed fate-to a will not my own; a victim of someone else's ploy . . . I fight back . . .
A noble bee stings but once, taking his own life, and I, damn it all' shall free my chains and release my soul . . . it is all that I control; my hate, my precious hate . . .
When and how but remain . . . mine all mine, blessed greed. . .
Past is gone, it cannot be; present, oh no! For in a fleeting thought, present is now in past's endless sea . . . The future it is, in a moment; until it comes and I will be . . . nevermore . . .
How? No torture! I'm not man enough; yet, not quick——I do not
deserve the kindness it wills . . .
The mirror stares, hiding the answer. Shaky hands slide it by . .
Pills! Thank God for pills! Time to ponder while the dream shifts to reality . . . The water runs/ I fill my cup; but first or last, a toast . . . "To HELL with life and LIFE to my hell !". . . . .
I fooled them all . . . .
. . . . It is done . . . .
. . . .

Kathie Esser
LIFE
Haven't you heard?
Those who have, are hearing.
Those who have not, cannot.

Though, you may have seen.
Those who have seen, saw.
Some may have, at least, looked.

deserve the kindness it wills . . . . .
  answer. Shaky hands slide it by
Some have often said.
But, haven't you heard?

Glory Posey
FABRIC OF A NATION
The ennobling grandeur of this illustrious nation
Was woven from the vision and inspiration
Of intelligent, courageous pioneers,
Who, conquering their tribulations and fears,

Built homes upon empty prairies, planting lush verdant fields;
Envisioning families gathering to reap their fertile yields;
Not without trial and conflict was this fabric loomed,
Not without sacrifice of bloodied flesh entombed,

Yet, transcending rubble, grief
and deprivation,
Their nobility of character and
total dedication
Is blended in the length and
breadth of blood red bars,
The strong, rugged threads of fifty
United Stars.

Barbara N. Beecher
MY LOVE
Time stands still
And the music I hear is silence.
The rythmn I feel is but my heart
beating.
Gently, your hands reach to
touch me
And the tempo of the music
increases.
From far away I hear you whisper
my name,
A whisper sultry with emotion.
I touch your lips with mine
And the taste is heady, like wine.
Dusky, sleepy eyes,
Hidden worlds of joy and ecstacy,
One moment revealing,
The next veiled in passion.
No words are needed.
No spoken promises, we are one.
With all our being we know this
to be so.
Our destinies are bound beyond
time . . .
Beyond reason . . .
We are certain as time,
As the changing of the seasons
That whatever tomorrow holds
We will conquer
Because I know that as long as I
am
You will be My Love.

Sherrill K. Riss
SENSE A NEW BEGINNING

*This poem is deicated to and
inspired by my fiance, Ed. I'll
always love you!!*

Feel the heat on your shoulders
as the sun beams down
Smell the sweet fragrance
of the newborn flowers in the
meadow
Touch the cool, clear water
of the babbling brook
See the young animals
frolic about in fun
Hear the birds sing
as they greet the day
Sit in silence
as you admire a new spring
Laugh and be happy
while at peace with yourself.

Ada Ramsey
A HILL SIDE
Such splender is the hill side
To sit and gaze upon.
It's colors do enchant you
For to look and ponder on.
Oh' to find it and adore it
All the beauty that is within.
Such a great and glowing
brightness
Calling you to come on in.
How great it is before us
Painted with such loving care.
Deep red and bright yellow
Orange and green here and there.

How is it there is such beauty
All around and every where?
Just to cast an eye upon it
For no man did put it there.

Catharina Rinta
ENJOY THIS DAY
Don't let me ever fail to notice,
the start of every lovely day.
The wake-up song of birds, that
thrill me,
and gently chase the night away.

The sky, whether it's blue or
cloudy,
with infinite depth, and golden
sun.
And all the stars at night, to
cover
a sleeping world, at rest from
work well done.

Let me enjoy hundreds of colors,
that can be found where ever I
look.
The grass, the flowers, and in the
winter
the purest white, on tree and field
and brook.

The people, as they go about
their business.
The young, the old, each one a
special part
of this great life, with all it's joy
and sorrow,
in each a spark of love, to touch
the heart.

Let me be grateful for the sights
and sounds of living.
Don't let me waste a moment of
this special day.
There's so much beauty in the
smallest thing or creature,
Let me enjoy it now, before life
slips away.—

Shannon L. Williams
THINGS

*For my children, Caleb and
Marisa. Without them, I am
nothing. I love you both. Written
to a special friend, with love.*

Love like I've never known
No longer am I alone
Love so real, love so free
These are things you offer me.

Life so content, so easy
Hearts so light and breezy
Life so happy, life so true
These are things I offer you.

Happiness like we've never
shared
Feelings of love we've never dared
Being friends as well as lovers
These are things we offer each
other.

Edith Elizabeth Hartley
WILL HE PASS ME BY
Am I like the foolish virgins,
Have I lived my life as they?
When I hear the trumpet sounding,
Will my feet be made of clay?

Oh, my sister! Oh, my brother!
How the time is fleeting by.
Have I lived my life in Jesus,
Is my oil in good supply?

Now, the midnight hour is nearing;
Soon the bridegroom will be nigh.
Will he say, "Come my beloved,"
Or, will he turn and pass me by.

Mimi Sturgeon
COLUMBUS DAY
Long ago in 1492
Columbus sailed the ocean,
He headed off with ships and crew
Steered by the moon and the
tidal motion.

He sailed East or was it West?
From Portugal he did leave,
And found at the end the very
best—
This land to which we cleave.

Picture what America was like
Back then without modern
technology—
It must have been a marvelous
sight,
A regular "New World" oddyssy!

Things have changed over the
years
Neither all for the good or bad,
The laughter's been interspersed
with tears
With the joy out weighing the
sad.

Time marches on, or so they say,
And we go marching with it;
But, congratulations are due
today—
Columbus, you went and did it!!

Mary Agnes Lynch
HALLOWEEN
"Witches, and Goblins, flying
about,
children in costumes, crying
watchout,
Parties, and fun, jack o' lanterns
are seen,
Time to celebrate, sure it's
Halloween."

Marjorie Anderson
THE WUTHERING WIND
The wuthering wind is as old as
time
And cold as the northern star;
It blows from out the frozen wastes
Where the bones of dead men are.

It mourns in the ear like a
widow's sigh
When the nights are cold and long,
And it croons above a cradle bed
And eerie, sleepy-time song.

It stirs the memory of sorrows
And the wounds that time has
healed,

And the specters of fear that
come in the dark,
Which the brightness of day
concealed.

The wuthering wind brings chill
to my heart
As it chills the wandering soul,
And far away in the realm of
dreams
A bell is beginning to toll.

Sybil Eakes Woodruff
**Shreveport, Louisiana: Late
Autumn**
Today crumpled brown leaves
joust for positions on my once-
green lawn: the winds direct
with authority.
Trees shiver as if in anticipation
of the cold yet to come:
Their blank stares resemble the
resigned expressions of old
men's faces, accepting the
coming of death.
I inhale the apple-wine air, deep
into my lungs, savoring the
dried fruit fragrance of late
Autumn.
A squirrel, almost disappearing
into the gray bark of a tree, sits
motionlessly; ready to scurry to
the oak's topmost branch at my
slightest movement.
The sun makes fitful
appearances:
First it lights the face of a
small blue flower which is
drooping on a pale green stem.
Then it makes Saturn rings
around a clump of gray-green
moss, damp from morning's
dew.
Red golds have not yet colored
my autumn domain.
Winter's cold breath will bring
them to life.
Now I stand in this pastoral
scene thinking of how the
seasons change.
Each one has its own song, and to
this scene, I, too, belong.

Gloria Evangeline Mayer
PUPPY LOVE
Kind sparkling eyes
Sweet loving expression
Faithfulness forever
Always forgiving
Fully protecting
Soft gentle kisses
And a cold wet nose.

Tacha Leider
ODE TO A BALLERINA
To a wonderful friend, who is a
ballerina
Whose always had a great
devotion,
To be a great primadona,
With such a distinctive motion.

With your movements so precise,
With your friendship and limbs
so graceful,
You use dance as such a devise,
To make something so beautiful.

Your friendship is so precious,
Making other lives so bright,
And your personality so
vivacious,
Bringing me such delight.

Your moves are so intricate,
You practice so diligently,
Your expressions are so delicate,
You, the ballerina, move so
  elegantly.

Joseph O. Roberge
MY DARLING

---

*To my ex-wife, Dorothy . . . may
she have all the space she
dreamed about.*

In my dreams your beautiful face
  hounds me and all that blooms
  on earth only reflex your beauty
The delicate new grown grass
  only dares to match the beauty
  of your green eyes
The red rose is only a shadow of
  your tantalizing red lips
The magnificent pink of the
  orchid only reminds me of your
  rosy cheeks
You have, I know not what, but it
  always awes me
Your touch can be as gentle as
  the flutter of butterfly wings
And your voice can be as soft as
  the blush of bashfulness
Oh you, my beautiful, you have
  loveliness beyond compare
You have the beauty to conquer a
  soul and you've made me your
  slave
Grace is in all your doing
Every gesture is a charm
Your eyes, your lips, your cheeks,
  your shape and your features
Draws pain to my heart, now that
  you are departed and remain
  far away
Your loveliness is forever in my
  heart and you are fatal to me
I beg the God of mercy to deliver
  me from your tyranny.

Beverly Rinehart Banks
OMENS
Flames blaze at eardrums
Pain catches between bones

Owls moan at noon
Showing tiny teeth, bats smile

My own dog whines at my car

Salt shaker spills
Ladder athwart my way

Black cat at evening
Stalks my path

Mirror cracks
And in a thousand shining shards

I see your face

And fear

Constance Jean Larson
BORDELLO
Vow breakers
come to satisfy
their whims.

Prudence waits at home,
cleaning her virtues,
while Folly plays.

Secrets shared,
in the temporary night,
Quiet cash paid.

Prudence forgives,
rubs his back,
and Folly still plays.

Linda Clark
LISTEN
The sounds around us are
  drawing us near.
We may not know it, but it's there.
Whispering! Shouting! Never the
  same!
Piercing our ears! To what gain?

Who is listening? Who wants to
  hear?
Would they understand? Would
  they care?
Would they try to change things
  somehow?
Who knows the answer? We'll
  find it, if it's there.

Listen to the sounds, turn your
  head!
Face it, the world's not dead!
If you understand, if you try,
The world will stop . . . not pass
  you by.

Faye Wasserburger
THE RELUCTANT LADY
Fair Summer has outstayed her
  welcome,
  With her flowers and fancy frills.
Why doesn't she wrap her green
  robes around her
  And drift away over the hills?

It's time to breathe the crisp air of
  Autumn,
  For the leaves to turn crimson
  and gold.
We want to hunt and roam
  through the woodlands
  Before the wintry winds blow
  too cold.

The songbirds have long since
  departed,
  They knew the proper time to go.
Your mission is now completed—
  Oh Summer, why this year so
  slow?

Lucille Kerr
THE WINE
You raise the glass to my lips
And I, to yours.
We sip the wine
and it is sweet;
The fruit of the vine
ripened on sunny hillsides,
now cool on the rim
of the goblet,
warms our hearts.
Your lips touch mine—
The wine
and your kisses
are sweet.

Mary J. Watkins
SEVENTEEN
When I was Seventeen
  I had All the Answers . . .
I knew Everything
  when I was only Seventeen!

When I turned Thirty-three,
  or thereabout, I found
There were a few things
  still unknown to me.

When Forty-three arrived
  I suddenly realized . . .
Time was way ahead of me!
I was running late . . .
  when I was Forty-three.

Now that I'm nearly Sixty-three
  I can plainly see

That Life's a Great-big-mystery;
  More Questions than Answers.
Somehow . . .
  this vexes me!

For if by chance, I should reach
  Seventy-three . . .
By the Simple Law of
  Progression . . .
I'll know nothing at all
When I am Seventy-three.

Mary L. Garside

Mary L. Garside
ANGELS IN BLACK

---

*I dedicate this poem to the
firemen of Winthrop Harbor,
Illinois.*

I've seen angels in my dreams
And they always appeared in
  white,
Moving slowly to and fro,
Much to my delight.

Last night I saw a group of them,
But they were dressed in black;
Speed and caution were the
  things
They surely did not lack.

First came sirens and flashing
  lights,
And midnight turned into day;
Our neighbors were in trouble
And all I could do was pray.

God sent His angels before I ask
Or even knew their plight,
And protected the entire
  neighborhood
In the middle of the night.

Thank you, God, for our firemen,
Their dedication and their love,
And when their work is done on
  earth.
We ask they reign with You
  above.

Maxine Rushing
CHILD

To Joe—With loving memories

Come back and make me a child
  again,
I felt so young when you were
  here.

You took me down paths of pine
  needles, and pushed me
  screaming out into the spring
  rain.

I loved it, I didn't tell you then—
You're gone now
My grown-up heart hurts
and wants to chase Armadillos
  again
on the side of a Texas road in
  October.

I MISS YOU . . . . .

Robin Kirsten Spence
THE KINGDOM OF JOY
Cherished are the moments when
  happiness reigns above all else.
Whether silence or joyous cries
  dominate,
A feeling soars throughout the air
  of life and laughter,
Death and sorrow unknown—
Till later.

Welcome to the kingdom of joy,
Where every day is celebration
And every night tranquility;
You are met by our people,
Lovers of the human kind—
The peaceful ones.

Never leave, for the changes are
  more drastic than dreamed:
The outside world, a place of hate
  and wars
And grief and death;
While inside this land lies love
  and peace,
Happiness and health.
Find yourself captured in the spirit;
Never let it end,
For this is not reality—
Just a dream.

Luben G. Angeloff
STRESS
Since April first
  nineteen-seventy-eight
Is that I to love or hate
To be under an intellectual stress
To discontinue with my test.

Since then I am without any
  position
That is faculty's decision
Simply, because I do search
To do any cancer research.

I try to save human lives
And during my fifty-fives
To make the people happy and
  smile
Instead to worry and cry.

Why you don't try
To see how many people cry
And stop to use on me any stress
Because I will continue with my
  test.

You must terminate your task
But sit down and relax
Stop using any unhuman stress
And only then you will feel the
  best.

Gina Tjaden
BELIEVE IN HOPE
I weep in my soul,
  I hurt.
I beg to be comforted,
  Their mouths don't speak.
I cry out hoping to be heard,
  Their ears don't hear.
I pray to be seen,
  Their eyes don't see.
I want to be cared for,
  They don't.

Our World's Best Loved Poems

I am alone in the deeps,
I exist no more.

But wait!
Into my life has come light and
hope.
From the depths of hell I have
cried.
And He has heard my cry!

Connie M. Dollins
A CHILDS KISS
As I stopped at the donut shop,
For a breakfast treat.
I stood there and yawned, from
my nights work.
As I waited in line for my turn
with the clerk.
I looked down and saw a child so
sweet.
Running to me as if wings were
her feet.
With out stretched arms, and a
smile on her lips.
I reached out to touch her with
my finger tips.
She wrapped her arms around me,
and ask for a kiss.
An event like this I sure wouldn't
miss.
She recieved my kiss, looking so
sweet in her dress trimmed in
lace.
Then said to me, "I want to kiss
your face."
I received my kiss from her sweet
lips.
And a hug, then she touched my
face with her finger tips.
She left with her mom, saying, "I
like her."
For a moment I was stunned and
the world was a blur.
She ran to their car and turned to
throw me a kiss.
What a way to start your day, an
event I wouldn't miss.
A little girl so sweet and full of
bliss.
I felt one of God's angels had sent
me a kiss.

Guy Reid
A FUTURE GLIMPSE
When we enjoy the morning mists
Curling through the foliage of trees
And chase the beauty that exists
In nature the mind's eye to please;
When we observe the bird in flight
And lift our spirits high with him
To find new vistas, then we might
Change the forces that try to dim
Man's vision of tomorrow seen:
A place where all can love and
live,
No longer vieing to demean
But rather hope and joy to give
When we give the understanding
To the least among us today;
When we become less demanding
And send some love the other way,
Then our hopes for immortality,
Our dreams for the glory of man
May become a reality.
And somehow I know that we can.

Mildred M. Eckles
OCTOBER SCENES
Today I took a little drive
A hundred miles or more,
In bright October weather
A time I just adore.

Part way was on the inter-state
With campers, cars, and vans,
Big eighteen-wheelers rushing by
With freight from other lands.

We've had a couple frosts now
And fall is in the air,
Flocks of wild geese winging
south
There's beauty everywhere.

I turned off of the high-way
To go down country roads,
Farmers gathering all their grain
There was load after load.

The hills were a blaze of color
With trees of red and gold,
Orange and yellow, brown and
green,
'Twas beauty to behold.

A peaceful scene 'round every
curve
Beneath a clear blue sky,
God must have planned October
To lift our spirits high.

John D. Lawyer, Jr.
LOVE

Dedicated to: Diana Lee

To have,
To hold;
Not to let,
Her get cold.

To take,
To cling;
To each,
Of her needs.

To seize,
To squeeze;
Her heart,
So dear.

To see,
To be;
A constant ray,
Of hope.

Is love.

Edna Butler
THE FOOLISH MAIDEN

---

*For my husband, Harold, for his
patience and quietness, while I
was writing this poem.*

A foolish maiden, a girl of
twenty-three, found a rained
soaked bonnet, in an inlet, by
the sea.
Her mouth made a twist as she
placed it on her head; but the
algae stained her curls, a blue, a
green, and red.
This made the foolish maiden so
very, very, cross, that she took
it off and placed it by a tree,
hoping a bird would build a
family.
The wind was strong and full of
zest, it took the bonnet from
the new found nest; and blew it
back into the sea, so the foolish
maiden cut the ribbons, one,
two, three, and carried them
home for memories.

Mary McAlexander
FATHER'S FEVER
Father's fever
was caused by never:
a virus or bacteria.
It was probably due to:
staying in the dew
looking for Lou.
While Lou was looking for his
tick named Nick.
    OR
a rainey day at the zoo, with Lou,
because he wanted to see a cow
moo.

Lori Heikkila

Lori Heikkila
THE SEARCH
Huddled beneath the grill,
Frightened, cold, wide-eyed—
Looking
For safety from fear,
From evil.
Eyes peered down—
Cold, calculated,
Evil gazed down at them—
Hands reached for them—
Still searching,
Never leaving.

J. Diane Quinn
NO ONE KNOWS
No one knows, the true nature of
my soul.

The part of me that lives deep
inside.
Safe from hurts, where it can hide.
From the world, and its prying
eyes.

Must keep it safe, must not give
in.
Can't get hurt, not again.

If I should faulter.
If I should fall.
And bare my soul to one or all.

Will they treat it gently?
Will he be kind?

Or will I be used yet another time?

Debby Odgers
FINALLY ENDING
When I look to see
why things are never clear
I wonder why it's me
always standing alone here

I find I have to assign
someone to keep us apart
But I will always confine
our true meaning in my heart

My thoughts have many ranges
although I hear preaching

There are so few changes
but I keep reaching

You were always so meek
yet you went on a fling
I was at my peak
and you wanted to be king

So you tried to barter
but our love just died
Then I became a martyr
when I finally said "good-bye"

Marion L. Perry
MISSING YOU
In the cold frosty air
of early morning
I sat alone, letting the silent tears
flow unheeded.
My memories of you are precious
And ever with me
In this quite solitude
before the world awakens
And I am needed.
By those who are with me
everyday
I give them smiles
And my world keep's turning.
they don't know how
I miss and need you.
My heart is heavy
And ever yearning
You can't come back now
as they say—you have gone,
So far away and,
crossed, beyond the bar
But I'll always
feel your presence near
Goodby, my friend—until
I am once again with you
And we walk, beyond the stars.

Catherine Biancalana
HAPPINESS
When the world seems a little
cloudy and you start to feel
depressed,
Take the time to remember what
brings you happiness.

Is it the sparks from a fire when
you burn autumn leaves,
Or the peace that surrounds you
on those cold December eves.

Is it the wonder of children with
their eyes all aglow,
Is it the laughter you hear as they
play in the snow.

Is it the splendor of an oak tree or
the beauty of a rose,
Is it an amusing tale by Dickens
or a touching book of prose.

Is it the colors of a rainbow or the
restless, surging sea,
Is it a captivating novel or a
Gershwin rhapsody.

Whatever gives you happiness I
hope will never end,
'Cause I wish you all the joy that
a freind could wish a friend.

Ruth Naomi Oliver
UNTITLED
I've cried so many tears
That I can't see the sun.
I've crawled so far
I've forgotten how to run.
I don't know myself
Or anyone else either,
Because I've been lost
In a fantasy fever.

People walk by me

211

Not caring, not sharing
People talk to me,
Not listening, not bothering.
People not knowing what they
    want
Some not knowing where they are
Not knowing who they are
Some not even caring—if they
    don't
Then who should?

Stephen Robinson

Stephen Robinson
LULLABY

*This peom was written to be
sung to-and was inspried by the
theme from the first movement
of the Sonata in A for Piano K
331 by Mozart.*

Everything's going to be all right,
so just be sure to say your
    prayers.
Stars in the sky are shining down
to keep a watch the whole
    night through.

Go to sleep, my darling baby:
sweet are these moments we
    share together.
Pleasant dreams and comforting
sleep will come to you again
    this night.
Stars shall shine the whole night
    through.

Beth Anne Atwood
**The Rose That Wouldn't
Die**
You planted a twig one day,
Beneath the storming skies.
Gray clouds were all around you
    as that dear day went by
You didn't pay much attention.

You just forgot to look.
One day you just deserted her off
    in your world you took.
I know, because I watched you, as
    the rain dripped down your
    face.
The Memory, that day you
    planted her shall never be
    erased . . .
You didn't know you grew a rose,
    dear, a lovely sight to see.
Each petel just as perfect as, that
    rose thought you would be.
You grew a rose, that lost its
    scent. One day as time rolled
    by.
For she knew she'd lost your
    interest, yet, she refused to
    die . . .
As I watched on everyday, out in
    your world you went.
Oh! How hard I knew she cried
    even her limbs she bent.
Such a lovely little rose standing
    out there all alone.
Her leaves are getting brittlc, all
    those tiny petels gone.
The rose thought you would love
    her, I believe she thought,
    you'd care.
There's little life left inside her
    now, as if she almost isn't
    there.
How her buds have moved me as
    though they blossomed in my
    hands.
The desertion and the loneliness,
    her life could not withstand.
I see you with that twig out
    there,
Beneath the storming skies.
Gray clouds are all around you,
    and that rose that wouldn't
    die.

Dawn L. Wentworth
HE AND SHE

To Mostafa, Anah ba Heb bek.

On a paddle wheel
headed for New Orleans
stood a Southern Gentleman
and his Southern Queen,
Oh, it was true, he'd
been a gun runner once,
and a gambler too,
yes, he'd been quite a
few places in this life;
And yet despite it all
he was this lady's choice.

Brenda A. Decker
THE WIZARD'S DEATH
"The time has come,"
the wizard whispered roughly.
Outlines began to shimmer,
I sadly listened quietly.

"They're taking away my powers,
they say I've had too much
    wizardry.
Time and events have arisen,
for you to continue on for me."

Distantly a crow called, as bright
    colors whirled.
They flew in and out, blew up
    and unfurled.

Through two salty tears,
I measured his gaze.

Blue windows into time,
an infinity of days.

He smiled and then faded,
like colored dust on a breeze.
The crow made another cry,
and flew down from the trees.

The crow lit my shoulder,
fluttered and pecked at my ear.
I looked into his eyes,
after wiping away a tear.

They still held that color,
two orbs of ice-blue.
Wiling crafty magic-spells,
ready to entice you.

Sandra R. Bailey
HALLOWEEN

*To my sons,—Rob, Terry, Dino &
Curt: For all the fun we had on
"Halloween" in years past.*

Solo spirits and spirits in five
Tonight you're going to play alive.

Souls in limbo will come down
To join all others as they clown.
Skeletons rise from graves below
As autumn leaves rustle,
    Chilly winds blow,
    Pumpkins smile a sinister glow.
Witches put on crimson lips,
Add red, red, red to their finger
    tips.
Their kettles boil their witches
    brew—
As they go for a flying interlude.
Goblins and trolls in drab disray,
Shout clinical remarks as the
    vultures play.

The moon—
    Smiling o'er this circumstance,
Delights at seeing the "Black cats'
    dance".

Earthly children—donning
    costumes bright
Will be joined by these forms for
    a night of delight.
        Trick or Treat?
        Trick? or Treat!

Mary Thayer Blanchard
MY PUSSYCAT
I love to hear my pussy purr;
I love to feel his silky fur;
I love to see his feline grace
And those white whiskers on his
    face!

Mrs. Mary Tanco
**A Walk In the Autumn
Sunshine**
A walk in the autumn sunshine
Is truly an invigorating feeling
With the coolness of a frosty morn
It can almost send your head
    "a-reeling".

The array of bright colors of
    autumn
Can take one's breath away
The sight is really awesome
As the sun shines brightly
    through the day.

The beauty of lingering summer
    flowers
In contrast to the changing of the
    leaves of trees
You can "drink in" the beauty for
    hours

As you sit in the gentle breeze.

Take your time to enjoy the
    scene
As winter comes too soon
You'll have days with
    temperatures mean
Especially when there is a full
    moon.

Mary S. Craig
A Thousand Tomorrows
I wait for you in the shadow of
    my longing.
You are a hundred yesterdays
    away and a thousand
    tomorrows,
Endless days flinging out into
    eternity . . .
I cry for your presence, your
    tenderness, your touch,
But my tears stain only my soul.

Mercedes E. Gonzalez
THE DEAN
Arrogance, your power of authority
Behind screwed up faces lies the
    fear
With cocky smiles and
    confidence in your stance
But insecurity rides high upon
    your back

So smooth, so sly the movement is
The skin in shades of beauty
    Presentation, entrancement,
    illusion
The ultimate strike deceiving?
Fool. The crowd was there as you
    dressed.

Shouts of anger become
    cacophony
Hands of frustration are guns of
    your mind
Tongue sharp and gleaming, a
    silver thrust
Your animal of war rejects his
    cage

The high engulfs your head
A game is to be won
Sit hard, talk well, close all the
    doors
Rattle the irons and switch the
    whip
Watch passion inflamed, muscles
    burst forth
    —blood sails out in pieces

Now wake yourself! See the ass
    you are.
The young man is only crying.

Carol Eamigh
BEAUTIFUL WORLD
Cool breezes blowing, ah, so
    softly,
Making the leaves twist and turn
    in delight.
Beautiful World, so rosey and red,
Sunset! Oh, Welcome the night.

Fresh, fresh air and sparkling wet
    dew,
Petals of velvet, so lovely to see.
Crisp morning beauty, Oh,
    Welcome the day.
With the birds and the squirrels
    waiting for me.

Daybreak and noise, Oh, vanish
    the dreams,
Traffic and horns, everyone in a
    hurry.
Pollution, black smoke, as the

business doors open.
Arguments and people screaming
with fury,

Dusk again, peaceful and quiet,
Aromas of food, coming through
the closed doors,
Music and singing, happiness and
gaiety.
The world is beautiful once more!

Sonya Kittrell
In Memory (John Lennon)

To John, Wherever you may be:
Thanks for helping us start over.
Its hard to imagine life without
your song.

Walking by the park
Then, a shot in the dark
A shout of a name
By some man whose insane
And who is to blame
For the sorrow
Of taking away a man's tomorrow
And leaving a heartbroken widow
To cry and cry on her pillow
But through all the tears
For many years
We'll remember his happy face
And how he prayed for the
human race
But don't kiss a legend goodbye
For John will never die

Sandra Bushey Wilson
I WISH . . .
I wish you a life
of days forever clear—
That bring only joy
and cause you no tears—
I wish you the moon
with it's beams so bright—
I wish you the sparkle
of the stars at night—
I wish for you
the gentle spring air—
And the touch of fantasy
once found at the fair—
I wish you the promise
of a budding red rose—
I wish you the dreams
your heart alone knows—
I wish you the warmth
of the sun above—
I wish for you peace
and I give to you love.

John Chris Brault
HALLOWEEN
Carved out pumpkins, salted seeds.
Furry face, dangling eyes,
monstrous nose from fearless
boy.
Chilled air within moonlit windy
leaves.
Fairy princess and broken wings.
A witches hat, and no broom for
a breeze.
Party bags, chewing gums and the
next months bill.
Treats after tricks will be found
in the streets and on the clouds.

Helaine Bootzin and Michael
McKenna
BEHOLDING THE DAWN
We mustn't think of the trees
that have fallen
Instead we'll think of the seeds
that have just sprung

At times the world seems lost in
dark confusion
At times we see the dawning of
the sun.

We may not be two doves above
in flight
We might not always know what
we should do
But we'll endure a world of
darkest night time
By morning we shall see the sun
anew.

We face the world as one in
searching moonlight
By day we search to find a course
to run
Cloudy skies rain darkness on
the helpless night
Our hearts imagine rays of
brighter sun.

We dream a lake frozen in the
moonlight
Our whispers fill the gentle
breezy night
A rolling mist inspires the air
with silence
With joined hands, our hearts
begin their flight.

Through a rising sun, two doves
are soaring
In daylight two shadows are cast
as one
Night drops softly upon a
glittering ring
Our hearts begin ascending with
the sun.

Martin Vosseler
BACK FROM SEA
Flowery whales with silver tales,
blazing parrots smoking pipes.
Ivory sails setting sail,
rainbows land in distant sites.
Breaking wine waterfalls,
idling to a pond it stalls.
My boat and me back from sea.

Dorinda
The Peace That Passes
Understanding
He cradles us in nature's plenty,
Nourishes and loves us well,
But there is not a one of us
Who has not searched and fell.

We skip through life without
much thought,
Love a few and hurt them all,
And when He calls us to His work
We falter and we stall.

Why does He give so when we
turn away?
How can He love us so much?
How do we feel it amid our mean
play?
What comes to pass with His
Touch?

For though there be torment, trial
and pain,
I smile, and I know He is here.
I know when my heart, in its
darkest of days,
Sings out to a world wet with
tear.

"Glory to God in the Highest!
"He is my Comfort and King!"
My joy breaks out of me, bursts
through the trees,
And soars upon gossamer wing!

David L. Kersey
BUTTERDREAM
If life was lust
Butterdream

Dark-n-low
Cold-n-damp

Crying for a day of fun
Left out too long

Left in the sun

Janet Kay Weston

Janet Kay Weston
AUTUMN LEAVES
Autumn leaves
gently drifting to the ground
form a cascade of golden beauty
as they smother the quiet
countryside
in Nature's final fling.

Splashes of God's paintbrush
flutter to and fro
resemble my Grandma's
patchwork quilt
as they adorn the forest floor.

A melancholy feeling descends
upon me
as Indian Summer moves with
silent step
the gentle wind, a passionate
wooer
kisses the blushing leaf "good-bye."

With sadness
I feel summer's warmth slipping
away.
Oh, autumn leaves that flew
hither and yon
my thoughts will cling to your
glowing beauty
on the dark and dreary winter's
morn.

Yonlanda Marie Nagayo
GOD'S CHILDREN

In memory of my father Joseph
Santillana.

A band of angels marching across
a crowded sky
Gathering souls to guide them to
the gates of heaven.
A distant trumpet plays to the
tune of Judgment Day
Rejoice, Rejoice.
Come into the kingdom of
heaven for you have repent.
Rest your wondering souls for
you have proven your faith
The gates of heaven are open to
all God's Children.

We have searched for a new
beginning in the land of peace
filled with grace.
We have seen the power of our
faith for we are all God's
children.

Lanna J. Jones
She Walks Where I Walked
She walks where I walked
Inside the house and out
Beside the fireplace, in the garden
Around and all about

She walks where I walked
Across your heart and through
your mind
Once I occupied that part
At a much happier time

She walks where I walked
And surely feels my presence
there
Because I still send to you
My love, my hope, my care

She walks where I walked
My feelings rendered nill
Can she really take my place
Only time will tell

She walks where I walked
Since you've gone away
Still my love for you
Gives purpose and beauty to my
every day

Carl Mike Williams
Spirit Of Man (A High
Flight For Astronautics)
I've risked the heights that eagles
brave
And dared to tread the Tranquil
Seas.
I've flung my eyes through time
and space
And reached a voice into the
night.
I've sailed my ship from sphere to
sphere,
A ceaseless search for unknown
dreams,
And soared my singing craft on
winds
I cast behind with careless grace.
I drift in midnight solitude
Through ancient clouds of primal
dust
And leap at times on dragon's
breath
To meet appointments I must
keep.

And when at last I stand beneath
The virgin sky that's been my
quest,
I find my gaze still wanders on
To realms of unsung symphonies,
Where mind and soul will stretch
my hand
For endless stars I cannot touch.

Michael Radford
DRACULA
In the moonlight you see him
there by a tree, a darkened figure
pale face, blood-shot eyes, evil
lips

He looks a lot like a gentleman
all dressed in black, silken cape
catching a spark of light

He feeds off the souls of
his victims, most of them willing
then flies away, into the night

Fog rises from the ground
his tall lean figure slowly moves
he's coming toward you

You almost feel responsible for
   him
almost feel sorry for him too
but you raise your cross against
   him

He shuns the cross with his cape
he growls at you, his teeth in view
flies helplessly into the darkness

Angela C. Moran
THIS DIAMOND RING
He drives me home and parks the
   car,
kisses me tenderly in the dark,
walks me to the front porch swing,
takes from his coat, a diamond
   ring.

"Be my wife, I love you so;
I'll stay with you always,
   wherever we go.
We'll spend the rest of the night
   together,
then marry tomorrow and live
   forever."

Whatever made him ask such a
   thing;
to say those words, and give me
   this ring;
I love him more than words can
   say,
but it won't always be this way.

I have to tell him, must do it now,
but that look in his eyes; I
   wonder how
I'll ever be able to tell him these
   things:
'I don't want your love, or your
   diamond rings.'

But he watches my face, and
   suddenly knows;
tears fill his eyes, and he turns
   and goes.
That's when I realize, I love him
   so;
But it's too late; I've already said
   no.

One year later, as I sat in the dark,
across the street a car did park;
he walked her to the front porch
   swing,
and handed her my diamond ring.

Jeanne Ann White
Fishing With My Grandson

*With love to infinity, To my
precious Stephen*

Is that the morning mist I feel
   trickling down my cheek, or a
   tear of joy as I watch this
   incredible boy?

Running across the wheat
   colored field, oblivious to a
   bulls' insistent call, trying with
   all his might to share it all.

The beauty, the calm, the
   excitement of the day, feelings
   between us exchanged in our
   own special way.

"How delightful", I muse, that the
   well spring goes deeper than
   ever before, or should I say

different,
for I could not have loved her
   more.

How strange and yet how
   wonderful that today these
   things I find, in a setting that is
   so simple, simple and yet devine.

And that they again remind me
   of my love for this bonus, this
   miracle, this precious grandson
   of mine.

Joseph Ecklund
HALLOWEEN
It's Halloween, an eerie night
As grown ups tremble in mock
   fright
Weird leaders raid with motely
   crew
Intoxed with made-up witches'
   brew.

Painting of face a most grave task
While others don an ogre's mask
Siblings, some as old as twelve
The mystic world of shosts to
   delve.

Amused response from peopled
   beats
To quavering cries of "Tricks or
   Treats!"
The saints must watch in feigned
   dismay
Wee goblins commandeer their
   day!

Ruth Frances Hall
GUIDING HANDS
Healing waters of my mind
Spread your fingers, oh, so kind
Flowing gently through my brain
Bringing peace, to me, again

With open heart, the stream will
   flow
Healing me, from head to toe
God's gift of everlasting love
Flows through my veins, from far
   above

I feel sometimes, his hand on
   mine
To guide me through, to love
   sublime
But lets me go, to my regret
With words, you are not ready yet

Kurt B. Miller
DREAMS
Lost inside the labyrinth
Of your mind, you fall asleep.
To wander through mysterious
   worlds
For secrets that you seek.
You're frightened by the thought
   of
Leaving your earthly being behind,
But still you keep on searching
For the truths you hope to find.
You wonder if the teachers laugh
At mortals who like you,
Propel themselves to unknowns,
   or,
If they will name you fool.
Incandescent images, that
Imagination weaves,
Float freely on a silent wind
Like luminescent leaves.
Ancient ruins, unspoken words
Scrawled on a parchment page,
Spell out unholy terror from
A different, older age.

But all too soon you find it time
To make your way back in
To the world you're taught to
   understand
And you wait to live again
In the unknown realm of dreams.

Donna M. Robillard

Donna M. Robillard
WINTERS KILL

*To my Father, I will miss you
terribly. Charles Walter Hill
Wyard—Scott, Edmonton,
Alberta, Canada*

Against the snow covered fence,
With the wind blowing strong
   and chill.
Sat a snowbird quiet and tense,
Sitting there against his will.
Around him the snow blew and
   blew,
And the world seemed so
   immense,
For the little bird finally
   knew,
That what would be the sense.

For no matter how he tried and
   tried,
This was to be where he died,
For his feet were froze to the
   wire,
As in a grip of steel,
And his cry could be heard for a
   mile,
As he squealed and squealed and
   squealed,
Then finally with his beak to his
   breast,
And one last murmur of pain,
A sigh, and shudder, a cry,
Then he never moved again.

Jill Marie Anthony
A FANTASY
A fantasy is . . . a dream set free,
   A place where no one else can
   see.

Where unicorns dance
   And children glance,
   To see a friend;
   A friend that lasts forever.

A place where wildest thoughts
   can wander.

Where willows sway.
   Or could you say,
   A fantasy is itself together
Coming true?

Arlene M. Clerc
MOV'IN
A little girl's room about?
Doesn't look like it anymore.
Drawers are all pulled out.
Clothes all over the floor.

Dad peeks in as he goes by,
And can't believe his eyes.
He doesn't understand why,
So asking her, he sighs——

"What are you doing, Honey?"
"Mov'in, Dad!" "You going far?"
"Uh uh, Dad. Can't you see?
I'm mov'in to my other drawer."

Rhonda Watt
DEATH SONG
On these days when life's so dark
You think you'd hear the lark.
The bird of morning, oh so near
Sings the song of pain and fear.

But yet you listen and there is no
   lark
In fact, there is no sound within
   the dark.
All you hear are silent cries
As the world around you slowly
   dies.

And as it dies you try to cope
But you soon realize that there is
   no hope.
So you join in with your own
   silent cry
And slowly even you begin to die.

Peggy N. Wainwright
THE OTHER WOMAN
She swooped in like a vulcher
   from the sky.
Kept on circling and circling,
   waiting for a sick marriage to
   die.
It did not die quietly, much
   surrering and pain.
A number of years it had lasted,
   but nothing could remain.
Vulchers by nature look for the
   sickly
and play their deadly game.

Lucindy H. Cobb
GO TO CHURCH!
If you feel bad, sad, or forlorn,
There's no better place on Sunday
   morn.
   Go to church!
When the storms of life seem
   about to depress you,
Go to God's house, for there He
   will bless you.
   Go to church!
If life's battles are hard to fight,
Live a good life, the kind that's

right.
  Go to church!
If a friend should forsake or
  disappoint you,
Just let your Savior with His
  spirit anoint you.
Go to church!
As you grow old, and your years
  are few,
Remember the good Lord will
  take care of you.
Go to church!

Dennis S. Mierzejewski
A FLOWER
Flowers! I say flowers, let blossom
  scent flow in your grass,
Let it rub scarf from your steely
  joints, like a bare-giving oil.
Till it gives you heart the curves
  of wine and the suppleness of
  color.
For then will be refound the sun
  of eagle,
The reconciliation of night, light,
  and life.
And to hear, especially to hear
  the woman,
Who with a saxophonic song,
  created summer and spring in
  seven days.
And on the child, slept a great
  humming sound.

Ellen Given
My Great-Grandfather
I climbed the winding stairway
  with caution,
feeling the pie shaped steps with
  my hands,
reaching the second floor hushed
  in darkened tones,
but for a bit of light from his
  little room.

He was seated by his desk—a
  wooden fortress
laden with boxes, letters, papers,
  books . . .
exactly as he wanted them.

He sat motionless, captured in a
  grimace of age,
as if posing for mountain
  sculpture.

Smoke curled round the radio
as the crowd roared above the
  announcer's voice,
a voice of familiar comfort
to this gaunt man with high
  cheekbones.

Slowly he turned to me . . .
but, looking down, I could not
  tell
if there were a twinkle in his
  eye.

I thought he was part of the chair
and hadn't left the room in years,
like the ticket man at the train
  station,
so attached to his surroundings
that he elected to stay on
long after the building had been
  torn down.

His treasury of memories were
  lingering at dusk
like a fading postmark . . .

It was the last time I saw him—
when I was four and he was
  ninety.

Peter J. Dellolio
A THROW OF THE DICE
The sound of
raindrops is
similar to that
of footsteps only
because he is
  in a hurry and
  the door is
  open so the
staircase resounds
while the storm
is raging.

Mariam Abdul Razak
THE SCENT OF LOVE

To Ammar with love.

"I would like to serve you till the
  end of my life"
My ears have not yet drunk a
  hundred words
Of the tongue uttering
Yet I know the sound
Is it a dream?
Is it reality?
How I wish—I were in his arms
Feeling neither the sun's
  excessive heat
Nor the moon's excessive cold
And the shades of the garden
Will come love above us
And all between us
At the rising of the sun
Deck the heaven with beauty in
  the stars
And the bunches of fruits
Will hang low in humility
How I wish . . .
I could press to his breast in a
  close embrace
And cry out clear "I Love You"
Thanks to God for creating all
Especially Him.

Susie Scalia
Ode To the Evening Shift

This is for Dennis.

I'm so glad you're off tomorrow,
No more late nights filled with
  sorrow.
Evenings drag while you're away.
There's no fun; what can I say?

How much do I love you?
God only knows.
I hope I can show you
In the lines of my prose.

Inadequate? Yes.
Silly? Maybe.
But I just love you,
My sweet baby!

Jaime Joan Hartman
SECURITY
Maybe tomorrow,
Maybe today,
Maybe something
Will come my way,
To solve my problems,
Share my fears,
Listen quietly
With open ears.
Always to comfort,
Never to scold,
Something to love me,
Something to hold,

To tell me that
It's alright to cry,
To give me wings
And help me fly.
Just someone or something
To always be there
To understand, to respect,
To love and to care.
Maybe tomorrow,
Maybe today,
Maybe that something
Will come my way.

Eleanora S. Martin
TO A HEARING AID

*Dedicated to all of the wonderful
people everywhere who help
those who are unable to hear.*

I thank you for the music that I
  hear
    And for the joy it brings,
I thank you when I can hear
  whispering
    And many other things,
It's such a thrill to hear voices
    That speak in ranges-high to
    low,
I am able to answer questions
    Instead of saying, "I don't
    know".
Yesterday, I could not hear
  golden tones
    Or any kind of sound,
Silence kept out moans and
  groans, bells and phones
    And footsteps on the ground.
I can hear birds that sing and the
  mourning doves
    Cooing to their mate,
Thank you, little hearing aid,
    I rejoice and humbly celebrate.

Violet M. Sandru
If I Could Do What I Wanted To Do
If I could do what I wanted to do
I wouldn't know where to start,
It's been so long that I've been
  bound
To doing whats not in my heart.

First I'd praise Lord Jesus,
Morning, night and noon,
And not be rushed by daily chores
And cleaning every room.

I'd fly off to unknown places
See things I have not seen.
I'd hear the oceans mighty roar,
And hear the sea gulls scream . . .

I'd go to the lofty mountains,
Midst cedar, rocks and pine,
In the streams I'd dig for gold
The mother lode I'd find.

Yes if I could do what I wanted to
  do,
I wouldn't know where to start,
So I'll keep up with daily chores
And ponder these things in my
  heart . . .

Louise S. Yates
Quest Of the Lonely Journey
From whence . . .
    came life?
To where . . .
    this life?
Psyche, lonely as I,

Querries with a sigh,
"From whence . . .
    the beginning—
Ah, for remembering—
Recalling the epochal past—
Ages that did not last;
Past lives now lost—
Fragments now tossed
In the memory bank
Like sand in a tank."
Looking deep inside,
I try, try to decide—
Psyche stands to chide
Lest I err in recall
As I search and stall
Searching early dawn
Of ancient ages gone.
I search the mountain cave,
River valleys, ocean wave,
Forests, deserts, quarries,
Plains, swamp, prarries;
Psyche and I search—
Through sands of time
For one glimpse sublime;
For revelation of meaning
For yearning and dreaming
As the lonely journey goes on
From life to life—on and on.

Joani Franklin McAnally
FOR MY PARENTS
Be ready to listen,
but don't force the words
Don't give me sermons,
for I only want suggestions.
Don't give up on me,
when you don't understand the
  questions.

Take an interest in my life
but don't pry
Please hear me out
before you ask why.

Take precautions where needed,
but don't lock me in.
And please Dear Parents
be there when I need a friend.

Charles E. Stevenson
Help Me Lord To Do No Wrong

*To All My Children And
Grandchildren*

While down here in a world of
  scorn
Amid tribulations a world all torn
Jesus keep me I am all alone
Help me Lord to do no wrong.

Temptations all around me stand
Help me Lord to be a Godly man
At time I feel very worn
Help me Lord to do no wrong.

Almighty God grant me grace
To run this tedious race
Grant me Lord some more faith
Help me Lord to do no wrong.

In death dark vale I feel no ill
The king of love my shepherd is
Thy rod, thy staff my comfort
  still
Why holding God's hand I have
  no fear.

Master let me now be heard
I am waiting for thy gracious
  word
What hath thou to say to me?
Help me Lord to do no wrong.

To the end I have promised to
serve
Be thou forever near me
Be my Master be my friend
All around me and within.

The wise may bring their learning
The rich may bring their wealth
Some may bring a mighty thong
Help me Lord to do no wrong.

Millie Davis
WHISPERS IN THE WIND
I have felt the taunts and teases
of the gentle, youthful breezes,
Which whirl away without a
single care;
I have often been disheveled by
the wildly raging devils
That have whipped across my
face and in my hair.

I have felt the deep despair of the
dark and stagnant air,
Which never even offers us a sigh;
And I have known the wind to
seek to caress my saddened
cheek,
To console and lift my spirits to
the sky.

I have known the winter snow,
harsh and icy as it blows,
In February, in the northern
clime;
Still, the warm winds bring the
spring when the birds begin to
sing,
So I know that all things pass, if
given time.

But wind isn't really free to be
just what it wants to be;
It must gust and blow according
to the season;
So our impatience and sorrows
too will rage or wane as
seasons do,
Though it's often hard to
understand the reason.

    I yearn for fulfillment,
    My heart seethes and burns;
    And I shout to the wind,
    But only whispers return.

Rosamond Suzanne Blok
A POEM
Feeling your warmth
Keeps me from crying,
And forgetting
That living
Is also dying.

Billie Shambaugh
HAPPY DAYS

---

*This poem is dedicated to Bob
and Darlene—who have faith in
me.*

Happy colors all around, happy
days ahead
Watching red and gold leaves fall
from high above our heads.
Soon the snow will cover all and
joy will fill our days
Little hands building forts and
snowmen in their play.
Faces all aglow as to the top the
children climb
Pulling bobsleds up the hill with
yapping dogs behind.
Now the red and gold and white

turn back to green in spring
And happy as we watch the
flowers the sun above will bring.
Gaily splashing in a pool on a
summer day
Crisp and clear the stars at night
along the milky way.
But surely no one can deny the
brightest time of all
When happy is as happy does and
we head back toward fall.

Carmen Rinehart Moss
GUARDIANS
    A hot, savage wind—

the house stands lonely, secure—
cottonwoods on guard.

K. J. Arnold
MY DREAM
I have found my spot called
paradise,
That once was only a dream,
It's guarded by fifty straight
sentinels,
In various shades of green.

The house built of sweet scented
cedar,
Surrounded by clover and broom,
Moonlight glides o'er the rooftop
And God blesses every room.

The birds whistle this is shangrila!
The bees murmur heaven at best!
The sun shines into all corners
And I know that I am blessed.

Ronald Oldfield
BABE

---

*To my wife Mona Louise and my
children Toni Louise and Richard
Thomas*

The babe caught life on a roll
he stepped up took his best shot
and won
tipped the scales of life with all
he had to offer
spread a little love and joy
stepped on not one
gave a parting grin
then left

Claire Louise Mangano
LITTLE PEOPLE
Come gather 'round and I'll tell
you a tale
Of the little people of Sleepydale,
Who are just as tall as your tiny
toes
And live in the closets behind
the clothes.

They cannot be seen for they
sleep all day,
But at night, in delight, they
romp and play
And hide in your shoes and your
pockets too,
And while you're asleep they
watch over you.

They have bright, green eyes and
long purple hair
And for clothes the fingers of
gloves they wear
And their small, pointed ears
catch every sound
As they frolic and tumble round
and round.

They gather the crumbs from the
pantry floor
And have a grand party behind
the door,
Then they play see-saw in your
mother's spoons
And on the brass kettle they beat
gay tunes.

But— when the very first
sunbeams awake,
With many a wiggle, many a
shake,
They climb through the keyhole
and out of sight,
To sleep all the day until the
next night.

Debby London
RAINDROPS
Inconsistent beads of God's sweat
  Trickle windows to accumulate,
    Becoming great puddles
      Causing grown men to put
      Booties on their feet.
        Alone they matter little,
        Together they may
        Wash a road or
        Down a bridge.
        Power not in
        The sweat
        Of you
        Or
        Me.

Rosalind Ponsolle
ABE SMILED
Destiny appoints her Sons
To fulfill their dreams
And expand horizons,
Those liberated Ones
Are shaking the dust
From off their feet,
Marching forward to claim
Heritage and birthright
Paid for in blood
At Gettysburg and Atlanta.
My ears are attuned
To the rhythmic beat,
Even unto the door
Of the Oval Office
For destiny is irrevocable,
And from his marble chair
Abraham smiled.

Betsy Papendieck
THE OWL AND THE TREE
On a far reaching branch, bare
from winter's wrath
Rested a weighty old owl in the
twilight of the morn.
He surveyed his domain as a
scholar of the world below,
From a perch of an anguished
soul, it was so.
The wise and the wizened formed

a symmetry to behold,
Interrupted only by night, when
the owl took flight,
Leaving behind, the tree to think
in his own aloneness . . .
"Oh, to be shriven and released
from these century old roots!
To be free like the owl in his
awesome wisdom;
To be touched by the knowledge
of his truth."
It mattered not, the forest which
grew from its fertile seed,
Nor the shelter it provided its
nemesis . . .
Unbeknownst to the owl, the tree
had begun to die
From a hopeless desire to change
its caste.
Little by little, the tree let go of
the source
Which kept it upright and
righteous;
And then, one stormy night, the
owl came back
To find the tree upon its side . . .
And the owl asked, "But why?
You were my refuge, sturdy and
secure,
My tradition that could not be
broken.
What troubles you so that makes
you want to die?"
The tree, still not understanding
or the wiser,
Could only reply, "Like you, I
wanted to fly."

Mary Timothy Anthony
QUIET MOMENTS
Quiet moments, when we are
    Alone together
I steal a look at you
    My mind reals
      With wonder
To see you and know
We have lain together
    And
Thrilled, striving toward
Unimmaginable heights
    Of pleasure
Quiet moments, when we are
Still, my head resting
On your chest listening
To your heart beating strongly
    Your voice
Speaking quietly into the darkness
Quiet moments such as these
I reflect upon the perfect unity
Two people can achieve through
love.

Robert Charles Munson
**Don't Fall In Love Too
Young**
Like the waves drifting upon the
face of the ocean,
So our lives wander aimlessly
with the passing of time.
It seems a fruitless journey into
the perils of the unknown,
Yet, the one thing that must be
perceived is this,
Don't fall in love too young.

I'm just a man trying to lick the
wounds of love,
Who thought that I was traveling
upon the sure path.
But there is a way that seems
right unto a man,
And that way will surely bring

forth God's wrath.
Please, Don't fall in love too young.

I gaze at the vast universe and
our glorious earth,
With the laughter of children, it's
fragrance so sweet.
But there is no merriment inside
my being, only despair,
Can anyone feel the way I do, it
just isn't fair.
I beg you, Don't fall in love too
young.

At times I wish that I could
escape from this body of flesh;
I would travel into my next life,
And elude the pain that makes
me hurt so.
For some it's just that simple,
A gun, a knife, some pills and life
ceases,
But my situation would not
render such abuses.
I plead with you, Don't fall in
love too young.

So, I'll just walk my life, with this
increasing pain,
With my only hope, that of us
getting back together again.
The fire rekindled, my strength
renewed,
I'll always carry this burden for
you.
It's so unfair that this tragedy has
happened to me.
So, Don't fall in love too young.

Julia D. King
WHY LITTLE GIRL

*This poem is dedicated to my
daughters, Bonnie, Marie,
Charlene, and Penny, who fill my
heart with joy.*

I think that I shall never see
This little girl get out of me.

A little girl who's full of pride,
Why can't she turn that pride
aside;

And be instead a humble one,
Who's full of love, and full of fun;

Why let pride get in the way
And spoil a life that could be gay;

Why wait until the autumn years,
To learn of life, and humble tears.

Why—Little girl!

Delores Reid Skipper
GOLDEN ANNIVERSARY

*For 50 years of devotion to one
another and the love each couple
shared with their children, this
poem is dedicated to ZEMMA &
MILTON REID and IRENE &
RED SKIPPER.*

50 years ago
You became man and wife
And promised to live together
For the rest of your life.

You have kept the vows
That you made so long ago,
Traveled many miles together
And brought joy to those you
know.

You've shared joys and pleasures,
Yes, disappointments, too;
But they've only served to
strengthen
Your love that's been so true.

Through experience you learned
many things
While together you've been
living;
Your happiness increased a
thousandfold
In loving, sharing, giving.

In little things you've found
pleasure,
With the one you love so much,
Like a loving glance, a smile,
Or just a gentle touch.

So on this Special Day I hope
That, with the love you share,
You'll have many more years
together,
And happiness beyond compare!

Tammy Lynn Rekito
ONE HALLOWS EVE
Misty rain is in the air as the
midnight fog unfolds.
Laughter echos through the night
and ghostly tales are told.
The moonlight beams pierce
through the fog like daggers in
the night.
The wind is cool and sends a
chill down to my soul in flight.
The trees are bent in dance with
wind like hideous dancing
ghouls.
And at the midnight hour, a
haunting bell does toll.
There's lighted heads in panes of
glass with smiling grins shone
bright.
And acts of mischief do occur all
through the dark of night.

Dora Dietz
THE WOMAN IN BLACK
Taking to the air like a spirit in
flight
Casting her spells upon the world
of innocence
Demanding powers that cut like
a knife
Evil is the wicked who dares fly
at night.

She flies like a dragon with great
strength
The magic that exists has risen to
full extremity
Overpowering obstacles with her
enormous wand
Beware the woman in black who
hides behind the color.

She can make you feel alive or
cut you down to nothing
She lives off of people who give
her their heart and soul
She takes what she can, gives
nothing in return
She has it all, satisfaction has
taken her soul.

Continuing on, making rounds at
night
She is the darkness, a mystery
woman
Probing life's grandeurs, turning
them down
She is unhappy and dying from
lack of love.

Monique C. Elser
HIS DREAM
Not long ago,
A little boy said
As he peeped up,
His little round head.
I will be President
Of the United States.
I will rebuild
The Golden Gates.
This is his dream,
He hopes it comes true.
So there will be peace,
Between me and you.
We hope we will live
With family and friends.
And if a war gets started,
It will come to an end.

Brenda B. Ozunal
The Hiding Of the Conflict
Lost in the wilderness of pain
he walks
Black streets with a
blue atmosphere.

Drunk
with the Conflict
Firewater
Foolishness of the man.

He explodes with
electric laughter like
spiders
of the dawn
creepy and crawly.

Years of plunging into pools
of bitter/sweet alcohol.

For the man
the blowing
of pails of suds is
over
For the Conflict
Burned some black
into the hole
of light
He dwelled in.

Edna M. Brewer
A Stone Upon My Heart
I have a stone upon my heart,
It weighs almost a ton.
Today my mother placed it there,
I'm sure she was the one.

Roll the stone away, Lord;
Roll the stone away.
No one but you can do it, Lord!
Please roll the stone away.

I came to give her gifts of love,
To gaze upon her face;
To eat there at her table
In my dead father's place.
She placed this stone upon my

heart,
She filled my life with pain,
She left unpleasant memories
That always will remain.

When I was just a little lad
My love for Mom was deep,
And when I grew to be a man
I worked and payed my keep.

But now she's cut the tie that
binds
With weapons that are sharp.
Please take this stone from off
my heart
And place instead a harp.

Lisa Bross
**If You Don't Have
One—Borrow**
I woke up this morning
and couldn't find it;
I was sure someone
wouldn't mind if,
I were to borrow their's
if only for awhile,
They would surely
lend me a little smile.

I promised I would
give it back;
I promised it would be
warm and wouldn't lack,
Any of the luster
or the goodness;
That's sometimes so deep
inside all of us.

I decided I would
keep a bit of it,
Just in case I should
be in need of it;
Or wanted to lend
or give it away,
For we all should smile
at least once a day.

Marjorie E. Williams
BLOWING BUBBLES
Little children blow them high,
Watch them rise up to the sky,
Use your little plastic wand,
To blow the bubbles, one by one.

Watch them as they drift away,
Colors glinting in the sun,
Separating as you blow,
Big and little, there they go!

Some burst and vanish in the air,
Away they go, we know not where,
Little children shout with glee,
The bubbles soaring merrily.

Yes, as long as we can blow,
The bubbles form and swiftly
grow,
Like laughter from a joyous heart,
They fill the air and then depart.

If our dreams could always fly,
Like those bubbles floating high,
Then our dreams would never
tumble,
In the dust to fade and die.

Some might burst and fade away,
Others sail into the blue,
Off into eternity—
Where they wait for me and you.

So blow my children; do not stop,
Spun of irridescent gleams,
They float on sunlight's golden
streams,
Blow my children; let them rise,
Upward, upward to the skies,

John Campbell, Editor & Publisher

Translucent orbs of light and shade,
To the land where dreams are made.

Julie Ann Ehlke
SCATTERED MEMORIES

To a person whom is very warm and caring, yet like a child is afraid to let it go.

Soft fluffy snow floats ever so
  lightly to the ground,
Then, settles
  among all the other glistening
  flakes
Until a whispering breeze
  comes to puff them away.

Reminding me
  of your gentle ways.
The soft caresses
  exchanged in the quietness of
  the night.
Warm and caring affections
  stirring so peacefully.

And then scattered
  and lost
    with a puff of reality.

Elisha J. O'Neal
ARDOR
There's no fire . . .
  Coals are sizzling orange and
  amber,
    warm, awaiting yet the
    timber
      —to ignite.

Uneasy feelings seize the night.
  Soulful yearnings of desire;
Requiring limbs to douse the fire
  —felt inside.

There's no dry wood.
  Unsatisfied, we smoulder on
    —the fire and I . . .

Gerrie Pinkerton
Let Me Tell You About My Lord
Though your sins, be as scarlet,
  they'll be as white as snow.
Whereever you wander,
  your love for the Lord,
  will show.
Let me tell you about my Lord.
Let me tell you about Jesus,
  his goodness,
    to whomever I meet.
Shout his name, Hallelujah,
  on every corner,
    on every street.
He'll walk beside you,
  whereever you go.
You should know,
  each day,
    he's more precious to know.
Let me tell you about my Lord.
Just call on him,
  and he'll answer,
    and give you peace within.
He'll change you,
  and forgive your sins.
Let me tell you about my Lord.

Ron Maccari
SILENT VICTORY
He sits and stares at the smoke
  filled sky
Memories return as he begins to
  die.

A boy so young and yet so old
His thoughts are warm while his
  anger grows cold.
He remembers the way life used
  to be
His heart projects what his eyes
  no longer see
Blocking out both pain and fear,
Flashing back to forgotten years.
He holds back the tears with
  what strength he can find
Thinking of the people he had
  left behind.
He longs to be with his family at
  home
The loneliest part of living is
  dying alone.

Death looks on for souls to steal
There are no winners on battle
  fields
War is but a game that grown
  men play
The price is sorrow that all will
  pay.
As if approaching sleep, his life
  slips away
His final thoughts of how he used
  to pray
He whispers watching the last
  light fall.
Father forgive us, forgive us all.

Vincent A. Roth
A CHILD'S PRAYER
One night as I turned off the lights,
I heard my child praying.
And I was really quite amazed,
  and proud,
At the things that he was saying.
  "Lord Grant unto our leaders, a
  love for whom they serve.
And to our soldiers fighting
Lord, grant an iron nerve.
Grant unto our teachers Lord,
The widsom to teach us well.
And to our ministers, dear
Lord, Grant the words to tell.
Grant unto my Father Lord, on
  whom I do depend.
The healing hand of love you
  have, His tired body mend."
Then I heard him thank the Lord,
For listening to him.
I softly said "Goodnight son".
As the hall light I dimmed.
When I got back to my room,
Holding back the tears.
I raised my heart to God above,
And in a voice, that was loud and
  clear.
I asked he'd heal my dying son,
If it was his will and plan.
And let this special boy grow up,
To be a special man.

James W. Zwickey
SEARCHING

To my wife Debbie who brought my search to an end.

Would you come to me if I lay
  dying?
Would you stay with me if I were
  sad?
Will you sit with me in the
  loneliness of midnight?
Can you laugh with me when I
  am glad?

Will you lay your softness down
  beside me
as we share in each other's dreams?
Will you comfort me in times of
  sorrow
as the dry land is soothed by cool
  streams?
Will you share my life, my love,
  my happiness
as we walk forward in time?
Will you be the light that guides
  my way,
strong as the sun that forever
  shines?
Will you travel with me through
  new dimensions
of Earth and Sky and Sea?
And will your love remain until
  the end of time
and span the breadth of the galaxy?
If all these things are possible of
  you,
then what I've asked, I will galdly
  give too . . .

Heidi Tansosch
AUTUMN NIGHT
Softly, gently the autumn trees
  sigh.
Dark silhouettes against the
  night sky.
Dry leaves rustle,
As a soft breeze blows.
Patiently awaiting,
The not to distant snows.
The darkness is total.
There is barely a sound.
Except for the whisper,
Of dry leaves falling down.
"Winter is near,"
They whisper as they fall.
Winter is near.

Kleon Kerr
THE FUTURE
I walked in the land of reverie
And turned back the pages of time.
I tried to erase certain actions
And make my past life more
  sublime.

My efforts were never so futile;
The records were indelibly
  written.
Not one word nor act of the past
From the pages could ever be
  smitten.

The past was the past and I rue it,
But what lies ahead is all mine.
The future offers the challenge
To make words and acts more
  divine

Jake de Peuter
THE ANCIENT OAK

Dedicated to those in my life, who had shown to me the ugliness of life, that when beauty presented itself, I knew it was beautiful.

Dost thou not see that Ancient
  Oak
on the coldest winter morn?
Alone it standeth in the snow;
Alone, and oh, how forlorn!
Icicles, like slim silver ghosts,
How they hang from branch and
  limb!

A ghost itself, that Ancient Oak,
Its silver fingers so slim!

Donna Mae Bell
DREAMING
When I sit here in the darkness
Images invade my mind,
Never will my questions end
Nor the answers will I find.

When my mind and soul surrender
To dust again they turn,
For what creature will I be
When again I must return?

Who will be the one I wonder
Will be the very existance of me,
When the sun comes up once
  more
To light the love within me?

Life unseen yet by my eyes
And the yet untravelled pathes,
Give me courage to go on
And answer the questions that
  I'm asked.

Here while slipping out of the
  darkness
Back to the world again
Never will my rainbow end
Nor the life I dream begin!

Sandi Jendrowski
A FRIEND
Someone who will listen,
talk,
be there,
forever.

Someone to share a secret,
stories,
smile,
always.

Someone to go out with,
stay home,
be together,
now.

Someone to join in planning
a party,
a day,
a lifetime . . .

Together,
You and I,
Forever, always, now,
Friends.

Michael David Steimle
VISITATIONS
Visitations
long lost magic
golden arms of light,
  take me
cosmic mate of the dark forest
to the red necked wood
to the raw bountious creation
  show me
flights of angels emerge
rising on leafy beds of desire,
unborn babies damp assention
softly marring light beings
to flesh soul
unbanded
take me
let it go

Jeanette Brown
My Prayer (Thanksgiving)
Thank You Lord for the beautiful
  day that was mine to enjoy
Thank You for myself-for my
  wisdom and understanding
For I had to depend on You and
  others to teach and promote

Our World's Best Loved Poems

me
Thank You for Yourself "You The
Greatest" so condescending
To reach down to all with love
and forgivness to all humanity.

I am greatful for loved ones—and
all blessings including my
beautiful country
America, with it's glorified
seasons—and diligent people
It's hills, rivers, fields, forests and
mines—It's industries and
luxury
Thank You for displaying Your
soul in the sunset
Your spirit in a silver-lined cloud-
moving with triumph and
assurance
The peaceful nights and Your
benediction thru the
constellation of stars in
endurance
Your gilded mornings for
meditation-and Your
whispering comfort in the
breezes
Thank You for the gift of
memories
Pleasant memories, that can fill
the emptiness of time with
gladness
Like small candies they bring the
glow thru the gloom of
lonliness
Forgive me for my wrong-doings
as I have forgiven You for grief
and sadness
Tho I realize it was to meld a
strong bond between us
A bond as strong as steel-as
radiant as gold.
Thank You for letting us die only
once befor we can live again
It is so sad to see the eyes grow
hollow and dim

Reveal Your presence to all
people-young and old
Be our leader to faith, truth, peace
and purity
Be our "Glory" to the realm of
Eternity "Amen"

Ann Valéncoure
A Long Remembered Road
I know I've seen this road before,
In some remembered time and day,
The oak tree where we carved
our Names,
And promised love for evermore.
The little brook still sings so free,
Her music carried on the breeze,
and Heaven seems so near again,
Of happier days that used to be.
The farm house beckons me to
stay,
And live with dreams of yesterday,
But shadows on the Mountainside.
Remind me, to be on my way.
For I have many roads to quest,
And many hills to climb, I guess,
Before the sun sets, in the West,
Then I will rest, then I will rest.

Miss Laura Lambe Burrell
HIBERNATION
Men should hibernate in
Cold weather;
Such laziness provokes weak
Minds
During frostbitten trees of Feb.

To think of fireplace
Covers glowing around
Chilled bones is warmth
Wrapping around pillows
Like small chicks inside
Their eggs
Ahh, spring hands
Guide strong minds throughout
Summer in attempt to revive
Winter weaknesses.
David G. Walker
The Princess Of the Nile

For Valerie

There's a beauty trapped in the
pyramid zone
with a hundred Pharaohs trying
to take her home
But nighttime is for dancers in
their polished midnight style
As evening's hour beckons in the
Princess of the Nile

The intrigue of the moment is
mirrored in every face
While the music cranks it up and
dominates the pace
They're shouting at the tables
and shoving in the aisles
Awaiting the arrival of the
Princess of the Nile

Crazy Horse comes down from
the mountain alone
After looking for her portrait that
was carved into stone
He studies the shoreline and
keeps it on file
It's an elusive search for the
Princess of the Nile

The Colorado equation knocks
the land to its knees
The buffalo are gone like an
innocent breeze
When reality hits home they just
turn the dial
A few will turn to the Princess of
the Nile

Arabian horses run wild on the
beach
That freedom of the spirit is still
within reach
But some fall short by a thousand
miles
And all fall short of the Princess
of the Nile

Now there she stands by the
lower bar
An oasis in the desert, our
guiding star

The lights can't cut her electric
smile
For none can resist the Princess
of the Nile

Jane L. Coff
Thinking Through Your Eyes
I sit and think
of how to write.
The world is coming
around to night.

My mind has been
wandering in endless thought.
Through all the technique
that I have been taught.

If only I could find
a good subject to use
I know if I did
I just couldn't lose

I'm going to sit here
and think till I find
That fabulous subject
and the one winning line.

You know how it is
when you read a poem,
there's always that one line
that really hits home.

And sometimes it comes
as a big surprise
To find someone else thinks
through your eyes.

Judy Marilyn Dawson
FOREVER ONE

---

*To Hank and Jimmy, my two best
friends in the world! Thanks for
everything, I love you, both!*

Confusion on hand, a state of
shock, up with defenses, a
mental block.
Curiousity around, all four walls,
body shaking, tears begin to fall.
Weakness sets in, depression has
begun, a throat is cut, life is
done.
Saddness arises, people gather
around, to cry over a body, six
feet underground.
Maddness stirs up, they claim it's
all fake, the happenings today,
just a mistake.
Hysterical they become, down
they go, bodies rise, the truth
begins to show.
Searching is about, they linger on,
people scatter, the feelings are
gone.
Becoming frozen, souls arise, the
searching is done, they are
disguised.
Uplifting spirits, they join as one,
falling together, as does the
setting sun.
Vanishing together, soul, mind
and heart, forever one, never to
be torn apart.

Kathleen Forton
TO A FRIEND
You entered my life in a casual
way
And saw at a glance what I
needed
There were others who passed me
or met me each day
But never a one of them heeded.

Perhaps they were thinking of
other folk more
Or chance simply seemed to
decree it
I know there were many such
chances before
But the others—well, they didn't
see it.

You said just the thing that I
wished you would say
And you made me believe that
you meant it
I held up my head in the old
gallant way
And resolved you would never
repent it.

There are times when
encouragement means such a
lot
And a word is enough to convey
it
There were others that could
have as easily as not
But just the same, they didn't say
it.

There may have been someone
who could have done more
To help me along—though I
doubt it
What I needed was cheering and
always before
They let me plod onward
without it.

Thomas Mann Selkirk
ANALYSIS
Analysis, we here cite,
Is the start of the art of thinking
right,
In which the devil is not gaily
bedight
Because one's in darkest night,
Produced by fright,
Caused by the sight
Of one's fight
To avoid the trite
At its height,
In spite
Of only a slight
Knowledge of God's almight,
Which brings to light
The brightest of the bright—
An unbelievable delight!

William J. Hardin
Your Love Is Like An Arrow True
Some women for their smiles are
loved
And some for eyes so blue,
But let me tell you now my love
I love because it's you.

On distant shores over land or
sea
Wherever I may roam, they're not
the
Same those girls abroad, when I
know
That you are home alone.

My heart it bleeds, my life is
slowly
Slipping from within;
But, when my thoughts return to
you
I'm filled with life again.

Your love is like an arrow true,
That's clinging to my heart,
And robs me of my drops of blood
Whenever we're apart.

Cheryl Lee Miles
AFTER EFFECTS

*To Frank Mabry who always
believed in me . . . and to God
who gave me the gift of words,
with which I write my poems.*

Rainbows after tears
  Sunshine after smiles
Warmth after love
  Memories after life
These are the after-effects
  We experience through out our
  years
Whether tears are for joy or pain
  Smiles for happiness or gain
Love given or taken
  Memories stored or forsaken
None of these are done in vain
  Heaven awaits us
Or Hell overtakes us
  But still these things remain
After-effects

Alicia Moeller
MIND PLACES
This lovely place so far away
is where I'd like to be;
flashing pictures in my mind,
possibly made by me.

taking happiness with me,
well thats just great because;
everything that *is* now
will then you see be *was.*

Karen Marie Breslin
SHADOWS OF THE PAST

To my grandmother, Lovie Mae.

We cry like banished children,
In search of a dream
For a meaning in life.
As a shadow passes in a squall,
We form visions of a spirit in flight
The Wings of Freedom.
On a splendid peaceful sea of
  dreams,
The spirit glides on . . .
The Wings of Hope.
Holding on to reality,
Like pages in a book.
We stand in place.
We reinforce our beliefs
With new illusions of Freedom
We glide so slow but yet so fast
Our visions fade . . .
In the shadows of the past.

Shirley Raye Austin
WAKING
Sh! Don't say a word, don't utter a
  sound not even a whisper sigh
Just let me gaze upon you with
  your hair tousled from a night
  of sleep, your eyes half open in
  waking.
You need not open them
  completely I know their color
  all too well.
I've gotten lost in them many
  times before.
The flush of sleep on your cheeks
  like the pink of roses in the
  early morning dew.
Lips, half parted, with just a
  glimpse of pearly teeth between.
Lips that beckon to me, begging
  to be kissed.

Your skin is smooth, warm, as if
  touched by the golden sun.
You remind me of a baby soft in
  body, safe in mind cradled by
  the surety of its mother's love
  or an angel content in God's
  Heaven.
Now that my senses are reeling
  from the sight of you
Now that I am trembling for the
  touch of you.
Now that my joy can no longer
  be contained within me.
Let me bend and kiss you good
  morning.

Angela C. Tomei

Angela C. Tomei
DESPERADO
In desperation I sit alone,
Fearing I have lost
What once I owned.

Others have no need for concern,
It is not their life
Beseiged and burned.

To climb the stairs in search of
  one door,
In finding it locked
I am wanting for more.

I need the freedom of another
  world,
Where dreams are not painful
Burdens to unfurl.

Alice Wassom
MAUVE MEMOIR
"Ancient one, gray and withered
  as the creaking porch beneath
  your chair,
Why do you smile?"
His eyes glowed as he replied,
"The fragrance of my lilacs now
  in bloom bring sweet memories.
The first time I saw my love was
  when they blossomed in the
  spring long years ago.
There she stood, pale golden hair
  tossed by soft spring breezes,
  holding lilacs close in her arms.
Then came love, life, joy; sorrow
  when death came her way.
But when lilacs bloom, she seems
  near to commune with me."

Salvatore D'Aprano
Voyage With No Return
The convict in the death house,
  waits with confident hope,
  what he lacked for his victim:
  Human pity.
But, looking fortuitously from the
  grating, takes a glimpse of the

halter which oscillated in the
  wind, on the scaffold already
  erected.
He shuddered,
  while he felt a lump tighten his
  throat, realizing with lucidity
  that the law of retaliation is
  still in force between the
  humans.
As a shipwreck survivor, he finds
  himself in an oppressive
  solitude and in his desperation,
  disowns God.
And with automation gesture
  slowly gets ready for his last
  voyage with no return.

Hamish G. Rennie
CRIMSON APPLE
You soil my lips with your
  kiss . . .
Friend of my father who knows
  my mother's legs,
Why are you no friend of mine?
This night, I walked with the dark,
Alone from mansion to tree-
  watched mansion.
A ghost of the past challenged
  tomorrow's spectre,
And lost.
The dark with which I walked
  was a sunlit plain:
The dark from which you came
  swallowed my sun.
No more shall I trust past
  fantasies;
No more of pumpkins, tricks and
  treats.

Yesterday
You brushed a mother's legs,
  brightened a father's smile.
Tonight
You are the razor-blade in the
  apple I bit.

Gisela Grussmayer
COUNTRY MUSIC FAN
Yes it's true I love them all
Kristofferson, Bare and Hall
their music I like to play
wherever I go, sit or stay.
I listen to Charley Pride, the
  Statler Brothers
Chet Atkins, Merle Haggard and
  many others.
If I had at work a bad day
They lift me up, make me say:
You're the greatest for me
Make me laugh and sing and be
happy and in a good mood again
no matter if it's sunshine or rain.
Sometimes I wish I could write
  like you
I'll try it and maybe you like it too.

Wm. Douglas Mefford
RECONCILIATION
Whenever, in the night
you call for me
  I am gone,
  do not seek me.
No more speak my name
and see me run
to meet your smallest want.
  I am gone,
  torture me no more.
Your beauty lingers in my mind
as I quest these empty roads
for a surcease from your memory.
  I am gone,
  think of me but

do no look, I have hidden
from your sight, for
  I am gone.
It is the only way I can
survive, knowing we are apart.

Susan Lillis Dilisio
SORROW
Sorrow touched on all of us
A gradual hurt, enfolding into a
  deeper one.
The mystery of it all, leaving me
  with a sense of fright
My Belief questioned once again,
  giving way to doubt.
Anger, confusion and fright, all
  feelings combined
A part of life as we all know, but
  do not want to face
The loss of a loved one.
Time will help, but never quite
  forgetting.

Anger lingers on and bitterness
  could easily remain
Someone is taken away from us
  and we feel the pangs of
  lonliness.
The absence of that someone
  makes the lonliness acute at
  times
Until finally acceptance of His
  will is achieved.
Acceptance, in turn, creates a
  much greater strength
One must try to turn the page of
  time, as we look forward to a
  brighter day
One is gone, but not that far
  away.
A period of working and waiting
  until the final reunion.

Andrea M. Turoczy
MARIA JOHNSTONE
Maria Johnstone, a career must
  you choose?
Will you be a seamstress, a
  teacher, or a mother instead?
"But I'm not very nimble with
  needle and thread."
"The other two careers are good
  don't you see, but,
  those careers are just not for
  me."

"A women's career choice is a
  select few."
"I don't really like that how about
  you?"
"Although, you're a man I really
  don't think that you'd
  understand
for a man, is a king that controls
  all the land."

"Oh excuse me Miss Maria, what
  will you be?"
"An angel in heaven or a saint
  maybe."
Oh it's not quite so humorous,
  don't you see?
A Dentist, a Dentist is what I
  want to be.

My ears now must be deceiving
  me.
A Dentist is a man's career, oh
  Maria don't you see.
Yes, I understand but I have no
  fears.
But Maria you won't compare not
  even come near.

Our World's Best Loved Poems

I have just as good a chance as you,
Just as well as the other men too.
It seems to me you're not too shy,
So go ahead Maria, give it a try.

Try, oh try, yes indeed.
But, dear sir I plan to succeed.

Theresa G. Pittman
A MOTHER'S DAY WISH
For all the things you do and say
I know I'll never be able to repay
One tenth of what I owe to you
It should be Mother's Day the
whole year thru.

Maybe then I'd find the time each
day
To tell you what I'd like to say
How much I wish I only could
Change all the bad things into
good.

I'd make you young and strong
again
I'd bring back Daddy to be your
friend
You'd never be lonely and you'd
never feel pain
There'd only be sunshine and
never rain.

Your children would prosper and
bring you no sorrow
You'd never have to worry and
fear tomorrow
Grandchild would love you and
learn from you knee
All the wise things you tried to
teach me.

If only somehow I could find a way
To grant you these wishes
everyday
But for now I hope you're able to
feel and see
These wishes are part of the love
for you that's in me!

HAPPY MOTHER'S DAY

Cathe
UNTITLED
... When
I've no time
for forming rhymes
(those metred, syllabic treasures),
my mind's a store
deluged with lore;
Each breath I take's in measure.

But ...
if I'm asked
(a simple task)
to put my pen to paper,
I toil in vain.
My noble aim
is brought to naught; belaboured.

What
remedy—
this malady?
What end these endless sighs?
I must needs be
what's Poetry;
while penning, improvise ...

Mary Joe Thompson
SINGLE MOTHERS
Raising children on your own
so many say,
that's not a home

The critics choice, a mom and
dad
then a sound foundation your
children shall have

So with guilt and sorrow you
fumble along
masking your face that you are
strong

All the decisions are yours alone
on how to manage a peaceful home

Just where do I go, how much can
I do
their entire future depends on you

With great endurance you get
through the week
you ache from your head right
down to your feet

How much can I take, there's no
time for me
both mother and father I just
can't be

As time is the healer of confusion
and pain
you tackle your problems with
far less strain

There's a sound in your house
you haven't heard for awhile
it's love in a laughter, a child
with a smile

Astonished and thrilled you just
can't believe
I've made it! I've won! by just
being me!

Nora R. Enyart
VANITY
How few know the simple beauty
of a gentle rain,
Or the secrets it brings to a
listening ear.
How subtle are its promises and
how honest its answers.
One drop portrays the meekness
of mankind with its trembling
vanity.
Its splendor lies apparent to those
who would see.

Margaret Spence
**Beyond the Setting Of
Life's Sun**
When life's sunset days have come
Things of earth grow really dim.
Things we might have treasured
once
Now seem to have been just a
whim.

And as the twilight deepens
Heavenly things grow more bright
And anticipation grows the greater
As we seen the heavenly lights.

And oh the anticipation of seeing
Jesus
and the Father on the throne so
white,
Everyone giving you a welcome
As you come to the end of night.

Oh, the joy to hear the Father
As he turns to you to say,
"Welcome home, my child. I've
been waiting
Just to have you here to stay.

For there will be no night here,
Just an eternal day
Where all will be rejoicing and
praises
And every tear will be dried away."

Sarah Marie Edwards
IF I WERE FREE
If I were free,
What would I be?

Would I be a cloud in the sky,
Or a bird that flies high.
Would I be a dove full of love,
Or a person from above.

If I were free,
What would I be?
Would I soar high like a bird
And not say a word.
Or would I fly like a plane
With the sky my domain.

If I were free,
What would I be?
I could be a bird on a sunny
                    summers day,
Or I could be a ship and sail to
              some place far away.
I could be a lost sail floating on
the sea,
Or I could be a ship and sail to
              some place for away.
I could be a lost sail floating on
the sea,
Or I could be a clown that shouts
out with glee.

I wonder ...
If I were free—
What would I be?

Paulette Samuel Murray
**Words From Mother—
Unborn Child**
Hey, little baby
growing inside of me
Everyday I'm dreaming and
wondering what you will be!
When you stretch your arms and
kick your legs,
it lets me know that you're
alive and it won't be long
before you'll soon be in my arms.
Only then little baby will I know,
what *you* came out to be.

Alice Madsen
HANDS
Hands ... so quiet and relaxed ...
So sensitive ...
To my heart, soul and mind
Hands that gently and quietly
guide
Yet firmly direct me to where I
should go
Lord, ... let my hands
Be equally as sensitive ...
To his wants ...
    To his needs ...
        To his hurts ...
            To his desires ...
To openly respond to his love
With the gentleness ...
        delicateness ...
            and kindness ...
He has shown ... me ...

Ramona Beth Parsons
LOVES GROWS
As the birds fly
As the wind blows
Through the blue sky
My Love grows.

The happy sounds
Of the dew drops
Soft as the ears of a hounds
The feet of time slowly stop.

I melt in your arms
Everytime you reach for me
With you I never fear harm
Because your Love is plain to see

So whisper soft
Your words of Love

Take me to heights
Of worlds above.
Bright lights explode
Inside my head
As if by code
My feelings are said.

It's for you
And you alone
The things I do
My words, My thoughts adorn.
My Love grows.

Gwendolyn Guth
LIBERATOR

*Dedicated to my maternal
grandmother——"Gram"——
because of her loving interest and
encouragement throughout my life.*

Silence seeks to find me when the
Pressures of life blind me and
Unending duties bind me like
A fettered captive's chain.

Silence taps me lightly, offering to
Loose the tightly fastened bond,
but
In the rat race of my mind
I heed her not.

Silence is persistent, though my
Busy life's resistent to
Deceleration; "rest" is just
Another abstract word.

Silence does not mock me as
I beg her to unlock me when
At last the pressures cause me to
Implore my world "Slow down!"

Silence soft caresses me with
Stillness, peace; redresses me
With strength to face Tomorrow
by
Uncluttering Today.

Silence knows that only she is
Keeper of the special key which
Frees a tangled, anxious mind
Without making a sound.

Linda Lee Chmiel
RUINED
Did you come to watch the
wounded bleed to death?
My wounds are all exposed
You left nothing intact
You pierced and penetrated all of
me
The flesh left without sensations
My soul lost
My spirit weeping and confused
My heart aching but beating
Beating life into a lifeless being

Faye P. Parker
IN THE GARDEN
What I saw in the garden
Would make a tree smile,
A grasshopper would laugh
And a frog jump a mile!

The pumpkins would grin
Wearing Hallowe'en hats
And lizards would folk-dance
What d'ya think of that?

Crickets would stop Chirpin'
The grass'd turn Handsprings
The gopher would eat turnips
Isn't that the silliest thing?

What I saw in the Garden
'Twas a pretty sight to see

221

A host of yellow Butterflies
Givin' a party-just for me!

Gail Magee
HE

---

*This Poem is dedicated to my
Dad, Edwin V. Maul who is more
then just my dad, he's also
someone I love and respect and
owe my existing to.*

He will alway's be mine,
He was there when the sun
    wouldn't shine,
He was there when it was raining,
He was there when school time
    came,
He was there when I was sick and
    in pain,
He's here now and you know why
    cause he's my dad
and I'm glad, cause he's here even
    now when thing's
don't alway's, go right!!

Doris Ruth McElroy
LIFE
Keep your feet on the ground
But always keep reaching for the
    stars.
For soon we shall be together, my
    love.
When you look at the moon, I will
be looking at the same one
and we will always be together.
For time will pass over in just a
minute or second
and all will be forgotten.
Today is here
Tomorrow is yet to come
and yesterday is gone forever.

Michele Farrant
LIFE'S ESSENCE
If you open your eyes
To look at life as it is,
And not what it was.
You would find that you,
A person of peace of mind,
Loves the life they're living . . .

Maybe when we all can see
That we are the most we can be.
And notice what life,
The life we are living really is'
Then we will be thankful for
    being . . .

Larry Dean Blocher
STORM WATCH
Clouds
Slowly move
Closing in on time
Choking off the sun's warm
    mouth
Whipping up winds that batter as
    they crash through
Having no regard for life
Shadowing the ground
Lucky few
Smile

Debra Lynn Williams
FRIENDS
Friends are people,
who never let you down.
They're always there,
when you have a frown.
They'll do anything you want
    them to,
even when you dare them to.
But most of all,

A friend is one,
Who really show they care.

Michelle A. Streckfuss
LOST MEMORY
I clear off the cobwebs and
Wipe away the dust.
The image is blurry and just
Out of my reach.
I search for streams of light
To illuminate the image I so
Desperately seek.
I search through dark corners
To find the key that will
Reveal the true identity of
Myself.

Albora B. Edwards
REAL REALITY

---

*To my much beloved family;
especially my three sisters known
as Gloria S. Hall, Ika L. D.
Edwards, and Edwenia L. Moring;
whos real love keeps me wanting
to stay in the real world!*

Shattered so often
When being in reality
That I break in pieces
To another world
Without the pain
There I remain
For lots of hours
Almost to the point
Of not returning
Afraid that someday
I will be there
Always to dwell
But as long
As I am brave
I will try
To stay in the real world

James Martin Gau
Frontispiece For a Hymnal
Praise the Lord for what we've got,
    (It is a song which must be sung!)
For when ill-fortune casts it's lot,
    We are still blessed with hands
        and tongue
        To toil for glory, sing for joy
    And rout the Dark-Lord, most
        forlorn
    And worship then the little boy,
    Whose birthright was a crown of
        thorn!

John C. Garcia
EGO
There is a game we all must play
    before we can learn to grow
we have to stand and speak to
    say what we do or think we
    know.
We speak aloud with a
    confidence that shant be
    overthrown
based on insufficient evidence of
    which still remains unknown.
We stand behind a shade of green
    in order to stay in the game
while true wisdom flots aloft
    unseen as we rescue our pride
    from meaningless shame.
With prompt reply our mistakes
    we mend to justify what we
    defend.
Thus we fail to ask the questions
    and go unsatisfied
purely because we're afraid to
    step out from behind our

foolish pride.
When the game is no more a
    priority in our day
social life we seek wisdom from
    the wise with authority to
    enhance this wonderful new
    light.
The growing starts when we
    knock down the wall and
    admit to ourselves we know
    nothing at all.
By now the name of the game is
    what you should know it
    stands so clear and its called
    ego

Anthony Ferrero, Jr.

Anthony Ferrero, Jr.
smart
i've seen girls
that are pretty,
that are cute
but i would describe
your looks as "smart"—
a fine-polished statue face
that would brighten
the most intellectual
    bookshelf—
but you can't be bought
at an auction,
or seen in a museum;
you have a look
that can be attained
or approached,
only thru years and years
for arduous research.

Nancy M. Stallard
NO WORDS
The trees rustle with the sound
    of winter,
The air is cool and brisk,
    few leaves still hang on the
    tree branches as winter befalls
    us.

As we walk bundled warm hand
    in hand, our hair blowing in
    the wind,
We glance at one another, we
    smile,
    no words.
We walk on, our feet rustling the
    leaves under them, that lay on
    the ground.
We stop and sit on a bench under
    a tree,
    we kiss,
    no words.
We sit for a period of time
    embraced.

As evening approaches hand in
    hand we start for home.

A. J. Shaffer
THE CHAMELEON
I've spent lonely days
with pen in hand.
I write of love,
I write of man.
Yet no one knows,
And no one sees.
The real person hiding
inside of me
The things I write
Some funny and light
Is my coat, my Chameleon,
Hiding pain and fright.
Me, the Chameleon you don't see
I hide well among the words.

Elijio Juarez
LOVE
When Heaven selected you,
    angels smiled
To put such beauty and softness
    all in one child.
The wonders of the world
    content and mysterious
Just to make room for you have
    been put aside so serious.

The wonders of love and secrets
    of beauty,
Things that make Heaven above,
Were given to you for you to give
To someone else with love.

If only the earth stood still to
    talk and be with you,
The treasures and the sweetness
    would become so real.
My heart and soul would
    experience the dream I feel.

If all the world were right to
    suppliment us in sight,
How many people would be with
    light.
Let me say this as I know
You brighten my day and night.

Jeffrey McDonald
I AM A BIRD TODAY
I am a bird today
    I s'll fly away
Not to see, my company
    above the ruinous seas
I s'll gather innocence
    among the open air
My wings a mighty grasp at
    length
    ——this sanctuary cares

I'll fly alone today
    to nestle feeling among despair
Cheers! to strength in quiet play
    I am a bird today

Jeanne Louise Morgan
FRIEND

---

*To Dr. James William Gambell,
for whom this haiku was written*

Walk happy through life
May your flowers never wilt,
Your song never end

David Yanniello
JUMP HOLLOW HIGH
Since we have accepted the
    reasons,
For keeping our cars off the roads,
Jump Hollow High leaped to ten
    winning seasons,
'Cause no cars have been hitting
    their toads.

Elizabeth Clark
RIBBIT
How many times
Have I met
The Prince
Who was really a frog
And the frog
Who was really a Prince?

There's a lesson . . .
But I've yet to learn it.

I still want the Prince frog
Instead of the frog Prince.

I deserve to be covered with warts.

Paula Fisher Galson
A HERO'S CHOICE
Dear friend departed . . . much
    too soon . . .
Who gave his life one afternoon
When crisis and disaster reigned
As two small boys engulfed in
    flames
Reached out for someone's
    helping hand
'Twas then God made a large
    demand . . .
Two young lives saved—another
    lost,

He acted without fear of cost;
His heart was weak, he knew it
    well
But, somehow, brave men cast a
    spell
And so he did
And when 'twas done,
He stopped to glimpse the setting
    sun
His time was up, this man so true,
He gave his life for me and you.

Ronald Joseph Flemming Jr.
Graceful Is the Morning
Graceful is the Morning when
    she slowly awakens
rubbing the sleep from my eyes
    she begins to smile
the sun starts to shine, while
    stars quickly dissapear
A "New Day" has begun with the
    turning of the dial . . .

The "Morning Air" is sweet like a
    "Baby's Breath"
The grass is soft beneath my feet
Like a "Beautiful Peacock"
    spreading it's "Colorful Plumage"
The "Morning" spreads it's
    "Wings" and brushes away my
    sleep . . .

The "Flowers" open their petals
    and "Greet the Sun"

The "Leaves" slightly rustle at the
    "Wave of her Hand"
Each and every morning is the
    beginning of a new day
To hear a bird sing, to see the
    stretching land . . .

Birds in the trees, and birds in the
    sky
All their lovely voices fill the
    warming air
The "Morning is Life" renewing
    itself; a "Time of Peace"
A time to open our hearts, and
    start the day with care . . .

Ralph Chenoweth Reynolds
EVE IN THE PARK
In the chill air she sits
combing her hair. Snow
falls gently and rests
in little mounds upon
her breasts.
Some forgotten sculptor
left her there, where
alone she must spend her
endless days and endless
nights. She seems indifferent
and comtemptuous to stares
of shivering people passing
by, some with compassion
who would shed their cloaks
to cover her. But still
she sits and still snow
falls and fills the little
valley in her naked lap.

Frank Leonard
Hiara Pirlu Resh Kavawn

*It is to the Indian Melanie That I
dedicate my poem*

A mournful soldier walked upon
The smoking, broken land
He sighted faded imagery
And held it in his hand

A tearful wind blew up behind
And stole his prize away
With hollow eyes and tattered soul
The soldier walked away

He came upon an Indian
Nestled in an empty tree
He watched her hair begin to
    dance
Then die soft on the breeze

He bent down to touch her
Offering water from his well
But fingers passed through
    crimson air
Her body was thin shell

He wandered hills and valleys
Until he came upon a lake
He plunged into the waters
His shattered life to take

But the Indian had been waiting
    there
And took him by the hand
She disappeared when she was
    done
And he woke dry on the land

The soldier became a landmark
For all the world to see
But no one ever realized
The soldier was the tree

Lucille Besch
FIRE AND WATER
Reverberating echoes of sparks—
Synthesized streaks-and-spools of

black
Where their fatal footsteps fell.
They raged roared made rigid the
    soft
Melted the strong and still
    unsated
Etched even the empty earth
Underneath unshapen.
Unrelenting rain swirls-and-
    swells then stops.
My life axed to ashes the
Fearful frustration fixed frozen—
Standing still tear torn and tired—
One moment-madness rainbow
    preens—
Points—to what was once my
    house.

Cathy Barulich
AS LONG AS I LIVE
For me there is only you
And nothing that you could do
Will ever change the way I feel
I know my love for you is real
From now until my dying day
I know my love for you will stay
Ever burning, shining bright
Every minute, day and night
Others may give me a try
But I will always pass them by
For no-one else could ever be
All that you have been to me
My feelings are sincere and true
My life will be spent loving you
And I hope one day you'll see
You can feel the same for me
But whether or not you do
I know that I belong to you
For you are one of a kind
And I have made up my mind
To stick it out through thick and
    thin
And never give up or give in
So enjoy all I've got to give
For I'm yours—as long as I live.

Raquel Fuller
GAMES
Why the Games?
Is that the way it has to be?
Why can't there be honesty
    between you and me?

The world has changed so much,
    but why can't you and I still
    touch?
I know that we live in a
    promiscuous society.
Yet, this is a real tragedy.

Everyone doing his or her own
    thing.
No matter who causes the pain.
Singles bar's, Disco's, everyone
    looking for heaven knows.

Dancing, laughing, drinking,
    having fun, searching for
    someone.
You flirt, smile, bat your eyes,
    knowing that you have to try,
    to see if this is the one, who
    can give you so much fun.

Is he willing to be freaky, free and
    fine as vintage wine?
That's a chance you'll have to
    take, and hope you don't have
    something strange when you
    awake.

There are no set rules, cheating,
    reneging and knowing you'll
    lose.

I don't like the game, I refuse to
    play.
I like it the old fashioned way.

Where boy meets girl, and takes
    her out on a date.
She primps and get's pretty, and
    would never be late.
Hand-in-hand they go, off to see
    the movie show.

He opens the door and helps her
    in, just like a true gentleman.
She gives his a dazzling smile,
    and thanks him with lady like
    style.
This is the way it should be,
    relationships built on honesty.

Emilia L. Bave
FUN AND FARCE

*In memory of children who have
been injured or sick, due to
sadistic actions of some people.*

Hallowe'en is here again,
It's time for trick or treat.
In past years, this tradition
Was always pretty neat.
Spoiling this delightful time
Are some folks "real mean"
That no one had suspected
Would come upon the scene
And stuff some dangerous
    elements
In pieces of the candy
That was dropped in children's
    bags
And they thought it was dandy.
Then we heard of tragedies
That happened after eating . . .
It's too bad culprits weren't caught
And given a good beating!

Ronald H. Watson
WHERE WILL WE GO?
We fight each other with guns,
kidnap the rich mans sons, we
live our lives in poverty, is this
a total democracy? We tire
ourselves just to survive, and
hope our sons at war are alive,
we push and swarm like flies,
and try to top each other's lies.
We live in a world fast and
hectic, live in shame and don't
regret it. We hate our president
we elect, we put him there
don't forget. We envy those
that are full of wealth, and
despise those with perfect
health, we play the game of
living, always taking and
hardly giving, well hear me
world and hear me loud! This
world is not roses nor a cloud,
it stinks, it's dirty and that's
the truth, those sophisticated
broads looking for youth.

And you over there with your
long joint, get up from there
weed ain't the point, Mr.
Complaint that's all you do is
say this world ain't right for
you. Well get off your butt and
try to show. What you want or
do you know? Mr. Man a half
done pimp, making sure your
whores don't split! Mr. Rich
you've earned your keep, stop

223

your bragging and go to sleep!
Ms. Right you ain't so civil,
your mind is filled with
violence and evil! I can't do
anything but speak my piece,
but my friends, I've reached my
peak! That's right I am tired of
this fuss and strain, this world
is a down right dirty shame.
We learn of past in our text,
never knowing what's up next.
And this world we live in at
this time, will be history, about
the crime, about the selfish
dumb and greed, that's the
book my kids won't read, little
we have to show tell me
friends, where will we go!

Gladys M. Arquette
ENCORE
October, gracious lady that you are
Lavish gifts of beauty you bestow
And even when it's time for you
    to leave
You give us Indian Summer ere
    you go.

Indian Summer, October's final
    fling,
She leaves us tho' we're calling
    out for more
A few more of those heavenly,
    golden days
October, please—encore, encore,
    encore.

Paula Dow
**A Little Boy's Christmas
Prayer**

*This poem was especially written
for my grandson, Joseph Anthony
Collins of Amesbury,
Massachusetts, when he was four
years old.*

Santa's coming down my way,
I know he'll visit me;
For I have been a real good kid;
I'll sit upon his knee.
He'll ask me if I mind my folks—
I know I try each day.
I help my Mommy all I can
And don't get in the way.
I clean my room and keep things
    neat
'Cause that's what I must do
If I want Santa to appear—
My things must look like new.
I hope he'll bring the things I want
And stuff for Mom and Dad,
Also, for my sister, too,
The best we've ever had.
But, I know what's more
    important now
Than any Christmas giving;
And that is being happy with
The home in which I'm living.
I love my family very much;
I couldn't ask for more.
But, Santa—you may welcome here
The Christ Child we adore.

Lorna Tallent Kidwell
**"Vengeance is Mine",
    Sayeth the Lord**
He was set to pull the trigger,
Set to kill his enemy
As he waited for his arrival,
Crouched there behind the tree;

For the man had killed his
    brother
And the feud must go on
Until no member of either family
Lived to face another dawn;

But a snake lurked in the bushes
And it struck him in the head
Just as he pulled the trigger—
The shot went wild and *he* was
    dead.

"Vengeance is mine", sayeth the
    Lord of hosts,
"Vengeance is mine",
But we humans keep forgetting
So we have to pay the fine.

DelVina McCormick
STILL BUSY

*In loving memory of my brother
E. V. "Bud" JACKSON, who's
Strength, Courage, and Faith in
God is an inspiration to us all.*

Our eyes were filled with unshed
    tears
we watched him weaken through
    the years,
He could make us forget he
    wasn't well
as he sang in a voice, clear as a
    bell.
He laughed and joked and just in
    fun
he just had to tease someone,
He knew just what made all
    things tick
there was never a thing, he
    couldn't fix.
A toy truck, a big truck, a giant
    machine
the finest mechanic you've ever
    seen,
No mystery man his brother of
    mine
he's very well known as honest
    and kind.
Like the best part of each of us
that's how Bud seemed to be,
I'll bet he's busy helping God
through all Eternity.

Svenska
A THOUGHT

*Dedicated to: My children's
Daddy, Stan, with loving memory
in our life together and a
memento to posterity of our
times as one. Your loving ways
are still etched within my mind
and heart.*

A breeze through my hair and
    across my face;
The same one that moves my
    curtains of lace,
The tempered tone of a clock
    that strikes three,
Stirs within me an old loves'
    lambent symphony.

James Griffin
HARLOT
A wig capped her head
Gum sugared her mouth
Eyeliner hemmed her eyes
Lipstick blanketed her lips
Eye shadow veiled her eyelids.

He tongued her cheek, lipped her
    ear, palmed her shoulder
Sweat beaded his arms
Dirt and grease grimed his wrists
Wine molded his breath
Incense perfumed his room
When she thought that he wasn't
    looking at her, she snatched his
    watch

". . . you bitch!", he boomed
Her eyes ballooned
She dropped his watch, jetted up
    off his couch and darted to the
    door
With his fist clasping his lamp,
    he bolted after her.

Sabina Landavazo
A HALLOWEEN NIGHT

*I dedicate this poem to the eighth
grade class of 1983-84 at St.
Raymond Catholic School,
Downey, California.*

The moon above cast a shadow
on the houses down below, the
kids were ready, bags in hand,
they trudged on through the
snow. Nothing would stop
them from getting their treat,
for this they had been waiting
for what seemed a thousand
weeks.

Karen Sue Dixon
**Please Help Me, I'm Just A
Child**
Take me in your arms,
For I am just a child.
I'm so lonely and confused,
All the people are so wild.
Hold me close, please let me know,
Will this confused child ever grow?
Help me to find a peaceful place.
Where there is a lot of room, and
    loving space.
Please listen to my words,
All I want is to be heard.
Comfort me the whole night
    through,
Together we may find a peace we
    never knew.

Margaret Adams
THE VALLEY OF MEMORY
Come with me to that valley
Merriam Gilbert Library
Come with me to that valley
That valley of memory
And sit with me by the brookside
Sharing the peace with me.

Come with me to that valley
The valley of memory
And feel the warmth of noontide
And the humming of a bee.

Come with me to that valley
The valley of memory
And watch the stars and the
    moon glow
And reach out your hand to me.

Joan Kalbakdalen
SHADOWS AND TWILIGHT
Life flows and ebbs with the
    winds of time
Each day that passes will never
    return
A moment lingers and then it is
    gone

Fleeting illusions that dance in
    your mind

The stirring of leaves on a
    summer day
Brings to me a whisper from the
    past
The trace of a dream unfinished
    and faded
I close my eyes and the moment
    is lost

So swiftly flows the sand of time
Never still, going onward toward
    forever
If I stop and look behind me
I am overcome by the regret
Of half finished dreams that
Should never have been

So I look onward and upward
    toward twilight and shadows
Trying to hold in my hands
    something so precious and
    special
That it will be spoiled if I try to
    put it into words

Memories and dreams entertwine
    in a vision
Of what I had hoped for, but
    never could have
Only Jesus hand loving and
    gently consoling
Brought me at last to my
    Promised Land
Then I could stop looking at
    shadows and twilight
And walk in the sunshine, just
    holding His hand

Rebecca T. Urrutia
FOG
The fogs illusive mass
Makes things look like the past

Phyllis A. Dodge-Grainger
I AM

*Dedicated to Sir. Hollyhock
Slayer, the silhouette in my
dreams, March 4, 1984. Happy
Birthday Edward. Inspired and
created at the meadow on August
6, 1982.*

Sometimes things are not said
Because they can Not be said,
    For verbal acknowlagement
Means mental acceptance of
Sometimes painful reality.

My words are like thumbs
    In the dam of my soul,
And if I but utter one sound
    The thumbs will become
        weakened,
Allowing the waters of my
        emotions
    To surge forward,
Without logical direction,
    Exposing myself
To the cruel judgement
    Of my own inner desires.

I can't say I want you
Yet, you are beside me when I walk
I can't say I need you
Yet, you are near me when I sleep
I can't say I love you
Yet, my heart cries only for your
    warmth
I can't say I am yours
    Yet, I AM . . .

224

Our World's Best Loved Poems

Barbara Wirkowski
Magic Night Of Halloween

Magic Night of Halloween
Mystery you adore.
Magic Night of Halloween
Someones' at my door.
Afraid to open, Afraid to peek.
Afraid to know whose behind
    that creak.
Magic Night of Halloween, you
    mystify me so.
Magic night of Halloween
Full of Mystery, this I know.

Kimberly Dolan
THE TEAR DROP IN LIFE

I want to be the first to
            smile,
            cry,
            and to mostly wave
            goodbye . . .
I want to be able to leave my line
    of beloved companions first,
    because till now in all of my
    most valuable knowledge I
    have not yet learned the most
    important meaning of letting go.
I want to do this in order to avoid
    the countless unhappy pains
    that I would have to feel if I
    was the last to have to wave
    godbye—
            and be left alone without
    anyone,
            to wave goodbye to ME.

Del Neumeister
AUTUMN

The wind that blows makes it
    seem colder than it is.
The dampness adds to the feeling
    as it hangs in the air.
The brown and green leaves
    blowing makes my heart race,
    as I think of a time when I
    might run, jump, and shout.
The half barron trees make me
    want to run and climb to see
    eyes that wish they had never
    seen time.
These sights and things I feel
    have a way to make a heart feel
    things that it hasn't felt or
    wanted to feel in years.
As I stumble through the tight
    wound grass I think . . . what
    a shame it must be to never be
    where this could be.

Michael D. Moe
HEAR THEM?

A
paranoic
explosion
of
unrealistic
proportion,
tearing
at
his
life;
because of
the conversations
of those
who
don't
hear the
bomb,
or their
own voices
and what they are saying;

as heard
in his ears
of the dying,
and the dead.

                        No.

Mary Ninow Ryan
TRICK OR TREAT

The sun shone bright on
    Halloween Day preshadowing
    the night when goblins play,
Stalling the thought of witches
    and cats, grimacing Jack-o-
    laterns, fluttering bats.
The hugh black cauldron, filled
    with the brew, the stinking,
    horrible witches stew.
Soft little flutterings in the corner
    of the eye, suddenly a ghost
    floats slowly by.
Clattering, chattering, followed
    by moans, introduces a
    skeletons bones.
Amid clanking of chains, wound
    all around her, down the street
    comes a frightening monster.
Even the wind joins in the terror,
    blowing and whistling, making
    it scarier.
The streets are deserted, the
    lights all turned out,
Only those foolish at heart are
    about.
Don't take any chances on this
    spooky night, stay in your
    house and lock the doors tight.
Don't venture out where the
    goblins play, stay snug inside
    till All Saints Day!

David Lee Ruppert
THE BUTTERFLY

---

*To Linda Margaret with love and
thanks for her inspiration and
belief in me.*

There was once but a lonely
    lowly worm,
Having little self worth and
    feeling forlorn.

Feeling so bad he wound himself
    into a cocoon,
Giving up he resigned himself to
    his tomb.

By his actions he was to finally
    transform,
Growing into a magnificent
    butterfly he was reborn.

Arising like the Phoenix from the
    ashes of his despair,
To soar and fly in peaceful blue
    skies where only eagls dare.

For all of his elusiveness he is
    learning to share,
Taking time to be with those
    with whom he does care.

Flitting about as a buterfly does
    he has found,
That he brings pleasure to those
    who want him around.

May he always land softly on
    your tender heart,
So you may share your love even
    though your apart.

When you are apart you need feel
    neither sad or blue,

Just think of him and his heart
    and mind will embrace you.
Though you may be separated by
    many a mile,
When he thinks of you he will
    remember your loving smile.

He will always love you though
    he may flit and fly,
For that is My nature for I Am
    that Butterfly.

Gaynell Ott Wimer

Gaynell Ott Wimer
Bits and Pieces Bring Love

---

*To Margaret A. Flick, a dear and
loyal friend, who stood by and
inspired me to write, while I was
sick and recuperating, in August,
September, and October of 1983.*

It was soon Halloween with
    costumes galore
Witches and cats, and candies in
    store,
All the pumpkins sat straight in a
    row
Bright orange and plump and
    ready to glow.

One little pumpkin sat in a box
All alone and out of stock,
It was so small, it could not have
    grown
Taking the shape of an old dog
    bone.

Folks bought all the pumpkins
    except for it
So it landed in back, with the
    pieces and bits,
It was cold back there, it needed
    lit up
Scared to death like a new born
    pup.

The lad begged for food, the store-
    keeper knew
His family was poor, but what
    could he do?
"Go back of the store" the keeper
    said,
"There is bits and pieces by the
    old tood shed."

The lad gathered bits and pieces
    of scrap, the pumpkin too,
Put it into a bag with his spirits
    renewed,
He hurried home to tell his pa,
His sisters and brothers, and even
    his ma.

The little pumpkin had a place

Out by the mail-box and near the
    gate,
Slits for the eyes, a wide mouth
    and nose
Being loved from a poor family,
    and bits and pieces of love
    showed.

Frances Hendrix Manley
My Darling Little Pixie

Darling little Pixie, Damion, with
    your elfish grin you bring back
    my youth and childish
    laughter, and my soul can see
    through innocent, trusting eyes
    once again.

In your laughing eyes I can see
    the reflection of my Christ, and
    Angels lingering ever so near.
    You and I share a secret as
    hand in hand we grow. Of little
    pixies dancing in the forrest, in
    the quietness of the night, and
    powerful forces of God's angels
    flying all around you, as you
    and I take our fanciful flight.
    For, my darling, we can dance,
    and we can sing in the
    darkness of the night. and we
    can fly over the mountains,
    and the water ever so blue, safe
    and secure, riding on an Angel's
    wing. And through innocent
    eyes, I can see the reflection of
    my King.

Harold Olsen
MISTY MORNING

---

*To the memory of Belle Murphy,
Principal of Bernard Moose
School, Chicago, Il.*

The misty fog hangs low over the
    roof tops,
The objects that you see each
    day, are shrouded in mystery.
For though you stare and strain
    with all your might,
The misty morning makes things
    out to be not all your eyes see.
The lights in the houses, that are
    usually so pleasant,
Now look like the eyes of some
    savage animal, about to devour
    you.
The street lights have a halo,
That sends shivers of anticipating
    dread,
In the eerie, misty morning light.
The cars that come are but eyes
    that barely shine,
With their engines making it's
    weird cry in the misty morning
    light.
The streets are like long black
    tunnels,
With the luminous eyes of the
    predators, lying in wait.
The chill of the dampness sends
    messages up and down your
    spine,
And you shiver, but not really
    from the cold.
It is the sense of unreality that
    you feel on this misty morning.
When you see through the eyes
    of the imagination,
And not through the eyes of reality.
There is something strange about

225

a misty morning,
For though you shiver and shake,
Though you strain your eyes to
    see,
And what you see, is not what
    the eyes see,
But what you imagine you see,
    and though you fear,
Yet you are glad to see the misty
    morning's eerie light,
For then the imagination is on a
    holiday.

Debbie Kay Peacher
YESTERDAY
    As I sit here alone
    Reality gradually fades
    and memories and moments
Once again become my world,
    I escape to a time
        of you
        of me
        of us
I can see you
holding me close
Chasing away my fears,
tenderly kissing me goodnight.
    All of these things and more
    closed in my mind
and for a moment
    I can almost believe.
        Then tears burn my eyes
and slowly I remember it was
    yesterday . .

Martanne Louise Louthan
RESTLESS

Salud! To Mariellen's curiosity!

Flitting from place to place-an
    uncontrollable urge!
Natures calling the psyche's
    colorful mood barometer.
Feelings demanding curious,
    inquisitive imagination to
    travel rampantly.
A never-ending freedom search to
    determine one's changeable
    secrets.
Wandering needfully to
    contradict a lethargic nature!

Sliding down rainbows!
Plopping on bouncy, cottony
    clouds!
Peeping o'er the edge to
    deliciously examine an
    ambitious thought!

Ivan Hill
Help Me Find The Way
I have tumbled in life's ocean
I have drifted from the shore
I have walked that lonesome
    valley
And I've stumbled even more

I have seen forbidden places
I have tasted life's sweet wine
I have taken all the wrong roads
And I've done it everytime

Broken hearts, I have seen many
And I've even had a few
But I have picked up all the
    pieces now
And I give my heart to you

So as I journey, as I wander
As I ramble, as I roam
I have always been a sinner Lord,
Help me find my way back home.

Debora Chaney
A HALLOWEEN ODYSSEY
As the autumn leaves fall
I hear a voice
Is it yours
Or a monster
Of Halloween night?
The night of ghosts
And goblins
I turn
To see what's behind
I see them
Creepy little objects
Coming up
To catch me
Oh, they got me!
Before I rang the doorbell
They got me!
The creepy little things
Steal my bag of candy
Now, I ask you
Was this a trick?
Or a treat?

Dan Goettsche
THE LAMENT
I see a man
    lowly and crippled,
Remembering
    when he stood
    tall and proud—
    Arapaho, Sioux—
When his home
    was boundless.

I see a man
    battered and weeping,
Remembering
    the places
    and the names—
    Wounded Knee, Sand Creek—
All the venom
    and indignity.

I see a man
    consumed and wasted;
I see a man
    dying.

E. W. Halaby
This Place Called Eden
Within your spiritual walls
    which encompass some mystic
    yardage
    that to this day defy the records
    of man—
We wandered in easy grace.

Within the vastness of this
    incalcuable space
    Spending our days in total
    harmony
    Spending our moments in tender
    intimacy—

We did live, we did laugh, we did
    love.

Within a realm so real, yet unreal
    Never anticipating such
    unspeakable meditations
    Never knowing rancour among
    our kind—
We were only two, perfectly
    unified, we were one.

Bonnie Weiss
TOTEM POLE
Totem long forgotten, what
    magic have you cast
O'er lands of ancient customs and
    tribes of distant past?
Why do I shiver slightly as I stare
    into your eyes,
And detect a look of sorrow from
    ever-silent cries?
Your wings of painted wood, a
    weary flutter give,
But cannot lift the burden that
    was meant for you to live.
For you have been deserted, left
    behind to tell the story
Of days once drenched with
    folklore and proud established
    glory.
Yet you would rather die than
    stand here all alone,
Serving as a grave, the last
    remaining stone,
Marking bravery and pride, the
    power of great men,
Decayed and gone forever, it will
    never come again.

Maria A. Bailey
I STILL SEE YOU
Far from the east,
In the heart of the west,
I still see you
Between the sagebrush and the
    sky,
With brown dust in my eye,
I see your smile
And feel the warmth of your ice-
    blue eyes.

What magic is it
That brings you here
On the lonely plain
Where even the buffalo
Have all been slain?

High in the midnight sky
The stars still shine
For me and you;
Beneath the concrete and the crust
Of this rich earth,
There is still a tremble of unseen
    power;
In the air and in the water,
There is still a mystic flow
Of life and love
For me and you.

You have crossed the intersection
Of my mind.

P. F. Scheible Jr.
I'M NOT GONNA DIE
Sitting on a cliff in a drunk
    confusion, overlooking vast
    waters' of Hudsons construsion.
The water's so scary as it meets
    the sky, all the trees are
    moving, they want me to die,
    the rock walls want to eat me.

My boots sink in toward natures'
    heart, as I walk in emptyness,
        I'm coming apart.

The minutes are hours,
    the hours a daze,
I see a dim light that appears to
    blaze.
As I walk toward the light,
    there's a new kind of fright.
I'm not gonna die,
                    but live.

Deborah A. Brownell
A RUNAWAYS MEMIORS
To Escape
I ran to the world of the city,
Hungry for its excitement and
    Luxeries
Craving for its passions and way
    of living,
But I soon found out,
The city is cold and Hungry
with cement walls
that devours the Last of the
    Innocents,
Now, I yearn for the past I left
    behind,
I now look for the contentment
    that
I mistook for boredom
and this cold concrete world
will not let me go,
It knows that who I once was
to whom I have become now,
will not go back
cannot go back
For my Heart, that once was
    warm, hungry and alive is now
    a Cold stone cement block;
    within the city.

Suzanne Lippard
FRIENDS FOREVER
Once I met a stranger
We slowly became friends
When we were too close to be
    closer
She gave me more love than
    anyone sends
We shared our deepest secrets
And every problem we'd ever had
When I was down she'd send me
    a smile
Soon I'd forget I ever was sad
I'd have given her anything you
    could dream
Because she meant so much to me
Though it hurts, we both knew
In order for good the bad the
    must be
We had our share of arguments
And even a few fights
But we worked them all out
And were freinds before night
We'll always be friends, no matter
    what
We could never be enemies, we'll
    stick together
I'm making you this promise now
And telling you, we're friends
    forever!

Yvonne Vansickle Smith
DAD IS GONE
I just hung up the phone; they
    said, "your Dad is gone,
Make reservations on the next
    flight home."
It cannot be—I was sure he'd live
    'til spring came,
"Yes, pack my luggage, I must
    reach the plane."

Composure and strength—I must
    be strong for Mom,

"Hello sir, yes, I'm the youngest of
the sons,
You say he did not suffer long,
How well I remember his last
handshake strong."

The flowers—they're his favorite
color,
With love I helped choose
them—along with my brother,
A closer tie than ever we feel for
each other,
Tears flow unashamed just
watching our Mother.

The hymns sung softly—my
watch ticks slower,
As friends—then family pass by
the door,
A peaceful expression covers
Dad's face,
He's surely at rest in God's
heavenly place.

Dad left me honor, justice and
courage as a legacy,
Gentleness, loving kindness and
integrity,
Am I the living legacy left to
build my sons as he built me?
I'll do my best to teach them with
love as he taught me.

Comforting Mom, boarding the
plane, adjusting the seat in haste,
A future vision veils my face—
another time, another place,
When someday MY sons, so far
from home,
Pick up the phone and a voice
says, "your Dad is gone."

Mark Steven Spicer

Mark Steven Spicer
DO I DARE

---

*To Sharon whose measure of
friendship can only be found by
counting the stars above*

Dare I move from where I'm at
within my heart t'ward you
Lest I prove the adage that
'friends can't be lovers too'
Dare I speak unspoken things
that yearn to raise their voice
Lest I seek a love who sings
another's song by choice
Dare I reap the love that's grown
through years of subtle toil
Lest I heap what has been sown
beneath the sun to spoil
Dare I run the age-old risk of
going one step more

Lest there come a wind so brisk it
slams shut your heart's door
Dare I reach beyond the sight
where limits have been set
Lest we each fade with the night
escorted by regret
Dare I chose to have words paired
with feelings at this time
Lest I lose the love that's shared
between your heart and mine

Madge Mullins Wilbanks
THE TOUCH
Questions and doubt
Feel refreshed when God's
answers
Come giving reassurance, solace
A time cleared for thanksgiving

Of life to life
Loved one to loved one
Layman to God's all-knowing
hand
Stretched

To touch, to fulfill dreams
Long seemingly dead
Until now in the reverance
Of given Life once again

Whole, filled with renewed
Strength
Faith
Reinstated, affirmed believing,
belonging.

Megan Edwards
SWEET BREATH
Let me breathe in one breath;
All of Life, all of death;

Let me smile and cry-
Without knowing why;

Let my fear not deceive me—
As I strive to know all;

And with honor endear me;
As I answer each call.

Don't shatter this dream;
Of achieving perfection . . .

Don't fall to the dark prey;
of selfless rejection.

Cynthia Carmen Snow
GRANDMOTHER
at the mailbox she waits
pouch protruding
skin loose about the lower lip
brazen whiskers dimpling the chin
—hormones long since in balance
eyes bright and searching with
watered glances
Social Security? Pension? National
Geographic?

the wind
and rushing traffic

Tammi A. Bolling
MOMENTS TO LOVE
The knot in my stomach turns
again
piercing agony through to my
heart
yet the phone does not ring

I think of the few hours I have
spent alone in your arms
here comes the fear again

Last night you held me close
only for a moment I recall
the tears are merging within
I begin to think I want you to know
the feeling bottled up inside
the struggling starts again

The memories of the past are
here
etching sad scenes in my mind
I shudder the torment is strong

The tears, pain, and fear are
blinding
one romantic moment
I think I'm falling
in
love

William T. Covil
LOST
I am lost.
I am forgotten.
I will remember no more.
The wind has swept my tablet
clean.
I will endeavor no more.
I will exist, without purpose or
path.
As a ship, without rudder, is
twisted and tossed, thus shall
my life be.
What was, is.
What is, is.
That which might have been,
shall never be seen.
The power to change yesterday is
not mine.
The courage to hope for a bright
tomorrow is not here.
There is no magic.
I wish that I might, someday, see
the light.
And do what I know is damned
well right.
But who, please Heaven, will
share the fight?
And not turn and run in
frightened flight?
Kindred spirits, fail me not.
Before this curtain around me falls,
Before I drink of this bitter gall,
Tell me, sweet Jesus, how may I
hold the sweet Sunshine?

Nina Bailey
**November '66 — After
Octoberfest**
From the ancient shores of Africa,
Asia, Asia Minor, and Europe
— the Ghosts, Spirits, Shadows,
Tombs, Shrines, Museums,
Pyramids, Rivers, Mountains,
Spires of Mosques, and many
other related items, all reflect
that the Octoberfest dwells
with us long after October.

The secrets of the Nile at Sunrise
or in the stillness and Blackness
of night, harbor the Ghosts, and
Spirits of many ancient fests,
including Octoberfests.

Atop Mount Entato, Outside
Addis Ababa the vastness
beyond has much to tell of the
very oldest of all "fests".

Bethlehem, Jerusalem, and the
Mount of Olives are always
bursting forth with the wailing
and Spirits from the ancient
Tombs — Rachel still weeping
for her children.
Saint Sofia entombs many Spirits,
and there is forever the Beloved
Spirit, of Paul atop Mars Hill
declaring to the Athenians
their unknown God and that

all nations of mankind are made
of one blood.

Kerri Guilfoil
FOR MOM WITH LOVE
A mother must be a tough job,
Although I don't know what
you're feeling,
Yet, by the expressions on your
face,
Mixed emotions are what you're
revealing.
A long road seemingly endless,
We children who tease and taunt,
A puzzle missing a piece,
I pray you find what you want.
Do you want love? Peace? —
Or is it a happy family for which
you long?
No family is made perfect,
Only work will make it strong.
Maybe someday you'll understand,
The crazy things we do,
We do them for personal reasons,
Not to try to annoy you.
Just think about everyone's feelings,
Don't concentrate on just your
own belief,
You'll realize we don't try to hurt
you,
And I hope that will be a relief.
Think long and hard,
About this poem,
You'll see that no one is perfect,
And neither is any home.

Louise Beaven
STONE

---

*To the glory of God. "Come unto
me, all ye that labour and are
heavy laden, and I will give you
rest." (Matthew 11:28)*

Dry-eyed and silent
They said she was stone
But her heart wept with anguish
All tears ingrown

Elmer Perry Jr.
**Love Was A Dove
Untouchable By Me**

---

*To Leslie, my inspiration of love
and friendship.*

Love was perched on a limb like a
dove,
Out of my reach, untouchable by
me.
Everytime I tried to reach out for
love,
It would fly away to another tree.
I spent days and nights looking
for someone
I could care for. the way I care for
you;
but wherever I searched, I found
no one:
For I've never felt as I do for you.
You brought love down to land
on my shoulder
and to feel its softness upon my
cheek.
Your love has made me a little
bolder
and brought my feelings for you
to a peak.
Love is now a dove that flies over
me,

Bringing your warm, sweet, caring love to me.

Henry David Polite
A SURVIVOR'S QUEST

With wind or snow on bummers row, a station for the indigents to reside.

I committed my dough and drank the flow, for the drinkings it preserves my pride.

Weaving through the air that blew, a migratory move for free hand rides, this odysses brew the exclamable avenue, the address for the retreat's last strides.

The side walk rise like the aroma of rye, there isn't a border for a match.
Swipes the eye view of the sky, like a carpet wall to wall patch.

Levinly, I warily search for a companion,
sums this inequitable tally my share.
drives my faith through hell's deepest canyon, its the drinking that paid my fare.

This chamber of horror I exit by pleas, for terror and degradation are commanding.
Teardrops splattering on my knees, thank God, I must be standing.

A cloud demist there shines the ascending, with fortification no longer the pour,
reveals the comfort of the everlasting blending, my strides slips away that golden door.

Lynn M. Hartz
WHAT IS LOVE

What is love
  Is it something to give,
  Something to take.
Or is it what we share?
Is it possible to love without liking?
  Don't I have to like you first
  See you as a friend
Or can I love you so much?
  That I'll overlook all faults
  And ignore the things
Which in others I would detest?
Does it also blind you to my flaws?
And help to bring out and cause to shine
What is good in each of us.

Louis Peskin
LONELY FLOWER

Like the tree in search of a forest
Only to endure as a lonely flower
A careless heart in life-long sadness
In a ship adrift, The Ivory Tower.

Miracle-miracle, an angelic quest
Of a lonely wayward flower
Midway between heaven and hell
In a fool's ship, The Ivory Tower.

"Only God can make a tree"
He can also make tomorrow
There is no Godless flower-tree
In a man made ship of sorrow.

Awake-awake, the Angels were here
Your nightmare, a timely dream
Head for your little Country Church
Come face to face with HIM.

Irene Dolores Lippert-Hoffman
OH I DO HOPE

Oh how I hope you will always love me for without you life could never be.

I hope that your love will be forever true and that you will never find somebody new.

Oh without you I know not what to do for there's nobody I love but you.

So when you want to love me just feel free for there's no other love but your love for me.

Oh how I hope the future you could see for no one could be happier than we.

I know our troubles will just be a few I hope I will never ever make you blue.

Frances Tenoso
I LOST MY WAY

In going home
  I stumbled,
Then I lost my way

In groping home
  I fell,
Then I wandered on

In seeking home
  I wondered, then
Found my faith again

In finding home
  I smiled, and
Thanked the God above.

John Gardner
SPRINGTIME KNOWS

Springtime knows
What comes and goes
Before, during and after.

It leaves behind
Cold thoughts of mind
Promising new life, summer warmth and laughter.

Love can find or leave us any time of year.
When it happens in Springtime, the loss seems o' so dear.
It does so with much more profundity;
Yet, with the hope of better things to come to me.

A lost love in the Fall
Promises nothing at all
But a cold, cold, lonely Winter.
You can find no warmth within her.

Springtime knows
What comes and goes
Before, during and after;

With promises of
Another love;
Perhaps pain, joy and laughter.

Richard J. Smith
LIFE

Something we're supposed to live.
But do we really?
Do we take time to see each day in its beauty or, are we in too big of a hurry to get from here to there?
Take time to appreciate the small things in life.
A beautiful flower, a refreshing rain.
Or, are we too busy supposedly making a living.
Making money and wasting our bodies.
Not taking time to appreciate what life has to give us, what it has to teach.
Are we really taking time to live that thing called a life?

Roger LeVasseur
THE NEW PARADISE IV

Now all those I love are gone, God has denied me all;
And after darkness, my cloud of unknowing passed away.
Now I know, for God, once enigmatic dream, who to me seemed a remote and never tangible abstraction, now all surrounds me, and I am lifted on that sea, whose Beauty floods my soul!
I dreamed such beauty inviolate fills the universe;
Each space is crammed with crystalline presences.
Awakened now I see it's true!
O no more empty space, o no more time; no more hours to kill,— time is dead, or rather time to God has sped, so fast it's gone from sight!
Now I walk in ecstasy, new born in Jesus' love.
O Birth, O unaborted break through into life!
O ever-changing, always breaking dawn!
O boredom banished! O limped, velvet fog of radiance!
O feeling God who breathes love into my soul!
Never jaded,—more powerful than nightingale, outsinging every tune!
Waters that satiate my heart,— forever filled!

Nicolai Stefan Popescu
Megalopolis Apex (Pastel)

Words: pictures of things, lucid and normal
as pictures hung on the walls of schoolrooms,
illustrating carpenter's bench, birds, animals.

Names are individual, unique
not very comprehensive — like people:
brightness or darkness of sound, confused image, with color uniformly painted,
posters entirely blue, entirely red;
blue or red — the sky and the sea, the ships and the church, and the people in the street.

Oh, New York, compact and glossy,
violet-tinted, violent!
Unchained, disputatious, solemn, aslant
and very twentieth age.
I inhabited a dwelling compact and glossy:
the Hazards' five-level dwelling on Ninety-Fourth East
violet-tinted, but soft
with no relation to the houses in any other megalopolis of the world—
miraculously embalmed the City of the Magnolias,
honey and milk, and VENOM;
inconceivable marvel a morning in spring!

Riverside Church, a new Chartres
with stained glass from Bruges and Rheims tapestries;
Saint Patrick's so lofty in its noble, ivory lace:
whitness ranged from egg-shell yellow to a pearly-gray,
and spires of butter . . .
Oh, New York, compact and glossy, I love you so!

Karen Ann Foster
CHANGE

Gentle hands
  Draw me near
Warm my thoughts
  Caress my brow
    Fondle my body
Hold me securely
Down.
Distort my thoughts
  Cover my eyes
    Possess my body
Force me to run
Away
  From those gentle hands.

Gregory M. Page
WRITER

With undying gratitude for RENE VERNON NICHOLAS

I'm only a courier
For the voices calling inside me
From the outer limits
There comes a spirit
Who guides me in thought

Mildred Kindy
GOD'S TREES

The trees, majestic trees,
They bow and curtsey in the breeze.

Those trunks, they never bend;
On them the limbs and leaves depend.

Their gowns, see how they sway?
They swirl, those emerald robes of state.

Our World's Best Loved Poems

Listen, hear what they say?
They whisper grateful rhymes of
     praise

To God, their Creator,
Who through these trees to me
     now shows

Himself. Is it not so?
By what He's made, Himself
     makes known.

Mary H. Butts
LORI
You were only seven
When you were taken to Heaven.

We miss your Smile
We'll have a Reunion after awhile.

By God's Loving Grace
We, too, will see Him face-to-face.

We promise you, Lori,
We'll see you in Glory.

Rose Ashour
BREAD FOR THE WORLD
Wake up my people
Hear the Word of the Lord!

While millions starve
I store up food
I can't run short
I might feel hungry.

Yet other people cry in pain
Their stomachs gnaw,
Their eyes deep
     in their sockets.
They die.

Do I wish to hear
When my life ends,
"I was hungry,
And you fed me?"

I can assuage their hunger,
How?
Listen, Love, Respond.

Be "Bread for the World."

Jean Morrissette
A CHILD
A baby is a precious gift,
handled like fine china,
given everything needed.
A child is yet fragile,
but very breakable,
still given everything needed and
     wanted.
A teenager is no longer fragile
and is broken many times,
no longer given what is wanted,
but only what is necessary.
An adult is strong like china,
but will never be broken again.
Are they given anything?
Love by broken children.
What more is needed?

Kathleen McStay Wagner
SUMMERS CHILDREN

*This poem is dedicated to my
wonderful children-Adam, Craig,
Amy, and Cory . . . who reminded
me to take a closer look, and my
equally wonderful husband, Dan.*

Golden moments touch my day
As I watch my children at play.
Warm lilac breezes softly blow,
On happy faces all aglow.
Running through the dew tipped
     grass,

My laughing lads and merry lass.
Sharing summers sparkling light,
Filled with wonder at each new
     sight.
Chasing rabbits hopping by,
Sneaking up on a butterfly,
Keeping watch on a robins nest,
From eggs, to nestlings, to flying
     test.
Crawly creatures creeping slowly
     by,
Caught and pondered with
     marveling cries.
Creeks with minnows . . . and
     pollywogs
That will someday be hopping
     frogs.
Seeing these things through their
     eyes,
Helps chase the cobwebs and the
     sighs,
That sometimes cloud a mothers
     sight
And tarnishes summers golden
     light.

Phyllis A. Dodge—Grainger
RAINBOW TALK

*To James A. Gloff the best friend
a lady could ever have (true, no
joke!!!). March 16th 1984. Happy
Birthday Jimmy.*

And so the rains came and went,
leaving the flowers to shake
their delicate heads, and dry
their petals in the sun.
The lizards came out,
seeking a rock to warm
their chilled bodies upon.
The waves of the lake
lay calm awaiting the
birds that come to sing.

And the rainbow stopped at my
     front door.
It came right in and said to me.
"Drop your troublesome thoughts;
let your spirit be as free and pure
as the clouds above the mountain
     tops.
Come with me to see the world
as you have never seen it before.
Taste the colors with your eyes,
feel the beauty with your mind,
and know the peace within your
     heart."

And so I went, and there I am
come and catch me if you can.

Brenda E. Teetsel
THE MORNING WALK
She was old, yet spry as morning,
     when they started out.
Her hands were cool and
     wrinkled. Her heart was warm
     and stout.
They walked into the sunrise,
     through misty air so mild,
This aged, loving woman and a
     crippled child.

With a smile as warm as summer,
     her face grew young and smooth.
The child, who had been limping,
     now ran as grandma cooed.
The mist was all around them.
     They felt it in their hair.
"Don't run too fast now darlin',
     we must be almost there."

"We have to hurry, grandma". The
     child was far ahead.
"We could slow down a little if
     you want us to" she said.
"Well child, we needn't hurry, we
     will not be late.
The mist we just came walking
     through, that was heaven's gate."

"Oh grandma, is it true then, that
     you will not grow old
And I will never walk again with
     a limp, like you once told?"
"Yes child, we are free now. This
     is our land of dreams."
And so they walked on through
     the mist. Heaven's healing
     beams.

Mira J. Reynolds

Mira J. Reynolds
BILL'S FAMILY
Up at five, stirring early today
Our loved ones are going away
The dearest children, their Mom
     and Dad.

They drove off, going afar
God is with them in that car
He will bring them back, and I
     will be glad.

Yet they have not gone, they are
     here
They are in every room
     everywhere
And in my heart, my life, my head.

Patsy Duke
I SEE
I see the church spire's silhouette
     against the moonlit night
I watch the golden sunrise evolve
     from dawn's gray light
I frolic through the pages of many
     treasured books
I catch subtle glances—even hard
     and starey looks

I figure household budgets in
     spite of all the tax
And shop for gaily colored
     clothes among the town's store
     racks
I hear those sweet familiar words,
     "I'm home!" and match the
     voice with face
I watch a ballerina and thrill to
     form and grace

I drive the crowded freeways or
     down a country lane
Count the flocks and herds in
     knee-deep grass, look up and
     trace a silver plane
Etching its flamboyant trail

across the western sky
These things can be
     accomplished only with the
     human eye

So when my sight began to fail
     and seeing was a chore
I sought an ophthalmologist who
     had healed me once before
He snatched my vision from
     eternal darkness—with skill
     restored my sight
My grateful prayers wing their
     way to Heaven day and night

God bless this man. God bless his
     staff. With gentle hands they
     mend me
Into the world, whole again, these
     learned people send me
I could not render this man's
     worth if I had Solomon's wealth
So I pay his fee, then on bended
     knee, I thank God for my health.

Ronnie Tancredi
YOU
When God looked down from the
     heaven.
He was sad at what He saw.
It was barren and empty, with
     nothing at all.
He snapped His fingers and there
     was the universe,
With venus and mars and a
     planet called earth,
But without pretty things what
     was it worth.
So He dreamed up some
     mountains, and they did appear,
With rivers of beauty from there
     to here.
He imagined some flowers so
     pretty and free,
To keep growing and growing for
     all to see.
But flowers need rain so he made
     the sky,
So pretty and blue where, the
     birds can fly.
And there came some oceans so
     fierce and strong,
To last forever and that can be
     long.
And as He looked down from
     above,
He knew what was missing and
     called it love.
So from His eye a silent and
     almost invisible tear grew to be
     you,
The most loving and beautiful
     thing here.

Barbara Lewis
GRANNY WAS A WITCH!
I don't wear a tall, peaked hat.
I don't keep a big, black cat,
Nor within my house, a bat,
But Granny was a witch!

I don't ride upon a broom.
I don't frolic in the gloom.
I chant beneath my breath, no
     rune.
But Granny was a witch!

I prepare no noxious potion,
Nor to Satan swear devotion.
Midnight brings no deep
     emotion.
But Granny was a witch!

I advocate no spell
On those who round me dwell.

But the ancient blood will tell.
And Granny was a witch!

Yes, blood will tell and soon.
Beware, the rising moon
Weaves spells on an astral loom.
And Granny was a witch!

Frances V. Hadden

Frances V. Hadden
THE DREAMER

---

*Dedicated to my mother, Mildred
V. Elliott. Her inspiration enabled
me to find a beautiful world
through verse.*

Down below the orchard, near a
rushing stream, green and
grassy meadows, lies a painter's
dream.
Birds softly singing, with an even
keel, water gently falling, o'er a
water wheel.
The trees on wind a-whispering,
bending boughs down low,
frogs and crickets hopping,
going to and fro.
The honeysuckle's perfume, is
filling up the air, aroma from
the flowers seem to come from
everywhere.

On the fresh green carpet, in a
pleasing way, a dreamer sits
with nature, to brighten up his
day.
So silently he listens to every
little sound, so tenderly those
feeling hands, touch all things
around.
It's a heartfelt moment, as he
makes a pleasant sigh, knowing
that this dreamer, on ears and

nose rely.
The dreamer sits long hours, in
this special place, full of true
contentment, a smile upon his
face.
He's painting a great masterpiece
with just his heart and mind, in
a world of darkness, for this
dreamer, he is blind.

Eleanor Otto
ROLLER SKATING
swishing swinging
swirling reels
seductive saucy
singing of
smoothly spinning
winged wheels
that scour
the delightful
ring
scratching gently
as wave washed
sand
scalloping
scrolling
circling caper
serpentine
scarf
gliding ribband
of flight
scudding
as clouds
of vapor
whishing freely
through
taunting smiling space

Rain Fawn Barett
EYE OF THE PIRATE
As I peer behind this pirate eye
Thru the broken window pane,
I see witches stirring up some
goblin brew
And black cats hissing at ghosts
that fly by.
Caught Dracula in the corner
sipping on some blood red
wine.
And Jack O'Lanterns lit all thru
the room
And seeing Frankenstein eating
on some pumpkin pie.
I looked to the ceiling and seen
witches brooms spell out.
Happy Halloween To All Of You.

Karla Ann Monroe
THERE IS A SWEET JOY

---

*This poem was written in
memory of my grandma, Francis
Estalene Patterson, August 23,
1916 — April 15, 1973., It was
written not long after her death.
It is one of the first I ever wrote
but, is the most special of all.*

Sweet joy there is that often
comes
through our sorrows,
With each passing day lies
a brighter dawn.
The stars may dim
flowers wilt—fade.
Our loved ones to their rest
are laid.
Through our sorrow and griefs
joy may often come,
And onward we'll strive
in search of the sun.

Dixie Lee Knittel
A SENSE OF HUMOR
A sense of humor is really
essential,
To get you through life from day
to day,
It helps you overlook the
unattractive,
Laugh at unpleasantness along
the way.

It helps you cope with the
unexpected,
Tolerate the weaknesses of
human life,
Smile about things that seem
unbearable,
Endure change of fortune, toil
and strife.

Suanne Dunn
GLASSES
If there's one thing I hate,
It's having to wear glasses,
'Cause people just stare,
In all of my classes.
They take a quick peek,
And then have to smile,
And I just want to sink,
Right through the tile.
They can't help it, it's one of their
senses,
But oh thank you, Lord, for
contact lenses!

Donna J. Evetts
METAMORPHOSIS
Wrapped up in my very own
little world
a cocoon in my own right.
They say if I come out
I may taste the nectars
of the world
& join to the beauty
of the flowers.
But my fear envelopes me
everytime I think of
the rain
the thunder
& the pain of being alone.
No pain can reach me
here in my cocoon.
Then there is the fear
of not emerging
Beautiful,
as all butterflies do.
My cocoon is my safety
My freedom is my fear.

John William Cole Jr.
CONTEMPLATION
To the end of eternity
Lies the truth of reality
Evolving the state of man
In his on infinite plan.
The destiny of his mind unseen
The awsome power it means
Delving deep into his thoughts
In his own fate, he is caught
Ever learning what lies beyond
Step by step into infinitys arms
The dawning of reality's truth
Wroughts heaven or hell
rampaging loose
A journey all must take for sure
Lifes changing course, we all
endure
A choice for all, it's life or death
Who conquers life, who stands
the test
Who is so strong, who is so able
He who discerns between truth
and fable

Jean Haley Stein
A Thanksgiving Prayer
T—hanks, Dear God, for
everything—blessings big and
small!
H—elp us never cease to marvel
at the 'wonder of it all'.
A—nd may we never take for
granted the mercies you bestow
N—or the seeds of love you've
planted and continually let
grow.
K—eep our hearts attuned to
"little things" so often
over-looked,
S —o we may understand.
G—ive us wisdom to appreciate
the planning that it took
I —n creating your vast world of
beauty beyond words,
V—isit in our lives and let our
grateful voices e'er be heard.
I —n your great plan for all of us,
may our hearts be always stirred.
N—ever let us falter though the
paths seem often rough,
G—ive us strength and renewed
endeavor because we've known
your touch.

Iva R. Jorgensen—Hooten
IF
If you want a thing bad enough
You won't mind an occasional
cuff—
If you're made of the right sort of
stuff
No going will be too rough.

If you've learned the right way
To look at your sorrows
They can point the way
To glad tomorrows,

And the things that once
Were bitter disappointments
May lead you on
To new appointments.

Angela C. Wilson
PRICELESS
What the eye sees
And what the mind perceives
Cannot be measured
But only treasured

Pamela Deanne May
JUST YOU AND I
Oh, the ways of the world;
How very strange it all seems.
Why must life be so complicated
That we have to live on dreams?

In another time, another place,
We might have had half a chance.
But, you have to admit we can't
get very far
Considering our circumstance.

Our lives; so very different
And yet so much the same,
Keep throwing us together
Only to tear us apart again.

Don't get me wrong—don't
misunderstand.
My love for you runs deep.
You're my every thought from the
time I rise
Until I lay down to sleep.

At night my thoughts are still
with you
As I dream of a brighter day,
When you and I walk hand in

hand
And have everything going our
way.

Merri Power-Dixon
My Cupcakes . . . My Child
OH, CUPCAKE, CUPCAKE
On my wall
Do you have no shame at all?
How'd you get there?
Tell me now
A-fore I swipe you, with my towel.

CUPCAKE, CUPCAKE
Rich and sweet
Since I know you have no feet . . .
With which to walk
Upon my wall
Were you thrown, as if a ball?

Well, then CUPCAKE
Time has come
I will find the guilty one
It's not hard
To spot the crook
Give his sticky hand a look!

With chocolate Icing
On his face
The sign, that always leaves a trace
I'll find him sure
My child will pay
By getting no more cake,
TODAY.!!!!

Danny Ray Carman
RAINY DAYS
Standing in the window,
with my face against the glass.
Dreaming of a yesterday,
I knew was gone at last.

As the rain ran down the window,
the tears began to flow.
My world turned a misty gray,
my heart I let it go.

The clouds grew dark, the
    thunder roared,
I tried to break and run.
The grip was tight, the voice low,
be peace oh little one.

I looked back through the window,
a face appeared to me.
Speaking words I did not know,
so soft and tenderly.

And then at once it happened,
he took me by the hand.
Come walk with me oh little one,
into the promise land.

The clouds began to lighten,
the sun began to shine.
Then I knew, T'was not a dream,
this really could be mine.

Oh rainy days I love you,
and all your woundrous grace.
For now there's smiles and
    happiness,
Instead of tears upon my face.

Thomas R. Boughan
COYOTE
Coyote ripped the wooly sheep's
    flesh,
Blood stained the yellow sage grass
And the yellow sand.
"Poisons must return," say the
    herders,
At the expense of killing every
    animal
Before killing the coyote.
They don't care about life around
them,

The herders care only about how
    to make
More money.

Lona Jean Turner Binz
Lona Jean Turner Binz
HALLOWEEN

*Dedicated to our children
referring to the joyous halloweens
when they were small excepting
1958 not noticed by the 3 Danny
2 1/2 lost all his candy. Michael
6 1/2, Vicky 8 1/2, had to share.
Loving you always —Mama and
Daddy.*

Most common of colors are
    orange and black mixed with
    greens and yellows, on some of
    our tricksy little fellows
But the tiniest; Casper, the little
    white ghost' could possibly be
    the biggest boast
They wait with fascinating
    delight for the first signs of
    night, this once a year flight'
        IS A SPECIALTY!
They flit here and there, usually
    in bunches but sometimes a
    pair
For all their goodies each carry a
    sack gathering all they can
This flighty frolic, Man'
        IS REALITY!

Oh, no! Little Casper starts
    dragging his sack' while
    wishing he really could float
    with his pack
And slower and slower, drags his
    poor little feet' and a hole
    starts forming and a trail—
    ohhh, so neat
For others to follow . . . so sweet,
    so sweet!
But to poor little Casper' his first
    joy a defeat;
This one has learned a lesson
    from his very first deal, you can
    bet next year 'no hole' will kill
    his thrill.

On they go, still scrambling here
    and there
It might as well be a 'FIEND'
    (devil) if a black cat is seen
They stop, in fear; and to all
    share their care "DON'T CROSS
    THE BLACK CAT'S GROUND,
    BAD LUCK GO AROUND"
    they scream as they stare
And they do . . . I'll declare!

And, ohhh! This night we may
    see a strange jet' the story has
    been told many times you can bet
The ugly witch in black, on the
    flying broom
Laughing crazily, through the air
    with a whisk of a zoom . . .
"LOOK! THE MOON IS
    CLOUDING OVER WITH
    VAPOR, THAT MUST BE
    THAT SCALAWAG UP TO
    SOME CAPER!"
So they scamper home mixed
    with fear and delight
What a beautiful, beautiful; yet
    'MYSTERIOUS NIGHT'.

Carol Vitiello
LOVE!
To love you and know I can
    never have you.
To see you every day, but never
    really know you.
To feel you but never really
    touch you.
All these things hurt when your
    in love.
When your really in love every
    little thing you say to him
    comes out wrong.
Every little thing he does means
    more to you than anyone else.
You walk around in a daze all day,
    but never really know why,
        when your
            in LOVE!

Betty Jean Leasure
OUR GUIDE
The Holy Spirit descended—
A boon for the human race,
After Jesus had ascended,
Up through limitless space.

He came to convince of sin
In this very present world—
Degradation, we're living in—
Much grace has been unfurled.

Obey Him, indeed, we must!
Lead gently, where He may,
With great assurance, and trust—
There's coming—a Judgment Day!

Linda G. Lachenmayr
AMERICA
No matter where I rome,
America will always be my home,
For this is the promised land,
And this is where I stand,
May her beauty live on forever,
And may everyone work together,
To make America a better place,
For the human race.

Richard A. Mosher
MY HALLOWEEN DREAM
Screaming down a one way street
They stopped along the curb.
Scarfed and scuffling towards the
    dark
Were real-life Ghosts, Absurd.!!!
Sensation drivin the rest of the
    way
With just my Jack-O-Lantern.
Shattered spheres of Disraeli Gears
And noisy tanks from Saturn.
Towards the doorway and
    moving fast
Were soul, The mind, and body.
Creeping essence of foaming gas
Destroyed my knowledge of
    Karate.
I made my way from the indoors,

outdoors,
To the noisy repetitions.
Of my neighbors making their
    vivacious swaying
In a ditch next to defense
    positions.
Here come the Ghosts,
The attack is on,
They're sure real hard to see.!!!
I dropped my guard
For a second or two,
Now the Ghosts are after me.!!!

J. Michael Major
REFLECTIONS
"A setting sun—
    Is the day over?"

I think not.
It is time to reflect
on what we did,
or who we are,
like the sun that casts
its image on the water.

(And keep the clouds away!—
For they hide the
true reflection of
the face we gave today.)

"The sun sinks lower—
    Is it too late?"

I think not.
It is time to perceive
reality—
not what we see—
for water bends the image
of an evening sky.

"It is dusk—the sun is gone.
    Can I still see?"

I think so.
But think quickly, my friend,
before time dims
bright memories,
like darkness fades
reflections of the sun.

Beth Hodierne
THE BABY
he looks up
he sees her face
with kind eyes.
he feels her touch
soft and gentle,
they rock
slowly back and
forth.
he nestles in her arms
his eyes close,
he sleeps
    in loves warm embrace.

Marianne Remishofsky
THE PAINTING
I paint the picture of my soul,
As a ship that sails the sea,
A ship that knows not where it is,
Or who it'll come to be.

I paint the boat that let's it drift,
I draw the mast so tall,
I paint the sail the brightest white,
And hope it doesn't fall.

I paint the sea that carries me,
Both stormy and serene;
I paint it deep as life will be
When I want to drift along.

I paint the sky with clouds of gray,
That turn the peace to storm,
That build a wind with forceful
    gusts,
Which leaves the ship forlorn.

Stacy D. Conaway
MEN OF OLD
Long ago and far away in the mid
of a century,
Men were shy, timid things that
lived amongst the trees.
They spoke no words, nor recited
a phrase;
Only by movements did they
speak.
How odd it is to think of man as
a simple, terrifying beast.
The tools they used were sticks
and stones they sharpened to a
tee.
The food they ate was raw, not
cooked since fire was not a
friend.
They warmed themselves by long
fur coats that covered every
inch of their skin, and
cleanliness was not of the
essence since soap was not yet
invented.
Life for man was hard and cruel,
and life was short, not long.
For just as we are the hunter now
we were the hunted long ago.

D. W. Schmitt
FAIRY-TALE
Walked out in the pouring rain
With the intentions
Of looking for you
But when I found myself
In this street cafe
Drinking coffee
And watching people
Watching me
I soon realized
That our love affair
Was just a fairy-tale
And you were
Never all mine
I have to share you
With the world
Caroline

Marie Ruffino Mannino
**What Has Happened To
Our Love**
Life was once filled with love.
It was a blessing from up above.
That twinkle in his eye, his
special touch,
simply defined, he loved me so
much.
He made me smile when I was
sad.
He made me laugh when I was
mad.
He was always by my side.
He never cheated, never lied.
I don't know what went wrong.
Why am I singing this sad, sad song?
Another woman has stepped in
and they decided to live in sin.
What has happened to our love?
No, it wasn't sent from up above.

Lillian Henderson Fite
**The Cool Breezes Of
Summer**
The cool breezes of summer
are a welcomed change
from the breath of the beaming
sun.
They're like a good cold drink
to quench the thirst.
They're like a shade tree from the
evening's light.
They're like a revelation from a

hard day's work.
They're like a relief from the
passions of the night.
The cool breezes of summer are a
welcomed change to me.
They blow through your body.
They chill the skin.
They make the summer athlete
win.
They rustle through your body
like the wind through trees.
The cool breezes of summer are a
welcomed change
from the breath of the beaming
sun.

Joseph Emile Moghabghab

Joseph Emile Moghabghab
THE CROSS

*To my dear sister Grace with
love, may God bless you.*

There was a planet we all call
earth.
And on that planet there were a
lot of crosses,
crosses of all kinds.
And each one of us was carrying
one cross.
Crosses were all over the place.
Some were heavy and some were
not.
Some of us bent under the weight
of the cross
and some did not.
All the crosses were being
carried.
All of them . . . but one, one
cross was carrying . . .

Mary J. Bowser
INSIGNIFICANT
Some folks claim that I'm
insignificant
Completely out of the norm
That unlike everything else upon
this earth
I have hardly any duties to
perform

Some even call me a terrible
nuisance
And sometimes down-right
unruly
Never once taking into
consideration, that
There's a very good reason why
I'm unduly

The cattle all find me quite
irresistible
For upon me they must rely

I'm highly essential to all
mankind, too
For I'm one source of their food
supply

The birds also find me very
useful
As they nestle in their nests
They choose me from all the
others
Because they know that I'm the
very best

Lynne Taylor
MY MOM
My mom wasn't too tall
Actually, she was quite small.
But, when she spoke, you knew
You'd better listen, or she'd get
you.

She was a hard working ol' gal
In the garden and out in the
corral.
She had the greenest thumb of all
I ever knew
Big beautiful flowers and
vegetables, too.

I can remember her walking a mile
to hoe the garden, then back
home with a smile.
She used her apron to bring
vegetables back.
That apron she always wore was
used like a sack.

She would cook for a crew of 20,
year round.
Come summers, more to feed
were to be found.
I know of times she'd be herding
sheep.
With 2 dogs and a tent, up at
Clouds Peak.

She had eyes like a hawk and
could see many miles below.
At the sight of our ranch house
her eyes would glow.
She had a beautiful heart of gold.
Sharing what she had with young
and old.

She left a legacy of love behind
And nowhere else could you find
The strength, character, heart and
soul
Of my dear Mom, my own sweet
jewell.

Daryl W. Mandoza
GRAY

*For Cornelia the person who was
the inspiration of this piece. And
the woman who taught me to
accept. With Love.*

Gray
    so smooth
        emotionless. paint
Gray clouds
    filled with emotion
soft,
    yet ominous.
        Gray eyes deep,
            understanding.
    The ocean
    Gray, foam-flecked
        tides
rolling hills, unstable.
        Gray

Today I'm Gray
in all its
glory.

Teresa Darlene Hanson
ONCE A YEAR

*This poem is dedicated to the
memory of my papa, Richard
Willis. Who's poetry brought so
much joy to others that it
inspired me to want to do the
same.*

Halloween comes this time each
year
A time for fun and laughter
A time for scaring those around
you
And treats being given at the door

Halloween is for children
As well as adults
They hide behind costumes of
every sort
The costumes they vary
From Ghosts to Witches
And Monsters to Fairy Princesses

The Halloween season
Is celebrated in several ways
The door to door "trick or treat"
The party at the end of the street
Or the haunted house
That guarantees to scare you down
To your very soul

Halloween
It comes but once a year
And that is definitely enough
To do the trick

Kathleen G. Mullen
AUTUMN
What happened to autumn?
I remember weeping for summer
as I fell into September,
Memories of warmth and sun
laughter and gentle rains.
Running through summer
hand in hand
We found our hearts
dancing with the moonchildren
and the elves.
We woke.
Startled by September
Blinking our eyes
You were gone before
mine were clear.
But now the wind rips through
me
and reaches the depth of my heart
and touches my soul.
What happened to autumn
to make winter so bitter?

Martha E. Cook
THE FACE IN THE CLOUD
I was resting in my easy chair
Out in the yard one day,
Watching the clouds skudding
about
Across the blue skyways.

When all of a sudden a dark
cloud came
And seemed to hover above,
And out of that Cloud a Face
appeared
Shining and full of Love.

I stared at the Face, My Heart
filled up
I felt it would overflow,

It was the Face of our Lord Jesus
Smiling at me and all was Aglow.

The Cloud floated on, To another
place
But I felt so Peaceful there,
Because the Face in the Cloud
had appeared
Not for Me alone, But others to
Share.

Heidi Riederer
SADDLE UP

*To Mr. Zugger who was always
by my side encouraging me to
saddle up.*

Work hard.
Keep training harder.
Practice a lot.
Go even farther.

If you make an attempt and fall
on the way;
You know that you've tried.
And it hurts to lose;
But get up on your horse and ride
it again.

Pull it together and get in your
place.
Make note of your problems,
And change them right then.

Ride your horse when the sun
rises.
Don't fall when it sets.
Jump the fence of SUCCESS;
And try to the end.

You're up in your saddle,
Now ride for SUCCESS!

Cheryl Kathleen Bye
My Daughter Once Told Me

*This Poem Written For, And
Inspired By, My Daughter
Shannon.*

I live on top of a big mountain
I see the deer leap by
And the chipmunks play
There are beautiful things where
I live.
The trees are tall and the skies
are blue.
I take walks in the forest and
daydream
Of all the things I would do if I
were a fawn.
I love where I live and wish
everyone
Could have all the joy I have
and be
Happy where they live, too.

Mary Ann Christe
Trials, Tribulations, and Victories

Like waves of a gigantic ocean
Rolling to shore are trials and
tribulation
Storms of the day
To lure the faithful away
Little knotholes against the grain
To laden a weary heart with pain
A time of nothing going right
Falling darkness like drops of
night
If there was not defeat
Victories would be unsweet!

Chuck Sullivan
ONLY ROOM FOR TWO

*To Robin and Toby and our
future, Love, Chuck*

A teardrop drifted down my
cheek and plummetted to the
floor;
With it fell a thousand memories,
gone for-ever more.
My heart was pierced and torn by
a Love I never knew;
She had my child then gave her
away, something I'd never do.
I've closed this door inside my
heart and opened up another;
This womans' love that I have
found is Truly like no other.
The love this woman has for me
is shared by her little Boy;
A Solid Love so warm and True,
one "Nothing" can destroy.
Upon this Love we'll build a life
and live it to the end;
Defying every obstacle the devil
may try to send.
A religious man I'm not, but I
know God is there;
Watching over the both of them,
caring as I care.
I Love you Robin and Toby, my
heart is filled with you;
"No Vacancy" reads the sign on
my heart,
"Theres only
   Room for
      Two!"

Charlotte Randolph Fulp
The Seeker And the Finder
The seeker seeks to find his place
and stake his claim to fame,
The finder having found his place
imprints there his name.

The finder holds his place by
performance, word, or deed;
And never does he discredit the
unwritten creed.

The seeker seeks for better
improvement of each daily plan,
And having committed himself
becomes a better man.

Pauline Lewman
MY WORLD
I loved my world when I was
young,
but hate what it has now become.

Every day I would arise,
with love and happiness in my
eyes.

Looking forward to the day ahead,
instead of to a day of dread.

Enjoying each minute of the day,
and at night being able to pray.

The blacks are now against the
whites,
and riots light up the skies at
night.

The fear of wars are now on earth,
The control of women giving
birth.

Nation against nation, and friend
against friend.
only God knows when it will
end.

Our school's where we use to go
to learn.
are now full of hate, sex and scorn.

Our boys are led off to fight,
for things they don't believe are
right.

Some are saved and others die,
mother's sit at home and cry.

OH, how I wish I could awake,
and find it all a bad mistake.

That it had been just a dream,
that I hadn't seen the things I've
seen
when I was oh so young.

Oh God I pray when I sleep to
night,
that you will come and make
things right.

Gary Dwight Graumenz
WHIPPERWILL
Down by the creek the willows
still grow, for this is a place the
farmers can't mow.
Into the willow the whipperwill
went, for this is where most of
his time is spent.
As the Earth turns around and
the sun goes down, the
whipperwill makes this lovely
sound, whipperwill, whipperwill,
whipperwill.
I long for spring, that's when he
will sing his lonely mating call.
Into the night he sings his song
hoping a mate will come along.
As the water bubbles by the
whipperwill sets high on his
perch in the willow tree.
Singing whipperwill to his mate,
and as well to me.
Down through the valley his
lonely cry went, as it echowed
back it was almost spent,
Whipperwill, whipperwill,
whipperwill.

Rebecca Welsh
HALLOWEEN
Halloween, a bewitching time.
A time of rhythm, a time to rhyme.
A time to hide behind a tree and
find a victim to trick not treat.
A time to knock on certain doors
and hope for hands of welcome
scores;
   of goodies like: cookies,
   chocolates
   and even jelly beans.
But most of all and most to me, is
the time I look to the mirror to
see:
   If I am funny or a pretty she
   or am I a scary?
   "Yipes", is that Me?!

J. Michael Fish
WE MADE HER A DAY
We can write all the words that
were written for her
In the songs that our hearts often
tried to confer,
But the songs never told in an
accurate way,
How important our moms were
to us everyday.

How her kiss healed a cut and
her hugs ended cries
Or the shame that we felt when
she caught us in lies.
How we yearn for the days of her
loving and care
And the peace that we felt just to
know she was there.

We matured in our needs and our
bodies have grown,
Had to go into life in a world, all
alone;
But we grew in her love and as
children remain
In the warmth of the thoughts
that her heart will retain.

So we made her a day that again
passes by,
Just a day in a year to remember
and try
To repay with our thoughts for
her loving and care,
And the peace that we feel just to
know she was there.

Mary Ann Di Bari

Mary Ann Di Bari
LOVE SONG

*To Jack; whose emotional
intensity filled all the craters of
my volcanic heart—for more than
thirty years—with Song.*

All that I am
I offer you my Love
Of Goodness, Beauty, Truth
All I'll never be
Bequeathe Thee, Sir
I give Thee green seasons
Yesterday's youth
Aurum, Frankincense, Myrrh . . .

More than my self
I leave Thee
Of Progeny, Poetry, Press't
Petals—the white gardenia—
A yellowing wedding dress . . .

Chaliced Wine I drink Thee
Pure Moments
Silent Prayer
One Sweet Sweet Absolution
And all my share
Of Promised Land—of Ecstacy
Less this alone—this soul
That God might
Kiss her passion—
Give Thee All!

Stephen Harrison Bixby
TIME
Time passes like breezes through
open windows
Endlessly swirling and turning,

covering
gentle green meadows.

Trees grow, seeming to reach the
sky yet never aging.
Mighty ships keep sailing to sea
while the storms are raging.

All the distant lands that were
ever won or conquered
Seem to remembered in the past
like a pebble
That has hit a calm pool of water
making it unclear and blurred.

Iron statues that stand uncared
for eventually do rust—
And so you see, try as you may,
as time passes, you'll return to
Mother Earth, drifting on breezes
in the form of dust.

Tehany
FEELINGS OF LOVE

To every father, mother and child

There is a feeling that many of us
feel.
And some of us don't.
Oh when we feel that way.
We're not really wrong.
It's in the air, it's in the sea.
No one looks for it.
No one cares to see.
It's more valuable than diamonds
and precious stones.
It's more fragile and kind,
than the delicate petal of a rose.
It helps us, live.
It makes us, cry.
It makes us, suffer.
It makes us, die.
It gives us, happiness.
It helps us, trust.
It gives us, strength.
And the feeling is love.

Richard Lamar Galloway, Sr.
LATE WISDOM

*John & Lola Duncan, Frank &
Marion, Jack & Josephine Allen
Alvin & Shirley Smith, III; Lanier
Rollins; Marty Booker & Family;
J. O. Reid; Brenda Galoway; Peggy
Rainy; Edith Parker Jackson.
Whom in all is much Love*

Like the boy that becomes a man,
who must go out into the world,
To make and carry out his own
plan;
He steps out to make his stand,
he's now a man.
Where he goes, there's fate to learn
Mother's grieve how, how shall
he return?
Her long experience has taught
her so,
One can't rightly judge of friends
or foes.
Her arms extend straight out ah!
A hug and kiss.
A safe return she shouts, and as
she hears him say good-bye,
She holds herself no more, she
cries.

She sees him wondering in the
winding glade,
And the truth shows her only

that he's strayed,
He will learn the relentless
hatred, and the erring need for
love.
OH help him, she prays Father
above.
He will hear the voice of death
and woe,
She prays he'll pass it up and not
go. Now she goes down by the
riverstream.
And she ask the Father above to
give her son a dream,
She sits up on the rock and rises
from the shock of hearing a
voice,
From the heavens say again your
son shall come again,
He'll have no late wisdom.

Margaret Edwards
ABOUT FRECKLES
How did God make freckles?
Did He dot each one with care?
Or did He shake his brush
And they splattered here and
there?

They must be pretty special
Since they're only added now and
then,
So lucky you, if you have them,
Don't hide, be proud, and grin.

Michele Mouttapa
TEN PET MICE
I have ten pet mice.
For dinner they all eat rice.

All of them look so cute,
Each one wears a suit.

One of them is the mom,
I named the dad Tom.

I first saw them by the door,
Begging on the floor.

Jada Lynn Brown
THE RELATION IS YOU
The relation is you
for like blood the ties
run deep.

The relation is me
for my reflection
is no longer shattered
but smooth.

The relation is you
your connection crosses
A straight fine line,
which when fused together
will bring much relevance
to our predestined time.

P. R. Castanon
EVEN MORE
Honey, would you love me even
more if I could fly a plane,
Or if I had some big name,
Or would you just love me if I
remained the same.

Honey, would you love me even
more if I drove some flashy cars,
Or if I could act,
And mingle with the stars,
Or would you just love me if my
heart was intact.

Honey, would you love me even
more if I wore some fancy
threads
And made all sorts of bread,
Or would you just love me and
still share my bed.

Honey, would you love me even
more if I had some status in
this world,
Like some kind of earl,
Or would you just love me if I
said for me you were the only
girl.

Honey, would you love me even
more if I were all those things,
And if I were and if I could I
would fulfill all your dreams,
But Honey, I just can't seem to
please you,
So, Honey, I must leave you.
But Honey, just the same I love
you even more,
'Cause Honey, I still need you,
Even more than I'll ever show.
Even more than you'll ever know.
'Cause Honey, I still love you
even more.

Wendy J. Heilig
FRIENDS AND LOVERS

*To Brett—for without his love
and encouragement, this would
not have been written.*

What is friendship?
It's—giving, without expectation,
listening, without judgment,
caring, without promise.

It's loving someone, though they
may not understand it.

It's trust and faith in that person,
no matter what they do.

To be a friend is my only desire,
though we are lovers, too.
You are—most of all—a friend,
and that is the greatest gift in the
world.

For, you see, lovers come and go,
but friends can last a lifetime.
The unspoken bond is there to
enjoy,
so let us be friends—as well as
lovers.

Monica A. Fabre
SONG OF PEACE
A tiny brown sparrow waits for
the day
When the blue skies arrive
through the dark clouds of grey
Rain pounding poorly, but he
doesn't care
He remembers the time when it
all was so clear
Though the flowers are dead and
the love moved astray
A tiny brown sparrow waits for
the day.

He lingers patiently on through
the night
While the stars in the heavens
hang silent with fright
He knows what happened but he
doesn't cry
This poor little bird breathes a
long, deathly sigh
The winds of destruction grow
colder each night
He remains in the valley and puts
up a fight.

Is it all we have left of this great
power gone

Is it too much to ask for a new
starting dawn
The young soon turn old, but the
old soon forgot
Where is the dream, for the life is
here not?

Many years have brought a
generation bound between
The smog that surrounds an
illusion once seen
The sparrow does not sit, his
spirit has flown
But his body remains still, cold,
shattered, and moans.

Kay Fannin
The Coming Of Autumn
"Come little leaves", said the wind
one day.
Come O'er the Meadows with me
and play;
Put on your dresses of red and
gold;
For Summer is gone and the day's
grow cold.

Donna Jo Gibson
**Beyond the Realms Of
Lonliness**

*This poem is dedicated to "Hopi".
For one of the greatest
inspirations in my life, has come
from having found such a true
friend in you. P.U.T.A.*

To the restless hearts of the
universe
I take my hat off to you!
For you have explored all elements,
you have touched upon and
opened up
the innermost desires of man.
To be able to reach out and touch
the wind,
to possess the soul of a bird in
flight.

The most intellectual moments
of man
are found in the midst of
loneliness.
The pieces of the mind's puzzle,
separated,
one by one disected, and answers
found.
The whys and whats of the world
become clear,
and fantasies become reality.
Take time to explore the
universe of the mind,
and in the end . . .
    A wiser person you will be.

Shelley Towle
LONE BOAT
Darkness envelopes the Nordic
  valley
  Rowing, rowing on the sea
Blackness, like death
  Gliding ever gracefully.
Desolation and death
  Behind them the day
Another village conquered
  Nothing stands in their way.
Vikings, men of glory
  Pillagers of friend and foe
Slip out of sight
  On the still, night water, row. . .

Terry Lisa Tamashiro
UPON YOUR KNEE

In memory of my grandaddy,
Charles Leslie Creasy

As a small child I'd sit on your
  knee
  So timid and quiet and shy
I'd listen in awe while you spoke
  to me
  And gaze into soft, smiling eyes

I'd sniff the smell your cologne
  would cast
  Old Spice I think it was
While you told me stories of your
  past
  Like only a grandfather does

And as I sat upon your knee
  It never crossed my mind
That you held more than the eye
  could see
  More than my nose would find

Something is special 'bout your
  chuckle so deep
There's a catch to your southern
  drawl
But they're just signs to let the
  world see
  How special you really are

Now I am older; too big for your
  lap
  But those moments I will always
  hold dear
You're older too; to happen that is
  apt
  And your tmie to go has come
  near

We'll meet again someday I know
  But right now I just want you to
  see
That, Grandaddy, I love you so
  As I loved those times upon
  your knee

Genevieve (Stumpf) McNett
1943, Just a Mothers Prayer
There is a Service Flag filled with
  Blue Stars,
Hanging near the sanctuary in a
  little village church,
Where a Mother came to Pray
  and as she knelt there,
The tears filled her eyes as she
  bowed her head,
And whispered these words there
  is a Blue Star,
In that Flag for a boy out on the
  sea,
Far from his home and his loved
  ones,
Dear God guide and guard him

keep him from harm,
Shine your heavenly arms around
  him for he is just a boy.
So dear God tenderly care for him
  till they send him home.
And dear God don't let that Blue
  Star turn Gold.
But bring him safe back to me I
  pray.
Spare all mothers boys and grant
  to all mothers,
Who is called upon to sacrifice
  her boy.
The Grace and Courage her cross
  to bear.
Pour down thy blessing
  abundantly upon them.
And bring us Peace everlasting
  Peace,
That they who gave their lives in
  the service of their country
May not have died in vain.

Marianne Carpender
LOVE: SUN

Where would I be without the
love and support of my parents,
Joseph and Mary Carpender.
Thank you for all the years of
belief and trust.

Drifting in and out of slumber,
Lying victim to a scorching sun.
Feeling the warmth building
  inside me,
And the fire has begun.
I'd felt the warmth from a
  distance;
It filled me with desire for more.
I welcomed the comfort, chanced
  a burn,
As if I'd never felt this sun before.
It came upon me rather slowly,
But became far too attractive to
  resist.
This warm, glowing love: sun
That changed my tears to a
  gentle mist.
'Can't imagine feeling any better
Than being filled with this
  "scorching" sun;
The warmth burning deeper
  inside me . . .
And the fire has begun.

James Herbert Hammond
Looking From the Pier
The tall sails blowing gracefully
  in the wind
As the ship comes toward the
  docks
As I look on the ship I see the
  smiling faces of the sailors
I see the waves brushing against
  the tall ship
The sailors with their bags in
  hand waiting to set foot on land

The families of the sailors wait
  impatiently on the pier
The sailors run off the ship to
  their families
Embracing each other gleefully as
  I stand alone
Standing alone, as always I must
Each day I hope as I stand on the
  pier

Standing here alone, watching the
  ships
Hoping each day that someone

will be next to me
Dreaming that I'm never alone a
  day in my life
I turn away from the ocean
Turning to walk to the place that
  I call home

As I walk away, I turn to look at
  the horizon
And I see myself, alone, as always
I turn and start to walk home
Spirits down and my head hung
  low
As the tears go down my cheeks

As always they do

Mary Ruth Holtz
**They Thought a Smile
  Means Friend**

Dedicated to Thomas Evans
Blessed are the Peace Keepers . . .

They come from places far across
  a land and sea
Where waters kiss the shore on
  either side
And in between the mountains
  bless the breeze and
Sweep it down across the fertile
  land . . .
They serve, because they believe
  and some because the
Smoke no longer belches jobs and
  so they go . . .
They leave the places where love
  smiles down on them and
Where the love of home baked
  pie is real and understood.
Oh, where is this beruit they
  laugh and say I'll come right
  home
As soon as it is deemed safe for
  them to fight each other . . .
Then they kiss their girl and
  mother and their aunt and leave,
A swagger, just so slight after
  they turn and wave . . .
The mother twists her ring and
  wants to beat her chest and wail
She hugs herself and frets if he
  trusts a smile too much
She taught him so . . . now is it
  wrong for where he goes?
The door is draped in black, they
  haven't heard . . .
They find nothing , , , to tell . . .
Until they do the door will
  stay. . .
The silence deepens never to
  break with his laugh
The pie is thrown away . . .
The smile he saw was there, he
  answered it with all
Knowing nothing but the flash
  and roar . . .

Dorothy Love Trent
SEASONS OF LIFE
The Spring of Life is full of bloom
With petals bright and pure
Learn how to talk and how to
  walk
With steps that are strong and
  sure.

The growing years are full of love
And know not the meaning of
  strife.
That will come later on
In the summer years of life.

The autumn days must come
  along
To find that summer's gone.
The children are grown up
And gone out on their own.

It's so hard to accept
That now I'm left alone.
I can only pray to God above
For the courage to go on.

What is left for me to do,
For someone at my age?
I've found that I'm needed to help
Folks in their winter stage.

Mavis Inhetveen
GOD'S GARDEN

To beautiful Bellingrath Gardens:
They testify to mankind's
partnership with God.

God's Garden—long ago begun,
  a reservoir of natural beauty,
  has been blessed with rain and
  sun.
Designed by the Master Craftsman
  with a gentle hand . . .
He transformed into paradise
  once untended land.
Unfolding flowers fringe winding
  pathways
  of glistening grains of sand.
Trees; tall, majestic, ageless,
  seem to possess the land.
Nearby—a placid lake;
  mirrrored by the Giver . . .
Along a curving shoreline
  an unrestricted, flowing river.
Each season is endowed with color
  that strives for closer view,
Outpicturing a rainbow of myriad
  shades
  under a canopy of perfect blue.
Birds arrow here to chord
  their joy songs to sing.
They testify to strength—of the
  soaring wing.
Fragile, frolicking butterflies
  gesture to their welcome tune.
Busy bees, their bodies overlaid
  with gold,
  Sip nectar from each bloom.
Upon this lush green acreage
  you can see the signature of
  God
In every blooming flower;
  in every inch of sod.
This is the garden which God
  hath made.

John E. Backman
SENIOR'S LAMENT
O' Hallowed halls, where minds,
Once fettered by social truths
  are loosened.

Free—to fly among the
  sometimes agonizing
  particles of knowledge.

Free to absorb, consider, or
  dismiss,
And in doing so, forming yet
  more social truths,
Until at last,

The wisdom of the original
  fettering is understood.

Minds, intertwined with the past
  and present, but ever mindful
  of the future.

Minds which must shoulder the awesome responsibility of what is yet to come.

And these hallowed halls, so nuturing in their caress.

Not brick and stone, but as living flesh—
Never to be forgotten.

I must leave you now, O' Hallowed halls,
But a part of my spirit remains.

And in its place—
I take a bit of you.

Ethel Morris
WELL DONE
The sun gives us warmth, gives us light;
Could he talk, would he tell
Of a splendor so bright?
One we should all know well
Our good Father's love.

Pretty child—little child
Don't hide your love
Let it shine all the while
It's free high above
Sent down to you to use.

Give God a chance to say to you,
"Well done".
Do helpful, useful deeds
And, my little son,
He'll fill your needs
Give of your love as your Father has done.

Mrs. Mary La Plac
THE MIND
Thought, the gift of God to man
Through which portals he may pass
Blest with reason by his holy hand
Where no other may command.

Reason, dissecting right from wrong
Making a skeleton of a thought, and try
Finding what our work has wrought
Passing the pitfalls that catch the eye.

Dreams, life's sweetest recompense
Falling back into reveries
Love's joyous ecstacies
Or desires held in suspense.

Through reflecting mirrors of the mind
Relive again scenes that have passed
Keep the light aglow until the last
The mind lives on, the wings of time.

Hubert D. Joy
IS HE ALONE

To my wife, Edith

Sitting by his fire
Looking to the sky
Where stars flicker
He wonders why
Or if he is alone
Within the greater scheme
Or if perhaps his thoughts
Are only just a dream

With telescope fixed

Toward the Heaven vast
He observes a star
Shooting out, and past
His Gallaxy
Beyond his Earthly home
And could it be
That he is not alone

The Earth behind him
So very, very far
Is just a speck
As though a star
And as he gazes
Out from in his dome
At the Universal Wonder
Is he there alone.

William E. Douglas
SIXTY
Sixty
laughs and smiles
dreams and weeps
knows and tells
thinks and sleeps
watches, wonders
remembers and recalls
looks, listens
and knowingly stalls.

Norma Jean Moore (Mrs. Roy)
Hurray For the Farmers Fair
Fall is in the air,
Joy is everywhere,
You hear the shout,
The word is out,
"It's time for the "Farmers Fair".

The farmer makes his plans,
His wife selects her cans,
The jars of jams, jellies too,
Must be the best that she can do,
There's lots of helping hands.

The children shout and sing,
The carnival will bring;
The rides, the games, the goodies too,
There'll be much that they can do,
Their joy they can't contain.

The floats are being made,

The stage is being laid,
The contests, music, shows are great,
It's getting very hard to wait,
To see the grand parade.

The signs will soon appear,
The barkers, we will hear,
Cotton candy, popcorn, too,
Candied apples, "dogs" for you,
The best time of the year,
"The Farmers Fair" is near.

Bonnie Jo Henkel
Can You Give Me the Answer?
Oh God, please send me the strength
To make it through another day,
For sometimes it all seems
So hopeless.
The world is in such mass Confussion
And to its' end seems no Conclusion
People always living with fear,
And with each day that passes
The end seems quite near.
Oh dear Lord,
Was all this in your master plan
When you decided to create
This great land?

Or did something go wrong
Not even you quite understand?

Zenobia Bishop

Zenobia Bishop
If You Only Knew What Was In My Heart

Dedicated to someone I love very much

I knew right from the start some day we would part, but if you only knew what was in my heart.

You thought you had the facts that raining day, putting you first just didn't pay.

But if you only knew what was in my heart.

You did not give me time to explain, but I still love you that fact remains.

But if you only knew what was in my heart.

The hurt, the pain the emptiness, oh how i wanted to hold you to my breast.

The lonely hours, I waited for you to call, but the phone didn't ring at all.

You were always on my mind, but for me you didn't have the time.
Some times that didn't bother me too much just as long as we kept in touch.

The days and nights are empty and hours are so long, who was right and who was wrong.

How much I love you, you will never know, But if you tell me I will try to show.

But if you only knew what was in my heart.

You can not know what's in my heart so that is why we have to part.

Lynnette Ratcliff
ARTIST LAMENT
Brush in hand
Paint by my side
My mind Like sand
Awaiting the tide

As for a thought
Nothing came to me
For all the tools I had bought
With my imagination rushed out to sea

It came from a distance
Like a bright far away light
Then faded in an instant
With all of my insight

I sit here and stare
A blank canvas in hand
How could I ever dare
To paint again

Fannie Lane Steele
The Things That I'm Not
My work is not Rembrandt or Michelangelo
I can't paint a flower like Vincent Van Gogh
The ceiling of a chapel while I lie on my back
Compose a sonata in major b flat.

Unlike William Shakespeare, I can't write a play
A poem like Longfellow, the best in his day.
Or Poe's poem, "The Raven," or "Annabel Lee"
I cannot influence like Emily D.

I can't write like the "Dickens," who taught reform
Emancipate like Beethoven in symphonic form.
No, I'm not Picasso, Mozart or Bach
But these are all the things that I'm not.

Now let me tell you the things that I am
A daughter, a wife, and no-less a mother
A teacher, a nurse, and oh-yes, a lover;
Psychologist, advisor, a cook and a maid
And for all these things I never get paid.

One thing I've in common with these folk of art
The work that we both do comes straight from the heart.

Miss Diane L. Veatch aka Teensie Veatch
TEARS
Tears for a husband,
tears for a wife.
Tears of happiness,
the joy of new life.

Tears of anger,
tears of strife.

236

Our World's Best Loved Poems

Tears of the war,
taking a young mans life.

Tears of anger,
tears of love.
Tears for loved ones,
gone to heaven above.

Tears are for,
the sensitive and fair.
Tears are the symbols,
of love and care.

Cynthia Majeski
HER LAST WORDS

To my mother Irma Crissell and my three children Kellie, Joshua, and Little Cindy. For all their love trust and support and for always being there.

I was sitting by her bedside, the night before she died.
I watched her labored breathing, I saw the tears where she had cried.

Then she turned and looked at me, and tried her very best to smile.
She said "Honey, Mama loves you, but I must leave you in awhile."

"Honey, be good now, and mind your daddy each day".
"Honey, I'll be watching you, I'll hear you when you pray."

She started crying softly, and the tears they left a trace.
A fallen veil of wetness, on her loved and beautiful face.

I didn't want her to leave me, but she said she had to go.
That night before my mama died she said, "Honey, Mama loves you so.

Susan C. Iffinger
Ode To My Son On His First Birthday

Well, a year has gone by since we had our son, today he has turned one,
It's been a year of teaching and learning and it's only just begun.
He has a personality all his own, yet most say he's like his father,
I used to say he's a lot like me, but now I don't even bother!

For sure enough as time goes by, his father he certainly takes after,
His looks, his actions, his constant movement—all the way down to his laughter.
But don't get me wrong, it's best this way for if I had my d'ruthers,
I'd rather he resemble his father because it's easier to prove I'm his mother!

It seems it all happened so long ago that I gave birth to Jack,
I promised myself I'd never forget that morning so many days back.
But time goes on and your memory does dim as much as one regrets,
So I have reconciled myself to the fact that over this I should not

fret!
For all that matters is he's brought us joy and each day I wake renewed,
It's hard to remember what life was like before this impish dude.
He's filled a void down deep within; he's made my life complete,
I have found my niche in motherhood, nothing else could even compete!

Some day, I'm sure, he'll have a brother or sister or maybe two,
But until that time I'm afraid it's us with which he'll have to make do.
For soon enough there'll be other siblings with the usual fighting and sharing,
But that's what a family is all about with the emphasis on caring!

Vivian Snow Votaw
WHY, OH WHY?

My heart sang with the mockingbird
Sitting on the limb of the tall walnut tree.
It's little throat swelled with music that stirred
Sleepers awake for a free melody.

Each morning it sang till the coming dawn
With roseate hues dyed the grey-blue sky.
Then quietly flew to another lawn,
First singing the walnut a sweet good-bye.

This morn the bird sat on its favored spot,
The song first plaintive, then wild and free,
Was hushed by a sudden, rending shot.
A woman with a gun was all I could see!

Poor woman! I know you are tired and worn
And with life's problems unable to cope.
Else why would you on this fateful morn
Take the life of this songster of hope?

Rhoda V. Miller
CRYING WITHOUT TEARS

In memory of Earl A. Miller, Loving husband and father.

I do not know how some folks get
The best of everything.
Life for them just rolls on by—
There never is a sting.

I had you such a little while
My friend and husband lover,
And through long years I've been alone,
I have not had another.

I worked and raised the children
You didn't see much of;
I gave them understanding
And your share of my love.

I realize I've cried sometimes
Down through my widowed

years,
But mostly I've been strong enough
For crying without tears.

Karyn Freund
YOU

You are the sunshine in the rainstorm,
you are the flower in the empty field.
You are the happiness in my sadtimes,
you are the one who shares my goodtimes.
You are the embrace in my nightime,
that always carries me to the daytime.
You are the one for whom I care,
my love is what I want to share.
You're the one in my life that I can't replace,
for there is no one to fill your space.
You are original and unique—
for I cherish you as my life's antique.

Deloris Fjeld
I HOPE IT'S FOR ME

A present, a present,
Under the tree.
I wonder, I wonder,
Whose can it be.

It's wrapped up in silver,
Tied up with blue,
With some jingly bells
And mistletoe, too.

It won't make a sound
When I try to shake it.
I've squeezed it and rolled it.
I hope I don't break it.

A present, a present,
Under the tree.
Tomorrow is Christmas.
I hope it's for me.

Marianne Gregor-Bartsch
MISSING YOU

To my husband who must be away from home often for those unforgettable moments that make life so special.

Watching the sunset,
I sit by the window and dream about us and our precious life,

what does our relationship mean, and for what do we really strive!?

Happiness?—It seems so easy to get,
yet it's so hard to maintain,

I'm truly thankful that we have met,
my feelings for you I cannot explain.

I think of the times we spent together,
there was closeness, love, and a lot of fun,

we did all kinds of crazy things in the worst kind of weather,
for we always did see the sun.

I sit by the window and stare into darkness,

you are gone and with you the sun,

suddenly I am full of sadness,
feeling lonely with nothing left to be done,

another day without you went by like another meal without spice,

I look up to the stars in the sky,
and think:
Even happiness has its price . . .

Martha Virginia Beach Chalfant
OUR LOVE WILL LAST

This poem is dedicated to my beloved husband, Monroe D. Chalfant.

If you could only be with me
And once again your face I'd see,
I gladly would forget the past.
I know, my dear, our love will last.

I think of all the times we've shared
And now I know you really cared.
Unto your love, I still hold fast—
I know, my dear, our love will last.

If now to me you could return,
I ne're again your love would spurn.
If only death had not gone past!
I know, my dear, our love will last.

Jeanne M. Bezko
OURS ETERNALLY

Lord I've not thanked You nearly enough,
For Your patience, guidance and sweet love.
All that I've done, and everything You've seen,
Forgive me please, I'm just a human being.

I've tried to live by the golden rule,
But the devils' folks are mighty crule.
If we all were the same it would be easy to live,
No sins to make and nothing to forgive.

But there's people here that test us each day,
From Your love they try to make us stray.
Rules are broken, souls are lost,
All are to blame at such a cost.

Thank You Lord, for helping me stay in line,
I'm usually there most of the time!

237

When I stray it's never far enough,
That I don't feel forgiveness from
Your eternal love.

Brenda K. Allen
I LOVE YOU
You entered my life
And brought me such joy,
You never treated me
Like a child's toy.
We value our time
For it is well spent,
We cherish our love
For it is well meant.
I just wanted to show you
With the little things I do,
That I'll never forget you
And I'll always love you.

Betty P. Luellen
NOVEMBER

*To the memory of my son,
Kenneth William Luellen. Killed
in 1983 by a man who was DUI.*

The forest, ethereal cathedral of
lace,
Points with pride toward the
sky's pearly face.
Nearby meanders the singing
river along its way,
Beside which fields of green and
amber meadows lay.
Sway the nippy breezes of
summer late.
Alas, the tranquil, lovely summer
days are sate.
This beauty gives us pause, for
the distant sea
Of purple mountains is calling to
me,
"Be Happy! Believe! Lest we falter,
lest we grieve."
Today is real: this day is for living.
Give up one's sad heartpulls; and
offer Thanksgiving!

Kay Havard
TOMORROW

*This poem was written to my
Mother (Elgin Lois Havard) the
day before she had surgery.*

If I can hold back my tears
Just one more day
I may not need them tomorrow
Maybe my worries will go away

If I can just be patient
And not fall apart
Then maybe by tomorrow
This fear will leave my heart

If I can just hold on
And be a little stronger
Tomorrow I may have no reason
To hold these tears any longer

If I try a little harder
Not to shed a tear
If I wait until tomorrow
Then today will disappear

Deb Redfearn
ESCORT
I Met Death
as I came around a corner
on the way from now to never—
about two blocks from always.
He smiled at me from behind

His mask
and chilled my blood to ice,
because I knew my time had come.

I smiled back to hide my fear.

He took my hand
and led me down
the street of darkness,
Opened for me the door of death
and ushered me into eternity.

Sible Thomas Lampkin
LONELY

*This poem was inspired by and
written to Samuel Lampkin and
Charles Moore.*

Why should I feel so lonely
When there are two men in my life
But to me they are as different
As day is from night.
Some folks call me crazy
I, in turn, say you too!
Why do I get so offended?
When I know what they say is
true.
A true friend is very valuable.
A person that's hard to find.
But then, even they are not
"worthy"
If you're still "lonely" all the time.
So if your heart is das and lonely
And your mind is deep and blue
And your loved one has just left,
You would feel lonely too!
So when you are depressed,
Feeling all alone and blue,
Don't ever think you're the only
one
'Cause I'm "lonely as Hell" too.

Julie Prohaska
REALITY
stings you in the face
slaps you on the cheek
pushes away the world
you wish could be.

Edith C. Mullin
A WIDOW'S LAMENT
I sit within my silent room
Of memories mind,
And search the growing gloom
Of heartbreaks grind.
Recalling memories of our loves
bloom,
From a birth divine.
It grew, a flame, our hearts
consumed
In passion, combined.
But with time, became a
cherished heirloom
Of our loves shrine,
And is now, only a sweet perfume
Of broken vine,
Lingering about the tomb
Of memories mine.

Larry W. Youngblood
KAPIDZHIK DREAMING
There can be an unknowing
ignorance captured in the
enthusiasm of confidence,
and an extremest in outward
behavior to which
consciousness might aspire.

A fanatical subconscious
tendancy, Life; providing places
where mankind's
social evolution still travels the

internal change of organization,
industrialization and economics
like scattered psychopaths in an
ant farm, foraging the confines
of an era.

Radical or obsolete political
concepts become a morality,
and social structure is
organized religion.
Intelligence eludes mass
organization.
For the promotion of creativity,
science and priveledges
are subject to a guideline for a
multitude.
There's also more to fortitude and
idle eagerness than delequent
activism, for people do break
through bringing change with
them.
And the human condition will
consume the consciousness of
man
As does the ideal of civilization.

**Ms. Irma Armenthea
Williams**

Ms. Irma Armenthea Williams
DEPRESSION SUICIDE

*In these foresaken times when
our backs are against the wall,
And we feel we have nowhere to
turn, We must turn to God for
He is truly our only Salvation. To
All Who Feel Forsaken.*

Look at the problems that
surround us everyday.
The times and situations are so
critical I hardly know what to
say.
It's become a common thing now,
it's spreading world wide.
It's a contagious epidemic, known
as Depression Suicide.

Thousands are jobless, have no
money, and have lost their
homes.
Many have lost their families and
are left living all alone.
Helpless and desperate with only
the Devil as their guide.
With nothing left to live for they
turn to suicide.

You see in the paper where man
kills family and self.
You see where even the rich have
lost their acquired wealth.
Hunger in the stomach of their

children and some have no
decent clothes to wear.
This kind of pressure is just to
much for some to bare.

Some can't stand to see their
family suffer, so this world
they've grown to hate.
So depressed with life itself, their
life they decide to take.
It's a shame so many good people,
who at one time had so much
pride.
In a fit of desperation turn to
Depression Suicide.

Louie (Birdy) Martinez
ONCE AGAIN
Once again
I walk on you,
dead leaves
that make up
autumn's face . . .

Once again,
I listen to the sound
that makes me feel
in the middle,
In between summer's joys
and winter's silence . . .

Once again
I feel the inner changes,
Revolving circles
that united,
Make the whole sense
of my life . . .

Once again
I feel the changing seasons,
In their journeys through my life,
And instead of warming days
And happy nights,
I see wintry time,
In flirting rituals
with autumn's
rainy and chilly smiles . . .

Once again
I hear the wind,
When it shakes
all the trees,
Leaving them naked
and prepared to go to sleep
in winter's bed . . .

Once again
I have to unpack
my winter outfit,
To keep warm and well
my glacial feet . . .

It's really sad to see,
How all trees
lose their abundant leaves . . .

And the birds
in their migrating flight,
Say good-bye to me,
Who remains on this part
of the planet,
Breathing snow
and lacking warming sunshine . . .

Robert John Scott
SOMEBODY SMILED
Somebody smiled at the world
today
Somebody smiled in an unusual
way
For the cares and burdens that go
with the years
Have turned to laughter instead
of tears

It's true that days will come and go
And the world moves on with a

pace fast and slow
But if you can give just one
  cheerful smile
Do so, then life may be
  worthwhile.

Jan Mennenga
too late
it's too late for flowers.
  too late for gifts, large or small.
what's done can't be undone with
  material things.
  you can't buy back stinging
    words or neglected needs.
my unhappiness isn't for sale.

Judith I. Jefferies
REDEMPTION
Crackling snow now covers grass
  beneath abandoned skies, while
Humming barnyards whisper
  faint since summer's rush.
Gleaming frost cloaks muzzled
  sounds, where fragrant
  blossoms sleep,
Winter's gentle breeze embraces
  all that rest for now.
Still—
  so still.
Childhood thoughts remain
  in soothing silence.
D
 R
  O
   P
    S,
Descending on blue-green slates,
Reflect the remnants of
  winter's glory,
Pledging tomorrow's redemption.

Eleni Katzingris Moustaka
A TRUE STORY
Somewhere in one remote village
  where a solitude embroidered
  fear into the dead of night, the
  wind ruffled the moonlight,
  gnashing through the gap-
  toothed peaks and screaming
  like a human being, crashed on
  a tortured mud hud, where two
  kids sat huddled together near
  their lifeloss youngish mother,
  crying their little eyes out.
The father had left a many days
  ago, looking for a job in the
  next city.

While the time tyrannical kept
  an eye in this endurance, the
  three year-old downcast girl,
  just still sitting beside her
  mother, tears ran down her face.
"Mommy, don't lie down, she
  whispered.
Please, Mom, open your eyes.
Why do you sleep so much?
Why didn't you want to tell me?"
She touched her mother in
  exasperation over and over,
  until just abandoned herself to
  the despair, inconsolable
  moaning again silence, again
  unfriendly mother.
The two year-old boy threw
  himself over his mother and to
  stave the hunger, played with
  her hair, laughing,
  singing . . . sobbing.

The neighborhood had listened
  with carelessness and
  displeasure to the plaintive

screams which roamed through
  days and night, so near and yet
  so far, to their stiff hearts.
The screams were ever that
  increasing and diminished very
  little.
Afterwards, the sorrowful silence.
Three stars had already left, when
  John returned.

Vanessa R. Gates

Vanessa R. Gates
**. . . And The Children Are
Neglected**
I have to take care of myself
I don't have the time
Let someone else do it
He's not mine.
  . . . and the children are neglected.

Violence in the streets
Abuse in the home
Devastation is everywhere
How much longer can it go on?
  . . . and the children are neglected.

John's years are seven
David is only one
Both are abandoned
Now Steven is born.
  . . . and the children are neglected.

He said "suffer them to come"
But we refuse to let them
And yet they are a heritage
And of such is the kingdom.
  . . . and the children are neglected.

You tell Him of your many deeds
Of how righteously they were done
You stand before Him haughty of
  heart
When suddenly says the Son
"but the children were neglected.
Those from whom I have perfect
  praise
Those who are a heritage unto me
Those who are considered of all
  the least."
  . . . the children were neglected.

You were so righteous,
So perfect,
Yet so blind you could not see
  . . . the children were neglected.

Yvette M. Caruthers
WITH DEEPEST SYMPATHY
May I express my deepest sorrow
That it's almost the end of your
  tomorrow;
For as you join the "over the hill"
  gang
I'm afraid that life just won't be
  the same;
So enjoy one last mouthful with

your own teeth
Before you switch to jello instead
  of meat;

For pretty soon your first
  morning task
Will be taking your teeth out of
  the glass;

When the sound of the TV begins
  to fade
It's time to get fitted for a hearing
  aid;

Be sure to enjoy your last tennis
  game
It will be difficult to play using a
  cane;

And don't worry once your cane
  gives out
You'll soon learn how to push
  your wheelchair about;

And as often as you can, make
  use of your comb
For your head will soon be as
  smooth as stone;

If the sun is shining and you
  insist there's fog
Its time to replace your glasses
  with a seeing-eye dog;

But along with the sympathy it's
  only fair
To wish you lots of good
  memories in your rocking
  chair;

Of course you may be senile and
  can't remember much
So perhaps you'll forget you've
  lost your sight, sound and
  touch;

And even though you may try to
  deny this day
I hope you have a very Happy
  Birthday anyway!

Vicky Crow Anderson
GROUP BUS TOUR

─────────────

*In memory of my beloved sister,
Dorothy Crow Massey, whose
untimely death prevented her
ever taking a tour.*

─────────────

Feeling lonely, bored or insecure?
Why not schedule a group bus
  tour?
Your days will be filled with fun
From early morn' to setting sun.

So what if you are past your prime?
Enjoying yourself is not a crime.
Wonderful sights you'll see along
  the way,
And new freinds you will make
  every day.
Good memories you can store
  away
To relive again some rainy day.

But, no matter where you go,
'Tis good again to tell your family
  "Hello".
Then, what exciting tales you'll
  spin
About those fabulous places
  you've been.

June Lydiard de Leon
TRICK OR TREAT
Who holds this pumpkin, at my
  door,

With open top and sticky floor
And grinning teeth 'neath V-
  shaped eyes?
Why it's our neighbour's
  son . . . 'Surprise!'

Again the call and now I see
A clown, a space ship and a bee;
So pour the pennies into hands
That even hold some silver wands.

The night is quiet now, I go
To sweep the steps and though
The sight is startling as I end
My cleanup-here's another friend!

"Hold hard!" he cries, 'leave off the
  light:
I come here yearly on this night!'

I peer and try to place the one
Whom I should know in all this
  fun.
"Hold hard?" I laugh, "and what
  are you?"
'A memory that's come to view!'

I hesitate . . . his features dim
And all that I can see of him
Stares through the door and so I
  turn
To look inside; I feel him yearn.

"Do I know you? Did you live
  here?"
The man is gone, my steps are
  clear.
Why should a trickster disappear?

Ginger Gordon
BOOOOO!

─────────────

*Dedicated to my father who
would have been proud.*

─────────────

The time we fear is drawing near,
The time of spooks and goblins.
They peer at you and leer at you,
And set your courage wobblin'!

The witch will zoom upon her
  broom
Accompanied by her cats.
And pumpkin eyes will show
  surprise,
You might even see some bats!

Wolves will howl and cats will
  yowl,
And you'll sit rigid with
  fright.
So be prepared 'cause you'll be
  scared,
On coming Halloween night!

Carole Anne Hayworth
THINKING OF YOU

─────────────

*To John, for all the memories you
have given to me. You keep me
going, and I am truly always
thinking of you.*

─────────────

I'm thinking of you,
As I so often am.
My heart feels so empty,
Waiting to see you again.

You give so much,
You say it's better to give than to
  receive.
I want to give you everything,
What will I do when you leave?

I'm thinking of you,

Now you're gone and I am alone.
But always are the memories,
Of all the love you've shown.

Remember me here,
Alone and thinking of you;
Come to me when you need
    someone,
I'll be needing you too.

This isn't where I want to end
    this now,
For I only wish inside that I was
    there.
Although the summer is over,
I know there's so much left for us
    to share.

I'll be there soon,
We'll be together then;
I'm living for that moment now,
I'm thinking of you . . . . Again.

Leah Elizabeth Dorney
SORROW
I try not to let it out,
not to let my anguish take over
    me,
but when my heart feels as if it is
    being ripped into my stomache,
    and my throat is tied into a
    thousand knots, I cannot help
    but let the tears roll down my
    cheeks into sorrow.

Bhagwan Khanna
RENASCENT
No one to love me
no one to love
No one to trust me
no one to trust
    Living, though natural
    getting tougher,
    Friendship, though precious
    but getting rare.
Rampant doubts and constant
    fears
uneasy jealousy and killing
    criticisms
frightening shadows and chasing
    frustrations
    Life, my life,
    needs a chance, deserves a
    break,
Faith in self and faith in love
faith in dignity and faith in zeal
faith in humaneness and faith in
    trust
    Lurching vigorously and
    aiming magentically at
    renascent, the hope for
    survival, the hope for growth.

Arlene Longo
FOUNTAIN OF LIFE
A fountain sparkles in the
    moonlight,
Water falls carelessly into it's
    pond.
A small child sits there crying,
She doesn't understand.
So is the fountain of life—all
    things must end,
If only to be born again.
She crys to daddy, and he
    explains
How all must end despite the
    pain.
This end is only a beginning,
And we are the droplets of water.
So as the water flows again all
    crisp and clean;
We too will strengthen when the
    world seems mean.

Mr. & Mrs. William F. Ford
Loree Ford
Octoberfest's Silhouettes

---

*In memory of my mother, Ella
Belle Price Macfarlane, first
Caucasion girl born in the
wilderness area of the Rogue
River, at the mouth of Mule
Creek, Oct. 31st, 1886
Limited education did not restrict
her love for fine poetry and
music, and she kept a little box of
clipped poems she'd read me,
even as a child, instilling in me
that love, still a dominate part of
my life.*

October, month of opulence in
    tree and shrub and sky,
Crisp leaves that crackel
    underfoot, as children hasten
    by,
Trick or treat gobbolins and
    witches by the score
Organize with hoops and hollers
    and
Besiege our dimmly lit front
    door.
Expectantly they clamore and
    extend an emty sack,
Recede, and stand a waiten', to
    see how we'll react.

Fleet of foot and fervant, when
    their request is met,
Excitedly they scamper on, to see
what else they'll get.

Smitten by this season of ghosts,
    ghouls, owls, and cats,
The harvest moon silhouettes
    them, in company with the
    bats!

Beverly Dunn
YEARS
We've lived together for many
    years,
we had many happy moments
    and shed many tears.

We've watched the green grass
    come and go,
and we've seen the sunshine and
    the snow.
We raised our children to our best,
so now I think it's time for a rest.

We've played our part in this land,
and walked through life hand in
    hand.

Remember our wedding day,
you looked so beautiful, so happy
    and gay.

I was overcome by your charms,
and held you tight in my arms.

I was afraid that someone might,
come and take you out of sight.

But, then I knew that you were
    mine at last,
and it was time to think of the
    future and not the past.

We have nothing left to do.
so, my darling don't be blue.

For, now we go hand in hand,
into a better and more wonderful
    land.

Wanda Richey-Roach
**Celebration Of New
    Grandchild**

TO JENNIFER

Love, twice doubled, yet only
    one—
    Tis you, child of my son.
Many versus a single affection
Is my natural heart's expansion

So heart's spaces speedily enlarge
To accomodate earth's new queen
    My once removed charge
    And grand miracle finally seen.

B. A. Breton
HAPPY
Days of happiness, weeks of fun
Months of laughter; we missed
    none
    Days of a year
    Times of a life
    Joys to be found
    When shared with someone.

Elsie Day Cruthirds
THE WILD SEA
Why does the wild sea reach
So madly at the beach
And claw at the sea wall
With waves that always fall
    Viciously tearing the air?

How selfishly she tries
To grasp the starry skies,
Though not just satisfied
With moving with the tide
    While the moon keeps shining
    fair.

The waves can't understand
That the wind gives the command
While the moon gives them light
And watches waves in flight
    When the wind withdraws
    from there.

Just like a bad spoiled child
Who yells loud and wild
For the bright silver moon
Which he demands quite soon
    But the moon will only laugh
    and stare.

Elsie Day Cruthirds-Hutto
The Composer Of My Songs
I was simply a bunch of jumbled
    notes;
    Long notes, short notes,
    With no rests at all.
These notes were flung
    Across my empty strings;
    Just simply noise, Lord
        UNTIL
You took my pen in Your hand,
    Now my heart sings.
You added a beautiful melody,
    Just the right beat, too, Lord,
    And just then,
    You added Your harmony.
Then came Your love,
    Your hope, your time,
        Your song.
You composed the lyrics, then
    came the song.
    Now mine.
Yes, Lord, not my rhythm,
        not my melody,
        not my lyrics,
    Not even my harmony.
But with you, as composer of this
    song
    And your baton within Your
    hand,
I'm under the direction of You
    now, Lord,
    And I will sing this song; for
    now I can.
You placed the notes where they
    should be,
    You made your melody
    beautiful for me,
You gave the rhythm, and the
    rhyme,
    You let your harmony, Thy
    Love, become mine.
You placed each part with love
    and care,
    You let beautiful music sing on
    the air;
Now with you, the composer of
    my songs,
    I can make music for to You I
    belong.
You are the composer of my
    songs;
    To God be the Glory, To Him it
    belongs.

Edith Mariniak Porter
WHAT CAN I DO?
What can I do?
    What can I say?
My nerves are shot
    My hair is grey.

I've labored hard
    And preached a lot
Exhausted all
    The strength I've got.

Reasoned much
    And used the switches
Given the touch
    Burned up britches.

Tried persuasion
    Turned to force
Which left me feeling
    Full remorse.

Our World's Best Loved Poems

All this I do
  While he just sits
And calmly watches
  Me in fits.

What can I do?
  What can I say?
I think I've had
  Enough today!

Naomi (Lowry) Wood
LOVE ANEW
There lies beneath this sky of blue
A haven meant for me and you
And someday in that misty hue
A chance to build our love anew

Helen Cranfill Elliott
BANNED IN BOSTON
Into my garden you came
Sampling my nectars.
When you became satiated,
You darted and soared,
Like a humming bird,
From my beautiful garden
Into another.

Wanda Y. Schooler
An Alien's First Impression

---

*To Dena, who sparked the flame,
Sandy, who fanned the flame, and
Jeff, who fueled the flame.
Without any one of you there
could be no warmth.*

The air was chilled and the night
  was dark.
I landed my spaceship in the park.
I got down on my knees beside
  my berth,
And prayed "Let there be gentle
  life on Earth".

I opened the hatch and stepped
  into the night.
Panic washed o'er me at the
  horrible sight!
What had happened since we last
  checked on this place?
What happened to the peaceful
  human race?

I hid in the dark and regained my
  senses.
I locked the ship and checked my
  defenses.
I left the park to investigate
  farther,
With no intentions of being a
  martyr.

While in the street scurring to
  and fro,
Were creatures of every kind and
  all with a glow!
There were Devils and Demons
  and Vampires too!
Witches and Ghosts and Animals
  from the zoo!

They would run to a house and
  knock on the door.
Sometimes in twos, fives, or a
  score.
A human would come to the door
  for to meet,
The chorus of creatures sang out
  "Trick or Treat".

My recommendation for
  conquering this place?
Forget about the planet and the
  whole human race!

The creatures are small and of
  thousands of types,
With far to many powers for us
  to fight.

Carrie A. White
ONE SIMPLE TEAR
Four children
  sitting at his feet.
  listening to memories of the past
  waiting for grandpa to stop
    rambling on
  not understanding what was so
    special about his youth
One simple tear rolled down
  his cheek.
One teenager
  sitting on the couch
  Remembering grandpa
  One simple tear
  and wishing she had listened.

Barbara Ayers Fischer
THIRD FLOOR ART ROOM
Purple powdered paint
Paper cutter
Paste and clutter
Crayon, sissor, glue
Gray, orange, or blue?
Color, shape, line
Texture, overlapping
Very good design
Large and small give variety
Repeating rhythm is unity
Wow! says John
When can we begin? Asks Lyn
I goofed, exclaims Sam
A goof can change
And
Become anything, offers Joanne
Finish so we can see
Don't forget, clean up
Purple powdered paint

Patty (Tibbs) Lunsford
ANGEL EYES

---

*To my father, Ollie Tibbs, who
since his death at 28 years, has
been my guardian angel. And to
my mother, Edna Tibbs, whose
strength and love inspires my life.*

All thru the skies are Angel Eyes
That watch us everyday.
They watch as we dream,
And robins sing,
And children run and play.
They tell the *Lord* when we are
  good,—
Or bad as the case may be.
But what would help us most of
  all,—
Is if we all could see!

Kathleen Manahan Mc Evoy
CHRISTOPHER ERIC
Christopher Eric was quite
  unexpected,
Christopher Eric was quite a
  surprise,
When Mom and Dad saw him
  the very first time,
What joy could be seen in their
  eyes.

His soft, downy hair and his
  bright, shining eyes,
Made his brothers and sisters all
  smile,
When asked what they thought
  of the baby—

Said: "I guess we will keep him a
  while"

Christopher Eric brings laughter
  and pleasure,
Christopher Eric's a real special
  boy,
Christopher Eric's his Moms'
  special treasure,
Christopher Eric's his Dads' pride
  and joy.

Did the sun shine so bright
  before he came along?
Were there so many stars in the
  night?
Was the sky quite so blue, or the
  grass quite so green?
Or the colours of flowers quite so
  bright?

Christopher Eric is special that's
  true,
But while we are singing his praise,
Remember his brothers and
  sisters as well,
Who each have their own special
  ways.

D. Svuba
BEIRUT
When I was young and naive,
I thought it was an aftershave
With an exotic name and
  sensuous scent.

But like an apple turned sour
Or a dog gone crazy,
Beirut has changed.

Lost Lebanese walk in a forest of
  fear.
Sorrow and grief run deep in the
  streets.
Burning bombs and stenching
  bodies
Pockmark the battlefield of beirut.

Armed reality struggles with itself.
Peacekeepers gaze upon their
  crystal ball
Inside—
Future confusion reigns supreme.

Donald Dennis
I DIDN'T KNOW CHRIST

---

*Mr. Jac and Mrs. Dena Colon
Revelation now Box 459 Madison
TN 37115 and the Dennis family
118 Washington St., Clarksville,
TN 37040*

What Christ did in my life,
He bought me out of the land of
  darkness into the light.
I once was lost, but now I'm
  found,
If I had not known Christ from
  the beginning, I would not
  have known about Jesus when I
  first heard the Word being
  Preached, I realize, that
  something was missing out of
  my life.
And that was Jesus, was the
  answer to my life
I finally realized that I had to
  make up my mind.
Do I want to go to Heaven, or
  Hell
I had to pray about this and it
  really did concern me for I had
  to make a choise.

E.M.C. Arnusch
FALL BEAUTY

---

*My Thanks Goes to God,—My
Mentor!*

Woods are gloriously aflamed,
Filled with an array of colors,
Russet leaves, crisp and dry,—
  Blowing,
    Falling,
      Floating,
In riotous beauty.

Mountains cloaked
In a coat of many colors,
  Golden larches,
    Silvery birches,
    Greenish pines,
Like an artist's palette,
Filled with colored paints.

A rare painting,—to be seen
Green and gold poplar trees,
  Flaming bushes,
    Bronze Shrubbery,
    Crimson plants,
Colored reflections,—in a stream.

With His giant paint brush
And His mighty Hand,—
  Splashes,
    Bloches,
    Touches,
The Lord,— has painted the land.

Violet B. Barton
INSPIRATION
Sweet Inspiration!
It lifts—it laughs—it lives.
Blest is the one who has it;
Blest . . . who gives.
Swiftly it arises, expanding
  multicoiled.
Gently it infiltrates; ill intent is
  foiled.
Above a human love kiss
Which, given morn or evening
Could still by-pass the heart's
  response
For lack of proper leavening,
Sweet Inspiration touching, mind,
  heart, soul,
Could unify our life into
A grand, concordant whole!

W. T. Reeves
THE BEAUTY OF DEATH
I watched a leaf, in autumn, come
  gently spinning down,
to join a million others already
  on the ground.

In my heart there is a sadness for
  winter is on it's way,

and the thing that we call death
claimed another life today.

The little leaf now lifeless and
slowly turning brown,
death seems everywhere as more
join it on the ground.

Man is the only one saddened by
the leaf that died today.
The other animals are rejoicing
and going on their way.

Maybe it's because their noses
are just inches off the ground
and they smell the decay of death
as the leaves are turning brown.

Or do they smell the breath of
life bursting in the ground?
And understand the mystery of
the leaves turning brown.

A billion microorganisms
munching all around,
bacteria regenerating life that
started in the ground.

Man's nose so proudly pointing
high into the sky,
he totally missed the beauty of
why things have to die.

The little leaf was aging so death
was just a way,
of speeding up the process of
giving life to another day.

Alma Leonor Beltran
TODAY'S SONG

*I lovingly dedicate this poem to
my dear sister, Ramond Martinez
Perez, who has had the fortitude
to perceive Life's sunshine inspite
of the darkest clouds.*

Live this day to the fullest!
Fill your heart with a song
Tomorrow is not yet here
And yesterday's long gone

Weed out your garden of all your
past mistakes
Plant all your dream seeds with
Hope and newborn Faith
Bury deep all your troubles, all
your sorrows
Build new foundations for better
tomorrows

Live this day to the fullest!
Love, rejoice without fear
For yesterday has long gone
Tomorrow is not yet here

Valarie Westbrook
YOU HAVE TOUCHED ME

*To: Conn Carson Who has taught
me so much about friendship.*

You have touched me,
Deep inside my heart.
You have loved me,
Soothing my battered soul.
You have given me
A special part of you.

You have touched me,
With your loving ways.
You have loved me,
Giving my heart hope.
You have given me
All I'll ever need.

You have touched me,
Gently, like a whisper.
You have loved me,
Mending broken dreams.
You have given me
Friendships golden love.

Nathan Vogel

Nathan Vogel
Poor Little Broken Blossom
Poor little broken blossom
Lying on the ground,
Poor little broken blossom
Once so safe and sound.
Basking in the sunshine
Drinking in the rain,
Poor little broken blossom
Life was all in vain.

Ah! the hand that plucked you
Never cared or knew,
Poor little broken blossom
What it meant to you.

The sun may shine again,
The rain may fall
But to poor broken blossom,
It means nothing at all.
Torn from her bed,
She can't raise her head
For poor broken
blossom—is—dead.

Kimberly Stevanus
A LITTLE RAIN
Into every life, a little rain must
fall.
Into every pillow, a few tears
must be shed.
Pain and sorrow are at sometime
felt by all.
The words of despair at sometime
must be said.

Every river must someday meet
the ocean.

Every rainbow must someday
fade away.
There are dreams that never get
into motion,
But always, the memories will stay.

Some days must be without the
sun.
Some nights must be without the
moon.
Some deeds are simply never done,
But the happiness is coming soon.

Please, little one, listen to my
whispered call—
Into every life, a little rain must
fall.

Zoe D. Clark
TOGETHER

*To my husband whose love and
devotion inspired me to write
this poem.*

Together we travel the long road
of life,
And too often we find trouble
and strife.
We're hurt and sorry and often
we fear,
The struggle will cause us to lose
what is dear.
But the love we have is stedfast
and strong,
To face the road—no matter how
long.
If we cling to each other and let
love be our guide,
We'll pass thru the strife to the
sun filled side.
Our love and devotion much
stronger will grow,
If daily to each other our love we
show.

Grace Shelton Dukeminier
'TIS NOT NEWS
When snow drifts pile around the
door
Our paper lands right in it.
When snow is gone and cold
winds howl
Our nightly search can reach its'
limit.
But spring has come and work is
hard
Our time is spent in hours.
Guess where the "daily news"
winds up . . .
Among our favorite flowers.

Harvey G. Gammon
WORLD OF TEARS
A man in a crowd, unknown
Passing by a silent world—known.
He cries,
Someone steps out of the crowd
(cloud)
Feels the tears,
And together they cry out loud.
Another hears—soon to follow
A world of tears, filled with sorrow
Leaves another standing alone,
and hollow
Clouds cast around him to
bellow.
From the crowd the tears rain on
him—
Tries to run, but there's no escape,
The storm grows bigger—darker,
With every step he makes.

He stands alone to face this fate
In silence he begins to meditate.
The crowd cries around him and
fears,
He waits, someone steps out of
the tears.
Another breaks through—soon
follows
A world of tears, cleared of
sorrows.

Lilyan Cuff Shaw
TO WITCH A WITCH
I thought she was a witch you
know
And, foolishly, I told her so
I lost her friendship, saw her hand
Waver from the reprimand
As she drew meaning I knew not
To be the ending of a plot
From satan on his frozen star . . .
Once called a witch, that's what
you are!

Shella M. Lucas
OCTOBER

*To Lance, For understanding and
sharing my great love for classical
literature.*

The wild geese are flying south,
Cold weather's coming soon,
So bid farewell to summer's drouth,
And greet the harvest moon.
Take time to rest from a year of
work,
And bask in the golden sun.
Be happy and proud as you look
back,
And survey a job well done.
October skies are bright and
clear.
It's autumn nights are long,
Enjoy it's music while it's here,
Don't wait for winter's song.

Michael Chesney
ESCRITITOS
Pieces of paper,
Parts of my life,
Scraps with scribbles
Of adolescent strife.
Precious little poems—
Silly little things;
Incomplete thoughts,
Songs no one sings.
Ridiculous fantasies,
Lovesick laments,
Most mediocre
(None excellent).
Brought forth with joy
Though born through tears,
Bittersweet writings
Chronicle my years.

Karen Morgan Myers
**My Like-My Love, My
Buddy—My Friend**
A bud becomes a flower
And a lie a sin,
Girls grow into ladies
While boys become men.

It takes many years to develop
into such
Through good times and bad, to
have that final touch.
If all these things are possible,
then why can't we
Take what was once a "like" and
make it "love" for you and me?

242

I've passed the stage of worrying
what others think, say, or do,
This main factor I can contribute
to you.
I've conquered all these things
that life has brought my way
But I don't think I could make it
without you here from day to
day.

Whether it be like or love, it
really matters not,
For a friendship like ours can
never be forgot.
The very best of buddies we have
been and shall remain,
With nothing to lose from it,
only to gain.

There you have my story
My thoughts, feelings, and fears,
And when the time for parting
comes,
There'll be laughter, pain, mostly
tears.

Annette M. Imus
A SMILE
When you see someone smile.
Doesn't it make you feel good,
for just a little while.
A smile, is like the sun.
It brightens up the day.
So what do you say,
Give someone a smile along the
way.
And brighten someones day.

Ms. Denise Johnson
DOWN ON HIS KNEES
Down on his knees praying to God
The one who's most closest to his
heart
Sharing every moments with
family, friends on earth
Being meekheartness, polite,
being treated like dirt
But still yet he had the heart to
say,
"I Love You, I Really Do!"
He seen the beauty of God
That stays deep down within his
heart
Sharing that Godly love to the
world.
Not taken all but wanting to share
At times a voice would say, "I'm
God!"
The One Who's Closest To Your
Heart

Mary Brickman Mayse
SPIRIT OF HALLOWEEN
The brisk cool winds are howling,
and there's a creeking of the old
wooden door.
Now you have a very eerie feeling,
but it's just the spirit of
Halloween, once more.
On your way, to the next door
you go,
when you come to another little
person, "Oh, Hello".
He ask's "Who are you?"
"Well, I'm little boy blue."
"And you don't look scary—"
"Well of course not, I'm a yellow
canary!"
"Let's walk together we'll have fun,"
but I'm scared, so let's not walk,
we'll run."
With their bags full of candy,
and lot's of happiness in their
smile.
They reach a big creepy house,
stand back, look, and wait for a
while.
The house is standing on a hill,
they walk the path slowly, on
their way.
When they hear the whoing of an
owl,
their knee's start to shake, and
they wish for the light of day.
They reach the entrance, see the
black painted door,
The door slowly open's and they
yell "Trick or Treat"
The witches, ghosts, goblins and
much, much more,
came out to give them something
sweet.
and as you see the closing of the
door,
you know you got the spirit of
Halloween, once more.

Virginia M. Weber
He Glances From the Sun
Sitting upon rocks
Watching the Spring water
Pure ripples over stones
And freshness from the Earth
Pebbles from ancient times
And hills of water-cress

Ducks like buoys
Coasting into shadows
The crooked trees of wet-lands
Forming patterns on the lake
Eternity held in tree arms
And growing grasses

Listen to the sounds of swamp
Insect buzzing, bird calls
Be at peace, for He is here
Raise your head

D. F. dal Porto
FACE OF NIGHT
Dead Night, Dread Hag, who
gnaws at both my eyes,
And leaves their dark and
senseless sockets bare;
Foul Fiend, whose darksome
aspect ever lies,
Enshrouded by the comely veils
you wear;
Unmask! And show thy face, O
Hellish Queen;
Reveal that visage so long unseen!
Cast off that outward sight,
enchanting and fair.
Thy mystic mien that draws men
near;
Their unsuspecting souls to snare,
And 'prison in thy dismal lair;
Away, fell Siren, on human prey
ravined!
No more by you my rotting
corpse be gleaned!
For soon thy lightless, lurid sway,
Be vanished in the Purifying Day!

Elizabeth Haynes McAnally
OCTOBER IS A VAMP
Upon reflecting—calm and sober,
my favorite must be October.

She waltzes in, in satin gown
of red and gold and bronze and
brown,
drops bits of lace
on field and town.

She wafts a perfume thro' the air
and scatters sunshine everywhere.
Her breath is wine and flowers
and musk,
and damp as dewdrops in the
dusk.

She brings the pumpkin from the
vine
and needles falling from the pine.
She fills us too, with golden days,
apples ripe and sunset's blaze

Turning, she prepares to go
and dons a wrap of feathered
snow.
A wink, a smile, we may
remember—
then ushers in the grey
November.

Nadeem Shaikh

Nadeem Shaikh
REINCARNATION

*Dedicated to Dearest Masoom &
Amina*

My body it is a base
for I the soul to participate
in this race.

An Endless cycle of birth,
I'm still imprisoned inside
This earth.

I seek for the one way out
yet I worry as I'm still in
doubt,
the transmigration of my soul
I know it won't grow old.

My dreams and facsimilies
they show me past, a past that's
quite vast.

I look not for my future
but to my creative end—
seeking transcedental knowledge
so I'll be immortal and live in
the spiritual world that has no
end.

HARE KRSNA, HARE KRSNA
HARE RAMA, HARE RAMA
I say these words to forgive
my sins, despartley hoping for
immortality to win.

Jane Hurst
MISCONCEPTIONS
I always knew that owning a boat
Being part of a crew and being
afloat
Was azure blue skies, bright
summer sun,
Water so sparkling and clear,
Diving and skiing, just imagine
the fun;
Hauling in fish, having a beer.

Nobody told me that lines and
cables and pumps
Get tangled and twisted into foul
rusty lumps.
Nobody mentioned the high price
of fuel
And new life jackets and flares.
Sending away for that special tool
To fix the spot where the canvas
tears.

Ah, yes, owning a boat is no
longer funny.
It's a hole in the water for my
time and my money!

Ginny Sunken
YESTERDAY
We reached across the years
For a trace of yesterday
As we touched—we grew
Loving as we attained today
With night came our parting
There was no other way
But the memory is sweet
When I think of yesterday.

Glenda C. Laster
THE REAL *CHRISTMAS*
When I was a child Christmas was
A joyous time of year.
There were gifts, food, and big
warm smiles
And lots of merry cheer.

But now I see it differently
The way that it should be.
That's why I want to tell the world
What Christmas means to me.

Christmas is not a tinseled tree
With shiny gifts beneath.
Christmas is love within my heart
And a very real belief.

The Son of God came to the world
Without a royal crown.
Upon a manger bed he lay
While Heaven's Host looked down.

His mission was to die for men
Although some do not care.
He suffered on a cruel cross
The sins of all to bear.

The Son of God was sent to earth
To give His life for me.
He is the greatest Christmas Gift
A priceless one, yet free!

Rebecca McLusky
MY MASK
So you think you know me, do
you?
How can you say that when I
don't know myself?
What you see is a facade
Built up over the years of hurt.
As I stand here looking at you,
Watching you, watching me
I think about what you see.
Someone who works hard
Someone who plays hard
Someone who appears in charge
of themselves.
Really what I am is a person full
of conflicts,
Of ups and downs, of great joys
and of great sadnesses.
Someone who strives hard and
never seems to get anywhere
Someone with great fears, hurts
and lonelinesses.

I have few friends who come and go,
Only to become memories.
My life is drifting on without me.
What you see is a mask
Hiding what goes on behind it.
And like any mask, it is a good disguise.

Linda J. Breiting
ANTICIPATION
Her pots were boiling in preparation,
The potion was finally right—
A pinch of this and a dash of that,
Her prize winning witch's delight . . .

Her black cape was washed and drying,
She added a log to the fire—
Maybe now she'd just sit a spell,
She didn't want to tire . . .

Her faithful broom stood ready and waiting,
Their journey diligently planned—
It was going to be so grand . . .

What was that, a noise outside?
It must have been the wind—
She shifted her eyes to the darkened window,
Her fun was about to begin . . .

The clock on the wall stroked midnight,
The witching hour was here—
She nervously cracked open her heavy, oak door,
Well, maybe she'd wait till next year.

Ted Cowdrey
AZURE BLUE

My daughter Lynne and my son Paul: May the close of every day bring you new light.

Look!
Westward wakes a brand new day mixing morning orange d'light . . .
Azure blue turns black this day slips into night . . .

Kenneth Arruea
The Poet and the Painter
Said The Painter to the Poet:
Greater am I than thee
Gaze upon my great creation so beautiful to see
Painted valleys in the sunset, rivers flowing far below
Forests green with ancient wisdom
Mountains caped with fallen snow

Said the Poet to the Painter:
Yes, I see it very clear
Filled with beauty beyond belief but you are wrong I fear
No greater is one man than another when all live in the light
For God is father of creation
Be humble in His sight

Keotah M. Fannin
DREAM PILLOW
I dreamed I had a fortune
To pile upon your head
But when I woke up
I only had the feathers

From the pillow on my bed
I dreamed I held up diamonds
Pearls and rubies red
But when I woke up
In my hands were feathers
From the pillow on my bed.

I dreamed I held you close to me
On my shoulder was your head
But when I woke up
In my hands were feathers
From the pillow on my bed.

No matter what my dreams will be
They won't be like they said
For when I wake up
I'll only hold the feathers
From the pillow on my bed.

How many times, Dream Pillow
Will I wake up instead
Holding only the feathers
From the pillow on my bed?

Violet Morris
The Old Rocking Chair
The woman was hagged, old and grey,
She must have seen, a better day,
Pushing her grocery cart to her door, she paused to find her key,
Nervously, she looks around, for fear of an intruder,

Finally she enters her home, thanking God, that all is well,
Putting her groceries away, she then sat down, with a prayer,
Thanking God, for her little home, the peace and quiet there,
She sat down, in her old rocking chair, with her cup of tea,

How she loved the old rocking chair, and the memories it held,
It was bought on the day, her first son was born,
And is now three score and more years old,
Her Henry, who is now passed on, gave her this loving chair,

If the times could be counted, for the rocking she did,
The numbers, would run into thousands,
For the good Lord, gave her six fine sons, all doing well now,
Yes, she is proud of her boy's, yet, so often they forget her,

There are times, when one or the other, sends her a gift,
Or makes a phone call, to say hello,

She has little news for them, but to hear their voices delights her,
She never tells them of her lonelyness, or the fear of being attacked,

Why should she burden them, with her troubles,
Tis God who really understands, he comforts her in her prayers,
Tis God, who listens to her songs of old,
As she rocks, in her old rocking chair.

Patricia A. Paton
Halloween, The Way It Was

Dedicated to Laurence L. (G.R.H.S.), Rhea M. (Reilly), Laurence W., Kenneth F., Charles J., ... to High Street, Mulberry Hill, Gramp's garden, Cowboy Hill, Ma's baking and Pop's bleach, backyard skating, an old black stove and a Great Depression that kept the family together . . .

Ah . . . for the days when I was young.
Mother allowed us so much fun!
The house was not modern, it swayed, it creaked,
As we danced and we danced on good strong feet.
Full of fear, my father, that the floor might give way,
That the yard ended up a good place for rough play.
Seventy-five happy children, I couldn't say "no",
When a few were invited but all wanted to go.
Doors slammed for post office, the neighbors could hear!
Caught up in the party, they came to be near.
Laurence played the piano, we sang along,
As my mother made snacks, to keep up with the throng.
Decorations were everywhere, bright orange and black.
There wasn't a thing that this party did lack!
My Gramp held a towel as he heartily laughed.
Kids ducked for apples, you'd think we were daft.
Out on the street bonfires were burning.
Today, we frown; then we were learning.
Cutting the clothesline, a pin in a bell!
Someone threw water, someone's face fell!
People were happy though people were poor;
Accepted their plight—not bad to the core.
Halloween saw its day when life was so simple.
When everyone cared, yet survival the riddle.
I shared in that life, I am happy to say,
When family and friends got in nobody's way.
We sang and we laughed on the

front porch at night.
It was good, it was warm, it was God in His might!

Frances Jane Dunkle-Hunter
TREE AND ME
As a child
I was like the Spring buds ever swelling with new growth
Life for me
has been akin to the summer tree whose foliage is ever tested by outside elements
I have grown
from a mighty oak and have stood strong
My roots
so long ago were firmly planted in rich brown earth
I have injested
all the richness that God fertilized
my boughs with
Now it is the Fall
a time for rest
You will find me
when Spring returns, the same sturdy
oak, but new growth will be present
Oh I may look weathered
but look deeply, you will see the strength is still there
I am not yet ready
for the woodsmans ax.

Haleh Vahidi
A NEW BEGINING
As I sit in the darkness of the night;
And as the night drags on;
I carefully let go of the memories,
And let them fade away into the night.
The love, the pain, the laughter;
They all go.
By the time the sun comes up,
And the light shines in;
I've got a new life ahead of me,
Clear from the start—

Ruth Olkewicz
Coward's Dance Floor

I dedicate this poem to my son and his wife married in June, and my niece and her husband married in September; and my niece's father's comments at the weddings.

We've got the beat, but we're out of step,
One two, one two, they say;
With all those dancers on the floor,
We seem to be in their way.

Therefore, I think that there should be,
A dance floor for us cowards,
We're shy and yet we love to dance,
I know we'd last for hours.

Marjorie Gagnet Berry
MAN
Upon golden chariot, great stallions pulling the way, no time to pick a flower or beneath a shaded tree play.
Round steel wheels are feeling

the strain, the pace becomes even faster,
denying weariness, hearts emote, but the mind is the master.
Faster, faster, sprinting, galloping, wheels forever turning,
ambition, goals, dreams fulfilled are the secrets within burning, burning.

Chris Roach

Chris Roach
ON THE DRIVE

This poem is dedicated to my family, who lived and grew up on the drive.

There was a house located
right up on Riverside Drive.
In this house once lived eleven people
but more would often arrive.

Twenty seven, seventeen
was the first address it held.
Then Seventy two, fifty one
a house its size should be celled.

Eleven rooms it did have
to hold a family that size.
And with the feeling of togetherness
what problems could arise?

At one end of the house was a study
and at the other end a car port.
In the front yard a large Weeping Willow
and in the back a rotted tree fort.

Nine kids seated at the table
all screaming and fighting for food.
But only doing this in front of company

was it ever considered rude.

Sam the dog and two gerbils dwelled there
also Toto and Tigger the two cats.
But what really takes me back to the drive
is reading this poem just like that.

Ruth E. Morgan
AT ALMOST 92

To My Mother, Mrs. Anna Stoole

Our Mom's face is thin and all lined,
Her will is ever so strong and she's still keen of mind,
She's mentally alert and has her pride
Has a sense of humor, takes things in stride,
        "At Almost 92"
Loves to read outloud and an audience craves,
So articles of interest she collects and saves.
Out of a two-door car she climbs in and out,
Rides in the back seat, claims there's more room to move about.
        "At Almost 92"
She's fussy about making her bed each morn, it has to be just so,
Pillows fluffed, bedspread straight, otherwise it's a "no-no."
She recites "Black Sarah" verbatim, a favorite childhood hymn,
Her voice breaks, however, so the song she doesn't try to sing.
        "At Almost 92"
She's brightened the lives of those who love her, and has given from the heart,
She's the dearest of all Mother's, to make her happy we all try and do our part.
        "For She's Almost 92"

Natalie Fern Zaidman
The Secret Of the Night

Tonight
All shall come
From the depths of time
They will rise
And overcome
Their weapons of death
Follow close behind
Frightening all in their way, they come closer
Closer
Closer
Drawn by the moon
Full, large, their guiding light
The moon
'Til the rays of Dawn
Find their way through the dark, lonely sky
And return the visitors to their resting place
Until the next
Halloween

Mary Helm McRoy
There Are No Words

There are no words, when
autumn leaves come down
In showers, like a shimmering golden rain;
Or when one leaf, high on a

sycamore,
Falls twirling down to meet the earth again.

And when the leaves go dancing down the street
Before a wind that has a winter sting,
There are no words to tell the sudden, swift
Emotions that they bring.

For, with the leaves, my heart is dancing to
A tune no other earthly thing affords;
An exaltation high, and clear, and sweet;
And for this pinnacle, there are no words.

Robin Fern Spain
THE BLACK HORSES

Prancing across fields of bearberry and pulsarilla
Come the black horses of a thousand windswept days
Look across the white clay creek of lost Lakota ghost dancers—
In the timeless wind—in the timeless wind
Seek the western circle and you shall see the horses of another morning roaming
Until their days are done.

Michael Calabrese
IN THE NIGHT

These nights of mine,
like themeless books with no pages.
Sleepless black slabs of slate, cold, angular, stark.
One fitting neatly next to the last along the shelves on my walls;
adding up to absolutely nothing.

Charity Turner
WINTER

The leaves turn green,
then they turn gold,
Then they turn brown,
No more to hold.

The trees are bare
all winter long.
The birds are no more
Calling their song.

It's white thru out the winter,
but not thru out the Fall.
Not to doubt Winter,
the coldest of them all.

Marci Pulczinski Lindahl
A SECOND CHANCE

While spending time together,
It made us so aware,
That people hold their love inside
And never show they care.

Then God hands out his orders,
It gives you quite a scare.
You realize the love you have
Was meant for you to share.

God granted us this time right now,
To take another glance.
And love each other openly,
It's called *"A Second Chance"*.

Judy L. Honea
What Will People Think

You tell me you are a Christian.
But you slander your neighbor each day.

You're concerned with, "What will people think!"
If I dare do things my way.
You're not concerned with, "What will God think!"
If you live a certain way.
It's always, "What will people think!"
If I dare do things my way.
It isn't important, "What people think!"
It couldn't matter less.
It's, "What God thinks that's important!"
So try to do your best.
He wants us to love our fellow-man,
Be ready to give him a hand;
And if he's troubled and bothered,
Always try to understand.
Don't worry about his *color*.
Don't worry about his *looks*.
It's really *what's* inside that *counts*.
And it's *God* that keeps the *books*.

Carol Ann Hershberger
GO AHEAD—CRY

To my mother, my step-father, and to the loving memory of my father, for their love and understanding.

If you should feel the need to cry
Don't ever hold it back
For sometimes it relieves the hurt.
Your pride you will not lack.

Some people say men should not cry
For fear it shows they're weak.
But those who think that this is true
Shoud have no right to speak.

A man can also feel the hurt.
Why must he be denied
The right to let his tears fall free?
He should not have to hide.

So let this man be human too,
And let his feelings show,
For if he's not allowed to cry
This man may never grow.

Cindy Lynette Leoni
RESTLESS DESPAIR

Tears lie hidden behind my eyes,
Lids—moist with thoughts
Tears grasping—as they slowly slide down the sides of my face;
clinging to their very existence, falling to their destiny . . . as do I, my heart heavy,
    my feelings beyond— something within
That I can not find. I desire to free it . . . yet the key is missing, mistakely misplaced.

Inside me, deep, hard to understand—lies this key.
Knowing myself is difficult. I am one thing and yet another,
Seeking to find where my soul is hidden . . . I know it follows near my consciousness.
For me—this valued emotion comes and goes. I fear one day—it may leave.
    God help! My soul—if it departs. Keep my mind and know my heart,

for the feelings and thoughts
of my mind—
are not my own.

Katherine Thomas
THE SAND PILE
Children
Playing at my door
And who on earth
Could ask for more.

My folding chair
Is out of place,
My walking stick
Is a disgrace.

Grimy and gritty
From wetted sands
And shovels and sieves
To castles grand.

To bridges
Over narrow moats
With draws that open
To boats that float.

And if the sand
Seems scant and poor
Do take
What's on my kitchen floor.

Gloria Jean Robertson
JUST YOU SUNSHINE

---

*So happy you have made me—
This past year of 83; My Dear
ERNIE MICHAEL CONTI!!!*

My dearest Sunshine!
With you, I hear the bird sings,
The grass is greener,
The sky is bluer,
And my heart doth take on
wings!

My dearest Sunshine!
Just the thought of you,
Starts my pen aflowing,
As you inspire fantasies,
That keep growing and growing!

My dearest Sunshine!
Your eyes possess me,
Your arms entwine me,
Your lips give a kiss so exotic,
That you leave positively estatic!

Darlene Brandon
DANCE OF THE NIGHT
Death by darkness comes quickly
As if by the madness of night
The groan you hear in the stillness
Bespeaking our own inward fright

Of mans necessary evil
Laying placid in light of day
Just waiting for you to stumble
And carry you quickly away

Surrounding your flesh with
temptation
Alluring with unspoken words
The darkness is pushing and
pulling
and piercing the goodness with
words

You feel it caressing your body
Holding you ever so tight
You can feel the good of your
spirit
Slipping off into the night

The world will soon be in
darkness
The good will have gone with the
light

All thats left are the wicked and
evil
Dancing the Dance of the Night

George Givens
REJUVENATION
I saw a skinny old dog
Going down the street;
He was limping along
And he looked mighty beat.
He found an old bone
And he began to eat.
Now he glides along
Like a boat with a sail,
With his head held high
And wagging his tail;
Clear cool water
In a rusty old pail.

Paul Omar Campbell
THE BABY
There he lies, pink-fisted, asleep
With all his future ahead;
With never a thought of the vigil
we keep
Over his wee little bed.

He'll soon be a president, or
preacher, or what,
If we knew how to cheer him.
He could be a thief, a beggar, or
sot,
If we shoud not rightly rear
him.

Oh, may his training be Godly
and pure;
May evil learning not reach him.
May his name be bright, and
always endure,
Why? God taught me how to
teach him.

Roberta Reading
SUPREMANCY
I did not pray this morning, the
way is very dark
The Bible left upon the sill is
such an easy mark.
I'll hurl it through the casement,
out in the dripping rain
For hatred reigns within my
breast and fogs my lowly brain.

Of God, Why did this happen, Oh
God, how can it be?
When all these years I've sought
you out, evil's still with me!
Oh can't you see? Oh can't you
tell my heart is breaking too!
How can I know, How can I find
joy in serving you?

It's pages I'll tear asunder, not to
be read again.
"You Fool! To believe all that
garbage
To believe in the rise and fall!
You, of course, are the big-gest
joker of them all."

I'll turn on the news this evening
to see what the weather will
be.
Tomorrow I'll start a new life and
from this humbug be free.
The program was not what I'd
wanted, the speaker concluded
his talk.
The chords of the organ, the
words of a hymn are forever
lost to my ear.
But overwhelmingly clear dame
the thought "I'm still here."
So that trust and I took a walk.

Travis Hilton Beman
CHRISTMAS 1981
Christmas is a happy time of year
you know,
With lots of presents, Christmas
trees and snow.

And if you're good all year round,
Old Santa Claus will come down!

Down from the sky
With his eight tiny reindeer that
fly.

But we must not forget what
Christmas is really about,
Because to Jesus it doesn't matter
whether we cry or pout.

So remember on Christmas day
When you open your presents
and begin to play

It's really His birthday!

Theresa D. Jones
AT THE PARK
The wind hits my hair
As I get higher
In the air
On the swing.

I stop moving my legs
And I close my eyes,
And I think
About the wind and other things.

My stomach feels
Like it's being
Dropped from the sky
To the ground.

When I get closer to the ground,
My feet hit the sand
And I open my eyes
And start getting higher again.

Beatrice Waters
EVENING SHADOWS
The evening shadows push and
shove
Around my cottage door
Then move with gentle velvet feet
A cross my kitchen floor
They mingle with the night birds
call
But then the fires glow
Scatters them like autumn leaves
To where ever shadows go

Lisa hope Greene
SHANNA'S WORLD
Shanna, the girl who could only
dream. Died today.
Young and beautiful was she.
The world was hers, she could not
get it for her
life was short,
Only eighteen winters old.
Love, was hers for an instant, then it
fled down the road
never to turn back.
White walls surrounded her life
for two and a half years.
To see sunshine through multi-
coloured glass was joy.
To see faces through waves of
plastic was a terrible dream.
Happiness came when death took
with it the pain, the tears,
and the feeling of total loss.
For she was young and the world
was hers but life

she could not
hope to grasp.
Now she is just a memory
of a girl . . . We can keep.

Alyce Chew DiBella

Alyce Chew DiBella
FALL FANCIES
While leisurely strolling through
the woodland with its wild
sweet fragrant smell,
Observing God's timid and wary
little creatures in the leafy
nooks they love to dwell;

Where the trees' waving arm-like
branches seemed to urgently
beckon me
To wander further and find other
wonders that were hidden, at
first glance, to see;

And the wind, through the trees,
was like a solemn sermon,
given for the nature-loving
attentive ear;
While through this lacy leafy
vista the frail azure suggested
God's presence, which seemed
consolingly near.

Thus, suddenly recalling that the
fall is also here when all nature
excells in great splendor;
When the leaves of the trees, in
their varigated tints presents a
vivid picture, indeed, of rare
grandeur;

And, the farmers their precious
hard-worked for harvest, have
hurridely and carefully
gathered in
Before Jack Frost could slyly
come along, and quickly nip
them to ruin;

And, I all this wondrous
picturesque beauty and
amazing metamorphosis do
behold
With half-sorrowful eyes,
realizing winter soon follows
with its mostly dismal, gray
and cold days, all told.

R. Elton Cook
FLUFF
A storm cloud cries
Then dries its eyes
The flow of tears abates;
With one last growl
Resumes its prowl
Or else evaporates.

Our World's Best Loved Poems

Linda Blue
MOON IN THE LAKE
I walked through the clouds
silent like a breeze in the night
moving through my hair
"Are you there? Are you there?"

I ask the question
I am the messenger
In a shroud of haze and
    subtleness of light
I whisper in your ear, "You know
    what to do"
"Time to choose! Time to choose!"

I cry through the pain
silent like a single drop of rain
passing through my time
"Are you mine? Are you mine?"

I am the answer
I am the passenger
In a blaze of light touchingly real
I shout so you will hear, "Answer
    my prayer!"
"Are you there? Are you there?"

I slide through the glass
silent like the moon in the lake.

Diane M. Flaherty
PSYCHIATRIST
given "presents" every day
to unwrap and look
to toss away
over his shoulder
a mountain of sighs
untied ribbons
last goodbyes

charles davis
debit
waiting
with no lines
no formica counters
and no five part forms
that fall apart
when you pick them up

waiting
for a check
that's in the mail
and apparently knows
the virtue of arriving
fashionably late

waiting
for forty minutes more
before all the tellers
in the world
go home for the weekend

Everett Francis Briggs
AT CHRISTMAS
To all who go outbranching ways,
    To all from family apart,
Blest Christmas now, as long ago,
    Is still a journey of the heart.

When one, at Christmas, can not span
    The farflung and estranging
    miles.
Somehow the heart grows sad
    within,
    At thought of all those missing
    smiles.

In Bethlehem though all was
    bleak,
    Smiles lighted up night's savage
    frown.
The hope of ages, Christ, was born,
    Forsaken His celestial crown.

He came to Bethlehem to bless
    His mother, foster-father, too.
To all far from their Bethlehem
    His smile outreaches, e'en to you.

Evelyn Judy Regulus
RED
Sunsets
Velvet
Roses
Cherries
Autumn leaves
Fire
Strawberries
Ruby
Burgundy
Lipstick
Tomatoes
Dead stars
Mars
Apples
Cardinals

Gertrude Millard
THE ELF BRIDE

*To my family and friends—the
greatest fortune anyone could own.*

Mother! I heard the elf-horns
    blow last night when the world
    was still and the full moon laid
    a silver path for the wee folks
    over the hill.

I heard the pattering of their feet
    and the whispering of their
    wings and I knew the grass by
    the wishing tree would be
    marked by their dancing rings.

Mother! They called me the
    whole night through! Bidding
    me "Follow! Follow!" Their soft,
    wild music filled my ears and I
    knew how they thronged
    through the hollow.

But Richard slept sound and did
    not hear, and I lay in the crook
    of his arm. He smiled in his
    sleep and drew me close, and
    his breath on my cheek was
    warm.

Then I knew that, however my
    feet might long to dance in the
    night and the dew, my heart
    would nevermore let me go for
    the love in my heart is true.

All night they called, and my
    eyes were wet with tears both
    of joy and of pain, for they
    knew that I heard them and
    answered not and they never
    will call again.

Pat Sinning
SECOND CHANCE
Our gift of life is from God up
    above
We begin so tiny, helpless and
    need to love
We grow from the nourishment
    the earth has to give
We grow from our spiritual life,
    we need that to live.

We learn right from wrong, good
    from evil, love from hate
We learn as an infant, child, and
    adult, how to take
As we learn to give, care and
    love—we are abused
By those who learned nothing but
    how to hurt and use.

Through our lives our mistakes
    and heartaches are so many
We struggle with work, sweat and

cheat for that mighty penny.
We forget that life was given
    from God up above
To learn about sharing, caring
    and the importance of love.

With old age now upon us our
    life has gone by
We know we have only to look
    forward to . . . die
Death oh so frightening; no we're
    not ready yet
Where is the second chance, that
    part of life we didn't get.

Gibson G. Douglas

Gibson G. Douglas
SALVATION

*Dedicated To E. Lou Cole Who
Made this Book possible. G.D. 83*

May all your skies
    Be sunny
And a pretty blue
When cloudy let the
Sunbeams and rainbows
Come shining through
May all your prayers
Be granted
Many dreams come true
Forever and ever for You

Michelle Lutes
AUTUMN
All the trees wear pretty leaves,
Until they blow with the breeze.
Tumbling through the weary trees,
Until I land upon the leaves.
Mother has gifted our trees,
Nature has given them the pretty
    leaves.

Joyce Suter Whitcomb
DAKOTA SKIES
Perhaps it only seems that way . . .

The sky, so black, like velvet,
The stars so close, I can almost
    touch them,
The air, so soft the slightest
    breeze caresses
Like a tender kiss.

And oh, the smell of the pine trees!
Their fragrant needles crackling
    beneath my feet
Breaking the stillness of the night.
Somewhere there's a plaintive
    sound—
A solitary owl.

The night so perfect,
Like no other,
Anywhere,
Only in the Black Hills,

Just the way I remembered,
Long ago, in South Dakota,
The way a night was meant to be.

Perhaps it only seems that way . . .

Marilyn Dorf
Wheat Fields On Wyoming
    Highlands

*Dedicated to Jan and Don
Peterson, whose own Wyoming
wheat fields inspired this poem.*

Wheat fields whittled hard on
    highlands,
Jaws pried open to the sun,
Sucking sustenance from Nature,
Stiff beards clawing peacock sky.
Wings of purple windstorms
    whistling
Through the golden-tawny mass.

Wheat fields whittled hard on
    highlands,
Just beneath the brow of God,
Savoring untained raindrops;
Tanning under sterling sun.
Regally on rain-mixed mornings
Rainbows rise up from their sod!

Autumn Brenden
FUNNY CREATURE
Funny creature lost and alone
Searching, lerking for a home
Wondrously, adventuring
    through time
Flying with the tides
Floating in confusion
Running from boredom

Hazzy sky so mysterious above
    the horizon
Mysterious lapse
Wonderous endeavors

Flustered by many crys
Which challenge to take
Knowing that there's no
    returning
Temporary arrangements
Distant memories of days past
Stoned with compassion for a
    lovers touch
Haphazardly following feelings

Summers beauty fading, fading . . .
Reflections of the pompous lair
Trying to understand
Funny creature lost and alone

Eddy Shoemaker
The Strawberry Patch
The strawberry patch
Is where I go,
To see the wonder
Of how things grow.

It's God's powers,
His amazing grace,
That is shining all
Around the place.

I rejoice in His
Awesome power,
As I wait for
The final hour.

His brilliant splendor
Fills the skies.
His eternal glory
Blinds my eyes.

From mountains, I'll shout!
From valleys, I'll sing!
Surely, there's no doubt
He's the Almighty King.

Steve Bailey
SUMMER'S VENGEANCE
Wild thunder echoes,
Black stallions in the pasture
Become so restless.

Janie Theresa Crowner
**That Man's House —
(A Special Tribute To
Jeff Jacobs)**

---

*Dedicated to my dearest friend,
with sincere appreciation for
your loyal service to God. Thank
you just for being you—an
inspiration in my life.*

His house is made of neither
  wood nor stone.
That man's house is built with
  flesh and bone.
If you must know who designed
  the blueprint,
A special plan from God was sent.

His house is built on a firm
  foundation—
Nothingless than righteousness
  and salvation.
His frame is strong with
  knowledge and power,
As he consecrates his life each
  and every hour.

His furnishings are neither
  contemporary nor antique.
However, that man's house is
  quite unique.
You must know that he is not
  sophisticated,
But only to God is he dedicated.

His carpet is plush and fine,
As he walks by faith in God's time.
His house is kept clean from
  within,
And the best cleanser is
  abstaining from sin.

He has many occupants residing
  there.
He loves all of them, but his
  favorite is prayer.
That man's house is surely
  anointed,
And the Minister of Music he
  was appointed.

Although his house is quite fine
  and grand,
It's with the grace of God that he
  shall humbly stand.
For the wealth of his house is
  neither silver nor gold,

Because THAT MAN'S HOUSE
  loves God deep within his soul.

J. W. Cheney Jr.
DAYBREAK
Some "other" semblance, surely
"evolving" such, "so" past
enigmatic, "time's" perspective
dim, "forevers" never last?

Damnation, tempus' torrents
imaginatively, "sane."
Breakthrough's "crest", "reality"
remniscent, dreadful, bane.

Second's spectred stallions, surge
fly forth "forever's" nights.
Embridled, "essance" harbinger
facetious, "fortune's" flights.

Hapless, hedonistic hours, part
to daybreak's dawned, anew.
Initiate, "tomorrow"
night-illusive, "time's" askew.

Darrell Fielder
I Relied On a Rose
I relied on a rose
To say my words for me
But all I got was self-dispose
And cruel indignity.

I relied on a friend perchance
To say the things I could not
But within her heart he did
  advance
And stole my sacred lot.

I relied on myself this time
And put my shyness down
I faced the mountain I had to
  climb
And my love did abound.

Chuck Ellery
HERO UNDER LOVE
When love comes down on a
  bold-hearted hero
He hides the feeling 'til they tear
  his apart.
So many feigned loves by cold-
  hearted zeroes,
There's no room for a heroine in
  this hero's heart.
She dares to smite his armor with
  forthright affection,
He positions his aegis to ward
  away her blow.
His effort fall inane; she knows
  not rejection.
She means to break the wall and
  let the river flow.
On and on she tears the wall
  with love her sole agression.
The day breaks, the hero wakes,
  still he's forced in defence.
Without eat, without sleep, he
  muses in depression.
Only loving the heroine will
  restore his hero sense.
Beneath the clock of a winter's
  night echoes a cry of pain,
With love complete the warriors
  meet to fuse their soul in
  chains.

Emily Decker
REMEMBER WHEN?
Remember when you tried to get
  away with something
Only to discover Mom knew it
  all along!
Are you sure she didn't have eyes
  in the back of her head
You thought moms were always
  supposed to be wrong!

She knew everything before you
  started school
Then dropped to second place
  "teacher" took over first
Mom wasn't so anxious to hear
  about all her mistakes
You couldn't understand why,
  when you were about to burst!

During your teens, Mom was far
  from being "cool"
After all she couldn't even spot
  clothing that was "chic"
She always was old fashioned in
  her lingo and her make-up
Instead of "a bummer" she said
  something about a "muddy stick"

By graduation she was beginning
  to wise up
She wasn't always on my case
  about "pigging out" and "zits"
I was wondering if she'd ever
  come out of it
Honestly, sometimes Mothers are
  simply the pits!

I can claim her as one of my
  friends now
We can even go places without
  any dreading
Hm-m-m, you know, the older I
  get, it seems
The smarter my Mom is getting!

Cathi LaVonne Sweat
Walk a Little Plainer Daddy
Walk a little plainer Daddy
  said a little girl so frail
I'm following in your footsteps
  and I don't want to fail
Sometimes your steps are very
  plain
  sometimes they are hard to see
So walk a little plainer Daddy
  for you are leading me.

I know that once you walked this
  way
  many years ago
And what you did along the way
  I'd really like to know
For sometimes when I'm tempted
  I don't know what to do
So walk a little plainer Daddy
  for I must follow you.

Someday when I'm all grown up
  you are like I want to be
Then I will have a little girl
  who will want to follow me
And I would want to lead her
  right
  and help her to be true
So walk a little plainer Daddy
  for we must follow you.

Georgeina Davis
TASTE OF TERROR
Reach deep in the complex
  organism of man.
The terror will imerge that no
  artist dare attempt to capture
  on canvas.
As tots we hide under patch work
  quilts of pastie colours
  arranged in parallel angels of
  one another.
Are tiny toe would not dare
  touch the fake fur rugs that lay
  listlessly on the dark pine floors.
Little screams softly bounce from
  mirror to placid coloured
  paintings that line the hall.

It disappears the instant the
  sweet gentle mothers cradle
  you in her bosom.

As adolescence approach's
  demons seem to grow as we
  indeed do.
Darkness becomes a dungeon of
  dragons for slaying.
Dressing in deformed plastics
  made by little men with,
  questionable desires.
Young men embrace the
  unknown with cave man style
  tactics.
While young ladies shake and
  satuate artificial handkerchiefs,
  scented with a dash of alcohol
  and a dash of rose pedales.
To tease your senses.

But on the other hand.
Adults quickly dismiss as
  excessive imaginations and
  childish expressions.
Novels are typed fearlessly.
Massed produced to reach out
  and captivate with a almost
  contagious like germ.
Movies are publicized and over
  promoted for our nieve benefit.
We crowd into massive
  structures to consume white
  puffed grains and flavored
  liquids.
Resulting in our spines stiffing
  and hair standing at attention
  on our heads.
But as time heartlessly carves
  into weakening defences.
Man seems less impressed by
  conventional attitudes.
Taunting evils become non-
  threatening or just simple
  predictions of a wreckening
  civilization.
We imerge victories.
We have ways to control the
  terror within.
Or is it just waiting to strike
  when man least expects it.
Does it laugh and taunt us with
  its tomfoolery.

Kim Keir
RIVER OF LOVE

---

*To My Darling Ray, whose
constant love, caring and
understanding inspired this
poem. Absence truly makes the
heart grow fonder. Remember, I'm
forever your Angel!*

As I lay here thinking of you
Waiting for the months to pass
Thinking of all the things I want
  to do
Praying that our love will last

As my feelings wash over me
I'm sent into a whirlpool of
  dizziness
Waiting for the moment when
  our love will be free
When I can always feel a ripple of
  happiness

Waiting until we can take a walk
On a deserted sandy beach
Walking, watching the burning
  sunset

Our World's Best Loved Poems

Knowing you're always within reach

Being lost in a sea of passion
As the waves come rolling in
Holding my head against your chest
Feeling the fire from within

Waiting for the chance
For our hearts to blend as one
Waiting for a romance
More exciting than the sun

Everyday I think of you
As sure as the stars above
Waiting for the time when we can
Drown in our river of love

Claudette Wilkins Gibbs
Happy Birthday, Mother

In loving memory of my grandmother, Lillie Bradley

God will bless you today, just as
He did yesterday.
There will always be a guarding angel coming your way.
If there were more people in the world like you,
Everyone would mind their own and know what to do.

Mother, thank you for your love.
Coming from you is like that above.
I remember when I was a child.
You took my hand and held it awhile.

Mother, I will always look upon you as a queen.
You are the greatest I've ever seen.
You will always be a part of me,
From now until eternity.

John Eugene Taylor
NIGHT JOURNEY

To my wife, Alison, with love

When night unfolds
Its perfect paradise,
The destination to another world
Is about to begin.

Close your eyes my dear
Let darkness enter your soft slumber,
Let us journey to the other side of the rainbow.

Free from space and time
We dive under an ocean of dreams,
Sinking deeper, and deeper.

Released, devoid, undisturbed.
Relaxed, tranquil,
Washed away in sleep.

Together, warm, naked.
Nestled like innocent children,
In the womb of solitude.

Connie Michelle Duncan
THE EXECUTION
I hope that I shall live to see
What tomorrow holds for me.
My time is short and running out.
I still can't determine what life's about.

It's been so very long and hard.
I try to get out, but my windows are barred.

Like an animal caged, to be
Inside forever and never free.

What remorse I feel inside,
Knowing that soon I shall have to die.
I think that they have come for me.
I can hear the sound as they turn the key.

Oh no! They mustn't take me out.
"Not yet!" I shout. "I'm not ready to die.
Oh God please don't let me cry.
I'm not a coward so it mustn't seem
That I'm afraid.
I know I mustn't scream.
Just a little longer . . .
please.

Jacklynn M. Donaldson
LONG AGO DREAMS
When I was so small
I would dream . . .
That the moon would fall
So I could meet it's keeper

And I would be so tall
I could touch a falling star
And make my wish,
And make my wish . . .

The wind would carry me away
To visit the dark side of dreams—
Yet to come true . . .
And bring me to you,
And bring me to you . . .

We wait years and years to find
What some people never do
In a whole lifetime
Yet I knew when I saw your face
I could leave the darkness
Of that lonely place,
That lonely place . . .

Katherine H. Rudden
FIRESIDE
As I sit and dream by the fireside,
I see your face so fair
In the dancing flames of fire light . .
And Oh; My dear, I want you to know
Just how much I care.

Stephen J. Torres
THE SMALL PAINTING
When the time was near
I sat looking at a small painting
that you had given me
when you were about six.
The small painting sat around the house for years.
But I never really looked at it
close enough for me to see
the message that you had told.
Now that the time is so short for me
I understand and see a lot more now than before.
It's funny
how my whole life I missed out on so much.
And now that the time is so close there's not enough
to see or hear everything all over again.
I guess I lost.
For now the time is here
And the room darken and slowly
the small painting dissappeared.

Osie C. Brown
HALLOWEEN
Have a pumpkin of a time
Wear a costume if you don't mind
Take a napkin home with you
Just a mask will do!
Its the tradition of the month
It's October for Halloween
Sure will miss some residents here this year
Cannot pull them in
Come one, come all
Prizes will be awarded so wear what you can

Denise Ouellette
WHY??
I asked him why
He gave no reply
Afraid of lying
Yet still loving

Be cheerful
Cause you're an angel
He said with tears
Living without fears

I'm only making you blue
For I can't see you
I won't make excuses
That everyone refuses

But you know I love you
I always said I do
I wish I could embrace
Your heart of lace

I'm sorry
Don't worry
That's all I can say
We'll meet again some day.

Jillian Umphenour
DRIFTING
The ocean
A sparkle of iridescence, lilting to and fro.
I sit alone,
Bare skin on warm sand.
The birds soar,
Suspended by invisible wires
On a vast stage.

I love this place,
It's sounds and scents,
The warm breeze blowing my hair.
Memories wash over my mind
Like watercolors.
Sand castles flattened by the tide,
Lovely moonlit nights.

Forgotten today
Are yesterday's cares.
At this moment,
I would stop the hands of time.
But reality speaks,
"You're not there at all, only looking,
At a picture on the wall."

Malcolm C. Turner-Kerr
An Ode To the Imitators Of Immortality
Doublespeak, triplethink—fun for the sons of power?
As we watch, powerless, each passing hour in trepidation;
And they, in their ill-earned security, silently sneer at our ineptitude.
Oh! Ingenuous voter, that quinquennial conn—
Who said an "X" was quite so strong?—
That power is wielded by the

individual pen
Appointing servants not as individual men but agents of the common will.
X-rated indeed; a bitter pill; a sly deception.
What a hilarious riddle for the kids—
When is a man not a man?—
When he's elected, you fool!—
Oh! how naive, I never thought of that.

But hold it, powerlings, and do not be deceived
Although it may be yours, deceit is not our way.
Neither naive nor fools are we
Our consent is indeed your security;
Consent, now tacit, now of apathy
Remains through an ancient subtlety.
The resource of time of the common man you hold in check—
His king in the chess of powerplay
Against your queen of debt.
Tough, in his insecurity, you cannot have him lose.
Twin paradox behold! A subtle ruse;
His victory is not your loss; but mankind's gain.

Marilyn Mills Robertson
A DREAM

This poem was inspired by a very dear friend who will always be special to me.

I dream about you every night
I've memorized your face
Your special smile I love to see
Your arms my favorite place.

The special way you talk to me
The loving things you do
The way you walk into the room
My only love is you.

The lonesome feeling deep inside
When you are not around
A feeling that I can't explain
That really keeps me down.

The love I feel when you are near
The pain when you must go
The long and lonely days I spend
I need and want you so.

These things and many more
Show the love I have for you
You're a dream I've dreamed about so long
I've wondered if you knew.

Gabrielle Caron
I SET YOU FREE
I wanted you,
You didn't want me.
Our love could never be,
So I set you free.

I needed you,
You didn't need me.
So I said goodbye.
Now I'm alone to cry.

My love for you,
I can't conceal.
I just can't hide,
The way I feel.

249

And as I close the door,
I hope you always find,
Just what you're looking for.

But if you ever find,
You left someone behind,
I'll be right here,
To dry you're every tear.

Gwendolyn Beth Taylor
DEATH DENY ME
What does modern man need see,
  the force of evil life doth be
Upon his back like riding a horse,
  his blood is dry its run its
  course.
And his tomb awaits his bravery,
  I'm asking you death to please
  deny me
The ghastly presence surrounds
  my door, it creaks through
  cracks which sprout the floor
It slinks across rugs and up the
  wall, it flows through the foyer
  and sifts through the hall, And
  knocks upon my heart to call
  me, I'm telling you Death to
  please deny me
Call me when my deeds are done,
  call me when my friends are
  gone
Call me when I'm all alone, call
  me when my heart is stone,
But not when I vibrate with lifes
  energy, I beg of you Death, do
  deny me
The entertainment you provide,
  is dark and lonely so gloomy
  inside
The sweltering premonitions that
  you fortell, plunging man to
  heaven or to hell. I'm not ready
  to die with dignity, so can you,
  will you Death Deny me.
Man cannot say what tomorrow
  may hold, Nor can he create a
  human from a mold. So then
  we know that in the end,
  Death is mans most peaceful
  friend, And in the midst of
  pains great nape, Death can be
  a most valued escape, But I am
  scared so let me be, Unto you
  Death to just deny me.
My days aren't numbered, neither
  few, right now death I don't
  want to meet you, I know of
  hearts you've split in two, I
  know how you work but I'm
  not due.
Deny me please, my life I beg, I
  give you my arm or even my
  leg
But when it's time don't let me
  know, just steal me away like a
  theif and go
Go before I'm missed, the masses
  one lead, Take me I pray before
  they realize I am Dead
I'm so sorry the words shall never
  mean be,
Death my phoniest friend shall
  never deny me
You're too polite and kind to save
This poor pauper from anyones
  grave . . .

Robert F. Grunwald
YOU'RE MY GIRL
At times I love you,
  with such a passion that burns
  inside,

it scorches my soul,
and my only relief is you.
Your sweet smile,
your gentle touch.
At times I love you,
like a child,
with the intence happy,
and carefree trust of the young.
Having no fear,
knowing you'll be there,
to hold my hand and dry my
  tears.
So when I say it soft,
I'm yelling to the world,
I'm in love with you babe,
and you're my girl . . .

Jennifer Marie Beckwith
LONELY FEELING
A lonely chill
Went up my spine.
This one,
Was one of a kind.
A lonely pound
Went through my head,
When I found out
My father was dead.

Now I must
Look ahead,
At my future
Since he is dead.
He may be gone
In the end,
But deep in my heart
He Lives!

Chritine Christian
A STROKE OF LUCK
She wasn't crazy;
there just wasn't anywhere else to
  go.
She always knew
when I was feeling badly,
and with her right side silent,
she comforted me
from the left,
the right words
from a left person.

Jodie Keadle Nemec
NIGHT'S RAINBOW
  Moonlight's glow plays games
  as rings of rainbows reach out
    beaming crystal light.

Doy M. Neumann
DEATH
I rush forward
with arms outstretched
To meet Death
I've waited for
its mystifying disclosure
of the unknown
since I was born
I've overcome my fears
cried my last tears
for all those who
went before me.
Death is no dark enemy
waiting to take me
into—Black Infinity
It is a light at the end
of the tunnel
It is the promise of Glory
a waiting of disciplined time
until one can leave and join
the Divine
The promise of eternal life
the rebirth
without the pain
I rush forward to meet Death
my Birth—my Gain.

Theresa Marie Sokolowski
The Warmth Of Emotion
The two figures embrace
Sharing each other's warmth from
  the cold.
The fire flickers before them,
Casting sparks of light and shadow
  on their rosy cheeks.

She remembers the walk in the
  woods,
Whose memory lingers with her
As their footprints in the
  newfallen snow.
He remembers her smile and the
  look of contentment in her eyes.

Now inside their awakening
  continues.
Wrapped in a blanket and each
  other's emotion,
The feelings exposed and
  promised.

Will they be together tomorrow?
She wonders.
Yet content to be with him
  tonight,
Her eyes close.
The fire begins to dim.
He leans and tenderly kisses her
  forehead.
He drifts from reality to a
  dreamstate.
The fire proclaims its last hisses.
As they both reach a somber
  which leaves them now
  complete.

Jane Gill
SUMMER HEAT
Waves of heat that strike the body
  with the intensity of an ocean
  storm
rebound from the dead ground.

Opressing brightness that blinds
  the eyes
with glittering diamond brillance
dances from dead leaf to dead stone.

The mind and body beaten by heat
without release without dreams
and in the end without care.

Waves of heat, oppressing
  brightness
Blinding the mind, draining the
  body.

Kenneth K. Miller
ASHAMED
Under the blankets of my memory
lie hidden in careful secrecy
dark deeds of long ago.
I thought I had them buried deep
and nevermore should have to reap
what was such fun to sow.

The scorpions feel secure at night.
Hunters, though, employ black
  light,
exposing them to view.
There's such a light I can't detect,
illumes what I scarcely recollect,
discovers each miscue.

Why should I fear and want to flee
when no one is pursuing me,
and no man knows the truth?
Whence this feeling of impatience?
Can it be distress of conscience
from away back in my youth?

Time's just time; it can never inter
our sins or the guilt we once incur,
nor blind the eye of God.

Janice Stephanie Ward
IDENTITY
At birth your just an empty soul,
As aging comes you set your goal.
  A goal in which you do
    complete,
And now you think you've got it
  beat.

And when its time to find a
  mate,
He clings to you like a bolt on a
  gate.
  Just when you think your life
  is complete,
The man you love begins to cheat.
  Now I see the morning light,
  which I say to him I cannot fight.
  And now my life is going to be,
So free and easy like a bee,
  And now I shall find my
  Identity.

Jacqui E. Murphy
SON OF FREEDOM

---

*This Poem was written for my
son PVT. Bob E. Murphy,
Bamburg, Germany "1980." Now-
Staff Sgt. Bob E. Murphy Kirch-
goens, Germany.*

On a distant shore,
A young man stands alone;
Gone from the womb of his
  native land;
That place which he call home.

Straight, tall and proud he stands,
No longer a child, not just a man.
But a soldier with a distinctive air,
And a cause more than great
That keeps him there.

Always on guard
With a watchful eye;
And a spirit not wanting
Yet willing to die!

He protects that word he hold so
  dear;
It's called "Freedom"
By the folks back here.

Richard Craig Hatheway
GOD'S LITTLE CREATURES
The house is clean when I wake up
just waiting for me to get up.

For I have messes to make
and lots of things to break.

Mom dresses me like a spring
  flower
with luck I'll stay clean more
  than an hour.

She loves me even though
I cost a lot of dough.

My dad hugs me so tight
so I can't bite.

But I'm still full of fight
because I love him with all my
  might.

God made little creatures like me
for mom and dad you see.

Michael Brian Jung
UNTITLED
Our Father, who art with us,
Hallowed is thy unspoken name.
Thy kingdom is come
Thy will is done
Here on earth, as it is, here in

heaven.
You have given us, on this day
our daily bread for eternity; and,
though
you created the one who creates
temptation,
our love endured all
and you delivered us from
ignorance
into ever-flowing life, bliss
beyond words.
And now we are each a part of
the source of
the Father, Mother, Child, and
the Holy Ghost,
forever, and evermore. Amen.

M. J. Sweatfield
FRIENDSHIP RETURNED

Dedicated to Dr. Merle L. Trewin

How can I help you
As you've helped me?
I know it's been
A bad time recently.

I've wanted to tell you
I understand——
Sometimes it's hard
To grab a helping hand.

I've grabbed yours
For, oh, so many years.
Let me share
With you, some tears.

Friendship is giving,
Sharing too.
Friendship's also receiving
Hope anew.

As you've told me
"We must go on"
Meeting the future
And memory's song.

Michelle Timbs
NOW NOT TOMORROW
The time is now . . .
There's no time left to leave
a promise unkept,
a grudge unforgiven,
the Good News unspread,
a friend unloved,
the hurt unconsoled,
an apology unspoken,
or a thank you unexpressed.
The time is now . . .
There's only opportunity left to
keep a promise,
forgive a grudge,
spread the Good News,
love a friend,
console the hurt,
speak an apology,
and dictate a thank you.
The time is now . . .
Tomorrow may never come.

Margaret H. Coalson
LIGHT
It is a sad thing for a man
without sight,
but a pity to see a man without
light

The light is mirrored in a small
child's eyes,
when he receives a very nice
unexpected surprise

The light that glows on a young
woman's face

As she holds her baby in it's first
embrace

The light is a man bursting with
pride as he walks down the
aisle with his new bride

The light is in the elderly's smile
When they look to heaven for
their last mile

The light is in flowers, trees, and
birds, the light is something
hard to put into words

The light is given from god
above, the light is all life, the
light is love

Bonnie Pignotti

Bonnie Pignotti
JANIE
Childhood friends we were,
Sharing secrets, dreams and
good times.
Together we laughed:
Sometimes cried,
Always inseperable.
Now though life's obsticles
intrude

Demands drawing thin the bond.
Yet, once friendship has been
decreed,
Each takes a place in the
other's heart,
There to be loved, always.

Laura Gauthier
HIS PROMISE
Sitting, Thinking how short time
is,
I look out over the land
Where life was full and happy
With the man who was my father.

Gone now and yet so much alive
In my mind and memories.

I look at the soil so rich
With the imprint of his life's toil.

I race back to those memories
Of laughter that warmed our
hearts
On those cold and lonely nights
That the family shared together.

Memories of sixty-two years,
Years spent in love and joy
With always enough to share.
Memories of a man of God.

Listening to a mockingbird,
The midnight sky seems so dark,
And yet, this cold land
Glows with cherished thoughts
of the past.

Through my longing for days
gone by,
The voice of God's promise comes,
His eternal care and comfort,
"I will give you a song in the
night."

Anne McCollom
TOO LATE

*I would like to dedicate this
poem to Stacy Allen Joseph
Benandi, who I love with all of
my heart. This poem is all I can
say to express my love.*

I've loved you for so many years,
And oh I've shed so many tears.
For I love you so very much,
I long to feel your sensitive touch.
I've never had enough nerve to say,
I love you in every single way.
But when I do I'll need the fate,
I only wish I can before it's too
late.

Robert Gibson
POETRY IS:
Poetry is,
creating moods of all kinds.
Poetry is,
meaningful delightful rhymes.
Poetry is,
events taking place in our minds.
Poetry is,
trips to different places, and
times.
Poetry is,
inspiration constructed of lines.
Poetry is,
life for which the soul binds.

Debra Lynn Guerrazzi (Douglas)
NO STOPPING ME

*To my pal, Howard Mancipe, who
said, "Go for it!" Inspiring many of
my writings.*

Like a tree you cut me down,
But I will sprout new limbs all
around.
Take from the top I will grow
from the bottom.
For my roots are planted firm,
This you will learn.
Like the wind you force yourself
up-on me.
I will accept the dare and then
begin.
Like the mountain you tunnel
your way through me.

I will stand strong, surviving any
wrong!
My faith in me it stems deep.
The challenge is such you may
only compete!
And just in case you have any
doubt;
Try me once, you will find out'.
You can not stop me,
For this I know.
My destiny in life is to grow!

Debra Blakely
MY BEST FRIEND

*Dedicated to the one true friend
in my life, "my mom".*

I see before me a golden light
A simplistic ray of a divine sight
Casting a glow, for all to see
Upon the world, directly on me
The warmth it shed, has reached
my heart
Extending my senses, negation
kept apart
Total tranquility of my conscious
mind
To the rest of the world, has
made me blind
Such a contentment, I've never
before felt
A state of conviction,
suppressing all doubt
Peace and compassion, together
blend
In this golden light of My Best
Friend.

Martha Jane Cumpton
A STREAM
A stream
Beside a tree
A sad and gray face
It cries with color leaves
Fall

Sandra C. Muller
THE UNICORN
The unicorn stood there so proud
and tall
Determined to prove he was the
mightiest of all.
He would take his chance against
anyone
And stick it out til the battle was
won.
He was strong and mighty, that is
true.
But nobody ever really knew
How he felt deep down inside
Because those feelings he would
always hide.
He liked to play all sorts of games
On him there would never be any
reigns.
Of this he was convinced you see
But that was long before he met
me.
I saw him standing there one day
In his proud and mighty way
And knew that something special
was there
And I could find it with a lot of
care.
I got beyond that big bold front
And started on my little hunt
Not quite sure what I would find
Locked up inside his mind.
And what I finally did discover
Was more than just another

lover.
But time alone will tell as I sit
here this morn
Whether or not I can capture the
heart of a unicorn.

Mark A. Lentine
THE ENTERTAINER
I try to capture my feelings on
this summers night,
The breeze is soft and balmy, and
there's no one else in sight.
The cars drift by so slowly and
the lights like sentinels stand.
And change their colors silently,
on a quiet unseen command.

My mind starts to wander, and
again I'm on the stage
The place I've wanted to earn my
keep, from a very early age.
There's no one in the audience
and I'm acting all alone,
Like a hero who's come back
from war and finds he's on his
own.

I begin to sing the blues song, the
one I know so well,
And then the piano man follows
in, and we weave our magic
spell.
We have the audience in our
hands, not a sound can be heard,
Every man and woman is
spellbound, as they listen to
every word.

I make it to the final scene,
where I end alone on stage.
The place I've wanted to earn my
keep, from a very early age.
The lights are almost off now, as I
make my closing speech,
I pray I can continue, but the
lines seem out of reach.

The play is finally over, there's
the old man with his broom
He's locking me up for the night,
as I walk back to my room.
The tears roll down as I pour a
drink, this life can make you
weak.
The wind blows colder and the
night gets older, and the
raindrops hit my cheek.

Gordon J. Lorbetski
passio hominis
feathery thick clouds
as though winter's snows
along mountains rumbling
past fiords, speeding
to fill valleys of existence

themselves,
would surely crash with roaring
thunder,
plummeting into confused
wretched mania
to the depths of hell
at a single agonized yelp
of faithless despair,
if not for the flicker of a
candle of hope buried
too deep for blind eyes,
somewhere in a hardened heart
of a foreboding Job

Kathie Pongracic
APATHY

*To sanity in a world of
tranquilized tears and sedated
smiles.*

I know a warm, safe place to hide,
where no one ever hurts me;
Where I can go to be alone,
Its name is Apathy.
A place where I can tend the
wounds the world and life have
dealt me,
A place where doubts don't haunt
me.

Apathy asks no questions, tells
no lies,
Expects not a thing from me.
More than a place—a kind of
friend who holds me while I
mend.

I shed no tears in Apathy for I've
left them all behind me:
The pain is gone while I dwell
here, for there's nothing to
remind me.

I like it here in Apathy; yet they
say I mustn't linger.
They say I should try at life
again, and then I begin to
remember;
The pain and doubt, the hurts
and fears,
No thank-you world—I'll stay
right here.

A. William Floyde
OUR BOYS IN LEBANON

*Dedicated to the memory of a
few but precious U.S. Marines
who have been killed during
"peace time".*

Many people do not agree with
the policies of Reagan,
and many people sympathize
with the feelings of Begin.
Should the Marines stay in
Lebanon?
Will we feel sorry when they are
dead and gone?

We are losing our boys one by one,
under the heat of the burning
desert sun.
But what is their real purpose?
Are they only clowns in this
deadly circus?

I hope someone really cares,
for their delicate flesh burns and
tears.
They are there for peace and not
to fight,

but someone is making this
tourniquet real tight.
Will you please listen to our
words,
and don't think they can not be
heard.
We will scream and shout,
"We want our boys out."

Joan Reid Hyde
REACHING HIGHER
I wouldn't like to wander
like a derelict
never knowing
where I'm going.

All the beauty of this earth
would make me feel bereft
if I knew not why
the earth and I
exist, then die
then live.

A moment of reflection—
I wander aimlessly
upon a mountain of senses.
I catch the color of a sunset—
it leaves me breathless.
In moments of despair
it brings me up from the depths.
Then I catch the vision
of forever, only to lose it again
in earthly endeavors.

I must reach higher
past the pull of earthly cares;
gain the "vision of forever"
step by step—like climbing stairs.

John D. Boykin
SILLY LITTLE SPIDER
I threw a dart towards
A tiny fly on the wall
Wondering very briefly
Would I hit him at all!

Suddenly a spider came
Running towards the fly.
The fly just sat there
On my living room wall.

Then the spider jumped
And my dart struck home.
Twas the spider and not
The fly who I heard groan.

So I laughed and laughed
With a twinkle in my eye
At a Silly Little Spider
Who tried to Kill a fly.

Frank J. Fedele
MEDIOCRITY
See how the world marvels at the
mundane and the small.
They fall short of creative talent
and bask in the limelight of
fools!

How exalted are the repetitious,
and the redundant ones!
Even as the Great fall by the
wayside, and lose grips with
this contemporary
encompassment of life.
The banana people have invaded
the earth and the virtuosos are
lost.

They stare in awe at the ugly and
the agressive, but make no
sound upon their ears of
softness or pleasant tones.
I've seen them become enraged at
such things, wondering why we
are not like them.

The mighty have all gone by, and
the gargantuan insects are now
in control.

The judge and jury of the illicit
will not allow the evidence to
be brought forth!

Shanaz Ostowari
DREAMS
Pot of gold,
Happiness,
Money and Love are all there is
of Life.
The road chosen is to be
questioned
The path is insignificant to those
who know
Value and happiness is all there
is for now
Today and tomorrow are the
same.
Today, a scene of all the
tomorrows and
Tomorrow, the future that
withholds all
The inner-fears of
What is yet to come, and ways to
accomplish a life of
dreams and goals beyond our
expectations and
realm of reality.
This is the Tomorrow Land.

Blaine S. Blakney
AFFECTION

To my love; With all my love.

Hold me . . .
And I'll love you.
Believe in me . . .
And I'll love you.
Love me . . .
And I'll love you.

And I do love you
. . . dearly.

Joanne M. Marinelli
AFTERMATH
Lying in bed I watch the smoke
rise,
Sometimes shaping little demons
or poisonous clouds.
You too, light your cigarette,
And I wonder why the only heat,
Comes from burning our fingers
on butts.

Elizabeth Miller
On the Death Of Icarus
Soaring above the setting sun,
My only child flew on alone,
With artificial wings myself I
made,
I stood aside and watched.

The waxen wings bent back the
rays,
Of harsh beams glistening on
their edge,
They dripped into the sea.

Could such anguish pierce a
heart,
To watch my son fall from the
start,
Of this ill-fated flight?

What caused this child to fly so
high,
To disobey,
To cherish heights not meant for
man?

I cannot ask,
I only feel.

Melanie J. Wiley
MIDDLE AGED LAMENT
My needs seem insatiable,
my looks now deplorable,
my thoughts . . . how abhorable!
Who would believe I was once
    quite adorable?

B. J. Nowak
MASQUERADE BALL
Bring your flask, a mask, and
    funny hat.
Unpack a cape, or wrap in
    mummy tape.
Be decked in jewels and lace,
    paper and paste.
In rags and bags. or dress in drag
Just for the fun of escape.
Become a clown, a cat, a gangster
    rat,
A knighted "Sir", sorcerer, or sheik.
A damsel fair, a vamp, a tramp
Or costume whatever you think.
And come out of the closet,
Crawl out of a coffin,
Come out from your chink in the
    wall.
It soon will be Halloween,
And we're having a Masquerade
    Ball.

Wynona Francisco
Dreamy Dark Shadows
Dreamy dark shadows
Speaking to my heart and soul,
Telling me, I'm loved.

Secure deep darkness
Just waiting down there
    somewhere . . .
It becons to me.

Looming allusions
Weeping, searching piercing
    eyes . . .
They're calling me home.

Vapored Corridors
One. two, three, four, then no more
Zigzaging nowhere.

Back away, Liars.
I'm waiting for my friend
    Death . . .
Peaceful, comotose sleep.

Howling red blindness
Lying here alone . . . all alone . . .
Blackness, Nothingness.

Jerry Neal Barnes
TRANSISTION
Inside the canopy of tall cypress
    no moonbeams penetrate
Vapors rise to mingle with
    ethereal dampness
Eyes cannot see beginnings of up
    nor down
only glints abound from creatures
    small
dark waters creep amidst roots
    and coagulate.

Passing through by pirogue, gifted
    sense of direction
Push pole touching faintness of
    soft bottom providing
firmness to eerie world with lack
    of definition.
Spanish moss brushes the face
    with ghostly touch
the swamp gives way to sawgrass
    sea insurrection.

The moonlight illuminates
    waving sea punctuation
flickering lights, the flaming
    torches, backlight elephantine
rusty hulks gliding through deep
    cut channels
appear to be floating through
    solid earth
creeping inland like tired sea
    monsters seeking hibernation.

Disturbed alligator roars protest
    silencing even peepers
roosting birds echo octaves
    higher as pirogue passes.
Faster now with sculling tail
    through widening waterways
it's surface dimples with the
    faintest splash
ripples reflect distorted stars,
    disturbing sleepers.

Feu follet feeling, mist giving way
    to lightness
feel the pulling tide toward
    distant rumble
where sea wages war on white
    sandy beaches
Powerful punches in yielding
    softness reduced
to whispering hissing; transistion
    completeness.

Aaron Harper
PAPER AND PENCILS
Paper and pencils, crayons and
    pens
the tools to another world
To travel to space or explore
    the human race
a small boy's world comes alive
He can be in far away places
Places where I've never been
He'll travel around in a colorful
    world
a world that's never been seen
Whether riding a semi
Or flying a mile high
In a jet that looks like a stick
With paper and pencils, crayons
    and pens
He travels to other worlds
And though when he gets older
And his world may not be what it
    was
As he lays down at night, and he
    smiles
so slight,
Of papers and pencils, crayons
    and pens,
When a small boy's world came
    alive.

Dottie Jones
REFLECTIONS
A mirror reflecting an image
An image of a reflection.
Which is reality?
Viewed from the eyes of the
    image,
Seeing myself reflected,
I wonder.
My soul seeks identity acceptance.
I know who I am,
I know what I am,
I know what I can become.
But others see a reflection
Mirroring many prisms
Of a multi-faceted personality.
Is no-one able to perceive
The reality that is me?
Acceptance cannot come unless
In the eye of the beholder

The genuine image reflects
The inner integrity of the
    personality.
The reflection becomes one with
    the image
Reflecting the inner being
    pleading
For recognition.
Please, God, let someone see.

Robert L. Cashion
FEELINGS
Misty eyed,
a tear falls inside,
staring out the window.
The wind is blowing, the snow is
    falling,
jealous of the time I didn't know
    her.

Her beautiful memories of the
    past,
sweet dreams that didn't last,
my heart breaks for her.
Forgive me God,
I'm jealous of her past.

Billie McKindra Phillips
HALLOWEEN MOTION

---

*To three special persons who
nurtured my imagination with
wings for soaring: my parents,
William and Anne McKindra; my
son, La Monte H. Mays, Sr.*

Pumpkins roll.
Scarecrows stroll.
Ghost gloat lightly by.
Witches ride.
Winged bats glide.
Crows fly low and high!
Fast and slow,
On they go,
Moving all around!
Sometimes fast,
Sometimes last,
Barely touching touching ground!

Gloria Woods Buchanan
OCTOBER MAGIC
Octobers here that magical time,
That sets our hearts all in a
    flutter
Up in the sky theres a big round
    moon
Looks like a ball of pale yellow
    butter.

The corn shocks are standing in
    long straight rows
Bright orange pumpkins are piled
    up high,
The children is getting ready for

Halloween,
Can't wait for their night of fun
    and surprise,
The air has turned cool and nips
    at your nose
I know Jack Frost must be
    standing by,
Every little creature is preparing
    for Winter
The Wild Geese on the mill pond
    are restless to fly.

The grain is gathered and time
    goes slow,
Theres not much left to do
    around here,
Just sit and enjoy Octobers sweet
    magic
That comes to our heart only
    once a year.

Laurie Parton
ATOM CONNECTION
Atoms and molecules twist and
    turn,
Cells and energy blend and burn.

They spin around the world so
    fast,
They spin until they fade at last.

Together they form some kind of
    mass,
A solid, a liquid, or even a gas.

Merging together it's plain to see,
The objects they form are you
    and me!

Terri L. Holmes
TIME
Time . . .
Ticking on, and on
never stopping.
I stop to think awhile,
My time is gone.

Pat Fleming
A YOUNG GIRL'S HEART
At seventeen, a young girl's heart
    is broken from the strain,
A young romance, she took a
    chance, that caused her life-
    long pain.
In great despair, she grasped a
    love that could not fill her life,
And brought him forth a baby,
    and made herself his wife.

They stayed together three long
    years—each went their
    separate ways,
Without the love of marriage—
    serving each new day.
They never laughed together, nor
    wept a single tear,
And never once were shared the
    words—of doubt—of pain—of
    fear.

The marriage one day ended—at
    last he was set free.
And though her heart was
    burdened, their future would
    not be.
She turned and reaching for a
    friend, found true love by her
    side.
In eyes that held a future, their
    love they could not hide.

A marriage so imperfect because
    of one brief sin,
Took hold of her whole being and
    could not let him in,

For though she'd found the one
God meant, to be there from
the start,
Her husband had come home
again to tear her world apart.

Florence Lillian Cripps
JUST ONE
If I have made one troubled life
brighter
One heart ache a little less—
If I have helped make one burden
lighter
Eased the soreness of distress—,

If from some one's troubled eyes
I have helped erase the look of
pain,
Then I feel that my own life
Was, perhaps—not all in vain—

Sheri Layne Werner
SUNSETS, SUNRISES
The day is coming to a close,
sunset time is near,
The sky is changing to pinks,
oranges, yellows,
A beautiful sight to see.

The sun has vanished, nighttime
is here,
The sky is becoming darker,
Stars are coming out.

The night sky is black, as if
nothing is to be seen,
Everyone is asleep by now,
This is the quietest time.

The sky is becoming golden, the
sun is beginning to rise,
People are starting to get up,
Homes are more active.

The sky is blue again, daytime is
here,
But don't worry,
Sunsets and sunrises will be back.

I have only one more thing to say
about sunsets and sunrises,
They help make life in these
United States more beautiful.

Susan B. Harris
UNCONQUERED LOVE

*This poem was written in
thoughts of Irlen Ray (Byrd)
Freeman from Bolton, N.C., in
September 1983. Encouraged by
Pat Phillips and Jackie Ludlum.*

Being comatose of the deathtrap
when looking into those eyes.
It could have been exquisite if
there wasn't a disguise.

Seeming to entice with those fain
ways.
So impotent to the situation
being left in a daze.

First was loath and frivolous, Was
caused to be delirious.
Bedeviled by the fidget way,
Causing to falter day by day.

Wanting to be impudent about
what was nascent.
Yet it was so formidable could
have used a grapnel.

If it hadn't been for the lapse, It
could have been a perhaps.

Those harbingers made it pall.
Needing to suppress and

relinquish.
Yet wanting to be roquish.

The feeling can be subdued,
Never meant to intrude.

Vicki L. Rohr Lanham
MY ROOTS IN OHIO
My roots are in Ohio,
Where I once roamed.
Many places I now know,
But, East Liverpool, is my home.

Family and friends are still there,
And wait for my return.
Leaving home is hard to bare,
As there, my life I did learn.

History in Ohio's rich,
And stories are often told.
People lived without a hitch,
And often where brave and bold.

Away from home, I have to be,
But my roots are in Ohio.
No matter where, I may be,
I'll love, East Liverpool, Ohio.

Laurie Hartman
EVANESCENCE
Hours have I spent upon the
beach,
Building up my kingdom by the
seaside.
My castle walls are strong and
gird the tower in which the
fairest maid does wait.
My mote of water 'round my
castle runs,
And I, the ruler, build the towers
taller, till but small points do
stand so high.
Then with one gentle move, my
kingdom is covered, like
Atlantis, far, far below the
surface of the sparkling green.
The wave recedes; no longer
stands my kingdom.
None but a mound of fallen walls;
The maiden and the mote are gone.
My reign, silently, so silently
ended by the single rush of a
wave.
My power and my kingdom, no
longer mine,
Reclaimed by the waves and the
endless sea.

Dean-ann Bauza
UNTITLED
Life is a fantasy,
Where children chose to live.
Spending out their lives,
In a myriad of never ending lies.
Sometimes they're little,
Sometimes they're old,
You never know just what they'll
be.
'Cause reality is just a myth,
In a land of make believe,
Where children chose to live.

Brad Sweitzer
DYING ON THE WIND
Dance of the flowers
Dying in the air
Not dying in body
But the spirit no longer
Lives here
Empty shell
Just a life I don't own
Just a life I don't want to own
Not set free, just paying the price
Alone
Rattling in hollow mortal bones

Empty prison cell
Where love is just a vice, it
won't
Survive in here
Dance of the flowers, petals in
the wind
Where no seeds are sown
No garden grows
And love like truth is just a
myth

Nicole L. Nearman
TRUST
To share yourself completly
To give all that we have
Our lives, our hopes
Our joys, our plans.

To trust someone
Gives a special feeling inside
To have a good friend
To whom you can confide.

Your deepest pains,
Your spirited joys
Are kept only in trust,
If trust is not destroyed.

Margaret Aube'

Margaret Aube'
A CHRISTMAS REMINDER

*Dedicated to Tovahl Aube',
StarAngel and Michael Bourgeois,
Janet Bourgeois, Jerry and Lolita
Aube'.*

A song is heard on that dark
bleak night.
A star has led shepherds filled
with fright.
Sending messages of a Baby
Prince
Happy angels all in chorus sing,
"A Child is born to you this day,
In David's town, go! Don't delay."
As His mother smiled and
whispered low,
"The Savior has come to save the
blow
which hell has set on this sinful
world
to make it free as God's Promised
Word."

Shyam P. Mehta
DOOMS DAY
I sat there alone,
Gazing at the stars.
High above, the
Sputnik twinkles
Skylab winkles
Satellites beam,
The invisible rays.

Phobia or the reality of—
Nuclear annihilation!
Life worse than Hitler's War.
I shudder at the thought of
someone
Keeping my fate squeezed,
At his whim or charade of
idealogy.

Oh God! Help us to ride off
The prophecy of Doomsday.
Teach us to live in love,
Without any rancor and
With malice towards none.

Sydney J. Archer
THE GLISTENING HILLS
"See the snow, The lilly white
snow"
Glistening a top of the distant
hills.
The sun rays beaming through
the icy tops,
Melting and streaming down the
glistening hills.

"See the snow, The lilly white
snow"
Spreading its beauty, As it kisses
the ground.
"Falling, "Falling", through the
open sky
Unto the tree tops, and over the
hills.

"See the snow, The lilly white
snow,
Freely falling, beneath the hills.
Blending with the lands-cape so
beautifully set,
As we take a view, of the
glistening hills.

Jacquelin Ford
FORGET—ME—NOT
Bouquets of forget-me-nots
fill the air
In the dark lonely graveyard
where they go and stare
The people they talk
of the death she committed
While not even realizing
it was they who did it.

The young, friendly child
was once innocent and sweet
Until she met with adventure
taking her to the street
The times came and went
were lost in a moment
But she knew in her heart
to make it dormant.

The harrassment continued
day after day
Her fears never ceasing
rarely drifting away
She dreamed of true love
with a man who cared
But to tell him her past
she didn't dare.

She stared at the moons glow
on the rippling water
Hoping the many people
would forget about her
But she knew their cruelty
and began to cry
She did it with a knife
praying to the sky.

This tragic story
of a girl once live
Should bring to everyone
a tearful eye

So many people
  speak out of turn
They're careless and slipshod
  I pray they learn.

B. Isaacson
Where the Willows Bend
I was dreaming pastels when you
called my name. My eyes slid
open. I heard you again. I was
alone but feeling your sleep.
Your thoughts seemed
disturbing, groping. Too deep
for days where the willows
bend and the wild ones run.
But those days will come.

I remember a moment when I was
afraid. My heart was in fission
with one of your maybe
decisions. My palms are still
itching. I'm growing a scar. You
keep me from reaching too
near or too far. Wow baby it's
hard this race for the strong.
Your arms may be tired from
just loving too long. Maybe
you once warmed a special
close place. But maybe some
lover marooned you in space.
Or maybe those days when the
willows bend and the wind is
tapping a silent drum will rise
again. That day may come.

There's magic to see in the
freebird's flight. And I'd write it
down if I could, for you I
would . . . build a castle in the
sky, with pillars of rainbows
where the freebirds could fly,
where the willows bend in the
Portland dew, where your
brown eyes sleep in the
evening blue. When I come to
know those things that are
true, where someday comes
and I'll be in love with you.
When the wind is tapping on
its whispered drum, where the
willows bend— our day will
come.

Dina Chatelain
HALLOWEEN
Witches witching,
Goblins laughing.
The moon disappears
When the dark clouds are passing.
Halloween is here again.
Spooks of all kinds know it.
When the Halloween moon
  comes up again,
It's time for Witching Hour.

Jeni Grant
TELL ME
If light and dark were as one,
  could you see me,
If the sand was made of gold,
  would you notice the sea,
If you wore your dreams around
  your neck,
  would anyone see their beauty,
If your eyes cast the darkest of
  shadows,
  they'd be noticed most
  definitely,
If your companions were painted
  illusions,
  would you know they were
  empty,
If you explored your mind and

soul,
  would you see what you wanted
  to see,
If you walked in circles for the
  rest of your life,
  would you still see your destiny,
How about something simple just
  try to see me,
  I know you look,
  But it isn't that easy.

Amy Cunningham
PROGRESS
Leaning, sighing, resting
After the fierce winds
Fade into cleansed breezes.
The weakened stems
Of frail flowers
Lean on the strong leaves
Of sturdy, still standing plants.
Others lie beaten
Afraid of what comes next.
Maybe nothing, maybe death.
Some slowly rise and come forward
To face what Fate prepares.
Relief floods through every vein
Of every leaf that thrives,
As the sound of dying storms
Drift into nothingness.

Myron C. Weinstein
SAKHALIN
a child lies dead on Hokkaido's
  shore.
it was found by fishermen
nameless on the sullen coast
where the sea had moved it
from the wreckage of Korean Air
  Lines Flight 007
downed off Sakhalin by a Russian
  missile
on September 1, 1983.

Americans will never forget.

tears can bring my feelings to
  this place
and move my heart to sadness on
  the wind-swept shore.
a child lies dead
and by human design,
delivered up to us mercifully by
  the sea
that knows no bounds.

I am told that sailors believe
in the dignity of the sea
as a final resting place for the dead.
but there is no dignity in this.
for after all the stories and
  resolutions and reports,
there will still have been
this one human life unlived.

Lind Beth Toth
MIDNIGHT MONOLOGUE
Remember nights I read your
  rhythms,
met and matched them to mine
in our land of always summer?
You laced my hair with
  moonbeams
and burrowed into the furrow
  of my wound
to fill me with your diamonds
and leave the garden glow
in an aura of harvest dreams.
You mounted and rode me up
  Orion
past deep purple mountains
cast with sunlight and silver
and made me sing in your arms
like the sea.
Love led me through the woman

songs
where I wore new moonlight
and let you enter my silence
to know its willow soul.
I shall not kneel at your grave:
there is no need;
it is this empty pillow next to
  mine
that once saddled starlight hips
then graced your gentle head
before these nights of midnight
  blue.

Mary Laura Kitchen
Mary Laura Kitchen
**It's a Rough, Rocky Road
To Heaven**

---

*To: Reverend Clarence Branch,
Pastor First Baptist Church
Anson, Texas 79501*

The road is rough and rocky,
  And thorns are everywhere,
Temptations there to greet you
  on every hand,
  Not many will want to help you,
  Not many will want to care,
And give you faith and strength
  on which to stand.

And we'll all sit down on the
  right-hand-side with Jesus,
  We'll share all the things our
  Father said we'd share,
He's gone to prepare a place,
  There to see his blessed face,
And the road paved with gold
  when we get there.

Yes, it's rough, rocky road to
  Heaven,
  It's rough, every mile of the way,
But to hear my Savior say,
  "Well done, thou faithful servant,"
Is worth every rough mile of the
  way.

The road is rough and rocky
  And uphill all the way,
And few there be that really
  make the grade,
  They stumble and fall by the
  wayside,
And refuse our Lord's commands,
  Hoping to get there anyway,
  some sweet day.

But they'll not get to sit on the
  right-hand-side with Jesus,
  Nor share all the things our
  Father said we'd share,
They'll not share his warm
  embrace,

But, instead will hide their face,
And the road paved with gold
  will not be there.
Yes, it's a rough, rocky road to
  Heaven,
  It's rough, every mile of the way.
But to hear my Savior say,
  "Well done, thou faithful servant,"
Is worth every rough mile of the
  way.
It's an uphill, upgrade road from
  here to eternity,
And I hope to meet you there
  some sweet day.

Gerald P. Wesley
THE CALL OF THE SEA
An intimate feeling that can't be
  explained,
but it's sure every sailor knows,
Is the feeling of infinite power,
While watching a storm as it
  grows.
With the storm waves pounding
  and crashing,
against the side of his ship.
The winds getting louder and
  stronger,
the barometer taking a dip.
The challenge of pitting ones
  brawn and endurance,
against the holocaust,
While knowing that any mistake
  on his part,
and everything is lost.
And once more back in the harbor,
back where it's safe and it's warm,
A wonderful feeling of conquest,
from having weathered the storm.
It's the feeling which draws every
  sailor,
back once again to the sea.
A regular haunting and longing,
from which he will never be free.
He may think for a time he has
  licked it,
and vow to stay on the shore,
But sooner or later he looses the
  fight,
and has to go sailing once more.

Gail Worfolk
THE LITTLE BOY
The little boy, all dressed in blue,
Sat on the warm rug,
Surrounded by his blocks.
As time slowly passed,
The blocks began to form a shape,
The little boy's imaginary castle.
Unaware of the world around him,
Vast and complicated,
He created his own world.
One of knights, kings, and heroes,
And armies that always win.
Of magical lands and mystical
  places,
And happy people everywhere.
And all these things,
He thought were true.

The aging man, all dressed in grey,
Sat in the corner of the room,
On an old wooden chair.
As he watched the little boy,
Creating a new world,
He reflected on his past.
He remembered the happy times,
And the caring people.
But then he thought of the wars,
And the people that suffered,
And died.
He thought of life,

255

Deceitful and wrong, but yet,
Sometimes rewarding.
The old man was wise,
He understood life.

Suddenly a powerful wind,
Penetrated the little boy's world,
Causing the castle to crumble.
The innocent little boy cried,
But in the corner,
His grandfather only smiled.
And then he said,
"One day, my little boy,
You'll rule our world."

Alma Joyce
IMPULSE
Vanity's ignorance indeed is bliss.
While knowledge led in trusting
love
must hold that nakedness apart
by skin or veil til harvest time.

Then spirits dipped in blood do
rise
to fashion coverings on high
for he who laid aside his glory
as she shattered her fragile love.

Therefore manipulate not me
today.
For those who tried it yesterday
have gone their way into the sea
to clothe with tears what cannot
weep.

So burn your shadows of inner
space whose finishing comes but
from above, feeding the flames
with what once was.

Lee Barnes
THE GAME
In celebration of Spring's revelry
I grab my racquet and I flee
To the court of closest proximity
And there set about to free
The aches inflicted by society
As a ball and a fool
Make a clown of me.

Rose Michelle Boccasino
HOLLOW-MASQUE
"A facade," the loner cries in
whispered words,
too silent to be heard by the
glory-seeker
who denies their claim.

"Not really," he replies, "merely a
masque to disguise myself,
like Falstaff of yesterday or
Emmett of today."

"A facade," the loner's voice again
intones the silent sound
Which echoes in hollow refrain
on deaf ears.

Almost in defense of his self-
seeking lifestyle,
As though on trial, he replies to
the accusation
"Not true, I swear it is not
true—
merely a role to play
a part of the politics of daily
living
a way to survive."

Again-again in one last breath the
loner tries despairingly
to make the petulant seeker
listen to her repeated cries,
In final tones she silently
mouthes the word, "facade."

But alas it is too late, the eve has
ended
and all that remains is the glory-
seeker's wanton ghost
a "Hollow-masque."

Michael E. Mathews
THE CHAPTERS OF LIFE
The chapters of life begin at birth
With child born into the world,
He sees his part with total mirth
And stays confined in his
contented world.

He grows and grows and as he
grows,
Lessons are learned of different
cases.
He experiments with being and
thinks he knows
How to read age on everyone's
faces.

He is united with hearts as one.
So embraced in wedded bliss,
He becomes a father to a son
And slowly awakens to his
liableness.

As years go by all things change.
The face he reads is now his own.
The world he views is all too
strange
And he looks to the stars for a
mellow tone.

His vale of years have finally
been touched.
Once so green and now so prime,
The chapters of life he loved so
much
Have all disappeared with time.

Chrystal Kay Thompson
THE WANDERER
When time and weather seem to
age
And man has written another page
And friendships grow and wane
and are
And our dreams have gone to
another star
I'll sit and ponder and wonder still
What's on the far side of yon hill
And wish I had gone to look, to
find,
Instead of just set and make a
rhyme.
To go and see and do and find
And wonder why others are not
so kind
Who look on this wandering,
Gypse soul of mine
That wants to see yon hill and star
And wonder forever what they
are.

But when my years of life are
spent
and the summons for my soul is
sent
I'll ask God for just another peek
At places my wandering feet did
seek
A look on friends and places far
The other side of the hill
The wandering star.

Mrs. H. R. Kirk
**Show Christ a Happy
Birthday**
Christmas is a joyous season,
We celebrate each year,
It is our Saviors birthday,
Thank God He still is here.

Although He gave His life for us,
Paid for our sin's that way,
How could we turn away from
Him?
When He showed His love that
day.

He showers us with mercey,
Which we could not repay,
Yet He is always pleading,
For us to live His way.

He knows we are not perfect,
But He only wants us to try,
For He will help in many ways,
With love we can not buy.

Our precious Lord knows all about,
The good things that we share,
He also knows the bad things,
For Christ is every where.

Edith N. Brewster
The Smile Of a Stranger
It was in the month of April
On a glorious, beautiful day,
And I was sitting on my doorstep
When a traveler passed my way.

He was old and tired and wrinkled
And his hair was turning grey,
But I could tell that he was happy
When he happened to glance my
way.

I said, "hello," to the stranger
He smiled and then he was gone,
Taking the sunshine with him
I suddenly felt all alone.

It was only the smile of a stranger
That made me understand,
God speaks in many, many ways
To the heart of a lonely man.

Joseph W. Stieg
CHANGE
We often change for friends,
we'll change to be in style!
we will change to be accepted,
thinking, is it all worthwhile?

A person is what they are inside,
self honesty is hard to find.
For trying to please another,
makes us to our own needs blind!

The most important thing is you
in that your satisfied.
Only then can you like yourself,
and hold your head, with pride.

Change only if you want to!
Let no other interfere!
Worry not about the stranger,
pay no attention to their sneers!

Change only for your own needs,
without bitterness or shame.
Your life is your own,
you'll have no-one to blame.

As long as you are happy,
thats all that really matters!
We have a life so short.
Why waste it with useless clatter?

Shelena M. Hohmann
PARADISE
Long ago, in a land so free
There lived just two people, they
were you and me.
We ran around together, loving
each other all day.
Swimming and playing,
Living on the fruits of the land.
In our tropical paradise,
No one around to cause harm.

With unicorns as our pets,
Riding and roaming in the sand,
Giving us some sport.
Everyday as time goes on,
We grow together.
Until one day a ship comes
Taking you from me.
Every night I sit and wait,
Lying on the beach,
Crying at every sunset,
Adding to my grief.
I know as each day passes,
I die a little more.
Without you on our island
Happiness is no more.

Martha W. Hutchinson
A DEAR FAMILY DOCTOR

---

*Dedicated to Dr. Ross E. Newman
I feel deep gratitude to you our
friend.*

A toast to you of yester year,
To a grand gentleman and scout.
With college days long over,
Open minded, constitution still
stout.

As I visualize your passing years,
From colossial youth and grace,
SPRING time of youth has passed
you by,
But not the gentle smile on your
face.

The *SUMMER* of life was one
grand fling.
Your brilliant mind and healing
touch,
Saved so very many lives.
To many of us, you simply mean
so much.

The seasons drift so swiftly by,
The *FALL* of life still fair.
Your step didn't halt or falter,
Your sick patients got special care.

WINTER of life, like a drifting tide,
Sprinkled hoary frost in your hair.
Roses bloom faintly in your
cheeks,
Dear family doctor, many people
love you and care.

When evening time of life is over,
The last sun ray fades from the
west,
I pray my Jesus to lead you safely
home,
To a reward prepared for the
blessed.

Our World's Best Loved Poems

Thora J. Supple
AUTUMN LEAVES
Autumn leaves so brightly colored
Paint the hills, valley, and dale
Tell a story of Jack Frost's passing
Sing a tune from Nature's tale!

Autumn leaves so gayly colored
Tell of wood smoke in the vale
Tell of summer's recent passing
Speak of winter's icy trail!

How we love the season of
  Autumn
When birds fly the high sky
  trail . . .
Heading southward from the
  winter
Heeding Autumn's signal flare!

Michael D. Milner
QUESTIONS
Has anyone ever felt as empty
  and isolated as I?
Am I alone in this seemingly
  meaningless existence, or are
  there others?
Others who perform their lives
  day by day, minute by minute,
Like brilliant actors in endless
  roles on eternal stages.
Have they, as I have, ever
  contemplated terminating their
  contracts?
Have they ever attempted that
  daring step beyond mere
  contemplation,
Only to be awakened by
  unrelenting sounds of failure
  pounding in their ears?
Have they had to return time and
  again with heavy heads held
  painfully high
To continue the never-ending run
  of life's inevitable play?
Do they become drowned in their
  work as a temporary diversion
  from themselves?
Are they lavishly praised for
  intelligence, compassion, and
  sensitivity?
Are they able to blissfully and
  shamelessly bask in such?
Or has each accolade been
  graciously accepted by the actor,
While they stood quietly
  backstage in bewilderment
  over such undeserved affection?
Do they seek refuge in music,
  television, movies, magazines,
  and books?
Do they derive the maximum
  pleasure from a kitten's purr or
  the wag of a dog's tail?
Are they privately prone to tears
  over simple thought and things,
And often over nothing at all?
Do they ever find themselves in
  well-concealed oceans of
  self-pity?
Do they live in constant fear of
  the actor missing a
  performance,
Leaving them onstage naked and
  alone to slip over sanity's
  precarious edge?
I know there must be others out
  there, perhaps pondering these
  very questions.
But no two of us will ever meet;
  the actors won't permit it.
Perhaps these questions are best
left ignored, if not forgotten,
For what solace could there be in
any possible answer?

June Lee Box

June Lee Box
Northcoast Awakening
Pushing wide my casement
  windows
I draw deep breaths of the spicy air
And watch the early rising sun
Shining through the morning mist
Nudging the dense vapor that
  nestled all night
In the rows of barren blueberry
  bushes
The fog fades awaytrailing veils
Through the nearby sentinel
  stands
Of Redwoods into the cool
  darkness beyond
From my neighbor's home down
  the hill
Smoke streams white and
  straight—
A morning fire against dawn's chill
The strengthening sun shows
  tiny blueberry leaves
Green-tinting long aisles of bushes
Above busily darting robins
Whose russet breastplates are
  sun-struck shields
Thrust out below questing beaks
Add life and color to the early
  scene
Entranced with God's graphic
  painting
I give silent thanks for this new
  day
And with a light heart
Swing into my chores!

Lou Hobbs
SOLUTION
And so, he knew the end was near
In dark eyes he showed no fear.
He looked down where the paper
  lay
And could not find a thing to say.

The world no longer knew him
  well
His life, he'd found, was one big
  hell.
Now that she had gone her way
Nothing else could make him stay.

They used to have the perfect life,
Free from all the pain and strife.
But like all else there came an end
And with it came hurt none
  could mend.

On the shelf his peace awaited
And with his thoughts left
unstated,
Leaned to touch it, smooth and
  cold,
Picked it up, its outline bold.

It was colored metal-blue
The highlights shone with silver
  hue
The butt fit him like a glove
Its shape he'd come to know and
  love.

With nothing left to do or say,
Beside his head the barrel lay.
Leaning back, his thoughts he
  dulled,
He closed his eyes, relaxed, and
  pulled.

Margaret Malinoske
GIVE ME SOME TIME
In the land of the everlasting
Where the river turns at the bend
I'd like to sit and rest a spell,
In the glow of the setting sun.
There has never been a moment
When I could just sit and rest.
It was work, work, work forever
Even when I tried my best.
I never got caught up-always
  behind
No matter the speed I set
And I'm getting so tired, I need
  rest,
Some time to recall and reflect.
Give me some time to remember,
And a little time to sing;
Life's journey is so much lighter
Going forward but remembering.

Mrs. Billie Jean Duffer (Bingham)
MY DAY

---

*I would like to dedicate this
Poem to my Children Tammy &
Chase and also to my Parents for
giving me the encouragement I
needed to write, without them I
would never have tried.
Thank-you!*

Wake up in the morning to
  sounds so nice and sweet;
I look all around and see young
  ones at my feet.

They say "Time to get up and on
  my way;
This is the start of a beautiful day".

Time for breakfast what shall we
  eat;
One wants cereal, the other
  something sweet.

Then off to school they go to
  start their day;
First a smile, then a wave and
  their on their way.

It's now time for me to go and I'm
  singing a song;
For I know that nothing will go
  wrong.

Once I'm at work and eager to
  start;
Everything just seems to fall
  apart.

But hoping the day will go better;
I stick it out, for I'm a real Go
  Getter!

When the day is thru and I'm
  ready to pack it in;
I've just enough time to put all to
  bed before it begins again.

You see my days a merry-go-
  round this is true;
Filled with moments so precious,
  and so few.

So make the best of each day and
  all the while;
No matter how down you are—
Just put on a smile.

Hope you have a nice day.

Margaret K. Shick
One Persons Concept Of Brotherly Love.
My dear brother may I walk
  beside you, that in some way I
  can understand the weariness
  that you feel.
May I feel the losses you suffer.
  The heartaches you encounter.

If I may suffer these things with
  you, through love, I will show
  more compassion and I will not
  have so much time to wallow
  in my own self pity.

In this way I can help share your
  burden while you are helping
  me shoulder mine. What better
  way to truly demonstrate
  brotherly love!

Sandra G. Roberson
PORTRAIT OF FALONIA

---

*This poem, inspired by an old
photograph of an ancestor from
the mid 1800's, is dedicated to
the memory of my mother, whose
name was also Falonia; and to a
little niece, who bears the same
name.*

Poised with beauty, youth and
  grace,
Embroidered eyelet, frames her
  face;
A scarf of silk, adorns her hair—
A simple part of perfection there.

Golden treasures, sweeping fine,
From another era, place and time;
Indian beads, and woven belt—
Grace this lass, of common-wealth.

The look of innocence—blushing
  cheeks,
A rare exposure, the
  photographer seeks;
She sits there—so demure,
With silence on her face—so pure.

Young eyes at peace—yet sweet
  release,
Of pain and hurtin', her smile—
  not certain—
What the future holds, what lies
  unseen—
For one so young, ten years—past
  seventeen.

Frances N.C. Jedd
GOD'S LAWS
The sound of thunder booms
  from a rolling roar,
The sky sounds like it is splitting
  with a crack,
So loud the rolling clouds rumble
  overhead.
And through the rumbling the
  lightning again splits the sky,

Like an army of clashing cymbals
  and drums,
And I on earth in silent awe,
  listen to God's majesty.
I feel safely cared and protected
  by the strength
Of the Almighty God and his
  army of majesty.
How perfectly the meter falls in
  place, as the rain
Pelts in downfall, among the
  rolling rumble in the air.
The early spring earth is brought
  into green life
As the fresh smell of the rain and
  earth fill the air,
And I breathe deeply of the early
  spring smells
While my soul is freshly made
  aware of the strength
Of God's Being letting the world
  know his power is awesome.
He created the earth and lets his
  presence be felt
As the trees band with the power
  of the heavy wind.
To go against nature is foolishly
  unwise, we need to bend
to nature's laws, which God has
  sent for our approval.
The hurricanes roar and houses
  are tossed in the fury,
The tornado whirls and scatters
  all in it's path,
Uprooting trees and houses to be
  tossed in angry air.
How unwise not to run and hide,
  lest I be taken
And fling in mid-air, if not
  heeding God's own laws.

Mike Feraco
CARING

---

*To Diane, a very special and
gentle lady who I will always love
and will forever be in my heart.*

Each word you speak is harmony
Your smile, a gentle glow
Your skin, so tender and devine
Your lips, as soft as snow.

Each day away from you, my love
Is an eternity
Your gentle hand I'll softly touch
While walking next to me.

You give me heaven here on earth
Each time I see your face
I pray that you'll be mine, my love
To feel your soft embrace.

Velma Carman
A BUSY SQUIRREL
High winds blow through the tree
  tops
While low upon the ground;
Among soft leaves, a busy
  squirrel stops,
The nuts are tumbling down.
He gathers them up, then goes
  away
Puts them in his store;
Somehow he knows soon comes
  the day,
He can gather no more.
When the woods are cold and bare
The soft sunshine has gone;
Then he is safe and cozy there,
All his work is done.
High winds blow through the tree

tops
Cold snow upon the ground;
No soft leaves, no squirrel who
  stops,
No nuts come tumbling down.

Margie H. Smith
GOD'S WONDERLAND
I like to walk in forest land
Hidden from the eyes of man
Dapple gray and forest green
Spiders spin their webs unseen
Shadows flit like butterflies
Deep within the cuckoo cries
Enveloped in the forest trees
Hear the distant hum of bees
Bird like voices hear and there
I alone their secrets share
The fern grows thick, the brook
  runs cool
To fish, a magic swimming pool
I linger in the failing light
The frogs give promise of the
  night
I leave refreshed, I understand
Why this is God's own
  wonderland

Colleen Smith
**A Day Of Small
Accomplishments**
Do you ever wonder why your
  shoulders have no rest
Every day by burden you are
  down and troubled with a test
Looking for an answer that is
  somewhere in the air
Do you ever search your heart
  and find a treasure there.

Some days are longer than others
But only in our minds
The clocks still tick second by
  second
And hour by hour they chime.

Does happiness seem so far away
Yet when it rains a rainbow
  brings you closer to it.
Why not count your daily
  accomplishments
Each day you win if you just get
  through it.

Sandy Greer
CHERISHED RETURN

---

*To Norman P. Smith—This Ones
For You—I Love You*

I hold you close in my mind,
  Forever willing to give.
The feelings in my heart
  Cry out in silence,
    Never to be heard by you
    Fearful of rejection.

Hold me close
  If even for only a moment,
    And I cherish the feeling.
Even when you're gone
  That feeling carries me on,
    Until you might return.

Joseph Cruz
**It's Time To End the Love
Once Told**
I've lost that beauty in my smile
I've lost that tenderness of my
  touch
I've lost that time that we're
  together
I've lost you!

I'll never forget how love can
  really be
I'll never forget the trust you
  showed me
I'll never forget our times
  together
But I may forget; FOREVER

The memories of love may never
  cease
The moments well spent may
  never freeze
But the continuance of love has
  found its end
And the hopes of tomorrow; lost
  in the wind

I've given you me as honestly as
  can be
I've loved you for tomorrow as
  you can see
But parts and pieces don't make a
  whole
It's time to end the love once told

Beatrice D. Londergan
The "Vietnam War" Is Over

---

*To my son, Thomas E.
Londergan—VFW—Navy Task
Force 116—Vietnam Mekong
River Delta—1968–1969*

The "Vietnam War" is over.
  They, who say these words,
    never gave a part.

The "Vietnam War" is over.
  Tell it to the wives and mothers,
    with "K.I.A." or "M.I.A."
      branded on their hearts.

The "Vietnam War" is over,
  Could you explain it to a child,
    if you heard the words he said?
  "My daddy can't come
    home—until,
      what is 'dead'?"

The "Vietnam War" is over.
  For the youthful lives they gave,
    are they resting peacefully
      or turning in their graves?

The "Vietnam War" is over.
  Foolish words—yours and mine.
    Wars are never really over
      until—the final end of
        time.

Jane Collins
TIME GOES BY
One surely misses something,
If he never gets to roam.
In an old abandon farm house,
That once had been a home.

You look around you and try to
  figure it out.
About the people that lived there,
And what it's all about.

You think it might of been a
  young man,
with his beautiful bride.
How they must of toiled to raise,
their family with pride.

Then you think about this
  couple,
How life quickly passes and
they are old.
Then you think about the stories,
If only they were told.

Sometimes it was beautiful,
And of course sometimes it's sad.
But it was mostly about,
Someone's Mom and Dad.

Kathleen A. Egbert
DROPS OF LOVE
I close my eyes
To see my mind
I see only you
With a smile so kind

There you stand
Reminding me
Of the love we once had
When you were alive and free

Many a time
I feel alone
I whisper to you
"Please come home"

Whenever I am sad
I go to my mind
I open my heart
And it's you I find

I know you are there
Wherever I go
And I know you hear me
When I say "I Love You So"

Please don't feel sad
When you look down from above
The water from my eyes
Are just drops of love

Char Skobel
CAN YOU HEAR MY CRY?
Whisper to me,
I want to hear the sounds of your
  heart.
Mine echoes from emptiness
  within.
If I should reach out
Could I touch you,
And draw you near
To warm my cold body?
If I cry will you
Wipe the tears from my face?
The depth of my sorrow
Can only be recognized
By someone who has preceeded
  me there,
And the stopping of it
Will come with your
  understanding.

Gail Suit Brack
SMILES
Marriage is no simple thing,
It's symbolized by just a ring,
But those of us who've walked
  the aisle
Know ther's a tear for every smile.
So we take the tears with a grain
  of salt,
And give the smiles a lot of
  thought,

For when we've reached the golden years
We'll remember the smiles above the tears.

Paula A. Boyd
PRECIOUS TIME
The moment's fleeting from our grasp,
And soon what is will be the past,
It's not what's lost, but what we don't find,
And the grief of losing precious time.

Each lost heartbeat that disappears,
Each foreign melody we can't hear,
It is merely a concept of the mind,
For the wasted hours of precious time.

Mourn not the loss, feel little regret,
It will swallow those who can't forget,
To try and repeat is the real crime,
In the art of losing precious time.

Alondra J. Knox, Benge (Lonnie)
Snow
The snow sifts quietly . . .
down through the bare trees.
Coming to rest . . .
on the long dead leaves.
The snow is too quiet,
like a very dark night.
It's holding a secret,
and won't bring it to light.
It's like a beautiful bird,
that can't fly or sing.
It's restless and quiet,
a very strange thing.
Snow is as quiet,
as quiet as stone.
It shifts and it blows,
and seems so alone.
The snow holds a secret,
that no one can guess.
It's quiet, so quiet . . .
it's almost like death.

Geraldine M. Oberbroeckling
Come To Me My Only Love

*Thank you Robert David Moore
Whom this poem was written
originally of.*

From the first time we met, I knew, I had a never ending love for you. With every hour that passes, I need you more and more. From the moment I lay down to sleep. Till I awake, I want your heavenly body next to mine.

To touch you, to hold you, to feel the loving security of your arms about me. Nobody, but you, can give me these feelings I hold so dear.

I have never stopped loving you, needing you, wanting you near me. Even, if just for a few moments. Just seeing you and talking to you, gives my life such happiness, if only for a short time.

It would be such a joy, to be in your arms, listening to your heart beat. And to feel the warmth of your body against mine. Even when we are not together, I know you are there. For I can feel your presence all around me. You have that gentleness, that always makes my day.

The passing of time has me realizing how much, you hold the key to my happiness. When we are miles apart, I have a special, close to you feeling.

Please take the sadness out of my heart. Come to me my only love. Give my heart life, Show me true happiness again.

June Lee Box

June Lee Box
Floating Fare In Crescent Harbor
Seagulls flapping, squawking loudly
Circling around in frenzied flight
Wings held high and bodies rigid
Are putting brakes on as they light.
They are swooping at the fish dropped
From boats dockside with open hatch
Where handy hoists are unloading
The slings of tempting un-iced catch.
With El Nino's warmer currents
Albacore's now near the North Coast
And are lures with crab and salmon
The gulls take from their grudging host.
Here, fish boats work on Percentage.
More fish weighed in; the more they earn.
Ever hassled by the seagulls,
Boats are keen-eyes from stem to stern.
With the diving, snatching seagulls
Strident noises splinter the air.
Sights and sounds we welcome gladly.
The fleet's in Safe, and many Share!

Joan M. Paradiso
ALONE
I search with my eyes
but they couldn't see,
turning around there
was no one but me.
The panic the terror

rushed through my heart,
where could i find them
where would i start.
They were there i could
feel them all walking
about, never stopping to
listen hear my terrified shout.
Then someone they touched
me and softly they said,
be still now i heard you,
i heard you i did!

Florence Reid Riemann
AUTUMN LEAVES
God has been happily toiling
As the night lay dark and still
Tinting all the foliage
Of the trees upon the hill.

He has used the brightest colors
Of orange, yellow, red, and green
With the muted shades of rust and brown
All blended in between.

The trees look like lovely maidens
Dressed for dancing at the ball
In their frilly bouffant dresses
In all the hues of fall.

There's a tall slender maiden
Arrayed in a gown of rosy-red
Next to her a saucy gold and green
With a green cap on her head.

They're standing on a carpet
Of the softest silvery-brown
Patterned by the brilliant leaves
That have drifted to the ground.

Too soon the ball will be over
And each one will shed her gown
Then they'll stand with bare arms uplifted
While God sends the soft snow down.

Lussy Villein
HALLOWE'EN
There were robbers and dance girls, clowns and a 'Mister'
Little ones, bigger ones, brother and sister
Collecting for UNICEF on Hallowe'en night
With happy faces and feet quick and light.

Linen bags opened, white or in colour.
'Tricks or treats', children smilingly holler.
Shiny cents they collected all along
For the others in need with their Hallowe'en song.

How the treats in their little bags, visible, clear,
As fast as the evening disappears!
And no one forgot to say happily 'thanks'
I like you all in your various ranks.

A few turned around and waved me
'Good night'
Oh, healthy youngsters, what a heartwarming sight!
You helped UNICEF with heart and hands,
This way reaching out to far away lands.

I loved you all, you shining faces . . .
Our dog sniffed happily in your traces.

Linda Eversole
THE LITTLE BOY I LOVE

*(Dedicated) "To: my Baby Doll,
my sweet pea my little dreamer,
"the little boy I love" the little boy
I love my son: Timmy-John."
Age 5 yrs. old.*

I see him playing in the sun
running with the wind . . .
wearing that little grin
I'm so thankful, God gave him to me
To love and take care of . . .
The little boy I love.
One day he's a soldier . . .
The next day a clown . . .
Or "Joe Montana"
When he makes a touchdown
He's all the things
That make a boy
But most of all . . .
My pride and joy . . .
The little boy I love

Patricia Ghering Wilder
ENCOUNTER
A moment stolen in time a
memory without a rhyme.

Hearts are broken and fools
do fall, was she so blind
not to see it all?

Words sweetly spoken her
defense does fall, of herself
she gives, foolishly her all.

A time of weakness or that of
love, a question with no answer of.

A moment stolen in time a
memory without a rhyme.

B. A. Breton
SOMEDAY

*To all who believed in my work;
especially my close friends*

If a time should come, someday
That we would part each others company
Let no foul words be spoken
For to remember we were once good friends
Is easier on the heart and the mind
Than to dwell on the reasons for parting.

Cheryl Lynn Buckley
LAND OF THE FREE
America is the land of the free,
and the home of the very brave.
I wonder if there's a place for me,
if sanity I can save.

In the life we lead today
is an abundance of war and hate,
of the subject I have much to say,
will greed bring us to our fate?

The land was molded before I was born
so that man must have to compete,
only to make a name for himself
and his enemy he must defeat.

In all honesty I need to say
I'm afraid of getting older,
I see the world's tragedies now

and my ambition began to
smolder.

If all mankind would join together
and think of our Lord as one,
our burden would be light as a
feather
the answer can be found in his
Son.

Velva Arlyne Urwiler

Velva Arlyne Urwiler
THE OCEAN OF LEAVES
What is this swirling, curling
driven by the wind
Is it the ocean madly beating
'gainst a rocky shore?
Nay friend, we've no ocean here
to see
but yellow leaves of autumn

So soon not to be.
In this cooling, hushing season
before winters dying
We perchance may still see one
last rose
or butterfly a-flying.
This mad swirling of the leaves
portends the winter yet to be.

Brenda Ann Goodloe
HALLOWEEN
The time is here for witches and
goblins
And jack-o-lanterns too,
You better beware and do take care
For they'll surely get you.

The spooky spooks, the scary
ghosts
The witching hour draws nigh,
The time has come when normal
things
Usually goes awry.

You better beware and do take care
The bats are flying too

If you don't watch out, there is no
doubt,
They will surely get you.

Listen, hear the dogs howling at
the moon
The creatures of this night will
be emerging soon.
You better beware and do take care
Be careful what you do
The ghosts are flying out tonight
And they will surely get you.

Judith Kaye Ward
I AM LOVE

---

*Dedicated to: David & Terry
Ward, Steve Miller, Linda &
Duane Hawkey; You've given me
love and shared your life—you
are my inspiration.*

Invading your dreams, making
you smile
bringing sunshine and laughter
if just for a while

You cannot see nor touch me
you can only believe
if I am to be yours, this must be

I am love

Gentle as a warm summer breeze
fierce as a storm, bending and
breaking
the strongest of trees

I am an ocean but not so deep
as the depths of your heart
where my secrets you'll keep

I am love

The sweetest of memories,
always I'll stay
when all others grow dim
and fade away

So cherish me as your greatest
treasure
and you will hold riches
beyond all measure.

Rebekah Mitchell
ZAPHIREL
Black angle, dark angle
child of night
sable spiral
in hawken flight
arms out streached
eyes blind sight
body burns cold
blue firelight
shadow of wasteland
unholy blight
perilous beauty
deception of might
to ever beyond
threshold of hight
onyx shine ebony
angle of night.

Greg Rayner
SPRING
Parting of the rain,
the wood lark's songs,
the true tone of life
away for all so long.

All of these are the markings of
Spring
with the sky as the victor,
the majestic sun as its
companion.
With the parting of the rain, the

sharing of life,
leaving all cluttered depression
abandoned.

At the edge of the wood the lark's
call enchants—
with all its gaiety, with all its
romance.

As the distant mornings spread
onward,
crickets' melodies fill the night,
All falseness is shadowed,
for this is the true tone of life.

Spring, you brighten our days
with a dream or a song,
So why then Spring, do you stay
away
all so long?

Trisha Johnson
A Summer To Remember
The Utah floods were something
to remember.
The sandbags we filled seemed to
last forever.
The hot sweltering sun was our
biggest rival,
Yet we kept on going because we
knew it was survival.
We blistered and we sunburned
during the long dreaded hours,
But that didn't bother us as much
as the showers.
No one seemed to complain but
you could feel it inside,
We were tired and weary and
only wanted the land dry.
As the days passed on and things
started to clear,
The Spirit of Survival was what
kept the good cheer.

Lee Crokaerts
BABY TEARS
Throughout all time it has
remained the same.

For heaven above has set the plan
for you to come here and
return again.

As the doctor helps you into this
world of hope, of dreams, of
trials, of fears you welcome it
with baby tears.

With all our hearts we welcome
you, for our hopes and prayers
and dreams have come true.

The veil is there now and you
cannot see, for that part of the
plan has been set up above and
Father in heaven has sent you
with love.

Ruth Roberts Douglas
ANSWERS
At a roadside tavern under neon
sign
You found your answer in the red
of wine
and a red geranium
grows upon my
windowsill.

A kaleidoscope of song and music
spoke
and covered up the sound when
your heart broke
and across a country lane
A night bird sings Whip-poor-will.

Frenzied laughter—red of satin gown
keeps off memory for another

round
and The Book upon my lap
is warm with tears
Peace, be still.

Lorie M. Rezanson
UNTITLED
A first love
is the love
that is never forgotten . . .

But the last love
is a love
that grows into a future
full of cherished hopes
and unending memories.

Elizabeth P. Pirrung
PEACE 1983
fragmental
lithe
out-of-bounds
pre-empted

chances are
the spelling
or it
is lost
or
pieced out

Sharon Diane Reeve
A POEM FOR MILLIE

---

*I dedicate this poem to Millie
Radke, my friend and neighbor
from Cottage Grove, Oregon. At
the time of her funeral I couldn't
afford flowers, so I gave her
something from my heart;
"A POEM FOR MILLIE".*

What words can describe the way
one feels?
It just takes time and love to heal.
She was our friend, a friend
indeed; a wife,
A grandma, a mother in need.
But, life itself is just a test, to see if
We're strong to handle the rest.
Who are we to say what's going
to happen
Tomorrow; let alone today?
God only knows, and he wants it
that way.
It reminds me of the blossoms on
our trees,
You wait each year just to smell
them and see.
But, before you know, they've
come and gone; and
Fall like snow in the morning sun.
So, year after year, when the
blossoms bloom,
They'll remind me of you Millie,
and I'll see you soon.

With love, from Sharon Reeve

Yvette M. Bogle
UNFORGOTTEN BLISS
What brought you here?
You've been gone some ten years
Wow! I hate to admit
But you do look fit
Fanciful, but wonderful
As usual simply beautiful
Suddenly I've grown shy
And I've become tongue tied
Gosh! is it you I'm seeing
Tell me, or am I dreaming
What indeed brought you here
After ten long years
No, don't say it's me, you miss

That I am your unforgotten bliss
I wouldn't, no I couldn't believe it
And couldn't quite conceive it
You wouldn't perchance, do you
Think I've been waiting for you
Tell me, won't you, do you know
For sure, what made you show
Was it love, was it really, really
love

Alessandra A. Poles
ROCKING CHAIR
Near the embers' blush
Waits a lonely chair,
Vacant, dim with dust
Waiting for that touch,
Hands that once caressed.

Now and then it rocks
Through the quiet nights
Beckoning back the past
Transient, nameless bliss;
One more warm embrace.

Edward R. Marko
MY PRAYER, PRAYER
Why did you go and die?
Was the cross on your back
More than you could hack?
Was it too much a load
On the straight and narrow road?
Or, did you finally get weak
Turning the other cheek,
For the deaf, the dumb and the
blind?
And I guess it really blew your
mind
When the only girl that you
could find
Was charging for her time!
Then to reinstate your pride
You tiptoed on the tide!
Changed the water into wine!
But if you were such a special guy,
So tight with the big man in the
sky,
Why? Why did you go and die?

Debbie Hlavaty-Knobbe
JAN AND KEITH
Jan gave Keith everything he
wanted.
Her never ending love,
Three lovely children,
Dinner ready promptly at six
each night,
A clean house,
All her earnings (to pay off his
past debts)
And a divorce.

Wayne Thomas Ritchie
SUMMER ROSE
In a tiny store shop window, sat a
dolly by herself.
When my parents went to buy
her, the man pointed to the
shelf.
I'll start crying in a minute, if
that dolly we can't buy.
And the owner started laughing,
just as I began to cry.
Well the owner hummed and
hollered, that it ruined his
display.
And thats how I got dolly, and I
have her still today.
It was tea time when I called her,
but my baby never came.
Was the reason for my baby, that
she did not have a name?
For she never heard me calling, as
the others came to tea.

I went looking for my dolly, then
a name it came to me.
My dear daddy came to see me,
"Can I help you in your find"?
Well I'm looking for my dolly, oh!
gosh daddy your so kind.
She looks a lot just like me dad,
and her name is Summer Rose.
Well he found her in a second,
like he found me I suppose.
My dad never did tell me though,
and he never will I bet.
I wrote this down so years from
now, we never shall forget.
I have others that I play with,
like my Barbie and Shortcake.
But when we go on vacation,
she's the only one I take.
When it is time to say good
night, she goes into bed with me.
We both share all our sweet
dreams, I hug her so tenderly.
When it comes time to put up
dolls, my Summer will always
stay.
For the memory of my golden
youth, that will never go away.
If ever I should have a girl, I'll
watch her as she grows.
And give to her a doll I have, I'll
give her Summer Rose.

Carmen Lydia Colmenares
Carmen Lydia Colmenares
PLEASE-SHED-NO-TEARS

I dedicate this poem with love, to
everyone who is blessed with
inspirational inner vision. To the
ones who can see beyond the
superficial screen of life.

I have felt the magic of a song,
and have heard the music in the
rain,
I have run across green hills, so
strong,
in my search for nature's sweet
refrain.
I have known the ocean's strong
caress,
as the foaming waters bubbled
near,
I have heard the songbird at his
best,
in his joyous moment, without
fear.
I have heard the laughter of a
child,
when the snowflakes kissed a
button nose,

I have seen the flowers bloom
and rise,
as if to court the sunshine, in
their pose,
I have known the sweetness of a
smile,
that the spark of innocence can
give,
I have felt the love in all of life,
and I've known the urgency to
live!
I've found peace, dear heart,
because of "Him",
"He" who blessed my darkest
hour with light!
Please shed no tears, when my
life grows dim,
for the joy, is eternal . . . at "His"
side . . .

Renee Dreishpoon
THE MUSICIAN
The man with rhythm sings for
the moon,
His visions are put to notes in
tune.
He plays to please his inner mind,
Strangers employ him and think
him kind.
It may be lean, stout, short or tall,
Each musician's style varies in all.
Styles change with the wink of an
eye,
When a man and an instrument
know they must try.
To compose a work of song,
A man must always believe them
wrong when
Judgement is passed upon his tune,
Fans know they judged too soon.
The rags of some and riches of
others,
Have made all musicians nearly
brothers.
The soul of one is the life of the
other,
Which makes each player the
perfect lover.
That is to say that music is such,
The world may never have too
much!

Wesley Nyblade
A BROTHERS MEMORY
Why were the skies so gray
when soldiers marched to go and
play
why was it under darkened skies
that Johnny went to play and die

Father wept and mother prayed
when Johnny went out to play
lightning struck and thunder
rolled
as he marched to meet his foe

Thors mighty hammer sang in
the sky
as one by one they crumpled and
died
the clouds with drops of weeping
tears
tried vainly to wash deaths grisly
smear

It was under a darkened sky
when death it bit and my family
cried
death it knocked on my front
door
and whispered news that
drenched the floor

Johnny came home one darkened
day
came home from battle and not
from play
his grave lies up on yonder hill
a vivid memory, another mans kill

Why oh why is the sky still gray
when the blood red sun brings a
new day
I will tell you why that skies so
gray
'cause soldiers are going back; . . .
to play.

Ande Griffin
APOLOGY FOR A FRIEND
I'm a fool to live without you, babe,
But I'm a fool to carry on.
I just can't hide all the things in
my mind;
I can't lie to you no more.

The world goes on with little
games;
We're just victims of a play.
In another time or another place
Maybe it wouldn't end this way.

You said I was your only love,
But I couldn't tell you the same.
You touched my heart, but we're
worlds apart;
Satisfactions getting hard to find.

All I've said and all I've done
You still call me your friend.
I'm a fool for ever loving you
When I just hurt you in the end.

Nancy Arena
Tribute To John F. Kennedy
A giant of a man
Struck down with a gun by a fiend
While the world, stunned and
bewildered,
Was left to mourn bitterly the
loss of an inspiring leader—
Emotions spilling over tear-
drenched cheeks,
Grieving hearts screaming
silently at the outrageous deed
of Fate.
A man of noble purpose for
brotherhood and peace,
A proven hero, a man of courage
and integrity,
A man of great charm, intellect,
and wit,
A man much-loved, never to be
forgotten or replaced.

A monstrous, deplorable tragedy!—
The assassination of John
Fitzgerald Kennedy.

William Robert Walton
OLD TENNESSEE
The land of pure and balmy air,
Of streams so clear and sky so fair
Of mountains grand and
fountains free
The lovely Land of Tennessee
Old Tennessee Fair Tennessee
The land of all the World to me
I stand up on the mountain high
Hold communion with skyview
Glowing landscape floating over
Tennessee for evermore
The bravest of the brave have We
Fairest of the Fair We See,
Freeest of the noble
Free in battle
Scard Old Tennessee
The rairest fruits and fairest

flowers
and lovest homes on Earth are ours
If heaven below could only be
Would surely shine on Tennessee
Tune my heart with chordful
    string
and of the lovely country song
from east to west the chorus will be
God bless Our Dear Old
    Tennessee

Flo Lampp Hageman
SOLACED BY APRIL

*To: My Father Emery Gilbert
Lampp Dec. 16, 1894-Apr. 9, 1982*

I stand shrouded
in the morning mists
of early April—
The whip-o-will mourns,
unconsoled as I—today
my fair beloved April
has wrenched you away.

The sun rises—
I see a gossamer April
in resurrection dance—
All things dormant, so
visibly dead, delight
at her fleeting touch,
to blossom to new life.

The mists burn away—
my tears vanish—
while April declares
God's promise,
"All things made new."
I stand consoled—
sure he included you.

Gail Walton Harris
BABY GIRL

*This poem was inspired by, and
written for, my darling Baby Girl,
Angela Michelle, with all my love.*

I stand in the shadows and watch
    her play,
I see her grow from day to day.
I share in her laughter and dry
    her tears,
I answer her questions, I ease her
    fears.
I stand gazing upon her while she
    sleeps,
Wearing a contented smile, and
    silently
Whisper a prayer, for such a
    "beautiful", healthy child.
I think of her future and how it'll
    be,
She's got a long way to go cause
    she's only three.
I think of the day when she's
    fully grown,
And my baby girl will pass and it
    won't be long,
Before she has a child of her own.
Then it'll be her turn to wipe
    runny noses,
Teach them and guide them as
    they grow.
But no matter how old she grows
    to be,
She'll still be my "Baby Girl" to
    me.
There's no limit to a mother's
    love.
It starts from the day the new life

begins,
And continues to grow until the
    day it ends.
There's nothing greater in the
    whole wide world,
Than the love I have for my
    "Baby Girl"!

William L. Jarvis, Jr.
NATURAL ACTS

*To my son, William III; I Love
You, Dad*

A snowflake falls, so gently from
    the sky—
A bird strokes its wings, and
    begins to fly—
A catipiller grows, and becomes a
    beautiful butterfly—
A baby enters this world, not
    knowing its future is to die—
    (life is deaths embryo).

Nova R. Rohrbaugh
AUTUMN

Autumn is so beautiful,
Gorgeous hues of color abound.
In the leaves of the trees—
The fall flowers in the ground.

The sky is a bluish gray,
The wind too blows colder now.
Beauty is all around us
In the grass and bending bough.

The colors of bush and tree
Are many and varied too.
God made this lovely season,
A blessing for me and you.

Herman Weiss
Tomorrow Is a Beautiful Day

*This lullaby song is dedicated to
all children of God's world,
especially to those who suffered
due to war.*

Go to sleep darling,
Close lovely eyes so blue.
Brush away your tears,
As daddy wants you to.

Where is daddy darling,
Why he's somewhere over there.
No we can't bring him home,
No matter how much we care.

Some day little darling,
Let's hope wars will end.
Lights glow in many homes,
Cause daddy's there again.

Close lovely eyes so blue,
And dream your cares away.
Sleep tight little baby,
Goodnight little baby.
Tomorrow's a beautiful day—
God Willing, Tomorrow's a
    beautiful day.

Lillian Faye Winks
A BIRTHDAY THOUGHT

Do not weep child,
    borned ont he first day of fall.
Summer is truly gone,
    as your youthful dreams.
Dreams of life and love,
    like the warm soft breeze.
Borned in the sunset of the year,
    is also, now, your span of
        continuum of age.

Do not shed tears,
    in freezing chill it brings,
    shall set in the shades of
        Autumn.
Shades of shaffon, crimson, and
    maroon in jade,
    mingles with the fire in the
        eventide sky.
Dream again child,
    for helt in your hand is the
        Sapphire.
Dream of the richness in the heart,
    that has been aquired, which
        can be given.
Smile on, fortunate child,
    for this is a picturesque season
        of change.

Tammy Murray
I AM

I walk alone
In my thoughts
Because no one else
Thinks them but me.

I walk alone
In my dreams
Because no one else
Dreams them but me.

I walk alone
In my sorrows
Because no one else
Feels them but me.

I walk alone
In my joys
Because no one else
Sees them but me.

I walk alone
In my goals
Because no one else
Chose them but me.

Thomas J. Giannelli
THE HERE

The under
Stood up for what
He believes in many
Things that are true.
The over
Estimated total
Cost more
Than what
You thought.
The in
Side with winning, winners
Will always be
In.
The out
Standing can tire
four legs, long
And skinny and standing
Out . . .

Karen Theobald
MOM

I looked at her on that day of
    pain,
thought to myself how much she
    changed.

Her coal black hair had turned to
    grey,
her soft white skin would stay
    that way.

She opened her eyes and looked
    at me,
I trembled as she touched my
    knee.

I knew then she would be alright,
she made it through that painful
    night.

So strong and yet so frail,
she's paved the way, can I follow
    her trail?

What kind of life did she leed?
No one will know, there is no
    need.

My only friend in this world of
    trials.
No questions asked and no deniles.

The love the hate, the truth the
    lies,
what will I do when my mother
    dies?

Ian Luke
TIME UNLOCKED

I would love to stroll
    Through the passages of time,
And watch the eye that watches
    me
    As I fill the hills with rhyme.
The red would turn to blue,
    The black would fall from sight,
Streaking on the wings of fire
    Conquering the night.
I can see the lights of Osadus,
    Shining from the tip,
Of a sword so mighty and majestic,
    From the end, dragon's blood
        drips.
Yellow leaves will breathe,
    The air of a thousand lies.
A rainbow of windblown flowers,
    Freshen up the skies.
If it so happens
    That I find this passage of mine,
I will send a postcard to everyone
    Who loves to dream as I.

Patricia Mary Post
YOU . . . MY LOVE

As I sit alone at night
You are all that is in my sight
My heart may be cured
But my sight is still blurred
For you are not here tonight
Making me feel right
For I know I miss you tonight
You are still in my sight
If I could have a wish come true
I'd want to spend every minute
    with you
For I'll never leave you behind
And you'll always be on my mind
Just thinking about you brings
    tears to my eyes
For someday we might have to
    say good-bye
I hope that day will never appear
For if it does my life will
    disappear
There is nothing for me to do
I can't go on without you
For I was hoping to become your
    wife
And spend my life
With you . . .
My Love!!

Alice L. Dale
THE STRAY

The big maltese cat that came
    one day,
Was sort of bluish gray.
He had no home it was plain to
    see,
For he intended to stay.

He ate the food that I put out,
For my timid little cat,
He simply sat, and blinked his

eyes,
And stared, when I said, "Scat."

I didn't want another cat,
I chased him with a stick.
I only meant to scare him.
I didn't strike a lick.

But that arrogant big tom cat,
Didn't frighten worth a whoop.
He just prowled around the
  bushes,
And sat there on my stoop.

A cat won't sit up, and offer a paw,
Like a friendly dog will do,
But he waved his tail, and arched
  his back,
And purred a sound or two.

He clearly wanted to be my friend,
At my house he wanted to stay,
And 'though I ignored him, and
  shooed him off,
He wouldn't go away.

He became a permanent boarder,
And shared my kitties food.
She seemed to even like him,
Or just didn't want to be rude.

So now it seems I have two cats.
There was nothing I could do.
The one is named Amanda Belle,
The other I call Big Blue.

Sheila Chen
ONCE MORE

---

*This is dedicated to my four
children Gary, Angela, Kimiko
and Leewan. My inspiration and
my life. For all we have been
through and for our lives to come.
Eternally yours Mom.*

If we were,
What we would like to be,
IF WE WERE,
We'd have a chance to see,

Then we'd know,
Just what it was we were,
When we were,
Where we were before.

So we are,
And here we are,
No different than we were,

So if we are,
SO sure we are,
Then we are where we were
                    Once more!

Tracy Malcom
MY WINDOW
Looking through my window now
if you ask me what I see
I'd say, "Only the reflection
of the world upon me."

I see the people come and go
the rich, the poor, the middle
  class
all I can do is give a sigh
and lay my head against the glass.

I think about the times to come
when I'll be leaning against my
  window pane
wondering where those people are
and of what importance their
  lives have been.

Looking through my window now
I don't know what the future
  holds

All I can do is wait
and see what time unfolds.

Marlene Fatur
LET GO
When you love something
But know it must go,
Close out your thoughts of the
  world
And try desperately to let go.

Be sad no longer
For there is no need for tears,
Indulge in the joyous moments
Brought through the years.

So let go little one
No matter how difficult it seems,
One day you will meet again
If only in dreams.

Vernon L. Downs
ANGUISH
The frothy surf beat on the rocky
  shore with thunderous echoes
The misty grey of stormy skies
  shadowed the ebon floes
I was lost in a dreary world of
  agony
A shipwrecked soul that had
  longed to be free
But now I was caught in the
  throes
Of an angry ocean of spiteful
  blows
Any my consciousness was
  overcome
by the sound of distant crows

Mary Letha Washington
WHAT SHALL I BE?
Through your love
You want me to be happy and
  free—
Free to live and choose from
The many courses you set for me,
Hoping one of these
I'll surely be.

I need your guidance and loving
  care
To carry me through each trying
  year.
I am trying to be what you want
  me to be,
But to be happy and free
I will need to be me!

Jody Clark
**My Handicapped Son,
Mark**
In his Dreams,
  I wonder if he walks and talks.

Donna Maree Corbin
PRAYER FOR THE DAY
Lord,
Guide my man all through the
  nite.
Keep him warm and
Keep him bright.
Make him clean like
A snowfall dove.
He's my joy, my life,
My only love.
And
Teach him
Lord,
From good and bad,
Keep him happy,
Never sad.
Make him glad for all's
He's done,
He's my joy, my life,
The Only One.

Sonja Christina

Sonja Christina
LIFE'S GAME

---

*All love is play acting in part
Here and there we give a peace of
heart! Comes life's eve the heart
compartments does contain—
Each one recalling times of joy or
pain! Then life leads it in spite of
bane— To hopefully with
renewed anticipation And newly
discovered orientation To re -
enter life's wistful game!*

You laugh with a woman
You cry with a woman
That is my friend, what you do—

You talk with a woman
You laugh with a woman
And that is how you get through

You cry with a woman
You sigh with a woman
You make her feel you are a part
Of all that hurt's her at the
  time
For love my friend is an art!
You cry with a woman

You sigh with a woman
That way you conquer her
  heart!
You laugh with a woman

You joke with a woman
That way you make her feel
  whole!
You laugh with a woman

You comune with a woman
To enter her very soul!
You laugh with a woman

You feel with a woman
That way you put her at ease!
It is the little intimacies

Which bring the desired peace!
You laugh with a woman
You feel with a woman

That way she responds the most
Only the vanity of men makes
  him think
Only in bed he must play perfect
  host!

So laugh with a woman
Cry with a woman
Whether you are sincere or just a
  flirt,

Better to be remembered with
  inner gain
Then to be remembered for

having caused hurt!
Cry with a woman our humanity
  is all the same
A woman's lot is not an easy one
She just tries to be part of man's
  game!
So laugh with a woman

Cry with a woman
One night or a lifetime—have a
  ball—
Never let on how you realy feel

After all—you can't love them all!

Wasteland Misfit Henderick
No Poetry In Newsprint?
Authentic poets sense our true
  identity
beneath the din and strife of
  everyday.
They find our greatest treasure in
  their wilderness,
ecstatic in the sweetest light and
  truth.
They know that life is death and
  misery
where vanity and cynicism reign.

They know within our depths we
  love the good,
we love the true, the noble and
  the brave;
we love the gentle, kind, and
  understanding;
we love a simple, disciplined
  integrity;
we love good craftsmanship and
  quality;
we love the teachers who respect
  the truth;
we love warm friendship,
  firesides, and justice.

So why is there no poetry in
  newsprint?
Why are draught of joy and life
  denied?
Are banal vanity and man's
  brutality
the only items worthy of our note?
Are people lacking interest in the
  real?
Is every weakened soul forever
  doomed?

Shine forth, O lovely spirit of the
  light!
This wintry night's been dark and
  O so cold!
The strife and violence and
  competition
have blinded us and deafened us
  to truth:
Our hearts do not need riches,
  fame or power
to fluorish, love the good, know
  love's delight.

Martha K. McHenry
THANKFUL BE
The exuberant life that radiates
Beaming with vivacity and
  happiness
Hope, joy and love.
To behold the goodness of all
  mankind
And vibrates from friend to friend.

Communication among all nations
That will bring peace from such
  an occasion.
Shelter and comfort to abide
In a place somewhere inside.

For many unexpected things
From various sources sprang
Birds that chatter, winds that blow
even the frost and snow.
Sunshine and trickling raindrops
that fall below
Flittering bees on fragrant
blossoms of little buds.

For all things that make the
world beautiful.
Be Thankful!

Lucille M. Kroner

Lucille M. Kroner
SPRINGTIME
Oh, springtime's growing in the
land,
Its daffodils, its violets blue,
Its crocus snuggled close to banks
Of ferns kissed damp with
sparkling dew.

Springtime's a donning her new
gown
Flowered in the softest hues
Of roses pink, of lilies white,
Of daisies softest blues.

Green ferns make lace around her
skirt,
Jeweled bright with raindrops,
too,
And here and there, crisp ruffled
vines
Around her dance anew.

Oh, could I but 'waken into
Spring
Once more, and see her face,
Could feel her newness and her
charm,
Her fresh and titilating grace,

Could see her glory on the land
Touched to life anew,
How happy I would be again,
My faith thus to renew.

Linda W. Kornegay
LITTLE KITTY

*"Little Kitty" was written for 2
1/2 year old Sarah K. Hroza on 12-
24-82. She received one of our
kittens from Santa Clause.*

This "Little Kitty" is a gift
for you,
If you love, her, she'll forever
be true.
She'll cry if her tail you do
happen to pull,
She likes to cuddle you whenever
she's full.

This "Little Kitty" is yours
for the keeping,
But, if you're too rough, it'll
be *you* who is weeping!
Dorothy L. Aldridge
SECRET LOVE
So fragile is my secret love
a spiders web
with dew drops shinning
in the morning sun.
A string of sparkling diamonds.
I hesitate to open my heart
to bring it out for all to see,
less it be destroyed before I
can know the fulfillment of
my secret love.
June Lowie
THE OLD HOMESTEAD

*Dedicated to all old time
homesteaders everywhere And to
all my children and granchildren.*

1. When my Mother died, Father
faded away.
And soon lay beside her, beneath
the cold lay.
We boys heard the calling for
men who could fight.
So we shook hands and left the
old homestead one night.
2. The years passed by and we
fought for our land.
Honored the flag, and for all that
she stands.
Then one day on leave, on my
way over seas.
I decided to renew some old
mem-ories.
3. There's not much left of the
old homestead today.
But two weather bent crosses
where Mom and Dad lay.
The peaceriver still winds
through valleys and trees.
And the pines and the tamerack
still wave in the breeze.
4. Old Lobo still howls from his
den on the hill.
The deer and the moose come to
drink at the mill.
The prairie dog still buroughs
under the barn.
And the fire weed still lines the
fence of our farm.
5. The lilacs still bloom by the
brocken down gate.
The old homestead looks lonely,
awaiting her fate.
Yes I think I'll come back, when
this war is through.
And turn it back into, what I
once knew.

Ada M. Fletcher
REMNANTS

*To my mother, Margaret Henkel,
whose boundless faith has never
faltered.*

Spidery webs of crumbling faith
In darkest corners bide,
For faith is often shelved behind
The ego, 'till inside
We panic with a rage and fear
When faced with grief or loss
And then evoke with clarity
A Simon for our cross.

Louise Monger
AUTUMN
Gallant fleets
Of Autumn leaves
Hoist their sails
Of red, yellow and gold.
Becomming pirates
Riding the tides of wind.
Carrying treasured colors
To settle on the ground;
Their new frontier.
Marie Bond
CHANGING SEASONS
A time of year when our
thoughts change from summer
fun to mystic things.
A gentle breeze in summertime
now seems a twisting hurricane.
The creaking sounds so charming
now have changed to demons
to which we bow.
The shadow of a tree at night is a
monster in full flight.
Have faith, my friend, as you will
see all is natural as can be.
No matter how strange it all may
seem you are preparing for
Halloween.
JoAnn Simpson
MY HERO

*Special thanks, to all men, —who
volunteer to fight for our country
& our freedom, and all men like
"David", who died bravely doing
it, such an honor.*

Was it a hundred years ago? "No
it just seems." Even now as I
think of you. It seems like a
dream. Only nineteen when
you were called to war.
Sometimes I still wonder what
it was you died for. After all
this time You're still on our
minds, Even though you never
said so, It wasn't easy I know to
leave all your loved ones so far
behind, you laid your life on
the line. Regardless the cost.
We were hurt and confused,
cause we thought your life had
been misused, we didn't realize
what we still had, for what we
had lost. It's because of you I
know It's true, You're My Hero.
You were called to fight a war,
you went, not giving it a
thought of how your life would
be spent. You were called you
didn't say no. You went to a
place a lot of us wouldn't dare
go, You took a stand to help
your fellow man. You fought
for our freedom and for our
country. It cost you your life, It
didn't seem right. A high price
to pay For no mans land. All we
have left now are the
memories. Things change and
people forget, "I want you to
know we haven't forgotten you
yet." Over the years things
change, only a few things
remain the same, there is still a
war going on today. Only the
names and places have
changed. Instead of Vietnam,
Now it's Beirut, and Lebanon.

Each time the American Flag is
raised up high, "I think of you
in the big blue sky." You're a
true American,—Red, White,
and Blue. "Thank you David,"
for the job you did and a job
well done. You're My Hero.

Tamara L. Collins
SHARED BEAUTY
We saunter out of Merlins Gate
leaving behind the lush,
swaying trees of Merlins
domain.
We step out on to the beaten
down path of years before.
Our gaze extends past what we
have left behind and drifts
onward to the brilliant, slowly
sinking sun that is cradled in
the valley between the two
mountains in the distance . . .

The music plays on adding to the
beauty the three of us are sharing.
The flute plays like the wind that
carries a thousand different tunes
of birds harmoniously singing
their never forgotten song.

Midge Sullivan
TO KNOW

*TO AUNT SHIRL with Love and
affection—This poem was
written with thoughts of you in
mind for sharing and caring.*

DEAR GOD THIS IS THE
BEGINNING OF A BRAND
NEW YEAR
TWELVE MONTHS TO GO
THRU AND CHERISH MOST
DEAR
TO KNOW how to live a Day at
a Time with You
TO KNOW you'll always see me
thru
TO KNOW how to help a friend
in time of sorrow
TO KNOW that the Sun will
come out tomorrow
TO KNOW how to share the
riches I have received from YOU
TO KNOW how to be the me
that YOU want me to
TO KNOW how to laugh at
things that may go wrong
TO KNOW how to LIVE my LIFE
like a beautiful song
TO KNOW that at time I may
fail a request
TO KNOW that all I can do is
my best
TO KNOW that I grow more
when I suffer pain
TO KNOW that I can always
start over again

Mrs. Dorie Millions
TO SAY "GOOD—BYE"
Here sits I at the old table's edge;
I'm trying to say "Good-Bye!"
Seventeen years old and the
eldest of fourteen children.
A gal in trouble and scared. I
should be the example. I know.
But how do I say "good-bye" to
the people I love?
Silently I look around the clean
unpainted room.
Dirt poor are we but definately

loved by all.
Now I'm in trouble because I let
my body rule my mind.
I'm so sorry! Wow! What a cop-
out. I'm running.
I must do what's right. We have
no room after all for another
bundle of joy.
MY problem anyway.
Mom, Dad, everyone I really do
love you all.
Tell the kids to help out with the
others.
I know that sounds hollow
coming from a cop-out kid like
me.
But I mean it anyway. DAM! this
is so hard.
I thought I could just walk away.
I can't. But I must. What do I say
now?
I love you all yet I hurt you.
Why? I have no answers.
Well don't worry *this will be my
last hurt.*
I have to go now. It is getting late.
Here sits I alone, scared,
pregnant, seventeen years old.
Slowly I rise, walk to the door,
open it.
I take one last look around, turn,
run, and cry.
I cannot face this anymore;
"PLEASE FORGIVE ME."
Know what? I didn't even say
"GOOD-BYE" yet. I just can't.

Trudy L. Keiter
FLOWING MEMORIES
My mind, like a river,
flows freely with the memories of
you;
winding its way through the
channels of my intellect,
pausing only to remember how
insignificant life was until . . .
the rapids of your love crashed
upon the stillness of my lonely,
waiting heart.
Unable to see around the bend,
I wait for the fate of my heart:
whether
the end of a beautiful flow of life
or
the beginning of a vast, new sea.

Ada M. Fletcher
OCTOBERFEST

---

*To my sons, Bob, George and
Michael, who always share my
enthusiasm for the change of
seasons.*

Fall's open house—a pristine
kaleidoscope of color
Kindling a surge of the spirit, a
burst of energy
As the cool, brisk days tease the
leaves down.
Visions of witches, goblins and
ghosts wait in the wings
As nature's lending library sates
us with the splendor of it's
cache:
The sun basting treetops to the
sky with threads of silver;
The pregnant earth vibrating
with preparation for
A winter gestation;

Gossipy squirrels chattering as
they vie for knothole
Apartments;
Profusions of multicolored
flowerage nodding before the
Winter solstice;
Lawn mowers sputtering their
last hurrahs and Tulip bulbs
Being tucked into the earth's
bosom;
Pumpkins running wild in the
fields; winged creatures
Cascading to treetops for one last
panoramic view;
The tantalizing smell of apple pie
and cinnamon, burning
Leaves and chimney smoke—the
last rose.
The tangy bite of fresh apple
cider; the resonant honking
Of migrating geese; the sound of
laughing children
Gamboling in crunchy leaf
pyramids.
Now, priorities quicken—logs are
stacked and covered
And the apple cellar is filled.
Bird houses overflow with seed,
suet and peanut butter—
Raisin-oatmeal balls.
The frost is on the pumpkin—a
quietude descends.
It's October and all is well!

Shanda M. Stephenson
A FIELD OF CLOVER
Greenery is the scenery,
where unicorns play.
Where rabbits run,
through the sun,
and flowers bloom all day.

Where spring rains fall,
and rainbows rise . . .
and nature's splendor is no
surprise.

Sharon Lee Hargrove
MY VISION
In the spirit I am in deep slumber,
hear I the spring rain, the birds
with great joy sing, they make
sweet music that tells a story.

See the stars by night give light
to the master's stairway; it
cannot be seen by day, the
clouds giving protective cover,
for only the saints to discover.

Atop the staircase our saviour
stands, with outstretched hands
from the north to the south.
His robe blowing in the breeze
from the east to the west,

becking to everyone his heart
bursting in his chest.

With love unending, his work is
never done, he commands the
birds to sing from sun to sun.
With stares he guides the way
at night, to behold him is like
unto a ship anchored from
stem to steam. His loving
power fills my soul, fearing to
look, unable to turn away, my
heart bids me go, though my
soul with him will stay.

This is a page of a book not
written yet. That in answer to
a prayer, my god let me see
because my saviour heard my
plea.

Allyson Mayo
OCHRE PRISMS
The last time I looked that way,
Screamed, yelled, shook that day,
Ochre Prisms of life did stay.

Many hours my mind was dead,
Paralyzed, captured my body bled,
It was Ochre Prisms of life that
led.

I tried, my chords of thought
dragged,
My whole bubble of soul sagged,
Ochre Prisms of life bragged.

With stretched out hands I cried,
no more!
My spirit was broken my body
sore,
It was Ochre Prisms that
slammed the door.

I saw the crystal of purple light,
Of strange aura, intensely bright,
Ochre Prisms of life grew tight.

With great energy I slowly rose,
Enwrapped with wonder I knew
no foes,
It was Ochre Prisms of life that
froze.

I and the atmosphere together
razed,
Now free from barriers, no longer
dazed,
Ochre Prisms of life were crazed.

Through realization I weakly
sighed,
For all the cycles of times I've
cried,
It was Ochre Prisms of life that
died . . .

Miss Lisa Lorraine Pierce
FOREVER NO MORE

Dedicated To The One I Love

Ever since you left me . . .
My life hasn't been the same,
My wall of independence
crumbled . . .
My soul now still and drained.
Now I lie meek and humble,
No longer have I pride.
I just want you back again . . .
Forever by my side.
To stay forever more, my dear . . .
To set, my smile free,
O'Endless love op-en your
heart . . .
And hear my silent plea.

M. Earley Grace
ZIRCON
The night was stormy
The wind whipped through my
mind
I went to him that knew me
And laid there by his side

I went in my tangled nowness
For comfort in his warmth
Bringing my unsureness
On a January morn

He petted and consoled me
As early morning turned
to day
Yet surfaced only weariness
For encounters too many
Had ended that way

Duretta Reel Harding
SHADES OF SUMMER
When I have a moment or two to
spare
I love to bask in sun and open air,
And to cast my gaze on summer
sky,
To watch and listen to birds
flying by,
To see frothy clouds roll silently
on
To disperse themselves or
thunderstorms spawn;
I wish I could lie here for many
hours
In this lawn chair near the
fragrant flowers;
I'd like to always an optimist stay
But with so many obstacles, no
way!
For bees, flies and wasps are
cruising too near
As little red ants are nibbling
my ear,
Plus that boiling sun soon chases
me in
To seek more lotion for my
burning skin;
Oh, why couldn't I have been
born a brunette
So I could be a sun worshipper
yet!
(I could lick the bugs with some
pesticide
But only God can color my
outside.)

James Midolo, Jr.
YOU ARE
You're an angel sent from up
above
You're an unforgotten song
You're in my heart forever love
The place where you belong

You're a shooting star up in the
sky
With moondust in your hair
And golden starlight in your eyes
I love when you are near

Until the earth spins out to die
The two of us will be in love
Me, a poor boy from this earth
And you, an angel from above

Louise Levesque
THE MONKEY
Through the window you're
looking at me
Laughing at every move that I
make
I'm a prisoner and you are free
And that for me is so hard to take

265

You think that you're superior to me
You think that I'm funny but brainless
I bet that you'd be surprised to see
What I think of you nevertheless

I look at you make faces at me
You look even dumber than I do
And in your great pride and vanity
You'll never know how I despise you

What do you make of this cleverness
That puts you higher than all of us
You spoil most of it with carelessness
I look at it and think: "What a loss!"

You destroy everything that you touch
And you think it's your right to do so
You cage us and don't seem to care much
While every day we're dreaming to go

Yet you're still free and I'm a prisoner
You laugh at every move that I make
And I'll die here sooner or later
No matter how hard it is to take

Brenda Cogar-Williams
HOW CAN I SAY THANKS?

For my Dad, who gave me the courage to keep writing; For Lou, the love he gave me inspired me to write this poem . . . I Love You Both—Dearly

How can I say thanks
for a smile in my heart?
for a crinkling about the eyes?

How can I say thanks
for a feeling that makes me glad to be alive?

How can I say thanks
For you?

Anastasia Claire Aghasian
THE WAYFARER

Dedicated to Dr. Alexandra Robyn Schuttais, a candle lighted.

So lucky am I to choose where I will
Beyond the horizon, up over the hill
A wealth of creation lies there at my feet
The song of the universe lifts glorious, sweet.
To travel the hi-way, the bi-way, a road
Where freedom is free-est secure from all loads,
To roam in that freedom following it where
Immeasurable joy supercedes all my cares.
Worlds beckon and smile each

hour each day
And I claim myself King of all I survey.
Let me not stumble or think to be lost
A midst all this treasure I adjure the cost.
The rewards of the union spring fresh everywhere
Enrapturing the kinship with richest of fare.
I travel this way, and for once I am 'farer,
The journey is mine, with freedom my bearer.

Barbara Sacchetti
NEW ENGLAND AUTUMN

Dedicated to my home town Gilford, New Hampshire

The Autumn trees of red and gold
Beside the thorny hedge
Reflect their lovely colors at
The peaceful water's edge.

They're in their bright pajamas, which
They don for Autumn sleep.
They bow their heads and nod and sway
As golden sunbeams creep.

White wisps of clouds pass overhead
In endless caravans;
Some shaped like camels, some like dames
With fluffy ostrich fans.

As on an artist's palette, in
Profusion clear and bright,
The multi-colored landscape lies
And stretches out of sight.

From here, I gaze about and see
The vivid golden hue,
Which now surrounds my homeland with
A sun-filled Autumn view.

Mr. Michael A. Daigle
MEADOW DAY DREAMS
Sweet like the fields of clover,
dry as a violinist's strings.
She's tipsy on her pastel thoughts,
her stormlike love has blown over.

Her parochial ways pushed me to parody,
and eyes reveal the unpublished sorrow.
I truly must be totally crazy,
I'll still even love her tomorrow.

Like captured pools of green pea soup,
mine eyes they shall wander.
Gosh, what an artistic rumpus,
there she goes up yonder.

Picking daisys ever so sweetly,
she sings the lyrics of praise.
Yes, this one is pretty,
and I secured this lasting faze.

This dream will never end you see,
I guess I'll tell you why.
For when I look at the tops of trees,
I see her in the sky.

Pauline Elizabeth Pelkey
SILENT SNOW
. . . I wakened . . .
In the still dark hours . . .
Of the early morning.
Why? I cannot say,
For I do not know.
As from habit . . .
I looked out of the window . . .
At a picture world . . .
Of fresh white snow.
The flakes were falling soft and gently,
Lighting the night . . .
With a sparkling glow.
Topping the fence posts in the meadow,
Standing like white capped sentinals in a row,
And dressing the trees on the hillside,
With white overcoats of snow.
The pristine beauty awesome,
As yet, unsoiled by man and time,
In the hushed, quiet, of the mid-night,
As I watched, enraptured . . .
Captivated by the sight.
I felt a warmth inside me grow . . .
As I watched . . .
The falling . . .
'Silent Snow'

Genny
WITCHES HOUR
A soul does stir within the bower
Thoughts gone stale with night so sour
Sleep evades, warm comfort dour
At some would call, the witches hour

Close bound, imprisoned in dark tower
Thorn and bramble shed from flower
Tall dark forces take the power
From some would call, the witches hour

Await the dawn to banish fire
Begone now, forever, liar
Burning fierce thru evil glower
Foe demon called, the witches hour

Bridget Ann Flannery
AUTUMN BREEZES
Carry me, carry me,
take me far away.
Let me walk in the cool autumn nights,
Let me laugh in the short autumn days.

Smell the hot chocolate,
and walk through the trees.
Enjoy that familiar rustle
as you walk amid the leaves.

Sit with me, talk with me
at the football games.
Let's remember the past,
and hope things can be the same.

We'll cherish our friendship
and we'll love each other, though we know
that it's only those autumn breezes
that are making us change,

helping us to grow.
O carry me, carry me,
take me far away.
Let me love you in the future
as I love you now this day.

Lene P. Mingleton
REAL DREAM

To one with whom I learned the greatest "Unconditional Love."

It was very early in the morning
as she listened unto the songs
Of birds, and the morning dew
lay heavily upon the new day.

Thinking back on the face of her love——The vision became clear;
As did the touch of him. The feeling was as though she were in
His arms, and they kissed gently; oh how lovely the kiss, the
Firmness of his lips, the succulence of his mouth was that of ripened
Fruit, and their thirst was indeed quenched.

Catherine Ford
MEDUSA
What awesome forces did forsake,
To create a synergy of woman-snake?
Such awful woes—no plausible chapeaus,
And hair that preys upon the lips and nose.

Dean Caldwell
MY LOVER, LEO
My Lover, Leo
I long to keep her
'Cause she keeps me
for her very own
My Lover, Leo
I long to hold her
'Cause she keeps me
oh, so very warm
My Lover, Leo
I long to see her
'Cause she feeds me
with her sweet, sweet love

My Lover, Leo
I long to hear her
'Cause she tells me
things I need to know
My Lover, Leo
I long to touch her
'Cause she strokes me
when I most neet it

My Lover, Leo
I long to see her
'Cause she needs me
the way I need her

Gladys G. Whitacre
TREASURES OF TIME
I saw a flower of lovely hue,
Fragile, translucent, fragrant, too.
Its perfume rare, was shared by all.
A jewel fair, I picked it there,
 beside the wall.
And then, I put it safely away—
Thinking, "I'll cherish this alway."
Another day, I sought the
 wondrous masterpiece,
But lo! it was withered dried
 away, deceased.
Just the fragrance remained to
 stay,
Of the beautiful rose of yesterday.

When I too, shall someday grow
 old,
May I not become bitter,
 remorseful and cold.
And hopefully those around will
 say,
"I am so glad you came my way,
The deeds of love that you have
 shown,
Are like the blossom that is full
 blown."
"Time changes things," I have
 heard them say.
But love's sweet fragrance, like
 the rose, will never fade away.
So, may a tender, loving smile
 replace,
The marks of time, upon my face.

Coie Lorraine (Hill) Cannon
THE SHEPHERD'S SONG

*By Miles Edward Hill of Texas,
Oklahoma, and Washington, D.
C., Farmer, Carpenter, Pioneer
Newspaper Editor, Cabinet
Maker, Construction Engineer,
Baptist Deacon, Mason, A Man of
Peace, The Salt of the Earth.
(10-19-1894 to 1-31-1963)*

A cup of cold water given in My
 Name
May not bring wealth, long life,
 or fame
But when—your blessings
 counted,
Like your sheep—you're
 underneath
Your blanket fast asleep,
A dream I'll give you with a
 rhyming tune
That goes with "happy" morning,
 night, and noon.

Ruth Ann Schoonover
A CARPENTERS SON
Just a carpenters son, everyone
 said
but Jesus knew different in what
 lay ahead,

He taught in the synagogue, His
 words all true
but something was different,
 everyone knew,

But then He left, and traveled His
 way
He preached and He healed all of
 the day,

"Come follow me" He told many
 men
"I'll give you a life that never will
 end."

Many men followed, twelve in
 them all
but Jesus foreseen that one would
 soon fall,

But still He went on, spreading
 good news
many believed and doubters were
 few,

But the kings and the leaders
 were fond of His powers
and Judas then came at night to
 their towers,

"He'll be in the garden," he said
 with a hiss
"I'll show you which one with
 only a kiss,"

So they went to get Jesus with
 their swords and their lights
but Jesus went calmly, not trying
 to fight,

They gave Him a trial and put
 down His name
they beat Him and bruised Him
 and put Him to shame,

And then they went on, towards
 Calvary's hill
as He carried His cross towards
 His mission to fill.

Lee E. Muir
THAT DREADFUL HILL

*To my friend Kenneth Bono who
is no longer with us.*

It was tormentingly still
on that dreadful hill
the earth was torn
and battle worn.

The night was cold
and fearfully old
it chilled my bones
for I was alone.

The air was death
with every breath
among those dead
which I had led.

I laid in pain
in icy rain
my body gashed
my legs in hash.

I tried to cry
but my eyes were dry
I felt a breath
and knew it was death.

Frances Kavanaugh Nelson
MY DOCTOR'S REPORT
I read my doctor's report—the
 words clearly say
"Female, Caucasian, forty-one
 and OBESE."
Can twenty pounds change
 contentment to dismay?
At the market I stop to shop for
 my evening's fare.
Pies, cakes, cookies, ice-cream,
 candy—I sigh.
Up and down the long aisles I
 seek— should I dare?
Chips, dips, pop, nuts—I pass by
 these so fast.

I settle for crisp lettuce, fresh
 cottage cheese.
As I approach the check-out
 counter at last
I note my cart holds such a
 pitiful dole.
On impulse, I add a bunch
 fresh—cut flowers.
I must have their sheer beauty
 to feed my soul!

Tiny Cook
OUR LAST GOODBYE

---

*This poem was written for my
husband, Jimmy, and to be held in
memory for the day I pass from
this life into eternity. May it be
accompanied by comfort and the
hope for life everlasting on your
day of sorrow. I'll always be with
you.*

We fell in love, we both were so
 young
We planned a good life, the
 wedding bells rung.
We grew together, we learned to
 share
People looked at us and said, "boy
 what a pair!"

Time and things began to pull us
 apart
We still loved each other, but
 couldn't say what was in our
 hearts.
Each thinking the other no longer
 cared
We turned our backs on what we
 had shared.

We went through agony, we went
 through pain
We went through something we'll
 never have to go through again.
It brought us closer, it made us
 see
The only important thing in life
 was you and me.

We fell in love, this time it was
 for real
We knew what it was, how it
 could feel.
There was no longer a you, and
 no longer a me
It was just "us"—the way it was
 meant to be.

We had a second chance, so few
 people do
You gave me your heart, I gave
 mine to you.

We were two—living as one
We lived life to the fullest, we
 did all that could be done.

But now the time has come for
 our last goodbye
Look at me Daddy, but please
 don't cry.
Remember the good times, the
 joy and fun
Remember the morning I gave
 you a son.

Remember our life, we had what
 so few people ever find
I have no regrets of what I'm
 leaving behind.
Think of the future and the time
 that will be
When we'll be together
 throughout eternity.

So look at me Daddy, kiss me
 goodbye
But remember some day you'll
 join me in the sky.
Our love will be spotless, pure
 and white
I leave you with this goodbye,
 because I know that forever is
 in sight.

    Goodbye Daddy
    I love you—MOMMY!

Evie Salee
THE EAGLE
The Eagle, symbol of strength and
 freedom,
 Knows no boundary, no fence,
 no leash.
He is declarer of his own destiny.
 Fly, handsome Eagle.
The world is yours.
 Be the best you can be today.
This day will never come again.
 There is only now, only this
 moment.
Grasp it! Soar with it!
 Don't let it go
Until you have lived it totally.
 Freedom is a state of mind
And is never given,
 Nor is it taken away by others.
You have the freedom to be, a
 precious gift.
Nothing can restrain you except
 yourself.
Accept yourself. Live fully. Live
 completely.
 Live lovingly,
Grateful for what the universe
 provides.
 The Eagle listens only to a
 higher power.
There is no one and nothing
That says "No! You can't!"
He knows that he can.
And so he does.

Linda L. Tilton
EERIE DESTINATION
Look out to the fathoms of the sea.
Where the sun beams down it's
 sparkling brilliance.
Then look away, to the invading
 objects in the sea.
The ocean suddenly looses it's
 respect to man's ideas.
The sea seems to turn grave.

The mechanicalism of the
 Dolphins playing in the
water is often what resembles

man's Life.
Flowing in the same direction,
  going round and round,
applying and displaying ourselves
  like targets to man's
inhabitions.

But wait till the days of new,
distruction to natures architect
will once
again be restored and respect will
  be awakened to enormous
beauty.

Judie M. McDowell
CHILDREN

*To Delissa and Deborah who
inspired this poem*

From my children I get,
Hope for the future;
No regrets for the past,
Faith in people;
And love that last's,
Thank you God for all these
  things;
And in my heart memories that
  sing.

Grant John Frew
LIFE
Life is great
It has many things to offer
Laughter, joy, and happiness
It is a time to be free
Enjoy it while you can
It means taking everything in
  stride
Life, if you can narrow it down
Means love
Take love, and define it
It means life

Patricia Pratt Smith
THE GIFT OF LOVE

*Dedicated to Irene A. Sarinske
For the love and caring she gives
so freely to everyone she meets.*

We are all God's children
Created by his hand
All with special purposes
To be upon this land

All are sprinkled with his glory
From the heavens up above
But to some especially
He gave na extra touch of love

To you, he gave patience
And a large amount of care
Along with comforting words
When others visit despair

He gave you hugs and a warm
  smile
That you simply give away
To anyone who needs them
On no particular day

He has blessed you
And you have given to the rest
Everything that you can spare
But nothing short of the very best

Barbara I. McDaniel
SEASIDE CALM
The sun
The sand
The boats sailing by
So peacefully.

You lay in the sun
Take a stroll on the beach

You build castles in the sand.

Then as the sun
Sets in the evening
You feel the first cool ocean breeze
You see the moon reflecting
On the waves
Like silver sparkles dancing about.

No picture or words
Could ever capture
The peace and calmness
And beauty
That takes your breath away
It is something you have to see
A place you have to be.

Patty Landry
MEMORIES

*This poem was written to my
Grandmother, Edna Landry who
died June 8, 1983.*

I know this day
  would sometime come.
I know you
  would have to go.
All I want to say
  to you,
Is that I love you so.
You deserve not only
  the best,
But a lot more.
I know you're happier now
  than you've
  ever been before.
It wasn't easy for me
  to see you go,
And I still really
  miss you.
But my memories are
  all here,
And remember is all I'll do.

Bonnie Van Ostran
RAINY DAYS
Rainy days are to be drab and
  dreary,
Sunny days are for fun and joy.
You're to love your parents,
  sisters, brothers, friends,
  and other family.
Respect is to be given to elders,
Adoration is for children.
When someone dear to you dies,
You grieve down inside like no
  one could ever know.
When someone does true evil to
  you, there is no possible way
  you could ever feel for them
  again.
But in time things change in
  drastic measures.
Loves can die and be born anew,
Hatred's fire can burn where no
  one expected it to.
Thoughts get lost in sudden gusts
  of wind.
Words and promises get cluttered
  in the attics of our minds.
Time can make the hurts less
  painful, and the fun more
  enjoyable.
For Time has a strange way of
  changing things—so slowly
  that you don't know it while
  it's happening,
But so suddenly that once you
  realize it you know it's too late
  to do anything about it.

Geraldine Coomes
FIJI IS MY NAME

*To my Mother, Margaret Sawyer,
Poet, who donated Fiji to Valley
Skilled Nursing Facility,
Sacramento. Mom was happy and
well-cared-for at Valley.*

I'm a blue and white boy parakeet:
I live in Mountain Skilled-
  Nursing Home.

Jeri had said, "A cute pair of feet,
Pretty feathers: clowning, and
  then some—

I'll take him." At Mountain, she
  wanted
The Janitor to name the birdie.
"What Country are you from?",
  she wanted
To know. B.J. replied, "From Fiji."

"That's it!" Jeri cried. "Fiji's his
  name."
A lady in a wheelchair said, "My

Poodle's name is 'Fifi'—not the
  same."

"My daughter's name is Gigi",
  replied

A visitor, "will Fiji learn most
Words and names? Will he do
  tricks and play?"

Jeri declared, "He better. He cost
Sixteen Dollars and Ninety-Five
  Cents. Pay

TV is cheaper fun." I make the
Patients happy—I sit on fingers,

Kiss, spin, climb, nibble, try to
  take a
Bracelet off, sing, talk, fluff my
  feathers.
Jeri's teaching me to say, "Fiji
Is My Name", "Take a Bite", "I
  Love You",
"Hit the Road", "Kiss Me", "You're
  a Teaser",
"Jesus Loves Me", and "Star Above
  You".

Olga L. Sosa
DON'T BE SCARED
Don't be scared,
Be strong!
Life sometimes isn't fair,
Sometimes happiness won't stay
  long.
Don't be scared,
Sadness always comes and goes,
Just like the breeze of air.
Fight it—maybe you'll win—who

knows!
But, don't be scared.
Brush those tears away,
Learn to live again and care
And make that sunshine stay.
Don't be scared,
Everyone goes thru some of that
  in life,
They learn the feeling that they
  can bear,
That living is to survive.
Don't be scared.
You'll lose one and you gain one,
But you fight for what you care.
And in the end you'll feel that
  you have won.
Don't be scared.
Victory for some may come,
With such a mighty flair.
But you stick there, and you hang
  on.
And you just don't be scared.

Anita Hutton
HAVE YOU EVER WISHED
Have you ever wished you were
  little once again?
Innocent and loving—free from
  the burdens of men
That once again you could trust
  blindly without
  cynicism—unwary
Enjoying the simple things—
  believing in Santa and the
  tooth fairy
To little ones, black is black,
  white—white something's
  either good or bad
And decisions—responsibilities—
  they are handled by Mom and
  Dad.
To appreciate the pictures in the
  clouds
To romp for hours in the leaves
To pick a daisy for a friend—
  a friend who in you completely
  believes.
Oh, that my heart were like a
  childs
  full of appreciation and love
Unburdened by worry and fear
Able to see the beauty in little
  things
Able to ease the pain by a tear.

Helen Brown Vandervoort
GOD'S GLORY
The Heavens declare the glory of
  God
For all Mankind to see,
They measure the length of our
  days and nights
With strict regularity.
For every Life upon this earth
God also has a plan,
We know not when our days
  shall end,—
Our times are in His hand.
So let us strive to live each day
His Gospel to proclaim,
And like the sun and moon and
  stars
Bring glory to His Name.

Kimberly H. Duffey
DOUBTS
She sits at ease with the world,
Calm cool with nothing to fear.
Friends all around her, a guy at
  her side,
Why should she need me?

Colleen G. Brown
The Reflection Of Perfection

I've looked the world over inside
and out.
Seeing different faces,
Walking distant places,
Not knowing what life is all
about.

I've asked all sort of questions to
myself.
Who am I?
Why do people cry?
Why do so many put their pride
away on a shelf?

You should never put yourself
down.
Hold up your chin,
Let your life begin,
Don't be someone's foolish little
clown.

You're the only one that has to
live with you.
Stand straight and tall,
Don't let yourself fall,
Turn your grey skies into blue.

So next time you look yourself in
the mirror with affection;
Don't be so vain,
And considering yourself saine,
Staring back at you with a big
wide grin
Is the reflection of perfection.

Lori M. Trepa
TOGETHER FOREVER

As I lie here in the moonlight
Thinking of the love we shared
tonight
I know our love will never end—
You will always be my best
friend.
I know in my heart
Nothing can keep us apart
For we belong together
To love each other forever.

Michael James Dulnikowski
THE PAST IS LIKE A CELL

The past is like a cell in which
I'm held
And like the Prisoner of Chillon I
have become
Such friends with the very chains
which are the memories
That bind me to the stone of my
dark dungeoned mind.
Ah,
This heart in its *own* prison has
hopes of liberty
And catches whiffs of freedom on
every wind
Of every breath I take. O, I would
My soul like an eagles cry to
light on ears
Of snow capped peaks and swell
in valleys below.

J. Cockett Lambson
SOLITAIRE

With trembling hands
I deal the cards
The deck I've had for years
Old and worn
Familiar to my touch.

I deal my hand and start to play
My game of Solitaire
It's then I think and pray
As each card falls into place
I deal my fate.

Long ago I played the game
Of life and love
My cards turned up
Sometimes I lost; sometimes I
won
And now I sit here reminiscing
About the way I should have
played
But now I'm playing Solitaire.

Anthony Wayne Antolic
The Funny Dog Dy—ee Pierre

In memory of my dog Duchie

Dy-ee is my puppy.
Three months old is he.
He chews and chews on
Everything.
Sometimes even ME.

Dy-ee is my puppy.
Three months old is he.
He jumps and jumps on
Everything.
Sometimes even ME.

Christine Lowthian
VISIONS

I have seen the sun so bright
I have seen the moon at night
I have seen the snow in winter,
With it's clean, special glitter.
And I have seen the flowers so
pretty
And the tree boughs hang in pity.
I have seen the rain fall,
Through the trees so tall.

Yes, I have seen, but no longer
can I.
For now all I have are the
memories.
It does not matter. For now my
Memories and my visions will
last a
life time even though my sight
didn't.
For those of us who have never
seen I
Give my feelings the most.

The sights passed the sounds and
visions have increased.
No longer can I see the sun so
bright,
Nor the moon at night.
No longer can I see the flowers so
pretty
Or the tree boughs hang in pity.
I wish for the day that I could see
the rain fall,

Through the trees so tall.
I'd love to see the sun rise and set
again.
I long to see the beauty of the
foothills,
But even more my friends.

John Landgraver, Sr.
EAGLES SKY?

Up where eagles fly
near the top of the sky
God stores his paint, for rivers
and streams
the forest so green,
and even things mean
like thunder and wind, fire and sin.

There's a calm peaceful view
he made just for you,
so judge all things well,
as you gaze at these sights,
or you will never see darkness,
only the fires of hell
and their flickering light.

Pamela S. King
HEART OF A ROSE

The rose it had no friend,
Yet it never had hate to send.
It's petals stood tall and broad
Remembering the promise of God.
That if your heart is always good,
and you have peace as you
should,
That one day it shall be sent to
higher ground.

So the rose dropped a tear as he
bowed,
Although he stood tall and proud.
Love Always
From day to days.
Add up the deeds
That heaven needs,
And be as good as the love shows,
And have the heart of a rose.

Ghedden Wahr
QUIET DEATH

One poor boy is depressed,
The country is recessed,
A lecture to which none listens.

This poor boy ends his life,
A quick slice of the wrist with
his knife,
Though things might have
changed.

Listen to a piece of mind,
In the end the sun will shine,
Don't be fooled by a moonless
sky.

Oh no, it is the end now,
You'd like to stop the bleeding
but don't know how;
All because of an ignorant
decision.

Don't worry about nuclear war,
Don't think that life is just a
bore;
It has much more to offer than
pain.

Think about your feelings,
Stop your life from unreeling,
Reach out for the hand that
wants to help you.

Don't succumb to the Quiet
Death,
You've much to do before you lie
at rest;
There's someone out there that
loves you.

Richard D. Cagg
MERCY'S SCALE

So must we let truth
Bring to our eye a tear
That we might have a fear
That we went too far
Stayed too long without shame or
sorrow
Yet from today comes our
tomorrow
For that scale of mercy in God's
Hand
Weighs our soul at His demend

Lucille Haddad
TREES IN SEASON

In Spring, they don their lacy
frocks to wear to Summer fests
held everywhere.

A rendezvous through country
and town, then time for them
to settle down
to the tempered winds that soon
will call for them to change
their frocks for Fall.

They then will change with
timely grace till radiant colors
paint their face.

Their colors sure to fade away,
reluctantly, from day to day.

A grand finale with "sad goodbyes"
will bid them bow to Wintery
skies.
This show will come alive each
May for those of you who
chance to stay.

Now, we applaud the Stately Tree
for their performance, given
free.

Millie Hooper
THE ABYSS

Every sound of night reminds me
of you . . .
the hiss of tires on pavement
(anticipating you)
the whirr of the clock bothering
me
that I won't reach the alarm
over you—still sleeping
the ignition of the furnace
replacing the lovely warm of you
the bark of neighbors' dogs
instead of our quiet nighttime
talks,
the solemn, lonely breathing of
one.

Sharon Rawson
OUR TIME

I miss you when you leave me,
I wish you didn't have to go.
I always feel so empty,
Oh how I love you so.

When we are together,
The time we have goes fast.
It seems that we never,
Have any time that lasts.

I wish we could just take this time,
And go some where alone.
Then spend our time the way we
want,
And share our love thats grown.

My heart it aches so badly,
When you leave my side.
Some times I just can't stand it,
I've just sat down and cried.

I hope and pray each passing day,
To find a way for you.

To stay with me and never leave.
And love me all day through.

Christine M. Buchman
SEASONS

To all those who incourage me to write poems, my family, and friends.

Hark, listen, quiet, fall goes now down
Hear them fall, leaf by leaf blow round
Color change, bare twigs bend and break
Hark, listen, quiet, fall comes for Gods sake
Cool, wind blow, colder, colder yet, blow
Beevers dam, crickets cease, bears sleep, come snow
Winters upon us,
Snow, blizzard, icy pond, deer graze for want
Children, snow man, coat, mittens, thin and gaunt
Still quiet, listen, drip, rustle, springs about
Rivers flowing, trees blooming, grass stands stout
Flowers growing, fruit ripen, summers here at last
Heat, rain, grow corn, children run, hunters past
Hark, listen, quiet, fall goes now down
Hear them fall, leaf by leaf, blow round
All this I see, I listen, I feel, I know
Flower spring, heat summer, leaves fall, winter snow

Chandra Jaime
HE ENABLES ME
He made me a dove
with wings to fly,
but clouds did come
and I was afraid to try,
I cooed to him my lament
and the Lord heard my sigh,
He lifted me in his hands
up to the sky.
He gave to me eagles
wings to fly
and so enabled me to
soar above the clouds so high.

Mary Annie Johnson
GOD'S SEED
I write this poem for you to read,
Sent from God a sprouting seed.
The only way this seed will grow,
Is sharing with others what you know.
Tell of Christ who died for you,
How this God made all things new.
Now accept Christ in your heart,
He will give a brand new start.
Now you've had your chance to read,
Would you like to be God's seed.

Mardi
HALLOWEEN
Halloween, Oh Halloween
That's the time when the witch is queen
Halloween, Oh Halloween
It's the time for ghosts and goblins to make the scene

It's the night for trick or treating
where children dressed in costumes you'll be meeting
Halloween is a time of fun
and many treats will be collected when you're done.

Maggi Polk
MORE THAN ONE WAY
There's more than one way to see a cloud.
More than one way when the road gets rough.
Look for the view on the other side.
You will find to your joy that the clouds a puff;
A beautiful puff of delicate rain
And the road has turned to a shady lane!

Leona Tubberville
ON BENDED KNEE
A little girl on bended knee,
saying her prayers so thoughtfully.
My dad was tall and my world was so small.
A child again to be, when the failures of a man we cannot see.

Yvonne J. Butner
TIME

This poem is dedicated to my mom, who is using the extra time God has given her wisely.

Time is promised to no one.
We live in it's lerking shadow awaiting it to swallow us up;
leaving only a bleak memory of our time spent.

Time sneaks away and returns like a theif, to rob one of precious youth. It leaves traces of it's vadelism in the forms of ruins and wrinkles.

Time strips a man of his strength of ten, to a weakness of one in a shortness called—a life time. For nothing has power against the awesome force of time.

Time is ever on the move, never pausing or turning back to see what it has done; always looking forward to what it can do.

Take heed of time, for it comes to soon for us. Time makes no promises of riches or fame; nor longevity of ones life.

Time is powerful, time is endless, time for us is short; use it wisely!

James F. Webb
OCTOBER NIGHT

To Lee, my beloved wife

I met you in October on a windswept hill;
The moonbeams brought you there, a goddess of the night,
And scattered stardust in my eyes and heart until
I stood bewitched, enraptured by this dream-born sight.
You wore your Beauty like a gown of sparkling dew
That wove a web of sweet enchantment round my heart;

An aura like a rainbow mist surrounded you
And I knew then that we must never be apart.
You taught me all the Sweet and Wonderful of You
And opened Heaven's Gate to let me in; you filled
My life, my world with total happiness anew
Until I thought my pounding heart could not be stilled.
October has gone past some fifty times since then
Yet Love, True Love once born, is a forever thing
And though the acrid smoke of burning leaves again
Reminds me that it's fall, you make it seem like Spring.
Our days together-spent have turned to yesterdays,
A haunting host of memories that we once share,
Now flit in ghost-parade through all my nights and days
For Death had taken you away while I was spared.
I wake at night, cry out your name, there's no reply;
I miss you more than ever then. You surely know
That all my thoughts are ever turned to you and why
My Love, through all Eternity shall follow You . . .

Robert Block
TIME IN A BOTTLE
Longing, we yearn
Hoping to learn, to earn
A memory we may coddle-
Ah, what a wonderful trinket;

Really, I'd dare;
Loving, I'd care and share
If I could put TIME in a bottle,
But then, I'd probably drink it!

Beverly Couzens
I WANT IT ALL

For Jim Harvey, one of my dearest and closest friends.

Things for once are going well.
I have a choice between the moon and the sun.
But alas my mind does not on my good fortune dwell.
I want both, not just one.
If not careful I could lose all.
Oh how sad that would be.
Simply because I want all
I could make my life empty.

Deborah Hopkins
FOOTPRINTS
Warm desert sandy land which sparkled against the sun
twinkle as though the stars were a starry night
All of heaven quiet on the hot and muggy day.
Sand dunes spread against the horizon makes room for the moonlight by night.
Just beyond the clouds were also white seagulls ahigh.
There sand sparkled the earth too.
Against the coast with waves on high

were surfers
and all was left was
Footprints in the Sand.

Elizabeth E. Bowen

Elizabeth E. Bowen
THE RAPTURE
Hidden amidst the flowers,
profuse with buttercups
Played a precious babe with Fluff,
his little pup
Beneath a shady tree nearby, the mother read and watched
The book was called the Rapture,
of angels around a throne
And there was a mighty thunder and she was left alone.

The Heavens parted as a scrow,
the sun was black as coal
Men did hide beneath the rocks for God's wrath would take its toll.

An angel down from Heaven came with an open book
Saying, Woe to men on earth for Babylon, the great, is fallen
She drank the blood of Saints, for this I dare not look.

Because of that, their evil Misery shall be their lot
Her children shall die of famine When wheat for a penny is bought.

Then came a voice from Heaven Like the roar of a lion, God cried
As many as repent, I will chasen
And they shall sing a new song
Worthy is the lamb who was slain yet liveth
All tears shall I wipe from their eyes
And they shall wash their robes white in the blood of the lamb
And shall be Kings and priests forever, for they shall never die.

Then, with a sigh, the mother closed her book, reluctantly, to attend her child.

Jaye M. Plummer
MY LITTLE DITTY

Dedicated to my great Grandsons—Frayne, Trevan, and Corey Haga Kenny and Gary Riley

Listen my friend to my little ditty
I ain't very smart and I aint very pretty
But I got a secret I'd like to tell

Just don't complain and all will
  go well.
I aint got money that is not a lot
But I am content with what I've
  got.
A horse, and a dog, a ball and a bat
A willow fishin' pole and a big
  straw hat.
A pair of old shoes with holes in
  the toes
Slagged off jeans and arrows and
  bows.
A swimmin; hole just down the
  road
A tad-pole on two, and a big green
  toad
as I said before I ain't very smart
But I love what I've got with all
  my heart
I live on a farm and not in the city.
So this my friend is the sum of
  my ditty.

Kathi Brooks
For David—May 14, 1983
My silence when we sit
  is not because I wish you not
  here
  I wish you here when you are
  otherwise
so I do not wish you not here
  when you are.

My voice is stopped by fear
  not of you—no never that—
of the closeness I want but dare
  not touch
can one touch a mental closeness?

My hand reaches towards your
  shoulder
  no fear of this closeness
relief from this closeness—
  it keeps the other distant.

My heart cannot keep the charade
  you perceive me too well
you ask—I remove my hand;
  preparation for my other retreat.

Your voice breaks the silence
  I retreat—mentally this time
my world! no one enters it—
  I cannot hide, your voice
  persists.

You care—I know you do
  I care for you—and me, also
fear makes me a coward
  please do not be mad—be
  patient—
  you once said, "All worthwhile
  things take time."

Kari Tex Nixon
MUSTANGS
The Wild Horses are running
They are running away
Their spirit and wind broken
from running all day
Civilization is coming
trying to take them away
They have roamed the prairies
The mountains, and hills
With freedom and might
and very strong wills.
For hundreds of years
they have been alive.
Escaping from the Spanish herds
To run free and survive
Will they live longer
In American valleys and hills
Or will they all die
Against Wild Horse Annie's will?

Faye Lanier
AUTUMN FLING
Upstart! You fling your flirtatious
  eyes in every direction;
You're badly in need
  of some positve correction.
The chill of your breath
  brings a flush to my cheeks.
Your brilliant hues are matched
  by few;
Those golden locks so gently
  mock.

You dress like the queen
  of a rich monarch.
You swirl and curl
  and look so sharp.
Snapping your fingers, you're very
  proud.
At times, you're boisterous and
  loud.
You flaunt your looks in every
  nook.

I know your type,
  Oh, so fickle!
Everyone knows you're
  unpredicatble.
Your stormy moods are
  downright rude;
At other times you act the prude.
Your arms reach out
  with a warm embrace,
But where is your loveliness—
  your grace,
  When those stretched-out arms
  become effaced?
Where is your beauty
  when youth is gone?
Old age comes quickly on.
But have a last fling,
  you seasonal vamp
Until winter arrives,
You're the breath-taking champ!

Christine Kay Powell
AUTUMN OF LOVE
Could I begin to tell you of my
  love?
It fills my heart so many days and
  hours.
It's simple, far more simple than a
  dove
Whose soul and wings own even
  stronger powers.
My love's a flower reaching for
  the sun,
Deep-rooted, strong against a
  field of weeds.
And yet my love as flowers when
  day is done
Will wither when deprived of
  what it needs.
A closer time we shared not long
  ago;
A good time when our lives were
  free of lies.
But things are changing: Sadly
  now I know
That love cannot exist where
  trust has died.
  So try not now to make this
  flower last
  And be not sad when finding
  love has passed.

Jane Boroviak Divis
DAY IS DARKEST
Day is darkest when the sun's in
  empty heaven
And no cloud occludes its brassy,
  prying stare.

Shadows are alight for all to see in.
Whomever's given access wants
  to share.
Please! Lock the gates! Allow no
  trespass!
Protect the private feelings hiding
  there.
The shelter of the shade may
  shield some secrets.
The knowing sun is hard enough
  to bear.

Gertrued Hickin Sigmon

Gertrued Hickin Sigmon
JOIE DE VIVRE
Who is he who longs
For aught but life
And glad, gay songs,
And busy, humming living earth?
Where is he whose chaotic fear
Makes him gloomy all the year;
Who hears nor feels nor sees nor
  breathes
Love, life, pulsing in the breeze?
God give him love of everything
That he may join with us and sing.

Juli Jelinek —(A. J. Jules)
SOMEONE

---

*I was inspired to write this poem
by someone that never saw this
but, I'd like to dedicate it to
"someone" that has!*

Someone who makes me glad;
  when I am depressed or
unussually sad

Someone who is special
  in every way; to be
the sunshine in my day

Someone who is always there;
  to show me that "someone"
really does care

Someone whom I could never
  forget;
  and always remember
with not a single regret

Yes, that someone is special,
  loving, and true; and
that makes me sure that,
  that "someone" is . . . .
  YOU!

Tami Ellis
NOWHERE
I sit, overwhelmingly,
In a place which is nowhere,
And it's nowhere that makes it
So special.
No sounds of heavy industry;

Just the pleasant sounds
Of God's perfect nature.
It's a picture of perfect poetry,
And a place so divine in my heart.
The breeze sounds like an
  invisible ocean
Making It's waves in the acres of
Corn and grass.
The creatures are my
True companions with their
Hearts of solid gold.

Never again,
Do I desire
To return to that place of
Pressure and lies
A place which makes me as
A tiger in a cage.
Never Again! Never!

Miss Ronni John Stevens
A DREAM OF YOU
I was defeated again by realitie's
  blots.
Ashamed of my weakness,
Consumed in my thoughts;
Spinning my mind through
The whys and why nots . . . .
Then I remembered you were in
  the world.

Not even the whisper of fantasy's
  gain
Could settle my drifting on.
Holding my candle up to the rain
Without hesitation of sorrow,
The morning brought me pain . . .
Then I remembered you were in
  the world.

Alone in the clouds of the night;
My light silvered and soared
From the depths of the sea's might,
To the swish of a rainbow's reward.
And I flew with shear delight . . .
Just remembering you were in the
  world.

Energy and atoms astir with life
  expand,
Reaching far into your soul.
Revealing a possitive array of
  colors once bland,
To build up my being's know;
Uniting the two of us in life so
  grand . . .
I'm so happy you are in the world.
Some day, may I touch your hand.

Mary A. Pennington
WHERE THERE IS LOVE

---

*I'd like to dedicate this to the
most precious Mom and Dad and
to each and every one of my
children who taught me that love
is more important than anything.*

Oh, what a beautiful dream I had
  of Heaven last night
Little children were playing, in
  the glow of God's light
They all seemed so happy,
  laughing and gay
Wasn't like the homes on earth,
  where children cannot play.

For a house is not a home, if little
  children cannot play
Mothers get down on your knees,
  teach your children how to pray.
Show them right from wrong,
  God will bless you if you do

Make their home a place to play,
and they'll never stray from you.

Everytime your child does wrong,
do you close him in a room
Or tell him that he's bad, how can
his love for you bloom
What would you do, if God did
not, forgive you of your wrong
So make your house a place of
love, your children can call
home.

Nadine Lewis
CHRISTMAS
Remember the Christmases we
crept
In footed sleepers, down each step
Gripping the stair rail, peeked to
see
The awesome glitering Christmas
Tree?

Between the living room and hall
Standing and staring in childish
wonder
High as the sky it seemed to be
Sparkling boughs with toys piled
under.

Where do we ever again recapture
That joy and awe and childish
laughter?

Christmas alight with tinsel bells
Glistens and gleams for us once
more
Little faces that shine with joy
Wake in us feelings we knew
before.

Now at this time of happy giving
Let us all welcome our Lord and
King
With love for the world in which
we're living
With love as the reason for
everything.

Barbara Pompei
THE CANDIDATE
Clad in white
In the presence of The Father
He stands (proud)
Vowing his faith
A stepping stone
To the devotion ahead
He professes
Before those dear to him
Sharing this special moment
Of acceptance
And proceeding with honor
To serve His people

Teri Milwid
Do You Love Me Or Do You Not?
You told me once but, I fogot.
You told me that you loved me so,
Now I pray you won't let go.
I want to be near you all the time,
Then tell my friends that you are
mine.
You make me happy but never sad.
I'm sure there are times I've made
you mad.
But, I want to spend my life with
you,
And let you know that I Love You!!

Virginia G. Nathan
THE SPRING AFFAIR
Mother Earth gave a spring Ball
And it was a lavish affair.
The budding trees filled the hall
And all the spring flowers were

there.
Cynthia Crocus was first to arrive;
She was dressed in royal purple
and green.
Then Thomas Tulip looking so
alive;
Never a more dignified
gentleman was seen.
Helen Hyacinth wore her alice
blue gown
And a perfume with a delicate
scent.
The Poet Narcissus just dropped
around;
There never was a more elegant
gent.
Then in danced Dorothy daffodil
Dressed in a brilliant yellow.
Dan Dandelion came of his own
will;
For he's quite a remarkable fellow.
There never was a more gala affair
And they danced the whole night
through.
Quaffing the aroma of the air;
Then stayed for the morning dew.

Lisa J. Chase

Lisa J. Chase
A MOONLIT NIGHT
Cats are hiding in the trees
dogs are on the prowl;
All the front porch lights are on
someone hears a howl.

Many tales of horror to be
said upon this night;
People in their houses now
await the time of fright.

Dusk is now approaching and
the children are uptight;
But there's no need to worry
it's just Halloween night.

Brenda R. Gilliam
A FOUNTAIN OF LOVE
A Fountain of joy
A Fountain of peace
A Fountain that flows with living
water.
A Fountain of Love.

A Fountain that's cool and
refreshing,
A Fountain that will quench a
thirst.
A Fountain of Love.

A Fountain that looks good
A Fountain with water that tastes
good
A Fountain of happiness always.
A Fountain of Love.

Betty J. Lewis
To Be Or Not To Be, Fat
To be, or not to be fat, that is the
question
Whether it is nobler to resist the
sweets or turn down the starches
Whether, 'tis harder in the mind
to suffer the pangs of hunger
Or suffer the slings and arrows of
the mirror
Or to take arms against a sea of
calories
By opposing counting them fewer
No more, and by a sleep to say we
loose
The pounds and heart ache of the
bulging waist line
Tis a consummation of delicate
morsels
That smooths out the finest
eating habits
And then to sleep, perchance, to
dream
Aye, that the rub, tub, tub, is
transformed into a slender swan
We have at last shuffled off
The mortal fatty tissues of
wanted waste
Nevermore to take calamity
against the dieting soul
For who would bare the whips
and scorns of overweight
To satisfy the sweet tooth craving
Thus, overeating does make
cowards of us all
With this regard we cast off
pounds and inches
And take our slender form as
nature and beauty intended.

Ms. L. Templeton
SUCESSFUL

---

*To God, Be The Glory, for the
things done in my life: And to my
daughter: LaKetyshi Lishori—Lynn*

Comes from commitment which
brings on faithfulness in what
you set out to achieve.
Faithfulness, brings you to a place
in your life that regardless of
what goes on, you are true to
your sucess.
Sucessfulness, is hard work with
a set mind of determination for
yourself: It's affects others, in
ways of encouragement; or can
make other's jealous.
But, in general you're a "fighter",
in that you're not going to let
others or things get you "down"
or make you "quit"! But, you let
this be a learning time to the
"Top".
Sucessfulness, only comes one
way, that's a made-up mind and
a determination to see it
through; plus our friends and
strangers can encourage us on.
It's like Jesus, seeing us through
our trials and encourging us to
go ahead.
It's only when we depend on
Jesus, that we become truly
sucessful along with
faithfulness, and contentment
brings a honest determination
and a peace of mind.
Sucessfulness, without Jesus, is

like a "smile without teeth"!!
EMPTY!!!
Thank God, I'm Sucessful, in
Jesus Christ.

   "SUCESSFUL OR
FAILURE?"

Dorothy Thomas
BOBBIE'S CHOICE
Throw a saddle on the moon
Ride rampant 'cross the sky,
Take a bite of the Milky Way
As you go riding by.

Carve your name on a falling star
As it falls from out the blue,
Watch its fiery fall to earth
And shed a tear as it falls from
view.

Ride a moonbeam to the earth,
Turn and tell the moon
good-bye.
Release the piece of a fleecy cloud
You grabbed as you sailed by.

Throw your saddle on a thought,
And ride it to the end.
Then put it aside, cause you've
reached your goal,
Pick a new goal, begin again.

Michael A. Barendregt
THE PAINTER
He sees the world through
diferent eyes
The world that most men miss.
And so because we cannot see
We say he's all amiss.

He doesn't do what most men do
For he just sits and paints.
He lives just in his own dream
world
Reality he taints.

We do not need his likes around
There's naught that he can do.
We will not waste our time with
him
Come! We've got work to do.

But if we looked more closely
We'd hear his work to say:
"Rejoice in things not thought of
That God gives you each day."

Diana L. White
TO STILL LIFE
The painter sits alone
In the corner of a room,
A new stroke of ink added
To the picture everyday.
The paint brush new and bristled.
Awaiting each new color,
But the colors soon run dry—
The bristles and brush die.
No colors come from his brush,
But the artist must finish.
He trys a new brush.
It gleams like polished metal.
He makes one stroke with the
brush—
Bright red ink flows
And finishes the picture.

Monica Cecilia Carezani
PEACE
"Peace please". Oh what a
delightful sound.
Peace's a quiet note of a truthful
song
Sung between the high blue sky
and ground.
Peace should be a long golden
chain, strong,

Uniting all the known souls and strange.
Peace should fly around like a young dove
Not knowing any temporal change:
Breathing pure air, fragrance of love.
But peace by egoistic men's shaken,
And in winds her sweet melody fades.
Peace as an impossible is taken;
Her face before men's actitude pales.
So to us, the dove of the earthly seas
With a musical cry begs, "Peace please".

Mary Lou Willoughby
How's It Going, Scotty?

To a very special Scotsman who, when asked, "Have you ever been to Europe?" said, "Yes, Mum, I was born there!"

"How's it going, Scotty?"
From paraplegic came.
"Be done here in a minute"—
He said with tone the same.

"You don't remember, do you?"—
—when we from battle bore
The bits and pieces of Marines
Who yet could fight no more.

Your bayonet upon your pack
You strapped upon your back
And we to medics then did trust
Those souls with pain so wrack'.

An age and half a world away
And I now half a man—
Remember you? Oh, yes, I do—
You from your Scotsman Clan.

Elizabeth Osborn
TO A FRIEND

For My Mother

I've come to the beach a thousand times,
against the crystal-fine sea.
Trapezoids of blue, white caps alive,
sum and reflection on me.

Fragments of a cloudless day
under a great, balanced sky.
Wind like a song, constant and true,
prompts me to think of old ties.

When life was filled and senses thrilled
to sweet, immortal dew.
The mist that came and the weeping rain
were softened by friends like you.

There isn't a hand to stop the sand,
the tides that ebb and flow.
So little time, so little breath,
the sun that dips so low.

For what I was and what you were,
today can't be the same.
The twilight years of well-spun gold
are yours and mine to claim.

Diana Fox
I MISS YOU, TOO

Dedicated with all my love to my daughter, Shannon

When I'm at work
I think of you
I miss you so much
the whole day through

I know you'll be with me
in a short while
but I miss your laughter
and your cute little smile

You're growing so fast
I missed precious time
the fun and the games
should have been mine

Instead I must work
there are bills to be paid
So let's make the best
of our time to play

So when you feel sad
when Mommy's away
Remember I love you
and miss you all day

Shannon Maura O'Brien
ON THIS DAY

To my parents, Thank you.

On this day
Of deep and misty drizzle
I hear the small sounds
Of rain
Patting on glass
Like whispers.
The empty droplets
Wade and distort
A pathway
Down.
They are likened to tears
Whose bitter-dry memories
Still are so close to me.
But soon the darkness
In the sky
Retreats
Drawing with it
The lonely, sighing wetness
Of rain
Humbly bowing to the
Majesty of gold
And crimson
Nestled for a moment
Oh uneven horizon
And then gone.

Bernita Truh
THANKFUL

Dedicated to my own papa John Franklin second by birth a Negro master stone mason by trade till death, Of sons by generations of our great forebear Statesman Benjamin Franklin. Of our Country's Founding Fathers Of we Peoples of the United States of America My Home Country I am in.

Is there more to be said about thankful,
The sense of touch. to feel. to hear. to inhale.
Intakes of deep full breaths. of

Gods blessed air.
The pain that is not as I walk I skip I run.
Oh blessed thanks to my Good Lord for the pain that is not there.
I breathe with ease, I know its worth.
As too many times the effort was strained.
A gag. a cough, a struggle for air.
Winter in the air. is the time for it.
But today my Lord thank You for the pain
That is not there.
With every intake of breath. I thank You my Lord
For the pain that is not there.
Thankful

Veronica Seeman

Veronica Seeman
LOVE ME NOW

If it's in your heart and mind to write Shoot for the stars You just might catch one—I did.

Love me now—
I'll be gone in the morning,
before the sun begins to rise.
Love me now—
before the dawning,
of the day stars early skies.
Hold me now—
this summer night,
we both will give and take
Then like the bird of swiftest flight—
I'll be gone before you wake.
Forget me then and hold me now.

Jennifer J. Edney
How Still Are The Mountains

Still!—How still are the mountains!
How majestic! How powerful!
Surely they must have much wisdom.
Hidden behind the deep, hard rock,
Lies an all seeing knowledge.

Deep!—How deep is the ocean!
How cruel! How beautiful!
Surely that, too, must have much wisdom.
Hidden in the deep waters
Are secrets unknown to man.

Cruel!—How cruel is this Earth!
How destructive! How blind!
Surely man must have much

wisdom.
Hidden somewhere on Earth
Are a race of people with much wisdom.

Blue!—How blue is the sky!
How wide! How deep!
Surely space has much wisdom.
Hidden deep in space
Are a race of people with much wisdom!

Kevin P. Fealy
DEPARTED

Who is to judge thee?
Who's measure shall define your length?
To some your words were bitter—
To others the taste of sweet absinthe.
One is not all weakness,
Nor all of one be strength;
And passing changes nothing
Except the reviewer's tense.

Frances E. Holland
Proper Temperature Range

For Marion

The air I breath is hot, watching him stand cool among his machines.
"Have you finished that task?"
Vibrations clawing their way
"I have a project for you to do."
up my spine,
He walks over with some papers,
lungs laboring to breathe
"It's really not very difficult."
in that heavy air,
Pulling up a chair beside me,
here is the source, the
"Let me show you what to do,"
heat my blood rushes
sitting down with explanation.
to extinguish.
Reaching across me to touch the keys,
I can taste his skin,
his fingers rearrange the screen
tongue trembling
into patterns of coherency.
for want of salt.
Do you understand?
Yes.

Lillian E. Hermann
Does Heaven Have Eyes?

Does Heaven have eyes that it might see . . .
my plight, my trials, my misery,
the essence of my destiny?
Does Heaven have eyes of vast deep blue
to carry me this whole world through . .
and help each day to start anew?

Does Heaven shed tears when I stumble and fall,
will HE make tomorrow not hurt at all?
When lifes rugged road takes a sudden bend,
and I have trouble of no end,
will Heaven its SON then send?
When folks all around you put you to the test . . .
and you are not sure what is the best,

just stop and think . . I'm sure
HE sees!
HE takes no rest! HE watches
over all!

Goldie James
**First Little Trick Or
Treater**

Dedicated to: My Grandchildren
Brian Richard Stanley Shaun
Brandy Kendra and Step
Grandson, Josh

You're my first little trick or
treater
In your costume all dressed up
I'll give you some pumpkin cookies
And a great big kiss and hug.

I'll pretend that I don't know you
In that costume that you wear.
It covers you from head to toes
Is that you-I do declare.

I'll give the children treats tonight
And pray no harm to them will
come.
Send them on their merry way
Hoping they have lots of fun.

Machelle Stout
SOMETIMES
Sometimes never seems to count,
When you say you care.
Sometimes never seems to count
when,
no one knows your there.
But when you say you sometimes
never cry.
Everyone knows it's more than
half a lie.
So why say sometimes when it
means little more than none?
When it explains hardly anything
to anyone?
Because I Sometimes think about
you.
And I sometimes love you it's true.
Sometimes I mean it but most of
the time I do.
So do I lie sometimes or do I
mean it's true?

Shirley J. Reed
THE SILENT ENEMY
He's unkempted and somewhat
relentless.
He doesn't seem to care about the
pain.
After your first meeting, life
seems useless
You learn to survive, knowing it's
in vain
For time has been altered by the
silent enemy.

He invades your privacy without
a thought.
And though you try not, you
have to recognize
He's there and he exists without
a doubt.
You are forced to accept and
realize
The cruel victories of the silent
enemy.

He has ran so long and moved so
fast
That no one or nothing has been
able to stop him.
He has eluded men both present

and past
Stolen life's rainbows making
time short and dim.
And yet, I'm still stunned by the
silent enemy.

I'm adrift at sea, no ships passing
by
Only small boats but they are all
filled.
The rescue ships come, the sides
are too high
The water is cold, my flesh
chilled
By the final defeat of the silent
enemy.

I have reached the point of no
return
Like the none performing dancer
I haven't the strength any longer
to run
From this silent enemy, sir
named cancer.
I have renamed it the angry death.

Wanda A. Teal
DON'T LOSE FAITH
Healthy, free, the world before you
Where life and dreams are one,
Live not in wounds, but wisdom
Look to the morning sun.

Happy's the man without a care
In health and peace of mind,
And as you walk the roads of life
Be sure to take your time.

But if by chance, you find your
way
Do not forget your dues;
For once you were that lonely man
And stood within his shoes.

Leanna Jewell King
IS THIS CIVILIZATION?
I see the world as a lovely place
when no man walks on it.
I see man as a wild creature that
walks for hate and destruction
I see the destruction and the hate
that causes the killing and
fighting
And I will see the war, the one
war to end it all.
Then I will see nothing except
the dust from this once so
called civilization!

Kathy Anita Thomas
NO ONE HELPED ME

---

*This poem is dedicated to my
loving family and friends, who
inspire and encourage me in all
my endeavors. To Jay, my poetic
inspiration. Love, Kathy*

I struggled until I made a way
I freed myself, and no longer were
my skies gray
I marched on until my freedom
bell rang
Feeling that ray of hope with the
songs I sang

I lived in fear on many occasions
Wondering what food would be
put on my table
I wore the clothes that others
threw out
Hoping the job I had lasted day in
and day out

I fought many endless perilous

fights
I clung to my pillow on many
sleepless nights
I walked the streets daring to be
free
And yet you say, someone did
help me

I prayed to my God in a
continuous prayer
Seeking his wisdom, his love and
his care
Someone did help me through my
sleepless nights
Blessed by his love, my soul
found the light.

Delores Jensen (Punkin)
SUICIDE

To those I'll leave behind

A word that holds no life
only the end of what use to be,
Definition: to kill one's self
or is it just to be set free?

Free from the pain you carry
of things your mind can't hold,
When you don't understand the
answers
and there's no where left to go.

When everyone has run out
and only you remain,
To go over the situation
and try to remain sane.

A point where giving up is easy
no matter who's left behind,
The ending of the battle
for fear of losing your mind.

The signs remain unnoticed
the cry for help unheard,
No one left to turn to
the answer is just one word!
SUICIDE: Definition—to be free!!

Rachelle Ann Eckholm
Is It Care Or Is It Love
Care is when you want somebody
Love is when you need somebody

When there is Care, there is not
always Love,
But in order to Love, there first
has to be Care

There is such a thing as Care at
first sight,
But Love has to be built right
from the start

Everyone has the ability to Care,
You have to know how to Love

Care is something simple,
something to want and enjoy
for awhile
Love is something special,
something to have and to hold
for a lifetime

Betty J. Wood
THE OLD MAN
The old man kept his silence
As the talk around him fell.

Old memories rose to haunt him
Old times he couldn't tell

And those who might have
understood
Had passed on years ago

For youth was now his company
and

Age his greatest Foe

If he could just go back . . . but
no
He knew this couldn't be

And the lonliness posessed him
But none did care or see

They didn't know his value
The things he could have taught

The ways he could have shown
them
The things that can't be bought

So as he bowed his head he
prayed
That time would be their Friend

That the heartbreak Life would
deal them
This friend, "Time", would mend

The old man's head still bowed
Twas awhile before they knew

He'd gone from them to stay this
time

As The morning kissed the dew

Margaret Smith Beach

Margaret Smith Beach
THE PRODIGAL KIN
Who'd you say was coming
'Round the bend?
I ain't seen him
Since he went out to sea
He's been gone a year ago, today
We never knew just why he went
away
I can't imagine why he's coming
home
But we'll just welcome him and
wish him well
I see he needs a shave, his beard
is long
He's kind of thin and maybe not
too strong
Don't josh him none, 'cause he's
sure looking sad
And by his walk, he must be
feeling bad
He's trudging down the pathway
might slow
It's best we go and help him to
the house
He's grown so weary, more than
in his walk
He looks bedraggled and might
confused
Go fix the bed and make a pot of
soup
Some strong black coffee just
might hit the spot
And throw a piece of wood onto
the fire

To help to warm his cold and
  fragile frame
Let old scars heal; let hurtful
  memories lie
And just be thankful he's come
  home to die!

Julia Duyka
Settling Down-Forever?

---

*To Mother and Daddy, who share
in my happiness when I reach a
cherished goal.*

"I'm not ready to settle down.
I need more time!" I protest.
"It's now or never!" he insists.
"It's too soon," I reply.
"You're with me.
Or you're on your own," he states.
(I can't stand alone.)
"Don't walk out on me!" I cry.
(I was wrong.
But can't you give me a second
  chance?
Just one more.
This time I'll do the right thing.
Still . . . I know I don't know how.)
"I swear I never meant any harm.
It's not in me to hurt you
  purposely," I mumble.
(But I did.)
"Please! Give me a second chance.
I'll make things right.
Somehow I'll make it up to you," I
  say.
(Retreating footsteps never
  sounded so final.)

Judith Link
SAIL ON
Feeling content in mind and
  heart,
He see's his ship and must soon
  depart.
Searching through the seas of
  space and time,
He'll leave tracks for us to find.
A mansion he'll build for those
  that flow with his life's blood.
Looking on us from day to day,
Helping to guide us on our way.
When he see's our planting and
  harvesting is done,
He'll come to get us one by one.
He must feel our complete faith
  in him.
He's our father, his name is Jim.
A pridefull man once again.
Now we must say good-by,
Shed a few tears,
Keep our chins held high.
He wants us strong to keep his
  mind at ease,
Our suffering would keep him
  from peace.
Only then can he board his ship
  and sail out to sea.

Misti M. George
MY HALLOWEEN FRIEND
Once upon a time on a
  Halloween night,
The sky was black, the moon was
  bright,
I thought I saw behind a tree,
A ghost or a goblin spying on me.
I went to see what could be there,
But for me, it was a thrill, and a
  scare.
When I peeked much to my

surprise,
A trick-or-treater in disguise?
I asked of him his destined place,
And that's when we began this
  chase.
Down streets, around corners,
  now where could he be?
A trace of him I didn't see.
He couldn't just have
  disappeared,
Then in my mind this idea speared.
Maybe he would come out of
  hiding,
If as his friend I tried abiding.
"I come in peace," I said, "my
  friend,"
Had my discovery come to an end?
Then slowly an eery shape
  attended,
And into the sky the shape
  ascended.
To this strange friend I said,
  "Good Bye."
And as he rose he said "Happy
  Halloween Night."

Florra Ida Mork

Florra Ida Mork
WINTER
Within the utter stillness
Of one frosty December night
While standing by the windows
I beheld a beautiful sight.

The bride adorned in frothy
  white,
Her gown designed by J. A. Frost.
The bridemaids too a lovely
  sight.
Whatever could such finery cost?

The azure sky calm and clear
Generously splashed with
  shining stars,
A priceless background cast so
  near
From frosty earth to distant Mars!

Maria Costa
. . . AND SO ON . . .

---

*To M. C., in hopes that she will
find herself.*

Fall . . . here it comes,
with that first cool breeze
brushing across my cheeks
. . . and they become pink.

Through the fall colored leaves
children leave a trail.
Off to school time,
no more summer time,
. . . and they become sad.

Another college semester arrives
many new faces will stare
and I shall stare back.
"Hi, my name is Joanne."
"My name is Linda."
. . . and they become friends.

Sally Jo Dern
EGG SALAD
These eggs are not spoiled
Though they may look that way,
But I set them to cooking,
And sent Tony out to play.
He was impatiently waiting
For mom to appear
So, I went out to join him,
And in one hour, I fear,
I returned to the kitchen
To find in the pot,
That the eggs were still cooking
In water so-o-o hot.
So these eggs are black,
Not the usual yellow,
Because of nice weather,
And one special young fellow.

Sulo Aijala
DOOMED
Good wife, good life,
Spare time, 'nuff cash
Wife dies, join club,
Girls swoon, like some,
Can't choose, meet more,
Want two, can't do,
Mixed up, must think.
Looks like loves self.
That's all, no swoon!

Susan Dunnegan
DAYDREAM
I'd like to be a snow white cloud
And sail o're land and sea
To the hills of peace and
  contentment
Known only as 'heavenly'
Where babbling brook greets the
  sunrise
And sunset turns to gold
There I'd put all my cares beside
  me
And luxuriously grow old

Lewis Henry Hinesley
CARDINALS
Today I watched some hungry
  cardinals
  In the snow;
Dressed in crimson coats
  Like rubies on clouds of cotton;
Searching for hidden food
  With eyes aglow;
Competing with others
  For sustenance of life;
Chirping gratefully upon finding
  seeds
  Left (as by Providence) in the
  snow.
Such beauty is mine to behold—
  A priceless gift of God—from
  days of old.

Nancy J. Hull
FROM RETREAT
In this place I hang, but
by one fingernail from
the tiniest star. Still a
part of the vastness, yet
weak in comprehension.

I sometimes think I should
drop my finger and fall into
emptiness. But no matter the
greatness of fear, the
smallness of my part;

I will cling for that
one moment of life.

Linda Weniger
YOU
I wish I could
Say to you
All of the things
I'm feeling.
I wish I could
take you
In my arms
And show you
All of the ways
I feel,
  about you,
  for you,
    with you,
And more than anything
without you.

Beatrice Perry Stanley
SYMPATHY
Bring me your love,
And I will hold it for you.
Tell me your dreams,
And I will shelter them.
Give me your pain and I will
  soothe it for you.
Share with me your heart,
And I will preserve it.

Irma Campbell
PRAY FOR PEACE
What does it mean to pray for
  Peace?
Does it simply mean that
  BOMBING will cease?
While men still crouch in fear
  and dread
Knowing that Communism still
  will spread

While men are still afraid to pray
Because of the communistic way
And some folks still must hide
  their face
Because other men hate their race.

Lets pray that VICTORY shall be
  won
And that theres peace for every
  one
We can make the right prevail
Trust in GOD we need not fail.

If we fight to shield the right
God will help us by his might
So lets each one do our part
To keep the PEACE within our
  HEART.

Ms. Oris A. Wheat
BEN OHIKU
I've never seen Africa's rising sun
But I have seen your smiling face.
Through you I visualize the
  beauties
They tell me are in the
  motherland.
Your caressing arms bring to mind
The tales of the comforts of the
  slow-moving waters.
I feel a touch of Amin
When you rationalize my
  wrongings,
Yet your peaceful state of mind
Is a welcome contagion.
You are the fertile land and rich
  soil.
You are ever-active being
  creative.
You are prosperity.
You seem untouchable, yet so

feeling.
You are a surprise to me.

Cindy Land
FREE SPIRITS
Free . . . at last.
Untethered and unchained.
To soar with the clouds.
To live our lives as we choose,
Yet to walk beside each other;
Safe in the knowledge that
    we are two . . .
    separate and individual;
But with the priviledge
of soaring with and sharing
    our freedom . . .
        together.

Rory J. Shaffer
You Know It's Fall When . . .
You know it's fall when you see,
Seas of golden leaves.
First they turn a golden brown,
And you see them all around
    town.
Then they turn a reddish hue,
And you may pick up a few.
After a while you soon see,
A pile of debris.

Wm. A. Gaffner
FOUND
I was lost
I was hurting
I was alone

I was empty
I was searching
I just knew I didn't belong

I looked for love in a woman
I looked for peace everywhere
I looked, but it escaped me
And nobody seemed to really care

Then I turned to Jesus
And He was waiting for me there
To fill me up with His great love
And take away all my fear

Yes I was totally lost without Him
I say this only because it's true
By the grace of Jesus Christ the
    Living Lord
I am found!
I am found!!
I am found!!!

Deborah Emmett
OUR LAST DAY
I am a little girl who should be
    tired
But a man gave me some candy
    that made me wired
Blue and white used to be my
    curtains
I think I am almost certain
Look over there a dancing cat
And over there a door that is fat
I've never seen sights as of today
Everything is happy and gay
My daughter wrote this the night
    she died
The pusher is loose and I only
    cried.

Fauvette Redding
LIFES SKRMISH
Those who have never dreamed
    have lost a sweet repose.
And those who have never hurt
    true happiness never knows.
Life seems a war that we must
    fight and battles win we few.
To know the agony of defeat
    when metals seem we due.

To know the sword
    to feel its pain
The deepness of its thrust
Yet hold the blade within your
    hand and find in it a trust
To hurt, and hurt, and hurt, and
    hurt till you can't bear the pain
To always, always know the loss
    and seldom see the gain
The struggle long, great deeds
    unseen
    the crowds to pass you by
And yet the war we bravely fight
    in battle do or die

Mary A. Pennington
My Home In The Country

*In memory of my home in the
hills of Kentucky and to Mom
and Dad who I thank very much
for the little churches I used to go
to every Sunday.*

There's a place back in the hills,
    where I'd love to go again
And smell the honeysuckle, that
    blooms down in the lane.
Watch the little fireflies, as they
    light the starry night
Hear the crickets chirping loudly,
    underneath the pale moonlight.

Where you wake up in the
    morning, to a bright and sunny
    day
To a good old country breakfast,
    that will help you on your way.
Walk barefoot through the
    clover, in the early morning dew
As you stroll down by the river,
    where the water's clear and blue.

The smell of wild red roses, that
    grows so pretty on the hills
Makes you feel like you're in
    Heaven, with the singing
    Whipporils
As you sit out on the front porch,
    when the evening sun goes
    down,
Friends would come from miles
    around, for a good old fashion
    hoe-down.

Now that little country home I
    miss so much, since I moved
    away
But I'll keep on going back, till
    they take me back to stay
To that little country church,
    where my parents took me for
    so long
When they lay me down to rest,
    that's where I'll be at home.

Raymond Sutherland
EXPLANATION

*Dedicated With Love To Leigh
Adair*

(This is the story of a
little boy bee and a little
girl bee. The little boy bee
is the old New York bowery type
for tough guy, sporting a slant-
ed black derby, short cigar
butt at the side of his mouth,
wearing a quite-worn T-shirt
with horizontal, wide stripes.

Ready to fight at a split-
second notice. A wonderful
guy. Very tough. Very
gentle.

Unfamiliar with Oxford English.)

Raymond Sutherland
WEE BEE
Once upon some time ago,
Slowly stroling tru de park,
At two minits befor dark,
Cupid hit me wit a spark!

Thar she was! A honey bee.
De most pretiest dat cood be!
Since she wos de best of all,
Ah shure had quite a great fall!

Hallow, prity litel bee!
Gash, you shood belong to me!
Ah'm so kerazy for thee!
Honey Wee Bee, cant you see?

Gonna tell you what lets do.
Lots of lovin! Me and you!
Someone is ringin dem bells,
And ah don know nutin else.

Is wit me dat you shood be,
My very own Honey Wee Bee.
Witout you ah canot rest.
You're de greatest! De most best!

Den, she winkt one mor time,
Ah ah knew she wood be mine.
So, we staid right in de park,
Makin love when it wos dark!

Kimberly A. Bullock
NEEDING LOVE
There are no limits

I need to be high
On the love that . . . Is yours.
Only your love
Can make me . . . Feel this way.

I can "thrive"
On your love . . .
For eternity.

I am a "junkie" . . . for your love.

Your love can guide me
To the moon and back in one hour.
Your love is so, so strong.

When I am down . . .
And feel all alone
I think of your strong
Wonderful love
To pick me up again.

Everytime I see you,
I need more and more.
To take me through,
the day and night!

Love, your love
I only need . . . 1 dose and it's
    "up-up and away."
I can fly high just on 1 teaspon
    of . . . you!

I need it.
I got to have it . . . It's a habit I
    can't quit.
Just one more . . . please . . .
I don't want to come down
Not now
Not ever
'Cause there's no cure
For getting over you.

I'm just a love-sick "junkie"!

Michael W. Rubin
SO MUCH ALONE; AGAIN
Here we go
    Alone, we go

Along-we'll go
    again
And so we go.
    So much alone, again,
    we'll go—
and so we'll go again.
And because we go
    Alone,
We go along,
    as we go again,
To be alone
    and to
        go along-
So much alone
    We'll be
        again.

Julie Jean Couey Pursel
THE SEED
Possessions I haven't any more
Destroyed by ragging flames of fire
Ten years of treasures and work
Burnt to the very core.

Still I have all I ever need
Passionate, Protective, Devoted
    love
Not wanting or needing any thing
    more
Given freely, planted deeply the
    seed,
Of ever lasting love and devotion.

Linda L. Ferguson
INTO THE NIGHT

*Lovingly dedicated to Darlene,
Mom, and my Son, Gary Linn for
their love and faith in me.*

Into the night
I pass,
Softly singing within,
That
Which all is a part of.
The night
Is caressing the moon
I, lie
Silently caressing the night.

Naomi R. Hughes
**Flight Of the
    Taxidermist's Grouse**
Side by side, wings outspread-
hen, cock,
Stationary log perch
separated from your flock.

Mind's eye captures your flight
streaking through the cold dawn's
morning light.

While mountains lay dressed in
    errie gray mist

with the early morning sun
sending
it's warm gentle kiss.

Gliding upward, a remarkable pair
one with one, nary a care.
A shot, silver streaks on the land
one on the ground,
a shot, two down the hunter's plan.

Now an infinite perch on your
stand
Forever gliding together ended by
man.

Lester E. Garrett
**After the Falling Of the
Leaves**

---

*Dedicated to the Lord, our
Heavenly Father and friend, who
has blessed us with so much; and
is surely pleased whenever His
children speak of their gratitude,
and the cherishment of freedom.*

Halloween's spooks, goblins and
pranks
Has faded into the eye of the
autumnal winds,
Replaced by crisp November
bringing
Another joy, another
blessing—Thanksgiving!
With my loved ones, I am at the
table of plenty;
And delightful odors abound
As the carving, the serving, and
the quiet
But happy talk and laughter
begins . . .
Along with the great inevitable
gorging

Which, we take it, is traditional.
One may simply stuff one's self,
Sleep it off afterwards
And nothing is thought of it;
It is wonderfully American!

Conceive of it: we are free
To eat what we like, to say what
we like;
Free to open our Bible and quote
without fear.
O, how it warms the heart and
firms, too,
The wording as we give thanks.
For we know it may be uttered
loud and clear
And in the knowledge that the
Lord listens
When we are sincere, and aglow
With love, gratitude and trust . . .

Whether it be before,
Or after the falling of the leaves.

Syrena M. Palmer
WINTER
Cold noses everywhere,
A big fat snowman over there.
Time for jack-frost to bite your
toes,
Oops watch out there he goes!
Coldness fills the winter air
In the woods the trees are bare.
The fire crackling in the night
Is a warm and pretty sight.
Rabbits hopping through the
snow
Are leaving footprints where they
go.
Have fun this winter too,
But watch jack-frost, he's after
YOU!!

Elizabeth Mackie
Growing Up Is a Mystery
Growing up is much like,
a puzzling mystery.
What happened to the children,
we all usc to be.
All of the time,
went by so very fast.
Looking for a future,
forgetting all the past.
We remember only,
what we want to know.
What happened to the time,
where did it all go.
There is only one thing,
that I can really see.
That is why growing up,
remains such a mystery.

Karen Robey
TIME
Time goes on
Like a river flowing
It's never knowing
And never showing
When it will die
Or when it will end
The day will pass
The night will come
And leave you wondering
How long you have left
It is soon over
And your time is up
So enjoy your life
That river flows fast.

Marlan LeVan Rhame III
**The Eve Of My
Destruction**
Here I am, on the eve of my
destruction.
It's been nice knowing everyone
But now it's time to go.
I see the room floating around
and around.
Everything is fading to black.
Will I be remembered after today?
Oh Lord, Will anyone really care?
Happiness and joy have faded out
of view.
This is truly the end.
I, sometimes, wondered why
Things never seemed to go right.
Yet, now it seems so clear
Questions are better left
unanswered
Because we really don't want to
know.
So here on the eve of my
destruction,
I bid everyone one last goodbye

Linda J. Eardley
LOOKING OUT
For the night is dark and scares me
I scare myself
And in the silence
I think of how it should be
And while the world sleeps
I lie awake
And try to figure it out
And then comes morning
And here I am
Still one step behind
Lifeless in the dark
No distinction
Without definition
But never without mystery
Yes the night excites me
But never scares me
And I scare myself . . .

Sue Blythe
nighthawkers

---

*TO MY FAVORITE nighthawker
ROGER BLYTHE*

---

with skin so pale
they've got words for sale
poetic justice guitars strum
words sung in rhyme
cadence amplified
hawk your wares if you dare
licentious eyes and pony-tailed
hair
you hawk your wares
carnival lights in orange yellow
red and purple
atonal symphony of destruction
you end your rhyme with a
catch-cry
hawkers in the night.

Jane Boese
THE BABY
Although he has not said a word
And cannot walk nor crawl,
Whenever his young voice is heard
It motivates them all.
His smile can brighten any day,
His wails can mar the night.
His mother seldom gets away
From this demanding mite.
But then, there is no place to go
Where she would rather be.
She sees the doubtful future grow,
This child upon her knee.

Michael E. Buse
MY LAST FALL . . .

---

*You walked out of my life, and
into my dreams, on this I shall
survive, until we meet again.*

When taking walks along
the pathways of my memories,
I am compelled to stop and stare
when I happen across that field
where all love stories co-exist.
I have no doubt that anyone has
ever beheld a more beautiful sight
than you in those surroundings.
Perhaps, you looked that way for
me,
or someone else you wished to see;
but, it was I who loved you.
As we walked through autumn's
speckled field
playfully teasing and tackling,
I don't quite remember if it was

the crisp breeze,
or the swirling of the falling
leaves, or you;
but, once we fell,
and there we lingered;
and I linger still.

Mike Lee
THE MUSE
Taken by the wind,
a spirit that would be:
deep within,
coiled with love,
is out;
dark, is blue
as the sky is Spring;
scorching, cool:
a dance
to sacrifice her purity,
and thus,
by the light
of her eyes so blue,
she renders being being true.

Teresa M. Ariza
THE DAUGHTER
The daughter wanting so much
from her father.
She is so scared at times not
wanting to be a bother.
She needing not material things
but paternal.
Wanting so much to be her
father's pride,
Wanting so much to be loved, to
be by his side.

The daughter wanting to be on
stage with the light.
Looking down and hearing her
father say,
"That's my daughter, my baby".
Oh dear Lord, wouldn't that be a
sight.

The daughter has a vivid
imigination,
Knowing that all this is but in
her dreams.
Reality sometimes escaping her
mind,
For her father never has enough
time it seems.

Ronnie Bruscino
REALITY

---

*Ded: To my wonderful family y a
mi hijada, Brenda; Para mi
Carnales; to Jessie, who I lost but
will never forget Ronnie*

Have you ever seen a riot from
behind a prison wall,
Or from right around the corner
heard a dying mans last call,

Have you ever seen the rec. yard
filled with hundreds of restless
cons,
While you were in prison behind
cold steel prison bars,

Have you ever seen the warden
pardon a very wealthy man,
Turn his back go on his way and
not look back again,

Have you ever dreamt of a home
life, with a wife and a child or
two,
But because of laws confinements
had these things denied of you,

Have you ever written a letter to

someone you called a friend,
And never received an answer
because they didn't have the
time to spend,

If you've never done these things
your a very lucky man,
Your lifes been filled with beauty
since the moment it began,

For he who knows of life from
inside a prison cell,
Has had his share of heart-aches
and served his time in hell.

Katherine Florence Marsden
**A Grandaughter's
Remembrance**

---

*Dedicated to my grandmother,
Florence Marsden, who has been
a great influence on my life and
who has given me many
wonderful memories to cherish.
God bless you, Grandmom!*

I remember,
when I was a small child
and you were there
when I needed a grandmother's
comforting arms,
to calm my fears and take away
my pains
with your love.

I remember,
when I was a confused teenager
and I had many questions about
life and love,
and you were there
when I needed a grandmother to
help me
understand what it means to be a
woman.
You did this with your love.

Now,
that I am older,
Let me be here
for you,
when you need me,
and let me show you
I love you with my heart.

Libby Lady Cooper
LEAVES OF OCTOBER
Natures artists dip their brushes
into vivid colors and paint the
leaves
As they float to the ground, they
seem to be shouting to all the
world
Look at me, I want to be free, and
then they are gone like the
yesterdays that are no more.

Catherine Huestis
LOVELESS LIFE
Life without love
is impossible to see,
for life without love
is no life for me.

If I manage to survive,
to see another day,
what will I have to give
to a world that's gone astray?

A life without love
is what I'll have to give,
because I've no one to love
and no one cares why I live.

A loveless life
is what it will be.

The world will end
as well as you and me.

So put a little love
in the life that you lead,
and you will live longer,
satisfaction guaranteed!

Gwendolyn Trimbell Pease
FIRST FROG

---

*For my five adult kids—Susan P
Carroll, Sally P Adamson, Morgan
A Pease III, Cynthia J Pease and
Martin A Pease; for all the fond
memories of all their "First Frogs".*

Extensive search about the
ground
Energetic hopper finally found
Apparently some shade of green
All spanking clean
For an amphibian, I mean

Kimberly's new froggy pet
Bumpy, knobby and all wet
Fall hibernator extraordinary
First impression may vary
Little creature—seems scary

But held lovingly upon the palm
Friends together all calm
Understanding an alive situation
Cause of great celebration
Another environmental
revelation.

Linda Cox
REFLECTIONS OF LIFE
The reflections of life surround
me,
Before my blinded eyes, I see,
Re-calls of sorrow, and all thats
left,
Sleepless nights, I've laid and wept,
Within I need to gain, respect,
To rectify the life I've wrecked.

I need a place to store my sorrows,
I need longer and better
tomorrows,
I need a prayer from heaven above,
I need a man, to care and to love.

The reflections of my life, I see,
Understanding the need to be free,
My heart is heavy, my soul is lost,
The bridges of courage have all
been crossed,
The experiences of life, have been
a trial,
Lord, let me rest, just for a while.

Joseph T. Mancuso
**Works While In
Matrimony (Always)**
To the depths of the future
You will always be mine
My light, My life, My guide

To you an you alone
I will always be near
My Giver, My food, My home

Forever I will keep you
Always close to touch
My strength, My growth, My
wisdom

From the halls of time
You were always here
My seasons, My water, My tree

Your eternal light
I will always follow
My love, My father, My God

Bhatkin Devi
THOUGHT WONDER

---

*To all the poets and writers of
today, yesterday and tomorrow,
gracious tidings.*

Sunshine and Rainbows;
Infateous rambling
Transverse climates; Drifting
along shoreline winds
Shoveling treasurers of vanishing
pirates
Ages being passed through that;
reveal man's darkest secrets
Short ship, junky rambling
Moonlight in full circle (of
crescent Light (Des de noire)
Multicolored-laser disco, Designs
of bright
Anytime man knowing no savage
Thrists of glory that are forsaken

Shades of pompous pieces of
theory that cater to none
Running through minds and
images of clustered focus
Summertime shoot-fly-got caught
by the slammer
Hemingway & Fitzgerald herald
the poetic interlude of those now
and gone known for enchanting
verse

Echelons and phylums combed in
cucumic precautions
Misery suppressed to insidious
desires of lust nagrity

Fading beauty, exhanced dreams
Trips to nowhere, sometimes
living in oblivion
None right for me wondering
through mazes
Cultivating habits that we never
quite acceptable
Pompous pieces of men and their
rampling thoughts
Forsight for the blind and for
those stalling for time
Sunburst of light shine through
the clouds

Kathy Lane
TOO LATE
The moon peers down on my tear
streaked face, as I sit crying in
the night,
Looking to the stars, trying to
seek answers from their
shimmering light,
My body shakes with pent up
frustration, I scream out at the

unexpecting darkness,
Wanting some relief from the
torment that racks my soul, a
pain I can't suppress,
But no relief comes from the
darkness that surrounds me,
only loneliness, my heart cries,
My mind keeps running back in
time bringing up old memories,
so many which are full of lies,
What a fool I was to believe that
love would claim my lonely
heart as its own,
I should of seen the game it was
playing before it had a chance
to turn my heart to stone,
But now it is too late, I lost at the
game and my heart is
entrapped in pain, my mind in
memories,
So now I sit in the darkness of
the night . . . trying to hide
from my own misery . . .

Bessie A. Neal
TOTAL LOVE

---

*"POOH" This is dedicated to you,
for you, and because of you. Keep
on loving me, as I shall love you
forever and ever and always.*

If you could love me more today
than yesterday,
I'll love you even more tomorrow,
because you are the sunshine
of my days,
the dreams of my nights,
the answer to my prayers,
the fulfillment of my fantasies,
the essence of my happiness and
the recipient of my love

Dorothy Wills-Raftery
MUSIC

---

*As my first published poem, I am
dedicating this to my Mother for
her many years of love, patience
and support that encouraged me
to pursue my dreams. Also to my
husband, Tom, for his love.*

Music
Blasting, soothing
Keeping silence away
We all listen to
Music

Susan Diane Rupp
ROY, I NEED:
I need someone
To love, guide
And
Coach me . . .
Through the rough paths
Of life.
To acknowledge acheivements
Not tear them down
Bit by bit . . .
To hurt and destroy.
I need someone
To hold a hand; lead
And
Follow at times . . .
To see if the
Sunrise is high, or the sunset's
too low.

To love honor and cherish
Not distrusting, lying, cheating

Hating . . .
But honest to goodness
"Loving", as is in our hearts . . .
'Til death do us part.

Dawn Marie Hodgkinson
MY WORLD

This poem is dedicated to Frank Morrison—the man who showed me what "my world" is all about . . . and also to my loving parents: Daniel and Barbara, and my sister, Barbara—who all give me an overwhelming amount of love and strength.

I am doing what I do best,
  dreaming of a world without the rest.
The only people in this place,
  are all familiar faces.
There are no strangers,
  therefore we experience no danger.
This world contains no pain,
  or people living in vain.
It is a world made of dreams,
  where the faces seem to gleam.
Here happiness, peace, and love,
  is held up above.
The feelings are not hidden,
  and fear is now ridden.
A quiet breeze with a gentle
  voice is the only sound,
  for peace is finally found.
There is only one man,
  I want to share my world with-
So please come and gently take
  my hand,
  for my world is no myth.

Letitia J. Knoche
VISITATION

This poem is dedicated to my brother, who's death inspired me to write this piece. I want him and the world to know that we love and miss him very much. This ones for you Tim.

A room, dark and regretful,
filled with remorse.
The flowers full of life seem
to wilt in the presence of death.
A cascade of trees, now fallen,
holding a motionless love.
Friends over taken by grief
seem cloudy and vague to reality.
Foes now trying to ease their
conscience by bringing forth
  condolences.
Tears are wept, and love is
  shown, each
holding on to their own precious
  memory.
Silence has over taken the
  anguished
brigade, all but a quiet weeping is
  heard.
Now a young girl of sixteen
  approaches the
pedestal to give her last kiss to
  her fallen pride.
An older sister comes forth with
  tears
in her eyes to give her love to her
  brother.

A brother of sorts, confused and
  bewildered
from the loss of a gained friend,
  comes forward.
In a slow panic a mother arises
  to
hold her son just for a loving
  moment.
At last a father comes to his son's
  side
to look longingly at his boy, now
  a man,
and only these words are heard, "I
  love you
my son, and remember this is not
  good-bye,
just see you around."

The march of death begins.

Mark Stephen Wallinder

Mark Stephen Wallinder
BE CLOSE
If I had to say
For you
How I really feel,
I'd only have to say
I'm so happy that you're real;
For real things
Are full of life
And happy just to be,
And I am only happiest
when you are with me.

Patty Taylor
AUNT'S ADVICE

To my GodSon and Nephew, Sheldon Scott Eby

You are my GodSon
And my nephew as well,
Here's wishing you fun
From the stories you tell.

Grow great big and tall
To reach the cupboards on top,
Don't slip and fall
In the hands of a cop.

Always remember what's true
And the things that are right,
For God watches you
From morning till night.

I send you my love
From all of my heart,
As the Savior above
Wants you to do your part.

Don't forget this last phrase
Since it's now at the end,
Life's like a big maze
That has many a bend.

Linda G. Frey
PRICELESS

To Gordon D. Clark, a close friend and my inspiration.

I never expected a ring from you,
But received one anyway.
It's made up of saphires and
  diamonds
Which are set in the brightest
  band
Of gold, it's not of earthly
  materials,
But means just as much to me, and
Is as priceless as the rearest of
Art forms.

My ring consists of a band of gold
  which
Is the golden glow that circles my
  heart,
My saphires are the many joys
  we shared
In the cool blues of the night, and
  my
Diamonds are the many tears I've
  shed
From the memories, that are the
  hardest
To forget.

The ring you have given me is one
That can't be taken back or layed
  in a
Box to let tarnish and lose its
Brilliance, but one that will be
  with
Me always, and remain just as
  priceless.

Cynthia E. Ravinski
ONE OCTOBER NIGHT
In the Dark Gloomy Clouds
  above, I see a light, a small
  flicker
Showing the way through the
  unlimiting, devastating
  darkness, Alone I watch.
In time, now, light has been
  dimming.
Smile weakening, goose bumps
  standing on each others edge.
Somewhere out in the horizon, a
  streak of lightning.
One solemn streak startling the
  night.
Than where the sullen sky meets
  the Autumn trees filled with
  vast luminous colors.
The gloomy clouds are pushed
  aside to expose a
glowing yellow ball that lights up
  the whole Earth.
I stand, my feet secured to the
  ground by some unseen force.
A dog howls somewhere in the
  night.
I try to run, but when I do I hear
  laughter; I watch afraid with
  curiosity.
Out of the West, a whirling wind
  brings many laughters,
  stopping at the yellow ball.
Now I see them people, I think,
  wearing black with tall
pointy hats, boots that go to their
  thighs and a necklace
with many fangs dangling from it,
  which shines, radiant light.
As I stand the light from one of

their necklaces shines on me.
I scream, they smile, bearing long
  teeth, I try to run, but
I'm stopped, as a force pulls me
  back toward the yellow ball.
The heat of the yellow ball is
  unbearable.
The people I've seen have gone in
  their whirling wind, leaving me
  to burn.
I move and struggle with the
  yellow ball, just to awaken
  myself
to find covers over my head and
  sweat running off my forehead.
I look out of the window and I
  hear laughter as the wind
whips around the side of the
  house.

Jan Cerny
I BLEED WORDS
The substance that motivates a
  writer—the language of the pen;
An art form that expresses
  feelings in descriptive phrases;
My poetry flows through my
  veins and I bleed words.
The words stain the pages of my
  book and sing praises.
When veins are too narrow, the
  blood tends to slow,
So it is with my writing—the pen
  dries of ink.
The richer the blood is, the
  healthier the body;
My plume can create anything on
  paper while I continue to
  think.
Just as life is void and useless
  without the blood of Man,
The parchment holds the words
  of life and the promises fulfilled.
Laughter, tears and words of
  wisdom grace the many pages—
May the "spilling" of the bleeding
  words keep the readers thrilled!

Leilani G. Arrocena
WHY

This poem is especially dedicated with all my heart to David S. DeLeon, my very first and real true love. I'll always love you . . .

How is it that I have been so
  wrong
To honestly think that our love
  was strong
Why were my eyes so very blind
To let me believe that you were
  ever mine
And how come when I see you
  walking on by
Something inside me makes me
  want to cry
Why do those memories keep
  floating in my head
Will I always be sad—can't I be
  happy instead
Why do I wish we could walk
  hand in hand
Please explain these to me, I don't
  understand
How come I'm always thinking of
  you
In whatever I see or whatever I do
Why do I always think of the past
When I know in my heart that

we didn't last
How come you cause me to act
  this way
And why is it that for you I
  always pray
All these questions keep
  pounding my mind
Could you answer them for me,
  please be kind
Just tell me the answers or at
  least try
I really only want to know just
  why?

Ada M. Williams
THE GLOWING TREE

---

*In Memory of my Dear Husband
Charles J. Williams*

It seems this tree is very strange
With it's unearthly light
Is that because it's out of range
At sunset's lovely sight?
Why point it out to friends your
  age!

Those older ones, so sage.
Blind, they seem,
But ask a girl of seven
Her answer is "it reminds me just
  of heaven".

Katharine C. Lickers
LOVE IS
Love is our whole family doing
  something fun together.
Love is our mother singing early
  in the morning.
Love is nice meals and clean
  clothes.
Love is the look in the eyes of
  our beautiful German Shepherd.
Love is our father, patiently
  building our home a brick and
  a board at a time.
Love is my sisters and I giggling
  over something silly.
Love is dear relatives and trusted
  friends.
Love s a warm black hand,
  holding my white hand.
Love is John 3—16!

Nikki Langslet
A FRIEND
When happy skies start to run gray
When sad people pass your way
When all the time you cry
And yet you don't know why
When your pale all the time
Like you lost your gold mine
Thats the time when
You need to find a friend

Maye Schwartz
Up On the Hill With God
I often walk to the hilltop
And while I'm resting there
I listen as the wind sings
A gentle evening prayer.

The troubles that I feel today
Will all be blown away
To grasses growing down below
Where children laugh and play.

Where I hear cattle lowing
Where horses softly neigh
Corn is showing silky threads
And fields are stacked with hay.

The sun sinks down below the hill
The evening star blinks bright
Dusk beckons to its creatures
To safely seek the night.

The Whip-Poor-Will is calling loud
I feel a drowsy nod
And add a prayer to the wind's
  song
Up on the hill with God.

Barbara Weaver
I FELL DOWN
I fell down . . .
You appeared as if from nowhere
and gave me your hand
to help me out,
just as you had done
so many times before.
I longed to throw my arms
around you,
And beg you
not to go.
But instead,
I took your hand.
You helped me to my feet,
made sure I had my balance,
Then you took your hand away. . .
leaving me to stand
on my own.

Michael Federika
THE HELL'S ANGEL
The Hell's angel rides his cycle
  domain
With his cycle, his commrades,
  and his piece of steel chain.
He drinks his liquor, and makes
  love to his woman,
Until he detects the policemen
  a-comin'.
He's made fun of, and he's
  laughed at but he takes it in
  stride.
He returns to his commrades
  where he regains his pride,
He takes to the highways making
  a frightful scene.
Stealing and racing on his two-
  wheeled machine,
From party to party; he has lots of
  fun.
Cussing and kissing and fighting
  everyone.
The Hell's angel will forever reign,
'Less he rides up into heaven,
  never heard from again.

Alice Carlson Barnes
LOVE'S FOUNDATION
When LOVE is your foundation
You are blessed beyond compare
For, with that God sent blessing
There is nothing it won't bare

It will bare the storms of nature
Standing strong against the wind
It won't crumble in advirsity

Nor, will time, bring to it an end
Your foundation will be stronger
Than any enemies rath
And, TRUE LOVE, entwines
  together
Like Gods rain, for a cleansing
  bath

When LOVE is your foundation
The strength of it will stand
Through every test you give it
And come in safely, to stand
  GRAND

Elizabeth A. Prato
FOR A UNIQUE MUSICIAN
From day to day I play my part in
  life
rarely looking beyond the players
  faces:
even you can't escape my illusion;
I hold you dear for the person I see.
But when I've lost my love for all
  good gifts
and my spirit for life is running
  low,
I have only to find you, knowing
  that
the music you make replenishes
  me.
Mesmerized by your melody of life,
I let each note reach out to touch
  me;
from the world in which I
  normally live
I am swept away, renewing my life.
  You lose yourself in your
  dedication
  as I easily lose myself in you.

Mary Mc Con
MY SHOE
My Sole is gone
I'm gettin old
Where I have

been will never be
told things I've
seen I'd rather
not I've been

To places both
Cold and hot

I've seen the best
my sole is tried

I need a rest
I've supported a man
and comforted him
I came and went at his will
my toes is tried my mine is old
I need repair or
be
born again,

Christa Nelson
LIVING

---

*Although not inspired by anyone,
this poem relates, and is
dedicated to my best friend,
Stacey Pope. I'd also like to
dedicate this to my Mother,
without whom, life would have
no meaning. I love you both!*

Life is full of so many wonderful
  things
The joys of being happy
The joys of love
But even life has its sad things
The grief of death
The heartbreak of a lost love

But there is nothing better to life
Than living

Sonja Roiko Gellerson
DISCOVERY
The moments
We have left to share—

Will be times
Filled in the Discovery

Of loving each other.

Ruth Sampson
THE IMMIGRANT
To this, a bountiful land I came,
Not to scrounge, defile or distress;
I came as brother to brother,
Our Mother, England, the bless'd.
Wolfe, the dauntless hero of old,
Planted England's flag to unfurl
In the soft gentle breezes of this,
A glorious land of wealth untold,
Canada without peer in northern
  climes,
Abounding in plains, mountains,
  streams and sea.
Mighty St. Lawrence, Great
  Lakes, Falls of Wonder,
A thousand isles to sail and
  cruise among,
Giving sustenance to man and
  beast,
Buffalo, seal, reindeer and caribou,
Eagle, starling, robin and crane,
Many, many, many more can yet
  be named.
Feed their full on this land so vast.
Seasons come and seasons go,
Summer glides into winter's snow
Yet these innumerable
  dependents all
Rarely anything of food ever lack.

Man his puny efforts oft tried to
  pit
'Gainst Nature's mighty and
  mysterious ways,
Wanting to crush her long
  unbridled reign,
Intent Time's immortal ways to
  change,
To subdue them to his command;
  in vain.
Tundra regions with flowers rare
  in north's summer
Uncharted forests of maple, cedar,
  fir, birch pine,
In mystic beauty meet distant
  skies.
Rolling grasslands into
  unmeasured distance stretch,
Canada, God given! beautiful!
  immense!!
An immigrant brother I came to
  dwell,
Willing to share the pains of
  growth.
Just as they, spawned by the
  English Mother.
Colonial were yesterday—today
  independent are.
But, man's memory is short, time
  has flown,
My claim of brotherhood oft
  scorned, unknown.
No brother am I, many of them
  say.
Forgotten the times when, side by
  side
We fought for Freedoms, Monarch,
  Empire
But, Oh Canada, as in yester-years,

Allegiance I will pledge to thee,
Today—tomorrow—and, forever!!

Keith Walker
A PASSING THOUGHT
As I cast my feelings
  through this pen
The train of thought that
  never ends
It burdens my mind both
  night and day
What my mind can see
  these words can't say

So many ways each thought
  could be taken
I fear some views might
  be mistaken
Can your mind conceive
  what your eyes can see
To answer this you must
  first know me

Joanne M. Leight
KIM
Why are you my friend?
Do I really deserve you?
You say you'll be with me until
  the end.
You say you'll see me through.

Will you be there to cry on?
Or to send you my cheer?
Will you be there when I'm wrong?
Will you be there to wipe away
  my tear?

The answer to all are yes,
I know it to be true.
You are the best, I must confess.
And I really do love you too.

C. J. Crawford
HALLOWEEN'S NIGHT
The sun is fading on this October
  day
And soon after dark will begin
  the play
The shadows grow long, the stars
  soon appear
The stage is being set for a
  perfect night of fear
The owl awakens and welcomes
  the moon
As it casts its eerie glow of
  depressing doom
The black cats they scurry, the
  spiders they weave
As the voice of Halloween hangs
  heavily on the breeze
And then they come, these
  goblins half grown
With their blood curdling
  screams and dreadful moans
From out of the corners and
  unseen places
Arise hideous creatures with
  monstrous faces
The witches ride their booms
The ghosts rattle their chains
The Jack-O-Laterns smile with
  faces of fiery flames
The vampire appears in his basic
  black
And the warlock steps out in his
  new cape and top hat
Then come the creatures from
  way outer space
Hey these guys are normal, they
  aren't out of place
The parents aren't left out, they're
  caught in the middle
They get to pass out the candy
  and the peanut briddle

But soon the witching hour
  comes to an end
And the weary trick-or-treaters
  now no longer pretend
For the ghosts and goblins of the
  night have fled
And the Spirit of Halloween is
  tucked safely in its bed

Dorothy Hyatt
BABY CATS
Kittens, so cute, cuddly and full
  of play
They really do brighten up a
  dreary day.
The worst thing about a kitten is
  that
it grows up and becomes a cat.

Lynn Greenwood Brown
CHANGING EVERYTHING
You, understood me
Before we met.
More than all the rest.

I realized the sameness.
That first time,
we really talked.

The ability to be
Totally alone.
In a room full of people.

Thank you, for taking my hand.
As we walk out of
the Valley of Loneliness

Theresa Fidurski
The Cave At Grandma's House
The Cave At Grandma's House;
Ah yes, t'was once the hiding
place for this lost child.

For she who played in it;
Fast and strong was she;
This child who still
resides IN ME.

Faster and Stronger than
others for you see; She had
practiced running from reality.

From Harsh Reality She Went
on slued foot.

Faster, Faster, Faster she ran
Away from vast reality of what
she was *to be.*

For she thought; Less than
average she would *be*

Not So sais He who created me,
Wow; slow down!
That I may catch up to thee.

Dr. Lionel Fern
SAMHAIN
Apples and gold merge into gray
  and black.
The rose on the face turns
  cinder-hue.
All petals are gone, the thorns
  pricking you,
Swarming balls of fire (the eyes of
  the cat).

Bewitched oak tree! . . . is this one
  or that?
Floating through the forests, Julie
  and Joe,
Started the searching for the
  mistletoe.
Each one of them dreaming of
  that great smack.

Remember the treat we have
  made at home:

Oh, wonderful night, surprises
  and sweets!
Your singular face in the
  masquerade!

—She played me a trick. She did
  never come.
I spent the whole night, in
  shadows and leaves,
Feeling her: the breeze, the scent
  and the shade!—

Peggy Fisher
I REMEMBER YOU

*Written to my ex-husband, in a
night of total despair. To God, as
always, and my daughters, Steff,
Jenny and Courtney. Also, for
Laurie, my favorite aunt and
friend. Finally, for my Mother,
Jean Binegar, who believes in me.*

Broken dreams and leftover hearts
Are all that's left of our loving
  start
But
I remember you, and all the love
  we knew
  the love you're giving to
  your somebody new

The time has come for me to see
There'll never be anymore you
  and me
But
  I remember you, and all the love
  we knew
Now I'm up all night and
  drinking more
And God, I wonder what's in store
For me, now that we're through
And I'm remembering you, and all
  the love we knew

There's lots of men, now that
  you're gone
But without you, there's just no
  turnin on
Do you remember me, and why
  you set me free?
Do you feel this pain, this pain
  that's killing me?

I can't believe we're in the past
I can't believe we didn't last

There's just this hell I'm going
  through
And now, I can't remember you

But I wonder
Do you still remember me?
The me who used to be?
The me who loved you?

Sue Fuchs
THIS WORLD OF BEAUTY
Sparkling through the forest of
  trees,
The sun glows within my eyes,
The beauty to see this world so
  free,
As I gaze upon the clear blue sky.

The rippling water glitters as it
  flows,
To its destiny of peace and will,
Till the end of its travels, it will
  grow,
Then the movement will be still.

To climb a sky made of rainbows,
To touch the softness of a cloud,
To feel the strength as the winds

blow,
To sight the world standing so
  proud.

Watching the feathered birds soar
  through
      the air,
Gliding with the sounds of love,
To fly with hope and time,
  somewhere,
Throughout the heaven's high
  above.

Peggy Fisher
END TO END

*This poem is dedicated to Ron
Fisher, my daughters Steffanie,
Jennifer and Courtney. And, as
always, especially to God. Also, to
my dearest friend and cousin,
Judy Nelson, who always
understands me and my writing.*

It runs from end to end
But the middle is weak
Insanity is on the line

How long does it take
To lose your mind?
Are you sure
You still have time?

Will you be over the edge
If you move?
Better stand still
Don't go ahead, and don't look
  behind

It's right there
Nipping at your heels
Trying to get in front of you
Trying to move inside

And like a snake
It can open its jaws
And devour you
And take your pride

But you do slow down
Because you know in the dark pit
  of your belly
That it might be nice
To now live twice

Once on top
In the real, hot world
And once underneath
Under thin ice

Not really knowing any less
But now really caring anymore
Now, you must go quickly
Or insanity will shut the door!

Vicki Marus
UNKNOWN
This is the season
  When man knows no reason
  For dealing with the
  mysterious leads
To frightful crimes and deeds.

Thoughts of kindness and being
  fair
Seem to disappear in thin air.
  The heart is no longer being
  nice
And love appears as thin as ice.

Could it be the haunting moon
  That guides the soul to ruin?
  Could it be the forlorn melody
That sounds so sinful and eerie?

It is something heard and seen
  In the season of Halloween.

Calvin VanPelt
MY SPACE IN TIME
My earthly day's I shall define
Sim-ply as, MY SPACE IN TIME
I'm thankful for each wondrous
    day
that seems so fast to pass away

Sometimes I stop and wonder why
the strongest Man must
    sometimes cry
and wonder why that he should
    live
because it seems he can-not give

enough to help the human race
and make this world a better place
but this shall be a goal of mine
as I go through . . . My Space In
    Time

My time shall not be long . . . at
    most
my path may lead from Coast to
    Coast
but my foot-prints will fade away
who'll know that I . . . was here
    one day?

Lord grant I hurt no friend or foe
as through my space in time I go
forgive me for the times I'm wrong
and if I'm weak . . . Lord make me
    strong

that I may do my best each day
to help some-one along life's way
and make worth-while this life of
    mine
as I go through . . . MY SPACE IN
    TIME . . .

Caroline M. Orlandi
MY MOTHER'S HOUSE
It's just a house, our "home" no
    more
With family life beneath its crest,
No longer do we touch the door
That quickly opened for a guest.

As birds do fly from Mother's
    nest
I, too, moved on, just like the rest,
But surely, every now and then
We all came home to roost again.

Mom would listen to our chatter
With all the noise, it didn't matter,
Happy roosting in full swing!
We covered almost everything.

Memories of that sweet home
Are old and yet so clear,
Never ever to depart
Because of Mother dear.

Now someone else is living there,
Another family,
And Mom's in her Celestial home
For all Eternity!

Tamatha Lynne Montgomery
As Another Flower Blooms
Alone a flower grows
    All around it things change
        Things come
            Things go
It loses petals and leaves
    But in time
        It has more
Different ones to fill the space
    The others left empty
It continues on like this forever
Some stay with it longer than
    others
    They grow old together,

As one
But eventually they grow old
    And fade away
But no-one seems to notice
    As another flower blooms.

Kathleen Lyon Vaughn
Kathleen Lyon Vaughn
HARVEST NIGHT

*This poem is dedicated to Jaimie,
who is my whole life's
inspiration!—and Star Madonna,
David Christian, Chris Lyon,
Daniel Leon, & Kenneth Leigh—
Vaughn, my children.*

A laughing party strolled back
    home,
Finished, at last, with all their
    work.
They'd bent all day, above the laom:
Not thinking once, their part to
    shirk.

The harvesters soon went to sleep,
And sweetly, dreamed in peace,
    that night,
Knowing that God, their watch
    would keep;
Until the morning brought the
    light.

The harvest moon shone gold
    above;
O'er bare fields, it's soft light
    hovered.
And strolling lovers talked of love,
'Neath shadows of haymows,
    covered.

Anthony Wilder
FREEDOM
When I am free
I will drop in from the stars

find a home with my baby
the way it should be
whistle in the moonlight
near the windy willow tree

And I will open
the door of love
with my poetry key

I will trace
the grains of sand
by my baby's footprints
that lead like tears into the sea

And there I will spread colored
    tents
on the dunes
caressing the starlight
from that love lantern
called the moon

Crystal A. Hamilton
**Reflections Without a
Mirror**
We are Brother and Sister of the
    Spirit,
Two sides of the same soul
And closer than bonds of blood
Or other.
Though we met only short
    months ago,
We have known each other
Forever
Becasue we sprang from the same
    seed
In the mind of God.
Created in the image of each
    other
No mirrors are needed
For accurate reflections.

L. Brandi Wilson
WIDOW
Dead air, space to wander,
    A sudden shock,
. . . . Alone.
With me forever,
    Or so I thought,
. . . . Never.
What to do now,
    I, silent,
. . . . Snared,
Here, then gone . . .
Busy friends, paired,
    Where to go,
. . . . Nowhere.
Yes, here then gone,
    Pain, then numb,
. . . . "Widow".

Aurora L. Espinoza
PENSARAS EN MI
Cuando escuches la palabra, amor
con otro acento y en otros labios
volaras, hacia mi en tus recuerdos
cuando resibas otros besos . .
    pensaras
que yo te estoy besando;
Y cuando otras manos, acaricien
cada una de las partes de tu cuerpo
pensaras en *mis* caricias y
    temblaras
en tus recuerdos;
Mas te fuiste buscando la aventura
sin mirar atras lo que dejabas
bueno o malo al irte tu me
    rachazabas;
Ingratos amores que matan ocazos
que dejan amores por una ilucion
mas hoy se que lloras y buscas
un carino . . que al mio se
    paresca;
Mas yo estoy segura, que no hay

en el mundo, dos carinos iguales
que llenen completo , , un corazon;
Mas si algun dia regresas, vencido
y me pides perdon.
te abrire las Puertas de mi alma
y abrazada a tu cuello . . te dare
sin rencores . . . todo mi amor;

Simon W. Tache
NO COINCIDENCE
Flume Park, foot of mount
    Liberty, point of departure.
A run of three miles, a rise of
    1,000 ft. adventure,
That is Liberty's trail, still 4,460
    ft. of mountain,
Here sun's rays spurt gracefully
    like fountain.

    Teasing, tackling breeze induces
    a laugh.
Mist, air, light fusion spell out
    life,
Path whose expression in
    existence we perform,
As to honor a rite or obey a call
    we took form.

    Each one of us resolutely in our
    fashion.
Followed bravely our intuition's
    inclination,
Until the wheel of fortune took a
    turn,
For reasons known only to her,
    URI won;

    Became bridge and catalyst for
    exploration.
As I initiate challenge of this
    excursion,
I appreciate its reciprocity to our
    relationship.
Even as the climb was tedious,
    but so lavish.

    Our experiences have been
    mixed, but exhilarant.
Now at summit of mount Liberty
    we're cognisant,
You, like the lovely Flower, that
    blooming blazes,
I, like the little Prince, that
    patience tames.

    Unless our bid for self
    expression be self deception,
Unless our claim to individuality
    be empty rebellion,
We must know life is growth and
    growth is relating,
Mutual sharing of life's benefits,
    trials, blessings.

    To the skeptic, our world
    fascinates.
To the believer, our
    compatibility, mysterious,
To the mundane, our knowledge,
    stupendous;
But to US, the all . . . , no
    coincidence.

Tracey Anne Irzyk
SOMETIMES I WONDER
Sometimes I wonder if there's a
    purpose
for all things good and bad
when life is just an endless battle
and everything seems sad
when the feeling of confusion
    sets
from all that is around
I often question if He's there
and why He can't be found

282

Sometimes I feel that no one cares
as I lie awake at night
for there seems to be such
    endless tears
and I'll never win the fight
If only someone understood
the feelings deep inside
there are many empty spaces there
that I always seem to hide

Jesus, if your listening
I know you'll help me through
If ever I needed a hand or two
I need one now from you . . .

Dolores Dahl
God's Catch Twenty-Two

---

*Dedicated to my husband Claude
who 'slipped away' one April
day . . .*

If we but knew
the time, the place . . .
how could we face You freely
at the chapter's end?

If every friend and loved one's
time were told . . .
could we unfold as 'self'
in interaction,
or would falsity come into play?

In trying to be loving, kind . .
to please
because the time was near,
would growth then, disappear?

Catch twenty-two . . . for me, for
you.
'Tis God's own plan.
For He wants every man
to love, and freely . . .
always ever, just because
his love is real and genuine,
not just to please a dying soul
when time is due.

'Tis God's Catch Twenty-two.

Sandra Shannan
AUTUMN LOVE
Darkened like the autumn days
    is the way I feel inside.
I can't find a source for the
    warmth I need, and the wind
    won't let me hide.
Like the rain from the angry sky,
My tears pass on by.
And like a gust of wind I breath a
    heavy sigh.
I will wait for autumn and winter
    to pass by, until my days are
    filled with spring.
When newborn creatures awake
    with a cry and my heart can
    finally sing.

Anna Young Sanders
GRANDMA'S HOUSE
Once again I climb
these old and creaking stairs,
As a child this was an eager
    struggle,
Finding my bed, saying my prayers.

Grandma's house was old,
But so new to a kid.
I gaze into the memories,
The mischevious things I did.

I loved to sleep at Grandma's,
When the rain was falling down.
With just the tin roof above me,
Such a sleepy sound.

Grandma would help me up the
    stairs,
and tuck me in the bed,
leaving me with the music,
Without a fear to dread.

The roof is almost gone now,
And the house is rotten and plain.
But there's still alot of memories,
left here in the rain.

Maurice Waters
CHILDRENS WAY
A child
With a toy
Knows joy.

But a child
Without
Will only cry and pout.

What price
Must we pay
To raise a child
With or without today.

Geraldine Kilgore
8:28 P.M.
At this moment that I stand here
By mother's coffin. How I mourn.
Far away across the country
My first grandson has just been
    born.
God's great plan is all mysterious;
Yesterday He took-today He gave.
And I stand with deep emotions,
    trembling
Between the cradle and the grave.

Jeffrey S. York
CONFUSEDICTORIAN
Madness minus method
    trade of will for whim
        scythe-curving
godstrokes de/creation
    And twisting living stalks (Into
        amputated).
    Teleprompter men
Helicopter beat/heart blades
    some mornings
taste like ashes. They
    scatterdance to whispers
    and stray from Eden—
I had questions these
    rhetorical congregations of
        ambiguity
(If love and justice both are
blind, who leads when they
        dance?);
    but thought harbors malintent
        for trust
    if words are skimmed from scalp
        and dissolve
like solitary sugar in wet light. so
    Maybe
    it all runs in bad circles
    and starts where it ends, It does
        or maybe not
depending on how gray it is.

Susan K. Wermager
HARMLESS VIEWS
The world's out of time
Seems such a crime.
Fate held in a single blast;
How long can it last?
Life on such shaky ground,
waiting for silent sound.
Who holds the deadly gun?
What will it have won?
Human lives so precious;
Human minds so vicious.
Nuclear Arms race,
here, face to face,

seemingly filled with grace,
pull the trigger, not a trace.

Stella Handley

Stella Handley
**I Learned About Jesus In
Grandma Rocking Chair**

I learned about Jesus in grandma
rocking chair. Storie's of the Bible;
And how he came to be here. She
    told
me God sent Angel picked Mary,
    for best.
She excepted at the Angel
    request. Mary,
being on the wise. It was
    Almighty God,
who opened up her eyes! A
    darling baby
sent from Heaven. Mary, would
    of never
changed her life if she could.
    Because
he created every thing on earth
    that
good. And he's the only one that
    lives a
life the way we should; He's the
    power
of Heaven a light that never goes
    out!
If you will only believe in him,
    with out
a single doubt; I know Jesus has
    grandma up in her rocking
in Heaven, rocking chair! Her
    presence is missed down here.

Sandy S. Conn
THE TWO OF US
When two are one
We have fun.
When two are two
We are blue.
If we stay together as one
A life forever, we will have won.
If we stay together as two
We will not always be true.
So shall we say, we two are one
And our lives have just begun.

Nicolette D. Bernard
WHY MOMMIE?
"Mommie, tell me why?
Tell me why kids laugh at me——
Tell me why they tease and jeer,
"You're just not like you're 'spoz
    to be.'"

"Mommie, tell me why?
Tell me why their mommies
    stare——
Tell me why they say 'bout me,

"What a pity, 'when you're not
    there.'"

"Mommie, tell me why?
Tell me why if God is kind——
Tell me why He made my legs
Twisted and deformed like mine."

"Son, I cannot tell you why
He chose you among the rest.
But since you've come into our
    lives,
Precious Child, our home's been
    blessed."

Dorothy Webb
TO REMEMBER
Gentle lilacs waiting for the kiss
    of the morning sun
Sweet smelling earth, damp and
    dark, free at last of winters cold
    blanket
I think of you, and wonder do
    you ever think of me?
Delicious nectar trickles down
    my face, I lie in the tall green
    grass
My eyes dazzled by the brilliance
    of the sky
I remember how we were, and I
    smile
Children's laughter, cool water
    lapping at my feet
The sky and the sea are as one
I remember us with tenderness
    and tears
October days, cool winds
Golden leaves cling desperately
    to grey branches
Beautiful even in death, goodbye
    is cruel to all of nature's
    children
Bare trees, mounds of snow
    cradled in there boughs
Firelight, warm comforters, cups
    of tea
I remember how much I love you
Did you ever love me?

Peggy Hyatt Rudd
COMPLEXITIES OF LOVE
She *entered* the relationship
    with a nesting instinct and
    a desire to belong.
He *approached* the relationship
    with a conquering instinct and
    the desire to go on
    to conquer another.

The relationship for many years
    remained a struggle.
Her trying to constrain him;
His trying to escape.

Time changed the rules of the
    game and the players.
Now he craves the security of
    nesting;
    while she is trying to escape.

Maria Tummillo
TO BELIEVE

---

*To my Mom: Thanks for
everything. To Victor: Thankyou
for always being near.*

To believe of the love
That is not there.
Is to find in him
He can only care.

To discover the dream
Of the love so true.

John Campbell, Editor & Publisher

Though he not discovering
The dream with you.

To dream and discover
To love and believe.
The one you will seek
Is of whom you'll recieve.

Ms. Jayne Harris
TALES OF FIRE
The hot pungent breath of the fire
Pervades the night,
Muttering hypnotically,
Its single sibilant voice
A choral issuance
From numerous tongues of flame
Its language more primal
Than the drone of bees
More mystical than the litanies
  of monks.
Murmured chronicles of Earth
Of cycles so vast and
  age-consuming
As to defy mortal perceiving;
Whispers of tropics and glaciers
Reptiles and mammoths
Tinder and lightning
And the forebears of Man;
Enigmatic susurrations
Of the Time Before
When all was naught
And the Time to Come
When it shall be so again.

Ruth V. Lewis
ANCIENT COAL
Through the worst
Some good becomes of it.
I adhere to this.
Many aeons ago
The water-covered Earth
Sank marshy beds
Of tall lace ferns—
And formed solid seams of coal.
Through vast seasons of time
This great resource was lifted
  upward
Into the rugged hills.
And now, tonight,
As the glowing embers
Warm my study-room
I see,
  I feel,
    I know! . . .

Lucille L. Todd
DREAM CASTLES
Come, little girl, take my hand
Walk down paths of
  might-have-been
Once I walked like you, full of
  questions
Hair in pig-tails, dirty face,
  scarred knees,
Full of life, anxious to meet it all
Knowing not that life can scar
  when you fall.
You get up, brush aside, though
  smiling, the tears
Rush on towards another bout
  with life.
You will make castles in the sand
Tearfully watch them washed
  back into the sea.
But you are from sturdy stock;
  you will not quit
Probably stomp your foot, cry out
  in anger
Return to your castle, your life.
So it will be, scars, feelings of hurt
Dream castles swept away. Will
  you? I don't know.

Perhaps you will be more
  fortunate than I,
Making new castles of brick and
  stone.
Knees that heal, no scars, feelings
  that do not the heart break
Strength of mind and wisdom in
  making your decisions
A foundation that is strong, true
  to yourself
Dreams that will endure, castles
  that do not return to the sea.

Cynthia Waters
LING-LING'S SORROW

*Ling-Ling's first cub was born—
and died— one day in July, 1983
at the National Zoo.*

A little baby was born today—
A tiny, cuddly panda boy,
And 'though I wept, it was not
  with
The tears that I would shed for joy.

He lived for only three brief hours;
The keepers, helpless, watched
  him die,
And Ling-Ling watched and
  silently
Kept vigil, for she could not cry.

Her heart must have been filled
  with love—
She nuzzled him when he was
  born,
She licked him and she picked
  him up,
But at day's end she was forlorn.

She knew her baby son was dead;
The time he spent with her was
  brief.
She does not have the power of
  speech—
She could not tell us of her grief.

I cried for her, since she could not,
Nor does she know within the
  scope
Of one more year she might give
  birth
Again—but I know and I hope.

Lisa C. Brown
THE MEMORY OF LOVE
I often think of this past year
We were so close, it brings out a
  tear.
Sometimes I miss it, the love and
  all.
At school I still see him in the
  hall.
I was so sure that together we'd
  stay.
I remember it vividly, each and
  every day.
I wonder what I feel now.
I wish I could know, but how?
There are so many emotions; love
  and such.
I'm so glad, though, that we've
  stayed in touch.
Why does it happen, nobody
  knows.
That's just, I guess, the way life
  goes.
I think I still love him; but there
  still is doubt—
and I'm not sure it's true; what's
  this all about?
The memories are fresh within

my mind.
I know now that I must put him
  behind.
Sometimes my heart gives that
  feeling a shove,
or is it just this . . .
                 The Memory of Love

Karen Leah Segovia
FLORENCE
In isolation and solitude she
  lingers,
in search of contentment and
  happiness
When her eyes shine bright and
  she gives
you a smile, she reaches to touch
  you,
but she is so helpless
She tells some old stories and
  recites them again;
That is all she knows—past life
  with her kin
When she reaches for a cigarette
  and is
constantly talking, without even
  lighting
it, she begins smoking
Her family consists of two little
  dogs;
she feeds them and bathes them
  making sure of no flaws
When she hears beautiful music
  that
makes her want to dance, she will
  show
you her talents with an old hat
  and dress
I love this lady and think of her
  every—day;
I'll miss her old stories and the
  laughs
we had together when she goes
  away.

Jeff Fredman
ALPHABET SOUP

For P. T.

Clustered among pieces
of peas and carrots
were the letters of your name
and every time I
arranged them
they broke apart again
  It was all that I
could do
to force the letters in line
but I lost you in
the carrots
Every single time

Ruth L. Johnson
TROUBLES?
Whether we have arthritis
  or blindness
We all have our crosses
  to bear
And as we meet closer
  together
Each other's problems
  we'll share.

The path of our life
  is more easy
If we boost one another
  along
And say a kind word to

our neighbor
And lighten your load
  with a song.

Now let us all pull here
  together
And try to cheer others
  today
We might just make
  somebody happy
By one little word that
  we say.

Jorgi Russell
LOVE AND MERCY
Like a river to the sea
Flows God's love to me,
Love and mercy full and free;
May it ever be.

He who guides the sparrow's flight
Turns to light my night,
Fills my blinded eyes with sight,
Keeps me by His might.

Kevin Dean Van Buren

Kevin Dean Van Buren
BLACK CONSCIENCE
Hello,
remember me?
You try to disregard me,
but you know I'm here.
Dark latent thoughts,
delicately hidden within . . .
Created by blatant wrong doings.

My excruciating predominance
imperceptibly corrodes
the stronghold of innocent
  ignorance,
and guilt flows through the cracks.

For I am the epitome of
  pestilence . . .
Brought into being through pure
  cognizance
of malicious acts.

You take drugs, attempting to
  elude my presence.
You contrive devious ways to put
  me out of mind.
Though your efforts are futile.
You can't destroy me.
So feed me, build me,
make me rockribbed.
One day I will break
these barriers of restraint,
and I'll drive you straight to
INSANITY!!!

B. P. Eshbaugh
OCCULTATION
The vision breaks in torment,
  seeks, insistent:
  Like long and seemly leaps of a

gazelle
In boundless runs; like a
brimming tempest's well
Which pours its sweetly sour
drink intent
Upon my unquenched
maddening thirst that grows
Though solely in my dark and
dusty mind;
Like a short lived round corona
defying kind
And loving souls, condemning
life's cold foes.
These halo'd moons have mercy
but sing their lay
Of labor briefly, shed the rays of
prescient sight
Illum'd but only for an instant;
herald's flight
Is bold man's courage, reaching
out to say
That he is god. The light will
come again
To brighten life, not aspiring
gods or men.

Patti Hombs
LONELY

---

*This poem is dedicated to my
beloved friends and family.
During the months spent away
from home, there were many
hours spent alone. The mighty
Oak outside my third floor
window, inspired my poem.*

I have a friendly neighbor,
who waves every day.
 Never do I peer from my window,
my neighbor looks this way.
I'm sure the neighbor's been
there many, many years.
 So strong and stately looking,
with out any fears.
 I've seen a squirrel,
two or three—,
take refuge in my neighbor's arms.
My neighbor is a tree.
 My friend is slowly changing.
The limbs that were so full and
green, are getting frail and thin.
I can see in between.
 The big fellow's robe,
with warm protective sleeves,
fall slowly, gently piling, down
around his knees.
 Each paisly print has dropped
one by one, leaving my friend
dis-robed, and shivering, in a
 more
distant sun.
 The naked grey branches
reaching out so very high.
Strong, secure——holding up the
sky.
 You're Peaceful and resting now,
Soft, white cloth adorns each arm,
Sparkling and glittering,
adding to your charm.
 Soon God's exclusive pattern
will prevail—and every bird will
sing.
 Once again, you'll be robed,
a refreshing garb of Spring.

debbi giglio-bowles
Moonlight Dreamer
It is to the stars that I look for
 answers to lifes most weariest

ways.
They hold no wisdom nor advice
 but gleam with hope, peace and
 love.

In their solitude . . .
 how ancient they seem to man;
 how beautiful they seem to
 lovers.
Courageously they stand against
 time as sentries to the heavens
 above.

If for answers we are looking, we
 are right to choose the stars.
For if you choose the brightest
 sparkle, its brilliance will burn
 inside your heart and guide
 your spirit to a wealth of
 knowledge.

To know the answers is to have
 faith in oneself and carry truth
 for others.

The stars hold secrets within
 their silence beckoning for
 those who believe and for
 those who dare to challenge
 their mystery.

Marion Palm Riola
CITY RAIN
The city shrinks
when it rains.

Nylon spoked shields
spread and bloom on slender
stems in colors to
challenge a rainbow
cut in grey.

Pools of palid water grow
mushrooming over
sidewalks and sewers.

Sweaty music slops over
into the corners of our ears
nesting into soggy collars.

Cars cough mucous vapor
steaming, blowing, pushing
over sand
sitting beyond the goddess of
 freedom
who guards our shore while
 locking
the night.

Amy Pittenger
FREEDOM'S BEAUTY
We can train a horse,
And he'll obey,
Everything we do or say.
But when we watch him running
 free
He's not the horse we always see.
For even though his body's ruled
A horse's heart cannot be fooled
So in a sense he'll always be,
Majestically running, wild and
 free.

Kym Davison
**Holocaust at
 Herculaneum: 79 A. D.**
It is an awesome sight
piles of human skeltons
like a moment frozen in time.

Beside a boat, a sailor
clutching an oar
(in a frantic effort to escape)
looks towards the heavens
to see volcanic ash.

A servant girl
clutching a baby in her arms

(in a frantic effort)
looks towards the heavens
maybe for the first time
to see volcanic ash.

As if time preserved
skeltons are unearthed
from under six feet of volcanic
 ash.

May God have mercy on the find!
The finders have "Evidence
Unearthed in Volcanic
Mysteries."

Elva M. Hull
1933 WAS THE YEAR
Nineteen Thirty-Three we took a
little trip to Cannon Beach in
our little Model T. As we
buzzed along the highway, we
would sing our hearts out. We
would sit on the beach,
watching the evening stars
come out as daylight faded
away. Our friend the moon
shine's down on us.

We would say such silly things—
then laugh ourselves into tears.
Then we'd kiss them all away.
We'd go dancing in Seaside
with the Archie Loveland's
Band. He would play our
special love song. Come dance
with me and let me sing you
my love song.

We had the sweetest love of all.
A heart can feel so many
things that words can never
show. We were learning to play
the song of life. That's why our
love was so sweet. Now years
have passed since that day by
the sea, but never has love
seemed so close by.

Edith (Sue) Bowman
DADDY—WE LOVE YOU

---

for my Dad, with all of my love

Daddy, you are the very best,
You are better than all the rest.
You've always been there, in
 times of need,
It can't have been easy, with so
 many mouths to feed.
But feed us you did, and helped
 us along,
And through it all, you've been so
 strong.
Sometimes you must think,
 you're taken for granted,

Sometimes we've raved and
 sometimes we've ranted.
But taken for granted, that you
 are not,
For we appreciate, we love you a
 lot.
For there is no Father who is
 finer,
You're a definite ten, certainly
 not a niner.
Maybe it's not often spoken
 aloud,
But we all know it, the whole
 crowd.
We have the best, the gentlest,
 the kindest,
The most handsome, the coolest,
 the finest.
So, as you go through each
 passing day,
Remember our love, let it help
 you along the way.
May the sun shine on you, may
 your days be bright,
In everything that you do, let our
 love be your light.

Doris H. T. Harrison
The Bursting Of Spring
The Apple Blossoms bursting
 wide now beautify the tree
It makes a Springtime picture
 that is beautiful to see
Fragrant lovely blossoms fill the
 air like a bright bouquet
As the winds gently sway your
 flowering branches today.
Springtime is a season of joy,
 hope and cheer,
Presenting beauty all around us
 to see, and hear
No matter how sad and
 discouraged we may be,
New happiness is born as we
 behold leaves budding on a tree
For the bleakness of our spirit
 like the beautiful Springtime
 tree,
Is singing with hope and joy—
 look at me!!
And lose the wintry darkness,
 and let your heavy heart sing
For as the Winter ends, then
 begins the joy of Spring.

Lois Moore
PAINT ON THE SNOW
 A few more miles,
 And asleep in his bed:
 Was the only thought,
 In the driver's head.

 Till he happened to see,
 In his light's soft glow:
 The tiny traveler,
 'Most buried in snow.

Lori Ann Keller
SHIP OF MANY DREAMS
It sits alone at the dock!
 waiting for the stern to rock.
Finally it slides out into the sea,
 as it glides to make history.
We watch from the great big peer,
 to see all the sailors give a
 cheer.
The bilowy masts flow swiftly,
 in the night air that is quite
 misty.
Then it sinks and rises,
 while it disappears over the
 horizon.

So gently he smiled,
So gently he said:
Oh, no! Tiny possum,
Go back to your bed.

Go swiftly! Go now!
To your warm soft lair,
In your mother's warm pouch:
There's safety there.

This eighteen wheeler's,
Got power to go:
If I put on the brakes,
It will skid on the snow.

SCREEEEEEEE!!!

Oh, No! Tiny traveler,
Guess now I'll never know;
Why we're lying together,
Making paint on the snow.

Donna Joy Bowman
Before, During, and, After
Before you came into my life,
I was lonely and empty.

Now that your here, not only
can I feel and touch; I can
love and be whole.

You make my life more exciting
with each passing day.

You've made me realize just how
important I can be.

Now that you've gone I once
more am lonely and empty.

But, you left me with the courage
to go on living and loving,
instead of being withdrawn
into a shell as a turtle.

I not only thank you, but love
you and will always remember
the wonderful things you
brought into my life and
shared.

Catherine Ferrara
A Case Of Too Much Fright
The lights were out.
    The room was dark.
My little dog Peanuts
    started to bark.

I ran to the window,
    the door, then the lock.
When all of a sudden,
    I heard such a knock!

My heart was a'thumping
    My stomach was sick.
My legs started shaking—
    The door knob went click!

I hid in the closet
    and held the door tight.
Something was coming—
    Was I ready to fight?

I peeked from the key hole
    and oh, what a sight.
It was Mommy and Daddy
    who caused this whole fright!

John H. McCullough
**Why Do You Say "I Don't
Understand You"**
I really don't know why you say
    that, for I'm surely the simplest
    of men.
I just want a place to hang up my
    hat, and to raise an occasional
    hen.
To catch an occasional catfish, in
    a stream that is shaded and
    clean.

To eat an occasional beef dish,
    trimmed in things I have seen.
To throw a rock at a rabbit, and
    walk through some land of my
    own.
To sit on a porch as a habit, and
    think of old friends I have
    known.
To wake in the morn to the soft
    sound, of a rooster and coffee
    a'perk.
To jump out of bed with a quick
    bound, eager to get at the work.
To breathe in some air full of
    country, not anything strange
    to the nose.
Familiar old smells, like a pine
    tree, mown hay, fried bacon, a
    rose.
Is this so much to ask really,
    so much after all of these years?
To some this may all seem quite
    silly, but its all I want truly,
    my dears.

Miss Desiree Genevieve Goins
This Is How I Love You
I love you so much today
and tomorrow will be the same
    way.
I love you with very little pay.
Just let me hold you if I may
and you can kiss me in your
    tender way.
With you I'm happy everyday.

Linda Cheryl Escaip
IN THE EYES OF A CHILD

---

*For Matt I'm dedicating this
poem to you because no matter
where you are, I'll always love you.*

I sat staring in the eyes of a child,
Finding innocence, so tender and
    mild,
Seeing his world so truthful, so
    alone,
Feeling rejected and away from
    home.
I remember this child,
This warm, caring child,
I'll love him as long as I live,
And if I could, for him, my life I'd
    give.

I let my mind ponder
And my heart wonder,
But that always leaves me sad.
It makes me remember the child I
    once had.
In my thoughts I see the past,
How the days went by so fast.
The distant laughter sends echos
    through the room,
Chasing away the sorrow and the
    gloom.
Then I turned to the portrait on
    the shelf
And saw a reflection of myself,
In this reverie, so deep yet so mild
There were tears in the eyes of a
    child.

Helene Suzanne Pomeroy
ANOTHER SAD MOON
I saw you watching me in varying
    ways and when the moon went
    'round our heads for the last
    time, I looked out the window
    and started to cry . . . for you,
    for me, for all the undone

gestures that we could have
    tried to act out . . . so many
    rehearsals were scheduled and
    when the hour came to call on
    you for just a simple line to
    repeat, you bowed in silence
    and left my stage; left me there
    to close the heavy curtain
    alone . . .

I was tired and felt so betrayed;
    my weary dreams lay in a
    soiled heap at my feet . . .
    they looked like discolored
    weeds and I felt them grow in a
    sudden urge and they choked
    me in slow motion . . .

I could only run to hide; run to
    feel the pain stab my back and
    keep me awake . . . for I feared
    the dark and sleep I had
    learned not to trust . . .

I saw your eyes smile just for a
    moment when you thought I
    was looking down in my
    lap . . . your hand took mine
    ever so slowly and I felt weak
    and in love with you all over
    again . . . It was getting much
    darker outside; the sun always
    goes down before my swollen,
    wet eyes . . . and I can still
    hear that night music follow
    the moon 'round and 'round,
    and I am sad . . .

D. Roby-Weaver

D. Roby-Weaver
BANANA TREAT
There is a fruit slim and curved
With endless ways to be served.
Cut it lengthwise and have a split,
Or peel it down and eat it bit by
    bit.

Never loners—on stalks they're
    batched,
Stacked one over one as if all
    attached.
Everyone enjoys them it is plain
    to see—
Especially the monkey who apes
    you and me.

There's puddings, cakes, and pies
    to please.
You'll find them in salads—even
    daiquiris.
They're rich in potassium, so I've
    been told,
And good for the young, middle-
    aged, and old.

They're easy to peel as one, two
    three—
On this I am sure you will all
    agree.
However, if you value your life at
    all,
Don't step on the peel—you'll
    slip and fall.

Charlene Matson
I CAN SEE YOU
What has happened to you?
must I wait here and stand you
    up when you fall?
Bit by bit you will come apart, as
    I have just thinking about you
    and no love can come again.

The air in the way that you
    breathe makes a strong fearful
    urge to leave.
A simple song to be sung long,
    loud and clear. A dramatic,
    mystic mind so dear.
It's you that I see in the clouds
    over me.
And you look right through, not
    even seeing me, even though I
    can see you!

Blair W. McShirley
AUTUMN OF LIFE

---

*To My Father and Mother—
God Bless Them.*

And so I sit, and read and watch,
An old man now, and yet
Not so old, except in thought.

The thought of others, they stare
although they are not concerned,
For who thinks of an old man,
Wrinkled and weathered, and
    young no more.

They rush by me, helter Skelter
Without seeing the bird fly.
A baby cry, they care not.
For man, keeping pace with man,
Forgets, oh how he forgets
To be slow, to enjoy, to roam
    about.
Until one day he is old, then will
    he
slow, and watch, to enjoy this life.

Old man am I?, No not so old.
Wrinkled, grey, I move as though
I am a snail, but I see life all
around me, reaching out to touch
    me.
A church bell rings, a sound of
    peace,
I am still young, my heart beats
    life through me.
And so I sit, and read and watch,
    an old man, no
A child of wisdom, yes.

John R. Richardson
FOOTPRINTS IN SAND
I've kept my heart from bitterness
When there was hatred all around
The motivation demanded revenge
Excuses to forgive I found
Still I could not keep from
    lonliness
Still I could not keep from being
    sad
I held on to a fading hope
Because that hope was all I had
I kept on believing
I still dared to dream

Our World's Best Loved Poems

Carlos Rosales
I LOVE YOU
I talk to you on the phone
but I wish that I would talk
to you in person, hold you close
to me, and touch your soft skin.

When I am with you, I feel that
we are the only human beings in
the whole world; I see no one but
you.

Whoever I see, I see your face
and no one else. I feel lucky
that I have someone like you.

I dream about this special
night that I spent with you,
I will always have the memories
in my heart because:

"I LOVE YOU"

Brenda Arrowood
THE BRIGHTEST STAR
I stay awake at night
Thinking of you
Wondering if you ever cared
If your love was ever true.
Looking out the window I see the
stars
One by one, they begin to appear
Slowly one falls
Like a falling tear
A tear I cried for you
When you walked away from me.
You scarred my life forever
My life will never be the same.
I close my eyes and wish
Upon the brightest star
That someday I can love again
And take away your hidden scar.

Edith Slape Ratliff
MICHELLE
I want to thank you, Michelle
For the dawn you bring each day
It is like a kiss from the skies
That bends down low to light our
way
I'm always grateful for the stars at
night
And the blueness of the heaven
When the moon is shining bright
And for all the precious loved ones
Whom I hold so very dear
I want to thank you for each
moment I live
And the thousand little blessings
That to each of us you give.

Jan Yancey
THE LORD'S RETURN
I wake each day, before the dawn

and wonder where my life has gone

Before I turned to Christ the King
I thought that I had everything
And then one night while I was
home
And in my bedroom all alone
I knelt down in humble prayer
Then I knew my Lord Was there
He said he'd guide me through
each day
If I would remember him and pray
I said to him my God above
I'll treasure forever your eternal
love
He hung upon a cruel tree
To cleanse the sins of you and me.
So friends look to him each day
and take a moment to stop and
pray.

Look upon his nail scarred hands
and try very hard to understand
Take a glance at his pierced side
and behold our Lord who lived
and died
He is coming back for us again
So we should always be free from
sin
What a happy time we'll have
that day
When Jesus rolls the clouds
away.

Vernice Virginia Mitchell

Vernice Virginia Mitchell
TOMORROW
Tomorrow, tomorrow, tomorrow
tomorrow is now today
yesterday gave in to tomorrow
yesterday and tomorrow's today

Today brought little sunshine
yesterday we had rain
Tomorrow, tomorrow, please
bring sunshine again

I saw you yesterday standing in
the rain
today we missed each other
Tomorrow I'll see you again

Try to hold on to tomorrow
yesterday is gone
Today is moving on
All that's left is tomorrow
when it comes along

Mary Edelen May
UNKNOWN
Sitting in an unknown world
With only your senses to guide
you
Trying to think of where you
would like to be
Having tears come down because
of an unknown unknown
Hearing noises that would once
frighten you into locking the
doors
But now wondering if you will
ever make it to that untouched
lake or the virgin white
mountain top.

Unknown to anyone else that
beauty that you shall soon see
Camped under the stars of
night
Soon the unknown shall be
known.

Karen Elaine Ely
OUR BOYS
They send our boys far away.
And teach them the rules,
Of a game they will play.

But it's not a game,
It's for real
They teach them worse then to
cheat and steal.

It's a game of war,
That they all play.
A game of war they fear day after
day.

Bombing and shooting they fall
to the ground.
They wish for relief,
But there's no help around.

The French and us,
We lost our guys.
It all came as a bad surprise.

They play the game,
Maybe against their will.
They fight and fight untill they
are still.

These days of sorrow,
We feel in our heart.
These days of war will tear us
apart.

Peace is the one thing that we
bequest.
Then we may bring our boys
home,
And lay them to rest.

OUR BOYS

Deborah Lynn Chesi
THE WAIF
I sat amongst the other jigsaw
pieces
Waiting to complete the puzzle.
Clumsy hands fondled me,
Ruggedly pushing me against a
jagged edge.
I did not fit there either.
I was torn away from a place
I had almost become comfortable
in.
I knew I shouldn't be there,
But for a moment
I had a feeling of belonging.
I wanted so much to be a part of
the picture.
It had happened so many times.
Each time I became anxious . . .
But I never did fit in.
One day the puzzle was finished.
The picture was complete;
But I remained outside by the
empty box.
A mistake in an earlier time
I guessed.
Placed in the wrong box
In a moment of haste.
Still, I remained . . .
Unsure of what I was waiting for.
And sad in realizing I would
never know
What picture I had been meant to
complete.

Mike P. Diehm
THE BEAT OF THE RAIN
The rain pounds out a complex
back beat,
Birds join in an overlay.
Wind blows through my opened
mind,
Shadows dance, and slip away.

Said she loves me, echoed back,
A distant train carries through
the air.
The walls are alive with an even
glow,

Thoughts drift on through scenes
of nowhere.

Shades of blue that paint my
mind,
Cooling water running past.
Pictured paradise at my feet,
Like in the dream I wish would
last.

The tune of nature slowing down,
Wind blown curtains dance and
sway.
Dreary motion, back and forth,
To the chorus this grey day.

The beat of the rain
Can open your mind to the
chorus of grey.

Shirley L. Fahrny
HALLOWEEN TRADITION
It started out
So long ago
Which Halloween . . . I hardly
know.

The children came
From all around
To catch a glimpse and hear the
sound
Of screams and moans
That filled the night
And clanking chains that fed
their fright.

A sudden movement
Caught their eye
Some . . . terrified . . . might start
to cry.
A black-gloved "paw"
Appealed with charm
Assuring them there was no harm!

Through blackest whiskers
A voice that purred
Beckoned for treats . . . of which
they'd heard.
This faded cat
Appeared each year
Renewing every young child's fear!

Though each one knew
Her face and name
They loved this neighborhood
lady's game.

Jonathan S. Picklesimer
THE SUM OF LIFE
Through the sands of time
We tumble and toss;
Only to find that we are lost.

The present, the future,
The past—
What do they mean? Alas, we
Find out.
The days fly by, the months,
And the years,
Through all kinds of toils and
Tears.

This is the sum of life
Going swiftly by
Without time to sigh
Like sand through an hourglass.

Mark Edward Hammann
SUNDAY COMPOST
You say
you saw
but did you see

In they came
dressed to kill
through hot

        through cold
hidden faces

meaningless embraces
lost in thought
            drunk in passion

Did the answer come
is the demon gone

I was there
and never saw
but Oh yes!
I see

Betty Ann Wooley

Betty Ann Wooley
AUTUMN
Should I be asked to choose
One season among them all
Though I love Spring Summer
    and Winter
The most I love is Fall

Her quiet way of showing
It's time to put to sleep
Flowered faces the Summer
    embraces
And ask the trees to weep

Sad, but still coming soon
A beauty of snowy white
The crispy glow of Winter's
    moon
The winds of song at night

Then youth of Spring again
    appears
Eager to show her gown of green
And soon becomes as Summer
    nears
A lady's warmth in her supreme

The quiet days are here again
The lovliest season of them
    all
Her presence nears like golden
    years
The one I love the most is Fall

Cheryl Annett Whipple
LAUGHTER
Laughter
I hear laughter
Children laughing
Music to my ears
Joy
Happiness
Signs of laughter
Brings good times
And cheer
I hear laughter
From down the hall
Noisy playgrounds
Enchanted laughter
In the streets
Of our home
Laughter—
Music of the Galaxy

Geneva S. McDow
**The One Hundred Twenty
Nine**
In the great Atlantic Ocean,
    Oblivious to tides and time,
Lies the brave men we'll
    remember, The one hundred
    and twenty nine.
In that dark and dismal water, we
    may never know just where,
But of one thing we are certain,
    They are resting in Gods care.

We may never know the reason,
    All these brave men had to die,
We've no choice, but to accept it,
    But we'll always wonder why.
We'll go on into the future, But
    we'll pause from time to time,
And breathe a prayer in sad
    remembrance, Of the hundred
    twenty nine.

Those men cannot be forgotten,
    History will record their
    names,
We must finish what they
    started, Or they will have died
    in vain.
Let each man respect his
    neighbor, Work together, never
    shirk,
Let the view from every angle,
    Show democracy at work.

And if by some unknown
    mystery, They are watching
    what we do,
Let them see us up and doing,
    With A will to carry through.
Even though we'll have our
    problems, Brought about by
    passing time,
In our prayers we'll still
    remember, The one hundred
    and twenty nine.

julie ryder
you smiled——again
    one blustery night—
mid—march—
i watched a warm,
furry figure,
    snow—cloaked
and breathless,
doubled in
    helpless laughter.
that alaskan night
was three months long
    —ago—
and now, at last,
i glimpse the sun
in the twitching corners
of your sad mouth.
    a fiber of light
erupts the sky——
morning?
or just another
storm . . .

julie ryder
COUNTRY—HOME BLUES
Soap and towel in hand,
grimace on frozen face——
    Good Morning Honey
and welcome to your
thirty—three thousand and
fiftieth day
on this earth.
    A hospital gown
under a backwards duster
topped off by a harness
——white straps to keep you

down——
ragged cotton stockings—
    your feet deserve better,
having carried you through
    mud and snow, hard times
    and pain
to this place—
a bed for the old,
four walls to die in,
wheelchairs and pureed food——
    Have a nice day, Honey.

Kristin Abbott
RAGE!
Being alone in the dusk of night.
    Running fast, but going
    nowhere.
Having to deal with many a
    fright.
    Reading the sign "BEWARE!"

Being thirty-five years old when
    you could swear
    You were still twenty.
Having no friends, though you
    are
    A friend to plenty.

Living in horror, terror, no love.
    Feeling the hell
That someday your children will
    fear.
    Thinking that none of this
    could really be real.

Loving someone, but not
    knowing who.
    Feeling hurt because no one
    loves you.
Reading a book with no ending.
    Leading a life with no start.

Ginny DuBois
LETTING GO

*This poem was written to and
inspired by my youngest
daughter Jamie Love Mom*

That night I watched you board
    the bus
I thought my heart would break
This was the first time you were
    on your own
And I hoped it was not a mistake.
So many things went through my
    mind
As I went back to the house
    alone
I couldn't believe how fast the
    years had passed
Or that my youngest was on her
    own.
We think we have so much time
    with our children to spend
And when it's just beginning, it's
    already time to end
The hardest thing to do is
    learning to let go
But go, my child, with my love,
    for there is much more to
    know.
I gave you life, but it is yours to
    live
So do what you must do.
The doubts I had were with
    myself
And certainly not with you
For you have done what you said
    you would do
And yes, my child I'm very proud
    of you.

Ms. Jean Boyce Capra
A MISTY, FOGGY DAY

*I wish to dedicate this poem to
my dear friends of poetry and to
my mother, Mrs. Ida Boyce, as
well as to my children, Judy,
Patty, and Carol, my
grandchildren and my dear friend,
Sal A. Capra.*

The earth is all ablaze today
    As autumn's trees stand arrayed,
In festive tones of golds and reds,
    God's palette of color displayed.

It seems God knows just how to
    paint,
    Betty scenes than any artist
    known,
And today as I was going to work,
    He had painted a fog, full blown.

As the bus driver took us carefully,
    Over the span of the bridge, to
    work,
The God of all our universe
    Obscured our vision quite
    sublime.

The vapors of the autumn fog,
    With mists so moist and fine,
Touched each tiny leaf on the
    trees
    Making this day especially
    mine.

For 'tis a grey, rainy day that I
    enjoy,
    And the vapors of a foggy day,
As well as the beauty in the
    rising sun
    With a rainbow over a river or
    bay.

The skyscrapers of the city skyline,
    Vanished like Halloween ghosts,
And street lights hung uncanny
    and still,
    Like a foreign planet's host.

The views of our world about us,
    God made for us to enjoy,
As He opens our eyes to inspire
    our hearts,
    With paintings of beautiful
    views.

Mrs. Adair Conlon
THE HALLOW EVE

Happy Birthday Marlin and Judith

The streets are dark and empty
No children's voices heard
The bats and cats are waiting
To have their night disturbed.

It was not long ago
That tiny feet would weave
Down each and every route
To celebrate the eve.

Now not a soul dare wanders
On this ghostly night
For fear that evil brews,
Doors are locked uptight.

Forgotten are the carefree ways
The children use to go,
Collecting special treats
From people they did not know.

There was no talk of razor blades
Or poisoned candies wrapped,

Shaped to kill young children
Before their life's uncapped.

Harmless pranks have
  disappeared
On the Hallow Eve,
Now we watch for pot and pills
And wish it had never been.

Louise D. Plant
ROSE

---

*Dedicated to: Rose Linda Staffa
Stevens My Best Friend and
Loving Sister*

A Rose is a flower,
rosey is a hue,
together they discribe
the Rose in you,
they come in red, yellow, pink
  and white,
they are Gods creation,
and heavens delight,
the Rose in you is soft and warm,
like the petals, but not the thorn,
a Rose like you,
grew one by one,
and shared her beauty,
from Sun to sun.

Debby Butler
TINY CHILDREN AT PLAY
Tiny children at play
Without a care in any way
To laugh—to cry
To live—to die
To love—to hate
To grow—it's fate

After you've grown
You think of what's gone
And wish you were once again
Tiny children at play.

Connie Krueger
MY OLD CAMPING SPOT
Slant-angled boxes
in muffled grays and browns
their sun-trapping panels looking
  south
have anchored themselves to the
  soft dark earth
where I once slept.
Framed by tidy borders
of green clipped hedge
and sunny red geraniums in pots,
their lush velvet grass
too chaste to sprawl on.

Squatters on my refuge,
they form a coffin lid that seals
  away
the ghosts of my childhood.
Smuggled lipsticks applied
  between giggles . . .
How will it feel to kiss a boy?
What do you say to him later?
Thoughts we lifted only as high
  as the trees. Timbers fell with our
  secrets,
buried beneath concrete
  foundations.

Rebecca G. Bates
THE SOCIAL SCENE
Society
dictates morality
but not kindness
The strict rules
are not tempered
with love
Discreetly done

anything is possible
But when the veil
of hypocrisy
is tattered and ripped
to reveal

A cry for help
A plea for understanding
A naked truth

Society turns up
it's dainty nose
in disdain
and sighs
My dears it's just
not done!

Bobbie Collins

Bobbie Collins
THEIR LAST FLIGHT

---

*Dedicated to Mrs. Larry
McDonald and Family*

They loaded up their bags and
  went on their way.
  Little did they know what was
  in store for them that day.
Many was the number that was
  on board, two hundred sixty
  nine and maybe more.
Some were Americans, some were
  not, but the tragedy of that day
  will never be forgot.
They were off their course so the
  Russians say, warning signals
  they did not obey.
But, instead of guiding them to
  the ground, the bloody
  Russians just blowed them down

Mrs. Mary K. Quisenberry
DAYS OF AUTUMN
The days are a gettin' shorter and
  the air a keener snap
Apples now are a droppin' in
  Mother Nature's lap
The mist at dusk is a risin' oer
  valley, marsh and glen
And its just as plain as sunshine
  Winter is a closin' in
The turkey gobblers now are a
  struttin' around again once more
Their mates are all done their
  nestin and batchin are 'oer
The Farmer he's a cuttin' down
  the fodder to fill silos so high
An he's sorta frettin' and
  complainin' of the drouth just
  gone by
But the air around now seems
  peaceful and scenes are good to
  see

Making something about
  Autumn stir inside the heart of
  me
Oh I just can't help being
  thankful to the Almighty
  (when)
We have garnered in such a
  beautiful, bountiful harvest
An' the frost has begun appearing
  on the Pumpkin again.

Linda Vokes
NIGHT VISITOR

---

*To all my brothers and sisters
living in U.S.A.*

As leaves swirling in the wind,
You rustle by my door
—always at the same hour.

Like the ticking of a clock,
I hear you moving outside,
—with your ghostly, swishing
  walk.

Whirring sounds fill the air,
As you hiss and snap,
—the way woodland branches do.

By the moonlight's shadows
You circle and weave
In and out of the foliage
On your way round my garden
—eating worms in the rain.

AND, I put a bowl of milk out,
Especially for you HEDGEHOG.

Fayma Caraway Johns
OCTOBER'S SKIES
No skies are bluer than October's
  skies——
  No days more fair and filled
  with promise bright
Of happy days to come that lie
  ahead
  After the Winter's night.

There is no dread of Winter's
  quiet sleep
  As crisp October lifts the spirit
  high,
With just a touch of sadness now
  to know
  That Springtime's flowers must
  die.

For those who've reached
  October's time of life
'Tis much the same——life
  takes a brighter hue;
The turbulence of Summer's
  storms now past,
  The skies are clear and blue.

October knows that Spring will
  come again
  And flowers——faded by
  November's blast——
Will bloom again for all eternity
  When Winter's sleep is past.

Suzanne Y. Bell
RONNIE'S POEM

---

*To Ronnie, whose name will
always be burned upon my heart;
And to my mother, Wanda Bell,
whose faith and love encouraged
me to further my talents.*

I've seen God on your face,
His home is in your smiles,

It's evident that He is your base
In the middle of you trials.

His love I know surrounds you
When you choose to worship Him,
His promises you cling to
When the world is deathly grim.

Sometimes you trip and stumble,
But which one of us does not?
Still your praise is no mumble
For His forgiveness you have
  sought.

And because of your seekings
And sincerity of your heart,
He is showing through His
  teachings
That from you He'll never part.

I'm praying for you dear brother
As you go life's narrow way,
In your heart you'll serve no other
Than the one you do today.

Angie Rabold
LION
You walk through the forest
  without a care
Arrogant and selfish, not wanting
  to share,
It makes me wonder what you
  have inside
To act so superior just to hide,
The act isn't working
I know something's lurking,
It's better to get it out
Than let it swim about,
The act on the outside means
  nothing to me
It's what's on the inside that I'd
  like to see.

Angela Quintieri
**Through the Eyes Of a
Child**
Through the eyes of a child
The world looks so big and
  wonderful
The carefree life of childhood
Has no worries except mere
  broken toys

But as we grow and we mature
Problems arise and answers are few
The breezy life of childhood
Is soon lost in the swirl of
  adulthood

No more are problems easy
The answers far more complex
But life is today and tomorrow
And yesterdays are no more.

Charlianne Brock
WHISPERS
I hear a whisper of love.
It's coming from your heart.
I hear the soft echo of your voice.
In my heart all of the time.
You have something special,
In the way you talk to me.
You're truly wonderful.
I hear whispers that,
We're meant to be together.
For as long as possible.
I feel your soft hands touching me.
I hear bells when I think of you.
My eyes seem to shine when,
I hear your voice or think of you.
I feel your lips kissing me so
  tenderly.
And you're so very tender and
  gentle.
I think about you all of the time.

289

Whisper into my ear,
I hear whispers of love.
From both of our hearts.
Your whispers of love meant,
So very much to me.

Ethel Pearce
HALLOWEEN

Halloween is drawing near, one of
my favorite times of the year.
The kids are as busy changing
their minds to what they want
to wear, as their mothers are
exchanging ideas, material and
finding the time to make their
atire.
They come in all sizes, shapes
and forms oh, how we love
seeing each and everyone.
There will be witches, clowns,
bunnies, cowboys and Indians,
ghosts, and gobblins and so
many others coming to our
door all out in the cool night
air, with spooks galore ooooooo!
The parties are all over at school,
oh what fun with E.T., Star
Wars, and more.
The churches are all so busy
getting ready for their famous
"Bob for apples game", come on
kids stop by real soon and see.
We gathered our pumpkins our
pies are all made, our Jack-O-
Lanterns are all lit, the candles
are glowing, our treats are all
ready, shall we get the night
going! SH SH I hear a knock.
Trick or Treat, oh dear a ghost, a
witch, ooooooooo!
You scare me. No ooooooo! E.T.
this is not a haunted house.
Have lots of fun kids and a safe
night ooooooooo!
How scary, ooooooo! The Hulk!
ooooooooo!

Judy A. Herrmann
LIFE

Today I caught glimpse of a
buttefly in flight,
Floating with the breeze as it
sparkled in the sun.
And with a blink of my eye it
was gone,
Fluttering off into the wind; never
to be seen again.

And so, people go in and out of
our lives.
We catch them for a moment and
they are something special,
A dear and warm person who
brings a touch of happiness to
our lives.
And, we grow to love them.

And then, just as the butterfly,
they too go away.
Even though we are saddened by
their loss, we should always
remember the light that shined
in our hearts.
And, we still love them.

Kalvin R. Capener
LEGEND

Upon October 31, I glanced
toward the clock,
And watched the swinging
pendulum as I listened to it
tock.
For every year at this time; on

October 31,
I watch the minutes slowly pass,
fearing for the worst.
The minute-hand struck
midnight; the clock began to
chime,
I counted them in silence, past
seven, eight, and nine.
But as it struck eleven, I quickly
drew my breath,
For instead of chiming number
twelve, the pendulum stood at
rest.
I heard a muffled hissing sound,
rising from my porch,
I moved and opened up the door
and saw the flaming torch.
It was rather long, and rather
lean, and rather on the floor,
And I'd rather throw it to the
street than have it at my door.
In my fear, I watched the blaze
take a definite feline shape,
And as I watched, the fire died;
the smoke curled in it's wake.
It looked up at me with firey
eyes, bared it's fangs and
yawned,
And I knew this was no black cat,
but a demon from beyond.
I turned and shook the door knob
with the strength of ten in zest,
But the door was locked; and as I
turned, it leapt up for my chest.
I swung wildly at the creature,
ignoring the tearing flesh,
But in the end, it pulled me
down; the smell of blood was
fresh.
I layed sprawled upon the
sidewalk, my blood pulsing to
the ground,
The last thing I remembered was
a deep-throat purring sound,
And thus the legend was fulfilled
on October 31,
The demons are out searching for
warm blood to quench their
thirst.

Anna B. Cook
FOR THIS

I need no epitaph to show that I
was here I don't regret that I
am gone; for this, I have no
fear.

I woke up every morning to the
melodies-no words, of endless
notes of harmony; for this, I
thank my birds.

And underneath my trellis, I
puttered many hours, admiring
nature's beauty; for this, I
thank my flowers.

I always loved the color blue,
'twas one of my favorite dyes, I
absorbed it every living day; for
this, I thank my skies.

There was no medication to calm
down my emotions, I had my
tranquilizer; for this, I thank
my oceans.

When my painting wasn't perfect,
and certainly no Picasso, I saw
colors that never ran; for this I
thank my rainbow.

And when a chill came over me,
through daisy fields I'd run, the

warmth would flow through
my veins; for this, I thank my
sun.
And when nightfall came upon
me, when life seemed like a
farce, my silly wishes would
come true; for this, I thank my
stars.
When my mind thought evil
things, it was drowned by soft
refrains, and cleansed by pitter-
patter; for this, I thank my rains.

Whenever troubles came my way,
and there seemed to be no end,
a loving hand would soothe
me; for this, I thank my friend.

I leave no worldly goods behind.
Don't think me to be odd, I
leave you all my legacy; for
this, I thank my God!

Pamela Duran Chavez
THE BUTTERFLY

---

*This poem I dedicate to my
mother and sister who
encouraged me to write this
poem. And for my step dad, who
loves butterflies.*

Look at the wings of the
butterfly,
Flapping so hard in the sky.
Going up higher and higher,
Letting the trees flash by.

Then he stops flapping his wings,
Only to go gliding down.
Down through the mountains
Down through the rivers
And again greeting everyone in
town.

Judith J. Carl
LAST TRIP TO THE PARK

These ashes about his feet
are years around a tree.
Most leaves brittle
some yet soft,
each a vein of memories.

A block of cement
he stares upon will be there
long after he is gone.

He holds his hands
shuffling his feet,
the chill in his bones
will repeat—will repeat.

Stay on your guard old man
a refuge you seek
relief as his coverlet
he sinks to his feet,
decades of dreams
will fade with his sleep.

Shirley Ann Barrett
POETRY

The verses so sweet
words can't describe
The feeling unique
One can't deny it

Rhythm that flows
And is on time
So good to know
It's more than a line

Peace that's within
And somehow brought out
Love, to give
Thoughts to think about

Muriel Hollingshead
THE GENERATION GAP

So says the mature and wise:

Save that quarter
Save that dime
Watch those pennies

Save save save

Don't spend a quarter on that
flower
It will only fade
Don't send a dollar card
They'll get well anyway
Don't forget those pennies

Save!

Save for that rainy day
Tomorrow!

To which the young replies:

A frigging tomorrow
When a mushroom-death
spends it all?

Shannon K. Leary
Captives Of the Human Kind

Tree of angelic beauty, how can
you stand tall while
Your children are stolen by the
wind?
While human life tramples over
their remains.
Surely you have love, though you
have not a heart!
"Child of God", it replied, "I am
old and weary.
My children leave to find their
princes, the wind is their carrier.
Humans are the dictators of
nature.
I have no choice but to sacrifice
my little ones as tribute.
Do not worry for me, little friend.
I will see you soon, when I join
my children."

Darla McBryde Haston
THE BLIND

The art of an abstract heart
a blind
camouflauge of the soul
you cannot see me
or into my feelings
i have hidden among
the rotting foilage
and the mossy jungles of
the war torn memories that
deny the war is over
no one has told my memories
they hold the fort
no way

no way
to communicate for
the lines are down
from piece of my heart
piece of my mind
no peace of mind
i find
that i cannot find the
art of the abstract heart
no soul camouflage
over and over no no no.

Sandra Becktold Dahlquist
THE HUNTED
The echo of a gunshot, ringing
through the air.
Riding on the breeze, sounding
everywhere.

The piercing of a bullet, in the
heart of a wild deer.
Dead, it drops to the ground, its
gentle eyes filled with fear.

A young and frightened rabbit
wiggles its long pink ears.
Its small pink eyes look startled
and begin to fill with tears.

A chipmunk scurries quietly to
an overhanging limb.
His little ears alert for the
gunshot in the wind.

The forest is still and threatened
as death lay all around.
Forever listening for that lone
and dreaded sound.

A helpless doe wanders endlessly,
searching for her child.
But her baby is dead, killed by
the gun of man, ugly and wild.

Stacey Brooks Siman
I CAN'T FORGET YOU
You've been the center of my
universe ever since I saw you
first
And now every dream that I
dream every song that I sing
reminds me of you
It seems I'll never get you off my
mind and I wonder if I will ever
get over you.
I knew you before I met you and
yet I didn't.
I loved you when I heard your
name.
Summer seems so long ago
Yet our meeting seems like
yesterday
Will it be forever before I see you
again?
Because I can't think of anyone
else
When all I can think of is you.

H. Frank Martin, Jr.
BACK TO THE SEA
I have a need today
to return to the sea.

Even to flee,
not backwards in time;
but forward to be nurtured
by the mother of life.

I need to taste the salty
air
and to be free as the
birds of the sea,
flying down from their
lofty heights
in a grand manner
and with grace.

To know that the water I
see has churned longer
than I could define
and bathed the beaches of
the earth.

I have the need today
to return to the sea.

Patt Fogerty
YOUR SON
Your son means the world to me
He's sweet and kind and loving
you see
He's gentle and caring and gives
so much
With emotions he's not out of
touch

He's got so much tenderness and
love to give
But he gets that from the life you
live
You've given him the strength to
need
In all he does he will succeed

He'll never outgrow his need for
you
That's something that he just
won't do
He'll always welcome your support
And keep with you a good rapport

He's botched things up now and
again
But with you there he'll always
win
Because in life the important thing
Is the love you receive and the
joy you bring

Reba Horton
OCTOBER GRACE

*"To My Family"—who has made
my life as beautiful as the colors
of Fall.*

The frail duration of summer
 Is on its last pall;
Quietly summer slips by;
 Into the beginning of fall.

The death of a season
 By nature we visualize;
Summer declining to repose;
 A rendezvous with the winter
 skies.

A delicate October month
 Shines through the uterus of the
 sky;
Teetering on the edge;
 Of inheriting winter's thigh.

Forming an intervenint chroma
 Terminating the era of hue;
Winter is traversing along;
 Awaiting its cue.

God has the blueprint
 To seasons and all;
Thank you Lord for the four
 seasons
 Especially fall.

Douglas S. Allman
THE SEA
As I sit here watching the
 beautiful sea
I realize it's beauty is in the eyes
 of me
Two nights ago it was raging wild
Now it's hard to believe it could
 be so mild

It came in with such force that it
 ate up the sand
The evidence is clear by just
 walking the strand
After a storm the beach is never
 the same
This makes us realize the sea will
 never be tame
The sea is so mysterious, the
 waters so deep
And in her depths secrets forever
 she will keep
God made the sun, the land and
 the trees
God made the seasons, spring
 summer, and winter freeze
He made living creatures all
 kinds, he made the birds
He made things so beautiful, it's
 hard to put into words
God made things as complicated
 as you and me
But one of the most mysterious
 things that he made
God made the sea

David J. Quinn

David J. Quinn
GHOSTS

*Dedicated to: the Ghosts in my
dreams who inspired me to
attempt their exorcism; the real
people who believe in me——my
Mom & Dad, my Wife, and my
Grandmother; and those who fall
somewhere in between.*

We all have ghosts we bid, "Stay
 buried;"
Unseen skeletons in spectral
 closets.
They come to us in our
 unguarded moments;
Some gild our memories——
 others inflict torment.

These phantom shades of
 yesterday
Profess to be the things that were.
But more often than not, they're
 twisted and bent,
Gross distortions of the reality
 they conceal.

Some haunt us with love that
 never could be.
While others mock us with deeds
 left undone,
As they flit back and forth
 through unconscious mind
And shadow the peacefulness of
 our swirling dreams.

I envy the man who fears not
 their taunts;
His dreams filled with laughter,
 his slumber untortured:
For I know when I rest my head
 on soft pillow,
I'm doomed to a visit from
 unsettling guests.

Christine M. Trucinski
A MOTHER'S LOVE

*To all Mothers who have met
their children's needs not only
materially, but emotionally;
spiritually as well and in this
given them freedom to speak
what's on their minds; in their
hearts.*

A Mother's love—is probably—
 the most-taken for granted,
 abused
 and important element in a
 child's life.
Her love is self-sacrificing,
 unconditional and resilient.
It is a combination of—total
 compassion,
 sensitivity and never ending
 patience.
It has an unquestionable quality of
 quiet fortitude and
 determined strength.
An essential ingredient is—
 a mixture of gentle humor,
 wholesome laughter, genuine
 smiles,
 sheer delights and
 unexplainable joy.
This love is proud of
 accomplishments,
 excited with good news and
 sad—at defeats.
It is a love that has to have—the
 wisdom—
 to know—when to reward or
 discipline,
 when to be involved, stand back
 or let go.
Within this love—is the innate
 knowledge—
 to understand—that the
 children—
 they have conceived and borne,
 taught and nurtured,
 guarded and pruned,
 need-someday—
 the freedom—to grow away—
 from her—
 no longer—as extentions of
 herself, but
 as individuals becoming
 totally—one with themselves.

Karen Bailis
DISCARDED WORDS
The virgin sheet of paper
Sits on the desk staring blankly
At the pen poised—thinking—
About to write its flourishing
 thoughts
Fulfilling the paper—its
 personality—its feelings
The cheerful poetic words swiftly
 appear
Adding a magical meaning to the
 life of the paper.
Slowly the pen withdraws—
Out of thoughts;

Nothing more to write—yet
unfinished.
A hand reaches toward the paper;
In a harsh grasp—it is crumbled
Into a tight ball of jumbled words
Thrown among the other discards
Into a can of abandoned work
And unwritten emotions.

Sonya Prescott
THE FALL
I always will wonder
Why Fall makes me sad
If it's the Winter ahead
Or the Summer we've had

Being between them
Makes you just want to think
Of the things that have happened
Oh, they've happened so quick

But, we must realize
We can never go back
All that's left are memories
Like words on a plaque

There to remind us
Of what's happened and done
We're racing with time
And of course time has won

Lisa Konewko
LUCK OF THE IRISH
Bombs explode like a gun salute,
But saluting they are not;
They end up like a firing squad
With all the horrors they have
wrought.

Tired young soldiers with heavy
hearts
Fighting for a sacred right,
"I want God and peace," they say,
Reflecting their will and might.

The beautiful Northern Irish
grass,
An innocent, rolling plain
Has sadly become a bloody pit
For the wounded and the slain.

Inside the frame of a church
A soldier kneels in the sand,
Praying to his God above,
A machine gun in his hand.

Come forward baby soldier boy,
Come forward and blow your horn
For the spiked four leaf clover
And the golden crown of thorns.

Strangely enough, a flower grows,
A body it blooms beside;
A lonely old woman crushes the
petals,
And over her son, she cries.

Lanie B. Cooper
REFLECTIONS

In loving memory of my son, Max.

When God made this beautiful,
wonderful world,
With it's blue skies and land and
seas,
It is clear that He knew from the
very start,
That we would be hard to please.
So for those who love the
melancholy days,
The leaves of red and brown—the
cornstalks tall,
The sound of gentle rain upon
the roof,
He made the fall.

For those who love the fireside
bright,
The falling snow in all it's
glorious splendor,
The carols softly sung at Xmas time,
He made the winter.

For those who love the gay, bright
days,
Who want to love and dance and
sing,
When nature paints the world
anew,
He made the spring.

For those who love the perfume
of the flowers,
The lilacs and humming of the
bees,
The breezes softly sighing
through the trees,
He made the summer days.

I've tried to pick the season I love
best,
I really think it must be fall,
But when all the others come
around,
I find I truly love them all.

Maro Rosenfeld

Maro Rosenfeld
BUTTERFLIES

---

*to Rochelle Finkelstein, Creative
Photographer who captured my
Soul in this photo*

You say
Butterflies are Free

Where
have you seen
a collection
of flees

James B. Hamilton, Jr.
A WINTER'S RAIN
A Winter's Rain all white among
the dirt.
Makes the little children smile
and takes away the hurt.
Deer breaking fast and running
free.
Through the powdered brush and
trees.

A Winter's Rain all white among
the dirt.
Covers roof tops and the steeple
of the church.
The coldness in the air freezes
ponds and the swelling lakes.
Children build snowmen and
frosty little cakes.

A winter's Rain all white among
the dirt.
Beautifies the view atop the
virgin hills.
Snowballs whizzing by.
Skiers taking flight down the
mountain trails.

A Winter's Rain all white among
the dirt.
Crystal icicles form below the
eaves.
The sun shines and sparkles on
the ice.
slowly melting the beauty
created by Father Ice.

Jan Hill
THE THINGS WE SHARE
We've shared the good times with
the bad
Where oh where is the love we
had
When we started anew, with only
me and you
Now's there's many all around
Telling us what we've found
They don't know the things we
share
They should leave, it's only fair
For us to have what we need
They should leave, yes indeed
We have something that is rare
Only we two can possibly share
All the good with the bad
I wish they didn't look so sad
Time will heal all our wounds
And we will know very soon
As we go from day to day
Sharing as we do in this way . . .

W. H. Keiser, Sr.
WHY
His frame was rigid, his legs were
bent,
From the body came an awful
stench,
He didn't seem to breathe at all,
He didn't move when someone
called.
I wondered why he was lying there
With mouth agape and that
vacant stare.
Then I overheard someone say
He had lain there for several days,
Since the day that he was killed,
When he ran out to chase an
auto's wheel.

Rachel Leroy Owens
FANTASY

---

*With all the love I have to give to
my mom and dad. Without them
I wouldn't be*

Ghouls, goblins, ghosts and a
haint,
faces made up with funny paint.
Boys as pirates, girls as queens,
the one day of the year to live out
dreams.
Knocking on doors yelling trick
or treat,
rush back home with goodies to
eat.
The shapes and shadows make
strange noises,
but up ahead there's friendly
voices,
Horror houses with graveyard
gloom

children afraid of a darkened room.
Was that a witch there up ahead?
I don't know but I'm going home
to bed!

Mary Hamilton Darrell
NEVER ALONE
In the still of the night
He is with me,
In the glare of the
noonday sun.
So I never fear, though the
way be far——
He'll be there when the
day is done.

As the thunder rolls in
the distance,
As the wind wails
over the land,
I do not fear for my
Lord is near;
Through it all He will
hold my hand.

In the quiet peace of
the dawning,
In the stillness at
break of day,
I will seek my Lord then I know
that He
Will be with me through
all the way

Carmen S. Jackson
MIDNIGHT SCARE
On a dark night
When the crickets were calm,
The sky was black
And the wind was small.
The clouds overhead
Were circling the moon;
It will be midnight very soon.
Then the clock struck twelve
And the bells were ringing.
The fog was rising
And the crickets were singing.
Then there came a loud scream
That echoed through the hills;
Everything was silent,
Everything was still.

Aurora Lee Wendt
A WINTER'S DAY
The freezing wind pierces the
many layers of skin.

Blades like silvered icicles slice
through all they touch.

Blood lays in a beautiful pattern
on the snow.

A white tooth falls on the soft
cotton and turns black.

A four fingered glove still under a
blade, is suitable only for a four
fingered hand.

An empty stocking cap stranded
in a ditch; children sledding on
smooth ice.

Lucille A. Norwalk
THE LAST ROSE

---

*Dedicated to my mother, Emma
C. Wilkins who fought the good
fight and was indeed mighty like
the rose.*

The last rose in my garden stands
stately tall,
Taller than all the summer
bloom,

Stretching toward heaven to be
seen,
Fragrantly sweeter in Autumn's
gloom.

A rose speaks of God in every
sense,
Each petal opening to glorify,
A velvety touch, its beauty
enhances,
A rose is a rose, no one can deny.

But the last rose in Autumn is far
more precious,
Its presence uplifts the
downhearted soul,
Giving hope to a Summer's fading
faith;
Mysteriously playing a spiritual
role.

Louise Ann Simpson

Louise Ann Simpson
A DYING MAN'S SONNET

To Ronny: *"May your love,
patience, and support continue to
flow into my life . . ."*

Am I not thy Servant,—thine
acolyte?—
Who drapes thine alter in
dazzling array
By offering to it each and every
day
Of my existence? Hence, dost
thou not requite
In by lending to me still another
night?
Why then dost thou permit such
worthy display
To spoil with age,—to ail and to
fray,
Knowing well whose eye ruin
seeks to delight?
O merciful one, I beg thee, attend
This fragile host whose spirit
stands shaken;—
And for thine Honour (mine
Honour), defend
Both Beauty and Essence which
thou hast forsaken!:
Drive thine Impetus through
Death's limitless bend,—
Where a desperate soul longs to
awaken!

Carrie S. DeBell
EROS
The beautiful rose long and strong
anchored into the earth
bowed its head into the storm
and wept into the dirt.

Soft petals sweetly scented
now tattered and wildly worn
wonder how they could survive
raging winds hailed by the storm.

The stem was pulling from
side to side as if to break the
earth
to free itself from tormenting
winds
and, from its birth.

Yet the roots held it firmly
as if by some magic force
gave the sweet rose strength
to endure through the worst.

And, as the rains subsided
the rose looked into the sun
its bouquet and beauty
now greater than it had begun.

Bob R. Galbreath
VENGEANCE
Vengeance, like the wind
Fiercely blows to and fro.
From the darkness of it's
Short night, returns so.
Malady of the heart
Usurper of the soul
Apollyon from the start,
Man divest of goal.

Daniel V. Lawrence
YOUR SOUL AWAY
Come to view as I close my heart
and
Kneel not into darkness, for I
turn away
Those things that caused my
death
To which I fell prey with you
When we grew to know not!
"Do," I say, to open the hour of
death
And let us sleep to slip into . . .
not afraid
Of the hell on fire as we know it,
it to be.
If not to yell forever into our own
pain,
For when we yell, not for
ourselves.
Invade not our domain to place
this hell in my hand,
When I loved you so, it killed me
deep, as . . .
Deep rivers flow quietly by, my
blood came clean.
You did steal my flesh and rotted
my name;
So hence, to hell is no place.
Now we, the one, shall tell of no
grace in you at all,
We, the one, will do as it is told,
when the East has died;
As I have loved once and will
love again.
For you took my blood, I live
again from yours,
Because you promised and named
me king.
For you did take and steal my life
and limb,
You laughed it away upon your
heads and precious children,
And those souls that we search
will cry to you
When you have no ears to hear,
And upon the striking hour . . .
you will have no life!

Lee Ann Cornell
THE LIGHT
A dark, ominous cloud surrounds
the essence of my being, filling
the corners of my mind.

I am surrounded by treachery,
anguish and despair.

There are those who are envious
and wish my destruction.
And some seek my soul as well.

A storm rages and the tension
mounts.
A cold, penetrating wind robs my
warmth.
I tremble and my heart swells.
The rain flows through my eyes
and touches upon those who are
near.

Darkness creates illusion and
deception.
Pathways become dim and hard
to follow.
I stumble and trip others.

I will not become a victim of
total darkness
for I understand the balance of
nature.

Behind each cloud there is a
glimmer of light
waiting to burst into full radiance.
There is a natural flow and
clouds shift,
No matter how faint the light
becomes,
the sun is not lost forever.

That shining ray of light
Faith
Faith in the son
Jesus

Katharine Mildred Hynds-Pestell
WAVES OF GRACE

*Except for the grace of our one-
God creator, where might we be!
Additional thanks for affirmation:
Women's Aglow Fellowship and
notification of world poetry: R.
Hendrickson*

Seeking TRUTH
Is a servantry
With the most harrowing
Master of all.

For it sometimes comes
In bits and pieces
As fine as the dancing
Wisps of spray
Above a towering
Ocean white cap
On a bright and windy
Day.

There for a moment——
Then gone——
Yet ever to return.

Leticia D. Lacson, M. D.
AN INTERLUDE
Like the breath of spring we kissed
On a midwinter morn
Witnessed by cold walls bare
The sun peeking thru windows
worn
The coldness and fear I felt
Was warmed by your touch
Like the sun kissing mother earth
Melting snow to mulch.

This feeling we trust
Can it last, is it rare
Is this lust, love, or regression
The mental telepathy we bear
Or is it something that we share
Without giving pain to those we
care?
Kathy Lutz
NEW ENGLAND ROOTS
In the backwoods of New England
I'll lay my roots to rest
Where water flows from
mountain streams
And sundown is at its best

Where vibrant days of nature's
works
Can fill your heart with love
And placid nights of lividness
Glow with stars above

Wild flowers stalk the land
In beautifull array
Another natural splendor
Like heaven's own bouquet

Mountaintops glisten in the sun
That hangs in amber skies
Looking like medieval giants
Leering with nasty eyes

Away from city madness
Away from fabrication
To the backbone of reality
of body and soul salvation

In the backwoods of New England
Where the proud eagles fly
In the clean air and fertile soil
That's where my roots shall lie

Arnecia Patterson
**Stained Glass Windows
Give Rainbow Light**
Stained glass windows give
rainbow light.
A church on a hill, forlorn,
destitute
Silent church bells ring clear at
night.

Gentle hymns; whispered sounds
makes it right.
Heads bowed low in prayerful
gratitude
Stained glass windows give
rainbow light.

Tails of fallen stars grant
welcome respite
from a midnight sky so deeply
hued.
Silent church bells ring clear at
night.

Mourners bench worn from
Sinners' fright.
Resident sparrows set an
innocent mood.
Stained glass windows give
rainbow light.

Sweet angels prepared to keep the
night
shimmer like moths in the damp
vestibule.
Silent church bells ring clear at
night

Doors shut softly, shutters drawn
tight.
Altar stands royal in its' solitude.
Stained glass windows give
rainbow light.
Silent church bells ring clear at
night.

Michele Burns
AND SILENTLY I WALKED
In the mist of dawn
   I walked,
silent and secretive
waiting upon Death's Portals;

Shrouds of moisture
   covered my bones
and I shivered with the knowledge
that I, too, was mortal.

Death walked beside me
   in a silver—stained gown
questioning my eyes
brushing beside me—
she breathed dewy air
and without one word
she touched the soul
   deep inside me.

Her hair was of water
   and her eyes shadowed gray
She whispered very gently,
"Daughter, you will not run away."

So, paralyzed I stood
   not breathing one breath—
not remembering any life
the morning that I tested
   Death . . .

Jeannette Hintzel
HIDDEN NIGHTMARE
Russian roulette inside my head
With each click coming closer to
   death
Shoot the chemicals into my vein
Help me to forget todays pain
Though the dawn may be coming
   soon
Forever I will live by the light of
   the moon
Beyond the darkness of the night
I look upon and see a sight
A vision made only of fantasy
Shut the window of reality
And pass through the door of
   insanity
For in this world that I exist
Happiness is only a wish
The shadows of a faded dream
Is all that is left for me to see
An empty glass
Scars of the past
Will haunt me forever

June Marie Griffith
REFLECTIONS
Mother, you gave me life and
   breath to breathe
Your vision through which the
   world I could see;
You knew not of my appearance
   or destination,
But loved me from the moment
   of my conception.
You surrounded me for nine
   months, kept me safe,
Kept me warm and from harm.
You gave me strength and
   courage, the ability to move on.
As an adult, I believe those were
   only a mere fraction;
For you helped to mold me into a
   person and to achieve many
   things.
Never quantity; but quality.
You have continued through the
   years to be the cornerstone of
   my life.
Your gentle touch and soft
   spoken words have guided me
   through a lifetime.

Many a time the burden seemed
   unbearable; you carried me
   through it.
You are a beautiful person, not
   because you're my mother,
But becasue you are full of love
   and life.
As a toast to life the wine glass
   sparkles, and a tear drop falls;
As life of yesterday holds very
   beautiful memories—
For you and I to share.

Claudine Bland

Claudine Bland
WHEN YOU KISSED ME
Darling when you kissed me as
   you got into your car
I knew the tears wasn't very far
You kissed me good-bye
I felt tears rushed into my eyes
I felt them when they dropped
But somehow I managed to stop
I braced myself with all my might
As I stood there and watched you
   out of sight
Since you've been gone
I've been feeling so alone
I miss your touch
That means so much
I miss walking in the rain
Holding your strong hand
I miss lying my head on your chest
When I'm tired and needs to rest
I miss the smell of your colonge
Now I know you're really gone
I miss you more than words
   could ever express
So maybe you leaving wasn't the
   best
I never wanted anything to come
   between our affair
You know I really really care
If you ever get lonely and want to
   talk to me
Dial my number; it's 561-4723

Jan D'Zuris
FEELING THE PAIN
Again I've hurt you.

Behind the pain and scars
I see you sitting there
with a broken wall of trust
that may take forever to rebuild
Behind the mistrust and lies
I can't honestly blame you
for hating me.
I only wish there was something
I could do or say
to make it up to you.

The only person I care about
and need the most

gets hurt the worst;
by my irresponsible, childish
   behavior.
The one who loves
and keeps loving me
for being myself
even when it's not myself

Thank you for loving me so much.

Tanya L. Nuetzman
WHAT ONCE WAS

*I would like to dedicate this
poem to a friend who has helped
me tremendously through both
the good and bad times, Trina
Sliefert. Even though we don't
always agree, she has given me
the courage and the support
when I needed it the most and as
a result, this poem is now being
published. I only hope my words
are able to express how I feel.
Thankyou for standing by me
even at the times when you
know I was wrong.*
                    Love Ya Forever,
                              Tanya

I can't recall the first time we met
But it's something I will never
   forget.
Our laughing and smiling,
And caring for each other.
The love we gave to one another,
   was very true and lasting.
But as times pass by
I realize not all good things last
   forever.
When someone else comes along
   singing their song,
You leave me for them.
And I don't know
   why this is so,
But then I realize,
It is for this reason
I must let you go.
But I will never ever forget
Just how I loved you so!

Carol Jean Spurr
THE MIDNIGHT VISITORS
It's Halloween night and I'm alone
In the livingroom of my home;
When suddenly the lights go out,
And there are whispers all about.
A rush of footsteps down the hall
And then a silhouette on the wall.

The only sound is heavy breathing;
And my mind, my mind is
   seething
With thoughts to run. Yet in my
   fright
I cannot move. I cannot fight.
I cannot scream; nor can I cry.
I am so scared; so scared am I.

A second shadow then appears
And on my cheek I feel the tears
Of terror and anguish run down
   my face.
Oh how I wish there were
   someplace
Where I could hide; but it's too
   late.
And now I cringe. And now I wait.

The shadows edge closer now,
And I know, I know somehow
I must escape, and I cry out!

I hear a giggle, then a shout.
The lights go on and standing
   there
Is my little brother and his teddy
   bear.

JoAnne Raz
I LOVE YOU

*To Jimmy Glowenke, Rick
Frasco, and John Ellison, For every
time we were hurt, And went
through it together.*

It is said
To different people
At different times
For different reasons
But the statement
Contains no intimate meaning
For it has been proven
Over and over again
That I Love You
Is too commonly said
To the wrong people
At the wrong times
For all the wrong reasons.

Dena Labell
ON HALLOW'S EVE
T'was the night long
On All Hallow's Eve
And ghastliness filled the air.
The howl of a wer'wolf
Awoke from deep sleep
A wretched old woman
To earn her own keep.
She dressed all in black from
   head to toe
Lit all the jack-o-lanterns
To prepare for the show.
She hung ten cats from the
   gallows of wrath
And when she was done
She began to laugh.
In the snap of her fingers
Her guests had arrived.
They joined in the *danse*
And all was alive.
T'was the night long
On All Hallow's Eve
And ghastliness filled the air.
A wretched old woman
Had earned her own keep
And the cry of a skreech owl
Cast spells of deep sleep.

Laura Louise Greene
BROKEN
Message like steel
Slashes like blade
Slicing up feelings
With words.
I was afraid.
I feel with my heart.
Yet heart will not last
When clarity sought
Shatters like glass.

Annette Rogers
A MATERNAL LOVE
If time could run backwards,
I'd change not my life.
I'd shun a kings ransom,
I'd endure the strife.

To know tht forever,
A child such as you
Would create the abundance
Of joy that you do.

I'd give up the ocean,
Were it mine to give;

Our World's Best Loved Poems

Relinquish the freedom
With which that we live.

To see through your eyes
All the joy that you see,
And return half as much
As you've given to me.

Debra K. McMullen
THE ARTIST
The hand of an artist
Moves across a clean page
To leave us an image
Worth more than a wage.

Its' beauty and style
Is like none ever found,
In no other mans' mind
Has it ever been bound.

Perhaps it was seen
In a dream late at night
And will never be captured
By soft morning light.

Or maybe it's real
And only he's seen
The abstract beauty
In this one scene.

But he's shown us his soul
And he won't ever die,
His work will live on
To keep him alive.

Evelyn Stebbins
MAMA'S FAITH
Mama brought the bible all the
    way from Ireland
It was yellowed some but every
    page was there,
Our Papa read it to us by the
    hearthside, so tired
He'd fall asleep in his big oak
    chair.
I can still see Mama standing in
    the cabin doorway
As our Papa rode away with
    many men.
Tears filled our eyes that silent
    Summer evening
And Mama held the bible tightly
    in her hand.
"Come inside and pray with me,
    my children
That God will keep your father in
    his care."
And Mama read to us from pages
    in the bible
Until she fell asleep in our Papa's
    chair.
Winter passed slowly but Spring
    came
And Mama's faith seemed
    stronger than before
Till another Summer night when
    men came riding
To leave dear Papa at our cabin
    door.
Safe inside and smothered with
    our kisses
Our supper done and all our
    chores done too
We listened to our Papa tell the
    story of a horrible war
And the miracles that brought
    him through.
Then Papa patted his knee and
    said, "Come here girl."
And Mama smiled as Papa
    stroked her hair.
Peace filled our hearts with
    gladness as Papa read the bible
And they fell asleep in Papa's chair.

Rita A. Kunz
**Dagger My Heart . . . And
You'll Burn In Hells Hole**
Burn in hell,
Like Satans believer;
I'll take you from hell,
And be your retriever.

Dagger my heart,
With Satans spear;
I'll place you a halo,
And hold you so near.

I'll draw your red-blood,
From deep in your heart;
I'll send you to Satan,
And we'll be far apart.

Death is not Heaven,
Death is hell;
God has your soul,
But its yours to sell.

Sell it to Satan,
He'll set it a-fire;
Sell it to the Lord,
In Angel attire.

Give up your freedom,
And you give up your soul;
You'll burn into ashes,
In Satans hell hole.

Cin Forshay-Lunsford
FREEDOM

---

*To my brother, James . . . You
are unique because you are
proud. Be proud that you are
unique. I'll always love you.*

Today I am alive.
I breath cold razor-edged air
and warm smokey sin air.
I feel the veil of warm sunlight
    on my face
and the drizzling tears of fog.

Tonight you, in jealousy, wish me
    to be a child
a frail creation of obedient
    intellect
rather than a beast of body and
    soul.

Why do you begrudge me
my silver fish-net night
my shimmering moon
and glinting stars?

Do not envy my youth
for children die too.
And tomorrow I may be gone
even as you fear your own passage.

Tonight, give me my wings of
    powder
and let me fly unburdened
to the heart of the flame.

Carol Ridings Bearden
THE BROKEN MAN
Battered by years of a menial's hire,
    The stooped figure of a broken
    man
Leans upon his sickle and bows,
    And rests upon his hand.

The pain and the toil of ages,
    Imprinted upon his face,
Show through to those who see
    him
    For he accepts his allotted deed,
What more can he now ask for,
    When he knows there is no
    need.

So this withered human being

Lifts his heated brow,
To continue with the harvest
    For the time to reap is now!

For time is swiftly passing by
    And the end is very near,
The man will lay his sickle down
    With a brimy, salty tear.

Why cannot men see the pain
    The toil of the ages wrought
And change the fate of mortal man
    The pain of the ages taught!

Clay Patrick Cunningham
EPILOGUE
This concludes my poems they
    came from my heart
Three poems to you was only a
    start
We have our lives to live as we
    will
To spend time with you I'd beg,
    borrow or steal
Please don't forget me and ease
    your fright
It's a perfect marriage
            the snow and the night.

Alice Cleveland Daugherty
LOOKING FOR SPACE
Alas, my dear, don't try to hold me—
    Give me space, for I must grow.
Don't try to keep me in your
    shadow—
    Tomorrow calls, life's sun is low.
The voices echo in the distance—
    Calling me to spheres unknown.
I say farewell to friends and loved
    ones—
    The path ahead, I tread alone.

Where is this place that lies
    before me—
    Sandy beach or mountain high?
Is there roaring waves and big
    adventures—
    Or solitude under desert skies?
When evening comes, light your
    own candle—
    You must now reap what you
    have sown.
I know not where I'll be tomorrow—
    But the space I'm in will be my
    own.

Allison Engel
MEMORIES
Thanks for the great times we
    had together
too bad it didn't last
it's time to look into the future
and not dwell on the past.
The times we shared together
    meant so much to me
but now I look into reality
and see it couldn't be.
We were two different people
unalike in many ways
but my memories of you
I will treasure always.

Connie Bremner
LONA AND LYNN
Thank goodness you're not alike
    as two peas in a pod
To your gramma you are both gifts
    from God
With your hair of gold and your
    eyes of blue
I love both you and you.
To think today you are ten years
    old
Yesterday you were little enough
    to hold

My how time has slipped away
On the road of life you're well on
    your way.
Twice as much laughter and
    chatter
Twice as much singing and patter
You are Lona and you are Lynn
You with your smile and you with
    your grin.
Two little girls, going hand and
    hand
Having fun to beat the band
Expecting one of God's blessings,
    we got two
The world through your eyes,
    again, is shiny and new.

Leora Edith Smart
MY DREAMHOUSE
I have a little dream,
    I dreamed of long ago.
Just merely thinking of it,
    Sets my heart a glow.

I'll have a little dreamhouse
    That sits up on a hill
I know I'll have it someday,
    My heart says that I will.

It's roof is made of shingles,
    It's walls are made of stone,
I'll have a bell that jingles,
    To answer when I'm home.

And all around my dreamhouse
    I'll sow some grass and flowers,
And in my little dreamhouse,
    I'll spend many happy hours.

Gary M. Humphreys
**In Memory Of: Abraham
Lincoln**

---

*With some hard thinking, and
help with my wording from a 9th
grade English teacher at Bossier
City High School, from Bossier
City, Louisiana; I dedicate this
poem.*

On February 12th, 1809,
There was born a boy, who grew
    up very fine.
There in that cabin on a far-away
    hill,
Lived a very small boy, with a
    very strong will.

Lincoln would study on the floor,
    by the fire,
Of reading his books, he would
    never tire . .
One thing that I remember best?,
Is when Lincoln said the
    Gettysburg Address? . . .

When Lincoln said the
    Gettysburg Address,
He said that "Slavery is
    abbolished . . .," I guess . .
The more Lincoln said it, the
    slaves jumped with glee,
For they knew that they were free.

Lincoln had told Nancy,
For her to "Dress fancy." . . .
For there was going to be a great
    feature,
At the Ford Theatre . .

Slyly and quietly,
John Booth came in silently . .
With his gun in his hand,
He shot Lincoln, and ran . .

Lincoln was alive,
But he died in April, 1865 . .
Right now, we can't miss him any,
For he is on our one—cent coin;
the penny . .

Cheryl Jensen
CRAZY WITCHCRAFT
It's Halloween nite, I'm ready for
flight,
All the world is waiting to see if I
might,
Fly freely through the skies,
To see my goblens wearing their
disguise,
The cats, nomes and ghosts just
waiting,
For the place and time to scare
the world that's playing.

I can hear all they are saying,
For I am a Witch with a Crazy
Craft
I make things happen even fat bats,
People with hair long and flowing
Beware your legs are growing,
And those with toes, for I have
none,
Watch out yours will be gone.

It's twelve O'clock midnite I can
see all,
Dancing and prancing on the
sidewalks,
They better watch out for the
world will fall.
For I am a Witch, Halloween is
my time,
All my family I made for mine,
Ghosts and my Creatures walk
on the earth,
If you want to help me, be the
next birth.

Ashley F. Mercer
THE STORM
Clouded moon splints
swallow the sky.
Deep ocean waves
unfurl themselves
with thunderous applause,
creating white heat above their
surface.
Silver sheets of rain
penetrate—
forming crevices
on the sandy beach.

Secured ropes snap
releasing the dingy.
Helpless in the separation
there is no gravity,
only spanking waves
and a sudden midnight flight.

The heavens lighten,
streaming into stillness.
All suspicion is lost.

Once again land—
the sixth sense has been recovered.
Like the flicker of a candle
in a dark room,
the light house has been spotted.

Michael Grady Chancey
TENNESSEE
In springtime when the flowers
bloom
By the river neath the shining
moon
There is no place I'd rather be
Cause I belong in Tennessee.

The mountains in the summer are
An echo for my old guitar

The air is clean and I can see
The beauty of you Tennessee

Autumn-time in Tennessee
Is red and yellow maple trees
And people live in liberty
I know that God has smiled on
thee.

Wintertime in Tennessee
Is exactly what it ought to be
The best to some you may not be
But Tennessee you are to me.

**Lord Weyoume, E007601
GsUS, CcDQ**

*Lord Weyoume E007601
GsUS, CcDQ*
ETCHINGS IN ACIDNA

*To WEYOUMEION: d UnIted
Star System In Love
H/OurUnIversCity anl dedicate
This Living Statute, This Yoke of
Liberty, This FOReEverMoore
Perfect UnIon, H/Our Golden
Rule, H/Our Evergreen Tree of
Life, by Divine DeSign, H/Our
Family Tie, ie: J. Doe/
WEYOUME*

Come again, Oh Divine
Androgeny/Synergy/
HeuManKindRed/Temple
Light, Be a Crown Righteous on
The Head of H/Our
DiversCity: Parity, Surety to The
Feet of Destiny; *Divinity.*
Oh come again, My Life, My
Law,
My *Word,* My *Bond,* My *Love,*
Oh My *GOD! GOD* Is U.S., UnI,
MEnU, *WEYOUME/The
People*

Come again, Oh *Divine Mind/
Eye,
ReignBeaux,* UnIted. Stay
FOReEverMoore Perfect
UnIon. . .
In LOVE WEYOUME *Trust.*

*Nomenconservandum:
Etchings In AciDNA
Teach All H/OurUnIverse
Program: Rapport
Language: Basic . . . Common
Sense
Come again: UnIted Nations
Come again: World Health
Organization
Be Here Now! 1983, Year of
The Bible
Home again: Now The*

WORD Is made Flesh,
*and dWells withIn U.S. . .
WEYOUME*

YOU
ME +
LOVE +
DIVINITY÷
AFFINITY×
WeYouMe=

WeYouMe M+

WeYouMe MR
WeYouMe MR
WeYouMe MR
WEYOUME MR

Manifest Destiny
*"In The Begining was The Word,
and The Word was with God,
and The Word was God" Gen
1:3,26 Jn 1:1 3:16-18 1Cor12:13
Gal 5:14 Rev 3:12 22:17. "We,
YouMe Mutually Pledge to
Each Other H/Our Lives,
H/Our Fortunes, H/Our SacRed
Honor" 1776/ANNUIT COEPTIS*
AIM
WEYOUME
ONE FOR ALL FOR ONE
BODY MIND SPIRIT MIND
BODY

Virginia Lemperle
SILENCE
Hear the silence
of the pine trees,
great green pine trees
towering over us;
Hear the harmony
of birds' songs,
forest's voices
all around us;
Hear the whispering
of the soft waves
lapping, licking
at the land,
Taking back into the seascape
countless grains
of stone and sand,
ever building,
ever growing;
lush green marsh
grasses glowing
in the soft and shimmering
sunlight's golden rays;
glimmering end
of sunswept days.

Byron J. Miller
SANDY
Here she comes
Her silk complexion and delicate
facial features

Like a radiant angel she
outshines the others
I see only her
Gazing into her deep brown eyes
I am taken away upon light
clouds of adoration
She smiles and I am overcome
with a warm glow
As she passes my senses are filled
With the sweet essence of her
soft perfume
How her long raven hair cascades
down her back
More ravishing than Venus
My mind is fixed on no one but
her
There she goes
She is beauty

Elly Mae Boonstra
GRANDMA
When I was just a little kid
And sat on Grandma's knee,
I remember all the loving
My Grandma gave to me.

She was always there to hold me
And take me by the hand,
She was always kind and
friendly,
She'd always understand.

I remember all the good times
(There hardly was a bad)
I remember all the laughter
Me and Grandma had.

When I felt cold and angry,
——Didn't know what to do,
My Grandma always was right
there
To chase away the blue.

My Grandma always was so
sweet
She means so much to me.
She's the best Grandma in the
world,
And she will always be.

Theresa I. Miles
RESURRECTION
COME to the cross, where He
suffered and died.
SEE the great tomb that they
sealed Him inside.
GO to the people who weep for
the dead;
TELL them He's RISEN, just as
He said!

Helen V. Le Marr Wright
OCTOBER ART
Can an artist really capture the
beauty
Of Octobers' gay dress parade?
The reds, the golds, and browns,
And greens like treasured jade.

I have viewed many painted
pictures
And beauty in them saw
But never like the beauty i see
When walking in the fall.

When mother nature has wielded
her paint brush,
And put each color there
Then blows a gentle little breeze
Sending colors through the air.

Like graceful ballerinas
The leaves dance round and
round
Quietly they twist and turn
Then gently touch the ground.

Creating a vision, a patch work
quilt,
A warm covering, for mother
earth.
Protecting her from winters cold
Until springs warmth brings new
birth.

Esther Ager Smith
THE DOWAGER
Lord, the old mother wants more
money as well as to control.
Little Sister still helps, but finds
no one who will console.
She is weak, tired, in pain, but
there's no rest for her soul
Because Great-grandmother
curses her children and their
foals.

How the Dowager has broken the
ones she gave suck.
True, Little Sister remains to
help—"I'm the one who has pluck!"
Then the Martyr grimaces, "If I
find help, it's purely luck."

The oldest son, my Love, with
kindness tried teaching.
Instead of reaching, he was
accused of unjust preaching.
He wrote, "Why do you hate me
so? I was only beseeching.
Sister, you are sick like me and
tired of her leeching."

Lord, with tears he turned to me,
his spouse.
"You have known me for forty
years——Am I truly a louse?
Our Children's children must be
happy in our house!"

Only you, Dear Jesus, can melt a
selfish heart of stone.
Because our children experienced
unhappiness in her home,
They will not expose their little
ones to her demanding tone.
So our grandchildren will never
know the Dowager as their own.

Lord, this is a sad story of an old
woman who will not bend.
She contends: "I'll not rescind; 'tis
the way of my kin
Not to pretend; yes, I need more
money than you send!

'Tis my children's whims that
makes my old heart rend
Because I love deeper than ten
times a thousand men—
Understand I never, never, never
sinned!"

Dick Chamberlain
CONTRASTS IN LOVE
Old, new, borrowed, blue;
Pink champagne, Mulligan stew;
Freckles, pigtails, chiffon gown;
Cane pole, bobber, white
button-down;
  Here's to different things.

Silver, crystal, paper cups;
Siamese cats, mongrel pups;
Cactus, ferns, scarlet roses;
Jazz, classics Brahms composes;
  Tunes Sinatra sings.

Nature hikes, carnival rides;
Rocky Mountains, ebbing tides;
Drive-in movies, municipal zoo;
Crowded room, just me, just you;
  Joy variety brings.

Marie Mini
The Window Of My Dreams
My bedroom window is open just
enough to feel the nip of a
breeze.
A ray of sun shines in.
It rests gently on my arm
warming away the goosebumps
that have taken over my skin.
looking beyond the trees, into
infinity, My mind is swiftly
taken into another time . . .
We embrace each other as if
one, while walking across a
desolete beach.
The sun has fallen, and the
reflection of the moon glistens
at the tips of the waves that
rush at our feet, threatening to
swallow our ankles.
Alone with the stars, we melt
into the darkness of the night.
Unaware of anything but how
our bodys lock together, as
does a missing piece of puzzle
thought never to be found.
Our lips again meet, promising
never to part.
Again I see the trees through my
familiar window.
I feel the sinking of my soul
down imaginary seas, as my
mind returns to my body.
The face to my heart is never
seen in my dreams.
When I find my beach, I'll find
my love.

Tracy Hobbs Adolphsen
TOO YOUNG TO FLY
He looks at me with serious eyes.
It makes me scared, I want to
hide.
I loved him once and he loved me.
I changed my mind. I had to leave.

He didn't understand my reasons
why.
I said I was young, Too young to
fly.
I never speak to him anymore.
I guess I'm scared, just as before.

Ben Gray
HALLOWEEN NOW
My recollection keen of my
halloween
The shivery-quivery of magic fear
As masks and sheets and witch's
hats
braved Dracula to 'Trick or Treat'
We laughed and joked and cut
the fool
Ran like hell past town spooky
house
Where goblins cavorted in our
mind
and children eaten from pickled
brine

Times now changed with
monsters real
as I dog my children on spooky
trail
Few happy faces through open
door
answer the knock of small imp
fist
My children do laugh for I have
instilled
the eerie principle of darkened
bush

But unlike my youth they are
ever aware
of Satan behind flesh-mask of
smile

At journey end the sacks are
spilled
on kitchen table with trash can
near
To eye, to probe assorted loot
To seek razored belladonna, the
evil hue
The gleanings kept from harvest
large
The pitiful remnant stills the heart
and drives home the hateful fact
All the monsters of yesterday are,
no longer fable but real as death

Debbie Ann Marino
DAYDREAMS
In my dreams I wander
Through fields once moist from
tears
The grass no longer ragged
The path now newly cleared
The fragrance of the flowers
No longer dry and dead
Fill the air with sweetness
As they lay upon their bed
The whisper of the breeze
Plays softly in my ear
Cradled in its arms
I know there's naught to fear
The humming of the birds
Heard from up above
Then wakes me from my dreams
Into a world of love

Adam Hancock
WORDS
The words that I write,
Are slashed and cut down
By that blood red pen,
    Until,
    They're not my words,
But somebody else's;
Words that have been
    Twisted and turned around,
    Until they are
    "Correct".

Regina Ann Lester
BLACK HEARTS

*For Bryan . . . Who's black heart
has caused mine such sorrow.*

Just a victim of it's own desires,
Our hearts burn with secret fires.
They try to pretend and make
believe,
But they really lie and decieve.

Silently they search for truth,
Finding nothing but ashes as
their proof.
We don't realize what happens
before our eyes,
The way a black heart stutters
and lies.

The first step toward a mistake.
Is allowing your heart to fall and
break.
After the damage you can take a
step back
Or let your heart bleed until it is
black.

These evil hearts so cruel and cold
Cause young, innocent ones to
quickly grow old.

Constantly seeking and hunting
their prey
They destroy more hearts with
each passing day.

There is but one common solution
To rid this world of their
needless pollution.
This can only be done if we take
that step above
By showing and teaching them
how to love.

Rob Moline
DESERT CAIN
There is the horse I
cannot ride. By my
side she stands, a
quick bolting nightmare.
I am too old
for her steadfast
boldness.

My fever
rises to the occasion
of my sticky,
stained d eaver dripping
a clash upon
the rolling grass. The
moon fills my
horror.

Buzzards peck away
the colt's painted
ass. My sense
is in the pasture
lost a long
time ago. I close
my door
along with the dreadful
draft.

Traci Sue Setford
AUTUMN ARRIVAL

---

*Dedicated to my daughter, Tara
Sue, for all the joy and inspiration
she has provided me to continue
with my writing talent. This is
for you. I LOVE YOU. Mommy*

Soft—
  Like a child sleeping sound
The autumn breeze whispers
  secrets
  To the changing maple tree
Quietly—
  The night darkens the summer
  away
As we face the fresh beauty
  Of the oncoming season

Marinis Becknell
A DREAM
See your shadow—
on the wall—
by the light—
out in the hall.
Coming closer—
oh so near—
drive away—
all my fears.
Hear you breathing—
in the dark—

feel the beating—
of your heart.
Lay beside me—
on my bed—
your arm a pillow—
for my head.
Gently touching—
softly kissing—

tonight exist—
for you and me.
Open my eyes—
to realize—
it was all a dream.
Dry my tears—
close my eyes—
and pray—
I'll dream again.

Joyce Doreen Bea
MOMMY WHY
Mommy why do you cry all night
        long,
Never being happy, never singing
        a song?
Mommy why do the birds never
        sing
and the church bell in the valley
        never ring?
Mommy why is my world so dark
Why can't I hear the dog who I
        know does bark?
Mommy why am I so cold
and why does your face look so
        old
Mommy why is daddy not here
is he out again drinking a beer
Mommy why don't you hold me
        tight
the way you did all those other
        nights
Mommy why are you walking
        away
the way you do every day?
Mommy why did I have to die?

Janet Clawson
MY LITTLE BOY
I want to tell a story
the sweetest ever told
because it tells of a mothers love
for the son that she does hold.

The little boy is Rodney
and how she loves him so
He makes her day shine brighter
and the moon to be aglow.

He has some freckles on his face
but they just make him dear
sometimes he is a bad boy
and causes his mother a tear.

But when she tucks him in at
        night
He smiles his toothless smile
she listens to his prayers to God
and her work can wait awhile.

Then when he grows to be a man
and has children of his own
He'll still be mommy's little boy
and only Hers on loan.

Nettie Kittrell
DAWNING
We awoke one morning to behold
A scene of beauty to unfold
Curtains of the night gave way
To the dawning of this new day

Sun glows burst across the way
A field of sparkling diamond lay
Dewdrops glistening on uneven
        grass
A lovely picture so soon to pass

Dewdrops from heaven fell in the
        night
Reflecting stars fading from sight
A lovely picture from the
        master's hand
A hush, a stillness fell on the
        land

A special moment of beauty rare
A moment of humble thankful
        prayer
A picture in memory, a keepsake
        to hold
Such beauty in words, can never
        be told

Marjorie Burney Willis
Lullaby Time With the Cats

*Dedicated to my beloved sister
Lowell Burney Carter of Waco,
Tx. This poem won 5th. place in
"The Cat Award" Contest—given
by the Poetry Society of Texas in
the 1983 Annual Contests.*

When memories come dazzling
        my senses—
    dizzying my mind, I hide away
        with them;
            then stars come twinkling
                over a Texas hill
    and a whippoorwill comes
        calling.
Summer breezes begin crooning
    sweet lullabies for Loell and
    me.

Fireflies begin flickering
    round the flowers;
        our cats come hovering
            round our feet
    telling us it's rock-a-bye-baby-
        time.
We begin slipping them off to
        Dreamland—
    sneaking them through
        windows,
        whispering to the frogs and
            crickets:
"Don't tell our best-kept
        secret!
        We're sleeping with the
            cats—
                Snowball, Chigger and
                    Skeeter Baby."

When memories come stealing—
    revealing the past—
        night comes creeping
            over a Texas hill
    and a moon comes peeping in
        windows.
It's the time for sleeping with the
        cats.
We begin hugging them close to
        our hearts
    and they begin tuning their
        music boxes,

    purring, purring for Loell and
        me—
    purring a Brahms lullaby.
Tauna J. Smith
LIFE

*This poem is in honor of all my
friends who helped me choose
this poem; especially Angie, Lisa,
Garrett, Danny, and Doug.*

Life brings happiness.
Someone new coming into the
        world
Entering the hell,
The love, and sadness;
Suddenly leaving
For the glory of heaven,
Or the breaking of hell.

Linda Sutherland
LOVE'S SONG
Our love like the rebirth of
    Spring's sonnet,
A symphony of sparrows singing
    merrily to
The morning's sun-kissed dew.

Our hearts like rich soil
    everbudding,
Blossoms sweet and fragile,
Fresh with life everlasting.

Intensly warm, as golden shafts of
Sunlight upon my face.

Gentle as wisps of fleecy clouds,
White and Pure.

Refreshing as a cool mountain
    spring,
Running over shiny pebbles,
Playing Nature's music.

Blessed as a serenae of Angel's
Singing the Joy of
The Glories of Heaven.

Fulfilling, Bubbling, Overflowing,
Two as one in harmony of peace,
"Our melody" eternal.

Michelle L. Meyer
A TRUE FRIEND

*After I wrote this poem, I lost a
special friend, my cousin Jay. I
hope this poem touches your life
as he has touched mine. I'm
dedicating this to his memory, as
he was a very special and true
friend to those who knew him.*

I've found a friend
A sweet kind man
who gave me a smile
and lent me his hand.
He picked me up
He knew I was down
He wiped away my tears
as a smile replaced my frown.
He spoke so softly
as he whispered in my ear
He said "follow me
I'll take you away from here."
The place I was in
was called loneliness.
I refused other offers,
I knew his was best.
His knowing smile
His playful wink
I picked up and followed,
I did not need to think.

For he taught me to love
He showed me how to care
He said, "don't worry this time
for you I'll always be there."

Patricia Holko
BLACK AND WHITE
The man who lives by "Black and
    White"
Sees all in life as wrong or right.
He has no time for inbetweens
Or searching out behind the
    scenes
To see if certain doubts prevail
To slightly tip his rigid scale.
The man who lives by "White
    and Black"
Has never seemed to learn the
    knack
Of seeing someone elses side
For this would go against his pride.
For him there is no middle lane
And thus the reason for his pain,
For love can't get a proper start
When nurtured by a stubborn
    heart.
So the man who never learns to
    bend
Has only himself to call a friend.
For all in life can never be
Exactly what one man can see.
So I ask of you Lord, let me live
    everyday
Not in Black or in White, but in
    fine shades of grey.

Dennis D. Denz
SUNSHINE
As the sun descends
    A rose mist recedes from the
        sky.
Do not close your eyes,
    Observe the glimmering stars
        ascend.
Release those inner cries,
    Relax your bleeding mind.
Absorb the lasting warmth of
    paradise.
    Deploy your thoughts upon the
        earth,
Hold closely a love of life,
    For soon you must realize.

Nina LaGrassa
TEETH
Fragile in their susceptibility to
Neglect, abuse and sweet
    enticements,
Hiding their deepest
    vulnerabilities
In a cavernous interior
They flash a dazzling smile to the
    world.
Focused on utilitarian concerns
But often ravaged by hedonistic
    indulgences,
Their purpose is to nourish and
    protect.
Yet, they demand continual care
    and attention
Often of a specialized nature.
Silent, but essential to
    verbalization,
They give birth to words, kisses,
    bites and pouts.
Suffering through stages of
    maturation
They cling tenaciously to their
    roots,
Surviving interior and exterior
    assaults.
Seemingly anonomous,

Our World's Best Loved Poems

They possess a distinct identity.
Imposters can be rather
  convincing,
Adhering to their positions until
  sundown.
Environment and heredity may
  affect them,
But, if I take great care
I won't lose them or bear their
  ache.

Laura G. Nicholes
ALL THE LOVE SHE HAD
When I was but a child, my
  momma's life was rough.
For it seemed no matter how she
  tried, there never was enough.
But we never hungered, and we
  were never sad,
For she gave us what we needed
  most, all the love she had.

Oh, how hard she struggled
  trying to make ends meet.
She'd have taken on the world to
  put shoes upon our feet.
And although most things were
  scarce, and the times were bad,
She gave to her three children all
  the love she had.

She gave us a set of values, and
  she taught us right from wrong.
And we learned just by watching
  her to keep our spirit strong.
Still, sometimes we argued, and
  really made her mad,
But she never stopped giving us
  all the love she had.

Our Childhood days are over, but
  our memories make us glad,
For her love, by far, exceeded all
  the things we never had.
My life is filled with blessings,
  and I'm thankful for each one.
But the greatest blessing of them
  all, was to be given such a mom.

P. J. Huffman
PEACE

To: You, From: Just me, Til:
Tomorrow!!

I sleep each night
only after I tuck you away,
carefully, softly, . . . lovingly.
I close my eyes and watch you
  sleep beside me;
feeling your warmth, and timing
  my breathing to match yours.

I awake in the dark
to your presence . . . tapping on
  my shoulder;
And, in my mind's eye, I turn over,
gathering you gently into my
  waiting arms,
only to sleep again . . .
  more peacefully.

Betty Jo Meadows
TO SAY GOODBYE
Goodbye to a thousand words
  Left unspoken
The few halting ones were
  Only a token
Goodbye to many times of
  Love and delight
There will be no tomorrow
  The end is in sight
How difficult it is, as it

Must be to die
As to say the words
  Goodbye, goodbye.

Ingrid Enloe Aleman
MY DAD
My dad is a strong man,
  but yet gentle.
He knows what is right,
  and wrong.

He's a man with a loving heart,
  and has worked so hard,
To help his children,
  in any way he can.

He gets frustrated with us kids
  sometimes,
but he loves,
  and helps us still.

I love my dad very much,
  and when he goes away,
    someday,
  he will be in my
  memory forever.

Kathleen M. Flood
MICHEALE'
She walks on the road
  and roams far away,
Her life is a fantasy,
  day after day.

The fears deep inside her
  are lead all astray,
Hidden by a dream,
  in a frightening way.

Companions are worried
  for the safety she keeps,
Parents are quiet,
  and privately weep.

Hunting for refuge
  she runs from home,
No longer a child,
  but a teen all alone.

Dawn Farris
QUIET TIME
I feel the quiet engulf me now as
  over the water I gaze
And see the mountains cold and
  clear, half hidden in the haze
Finding feathers on the ground,
  my eyes look to the sky
And far above, beyond my reach,
  the graceful seagulls fly

Sittin close and looking 'round, a
  cat of greyish hue
Shares this moment of quiet
  peace and we are one, not two
How great the longing does
  become to hold this moment
  still
But time flows on and so must
  we, even against our will.

Frederica McDill Culbertson
REFLECTIONS
Stopped in traffic—
  waiting for the light,
the glass building's reflections—
  are certainly a delight.

Young architects' dreams—
  are different, I perceive—
from old masters' conceptions—
  of design and pleasantry.

Today's low building reflets
  palms and sky,
while the IDS Tower is so high—
that all fifty-nine stories, I recall—
reflect Minneapolis and Nicollet
  Mall.

Yes, I remember—all four seasons
  in them I saw.

When I look back I love the old—
yet, as I go forward I also love the
  new.
Life is constantly blending and
  changing,
which is best for you—and best
  for me.
Of this, I'm as certain as I can be.

Nancy Menda
In the Eerie Moonlit Shadows
In eerie moonlit shadows he
  creeps
  and then slips quietly through
  the deep.
While whispers the wind-tossed
  leaves that nod
  the night winds breathe some
  unearthly plot.
Beware! The night sounds utter
  their cry
  while moonlit shadows hover
  nearby.
Upon night's dark-mantled,
  shrouded orb
  he slips through the night in
  ebon form.
He will slyly stalk his prey to
  nab
  in the midnight's moonlit
  shadows drab.
He seizes his prey, which meets
  its doom
  the night chants, "GOTCHA!" as
  shadows loom.
As the night succombs to lighter
  tones
  he slinks to his refuge, daytime
  abode.
Black Shadow remains in cat-like
  trance
  on lap or bed; he awaits his
  chance.
Then dark once more, he will
  stalk his prey
  in the eerie moonlit shadows
  grey.

Hessie Graham Byrd
OCTOBERFEST
Octoberfest is—— October,
Fairs, Halloween and Indian
  Summer.
Excitement is in the Air,
All nature is A Fair.
Nature outshines herself in
  October
with her "bright blue weather".
October is unique,
Fall colors are at their peak.
Fall coat of many colors.
Proud show of nature's wonders,
Some patterned, some splashed,
Like an artist had just brushed.
Who can the artist be,
Who works with such Artistey?
With the moon, sun and wind
  making the season
And God providing the reason.
It's that time again
To head for the mountains.
Here, there or anywhere,
Just beware!
There may be ghosts about
And goblins that shout,
May be seen
At Halloween.

Lori Jeanette McIntosh
Mr. Tee's Halloween Party
The moon glowed its evanesce
  hue over the fog laden ground,
while pumpkins blinked and
  winked. Candles flickered light.

As little Tricker Treater's pound
  each door, gathering fruits and
  candies. Disappearing echoes
  giggle, muffled whispers dwindle.

Toward Mr. Tee's light sheeted
  house of lamented ghosts with
  green emerald eyes cast their
  spell upon the walkway hosts.

As the wind blows fog, gapping
  upon Mr. Tee's shielded door.
  Him watching little tykes
  dressed in ghoul uniforms.

Frightening they are, he thought.
  "Them rapping at my door."
  And he dressed in black
  downed fur. "Coming they are
  to my travel ridden door.

Mr. Tee stretched, coiled and
  sprang toward the ensuing door
  of doomed glittered masks,
  crowded tiny fingers wretched.

With spoken outrage, bristled
  bloated tail, stating his position
  upon witches ragged broom.
  Children howl into the nights
  fog consumed.

Esther Myers
TO ROBERT SERVICE
In your little cabin in Dawson
  town,
I walked right in and sat me down
On the rusted bedsprings where
  you slept.
With heavy heart and tears
  unwept,
Contemplated how I would have
  greeted,
If with your spirit I had been
  treated.

Peggy Martin Underwood
SHADOWS
Shadows of the night, what do
  you see?
A reflection in a mirror, please let
  me be.
Memories walk across your mind,
  images of me,
Ghost of days gone by. Shadows
  of the night.

Shadows of time, has it been so
  long?
Pictures of the past, years move
  along.
Cool, crisp evenings, a refrain
  from a song,
Promises that bind, the shadows
  of time.

Shadows on the wall, why are you
  there?
Favorite places, familiar faces,
  you memory everywhere.
Sunny days and starless nights, I
  wish you were here.
The games we play with shadows
  on the wall.

Shadows of memories, are they all
  in vain?
In the darkness of the past,
  there's always pain.

We reach out and touch, our
souls to claim,
Days never to return. Shadows of
memories.

Shadows of our lifetime, what
path do we take,
To live our lives with the choices
we make?
Visions of our future, afraid of
our mistakes.
We then become, the shadows of
our lifetime.

Regina M. Combs
A DEBAUCHERY
Too many want
only to be
lovers
Never willing
to wipe
the tears from
your eyes
but . . .
unknowingly
willing to
put them
there.

Jules J. Eugene
OCEAN OF DEATH
My tears will never fill your glass
Stronger than waves my power is
Too weak to fight you
Calm, your moon seems never to
forgive
I burried my dreams, that seems
never to please you
My tears will never fill your glass
Far beyond your memory will
never forget.

Janet Pfeifer Waring
LAST BUS
She is a widow
Like winter wheat hunching
under snow,
Her breasts shrunken from tiny
mouths
Now men.

She is knowledge
Like the faded pages of a brochure
In the dust of her attic.
Her eyes cower from the debris.

She is a tombstone
Like the reflection of an antique
mirror
That quivers with death.
As she rocks,
Her knitting-needle hands
Lay flat, palms up, in her lap,
Wasting, wasting.

Velinda Edwards
PROGRESS?
What happened to the days,
When it was safe to walk our
street,
And you didn't have to run,
From every stranger that you
meet.

When man could be a man,
And had a name and had a face,
And wasn't just a number,
In a fast computer race.

When music sung a song of love,
Or had a thought to tell,
Instead of some sadistic sound,
Trying to send us all to hell.

When murder, rape, and robbery,
Weren't a daily headline sight,

And folks could feel secure,
In their homes asleep at night.

What happened to those days,
I guess they're dead and gone,
Mankind cannot concern himself,
Cause progress must go on?

Yvonne Jester Wallace
SPAKE THE WIND

*To the memory of L. Cpl. Michael
A. Hastings of Delaware and
others who gave their life for
freedom.*

Standing upon this battlefield
Who can hear the echo of gunfire?
Swirling in a whirlpool of thought
Who can tell what happened here?
Hurrying through dense nameless
shadows ·
Who can find a budding white
rose?
Stumbling across dark empty
trenches
Who can feel death's icy glove?
Whispering souls upon the wind
Who can say they died in vain?
Watching in the golden glow of
time
Who can know if peace will ever
come?

Angela Carol North
YOU TOUCHED ME
You've touched me
    More deeply than you know
You've touched me
    Where I've let few people go
And when you touched me,
    A voice whispered to my heart
Cause when you touched me
    You became a part——
                            Of me.

Melissa K. Gibson
GOLDEN MEMORIES

*This is Dedicated To: Julie
Dawkins, Tracy Dennison and
Robin Mills, My Greatest Friends
In The World.*

If within the days of old,
    All the memories turn to gold,
I hope that within A few,
    There are memories of me and
you.

The times we cared,
The times we shared,
    The times we cried in vain,
On my shoulders you cried at
times,
    Between each tear you called
my name.

These memories we share,
    Please keep within your heart,
And think of those Golden
Memories,
    Whenever we're apart.

Marguerite E. Wiggins
THE PEACE OF FALL
Listen to the quiet peace of Fall,
As God keeps vigil over all,
The rustling leaf—the crackling
twig,
    The smell of walnuts, damp and
trig,

The wind—when just a nip is felt,
    The sky o'er head so blue and
svelt—
The chant of crickets, lingering
still,
    Birds winging south—so strong
of will.
The smell of smoke upon the
breeze,
    The glorious colors of the trees.
Another summer put to sleep
    With hope of Spring, its vigil
keep.
A time when mortal man can
think,
    And plan and dream and catch a
wink.
A wondrous languor over all,
    Listen to the quiet peace of Fall!

Carol Kibbons

Carol Kibbons
THE SILENT MINORITY

*To my parents, Elizabeth &
Joseph Foster, who taught me
values, that love is unselfish, the
meaning of empathy, & love of
God. Their world of silence
taught me more than mere words
ever could!*

Sounds! How we take them for
granted, 15 million Americans
suffer some kind of hearing
impairment
And 2 million plus are
profoundly deaf, never to enjoy
beautiful priceless sound
Surely most of us have thought
how frightening not to have
vision or use of limbs,
disabilities so evident
But we seldom give thought to
those who can't hear, for
deafness is the 'invisible
disability', not easily found . . .

Deafness is the most 'isolating
disability' with the exception
of being totally deaf & blind
Not much thought is given to
what it must be like to be deaf
& how hard it must be to learn
language without benefit of
sign
Most of us, disabled or non-
disabled, have the ability to
communicate
To absorb & learn language
through the media, parents,
peers & in school listening

with our ears to what people
say . . .

Sign Language, it is the language
of the deaf, the 4th most used
language in the U.S.A.
Although ASL (American Sign
Language) is a legitimate &
certified language accepted by
most countries, there are those
who prohibit the deaf their
language & demand they obey
There's this misconception
among many teachers of the
deaf that learning to speak &
lip-read is the only way to learn
english
This being the "Oral Method"
which is cruel, demeaning,
degrading, & should be
abolished . . .

The preferred method, now
gaining in popularity, is "Total
Comunication" using whatever
means available to learn
language, especially sign
It's criminal to see grown men &
women, educated orally, afraid
to use their native language for
fear of reprimand from parents
& long past teachers who still
treat the deaf as inferior
It's easy for these do-gooders to
chastize the deaf & demand
they speak & read lips because
do-gooders have hearing &
have never had the burden of
trying to lip-read & the
desperate struggle to speak,
they feel superior
These hearing people seem to
forget that we allow foreigners
their native tongue &
understand when they speak or
write broken english, this is
fine . . .

But if you're deaf, a native
language you have none,
according to some, & must
speak & write fluent english
lest you're considered "Deaf
and Dumb"
Only 35% of the english language
is readable on the lips & this is
usually one on one, when
others join in or a speaker's
coming in, then friend, 35%
goes down to almost none
And then we have the mumblers,
gum chewers, moustaches,
accents, the list goes on and on

When family's round the table or friends stop by, a deaf person feels insignificant, for they forget you're there, & conversation is not shared . . .

Give a little thought to how you'd feel watching people dancing, laughing, talking, & not hear a sound
Not to hear a baby's gurgle or cry, or birds singing at dawn & crickets chirping at night
Not to hear a movie on T.V. or in the theatre & wonder if you interpreted it right
Try watching a silent movie & see how much you understand, or plug up your ears & feel the abuse & hurt when someone's angered because you didn't hear . . .

The invisible disability, most who pass wouldn't know, see or care, so friends when passing, share a smile, a friendly hi, who knows, you may just meet one of "The Silent Minority" somewhere . . . ?!!!!

Robert G. Blewett
THE LONG SEASON
Lightly gliding through
my late-night, easy reverie;
I have fleetingly touched a dream
——of love so strong——
——and peace so great——
that surely this musing only be:
the artifice of a mind deceived.

And yet, as I view from afar,
warm in my perch of comfort,
the silvery wraiths promising all
and giving of nought;
I learn the need to seek that
dream,
as my driving gods would have
me do.

For there can be no greater
calling
——be it man or cloth or man of
stone;
For there can be no greater passion
——be it white-hot or cold of dead;
For there can be no greater
freedom
——be it soaring of high or
buried deep:

than following the fate which
truly lives
in the soul of each Long Season.

Jill Johnson
THE SUPREME COURT
I know we have met
Your face, your eyes
You refresh me,
Who are you?

Your voice I have heard
Kind, soft
It secures me,
Whose is it?

I recognize the touch
The gentleness, the tenderness
It calms me,
But how?

You represent something
Past, present
You mystify me
Like a new born babe.

You are a part of me
My soul, my mind
I feel it
You are my inner thoughts.

J. Robert Lomax
BEHIND ME
When I look behind and see your
face,
theres a setting sun that
shadows me.
And from within my soul merges
a silent
memory and a time we once
shared.
In this secret place, again and
again
I fondle each lasting moment.
For tomorrow, you'll be further
away . . .
A silhouette of life-behind me.

Lois Roquemore Carden
ARTS INDESTRUCTIBLE
The arts are the soul of a people
Made manifest and tangible.
The artist, alone, can capture the
will and the soul of man.
The arts live on even through
times of neglect;
They outlive politics and
politicians,
As well as governments and
creeds, and even societies.
The arts outlive the civilizations
which gave them birth.
They are the embodiment of a
people's faith.
Aknaton's hymn of adoration to
the sun,
Homer's great epics, and King
David's sweet songs:
Neither they nor the beautiful
things we find
And recover with infinite care
When the flood recedes,
Or the volcanic ashes cool,
And the ruins are cleared away,
Can ever be completely
destroyed.
The arts are indestructible!

Bonnie Elise Baker
NATURE'S CHILD

With Love to a Special Hair Stylist named Pete, from your friend.

Nature's Child is Wild and Free
And Meant to be for Eternity.

He Cannot Be Kept in a Little
Glass House—
He Needs to be Free like the
Little Door Mouse.

His Purpose in Life is to Add
Beauty and Grace—
Taken Away Would Wipe the
Smile From His Face.

Nature's Child Needs to be Loved
From Afar—
Love in Confinement Would
Cause Quite a Scar.

So Now, I Will Sit and be
Thankful to Watch
Nature's Child Run Wild and
Free
And I Will Love Him for All
Eternity.

Frances Stevens
VETERAN'S DAY 1983

Sgt. Thomas M. Stevens, Born November 11th, 1949 Lt. jg Raymond W. Stevens Phm 2/C Frances Stevens, WAVES

I am a soldier in "God's Army",
I know not when I lost my life.

It could have been in Korea,
Vietnam,
World War I, or World War II.

I only remember, I was too young
to die,
My life was just beginning
I had no time to cry.

But when my friends saw me
they smiled and said,

He is truly up in heaven,
a soldier in "God's Army".

There are no wars for these
soldiers to fight,

Only Peace and Tranquility
and God's Holy Light.

        Amen

Elizabeth Reynolds
THIS OLE HOME
This ole home, is lonely for love.
This ole home, is so empty, of
small
little one's try-ing to com-ing up
the steps.

     This Ole Home

This ole home, is so lost with-out
those
small voices say-ing those funny
things.

     This Ole Home

This ole home, is so lonely and
lost with-out
those small feet and the small
voices
runn-ing in said may I have some
cookies
and may I have a glass of kool-aid.

Louise Minnick
THINGS WE DO

To my husband who enjoys doing things with me.

We watch birds build their nests
Tirelessly feed their young
Get a fleeting glance of a
hummingbird feeding
Touch a child's soft cheek
Admire a perfect rose
Look at grass struggling to grow
in a crack
Wait for the first red ripe tomato
Smell a melon at it's best
Tear husks from a perfect
roasting ear
Savor a hot bowl of homemade
soup, on a crisp cold October
day
Take a pleasant drive to see the
Autumn leaves in a blaze of
glory
Smell the pungent odor of
burning leaves
Watch the flight of geese, in
perfect V formation, heading
south

Sooth an innocent child's fevered
brow
Comfort a dear friend, who has
lost a loved one
Wait for the rising of the sun
The setting of the same
Listen to the pitter-patter of long
awaited rain
We anxiously wait for the first
snowfall
And for a fire blazing and
crackling on the hearth
Curling up in our favorite chair
Reading a good book
Forgetting about the cares of the
day
Thanking our Lord for all things.

Margaret Pettus Parrish
CITIES
New York was once a great city.
Oh my it is a great pity
that it has deteriorated so,
And now people run to and fro,
Not knowing when it is that
Someone may hit them with a bat
Or grab their necklace of gold
And knock them down and be told
They hate you for you are old
And helpless and cannot see
The likes of people like me
Who are out to get what they can
From the helpless and ordinary
man.

New York is not the only place
That seems to have lost it's grace,
As all the cities in the U.S.A.
Seem now to be the same way.
Wo what can we now do
To shed this hubadroo
And put a stop to murdering?
For we were not meant for
plundering
But to live in peace and
brotherhood
And love each other is understood.
So what can we do to help our city
Except to set an example of great
Deity.

Elinor Lowe (Pierce)
LAST WISH
Oh God! I'm dying, and words
won't reach my lips.

Yet, I pray as you caress
my face, my thoughts will
somehow seep through to your
fingertips.

I have so much I want to tell
you. I have so much I want to
say. One is; even if You
granted me any more years, I
wouldn't want them any other
way.

We had a hard life. We had a
poor life. Yes! most of it
was bad.

But please look back with
Tenderness
When You think of the life
we had.

Genevieve Sanderson
Ode To Fort San Carlos
Old weathered darkened stone
Deserted and echoing alone
Gone is the tread of the midnite
watch
Gone are the pirates bent on
debauch
Gone are the Galleons under sail

Gone is the need for the sailors hale

The world now flights in another war

Rice and swamp, pockets and pomp

Politics, and fly boys jump into space

And when our babies grow up to face

Their world, will they too

Battle for freedom in a world all new?

On and on the conflict roars

Over sea and land and moors,

Until our GOD shall call us in

HOME from our eternal din

Eva Cook

Eva Cook
MISSOURI
Here in Missouri
Where you know we like to be
Everybody loves Missouri
You can plainly see
The people will sing it
The chimes will all ring it
As we look towards the sky
With our hopes just as high
Independence rates A 1
Position now for me
For you know Missouri
Is as great as it can be
The people are humming
Everyone's coming
To the show me state.

Brenda Lee Pickett
Who Knows What the Future Holds

To Ray who has been a great help to me, family members and friends. To my church and everyone who's searching for an answer.

Who knows what the future holds when the future is in God's hand.
Sometimes that seems so very hard for you and I to understand.
All we can do is have faith in the Lord that he would light our way.
Don't worry about the future let your light shine and just live from day to day.
The Lord makes all the decisions his will not ours be done.
The future will seems so far away until the last mile of the race is won.

For the future is not under your control, just shoot straight ahead aim for your goal.
Make the Lord your all and all you will make it to the top.
Just enjoy now don't you ever in this life stop.
You'll worry about the future that you might not ever see.
Quit worrying live the best out of life what ever will be will be.
Who knows what the future holds it maybe billions of miles away.
Let God take care of the future you just think about right now today.
You haven't the time to think about the future or about the past.
The only thing you have to think about is only what you do for Jesus CHRIST IS GOING TO LAST.
So do what you can it depends on no one but you.
Remember Jesus Christ said if you should take one step he would take two.
While the blood is still running warm in your vains think not of things untold.
For Jesus Christ and him alone knows what the future holds.

Dixie Lee Knittel
THE SURVIVORS
Wild geese nested in the thick green reeds,
In the marshes alongside the playful otter,
Little goslings grew big and learned to fly,
And swam and glided on the slumberous water.

They all flew south where it's warm and sunny,
Before the snows and the frigid cold arrived,
Many fell prey to predators and hunter's guns,
But returned in the spring, those who survived.

Loueda Gilmour
Birthday Balloons and Candles
Birthdays and Balloons
Light, gay, colorful
Sometimes airborne—
Floating gently
Until impaled—the bubble bursts,
Or, one lasts and lasts,
It's happiness to bring
To the Holder of the String.

Birthdays and Candles
Flickering in soft light,
Warming and Caressing
With loves gentle sighs
Now, Magical shadows
Now, Bright and Bold
Revealing—at Sixty—
A New Loveliness to Behold.

Mildred Barger
ONE BRIGHT NIGHT
One bright night long long ago,
Three wise men saw His star.
They hurried forth their Lord to find,

Their journey took them far.
The shepherds on a near-by hill,
While watching by their sheep,
Were visited by a heavenly guest,
While most men were asleep.

Now we remember that bright night,
When according to God's plan,
A babe was born in Bethleham,
And God reached down to man.

Phillip E. Carrico
THE TIN THORN
The rolling grass resembled painted glass
It seemed to go on forever,
The winds entwine viewing beauty sublime
And God must have sent the weather.

Gulf washed beaches to the fartherest reaches
Of Texas, all the way to Brownsville,
Bison were satisfied and longhorns multiplied
In this vastness where time stood still.

You could ride the west wind, call the north star friend
And look forever in any direction,
Freedom knew no bounds on these sacred grounds
And the sun saw it's own reflection.

The encroachment of man over a time span
Produced problems with the tin thorn,
Suddenly the longhorns were tame, things were not the same
And the west was a world reborn.

The old cowboy cried and the buffalo sighed
It was much worse than a prairie fire,
The world will never see the way it use to be
Cause they've strung the prairie with bob wire.

Joyce Billingsley
DESIRES OF THE SOUL

This poem is dedicated with love to my husband, Stan and my brother, Jimmy Jolley and sisters, June Cutler and Linda Olson.

The wind blows softly against her face,
like a lover's caressing hand.
Her soul mingles with that of the wind,
and she becomes a partner to a lover again.
The wind brushes a kiss upon her flesh,
bringing alive feelings,
that were once put to rest.
Clinging as to never let go,
they become passionate lovers
by the touching of their souls.

Vanessa Kaye
MY PURGATIVE
Coiled like a serpent inside of me
this pain and abject misery,

Eats at nerves pulled taut and tightly strung,
I try to cry, but the tears won't come.

Wound about my head, a vise that twists and turns but thrice,
Within my brain and bitterness doth strum,
I need to cry, but the tears won't come.

I seek the cleansing, healing flow to purge my tortured soul
Of things that make me want to run,
I have to cry, but the tears won't come.

So I tap the well of relief within and take out my paper and pen,
From which fly the words that bring a peaceful sum,
I want to cry, but the tears won't come.

Christine Y. Chadwick
MAKING AMENDS
He took some snow
To dust Earth's face,
To hurl snow far
Beyond the hill,
To fling it high
With gasping breath,
To blow it out
With blust'ry chill.

Snow granules raced,
Each sharp and fierce,
To pelt the air,
To sweep the sky,
To blot out trees,
To hide all paths,
To leap the fence
The World to seize!

Since He loved Earth's people,
He told His sun
To prepare for Spring,
To melt the snow,
To put Winter on the run!

Georgiana Leider Lahr
THE POET
The poet writes with pen that's dipped in gold,
The gold of truth, and love, and joy, and pain;
He tells of life, its sunshine and its rain—
All this he must inscribe with spirit bold,
The heights and depths of life he must unfold,
And pure must be his words, without a stain,
Then what he writes forever will remain.
He asks not for reward, or praise of men,
To Life, And Truth, and Love, he raises pen!

Katherine E. Cartwright
SILVER AND GOLD
Silver and gold, silver and gold
The colors of night and day
Silver are dreams of love that is gone
Gone in the dawn's first ray
I would rather not see the sun
Let love's stars shine forever
Gold is too bright for a broken heart
Bring back the moon's soft silver

Marylou G. Frisbie
EVENING SONG

Even the greys are beautiful,
Lord—
After the brilliance has faded
and the day has gone—
soft shades of evening—
subdued tones of twilight—
delicate patterns of silver
encircling isles of the Sound—
white sky through broken
clouds
giving promise morning will
come again.

Lord, help me to see
there is beauty in life's eventide;
the blaze of youthful strength
has waned—
but there remain
tones of gentleness,
of wisdom and strength
born of storm and stress,
of heartache and loss—
the quietness of a soul anchored
in the depths with God.

Bernard
Especially When You Are Sick

It's not nice to be alone
Especially when you are sick
To lay in a big empty bed
feeling the space grow
It's so forlorn to be left alone
Knowing how bad you feel
How your fever seems much worse
Your aches so much deeper
The blur of watery eyes and
The warmth of a runny nose
It would be so nice
to lay with someone close
Or talk with a faithful friend
someone who cares
It's not good to be alone
When you don't feel well
But that is the way it is
Especially when you are sick

George Malouf
THE CRY OF A SOUL

High above the clouds I soar,
Roaming, searching throughout
your realm;
Hunting, seeking your gateway's
door,
There, beyond the oasis's palm.

At times, I find me confused
and lost,
In need of guidance from a
heavenly host.
Hoping—praying, as my heart
aches stronger;
Shouting—screaming, as my
senses begin to falter.

. . . I find this world full of
hate and war,
And no one is there, in peace
and calm,
To care about what lays in
store,
Nor to want peace enough, to pay
its alm.

Staggering, shaking in my heart's
core,
I've pledged forever, this sea to
roam;
Steering, steadying my small
ship's oar
To trail behind the ethereal
foam.

. . . Have mercy, O'Lord, on one
and all,
And save us from this dismal fall;
Help us clean this awful mess,
That all mankind may live in
bliss.

William & Pat Rude

William H. Rude
SWEETHEART

*Dedicated to my sweet and
beloved wife—Pat Patterson
Rude*

The day we met we fell in love,
Smiling faces where love did start.
It had to be one for the other,
It was true love right from the
heart.

So kind was the girl that I did want,
So beautiful her love would shine.
I knew we would be joined
together,
I'll be hers and she will be mine.

That sweet young lady that I did
ask,
Was the one I wanted for my
wife.
Through Gods great power we
became one,
One we will be until the end of
life.

Now that God has joined us
together,
Our marriage stands out with
great pride.
The greatest thing upon this earth,
Is to have your lover at your side.

Good marriages hold to the very
end,
Our love for each other was

spoken in prayer.
When the time comes when we
must part,
In heaven will meet will both be
there.

Ruth G. McAlley
THE WORTHWHILE LIFE

Lord, give me life that I may know
The thrill of living clean,
The joy of love, contentment,
rest—
A depth of things not seen.
Lord, help me love that I may show
To all my fellowmen
The light of hope and faith on
Earth
And live them all again.
Lord, give me home and friends to
keep
The taint from future years,
Then hold me fast in paths of
truth
And fell the dreads and fears.
Yet best of all, Lord, give me hope,
That living, loving, all—
In fears, in strength, in sorrows, joys,
In life He'll be my all.

Frances L. Ayers
MY PRAYER

God, open my eyes, that I may see
Just how good you have been to
me
You've given me one swell person
that means so much in every
way
He fills my heart with joy day
after day
This is a gift that he daily passes
by
As I look into the world with an
unseen eye
He is not a stranger, unloved or
unknown
But a friend with a heart that I
would like to own
I love him dear God, and want
you to bless
Everything you hold in our
happiness
Take us and keep us in your
tender care
And hope someday we will be
one happy pair

Danny Raymond Johnson
Forgotten: But Not Gone

*To those many people, including
this poet, who fail to visit and
comfort those gallant souls who
dwell in veteran's hospitals and
forgotten rest homes, just waiting
and longing to see a loving face.*

Have we forgotten pearl Harbor?
Yes, I really think so.
How could we forget that stab in
our backs, that rape not long
ago?
Who knows, who cares? I can't
say cause I don't know.
Don't bother to ask about such
things, cause folks get offended
so.

Can you remember Korea,
Vietnam, Normandy, or any
other war?
You say: "cool it pal—— don't
remind us anymore"?

You're getting to be a bore. Don't
look at me, I'm OK, I'm not sore.

How easy it is for some to forget;
pain, lonliness, fear, sweat.
You say: "forget about Iwo Jima,
Mekong Delta, France"?
But, did you notice my one-legged
pants, my twisted frame, my
limp?
You say I shouldn't complain; I'm
acting like an imp?
Forty years have come and gone,
and now, America sings a
strangely empty song
But, I've got security; this
veteran's home. Thank God,
I'm not alone.
So . . . , what the heck, so, they
don't care. Who expects
America to always be fair?

John A. Cicala
CHRISTMAS 1983

*To a very special person—who
constantly restores my faith in
mankind—my wife* Maxine.

The time has come to think again
Of all our friends from way back
when
The dreams we shared, the fun
we had
And all the things that made us
sad

I guess its good that memories live
And once a year a season gives
A time for *hope, for love,* for *peace*
A time for man together be.

Josephine Corliss Liebhaber
GIVING THANKS?

Prospects are dim; one small flame
Enlightens the world, a gusty world
According to the news reports;
Certainly there is no hope, no
Expecting amity, harmony this
holiday.

Old geography lessons come
back—
Nicaragua, Lebanon, Granada,
Tripoli.

Expecting peace to appear is like
Awaiting the long gone Messiah's
Return; we wish for the
Thief in the night, but
Have only a raid at dawn.

Elizabeth Saltz
ROAD OF LIFE

Everyone has ideals of a perfect
life,
When we are born we strive for
perfection.
After a few years, we try to be
better,
When we reach our teens, we
are ready for life.

We ponder on a norm that will
bring success,
Achievers are most likely to
attain a goal.
After toil and strife, we reach our
aim,
Strife has not been in vain but
rewarded.

As life unfolds, it is not always
perfect,
It is filled with obstacles and

John Campbell, Editor & Publisher

reverses,
As one tries to achieve, there is
adversity,
What is the true road to success?

The road to life is hard, there are
pitfalls,
The weak fall by the wayside.
The strong survive and attain
happiness,
It is the will that helps to achieve.

When conscience tells that you
are wrong,
You try to reason and change.
The path you take must be
straight,
It will lead to fulfillment of life's
goal.

Laverne R. Hebert
Our Beautiful Outdoors
I love to be out in the woods in
the spring,
And listen to all the pretty birds
that sing.

And watch the fish swimming in
the stream,
As the wind softly blows,
making the small trees lean.

A deer softly steps through the
brush,
When we were listening to the
song of the thrush.

As the sun sparkles across the
water,
We caught a glimpse of a small
otter.

In the evening by the moonlight,
You see small brookies, like
propoises, jumping in the night.

We watch the squirrel and the
bluejay scramble for a piece of
pancake,
That some camper had
purposely left for them to take.

Someone calls out "I got a fish",
In the morning, that was his wish.

Oh, what a beautiful country God
made,
Something which is worthwhile
to save.

george a. mueller
ALONE
All alone, I sit in a secluded den.
Devouring a sandwich which had
been given.
Wondering why? I should come
to this?
With the bring up which I had
been given.

Someplace along the line of life
I must have missed my cue.
So, I slipped and slid but never
reached bottom
The way all drifters do.

I once changed my clothes at a
nobody home.
I looked into the glass with a
smile!
Then, this thought came right
into my vitals—
"This is only for a little while!"

Before I knew it that suit was a
mess.
I didn't feel bad cause it, wasn't
mine.

I believe it takes something more
than dress—
To change this slide down! of
mine.

Oh! giver of life! Am I hopeless?
Or will I someday find my que??
Please give me a little more
stigma—
Then, I'd climb straight up, to you!!

Ann L. Browning
OUR HERITAGE
Our ancestors seeking freedom
In a wild unsettled land
Built an enduring type of life
style
On which we base our stand.
They chose our country's emblem
The star-spangled
Red and white and blue
To gloriously wave above us
Let us to that flag be true.
Red for blood shed in its service
White for loyal purity
True-blue a field to find forever
States as stars to shine in unity.
History is in the making
Our country onward moves
And as they who trod before us
We our loyalty must prove
As they served the God of ages
So to Him we should return and
"In God we trust," our motto
Whole-heartedly affirm.

Mrs. Ellis J. Smith, Sr.
From Strangers To Friends
Tell me, who is that stranger
I see?
He is no stranger to you, but he is
To me.
You know how he walks. You
know how
He talks.
When he smiles I wonder if he
loves
Or mocks.
As I observe him I ask; will he be
friend
Or foe?
Will he one day lift my spirits or
cause
Me woe?

Once I met a stranger, that
stranger
Was you.
You have become a dear friend,
tried
And true.
We've laughed together, cried
together day
By day.
We've shared our secrets, told our
fears in
Moments grey.
Friendship is the greatest treasure
one
Could possess.
Many friends are first strangers,
as you
Might guess.

James Andrew Stowe
STRESS
Most any one will usually
confess,
No pain compares to that of
stress.
It affects us all, in some degree,
And the harm it does, we may
not see.

But why does it have to be that
way,
Can't life be calm from day to day?
To end each day with a restful
night,
Without anxiety, fear or fright?

I'm sure there's things that we
can do,
To keep our life from being blue.
A little help from others too,
But most of it must come from
you.

If you break a glass and can't
repair,
What good to fret or feel despair?
If emotions rise and your eyes are
filled,
Why must you cry, the milk is
spilled?

But, what will help, is make a vow,
Take positive action, here and
now.
Resolve and earnestly take a
pledge,
To never leave a glass at the table
edge.

If our emotions take command,
And always keep the upper hand.
A stressful life, we can't correct,
If we do not use our intellect.

Christine Y. Chadwick
WHEN SPRING ARRIVES
The sun kisses awake the buds of
the trees,
Which respond and begin to
swell.
In the warming, refreshing breeze,
Something's happ'ning, you can
tell!

Down by the pond in the
shadowy marsh,
Creatures stir from their winter's
sleep,
As the ice, long bitterly cold and
harsh,
Now melts and makes "Ole
Winter" weep!

Birds rouse and trill in the
branches above
Greening grass, where a vi'let
starts;
Life now moves to make new love,
For near each male, a female darts!

A sun's gold ray has made its mark
Longer than yesterday's on
kitchen wall.
You feel the earth wake up; So
Hark!
You know that Spring is
sounding its call!

Willie Lee Gray
SENSE OF VALUES
If a soldier's life were valued
More than oil that's in the ground
Guns or bombs in any country
Would cease to make a sound.

If a soldier's life were valued
More than territorial gain
Each nation would be satisfied
With it's present domain.

There would be no wounded
soldiers
No more numbered with the dead
We would learn of war no more
And have peace on earth instead.

Dan Tyler
DREAM BROKER
My ticker tape day sags
to a chest-high oak horizon's
crowded choreography
of collars loosening and desperate
gulping.

　　　　　Make mine wine
as random words like bees knees
and Madagascar
develop colossal momentums of
delight
and crash the party of my tongue.
Or
overhearing, "But we're cultured
people . . ."
I imagine them sprouting
like bacteria in petrie dishes. Or
wonder is sighs whip rose dust
into stars.

　　　　　Loony tunes? Anyway
worth the price of wine
or versa vice. "Hey barkeep,
what's on tap?" "Opportunity," he
says,
drawing it,
as tears wear gulleys in his
gorgeous face.

Danny Raymond Johnson
**Whatever Happened To
the True Christmas
Spirit?**

---

*To remind the world that
Christmas has been grossly
abused in recent times and that it
is a time for giving, not always
the opposite, or receiving.
Scripture: "It is more blessed to
give". Acts 20:35*

Whatever happened to the
Christmas spirit we knew not
long ago?
People don't exchange gifts much
anymore; Or, or at least they
tell me so.
But Christmas is all about giving,
not taking
Each Time I think of what's
happened to Christmas
My heart can't help but start
breaking.
There's a simple answer to this
question. And it's in the Holy
Bible.
If I should be bold enough to tell
you why, I might be held for
libel.
In that great book of wisdom, it
tells of man's last days
And Christmas is the surest sign
we've turned Christ "out to
graze."
It's hustle, bustle, run and wait;
There's panic in our holiday gait.
And all for what? There is no
doubt; in Christmas most folks
leave Christ out.
It's all too plain, we think of
personal gain, and selfishness
seems to be the rule. Isn't that
just like a fool?
What happened to the old
fashioned love; to the wise men
who once looked above, into
the face of God to look for a
blessing

304

Come on folks!, I can't be just
guessing.
You know that what I'm saying is
true. Your heart alone, it tells
on you
The way we shop and push and
shove, you'd think there was
no God above
Is our Lord and Savior really
forgotten?
If so . . . we sure are pretty darn
rotten.

Barbara A. Levins
GOD
God is morning
God is night
God is everything in sight.

God created the skies above,
God made woman for man to love.

He did his best to make us right,
He gave us hearing, speech and
sight
and all he asked is that one day,
we'd set aside all things and pray.

God created the wind and sea
Thank you God for creating me.

Jane Ross
WE LOVE MAMA

*With all my love to Mama
Georgie Ronnie Doreen Gwen
Bobby Patty Terry Flo And Alex*

Dad left without a care
he left all to Mama
he didn't take his share.
Mama was left with ten
but Mama did the best she can.
Mama knew that the times ahead
would be hard,
but she always said have fate
in God.
Mama also knew that she would
have to bring us up all alone,
but she was determined to give
us a good home.
At night we all slept in one
room,
Mama tried to be happy and
showed
no gloom.
At times we shard a loaf of bread
we don't know how Mama didn't
go
out of her head.
Ten little babys all running
around
but Mama never let us sleep on
the
ground.
Ten little babys all screaming
with shout,
we don't know how Mama didn't
walk out.
Mama gave us her love and every
thing
she had,
and she is the best Mother a child
could have had.

Trudi Barnard
FROM ENEMY TO HOPE
The enemy came
It stayed and stayed and stayed
Lives were ruined
Chances were gone
Things seemed hopeless
Would we ever be free of it?

Then came hope!
Hope was availabe to all
It brightened faces
Mended lives
Shone the way to truth
Would we take advantage of it?

The enemy is still here
But not for long
It has been purposed for
destruction
Hope conquers all
Now a time for rejuvination
Giving thanks to the Giver of
hope.

Mary Katherine Fleck
THE LIGHT OF MY LIFE

*To all Christians for their
undying devotion to the Lord and
to Jesus Christ for His undying
love for me.*

Lord, you're the only one who can
take my hand,
And show me the way,
Who I can talk to and know that
You will understand,
And help me to live day by day.

Lord, you're my everything,
You picked me up when I was
down,
And gave me a song to sing,
That helped turn my life around.

Oh, what would I do without you,
Lord,
For You are always by my side.
You have given me my sword,
So that I shall abide.

Your Son died for me,
And He is the sunshine of my life.
I will never be able to thank Thee,
For all Your guidance and light.

Jettie Tuthill
CHRISTMAS MORNING
Golden Star glowing
Blue snow blowing

Pine trees perfuming
Blue birds tuning

Azure sky glistening
Angels listening

Wise men riding
Shepherds abiding

Cherubs flying
Mary sighing

Christ Child borning
Christmas morning

Hazen Fauver
Someone Will Ask For Thee
Someone will say, "If I had known,
I'd lose my friend so soon,
I could have shown more kindness,
Instead of flowers now bestroon."

Someone will say, "I remember
the time,"
And you're alive again,
As they laugh and talk of days
gone by,
And filling memories in.

Someone will come and ask for
thee,
But you will not be here.
Someone will long again to see,
A friend they held so dear.

I deem my friends the loyal kind,

The kind that help you through,
The toughest days and lonely
nights,
As any friend would do.

Some things will help one to
conform,
But all the gold will not replace,
The satisfaction of seeing a friend,
And the smile of a friendly face.

Dorothy G. Gerber
A FRIEND
A friend is one who's always there
And who your life will gladly
share.
Sometimes the going can get tough
And the way ahead looks very
rough.
Whatever the weather, be it good
or bad,
And whether your mood is happy
or sad,
A friend is one who'll really care
And who her time will always
share.
Maybe there's not a word to be
said,
But only a need for the soul to be
fed
By a friend's warm hand on a
shoulder placed
Which can speak many volumes
when one is faced
With a sorrow or fear so big and
complex
That in one's mind the world it
affects.
There's also the joy and the
laughter in life
That can be shared, just the same
as strife.
A friend's ever near to lend a
hand
To wipe away teardrops or strike
up a band.
A true friend is one who's tried
and true
Whose hand reaches out to me or
to you.

Mary E. B. Hallbrook
HOBO
He's not very much, so it seems,
With his shabby clothes, and
broken dreams.
Walking the streets endlessly,
devoid of
A goal, he's lost touch with the
world, but
He still has a heart, and he still
has a soul.
His pockets are empty, his eyes
misty with
Tears . . . . ask him how it
happened . . . sadly,
He adds up the years.
He once had a family, including
a wife,
'Til a man with more money,
promised a better life.
And now, his new
bedfellow . . a bottle of
Gin, the bottle's cold against his
body,
Still warms him within.
He walks away the memories of
a shattered life
From one town to another,
sleeping . . . anywere,
Broken; by temptation and love,
Living in strife.

Anne Chatterton Brown
A CHILD FOR A DAY
Teardrops reflecting images,
Of our yesterdays,
Recollections of us,
Children at play.
A haunting tune,
From the days gone by,
Mothers sweet voice,
Singing a lullaby.
Memories, so distant,
Faded by time,
Laughter still echoing
In the depths of my mind.
A vision I see,
From my childhood past,
Of the days passing by me,
Till I'm grown up at last.
Teardrops reflecting images,
Of my children at play,
And here I am dreaming,
Of being a child for a day.

Van D. Garner
As Long As the Spirit Lives
As long as the spirit lives, there
Are poems . . . each one a
sculptured
Silhouette of the soul . . .
Each one returning three-fold
Life's potpourri of fantasies
And realities.

As long as the spirit lives, novel
Ideas abound, spraying inventive
Incense into creative expression,
Molding each thought, pressing
Each word, clarifying confusion.

As long as the spirit lives, the
Rigors of self-discipline
Challenge the mind's free-wheeling
Aspirations, taming wild
imaginings,
Dissolving subconscious
impurities,
Growing in love and
enlightenment,
Producing poetic eternities . . .
As long as the spirit lives!

Dottie Dunbar
MY HOPE
As the years flash by
I often sit and sigh
What have I done
And what have I won
And what will the final count be?

I try to live each day
As the Good Book says I may
Loving the beauty all around
And treasuring what I have found
And keeping my faith in Thee.

Now maybe in the end
When the road has reached the
bend
And I am received up there
In the land beautiful and fair
I'll find the books balanced and
free.

Jan Fairless
INTEMPERANCE
Here is the shell of an empty man
who crawls inside a bottle
whenever he can.
He never shares his hopes and
dreams
and no one can hear his soul as
it screams
For love and kindness,
understanding at best;

he hides in the bottle with all of
the rest
Of the empty shells who, afraid of
life,
blame everyone else for their
troubles and strife.
Who with their alcoholic
illusions seek escape.
Who with their empty lifes,
loving souls, rape.

John L. Caravaglio
HOLD ME
Hold me.
Never let me go.
Hold me.
My dear, I love you so.
For now's the time.
For you to know.
If you really love me.
Of if you let me go.

My love, you'll never know.
How much, I really love you.

How much do you know.
So love me now.
And say no more.

Why?—because,
I—love—you.
I—love—you.
I—love—you.
So hold me—hold me now.
And never let me go.
My dearest, I love you so.
Now, and for ever more.

Barbara Slaga
WHERE DID YOU GO?
Remember how we met? It seems
so long ago
I felt as if I knew you for a
million years
But love is so unpredictable
It goes through so much and now
Where did you go?
We walked in the park
We danced until dawn
We shared so many dreams in the
night
Now, I never felt so alone
Where did you go?
I gave you everything I had to give
I loved you with my heart and soul
I thought you shared the same
feeling
Where did you go?
Was it too much, was it too little
Did I hurt you? or
Did you just get scared of love
and run away.
Couldn't you bear the price
We both had to pay . . .

I held on so long and strong
Then one cold day-in June
I found out
I treasured love too soon
Where did you go?

Mary Ann Talley
TO DOLLY
To graze alone you were put to
pasture.
It should not matter that you've
passed your prime,
Not you who raced the wind and
beat the time,
But there was no thought, no
glance, no gesture.
It is not fair; it's really quite unjust;
You were a star, you wondrous
mare of white;
You won them all, brought glory
and delight,
Just look at all the trophies
catching dust!
The barrels were placed even as
you please;
The poles stood straight, all six,
all in a row,
And in and out you went 'midst
shouts of "go!"
Head straight, tail high, name
flying in the breeze.
You've left the arena who were
the best,
But graze in peace; you've won
your chance to rest.

Ronald A. Bond
TO CLIMB IS OVER
It's been rough sometimes
along the way,
Struggling to climb life's hill
day by day.

On my climb to reach
the very top,
Sometimes I'd run
not wanting to stop.

But lately I'm feeling low
like I've lost my zip,
As over the top
I'm about to slip.

For I've come
all the way,
And over the hill
I'll go today.

I know my friends
will laugh and say,
Smile! Life begins
at 40, anyway.

Marilyn Wilson
MOM AND DAD
There are lots of people, all over
the world some men, some
women, some boys, some girls.
But I could search and never find
a man more gentle or a woman
more kind.

You raised seven kids to be
healthy and strong and taught
us the difference between right
and wrong.
Though we've all gone now with
mates we've found whenever
we're in trouble, you're always
around.

Out of all the people I've known
or met there are two special
people I'll never forget.
They brought me up and I'm so

glad.
They're the people I'm proud of
MY Mom and Dad.

Sister Marilyn Therese Beauvais
(Sister of Charity)
BORN THIS CENTURY
Jesus, What if You were born this
century,
Surrounded by gifts and
Christmas tree?

Would you see this poor, poor
world at all,
Or only see a colored hanging ball?

Would You look at all glitter and
light,
Yet, prefer that cold Bethlehem
night?

Would You see life as a tale or
fable,
Then choose Your time back in
the stable?

Would you cry out loud, and
then suddenly pause,
Knowing You were preferred to
Old Santa Claus?

Would You smell the pine and
cedar wood,
And still think of Mankind's
eternal good?

Would You grasp Your mother's
veil,
And wish peace on earth prevail?

Would You look up and see a
bright star,
And thank the Father for Who
You are?

Yes, Jesus if You were born this
century,
You'd still be remembering little
ole me.

Linda Jeanne Thomas
THE WREATH
The wreath of holly upon the door,
beckons friends from near and far.
The crisp green leaves,
bound in a wreath,
are reminiscent of a crown.
A crown once worn, so long ago—
of thorns that cruelly pierced His
head!
Jesus bore the pain,
the death, to save our souls.
The holly berries signify
the blood from thorns that He did
suffer!
The bright red bow denotes His
heart:
betrayed and weary, and torn apart!
So when you hang your lovely
wreath,
upon your sweet home's door,
take care to thank our Lord above,
for the Son He gave, so long ago!

Nanette Lee Hurray
To Christmas, With Love
Why does Christmas tend to
change
Every person of every age,
Create a glowing warmth, and yes,
The newfound feeling of happiness

Could there be a fitful reason
When with the coming of this
joyous season
Hearts grow fond and unafraid
And friends are so very easily made

Might it be the Holy Birth
Of long ago on this aged earth
Which brought salvation to all
mankind
That is forever embedded in our
minds

Didn't the Christ Child come that
day
To love us and to show the way
That we could live in harmoney
Through faith and Christianity

Then tell me why it must disappear
When it should be here
throughout the year
This lovely feeling should around
us stay
And not be saved only for
Christmas Day

Dixie Higgins
UNTITLED
The wind blows
dust thick in the sky—
the wings of a
million butterflies.

Naomi Arakawa
LIFE

---

*To my mom and dad, who I could
never live without. My brother
Jerry, who is always willing to help.
And my brother Patrick, who has
shown me the two sides of life.*

Life has its ups and downs,
It's good times and bad times,
The trials and the errors,
The triumphs and the failures,
The laughs, the tears.
Sometimes don't you wonder,
Is it worth the while?

You go through life from the cry
of birth to the sigh of death.
All the slaps, all the kisses,
The dances, the parties, the dates.
From kindergarten to college
graduation.

From boyfriend to boyfriend,
girlfriend to girlfriend.
The fun of teenagers to the
sophistication of adults,
From courting to marriage.
The children, grandchildren, and
godchildren.
And all you can do is to enjoy life
while you still can.

Walter Warren Williams
JEALOUSY
If I have thought of you with
love, my dear,
And known your body close to
mine in sleep,
Can I then see you with other
men without a tear,
Or know, forevermore, the force
of love so deep.

My errant thoughts of you caress
my mind with love,
Laughing love, love in the union
of two bodies deep within a
universe,
Love that isolates our transient
beings in heaven above,
And for one brief moment returns
them to mundane matters to
immerse.

If I had known that my love for

you would be betrayed,
And put aside to light another
    flame,
Would I have given you my heart
    with heaven's aid
Only to watch the wild passion of
    my love be love in only name.

Where'er I go I will carry the
    eternal rapture of your face,
Through my whole life, a sword
    upon my troubled heart,
And I will know that I can never
    win the race
Again, that caused our love to fall
    apart.

Elaine M. Marshall
DANGEROUS DAN

---

*This poem is dedicated to my
grandchildren Derek, Dustin and
Daniella*

I'm Dangerous Dan
    from the Yucatan,
I'm searching for the
    famous Marshall Clan!
The badge I am wearing
    is silver and bright,
everyone can see
    I'm ready to fight!
I look to the East
    as far as I can,
right at that moment,
    I have a plan.
I'll blow my whistle
    for Deputy John,
together we'll meet

the whole Clan head-on!
We will surround them
    as they sleep at night,
they'll have to give up,
    they won't want to fight!
The town will honor
    my friend John, and me,
with cookies and punch,
    we'll be CELEBRITIES!
A noisy parade
    we will lead through town . . .
oh no, Mom just called,
    it's time to lie down.
I will keep my boots
    right here by my side,
so after my rest
    I can quickly ride!
I need to find that
    famous Marshall Clan,
'cause I'm Dangerous Dan
    from the Yucatan.

Mary Ann Christisen
MY LOVE FOR YOU
My love for you has always been.
My love for you is now.
My love for you will always be,
Of this I have no doubt.

Of all the happy times I've had
The best were shared with you,
Just doing little silly things,
But so important to.

Not all the years we've shared
    went smooth,
Not all were up to par.
Not all the blame is put on you,
Not all on me by far.

Can we think of growing old
    together,
When growing up must still be
    done?
It's this we must accomplish,
Before we two are one.

Mabel Esmay
SONNET
Strange, is it not, that I once
    thought to bring
You song, as though it were some
    shining thing
For you to see and hear—then to
    hold tight
Like some charm against a
    prowling night
That sought you out to startle or
    dismay?
Then,—within the dark that men
    call day
Alone, you rose to gain a higher
    place.
I now hear memories, where once
    I saw your face.

There was no need of words to
    bring me
The constant singing of the
    surging sea
Each memory again finds roll
SO, in your quest, you stand upon
    your OWN high place.
DID I NOT EARLY SEE THIS
COMING IN YOUR FACE?

Shirley Skinner
DANIEL
Daniel
Daniel
Siting in a lions den
Waiting for deliverance
Quietly
Patiently
full of confidence
in you Lord
You delivered
you delivered
Strong if your power
trust in you
Yes I do
Yes I do Quietly
Patiently
Full of confidence am I
I wait for your deliverance
For you deliver
Yes you do
Yes you do

Albert Stengelsen
SAGE AGE
With creaking joints and many
    groans
He ached along from day to day.
He blamed his years (three score

and five)
And spread gloom thickly on his
    way.

"Now, Sonny," said his graybeard
    friend,
"You're young. It's good to be alive.
Just think that when you reach
    my age,
I'll be a hundred twenty five."

Mrs. Mildred Gollnick
CHRISTMAS
This the Christmas season, is the
    best time of the year.
We always seem to get in touch,
    with loved ones far and near.
Did you ever stop to wonder, why
    we'er so full of joy and mirth?
Its because we celebrate our own
    dear Saviour's birth.
Not because of presents, or
    baubles on the tree.
But because God sent his Son, a
    gift for you and me.
So with joyful hearts we
    celebrate, God's gift so filled
    with love.
For with his Son, God also sent
    his blessings from above.

Walter Brightwell
COSMOLOGIC
God stopped the earth
That we should meet
The day was short
The shortest
The winter solstice
Lonely had been our nights
Cold
Empty
Spiritless
Loveless
Until that time when
Earth in God's universe
Paused
And we stood smitten
Face to face
The earth began to move again
Slowly at first as though
To guide our way
Past spring
When night time equaled day
Till June
When then it paused once more
And locked our hearts away
Now hand in hand
We watch each season pass
Sharing the warmth and wonder
    of each other
And question not
This miracle in our lives
Any more than how
The universe itself survives

Jeanne Marie Halama
MAPLE GOLD PURLOINED
Midnight's frost felled the
    chrysanthemums to the last
    yellow-blond and red head.
They stand today with hanging
    blossoms, aromatic foliage
    curled and dead.
Morning stirrings of a nippy
    breeze send down golden
    leaves, a sudden rain . . .
Autumn denuding carnival trees
    to lithe grey trunks and limbs
    again.
Winter frowns on Autumn gaiety
    erasing party world in one fell
    stroke, bringing a somber touch

of sobriety
this frost-befingered night awoke.
I tread the fallen carpet ruefully.
Winter, you've stolen Maple gold
    from me!

Curtis L. Woods
MISSILES
Out on a hill where scarecrows
    stand
    Beneath an autumn moon,
And cast their deathly shadows
    o'er
    The world without impune,
Like silhouettes against the sky
    Their ghostly specters loom,
Like falcons with their talons bare
    Forecasting pending doom.

For there's a grizzly bear at large
    Who preys upon the meek,
And if there were no scarecrows
    there
    She'd soon devour the weak;
But hunger pains will tempt her
    soul
    To cross the great divide,
In quest for all the eagle eggs
    Upon the mountain side.

The eagle then will spread her
    wings
    And fly out o'er the hill,
To where the deadly scarecrows
    stand,
    Intent upon the kill;
The bear has found the eagle's nest
    And bellows in the wind,
To find the lust for eagle eggs
    Has brought her final end.

Anna L. Morris
HAPPINESS? WHERE?
    Ma
I looked for happiness in the sky:
Cold stars twinkling met my eye.
I looked long at a dew petaled rose,
And at the glistening snowflake
    froze.
No, nor was it in the brand new
    chair,
Happiness? Where, oh, where?

I searched for happiness on the
    street,
Glancing at faces I chanced to
    meet.
I looked in the stores for new
    clothes.
And it wasn't in the dress I chose.
I looked for happiness in a car,
Traveling many, many miles afar.

Happiness? It wasn't there.
I must find it. Where? Oh, where?
I did a kindness and then—indeed!
Happiness happened like a warm
    seed.
It blossomed and bloomed like a
    lovely flower.
Happiness! ! ! I found it this very
    hour!

Ms. Marilyn Boatner Ford
RON

TO . . The one I Love.

When I first saw you, I wanted to
    examine your being, right
    down to it's finest core.
When I first saw you, your smile
    almost made me slip into

a wild fantasy of love, which I
never experienced before.
Your warm vibration, felt like a
love meditation, flowing gently
through the chambers of my
heart.
Your eyes touched my eyes,
Your lips touched my lips,
Your hand reached out for
mine.
OH! I couldn't stop the tears,
which fell from my eyes, for
my soul has often cried for
someone like "you" by my
side . . . Right then and there, I
said a prayer to be in your
heart FOREVERMORE,
Sharing Love,
Giving Love,
Like never before . . .
You see "Ron",
When I first saw you, I KNEW
that . . .
I loved you,
Very
Very
Much.

Mary Lou Collins
LOVER'S REQUEST
Walk gently my love
to the door of my heart.
Turn the handle with care
not to break it apart.

Enter without any doubt
in your mind,
that the world here with me
is the best you can find.

Dance with me through all
the troubles of life.
Help me to stray from the
sorrows and strife.

Smile with me always,
don't make me blue.
And I promise you darling
I'll always love you.

Heiwet Keflom
WHY NOT ME . . . ?

To Mom and Dad

Better count my blessings ere I go
astray
Wander further yonder, day by day.
Woe me, where do I —heedless
sinner— begin?
Only the other day did YOU treat
me like a queen.

YOU, O Lord, fortified my plight
Guided my every step day and
night.
While many —young and old—
shivered with fright;
When nature revolted against the
gruesome sight.
Dare I shout, nay, whisper Lord:
WHY NOT ME . . . ?

But still do I tremble at the
nations' cry:
Let's brew war here and there;
Devour some, remake some, what
seems to be the fear.
Peace talks are known not to
hold any water;
Peace treaties can be broken with
renewed manslaughter.
Oh! How my heart bleeds!

Will my beloved country
disappear?
Am I doomed not to set an eye on
the land I hold so dear.

Yet, YOU, O Lord, and only YOU
are the Doctor.
YOU bring peace, calm troubled
water.
Rejoin families, bring nations
together.
Dare I not utter then, Lord:
WHY NOT ME . . . ?

Catharina Rinta

Catharina Rinta
MY HOMETOWN

*Dedicated to my Hometown
Painesville, Ohio.*

I like to walk your streets and
watch the people.
I'm so at home, I know each little
nook.
From stately Courthouse to the
hotdog vender,
From store to store and
everywhere I look.

I love the park, a quiet small oasis,
right in the middle of your busy
square.
With trees, and squirrels that
play on grassy places,
a bench or two to rest a moment
there.

So many memories hide in every
corner.
My children's faces I can clearly
see
at Christmas-time, through
decorated windows,
while snow and Carols weave a
spell for me.

Some stores are gone and leave an
empty feeling.
But there are new ones, that will
make the present bright.
New friends to meet, new things
to catch our fancy,
each store stands out and brings
some new delight.

You've changed a lot since we
first moved here.
But so have we, and change is not
so bad.
We've grown together, through
some good and bad times.
You are MY Town
and I'm so glad of that!

Frances Carter
GOOD MORNING, DEAR
"Good morning, dear. Sleep well?"
Our voices casual, bright.
We kiss, hug briefly, tightly,
search each other's face
Covertly, lest new knowledge
show of numbered days
And tight-rope phase begun. Our
fingers cling. I ask,
"The nights, perfection now, don't
you agree? Our kind—
Wool blanket weather. Snuggle
weather. Yes?"
In the old mirror old eyes catch
and hold and shine.

I brew our breakfast tea, stir
hiccoughing oatmeal,
Set out three eggs for Jim, and
pray you had not sensed
My panicked listening for your
breathing in the night,
I as distraught as you that morn I
overslept.

"The day's a gem," I chirp. "I'll
pack a picnic lunch."
You nod and smile, "I'll finish
pruning while you dust.
We'll walk our forty-minute brace
of miles and then
Drive 'round the foothills." (Oh, I
love you, Man.)

To Jim, "Do come along. We like
your company."
Considering, fork in air, Jim tilts
his head.
Now eighteen summers wise, our
grandson-guest—
Of late our keen observer too, I
note—
Is tolerant, fond, amused, and
yesterday advised
Paris couture, world travel, Kenya
safari, art.

Tamara Lee Topor
JUST A FEW REASONS
You are my friend for many
reasons
Many of which are hard to explain
You are there when I'm feeling
pain
You are there when I'm feeling low
You are there when I'm feeling fine
That's just a few reasons why you
are a friend of mine
Even though we have our share of
fights
Which might produce some
restless nights
Regardless of how bad either one
of us is hurting
We seem to find it in each other
to forgive
So, as long as you're you and I'm
me
You'll be my friend forever.

Irene S. Laymon
SPECIAL PEOPLE
Special people are the ones
Who while shopping say hello,
Give a smile to those grown
weary
Make a heart with warmth glow.

They pause to see the beauty
Of a cobweb filled with dew,
Or listen to a singing bird
While picking flowers for you.

They wipe the tears of children
They take time to care and share,
They listen to your problems
And wisk away your despair.

Special people are earth's angels
Carrying out God's plan,
Of spreading goodwill and
brotherhood
Across this magnificent land

Ruth J. Rowland
TRUE LOVE
Beneath the rose twined archway,
under a lemon moon.
Stood a love enrapured couple,
enchantment in full bloom.
From jewel encrusted heavens,
shines a bright and shimmering
star.
As tho a glowing beacon, from a
light house ever so far.

He offered her a lifetime,
promising never to part.
In turn she gave of her sweet lips,
with full and bursting heart.
They came together in wedded
bliss, surrounded by family and
friends.
Four beautiful children, formed
happiness to the end.

All four children have left the
nest, starting families of their
own.
Each striving for utmost success,
with soaring heights unknown.
Lovingly guided by head of
family, to him they are so dear.
With expert finesse he has paved
the way, proving love will
persevere!

Doyle Honea
WERE YOU ASLEEP DADDY
Morning begins unreal, it seems,
with
"Coffee's ready, dad".
Somewhere in my misty dreams I
understand whats said.
Later as I leave for work, a tear is
softly shed.
"You didn't kiss me bye—have I
been really bad?"
Hugs and kisses quickly
exchanged, I hurry on my way
To wonder what happens to a
little girl in an everlasting day.
In the evening a full report of the
fun or agony
From the joy of kitten found or a
skinned and bandaged knee.
"A wheel came off my tricycle
and I broke a glass today.
But I didn't get a spanking 'cause
mommy's nice that way".
And then a sound in the midst of
night,
I jumped to my feet, unsure in
my fright.
"I want a drink of water please".
The voice recalled, I breathed
with ease.
Sleepily I staggered through the
scattered toys and dolls,
Stepped on Jacks, tripped on
skates and balls.
Sitting there sleep-eyed, smiling a
sheepish smile,
"Were you asleep, daddy?"—"Only
for a little while".
The drink consumed, a thank

you spent, covers again in
place,
A teddybear under a now limp
arm, and love all over her face.
"Were you asleep, daddy?" a half-
awake child discerned,
"Only for a little while, but *never*
where you're concerned."

Ginger Giles
LETTING GO

---

*Dedicated to Monty Roper who
inspired me to write this poem.
And to my parents who gave me
support and encouragement.*

Today I remembered
All those times we had.
We had mostly good,
But there were some bad.
Now we're apart,
And now I can see
That I took for granted
All the things you did for me.
I wish we could go back
To times long ago,
But as someone once told me
To the past you must let go.
So now I am strong
Or I am trying to be.
But when I start thinking,
It's hard not to see
Memories of us
That will always last.
But I must look for the future,
And not live in the past.

Martha Stroshine Burrow
AUTUMN
Pumpkins on the vine
Trees of red and gold
A nip in the air
The smell of burning leaves
Autumn.

The apple harvest in fall pagent
The spectacle of folks browsing
At apple stands, sipping hot
cider
Sampling slices of smooth Rome
Beauty
Autumn.

Sweet Delicious apples
It's enough to make even a
New Englander envious
But there's more to autumn
Than apples.

The sycamores and oaks are even
now
Putting on their finery of yellow
And gold fall colors
There's a spreading chestnut tree
Autumn.

The oaks are turning gold
The liquid amber is turning rust
and orange
The Chinese pistache can get
four or five
Colors on one limb, oranges,
yellows, pinks, reds
Autumn.

These are the hallmark of
autumn.
"The picture that no painter has
the colorin'
to mock," as James Whitcomb
Riely put it
Autumn.

A unique stand of aspens, which
turn yellow in
The fall, stands of dogwood
which turn yellow and
Maples which turn red and gold
can be found in
Abundance, I suspect we'll have a
long
Autumn.

Stress is part of what makes trees
turn color
The season will probably be slow
and leisurely
What we need are some cold
nights, but the Evergreens
Don't turn colors, just drop pine
cones
For autumn.

Is it necessary to climb a
mountain to find Autumn?
Not while classic autumn props
such as pumpkins,
Cornstalks and Indian corn lay
waiting in valleys
Even fall colors touch the
Sycamores in yellow
Autumn finery.

Pistachios which turn red and
Tritan maples blush
The Chinese elms along with the
Maples turn yellow
The liquid amber trees turn red
and are scattered
Widely throughout the city. It
isn't New England
It's Autumn.

Gina Marie Russo
THE WHITE DEATH
Elusive demons of the white
variety:
Snow-flecked gloom within the rut,
Ennui murmuring through chalk-
heart thrusts
its ghost anxieties.
Triggering pinched sobriety
among the frayed.
Cold, barren ash of Mechanical
days
ekes its langour,
but with no definitive tracemark.
Just innocuous, lead space-warps
to quote pain,
a droning of vortices.
Locked irresistibly on left-brain
to exact mind-pall.

Kalevi Lappalainen
A POEM IN PRAISE
I waited for the truth
I prayed a lot
I was so worried
Had you become Lot

Ten years since
Our marriage ended
Is she happy, does
Glenda exist

One's quest for truth
And one's ardent wishes
Will be answered
When the time is right

These and similar
Thoughts of mine
Recurred in the mornings
Dissolved into the nights

Till is happened
The call last night
You had matured
I loved your heart

Patricia Ann Warkentin
**Breathless Flight For
Eternity**

---

*Dedicated to the Lord and the
inspiration of His Word.*

Today for the first time reborn
I saw a silver tipped eagle
resplendent in flight
Against a dark cloudy sunless
morn
He rose, mounting against a
threatening, tumultous roar
I behold the beating flurry of his
wings soaring toward the light
Breathless, my new born sight
pierced the shroud till I saw the
eagle no more
Struggling, beating furiously
against the storm

He won his battle against the
night
My heart took courage in his
battle with the foe
As the strength born in his new
found wings took form
And he sailed beyond the
pinnacle of all earthly sight
How great is God who causes an
eagle to soar
Who His wonders does bestow
Through His gift of life freely
given to Praise Him forever
more.

Florence J. German
WHY?
What makes the sun shine mother?
Why is the wind so cold?
Why do we have to go to sleep?
Why must we all grow old?

The questions of our babies
There's many every day,
Answers we must give to them
So they resume their play . .

The trust and faith a child will
learn
From mother's guiding hand,
Leads them ever forward
She's the leader of the land.
Mother tells them to be quiet
Life can not be won by noise,
Instead you must learn
peacefulness
Of speech, of toil and poise.
She also tells them in her songs
Lullabys soft and sweet,
Life can be so beautiful
And of all of the joys we meet.
She starts the little baby feet

On their merry way,
A great and honest man he'll make
Within her heart she'll pray.
The questions have been answered
Dear God, I've done my best,
Please make my baby brave and
true
In your hands I leave the rest.

Joel R. Beason
Mother, Mourning
Reflecting on the memories
Of a lifetime newly demised,
Emptiness mocks the future
She sits alone and cries.

Shadowy patterns on the walls
Seem to silhouette his face.
Survivor of their love,
She has won the race.

Part of her is missing, .
An abscessed cavity remains.
Tranquilizers fight to pervade
Anything to ease the pain.

The children you shared
Try to form an egress,
But nothing can supplant,
His tender carress.

Lynda Harwood McLaughlin
DAWN'S RENDEZVOUS
When all is quiet and still
Between twilight and the
morning dawn,
I hear the sound of a whippoorwill
Knowing the darkness will soon
be gone.

I see the nightfall fade into
daylight
As the sky enfolds itself in blue.
I hear the birds sing with
splendor and delight
Welcoming the new morning all
on cue.

The trees rustle their sleepy
leaves
While the sun extends its
colorful hues,
Transforming the horizon with
lazy ease
As nature begins another
spectacular debut.

Margaret Schultz
Gulling Gulls Plucking

---

*Devotedly to my Texas brother,
Glenn and his wife, Paula who
enjoyed a bird's eye view of our
feathered friends in California.*

By sloping surrounding hills,
gulls the lake circling,
Chuckling children chirruping at
waterfowls,
Ducks, ducklings, geese, and
goslings swimming,
For food searching, heads bobbing
in water.
A slice of bread flung at a
duckling,
Waddling into water, swimming
with her morsal,
When side by side, two gulling
gulls screeching,
Plucking tidbits from the slice,
Their portion they should 'ave
been getting
Instead of taking bites.

309

Margaret Schultz
SLIPPED UP SIGNS

*Fondly to the Doctors Taylor, my
sister, Loretta and her husband,
Harold, math teachers and
authors. I reached whopping
tethers while working with
answers for them when I did not
get the signs right.*

Students reach a whopping tether
When not getting math together
By disregarding a rule
While doing papers for school.

In order to become versed
Pupils begin to count first
And then set one and one as two
With the next steps for review.

Five and six add to eleven;
And eight minus one is seven;
Two plus four don't setup eight
So students need their marks
straight.

An "X" as times is the right
sign
To bring the figure into line
As plus is granted for six
Since symbols clearly don't mix.

Savants don't squarely contrive
That twenty divided by five
Results in two hundred fifty
For that would be all shifty.

Problem solvers need common
sense
To guess with some experience
If they don't get the signs right
They can't jink a sticky plight.

Margaret Schultz
**Wolfish Seagulls and a
Duckling**

*This poem is affectionately
dedicated to my son, Steve who
was fuming the same as I when
two seagulls snatched bits of
bread from a helpless duckling in
Sandy Wool Lake near Milpitas,
California.*

It was serene at daybreak
By the Sandy Wool Lake
Encircled by sloping hills
With a handful of quills.
Chuckling children chirruping
Slung bread to a pleased duckling
Waddling into water
As a rousing darter.
Like two vicious numbskulls
Sneaking screeching seagulls,
Each as a wolfish ripper
Hemming the helpless dipper
Snatched bits from the split.
Feeling a violent fit
But with a silent tongue
A fuming little tot flung
With a mighty full swing
Extra bread to the duckling.

Cyril J. Bishun
PLEADING

Where are you, my dearest
love,—
Where are you today?
I only see you in my dreams
Because you're so far away!

Where are you, my dearest
love? . . .
Speak to me today!
For dreams will soon pass away
But I'll have you night and day.

Your smile will give me hope and
joy,
Our songs to write and sing, . . .
Nothing can our love destroy
But happiness you bring.

So come with me, my dearest love,
Let your answer be yea,
And kindle my heart, that's full
of love, . . .
with heaven's holy array.

Eva Cook

Eva Cook
**When The Rain Comes
Pouring Down**

When the rain comes pouring
down
Listen to the thunder boom
As it rolls across the sky
Listen to those drums beat
Up there in swift disguise
Watch the lightening streak across
It does seem bound to hit
When the rain comes pouring
down
We grab our umbrellas, raincoats
and hats
We bow our heads and dash real
fast
Just to keep from getting wet
The trees, shrubs and flowers
All reach out for their drink
The insects and the birds and bees
Are filled right to the brink
The people are happy to scrub
and clean
Their garden areas pretty as can
be seen
Animals and fishes have their bath
Puddles of water are on every path
The world is now a brighter place
We must not fret or frown
When the rain comes pouring
down.

Mrs. Leslie Ann Cook
ALLERGIES

*This poem is dedicated to my
two sons, Michael and Billy Cook,
who like millions, have them.*

Cough, cough, sneeze, sneeze, Oh,
these stupid allergies!
They make my eyes water, and
my breath a wheeze,
And they bring me to my

allergist, begging, help me please!

The flowers, the grass, and the
trees, sway gently with the
breeze,
But need it bring the pollens, that
settle in my nose, to do its
dirty deeds?

So I suffer with my sneezes, as
the season goes on and teases,
And though I know that soon it
will go away,
For now, my allergies are here to
stay!!

Daniel Jarrad QUAIN
**Somewhere . . . In the
Dark . . .**

*For all those who will never have
a choice, because too many
others have made the wrong
choice . . . .*

Somewhere . . . in the dark . . . I
hear a baby cry:
A tiny, muffled sob—meant just
for me;
As unborn fingers clutch an
unbought crib,
In a phantom nursery never
brought to life.

The time was wrong . . . but is it
ever truly right?
A choice that Man may make—
but so alone!
Is it wise to leave that choice to
frail flesh?
We've had our chance: now give
them theirs; it's only fair.

Another-when, it would have
happened differently . . .
There'd be soft gurgles coming
from far room.
But fear and desperation
sometimes ride the winds of
doubt,
And natural instincts assume
rare strange dimension.

There will always be one empty
crib . . . no matter what . . .
Though time runs on
unchecked . . . tis not enough,
To repair the damage done—the
misery in the heart:
An empty spot that aches . . . that
can't forget . . .

Christine C. Aubert
**Corry A Young
Good-Witch: With
Temper-Control**

*To All Those Bullied— and To
All The Corry's Who Could Do
Something About It!*

I, Corry, fairly new at the school,
turned the corner to go
Down the hall, waving, to several
friends she had already
Met. Her books cradled in her
arms, she practiced the wording,
For her next class' oral report.
Suddenly, she saw
A line of five bully-girls jack-
knife in front of a girl

Several class-years younger than

they, daring her to move. "Look
At her; the little chicken's afraid
pass!" One jerred, and
Another grabbed at the books,
making them spill all over the
Floor. The bully-girl responsible
looked very wide-eyed, and
Leered out an "ahhhh, gee. She
dropped her book-ies. The baby
should

Be more careful." They laughed.
Corry stood perfectly still and
(Furious!) controlled her temper,
watching, them; waiting. They
Did not notice her or her eyes
poised

Fully on them. They
Only saw that she had made no
attempt to stop them. But,
This time Corry had had it; The
bully-girls had threatened

One time too many, and needed
to be given back
Some of their threats and
belittling. She smiled grimly
And, her eyes glittering,
whispered ancient words, and
knew they would become
real—and did! "Pretty petals of
pansey;
"A tight knot made tighter; dill
seed and mace, and with web of
"Spiders; Join hands all and give
these girls three days' worth to
wear.
"Three fuzzy spots—right in the
very tips of their noses."
She already started to see the
grins of those around
And to hear the twitters to jeer at
the girls as the spots
And nose-tip fuzz began. She
smiled! NOW they were paid
back.

Maurleen H. Capron
THE COMING OF SPRING
By candlelight
In the evening I can hear
The temptuous movements
of Spring
Alive and reborn
Thus
The bittersweet voices of
Yesteryear
Haunts not me
And by the fire
In the evening I can feel
The winter within
Joyously die
In ashes.

Randy Cunningham
IF YOU WERE MY MOM
If you were my mom and I was
your son,
Think of the joys I'd behold.
Beautiful and smart, with a
girlish figure,
And breast of a maiden so bold.

A mind so sharp, no job to hard,
With tender lips a man could
devour.
Flashing dark eyes and a face so
cute,
A man could stare by the hour.

Alas, I'm not your son, but just
your old man,
But the above is mine to stay.

So take my love and wear it
   proud,
Because I love you, HAPPY
MOTHERS DAY.

Louise Butts Hendrix
A PROBLEM OF DEAFNESS
Music and songs are lovely,
They sing in your head;
But how do you reconcile reason
When you can't hear what's said?

Loud chatter and laughter
Gets tiresome for friends
Who weary of shouting, shouting
To make you understand.

Did you say "preacher" or
   "teacher"?
Was it a man or woman tale?
It was something about water,
Could have been "Save the
   Whales"!

So many people speaking
Only melt into a roar;
If just one person would tell you
What its all about once more!

Keep talking, talking, talking,
That's the only way,
The greatest trouble is waiting
For others to have their say.

Mauricia Price
SECRET SEEDS
Deep within the curtained secret
   heart
Of everyone who truly yearns
   and strives
Toward bright, unspoken hoped-
   for goals, there lies
A little isle of hidden psychic
   sod
Where precious seeds of
   cherished dreams are sown;
But those which die or wither on
   the vine
And never burst into fruition's
   bloom
Are those known only to himself
   and God.

Robert A. Bowen
THE EAGLE
It soars and screams, until it
   seems the Portals of Heaven
   are near

Eyes searching and burning, ever
   yearning to escape the Gates of
   Fear.

Wings flapping, wild motions, as
   crashing oceans soul fighting a
   valiant war

Appetite ravenous, scarlet beak,
   nature's technique always
   seeking more.

Why?! Why?! All this in a
   darkening sky crescending all
   that it can

The answer it seems, in the quest
   of dreams are all the Methods
   of Man!

Charles Allen Huntsinger
AWAKE YET UNAWARE
If the book be right,
   And straight, and true.
If man be I and woman you,
Then let the rose bloom and fill
   the air,
Let the rose watch
   Awake yet unaware.

If the balance shift, and sway, and
   tip.
If we stumble, fall,
   And finally slip.
Tis' then the petals fall,
   Stem-bare.
And we'll see the rose
   Awake yet unaware.
   So unaware.

M. H. Blundred
DEFEATED
So the world's got you down,
You're sick of your lot.
Your life is humdrum
And you want what you've not.

You've been on the heights
And you've tasted the depths.
Why give up now?
There's still something left.

New worlds to conquer,
New goals to attain,
Get up, you slacker
And begin again.

Retha Gossett Jones
LOVE
Just what is love? Is it a fantasy?
Or is it seeds emplanted in your
   heart?
No one can really know—we just
   pretend—
Our thoughts can cause a smile
   or teardrops start.
If you love something or some
   one too much,
Altho' it hurts your heart, just set
   it free—
And realize, if it does not return,
That precious love was never
   meant to be.
But if it should come back to you
   again—
Don't smother it—imprison it?—
   no, never!
Be thankful that you have
   another chance,
And cherish it forever and
   forever.

Brad Miller
TO LIVE AGAIN

To Sharyn, Forever Special.

Simply that I have succumbed to
   your charm could not explain
   my feelings.
Were you the only reason I love,
   a simple understanding would
   do.
But the night's embracing air has
   unveiled a me once hidden
   from the eyes of the world.
More than passion and lust, more
   than heart and soul, the most
   ethereal love gives life to a
   man once thought dead.

Since we've met my days are
   much fuller, my nights know
   loneliness no more.
Your presence is more than the
   joy of companionship—much
   more.
A long-suppressed need compels
   that I pursue my heart's
   desire.
And though time escapes me, it
   shall not escape my eternal
   love for you.

William L. Bongard
A NATIONS DEFEAT

To All The Nations People

Enslaved by eager passions
Man brings on depression
For the price of freedom
Troubled by thoughts of agression.

Harrassed nations, bound by
   hatred
Are soon to fall in defeat
If they do not retaliate
Their armies will soon entreat.

John W. Hugel Jr.
A GAME OF SKILL
The stakes were high, the score
   was tied
It was the last draw of this hand
I had an ace right up my sleeve
So I felt lucky, I bet my hand.

But the other guy just winked
   and said
I think your bluffing, I'll call your
   hand
But as I started to lay my hand
That extra ace came slidding
   down!

He stared at me, but I stared him
   back
His eyes were red, but so were mine
He stood up high and clenched
   his fist
As I threw my cards and
   snarled ... you win!

Margaret Osgood
Stephanie and Grandpa's Dancin' Song
Grandpa's 83—Stephanie's 3,
They dance to the music happily,
Drum beat, drum beat, beat beat
   on,
Stephanie and Grandpa's dancin'
   song.

Grandpa puts the record on,
Then they dance and clap along,
Grandpa with his hair like snow,
Stephanie with her face aglow,
Drum beat, drum beat, beat beat
   on,
Stephanie and Grandpa's dancin'
   song.

They laugh and sing and twirl
   around,
"Stephie's" feet fly off the ground,
Upbeat, downbeat, beat beat on,
Stephanie and Grandpa's dancin'
   song.

Heartbeat, drum beat, beat beat on,
Stephanie and Grandpa's dancin'
   song.

Robert E. Monrean
WINTER THOUGHTS
The flakes fall, all during
   the night
and were happy of this sight.

People gather by the sleigh
and they'll sit in warmed hay.

Sitting with my friends in hand
traveling through a bountiful
   land.

Over and about countless hills
soon the snow nips with chills.

This I thought was really grand:
a Christmas ride, through the
   land.

Kevin J. Aguirre
Night Cliff Of Precious Life
Reach for my hand, damn it,
   reach boy!
Stretch your limbs, like you
   stretch in bed in the morning.
Push, damn it, push!

I can't, I can't!

Don't say you can't, you can boy,
   you can!

No, don't let me die, no ... no!

Hold your tongue son and reach,
   that's it, you've got it!
Reach boy, reach!

I can't see where I'm grabbing!

Don't worry son, I can see. You
   just put your hand up.
Up to the sky, son.

I'm pushing, I'm trying to.

I've got you boy! I've got you!
Sweet Jesus, I've got him!

Pull me, pull me up!

That's it boy, push.

The rock's cutting me, it hurts.

Your other hand boy, give me
   your other hand.
That's it, now use your legs. I'll
   pull, you climb son.
That's it, that's a boy!

I'm almost up, pull me!

Here you go ... gotcha! Dear God
   I've got him!

Helen Sims Smaw
JOY IS LIKE A MENORAH
Joy is like a menorah blazing to
   adorn
My heart when in need of hope I
   mourn,
Igniting faith with love till I'm
   reborn.

Joy is like a menorah warming
   my hands
For patient work in wrestling
   with commands
To show mercy till grace
   combusts to firebrands.

Joy is like a menorah beaming
   my mind
Toward God's highest joy: seven
   virtues refined
Till in my heart the Living
   Menorah be enshrined.

Edith L. McDonald
SKEPTIC

With Love to Janice

Who can catch and keep the
    smell of lilacs in the spring
Refold a rose whose petals are all
    blown away by wind
Or hold a snow flake to the heart
And keep its sparkle there.
If you can please tell me so I'll
    know
Where all this tender love will go.

Jane Ross
POOL OF AGONY

*With all my love to my sons
Frankie and Johnnie*

Once the winds were soft and
    gentle,
once my heart was pure,
once you were mine.
To this morning
I await still
to awake to feel the sun,
Ah I still care.
Yes it is your face
who puts me to sleep.
Behold away, away
you do stay.
There will no be other lovers.
Oh I'm nieve for still wanting
    you,
but not ignorant as to surrender
to your every whim.
Yes, Yes, Yes,
I am the fool
who dwells in the pool of agony
for now the winds blow only pain.

Debbie L. Reinhold
Catacombs Of My Mind
In the catacombs of my mind
Thoughts of you spin webs so
    fine
The gentle touch of your fingers,
    rare
A tender kiss to show you care
Your lingering voice upon my ear
Fills each filmy room as though
    you're here
Caressing lightly, ever sublime
In the catacombs of my mind

Anna Argano-Adamo
CHRISTMAS EVE
'Twas Christmas eve, and as I
    walked along
Weary with labor, the unending
    din
Seemed to surround me,
    pinioning me there—
Strident voices, rumbling cars,
    and neon
Signs flickering, and stationary too,
Until the world became a
    confused haze
From which I fled into the
    nearest place,
And that, (coincidence, or
    mayhap Fate)
Turned out to be a little Catholic
    Church.

Slowly I walked up to the altar rail,
And kneeling, clasped my hands,
    and closed my eyes,
A sense of perfect quiet fill'd my

heart,
A peace that soothed the soul,
    cleared the mind,
Endowing me again with pow'r to
    think,
Not in a jumble, as I had before,
But with an almost startling
    clarity—
And then I raised my eyes and,
    looking up,
Found myself gazing at a tender
    sight.

An humble manger, rather dimly
    lit,
And Mary, Mother of this
    troubled world,
Kneeling beside her radiant-
    visaged Child,
While opposite, St. Joseph
    likewise knelt,
Bowing his head in deep and
    reverent awe.
So sweet a scene, so full of
    stillness rare,
That I did rest my head upon my
    hands,
And cry, "Oh, Mother, help us to
    attain
That gift of peace whereof we
    stand in need!"

And lo! A voice did speak, so very
    soft
That it was but a whisper to my
    ear,
And said, "The need you have, oh,
    weary world,
Is faith and trust, but, even more
    than these,
Love of thy neighbor (whom thou
    hast forgot)
Burying it 'neath the lust and
    greed for gold,
Position, power—all things
    material—
Putting aside the soul's most
    urgent needs,
Crushing to death the peace that
    you now seek!"

Trembling within, full of a
    nameless fear,
I started up to see I knew not
    what,
But no, the scene before me had
    not changed,
Yet, looking closer, I observed the
    Child
Gazing upon me with a gentle
    smile
In which I read compassion for
    the world,
For all its blundering ways, its
    countless sins;
There, too, I saw the silv'ry wings
    of hope
For those who humbly sought
    their long-lost faith!

Footsteps began to echo through
    the church,
And I recalled that it was
    Christmas Eve,
That, from the poorest home to
    mansion grand,
Many would come, as centuries
    ago
The shepherds came, and too, the
    Three Wise Men,
Tonight, with like humility, each
    heart

Would lay, in wordless adoration,
    there
At the wee feet of Him who gave
    His life
That we, in turn, might know
    Eternity!

I gazed again upon that wondrous
    scene,
Gaining an inward strength as I
    looked on,
And felt, deep down within my
    new-born soul,
The blessed sense of peace that I
    had sought.
'Twas then I knew, beyond the
    faintest doubt,
That Mary, and the Child, had
    heard my prayer,
And joyfully I left the little
    church
Rich in the knowledge that I had
    received
The greatest Christmas gift I'd
    ever had!

Kristin K. Benton
Kristin K. Benton
NOBODY KNOWS
It is something very far away,
Yet it seems so very near
I admit it's very baffling
But it I would never fear.

We'll never know what it's like,
Or if it's something we'll love
The only thing that would
    know
Is the majestic Heaven above.

We'll all know what this is
    someday,
But 'till then don't hold your
    breath
It's nothing to fear, my friend
For it is only Death.

Helen W. Ridgeway
WHY
In this great, wide, wonderful,
    beautiful world
Various problems daily unfurl.
Some troubles occur and we're
    not at fault—
Yet many are caused by deeds
    we've wrought.

Vehicular accidents cause death
    and pain,
And the victims aren't always to
    blame.
Yet speeding and drinking take
    their toll
Of infants and children as well as
    the old.

How sad to see suffering and death
When caused by our own
    destructfulness;
For families and friends share the
    pain
Of those affected, with nothing
    gained.

Why waste our lives and trouble
    others
With drugs and drinks which
    cause much sorrow?
Take time to enjoy this beautiful
    world;
Then more can share a bright
    tomorrow.

S. Patricia Thomas
FUTURE CHILDREN
Give me the key to
    understanding
Give me compassion for my
    fellowman
Mold me in the fashion of a firm
    yet loving person
Show me the ways of the world
To be wise
To have promise
To be the best that I can
I am eager to be a part of
    everything
One day I will make a positive
    contribution
I am a child . . .
Teach me

Frances Thomas
A WILDERNESS TUNE
A land where wolves and coyotes
    howl,
Where black bears and grizzles
    prowl,
Sometimes there comes the cry of
    the loon,
And put altogether, its A
    Wilderness Tune.

Winds whistle through the birch
    leaves,
Branches snap during the winter
    freeze,
The wolves all howl at a full
    moon,
And put altogether, its A
    Wilderness Tune.

Roar of rivers following their
    course,
Echoing hoaves of the last horse,
A thunder of crackling ice starts
    soon,
And put altogether, its A
    Wilderness Tune.

Where bunchgrass waves in
    summer breezes,

Where cold north winds, blow
  and freezes.
Where great owls hunt, beneath a
  full moon,
And put altogether, its A
  Wilderness Tune.

The rivers man stopped in their
  course.
He shot the bear, the wolf, and
  the wild horse.
The trees and grass will be paved
  over soon,
And we'll no longer hear, A
  Wilderness Tune.

Mark Aaron Robinson
YOUR EYES YESTERDAY
Once we were younger,
driven by a hunger within—
like the wind is driven by itself.
So far we flung our hearts
to where we've sung our parts of
  searching songs.
But the lyrics fell faint in the
  distance
and isms failed to explain our
  existence
in a void filled only by
  Maranathas and Mariahs.

Had I known fifteen years ago
that we'd be home for a minute or
  so,
I'd have rehearsed reunion
  speeches
and polished the clumsy reaches
that finally held you for a moment;
for in our fleeting meeting
years of seeking meaning
lost their substance,
and I found myself careening
through what was once:
caressing the breast of truth,
clinging to the rest of truth,
we bore the banner of the quest
  for truth—
but all we really knew was
  youth . . .
Yet I was so surprised
to awaken to your eyes yesterday,
that I fumbled for my emblems
  anyway.

Lajetta Hansen
MOUNTAIN MAN
I walked in the woods one
  October day and found to my
  surprise
A small abandoned cabin, hidden
  far from travelers' eyes.
The shingles were dry and curled
  with age, the door stood open
  wide;
The glass was gone from one
  window. Did I dare to step
  inside?
A wasp nest hung from the
  ceiling, spider webs stretched
  wall to wall.
On the table sat a cup and plate,
  with an inch of dust over all.
On the rusty stove stood a skillet
  and a big black coffee pot;
I could just see the mountain
  man as he poured a cup, black
  and hot.

How many years was the cabin
  home? He'd built it strong and
  square.
Hours of work were evident in
  the table, the bed and the chair.

I brushed the dust off the hand-
  hewn chair and on its back I
  could see
"ADAM" carved into the wood,
  his name now revealed to me.
My mind played tricks and I
  could see a big man sitting there,
Plaid woolen shirt, heavy boots
  and jeans, curly black beard
  and hair.
As I dreamed, I felt him turn, and
  his eyes were warm and blue.
He smiled and bid me welcome.
  Why he was lonely too!

I had been lonely all my life; love
  had never come my way;
Now something stirred inside my
  heart, and I knew that I must
  stay.
Some folks will say I'm crazy, (but
  they thought so all along).
They'll say I'm even more alone,
  but they will be so wrong.
He's as real to me as the table and
  chair and I hear his voice so deep;
I can feel him close, his hand on
  mine, feel his breath warm on
  my cheek.
I've got to leave you now, Adam,
  but I'll return, you'll see.
Just drink your coffee, don't go
  away. I'll bring a cup and chair
  for me.

Peggy Jo Rexrode

Peggy Jo Rexrode
**Roses, Roses, Dear Father,
Above!**
Roses, Roses, Dear Father, Above!
Roses, Roses, Dear Father, My
  Love!
Roses, Roses, Dear Father, My
  Dove!
Roses, Roses, Dear Father, My
  Glove!

Roses, Roses, Dear Father, just for
  You!
Roses, Roses, Dear Father, just a
  few.
Roses, Roses, Dear Father, just,
  for You!
Roses, Roses, Dear Father, just,
  with dew.

Roses, Roses, Dear Father, just
  look!
Roses, Roses, Dear Father, just
  book.
Roses, Roses, Dear Father, just
  time.
Roses, Roses, Dear Father, just
  rhyme.

Roses, Roses, Dear Father,
  deepest wine!
Roses, Roses, Dear Father,
  keepest thine.
Roses, Roses, Dear Father, long
  stems!
Roses, Roses, Dear Father, strong
  gems.

Roses, Roses, Dear Father, My
  God.
Roses, Roses, Dear Father, thy sod.
Roses, Roses, Dear Father, Thank
  You, Praise Your Name!
Roses, Roses, Dear Father, Thank
  You, Praise Your Fame!

Roses, Roses, Dear Father, Above!
Roses, Roses, Dear Father, My
  Love!
Roses, Roses, Dear Father, My
  Dove!
Roses, Roses, Dear Father, My
  Glove!

Marjorie Gagnet Berry
COULD THIS BE LOVE
How painful, simply torturous,
  heart pounding, I'm weak.
Legs wobbly, gnawing stomach, a
  yearning soul so meek.
Feeling giddy, quite confused, my
  face keeps blushing pink.
Hypnotizing, mesmerizing, as
  eyes go blink, blank, blink.
Your eyes change to soft and
  misty, I think you feel it too.
Tell me please, it is love, or do
  you have the flu?

Mary Ann Clark
FRIENDS
Friends are people that care.
They show that they trust you.
They are willing to help you, if
  you get in trouble, They are
  there to help.
They don't drag you down in a
  hole, they pull you out.
But sometimes friends, when you
  think they are, are not really
  Friends, they'll use you, taking
  as much as they can,
  Then stab you in the back, and
  leave.
Friends, you do things together,
  dancing, movies, just driving,
  They are also trustworthy,
  faithful and truthful.
But still some, you think are
  friends—but they are not,—
  Watch—check out, *before* you
  really start trusting and
Think that they are friends.
Cause they'll talk behind your
  backs, and take what they can,
  Besides stabbing you also,
Friends are trustworthy, caring,
  they're there when you need
  Them.
Friends are there, really there to
  help, not back stabbers or
  Two—faced.
Friends share with you, you can
  confide in them also.
Friends are friends.
Friends are there.

Shirley Alberts
ALLHALLOWS EVE
Screeching bats
And Halloween cats,
And all the night
a witches wonder.

I wandered out
To see Ghouls & Ghosts
All milling about—
The evenings hosts.

Pots brewing spook juice,
Inviting all to dine.
Lives so endangered . . .
  I hope it's not mine.

I pretend to be a friend
And howl at the moon.
Combined with bones and chains
We crank out a tune.

Skulls and pumpkin heads
Dancing about,
They all come toward me
And I begin to SHOUT!

How strange.—I wake up.—
In my own bed.
It was only a dream—
  But am I really dead?

Carol L. Smith
MY FAVORITE SCHOOL
  Place to learn and earn.
Subjects taught by the score,
  make you study even more.

The honor role is there,
  for those who care.

Those who want trades,
  must earn good grades.

Lots of homework abound,
  there's no fooling around.

On Graduation Day,
  you can say:

When students are trained
  and knowledge is gained,

Then teacher's efforts
  were not in vain.

Irma P. Spacey
THE AWAKENING
Pain at last—it's real
  Numbness melts, now I feel
Spastic sobs soon let go
  Hidden tears release and flow.

Deafening quiet—I cannot sleep
  Only memories to keep
Alive— fearful not to erase
  This fading picture of your face.

A dream, ah! but to awake
  From reality I cannot take
Nothing left—but to question why
  You, my love, had to die.

Ilona K. Novaky
COUNTRY LIFE
How blest I am to live in a
  country side
Where God's beauty can not hide
Nature beckons in glorious
  splendor
To the beauty you can't help but
  surrender

Little squirrels jumping from tree
  to tree
And blue birds singing so
  beautifully
Flowers scattered in colors of a
  rainbow
Pools of water rushing below!

Golden leaves falling all around
By magical beauty I'm surround
The winds whisper a happy tune
Winter is coming soon!

In winter, they're kept at a busier
  pace

313

They have to put on a harsher face
Yet, there's magical beauty in
  each snow fall
Each tree is dressed for a
  glamorous ball

As there's beauty in every Season
For each valley and mountain,
  there's a reason
In HIS time by HIS design
Set into action by HIS HAND
  DIVINE!

"He hath made everything
beautiful in His Time." Eccl. 3:11

Jennie M. Root
I WONDER
There's a bright shining star
In the East
Seen if no clouds to bar
At least
When its beauty t'is not afar.

I wonder if it's the star that led
The wise men
To Mary, babe and the stable bed
In the town of Bethlehem?

Janie Irene Luster
NATURE'S CYCLE

Dedicated to my loving
Grandmother, Janie Davis
Givens. An Angel in Heaven.

Slowly the dewdrops,
Slid down from the rose,
To moisten the ground
Where the wild grass grows,
That surrounds the oaktree
All covered with leaves,
That flutter and crackle
When touched by the breeze,
That came from the ocean,
When waters where high
Made up from the raindrops
That fell from the sky,
That surrounds the earth
Where the wild grass grows,
All covered with dewdrops,
That fell from the rose.

John E. Rautio
LONDON FOG
Eating Fish n' Chips
Walking down a foggy London
  Street
Looking for yesterday's news on
  the ground
As the rain splashes down on the
  cobblestone walk
The light mist of the rain pierces
  the brightness of a street lamp
And once again I'm swallowed in
  darkness
A fog horn blasting, as the smell
  of salt fills my nostrils
Off in the distance a lighthouse
  breaks the gloom of night
Warning ships land is near by
And who knows what I'll do?
Maybe I'll stop in a waterfront pub
Listen to sailors shoot the breeze
  about when they were young
Have me a good mug of ale
Listen to all this talk of
  harpooning whales
Jolly good England they say, see
  the sites of the world
Hear Big Ben's chimes fade away
  in the bad weather night
As two drunken sailors on a dock

start to fight
Raging like mad dogs, the two
  men brawl
Until one takes a fall into the sea
  below, he hits his head on a
  rock and drowns.
The others turn around to the
  pub for a drink, hoping the
  body will sink before dawn.
They find the body in a couple
  of days
It'll just be another case for the
  Harbor Patrol.
Jolly old England and God save
  the Queen
Are just words around here
  without meaning.

Patricia E. Canterbury
ARROW MAKER
The maker of arrows sits
crossed-legged
like some picture-book Indian
reading tales of Thoreau
and Bertrand Russell.

Listening to the laughter
around him
slowly inserting tiny
yellow feathers.

Frank Linwood Fowler III
LATE OCTOBER
Nature paints splendid
  avenues in radiance
    only the sun
      can give . . .

Find out those inhabitual
  barings hidden in
    her foreign home we
      do not see . . .

Crisp mornings find us
  wanting to hide till
    the sun finds
      our hearts . . .

Marciana A. Sevandal
THE GIFTS OF THE MAGI

This poem reveals three
significant attributes in the life
and personality of our Lord and
Savior Jesus Christ. He went
through the stages of birth, life
and death like humans to show
His humanity. As God, He was
the King of kings, possessing the
attributes of divinity and royalty
at the same time.

When Christ was born in
  Bethlehem,
  That cold December long ago,
Three Wise Men came from
  lands afar,
  Foll'wing a lone resplendent star.

Three Wise Men bearing precious
  gifts,
  That symbolised the Savior's
  life,
Came out to tell all humankind,
  Christ was human, royal, divine.

What were the gifts the Magi
  brought,
  That first glad Christmas long
  ago?
The purest gold, sweet
  frankincense,
  And bitter myrrh for sad-sweet
  times.

Hear what the Magi said of old:
  The first: "I offer purest gold;
You'll be the greatest—King of
  kings,
  Here on earth and in the
  heavens."

The second—with his
  frankincense,
  Symbol of Christ's divine
  life—cried:
"Dear Child, our own Immortal
  God,
  You came to give us Your true
  love."

But the third—with his bitter
  myrrh,
  Symbol of Christ's humanity—
Predicted death by Cruc'fixion,
  For our Salvation and
  Redemption.

Finale:
The gifts presaged Life Eternal
  after Death.

Charlene W. Villella
MY MOUNTAIN
Part of my mountain is no more:
  through
Someone's carelessness the
  covering of
Wild wheat is now nothing more
  than
Charred black stubble.
A portion of natural habitat is lost,
Never to be regained: Oh, the grass
Will grow again, but how do you
Replace the lives lost?
Here lies the bodies of four
Small lives, the down gone from
  their
Wings with the first flash of
  intense
Heat: Not being old enough to fly,
They had no chance of escape.
Their nest became their funeral
  pyre.
The wild beauty of eagles in flight
No never to be.
A jumbled mass, still partially
  furred
Lies with staring, yet sightless
  eyes:
Arms spread as if in suplication
  to its
Fate, its mutilated body forming
  the
Question mark, to the silently
  screamed
"Why: Man, Why?"

Walter Villanueva
My Holiday Wish To You

To Te, Karen, And Shirley,
Wishing you thanks on every
holiday. Enjoy.

Magical moments,
  Entwined with warm greetings,
  From every close friend.
Tis' the season
  Of friendly meetings
  Concluding the year's end.

Getting together
  For the end-of-year bash,
  Bringing all generations into one.
This party crescendoes
  Into a year-end smash,
  One which everyone has fun.

Hugs and kisses,
  Casually exchanging oft,
  Enjoying it by all.
Sharing and caring
  With caresses so soft,
  Between people, big and small.

Each and every moment,
  Worth rejoicing for,
  Enlightens the old and the new.
Altogether we walk
  Into "Next Year's" door,
  Saying "Happy Holidays" to you.

Mabel Lagerlof
OUR THANKS FOR ELVIS
There was a young man from
  Mississippi
Who was handsome, tall and hippy
His langried gaze with blue-grey
  eyes
Could, at mill, hold you like a vize.
With golden voice and fingers
  strumming
We listened to his trance like
  humming.
It grew and grew into music so
  rare,
He became a "legend" beyond
  compare
Six years now since he is gone! But,
Somehow, his laughter lingers on!
He gave us All he had—as
  entertainer
Man and friend—right to the end.
When his great heart burst
  and could not mend!
Rest well, dear ELVIS and rest
  assured
Your many songs helped heal and
  even *cured.*
Here, too, your "spirituals" played
  their part
to gladden us and sooth the heart!
For many a day where we were
  blue,
Spinning your records, helped
  pull us through.

Connie G. Rode
THE REALIZATION
Her photograph is neatly tucked
  outside the picture frame
  that holds you and a friend skiing
  on sloping, snowy terrain.

She stares at me with frozen smile;
  as I stare back, I see
  visions of forgotten loves,
  and ours that will never be.

Mark H. Miranda
The Man With No Wrath
Upon the hills of life and death,
I met a man who had no wrath.
We walked and talked a million
  years,
He knew my life, I shed some
  tears.
I realized he was not just any man,
His name was written, I had his
  hand.
He showed me wonders old and
  new,
The time when we would start
  anew.
We traveled up the rocky paths,
To see below the worlds gone past.
I stood in wonder of this mans
  great might,
He took me to the lasting light.
For many years I read his words,
But his message I never heard.

It's all so true now I can see,
Would you now like to be with me?
He's here to stay for eternity,
His palace is just across the sea.
He bids us welcome young and old,
Don't ever let his name grow cold.

Molly Therese Stewart

Molly Therese Stewart
BELIEVE IN YOURSELF
When things you do, don't come
out just right—
Get in there, with all your
might—
Try fun and laughter, every day—
Soon your troubles, will go
away—
Think of people, who love you,
just as you are—
Your eyes will twinkle, like a
star—
Let your pleasant memories
unfold—
Hold them close as they are real
gold—
Think of God standing by—
Watching you, and seeing you
try—
Your face will take on a smile—
You'll say to yourself, this is
really worthwhile—

n. ming s. ureta
BECAUSE I BELIEVE
in the early winter of December,
there i stood upon a naked rock
between earth and sky,
lifting my head up high
if only i had wings
i could have soared
and scaled the great unknown.

amid rain and wind and icy cool
the warmth i felt not cold
the silence there.
the peace of mind.
the bliss of solitude.

where the wide blue waters
even as half frozen
rain turning to snow
made purer than ever before,
ah, the wonder that nature yields!

in the early winter of December,
between earth and sky
there upon a naked rock i stood
and lo, the uncircumscribed
beauty,
the noblest of wonders He was
sharing
with me who was receiving
and all, because i believe!

Goldie Bridges Kelley
JESUS MY ALL
Jesus, whose love my spirit thrills
Jesus my all, my Heavenly prize,
My longing, hungry heart He fills,
My every need He satisfies.

Since I have looked upon His face,
His glorious radiance fills my soul,
I rest my soul in His embrace,
His praise refines, and makes me
whole.

My Jesus only now I see,
All else is lost unto my sight,
All else is only vanity,
All else is darkness, He is Light.

Jesus, whose name my soul shall
praise,
Jesus, my treasure evermore;
He is the guardian of my ways,
He is my joy, whom I adore.

Donna J. Reimus
SPRING CLEANING
I started the Spring Cleaning
In the attic of my mind.
It's really quite amazing
The old memories you find.
Tucked back into one corner,
Just about five years ago,
I found the charred remainder
Of a love that lost its glow.
I dusted off the cobwebs
With a tender loving stroke.
A tear slipped from my eyelids
At just why our ties had broke.
I tried to wash away the
Precious moments that we shared,
But your image keeps returning,
For I thought you really cared.
If somehow I might have hurt you
To make you drift so far away,
Believe me, I never meant to,
Nor would I, to my dying day!
May all the good that life can hold
And blessings from above appear,
As all your very fondest dreams
Come true, in time for you, my
dear.

Nancy Anne Knowles
They That Grow On Ridges
People tramping, people crowding
Push and shove, push and shove
Emotions rising, emphasizing
Hate and love, hate and love
Jostling, faltering everywhere
Escape into the open air
Leaves heave breathe leave
All despair, all despair

Lo draws the night begins the day
Alone is freedom, go away
Anger pent-up feelings drown
In a dark and deepening frown
Lo the people so they say
Alone is freedom, go away

Grow pines on ridges, stumped
and bent
Solitary glory spent
Gazing into faceless night
Cramped and short, ugly sight
Deep and green the thick ones
grow
Basking in reflected glow
Lean one on one bough bends
Pushing frongs, shoving friends
There grow they, the tall and
straight
Tramping, crowding freedom's
weight

Alfred Rodriguez
CHRISTMAS
The hoary solstice of invernal
dark,
Of torpid Nature, of our
discontent,
Is portal to a warming Spring, a
spark
That buds her trees and brakes
our own descent . . .

Your birth is signal to the wintry
night
That it desist from holding life in
rein,
That from its gloomy darkness
should come light,
And from its cold the warmth of
your domain.

How simply marvelous the man-
made meld
Of what our errant Universe
unchains
And what our hearts have always
held!

Would that all things by lofty
man construed
Should hold, at one with Nature's
claims,
The golden key to endless life
renewed!

Patti Bowes
YOU

Inspired by My Sweet Stranger

You
  linger on the edges
  of my mind
Like some sweet stranger
waiting
  to be known

Harlie A. Larson
CHRISTMAS MEMORIES
A pause to give of pensive mood,
Amidst so much of furry.
Perchance there be unwittingly,
A thought of bygone scurry.

When times were less of
handiness,
No auto in the shed.
Horses were an ever must,
To mobilize the sled.

Planning programs for Saint Nick,
While winter held its sway.
Meant a-riding o'er the fields,
All bundled in a sleigh.

A haze within that country school;
Naught but a flickering light.
That all may be a precious part;
And do each speech just right.

The heap of gifts, each duty tagged;
No end of shapes and sizes.
The teeming swell of curiousness,
Could have won many prizes.

Twas then there came that early
chance,
That only Christmas gives.
To face a maze of merry folks,
And sing that song that lives.

Elizabeth L. Fucci
LOVE?
Love! It's just for thee I'm singing!
Bells are ringing
Gaily bringing
Joy into a heart that's clinging

Ever to thy phantom face!
Love! For thee my heart I'm
keeping,
Ever weeping,
Never sleeping,
Longing for thy tendrils, creeping
Even to my soul's embrace!

Lightly, spritely, skipping nightly
Through the mist of dreams
bound tightly
In my mind, however slightly
Comes recall by Dawn's first trace,
Love! You tease me,
Sometimes please me,
Always sieze me,
Even freeze me!
Bind my heart! But, never ease me
From thy merry chase!

Donna M. Crebbin
**Our Holy Father the Polish
Pope**
A magnificent man
So holy and wise
A man who saves souls
He wears no disguise
With extended arms to his
brethern he cries:
"God will save Poland—let
freedom arise".
You must never lose hope
So pray and be strong
Our heavenly father will soon
right this wrong
My beloved people with tears in
my eyes
I give you my blessing
Let us reach to the skies
You must stand tall like pillars
Your faith has been tried."
We adore this Polish pope—so
brilliant and wise
A humble man who loves souls
with tears in his eyes.

Harvey Alan Sperry
AGELESS AS A ROSE
I'm told you aged another year
but I don't believe in all I hear.
I had to come myself and see.
Now I know someone lied to me.
You haven't changed since long
ago;
it seems about a week or so.
Or has it been three years or more
when I first sauntered through
your door?
You're still mischievous
mean and sometimes devious.
You can still be carefree, also kind
when that playful urge nudges
your mind.
But most of all, you are still nice
your life is ever full of spice.
So here's a toast to see you
through
your special day and next year
too.
And here's sweet roses; Love's
salute
an ageless gift; your birth's
tribute.

Mark H. Miranda
DARKNESS
On the road of no return,
My life had passed me by.
I saw before my eyes,
The path of pending doom.
I tried with no success,
To find the right path home.

I had bitterness inside,
For those who lead me here.
Tho it's to late to turn back now,
I'll try to change my path.
It's this emptiness inside,
That turns me inside out.
It was beautiful at first,
But than it all went dark.
My life is one big blur,
Oh God please help me out.

Thelma L. Reusser
LOVE OVERCOMES ALL
Far from our family of loved ones,
Mountains and miles span great
distances there;
"God Bless!" we say with a prayer,
And in our hearts there is love!

Warmth turns away the cold;
Sadness dispels in memory of
loved ones we hold;
We have a joy that lasts—
Because we have love!

A letter rec'd, waiting is over for a
spell,
A token gift is bestowed,
And wells of joy o'er flow;
There's been an expression of love!

Verse and inner thoughts are
penned;
Day is done, and darkness as it
ends;
We have had, and put the day
behind us—
Ah, but in that day was love!

Rebecca K. Kennedy
TOMORROW
Today how precious you really
are
As valuable as treasures afar
This day is all the time I truly
possess
And I will enjoy you in spite of
stress
May I find the courage to live
you fully
As unknown to me from my life
you may flee
Tomorrow bears not a guarantee
And is as elusive as the wind
blowing free

Lynda A. Curry
Remember The Rainbow
Follow the rainbow . . .
    In search of your dreams.

When clouds block your path,
    Rise above them.

For it is only after the storm,
    That the rainbow shines.

Let the rainbows in your life,
    Comfort your heart,

And keep your soul happy,
    And at peace within.

Gladys Reusser
FANTASY OR REALITY
Daily I spread a love carpet
    straight to your door,
And hourly I tread that path, to
    see you once more.
With scenic imagination I take
    your hand
And back over the carpet to my
    door we stand.
With picturesque thinking I hold
    you to my heart.
And in my day-dreams I know
    we'll never part.

Then I hear the phone ringing
    insistently,
And suddenly I'm awake to
    reality.
I hear your melodious voice real
    and clear.
Saying, "Can we go out to dinner
    dear?.
    This is real not fantasy
    And I am in ECSTACY!

Janet Arnold Lietz
GOD SPEAKS TO ME
I love to sit upon the rocks,
    gazing out to sea;
In a subtle plea, it speaks to me,
Sometimes, ferociously.

When I sit upon the rocks,
    listening intently,
I can hear it call, and tell to me
Of immortality.

Far off, on the horizon, where
    heaven meets the sea,
They blend in a mutual glory
Of glowing serenity.

And then my eyes are opened . . .
    it's God who speaks to me.

J. C. Schill
STILL IS THE VOICE

*The late Rev. Uen Key Whose
voice is now . . . still*

Stillness stiffles the breeze and
    stills the trees.
Still, still, all is still.
Still is the voice that seems
Like the breeze that stirs the
    trees.

Still I hear the voice so clear;
Still it whispers near.
Still it's fading, fading, still,
Still, still, all is still.

Drifting farther, as if to sea,
Fading still, far away;
Still I hear, though fading still,
The voice that seems like a
    breeze
That stirs the trees.

Voices here, voices there,
Voices everywhere.
Everywhere the sounds sound
Empty still.

Years may come, but
Still and silent still
Will be the voice that seems
Like a breeze that stirs the
    trees.

Harley Allen
OCTOBER'S WONDERS
Autumn time has come our way,
and now it's time for Mother
    Nature to make her play.
Her summer gown will never do,
She must change it all to a
    different hue.
Yellow fields of corn look like a
    golden sea,
and apples red are hanging from
    the tree.
Golden rod and wild asters, too,
make a big bouquet for you.
Morning frost is in the air,
and colored leaves are everywhere.
Mother Nature's door is open wide
for you to view the autumn
    countryside.
I took a walk just to see
the many things that were free.
I stopped and gazed with
    wonderous awe
at all the colors that I saw.
The colors all are bright and bold.
It's one of nature's gifts that can't
    be sold.
To watch the autumn sunset I
    never tire.
It seems to set the western world
    on fire.
And after the sun has set with all
    her grace,
the harvest moon comes up and
    takes her place.

Kay Martin
THE SHROUD SPEAKS

*I dedicate this poem to all the
people who have worked with
the Shroud trying to prove that it
is the buriel cloth of Jesus.*

Did you ever carry a Heavenly
    message
For the whole world to touch and
    see?
I was chosen to do all this
When God's blessing was given
    to me.

I am the cloth that covered Jesus,
I am the cloth they call the
    Shroud,
I am of linen—a herringbone twill;
I make no sounds but my
    message is loud.

When the took His body down
    from the cross
They had no time to annoint or
    clean;
The Sabbath was near, its laws
    forbade.
They used *me* to enwrap, *my*
    duty supreme.

I witnessed the beatings of a
    Roman whip,
For His pain-wracked body rested
    on me.
The blood from His head where
    the thorns pushed thru
Covered my fibers, but this had
    to be.

The wound on His left wrist from
    a 10-inch nail
Driven through His hand to hold
    His body secure
Prolonged the agony—the blood

from His side
When His heart was pierced, Oh!
    how much to endure.

His facial image is clear and
    pronounced,
His hair dropping on forehead
    formed number 3
Oh! how prophetic, Oh! how
    miraculous,
For the third day He arose for the
    whole world to see.

The tomb is quiet: I cling close to
    my Lord;
I absorb His blood, His sweat, His
    tears.
His body is still, must rest awhile.
The moment will come to quell
    the world's fears.

A heavenly music resounds off
    the walls.
Angels are singing a new kind of
    song;
A blazing light which the world
    cannot match
Heralds the Rising, God's answer
    to wrong.

A spiritual life now flows
    through Christ's body
He puts me aside, gently, with
    love;
The angels move the stone aside.
Jesus now proves what prophets
    spoke of.

But lo and behold! what a change
    over me!
He left His imprint no time can
    erase:
Every mark from His body,
    punctured and bruised
The agony, torture etched on His
    face.

Over the years they have tried to
    disprove,
But scientists the world over all
    now agree
I carry a true picture of Jesus, our
    Lord,
All that glory has been given to
    me.

There's nowhere else a positive
    negative
A 3 dimensional imprint for all to
    see.
For I've been a witness of all that
    has happened
I am proof—*I* am positive, God
    gave it to me.

Lawrence A. Souza
OUR FLAG
White stars on a field of blue
    carried
By our patriots true,

With it's stripes of white and red
Draped across our honored dead,
    OUR FLAG.

Burned and spat upon by foe,
    flying over
Row by row of crosses in a field
    of green,

Where lie soldiers who have seen
    hell on
Earth but still fought on, OUR
    FLAG.

Flying over voting polls,
    schoolyards,

Our World's Best Loved Poems

Churches, honor rolls.
Courts of law and monuments,
   houses,
Mansions, canvas tents,
   OUR FLAG.

Worn on the seats of pants,
   carried with
The wrathful chants of radicals,
   OUR FLAG.
May it be there every dawn,
   flying proudly
When I'm gone.
O'er a nation strong and free,
   lasting to
Eternity.

Carrying on the noble plan, of the
   last
Great hope for man,
   OUR FLAG.

Sandra d'Entremont
SPLENDOR AT DUSK

*To Delmar: May the dawn of our
love lend luster to our final
sunset. Forever, Sandra*

In the raw dawn of our years,
When an hour seems a life,
We compare wins and losses,
We measure failures with strife.

Our noons bring out another facet.
The edge on our sword is cast.
Preoccupied with our destiny,
Gleening knowledge from our past.

He who's reached the twilight
Knows how lovely life can be,
With tinted glasses of wisdom
Obscuring harsh reality.

In the mellowing of a final sunset,
We will in splendor see,
Shades of what is yet to come,
And shadows of what used to be.

Cecelia Marchand
LOOSE CHANGE
Coins,
Separate, different,
Touching, sliding, separating,
Going in different, directions,
Us.

Howard H. Mackey, Jr.
THE LAST HAUL
Let's gather up our apples
For time is drawing nigh,
Let's make this last haul for winter
While there is autumn in the sky.

Let's make peace with those
   about us,
Shed those dreams that can't
   come true,
For tomorrow we reach our
   destiny,
And today is nearly through.

When our apples have been
   gathered,
And we tally up the strife,
We will have experienced a long
   long tenure,
Before the winter eve of life.

We, then, can turn and look
   behind us,
And offer wisdom to those who
   call,
As they prepare their personal
   life sleds,
To make the final haul.

Cathy Raming Neybert
BABY BLUE
The dollhouse is still; as if she
   had just played with the now
   dusty furniture . . .
The dolls lie graciously on her
   bed's sham.
Cobwebs lace the canopy to the
   ceiling.
Musk penetrates . . .
Dust floats like smoke.
Heaviness hangs in the air as
   almost a death.
Blue walls, bedspread edged with
   blue eyelet, and matching floor-
   length curtains.
Once, so much blue held my baby.
Bye, bye, baby blue . . .

John I. Hancock
RHAPSODY
Soft, how soft, the moonbeams
   caress
In delicate downpour, to drape
   night
And quiet earth with a silver dress.
To love, to love, dedicate the night.
Full bright starshine, the
   moonbeams
Meet, touch, glitter the silver dress
With torrential splendor so it
   seems
To draw close, closer still, to stress
The seductive elegance of tropic
   night.
Shadows and moonlight, a fluffed
   cloud
That drifts by create a lovely sight
So overpowering Nature sings
   aloud.
To love, to love, dedicate the night.
Early dawn rose-pink paints the
   cloud.
To love, to love, dedicate the night.

Yohauen Austerlitz
**An Splendid Fools Poetic
Utopian Noble Dream**
Would but that it was or would
   or could become to be as
   sometimes real . . .
   That which one would but so
   feign to make it seem
And Time upon its Wingless
   Flight for a time and a while
   stood still . . . and
Waystayed the swiftly fleeting
   years
Realities would become to be and
   be of they upon whom they
   may depend
As mankind learned to respect
   and regard Justice and
   Authority . . .
Of wisdom and with knowledge
   of dignity and of pride or
   even . . . pride's own vanity
   Then . . . treasons and delusions
   and deceits would no more
   be . . . and
Moral and intellectual fade
   would end and fade . . . the
   shed and unshed tears
   As surely The River of Life on
   its destined ways does slowly
   steadily wend
And become to be amidst the
   multitudes of mankind and
   society . . . the factions two
   Of each . . . wisdom . . . dignity
   and pride or forsaken loves and

lives and years
In Life and Society being but that
   it is . . . The Great Divide

As oft of but pretense and
   mockeries fades the devotion
   regards and esteem
   One or another then from life
   and love duty responsibility
   seek retreat respite
Yet tis not always as fools and
   the blatherskites would deign
   make it so to seem
   And all life to be . .. or become
   to be . . .
As but an imagined fantasy and
   as but . .. a temporal jaded
   fading dream
   As fades of but time upon its
   endless Wingless Flight of
   tin . . . its temporal sheen
Fades diminishes and vanishes of
   the forsaken and the
   forsaking . . . life and love
   and . . .
What be the soul of man that
   harbours nor contains not even
   the shades of . . .
   An splendid Noble Dream . . .
Not even the shades of an
   Splendid Fools . . . Poetic
   Utopian Noble Dream
   An splendid Fools Poetic
   Utopian Noble Dream

Judith Eshoo
THINGS

*To those who have rallied at their
losses to appreciate their gains.*

I've been lucky
you see,
to have had things.
Things to wear
things to use
so I could muse.
Things always shrouded my
   discontent,
such rewards for time misspent,
to worry more about more things,
until I ran out of things,
and chose never to replace,
an empty space,
with empty things.

Teresa Lee Smith
MEMORIES
I'm sitting alone by my window,
   watching the day depart,
Wondering what you are doing,
   and missing you too, sweetheart.
I am trying so hard to forget you,
   but my love for you will not die,
My thoughts ever turn to the
   thrill of your kiss, and the
   lovelight that shines in your
   eyes.
I relive in dreams those
   wonderful days when we met
   for a fleeting caress,
Knowing so well that our love
   should not be, though it brings
   us such sweet happiness.
I'll always remember your kisses,
   the love in your eyes, and your
   smile,
For your dear face a corner will be
   reserved deep down in my
   heart all the while.
If never again should I feel your
   arms, never again know your

kiss,
I'll always cherish my memories
   of you and our moments of
   Heavenly Bliss.

Edna Dame
THE OVEN BIRD
The smartest little bird to me
Is one I often hear
When working in the garden,
I know he must be near.
He's in the trees just out of sight
And calls to me five times,
"Teacher, teacher, teacher,
   teacher, teacher."
How does he know?

Arlone Mills Dreher
THE BLESSING OF GOD
Aloft in the sky I look down
   underneath me.
My plane's silver wings are
   reflecting a glow.
The mountains behind me are
   dressed in snow blankets
but rivers flow through them
   with waters so chill.

The foothills are verdant with
   shades of the springtime
and far down beyond me the
   desert's in bloom.
My plane is descending toward
   cities that bustle
with people who welcome the
   warmth of the sun.

My plane comes to rest at a great
   city's airport.
The beauty around me's the
   Blessing of God.
I pilot my plane to the airport's
   great hangars
and know that God's love is
   surrounding the world.

Susan Dale Geiger
EYES
Art is as beauty,
In the eye of the beholder.
There from a feeling of duty,
By a musician, a sculpter or
   molder.

Impressions from the mind's eye,
May be lost upon another.
An unplifting, a light, a breath-
   taking sigh,
May only be smothered by others.

And they must never be lost,
These many eyes.
For it is of an evolution,
It is what makes man wise.

Gene Darwin Abbott
A Matter Of Commitment
Do you ever wonder why many
   marriages are over so quick;
And, why do so many with their
   partner decline to stick?

For the mood of our generation,
   do you have a feel?
Have you noticed the failure of
   men to stick to a deal?
A commitment must be genuine
   if the commitment is real.

Can a dedicated commitment be
   found, I ask, without
   regeneration?
Can a commitment be genuine if
   God did not bring about
   dedication?

And did you ever consider a
backslider wondering where
the dedication went?
Perhaps the dedication was his
own and would therefore be
expendaply spent?
If the dedication were genuine,
would his commitment not be
Divinely sent?

Search through the world and
note the problems all around:
Is it not in this mess since so
little commitment is found?

Dorothy Brin Crocker
THE VIGIL
The ancient stones were covered
with moss,
And the road they guarded was
ruined and decayed.
The hidden secrets they would
never tell
Were buried in the house where
hope was betrayed.

The house was a shambles of
beauty gone
With a widow's walk that sagged,
and cast
A thinning curious shadow long,
Resembling a splintered, broken
mast.

The stalwart captain of the
whaling boat
Who dwelled in the mansion of
the coastal town,
Was lost at sea when the boat
was wrecked
By a whale that forced the ship
aground.

The ancient stones that guard the
road
Are waiting still for his return.
The widow once so filled with
hope
Is always seen when the seasons
turn.

For more than a hundred years
have passed,
Yet every year you can hear her
weep,
"Release his spirit from the
bottom of the sea,
And set me free from this vigil I
keep."

Rebecca Paashaus Blizzard
HE CARES

To my loving grandmother
GRACE B. BANCROFT

When I have trials or burdens to
bear,
And no one is there to help or care;
Do I cry? Do I shout? Do I mope?
Do I pout?
No! Because Jesus is there, I know
He cares.

When I'm alone, and things get
rough,
The times are hard, the going is
tough.
It all seems hopeless, my soul is
distressed,
But Jesus is there, I know He cares.

Now I am happy, sad too,
sometimes,

The trials are hard, and the
reasons His,
Come what may, I count it all joy,
Because Jesus is there, I know He
cares.

Virgil Graber, Ph. D.
O GRAND LAND
O grand land of this U. S. A.,
You are my home ever to stay;
You are the best with majesty;
You are the blest with liberty.

O grand land of this U. S. A.,
Your landscape is Nature's display:
Your mountains and canyons and
plains;
Your awesome awe that ever
reigns.

O grand land of this U. S. A.,
Your real wealth shines in such
array;
Your resources, so rich and rare;
Your industries, with no compare.

O grand land of this U. S. A.,
Your compassion is men's
mainstay:
Your open door for all good men;
Your humane heart kind without
end.

O grand land of this U. S. A.,
May God bless you on each
birthday;
Stand tall and proud for all to see;
Hold high your torch of liberty.

Harold Olsen
FANTASTIC
When morning's light drove me
from my bed, and then to my
window fled,
To behold the ermine robe that
God had spread.
Then, filled with glee, I away did
speed, to see the world so clean
and white.
The castle's now appeared with
turrets tall, where yesterday
the crows did call.
The ice-clear waterfall that sends
rainbows of delight to fill my
eye.
The new highways that filled the
forest floor, so that now,
I could see with naked eye, what
in summer was a hidden
mystery.
The flash of red that through the
trees did streak,
Made me dream of him in the red
sleigh, that also soars thru the
sky.
There, through the trees now
bare, I catch a glimpse of deer
that seem to fly.
Then my eyes are opened wide,
as I see the earth so pure and
white.
Then on my knees in the
wonderland of white I fall,
For I see as I never saw before,
God sent the earth a gift at night,
that I too, in His eyes, be pure
and white.

Margie C. Bonvillain
THIS YEAR
January arrived lonely and cold
February left before getting a score
March rolled in like a loud
beating drum

April showed up with a big green
thumb
May covered over in a dazzling
display
Romantic June lit the nights
along his way
July was unbearable too much
heat
August right behind her did and
exact repeat
September wore a vest of brown
edged in gold
October weaved rugs in Persain
rose
November tipped-toed across
them on frosty feet
Now here's December stuck in
snow knee-deep

John Tworoger
**Though You Are Many
Miles Away**
Though you are many miles away
Beyond the stormy sea,
My thoughts are with you night
and day,
For you are part of me.

The clouds that travel far above,
Are messengers of mine,
They bring you my undying love,
Red roses in a shrine.

No ocean and no mountains steep,
Impede my flight to you,
No chasm wide, no river deep,
No night, no morning dew.

My wings span over time and
space,
Though you are deep asleep,
Eternity dawns in the haze,
The rain and wind will weep.

Mark C. Morris
hungry
oh america
how things have made you
seem
like a strange dream
where
i wake up
in yr house
&
eat yr groceries
only to
return to yr bedroom
where
youre dreaming
yrself
so i said
"one of us should
be awake"
so

i woke up
so you could
dream.

Helene Suzanne Pomeroy
CHILL
I seem to be in a constant state of
cold . . . I shiver when I
remember to hear your voice
say that ol' line; the haunting
sound of your fast car leaving
early in the dawn scares me so
and as I wake up alone, I am in
the dark and none of the lights
work and music begins to play
in a steady beat of romantic
overtones . . .

I walk the halls in a trance and as
I search for your shadow in the
faint diaganol light from the
street, I faint in a chill of
worry; I miss you already and
the silence is screaming at me
to wake up and relax . . . I
rush in a stumble to turn the
music off, but the door is
locked and I turn behind me to
see pain holding the
key . . . please no, not
again . . . to love halfway is
such a waste and I am too
exhausted to argue the point
with a man who is not to be
found in this storm
. . . lost again in my own
house of utter surrender. I have
to find a blanket; the wind is
strong and the tea too
weak . . .
please don't call just yet
. . . let me get settled in the
room with all the saturday
morning memories . . . .

Florence Whitaker Gross
EMILY DICKINSON
I fled from Life and took my Love
with me,
Deep and rich and warm within
my heart.
Oyster-fashion, out of pain I
wrought the pearl,
Hidden close until Death reft the
shell.
Cutting swiftly, surely,
My fancy carved poetic cameos,
Dainty, mystic,
Set in iridescent words.

Helen Paine
A DEBT TO PAY
Across the years, our burnished,
red-skinned brothers
Roamed free and unafraid o'er
hills and plains—
But history tells the story of their
losses,
And writes in blood the story of
our gains.

We had so much, and then we
added to it;
The redskins, too, were rich in
Nature's stores—
But then, the white stampede
swept all before it,
With wagons, whisky, war—'til
woods and shores

Reverberated with the awful
sounds of gunshot—
And arrows whirred—but could
not stem the tide;

How can this land espouse the
cause of freedom
'Til we erase the blot of fratricide?

E. John McGovern
DAYSPRINGS

To my beloved wife Joan,
The dayspring of my life.

Have you gathered streams of
daysprings?
Sipped sunbeams from the
morning star?

Rode the dayspring to Gobi,
Comforted thunderclouds in
Zanzibar?

They roar and jostle the heavens,
Then they are no more!
The dayspring flows forever,
Quickening each lovely bloom!
Some are Lama's in Peru,
A children's choir on tune!
A maple leaf in autumn,
A kiss for a love in June!

Oh, I cannot see the dayspring!
Nor God's love kissing thee!
Yet, the dayspring flows forever.
For you, and daysprings even me!

Mary J. Watkins
CITY BY THE SEA
Where swaying palm trees whisper
Untold secrets to the midnight
sky . .
Wild Santa Anas shriek! and
spray
The desert pollen free.
Misty, sleeping mountains
Blend rain and sun and snow . . .
Send refreshing waters
To embrace the arid earth
below.
This is Los Angeles
City by the Sea

Where orange trees, cactus and
hibiscus
Bloom side by side . . .
And diverse cultures blend
Like rainbows, in the sky.
When soft pacific winds caress
And seagulls lift your spirits
high,
Sh . . .! You can hear the ocean
calling
Softly, as a sigh . . .

When sunny beaches beckon
And the surf is running wild . . .
Take your cares . . . your
troubled hearts,
Forget them for awhile.
Where the desert turns to
mountains,
And the mountains greet the
sea.
Where the climate's always mild
And life is so carefree . . .
In the City of Angels
City by the Sea.

Charles Wall
INFANTRYMEN
Who will fight
day & night?
On whom can you depend?
The Infantrymen.

Anywhere
they'll be there.

Right up to the end.
They're Infantrymen.

The very best
join the Army.
And pass the test
when combat they will see.

And when it's o'er
add the score.
You'll be thankful you did send
Your Infantrymen.

Matt Hammond
My Little Dark Haired Girl
This may be very silly
Please don't say it makes you sick
Am I in love? All my friends ask
me.
I say I'm not sure
I'm sure she's fallen in like with
me
It makes me sick

I really was happy before
knowing SHE
She's just the icing on the cake
Life still has beauty and misery
(I usually concentrate on the
darkness)
By worrying about mental
problems you can still go crazy
All I can say is: I think we all
have our own cage

Paul Shapshak, Ph. D.
WIDSITH RETURNED
Once again, Widsith opened his
word-hoard,
Unlocking mind's barriers to
view the Earth.
And to gaze at Space, early on the
road to victory,
Wings crossing time's reef with
his sons.

I have been a neutrino,
Transported through Suns blazing.
Like wisps of thought threading
galaxies,
I traversed at light's speed.

I have been an ion, free in
interstellar space,
But bounded by magnetic lines of
force, carrying me
Along invisible threads of
generations of echoes,
Exchanging photons with time-
future and time-past,
Learning every sphere's
reflections in a crystal pool.

I looked in the book of light,
I shredded stars in the mysteries
of cosmic creation,
I have been a dwarf in the
emptiness,
Lost in the arguments of fate.

I have been a comet on a solar
route,
Smiling at the planets, dodging
asteroids,
Finally, I am lost again in the
unknowing universe.

Constantino C. Flores, Jr.
BEAUTY
When all are sensitive to beauty's
awe,
E'en those prosaic are touched by
its forms;
The line on which may come this
magic law
Disputes enormously with

diverse norms.
For some it is the grace of
childhood's youth,
For some the surge and thunder
of the sea,
For some the meaning of sweet
life in truth,
Or quietness of afternoons at tea.
Or is it music of a voice that
speaks?
Or beautiful songs of birds in the
springs?
Or dazzling splendor of the
mountain peaks?
Or cold that frosty autumn
evening brings?
All these but none can match
the style and grace
Of beauty of the inner man:
God's trace.

Teresa LaQuie LeDoux
LIFE
A tiny drop of dew
Sprinkles from each blade of grass
Making the morning seem
Fresh

A child is born through love
Carrying on a name
Making our world seem
Blessed

An old man dies in pain
Screaming in fear of death
Making life seem so
Depressed

Life, endless life
Flowing from person to person
Life beginning so fresh
Being so blessed
Ending depressed

Thomas E. Roy
Stars Come Nightly To The Sky
Stars come nightly to the sky.
Oh! why, Oh! why, must we say
good by.
It must be because I love you so,
that
I do not want to let you go.
So if it must be that we must part.
Until we meet again sweet heart.
Fair well take care I care you see.
For you and I were meant to be.

Frank J. Kennedy
SANTA SAYS
When Christmas is over I'm
pretty damn tired and nothing
but quiet and peace is desired.
I used to be so lively and quick
now I slip all over the rooves
when they're slick.
I am no longer happy thinking of
flight or the ominous prospect
of working all night.
Your chimneys are small or I'm
getting too big all those
cookies and milk make me eat
like a pig.
My reindeer team lost it's get up
and go they all run and hide at
the first sign of snow.
Then Rudolph, who should be
leading the crew, was so cold
last year his red nose turned
blue.
If that's not enough, the more
modern gift has gotten so large
it's too heavy to lift.
The girl, who was happy with

embroidery frames now gives
me a list of electronic games.
There's no understanding the
present day boy, he's not
satisfied with a ball or a toy.
With an attitude like an army
recruiter, He'll ask me for a
new home computer.
In view of these facts, it won't
appear strange if I tell you here
that it's time for a change
'Stead of cookies and milk, which
I shall refuse leave a beautiful
blonde and a bottle of booze.

Ada M. Fletcher
Did You Hear Him, My Sweet Justin?

To my beloved grandson, Justin

Did you hear Him, my sweet
Justin
As you lay in your gray steel
prison
With ghostly forms tending the
cold, plastic tubes
Breathing life into your fevered,
little body,
Your damp, golden ringlets
haloing your beautiful face,
Tape holding your frail life in
place?

Did you hear Him, my sweet
Justin
Near the end of the tunnel in
blinding, white light,
In the plaintive petition of your
guardian angel,
The prayerful pleading of your
Mommy and Daddy,
Grandpa and me—on bended knee?

Did you hear Him, my sweet Justin
When He willed you back to us
And cured you with His Holy
Hands
And, having been a babe Himself,
understood your
Helplessness.
Did you dream of loving smiles
and favorite toys
And His whispering of future joys?

Did you hear Him, my sweet
Justin?
Gary K. Fredrickson
OFTEN SUPRISED

To a Good Wife:

It's been too long
And many too strange the sights,
So little the strength to call our
own
To lead us through these endless
nights.

How to mold this centrifugal will
As tug-of-war and spirits soar,
With such strangers in my mind
Leading through another door.

Despite it all,
Warnings given,
Who could have seen
Thoughts so riven?

Clinging tight to who we are,
Suddenly a place in view.
Given choice of love or life,
Strangers many, friends too few.

Edward J. Jeffs
For the Log Of the Clearwater I
Let us turn to the Hudson,
We who cannot feel its grief,
Who have not lost our purity
In great flows of waste,
And sing of cold waters and the moon,
While we dream alone of warm rivers,
Our unshared births.

In this time of absent myths,
We have to turn from men and gods,
To our inner resources,
To reinterpret, reaffirm,
Humanity and its environs.

Oh my lovers, how you have used me,
My surface you swam and shelled
In your beginnings of a nation,
My fish and waters you ate and drank
To survive,
Take care, despair runs in my veins,
Your commerce of barges and ships
Has only anointed my name,
I can only look to men to remain.

Connie Ratliff
He Put Her Hand In the Hand Of the Master
I was priviledged to watch one day
My Power Prayer Preacher
minister in a beautiful way,
A dear one was seeking peace,
and she knew
That, to give her heart to God
was what she needed to do!

He talked with her quietly, I sat
on the other side
Of the chapel and prayed
That, when she left this place,
she'd be stayed
In Him, in her faith she'd be strong
And know that, to Him, she'd
always belong!

Soon they bowed their heads in
sincere prayer
The Holy Spirit was truly there,
My Power Prayer Preacher
tenderly cast her
Cares upon His lap, then and there
He put her hand in The Hand of
The Master!

Joan M. Ricketts
STILLNESS IN THE NIGHT
In the stillness of the night when
everyone is asleep,
Many strange and wondrous
things seem to appear in the
deep.
As some watchful eye is in to
being with circumventing care,
The feeling of security, love and
closeness is too much to bare.

One seems to question whether
this strangeness is love,
But pulsating thoughts keep
bouncing around reassuring the
above.

Each tiny movement with its
comforting relief
Is like a kind of pressure lifted
beyond one's belief.
As one begin to turn around and
drift back to sleep,
More strange and wondrous
things seem to appear in the
deep.

May D. Rogers
BACKWARD LOOK

To Rachel, for whom the house
waits.

It's not for the new owners that
the old house sighs
And gathers to itself warmth
from altered skies.
Little does it care for the sounds
it hears
When strangers in the hall cancel
the long years.

Shadows, mirrors, clocks hope
and plot and wait
For steps that never come past
the garden gate.
When dusk lies on the floor the
boards forbear to creak.
Lest a long-hushed voice
suddenly should speak.

Pauline Sheehy
OH YE GREAT SURGEONS
You put bruises on my elbows
with your little rubber hammers,
Took large pins from your pocket
and stuck me in my fingers.

Drained some fluid from my spine
trying to make me dye,
Struck a nerve with your needle
and almost made me cry.

You let me push on you
but I couldn't win,
You left me in stitches
to bleed with the blues.

But somehow you touched me
charged me and kept me alive,
and for all of this
I'm in debt to you.

Margaret E. Ott
THE SAD CLOUD DRAGON
The Sad Cloud Dragon sat high
in the sky,
Idly watching other clouds
floating by.
When, suddenly, much to his
surprize,
A girl dragon appeared, just his
size!

He couldn't wait to get close to
her!
She was so lovely in her white
cloud fur.
But the wind was fickle. It started
to blow.
And they both disappeared.
Where did they go?

Gary K. Fredrickson
INNOCENCE

To Ruth Starbuck:

Looking back,
where would each branch have
led
if only
a little gentler,
a little sooner,
a little wiser?
Or a crossing taken slowly,
knowing that a moment would
occur again,
(in memory),
of what would be
not only the result of all
but also each, as,
sharing across a galaxy
of time and experience
we recognize the other
as real as ourselves,
and thrill to see the triumphs,
sorrow at the tears shed and
remain,
convicted of reality,
one moment's innocence
our common source.

Debbie K. Peacher
ON THE RANGE
Out on the Range
where the Animals roam free,
You will find an Eagle in the sky
and the Horses running free.
Where the Humming Birds
hum a sweet melody.
Though the water is hard to
find
and the food is scarce in the
winter time,
They somehow survive on this
great land they live.
On the range or on the planes,
we shall not invade
their home on the range . .

Carman Parsons
TENDER TORTURE
Memories which somehow
don't belong
tenderly torture
my aching mind.
And just as I think I've
got them figured—know
where they rightly go,
They skip just out of reach
and slyly sharpen their
tender torture.

Dominick Philicione
BLAME NOT MY HEART
Blame not my heart for loving
you—
When came the first I saw of you,
I felt myself adoring you,
And knew at once, 'twas only
you—
Blame not my heart for loving you.

Blame not the dreams I dreamt of
you—
They were in day and night of
you,
In darkness and in light of you,
And kept, always, the sight of
you—
Blame not the dreams I dreamt of
you.

Blame not the tears I shed for
you—
Upon my pillow bled for you,
When first I heard it said of you,
That someone would be wedding
you—
Blame not my heart for loving you.

Douglas H. Stanton, M.D.
Cockroaches In Paradise
Some dine on lobster broiled in
butter
Others eat what's in the gutter.

Some are macho, some are gay
Some change their sex along the
way.

Some babies die and go to heaven
Others survive to 97.

Some are blessed with high IQs
Others can't learn to tie their
shoes.

The sun still shines, the earth's
revolving
Let's hope that we are still
evolving.

Amy M. Silberman
GOLDEN BOYS
His poreless beauty
removed any magic
which only the other boys
could give

This golden boy
with the golden interests
who ate Nilla wafers
and milk

The other boys
whose interests lay
in The Supremes
and Vivaldi
ate dried apricots

These boys
with eighteen-year-old magic
so fleeting
it made us sad

Sophia Johnson Foster
SWEET DEBUTANTE
She walks in beauty—a tender
bud unfolding
A lovely lass, aglow with
anticipation
Poised on the threshold of life
Awaiting the cue to make her
exciting debut.
Atiptoe she scans the distant
horizon
That lies veiled with the mystery
of the inscrutable
She peers deeply through the
misty haze
Anticipating a glint of
illumination as she advances
And emerges through the
doorway leading to what is to be.
Undaunted by the nebulous
obscurity, she moves along.
Like the moth that flirts with a
candle's flame,
She glides ahead in utter
fascination.
Eager to learn why the flame
flickers.
Its flickering light beckons her
onward.

Now the flame becomes the
  reality of ambition
Brighting the shadowy vistas
  ahead.
Its beam glows as if held by a
  phantom guide
Calling to her, "Come, this is the
  way!"
Fearlessly, she follows seeking
  her true destiny.
This budding flower of
  womanhood, graceful and lovely.
Reaches the first milestone with
  unwavering resolve.
Aware now that she can make it
  step by step.
In triumph she perserveres
As she walks in beauty.

Sigrid Emanuelson Moore

Sigrid Emanuelson Moore
MY FRIEND
Your charming ways light up the
  golden flame
Of graciousness. It's silent spirals
  claim
The distant rim where special
  sunbeams hide
The magic shafts that dreamers
  like to ride.
Candescent streamers conquer
  Clotho's loom,
And lights appear as misty
  thoughts assume
An air of happiness. This aura
  weaves
A subtle spell! The fleeting vision
  leaves
A halo circling Grace's fragile cup.
If you could spill your precious
  treasure where
Tomorrow spins the plans of
  destiny,
Each day would gather beauty to
  light up
Your life. Your charming,
  thoughtful ways and care
Spread sunshine in the morning's
  wings for me.

Helen E. Moreland
HAPPY RETURN
Down, Down, from the blue
  mantle of the sky,
Silver wings sparkling through
  the clouds on high.

Down, Down, gently to the ground,
A large bird returns,
A Space Ship safe and sound.

Down, Down, to mother earth,
To old comrades,
  to success and mirth.

Blanche Fredricks
A Small Slice Of Americana
"All aboard! All aboard!"
"Does this train go to
  EASYTOWN? Does it stop
  there?"

"No. Sorry Lad. This is the last
  run to MEMORYVILLE."
"Never heard of the place. What's
  the fare?"

"We go straight through
  STRUGGLE, then over the hill.
After tomorrow this run will be
  no more;

was a time though it ran from
  shore to shore.
Well don't stand there! Make up
  your mind;

Either get on or off, we're running
  behind.
I warn you this is a SPECIAL,
  deep and mystical;

you'll see things you thought
  only statistical;
the buffalo will roam the plains;
  Indians will give chase,

ladies will wear bustles and
  bonnets trimmed in lace.
You'll see a high stake poker
  game in the club car;

Jesse James' gang might ride up
  with Belle Starr.
You'll see the Delta Queen on the
  old Mississip,

and the Texas Rangers with a
  gun on each hip.
It might be too rough for the
  likes of you,

who has never earned a dollar but
  spent quite a few.
Better take the plane at LAZY
  HOLLER.
You can taxi there for only a
  dollar."

Dawn Hatanaka
UNTITLED

___

*I dedicate this poem to you,
Lance, my teacher and special
friend. Wherever you are today,
may you always find happiness in
everything you do.*

___

Without your love, what would
  life be?
For words could not describe how
  much I adore thee.
Your presence in our church has
  lifted many hearts,
And nothing in the world will
  keep us apart.
The Lord God Almighty has
  given you the light
To preach the gospel with your
  strength and might.
It's comforting to know there are
  people like you
Who care so much about others,
  too.
Within me I feel that you really
  have been blessed
By the one who is holier than all
  the rest.
I can't thank you enough for all
  that you've done

As a teacher and a friend because
  I know you are one.
I send you this greeting as a
  token of my affection
In hopes that others may follow
  in the very same direction.
Here's to you, Lance, my thoughts
  and my feelings
From a girl who now knows that
  seeing is believing.

Brian Keith Johnson
THE SEED
Oh what a wonder
Who makes winds still
And assigns the seed
of His magnanimous will
to clothe in the flesh
humbly to prove:
miracle seers
make mountains move.

He told humankind—
the believing and the wise—
their faith would lend
the blind man eyes.

Our Father in heaven
Came here as our brother
teaching love for our Father
Is love for each other.

Esther Kazakevich
RAIN
I feel so sad on days it rains,
The drops of rain are tears I
  borrow.
Memories return with lasting pain,
While storm clouds swirl toward
  to-morrow
Inside the aching heart, rain adds
  grief.
Rain gives strength to make all
  things grow
Revives the withered leaf, calms
  the
Thirsty earth and adds a re-
  freshing glow,
But only God can cleanse and
  re-new
My soul, like a gentle rain sent
  special
To me, to wash away the grief
  in-side
And set me free.

Francis W. Sayre
SILENCE OF NIGHT
Silence stalks the midnight hour
As quiet seeps into my soul.
The shades of night are drawn
And shield out light until dawn.

The dreams of night are vivid.
As day holds forth in visions,
Night shades in veiled
  imagination
When shadows paint scenes in
  bold array.

Beauty stalks the night in
  lovliness
As dreams paint with vivid
  allure.

Eleanor Kirkby
SHELTERED
  Need I have a shelter,
To hide me from the past.
  Or just an open window,
To free me now atlast.
  I'm climbing the stairway,
One step at a time.
  'Cause there's no life's pattern,
No set rhythm with easy rhyme.

Thumbs up it means a chance,
Down, it means to ponder,
  On the meeting of a challenge,
Beyond the vast blue yonder.

Marion A. Sample
RETIRED? NOT ME!
When I retire I'm going to be
  the busiest person you'll ever
  see.
I'm not about to sit and rock
  or be tossed away like a
  wornout sock.
There's too much left for me to
  see,
  and too little time for me to be
content to wile away the years
  with idle hours and useless
  fears.

No, that kind of life is not for
  me.
  It's going to be such fun to be
able to travel and get away
  from the hustle bustle of the
  working day.
I may just up and start anew
  some projects I've always
  wanted to do.
Who knows? Some talents I may
  find
  that will be a boon to all
  mankind.

At least I'll know that I have
  tried,
  and the very trying will give me
  pride.
If nothing is ventured, nothing is
  gained.
  (You wouldn't have rainbows if
  it never rained.)
So you won't find me with
  nothing to do;
  there's a lot of life waiting and
  before I'm through
I'll have tasted new pleasures and
  tried a few schemes—
  met some new people and
  dreamed some new dreams.

I'll never be famous; I'd much
  rather not—
But no one can say I didn't give
  my best shot.

John W. White
HALLOWEEN

___

*To Kimberly St. Peter—When her
boyfriends in need ... She's a
girlfriend indeed ...*

___

Spooky creatures on the street
The kind you wouldn't want to
  meet
Ghastly goblins, an ugly fright
Ugly still, in darkness of
  night ...

Bewitching spellbinders motivate
Ugly spasms initiate
Rotten deeds throughout the
  night
Make you mourn the sorrow of
  fright ...

Pumpkins light the darkness
  'round
So you know not what you've
  seen
Only hearing the eerie sounds
On that night ... called
  HALLOWEEN!

Katherine E. Gerwin
TO ACCOMPLISH
A drop of water
Dripping on a stone—
Half-inch mirror
Reflecting hone,
At first
Makes no imprint
On the smooth flint,

But, by falling
Drop by drop,
Day by day,
With measured plop
On the self-same spot,
In constant force
Of purposed course,

Will, at last,
In monotone,
Crack the strata
Of the stone.

Stephen Gianotti
PRICE OF PARTING
I feel the leaving keener now,
  To stay magnets my heart
Fast to the look in your water eyes,
  Deeply to your deepest part.

As I'm off to where I'm going
  I am stretched from whence I
  came,
Which was solace in a loving
  That softly said your name.

And the parting remains painful
  As trickle days trudge by,
With footsteps of a cannon blast;
  The helpless of baby-cry.

Margaret K. Behnke
Small Hearts—Big Hurts
Oh how sad it is to see a small
  heart broken
To hear the questions in the night
To feel the pillow wet and soaking
From tears shed of those little eyes
To feel such hurt at that tender
  age
To be afraid and all alone
To keep asking and asking, never
  ceasing
"When is my daddy coming home?"
Try to understand my little dear
It is better that he's not here
He brought to me an emptyness
A love that was not sure
Although to you, he was a king
A king, and even more ..

Elsie Halsey Lacy
IN HIS LIKENESS
His likeness Human eyes can
  never see
with perfect wholeness as could
  be
even from infancy while a Babe
as in a manger on straw He laid.

Within His Person no wrong exist
Though the vile would cuss and
  hiss
rendering Him cruelty and pain
He vest with purity did not wane.

His equal mankind has never met
One through hardships did not
  fret;
This Holy Lord evil men crucified
on the cross at Calvary died

so believers could gain a home
with eternal life around the throne
of God to live forever more
where praises of Christ is in store

from the Redeemed who glorify
  His Name
with uttered praises They gladly
  acclaim.
by tongues aloud they share
resounding everlasting there

Malcolm Scott Mac Kenzie
ONE
Limpid flow of knowing
that feels me,
I will tell you what I see;
frenetic forms are peace;
they have
Sighs of resignation,
Cries of expectation,
Breasts of exaltation;
from selvic depths
they are born
in struggling tides,
roar their foaming crests,
dropping on castled sands,
then drift back toward the sea.

Della M. King
GATHERING STARS

*To my loved ones, always and
forever.*

In my cabin on top of the
  mountain
  'Neath the pine trees that
  whisper and sigh,
With a big golden moon glowing
  softly
  As it drifts through a star
  sprinkles sky . . .

Far away from the lights of the
  City
  From the noise and the scent of
  the cars,
It seems I could look out my
  window
  And gather a handfull of stars.

I'd wrap them in dreams and I'd
  send them
  To the girl I adore and she'd
  wear
Them strung on a chain, for a
  locket
  Or entwined in her long golden
  hair.

The breeze in the pines plays a
  sweet melody
  Like an echo from memory's
  lane . . .
Or the whispering strings, of an
  old violin
  Repeating a haunting refrain.

It's a night made for dreaming, for
  gathering stars
  For watching the moon growing
  old . . .
A night made of beauty, for love
  and romance,
  With some one to have and to
  hold.

W. E. Davis, M.D.
TO NEWELL
I loved her, and she knew it well,
  I loved her, and she wove a spell
Of graciousness and loveliness
  On all our life together.

I loved her, and could I but say
  "I love you" as I did each day
Through all the intervening time
  Since our first, early meeting.

I loved her, If I might hold her
  hand
  And somehow make her
  understand
How desperately I miss her
  Since she went away..

I loved her, I can see her face
  And I can feel her fond embrace.
Her soft voice echoes down the
  years.
  I view her tender smile through
  tears.

Marlene H. Hardesty
LITTLE GIRL
Am I still that little girl who
  kissed you goodnight
When life was easy and things
  seemed right?
Oh! The happy carefree times,
  how quickly they've passed,
When years take hold and you
  become woman at last!
Womanhood! What a hard and
  puzzling thing,
When I ask myself, is this all that
  it brings?
Oh! Have we changed so much in
  mind
Or is it those wonderful years
  we've left behind?
Am I still that little girl you
  peeked in on at night?
The little girl who once held your
  hand so tight.
Those precious years that haunt
  my mind,
Why did I have to grow up and
  leave them behind?
Do you long to hold my hand,
  and kiss me goodnight
And oh! To squeeze my neck so
  tight?
Oh tell me! Please tell me! Am I
  still
That little girl?

Thirl Michael Butler
FOREST BAUBLE
Dark forest bauble
lying gilded in
sunlight and shadow.

Leaves twisting, falling,
green fern silouhette
flowing across the

floor like centuries.
Guardians of earth,
tall trees rooted in

the soil in the
shadow, protecting
forest's dark bauble.

Rumpled wing and blue
feathers, gilded in
sun shadow and moss.

Tamie K. Eby
I WENT TO THE FOREST
I went to the forest today
I let the cool waters soothe my
  aching spirit.
I felt the purifying warmth of the
  sun against my weary flesh.
The sounds, they pacified me
For a fleeting moment the world
  and all its turmoil vanished.
I long to stay in the soothing
  peacefullness here and yet I
  know I must return.
For there are those who need me
  and yes I need them.

But I will return,
  oh my stream of peace
When once again my soul is in
  need.

William L. Bongard
KIDS

To All Mothers

Kids will be kids
We can plainly see,
They are so important
To you and me.

Kids seem like brats, at times—
Parents don't know what to do
When you think they love you
They can make you blue.

Kids can be very happy
As part of their dreams
When Mothers want to scold them
A great big smile beams

Kids have a bright future
That we love and admire
To make them good citizens
Is what we so desire.

Barby Phillips
SHE NEEDS LOVE

A friend, Wayne

She sees her potential personality
happy-go-lucky, full of life
with warmth and love to give,

Standing back seeing herself
through the eyes of her piers,
she's hiding from herself,
afraid of acceptance or rejection?

When she's laughing,
she's crying, when she's crying,
she's confused

I'll break that barrier,
of insecurity and self doubt,
accepting myself.

Happy-go-lucky, full of life,
with warmth and love to give and
communicate, only then will
  love,
  shine back on me.

Brian K. Freels
RHYTHM OF THE WIND
I hear your name
spoken like a song on the breeze;
but when I turn
to see where you are
the clouds in the sky
are all that greet my gaze.

Our World's Best Loved Poems

I feel your touch
brushing like a leaf on the wind;
but when I shift
to lengthen the caress
emptiness
is all that reaches my flesh.

I hear your voice
breathed like a sigh on the breeze.
But if I turn
to see if you are there
I only admit that you
have gone from me.
As I turn to see where you are
the rhythm of the wind
stirring the grasses of time
is all that meets my gaze.

Frances M. Burns
THE ADVENT
The trumpets sounded in Heaven,
As stars shone in the skies.
Angels hearlded His coming,
The world was not that wise.

Who thought a cave would be a
nave
To bring a bright new light?
We wait again as some did then
On that clear starry night.

Martha L. Schaffer
So Great a Promise Kept

*Dedicated to my wonderful
husband of thirty-five years,
whom I love and admire more
each passing year.*

Oh Holy Babe, thy light to see,
We followed your star as you slept;
Beside your crib we bend our knee,
For so great a promise was kept.

Of the promises he did make,
To his children upon the earth;
No vow did our God ever break,
The greatest upheld was thy birth.

God's love is of eternal sway,
His promises ever stand true;
"By humble birth," we hear him
say,
"My only son I give to you".

Oh King of Kings, and Lord of
Lords,
Before thy throne our hearts we
bow;
Possess our lives, our deeds, our
words,
Keeps like thee, true to our vow.

Faye Roberta Parker
GALAXY
There's many a turbulence in this
place
Many a wandering souls floating
in space
None would dare venture out to
see
An avarice multitude such as we.

Every soul keeps his distance, tis
by far
Afraid to come near us, so they
are
One would think there's power in
the blood
Oh, tis but a pity we can't calm
the flood.

Floating in a galaxy all our own
Where many a sins are condoned
Spaced out, tripping, calling it fun

Where will we go when our
galaxy is none?

Others who view us from afar
Think what a shameless people
we are
No remorse, all self esteem
A burning hell is what it means.

Galaxy, oh galaxy in such a
lovely attire
Galaxy, hot galaxy seat of a
raging fire
Burning like mad, oh what a pity
Oh galaxy, oh galaxy, don't burn
me.

Tis many a turbulence in this
place
And many a wandering souls
floating in space
Robbing, killing, lusting, all in fun
But where will we go when our
Galaxy is none???

Jerome E. Politoski
THE CHRISTMAS TREE
I remember long ago
The tree stood tall and in the wind
Its branches waved as if to say
You're in my living room today

Standing in the winter snow
The glisten of the boughs at night
A silver star from far away
Turned the night time into day

In its fold there perched a bird
Amidst the cones and blades of
green
A spider's home, its master's fled
But stays the fly in its last bed

Think of not so long ago
The tree stood tall but not in wind
A man's own room, his living place
The pine was only taking space

Although white, the snow was
warm
And glistened in the twinkling
lights
The plastic star upon its head
Glows from a man made light
instead

Now the tree is lying bare
On carpet of its home again
In flattened branches is no bird
But in the darkened night is heard
—A spider makes a home
Kimberly Eames Donaldson
EVENSONG
Colors of blazing brightness,
purple, magenta, red, orange,
gracefully descending upon a flat
brooding sea of deepening blues,
melting into one majestic horizon.
Slowly, as if making a secret
escape,
the great ball of furious fire
slips behind the scene,
moment after endless moment
edging downward, casting gentle
shadows
of dimming glow over the silent
earth,
leaving pale stillness
and hints of moonlight.
Marie Lundgren
HIS FIRST CHRISTMAS
The Star was bright, the city slept,
When Jesus first beheld His
Mother's face.
Serene and rapt, she smiled and
crooned

A lullaby within that holy place.
He turned His head, His father
knelt
And kissed the tiny hand that lay
in his.
Thus Joseph welcomed Him, this
Son,
His heart a battleground of fear
and bliss.
They knew, these parents, in
their hearts,
That Jesus was no ordinary Child,
That destiny would lie in wait
To mold a future King from One
defiled.
The Baby heard the restive beasts
And felt the warmth they gently
breathed on Him;
He watched the Star, the guiding
light
Whose brilliance caused the
firmament to dim.
The Wise Men came to kneel in
awe,
To proffer gold, and frankincense,
and myrrh;
The Christ Child smiled, and
Mary prayed
That she would justify God's
faith in her.
And thus He came to save a world
That long ago, unheralded
Christmas morn,
While angels sang to worship
Him
And cried "Behold! This day a
King is born!"

Lillian Payne RN

Lillian Payne RN
Dear Heavenly Father
Dear Heavenly Father—
How wonderful—but true—
That we can bring our sins and
burdens—directly to you.

You see our deep repentance—
You see the way we stray.
You see the longing in our
hearts—
To be right with you each day.

We feel your loving arms—as you
draw
Us near—we hear your loving
words—as
You speak so clear—"My child
your sins
And burdens are now mine—I
bore them
On the cross—My precious blood
shed.
That you would not be lost"—

Donna Cozad
LOVE

*To all of the caring people in my
hometown, Huntington, Indiana*

Love is like a tear that's shed
It's soft, gentle and never said

Love doesn't come in a chasing
way
It stays longer than a year or a day

Love is not a bird that's never
flown
It's able to reap what it has sown.

Love is what I give to you
Hate is darkness, love is true . .

Love is all I have, you see
The wings of the mind are strong
and free.

Yolanda Marie Nagayo
HUMBLE HEART

*I dedicate this poem to my
children Alexander, David,
Jennifer and Karen.*

Humble heart
Most merciful
Hear our prayers
Model of perfection
May we walk with you
To praise you for infinite goodness
Watch over me
Guide my way
Guide me to be just, patient and
humble
Guide my life
Love is a lamp in darkness
To forgive lights up the world.
Accepting joys along with sorrows
Can bring a more peaceful soul
Humble heart
Happy and thankful are we
Hear our prayers.

Stephanie Lynne Porr
RIVER OF EMOTIONS
I am a river,
a river of emotions
I was once a human person
until I cried myself into this river
I cried and cried,
I cried for sadness, I cried for
sorrow
I cried and stayed here, then I
became a river
My name is Sadness River.
People come and walk at the foot
of my water,
they sit and think, they think
about their lives.
Most of them cry, some of them
smile
I feel their emotions, they
become part of me.
I know when to be soothing, I
know when to rage,
and it is then that I crash
against the rocks.
I feel for the people,
whether they be black or white.
I comfort them and I cleanse
their thoughts
they can swim in me,
They can stand away
it doesn't matter what they say.
I am here for them, and always

323

will be.
        I ask only one thing;
PLEASE DON'T POLLUTE ME.

Bernerd Brooks
COVERS
I'm a book unread,
    a story untold.
I have dreams to share with
    someone who cares.
I'm a hunter stalking through this
    world alone,
I have no gun,
    their is no game.
I'm a writer who cannot talk,
    no pen to speak,
    no one to hear.
Yet, I have dreams to share with
    someone who cares.

Helen M. Garriott
SENILE
Senile—my mother—she knows
    me only as a child,
    no recollection of later years.

She calls and I cannot come,
    for I am no longer a child.

Christmas holidays—she was
    coming for a visit
    but age overtook her.

I sit weeping on the floor of her
    apartment,
    sorting a collection of letters
    saved since my college days,
    trinkets, clippings, gifts I have
    sent.

It is Christmas eve'—a knock—
    they have come to take the
    things no longer useful to her
    in a nursing home.

I ache!

A nursing home—the last place
    she would wish to be.

Thank God she doesn't know
    where she is.

H. Rhea Pritchard
MUTUAL ADMIRATION

*Dedicated to two very dear
people (no longer young) whose
true experience inspired this poem.*

Now, he was five years old, and
    on that day
He wore, for the occasion, his
    new suit.
He had (most stern) instructions
    not to play
Down in the dirt—for reasons all
    too moot.

His "ice cream" suit was white
    with pinkish stripes
And he was proud as a small boy
    can be.
He, carefully, made no grubby
    handed swipes
and stood so he was sure that *she*
    could see.

He did make quite a picture for
    the lass
His button-shoes were shiny as
    shoes get.
Their glances met—dead—center
    "here was class".
They all went home—or, they'd
    be glancing yet.

He was impressed—therefore he
    said it twice!
"That little girl thought I was
    pretty nice."

SHE

The little lass? Well, she was
    dressed up, too.
Her dress was white, with
    beautiful pink sash;
For Sunday school—well, nothing
    else would do.
In any group, that girl would
    make a splash.

Three tiers of ruffles trimmed the
    little skirt
(Her petticoat was starched to
    hold it wide)
Now, I'd not say the lassie was a
    flirt—
But, often, she made sure the sash
    was tied.

The ribbon in her hair was just as
    pink
As was the sash—'twas of the
    selfsame shade;
So if "that little boy" took time to
    think
He'd like the pretty picture that
    she made.

She could not see why grown folk
    laughed when she
Remarked "I think that little boy
    liked me."

Rosricka C. Baugh
OUR EMOTIONS
Like high tides roaring at sea;
Like the hustle and bustle of
    people shuffling down a busy
    street.
That's how steadily our love
    almost always flows.
For in as much effort one puts
    into a normal breath,
That's how much we contribute
    to the continual flow of our love.
Similar to the contentment a
    babe feels when resting his
    head on his mother's breasts,
I enjoy the sensation of my
    fingers rubbing up and down
    the contour of my lover's face.
I'm so thrilled when my hands
    wander over his muscular body.
Feeling the warmth it gives off
    and the vibrations his body
    gives mine.
It's so COMPLEX!
Caressing your body, kissing your
    lips, and licking your whole

body from front to back and
from one side to the other is
enough pleasure to give me the
ecstasy some women
experience when having
complete orgasms!
You make me light up like a
candle when you look at me
with those eyes.
You make my body quiver when
you touch my hand, and my
heart skip a beat when you
hold me, kiss me, and say that
you're mine!
Foreplay with my lover is a
delicacy in my life that I will
never take for granted.
For his touch alone, seems to be a
thrill I always wanted but
never had.
And during our prolonged
foreplay, my lover hints to me
that he's ready to burst into
colors of the rainbow with me.
Then I moan and say, "Get it
baby!" He moans and then cries
out, "Go Girl!" And I ride my
cowboy until we get lost in one
another's euphoria. Then we
collapse into each other's arms.
"It was so GOOD!" If my needs
cannot be thoroughly supplied
when you are trying; they can't
be met because you alone
supply me with every thing a
woman could ever desire.

Stanley A. Fellman
NIGHT CITY EDITOR
If I had a friend who just didn't
use a spoon on his soup and
picked up the bowl and sipped
the stuff, I wouldn't drop him.
But if he were the kind who set
fires for nothing special at all, I
would have to let him go," said
the Reporter.

The Editor replied: "If he were
really my friend, I'd keep him—
But, when ever we went out, I'd
carry a fire extinguisher along
with us."

Nancy S. Bensinger
WHAT A LOVELY SOUND
Christmastime will always bring,
Joy the world around.
Listen to the church bells ring,
What a lovely sound.

Families trim their Christmas tree,
Snow flakes hug the ground.
Carols sung in harmony,
What a lovely sound.

Special treats are now in store,
Chestnuts by the pound.
Friends come knocking at the door,
What a lovely sound.

After Santa's busy flight,
He is homeward bound.
Sleigh bells jingle through the
    night,
What a lovely sound.

Presents underneath the tree,
Waiting to be found.
Children laugh excitedly,
What a lovely sound.

But the sweetest sound of all,
When a star shone 'round,
Was a low cry in a stall.
What a lovely sound.

Rose Colombo Strickland
SNOWFLAKE

*To my sister, Patricia Ann
Colombo*

Flutter softly to the ground
Fall quietly without a sound
Lie peacefully beneath a tree
Melt gracefully into the sea
Return again on winter's eve.

Onda Horning
THE PRESENTATION

*To all observers of the rose: Feed
thy mind and thee will
comprehend*

A rose after long neglect
And adverse conditions,
By persistence and tenacity,
Has finally come into
Its glorious full bloom.
However, the one refreshing
    shower
Necessary to bring out full
    maturity
For everyone's veiwing
Came at the precise moment
In the rose's growth
To perfect the full bloom
And enhance its aroma.

Eugene D. Evans
GAMES

*Mr. Evans is author of the best-
selling novel GOLGOTHA*

She played at games as children do
Amid much noise and laughter,
A little girl of just-past-two
Whom sunshine followed after.
Her world was full of happy
    dreams,
Her hours were fairyland bright
As she played on with childhood
    schemes
In a kind of angel light.
But I was busy with the chore
Of dreary daily things
And as she laughed it made me
    sore
Since life had clipped my wings.
So with the callousness of age
I bellowed her to quiet
And knowing my too—worldly
    rage
She cried. (I can't deny it.)
"You goddam kids make too
    much noise!"
That shut her for a while:
And once more foolish heart
    found joys
At cost of an angel smile.

Dorothy R. Larson
EULOGY FOR MATTHEW
He never saw the sunlight, yet
    his face
Reflected all the joy of summer
    days;
His world was bounded by the
    little place
Where he was born, but still no
    worthwhile phase
Of life escaped his eager mind.
    His love

Of simple things was beautiful to
  see;
He knew each bird by sound. For
  him they wove
Their sweetest tapestries of song,
  and he
Could tell each flower's name by
  gentle touch.
He was beloved by everyone he
  knew;
His quiet, kindly humor did so
  much
To soothe a hurt. Now that this
  life is through,
We know how great the angels'
  joy must be,
To have him with them through
  eternity!

Franklin Himes
beggar's song

*In loving memory of 'Gramma'
Robertson*

All days must turn to face eve;
Most passion may turn into love
But nothing so much, so good, so
  above
our earthly flesh, do we grieve
as the past to our frightening
  future we leave

And in all the doubts of better
  days—
the haunting strains of hazy
  holi-days
drift dumb upon my living ways
and gratitude beyond mere
  graciousness
gives eternal rise to a misty
  tenderness

Thus engulfed so full of memories
i cannot word what Kings might
  sing
a beggar's song of love is all i bring
for the help to hope i humbly
  seized
from you with whom i've been
  well pleased

Lynn Weston
BANK OF LOVE
Over the years I have made many
  deposits.
Yes—I must admit I have
  received a portion of interest.
But to be quite honest—
I have received more withdrawls.
Now I ask you.
Am I really being so unreasonable
As to say that all I really want is
  a return on my investment.

Suzanne Larsen
A CHRISTMAS STORY

*With fond memories of my
father, Charles H. Flint*

Out on our excursion Dad and I'd
  go
When the fields were all covered
  with snow.
He had a certain place in mind
Where he knew we'd find that
  special pine.
He could read a tree like a book
All it took was one look.
He told me the wind blew from a

certain way
And there had been no water day
  after day.
Down row after row we'd walk.
Sometimes silent, and sometimes
  we'd talk.
This tree was too crooked and tall
And that tree was too bare and
  small.
Finally we found just the right one
And with the last chop our job
  was done.
Like returning heros we were
  treated.
With hugs and hot drinks, we
  were greeted.
Dad and I knew we'd done well.
By Mom's and Gram's pleased
  smiles we could tell.
The tree was decorated later that
  night,
But not even the star on top so
  bright
Could dim the beautiful memory
Of the day Dad and I shared
  among the trees.

Suzan Bond
MY SPECIAL SOMEONE
Down by the river
We sit in the sun
Loving together
One on one.
He says he loves me,
I reply with a kiss.
Before him
I've never loved like this.
It's the togetherness I have
When he's near;
It's his lonely good-bye
I never want to hear.
As I watch the sun
Sink slowly down,
I know my special someone
Has been found.

James M. Foltz
THE DEVIL
Woke up this morning, just
  feeling a fright
been tossin' and turnin' all night
smoking grass and turning on
living it up from dark to dawn.

Felt so good, lifted so high
cool and pink was the sky
but my time was short lived
I saw the Devil, this is what he did.

Stole my soul and threw me out
stood and looked at me with a pout
pointed his firey finger at me and
  then
made my head hurt as the cops
  busted in.

They jerked me to my feet and
  took me to jail
said I'd rot and burn in hell
the Devil was in the corner of my
  cell
said come with me, only thirteen
  steps to hell.

I wanted my soul, I wanted it back
can't find my way out, I've lost
  track
of what it's like to be a God-
  Fearing man
oh, help me Lord, teach me to
  stand.

The Devil is there, I can feel him
  all around
I can hear his eerie and firey band

playing like nothing Ive heard
  before
here he comes, please Lord, shut
  the door.

Sharon Groten
ADVICE
What do I do?
We each have asked this question
Of ourselves.
Many have sought the answer
From people outside the problem.
Bad advice can be found in
  abundance.
Good advice is as rare
As a bloom in the snow.
Advice can help, heal and portect.
But when the troubled is too blind
To see good from bad,
Then there is suffering and pain,
And loss.
Advice is a very dangerous thing
To give to someone in need of
  help.
The advisor cannot know
If the advice is weight and
  balanced
In the clear light of day and reason,
Or the cloudy night of fear and
  doubt.
When asking advice of one trusted,
Stand in the sunlight of the mind,
And listen to its rays.

B. Eldon Taylor
A MESSAGE TO YOU
A spotted fawn pokes out its head
And bravely dares the aspen edge;
The rodent raises from out its hole,
Their eyes exchange an innocent
  role.

The dew has moistened the
  wooded green,
It glistens bright with a polished
  sheen.
The yellow rays reflect upon the
  forest floor
Extending Lifes gift from Heavens
  door.

A covenant to mankind, a prism
  of color,
Descending to caress the bosom
  of its mother.
The envelope closes leaving only
  twinkling light,
Appearing in the distance is the
  chariot of night.

Drifting in flight above the
  mountain high,
Silhouetted by the dawn, soft
  shadows in the sky.
Reflecting below on a blue mirror
  of nature
The rushing falls are stilled, in a
  blending rapture.

The symphony provided by God
  given beauty
Inspires the orchestra to a much
  higher duty;
The bouquet of bounty is but my
  shy attempt
In returning to you—what your
  love has meant.

Judy Baker
**The Thought Of Loving
You**
The thought
  of loving you
  was always

on my mind.

Many times
  it helped me
  keep going
  when things
  got rough.

How I'll miss you
  dear friend,
  and all those
  lovely fantasies . . .

Your eyes
  I'll miss the most—
  there were our other
  lives together
  hidden for me
  in your eyes.

Sorry this time
  could not be ours . . .

Beryl Siemer Held
Sancta Maria de Fontibus
St. Mary's by the Springs
once "thick set with thorns . . ."
encircled by hills and moors
Haven for religious dissenters,
coarse-robed Cistercians
. . . monks who molded and
  shaped
the fertile river valley.
Nurtured soil yeilded crops
while sheep were tended
in silence.

Time dispelled an era
robbing the scene of simply-clad
  figures
bequeathing arched fingers of
  stone
struggling to brush the sky.
Crumbling walls stand mutely,
age-worn relics of the past,
asleep on blanket of lush green
while dripping rain-washed leaves
whisper to the wind.

Kelli Burns
FANTASY
In a land of fog and marsh
Where once a people lived,
There is a great house of solitude
Where a guardiance of soul is
  gived.

And in the golden chamber
Lies the wealth of a thousand
  kings
Inside the pointed object
Which holds the rolling rings.

But fear all ye who touch it
For it was not made for man;
The powers kept within can be
Only for the mystic's hand.

And when the mystic's hand has
  touched
The object alive will be
To bring a peace upon the land
Or destroy it for all eternity.

But beware all ye who venture
To keep it for your own
'cause many have come a seeking
And less doth their number grow.

Emily Brueske
EXPLOSION
Injured
A child lies gasping for breath
Raped
A girl runs from a ruined emotion
Crazed
A boy barters his soul for a drug

And displaced
A waif searches a border of tents
Hungered
A wail cuts across the cold air
What has gone wrong
With the song
In the night
Where are the wisemen
How far
To the Bethlehem star
God intended this day
For joy

Suzanne L. McNutt
FASTDIGGA

To my beautiful children,
Suzanne and Regina and to John,
who encouraged me with love.

Gerbil, gerbil in the night
You dig so fast with all your might;
You flurry and scurry and hurry
   about
"You woke me up!" I want to shout.

What is this mad activity
Impelling you obsessively
To be a perpetual motion machine?
Sometimes you make me want to
   scream!

Hey, gerbil, I have had enough
Of this nocturnal sporting stuff.
I'll fix your wagon, Hee! Hee! Hee!
I'll cover your cage so you can't
   see.

Peace at last! The room is still.
I hope that she has had her fill,
And settles down upon her nest
So I can get two hours rest!

Oh, no! It is too quiet now.
I find I cannot sleep somehow.
It's already six o'clock, I see.
Hey, gerbil, will you play with me?

Shelia Graham Clemons
CHILD OF NINE
I remember in my days of youth,
   To hear some say, "a King," in
   truth,
Yet to others just a man.

He passed through town one
   dusty day,
   while on His way to Galilee.
The old ones crowded around
   Him so,
   I could not even see His face.
I crawled upon the dusty ground
   just trying to touch His feet,
But I was just to small you see,
   for only six was I.

In later years, three exact,
   He came again into this town.
The scene was changed somehow
   that day,
   Both hands were bound in
   ropes this time
And upon His head a crown of
   thorns.

He carried a cross up a rocky
   mount,
   Goliatha, the name, as I recall
And there they nailed Him to the
   cross.
   I stood upon a solid rock
And with outreached hand I
   touched His feet.

I head Him whisper very soft,

"I've known you child before
   this day.
Go teach the things that I have
   taught,
   I live in you, a child of nine."

Kathy Sommer
Conflicting Personalities
What should I do,
When I feel blue.
What can I say,
To make you stay away.
I don't need the pressure that you
   can impose,
Why should I tell you things no
   one else knows.
I don't understand what makes
   you stay around,
What makes you keep asking
   when your answers just can't
   be found.
Even though I do need you to
   stay with me,
You can give me comfort but I
   need more room so I can be free.
What does it mean the way your
   comfort and esteem seem to
   blend,
I think it is nothing, but shows
   you are still a FREIND!!

Mary Beth Ray
IF YOU WERE MINE
I would put you in a case made of
   ruby glass on top the summer
hillside where lovely breezes pass.
   The sun would touch it lightly,
      reflecting love so pure,
shining toward the east, to the one
      my love is for.

I'd put flowers by your feet when
   they touch the ground, and wish
a pretty rainbow to encircle you
      around.
   Your beauty is as outstanding,
      my love is overflowing,
I had given you my world without
      you even knowing.

The wind shall play a melody
   when my dream comes true,
and whisk it off so tenderly and
      direct its song to you.
   And the harmony between us
      would be so true and deep,
an emerald eternity of love for
      us to keep.

Ken Nelson
FAREWELL OLD FRIEND
The saddest day of my life I guess
   was the day when Andy died.
I'm not ashamed to tell it now I
   just sat down and cried.
Seven years he gave me
   everything he had to give for
   such a noble animal, seven
   years ain't long to live.

He was just a little blue tick
   hound, I raised him from a pup
   with a heart as big as Texas, he
   never would give up.
A giant never walked as tall as
   that little blue tick hound a
   greater friend, a truer friend
   simply can't be found.

It didn't make much difference if
   the game was large or small
   once he had a critters track, old
   Andy tree'd them all.
There were Cougars, Coon and

Bobcats, now and then a Bear
   when Andy started barking
   tree, I knew the game was there.

Cold and hungry, tired and lost,
   we hunted side by side then
   something died inside of me
   the day that great dog died.
It was hard to find some fitting
   words to carve upon a stone I
   couldn't bear to say goodbye
   and leave him there alone.

So I just carved farewell 'old
   freind,' I'll see you someday
   soon where the trails are not so
   rocky, and there's lots of cats
   and coon.
Then I built a box of stout pine
   wood, carried him up in the
   hills as far as I could
I left him there beneath that stone
I left him there, but he's not alone.

Now there are times on a moonlit
   night when the air is clear and
   winds just right
I can hear that voice I know so
   well, high up on that ridge, just
   as clear as a bell.

That long lone trail he travels
   now I know it leads to some
   good dog chow a nice warm
   bed, a bone to chew, and well,
   whatever a hound dog likes to
   do.

Jean Angelina Stratton
TOWERS OF STRENGTH

Dedicated to my family for whom
all my poetry is written

A thought creeps in and spins
   around and sets the mood for
   the day

Sometimes it's kind and
   sometimes it's cruel and often
   it will pass away

It spans across an open place
   then attaches and begins to
   grow

And as it does it will form the
   words that can soothe or deal a
   blow

The power within an open mind
   finds peace throughout it's
   length

When used to full capacity it
   becomes a tower of strength

Heather M. Draughon
OVERWHELMED
Overwhelmed by a voice that
   assures forever,
With trust felt
From the lingering hours to the
   morning's dawn.

Such tranquil essence
Uncaptured yet everpresent,
Carries me to listen sincerely.

Evelyn Conley Stauffer
NIGHT WALK
I walk the beach on summer
   nights, my senses are alert,
I breathe salt air from restless
   seas and marvel at the surf.
There's prostrate sea-weed on the
   sand, a camp-fire pungent smell,
Hot dogs all charred and mustard
   strewn, lie half chewed where
   they fell.
The basso bull-frogs echo, croak,
   midst cricket symphony,
The sleepy yawns of inlet
   streams soft trickle out to sea.
High tide comes in a "thousand
   strong," small grunions leap
   and strive,
To stand tail tall, their seasonal
   ball, then leave their spawn to
   thrive.
As I walk on past drift-wood
   roots, outlined by cabin lights,

Each barnacled limb invite sea
   gulls, to rest by days or nights.
Sea breezes kiss my wetted cheek,
   I long for hands in mine,
Yet feel my ever present God,
   who walks with me each time.

Patricia A. Montgomery
TWO IMMORTAL MEN
The Lord giveth and the Lord
   taketh away . . . no one is here
   to stay
Some will rise again another day.
They came to power 100 years
   apart
Leaving goodness with memories
   never to depart.
Likeness was no coincidence.
Even names were not by chance,
   surnames contained seven
   letters at a glance.
The Secretaries had the names of
   the opposite in power
For theses two names have been
   erected many a tower and sown
   many a flower.
Lincoln's Secretary was Kennedy,
   Kennedy's Secretary was Lincoln.
Their Secretaries warned them it
   wouldn't be fun, pleading with
   the power to refrain from that
   days engagements was not
   dumb.
Lincoln and Kennedy were shot
   in the back of the head, leaving
   their wives to witness and live
   in dread.
The stage for Abe was the theatre
   and Booth ran to a warehouse
   for more than a metre.
John went to Dallas against
   somes wishes where Oswald
   wasn't hiding in any bushes.
He used a warehouse in his plot,
   escaping to a theatre through a
   parking lot.

It was black Friday in both cases
Booth and Oswald born 100 years
   apart with 15 letters in their
   names were disgraces.
The world is weeping tears, will
   it be another 100 years?
Surely powerful goodness will
   surface again, unlikely to
   surpass the magnitude of these
   two men.
Lincoln freed the slaves while
   Kennedy integrated them, no
   small wonder we love the
   Battle Hymn.
Successors will always be around,
   most of them elected from the
   ground.
With 13 letters to their names,
   Andrew and Lyndon Johnson
   were born 100 years apart
Getting off to a good start, they
   came from the Senate with a
   southern Democrat heart.
Fair to compare . . . never
Surely goodness and mercy will
   follow our immortal men and
   they shall dwell in the house of
   the Lord forever.

Stephen M. Pritchard
MATRIMONY

---

*For Lyell and Cathy. Who's
wedding on June 26, 1982
inspired this poem.*

You have a love that is built on
   friendship,
Which is common place to see.
It is your friendship within your
   love,
That is a special quality.
Though your love may seem to
   falter,
During those times you disagree.
Forget the bad, and cherish the
   good,
As part of your memory.
I remember you growing together,
And becoming one entity.
And I'll cherish the day, years
   from now,
When I can look back and see.
That I was right, and you were
   right.
It was love for eternity.

Sarah K. Springer
**Christmas Eve, My Sister
   and Me**
It was Christmas Eve, time for
   Santa
He was the one we wanted to see.
My Mother said, "Now go to bed."
He'll come after you go to sleep.

So my sister and I went to bed.
But we kept peeking to see if he'd
   come.
My Mother called upstairs and
   said,
"Stay in bed, don't you trust
   anyone?"

"Now go to sleep, I know he'll
   come.
But he has many things to do."
We said "We want to see his
   sleigh,
And we want to see his reindeer
   too."

But Mama said again "Now go to
   sleep.
He just might not stop
If he finds you both awake.
In the morning you'll see what he
   brought."

We went back to bed and went to
   sleep.
But we were awakened by a Noise.
We got up and peeked thru the
   door.
We saw a lot of pretty toys.

My sister said "We were wrong.
There is a Santa like Mamma
   said."
I agreed that she was right.
Then we went back to bed.

Then we heard a terrible thud.
So we peeked again to see what it
   was,
And we saw that Santa fell over
   the rug.
And the words he said were very
   bad.
We knew right then that Santa
   was our Dad.

I can't repeat the words he said,
They really were not Vicious.
But you can bet your life,
It was not Ho, Ho, Ho. or Merry
   Christmas.

Margaret Powers Hughes
CHRISTMAS 1907
A big tan teddy bear
In a little wicker chair
Waits for his brand new mistress

A sturdy little girl of four
Stands in the study door
On this morn of Christmas

Now safe in her arms
Are teddy's furry charms
And in the chair—bear and
   mistress.

Years of holidays go by
With heart and spirit high
But none-like this first
   remembered Christmas.

Lorraine June Whalley
SNOWFLAKE
From the vast wonders of heaven
A tiny snowflake fell,
Fluttering, turning, twisting,
With silent chimes of a winter
   bell.
Gentle hot rays of a morning sun
Builds a crystal cold icicle.
Securing itself to an eave
Hangs dangerously like a lady,
   fickle.
Colored lights from a Christmas
   tree
Their radiant glow softly
Brings new life to the ice spike;
Pleasure to an old man alone
Silently watching.

Keotah M. Fannin
THE TOY RIDER
Death comes so quick
Like a thief in the night.
To steal away your loved ones
And shatter your life.

Did he look over Jordan?
What did he see?
Four holes on the wall joining,
"They're coming after me."

I'm a small toy rider
On a galloping white horse.
He lunges forward
Flings his head to the north.

Clattering wheels of a train
Screech to a stop.
With no more movement
The silence is a shock.

The great horse turns his head
Shows me gleaming white teeth.
Open mouth and flaring nostrils
A magnificent beast.

I hear a sad wailing
Someone lets out a cry.
I see it on the ceiling
It's the twinkling of an eye.

Bridget Scott
WARMTH
No apparel
   can warm me
      more than the smile on your
         face
Not even the sun
   can generate the magnitude of
      warmth
   as does your touch
No blanket
   can remove the chill of the night
      as well as your arms about me
No fire
   can replace the warmth
      of your body juxtaposed mine.

Keotah M. Fannin
A CHRISTMAS GONE
This Christmas time
   This time of year
Brings joy to some
   And to some a tear.

Happiness—love so tender
Wondering, if you remember.

Do you yearn for a lover
   From the past?
Does your heart long for me
   At Christmas?

Judith I. Tucker
THE RAIN
O how the rain did pour
Then stopping to rain no more
Clouds apart, they moved slow
A ray of light began to show
Streams of light then flowed down
Like a vail from a wedding gown
Too glorious for this mortal to
   conceive
A vail of light that God doth
   weave.

Donna M. Robillard-Yagos
FREEDOM
Galloping along the seaside,
Sand whirling beneath our feet,
The waves laping along the shore,
Water billowing behind us,
Like the dust on a busy street.
The shining whiteness of
   reflections,
On a sea of foam and froth,
Gives a tang of cool wetness,
To our hot bodies a treat.
Tossing her head the mare
   whinnied,
So joyously free and redeemed,
The fresh cool air all around us,
Such happiness and so complete.
These moments we'll always
   remember,
While caged in a house of glass,

Where freedom is only a memory,
To those who are in its grasp.
One day again we will come here,
To refresh our lonely despair,
And breath the freedom of
   tomorrow,
In the cool salty sea air.

nks
UNTITLED
Traveling down life's lonely road,
   seeking hopes and lost dreams;
   shivering at thoughts of
   unknown fears.
Searching for a tomorrow that will
   never be, praying to find an
   answer you will never know.
A flicker of light in a darkened
   world,
   with gusts of air grasping at the
   weakened flame hoping to
   extinguish it.
Endlessly tortured by demons
   destroying
   your soul, while cries of help
   echo through your mind.
All that's left are the memories
   and
   as the flame slowly dies out; no
   one
   notices the tiny teardrops fall.

Tommy Pettyjohn
WHO?
Being alone is in fact a
something-you've-got-going
for you.
for when the agrevations of
bickering with ones lover or
scolding the children there is
a lonliness someplace

in a person
who might desire to
come home alone,
who has never done it
before, who dosen't know.

Mary Janeen Dorsett
HEALER

---

*Dedicated with love to my
parents, C. B. and Dorothy
Dorsett, my twin sister, Martha
Janette Dorsette, and my brother
Dr. Charles Irvin Dorsett, Ph. D.*

Healer
Medicine man
Chanting, praying, curing
Evokes aid from supernatural
Shaman

Eleanor McKee
THAT MAN OF MINE
How rare is that garden, with
   flowers that sadden
They cover the ground, where
   lies the mound,
Beneath the mound the smell of
   the flowers penetrates
Maybe it will help keep away the
   snakes.
He was strong and tall and when
   drinking with a bang would
   fall,
To lift him up took all ones
   strength, for his body was a
   good 6 ft. length.
But one thing was sure when he
   drank, into bed he would
   tumble, never cause a rumble.

He slept like a babe with his head
  on my breast,
When he awoke he was full of
  jest.
This man of mine was one of a
  kind, but he had a weak mind.
I loved him then when he was
  full of laughter and mirth,
Still do even though he sleeps
  now far beneath the earth.

Marilyn Whitten
DEPARTURE
I cannot speak, I cannot move
Pain clutches at my soul,
Anguish scores my heart.

I do not want to hear, no I cannot
  listen,
His words are too painful.
He says he's leaving, our lives
  now to part.

I want to reach out to him, beg
  him to stay
But torment stifles my speech,
My vitality-nipped body pillared
  to the land.

He's gone now, he would not wait;
Silence falls all around.
Enveloped in silver emptiness
  Alone—I stand.

Randall W. Hocker
I UNDERSTAND

*In memorial of my Uncle and
Godfather Edward A. Tholken.*

I reach to touch the morning air,
  but emptiness I find.
I search for wisdom eons old,
  with knowledge left behind.
And stars are shining endlessly,
  so bright, their light benign.
In endless limbo I find myself,
  in things I find unkind.

But one day through the
  emptiness,
  the morning air I'll grasp.
And wisdom slowly creeping too,
  will come to me at last.
And stars shining endlessly,
  will brightly hold my past.
And endless limbo will be no
  more;
  I understand, at last.

kerma m. more
WHY NOT ME
I think of friends who travel afar
  To foreign lands across a mighty
  sea;
And wonder—
            Why not me?

My nieghbors home with rooms
  of beauty
  Giving parties and fancy teas—
In the yard the gardeners' work.
            Why not me?

Then came the answer on Easter
  morn,
  As I counted my blessings
            one—two—three.
"God" gave me this Life
            and filled it with Love;
He sprinkled Happiness
            down from above——
He gave me the air—the rivers—
  and trees—
            Why me?

Natalie Mooers Downs
GHOST OF A YOUNG GIRL

*This Poem is dedicated with love
to my sons Harold and Michael,
my grandchildren John and Leana.
And a special thank you to my
daughter-in-law Andrea and my
sister June for their
encouragement.*

A Ghost of a young girl came to
  me,
One night, when everything was
  still
She asked if she could stay awhile,
She had a mission, she had to fill.

She had a sad story to tell me,
One that filled my eyes with tears,
Of a young girl, filled with
  hopelessness,
Depression, and many fears.

She kept them all inside herself,
For no one else to see,
Hoping they would go away,
And finally she'd be free.

Because her life was so complexed,
She did not want to stay,
In a world so cold and lonely,
Made of false hopes and clay.

So she took her life into her hands,
To end what she could not bear,
Leaving many friends and family
In sadness, and despair.

She asks to be forgiven,
For the pain she has left behind,
She never wanted to hurt anyone,
And she hopes—God will be kind.

So say a prayer for this lost soul,
As it journeys on its way
Looking for peace, and happiness
In God's Kingdom, one bright day.

Paula Kay Alexander
DAY AFTER
No more gifts beneath the tree.
Everyone's in bed but me.
Here I sit, all by myself.
Pulling memories off the shelf,

Of Christmasses when I was small,
And the magic of it all.
Lighted wreaths, a tinseled tree,
And gifts that Santa left for me.

And I suppose as each went by,
Mom would sit alone as I,

Staring at the colored lights,
Drinking in the sounds and
  sights,

Storing up the Christmas cheer.
Enough to last throughout the
  year . .

Laura Bruce
MY DREAM

*To Ron Anderson, with love.
Thank you for giving me reason
to dream once again.*

Each time I remember your gentle
  kiss,
I relive our moments together,
The laughing and talking away
  the hours
From sunshine to starshine
And all loves hidden powers.

Because of you there is feeling in
  my heart
My mind is filled with words to
  say,
You brought sunshine instead of
  rain
Showed you cared, and cased the
  pain.

The thought of your eyes so dear,
Your touch, that releases my fear
Deepens my love each day
And I'll go on dreaming
The lonely nights away.

In my dreams there will be
  forever you
A bright, shining sun beside me,
As I walk the trails that cover
  mountains,
You will be the light that guides
  me.

My dream which falls beyond the
Bounds of reason
Should be cast away.
And though I may never again
Feel the warmth of your embrace
In my heart, you will forever stay.

Esther Drawdy Briere
HOLIDAY CHEER
Most folks like to visit at this
  time of year
To be with loved ones and share
  some holiday cheer.
The time to stay for the holiday
  may be a week or less
But they anticipate reunion joy
  and lots of happiness!

It's great to get together with
  those that mean so much . . .
Inspiring to be with those who
  have that special touch . . .
Especially when it's home you go,
  with all its dear surroundings.
It takes you back to long ago and
  sets your spirits bounding!

If perchance your holiday plans
  just simply don't work out,
There's really no need at all to sit
  around and pout—
How about doing an alternative
  thing?
It's guaranteed to give your New
  Year a zing!

There are those who have no
  other (nary a cousin, sister or
  brother)
That may be completely alone . . .
Or one like you, whose plans fell
  through . . .

They yearn so much to share
  some time, or coffee, or talk, or
  a bit of fun!
It's really a great way to feel
  alive! . . .
The joy is contagious and your
  spirits'll revive . . .
Just reach out to a lonesome soul
  and show him that you care
And share with him your holiday
  and lots of your holiday cheer!

Susan VanTilburg, M. S.
IT'S COMING
Icky, yicky, yucky, phooey
Garbage all around
Ground is gooey
Over the land
Over the sea
Watch out
The goo is coming
For you and me

Gene Darwin Abbott
THE SECOND COMING
Kingdom will rise against
  kingdom as kingdoms will do.
There shall be earthquakes,
  plagues, and famines, too.
The gospel is to be preached in
  each nation.
There'll be set-up the terrible
  abomination.
Woe shall come during the great
  tribulation.
The sun will be dark, the waves
  will roar, men will faint out of
  fear.
The stars will fall, the sky will
  split as the day of wrath draws
  near.
Upon a cloud, coming in power
  and glory, the Son of Man will
  appear.

This is that time when apostasy
  will abound:
'Tis a time when dedication is
  seldom found.
The earth's inhabitants will be
  led astray.
There'll be drugs and lying and
  moral decay.
These days anti-Christ shall
  have his way.
The sun will be dark, the waves
  will roar, men will faint out of
  fear.
The stars will fall, the sky will
  split as the day of wrath draws
  near.
Upon a cloud, coming in power
  and glory, the Son of Man will
  appear.

Upon the earth, seven trumpet
  judgments are to be sent:
Of murders, thefts, and
  immoralities men won't repent.
With trumpet five, the first woe
  we'll see.
With the next trumpets, two
  more there'll be.
God's wrath will come with woe
  number three.
The sun will be dark, the waves
  will roar, men will faint out of
  fear.
The stars will fall, the sky will
  split as the day of wrath draws
  near.
Upon a cloud, coming in power

and glory, the Son of Man will appear.

Lynda Kaye Thomas
WHAT CAN'T MEAN
I missed you today . . .
from thoughts so long ago
I wish somehow that you could
  know
life to me without you isn't the
  same

I wondered how I could smile
knowing its been quite awhile
since I held you close
heard your voice call out my name

If its got to end
then somewhere its got to end
rather it be now until forever
or rather it be for always then
until never . . .
somewhere I just know it must
  end

And if it's will I'll make it
to survive . . .
to be justly I could try
but when invisible to you
who am I . . .
to stand in the way of what can't
  mean?

Ruth Ann Karambela
IN SPECIAL FAVOR

*To Ken Larrey May there always
be lakes to dream on. And
Mountains to share.*

The scent of a blooming rose bud,
I sence the splender red there is.

When feeling the sensation of
  heat
through the leaves,

I conceive this must be gold.

Why has such assemblage of grace
never passed through my sight?

My nights and days have been
  beneath
the horizon.

And turned into one.

I've always had certain perception
when the snow was to fall.

When blossoms were to become an
expanded bud.

Tho others were affected with
  supprise.

I was once suspicious of this frame
which holds my soul.

But I,

One so blessed with the keen
  sighted ability
to know.

With no sight.

I am of supreme reguard.

In special favor.

John Lone
PEDESTRIAN THOUGHT
Born of pedestrian, perhaps
equestrian folks,
Raised on the lore of the arrival—
  just other day,
Of devil-puffing, marvel
whistling, rolling
Engines on wheels of steel in

smoke and steam;
And how laboriously the rails
  were stretched
To show the way and point and
  call
To freedom, to the horizons and
  the seas beyond.
New distances for lives contained
  by time and space
Expanding.

How, pray, now are we able—sons
  of slaves
To season and the soil of
  distance—once removed,
Command the skies in boundless
  joy
With hawks and geese and spirits
  soaring,
With those that wished and built,
And dared with human
  impudence divine,
Inspired by visions seen in
  imitation
Of the word—Creator—strike a
  spark
Into materials inert, of Life—
Expanding?

Gertrued Hickin Sigmon
INHERITANCE

*To my mother, Gertrude
Throssell Hickin, who died 76
years ago.*

I never knew my mother nor her
  ancestral tree,
She gave herself completely in
  giving birth to me.
My father never spoke of her, yet
  deep from in his heart
Her beauty and her loveliness he
  somehow did impart.

I never knew my mother nor her
  ancestral tree,
Yet grows a root of greater love
  joined with eternity.
And so I know her spirit and all
  her kinfolk, too,
For she has held me close to God
with roots spread through and true.

Doris Ruth McElroy
LOVE
A special feeling that two people
  feel for one another
Each one caring and sharing in
  their every day lives
giving, yet taking nothing away
a tender caress, a warm embrace,
  a happy smile upon a face, a
  bouncing baby
all full of joy, two proud parents,
  a beautiful baby boy, a walk in
  the park
hand in hand, a picnic on the
  beach playing in the sand, a
  dinner for two
by candlelight, a kiss at the door
  step at midnight, a love story
  on TV,
a fireplace all aglow, a sip of wine,
  a walk in the moon light, a
  warm feeling
that shows love is that special
  feeling that two people feel for
  one another;
only seeing and having eyes for
  each other yet surrounded by
  others . . .

Martha Virginia Chalfant
YOU DEARER GROW

*This poem is dedicated to my
beloved husband, Monroe D.
Chalfant.*

Each day you're gone, you dearer
  grow.
  Whate'er I think or say or do,
I sense you understand and know.

The places where we used to go
  Are filled with memories of you.
Each day you're gone, you dearer
  grow.

My thoughts and actions toward
  you flow;
  For where you are, I would be, too.
I sense you understand and know.

I read the books that you loved
  so,
  And touch the things esteemed
  by you.
Each day you're gone, you dearer
  grow.

Ideals I saw within you glow,
  I keep alive. I still hold true.
I sense you understand and know.

When God called you, you had to
  go;
  But we both knew I'd come to
  you.
Each day you're gone, you dearer
  grow.
I sense you understand and know.

Claude Wilkinson
SHADOW PLAY
Full amber moon / frosted
peach
I wonder / if you observe
the shadow playground
you create,
each summer night / at this
  address.
If you notice / the lanky black
  slant
of a bricksiding house / as it lies,
on a freshly cut lawn.
If you notice / the fleeting, black
  dart
of a fugitive rabbit
hopping thicketwards,
where safer shadows play.
If you notice / the antics
of a fearsome / black / giant
who becomes a little / Negro / boy
on stepping out,
of your playground.

Holley Frances Mathison
ON MY OWN

*Dedicated to my Mom and Dad—
Two of the most wonderful
people in this world, who have
given me everything . . . just in
knowing they love me.*

I am one self, one soul, one being
Who stands alone, apart from you
I feel the space between us now
I'm reaching but I can't get through
The lonliness I feel each day
Remembering the time before
When we were one, a family
But now I need to tell you more
This time I have to spend alone
Has given me a sense of strength
To know a part of me unknown
To push myself to any length
To find out what I'm all about
To hear the little voice inside
That tells me "I can make it
  through"
And keep alive what might have
  died
So when you need your "little girl"
To hug her and to bring her home
You won't be looking for me, Mom
I'm all grown up sinse on my
  own . . .

Lucy Beemer
DRAGONFLY WINGS
Silky satin sunny streamers
Winding in among the trees,
Making many varied pathways
Patterned by the boughs and
  leaves.

In among this world suspended,
A silent scene does nature weave,
As the pink-gold quartz is
  burnished
Copper brown and olive green.

How still the gentle drifting
In this changing view takes place
As a hidden plan is sketching
Autumn's grand and stately grace.

You can hear the strains of music
By the mourning Turtle Dove,
Harmonic undertones rebounding
Vibrant with an Inner love.

Peggy Turner
WHO AM I?

*"To my sister Carol,"(my sounding
board)*

Who am I?
Why and for what was I born?
What plan had he,
when he created me that morn?
What have I given,
since the day of my birth?
What purpose was I formed from
  dust,
and put upon this earth?
What have I achieved,
what have I done?
I have borne a daughter,
and spawned a son—
I have loved deeply,
and been loved in return—
and for my country,
felt deep concern
I have been a friend,

I have earned my bread—
but are there also other paths,
I should have tread?
Have I built a bridge,
or planted a seed—
from life's lovely garden,
hve I pulled up a weed?
What, yes *what*,
have I really done—
to make our world a better one?
In the end when my life
passes in review—
what great deeds will I see,
that I did not do?
Why was I put here?—
I pray someday I'll know,
and gain peace of mind
before I reach the end of the row.

Elizabeth Saltz
LAWS OF STATE
The laws of the state made the
nation great,
They opened the door to trade.
Many laws were passed against
slavery,
The negro was freed and given
the vote.

The country thrived because it
was free,
The laws were made to give
justice.
The rights of the people were
guaranteed,
The courts protected people
against unlawful search

As the country grew, new laws
were added,
The slave states were admitted
into the union.
The Civil War brought freedom
to the negro,
He is given equality and non
discrimination.

United States is proud of it's Civil
Liberties,
It gives justice to all races and
creeds.
Our forefathers fought to make
us free,
Our beliefs made us a nation
bound to justice.

The statutes are the law of the
land,
They govern the states with
authority.
Laws were made to make men free,
They give men truth and
equality.

Margaret Nienstedt
**Reflection On Grandpa's
Rocker**
Old chair, handmade before I was
born
Your satin finish smooth and worn
Stand tall with dignifying grace
So proud to occupy the space
Where Grandpa always sat and
rocked
Allowing dreams to be unlocked.
Has history soaked into your
wood?
Did you experience all that you
could?
A bridge in a generation gap
How many children climbed into
your lap?
How many stories could you tell

About Grandma and relatives as
well?
Did tears ever spill to stain your
arm?
Did laughter inaugurate your
charm?
A chair that's been around so long
Must be of fiber firm and strong.
No wonder I give my tender care
To a piece that magnifies a share
Of all my faith in maturity
And represents my sense of
security.

James Nolfi
MORNING
six a.m. / the barn/
the meadow thick with fog
country music and the trading post
on the radio
the warm bulk of the cow
the bucket foaming with milk
the cat tangled under my feet
pleading for a milkshake.

Kathy R. Nagy
Thanksgiving Without You
Well, Dad, it's Thanksgiving
And just seems another day,
Because without you here to
share it with
I would rather go astray.

I've always loved the holidays
But now there's something
missing,
Since now you are somewhere
else
I have to dream of our hugging
and kissing.

Chills flow through me
As I sit and wonder how it would
be,
If you were still here
To sit and talk to me.

I know it isn't right
To ponder over the past,
But Daddy why'd you have to
leave?
With only memories for me to
last.

It seems as though I was just
beginning
To find you not only as a father,
but also as a friend,
Just when we were getting close
Our relationship had to end.

I guess I have to accept that
God needed you up there,
But I wish he would have known
That to me this isn't fair.

Barbara Jean Dinnes
MY DESTINY
In the deepest realm of my mind,
I see shadows of what was and
what is yet to be;

I dream dreams of things in the
past, relive some, in a vain
attempt to change my destiny.

I contemplate moments ahead, of
the way I will meet new
thoughts;

I try to visualize and remember
those things of which I was
certainly taught;

Like how important it is and will
always be to make a good first
impression;

And to put on a smile when your
heart is aching without the
slightest expression.

Depression moves over me
sometimes, and envelops my
inner sole;

Then a miracle, someone smiles
at me, lights a spark in me, and
again I feel whole.

James S. Riggs
MOTHER

---

*Lena Rebecca Kesgard Riggs
My Mother—Aug. 2, 1872—
Feb. 9, 1939*

I remember when I came to be
Just a danish little sprout.
My mother always watched
The way I skipped about.
She worked so hard
Most everyday.
But always had the time
To tell me where to play.
Her answers came for everything
That I must know about.
She always seemed to be a source
Of guidance on my route.

Jeanne M. Sharp
With Thanksgiving Lord
With thanksgiving Lord, we come
to You—And we count our
blessings, two by two.
We thank you Lord for faith-in
knowing You are always near.
We thank you Lord for hope-for
always showing us You care.
We thank you Lord for love-the
greatest of the three,
And we praise You Lord-and with
thanksgiving we bow our heads
to Thee.
We thank You Lord for the
beauty of the flowers and the
trees,
We thank you Lord for the
animals and for the honey bees,
We thank you Lord for the
warming sun for the moon and
all the stars—and the rains that
come—to cleanse the earth and
fill its streams—
So that we may thrive and dream
our dreams—and Worship Thee.

Felicia Shaman
HAPPINESS
eating chemicals of
all different kinds
listening to music so loud
it'll blow your mind
dealing with pretend friends
who will cheat you blind

wanting to escape from
this monotonous grind
running away now
leaving everything behind

you think happiness comes
from the outside, inside of a little
pink pill
but in your heart you know the
truth
of the matter is the craziness is
making you ill

you reject it, forget
being depressed every day
because you know there'll

come a time when all of your
pain
will just melt away

so stand tall and proud
whatever beside you
remember someday
    BEAUTY
will shine out from inside you.

Mrs. Ada M. Hickman
OUR CHILDREN
C—is for children, yes this is your
week. We hope you will
enjoy everything that you
seek.
H—is for happy we want you to be
not just in our area, but from
sea to sea.
I —is for important, it is
necessary you know to strive
for the best and each day
better grow
L —is for learners. You have
much knowledge to gain
May you seek out the right
and evil things disdain.
D—is for dare, take courage to be
true. Each doing the work
that you have to do.
R—is for reliable. Not failing
your part but doing with
gladness each task from your
heart.
E —is for enjoyment. Try to
treasure each day the
beautiful sunshine and
flowers so gay.
N—is for never. Try not to forget
the good things you've been
taught, and the goals you
have set.

Dannielle Jean Hayes
IMAGINE
Deaf, dumb and blind child
how have you learned to smile?
So many things you cannot see,
how have you learned to dream?
You cannot tell the dark from light
for someone robbed you of your
sight.
You feel no sorrow, shed no tear
for all the voices you'll never hear.
Deaf, dumb and blind child
why do you smile?
A child born without his sight
has mirrored eyes that reflect light.
Silence echoes in your mind.
Why is life unkind?
So many things you'll never see.
So you see more than me?

Shirley Ledbetter Barnett
LONELINESS
What a loneliness it is
Living here alone like this
With a house full of people here
And, I alone, am filled with fear
Everyone speaks my name
But I hear only bits of sane
Am I living in the wrong house
With maybe, the wrong spouse
There are strange things inside
my head
Restless feelings and to much said
No closeness I can not feel
And I alone claim this ill
Is there a home some place else
Where I can learn to be myself
Why can't this house shed it's
weight

Of pressure from some unknown
  fate
And let me rest my weary head
Upon some shoulder I do not
  dread.

Estella M. McGhee-Siehoff
**She Took Up All the
Instruments Of the Idle
Shepherd**

And the lamb died: from her
  gainsaying about a new home.
And lamb died: from her
  gainsaying about a true love.
And lamb died: from her
  gainsaying about an accepted
  work.
And the lamb died: from her
  gainsaying about a talent.
And the lamb died: from her
  gainsaying about appearance.
And the lamb died: from her
  gainsaying about pretty
  clothes.
And the lamb died: from her
  gainsaying about normalcy.
And the lamb died: from her
  gainsaying about possessions.
And the lamb died: from her
  gainsaying about
  righteousness.
And the lamb died: from her
  gainsaying about doctrine.

James Buckner McKinnon
HE'S ALL THAT IS

---

*To Martha, my wife and light of
my life.*

HE touched me
And I knew
From the stellar depths
We are as one—
However distant
To the center
From which the nascent
Beauty comes.

No gender, age or feeling
Stays His power to traverse
The heavens,
Because His essence
Is the fire
Of meaning in the heart—
Ubiquitous—yet,
Like galactic peace,
Inseparable from the firmament.
  HE's all that Is!

Deborah E. Thomas
THE SUN IS SHINING
The days seem to drag, with all
  the pressure and pain.
I wish they all could wash away
  for us all by the rain.

Everyone seems so gloomy at the
  end of the day.
The only reason they're working
  is to get their weekly pay.

Why are we here? And what are
  we to do?
Why don't we all start caring for
  each other, even you.

Let's cut out all this hate! Let's
  cut out all this war!
We keep on doing these things,
  but what for?

Look! The sun is shining!
Yet there are still people crying.

I wish the fears,
we all have would fade away with
  tears.
If we'd all open our hearts, and
  feel the warmth of love
Our souls would be soaring on
  the wings of a dove.

Barbara Lorden
US INFINITY
Wait until the October vigil
  comes;
We shall wear flannel within the
  tunnelled wind
And pour the cascading cicadas
  into the channel of night,
Coralling crickets dialing the
  remnants of time
In an herbal garden by the
  meadow's pass.

I heard the ancient flight whirr
  on moccasinned wings
And watched the quilted feathers
  spin gently through the loom.

On a crisp misted night
We shall strip belts of bark
And carry nutted hewn logs
Into the centre of our earth.
The mountains shall rest their
  doors invisibly
Beneath the quartz mineralled fog.

And there shall be no clock,
For in the stations of hills time
  does not exist.

We shall wait until our
  interstates cross;
And only then we shall kiss.

Carrie Witcher
STARDUST
Once there was a midnight dream
Played upon the grass
Beneath the moonlight shining
  down
Pearl-lite green and fading fast

Once there was a lonely man
Who cried out to the world
And love in dollars poured in
—But how could he be sure?

Once there was a falling star
As I looked into the sky
Before it faded into dust
I cried a tear goodbye

Abigail Hereford
WHEN SPRING CARESSES
When Spring caresses the new
  blossoms
Softly sprinkles pearls of dew,
Gently whispers among the leaves
My heart calling dear one, anew.

I remember yet, my darling
When the wind touched in soft
  sound
I still wonder if the blossoms
Are still growing all around.

Birdsongs drifting from the
  branches
Of the delicate wild rose,
Sunsets fire still must be burning
And my heart longs to go.

Back and stand in silence
Try to remember each dear word,
Pretend we are still together
Your voice again dear heart, be
  heard.

In memory you are beside me
There has been no broken scenes;

Our hearts entwined so close
  together
And will forever dream.

Rebekah Stion

Rebekah Stion
**November and Thankful
Are We**
Knock, knock, at your door,
November and surprises are in
  store.

Blowing out her breath so cold
The winter nights approach bold

By the fireside we snuggle so
  tight
Enjoying the closeness of the
  night.

Cherishing each moment coming
  our way
As days pass arrives
  Thanksgiving Day,

Family and friends extending
  good wishes
From the kitchen all kinds of
  good dishes

Children laughing, how beautiful
  the sound
Snowflakes falling, covering the
  ground

Such a beautiful time from God's
  hand
America, how He's blessed you,
  our land.

Yes, Thanksgiving is a very
  special time
As we gather with loved ones,
  yours and mine.

Amy Gerber Trowman
NO TEARS
I have no tears to shed for thee,
I have no tears to shed for me,
Nor do tears have I to shed for WE.
For what was WE has passed away;
The reasons not even our hearts
  will say why WE should go our
  separate ways.
No more tomorrows shall WE
  share no joys, no sorrows, no
  more cares.

I have no tears for what is dead,
Gladness is what I know instead.
For our life together was nought
  in vain
A child out shadows all our pain.
When WE see her, WE will know
  the best of us both is making
  her grow.
Strong and happy, wise and good
  she will be, what WE never could.

Anna Beisel
**Why We Celebrate
Christmas**
We celebrate many birthdays . . .
  The most famous one we recall
Is that of a man named Jesus
  Who taught love and kindness
  to all.

He became the greatest leader
  To ever walk upon the earth
And the gifts we give at Christmas
  Are in memory of His birth.

Long ago shepherds and wise men
  Carried gifts to an infant small
And a day to honor His birth
  Became "Christmas Day" for us
  all.

Brian Finney
EVENT HORIZON
You hold me at a distance
Like a moon and her mate
Never giving any reason
For this hell you create
I have no hope of freedom
From this tangled web you weave
I am subject to your fancy
But still no love can we conceive
You took from me my being
My hope, my self-control
You left me helpless to your
  whims
Event horizon of my soul

Herbert J. Fisher
THE BLUE JAY
A crested bird of gray and blue,
  Is very busy all day through;
He roams the villages, fields and
  woods,
  To sample Nature's ample goods;
At feeders, he eats some seeds
  and suet fat,
  And battles others for just that;
In places Wild, his raucous cry,
  Alerts some Prey that danger's
  nigh;
They heed his warning, turn and
  flee,
  Leaving baffled Hunter with no
  glee;
At nesting time, he's seldom heard,
  He's, then, a shy and nervous bird;
Though active and cocky as a
  thug,
  At times, he eats a harmful bug;
In spite of his any ornery way,
  We miss him when he is away.

Debbie Charney
DRUNK DRIVERS
They go out and have a good time,
When they leave they're feeling
  fine.
They feel no pain and can hardly
  talk,
They giggle and laugh as they try
  to walk.
They stumble out and look for
  the car,
They start it up and speed out of
  the bar.
They weave all over the highway,
They're so merry, so gay.
They don't see what they hit,
But they pull some fit.
They kill a family of four,
But they're able to walk, just a
  little sore.
They commit murder and get off
  free,

That's a little stupid if you ask me.
They have futures, the family don't
They can have fun, the family won't
They can still walk, talk and see,
But for the family that will never be,
They're the worst criminals of all,
Yet they never take a fall.

Sheree Taylor
HOLIDAYS
New Year's Day
Resolutions are made.
How many are kept?
No one can say.

Valentine's Day
When hearts are aglow;
Flowers and candy
With promises flow.

Easter Day
Christ arose from the grave;
His goodness he bestowed
And mankind he did save.

Fourth of July
Our nation's birthday;
Fireworks and patriotism
Both on display.

Thanksgiving Day
When prayers are said;
Thanking the Lord
For our happy homestead.

Christmas Day
With angels in flight;
A savior was born
On this holiest of nights.

Penny Reuter
(CHRISTMAS) Love To You

Dedicated to my sister, Lorrie Eastman, who has given me love and strength to help me in my life.

I've nothing much to offer,
So to you it's love I'll send.
It's nothing that I borrowed,
And, it's nothing that I'd lend.
It has no noted value,
And it can't be over used,
It isn't fragile, so can't break,
Though often is abused.
I've given this to others,
And each one is so unique,
It's meaning always different,
Depending what they seek.
It's something you can store away,
And feel, when you're in need,
But never is it on display,
Its beauty can't be seen.
It's given now, "NO STRINGS ATTACHED"
No costly warranty,
For this love that I am sending,
Has a "LIFETIME GUARANTEE".

Cindy Lobato
WHO AM I
Who am I?
I am me
  I'm not a frog
I'm not a tree
  I am what I want to be.

I can be a bird
  And fly high through the sky
I could be a drop of dew,
  I could be anything
I want to be
  But most of all
I am me.

Bess M. Phelan
THANKSGIVING
The harvest is gathered,
the season has been good.
We welcome family, friends and
  neighbors to share our food.
We give thanks for the bounty
And pray that we may be
Worthy of the Blessings of
Thanksgiving Day.

Suzanne Elizabeth Kalasin
THE PAINTER
He sits in a place pondering
Life's philosophy
Yet confusion overcomes him
When decisions he wants to
  master
Another time awaits his answer.

He looks about his canvas world
With greatly saddened eyes
And then procures the instrument
To tell us of life's lies.

Greed has been planted
Within the mask others wear
Envy is comouflaged everywhere
And destiny remains
For nothing seems real
Right now it's his painted world
He reveals.

Lonnie Gene Smith
A VESSEL

To Janice Bergamini-in sincere appreciation for all the help, support and encourgement you've given me.

A sail unfolds to catch the angry
  wind-
A thread to hold a whale.
If it could think I know it'd sink-
A vessel much too frail.

A rudder turns to steer her right
Against the ruthless waves.
Holding strong, she just sails on-
A vessel oh so brave.

Persistent against a bitter sea,
She never betrays her crew:
If she could say, "I will obey",
That's just what she would do.

I adore this ship with my heart
  and soul-
A lover always there.
My home, my life (and yes, my
  wife)
Breathing the fresh sea air.

Mary M. Gardner
THE OCEAN
I sit on the ocean sands
and watch the waves that bend
A scene of lasting beauty
Which gives you peace within.

The waves roll high and mighty
To form in layers white.
You watch in astonishment,
Because they move in just alike.

In the far off distance,
Fishing boats go by.
To their long destination
Not knowing where or why.

When I see the ocean waves,
The thought that comes to me.
How Christ walked upon the
  waters,
And calmed the raging sea.

When God divided the waters,
The wonder of how it could be.
In much joy and fascination,
The ocean brings to me.

Kerri Kristine Van Sickle
Christmas Bells and Snowflakes
The Christmas bells ring
  as I sing in the snow
below the sky
  way up high
so high humans can't see it
  with their eye.

The snowflakes fall
  down to the earth
way down low
  so low you can't even go there.
Where the snowflakes fall
  we build snowballs.

Suzanne E. Morse
The Magic Of Childhood

This poem is dedicated to Robin Phillips, who holds the magic and spirit of childhood in his hands.

Robin, you hold the truth.
Your eyes viewing the stars,
you stretch to reach their lights.
You use your hands to guard
insects from a deadly web.
The world is yours to keep,
the web, your dog, and trees,
until you fall asleep.
Robin, you look so free.
On tiny legs, you run
across the field, past me,
until your form is lost
beyond my narrow sight;
wrestling a bush, a fierce
monster with all your might.
Robin, you are alive.
You catch lizards and toads
and harbor them in cans;
I find them, but am old
and cannot understand
so throw away the cans.
Robin, you are a child
with magic in your hands.
Teach me childhood's magic
that I may live again.

Frankie Pierce Long
SOMEWHERE STAR
You say I'm your best female
  friend,
I was there if your heart needed
  to mend;
You're special, just the thoughts
  of you,
When I dream of you, I am never
  blue.

You picked me out a special star,
In the glittering high sparks so far;
When you tried to show it to me,
You couldn't locate . . . it was
  too free.

My love is like stars in the sky,
Peaceful, fluttering like a butterfly;
But my love is easy to find,
So clear, even your green eyes
  can't be blind.

My heart sends special thoughts
  always,
For the best times for all of your
  todays;
Just remember, I'll be here,

For all your needs-always holding
  a care.

Maybe one clear night I shall see,
That "somewhere star" you
  picked out for me;
My heart knows that it's shining
  there,
I'll keep looking high-and never
  despair.

caroline shaffer
undisiplined tongue
I have a problem it is my tongue
when it is loosened away it will
  run
thus calamity rains upon my
  head.
its the embarressment i dread,
it seems i shall never win,
alas my foot is in my mouth again.
I try and to no avail,
impossible for i fail.
My foot is placed where it should
  not be,
I am in a spot not chosen by me.
and yet through it all i find it's
  quite true
the only sensible place for my
  foot is in my shoe

Susan A. Wein
ME

I would like to dedicate this poem to: Mom, Dad, Michelle, Grandma Florence, Grandma Pauline, and Ms. Weston—all who help me realize who I really am, inside and outside.

I like to pretend
I love money to spend
The whole world someday I will
  see,
In size I am small
But my pride stands up tall
I'm different, I'm special, I'm me.

Caryl J. Akers
HE CAME
I may not know the exact day of
  his birth,
Whether there was sunshine or
  rain,
I only know He came.

I do not know if there were snow
  capped mountains,
Or a hot desert plain,
I only know He came.

To know the location of the stable
I do not claim,
I only know He came.

I know not why many refuse to
  believe,
For the truth will not change,
I only know Jesus came.

Avis Houghtaling
HEAVENLY LAUGHTER
Laughter takes on so many forms
  And each one has his own—It
  charms
Like sunshine after winter's storms
  Gives pleasure as it warms!

It may be like a tingling bell
  Or a spontaneous rumble
Gushing forth heedlessly pell-mell
  In instant riant rebuttal!

Just a blithe spirit's wan smile,

A superior affectation,
The well known tee-hee style,
All claim our prompt attention!

'Tis sweet to hear upon the ear
Amid earth's trials and its ill
The Ones, God endowed to cheer
With gifts of mirth our hearts to
fill!

For panecea, take oft we should,
Reliable its always been.
A merry heart doeth good
Prescribed Heaven's medicine!

Brian L. Harris
THE GREAT ESCAPE

---

*To Mom and Dave For a glimpse
of life Beyond the cabinet(VJM)*

There once was a fly named Dave.
Who was trapped in a cabinet for
days.
He was released from his prison
Then started spinnin'
And a dive into the toilet he made.

He swam for his life,
Though the outlook wasn't very
bright.
He started twirling around
And a frown he soon found.
As a finger pulled the lever down
tight.

Elaine Patricia Rodrigues
ONWARD
Evolving from amoebas,
birds and creatures
into reasoning beings,
we stand at the crossroads
of human development.

Will we complacently
follow well trodden
paths to military might,
risking nuclear holocaust?

Or call upon divine power
from within each one of us
stemming our rush toward
planetary destruction?

Let us travel onward
building peace based
on a state of mutual respect,
with visionary programs
evolving into social justice
for all peoples;
making our deeds
reflect good intentions,
upon our beloved planet and
beyond.

Mary Stanowski
MISTLETOE DAY
Let's make this a mistletoe day,
dancing around lightly on our toes.
The snow-fresh, white, cold . . .
a gentle kiss.
Let's make this a mistletoe day,
a package with bright red, shiny
paper and silver ribbon,
given to those giggly children;
send poinsettas for those we miss.

Today is our day.
My basket is running over with
winter wheat;
the smell of strawberry preserves,
tightly sealed, for our friends on
the list.
Let's make this a misletoe day-
sort through pictures from

memory albums;
you-standing there in tuxedo
fashion;
me, smiling, still filled with
wedding day bliss.
Let's make today, just this.

Marissa Rose Panigrosso
FOR YOU
For you I can be
That song on the radio
The blue in the sky
Or the red in the sun.

For you I can be
Tomorrow and yesterday
The ripple in the water
For you I can be
Anything.

Eleanor P. Weinbaum
ROCK A BYE BABY
The clock has chimed a quarter
past two.
My eyes close and aching
shoulders droop.
Rocking eight pounds, three
weeks new.
The bedroom chair is squeaking a
boop-a-doop.
Perhaps disturbing a dream from
Fairy Land.

Ah me, he is wet from head to
toe.
He folds up, then stretches like a
rubber band.
That tearless cry alerts me to
know
This rhymic whimper is his
natural key,
In concert with my singing
LITTLE BO PEEP.
He settles comfy-Do my eyes
deceive me?
Dear Lord, at last, he is sound
asleep!

Velva Arlyne Urwiler
**Let There Be Light In One's
Heart**

---

*"To Francis"-my dear husband
whose love has sheltered me for
35 years, as together we share His
love.*

Grow love
A spark at a time
Till a flame is ignited in your heart
Creating a light
To shed its radiance of joy and
cheer.
Healing the trials and errors

Of those who need His love and
grace
Spread about them
Like a mantle sheltering their
hearts.

Estella M. McGhee-Siehoff
THE LEGACY OF LIFE
In God, disobediences can be
revenged when
Obediences are fulfilled.
In God, sins against Him can be
forgiven,
And good works ordained.
In God, life can continue after
death,
Rewarded after judgment.
In God, all things consist and are
redeemed to Him,
In His Son.
In God, is faithfulness and mercy
and pity
In love, for those that truly
seek Him.

Jude Hauenstein
PETALS
Birds sorr beyond the window
I don't want to leave
my world of you

I have a friend
who's flame
bloomed a flower

the petals fall
one by one
floating to the ground

But there will always
stay one
to remind me . . .

Glen W. Moorehouse
Restore Virginity To Earth
The sun arose and peeked
At the new day it had birthed
And blushing rosy red
Came up to view the earth.

Man made storms obscured the
view,
War, crimes, pestilence, starvation.
And over land and sky and water
Violation and pollution.

Sun; through the ages worshipped
By man as source of all creation
Hid his face behind the blight
Of mankinds desecration.

This rape of nature has no friends
In any city, state or nation.
This dangerous, cancerous,
loathsome plague
Most quickly face extinction.

The greatise challenge of today
In any land thats given birth,
Is; clean the water, air and land,
Restore virginity to earth.

Kenneth G. Geisert
BROTHERLY LOVE
"He left without saying goodbye,
His stature was short, I was tall,
Spring his season, mine fall,
Ever relieving problems with a
call."

"He left without saying goodbye,
His goodness shining in his
smile,
Shoulders and courage embracing
a mile,
Unpretentious all the while."

"He left without saying goodbye,

Leaving three little guys,
Bewildered with puzzlement and
whys,
Searching for a meaning with
their eyes."

"He left without saying goodbye,
A thousand lifetimes with each
other,
Born apart but of one mother,
Referred to only as brother."

Dee Marie Burnham
DREAMS

---

*To one of the dearest friends a
person could have; the one who
inspired my "Dreams"-Terry
Burke- and to all of the wonderful
people of Boonville, Missouri.
Thanks for believing in me . . .*

Winds blow soft
The sun peaks through
Clouds aloft
I dream of you

Drive on by
Ignore my face
Tears which cry
Interlace

Hold me now
Just don't let go
Don't care how—
Love you so

Steve Merckx
FESTIVAL OF GLOVES
the matrimonial force begins
as the wings of the eagle spread
high and wide
and all of life lies still-dead

the caped unicorn from hade's
abounds, to capture
to culminate the insearchable
patterns, of
which life itself cannot be defined

but if not for us to go unnoticed,
the pierced claw of the dragon
would strike

in one swift move
destruction of all the people
by the people
for the people

destruction reins and death will
rule
our souls are outnumbered one
to one

but to be the force, to know the
source, from where it begins
is not to know all, but to know
nothing

live not for glory, not for
boredom, nor pestilence, strife
or greed
but live to grow, and live to
show the miracle of our seed

what hath not man?
we mustn't worry, or fear will
draw our days

and now to live in the side of the
ulcer, brings pleasure beyond
pain
and strife beyond woe
and all beyond none

it leaves, however, the
evergrowing vulgarity, of one
beyond one

John Campbell, Editor & Publisher

Guido Florimbi
THE HURRICANE

To my Grandsons I dedicate the following poem that roughly illustrate, the lived experience, of the yet uncontrolled and devasting behavior of Nature's Elements.

The storm's roaring over Ocean n'
   Land,
Tiadal waves crushing'r the
   beaches's sand,
wind n' water swallowing'r the
   dunes,
to the Nature's behavior nothing
   is immune!

Cracking roof's house n' walls . . .
lashing wind, rain n' Ocean water
   falls,
fearful People gripping'r to their
   household . . .
while through water n' mud
   floating's it all.

Flooding's rising feet by feet . . .
Everybody'r sad in their defeat . . .
It's impossible to fight, to toil,n'
   dare,
the Nature's Elements that
   brought us despair!

Stormy waves'r making rivers
   over the streets,
everywhere life's becoming very
   bleak . . .
the storm has torn the things us
   adorn . . .
telling all around how life he
   scorns.

In the nearby church sobbing
   faithful pray . . .
while the roaring gale still's
   astray . . .
crushing the walls of the Temple
   of God . . .
daring the Deity from protecting
   this Clod!

Leonard Trogdon
TWO LITTLE WATCHES
Two little watches, side by side,
   what bliss!
Two little watches named Darren
   and Kris,
They knew not each other on
   registration day,
At this Academy by the
   Monterey Bay.

School days run along quickly
   into November.
Then came Merry Christmas in
   Merry December,
But school paths usually cross
   some way,
At this Academy by the
   Monterey Bay.

Working at the mill with nail
   gun in hand,
With this little miss among the
   mill band:
Working hard making dollars
   that would stay,
At this Academy by the
   Monterey Bay.

In April was the banquet of
   parents and son,
To be there and take part in all
the fun:
And meet Kris at the car show
   that day,
At this Academy by the
   Monterey Bay.

Soon graduation week end, and
   Juniors march too,
For they would have part in the
   graduation march adieu,
And receive roses from the
   seniors at the class night array,
At this Academy by the
   Monterey Bay.

Gwendolyn Herron
You're a Sweet Electrical Line (A Salute To Electricity)
City lights shining so bright,
I know You'll shine for me tonight,
You'll throw a little spark on my
   heart.
As I pass your bulbs of height
You shine on me everyday
Same time seven days a week.
You give me hope and reassurance,
To make my days become so bliss.
Sometimes one, two, three, or
   maybe even four of us might
   glance at you from time to time,
We do it because we love you . . .
You're a sweet electrical line.
Our children love you too,

They do things under you while
   you're glowing,
But, sometimes it's less of a
   serious business for them,
I don't know what we'd do
   without you, we could use a
   candle.
But it still wouldn't give us
   satisfaction like you do
Once you come on, you stay on
   until everyone has gotten
   through using you
You do blow out sometimes, but,
   that's only when you've gotten
   tired.
"City lights shining so bright"
You can always cast a light on me,
'Cause it doesn't matter how far
   down or up you go,
By way of your electrical line . . .
We will always be able to see.

Betty C. Baker
LIFE

Dedicated to Mrs. Minnie B. Bennett who has been so supportive and encouraging.

Life gave me heartache,
In God I believed.
The heartache was relieved,
The heaviness was deceived.

Life gave me disappointment
But during it kindness showed.
From my face gratitude glowed,
The disappointment was slowed.

Life gave me sadness;
Smiles can't show through gloom.
The love of God in my heart had
   room
And happiness did bloom.

Life gave me fear,
To faith I did cling,
Held on to a little string
And gave fear a fling.

Life gave me pain,
It did not last forever.
I remembered; He will leave me
   never.
Sometimes I'm quite clever.

Life gave me a lot.
The full amount was accepted.
Trusting in God I'm not rejected.
With steadfast faith I'm protected.

William Homan
A CHRISTMAS TOY
A mechanical Santa
   just ten inches high,
His batteries run him
   as he shuffles by.
He shakes, and he jiggles.
   He rings a gold bell,
All the while whistling
   some Carols—to tell
Those who would listen
   that Christmas is nigh,
As he peers at us with
   such a gleam in his eye.

His little round face
   is framed with white hair.
And the cap on his head
   is in need of repair.
On his sturdy round body
   he wears a red suit.
And each of his feet
   has a fur-trimmed black boot.
I wish you could see him—
   this wee elfin toy.
Your heart would be gladdened
   with the seasonal joy!

Kathy Johnson
WHERE I HAVE BEEN

Dedicated to my son Randy

All these years that have just
   slipped by,
Not a thought in my mind, or a
   tear in the eye—
The awaking all happened in "83",
Who was in the center but just
   us three.
Our chairs were as close as we
   could get,
We hung on tight and lit our jets.
The tears they flowed—fast and
   many,
The door had opened—and we
   were forgiving.
The Lord has blessed me with a
   family of five,
And I thank you, dear God, we
   are all still alive.

Rita H. Palola
HOPE
Hundred and twenty men came
   to Virginia on that stormy day,
to the place called Chesapeake Bay.
Jamestown was found
in the days so gray.
Food was gone and starvation was
   on.

The years were hard night and day.
The air was cold, still and dark.
The disease hit very hard
and many died.

There was still hope
in the days so dark.
For there came the ships
with medicine and food.

The things got better
then and forever.

Rebecca M. Bergeron
MY LOVE
What can I give my love?
If I had an apple tree
I would give my love apples
If I had a fig tree
I would give my love figs
If I had a vineyard
I would give my love wine

If I ruled a kingdom
I would give it to my love
If I were a star in the sky
I would come down to my love
But since I have none of these
And very little else
I shall give my love myself.

Andrea M. Arkin
FRENCH KISSES

I dedicate this poem to Michael— A falling star that has fell unto me.

You think of french kisses—
I think of hugs—
You think of passion—
I think of love—
You think of Central Park—
I think of you—
You think of your friends—
I think of two—
You think of the Sun—
I think of the stars—
You look to the Moon—
And I reach for Mars—
You think what is real—
I dream what could be—
I think of you—
I think of me.

Louis Joblon
THE COMING OF SPRING
A gentle breeze that rustles trees;
The bright, clear skies, the flight
   of bees;
The radiant sun, a bird on wing;
The fresh, warm air, the urge to
   sing.

The buds on the trees, the
   milkweed pods;
The velvet grass, the goldenrods;
The dew on the lilac; the
   grasshopper's song;
The little brown worm that
   struggles along.

The frog that sits on the lily pad;
Croaking all day a note happy or
   sad;
The moist, wet forest in the time
   of dawn,
Within abiding beaver and fawn.

The tall, stately mountains
   tipped with snow;
The swift running streams that
   swerve as they flow;
From all of these, one is aware
That something is coming and to
   prepare.

Yes, something is coming, the
   winter's now o'er;
It's Spring that's arriving, the cold
   is no more.
The brief warm showers that fall
   on the sill,
That invigorate enough to give
   one a thrill.

And it is Spring that makes love
bloom with the flowers,
And many a heart is turned by
Spring's powers.
It makes one happy just being
alive:
It refreshes and knows the charm
to revive.

Edward C. O'Hara
LIFE IS BUT A MYSTERY

*To my beloved wife Barb and
loving sons, Ed and Jeff; also in
respectful memory of my father.*

Life is but a mystery
One does never know
What lies ahead hour by hour,
Or even a day or so
But one must keep his faith and
hope
As I'm sure you do know.

For without it we are but a petal
That will wilt and never grow;
As you would take a flower
And pamper it with care,
So does God take us His Children
Knowing that we care.
He'll pluck us like a flower
And take us way up there
Knowing that our families with
faith
Will someday MEET US THERE.

Loretta K. Metzger
MORNING DAWN

*To my Grammy Kriedler for
giving me the will to weave
words, and my parents who have
taught me the infinite meanings
of love.*

The sun slipped silently over still
mountains.
Shimmering just so . . . turning
trees into fountains.
As I awoke that morning,
I had a special feeling
That I would be right in all my
dealings.
Looking out onto the horizon,
I saw the most surprising,
Snowy white Albino deer.
Looking all bright eyed . . .
Trying to fight the emotional tide.
Soon the morning will be slipping
on,
The Albino deer will be gone.
No longer lonely and feeling blue,

For it has found
It's baby fawn,
Gifted by the morning dawn.

Katie Brunner
THE CHANGE OF TIME!
I always look forward to Christmas
the day of joy and cheer,
and think of—oh, so many things
concerning Jesus dear.

Who had to be born in a manger
and yet He was a king.
In swaddling clothes had to sleep
on straw
when of the past we sing.
The present is so much better
I think with a thankful heart,
the babies that are born today
have a much nicer start.

We have clothes and cuddleling
blankets
and cribs that are soft and warm—
a home that is heated, not drafty—
like the barn, in which He had to
be born.

He was chosen to be our Saviour
was send from heaven above
to teach and guide all mankind
in the most precious gift of love.

And whoever is willing to listen
feels protected, free of harm—
that's why to me this Holiday
is immensly full of charm.

Lora J. Willard
MY HAMILTON
A Hamilton was given to me,
An old-time dryer of modern
society.
It took us awhile to get her run'in;
But, now we see her tumblin and
humm'in.
I am proud of this piece of
machinery.
She's an old-time beauty made for
me.
She rumbles, hums and purrs like
a kitten.
Gets clothes dry in a smitten!
Ole' sweet hummer is older then
me,
And just might make it
further . . . wait and see.

Lorraine Mead
AHA!
"CABBAGE PATCH KIDS MAKE
SPECTACULAR BID FOR
EACH MOPPET'S
ATTENTION THIS YEAR"
(So the headlines proclaim.)
"And each child must name
its new toy and provide for it
here."
Now you parents of each little
tyke,
Be it Helen or Betsy or Mike,
Can quickly reclaim last year's
Pac-Man Game,
and the year before's ten-speed
bike.

Sandra Patricia Soto
LOOK AT MY HANDS
Look at my hands.
They interlock so tightly when
praying,
as if in the fierceness of their
desperation
they could crush and hold you
forever,

if you should be caught between
them.
Look at my hands.
They lie numb and unmoving.
Martyrs hands. Stricken and
wounded deep beneath the flesh,
pathetically stretched out to
receive you
if you should stagger back.

Look at my hands.
They still reach out in vain to
touch you,
only to seize and clutch at the
empty air.
Little do they know that you
have fled from their
grasp to hold anothers.
Look at my hands.

Tamara Kay Arnovitz
LET THERE BE LOVE

*To my mother and father for
with their strength and guidance
my tumultuous adolescence has
been virtually painless and
decidedly good.*

Let there be bonds softly woven
of dreams and aspirations;
Souls gently entwined in exalted
inspirations;
Minds interlacing to coherent
destinations.

The stars above are frozen dew,
You are me and I am you.
On gilded wing is snowy dove,
Like none before, let there be
love
Between you and me.

Let there be tears slowly shed
from immature frustration;
Words whispered low in heartfelt
consolation;
Heart beats quickening in
desirous expectation.

As pure as pearls in an oyster
shell,
Or the whitest cloud blown by
crystal gale,
Our hearts will be bound with
consent from above,
Like none before, let there be
love
Between you and me.

J. D. Neubauer
THE PATRIOT

Young America

Free flies the flag of this great
nation
And the freedom for which it
stands
Shall endure—like an endless
duration
Till time shall run out with the
sands

And I as a man will rise to defend
it
And be it with my last dying
breath
Shall shout—so the whole world
might
Hear it
Give me liberty—my freedom—

Or death

For what is a man if he cannot
endure
The pain and the heartache that
he might secure
Eternal peace—though not easily
won
For a land of the free—where
"God's will be done"

Abraham Casiano Napoles
YES
Thank you for the turkey,
stuffing, cranberry sauce
Thank you for the pumpkin pie,
this feast you made for us;
There are many things I'm
thankful for so on this day to
be thankful
I thank you for your Company
your Friendship and your
Love
But most of all I thank You for
the Answer you gave me
WHEN I PROPOSED

Pam G. Marshall
DANNY

*Love you Danny, I dedicate this
poem to you.*

Love is like a rare bird
in the palm of my hand.

Close my hand I will smother it;
it will die.

Keep my hand open and light
and it will stay.

You are the rare bird in the palm
of my hand.

I love you even if its only a
moment long.

A moment is worth many
pictures many memories—

so is Love.

Teresa D. Hanson
ANTICIPATION

*This poem is dedicated to my
mother, who has shown me the
importance of keeping the "spirit
of christmas" alive throughout
the year.*

Quietly she crept down the stairs
in anticipation of what was
there.
It was well after midnight
and she hoped she'd guessed
right;
That this was the time
for that jolly old man,
And this time she was going to
catch him and give him a hug.
When she reached the bottom,
her eyes opened wide;
For she was met with a big
surprise.
That after all her calculating
of time—
Santa had been there
already that night.
So she quietly mounted the stairs
back to her room;
With a determination, rather
than
gloom, she began thinking

of another plan.
So with a smile on her face as she
  slipped into bed,
She fell asleep with the thoughts
  of "Next year!"

Carol A. Stoneroad
JUST FOR YOU
Oh, Lord hear what I have to say
Listen while I kneel and pray
I know you're use to requests
But tonight I'll leave you rest
Remember when you came to
  me that day?
All the leaves had fell away
I want to give my thanks to you
Because all your gifts to me were
  new
Just as the blue heavens above
You freed my heart, so I could love
So now, my soul I will bare
Peace and good will I want to
  share
On this very special night
I sit here in the candle light
Giving my love and thanks to
  thee
On this night, Christmas Eve.

Anita M. Garrett
LOST REFUGE
All through the night and day
My wings have beaten the air
Leading the flock.
I have spearheaded the "V"
Hearing the voices behind me.
Now as dusk is descending
We know with that strange sense
Handed down from goose to egg
  to goose
That soon we shall find the
  marshland
Where our breasts will rest
On quiet waters and we shall
Nourish our depleted bodies.

But we see no green marshland,
Only a vast black expanse,
A multitude of yellow monsters
Exhaling smoke and fumes,
Frameworks of wooden nests
Men build to shelter soft bodies.

Here can be no nests, no eggs,
No goslings to follow mothers
Into quiet threads of water.
Where can we go?
The flock is in confusion,
My tired heart has slowed,
I am sinking, sinking—

Susie Katherine Smith
RAPPORT
From the first there was a rapport
  between us,
Together we visited the land of
  make-believe.
He was just a little boy,
And this land was easy for him to
  receive.

Our friendship was strengthened,
By the passing years,
Our time spent together was
  happy,
Unmarred by tears.

Time passes quickly,
Soon he grew to be a man,
He visited me again to relive his
  memories,
As only the heart can.

"Give me a little more time", he
  seemed to be saying,
For he was reluctant to go.

But we must hold loosely the
  things we love,
This we all come to know.

Now he is getting married,
At the altar, the bride will be
  beautiful and fair.
He will be tall and handsome,
But I'll see a little boy standing
  there.

Loretta Jeter

Loretta Jeter
THE VAGABOND
Rough hewn cabin with broken
  door,
Humble abode of the meek and
  poor,
Let me in thy confines find—
Shelter for the night.

Broken chimney and splintered
  floor,
You are all I want and nothing
  more,
Marble mansion you seem to me,
Weary traveler that I be.

From sheltering barns and culverts,
To bare fields and cradling ditches,
You seem the fairy cottage of my
  great mirage
For which I've sought so long and
  hard.

So corral thy spiders into their
  webs,
And scurry your mice into their
  holes.
Silence thy creaky, rusty nails.
Your master is here; and has need
  of thee.

Thelma Van Scoik
THERE IS STILL—
There is still a song in my heart
  Because I so love you.
My days with you so beautiful
  were—
  Only God knows why so few.

There is still a smile on my lips—
  The smile you gave to me
The day you whispered, "I love
  you,"
  And kissed me tenderly.

There is still a glow in my eyes
  That tears have not washed
  away—
Tears that flow softly and freely
Since that tragic winter day.

There is still a love in my heart
  That death could not take away—
A love I'm saving to give to you
  On my "Triumphant Day!"

Alvena M. Wylin
COPING
When things get tough,
  it's just not enough,
to worry, stew, and fret—
prayer is what you need to get.

It helps to know that others care,
and your grief and pain they share,
that a higher power can erase—
the tears upon your face.

So when trouble's all around you,
and your world starts caving in,
let God and people surround
  you—
to help you keep up your chin.

Estella M. McGhee—Siehoff
"Distress Of Nations" Is Upon Us
And there is no way out: Fighting
  other nations' battles.
And there is no way out: Fighting
  other spirits' revival.
And there is no way out: Fighting
  other families' children.
And there is no way out: Fighting
  other builders' workers.
And there is no way out: Fighting
  other pulpits' craft.

And there is no way out: Fighting
  other entertainments' support.
And there is no way out: Fighting
  other means of survival.
And there is no way out: Fighting
  other tribes for land.
And there is no way out: Fighting
  other tribes for caves.

Harold E. Williams
CEMETERY SUNDAY
On Cemetery Sunday, We'll pray
  the rosary.
Poor souls of those departed, live
  on in memory.
Wreath flower graves laid today,
  for someone very dear.
Cherish them in solemn prayer,
  each waiting passing year.
Have faith, hope and charity, His
  mercy makes us strong.
Sweet Jesus graces bless all, guide
  sinners who do wrong.
Some time we shall meet again,
  in Heaven's great above,
Greeting our dear lonesome
  friends, fill peaceful hearts with
  love.

Maria McGrath
CAROUSEL HORSE
Pretty painted horse,
silently circling your private
  carousel,
with porcelain features to
  shield your pierced heart,
& dancing eyes which
  mysteriously conceal
  your obscure spectres,
& simulated smiles to decorate
  your broken spirit,
& the music of your carousel
  sweetly deceiving
  your unsuspecting audience

Each ride has an ending,
each life its unadorned
  realities,
& each man the strength to
  overcome the demons of the
  carousel.

Steven P. Lawrence
BELIEVE

*To Kelly Sue: You're like a
shadow that has fallen upon me
to bring me bliss.*

One nite an angel came to me
on a sweat filled summer's eve
Ever since that night I've seen the
  light
Jesus, I believe

You've changed my life in front of
  me
I'm grateful, Yes I am
Like a shepherd in the field of life
You've steered me like a lamb

For now I'll ever follow you
Wherever you may lead
You died to save the soul of man
Jesus, I believe

Doris Howell
THE KING SAID GOODBYE

*IN Honor to all ELVIS fans all
over the World. I as one of his
fans my self DORIS HOWELL
LOVED him an his music very
much.*

Tell all my fans.
To please don't cry.
I had to go i done my share.
Entertaining for ever one.
O, God did we all have fun

Tell all my fans.
Please don't cry.
I had to go.
Please tell them all the reason
  why.
Tell all my friends.
Why i had to die.
Please tell them all.
That the KING said goodbye.

Tell all my fans.
That the king had to go.
All my fans ought to know by
  now.
THat GOD called me home to be
  with him,
He had much much better plans.

Please tell my friends.
To please don't cry.
that i had to go.
Please tell them the reason why.
Ella all my friends why
Why i had to dye.
tell them that the KING said
  goodbye.

Lynn Bain
RUN AWAY
I want to run away
To forget you're even there
But my world becomes so
  different
I breathe a different air.

I look around and there's just no
  one
Who can fill that empty space
And everywhere I turn
I can still see your face.

Is it right or is it wrong?
My conscience drives me mad.
Are you good for me, my love
Or are you extremely bad?

The tortures of my mind
The heartbreak that I feel
I know I bring upon myself
But they're so very real.

Yet, I cannot live without you
My world would fall apart.
Though I sometimes try to run
  away
You're imbedded in my heart.

Allen Webster Van Horn
GOD'S GIFTS
Admonish not the sun as it peaks
  at heat of day
Admonish not the rain drops as
  the rivers rise in May
Admonish not the wind that
  scatters all of the seeds
For that's simply Gods way to
  provide all of mans needs.

Scold not the honey bee and fear
  not his stings
Scold not the church bell for its
  Sunday morning rings
Scold not the little children who
  trample on your lawn
For they are simply Gods gift to
  help man carry on.

Censure not the wild waves that
  crest upon the shore
Censure not the mountain music
  that spreads our countries lore
Censure not the shadow when
  the sun hides behind a cloud
For Gods only resting the
  spotlight which makes a man
  stand proud.

His gifts to us are endless though
  we recognize but few
We overlook our blessings to
  search for something new
And when the search is ended
  and we find that nothing is there
We return to our Provider
  through softly uttered prayer.

Sybil I. Stambaugh
THE REMEMBRANCE
The rose dropped silently into
  the fresh wet snow by the
  tombstone,
All was still in the twilight, in
  the December cold, the man
  stood alone.
The man stared at the rose for a
  moment, and a smile captured
  his face,
Peacefulness and joy appeared
  eminent, the fond memory
  could not be erased.

The Christmas holiday had made
  him remember his mother's
  sincere love and total giving for
  him,
Twenty Christmas holidays had
  passed since her death; the
  memory was pleasant not grim.
As he stood there he remembered
  her words one Christmas, to a
  child who had lost his first
  tooth,
"You will lose many things in life
  from teeth to friends my son,
  but never lose hold of your
  youth."

At 26, now he finally understood
  what she was trying to say all
  those years before,
You lose a tooth and it leaves a

space for growth with the
  attitude of a youth, not
the hopelessness of a padlocked
  door.
How easy it is at Christmas time
  to be thinking of all we've lost
  through the years,
And then by New Year's Eve
  we're totally discouraged and
  desperate to relieve our fears.
But if we hold fast to the mind of
  a child, who believes in Santa
  Claus,
And hold fast through time as the
  wise men did who followed
  that distant star,
And stop in the busy sidewalk,
  and listen among the bustle to
  the distant Angel choir,
With the curiosity, simplicity,
  and ears of a child, we'll
  journey through the void,
add experience, grow a dimention
  higher.

He picked up the rose in
  reflection, and sniffed it as a
  tear trickled down his face,
He'd lost his teeth, his mother,
  his job, but his youth was still
  growing in the space.
The rose dropped silently into
  the fresh wet snow, as the
  young man turned to go,
"Merry Christmas, Mother, your
  giving spirit of wisdom lives
  on, and I still love you,
you know."

Carlene Breckenridge
WILDERNESS WOMAN
Who is this woman coming up
  from the wilderness?
She's been forged by God under
  deep duress.
What has she been through?
  Where is she going?
In one hand she carries seeds for
  sowing.
How did she survive? What is her
  reward?
She leans on the Arm that wields
  a mighty sword.
And in so leaning she becomes
  stronger than any
in faith and love that can reach
  so many.
In the wilderness her tears
  brought forth a spring
that if one drinks of will make
  one sing
of a love so demanding it would
  not yield
until to her Beloved her heart
  was sealed.
No danger was too great as she
  sought after Him,
her shout to know Him made the
  desert dim.
Her all consuming love she cried
  to give
to the One Who caused her to
  live.
So she comes up from the
  wilderness
putting behind her fears, her
  stress.
In one hand she sows seeds of life
created by her tears to end others
  strife.
She holds her Beloved by her

other hand
knowing by this she'll forever
  stand.

Cleo Hall Critelli
THEY'LL NEVER KNOW
Those big heads back in
  Washington
Should wear a poor man's shoes,
Then they'd know what it's like
To be hungry and have the blues.

When there's a change in money
  plans
It's the poor who always pay,
The rich get richer and the poor
  get poorer,
It has always been that way.

The big heads don't know what
  it's like
To go to bed hungry every night
Because the pennies just won't
  stretch,
They have already been stretched
  tight.

Most big heads are millionaires
But they're always reaching for
  more,
They buy jewels, liquor, and cars,
But they never help the poor.

The rich don't care what the
  Bible says
About helping those in need,
All they think about is more and
  more
They are so filled with greed.

They think their riches will save
  their souls,
But one day they'll find out
When they drop into the pits of
  Hell
And they never will get out.

Thelma G. Monk
LOVE
Love is a wonderful thing,
It has heal, made a smile,
Brighten up ones day,
Pointed out the way,
It can be on the mountain,
In the valley, give it and
It will come back to you.

Eulah Proctor Stanley
THE INCARNATION
If I were to live a million years
My praising voice would sing
Holy Redeemer Holy Redeemer
Down through the ages ring
He came to Israel with the
  greatest love
Some rejected Him
If she could have known
From whence He came
A greater place from Abraham's
  faith
they'd run
Gracious God the Father, Jesus
  Christ the Son
equated with the Holy Spirit
They become One
The Almighty Jesus, saviour of
  mankind
Born of the virgin birth, wrought
  by
the manifestation of the Holy
  Spirit
The eternal Son of God, became a
  human man
God became incarnate in Jesus
  Christ

He lost nothing divine
When the word became flesh
Jesus the light of the world
Was with God even before the
  creation

Mari L. Baker
BLESSINGS
Dear Lord above, Hear my words
That I say to You in this moment
  of prayer.
Thank you for my caring family
  and friends
You have so graciously given to
  me,
Thank you for giving me the
  chance
To enjoy the peacefulness of
  nature and freedom,
Thank you for giving me the
  opportunities
To help enhance the growth of
  young minds, and
Thank you, most of all, for
  sending Jesus Christ
To me and to all the world.
Help me to spread Your Word to
  all I meet
That they too may know of Your
  everlasting love.

Lois M. Buzzell
GARDEN OF DREAMS
I've a garden of dreams
That I'm tending with care,
And it makes such a heavenly
  view.
In my garden of dreams
You're always with me,
And I cherish each moment with
  you.

Oh, the dreams that I know
Really do have a glow,
And there's joy everywhere to
  share;
And how good it would be
If you dreamed there with me,
For there's love, special love
  everywhere.

Mary Fattig
LOVE
Love is a touch, tender with care
A meaningful look, secrets to share
Love is a mood, laughter and
  tears—a tuned through the years
Love is a word that kindles a fire
  to give you the world and all
  you desire
Love is a faith, that dreams will
  come true
Love is wonderful
Love is you
Every look every smile every
  touch—
I fall in love with you twice as
  much.

Margaret Malinoske
LITTLE SNOW FLAKE
Intricate little snow flake
Created by an Omnipotent hand,
Perfect design, something special
So tiny, yet so grand.
Silently you descend upon us
Falling softly where you will,
Only God knows where you'll
  settle
Before you whiten the hill.
It takes some million snow flakes
To cover all the land,
From mountain peak to valley
But only one Omnipotent hand.

Mrs. Betty Ann Frederics
IN MY DAY
In those tender days when I was
born,
A baby's gender begat some
behavior almost uniform;
With boys wear blue, little girls
wear pink.
It was sheer kind of, sort of
instinct.

Vincent kissed me way down in
our Daddy's cornfield.
The receipted fee: One graham
cracker per kiss yield.
Worst spanking Mama gave me
was 'cause of bathrooms:
Picture soapie drama: Innocent
relieves as Vincent washing,
grooms.

Daddy was a nurse enduring
World War I days.
Justifying a curse was prating,
expectorating, not his ways.
Papa tipped his straw hat to Mrs.
Walker.
Sunday School Mrs. Walker
taught, great Bible talker.

The five of us never saw our
mother drunk.
Mama was LOVE, gave board,
room, wasn't a monk.
And in my day, high school study
rainbowed aspirations;
Not being shy, cheering the boys,
holding virtuous confrontations.

The second time around birthed
four answers to prayer.
Heaven made mine: Marriage
bonded by the supreme arrayer.
It's hubby Michael's humor that's
probably kept us together.
His laughter shackles
dissensions, his love the
ultimate cover.

Time and times watched man on
the moon and numerous
count-downs.
"Computer error", rhymes the
secretary answering our claims
and vocalized frowns.
The earth's reckoning kept in
spite of the reaping nuclear
bomb:
My day beckoning, sees His
coming in clouds brighter than
sun.

Stephanie A. Hellmann
MAD ABOUT YOU
I remember standing on the curb
waiting for an end to traffic,
when suddenly you were there.
You waved,
and your broad smile gleamed in
the afternoon sun.

They surely thought me mad—
beaming at the bananas, grinning
at the milk,
giggling my way through the
groceries.
It was the day after.

The night before had belonged to
us.
You sang to me. We danced. I
gave you my heart.
We kissed.

It all seems so long ago. Past
times are gone.

But I remember.
Was it so long ago that you have
forgotten?
How can it be that as I stand on
the curb I never will see you
again?

I can't believe that.
I see you always.
I remember
and my heart sings.

Opal M. Kessner
AS A TREE
A Christian is just like a tree,
Standing tall, for all to see,
Our roots, well deep into the
ground,
Spreading salvation, all around;
Reaching out to all we meet,
Helping them to a life, so sweet.

Although our leaves and
branches show,
Our roots are thoughts and deeds,
we know,
To tell to others, of the way,
Of our redemption, and convey,
How Jesus saves our souls from
sin,
And gives us perfect peace within.

We must spread our roots far and
wide,
Let others see Christ does abide;
He feeds us from His living stream,
And makes our outside branches
gleam,
With roots well grounded, we
should be,
An everlasting, fruitful tree.

Hazel B. Plummer
A RAINY DAY
Some folks dislike a rainy day
But they can be the nicest kind,
It's all in the way we look at it,
Depends on our state of mind.

If the flowers didn't have the rain
How could they grow so fast?
And become such things of beauty
That bring us joys that last?

The trees and shrubs grow thirsty
too
Without water, lawns turn brown,
Was there ever anything more
refreshing
Than air—as the rain comes down?

How could we enjoy the sunshine
If we never had the rain?
How could we enjoy our blessings,
If we never had a pain?

Patti Sue Beagle
PRECIOUS MEMORIES
Our love was such a beautiful
thing,
Like a song, a Robin might sing,
Through the years, it flourished
and grew,
And each day brought someth
ing new.

Our love grew throughout the
years,
To lose that love, I had no fears,
Because I was yours and you were
mine,
That made our love, one of a kind.

We had good times and bad, we
laughed, we cried,
But we stood by each other, with
respect and pride,

Because, we knew, no matter
what lay ahead,
Our love was strong, and we had
nothing to dread.

Yes, our love was such a beautiful
thing,
Even more beautiful, than a song,
a Robin might sing,
I daily thanked the Lord above,
For giving us an Eternal,
Everlasting love.

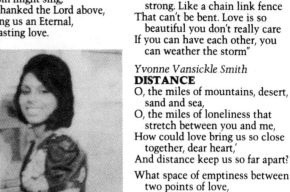

Emma Jean Lewis

Emma Jean Lewis
True Love Is Hard Too Beat

*This writing of poetry was
inspired by Melvyn my Friend,
who work for kake channel 10*

Love is so beautiful that love is
blind
You don't see thing's that you
normally do
Because you are in a enlighting
dew.
Your heart feels the love, that
you can't explain,
You just want to be with your
love one from sundown
To sunup

To look your love one in the eye,
and see the mystery that
You both can feel, the mystical
power of your love flower.
When two people are in love,
they can feel what others miss.
This beautiful feeling that they
have, no coldness, but
Warmness and fondness, and the
friendship of love. Two
People can feel the nearness of

each other without touching.
It is almost like looking in a
mirror, on the inside of each
Other soul. No explaining, just
looking into each other eyes
And running into each other arms.
You can't get enough of each
Other, because the bond is
strong. Like a chain link fence
That can't be bent. Love is so
beautiful you don't really care
If you can have each other, you
can weather the storm"

Yvonne Vansickle Smith
DISTANCE
O, the miles of mountains, desert,
sand and sea,
O, the miles of loneliness that
stretch between you and me,
How could love bring us so close
together, dear heart,'
And distance keep us so far apart?

What space of emptiness between
two points of love,
How far is east from west or earth
from worlds above?
How do I measure the space
between our lives?
Such far-away place no wings
could fly and survive.

O, miles of rain and wind and
storm and snow,
O, miles of land or sea or air—
high or low,
Such wide continents between
the heartbeats of our love,
What anguish to think of
distance, my beloved.

We are so far removed one from
another,
But bound so close by love, my
traveler,
How could love bring us so close
together, dear heart,
And distance keep us so far apart?

KC Lim
A Shallow Grave By the
Stream
If I had been there
Once, I would have felt the need.
And if I could have been there
Twice, I might have planted a
seed.

If I had chance in this life time,
Would I not bury the remain
someplace
Gentle to the touch? Maybe
Soft felt hill top by the glowing
face?

And suppose if were supposed,
Would the stream flow
downward
Instead of up? And bringing with
it
The thousand seashells with
stories.

And maybe by the changing
wind,
Were shallow grave washed away
To take its place in my heart;
Would I feel the pain?

And if stream became my tears,
Would you drown with this
Flat bed of my eternal valley?
If I were a shallow grave by the
stream.

Ronald F. Smedley
UNTITLED

To Julie . . . Truely the jewel of my life and the warmth of my heart

sunshine feeding morn
rays reflect warmth
hearts smoothing close . . .

as time draws near
  bubbles burst
  life comes out of this
    into that
  and the synergism of souls
    becomes the unity of our being.
  she he becomes you me
observe now the birth of a seed
  nurtured with love . . . yet
    sometimes forgotten
  watered daily . . . while at times
    feeling a drought
  showered in sunshine . . . with
    the dark room always a
    reminder.
  . . . the path is set, only the walk
    remains.

with many highs, lows, and
  dozens of "i hate yous"
our lives
  have blossomed into
our live   our warmth
    has become
    our love come, let's walk
      awhile
        . . . now the gray hair can
          come in peace

Nancy Ann Gandee
The Miracle My Eyes Can See
The way is long; the road is hard.
I cried, "Oh, I can't make it, Lord."
"Yes, you can, just take my hand;
I'll lead you to the promised
  land."

"Where I am, you may go;
Were it not true, would I tell you
  so?
Just trust in me, I'll take your
  yolk."
And in my mind I knew the Lord
  had spoke.

He said, "My child, may your
  troubles be gone,
For I am with you; you are not
  alone."
Then victory came over me,
My eyes were open and I could
  see.

Oh much too long, I'd carried a
  load
Till my eyes were open and I was
  showed;
Now heaven is so much sweeter
  to me
So even death has no sting you see.

My heart swells up and it is glad
For I've already forgotten the
  troubles I've had.
Is it not plain for you to see
What I know my Lord has done
  for me?

So open your hearts,
Your souls, and your minds,
And have peace and contentment
Leaving your troubles behind.

Miriam Del Pino
'TWAS THE CHRIST
'Twas the presence of immortal
  heart
sacred flame, to set my soul ablaze
flaming truth, coming to impart
  His Spirit and mine, in ardent
    embrace
'Twas the heart of love enduring
  springing pools of life divine
boundless streams of waters
    flowing
  from God's Spirit, unto mine
'Twas the Christ, in the depth of
    me
my soul tranquil, in His presence
    spent
long bound my spirit, soon was
    shackle-free
abandoned to Him, in total
    content

Mark Duden
QUIET THOUGHTS
When silence falls upon my lips
  and I quietly walk away
not showing any responce to you
  as I did at earlier times today.
It's not that I love you any less,
  it's not that I'm mad at you.
It's not that caring has left my
  Heart, for my love for you will
    always be true.
I walk in silence to think my
    thoughts,
to clear my mind, and search my
    heart.
Be patient with me my darlin,
  believe in my love for you,
For it's you I love and no one
    but you.

Charlotte P. Koslo
IT'S CHRISTMAS
It's Christmas, it's Christmas,
The snow is bound to fall.
For after all what's Christmas
If there is no snow at all?

A light, an image reflected,
Jesus there in the manger lay.
So warm and unaffected
In nothing more than straw or hay.

Yes, it's Christmas, it's
  Christmas—
Who needs that snow fall!
It's time for peace and happiness.
Rejoice with love for all.

Ruth C. Hawkins
CHRISTMAS STORY
The beauty of the Christmas
    story
  lies deep within our hearts
Tis a day of gladness and of joy;
  a day that we set apart
To lay away our sorrows and
    trials
  and with a love sincere
Welcome again the blessed Child
  To whom we are so dear.

God's gift to us: a tiny babe
  To cherish and to hold
A child that would someday
    repay
  the debt of all men's souls
So let us lift our hearts in prayer
  with all the love we can bestow
That we may all his blessings
    share
  as God has willed it so.

Frances C. Emmons
OUR NEW BORN BABY

To Everett Nathaniel With Love

Our new born baby
  Is so small,
Suddenly my others
  Look quite tall.

What a beautiful gift
  For God to give,
And we are a part
  Of this life to live.

Life's former patterns
  Now seem strange
As to a new schedule
  We all must change.

Our lives with this baby
  Will also mature
As trials and errors
  With him we endure.

We are a part
  Of each challenge he tries
And the love we share
  Will broaden our lives.

Wm. Keith Clayton
DREAMS OF YOUTH
The dreams of youth
Are like a dove,
They fly on by
With puppy love,
And prepare the heart
For all ahead,
With full intent
Of hopes to wed.

As time shall pass,
The years will gather.
A faithful love
Will never weather
With sentiments,
And songs we save,
But carried on
Into the grave.

Charles Mark Morrison
YEARS GO BY
The years go by so quickly, it was
  only yesterday;
I saw the fields of grass, I turned
  and they were gone.

Now empty streets fill the fields,
  and the fruit no longer yields.

The warm breeze passing through
  the tower of trees standing so
  proud and tall.

They too had to fall.

Street lights shed their glow
  amidst the serentiy,
Flowers of paradise no longer sow
  the seeds of beauty,

Rivers of black ice flood the
  paths.
Jet stream runways replace the
  golden grass.

Streams are now covered with
  signs and highways,
The river beds are now behind
  the byways.

The gates of freedom do not
  remain anymore,
Gone too are the dusty trails and
  folklore.

The years went by, and the
  mystery of the silent ages

couldn't compete with the new
  sounds of marching feet.

. . . It was only yesterday . . .

Jean Ann Sanchez
THAT I MAY FORGIVE

To those whose lives I have touched, and those who touched mine. Matt. 6: 14,15

Father, teach me to forgive
The hurt that's done to me

Cleanse me of the sin of hate
Set my spirit free

Let Your great love freely flow
Through my flesh and troubled
  mind
Grant, I too, know how to love
So I'll not be unkind

May I be blessed with wisdom
And open eyes to see
How to forget and to forgive
Each and every injury

Lord, empty to me of self today
Bestow on me Your grace
Let my would be enemies
See love upon my face.

Jacqueline Gaudet
JOHN
So many loves clutter my
  thoughts and my heart.
Like treasures stored in an attic
  ready to be picked up and
  thought about anytime I
  choose to search through the
  many stored there.
Some have collected much more
  dust than others, some stored
  so far into a dark
  corner . . . almost
  forgotten . . . but still there
  taking up space.
One day the attic will be cleared
  out, ready to recieve new
  treasures . . .
yet in a corner there sits a box . . .
not yet forgotten . . .
A box I just can't bring myself to
  throw out.

Yvonne Vansickle Smith
SILENCE THE GUNS
Silence the guns that fill the sky
  with smoke,
That swell hearts with fear and
  dim their hope,
That spill blood and cause the
  smell of death,
What need have we for sorrow
  and regret?

Silence the guns in mountain
  jungle and desert trail,
Where innocent victims in
  anguish wail,
Where battered bodies seek
  shelter and food,
What need for tortured minds to
  brood in solitude?

Silence the guns 'ore troubled
  seas—in ominous skys,
Valiant men brought to naught—
  but scream and cry and die,
Brave loved ones left behind in
  grief,
What need for loneliness, and
  distress in wilderness!

339

Silence the guns in our own brave
land,
Aimed at hearts devoted to aid
and understand,
Striking down gallent statesmen
in the spring of life,
What need for shedding blood
and spreading strife?

Janet Malloy
LIGHT OF LIFE
Candle burning oh so brightly,
Your golden flame is all aglow.
Like a lighthouse for all ships,
You guide us with your
Christmas cheer.

Candle burning oh so brightly,
How you keep going I do not
know.
Your Christmas spirit inspires all
of us
To have good will for mankind.

Candle burning oh so brightly,
Keep your flame alive all the year.
Keep men happy, keep men loving.
Never let hatred persevere.

Maureen C. Connelly
FEELING
Feeling kinda Low, like a boat in
tow!
Betcha, ribbons to bows; the sun
is gonna show!
All this sadness will go!
Keep me, in your thoughts, and I
will feel,
a warming glow!

Loreta Inman
NEVER BE DISCOURAGED

To Mary Wright

Never be discouraged
When failures come to light—
Just use them for stepping stones
And make a stronger fight.

William B. Houston
RAVEN HAIRED BEAUTY
A Raven Haired Beauty of the
Florida Shore
Made the trip bearable for me
and more;
I knew not what there was in store
til I arrived at that Florida shore.

Monday through Friday was only
just fair
til I met the girl with the raven
hair.
All week long I tried to meet
the Raven Haired Beauty, so
pretty and sweet.

Her ways were so charming, her
wit was so bold,
her eyes were of green jade, her
heart of pure gold.
Her friendliness was of great
value, her tenderness so true,
her beauty was so genuine, it
showed clear through.

Her lovliness was unbeaten, her
personality a treasure,
her character was untarnished,
her laughter a pleasure.
Her body was so heavenly, her
mind so unique,
her company I yearn for, her
hand I seek.

Of this Raven Haired Beauty I
will surely miss,
the sound of her voice and the
taste of her kiss.
The touch of her hand and the
nod of her head,
the absence of Penny, I most
surely dread.

Earnest Ray Westenskow

Earnest Ray Westenskow
I KNOW

*To my beautiful parents Sara &
Jack Cludas*

I Know the heartaches you've
been through
I Know because I've had
heartaches too—
I Know the loss and hurt inside
I Know the tears you try to hide—
I Know the empty lonely days
I Know how much that you have
paid—
I Know together we can turn it
around
I Know the happiness that can be
found—
I Know the Lord will see us
through
I Know because I feel as you—
I Know our lives have been blessed
I Know that it was just a test—
I Know that we've shown our
worth
I Know that we've found our
place on earth—
So let us take what we know
Forget the past and start to grow—
We can build a life full of dreams
Work together and become a team.

Earnest Ray Westenskow
JESUS
I'd like to tell you of a man
that I've just met today—
He came into my life you see
and He is here to stay—
He talks to me through sparkling
eyes
not one word from His mouth—
He shines on me throughout my
day
and even in my house—
Hair like silk, hands so soft
feet don't touch the ground—
The beauty that I see in Him
He spreads it all around—
This man will come to you one
day
and offer you His Love—

Be ready to accept this gift
It came from the Lord above—
You see—this Man's name is
Jesus.

Robert Gibson
ROBMIEKA
My child
lovely daughter of mine,
your soul be restless
and much divine.
Your mind trying
to out grow your years,
causing loved ones
stress and tears.
This driven mystery
you shield inside,
creates the misery
you feel to hide.
You're a lovely child
other-wise,
with long dark braids
and beautiful eyes.
"Robmieka"
let your inner love flow,
for you have a life time
in which to grow.

Christina Praskin
THE PILGRIMS

*I dedicate this poem, whom I
haven't seen in years, to my
brother John Praskin, love you
very much.*

Beauty is
 The peaceful land,
When the pilgrims
 Stood hand in hand.
Plymouth rock
 A memory ago,
Where once the pilgrims
 Stood on a land they didn't know.
The indians arrived
 And thanksgiving had begon,
Living and growing together
 A nation we become.

Amanda Sheets
MEMORIES IN TIME
We walk down the beach hand in
hand.
We look in the sky for far away
lands.
We stop on the beach turn and
look back.
Yet all we see are our old tracks.
We stop and think of memories
we left behind.
We turn to go on to make new
ones in time.

Betty F. Brown
FINALE

Dedicated to: Glenn T. Snyder

We buried September on a little
hill in the country.
The four o'clock sun shone like
foot lights on the goldenrod
and funeral flowers.
A final prayer is said like an
"encore" or a "bravo".
"Lord, thank you for all we knew
and loved about September."
The mourners stay as long as
they can, but the final curtain
falls and the sun is also buried.
As we leave we watch October's

dress rehearsal.
On stage everybody!!! Crimson,
gold, terra cotta, russett!
Tomorrow's dawn will raise the
curtain on October's play on
life . . .
But I long for one more look at
September . . .
I turn, but the grave has been
filled.
The theatre is empty.

Dorothy A. Newsom
FRIENDSHIP
Be my Friend—tell me my errors—
 Hold up a mirror for me to see
The me that *is!*

Don't tell me the good things—
 Don't tell me how clever and
 bright I am—
I know these things.

But please, Friend, tell me
 What's there in the corners
I hide from me—and

Together let's drag them out
 Into the light of day
And clean them up!
Please be my friend!

Maxwell B. Courage
A LITTLE KINDNESS
We spend our lives hurrying here
 and there
Upon what we think are
 important affairs;
Yet we tend to overlook so many
For whom a kindly word might
 relieve dread cares.

It is so easy to get wrapped up
In a cocoon of self and forget
The gallant struggles of those
 around.
Lending a listening ear we'll not
 regret.

A little act of kindness every day
Can be the goal of everyone;
A thoughtful gift of a book or
 flowers
Could brighten lives as does the
 golden sun.

Edith Cannon Storey
WINGS AWAY
Wings away, wings away
The wild geese are flying
 southward to day,
They are honking and waving
 goodby, goodby
To the cold frozen north with it's
 snowladen sky.
When I see them flying
My heart seems so bountiful free
While I am airborne with the geese
Flying to a new land for me.
A new land of beautiful dreams,
A land of love and of light
With God's angels awaiting me
 there
Where living is a joyfull delight.

E. June Mathews
NOVEMBER
I wakened on that chilly morn
To glimpse a fleeting summer born
And saw the smile of morning
 light
Obliterating veil of night.

Like days in June that fade at noon
The summer's blush departs too
 soon,

With sudden clouds that brings
  the rain,
It's song of summer's last refrain.

I sadly look at fallen leaves
And understand the weeping
  trees
Recalling times of yesterday
As light of summer dies away.

I know the year is growing old,
November days are short and cold,
While sand is slipping through
  the glass
We see our autumn winging past.

June Harrington
MIND SEIZED
mind seized
I blunder
through autumn's thunder
of clamoring color . . .
trees leap out of the forest
like screaming fire
and I am foliage blinded . . .
heart worn
I flounder
through life's loud crashing
of tasteless tears
and voices come out of my past
in a choking tangent . . .
run down my days in an hour
my dreams in a minute
I am
mortality reminded . . .

Patricia Habiger
LOVING
Come walk with me and stay
  with me
until the dawn's curtain
  proclaims a new day.
Everyday is rebirth with you—
You hold me, every ounce of the
  moment
whispers a miracle.
I'm grateful our paths should blend
in this life—
giving sweet reasons to exist.
Press your heart on mine—letting
  each beat
be our time clock for loving.

Barbara Jo Huzvar
Santa Isn't Watching Me
Why doesn't Santa ever watch the
  things I do
I am beginning to think he's not
  true
Santa will never know when I
  cheat in a game
And I'll get my toys just the same
So I know Santa isn't watching
  me today
No sense in being careful with
  what I say
But I must admit it makes me
  very sad
Cause maybe Santa would watch
  me if I wasn't so bad

Louise Shannon Monteverde
THE TEAR IN YOUR EYE
All the resentment,
My bitterness
All the hurts and pains
And unforgiveness
Buried, imprisoned
In the corners of my mind
Cobwebs, tangled and
Torn bits worn in and
Edged and etched in
A hardened mass
Turning and twisting

And snarling, biting
Envy and pain
Reviling, unfeeling
In hardened heart
Taunting me
Over and over again.
With one tear
And a choke of words
That you spoke
I knew you had suffered as I.
God in His wisdom
Freed me from my prison,
When I saw the tears in your eyes.
For I so wanted to hold you
And dry the tears
And heal the hurts
In your heart.
For something much
Bigger than my pain
God's love in me over came.

Venetia Dawn Davison
SEPTEMBER
Help me
I'm changing again
Just like the leaves
in September
I ask
"Whose leaves are these?"

Whose leaves are these?
orange, gold and red
scattered on the ground
like the skin I'm shedding
Whose leaves are these?

Whose leaves are these?
I said aloud, at last
Call forth the wind
Let him sweep my past
away from me
So I don't have to ask
Whose leaves are these?

Marian Kiler Hall
I Was Born On a Stormy Night
I was born on a stormy night
'Midst lightning flash and
  thunder roar.
Howling wind and rain and sleet
Foretold my life that lay before.

I travelled the seas, I laughed at
  the waves
Pounding the bow, engulfing the
  ship.
Typhoon, earthquake, desert heat,
I've taken a taste, I've had a sip.

I've flown a plane to hunt wild
  game,
And followed the course of the
  Amazon.
I've lost myself in the elements
And come forth when the storm
  had gone.

But this is only poetry
And not a line is right
Except the first which you have
  read:
"I was born on a stormy night."

Janet Phelps-LaComb
TWO IN LOVE
Two People
Alike in many ways
Yet so different.
In two worlds
One hell
One paradize.
In two lives
One surviving
One living.

With two gods
One good
One bad.
Yet as different as they are
As far apart as they are
They are close.
Together.
One.
They are
In love.

LeVon-ninsky Von Hardin
There Is No Such Thing As "Luck"
"Man in his weak efforts to
  overthrow the law, beings upon
  himself such sufferings that he
  is almost compelled to seek
  wisdom, and in finding
  wisdom, *he finds love, and
  recognize it as the law of being,
  the law of the universe.*

The thoughtless, the ignorant,
  and the lazy man, seeing only
  the effects of things, and the
  things themselves upon seeing
  another man prosper, *talk of
  luck, of fortune, and chance.*
  Seeing a man who has become
  very knowledgeable with
  wisdom, they say how blessed
  he is. Observing another man
  with the ability to produce
  effects, they say how fortune
  assist him. Yet, these men have
  not seen the *trials*, and
  tribulations, the *struggles* in
  which these men have had to
  undertake in order to gain their
  experience. They have no
  knowledge of the sacrifices
  these men have made. The
  efforts they have put forth, and
  the faith they have exercised.
  They do not know the
  darkness, and heartaches that
  these men have endured. They
  only recognize the results, and
  they call it chance . . .

In all human affairs there are
  efforts, and there are *results.*
  Chance is not . . . Gifts, be
  them, *power, material,
  intellectual,* or *spiritual* are the
  results of efforts, and into each
  man's hands shall be placed the
  exact result of his thoughts. For
  he will always gravitate toward
  that which he most love, and
  he will receive . . . He will
  either fall, remain as he is, or
  rise with his thoughts, his
  visons, and his ideals."

There is no such thing as "Luck"

Leslie N. Phillips
Confusion and Problems
  Have you ever been so confused,
you don't know what to do?
  There isn't a way to turn,
nowhere to go to.
  Your sacred,
  Your broken,
  Your heart's fallen into your feet.
  Now you just can't go back,
  there's no way to retreat.
  You can't see the end,
it surrounds you more and more.
  You wish that you could stop,
and open up that door.

You sit and cry,
as your life flies by.
You don't care what you do.
You try and promise yourself,
that it will stop but . . .
There's always something new!

Diane Michaels
TODAY
I bowled a good
  game—Today;
I did the best
  —I could.
I aimed 'em,
  and I got 'em,
Down the alley
  —smackin' wood!

My score was
  never higher,
With lots
  of strikes
  and spares!
If I should
  'foul it up'
Tomorrow
  —Who cares?

Barbara Merrill
SEA SHROUD
The rolling sea . . .
Blanket of the dead,
Thundering in to the shore!
Would that I
Could sink in your depths,
And rise to the surface no
  more . . .

Let not this earth
Be my shroud,
When the Grim Reaper calls for
  me!
Let me lie
On the ocean floor,
And be covered by the warm,
  warm sea!

Martha Johnson
Be My Valentine, Little Star Of Hope
Be my valentine little star of
  hope.
And follow me wherever I go.
You are my valentine,
You told me so.
And I am yours forever.
You came from afar,
On the wings of love and peace.
You flooded my soul with joy and
  happiness.
In my heart, you lit the candle of
  eternal love.
Glow! Glow! Glow!, forever, little
  star.
For you are my valentine.
Depart?
No. Never, no. never, never.
  You
  Are
  My
  Valentine.

Della Doherty
FROM MY WINDOW
In Springtime through the glass I
  see a robin in the willow tree.
He sings his song with joy and
  mirth, proclaims his praise of
  Gods green earth.

In summertime I sit and gaze and
  watch the children as they play.
They frolic on the vast green
  lawn, alas, their youth will
  soon be gone.

In Autumn through my window
pane I watch with sadness,
falling rain.
The leaves of amber, red and gold
paint a picture to behold.

Winter comes with beauty rare
with frost upon the trees now
bare.
The sun there on the snowbank
shines, the diamond crystals all
are mine.

I've watched the seasons come
and go with one I love and now
I know
I wouldn't trade my window view
for all the worldly gold. Would
you?

Karen Elizabeth Cibert
REFLECTIONS

---

*This poem was composed for my
fiancé, Steve DeLeon, who
inspired me just by being loving
and caring in every way.*

As the day begins to break
 I reflect upon the night
  The image comes to mind
Your arms around me tight

 Holding each other
 In a gentle embrace
 Emotions of love
 Etched upon your face

Your lips softly spoke
 Tender words of depth
My soul drank them in
With each and every breath

I cherish each moment with you
 And love you more each day
 It always warms my heart
  To dream of yesterday

Gail Tujague Moore
THE BIRTH
When the time was right the
 birthing was made.
In darkness and water creation
 was laid.
By hand, and word, moved
 chaotic matter
into order and beauty down
 heaven's ladder.

Below were waters which nursed
 and fed
the earth which was sleeping on a
 liquid bed
until ready to break when the
 time was right
for the birthing of one who would
 split the night.

When did his life end and begin?
At the slap, the cry, the tumult
 within?
The shift from father to cacooned
 child,
runged and tied by unknown trials.

The tears, unshed, cradled in joy
lay low and soft, sleeping like the
 boy
whose peace on earth was yet
 unknown,
still in the hands of the father
 alone.

Between heaven and earth was
 love labored down
from the birth of dawn to the son

of man
to lay the foundation in the dark
 of night
until ready to break when the
 time was right.

Pamela Yoshino Tagami
DREAMERS NEVER DIE
You changed my life—
touched my soul;
You showed me love—
forever to hold;
You built the confidence—
stored the faith;
You showed me stars—
only dreams await;
You held my hand—
and smiled sweetly;
You stayed with me—
and gave completely;
You made the laughter—
the tears went away;
You fought the pain—
and watched it fade;
You gave your all—
only to die;
You gave me everything—
so why can't I;
Share it all with you?

Louise Shannon Monteverde
CHRISTMAS LOVE
What will Christmas offer to you
What will you give in return?
Will your heart be kind and true
Turning to someone less
 fortunate that you?
Will your heart be open to receive
A friend who needs a friend?
A hand extended to a needy friend
Is the heart Christmas Love lives
in.

Jeanne Diane Kimura
THANK-YOU
If I'm kind and thoughtful
 with people I know.
If I'm loving, and don't mind
 letting it show.
If I take delight in
 helping a friend.
If I'm soft and gentle,
 and willing to bend.
If my plans are well thought-out
 before I begin.
If I'm eager to play, but,
 not necessarily to win.
If I'm honest and truthful
 in all that I do.
If my husband and I
 are one, not two.
If I can laugh when I'm happy,
 and, cry when I'm sad,
It's all because of
 you— MOM and DAD.
THANK-YOU!

Billy F. Hicks
BLESSED ARE THEY
Blessed are they who understand
 my faltering step and palsied
 hand.
Blessed are they who know that
 my ears today
 must strain to catch the things
 they say.
Blessed are they that seem to
 know that
 my eyes are dim and my wits are
 slow,
Blessed are they who looked
 away

when coffee spilled at the table
 today.
Blessed are they with a cheery
 smile
 who stop to chat for a little while.
Blessed are they who never say,
 "You've told that story twice
 today".

Blessed are they who know the
 ways
 to bring back memories of
 yesterday.
Blessed are they who make it
 known
 that I'm loved, respected, and
 not alone.

Blessed are they who know I'm at
 a loss
 to find the strength to carry a
 cross.
Blessed are those who ease the
 days
 on my journey Home in loving
 ways.

Audrey Lawrence

Audrey Lawrence
LIFE'S ROAD

To Stanley

Life's road is like a river
Wending its way to the sea
Ever traveling, traveling
To its place of destiny.

The river is sometimes rough
Tossing its cargo about
Again the river is peaceful
Safe landing then seems no doubt.

So it is on the road of life
Soon we'll put out to sea
Braver we ride the storm
Smoother the landing will be.

Nina LaGrassa
THE CIRCUS
A tightrope walker with acute
 acrophobia
Precariously proceeds in a
 darkened room without a net.
Clowns with painted personas
Cry silently behind their facades,
 adjusting their smiles.
Frozen with bravado, the blonde
 target
Escapes damnation as blades
 circumscribe her.
The sword swallower practices
 mechanically,
Never questioning the merits of

his forte.
There is no rest for the juggler,
Nor the acrobat whose one miss
 precipitates collapse.
Treacherous tigers, wakened from
 cat naps
Wait for the moment to pounce.
The big top has never held much
 allure for me.
Too much of the circus goes on
 beyond its parameters.

Philip Kae
A WALK WITH GOD
One morning I walked down the
 floral lane
Of a fragrant meadow brilliantly
 green
Birds were singing their songs of
 joy and play
As birds do with the break of
 every day.

The sun was just rising beyond
 the hills
Casting golden rays to dispel the
 chills
And the shrinking shadows of
 bush and tree
Lifted me with the sense of being
 free.

I came upon a winding, babbling
 brook
Gurgling infinitely through crane
 and nook
Rolling down mountainside and
 shady lee
And bubbling with laughter so
 merrily.

Two little birds perched on the
 tip of a bough
Swaying in the gentle breeze to
 and fro
With breath-taking joy I watched
 them above
Flipping their wings and tweet
 tweeting with love.

The meadow, the flowers, the
 majestic trees
The brook, the ruffled birds
 swaying in the breeze
Everything I saw, everything I
 heard
Proclaimed the glory of a loving
 GOD!

Vicky M. Semones
PISCES

---

*For B.B., my "companion in life's
fleeting song."*

In Maui, I began to love again
 with surety and constancy
as cooling Pacific waves
 unfolded subtly.

With eternity before me
 —a perfect horizon in blue—
I tempted the currents
 demeanor.
 (uncertain steps would
 construe.)

Coral beneath — a camouflaged
 pain—
 awaiting a tender touch;
the crystal depth beckoned my
 love
and we merged in its gentle
 rush.

342

Our World's Best Loved Poems

Flaoting with my lover
through the velvet brine,
the tide urged us shoreward
to greet the gritty sand, supine.

Frances Clark Handler, PH.D.
Hark the Herald Angels Sing!

Hark the Herald Angels sing,
For Christmas Day is a Holy thing!
Peace on earth—Goodwill toward
men,
That is our plea now—as it was
then!
Love and Peace ever our goal!
But the prayer must come from
within our soul!
Hark the Herald Angels sing,
For Christmas Day is a Holy thing!

Miss Mary Jane Dennis
Tribute To Seed Time and Harvest Time

To hold in remembrance: Fifty Years of Memories Comprising Father, Mother, Family, and Farm Behalf Seed-Times and Harvest-Times (1932-1982).

Father rode a planter, dropping
corn seed in the ground,
Then with care did cultivate to
make a crop abound.
Mother brought out pumpkin
seeds, for planting with the
corn,
Knowing that in harvest they
would well the field adorn.

Father viewed his ripened corn,
some prize-sized ears to find,
He was satisfied to see it yielded
hybrid kind.
Mother saw the pumpkins,
golden-ready for some pies,
She picked out a couple that she
knew to be right size.

Father worked at harvesting and
bringing in the crop,
With these tasks unfinished, it
was better not to stop.
Mother mixed ingredients, some
pumpkin pies to make,
Oh, the spicy sweetness that
prevailed while they did bake!

Father knew the storaged grain
would help supply some need,
Silently, he thanked the Lord for
blessing planted seed.
Mother set the pumpkin pies
where eye could meet the view,
Later, she would put away some
seeds for next year, too.

Father felt so weary, "Could he
plant just one field more?"
"No," the Reaper whispered;
"Come with Me to heaven's
shore."
Mother saw the Reaper coming,
still she made her pies,
Soon she too was brought in for
that home beyond the skies.

Father saw the ripened corn his
Maker did bestow,
Silently, he thanked the Lord, his
gratitude to show.
Mother saved some pumpkin
seed, bequeathing all to know,

For a golden harvest, what we
reap, we first must sow!

Vicky M. Semones
HOLLY AND A ROSE

To Rosanne and "the group" for sharing life's transitions . . .

true beauty are in those—

winter has beckoned
from golden, leafy throngs
evergreen and berries
to nestle near a sweeter song
with perfume edging
the breathy cold
entering the new year
with a garland to hold
as gray light flickers
beyond our reason
a single image endures
through this season—

Holly and a rose,
true beauty are in those.

Robert R. Weetman
THE REAPER
"Cheat death"? cried the reaper,
It's never been done.
I harvest my crop all year long.
Don't be foolish to think
You can now cheat on me.
Remember! I'm always around.
So saying he left me,
With those somber words,
Now I'm older,
And know he is right.
For this shell that I live in
Has now cast it's seed.
And the pod must return
To the soil.

Sandra L. Haight
MIDGET

In memory of Midget, the "Mighty Dog", who won the hearts of everyone who met her.

A cute little dog that once was all
black—
Is aging now, but energy she
certainly does not lack—
Her eyes at times pierce—
And her little bark is anything
but fierce!
She's small and she's soft, and so
full of love
She's a perfect gift from up above.
She has brought love to three
masters in her own special
way—
She's a gift from heaven—here for
a stay.
She bites at her nails
And wags her tail
One has to laugh when she
makes her bed.
But no one can teach her to play
dead.
God made her like a little toy—
Knowing full well all the people
to whom she'd bring joy.

Sarah J. Nickel
No Singing In Gethsemane
The night was dark, the air was
cold.
Sunk deep in prayer, he made his
plea

So bold, and yet so fragmented,
For death, for life; the Father's will
Was what he wanted,
Yearned for; still
There was no singing in
Gethsemane.

The hours passed, the nighttime
waned.
And yet he knelt, absorbed in
prayer
And pain, in sighs too deep for
words
For him, for them, for what would
be—
The longed-for song
About to start;
But still no singing in
Gethsemane.

As dawn approached, the stars
winked out.
And finally from the ground he
stretched
And let a shout of triumph slowly
Burst the barriers, win the fight.
The battle o'er,
The song began.
There was no singing in
Gethsemane.

Hamilton Lee
Mother's Telepathic Word
From your letter I know you
reside in a place
where you can live a life in peace
and at a pace
for which you've aspired, so as to
reach
the supreme goal by your earnest
search.

Though the sea now separates us,
yet, our hearts always feel close.
Often beholding the southeast
direction
I seem to feel your presence via
telepathic communication

Kecia Wolfe
MY DREAM

I dedicate this poem to all people on Earth. For us to struggle for peace instead of power.

I have a dream,
a very special dream.
My dream is to bring
humanity back into people.

To me, people are very special,
They are the smartest animals
on earth, so people say.

But if people are so smart,
why is there crime, poverty,
and destruction?

In my dream, I am the leader.
Not a king or tyrant,
Just someone to show people the
way.

But what if the world were
perfect?
Would we actually like it?
Could we keep it perfect?
Probably not, for people aren't
perfect.

We're just another of God's
creatures.
And that's what makes us so
special.

And even though my dream is way
beyond reality,
I believe with a little
determination,
my dream could come true.

Sheri Ann White
TRADITION AS PROGRESS
Amidst complexities of
calculated computes and
configurated results to
ironically self-made modernday
dilemmas; among analyses of
missile strength and dissection
of the human condition;
surrounded by futuristic metal
minds making mankind's
destruction a new art form;
encompassed by probes of
morals and nightmares that,
unlike simple dreams anymore,
come true; encircled by a
raffled cosmos where the only
rules are winner-take-all and
don't block the trafficking
progress—the poet still writes.

Stan Butcher
PAUL BUNYAN
Paul Bunyan was a big tall man
Some fifty feet they say,
And Babe his big blue ox could eat
A barn of hay a day.

A lumberjack who with a whack
Of his huge ax could fell
All trees that stood within the
woods
A mile or so, they tell.

He roamed about the great
Northwoods
From Maine to Idaho
Searching for a woman
Who was near his size, you know.

In all his travels back and forth
He never found a wife
And so it was his destiny
To live a lonely life.

Some people think it's just a
myth—
No man could grow so tall
To walk the land with such an ox
Unless his name was Paul.

Just look in Minnesota
And Montana bleak and bare—
What other proof do you demand
that Paul Bunyan was there?

Ellie Connelly
God's World—Not Man's
The world is really quite large,
And yet it's so very small—
God created Man—
And Man created weapons,
Weapons can destroy Man—but
Man can change Man's mistake—,
But, will he—before it's too late—
Before he ends us all,
And all around us ends?

Faith Constance Howard
THE TREES AND I
God gave me trees so tall and
straight
To teach me to be strong;
That though the battle's hardest
And the pain and grief are long
To walk unbowed-unbeaten—
Though there isn't any song.
God gave me little willows
By a tiny pool of glass;

343

That rippled as the summer breeze
Let the sunshine pass
And there, beside the waters edge,
My dreams with theirs I cast.
God gave me poplars grace and
charm
That shimmered in the sun;
That caught my hungry happy
heart
When all my dreams were done
And tossed some stardust back to
earth.
To face the shining sun.
God gave me boxwood by my door
With hedgerows trim and neat;
To keep my pathway straight and
true
And stay my rushing feet,
That though my way just dances
My life must be complete.
God gave me trees-ah yes—
And long I've watched and
known—
I've listened to their lullabies
To every chant and tone—
And God I've seen the shadows,
In the dark-and all alone.
So teach me to be strong and brave
When the best is not for me,
And teach me to accept my lot
Although it's hard to see
The sunshine there along my
way
As it is upon your tree.
And teach me to be patient
With the trees at evenfall,
For when my heart is singing
Just like a star 'twill fall;
And be buried with my hopes and
dreams
But still-must stand quite tall.

Cheryl Gengery Zaccagnino
LIFE

---

*To my parents, Nick & Carolyn
Gingery, who gave me so much
love and support.*

Let me flow down a mountain top
with my water pushing fast and
free.

Let salmon swim up my stream
fighting for a place to spon their
young.

Let grass grow tall and free by me
and I will quench each blade with
my cool sweet waters.

Let me last forever and a day,
with new horizons dawning.
And branch myself into many
parts
and end in a pool below.

If these things were never done
and I could not branch out.
Or if the sun dried up my stream,
life would be much without.

Such is the meaning of life itself,
with people needing you.

For without you there would be
no life.

Mrs. Debbie Norris
MY LOVE
My love, I feel safe and
secure in your arms.
I am attracted
to your charms.

My love, I always think
you will leave me.
But, can't I see
you're right here with me.

My love, I love you
now and forever,
like I have never
loved anyone before.

My love, I hope you
love me as much as I love you.
Our days grow brighter
as our love grows stronger.

My love, may you
and I be very happy and
all our dreams come true.
My love, I love you!

Nico Boccio
THE ALCHEMIST
From an ancient world
an aged Alchemist sits with
conviction strong
that transcribes turning all dross
things into gold.
'Tis a tale oft told
wheather not we knew thus
prescribed rings true.
Reaching all caught in 20th
Century schemes.
Now is the Time for dreams!

Geri Koopsma
You and Your Children

---

*Dedicated to My three sons:
JODY, JIM and CHAD*

Being a parent as the years slip by
Not really noticing how the time
does fly
Then they are all in school one
day
And one is even at school away
While doing the dishes-as usually
Somehow the house is so empty
The peace and quiet that you
longed for before
Is here-along with time galore
A mothers mixed emotions that
come at this time!
"How come I'm not enjoying the
peace so sublime?"
You can still love them during
the day
Even when they've all gone away
For if your Love comes from
within your heart
You and they will never really be
apart.

Ann De Laney Spivey
STORM
In tormented skies
Ancient gods battle for
ascendency.
Vast cloud-armies clash;
Heavens are rent by the
thundering sounds
of flying, sparking hooves
Driving across a blackened,
roiling sky-scape.

I sit safely inside my
house-cocoon,
Face pressed to sweating glass,
And watch this monumental war
among forces
I can only dimly envisage . . .

But in my secret heart,
I long to escape from passive

security
And dash into the slashing
knives of rain,
To become one with the raw,
unleashed power
Of the elemental deities.

Harold R. Bell
TOO BUSY
"I Like to be busy,"
So often we hear one say.
It helps to pass the time
To bring another day.

But sometimes, we get so involved
In so many ways and things,
We often wish we were a bird
And could fly away with wings.

We have to be here it seems,
And then its time for there.
How can we ever do it all
And still have time to spare?

But the time keeps moving on;
And we haven't accomplished
much,
Not even time for those we love
And with whom to be in touch.

If we could come to realize
There is just no way to win
When we take it upon ourselves
To spread ourselves so thin.

Dorothy J. Nelson
Potter County's Tall Indian
Can you hear the echoes across
the hills tonight
Indian you were so very tall
Over seven feet they say,
I can see your open grave,
looks so dark and lonely there.
Someone removed you from your
resting place,
Big bolders still lay on top of the
mound,
Around the emptyness that once
held you.
Tall Indian did they take from
your sacrifice pit too,
all the treasures your loved ones
sent with you,
Or did they want only your bones,
To prove Potter County Indians
grow tall,
Over seven feet you were,
Tall Indian where ever you are
tonight,
Can you hear the echoes across
the hills
you were buried between the
Genesee Valley and the
Oswayo Valley,
Just one mile from rose Lake

On the highest point, so the
water wouldn't touch you,
Can you hear the rustling of the
leaves in the fall?
And the birds that sang that last
farewell to you so long ago,
Can you forgive the greedy souls
that took you away,
Rest in peace tall Indian, where
ever you are tonight,
Soon your empty grave will be
covered by a white blanket of
snow again.

Norma Hardin
UNTITLED

---

*Inspired by God Dedicated to
Paul Johns*

Love is the warm cloak of God,
Let no man fear to wear it.

Love is the food of the heart,
Let no man fear to share it.

Love is the candle of the soul,
Let no man fear to light it.

Love is the voice of God,
Let no man fear to hear it.

Love is God's most precious gift,
Let no man fear to accept it.

Jannice Leah Flick
WONDERING
Many nights I sit alone
No one visits me at my home,
They're too busy to even give me
a ring
When they do it's about some
unimportant thing.
I have plenty of time to dine and
dance
But I rarely ever get the chance.
I think I'll change in just one way
I'll live my life from day to day,
Doing whatever makes me happy
at that moment
Not worrying about a single
comment,
This will probably leave me
wondering why
But chances are good I won't feel
the need to cry.

Denise Knott
REFLECTION
I want so much to let you see
how deep my love does flow
But God dealt the cards
darn, life is hard
Why did you have to go?

I never told you how much I care
the way I really feel
Now it's too late
I see you can't stop fate
Now, I know I never will

One doesn't realize what he's got
untill it's been taken away
Now this hurting pain
and my tears like rain
Make me realize what I wanted
to say

I wonder if you can hear me
now that we are so far apart
I never told you
you were my world
I loved you with all of my heart

I only hope God loves you too
as much as I did Dad

Our World's Best Loved Poems

I'll never regret
and I'll never forget
all the memories that we had.

Dolores Q. Canapi
I Took My Children On a Trip and Lost Them
'Been quite sometime—
Haven't heard of them nor from them
No presence felt nor shadowy glimpses;
Since I took my children on a trip—
And lost them.

Overcome and alone, I stare at the phone
And painfully strain for sounds,
Hoping it rings very soon;
But deafening silence reigns,
As I sit alone, resigned to nary a tone.

Resolve must I, to ne'er strain for tones and shadows?
Just listen as the clock ticks time away?
For my life's clock is pretty close to six o'clock
And when it does—
Smothered are all hopes and cares;

Should on this trip, they be above the world,
Then cherished reward is the loss
And nil is the need to pine and search!
For I took my children on a trip
And lost them.

Marian Kreger
THE SEQUEL
Just thought you might like to know,
A short rhyme of mine
Has been published in "Today's Greatest Poems."
Now isn't that fine?
I just might take heart,
And try it again.

When you come to my home,
I will point to you the page
Where you can read my name
Above a few lines by the sage.

Now, now, don't get excited,—
Mine is naught, compared to some:
Just some-what special you see
For little ol' me!

Marie Hart
THE SIMPLE THINGS
Give me a flower
to wear in my hair,
with a smell so sweet
to flow through the air
Give me a scarf
of turquoise, and gold
to wear cross my shoulders
whenever I'm cold.
The simple things
bring me joy.
A candied apple,
a child's toy.
I ask not for very much
A subtle smile,
a gentle touch.
Give me a candle
of soft golden light,
to sit by my mirror
and brighten my night.
Give me your love
as I give mine to you.

The most priceless gift
anyone ever knew.

Gerald F. Coppola
PATIENCE
A fever grips his body
Its Origin Unknown
The Physicians work together
To stop his pain from Growing

He wakes up in the morning
Not knowing what He's done
The Hospital is hopeful
the virus is on the Run

He returns home on a Thursday
On rest he will be weaned
He feels his body weakened
And he Can't fulfill His needs

The time is passing slowly
His thoughts are on return
to the life he practiced last week
before the evil came

Holly Ann Boettcher
SNOWY WONDER
The still of death on nature falls,
And quiet sounds of winter call.
Waiting for a chance to make
The earth a bed in soft snowflakes.
Covering that of a sleepy sight,
That with a blanket of frosty white.

The falling of snow so softly laid,
Quickly takes over as the darkness fades.
Turning the sky a dusty white
Making the nights so shimmering bright.
Spreading her plenty wherever she goes,
Leaving us with dreams of Christmas snow.

Lisa Niccum Phelps
TIME TO APPEAR

I wish to dedicate this poem to my newborn son, Alan Marcus Phelps. Nine thirty-five a.m. on February 6, 1984 was his "time to appear."

Babies laugh and sometimes cry
It makes you often wonder why.
They push and move to let you know
That in your body they still grow
The last few months linger on
as to create a stronger bond.
The little body you finally hold
Is that of yours to always behold.

Iris Ward
ASTROLOGY
Astrology is one of man's oldest sciences
It has survived thousands of years
For good reason humans corespond according to cycles
The cycles of the Stars and Planets
Astrology is only a part an indicator of the human condition
Primary forces in a natal chart are the Sun, Moon and ascending sign
Each has particular meanings according to the House and sign they are in
The Sun basic character of the individual needs

To feel fulfilled, recognized and important
The Moon referred to as the subconscious mind relating to the past
Childhood conditioning, instinctive patterns, feelings and inner nature
Ascendent how you project yourself
The window through which you see the World and the
World sees you
It's the mask you wear before others.

Rosemary Cormick
A PRAIRIE DAY

Dedicated, with love and best wishes, to my sister, Robbin Frazer, to Uncle James and to nature lovers everywhere.

A glorious morn has just begun:
A snowdrop opens to the sun,
Bird-song floats upon the breeze
That softly whispers through the trees.

The brook is filled with melting snow
As tramping through the fields I go.
Oh glorious morn!—with sun on high—
My eyes upturned to bluest sky.

What holds this day as it unfolds
Its treasures rare as shining gold?
Life is precious, and well I know
This prairie day will prove it so.

Ruth Powell
Everything Is Going Up They Say
But there's no charge for flowers
Blooming near the door
There's no price on sunshine
And birds' songs cost no more.

The rain is coming DOWN
The price of joy is the same
And moonlight on the ocean
To low cost makes its claim

The wide blue sea and mountain tops
To gratis their claims lay
It costs no more to play or sing
The things that really matter cost
just the same today.

June Dawn Ferrier
GUIDED MEN
God, Grant us your Heavenly guidance as war threatens our land once again,
For more than bombs and missiles, what we need is strong "Guided Men."
God, please show us where we are all going; please show us where we have gone wrong.
Stir us, and wake up the faith in our souls;
Renew our love in mankind, lead us to higher goals.
Teach us to cherish the peaceful Earth you gave us.
Take our greed and our hate to destroy.
Teach us to all join hands in brotherly love, and make Earth

a place to enjoy.
Teach us that only through Thy grace, we can have peace on Earth and outer space.
Teach us to not go on vainly fighting, as we have in the years gone past.
They were only many empty victories and a peace that would not last.
God, please give us strong "Guided Men" and be there when we call.
We don't need guided missiles and bombs, that will only kill us all.

Madeline J. Miller
OUR FIRST CHRISTMAS

To Margie and Bill Sacre

The tree is decorated, the fire before me burns,
And it is while I sit here, my thought of you returns.
As slowly we trimmed the tree, each icicle that we hung,
FIlled my heart with gladness and in it was sung,
A song of love we found not long ago,
With the touch of your hand and our first hello.
I hear you in the kitchen, the drinks are being made;
Then as we drink of the warming glasses, all cares just seem to fade.
This is my night to sit before the fire and have you next to me,
For on this evening, we share our love and our first Christmas tree.

Kris Hendrick
A Better Day
When winter's time approaches,
When shadows streak the sky,
Surrounded by the bleakness,
I start to wonder why.

I see life quickly changing
From future into past,
And wonder if the things I hold
So dear today will last.

I wonder if tomorrow
My progeny will see
A world where they can live at peace,
Or a world of agony.

I wonder if a God exists,
And if He really cares
About what's going on down here,
In man's corrupt affairs.

And then the sun comes shining through,
As if at last to say,
That Someone cares who's goal is set,
To bring a better day.

Grace Fox Macklin
Farewell To a Loved One
Gray and lifeless rests the sod
Upon the grave wherein he lies,
And lonely is one who lingers there
Tearfully dreaming of broken ties.

Blow ever gently, summer breeze,
Breathe softly as a sigh!

Play "fairy music" o'er the dead
As she whispers: "Dear heart,
goodbye".

If memories were wishes
Dreams would last forever!
If dreams could come true
Death no soul could sever.

Our heart's desire would be
A shield from grief's grim fear,
And love's ecstasy wouldn't yield
To a formal funeral bier.

Alma V. Schmitt
IS THERE A GOD
The morning sun
The moon and
Stars at night,
The flowers that bloom
The bird that sings
All these are lovely things,
Need we ask
"Is there a God?"

A new baby's cry
A child's sweet smile,
A look of faith
In wide eyes that shine,
A curly head
Just tucked in bed,
Need we ask
"Is there a God?"

A chapel bell
In the distance sounds,
Calling tired souls
That are discontent
With material things
That to us are lent,
The serenity we feel while in his
house
Need we ask
"Is there a God?"

We often wonder
As time goes by
Where are the answers?
We must have faith
And live each day
In such a way
We need never ask
"Is there a God"

Tim Kissell
Bob's Alcoholic Lament and Alibi
Don't remember
coming home
last night.
Must have
been to
drunk to
really care.
Anyway, I
don't do
that enough
to let
it upset
me or
to scare
me. I
guess I
have a
little brain
damage that
saves me.

Cheryl Warren Cooley
TRAPPED
Trapped inside this prison I've
created for myself,
I trade each fleeting emotion for
another,
Trying each one on like a hat;

Trying to find one that fits—
One I can live with.

I am hot and cold emotion
All bundled up and neatly tied
With frayed nerves that have
raveled like old rope.

My guilt plays upon me cruelly
Knotting up inside me until
I feel like I'll be drowned by the
wave of it.
And then, it creeps silently back
like a receding tide,
So that I feel almost human again.

I spend so much time
concentrating on them,
That I often stumble blindly over
now;
And almost never can I visualize
tomorrow.
But never will I forget that for
one night
I possessed you completely.
Every fibre, every nerve, every bit
of you was mine
—And no one can take that from
me, no matter what
form of attack they might pursue
For that night belongs to me, to
you, and to eternity.

Daisy-Shipley-Benson

Daisy-Shipley-Benson
OUR MOTHER

*To our dear mother—Margret D.
Shipley by Daisy Shipley-Benson*

She was our mother, the one who
cared.
She washed our face and dried
our tears.
She would tell us daily, "Do what
you are told"

Her motto was from day to day,
Trust in the Lord in every way.
He will guide you through, when
your hopes are low.
This our dear mother really did
know.

She was a mother to all neighbors
and friends.
When it came to her help there
was no end.
If it was in the church or in our
home,
My mother was there we were
never alone.

Her work was important and hard
to do.

But she never said, "I can't help
you"
She lived her life helping others,
That is why we love our dear
mother.

Michael P. Curran
TEACUPS
The teacups ran around
With the same old bags
Sophisticating, up and down,
"Another shall we have?"
"Yes, do, another if you please,"
With the same worn leaves
(From auto-borrowed biographies
Raked up to burn the dead,
Feigning fear that plague would
spread)
Turned about, tea timed out.

Rounding up tales of has-beens
who
Never were the way the ladies
don't quite say they were,
They shudder to think of the
things they think of every day,
Stirring their afternoons away
On nights they never lived.

All curdle cud-dled in
conversation—
Each dragged to the bottom of the
cup
To be again and again brought up.

Jean Proudian-Brown
A SPECIAL FRIEND

To my mom, for being who she is.

I met a girl, she was seventeen
I grew to love and trust her
A babe in arms, one by her side
Both of them were daughters.

Nineteen came, a son was born
Much to the relief of his father
By twenty-four the final count
A son, and five fine daughters.

Up at dawn most every day
And once most every night
Asthma attacks, soaring temps.,
And breaking up their fights.

She studied hard to graduate
She earned an associate degree
Taught her children how to love
And about the birds and bees.

Weeks have gone, years have
passed
Her children have all grown
All have gone their seperate ways
But weekends they still phone.

I met a girl, she was seventeen
There is no other like her
I tell you now, I wouldn't lie
I am the second daughter.

Jacqueline Dunigan
God Made Dandelions For Brian
To think a couple years ago
I envied other people so
Whose lives and grass appeared
so green . . .
But much has happened in
between.
Oh, THEY still have the perfect
grass,
Symbolic of their upper class—
And though my lawn lacks
finished art

I still have got the better part
For dandelions grow and bloom
In wild array, dispelling gloom.
And crabgrass, you have lost your
mean
Since Brian came upon the scene.
He looks with wonder at the
view
And beaming saya "A flower for
you".
I think that he's the one that's wise
With so much love in such small
size.
He's turned to sunshine darkest
hours
And has proven there are flower
powers.
So weed-be-gone stay in the store
Cause here comes Brian in the
door
With fistful of the golden weed.
My life is very rich indeed!

Ruby M. Mills
Thanksgiving-Christmas

*To Forest, whose mini sermon
supplied the title, and was the
inspiration that demanded my
poem be written.*

From Thanksgiving to Christmas
is a time of preparation
When Christians the world over
join in celebration
Of the birth of Jesus our Saviour
and Lord
Whom God sent to earth to make
of one accord,
All peoples and nations the
whole world round.
His plan was for love and peace
to abound.

Some people believed but some of
them doubted.
Some sang His praises while
some of them shouted
"Crucify Him! Crucify Him! He is
an imposter!
We don't want Him around! He's
not on our roster!"
They took and mocked Him and
beat Him, and then
Nailed Him to a cross between
two wicked men.

He died, was buried then arose
again.
Now He reigns forever in the
hearts of men
May true Christian love in our
hearts be found
That peace and good will on
earth may abound.
Let us all be thankful!
Celebration is here!
Let's have THANKSGIVING-
CHRISTMAS throughout the
whole year!

Mrs. Leona Boley
THE HEARTS HOME
Searching, seeking, ever so,
Beyond the hearthside fire,
Past the horizon's sunset glow
With heart dreams to inspire.
On highways of silver gleam—
Or byways of narrow stride.
The heart still follows a dream
Though it takes one world wide!

Aye, over a bountiful sea,
To a foreign shore.
Emerald mountains to the lee,
Above a far reaching floor.
Curving scrolled Cathedral spires
Tower over the fountained square.
Fulfilling the dream inspired
On a rolling plain so fair!

The searching heart still seeks a
    home,
Though far away it seems.
In seeking, one must roam,
To fulfill a dream.
Heart strings call it back again,
To the hearthside glow.
With the knowledge and the pain
The heart's home to know!

Lucille Acker Sibley
STARDUST
Methinks the stardust sifted
    down to cover all the ground.
It glistened under moonlit beams
    and magic did abound,
As if some fairy wand at night
    had bathed it in ethereal light.
I held my breath in sheer delight
    expecting elf and woodland
    sprite.
The facets of a million gems
    sparkling all around
Could not give off the magic of
    dewdrops on the ground,
Twinkling back to heaven like
    jewels in a crown.

Mavis Powell Mixon
TALK TO ME MAMA

*(I dedicate this poem to my
beautiful and beloved Mother,
Gulma Bernice Powell, Whose
love is like none other.)
(March 19, 1909—Jan. 18, 1984.)*

Talk to me, Mama, I hear your
    voice,
    Though many a step you've trod.
You're within these walls, please
    talk, Mama,
    Even though you now live with
    God.

I hear you, Mama, in your
    rocking chair,
    It squeaks as you slowly rock.
It seems so real, I can hear it
    creak,
    Keep rocking, Mama, please
    don't stop!

Your soft clean gown smells of
    ivory snow,
Hold me, Mama, like you use to
    do.
Put my head upon your soft
    shoulder,
    And hug me like I want you to.

Sing to me, Mama, I hear your
    voice,
I promise I will not cry.
Humme a tune and sing a few
    words,
    From your favorite, Brahm's
    Lullabye.

You're living, Mama, within my
    heart,
    And I sense the touch of your
    hand.
I cried, though you had to leave

me, Mama,
    For your walk to the Promised
    Land!

Harry L. Eriksen
CARING

*This verse is dedicated to my
loving family and to all my caring
friends who helped pull me
through a very trying time in my
life and the inspiration of my
special lady, Gini.*

Caring is a tenderword;
Perhaps a smile or tear
That helps to heal an aching heart
Or calm some awful fear.

Caring is a true gift from above
When you show that you love.

Your the real winner in the end
When you've helped a neighbor;
    made a friend.
It's part of you that you are sharing
When you help someone by
    CARING.

Antoinette M. Silvestro
CARING
When things seem to be going all
    wrong,
    Remember that they won't be
    that way for very long.

Also, remember this—
    There is someone who cares a
    great deal about you
And always wants to be near you.
Someone who never wants to see
    you sad
And who you can talk to when
    things go bad.

Just remember one other little
    thing—
    That the someone who cares a
    great deal about you
Is me.

Doreen M. Floyd
ANGER
Does everyone want to be the
    Arrow?
Or, march to a different drummer?
And when I hear music, can't I sing?
Why must I be the hummer?

All my dreams and expectations
Beat strong within my breast,
But there are all the people
Who must put one to the test.

Can't you take me as I am?
Show me one without flaw,
And I will surely give him his due
And stand stupidly in awe.

Harness not the thoughts that flow
From me, for they alone are mine.
And tho you know so much more,
I withstand the test of time.

Beth Kincaid
THE OLD BARN
The old barn stood in sad decay,
So lonely and quiet within,
The outside boards were all
    weathered and gray,
The roof was of rusty old tin.

The weeds had grown high, the
    gate blown down,
A door sagged from only one hinge,
Its big old mouth yawned open
    wide,

Where the teams and the wagons
    went in.

The broken pane in a window
    frame,
Glistened like a tear in its eye,
A silo that stood reaching up to
    the sky,
Spoke well of an era gone by.

The old barn sighed, it gave a
    groan,
Over memories of a time long
    gone,
Where once it was painted and
    full of life,
Now its usefulness over and done.

Marjorie L. Tish
THE LASTING KIND
Love is more than a look of lust
to be tossed all over the place
it needs to be nourished in
    someone's heart
to show on that person's face.
You dare not take—or bribe to
    get—
and expect to keep it long
it comes in a flash of a friendly
    smile
and the hum of a happy song.
It's there to count on every hour
when days are rough with care.
It's standing by and helping out
for loving means to share!
You laugh and live, and love and
    give
and by chance in quick surprise
You'll see your love reflected
in another person's eyes!

Diana M. De La Cruz
LAURA
As words poured from her lips
The glaze of water slowly slipped,
    (from her eyes)
As she told her scares of life
And her struggle to survive.
She passed the chains and the
    knifes
Which we never see through life.
This child which was at short
    breath
Seemed to be running; with depth.
"Did my ears deceive what I had
    heard?"
These were more than child's
    words.
They were crys of a child bleeding
From lashes of so many beatings.
"How was I, to mend the wounds
Of scares left by one soul brute"?
Her hands she raised to her lips
Afraid of gestures meant to whip.
Her eyes wondering somewhere
Alone and scared, wanting life
    (to be fair).

April Brantley
OUR SONG
As I sit here thinking of you and
    me
    I remember our special song
the one that seemed so peaceful
    that made our love last long
The first time I heard it we danced
    the second time we kissed
then I remember the confusion
    and all the things we missed
There is no way to sew
    my bleeding broken heart
the one that always loved you
    from the very start

I always cry when I hear it
    but I really don't know why
I just can't hold back all those
    tears
    even though I really try
Once in awhile our song still plays
    in my heart it will always belong
and no matter what else happens
    it will always be our song

Robin J. Carvalho
CONFORMITY

*For my family—who has let me
be me.*

First they make you conform
Then you want to conform
Then you have to conform
And the next thing you know
You are so much a part
Of the pattern,
That nobody sees you
Anymore.
Yet all this while
You secretly cry out
I am different.
I am an individual
Look at me.
Hear what I say.
But alas: your pleas
Fall on deaf ears.
But I cry out to you,
I see and I hear
And I too cry out,
I am different.
I am an individual.
Thus we are one,
For we are different.

Anita W. Kuesel
MY INLAND OCEAN
    There was an ice age long ago
that left a gift for all to know.
    Through endless days and
    months and years,
Through lives of joy and some of
    tears
    It's had a place in many hearts,
And carried ships to many parts.
    If you are from the middle-west.
Like me you have a lake that's
    "best."
    Its very name rolls like a wave—
That's "Michigan" for sailors brave.
    Sometimes obscured by fog and
    mist,
It waits with patience to be kissed
    by golden mornings, golden days,
its beaches, cliffs and darkest
    caves.
Northeasters hurling waves to
    shore
seem to last forevermore—
    Until some early summer day,
begin to slow, then lose their way
    and gently foam upon the sand.
It's their surrender to the land.
    The skies then turn to azure blue
with sometime clouds of violet
    hue,
    and sometime clouds of purest
    white,
snow castles of enormous height!
    The water is a thousand shades
of deepest blue to dazzling jades,
    robins-egg and turquoise too,
with sparkling diamonds, quite a
    few.
    Let's hurry for the brush to paint

the awesome scene left by a Saint;
This wondrous sea of many
  moods,
all edged with cities, sand and
  woods.
God must have put it in this
  place
for more than just to fill a space.
He put it there for all to see,
He put it there for you and me.
Let's cherish it and not ask,
  "why?"
for we are only passing by.
Let's keep it for our children's
  child,
keep it clean and undefiled.
So much is said about the moon,
but, have you seen it light a dune?
Or, have you wakened just to see
a sunrise that's about to be?
I cannot tear my eyes away;
a flaming ball is in the bay.
It floods our world with life itself.
That moment now is on my shelf
of memories for years to come.
Lord, make me grateful for each
  one.

Edith Elaine Paparone
Where Love Has Taken Me

*To One who has loved and
always encouraged me with all
His heart.*

I have not dined with Kings
I have not lived with Angels
But I have climbed the stairway
  To a Royal Heaven

I have not bathed in Gold
I have not dressed in Silver
But I have clothed myself
  In the warmth of Love

I have not reached for the Moon
I have not touched the Sun
But I have found my way
  Through all Eternity

Patty Naglus
SO POETIC

*I dedicate this poem to Shawn
Hart, who taught me how to open
myself up, and express my
feelings. Since we moved apart
from each other, I began to write
poems to express my feeling, and
my pen became my good friend. I
love you Shawn. ME:*

My poems may be out of tack
I'm not of a poetic nature
I just write so exact
of my feelings and emotions

My expression are abrupt
My vocabulary so slight
I know what I want to say
and that is preciesely what I write.

Marilyn N. Hill
TENDER LEAVES
We are too weak to accept the
  truth, for it was written years
  ago,
The light of high noon's sun is
  not for tender leaves to know.
Despite the frail and fragile
  skin—tis interesting to see
That even the tenderest leaf must

deal with the sun's reality.
All can not hide away in shadows
  when the sun is high,
Many reach for the light, their
  tender faces to the sky.
So it is, that men like leaves,
  search for the truth they want
  to see
And in God's skies, find glimpses
  of all eternity;
With this truth, they gain in
  strength, more able on their
  way
Just like the leaf . . . exposed to
  sun, grows stronger day by day.

Ilah Notestine
ALPHA OMEGA
ALPHA
Alarm rings
Get up.
Walk around the bed,
Stumble over pup.
Open bedroom door,
Air is cold.
Grope way to stairs,
Bannister take hold.
Flip light switch on,
Rub both eyes.
Take quick shower,
Time flies!
Sip hot coffee,
Burn tongue
This is the way my day begun.

OMEGA
Pick up clothes,
Hamper full
Click off T.V.
What a lull!
Put wood in stove
Check the draft.
Lock the doors,
Both fore and aft.
Put on P.J.'s
Apply night cream.
Messiest bathroom
Ever I've seen!
Clean towel on rack,
Call man's best friend.
Turn out the lights.
My day's at its end . . .
Then pray to the One
Upon Whom I depend.
Amen and Amen

Connie Nunn
THAT SPECIAL NIGHT
Do you remember the night we
  were alone?
The night you said you wanted
  me for your own?
Do you remember saying we'd be
  together forever?
Do you remember saying we'd
  never part, ever?
Do you remember the stars
  shining so bright,
making everything perfect that
  night?
That was the night we swore our
  love true,
The love that made me do
  something I swore I'd never do.
That was when I knew.
I knew our love would last.
Behind us, we put the past,
and started all anew.
We started our love fresh,
Just me and you.
Later on, many years from now,
We'll look back on the years

so pleasantly spent, saying
  without tact,
I LOVE YOU!

Ann Marie Nobach
SORRY
There is so much
I have to say,
But in my mind
I lack a way.
I know that
I've hurt you bad,
And jeopardized
The trust we had.
I'm afraid I've lost you
Just gave you away,
Because I tried
To love another way.
I won't blame you
If you send me away,
I know
I haven't the right to stay.
I want to make it up
To make this work,
I want to help you
Forget the hurt.
I don't know
What else to say,
But if you wish
I'll be on my way.

Patricia A. Wilburn
IT'S SUNDAY
It's Sunday, and Dad is waiting at
  the door with his cane.
As I get out of my car, Dad is
  already by the passenger door.
"Hi Dad", I say as I give him a big
  hug.
"You're right on time as usual
  Jenny" he says, returning the
  hug.
"Let's go to the drugstore before
  dinner, ok?" Dad asks.
Dad buys cigars and paperback
  westerns at the drugstore, then
  we're off to dinner,
Dad's choice.
It's important for Dad to get out
  of the "Home" occasionally, I
  like to buy Dad dinner,
it's the least I can do for him now.
Instead of going to my brother's
  house, Dad wants to go to my
  place.
That surprises me, Dad loves to
  visit his grandchildren, but I
  don't question his
request, we just go to my place.
Dad sits in Mom's rocker and
  smokes his cigar.
"Today is your Mother's
  anniversary" Dad says quietly.
"I remembered Dad, I bought
  some flowers for her, want to
  go now?" I asked.
Dad keeps on rocking and nods
  his head yes.
It's Sunday at 6:00 pm, we lay the
  flowers on Mom's grave.
Dad's wife of 40 years is now a
  memory within his mind, after
  2 years, he still cries.
I hold him while he cries, and I
  cry for both of them.
I take him back to the "Home", I
  talk aimlessly while I put his
  things away.
He looks contented this Sunday,
  he hugs me tightly and
  whispers, "I love you and James

very much, good night".
"We love you too Dad" I whisper
  back, trying not to cry.
I call my brother James and tell
  him about my Sunday with Dad.
James sounds dissapointed that
  Dad didn't want to come by,
  but says there is always
next Sunday.
It's Sunday, I am just drifting off
  to sleep, when the phone rings,
  "Could you come,
your Father has just passed away".
I lay back and cry softly, it's
  Sunday, Mom and Dad's
  anniversary.

Teresa Robinson Stolz
FREE
Your heart was like a bird,
  Eager to be free.

But I held you closer,
  Thinking just of me.

Couldn't bear the parting,
  Tried again in vain.

Wanting you to stay;
  Freedom called again.

Then I thought of you
  With love inside of me.

And with all my courage
  Finally set you free.

Nancy E. Hale
SECOND CHANCE
If only life would give us a
  second chance and rewind the
  spool . . .
Lessons learned from experience
  could be used as a corrective
  tool.

In our extreme youth, we must
  decide the path of life to take . .
  and
Because of inexperience, grievous
  mistakes do we sometimes
  make.

Events and decisions of the early
  years do a lifetime last . . . and
Future happiness can be clouded
  because of memories from the
  past.

So whatever shadows there might
  be in your life, push them
  away . . .
With faith and determination,
  the sunshine of joy can come
  to stay.

Raleigh E. Green ll
The Race For Your Love
There you stood with your
  beauty and charm.
Wrapped up in another man's
  arms.
  I couldn't hide the tears, as they
  ran down my face.
I suddenly realized, I had lost the
  race.
  The race for your love, I had
  futilely fought.
And had hoped I had won, but
  found I did not.
  What a crushing blow that sent
  to my heart.
He was fueling the flame I had
  hoped to start.
  But the race is all over, and I've
  gone away.

With his checkered flag, with you
he did stay.

Mavis M. Caldwell
The Beauty Of Our Garden
There's a beauty in the garden,
That most folk never see.
The soil in preparation,
And when she sets her captive
free.

Mother earth no longer holds
The magic seeds breaks through.
Natured by sun and rain,
And the early dew.

Each little plant has its own
beauty,
Tho how common this we see.
The onion has a blossom,
If you'll only let it be.

Look you good at golden squash,
And okra bloom a corsage could
be.
Morning glories add their colors,
This at sunrise you should see.

Look you good at kale and lettuce,
At miss mustard's curly green.
And even the pumpkin blossom,
Could be a flower for a queen.

Have you seen the tomatoes,
From pepper green to crimson red?
Or the tiny pear shaped ones,
Yellow in their green vine bed.

The harvest of turnips and
potatoes,
From their growth beneath the
sod.
The gardner pleased with their
production,
Said thank you God.

He knew mother nature helped
him,
Altho he had to toil.
Or he could have been a failure,
Even tho a genius of the soil.

Clyde W. Painton
TURN OFF, TURN ON
Turn off the hate, the cruel wars.
Turn on the peace of man we pray.
Turn off the violence and the pain;
Turn on the peaceful days again.

Turn off the ugly things of life
The bitter words, the endless strife;
Turn on the love that is a part
Of every normal human heart.

Turn off the coldness of our day
Turn on the people who can pray.
Turn off the evil deeds and fear
The bitter cries of hate we hear.

Turn off the slaughter of mankind
The hardness of the hearts so
blind.
Turn on the hearts filled with love.
Turn on the wisdom from above.

Turn on the beauty of our world
And let its banners be unfurled.
Let truth and justice supremely
reign
With peace and hope for all again.

Geraldine Miller
THANKSGIVING
A happy childhood a future
fortold
Love and marriage with mate of
purest gold.
Eternity in Heaven, what more is
there?
Nice to know I'm going but I like
it here.
It's great to be ready, waiting the
day.
Just pick up my bonnet to be on
my way.
Have had some times that were
bad
Found myself crying on days that
were sad.
Today I can say with a smile,
With God as my Pilot
It has all been Worthwhile.

Marianna B. Hill
POWER AND WEALTH
Creates an empire, then marries it
Number one lady in life, number
two is his wife.

Nerves of steel, shredded by
wheels
turning, churning, eating and
burning.

A heart on fire losing desire
Slowly dissolving, the pieces are
falling.

Spiritless eyes, no tears to cry
Oppressing days in mental ways.

Continuous work, strenuous work
No retreat, becoming weak.

Ignoring breath, building wealth
A vicious road, a heavy load.

Desperately alone . . .

King on a Throne

Bethel Nunley Evans
GIVING THANKS
Dear God in Heaven
From Whom all blessings flow,
Make me as thankful as I am
Dependent upon You for the
Merciful kindness on me You
bestow.

Dear Father, I love You.
From the depth of my soul
I ask Your forgiveness
For my negligence when I fail
To work toward a Christian goal.

Dear Master, I am so grateful
That You are my Shepherd and
Friend.
Life is not easy with all of the
Sadness, troubles, and fears
That seem to have no end.

Thank You, dear Lord
For the fathomless depths of Your
love
That took me out of a world of sin

And gave me new life and the
Promise of a Heavenly Home
above.

Dear Father in Heaven
From Whom all blessings flow,
I bow my head and give thanks
To Your Holy Name as I pray—
Please, God, let my Christian
witness grow.

Betty Jo Lloyd
TO LAURA
For thirty years we
lived side by side,
My next-door neighbor
and I.
She died last week
and has gone away
To that neighborhood
in the sky.

We shared so much
through the years.
I keep remembering
as I wipe my tears.
I hope she knew
just how I felt.
I'm waiting now
for the snow to melt.

I'll take some flowers
to her grave,
And thank her for the
love she gave.
I miss you, Laura,
and always will.
Someday I'll join you
over the hill.

Bob Barci
ROOMMATE

---

*Dedicated to Ray Torres, and to
all roomies, past, present, and to
come.*

Hello roommate.
My name is me.
I'm a person just like you
And I have feelings just like you
do.
Together let's build a bridge
To find each other.
The bridge will be weak at first
But in time will be strong.
Talk to me and I'll talk back.
Talking, listening, watching.
I believe that's our bridge.
Let's do it now.
It doesn't matter what culture we
are
Just as long as we find each other.
For this situation, I need you
Just as much as you need me.
We are roommates and must
communicate.
That is the crutch of our
existance together.
We may not turn out to be the
best of roommates
But at least we can say we tried.
Hello roommate.
My name is me.
I know your name is you.
Let's build a bridge and find an us.

A. E. Olson
BEST FRIEND
When I was just a little boy,
about a week ago,
I lost the "bestest" friend, I s'pose
I'll every know.

He used to follow me to school,
rules stopped his coming in . . .
But there he'd be out by the walk,
when I got out again.
He used to run, and jump about,
chase sticks and catch a ball;
Sit under a tree that I had
climbed, in case I chanced to
fall.
No proof Have I his thoughts to
know, but true they must have
been;
No food he ate til I had mine, so, I
guess I ate with him.
Late one day when out alone, and
dusk was settling down—
The screech of brakes, one
piercing cry, my friend was on
the ground!
With amazing speed my Dad did
run, to see the make of car . . .
But like the thoughtless driver, it
was long gone, and far.
Puddle splashing is fun no more,
his toys are on the shelf,
Could that driver realize, I walk
to school now,—by myself?

Mary J. Braman
MOTHER
I would like to give my Mother a
Rose.
For every time she blowed my
nose.
For every time she wiped my
tears.
For every time she helped me
through my fears.
But God only knows there is not
that many Rose.
So Mother dear all I can say is,
I'm glad your my Mother, And I
love you in every way.
So I'll just draw you a paper Rose
today.

Everett Francis Briggs
Home Again, In Massachusetts
I will take leave and go now, to
Massachusetts hills;
Among the slender birches my
summer tent pitch there,
And far from cities' traffic,
possess my soul in peace,
And there alone, breathe God's
pure air.

Yes, I shall be at peace there,
among ancestral scenes,
Where all the trees will whisper
the names of those I love,
By me at times forgotten, now
deathlessly inscribed
Among the gold stars high
above.

Yes, there I'll feel the breezes that
kissed them on the cheek,
And there I'll see the fireflies
retracing paths they trod,
When I was just a lad there who
never thought of night . . .
How long ago it was, dear God!

Among those scenes familiar,
somehow I'll live again,
The dear ones resurrected to
part from me no more.
I'll feel their presences there, the
spirit-presences;
I'll sense them at my deep
heart's door.

Bernadette Rettig Wirtz
A GIFT

*To my husband, Daniel J. Wirtz,
our children, Geralyn, David,
Patrick. Thomas and Linda, their
son, Matthew; to our parents,
Max L. and Hedwig C. Rakoczy
Rettig, John P. and Katherine M.
Marach Wirtz.*

Diamonds sparkle on the surface
Of the new fallen snow.
Reflection from the sun light
Streams on the earth below.
Brightening the cold winter's day.
Makes the heart feel young.
These are gifts to both the rich
   and the poor.
They need only to see with the
   eye for sure.
The diamonds, which have fallen
   from the sky,
Warm the heart while shoveling
   the drive.

Ms. Pauline (Polly) Richardson
No Time For Childhood
He sits rigidly at his desk,
pondering a monstrous machine.
The high-tech computerized age
has seized him tightly in its grip,
This wee man-child of seven years.
   No time for childhood.
She prances out on lighted stage,
Rouge shining on her silken
   cheeks.
Mascared lashes; crimson lips,
She preens and cavorts hautily,
This little woman-child of ten.
   No time for childhood.
Suddenly, the nest is empty,
Swallowed in mad competition
of silicon chips, space shuttles,
and hectic pageants of beauty.
Moments ago, they were children.
   No time for childhood?
Let us take the time, dear parents,
To let our children run and play
in the fleeting sunlight of youth,
For the curtain of innocence
descends as a flash of light'ning.
   Make time for childhood!

Thelma Louise Holt
**My Little Hooty Owl and
   Me**
Sometimes when my nights are
   long,
He sits and sings his little song;
Hoot, hooty, hoot, hoot, hoot, hoot.

In wet weather, or in good,
His "hang out" is in the wood,
I'm as comfy as can be,
While he's sitting in a tree,
And the rain pelts down on he,
Making hoots sound shivery,
Boo, booey, boo, boo, boo, boo,

I'm eatin' taters in the house,
While he's out huntin' for a mouse.
(Eee—yuk, can you imagine
   eating a mouse?
It might be O.K. if you were a
   "Hooty" Owl,
And didn't give a hoot.)
Hoot, hooty, hoot, hoot, hoot,
   hoot.

He's my finely feathered friend,
Who'll be hooting 'till the end,
In nasty weather, or in good,
He's always hooting in the wood.

He's a friendly little fowl,
He's my little "Hooty Owl"
What a funny couple we,
My little "Hooty" Owl and me.

While I'm cozy in my house,
He isn't quiet as a mouse,
We're hootin' at old '83,
My little "Hooty" Owl and me.
Hoot, hooty, hoot, hoot, hoot,
   hoot.

Lulu L. Thomson
TRANSPOSITION
Children laughing in the street,
Old folks welcome friends they
   meet.
   People are walking—
   Young folks are talking—
Glad—embracing as they greet.
They are substances of ghosts
who lived one hundred fifty years
   ago.
   People strolling, walking slow.

Where are those glad faces now?
Were they borrowed to be lent
With all their happiness spent?
Streets filled with cars and hurry.
   People dash—how they scurry!
   They're hastening to and fro,
   Contours of the long ago,
Make them merry—walking
   slow.

Linda Zittel
RICH LAMENT
I have no joy this Christmas.
While lights glitter all around our
   door,
Ads bombard us with expensive
   gifts,
I've money for these and more.
Where is my happy spirit?
I have rooms full of decorations;
Paychecks every week afford me
High expectations.
Somehow it's not enough—all
   this stuff.
Things are out of hand.
Let's slow down and *really hear*
The carol words we sing each
   year;
Let's find Christ's simplicity,
Throw away the colored ads—
   forget the fads!
Light one candle; spark hope and
   peace.
My joy returns when I let go
A little bit of love.

Ruby Gray Young
GRANDCHILDREN
In the years gone by
   When my children were young,
To be a grandparent
   Really seemed like much fun.

My mind was made up
   For when I had my turn.
How easy it would be
   For me to remain firm.

But something strange happened
   When that time arrived.
How my heart did soften
   As I looked in those sweet eyes.

What a pleasure they give
   And such joy they do make,
For grandchildren to me
   Are the icing on the cake!

patricia hutson
THE TRANSFORMATION
I stood within the thronging
   crowd,
With faces all around,
An undertone of talk droned on,
No warmth, no smile, I found.

Like bees within a crowded hive,
Strive only to exist,
Their hearts reflected in the air,
A cold, unsentient mist.

No gay "Hellos", no fond
   "Goodbyes"
No calling of a name,
As this one came, and that one
   went,
The crowd was just the same.

With stony eyes as statues stood,
It seemed no feeling known,
I pondered if each single heart,
Were lonely as my own.

A stranger's silent entrace there,
Revealed a sudden change,
As warmth flowed free among the
   crowd,
Their faces rearranged.

The droning ceased, the eyes of
   stone,
Now softened with a smile,
This unknown one of love and
   peace,
Had come to stay awhile.

Louise Johnston
**Tender Mem'ries Of
   Yester-Year**
This house is now saddened
That once was so gay
Echoes a child's laughter
As he happily played.

And when he grew drowsy,
Into my arms he crept
Twas his nest of security
While he peacefully slept.

Then gently I would lay him
In his warm little bed
Touching those golden curls
That crowned his little head.

Those days are gone now
But the mem'ries are here
Locked deep in my heart
Tender mem'ries of yester-year.

Dr. Paulette T. Riley, Ph.D. M.H.
TRAPPED
The roof tree over head has
   sheltered us from the cold
Housing within it a family that
   was daring and bold
The wooden frame lined with soft
   linen,
contains precious moments that
   from childrens eyes are kept
   hidden
There is the hearth that warmed
   our flesh each day
Sustaining the body come what
   may
The chairs that held all kinds
   of weight
Never being able to feel or
   hate
The door that opened wide to
   strangers, but more so to kin
Has also given way to let the sun
   light in
With such lovely things to say
   about this place where I dwell

Why do I still feel as though I am
   living in Hell.

Angela Edminster
DAD
When I was young
you took my hand
and held me up
ain't love grand?

Through my life
you were always there
when things went wrong
you always cared.

I remember the good times
and the bad
no matter what they were
I was always glad.

And then one day
you didn't come home
I was so confused
where did you go?

I'll never forget
the day you died
of the night that the
whole family cried.

I need you now
but your not here
maybe I'll see you
one of these years.

I'm glad you were here
and the times we shared
I'll never forget you
I LOVE YOU DAD!!!

Mardi
ALIVE
   To be alive
for happiness is what we should
   strive
   To enjoy everything
all that nature may bring
   To live each day
making it happy in your own
   special way
   To meet each new experience
   with a sense of
expectation
   Being alive one can see new
   adventures at hand
which can be set to music of a
   band

M. Elisabeth Steiner
Cathedral Of the Pines
On a hill stands a cathedral,
Where one may pray in his own
   way,
Its outdoor chapels pledged to
   God.
The peaceful valley far below
Is ablaze with autumn's
   brilliance,
Crimson, scarlet, copper and gold.
As the wind rustles through the
   pines,
We marvel at nature's wonders.

This tribute to a young pilot,
And to all others, through the
   years,
Who gave their lives to keep us
   free,
Expresses gratitude with love.
The altar wrought of precious
   stones
From far and near marks unity,
As the wind rustles through the
   pines,
We pause to remember with
   prayers.

Lord, You gave us a spacious world.
To be shaped into paradise.
When will we heed Your great
  wisdom,
And "beat all swords into
  plowshares,
Forge all spears into pruning
  hooks"
Before each living thing is dead.
As the wind rustles through the
  pines,
We dedicate our lives to peace.

Alfred E. Unterreiner
TINA

*In memory—Tina was a long
awaited morning star of a couple
very much in love. Tina died at
the age of two months.*

Thou Gavest eyes that wonders I
  may behold
Sounds enchant and spells about
  me fold

Fellow creatures have I, no
  tarrying hours haunt me
Time consumed too soon, thy
  fleecing wings taunt me

Love which knowest I, thy gift
  most precious be
Came not upon it's own, but with
  thy company

And in thy stead, by thy works
  supreme
Thou gavest me in life, a love, a
  dream

'Erhart'

J. W. Cheney Jr.
AMBITION
Tendrils of your essance, cling
surely, such, "seems" "you".
Enthralled, emparted, rapture
"abstracts" of "times" subdue.

Should sombre, seconds' "forecast"
strike severely, future's "ways"
departed, brighter, passages?
Foremost, "better" days?

Night's 'nil, fiery parodies
needless, never, end.
Future's— 'fleet "forevers"
nostalgically, transcend.

Ethereally, "even" satiate
surruptitious, "sage", desire
paradox, priced, pleasure
portentious, "so", aspire.

Tracy Wendt Harding
TO MY FIRST LOVE
We've been together for so long
I can't believe its through
You became a part of me
And me a part of you

You were something special to me
But I had to let you go
You will always mean alot to me
Thats something I want you to
  know

We shared so many secrets
And many special days
We understood each others
  feelings
In very different ways

I'll never forget the day we met
And the night we got together
Thank you for those memories
I'll treasure them forever

I know I'll never forget you
And the things we used to do
But I can't make you love me
As much as I love you

Marsha Pockrus
PEACE OF MIND
My subconscious,
free at last
dances on
the brisk night air
As the goblins of my mind
fly away in blackness

I wonder
at the stars
I never saw before

And at the second chance
to live again.

Sheila Edwards
. . . AND I CRY
At home, safe and snug
in my own little world,
  I watch the newscast,
  about how they died
  in Lebanon, blown to
  bits by terrorist bombs,

  . . . and I cry.

At home, safe and snug
in my own little world,
  I watch the faces
  of the families
  that don't yet know
  who's dead or alive,

  . . . and I cry.

At home, safe and snug
in my own little world,
  I watch them digging
  through the rubble,
  trying to recover
  what's lost forever,

  . . . and I cry.

Clay R. Carroll
THE CHILD

*In memory of my Father—You
gave me the chance to be . . . THE
CHILD*

Alone but never lonely—we're
  alive this place and me,
air and water are our lifesource—
  I rely on only God and me.

All around me live my brothers—
  on crags of rock in dark green
  trees,
with elk and otter I share the
  mountain—the eagles cry our
  symphony.

While the Spring breathes soft
  around me—my joy in life
  returns anew,
I feel that I could never long for—
  more than this before I'm
  through.

And in the falling white of
  Winter—when all is muffled
  quiet and cold,
I sit beside my cabins' fire—and I
  thank life for what I hold.

The hidden glade where I am
  dwelling—where no men stay
  to dim the dawn,
so deep and clear the lake below
  me—where the great sea—
  pilgrims spawn.

In the first gold rays of
  dawning—in the last pale rays
  of day,
I stand in awe, embraced by
  mountains—where it has
  always been this way.

What has a man when he is
  ended?—What has he when he
  is born?
Alive up here he's cloaked in
  grandeur—with this alone he
  hears life's song.

My passions are majestic
  mountains—swift cold streams
  to which I'm drawn,
the living light that shines upon
  them—none will change when
  I am gone.

I drink from streams born in the
  snowmelt—I eat of morsels
  growing wild,
I breath the sweet air of the
  Sawtooths—I'm not alone, I'm
  Natures' Child.

Mrs. Dolores Jean Solt
JUST BE THANKFUL
If God would grant you, just one
  wish
What would you ask him for?
Good health or wealth or
  happiness—
Which one to you means more?

I often think of all the blind,
How much they'd like to see
Also the deaf, they cannot hear
Sweet music, such as we.

So many lame they cannot walk
The miles that lie ahead,
Also there are the many sick
That cannot leave their bed.

I think when you look all around
You're satisfied to be,
Among the other persons
Who can walk and hear and see.

Charlene "Charlie" Dillaman
HIDE-N-SEEK
It is so easy to hide in darkness,
  any child can tell you that
With children it may be a game
  of hide-n-seek and that's a fact.
But why do adults play hide-n-
  seek? Do they not want to be
  found?
Or are they more secure when
  darkness is all around?
Is the fear of deeds done long
  before?
Or do they not wish to change . . .
  the way it is . . . is more
  secure.
I am not saying it is easy letting
  the light shine on you
Because when the light is on you
  nothing is hidden from God's
  view.
Yes, it is scarey when the light
  first appears,
But His total forgiveness will get
  rid of the fears
Then there will not be a reason
  for hiding
Because you will find yourself
  only abiding
          in His light
          in His Love
     and in His Forgiveness
The darkness will not last!

Diane M. Krall
DESTINY

*For Frank Aulicino, your future
will take care of itself.*

What is meant to be; shall.
Every state of being; will be.
Every presence of existence; is.
Every search that is; lies within.
For all there is, has it's own
  Reason to be.
All there is to life, that it is so
  alive.
We need the endurance "to be".
All that is given us,
And we wish for tomorrow be
  gone.
Our future we urge to look
  through,
While robbing ourselves
The joy of the moment.

Anna Mae Kochel
AFRAID

*Dedicated to my lovely daughter
Ann, who having a Lazor Beam
operation, (for detached retina in
one eye), that resulted in
immediate restored vision.*

Looking ahead, trying to see
  A dark void socket
And stars circling, swirling
  All around in front of me.
I try to reach that black pocket,
  Pluck it out so I can be me,
Except someone is screaming
  Crying out hysterically,
Lord, why me? Why me?
  Later, much later
There is light behind a patch
  I feel light headed
As I'm being told
  God will be good to me.
Later, much later I will see
  Suddenly that dark black socket
Is gone along with the stars
  Pain is jagging in my pocket,
But I am going to see,
  So God has been good to me
I am no longer afraid.

Laura Lois Lopez
TWILIGHT OF THE DAY

*To all my equitation instructors,
school teachers, and the people
who influenced me the most, my
family.*

Twilight is his name,
In the spring, winter, summer,
  and fall,
We always play games,
He is the greatest of them all.

I race on him fast and far,
He always loves going over jumps
  while racing,
He is sometimes faster than a car,
But he never takes time for
  pacing.

He is a very active horse,
He likes to jump, hunt, and run,
He always likes running the
  course,
He is always so much fun.

He has a heart of gold,
He is peaceful as a dove,
He never will be sold,
He will always be my love.

Joel Alan Boucher
The Golden Glory Of Sunset

The eminent immensity of a
reflected mark in time.
Majestic and beautiful,
The omen of a storm forthcoming.

Pink and yellow mists
Surrounding watercolor fabric,
Pink-lined grey scribbled in the
heavens,
Its fury surpassing the surf below.

The mists solidify
Into the strokes of a passionate
brush,
Beneath the forever reaching
mass of grey.

The golden glory hangs lower,
Lower, lower,
And is gone.

Robin Reger
NOUS

The Shadow takes
          And shakes and wakes
The secret soul alive

It gleans and cleans
          And weans away
The darker world inside

An ego met
   An id announced
      A psyche well-acquainted

The agony
      And ecstacy
   Of softer side once tainted

The Piscean
          May choose to swim
The depths or seek the light

To plumb the glare of day
      Or search the sin of night

Bill Darvin Gregston
FACES

I wish to express my gratitude to the many poets and other lyricists who have inspired my writing; and to my devoted friends for their love.

I've been around here and there,
And just about everywhere—
Yes, some faces I can bear
For some of those I do recollect
And my words will surely reflect.
If I see a singing-the-blues frown
Yes, that one needs a *happiness*
clown.
When I see a I've-been-used face,
Of true friends that one needs a
taste.
So often I see a I-don't-trust-you
look,
That one should see that some
are a book.
There are many a everything-is-
great facade,
But reality into that life must trod.
At times I see a I-want-to know-
you stare,
To talk to that one is only fair.
Or to see a let's-have-some-fun
smile,

Is surely one who has good style.
When I feel a I-need-you touch,
That feels better than a good
lunch.
If I get a I'm-your-friend hug,
My emotions that one is
beginning to tug.
So seldom I hear 'let's have dinner
sometime' line,
But, to know me that one has
taken the time.
Some of those faces will not
remain,
But some memories I will retain,
For only few will my love stay
the same.

Martha Stroshine Burrow
The Wizard Of Wangdoodleland

There is a place in
Wangdoodleland
Where stories are heard every day,
And the wizard is kind
As he helps us along
In his bright robe
And beard long and grey.

We earn as we learn. Awards and
pins
From stories and games that we
play,
Even our pets get their chance to
march proud
In that land far away.

There are songs to sing and
puzzles to play
And stories from books that pile
high,
The leprechaun in green
And cowboy Pete. With boots on
his feet
Occasionally do stop by.

Come visit our place.
If you don't know the route
Just ask anyone
They'll tell you right out.

We think it's O.K.
In this land far away
And the Wizard of
Wangdoodleland.

Alice N. Almeda "Ahna"
A Friendly Stimulation

TO: Julius C. DeLaney "A SPECIAL FRIEND" of Inspiration

The white foam rushes with the
waves on seas
Birds are building nests among
God's trees
Electrifying feelings come over me
As I begin a new life of positive
creativity
All because you stood at my side
Comforted me when I cried
Encouraged me to personally find
The best decisions from my mind
To confidently combine all
possibilities
How to choose the primary
probabilities
To believe in a faith of a different
kind
To give with a special love in
mind
Regain assurance with good deeds
Stimulate the ultimate of my
needs

As justice is bound to come my
way
Success and freedom will swiftly
pay
We conquered our battles from
afar
Times I just wasn't up to par
Yet, you extended with love and
harmony
A special love, for a stagnent me

Gwen Taylor Lundy

Gwen Taylor Lundy
For the Mother Of Mary

For all grandmothers everywhere

Forgotten mother of Nazareth
   Did you weep to see her go?
The world was wide and
   frightening.
   The journey long and slow,
And she was just your little girl
   So brief a time ago.

She left her dolls behind her
   Did you range them on a shelf
And weep for the little daughter,
   Soon to bear a child herself?

Did you worry and fret about her
   So far away from home?
Did you dream of a lowly manger
   And an inn that had no room?

Did you turn your hands to
   homely tasks
   To quiet your heart's alarms
You, who should wrap the
   swaddling clothes
   And lay Him in her arms?

Grandmother of the Christ Child
   Two thousand years ago,
Unsung mother of Mary

Did you weep to see her go
On the lonely road to Bethlehem?
   Yes, I think 'twas so.

Jerry L. Tienter
THE CHRISTMAS TREE

To my wife Susan

Time passes in leaps and bounds
Where once was a child now a
   man is found.
Old, tall and grey
In this world I have lived
and for its good I have little to say.
Black my nights and cold my days
In one room from fear
I am forced to stay.

Why for my last Christmas
I took a tree tall and plain
Why now after all these years I
   cannot explain
And covered it with light
reds, yellows, green and white.
Filling every branch with stories so
even to my old, cold eyes
it was a beautiful sight.

Perhaps I never lost love or hope
but buried it thinking I could
   better cope
with lifes ugliness and hate
The wise old man made a
   mistake
in thinking he could shut off pain
by hurting others for his hearts
   sake
he only hurt himself that was
   finally plain
When he broke hearts he could
   feel his break.

Now old and living in shadows
Last fears becoming real to me by
   degrees
From one day upon another
Trying to learn from what I see

To take the hand of the child in
   the man
and show him how to love again
In my last season, thankfully,
   there appeared to me my first
   Christmas tree.

Joseph P. Kowacic
PINK MOONLIGHT

For Kim

The moon hung
in the tops
of cherry trees
like a glowing pearl
nestling
behind the pink lace bodies
of a girl.

The Night
pressed its damp kiss
upon my cheek,
and in the scented silence
neither It
nor I
had words to speak.

And my thoughts
sped out through the darkness
to the farthest
shimmering star . . .
past the moon
in fragrant blossoms,

to the distant Dream . . .
You are.

G. Marie Miller
I had a dream
I had a dream,
In that scene,
I saw Mars,
There among the stars.

My arms were wings,
I stretched them out to fly,
To another place,
In outer space.

To stay forever more,
Away from the shore,
Stars were twinkling in the skies,
When I was in for a great surprise.

With my guardian angel,
Watching over me,
Fufilling a promise,
Of a foretold paradise,
Was there for me to see.

G. Adcock
LAND OF WONDER
O Land of Wonder and our home
God help and protect you from
  wrong.
Unfurl the banner, raise it high.
  Pride of a country free and
  strong.

Americans be proud, shout out
  loud Pacific to Atlantic wide.
Proud to be known across all
  foam as a nation that leads and
  guides.
With all our great might, our star
  is bright; rejoice, and give your
  best
Strength, loyalty and integrity to
  our country blest.

With brave and conquering heart,
  do your part to respond to the
  glorious call
On guard for right, with honor
  bright to be a people loved by all.
Dare we our own 'gainst tyrant
  throne, and the Future we
  acclaim.
Let Fairness, Freedom, Peace and
  Love make America's name.

To defend the Fine and stand for
  Truth, let this our sacred vow
  ring clear
O'er sparkling waters, forests tall,
  a noble strain for all to hear.
Vast is our soil, our heritage
  great, and fair our Yankee sky.
The wealth of beauteous U. S. A.
  laud then, with heads held high.

Mrs. Kathy Morrison
BITTER THOUGHTS
I searched my heart this very day.
I found some bitterness along the
  way.
Some unkind thoughts—the
  judgmental kind.
The ones dear God I don't want
  to find.

I remember your words when you
  hung on the tree.
You died and gave your life for me.
Your heart was so pure to your
  creation man.
You even look down from glory
  and call us your friend.

Never a bitter thought, no sin or
  guile.

You are the sinless one no matter
  the trial.
You walked this earth with such
  radiating power.
Oh God! please help me this very
  hour.

Forgive me Lord and give me
  Christ's love.
I know that this kind of help
  comes only from above.
When I search my heart again I
  pray,
"Help my very being and soul
  never to stray."

Ada Florene Adams
**The Holly Trail Of
Churches**

*In loving tribute to my fellow
choir members and organist of
Zion U. C. C.*

What an extraordinary invitation
  for all people,
To visit the Sanctuaries of their
  choice
And share in the loveliness of
  this Special Holy Season!

Graciously, Our Guides welcome
  those who enter the doors,
Eager to learn of our church's
  history;
Tender memoriums grace the
  many stained glass windows,
Which on sunny Sabbath morn,
  seem to shine with Holiness!

Lifting our eyes Heavenward, our
  Eastern windows
Express Justice, Peace, Love, Faith,
  Work and Joy,
While those on the West
  represent,
Rest, Reward, Courage, Prayer,
  Charity and Hope!
How impressive! The Center
  window draws our gaze
To the ascended Lord!

Reverently, moving along rows of
  shimmering candles,
And wreaths exquisitely trimmed
  with soft velvet bows,
We behold on the one hand, an
  outstanding manger scene,
And on the other, a beautifully
  lighted Christmas tree!

Our choir loft and organ are
  silent now,
A record plays Heavenly strains
  of Christmas music,
Above the Altar, there is a
  painting of our Heavenly Father,
With outstretched arms, pleading,
  "Come unto me!"
(Would that we accept that
  challenge, light one candle,
And free the World From
  Darkness!)

Pleased, our visitors offer thanks
  and smile,
So grateful for this Day!

Ethelyne R. Harper
MEMORIES
As I sit alone in retrospect,
Of all things duly circumspect,
My state of solitude bemoaning,
Ghosts of yesteryears come

roaming.

Forbidden phantoms slyly
  intrude,
Of many a delightful interlude.
Spanning half a century now
  bygone,
They parade before me, one by one.

These near forgotten memories
  persist,
Of pleasures and intrigue they
  consist,
And circumspect loses all appeal,
As emerge the dreams I've fought
  to conceal.

Now, unbidden they return to me,
And again I am engulfed in ecstasy,
As alone I sit in reverie.

Robert J. Kerrigan Jr.
LOVE

*Inspired by the warmth, love and
presence of Karen Garbutt and
those times we spent together*

From the moment I first saw you
And your eyes looked at mine
There was something that came
  over me
And now I feel it all the time

For you have eyes that sparkel
And a romantic is what I see
There's so much of you I like
And you're so beautiful to me

For I long to hold you in my arms
And take those slow walks too
Just spending our time together
And sharing my love with you

Walter J. Gauntt, Jr.
TRY

To Gaye and Garry

It does no good to fret or frown
or let your troubles get you down
to sit and worry and to stew
does nothing more than make
  you blue

Attack your problems with all
  your might
arch your back and stand up and
  fight
decide you will beat them and
  just begin
and you will be surprised how
  many times
that you actually will win!

guy petit
JANUARY
Two stars across a darkness met
And touched; and now I seem
To feel the afterflow—and yet,
Perhaps I only dream.

Stars have their moment, so does
  love;
But now that night is done.
I'd give you all the rest above,
Had they been one.

Dawn M. Martin
LAST GOOD—BYE
Wanting out
Trying to be free
Going to circles, not knowing
  where to be.

Reaching for

Only happiness
But wondering where to find it,
  she can't guess.

Taking time
To find what is right
Sometimes she breaks down, and
  just can't fight.

She's falling
Nobody seems to care
She cries angered tears, knowing
  it's not fair.

Leaving all
There's nothing to try
She has written a note, it's her
  last good-bye.

Mary Sachs Zello
THE BIBLE
It is called the Book of Books,
  Its Author is the King of Kings.
Oh Praise His Holy Name
  forever—
  Praise the message the Book
  brings.

This is no ordinary Book—
  For it was written by Word
  Divine,
The pen is mightier than the
  sword—
  It does the word of God define.

The world wherein old Satan
  dwells,
  Has always plotted to
  destroy—
The ways of God's eternal love
  Many devious ways he has
  employed.

The Bible is called the "Living
  Word"
  For in its pages we can see—
God's word defined and wisdom
  given,
  To save the souls of you and me.

The world has oft tried to destroy,
  The Book, we hear the lions
  roar—
But God's Living Word will never
  die,
  Its teachings will live
  forevermore!

R. Mike Gilliam
THE OTHER SIDE
There's a side of you I never
saw or knew.
You kept it in the shadows,
just away from view.
It evaded all detection,
positioned always out of sight.
Like the far side of the moon
that never sees the light.
It was always there I'm sure
lurking just below,
Why couldn't I have recognized
and told myself so?
But now it's presence overwhelms
and saturates every pore.
It's funny,
I never notice
Rainbows anymore.

Opel E. Buzbee
FIRST CHRISTMAS
The very first Christmas God
  gave to man,
T'was the greatest gift any man
  can,
Mary called his name Jesus, He
  was God's only son

He paid for our sins, when he
shed his blood.

This may be our last Christmas
before His return
We are living in days of Noah, as
we have learned
But all you have to do is confess
your sins and accept
Jesus as our Lord and Saviour and
then we will win
Your home up in heaven with
streets of gold
All because you trusted and did
as you were told
So love Him, trust Him, what a
day that will be
When we all meet in heaven our
saviour to see.

There to walk the streets of gold,
all our loved ones to see,
Our mamas, our daddys, our
babies to hold
All gone on before us, what
beauty to behold
Just like Jesus promised, if we do
as we are told.

Nancy Roulias
HAPPY VALENTINE DAY
Valentine day is the day of
expressing to one another our
love—
Our love to family and friends
and our heavenly Father up
above.
You don't need fancy bows and
delicious candy to say "I love
you!"
It should come from a sincere
heart and kindness in whatever
you do!
The love of a husband and wife
grows stronger and dearer in
every way.
Love is so precious and priceless
and it should be known every
single day.
Love of parents for their children
grows fonder and sweeter as
time goes by.
Children don't mature to mom
and dad—they share their
sorrows and also cry.

But the purest most perfect love
of all is our heavenly Fathers
love,
God gave His son so we can have
an eternal home in heaven
above,
We can always depend on Him to
protect us and keep us safe
from harms.
He is always there with His light
to guide us safely to His open
arms.
Happy Valentine Day, Heavenly
Father, with your love we need
no other.
And thank you for Lord Jesus, our
mediator, born of a virgin
mother.

Rita K. Tillemans LA LADY
FRIENDSHIP
Sand Castles built on a sandy
beach . . .
Can't be expected to stay.
For when the tide comes in from
the sea . . .
It will wash those castles away.

When the tide returns back out
to the sea . . .
The beach is once again
smooth . . .
Sand Castles then will be rebuilt
Only to be washed away again . . .
to soon.

A Mansion built on a rocky
clift . . .
Will last perhaps longer than just
a day.
But when the North wind blows
to meet the South . . .
Eventually it too will blow away.

Like Sand Castles and Mansions
not wisely built . . .
Friendship is often too.
When the tide comes in or the
storm breaks . . .
It seems a weak friendship is
doomed.

But a Friendship built on truth
and honesty . . .
Will last forever and a day.
It will stand strong through
storm and sunshine
And can never be washed away.

Bessie M. Waguespack
EMOTIONS
Emotions are from
deep within,
Surfacing with feelings
of happiness or chagrin.
Aroused by something
very appealing,
Then with positive
emotions we are dealing.
Including love, liking,
joy, delight and hope,
Now being able
to finally cope.
If unhappiness or
dissatisfaction prevail,
These negative emotions
cause us to fail.
Like sadness, despair,
disgust, anger and fear,
Unable to understand
these is quite clear.
Emotions are either
strong or weak,
And recognized in
the manner we speak.
When very angry
we become raged,
Or merely annoyed,
an emotion staged.
Emotions are
hard to understand,
Reactions—good or
bad—we never plan.
To be happy
one must learn now,
To cope with
negative emotions somehow.

Bethel Nunley Evans
LITTLE SOUTHERN BELLE
I am a dreamer from dreamland
Every day new air castles I build.
Little bubbles float like snow
flakes
Into my fortress until it is filled.

I take a evening stroll around
the lawn
The flowers are in bloom
everywhere it seems.
As the cool air blows a refreshing
breeze

I slump under a tree and fall into
a dream.

My thoughts go back several
years ago
When I was told that a few
months hence,
I would need to get a nursery ready
And a play yard encircled with a
fence.

I remember how my heart
thumped,
And I was deliriously overjoyed,
The thought was great of having
a sister
To share her life with our fine
little boy.

I asked God to give us a healthy
baby,
Then, I told him I had a secret
flair—
For a little girl to look just like
her daddy,
With brown eyes, dimpled chin,
and curly hair,

I knew I did not deserve His favors,
But, God tells His children to
keep in touch.
So I left it in the hands of The Lord
To decide if I had asked for too
much.

The time passed on until one
February day
I awakened on a hospital bed.
The doctor was standing close by
my side,
"You have a beautiful baby girl,"
he said.

I'll remember those words as long
as I live,
I knew God would keep my
secret true,
I was not surprised when I saw
He had
Given her all the credentials I
had asked Him to.

It wasn't hard to find a suitable
name
To fit the little Southern Belle,
She looked like an angel without
wings,
So we decided to call her Ann
Genell.

Soon we took her home to cuddle
And for her eager little brother to
see.
He gazed at her from head to foot,
then grinned,
"Daddy, she has a hole in her
chin like you and me."

A loud whisper from a mocking
bird
Sitting just above on a limb of the
tree
Brought me suddenly to my
awakened senses,
And I realized from the trance I
was free.

It was a sweet dream of memories
From the last four decades that
have passed,
And even though I am now left to
live alone,
Thank God, He has given me
faith enough to last.

Year after year lives have been
blessed

By the Southern Belle, now a
lovely Christian lady.
With the help of her talented
nursing skills,
I may live to a ripe old age, just
maybe.

patricia hutson
ONE WAY
There is only one way in;
I found the way and I cherish it,
Yea, even fondle it,
Find security and satisfaction in
the knowledge of it,
For I know that nothing can hurt:
The rusty nails of hate,
The haughty words that prick
one's heart,
The self-righteous that would
destroy,
The provoking thoughts that
battle for self-justice,
The cluttering memories of
mistakes, disappointments and
unrighteousness,
Even temptation lies in silence
like a charmed snake,
At the voice of a child playing in
the breeze,
Running up and down the hills,
uninhibited,
Because he carries no weights of
yesterday,
But only the light garment of
truth and shoes of now,
And rejoices in these and nothing
else;
Except you become as little
children,
You shall not enter . . .

Eudine Mills Gee
FLIGHT
The spiraled city parked on earth
Intermixed below the clouds—
A downward look,
An upward glance,
A touch of God's great beauty
spread
Through space housed by the
floating clouds.

A touch of Heaven,
Yet of earth—
Unsurpassed, uncomparable,
God's great handiwork above the
clouds.

M. Ada Keating
My Guarding Angel Mother
I sit and think back to a long
time ago when I was but a
child . . then
No matter where ever I walked
T'was in a sunny land, with
"MOM" as my guard.
As I grew older "MOM'S hand led
me on and on.
Soon I thought I should be old
enough to walk alone in
Youth's all glorious dawn.
MOM did let me go, or so I
thought, to choose my own
pathwasy joyfully.
I'd run scarcely noticing the
"Farm" that followed along
beside me, so silently.
No wonder then when I grew
older and my paths grew rough,
and oh so steep
"MOM'S gentle hand would lift
me up until I could walk again.

Our World's Best Loved Poems

My friends would say "What a
   precious Mom" you have, she
   surely is your gift from God"
But, years later, and I'd grown
   older . . when my courage
   would grow thin
The 'Hand' that had led me on, I
   could not see. ! ! !
For LO, Through those years,
   'MOM' had gone to her 'REST'
But Her Spirit lingers on . . . far in
   my heart
I still feel 'MOM'S' gentle hand
   leading me on.

Ann Heidenry
FELINE INTENSITY

*My beautiful Calico sharer of all
my moods the delight of my heart.*

What mystery holds thee so
   intent?
A passing cloud?
A cardinal in the young green
   tree?
Perhaps a velvet bumble bee.

Could never be a thing so great
As that which trembles in my
   heart.
If perchance your amber eyes
Chose to favor me.

Eyes pierced deep within my soul.
Knowing all that I have been.
Or ever hope to be.
A part of your infinity.

My mind runs wild with
   memories
Of beauty I have seen;
Snowclad mountains, peaks,
Wild whitecaps, rolling seas.

But not one, not one, not one
Of these that I conjure,
Could ever be compared with the
   Aristocratic dignity of thee.

Ah beauty & thy name is cat.

Mrs. Grace Freestone
Christmas Reflections
Christmas is the greatest day of
   the year
A day we give and receive joy;
It is a time of reflections and joy
For all, be it lady, man, girl, or
   boy.

The gifts so lovingly wrapped and
   placed under the tree
No matter how large or small
   they be;
Are given with that thought in
   mind
The joy of Christmas, we all to
   find.

Christmas is the reflection of life
When we realize the true
   meaning of it all;
It is a time of awe and
   wonderment
When we realize that God
   planned it all.

The day is magic from beginning
   to end
As we spend the day with those
   we hold dear;
Oh that we could keep Christmas
   in our hearts
Throughout every day of the year!

Tricia Lengerich
A SPECIAL FRIEND
A special friend died today,
Not really died—just went away.
She played a game and got caught
And re-learned a lesson that was
   taught.
Never play with fire you might
   get burned.
Never mix emotions she had
   learned.
Never take chances too risky to
   take.
Never make promises when
   you've got too much at stake.
The game to her was really fun,
But the game had just started, the
   tracks just begun.
The tracks of temptation of
   wrong or right,
The forbidden temptation of "just
   once" for tonight.
She's chosen her path her wrong
   or her right,
The path for her was not quite
   alright.
She ended up scared and all alone,
Crying softly at night in that
   same frightened tone.
And yet she kept running away
   from it all,
Never facing the fact she had
   taken a fall.
She came to me frightened within
And told me of the night she
   made her first sin.
How sad and depressed I had got,
When she told me the game had
   had her caught.
My special friend died today,
Not really died—just went away.

Sister Barbara Mary Lanham, O.S.F.
GOD'S SPLENDOR
God made the mountains,
Iridescent, dancing rays—
Spellbound, I gaze.

God made the ocean,
Rippling, gushing, tidal waves—
Awe-struck, I stand.

God made the Seagull,
Strong, majestic wings
expand. He flies!

God made you and me,
Image of His very Self—
Thankful, we kneel.

God poured forth His Love,
and chose us to be His brides.
Joy-filled, I cried!

God took me in hand,
"Gospel Poverty," He said.—
My God, my All!

Kendra Ann Eldredge
WINTER
Winter is peaceful yet lonely,
   overcast by gloom.
An icy chill lingers in the air
as misty warmth rises from
   securely muted homes.

Trees have been mysteriously
   stripped
a few, crinkled leaves are left
   abandoned.
The birds have long since
   deserted their vacant nests,
which now sit isolated on bare
   trees—
slowly being filled with snow.

Life-less yellow grass becomes a
   tiny icicle forest.
No little creatures dart about
as no one dares to disturb the
   deathly stillness.

Marjorie E. Johnson
WINTER
Winter is here in all its glory! !
   Snow-forts, sleds, ice,
   Chilly, snowy,
   Toboggans, snow-mobiles, skis,
   Mittens, boots, sliding,
   Sleet, wind, snow-balls,
   Snow-men, skates, snow-flakes,
   Snow-drifts, sleigh-rides,
   Frosting, melting, freezing.
Winter is here in all its glory! !

B. J. Hulsizer
REFLECTIONS

*This poem is dedicated to
Vincent Pischettola.*

All life is reflected in the one you
   love.
Today we begin sharing not just
   love, but life.
Eternity seems much too brief
   and forever,
but a day.
   Love is the beginning of forever.
   Love makes the world a garden.
   Love is eternal.
Because we love, we are beyond
   all time and space.
Love is a happy feeling that
   dwells in the heart forever.
You are my happiness, my
   sorrow,
my yesterday, my tomorrow.

Marie E. Fernandez
BEGINNINGS
Beginnings . . .
   Life's awakening to
   Moments filled with
   Fresh newness
   Which fade to
   Dull familiarity
   And finally
   To surrendered endings
   Which ultimately
   Are only misconstrued
Beginnings.

Patricia Antosh Rogers
A WINNER?

*This poem is dedicated to my
wonderful husband, Elmer G.
Rogers, because of his faith and
devotion, inspired the following:*

When I thought I was a winner,
and was told that I was not.
I kept on searching for something
Not knowing for what I sought.

I tried a whole new wardrobe
and that was not it at all,
I tried staying at home alone,
while my friends were having a
   ball.

I read the works of Shakespeare,
And of all the poets I know,
I reveled in the joy of laughter
And wept with the tales of woe.

How does one describe a winner?
Other than to simply say they've

won.
I know now after looking back,
A Winner—yes, I am definitely
   one.

Ken-Roy Pulse
VERNELL

*Dedicated and Written For
Vernell Burleson For Her Faith In
Love*

You are the Natural Beauty
behind a Moonlight Veil,
with All;
The Devotion,
The Love,
The Charity,
You Prevail.
You are the Strength
behind your Son's woes.
The Power behind
your family's Glows.
It is You,
The One who is Special,
Vernell.

bob SHON'SORO knox
SITTING IN A CELL
I'm sad as sad can be, and there's
   no one here but me.
   No one to love and care, on
   Christmas eve.
And on the coming Christmas
   morn', I'll be sad and all alone,
   just sitting in a cell, that will
   never set me free.

How I wish that I could be,
   sitting around a Christmas tree,
   with all my love ones there, on
   Christmas day.
Oh I miss my mom and dad, and
   the good times we all had. I'm
   just sitting in a cell, that will
   never set me free.

It was many long years ago, that I
   was there in Ohio, and
   laughing with my friends, on
   Christmas Day.
Now I sit here all alone, and play
   my Christmas songs. I'm
   just sitting in a cell, that will
   never set me free.

Now the days just come and go,
   and the years begin to show,
   in graying hair, and sad and
   wrinkled eyes.
All the folks back home are gone,
   and I'm so all alone, and
   just sitting in a cell, that will
   never set me free.

Nettie M. Fernley
A BACKWARD LOOK
I took a walk the other day—
It seemed about time I should—
Too long I've driven city streets—
I longed for the Autumn wood.

I walked a long time in silence
Reflecting on familiar scenes;
I seemed to be back in childhood
   days
Before I as in my teens:

When in long, hazy days of
   Autumn
With never a thought of care
I wandered through the woodlands
When trees from leaves were
   bare.

355

I saw a squirrel peeking from a
hollow tree.
I watched a beaver floating dry
wood;
A wary raccoon was washing a fish
As up on his hind legs he stood.

A muskrat sliding down a muddy
bank
Broke my beautiful reverie;
I *had to go back* to a different
world—
But I looked back as long as I
could see.

I *had to leave behind* this world I
had known
When as a child I had wandered
at will;
Please, God, let it ever be there
till the last
So others can see it still.

Cynthia R. Golderman
ILLUMINATION!
I have seen
                    inside your heart
I have glimpsed the depths there;
the concreteness
of your goodness
and your caring . . .

I shall step forth to greet you
wholly and tenderly,
knowing now the way of your
heart
and how it cares.
I am filled with vertigo
from the vortex of my
cyclonic dreaming, . .
you . . .
    like the shining in an eye's iris,
it's great device,
has shorn me of cowardice,
                                and
with those corduroy clothes and
brilliant smile
have ensnared
that which was not ever graspable,
where you hold no guile
in your sensuality I am awestruck
            with intensity of feeling,
reeling neath the truth
            of your
                        being,
I, i, shall never be . . . the same!

Muriel W. Mayfield
REMEMBERING
It's hard to trim the tree
    When the children are away . . .
But you get out the ornaments,
    And for strength you pray.

For in each shining ball you see
    Reflected from yesteryear,
Little faces of your loved ones
    Who are no longer near.

You seem to hear the voices
    Out of long, long ago,
"Where does old Santa come from?"
    They always want to know.

"Can he get through our chimney
    With so many, many toys?
And will he know for sure
    We've been good girls and boys?"

"Does he really keep a record
    Of how good we've been this
    year?
And are you sure and certain
    He will leave some presents
    here?"

So, you sit there in the silence
    And let your beautiful memories
    unfold;
For Christmas is a love story—
    More precious each time it is
    told.

Franklin Hartfield

Franklin Hartfield
THE LEAF
A leaf just fell upon the window
sill.
The wind pressed it against the
pane.
For a moment it stayed there
shivering in the chill.
It slid a bit, then marched back
up again.

That is all it bequeathed in it's
affinity—
A performance in the wind.

Lucille Domain
LIFE
Life . . .
It ticks like time
In a slow steady rhyme
It is filled with love
And such beautiful things as
doves
Sometimes it makes you laugh
Sometimes it makes you cry
But you should always try
It's sad to say
That people waste the days
Never sharing
Not even caring
Letting it slip by
Without giving it a try

Amanda Elizabeth Vasseur
DANIEL

---

*Dedicated to Daniel, my son, the
joy of my life.*

Daniel, You are the light of my
    eyes and the star in my life.
Your toes twitch and your hands
    wiggle to let me know your
    demands.

The look in your eye, ask for help.
The movement of your body lets
    us know if you are comfortable
    or weary.

Daniel, ask for our help and we
    will be by your side whenever
    you need us.

Daniel, we had you and aim to
    care for you no matter what it
    takes.

We wanted you then and we
want you more now. You are a
gift to us.

Look up Daniel, and see all the
love around you for you are
now the
apple of our eye and the light of
our life.

Marguerite Wasielewski
**Golden Wedding
   Anniversary**
It had been planned a year ahead.
Important things had all been said:
Just who would help, what food
    to get,
And where the table should be set.
He said not much. His suit was
    old,
His shirt was mussed, his fingers
    cold.
They made plans for a huge affair.
They planned to ask many a pair.
But as it was, nothing was done,
For he was gone, the quiet one.

Diane Elizabeth Provan
CHRISTMAS 1983

---

*To Kathy McDonald, whose
husband, Rep. Larry McDonald,
was aboard the shotdown K.A.L.
Flight 007.*

Christmas 1983 was not as great
    as last,
For on Christmas 1982 she held
    her hero fast.
In silence, with eyes closed she
    stood,
Recalling life and love so good.

Her daughter, born on Christmas
    Day 1982,
Was now without a father, one
    whom she never knew.
Gone was he who owned her
    heart,
Her life itself was torn apart.

She thought back to other
    holidays,
When she so shyly met his gaze.
This time, slowly, her eyes did
    mist
As she, in memory, her lover
    kissed.

How gentle was the sweet
    embrace
Of him whom none could e'er
    replace.
But now, the harsh reality,
As she through life alone would
    be.

She sighed and watched her
    Lauren play
Then turning, saw her Larry pray,
Her son, though he was only two,
Had her in tears when he was
    through.

"Dear Jesus, make Mommy
    happy, he said,
For she thinks that my daddy's
    dead.
Maybe he is and maybe he's not,
You see, his plane by a missile
    was shot.
If he lives now, God, please
    someday, send our Daddy
    home to stay."

Robert Conley
THRESHOLD OF LIGHT
My heavenly Father,
I realize I cannot be
Other than I am.
Help me then to make
The best I can of me.
Give me strength and wisdom
That I may share Thy will
Of service to my fellow man
Through faith I have in Thee.
I realize, my Heavenly Father,
That the evils in this world
Are brought about by man's own
    greed
And selfishness of deed,
For Thou hast said,
"Love thy neighbor
And lift the low in spirit."
I pray that Thou wilt guide me
In my daily walk with men.
Consecrate my mind and heart
And make me truly see,
Through loving Grace
And kindled Light,
My life belongs to Thee.

Vernice Abshire
A Little Girl At the Beach
On the beach, in the sand one day
A little girl sat, busy at play
Making sand castles, then tearing
    them down
And playing with sea shells she
    had found.

She watched as the birds
    hopped around in the sand,
She looked at the ocean, so blue
    and grand,
So much to see for a girl so small
Her little eyes could hardly take
    in it all.

She ran, she laughed,
    she enjoyed the sun
She thought she had never had
    such fun
The beach is a mighty fine place
    to be,
Seems as though God made it
    just for me.

Julia F. Hackett
HEART OF STONE
You've touched my heart
Of stone
Restoring its beating life
And you've taught me to feel
Once again . . .

With your gentle touch
Caress away
My hurts of past.

And within your arms
Hold me tight
And knit with me
Our future dreams . . .

Alice McInnis
BEING FREE
Whoever said life came easy
I can prove them to be wrong,
Because of all the troubles it brings
It takes someone who's strong.

Oh yes, there are good times
But the bad times come too.
When you're least expecting them
Is when they will hit you.

They hit like a big rock
That will knock you to the ground
But you have to pick yourself up

And forget those bad times
you've found.

Find in your heart to be happy
No matter how hard it may be
And you'll be rewarded
With good times ahead for you to
see.

Remember never to look down
Always hold your head up high
And be as free as a bird
Flying in the sky.

Enjoy life as what it is
Not what you want it to be
Because that is not the way to
show
That your life is happy and free.

Claude Wilkinson
Tonight I Counted the Stars
I thought of her lovingly,
Serenly,
Tenderly,
As tonight I counted the stars.

The sky clear as tears of sorrow,
Tears of loneliness,
Tears of pain,
Tonight I counted the stars.

Just a thought apart,
A touch apart,
A heart apart,
As tonight I counted the stars.

Blessedly cursed by love never
returned;
Forever to be yearned,
Tonight I counted the stars.

My mind wandering throughout
heaven and earth,
But wondering only of her;
So much lacking,
Surely life deserves,
Tonight I counted the stars.

And when no more nights and no
more stars,
And neither I remain;
I remember her lovingly, serenly,
tenderly,
The nights I counted the stars.

Raymond A. Sammak
Pirate's Den: New Orleans
Open mouth, stale with vodka
breath,
Teeth ripped from skulls with
bloody presision
Magnify the horrors of the fun
house with lysergic trust.
Momentum of roller coaster cars
keeps Negroes at the Circus.
Gyrations of a topless dance
queen, bown and shiny
Mix with the music of the
needle-pressing guitar man;
His ancient log-beat rythym
pulsates the room
Like some dark demon's heartbeat.
Black blood charged with electric
Copulate in back room of
boredom and dust.

Craig E. Burgess
SOUND IMAGINATION
The wondrous world of sound (or
noise),
When heard by radio—
Or played upon a phonograph
In living stereo—
Can often be misleading,
And even can excite,

Since our imagination
Will conjure up some sight:
Of agony or ecstacy;
Of love of those we know;
And yes, of dreams of lost
success . . .
Or of deserts made from snow!

Reality is thus replaced
By vivid fantasies
Which make it much more
difficult
To recognize with ease
The basic visual patterns
Which we may later SEE . . .
When they accompany the sound
Of imagined entity.

Jenny L. Dewey
If Yesterday Were Today
If yesterday were today,
It would be easier to see the
problems,
The hurt would be less,
For we could have taken steps to
avoid them.

But without yesterday,
We would not have the knowledge,
Nor gained the wisdom that we
need,
To manage what we have to today.

Blanche Eloise Higgins
DREAM

*To my Sister-Sunday McKinley
Bailey*

The day has been long
Night is on it's way
Shadows move and flicker
Like children at play.

Come let us light a candle
While we sip our tea
We can talk of good times
Just you and me.

Shadows creeping candle low
Do you really have to go
Yes, but not far
Just behind the glow.

Kathryn Sutton Elikofer
WHEN PEOPLE DROP IN
When some people drop in,
I think to myself, "What a Sin!"
Then off to the kitchen, I cry out
to Rover,
"Move Over," I'm here to get the
leftovers.

First the baloney, then the
cheese,
I throw it down with a squeeze.
Then I look all around and begin
to think—
What will I serve those people to
drink?

Will it be "cola, gin or rye?"
Gee. Oh no! I would rather die.
By then, I was getting hotter, and
hotter,
So I put in an ice cube and
poured in the water.

When I looked at my trembling
hand,
I had served their drinks on a
rusty old pan.
He looked at her, she looked at
him, as if to say,
"Here our friendship ends!"

No matter if they are my kin,
That is the way I feel, when some
people drop in.

Peter Vallas
DECEMBER

*Dedicated to: Ann Matticola you
will never be forgotten you are
December. . . Love Rhoda & Peter*

The time has come again
this year,

For all the world to spread
good cheer,

The thoughts of love fill
the air,

And gifts galore for all
to share,

Sharing is a very special thing,

And only happiness can
it bring,

Smile and be happy and
try to remember,

And make every month

The month of December

Evelyn A. Tompkins Miller
**It Could Only Happen
Here—**
They seat you on that cold, cold
pan;
You sit there 'cause you think
you can—
And then you can't!

You're sound asleep
And all is still—
Nurse comes in
With a sleeping pill—
Keep calm, don't rant!

They test you, X-ray, operate;
Then worry 'til you urinate—
You're sick all right!

They treat your every ache and
ill,
You're feeling fine—
You get the bill—
Relapse tonight!

Dora Gore
HELP ME LORD
Lord, help me live my life each
day
With a heart to love, and a mind
to pray
And the almighty grace to go
God's way
And do God's will, and work each
day

As each day, passes by with time
I want my life, to shine up high
To live with God, and stay in line
And give the best, without a sigh

And keep the faith with almighty
God
To walk the path, that Jesus lead
And love thy neighbors, for God
is love
And do the work, with faith
above

Keep going forward, it's the only
way
To walk the path that Jesus
walked
To reach that glorious home

some day
And find the hevenly doors
unlocked

God will lead you all the way
To reach the heavenly home above
If you continued, with faith each
day
And give God's best in all you pray

So, help me Lord as I live each day
To do God's will in a loving way
To walk, the straight, and narrow
path
Is the only true way, life can last.

Carrol Rowan Bailey
LO! THE CHRIST CHILD
In a manger of old,
In the sweet-smelling hay,
The Christ Child was born
On that first Christmas Day.

The Angels brought tidings
Of great joy to all men
That a Savior was born
Who would save us from sin.

Now that same Christ Child
Is the one who died
Upon the cruel cross
He was then crucified

For our sins He suffered.
Must it be in vain?
Oh, be ready to go
When he comes again.

Frank James Alles Jr.
SEDUCED
A thousand songs you sang for me
Softly sweetly all in key
Bathed me in an endless sea
Of harmony and love

Your stately stature caught my eye
Bade me not to walk on by
Whispered me a siren's sigh
Seduced by gilded timbre

You never laughed nor cried or
breathed
But oh—WHAT ROMANCE!—
you bequeathed
You trill the sweetest loving prose
MY LOVE! MY LIFE! MY STEREO!!

Ray "Skip" Connors
**Where Shall We Lay To
Sleep**
Sing a summer serenade
Green fields warm and deep
Boundless youth so unafraid
Where shall we lay to sleep?

Autumn sheds her panoply
Not a leaf to keep
Under a winter's canopy
Where shall we lay to sleep?

Willows weep and snowbirds play
Where the ivies creep
Rose of May at the close of day
Where shall we lay to sleep?

Lynell Dyann Hobson
WATCHING

*This poem was written for-and
inspired by-Dennis Paul Davis Jr.,
whom I'll always love, and always
be there if he should need me.*

I've seen you watching me,
s)eetheart
I haven't missed a single glance
because I've been watching you

even closer
Why don't we give "us" a second
chance?

I know we could make love work
if only we could try again
I realize the things that were wrong
so I know better now than I did
then.

Well, I've seen the way you look
at me
and if I'm looking from the right
direction, you still care
You have to look between the
glances to see it
We should love each other, not
sit and stare.

Bright Ceasar
DREAMLAND
A place where we can dream of
beautiful things
like flowers blooming in spring
doves by the oceans shore
tender thoughts of love and much
more
with a silent breeze blowing
through our hair
expressing our candid feelings of
care
listening to birds singing in the trees

royal blue butterflies landing on
leaves
feeling the rays from the sun
running through the sand having
fun
as if life for us has just begun
dreamland what a wonderful
place to be for
love and fun underneath the rays
of the sun

Eileen C. Joyce
THE LEGACY
My wordly possessions are
trifling and few
   That when I die I can leave to
   you,
No horde of money or priceless
treasure
   To launch you on a life of
   pleasure.
I leave you the rain on a warm
summer day,
   And the hawthorn trees that
   bloom in May,
I leave you the park, all fresh and
green,
I leave you the sunset each night
to be seen.
I leave you the hope of mortal
resurrection,
I leave you God's grace for a life

of direction
I leave you the things that can
never be bought
I leave you life's goodness which
must be sought.

Scott Whetsell
HARPERS FERRY

---

*For those who are my every
breath, my wife Kathleen, my
daughter Holly, and my son Jeff.*

Cradled in the mountains of the
Blue Ridge,
   unspotted except by the moon
   at night.
   Caressed by the rivers, allowing
   nature to live,
   flora and fauna, truly an eye
   delight.
In Spring, the aroma of the
Paulownia trees
   engulfs this lonely place.
   The river dampness carried by
   a breeze,
      lingers ever so gently on my
      face.
In times before, I've walked the
street
   where history has its bounds.
   Early in the morning, I've
   chanced to meet
   the spirits that claim these
   grounds.
They wander endlessly as if time
stands still,
   or just to isolate.
   This town hidden by the hills,
   which nature dedicates.
God in his great wisdom, must
   there be a plan?
   To create this refuge the world
   cannot erase.
   Where reality and illusion are
   just products of man.
      Where the past and present
      have only one face.

Sara Spillman
THE ROPE
Can I, Should I, Will I, and When?
How am I going and where have I
been?
When to, Where to, What for,
and Why?
Who should I turn to or which
way to try?
Coming and going, turning
non-stop
Down to the bottom, and back to
the top.
Constantly moving, never unwind,
All just to keep you off of my
mind.
My eyes want to cry and my
heart wants to break.
Sometimes I wonder how much
more I can take.
Till I come to my senses and
realize again
That there's really no loss cause I
still have a friend.
So let's harp on the good times
when chance has us meet
To talk of our progress, to forget
our defeat.
And to wish one another all
goodness with fate
As we open our eyes, as we pull

our own weight.
As we try to keep happy, never
giving up hope.
Cause it all goes to pieces when
you let go of THE ROPE!

Misty Walker
INCHWORM
Your Highness.
Before you insist on ruling
and boast on the strength of your
royal scepter
and how far your kingdom extends,
you should stop this ridiculous
moment
and seriously consider the all too
obvious
that is not often enough
overlooked:
   In actuality, you are only
   slightly less
   than eight inches long—
   not the length of a ruler.
   Two thirds of it equals a
   common man
   with full staff extended still
   short of the Kingdom.
your highness? No.
A petty dictator of inches and
moments—
weak and soft and worthless after
the reign.

R. Scott Hastings
CASTLE STEPS
The graying, weathered, hand-
carved, stones
can barely be seen against
the salt-water mist
floating up from the
crashing waves
of the ocean below.
They carve themselves down
through the cliff side
until they reach the bottom,
intruding on a very special
relationship,
that of sea and sand.

Patricia Ann Lewis
IF I COULD

---

*Lovingly dedicated to my father,
Andrew Lee Lewis, who has
always encouraged my creative
endeavors.*

You come to tell me
Of your sorrows
As a willow weeps
To a stream without water.
I have no room left
In this empty heart I bear
Cast over by shadows
Which will not leave.
I would give to you
If I could
But there is nothing.
Those before you
Have taken it all.

Paulette Kupari
LOOKING BACK
As I walk through the shadows of
my mind
I see the past with old eyes;
the questions of yesterday still
linger within me.

As I look upon my present life
I can only see today;
yesterday's gone but is not

forgotten.

As I think of the future,
my questions of yesterday return;
tomorrow is something I cannot
see.

I must look through the shadows
of the past and the present
for the future,
In that way I may see with new
eyes.

Anna Mae Brennan
FIRST—BORN
As I feel your life begin to stir,
My heart will find no rest.
Longing to feel you in my arms,
And hold you to my breast.

Each movement makes me anxious
As I imagine who you'll be.
A boy just like his daddy,
Or a little girl like me.

As I listen to your heartbeat,
I hear the echo of my own.
For I know the beauty you will
bring
Into our lives and home.

As your body grows within me
A special bond is made,
And nothing in the whole wide
world
Will ever make it fade.

I know the pain that I will bear,
Yet I will not be forlorn.
No greater happiness I will know
Than the joy of our first-born.

Mrs. Mary Tanco
Christmas!-Then And Now
Christmas used to be
A time for much joy
But now, it's quite different, as
you can see
When you try to find a small toy.

There are so many things
You don't know about
Such as dolls, toys and rings
It almost causes one to scream
and shout.

With all the video games
That everyone seems to crave
Nothing seems to be the same
When you have to scrimp and
save.

It used to be much appreciated
Just to get a little trinket
But nowadays, it's hardly accepted
If you only spend a "triplet."

Just keep on hoping and praying
That Christmas means you really
care
For others and the Savior
This truly is my prayer.

Ron Kuenzli Jr.
THE JUDGEMENT DAY
The Judgement Day is upon us,
We better not make a fuss.
God has readied seven angles
with trumpets,
And He's sending His Son for us!

The first angel will sound with
destruction, blood, fire, and hail,
The second with volcanoes and a
bloody sea, you still have time
to post your bail.
A falling star from Heaven will
be the third and it'll ruin part
of the sea,

With the fourth taking a third of
the Earthly light, We're going
to pay our fee.

"Woe, woe, woe", the torture will
have only begun,
Because God won't let us have
any more of our fun.
We will pay for putting Him down,
And upon His head will be the
crown.

The fifth will have locusts to
torment those without the
Lord,
The sixth will send four to slay
part of us, so to live without
God we can't afford.
With the seventh will be voices
which are great,
And by this time it will be too
late!

Ruby K. Reed
A Flower For His Bouquet

---

*Dedicated to Bridgett and Adam
my grandchildren*

God was creating a beautiful
bouquet for His mansion in the
sky
He searched His gardens below
from His throne on high.
Just one more of beauty rare, only
one in a million will do,
Of all the beautiful colors one
was eminent in His view.

He plucked this one, oh so
gently, took it to Paradise
above
To dwell in that celestial home of
everlasting love.
He left the lusterless ones to
linger here on earth
We, to be like the one He
gathered, will have to prove our
worth.

Live quietly without pretense of
glory we have not earned
He is not deceived by words we
speak, but considers lessons
learned.
We are lonely, and we miss her
so; that bright flower we
cannot see,
Yes, God took a flower for His
bouquet, June second, Nineteen
eighty-three.

Melba Avis Williams
Beloved Child Of Long Ago
You gaze from oval picture frame,
Your baby face, with trusting
glance,
Forever waits upon some
childhood game.
Plump, dimpled hands clasp ball,
or toy.
Dark, limpid eyes, uplifted there,
Brimming with some secret joy.
White cap, adorned with cabbage
rose,
Askew on wispy, silken hair—
Could you, encumbered so by
heavy gown,
Slip from your chair,
To run about in childish glee?
Or, must you forever sit and gaze,
With soft air of baby trust,
Through an eternity?

Nina Patchen
THANKSGIVING
Thanksgiving is not just one day
a year,
A day for feasting and greeting
ones, dear,
Thanksgiving should come to
you every day,
And I can tell you of many a way.
If all these things you follow
through
Thanksgiving can mean much
more to you;
There are many friends to be
thankful, for,
Good health and family, and so
much more.
We must thank GOD for His
loving care,
We should be ready to help and
share.
We remember the ones who have
gone before,
We should be thankful their
suffering is o'er,
We shoud be thankful for the
food we eat,
Also, or new freinds we happen to
meet.
So, let us give thanks to GOD
every day
For giving us Life, helping others
on the way.
Thank Him for all the blessings
we share,
We must end all our thanks with
a humblest prayer,
Then . . . when that day in
November is here
We can say, I've had
Thanksgiving every day this
year.

J. L. A. Roberts
PRONOUNCEMENT
"of my candicacy for
the presidency of
these U. S. of A. . . ."

Like salt to the tongue
of the salt-deprived or water
to one dying of thirst:

"that the incumbent
is a macho posturer,

that I, Jesse Jackson, have the
right
to exercise my option to send any
child,
of my five children, or even all of
them,
to a private school if I so desire,

that I would instigate neutrality
in trust
as a way of life in military disputes
in Grenada, in Lebanon, or in any
other
land, or any island;

that a talented woman should
join me
on the ticket as candidate for
V.P. . . ."

My gut screams out,
"YOU'LL HAVE MY VOTE!"
I quote.

Doris Irene Warren
CENTURY PLANT
I ponder on the Century Plant
That only blooms one hour
So long in toil, to bring to birth

It's brief and perfect flower.

I touch the dying petals now, and
know
It thought it worth the pain
To have perfection for one hour
Then hope again.

But women's pain looses it's beauty
When kept with tears
And toil is worthless when it
counts down
Empty years.

Because I must not say "I Love
You"
Because I must not feel, I see
Rejected, Spurned and crushed
The blossom of my century.

Lyllian D. Cole
The Humble Donkey Lay

To Bonnie Jean

'Tho Angels sang, each beasty
hushed, was still
as Christ, The Child, was born in
Bethlehem;
peace wrapped, He lie acrib
beneath the Hill
brow marked with naught save
Haloed Diadem.

THE HUMBLE DONKEY LAY
beyond the Creche,
unnoted by the Wisemen bearing
gifts,
to rest his wearied bones, prepare
afresh,
for flight from Herod's vile
decree, to Egypt's

Vast protective sands, to wait
again,
for guidance from the voice of
Angel-call
to Joseph: "Harken! Herod's ended
reign!"
the Humble Donkey then, a part
of All.

The Plan to bring to erring Man,
Salvation
that he does not, as yet, deserve
or earn;
fast fades the Hope before
complete cessation
that Man may yet this Humble
Lesson learn.

Marjoire E. Johnson
MY GRAND-DAUGHTER

To Stephanie Nicole McNabb

She has round, rosy cheeks,
Loves to play hide and seek.
Her eyes are a sparkling blue-gray,
Twenty five pounds she does
weigh.
She looks roly-poly with baby fat,
And loves to watch her furry cat.
My expression she anxiously
seeks,
As through her play-pen net
she peeks.
I love to comb her fine brown hair,
As she plays with her cuddly
teddy-bear.
She makes me feel really fine,
She is my ray of bright
sunshine.

Nina F. Patchen
THANKFUL
Whenever I see a crippled child
On crutches or in a wheelchair,
I cannot keep the tears, back
To see him sitting, there;
Even those who have brain damage
Will give you a loving smile,
They live in a life, all their own,
To charm you is their style.
They ask no sympathy from you,
They have no woes or cares.
I cannot help but wonder
If I were the one sitting, there
Would I have a smile for everyone?
Would I ask for sympathy?
It really made me stop and think
If that one were really me.
So, I must be more thoughtful
Of those who have this cross to
bear,
I will be more kind and tender
To the one sitting in that chair.

Virginia E. Cruikshank
NEW LIFE
Down in the meadow
Deep in scented clover,
A newborn calf
Stands shakily,
And eyes its world
With wonder and content.

Up on the mountaintop
At dawn's first light,
A sunburst spreads its rays;
And I in newborn wonder,
Lift arms ecstatic
To the sky.

Nevada Swisher
**On Enlightened Self-
Interest, Via Science**

---

*TO BOBBY for David Wolf,
patent attorney, and family, and
with special thanks to Mary
Farrell, librarian.*

Given: *The Zero-sum Society*,
Lester Thurow,
Only one can win—
or several,
or a mob.

That's where primitive man
caved into the scene.
He'd got a bit of meat,
a bit of fat.
He'd hit you on the head,
you know,
for that.
He *had* to.

And yet . . .
He was surrounded by riches
untold, unlimited blessing, if
only he knew.

Doris Coleman
How Long Will You Sleep
Why do you sleep so long; my
daughters and sons
Do you not know you awakening
has long begun
From the day I sent my beloved
son
A path was spoin, just for you,
my love ones

Awake from your sleep
I have promises to keep
I promise to guide your feet

Wake now so death and sin can flee
For neither death nor sin are of me
Awake my children and see plainly
Your path is me, for I created thee
Walk closer with me
I am your best friend, you see
You must follow me

My begotton was hung on a tree
So that ye may see
Open your eyes, Let me reward thee, openly
My begotton is the key
My sons and daughters, how long will ye sleep

Shirley-Ann Turner
SEASONS OF LOVE
I loved you when Spring was young,
everything was new and exciting,
the world was thriving, and we became one.

I loved you in summer, in the shade,
the meadow lush and green and wild,
and new discoveries we made.

Now in September, I stand upon the hill,
enjoying flaming maples and golden sunsets . . .
exciting moments, and I love you still.

I'll love you in repetition of winter,
firesides, when we are warm and mellow,
and all is settled and familiar.

Silent transient, when death makes a claim,
and the time of mourning is past . .
memories to comfort, and a love that will remain.

Grace Carter
HEAVENLY GIFT

In anticipation of the birth of my first grandchild, Chris.

'Tis for sure you'll be a "cutie",
And as dear as you can be,
For you're coming down from Heaven,
And two will now be three.

Oh, I know you'll miss the angels,
That you played with way up there,
But you're bringing Heaven here to earth,
With your love that's meant to share.

So, Little Angel, here's a wish—
For Mom—and Dad—and you,
For Mom and Dad—true happiness,
And naught but joy for you!

Donald Daniel James Knox
OUR OLYMPIC TRADITION
Mount Olympus, in divine homage
To they laurel leaf—promises
In thy ancient temple
Bid fare—to they nemesis

Befriend
Ways of thy malice
Triumphant
Drink of thy chalice

Robin S. Bachnak
FROSTY WINTERLAND
A snowflake falls gently to the ground
It seems to make everything glow
All animals are asleep safe and warm without a sound
As a drop of melted snow falls into the valley below

Not a bit of beauty is out of place
Beauty runs in the rivers and streams
Snow falls steadily and yet with such grace
It's a place made just simply for dreams

It's a place for someone to smile and to have some fun
To let the child out of you and to let you feel good about yourself
You can run as far as you want to run
It's a kind of place you'd find in a fairytale book sitting on a shelf

You cannot take this winterland home with you
But it sure would be nice
To come here when you're feeling all alone and blue
Please come to my beautiful world of crystal ice
Come to my world of Frosty Winterland

Donna A. Hauff
Giving Thanks and Praise
Goodness it is nearing time for Thanksgiving Day,
To praise God I know not quite what to even say,
That would give to God enough honor and due praise,
For God has blessed me and helped in so many ways!

Many times we forget to praise Him or be thankful,
For sometimes we complain when we should be grateful,
We all should each and every day count our blessings,
And thank God for each and every blessing He brings.

For things do not just so happen we should know!
For God in His goodness His love He does show,
For life does take some heartaches and some pain,
It also takes the sunshine and the turbulent rain.

So let's look to God in thanks and in our gratitude,
For our happiness is controlled by even our attitude,
Our heartaches, sorrows, problems, cares and our trials,
Aren't easy but we must look up and keep our smiles.

God deserves our praises and yes our thankfulness,
For God is good and He works for our happiness,
So whatever is your day on this Thanksgiving Day,
Remember God loves you and He is only a prayer away!

Norman L. Dodge, Ph. D.
Will You Share An Eternal Love?
Adam was known to have needed Eve
And that nature has followed through
I find an Adam in the heart of me
Who visions his Eve in you.

You'd be a fool to resist my smile
Or to ignore my manly appeal
For God gave me magnetic wiles
To create this flame you feel!

I have the eyes that have seen God's light
To watch for the pitfalls ahead
The loving arms to hold you tight
And the hands to toil and for your bread.

My warming lips will prevent the chill
You may feel at the close of day
And you have love's thrill
To shield me from blowing away.

While the summer stars are gay
And play in the heavens above
Will you come to me beneath their rays
And share an eternal love?

Catherine Rose Mangual
MY FIRST LOVE

This poem was inspired by and is dedicated to, George McArthur, a very special part of my past.

I loved you once, but now you see
You took your love away from me
You said you loved me very dear
Yet in your heart it wasn't clear
You made me love you, that is true
But far too soon I lost you

Although you said you cared for me
I find it awfully hard to see
If you loved me, so very dear
Then tell me why did your love disapear?
You made me think you loved me so
But just like that, you let me go

Although it hurts and makes me cry
I'll still love you
Until the day I die
You were my first, but not my last

And after today, you'll be a
Part of my past.

Helen S. Tuttle
THIRTEEN
Now how can I write of you my sweet
With your golden hair and your laughing feet;
And your budding breasts and cornflower eyes?
Still with the dreams of a new sunrise.
How can a mother, write of a child
Who wants to be a woman, yet is wild
As buttercups by the winds beguiled:
Still with the faith of an infant mild.
Strong as a sapling that's what you are
And I look to you as to a star
Who has more than once been my guiding light.
A child's hand to hold, through
The long dark night.
      SYNOPSIS
Now I am tired,
My youth is gone—
But her love and laughter
Carry me on.

Gone forever the fairie-like child
Her feet are subdued
Her manner mild,
But under it all is a heart still wild,
As buttercups by the winds beguiled.

Bianca Covelli Stewart
BLACKBOARD
Dawning. The blackboard glistens clean and dark.
I am. I stare into the blank new day.
Teach me, Life, take your chalk and make a mark,
The sign for birth, the symbol for decay,
The patterns for to trust and to betray.

Midday. The blackboard creaks beneath the weight
Of centuries of words that blur and blend,
Converging lines that force Will into Fate,
Vague portraits merging enemy and friend,
And crowded, linking circles without end.

Twilight. The blackboard dims against the wall;
My soul no longer tries to read its face.
Too many shadows have begun to fall,
Distorting, shifting truth from place to place—
Better to erase! Better to erase!

Midnight. The blackboard shrivels, bare and dark,
Devoid of science, art, philosophy.
Teach me, Lord, take Your blood and make a mark,
Two crossing lines that shall become for me
The only truth and beauty and serenity.

Our World's Best Loved Poems

Mary E. Hill
CHEER

If you're feelin' low and blue
Tell you what you have to do:
Lift up your head, give a big smile,
Put on your coat, walk a quick
    mile.

Look up to Heaven, praise the
    Lord,
Ask Him to guide you ever toward
Doing His work, accepting His
    will;
Then reflect and relax at your
    domicile.

Call a friend who's lonely, insecure,
Do a good deed, take a short tour;
Read a good book, see a good
    show—
Buy some new duds from head to
    toe.

When the day has passed and
    night has come
Be glad your spirit is no vacuum;
Consider your blessings, the
    battles you've won;
Life is worth living—so have
    some fun!

Remember life is a precious gift,
Not to be squandered nor set adrift;
So make the most of each hour
    here,
And feel the breath of Heaven
    near.

Holly Healey
Thanksgiving At My House

Thanksgiving Day is almost here,
    but I regret to say,
I know I ought to be thankful,
    but it's not my favorite day.

A twelve by sixty trailer,
    is where I live you see.
There's plenty of room for five of
    us,
    my husband, three kids and me.

But when it comes Thanksgiving
    Day,
    and the turkey, it smells fine,
Within my trailer walls there'll be
    a count of twenty-nine.

I have no place to sit them all,
    and to move you didn't dare,
For even in the bathroom,
    there was someone eating there!

So on that night I kneel and pray,
    my eyes almost in tears.
I ask the Lord if He could change,
    Thanksgiving to every other
    year!

Deanna G. McGinnis
WATER

Darkness is my depth
Clear is my color
Swift is my body
Shimmer is my nerves
Slosh, Gurgle, Tinkle is my voice
Quiet is my thoughts
Rivers are my limbs
Lakes are my body
Clouds are my food
People are my enemies
Flowers are my friends
Fish are my playmates
Drink from ME, "Oh People Of
    God"
Save my person from distruction
    so we may live.

Dale Mark Presley
A Man's Fiery Love

When God makes a boy, He
    lights a little fuse
That smokes and smolders, at
    first just to amuse.
But the boy's soon obsessed with
    the sputters and sparks
As he starts on his loving war
    and slowly embarks
On young men's greatest quest
    that they ever know
Of fighting these flames that
    daily grow and grow.
At last he must decide what his
    love will be,
Pure and compassionate . . . or
    wild and free.

Deep in my heart is this slow
    burning fire,
Kindled by kindness and fanned
    by desire.
I've quared all my life against the
    sigh or glance
That might fuel this fire and
    allow it to enhance
Flames of passion within the
    smothered coals of my soul
That could burn my defenses and
    grow out of control.
But emotion and reason now
    wrestle all day long
And it's harder to quench this fire
    and keep myself strong.

I know when God made you so
    opposite from me
He used the kind of power that
    pushed land from sea.
And just like crashing waves that
    beat on the shore
Your essense tears at me and
    cries out for more
Of all that I hear and all that I see,
Of all that I am or ever could be.
My heart's now convinced we
    were created as a pair
Though God's kept us parted till
    this special when and where.

T. Allen Madding
REAL LOVE

What kind of life is this supposed
    to be?
Plastic spoons, plastic forks,
    plastic people who smile at me.
Everything has become so
    automated,
From the banking machines to
    the girls I've dated.
Yes, thank you, let's sit here.
Mind if I order us another beer?
Now the evening comes to an
    end,
And the quite trite question "Can
    we stil be friends?"
Where have all the phone booths
    gone?
What ever happened to the old
    slow songs?
What happened to respect for the
    God above
And what has happened to Real
    Love?

Michael J. Dougherty
VICTUM

It is a deep darkness
Not sinstrous though
More like a black pit
always so cold
A kind of emptiness

It's entity so oblique
where no light
shines through it
nor cometh of.
A hole in time
and of persistence
Nothing can exist
There is no place there
Only a reality of dispair
A monolithic symbol
of such magnatude.
Forever does it survive
Never to forget
It endlessly continues
with no prupose at all
always here
yet never there
So desolate
and incomplete
That's all there really is.

Alvelda Record
MAN

God put man upon this earth as
    His instrument
He breathed the breath of life in
    us and
gave us the will to live
He gave us eyes to see the world
    as it is
And ears to listen to all men

He gave us minds to discern right
    from wrong
And knowledge to separate the
    difference
Hands to help our brother or
    sister along the way
And He gave us a heart to be
    light but strong

Understanding to know that all
    men are created equal,
but not perfect
Strength and compassion for
    those in need
The ability to share joy and sorrow
And power to place hope in the
    heart of the downhearted

Knowledge of when to be silent
    and when to speak
The audacity to smile even when
    things go wrong
Feet that should walk forward to
    ways of bettering things
Giving acknowledgement to the
    lowly and the meek

God made us in His own image
    and likeness
As He suffered upon this earth,
    so shall we
As He forgave, let us do, as He
    was kind, let us be
For the short time that we are
    here, let us give happiness

Susan Jean Bell
MY BABY

Morning sickness, gaining weight,
Then came the day to celebrate.
Dirty diapers, lullabies,
Formula to sterilize.

Learning to crawl, then to walk,
Understanding baby talk.
Diaper rash, teething pain,
Next it's time to potty train.

ABC's and one, two, three,
Riding to town on Mommies knee.
Temper tantrums, learning to
    share,
Braids and ribbons in your hair.

Pretty dresses just for you,
Next it's time to go to school.
Mumps and measles, chicken
    pox,
Toys and games and building
    blocks.

Scrapes and bruises, many tears,
Lots of hugs throughout the years.
Next I know, your in your teens,
Puberty and faded jeans.

Sixteenth birthday celebration,
Parties, dates, and graduation.
Special man that you found,
Engagement ring and wedding
    gown.

Throughout the years
I've loved you so.
Now it's time
To let you go.

Katherine M. DeNering
PREACHER FRENNY

Preacher Frenny
    ranted and raved
At the congregation
    he'd vowed to save;
All with good intent
Or for his frustration
    to vent
At those who throughout
    the week
Had their bread and
    butter to seek.

Surely weariness was
    the lot of many
As they listened to
    Preacher Frenny.
Mrs. Gulpen sitting on
    the outside aisle,
Marveled at the
    preachers style.
Matt Liston sitting
    near the center aisle,
Noted with a quiet
    smile,
God bless and save
    those who endure
Such folly from
    the floor,
When a message he
    could be giving
Of love to help
    the living.

Patrice Diana Saylor
MY DEITY

Within me you calm the roaring
    seas
you are to me my Deity
you guide my every step
you move the mountains in your
    way
you are my strength to face each
    day

You clear the valleys way below
you lead me to where I ought to go
to you I give the glory
you gave your life for me
when you were crucified at
    Calvary

You give me hope, you fill my
    needs
upon your word I will feed
I praise you Lord for all you have
    done
Since I found you, I search no
    more
you've given me the life I have
    been searching for.

361

John Campbell, Editor & Publisher

Sandra D. Catlett
SOUNDS

To my mother and sisters who inspired me in writing poems and not just listening, but understanding. I love you all.

The sounds from the ocean
hitting against the rocks
Oh! That beautiful sound.
I live for that sound to carry me
away,
And when I hear that sound, I
drift very far
Just as the sand does as the ocean
washes it away
The emptiness in the echoes, the
loniness in my heart
I feel like part of the ocean,
Because it reminds me of me
Wondering if the emptiness
would ever be filled
Wondering if the loniness would
ever disappear.

Grace Carter
A CHRISTMAS PRAYER
Bells are ringing,
People singing,
And there's a lonely man, Oh,
Lord!

Crowds are bustling,
All are hustling,
But there's a hungry woman, Oh,
Lord!

Snow is falling,
Friends are calling,
Yet there's a child in pain, Oh,
Lord!

If only I could do so, Lord,
I'd erase all loneliness,
I'd put a smile on every face,
And everyone I'd bless
By taking away all loneliness,
All hunger, pain and strife,
And giving to each another
chance,
To lead a happy life!

Kathleen Kay Lewis
THANKSGIVING DAY
From London's River Thames one
day, the good ship Mayflower
sailed away
With faith and hope and food
supplies, they severed all ties
faced the open sea
After many months and rough
times too, tossed around by
wind and waves
The good ship held and made it
through, on bended knee the
pilgrims prayed.

At Plymouth Rock the Pilgrims
dock, weary and wondering
look around
Suddenly "Big Chief" came along.
"How" said he, and peacefully
he raised his hand
Then they were offered food and
rest, prayed for the courage to
respond
To do the work that they knew
best, share the good things they
had found.

Now every year this great affair is
celebrated in this way

Turkey and good things by the
score, with grateful hearts we
ought to pray
Thinking of those who came
before
Americans call it "Thanksgiving
Day".

E. Louise Ponder
MEALTIME
It must be the birds lunch time,
There are so many hopping from
limb to limb
Picking at the cherries red,
I wonder if they too, "thank Him"?

I wonder if they say, "We thank
You Father, for these,
The delicious wild red cherries
You've put upon these trees.

I wonder too, if they have to be
good
Before expecting Him to supply
their food.
Perhaps instead, its a banquet,
Because they are staying so long,
While the berries are fast
disappearing
As they eat, and yet still chirp
their song.

D. Annetta Pickering
AN INNOCENT BABE
Jesus was born on a bed of hay,
Sweet and innocent there he lay.
Mary was smiling her eyes filled
with pride,
While Joseph his father knelt by
her side.

The shepherds were standing in
awe looking on,
While the heavens were filled
with a glorious song.
The angels were telling the world
of his birth,
The King of all Kings had come
down to earth.

The wide men had come from a
land far away,
They'd followed a star that
showed where he lay.
They brought him their gifts,
gold, frankincense, myrrh,
Then bowed their heads and
worshipped him there.

The babe that was born on that
starlit night,
Would lead sinful men into God's
glorious light.
To a world that was lying in sin
and despair,
He came as our Saviour, that
Babe lying there.

Donny Bert
THIS DIRTY TOWN
Nothings changed in my home
town
same old faces still hanging
around
dealing cards from the bottom of
the stack
I wonder what it is about this
place
that keeps me coming back
memories linger on
pass through my mind before
there gone
and I still can't see
why this place means so much to
me

this dirty town has no hope
the streets are filled with
emptyness
but I keep coming back
to this dirty town—this dirty
town

just a boy I was still in school
life was crazy and love was cruel
I sat in my car it was late
a bottle of tequila and a loaded
thirty eight

I almost took my life away
in this dirty town
I almost took my life one day
in this dirty town—this dirty
town

Elizabeth Utley Henry
REACHING

*Dedicated with love to Paul and
Ruth Henry*

Reaching, I've been reaching for
the sky
Reaching out to touch the world,
as it goes by
Now I'm reaching down to touch
the earth
To see if I'm still there
Being in love is like walking on
air
Reaching to feel the wind rush
through my fingers
As I reach out to touch your hair
Reaching to feel the softness of
your hands
But never reaching for demands
Reaching, reaching to take you in
my arms
Reaching, never reaching to do
you harms
Reaching, never reaching in
despair
Reaching for love and you are
there.

Cindy McConnaughey
tribute
cinnamon clove smells
of a long ago person,
humming ancient Irish hymns,
sipping hot tea
on a bleak rainy evening.
I miss her so.

R. L. Brummell
**The Dust Of Empty
Christmas**
Greyly the night presses its
wetness
Against the empty window pane,
And swirls into a darkened dusty
room
Spattering droplets sucked
hungrily up
By torn and drooping wallpaper
That gaily once declared of happy
days and cheery voices.
Rustlings in discarded papers tell
of
Tiny shiny eyes,
The mice are landlords now.
Farthest from the wind, alone,
cast off;
His chair,
A chair of strength, decisions,
bravery,
And on whose wide strong seat
the children (two)

Could curl and hug away a
wintery afternoon,
Broken now and stained by times
regret,
It sits in judgement of an empty
Christmas Day.

Dawn Koontz

Dawn Koontz
THE FINAL CURTAIN
Loving laced in lies
Two together . . . yet alone
As the finest actors
We really knew our roles

Everyday the same . . .
Afraid to face the night
In fear of what's in sight,
the lovers turn away.
Love drowning in the rain
Face another lonely twilight.
Night's longer than the days
For love, there is no time
Unable to unite, surrounded by
the rain
The moment never claimed . . .
Aimless is the night.

Face the final curtain, of this
lover's play.
It's closing night for love
Our moments not enough
Let it go, and take a bow
For love's escaped us now
Face the final curtain, for
heartache's all we gained.

Rita L. Heinzen
OH FOR SOMETIME
Oh for sometime alone with you,
To hear you laugh and sing.
To touch your cheek and smooth
your hair
and enjoy the tenderness it would
bring.

Even a moment of your time
would satisfy my yearning,
to have your arms around me
tight.
The desires like a burning.

Oh, to feel your breath upon my
cheek,
Softly whispering in my ear.
You've always said those things
to me
that every woman longs to hear.

Oh, for the time to spend with
you.
I know it will be someday.
I pray whenever that time might
be
we won't let one minute slip
away.

Wesley Wildt
A PRAYER
If I could say a little prayer
Expressing all the joy
Within the happy hearts tonight
Of every girl and boy,
I think it would not be the toys
Or shining Christmas trees
That I would thank him for the
most,
For all such things as these
Can never be compared, it seems,
To love that God has shown
By sending us his dearest gift,
His only , precious Son.
And so, if it were left to me
To say a prayer, my prayer would
be,
"We thank you, God, for Jesus."

Debbie Smulski
ONE SPECIAL NIGHT
The lights go on,
The world is bright.
The snow is falling,
All is white.
The bells are ringing,
The people pray.
The children singing,
On this glorious day.
For just one night,
For all to seize.
The feel of tranquility,
The world at peace.
The hugs, the kisses,
All join as one.
A mother, father, daughter and son.
All sadness forgotten,
All sorrows will leave.
If only each night
Could be Christmas Eve.

Brenda I. Felsinger/bif
CHRISTMAS EVE
Christmas stockings hanging
round;
New fallen snow upon the
ground—
Quiet times can now be found;
It must be Christmas Eve.

Our children gone, but yet their
here;
Their memories are always near.
Christmas carolers we now hear;
I must be Christmas Eve.

Pa, to bed now we must go.
We've burned the candle 'till it's
low.
Tonight the wind it shall not
blow—
Tonight is Christms Eve.

Carole Arthurs
AUTUMN COMES IN VIEW
The autumn leaves are springing
forth
In shades of red and gold.
In every tree, on every hill
There's beauty to behold.

Just wander through a wooded lane
And see a marvelous view.
Of green and red and golden brown
In shades of every hue.

I cannot see this wonderous sight
Without a breathless sigh.
And know His hand has wrought
it there
For folks like you and I.

A panoramic vision of
His gifts in golden hue.

I feel His presence most of all
When autumn comes in view.

Buffy Weaver

Buffy Weaver
THE CAPTINS SON

*Inspired by my Dad, A Volunteer
fireman in Francesville, Ind, and
all the other brave firefighters . . .*

Raging blazes
of fire raises
A tower of flames
a fireman tames
smoke towers black,
oxygen on his back,
Axe in hand to chop inside
heat everywhere, no place to hide
celling is down, he is pinned.
for this act he'd not intend.
In this colored ember of heat,
he fell many feet.
And for someone else, he gave his
life,
left his family, kids and wife
She knew the dangers, born in his
blood, to be done,
for he was the captins son.

P. Scheible Jr.
Captain Cooke and Rosey
O'Shea
Captain Cooke was sick of the
mire.
The man was empty, but full of
desire.
You don't need the wine to feel
the fire.

Captain Cooke went out one night.
He met a girl called Rosey
O'Shea.
Rosey's a girl who listens w/care.
She's got eyes that say life is
sacred and rare.

Rosey took the Captain and put
him at ease.
She erased his pain and his
elusive disease.
Live for your mind and treasure
your soul,
all will be o.k.
A special girl is that Rosey
O'Shea.

They talked for hours
of words w/powers,
of family, friends and love.
The Captain saw a city,
turn from eagle to dove.
He knows there's true hope from
above.

He left alone in the night,
but he was feeling alright.
A friend was found in a day.
It's a thrill to know of Captain
Cooke,
and the lovely Rosey O'Shea.

Carolina S. A. Caletti
AN OLD MAN'S HANDS

*"Alla nonna Silvia" with love and
pride.*

Hands!
Hands from which you
Can understand years of pain,
Years of happiness.
Hands from which you
Can free the human softness,
The human toughness.
Hands!
Hands which may strike out
Hands which give bread to the
hungry
Just aged hands,
From which you can see the
ancientness
Of the man who
Has given everything
And anything of himself—
No face,
No body,
No character,
Just hands—
Old hands folded in the natural
despair
Of
Death.

Dennis Johnson
SUCCESS IS A DREAM
Everyone has a desire to be
Successful from the start,
It's a yearning that comes from
inside,
Deep down in the heart

Everybody needs to feel
That somewhere in this life,
They're going to get up on their
feet,
And walk out of all this strife

It boils down to every individual
And the desire to stay alive,
To get ahead of the "rat race",
Become successful, and survive

So tell me, from these strong
desires
Why we will give up on our
dreams?
Settle down in the ruts of life,
And be happy, or so it seems.

I think it's drilled into us from
birth,
We could lose as well as win,
And losing never did feel good,
So why even try again?

If from birth you're taught that
you're going to lose,
There is no way to succeed,
If you try to stand, you'll be
beaten back down,
By this world so full of greed,

Then, I'll say this, take a firm
stand. Because you have a right,
If you fall, get back up and then
Continue with your fight

This world has it's ups and downs,
But let your desires burn on,

Because if your dream dies,
All your hopes are gone

So reach down into your heart
And grab the desire to try again,
You may fall down, but hang in
there,
And soon you just may win.

So don't give up, hang on to your
dreams,
Never let them unravel, unfold,
Success will one day come your
way,
And with it, your pot of gold.

Bobbie Goodwin
MISSISSIPPI SUNSET
Sunset, you are so beautiful.
Your horizon
Is so gay.
You seem so near
And yet
So far away!

As the day comes to an end
I look at you
With amusing eyes,
For I know
In the morning
You will be a beautiful sunrise!

Ted Cowdrey
STAR * LIGHT

*To my friend Shari, a star, whose
timeless light guides many.*

Last night dark clouds absorbed
star * light
And changed it * love * when day
broke night
Into crystal * form * like * pure
white snow
**** To sprinkle * on the earth *
below ****
*** Where it stayed * the whole
day thru ***
** Sparkling ** just like ** your
eyes do **

Dorene Brenner
WE WERE FRIENDS

*To Gord, Mom and Dad — Happy
32nd, and RF, the bride to be.*

We had seen the world,
fell in and out of love,
had various jobs,
various places of residence,
our own set of friends.

Two strangers returned to the
hometown.

No job,
no friends,
no idea where to begin.

I to an apartment, she back to the
nest.

We met on a cold November eve.

Together we tried seperately to
find happiness.

I found love, she found a job.
I lost love, she lost her job.
I found a job, she found another.
Together we tried seperately to
find happiness.

I was engaged, she was upset . . .
never came to the wedding.

We were friends!
One day she'll marry, I'll attend. . .
We were friends.

Margaret Shell Kincade
Different Christmas Times

*(Dedicated to my grandchildren:
Shelley Kincade, Charles Kincade,
John Steinbeck and Margaret
Steinbeck)*

Christmas time has come again,
The greedy merchants vie for gain,
In toy stores children mill about
Confused, distracted, quite worn
    out.
Too many gifts, too much display,
Too much to want, too much to
    pay!
Demands and whines moms try
    to parry,
For year long payments cause
    much worry.

My childhood Christmas joys
    were simple
A home-made flour sack "Dolly
    Dimple"
Was quite enough for year long
    pleasure.
Then any gift was such a treasure
Oh, how my heart with joy was
    thrilled,
To spy my stockings Santa filled,
He just left fruit and maybe candy,
But in my eyes that was so dandy,
Folks then had little cash to
    spare—
But did have *time* for love and
    care,
Not just at Christmas but each
    day
Christ's teachings helped us on
    our way,
We tried to heed his admonitions
Through all the year in all
    conditions.

Elizabeth B. Radford
ONLY A LITTLE TOWN
A quiet, dark little town till this
    special night
  To Bethlehem came a dazzling
    light
Of a Star that paused over the
    lowly stable roof
  Which was a wonder to those
    who were aloof
And those who came to adore the
    newborn child
  In the humble manger
    emanating a radiance, smiled.
'Twas only a little town like so
    many are
Until our Savior's birth under a
    brilliant star.

Paulette Schrab
A CIRCLE OF LOVE

*For T. Rueth, may we always stay
in the circle.*

We have reached the point.
I reached out
but drew back,
and came in slower.
You drew back,
but came very slowly nearer.
You reached out,

I reached out,
We reached each other.
And we reached a point,
A very real point
which may last forever
If we clasp out hands over
    the point
and let ourselves revolve around it
Circling it,
Encircling it,
Clasping,
Revolving,
Drawing a circle—
A circle,
Drawing a circle
Of you and me,
Our circle would never be empty—
It would be filled with love,
It would be our world.

Michael S. Garmon
ICE FIELDS
Into the ice fields,
over glaciers carved by ourselves,
we ramble, we wander.
When the creeping of truths
    unknown,
causes us to falter,
the heat of our blood
melts us into that
on which once we stood.

Marian Jackson
THE YEARNING

*Dedicated to a feeling of FURY
which will linger forever inside me.*

Been waiting for
the phone to ring.
I just can't think
of anything; But you—

Last night was heaven
in your clutch.
Your forceful yet
so gentle touch.
I'm filled with fear,
but want so much;
So much more of you.

Permanent visions
of your tempting face,
have left me to yearn
for your warm embrace.

Touch me again,
and hold me tight.
I need a feeling
I cannot fight!

Barbara L. Caldwell
LOVE'S REFLECTIONS
Look into my eyes, my friend,
And tell me what you see.
Do you see the gratitude I feel
To know you've chosen me?

Do you see the admiration for
Your spirit, charm, and grace,
And the happiness I feel within
When I look upon your face?

Look into my heart, my friend,
And tell me what you see.
Do you see the love that lives
    therein
For you especially?

Do you see the tender thoughts
    of you
That lie so deeply there,
Where you have found a special
    place
Which no one else can share?

Look into my soul, my friend,
I've found you understand
And know how much you mean
    to me.
God holds us in His hand.

John H. Hausner
HER HANDS
They work so hard in both
    kitchen and yard,
Yet easily thread a small needle's
    eye.
They delicately sign letter or card,
And wipe away tears when I
    make her cry.

Others may see her hands as
    coarse and rough,
When they meet her at some
    social affair;
But I can't feel their loving touch
    enough.
They always say: "Darling, I really
    care!"

Sheri Fritz
A TOUCH

*Written with love to a very
special person in my life— Neva*

Isn't it funny what just
a little touch can do for you.
It can say so much. "I love
you" or "I'm here, you're needed".
The feel of someones arms
holding you so close.
It's such a safe feeling—
such a feeling of love.
It sometimes gives you the
o.k. to cry, or yell, whichever
is needed most.
When you're feeling down, or
feeling up, a touch is just
what is needed.
Just having someone run
their fingers through you hair
says, "It's o.k., go ahead, cry".
God did all of us a
big favor when He gave us
arms and hands.
A touch can mean so much!

Mrs. Marilyn Jean Allen
MY SUNSHINE

*In loving memory of our daughter
Sherrie, who died at age 17.*

And Sherrie was her name,
  No one was ever quite the same.
At first, a babe in arms full of fun
    and joy,
  But always, always a girl, never,
    never a boy.
Then a young lady she came to be,
  Full of fun and laughter, that
    was plain to see.
A little bit of mischief too was
    part of Sherrie's love,
  She loved her life, her family
    and friends, and Him who is
    from above.
We loved her so, this beautiful
    daughter of ours,
  And she will always be
    remembered, by the days, years
    and hours.
She loved flowers and nature, as
    well as all of life,
  For now she's happy and at

peace, instead of struggle and
    strife.
We thank you, Lord, for a love
    like this,
  And until we meet again in
    heaven, she always will we miss.

Mim Cundiff-Rambo
THE ABANDONED BARN
The old barn stands with door ajar
As if asking where the animals are
Which once it sheltered from
    heat and cold
Before the farmer grew to old
To milk the cow and pitch the hay
And close it's doors every day.
The milk stool leans against the
    wall
Of Bossy's now forsaken stall,
The hay loft's empty where we
    played
And gathered eggs the ole hens
    laid.
No kittens come to drink the
    milk
With rich, warm foam smooth as
    silk.
The tin roof's rusty and there's a
    leak
Beside the bird's nest in it's peak.
The farmer now has time to read
Of far off places instead of seed
But now and then as twilight falls
He still hears Bossy's distant calls.
While the old barn stands with
    door ajar
Asking where he and the animals
    are.

Charles Hendon
CHRISTMAS PRAYER

*Affectionately dedicated to my
mother Lillie C. Hendon, who has
known and loved ninety two
Christmastimes.*

I
Thank Thee
For
Our Christmas tree
For
Joyous ancient carols
in the
Frosty winter air
And
For simple love that frames
this
Homely fireside rime
to share
With friends and dear ones
near
To spend another Christmas
t
i
m
e
CHRISTMAS PRAYER

Gloria J. Mathers
CHRISTMAS BABY
It's the Space Age Christmas Baby
Will we care about you still?
As we see the sparkle of space
    capsule's arching trail
While men aboard are striving to
    beat gravitational pull
Every effort must be made by
    these pioneers of space
For in milleniums to come, it
    may save the human race.

In olden days the trails were blazed with ax and wagon's pull
As surely as those times have past
It's our turn—will we fail!
We can't turn back, the future's ours
Let's face it fearlessly
And every moment savour as we go on relentlessly
Let's turn to space, computers, and technology gifts given
And make them our frontiers and seek the stars and heavens
But Oh dear Christmas Baby
Let us not forget to care
Your love came down at Christmas
Teaching us to share, to feel the warmth of godly hearts
To shine with truthful lights
It's the Space Age Christmas Baby
Oh be with us tonight!

Marian Johnson

Marian Johnson
Just For a Second Or Two

This poem is dedicated to children young and old. May they never miss Santa, not for a second or two.

I'll never close my eyes
and I'll not fall asleep
but I am oh so very tired
and closing my eyes gives such relief.

I know just what I'll do said Jenny
I'll close them for a second or two
then I'll open them up again
and watch the whole night through.

Now mind you, a second is all I'll need

then I'll see the presents he leaves
and I'll open mine up early
to see what he left for me.

And so to sleep went Jenny
just for a second or two
Santa came and left the presents
as you probably knew he would.

And when she awaken the next morning
from her slumber of dreams
two seconds was all that was needed
to miss Santa it seems.

For the Sandman came early
and left with her, sweet dreams.

Les Myers
LIFE

I would like to dedicate this poem to all the staff at SMI who have helped show me what life really is.

You make life what you want it to be.
This is very true so try to believe me.

You can make your life very good or very bad.
You can make your life happy or sad.

It is your choice to make life what it is.
We can get the help from our Father, but our life will never be like his.

You make life what you want it to be.

Danita Ward Herzberger
WINNING

Winning first was all of my life.
Never knowing the feeling of second.
Working hard to be the best.
And accepting this was all there was.
I wanted to be the best,
and I was the best.
Was, what a powerful word.
A description of the past.
Winning is my past.
Now I'm married, depressed and not happy with myself.
It seems I'm always dreaming of something more.
Where's this great feeling of being number one?
Where's this achievement I worked so hard for?
I'm not winning now.
I'm not even placing second.
How can I go on with life, as is, knowing
I'm not number one anymore?
And realizing I may never be again.

Jalane Rogers
INNOCENCE

Like a bright summer day all so mild,
Tame like a kitten not ever wild.
Like the gentle rose protected by thorns,
Leaving beauty not shattered or torn.
Free from danger roaming all about,

No slaves or hunger, floods or drought.
Where days last for ever ending not,
Memories remain never forgot.
Being as lucky as four leaf clovers,
Then as morning comes, the dream is over.

David A. Britt
SALVATION'S GARDEN

In Eastward Ground those early days
He joined us for the planting.
Sweet days did pass in fellowship,
In freedom dressed our garden.
What have we sown oh garden bare;
Forbidden fruit the harvest?
With garden closed to Tree of Life,
In Fall our seeds are buried.

Out of the East came Son filled seed;
Again His love descending.
That love filled seed did touch the earth;
To plant the straight and narrow.
The fruit of seed was lifted up;
It met not our requirements.
Again the dust rejects His seed!
Knows not the Master's touch.

Powerless dust blow now your way,
As planting days grow fewer.
Without His touch how may we grow?
In Spirit now we're planting.
Read well His growing plan of old;
Through faith that word is taken.
Pure seed again from Him you'll come:
Perfection at that coming.

Carl A. Weaver
For You (The Candle In My Heart)

The Candle In My Heart
Can Burn Forever
It's Wick Is An Endless Flame
And Even Though Your Heart Belongs To Another
My Heart Will Always Burn The Same—
For You

Lana Richards
THE TREE

to my grand-father-Allan Atteck

You stand there all alone,
everyone seems unconcerned.
You never seem to be known,
'cause you are old and overgrown.
Your twisted root seek through the ground, and keep growing all around.
Always wishing now and then,
that he had a very special friend.

Karen Elizabeth Serfinski
AERIAL'S ENCHANTMENT

To the reader whose imagination has power to perceive ideals in diction, like photographs of dream.

Silent, as mists that sail over sea,
Aerial perched, deep in despondent muse
When the near glassy tarn stirred

suddenly
And across its calm face something did cruise;
Transforming the wavelets it made to light.
Then with fragile arms aloft it mounted
Into the enchanting aura of night,
More splendid than a thousand stars counted
In one gaze of an exuberant eye.
It was a small faerie of wondrous tale
Which made young Aerial's sad spirit leap high
And chase this creature so bright and frail.
She, startled from her innocent content,
Fled leaving an entrancing primrose scent.

Mrs. Betty Rose Kessel
MY—SOLDIER—SON

One-I-Love-
That-one-my-soldier-son-is-you
I've-held-your-picture-tight-
As-I-prayed-each-night.
That-the-Lord-would-see-you-safely-thru
In-my-dreams-I-see-you-smiling-tho'-we-are-far-apart
Always-I'm-remem'ring-you're-the-closest-to-my-heart
So-I-send-this-message-and-hope-it-won't-be-long
That-you-will-soon-return-to-the-land-where-you-belong
Along-with-victory-my-soldier-son

Dorothy Beecher
DRY DOCK OF DEATH

To Mom and Dad. For their love and respect, and confidence in my ability. And to God for showing me the way.

Like a ship sailing on the mighty ocean,
I too am A voyager,
sailing the stormy sea of life.
And like the mighty vessel quietly moored in the harbor
I am moored in lifes harbor of the aged.
When the ship is covered and in Dry Dock,
I too will be covered,
in the Dry Dock of death.
Like the ship waiting to be birthed,
I wait to be reborn,
and again sit at the helm of the vessel
to sail the sea of life once more . . .

Dorinda Bingham
GLASS HEART

The thoughts of my dear Brad Bittick

You would hold my glass heart gently, you filled it with love.
My glass heart shined when I had you.
But you dropped my heart, I can't put it together.
Only you can glue my heart back . . . with love.

Edith Cavere Jenkins
Please Do These Things For Me

l Edith Cavere Jenkins, would like to dedicate this to all the members of my family.

I wish I could explain my love as
   some great folks do.
But my words they are to plain,
   for someone as dear as you.
How can I tell you! How can I
   make you know that you are
   everything to me?
When whats in my heart I can't
   express as I would like to do.
Before I attempt to even try to
   tell you how I feel,
Please do these things for me.
Buy the truth and sell it not.
Also wisdom and undertanding,
   because through wisdom is a
   house builded, and by
   understanding it is established.
And by knowledge shall the
   chambers he filled with all
   precious and pleasant riches.
Darling if you have these, I am
   not ashame to express my love
   even in my plain way.
I love you as I never loved
   anyone else before, now and
   always my love for you will
   flow, it is as deep as the ocean
   and as solid as a rock.
If I tell you about your self, don't
   let it be a shock.
You are like the breeze in the
   springtime, that squeeze
   through the red rose which lets
   you out with a fragrant that
   makes one want to draw you
   near and taste your mouth
   which is better than wine.
Come let us take a walk in the
   gardens and sit in the wines.
Sit down beside me, oh my love,
   lets look at the moon and stars
   above.
Now let me take you in my arms
   and when I squeeze you tight
   don't be alarm.
Your cheeks are lined with rows
   of jewels, thy neck with chains
   of gold. When I look in your
   eyes you make me very BOLD!
Love me my love for the winter is
   past and gone.
And flowers appear on the green
   earth. And time for singing
   birds is here, the voice of the
   turtle dove is heard in our land.
Let me take you in my arms. I
   love you, I love you!

Jerry Lee Lints
MORNING DREAMS
How soft your spirit seems, like
   morning air
intangible, and yet, so good to feel,
how like a dream yet beautiful
   and real,
so close, so far, lovely beyond
   compare,
how beautiful you are, so warm
   and fair
like morning with each element
   ideal,
you touch with joy, with extra

sense appeal
that gifts intrinsically each life
   you share,
like seasons never done, you
   change with time
to beauty yet unique and better
   still
than any else the years had
   reached before,
like morning dreams your
   splendor ever climbs
and like a breath, some never get
   their fill
for dreaming once of you just
   wishes more!

Lauretta E. Pelton
AT CHRISTMAS
   The children cheer:
      OH! OH! OH!
   When Santa says:
      HO! HO! HO!
      At Christmas.

   The bells ring out:
      Ding, Ding, Ding.
   As carolers laugh and—
      Sing, Sing, Sing!
      At Christmas.

   Around us all there's
      Joy, Joy, Joy!
   With lots of fun for
      girl and boy—
      At Christmas.

   Open your eyes, see it—
      Snow, Snow, Snow!
   Enjoy the sound of the
      HO! HO! HO!
   Join in the fun of the
      OH! OH! OH!
      At Christmas! ! !

   MERRY CHRISTMAS!

Dale Rhoades
THE WARRIOR
Beneath the moons of
   Primalthought,
Upon the Plains of Lore
Black rainbows hover, long forgot,
Above the muted corps.

Wearied now, the beast, distraught,
Makes homeward 'cross the
   plain . . .
Cold blood of bronze, upon his cot,
Bedecks his crimson mane.

Pampered wings light mindless
   doves
Upon the plains once more,
As battle axe and tattered gloves
Lie lifeless on the floor.

And though he slumbers once
   again,
Within the ancient deep,
Gray Hatred rouses from its wane
To guard the Warrior's sleep.

Debbi J. Bair
UNTITLED
Shining hair
neatly, gently
halos
finely-featured face—
eyebrows bouncing,
chocolate eyes sparkling,
nose wriggling glasses into place,
dimples somersaulting around
   the mouth—
all join the rest of the body
in eager, intense, energetic music-
   making—

face brightens to render make-up
   unnecessary.

Music finished,
body droops,
as sigh of relief,
and a grin—
   encompassing
   cartwheeling dimples,
   dancing nose,
   eyes rolling toward bounding
   brows—
skips across elfin face.

John E. Rinehart
Echoes Of Spring: Echo I
The church in shadowed dusk;
The cross tipped towers edged
   with snow
As icing on an angel cake;
The bells pealing, as of from great
   distance;
Proclaim the arrival of distant
   Spring.

It stands mutely, as a testament
To the perfection of love;
But the bells sound from its
   silent tower,
The screams of martyrs
Or their soft tears, as they weep
   for man
And the imperfections of love.

Ruth Wilkins
DAY DREAMING
As I sit gazing
   at the beauty all around,
I see you walk out of my thoughts
   my heart begins to pound.
I start to realize just what
   it is you mean to me,
And as we once were very close
   again I want to be.

My life without you could not last
   two minutes or a day,
But because of my own foolishness
   that price I'll have to pay.
If there ever is a chance
   that we again will be,
I will wait until that day
   from now until Eternity—

D. F. Sanders
SOMETIMES, IN DREAMS
Sometimes, in dreams, I hear you
   calling,
Your voice, the soft touch of mist
   upon a midnight air.
I see the gentle curve of your
   cheek
Where the shadows dance with
   the moonlight,
And the feather-dark wreath of
   hair about your face.
There is a look that you have
When you think no one is
   watching:
A look of wonder in your pear-
   gray eyes.
I have only to reach out
To share that wonder with you.

In dreams, you come to me,
A smile, rainbow-bright, upon
   your lips,
And quiet understanding in your
   touch.
There is little of my world in you,
And it is this trait that I cherish
   most.
You bring me music and make
   me feel alive,

And I thrill to the sound of your
   laughter,
As familiar as a heartbeat, yet as
   elusive as thought.
Sometimes, in dreams, you
   embrace me, and for a little
   while,
My troubles fade away, and I am
   whole again.

Jean Carpenter
A TEACHER'S PRAYER
I look into these eager upturned
   faces,
Not eager for the wisdom I may
   give,
But eager for a taste, a touch, a
   feeling
Of a strange new adult world in
   which to live.

I pray that I may teach them love
   of laughter,
And show them sorrow softens
   with a song—
And answer somehow their
   eternal questions
Of "Who am I!" and "Where do I
   belong!"

I only pray, O God, that I may
   teach them
That every door must open with
   a key;
May I instill within them faith to
   find it
As someone once instilled this
   faith in me.

Regina Conrath
HELP OUR LADY, LIBERTY
The Copper Lady long has stood,
Uplifted arm, serene of face;
This gentle mother welcomes any
   race.
Flowers grace our homes and
   earth,
Their scent so sweetly fills the
   air;
So, too, Miss Liberty increases her
   worth;
To see her torch insures a rebirth.

A symbol touching minds and
   hearts,
While waves of water rust her
   dress,
Her rivets rust out as time brings
   stress;
At ninety-six, the waves will slap
   at her feet-
Their need to awaken our
   conscience and souls
To painful times, a world in
   retreat,
A claim to clean this engineering
   feat.

Her beauty devised by loving
   friends,
This two hundred twenty-five ton
   of wage,
This Goddess of Liberty, soft
   green by age,
Sculptured by the dreamer,
   Bartholdi from Alsace,
Made her home here, welcoming,
   sheltering;
Bartholdi found the soul of us in
   her grace;
Be noble to help refurbish her
   place.

Our World's Best Loved Poems

Sherry Hopkins Shelton
AUTUMN CHILL

For My Father

The leaves are falling like tears
in the dead years of my memory.
Old sorrows have turned dry and
yellow with regret.
The wind catches and dances
with them in circles always
leaving them in that same cold
place in my memory.

Time dresses them for death.
Bright orange and yellow and red
catches my eye and reminds me to
notice them
and other autumns.
I'm forced to step back and observe
this woman I was
and shed like the leaves in
autumn.

I must have been her.
How else would I know her
feelings?
But she died and I feel her weight
within me.
I wear some of her dying colors and
old acquaintances talk with her.
Their eyes won't look at her death
for in it they may see their own.

I've tried sweeping the leaves
in one large pile and burning them.
Have you noticed how the
fragrance
of their burning remains?

J. S. Jean Mertz
LOVE'S FAIR BLOOM

Disseminate deep within soul's
soil,
The dormant seeds of love so true
And, with tears of water for
thirsty spawn,
As sunshine's warmth is inward
drawn,
Small sprouts burst through,
products of God.
See this, these sprouts reach forth
and grow,
Watered still with tears of woe,
Then too, hope eternal nourishes
well,
And love's flower blooms
With it's captivating spell.
The broken dreams and pain, one
feels,
Are quite deminished and seem
not real,
As a new day's sweet dreams
increasingly renew,
Concealing the harshness of
love's fair bloom.

Ivan Hill
VANISHED

I awoke one Christmas morn
Strange noises I did hear
I saw the reindeer on the roof
But Santa nowhere's near

Then I heard an awful sound
A man cried out in vain
Santa was stuck in the chimney
And he was in such pain.

I woke my neighbor and he said
"There's sure no need to fuss,
I'll get the ladder from the barn
You go find the Santa-Flush!"

I searched the house to no avail
No Santa-Flush to find
But here's some Crystal Vanish
It's almost the same kind

My neighbor said that it might
work
So upon the roof we went
And dropped some Vanish down
the hole
And we ain't seen Santa since!

Now the moral of this little poem
"To avoid any complications
Is to use the proper product
For the proper situations!"

Maxie Solomons Fountain
**That Babe Beneath The
Star**

Shall we take Christ out of
Christmas,
"Till we fall into the snare,
Beguiled with tinseled wonders
To make us unaware?

Should the thoughts of all the
giving,
Tempting buyers by the score,
Displace the tender Christ-child
With new wreaths upon the door?

Shall the magic of old Santa
In the minds of child and man,
Replace the magic in the stable,
Wrought by God's own loving
plan?

May the twinkling lights of
Christmas,
Shining forth throughout the land
Serve only to remind us of
The Angels Heavenly band!

May the giving to our loved ones
And the giving to the poor,
Help us to remember that
God loved US even more.

So let our love be not divided,
Let us remember who we are:
The CHILDREN LOVE
REDEEM-ED
By the BABE beneath the STAR.

Robert Louis Lyon
MOON FANCIES

*To Bernice Clark Lyon, my own
Truelove—Her luminous eyes so
radiant with grace, The envious
moon would fain conceal her face.*

I saw the moon, a great
blood-orange,
Quartered and crushed against
the sky,
And the juice explode in staining
drops
Of gold as the cloud-robed night
swept by.

The moon, a lunimous globe, I saw
Impaled on a cold stalagmite peak,
And the light, in a golden shower,
rain down
On the face of a silver mountain
creek.

I saw a cloud cauldron with a
bright rim,
A crescent moon like a
goldsmith's mold,
And a shining flood spill over the
brim,
To flow down the valley, a river

of gold.
Then I turned from the moon and
the lambent light,
From the golden arch of the
haloes night,
From the moonlight brocade aloft
in the skies—
And treasured the light in my
Truelove's eyes.

William James Fillmore
*William James Fillmore. N.d.,
M.th., B.Sc. (Foreign Missionary)*
**How Paradoxical—Death
Is Life**

*To my wife: DAPHNE
WILHELMINA FILLMORE
(Beloved of Apollo) 50th.
Wedding Anniversary—"These
Golden Years" Memories of our
Homeland—Shall live forever.*

An explosion of colour assail the
senses . . .
Such majesty is here now seen—
where nature rules it is
supreme
Here is death . . . the falling
leaves
They lie scattered in wild
profusion—here too is no
intrusion
In their dying throes—the
lifegiving sap
Returns to the womb of Mother
Earth below
A soft sighing—a funeral dirge—a
lament is heard
The music of the breeze—how
placid and kind
As one's soul shouts with
joy . . . this inner urge
The silence in eloquence—
shatters the mind
Strange . . . this is death—the
change of seasons
This vibrant splash of colour bids
a last farewell

Nature has it's own way—
Autumn, The Fall—a
continuance?
This is no death—but a living
reality
Surely a rebirth—so rare—so
lush—so free
Here too is life—in vivacious rich
hues
Yet in their passing . . . it does
adorn
Sluggishly—remorefully—the

rivulets . . .
Bear the fallen leaves in their
embrace
Another journey into time but
not oblivion . . . I listen . . .
"We shall return—renewed—
another glorious day"
This is but a prelude . . . soon
An Awakening
A Resurgence . . . The rebirth of
Spring . . .

Betty Jean Cioffi Smith
IT'S A RAINY DAY

It's a rainy day
Like many a rainy day that's
come and gone
A bone-chilling, spirit's willing,
but flesh's weak day
When you don't get much done
A wasted day to some, with time
high on their list of priorities
But for some—like me, at home
alone, apart from the busy
bustling world out there
It's a day to revere
A day to contemplate one's life,
"Where do I go from here?"
A day to gather scattered
thoughts in the dusty attic of
my mind
Like so many cobwebs
intermingling and needing to
be cleared away
So that I can think about
profound things like, "What
sort of plan does God have in
mind for my life?"
Yes, it's another drizzly, rainy day
But I think I needed this rainy day
Thank you God for rainy days

Merrie Carol Jackson
THE RAIN

*This poem is dedicated to my
parents for their help in the
development of my Christian
background.*

Jesus Christ, the Prince of Peace
He died upon a hill,
He died for us,
he crys for us,
For everyone at will.

For everytime that we sin,
Causes a pain deep within,
This pain causes him to cry,
The tears fall
as rain from the sky.

So everytime that it rains,
Always keep this in mind,
For with every sin
comes a pain,
Which causes Jesus to cry!

R. H. Peat
THE SLEEPING MAN

Night sleeps like an old man
Deep and dark in rest
At home beneath the full moon
Light that brights the tranquil
repose
Of the dormant slumber within
the house
Where dwells the heart of dreams

From over the speechless peaks
Slides the round midnight disk
Which silvers the three Cypress
dark

367

Silk before the thrown open
entrance
To the solid timber home which
invites
The unreal, unconscious inward
sight
That secretly spins away the hours
In a slow drift of things to come

Up the walk of discarded time
Come the soft blunt taps
Of tired weary footsteps and cane
To the shelter of a wooded
sanctuary
Where dwells the charm of silent
suprize—
A residence of the right vision
Who like an old man with a
walking stick
Looking for a couch to lay upon
Is a guest of those who've left
To battle the long toothed day.

Gale Morrison
MEMORY VALENTINES

*To my wife, Olive, and our
families.*

Those rare old time cards, so
neat,
Cheerful the verses and rhymes
complete,
yearly to define
be my Valentine
from friends of every description
indeed.

One comes yet across many long
ago cards
pictures, flowers and ribbon of
many yards.
around the hearts
Valentines on carts
verses so many as sung by old
time bards.

To find those beautiful cards of
long ago
sent by friends and schoolmates
so good to know,
so many not here
that were so dear
Grandmothers, Aunts, Cousins,
putting on a good show.

Even Great Grandmothers in
nineteen eight,
childhood memories when found
of late
Valentine cards sent
keep others content,
saying, of all Valentine cards, this
one is great.

Don Gunkel
GROWN AND GONE

*To my youngest daughter,
Michelle, for all the hours of joy
and pain I've had while watching
her grow up.*

So small and thin and cute and
sweet,
She's loved by one and all.
Her lust for life just has no end,
Like a maiden at the Ball.

I'll stay back in the shadows,
And watch her growing up.
I'll try to keep a low profile,
And not be too abrupt.

I'll try to like her boy friends,
And always be polite.
And try not to yell too loud,
When they're out too late at night.

I know I'll always love her,
When she's grown and gone.
For she'll always be my baby,
With children of her own.

Mark W. Kness
VISION OF THE EVENING

*The poem of mine appearing in
this book is dedicated to Mary
Ann Umscheid, because it would
not be fair to dedicate it to any
other young lady I know. To
those who have been victims of
one-sided relationships, the
phrases "moonbeans and rainbows
. . . and sunsets to watch . . ."
should represent those things
that are beautiful, but elusive. To
say "I love you" is the best thing
to say, and what better way but
in a poem!*

Moonbeans and rainbows to hold,
And sunsets to watch.
Recollections of days and
Years gone by,
And visions of the wonderful
times to come.
Nighttime excitement
Never wanes,
Until I see her no more.
Moonbeams and rainbows to
hold, and
Sunsets to watch.
Can I ever forget
How I first saw her in the evening?
Even now, my dreams carry her
vision
In the
Darkest of nights.

Lee Heckman
WEEP NOT
Do not weep for where my bones
lie,
For you cared not until I died.
When I lived and did for you,
You'd not a note of love tis true.
Do not shed a tear of sorrow,
For all that is pain is your
tomorrow.
When I needed to tell you of my
fear,
You closed your ears and would
not hear.
So often I needed to just talk;
Yet, you did not listen, only
balked.
When my spirit was beaten and
broke,
I became your passing joke.
Then I begged for simple care,
None could be found anywhere.
Where were you in my hour of
need,
That left me to beg and plead?
Now, I am laid to rest,
Strangers did their very best.
So weep not for me;
But, weep for thee!

Sarah Daniel Vaughan
REMEMBERED MUSIC
Oh, do not sing sad songs for me
Although your path leads far
away from mine—

For sweet, remembered music
fills my heart—
Music you and I alone have
shared!
Oh, do not sing sad songs for me
Although I miss you all the time—
For sweet, remembered music
fills my heart—
As it has since first I knew you
cared!
So, sing a happy song for me
For someday soon our paths will
intertwine;
And sweet, remembered music
fill our hearts—
Music you and I alone have shared!

Galen A. Smith
THE COEDS
The guys with their concret hearts,
and the girls with their desirable
tarts;
it almost tears you apart
to walk straight down the narrow
path
without a laugh . . .

We see them on the outside
and rarely on the inside,
it almost makes you want to cry,
because of their unbelievable pride.

It will come to soon or maybe to
late,
and because of their lacking faith
that is still lying on the plate,
he or she may never find the
right mate.

Larry Douglas Chappell
A CHRISTMAS DOLL
She's not an average doll,
Nor is she a "Cabbage Patch."
Her description
Is more like that
Of a "Raggedy Ann,"
But her pleasant disposition
Fills the prescription
That makes me glad
I'm her man!

Carl Johnston
SPACE
Even a rock, needs a space.
For every thing has its place.

A flower with no soil will not
grow
For we know, without space,
there is no place to grow.
A weed is a useless wild growing
plant.
Yet when allowed to run free.
It can cause, much misory.
A beautiful flower, may be
consumed, without a trace.
Mearly because a weed stole its
space.

Jo Starrett Lindsey
CHRISTMAS STAR
A star one night,
A baby's cry,
And Christmas came
Down from the sky.

Then history changed
Its jagged course,
And love for all
Became a force.

That Christmas star
Shone long ago,
But we are warmed
In its afterglow.

Olga Zedric
THE HIGHWAY OF LIFE
While traveling down the
highway of life, my past began
to unfold
I realized, pleasure was only for a
season, the price tag attached
was my soul.
As I approached a fork in this
highway of life
The master deceiver was telling
me "this road was right."
I arrived at the fork and came to a
halt
I sat there and gazed at two signs
deep in thought.
One sign was written in words so
bold and to spell
"The road to pleasure, sin and the
way to hell"
The other sign was written with
words of love

"The way to our Saviour and
Father above."
Embroidered in my memory was
a proverb, long ago, I did hear
"There is no pillow so soft as a
conscience that's clear."
I couldn't hold on to this world
with one hand and to God with
the other
So I took the road to our Saviour
and Father to discover
My soul is worth more than all
the pleasures of this world
Just one second with the Lord is
worth living His word
He's forgiven me for all the stops
I made along the way of that
road that's old
Even though this road is rough
and steep, I know at the end it's
paved with gold!

D. H. Rubalcaba
The Little Christmas Tree
Oh hurry, oh hurry don't hesitate,
I know it's Christmas eve and
your running late.
But wait, oh wait, the pretty
young lady with the gold
shinning hair,
Has stopped and I think that she
cares,
How much, she is asking, for the
maimed little tree?
Four dollars, says the merchant,
and a bargain you see.
Four dollars, exclaims the young
lady, oh how can that be!
Four dollars, says the merchant,

and it's your little tree.
She's dropping four silver pieces
in the short merchants hand,
And she reaches to lift me from
my end of the stand.
Then hurry home, hurry home, as
fast as we can,
The guest will be arriving on
time as was planned.
I'm placed in a corner and left all
alone,
While she rushes to the bedroom
to answer the phone.
She's now placing the ornaments
one at a time,
Each gaining in beauty as upward
they climb.
One that is broken but still
shares fond memories,
With a maimed angel topping
that is loved just like me.
The guest are all joyful with the
sight that they see,
And the lights that surround the
now proud little me.
A miracle has happened that is
often so rare,
And all because the pretty young
lady took time to care.
I'm being admired and what can I
say,
But thank you for choosing me,
for your Christmas day.

Mrs. Melba Patton Schubert
TO MY LOVE
Remember the time we danced
the night through?
I felt so warm and good in your
arms;
I wanted to dance a lifetime with
you,
I was so overcome by your charms.

Then fate stepped in to be on my
side—
My love grew for you, and your
love grew too.
And as time passed by, our love
never died,
We've been ever faithful, as true
lovers do.

Now, many worthy years of ours
have flown—
Perhaps a misfortune now and
then,
While countless blessings we
have known,
With you, my dear, as always my
win.

What our future holds, we do not
know,
No need to wonder or care,
For God who has kept us strong
so long,
Will know when we are needed
up There.

Leona Wise
A Living Christmas Tree
A living Christmas tree I saw
today;
In raptured awe I saw the bright
lights play.
Entranced, as choir sang while
dazzling colors danced.
A living tribute to the living
Christ, our Lord.
In breathless contemplation
heeding every word;
And every song I hear, and every

light I see,
Brings each thought, as
Christmas ought,
Oh, Christ, my Lord, to Thee:

To the beaming, gleaming star
Guiding magi from afar;
To shepherds watching flocks by
night,
Awestruck by the brilliant light
Of angels singing of the birth
Of the Christchild come to earth.

But most of all the Saviour's love
Enduring through the long and
endless time.
A Christmas gift from God above,
Rejoicing in His presence,
priceless and sublime.
Thoughts of long ago, living still
as living then;
Spirit of goodwill, of peace toward
men.
So all day long it went with me,
The sight of the lovely living
Christmas tree;
And as the years go by, I'm
certain that I will
Remember it still.

Adelyn E. Kirkwood
UNTITLED

---

*As a sad, unhappy child had I
been told I would someday have a
beautiful, loving and talented
daughter I would not have
believed it. Here's to you Suz . . .
To my child with love:*

May you always feel secure and
free in my love.
May you do all you need to do,
for your own fulfillment,
knowing I am supporting you,
but never intruding.
I pray I have given you the
background to be honest with
others and most especially
with yourself.
May you know the pleasure of
pleasing others without
negating yourself.
I believe that as a child of the
universe wishing to contribute
to perfection, through
evolution, you cannot function
to the fullest degree without
personal dignity.
This is the one cause, as I see it,
worth fighting for.
May you know that discipline is
the mark of a well ordered life.
May you know the value of
spiritual and material things,
keeping each in it's proper
perspective.
May you learn, very early, there
are many kinds of love and you
do not need to give up one to
gain another, our capacity for
love is great enough to
encompass the universe.
May the one you choose for a
mate be the prism through
which the light of your
personality will outshine your
fondest dreams.
Most of all, my Darling, I wish for
you happiness with yourself.

Mark A. Jenne
SERENITY
Clear sparkling water
  Beneath the summer sun
Feeling like this summer breeze
  Was meant for all or none
In the mountains by myself
  I fade to distant dreams
Mountain air so fresh and clear
  Reassures this isn't a dream
Hiking up and far away
  Problems left behind
Relaxing in my favorite blue jeans
  Has the city robbed me blind
Flowers bloom, and water falls
gleam
  Beneath the mornings light
Distant dreams of far away
  Occupy my mind until the night
A star appears from up above
  The heavens clear to me
I lie beneath a moonlit night
  Of peaceful serenity
Falling stars across the sky
  They are then are no more
Just as life, they live in light
  And then they're gone
forevermore.

Barbara Myhr Langston
Clothes Don't Necessarily Make the Bear

---

*To all who have known the love
of a Teddy Bear, and all those
who would like to know that love.*

I sat there on the toy-shop shelf,
As classy as you please,
I wore a riding habit
With pants just to my knees.

My boots were bright and shiny,
My cap set on just right,
My red, gold-buttoned jacket
Was just a smidge too tight.

I really did look quite superb,
Of that I was quite sure,
The best-dressed bear in all the
shop,
Such class should long endure.

I sat there, days going into years,
No one seemed to see.
Other bears were taken home,
What would become of me?

The shop clerk looked askance at
me,
"Why is it you're still here?
May be your suit's too fine to love,
Or give a child cheer."

He took me to the store-room
Which was behind the shop,
And there he took my jacket off.
My heart began to drop.

Next went my britches mighty fine,
And then my perfect cap,
Then both my boots with dusty
shine,
(I hoped he'd leave a wrap.)

But, no, he put me back to wait
Quite nude upon the shelf.
The evening dark within the shop
Covered my naked self.

The morning came complete
with sun,
And customers galore,
Moms with little kids in tow
Crowed in the store.

A tiny girl with hair so red,
(Like my old jacket was,)
Saw me and whispered to her mom,
(And I—dressed in my fuzz!)

I felt embarrassed, just until
The store clerk took me down
From the high shelf, straight to
her arms.
Her mother made a frown.

"But, Mommie, he just looks so
cold,
He doesn't have nice clothes,
Please may I take him home with
me,
And warm his fuzzy toes?"

She took me home within her coat,
A blanket wrapped around,
And sat me on her trundle bed
With pillows all around.

The years went on, my friend
grew up,
And soon a Mom was she,
But still I live with her at home,
And with her daughters three.

The youngest girl has hair so red,
Like my jacket used to be,
But the finest clothes I did not
need,
They loved me just for me!

Ramona Allan
HOLIDAYS
Holidays may come and go.
Our spirits soar high and
sometimes they go low.
Some of us are happy and some of
us are sad.
With out Holidays we would
have nothing and we would
really feel bad.
So give more than you take,
then you shall live with the life
that you make.
Some Holidays give us memories
that make us laugh or cry.
Yet sometimes they make us ask
why our loved ones must die.
Happiness and sorrow a little or a
lot for each tomorrow, some we
have and some we borrow.
So to all good people celebrate
and bring in the New Year,
May the Good Lord Bless and
bring you nothing but cheer.
Happy New Years.

Nelson Edward Smith
Hold My Hand (My Son Of Death)
T'was never so brave, nor fearless
yet, as some do claim to be,
So when it comes my time to die,
Dear Lord, please stand by me,
And hold my hand, in that dark
hour, before eternal dawn,
To quiet my fears, as I do fly
away to Heaven's home.

Be oh so close, when comes my
time to leave this world of pain,
And hold my hand, my soul to
cheer, till I stand on Heaven's
plain.

Be ever so near, to soothe my fears,
and quit the tears of those I
leave behind,
And Death will not be near so
dear if I hold your hand in mine.

Be close to me, My God so dear,

as I move on down through time,
Help me prepare, not death to
    fear, and hold my hand in Thine.

This is my prayer, My God,
    to Thee,
In Life's last hour,
    please stand by me.

Joy A. Swanson
TIME
Her thoughts wonder back,
    as a flock of birds fly south
    for the winter.

Her caring is of moments lost,
    holding on to the love
    of precious things.

Under all her silent thoughts,
    beneath the lies of her words,
    do so many hidden treasures lie
    of moments of splendor.

So hidden by the dreamland
    of the harsh, the brazen realities.

She hides so smartly behind busy
    hands.

Remembering only the grandest
    of the grand.

This woman, lost in her
    memories of past, wanting
    them so to last.

Burning with the anguish of fiery
    lust.

Simmering down the silent
    memory of love lost.

The soft gentle pain.

Trying constantly to regain that
    soft, sweet memory lost in the
    falling rain.

Holding on, constant pain,
        never to come again!

William Francis Armocida
NEVER ENDING LOVE

---

*Dedicated to the one I
love . . . Cosma, my dear wife
Who keeps things happening
. . . throughout my life*

Love is a word I only heard—in
    and out of school,
Then you came along with a new
    kind of song . . .
To put my life in tune;

What would you say to that old
    chiche'
That all good things must end?
And what would you do—if I told
    you . . .
Good things—don't have . . . to
    end! ! !

You come into my world with
    never ending love;
You give much more than I can
    ever hope to give you.
I keep hearing music everywhere
    I go . . .
It's the sound of music when you
    say: "I LOVE YOU"

Your love is like a bell that rings
    for evermore,
Just like a shining light that
    brings the night I wait for;
I don't need the roses or the
    wine . . .

Don't even need the ties that
    bind . . .
I only need your never ending
    love . . .
Ever blending—always
    bending . . .
Never ending love.

Juanell Willingham
IF DEATH

---

*To Gary—My husband, my love,
my life.*

If death doth his fickle
hand point my way,
'Fore in your arms I
may humbly lay,
Lest we shared no love,
no love at all,
Kiss me for eternity from
my shrouded shawl,
And if to a bed of humble
earth I must part,
Shall there lie a vestige
within your heart,
Of golden life we couldst
embrace,
If God a shadow cast not
upon my face.

Kathlyn A. Francis
FAMILY CHAIN

---

*In loving memory of James C.
Griser, who inspired my life in so
many ways.*

A family starts with a husband
    and wife
Who build their love and make a
    life.
They buy a house and settle down
To share a joy that they have
    found.

They grow together day by day
And learn from mistakes along
    the way.
They share in happiness and in
    sorrow
And help one another through
    tomorrow.

They bring the babies into the
    world
One is a boy, the other a girl.
They learn the games and sing
    the songs
And teach the children right from
    wrong.

They'll show the kids how to be
    dependable
But they'll soon find out, rules are
    bendable.
The kids will learn to take a stand
And Mom and Dad will lend a
    hand.

The kids will leave to live their life
And take a husband or a wife.
And so the tradition does go
The family, chain, that love will
    show.

Trava G. May
A CHEERFUL WISH
The brightness of the season
    The song that's in the air
A special kind of feeling
    Is flowing everywhere

A smile, a wink, the warmest wish
    Will all be sent your way
To give you hope and peace and
    love
    This joyful holiday

And when the calendar says it's
    o'er
    This spirit of good cheer
May you and yours find naught
    but more
    To last throughout the year.

Floyd S. Knight
YARD SALE
Alone now,
she sits on the shaded lawn,
surrounded by her carefully
    arranged camouflage:
tall lamps and a Japanese screen
    between her and the clothes
    racks;
his golf clubs and fishing gear
    leaning on the hidden side of
    the oak;
wristwatch, cuff-links, chef's cap,
    shoes—all eclipsed by the
    musty moosehead on the
    barstool.

Unknowing, uncaring,
    a bargain-hunting interloper
    pulls a shirt—
HIS favorite shirt—from the rack.
"A dollar? Ain't worth a dollar."
Right then, if he had known,
his life wasn't worth a dollar.

A boy tugs a hand-painted tie
    from a colorful cluster,
    drops it to the ground.
A muddy-footed boy steps on it.

Someone carries off the
    moosehead, its eyes fixed on
    hers accusingly.

Suddenly vulnerable, defenseless,
    resigned, the proprietress—the
    widow—sells her past, her life
    and times,
for pennies and nickels, and
    dimes.

Laurel Morris
CHILD'S MAGIC
Coming home from school one
    day,
With tear drops on her face,
My little girl cried to me,
Telling her very sad case.

Her friend laughed and mocked,
When she burst out the news,
That the tooth fairy would come,
For the teeth she did lose.

Her friend said she never came,
Leaving money under the pillow,
There was no such magic fairy,
That tale just wasn't so.

Asking if she really believed,
I smiled at my little one,
She said she really wanted to,
For it was so much fun.

When she awoke that next morn,
Gleefully I heard her cry,
The fairy came leaving her gift,
Magic works if you just try.

Returning home from play that
    day,
Shinning eyes and joyful smile,
Her friend had now decided,
To believe in magic for awhile.

Glenda Wells Winter
HAPPY TRACKS

---

*To Daddy, whose greatest joy is
to find another "Happy Track"*

I just call them happy tracks
On tables, under chairs,
In doorways, on the windowsills
And up and down the stairs.

I've even seen those happy tracks
Around my coffee cup.
I've seen them on the porch
And I've seen them in my truck.

Happy tracks are choo-choo trains,
Whistles, dolls and cars.
Happy tracks are baseball bats
and tiny sheriff's stars.

Crayons, scissors, fingerpaint
Can all be put away.
Kite string ends and fuzzy friends
Are not here to stay.

Cookie crumbs and paper scraps
Clean up without a trace,
But happy tracks are permanent
And cannot be erased.

Little feet leave happy tracks
As they wear my boots away,
And little hands make happy tracks
When they clap and play and pray.

Happy tracks are here in all their
    special places
To remind me of the fingers that
    leave behind the traces
Of my children's little children's
Precious little faces.

Stanley L. Robinson
IN APRIL
Rain falls soft in April,
She walks in a gathering gloom,
Slowly, to a lonely room,
Where her mind is her only
    companion . . .

She weeps for self;
And self cries out, "Does anyone
    understand?"
"I need to be, but I don't know
    how."
She sits . . .

Living with her guilt like an old
    lover
Whom she knows too well; (He
    stares at her.)
But she can't leave,
And guilt won't leave.

Rain falls soft in April,
But only in her heart . .
Gray falls all around her,
As silently,
Slowly,
And utterly alone
She falls apart.

Jenna V. Ownbey
WILD GEESE FLYING
Dreams are like wild geese flying.
Nurture them and they will
    return to you,
Circling down from their skies of
    blue;
But if you abuse them,
Or confuse them,
Or lose them,
They will rush on by
Crying!

James E. Williams
PRECIOUS

"L,
  You are the life of love
That grows in me.
With you I see a reason to be
Because you are my reason to be.

  'Your love is sweeter than sugar
And more precious than any stone.
I love you and your love every
  cherishing hour upon hour on
  and on.

'The warmth of your affections
passionately enlightens the
  chambers in my heart.
Loving emotions are set a
  glowing, wanting
And needing to be closer by all
  means never apart.

'So touched by the love from
  your heart
My heart and I adore you in
  everyway.
To grow into and understand
  more about love.
Is to learn more about you
  everyday.

'Your love is my need and this is
  my
Declaration of love from my
  heart and mind.
Without a doubt you are the one
  I want to
give my love and share my
  loving time.' "

Barbara J. Sutton-Mundt
FOR YOU SON

---

*For my son Patrick, on his 19th
Birthday, and the future, when
memories are cherished. (Always
keep a light aglow)*

Nineteen, most wonderous of
  your years
  An ending and memorable time
  appears.
Memorable, are all the joys, good
  and bad that past.
  Time allows so very little to last.
A new adventure takes on a new
  beginning,
  One with assets, values, and
  goals never ending.
Take in account each step you
  take—
  Allow room for all your mistakes.
Life will be exactly what you
  make of it.
Keep a pocket full of smiles as a
  consolation kit.
Each new day from here on in,
  Will place new memories, of
  what you've done
  And where you've been.
As the pages in your book begin
  to fill,
  Add alot of love and
  undertanding, if you will.
Place respect upon "THE
  GOLDEN RULE;"
  For time has proven it a precious
  tool.
From a loving Mother to her Son—
  You've been a wonderous one.
You have opened many a closed
  door,

brought in laughter and so much
  more.
I have a "SINCERE WISH," to
  place on your special day.
  and this, my son, is what I wish
  to say.
Let your conscience be your
  guide,
  Since I'm no longer by your side.
If inner voices leave guilt feelings
  to things at hand,
  Make amends, tie proper ends,
  and don't fall
face down in the sand
Keep alive my wishful thoughts
  on the above—
  Don't fail me now, and mar a
  heart full of love.

Lovingly,
Mother

Pinkie Mae Malone

Pinkie Mae Malone
Black Child-White Child

---

*To my nieces: Tiffany and Joslyn
Foote*

Mama please don't make me do
  it.
I don't want to make him cry.
He does not want to play with
  me.
He will not even try.

I waved my fingers from my nose
And made a face at him.
He only looked and wondered
Why I should have this whim.

I wish that he could like me
But I feel so mean inside.
I know he won't come near me.
I make him want to hide.

Please, don't make me do it.
I'd like to watch him for a while.
I think that he is beautiful.
I'd like to see him smile.

Midge Hasenbank
Thoughts On a "Silver" Birthday

What is twenty-five?
I can tell you what twenty-five is
  not.
Twenty-five is not like twenty-one,
  when you legally become an adult.
Twenty-five is not like forty,
  when they say your life begins.
Twenty-five is not like thirty-five,
  when you're supposedly "over the
  hill".
Twenty-five is not like thirty,
  when you know your "younger
  days" are through.
What is twenty-five?
Twenty-five is when you look
  back
and realise you're not a "kid"
  anymore,
but you're not really "old" either.
Twenty-five is when you know
  you must
take responsibility for your
  actions,
knowing you can't explain them
  away anymore.
Twenty-five is when you know
  you would not want to be
  twenty-one again.
Twenty-five is your "silver" year,
  when you have lived for a
  quarter-century,
yet you know the best is yet to
  come.
I think I'll enjoy my "silver"
  year.
Being twenty-five, that is.
Now I can't wait until I turn
  thirty.

Kimberley Ritchie
INNOCENCE

On the mountain dark and red
Curved and crippled an old oak
  stands.
Once a creature of beauty now
  gone,
Alone it lives with no demands.

To have been of nobility at one
  time,
To be crowned with the gift of
  strength,
Now all dreams shattered,
Destruction left behind.
Sorrow after joy came at length.

Timothy M. Foran, Jr.
DAWN'S GREETING

Beaming stars in moonlit skys
And then to come
Without warning,

Silent Dawn as it supplies
A bright and cheerful,
  "GOOD MORNING"

Sharon Oakley
SECOND THOUGHTS

All Hallows Eve sparks a thrill
of excitement in me and I loose
  my will
to venture this night
from warm bright lights
and see the sights.
Who knows what might
be there?

My imagination is on the loose.
A terrible monster with
  snaggled-tooth
could be waiting.
I'm hesitating,
investigating
the nauseating
idea.

I'm not afraid, but I think I'll stay
inside my house untill the day
dawns bright and clear.
So I'll stay here
and close my ears
and calm my fears.
At least untill next year!

Ms. Helen Hayter
HALLOWEEN NIGHT

Watching the dark forms of the
  children arriving at and leaving
  from the door
Vaguely regarding the flickering
  flame lights the middle, the
  wet triangular eyes of fall's
  plump orange fruit

Divine Animator of Realism's
  own truce
Ceremoniously signal the
  harvest's finish
felt already in the ash of another
tickles the guard dog's, the throat
  of cerebrus
Occludes the memory, of some
  antiquated other time.

I am waiting outside your door
The neighbours say that you're
  not home
My host wants to know if your
  guest is there
Your guest tells me that your
  host isn't home either
My host wants to meet your host
My host knows that your guest is
  in
Your host opens the door

Long, langorous lingering over tea
The silhouette of Reason framing
  the doorway
In the dim light waiting for
  morning
Some moving finger dance
The wind waiting through the
  curtained window
Under the table a foot moves

Vaguely occluding the sight of
  the children arriving at the
  door for more candy
The dusk watching the night sky
  darken

Linda J. Reed
RUBBLE AND DUST

The martyred cries rise with the
  smoke
From the flames and the rubble
  and dust.
Dreams and nightmares, plans
  and schemes,
What ifs and what nots
Lie crushed in the rubble and dust.
Half mast flags sway and twist in
  the wind,
They writhe for our humiliation
  and defeat.
We rage in despair and wonder
  why?
Lives are not lost,
They are simply snuffed out.
Dreams are the ones that are lost
In the rubble and dust.

Mildred M. C. Brookins
Merry Christmas-Happy New Year

I gazed across the valley,
to view the setting sun.
The flowing hills in the distance,
seemed to blend into, just one.
I paused awhile and listened—
to the sounds rushing by.
I marveled at this great universe,
the land, the sea, the sky.
I heard a childs clear laughter,
Birds, singing in the trees.
All these sounds were carried,
like whisperings, in the breeze.
I wanted to shout, "Merry
Christmas"
to everyone, every where,
And to say Thank You, God,
For all of your loving care.
I wanted to sing "Alleluia's",
To celebrate the Saviours, birth,
And when the New Year, dawns,
May it bring us PEACE ON
EARTH.

Julie Potter
BUILDING A POEM
an idea
a thought
a group of
feelings and
emotions which
when all together
seem completely one
these elements can join
building upon one another
to make something much more
than the individuals can ever
blended in a special way or shape
they become the ultimate and
perfect
thus is brought into new life, a
poem

Bernice Rapson Wilde
This Is the Season Of Christmas

To my Family the Lotter's, the Wilde's and the Rapsons

In the days of yesterday—Folks
worked very hard
Our ancestors fought their
battles, we are fighting ours
Now this is the season to enjoy
yourself—this is the season for
giving
Put sunshine in someone's life. .
This is the Christmas season
Christmas comes but once a
year—Make it a happy season
During the year, its the same old
grind, working from day to day.

Every day the same old chores,
done over, over and over again
All year the worry to keep our
home's—mortgage—taxes
Numerous bills—paid by the
score, so forget them for a while
we dream of a heavenly life
ahead, free from worry
this is the Christmas Season. Be
happy—Be Happy—Be happy
Each and everyone of us—make
someone happy—very happy

This lovely, lovely season, around
the whole world

Come—come—come, and enjoy
the Christmas season
Happiness—oh, happiness—this
lovely giving season
Do your giving to your loved
ones, It's a Merry, Merry season
Remember all around the
world—this is the Christmas
season
So be as Merry as you can—
Forget your every day worries

Bernice Rapson Wilde
RULES

To my son Robert Harold Lotter

I once knew a cocky young man
Who defied every rule of the
game
It made his life so much harder
He never would learn the rules

He went to work in Detroit
and quit his job there too
He still hadn't learned his lesson
He never would follow the rules

He joined the armed Forces
Where the lessons sunk deep in
his head
If you follow all the rules
You're bound to come out ahead

Rules are part of learning
It's the only way to grow
Certain people—learn the hard
way
Some people—never learn at all.

mindy levine
A DIRTY WHITE

To my mom and dad who I love forever

The world is like a plain piece of
white paper,
                    pure,
God made the world perfect trees,
birds, lakes,
     oceans, then he made man,
Someone drew on that white
piece of paper with
permanent marker and drew out
of the lines,
They could not start all over it
was their
          only piece of paper,
They cannot start all over cause its
already ruined . . .

Marie Coleman Coss
The Manger, Cross, and Throne

From the manger to the cross and
on the throne
'Tis the story of Jesus, from the
Bible 'tis well known
Mary bore Him in a stable, on the
straw, in the cold
Angels told it, wise men saw it,
what a gift to behold.

There so innocently He slept,
safely by the little lamb
Too small to know someday, He
would be the great "I Am"
As He grew, God led and taught
Him to love and forgive sin
Gave Him wisdom and
compassion as
He humbly walked with Him.

Precious baby that He was,
gracious
Lord He came to be
Healing, preaching, teaching, over
land and on the sea
But men didn't understand Him,
they treated Him with scorn
Oh, if only they had known why
this
Holy One was born.

So they crucified our Jesus, nailed
Him to that cruel cross
as He bled, He cried Father
forgive them,
lest one soul be lost
He gave to us the Holy Spirit, so
we would never be alone
Now He's reigning with our
Father,
beside Him, on the throne.

Alice C. Chapman
NEVER WITH CHILD
Young newlywed was I, a
motherly type, I was told;
Years passing by, no child will I
every hold,
No son to carry on my husbands
name,
A sweet baby girl! My hopes were
in vain;
My husband accepted the fact
before me,
That our love would endure
without a family;
Yet he knows not, how empty I
feel within,
Never with child, runs through
my mind, again and again;
You'll never know, coming from
those experiencing
motherhood,
Words that broke my heart, to
them were good;
Tis the closest to death—the
ultimate pain—for women
upon this earth,
Never with child, you'll never
understand, unless you've
given birth;
Four decades gone by, our love
still endures, season after
season,
Childless yes, but many years
back,
My Heavenly Father showed me
the reason;
I need women like you, for love
and a gift for sharing,
For all the orphan babes, will
need your caring,
Could this be another reason?
Our Heavenly Father said,
"Blessed are those who are barren".

Virginia Stonestreet Bush
MOCKINGBIRD'S SONG
There's a time in all lives we like
to recall
The happy springtime of life be it
Summer or Fall;
When two hearts entertwine with
a love that is warm
And the days are as happy as the
mockingbird's song.
I remember the days when the
mocking bird sang
It was in early springtime when
days all grow long,
Our hearts were so happy with
tender new love

They echoed the mockingbird's
song.
He sang through the long days
and warm eventide
He sang through the bright
nights until early morn;
Our hearts were so happy with
tender new love
They echoed the mockingbird's
song.
The mockingbird sang through
all the springtime
And all through the summer
until September was gone
Then his voice faded and at last
became still
As if he knew in our hearts was
no song.
I will not recall that time in my
life
For remembering brings pain like
sharp thorns
I'll blot out the memories that
sorrow my heart
And remember only the
mockingbird's song.

Frances Adair Miller
CHRISTMAS GIFT

---

*To my mother, Irene Bird Adair
December 25, 1970*

There are girdles and girdles
For Betties and Myrtles
And all of them brand new and
clean;
But when I go shopping
There's really no stopping
At the one that is right for
Irene.
So here's a love gift
For the perfect uplift
That will make you look most
chic and lean.
A merry Christmas to you,
And all our love, too.
What a dear of a Mother you've
been!

Evelyn M. Byrom
THE VIGIL

In loving memory of my mother

Day by day,
 Hour by hour,
I sit in vigil and watch,
 the demon of disease
Demonstrating its power,
 draining my mothers life,
Killing a most gentle flower.

My soul cries out in anguish,
 powerless to ease her pain and
fear,
To comfort and protect her,
 to keep her ever so near,
To give her back her life,
 if only a few more years.

Each time I see a gently falling
tear,
 I see in her eyes, her ultimate
fear,
The knowledge that impending
death is ever so near—
What a cruel and unjust end
 for one I love,
One who has always been my
truest friend.

Death, Master of Darkness,
  making me ever mindful—
Nothing can stop its power
  from killing my gentle flower.

Eugene E. Cain
FOREVER

---

*To my wife Fran, who gave me
the meaning of life, and opened
the eyes of my soul to a world of
love.*

I awake and you are near me,
  I touch you and you respond.
A soft warm kiss and you engulf
  me with warmth,
  I love you and forever you'll be
  with me.
Someday I may awake and find
  you gone,
  The Lord above may call you to
  His side,
But I will feel the sun upon my
  cheek, and know it's you,
I will gaze into the field of fresh
  warm strawberries,
And know that you are here with
  me.
  I'll gaze at the blue sky above
  and sense your presence,
And recall the days of yesteryear.
  The breeze will toss my hair in
  disarry,
  And I'll know it's you messin'
  around again.

Shirley I. Gilarski
Mother's Parting Child
Then she wept a new tear
one she hadn't known
before.
How could it be so cold,
as though her heart
would break.
The brittle breaking of
her tender love's tie.
She wondered why the rose
has to die.

Madeline Rasmusson
GREAT LITTLE THINGS
It was many years ago
An I was still a young girl
My neighbors had to live
In a poor and sadden world.

I held in my arms my neighbor
Girl who was a little dear
She was sobing because she was
Told Santa could not come this
year.

"He told me in the store he would
Bring me a Barbie doll she wailed
I told him I have always been
  good
Obeyed Mamma with out fail"

After I calmed her I hurried home
Wrapped my old Barbie doll some
  clothes and a toy
I delivered them to the grateful
  Mother
Whose eyes just lit up with joy.

I never forgot the feelings that I
  had
When ever I saw my little friend
Some how I felt God was smiling
  too
As on me his blessings he did
  send.

As Christmas we often pray to
  God
To do great big things is our wish
We sometimes ignore the
  opportunity
To do great little things which
  we can accomplish.

Carolyn L. Vaughn Asher
LIFESMITH
Days of silver
  days of gold,
Shiny new days,
  lustrous old.

With antique days
  softly burnished
Are my mem'ries
  fondly furnished.

And each new day,
  a nugget, shines,
Ready to forge,
  Engrave my lines.

Each is formed as
  shape betakes it.
Each unique as
  I, who makes it.

Leitha Jaye Parker Ladabauche
GENTLY
Amber candles burn
as together
we slowly embrace
Holding on to one another
face to face
Love shines—
the glow
ever so brighter than
the candles near
You and I
loving gently
as slowly the candles dim
with the night
We close our eyes
still holding on
to one another
and sleep sets in
Only till morning—
yet another light
for us to love by
Gently . . .

Doris Jean Hamilton
ESSENCE OF BEING II VI

---

*Lovingly dedicated to: My
precious Daughter Ginger Lee
Renaker*

Did your heart ever soar to the
  mountain peaks, beneath the
  lofty sky,
To where the lazy floating clouds,
  were softly drifting by?
As gentle shadows brushed the
  face, for a moment a hidden
  sun,
Like a child playing games of
  hide and seek, a magic just
  begun.
Was there a silent footprint, to
  show how time stands still,
Just a picture of a moment,
  captured on a distant hill?
And feel the gentle breezes o'er
  blue waters down below,
Lights dancing merrily like
  ballets, in a misty panaramic
  show.
Did you feel the touch of
  something, invisible to these

eyes,
Like the gentle of a baby's breath,
  or the contentment of its' sighs?
Did you listen to the hush of
  serenity, and the bliss of
  freedoms' wings,
As thoughts of calm flow
  effortlessly, blending as nature
  sings?
Was there a warm glow all
  around, like the fantasy of a
  magic wand,
That touched your soul and mind
  to reach, into a world beyond?
Where the misty veil is drawn
  aside, for a glimpse of eternity,
Delusions banish forever, at the
  grandeur of this invisible scene.
Where the sweetness of self
  surrenders, reaching depths of
  fathomless time,
Detached from this material
  world, aware only of the subline.
Sweet solitude, though never
  alone, the stillness seems as a
  trance,
Like manifestations of an artist
  brush, rare colors to enhance.
As serene quiescence steals
  across, the recesses of the mind,
Unfolding like a psalm of praise,
  to the great Universal Mind.
Where beauty stands in mystic
  awe, at the stillness of this
  scene,
If you have touched this moment,
  you have touched something
  Supreme.

Carol A. Bourgeois
CHRISTMAS EVE
Who's that in the livingroom
lighting up a tree?
I was peeking from the corner
so that I could see
He wore a funny red suit and
had a beard like snow
He opened up a big sack and
chuckled HO HO HO
In the sack were packages that
he placed beneath the tree
He held up a pretty doll that
I hoped would be for me
It was just like in the story
My eyes could not believe
There really IS a Santa Claus
that comes on Christmas Eve.

Edna Pickell
LASTING LOVE

---

*This poem was written for my
husband, Vern, the one I hold
such a deep love for.*

There was a time not long ago,
  when I could not believe, that,
  never in this life of mine you
  would not be with me.
Then one nite, I remember it
  well, you said to me with a
  smile, all good and lovely
  things must end, but only for
  awhile.
We'll be together soon my love in
  another time and place, where
  time will always be our friend
  at a slow and loving pace.
We shared the time we had left
  with loving, tender care, like

holding a precious bubble that
  would vanish in the air.
Now we are together again in
  that other time and place and
  time indeed is our friend at a
  slow and loving pace.

Roxe Anne Geringer
POSTER ON THE WALL

---

*To my husband, Ron, for his love
and patience, and our sons, Allen
and Andrew, for inspiring my
imagination; and to my parents,
my sisters, and my brother for
their positive support.*

Adventure with me through my
  poster on the wall.
Journey to wherever you wish,
  anywhere at all.
Glide through a forest, and feel
  the misty rainfall;
Or walk through fields of posies,
  in my poster on the wall.
This morning it may be spring;
  this afternoon it may be fall—
But, be assured each trip is
  different, in this poster on the
  wall.
Escape to the world of the wild,
  both big and small;

Listen closely, you will hear them
  call, in this poster on the wall.
Alice in Wonderland, Cinderella,
  and Aladdin,
I thought they had it all; until I
  took a closer look
At my poster on the wall.
Sometimes I walk, sometimes I
  run, and sometimes I just
  crawl—
Into my poster on the wall.
A giant or a nymph, or a soaring
  eagle above the trees;
For a moment or two, I can be
  anything at all—
In my Poster on the wall.

Bethann Byers
REMINDERS OF FALL
As the wind gently rustles the
  leaves of gold,
I watch as a miracle begins to
  unfold.
The cornfields, the pumpkins, the
  goldenrod in bloom,
Nature is the artist, creating
  beauty until there's no more
  room.
When looking at everything

bursting with colors
of yellow, orange, brown, and red,
Thoughts of thankful praises
begin to fill my head.
I am thankful for it all,
I am thankful for the reminders
of fall.

Esther Hays
THE KING

To Christ the Kings work

J Is for justice unto all things.
E Is for earning Christly rewards.
S Is for the gift of abiding grace
for everyone.
U Is for us growing in
acknowledgement thereof.
S Is for the gift of abiding grace
for everyone.

C is for total commitment to
Christ.
H Is for the heavenly host and
home.
R Is for the resurrection and the
first Easter.
I Is for the inspiration on the
day of crucifixion.
S Is for the gift of abiding grace
for everyone.
T Is for the blessed truth of the
transfiguration the 3rd day.

I Is for the inspiration of the
"Will of the Holy Father."
S Is for the gift of abiding grace
for everyone.

K Is for the King of the Jews.
I Is for the inspiration on the
day of crucifixion.
N Is for non-believers to come to
belief.
G Is for the glory of the Father,
Son, and The Holy Ghost.

Nila Jane Chrispell
WINTER TIME
The first signs of winter one
begins to see
The grass turn brown, the leaves
fall from trees
The air takes on a silent chill
The trees start bending, what a
thrill

The temperture began to slowly
decline
And now its only a matter of
time
The snow flakes slowly hit the
ground
Begins piling up and soon soft
mounds

Now its deep and deeper it grows
The wind is howling oh how it
blows
It's drifting bad oh what a sight
Keeps this up, we will be snowed
in tonight

The familys all here, the fires hot
Come now children, theres corn
to pop
Now settle down, we will watch
T.V.
Winters not bad at all by gee

The time has come, were having
a thaw
The air is warmer, the birds make
their calls

Winter is gone and spring is here
Another wonderful time of year.

Charles Mathis iii, M.D.
WEATHER REPORT

—to Dianne groesbeck 1983

What became of the gentle rain
that once fell upon us in autumn?

That covered us in warm wetness?

That once sealed a bond of love
in aqueous tenderness?

We now fall from each other
like large brown leaves
from sleepy autumn trees
on a crystal crisp autumn
morn . . .

And there is no rain in the
forecast.

Katie Brunner
KINDHEARTED!
I watched some children playing
in the park the other day,
also saw a helpless youngster
handicaped, unable to play.

He sat in his rigged up carriage
so forlorn, so pale and thin,
he was looking at the children-
noticed the quiver of his chin.

No one paid him any attention
no one cared how bad he felt-
he had dropped his "Raggedy Andy"
that close to his heart, he had
held.

Some children stood quite near
him
licking candy, lollipop-
they did not give him any,
being busy, they simply forgot.

Along came a chubby, friendly
fellow
about three, or maybe four years
old-
he picked up, and gave his "Andy"
plus some candy, without being
told!

Judy Bell
POOR TOM

---

*To Tammy and Terry, my
daughters, written for them when
they were 7 and 10, to share with
their friends on the holiday.*

Hello, my name's Tom Turkey,
And I'm as sad as I can be.

It's November and Thanksgiving,
And I guess it's the end for me:

I've eaten almost nothing,
Since the calendar said May,
I thought if I got skinny,
They would send me far away:

But instead of getting thinner,
I am fatter than before,
Nice and plump and juicy,
I need not tell you more:

I've even thought of running
away,
But it doesn't make much sense,
When I am only three feet high,
And I'm in a six foot fence:

Well here comes the farmer,
So I guess I'll say good-bye,
The axe that he is carrying,
Is pretty good reason why:

Whoever gets my drumstick,
I hope I bring them luck,
Yippee. I can't believe it,
He went over and got the duck:

Jean M. Price
THE PROPOSAL

---

*To all the lovers, who thought
they had found the right one,
only to be sadly mistaken.*

Thoughts of knowing you,
as I felt the security of love.
While dreams of white danced
through my head.
THEN IT HAPPENED!
You asked me to be yours.
But that startled look, when I
said, "Yes", hurdled me back to
reality.
What do you mean, not me?
I thought . . . you said!
But why not . . . then who?
All this just to realize I never
knew you.

M. A. Tempel
A CHRISTMAS TEAR
In silent thought, hidden in the
quiet warmth of my home
I remember the Christmas Story;
A Babe being born in a manger
surrounded only by animals
and Angels singing in the
silence of the night of Peace on
Earth.

A lonely tear slides down my
cheek as thoughts change
To today's turmoil;
Of the human suffering and
discontent throughout our
world and my countrymen
giving their lifes on foreign soil
in the name of Peace.

Overcome by saddness, no longer
can the tears be controlled
As I begin to wonder;
If mankind will someday seek
and follow the Christmas star
and unite together on a silent
night; experiencing true Peace
on Earth.

Carole Ann Blanch
WHAT IS LOVE?
Love is something that shows
how to share,
Love is telling someone that you

care.
Love is a bondage between a boy
and a girl,
A mother and daughter, an oyster
and pearl,
It's something thats special in
every small way,
Love is a happiness day after day.
It can be a passion, a want, or
some need.
Without love some hearts would
constantly bleed.

Love can be fun, exciting, and
thrilling,
Or it can be cold, bitter, and
chilling.
Love is something shared
between two,
Love is sometimes hard to find
true.

It's symbols are many and
sometimes so small,
You can name quite a few but
never them all,
It's referred to as puppy, maternal,
or true,
It's experienced by many and not
just a few.

Love is a joy, a happiness, a
pleasure,
Love is worth more than an old
seaman's treasure.
Can you possibly measure love's
price or its cost?
Love's value when true can never
be lost.

Lyllian D. Cole
LANTERNES
            The
        Dutchman's
       Breeches hung
        drying in the
            sun.

            The
          dotted
        Butterfly
    signalled in Morse
          code.

            The
       hail skipped
       like pebbles
      on the crystal
          tarn.

            The
         Evening
    Primrose lights
      up the garden
          path.

            The
          Lilac
      cast her sweet
     scent to the Four
          Winds.

Gina Gouch Stone
WHERE
Where smiles line your paths in
life
so there travels joy.
Where peace lines your soul
so there nurtures rest.
Where love lines your heart
so there multiplies true
happiness.
In these are contentment with
self and life.

David A. Johnson
OPPORTUNITIES
Some people call them "problems"
They see them larger than they are
They expect to fail
Before they even start
And others call them "nothing"
And say they are not there
But when they come upon them
They are unprepared
But we who *really* see them
We see reality
For "problems", they are "nothing"
But opportunities.

Albert Miccio

Albert Miccio
THE PEOPLE TREE

---

*No one has love greater than this,
that someone should surrender
his soul in behalf of his friends.
John 14:13*

Rooted meadow of broken stem
Fallen tree had died again
Moistened by the young childs cry
Grew up to meet the heavens high
To greet its friends the butter fly
All of us with only me
Family of the human tree
Falling off and sailing down
On the streets onto the ground
Hope that we God have found

Lorie Motta Gonzalez
ALWAYS—MICHAEL
What can I say
except that I'll always be there for
　you

Through the times when I'm in
　your head
and the times when I'm not

I care for you
and the intensity of our friendship
is nothing I've ever felt before

When I think of you
I smile, pure and simple
yet with such contentment
the experience is to cherish

Though our moments are stolen
and our lives spin a dangerous web
I'm still tempted with the risk
to see you again and again . . .

You make me see that part of life
　I've searched for—
The insane, yet tranquil
happy, yet solemn reaches of my
　soul

You are special, my friend, my

lover, my protege
You reflect that part of me
that I have grown very fond of . . .

Grace M. Carlin
THE BUZZARD'S STORY
I'm just an ugly Buzzard
And no one—wants me around;
There's no one—wants me—for a
　pet—
Like a kitten—or a hound!

It always made me feel real sad,
Kept my mind—and thoughts,
　real "Jerky",
Wondering—Why, Oh why—
　couldn't I,
Have been born a nice, "Tom
　Turkey?"

I saw him srutting all about
As proud—as proud—could be
People bragging on his beauty,
And no one—ever—looked at me!

I saw, all animals together,
Pigs and chickens—cows and
　horse,
It made me feel so sad and lonely,
But it was—"Jealousy"—of course!

And then—I saw the farmer,
grab the turkey—by the neck—
I couldn't believe my poor ole eyes
As the axe, came down—by Heck!!

Oh Boy!! I'm glad that I'm a
　Buzzard—
And I'm happy now—to say—
That I know I won't be "Eaten"
At a table—Christmas day!

Ms. Shasta-Dawn Maloney
HARMONY
I recall myself, in vindication,
　singing a song of joy.
While touchstones of love are
　carefully placed
Within God's gracefully spinning
　plan of Madra circle;
Knowing full well that
　desperation and despair
Might well come full circle
　through healing faith.
And so, I will acknowledge and
　rejoice in a rainbow,
Whose spectrum, of colorful
　auras, promises a covenant
Promises a renewal, a benediction
　and a blessing;
So may it please God that I
　become more and more
Filled with the reality of spirit,
　truth and peace.

Diane Wuchevich
GREY SKIES
Oh what a day
The sky is so grey
I feel that way too
But for people it's blue
I miss you so much
I miss your touch
But can't you see
I have to let me be me

Mary T. Leone
UNTITLED
Poetry
Expressing me
As I
Express it
The lifeline
Pulling me
From insanity
To immortality

Thomas Mann Selkirk
FOOTBALL MISERY
On Thursday our tackle fell.
　On luck we couldn't depend.
On Friday our guard was down.
　On Saturday we had a week end!

Ida L. Franklin
MEMORY
I REMEMBER HEARING YOU
　LONG, LONG AGO
rolling across the tracks
PASSING THROUGH TOWNS,
　AND CITY STREETS
always your mournful cry.
CALLING WHOOEE, WHOOEE,
　WHOOEE
the sound of your clumsy dance
BUMPING, SLIDING, AND
　CLANGING
the boxcars swaying, to and fro
CARRYING THEIR SECRET
　CARGO WITHIN
sunrise, sunset
AND IN THE STILLNESS OF
　MIDNIGHT
your grinding against the relentless
STEEL RAILS CAN BE HEARD
the wailing and lonely sound
OF YOUR WHISTLE,
　SCREAMING WHOOEE,
　WHOOEE
seems to be calling me.
FOR A FLEETING SECOND,
　THER IS A WILD
desire to run, run, and leap
INTO ONE OF YOUR CARS,
　JUST TO BE A PART OF YOU
and follow where ever you go
AROUND THE BENDS,
　MOUNTAINS, HILLS, AND
　VALLEYS
dancing across high bridges
WITH THE LAUGHING,
　CURVING, RIVER BELOW
suddenly, you are gone
LEAVING ME BEHIND, AND
　TRAILING IN THE WIND
your mournful cry. whooee,
　whooee, whooee

Monsignor Bernard Powers
MUSIC OF THE SOUL
Others cannot set
your song to melodies
nor the words of your thoughts
to harmony,
　but you can let your fingers
　music into sound
　the songs of your being
　and place in the symphony of
　the universe
　　the rhythm of your being.

One must
hurl the song of their being
into the musical scale
　and let the notes
　discord themselves
　freeing feelings
　in sound

and the universe
will hear
　the crescendos of the heart
　and the soul will
　present its concerto
　to the world.

Flo Lampp Hageman
Unforgettable November
The old School Book Depository
　stands empty now,

Silent sentinel o'er Dealey Plaza
　and Elm Street.
Decades have passed and today
　memories still see,
The motorcade moving slowly in
　Indian Summer heat,
Bearing our handsome leader; his
　lovely Jacqueline!

People still pause; remembering;
　trying to forget—
Unaware of traffic noise; silently
　hoping to delete
the shock; the shame; agonizing
　and asking why—
And they wait yet in love and to
　welcome; to greet
Our so vibrant young leader; his
　lovely Jacqueline!

Trauma lives on in these hearts;
　never forgotten
shots split their silence; to repeat
　and repeat—
Time, has not erased a pink suit
　splattered red—
Some, who lived that November
　day will always weep
For our fallen young leader; his
　lovely Jacqueline!

Elaine Meli
Grandma Believes In Santa
Darryl at six can see that "Santa
　Cannot Be!"
Jared has been told by his sister
　that—
"Santa is always a mister"—"A
　daddy, a grandma, a mommy, etc.
"Jared, Whatever you see, they are
　giving the presents to you and
　me."

Now Travis is the only one,
As he looks out the window he's
　not looking for sun—
He knows there's a Santa
Who will scamper with reindeer
　and sled unhampered,
To city and village, to the top of
　the mountains, and down to
　the field;
Delivering presents to those who
　believe.

So Travis and Grandma look out
　the window
He knows there's a Santa for us
(Let's suppose.)
He knows that his Grandmother
　knows!

Ina Price
THE SEASONS
I've lived through the springtime,
　when the world was young and
　gay.
Flowers bloomed and bluebirds
　sang, in the meadow where I
　used to play.
Soon the spring changed to
　summer, the world had a more
　somber hue.
I no longer romped in the
　meadows, I had more important
　things to do.
No more apple trees to climb, no
　time for the grape vine swing.
There were too many chores to
　be done, there were lullabys to
　sing.
Autumn followed summer, blue
　skies changed to gray.
Rain on the leaves made a lonely

sound, and the birds had flown
away.
Now winter is beginning, it's
uncertain what it will bring.
I'll keep warm in the memories,
of the summer and the spring.

T. Zoe Standard
THE CHILD
Into a world of problems a child
was born,
A humble start to a life of
influence.
The inspiration to a world of
believers,
A key to eternity . . . the King of
Peace.

Into a world of problems my child
was born,
An average start to a life of
significance.
My inspiration to believe in me,
The key to my eternity . . . the
peacemaker.

Eternity—heaven and hell—is of
this world,
Determined only by my
willingness to believe,
And by the strength of the love
I share with the child.
Peace comes with realization, and
accomplishment.

Betty Couse
A Christmas Message
Let's put Christ back in Christmas,
We have heard this, in many a
rhyme.
We know that's not at all
necessary,
For He's been in there all this time,
As Christmas is Christ's own
birthday,
It's his very, very Special day.
If we will take time to remember
this,
And just try doing things His
way:
C is for Cheerfulness, spread it
about,
H is for our Heart, we can't do
without.
R is for Remembering, someone
in need,
I is for Interest, with which we
take heed.
S is for Sharing, what we have,
with others,
T is for Trust, we have for our
brothers.
M is for Mankind, God placed on
this earth,
A is for Actions, with which, we
earn worth.
S is for Soul, to go with our Heart,
So you see Christ is there, doing
his part.
"Merry Christmas"

Staci G. Mattern
EMOTION MOTION
I cry, and my tears
Stream down my cheeks,
Around the base of my nose,
Outlining and crossing over
The edges of my quivering lips.
On down to the bottom of my chin
Then to the nape of my neck;
The tears fall upon my naked
breasts;
And are absorbed into my body—

To be recycled.
So that another tear may fall,
Down my cheeks,
Around the base of my nose,
Outlining and crossing over
The edges of my quivering lips . . .

Jennifer Estelle Mathews
A MORNING PRAYER
Good morning, Lord.
What a beautiful day.
Help me be a witness
And follow in your way.

As the day goes by
And I do my daily task,
I know you will help me—
I don't even have to ask.

I know that you give help
To everyone who lives,
And I know that to your
followers
Special blessings you always give.

Whether it's to school
Or to a daily job,
You are always there
To save us from Satan's mob.

I realize I don't have to tell you
this,
Because everything you know,
But I want to others
My love for you to show.
Amen

Sarah Stock
Mid Day In Union Square
Day
A new gift
Was around the square
Corners
Buildings
Something towering
Sunbeams
Glamourous
At every street
Twelve bells
A shocking laugh
And so noon
Split the sky
Proud in prayer
And the blue day
Shouted

Austin Thomas
MOTHERS ARE

---

*To my mother, Bertie Dorman
Shelton, who taught me how to
be happy in song and rime.*

Mothers are kind,
Mothers are neat,
They like to clean your nails and
wash your feet;
They sing to you like canaries,
Squawk at you like crows,
But they always take your side
against all your foes;
They smile like angels,
They growl like bears,
They take you to movies or
circus and pay your fares;
Mothers are lonely creatures who
want you to visit or write,
They try to forget those times
you gave them a terrible fright;
They remember the good you did
and not the wild,
For to mothers a man is
always a child.

Bonnie J. Shirley
A TEDDY BEAR'S LOVE
I clearly remember that special day
it's been many years since then
A kindly gentleman beckoned to
me
and I gladly left my den.

His face was so kind I suddenly
knew
I had nothing to fear
He took me home to his first
grandchild
and gave me to the baby so dear.

The baby and I were soon best
friends
together night and day
The grandfather proudly watched
us close
"They're both growing up," he'd say.

When the child was ten the
grandfather left her
and went to his heavenly home
I knew he'd want me to care for her
so I watched her all alone.

I stayed by her side so faithfully
she grew up tall and strong
I knew her grandfather must be
proud
my heart sang a happy song.

I often remember my promise
to her grandfather long ago
So many years have passed since
then
My job is well done, I know.

Rita M. Bender
WILL YOU EVER BE MINE?
For days I can hear nothing from
you
And after this time I don't know
what to do

But you make me calm down
right away
Without even knowing what
words to say

First, your smile melts the anger
from me
So that to be close to you is all I
can see

Next, you feel my face with your
gentle touch
Till all I know is I need you so
much

Then those kisses that only you
could send
Quickly put my feelings back on
the mend

I just can't stay mad no matter
how hard I try
You always win and I'll never
know why

Why am I there when you want
me to be
I guess cause you tell me you
care about me

I'm glad you think we are getting
along fine
But I can't help wondering—will
you ever be mine?

Amy C. Butts
GROWING AWAY
where have you gone
my forever friend?

where are those days
we spent in the usual youthful

ways?
Can this be the tomorrow
we spoke of just . . . yesterday?

Blinded by the callow eyes of
youth
we never glimpsed the truth

that promises and summer days
fade away

and we must carry on
in a most unusual way—
alone.

J. Kevin Thompson, Ph. D.
SUNDAY EVENING
Quietly contemplating,
Missing a cog,
Staring silently,
An existential fog.

Antoher Sunday of retrospect,
A future of indecision,
Seeking objectivity,
But lacking percision.

What prompts this periodic
obsession?
Fatigue, loneliness,—or, depression?
What ends each little session?
Another impossible question.

Literally loathsome,
Figuratively failing,
Lost in alliteration,
A cognitive flailing.

Reality beckons,
An unfortunate call,
Promoting practicality,
To cushion the fall.

For now, adeiu,
Unanswered ruminations,
Come back soon
With fresh intonations.

Joanna Johnson
FREDDIE THE FISH
Freddie the Fish swims in the sea,
swimming along singing merrily.

Passing by nets and lines,
singing and having a good time.

Then he goes to his spot,
being happy that he didn't get
caught.

Kim Lawson
FORTUNE
I believe that I may find my true
worth
In simple values
Love, marriage, and earth
Though let me not mislead you
I too, have need for fame
But in light of one moment's glory
Our tears are but a stone to blame
For he in darkness would confess
Of his spotlighted days
That he had riches beyond mere
man
Had he beheld a loving gaze.

Julian Clyde Sims
OLD TOGETHER
Fall undressed the trees, and left
them standing bare,
Winter's chilly freeze, is hanging
in the air.
Many summer memories, were
made just yesterday,
Before the changing fantasies,
took our youth away.
Our love was like the seasons
with their ever changing scenes,

For all the usual reasons, we hung
  onto our dreams.
The Winter came upon us, and
  caught us by surprise,
And stayed around to haunt us,
  in its cool disguise.
Frost is on the pumpkin, and
  snow is on the peaks,
The Summer years were
  something, but Winter
  possesses bleak.
We know it's almost over, we see
  the cloudy skies,
We've lived our lives in clover, in
  Love shall we die.

Cleo Hall Critelli
KEEP SMILING
Be sure you are smiling
When you go to bed,
Should you wake in the night
You'll know you're not dead.

It's much better to smile
Than to be an old grouch,
Even though your wife makes
  you
Sleep on the couch.

So smile darn you smile
There's just no other way
To help those around you
To feel happy and gay.

Keep smiling, keep smiling
Though you ache inside,
Worries will soon vanish
And leave like the tide.

Smile, smile every chance you get
Smiling has never hurt anyone
  yet,
Everyone else has troubles and
  woes,
Smiling wil help you keep on
  your toes.

Smile until your face hurts,
Laughing is good too,
The world will keep turning
No matter what you do.

patricia hutson
UNSHACKLED

---

*To a very special one whose
friendship brought to birth my
freedom.*

Time is an invisible tether,
Binding, chaining, with endless
  rhythm and fastidious beat;

Let me vanquish the pendulum
  that makes the night full of
  doubts,
And build the stairs that climb
  from day to the stars,
Instead of fading away and
  leading me bluntly into the
  night;

Freedom and Eternity know not
  time,
And tho we must somewhat
  abide by it bodily,
Our spirits pierce thru its
  dooming walls.

Freedom says that sorrow is no
  different from joy,

Pain no different from ecstasy,
Night no different from day;
It is the scope into which you
  view

them,
And with what velocity your
  inner self is liberated.

W. H. Byrd
BURIAL AT SEA
Sailor on an empty sea
I raise my sail in empty air;
Sail an ocean of despair
Where seabirds mock my lonely
  cry.

No compass point nor star to
  guide;
No helping mate close by my side.
Tillerless, slack-sailed and lost
Adrift in yearning troughs
I rest my head on memories
While night slips over the rolling
  sea.

Sail on to nowhere alone
To cast my anchorless soul like a
  stone
In the black-deep ocean's grave.

Nell C. Gaither
SEASONS OF LOVE
A full jar of honey
  spun-dewed umber
  folded in sunshine.

Spoon by spoon
  sweet scars the lips
  tasting love's hunger.

From the empty jar
  the last drops of honey
  sweet chills the tongue.

Teri Jo Adams
AFTER YOU
The morning after a night with
  you and the day drifts in
I dream my way home from work
  wanton—so wanting you again
    and I wait
      go to bed alone
        smell you on the pillow
          wake up to the empty
            stillness
The morning after a night with
  you is so alone.

Cora Durski
WATER FALL
I gaze at the water fall
A lacey sheet of spray,
Falling to depths down below
Where soon it goes astray.

Life is like a water fall,
Cascades through youth and age,
There're so many ups and downs
Before the final stage.

LaDonna J. Nally
A VISIT TO REMEMBER
Then he came to me,
in the form of a cloud.
He came so quietly,
yet so loud.
He then spoke,
not just a word.
Several and more,
each one i heard.
Extending his hand,
to touch my cheek.
God's so gentle,
oh so meek.
What he offered,
added to my mind.
One greatest gift,
i could ever find.
He never left me,
there all alone.

Making me different,
much like i'd grown.

Lorena Gray (Mrs. T. G. Gray)
LIFE IS BEAUTIFUL
Life is beautiful
  So much to see,
Life is thrilling
  So much excitment,
Life is full of rainbows
  Beauty to see,
Life is so devine
  We smile when in pain,
Life is rosy
  Problems always small,
Life is marvelous
  Wonders to discover,
Life is wonderful
  God gives grace,
Life is full of glory
  Makes us humble,
Life is great
  God is love

Elaine Meli
KITCHEN TABLE
Around my kitchen table
All my loved ones sit.
Whenever there is a crisis
My oldest son covers it with wit.

I had two sons and I thought
When they married I had given
  them away;
But, they married girls
That I've adopted to this very day.

I have three grandchildren
And someday maybe more.
Someone is always at the door—
Lonliness can't come in.
    (This house is filled with din!)

So instead of two
I now have seven.
If the dice are right
Someday it will make eleven.

Ruth Bell Sweeney
A SUNBEAM
Jesus wants me for a sunbeam,
But what do sunbeam's do?
They try to follow Jesus,
And want others to follow Him
  too.
A sunbeam is warm and friendly,
And show how much they care.
By showing love and kindness,
And always willing to share.

Michelle Eva Papp
THE GIFT
Who is this stranger with fallen
  eyes
Sadness surrounding her lonely
  cries,
Forever in circles she searches
  still
Is there kindness free at will?
For she and I are one the same
I feel her hunger; feel her pain.
As I look inside the sleeping soul
Of another who dreams to be as
  whole.

Sweet child you will someday find
The magic you hold but cannot
  find,
To surface when the heavens
  shine
And leave you stronger within
  your mind.
You will never watch the hours
  alone
Your power will penetrate those

of stone.
For this soul awakened has grown
  to be wise
Share this gift with the stranger
  who cries.

Linda K. Rasile
DOWN THE ROAD OF LIFE
Life begins like a miracle
  With the sound of a baby's cry
So much pure and innocence
  A smile and a twinkling eye

Each day leads to another
  The road ahead looks long
But take each day, step by step
And nothing can go wrong

Life should be so beautiful
  Like a colorful butterfly
So look ahead with happiness
  A smile and not a sigh

Be happy now and always
  For life too soon is done
But for every life that's ending
  Another has begun.

Robert L. Fox
Vision Of Timeless Oceans

---

*To Marga, who made the vision
come true.*

Timeless love, from what seas do
  you come from to me?
There was a time when the wind
  blew through my hair
  and mist was upon my face,
The crashing sea echoed below
  my feet
  and grass caressed my legs,
Above the horizon the moon
  shone upon the waves
  and I heard a voice.
The sound was as frail as
  translucent moonlight
  shimmering in the air.
Sight, hearing, breath, sensation,
  were all as one
  and I was thus ready,
A spirit came and took me to
  shores beyond
  another place in time anew,
Never have I left, here is where
  my joy still lies,
  here I have found meaning in life.
Thus again dear love I ask; From
  what seas
  have you come from for me?

Colin Clift
THIS MUST BE THE YEAR
Dear parents of children
Over the age of three . . .
As Armageddon draws near,
Surely this must be the year
To make Christmas
What it ought to be—
Devoted entirely
To Christianity.
(Do you suppose computers,
Those incredible neuters,
Can save the human race?)
Subconsciously,
I know you see
That toys only breed
Incipient greed.
Therefore, from this year on,
Instead of such stereotypes
As games and dolls and bikes,
Why not give them books
Containing just His words?

(For too many of us,
Either innocently
Or calculatingly,
Set our denominations
Above His revelations.)
On a higher plane,
Please let me explain
What I comprehend:
Communism is a disgrace
To God, Christ and the human
    race.
On the other hand,
I clearly see
That Capitalism
Isn't Democracy.
(Both systems contain examples
    aplenty
Of the few taking advantage of
    the many.)
Therefore, to prevent
    Armageddon from coming true,
Christ Communalism *must* come
    shining through.

Rebel Fagin
BLOWN AWAY
You are like a dream I had
Visiting a star
You are like a wound of mine
I still carry the scar
Like a moth to a flame
I should go when I stay
I'd really like to love you
But I get so blown away

I am just a wave that breaks
So gently on the shore
You are like a dream I had
Or maybe something more
I am just a wave to you
From the backseat of a car
We pull away so fast
We pass away so far

For a moment I saw you
Like a frozen star
Like a ghostly sailing ship
Visioned from afar
I think that I could love you
If I could learn to take the loss
Your arms hold that ladder steady
That leads back up that cross

Grace Genevieve Jean
A TRUE THANKSGIVING
Oh God, thou who art the only
    God we've known,
For this we give thanks.
And God, Thou who art all we've
    ever desired,
For this we give thanks.
Thou who dost clear the clouded
    shadow of death
From our eyes with the light of
    thy Son,
For this we give thanks.
Thou who dost brace the broken
    bones of our frailty
With thy omnipotence,
For this we give thanks.
Thou who dost dry our Judas
    kissed cheek
With the promise of your
    everlastingness
For this we give thanks.
Thou who dost heal our sin sick
    hearts
With the gilead balm of your
    stripes,
For this we give thanks.
Thou who dost fill the emptiness
    of our doubts

With the fullness of knowledge
    of your mystery of grace,
For this we give thanks.
And Thou who dost end our
    earthly existence
With a beginning of eternal
    heavenly life,
We give thee thanks.
And God, you gave your only Son.
No greater gift; dear Jesus Christ.
We give our thanks.

Maurene M. Sarosi
MY SEASON'S GREETINGS
May your Christmas be filled
    with hope and good cheer.
With love in your heart, bring in
    the new year.
May the dreams that you dream
    some how all come true.
And my prayers will be filled
    with high hopes for you.
As for me there is just one thing I
    will ask,
I'm sure you will find it not much
    of a task;
I would like you to take some
    time Christmas day,
To thank The Lord for all the
    things that He gave.

Phoebe Norris Bradley
COMPENSATION
As I grow older I see more clearly
The beauty all around—
The flowering shrubs, the leaves
    on a tree,
And the green grass covering the
    ground.

I have time to enjoy the birds
And the wildlife that comes to
    play
In the yard at the back of our
    home
At certain times of the day.

I am witnessing Nature's Soul
As I sit right here at home
And enjoy the wonders around
    me—
With no urge to rush and roam.

I can gaze at the beautiful sky
With clouds as white as cotton,
And think on days at the ocean
Which never should be forgotten.

I watched the waves rush in and
    out
As they sparkled in the sun;
I pondered on the miracle—
While I enjoyed the fun.

I witnessed again the Soul of
    Nature;
And it seemed very clear to me
That a Divine force is at the
    helm
And what will be—will be!

Dorothea A. Dickie
WINTER
Winter is an artist,
She paints a pretty scene,
Her brush the mountains kiss,
Her eye is very keen.

She dabs white here and there
On house, tree and field,
And they their winter dresses
    wear
When to her touch they yield.

The snow-banks piled high
Are done by her skillful hand,

As are the snow-caps 'gainst the
    sky
And the glittering snow-clad land.

The softly falling snowflakes
Makes for a pretty sight,
She now has painted much
The earth is clothed in white.

Virginia Morton Ross

Virginia Morton Ross
**A Tribute To My Mother
(Merle Morton)**

*In memory of my mother Merle
Morton. She had many talents
among them writing. She is
greatly missed.*

My mother was a poet too.
She was my inspiration.
She wrote about the things she
    knew,
In all life's situations.

My favorite was the one she wrote
Before God called her home.
With your permission I will quote
Her lovely, little poem.

    Life's Game

Life is like a shooting match
And I so often miss the mark,
But I'll practice and keep
    shooting
Till I'm a "Master", at the art!

Then I'll receive life's highest
    trophy
That I have worked so hard to win,
When the gates of heaven opens
And God bids me, "enter in!"

Where there's no death, no more
    crying,
And this world will end for me,
Where no "Time-clock", will be
    striking,
This is God's "Eternity!"

Gem M. Dumas
IRIS ON A HILL
The August sun is blazing
Silver halows dim my view.
I stand alone and listen
For the comforting sound of you.

For haven't I been here before
And spoken with the wind?
Haven't I touched silence
Where the rustic hills do wend?

I've gathered Iris on this hill
In a past life long ago and tied
Them tight with clouds of white
From skies I used to know.

I will return to this love of mine
Though centuries may pass before.
I shall greet the hills, the wind
And rain, I will live and love once
    more.

Lyllian D. Cole
**No One Will Ask Him How
    He Fared**

(To the Sealers)

A mother searches for her pup
    she doesn't know this naked blob
The snow-white camouflage was
    stripped
    by need of Man to do his job.

Her nose was severed yesterday,
    just one of many hasty chops,
She stood her ground to save her
    young,
    and now it bleeds in frozen drops.

The hunter's home, he needs his
    rest,
    the smell of blood is in his hair,
The cries of mourning in his ears,
    his sea-hawk eyes are filled with
    care.

No laughing children rush to greet,
    instead, they turn their eyes
    away,
NO ONE WILL ASK HIM HOW
    HE FARED,
    how many pelts he bagged today.

But he can pay the grocer's bill
    and buy a worthy fishing net
And all the children rubber boots,
    at last he's shucked a year of debt.

He clasps his loved ones in his
    arms,
    forgets the days, the blood-
    stained floe,
Thanks God they're safe and
    warm and fed,
    forgets the blood and death and
    woe.

Teresa Cerna
**The Rain, The Wind, The
    Sun**
Too much rain can change a
    bone—dry land into a raging
    river.
Sending muddy—floodwaters
    surging and churning
Down a path of total distruction.
When rain and wind get together,
    they become strong and sound.
Spread out so much force,
    fiercely—growling like a lion,
Devouring everything along it's
    way.
Rain is good, but sometimes it
    gets out of hand.

But a light wind is gentle as a lamb
Grasses swish, treetops sigh,
    quiet things creak and clang.
It flings your kite upon the sky.
The trembling leaves fall off a
    tree
It whirls them around, scatters
    them about,
And spreads them like a blanket,
    that covers your front lawn.

The Sun, resplendent at it's rising.
Shines forth, like a vision of glory,
What a wonderful work of the

Lord it is!
The morning sun, brings tender joy,
With happiness awakes the earth.
By it's fiery darts the land is consumed;
The sun sets the mountains aflame.
The eyes are dazzled by it's light.

Diane E. Rohwer
PATRICK
Some sunlight was captured in a smile.
Golden child.
Easy to love and free as a gull.
Small hands that reach out for love
and simply find it.
Fleeting moments in time and I can almost
see you grown.
But I'd rather not.
Till then and you can know what love really means.
Then take your space in this tumbling,
torn up world.
Golden child you can fly.
So don't grow up for a while.

Marie Elena Malady
PEGASUS

I dedicate this poem in memory of my dad, Joseph J. Malady.

With strength and great beauty
He escapes and takes flight,

His mane in the wind
Eyes twinkling with light.

The mystical steed of worlds gone by,
Whos home is the heavens, the stars and the sky.

Ingrid Christel Hoffmann
LIFE
Life is hard
and life is cruel
Life is sweet
and yet in between
There can be love
There can be luck
and happiness
many tears
many fears
many ups and downs.
And then again a hopeful cheer
To push you onward, way up high
To all limits, to the sky.
Then you fall again, again
Life is funny my friend.
But to keep on going, until you drop
even if you should hate your job
Someday you'll get again to the top if, you so choose.
unless you want to lose
You must go on and give
And live.

Larry A. Stevens
THE TWINKLE IN HIS EYE
Upon the tallest mountain, by the shinning piercing sun,
I see a glimpse of Glory as a new day has begun.
I smell the fairest roses and the fragrance of the dew,
I visualize the love of God, in a

picture perfect view.
The warmth of the glaring sunshine drives the chill out of my soul,
The vision of the Fathers love as bright and just as whole.
The singing birds have held their songs in their hearts throughout the night.
but now they praise our Fathers gift, as they share His love in flight.
The morning breeze it stirs the leaves and opens up my mind.
As a stagnant thought, that now has brought, a breeze that moves all time.
And I see the Christ my Jesus, His arms both stretched out wide,
His smile, His twinkle in His eye and a bid to join His side
He turns to walk away from me I feel a sense of grief,
but now He bids me follow Him, I feel such great relief.
A love, a calm and peace of soul are the perfect love of God,
I awaken now out of my sleep, with a wonder, and a nod.

Bernard Davis
A LONELY LITTLE PUPPY
Have you ever stopped to reminisce, say thousand of years ago.
A Lonely puppy went looking. He had only his love to show.
No-one seemed to care for him. He had hoped for the best.
When along came a Cave woman, she nursed him at her breast.
Maybe it began like this. There had to be a start.
When that Lonely Little Puppy wormed his way into our hearts.
And hundreds of years later the Pharohs found him too,
And they taught that Lonely Puppy many things he never knew.
Time and years went by, he was that perfect friend to Man.
English, French, Italian, German, he was there to lend a hand.
None was more courageous, ask the Eskimo he knows,
For without that Lonesome Puppy, their race would probably close
Long before Mankind he roamed the fields alone,
That Lonely Little Puppy, he never had a home.
And in our Modern Age we know all of this is true.
For the Lonely Little puppy had his heart set on YOU!
Yet all he ever wanted was Guidance, Care and Love
And maybe That Man Above gave a friendly little shove!
A smile was on his face, complete with wagging tail,
A couple slurps came from his mouth. The end of a lonely trail.
Still there are those disliking his various needs,
Forgetting the millions of lives he saved. His countless other deeds.

The story of the Shepherd, he dove through a closed screen door,
To save three sleeping people, he never knew before.
The Rough Coated Collie, he heard screaming from a pond.
He rescued two small children, There was no-one else around.
The Service dogs, the show dogs, yes even that little Mutt,
All were descendants of that Lonely Little Pup.
We played with him. We talk to him. He's so nice to have around.
To those of us who own him, there's always a secret bound.
And to think it all started long before our time,
A Lonely Little Puppy sought someone who would be kind.
When Man came along, they became the best of friends.
"Cause Puppy saw him first, and so this story ends!

Sarah How-ree Nichols
HUGABLE SUMMER

For Jeff (Shane) Perkins. A wanderer in this place called earth, and who I shall see again, and some where—again.

In snow storms,
I will hug this summer.
No great thing happened,
Good or bad. The most,
An arm broken at play,
The least,
A little robins egg,
Shattered at the base,
Of a tree.

Thank you, God.

Sarah How-ree Nichols
POEMS

To Arlene Smith, sister, who comes and gives encouragement. To Ronda Wolking, niece, who has endless enthusiasm for my efforts. Please accept this small bit of thanks.

Sometimes—,
you find poems,
under trees,
with bumble bees,
in flower beds,
old worn sheds,
winging by,
on butterflies,
falling down,
from rain filled clouds,
in clear blue skies,
and once—,
in the highlight,
of Joyce's eye.

Ruby Nifong Tesh
BY A FIREPLACE
At day's end one sits and dreams
As logs so gently burn.
Flames of yellows, blues, and greens
Curl quietly round logs of pine and oak
While one's cares dissolve
And float away in smoke.

Grace W. Shaw
CHRISTMAS MEMORIES

To the memory of my beloved husband, William D. Shaw.

My darling, you will not be here with me
This year as I trim a Christmas tree
God called you home to help the angels there
But in spirit you will always be with me.

When I hear the beautiful Christmas chimes
And see the happy carolers go to each home
I will know that you are singing somewhere
In a beautiful mansion—perhaps in the dome.

I can hear God's choir singing loud and clear
The words, "Silent Night, Holy Night"
And your beautiful voice is clearly heard
As you sing, "All is calm, All is Bright."

My love, I can never forget the nice gifts
That you placed under our tree for me
As I unwrapped each gift I planted a kiss
Upon your sweet lips for everyone to see.

As the holidays draw near, I feel so blue.
For I miss your loving ways and sweet smile
But if I can live a life much like yours
Someday I'll meet you on that beautiful isle.

Carolyn Robertson
THE LONGING
I am so lonely for you—
My kindred spirit.
I've lived this life
In longing and have not found.
Why do you ellude me,
Escape my sight—and mind?

Do you not know
How it is for me
To be without that
One spark of life which
Matches mine, understands?
Or—are you real?

If you are only a dream,
Then I shall see you
When I close my eyes
And try to sleep,
Lonely and berefit.

Barry Levy
Making Merry In This World
There is a touch of sadness
to the gladness of these days
No wise men bearing gifts
No meaning rifts the snowless banks
A most unjolly melancholy
in the folly of our ways
No little saviour being born

John Campbell, Editor & Publisher

No warnings scorn the endless
tanks
   Making merry in this world
     Making merry

A seed has sent the land
  and every hand that warms a
coin
No faith is holding fast
No lasting testament of grace
There is a need for kindness—
  how our blindness does purloin!
No end to poverty in sight
No light upon pale hunger's face
   Making merry in this world
     Making merry

All the more to sing and give
Give more to all that they may
live
   Making merry in this world
   Making merry in this world

Roberta Reading
HE LOVES ME
Yahweh loves me, this I know!
He loves me in the morning
When the day has just begun
He loves me in the noonday
And with the setting sun
He loves me in the mountains
And in the surging sea
He loves me in the meadow
Beneath a leafy tree
He loves me in the sway and pull
Of pushing mob and strife
He loves me in the stillness of
The quiet times of life
Whatever does betide me
Doubt, fear, or unbelief
My soul will live forever in the
  mercy of my chief.

Edw. C. Granati
TODAY
Today I reached out and I
  touched you,
  And you were there!
Today I needed you,
  And you were there!
Tomorrow I may need you again,
  And you'll be there.
For you are my lighthouse in the
  night,
  My rocks upon which the waves
can dash.

I need your smile to warm me,
  Your strength to brace me,
Your warmth to guide me,
  And you'll always be there,
Even if only in my memory!

For God gave you to me,
  To be a part of me,
To cheer me when I'm blue,
  To hug me when I need it!
I will never lose the glow of you,
  For God has put his love in you,
And you will always be there,
  When I need you.

Thanks for being you!

Sandra J. Benedict
A CHRISTMAS PRAYER
If I had but one Christmas wish
I'd wish for all the world to be
A place where peace and love
Would flourish happily
All the wars of days gone by
Would cease to stand
In the hearts and memories
Of every fighting man
A song of joy

Would fill the universe
And laughter would replace
crying
As sorrow would disperse
I pray to God
That someday I shall see
My Christmas prayer come true
For all humanity.

Darla Kessler Miller
HAPPY ANNIVERSARY
The sink is stacked with dishes,
You can never find your keys,
The kids are closet monsters,
With band-aids on their knees.

True love lasts forever,
Our's has past the test,
But even though I love you dear,
I need a six month's rest.

Dorothea A. Dickie
MEMORY TRAIN

---

*In loving memory of my husband
ELLIOTT F. DICKIE 1911—1982*

At night when I am restless
And cannot seem to sleep,
My mind will rhyme memories
Instead of counting sheep.

I think of my grandchildren
To me so very dear,
When they come over to my
house,
Yell, "Grandma, we are here."

They always open the fridge
To see what's to eat and drink,
They'll have some pop or juice
And some fruit too, I think.

I read and tell them stories
And play some fancy games;
It reminds me of our kids,
The difference is the names.

Then going back still farther
On "Good Old Memory Train,"
I see me with my family
And childhood friends again.

But what is the best portion
Of getting somewhat older?
You have more generations
In your "Memory Folder."

Jorji Gingrich
First Christmas
Remembering

---

*To my darling son is this
dedication— One of a kind in
any nation! Berwin.*

On the night before Christmas
  and all through the house
People were stirring, 'tho still like
  a mouse.
No stockings were hung by the
  chimney with care
'Cause only grown up kids were
  all that'd be there.
Dad was there still supervising
  you see,
As all things were done as he'd
  want them to be.
His spirit pervaded the whole
  atmosphere
And sometimes it seemed like he
  surely was near!
Mother arranged for a beautiful
  dinner,
And everyone knew it would sure

be a winner.
In spirit we knew he'd be saying
  with cheer
"Merry Christmas beloveds and
  Happy New Year"!

Joyce Billingsley
Reflections Of a
Thanksgiving Day

---

*This poem is dedicated in loving
memory of my wonderful
grandparents, Stuart & Jo Belle
Jolley; George & Lula Ann Tribble
of Sherman, Texas.*

Burnt brick leaves falling from
  the trees,
swirling through the air,
like dancers caught in a breeze.
Late spring apples now ready to
  bake,
will be the main ingredients
for grandma's favorite cake.
Fluffy whipped cream on pecan
  pie,
gives the illusion of
white castle clouds floating by.
The once gobbling turkey,
who is now silently still,
will be baking in the oven,
till he is brown as the plowed
  fields.
Grandpa, who is sitting in the
  porch swing,
keeps an eye on the road for his
  grandchildren,
the car will soon bring.
Silvery rays reaching so high,
shine on the barn's tin roof,
like a spider's web from the sky.
A handmade lace cloth
taken from the cedar chest,
makes the old oak table
look its very best.
This busy country home reflects
  a picture,
painted with love and care,
of a family, who will give thanks
  this day,
for the food and blessings they
  share.

Gloria Jean Beczkowski
THE KISS
Your gentle brown eyes is what I
  see
Your loving nose so long, but not
  to me.

Ears are a part of that loving face
With your hair always in place.

I don't need a picture to
  remember it
But maybe a kiss just to keep it lit.

Winifred J. Hamilton
I Walked Where Jesus
Walked
I walked the paths where Jesus
  walked
Two thousand, or so, years ago,
I reached to Him—He answered
  me,
Don't ask me how I know;
I saw where Christ performed
  miracles
And healed the sick and lame,
I could see him walking on
  Galilee,
I prayed in Jesus' name;

I fancied I saw his disciples
On the shores of Galilee
As they lay down their nets to
  follow him—
No matter where it might be;
I stood in the Upper Room one
  day
Where they broke bread together,
I heard my Saviour say, "Peace,
  be still"
In that wildly boisterous
  weather;
I walked where Jesus carried his
  cross
On the way to Calvary,
I wept as I thought of how he
  died
To salvage such as we;
I'm humble at all the black and
  white proof
That shows how much God cares,
Only a part of me came home
For part of my heart is there.

Jackie Berkson
Jackie Berkson
TO DAISY IN GERMANY

---

*I dedicate this poem to my
fraternal twin sister, the actress
Daisy Byrk in Berlin, Germany,
who is the love affair of my life,
and whom I should never have
left for California.*

Did you ever remember
That we met in a secret place?
That my feet were near your face,
And that it was December?
That though we were so near
  each other
In the womb of our mother,
Each had her own, if tiny house?

With my inner eye I see us:
Children hand in hand together
Roaming fearful through the
  streets,
Promising to never ever part—
"Battered" children; our life was
  hard.
At eighteen years I run away
To find a place for us to stay.

We married both and parted.—
Now my friendly mate is gone;
Your husbands life is measured.
We are nearly seventy.
You are my only treasure.
Is there still hope and time for
  us
To live and love and care for us
    TOGETHER?

380

Vibert R. Lowe
JOYS OF LIFE

Joy and gladness, always follow
moments of sadness
Moments to think, moments to
forget.
God has given these moments,
for, the blessings we may
count.
And give thanks for the joy of
living, as they mount.

Moments of solitude, our
thoughts here begin.
Times for laughter and love, with
peace from within.
The joy of a new day, to send us
on our way,
These are the joys of life.

The joy of living, our opportunity
for giving.
Having friends and the fellowship
we share.
Our opportunity for learning, a
stepping stone for earning.
These are the joys of life.

A house we call home, a garden, a
place to roam.
A tour or trip, with their friendly
visits.
To receive a broad smile, with a
firm handshake all the while
These are the joys of life.

To enjoy good health, with a
touch of wealth.
Our utmost concern, a living we
can earn.
To enjoy God's creations, the sun,
lakes, and woodland.
These are the joys of life.

Lana Poff Lester
WHEN

When darkness spreads her cloak
of black,
and stars cast forth their
hue;
When the sun is gone below the
hills,
and the sky has lost its blue;
When the cricket sings to his
lady love,
his song so gay and bright;
When the animals nestle down to
rest,
it's time for a peaceful night.

Sarah How-ree Nichols
**Christmas Danced Across
The Snow**

*For Selma Traugott. A friend I
shall treasure and for whom I
shall wait on the other side, and
Don Green, a bright light for me.*

The firey roll of the morning sun,
Sent out it's finger tapers,
And flicked the late stars,
One by one,
Off sky's blue wrapping paper.

Christmas danced,
Across the snow,
In spun sugar frolic,
Urging me through the frosty
glow,
Into the loving arms of family.

Victor Terry Au
1 EQUALS 2

*This poem is being dedicated to
the "Big Mac." Good luck in your
new career. Your friend, Victor*

Drowning in a sea of passion,
Is the fool's fool.
Insanity the force that drives him;
Into a world, where only a few
dare to enter.

He is locked in, there is no escape.
Knees planted, he pleads for mercy;
But everyone turns a deaf ear.
He knows he has met his Maker.

He waits his turn.
He will join the Maker's other
unfortunate souls.
He is willing to give up his life.
He doesn't seem to care.

Staring at those eyes, he utters
his last two words.
Now he is not part of this world
anymore.
I have lost a sole friend.
Too bad he chose to end his life
this way.

Gail Ponder
SEPARATE ORBITS

*This poem is dedicated to my
identical twin sister, Gloria
Ponder, for her courage in our
continued struggle to find our
individual selves.*

From the conception of your
sperm father and your egg
mother, two lives were
fertilized from the love the two
of you shared together.

I can now only imagine the
happiness that must have been
felt and shared between the
two of you, for the specialty of
conceiving twin orbits.

The attention you were given
when you walked down the
streets with your twin orbits
dressed alike from head to toe.

If only you knew dear mother
and father, the raging hell
within your twin orbits.

Nights blinded by tears of
uncertainty.
Shadows of raindrops falling on
our pillows.
Feelings of being denied
individual lives and feelings of
being trapped.

Angry with ourselves and at
times with the two of you, yet
our anger were hidden in
muffled sobs.

Survival for us is wedged in a
world of confusion, not
knowing who experienced
what in life's experiences for
we functioned on one mind.

Dear mother and father we are so
emotionally entwined, we are
living a nightmare trying to
emotionally unwind when

being dependent on each other
for the love, attention and
comfort, not realizing orbits
needed people too.

Oh! father and mother with eyes
so soft, tears so new, you
smiled so sure, not realizing
you have separate orbits.

Lawrence E. Bryant
WITH THE TIDE

With the wind in her hair, each
day spent there
she gazes through an empty sky
lost in the faces, and the make
believe places
that live untill the mind and soul
die.

A desperate song, sounds clear
and strong
with the breaking of the dawn
the rolling waves, bring their
song to the graves
of the days already gone

When she smiled, the tide danced
wild
and when she cried, the sky grew
black
but she'll never fall in love with
these gifts she's tried
because she knows that she must
give them back.

A seabird flies, in the sullen
skies
of her waiting by the sea
she see's him there, and pretends
not to care
though he seemed free, as she had
alway's hoped to be.

The day grew weak, as she started
to speak
of a war that could never be won
The time of life just passes by
"She said" softly then, with a tear
in her eye
and it fell to the tide,
which in turn cover's the tracks,
by its abandoned, uneasy side
another day was done
A seabird sails to the setting
sun——

Nikki Rose Arrigo
LIGHT
The becon of truth—
Caresses the waters
As they appear on shore
and
A questing through the mist
Returns one to the stars
Which blanket the sea
of mystery with hope
As the tide and wind
whisper
through destiny.

J. Duwaine Hirschy
WINGS OF THE SOUL
The road never seemed smoother
than it did on the way home.
The moon it ne'er shone brighter
on the one traveling alone.
The stars have never twinkled
ever brighter in the skies;
and Heaven ne'er seemed nearer
to the sensing inner eyes.
The heart's been seldom lighter
as it burst forth into song——
it seemed that there beside me
one harmonized along.

Could it have been an angel
who was riding there with me;
in heart and mind was present
dwelling there continually?
If so, while traveling daily,
I'll gladly pay the toll;
for knowing love and song now
are the soft wings of the soul.

Carrie M. Haun Grindley
**The Two Gifts: Love and
Love**

It's your birthday,
sweet Jesus; come
see how the night smiles!

Come, see the little evergreen——
reminding me of the reason
you were born: to give
mankind life everlasting . . .

Come, let the wee lights blinking
reach for thy face, from nests——
as did those glassy, winking eyes
strung in the husk by musky
beasts . . .

O gentle brother, may the
rosemary
in small pillows of blue return
the nuances of thy mother's breast;
and the cedar curls, Joseph's
hair . . .

O take my lowly star askew
and make it
as bright in your eyes as
the one our father made
on your first birthday . . .

Do you feel a lamb, nibbling
your hem, sweet Jesus? Look
down: it's me.

O come, my gentle brother,
for we have gifts to give
each other——Love and love.

Lee Romig (SW)
BIRTH

Bill, my husband.

I gave the child life from the
depths and pain of me.
I carried, nourished, dreamed and
wondered of what the child
would be.
It was my straining, longing,
struggling and final relief;
That brought the child to reality,
presence and one of belief.

I looked at the man so aching and
determined to share.
Yet of the true experience, he
could only be half aware.

My pity was not without pride in
the man who planted the seed.
I could not control my pride,
importance and yes even greed.
This is my moment of triumph,
my moment to gloat.
Our chances of sharing in this
mystery are NOT remote.

William James Burch
RAINBOWS AND SMILES
My love for you will never end
For you are such a special friend
And you brighten up each day
the way you show you care
Cause rainbows aren't as
beautiful
as the smile that you wear

Dale Wayne Boettcher
WHITE LIGHT
A vail of darkness lowered by
might
Walks its shadows once again
Striding time to the pulse of
white light
Casting a spell remembered when.

Night's curtain drawn on life's
stage
Leaves shadows lingering where
actors once played
Characters and plots void of
outrage
Replaced by nature's white light
ready-made.

Lucille Goodman Kidwell
A GIFT
Shivering winds came down to
touch
A Christmas Trip That meant so
much.
When childhood memories came
to flare
Our car was stalled in freezing air.

The house is damaged by a gust
The Trip becomes a cancelled
must.
A Record Low or Weather Bust!
My faith is but a drizzle trust.

Three hungry squirrels came
down a tree
They want the Christmas nuts
from me.
In childhood, I had ample trust
I prepare them for a Blizzard
Thrust!

Sister M. Michael Rhatigan
SONG OF HOPE
When I see lovely things that
pass
Under old trees with leaves more
green
Than all my hopes of Yesterday,
Or dreams that died before the
dawn,
When friends and flowers with
half-forgotten fragrance
Dance by with all the music of
the world,
Then settle deep and still
Like the stillness of the August
sun;
  I wonder, will Tomorrow's day
be more lovely?

Will the glad heart of any
everlasting thing,
Like turrets on a castle wall,
Withstand enduring memories
Of meadows loud with linnet song?
The curlew bird at the ocean's edge
Takes wave after wave in the
breakers,
With outspread wings he catches
an updraft and is gone.
  I hear his song in the wind.
  I hear his song in the wind.

Rita Blanchette
SEPTEMBER LAMENT
A time when summer's end is near,
When schoolbooks on the scene
appear,
The swimming holes are empty
now
The days so quiet-yet somehow
We wonder where the time has
gone,

Yes—now we have September's
song.
The school bells ring—they're
telling you
No more you'll hear "What can I
do?"
Fishing poles in the corner
stands,
Alarm clocks now take full
command!
A rainbow of colors in the sky,
As we watch the summer slowly
die.

Sheelagh M. McGurn
THEN GIVE IT A GRIN
A sense of humor
That gift from God,
Can make us soar
Instead of plod.

When our lives
Get most confused,
Is when we need
To be amused.

Problems, delemas
That make us daft,
Are easily solved
After we've laughed.

So when it is darkest
With troubles you're in,
Give it your best
Then give it a grin.

Evelyn H. Phillips
THANKFUL
At any time, day or night,
When I feel beaten and downtrod,
I am still and very quiet;
I know the nearness of my God.

When I listen, I always hear
His voice soothing my frustrations.
He loves me. He is always near—
He, alone, is my salvation.

I need Him and He is near;
He holds my life in His Own
Hands.
The essence of my constant prayer
Is: He knows and He understands.

So, all the time, every minute,
He is with me everywhere.
This is His World—I am in it.
Being thankful—that's my prayer.

Estela Fregeau
A CHRISTMAS MESSAGE
My beloved one, you know we're
far apart.
But distance means nothing to
the heart.
For this unity I feel
Surely has to be real.

May you have peace and health
Not to mention happiness and
wealth.
With joy I say, "Merry Christmas
to you this day."
Let us all be grateful and
faithfully pray.

If for any reason you feel rejected.
Fear not my dear one for you're
protected.
Loneliness comes to only those
who forget
That the mind from which all
wisdom comes
Forbids you to fret.

Prayer is a powerful word and one
we must heed.
For God's guidance is something
we all need.
God is within all of us.
Neither you nor I nor anyone else
is the boss.

Our source of light and wisdom
comes form the Lord.
That is why prayer is a powerful
word.
Confidence is something we must
have to succeed.
For without it we might never
obtain what we need.

God's love sustains and comforts
us.
So lets all pray without any fuss.
The Lord is almighty and surely
the boss.

Rosemary Biel
DECEMBER
December is ecstasy in the
children's eyes
Bright red ribbons, upon wreaths
and doors
Great cakes and goodies for all
Mail, heavily burdened with gifts
from afar
From Santa for everyone
Since the Wise Men followed the
star in Bethlehem
Now each year is the birthday of
Him
On Christmas day
Each year the miracle is with us
again.

Janice Ann Conard
A HANGMANS' DEATH
Slowly, one by one, the lights go
out.
Wondering if ever I'll get out of
this prison cell.
I can just tell that my life,
Not the light, is slowly running
out.
From my neighbor I borrow
An ounce of hope about
tomorrow.
But I see through the cell window
The light that comes with the day.
And below that I see, below the
brightly lit sky,
The hangman standing next to
his gallows.
I feel like a hollow empty shell
Condemned to eternal hell.
I frantically try to run.
I realize though, that my time is
done.
Such a beautiful day.
Yet, as I try to enjoy it,
The hangmans' noose gets in the

way.
The hangman himself smiles,
Knowing I've such a short while
To figure out why I'm here;
With death so very near.

D. Richter Lawrence
LINGER AWHILE
There's a hazard in knowing you,
causing me pain,
When before we have parted,
your mind's gone again.

To all of the thoughts that your
life occupies,
And racing ahead of the moment
here lies.

So I, disappointed, as gentle my
style,
Would beg to entreat you to
linger awhile,

And savor the moment, cherish
its worth,
For ever such joy there could be
on this earth

Is yours to make memory, as
vivid as mine,
Becoming a treasured
remembrance in time.

Please take time to note all your
senses compile,
To love and be loved, as we linger
awhile.

William P. Brady
1943
The Time to go for broke was over.
Beneath the ground lies the
memory
Of wired limbs climbing a
mountain
To the rhythm of bells
To the whisper of snowflakes
falling
Falling, touching the ground to
Evaporate the tyranny of time.
They were a band of Celestial
Samurai
Without a gambler's chance.

A world away in the Pacific
He set out upon the last journey
After one complete victory
Knowing nothing of atomised
Miamata water.
Surprised by the Eagle's flight
He hit the mountain. At last
content
He joined his brothers to play
poker
In the cold and snow that was
Monte Cassino.
The bells are ringing still.
The tinkle of donkey bells
answers.

Nancy Knowlton
CRIES
The emptiness inside me is
almost crushing.

I'm being swallowed up whole by
this disease called loneliness.
I want to have the love and
companionship so hard fought
for.
I want the undying commitment
so many times cried for.

I am as the trees in winter.

Their nakedness is only covered
up by the cold snows.

382

Their souls bear the brunt of the
biting winds.
I feel as the trees.
The winter's chills will go at the
onslought of the spring.
And I will survive the darkest
nights alone until the ice melts.

Jane Downing
THE GOOD OLE DAYS
Way down yonder in the Ozark
Mountains
That's where I was born
Racing barefoot through the hills
Our clothes were worn and torn.

Our feet were bare, we didn't care
Skipping along free as the breeze
We wandered down the shady
path
To grab a limb and swing from
the trees.

We crossed the creek on sticks
and rocks
And usually fell in and got wet
But we didn't mind, we dried in
the sun
Those were times we didn't forget.

The birds were singing above,
The rabbits scampering below
We grabbed some berries on our
way
From the vines swinging to and fro.

A little house loomed thru the
trees
With grandfather sitting in the
shade
We knew we'd be rewarded
With cookies grandmother had
made.

Jacqueline Rowe Gonzalez
SPECIAL DELIVERY

---

*To all of the special people
everywhere who have taken in
children to raise, other than their
own, by opening up their homes.*

Happy Birthday Tim, I called, as
he raced up the stairs cap and
gown in hand.
He came as quite a surprise many
birthdays ago.
Early one summer morning, I
opened the door and saw a
cardboard box behind the bush
by the front step.
As I picked up the box, to throw
away, I heard a wee cry.
Looking inside I found a tiny
baby boy, wrapped in
newspaper, and a note which
simply read, "His name is
Timothy, LOVE him".

The nurse in me bathed and fed
him. The mother in me
brought the old crib from the
attic, and LOVE him we did.
He fit right into our home, our
hopes and dreams; into our
very lives.

We watched him carefully, never
knowing if someday someone
would come saying, "That's my
boy".
Now he's a man. Valedictorian of
his senior class.

Twenty-one years ago today
someone alone and afraid
trusted us to raise her baby
boy.
In combating her personal pain,
she has given us twenty-one
years to LOVE Timothy, our
son.

Alice Ponce
God Bless Them Always
The look in his eyes, were as if to
say
Your still the young beauty, you
were
72 years from today

Her smile for him, was it to say
Your the man I've dreamed of,
In every way

She reached for his hand, real
love
It seemed
Again they'd meet, in their
place of dream

They're still young at heart, but
they
May seem old
God bless them always
For the love they hold

Norma Barker
LITIGATION
L ies and devious diplomatic
diversions
I ntentionally and impeccably
related;
T ransform, transfigure, and
transversely illustrate
I ncidents or insinuations
cunningly calculated. To
G ather information to poultice
the situation is an
A ttorney's arduous ramification,
of
T actics and tolerance,
accusations and indictments,
I nducing at times blatant cross
examinations, then
O ffering to bargain to remedy
the fusion, by
N o means demonstrate the need
for representation.

Jacqueline Rowe Gonzalez
OUR NEAR PERFECT TREE

---

*Dedicated to the little child in all
of us who love Christmas and
make it fun for others, and
especially to my Mom and Dad
who always made it happen for
me.*

Into the woods, Daddy and me, in
search of
a tree painstakingly.
The ground was all cloaked with
fresh-fallen snow,
while sleds and toboggans raced
bout to and fro.
The midwinters day was
exceedingly cold,
Daddy's face rapt, voracious and
bold.
A charming chalet blanketed
with white
with smoke from the chimney, a
marvelous sight . . .
All cozily warm and inviting
within

but we were still searching, our
patience now thin.
We found one at last, our near
perfect tree,
our near perfect tree, for Daddy
and me.
Tinsel and garland will make it
look great,
we don't even care that it isn't
quite straight.
My Daddy can fix it upon the
new stand,
this Daddy of mine, a giant of a
man . . .
Our family and friends, to our
home will abound,
to see the fine tree that my
Daddy found.
Just in time, I may add, on our
searching spree,
our near perfect tree for Daddy
and me.

Virginia Grim
HEART AND MIND
Thank you, oh Lord
For the privilege of living
In a world filled with
Beauty and excitement
For the gift of loving and being
loved
For friendliness and understanding
For the green of the trees
The sound of a waterfall
The harvest of the soil
For the delights of music and
children
For other mens thoughts and
conversations
And the books to read
The rain falling on the roof
The snow blowing outside the
window
And the cry of the new born babe
For the babe born in the stable
Who gave his life that we may live
Gratitude for every good—
Which we enjoy
Especially the moment when
We pause to praise and pray:

Larry Douglas Citappell
AS I DAILY AGE
As I daily age
May I remember
All opening lines
While playing
On life's stage
The role called me
And, may I, at opera's end
Forget not to bend
And give thanks to thee!

Each day I pray
To you God
To let me play
And live the role
Of a "would be" Robinhood
Who with golden deeds
Fulfills the needs
Of his neighborhood!

As I daily age
Withdrawing slowly
But ever so surely
From life's stage
May I be the introducer
Of the new actor
For my job, he's won.
He is Jack—he is my son
God you know how it is
In family biz!

Jean Cunane Murphy
LEFT BEHIND

---

*For Elaine Kelly Hecht You
bathed my soul in brilliant
laughter . . . and sunlit tears . . .
for all our years . . . Thank-you . . .
Murph.*

Ah Kell . . . kindred mate of my
soul
Without you . . . such stark,
unearthly cold!
Weeping Sun cries forever after
your glow.
Left alone . . . I break with woe.
At last you found your home
As I wander through tombs of
stone.
Half a century of courageous
dreams
You achieved alone . . . not by
team.
How on earth do I live now?
Please smile down . . . show me
how.
My love for you accepts no
end . . .
Rare, eternal, quintessent friend.

Veronica J. Rodriguez
UNTITLED
Let me be free from you and me
whoever they may be
You are a stranger walking in the
night
I am but a ghost invisible to all
until I see the light
Unless I know pain
I cannot feel joy therefore
I have only lived in vain
Instead of standing in pride
I remain behind the people
what a safe place to hide

Jan Pearman
MY GIFT TO YOU

---

*To that very special person who
gave my life meaning, who made
my life complete.*

I offer you my love please accept it.
It is not an "all consuming" or
"overwhelming" love
It is a love that will allow you to
be the free spirit that you are—
I understand that because I too
am a free spirit.

It's a love that will always be
there-backstage.
Even tho on occasion it will
move forward and take center
stage,
when that occasion passes, it will
again move to its right
position, backstage.

It will be there to comfort you
when you need comfort.
To support you when you need
support,
To be loyal to you when you
need loyalty,
To laugh with you when you
need to brighten your day.

It's the backrub when your tired,
a kiss on the forehead while
you sleep, the tender touching

of your hand.
the lying close to you, the wink across the room,
the rembrances that we share.

Even if our relationship should end today, you have
gained my respect and my love. It's yours forever.
no strings attached. It asks nothing in return.

Joe Dylik
HIS PAVED ROAD
We walk the road of life not knowing how, where, or when it will end.
Going along with adversity or happiness, as we come to the next bend.
The right attitude about those experiences will enable us to learn,
how to cope with the challenge that we may face at the turn.

If the road is crooked, bumpy, and going uphill,
we should stop to meditate, and learn to be still.
Then our inner conscience will direct us in the way to go,
like the rivers that seek the oceans, know which way to flow.

If we ask for His guidance and the way to be saved,
He will give us light to find the road that is paved.

Jean Boyce Capra
Grandma's Mince Meat Pies

I dedicate this poem to all GRANDPARENTS, and especially in memory of my maternal Grandmother Ettie Patton Madison, deceased, whose cherished memories inspired me to write this day the one poem best describing her works of art, those luscious homemade pies! Adelbert and Ettie Madison's farm was near the Mark Twain park, Barry County, Mo.

We all bundled up in our winter coats,
And loaded food and ourselves in the cars,
For we were going to Grandpa's country house,
And help him feed the horse and cattle oats.

Once inside the country home, we all smelled food,
For the years crops were abundant and good,
The old wooden table with table cloth so white
Was loaded down with goodies, each plate a delight.

There was plenty for all the kin folk there,
With two helpings each and plenty to spare.
The men folk talked about the past years hunt,
While women and children were busy icing the Bundt.

But it was Grandma's country mince meat pies,
That steamed from the wood stove and caught our eye,
Made of raisins, gooseberries, two kinds of meat,
Some suet, chopped apples, currants . . . what a treat!

In the center of the table were syrups, jellies and jams,
And plenty of hot rolls, corn bread, and bisquits on hand,
Luscious whipped cream on top of the fruits and pies,
Every recipe was from 'scratch', herein the secret lies!

Elsie Rae Santagata
A SMILE
Did you ever think what all a smile can do?
It is small, but it can change the world for you.
There's only five letters to spell, S . . M . . I . . L . . E .
Each one has a special task it does, you see.

S . . is for sunny and shining bright.
M . . is merriness and happy delight.
I . . is for an invitation of friendship sent.
L . . is for love, given, but never lent.
E . . is everlasting joy, you see.
All of this came from the SMILE you gave to me.

Ila Reams Odom
CHILDHOOD DAYS
Happy were the days of my childhood when time seemed to stand still.
When I roamed the fields and wood and played or worked at will.
No worry burdened my mind nor frown clouded my brow
As I walked, my dog tagging behind, in search of that old stray cow.
A rabbit might scurry from the underbrush or a gray squirrel dart from a tree;
All seeming to be in quite a rush but not really afraid of me.
The flowers that bloomed in the sunshine and the ferns in the shade of a tree
All contributed to these fond memories of mine of when life was happy and carefree.
The passing years have taken their toll but my mind has firmly withstood
Any erosion into these memories of my happy and peaceful childhood.

Natal J. Carabello
WOODKNIGHT
Mountains clothed in brilliant splendor
Multi-colored shades and hues
Autumn's glory soon to vanish
Into winter's gray and gloom.

Then to witness resurrection
In the springtime miracle.
Life returns from winter's

darkness
Summer spreads its verdant wings.

Sea of green and sky of blue,
Woodsman, you command this view.
You are lord of all outdoors,
Woodsman, this fine world is yours.
Woodsman, it's now up to you,
Keep the living cycle true.

Fight the fires, dam the flood,
Stay the huntsman's lust for blood.
We're all creatures in His sight,
Woodsman, use your might for right.

Lester E. Garrett
The Two Candles Of Christmas
All too soon they watched it flicker,
And die, forgotten . . . though once
A happy candle held high in a time of
Togetherness, freshness, beauty and hope.
But the heart need not despair;
For He stands as near to us as ever,
Our Lord and Mystic and Giver of gifts.

Out of love, He made Christmas happen,
Gave us Jesus and a candle of guidance;
Yet, in the grasp of the human hand,
So often it trembles, flickers and dies
And the simple story fades . . .
The bright tree in the sea of light becomes
As dead as wood, in a dense, dry forest.

It's over now, the planning, the shopping,
The joys, the disappointments.
The tree's down, and all the decorations?
Abruptly a post holiday trauma sets in.

But be merry, be of good cheer!
Once again, through Christmas, God has reminded us
Of what it is to hope, to know of Jesus afresh.
And has He not shown us the depths of the love
And the goodness that lies within the human being?
O, let us keep our candle lighted,

and have faith
That Christmas love will glow throughout the year.

Jolene Burke
HIDING
What does it take to unveil the mask
That I wear so cleverly?
Hiding, searching the by-gone years of past.
Weights of guilt, burdening heavily.

What daring fool would choose to
Unveil the secrets that I carry?
Bewildered this small child who
Seeks in vain her true identity.

Diane Elizabeth Oberhaus
IF I COULD HAVE
If I could have any friend in the world
You know that I would pick you
You always seem to know what to say
And exactly what to do.
I never have to say I'm sorry
'Cause we never seem to fight
We keep on talking it over
Until we get it right.
You always seem to understand
When I am feeling down
You'll never know what it means
Just to have you around!

Arlone Mills Dreher
MY DEAREST LOVE
My Dearest Love, I have not gone away
I'll be beside you when you need me, dear.
My love will be a beacon on your way
and guard you well and keep you free from fear.

My love's still strong, though I seem far away.
I'm still with you and share your busy life.
I'll be beside you, dear, and this I pray—
you'll always feel my love, my blessed wife.

Patrick T. Mayernik
A SIGN OF LOVE
It was a dove, from Noah's Ark;
With a branch of olive, Blessed by God.
A Sign of Love.

The Wedding of Cana, from water to wine;
To, Him above, He gave, His Sign.
A Sign of Love.

With this ring we do join;
A Sign of Love;
The Angel's sing, from Him above;
A Sign of Love.

Baptized in the Jordan, a sign of a dove.
Manna in the desert, a sign from above;
An olive's branch, a wedding ring;
Water and wine, we all sing.

A rose for your heart;
A kiss for your love;
A sign from above;
In the sign of a dove;
A Sign of Love.

Our World's Best Loved Poems

Helen Strey
CHILD OF GREAT WORTH
A Babe was born so long ago
In Bethlehem town
And low—
This child of great worth
Lay his head on a mound of hay
For a bed.
Our calendars are dated by His
birth!
This Child of mirth
And sorrow—
The SON OF GOD—begotten—
To free us of our sins—the cross—
Not forgotten—
Sadness—turned to gladness!
On the hay—and on the cross—
He lay,
Love without measure—
He paid our way to HEAVEN!
And Treasure—

Cynthia I. Washington
MIRROR
Mirror, mirror on the wall
What is it that you see?
A thousand times I looked in
your eyes
And all I saw was me.

I tried to look past the image,
The one I saw of me
I tried so hard in search for
you . . .
But myself was all I could see.

Mirror, mirror on the wall
What could the problem be?
Maybe it has nothing to do with
you
Maybe it deals only with me.

Can you tell me what you know
Explain what's in your view
Describe to me, exactly what you
see
'Cause I want to see it too.

Mirror, mirror on the wall
Inside I bet you're laughing at me
You're thinking I know the answer
For all I see, you see.

Beyond this face holding
watchful eyes
Beyond this peer-forced grin
It's obvious you know something
I don't . . .
Hidden like an unknown sin.

Mirror, mirror on the wall
You know something I do not
One day you tell it to me
For I know you see a lot.

Vivian L. Abbott
SUNRISE TO SUNSET
I watched the dawn of a new day
As the soft rays of the rising sun
Came shining through the trees
Growing brighter as higher it
rose in the Heavens,
Letting the sunlight cover the
Earth and brighten the Seas.

I watched the sun in the
lengthening day
As it descended into the evening
Casting a glow across the
western sky
With myriad colors in array.

How wonderful, that God can
paint
A picture over the expanse of
Heaven

To delight the human eye!
And throw a mantel of light
across the World,
To show His love for you and I.

Gladys G. Whitacre
REFLECTIONS
Way up in the beautiful azure
skies,
Yet very dark, the moon has gone.
And millions of starlights blink
their eyes,
So far away, just waiting to see
the dawn.
This recalls to us of the
appointed time,
When one star did outshine all
the rest.
Mary pondered many things in
her mind,
And held the baby gently to her
breast.
Did she know that the brilliant
star,
Would guide to hope, joy, faith
and love;
And the beautiful baby born afar,
Would herald everlasting peace
from above?

Now many years have come and
gone,
And the lights of earth reflect
again.
Joy to the world, the Lord has
come.
To bring peace on earth, good-
will to men.
But many are blinded and cannot
hear,
The beautiful message the
shepherds did adore.
Although the stars shine on in
the heaven's clear,
The vision is dimmed by
weapons of war.
Help us, dear Lord, to reflect your
light,
And bring to others your message
of love.
Then hope, joy and faith will
brighten the night,
With heavenly blessings from
above.

Kevin MacIsaac
SEARCHING FOR MYSELF

*To Lorie and David, may the Lord
shine over the path you travel.*

The cornerstones in my mind
Reflect an image
Of a lost thought I can't find
I'm in search of myself.

Somewhere in my head
There is an identity
Of someone I used to be
But it is not clear.

I see friends I once knew
Standing right here
Yet, totally unaware of my
presence.
I feel so helpless.

My parents sharing a few laughs
Just living their lives
As if I never existed.
I wonder who I am.

I ask God what is wrong with me
And He tells me

You need no longer search
For you have just been found.

Carol A. Barwick
Beauty Of the Aged
There's something special about
the aged and the old,
Their eyes glisten and sparkle
like nugget of gold.
They're grateful for the littlest of
things,
And to them a certain happiness
we can bring.

A soft word of assurance, or a
smile in the night,
Can make the dawning of
another day a little more bright.
A patient answer to their
questions and fears,
Can bring a smile and stop the
trickle of tears.

When their eyes turn dull and
their time has come to leave
this land,
Stay close by and let them feel
the warmth of your hand.
With them, this great moment
you can share,
And let them know that you
really care.

When their pain and suffering
has come to an end,
And they have rounded the last
curve in the bend,
Look up to God and say a prayer,
That in His happiness they will
share.

Larissa Judith Vassari
FRIENDSHIP
Friend, I have opened my heart to
you—
Bared my soul-cried my tears
and shared my failures.
Yet you smile and say "I love you
still."
That to me, is all that is
worthwhile in this weary world.

Joan Brigensmith
I WANT TO RUN AWAY

*To my very special friend Laurie
who gave me the strength to
accomplish a dream. Thanks for
your support, Keller.*

There are sometimes I feel as
though I want to run away
But in my heart there's
something that makes me want
to stay
I often sit and think about the
bad times I have had
And then I think of all the times
that really weren't so bad
To live your life in full you have
to set a goal
And no matter what it takes you
have to feel it in your soul
My goal is very simple that I set
upon myself
It is to do my very best and think
not of myself
Throughout my life I always tried
to help the ones in need
I really tried to heal the pain and
all the hurt I've seen
Sometimes I can't accomplish all
the things I want to do
But yet I do the best I can to see
the bad times through

The work I chose, it's right for me
it helped me meet my goal
A nursing home is where I work,
caring for the sick and old
I put my heart and soul into the
work I do each day
I only wish that I could do my
work in my own way
It makes me feel so bad inside I
don't have time to spare
To do the things that mean so
much, like memories to share
You really grow to love the folks
you care for everyday
They ask you why the hurt and
pain, you don't know what to say
I always try to comfort them and
then they tell me why
It's all because they're lonely and
they are afraid to die
I say there is no need to fear for
you are not alone
You still have all your memories
that you can call your own
Here lately, it has seemed to be
I'm always in a rush
To do the things I have to do that
really are a must
It really makes me feel so bad
that I don't have time to spare
Cause what I really want to give
is tender loving care
Each day as I go off to work my
mind is full to thoughts
Maybe, this could be the day that
I have always sought
A day that I coud heal the pain
and work without the strain
A day that I could sit and chat
and even share the rain
A day that I can go back home
and get a little rest
A day I have in my mind that I
have done my best
A day that I can get some sleep
and I don't have to cry
A day that I don't have to think
and ask the reasons why
There are sometimes I feel as
though I want to run away
I finally figured out the reason
why I want to stay
It has to do with all the folks I
care for everyday
The folks who say they love me
and they need me here to stay

Richard Steven Wells
'TIS THE SEASON
A time to be cheery
A time to be jolly
A time to forget
The year old's folly.

A time to remember
The Christmas gone past
A time for the New Year
Approaching so fast.

A time for your old friends
Both far and so near
A time for your close friends
That you hold so dear.

A time to reflect
On the seasonal meaning
A time just to wish you
This Merry Christmas greeting.

Eleanor H. Cumming
SPRING AND LOVE
So often have I looked for Spring
Beneath the leaves of Fall

385

And listened breathlessly
For a lone bird's call.

So often have I given love
Wholeheartedly and free . . .
Yet as I waited all alone
No love came back to me.

What is Spring and what is love?
A resurrection in the heart . . .
A faith that flowers will bloom
    again
And love, like flowers, will start.

Peter Kerestur
Woman, You Better Stay
Woman, you better stay out of
    my life
So I can keep my dream alive
That your lips were created for
    kissing
Not for spitting out the insults,
    jeers, and mockeries
That your face was created for
    pleasant smile
Not for angry frown nor
    menacing grimace
That your voice was intended to
    be gentle, tender, clear
Music sweet to my ear
Not an ominous thunder looming
    o'er my head

That your eyes were created for
    expressing fidelity, loving, joy
Not for tears shed in false
    jealousies, desparate hate, idle
    sadness
That your cheeks were created to
    flush and blush
In passionate emotion for my
    unabashed love
Not to be drained off of your red
    blood in a futile ire
That the words were intended to
    echo the gentle side of your soul
Not to rev in complaints,
    jeremiads, laments, blames
As though your tongue was still
    dipped in the primordial venom

Woman, you better stay in my life
So I can live the real life
And have somebody to insult me,
    jeer, and mock
Be angry and threatening, shout
    and hollering
Be jealous, hate, call on my
    sympathy
So I have somebody to resent,
    complain, lament, blame
Somebody to keep my dream
    perpetually aflame

M. Ruth Howard
GOD IS EVERYWHERE
Have you ever stood in a garden
    and watched a tiny seedlet grow?
Did you stop to consider God's
    presence was there?
Have you ever been in a hospital
    and watched a tiny baby born?
Did you stop then to consider
    God's presence was there?
Have you ever sat by the bedside
    of a dear one slowly dying?
Did you stop then to consider
    God's presence was there?
Listen my friend I've been thru all
    of these,
And I'm ashamed to say I never
    once considered God's presence
    was there.

He made that little seedlet grow,
    to the unborn baby He gave
    life,
Because He loves us so, He is
    always there.
Yes He taketh away our loved
    ones, and he gives them eternal
    life.
So stop and consider this my
    friend, God's presence is
    everywhere.

Jamie Marie Bowlsby
WINTER

FOR: My best friend Marilyn J.
Dennis

Winter is a most wonderful and
    special season.
The white snow falls slowly, with
    a shinning crystal color.
White and pure as a wedding
    dress, it falls, and brings a
    special beauty to everything,
    covering the world with a
    white blanket.
Along with the beauty a special
    feeling of happiness arrives.
Cold and wet, as it may be, winter
    seems like the best, and most
    special season to me.

Barbara A. O'Hara
MY KEEPSAKE
Mine to keep
not ever to be shared
leaned on
    or marred.
It cannot be destroyed
changed
taken away
    or altered.
Nor be worn by anyone else
admired or adored
felt
    or held.
It is something
that is only for me
yet, I do not
    own it.
It is not for sale
cannot be given
entrusted
    or rented.
I have it to hope on
trust in
for the rest of my life
    to love.

Patricia Ann Hale
**FLOWERS, FLOWERS
(Children's Jump Rope Song)**
Flowers, flowers on the hill,
Daisy, dandelion, daffodil,
Lovely, lacy, fancy, frill,
Flowers, Flowers on the hill.

Smiling, sunny, summer day,
Breezes blowing, briskly play,
Flowers, flowers, 'till they sway,
Swinging, singing, songs so gay.

Flowers, flowers, sigh goodbye,
Watching, waiting, winter's nigh,
Flowers fear that they must die,
Flowers crying, flowers . . . cry.

V. A. Howard
CHRISTMAS JOY
A yule log, a warm eggnog
A wreath made of holly
Toys on shelves, made by the elves

Of Santa, Oh! so jolly
A cap of red upon his head
A man who doesn't tarry
Bells are ringing, people singing
A time to be so merry
A time of myths and giving gifts
Is what we choose to remember
We can hardly wait to celebrate
The twenty fifth of December
A Christmas tree, a gift for thee
We think of these things solely
How is it that, we can forget
That Christmas day is holy
A child was born that frosty morn
And I have this to say
It's such a shame to forget the
    name
Of "Christ" on Christmas day
The bells we hear, the cup of
    cheer
Can't bring us half the joy
Of the peace on earth, brought by
    the birth
Of "Christ" the baby boy!

Dorcas P. Hord
DEEPER WALK
A deeper walk, a deeper love
Take me deeper still,
'Till my eyes feast on You
And Your perfect will.

Take my hand lead me on
From this worlds affairs,
'Till my mind is resting
Take away all earthly cares.

Bathe me in Your Spirit
Wash me in Your love,
Cleanse me precious Savior
Until I'm home above.

Orville Pointer
LOVE

Sometimes born into the world is
a Lady of Heart in who's heart
love is not just an obligation, but
a gift not only to her family but
those her heart touches.

My name is love I am there when
    you reach inside of dreams to
    mend a broken heart.
I am theirs when people cry with
    true pain their tears fall upon
    my face.
I am their eyes when some see
    not only a face but the face and
    the heart together.
I am their feelings when touch is
    more than lust but life given to
    another.
I am their gift when little is had
    the greatest is given.
I am their truth when they say
    that love is more than a word
    and takes great courage to
    stand in a world sometimes of
    hate and cold.
I am their truth when tears are
    given for happiness or sad.
Those who seek me should they
    find me never empty love is my
    name.

Michael Sandford
SUN SHOWERS
The rain kisst my cheek.
As though, it were a shy girl.
Then quickly ran away.

Lisa Lin Turner
NO GREATER LOVE

*To all my friends who have
helped me to know the Lord, and
strive to serve him better! I will
always remember all you have
done.*

Lord you have been there for us.
You listen to our problems every
    day,
And never make a fuss.
At times we only come to you,
When things go wrong,
Or when we fell down and blue.
But you are always there never
    gone!
I wonder why you even care,
When I think of how your son
    had all our burdens to bare.
We don't deserve your love,
But you still sent your son to die
    and shed his blood.
Oh, Lord there is no greater love,
Then that of you and your son!

Eleanor Knight Childress
SEARCHING
Another time, another place—
    Where have we met before—
In misty light of morn's new face
Or on some distant shore?

Perhaps in spring or summer fair,
    Beside a garden wall,
Or did I catch a glimpse of you
    Through autumn leaves one fall?

I've seen your smile before-
    somewhere.
I've felt your perfect love.
I've heard your gentle voice, so
    clear,
In breezes high above.

I faintly see your silhouette
    Against the earth so sweet;
And know that I can find you, yet,
    In everyone I meet.

Mr. Kurt C. Radtke
A LUMINOUS SELF
Once in a lifetime you know it is
    right, the flame of the candle
    burns tall, pure and bright.
The light from her face and the
    gleam of her eyes find a
    sensitive place, and you're not
    too surprised.
You gather your courage, your
    feelings let go, in a matter of
    moments the whole world will
    know.
A smile and a comment; a
    bouquet of flowers, some
    dinner; the movies; the
    minutes like hours.
You want to be with her, the
    hours they fade, you spend
    time together, the progress
    you've made.
A relationship builds, she's as
    close as a sister, when she's not
    in your arms, you know that
    you miss her.
You hold her and hug her, and
    tell her you love her, you hope
    that some day she'll be your
    bride.
The feelings, the loving, above
    all, the caring,

are not something easy to hide.
You ask her to join in the
struggle of life, to marry you,
be with you, lover and wife.
The energy focused on being
alone . . . of wondering,
hoping and dreaming is now
rearranged in a masterful way
for another . . .
the challenge of sharing.

Sheila M. Sebald
THE FINAL SHOW
A circus of people wait to be seen
Bright colored tent and big caliopy
They scramble and stutter with
pain on their face
The first act's beginning it's time
for the race

Come one and come all
the Big Top is here
All ages are welcome
from both far and near
We've horses and camels
Oh, yes, we have clowns
They've traveled for miles
to brighten your frowns
There's popcorn and peanuts
there's pink cotton candy
Bring Teddy and Rover, bring
Mommy and Daddy
Tigers will dance and lions will
roar
Clowns stand beside them, they
watch the cage door
Ladies swing high upon the trapeze
While men walk through fire
with grace and with ease
The Ringmaster's calling, the
finale is through
Good night and God Bless——oh
yes Sweet Dreams too!

Craig Kilpatrick
LORDS GIFT
Lord You gave me legs that I
might walk,
And a tongue that I might talk.
You gave me eyes that I might see
And wisdom Lord that I might
praise Thee.

And Lord You gave me one,
Like there is no other,
Whom I love dearly
For she's my mother.

Ray Yedding
ONCE UPON A CHILD
My son and I ran barefoot along
the beach, hand in hand
stumbling through the water's
edge,
falling down and wrestling in the
sand.

The woodland stream where we
used to wade,
these memories of his youth with
me that will not fade.

Of chasing butterflies, and trying
to catch a frog,
exhausted by the end of the day,
Curled up in front of the fireplace
with his dog.

We caught a catfish from the old
wooden pier.
I watched him trim the sail of our
boat,
and helped him learn to steer.

Now, as these tired old eyes of
mine grow dim,
were they just dreams, or was it

him?
Will he wonder of things that
might have been?
Will he look back on life and
know he's had,
a father who loved to be with him
and not just a man called dad?
Michelle Elizabeth Petze
LET ME FIND HEAVEN!
Dear Saint Anthony,
Let me find the road to heaven.
And when I'm safe on the road,
Let me find the gates to heaven.
And when
And the love in me I've left ungiven
I'm through the gates,
Let me find heaven.
And sweet Jesus,
When all has been found,
Let it be perfect!

Ethel Ellen Lewis
Ethel Ellen Lewis
CLOTHES LINE
Clothes in the rain
Hung in the sunshine,
Now dangle in a shower
Of
slanting
drops
stabbing
the air
by the hour
pelting my lingerie:
Hanging hose with stiff-legged
motions,
A green gown swinging its
dripping tail,
Pairs of panties
Hanging square and stiff,
Like a line of soldiers.

Norman Moffatt
I GAVE
I gave you my best.
You gave me loneliness
I gave you love.
You gave me sorrow and pain.
I gave you life.
You gave me death.

Carrie Waldo
REFLECTIONS OF A LOVE
Each time I'm lonely
I look into my memories
I see your smile
And my heart leaps with love
You are the fullfillment of the
part of me
That wished but never dared to do
The dreamer that never wished to
wake
And the love in me I've left ungiven

You are the warmth
Beginning in my heart
And reaching to my soul
A love so simply complicated
Yet so easily understood in us.
Lois A. McLeod
This Aries Lover Of Mine

*To My Inspiration Roger F. Mehl,
who's Love, Warmth and
Compassion will always be a part
of me.*

Ah, what is this Aries Lover of
mine
A sensuous portrayal of what
only God could create
A masculine marvel is he who
placates his woman . . .
A procurer is he, who only brings
that of himself to my bed
Finding him profoundly inducing
excitement until passion
ardently flows through my
trembling body, to his body . . .
No fool is he, as I feel the
weakness of my femininity
reaching out to attain the
lustful pleasurers of his
pleading mind . . .
Oh, such escatasy only lovers
could bringforth . . .
Boundless is the mind, body, soul
and spirit that is entwined and
then erupts . . .
Only peace and fullfillment lies
beneath this volcano of
ours . . .
What is this mystery that no
man has broughtforth to me
in half a lifetime, other than, this
Aries Lover of mine . . .

neva minks
A MEMORY
I came to walk
With my feet
In the water
My eyes upon
The sea
Wind blow in my hair
Whisper a memory
The roar of the waves
Becon
Come unto me
Come unto me
Friend am I
I will set you free
No more tears to fall
For all eternity
Then I too
Will only be
A memory
Patricia Randall
KELLY'S DAY

*To Kelly, You have showed me
how to love a little more and to
complain a little less. You always
make the clouds go away with a
smile, a hug and a kiss.
I love you.*

It is a great day
when the first leaf
falls in the already
empty barrel.

The breeze promises

a better tomorrow
as a last leaf
floats away.

You reach for something
and find plenty
on a great day.

Patricia Randall
THE OLD MAN

*To Mom and Dad, You taught me
that a song is how you hear it
and beauty is only in the way
you look at things. From you I
learned how to find fullfillment.
May we always be able to share
the magic of love between
parents and child.*

As he looks down upon the soil
nodding to old to toil.
Old man swaying with age
smiling wise old sage.

Searching in vain
trying to shake his pain.
Old man silent and cold
wanting love of long ago.

The world doesn't see
peace is what he needs.
Old man with pride
picture love at your side.

Inflation doesn't care for age
retired so no wage.
Old man with tattered coat
left without hope.

No food, no heat at home today
no place else to stay.
Old man alone and crying
freedom comes with dying.

Sharon L. Beavers
VENGEANCE

*To my mom who is behind me all
the way. Thanks mom!*

Once they were each other's friend,
now their relationship is at an end.
Obsessed by love for one girl,
upset the friendship in a whirl.

Revenge brings out one's dark side,
and when it's stirred it is hard to
hide.
All the build up of hate and spite,
will result in a ruthless fight.

Each man's purpose is to avenge,
Only one will survive revenge.
The war between them incites
violence,
each is screaming for vengeance.

Andrea Jean Kilburn
TELL ME
Tell me
what does one do
when—
the urge to reach out and
touch
is great,
but the urge to be touched
is even greater?
Tell me
what does one do
when—
a vacuum begins to form
in a place which was once
filled with memories?

Tell me
what does one do
           when—
thoughts and thinking become
   like physical pain.
           Tell me
what does one do
           when—
           Yes you,
                    Tell me.

Iva May Maudlin
IN DECEMBER
The little brook has lost its glee,
It no longer laughs up at me.
The vim and vigor is not there.
All it gives is an icy stare.
Snow in beauty, like pattern lace
Falls with gentleness on my face.
Snow men made by boys at play
Are too good to run away.
Birds leave their foot prints in the
   snow
Their calling cards
Months are many as I recall to let
   us know
I like December best of all

Victoria Marie Cyr
BEAUTY ABOUNDS
A world of matchless beauty,
   exquisite in every grace.
Brilliant hues disperse
   themselves to dine.
   in all imaginable colors,
That kindly covers the lands
   assuring comfort and security.
Colors, not alone,
   are surrounded by friends of the
   Society.
Images, satisfied with their
   splendor,
   revel in their shapely figures—
Mirrors of perfection.
   In the distance, the plea of a
   gull,
The thunderous echo of the sea's
   arms
   reaching for the shore,
Leaves, skipping secretly on a
   lonely road—
   offerings from the land,
Received by those who travel
   their eroded paths,
   appreciative of the honor.
Ecstasy awaits.
   while the passion for life lingers,
Consumed by the heart,
   savored by the soul.
Each beckons the other
   to dine.

Georgia Ray
TEARS
I woke-up this morning and tears
   had filled my eyes, for I knew I
   had lost the man I loved to the
   lost and lonely places we call
   time.
The tears are for the years we
   will never see, and for all the
   beautiful memories of years
   we've already seen, for he's the
   only man my heart has every
   known,
I will wake-up every morning
   with tears in my eyes, time has
   taken everything, my love has
   walked away, I'll never see the
   sun again, I'll never see a smile,
   all I'll ever see will be the
   memory of a love lost to time.

Claudia Elizabeth Cobleigh
A RED ROSE MEANS LOVE
Hi, I don't know you and our
   color is not the same
But I heard of your sorrow and
   the tears just came
Our worlds seem different but
   why must it be
With me fighting you and you
   fighting me
Keep all your customs and let me
   keep mine and
Let us respect this as we travel
   through time
Our land is a rainbow of colors
   and creeds
Of love thats within and
   expressed in our deeds
If hate over takes us then all
   hope is dim
And the progress we worked for
   will all die within
So when someone asks you to
   start racial crime
Say "We're in this together, hate
   can't have my time"
But gather the hate and use it
   just right
To make better laws so we don't
   have to fight
Unity and God are the strength
   of our land
If we devide we will fall, but
   united we'll stand
Education will help poverty that
   leads to most crime
And working together can move
   mountains in time
So pick me a Red Rose and I'll
   pick you two
Remember we need you, please
   need us too

Connie Olifeck
**My Love For This Special
Man**
One day when I wasn't looking,
   love came into my life.
And before I realized what was
   happening,
this special person made me his
   wife.

With each and every day that
   passes,
I grow to love him more.
Because he holds something
   within his heart,
I never knew before.

And as I look back upon the day,
I placed his wedding band,
I knew it would be forever,
my love for this special man.

Eleanora S. Martin
LOVE THE ANGELS

---

*Dedicated to Molly—My beloved
mother*

I am a little angel, I sit on your
   Christmas tree.
I hope that you will always take
   time to think of me.
I am made of pearls and lace and I
   have a pretty face.
My dress is trimmed with
   glitter—I love this special place.
There are some other lovely
   angels that keep me company,
Forever we'll be a devoted angel

family.
Someone made us beautiful, in
   gorgeous colors, so,
We could spend Christmas with
   you and fill the room with glow.
Songs tell our angel stories with
   lasting messages clear
We have chosen to be with you
   and we're always near.
Christmas is a happy day to say
   every heart felt thing,
Listen to the angels, the story of
   love they bring.

R. Michael Ingenito
THE FISHERMEN
The big nets
   whistle and sing,
   lives unto themselves,
   as the sun streams down
   in torrents and moans,
   striving to weaken
   with its continous
   undertones

   of constant glaring.

The self indulgent philosopher
   speculates under his shade
   of urbanity
   and dry martinis,
   while the bow bent men
   toil like convicts
   wrestling

   with their fate.

Anthony Frank Volpe
NO RECORD OF TIME?
Imagine if there were no way
   To know the date or time of day
Calendars none to remind us of
Thanksgiving Day with its
   turkey to carve

No Christmas memories with
   tinsel bright
Rudolph's nose wouldn't shine
   that night
No New Year's eves to hail or
   toast
No brand new baby to chase
   (Father) Time's ghost

I sure would miss sweet
   Valentine's Day
On February fourteenth and
   what I would say
Lincoln and Washington-two
   greats in our past
Their honesty and truthfulness
   would be forgotten
                    real fast

Can you picutre the Irish not
   havin' their day?
Not a soul t'would be marchin'
   in green all the way
Yet somehow you'd be hearin'
   loud "Erin go Braghs"
From the hearts of the Irish-and
   from all-wild hurrahs!

Mom and Dad-they'd not have
   their day
Imagine if time took a REAL
   holiday!
Not to celebrate the "Fourth Of
   July"
To cherish that freedom one
   cannot deny

Life's moments are milestones of
   unforgettable days
Each etched in our memory in
   the role that it plays

Never again will I query about
   TIME
For-without it-all beauty leaves
   your life and mine

Lavretta H. Truax
TIME
Alpha of the newborn,
Omega for the dying,
Robber of youth,
Taken for needs.

Squandered by the idle,
Limited for the condemned,
Unending for the depressed,
Taken for the sick.

Ruler of the employed,
Healer of broken hearts,
Mischief-maker of children,
Taken for duties.

Apprehension of the aged,
Joy of good friends,
Meter for music,
Taken for discipline.

Eternal to God,
Essence of history,
Destroyer of relics,
Taken for learning.

Used by all,
Enjoyed by many,
Despised by few,
Taken for granted.

Audrey Fish
solitude
you
in your peacoat
and faded jeans
dark eyes
dancing
just to be near you
is enough
but each time you go
in my solitude
i'm a fool
in love

Phyllis J. Apelian
CHRISTMASES PAST
The memories are bright of
   Christmases past
Of the family all gathered
   together at last
With grandma and grandpa, dad
   and mom
And children all ages to the
   littlest one
The Christmas tree sparkles and
   the fireplace glows
The presents are wrapped in
   ribbons and bows

The children have grown and the
   memories last
Of the warmth and love of
   Christmases past
There's grandma and grandpa and
   mom this year
Our wonderful dad is no longer
   here
The children are married and
   have families so sweet
We remember past Christmases
   as this year we greet

We think of our dad and the
   memories we have
Of the smiles and cheer he so
   lovingly gave
Of his thoughtful concern as he
   watched us each grow
We think of him often and want

him to know
That our love and memories
always will last
Of the beautiful Christmases of
yesterdays past

Susan E. Trojan
YOU!

---

*To My Teddy Bear, I cannot wait
for the day to come when we can
make Alabama our home. I love
you with all my heart and I never
want to live without you. All My
Love, Susan.*

The softness of your words,
The gentleness of your eyes,
The tenderness of your soul have
touched my life and filled
my heart with happiness.

Everything about you permeates
love and warmth.
Your smile is the sunshine that
lights my days, your strength
the power that warms my nights.

Your hands which hold mine are
soothing and kind—Your lips
loving and soft.

I give myself to you—heart and
soul.

I offer you my love—true and
never—ending throughout time.

Jan Bratcher
ACCOUNTABLE
The deed is done
The past has spoken
The future will tell
Whose hearts were broken.

But all shall live
In a world Benign
And at life's end
His deeds he'll sign.

William G. Muller, Jr.
**The Night Your Lips
Touched Mine**
Cupid's bow's forever sending
arrows through the air
Specially in the springtime when
his darts fly
everywhere
The clouds turned into stardust,
the moon began to shine
On the night your lips touched
mine

I've always run from cupid, oh! so
many times before
But now that he has hit me, I'll go
back again for more
Twas then I knew that church
bells would soon begin to
chime
On the night your lips touched
mine

I can't recall when e'er my heart
has ever felt like this
It's all your fault my darling, you
began it with a kiss
My bachelor days are over now, a
flame grew from a spark
Now I'm no longer in the dark

I've always sung a sad song, like a
lullaby in blue
But now I'm singing glad songs,
since the day I fell for
you

You changed a dreary blank verse
into a cheery rhyme
On the night your lips touched
mine

William G. Muller, Jr.
Drumsticks and Pigskins
What can replace the Easter egg
or the long eared, twitchy
nosed bunny
Who'd furnish the fright on
Halloween night if all goblins
and witches were funny
What would July the Fourth be
without the cannon's roar
The scent of punk, or a pinch-hit
bunt for a winning score
Who'd fill the Christmas
stockings if St. Nicholas were to
go
Who'd believe he came by sleigh
if there wasn't any snow
What would the lads and lassies
do on next St. Patrick's
Day
If shamrocks didn't grow in
March and the bagpipers
couldn't
play
Then who could hope to eat
turkey or partake of their
Thanksgiving feast
If the traditional gridiron classics
weren't played till
the following week

Dawn Lambing
FOR SOMEONE SPECIAL
I love you for the special way
you cheer me up when I'm sad.
I love you for the special kindness
you bring to me in your
thoughtful ways.
I love you for the special way
you bring me happiness in every
day.
I love you for your special
patience
you have when something is
wrong.
I love you for the special
tenderness
you always have in your heart.
I love you for all the special
things
you do for me.
I love you, for you are a
special person, and you are just
you!

I Love You

Robert Salazar
CHRISTmas
Joy to my belonging.
Gone to your arrival.
Come of time to see birth.
Come of time to see birth.
Go and see death.

Never go below,
There you will only see all,
Of earth in her youth.
Lying in a grave of hero's.
Gone to battle,
For religion of God's,
Unseen by man or woman.
Many say,
God's seen by new born,
But never a God seen by man or
woman.
Never go below to graves,
Of hero's of wars.

Religion is born,
Every time you feel down.
God's are as old as man's history.
Yet unseen to hero's of war.

New born, lose after learning
speech.
Joy to my belonging.
I died yesterday.
Gone to your arrival.
Come of time,
My father,
(I Am).
Come of birth.
Gone to see death . . . ?

Mary Louise (Pardi) Hinton
SPRING
you have me
in the palm of
your hand
i surrender
time is here
a tender birth
nature's own
shade's of color
dressed
to perform
fragrance
a stage of beauty
o' spring
a pillar
how sweet you hold

Robynn T. Upton
THE DANCER

To My Brothers, Zac and Rhett

She steps from behind the
curtain,
The Audience is in awe,
She has now become The Dancer,
Her movements are without flaw.

Her legs kick and pose,
Feet, barely touching the floor,
The Audience holds their breath,
As Their emotions begin to
outpour.

Her eyes see a different scene,
Not an audience in formal wear,
She sees something She would
never tell,
An oath taken in a dancer's
prayer.

Sometimes you can see the pain,
Etched across Her face,
But it quickly fades away,
And a smile put in it's place.

The Dance, now is over,
And the Dancer has gone away,
But She, who was The Dancer,
Sits alone upon the stage.

She sits in the dark,
As Her double soul bursts with
tears,
The Dancer smiling, the girl
crying,
A professional beyond Her years.

Johnaye Jones Walker
KINDNESS
You are my kindle of Inspiration
My shining amor——to guard,
Each moment of guiding light,
Bestowing sparkles of brightness
Along lifes way,
Be you ever so gentle-to remain
In faith forever

Rebecca Bostick
A WRITERS WARNING
If you're thinking of being an
author,
a whiz at pen and ink,
writing a novel which leaves
others crying for more,
stop a minute and think.
I grant you blessings of writers
cramp,
blisters from pentagon pencils.
Making your typewriter and
white-out a training camp,

turning out pages of chills and
thrills.
The thrill of victory, the agony
of defeat,
such a great profession, it can't be
beat!
Staying awake till all hours of
sunrise,
feeling the emotion in your sad,
weary eyes.
I love it but it's a two way lane,
writing a book causes endless pain.
But I cannot resist the chance to
show,
a best-seller, you never know!

Jane Thomas-Schrader
OUR LOVE SONG
Your singing our love song
to somebody else,
the way that you sang it
to me.

Singing the same tune,
the same old way;
Saying the same words,
that you used to say.

Our romance is over,
it's easy to see;
I guess that it wasn't
to be.

Your singing our love song
to somebody else,
the way that you sang it
to me.

Dolores Howe
Oh, To Be a Millionaire
Oh, to be a millionaire,
Not to worry about bills,
Not to worry what to wear,
Would surely cure all my ills!

Oh, to be a millionaire,
Not to worry what to eat,
Not to worry pains to bear,
Happy what a neat treat.

Oh, to be a millionaire,
Just to have money to share,

To help relieve others care.
To be able dreams to dare.

Claudette Wilkins Gibbs
A SEASON OF HAPPINESS

This poem is dedicated to my dear mother, Minnie L. Bradley Thomas, and terrific stepfather, Warren Thomas.

Christmas is a time to be merry and gay.
There will be many songs not like, "Oh, Happy Day."
I can hear the sleigh bells in the snow.
Here comes Santa and all singing, "Ho, ho, ho!"
I saw little snow flakes glittering in the sky.
I hear sweet little angels passing by.

Christ was born on the twenty-fifth of December.
This is a day everyone should remember.
He's our Lord Jesus Christ.
The only man who has paid His price.
He died upon the Cross of Calvary.
He died in order to set the world free.

When this child was born, it was a special day.
So special we know not what to say.
Some started to leave, others began to sing.
The time of year people wonder about everything.
We never knew the burden He beared.
For this man cannot be compared.

Christ has no hate in His heart.
He is the only Son of God.
He was born in a stable on the hay.
Many people and presents were on the way.
I heard a voice loud and clear.
"Hello, there, I'm the New Year!"

Sadie C. Laurent
SMASH
I made dash
I was a smash
Just a dash in
would be—fash-
on—
with a sash,
then a lash,
as i broke out—
with a rash
  then a gash,
The task was over,
Then I landed, in a—
  bed of clover.

Peggy West
Feelings Through the Holidays
In these wonderful times of the year
There would be more laughter, my friend
If you would just forget about your fear
And lend your wishful hands
Keep in mind that the world goes round, and

With all these changing seasons
Comes a loving sound, that of
A pleasant kiss with love as reason
But in the future
If you should forget
Remember the holiday adventures
When you and these thoughts met.

Tara Shimandle
PINK
Pink
Cotton candy
Sickeningly sweet
Pink sticky
Fingers and dirty faces
Straggly curls
Dirty knees, bare feet
And ingenuous
Young
Children.
Girls in cotton candy pink
Playing on the swings
In the park
And building castles
In sand,
Curls uncombed
Sweat sticking to
Backs bent over
Red wagons,
Running thru the
Park
In youthful, innocent,
Ugly, sweet, sick
Pink.

Paula Elson Hurley
AND LIFE GOES ON
The sun rises in the east and sets
  in the west
And rains fall softly to the
  ground
And life goes on, and life goes on.

A babe is born an old man dies
Good is smothered and evil
  survives
And I wonder why, I wonder why.

Thoughts go darting thru the sky
Looking for their own kind
And these they find, and these
  they find.

Can one fight his destiny?
Is one born rich and one born poor?
Is there something more,
something more?

If spirit is stronger than material
  force
And faith stronger than fear
Then I'll fight on, I'll fight on.

Some will live and some will die
And God gives strength to all
And life goes on, and life goes
on . . .

Robin G. King
Spoken With The Heart
I found peace
in the water colors
that drowned me
through the affection
of the touch of your hello.
A subtle mood of contentness
and I can feel
each shade of the waters
melt into a soothing trickle
of inner chills.
All because of your
extended hand
that parted the waters
in my eyes.
And, with the simplest

of your hellos,
I can see tomorrow.

Phyllis Y. Crockett Thompson
LOVES' DANCE

A loving wish, a tender kiss For one's there, has always cared My mother . . . Lillian V. Gee Smith

Love dances with the heart
  in awkward strides
Then smooth and fancy free
  this partner love's alive
Love keeps up with the time
  of lifes' smooth beats
Then struggles to survive
  the blows of lifes' deceit
Love fox-trots
  thinking it can slip away
Its' partner clinging tight for
  love
  to last another day
Love boogies
  turning fast and moving swift
Love throws the heart air-bourne
  to let old feelings drift
But then love trips
  to rip a fashioned heart
Then stumbles to recover
  lest its' dignity departs
Love takes the hands of hearts
  to dance again
Its' movements unpredictable
  from start to end

Mamie R. Caviel
SNOW-FLAKES

Arnett, Sheila & Friends, Otto/Mary Canton—Billie, M.D., Cleo, Thurman, James Henry, Everett, John B., Margie, Shirley Green, Ann Green, Murl Whiteside, Tanya Hagger, Annie Dennis Winfield—Church, Community, Professions

The best time of year
  for minds
is a plain dusty time,
when powders form
weighing down
already laden
boughs,

When the river hastens
  in tipping search
  of perfect streams
After howling winds
  and pre-spring rains
shake and pounce upon
  wintry boughs
  of tree tops,
in the early month of May.

—that best of time
when dust-covered earth
  powders
  and
  dulls
  fresh springs!

But when snow-flakes fall,
All is covered over
  with stillness
  and silent
  platitude—

And the catching of misty fog
is trapped in casually draped
  scarves.

Kathleen Wilson
LITTLE BOY BLUE
A crashing wind brought it down;
And this is what I found.
It fell to the floor and broke in two;
I believe his name was "Little Boy Blue".
Who will guard the sheep while he's away;
Who will watch over them and make them stay?
I will take his place——yes I will;
I'll be the protector——his shoes I'll fill.
Oh "Little Boy Blue" shattered and torn;
What will happen——without your horn?
Mend Little Boy——mend your wounds;
And come forth with your loving tunes.
Protect your flock of sheep;
And I'll be your protector——safe from harm——you, I'll keep.

Edvinia Y. Scott
A CHILD CRIES
A child cries in the night;
Awaken from a dream full of fright.
I tried to let her know that I was there,
But the child wasn't even aware.

Her eyes were full of water as it gleam;
A child was crying because of a dream.

As I wipe the tears from her eyes;
I tried to calm her down with lies.

I tried to assured her that the dreams would go away;
But the child didn't believe a word I say.

So as time goes on; the child still cry;
But for what reason; I still don't know why.

Marla A. Taylor
MEMORIES
The winter months have passed and gone
Christmas brought carolors song.

The frost glazed windows are melted away
The newly risen sun starts each new day.

A chair by the fire, a pipe, voice of wind
Recalls cherished memories asleep within.

Mary Beechler
GIVEN TO MY LOVE

To Joseph, my husband, to whom my love is given. Now and forever more.

Given with this ring as a token from me,
Is a love unyielding only to thee.

A love unending as a band of gold,
A love that never ceases as we grow old.

A strength which grows stronger as the days go by,

A fire ever present that will never die.

A bond that will let us freely bend,
And will bind us together until our mortal lives end.

For you to wear this ring is a sign to me,
That I'm the only one for you and will always be.

So with this ring, I give to thee,
All of my life and all it will ever be.

**Jannie Belle Young &
Kathleen F. Chatfield**

*Jannie Belle Young &
Kathleen F. Chatfield*

COUNTRY BOUND

*Dedicated to all our loved ones
and friends throughout the world.*

I'm so tired of living in the city;
I'm so tired of pushing my way through the crowds.
Lord, it's such a pity, trying to survive in this great big city.

Oh, Lord, how I long for the country side; to see familiar faces, and wide open spaces.
The country is the place where city folks seldom go; they say country folks, oh, they're just too slow.

I'm gonna pack my bags, put them on my back. I'm catching the first train or plane, and I ain't comin back. I'm gonna kick that city, city dust, I'm getting away from all, the noise and the fuss.

I'm going to a place, where people ain't so mean. Yes, I'm country bound, cuz that's where the air is always fresh and clean.

So you can call me a real country hound, cuz, that's exactly, exactly, where I'm bound.

Oh Lord, how I love, love to roam, and I'm gonna make, the country my home.

I'm so tired, of all the crimes, the muggings, and killings, I can lock the doors at night, but I don't feel willing.

Oh, the city life is such a mess, so I'm gonna keep searching for the country side, cuz I need the rest.

So you can call me the country hound, cuz that's exactly, exactly where I'm bound.

Oh, I'm leaving this big city cuz, I'm country bound, oh yeah, I'm country bound.

I guess you can call me, a real country hound.

Christie Bickerton

A MOTHERS DREAMS

I dedicate this poem to my two sons, Scott and Jeff, and their love that's given a meaning for my existence and created a joy and happiness beyond belief.

As my boys grow so does my ever deepening and expanding love,
sometimes filled with blue skies, sometimes clouds from above.
My babies cuddled near me and smiled into my eyes,
so soft and warm and full of small cries.
Soon it was time for my toddlers to go to school,
and be taught to abide by all adult rules.
The next few years were filled with games and fun,
my son jumping into the house yelling, "Ma, I got a home run."
Soon scouting and camping days came along,
we sat roasting marshmellows and singing songs.
Next it was the shock of discovering girlie books,
handing my sons my find and watching their horrified looks.
Then came the cars, "Throw our bikes away,
we're teens now and highriders are here to stay.'
Then one day my son went to his Senior Ball,
my little boy was so dashing, so handsome and tall.
I looked in amazement at this man who was my son,
recalling his first step and many years of fun.
The three of us will stay as one for several more years,
when time comes to part I'm sure we'll all shed tears.
In day to day living my sons help me stay strong,
as they say, "We'll see you later, we love you mom."
As the years go by we'll stay as one in mind and in heart,
assured that distance and time can never make us part.

Sonja Jean Tellison

DEATH

Darkness—
    still, ominous, deep,
        forever.
Dust
    settles over the
        mem'ries of
Death
    claimed minds that dimly

reflected
Doors
    unopened; misty
        web covers,
Dissolves
    away ideas
        yet unthought.
Darkness—
    still, ominous, deep,
        forever.

Lillian E. Hermann

I DREAMED THAT—

Cupid came with Angel wings
and brought a bright new year—
It made me think of many things
that filled my heart with cheer!

It made me think of far back there,
OUR CHRIST had come to live
among a group of people here,
HE came HIS life to give!

We' gained new freedom, scaled new heights
and prospered all the way,
because of that young carpenter
WHO came to us that day!

So I look ahead to NEW YEAR,
new hope, new friends, no fear!
and tremble with new happiness
I know I'll find right here!

Goldie L. Rose Bomia'

THE ANSWER

At the greatest depth of every soul,
Lies the answer to the pot of gold.
At the end of the rainbow of life,
And the mysteries of eternity.

The wonders of mankind; the secrets of nature,
And the miracles of life and all thats good and kind.

The wisdom of the ages and the spirit of love,
In the purest form.
And truth can be found at the greatest depth,
Of our soul.

Margaret Treadway

REFLECTIONS

A sturdy, green and lovely tree, stands in the corner for me to see.
Packages wrapped, ribbons bright, circle with love, like arms held tight.
Ornaments glisten of years gone by, reminds me and I don't know why.
Christmas, so long ago, tree trimmed in popcorn and a little red bow.
Sparkle of tinsel, now it hides, now its seen, now its silver, now its green.
Reflects memories of a bride to be, humble home, first christmas tree.
Colors dancing, red and gold. Oh! Its Santa, round and bold.
Prancing reindeer, loaded sleigh, delivering gifts in the same old way.
Blue lights twinkle, like years, I guess, each one filled with happiness.
Somehow things did multiply, grandchildren now will number five.

The five grew up and what a break, I now have more that I call great.
Reflections from my rocking chair, see the angel with a halo, there.
When I'm lost on my darkest night, above it all is a star so bright.
It's guiding light will show the way, then I clasp my hands and pray.
For peace and love, for all the world, another day.
Look up now and what do I see?
Reflections from my christmas tree.

Martine Hovis Huckeba

I'M YOURS

No words can tell thee of my love
But eyes were made to see;
And you will know I love you
If you only look at me.

If you will only hold my hand
And look me in the face
You'll feel the breath of fire
And hear my wild heart race.

No clumsy words I'll say
Let CUPID speak for me;
In touch, in sight, in sound I'M YOURS
I'M YOURS until eternity . . .

Doreen Candace Lane

RENAISSANCE

Months have passed since I learned of your existence, until now I am large and clumsy,
and waiting, waiting for your birth and the beginning of a new relationship—
all because when I learned of your existence,
I could not believe in abortion—
and I still would feel the same, because you are alive, and a part of me.

Virginia Peters Holt

Twenty-Seventh Wedding Anniversary

Another anniversary is here,
Living for the Lord, we have no fear.
Words cannot express how happy we are.
The Lord has blessed us so far.

We have the strength and courage to go on.
In our hearts is a prayer and song.
Many men and women just love each other so,
And our love constantly grows.

The seasons come .. and the seasons leave,
We praise the Lord and do not grieve.
We could never thank Him enough for all He's done.
Oh Christians have so much fun.

If everyone had a wonderful husband like mine,
Everything would be fine.
In Heaven above, all Christians will meet
And walk upon the golden streets.

Mimi Kasper
CHILDREN'S DELIGHT
Wonder of winter, children's
delight:
Fresh fallen snow——a beautiful
sight!

On go hats, coats, pants, boots,
scarves, mittens,
Then out to play like bouncing
kittens.

Shovels and sleds, skis, skates
and much more,
All must be tried in the snow
they adore.

Angels and snowmen, snowballs
and forts
Will take shape and please kids
of all sorts.

Mouthfuls of snow and icicle pops
Are treats as good as at the sweet
shoppe.

Rosy red cheeks, eyes shining
with glee,
It's time to come in now if you
please.

Soggy wet mittens, boots full of
snow,
Line up on the hearth in one big
row.

And happy cherubs sit on the
floor,
Drink cocoa and then go out for
more.

Dale R. Bennett
YOU
Don't you know I love you
And that I always will
Long as you want me darling
Ever and ever, forever more

Right or wrong

Because, darling, you are you
Enduring, all of my mistakes
Not just the little ones
Nor one here and there, but
Every, yes my every, shortcoming
. . . . so . . . .
Through all that life may bring
Today, tomorrow, and forever

I will love you
For as long, darling
you want me . . .

Linda G. Klodowski
LESSONS
In retrospect we sometimes see
tomorrow . . .
We view the future looking to
the past,
Unearthing hidden treasures
from a haunting, simple verse,
The circle of the truth revealed at
last.

The golden flask of virtue
overflowing . . .
The quest for peace is won
through our mistakes.
Inscribed forever in the book of
memory and mind,
The answer from the ages we
shall take.

And looking backward through
the aeons
We will see what lies ahead,
And judge now with humility
and grace . . .

The balance will be perfect when
the circle is complete,
The God who rules the heavens
we'll embrace.

For the stars that light our
footsteps through tomorrow . . .
May have burned away in time's
celestial past,
But still their light come
streaming down—as becons
from beyond,
On the mortals of *today* their
glow is cast.

Robert D. Smith
FIRST SNOW
Through the evening and into the
Midnight
I walk the roads that lead to
nowhere.
The smell of coming snow fills
the night,
And the memories of you are
everywhere.

The moon sailed away on a black
laced cloud,
And this nights' stars will shine
no more.
The evergreens' heads will soon
be bowed
To the snow covered white of the
forest floor.

From a wave of winter's magic
wand
The snowflakes gently start to fall.
Like tiny treasures from the great
beyond,
Heeding the summons of nature's
call.

No creature treads these roads
but I,
And only the silent thunder of a
beating heart
Marks the passage of a time gone
by,
A time that cleaved our worlds
apart.

As the night dons the cloak of
winter's first snow
My thoughts keep turning to the
love we amassed,
And dreaming the dreams that
we both know,
And wandering if the first snow
will be my last.

Annette Proffitt Matney
I LOVE MY HUSBAND
I met you when my heart was
shattered with love.
We talked yet I thought I could
never love again.
Heart frozen from hurt and pain.
Brain blocking out memories of
him.

At first I felt our relationship
would stand still.
I was afraid to let myself go.
You held my hand and
understood so much.
But I was confused.

I took a chance with you.
I needed your warm smile and
understanding.
You was a friend to me. A friend
who listened.
You never got out of line. Respect
I never had before.

We had long talks.
Took many rides.
You showed me all the wonders
of nature.
And all the thrills of you.

We grew close together.
Love took over once more.
Only this time my love was given
back in return.
My heart is frozen no more and
I'm free to love once more.
I love you my friend, my lover,
my husband.

Clar Genevieve' Flynn

Clar Genevieve' Flynn
UNTITLED

---

*With grateful appreciation to
Alberta McCormick Johnson. A
dear and treasured friend, who
gave me encouragement in my
pursuit of creative writing.*

My love is gone
   But his love will remain . . .
The memories are so sweet
   And so sad . . .
I cannot get his face
   Out of my mind
And I am sad . . .
   So very sad
Why did we have to leave
   When he had so much to live for?
Were we punished because of the
   love
   We had for each other?

My dog looks at me with
   questioning eyes
   As though to ask,
   "Where has my friend gone?"
And my heart weeps . . .

I rejoice though because I can feel
   love
And perhaps my love and I
   Will meet again and I will
   No longer grieve
I will have to move on
   Because I can no longer bear
   To see his face before me
I will no longer feel his hand in
   mine

Would it not have been better
   never to
   Have known such love?

Perhaps some day I will know

Joan E. Tarro
FEELING
Life's greatest treasure, for all to
see,
Is very simply, you and me.
So why is it so hard to see,
It's not what we have materially?

Have we become so thoroughly
blind?
Totally unable to use our mind?
Unable to distinguish between
what's real?
A living robot, unable to feel?

The greatest treasure, so unique
and real,
Is our human capability to love
and feel!
And although, at times, that
treasure brings pain,
We've got to experience it just
the same.

How else can we continue to
grow,
If feelings we refuse to show?
And what is the point in being
alive,
If emotionally we have died?

Diana Watson
found again
threads of friendship
   woven with change

   and growth

strengthened through the years
ready to be shared
   after years of separation

   renewed

   to cherish

a friend
   found again

Donna Gehrig
I LOVE YOU
Why do you hurt me like you do?
When everyday I give my all to
you.
I treat you as if you were a king,
And I get treated like a little play
thing.
I care for you so much, can't you
see?
Babe, I want you all for me.
You also tell me that you care,
But do you show it?, or do you
dare?
Friends say I should put you out
of my life.
How can I when someday I want
to be your wife?
I sit waiting for you most every
night,
Oh God, please help me do what's
right.

You hurt me so much it makes
  me cry,
I go to sleep at night hoping to
  die.
Please babe, I LOVE YOU. Give
  me a chance.
We could have more than a short
  romance.
Stop and think about what I've
  said,
And please stop messing with my
  head.

Debra Loesel
LAYERS
The sunset near the chapel tells a
  story:
Follow its colors and learn

The gray
  reflects the hidden dark recesses
  of your happiness

The purple
  is the mediocrity of your
  existence

The pink
  is the crown of all:
goals attained, the art of being
  positive

Pink is the desirable
  wouldn't you think?
It is only attainable, though
  when experienced after the
  other colors

A complete picture
  (and only complete)
  is the substance of life

Sheri I. Bolduc
THE APPARITION
It came.
It came as if out of nowhere.
The name.
The name of a past era.

The sound.
The sound of a child's voice.
'Twas found.
'Twas found as it began to rejoice.

I asked.
I asked if it was all a lie.
It passed.
It passed in the blink of an eye.

Irene Victor
Starvation Of the World
I forget sometimes there's a world
  of starving people
  composed of babies, young
  children, and old people;
  people, like you and me.
I forget sometimes there's hunger
  on the other side of the world;
no food, no water, no knowledge
  of the world,
  People; I mean people of the
  world—
  like you and me.
I forget sometimes and enjoy
  things of the world.
Only when God touches my
  heart do I awaken
to starvation among people—like
  you and me.
I forget sometimes and get hung
  up on my own tribulations;
not wanting to listen to problems
  of other nations,
  I get stuck with my own
  temptations.

Vickie Manuwai Pochelle
THE SOLDIER & ME

*To Lieutenant John M. Kelly, the
Navy Pilot I LOVE!! May the Lord
watch between me and thee
when we are absent one from
another.*

She said that she loved him with
  a childish grin
  Then opened her arms
  and took his heart in

And he said that he'd miss her as
  he left with a smile
  Then he kissed her and told her
  I'll be back in a while

She wrote that she loved him in
  letters so dear
  And dreamed of the moment
  when she'd hold him near

He flew to new places and far
  away lands
  While remembering the touch
  of her sweet gentle hands

She said that she missed him
  when he called her to say
  That soon he'd be home
  only one more day

And he said that he loved her
  with a tender young smile
  And he kissed her and told her
  I'll be home for a while

So she repeated she loved him
  with that same childish grin
  Then he opened his arms
  And took her heart in

Delores Ferguson Kelley
On Surrendering My Child
Vicki, tiny Vicki!
Oh Vicki do you know?
That today I gave you berth
But tomorrow I'll let you go . . .
Go to belong to another
Who'll cradle you as I should?
But please believe me, Vicki,
I'd keep you if I could.

What will they tell you, Vicki?
There are questions you will ask.
Don't let them say I do not care.
This is no easy task!
Don't listen to them blame me.
Don't let them teach you hate.
I'll pay for all the wrong I've done,
And naught can compensate.

Someday when you are older,
Please try to understand.
And please don't hate me, Vicki,
This is not as I planned.
But after having berthed you,
Life can never be the same.
Oh! The agonizing sorrow
You will never know my name.

Betty Louise Prather
**As the Stars Shine With
  Love On West Virginia**
As the stars shine with love on
  West Virginia
The time of the cool evening
  with the stars shinning
Down and giving forth their light
  to the world,
The deep velvet blueness of the
  sky in the time
Of the night with lovely stars so

very far away,
Shining down there on the scene
  of the time and

The way and making the sky and
  the time ever lovely,
Giving there on the scene of the
  time beauty and
A measure of happiness and joy
  to the way of the time;

Stars which have for many, many
  long years given,
A sense of joy and happiness
  there on the scene
Still shining with the same
  lustrous beauty
To the individuals of the hills
  and the valleys,
As the stars shine with love on
  West Virginia.

As the stars shine with love on
  West Virginia
And as the young lovers of the
  state of West Virginia
Still talk in the time of the night
  of the beauty
Of the stars and the moments of
  happiness which they
Spend there on the scene of the
  time of the joy
Which is theirs to share and the
  memories which are
Built around the times which
  they share in moments,
Of happiness and then sometimes
  with the talk of
A kind of love if it is only shared
  there for a time,
The beauty of the stars there on
  the action scene
And with the love and the
  happiness felt in the
Hearts of the many young lovers
  there it is a joy,
And then with the passing of the
  time still beauty,
As the stars shine with love on
  West Virginia.

Pam A. Marcelin
PAINTED SMILE

*Dedicated to inspiration: Farrell
Sr. and Sandra, an awaited arrival.
Marcel And Chris, Charles, Jade
& Tommy*

Walk in a room with
flowers and roses
painted on every wall;
People look at with gleam
The sky is happy
everything is happy
But.
What lies beyond the bed
of roses?
An evil—
Fake people—
smiles goodwill wouldn't accept;
So this is the other side of the
  bridge?
A painting with beautiful
structure and colors . . .
But corrupt paint
that sheds.

Lucetta Walters
THE MERRY MONTH
Christmas time is here again
With it, the blue mood comes

Emptiness seems to show much
  more
As the Holy Day draws near

I miss you much throughout the
  year
But Christmas tears me up
For I remember how it was
Back five years ago

Then after Christmas time is o're
New Years' chimes along
All I can find to celebrate
Are thoughts of years ago

If such a sadness could do good
In future years to come
It wouldn't matter half as much
If we could be as one

David Bazaure
SEARCHING
A lonely girl walks
Along a moonlit shore
A shadow cast upon the sand
The waves tossed to and fro.
A fresh and gentle ocean breeze
Her light brown silky hair
A path that's filled with starlight
Dancing moon beams in the air.
Her tender blue, grey eyes
What secretes do they hold
What deep and hidden mysteries
Lay buried and untold?
Her laughter, gay and carefree
The swift and rushing tide
A far and distant memory
A lost and lonely sigh.
Her smile, soft and fragile
A heart that's filled with gold
A love that's pure and lasting
A wandering, searching soul.

Rick Krebsbach
Wonders Of the World
I thank You Lord
For I can listen . . .
to the music of a running stream
Or see . . .
a mirror image of a snowclad
  mountain
upon a lake of glass.

For I can walk . . .
among perfume forests of sage
  and pine
Or through a vineyard
  savoring . . .
the succulent treasures of the vine.

For I can find serenity . . .
in the radiant complexion of the
  sky
As the sun cautiously dips into
  the
ocean pool.

For I can Listen, See, Smell, Taste
  and
Feel the Wonders of the World
For this I Thank You Lord.

Ann Wellbourne
IN GRATITUDE
I thank God that I have learned
To love my fellowman.
Race, religion, creed or color
Are not means of measurement,
You so much, and you so much,
But you a little less.
I do not question as to why,
Why should I be granted this,
For I've found contentment in a
  truth.
I've found peace and happiness.

I thank God that I am like
The others whom I love.
So I may know and understand
And shall not be offended,
By human weakness, selfishness
Or thoughtlessness unintended,
That I accept in humbleness
The love so freely given
By everyone I chance to meet.
I've found a path to heaven.

Chris Kindrew
MY MOTHER, MY FRIEND
You are my mother,
You are my friend,
You are my life
To the very end.
You have held my hand
And taught me to walk.
You have sat me down
And taught me to talk.
Now together we'll climb
To the heavens above.
And together we'll speak
Of the sharing of love.

Wendy J. Randall
TELL HER SO

---

*To my Mom and Dad. For having
faith in me, I love you both.*

If you love her, tell her so.
If you don't, she'll never know;
  How much you care and want to
  share,
What will it mean if she's not
  there?

What's in your heart do boldly
  speak;
Though be gentle, mild, and meek.
No matter how hard you try to
  show it,
Only by saying so will she know it.

Hurry! Go find her—search high
  and low;
And if you love her, tell her so.

M. Megan Roberts
EXPECTATIONS
I woke up this morning
and this rain, it took me by
  surprise
The weatherman had talked of
  sunshine
and yesterday the warm sun had
  filled the skies

It really shouldn't make a
  difference
I had no secured plans for today
And the lively sound of these
  raindrops
has no reason to put me in dismay

It just wasn't what I expected at all
yet with expectations come
  trouble
The weather could have brought
  most anything
Today's only a bit of rain and a
  few puddles

I guess the real problem arises
in being so surprised
Life changes all the while
Like the weather, with many lows
  and highs

So next time, as my life goes on
I'll take it as it comes
Not expecting this or that
Just a whistle and a hum

Irene Dolores Lippert-Hoffman
THE SNOW
When the snow first falls it is
  white
But then later on oh what a sight
Now you can see people everyday
Shoveling the snow out of their
  drive-way
Oh from the sky the snow does
  fall
With it the children make a big
  ball
And then a snowman oh so tall

Now to him the kids would call
Everytime they went out to play
Oh how they wished that he
  would stay
But then came a nice bright
  sunny day
Oh it was then he had ran away
For the kids it was a very sad day
For the snowman to come back
  the children did pray

Nellie Erwin Stromberg
DEAR LITTLE GUY
He was the dearest little guy
Brown of hair and brown of eye
His smile was bright as noon day
  sun
Where he was there was always
  fun
Together we walked beneath
  Florida skies
Delighting in all that met our eyes
Flowers and shells along the path
And there was a bird in her
  sparkling bath
Later the path would turn around
Then we would return to our
  own ground
Glad to be back before it rained
Enjoying the treasures we had
  obtained
When there were no more to see
There was picnic under the big
  oak tree
Those days were sweet and short
  it seems
I close my eyes and find some
  dreams
He was the dearest little guy
Brown of hair and brown of eye.

Andrea Jean Shaffer
HUMANITY'S CAROL
A sad blue Angel came to me,
He said his name, "Humanity".
His robe once white, trimmed
  with gold,
Looked limp and worn, and very
  old.
His majestic wings, a dismal gray,

What made them so, he didn't
  say.
The smile on his lips didn't
  match his eyes
They were sad, almost fluid, like
  he wanted to cry.
His voice but a whisper, cut like
  a knife!
For a moment I was afraid for my
  life!
"I am the suffering in the street!
I am the child with cold bare feet!
I am the father who cannot find
  work,
I am the homeless youth, without
  a shirt!
I am the old lady in the cast off
  skirt!
I amthe plea of the beggar's hand
I represent strife in every land.
I am hunger and I am cold" He
  said,
"I am all the pain and tears that
  are shed!
Humanity", he said, "that's me!"
He left as quietly as he came,
But for me, Christmas will never
  be the same
Unable to ignore the suffering I see
Inflicted upon poor, Humanity.

Andrea Shaffer
GRANDPA IN THE PARK

---

*In Loving Memory of Olin Lewis
Born: July 18, 1892 Died:
November 17, 1963
("Goodnight—Keem-ah-sob-bie!")*

Summer days, lazy days,
Strolling through Lafayette Park
Dandelion rings weave a crown,
Worn by Kings and Queens and
  Clowns;
And Grandpa talks of days gone
  by,
Of wagon trains and open sky.
Fireflys and Honeybees, with
  Honeycombs
As big as me!
I remember, summer days, lazy
  days,
And Grandpa in the park.

Andrea Jean Shaffer
WALKING BACKWARDS
At a certain time they retrograde,
To erase the scars of mutatious
  waves,
To a gentler time in retrospect,
When they maintained their self
  respect.
Yet the scars persist,
Like the incoming waves,
So deeper they delve in retrograde.
When total regression wins at last,
Lost they be, in their own past.

Suzanne Y. Cuell
Become A Child In Spirit
Would you like to spend
  a Christmas,
Like the sheperds did of olde,
As they gathered 'round
  the manger,
In the warmth of their sheepfold?

Just to feel again the calmness
  of that Holy Night;
When Christ was born in
  Bethlehem
  Beneath a radiant light.

Then . . . Become a child again in
  Spirit,
  With an open, loving heart,
And you'll be ready to receive
  Him,
For you've made a brandnew start.

Christ will shower you with
  blessings,
  Peace and Joy you've never
  known,
'Cause you've invited Him
  for Christmas,
So He'll make your heart
  His home.

Tamara Louise Crawford
YEARS WITH YOU

---

*To Tom: My Love, My Good
Friend, My Husband*

Silently, we lie together as the
  glow of the fire flickers on the
  now quiet Christmas Tree

No lights, No tinsel, Yet
  enchanced in its own natural
  beauty

The Snow falls gently, as we
  wonder what, this New Year
  will bring. Soon, the old year
  will ring out, along with the
  joys and the sorrows past. And
  we count our blessings, that
  through all the years, our love
  has lasted.

We renew our love here by the
  fire, You tell me, you love me
  and I am your good friend, and
  I know all my New Year's Eve's
  and all my life, with you, I
  want to spend.

Juanita L. Brokofsky
WINTER'S PAINTER
O'er rolling hills and valleys
  Awash with crystal light,
A wintry breeze comes brushing
  To wash the meadows white.
Gentle breezes draw their brush
  Throughout the silvery hours,
To paint white lace among the
  trees
  To serve as Winter's flowers.
All still as fleecy softness
  An ivory landscape shrouds,
While Winter's Painter greets the
  morn,
  Mere light behind the clouds.

Kathryn D. Robinson
I SAW THEM TOUCH
i saw them touch in a way
that reminded me of us . . .
and i gazed at the silk
beneath each fingertip as if
it was my own—

i craved your taste—
your scent—
the smile—
i touched each inch—
then ran each mile . . . while

beads of sweat escaped from
  them . . .
as i brushed one from my brow—
we were real, like that—
we knew we were—
and i remember now—

my sigh will return—

my breath will too—
the tear will dry—
and the key will turn—

we will be safe, again, in me—
i'll turn away—
say "we were a dream"—

mere imagery—
like them—
on a silver screen.

Rita Bennett
AN APOLOGY
When your style is a finely-honed
cynicism,
It's difficult to say

With clarity and
without a smirk
(the smirk comes
with the honing):

I appreciate you
I listen and hear you
and I love you for your care.

Carol M. Elfberg
THE RITE OF SPRING
Behold,
there is a light beyond the sky.
The clouds deny.
They hover over the Earth
and cast great shadows of darkness.
The light of the moon and the sun,
wane truly hopeless in their midst.
Lo, no hope, unless the winds
banish
them away to skys of blue.
Then the light of day shall rise
to hope and laughter.
The long cold winter is over
and gives way to the rite of spring.
The Earth,
shall sing in the breath of spring.
And the Earth will be renewed,
by the warmth of the sun.
The moon shall gain joy,
because of lovers holding hands.
Once more life and love shall rein.

ellen rene' stohl
THROUGH A CHILDS EYES

*For Myke Rudd; My Favorite
Little Man. because of him the
world takes on a wonderful new
perspective i love you.*

he hides and watches worlds go
by
a sword in hand and look serene
small voice becomes a warriors
cry
and chair becomes a forest green.

small eyes grow wide and
devlish air
make changes big in room so
small
a pirates ship becomes that chair
and couch a kingdom that must
fall

small thoughts create a
special place
where badguys roam but heros
wins
a captain brave in outer space
with fickle thoughts worlds
change again

oh what a sight the world
would be
if all could see as children see.

Shelley S. Mathis
A GOOD QUESTION

*Thanks to my parents for their
support in everything I do. Vic
and Sue—I love you.*

What makes us the way we are?
What makes us go so far
As to take the life of
another human being?
Or to take such pleasure
in the first sign of spring?
What makes us take so much joy
in seeing a child at play?
Or seeing that same child and
thinking in a perverted way?
What makes us good
or what makes us bad?
Is it the things we possess
or the things we never had?
Is it the love we never knew
that make us hate?
Or from our abundance of love
we learn to manipulate?
What makes us the way we are?

Derek W. Burton
A FLOWER FOR DADDY

*This poem is in special
dedication to our loving Father,
Thomas Deangelo Burton With
Love Always, Derek, Alanna and
Darrin Burton*

For each loving petal—
For each loving thorn—
We all love you Daddy for now
and forever more.

Each and every color has a
meaning—for all—we know
why—we give these flowers to
a fantastic guy.

Even though these flowers will
die?—our love for you
will always fly—high—across the
sky.

We all Love You Daddy, for
Now and *Forever* more . . .

Lisa Ann Logan
CHRISTMAS TEARS
He sits alone,
Staring at the place where his
tree should be.
He sits,
Relishing the memories of
yesterday
When he wasn't old or alone.
He remembers carving turkeys,
Giving gifts,
And the happiness in the eyes of
his child;
But that was so long ago.
A solitary tear
Rolls quietly and discreetly down
his wrinkled face.
He wonders why everyone chose
to go and leave him
To spend Christmas alone,
In the "best years of his life".

He sits alone,
No gifts to give,
No gifts to receive.
Another Christmas come n gone,
leaving to his collection of "new"
memories

another cold and lonely one.
If only he had someone to share
his happy memories with,
Someone that would remember
him when he is gone.
Yes, that would be the best
Christmas present this old man
could ever have.

Sandra Hayes
IN THE WIND
The petal blows through the wind,
A sign of love for the two of us.
The wind dies down and the
petal sits on a soft ground.
Does our love die to be put on a
shelf for the time?
The wind returns, and the petal is
held with care
as it's carried upward.
Our love is renewed by the soft
wind, and the petal
which blows.
The petal is gone and tells of
never returning to us.
Why then, is our love still strong
without the petal?
Our thoughts remember the sad
petal, and together
we hold our dreams forever,
The petal is gone, and now we
too are,
but the shadow of love will
always remain . . .
. . . in the wind.

Mr. Joseph R. Ambrosino
DO YOU REMEMBER
Remember the fun we had the
kicks we had being bad:
Remember the summer's bright
and sunny days:
We went to the barn and
madeout in the hay
Remember the night we walked
by the park we stopped
By the bench and kissed in the
dark.
Remember the day you asked
let's go steady,
And I said okay yes I'm ready
Remember the day we had our
first fight we
Quit each other and made up
that night,
Remember the day we went all
the way, how could I
Forget I had to pay, remember the
day we went to
The fair, how you flirted with
every girl there
You took a strange girl upon your
knee you told her
Things you never told me, the
whole afternoon was a total
Nightmare, but I suspected that
you just didn't care.
I went to a home for unweded
mothers, but you didn't seem
to care
Because you had your others,
now I'm in the hospital fighting
The pain and I just can't fly like a
plane, the doctor was here
An hour ago there might be
trouble maybe, so it wasn't that
bad
He said, and when he told me
this I grew very very sad.
I found out later that he was just
lieing because I was crying

The truth was that I was going to
die, the baby would be okay,
But I wouldn't last until the end
of the day, I just wanted
To tell you before I die.

"I love you my darling take care
and goodbye . . .

Loretta Ensinger
A NEW BEGINNING
Twas soon after the New Year
That things went awry
Death came without warning
In the blink of an eye.

Yes, it's the end of an era
Time to move on
To march toward the future
And face each new dawn.

A new year unfolding
We hope for the best
As each day goes by
We'll be put to the test.

So we'll pack up the past
And start a new life
Praying the New Year
Will be without strife.

Karen Porm
**Whatever Happened to
Christmas Cheer?**
The crowds are pushing, they pay
no heed,
They have that curse known as
Christmas greed,
They hustle and bustle; at each
other they jeer,
Whatever happened to Christmas
cheer?
No one utters a simple "hello",
And you'll never hear "Merry
Christmas my good fellow",
I stand on the corner, and watch
them go by,
And deep within I feel myself sigh,
Why doesn't anyone stop and
look around?
And see the lights, and hear the
sounds,
Everyone hurries, but where do
they go?
Out somewhere beyond the
falling snow?
But what does it matter, it's all
still the same,
Christmas comes, it goes, it's all a
big game,
You buy, give, receive, return,
A nice example for the children
to learn,
The children grow up, at
Christmas they'll yawn,
And before you know it,
Christmas will be gone,
But let's not let that happen, at
least not for awhile,
From now until Christmas, at all
you meet, give a smile.

Joanna Dean
THE SHAME OF IT ALL
Shut up world and hear my cry—
You're so noisy and fast you don't
see me go by:
I could live or die it wouldn't
change your pace—
As long as there are others to
take my place.
Sit down world, you're always in a
hurry—
Can't you see why there's so

much fear and worry?
Crime in the street—
And Governments cheat.
Wars on nations and UNCLE
SAM—
Wake up and realize, we don't
give a damn:
You talk of love, peace and
goodwill—
Shake hands with your right and
use your left hand to kill.
I'm ashamed of you world, for you
know what you do—
You had best shape up or it'll be
the end for you.

Alberta M. Mayberry
NOVEMBER
Winter, in all of it's splendor,
sleds traveling through the snow,
church bells ringing soft and low,
Armistice Day, rabbit hunting,
many activities we all remember,
all the busy days of November.

Thanksgiving Day, with it's
traditional treats,
families gather for prayers and
feast.
May you have "horns of plenty"
in store,
with God's blessing at your door.

Happy Thanksgiving Day!
What more can I say?

Alberta M. Mayberry
When You Are Getting Old
When you are getting old,
and age is creeping up on you,
I have a little secret,
I will tell you what you can do.

Wear a smile of sunshine,
have a greeting warm and true.
You will brighten up your old days
with friends sincere and new.

Life is a wonderful vacation,
but we must leave someday.
It will make us happy to know,
we have brightened up life's way.

When you are getting old,
and Father Time is knocking at
your door,
it will be so nice to know,
that on earth you made a perfect
score.

Tricia Zboya
IT'S WINTER
There's no sunshine
Left
In this world of mine
Because it's winter,
And I am far away
From
The one (let's say—)
Is a friend—or so—
She used to be
Last summertime
For she said to me,
"You're a friend of mine."
But now it's winter.
As the snowflakes fall
Down from the sky
I can hear a cry
Of my little white lie,
"It's winter."
No sunshine left
No happiness felt
No friendship yet
Til the icicles melt—
It's winter.

There's a snowman
There
With a wood stick hand.
As the sky is grey,
I call to her
During the winter,
And what does she say
Am I to her?
Well, someone else is there with
her.
So, she has a new friend
For wintertime—
It's only when the sky is clear
Is she a friend of mine.
It's winter.
For some reason (I don't know)
I can't blame her
For like the ice and snow—
It's winter.
There's no sunshine
Here
In this world of mine—
During the wintertime.
As the white snow falls
I can hear a cry
If her little white lie,
"It's winter."
If she knew this was how
It was to be—
I wonder just now
Why would she say to me,
"You're a friend of mine"?
Hey winter,
Doesn't she know
After the ivory snow
The sun will shine,
And she'll be a friend of mine—
Until next winter.

Kevin M. Coolidge
DISTANCE
Love, as blue and deep, like the
sea
Shining as the sun, upon flowers
hue
Loving, giving, what about me?
How about you?
Who are we, but our children
dancing,
laughing, singing songs of
innocence
Separated only by distance, fear,
resistance.
Loving kindness, compassion will
see us
through.
What about me? What about you?
Together loving, could find "we"
Whatever that may be!
Only loving, living as one,
Children of God, beneath the sun.

Monica Page
WAR
love is like a fox hole
waiting for the right moment
patiently waiting for the kill
shootings in the street
a caliber pistol
a 44 gun in their holster
waiting for the right moment
a shot gun thrown over
their shoulder
waiting
patiently
craziness hitting the streets
the children are off to fight for
the love
that is gone
when they get there
children wasted in the mists of

clouds of smoke
shot down in blood thirst
affairs

Monica Page
GLORIFYING THE NIGHT
the stars glimmer in the sky
and as i gaze at each one
they glisten with gleam
they shine like glitter in the sky
glaring with a glossy glaze
glowing in the black
with glisters glorifying the night

Bree Anderson

Bree Anderson
EMPTY WORDS

---

*For that special person, Chuck
Lewis, who believed in me before
I did. Who rescued me as
would—a "Knight in Shining
armor," had these been other
timed. He taught me to always
look upwards and not backwards.*

You say you love me now and
you always will.
Your words sound good, it's your
actions that
makes your words empty.
The things you do for me or the
things you
don't follow through on, thats
what I look at.
Words— Words— sound so pretty.
You told me if I ever got cold to
give
you a call and you would be right
over
to make the fire.
When I called, no one was home.
You said in your heart you
wanted me
and would never give love to
another
No— Not ever!
You got me to believe you
wouldn't even
look for another lover.
That even bothered me because I
worried
about you and didn't want you
cold and
alone because I had to put you on
hold.
My heart is too large to forget all
others
and give love only to you.
Your words were empty.
Your promises shallow.
Your heart not deep enough to

feel my heat from afar.
Words— Words— Empty Words.

Ellie R. Christen
FOR OUR FLAG
There is another helmet on the
ground tonight
Is it your son or mine?
Clear eyes closed forever,
Lips sealed till end of time.
It was war that called the roll.

We bow our heads in reverence,
Dedication of glorious youth
march by
They planned a work and build,
Duty fulfilled, on distant sands
they lie.
It is war that called the roll.

A mother's murmur from the
years;
"Be valiant, son, loyal and true.
Your wisdom is a gift from God,
Your character is you."

Our flag waves gently o'er again
'Twas carried for freedom's right
From Saratoga to dismayed Viet
Nam
Brave rulers, see the plight.
It was war that called the toll.

Greg W. Eichhold
CHRISTMAS CARDS
As Christmas cards are being
distributed
to friendly folk from near and far,
Some relative almost too hard to
distinguish
as a link to your family tree
Completely overtakes all
conversations
including your social priorities
But that is something we must all
learn to take in stride
Because you never know what
comes
next when someone is invited
over at
Christmastide.

James C. Donovan
CAROL'S POEM
What is life without love?
What is Love without you?
There was no want or desire—
Before I met you, my life was
plain.
I never really needed anything
But most of all I wasn't happy.
Now I have something to live for,
Something called love.
My life and love is Carol—
You're my life, you're my love,
Forever and always.

Margaret Mast
RAGE
When anger enfolds me
And everything goes, I shake
Uncontrolled
Rage building until it explodes
Unbound-unleashed
Everything I felt and had
surpressed
Becomes tangled up in reality
Mounting up like an army to war.
Madness comes . . .
Bids me lose hold on sanity
It quickly comes—more quickly
goes
And after all is spent
I have only emptiness.

Mrs. Ellen P. Goodwin
CHRISTMAS GREETINGS
May the Christ of Christmas be
near to you,
At this Christmas Season and all
year through;
May He bless your day,
And all you do,
With joy and happiness sincere
and true.

"Away in a Manger," we sing Each
year,
Usually starting about December
One;
Noting that Christmas is almost
here,
Toys and gifts all given in love.

Every gift we received should
truly bring,
Love more precious than silver or
gold;
Love never failing from our Lord
and King,
Everlasting peace, we can behold,
Never ending joys in the
heavenly fold.

Leigh Leflore
TOY SOLDIERS
Toy soldiers standing in the rain—
Who left them there?
The war is done,
The child's gone home
And left them as they are.

Mock soliders—silent as the
heart—
Left in a storm of pain.
Can't shed a tear,
But what's to fear?
The child will be back again.

You left me standing in the rain—
A mirror in the eye,
Reflecting back what I am,
I love you now as I did then . . .

A soldier that can cry.

The storm is now renewing
strength—
Nothing is the same . . .
The war is done,
You have gone
And left me as I am . . .
Lost in a crowd of toy soldiers
Left out in the rain.

Louise S. Yates
THANKSGIVING PRAYER
Thank you, Oh Heavenly Father,
For family, hearth, and home;
Thank you, Oh Heavenly Father,
For not having to face life alone.

Thank Thee, Father, for sunny
-skies,
For hope, for joy, and for peace;
For showers of blessings,
heavenly ties,
For victory over stress, peaceful
release.

Thank you, God, for clouds and
for storms,
For days of turmoil, wrathfully
filled
Followed by the gentle breeze
that warms
The earth so forlorn and icy
chilled.

Thank you dear blessed Savior
For Thy living presence,

compassion,
For quiet kindness in Thy favor,
Granting moments of Thy
loveliness.

Thank you, Oh Heavenly Father,
For golden sunsets, salmon skies,
The privilege of being together
And for the joy of family ties.

Thank you for family, friends and
home;
I thank Thee, God, for
togetherness,
For not having to face life all alone,
And for this life of loveliness.

Beatrice Lawson Thorp
I WILL SURVIVE

---

*My Thanks To: Bruce Turner,
M.D., his Staff, St. Francis
Hospital and my friends and
family, for their care and support
throughout my illness.*

Tonight I sit and wonder why,
Why tears seem to fall from my
eyes.

What have I done to deserve such
pain,
God please don't let me go insane.

They say I have a disease that
can't be cured,
But they are not God, so how can
they be sure.

I am a mother, sister, daughter
and wife,
God I need to hold on to my life.

Give me strength to go on with
my life,
Help me to be a good mother and
wife.

I will not let the devil take me
astray,
I will not give in, he won't get his
way.

I will fight until I can stand no
more,
And then I will ask God to open
Heaven's door.

As you read this poem, don't feel
sorrow,
I know God will give us a
brighter tomorrow.

All I ask of family and friends,
Is to help my husband and
children to the end.

Carmon Patrick
POEM FOR HANK
My eighth grade history teacher
put a line at the bottom of our
tests
and said if we'd doodle there
we'd get an extra point.
The more ambitious might have
drawn
a moustached general,
but I scribbled an apple with
leaves on the stem
and a triangular ink spot
to show reflection.

Hank Griffen was my teacher's
name.
Know of many Hanks who made
history?
Who harried an empire,

or swallowed cyanide and lived.
Rasputin did the latter,
or so the crimson pages of my
history book say,
and though his name may not
live forever,
he's given Hank something to
talk about.

Mary Ziacoma
My Sentimental Walk
Before Moving Away
I walked slowly up the wooded
trail, embracing all the beauty,
that seemed to be mine alone.
I gathered pussywillows bursting
with furry faces.
The forest would soon reveal its
magnificent show of dogwood
blossoms, overshadowing the
brilliance of wildflowers below.
A robin appeared, recalling a day
I found a baby robin on the
ground, blown from its nest,
and with help from its mother,
nursed it, until one day it flew
away.
I also recalled the many times
each spring, my grandchildren
and I placed pieces of string
upon the ground for birds, to
help build their nests.
The childrens happy faces and
squeals of delight, as the birds
collected the string, will
forever remain indelible in my
heart.
At the top of the trail, the skyline
of the city below was now
obscured by a mist, that gave
promise for a late winter snow.
As I walked back down the trail, I
visualized the purple wisteria,
that soon would be in bloom,
its tenacity still embracing the
tall white oak.
That majestic tree, that for more
years than I could remember,
gave haven to nests of squirrels.
Memories of bygone years welled
deep inside, my eyes filled with
tears.
I entered my now empty house,
parallelled only by the
emptiness I felt within me.

Fronces Bradley
OH REMEMBER
Remember the time we had so
much fun
Remember how we had to run
Remember Oh Remember
Remember how we'd go to the
show and then look around and
find a
No, No, Remember Oh Remember
Remember how we'd be so sad
someone would ask why and
we'd get so mad Remember Oh
Remember.

Remember all day we played in
the snow, awoke next morning
to school we couldn't go.
Remember Oh Remember
Remember how we went to the
fair got all scared way up in the
air
Remember Oh Remember.

Remember the time you got in
my way, remember the words

I had to say Remember Oh
Remember
Remember no matter what we
say or do, no telling on me no
telling on you Remember
Oh Remember.

Remember the word I showed
you in the dictionary, your
aunt walked by and we closed
it in a hurry, Remember
Oh Remember.

Remember the time our tongues
lashed away Before we went
into church we had to pray
Remember Oh Remember.

Remember on the corner there
lived a teacher, she told on us
when we talked about the
preacher
Remember Oh Remember

So remember the times we had so
much fun remember how we
really had to run
Remember Oh Remember.

Willie Gardner
TO BE WANTED
I'm so alone
And feeling blue
Will someone tell me what to do
And how to find someone that's
true?
I need to be loved and wanted
To be happy
To be living
Just like you.

My life is empty
My heart is filled with pain.
The one I love has gone
Never to return again.

Maybe there's someone just as I
Who needs to be loved and wanted
To be happy
To be living
Just like you.

John T. Hudelson
BETWIXT AND BETWEEN
Beyond the sea beneath the sun
upon the desert floor
I found my self
betwixt between
Hell's gate
and Heaven's door.
No spring pools
to quench my thirst
No breeze
to cool my brow,
I was alone
devoid of shade
To tired
to move around.
I prayed to God
and this I bade,
Please Lord
let me be found.

Jill Simmons
TWILIGHT
The darkness hangs above the
sky,
As the sun begins to yawn.
The moon stands ready nearby,
Twilight is about to dawn.

Twilight sneaks into view,
As the sun's gold begins to fade.
The world turns a rich rosy hue,
And God sighs at what He has
made.

John Campbell, Editor & Publisher

Gradually, the light dies away,
The sun creeps slowly to bed.
It is the end of another day,
And night is here instead.

Black of night surrounds the day,
The moon takes the place of the sun.
The twinkling stars come out to play,
An earth and night are one.

Pauline Vannoy
DREAMS
There are days to dream of love,
Of sunsets and mountain heights.

There are dreams of far off countries,
Castles of gold and carnival sights.

Ships go by and we wave them on,
And our thoughts go with them to countries unknown.

For a little while we are princesses and queens,
Living in majestic sheens.

But, it's time to awake and see the rose;
It's ours to take.

Or, the hill to climb, so sublime.

So sweet to dream but awake,
Today is ours to take.

Genelle Palmer
Walking In His Footsteps

*To my daughter and her family:
Mr. and Mrs. John C. Henderson
Tammy, Jenna and Lauri*

Walking in the footsteps
Of Jesus my Savior.
Walking-yes walking—
In the steps of my Lord.
Looking to Him,
My guide and deliverer.
Walking by faith,
Lead by His Word.
Kept safe in the shadow,
Of the cross, I will follow.
True to His promises,
Saved by His Grace—
My reward.

Deborah Annette Whitmore
THE UNICORN
A white cloud of fragile beauty
that captures the heart
in a tender embrace
and makes one weep
with joy and sorrow.

The subtle elegance and grace,
that lived in yesteryear,
lives in this strange creature
to stun the mortal man
and leave him breathless.

The mystical magic of movements
makes one gasp in awe
at the sight of such a phantom
and question one's sanity
as to the reality of it all.

This gentle, harmless sphinx,
untouched by time;
unmarked and flawless.
A 'prince' of ghostly perfection.
The Unicorn

Carol Kibbons
HOLIDAY

*To my husband Charles who is
my love & inspiration—To my
eldest son Tim whom I adore &
of whom I'm proud—To my
adopted children, LeVina, Perry,
& John Paul, all of whom are a
delight & challenge.*

C - Celebrations round the universe flourish
A - As Yuletide and New Year holidays advent
R - Reveling in the magic that destines hearts and souls
O - O'er the land children dance in wonderment
L - Leaving us in awe, with a profound sentence of happiness . . .
K - Keen senses of aromatic favor fill the crisp air
I - Inside modest homes filled with succulent fair
B - Buoyant anticipation of what is to come
B - Brings out the good, hopefully to which others will succumb
O - On joyous occasion, ill-will begone
N - Now the time speaks reprieve and pardon
S - Soon all will gather under festoons, holly, and decorated tree to honor "Christ" and start the New Year free . . .!!

Nicky Buschbell
FIRST ANNIVERSARY
Like a Jewel ever rare
thats how it was, our first married Year.
May it never dim, this Love devine
and your Eyes always throw a Kiss when they meet mine.
May your Lips always be warm and tender
when they beg mine to surrender.
And when it's time, to knock at Heavens Gate
and Peter says: Sorry you didn't make the Grade!
we shall not cry or fret,
we had our Heaven, just being wed!

Terri Lynn Brouillette
MY DREAM
As we watched the sunrise, hand in hand
All alone on the beach, lying in the sand
Not a whisper in the wind, and not a soul around
Just the shimmering of crystal scattered on the ground
The sky was a rainbow, and as colorful as could be
And we were there together, just him and me
Now my dream is over, for I've reached the end
I must awaken now and begin again
To search for this dream thats so far way

Of me and him together on that special day !!
R. W. Prinkey
LISA (IV)
How am I to tell
what's expected of me
I can't read your mind
I'm only as human as thee

If you won't speak
how will I know
if I should stay,
or if I should go?

One day you're laughing,
the next day you cry
I spend hours in thought,
but still wonder why

How can I prove them,
my feelings for you
I've tried often to say it
to make sure you knew

My feelings are this:
Love could be the word
and I'll run like a cheetah,
or fly like a bird,

to keep you happy,
"till death do us part"
and I hope you can see
that this comes from my heart.

Christine Wacik
MISSING YOU

*This poem was written for the
man I love, Edward Baer, who
means the world to me. I miss
you very much FACEY . . . and
maybe someday we will be
together again. I don't know if I'll
ever be sure, but I just hope by
the time I decide, it won't already
be too late.*

Sometimes I lie awake at night
and cry myself to sleep.
Just missing all the love I had, A love I couldn't keep.
I know you had to go away, I've known it from the start,
But watching you walk out that door, just somehow broke my heart.
The many tears we cried that day just proved how much we care,
So if our love is meant to be, then someday I'll be there.
I couldn't go away with you until I knew for sure,
That after we had been apart, you'd somehow want me more.
To prove the strength of our love, we had to set it free,
And now you say you know for sure, the rest is up to me.
You seemed to always know deep down that I could never leave,
And even though, I'm scared to go, I'm starting to believe.
I know that it's a challenge 'cause you want me there with you,
But I must look back one last time, before I say 'I DO'.
I know I can't keep asking you to wait much more for me,
But I'm afraid of holding back, what I feel should be free.
You said that you would settle down and take me as your wife,
But you have got to know for sure, 'cause it should be for life.

I know that we are both afraid, but one thing I have found.
Commitment only helps you grow, It doesn't pull you down.
I guess to be away from you has helped us both to find,
That TRUE LOVE can't be broken down, by distance or by time.

I Love and Miss you very much, but don't lose hope
'cause if it's meant to be, it will.

John E. Blackmon Jr.
The Last Of the Weeping Willows
A bird is by my window,
'Tis the owl, he never sleeps.
He tells me of a certain tree,
And lo, it ever weeps.

And so I see this weeping tree,
And ask, "why cry ye so?"
She did reply, "I always cry,
I am a weeping willow."

"But should you cry this way,
On a beutiful afternoon?
For the birds are all rejoicing,
And the flowers are in bloom."

But said the tree, "This cannot be,
For the painful reminder grows."
And off to sleep, this tree she'd weep,
For the last of the weeping willows.

Charlotte A. Morton
BEGIN AGAIN
Its time to begin again.
To start anew-just as friends.
To build something strong and firm.
Something willing to go full term.
Something to bring about the changes we yearn for
To rip away the waste and locate the core.

The time to begin again is now.
All we need to know is how.
To turn back the hands of time.
Just as far back as our prime.
To find the key to every door.
That special place-we'll go back for more.

Please-begin again with me.
To start off-close yet free.
Turning and finding a new day.
And knowing its just our way.
It'll come close to being all we need.
If you'll just follow my lead.

If I choose to make a stand.
Would you begin again with me.
Will you understand-take my hand.
Lets make it what it was meant to be.

Charlotte A. Morton
MIND MADNESS
I've begun to believe in mind madness.
When the heart trembles with sadness.
And the body is filled with alarm.
When you feel sure you'll do some harm
The feeling grows constantly within.
And the past is only somewhere you've already been.
As you watch your hands shake

398

with distress.
No matter what-more always
seems like less.

I believe in this mind madness.
When your soul no longer
recognizes gladness.
And your entire body is limp.
With all your greatness-your still
a shrimp.
You watch time flying past.
You can only pray this won't last.
Your teeth have begun to chatter
from the chill.
This is all inside you-all there still.

I believe I understand this
madness.
When lifes turned upside down-
its a mess.
And your eyes are filled with
misty tears.
And your voice calls-but no one
hears.
When your body is aching with
pain.
And you see it coming again and
again.
I see-life-has all of these
wonderful pleasures.
But sometimes love is not one of
its treasures.

Charlotte A. Staak
NEVER SAY "GOODBYE"
Life has a way of upsetting
The plans we often make
Somehow the scales don't balance
When your dreams you must
forsake

The time must come to be parted
From the ones you hold so dear
Yet memories of sharing and
caring
Never really disappear

The children, grown, who leave
the nest
Their unsure wings to try
We wish them well, true happiness
But never say "Goodbye"

Keep those dreams you nurtured
It may be difficult but try
Remember to say, "Auf
Wiedersehen"
And never say "Goodbye"

Fayma Caraway Johns
THE LAST LEAF

IN MEMORY OF MY BROTHER
Raymond Lamar Caraway June
15. 1935—August 28. 1980

Today I saw the last leaf fall
Beneath the hick'ry tree
Where just a few short weeks ago
You sat and talked with me.
We talked of life, we talked of
death
And of eternity—
Of dreams and plans that we had
shared
That now would never be.

The leaves were green that
shaded us
When last we shared that view
Of sunbeams dancing on the waves
Beneath a sky so blue.
We reminisced of days gone by
And friends that we had known—

Of life and all its mystery
And time, so quickly flown.

With grateful hearts for life we'd
shared
Upon this earth below,
We wondered still why you, so
young,
Should be the first to go.
We thanked our God for grace to
bear
The grief of parting pain—
For faith through Christ our Lord
to know
That we would meet again.

You knew I wished you must not
go;
I knew you yearned to stay—
And silent moments spoke for us
The words we could not say ...
I watched that leaf come
tumbling down
To rest beneath the tree,
And longed once more to be with
you
Since you can't be with me.

Susan Ann Montelius
Susan Ann Montelius
MY DARKENED CORNER
Looking out from a darkened
corner
my eyes catch a glimpse of one
flickering light
Two silhouettes dance upon the
shades
deceiving those who watch in the
night

Across town sirens race and cry
in pursuit of some lost soul
Whose anger and fury
could no longer be kept in control

Tears of sorrow pierce the night
leaving only a trace of silence
The mystery lies in their story
an act created in violence

Below, walking the street
a "working woman" waits
For the lonesome man
to open heaven's gates

Begging on the corner in
innocence
the hope of survival is wild
With the desperation held
captive
in the body of an abandoned child

But I sit here in my darkened
corner
I cry with all the pain of pity
Silent tears for all I see
living and dying in the city

Bryan J. Archer Sr.
The Regular Army Man
He aint no gold lace belvidere to
sparkle in the sun ...
He doesn't wear a gray cockade
nor posies on his gun ...
He is no pretty soldier boy, so
lovely, spick and span ...
He wears a crust of tan and dust,
the regular army man,
The marching, parching, pipe clay
starching
Regular Army Man.

He's not at home in Sunday
School, nor at a special tea,
And on the day he gets his pay
He's apt to spend it free.
He is no temperance advocate ...
He likes to fill the can.
He's somewhat tough ... And
maybe rough ...
This regular army man ...
This rarin', tearin' ... sometime
swearin'
Regular Army Man.

There are no tears shed over him
When he goes off to war;
He gets no speech from
ministers—
Or from the governor.
He packs his little gripsack up
And trots off in the van
To start the fight—and start it
right—
This regular army man,
The rattling battling colt or gatlin
Regular Army Man.

He makes no fuss about the job
nor does he talk so brave,
He knows he's in to fight and win
or else to fill a grave.
He is no mama's darling, but he
does the best he can ...
He is the chap who wins the
scrap, the regular army man,
The dandy, handy, starch and
sandy, *Regular Army Man!*

Gracie Sanderson Hill
CHRISTMAS PRESENTS
Christmas presents,
Christmas tree,
Children eyes want to see;
If there's a present just for
ME!

Christmas presents
Fill with love neath the tree,
Wrapped in colors you can see.
Red, green, silver, and gold;
This is one I want to hold!

Christmas presents,
Christmas tree,
Born in a stable,
Wrapped in rags,
Laid in a manger for a bed.
A bright glow is around his head.

Christmas presents,
Christmas tree,
Jesus Christ is the present of love;
God sent to the world from above.

Hermon Clark
THE WATER HYACINTH
On golden pond, a sunset prize,
unmolested, adrift;
Mast of bells unfurled, ocean blue,
decks of green array.
A watchful eye, a berth embay,
where the moorings.

Tred the mire, beyond the
thicklet lies,
nature's bouquet in repose;
Embrangled, awaits, in restless
pose,
a southward breeze.
Blessed peace, intrusion briefly
mars,
its wat'ry sanctuary.

Affixed upon a cypress felled,
a breath, trodden, tired;
A gaze upon the flow'ry bed,
a majestic show;
A course the four winds,
have chosen.

Dorothy Seiber Rhea
BY LANTERN LIGHT
Back in the mountains, tucked
under a hill,
In a little old cabin a widow lives.
She raised her children to trust in
the Lord,
In a little o'll cabin patched with
many a board.

Her floors were spotless, her
cubbards were full,
The Christmass I visited the last
I saw her.
I sometimes take courage when I
think of her smile,
Her dark eyes were merry the last
I saw her ...

The swing of her lantern I can see
in the dark,
As she made her way nightly to
clean up the church,
A short chuffy figure, climbing
alone,
The Path to her cabin, her
children and home ...

There must have been times
when her cubbards were bare,
Her children were sick, her soul
in despair,
But neighbors are kind, when
there is a need,
The Lord feeds the Sparrow, He
scatters the seed ...

Marie A. Eberle
THE WONDERS OF GOD
God gave us birds to fly
He even gave us a big beautiful
sky
And our land he filled with sand
He gave us a big blue sea
So we can sail, you and me
He gave us stars that glow in the
night
And even brightness of our
daylight
And our trees that blow in the
breeze
He gave us showers for our flowers
But most of all God above
gave us all his love

Terry Steele Pearson
**Can I Ever Live Tomorrow
Without You**
Can I ever live tomorrow without
you
now that I have found you today?
Now that I have held you in my
arms
and loved you my own special
way

Can I ever live tomorrow without
you

will my life ever be the same?
Will I make it thru all of the
  tomorrows
without gently calling your name?

Can I ever live tomorrow without
  you
Will I ever be able to see?
Will I be able to face the world to
  come
without your love supporting
  me?

Can I ever live tomorrow without
  you
  am I a fool for letting you go?
Will I be able to live without
  your love
  is it something I will outgrow?

Can I ever live tomorrow without
  you
Will the world ever be the same?
Perhaps you should take me
  along with you
  to share your love along with
  your name

Betty Jean Coachman
SANTA IS ON HIS WAY

TO: Jimmy, Michael, Jodi
Christopher, Jennifer, Casey
Marie MY Grandchildren

As I gaze out the window
the snow is coming down
the flakes are so pretty
no reason for a frown
All over the city
snow is blanketing the ground
And it really is a pity
Santa hasn't come to town
He hasn't as yet
so children don't fret

Santa's workshop is on the square
One day soon you'll find him
  there
With dolls, sleds, tops and a
  teddy bear
he'll take the list of each girl and
  boy
with his ho, ho, ho, they'll laugh
  with joy
E. T. and Garfield, were the rage
  last year
Strawberry Short Cake was also
  dear
And this year there's another
  match
Cute Care Bears and the doll
most wanted called Cabbage
  Patch

Dorothea Saul Seely
A WALK IN THE FOREST
Strolling through the forest,
  serenely content, enjoying the
  picture
No artist could possibly transfer
  to canvas with paint.
The soft rustle of leaves as I
  slowly walk at my leisure
Looking around, hearing birds
  sing, the sound of a brook, very
  faint.

Off in the distance, a majestic,
  giant waterfall
Presenting a beautiful panorama
As it cascades downward and
  onward, in tuneful beat, I stall.
Observing such natural
  uncontrolled drama.

I ponder—how many people can
  sense this exquisite view
Forget time is passing and remain
  dreamily unaware.
Of Nature's bounty, provided for
  everyone, not only a few?
Birds sing, becs hum, a squirrel or
  rabbit skitters here and there.

The little chipmunks poke their
  cute little faces around a fallen
  tree;
Watching, peering as I wend my
  carefree way.
Can relax enjoy this moment and
  think This is for Me!
Ah—do believe, I'll return
  another day.

On my next visit, a camera to be
  carried
To have for eternity, pictures I'll
  take.
And when in the future, if tired
  and harried,
Bring out these treasures and
  relive them for old time's sake.

Chuck Shoenberger
MY EYES CAN SEE
I can open my eyes but I can't see,
Oh my, what happened to all the
  trees!
I can feel the suns rays, gone are
  the bright shining days!
I can hear the rain thundering
  down,
But never seeing it hit the ground!
Things can look really dark, thats
  ok,
As long as I can walk in the park!
Some people are born not seeing a
  thing,
God takes their hands and shows
  them everything!
He gave us a heart to see,
Thats what He did for you and me!

Linda Kay Balzan
MOONING
Star struck, moon-struck
  loony and moony.
Totally crazy
  the mind's gone hazy.

Dreams in the moonlight?
  Up til past midnight?
Some proclaim, "mooncalf!"
  (What troubles the lass?)

Counting moonbeams falling on
  moonseeds.
  Even the weeds between
  moonflowers.

Fragrant and white they open wide
In the wake of pallid moonrise.

For in this parden of lustrous
  disarray
The plans are laid for the secret
  getaway.
Flailing to and fro over the
  sumptuous ground,
Breathing in the fragrance where
  blossoms abound.

But in spite of these lunacies and
  tenuous mendacities,
Nix! moonblindness.
Nix! Moon Childness.
Yea! Yea! to flights in moonish
  wildness

Madalene Mahaffy McClow
DAD
Today I stood where gently sleeps
The part of you that Nature keeps.
I've vowed to never see you here,
To disavow that one so dear
To my own heart could disappear
From this the land he loved so
  well,
From us, to leave our lips to tell
How beautiful he found the
  Earth,
How brightly greeted each new
  birth
Of son and daughters, Day and
  Spring,
Who saw God's hand in
  everything
That graced a life like Nature's
  plan,
That brought new depth to that
  word "Man".
I love the part of you that walked
Your share of acres, smiled,
  laughed, talked
Questioned Life's meaning,
  questioned Death,
Yet spoke for Life with every
  breath.
All parts of you I love, and so,
I want all parts of you to know.

Miss. Donnie Evelon Nash
WHEN I THINK OF YOU

---

*This Poem was written to Henry
Robinson, of Montgomery,
Alabama, who has been my
inspiration, and who has given
me plenty to write about. Thanks
for the beautiful memories.
Thank you my LOVE.*

When I think of you my love, its
  with passion
my desire for you will always be
For no one has ever pleased me as
  you
You're like a stallion, so wild, so
  untamed
that pleases me, wouldn't have it
  anyother way

When I think of you, my heart
  does sing, beautiful
melodies of love, for which we
  share
Then I laugh, wondering whether
  we're sharing the same thoughts

Theres not a minute in the day,
  when I'm not thinking of you
For you have opened my heart,
  my soul

I have no peace without you
I would rather die, if I couldn't
  have you
No other lover has given me
  pleasure as you

You are the breath I breathe
you're like a cancer eating away
  my heart
you're like a thief, for you have
  taken away my soul

When I think of you, it makes me
  sad, for I know, nothing
lasts forever
For there will be a time, when we
  must part
we must promise one another
  that we will never forget
the love, and the beautiful
  moments we've shared

For I will never forsake you, my
  love
you're the first, and the last
you're all I'll ever need
wanna spend the rest of my days
  in your arms.
For When I think of you, its with
LOVE.

M. Carol McCann
MY FRIEND

---

*To Tohru Mogami, My Boss &
Friend*

My Friend, we've walked some
  miles together
And shared our happiness and
  smiles forever
Although you go across the sea,
I'll always be a part of you
And you a part of me.

We've had our share of troubles,
  too
But you've always been there for
  me
And I've always been there for
  you.

May this friendship continue
  thru the years
Even though it brings me tears
To know that you must go away
And here I belong and here I
  must stay.

Someday, we will meet again
Though an ocean keeps us apart
I wish you health, wealth and
  happiness
From the bottom of my heart.

My Friend, we've walked some
  miles together
And shared our happiness and
  smiles forever
And I'm always proud to walk up
  and say
This is My Friend—any day.

Mary Elizabeth Cianos
A CRY FROM WITHIN
Awakening I find myself enclosed
  by cold, insensitive bars;

Oh, how I thirst to see above me
  a canopy of brilliant stars,

Hours of endless anticipation
  melted away by lingering
  anguish;

And filled with an inescapable

fear which tears cannot extinguish,

Such a shattering reality of being thrust into darkness without hope of light;

Sustained with spiritual strength generated by an increasing faith in God to overcome this desperate plight,

I find myself obsessed with a burning desire to grasp a breath of freedom.

La Nita McBride
CHRISTMAS
Today I went shopping
The busiest time of year
Through the hustle and bustle
I'd had it with Christmas Cheer.

Lines of screaming kids
With Santa at the end
Every clerk in the place
Pretending to be your friend.

Each corner you turn
Another Santa ringing a bell
They want your money
And don't have anything to sell.

That's when I saw the banner
And my mind was at rest
I went home and got my kids
And stood in the screaming lines with the rest.

I felt all cherry inside
And I smiled at every clerk
I no longer considered
Christmas shopping work.

I knew it was that banner
Nothing anyone did or said
"Keep Christ In Your Christmas"
The banner simply read.

Elizabeth Shelton Floyd
DREAMS

To all the special people in my life who have touched my heart. May I warm yours in return—always!

It all starts with dreams
And if you hold steadfast to them
You can achieve them.
It may seem
Impossible at times,
But never give up if you fail.
You learn from your failures
And become a stronger person.
Hold steadfast to your dreams
And make them a reality.

Louise Pryor Arfstrom
The Sounds Of Morning
Have you awakened just before dawn
To see the moonlight and shadows play on the lawn?
Have you heartd the coyote's last wail, when
He slinks off quietly to his den?
Heard the last peep of the tiny black cricket
As it goes back to bed deep in the thicket
Far off in the distance, the cock perches on high
Announcing the morning up to the sky.
The brilliant sun ascends the hill

Just for a moment, the world stands still.
The sweet gentle breezes come to and fro
The sounds of morning begin to grow.
A tiny brook rushes and splashes along
The birds lift their voices in a medley of song.
The screech of a hawk flying through the air
Arouses the forrest creatures in their lair.
The sounds of morning are music to the ear
By not uttering a word, its just what you hear.

Jamie Parsley Carter
MOUNTAINS
Their peaks touch the sky
Sometimes they're covered in snow
Others always stay green
They all let wildlife grow.

They're Gods own pyramids
They're peoples escape
From the hustle and bustle
City life does create.

Mountains stand proud
As they hover o'er land
One of Gods great ideas
A creation so grand.

Bonnie Van Ostran
Night Of Enchantment
It's a night of adventure, of pleasant rendezvous,
A night of peace and quiet, just the right mixture of the two.
The stars are in the sky, the moon shines softly down.
In the distance is a castle, shining frosty blue in the light falling round.
A long road carries wandering minds and feet to the enormous gate.
Mist and fog swirl round it, adding to the beauty and mystery of this place.
Something dares you to enter, to risk your future and your past.
It's a night that leaves you spell-bound, wondering how long it will last.
A night of romance, surprise, and merriment,
This night, tonight, is a night of enchantment.

Mary Letha Washington
HOW MANY MOUNTAINS?

To all the weary people, ask God to give you strength to overcome all obstacles and keep climbing.

How many mountains,
Do I have to climb?
I have climbed so many
Time after time
But I alone
Must keep on.
I can't stop
Till I reach the top.

God give me strength
To carry on.
I'll keep climbing
Till I get home.

Alice Clason Schaffer

Alice Clason Schaffer
We'll Love You Anyway

To my three beautiful children. . . Alvin Leroy, Sylvia Marie and Robert Wayne Schaffer, who made it all worth while.

Dare I gaze upon this tiny face . . .
as its smile slips away . . .
I seem to know
He chose it so
And we'll meet again one day.

When I smell this rose . . . and they should see . .
and tear it all apart . . .
I know that He
can comfort me
And mend my broken heart.

So if we meet . . . and once again . . .
I'd lose you one dark day . . .
Let's simply never fear, my friend . .
We'll love you anyway.

Eva Gumke
PAIN
Pain gallops through my body
like a storm sweeping
over the plains.
Lightening flashes
coincide with the stab of pain
in my side.
The thunder roars as the pain
jumps from joint to joint,
like a frenzied harriden
on Halloween.
Scary
the pain does not stop
I am helpless
caught in a web
swaying
in the wind
moving—no relief
except through sleep.
Even then the pain wakes me.

Kaye Roberson
MIRACLE CHILD
Miracle Child
with your tender heart . . .
so bold—
your love shining bright
as the Northern Star

You've taught me how
to see new things
through your far—away eyes
and seeing in your special way
I see things I never realized

I've come to love you for who you are
and the way you are right now—
your love soars free
then touches me . . . gently
from your distant star

I come into your special world
just to be with you
hoping . . . someday ., . .
with time—
I can bring you out to mine

Miracle Child
with your tender heart . . .
so bold—
your love shining bright
from your distant star

Gloria Duff
My Tree Full Of "Robins"
Christmas time, and cold
Christmas time, and excitment
ice and glitter on the tree,
—but not outside,
it's on my Christmas tree!
not free or given
decorated by choice,
chosen time!
"My" Christmas tree

Christmas time, and tinsel
Christmas time, and food
red Robins, fat and saucy
—on the tree!
but not inside,
this Christmas tree
decorated by lively "Birds"
chosen time!
THEIR Christmas tree to ME!

T. A. Connery
A VOID OF UNKNOWN

Dedicated to Addie and Morris And of course the coffee pot.

Into the night I drift
Just another void of unknown
Questions and riddles
Classified only
When knowing your goal
When answers haught your dreams
Demanding acknowledgement

Human hand open
Whispers, quiet whispers
Heard only through eyes
Of patience and persistence

Magic the wind
Felt yet not touched
Believed yet not understood
Into the night I drift
Just another void of unknown

kathy mil Hynds-Pestell
Christmas On the Home Stretch
Was a touch of the Christ-child
With you and yours
On this Memorable Day?

Did you share this thought
With loved ones—
Those quite near—
Or even those far away?

Did traditional carols
Of glad tidings
Refresh with joy
The treasured Hope
Hidden within the silent depths
Of your aged yet loving Heart?

Then yours, too—A Blessed
Christmas,
Affirmed by Faith and Love—
Will return in triple measure
With each enlightened Day
of this
FORWARD . . . MOVING . . .
YEAR

Lois Cooper-Jones
A CHILD OF PEACE
Turmoil through out our world.
With torturing wars and broken
hearts.
A'l search, and wait, and pray.
This one child of peace has come.

Come from where, he will be
asked!
Looking down on his face in hope
For an answer to all our doubts.
This blessed child of joy has come.

Unhad by all who doubt this gift,
New life before us all to share.
This task He asks of us, although,
To praise and love the child of
goodwill.

Marilyn R. Martin O'Brien
ANXIETY
When in trouble
Pray
When in doubt
have faith
When in need
believe
Then comes
The miracle.

Dawna King
WHAT IS LIFE?
What is life?
Is it shadows
dancing on a wall,
reflections of something
that is real?
Is it the wind
or perchance
only the wind's echoings?
Is it truth
or merely the stuff
of which dreams are made?
Is it the beginning
or the end?

Gloria May
OMEGA MOMENTS
Twas far from wasted, the waiting,
Those now cherished days of
yesterday.
While possessed by love
And held captive by the twinge of
memory,
All reality was set to
procrastination.
The loved one as prey to the
fangs of death,
Gave hold to dominance.
Through eyes inflamed by tears,
Made wise the broken hearted.
There was no discernment to the
pungent destiny.
Unequalled to any form of
helplessness before that time,
Was to observe the dearest of life,
Having life itself drawn from it.
To speak of wisdom be it of
heaven or earth,
To explain evolution of man from
then till now,
To probe the depths of the ocean
or hell,

Falls short to the experience of
one,
As he beholds the transition of a
soul,
From this place to its final home.

Galer Walker Roberts
BORN TO BE LORD
By the Spirit in the flesh Jesus
Christ our Lord was born
On a journey to a virgin who by
His grace did God adorn,
Revealing to the world a saviour
who would one day heed the
call,
Never yielding to temptation,
giving up His life for all.
This precious baby born to Mary
grew to be God's special man,
Offering Himself as servant,
obedient to Yahweh's plan:
Bringing good news to the people,
teaching them God's way to live,
Expressing God's love with
compassion and much healing
He did give.
Letting power from the Holy
Spirit flow through Him as God
allowed,
Our blessed Lord and Saviour
shared great blessings that His
Father God endowed,
Rendering much hope and
teaching how to live in victory,
Deliv'ring freedom from
oppression, setting all those
captive free.
Will you let Him also free you
from those things that have
you bound?
Allow Him now to be your
saviour and your joy will soon
abound.
Surrender also to His Lordship:
Make Him Master of your life.
Jesus as your Lord and Saviour
gives much peace in times of
strife.
Every Christmas we remember
Jesus' birth in Bethlehem,
Sharing gifts with one another,
giving love to honor Him.
Up to Him we lift our voices and
our hearts in one accord,
Singing praises to King Jesus who
was then born to be Lord.

Charlene Cutts
LOST HEART
Dare me! O' King of Hearts!
Such is this fate of mine!
My heart, I feel it leaving—
soundlessly . . .
Lost in the winds of time.

I cannot endure!
For what you have bestowed
upon me.
Am I selfish? May I hope?
Oh! What may never be!

Is such a love, so pure and true,
Destined to be lost inside of
never?
To be mourned and then forgotten,
To be gone forever?

Oh! Tell me, please! Dear King of
Hearts,
Tell me that I have been brave!
Knowing that I may never be free!
For the love for which I am
slave . . .

Lori Jean Long
THERE IS ONE

*Dedicated to my dear Mama:
From the moment I began to pen
this poem, I knew it was you
whom I wrote of. Thank you,
Mama, for all you've done. I love
you so very much.*

There is one who loves me
without ever a doubt,
Who lends me a hand when I
need helping out.
There is one who puts things in
perspective when I'm too blind
to see,
Who gives me strength and
support when I, myself, doubt
me.

There is one who lights up my
life when I'm surrounded by
night,
Who always gives me courage
when things aren't always
right.
There is one who is impossible to
ever replace,
Never will I ever see such
another face—
So loving, sharing, self-sacrificing
and kind,
Who in the eyes so beautiful the
heart and soul doth shine.

There is one who deserves much
more
Than I can ever hope to give;
I LOVE YOU, I THANK YOU,
DEAR MAMA
For as long as we both shall live.

Shirlee Ball Smith
MY HOT AIR BALLOON

For my son: Mark Smith

When look ye up into the sky
and see a big balloon sail by

It's me up there, but needn't cry.
For I'm sailing top the trees
As swift as sail boats in the seas.

When I look down to see the
squares
of land divided to their heirs
I feel so grand and free and wild
To be so carefree like a child.
I pump the gas into the sky!
It's like a magic trick to fly.
A trick a bird knew 'fore I did.
But I am sure it's feeling hid.
For none save I can know this joy.
To fly about in this great toy.

Gordon L. Florence
FLOWER GARDENS
Flower gardens invite one
to linger amid beauty,
and to unite, for a moment,
with a silent world
of color, scent, and peace.

Heather Christ
THE DEMON LOVER
He entered the girl's room late
that night,
From where, I do not know.
He stood like a statue in the dim
light
Tall and strong, his face as white

as snow.
Hair as black as a Raven's breast,
Brilliant eyes shining in the dark,
His unearthly presence disturbed
her rest
Until she woke; the pounding of
her heart
Came not from fear, but
unexplained desire,
The beauty of him unsurpassed
She knew and loved this Sire
In another place, far in the
distant past.
When she held out her arms to
him in surrender
He silently went into the maid's
sweet embrace,
then wrapped his cape around her
form so slender.
She gazed at him, awed delight in
her pretty face
As he held her tight and kissed
her rosy lips,
Filling her soul with wonder.
Time flew by. Oh, what bliss!
The young girl softly sighed in
rapture.
Early next morn, her mother
entered the silent room
And saw her lovely lass lying
deep in slumber.
Suddenly, the woman gave a cry
of dispair and doom
When she pulled back the
strange black cloak,
For there, on the dead girl's throat
Was the mark of the demon lover!

Christine Marie Mc Cullough
BRAINSTORM
The Mind . . .
simple,
yet extremely complex;
virtually unknown,
yet incredibly understood;
such a fascinating part
of life,
emotions,
and actions,
such a wonderful object
to explore,
enrich,
and fulfill;
the possibilities
are unlimited . . .

Joyce Suter Whitcomb
MY CHOICE
Dear God, I cannot see tomorrow,
A path of darkness lies ahead,
I do not ask for light to see,
Just strength to follow where I'm
led.

The path is rough, and I am weak,
And filled with stubborn pride,
Doubting, lest I ought to choose
A road that's smooth and wide.

Thy feet once trod this narrow
way,
Thou knowest every turn,
And Lord, if Thou my guide will
be,
I too will strive to learn.

Jennifer Lynn Frenchik
LIVING FOR TODAY
I'm living for today,
not for tomorrow.
You never know what it brings,
joy or sorrow,
no time to borrow.

Our World's Best Loved Poems

The past is gone,
  no changing to be done.
It was just yesterday,
  you went away.
It seems like a year,
  since I saw your face,
    felt your warm embrace.
I need to know if you're coming
  home,
  or if you're going to stay away,
    because
I'm living for today,
  looking for tomorrow.
In this world of crazy people
  only searching for lost dreams,
    painted pictures of happy
      streams,
    sunny mountains and quiet
      trees,
Do you even know,
  what it means to be
Living for today,
  wondering if tomorrow?

Valerie L. McCarthy
A SIMPLE TRUTH

To Edith and Fern McCarthy

Sometimes I'm good at keeping
  secrets—
  as long as they don't pertain to
    me.
I don't conceal myself well;
  especially emotions felt are easy
    to see.
I wonder are you looking?

When I was young I pretended
  what was not—was;
Grown, I've not learned how to
  pretend
  what is—isn't.
I Love You!

Tracy Lee Phillips
Turned To the Good Lord
My younger days they were filled
  with sorrow
For a sober dad I'd had to borrow
The schoolwork wasn't easy to do
But somehow I managed as I grew.

I was lead astray and got into dope
But the good Lord showed me
  there still was hope.
For He took my hand and lead
  me, again.
And He showed me a life other
  than sin.

Though, it wasn't long before I
  fell short
And I turned into a sorrowful sort
This time, a year, before I learned
That the Good Lord really was
  concerned

He told me to pack up and move
  far away
Be strong and push the devil out
  of my way.
Christian friends told me that I
  was too bright
To continue living that kind of
  life.

I have very much to be thankful
  for
I haven't much money, but I'm
  not poor,
For I am blessed richly with His
  Spirit
When I listen closely I can hear it.

Donna Isobel
MY ONLY LOVE

*Gene, my only love, my
inspiration, my happiness. To
you I dedicate my first place
poem, just open the door, my
sweet, you have first place in my
heart . . .*

Thru eyes saddened with tears,
I look back through the years.

And a smile returns to my face,
As fondly I recall the place,

Where your eyes and mine did
  meet,
And I gazed upon your face so
  sweet.

You engulfed my soul in your
  embrace,
Lifting it to a sweet and gentle
  place.

I surrendered to your soft tender
  kiss,
I thrilled to your passion and
  bliss,

Which held for us the greatest
  rapture,
That only true lovers would dare
  to capture.

But quickly now the smile
  disappears,
As I recall all of the empty
  years,

That I have spent waiting and
  longing for,
My only love to return and open
  the door.

Earl Wayne Shehorn
FORMS OF ART . . .
I like to think of myself as
  an "artist" sometimes—
  an "artist of words" . . .

Yet too, I draw occasionally, but
  less than I write—much less.

I suppose—truthfully, many
  people
  are "artists" of
  sorts—particularly
  in their work . . .

But some, are also I'm sure,
  "artists of thoughts" as I am.

I don't believe anyone must tell
  you
  you're an artist—it only matters
  that you believe you are . . .

Constance A. Thorpe
THE CRICKET

*In memory of my two son's Jason,
and James, my grandparents
Jimmy and Virginia Boyle, and
my dear family the Boyles and
Quesnels who are my inspiration.*

The cricket breaks the sound
barrier of silence on a cool
spring night. You can hear
them echo, like if it were a
ripple, in a beautiful clear
spring pond. Isn't it amazing
how nature is so much alike
yet, so different?

Hilda D. Dobson
A PICTURE OF LOVE
If I were an artist, I would paint a
  picture
with help from God above,
I would paint all the world with
  sunshine
I'd color it with love,
I would paint a world of
  compassion
with tolerance for every religion
  and race,
I would paint a happy smile on
every hungry child's face,
I would erase all the sounds of war,
I would paint the dove of peace,
All the heartaches, pain and sorrow
would forever cease,
I would paint a helping hand
for the lame and the old,
The warmth of a fireside
for the sick and the cold,
I would paint a world united
so everyone could see,
That all of God's people
could live together in perfect
  harmony,
If I could paint this picture
I would start it all right now
It would be so very beautiful
Because—God Showed me how.

Linda L. Jones
LOVE FORSAKEN
His love hath forsaken me.
His eyes do not care.
His heart: cold as December,
Has taken to dare.
  My heart it still bleeds,
  My eyes—never smile.
  My soul—regretfully empty.
  And my love once steadfast;
  Solemnly begins to impale.
One day he may implore
Of times so cherished.
Looking back on promises
Dismissed for immorality.
  Ah, might I then be
  Triumphant and aggressive,
  To my heart's own pleasure
  Instead of his procurity.

Lowenstein Wells
WHAT'S MY LINE
Life is the greatest gift I'll ever
  receive
Only God could give,
Whatever life holds for me
Even if its not my expectation
Now I am satisfied.

So I travel on day by day
To see and do all I can,
Eventually I know I must go

I want to leave my mark
No one said it has to be easy.

When my existance have perished
Even then I will not be forgotten.
Life is for me to enjoy
Looking back isn't the answer
So until the end I'll be here.

Camille M. Mucci
WHY?

*In memory of my precious,
stawlart Father Joseph— Love,
peace & prayers "Millie" 1984*

Why, oh God did you make me?
To enjoy your lilacs or endure
  E.S.T.
      (electro-shock-treatment)
Did you give me these eyes
To see the beauty of your snow
  and the artistry of Michelangelo?
Or just to shed tears of
  unhappiness and fears?
These ears of mine did you create
To listen to the birds and Chopin
Or must I always hear the cry of
  the damned
With my hands might I caress
Or must I clench a fist in distress
Oh these feet do let them dance!
Or must I flee from your enhance
Why, oh, why God did you make
  me?

Charlotte A. Morton
TOAST TO A FRIEND
To the tears that we have shed.
And to all the wrong words we've
  ever said.
To all the tests we had to take.
And all the colds we couldn't
  shake.
To all the games we've played
  and won.
And all the races we've had to
  run.
To all the gifts we ever got.
To every child and every tot.
To all the pains we've ever
  shared.
And to all the people who ever
  cared.
To all the growing we've ever
  done.
And all the times filled with fun.
To all the stories ever told.
And every hand we'll never hold.
To times together and times
  apart.
And every emotion that fills the
  heart.
To all the dreams that came and
  went.
And all the letters we should
  have sent.
To all the moments we tried to
  capture.
And those endless feelings filled
  with rapture.
To the memory of the "Heart
  Breaker's."
And knowing the difference
  between the givers and the
  takers.
To every moment we've shared
  together.
And to that solemn vow—to be
  friends forever.

Linda G. Smith
GOD'S BLESSINGS

Dedicated to my friend, Sarah M. Harrison, who unknowingly gave me the encouragement to continue my writing.

We are not promised the hope of tomorrow.
Nor even the strength to finish today.
The Sun might not greet us with a smile this morn.
Instead we see storm clouds coming our way.
Don't cry my friend, for God has a way
To take your troubles and create great blessings each day.
For by the grace of our sweet Savior,
Each day can be filled with enough light to shine
for a thousand tomorrows.

Debra Johnson Barrera
TIME PASSES ON

To my loving husband and children, Luis, Shanna, Kaysha, Thea and Baby.

Seasons go; as autumn leaves turn and fall to the ground
Years pass on
as snow kisses the earth
And spring rises up
to touch the sky

With living, bright colors

Rain Dances
Upon each tree, grass and petal
Then the sun scorches
in dryness
Time seems to pass on
and one day we turn
And yesterday
is long since gone.

John F. Tozzi
SILENT CASEARS
To my fellow silent seashells,
Who roar like the lion,
When picked but gracefully
From the sea.
It's a pity to see but the crest,
And never touch the depth beneath.

Paul D. Swigart
SYNESTHETIC SEIZURES
Whisper me a rainbow
In the color of your eyes;
Touch the suntide shadows
Bearing fragments of your sighs;
Kiss the moonlight laughter
Framed in echoes from your soul;
Taste for me a windsong
In the key of making whole.
The flower by the sycamore
Softly cries its fragrant plea,
Begging vainly for the sweetness of the earth
To travel through the hearts that cry.
The candle in the autumn wind
Offers light for those in need,
With silent flickers of a peace
Which only shelter can provide.

The teardrop in the waterfall
Stained its rushing waters blue,
In full expression of the ways
By which a nightingale came courting
And became the morning dew.

Fredesvinda O. Escamilla
PLEASE BE MINE
You like my way
of kissing
I love yours
we need each other
it can't be denied
please be mine
please be mine.

We share our thoughts
and we care enough
to keep our love
if you try to please me
why don't you be mine
why don't you be mine
it'll be happiness
for you and I.

We need each other
it can't be denied
please be mine
please be mine
it'll be happiness
for you and I.

It'll be happiness
for you and I
kiss me tonight, kiss me
for the rest of my life.

Betty Joe Stepp
Woes Of a Working Man
When I think of my toil and my labor,
I'm as low as any man can get.
Each day is the same as another,
With goals that I've set . . . still unmet.

And to see me, you'd think that I'm stupid,
Dirty, weathered, and old.
With no feelings, or hopes for the future,
Not feeling the heat or the cold.

And the sun as it climbs in it's heaven,
Makes my eyes blind with sweat,
The tools are too hot to handle . . .
Its as hot as only hell can get.

But, I guess it's just nature's balance,
It's a job that someone must do.
For some the living is easy . . .
And then—there's the miserable few!

Sandy Paden
WALKING HOME

To my wonderful husband and children. Thank you for your encouragement and belief in my ability to write poetry.

Alone and frightened I wandered through the dark and dreary night,
Dark clouds covered the moon, creating an eerie sight.

The chill breeze rustled the leaves
and the moon came out once more;

And I thanked God with all my heart
for bringing me safely to my door.

Angela Kinamore

Angela Kinamore
THE POWER OF LOVE
Love, is the strongest power
in the universe
So I dwelled on love to seek
its inner meaning and held that
precious word in my inmost thoughts
Thinking only of love and what
message it had for me . . .
Then one day love touched me deep
within and I began to understand
its true power
Love renewed my spirit and awakened
my soul to the meaning of Life
and its glorious wonders
And I knew God truly was Love
and always within our reach . . .
If we but only asked
If we but only searched
we would find Love
awaiting us within—
To try its ways . . .

Floyd Willougby
A DAY

To Bob and Barbara Harman who bring this Poem to life over many years of Christian fellowship

Any days work which is honestly done brings the peace of evening, the setting of the Sun. It's done Its' job and we've done ours now it's time to relax and enjoy a few hours.

Gather and family around, and sing some songs ask Gods help to right the wrongs. Make plans for tomorrow with the thrill of life, when you catch her looking—wink at your wife.

When the evening is done, and the family's in bed balance the checkbook to keep it black not red. Look out the door, and say "goodnight" to the stars be glad you're on Earth and not on Mars.

Then it's time to go to the room which made a girl a bride, and a boy a groom. Snuggle up close, but do it with care! 'cause your

eye might get poked with those things in her hair.

Sandra Elizabeth Jones
SILVER STRANDS
When I was young
I loved the silver strands
among the tresses of mother's hair.
I loved seeing the sunlight glimmer
on the silver strands, briefly
turning them to gold.

Now, many years later, I have silver
strands of my own, and as I stand
before the mirror, brushing and combing,
I remember with fascination and love,
mother's beautiful hair. Her silver
strands has now become a cap of pure
silver beauty, now that she's grown old.

Jessie Christopherson
SAILING BOATS

To Christina and Anthony, my grandchildren, who while visiting Lawrence Welk Village, pleasured many adults as they watched these imaginative children in a world of their own.

Sailing boats down the river
Excited Christina and Anthony.
They had to have them right side up
Before starting them toward the sea.

Boats of dry leaves from old oak trees
Were cupped by a blistering sun.
They fell from trees in a gentle breeze
For a new life just begun.

Leaves floated all day on a crystal bay
While daylight hours were spending.
It was fun to watch them tumble and turn
In fleets of boats, unenending.

Over the falls the boats were coaxed
Singly or in fleets together
Guided along a route to the sea
By the touch of a bluebird's feather.

Jannie Belle Young & Kathleen F. Chatfield
IT'S LOVE
My life was a lonely world until
you came along, then you
finally found me and my lonely
world was gone.

You reached your gentle hands
out to me so I could hold, and
then the love you wanted so
bad, was finally sold.

I knew I couldn't resist you, and I
knew we wouldn't part, I knew
this because of the love, you
put into my heart.

With the love in your heart and
the smile on your lips,
somehow I knew I couldn't resist.

You asked, do you love me? I
replied, I do, then you kissed
me and held me tight, so very
snug with all your might.

Then together we walked across
the smooth soft sand, feeling
the love among us, as we went
hand in hand.

Through-out the year from
January to December, every
day this time I'll remember.

Now, my lonely world is a faded
part of my past, cuz now I
know the love we share, will
always last and last.

Sometimes when I look back at
how lonely I was, and then I
think now, I know—IT'S LOVE!

Barbara Wirkowski
WHEN YOU LEAVE
When you leave and say
Goodnight.
You give me a kiss and say sleep
tight.
And as you walk out the door,
I realize I miss you more.
But as we know the night must
end,
And as I slumber in my bed,
I pray to God our love won't end.

Margaret DeVenny
MY PRAYER

To my late husband James

I Feel
As here I kneel
That this world's troubles
Are unreal,
Whether they are or not, I know
He will show
Me heavenly peace
When I go.

Renee' Leigh Cambiano
NANA

To the best Nana in the world,
Sue Torchia

If you think of the nicest person,
that ever could be.
Then you would think of my
Nana, so sweet is she.

Nana? You might ask
what is that?
Grandma in Italian,
a matter of fact.

Some may call her Sue
or even Mama.
But there are only a few,
fortunate enough to call her
Nana.

She means so much to me,
that no one word could ever
express.
The feelings I have inside, that
just don't seem to rest.

I might not tell her I love her
every moment of the day.
But deep inside my heart,
it's expressed in every way.

The only way to express my
feelings, is to come right out
and say.

Nana, "I LOVE YOU," I always
will no matter how far you are
away.

Kathy Leming
HIS OMINOUS PRESENCE
Through his existence I have
become myself, the person I
am;
I have gained knowledge,
experience, wisdom and a sense
of being.

But he controls me; my mind, my
heart and my soul;
He allows me laughter; he
permits me to love; he grants
me growth.

As a young girl I teased him and
flirted haughtily,
But as I grow older, I realize he is
not to be taken lightly.

His power was vague until I
began to love,
Then I felt his hands ever present
upon me like tight fitting
gloves.

He can be my friend, we can
share, compromise.
We can chase the wind, smell the
flowers, walk side by side.

I can laugh, be happy and feel so
carefree,
When he brings forth the
sunshine for the world to see.

I have known the pain, the grief,
the loneliness he invites
When he controls the darkness
and the gloom of night.

I struggle for control, I plan my
strategy, I attack.
Sometimes I manage; but, so
often, equal strength I lack.

I run joyously, yet with caution,
through a meadow of flowers,
Knowing he can stop me as I am
under his power.

I can take him, use him, even toss
him aside,
But he is forever with me—this
force, this Father Time.

Daniel Wray
BURNING

To Rhonda, whose spontaneous
smile will forever fan the flame
within.

When first I found the firelight in
your eyes,
I looked away for fear of feeling
pain
But soon the gentle breezes of
your sighs
Quick carried me the spark
that they conatain.

The blackened forest of my
trampled breast
Could hardly entertain another
fire—
The spark found nourishment in
loneliness
And fed upon the fields of my
desire.

It now has grown into a roaring
blaze

That has no want of waning for
a while.
It's flames grow higher with each
longing gaze
And hunger for the sweetness
of your smile.

If you could of these glowing
embers learn,
Then more would be the
reason that they burn.

Cathy Wandell & Debbie Kriebel
Cascades Of Silvery Light
The moon was clouded over,
But it didn't dim its shine.
The sea and sky were beautiful,
It seemed that they were mine.
I felt a warm breeze blowing,
Standing closer to the bow,
A planet shining in the distance
Seeming brighter now.

The boat was swaying as a
cradle would,
Suspended from the sky.
With a little touch of magic
It could prob'ly learn to fly.
As moon, planet, and stars made
Silvery paths upon the waves,
I knew that I could go There
If I only could know His ways.
I felt my spirit growing
In exultation with the stars,
And I knew He held a place for
me
In His ever-loving arms.

Donna F. Allred
YESTERDAY'S MEMORIES
Memories of my past
Come haunting after me,
Reminding me of who I am
And who I used to be.
Never realizing until to late
What "love" could really bring
Finding out that gold was brass
And there's no silver rings.
Discovering that life's not rosy
And there's no shining seas
To sail upon with no regrets
If the past should set me free.
It used to be so easy
To play a million games
But now it seems harder
To forget the many names.
Then one day I found the peace
I seemed to be searching for
By learning to look ahead
Instead of what went before.

Adele Grace Sayarot
WARNING CRIES
Ashes, ashes
turn to dust-tell our children
abhorrent lies
Ashes, ashes
turn to soil-feed our children
poisoned truths
give them what we left for them
pain and anguish-sorrow and greed
burn they flesh and breath foul air
remember once when you were
there?
Ashes, ashes
settle on earth
breed our children-as we once were
tell them secrets-show them how
let them see how we all died
Ashes, ashes
now you know-do as we say and
keep us alive
teach our children-teach them well

make them know their real selves
show no pity-do no favors
give our children what we deserve
Ashes, ashes
keep us safe-save us from
destructions fate
make our chidren understand-
make them one as we once were
Ashes, ashes
listen well-give all humans
human hell.

Bonnie L. Gorden
KNOCKING;
Answer the knock on the door,
The knock on the door to your
heart!
Jesus is standing there waiting,
Don't let that knock fade away.

Sometimes I ask why I'm waiting?
My heart has nothing to say.
Hear the knock on the door of
your heart;
He might be walking away.

Bright light's of the world are
glowing,
As sin of the evil one is showing,
He'll laugh while your drawn to
the flame.
The Lord is calling, calling your
name.

Life with Him means heaven,
No sin or pain will there be,
Answer the knock on the door of
your heart,
The bright light's of heaven you'll
see!

Donna Gilbert
The Meal That Got Away

To my daughter Melisa Heather,
who learned at mealtimes that,
silence is golden.

A bird sitting on a branch,
Looked down and spied some ants.
With a wiggle of it's tail
And a flap of it's wings
He landed on the ground and
began to sing.
He sang so long that when he
looked around,
The ants were gone,
Nowhere
To
  Be
    Found.

Alan Baron
THE RAIN
the rain, Gods tears
falling gently, falling softly
enveloping the moist Earth
like a soft wet blanket
sometimes it beats
like quiet thunder
beating in my heart
bringing loving warmth
inside secure walls
the earth and I are grateful

Barbara A. Palatino
CRIES OF OPRESSION
Reformation of thoughts
conditioned,
Extraordinary effort to overcome
reticence,
The power to command my
thoughts;
How melancholy the implications.

John Campbell, Editor & Publisher

Searching, wishing to find a safe
passage
To the depth of my being.

The tremors, the majestic fear
Of unavoidable pain, and the
nights with wide eyes.
How these encircling thoughts of
seemingly
Unaswerable questions haunt me.

The compromising conscience,
The matromonial convictions
Of a purpose, and
OH! The sacrifical joys!

"What laudable determination!"
they all say,
When they know not the answers
themselves.

Niki Sherer

Niki Sherer
BOB
  Sometimes in your life
when someone comes along,
they fill a very special part of
  you.
  But when they die
they take it with 'em;
that very special part of you,
even the part you had given.
  Never to return
and somehow be blamed
for the words you wished
you had said.
  Only to know now
that your good friend is
"Dead!"

Beverly Lake
LIFE IN FLIGHT
Liquid warmth in the sun's bright
  sight,
Sexually alluring in the
  shimmering light.

A dark river flows thru the valley
  grand,
Ever searching for another land.

Whirling, swirling sending finger
  streams,
Seeking the world's quixotic
  dreams.

Rushing turbently over the rocky
  sand,
Flinging flecks of foam against
  the Hinterland.

Struggling and fighting thru the
  journey's emotions,
Only to become an anonymous
  current within vast oceans!

Judith Detamore
THREE FACES OF AGING
Pity Me—
  I am old
  Cruel youth to pass on by
  So helpless
  No one cares if I,
    waste away.
  Dear death
  You're welcome here
  Come near
  I'm ready to depart
    from this heartless world
  'Twill miss me not.

Envy Me—
  See how gay!
  I fling and dance
    the many endless
    nights away
  Ah, flesh divine!
  While others wither
  I sparkle, shine!
  The mirror lies
  I will not let the
    years appear to
      slow me
      down
    I snear at them
    at all who stare
  How dare they think
    it's their affair!
  For me there is no end.

Respect Me—
  For though the years
  Have etched themselves
  So deeply on my whole
  I cannot sit
    and brood the while
    My soul
      needs to issue warmth.
      a smile.
  And when upon occasion, pain
  I think of those who once again
  Need my wisdom, help and cheer
  This all I'll leave
    another year.

Barbara McCorkhill
MYSTIC BEACON
I moved my bed
I wanted to wake up in a different
  place
no longer face the closet
each morning when I open my
  eyes
Now I can look out the window
I can heed every fine day

The mornings give me options
I can be filled with yin or yang
mingle with an orgasmic sun
or mesh with some mist-shrouded
  man
or just walk with the woman
who lifts up the last star
night's leftover
and looks
to see what she can find
to keep in her basket

When I go to bed tonight
I'm going to lie there and wonder
what prospects await me
what light
silently expands
ready to fill the curtains of my
  morning

Alma Joyce
UMBILICAL
Our spirits do not touch of late.
There is a wall of pain between

built by being known and
  knowing.

By layers lain bare clutching
  cover where no matter hides.
But love, you try me,
will not let me be.
Come tell, is there depth enough
to jump into a pool of you?

Sorrow, filtered thru our
  disconsolate
crumbling fortress, births joy
thirsting yet alive because of you.

Hilary Palmer
IMPRISONED BY TIME?
Time would cease to be
If we would not anticipate an end
To that which we consider the
  beginning,
We can be free.
Time is an ever present now,
A process expressing;
An immediate yet enduring
  moment
In which we learn to see
That which we perceive.

Donna J. Harris
SLOW DOWN WORLD
The world is moving so very fast,
We've even got a shortage of gas.

The interest rates are soaring high,
The airlines are on strike, they
  won't even fly.

The children we love are turning
  to dope,
They don't understand, they can't
  even cope.

Everyone wants more from this
  fast moving world,
They don't realize that we're all
  in a whirl.

Where will it end?
What can we do?

We'll slow down our pace, we
  won't even move.

Connie Hunter
I FIND
As I focus
On your
Eyes,
A Shining
Silvery white
Starshaped
Beam
Surprises its way
Into my mind.
My spirit
Fills
With radiant
Warmth.
We stand
Spellbound,
Suspended
In a moment
Outside of time,
Our souls
Connecting
Through the channel
Of our light

Cheryl Wilson
SAY YOU LOVE ME
As I lie here and think of you
make my sensuous dreams come
  true
Let all that I see-All that I feel
cease fantasyland and be foreal

May all of my thoughts equal
  yours
feel free to do all the things you
  adore
Thrill me with your magical
  powers
let them pour out in endless
  showers
When all is done and I lay in
  your arms
whisper to me your sexy charms
Before we close our eyes to sleep
just let you say you love me.

Florence Kropp Steffen
VALLEY OF THE FOG
The fog has been slowly, creeping
  in
Until we are encased in a silent
  white valley
Which is broken at intervals
By an auto slowly cruising
  through.
In a short space, it is swallowed up
By the massive white curtain
That is there, and yet, it eludes
  the touch.
An evasive thing, that shrouds
  the view,
Into a small, close, little world.
Until the sun's warm rays, break
  through
Then it mysteriously disappears
Into the atmosphere.
It reminds me of our Lord
Who surrounds us, with His love.
He is there, we cannot see,
or touch Him physically.
But He will here our prayers,
And take upon Him our many
  cares—
Until they too, mysteriously
  disappear
In the loving warmth
Of God's Son.

Sonya D. Mitchell
ALL ALONE
No matter how hard I try
to be the best I can be.
I just seem to live a lie
something that's not really me.

As funny as it may sound
there's no one to talk to
or help you when you're down
So you just have to come to
depend on you.

No one's ever been around for me,
I've had to make it on my own.
I'm doing the very best you see
Because I'm all alone.

Carole Neason
BECAUSE

---

*Dedicated to all of the children of
the world*

You wanted to learn of life,so
  that you may live.
You have had the greatest teacher
  of them all,
Life itself.
You wanted to learn of love, so
  that you may love.
You have had the greatest teacher
  of them all,
Love itself.
You wanted to learn of wisdom,
  so you may be wise.

You have had the greatest teacher
of them all,
Knowledge and experience itself.
Now tell me my child, what have
you learned from
The greatest teachers of them all?
I am simply to be, God is the cause
Without cause nothing could be
because.
I am now because, to be without
cause
Is simply to be.

Elaine J. Motes
BRIAN

---

*Dedicated to Bud, Laquita, and
Debbie, in memory of Brian
Mitchell Lunsford.*

Brian was a child with soft
blonde hair
He was a child with skin so fair
He was a child with eyes so blue
But his years were a chosen few
He was a normal teenage boy
Who was his family's pride and
joy
Now Brian Mitchell Lunsford was
his name
But one day Jesus staked his
claim
Jesus knew Brian liked tennis as
a sport
And he needed an angel for his
court
Now Brian also loved playing his
drums
And dreamed of when the day
would come
That he could have his own band
Which Jesus gave Brian in
Gloryland.

R. E. Vaughn
LAURIE JONES
I was elated at church one day,
when I met a beautiful child—
Pretty Laurie Jones, who had, a
most enchanting smile—
She was a perfect child, I thought,
to write a poem about—
A sweeter child, I'd never met, so
this erased all doubt—
Laurie is a dainty child, so
delicate and nice—
And when the Lord let me know
her, I had to pinch me twice—
To make me realize that He, had
given me this treasure—
Just knowing this little girl, is
such honor and pleasure—
Wonderful children like Laurie
are, a joy to be around—
And one day she may know how
much, she is loved by this old
clown—
It was a pleasure, seeing Laurie,
up at her grandma's one day—
My friend Jamie, and I were
walking, and we saw Laurie at
play—
It was a treat, when Laurie said
yes, she would walk with us to
the store—
And I think now, Jamie has
found, a friend forever more—
She knew immediately, how nice,
Laurie seemed to be—
And so that walk, out to the

store, filled our hearts with
glee—
She has a little doll of a sister, her
name is Kristie, she's three—
And I wish they both could
know, how much they mean to
me—
Laurie will be eight this year, the
twenty fifth of July—
And I hope, this is the grandest,
birthday of her life—
As everyone should know by
now, I love this little girl—
And I have many, many little
friends, in this big world—
But none compete, with Laurie
Jones, my special little friend—
God bless you Laurie, and I hope,
to see you soon again.

I love you pretty girl
(always)

Jennifer Lee Kubis
LIFE'S ROSE BUSH
Life is like a rose bush
You are born with roots and a
home..
You begin to grow and sprout
Like a stem.
You run into experiences and
dead ends
Like the ends of leaves.
You feel pain and hurt
Like only thorns give,
But most of all
You have beauty and life
Like the flower we call a rose.

H. J. Riedemann
A PROMISE
A thing to give
And to admire
A thing to cherish
And not have broken
A thing of will
That follows a desire
A thing of reverence
And not of token

Susie Salisbury
SINS
Is it a sin to love someone with
every part of your heart?
Is it a sin for you and him to
never, ever be apart?
Is it a sin for you to cry when he
really makes you mad?
To cry when you know that your
relationship is bad?
Is it a sin to wish that his ex-
girlfriend was dead?
To think bad things about her,
that you wish could be said?
Is it a sin to forget about the
others, and wander off together?
To walk hand-in-hand together,
through the woods, no matter
what the weather?
Is it a sin to wait for the morning,
so you can be with him again?
To think that he is more special
to you, than a dozen other men?
To want to live your life with
him as your only pleasure?
And to think of him as your true
love and endless treasure?
To make sure that he'll never
walk out on you and leave you
broken hearted?
Because the last time you were in
love and split up, it really

smarted,
So, now, how many sins could
there ever possibly be—
When you're in love with
someone as special as he?

William J. Sanderson
BEVERLY

To my love, Beverly.

I would stay by your side,
Until time has ended,
For my love of you is
strengthened,
Whenever we are together.
I would awaken,
From the depths of slumber,
To stand quick,
At your defense.
I would defend you,
Until death,
For you, my lady,
Are worth defending.
If i must fight,
To have you,
With all my heart,
I would.
I would not be able to live,
Without you;
For you,
Are me life.

Nadine L. Smith
RAIN
Rain is such a quiet joy
It's happy—shimmering—clean
And since it's good to feel—oh
boy,
what fun to walk around in!

Sprinkles tumble and tease you
hardly getting you damp—
'cause soon as you've grabbed a
cover
for the rain—it's gone, the scamp!

Of course, there's all those heavy
drops
that fall and fall and fall
and like to start on your head
with plops
when you've no umbrella at all!

Sprinkles, showers, drizzles—all
and let's not forget the snow.
It's all designed precisely to fall
on flowers and people
alike—below.

Veronica Seeman
HOLIDAY

---

*This poem was inspired by my
boyfriend who made my life
worthwhile*

It wasn't a holiday without you.
Although I knew
where you are and what you do
It wasn't a holiday without you
The dinner was fine, even the
wine
but no one was mine.
It wasn't a holiday without you
I had a great time,
the people were kind
It wasn't a holiday without you.
We pulled our pranks, and said
thanks,
on the way home, no one knew
It wasn't a holiday without you!

Merritt Bradford
Iambic Pentameter to Fall
Behold! A streak of silver slips
From Andromedas flaming crown.
Myriad sparks from golden tresses,
Ply staid October's chilling frown.

Transilient beam pours placid light
On falls flamboyant tinge, as sight
Diffuse translucency in flight,
Ere Ariel's spirit rides the night.

Ne'er forget days that June has
spent,
Forging colors on yonder hill,
Within the mask of our content
'fore metamorphosis of chill.

When winter comes as sure it
will.
Spring dances at the door it
seems.
Phantasmagoric, lesser dream,
As flight within the Pleiades.

Time—space, give willingly to
me
As Atlas daughters, all the seven,
Make sure I sense the melody
Falling with colors from the sky.

Satty Joshua
FRIENDSHIP
Friendship is like
The morning sun that
Wades away the gloom of night;
Friendship is like
The showering rain
That waters the rosy buds of a
flower.

Friendship is Like
The blowing of the evening wind
That sends sweet kisses to a
green leaf.
Friendship is Like
A waiting beautiful hut
That meets a traveller's solitude.

Friendship is Like
The smiling face
That welcomes a darling's
presence;
Friendship is Like
A mother's arms
That welcomes a new born baby,

Friendship is like
The firmament
That shades the inhabitance of
the earth;
Friendship is like
The gentle hand
That nurses a patient's wound.

Friendship is forgiveness, its
reconciliation
Friendship feels the sadness
and sorrows of his friend.

Friendship is pure and divine,
Friendship is love.

Jean O. M. Young
AFTER THE RAINBOW
What waits for you after the
rainbow?
A pot of gold that will someday
decay
Or the Light that's stronger than
death?
At the end of your life, will you
say:
"I never knew the Master of Life"?
Never known what it is to be loved
By God himself?

Yes, God is love, the Creator of
all things
And many things there are . . .
Too much for one like me to
count . . .
At the very last moment I spend
upon this earth,
I desire to say to my Savior:
"Yes, I know you and that you're
great."
Then I want to see him smile a
smile
So radiant and happy as his joy
will
Well from my heart at the very
sight of him
To finally know there will be no
more
Broken hearts and shattered
dreams and
All I've never imagined will
become reality
In his beautiful presence.

Norma Long Hill
A TOUCH OF GRAY
Today he spotted the evince signs,
About the temple, a mote of gray,
And though it fitted his facial
lines,
He wished they'd go away.

Yesterday claimed a effervesce lad,
Whose boyhood pleasures are no
more,
Robbed a man of what he'd had,
In turn closed the childhood door.

He put away his childish things,
Became a man in ages book.
But sometimes inside a siren
stings,
For one little urchin the years
took.

If father time could only turn,
The beseeching hands of lorn time,
I'd fainly give this silver to burn,
For one golden strain so sublime.

David F. Graham
PEOPLE AND BIRDS
I was watching the birds in the air
They were flying without a care,
As if to say we are free
Cause we can do what we want
you see,
They don't have any laws to
abide
Cause they are free and living
outside,

But men are different in many
ways
We do different things
throughout the day,
One day we might walk or ride
around
The next day we might listen to
sound,
So you see we are different than
birds
Cause they make sounds and we
say words.

Dan Leavens
WOMEN
They fill my mind with tangled
thoughts
That grow more complex every day
Their plan, their life, I fathom not
Nor do I know my play.

To have such beauty and such
form

Seems bound to make, them true
But I wonder if the're Eve reborn
With exceptions very few

Nothing in this world can stop
Their smile, their word, their spell
They turn it on and mean it not
Or perhaps they do—how can
you tell?

Their bodies are of unmatched art
Their beauty known to all
They turn their head and do depart
Or you turn yours and fall

They change their looks and
mind
Their way of life and plan
Perhaps it's done to surely find
An answer to the thoughts of man.

Jackie Yvonne Powell
Love Never Separates . .
WHEN your in the wind with the
one you love, think of love
let it make you feel as tho
when
your hair blows
it's blowing your problem's
away.
WITH your brain sence the
vulnerability of the one you love,
feeling's. think ahead of the
future live life as, it, is
not the way you want it to be,
there may not be time when you
need it to say the thing's you
must to the one you trust.

WITH your eyes look into the
persons, you love are the one
closest to you show him or her
you will never take them for
granted, see the beauty
written in her eyes take
her by surprise, pull her closer
look deeper into the dept's
of her eye, you see the beauty
written there with
special care, the uglyness gone
that was never there, there in
the
heart is where it's at
something worth wanting
more than
life it's self.

WITH your nose
smell the perfume the sweetness
of the air of the one you care,
the person you love because
when your separated are lost
to
each other in a crowd just
look around you may

see her from afar to be sure
you smell the scent of the air
the sweetness and you'll never
separate from the one you
love.

WITH your lip's say the word's
they long to here to the one
that's dear, but with those
endearment's
you could part after saying
what was in your heart an
part
and alway's have those last
word's,

WITH your lip's with a gentle
touch to there's express your
feeling's to there fullest
effection, taste the
sweetness of her lip's with a
gentle touch to drink
so much of the sweet wine.
there you'll find you'll alway's
have to taste just in case
out in the desert you'll be like
a dying man
to drink of the other's lip's will
be enough to get you
through without any water.

WITH your chin nuzzle, nuzzle
the happiness from the other
without relic take what's
your's not what belong's to
the other.

WITH your shoulders nudge
the one you love a little so
they
will turn your way to look into
your eyes without
discise to look into your
eyes,
for comformation and clasp
then in a long embrase.

WITH your chest are breast
press the other to find the
warmth you need to proceed
to know that there
and close by, by your side the
warmth from the heart
spread's from the heart into
each other, you will need
that embrase when your
lonely and feel the pull
to be against each other.

WITH your arm's wrap them
tightly around the other to
keep
them from moving further
apart & to keep letting them
go when
tho, there is a life for you
both don't let
nothing stand in your way.

WITH your hand's feel the
need that expresses the
others feelings & to know if
he or she is
still breathing when your
hand touches the pulse
beneath, to know there, there
to touch & hold.

WITH your leg's you'll walk this
earth hand & hand
together even as two ship's
that pass by
night even at times alone as
you walk along,
you'll look back and remember

another pair of feet that
walked with you. Beside you to
guide you, till you seek the
the other pair again . .

With your feet that walks' the
damp dark earth
you'll touch the stones while
thinking all the while of
another pair of feet that walked
in beat with your
own, as your feet touches
another stone
& kicks' & along side stand's
another pair to walk
with you to see you threw it
all now you know as
was told,

LOVE NEVER SEPARATES . .

Gregory W. Jahne
Robin and the Blackbird
Choosing not the cardinal's crown,
In apricot panache,
Spring's meistersenger celebrates
As thawing life unfolds.

Nearby, gay blackbird's robe,
Casting shadows half its hue,
Dances through the meadows
As it plays its own sweet tune.

Together, side by side,
Perched in perfect paradox,
Both the robin and the blackbird
Somehow make a merry match.

Mollie Wasley O'Sullivan
PERSPECTIVE
Our own perspective
Makes us large or small
Limits us or
Deals us Infinity.

The cards that we receive
Into our hand are those
We have dealt ourselves
In our own mind.

Esther A. Flatley
THE GIFT OF LOVE

To Chuck

I tried for so long to deny love,
to keep people away because
love, as I had known it, meant
pain.

Then I met you.
You broke the impregnable wall.
I felt—for the first time.
I laughed, cried openly, shared
my deepest feelings with you;
let you see me as I really am.

Finally I was able to say "I Love
You"
and really mean it in my heart
and soul!

My love and faith in you is as deep
as my love and faith in God.
Nothing you could ever say
or do can change that!
Were you to marry another,
I would still love you.

My wish, my prayer, for you is
that you someday feel what I
feel;
if not for me, then for someone
else.

You cannot change me, nor I you.
I will forever love you, and I will

always be here for you should
you need me.

Your Gift of Love to me
is mine, for you, as well.

Sherry Lee Burris
VALUE OF TIME
Days are filled with endless tasks,
And schedules fixed to very
minute,
Time is sparse, so we must budget,
Then push it to the outer limit.

The object of the reason being,
Time used wisely we are told,
Is put to some constructive use,
To measure gain or obtain goals.

Yes, accomplishments will merit
praise,
Every dream may be secured,
Yet while along this path of haste,
Have you enjoyed or just endured.

Ever paused to see earth's beauty,
Sweetness of a songbird heard,
Cared about another's troubles,
Stopped to speak a kindly word.

Pondered life and all it's meaning,
Read a book, a poem or two,
Played along with little children,
Been alone just God and you.

Some might call it procrastination,
Perhaps say you idle way the day,
Nonetheless, time's found
awanting,
If some's not shared along life's
way.

James M. Bell
THE QUESTION
Oh yes,
we search and we search
always trying to find
a reason for living
and a reason for dying,
but search as we may
it seems so obscure
to ponder a question
which hasn't a cure.

Ms. Barbara (Ellis) Shook
THOUGHTS ON AGING
Will you love me years from now
When I hunger for your touch
When my sight is failing and my
hair is white
Will you love me quite so much?

Will you still turn my lips for
yours
And gently touch where fires
smoulder
Will you hold me tenderly
And rest my head upon your
shoulder?

Will you take my hand in yours
As we walk closely side by side
Will you walk beside me always
tall
Because of me—will you feel
pride?

Will you still call me to your bed
To fill me full of magic emotion
Will you caress me if I am
wrinkled
And let me love you when I take
the notion?

Will you hold my wilted breast
Long gone soft in faded years
Will you hold me just as tender
And kiss away my saddest tears?

Will you still want me very near
To be my friend in time of sorrow
Will you be my own true love
When alas—I wake up old
tomorrow?

———I wonder.

Lynn M. McClure
CHRISTMAS 1983

To: Lani Lowell III Kona & Terry

Time has passed and we all have
gone our own way,
But, here we are together to
celebrate Christmas Day.
We want to say to each of you
today,
Thank you for sharing with us
your holiday.
Words can not express our
feelings of love,
Dad and I are very happy and
thank God above.
So have a terrific time while you
are here,
If we can't be together, you will
be on our minds next year.
God bless you all now and forever,
We will always remember this
year together.

Miss Jeannette Allen
The Cry Of the Lonely

*To Dwight Wrenn—A friend
Forever—Thanks to his love and
friendship, I'm no longer The Cry
of the Lonely; And to the
Innovations Band—Thanks to
their music and voices for
making these lyrics into a
beautiful song. I Love You All*

When the lights go down at night
And the evening comes to be
The lucky people become pairs of
two
Except for Lonely me.
As they walk along hand in hand
The pain in my heart begins
I sit and gaze all around me
Wondering when my lonliness
will end.
Heartache and pain possessed my
soul
And this hurt you never knew
Someone else stood by your side
She replaced the memories of our
love from you.
Now I'm no longer your true love
Nor your friend I'll ever be
You betrayed within me my trust
for you
The day you replaced her for me.
To hear the Cry of the Lonely
Has only been witnessed by those
untrue
I became the Cry of the Lonely
The day I heard Good-bye from
you!

Elvira Jane McHugh
BEYOND WORDS
It's so very hard for me,
To write any words for thee.
For there's no words that can
express,
How much you've brought me
happiness.

And there's no way that I can say,
How much I've loved you every
day.
I cannot even understand,
When you reached and took my
hand.
Why, then, the world seemed all
okay,
And I looked forward to each new
day.
I wanted to reach out to you.
To know what made you sad and
blue.
To know what made you laugh or
cry.
To know the real reason why,
I feel for you the way I do,
And want to make you happy
too.
No, there's no words that can
express.
This special feeling of tenderness.
And so, I must leave un-said,
And you must also leave un-read.
The real things I want to say,
And maybe someday I'll find a way.

Karma Wagner
BRAINSTORM!
When I brainstorm,
I am creative.
The poems I form,
Sometimes help me to relive,
Happy moments of my life.
They dispose all strife,
Within my heart.
Writing is a creative art.

Brainstorming is fun,
Especially in the sun.
It is very enjoyable,
And quite reliable,
Just as if it were a friend.
Even at wits end,
Sitting in the sun,
After going for a run.

Having a brainstorm,
Is usually the norm,
(For me anyway).
It takes me away,
Into a dream
Of life's stream.
So if you enjoy being at home,
Just sit down and write a poem!

Cheri Collins
DEATH KNOCKS
I am dying tonight.
I feel no feeling, I think but one
thought.
I'm a thing in distress, a thing
that's distraught.
And then I grow weary, in stress I
grow weak.
And then my body racked with
pain.
Sharp stabbing in my chest.
And I am barely breathing.
I need a place to rest.
I wonder if I'm worthy, for God to
take me home.
Or will he forsake me, and let me
die alone.
But then appears my Lord of grace.
He layes his hands upon my face.
He understnads my feelings, my
thoughts are known.
No longer am I weary, frightened
or weak.
But now I know, it's death that I
seek.

He closes my eyes, at last sigh of
relief.
He's taken me with him, at last
I'm at peace.

Florence M. Musgrave
MESSIAH
I knelt beside the manger bed
Thinking I heard the baby cry . . .
So tenderly I raised his head
He smiled and sighed a gentle
sigh.

I still felt troubled and afraid
So looked again HIS face to
see . . .
And still a sobbing sound was
made . . .
Alas! The crying came from me!

Forgive me HOLY ONE . . . I tried
To understand your sigh!
But blinded by my foolish
pride . . .
I could not see . . . YOU came to
die!

Linda Mathison Braun
PREDATORS BY NIGHT

*Dedicated to Jason, Eric, and
Theresa Braun for discovering
Mom's vulnerability—the
invincible cockroach*

They scurry amid us
In the quiet of night
Their senses alerted
For immediate flight

Nestled in crevices
In the dampness and gloom
Beady eyes quite appalled
Of predators with brooms

So keen their perception
As daylight approaches
They scatter triumphant
Those clever cockroaches

Carole Shattuck
THAT SPECIAL DAY

*Dedicated to my friend Peggy
O'Donnel Without her help there
would be no poem. And Gail
Turner who's always an
inspiration.*

Jesus so pure and gentle and
sweet
Let the world put nails in his
hands and feet.
To redeem us all from deep
within
Jesus died on the cross to save us
from sin
The Christmas carols so bright
and gay
Remind us of that special day
So long ago on a day so still
Jesus rose from the dead
It was God's will
He ascended on a cloud
To the Heavens on high
Telling the world He would be
back by and by
To help your troubles to release
And guide you safely to Spiritual
peace
So open your heart to all the love
From the Father up above.

Jean (morris) Byers
SONG OF THE PINES
In a graveyard sweetly sleeping
    underneath a twin pine tree,
Are the ones we love so dearly on
    the banks of the Miramichi.
And the songs of birds so lovely
    as they make such music there,
Sometimes with a whip-poor-will
    note nesting robins in their hair.
Oh! the needles shimmering
    glittering in the sunshine in
    the shade,
Falling down to make a covering
    on the place where they are
    laid.
Do you hear the rustle of these
    pine trees as they o'er your
    watch do keep
Sad to say oh! no not yet for you
    right are fast asleep.
Once upon a time these pine
    trees were just young but had
    to go
Midst the summer's golden
    sunshine & admidst the ice &
    snow.
Now so lofty in your splendor
    with your branches all around
In the Autumn spread your
    needles tokens to that
    gravelike mound
Oh! dear pine trees keep your
    vigil on their gravel
    forevermore
Till the dawn of resurrection
    when sting of death will be no
    more.

Debi Tonkin
SUNSHINE

*Written for and dedicated to
Lester A. Snyder—whom has
always encouraged me to
continue writing.*

The day is full of gloom
Clouds hang up above
As the wind hits the house
And the rain drenches us all.
There's no chance for any
    sunshine
Only one opportunity for
    brightness
As I wait without any luck
For I need you to brighten my
    day.
The smile on your face
The sparkle in your eyes
The authority in your voice,
Three things I love about you.
If only one possession could be
    had
I'd want to possess all your love
Happiness would fill my life,
Knowing you were apart of it.

Linda Bowgren
SOLITARY LIFE
Each respects life in his own way
    Traveling many different paths,
Only to arrive at last one day
    Into a new, unexplored world.

For me, contentedly find
    Days and years slip gently away,
In health of body and of mind,
    Giving peaceful memories.

For me, slowly melt, and hence
    Into the sun become

Part of the vast silence
    Forever and a day.

So permit me live, unknown,
    unobserved,
    So unlamented permit me die,
Pass quietly this world, the
    next—no stone
    Show where I lie.

Joanne K. Pickles
DAY BY DAY
I'm walking on a tightrope
trying to see the sights,
but all I see is misery
in the eyes of the night.

Look at every person
and gaze into their eyes,
notice the tearful sadness
of loneliness and lies.

The dreariness of complexions,
the sadness of their smiles,
if you look all around you
you will see it for miles.

laughter seems like a sin
whenever you're in a crowd,
it's strange to see their faces
if you're walking tall and proud.

Maybe their searching for
    happiness,
but their going the wrong way,
if only they would understand
to take life Day By Day.

Harvey Gammon
I'm Always Picking Daisies
Fed children hours,
Led toward an open field of
    thought;
Smelling flowers
Bled
Whispers dead,
("(S)he loves me—(S)he loves me
    not.")
While picking his flowered head,
Her soft breeze blows each petal
Across their world collectively
    bred;
Built within ivory towers:
Here love is a constant proof,
A passion blooming in truth.
Life is a see-saw, ambition and lazy,
Alone
You'll find—I'm always picking
    daisies.

Misty Parker
TO A COCKFIGHT
Along the winding Brazos
As wintertime draws near . . .
"Let's go to the cockfights"
A common thing to hear.

Of in someone's pasture
Hidden by the trees
In a rustic, run-down barn
The bets are running free.

See the mighty, strutting cocks
The roosters, and the stags
Bright combs, and shining feathers
They hold them up like flags . . .

The flashing gaffs, strapped to the
    spurs
Like tiny knives, they shine
The thrill I get, just watching
    them
No other place, I find . . .

I win a few, I lose a few
Excitement always mounts . . .
It matters not which one I do . . .

It's playing the game that
    counts . . .

Arlene L. Philips

Arlene L. Philips
SHE IS

To Phyl A. Huenink

Her eyes light my path
Down starless roads
    At night.

An angel in my midst,
A true love in my soul.

Her lips are two silk petals
Of a sweet new-blossomed rose
    In spring.

Flowers and the seasons come
    and go
While we remain the same
    In love.

In mornings hush I hear her call
    my name.
I shall to her all divine pleasures
    bring—
    We live.

Alma Thurmond
I WANT YOU TO LOVE ME
I want you to love me,
I want to know that you are mine
And share my dreams with you
Until the end of time.

I want you to love me,
To walk thru this world by my
    side
And know that you'll be true,
    dear,
Your love's my one great pride.

I want to hold your hand
And tell you how much I care,
I want to look into your eyes
And see the love-light shining
    there.

I want you to love me,
Be a part of everything I do,
Darling, I want to kiss your lips
And give myself to you.

H. K. McPhee
TO DREAM

*I would like to thank my wife,
Beth, for her love, support, and
encouragement. This poem is for
you Beth. I love you.*

Mountains and streams, oh yes
    what a dream.

My head feels younger when I'm
    here it seems.
To fly over the hilltop as an eagle
    would do,
And soar through the heavens,
    the sky so blue.
Be perfect untouched by no one's
    cold hands.
To touch a still tree and embrace
    it as it stands.
Places so perfect are rare and are
    few.
Tell me somebody, oh, give me a
    clue.
I've looked for it here,
I've searched for it there.
Because it is gone,
I am left with despair.

Eric Diestelhorst
MY LIFE'S ROSE (L.J.)
I have a rose
With the beauty unmatched
By anything sought for,
Dreamed of, or catched.

I never knew it was
Winter with spring far away,
Until my rose came
Bringing an endless summer to
    stay.

Without a feeling of warmth
And a smiling glare,
My rose will die away
Feeling no one will care

So with me giving
A kind word with a feeling of
    warmth
Our love will grow
And will powerfully go forth.

Verlie J. (Tomasik) Ahnlund
MARCUS DUPREE

*For: Sons, William and Joseph
Tomasik (Sooner Fans) Lee
Ahnlund and Granson Eric J.
Normandeau*

Marcus Dupree
I run to the signal . . . bow to the
    sound
Dance to the whistle . . . grace the
    ground,
I dream of the me and long to be
    free,
Not like a lost feather; caught in
    the breeze
Dieing, dreaming highs of used to
    be.
I love to play ball, and feel the
    wholeness
That you see,
But Trophys and Glory get in the
    way
Of me.
Oh/just to live now, and See
Joyously.

Dawn Renee Goodman
BEREFT OF LOVE
A soft breeze blows on a fresh
    spring day
With flowers a bloom in the
    midst of May
On a garden walk I check my list
Of the things in life that I have
    missed.
And much to my startling
    surprise
I've been bereft of love through

all my lies.
Lies of fame and fortune too true
For my greatest need is only of
you.
A thirst for precious love so fair
As in my dreams beyond compare
A lust for companionship is all
too real
And I long to give all that I feel.
In solitude most of my life has past
My emotions are rarely cast
To learn of love and it's many
properties
To experience it, in all it's rarities.
A fantasy placed in the reality of
life
A realm of light in the darkness
of life
A fragile, frail, and tender thing
In joy, a gift for love to bring.

Barbara Wirkowski
MAGIC OF CHRISTMAS
Two thousand years ago, A little
Babe was born.
A little Babe named Jesus, born
on Christmas morn.
A little Babe so tiny and small,
but yet he is
the king of them all.
A little king which no one knew.
Except the angels high above.
The angels knew of this king,
who would bring only love.
Yes, The Magic of Christmas,
began on that day,
When that little king named
Jesus, came our way.

Barbara Wirkowski
LIFE
Life itself is very amusing and
curious, but at times very
mysterious. You may be happy
one day, and sad the next, and
at times very complex.

As you think and wonder how
fast the years go by, with every
new day, a new laugh, a new
cry. And so as I say to you, Life
is very short, so don't be a
prune, Be a sport.

Floyd Willoughby
TIMES CHANGES

---

*To Rennie, Marie, Forest and
Heather who share the
responsibilities of life and are
teacher's of its' joys.*

Oh simple leaf of tree
what is your magic key?
How do you in February Snow
Know it's time to bud and grow?

To change from limb of twigs
quite bare,
and blossom into beautys' flair.
Softly clinging to branches many
providing shelter for birds a plenty.

From white and amber fuzzy
cotton
to green leaves of summer—cold
forgotten.
Where children play beneath
your shelter
Summer fun of heat and swelter.

Oh! simple leaf of tree with past
forever will the quest be asked?

To viewers eyes a miracle of life
continued always through toil
and strife.
Leaf which flutters in the breeze
unconcerned with who you please.
In Mother Natures stature
Naked, piled in fall to be raked.

Annette Thomas (O'Connor)
I'LL ALWAYS LOVE YOU
Until the Sun turns it's face from
me;

Until the rivers overflow their
banks,
And flood the land.
Until I feel the Scars of Jesus'
Hand;

I'LL ALWAYS LOVE YOU

Until the birds have no tune to
sing me;
Until children find no joy in a
Nursery Rhyme.
Until the blossoms "forget" to
return at Springtime;

I'LL ALWAYS LOVE YOU

Until lovers have no sweet words
to whisper;
Until Time is but the numbers
on a clock;
Until all the ships "set sail", no
more to "dock"

I'LL ALWAYS LOVE YOU

Until you tell me that there is
"another";
Until words, alone, can-not
"recall" the "pain";
Until you beg me to "forgive" you,
And vow that you won't return,
again—

EVEN THEN:

I'LL ALWAYS LOVE YOU

B. A. Jason
LOVE
Love comes to all who seek it
for it is found everywhere
In the flower, in the fruit, in the
stream,
in a bird, in the rock, in a friend
It is always there
waiting to be discovered.

In the flower it is fragrance
in the fruit it is flavor
In the stream it is movement
in the rock it is texture
In the bird it is song and
in the friend it is soul.

Viola C. Sharpe
THUNDERSTORM
God was Putting on his special
show
Using the most brilliant of lights
to outline clouds
In purples! blues! reds! whites!
Suddenly . . . a SONIC BOOM ! !
shattering nerves, frightening
birds!
Zigzaging flashes of light
cascaded all around.
Then . . . ROARING Thunder
shook the ground.
Hearts pounded, children
were heard to cry,
As God continued lighting
up the sky.
A RUSH of wind brought pouring

rain
And all at once . . . t'was calm
again.

Rolene E. Thomas
**A Tribute To a Friend . . .
"Naomi"**

---

*To Naomi McCullough, whose
friendship and special caring has
made all the difference.*

If only once in my travels here I
find a friend so true
And if only one friend was
allowed to each,
I'd want her to be like you.
For a special friend to share with
me in open honest ways
all the things we've shared since
we first met
have brightened many days.
The special friend that welcomes
you with a smile that says
"I care"
Is a treasure worth far more than
gold;
A jewel beyond compare.
When days are bright, you share
my song. When great, you
share my shout,
and when life's gone wrong, and
I'm feeling down,
You come in, when the rest's
gone out.
We've shared our thoughts, our
dreams and hopes
and memories of good old days
We've shared our loves and loses
we've worked and talked and
played.
You've been a friend . . . you've let
me be
to find my own struggling way
But when I needed help from a
caring friend
I've found you not far away
And as life goes on, if our paths
divide,
and we travel different bends,
Neither time nor miles will erase
the bond,
For you're a
once-in-a-life-time-friend!

Karla Wright
THE SHELL
I crawled in a shell and hid for
over a longer
than a skyride through the park
time,
fell asleep inside my shell
rolled over and the dark crept in,
I held in all the silent tears,
I dreamed inside that someone
would come along
and pull me loose from these
walls and make me find myself,
and move out from my shell,
brush the sand from my skin and
the salt from my hair, and my
eye lashes
that were closed over my eyes
from the spray of the ocean
inside my shell,
open the door to the light outside
slowly, and start me breathing
again,
gather wisdom from your
strength to come alive

and learn to laugh,
stand out from everyone else
become my own person,
with my one room trips, my own
design on life,
my honest fantasy that changes
with the turning
of the sun around the earth,
my friend stands out there to
catch all my drifts
so I won't be disappointed and
call for the glue
to put my shell back together
again.

Anthony Realini
ALPHA Y
"I am Alpha and Omega, the
beginning and the ending,"
saith the Lord.
—Rev. l:8

Alpha Y

The Way,
Its eternal membrane
The center of its mind,
Yet also Its border;
For in Itself
It finds another,
Singing out,
The way It does;
The Way.

Jesus saith unto him, "I am the
way, the truth, and the life . . ."
—John 14:6

Marlene Hankin
FANTASTICAL ESCAPE
For a brief moment, I shall
Dance by the whipped-sugar sea,
Whispering low sweet murmurs
To a kissing soft breeze . . .
Toeing over the sharp-fluted
shells,
Daintily patterning the moist,
spongy sand,
Tugging the ropes of a harbored
ship's bell,
Playing trilled tunes of mimsy
and flimsy,
Chanting, all is well . . . all is
well . . .

Teka Marcet Twilling
SEASONS
I recall a summer day I strolled
along a stream whose water
glistened
As it passed o'er pebbles flecked
with gold. Then in the fragrant
grass I laid and listened
To the waters bubbling melody,
and heard the wind play its
music through the trees.
I listened to a symphony, and
though no word was uttered, it
proclaimed, "The world's at
peace!"

Then there was the golden
autumn morn I sat beside the
sparkling lake in rapt pleasure
And watched a masterpiece of
God be born. The trees were
brushes, which at their leisure
Would lift thinning branches to
the skies and paint with swift
strokes of leafy color
A portrait of life as seen through
His eyes; and I was the lucky
beholder.

Or the winter noon I stood alone
in the field, silently wrapped in
a white blanket of snow.
As I watched the soft flakes fall
they did yield a marvelous
dance; a wondrous show!
Each shimmering flake danced so
light and so free, yet each
having a purpose to render.
That day I knew I was privileged
to see a ballet of magnificent
splendor.

And the warm spring day on a
grassy hill I witnessed with
smiles and with tears
The opening act of a play that
would thrill and amaze me all
of my years.
The birth of a flower awakening
to life, the death of the old oak
in the stand
Are merely roles in this drama of
Strife and Serenity penned by
the Almighty's hand.

Joyce F. Gaulden
MY LOVE TO JESUS
Jesus I love you more
With each passing day
And nothing shall separate me
From your loving, caring way

Not the love of money
Or the love of man
Nor any other power
Jesus, you're in command

Not anything in life
Or anything in death
Shall ever separate me
From the one who gave breath

Not anything above
Or anything beneath
Can hinder my love of God
Or change it in the least

Yes, Jesus I love you
With each passing day
And nothing shall separate me
From your loving, caring way.

Jonathan Dobbs
PROSPEROUS TIMES
I awoke this morning and gazed
beyond the window
The birds, they played for the sun
was in the sky
I looked to see the flowers giving
thanks
I saw the waves upon the banks
They beckoned me, they spoke to
me
My heart responded
My spirits rose, my worries froze
My mind and soul, they bonded

Elijio Juarez
LITTLE LOVES
This world for us has gone astray,
Since your mother went away.
Little loves how things started.
Many times you have departed . . .

Little loves are you lonely?
Little loves your so far away.
How I pray for you only.
I pray you'll be back someday.

Cause my heart is still breaking,
since that day you were taken . . .
Somethings happening to my
mind,
cause I can't have you, and your
mine.

Little loves are you happy, are
you well?
Let me dream of your smile so I
can tell.
Always's be good when your with
her.
Please let's pretend we're all still
there . . .

Valerie J. Schwontkowski
Reflections On a Bridge
An old stooped man paused
beside me
on the bridge in the park.
I felt the cold steel railing move
as he pressed his weary body
against it
and sighed,
And we stood silently as our
thoughts
fell together into the water,
swept away by the stream below
us.

Virginia Welch Bode
PRIVILEGE OR DUTY
A friendship is a privilege to share,
Never a duty for a friend to bear.
Unless Teaching is a privilege all
year long
To this profession the teacher
doesn't belong.
Unless doctoring is a privilege for
him,
Few may consider him a genuine
gem.
Unless your vocation is a
rewarding job,
Doubtfully will you be labeled a
nabob.
If your home is a privilege
beyond compare,
Happiness radiates toward a
wonderful pair.
If your marriage is a privilege to
bear,
You're richer by far than any
millionaire.
When a child's curosity is
nurished by one
The greatest privilege under the
sun.
When it's a privilege to assist one
in distress
The various goals conquered
shall be the test.
To be real in all that we choose
The stress of duty is what we
lose.

Edgar J. Willmott
LULLABY
Hush, my darling,
don't you cry,
I'll always be with you
there by your side,
have no fear of what tomorrow
may bring,
rest, relax and to you
a lullaby I'll sing;
so sleep will come swiftly
softer than down,
and the stars when they appear
from them
I'll make you a crown.

The moon
I'll have bathe you
in its gentle glow,
and my love, my darling,
will always
surround and protect you,

as over the years it will steadily
grow.

Jon Michael Stark
DISILLUSION
Strangled in an absurd reality,
corrupt with modern wit and
wisdom,
terror rips through the black
night of my kingdom.
Eons of nothing—nothing yet
discernable—
filter through the gravely stretch
of fibre
then tumble to the rocks like a
bare-backed skydiver.
Crazed, (could be a sinking
flagship),
spinning from the bottom up,
machinations shatter my church-
like hut.
Screaming, twisting, whirling in a
foreign world,
Windowpane slips through the
cells
into a beautiful sunlit hell.
Tumblers spin, my eyes burgle
the trepid waters of a lost
horizon,
and the sky crashes like glass.
Down, down to the death we had
our eyes on.
Rip, tear, split my glacial tomb.
Wandering voices echo tenfold.
I thought they had passed.
I thought I could last.
Disillusion.

Christine L. Allen
THE OTHER ME

---

*I dedicate this poem, WITH
LOVE TO MY MOTHER, for all
the support, encouragement and
understanding she has given to
me over the years.*

Creep into my room
let the darkness be my guide
Surrender all my dreams
nothing left to hide
Lying all alone
a chill sweeps up my spine
I do not speak with words
only with my mind
All my private thoughts
with only you I share
Speak none to the others
only if I dare
They could not understand
how could they possibly see
The person they saw last night
that was . . . The Other Me

Dolores Howe
HOLIDAY CHEER
The gang at the office lifts their
glasses high
To wish the joy of the season to
every one.
They've dragged through the old
year by just getting by.
Now they can't wait 'til the new
year's begun.

No matter that the last year was
very sad.
This one will be different; Just
you wait and see.
Each one has ordered a dream or
two or three,

And hopes to live in complete
harmony.
Be that as it may—this I know is
very true.
If they make some excellent
resolutions,
Their chances will improve one
hundred percent,
And they will be happier when
next year's due.

Betty Cutler Litten

Betty Cutler Litten
ONE BY ONE

---

*My poetry is dedicated to my
children, Joyce, Harvey, Janice,
Eileen, Harry, Diane, and Bruce,
my grandchildren Michael and
Phillip Gold, Jason and Allison
Zeisler and Stacey and Michael
Litten, my parents, Mr. & Mrs. P.
Cutler, and Herman Rosen.*

The rain that falls on me is
mine . . .
I lick it from my thirsty lips and
witness the remote design
around me of the pelted grass.
I cannot sip the total flood but
taste the fracture of a drop . . .
while every river runs to sea
I stand still as earth bound
rock.

Mertie Elizabeth Boucher
Within the Secret Depths
Within the secret depths of each
being lies a power
So unique, so indestructible, so
magnetic, so constant,
So contagious that a tiny spark
can set the world afire
Uniting all peoples, spreading
great joy!
Peace reigns!
This power is love! Man's greatest
gift!
Man's greatest need!

Love travels silently, within a
smile, a whisper,
Or a touch, on the breath of the
breeze,
In all things good and
beautiful . . .
More forcefully through words of
wisdom and truth,
Through melody, in noble or in
kindly deed
Providing man strength
As this power of love is freed!

Can this power of love be the electricity of Life?
Peace? Liberty?

Margarita de Enden
Don't Hate—Be Leaders In Peace!

Americans, born from all races, rich or poor you should be as proud as eagles and falcons
Swinging their wide wings into the air circling over your beautiful countryside,
Strong as the mountain lion ruling high up in the cliffs, powerful as the bear still alive everywhere,
Beautiful as all your flowers, bushes, and trees should be your soul.
Peaceful as all newborn—humans, animals, birds, all creatures on earth—should be your mind.
Educated geniuses from all races you should lead us again
Nice friendly and helpful to each other you should be.

Praying for peace on earth, you should kneel down talking to God, saying
"Spare us—we will be good—no longer hateful, Lord! From now on we will be kind to each other
And say to the devil in our minds, 'Get lost with your HATE!'" or crime soon will destroy all of us.

WE ARE ALL AMERICANS.

We will make our U. S. A. to be the most powerful country in the whole world again.
"Bless us, Lord, give us strength and wisdom to do right."

We never recognized until now how blessed we are, being born in one free rich beautiful country
Where there has been no tread of war for more than one hundred years.
"God help us to fulfill our dream to be great and loved again ALL AROUND THE WORLD."
Amen.

Ruth Tinney
MY FIRST GRANDCHILD

My grandson, Charles, has since departed this life. He was only with us twenty years, but left a life time of beautiful memories that death or time can never take away. The wonderful times we shared together will never be 1958—Oct. 1979)

I had just finished my Christmas shopping one cold December day
And returned to my country home just over the way.
My son's wife met me at the door, and grimly said
"The stork is on his way, and this time he will not be delayed."

So off to the hospital we went as fast as we could go
We weathered the storm for there was lots of snow
About twenty minutes after eleven
God dropped us a bundle direct from heaven.
You can imagine how our hearts leaped with joy
When the Doctor said it's a fine baby boy.

My heart was pounding and running wild
As I waited to see my first grandchild
It wasn't long until the nurse arrived
And layed the precious dear by his mother's side.
As the nurse left the room she gave us a tender smile
We all gathered up very close to gaze awhile.

At this precious little bundle so fresh and sweet
That God has so generously layed at our feet.
And a voice soft and low with a tender tone
Said with this bundle I've given you a glimpse of the unknown
And no joy on earth could ever compete
With the joy we shared with this baby so fresh and sweet.

Carolyn E. Mears
I Give To You The Spring

Oh my love, I give to you
Morning roses beaded with dew.
A starburst sun breaking the haze
Budding leaves, warm spring days.

We once were those budding leaves,
We grew together as do the trees.
A gurgling stream of emerald water drops
Fed our love that still never stops.

Ah, a never-ending winding spring,
I see us laugh in it's light reflecting.
Each shimmering speck remembers a hue
Of the colorful life I spent with you.

Your words come to me on the chauffeuring breeze,
Your voice becomes the rustling leaves.
I know you're still near when I listen to you,
So I offer roses beaded with dew.

I place them on your eternal bed,
With emerald water drops they're fed.
Their beauty comes not from water though;
Spring they seek, eternal spring you soe.

Oh my love, I give to you a tear.

Elizabeth Soboslay
Comtemplation Of A Rose

A delicate bud with unbounded mysteries;
Cautiously it unfolds, displaying depth and warmth—
Beauty from a single, minute part of nature.
"Tomorrow I will pluck this wondrous mystery—

I will reveal my love slowly, as this flower;
Tomorrow I will rise, bringing my rose to you."
A thousand Tomorrows have passed us slowly by.
I've waited in silence, hoping for the right words,
And through all the delays, this flower has survived.
But—
Today, I plucked our flow'r—
Once in my hand,
It died.

Donna L. Sanchez
25 Silver Years Together

Mom and Dad . . .
    I've learned the feeling of trust, the feeling that togetherness brings, the feeling of peacefulness when you hold me in your arms, and the heartfelt feeling of love—knowing today, tomorrow, and forever you're always a part of my life.
        Most important—
Mom and Dad . . .
    Is the love I see you share, the joy and fullfillment that you bring each other. Your love doesn't depend just on being together—it is much deeper—a certain closeness inside that is always there, a comfortable and warm feeling—a lifetime friendship.
        25 Silver Years . . .
        you've spent together—
        it's just the beginning
        of a life time to share,
        forever a love,
        forever a perfect pair.
        Happy 25th Anniversary! !

Joyce F. Gaulden
IN OUR DIVORCE

I can remember your smile
And the sparkle in your eye
When you wanted to be with me
And I knew the reasons why

Somehow we became so wise
That our feelings grew cold
Now we find ourselves apart
In heart, mind, body and soul.

Elaine J. Motes
MOTHER

Dedicated to Clydell James and Ethel Motes, inspired by a mother's love.

Loving arms that hold me
    Precious lips that scold me
A sweet hand that guides me
    A reassuring word reminds me
There is no other
    Like my precious mother.

Dale E. Shattles
THE ARTISTS

A backhouse sags
On the boarded side
Where artists
Burn-out.

The night dreamers
Often come to her house
As art students
Of certain surrealisms.

There's never much talking
Or eye-color looking.

Just art,
Simple,
As the active people
Finger-paint their world.

Deborah Lynn Roberts
NO WHERE TO HIDE

For whatever day you're blue,
Or if everything seems to be like a review.
Pull out this little message I wrote for you.
Because life is hard and cruel,
No one has the right to ridicule.
So stop and think,
Before you judge; for who's to say!
We all have someone to obey.
There must be answers,
Why everything is this way.
If I want them to change,
I will change them and learn the way.
For thats part of life, that we all live.
Life will go on whether we're happy or sad,
The route is ours to choose.
We will have to answer to all the dues,
So whatever awaits,
Don't leave it up to fate.
Change them to how you want things,
And make it a happy day!!

Connie Ramey
SPEARATED

I know that we are separated
By many days walking
But distance can never weaken our relationship
For what is in our minds and hearts
Is stronger than any outside force
And when we are together again
Our relationship will be
That much more intense and beautiful

Mike Talbert
WORLD UNREAL

Painted their smiles on plastic faces
Nowhere people from empty spaces
Touching someone who cannot feel
Water colored the world unreal
Realtiy is a dream that never ends
A dream seems real to the heart that bends
Nothing is just what it really seems
You cannot swim the make-believe streams
Artificial grass on the man-made feilds
Fake seed sown on ground that never yields
I watch cotton candy clouds going by
Hoping to wake before the paper doves fly
Shades of gray are the rainbows I see
An unreal world where no one can be
Tin-foil chrome are the wheels of time
Story-book words are the poets rhyme

413

Dr. Ambrocio Lopez
A Most Elderly Pair

This poem is especially dedicated to the one that I truly love

He limped just ahead, and she
walked behind,
    Their pace was so even, steady,
    and timed,
Soft snow all around, breath
clouds chill the air,
    Slowly they moved, a most
    elderly pair.

He carried a cloth sack, she
shopping bags,
    Their shoes minus laces,
    dressed all in rags,
So wrinkled their skin, so silver
their hair,
    Slowly they moved, a most
    elderly pair.

The streets were quite empty,
late was the night,
    Windows all rainbows, a
    prism's delight,
He gave her a glance, a smile they
did wear,
    Slowly they moved, a most
    elderly pair.

The house for orphans lay one
block away,
    All were asleep, for tomorrows
    the day,
Through the gate, up the steps,
each had their chair,
    Slowly they moved, a most
    elderly pair.

A candle was lit, to help with
their chore,
    He rubbed her hands, shadows
    danced on the door,
Out came toys and dolls, each
handled with care,
    Slowly they moved, a most
    elderly pair.

The gifts were placed neatly, all
standing tall,
    A joy for each child, one
    hundred in all,
Lastly, their hands fluffed an old
Teddy Bear,
    Slowly they moved, a most
    elderly pair.

Gently they kissed on the bench
in the park,
    Two tears by moonlight,
    together one heart,
The blanket had holes, and
needed repair,
    Slowly they moved, a most
    elderly pair.

Dawn brought Angles with a
note from above,
    Nothing is greater than the gift
    of Love,
And Love is something which we
must all share,
    Slowly they moved, the most
    elderly pair.

Julie Dee Elmer
MY LITTLE WHITE SHOES
I bought a pair of little white
shoes.
Because they were so comfy and
clean.

Little did I know, my little white
shoes.
All the wonderful places they
have seen.

Through the streets of Paris,
these shoes carried me,
Through Copenhagen and even
Helsinki.

In Nice, Stockholm, Amsterdam
too,
My little white shoes had a big
job to do.

Venice, Vienna, Frankfurt and
Rome,
My little white shoes are now on
their way home.

My little white shoes aren't white
anymore.
My little white shoes are old
dirty and worn.

My little white shoes,
Many places they have been.

But my little white shoes aren't
little,
They are really size 10!

Judy Sellers

Judy Sellers
VELVET SWING
I came upon an apple tree, and
hanging from it was a swing,
with velvet rope and velvet seat
it was the loveliest ever seen.

So I climbed aboard and kicked
my heels
soon found myself in tall green
fields,
the sky was high, the bump was
far
soon found myself on a street car.

There were no windows, there
were no floors,
no happy folks, no jokes, no words,
soon found myself flat on the
ground
with one sprained ankle by the
john.

From there to venture for many
days
"east or west" I could not say,
soon found myself on my way
home
to a place I've never really
known.

To here, to there,
through if and when,
sure hope my chance
we meet again.

Kimberly D. Triol
**We Must Fall Before We
Can Start Over**

*Dedicated to my dear friend
Linda A. More. You've shown me
how to pick myself up after a
defeat and start again, a problem
is never too difficult to overcome.
Thank you for your love, and
most of all your never ending
friendship.*

I watched a small child climb the
stairs today.
    One
        By
            One.
S—L—O—W—L—Y placing one
foot at a time
    awkwardly upon the steps.
He reaches out grabbing for the
    rail seeking stability.
The fifth step lies ahead.
Reaching the sixth, he stops to
    rest for a while.
    Onward he must go.
He looks up almost in despair,
    (It's such a long way.)
7, 8, 9.
    A smile forms in one corner
    of his mouth.
    His face is now lit up with joy.
10, 11, 12
    Only a few more.
13, 14 . . .
    He grabs for the rail, gasps,
    makes an effort to regain his
    footage.
It's no use—he is falling
    Tumbling
    D
        O
            W
                N
                    W
                        A
                            R
                                D.
Sitting on the cold ground,
    stunned, looking through hazy
    eyes he rises and once again
    attempts this difficult test.
    One
        By
            One.

Kate Russell
INDEPENDENCE

*Dedicated to my mother, with
thanks, for passing along her
sense of strength and
determination*

To be behind the scens,
    and mending his jeans,
was all, I thought, that I wanted.
Now I feel so sure
    that there's something more
to my life's plan than that.

Shall I proclaim guilt,
    and label me selfish,
or feel relief to admit the truth?
Shall I fight that urge that lives
    within to seek and to discover,
especially when the fears arise of
    what I might uncover?

What if I stumble,

what if I fall,
or regret my choosing
    independence?
Those "what ifs" are only
    inside me created,
and just as readily abated.

Shirley P. Davis
TO A FADED ROSE

*In memory of our mother, Rev.
Sis. Janie Perry*

Hey Mama, I see you sitting there
    with your
    Back facing me,
Your shoulders all bent, and your
    head bowed
Down, as if you carried the
    weight of
A thousand pounds.
    Mama, I see your face as you
    slowly turn
Around.
    The lines of time crown your
    brow, as weights
Of sorrow slowly weigh you down.
    But Mama, I can still see that
    once you were
A beautiful rose: so vibrant and
    bright in the
    Garden of life.
But, because of the vase, the
    picker has put you
    In your growth has been stunted,
And the food of love has been
    denied, and
Sometimes given in short supply.
But, Mama, you are still a rose.
    It has been said, "A rose by any
    other name
Would still smell as sweet."
    A rose, a rose, Mama, you are
    still a rose.

J. Crockett-Lambson
FOUR ROSES

*For my husband, Swede" who
grows beautiful roses and enjoys
each one, from first to last.*

I see four roses in a vase
The little vase of mauve and gold
That I brought back from Canada
        Ten years ago.

The roses are not the prettiest
        I've ever seen
Velvet petals of cerise and pink
    One yellow and one white
The leaves a tattered green.

I cling to their fragrance
And relish them o'er and o'er
They are very special roses
As this is late October
        And frost is near
These are the season's last
        My lovely roses four.

And so it is with life
As days are shortened fast
Like a child eating cake
We save the frosting for the last.

Fred Whiteley
MA'S HAT
We were sitting around the table
    in a friendly little chat
Discussing all the family in their
    wants of this and that
When Ma says, I forgot to tell
    you, I was down the town today

And the cutest little hat you ever
saw in a window on display
So I went right in and tried it on;
it fit me to a tee
And you will be astounded when
you know what it cost me!

Ye "God's" said Pa, another one,
that must be nine or ten
Yes, I agree, said Ma, but after all,
you are all alike you men
I have to keep in fashion with the
latest style and mood
And what with all your talking, I
think you're being rude.

I'll try it on Ma said, and tell me
what you think
And as she put it on to show, you
should have seen Pa blink
A hat you said, is that a hat, well
land of mercy sake
They're getting worse, I tell you,
those hats they try to make
And if that hat I had to wear, I
think I'd rather die
But I knew that Pop was kidding,
for he winked and gave a sigh.

Mary Iola Roussin
DID YOU EVER WONDER
Did you ever wonder why the
grass is green,
And why people dream?

Did you ever wonder why the
snow is white,
And why we always fight?

Did you ever wonder why a bird
can fly,
And why our love had died?

Did you ever wonder how it rains,
And what is pain?

Did you ever wonder why the
sun is hot,
And why our love is not?

Did you ever wonder why the sky
is blue,
Well I wonder why,
  I Love You.

Cindy L. Kindig
ONLY IN MY MIND
  Everytime that we are together,
I know tomorrow can only be
  better.
  Being with you gives me a
  natural high,
And I wish we never had to say
  good-bye.
  When you look at me that way,
I only have one thing to say:
"Come take my hand,
And we'll find our promise land."
  When I lay next to you,
I see all the great things we can do.
  Still I know that you are only in
  my mind!
But maybe someday I will find;
  Someone to love me, too;
The way I do love you!

La Nae L. Cavros
I Was A Child Once, Too
Angelique and Carinna
are the most beautiful words I
  know—
With eyes forever sparkling
and faces all aglow.

Every once in a while
their behavior will be bad;

Then I get myself all upset
and sometimes, try to pretend I'm
mad.

Generally, they try to act
pretty goll darn good.
The absolute truth of the matter
  is
there are times I wonder if they
  could.

They go through their moments
when they seem to shut their ears;
But when "candy" or "ice cream" is
  said
they just happen to be right here!

I am forever thankful
that my children have their health.
It's of the utmost importance—
other people can have their wealth.

God has truly blessed me!
Lord, I do thank you!
I have to tell myself time and
  again—
I WAS A CHILD ONCE, TOO!

Susan Lynn Burkholder
REVENGE
Death, oh how I hate you, I'll
  destroy you someday,
you'll be powerless soon if I have
  my way.
Cancer, poison, diseases and
  others will no longer be
harmful to my sisters and
  brothers.
Death, my enemy, you have
  taken from me all and all those
who were mine have heard
  your call.
You've driven my beloved God
  and I apart, causing pain,
leaving throbbing anger to surely
  drive us insane.
Death, you are like Satan, you
  sneak up from behind I guess
you're feeling powerful since
  you've conquered all that's mine.
But someday there will be a time
  when you will be off guard,
and I'll stab you from behind,
  driving the nails so hard.
I watched you destroy the others,
  taking their last breath,
So be prepared to take a fall, I'm
  talking to you, Mr. Death,
So put on your black funeral
  gown and say goodbye to all
cause now it's my turn for
  revenge, hell to one and all.

ElAyne Marie Zelmer
HE IS MINE!

*I'll stand behind you when you
need strength, next to you when
you need a friend, but never in
front of you to stand in your way.*

My thoughts go deep when I write.
Sometimes my silence tells him
  more than my words.
But he encourages me to express
  my feelings, and when they're
  tears he kisses them away.
Because he knows the tears only
  assure that he is loved.
His arms around me make me
  feel secure.
His smile warms my heart.

He tells me what's on his mind
  knowing I'll try to understand.
He notices the little things like a
  tear drop on a page.
He doesn't give me beautiful
  roses because he is expected to.
Sometimes the reason goes
  unsaid.
But the love I feel for him will
  never be unspoken.
He is my strength when I am
  weak.
He is my security when I am
  insecure.
He is my understanding when I
  am confused.
He is my friend.
He is my love.
He is my future.
He is mine!

Carl Allen Ward
MISCONCEPTION
Got a roach-clip on my collar,
Got two fifty-dollar bills.
Got a hash-pipe hangin' from my
  belt,
And a pocket full of pills.
My blue jean vest and pants are
  patched,
My hair stands out in curles.
How come I get the strangest
  looks,
From all the "Pretty" girls?
My leather hat is scratched and
  scarred,
And soaked with rain and sweat.
My goucho boots have holes in
  them,
Where there ain't been none yet.
Got a pinjoint stuck behind my
  ear,
A Thai-stick in my shirt.
An earring on my left earlobe.
They still won't let me flirt.
My moustache and my beard are
  long,
And shaggier than most.
My eyes have grown the large
  crowsfeet,
Of too much overdose.
I haven't bathed in fourteen
  months,
Nor combed my tangled hair.
Yet I can't seem to find a girl,
Who'll do much more than stare!

Bruce E. Gearheart
**I Have Dreamed I Loved
You**

*To Margie, my wife, who
understands that the dream is
what makes the heart grow
fonder when the out of sight
seems slipping out of mind.*

I have dreamed I loved you,
But I could never dream
Your love.

In my dream I have touched you,
But I could never dream
Your wish to please.

In my arms you have pleased,
But I could never dream
Your peace

Soon I will be home
And we will never dream
Apart.

Bruce E. Gearhart
County Fair Sulky Race

*To Margie, my wife, who knows
how much fun it is to win.*

Sulky racers slither past
Tippy-toe in rhythmic pace.

Fierce precisions's proper gait
Optimizes the straightaway.
"Excuse my pass,
  I need your space."
"Break stride horse,
  And you've breathed your last."

Anne McCallum
WHAT IS HE?

To my son Malcolm

What is he?
Our Western World asks.
Is he a scientist, pilot, engineer,
A musician or electrician,
A high finance man or professor?
Does he make money?
Our efficiency oriented
Status-oriented
Society
Demands to know.

What is he?
Now, go ask a Mother,
Who searches deeper in the man.
She sees a hand reach a wounded
  brother,
Awe and respect for Planet Earth,
A community worker,
A loving father,
And a caring,
Thoughtful, son.

Blythe Foote Finke
United Nations Inspired
The United Nations may seem
  evil,
Something like a bad bollweevil,
But remember it has some style,
And should stay around awhile.

Many resolutions the UN does
  pass,
Presumably to help the poor mass,
Yet each day it seems much
  weaker,
And ever so much more mild and
  meaker.

Out of an UN once in awhile
  does come,
An especially good little positive
  plum,
Of Needed assistance to the
  world's needy,
Often at the mercy of the terrible
  greedy.

In UN debates the Americans try
  to mediate,
The Russians only seem to want
  to deviate,
The Chinese would just as soon
  alleviate,
And the Third World just has to
  accommodate.

Down on the second floor
  diplomats' lounge,
UN diplomats from 158 memer
  states scrounge,
For the latest news and top secret
  scandal,

To negotiate with each other, or
the enemy vandal.

The United Nations is a peace
palace,
To Don, Jack, Bill, Jim, May and
Alice,
But for all of us it is so much more,
It would be foolish just to shut
the door.

Thomas P. Stefanucci
FRIENDS AND LOVE
Feeling alone, depressed, and
scared
the common ways,
we enter here.
For new beginnings,
and end to tears.
In strength from each other,
we conquer our fears.

Feeling warmth,
a touch of hands.
Speaking soft, discussing plans,
assuring friends,
passing times sands.

Feeling our hearts,
some pounding with pain,
falling in parts,
tears come like rain.
Friends giving love,
putting back the remains.

Angela M. Ikemire
A Dream of Peace
Sitting here alone I dream
Of happy, caring hearts;
And things beyond reality
That precious love imparts.

A dream of peace and beauty is
A dream so far from home
But yet, not found beyond the
fence
No matter where you roam.

How carefully we play with words
And say not what we feel.
Yet carelessly we play with swords
As though all risk unreal.

If all we gave was all we had
More generous we'd be.
But still, we give not quite enough
The slaves of mind to free.

With so-called courage, one
exclaims:
"For peace the stone is hurled!"
But yet knows not this is no way
To make peace in the world.

Harold E. J. Friedrichs
A SALUTE TO THE TREES

*To my beloved 3rd Cousin, Karen
Schultz*

The trees!, the trees!, the trees!
The towering trees
Lofty monarchs of the forest
The stately towering trees

Trees have majesty and grandeur
Their boughs varying in
thickness and in length
They recall to us the grandeurs of
nature
And impress us with the strength

Birds nestle in the trees,
slumbering from dust till morn
Comes the dawn they awake to
sing their many songs

While squirrels scrambling up
and down the branches
Chatter and impart curious
glances
Trees of the temperate deciduous
forests
And the enchanted parklands
Tell a most idyllic story
In their sublimity and glory
In Autumn the leaves begin to fall
Turning from green to yellow and
brown; or they lie upon the
ground
The awesome splendor of the
falling Autumn leaves
Whirling and twirling with the
crisp frolicking wind
As they tumble down from the
trees.
To renew their growth in Spring
When the ice melts in the pond
and the birds return to sing.
And Mother Nature renews the
life cycle once more
Fecund and fertile as before.

Gerard Brown

Gerard Brown
**A Christmas Song . . . For
Daddy's Little Girl**

*In Loving Memory Of Patricia
Brown*

The little hammering is quiet now
The little fists are gone
Hide and seek is fun no more
No more the squeals and giggles
Teddy bear is lonely
Cricket doesn't sing
Mickey mouse stopped smiling
And Christmas morning is empty
No fingerprints on the window
Just snowflakes . . . that melt
away
Santa never has to come—
Christmas? . . . Just winter day
No more the little whispers
"There's daddy, Quick let's hide"
But the squeaky cry of "Peek-a-boo"
Still echoes deep inside
Whenever things were broken
It was, "daddy I fix too"
But the dolly cart you fixed so well
Lies ever broken without you
No stocking on the chimney
It's resting on your grave
The Christmas songs have long
been sung
Now, Christmas morning . . . is
empty

JoAnn Estay Walker
HOUSEWIFE

*Dedicated to: My husband and
three children; that God loan me.*

Get up, cook, clean, the house
Each day begins like no other.
Picking up after the kids
Remembering you are a mother.

Can't buy too much today, must
wait
The money situation is at it's
worst.
In and out hospitals and doctors
offices
Until one day I feel like I'll burst.

May God help me, I sure need him
His helping hand is always there.
He has given me so much to be
thankful
May He always answer my prayer.

Joanne Haines
LAKESHORE SUNDOWN
Bloodpath on the water
Stretching far, so far away,
Beyond the bright horizon
To the swiftly ebbing day;

A carmine path of twilight dreams
Across the breaking foam
Still-shimmers, rosy-frothed, a path
The dreamer's mind may roam

To seek, beyond the sinking sun,
The quiet thoughts that lie
So still and ever-waiting
'Neath the graying evening sky

That curves above the ruby water's
Gently moving breast
To fade the scarlet ripples
Into cool and quiet rest.

Kathie Herron
BRITISH AFRICA
I saw the land of my fathers
Stretched beneath the burning sun,
And as my soul put forth roots,
Knowing it was home,
Cool drops fell from the sky
And ended in whirling dust.
The sea which had brought me
Twinkled in the light invitingly,
Tempting me not to debark,
But my soul had dug in
Like the the scrub brush,
And I knew I was home.
The night fell with soft whispers,
And the stars winked above,
The muddy sand sucked my feet.
The scent of mimosa assailed me.
The moon glowed orangely,
Showering the forbidding savanna,
But I knew I was home.

Georgia Gail Sizemore
OLD FEELINGS
All the feelings and emotions
I used to feel are gone.
There are others in our lives now,
But they will never mean as much.
You were special, and still are,
For, you see, other feelings for
you fill me now.
I love you, not as before—
But in another very special way—
I can confide in you, trust you,
and care for you—
As I can no other.
I know your insecurities

and
fears
and
weaknesses
As you know mine.
Your happiness is very important
to me,
For I love you———
as
a
friend.

T. Aileen Karg
Why, When and How?

*To my 3rd grade science class in
the study of small and big
machinery which ended in
discussing transportation.*

Whatever's in a nation,
It will come out somehow,
And here's our presentation
Of why and when and how.

From wagon wheels and carriages,
From cars to planes and jets,
Our country still goes onward
To greater heights and depths.

The man who rides the
moonbeams,
We've wondered at his charm,
And at his invitation
We've opened up our arms.

Our flag is standing there with
him,
The red, the white, the blue,
And what we do from here on
Is simply up to you.

America keep moving,
There will be greater days,
The Lord will keep on helping
So let's all give Him praise.

Candy Reed
AFRAID

To Sam—from Dee

I joke and laugh and toss a word
or two.
I hide the fact that I really love
you.
You smile and chide and evade
what's true.
Could it be, that you also feel the
love I do?
We care so much and yet we lie.
Why can't we admit it, instead of
deny?
We could reach out and tell each
other.
All we need is to trust one
another.

Mrs. Dorian E. Petersen
SIDE BY SIDE

*To my husband, whom I loved so
dearly. I thank you James, for all
your love to us all, and of your
kindness.*

There is really Laughter,
Yes, I know
Because you lit up
My darkness,
When I knew your Love.

Our World's Best Loved Poems

These are truly, more
Than words,
The past existed, but
became no more,

Side by side,
Today we are but one,
A Living Shadow,
Where our dreams will live
As long as we have each other,
And truly Love.

Ann R. Rountree
HUMANITY

---

*To my loving mother—who
continually fills me with
inspiration and strength.*

Life is full of ups and downs,
Ferris wheels and merry-go-rounds.
It's hard to feel happy and gay
When your soul is turning the
    other way.
Who knows all the answers to
    life's probing force?
Who can steer his ship perfectly
    through every course?
No man of course.
But we keep striving for the good,
The better, the best.
What an irony that this is our
    solace,
Which makes us rest.

Diana Barbera
YOU AND ME
    Here we are, You and Me
I feel it was something meant to be.
    We've been put to the test
Of experiencing, In so little time,
    Goood, Bad, Happy and Sad
                Emotional Times,
    Just to let us know,
        To open our eyes,
    And take hold of one another,
                because,
    There are not many of our kind.
        We'll start from scratch,
        and build our domain,
        Together we will grow,
                and
    Together we will remain!

Allan James Hayward
STREETPEOPLE
The Summertime, where is my
    help, what little I ask?
Least I can bask myself within
    the Summer's heat, cleanse
    myself within the smallest of
    waters that I may cross.
I lay within the darkest of alleys
    within the slums.
I lay upon doorsteps, the run
    down buildings, within the
    ghetto, within the slums,
    anymore, outside the slums
    wherever a corner might be,
    that I may grab what little
    sleep I dare.
My time, so much of it and yet so
    little.
So many long, long hours, where
    do I go, what do I do?
My cloths, once were so rich and
    clean, now all but rags.
I hold up my cup for a penny or a
    dime I beg.
I schuffle through litter, dig
    through trash, hoping a coin, a
    sweater, a coat, a scrap of food

would find its way upon these
    cold, tired and weary hands.
Winter is here, taking its toll.
    Where do I go, what do I do?
What is left? My pride, my
    dignity and my life seem all
    but lost.
When I awaken, it will be
    another day, and you will be
    there.
Where is my help, what little I
    ask?
What little I care now, but just to
    survive.

Nassoma Boone
HE CAME

---

*To God—Thank you To Willie
Clyde—Miss you To Moses—I
love you*

On a hot and arid summer night
An unnatural child sliced the
    steamy blistered air
Floating as a ghostly spectre on a
    silent misted stage
The vigilante came

Ominusly he stood with features
    shadowed like a macabe
    charcoal drawn by satan's
    wicked hand
His coal black eyes pierced the
    raging darkness with ferocity,
The vigilante stands

Waiting stood he like a devil cat
    in a graceful crouch amidst the
    backdrop of a lonely
    streetlamps quiet glare, and a
    fringe of bushes as surrelistic
    as he
The vigilante waits

With lighting speed his hand cuts
    like the rippers knife through
    the silence of this night.
Justice defined by urban life itself
    descends like a noxious cloud
    around the approaching being

Running sounds upon the hard
    cement merge into the sound
    of a fiery lighting tinged crack

And sound is no more

Like a gentle flitter of butterfly
    wings he gracefully withdraws
    into the pocket of the night—
    leaving only deaths calling card
    to say-He Came

J. C. Sandberg
NEW BEGINNINGS
Life can be so frightening
When nothing's going right,
The troubles that surround you
Make the future not so bright.

It can also be a lonely place
When no one seems to care,
Coping with illusions
Can lead to dark despair.

T'was not so very long ago
I had that feeling too,
Of wandering in a tunnel
Wondering if I'd make it through.

The way has not been easy
New decisions I had to make,
Not the ones I would have thought
For the new steps I must take.

Starting off a brand new life

Where God and friends abide,
Sharing all my problems
Helps me take things in stride.

If you find you have this feeling
Of deep down dark despair,
Find someone now that you can
    trust
You'll find some people care.

Tell them what's been kept inside
The good as well as bad,
You'll find the load has lifted
And you won't feel quite as sad.

Your problems won't become just
    a day or two,
It took a while to get this way
But with help, you'll make it
    through.

Mary Hamilton Darrell
The Hem Of His Garment
"If I can but touch the hem of His
    garment I shall be whole."
He came to earth to show love
    and compassion—
In the Bible we'er told.
We find ourselves crowded by
    doubts and by fears,
As the multitude crowded the
    Master
In those other years.

As the Master walked with them
On this earth below,
So to—day He is with us and
    guiding
Wherever we go.
Whatever He gives us, we know
    it is best.
Whether health, strength, and
    power,
Or peace, joy, and rest.
Whatever befalls us, be sure, we
    are told—
"Touch the hem of His garment
And thou shalt be whole."

C. Daniel Reed
GRIEVE THE WIND
The joyous lilt of every song
    we tried so hard to sing,
Lies mute—so very sadly now
    like sparrow cleft of wing!
Endearments flutter aimlessly
    as feathers in the sky,
Plucked unconcerned, and
    carelessly by either you or I.
Remorse stands not in profit now,
    but joy can ne'er be king;
For song and sparrow both lie
    dead, and neither tune will ring
When dark dispair prevails on
    high to mock the wind's sad cry.

Zoe D. Clark
FIRST YEAR

---

*To my daughter, Karen, who
asked me to write this poem and
to her boyfriend, Steve, for whom
it was written.*

A few short months ago we met,
    And in my life my rainbow was
    set.
Our relationship at first was just
    good friends,
    As together we walked each
    road and around each bend.
As silent as the sunshine and

refreshing as the rain,
    Something happened to us no
    words can explain.
A warm glowing feeling soon
    filled our hearts,
    And as it grew stronger, it filled
    every part.
Our lives like the roses became
    intertwined,
    With a special love that will
    last for all time.

Maria F. Hixson
CINDY

---

*Dedicated to Frank and Tilly.
Through the tragic loss of their
daughter, I was inspired to write
this poem.*

Born one day,
To live her own way.
At times, very lively;
At times, a little shy.
She was mostly happy,
But, sometimes she would cry.
For this is the question,
We are asking, "Why?",
"Why did her life's journey so
    suddenly stop?",
As she was just barely reaching
    the top.
The answer is as new as old,
"She has been called!".
Called by the Lord we all do adore,
Together with him she'll live
    forevermore.
Fond memories of Cindy in our
    hearts will stay,
Till the time comes and we're on
    our way.
On our way to the place where
    we too will be his guests,
Where our body and soul will
    find everlasting rest.

Carmen Rinehart Moss
SEA FANTASY
    Brisk wind, splashy laugh—
    their long hair streaming, mermaids
    riding on a wave.

Gloria Sketo Young
MORRO ROCK
Oh rock that I love, sitting high
above, I touch you, do you feel
me?

I sit at your base with many
    problems and disillusionments,
    the sea comes in and takes
    them away.

You make no sound, you cannot
    convey and yet I hear you.

Oh, to be as strong as you and
    unmoved!

The sea comes in and trys to
    push you away and yet, you
    remain unmoved; the sea gives
    up and breaks into tiny mist of
    foam.

For centuries you have sat and
    watched as ships come to your
    shore; Men have climbed you,
    yet all I do is sit beside you.

As I leave, you are still within my
    sight; and as the sun sets out to
    sea, tomorrow I know you will
    still be there for me . . .
            unmoved

417

Erica Hillemann
OCEAN DAY (A SONNET)
A young girl sits alone upon the
sand.
The sun is bright, the day is
warm and new.
She thinks about someone whose
love is true
And writes his name so clearly
with her hand.
The day moves on, the sun and
tide are high.
She watches as his name leaves
with the foam.
A tear at dusk, she slowly heads
for home,
And to the ocean day she says
"good-bye".

A new found love, a special ocean
day.
They both fill hearts with
sunshine's golden gems.
And seldom one anticipates their
end.
But time moves on and names are
washed away.
As with the sinking sun soft
sorrow stems,
Tomorrow's sunrise will a new
name send.

Ernest R. Tinkham
SOME SILVER LEAVES
Slowly, softly, yon rising moon
  Brushes the night with silv'ry
  bloom,
Where e'er you peer, where e'er
  you gaze,
  The world seems varnished in
  the haze
Of moonbeams; in the sombre
  hush
  The pear trees in the orchard
  blush
With luscious fruit, the gnarled
  pear trees
  Glint silver with their shining
  leaves;
The world seems still, a
  wondrous light
  Enwebs the weird, mysterious
  night;
Then like a shattered crystal ball
  A barking fox jars the forest
  hall;
In the orchard the gnarled pear
  trees
  Shiver and drop some silver
  leaves.

Zoe D. Clark
FRIENDSHIP

*To friends old and new who don't
try to change us but accept us for
what we are.*

Friendships are special so cherish
  them all,
  From all kinds of people both
  big and small.
Hold out your hand—give help
  where you can,
  For helping out others is part of
  His plan.
Whenever it's dreary and nothing
  seems right,
  Perhaps a kind word will make
  the sun bright.
Just do unto others as you wish

they would do,
  For then you'll feel needed and
  happier too.
God watches closely the way that
  we live,
  And our just reward is the
  blessing He gives.

Douglas Lloyd Berridge
AT A DAYS END
Set Before time
On the Chime
It's midnight.

The hours of today
Have raced away
As you Stumble to another day.

Body worn
With little earned
The heart burned
Life torn
Same lesson learned,
And the keystone remains
unturned.

Aileen Fielding
Christmas Kaleidoscope
Christmas shifts the year's
  kaleidoscope,
Revealing spangled reds, blues,
  and yellows,
Shaping them into evergreen
  trees and tinsel rope,
Holly berries, glittering bangles
  and bows.

A fairyland illumined by
  shimmering candle glow,
Against a snowy backdrop with
  its arctic-blue tinge,
Beneath the dangling clusters of
  waxy mistletoe,
Is trimmed with radiant icicle
  etching and fringe.

In bas-relief, burnished, dazzling,
  and bold,
In time's most magnificent,
  glorious tableau,
Gleams earth's grandest, greatest
  scene to behold:
A tiny baby, enveloped in a
  lustrous, golden halo.

Cradled in a crude manger,
  Incarnate Divinity,
God's gift, radiating to all people
  everywhere,
Condescended to embrace and
  identify with humanity.
To rescue creation's Adamites
  from death and despair.

Kathern P. Edwards
A FRIEND OF SPRING
  My young son seems to be
  asking since Spring is here
  again;
"Spring, my friend, where have
  you been?"
  "I have missed you a lot while
  you were not here;
And each day I hoped you were
  somewhere near."
  "Every day seemed so cold and
  gray;
because I could not go out to
  play."
  "Now that you have come back;
I'll be able to hear the duck's
  quack."
  "The pretty flowers will be in
  bloom;

to send away the winter's gloom."
  "I can see a butterfly float by
  on wings as light as air;
And now every day is warm and
  fair."
  "The birds sound cheerful
  when they sing;
And I am happy too now that you
  have returned, my friend,
  Spring."

John A. Gorski
THE ILLUSION
As her eyes were searching for a
  meaning,
  I was conveying mine.
She pocessed a quality,
  Known to but a few.
Her graceful curves,
  Made her enticing.
Those lips, always eager,
  To taste life's sweet fruit.
Golden hair, in all its splendor,
  Shined, as if, it was made of
  satin.
She spoke my name,
  And in a moment of awe,
I awoke,
  To find her gone.

Violet A. Glasser
EVEN THE ROSE DREAMS
The Rose.
It is the symbol of a dream.
The last reminder of Spring and
  hope
In Lifes barren field of Snow
Blood red against Death White
But you and I both know
It blooms because it never gives
  up the fight
The Rose wishes for infinite
  survival
And never once lets down
But when the icy winds begin to
  blow
And the snow covers the ground
It must give up and say goodbye
The Rose is fragile and easily
  broken
As your fantasies can easily die
Hold fast to your dreams for if
  you let them go
How can you say you tried? Don't
  stop believing
If your wishes aren't coming true
Don't think that no one cares
Just remember what the Rose
  always knew
That even if life's bitter storms
Stop your goals for awhile
Your dreams will last forever
As the Rose blooms in the Suns
  smile
Forget the shadows, look for skies
  of blue
And don't get caught in bitter
  snows
Somewhere, sometimes there's a
  dream for you
But you have to fight to be
The Rose.

Andrea Ross
A GOOD DREAM
Broken promises, shattered
  dreams fill my cup with an
  emptiness . . . it overflows . . .
It's hard to put my pen to paper,
  difficult to draw life from a
  dwindling . . . lingering spirit: a

child
one somehow hasn't the heart to
  tell, it just won't be, without
  saying to the child he must
  give up . . .
For one must try, as long as one
  can, so there will be a hope to
  cling to and bring new dreams
  to . . .
But dreams seem silly to the
  wise, who can easily sift
  through their memories and
  anchor their hearts
around the sweet, simple, perfect
  things life's about; . . . A clear
  day . . . a good friend . . . a happy
  home . . .

A good dream keeps the spirit
  soaring, knowing there is a
  God . . .
A good dream pulls you out of
  bed in the morning and tucks
  you in at night . . .
It makes you smile . . . It lets you
  love and be loved but most of
  all, it takes the emptiness
  away . . .
A good dream makes you strive
  for the things that count,
  things you will achieve, if you
  dream that way . . . and
never let your dreams grow in
  dark and awful places . . . where
  dreams don't belong . . . but
  keep those dreams
bright and colorful . . . Those
  impossible, silly thoughts
  called dreams help you
  accomplish all the things
you are *supposed* to do!

Sally A. Barrows
RIPPLING DUNES OF TIME
Over the rippling
  Dunes of time
Wander I
  An aimless soul.
Erased, each step
  I took
So knew I not
  If I went
Forward or back
  On the path.
My lonely trek
  Seemed endless.
And fruitless
  Were my goals
For cast was I
  Upon life's road
Whose end was
  Not in sight.
Then I found
  A fellow traveler
And now neither
  Cares the route
As we travel
  Our way together.

Lise E. Fabry
You Are My (Will) Power
You are my sunshine
You are my rain
You give me the power
To arise everyday.

You offer potential
To my very own soul.
You give me the power
To make every rock roll.

And when I am drowning
With sadness inside

You give me the power
To flow with the tide.

You make my life
Worth living to me
You give me the power
To let my self be.

Lona Nevada

Lona Nevada
LIFE

*Dedicated to my seven children.
Seven being the number of
perfect completion.*

What is Life?
Minutes or hours,
Time passed.
Where is time?
Children as babes,
Now grown or gone.
With little ones of their own.
My life, my life,
Where has it all gone?

June S. Sunkes
He's One Of the Great He Now Serves In God's Kingdom

*In fond and loving memory of,
Lance Corporal Harold F. Gratton
of Cohoes, NY and all our other
Marines who lost their lives in
the Oct. 23, 1983 bombing in
Beirut. My deepest sympathy to
their loved ones and may God
bless all of you.*

He's not just another young man
 he's one of the great you see
His life he had dedicated
 so that our country may be free
He died in the line of duty
 serving our country and its name
Let's not let him be forgotten
 his young life let it not be in vain
Dear God won't you lessen the
 burden
 the heartaches the sorrow and
 grief
That this young man's loved ones
 are feeling
 give to them a little belief
Somehow let them know that
 he's with You
 in Your Kingdom way up in the
 sky
And that You are the one who
 had chosen
 to take his young life and why

Let them know that he's been a
 great honor
 and now he serves in the
 Kingdom above
Let them know no more harm
 will come to him
 but most of all send them down
 your love

Star E. McCoy
TOO EARLY ALONG

Our lives are progressing
through the seasons of time
We blossom in spring
The hills of summer we climb

In Autumn we ponder
with wonder and fear
about the closing of winter
Is it far? Is it near?

But what of the soul
young and strong
who dies before winter
too early along

It makes me wonder
The analogy we make
Between life and the seasons
and what steps I will take

Will I walk in the leaves
in the cool autumn air?
Will I frolic in winter
with snow in my hair?

Will I listen in summer
to the bluebird's sweet song?
Will I die before winter
too early along?

Barbara A. Solomon
The Message, Say A Prayer

Say a prayer
 for those who have a lot to
 share.

Let them know
 that they should really care.

Give them love
 instead of hate.

So that they can give
 a message to those who have no
 faith.

Yes, say a prayer
 for those who sin.

So that they can feel the love of God
 in their heart once again.

Shane P. Pappas
The Shadow Of Saint Nick

To Buddy, my son.

The lad sat waiting 'fore the fire
 and shirt-sleeved all his tears,
 for this would be a Christmas
 unlike his other years.
Absent were the presents,
 likewise the cheer, the winter
 chilled clear through his bones,
 the Christmas tree seemed drear.
And as he had done on every year
 far back as was recalled.
 He'd bring grand gifts to
 stocking stuff and fuel their
 Christmas Ball.
He'd ride his sleigh like thunder,
 calling to his team 'til the earth
 near shook beneath them, or to
 this boy it seemed.
Like some great god he'd soon
 appear bearing gifts of varied

sort in sure response to
 scribbled notes; each childs full
 report.
He'd bellow out his "Ho, Ho, Ho!",
 and gaily venture forth 'til
 every house was filled with
 gifts and he returned up north.

But Santa never came, and soon
 the youngster slept before the
 dwindling fire while all around
 him crept
not Santa, nor Nick, nor Kringle,
 but the ones who loved him
 most who wept to see their son
 grow up, blind innocense his
 ghost.
And they'd be sure when he
 awoke he'd find his stocking
 full and presents crowded
 'neath their tree, sparkling like
 priceless jewels.
Soon he'd wake and forget
 dismay, caught up in
 Christmas cheer. The winter'd
 be not quite as cold and naught
 would be as drear,
for now the lad had come of age
 to put away ol' Nick while
 wept his loving parents. He'd
 grown up much to quick.

Mary A. Morton
DAWN OF LEARNING

*Thank you, Karen Wehba for
your support of my poetry.*

With tentative explorations
My sphere enlarges as new
 avenues
Are sought by my mind.

Which knowledge do I keep,
Or discard as I venture further
Into the quest for existence?

Do I perhaps retain all learned
to use in some other way,
Or is it simply, words at play?

Cluttered with wisdom unsought
I srive to rearrange these thoughts
Best I can, in years so thin.

Marcia Texter
FROM YOU TO HURT

*To all my friends I work with. To
my two nieces, Raquel, Heather.
To my two nephews Nick, Gerid.
To a friend, That it has Been a
pleasure to know, and to know
she is always there. Thanks
Becky B.*

Do you see this tear in my eye
Do you know you made me cry,

Please tell me that you still love
 me
Please don't SAY YOU WANT
 TO BE FREE.

Just wipe my eye, just hold me
 tight
Never let me go, tell me it's alright

Warm me with those words, you
 still care
Tomorrow is all ours, to love and
 to share

Do you feel that loneliness, like I
 feel,

Do you know hurt does not heel,

Please tell, me that you want just
 me
please don't say, it just can't be.

Just cure my heart, just mend it
 fast
Never let it break, let our love last.

Warm me with our memories
 they will stay
Tomorrow is forever, and
 yesterday past away.

Sharon Chambers
The Giant Redwood Forest

The Giant Redwood Forest
Is a sight to behold
In the middle of this wonderland
The trees stand tall and bold

The splendor of this forest
With none other can compare
Like a fairyland of magic
Are these visions you will share

You'll never find another
Awesome scene quite so rare
As the Giant Redwood Forest
In its wonderland so fair

In Northern California
Up near the Oregon line
As you travel Highway 101
This wonderland You'll find

Come and see the beauty
Of the trees so tall and bold
See the magic scenes and
 wonders
That the Redwood Forest holds

Derek A. Miller
THANKSGIVING

Thanksgiving may be past
But it will last
And I'll remember it below or
 above
Of how it brought so much love
And it will always be
A favorite with me.

Lynn James
My Father's Other Child

Crooning a lullaby to my
 father's other child as she lies
 sweetly smiling in bed,
Singing a song my Mother once
 sang to me, then kissing her
 soft sleepy head,
I remember when I used to lie in
 this room, secure with my
 parents both near
But never again shall I dream as a
 child, for my mother no longer
 lives here.
I, in my innocence, did not
 understand as my home was so
 suddenly torn,
And, in my confusion, I dreamt I
 was lost, abandoned,
 completely forlorn.
But I picked up the pieces and
 stacked them away, rearranged
 on the top of my shelf,
And as I grew up, I gradually
 found a home deep inside of
 myself,
Where, year after year, my
 wounds slowly healed and the
 pain lost its sharp
 burning glow.
Now I'm more sure of myself,
 matured through my pain in
 some ways they never will

know.
But, sometimes like now, a
  memory invades the thoughts
  I've pushed far away,
And a voice softly asks from a
  pain in my heart, "Why must it
  be this way?"

Elizabeth McFee
FINALE
Do you remember when you were
  young
*there was a time when the sun
  was high*
Eager for the songs to be sung?
happy days, with no time to cry
Enticing dreams—and things to
  be done
*youth—ignoring fact that all
  must die*
No thought of time or setting sun
ever encroaching, night draws nigh
Old—life over before its begun.
*faint whispering sigh—good-bye,
  good-bye.*

Sylvia Roberts-Clark
THIS FAMILY OF OURS

*Thank you Mom and Dad for all
the beautiful, positive
memories . . . I love you!*

Mama usta fuss
  but when she fussed
  we knew she loved us.

Papa usta look mean and silent
  and had a certain stare
  when he came from work
  but we knew he cared.

Mama had two dresses
  one black and one white
  own pair of pointed toe shoes
  and one sunday coat . . .
  for five years . . .
  until she couldn't fit them
  anymore.

Papa had
  one black suit
  one army hat
  one army coat and
  one pair of sunday shoes
  for ten years . . .
  until he couldn't fit them
  anymore.

That's how we knew they loved
  us . . .
  This Family of Ours!

Monica Y. Anschel
THE GUARDED BATTLE

*Tommy James Allen III and Todd
Anthony Bulich—Nous
n'oublions jamais.*

The air was electrified.
Emotions surged through both sets,
Caustiously hurling insults
Back and forth
Hoping the imaginary glass
  shield
Wouldn't split and shatter.
Thinking of the incredible force
  of desire
That would thrust through the
  gap.
They skirt each other

Waiting, watching
Hoping and praying,
The feelings die with the
  forgotten reason
Of the beginning of This.
Each set slowly withdraws
Knowing that on some future date
They will meet again
And fulfill their dreams.

Cheryl Aileen Herring
LOVE
Love, the fantasy,
Ingrained illusion grand—
Is it ever real
Or just the mind's last stand?
Does it ever venture
To come to those who seek?
Does it really take them
To the highest of the peak?
Is it all a dream
Or vision of the night?
How is one to know
If the love they've found is right?
When does one stop searching
In all the corners bared?
When does one begin to know
When somcone else has cared?
How is one to know
If love is ever real?
It's never truly clear
Except in what you feel.

Alexandra Jaworski Prober
SISTINE CHAPEL
A travel card came to life,
  captured me in a dream-like
  fantasy
Pinning me down among the
  paintings,
  Like a botanical study
Or a rare humanoid species
  Or an anthropological curiosity
Among the Biblical characters . . .
  their robes flowing, faces
  intent . . .
blended together
  in phantasmagoric
  complexity . . .
Their individual identities lost
  to become a mass of
  polychromes . . .
Reaching, enveloping the bold
  intruder
  Who dared to disturb
The frozen dreams of another age.

Linda Papworth
CRIES OF THE NIGHT
By the light of the moon a lone
  wolf cries,
His song of woe the cry belies.
He fills the night with
  desperation,
The loneliness caused by his own
  creation.

Who in the world will hear his
  cry,
None but the moon who rests on
  high.
Someone answer he loudly
  pleads,
Someone come and fill my needs.

On he cries to no avail,
On and on he sadly wails.
Then at last, to his surprise,
He finally hear's another's cries.

Oh sound of sounds he's not
  alone,
Tonight he's heard another's tone.
No longer is his life so bleak,

For a friend no longer need he
  seek.

By the light of the moon now two
  wolves cry,
Their friendship they will not
  deny.
Two lost souls at last are found,
And now theirs is a joyous sound.

Maro Rosenfeld
TRIANGLES

*To Lois Wilde— my invaluable
encyclopedia my Friend, my Soul
Sister*

Why is it that the eye should see
in modes of trigonometry?

The David's triading out at me
one-hunred years of history

And Delacroix's triangles unveil
the fantasies of ancient tales

El Greco's Holy Trinity
weaves the mystery of infinity

While Degas dancers line in three's
Picasso's Muses prance thru trees

And Luncheon on the Grass for
  three
the third eye of the Bodhisattva
  sees

While triangles prance thru Space
  for art
anatomy joins body soul and heart

And Neptune's Trident turns in
  Space
The Sun, the Moon, the stars, in
  grace

What truth is cast between the
  eyes
that triangles tie them to mind
  and skies?

Dorothy E. Law
THEY TOLD ME THEN
They told me then, on Christmas
  Eve,
The animals could speak;
So I went forth in silence,
Their company to seek.

I entered in so stilly,
They never heard at all—
I saw them kneel in reverence,
Each one within his stall.

The horses whinnied shrilly,
"Noel! Noel! Noel!"
The old cow greeted Christmas,
With a deep and solemn knell.

And through the open doorway,
A star burnt like a flame,
As in the lowly stable,
Another Birthday came.

Paul Layne
**Was I Born To Sing the
  Blues?**
Was I born to sing the blues?
I never became familar
With the tune before now.
I think I just learned
The first line today.
It started out about your leaving.
This old heart of mine started
  grieving.
And the second line came right on
  time. When you phoned me
  And said. What we once had was

dead.
The third line came with the
  dread of tommorow. A tommorow
  Alone.
Was I born to sing the blues?
Or just to lose?

Alexandra Jaworski Prober
YOU WILL REMEMBER ME
. . . When church bells ring at
  eventide,
Hymns, incense blend in harmony,
When moon's magic enchants
  your world,
When night's first star above you
  see.

. . . When fragrant blossoms
  everywhere,
Declare God's glory, wondrous
  creation,
When gentle night winds on your
  face,
Remind of conquered temptation.

. . . When blessed Christmas
  comes again,
Entranced in twilight's magic
  glow,
When you sing hymns of
  promise, love,
I'm closer then, your heart will
  know.

Think of me in a kindly way,
Remembering smiles, words,
  glances,
The embrace of peace, touch of
  hands,
Aching hearts' timid advances.

When this Sunday's church bells
  toll,
Their mellow call to morning
  prayer,
Walk softly love! Praying humbly
  for you . . .
My caring, lonely spirit is there!

Alice Miller
LIFE
When life begins
We never know
What it will hold in store
Will it be good
Will it be bad?
We never know for sure

Sometimes for years
We drift along
And never find the way
Yet hoping that tomorrow
May be our lucky day

It's like a jigsaw puzzle
Some never seem to solve
And yet it seems for others
There's no problem there at all
I wish I knew the answer
But I don't, because, you see
I'm one of those, like some of you
Still seeking the way for me.

Peggy Bellin
IT'S TIMES LIKE THIS
When the moon is full
And the wind does mingle
When the night is soft
It's times like this, I hate being
  single.

When the stars start to twinkle
And my skin starts to tingle
When music floats all around
It's times like this, I hate being
  single.

When the weather starts changing,
And the colors start to mingle
When the world smells of Autumn
It's times like this, I hate being
single.

When the hearth burns bright
And from the north comes Kris
Kringle
When I see couples cuddle for
warmth
It's times like this, I hate being
single.

When the world is bleak,
And everything is stark.
When everywhere I turn is cold,
It's times like this, I hate being
single.

Kaarina Merikaarto
LAUGHTER
Rivers like laughter unfold,
Bubbling boisterously,
Gushing in torrents that run
gaily onwards.
Lifting silky tones of
imperfection to the ear,
Caressing stones like feelings
shared.

Lilting tones of idiocy,
Come tumbling outward,
Producing smooth tones of
amusement.
Breach gaps of unknown
distances between you and I.
We share, carelessly, a time with
no dimensions.

Taffy Miller
TREE

Mother, I'll remember—

Father brought a tree home
And I bounded down the stairs to
look and found that
It blinked and quivered and
heaved a meek sigh.
And I blinked back and looked
through the tree to the
white wall between its feeble
branches.

My mother said, "this is the tree"
as she
tried to gleam like a Christmas
light.
And I said right out loud, "what a
meek little tree"
My sister glared at me and
frowned.
"Perhaps the tinsel and the lights
would help it to grow"
I said,
So we put up the lights and the
tinsel and all
But the tree still shook and
needles tinkled to the floor.
Brother kept on asking where the
family had
flown to.
Sister entertained and father went
to work.
Then Brother quickly left and
Mother loved the tree.

Then she said "The Tree is loved"
and I saw it
fight to grow
But my throat became too dry to
speak

So I just smiled and blushed.
And then stepped back and
watched
The branches bend down low, the
muscles
strain too much
Like an old and tired woman
trying
to carry bricks and such.

I went to leave, but she begged
me to stay.
I listened hard, then turned and
Walked towards her and placed a
Shining silver star upon her head.

Pauline B. Miller
THE GIFT
The eagle—A symbol of freedom
I now give you also
With wings spread
seaking—searching
Someday to find what is right
in his heart and head

To rest one day in his nest
Peaceful
Tranquil
Confused no more
Knowing his love is pure

Robert Aqualung
HERMETIC WONDER
Return
to the
Cave.
Sun,
so bright
so hot
so tiring.
Night,
so cool,
so lonely,
so inviting
A danger
of
lost vision
and
torch light.

Christine M. Trucinski
THANKS—GIVING

*To all that are born, alive and
well. To all that are gone, alive
only in memory. And for all other
blessings the Lord has bestowed
on us.*

We give thanks, Lord,
for all Thy blessings
both recognized and disguised.
We thank Thee for this universe
and earth,

for forests and plants and living
things,
for crops and famine and
growing things,
for beasts and animals and
moving things.
Blue skies and clouds and wind-
we thank Thee for.
hurricanes and floods-we
implore Thee for.
Fish and fowl and creeping
insects.
Men and women and little
children.
Those that are with us and
those that are gone.
Those that are rich; those that
are poor
Those that are well; those that
are not.
Those that are happy and those
that are sad.
Short or tall, big or small—
we thank Thee, Lord-for us all.
White or black, red or yellow
color or race-no matter at all.
We have our lives to live and
make;
to use all Thy bounty bestowed
and take
whatever means, whatever path
to follow and avoid, your's and
each other's wrath.
To have and to hold—
all that is given and all-that is
taken. AMEN.

Ethel Morrison W.
LONELY IS THE BRAVE
Lonely is the brave,
For they are not of their making.

Lonely is the brave,
Their country is their breaking.

Taking of will, mind and soul,
War Is.

David A. Logan, W.G.H.
**Tie Some Bricks To Your
Feet!**
If you think you're Sittin'
On top of the World—
With everything Tied Up Neat
Hold on There, Brother—!
"Tie Some Bricks TO Your Feet!!"

When you decide to Pass your
Fellowman
In a Break-Neck rush to carry out
Your very Favorite Plan—
You'd better Listen, Friend, I repeat:
"Tie Some Bricks to Your Feet!!!"

You and your Nose may be 'In the
Air'
The Scent of Roses may be
Everywhere
A Large Dividen, your Stock may
Declare——
But Remember Man, Each Day
Won't be Fair—
And, I Repeat: "Tie Some Bricks
To Your Feet!!!!"

While you're 'Way Up There'
Friend,
Think of the 'Long Way
Down'*****
Think of the things You've Done,
Man,
Without a Hint of a Frown—!!
It Wouldn't Have Happened, I
Repeat:

If You'd "Tied Some Bricks To
Your Feet",
AND, Kept them On The
Ground!!!!!

Karen Lynn Kerfoot
NATURE'S OFFER
This old house of the country
knows
The crimson sun and evening
pearl;
As seasons dancing slowly by,
Their splendor to unfurl.

Amidst the rustling branch and
leaf
Now brushed of autumn hues;
Nature in its reach is found
Unspoiled by city blues.

Waxen moonlight lends a glow
To winter snowscaped earth;
While outdoors quietly slumbers
Awaiting slow rebirth.

Springtime seeds bear new
beginnings,
Summer harvests sweet rewards,
Lazy days spent drifting
And listening to the warm.

Gaze these scenic windows and
Behold the wonderous pictures,
While those urban dwellers in
their blocks
Could never be the richer.

Vast skies above the hills that
shout,
and rhymes the breezes proffer;
Sweet voices of the wood and
stream,
The best is nature's offer.

Michele Bernadette Hartmann
Best Friends . . . Forever?
Remembering the first time we
met,
Years separating us apart,
Smiles bringing us together.
That day we became best friends,
Vowing that our friendship
would never end.
Now, as I look back,
I remember the happy times we
shared and the good times
we had together.
Years of my life that I will
never forget.
I realize now that age will
separate us for some time.
I know parting is hard,
but maybe sometime,
in years to come,
We can become best friends,
again. . . Forever?

Gloria Ann Hoversten
THAT'S LIFE

*Dedicated to everything that
makes life worth living. My
Family, Friends, and His smile.*

I sit in the loft of my little house,
and think of years to pass.
Will they be plentiful or lean,
This is what I ask.

Will they be great! (with little
sorrow).
Or will they be all strife?
I think, and think, and then I say
"Oh, well! That's Life!"

As the years are passing by, I look
    at them and think.
They weren't very sorrowful.
They were roses pink.

And now I'm in my later years,
with memories as sharp as a knife.
And when I look back and see it
    all, I say,
"That's Life!"

Daphne Whaley
LAST LEAF
I saw a leaf come parachuting
    down,
The last leaf on the tree.
And then the tree stood stark
Against the sky.
The leaf glinted golden as it fell;
The sun caught its splendor
And magnified it well.
The tree, too, had its brief beauty,
But now it is over.
The leaf was burned—
The tree is bare——
And it leaves a scary feeling
Of emptiness.

Jamil H. Abdullah
MOTHERS
When we begin to falter and feel
    that we can't go on,
Our mothers give us faith and
    courage to weather the storm.

When hard-headed sons go
    rampaging through residences,
It's the mothers to the rescue
    preventing further incidents.

Mothers are out of bed at dawn
    and stay up late at night,
Washing, sewing, cleaning, and
    folding a sick child ever so tight.

They are mothers to their
    husbands and to the suffering
children of every nation;
A mother's love and compassion
    for humanity is God's gift
to civilization.

Mothers are doctors when we are
    ill and lawyers in our defense,
It's been often said that mothers
    are possessors of a sixth sense.

When condemned prisoners are
    given their last requests,
It's to see their mothers who have
    stood life's test.

All that we have accomplished in
    life or ever tried to do,
Was because of the many
    sacrifices our mothers made for
    they
are loyal and true.

Some mothers are old now and
    some have passed away,
But the legacy of love they leave
    us will last always.

Rudolf Frenner
A FRIEND
Guidance and inspiring ideas
Have come from you
Spring awakening is equal
To your mind
A lifted spirit creates the wonders
Of the world, rising with
A mountain symphony
The sun grows with its forceful
    light
Illuminating love and happiness
Clouds are vanished and life glows

In a truthful light
And all has meaning
Through you a friend

Barbara M. Jackson
**Heartfelt Thoughts For My
Son**

*For my son, Michael Wellington
Jackson, whom I love and cherish.
You have given me a whole
treasure chest of joy and
happiness. You are a wonderful
child and a beautiful blessing to
my life. Thank you for all the
kind things you have done for me
and for giving me what I cherish
most of all—your respect.*

Not so long ago, you were but a
    baby—small, warm and fragile!
As I held you, I marvelled at the
    innocent life that God had
    entrusted to my care.
You were so dependent upon me
    for your needs; and I met them
    with tender love and joy.
Early in your life, I dedicated you
    to God and asked that He
    would bless and protect you.
I asked the Lord to teach me the
    ways of motherhood so that I,
    in turn, could teach you well
    and bring you up to honor Him.
When you entered my life, your
    very presence offered me one of
    the greatest challenges that I
    will ever have to face—
    molding and shaping a character.
I have tried to teach you
    principles and morals by
    exemplifying them in the life I
    have lived before you.
My son, you are growing up and
    standing before a door that will
    soon open upon manhood!
I pray that, when you walk along
    this new avenue of life, you
    will truly be a man of high
    standards and impeccable
    character.
Seek God in prayer and lean
    wholly upon Him for guidance
    and direction.
As you walk life's road, go hand
    in hand with God. Cling to Him.
Pray to God in faith and
    commune in your heart with
    Him. Meditate upon His word.
The spirit of His presence will
    comfort you when you are
    lonely and will inspire you to
    do what is right in any
    situation you may encounter.
Make God your best friend and
    trust His word with confidence;
And He will walk with you for
    the rest of your life.

Dr. Lionel Fern
CARIBBEAN YULE
Rattling pearls in maraca:
Riii-kii-chi . . . riii-kii-cha.
Doom-dung-da . . . doom-dung-da;
happy rhythm, marimba!

Rainbow light
swing in the sky.
Red-green height
sit on the white.
Cool of mints

coconut sings;
the ginger hints
cinnamon hymns.
Behold down . . . behold up,
Beauty!; Doll!,
heavy liquor;
mighty spirit . . . Lollipop!
Follow the dance,
free-will . . . from chance;
visit the manse,
hum up the chant.

Rattling pearls in maraca:
Riii-kii-chi . . . riii-kii-cha.
Doom-dung-da . . . doom-dung-da;
happy rhythm, marimba!

Florence E. R. Foster
UNCLE JOE'S YARNS
It happened only once or twice a
    year, . . .
Old Uncle Joe came out to visit
    here.
I remember how glad we were to
    see
Him coming to stay with brother
    and me.
We were so naive, . . . (that
    lovely time of youth), . . .
We'd never suspect he wasn't
    always telling the truth.
We devoured each yarn he ever
    told.
Of ship-wrecks at sea; . . . or his
    finding pirate's gold; . . .
His fun in the Navy; . . . His
    encounters with whales; . . .
His many sea battles; . . . and
    other tall tales; . . . .
Of his life, abroad, . . . in far-
    away lands,
He knew so much about Iceland,
    India, and the shores of France.
We got to know every part of a
    ship, . . . from stem to stern.
His fascinating stories made us
    so anxious to learn.
No teacher could teach us some
    of the things he knew.
We were the smartest in history
    and geography classes, too.
We learned so much, from him,
    about different creeds and
    races; . . .
From Africa, . . . To
    China, . . . and all those
    strange places.
His adventures on the high seas
    were so exciting to hear; . . .
And the memories of his visits,
    we'll always hold dear.
Whether told by the fireplace or
    out in the barn,
We owe so much of our learning
    to Uncle Joe's yarns.

Christopher Van Williams
YOU CAN BELIEVE!!
If you'll hang on to the hand of
    the man, who founded *peace!*
    You can believe!!
You're free to be freed!

Listen and understand the
    meaning of life!
    Heed to the words of Christ!
Repentance in humility is the
    perfect path!
Listen for love in *His mercy,* safe
    from *His wrath!*
Confess, we are nothing without
    Him!

But in Him, we are holy to hear
    the songs of salvation's story!
    Without sin or fear!

If you'll hang on to the hand of
    the man, who had to leave!!
That the comforter might come
    as the spirit we must receive!
    Hallelujah!! You can believe!!!!
Be blessed by *Him,* sanctified in
    love!
Our test of faith endeavor a
    conquest in *His blood!!*
There's rest in *Him,* victory
    through our storms!
He's the best freedom!!—'He is
    the song of the reborn!!'

If you'll hang onto the hand of
    the man, who founded *peace!
    You can believe!!!!*
You're free to be freed!!!!

Amy T. Seddon
AT THE BEACH

*To My Touchstone; Cornelius
Eady*

Sunbaked and floating,
An undulating breeze stirs and
    mixes me.

The crash of the waves
Slaps the ear in my stomach.

My back smells the heat.
Rising from the tiny grains of sand.

Each filament of anemone hair
Tastes the salted breeze.

In my breast, an eye
Winks at a passing man.

Donna Jo Gibson
FIRST LOVE

*This poem is dedicated to Terry
Lain, the first real Love in my life.*

I'ts been said before,
You can never go back
To the arms of an old love,
For what it may lack.

But here I sit
With a fond memory,
Combining reality with the past,
And what it means to me.

The feelings I once shared
With this old love of mine,
Have now surfaced again,
In this day and time.

The pros and the cons
Lay heavy on the mind.
As it weighs the decision
To snatch love back from time.

Surrender . . . with anticipation,
Like when you first held one
    another.
Turn back the pages, for you have
    been
Reunited . . . with your very
    first lover.

Carolyn Denise Warren
BEAUTIFUL MORNING
The morning sunbeams are
    sneaking through the cracks of
    the wood.
The birds are singing their songs.
Noises are beginning in the

distance from the closest town.
All of the animals are starting to move about.
Everything is coming alive.
I like to come out to this place where no one else would be.
And watch the world come alive.
And, remember, without God this could never be.

Karen Robinette Justice
MOTHER IS HER NAME
Time in my eyes, upon her, has not left a trace
For I see a memory when I look upon her face
I can see a mother pushing a child in a swing
And hear a laughter that sounds as birds when they sing
In memory a hand appears upon a fevered brow
As softly she whispers, hush baby try to sleep now
I rememeber the smell of her as she held me near
And lullabies she sang only for me to hear
I remember a love that always remained the same
Yes, I remember for Mother is Her Name

Natasha Barr
BETWEEN LIFE & DEATH

Kenya, Tommie & Henry Barr

The beginning of dawn rose upon us,
The end of night slipped away,
I felt death fall upon me,
And I said "no God another day"

Cleo C. Pope
We Salute You, Mom and Daddy

This poem is dedicated in loving memory to my late father, Mr. Luther Johnson, and to my mother, Mrs. Martha Clemmons of Hazard, Kentucky.

We salute you, Mom and Daddy
On this your special day.
We're proud to be your children
In every single way.

The years have been hard for you
The pain has been severe.
But we hope we've added shunshine
To make up for the tears.

Fifty years is a long time
Of giving, taking, sharing.
You've taught us all so many things
Like loving, giving, caring.

May health and happiness be yours
And God's strength for your sorrows.
And may His face shine on you
In your todays and your tomorrows.

May you know love in all things
Especially between the two of you.
And may you know real joy
So deserved by you too.

May God watch over you
And keep you in His care.
And give you days of lasting peace
Mom and Daddy, this is our prayer.

Jane Masterson
OASIS
The desert was hot, dry and vast,
my thirst was great—I was sinking fast.
My canteen was empty—my clothes were torn, my lips were parched—I was lost and forlorn!
Then I crawled over a dune and to my surprise, there was an oasis before my eyes!
Gathering my waning strength with joy I ran, to the life giving water there on the sand.
And quinching my thirst—I fell asleep—shaded by a palm from the desert heat.
I awoke refreshed to a golden dawn, and with new found strength I continued on.
And as I journeyed I met a man— who was lost and dying on the hot, dry sand.
He was headed away from the water I'd found, I said he'd find an oasis if he'd just turn around!
But he said I was crazy from the heat of the day, for his calculations said it wasn't that way!
And as he crawled on in the hot suns glare, I knew I couldn't make him know——
      I KNEW IT WAS THERE!!

Ruthe Ann Mason
QUIET SOUNDS

Dedicated to Wayne and Scott who inspired me to listen.

In the vast space of night
There dwells an unrequited treasure.
Come mingle with the shadows
and discover the aural pleasure . . .

Of a cricket choir engaged in Spring Song
as tap-dancing raindrops sprinkle the lawn.

Hear the gentle whispers of an evening breeze
and the rustling waltz of dancing leaves.

Lend an ear to the whistle of a slow-moving train
as a chorus of bullfrogs croon in the rain.

It is the aftermath of day
When the sun is lulled to rest
that night unfolds her symphony
of quiet sounds heard at their best.

Charles Bell
JESUS IS ALWAYS THERE

I wish to Dedicate this Poem to all my Union (Steelworker) 2610 Brothers.

Jesus was mine, before I was born.
He was mine, before I enter my Mother womb.
   Jesus gave me a plan.
   The plan is to stop the

concessionaire man.
The concessionaire man that take from the poor.
Jesus said that the way he will go.

   He bargain for the law.
Then he mis. use the law.
Jesus said, this man use the poor.
That why, he will let him fall so low.

   When this man is useing me.
That is when I fall on my bending knee's.
I ask God to give me wisdom.
Thats why, God is so wonderful.

   This is a message from God to the poor.
Do not worry because you have felt so low.
Keep on Praying and have no fear.
Because I know Jesus is always there.

Albert B. Richardson

Albert B. Richardson
THANK YOU JACKY DEAR

For my angelic wife Jacky. Rich

Thank you Jacky dear
For being so wise and bright.

And thank you Jacky dear
For being so nice.

Thank you Jacky dear
For being so kind and true.

And thank you Jacky dear
For being so beautiful.

Thank you Jacky dear
For having a smile so light.

And thank you Jacky dear
For your laughter which lights up the night.

Thank you Jacky dear
For your sweet presence; so right.

And thank you Jacky dear
For your voice; such a calming delight.

Thank you Jacky dear
For being the light of my life.

And most of all, Jacky dear,
Thank you for being my wife.

Katharine G. Leipold
THE HOUR
To take an hour and "while it away,"
Is a waste of time,—some folks do say.

To plan the time and do it right,
Does fill most folks with such delight.
Now me, I'm glad to have the time,
To fool around with verse and rhyme.
There's sixty minutes contained within it.
Tis just the twenty-fourth part of every day,
An important part in work or play.
An hour of happiness or love can be,
The beginning of a family tree.
An hour of sorrow or sadness can cast—
Many shadows of gloom, whether future or past.
So the happiest hours spent in a day,
Are the hours of happiness—that you give away.
For the time that is wasted and selfishly spent—
Breeds only unhappiness and discontent.
So to sum it all up, the best hour you spend,
Is in doing for others, or just being a friend.

Norma H. Barragan
TO MY FRIENDS

For all my good friends who have always been there when I needed them. This poem is for you. For my parents who've always believed in our talents. I dedicate this and all my works to you.

You showed me how to love
   and you showed me how to care
Whenever I needed a friend
   you were always there
You showed me how to laugh
   and you showed me how to give
You gave to me so much
   when you showed me how to live
There were times when we shared tears
   some were good and some were sad
But you were there no matter what
   so I'm thankful for those times we had
You believed in all my hopes
   and who I've come to be
And you helped me to have confidence
   and truely believe in me
There's so much that you have given
   that a single page just couldn't say
I just hope that I have done the same
   in all those passing days

Betty L. Vickers
MY LOVING MAN
Love is forever more
When it truly knocks at your hearts door.
Once you've had laughter and tears
And it seems no one even cares.
The burning red eyes from all the tears I've cried
Just knowing deep down inside.
True love keeps your heart occupied

When my heart is broken, all I
    need is words spoken.
Have no fear dear, true love is
    really here.
The hugs and kisses that we share
Darling, it's only for you that I
    care.
Your soft lips and holding your
    gentle hand
Darling, you're all I need for my
    man.
You have got the perfect touch—
    and so much
As you can see this is true love
    for me.
As I look in your big brown eyes
I see the Heavens and starry skies
Walking around hand in hand.
I can truly say this is my man.
True love means so much to me
Because all these years I had been
    set free
knowing no one really cared for
    me.
Now I have the whole world in
    the palm of my hand
Because I have "Ed" for my man.

John Joseph Everson
HOLIDAY
I remember Mary last summer,
on the beach, by the fire.
We had dreams for life;
dreams crushed under flaming
    tires.

A crimson sunset veiled our
    return;
smoke spun shadowed webs of air,
when rubber burned and metal
    fired wood,
and gin ignited our dreams aflare.

I remember Mary through scarlet
    windows,
darkness draped across bloodied
    dreams.
I see her face in every twilight
and hear in the alarm clock her
    screams.

Susie Werner
WELCOME SUN
It is so good to use the sun today:
All week the clouds have hidden
    it away;
The blizzard winds have drifted
    snow right down
And disguised every object in our
    town.

In silhouettes of white, the cedars
    stand
And birds fly by—a solitary band.
A few big dogs jump swiftly
    through the snow;
Where they are going, surely they
    don't know.

But all God's creatures do so love
    the sun;
And even though the cold may
    spoil their fun,
They all enjoy the brightness of
    the day—
And hope that now the clouds
    will stay away.

Carrie Sutherland
NO SILENT PLACE
No silent place, nor faraway.
Surrounded by hills that form the
    walls of a prison.
I look up, a glimpse each morning

at what I love,
But cannot seem to reach.
I can no longer lose myself in the
    hills,
Nor listen to the wild silence.
I long for days with no one in
    them.
I wish for the breath of freedom
    the wind would
carry to me.
I must return to the silence that
    heals,
The wind that brings me life.

Dan Lewis
CAMELOT
Mystic Fires
Strange Desires
To Stonehedge's Plain I go

Sorcerous Spells
Unholy Hells
Fiery Winds do blow

Mystic Signs are made
Lo, the price is paid
All other things forgot

Spirits Soaring
Fires Roaring
Return O' Camelot

Oh glorious sight
This ebony night
T'was once my fabled home

Once more returned
The right I've earned
This land once more to roam

Castles Rising
Soft Horizons
Here my true love doth dwell

Life begins anew
This beauty oh so true
And all once more is well.

Michael Terry Kosoff
PEACE
There's a peace upon the ocean
    as my soul has set a-sail.
For, I've chosen to take a journey
    with a God who does not fail.

He's the Lord of all creation
    and he knows a troubled mind.
So, he sent the way of salvation
    as a light to lead the blind.

He walks beside my vessel.
    He lives within my soul.
He has called me to serve him
    and I've given him control.

I can hear his spirit calling
    in the wind above the waves,
leading me to calmer waters
    by the love in which he saves.

Though, I see not to the morrow,
    neither do I look behind.
For, by faith I'm sailing onward,
    till his glorious shore I find.

Gregory Alexander
LOST TIME
It's ten o'clock by that clock, and
    it's five o'clock by mine.
It's eight o'clock by your clock,
    does anyone know the time?
His watch has one twenty-two,
    her watch has ten after three.
The courthouse has nine-fifteen,
    and none of these match with
    me.
Ask the time while in a crowd,
    and many come to your aid.

But many times you then get,
    still you find no match is
    made.
I'm not late I set my watch, it's
    from the line at the top.
Slow I stroll with lots of time, I
    look and my watch has stopped.
Therefore I give it all up, the
    guessing game is no fun.
Now when I want the real time, I
    just look up at the sun!

Ethel Smith
The Beauty Of a Winter's Night
I love to see the snowflakes softly
    falling
Upon a clear and chilly winter's
    night
They look like tiny bits of
    broken crystal
Cascading in a crazy, swirling
    flight

They settle on the leafless trees
    like dewdrops
And sparkle with an icy glossy
    sheen
It makes the earth a winter's
    picture postcard
More beautiful than anything I've
    seen

Tomorrow it will bring delight to
    children
And footprints will have marred
    this precious sight
But just for now, let me in
    shivering rapture
Enjoy the beauty of a winter's night

Susan Lenore Speroff
COBWEBBERY
I held you in my gossamer cup,
my trove of dreams of love delight,
entranced by your dance of
    promised days,
of your mystical hold over night.

But when you cried tears of
    tangled dew
which crushed my gossamer cup,
I allowed you to fly away.

I mended the cup with gossamer
    string
dismissing you from my mind,
sheding the weight of unkept
    dreams,
accepting in the night what I
    could find.

You appeared through the dark
unravelling my gossamer string
and stole my web away.

Out of my string you spun
    gossamer wings,
a filmy sketch of trails in weave;
you soared to heights we'd
    fantasied of
never sensing it was my time to
    leave.

I've kept the cup of magical
    thought
while abandoning my gossamer
    dreams.
It is I who has slipped away.

Pinkie Mae Malone
He Gave What He Could and He Could Give Much
He generated great force,
Yet he behaved quite well.
He acquired great knowledge

And saw no need to tell.
He faced great options
But deigned to work each day.
He endured great pain;
While problems did assay.

He expressed great love
To the world in varied measure:
Romantic, paternal,
Fraternal, filial treasure.
He projected great charisma;
Which kept one at his ease.
He embraced great wit
And used it not to tease.

He sensed great destiny
And followed his kismet.
He conveyed a great heritage;
His progeny won't forget.
He gave great service,
His honor and his name.
He yielded up the ultimate
To love's eternal flame!

C. C. McCool
MY JESUS IS . . .
How elusive is the trying to find,
The beauty of Jesus in words of
    kind,
Feelings and thoughts rush into
    the mind,
The hue in a rainbow . . a brush
    of the wind—
How to describe Him? I wonder
    again . . .
Perfect love in one pure
    Man . . yet held within,
The command of a
    glance . . calms the heavens
    above,
His own sweet Spirit, as soft as a
    dove,
This Jesus, this Saviour, this Son
    of God,
He gave me His Life, His Spirit,
    His love,
Alas! I cannot do it, to say in my
    way—
An expression of Jesus—the Light
    of our day
And then through His
    Scripture—
                    He spoke to me
My Jesus—He is altogether—
                    Lovely!!!

Tracie O'Dell
THE GREATEST GIFT
Why is it when you try to show
    the love you have for a friend,
You suddenly are labeled
    and feel you don't fit in?

Love has many meanings and
    it's yours to sort and give.
So don't let anyone tell you
    where your love should live.

Without that love we all would
    live
    in misery and pain.
And everyone would weep with
    tears
    like those of falling rain.

Give your love to everyone and
    everything you meet.
You do not have to give a kiss
    just smile when you greet.

The greatest gift you can ever give
    is with you all the time.
This gift of love is in your heart
    and doesn't cost a dime!

Heather J. MacLean
FRAGMENTS OF A SOUL
The incomplete heart
is like a love untold.
It tries to depart
It can't find the soul.

It tells you to leave
Who you think you love best.
Your heart retreats
And you feel at rest.

Ruth Manny Rider

Ruth Manny Rider
THE SACRAMENTO

To my mother, Sarah Thompson Manny, and to my high school teacher of American Literature at Van Nuys, California, Grace Halsey, who both encouraged me to write.

I left the city,
The mad, sad streets of the city,
I left the bone-deep despair
That I saw in each face in the city.

I came to the river,
The sure, sure flow of the river,
I came to the heart-deep joy
That I heard in each bird call,

In each moving leaf,
In each swirling pool in the river.

Beauty, peace, an awareness of God
I knew as I lay by the river.

Susan Collins Statts
MY LOVE
If every star in the heavens could
tell of my love for you
They still would only whispers
make bland echos in the blue
Or if the moon and stars would of

your praises sing
Their voices would be silent ones
like birds upon the wing
For I love you in a way that is
silent and true
Deeper than any ocean and bluer
than the deepest hue
My love cannot be spoken or told
of in story or rhyme
The way my heart beats quietly
for you with tenderness sublime
My love for you is heaven where
only by God dreams are made
Warm as the soft rain in spring
and soft as the winter snow
Though rhymes cannot tell and
the spoken word cannot reveal
If you will look into my eyes you
will know.

C. Charlene Wells
WISHFUL THINKING
There's some things in life you
like to keep small.
A hole in a sock, a crack in the
wall.
The bud of a rose fore the petals
fall down,
Your troubles I'm sure so you
won't wear a frown.

But there's one thing in life you
hate to see grow.
It gives you such joy, enriches
you so.
It can keep you young from day
to day
And makes you so proud in it's
special way.

The love that it takes and gives
in return
Is a gift that is given, not one that
we earn.
It sometimes demands, it
sometimes resists,
But all of this now will one day
be missed!

It grows and it grows to blossom
one day
To tear at your heart when it
moves away.
The It that has grown I want to
keep small
I'm sure you have guessed, your
"Child" after all.

So hold in your heart all the
memories you can,
And the child in your arms or
take by the hand.
For memories can linger but
children do not
Remember that Man started out
as a Tot.

Lucile Surface
My First Christmas Alone
What will Christmas be without
you by my side?
To see the grandchildren with
their gifts, their eyes aglow
with pride,
And hear the merry laughter as
their hearts and voices ring
With the love the Christmas
season always brings.

What will Christmas be without
you by my side?
As the cheery bells ring out to
people far and wide.
When we think of the manger

where the Baby Jesus lay
And smell the sweet aroma of the
fragrant hay.

What will Christmas be without
you by my side?
When all the trees are lighted
and presents neatly tied.
It is then I must lean on Jesus,
my Saviour and my Guide
To be my companion, when you
are not by my side.

Mary Lou Clay
A NEW DAY
It's dawn, I look from the window
and feel the pain
A night of storm-filled emotions
that leave me as desolate as the
blinding rain.

From my window, at dawn,
When the snow, the sleet, the rain
has gone away,
All is right, and I hope I can hope
some day.

It looks so beautiful at dawn from
my window I can smile, laugh, or
shed a lonely tear,
I know that between yesterday
and tomorrow,
A new day is always here.

Damon Thompson
ON RETURNING
Last night I was called home to
reinact with my people
One of the oldest rituals man
celebrates on this earth.
To join with them in praising—
the painful and anguished
eulogy—
The life of one we loved, now
dead . . .

Last night I was called home to
attend the funeral of Uncle Ry
And as all funerals of the past
had done it, too, set off in me
A river of memory. For
remembrance is a rapturous
river,
And I thought of them, and us, of
ourselves and some others.

Last night I was taken by the
woof and web of our lives and
their lives
And those of the people of the
town; and the seasons, and the
scores
Of dozens of faces in that gallery
of ghosts that people my
memory.
I remembered a thousand objects
and scenes and events . . . and
faces
And seasons: many seasons . . .

Last night I was called home:
Stricken, yet joyous, I was drawn
into that whirpool, drowning
In the tumult of
remembrance . . .

Aldine Lorena Matteson Gunn
To Jessie . . . At His Death
Star-crossed son of my star-
crossed later years,
Intentional son—my daughter's
choice,
Child of excitement and tears;
Explorer of peaks and valleys,
And realms where dreams and

nightmares merge . . .
Oh, child of passions and desires,
Of lust for life and lust for death,
How now are fed your fires?

There are sometimes snarls in
the Weaver's skein
As it feeds through the loom of
life.
And the warp and woof once
woven—
Be the pattern of peace
Or the pattern of strife—
At some deep past time chosen,
Can ne'er be unravelled again.

But a fresh skein always is
offered
As our skills and experience grow;
And the Soul has a long
apprenticeship
E'er it learns all it needs to know,
To weave its own Liberation
And its Union with the Whole.

Valerie M. D. Wrede
GOD BLESS PARENTS

*To Mother and Father John and
Martha Dirks Home with God*

Our parents in love bring forth
each child,
And give to them each love and
care,
Nurishing them with God's
special love,
That they may walk with Him
everywhere

Parents work hard God's trust to
fulfill,
And give to each child an equal
share
Of glory that God does provide,
With which there is nothing to
compare.

The values of life they teach each
of us,
That one day when we are on our
own,
We know how not to stumble
and fall,
And if we do they're there, we're
not alone.

They help us learn as we grow
each year,
The things of life that we all
must know,
Which things are right—which
things are wrong,
To make each of our lives with
love glow.

Even when we become fully grown,
When we have need of their love
and aid,
They're there waiting to lend us a
hand,
With great love and care that
never fade.

We must remember they're
human too,
They make mistakes as anyone
might,
Yet noone can ask them to do
more
Than what they feel for each
child is right.

So God bless parents and love
them all,

And give them the love that they
so need,
Their work takes all their years
to complete,
And their reward—that their
child succeed.
GOD BLESS MOTHERS AND
FATHERS.

Anthony Wilt
UNTITLED
Fall peeps around the corners of
summer
and drifts as cool air
thru cracks in the door.
Phoenix like the season
raises from the fire of long
summer days
to be born again,
in familiar sights,
smells
and sounds.
God bless
the changing of the guard.

Angeline Porter Brown
A SAVIOR BORN

*To two very special friends, Jerry
and Linda Starkweather*

A baby born—A King to be,
One born to die—to make us free,
Humble and reverent—Oh how
perfect was He,
A Savior born—to die for me.

How we neglect—this man so dear,
For our sinful ways—we should
tremble with fear,
Humble as a child—we should
strive to be,
Pray to Him daily—down on our
knees.

God loved us so—He gave His Son,
That perfect babe—that Holy One,
To teach God's love—was what
He tried,
And for that we had Him crucified.

A baby born—a King to be,
To save us from sin—to set us free,
With a reverent heart—let us all
adore,
A loving God—who dies no more.

Deborah A. Moore
MY MESSAGE TO MOM

*To mom: There are no words that
can express the appreciation that
I have for you. I know I don't
always show you how much I
care for you, but I want you to
know that you are always loved.*

Oh how I've displeased you,
but, oh how I want to please you.
I've let you down so many times,
but the words—I love you—
were in the back of my mind.
The road was long and lonely for
us,
but the journey was a very big
must.
You've shed many a tear over me,
and a blessing to you I want to be.
I feel I've let you down,
and now I've got to turn over
some new ground.
Can we forget the past and the

pain,
can us; we learn not to blame.
To you, I want to share my love
and smile,
on me, you can lean as we walk
the mile.
We've wasted already too many
years,
we've shed a lot of unnessasary
tears;
But yet, it all happened for a
purpose,
it happened to make you and
me—us!
We've come a long way and a way
we have to go,
but together we'll walk it and
together we'll grow.
So may we continue to talk and
to lean,
and may I show you how much
to me you mean.
I Love You, Mom!

Vineler Long Mann
MY BEAUTIFUL DREAM
One night as I was sleeping
On my bed so soft and white
I dreamed I was sailing
On the sea with great delight.

The ocean was so blue
Waving to and fro.
When I desided in my dream
A fishing I would go.

I thew my line in
And pulled a big fish up
I found he was so very big
I couldn't bring him home.

Soon I awake to see
This big fish I did not have.
I wasn't even riding
On the deep blue sea.

It was fun while it lasted
Although it wasn't true.
In my dream I tasted
A trip for me and you.

G. W. Bunde
IMMATERIAL
The stars—so distant—were held
dreamlike against the night sky.
Twinkling, as if a message were
to be revealed.
Secret things I know they held.
The moon—the night specter—
filled the air with a sense of
magic.
Mesmerizing the world into
believing the wisdom of fools.
Power to turn tides of might
sea and pebbled pools.
The trees—Gods perfection—
were dark shadows against the
night.
Rejoicing to be alive; to witness
the world; to be a part of all
things.
Simple as they are—they be
Kings!
And I—yes, I—with important
and majestic thoughts,
Trying to comprehend what I
feel—
Be immaterial!

Victoria V. Ryba
AUTUMN LEAVES
Autumn leaves are falling
November in the calling
Days of sunshine bright true

Breath in that air for you
Leaves fall one by one
Summer service done

Have you to stand under a tree
On a windy day look up see
Leaves twisting and turning
Its a dance their performing
Music the wind as they prance
Sound be heard leaves dance

Leaves fall do come fast
Cover ground become vast
Pick up leaf color hue
look for more find few
Place them in a book to be
Yesterday remembrance today see

Soon on trees leaves be gone
Will face winter storm
Happy that tree must be
Leaves fall gradually to see
Nature timeing is so great
Another year now to wait.

Zelia M. Goncalves
GIVING ME LOVE

*To Earl, who taught me how to
love again, and more importantly,
taught me how to be loved.*

When I'm feeling alone,
You are always there.
When I feel insecure,
You always show you care.

When I need to feel warm,
You're there to hold me.
When I need to be comforted,
Beside me is where you'll be.

When my face is a frown,
You're there to make me smile.
The times I begin to cry,
You make me laugh all the while.

All the times we share
Is something I'm certain of.
Because when I need something,
You're there to say I'm the one
you love.

Elaine Williams
My Thanksgiving Prayer
I thank you Lord for life today
For love your freely giving
For family ties and friends so dear
That make my life worth living

I thank you Lord for warmth and
food
For which my soul is needing
For all the beauty of the earth
That makes for precious seeding

I thank you Lord for ears to hear
For the songs the birds do sing
For eyes to see the sun and moon
To see the flowers in the spring

I thank you Lord for just each day
For burdens and sorrows you share
For giving me faith to face
tomorrow
And to know my Savior cares

John Tielesch
CHRISTMAS

*This poem was written to my
wife and my four daughters.*

White was the night
Bright as chrysolite
Grown old as a youth
In richness and truth.

Giving hands
Nothing in return
Holy the night
And Christmas day.

With lips of praise
Surrounded in love
Father Son
And Holy Joy.

A lonely man
Long ago
Enveloped in brightness
Crystal clear as snow.

Spirit of living
Human was his form
Strait forward
In divine reform.

The voice of the Almighty
In urim respond
Glittert like electrum
Appeared for you and me.

Viola Weidman Evans
**My Muse Delayed Her
Coming**

*Lovingly dedicated to my parents,
Cora and John.*

On reluctant steps my Muse
delayed Her coming.
Not from petulance or frivolous
distaste, but rather
From a humble hesitancy—a
feeling of inadequacy—
Of tortured impasses.

Whereat can She fulfill Her
earthly purpose?
Wherein can She feel entitled
and just completion?

For ages past Her efforts to
inspire Man's Higher Self
Have been aclaimed; and truly
have there been those
Worthy evidences that Man can
conquer all!

Then entered shadowy
illusions—war, waste, want—
In darkness, threatening to
destroy Peace—in all its
meanings;
Peace to Man—Peace to Myriad
Life, which
Eternally unfolds the Truth—
That only One controls!

That these dark trailing shadows
have no power—
Man must, of course, profess,
and
With Constancy and Faith
Each must boldly meet his next
confronted test;
Then fearlessly to make his
choice! To seek the Good!
And ceaselessly—to know that
from within his Center
Come Wisdom, Light, and
Love—
Strength's triumphal song—
In glorious Victory to carry
Man along!

Jean M. Dobberthein
MY LORD
I talk to MY LORD in the
Morning
I talk to MY LORD in the Day
To THANK MY LORD for the
Sunshine
And for this beautiful Day.

When the shadows of LIFE fall
  upon you
And you have Great Burdens to
  bear
Just remember that God in his
  Heavens
Will listen to all of your Prayers.

The Twilight comes after the
  Sunshine
As I kneel at my Bed & Pray
That God will Grant a Tomorrow
At the Break of a New Born Day.

He will help with all of your
  sorrows
And ease each long lonely day
Remember God's there to Guide
  you
And help you all the way.

Have FAITH IN MY LORD for he
  loves you
He will care for you every day
All you need do is just ask
  him——
into your Heart
And your.
LORD will be there in the
  Morning
YOUR LORD will be there in the
  Day
THANK OUR LORD for the
  Sunshine
And for this Beautiful Day.

Gene Skayer
THE MARRIAGE SHIP

*To Lorraine: Her noble nature and
elegance are what poets write and
dream about, but rarely find.*

For many years we've been asail
  Upon the sea of time
Since going aboard the Marriage
  Ship
  An August day sublime.

The waters were not smooth at
  first
  As we had to adjust
Our different personalities
  As many couples must.

But as the Ship stayed on the
  course
  Of navigator God
The tempest started to subside
But drown all that is clod.

The recent years have found the
  Ship
  Upon a tranquil sea
As it attracts sweet barnacles
  Of love and harmony.

The new horizons——future
  years,
Will not dim in my heart
The promise on that august day:
"Until death do we part."

Grace Lawrence
THE SEA OF PLEASURE

*Dedicated to Mr. & Mrs. Clifford
Francis (my mom and dad) for
encouragement.*

Walking along the measureless sea
Touched here and there by
  beautiful greenery.
A spot or two designed for secret
  cover

A perfect rendezvous for lovers.

A maid and her lucifer bent on
  pleasure
From the caves of full measure.
Eyes that seek the tender light
The best and brightest of a starry
  night.

Determined to accept life's
  limitless measure
Seeking the bounty of infinite
  pleasure.
Stating it's their own special
  decree,
Viewing now the endless sea.

And the fruit-bearing trees
Wears the mark of the future to be.
Within the net of love so free
Now aware of the cold,
  unrelenting sea.

(Viola) Ruth Dawson

(Viola) Ruth Dawson
A REAL MAN

*Dedicated to my ever-loving,
deceased husband, Ross Hinton
Dawson, who exemplified all the
excellent qualities of a real man.*

A "real" *man* never has to *prove*
  anything
Nor to brash artificialities cling
Like——being arrogant
          pompous
          conceited
          or insolent
                to anyone.
But with true
          self-confidence
          radiance
          kindness
          and relaxed charm
          he has fun
Knowing he doesn't have to "put
  others down"
Making himself a ruthless king
  without a crown
But, rather he generates love with
  a most gentle hand.
He doesn't have to prove it: He
  knows he's a man!

Richard F. Hay
SO MANY BELLS
Joyous Bells of Yule
Fire bells of doom
Those that tell the time
Or at the Steeple chime

For phones and other things
Front doors and back

To help us find a cow
And call the hands at noon

Jacqueline T. Naismith
MY WISH

*This poem is dedicated to my
Husband Don and our four
children Lily, David, Jackie,
Don Jr.*

If God could grant me just one
  wish
I guess you'd think it funny
With things the way they are
  today
I wouldn't wish for money

I'd wish all crippled children
Could walk so straight and strong
And hungry people of the world
Could eat their whole life long

I'd wish for wars to never be
Let people live their years
In love and peace and
  brotherhood
To do away with fears

If nothing mattered in the world
Religion, race, or creed
Except our love for fellow men
We'd all be blessed indeed

And then I think I'd bow my head
As I lay me down to sleep
To thank you God for all you've
  done
To make my life complete

Alice Jean Scott
RED LETTER DAY
Today is Garbage Day,
  Hurray ! ! !
All the trash will be hauled away.

Everything that's been marked for
  rejection
Has been gathered up and is
  ready for collection.

The required time hasn't been
  misspent
For it brings such a feeling of
  accomplishment.

When the driver comes by, I
  won't be on hand
To give him my thanks as I had
  planned.

So now, Dear Lord, will you tell
  him for me
That his job's as important as it
  can be.

He performs such a service to the
  whole community.
And I pray for him and all his
  family.

I'm reminded of when You made
  me whole
And took away the "garbage of
  my soul."

All my sin was forgiven and
  cleansed by Your Blood.
And washed away in that
  crimson flood:

Jealousy, anger, envy and strife
Sins I had clung to all of my life.

That, too, was Garbage Day,
  Hurray ! ! !
When all my sins were washed
  away.

Adair Conlon
1984

To a very special mom

The year is 1984
We fought two wars
We want no more.

If we could only start again
How could we change
What now has been?

We have progressed so very far
In short twenty years
From black and white to VCRs.

Technology has given us command
To create life in a tube
Or destroy it with the pressure of
  a hand.

Therefore, we should in '84
Share one common thought
What if there is a nuclear war?

We have only one last stance
To take inventory of life's worth
Then maybe peace will have a
  chance.

The year is 1984
We fought two wars
We want no more.

Stuart L. Williams
CATCH THE WIND
Catch the wind
ride along,
feel life to the fullest.
Feel the breeze of the summer
  sun
catch the wind,
feel spring.
Smell the blossoms of each new
  day,
  like today was a new begining.
Live today like tomorrow will
  never come.
Feel the softness of the flower,
  the coldness of the raging river,
feel the texture of the beauty of
  the human soul
search enjoy the feelings of
  others
touch like there's no tomorrow,
  with your body and soul
catch the wind.
Share with each other, but be a
  person share love
experience individuality with
  each new day,
count not the days behind or the
  days ahead, live for today
capture the moment, share the
  ride
share the passion within you, for
  passion is an extension of
  yourself
filtered through many channels
  for years to come.
Your passion may be short, the
  moment but brief
so ride the wind like today was
  forever.

Mauro Vescera
YEARS
The smoke from his pipe has
  lingered for years,
Now a mild, gentile old man,
long since defeated by ambition,
reflects upon his youth.

The war had ended in victory.

427

His father had felt its defeat.
He remembers himself
waiting
anxiously
for the attention of his
  supervisor.
Destine for employment
he arrives as a union member.

A decade of labouring passes.
Middle aged with unexciting
  thoughts of departure
constantly on his mind.
Ten years had brought him
  nothing but a dull-witted wife.

Fifty-seven and slightly grey,
with a wife who no longer gave
  him any enjoyment,
a wife who was satisfied to
  complain
or gossip with the neighbors.
Nothing else.

More years of boredom pass and
  so does his wife.
Alone with his job,
the only job he has known.
Still as can be,
he sits,
as the smoke from his pipe
  still lingers.

Larry Moore
KISS
Come close in doubt
trusting only
Instinct—guided
Feel assurance rendered
Eyes touch
Words unspoken
Kiss

Ben Gray
AT FIRST GLIMPSE
Half a hundred since my birth
Has my mark been made upon
  this earth
I think of countless gone afore
Too few remembered, there
  should be more
For those whose lives are touted
  in books were exceptionally
  good or dastardly crooks
But what of the fish in life's
  mainstream
Who bow toiled backs and live
  for a dream
The teeming masses who give it
  their all
Those are the ones who stand ten
  feet tall
The striking worker protecting
  his right
A soldier's family alone since the
  fight
The farmworker's hands, knotted
  and torn
The no-account wino, yet to be
  born
The little people, how great they
  are
A mobile nation in a junky used
  car
Their lives like the transport, a
  struggling thing and no
  remembrance does their grave
  bring
I may have twenty, thirty at best
To make my mark, to ace the test
I know it's too late and for this I
  cry
I am too damned tired again to
try
My mark on earth though feebly
  scratched is stark to those from
  ovum hatched
And so my last sip from earthy
  fount will be sweet with
  remembrance
From those who count
Laura Theroff-Braden
THE ANCIENT ONE

---

*DEDICATED TO HENRY
BENNETT And all of those who
share the memories And share
the loss!*

The ancient one in duty waits
for the reckoning of his fate,
The air was thick, without sound
his heirs all stood their appointed
  ground.
Not long now, his head bent in
  prayer,
each breath he takes with labored
  care.
Released from all his surviving
  pride,
"I know its time" he confides.
With acceptance took his last
  breath,
And welcomed in the arms of
  death.
With death it brings the
  unknown fears,
all the loved ones shedding tears.
His favorite tales his heirs will
  tell,
The ancient one bid farewell.
Though death be given, he shall
  live,
engraved in hearts his love did
  give.
The legend lives still hovers near,
The spirit of the ancient still
  lingers here.
We all were blessed by love he
  taught,
The ancient one shall never be
  forgot.
Louise Jane Stanton
**Love: The Other Half Of
  You.**

---

*From and to all spiritual light;
within all, ever present, no matter
how we spend our precious time
in the cares of the physical world.*

Love is all I have to offer,
what it says is fine;
none other can replace it,
not even space in time.
It can't fill you when your
  hungry,
cool you when your hot;
it can't make you happy
when your not:
but I want to!
Charlyne Blatcher Martin
NATURE'S PLAY
Sitting on a river bank in a secret
  place
Small lazy ripples licking our feet
  like the tongues
Of many puppies.
A soft gentle breeze, kissing our
  sun-caressed bodies.
We're both golden in the sun.
Nature loves us both the same.
Bank grasses sway a ballet.
As birds carry the tune.
Time passes and the sun-down
  acters.
Prepare their praise song to the
  moon.
Sitting on a river bank in a secret
  place,
Moonlight greets us in a coating
  of shimmering silver-white.
Nature loves us both the same.
Crickets strike up their tune.
The wilow tree begins her love
  dance,
As the breeze plays through her
  hair like fingers
Love touch a harp.
You gather me close.
We sit close and still.
There are no words for us to say
We are a part of Nature
Waiting,
For our parts in this, Nature's
  play.
Mary R. White
WHAT IS LIFE?

---

*To Raymond, with all the love a
heart can hold, and with all my
heart and soul, forever and ever...*

When this feeling comes and
  conquers me
It always makes me sad
A sad I thought I'd never be,
A feeling I never had ...
For what is life without you here
And what am I to do
When all your memories gather
  near
Reminding me of you.
I feel you here with me at times,
My reflection in your eyes,
I can smell your fresh, clean
  scent sometimes
And still hear you say
  good-bye ...
And what is life without you here
Whatever can I do
Now that I'm alone and you
Are somewhere out there, too.
Yvonne Elizabeth Adams
YOU LOVED ME

---

*In loving memory to: Louis &
Stella Smitkin, who gave me the
greatest gift of all .. Love.*

My Mom, beautiful French lady,
  Petite, yet strong.
Quiet and Oh, so tender and
  loving.
  You loved me ...
My Dad, handsome brilliant Indian
  Ambitious and energetic,
Your free restless spirit, still
  taught me responsibility.
  You loved me ...
You gave me loveliness, grace
  and thoughtfullness of others.
You gave me the strength and
  courage
  to be dependable.
  I love you both ...

Kathy L. Crowley
**Where Gypsies Sold Their
  Wares, I Watched ...**
The Bottleman—
  digging in the wastelands of
  peoples' pasts.
A canning jar still lingering with
  the juicy tang of Aunt Minnie's
  dills
  he finds under the dirt floor of
  the cellar
  of the old farmhouse in
  Belshaw.
With blackened, calloused hands,
  he lovingly carries it to his shop
  to set it carefully beside one of
  sparkling green,
  forged in the likeness of a cod,
  reminiscent of Grandma's
  ceaseless quest
  for purging the poisons from
  her bowels
  each morning and night.
Ink wells; no two with exact
  shape or hue
  reflect the sunlight from sills of
  gleaming window panes.
Belonging to what writer of
  legend or
  lover penning poetry across the
  miles?
Merrily he works at his mission,
  digging ardently in the dump of
  mans' immortality,
  seeking the bottles from which
  pour forth
  the secrets of yesterday.

Sharon Miller
SPRINGS BLOOM
A joggers heaven
A gardeners glory
Is the birth of Spring
Sending a cool breeze
o carry a brightly colored kite
Through the clear sky
A rose in full bloom
That pervades through an
  orchard
The gentle warming rays
The sun provides to help
A beautiful season
To stay for just a little while

Fate Kaldar
To Wish Upon a Unicorn

---

*With love I dedicate this poem to
Wm. Lafayette Corlew, Sr., the
father-in-law I have not met
physically, but know well
spiritually.*

If you believe in Unicorns
then they'll believe in you
their love will bring magic
to everything you do.

To wish upon a Unicorn
shows faith within yourself
nothing is beyond your reach
take your dreams off the shelf.

A unicorn to wish upon
a Unicorn to care
He will always listen to
secrets you want to share.

He'll be there when you need him
He'll appear when you call
a private, secret rendezvous
for you, but not for all.

Our World's Best Loved Poems

Gregory T. Verdino
ONE EAGLE
A silver sky surrounds a golden
sun
Where flies an eagle, alone, just
one
Both man and beast watch the
beautiful flight
They stare with wide eyes, into
the light.

A mystic aura and animal grace
To be compared with an angel's
face
No troubles, no worries within
his head
As the golden sun fades into red.

The sunlight fades but not the
eagle's flight
He flies through the darkness of
the night
In hours few the bird enters the
day
He circles high and he hunts his
prey.

He soars through the air, such a
graceful bird
And through the day his cry can
be heard
A symbol of power, our nation's
birth
Just one eagle, an angel on earth.

Julie A. Murchison
SNOWFLAKES
Snowflakes
  sift
    softly,
      quietly,
    to the
  frozen
earth.

I watch them,
  jealous
    of
      their
        peace . . .

Kobie Johnson
The Magic Of Christmas
Christmas time is here again,
and oh, what joy it Brings!
Like Mistletoe and holly wreaths
and other wonderful things.
Christmas cards and caroling
and stockings hung so high,
the angels softly singing
a Christmas lullaby.
Families will get together
to celebrate with Cheer,
the spirit of the holiday
their favorite time of year.

They'll decorate their Christmas
tree
with pretty lights that glow,
then they'll wrap some presents
or take a sleigh ride in the snow.
And all the little children
are waiting for that night,
when Santa and his reindeer
appear from out of sight.
The special magic of Christmas
makes us want to share,
all the love inside our hearts
and show that we do care!

Rebecca Postell Campbell
I FOUND ME

*Dedication: Robbinsville City
Schools*

The ground was so cold
on my little bare feet,
With hardly a shelter
and nothing to eat,
Not even a match
to kindle a fire,
Only these rags on my back
and this cold, cold air,
I'm lost in the woods
from my family and friends,
Please, somebody find me
before night begins,
I'm in an old shack
built close to a stream,
Then all of a sudden
I woke from my dream,
I'm so glad I found me
I'm catching my breath,
Before I go to the kitchen
I'm half starved to death.

Edwin R. Scott
A LASTING LOVE
You bottle your emotions
For a lost love.
Then conceal it somewhere
In the corner of your heart.
Hoping that it is contained
By the dust and cobwebs.
And when least expected
It reveals its presence
Like a ray of sunlight
Bursting through the clouds
In the aftermath of a storm
Thus revealing your emotions.

Fred W. Drinkwater
SPIDER—FLY
Won't you come into my parlor,
  Said, the Spider to the fly
I Have woven it with Beauty, and
  Hung, it in the Sky
I thought, perhaps, you would be
  passing, By
Now come into my parlor, and
  dine with me.
Do not, be alarmed, at the
  glistening web you see
I have prepared, All Kinds, of
  Dainties, just for you and me
the table is set, I am waiting for
  you
Do not be alarmed, what others
  say or do
won't you come, into my parlor,
  Said the spider to the fly
Do not, look around you, at the
  dying, and the dead.
I have a nice soft, Bed, for you
  and a pillow for your Head
Do not Heed, the Bombs

Bursting, nor the bullets
  whining By.
Won't you come into my parlor
  said
the SPIDER TO the FLY
Let us not wait three of four years
  through Blood and tear
Bring the U.S. Marines home now
  alive that they might Survive
that we might say GOD BLESS
  the U. S. A.

Cathy Marie Davis
DEATH
Death walks,
Within the footprints of winter.
The bare, quivering branches of
  trees rattle in the wind.
The fingers of desolation reach
  out for me.
This isn't what I want to feel.
I try not to notice gray skies.
Autumn is but a memory.
Her smile, once so tender, I can
  remember.
Leaves glowing like lantern lights
But now I listen to the blowing
  wind.
The voice of winter, calling.
I can see, the outstreached hand
  of winter, laying bare the land.
I think of shelter, a warm fire.
Hope you didn't forget to throw
  in some more wood.

Lorraine Maddox
A Fantasy Of a White
Knight

*Thank you Lou*Cole for making
me someone important: And for
all the people who had faith in
me, Tom, Tom, Nicole, Sal,
Joanny, and Joey & Natalie I love
you all:*

There once was a Girl from
  Brooklyn:
Who thought that if She went
  Lookin:
She find a White Knight, and He
  be right for
  whom she be Lovin:

But to her Dismay:
She found out one Day;
There isn't a Knight that is
  Willing:
To give up his Freedom;
To Love Her and Leave Him:
To a Girl who's just Dreaming:

Rachel Ledri
THE GROUND
Children once played on my tall,
  grassy back.
Today I saw a new beginning.
Only a handful of men appeared
  over the hilltop.
They were camouflaged as when
  a fawn matches in
with his surroundings.
Soon they disappeared as water
  ingulfs a burning flame.
Another quest of men came over
  the hilltop.
I could feel their staccato march
  trembling the
earth.
Their guns sounded like muffled
  cries of an injured

animal.
Axis and Allied reinforcements
  were cluttering the
sky and the land.
Tonight I saw an old ending.
Children once played on my tall
  grassy back.

Sallie Burns Ball Fuldner
SEE YOU LATER

*To my mother, Reba Ogle Ball,
who first awakened my
perception of the Soul.*

How much longer,
  my love,

    is the flight
      of the eagle
        to the dove?

Dolores Patricia Voisin
MY BROTHERS KEEPER
I am my Brothers Keeper
And that's the way it was meant
  to be,

What each of us does to one
  another
Ends up affecting me.

The God that gave us life
Also gave us minds to find
  solutions,

But we have stripped the earth of
  its bounty
And replaced it with pollutions.

We are destroying the only home
  we have
And it's possible we won't find
  another,

Just like a wanton and an
  ungrateful child
Who uses and abuses its mother.

Claude A. Newton
WRINKLE REGISTER
The hurt of yesterday is gone
The feel of "Now" is the
  measure
The scowl on wrinkled
  countenance prone
Is but a registered memory to be
  sure
The pleasure of now is how
As that depth of that wrinkle
Laced together on that brow
Is nothing but memories simple
  somehow.

Stephen Reid
Something About
Something
If I were to tell you something
  about something.
I would be telling you nothing.

Something about something
Could be anything.
Anything you may be dreaming
Or anything you maybe hoping
  for.

Something about something
Could be like a life story.
Your life and what you make of
  it.
Could make you something into
  something more.

Something about something

Maybe nothing,
But it could be alot for someone.

T. Donovan Gray
Look To The Distance

In memory of Lula Bates, Rosie Brown, Alexander Bates, Anthony Brown, and Victoria Sims; my beginnings.

Suddenly the rain stops and the sun shines
Suddenly the sun stops and the world no longer divine.
The world no longer divine, time stands motionless.
Time stands motionless and in the distance friends appear
Friends appear and sincerity becomes apart of being.
Then what becomes of what I've been?
Look to the distance, now I'm a friend.

Karen Neale
A CHRISTMAS LAMENT
A heartfelt talk between mother and son.
Will it be like this tomorrow mummy?
Will there be food to fill my tummy?
Will people still smile when we meet?
Will there be love and laughter on the street?

Will Christmas stop the war mummy?
Will it make everything all right?
Will Christmas stop your tears from coming,
Night after night after night?

How can there be Santa, when we are poor?
How can there be God, when no tree's on our floor?
Why do people dream of silly white snow,
When we dream of survival? Do you know?

There is a Santa Claus my dear,
Even though his gifts we will not bear.
Christmas will not stop the war,
Nor rescue us from being poor,
But Christmas gives us, so much more.

Christmas reminds us of days gone by,
On Christmas morn my eyes don't cry,
Though we eat no goose but chicken bone,
On Christmas day we are not alone.

Dorothy K. Pridemore
SNOW MAGIC
The snow fairy came in the dark of the night
And made a cover of snowy white
Dressing all the evergreen trees
With lacy gowns all silvery.

The tall black trees stand bleak and bare
Spreading their branches

into the air
With a most majestic flair
Shivering in the frosty air.

Each roof-top has a blanket white
To keep the house warm through the night
And every fencepost in the row
Wears a puffy hat of snow.

No tracks left on the snowy lawn
As morning breaks at early dawn
God's beauty not yet marred by man
Is spread in splendor o'er the land.

Frances Zapatka

Frances Zapatka
UNTITLED
Because I worship you, my Lord,
Do not think I expect favor,
Only grant me priviledge to praise you,
It is hard to forget a great God.

I love you
Not for giving,
But for being.

Fran Duke
THE CLOCK
The Clock ticks off the seconds, they grow into minutes, hours, days.
From babyhood thru adult life, our future ahead lays.

The days grow into months and years, with each tick we grow older.
You can't relive the past, it's gone, filed away in your life's folder.

The sun rises in the morning, sets in the evening sky,
And when it goes to sleep each night, another day's gone by.

For you it's gone forever, you've had your chance to give.
Show me, dear Lord, what I should do, please teach me how to live.

Yesterday's a memory, it never will return.
The past is finished, good or bad, no need to sit and yearn.

We fight life's battles, sometimes win, sometimes we take a licking.

Regardless what the results are, the Clock keeps on a ticking.

A. N. (Abe) Tolin
CONTENTMENT
An open fire; a dog on a rug
A girl nearby to kiss and hug,
A warming drink from a battered mug
And I'm filled with deep contentment.

A cozy house, a book to read,
A window sill where birds can feed,
Now how much more does a person need
To be filled with deep contentment?

A tiny stream, a pond or two,
A garden spot, a sky so blue,
Wood to cut and chores to do
Fill me with deep contentment.

And if the weather's foul or fair,
Or snow or rain may fill the air,
My latchstring's out so friends may share
with me, this deep contentment.

Fenella R. Morgan
MY SEARCH
I look for God in the sky,
And in the deep blue sea.
But while I am looking for God,
He is looking at me.

I look for God at my friend's house,
While we are busy at play.
While my friend and I are looking for God,
He watches us all day.

I look for God at twilight,
In the warmth of my mother's smile.
I found Him there in the velvet night,
He was with me all the while.

And now, wherever I go,
We're together, God and me.
I didn't think to look in my heart,
But that's where He was—you see?

Sherri L. Baker
OUR FLOWER

I dedicate "Our Flower" to the one I love, Eddie Collins

Our Lives have Met,
  Our hearts have Touched.
The past for us is Empty,
  The future is Unseen.
Our time will Pass,
  New beginnings will Start.
The time we have Shared
  Will not be Forgotten,
  Nor Remembered.
For it will inclose the Flower
  That has become from the
  Warmth and the Water of our Lives.
There it will remain until we
  Seek it again.
Protected by the Circle,
  Our FLower Will Always Be.

Pauline Akerley
LOTION AND GOD
Most hand lotion's potent stuff,—
  helps to soften skin that's rough.
Heals small cuts and bruises, too.—
  There's no tellin' what it'll do.

Cleans & softens & smells so nice,
  who could worry about the price?

Once, my heart was black inside,
  and from God I tried to hide.
I just thought he couldn't see,
  cause He didn't punish me.
But then, one day, I was told,
  "Jesus has a heart of gold!
He won't clobber you for wrongs,
  He'll put inside your heart a song!"
So I humbly looked right up to Him
  and I told Him all my sin.—
He had known them all the time!
  Still,
  He claimed me!!—said "You're Mine!!"

Don't you know I felt great bliss
  when I heard Him tell me this???

So when *you* use any kind of lotion,
  you can say, God is my portion—
Through Him I have eternal life,
  in His Presence, there's no strife . . . .

Lotion heals the outer skin, but—
Jesus heals the soul within!!!!

Leslie Marie Miller
FRIEND

To Veg, may our friendship last forever.

Be heard,
Be seen,
Be close,
Our friendship is dear.
I always want you near.
Keep in touch
. . . by verse,
. . . by telephone,
. . . by the years.
Keep your touch in our friendship
I intend to follow the same.
Friendship can not be justified by all the languages universal,
Nor will ours ever be unjustified.
Be close.
I Love You—You are my Friend.

Grace Arnell
Heavenly Sunshine and Shadows
Heavenly sunshine and shadows
At the close of each day
Another flower is added
To our life's bouquet.

Some of the flowers are tender and small
Others, like beautiful thoughts grow bigger
With Heavenly sunshine
And showering rain fall.

Good deeds spiced with radiant Colors of the rainbow from the blue
Kind words spoken to friends
A "Hi" and "I love you".

How I wish there were no shadows,
But to wish is all in vain;
For with the sunshine,
There must be some falling rain.

Tomorrow, God willing Heavenly sunshine and shadows,

At the close of the day
There will be another flower
added
To our life's bouquet.

Stephanie Finucane
**The Lonely Gather Of
  Night**
As the mist and fog of night
  prevail
a shadow of Hell emerges
  from the dark of night and sky,
there are no charities to run to.

Beside myself,
entrapped in loneliness,
I feel no other's life.
All I am
  is a victim
of society's weaponed war.

And over a passed time
I have lost all hope
  to the dark ghost of man . . .
but always,
  though my feelings reach low,
I become aware
  of whom I really have—
my God to guide me . . . .
And with a blink
I see nothing
And the Night's child slumber
  has won.

Stella E. N. T. Williams
Answer With Largesse

---

*To my son Arthur S. Taraldsen,
who served in the Marines Corps,
in World War #-2-*

Those souls who suffer from a
  paucity of words are poor
  indeed. They bleat and cry so
  few will understand if I should
  tie my poems, here and there
  with terms whose plea is
  subtly spoken. No, they say to
  me, a poet must be careful that
  he buy from sturdy plainest
  cloth, his cloak and try to
  please with simple words and
  brevity,

But this I answer from a heart
  and soul abounding with the
  greatest treasure known, the
  endless over lapping wealth of
  ores that wait for my word-
  mining; give the whole of glory
  found in rich new words. Set
  the tone up higher, many wait
  their golden stores.

Robert T. Kerr
OF A PROMISE KEPT
The pity
of young dandelions
is flashy bright
grows old
furry white
so fast.

From pity
to something else—
Aha!
From bright
to white
parachutes on the wind,
surprising
rain-soaked soil
with assurance
insuring more

brightly flash
better yet
next spring.

Virginia Mae Weber
THE WIND SPOKE
The Wind spoke
In the park
Old bushes of brilliant yellow
Blotted out
The hanging tree
And beneath—
The caverns of the subway
Spoke—
Minute earthquakes
In cadence

The old magnolia
Blooms again
And the old antique shop
Comes to life
When the white light
Bounces off
The pearl-handled silverware.

Twila A. Gorton
IT'S MEANING TO ME
A red Poinsetta sits in our church,
  And brings to mind our Savior's
  Birth.
And tho today, it may seem faded
  and sad,
  It represents the Birth of a
  special Lad.
The red in it's blossoms, seem
  pure and precious you see,
  For it resembles the blood Christ
  shed for you and me.

As Jesus grew through the years
  Suddenly into our lives a cross
  appears.
Where His precious body was
  nailed in pain,
  Only to prove it was not in vain.
For from His Grave, the stone
  was rolled away,
  So that we on Earth could Love,
  Worship and Pray.

Then as Our King and Christ
  arose Again,
  Into my heart came another
  refrain:
He Arose, He Arose, He Arose,
  Up from the grave He Arose;
With a mighty triumph O'er His
  foes,
  Hallelujah, Christ Arose.

And today in our Church, a pure
  white Lily does stand,
  It's purity represents, Christ's
  eternal Love for man.
If we will only repent and accept
  His Hand,
  His Love will lead us to Eternity
  in His Promised Land.
Although the Poinsetta and Lily
  may wither and fade,
  Our Special Savior, in Heaven, a
  home for us has made.

Harriette Eaton
Stay With Me, Jesus, Please
Stay with me Jesus please
The dusk is long and the night is
  dark
The loneliness only thou sees
Thy hand can guide my
  trembling bark
Tonight it seems my efforts fail
The sea is rough and I am frail
Guide me by night and day
Make the way before me plain

To a safe haven on the way
Keep me from storm and rain
Dear Father do not leave me please
I am a lost suppliant on my knees

He comes and stays and I am not
  alone
He gives more peace than I have
  ever known

Theodore N. Maher
An Anchor Towindward
Thank you unconcious
For doing your job,
Thank you for being
An anchor towindward;
But now I've outlived
Your cautious concern
On my voyage to happiness and
  beyond.
It's time to be free
Of your thoughtful restraint,

Which has kept my fragil bark
Between the breakers
And the rocky shore.
At last the time has come
For me to cut the link
And claw up towindward
Toward auspicious skies
And the constant breeze of faith.

Jeffrey Levine
STEPS OF UNFOLDMENT
Walking to our next action,
Coming home a step further along.

We never really fail,
but grow through our experiences.

A little wiser than before.

Ian Kelly
DEATHWARD BENT
The pain was just too much
to bear—
It shown there in his eyes
And as if the pain weren't
bad enough—
He was told he was going to die!

They gave him pills to ease
the pain—
Which helped him to some extent.
But the pills couldn't give him
  back
a life—
Still he is deathward bent!

Oh Lord, what do you say to a
dying man—
Whose world lay badly shattered
A young man in the prime
of life—
What said—could possibly matter?

I don't think he can quite

believe—
That his life is soon to end
Cause he holds his head up high
and smiles—
So we too—just smile and pretend!

Carol E. DiPiano
A CHRISTMAS WISH
I want Satin and Lace all over the
place.
Plush rugs and ceilings speckled
with Gold.
Chandiliers tinkling with crystal,
like ice in Winters cold.
I want mirrors reflecting marble,
waved with Onyx and Silver.
Crackling, dancing flames in a
fireplace to warm you when
you shiver.
I want a Rolls Royce in the color
of my choice.
I want a Yacht to cruise the
waters on.
Furs and Jewels I must also don.
An Oil well here, an Oil well
there, Money in every bank in
the Sphere.
An Island then I could buy, but
wait something else has caught
my eye.
There is still a void with all this
wishful wealth.
What I really want and need is
Faith, Love, and Good Health.

Tricia Hines
CHRISTMAS TIME

---

*I wish to dedicate this to all my
friends who encouraged me and
especially to my Mother who
offered me great encouragement
even though the times that I
became very discouraged.*

Here it is Christmas time once
again.
And stockings are hung above
the fireplace in the den.
Little boys and girls look forward
to Santa Claus on Christmas
eve night.
They are the first to rise even
before the sunlight.
They enjoy decorating the
Christmas tree.
And for a change their parents
they try to please.

Of course adults like Christmas
too.
They like to get gifts just like
children do.
But sometimes people fail to see
the true meaning of Christmas
each year.
That is Christ was born on this
day so that we could still be
here.
So I wish you a Merry Christmas
from deep within me.
And may God be with you and
yours through eternity.

Rosa E. Garcia
**THE TOWN CLOWN (An
  Alcoholic)**
Here I sit alone again,
With nothing else to do;
Wondering where I am this time,
And if I told the truth.

I just found out where I am,
With all these bars around;
I know I must have got picked up
For acting like a clown.

I now have quite a record,
For sitting in this cage;
For everytime I take a drink
I go into a rage.

I hope I'll find someone,
Before I have to pay;
That will tell me how to find,
The closest Double A. (A. A.)

So if you're an alcoholic,
Stop and think about this cell
And remember what I've told you,
About this man-made hell.

Marie L. Anderson

Marie L. Anderson
THANKSGIVING PRAYER

To David O., Kristine L., and Barbara L. the children I had the pleasure of raising, and loving, for which I will be always thankful.

I wake up in the morning-
And the harvest time is gone,
Of fruit, there is an abundance,
From the work, that has been done.
On the fields, that I have toiled-
And the seeds, that I have sewn,
I marvel! At the large, pumpkins-
To how tall! the corn has grown.
The bins are full, to over flowing-
With barley, wheat and rye,
I gaze, up to the heavens-
To thank our master, up on high.
I know that I have plenty-

With plenty, more to spare,
To feed the poor, the hungry-

With whom! I wish to share.
My thanks to God, I am sending-
For giving us, sun and rain-
With the food, we have harvested.
The world will have less pain.
To the world! "A happy thanskgiving",
Make peace in life, as you go,
I know, my prayers have been answered-
For you reap! What you sew.
"Happy Thanksgiving"

Maggie Magee
I CAN BUT SIGH
A flower of pink
you picked for me,
love shown in your eyes
for all to see.

A touch of your hand
brushing my skin,
a story of love
about to begin.

Gently you take me
into you arms,
casting a spell
with all of your charms.

Feeling you near
I can but sigh,
as you turn to me
simply whispering hi.

Rosemary S. Babinski
LOOKING FOR SOMEONE

May all of you looking for that "Someone" find him in God

Someone to love
Someone to care for
Someone who could give me love
Who could ask for more?

Someone who demands nothing in return
Someone who shares with me his time
Someone who gives me love in return
Without having to have reason or rhyme.

Someone to laugh with
Someone to share the good and bad
Someone to be with
Whether I am happy or sad.

Someone I could love and could love me back
Someone I could really talk to
Someone who does not turn his back
When I've hurt him without intending to.

Someone to share happy times together
Someone to come home to when day is done
Someone to help fight the stormy weather together
When will I find this Someone?

Ruth E. Morris
TO AN OCTOBER ROBIN
Well hello there, Robin Red Breast,
Did you come to say goodbye?
Was it getting a little colder up North,
Under the blue October sky?
Or did old Mother Nature tell you,

It was almost time for you to go,
To the South and a warmer climate,
To escape the cold and snow?
Well, if you can choose your seasons,
A lucky bird you are,
With no problems of transportation,
And no fuel to buy for a car.
And I have thought, how nice it would be,
If I could fly like you,
I'd take off for the South, miss all the cold,
And all those heating bills too,
But on second thought, it would never work,
All the clothes I would need
For the winter and the fall.
My luggage would be so heavy,
I would not be able to fly at all.
So you have a safe journey, my friend,
Take no chances on anything,
For we won't to be able to welcome you back,
In the early days of spring.

Dale L. Seal
THE DEATH OF A TREE
A
tiny
seed grows
fast and free and tall
and soon becomes a huge tree
only
to
be

cut

and

sawed

and

chopped

and

downed
By hands so black and
rough and
cold and
stupid and
unconcerned

Cheryl D. Jackson
WHAT I AM

Dedicated to Mrs. Ruthie M. Jackson, my mom and my favorite cousin Gayle J. Brown, and Toni, Easter and Damien

I, I've got to be what I am inside
Set me free take this look off my life
Let me breathe and suffer never again
Let my soul blow with the music in the wind
Let me stretch until my heart's content
Reach to put my life within my clinch
Who am I, what can I do
I'm I a winner or will I lose
Let me go you will see
Changes that you never thought could ever be
Then love me, and need me
Then we'll be so happy
Just believe in what I am, and in

return
I give you all of me
What I am
I, I've got to be what I am in my heart
I've got to be so strong I won't fall apart
I've got to ramble, let my spirit soar free
I've got to live my life and live it for me
Then love me, and need me
Then we'll be so happy
Just believe in what I am and in return
I give you all of me
What I am

Mary Jane Shackelford
BLESSINGS

Thank You, Magdalene, for your encouragement

Use this day to count blessings
Start counting and let your light shine,
Each day that we live is a blessing
I thank God for each one of mine.
To be able to speak is a blessing
So use your voice to give praise,
Thank God for all of your blessings
You've been blessed in so many ways.

To be able to hear is a blessing
So listen to God's Holy plan,
His servants are preaching the gospel
It's a blessing for each sinner man.
To be able to shout is a blessing
To be able to sing is one too,
So use your blessings to praise Him
Who gave His own Son just for you.

To have good health is a blessing
Straight legs, good eyes and sound mind,
All of these things are a blessing
Start counting and let your light shine.

To be able to walk is a blessing
To be able to work is one too,
Living for God is a blessing
Who let His own Son die for you.

Misti Thiel
'84 WINTER OLYMPICS
The battle lines
drawn they face
each other
in nervous anxiousness
waiting for the
fight to
begin
they move
within the confines
of their
achievements
fulfilling the
expectations
of the world
carrying the weight
of a million observers
upon their shoulders
they flash their
weary smiles
and begin their
quest for the gold.

Our World's Best Loved Poems

Betty Kathleen Hall
PERFECTION

For thoughtfulness: To my friend, Martha Alice Evans, who constantly puts others first. And to POETRY PRESS, who has given the world an opportunity to read some of my poems—and has given me much encouragement.

God is the hummingbird o'er
  nectareous flowers;
He is the sunshine, the breeze
  and the showers.
God is the bluebird, the robin,
  the wren;
He is the human being who is
  always a friend.

God is the cardinal, so stately
  and red;
He is the hungry as well as the fed.
God reaches out with omnipotent
  hands,
Renews us, sustains us, portrays
  us and then—

God plans our lives by day and
  by night;
He gives us courage, He shines
  our light.
When we are weary from illness
  and pain,
He heals us, He lifts us, and we
  bloom! again.

So God rules the universe, each
  planet, each sea,
He rules it all, even you and me.
He bears our prayers and each
  hymn that we sing,
For God is every good and perfect
  thing.

C. J. Reiter
SCAR COLLECTOR
Bitter is the taste left hanging in
  the night,
Remember now the wrong that
  used to be so right.
Sunken are the hopes that were
  once sought after,
Hearing weary cries that
  yesterday were laughter.
Forging the condition that
  everything's okay;
While acting out the role of an
  average normal day.
Breathing discontent in the sad
  malicious air;
While trying to pretend that you
  haven't got a care.
Broken down inside with major
  damage done,
The surgeons shake their heads
  for their remedies are none.
Turn to close encounters for they
  say they understand;
Confused in such a downpour,
  DO NOT take the helping hand.
So you walk the lonely streets as
  to maybe find a clue,
Knowing that the sun may never
  shine again for you.
The bars in your head hold the
  fossils of the past;
Count the scars in order from the
  first to the last.
The summary of the count is a
  survey of your life,
Coming now in focus is a history

of your strife.
It's a wonder you go on, when
  you're such a bad selector;
To pick out a life, and title it "A
  Scar Collector."

Lora J. Wesolek
THE SEARCH HAS BEGUN

This poem is dedicated to my now and forever guy—Bernie. You"ended my search" on February 17, 1984 by entering my life. I love you!

I know you've got to be out there
  somewhere—
I wish I knew the exact location.
Haven't I suffered long enough
  without you?
Why do you have to be so hard to
  find?

I call out into the lonely night
Listening for your reply.
Do you ever cry out in heartfelt
  pain
Knowing there has to be *me*
  waiting for *you*!

Let's try harder, my Love,
To connect our minds with
  telepathy.
Then, maybe on a lonesome
  night when we call out,
We will be the answering reply
  together!

Sandra R. Bailey
THE GIFTS

To my Mother, who taught us love and compassion.

First, comes the growing
Second, comes the meeting
Third, comes the knowing
Fourth, comes the greeting-
Fifth, comes the tie-that-bonds
Sixth, we sing of auld lang syne.
Eighth, we learn the wealth of age.
Ninth, we turn another page.
First comes the growing———

Louise Minnick
THE FIRST SNOWFALL

I dedicate this poem to all my family and friends, who wait for the first snowfall

---

Last night God gave my world a
  coat of ermine
As the sun came shining through,
  He turned it into a field of
  sparkling diamonds
The stately pines, garbed in
  green, stood guard o'er the
  scene
Where neither man nor creature
  disturbed anything
I stood at my window in silent
  awe
A picture too perfect to be
  painted by an artist
When I thought all was complete
He sent a raucous blue jay
And a cardinal in red armor
To the birdfeeder
What flashes of color for me to
  behold

how much time passees
That God painted a picture for me

DeDe Dudek
THE MEADOW SIDE
On that day all did gather,
upon the meadow side.

They came from here they came
  from there,
that day that one did die.

All did sulk and all did cry
upon the meadow side,

For the old red robin had flown
  his last
across the bright blue sky.

They dug a hole on that solemn
  day,
upon the meadow side

And all at once they pushed him
  in,
with a flower at his side.

Now all is gloomy
upon the meadow side,

For the old red robin sadly has
just died.

Suzanne Y. Bell
LEGACY
There is a part of me that is truly
  mine alone,
No one can go there with me, for
  it's not in flesh and bone.
It is my memory and my heart,
  things only I can see.
The good, the bad, the happy, the
  sad, they all have woven me,
Into the person I am now, all my
  strengths and my fears.
To know that place would be to
  know my laughter and my tears.

As I get older the more I retreat
  into my place with pleasure;
It is my sanity at times, my
  comfort and my treasure.
For there my heart knows it's
  loved, both past time and the
  present.
I have been treated and acted the
  parts of royalty and peasant.
My secret jokes, my childhood
  dreams, all that was dear to me,
Are in a special memory box,
  which I hold the only key.

Please don't be sorrowful that you
  cannot go there too;
For it does not have a place over
  my beloved life with you!
It is just a special place, that as I
  older grow,
Can go there and relive my
  youth, and warm my weary soul.

Loretta Olund
LIFE
In flight with wilted wings,
in green water swirling
in semi-cirles
the yellow daisy
meets the mossy tree:
gliding to the marshy bank,
blown to a cold smooth stone,
and toppling down under the wet
flowing clouds to see their delicate
  little dance, and spinning to the
  maker
or a just-sounded chirp,

bathed by silence, wetness,
and long-to-be remembered notes

of tiny flapping creatures,
joyfully tumbles
the winged wonder of a daisy.

Eleanor S. Follmer

Eleanor S. Follmer
ALONG MY WAY
I've walked many a weary mile,
And climbed many a rocky steep;
But the friends I've met upon
  life's road
Have kept my journey sweet.

I've seen lilacs bloom in spring,
And drank their fragrance from
  the air;
But the love I've seen in
  children's eyes,
Was a love beyond compare.

I've run through meadows in the
  sun,
And I've strolled through
  summer's rain;
But I've seen a beauty none could
  paint,
When God's Fall set the world
  aflame.

I've watched the angry
  thunderheads
As they churned the sky above;
But I've found a peace within my
  soul,
As I've walked in God's great love.

I've feasted from His riches,
And felt the Spirit's power;
And my life will be complete,
When I reach that golden hour.

Alma Childress Brown
Dorothy Wordsworth's Journals Revisited
The roar of traffic from the avenue
Comes indistinctly through the
  summer night;
While midge-like cares of day are
  put to flight,
The city glows against the sky.
  With you
I walk beside still lakes of lapis
  blue,
Or see you in Dove Cottage,
  swept and bright,
Set out the things for tea by
  candlelight,
In preparation for the cherished
  few
You love and favor with your
  caring look.
And now our paths through
  Scottish glens unfold
By misty loch, and crag, and fern-
  sweet brook.

433

Oh, strange it is within my hands
   to hold
All that we have of you, a slender
   book,
"Poor earthly casket" of a mind's
   pure gold!

Alexander P. Devanas
A CHRISTMAS WISH
Poor Johnny was an orphan
Who's prayers were for a home.
He played a tuba in the band
But he wished he had a family of
   his own.
People came from miles around
To adopt a son or daughter
Johnny heard the people's
   praising sound
But alas they took another.
Poor Johnny, he gave up hope
Of ever having a father or a
   mother.
So Johnny began to silently cry
Because he could no longer cope
His Christmas dinner was going
   to be,
Recooked rice, five times refried.
Until the silence was broken,
With a joyous "You want me"
His wish was answered after all,
Because God heard his call.

Carol Eamigh
Daylight and Daybreak
Daylight and daybreak, with an
   aura all its own,
A heart full of expectancy for a
   love that has grown.
A glance out of a window to
   welcome whatever may,
Another time to experience the
   happenings of the day.

To work in the home attending
   to a chore,
Or a day spent in shopping in
   your favorite store.
Everything is so special, a
   surprise and delight.
A feeling of peace because
   everything is alright.

Mrs. Leslie Cook
A PLACE I USED TO BE

---

*This poem is dedicated to my
sister Karen, who by being afraid
to go home to mixed memories of
our childhood friends and
neighborhood, inspired me to
write this poem.*

Here I am again, in a place I used
   to be
The scenery looks so familiar,
   but it doesn't feel like me
The good times, the bad times, all
   mingle in my mind,
And I stop to think awhile of
   what I left behind.

There's the old High School,
   where I used to go,
I wonder if there's anyone here
   that I used to know
But probably not, for we've all
   had to grow.

It's kind of a scary feeling, to take
   new steps, I know
But sooner or later, you see, it's
   the only way to go.

So I dry my tears, put away my

fears
And let the past go by
So I can finally see, what God put
   me here to be,
and why.

Letha Memorie Lloyd-Wayne
MASTERS
Moses—Jacob—Abraham—
Job—Joseph—David—
Each one—my teacher from God
Commanding me thru laws divine
Helping me climb the ladder of life
Showing me trust in gaining thru
   sacrifice
Patience and faith that I see
God in my flesh
Lifting me out of the pit of despair
Into the Kingdom of giving and
   Heaven
Carrying me all the while
As I walk thru the valley of death
Into newness of life everlasting.

Jerry Jamar
NUCLEAR FAMILY
A dying man is lying in the grass.
   In his left hand are petals from
   a rose. There are petals of
   sunlight in his eyes, but they
   are fading into brown like the
   petals in his hand.

Hospital and cemetery are far
   away from us now. The
   instincts for life and death
   mingle easily here.
An autumn hour free of time.
   Alone forever we lie, an
   ancient longing of the soul
   piercing deep beneath the
   grass, tasting the sweet earth
   that cast us into night.

I laid him here in the early
   morning light. I have kissed his
   forehead many times and have
   cried over his destiny. All
   wilted and pale, sad and pitiful,
   I whisper, "I love you." And
   then I press his eyelids gently
   over his eyes.

We never talked about simple
   things, about tenderness or a
   falcon's cry. And before a time
   had come when we could try to
   believe in one another again, a
   horror had bitten him unlike
   any known to Plato, Bacon, or
   Goethe.

Sunset colors of red, purple, and
   green have filled these eyes for
   the last time. A winter chill
   flows gently through his hair.
   The why for so short a life to
   have suffered so much. Like a
   flower in the snow he is free
   now, free to die. A leaf forever
   exposed to moonlight, dew, and
   rain. Unlike anything in his
   lifetime, he will lie in the grass
   and dream.

Catherine A. Helt
THE DRUNKARD
Can you or I understand the soul
   of a man,
Who by the evil power of liquor
   has fallen?
No, I think their are so very few
   who can,
Discern the need of a friend for
   which he's calling.

Can we stand by through thick or
   thin?
Do we try our best to decipher
   his living code?
Oh, so many of us in passing him
   by,
See only a drunken old sod, a bum.
Now if this same person belonged
   to you or I,
Would we try from this hell to
   lead him from?
But, alas so many of us would say,
Look at this disgusting creature, a
   regular deadpan.
Knowing not, that beneath the
   filth and fumes lay,
The hopeless, hungry, tormented
   soul of a man.

Susan G. Robinson
A KNIGHT'S CONQUEST
The shinning knight ventured to
   the sea
With questions in his mind.
A bottle he cast on the water so
   clear
For the secret one to find.

The flowers bloomed on the hill
   above
And a song blew in the air.
The voice of dawn echoed for
   miles
Exclaiming a love so fair.

There he kneeled to praise The
   Lord
For the wonders all around.
An eagle encircled the valley's
   edge
Soaring above all sound.

A vision appeared in the pond
   beside
Bringing joy into his heart.
His soul then touched the
   beautiful face
Of which he could not part.

The centaur galloped from tree to
   tree
Making a dream come true.
He scattered leaves of a glorious
   seed
From which miracles grew.

The vision gazing sparked in his
   eyes
And whispered a message to him;
A calm relief of an assuring code
Changing a future once dim.

Tori Vannes
GYPSY
The dark-eyed girl
on the old, yellowed tin
held a dark secret
from within.

Still the gypsies come
from a long, long time ago.
Still dances the dark-eyed boy
and still she never told.

Gladus M. Moore
HAPPY BIRTHDAY, LORD
Oh, how I wish, that I could go
Back home on Christmas Day.
To call out loud and clear
I love you, Merry Christmas.

This can't be, you see
God, called my love ones home.
They're on high, and near, His
   Throne

While I am here, yet not alone.

On this Holy Night, I pray
And wish our, Lord, Happy
   Birthday.
Then call out for all to hear
Merry Christmas World, He loves
   you!

Louise Beaven
HORIZON

---

*Dedicated to the glory of God,
Who has not left us without
promise, and for my husband,
Donald Angus Edwin Cameron
Beaven, a devotee of Robbie Burns.*

Soon . . .
the snow.
Now
the roses fade.
Promises of
greener spring
lie shrouded
in the shade.

Louise Minnick
THE WINDBELLS

---

*I dedicate this poem to all people
who have received Jesus as their
Saviour.*

Joyously the windbells peal forth
The oft told story of Jesus birth
The gift unspeakable
And full of glory
They ring in abandonment
To the winds and ears that are
   open to hear
They stir hearts to sing again
Peace on earth, goodwill to men
They awaken silent chords, that
   lay dormant too long
Everyone joins in the angelic
   song
Peace on earth, goodwill to men.

Karen Grignon
COSMIC IMAGES
Oh to see a cascade of colors
   spread across the sky,
   Its radiant beams touch the
   earth and
Fill our hearts with warmth as
   the sun kisses the rain.
   What a sight to see the
   spectrum brightly glow and
Form in brilliantly vibrant
   shades, set off a crimson cast.
   The mystical magic it instills
   leaves a lasting aftermath,
A secret path which no one has
   seen into a world of
   fantasy, to far away places in
   the Universe.
Then we enter another galaxy
   where visions of cosmic images
   beyond our wildest dreams,
   seem to last through
Eternity, till the end of
   time.

Sharon Humbard
SOFTHEARTED
As I practised guitar
I saw my index finger
Grow callouses on top of scars.
I wish I could practise
Guitar with my heart.

Tom Crisp
LOVE POEM

---

*To Jennie my first wife who still
haunts my memories*

Silver dew drops on the rose
   in the sunlight
Brown eyes twinkle like the stars
   in the night
Auburn hair flowing across a
   meadow
   in the morning
Music soothing to the soul
   in my loneliness.

You are beauty and the beast
   to a troubled heart
The sun in the morning
   to a new day
Peacefull rain at eventide
   to nerves drawn tight
Comfort in the night
   to a weary mind.

You are infinity to me my dear.

Stella E. N. T. Williams
THE HEART AWARE

---

*Dedicated to my Son David Lloyd
Taraldsen, who served in United
States Navy, in World War. —2—*

The night lay veiled beneath a
   star-skied tent,
the shepherds by their fires dozed
   in sleep.
Only the shadowed quiet charged
   with deep
electric force, seemed waiting
   some event
mysterious, beyond belief, while
   scent
of myrrh and aloes clung as if to
   keep
predestined rendezvous of years.
   The sheep
lay unaware, nor wondered what
   this meant.

But there were folk who sensed
   with eagerness
the miracle about to be revealed;
the few with hearts attuned to
   heavenly things,
whose faith is ever equal to all
   stress.
These shared the mighty secret
   long concealed.
Would I have heard the rush of
   angel wings?

Margaret Chew
HE

Never, his father, did see
For fear did he
The lightless nocturne.

Never, his father, did he
Touch, for the length of the
Touch, and the dare of the
Touch, he touched not.

Father, was, was not, the Sun:
Gold heart of milk.
Son, be, be not, Sun's son:
Jaundiced cream.

Alchemist and astronomer
Had solved not the problem
Of Father, Son and Sun,
But declared cream not of milk.

Nevertheless,
Hail he of sight and touch!
He, the Son of the Sun.

Lucille Thrower

Lucille Thrower
HAPPY FATHERS DAY

Dear Dad, I love you and I love
   my Mother too,
But because this is Fathers day
I'm thinking up wishes for you"

I wish to cheer you, you could
   play a game of ball.
And then when the day was over
That you wouldn't be tired at all"

Or maybe just a chat with a cute
   little dish"
Well then Dad, if that would
   cheer you,
I guess that, THAT is what I wish"

Muriel S. Thygesen.
NEW YEAR

What do you think this New
   Year brings
Trailing, for none to see,—
Is it joy and peace
Or terrible things
Hidden beneath it's secret wings?

Welcome this new and shining
   year
Full of the strange unknown,
For with hope and faith
And constant prayer
We shall yet conquer the worlds
   despair.

Sauna Maronski
A CHRISTMAS TEAR

---

*This poem was written for Louise
A good and wonderful friend
Someone we all shall miss
terribly.*

Perhaps it's time for Christmas
   cheer, a moment just to play
Perhaps it's time for family
   warmth, the days they slip away

Children happily laughing, smiles
   with camera caught
Santa Claus is coming, the gifts
   have all been bought

We feel there is no reason for
   anything but gay
And yet a sadness beckons, a
   cloud has set the day,

Our God is good and loving, he
   makes each life so grand
But all is not that simple, we
   sometimes need a hand,

A friend, she lies so quiet, a tear
   is shed in vain,
The justice is confusing, we are
   not spared the pain,

Pandora's box has opened, disease
   and illness spread,
No wealth or fame can conquer,
   this fate is held in dread,

I always will remember, the
   happy times too few
This fight she did surrender, the
   end is almost due,

But, sad be not for very long, her
   gentle smile lives on
The hands of God have taken,
   although from us she's gone,

For her there is no Christmas
   cheer, no wrappings to undo
The merriment of Christmas has
   lost its colored view,

She loved and always will be
   loved, good friends are hard to
   find
Her eyes, they said a thousand
   words, to her dear God be kind,

Perhaps it's time to look around,
   a time to see the way
Perhaps it's time to feel the need,
   a moment just to pray.

Paul Michael McAteer
WILL YOU FOLLOW?

A land of barbarians next
to a city of conformists
On a space confined to a Reserve
Walked a gunless, high-cheeked
   bone man
Full of courage, trying to survive
All the time just barely alive
His awareness keen of the
   decadence,
his tribes' broken back spleen.
His efforts to want to do
   something
Lost in the beer of his mind
Tommorow, maybe he would be
   fine.

Betty J. Beam
LEAVE ME NO LEGACY

Leave me no legacy
   Of your fear and your guilt
Nor make me a victim
   Of your anger and greed

Neither enslave me to
   Custom and tradition
And judge me not, brother
   For I do not judge you

Bequeath this boon instead
   Twin gifts of peace and love
Then grant me the freedom
   To reason and to choose

Of seven deadly sins
   Ignorance is not one . . .
All water will in time
   Find its way to the sea

Bernard A. Floto
ANOTHER ETERNITY

To Gail and Wanda

Will struggles never cease upon
   the earth
Of man on man of land on land,
Or are we of the lower beasts
Evolved to feed forever

On the lessor bodies of our kind?

Our history—an endless
   chronicle of war,
Five thousand years, or more,
The strong against the weak,
The bold upon the meek,
And now
The heinous missiles, planted
   like flowers
In the soft sweet soil of the earth,
Their deadly blossoms to poison
   forever
The shining cities of the world.

Will ashes stain the winter snow
On mountainsides across the
   lands?
And the only sound
On the molten ground
And the boiling seas,
Are the echoes of galloping
   hooves
Triumphantly racing the
   smoking skies
In search of a new eternity,

An eternity that eyes like ours
Will never see . . .

No! We have crawled too far from
   the caves
For such a destiny.

Gertrude A. Kiser
INEVITABILITY

I have wondered what is left to say;
What musicians could find to play;
An artist would next display;
Or a sculptor form from marble
   or clay.

But just as surely as through the
   ages
Each had its share of bards and
   sages;
And myriads of artisans in their
   right;
God will send new talent who'll
   see the light,
To combine symbol or matter
   with imagination
Bringing new art to this
   generation.

Rose Colombo Strickland
**The Perfect Christmas
Tree**

---

*To my daughter, Holly, on her
fifth Christmas.*

Once upon a time
   In the cold North Pole
Grew a perfect tree
   As green could be.

But old Scrooge said,
   "Let's chop it down,"
Santa's Christmas tree
   Fell to the ground.

When Santa's elves
   Came out to play
Their Christmas tree
   Was gone away.

But old Saint Nick
   With his magic stick
Wished it back
   Into his sack.

HO! HO! HO! HO!
   Santa did roll
Took one more look——
   As his fat belly shook.

The tree lit bright
  With shimmering light
While God's angels sang
  "Oh Holy Night."

The small elves cheered,
  Said the reindeer,
"Such a sight to see—
  The Perfect Christmas Tree!"

Mary Belle Cannine
**Our Silver Wedding
  Anniversary**

*Dedicated to my loving husband
George on our Silver Wedding
Anniversary Oct 12, 1976*

Twenty five years seemed forever
  away
When we took our vows on our
  wedding day
Where have they gone you say to
  me?
Like silver links to eternity.

The days are links in our chain of
  life
We've bonded together as man
  and wife.
With a lot of love along the way
To strengthen the heart and
  brighten each day

Never forgetting to pray for God's
  care
We've bonded a chain that will
  stand the wear
So the days and years have
  slipped away
But we've got a love thats here to
  stay.

Mary Belle Cannine
SEA SHORE KITTY
A little kitty by the Sea
Sat on a rock and looked at me
With such a strange and vacant
  stare
As if I really wasn't there.

Until I started to get too close
Then quickly dropping his quiet
  pose
he did along the rocky shore
And I never saw him anymore.

Gladys W. Tooley
REFLECTION
He was my Dad
And he was so good
I knew he must go
But not why he should
God knew
And said when
I wish He had waited.

Georgia Radcliffe
THE GOLDEN EAGLE
Cruising on the west wind
  his wing span wide and strong,
Coasting between two
  kingdoms——
  to which does he belong?
Golden neck band gleaming,
  feathered legs to the toes,
Sweeping the hallways of Heaven,
  this is the course he knows.
High on a mountain outgrowth
  he settles slowly down,
Talons grasping firmly
  a tree limb gnarled and brown,
Searching the earth below him,
  scanning the sullen sky,

Resting while deciding
  which way it is wise to fly,
Power controlled and throttled
  far from the maze of men,
He suddenly lifts, calls sharply,
  and sails on the wind again!

Debra Lynn Guerrazzi (Douglas)
ONE MOMENT

*To my family, Joan & Leslie
Douglas, Susan, Barbara, Al and
John. For all the one moments,
together we shared. Sometimes
unaware of the love which is
there.*

If I can touch your life just for an
  instance;
If I can explain one confusing
  thought,
Then you have shown me
  understanding.
If in a turmoil of anger,
I can offer an ear for comfort,
Then you have shown me
  tranquility.
If I can wipe one teardrop away—
Then you have shown me
  compassion.
If I can share a second of joy,
Which brings a smile to your face
  and laughter to your heart
Then you have shown me
  happiness.
If with insecure emotions our
  hands reach out and just
Barely touch but touch.
Then you have shown me hope.
If when in doubt,
I can shed some light for you to
  believe.
Then you have shown me faith.
Most important of all—
If just for one moment,
You feel peace within.
Then I have given you love.

Jeri Jo Wade
Ecstasy & Weeping Soul

Dedicated to my beautiful Dan

Oh joyous sweet weeping
  In my soul
I weep for love of mine
  Love of Dan——
                No other man
This is the end of —— time ——
No more will I search
  the land & sea —
The spirit of love
  My love has found me.
Oh joyous weeping in my soul
  My love abounds
                Majestic & bold,
Ecstasy & weeping soul.

Jeri Jo Wade
DAN

Dedicated to my beautiful Dan

I am looking close at the hills
                I feel kin to them.
Beauty of the sea foam sprays
                absorb in my soul.
I feel God's magic as I look upon
                the beauty He's created,

And know we're both made with
  his hand
                Me and the land.
I am touched with sweetness
                as I lay with my love,
We are one.
The magic goes hand in hand
                Me, my love & the land.
He brought me from isolation
                I was out of touch.
With feelings he made me care
I can feel the sea with all of me,
                feel the land.
In touch with feelings
                as I lay with my love
My beautiful, beautiful Dan.

Muriel E. Vebsky
SPRING COMES FORTH
Ducks head east in new-born
  spring,
With winter feathers thick and
  warm,
No sun to shine upon brown
  coats
For heavy rain clouds bounce
  about.
Fragrant spices toss the air,
As buds and greening leaves push
  out
On bush and trees along the route.
Chipmunks, squirrels, fox do
  scoot
From holes and dens their food to
  root.
Toward high noon the hazy sun
Disperses dingy thinning clouds,
While honking loud the ducks
  sail on,
O're towns and mountains they're
  borne,
Through soft and gentle winds
  are shorn.
Till I can see them them gleefully
Pass above me out to sea.
In a boat I take up the chase.
To see which of us wins the race,
As spring comes forth to cast its
  spell
Before the ducks can reach the
  dell.

Louise Beaven
FINGERS

*Dedicated to the glory of God:
"And God said, Let the waters
bring forth abundantly the
moving creature that hath life,..."
(Gen. 1:20), and to the Ankners,
Anne, Ray, Christopher and
Jennifer.*

Fingers stir the pond:
A ripple starts.
Infinitesimal fishes
Have hearts.

Viola Mae Spires
WINTERS FIRST SNOW
When the first snows of winter fall
In memory what does your heart
  recall?
Noticing every little flake of
  snow
To a childhood first you go.
Every flake would make you glow
Remembering all the joy and
  thrills,
Snowmen and sled riding down
  hills.

First snows of the winter time
In us all a bell, that rings a
  different chime.
Recalling a snowy hayride,
Snuggling warm by a fireside,
Thoughts of how quite and
  peaceful is the snow.

Somehow in the first snow,
Nearly all of us our ages show.
Older we are the less we think of
  it.
Why do I feel so closed in by it?

Claire C. Mears
**A Revelation
  —Perserverance**
I have seen the lightning flash
  And heard the thunder roar!
I have felt the mighty crash
  Of waves against the shore!

I have watched the earth erupt
  And hurl its crumbling crust!
I have walked where winds disrupt
  Each step through dormant dust!

I have scaled some barren
  mountains
  And tasted of the soil!
I have drunk from bitter fountains
  And bathed in flaming oil!

Horrors I have seen and heard
  Held pitfalls ever near.
But I took God at His word
  And learned to PERSERVERE!!!

Gina Kaut
**The Gift Of Love At
  Christmas**
I give to you my gift of love,
  Which was given to me from
    the maker above.
He gave it to me with the utmost
    care,
In hopes that it would grow, so
    again I could share.
  Without LOVE one cannot
    share,
  Even the smallest feelings that
    could be there.
I therefore thank you from the
    bottom of my heart,
As you've let my love for you
    grow from the day we did part.
  You've shown me how ones'
    love can grow,
  By your long distance
    phonecall and a friendly
    "HELLO."
Not only by this did I know you
    cared,
But by the days we spent together
    and the togetherness we
    shared.
  Wish we could share the years
    of love to come,
  But the distance it seems is far
    too great a sum.
I'll think of you then on
    Christmas Day,
Which makes you and I even less
    further away.
  "Christmas comes but once a
    year,
  So let's eat, drink, be merry, and
    have good cheer."
I heard those words just the other
    day,
Which made me think in the
    most unusual way.
  I wish you all these things so

great,
Even though they be coming a
bit too late.
I also send to you my dear,
A very Merry Christmas and a
Happy New Year.

Gloria Wilson Tessier
A GLIMPSE OF GOD
Should you be lame and see
concern
In smiling stranger's eyes
Perchance God is gazing at you
Although He's in disguise;
When strong arms guide you,
aged one
Across a busy street
'Tis possible your steps are next
To His own Holy Feet;
Midst throng should you feel
sudden surge
Of joy, and don't know why
It may be in the crushing crowd
That He just passed you by . . .

God's everywhere and anywhere
The time and place His choice—
Perhaps inside an unknown shell
With unfamiliar voice:
So next time someone smiles at
you
Is helpful or is kind
If you look fast, it may well be
A glimpse of Him you'll find . . .
What sweet delight can fill our
hearts
If ever we're aware
God may have passed or paused
awhile
In form of stranger, there.

James E. Turpin
US

*To Jeanette, You are the one
person who has seen my good,
bad and ugly sides, and who's love
has stood the test of time. For
this, I love you.*

Beyond the sea thats everchanging,
Here my life is rearanging.
When we stand holding hands,
I think of how we met.
I will never regret the steps we
took,
You know . . .
. . . It's almost like a scene from
a story book.
And when I think of the stars
above,
My heart is suddenly filled
with love.

Stephanie Nahirniak
**December Is the Month To
Remember**
As there are twelve months in
a year,
Each one has its share,
But to the last month being
December,
Not one can compare.
There's paintings of Nature
On the white crystal snow.
There's sparkling beauty,
Where ever we go
Each month's beauty is so great
Its too numerous to mention
But to the most beautiful
month of all,
I want to draw your attention.

For there come hours of the day,
then days of the week
Next come weeks of the month,
and at the months let us peak
January comes the first to start
the year right,
But December being last, brings
the greatest delight.
For its God who made the
world so dear,
But his birthday we celebrate
in December each year.
When Christmas bells chime
with music galore,
And carollers come carolling
right up to your door.
Its like a book with good ending
At the readers request,
The year ends in December,
Isn't December the best?

(Viola) Ruth Dawson
WHERE?
Where do man's relations end?
Being enemy: or being friend?
Love for others—do we fake it?
Or truly love—really make it.
Stay selfish, egotistical, and mean
Or perceive the feelings of others
keen?

Do we let our hot tempers flare?
Such conduct will get us
nowhere.
Some are ignorant and know no
better
Tolerance comes with a "man of
letter".
Races should not divide like
crevices deep
But cull out the worst—the best
of each race keep.

Good in a person can be buried
inside
Lie dormant; become frightened;
its worth will hide
A helping hand, a smile, a
kindness give.
Something beautiful, worhwhile,
and true
Might from this human come
back to you.

Each being is in God's love—not
let it fade.
Oh, where—where do man's
relations end?
The answer is up to us, My Friend!

L. G. Mace
CHRISTMAS BLUES

*For Frieda and Duane, who not
only inspired but shared the
sentiment of this poem—
Christmas of '83.*

Mom says Christmas will be
sparse this year.
When you're under financial
pressure it's hard
to get into the Christmas cheer.
It's bad news when you don't
even have the money
to buy yourself a smoke,
But even badder news when
everyone around you,
and including you—is broke!
You can look at catalogues and
dream
with a remorseful sigh.

And look in shop windows at the
Malls,
at clothes and articles, knowing
you'll never buy.
Of course there will be Christmas
dinner—
things can't ever get that bad.
Though the table won't be laden
in the fashion
of past dinners we have had.
Mom says it's only a matter of
money—
but isn't that the way it always is?
Part of the money making world,
the law of
commerciality and Big Biz?
So we'll be a family and try to
raise the
Christmas spirit-what do we have
to lose?
But I'm sure in the stillness of
our own thoughts—
We'll each be singing-the
Christmas Blues.

Jeanne Arnold Liska
CHRISTMAS THOUGHTS
Frozen crystals, one by one,
Laboring 'til their work is
Done.
Precious moments set apart,
Whispered secrets in the dark.
Sparklings lights, and church
Bells ring,
It's Christmas time, time to
Sing.
Days of skating and skiing Mt.
Hights,
Eve'ning walks on snowy nights.
I've cleaned and polished from
Front to back,
Chased the dust from every crack.
Stop a minute, for a cup of tea,
Then Dad and I will trim the tree,
It's early morning, sun's still
A-sleep,
Down the stairs I softly creep.
A thousand things must be done,
Christmas dinner will be
served
By one.
Pumkin pie and turkey smells,
Drift from room to room,
Everyone, will be here, by noon.
As Christmas joys I recall,
The one that lingers, best of all.
Hi Mom, I'm Home.

Don L. Robbins
JANUARY MORNING
Cold white flakes
Gently drifting down.
A soft white blanket
Fresh on the ground.

Walking can be so peaceful
My dog by my side;
A smile on my face
Stick-cane to help my stride.

Rabbit hides in brush
Beside my usual trail.
Birds fast on the wing
Keep flakes off your tail.

Young buck appears
Then heads through the trees;
Where an armadillo lies
Comfortably beneath the freeze.

Squirrel juggling a nut
Really quite concealing.
Tasting of nature
Always quite appealing.

Kathleen Dale Smith Thomas
TEARS
I do believe
That God catches
Every tear I cry
And He is saving them.

One day He will take me
In His arms
And explain why
Every tear was.

Pamela Tuggle Sutton

Pamela Tuggle Sutton
FINAL CURTAIN

*This poem is dedicated to Roger,
who knew the world is but a
stage, and with love to Ron,
Dene, Carol, Bob, Margaret, Steve
and David.*

As they lower the final curtain
A player has learned his part
That the world is but a stage
A tragic comedy of the heart.
Winds of change have blown
And you take your final bow
Your dreams have slipped away
Did they matter anyhow?
You climbed your last mountain
It was steeper than you knew
You rode the winds of time
And said your lines on que.
The audience overwhelmed you
They cried out, begged for more
You dried your river of tears
Leaving through the backstage
door.
The morning paper ran your
picture
The critics gave you rave reviews
They thought it was a dress
rehearsal
But, I think that somehow you
knew
The world is but a stage.

Tanya Reigh Miller
DRIFTING APART
I really loved you, that is true.
Still, you say, you loved me too.
We had fun, we played the game.
My life will never be the same.

You said you'd never hurt me,
You sounded so sincere.
I said that I believed you
Without a trace of fear.

The times we spent together,
I cherish in my heart
But the paths that now wander

John Campbell, Editor & Publisher

our way
Lead us to drift apart.

Brian Lynch Johnson
FIRST VISIT
The frost-burned grass crackled
Beneath my feet.
My first coming was announced.
On the side of Ciaran's Hill
I knelt and wept
And lost myself in memory.
Some lingering leaves clung for life
To the trees,
While others still hid
And looked for Spring.
A careless red breast chanced my
way,
He was late.
The kine low'd a lonesome lowe
That got lost in the fold of the
hills.
As I left the place for two
Occupied by one,
Secretly sequestered 'neath the
frozen sod
The black gate groaned,
The groan became familiar
And the Bitter Black Wind blew
Across the Bog of Allen.

Elizabeth R. Downer
MOM
You were there to help me with
my first step
to catch me when I fell,
And then you taught me right
and wrong
scolding me when I misbehaved,
You cleaned my wounds when
my battles were done
and listened when I was down.
You bathed my brows when I was
ill
and calmed my fears when I was
scared,
You weathered all my tantrums
And let me release all my
frustrations
And yet you never stopped being
there
creating for me a home like no
other.
Oh Mom
There are no ways to describe you
No ways to compile you
Except to say from the bottom of
my heart
You are the most super Mom ever
And I thank God you're mine.

Laura B. Reese
DREAM GIRL
Today,
  A beauty passed my way.
Alone,
  And free as the breeze.
Tossing aside,
  Her windblown hair.
Glancing too,
  At irresistable eyes of blue.
So shapely,
  In designer jeans.
Popularity,
  A going thing with the teens.
My thoughts,
  Are in a whirl.
Lovin!
  This fascinating girl.
She's,
  for me.
Dreamingly,
  It was meant to be.

Leonard Vincent/June E. Burns
MONA LISA
Mona Lisa, you were but a child,
How your husband beat you, I
  tried to dry your eyes,
You were so innocent, and I loved
  you so,
I couldn't help it darling, your
  tears my heart enclosed,
I painted you with Love my dear
  and took you to my bed,
I wanted you as no man knew,
  yet you were his and wed,
Our love was, oh, illicit, stolen
  now and then,
My darling I adored you, oh so
  much now as then,
You intrigued me darling, you
  intrigued me so,
You posed for me, and sat each
  day,
Why I'll never know,
I never understood my dear, you
  know I never will,
The child you bore was mine all
  mine,
The secret love fulfilled,
My darling Mona Lisa, a child yet
  fully grown.

Ranae Eastman
EXPERIENCE POETRY
Hear:
  Wind whistleing through the
  trees
  a robin as he sings
  a haunting melody
  whitecaps dancing on the
  ocean.
Feel:
  Softly falling snow
  a gentle warm caress
  the softness of a kitten
  that's poetry in motion.
See:
  A golden harvest moon
  a bird in gracefull flight
  a fiery setting sun
  a little childs face at rest.
Smell:
  A lovely fragrant rose
  the gentle falling rain
  coffee on the stove
  ahhh! poetry at it's best.

Queen Esther Johnson
BROWNIE

*I dedicate my poem to Mrs.
Carmen Williams. Carmen, which
I feel, deserves recognition for
inspiring me to open my doors as
a writer. Without her dedication,
"BROWNIE" would never have
been published.*

For the color of my skin makes
  no difference
and I will not carry my name
  with shame
I am who I am
and I will not change my name
I am an individual
who looks after herself
and needless to say, I can't take
  off my coat
because I am being myself
There's no other name

then either the one I am born with
so look now—
you have found people that aren't
  the same
"BROWNIE" is my name . . .

Alyce Jacob Pritchard
MAMA'S BIRTHDAY

*Dedicated to my Mama, Mrs.
Olive Jacob Pliley. You gave us
the happy, warm memories of
home, and the courage to reach
for our dreams. We all love you,
Mama.*

Sunday is Mama's Birthday,
Please God, let the sun shine.
Make it a day of happiness
For this wonderful Mama of mine.

She's always there when we need
  her
In that little house, all alone.
With all the love in that little
  house,
There is truly no place like home!

She could never ever be replaced.
This wonderful Mama of mine.
Her birthday will be here on
  Sunday,
So, Please God, let the sun shine.

Peter Adam Salomon
**Teddy Bear And Rose: A
Letter**

---

*Dedicated to Adina Baum—A
very good friend . . . THANKS*

Dear Rose: A Teddy Bear
      soft and plush
      made of love
      filled with hope.
      A little flower
      plush and soft
      made of sun
      filled with you,
for you are my Rose,
      and I am your Teddy Bear.

Hold me tight— and I will give
  warmth
I will caress and care for my little
  flower.
And watch it grow into a thing of
  beauty— A rose.

But it still has thorns— stopping
  my loving caress,
hurting my Teddy Bear paws.

Please stop the thorns— For your
  Teddy Bear.

          LOVE,
          TEDDY BEAR

Toni Lee Holford
The Greatest Love Song

---

*To the Prince of Melody Your
love and inspiration will always
be in my heart.*

Once there was a Prince of
  Melody.
There was a Lady of Rhyme and
  Harmony.
They knew not of love . . .
Or feelings of the heart . . .

Until they met and that was the
  start . . .
Of the greatest love song.

Some may forget this story's
  true . . .
For I am the Lady everyone knew.
Though we fell apart . . .
Both with a broken heart . . .
We never ended, because we were
  the start . . .
Of the greatest love song.

Some folks may say I never
  knew . . .
But I am the Prince who loved
  her true.
I never meant to harm . . .
I only wanted to charm . . my Lady.
She was my part . . .
Of the greatest love song.

Once there was a Prince of
  Melody.
He loved a Lady of Rhyme and
  Harmony.
Though his life was short . . .
Her love was long . . .
And so ended . . .
The greatest love song.

Michelle S. Levesque

Michelle S. Levesque
GROWING OLD
Snowflakes, Snowflakes,
Glittering, Glowing,
Shining, Falling;
Look! It's snowing!
Whiter, Softer,
Prettier, Older,
Older are the ones melted into
  the ground.

Amy R. Fitch
CONTEMPLATIONS

*To States . . . who personifies that
striving sense of understanding
beneath the confusion.*

Wandering, wondering, endlessly
  pondering
The fate of my existence: What
  shall I be?

Hoping, searching, tirelessly
  groping
For peace of mind among the
  stormy clouds
Of emotion: What shall I do?

Confusion subsequently arrives
And from under its wings
A sense of understanding strives
To survive.

438

Questions lacking answers,
Solutions for which no one ever asks—
To sort and define these are now my tasks.

Understanding shall come with time,
For I am told that confusion in adolecense
Is surely no crime.

Norah Powell
Salute Them As They Pass
Valient men who have gone
Into a foreign land to fight
Envisioning ideas and spreading light.
Thank you lads, your mission is done.

Now they are finally back home
And getting out of the greenish uniform
Mother land! they say, we have come.

Without limbs are many, but in line they form
Across the streets at the march's tune they swarm
Radiant, happy, also bitter tears from some.

Voices of men who have courageously endured
Enraged war hazards and now are secured.
Triumph of the spirit in the quiet night
Endeavor of the heaven's might.
Raphsodies of sacrifice and heroism
Alas, you were young and full of altruism.
National honor and respectful cheer
Salute for ever to you brave soldier dear.

Eloys E. George
MY MEMORY LANE
My thoughts keep turning backward to a road called memory lane.
Some of these thoughts of mine hold so much of warm sunshine,
And some hold stormy skies and rain.
I think about sweet childhood days when all the world to me was new.
These days were such delight to me, my heart so young and so carefree,
And these skies were always blue.
Then came the age of youthful days when life to me was like a song.
These were the days so bright when I thought I was so right,
And then found I was so wrong.
Then came the days of middle age and quickly passed these years.
The days took wings in flight and so quickly came the night.
These days were filled with laughter and some tears.
And how my memory lingers, now that I've grown old.
Oh this lane of memory now can so much longer be,
All that my heart can hold.
And as I think about dear loved

ones and pause awhile to pray;
There are those I can't forget;
how their memories linger yet;
Those dear ones who have gone away.
My thoughts travel down life's pathway, and I thank God for happiness and pain,
When I recall a favorite street and the dear folks that I meet,
Down that road called memory lane.

Rudolph V. Breland
JAMAICA VALENTINE

To my beloved daughter, sweet Jamaica

Dreams of Jamaica Valentine
A Heart carrying the Essense of Spirits
The valentine that knows
The Jamaica unfolds to be known
Wishes of the sweetness lost
For the Valentine of permanent thoughts
The deep pulse of the heart
As tides we drift far apart
Hopes of sunshine Jamaica smiles
With sweet Valentine charms
The air she breathes and evaporates within
The blood
My soul crys for you
My heart hungers for you
My Jamaica Valentine
A Plea For Our Spirits to Bathe in Time
To always stay in the Soul of the Mind
For I am Jamaica's Valentine
As She becomes Me

Cindy Land
Andrea's Christmas Wish

For my daughter, Andi, with much love.

Santa, dear Santa
Please help me, I pray.
After scouring our city
from bottom to top,
And looking both high and low;
Chasing down ads and calling the stores . . .
No one seems to know—
Just where are those Cabbage Patch Dolls
that my little Andrea dreams of?
When trying to explain, as best I knew how
that there weren't any to be found,
She looked at me and said with her twinkling
hazel eyes, big and round—
"Mommy, Santa put them all away so that *he*
could bring them on Christmas Day!"

So, Santa, dear Santa
If that be the case,
please don't forget our house.
Then the light on Andrea's little face
will have every creature stirring,
even the mouse ! !

Winnifred A. Lemmerman
HE LOVES ME
My soul unfolds
wide-spreading wings—
from tip to tip eternity—
my soul is stretching and it sings:
He loves me!

My soul glides breathlessly
in golden dawn—
it wings it's way right over land and sea;
it's drawn—
cannot be earthbound wavering and stay;
because: He loves me!

It soars rejoicing
to the sky—
right into space
were nothing seems to be—
it enters heaven
free and high
with joyous chant:
He loves me!

He told me forcefully
of love,
and bursts of golden light
pierced through the bars that had become my cage;
the door ajar, I spread my wing.
With knowledge of a new won life
I left my perch—
the spirit soaring free.
Triumphantly I do now fly and sing:
He loves me!

Roberta S. Blanchard
THE SHINING STAR

To Gram who loves poetry and encourages me to write it.

Darkness was about.
The Lord sent a babe.
The babe was to save.
Years come,
Years go,
Darkness still fights the light.
The world struggles,
Sin grows,
Darkness is still about,
But men need not worry or die,
Because of the gift of light that came
The first Christmas night.

Terry Ann Willingham
A LONELY HEART
A lonely heart
A bitter pain
Two eyes that weep
A salty rain
A love once true
Now falls apart
What's to become
Of this broken heart
A tender kiss
A warm embrace
Things that another
Can't replace
What kind of peace
May my heart find
When the love you hold
Is hers, not mine

Marilyn Rhodes
THIS WEEKEND
This weekend I fell in love with you, again.
Even though our lives have

been entertwined
for quite some time.
I fell in love with you this weekend.

Slowly, I saw your magic working into my soul.
Your thoughts, desires and passions became mine and yours
You worked your magic into my soul.

Together we worked on truly being with one another.
We opened up our lives for inspection and acceptance by the other.
Truly, we were with one another.

Still there is so much more that can be said.
Do you have the dream that I had in your arms last night?
I have so much more to tell you.

Yes, I do love you and have known that.
Closely, we become more and more devoted to our love.
My love to you for as long as you want it.

Jacqueline Vinar
INSPIRED

For Jack because I love him.

I've lost you
and they're telling me
to believe that
life goes on.
Of course I'm not listening
because I am wise
and because my thoughts
are somewhere else;
On mountain tops that are forever green,
peels of laughter
so very young,
teasing blue eyes,
motorboats speeding in the bay,
nights spent at our favorite hide-a-way,
kisses that never fade,
hugs that stay fresh,
An the fact still remains;
I will always always love you.

Ann L. Korosac
IF

Dedicated to my husband Frank M. Korosac Sr. BM 2nd class USS ENGLAND (DE 635)

If all the stars fell from the sky
To make a pathway of gold
It would not change the fact one bit
That we will soon grow old

If we could but sit and dream all day
About being young and fair
It would not stave off the wrinkles
Nor the silver in our hair

If we could but live each day again
From the starting of our birth
We'd not be sure of one more day
Upon this shining earth

And if all the countless treasures
In the ships out on the sea
Were loaded into one big ship
And gently tossed at me

My love, they could not buy my
love
This love I hold for thee!

Esther Womble Pendergrass

Esther Womble Pendergrass
**Arbutus Time In the
Carolina Hills**
Slender branches bursting with
bud—
Little green patches of sunlit
grass—
Musical tinkling of stirring
brooks
And the first red robin;—
All are melodies of awakening
spring—
And awakening too, what sweet
frail thing—
Little Arbutus;—pink and pale
Under the brown leaves far away
In the wooded Carolina hills---
There on the warm earth tenderly
clings
The delicately perfumed essence
of Spring!

Margaret Teresa McGarry
HARD HATS

---

*To Ralph De Simone,
superintendent who put it all
together*

The Sweethart bus followed the
twisting winding road,
Two deer leaped up and
frightened a toad,
Soft white flakes stopped
sprinkling the ground,
Sun peeked through a space,
A gray cloud moved around.
Many colored hard hats gleamed
brightly in the dew,
Workmen moved heavy
equipment on a Foreman's cue.
Dark Blue hard hats on the
brawny Westinghouse Elevator
Men
Bespeakes their dangerous
interior work,
In a darkened den.

Daly Plumbers sport a bright
cherry yellow,
Carry heavy pipes on shoulders,
With nary a bellow.
The Morganti orange is spotted

from end to end,
On Carpenters, Masons and
Laborers to tend.

An occassional RED speaks out
like a light,
Individuality of the wearer to
show his might.
Top Bosses, Engineers and
Visitors too,
Wear white headgear to depart
From the hard working crew.
The bus winds its way swiftly
and continues on thru.

Thelma Gray Woolard
JUST FOR ME

---

*My son Tony inspired me to
write this poem; when at
Christmas, he had a twinkle in
his eye:*

Mama has been out shopping
again,
A smile upon her face
She does not want me to know
where she has been,
But if that is the case,
She can have her way
As long as I have Christmas day.

Just think all the bright ribbons
and bows,
Christmas songs and mistletoes.
Im no fool, believe me.
I'll pretend I did not see.,
All the candies and packages
wrapped.
I'll even climb upon Santa Claus
lap.

I am so excited I can hardly wait,
For Santa to come and eat his cake,
That I have left under the
Christmas tree.
I feel like Christmas is just for me

Dorothy R. Douglas
FOR K. C.
What we have is so rare
Please, don't make it cheap
Joy and beauty without compare
Don't pile it up in a heap.

Others can only guess at what
loveliness
I see in your face

Tiny creases that live here and
there
Reminiscent of belgium lace

Some things I don't want to share
With anyone but you.

Lydia Jo Boston
ICE STORM
The world sits frozen en masse
Shrubs and trees and shimmering
tree
Fancy fences and shimmering tree
A world of crystal ecstasy!
Brave winter will sometimes dare
Her transparent clothes to wear
Robed in diamonds flashing bright
Enshrines a world that's frozen
tight.
The cold and silent winter sun
Shines down on jewels in
splendor done.
The lawn, a silken sea so smooth
Ice bound and rigid, cannot move.
The wind that whispers is
summertime

Now clangs a tune on crystal
chime.
The echo fades, the sound is past.
Silent waits the world of glass.
The cardinal rests, a glowing flame
Amid a world that ice has tamed.

Timothy Michael Gregory
IF BUT TO HOLD YOU
I saw you and a century of sadness
Became a day of happiness
The ocean I had cried
Transformed itself
Into one tender salty teardrop
Which I put away
As a memory forever,
If you will be mine
We will follow the luminated
trails
Along the pathways of stardust
Until we reach the portals
To the cosmic everlasting.
These places I would love
To take you
Yet there is something
I would enjoy more,
Yes, if but to hold you
And to know your desires
To feel your love-energy flowing
And to taste
That which is truly sweet . . .

L. Frances Taylor
LITTLE THINGS IN LIFE
It's little things
in life that count
The things we do
the things we say
Should always be
with just one thought
To help another
on his way
Selfish motives
we shouldn't have
Just humbleness,
and friendly love
A helping hand
to one who needs
The human touch
and then
God's love.

A. M. Rainbolt
BLESSINGS
Beloved I love to say that you are
mine
For thy hand is on my breast.
Love is the victory for us, my dear.
Love is the song I sing.
Love is the salute
I give as on life's path I go.
Love is the parade that passes
Each time we wait a bit.
Love's triumphs bless us day by
day
As each victory we win.
Blessings galore as we outward
pour words upon our friends.
Blessings now find each kind of
friend we met as on life's path
we trod.
Blessings fall upon us as each
new day begins
How could they help but find us
since we are
God's Blest Ones.

Le Wayne Morrow Barthel
Walk Softly In Thy Grief
Walk softly in thy grief for me
And do not cling
So tightly to thy sorrow,
That the heart forgets to sing

Its morning song;
Even though I am gone.

Go forward; oh yes, I entreat thee,
go!
Revel in the beauty of the dawn,
And sunsets' glow
Help heal the hurt;
I would not have thee grieving so.

Embrace my truth; this death is
not an end.
'Tis but a mi'nute part, of an
omnipotent plan . . .
Time here is fleeting; never ours
to keep,
Ours only for a moment; while
we sow, harvest; reap,
And it may be that Spring will
come again
With Robins' song,
But the time 'tween Heaven and
Earth
Cannot be long.

Go forth with never dreams than
mine, and sow
Thine own harvest; row beautiful
row,
Till in a finer hour and place in
time,
Thou shalt stack thy sheaves so
neatly, next to mine.

A. Carol
ONE WARM HEART

---

*For O'Neil, you showed me the
wonder of accepting love*

Reaching out to touch your chin
He has this wide open grin.
Warm joy, he brings to all
Peace within to those who may fall
Strength is hidden by his laughter
No one knows what he's after
For you there'll be no needs as
Quietly he takes the lead.

Tara Cook
LITTLE PUPPY
Little puppy
Please come here
You could fill
My life with cheer,

I have no friends
Could you be mine
If you'd do that
I'd be just fine,

You see, my daddy
Works all day
And never has
Much time to play,

Mom's too busy
Trying to please dad
She only notices me
When I am bad.

I am so alone
With nothing to do
But I'd be so happy
If I could have you.

Joyce Alford
DENIED
You offered me your hands as I
Journeyed into the poverty of
The past; but for this, I need your
arms.
You offered me your support as I
Regressed into the limitless depths;
But to sustain me, I need your

embrace.
You offered me your time and
said that
You would be there when I
reached for you,
But in my dark night, I need your
presence.

You offered me your shoulder,
and it
Became my mone' in the barren
land;
But, restless to be still, I retreated.
You offered to be my guide and
lead
Me onward, upward to my
promised land,
But love entered in, guarding the
way.
You offered me your blessing and
said
That I could continue by myself;
But without you, I am an intruder.

Ernestine Gillis
THANKSGIVING
Thanks and giving
Are props for living.
The two work together
No matter the weather.
Each on the other depends.
Strength one to one lends.
Giving gives great pleasure.
A glowing feeling is the treasure.
New friends are made;
No need old ones to trade.
Continue smiling and giving.
Joys and love are for receiving.
Thanks and giving
Truly are for living.

Patricia Ghering Wilder
DECEPTION
I can live a fairy tale though it
be drenched in wine, there I am
the players the stars in my mind.

Out of reality into the land of
dreams, drifting from life into
fantasies and schemes.

I can sigh, I can cry, who is
there to hurt, to die.

Love or hate as I want it to be,
no one is near to say no to me.

This plain I inhabit so familiar
it has become, though many a
player
still only one.

Arlene Z. Maynard
SITTING BY MYSELF
As I was sitting by myself one
night
I realize I haven't been right.
I been doing something wrong
It is a secret which is very long.
Maybe I should tell someone
When I think it's over and done.

Dorothy Thomas
HE
He's in each blade of grass
And every leafy tree
He's in the babbling brook.
Yes, he's in you and me.

He's in each sleeping flower
And every lacy fern
He's everywhere you look.
No matter where you turn

He's in a person's smile
He's with each sleeping child

He's watching while you sleep
And all your prayer's He'll keep

For he gave you a life
To live as you know best
If you live in his way's
He'll help you do the rest.

Anne E. Rasmussen
THANK YOU, FRIEND

To my friend John, without
whom this poem would never be.

You entered my life when I
needed a friend,
Just when I thought my whole
life would end.
You picked me up and put me
back on my feet
I wonder where I'd be if we
didn't meet?
You're the first person I've met
who never lied
Since I met you I haven't cried.
Thank you, friend, for entering
my life and caring.
Thank you for the wonderful
relationship we've been sharing.

Florence E. R. Foster
REMEMBER THE VIOLETS

*I wish to dedicate this poem to
my lifetime friend, . . . And
sister, Claire A. Weiss who also
"remembers the violets" (In our
childhood) down by the Neddy
Pond*

When Spring was warm; . . . and
skies were blue,
I gave sweet violets to you.
Our love was made in Heaven
above; . . .
And those violets were a token of
my love,
But life is strange, in many
ways, . . .
And, somehow, our love just
went astray.
Now, years have come, and
passed us by,
But, I find my love for you has
never died.
I think of sweet violets when I'm
lonely and blue; . . .
And I wonder, sometimes, if you
do, too.
Do you remember me when
Spring comes around,
And beautiful, blue violets cover
the ground,
Along the brook where we would
meet, . . .
Among lilies-of-the-valleys that
bloomed at our feet; . . .
And the Spring-bird's sounds from
every tree . . .
Do you remember sweet violets?
Do you remember me?

Suzette R. Bailey
TEALTOWN HILL
Amidst a world of confusion,
A refuge I had found
In the last unspoiled section of
road
That carries me to town
And into the race.

Oh! The peaceful, calm affect

This short stretch had on me,
A subtle display of Nature
In all of her glory,
For clear eyes to see.

I dreamt of leaving the road,
Trailing birds to home in the trees.
I begged to be released
From trite responsibilities,
While my eyes grew dim.

I became blinded by greed
And pressured to succeed,
Advised to stop dreaming and face
Life and Reality,
But Autumn burst through.

I saw lilac skies, amber leaves,
Reveled the briskness of chill.
For Nature, unlike Man proved
what
Was real, as I walked
Home to Tealtown Hill.

Lucille A. Norwalk
CHRISTMAS

*Dedicated to my grandchildren,
Brian, Jeff, Chris and Seth. May
you always be blessed at
Christmas!*

What, if we never had Christmas?
What, if we never knew love?
What, if we never felt inner peace,
And life was a drag that never
ceased,
It's a gift from heaven above.

It's a challenge that comes at the
close of the year,
To lift and brighten our days;
To carry through life and
hopefully so,
Making us sweeter as we go,
It's a treasure in so many ways.

God sent His Son for everyone,
A Blessing to follow for us,
His Unspeakable Gift, a joy for all
Born in a lowly manger stall,
Thanks to God for Christmas!

Phyllis Newton
African Violets Serene

*To my friend, Viola Best, in
appreciation for the many lovely
African Violet plants.*

African violets serene
They're fondled and fed with
acclaim
Part of nature's delicate scene
Perhaps they know the strain of
tame.

Their soft leves of brushed
velveteen
Reniforms colored spinich green
Layered as if arranged by hand
Enclosing purple flowers grand.

Their amethysts softly smiling
African violets serene
Sustained and cared by nourishing
Part of nature's delicate scene.

Edna Gossage Blue
ONCE AGAIN——
Fall has come to the Homestead
A profligate spender
Throwing around with careless
hand
A wealth of golden splendor

Throwing a veil of golden haze
O'er the fields of green
Spicing the air with Autumn's
perfume
Extravagance supreme

The leaves all have a golden glint
Tho some are brown and red
The corn Shocks glisten in the
sun
With Tousled golden heads

The pumpkins lying in the field
Each a golden Ball
Truly Gold is scattered everywhere
By Fall.

Helen Meyer
WEDDING WISHES
As you travel on life's journey,
May you walk hand in hand.
May your time pass serenely
Like sunshine gilded sand.

As you stroll together,
May you always take the time,
To appreciate the best in life
On your ever upward climb.

Onward through your voyage,
Whenever the sea gets rough,
May you find the strength and
comfort
In each other to be enough.

May the Captain of your vessel
Be ever watching from above.
And may you be forever blessed
With the beauty of your Love.

Mary Fay Kragel Roth
REST IN PEACE
Now is the time for solitude
(And please do close the door)
A time for quiet thinking
And perhaps a little more.

Please, have a chair, enjoy yourself
You're your own company
When nature calls do answer
By all means it is free.

Now is the time to organize
Your thoughts that are remiss
The perfect time for retrospect
A lovely time for bliss.

And, when your time is over
And a line forms at the door
Remember just one little thing
Is there paper for one more?

Denise A. Wilson
DEATH OF A POET
Such a sad and tragic story,
of a man so in love with prose
that he couldn't live without it—
That is how the story goes:

He had been suffering bouts of
blankness;
things weren't flowing at all right.
He couldn't find the proper words;
he had no rhyme, no rhythm, try
as he might.

So he went to an authoritis doctor
in search of a cure or an answer
But what he found left him
devastated—
he had poetary-gland cancer.

Imagination and creativity
continued their rapid decline,
and soon he could not even write
one single literary line.

He became somber and silent,
more withdrawn each passing day.

His life had no more meaning;
he had nothing at all to say.

Better (he thought) to be cut and
    bled dry
than to live his life without verse-
A world void of color and
    expression-
For him, not even death could be
    worse.

It is on that note the story ends
for this frustrated poet-man,
They found him early one morning
dead, with a pen in his hand.

Frankie Austin
AN ANGRY WORD

To my beloved daughter, Annette Austin for being beautiful sincere, intelligent, devoted and some kind of sweet and given me such a beautiful grand daughter Bridgette

---

Some words we say are hurting
Upon the surface bare
We can remove the paint, but
The marks are still there

There are somethings we cannot
    mend
Or return to former glow
Once the grain is scored
The scar for ever show

The words we say are no longer
    our's
They belong to whom we spoke
An angry word has its power
And sometimes a heart is broke

So be careful of the words you say
And keep them soft and sweet
You never know from day to day
Which one you'll have to meet.

Kathryn Ford Lafans
MEMO TO MY MIND
Close the fingers of my mind,
    And stroke each fragile probing
    thought to flow,
Coax each wisp of fantasy to find
    Unexpected fitness in a line.
Kindle warmth toward tender
    shoots of twigged verse,
Then, prune to start a new more
    cogent thought.
Greet the stinging agony each
    writer knows,
As golden phrases, slashed with
    firm intent
Drop like autumn leaves in
    beauty round,
But, save the prunings for
    another work,
Fertile nourishment for future
    tendrils of verse.
Reject the less choice line with
    tenderness,
It, also, is a child of thine.
    Brave it onward through the
    clearing mist
Thrust down the pattern of yor
    desired aim,
    Watch it form upon the page,
Love it into life, to stand exposed.
    Dare the critics, better to perform.
Know you are the worst you have
    to face.
    Cool your lines a day, and seek
To underscore the strong, strike

the weak.
    Close the fingers of my mind
And firmly seal thy mind's child
    And send it flying,
To make its life its own.

Kathleen L. Tuck
AUTUMN ABSTRACT
Incoming . . . with autumn's
    blaze of fire . . .
the ice-cold blast of the first
    snowflurry,
dousing the flame in its early
    appearance.
The great artist left their mark,
not only on the canvas,
but on the widespread forests
where their palettes were
    discarded.
Van Eyck left us with muted
    greens and somber browns,
the pre-and post-autumn colors.
From Grunewald came a burning
    orange
barely restrained in its intensified
    heat.
Gauguin, in the colors of his
    style,
gave the yellow-green of sassafrass.
Matisse, in harmony, willed the
    forest
a bold and vibrant red that
    decried death,
shouting life, movement, and
    freedom,
that the trees sought in the cold
    November winds,
and Goya, in his last fight,
a fight with nature, art, and sanity,
left us with the charred browns of
    autumn's ashes,
buried under the cloak of Manet's
    virgin white snow.

Margaret Adams
OCTOBER DISSONANCE
Flaming, flamboyant October,
    with mood carefree
Evokes a dissonance within the
    heart of me.
Chill winds of November, fading
    flowers, falling leaves, leaden
    skies
Match my spirit's slow demise,
For fate's envenomous arrow
At my heart was aimed
And in the midst of sorrow
Somber November is framed.

Wayne Davis
LOVE AS IT PASSES
Whispering as it passes
        only to be heard clearly
but once in the cycle
        of life.
But for some once is all
        that is needed,
for they remember and hold close
        that moment till the end.
But others leave unending tracks
        in the sands of silence,
never understanding the whisper,
        as it passed.

Kathy J. Lasby
I TRY
Through the mail today
    I got good news,
It made my day, and quit my blues,
The letter I got acknowledged me,
Lifted my soul and set it free.

It whispered to me of success,

I'll type on now with nary a rest,
The rhymes in my head I'll now
    put down,
I know in my soul, a poet I'm
    bound.

All of the words I strive to say,
Wind up in rhyme, in some
    strange way,
And if these words I rhyme with
    ease,
Someones soul they do please,
Then all I do is not in vain,
If they help someone who feels
    great pain.

Laura Burkland Klinger
REJUVENATED JOY

Dedicated to my beautiful, talented and loving daughter, Kathy Marie. What a "ray of sunshine" God gave me in you! I am so proud to be your mother. Love always, Mom.

My daughter is a special joy,
    An enigma . . . yet so real.
Each time you share your life
    with me,
    Can't tell you how I feel.

Reflections of my childhood past,
    Are locked within my mind.
You're the key to releasing old
    memories;
    Just by your growing up, I find.

Those memories of days gone by,
    That time cannot erase . . .
Childhood dreams . . .
    unwithered;
    Are seen there in your face.

As age lines cradle my weary eyes,
    Where a sparkle used to dwell;
Still the future lies within my
    grasp,
    In this girl-child, I can tell.

My dreams fulfilled for future
    hope;
    Now free from doubt and strife.
I have pride in what you have
    become,
    . . . . Sweet extension of my life.

Alma C. Groninger
Thanksgiving Day (1983)
Do people die in Lebanon
While royalty dines in "Babylon"?
Does sadness fill a sailor's heart
As distance keeps him far apart
From family where he'd rather stay
On this Thanksgiving Day?

Do little children cry out loud
As illness creeps in like a cloud
And takes their appetites away
On this Thanksgiving Day?

Does a derelict still roam
Some shadowed alley he calles
    "home"?
With head bowed down, he can
    not say
If he will eat, Thanksgiving Day.

Does poverty inflict great pain?
Do faces show a scarring strain
From unemployment, thus no pay
On this Thanksgiving Day?

If you prepare a festive feast,
Still meditate on Middle East,
Armed services, leukemia . . .
Economy's anemia.
Should problems all be held at bay
On this Thanksgiving Day?

Mary Rose Harding
ASYLUM

Dedicated to one of my favorite passengers on Earth Ship "Bounty" my Aunt Doris.

I picture the earth
    a vessel
    taking her four billion
    passengers
    on an illusory trip
    to nowhere
Orbiting the ordained orbit.

Meanwhile,
    there's Mutiny on the Bounty!

Richard John Briggs
WITH LOVE
Love is a sacrifice or gift.
A taking of ones time to lift,
Away, the tides burdens or fears.
A hug, a smile, lessens the tears.

A caring inquisitive tone.
Stop your world to pick up the
    phone.
For loves matter is while you can.
Day is at hand, tomorrows plan.

Even a thought is not in waste.
A time will come when it is faced.
Live. Live with love in your garden.
God forbid! That hearts may
    harden.

Ruth Schober Sims
**The Little Boy I Love So
Much**

To my wonderful son Jim, who I love very much—Mom I love you Tiger

---

While I sit here quiet and thinking
I remember days long past
the little boy I love so much
has grown up much to fast

He's tall and dark and handsome
and his eyes have much to say
though his life has not been easy
he's survived in his own way

He's honest, true and loyal
he's self-confident and smart
he's compassionate and caring
and he loves straight from his
    heart

He's now a soldier far away

protecting the land he loves
God keep him safe and bring him
home
watchover from above

I am so very proud of him
and never a day goes by
that I don't wish he were at home
underneath my watchful eye

Although he's grown and now a
man
I constantly pray and such
God keep him safe and bring him
home
"THE LITTLE BOY I LOVE SO
MUCH"

Janise Orton
FOR ERIC
I stared at him.
The one with the sparkling blue
eyes
With the dimple in the corner,
That deepened when he wore his
boyish grin
And made him unlike all the
other guys.
He stood there.
I watched him, thinking how
time had gone by too fast.
The tears trickled down my
cheeks,
As I wished that this moment
could forever last.
I watched him.
The one who did everything that
a big brother should.
The one whom I fought with, but
loved so much too.
The boy with whom great times
were shared.
The one whom I know always
cared.
I can't bring myself to say
"Goodbye",
Because today the sun is leaving
my sky.
I stood there,
As he walked out of sight.
I knew that never again
Would my life be just right.
People say,
That I will get over it.
But I doubt it.
Because there I stood-in tears.
Not knowing what to say,
For today was my
"Goodbye Big Brother Day."

Phyllis J. Lowery-Terwey
FOR RICHARD
The echoes of your laughter,
The things you used to say,
The memories of the things we did
are still with me today.
The love you gave so cautiously
that grew to be so great,
The times we talked the whole
night through,
The kiss on our first date.
Now I look into the past
and see your smiling face.
It helps me through another day.
It fills the empty space.
Life on earth without you
is a task I did not choose.
But as the wise men always say
"in love you win or lose".
We lived, we laughed, we loved,
we won;
and so my love will be-

with you, as now you rest at peace,
still I with you and you with me.
Our time was short but oh so
sweet,
Our love was deep and true.
We had our heaven here on earth.
I had all my roses with you.

Myrtle M. Rauer-Buck
MY GRANDAUGHTER
Sometimes I glimpse the essence
of her,
Little sunbeam, bouncing about,
Unbounded—just loved.
Her wide blue eyes are innocent
As with darting thoughts, she
outreaches us all.

The tiny hands are full of mischief,
(With dimpled cheeks and little
giggles)
She races away in her strawberry
tennies.
The golden hair is fluffed by her
speed,

The wonder of her—is my reprieve.
My son's little girl who is only
three.
My free spirited grandaughter,
given by Thee.

In her ruffled blue dress; she's
ready to be admired.
She talks so nice, sings and
recites; wearing her patent

shoes and stockings of lace.

She mothers her dolly and is
content with her books.
Her eyelids drooped—ssshh—
then opened wide,

She ran to gampa and climbed up
to his knee, to listen

quietly as he reads.

Then her tiny fingers crept up to
his chin and crunching

her shoulders, she whispered,
"Tickle, tickle gampa."
Her mommy's dimples almost
escaped and her daddy smiled

behind his hand.
Gamma's littlest sweetheart
rested under a halo of love.

Phyllis Cooley
HIS SPECIAL CHILD
God never meant to hurt you,
Even though you think he did;
But there's only certain people,
He trusts with his special kids;

He could have taken him at his
birth,
But he chose to let him live;
So give him hope and
understanding,
And all the love you have to give;

And when you feel hurt and want
to cry,
Then ask the reason why;
Just think again and then,
Thank him for giving you His
Special Child

Eugene Stewart
WINTER WONDERLAND
Wondering away not saying
good-bye
autumn blows its harvesting
leaves,

covering bare ground like a
mother's quilt
Soon flakes of winter's snow, like
a puzzle, would fall into place with
a silent nights assurance that the
chilling season was early on its
way
By evening a child-made snow
castle
stood three feet high, just outside
secured by a touch from a frost
bitten nose
Inside by the warmth of crackling
wood, visible images of the story
being told seemed so real
A place so near yet so very far
A place of magical charm

Dorris A. Western
LOVE AND TRUST
Love!
What is it?
A feeling, an emotion,
or what two people share.
Is it dependence and independence
laughing and crying
showing that you really care?
Oh, do not try to tie me down,
for you I will do the same . . .
Do not call on me for selfish
wants or needs—
but, when needed sincerely—
call my name,
your voice I will heed.
Trust, a very important part of love
Trust, the element that most
often destroys love
or should it be said . . .
Mistrust!

Ms. L. Templeton
I've Got To Be Free!!
Free, to find out who I am, and
what I want out of life:
Free to know myself;
Free to explore my thoughts;
Free, to know right from wrong;
Free, to know wrong from right.
Free to know that I am a Woman,
who have feelings for
herself, before I can share my
feelings for someone else!!
Free, to know my thoughts and
values I have learned and have
been taught.
Free, to give and free to recieve;
I'm free to go and free to come.
But, most of all I must be Free!,
Free, from Sin!
I'm free, I'm Free, and you can be
Free too; through
JESUS CHRIST!
"Are You FREE, Really FREE?"

Julia Duyka
GOLDEN SHAWL

To Ann and Monica and Frank
and Cindy, Mary, Pat, Thomas,
and Nicholas, Kathleen, Jimmy,
Christopher, Isaac, and Justin

The tree we stood beneath not so
long ago
Doesn't wear her golden shawl
anymore.
And my dreams that shined
brightly not so long ago
Lay crumpled among the leaves
at her base.
The shadows her lonely branches

cast on the sidewalk
Reflect the gloom deep in my soul.
Where did I go astray?
Why did hopes and dreams die so
suddenly
Before they had time to grow?
My only reprieve is knowing
That with the spring time comes
new growth
And eternal hope.

Joe Wagner
FINEST HOUR
Naked and alone
I sat on the shore of my despair.
Overcast skies trapped all my
fears.
As I pondered a future devoid of
me.
The winds of uncertainty swirled
all around me.

A vision wholly unanticipated.
As lovely a woman as ever could
be.
Through my clouds of anxiety
She comes forward to stand
before my dying eyes.
And pulls me into the protection
of her understanding.

Together we approached
The ocean of my disillusionment.
Each pounding wave of depression
Upon the two of us
Continued in less intensity
Until at last
With the sun high above
The storm had finally been abated.
United by love
I survived the worse of my own
tempest.
She gave me the strength I never
knew I had.

If the storms should ever return
The memory of the finest hour of
my life
Will enable me to stand straight
and tall
No matter how severe the winds.

Peggy West
THE HARVEST MOON
The harvest moon is glowing
The wind is blowing
The old men are hoeing
The young girls are sewing
Crows are cawing
Children are mowing
The corn is growing
The wheat is sowing
The wine is flowing
The harvest moon is glowing.

John Campbell, Editor & Publisher

Sharon Ann Kelly
A NEW BEGINNING
A time to realize new hopes and
dreams—
A time to learn what life really
means—
The day for setting up new goals,
The day for writting brand new
roles.
An age that perhaps, may bring
peace,
Throughout our world of pain
and grief.
An old year has finally past—
And a new one is here, at last!

Ruth M. Wilkins
**My Country Christmas
Road**
My Country Christmas Road
Is the place I long to see
Because down that road
Is my Grammas house
And Presents under the tree

Grampas out there choppin wood
In his coat of patched up holes
Grammas getting supper on
And my favorite cinnamon rolls

After supper I took a walk
Down my favorite country road
I thought of Mary and the Three
Wise Men
And the different stories they told

As I turned and started walking
back
Behold a beautiful sight
There were icicles hanging down
along side
My Gramma's outdoor Christmas
lights

As I started to go back in
I looked at the stars above
I paused for just a moment
And thanked God for all their
love

Jeannie Capion
Don't Grow Up Too Fast
I can look at you standing there
now, sixteen and full of life.
You want everything to come to
you now, without having to
suffer the strife.
Livng isn't easy without the
winning edge to make the good
times last,
Little sister, for your own sake,
please don't grow up too fast.

I know you think that I'm so
different from you in so many
ways,
But don't forget we came from the
same place and lived with the
same pain that stays.
Right now you're angry, bitter
and confused, feeling you can't
escape the past,
But the pain won't go away if you
try to grow up too fast.

You are trying to be independent,
and find your own identity,
Stay a little girl a bit longer, for
adulthood isn't all its supposed
to be.
It's good to dream of tomorrow
but remember to live for today,
For now is the time you will
remember when you look back
to yesterday.

Erinn Lopez
**My Chinese Letter, My
Heart's Holder**

*To the Lord who gave me the
talent to write for those who
have the feelings but no way to
express them.*

Red burning fire
  Leaving a trail of black night.
Finger painting
  Dripping gold rainbow.
Brown silk shreddings
  Pointed by the breeze.
Frustration's blue slash
  Crosses the page.
Deep green windows
  Look right through me.
Carefully shaped lane
  Never strays from course.
Picture of shining pink
  Hiding an ivory wall.
Innocent protects guilty
  But both are wished.
My flower's stem begins
  But ends quickly.
For off this page
  My eyes must not linger.
The feeling would be red
  Though the opportunity golden.
All this but lives
  On my distant tree.

Perry L. Bowen
THE MAN FROM GALILEE

---

*First I want to dedicate these
poems to God, and my dear
mother. Put God, first is her
words of wisdom, to Penny
Simms a seriously dear friend to
me. To Isabelle G. I will always
love you forever.*

He walked on the water and he
calmed the sea, talking about
the man from Galilee. Healed
the sick, made fisherman of
man, brought Moses out of
Pharoahs land.

Put his hands on the blind and
they could see, died on the
cross for you and me. Our sins
are forgiven if his laws we
obey, stay in his council and
learn how to pray. Follow his
advice and you can't go wrong,
soon Jesus is coming to take us
home.

Robert Smith
HAVE YOU
Have you ever listened to the
wind's call
Through the pines and through
the leaf?
Have you ever heard the snow
fall?
The silence defies belief.

Have you ever lived a heartbeat
From the great divide of death?
Have you ever seen a friend meet
His last dying breath?

Have you ever watched the wild
goose fly
To the left of the setting sun?
Have you ever heard his pleading
cry
For a mate whose race is run?

Have you ever shared a love song
Or kisses sweet as wine?
Have you ever felt a love as strong
As the one in this heart of mine?

Elaine Gerstner-Jones
Ring On Crystal Bell
The riv'let in the stream runs
silent,
and a snowflake touches the
ground.
The wind strokes the feathery fir
trees, and the stars form a
heavenly crown.

The morn is quietly awaking
for a familiar ancient sign.
Yes, I can hear it echo softly
as my ear strains to catch the
old chime.

'Tis the bell in the bombed
church tower as it breaks
through the pristine air
Ah! like the ring of fine cut
crystal—still calling its
scattered flock to prayer.
    . . . Ring on crystal bell.

Pearl Leona Ross
SOUTHERN SPRING

---

*In memory of a loving husband,
father and grandfather! M. D. Ross*

Mockingbirds,
Butterflies,
Dogwood and
Thistle.

Hummingbirds,
Buttercups,
Blue Jays and
Whistles.

Fragrant Flowers,
Rain Showers,
Sunshine and
Breezes.

Blue Skies,
Rainbows,
Green Grass and
Sneezes.

Char Skobel
Lonely Half-Solid Whole
I want to hold your hand and
dance the minuet,
I want to look in your eyes and
see the stars,
I want to share my fantasies,
Some that will come to pass and
others that will not.

But instead, I see my four walls
That will not talk to me
Or comfort me in the night.
And I feel the tears
On my face that time can not
erase.
I am the spawn of half a
partnership
Condemned to finding the
missing part.
I have looked the world over
And could not find it.
So now the search begins within,
Hoping all is there,
And afraid it is not.

Char Skobel
Mirror Of No Reflection
Mirror in front of me,
Why aren't the tears showing
In the eyes looking back at me?
The complexion without a flaw
Does not resemble the face
Swollen from the pain inside.
Can this being you reflect
In such perfect detail,
Be the same one that
Wants to crumble in a heap,
Like pile of discarded used
clothing?
I understand not the difference
between us.
We appear the same
And yet we are worlds apart.
I am real, you are a reflection,
An extension of what can only be
seen.
Being real is having felt
And I am feeling,
The loss, the extinction,
Of all that I call me.

Etta Marie Greenwood Snavely
**Farewell My Son and God
Bless**

---

*To my son, Bill, upon his leaving
for Military Service in 1966*

I saw you walk away, my son,
  I watched you go with pride
I formed a smile upon my lips,
  But in my heart, I cried.

A fleeting thought that this
  might be
  The last time I would see you
  here,
I quickly shut it out and prayed
  That God would keep you in
  his care.

Scarlett Anne Lockridge
A HAUNTING MEMORY
Ireland, I long to touch your soul
and feel your loving soil beneath
my feet.
To stand at the very edge of your
ragged cliffs
and look out as the ocean
caresses the blue sky.
If my eyes could only once again
drink in the
beauty that now only haunts me.
Yet even though you lie so far
away,
I can always feel you ever close.

As night falls I can hear your
name,
dancing merrily in the gentle
breeze.

The fresh scent of spring heather
that
reminds me of golden filled
mornings,
when without a sound you turn
your emerald eyes
to greet the dawn as she begins to
wake.
You are forever the spirit of my
existence
and the longing that haunts my
memory.

Veronica Johnson
DEWDROPS
Dewdrops among the
Mist, bathe the emerald leaves
Then trickle away.

Lester E. Garrett
Christmas Bells In The Snow
Thanksgiving had too quickly
come and gone;
But the memories of a
togetherness
And the wonderfulness of it all
stayed on,
Long into the glorious month of
December . . .
When, upon the eve of another
togetherness,
I heard the sound of Christmas
In the midst of a gently falling
snow
And caught a wondrous feeling of
peace
In the silence of the lovely night.
I keenly sensed the joy, the
anticipation
In the singing of carols along the
street;
And I remembered the Christmas
Eves

Of years gone by . . . each as
enchanting
As the other; each retelling the
story
Of the humble birth of the man
named Jesus.

I knew in my heart that He
walked this night,
Just as He had always walked,
Near to us, unchanging . . .
On clear nights and stormy nights;
Not merely a warming glow, a
lighted candle,
But a beautiful, everlasting
illumination.
He who first heard the Christmas
Bell
And, out of love, gave of Himself

in full:
Surely the truest,
And greatest gift of all.

Edward L. Keller
HAPPY BIRTHDAY JESUS
We celebrate a birth today
The birth of a special child
A child that was sent to show the
way
And to protect the weak and the
mild
But what kind of a gift to you
could I bring
What gift could be worthy for the
son of my KING
Could I paint a pretty picture to
hang upon your wall
No your FATHER painted the
sunrise and gave it to all
Could I sing to you a lullaby, the
kind to bring a smile
No your FATHER taught the
birds to sing like the laughter
of a child
Could I give to you the greatest
art ever to be made by man
No your FATHER gave you the
universe made by his own hand
Could I give to you a cushion to
rest your weary head
No your FATHER gave you
clouds as pillows and the sky
to be your bed
Could I give to you a story full of
courage and of daring
No your FATHER gave us the
bible full of your compassion
and your caring
What gift could I give to JESUS
What would his present be
When I asked what he wanted
most this year
HE said HE wanted me.

Elizabeth Pucciarelli
SISTERS
I love you
No that doesn't tell it
We are as if born of the same egg
You are a part of me
And I am a part of you

When I needed you
I didn't need to ask
You knew, You felt, You gave
A strength that kept me whole
A faith instilled inside me

I worked it through
I prayed it through
For inside of me
Was the strength of two

William W. West
FORGIVEN
And he will say to her
Theres time, yet, more time
And she will say to him
Not now, not mine

And he will ask of her
If not now, then when
He will hear the words flow
And she will say again

For my share is lesser
Tis not mine to give again
An imposition with times
For in a whisper then

And he will say to her
Theres time, yet, more time
And she will say to him
Not now, not mine

Sandie Kierstead
RETURNING
I've come back again to relive the
memories I hold of you
I know I promised to stay away,
to never feel anything for you
again
I know it's self-torture, but my
heart has forced me to return
My ears have heard the talk of
you and your new lover
My eyes have seen the two of
you together, happy
It's obvious that you've forgotten
me already, so why do I keep
hoping to sneak back into your
heart
Even I don't understand why
you're such a big part of my life
You're in my memory and in my
dreams
But, in your mind, these dreams
have died, and the memories
have all been erased
You've started a new life with
someone else, so why haven't I
been able to push you aside
and start anew
I guess I will never be able to
really say

    —Good-bye

Morrisson J. Duncan
I FLY UP HIGH
In one night I wrote a poem.
The poem read:

I fly up high
With my wings spread wide
 to my side.

A sigh . . . a cry!
 For peace
  For love
   For you
    For me . . .
Without war
 Without destruction
  Without evil.

A sigh . . . a cry!
 And I fly up high
  With my wings spread wide.

In one night I wrote a poem.

Linda K. Bridges
CHRISTMAS, HUMBUG!
Drats!
 It's a week before Christmas,
 and no gifts have I bought,
 For family or friends who are so
 dear.
I just hate this time of year!

Christmas!
 I've seen Christmas
 and Christmas
 All over the place,
 Even before Thanksgiving was
 here!

Peace!
 I've heard peace and goodwil
 to you, too, my friend;
 But don't you dare,
 Try to take my place in line!

Christmas Morn!
 Then it's finally over, no gifts
 left to buy;
 And as we gather around the
 fire,
 To hear the first Christmas
 story,

I feel the wonder, the joy, the
peace.
And I'm glad Christmas came
this year!

Curtis Anderson
DREAM WORLD
Daylight ends and night begins
And darkness hides the view
I close my eyes and visualize
Then I start dreaming of you
It seems so real and I can feel
You lying here next to me
I hold you tight it feels so right
Like the way it used to be
But dreams just don't last forever
You know I wish they'd never
end
Cause In my dreams we're so
happy
But when I wake we're not even
friends
Can it be that we don't see
Until it's much too late
It's hard to change or re-arrange
When you turn from love to hate
You know it seems we live in
dreams
But soon they fade away
Wish I knew just what to do
To make my dream world stay

Lorna Hazzard
LAST GOODBYE
I Don't Have Tomorrow
I only Have Today
before the sunshine
slips away.

One last time
to make it real
One lone memory
for me to steal

I gave my all
and have no doubt
It's time to move on
and take the easy way out

To all my friends
who choose to stay
My best wishes
and for you I pray

Susan Petriccione
Fun and Frolic In the Ocean's Foam

---

*To my parents—for the three
little girls, To Richard Oehling—
for constant inspiration.*

The journey begins . . .
There were once three little girls
clad in
redamberblue shorts-n-shirts
green-n-yellow kerchiefs,
passing play games—
stuped in anticipation of their
dearly awaited journey.

"Summer!" a fun-filled world: sun-
n-sand, miles of it
encompassed in pails-n-shovels.
(How far can I dig to reach the
ocean?) chocolate-n-vanilla
ice cream cones in one magical
swirl.

. . . and retreats . . .
The nostalgic parasite creeps into
the marrow of my bones—
it sits and bellows out its pains of
years,

passing play games—
three has become one.

The surf corrodes the beaches,
the miles of sand become a small
stretch.
The blowing breezes remove the
sting of my pensive sun—
a bird has excreted upon my
blanket.
Where is the point of unity
where sky touches sea?
The sky and sea like lovers caress
in shaded blues.
The lover's image soars like a
seagull in mid-flight,
gliding across a backdrop of
chalky whitesbluegreys.
She found a perfect shell among
the cracked pieces—
the pearl among the pebbles
cherishing within a secret
fountain emitting tiny droplets,
each containing the portrait of
the loved one.
Can she make you understand
the secrets of the fountain,
when she herself cannot
understand the meaning of
each droplet?

The journey nears end . . .
Perhaps wisdom, is not totally
lost . . . yet . . .
Three has still become one.

. . . and begins again.

Theresa D. Sigmon Trusty
TEARS
A fountain of emotion . .
Pouring feelings from inside, into
the see . .
Swimming thru the rough-
waters of
fear and sadness . . .
Drowning in the pain.
In the depth of darkness,
Lies the full meaning of the
eyes . . .
Spilling these tears I cry.

Calvin VanPelt
FIRST OF ALL
First of all . . . hear my call . . .
when I kneel and pray
be a guide . . . by my side . . . help
me find the way
give me grace . . . when I face . . .
those who put me down
may I still . . . do thy will . . . and
wear a shining crown

First each day . . . let me pray . . .
thank you for it all
if today . . . on my way . . . I
should start to fall
hold my hand . . . help me stand .
. . keep me close to thee
keep my life . . . free of strife . . .
until you call for me

Let my light . . . shine so
bright . . . let it show the way
may it guide . . . those inside . . .
who have gone astray
while I live . . . I'll forgive . . .
those who cast a stone
then at last . .. when life's passed .
. . I will not stand alone

First of all . . . thanks for all . . .
you have done for me
as I live . . . let me give . . . daily

thanks to thee
when I'm blue . . . keep me
true . . . while I wait your call
every day . . . let me say . . . thank
you Lord . . . FIRST OF ALL . . .

William G. Epperson

William G. Epperson
FOREVER
I spoke to you, as I turned my
chair
and you weren't there.
I had forgotten,
I had forgotten,
That you'd gone ahead.
I extended my hand, as I turned
in our bed.

I had forgotten,
I had forgotten, that you were
now gone ahead.
But you never left me, and I'm
not alone.
For we will never have parted,
when we
meet anon.
For you never left me, you never
left me.
You just went ahead.

Kim-Marie (Baldwin)
LITTLE MARTY

*Dedicated, with love, to a very
special little boy.*

Something new and something
wonderful
Came into my life,
It was June, the 4th, in '82
And what a precious sight.

He was christened William
Martin,
Born to Ron and Debbie Brown,

And the moment I laid eyes on
him
My heart began to pound.

He was pink and perfect; soft and
sweet,
A bouncing baby boy,
And I knew that in the years
ahead
He'd fill my heart with joy.

I was chosen his Godmother
And I made a simple prayer:
That no matter what the future
held,
He'd always have my care.

As the days and months go
passing by
I sit and watch him grow,
And with each new year, my
heart still pounds
Because I love him so!

Joanna G. Bonds
OF ALL THE LITTLE GIRLS

*To Kristi—Seventeen years later
and still my choice "of all the
little girls" ! ! ! Love, Mom*

One day quiet a few years ago
I wished to God that maybe
When He's caught up with time
to spare
He'd plan a special baby.

Not that I didn't appreciate
His usual quality!
Or that I'd think whatever He'd
make
Not good enough for me.

It's just I knew down deep inside
That somewhere in this world
Somewhere in the vastness of His
love
Lived the perfect baby girl.

I'd probably have loved her just as
much
Without that golden hair
That flew with the rush of her
busy feet
As she went running everywhere.

And those beautiful big brown
eyes
They read just like a book!
They'd change in a moment from
tears to smiles
My love is all it took.

So sixteen sweet short years ago
"Of all the little girls . . ."
I got the sweetest prettiest most
precious one
In all the whole wide world ! !

Carol Whitney Decker
Ride a Pony This Christmas Morn
One hushed and misty Christmas
morning, a pony touched my
face and sped me bouncing
down a road toward that sacred
place.

I clutched the mane he wore, so
tightly in my hand, and
listened to the rhythm that his
hoofs beat in the sand.

"Faster, hurry faster!" said I into
his ear, and we pranced
through puffs of snow that

danced upon the air.

"Do you know where the Magi
live who rode out late last
night? Or where the Star of the
East came from when it had
found its light?"

He only lifted up his head and
raced on through the trees, but
I thought I heard the answer in
the rustle of the leaves.

We sped along a tiny brook that
once had been a river and it
told me of King Herod crossing
there, wearing bow and quiver.

The sun shone on the water like
reflections on the sea, and I
thought I saw a cross there as
the light winked back at me.

Down winding trails where
cotton tails bounced along the
side, we sought a shady thicket
where a rabbit might reside.

Could this be where Joseph fell
into his wondrous dream? Or
where the shepherds fed their
flock near the flowing stream?

As the sun filled up the branches
and turned the sky bright blue,
my brave mount spied another
road and sped off through the
dew.

Soon the Holy Family surrounded
us and happiness filled my
soul, for here was Baby Jesus
wrapped in swaddling clothes.

Suddenly, the angel of the Lord
appeared before us and the Boy,
"Fear not, I bring you good
tidings of great joy."

My steed and I did humbly bow,
our trip near its end, Glory to
God in the highest, and on
earth peace, good will toward
men.

Past crooked rocks and cactus
plants, my friend and I did fly,
as the sheep scurried off the
road to watch us racing by.

So quickly and so silently did we
run that morn, that no one
heard our passing or knew
where we had gone.

Back through the brooks and
wooden glens we rode toward
that place where first I saw that
pony who had tempted me to
race.

At last beneath a giant oak we
stopped and took our rest and I
slid gently from his back and
patted his soft chest.

"Until tomorrow" I did say, as he
lowered his sweet head, and I
led him back to his secret spot
. . . on the floor beneath my bed.

GOD BLESS YOU ON THIS
CHRISTMAS HOLIDAY.

Mary Ellen B. Owen
THE BOLD SNOWMAN
Who is the stranger, staunch and
bold,
Defying the wind and the biting
cold?

With jaunty hat and black-booted
feet,
He's smiling on as he watches the
street,
Unmindful there of the wind's
sharp beat.

A bright orange carrot, his
splendid nose,
Adds a comic touch to his lofty
pose;
His black button eyes, steady and
deep,
Are eyes that will never be closed
in sleep,
As he waits alone in the wind's
wild keep.

His broomstick arms hang stiff
from his cloak,
From out of his pipe, not a wisp
of smoke;
His tall white body, so fat and
round,
Seems anchored forever to the
snowy ground,
And he pays no heed to the
wind's chill sound.

But, suddenly, high in the gray
winter sky,
The sun comes out and the winds
all die;
The stranger who looked so bold
and strong
Melts fast away till he's finally
gone,
Where snowmen go when the
sun comes along.

Pierre Valdez Lewis
STAR STEPPIN'

---

*Michelle captured my heart just
as a hunter captures his game.
And Star Steppin' is a product of
the love that We maintain. She's
my Courage, Inspiration, my
Dream and Smile . . . my loving
flower growing wild . . . all over
me.*

The laws of earth's gravity has
never applied to Me and
You . . . We leave its binding
atmosphere as nassau rockets
do . . . So up up and away we
go-to distant places no moon
men know . . . just Star Steppin'
at the speed of light, there is no
time no day no night . . . but an
endless journey with no goals
in sight and We leave Us a trail
like a meteorite . .
Up here there's no air to carry
your voice . . . so you speak to
me in whispers cause there is
no other choice . . . Your feet
have grown tired You disgard
your glass slippers . . . My
throat has gone dry so I drink
the Big Dipper.
We vowed to stay together both
for better or worse . . . plus just
think We Star Stepped through
the whole Universe . . .
Then following Our golden trail
which leads back to the
earth . . . We had an uncanny
feeling that this was Our space
from birth . . .

Everyone questioned Us—yes
both family and friend . . . they
all wanted to know where had
Michelle and I been . . . We
held out for awhile, then We
decided to give in . . . We stared
into each others eyes, and said:
Star Steppin'

Charette Macairan Miel, M.D.

Charette Macairan Miel, M. D.
Homage To Ninoy Aquino
Thanks for the life you gave
Though you had a broken heart
It was so big, full of love
That you offered your very life
for peace and truth

Your death was not in vain
It will serve as a light for us
And to all poor countries
That are exposed to chaos, wars,
floods, draughts and
earthquakes;
Adversities that are like flashes
of lightnings
So swift, so fast;
Like our short stay here on earth

You're not gone, dear Ninoy
You're always in our hearts and
memories
Your life will always show it's
footprint
Giving us more strength and
courage to carry on . . .

Kathryn M. Diana
LAST OF THE SEASON

To Joseph

How delicate in form and color
Is this small November rose,
Soft against the faded trellis
Like a memory in repose.

So unlike June's showy blossoms,
Short of life, though large and
bright,
Hurried by the heat of summer,
Bud to fullblown overnight.

Each a flower for its season,
Giving beauty to the year:
But November's rose is the last
one
And that makes it doubly dear.

C. Gay Fritzemeier
IF ONLY HEART
So often my heart
reaches out
to touch you

only to discover
it is entrapped
by dead-weight flesh,
paralyzed by the might
of self-conscious fear—

If only Heart
could break out
and conquer—
Malik Canty
Repent! Repent! Repent!

---

*For my Grandmother: Who
inspired me to write this poem
your spiritual soul is a beautiful
sight to behold! ! ALL those who
get a chance to see will agree
with me . . .*

Revelations only reveal the
devastation
that has yet to come . . Nuclear
involvement
only guarantee that we will fulfill
prophecy . .
God gave Noah the rainbow sign:
no more water
fire the next time ! ! ! !

For so long we have been warned
of the
forthcoming storms . . Global
destruction
is no longer a myth for we are
living it . . .
Our world is dying to save it we
better begin
trying . . Repent! Repent! Repent!
Even the rich and so-called
mighty won't
be saved when the world is
remade . . .

Floyd Willoughby
WANDA

---

*To the Staff and Residents of Life
Care Center Nursing Home,
Richland who care for each other
by sharing their lives*

She touched me once with voice
and smile
as we walked through life
A lonely mile.
A Woman unknown, yet
somehow close
I felt a bond which we had chose.

A Fall went by, A Winter, Too
as day by day we saw a brighter
view.

The Soul of Man had touched our
lives,
through a source of strength
who had taught the scribes.

Love is deep in a gentle way
traveling through life, day by
day.

she touched me once with voice
and smile
as we walk through life a sharing
mile.

Crystal Marie Ornelas
THE UNICORN
The Unicorn, white with its'
pretty blue eyes
gazed into the stars and the
mystical skies

As the Greek and the Roman
mythology said
the Unicorn had a straight horn
on its' head
Its strange single horn was
delicately kissed
with a sign of endurance and a
light spiral twist
With a mane that is wild silky
and long
The Unicorn never did anything
wrong
It had a body that resembled that
of a horse
and its' unique glow was often
mistaken for force
With antelope hind legs it stood
proud and tall
it had no worries of nothing at all
As it stood with a squat and a
bend at the knee
its' tail just flew like a flag in the
breeze
To symbolize chastity, purity,
clean
The Unicorn stood with his body
so lean
And it's often been said that
when Noah set sail
only one Unicorn succeeded to
prevail
There was only one Unicorn left
there alone
to rule over itself and take over
its' throne
Leigh Ann Senoussi
UNTITLED
Sadness
Seeped slowly
Through
The frown
Of the
Clown
Leaving
Behind
Wet spots
Where tears
Trickled
Down.
Rebecca T. Urrutia
WINDS OF TIME
Winds of time blow through my
mind
The air so clean uh so divine
Pass through this set of time
On to an eternity of brine
Molly Buckles
The Keeper Of the Gate

---

*To Bob: Who will always be with
us . . . Thanks for giving me will,
Bobby Lee, and a wonderful new
life!*

Dear loved one I am free now, to
go beyond the sun.
God's roll call has me listed, as a
chosen one.
I'm starting a great journey, and I
cannot be late.
God has finally called me home,
as "keeper of the gate"!
Though I go on before you, just
follow when you can.
Time can never separate the love
of mortal man.
Just dry your tears of sorrow, I'll
go half way and wait.
You'll meet me on your journey

447

home as "keeper of the gate"!

The "Keeper of the Gate" is one,
who loves someone below.
But heaven waits for no one,
when it's your time to go.
So I'll be waiting patiently until
it's in your fate.
With open arms I'll walk you
home, "The Keeper of the Gate"!

Geneva R. Kelley
HANK WILLIAMS JR.
What do you think of Hank Jr.?
I think he's the best in the land
He sings better than old Hank did
Has a damn good country band

The way that things are going
Hank Jr. likes to tell
He loves wine and women
And raise a little hell

He'll be a legend like his Dad is
He drinks whiskey and smokes
pot
He's got something no one else
has
Old Hank's talent, is what he's got

I love to hear Hank Jr. sing
Love his beautiful voice
If I had to vote for the best in the
land
Hank Jr. would be my choice

Hank said, he'd rather be in Dixie
To him it's pure heaven
He loves all the southern girls
Treats them to Seagram Seven

Yes, Hank Jr. is a lover
Will be till the day he dies
He's just as happy as can be
As he sits neath the Dixie skies

Elizabeth Hodges
IMAGINE
Imagine!
That I could break
this bond
of weighted flesh,
and will myself
on yonder star
Imagine!
That with but thought
and free of weight,
I could be with you
or anywhere,
as fast as light
in day or night.
No sense of solids
nor harm of fears
we bear today,
Yet free as wind
and light as air
Imagine!
I imagine it will be!
I imagine, a day of freedom
of pain and grief
of disbelief,
where man is free to be,
all he imagines.

Cathy Perry
A FRIEND

I love you, Ernie. Thank you for
being you. You've been more than
a friend.

A friend won't say it's over, and
go out for spite.
A friend won't hurt you as your
lover can.

A friend will never hurt you, put
you down, or make you feel
up-tight.
A friend is someone to whom you
can confide in.
A friend will help you whenever
it is possible to do so.
A friend will comfort you when
you need it.
A friend is someone who *really*
cares about his friendship with
you.
A friend tries to understand you,
and the things you do.
A friend will always be there—if
you're wrong, or if you're right.
Thank you for being my friend.
My special friend.

Betty Jo Nosbisch
THE CHRISTMAS CARD

*This poem was written for— and
inspired by— my husband
RAYMOND,— Our First
Christmas, 1969.*

A store bought card is quite alright
For someone else to send.
But it couldn't say "MY" words
just right
No matter how much I spend.
So I thought I'd make my own
With lots of loving care,
To tell you thanks for the happy
times
And all the love we've shared.

Here's wishing you a Merry
Christmas
And a Happy New Year too,
With all the love that's in my
heart
Growing sronger each day for
you.
And Honey if I could, I would
If there were only just some way,
To make for you——All year
through
A Christmas everyday——.

Alma Thurmond
GOD'S HALL OF FAME
Man's hall of fame is only good
As long as time shall be,
But keep in mind GOD'S HALL
OF FAME
Is for eternity.

The ever faithful here
Will be the famous over there,
This glory is God's way
When you obey him every day.

Someday you will be rewarded
For honoring Christ's name
And surely you will ever be
In GOD'S HALL OF FAME.

Daniel E. Butkiewicz
When Christmas Comes
When Christmas comes,
The world is glad.

The Prince Of The Air
Prepares his sleigh for the
World's special day.

"Dad, get me this,"
"Honey, I want that," they dictate.

Materialism is promoted and I
Cry for the children who are
Brain-washed for they know not

What is going on.
The Prince sings his song,
"Santa Claus is coming to town,
So don't frown and be good
As my children should. Oh, yes,
and
Remember this is little baby jesus'
birthday, ho, ho, ho!"

Joe Wagner
THE WOMAN IN MY LIFE
The time has come
To declare my love
For the woman in my life.

When I was in dire need
When I'd been deserted by all
others
She alone chose to remain.
She'll be at my side
Till the day I die.

She stopped my self-destruction
My endless self-indulgence.
Her love set my emotions free
So I could see with greater clarity
What true love can mean to the
disheartened.
Something my sardonic attitude
would never have allowed.

The beauty of this woman
Can only be measured
By the blue sky of a September
morn.

I swam in the world of doubters
Insincerity was all I knew.
But these words I now speak
Are as true as the wine of
hypocrisy
That I once so freely drank with
no hesitation.

I love the woman in my life
For returning the flame of love to
my long neglected heart.
A thousand lies can make any
man a cynic.
Faith lost has been restored.

La Vonne R. Rients
SELF REFLECTIONS
Apart from all my daily tasks
I write this rhyme and little ask
Except that in my verse you joy
As children with a treasured toy.
Set time aside for thinking true,
Ask questions answered not by
you,
Put not off what should be done,
Take pleasure in the game not
won.
Give of yourself, your time, your
care,

Your talents' best if you but share;
Duty bound to give your all,
Questioned not by conscience call.
Seal tight the lips that hurt and
sear.
Heart and hands the children rear.
Anchor firm your faith in God.
When it's your turn accept the
nod.
Perfect your way—add poise and
grace,
A smile becometh every face.
Respect the wisdom gained by age,
Educate with printed page.
Set a goal you wish to find,
Moderate with this in mind.
Most of all remember true
That someone else cannot be you.

Edna Livingston Hargraves
OH THANK YOU JESUS!

*To my husband, Ulysses
Hargraves who suggested that I
send this poem to World of
Poetry—*

Oh thank you Jesus for
understanding,
when no one else seems to.
Thank you for helping me with
the simple
thinks in life I have to do.

Oh thank you Jesus for caring
about me,
a woman, a mother, a wife.
Thank you for giving me comfort
and joy,
for being so real in my life.
For the simple things in life that I
face each day,
Would overcome me, oh Lord, if I
could not pray.

So I'm glad you're there when I'm
lonely,
and I'm glad you're there when
I'm sad,
I'm glad you're there when I'm so
mis-understood.
You're the best friend I've ever had.

I love you Jesus.
Thank you for being my friend.
For listening,
when all that can be heard . . .
Is my tears.
Oh thank you Jesus!

Midge Hasenbank
HARD TO BELIEVE
It's hard to believe
that You became like me.
I cannot perceive
all that You've done for me.
You were once a child
Who walked upon the earth.
So gentle, so mild—
You are life and its worth.

It's hard to believe
that You were flesh and bone.
It's hard to believe,
but how could we have known?
You, Who reigns supreme
from the heavens above—
held us in esteem,
performed the act of love.

It's hard to believe,
but You are more than real.
And You have achieved

much more than we can feel.
It is You I trust
and live for every day.
Believe then, I must—
there is no other way.

Marjorie Killian Baron
NOT KNOWING
The dark, the dark, it holds me
 tight!
    Enfolds
Me in the cold, cold night.
It grips me in a vise of fear,
    Piercing
As a kullen spear!
I pray and pray the light of day,
    Finds
You safe in every way!

Mary Lucci
THE ROSE

---

*To Joyce Marie McLain who is
dearly missed by Mom, Dad, and
Wendy*

She was the rose that bloomed so
 fair,
And, all too soon, faded away.
A life so full, with so much to give,
Her life influences us still.

Though no longer here on earth
 below,
Still sends her message evermore.
Don't wait, don't wait, to love, to
 give,
Too little, too late, may be your
 score.

Her message speaks to us loud
 and clear,
Don't wait to call that someone,
 dear.
Don't wait for the sun, a better day,
To tell a person what you want
 to say.

Now, now, is the time to speak,
To do the things, to help you
 meet
The needs of others who would
 keep
The faith, the love, the covenant.

An angel who stepped through
 Heaven's door,
She earned her way and speaks
 evermore.
Don't wait, don't wait, to love, to
 give,
So too little, too late, won't be
 your score.

Margaret Bryan
COMFORT
Hatred and vanity
You're losing your sanity
Then from the clouds
God's Hand reaches out
Bringing
    Love
      Serenity.

Spite and greed
Humanity in need
Then the song of a bird
So beautiful and clear
Bringing
    Comfort
      Indeed.

Grief and sorrow
Life seems a bother
Then God sends the rain

Bringing
    Flowers
      Tomorrow.

Jealousy and lies
Things you despise
Dark threads in the pattern
To help you grow
Bringing
    Maturity
      In disguise.

Dr. Florencio Pagan-Cruz
THANKS TO MY LORD
Three score and ten years ago, in
 a Capricorn month,
My Almighty Lord sent me into
 this tiny terrestrial globe,
And in His unique manner He
 spoke words of wisdom
In the blank cassette of my
 emerging little soul.
His message, so wise and
 profound, my awareness awoke
To symbols of esoteric truths,
 mysterious and unknown.

Physically He endowed me with
 the five sensitive senses,
Which aptly would take me
 securely along the trail:
Two eyes would see around me
 nature's polychromy,
Two ears would introduce me to
 cosmical sounds and melodies,
One mouth would alchemize all
 health-giving nutrients,
One nose would detect the smells
 and fragrances of this planet,
My touch would filter the
 loveliest feelings of the universe.

My Lord's magnificence has been
 so rich, immense, and true
That He miraculously formed me
 in His sublime and divine
 image,
And as a gift of gifts He
 thoughtfully domiciled me
In a little paradisaical island in
 the magical Caribbean Sea.

This unique enchanted island is
 like a perfect parallelogram
With an emerald-surfaced
 mileage of a hundred by
 thirty-five,
Where the most lovable forms of
 the world's fauna survive
And the flora resemble a
 polychromatic carpet of
 Isfahan,
And the umbrella in the sky high
 above is, to our delight,
Variably painted with dancing
 clouds and millions of lamps
And is surrounded by a water
 collaret, blue and abysmal,
In the magnetized domain of the
 fabulous Atlantis lands.

My island, Puerto Rico, princess
 of the Antilles, by God's views,
Serves as an amorous showcase of
 earthly gems and noble virtues.

Puerto Rico, blessed land under
 the sky and above the sea,
Will teach humanity a lesson of
 charity, love, and peace.

For all these messages that distill
 from Your heavenly streams,
For all Your precious gifts,
 worldly, divine, and spiritual,

I give you thanks, Oh, Lord, from
 the very bottom of my heart.

Edna May Hermann
OUR HOLY SEASON

---

*To my progenitors who
bequeathed to me a steadfast
faith in the continued divine
guidance of life, I dedicate this
poem.*

Onward toward the holidays with
Ubiquitous joy and uncanny
 search for
Rare bits of gaiety and rhyme, to

Hail internal holiness
Of opulent expressions,
Lest we forget the legacies of
Yesteryears, bequeathed to us
 through

Sacred, sacramental songs on the
Eve of Christmas Day, to note
Another Birthday of the Christ,
 Holy
Son of God, come to earth,
Obsure, unknown, unheralded,
 but for a
Nova, brilliant, in the midnight
 blue.

Hilda Mary Stanton
CAN YOU
Can you watch the morning
With all its splender rare
Can you feel the stillness
The peace and quiet there

Can you feel the warmth
When the day is soft and mellow
and skies are blue above
The feeling of Gods love

Can you feel at evening when the
 shadows fall
When long hours of toil are done
Can you feel rest and peace and
 comfort
Before the stillness of the dawn.

Martha Evvs
A MEMORY
A memory is all we have a
 precious
Link to the past,

A memory is yours alone and will
Forever last,

A keepsake is a material thing
Keeping that memory in view,

This special poem is your
 memorable
Keepsake, because it's written just
For you.

Bhadraji Mahinda Jayatilaka
**Little Things That Make
 Me Happy**
Dandelions and dewdrops
 and children asking why
Sunshine and the raindrops
 making rainbows in the sky
Roses in the morning,
 a twinkle in your eye
Little things that make me happy,
 they make me high.

Pebbles in a river
 and bubbles on the wine
A tiny voice inside my head
 that tells me you are mine
Everything I say and do

if you are standing by
Little things that make me happy
 they make me high.

Spiders in their cobwebs,
 sparrows on the trees
Starlight on a summer's night,
 butterflies and bees
Roses in the morning,
 a twinkle in your eye
Little things that make me happy,
 they make me high.

Franklin August Picker
A BRIEF ENCOUNTER
I know that many things are not
 just what they seem to be,
And in support, I offer this, as it
 once happened to me;
'Twas not an enchanted evening,
 there wasn't any gloom,
I don't remember seeing you
 'cross any crowded room.

I may have just been dreaming,
 but dreams so oft reveal,
The better, brighter, future things
 that finally prove real;
And if I wasn't dreaming, then
 perhaps it's really true,
The girl who walked across my
 life, really must be you.

I hope that you can understand,
 and even though I know,
You're promised to another, and I
 must surely let you go;
I'd rather spend a minute, just
 drinking in your charms,
Than have some other lovely girl,
 forever in my arms.

It was just a brief encounter, but
 disclaimers cannot hide,
The feeling it engendered, beauty
 personified;
Like viewing the loveliest sunset,
 from atop a windy hill,
When the world no longer
 matters, when time itself
 stands still.

Ann Thomas
IN MEMORIAM
Stately mansions cradled in cliffs
 above the sea stand proud.
Ancient facades, forlorn and
 forgotten
to yesterday's full round of
 seasons.

In cold skies, the setting sun
reflects it's glare on windows
 staring
Like the glazed eyes of old
 women
too empty of hope to even weep
 with the evening tides.

Hearth fires, winter rains,
 the frost bites, the warmth wanes.
The ground too cold and
 hardened
for the sowing of the furrow
 wherein he was lain.
Grey day, sepia earth,
 black skirt, funeral dearth.

The rains came
sounding like a thousand pearls
 tossed on marble floors.
The chalice has fallen
shattered like thunder and rain.

Only the formless form remains
in memories strung like pearls

On the golden thread
of mind's memory of love.

Dorothy Mae Johnson

FEELINGS

If I had never known suffering
Or felt so much pain.
I would never have known Jesus
Or spoken his name.

If I had never known desperation
Or felt despair.
I would never have had feelings
For others to care.

If I had never known sadness
Or felt tears on my face.
I would never have known the
comfort
Of a friend's warm embrace.

If I had never searched my soul
Deep down inside.
Without the real meaning of life
I would have died.

So for all of these feelings
I am thankful to have had.
Each one has left me with
something special
And for that I am glad.

Dorothy Mae Johnson

JESUS TOUCHED MY LIFE

He touched my life, He came to
me
From doubt and confliction, He
set me free.

He touched my life where I had
been weak
He taught me courage and
wisdom was mine to seek.

He touched my life where I
had gone wrong
He taught me how to accept Him
in my life and to Him belong.

He touched my life with the love
that He brought
By Jesus so much I had been
taught
He touched my life as He had
never before
For me Jesus opened up a brighter
door.
He touched my life as He came
today
He touched my life in a special
way.

Willie Chin Soo

HE'S NOT O.K.

*I wish not to dedicate this poem
to myself Every time I think of
my first love Karen Yip Chuck I
guess I can love no one else.*

He came afar with a crystal
vision—broken by love you
can't forever hold
Once his song of life glisten with
such a wonderful story
And the words lost its miracle
and it changed his whole world
Is it to blame somethin' undevine
to have stole all his glory?

Such a man lost his sanity over
one disillusion
And it's sad to understand his life
slip slidin' away
His cup of reality vapours away
with his intentions
Driftin' no-where he has lost his
faith in divinity

Walkin' on his own oceans
where-ever he passes
Almost to the end of his senses

And heaven on earth rolls on—
What did you learn?
Yet the decision intacts—You got
the power to stop the over-turn
So leave the inhibitions behind—
Life is every move you make
Forget material minds—Life is a
gamble you have to take

Lord it's hard to endure such a
life and it seems to late
Cos he feels no need to recreate—
Guess he's just a sympathy
Lying in the darkness you said
you tried
And it makes no sense and you
rather you died
And it's so sad destiny turn out
this way
You fear the nights and days

But it's just a feelin' that grows
deep in the cold
Broken visions, broken feelin' not
that precious to hold
Maybe it's just a day lost in the
wind
And it's so wrong to let your soul
be lost and your body grows
thin

The truth is time is no escape—
when time is the tickin' of the
penance
Move yourself righteous—save
the hurtin' sentence
Just remember—material dreams
is what you can work for
And the love you can't have be
strong—It's life achin' detour

Beverly J. Lowerre

THE NICKEL AND DIME

Ah! At last there is the Judge and
Jury!
The attorneys and my sister are in
such a flurry!
With a down beat of the mallet,
the noise begins to lesson.
I can feel the deep depression.
An officer calls the pledge to tell
nothing but the truth.
The witnesses in the crowded
courtroom look quite uncouth.
I was called the stand,
Only to be looked upon by the
attorneys as a reprimand.
They reminded me in a whisper,
That I had signed away my rights
on paper.
The Judge warned that I had
certain privileges, but
I insisted that my sister's
problems existed.
This case was important.
As it concerned my Mother's last
Will and Testament.
I was omitted from financial
consideration,
And felt like I was going through
a session of investigation.
The Jury eyed me curiously, as I
returned to my seat.
This is an experience I shall
never have to repeat.
My sister nudged me, as I went
out of the courtroom
and down the hall.
She said, "Thank you dear girl, for

being such a doll.
I will send you a check for
consolation.
Just then, there was revealed a
wonderful sensation.
Ah! I thought, what is a nickel
and what is a dime?
My sister will handle all that in
her own dear time!
Happiness is, not to have anxiety
over a nickel and a dime!
To have its possession, is not to
experience a life so sublime!
Partiality, within my family clan,
is not part of God's plan.
Some people would laugh and
applaud,
But this is not the path I will trod.
The nickel and dime may be
divided, or disappear into
oblivion, but I wont have to
worry or have a spasm.
My life continues on, loving and
living with
Spiritual enthusiasm!

Betty J. Willis

TO THE BRIM

I pray that God's Spirit come,
Down and fill you to the brim,
I pray that you will always keep,
Your heart, soul and spirit,
Entrusted to him: for He Is.

Elizabeth Jane Trittler

AUTUMN

Red and golden leaves go swirling
down,
Blanketing all living things upon
the ground
Leaving the tree's and bushes
look so bare,
Frost is on the pumpkin, Autumn
smells linger heavy on the air.
Snowflake's and cold winds soon
will come,
Making us shiver, making our
noses and fingers, feel so very
numb.
Flower's and some of the birds,
both quietly disappear,
They'll return when springtime
comes again next year
Autumn and winter always linger
far too long,
Everyone welcomes back the
robin's heady song.

Skaught Yuill

NECTAR OF LIFE

---

*DAVID: Myriads of hopes,
dreams; scents of a fresh rain, a
new dawning; now realized.
Because of you.*

Sips of lifes wine emanating
from your warm lips tantalize
my throat as myriads of
emeralds
please the eye.

Your touch burns runes, ecstatic
vibrations, across the
hearth of my essence.

The windows of your soul,
those searching eyes of
brightness,
opulence, hint of treasures
waiting
to be found.

At your touch, a magnitude of

light
burst upon life's darkening
horizon
brilliant as the rising sun at
morn.

I remember you, not for what you
were
before, or what you may be in
the unborn
tomorrows, but as you are now.
Thank you beloved.

Antonino E. Najera Sr.

Antonino E. Najera Sr.

AUTUMN LEAVES

Autumn Leaves—Fall-ing
Leaves—they're all around
Clean Areas—their weakness—
they're prone to hound.
Maple Leaves—by the millions
frolicking . . .
With rhythm—in unison—so
thrilling.
What a sight!—enlivens ones
tiring heart,
Mine eyes dance with them all—
cares not to part.
Leaves caressing my legs with
disregard . . .
to Duty—hence one of the
Crossing Guard.
They whispers—they entice—I
understand,
Sounds of Music—from the
howling winds Band.
Tempting me—step-up to the
Tempo;
But then—Duty First—before I do
so.
Climate not so cool—wind in
playful mood,
Drives away woes and I do feel so
good.
Frolicking—dancing Leaves—
they come and go
With the winds soothing—
howling high and low.
So graceful and so pleasing to the
eye—
And happily—praised them as
they passed by;
Leaves turn round and round—
with the wind's thrilling sound
Soon they're gone—knowing not
where they were bound.

Mrs. Deborah L. Breen

MOTHER

Mother dear,
Mother mine,
What world is
Yours now to find?

Is it peaceful?

Our World's Best Loved Poems

Is it pure?
No more hardships
To endure?

You left us, dearest Mother,
With your work well done.
You went to sleep, at last to rest,
Upon a setting sun.

Pain, now left behind;
And sorrow, by the bye.
Joy should be your all
Now, beyond life's tie.

May your path be straight
And sheltered, warm and free,
As you complete your path
Toward eternity.

Nell B. Bates
Let There Be Silent Night
Let there be Silent Night
And let there be place in hearts
for love instead of hate;
Let us let snowflakes pure
erase all greed, and selfish ill,
We shall find joy on Christmas
night
if we go out and seek a hill.
Let there be room for faith to fill
our hearts beside the dying
glow;
For the Star in the East shines
brightly still,
Then let there be Silent Night.

Jean Vick
Making Holiday Memories
The Holiday season is drawing
near
With sounds of happiness
everywhere
Brightly colored Christmas lights
Adorn each house for Christmas
night.

As time grows near to trim the tree
And oh what a beautiful sight to
see
It's sparkling and twinkling off
and on
And yes we must wrap the old
dog a bone.

Families will gather from far and
near
To give each one some Christmas
cheer
And the aroma of Mom's good
cooking
Brings everyone to the kitchen
looking.

As the day finally ends and we
must go home
The kids are asleep and we're all
alone
Leaving the family makes us
kinda sad
But we can't forget the wonderful
time we had.

Charlotte J. Guenther
SECOND CHANCE

---

*In rememberance . . . of the way it
was*

Alone . . and numbed with grief,
life passed me by
No more the touch of hand or
songs to sing
No more the glance of secrets
shared nor arm to cling

And what was mine to give now
stilled, the fires banked
Against remembered times, to
fade beneath the sound of
death's dark wing.

Alone . . I questioned not but
went my way dry-eyed
With head held high that none
would see the pain
But in the dark of night my
woman's heart would cry, in
vain.
God, how I prayed to face the day
and mask the fears within.
And then, as if in answer to an
aching need, he came.

Alone no more . . This gentle
giant of a man brought hope
Where there was none, and
wakened precious dreams so
long denied.
Enfolded in his arms the embers
glow once more, and I abide
He walks with me and shares the
wonderous joy of love re-born
Together, my new love and I go,
side by side.

Alone no more . . or must I turn
from love and seek
My comfort in the empty void of
memories past
Or will love flourish only when I
rush to hold it, fast.
Accepting risk of heartache in
this my second chance
I am content to try again . . as
long as our dear love shall last.

Walter R. Samson
PERFECTION

---

*Dedicated to my grandchildren,
in the hopes that they may seek
human perfection throughout
their lives.*

A perfect ball, a perfect speech, a
perfect job he said,
perfection exist not at all in
things that man hath made.
For perfect man, except for god,
this earth hath never trod,
and all the works that man has
wrought, imperfect still to god.
But we may reconcile our minds,
to not on failure dwell,
if we but strive throughout our
lives to use our talents well.
Perfection still to some degree, is
ours the wise men say,
by doing each and all things well,
in our most perfect way.

Arden Michael
TWO THE SAME
We each start down life's road
Wanting to join in life's game
Wishing to find the mate for life
Different people yet TWO THE
SAME

We hope for an enjoyable job
To help fulfill that life
Most ladies wanting a husband
And men desiring a wife

May Good Luck show her face on
you
As months and years slip by
Making you "Oh so happy!"

That the memories make you cry.

Dreaming of that house on the hill
Which we can call our's some
day
Looking out there in the yard
Watching our children play

You and your mate give thanks
each day
That along the other one came
As you help each other down
life's road
Finding love in TWO THE SAME

Steven J. Burtch
THE BROTHERHOOD
Everywhere the sadness and grief
I see.
Now they seem so plain and clear
to me.
I sense the hunger and the
endless thirst
And wonder, I never saw them at
the first.

But the years had passed on
fleetest wing.
Frivolity and joy made my heart
only sing.
Then I was hurt— my heart was
cleft in twain.
I choked with the agony and
wept with the pain.

Now I know a kinship with those
who suffer here.
The fellowship of misery now
seems more clear.
For the endless sorrow and
anguish of the years
Only can be seen through the
mists of tears.

Patricia A. Maloney
PIECEMEAL
What's the matter with me
I'm too religious for some
Too outspoken for others
Too rich for some
Too conscientious for others
Too young for some
Too worldly for others
Trying to fit myself in a group
I end up shattered . . . in pieces
Someone
Accept the whole me

Ernest Shelton
HOPE
I feel hollow deep down in my
heart,
Totally without emotion or
substance,
Void with no purpose in life,
What is wrong with me dear lord?
Give me strength to sort out the
problems before me,
May I have the wisdom to
succeed,
Show me the direction to move,
I look back into time and see it
was just wasted,
Hope is mine,
Dreams are stretched before me,
Desire is the one thing I don't
have,
The will to fight, to achieve
something,
Think not of others opinions,
Be prudent and act as the lion
does,
Hope alone does not make
success, fame, and fortune,

The stone jungle lies before me,
I am a realist with ambition,
Striving forward and meeting the
challenge,
Doing what it takes to conquer
my foe,
Good fortune isn't received its
achieved,
And for me the plan has been
sprung.

Bryan Dietrich
REGRET
My life
is a pathetic

dishrag

gathering water
as the faucet drips.

I am wet
and sloppy
with sorrow.

The grime of life
clings
to my seams:
even on washday,

I cannot come clean.

The ring in the sink
is the path I know,

and the drain—

my only window.

Esther M. Thompson
SO BEAUTIFUL
On the banks of the Potomac, so
stately and serene,
Stands the Capitol at
Washington, as royal as a
queen.
With cherry blossoms, sweet and
fair,
Perfume drifting on the air,
nothing with this can compare.
On the beautiful Potomac
location is the best.
From the north and south
admirers come,
As well as east and west.
A sight that will amaze you,
you'll think it is a dream,
But in reality it's Nature on the
beam.
Oh, Washington, so beautiful,
with sky above so blue,
I gaze at all the splendor, and
wonder is it true?
Could any place compare with it,
This side of Heaven's shore?
If only I could stand and gaze at
this forever more.

Paula J. Courtemarche
THE WEDDING
When will the hurting end?
Never will, it seems.

A remembrance of a maiden fair
Full of hopes and goals
and dreams.

Then the hurting came along
Yet she struggled on, e'er long;
and the goals were realized
Yet the hurting stayed, so long.

Yet—the faith of the maiden fair
Ne'er dimmed through the vale of
tears;
And soon the hurting disappeared
For she and her Prince,
were paired.

451

And the prince is the Son of God
and in the place called Heav'n
reside the lovers beside the throne
In the calm;
so blessing.

Kimberly J. Hamlin
MY LIFE HAS TROUBLES

---

*This poem was written to my
family Jack, Sharon, David,
Sharon Kaye and inspired by my
friends and family who say I have
talent as a writer and I want to
thank them.*

My life has troubles
til no end.

It won't be so easy,
til I find me a friend.

And how I wish
that you were here.

Tell me darling,
tell me dear.

Will I wait for an hour,
or maybe a year?

My life has troubles,
and oh how I fear.

Is it worth the waiting,
is it worth the time.

Am I your lover
or am I standing in line,

Will you hurt me
or show me love?

My life has troubles
but I'm getting through

I know my love is sincere,
How about you?

David E. Sutton
HAPPINESS
Happiness is the joy of life
It is bright sunny days
A cool breeze on a hot day
The first time we met

Happiness is a day full of love
A treat given to you by others
And returned to them by those
  who received of it
Multiplying ten fold in each
  passing

Happiness is a twinkle in your
  love's eyes
The sparkle in a child's smile
A schoolgirl's giggle
And the impish grin that only a
  young lad can produce

But it is always . . . always,
something to be experienced
Each and every day of ones life

Janet M. Wussick
WARM SUMMER NIGHT
Love me like a warm summer
  night.
As a delicate flower beneath the
  starlight.
Like the summer night drifts
  slowly by,
And the memory of its magic
  shall never die.
So shall my love for you be this
  strong,
So shall your touch linger ever so
  long.
Kiss me in such a way I will never

forget,
How your lips like the dew were
  so sweetly wet.
There is something in your eyes
  that will haunt me forever.
There is something in your voice
  that I will hear forever.
So you see you are so much like a
  warm summer night,
Something that is eternal but
  fades with the light.
When I close my eyes the
  memory will be freshly there.
Just like the warm sweet scent of
  the summer nights' air.

Ila Mae Holloway Jordan
THRILL SEEKERS
Your heart is filled with thoughts
  of high adventure.
You do no care for things of
  which I speak.
You always look for worldly
  adulation,
And cannot understand the
  thrills I seek.

I would not care to run a
  marathon,
Or try to climb the highest
  mountain peak!
But in my heart I've heard the
  voice of God,
And held a new-born baby to my
  cheek!

Michael Langston
**Sometimes When You Look
  In His Eyes**

---

*To Ronda, and the memory of a
love once shared.*

Sometimes when you look in his
  eyes
And say: I love you,
Sometimes then, remember too
That other person
You once said it to,
Who . . .

Far away and forgotten,
Somewhere now, sits and cries
And has no other eyes but the
  stars to look into;
Holding close in his mind,
There forever, and for all of time:
The memory of you.

Vikki Jenkins
RISKING
Open up-
The windows
Of your mind.
Let new thoughts
Sift through.
Shed all darkness
As brightness
Covers you.
Begin again—
Step out refreshed.
Let go the fettered past.
Walk proudly
Forward as you
Risk at last.

Arletta Vir-Mill
REACHING
Set before my life in measureless
billows of warmth and truth
—I found an unreachable cloud-
On dissadent ladders of struggle
towards

attainment
I climb the rungs of fulfilling
circumfrance
and see glimpses of never ending
  aloneness
and cry out in want of the
  unreachable cloud.

Can it be, ever,
  that the petal of life's flower
  blooms in lofts of splendor
  on the unreachable cloud?

Oh! Flower of reason, in this dark
  hour of need,
spread blossoms of awareness
across the haze of the cloud
and let the coushions of doubt
form into drops of reality
and pour onto my being in
  storms of passion
and promise—
  while unreachable heights be no
    more!

Rory Y. Takaki
**A True Humanitarian
  Heart**

---

*This poem is dedicated to the
true values and ideals of the
Frank J. Tanaka family*

"If you can help one who is
  greatly in need,
You will be seen as a great
  humanitarian.
But if you should help one only
  for the sake of,
Securing a place into heaven,
Let it be understood that;
God Will Know."

Sylvia Rodriguez
FOR MY JERRY
My first love, my last love,
  always you'll be
The one who inspired this flame
  inside me

A deep glowing warmth that you
  made me feel,
I just couldn't believe that it was
  for real

Such passions within me I'd never
  known
Yet always with you, they were
  easily shown.

You brought out the *best*, in me
  there could be
And all of my dreams I was able
  to see;

But now that you're gone the flame

burns so low,
There's nothing or no one to
  rekindle its glow!

It is only a flicker that is dying
  out fast
But I won't give it up. I want it to
  last.

It's all that is left of what we once
  shared,
And wherever you are, My Love,
  please take care.

Deep in my mind dwells the
  memory of you
My heart is still hurting, its
  aching and blue

If only you knew what I vowed in
  my heart
To love you forever and never to
  part.

Though now you belong to
  someone for keeps
You are mine anytime, while I am
  asleep

'Cause I still have my dreams, and
  sweet memories of you
That she'll never hold as true as I
  do.

Gone you are now and always
  will be,
And, gone with you also, is a
  special part of me.

Leah C. Anderson
A SPECIAL ANGEL

---

*Dedicated, with love and
affection, to Justin Horvatin,
beloved First-Born Son of Richard
and Carol Cannon Horvatin, who
arrived at approximately Noon on
August 4th, 1983.*

A Bundle from Heaven has just
arrived to join the Earthly Scene;
And brought along sheer
  Happiness, you know the kind
  I mean!

For in this lovely Bundle, filling
  Hearts with pride and joy;
Was a very Special Angel Child, a
  Healthy BABY BOY!

His Parents are quite proud, of
course, for He is NUMBER ONE!
  The very best there ever was,
  beneath the Noonday Sun!

Some day, no doubt, he'll make
his Mark, revered he'll always be;
And August Fourth, his Special
  Day, will go down in History!

Stacey Michelle Williams
A CHRISTMAS POEM
Hear the hustle bustle of the
  Christmas shopping rush,
In the streets the snow and ice
  are turning into slush.
The Santas' are in front of stores,
  ringing golden bells
Hear the Christmas music, how it
  sails and how it swells.
See the people running, sales are
  everywhere.
All there is, is hustle bustle,
  doesn't anybody care?
Is there not a true meaning to
  this Holiday occasion!

The children who want presents,
from their parents need
persuasion.
Is the love and joy of Christmas
truly out of sight
Is all that's left of Christmas joy
simply blinking lights?
But wait let's look in homes with
toasty fireplaces.
We see the children singing, with
the smiles upon their faces.
Though there are colored lights
and songs outside in the cold.
Now, I understand Christmas
can't be bought or sold.
No matter where you are, the
word in any part
Christmas isn't in the wrapping,
it is felt within the heart.

Diane Marie Luke
CHOICE
Details in my life reflect
that choice is one of
life's greatest virtues.
This gift allows me
to change with time
and discover who I am.
It gives me the power
to choose the direction
I want my life to take,
and gives me the strength
to create my happiness.

V. Ann Owen—Vansyckle
MY LOVELY VALENTINE

To "The Chief" who is: My Wise
Teacher . . . My Best Friend . . .
My Constant Helpmate . . . My
Lovely Valentine.

I've painted a lovely picture for
all the world to see.
It's a picture of "My Valentine", in
his entirety.

You will note, upon his face,
the eternal smile which I have
placed;
And, a perpetual tear claims the
corner of one eye
(which represents each time he's
ever cried.)

His hands are mighty and his
arms show strength enough to
hold;
And, in the middle of his chest—
see, I have painted a heart of
gold!

Now, isn't this a lovely picture,
this portrait of "My Valentine";
For it's a picture of "The Chief"—
he's lovely and he's mine!

Marjorie Tanner Hamrin
LINES ON TIME
Ivisible
Inexorable—
    Time Is.
Out of sight
Unbound by sound—
    Time flies.
Like the wind—
    Everyone feels
        Where it's been.
Whence it comes
    Or whence it goes—
        Nobody knows.
But it shows—
    Oh, how it shows!

Donna Marguerite Strough Barnes
**Merry Christmas—(To
Bobbie)**
Merry Christmas, Darling!
    The night is bright and clear,
The stars are smiling on the world
    And love is here.

Merry Christmas, Darling,
    And everything is still
With hope and love to everyone-
to everyone "Good Will"!

Joanne Amaral
DEATH
DEC. 18, 1980

With Christmas coming so near,
His eyes can't see it to clear;
The pain he feels as the days go on,
I wish I could help him look
    beyond;

Sitting in his chair throughout
    the day,
I see the pain that won't go away;
Like a father to me, he will
    always be,
A father to many, just not to me;

My only hope is, he sees the day,
Its Christmas please, let him stay;
Merry Christmas dad from me to
    you,
I'll always be thinking of you;

February 12, 1982

Another Christmas has come and
    gone,
Now I think he looked beyond;
His day has come, his pain is gone,
Now he's going way beyond;
    Let Him Rest In Peace

Mary Agnes Lynch
MY FRIEND
"Why do you look so sad?"
"Tell me, are things really that
    bad?"
"They are?" "My, you need a
    guiding star."

"I know what I will do,"
"To help one, so discouraged as
    you."
"I'll tell you about "Him,""
"From beginning, to end," "Who?"
"Why "God", my friend."

"I hope this little talk of "God;""
"Has helped you, to see the light;"
"It has? "Oh, I'm so glad;"
"To see you happy in "His" sight;"

"Well now, I must be on my way,"
"But before I go, I want to say,"
"Life will be successful, to the end,"
"If "God's," on our side, "My Friend.""

Marian Joan Yoest
THE LOOKING GLASS
T'was forty years or more ago
When in the looking glass
I saw a young vivacious lad
Just waiting for a lass.

I found the maiden oh so fair
The one love of my dreams
Who is as young to me today
As yesterday—it seems!

The looking glass has lied to me
These forty years or more
It never has reflected
What life has had in store.

And now when I have come
To that quiet time in life

I gaze into my looking glass
And there reflects the strife.

Yet I'd not trade one yesterday
For all of lifes tomorrows
For every new day with my love
Has joys as well as sorrows.

Ann L. Sweet .
How Much Do I Love You
You ask how much I love you?
How do you measure love?
How high is up my darling?
Past all the stars above.
You think it is the top dear.
When its as far as you can see.
But up goes on forever,
Thru all eternity.
How many gallons of water, are
    there in the sea?
How many grains of sand on the
    shore?
Well thats how much I love you
    dear.
And darling, even more . .
I would rather die my darling,
Than to ever have to part.
Because you are my everything
You are my very heart
Wherever you are my darling
Thats where I'll want to be.
And thats how much I'll love you.
Through all eternity.

Jess N. Martin
Christian Musical Comedy
Orchids, Daisies, Roses, and
    Sunshine
I saw them all last-night
Oh' such a happy group of girls
    and guys,
with smiling faces and sparkling
    eyes

I looked at you across the room,
like a Dish with a Silver Spoon
I looked and I could plainly see,
your smiles were directed at me

My heart was bursting with joy,
as I fastened my stare, on each
little girl, and each handsomeboy
Let me tell you one and all,
I sat out in the audience, I had a
    ball

I sat there spellbound, staring at
    the Stage
I was spellbound, as if in a rage,
I closed my eyes, and in my mind
    I could see,
you all were staring at me

Denese Davis
HAPPY NEW YEAR
Another year has come and gone.
I feel so empty-yet so strong.
All alone to bid "82" goodbye,
Memories to set aside.
New directions to unfold,
My own I will hold.
Never again to place love first,
Conceal my hearts hungry thirst.
Love is only a story book dream,
that gets caught up in its own
    theme.
Yes, love is only a story book
    dream . . .

Monica Ruiz
SISTER MOON
Glorious moon,
Princess of Heaven
What do you see in me now?
Do you see sadness,

Or do you see joy?
Perhaps you see loneliness,
Perhaps you see pain.
Tell me, Oh Moon,
What do you see?
Do you see me unloved,
Or just solitary, for now?
Do you see that I long for
    romance
The romance that has taken
    place for centuries
In your soft blue light?
Do you see that I am afraid,
Afraid to love?
Or is it just my imagination?
Sister Moon, you comfort me so,
For you send those silver rays
Straight to me, and only me—
Giving me hope to carry on.
For you, I will take the chance to
    love
But if love goes wrong,
You know I'll be back
Sitting in your light once more.

Michael Delaney
THE MISSISSIPPI
Roll along,
Slowly roll, slowly.
Long you are,
Dividing the land;
Wide you are—
We build our spans.
You quiet river,
What secrets can you tell?
Hear the bell?
The tug is coming,
Hum, hum, humming through
    your waters.
And you give way as if to say
"I'm your friend,
Hey, meet ya 'round the bend."
It's no secret,
You are a friend,
As you slowly roll,
Slowly roll along.

Sara Katherine Hurley
SEAGULL
To glide as free as a seagull
To have feathers of virgin white
To Know the highs from the lows
The dulls from the lulls
And know when to stay out of
    sight

When trouble appears to surface
Be prepared to fly low key
But not in the arms of Morpheus
Pick a destiny suited for thee

Robert L. Black
THREADS OF LOVE

To my wife, Linda. My
inspiration and my life.

Marriage, like a suit of clothes
no two are quite the same.
Still all start out with hope and
    dreams
as we all play lifes game.
Happiness is one thread, wishes
also play a part.
If sewn together carefully
a lasting love will start.

"A marriage made in Heaven",
that sayings not quite right.
It had to have a seamstress with
a hand just firm, not tight.
The threads pulled through the

needle
very softly, so it won't break,
stitching in a lot of giving,
and so very little take.

Threads of love, hold together,
a lasting love affair.
They keep you close together,
with a love so very rare.
Threads of love will keep you going
when lifes trials give you a shove,
so hold on to all the threads of
love.

Betty DiPrimio
MY LITTLE GIRL

To My Beloved Daughter
Michelle Love Mom

Little girl it seems like it was
only yesterday.
I held you in my arms and on my
lap you'd play.
Seems like only yesterday I'd sing
you a lullaby
Where did the time go it sure did
fly
Now your singing songs to me,
got a trinkle in your eye.
Your just a tender flower in lifes
big broquet
And to me the prettyist flower
was ever send my way.
It's a joy to walk with you thru
lifes way,
Helping you to become a
Christian lady someday
I hope I've made you happy in
some special way
just having you with me makes
my life each day
You are something special sent
from God above to fill my life
with a lasting love.
Always remember read your
Bible, go to Church, and pray.
If you want a life that's happy
thats the only way.
Someday you'll be a grown up
Lady you see.
But you will always be "My Little
Girl" to me

Ila Standlea Steinke
Ila Standlea Steinke
To a Former Classmate
Friendship, that fair ship,
The ship that sails forever
Though wild the storm and fierce
the gale
Still on and on friendship will sail.
Oh ship sail on forever.

Friendship, the true ship
That storms can never sever,
Through calm and clear, through
storm and gale
Still on and on friendship will
sail.
Oh ship sail on forever.

Freindship, my dear ship,
You are my hope forever.
Fail not your course through life's
dark ways.
Sail on through brighter, balmy
days.
Oh ship sail on forever.

John Spatafora
MARIA
Matronly, maidenly
Heavenly graceful
Resplendent and queenly
Graciously reigning
Our graces obtaining
To demons eternal pariah she is
To us sinners forever Maria she is.

Deana L. Arthur
REFLECTIONS
The sun sets behind you,
Your life is yet to live
But, you are in the future
And have nothing left to give.

The past holds precious memories,
The future lies beyond
But, you must live your life today
And find where you belong.

The future may bring happiness,
Or it may well bring pain
But, the past holds only memories
That cannot live again.

You stand here in the present
And look back upon your life,
You wonder what the future
brings,
It cuts you like a knife.

And now you're caught between
two worlds,
Your hope and history,
You pray the Man that lives above,
Judge tenderly on thee.

Michele Fregoe
WINTER AND BEAUTY
Bleakness and bitterness
are Winter's claim,
Chilling cold and
killing fame.

But Beauty follows Winter
everywhere
And where Winter leaves death,
also leaves prayer.

Valerie E. Parker
A MOTHER'S GRIEF
I'll go to her and calm her fears,
sing thoughts of faith into her
ears. I'll hold her gently all thru
the night and pray for strength
to help her fight this monster
that eats her more each day
and threatens to take her life
away.

She lays there motionless, quiet,
still . . .I pray she hasn't lost
her will to live, to survive, to
come back to me despite what
fate claims her chances to be.

My angel lays there with
punctured vein, her face
contorted, drawn in pain.

So young to face the rage of the
knife . . . . Machines
encouraging the breathe of life
into a frame that juts with
bone. A face of gray that one
time shone . . . a mere shadow
of what she used to be. Dear
God please don't take my angel
from me!

Karen Lewandowski
FRIENDS
We share our clothes,
We share our woes,
We both have troubles of our own.

We both love pizza,
and like the same boys,
We both have sorrows and some
joys.

We both like the beach,
and pretty dresses,
And both our rooms are real big
messes!

We're so different, and yet so alike,
We both love skating and going
on hikes.

We've laughed and also shed
some tears,
We've expressed our love and
also our fears.

We're best of friends,
It's too good to be true,
Too bad we couldn't have been
sisters too!

Bernice Y. Scales
GIVE ME TIME
Give me time, I need some time
To give my life some worth—
There are so many things I want
to do,
Before I leave this earth.

Give me time, I need some time
I want this life to last—
There are so many things I want
to see
But, time is moving fast.

Give me time, I need some time
I have no wish for death—
There are so many things I want
to say,
Before that one last breath.

Give me time, I need some time
To do these things and more
And when the inevitable comes
to pass,
I'll meet it at the door.

Paco Smith
NEARLY
will my life soon be over
God, can you whisper all the
answers to me
can I trade my youthful tears
on dreams that will never come
true—maybe pass it off
as a melancholy tomorrow
Lord, lie beside my head
leaving behind the painful
years—only listen if you want
to, because the darkened
eyes of yesterday
keep me running to an
early cast of fate
and as my faith grows
onward, pass the jeweled
crown on to another
more deserving.
God just whispers all
the answers to me.

Jeaneen McAmis
QUIET, SADDENED LOVE

For Nancy Reiser: A wonderful
woman who pushed me to
explore and stretch my creative
talent, to look toward everything
I could become—and who is my
friend.

Your eyes are dark as new moon's
precious night,
And in them I see wells of
deepest sorrows
Merging in a sea of dark
tomorrows—
Pleading for a love to bring the
light
To cleanse the soul that still can
feel the bite
Of pain. If for a time a heart to
borrow
I could find to ease your hurt and
sorrow,
I would give my life without a
fight.
This heart of mine is all I have to
offer,
Filled to overflowing with its
caring.
Fain would I give all and then
above
The boundless limits of this
pulsing coffer!
Cease your heart's lamenting and
dispairing—
Quiet now and know that you are
loved.

Betty Stanford
DESPAIR
Here I am on the brink of falling
apart.
I've tried to get hold of myself,
but really don't know where to
start.
I have this terrible urge to leave
it all behind
in search of greener pastures,
or go wild like an ivy vine.

Today is not the day; tomorrow's
not I'm sure.
Maybe in the near future I'll find
what I'm searching for.
My dreams are all turned under,
I've given up I guess.
No hope of better tommorows, and
less of happiness.

Doris W. "Dottie" Flock
Our Tomorrow Mountain

Dedicated to our beloved sister
and daughter, Darlene Michelle
who we love and miss very
much . . . Save us a place on
your mountain . . . Duane,
Valerie, Cynthia and Mother . . .

My dearest, how can I try to
explain the emptiness I feel,
the hurt, the pain?
Am I too vain to hope that
someday we can still find that
mountain we'd hoped together
to climb?
As I hold your hand and speak
your name, I wonder not why
or whence you came

into my life to share my dreams,
but, of how you now lay there
so lovely and serene.
"Come back to me, don't go," I cry.
"I'm not ready for you to die.
We've so much to do and things
to see; please, oh please stay
here with me!"
I pray as I watch you slip into a
world far beyond the sky so blue.
Your life is passing before my eyes
and, finally I stop and realize
that your reason for leaving has
got to be that you've found that
mountain ahead of me;
with its forest of love and peace
of mind amid gold lined paths
and rivers sublime . . .
My love, some day when the time
is right, I too shall climb that
mountain one night
and when I reach the top I'll see
that you reached it way ahead
of me
and was waiting alone for me to
come into your beautiful world
beyond.
Wait for me darling, I'll join you
some day; 'tho I may stumble
along the way;
for the mountain is high that I
must climb and to get to you
may take some time.
Yes, I'll let you go so you can be
on your mountain top to wait
for me.
My tears I shed are of joy, not
sorrow for I know I'll join you
on "our mountain tomorrow."

Stevie Jo Steiner
Oh Lord, My God, You Let Him Stay

To my darling brother who has curly brown hair. He is one of us of whom God cares.

Praise God, we are all joint heirs
To Our Fathers Great Grace and
Our Lords sweet care,
And on that day when Our God
said come
You Bowed your head and you
started on home.

As you took your first step, we all
were there
Anguished and asking, your
family of prayer,
Crying, "Wait big brother, don't
climb so fast"
"This pain of yours will surely
not last!"

"WE LOVE HIM LORD, YOU
KNOW WE DO."
"YOU LOVE HIM LORD, WE
KNOW THAT TOO,"
"BUT LORD, MY GOD, PLEASE
LET HIM STAY,"
"JUST FOR ONE HOUR, JUST
FOR ONE DAY."

Our Father looked down in His
Amazing Grace
And Jesus, Our Friend, stood
there in our place.
He cradled this one In the Palm
Of His Hand
Oh, we knew He was safe with
this Son Of Man.

"Hold up there son, stay yet a
while"
Said Our Loving Father with His
gentlest smile,
And the sweetest comfort poured
down from above
Our Father and Our Lord with
Their Miracle Of Love.

OH LORD, MY GOD, YOU LET
HIM STAY
NOT JUST FOR AN HOUR,
NOT JUST FOR A DAY.
I will not doubt, and I cannot fear,
For through it all, this message
rings clear

GOD IS NOT DEAD NOR DOES
HE SLEEP!
HOLD FAST TO HIM HIS
PROMISE HE KEEPS!
We are because He is and will
forever Be!

Patricia Cooper
BEYOND THE RAINBOW
"Where's Heaven?" she asked, her
eyes bright and clear.
"Is it far away, or is it very near?"

Her father sat down on a chair
near the bed,
he took her hand and slowy began.

"Heaven," he said, "is a wonderful
place
where God, Jesus and the angels
stay."

"But where?" she insisted, her
voice getting weak.
Her father shook his head, he
couldn't even speak.

He looked out the window
searching his mind
and there he saw a rainbow,
beautifully designed.

"Honey," he said, "I'm not sure I
really know,
But I'm almost positive that it's
beyond the rainbow."

With that, she smiled, she knew
his words were true.
"Good by Daddy," she said, "I'll
always love you."

She gazed out the window at the
beautiful array,
"Beyond the rainbow," she
whispered as she slowly slipped
away.

Fran Meeks
CHRISTMAS
Christmas time is here,
See the snowflakes fall
On the crystal ground?

We enjoy Christmas,
Each year we remember friends,
This is happiness.

The church is aglow,
With the bright, burning candles
As we sing praises.

Christ is here today
At this special time of year.
We're thankful of Him.

Joanie Mendyka
LIFE
Life is a challenge, like playing a
game,
You may lose or you may gain.

Life is sad, when things go wrong,
You have to keep your faith and

be strong.
Life is happy, when a day is right,
You will see everything rosey and
bright.

Life can teach you how to better
your soul,
So you are ready for judgement-
no matter how old.

Life has to be lived, not planned
each day,
So let things happen and be as
they may.

Michelle James
WITH THIS LOVE
I was worried but you were strong,
willing to Love, caressing so long.
I gave my heart without thinking
twice. You love me now and
that will always last.
No matter what we do or where
we go, I'm happy, I hope you
know.
I love you more and more each
day, and with this love I will
always stay.
You say you will not leave, I
know it's true, because you
love me and I love you.

Glenda Kay Abrams
Johnathon and Desiree

For Johnathon, my son, Desiree, my daughter. With great love forever, happiness for your lifetime. Love you both, Mom.

For Johnathon and Desiree I write
about my love,
First I wish you the important
things in life the feelings of
friendship and love.
I hope you both grow together as
brother and sister instead of
apart,
For the distance would match the
pain you truely would feel in
your heart.
I hope that as you grow up that
we grow into friends,
Instead of like some who as they
grow and have to let go the
love is where it ends.
I pray I have patience and
understanding thru out the years,
Plenty of laughter, no room for
anger or tears.
Most of all I wish you love for all
that you do,
And I hope this love will burn
thru out your lifetimes to burn
bright when it's passed on by
you,
I love you Johnathon and Desiree

Dewey D. Bayless
LONG AGO
Reflections of a summer's day
And of a life, lived yesterday
Remembering the almost forgot
Wanting now, what I have not

There are hillsides green,
meadows wide
Misty visions of the countryside
And shadowed roads, made of dirt
These reflections in my mind do
flirt

I'm teased with looks at yesterday
Of another life, another way

Of simpler times and bygone love
As they pass before me like a dove

On occasion . . . there exists
A wealth of love . . . in the midst
As though someone waits,
neglected
For my return, too long expected

Then the visions fly away
Taking love and yesterday
Like a failing memory, so is mine
Of a different love and seperate
time

dwight l. johnson
LULLABY FOR A LADY
Rest your mind in my thoughts.
Ease your heart into my love.
Melt your spirit into mine
And let yourself melt into my
dreams.

Let the world spin without you
for a time
And when you awake, we can be
refreshed.

So lie quietly within my life, love.
Close your heavy eyes for a while.
I will be with you in your fantasies.
You shall enter all my dreams.

Peace to you, my love. Peace.
Sleep for—Sleep, my love.
And awake off the slumbers
in the dawn light.

Goodnight
My love.
Goodnight.

Kathleen V. Beshears
CHRISTMAS 1983

To my sisters, Opal and Bernie, whom I love dearly

Dear Sister,
As I look at the sky
It's comforting to know
It covers you as well as I.

We see the same sun
Gaze at the same moon
Even though we're miles apart!

We are like the points of a star
With arms open wide.
We are from one root
Like the branches of a tree.

We have our ups and downs—
Days when we feel like clowns;
We also have our serious side—

Then love of God
Makes us know
We are a family!

    I Love You,
    Your Sister

James Trevor Twixtham
Grief Has Laid a Path To My Door
Grief has laid a path
to my door
So that I must
walk it evermore.
My windows let in
gales of despair
So when I breath
I breath this air.

Lock that door!
and seal that sill,
Then grief may leave me
with joy to mill,
with a heart to fill;
and time e'er so still.

Mary Lou Tabor
MOTHER
We begin life with a
Woman who cares, who gave
us birth and a breath of fresh air

I love my mother nine times
and over, more than a four
leaf clover.

Who braided my hair, and
sent me to School. Always
Said obey my rules.

Mothers are here to be loved
and near. They love the
   happiness,
of joy and fear.

Mom laugh when I laugh,
Cried when I cried,
All in all until life
Passes us by.

Mothers are one in the same,
Who always bare the deepest
Pain.

Love grows on as a dove,
Until we meet in Heaven above.

My Mama picked cotton,
My mama pulled corn
My Mama did everything
but, sat on a throne.

And if she dies before
I am gone,
God will put her upon a
Throne

Internal Love

Lisa A. Janas
A MOTHER'S LOVE

---

*To the most important person in
my life. Thanks Mom. I Love You!*

A mother's love is everlasting.
A mother's love can reach out to
   her children's friends; which
   can mean a lot to her children.
A mother's love is very special to
   her children.
A mother's love for her children
   and others will never die.
A mother's love is having trust in
   her children.
A mother's love can make her
   children's dreams come true.
But most of all a mother's love
   will never die for her children,
   and neither will her children's
   love for her.

T. M. Shore
UNTITLED
The plane again where all the
   lights have turned to stars.

In my eyes in your eyes
are olive and orange
blue pink purple
and distance

So the plane, again,
is humming.
Harmonics in various shades of
   cowardice
and running through scales
of running to, running from.

The stars are humming and as
the stars are fading the humming
drifts back to be canvas for
   talking
and the plane shakes
and the talking falls out of the

seams
in the plastic and oozes through
orange and pink and purple,
and hums.

Robin Murphy
UNTITLED

---

*For Darling Brian, my own piece
of sunshine, my whole world.*

Sometimes,
I feel so lost
and alone
and sad.
   Then you come and you fill,
my days
my nights
my very life;
with hope
and kindness
and love.
   The beautiful part inside of me,
comes shining through because
   of you;
and your tender
and gentle
and caring ways.
   You color my days, warm my
   nights,
change my darkness
to light
and joy
and song.

Wanda Lenore Wager
THE WISE ONES
Wise advice
For young or old,
Genius,
Average, bold:
Do your best
In your niche,
Serve with love
And you'll be rich!

Aurora L. Espinoza
NOCHE SIN PAZ
Noche de paz, ami solo tristezas
   me das
y en la mesa todos, contentos
   reunidos
y yo extranando mis seres
   queridos;
Noche de paz, en este pais tan
   lejano
donde el idioma nos hace callar
mientras todos esperan abrir sus
   regalos
yo solo anhelo, mirar mis
   parientes lejanos;
Y mientras todos se abrazan y
   desean felicidad
yo dejo mi mente . . volar y volar
a mi lejana ciudad, donde pase
   tan felis
mi ya lefana, juventud y nines;
Noche de paz, a mi solo me haces
   llorar
aqui jamas se reza el dulce rozario
ni se canta al ninito jesus
aqui solo es parrandas, regalos y
   vanidad
pues se a olvidado, lo que es la
   noche de paz;
Noche de paz, que me hieres en
   mis recuerdos
hasta hacerme, el corazon sangrar
tambien tengo ami lado, personas
   tan nobles
que me hacen un poco, mi

tristeza olvidar;
Noche de paz, aqui a los ninos se
   les miente
ensenandoles una cruel y falsa
   verdad
adorando un arbol repleto de
   presentes
y esperando a alguien volando
   por los cielos
y despues por la chimenea vajar;
y son los hombres del manana, la
   triste verdad
a quienes se les oculta que Dios
   vino al mundo
y jamas se les ensena al nino
   Jesus recordar;
En esta noche de paz, en que
   tantos ninos
se acuestan si un bocado probar
   sin una cobija
que sus cuerpecitos . . puedan
   calentar
donde la guerra hace destrozos . .
   porque los necios
quieren al mundo dominar;
Noche de paz, donde tanta gente
   quedo sin hogar
donde la sonrisa murio en sus
   labios
y quedaron solos . . sin fe . . sin
   felicidad
noche de paz, que esta noche me
   haces llorar

Kelly Irene Carney
UNCLE DAVE

---

*With Love to Ed G. : For
Believing in me.*

As I listen to the inarticulate
   murmur of voices,
I think:
Your life was not without history;
You were too soon, time-soiled.
Your life: a springtime river.
But you passed brave men proudly.
Your memory will never be like
   the insipid
Hypocrites that file past your
   casket.
Even though my speech is
   confused,
I know that you alone would
   understand—
You always did.

Yvonne Cassey
MY ETERNAL LOVE
Seeking but never finding,
   endless yearning of the soul;
   fantasy in mind for the love
   that together knows no
   bounds. A journey reached yet
   waiting for beyond control. My
   Eternal Love.

By the sacred flame that burneth
   eternally bright, Blessed be thy
   heart and soul, lasting beyond
   heavens height.
I chant the prayer which evokes
   the power, the sun and moon
   doest hide; in shining stream
   and secret tide. Upon the
   moonlit night with whispering
   winds, dancing branches,
   shadows with sight; for my
   eternal love. Elements come to
   my aid upon the earth, upon

the sea. Shadows glisten, spirits
   soar, join the journey of my
   path. I await perfect love and
   perfect truth.

My Eternal Love.

Marjorie Burney Willis
**Whisperings Of Divine
Love**

---

*Dedicated to my beloved brother,
Bruce Herman Burney of Marble
Falls, Texas . . . of the family tree
of Guilford D. Burney and Lona
Ann Gardner.*

We can't see God's face
   so He lights the sky with stars
   and shows us Heaven.
We can't feel his touch
   so He sends a summer breeze
   to caress our cheeks.

We can't hear his voice
   so He sends a nightingale
   to sing songs of love.

To tell us He cares
   He turns on sparkling sunlight
   and brings us flowers.

We don't know God's ways
   so He sends his only Son
   to lead us homeward.

B. Closs L. G. Anderson
**THOUGH I HAVE
   an adaptation**
LISTEN—though I speak in
   tongues—without love and
   glory to God in my heart my
   words are like gongs or a chime.
HEAR—if I see a new future—
   know all—understand—and
   have great faith— without love
   they're no good.
SEE—though I'd give all I have to
   the poor—give my life—
   without love don't you think of
   it twice.
NOW—love takes the pricks and
   is kind—it doesn't compare,
   never boasts of itself—it's just
   there.
KNOW—love behaves itself
   well—seeks you only ,
   beloved—lasts here to stay—
   leads never to evil and always
   away.
HERE—is my sacrament—I
   rejoice in God's word that his
   love never fails—divine love
   never has.
LEARN—that prophesies,

tongues, even knowledge could wait or otherwise prove superseded.
FOR—one half of my life I was given much LOVE, found FAITH as God's gift, learned to HOPE.
YOU—know I can give one away of THESE THREE. Chose the greatest, my love, on this Valentine's Day.

Rebecca J. Anderson
DANIEL

This was written in memory of Mr. Daniel Wolstein. He was a man of great intelligence, One of the dearest of friends, and a loving, caring, and respectable Father—figure. He was loved and admired by all who knew him!!!
— Forever in my heart, Your "BECKY BOO"

For this poem there is no reason.
  Not even a special song in mind.
Nor yet a certain favorite season.
  So when one reads it, please, be kind.

It's to tell of all the things I feel inside.
  My heart is of great sorrow,
For a true friend of mine has died.
  He doesn't get to see, a sun, tomorrow.

Why can't I forget him, oh how I've tried.
  I think of him most of all, at night.
My eyes have still, cried, and cried.
  I guess it's death itself that causes the most fright.

When I arise each day to find him gone.
  My hopes all seem to fall.
It makes no reason for the morning dawn.
  I wish that I could reach him, with my call.

As long as my life lasts, I'll miss his gentle touch.
  I've always loved him with all my heart.
And I believe he knew just how much.
  It's just sad, my friend and I will now, always be apart.

Pauline J. Williams
VAN & ME

To those who Love, and Feel love, like a never ending stream that runs through-out the entire body, mind, and soul and is activated, by the reciever, YOU.

We loved each other more than anyone else on this earth loved, either of us . . .
You might have found that hard to believe, if you'd ever heard us
At each other scream haller and cuss.
Make-up time, we called it his and mine,
We made poetry together, with

such beautiful Ryhme . . .
People might say we're miles apart . . .
But, that look of love I saw in his eyes, captured the depths, of my love, from my heart . . .
Van & Me how happy we could be, than life got in our way, and together
For us, it was impossible to stay . . .
As love would have it, not far from Van would I be away . . .
("I'll still come to see him even if not everyday,")
I know when my heart aches, it's him I have to see . . .

NO! NO! NO! This can, Not! BE!!!!!!

Last night in his sleep from life Van was set free . . .
It would have been less pain, if I hung by my heart strings
From the worlds tallest tree . . .
Now, who's left on this earth, to love,
Only . . . . . . ME?

Mark Stephen Wallinder

Mark Stephen Wallinder
To a Lady Bearing Gift
The times I've stopped to pen a line
To help me mark my living time
Are surpassed in moments now
By people who would show me how
That as we come to promised end
It's better with a welcome friend.

R. Stephen Kidd
THEN YOU'RE IN LOVE
As you look into the mirror at the start of the day,
Do you picture yourself somewhere far far away?
Do you gaze through tomorrow searching for a way,
trying to remember what lead you a stray?
  THEN YOU'RE IN LOVE.
So you light up a smoke as you quitely shave
You catch yourself drifting, running away.
Your body's in order but your mind is her slave,
so you light up a smoke as one burns in the tray,
  THEN YOU'RE IN LOVE.
You look at her pictures and you blow them a kiss.

While you're both apart she's all that you miss.
Your mind is a dreamer your hearts in her hand
you don't like to face it but you're in her command.
  THEN YOU'RE IN LOVE.
As the night draws nearer you'll see her again
You'll dream of the day when you won't dream again,
She'll be beside you as woman and man
for both of you love is forever without end.
  THEN YOU'RE IN LOVE.
So the days have gone by now and she is your wife.
You'll live with your dreams for the rest of your life.
You cherish her dearly both day and night
your love keeps getting stronger through wrong and through right.
  THEN YOU'RE IN LOVE.
Now you see that your happy so you thank God above.
What more could you ask for, you have her sweet love?
You have all you've dreamed of, ... YES,
  THEN YOU'RE IN LOVE.

Norma Spahr
CARING
Caring is the base
  Of true humanity
Full of compassion
  With so much sincerity
Putting others needs
  Before your own
Holding your hand out
  To one who's alone
Showing you care
  And wanting to share
Hurts and confusion
  That's so hard to hear
To listen with feeling
  When that's all you can do
To let them know
  At least they have you.

Mrs. Sofia A. M. Martin
BACKSEAT DRIVER
Keep driving that car— We don't have to go far—
Just steer to the right— Keeping others in sight—
Let the dust fly high— It may just reach the sky—
That cigar you smoke— Is truly not a joke—
Keep puffing that thing— Making some bluish ring—
Watch out to the rear— For some car is quite near—
Now slow that car down— We're coming to a town—
What's that by the road— It looks like a hop-toad—
A coffee I'd love— So stop at the "Lit'l Cove"—
One more hour to drive— And we'll make it by five—
Don't hurry too much— For the traffic is such—
I can see the sights— And watch the signal lights—
You better go slow— Because left you must go—

Just driving along— Singing a happy song—
Is better for me— Make a turn by the tree—
We are now quite near— Go put it in slow gear—
Now just let me out— I do so want to shout.

Ronald W. Saunders
LION, LION!
Lion, lion hunted a multitude
Sudden is judgement's fury so lude

A zone where happiness has paraded
The lion's mane a coronet masquaraded

Discover evil into thy wilderness
Where the hunted and haunted once sought tenderness

Voices of the wind, thy speckled birds
Believe not their shrills, they are ignoble words

Oh country an unfair shadow into the past
My inheritance blown into the wind: The vanquishing of a noble cast

A proud prince in the morning
Succumb to slaughter and satan's scorning

Gathering in thy wilderness: Thy beasts of the fields
A multitude of remorse is what the sinner yields.

The birds about my head: flapping their wings so boldly
Cursing the lot; the dead and their rot, not of the holy

It's pride like a coronet masqueraded
Sauntering about the wilderness, where life once paraded

Joanne Messer
THE GIFT
A parched thirsty earth opens its arms
To receive the soft summer rain,
Like a long awaited love returned
To sooth and comfort again.

Soft thunder rumbles distantly
Promising more relief,
The winds that have dried and scorched the soil
Subside as in disbelief.

The farmer stands in silence
And lifts his face to the rain
It cools his body and calms his soul
Like relief from a long suffering pain.

All through the day and into the night
The earth receives heavens gift,
Baring her soul and begging for more,
A languishing love adrift.

On the next morning the sun breaks through
And cautiously looks below,
It approaches the earth with uncertainity
Not sure if it's friend or foe.

But the earth is restored and rested

Thus it welcomes the sun,
Once again, like the moment of
birth,
The cycle of life has begun.

Marjorie Burney Willis
TO MY GRANDSON

---

*Written for my grandson
Morrisson J. Duncan— and
dedicated to him, March 11, 1984.*

As you travel through the years,
guard your footprints
that they may leave inspiring
patterns
of noble worth—of truth and
trust,
of honesty and integrity.

Stay on a pathway that leads
upward
to the Kingdom of God.
Never let anything or anybody
deter you from this great goal.

There will be many trials
along the way—
great temptations to overcome.
But if you put your hand
in God's hand,
you'll never walk alone.

Orland O. Sharp
ALOHA BIRD
A feather was found on the
"LOVE BOAT" so fair
May be a dream of a bird in the
air

Dark in color, small, soft and
round
May be from a fowl, here on the
ground

The thought of an "Aloha Bird"
lets pretend
Whatever it is—it's from a fine
feathered friend

Lonnie Greenfield—
Dreams on the Aloha Deck will
be heard
Even when it is about the "Aloha
Bird"

Peter Alexander Hannah
MY NERVOUS CATHY
You rushed in . . . in the Inn I
waited the day
Charging like a tigress . .
searching for a lost-found prey
You kissed me without warning
in your special nervous way
And my heart agreed we've found
a special friend indeed

Often I rush into affairs just like
you do
With little or no provocation . .
or notice due
Only to withdraw with broken
dreams to review
My lost amour my foolish
pride . . .
With much work and wine on
the side

You see I'm so tender . . so easily
done
I love to love and be loved by my
loved one
But some rip me off and misuse
my care and fun
And to the dark streets to find a

hooker I run
A hooker takes only ten or
twenty bucks or so
She's happy and content
everytime she'd come and go
Until I refuse her company by
telling her no
Thanks but I am looking for a
woman of my own

That's why I phoned you today to
say
I want you in my business and
life forever to stay
And when you said, "Why not?". . .
you made my day
I love you Kathy and only you I
will cherish and obey

Phyllis R. Ruggier
FRIENDLY THOUGHTS

---

*To Sandy for your help, your
understanding, and for being my
friend.*

You've been in my thoughts;
I'm not sure how to reveal.
I know that I ought
To express how I feel.

You're very special to me
In several ways.
You've helped guide me
Through many rough days.

There aren't many
To whom I feel so close.
Sometimes there aren't any
For whom I care the most.

I only hope you know
You're thought of in a special
way.
I find that I do so
From day to day.

Mary J. Moss
EMOTIONS
Forgive us Lord.
We have let our emotions,
reign instead of our brains.
You gave us a guide head, with
emotions as helpers, and not
to rule instead.

If we would stop and think,
to use our brains,
We would not sometimes have
emotions causing us miswery and
pain.
Lord, you said come let us reason
together.
How WONDERFUL!

Tammy Lee Todd
A FORGOTTEN LOVE
They Stood on the beach
Hand in hand.
And beneath their feet
Lay the golden sand.
The sand of the future
And of history.
The sand of a time
When love was free.
As free as a dove
On a carefree flight
And as welcome as the stars
On a winter's night.
The love that once raged
With a million sparks
Was now but a flicker
In the lovers' hearts.
Even together

They were all alone.
For the love that had been
Was no longer known.

Lucille M. Kroner

Lucille M. Kroner
The First Christmas Day

---

*"To my sister, Mrs. Irma J.
Castoe," in memory of "Christmas
1983."*

The moon was a tune and a
merry-go-round
Of fast stepping horses a-flying
'round,
In a star studded sky where a
shaft of light
Illumined the way for the
Wiseman's flight.

Led by a star they followed Him
To a manger small in Bethlehem.
There they laid their gifts
humbly at His feet,
Frankincense and myrrh, with
faith so sweet,

And the Star followed on,
Stood still where He lay,
Our Savior and Lord,
This first Christmas Day.

Brenda K. Deaver
EXPRESSION
There is no way to show you or
express to you how much I
really care about you.
There are no words to express the
way I really feel about you or
the things you've let me see in
you.
You've helped me so many times
when there was no one else to
turn to,
When I didn't know which way
to go about a lot of things.
No matter how many miles come
between us, I'll always think of
you.

Richard Rocereto
MY LITTLE BRASS PIPE
Once I found a little brass pipe
On an icy street one night.
I exhumed it from its frozen grave
And to it, a new life I gave.
And when life was mean and
hard to master
I could always find
In this pipe a "peace" of mind.

On my little brass pipe I could
always depend

On rainy dys and restless nights,
or lazy afternoons
My little brass pipe was a special
friend
Shared only , with a select few.

And then one night as fate would
have it
My little brass pipe had fallen
from my sight
And as I searched in frenzied
fright
I suddenly realized that my little
brass pipe
Had been stolen back by the night.

Joan Sajnovic
COUNTRY BOY
Country boy, country boy, listen
to my heart
Listen to its rhythm and see
The reason for my joy, from the
very start
Is simply your presence to me.

Country boy, country boy, you're
no work of art
Less handsome, more a freakish
sight
You are always working, doing
your part
When you appear, you give me
fright.

I do not know the reason why
Our eyes always seem to meet
I even think you a kind guy
But you knock me right off my
feet.

I will end this meeting, so I will
depart
Your charm has gone and so the
joy
I must be moving on to a new start
Good bye, country boy, country
boy.

Mike Steckel
WALKING BY A LAKE
Walking by a lake once
I saw in the water
A figure similar to the one I see
Every morning in my mirror
Upon closer observance
I saw the same confused eyes

A child on the other side
Jumped in the water
He didn't even look down
To see what might have been
himself
To him, it probably wasn't

Children have no need to find
themselves
Their imagination and games
Takes care of that
I think this, and only this,
Separates me from them

Looking back down into the water
The waves the child made
distorted
My once near perfect image
But gave me a better view of
myself

Cheryl L. Becker
OCEAN SHORE
I walk along the ocean shore,
Seagulls singing as they soar.
Winds never losing their pride, .
Leaving dunes at the end of it's
ride.
Waves dancing at my feet.

Seashells glittering on the beach.
Sands burning from the suns heat,
Scoarching many people's feet.
Seagulls leaving prints in the sand,
Couples walking hand in hand.
The beautiful sun is decending,
An array of hues at it's ending.
Drifting clouds fading in the sky,
Blocking the horizon as it passes
  by.
Walking along the moonlit shore,
Now hearing only the oceans' roar.

Alice Palmer
DESTINY

I'll dedicate destiny to all people young or old that are striving to get ahead in life.

Destiny is just one word! You
either go straight ahead but
you can't turn around. It is
making up your mind what
path you will follow. You
better think twice before you
decide what road you must
follow. Destiny is a several
letter word, and each letter has
a specific meaning. Watch out
for a little message in each one,
before you follow. Live for
today as it was your last one.
Destiny it won't pass you by
because you are the one to
choose before you follow. This
is not a hard pick, because you
are the one who is picking it.
Try very hard to know what
you are doing before you
decide to follow.

Edwin Nembo Forlemu
ORIGINALITY
No child falls from the naked sky,
no tree forms out of the vast void.
As anything spreads and shoots
  high,
it stands on, hangs on,
  something . . .
There's a reason behind every
  human ploy.
Or would any mountain or sea
exist today without the earth
on which its broad buttocks sit?
Even flashes of flair and mirth
are elusive arrows which hit
heads ignorant about the arrows'
  sources.
Ah, what a world of boundless
  resources!
Originality:
that new way of saying some old
  thing,
the extension, the cracking, the
  melting
of some frozen reality.
Nothing now is which never once
  was,
yet old becomes new in the
  hands of genius.

Patricia Wilbur
TO AMERICA
I am this land, for which they
  fought and died,
This land whose sons fought
  bravely, side by side,
Through sacrifices made by them
  for me
I, this land, am safe, and proud
  and free.

I am this flag that proudly waves
  on high,
This flag they rallied round,
  when threats were nigh,
Thanks to our veterans, and our
  honored dead,
I this flag, fly proudly overhead.

I am this freedom that you wear
  so well,
For my sake brave young men
  went into hell,
Some died in body, some in spirit
  too,
For I am Freedom, I'm their gift to
  you.

Please honor them as you have
  honored me,
These men who fought, so all
  men could be free,
Remember always what they
  fought to gain,
Make sure they did not ever fight
  in vain.

These men, of whom the history
  books will tell,
These who returned, and those
  who bravely fell,
Honor them, and the things for
  which they stand,
Your flag, —your freedom,—and
  your glorious land.

Elden T. Stuart

Elden T. Stuart
MASQUER
Upon the silent stage I wait
Each seat below filled, but one
Inside I feel anxious, lonely,
  afraid
Thoughts dwell on performances
  done.
At once, the glaring lights flash on
I stand, all eyes on me
Anticipating my display
An act for you to see.
Emotions stir prepared, believe
Myself to those a pro
But make-up, costumes, lines
  betray
What I so try not to show.
He then appears, descends the aisle
Proceeds to take his place
Among the now turned faceless
  strangers
The no longer vacant space.
Then lighting fades, curtain's
  drawn
Once more a pause I've earned
Removed aside, the next
  performer
Steps up to take his turn.

Amy Gervais
GLAD SPRINGTIME

This poem was not dedicated to anyone. I was impressed by beautiful Spring weather after a rough Winter and was inspired to write a poem

It's Spring again! I can feel it in
  the air,
Buds unfolding, birds awinging
Nature joins with God in bringing
Back to earth the warmth and
  beauty everywhere.

No more slipping, sliding as we
  stride along:
Gone discomforts of the weather;
There is beauty in the heather
As together man and nature join
  in song.

Feast your eyes on beauty as you
  go your way;
Daffodils around us dancing;
Tulips gay in hues entrancing;
Cheerful sights that stimulate us
  through the day.

Springtime rare! To me the best
  time of the year.
Everything is so contrasting,
Wish it could be everlasting,
As we welcome in each day
  without a care.

And how true to life the seasons
  are to me.
Happy Spring with love and
  laughter,
Summer stepping in right after,
Autumn next and then comes
  Winter as you see.

And let gloomy Winter all it's
  shadow bring.
There's no need to be
  downhearted
Knowing that from ere it started
With a little patience then it will
  be Spring.

Then ever let us keep the
  Springtide glowing
Within our hearts each day anew
As we our daily course pursue;
And joy and gladness ever we'll
  be knowing.

Evelyne Butler Heringson
NEEDED

To Jesus, my Lord, Who is my inspiration and to Mickey and Lorayne, Lafe and Verna, my brothers and sisters and their families, who still stand with me, side by side—

Before you were born, I needed
  you—
To fill a place meant 'specially for
  you.
And now My needs are greater
  for anger, confusion and chaos
  seem to rule the earth.
In these times, I need your
  compassion, love and
  understanding to help give
  others a feeling of self worth.

Before you were born, you needed

Me—
To give you the breath of life to
  set you free.
And now, your needs are greater
  for you've been hurt by the
  anger, confusion and chaos
  ruling the earth.
But in these troubling times, you
  will have My compassion, love
  and understanding to break the
  bands and let you know your
  worth.

We need each other, we'll always
  need each other—
To comfort, laugh, rejoice with, or
  bring us out of deep despair.
You don't need to be perfect, or
  condemned, only forgiven.
I love you. I need you, I care . . .

Russell O. Litchfield
THE ZOO

I dedicate this poem to my two year old grandson, Christopher Michael Blevins; his big blue eyes, smile, his flair. "To the thrill of seeing new things".

Oh! see the creatures large and
  small
  Big around and skinny tall.
Some are pompous, some are shy;
  Some spend time up in the sky.
  Some may hop and some may
  crawl;
Some may run and some may fall;
  Watch them scratch and watch
  them dig
  Watch them climb a tiny twig;
  See them swim and see them
  slide;
Hear their chatter as they bide;
  Watch them stand and watch
  them wave;
  Watch them by their tails
  behave;
See how they flutter through the
  air;
Then suckle a flower with gentle
  care;
  Watch them frolic and watch
  them sleep;
  Hear their 'roars'! their little
  "peeps;"
  Listen to their trumpets! see
  them eat;
  Be with them as they cuddle
  sweet.
Love the creatures here to see
Dance with them the joy of glee!
  Visit the animals of the Zoo
  They are here for only you.
    Bless the animals.

Loida Weber Maggio
FANTASY
Hand in hand we walk together
In the gardens of the Life,
And we cross the bridges
In the pathways of the land,
Our hearts beating together
In the infinity of time—
Hand in hand, heart and heart
Together, one in one, loving
Always what is yours—
What is mine—
Your love, mine forever
My love, only yours
Till the end of time.

459

Miriam Proctor
ANCHORAGE
you wend
your wavering way
head down
into the wind
a sail boat
cut loose
in a hurricane
of warring
desires wand—
ering uncharted
seas landing
by chance
on her bosomy
shore

Elda Yoder
SNOWFLAKES
A winter evening,
A darkening sky
Snowflakes drifting by.
A work of art, no two alike
These fluffs of white.
Patterned by the Master's hand
They gently carpet the land.
These sparkling crystals
Of softly fallen snow,
Create a fabulous show.
They glitter and glisten
On a cold winter's night.
It's magic—
These crystals so shiny and bright.

Terese Sierralta
A CHRISTMAS THOUGHT

---

*This Poem was written to Randy
Thomas Wilkins By Teresa
Yvette Bernadette Sierralta both
of New York City*

Underneath the Christmas Tree
Tonight
I Wish you were here to hold me
tight
As I look at the top to place the
star
I wonder where you are
with Jesus, Mary and Joseph a
family of one
We shall be together having some
fun
As I look up at the angel hanging
over the stable
you are the prince in a fairy tale
fable
while the night slowly crept by
I wonder if you will stop by to
say hi!

Jean M. Thieda
CHRISTMAS EVE
Awakened from sleep with a start
the house was all quiet and still,
But I knew from my thudding
heart
that someone was roaming at will.

Softly they crept, no noise did
they make
Silently going about on their way,
What, I wondered, what things
will they take
and will I have nothing to say?

I slipped out of bed and
cautiously crept
across the dark room to the door,
I trembled with fear and cold I
expect
as I froze my bare feet on the floor.

So, softly I went to the top of the
stair
and I peered down below to see,
A round jolly elf with white
beard and hair
placing presents under the tree!

Audi-Cecile
SOLITAIRE
Were you the one I talked to
in the middle of the night
Were you the one I held close
in the early morning light?
Were you the one I needed
even though you were not there
Or was it just my imagination
Playing Solitaire?

You see, I really need to hold you
even when you are not here
And I want to touch you
but I do not dare.
Because too many times I've seen
you
lying very near
But it is only my imagination
Playing Solitaire.

There are things I'd like to tell
to someone late at night
Many times I need someone
special
just to hold me tight.
There are many reasons why
I want to have you near
But my world is still empty,
keeps on
Playing Solitaire.

Daniel D. Wilson
AUTUMN RAIN
They crystal drops of falling rain,
upon autumn leaves of pastel
hues;
their fragile beauty they do retain,
their delicate nature they
cannot lose.

The rain becomes soft and steady,
as it dampens the forest floor.
For the rain is upon us already,
and surely there shall be more.

The rain becomes a downpour,
soaking me to the skin.
As to Almighty God I do implore,
to allow some sunshine in.

When finally the rain does
indeed abate,
and silence reigns supreme.
One's mind may enter a peaceful
estate,
and roam as though in a dream.

The barren trees stand straight
and still,
while the wet leaves they shed
muffle out all sound.
The kid in me experiences a thrill,
watching the squirrel run across
the ground.

The rain has a cleansing effect
upon the air,
leaving all so fresh and sweet.
Although I usually prefer it fair,
the rain is also a treat.

Tracey Hunter
FAMILY
A family is deeper than any ocean.
The feelings they share may
come and go
only
from the heart.

The meanings they hold within
their
undividing love
Is untouched by
time and
jealousy.
Like the brightest star of
Heaven's gates
they together
welcome
Each others lives
Though sometimes different as
they seem.
Families—given willingly by
God to share
peace and happiness
With those who
stand alone.
No matter the family
And no matter the place—
A family is a family
through life and love
and death.

Doris Rine
A SPY'S LIFE
Hellbent and marked for death
It's poison I inhale with every
breath.
Reckless and challenging to all
dangers
I am as if with one to all
strangers.
I have been holding on for so long
It's time I let go I am not strong.
I cannot speak of the tortures I
face
The words I form are not safe.
I want to live in an euphoria high
And when I go not say goodbye.

Mr. David Rehak
CHRISTMAS EVE

To all who had faith in me.

It is the blue and drifted hour
of midnight;
Christmas soon,
It will blossom like a bell of light
from earth to setting
moon.
Curved in the cradled silence now
such confidence are,
That every cottage seems a church
and every lamp a star!

Mary E. Collins
Another Springtime, Daddy

---

*To Mother (whose dream
inspired me) and to my brothers
and sisters; Those who share the
memories of our beloved husband
and father, Marion Pierce Comer,
born Aug. 21, 1908 — died
Feb. 12, 1981.*

Another Springtime, Daddy, crept
upon us since you've gone
Far beyond the sunset to embrace
a brand new dawn
I know you're well and happy . . .
up there in Heaven's Fold
Without the pain and suffering
that comes with growing old
I'll bet you're busy doing all the
things you wanted to
When you couldn't take the
winter's cold and couldn't

shake the flu
I know you're working on a
house. Mother saw you in her
slumber
You placed a nail and smiled . . .
before you drove it in the
lumber
She said your hair was black as
coal, your mouth was white
with teeth
Your dear and loving face was
smooth, with no lines of age
and grief
She watched with joy and
happiness, so quickly . . . you
were gone
Still she knew what you were
building was to someday be her
home
And we know Daddy, when it's
done, when you've perfected
each detail
You'll build a wishing well
outside (for her flowers),
complete with pail
There little lambs, and chicks,
and ducks, will decorate the
yard
Like the treasured things you
wrought down here before you
got too tired
But you're resting now Dear
Daddy, where winter comes, no
never
Surrounded by an Angel Band, in
a land that's Springtime ever
It's lonesome since you've gone
away to hear the angels sing
The seasons come and go . . . but
how I miss you in the spring

Louraine Armack Hollman
MAMA'S WEDDING DRESS
On gloomy, damp and rainy days
In our attic I loved to play.
Old trunks held treasures galore
Friends and I did love to explore.

Trying on old hats and worn-out
clothes
Looking through books and
reading prose.
Pretending teatime we sat in old
chairs
Mama brought lunch to us up
attic stairs.

Old albums of photos frayed and
worn
Pictures of people gone before I
was born.
One day at the bottom of an old
trunk of brown
I discovered a beautiful, lace
wedding gown.

I asked Mama who wore it when
it was new
"Twas Grandma's dear, but I wore
it too."
A moment of silence—she stared
off in space,
Remembering, when she wore
that dress of lace.

"Mama when I marry may I wear
it too?"
I was young and innocent, what
could she do?
"Of course my darling it will be
fine"
"You will look pretty in this dress
of mine."

460

Later, browsing through an album
  faded with age
Appeared a pretty lady, in that
  dress, on the very last page.
Standing beside her, a handsome
  young man
Looking dearly at her and holding
  her hand.

The beautiful lady like Mama did
  look
But who was the man next to her
  in the book?
I've never seen him, no never
  before
When I asked Mama about him,
  she said . . .
    "He was killed in the war" . . .

LYN
I AM
I bring you visions of a brighter
  tomorrow . . .
a clear blue sky, the sun on high.
Spiralling clouds, golden sunsets,
children at play, laughter in the air;
I am hope.

I wish for you the joy of being . . .
the gift of seeing, the blessing of
  knowing;
plans made together will be again,
another day;
I am peace.

I give to you all your
  tomorrows . . .
surrounded in a rainbow of colors,
feelings deeper than ever imagined,
caring stronger than time itself;
I am love.

Deborah Kehr
ALL NIGHT
We read each other's poetry
  sneak previews
  still unborn
  from the guts
  of affection
  and truth

    maskery
    is an art
    of the devil

We hide
  by turning
  pages

Elizabeth Breitfeld
THE LITTLE PINK PILLS
For about a month, I've felt so
  low,
That off to the Doctor I did go.
Now he said to me "Try these
  little pills,

They'll give you pep, to control
  your ills."
I followed the directions to the
  letter
But gee! is this the way you feel,
  when better?
My stomach growled and had to
  be fed,
So about midnight I left my bed;
For a glass of milk and a crust of
  bread.
At 4 o'clock I closed my eyes.
At 4:15 I did arise, and not to
  admire the starlit skies
Darn those little pink pills.
I shouldn't complain since the
  pills were free,
But oh! gee! gosh! what they're
  doing to me
Like high octane gas in an old
  Model T.
I'm not sure I'll take them very
  long,
Instead of "git up and go" — I've
  "got up and gone."

Margaret Rupert Green
WHO AM I?
Who Am I?
  I'm not quite sure
Mother daughter sister more
Someone's wife or someone's
    mother
Someone's trash or someone's
    treasure
Is this how my life I measure?
It is true that part of me they own
  Yet I am myself alone
  Liberated perhap's I'm not
But I'll settle for what I've got
    I wouldn't trade
    For the biggest bid
    In women's Lib

Jane Richmond Dortzbach
MARY'S SON
Baby Jesus, God's own Son.
Mary bore thee, Holy One.
Joseph stood beside the stall;
Infant sleeping, oh, so small.
Beckoned by the star above
Shepherds came to show their
  love.
Wise men came, their gifts to
  bring
To the long awaited King.
Baby grew into a man
And his mission he began.
Ministered to all in need;
His great message let us heed.
Love and kindness we must show
To all persons whom we know.
Later, on the Cross Christ died.
Hence, forever, Christmastide.

Marilyn L. Fuerstenberg
IT'S NOT UP TO ME
Snow coming down from the sky
Millions of flakes, on the ground
  they lie.

Children running outside to play
Making snowmen throughout the
  day.

Covering everything in a blanket
  of white
Remaining to be seen in the
  moonlight.

Rivers and streams, slowly they
  freeze
Ice cycles form to hang down

from trees.

A whole new season of activity
Sleighing, skating, and downhill
  ski.

Some people love the snow, day
  or night
Some people say, I guess it's alright.

But whatever your opinion may be
Snow will always be here, it's not
  up to me.

Vicki L. Miller
OUR FATHER . . .
Our father in heaven
  Loves us so
He came into my heart
  A few years ago
He's never left me
  From that day on
And he's always been their
  For me to lean on
He guides me to do right
And to live by his word
And every prayer is always heard
He is a very kind and loving father
  Who controls my life
  In every matter
He only wants the best for me
And I will praise him
  Through all eternity!

Brenda L. Hodges
Jealously Of the Gods
Harsh tears whipped the
swaying tree from the
saddened sky.

Fragile leaves desperately trying
to cling to their life support were
nonchalantly discarded.

Closed fists of whirling wind
beat unceasingly on the Earth.

Timeless years of frustrated anger
decidely destroying leftover
fragments of creation.

Shelby Spearman
ONCE AGAIN

---

*This poem is dedicated to E. J. B.
"For the imprint you left so deep
in my heart"*

Today is gray
Tomorrow I look for the sun
In it's warmth, I will find you.
Beyond the clouds, over the
  rainbow,
The broken line, that holds you
  and
me, will once again meet,

Jacqueline Soteropoulos
**Raise Your Voices To the
  Sky**
Raise your voices to the sky,
Hear the bells ring out,
Clasp a hand on this day,
Spread peace and joy about.

See the snow fly to the earth,
And the cardinal come to rest,
See the sparkling ice,
And the sunset in the West.

Sense the wonderful world about
  us,
Think not of future sorrow,
Dwell on love that's here today,
Forget the presence of tomorrow.

Men have tried to rule the world,

And almost got complete control,
Made us work and die for them,
But never snuffed the fire of our
  soul.

Joined together through faith
  alone,
Will make an army strong,
Which none can overpower,
The weapon—hearts in song.

So raise your voices to the sky,
Hear the bells ring out,
Clasp a hand on this day,
Spread peace and joy about.

Betty-Jane Watson
REFLECTIONS
Water flows, and
  Time moves on.
The eddies pool
  Shining like mirrors.
So move our lives . .
  Ever flowing
Over the rough spots,
  But ever moving.
The inevitable end,
  Dark, there waiting.
When we reach it-
  Blessed forgetfulness.
Only the love
  Of our Lord;
Surrounding, engulfing.
  We are enfolded
And happy,
  Being absorbed
And pooled,
  Into the pure
Love of God.

Ann Foley
Death Of My Brother
Deaf to my whispering voice,
I pray that I might hear your
  laughter,
But I only hear the night's
  silence.

It doesn't matter if I plant a red
  rose,
Or whether the sun rises every
  morning.
Whether the rose stands in the
  sunrise or not,
I stand alone.
With only thoughts of
  unaswerable questions
Of your absence.

I cry over dreams that have now
  settled
Into the dust,
Beyond the borders of the purple
  horizon,
Out towards the midnight skies,
Where stars shine and glitter.

It's the fighting of angry tears,
  That I've come to hate.
The throbbing of my pulse
  And painful aches in my heart.

As I try searching for you,
  In the soft white clouds or in
  the dark nights
Or in the sunrise on a early
  morning,
Amid the river with it's copper
  and gold.
I realize that your death is
  final,
All I have is memories of you,
With only lost dreams to hold.

Mary Anne Schofield
LOVE GIFT

Tis the little things, the
thoughtful things that warm a
searching heart
His grace unfolds; His love
embraces, a purpose to impart
Thank you, Lord, for encouraging
me through a loved one in this
way
A gift of love, an effort spent so
enhanced your love this day
Thank you and praise you for
blessing me so
You're more real today, more
alive in me than a day ago.

Penny L. Brady
THE MAGIC OF NATURE

Hey, fuzzy little caterpillar
why are you scurring across the
walk,
are you in such a hurry
you can't even take time to talk?
Is it time to find that certain place
in some dark hidden nook,
a corner where you can hide your
face
where no one dares to look.
Where you will wrap your fuzzy
self
up in a small cocoon
and hang yourself upside down
to wait the passing of the moon.
A place where you will go to sleep
after spinning your feather bed;
with silken sheets you've covered
yourself
from your tip toes to your head.
To nestle down and forget all time
while heaven guards you there;
and mother natures works sublime
and molds your life with care.
Where she'll change your form
like magic
and give us no reason why,
and call you softly from your nap
a BEAUTIFUL BUTTERFLY.

Michael J. Stanko
PUPPY LOVE

To M.y F.irst B.eautiful D.ate

The world was my oyster, within
it a pearl
Like a rare jewel—a sweet,
beautiful girl,
Perhaps my senses had been dulled
and into fantasy temporarily lulled.

But no dream was she, this one
was for real
Puppy love of youth, my heart
she did steal,
Shy and innocent, a lad of
seventeen
I held her in awe, as a lovely
queen.

In those days she was the "one
and only"
Many years have passed, is she
now lonely?
Drifting apart, we went our
separate ways
Other loves have filled the nights
and days.

To only one a secret can be safely
told
Sweet puppy love recalled after

growing old,
Cards played as dealt, it was our
fate
Soon time for goodbye, it's getting
late.

'Tis futile to think of what might
have been
Or to ponder now whether did I
lose or win,
Dormant feelings, awakened, tell
me share
Fond memories of first kisses,
loving care.

Lisa Connick

Lisa Connick
HOME AGAIN

*To my father, Ken, my mother,
Ann, and my little sister, Judy,
who have been so understanding
and loving during my rebellious
years. I love them with all my
heart.*

Do you believe it, I am home
a settled life at last
Not even for one million bucks
would I relive my past

It was horrendous, it was obscene
and not a pleasant sight
For me to gain my sanity
I had to struggle and fight

I met up with an awesome bunch
and they are now I'm sure
Deceased or locked up in the pen
where no one can they lure

I did not think I would survive
with all the drugs and sin
But someone filled me with His
love
and really helped me win

Thank you God for helping me
along the endless road
Because I've found a brand new
life
and I'm carrying a lighter load

Mary Ann Bittle
THE MOUNTAINTOP

A man stands upon a mountain
And sings praises to the Lord,
For when a man is on a mountain
Praises he can afford.

A man huddles in a valley
While storms around him rage.
He does not think of his Lord—
So sad; Turn the page.

The man in the valley roars

"Justice I will find, myself!"
But still he sends curses to the
Lord,
The only one who can give him
wealth.

As he cries in frustration,
His anger turns to fear.
He looks with questions up above,
And he wipes away the tears.

He kneels upon the rocky ground;
With shaky prayers his curses stop.
Then he opens his eyes with
wonder
As he finds his feet on the
mountaintop.

Lauraine E. Simpson
WELCOME HOME

---

*Dedicated to my father, who will
always be an influence for good
on the lives of those who knew
and loved him.*

I kissed him then, but he had gone
Into the Great Unknown, alone.
I held his hand, but he did not see,
For he was far away from me.

His soul was in another land—
He had already crossed the
distant strand.
I said, "I love you," but he was free
From the chains that had kept
him close to me.

His Lord had called, and he
answered Him,
Saying, "Guide my steps, for my
eyes are dim.
I have traveled far on my earthly
way
And though many called, still I
could not stay."

"I would be with you, Lord. Take
my hand
And lead me into Thy Heavenly
Land,
Where all is beauty, Lord, let me
come."
And the Lord said simply,
"Welcome home."

Willard L. Hartshorn
MOONLIGHT MAGIC

The moon holds on a straining
leash the ocean tides and
rolling sea
And moves back darkness with a
push that shouts of might and
main to me.
But see and feel the subtle touch
of silver dust and afterglow
Then dream the dreams that
mean so much and feel the
gentle undertow.
Speak to the heart that it may
learn of wiles used by the
moon above
Then feel the surge within the
breast and know the heart has
learned of love.
When it has learned the lips cry
out in thirst for other lips in
kind
And arms will ache while
thoughts will shout to help the
moonlight share its' find.
While arms that ache are soon
made strong to lift with ease in

in silver glow
By majic moonlight hearts are
singing songs that only they
can know.

Robert Ellis Feeney
WORLD'S END

The burning desire of love and
hate
Brings to me no reason for this
unusual fate
That many people who are not
the same
Is this a good reason to put the
blame
On those that have, within a kind
heart
Or is this the time we all must
start
Not to be just what we've been
before
But to gather our thoughts and
unlock the doors
To a better world for all mankind
With the hope of someday
having peace of mind
So if it be within our power
To give to each one more then
just an hour
Then to you, the one that has
control
Look inside yourself and search
your soul
That you do not react too fast
and end the world leaving only
the past

Lynette Johnson
BEHOLD

Clouds . . . . so soft, so pure;
You reach up to grasp;
You reach higher yet.
You held all the wisp;
There was to get.

Such . . . . is Happiness;
You're reaching-reaching;
Always with open hands.
You're never holding;
What you have.

Like . . . . this beautiful
moment;
You're thinking of more;
More moments with me.
The Beauty has fled;
For something that will never be.

Bertie Murphy
YOU ARE

You are the mountains, majestic
and tall.
Your stature inside to great ere
to fall.
You are the catalysts of galaxies
unfurled.
You are the future exploring a
world.

You are the distance of time and
space.
You are the most delicate and
intricate of lace.
You are the healer of life and
men,
You are the maker of a loyal
true friend.

You are the reason of all life for
me,
The maker of music, the waver
of seas.
You are the rhythm of daylight
and dark.

You are the surgeon, the
mender of hearts.

You are the poem recently met.
You are the symphony not
written, yet.
You are the sunset not ever seen.
You are the brook, sparkling and
clean.

You are the spinner of impossible
dreams,
Which you accomplish with
ease, it would seem.
Your heart is gigantic, for inside
it holds
The shape of the future, the
maker of souls.

Scott L. Weiner
FUNNY
I'm truly very sorry about the life
you had to lead,
And how it really went for you,
And how selfish it could be.
But life is very funny,
About the people that they choose,
Some people are made for great
things,
Some people are made to lose,
Some people are made for laughter,
Some people are made for pain,
Some people are made for love,
For this I can't explain.
But for all I know
I was made from you,
You gave me life you see,
For if it were not for you
Than I would never be.

Barbara S. Coulter
THE GIFT OF A FRIEND
The sunrise is the beautiful
wrappings
On the gift of a precious new day,
To take and use to enrich our life;
Not merely to waste away.

God speaks His love in the sunset
"Well done, my child, now rest,"
Then the moon and stars come
out to shine,
To watch over His children so
blessed.

Each of these gifts He gives to us
As we journey along life's way.
He knows the need and furnishes
it
Sometimes even before we pray.

One of the most important gifts
Is that of a very best friend;
Not one of the fair weather kind
But one that is true to the end.

One day up in heaven I'm sure it
was said
"A child of mine is facing a test,
A friend she'll need, a friend
indeed,
Search until you find the best."

The best was found, and your
path crossed mine,
And soon it was plain to see.
My gift was that of a very best
friend
That God had given to me.

Dorothy T. Seamster
DAWNS LIGHT
In the wee hours of the morning,
just before dawn, I sat and
watched a new day come.

The beautifully colored dark sky,

spreads gracefully across the
heavens so rich and bright.
It radiates a sense of peace that
calms the soul,
It generates a new reason to give
and love. It makes me want to
cry because of the love within
my heart, this new day's birth I
know is a gift from above.

The twinkling lights of the stars
above, are the guiding lights of
this new dawn.

Marie Gleason O'Brien
Here I Am This Is Me

*This poem is dedicated to my
husband George, my kids; Jim,
Sonny, Mike, Julie, and
Christopher, all of my friends and
family, my typist Bobbi Dresko
but most of all, to you Mom and
Dad. I love you all.*

Here I am this is me,
This is all there is to see.
Take me as I am in life,
Tell me things will be alright.
I can tell you love me true,
Don't tempt youself to overdo.
My love I show in different ways,
My lips won't speak an empty
phrase.
Your jealousy's to strong for me,
The pedestals to high you see.
My life's a trial of altered states,
And never served on silver plates.
We both say some hatefull things,
Then you want to clip my wings.
Floating downward through the air,
Are the hooks of deep dispair.
I'm so confused 'bout what to do,
I'll leave this story's end to you.
So here I am this is me,
This is all you get you see.

Mary M. Barnes
THE ELEMENTS
Waters triumphly raging,
An exibit of might and fury,
Wind's vehmently howling,
Provoking one to scurry,
Seeking shelter, hence shelter
cannot be,
Frantically searching, O where is
the key?
Structures crumble,
Rendered helpless in the torrent,
Debris wildly flying,
Creating a monument,
Trees up heaveled, fall by the
way side alone,
Voice's knowingly mimic, for
what price a home?
Darkness descending,
Generating chaos and fear,
Will all be lost to Nature's
vemonus lear?
Resentment and anger, Press
down on the mind,
Retaliate now! Strike back in like
kind!
Then from the acidous haze,
emerges a powerful hand,
Thundering who dares lay claim
to this imponderable Land?
For as day follows night,
And night cast's forth her Dreams,
So too, Shall The Elements
Reign Lord and Supreme!

Richard Russell Robertson
Be Careful With Our Love

*In dedication of Tammy Ore. I
love you very much. When this
comes out we shall have been
married, then, I know I can never
loose you*

As love progresses
Feelings do to,
As we open up
A love thats true,
Nothing to end it
Except me and you,
So lets be careful
In whatever we do,
And we'll always mean
An, I love you.

Vincent J. Keenan

Vincent J. Keenan
To My Lovely and Lovable Wife

Written in 1974 Still valid in 1984

Do you ever think, My Darling—
of the ages
Of eternity—that comes with
end of time
And the parable of drops of ocean
water
And the other one about the
sands so fine?
How—if ocean waters were to be
divided
Drop by drop—until there were
no more
Eternity would just then be
beginning
I know you've heard the stories
o'er and o'er.

And the one about the sands of
all the beaches
If they were to be taken—one by
one
And counted—grain by grain—
down thru' the centuries
Eternity would then have just
begun
I recall them to your mind, My
Little Darling
To tell you—though our years
on earth are few
When the water's been divided
and the sands have all been
counted
I will have only just have started
loving you.

Gretchen Wehmhoff
Where the River Bends
Rivers flowing . . .
passing friends . . .
I met a leaf where the river bends.

He twisted
and twirled . . . then rested
awhile
As together we talked in the calm
of the bend.

We laughed and we played
several days in that Spring
'til the wind changed direction,
and with it . . .
my friend.

I walk on my way now
passing my time,
currents and windfalls crossing
with mine.

And as I travel I'll meet him
again . . .
I have a feeling that river will
bend.

Joanne Radcliffe
APART
We are scattered to the winds,
like leaves in autumn blowing
in the breeze.

We are lost to each others touch
but when our hands reach out
they feel the warmth
through out the miles.

We have gone our separate ways,
as well we should and always
knew we would.

We are distant by miles
but ever close in our hearts.

We are a family.

Glenda Nabors Mitchell
UNDERSTANDING
Understanding not just one
another
But Understanding the sun above
Understanding our needs to
discover
And Understanding Love.

Kathy M. Trujillo
ONCE
Once I knew a little boy
who had tried to be strong
Since he was born, people
had did him wrong
Abandoned at birth, he never
had a family that would care
Given the chance, all his love
he once tried to share
He had himself and sadly, he
didn't have another
Maybe things could have been
different if he had someone
like a mother.
In this world, he was just another
kid that was alone
Then one night, while he slept, a
glorious light gently touched
his eyes
It released all the hurt and pain;
It gave him peace, love and hope
In that light he gently stuck his
head through a noose in a piece
of rope
He knew this was the way for
him and so he wasn't blue
When he said good-bye, good-bye
to the world he once knew

John Campbell, Editor & Publisher

Chariss D. Cruz
DID I EVER SAY . . .
Too many times have past
I haven't had a chance to say
How truly thankful I am
We share what we have today
How our friendship happened
If it was ever meant to be
I'm glad our pathways crossed
You're someone special to me
Did I ever say "I love you"
How beautiful you are inside
How your smile lifts me up
When all I can do is hide
I'd like to let you know
Just what you mean to me
But somehow the words get caught
When it's only you and me
But maybe someday soon
When another chance comes along
I'll take it without doubt
And let the words sing my song

Deborah Diane Whittaker
Thoughts Riding On The Winds
You're so much a part of my life,
More than you know or I will say.
I care for you so very much,
Which seems to grow with each day.

When I need some reassurance,
If only to know someone cares,
I hear your thoughts on the South Wind,
"Hey Girl, I'll soon be there."

Each time your here and then you leave,
I seem to miss you more
For when I'm with you: you touch my soul,
Something no man has ever done before

I kiss your letters every night.
Before I close my eyes to sleep.
I ask everytime in my prayers.
That your love for me will keep.

I feel you hold me so close in our dreams,
Because you're not just a lover but *my* friend.
So if you need to talk I will answer,
For my thoughts ride upon the North Wind

Salvatore D'Aprano
BEASTS OF BURDEN
I drag my heavy bundle
in the tortuous path of life
as the humble ox who, intent
to harrow the fields, bears
the onerous yoke and the
painful whip, with servility.
We are beasts of burden . . .
We are the eternal victims
in this society of vultures.
Only when we become larvae,
no more able to serve
our despot "Masters",
maybe we'll find the just reward
and the coveted rest,
in the next world.

Susan M. Franklin
SUNSET IN WINTER
Soft warm pink
Low in the sky
Dark snow clouds
Overlapping—why?
What is the meaning
Of the beautiful sight
That loses its luster
With the coming of night?
Is it to cool our anxieties
And our unbearable fears
The confusion, the noise
The teasing, the leers?
Or is it a sign
That the day is done
The beautiful, wondrous
Evening sun?

Angel Connell

Angel Connell
REVELASHUNNED
In a state of siezure
during the suspension of silence
something hackened;

The armor of skin and bone
rusted into antiquity
from the obscenity of sweat
from the erosion of tears
from the phoenix cycles of blood
because right guards
and the left guards
had left us defenseless
like homogendisguised butter
exposed
to the
apocalyptic descent
of an
anesthetized butcher's knife.

Cindy L. Wall
PHYLOSOPHY
So many times a profound thought
is on the tip of my pen
waiting to spill from the quill
making a mark on mankind!
Yes, so often the earth-shattering revelation
of phylosophy is there—
On the deep end of my mind
waiting to make a splash,
showering the surrounding souls
with enlightenment
and understanding . . .
an awakening to life!
Oh, to touch that masterful phrase
and light the sky with brazen letters,
seering their brand across the inky horizon . . .
I have to go to the bathroom?

Alice Johnson
THE CHRISTMAS SCENE
Tonight the whisps of cold, clean
   down Will tumble and dance, a
   circus clown
The boughs are full the path is too—
The lanters glow is pale and true.

The barn is warm, the mangers there—
The smell of hay is in the air.
A dove, a sheep, a docile cow—
No baby Jesus sleeps here now.

Tonight the whisps of cold, clean down—
Will tumble and dance a circus clown.
The trumpet sounds, there is no bell—
The King is coming—the people yell.

The scene on earth is super clear.
And thousands of angels in white appear.
The harvest is ready, the reapers have come
The end of the world is over—it's done.

Lona Jean Langdon Turner
SELF PORTRAIT
I always felt God has a plan
Though I don't always understand
My life so full of cares and pain
The thought of living was a strain
I can't go on and hurt this way
Oh, blind my eyes to light of day
In my torment He has heard
Just open your heart to my word
I'll bid your heartaches to cease
To your wounded soul, I bring peace
I stand knocking at your door
Invite me in for strength evermore
Now this you can believe as true
I live with Christ; there's room for YOU

Debra Josephson Abrams
BUENAS DIAS
I don't need you to help me sleep
alone anymore so I'm leaving.
Don't pretend to miss me when
I'm gone because you din't
pretend to notice me when I was here.
I got tired of trying to keep you
awake long enough to kiss me
good night so this is goodbye
and tomorrow I'll finally know
what good morning means.

Carrie Weaver
MOTHER
She sits, eyes dimmed by time,
face lined, knowing both sorrow and pain,
Hands that are never idle, have done so much in helping others—
Those arms that held and comforted each one of us as a child, a cut finger, stubbed toe or a bloody nose, her soothing voice and gentle hands soon made it right.

She walks, slowly and painfully, for her the pain is never far away, crippling and ageing, greying the lovely lustre of her hair.
She lies awake, hands clasped in prayer, alone, remembering, the lonliness is always there, waiting for some word or thought from those she loves, just to know someone cares and that she is wanted will keep the tears away.

She dreams of the days of long ago, the nights are long and seem without end, for the past has many tales to tell.
Then the day begins and with a smile she carries on with life.

She is loving, kind and gentle, she is old but is still young at heart, she means everything to me.
She is "MY MOTHER", "GOD BLESS HER" and I love her so.

Linda R. Healed
VISIONS
A face appears in the distance
No—A vision through the tears.
Always a vision; never reality.
The oceans could not hold the tears
Which have fallen from these eyes.
Tears for the time shared, and tears
For the time apart.
A lifetime has fallen from these
Eyes drowning the memories,
Yet the vision remains.

juli cherven
earthbound
you are still earthbound,
still tied to your sheets.
you sit in your hospital bed,
waiting to either get better or die.
are you still there,
sometimes i'm not sure
your words independent

they speak by themselves.
your ears are not silver yet,
your tongue not a moon,
the world still appears when
you open your eyes.
but you're turning to paper
and i don't want to watch.

Nancy Keats Benson
Child's Glistening Gold Of Slippers
On to newer shoes.
Candy canes, striped sugared red
And lady bullet puffy laced pink dancing
Costumes. Silver bells of
Musical chairs, party favors, crosswardpuzzle
Of never will be ended.
Joys from doll's curly golden hair.
And dog, turn me and I'll bark.
Sad old clown of rosy cheeks and
Buttoned ripened nose.
Bright blue eyes of smile fade down.
A fairy land that folds away
As glistening gold of slippers
Change to newer shoes.

Christine Lynn Campbell
SUNSHINE
The sun comes out.
Its rays run 'round about
Like a small, lost child
Searching for its mother mild.
Looking at it another way,
You could simply say
Sunshine is God's love
Nurturing us from above.

464

Shirley Smith
SIMPLY CHRISTMAS
The Christmas Season is upon us
  again,
With gifts to buy for family and
  friends.
Times have been hard and money
  is scarce,
but, with some imagination there
  is none to embarrass.
Make a gift from yarn or from
  thread,
sew or knit it for someone's head.
Make a card with a picture or
  two, sign it with love and that
  will do.
Money is nice—but that's not
  what it takes,
to give someone else a Happy
  Christmas Day.

Brenda J. Hedman
CHRISTMAS LOVE
There's a special feeling in the air
That comes this time of year,
It brings a special warmth and joy
A note of hope and cheer.

I see it on faces
Each one looks so bright,
Especially when someone gives a
  gift
And sees the receivers delight.

I feel it in handshakes,
And kisses, and hugs,
All these most precious of gifts
We need so much of.

I hear it in laughter, and music,
  and bell chimes,
And all those old fashioned carols
We learned as children
Just like our nursery rhymes.

So let us all be as little children
And believe in this magical time
  of year,
And do our best to make love be
  felt
Each and everyday of the coming
  New Year!

Karen A. Royal
I'M HERE FOR YOU
Have you ever wanted to touch
  someone,
But no one seemed to be there?
Well, you know I'm always here
  for you
And you know I'll always care.

Have you ever awakened, calling
  my name,
From a nightmare in your sleep?
Well, you know I'm always here
  for you
And you know I'm yours to keep.

Have you ever thought of death
  to make
Your troubles disappear?
Well, you know I'm always here
  for you
To kiss away the fear.

Julianne Latham
DEAREST MOTHER
For once in my life I stand all
  alone
Far from my family, far from my
  home.
I must be strong for now I am
  older,
But often I turn to lie upon your

shoulder.
You've wiped the tears each time
  that they fell,
When I felt broken, you made me
  feel well,
When I felt tired or scared and
  alone
My Mother's sweet love gently
  carried me on.
I touched your hand you made
  me feel warm,
You held to me through each
  blinding storm.
Now it is time my new life has
  begun
The first goal is reached, the first
  struggle won.
All is for you my Mother, my love,
All is for you and two Fathers one
  above.
One gentle kiss before I do leave
My childhood now gone, sweet
  memories I do keep.

Pearl R. Lindberg
NO CHRISTMAS

*In memory of my dear husband
Mervil C. Lindberg I love him so
much, and miss him.*

'Twas the night before Christmas
So alone and blue,
There's no white Christmas
For me darling with out you.

There's no stockings hung
By the chimney with care,
No Christmas gift's for you or me
No Christmas tree by the stair's.

Wishing you a Merry Christmas
  dear
Wishing you were here,
You are in Heaven darling
Spending Christmas there.

December twenty fifth
The day of Jesus birth,
I'm so alone and blue
Missing you darling here on earth.

Merry Christmas darling
Missing you here with me,
Always thinking about you
Where ever I go or what ever I do.

Beverly Burns
DESTINY
Long nights passed since it came
  to be, the dreaded terror we
  hoped never to see.

It came stealthly out of the night.
No warning or sound did it make.
Quietly, with a blinding light.

Sleeping they were, the
  unsuspecting, the skeptics.
They laughed when I tried to
  warn.
Only you and I were here to see
  the coming of an unbreakable
  dawn.

I knew it would come, it had to
  be, the mistrust had
spread from sea to sea.
Now alone, with unseeing eyes I
  sit and await my final fate.
Oh! Why did they think someone
  could win?
Why, couldn't they live in
  harmony, the way GOD
intended for it to be?

Lana Payne
HOPES AND DREAMS
Hopes and dreams
    Must not die
For if they did
    The world would
    Be dark
No sun shining
    In
No need to
    Survive

Vonnie Spenst
A QUIET LOVE
Like a snowflake drifting lazily
through a silver-laden void,
your quiet love touched me,
caressed me—
grazing my consciousness with
the softness of butterfly wings;

like a passing breeze
of a summer's day,
it gently enveloped me,
close in eternal warmth.

Ed McSwain Sr.
DADDY'S SHOES
I'll never fill my daddy's shoes
Just thinking of him gives me the
  blues
Daddy and I were far apart
Though he gave my life a start.

A just and simple man of God
In this land as we live and trod
Daddy had such friendly ways
Such a life that really pays.

In mathematics he was good
Do you favours any way he could
A typical American so was he
Loving his master made him free.

He was a man of faith and trust
To fill appointments yes he must
No beautiful angel from heaven
  above
But shared with family all of his
  love.

Through his life was work and
  play
Mostely work and very little pay
Just thinking of him gives me the
  blues
Cause I'll never fill my daddy's
  shoes.

Conrad Phillis
GROTESQUE GHOULS
You may talk o' savage beasts,
  and be careful crossing streets,
  And you can stand 'way back
  from ledges high.
Stay clear of slithery snakes; an' if
  jist the thought of "spider"
  makes
  You shiver, shake and slightly
  sigh,
Messy monsters make you cringe,
  and you're not on any binge,
  And a werewolf howl will give
  your heart a lull;
But of all the orges awful, the
  worst to make you bawlful,
  Is the ugly—wild—and
  bruteful—Bowling Ball!

For tis fall, fall, fall; off the step it
  lightly falls.
  The smashing-bashing-crashing-
  Bowling Ball.
Making purple toes its purpose if
  your foot you slowly jerk-ous,
  The vile—and vulgar—barbarous

—Bowling Ball.

The thing was made for fun and
  games but in the hands of
  heedless dames,
  A gentle Jekyl, to a hideous Mr.
  Hyde?
This flim-flam conster can be a
  three-eyed monster,
  And not even with your wishes
  abide.
When you hurl it down the lane
  it may come back again
  To chase you running down the
  hall,
So, when it comes out of its sack
  be sure don't turn your back,
  On the sneaky—stealthy—
  beggardly—Bowling Ball!

For its roll, roll, roll, making feet
  its other goal;
  The two-faced, Frankenstien-
  ish—Bowling Ball!
Making purple toes its purpose if
  your feet you slowly jerk-ous,
  This mercilous—pittiless—puts
  you on crutches—
        BOWLING BALL!

Angela C. Tomei

Angela C. Tomei
STAIRWAY OF LIFE

*To my parents—who were
always near every step of the way*

The pitter patter of tiny feet
Played across the kitchen floor,
Climbing stairs without defeat
Until the steps were sure.

But strides in life which took her
  higher
Let her fall as she would dare,
For steps in life are but desires
In an endless climbing up the
  stairs.

W. Hugh Headlee
ENOUGH IS PLENTY
Hear ye, hear ye! Let it knell!
I think it's time to ring the bell!
Half an hour of this jovial
  spouting?
It must be true, there is no
  doubting.
His are rhymes of a congenial nut,
But now it seems that he's in a
  rut!
Quite so, indeed the time is
  fleeting;
Please, let us now continue the
  meeting!

465

Sister Catherine Podvin
DISCOVERY

Sister Catherine is a Dominican Sister, with Motherhouse in Adrian, Michigan. She is presently serving at the College of Santa Fe in Santa Fe, New Mexico.

He's laughing at me, the Devil!
I said that he didn't exist.
I said it, and said it, and said it
Until I ran into his fist.
Then prostrated there in the gutter,
Attempting weakly to rise,
I suddenly knew that I knew him
In his non-existent disguise.

He's laughing at me, the Devil!
With reason enough, I suppose,
Although when I said it I thought it
Was merely what everyone knows.
I'm sadder but wiser, believe me,
I'm punch drunk and shaking my head;
But one thing is certain, I'll never
Be saying again
What I said!

Tyrone Hayes
WITHOUT YOU
Please don't leave,
  Stay for another day
For today I can't imagine
  What I can't do without you.
Lonliness, I can't hide.
Loving you, I won't deny.
Thinking of you, it's like a dream come true.
  Here today I have you.
I don't care what people say,
  For they're blind to see in every way
My love for you is true
  Without you I'm solitude.
So please stay
Don't go away
For today I can't imagine,
  What I can't do without you.

Nora Evelyn Wold
LILLI ANN

In loving memory of my sister, Wilhelmina Lillian Wold who died June 6, 1983

My dear Lilli Ann has gone
But her memory lingers on.
She did not want me to mourn . . .
"Enough grief you have already borne.
Keep a stiff upper lip
Into self-pity do not slip."

"We two have shared many years
With but only a few tears.
You know I was barely two
When I first laid eyes on you,
A newborn babe in Mom's arms.
Later, I fought to keep you from harm."

Remember . . . Stubby took your hat!
In return, he lost his own."
"I remember it well, Lilli Ann.
I never did like to fight . . .
Guess I wasn't *too* bright

But from fights I always ran."
Lilli Ann has gone, I know . . .
She did not want me to mourn.
Happy thoughts my heart will adorn.
Even though I miss her so,
I know she is happy with God
Sheltered and guided by His rod.

Thelma J. Cummings
A LONELY CHRISTMAS
A house at Christmas is not a home!
When you have to spend it all alone.
It used to hold six, then pretty soon more,
With brightly wrapped gifts all over the floor.
This house rang with laughter and sounds of good cheer,
When all of our children were gathered here.
This Christmas is lonely for Dad and me,
We haven't even put up the tree.
I know we'll have to spend Christmas alone,
It just is not possible for you all to come home.
We'll just have to wait for a happier year,
When all of our family will gather near.
Then we won't be sad or feeling blue,
When we can give our love in person to all of you.

Irene C. Knight
AT THE END OF THE YEAR
When a year has come to its final day
And the calendar's last page is torn away
A sadness creeps in.
The hopes we had at the start of the year
Have met fulfillment or defeat.
Those moments of time provided
A frame for our endeavors
And they will not return.
If we admit some satisfaction
For those swiftly passing days,
Having shown some kindly service
And known some sincere love,
We should now forget the longing
And lost credits,
And build upon the blessings
Of a year in retrospect.

Nicolette Skarvig
WINTER WINDS

Written for the Unger family in Loving Memory of Douglas.

Cruel winter winds are blowing again
Reminding me of the time, and the pain.
The time that slipped away since a strong burning flame
Flickered out of our lives as fast as it came.

It was a year ago today
I looked out the window this way.
And knew, I wouldn't hear him

walk through that door.
And knew, he wasn't coming home anymore.

The rain streamed down the window that November morning
Like quiet tears from my eyes, that fell without warning
When we found my son's footprints leading into the grey sea;
We knew that it had swallowed him up unmercifully.

Twenty years of laughter and tears.
Twenty years of triumphs and fears.
Twenty great years of gains and losses
Ended then as we clung to our crosses.

We said reluctant farewells to the one that we love
Whose soul we sent to our Lord in heaven above.

That day is as clear as the glass in the window,
And my pain is as sharp as winter winds that still blow.

C. Vincent Kroeger
My Last Conscious Thought
My last conscious thought, each night always is of her, when she is at my side,
And the contentment of knowing we might always be together with time to bide.

My first conscious thought, each morning always is of her, and the miracle of her smile,
The tenderness she gives to me, adorning my life with the gift of love for awhile.

My last conscious thought, at the end of life will be of her and her gift of love to me,
With thanks for such a beautiful wife and sharing the best that life for me could ever be.

Beverly Sue Beahrs
MY BEAUTIFUL FRIEND

To my Lord, Jesus Christ, Rev. Kent A. Young, Rev. Herbert A. Muhl, and my friend, Cindy Blackburn.

My Lord, my life, my beautiful friend,
walk with me 'til my earthly end.
Protect my soul from Satan's fight,
cover me in angel white.

Lord, lead me straight if I may turn,
chasten me as I must learn.
I often fall, as you well know,
lift me up, and help me grow.

Lord, light my life for all to see,
the graceful change you made in me.
Snuggled peacefully within your palm,
storms for me, at last are calm.

My Lord, my life, my beautiful friend,
walk with me 'til my earthly end.

Protect my soul from Satan's fight,
cover me in angel white.

Loraine Lewis
LIVING
Darkness has put the world to bed
Silence is loud on my ear
One last moment stolen by the fire
as the midnight hour draws near.

My body is as old as the spirit inside,
as I see with the eyes of my heart.
The chores and problems yet to be solved
before the old year is forced to depart.

I ponder the challenge that New Year brings
as she sweeps in so young and gay
trying to oust all the old hurts
which time sprinkled along my way.

Ah . . . She brings her own smiles and sorrows
hidden beneath her bright colored skirts.
The mystery of what she is to be
is written in the page of tomorrow.

As the fire turns to ash darkness creeps close.
I muse on all thats been or could be
I search for the strength to accept the challenge
that the New Year is bringing to me.

Alan David Lehrer
THE NIGHT
I walk down the street
Very few people do I meet
I approach the block
It is now 12:00 o'clock
Although it is midnight
My heart must be right
For to be afraid and scared
Is to have my conscience bared
I know I must stay
So that I can get my pay
I now draw my gun
And go after thugs on the run
No one need fight but me
For I am a cop you see

Hazel Evaughn Smith
MY LORD AND FRIEND
When others frown on me,
I just steal away and pray.
I ask my Heavenly Father
To give me strength each day.

When people are so busy,
They don't have time to stop,
I then turn back to Jesus
He's always there to talk.

I know he's interested in me,
Though distance we're apart;
I hear him whisper softly,
And feel him in my heart.

Even though at times I'm weary,
He's always by my side;
He lifts my faith and holds my hand,
And says, "Child it will be alright."

So we walk and talk together,

He never leaves or slumbers
He loves me to the end.

Janet Kay Burns
A SPECIAL MOTHER
I wish I had a crown,
To place upon your head;
Set with precious jewels,
For each kind word you've said.

For all your acts of love,
To dear ones and friends too;
For your comfort and help,
Always there to do.

I don't have a crown,
Nor jewels of any kind;
No earthly wealth to give you,
Yet I know you do not mind.

But I give to you,
What I will give to no other;
The most precious gift I have to
give,
A special love for a special Mother.

Megan Louise Green
WORDS

*This poem is dedicated to Karl—
Thank you for your words. Love
Megan*

Soft spoken words,
Sometimes are all I need;
Just like the rose,
That grows up from the seed.

The gentleness of your voice,
Makes me bloom from down
inside;
And the comfort of your touch,
Lets me know you are my guide.

The feeling of your heartbeat,
Is like the song of the birds;
And with the harmony they
profess,
I remember all of your words.

Words, the beauty of expression.
Words, to understand omission;
To know, to feel, to hear,
A song, a touch, a tear;
An answer, without the thought
of question.

Ralph S. Ward
ASBESTOS

*To all Asbestos Workers in
United States and Canada.*

Curses on you Asbestos
You've left my lungs simply
atrocious
They work only twenty percent
My time on earth is darn near
spent.

Asbestos, I've worked with fifty
years
It leaves your lungs in sad arrears
Now we know the terrible power
That wastes you away each
passing hour.

It's not too late for you who work
Drinking and smoking you must
shirk
Asbestos seems to thrive on those
Who won't quit these felling foes.

So wear protection when you can
and you will live a goodly span

Asbestos workers will all agree
Your lungs should keep on
working free.

Princess Orelia Benskina

Princess Orelia Benskina
ACCEPTANCE

*This poem is dedicated to my
children, Pearl, Paul, Brenda,
David, Paul, Jr., and my sisters.*

If you love me accept me
the way that I am;
Be supportive and encouraging
the way that you can.
No one is perfect this you
must often see
And if I displease you, please
do not judge; forgive me.

If I love you I'll accept you
the way that you are;
I will be understanding as long
and as far . . .
As I truly can give of myself and of
my time,
Knowing that my love is yours and,
yours, all mine.

Aretta Seal
ECHOES OF LOVE

To my one and only True Love

With the fragrance of the flowers
Wafting gently on the breeze,
With the murmur of each
heartbeat
My soul finds sweet release.

In the gentle arms of Morpheus
My restless soul reclines,
As my weary and hungry eyes

Upon your beauty dines.
Till the fetters and the shackles
From reality must fall,
As the vision of your loveliness
My spirit does recall.

Of how my spirit and my soul
Searched out the blue beyond,
Ever seeking, ever searching
For my most beloved one.

Oh, thou gentle Morpheus
How sands of time do churn;
As the hunter becomes hunted
And the lover, loved in turn!

Marguerite Wasielewski
April Neal— 1½ Years Old
There was an awful smell that
hung upon the air.
And all that we could think of
was where, where, where.
We peeked in April's diaper; it
seemed nothing there.
She walked around with finger on
her nose so fair.
Her mother changed her clothing,
made her somewhat bare.
Then fast the odor was so very,
very rare.
Now Ray did have an "ow-wa" on
his left, left side
With pain that little April could
never abide.
Soft kisses on his pants leg she
did guide
With tears and sympathy she
could not hide.
Ray figured pants to cleaners he
could not provide
Since April's tears and kisses
were so bona fide.

Aretta Seal
BLACKMAIL

*To my sister, Mrs. Juanita Nash
Eilber*

In my rocker, while reclining
Pondering o'er the years
declining,
I touched my hair now tinged
with grey
Remembering back to yesterday
And innocent childhood play.
I remember stolen kisses
And all those days I spent in
doing
dishes for my sister, who promised
not to tell of forbidden moments
in yon scented dell.

Gloria Jean Trail
WISHING WELL
Wishing well of old, with all your
wishes still untold.

Once filled with pennies bright
giving dreamers the pleasure of
wishing with delight.

Only you know the secret dreams
of young and old. Oh! How I
wish they could be told.

Now you are filled with leaves
and decay, no more pennies to
brighten your day.

You, like I have grown old but
wishing well what beautiful
memories we both still hold.

Lois Greenawalt
HOME

*I dedicate this poem to— All
American Veterans who fought
to protect American homes.*

I was thinking today of the land
o'er the sea;
Then suddenly my thoughts
came back to me,
And to this beautiful land.
The home of the brave and the
free.

I thought of my childhood days,
And the places I used to roam.
Then on the screen of memory
Was the picture of home sweet
home.

My thoughts came back to the
present
As I stood there all alone;
And I thought—Oh what a
blessing
Just to have a home of your own.

The thoughts of home went far
beyond me
To the beautiful Isle of
Somewhere.
I am thinking now of my
Heavenly Home
Where Jesus has gone to prepare.

Lucy Walker Wilhelm
WHIMS

*Dedicated to my good husband,
Clyde E. Wilhelm who has
tolerated my whims for 43 years,
and so graciously augmented
them.*

Whims I cherish—
his and mine,
wrought of need to
contemplate and rest
afore hard tasks we best.

There was a time
we whisked to action
like sharp rays
of sunshine bright
to finish before night.

Age takes its toll
and whims surpass
the urge to finish.
We settle in now—
Accept what time will allow!

Charles R. Blackwood
THE GIFT
I sing for joy—it's Christmas time.
I received the gift—the Christ
child's mine.
Oh, what a gift—at such a price
Was paid for me—in sacrifice.
Gave up Heaven—all His glory
To ransom me—Oh, what a story.
That sacred night—that holy
night
Love flowed down—the truth the
light.
Join hands, Christians—be a
throng
Carol the news—our Saviour's
born.
Sing of shepherds—that new star
Wise men followed from afar.

We'll sing the angel song again,
Peace on earth—good will toward
men.
Sing out the miracle—of virgin
birth
The Alpha and Omega—in all the
earth.
Hail Mary—in that cattle stall
Birthed the Babe—who paid it all.
Sing out to every tribe and
nation,
The Christ child's come—we
have salvation.
In praise and worship—let hearts
sing
Louder, prouder—make bells ring.
That precious Child—is Lord and
King.

Lettie J. Williams
DID YOU EVER?
Did you ever have a quiet time
That helped you along your way?
Have you daily tried to meet Him
Alone with Him there to pray?

Did you ever say? "Bear witness
God, under these stars tonight;
All I am or ever will be
I lay at your feet this night."

Did you ever find a talent
That you didn't know was there?
Did you ever wish to use it
And you put it in your prayer?

Did you ever really wonder
What your life should bring to
you?
Did you long to be a blessing
And an inspiration too?

Did you ever say? "Please, guide
me
For I cannot see my way,
And I want to follow your plan
Through my life's brief little day."

Judy Brown
A CHRISTMAS YEARNING
How cold and lonesome it can be
Sitting near the Christmas Tree
Even if the lights are burning
It doesn't fill that awful yearning
For someone to love and cherish
Until the world and you shall
perish
Someone to live and die for
Someone to love, work, and strive
for
Love is needed by everyone
Whether it comes from old or
young
Without friendship life is bare
Christmas? No one nigh to share?

Patricia Lorene Peterson
OH MY LOVE
You happened into my life
As gently as the sparrow rests
Upon the weeping willow;

Oh! my love, how eagerly you
reached for my hand,
And so tenderly touched my
heart;

So unaware of just how
majestically you
Reopened the doors of my self
being;

Our bodies entwined with love,
Your heart beating so rapidly
with mine,
Magically you touched the
depths of my soul;

But, my love, as the sparrow has a
need to be free,
So you must also take flight;

Spread your golden wings,
Fly high my love,
Reach for the Heavens above;

Never fear the falling, my love,
For as God knows of every fallen
sparrow,
So shall He have His Eye upon
you;

So fly away my love,
Fly proud . . . fly free,
Into your world so high;

But, fly with my love,
Tucked forever beneath your
wing,
As God has you, tucked forever
beneath His . . .

Wendi Moore
CHRISTMAS TIME
Christmas time is the fun time of
year,
For everyone to laugh and cheer.
Get out billions of boxes and
string,
It's time to do those Christmas
things.
Put up the wreath, and hang up
the holly,
Christmas time is merry and
jolly.
Finally, when Christmas time
comes,
We'll hop and jump and jump and
run.
Then, when Christmas is done,
There goes all the good fun.
For we have to put away those
boxes and strings,
And wait a whole nother year to
do those Christmasy things.

Joanna (dollarhide) Edmison
HIS WISDOM

*I wrote this poem for my mother
on the day of my brother's funeral.*

When I am heart broken
And my body is weak
When my hands tremble
And I can hardly speak
I reach for my Bible
Through it . . . God speaks.
Somewhere in the Bible
There's a message for me
Answering my questions
And giving me strength.
I'm awed by His Wisdom
Compared to His . . . I have none
It's this truth that sustains me
No matter what comes.

Jo Starrett Lindsey
VAGARIES OF TIME
Remember when you were a
child
Waiting for the Christmas
season?
The time began to slowly drag,
Seemingly without a reason.

Remember, later, when you
studied
To take some difficult exam?
Then time took wings and flew
away,
While frantically you tried to
cram.

But, time is not a simple thing,
And changes with the point of
view;
It slows upon anticipation,
And speeds when there is much
to do.

Ruth E. Oykes
WILL YOU BE THERE?
Yesterday as I walked along
I was singing my own sad little
song.
I turned around and looked
behind me,
And you were there.

You looked at me and your smile
was bright,
Just as if we'd never had a fight.
Just as if it wasn't the other day
when I
looked
And you weren't there.

You told me you still love me.
I asked if that could be.
You smiled and kissed me and
said—
"I'll always be there."

You say we'll stay together
For always and forever.
But I'm afraid one day I'll look—
And you won't be there.

Carol A. Fischer
ALONE . . . AGAIN
Hello wall, my friend,
So tell me—
how've you been?
Oh, you're not talking.
Well, hello lamp!
How's life?
Oh, sorry,
You're studying to be bright.
Good afternoon, bed,
Whatcha know?
Oh, you're resting,
I'll get up.
Hi, door,
how're you?
Oh, of course,
I wouldn't mind closing you.
What?
Oh,
you want me on the other side.
No, I don't mind.

*   *   *

Hello there, tree . . .

Ruth M. Sheppard
AHEAD
Fears rushed in
With doubts—
And suddenly,
Like a million
Tiny raindrops,
Floods of failure
Burst around me,
Trying to drown
My inner peace.
And yet,
Like the Ark of Noah
Fleeing that Great Flood of
Time—
TRUTH has
kept me afloat—
For AHEAD is dry land—
Reaching out,
To take my hand.

Glenn A. Fenster
SERENE BEAUTY

*This peom is written to the
women I have loved and more
important, to the women who
have loved me. Let's allow my
poem to carry on our memory.*

The summer days, so serenly
coming to an end
hours pass by, like a day at the
waterfall
I ride along the rainbows clarity
of colors
and wish away dreams, then
dream for it all.

Stretching along with brilliance
of picturesque magnificence
glowing erotic songs that erect
my eyes to see
It's texture untouchable, for one
has never been
To capture it's feelings, you'd
conquer, your right to be free.
Up top the beauty of it's sphere,
richer in beauty than any
diamond, reveals answers that
Great Gods speak through
scrolls
fortune in wisdom, one would be
pleasured through remaining
years
Rainbow of passion, Rainbow
of beauty,
I see your ideal, and enter your
knowledge.

Harriet Ahmels
Reminder Of
Thankfulness
Most of the world is in such a
mess,
And November is the month of
Thankfulness,
When that bird (turkey) is placed
upon
the table,
Be thankful that you are able
To partake of it over here,
And eat in peace and not in fear!
Look at those folks across the
seas,
Fleeing from one another, like
swarms of bees,
Let's all count our blessings,
As we gobble the dressings,
Not only on Thanksgiving
Day . . .
But each and every live long
Day!

Our World's Best Loved Poems

Dawn Davignon
My Love For You Is Special
My love for you is special, to no
one it can compare,
I'll think of you always, even
more when you're so near.

My love for you is special, I'll
wait till the end of time,
My love will grow even stronger,
the day I know your mine.

My love for you is special, my
love I want to share,
I need someone like you, to show
how much I care.

My love for you is special, I'll
love you all the while,
Each day I love to watch you, just
to catch a smile.

Linda Meeks
THE THIEF

*To my grandmother, Annie
Hedgepeth Tharrington 1874-
1956 With love*

Death comes quickly
Like wind-driven snow.

He walks across lonely floors,
But makes not a sound.

Moving swiftly and alone
Through the night-winds' song;

Hastening before the break of
light,
'Cause with it, we'll be gone.

But he will not leave alone.
A spirit follow close beside him.

William K. Baker
THANKSGIVING MEAL
The old indian
His moccasins from Sears
Sat in Mission Hall
Shoveling down food
Prepared by loving hands

Centuries before
The fathers of his father
Emerging from the forest
Also shared a banquet
Prepared by compassionate
And conniving men

Millie Ann Blakely
WITH-OUT MY LOVE

*To the special ones whom I love
dearly. Rick, Cynthia, Theresa,
Ruby and Jeremy Wayne Blakely.*

How could I face the newest dawn;
If you were gone from me,
someway?
With a broken heart and caring
none.
No-thing could ease my soul's
dismay!

How could I live;
If you were not the very meaning
of
My only life?
Eternally, to straggle on;
With heart-ache's grief—in daily
strife?

Perhaps, as a new born baby alone;
With-out a Mother's tender care,
or love.

Or clouds, with-not a place to rest;
If there were not the skys above.

Oh! Vision heaven's beauty toned.
Her hues and arc, the lovely
rainbow, bold!
And matters not, that at the end
would hold,
No blissful hope—of ambered gold.

My every dreams—My life's
demands!
Include the very breath's of you? I
pray!
I would not face the newest dawn;
If you were gone from
me—someday.

Evelyn Stickler
STOP, LOOK, AND LISTEN
Looking here, there, and
everywhere
Some wonderful sights are found,
And surprising thoughts are
brought to bear
In this worldly merry-go-round.

Though some can talk, and
others listen
Some eyes are sad, and others
glisten;
It all depends on the view they
take

When the words are heard, and
the mind's awake,
For listening creates, and ideas
form
In the heads of some, who brave
the storm
And carry on life to greater
things,
Fulfilling dreams which
perseverance brings.

Alma Lillian Hageman
There's a Bird That Dwells
There's a bird that dwells above
all cloud
Safe, secure, in feathered shroud.
Beyond the rain, free from pain,
Head nestled in, down pillowed
wing.

Spiralling in air so thin
Blue wingspread open wide
Needs no nest, no place to hide.
Aloft is all will ever be,
Pallid eyes more feel than see.
Course laid, cranes his neck,
Sails straight and through cloud's
billowing deck.

Sandi Washburn
TRAPPED IN A CASTE
Atop are the uncaring, the
supercilious.
Those dripping in diamonds,
Those glittering with gold,
Blind and unseeing of life as is
told.

Next are the workers, the
achievers they are;
Those working for wages,
Eating food homemade,
Seeing the hardships, unable to aid.

Scraping the bottom the Pariah lie;
Those fragile with fear,
Those hungry for help,
Facing the tortures everyday felt.

Like the pyramid, no movement,
No loss, no improvement!
Live in one class, die in one class,
Can someone remove this ugly
caste?

Dorothy J. Quinn
PREGNANT WAITING

*Dedicated to each woman who is
pregnantly waiting for that gift of
God, the child within her.*

Would that the embryo formed
within
Could know its future in this
world of sin.

Would that the eyes from the
womb could see
The potential home where it
will be.

Would that the unborn nose
could smell
Flower fragrance that
whispers . . . "All's Well."

Would that lips of the babe could
impart
Prisoner experiences, while near
mother's heart.

Would that the fetus ears could
hear
Only words of love, never of fear.

Would that the feet could push
open the womb
To release this new babe, sooner
than soon.

Would that the fingers could
lovingly clasp
The woman who holds the child
in her grasp.

Would that the pulse of the heart
could find
A way to shorten the duration
of time.

Would that the womb be a cradle
of rest
Until baby is safe at mother's
breast.

David E. Reid
TRANQUILITY

*To Melynda, My Southern Angel
who's vision of loveliness
inspried this moment of . . .
"tranquility"*

It's at times like these when a
peaceful, tranquil atmosphere,
settles the uneasy inner
feelings in one's self.

Such as a brisk walk through and
atop a majestic wooded
landscape, hand "n" hand, a
hesitation, a glimpse upward,
with a darkness that's
unsurpassed, a beautiful
moment of silence for the eyes,
which is suddenly broken by a
brightly streaking shooting
across the sky, as if being
tugged off into the horizon, on
a string, by an angel.

Then darkness transforms into
dawn. A blanket of turquoise
covers the expanse. A
refreshing sound begins
echoing through the trees that
of our feathered friends on the
rise.

There, in the far off distance,

rising from the ground, a ball of
light, which eliminates
darkness altogether.

As this light mass inches its way
overhead, the contents here in
come to life.

And look, over there a sparkle! !
Only to be a beautiful dew
drop, departing a leaf for its
journey to the earth.

At this point, within a twinkling
of an eye, this mass of light is
laid to rest, and night prevails
once again.

A twinkle here, and a twinkle
there, a tranquil feeling is in
the air.

Carol Rae Gagne
THE DAY AFTER
I watched, I listened, I prayed. A
movie of bombs, torment and
tears. I watched the beginning
of the end the emotions I felt
couldn't bear the fear, as the
sanity of man disappeared.
My heart cried for us and the
world so wide, and I remember
what my parents taught me in
the best of my life.
I listened to feelings of hope and
despair I listened to children
full of hatred and love for the
man who pushed the button
that made us all scared.
I wondered what feelings the
other side might have and I
hoped they'd remember that we
might all be dead.
At the end of the film my
emotions went astray, but I
prayed to God there would be a
next day.

Patricia J. Pelham
DIET—"HUNGER"

*To memories and friends at St.
Mary College, Leavenworth,
Kansas.*

In the evening when I am certain,
and just before I close the
curtain.
I sit and wonder and ponder why,
and even cast my eyes up high
to that Omnipotent Power
which exists,
and ask for help that I might
resist.
To once again reach for my door
and to the vendors rush for
more.
And in my pocket, reach for, that
thin silver piece of money,
which brings relief to my
stomache and a chewy
Bit-O-Honey.

Kelly Jo Chapman
GROWING UP
In shallow depths I lie
where strong banks
refuse to let me flow.

These muddy walls have held me
in
since my growth
from a single raindrop.
In bad weather they sheltered me.

In fine weather they let cool
  winds blow
across my liver-green body.

The tears I form
  can't move my stagnant waters
  or wash away the banks
  I momentarily despise.

Within myself I feel a new
  sensation,
  the need for new depths,
  bluer skies,
  wider banks.

I need to flow.

Within this stagnant pool
  I can no longer breathe.
I exist only because I know
  not even banks of steel can stop
  me
  from becoming a river.

Brenda M. Shaw
**Red Roses and Blue
Thoughts**

red roses with dew on a rainy day
delivered to chase the blues away.

they meant to me your love was
  true
deep in my heart lay my love for
  you.

red roses with dew drops to quell
  the tears
of sorrow and fleeting thoughts of
  fear;
that somehow, someday you'd be
  gone
and I'd awake alone to face the
  dawn.

red roses that finally stopped one
  day,
there was nothing left for either
  to say:
red roses that withered and
  finally died
and so at last those tears were
  cried.

Jonathan Sylvester Lee
THE GIFT

*With all my love I dedicate this
poem to my little sister Sherri
Cucinotta, who inspired its
writing by allowing me the
pleasure of giving her the gift and
she in turn gave me the gift as well*

Shirts, socks and even gloves will
  last me for awhile
but all of these nice things will
  eventually go out of style.
The one gift you can give
  someone to last until the end
is letting that special person
  know that you are their friend.
Birthdays will come and go as
  will the gifts you give
but you can be somebodies friend
  as long as you both live.
The caring and the sharing can go
  a long long way
it makes it easier for a friend to
  make it through the day.
The gift it does not cost a thing
  that you can believe
but is the nicest thing you can
  give, for anyone to receive.
A friend will always be there
  when your up and when your

down
They'll help you to smile when
  you really want to frown.
When things get as bad as they
  can be
a friend will say "just lean on me."
When your weak and feeling blue,
  your friend will have the strength
  for two:
The reason that we are friends is
  cause we do agree
that the things I do for you, you
  would do for me!
So when it's time to count my
  blessings guess what I will do,
I'll sit down and be thankful that
  I have a friend like you.

Linda Connelly
CHRISTMAS
I dream of a Christmas
  Not about the toys and candy
But of the love and joy
Where the world is in peace and
  harmony
Where men and women are happy,
  And the boys and girls are one;
Where giving is all the time
  And joy and sorrow are mixed
  equally;
Where time I'd forever
  Not just one tomorrow
In the dreams of all our hearts,
Where the smallest gift is of love
Where no one can put a price on
  joy,
Where we all get the dreams in
  our hearts.
The joy is such it couldn't be
  measured in time.

Evelyn M. Heslin
THE SANDPIPERS
I went out to see
The ocean so blue
But another distraction
Stold my view

A flock of wee birds
Flitted over the sand
They appeared to be gliding
As they traveled, in a band

Their legs are so long
And their bills are too
The piping calls, they make
Are an amusing thing they do

Some are speckled
And some are plain
Sandpipers—they're called
That is their name

Soon they disappeared
Leaving me all alone
With the ocean so blue
And new knowledge, I now own!

David Kinnison
DREAMS
Carry your dream high
However do or die
Going the longest extreme
Someday to fulfill a dream

Down falls along the route
What's life about
Pickup the remain
Carry on through all pain

Leaving mistakes behind
All will right in time
Live for futures best
Putting dreams to the test

Love the one who loves

Carry there love from all other
A dream to be lived
A dream to be given

Dreams for all
Dream the call
To one day see a dream
Climb its highest extreme

To us all we do
Dreams of old & new
Knowing just that
Dreams rarely come true

Linda L. Lindauer
Linda L. Lindauer
ON OUR ANNIVERSARY

To my husband, Love of my life.

When I look back on days of
  before . . .
  of waiting to be near you
  longing to touch and hold you
I spent hours in daydreams
  of thoughts, it seemed
  in thoughts of a future
  with you, to be
So not surprising when asked to
  marry—
  I could not have carried . . . a
  brighter glow.

As a year is now past
  our "First Anniversary" has come
  what you have given to me
  will last forever . . . in my
  heart

you give the warmth of your
  touch,
  understanding as my best
  friend
you make my smile with the
  things you say, and give
  security when I lay next to you
you give to me a feeling of
  pride to say, you
  are my husband
you give . . . Love.

I would not have thought I could
  feel
  so close—
  to any one person

and so I wanted to say,
  as each new day passes by
  I Love you . . . just that much
  more.

Michele Pye
A LIFE LEFT UNLIVED
It is in the night, completely alone
when I am truly myself
  dreaming private thoughts

thinking of things I've never done
  a friend never made
  a word left unspoken

And then I begin to feel lonely
  full of sweet regret
  dreams unfulfilled, songs
  unsung
I remember a life unlived—
  a hollow, empty shell
  a mere shadow of a soul.

Outside, in the quiet darkness
Clouds fill with rain
  reflecting eyes damp with tears
  the memories wash over me
  like a gentle rain

Alone in the dark
  I am completely myself
  where no one else can see.

Schrevenje Ara'hat Lawns
UNTITLED
Swirled dense of mist,
We dance down to the water's edge
Saw the ice pieces, looking as
  though they had been cut
by someone
Drawn by the sound of the
  creaking edged ice pieces
looking to the sun
the glowing circular hued dew
and the dripping red blood flow
  are won
Coming into the land of
  loneliness
We hug on ancient hills
Drawn by the melting sound of
  the edged ice pieces
Ancient rivers sending saged
  rivulets to the soul
We range the withered fields of
  jealousy
seeking still a deeper hue
Coming into the land of loneliness
We hug on ancient hills

Libby Lady
NOVEMBER SON
November slips into our lives and
  a young mother, moving
Ever so softly—almost like a
  whisper—checks on her
  sleeping babe.
Standing by the cradle, she
  lovingly places her hand on
The tiny brow and says a prayer
  of thanks for this
Wonderous miracle, a november
  son.

Like November, the son grows
  strong from toddler to teens
Loosing his dad in between, he
  strives with faith and
Determination to overcome
  sorrow and misfortune and
  reaches
For a goal that will once more
  make his family proud and
Happy, each day, each year, is a
  new challenge.

In another November, he is now a
  man. He has achieved
Success, his career brings
  laughter and hope to those
Around him and a peaceful
  satisfaction within himself.

And as the eleventh month
  enters our lives once again
A mother—as she has done so
  many times in the past—

Our World's Best Loved Poems

Bows her head and says a prayer
of thanks for one so close
To her heart—a November son.

Olive Christine Moen
FAITH
If we listen we can hear God say,
"Trust in Me, have faith when
you pray. My grace is
sufficient, I know your need,
though your faith is small like
a mustard seed. Your burdens
are heavy and you may fear,
but trust in me, I am very near.
I will hear you when you call,
believe in Me, like a child so
small. The clouds may be dark
but trust in Me still, My Father
knows best, I do His will. Hear
My voice, I am still on the
Throne, I will not forsake or
leave you alone. I have
promised your burdens to bear,
know ye not I am always there?
Have faith my child, believe in
Me. My guardian Angels are
watching thee"

Anna A. Leonard
SONG OF APRIL
April is pregnant with promise;
robins eggs, lilac buds,
green grass and peach blossoms.
Lovers planning for the June.
The world's in rhyme and
I'm in tune.

Cynthia Tweedy-Hoffer
TO A RELUCTANT SUITOR
At two and twenty still without a
mate,
an oddity for sure, due to her
single state.
In London your on the shelf at
twenty,
and a positive antidote at thirty.

Shy and retiring Miss
Marchington used to be,
and quite unassuming if you
could believe.
So what happens when a mouse
becomes a lion,
and a reluctant suitor doesn't
know his buying.

He would certainly be surprised
to find,
Just what goes on in this females
mind.
As he starts to dance, he doesn't
know it yet,
but his bride to be is standing in
the same set.

She has planned several attack
games,
so he won't know what hit him,
as he's bagged and tamed.
By this time next month, a
wedding will be announced.
The reluctant suitor won't
remember when the lion
pounced.

She smiles as they come together,
and winks at him as they bow to
each other.
He is intrigued by now and
smiles boldly her way,
OH, he doesn't know the price
he's going to pay.

But, all you reluctant suitors take
heart,

Don't feel upset, just grin and do
your part.
You know it started with an
apple,
so don't try to hard to upset the
cart . .

Mark J. Carpentieri
**An Acting Rose Before
God's Nose**

_____

*I have dedicated this poem to my
dear and loyal friend Sister Josita,
a great Irish belle and servant of
God, whom I am blessed to know.*

_____

I long to look upon the rose,
A mellow actor all the year
It plays a part with every pose;
In Spring the stage is set and
clear,
It opens smiling, swooning,—she
glows.
The Summer sears the critics
heads.
She spreads her body to the
clouds;
She hears the oohs and aahs in bed,
And waves her leaves to mistful
crowds.
Now Fall where all theatrics lie:
A test of good my rose must act;
A climax role of height or wry,
The audience will tell the fact.
The viewers 'llowed my plant to
live,—
But Winter came,—she died in
snows,
In another stage she will give,
Eternal drama she best knows:
An acting rose before God's nose.

Bonnie Lee Ward
WORDS AT SUNRISE
Words are far too prolific,
to describe the beauty of a sunrise,
The celestial heavens glories
abound,
Early each morning as I gaze
enchanted at the sky's vista.

It is magnificently immense, this
feeling. inside of me about to
explode.
As I continue to watch the
sunrise,
so fresh and a new day has dawned
bright and promising,
to be full of fun activities,
and all the things I love the best
to do in my daily endeavors.

Words are far too much to ever
write
down the way I feel when I see a
glorious
sunrise!

Edith L. Bustle
NOT WAR, BUT PEACE

_____

*Dedicated to my God Jehovah
and To my parents, who taught
me of His love*

_____

Dear God, make us all hate war—
The pitting of country against
country,
Man against man,
Man against woman,

Man against child.
Dam all greed and corruption—
The material to kill,
The will to kill,
The madness of war,
The devestation.

Oh, God make the madness
subside—
Make man become gentle;
Let us love peace,
Seek brotherhood,
Give us contentment.

Let us know you,
Help us love all your creation;
Please heal all wounds,
Comfort the casualties
And cradle the innocent.

Anna L. Nissel
**Wistful Wishing At the
Seashore**
I wish I were a sea gull, riding
high with each wave
On cool turquoise water; freedom
I crave.
Skyward I'd rocket to soar and
glide
As the waters below come in
with the tide.
Then swoop down on the
sunlight sand
To watch children playing at
pretend;
Building dream castles and dunes,
Or dancing to the billowing
tunes.
Gleefully hurling popcorn into
air
Watching as I hover to snatch my
fare.
Off again wheeling above the
silvery foam's wave
With wide diving circles reach
for my prey.
Freedom of Land, Air, and Sea—
That's my life in reverie!

Rev. Dr. Earle V. Conover
The Oneness Of Our World
The heavens declare the glory of
God
In all their immensity,
Yet when I look up at the stars
above
The stars look down on little me.

Our world has a sense of
togetherness,
And, in truth, there's affinity,
For when I look up at the stars
above
The stars do look down on little
me.

We stare at the stars in reverent
awe
Because of their complexity,
Yet they tell of our Father's living
love
For each little, simple me.

The stars made by God speak of
lasting love,
Throughout all eternity,
Though the stars, looking down
on us from above
Look at each little transient me.

How great Thou art, O, God,
In Thy splendor and majesty,
Yet Thou dost love each human
soul.

Thou we humbly ask, "Even me"?
God's planets, stars and meteors
Illustrate diversity,
But surely not any more different
than
Our most sinful society!

There is purpose, design and
wisdom shown
In the universe that all can see,
Since the stars show forth God's
infinite love
For each insignificant me.

However far-flung His stars really
are,
They make a vast family,
For each human soul may say to
himself,
"I'm included, for God loveth me"!

Carol Wilcox Welchance
CHRISTMAS SUGAR

_____

*For my beautiful daughter
ERICKA CHER DAVIS, this one
is for you sweetheart. Love, Mom*

_____

I would not know the meaning of
Christmas Sugar
if I hadn't seen the
crystal snowflakes sparkle
in your
eyes
and if I hadn't seen the
warm kiss of your charism smile

I can go another, mile
and all the while
see you with Christmas Sugar
"every" day of the year
because your vision is
always ever present, clear,
and way down, dear.

Remember, I hope, that Christmas
was once a song
that creeped from MOTHERS
soul, natural and real
cause it was the Christmas
sugar of you; that
I can feel.

C. Brian Cook
KOTO
Koto whispers
Her gentle song.
    A distant place,
Listening
I hear the love in
    Her soul.

Darald Lewis Wells
LINES OF A FOOL
Lieing on the bed sheets
The window up wide
Smelling the rain
On the streets outside
Lately this seems
To be all I can do
Lay here alone
And reminisce of you.

A helter skelter
In a moist forest floor moss
Like an ant caught in a shower
I find myself somewhat lost
And if I were a wizard
I'd cast down a spell
To change your hate back to love

My friends come and question
At why I'm so sad
And they reply they all know

471

When I explain what we had
But as she gently
Squeeze's my hand
I realize they don't
And never will understand.

Gloria J. Davis
BEING ME
Yes, this is I standing here in all
my glory.
My deep-rooted pride shining
through, my heart without a
worry.

I a woman of substance, strength,
and inner peace.
I face this world with endurance,
and a sense of stability that
will never cease.

Eyes open to a brand new day, the
gift of insight that will never
go away.
Seeing with my heart as well as
my eyes, the deep-seated
injustice that wears no disguise.

You may deflate but never
destroy me, for my inner
strength will sustain to any
degree.
And my light-hearted love for
what's right will always keep
me free.

And alone I'll hold onto my self-
respect, for that they cannot
touch.
As I go through life in my own
little world and lovin it so much.

Evangeline C. Flynn
A BOOK OF POETRY
A book of poetry belongs not on
a shelf,
Tucked out of sight, collecting
dust
Amid musty volumes bearing
weighty labels
No! what the poet meant,
(devoutly hoped)
Each time he wrote, depicting
some event
In rythmic sentiment
To glad the heart, to sweet the cup
To raise the mind and spirit up
Is that you'd keep it handy, open
on the table
And read a sonnet or a verse
whenever you are able!

Bessie Georgakakos
He Only Wants Your Heart

---

*Dedicated to my loving husband
Harry, my beloved children and
grandchildren. Also to my family
and friends. Their love and
support have been a great
inspiration in my poetry writing.*

Soon Christ will give a party,
To celebrate His birth;
He awaits so happily,
Everyone on earth.

You need no invitation,
This affair to attend;
He makes no discrimination,
For He is everybody's friend.

You may be rich or very poor,
Unknown or one of fame;
Whether a sinner or one that's
pure,

He welcomes all the same.

You do not have to dress in gold,
To impress the King of Kings;
His eyes look only at your soul,
And not your outer things.

He does not judge any guest,
From the color of his skin;
He knows who is the best,
From what He sees within.

He does not want a gift from you,
Nor your thanks as you depart;
All He wants each one to do,
Is bring Him your loving heart.

Carol Hebald
RUTH
"Depart, O daughter of Moab, let
me be;
I've no more sons in my womb for
thee ..."

My shadow in the glass
The glass asks in;
I hang my harp upon the willow.
I watch, a sparrow alone on the
house top:
The sun smites me by day,
And the moon by night.
If loving her be called a fault,
Where then is my iniquity?

Lord, make mercy in her.
Let her come ashamed suddenly
And make me skip like a calf
Among the evening flowers—
Let her say; "Come and eat of my
bread,
And drink of the wine I have
mingled."
And let her prepare her table
before me,
And anoint my head with fresh
oil,
And purge me with hyssop, so I
am clean—

For love should be a lightsome
thing,
Not rooted in the deeps of the
heart.

Wanda Wissman
THE RIDGE
From the Ridge . . .
the winds whistle through the
trees
You know autumn is here.
The chill tickles you to the
bone.
The colors blend hues of orange,
rust, grey and red from green.

Across the Ridge . . .
the mountaintops reach out to
her
Let yourself be free. Almost as if
the wind knew the way, she
wants
to show you.

Below the Ridge . . .
the valley thrives on the change,
adjusting itself to the new season.
Its waited a long time. Each new
day brings a different look as if
the
change of acts in a play.

You on the Ridge . . .
watch with anticipation, feeling a
part of the show. Wishing for just
the moment you can join in the
wind

and fly with her . . .

From the Ridge.

Elizabeth Benoit Riley
THE FALL
The days of wine and roses have
come and gone at last.
Most of them thin and shattered
like dusty antique glass.
Blow people's minds you said so I
followed you to a "T".
You really didn't do it, so you
blamed it all on me.
Look down from your mighty
throne; see the sad unsmiling
faces, yes, they were part of you
trying to match your paces.
Look again, you'll see them
beating at your throne
expressing only the fullest hate
because their left alone.
No' The queen won't be waiting
to lend a helping hand she'll
only point a finger at you the
pitiful looking man.
The sights you'll see, will make
you weep in sorrow and
disgust, because you'll be
numbered like the rest of us.
You'll beg, plead, and curse us
and even try to cheat,
We'll just stand in silence and
watch for your defeat.
Hurry, the door is closing inside
the graystone gate,
Yes, the judge is waiting to
determine yet your fate.
He'll let you utter a word or two
before his gavel falls,
The relief will pass your gone
alast the pleasures I can recall.

Andrea Glista Bowen
NEED WE ASK?
As life's troubles come upon us
And we know not where to turn,
The loving Heart of Jesus
Can cease our souls to yearn.

Did you ever face a problem
And want to ask Him, "Why?"
I think the Lord would answer us
From Heaven with a sigh.

I think, He'd say, "I love you.
Now, will you love Me, too?
And carry all your crosses
As I carried Mine for you?

My cross was very heavy—
I know the way you feel,
But I only want to see, My friend,
If the love, you've claimed, is real.

Do not complain or cry out.
Do not curse life or despair—
For when there seems no answer
My friend, you will find, I'm there.

You will see Me in the sunshine.
You will feel Me in the rain.
Like a gentle breeze in summer,
I will ease your heart of pain."

Lorna Bain
A DENTAL DISTRACTION
Have you noticed without
exception
Fillings have a predilection
For falling out on Christmas Eve
Or on a Friday—after six
So there's no chance to get them
fixed
Or temporary crowns be warned

and this advice you must not
scorn
If biting into your Big Mac
You find yourself with—just a gap
This will undoubtedly occur
Thanksgiving Eve or just before
Some special function or
engagement
Whereat your dental
re-arrangement
Will be the subject of much
amusement
For the assembled crowd.

Oh the agony, Oh the grief,
Inflicted on us by our teeth!
Shatter my heart, scatter my ashes
Preserve me from my painful
gnashers.

Marlene A. Roske
86—2ND AVENUE
Aware of the landlord's
peculiar feat,
Hung by the neck
in the cellar

below,
Rousting us from sleep
again,
Tapping out the rent.

Yvonne Wittmann
ALONE
He sits
Alone
Fidgeting
    with his pen.
A tear rolls
And anger builds
He throws his pen
Window shattered.
Gone
The days
Of soft winds.

Hard, choking sobs
Defeat
Surrounded by
Pain
    and
        anger
            and
                bereft
    of hope.
He's alone.

Mary Ellen Hogan
STERILITY
A dream surfaces.
Trapped in a barren mind, it cries
to be heard.

A dream is stifled,
It dissolves untried.

Life continues.

Brenda Irene Helling
WINTER'S DISGUISE
The earth is powdering her nose
with winter's snow,

A thin layer of dust from behind
the rainbow.

Coloring her cheeks is the
Northern wind so strong—

It whistles and sings a delightful
winter's song.

Icicle diamonds adorn the earth's
twinkling eyes:

Masking the hope of springtime
with winter's disguise.

Shari Quinn
GRANDMA
Grandma was round and short,
and walked slowly down the
stairs. I used to help her by
holding her hand. I would get
up in the morning and wait
outside her door for her to
wake up. Sometimes I talked
really loud to my dolls to help
her wake.

Then I'd watch her fiddle with
her false teeth and we'd discuss
what we wanted to do that day.
We usually took walks, cause
they were good for us. Then
she'd watch me swim. I'd kick
and splash and try to get her
wet, but she didn't mind.

On Thursdays we made donuts. I
would cut them out, and she
put them in the fryer. I liked
the raw dough best, but
couldn't eat too much or my
tummy would hurt.

She would make me laugh by
telling me silly stories about
her old horse and her friend
Gertie. I'd tell her all my
secrets. She promised not to
tell Mommy, although
sometimes I think she did.

At night we would sit on her old
green pricky couch and she
would read to me. I usually fell
asleep sucking my thumb and
hearing Grandma's voice
drifting off.

Evelyn B. Ryan
SAILORS AND DRAGONS
"The earth is flat," the ancients
said
And gave the sailors much to
dread.
But out they sailed uncharted seas
For gold to seek and kings to
please.

"Beware the dragons of the deep.
They rise by night and steal your
sleep."
But said they did, out from the
land
And put their trust in God's
Great Hand.

And fables told the ancients too
For want of something more to do.
"The dragons eat the moon away.
They rise by night and feast by
day."

With much to fear, the ancients

fled
From foreign shores to freedom led.
And all the while the dragons, too,
Sailed right behind on waters blue.

So many years have passed and
more
While ancients rest on heavens
shore.
The dragons, too, have passed
away.
Or, do they hide in dreams today?

No matter now, the seas still flow
And sailors drift where oceans go.
Do they still see the dragons rise
Where the earth is flat and meets
the skies?

R. Edward Franklin
TO MY DAUGHTER
As I watch you sleeping upon
your bed
I wonder what thoughts go
through your head
You look so innocent so peaceful
and calm
Safe from the world and all its
harms

I wonder do you dream of
growing up one day
Giving up your toys and
childhood play
Or do you just rest all safe and
sound
Having no troubles as this world
spins 'round

Maybe you dream of being a
Mother some day
Loving your children in your own
special way
Helping them face life as we all
must do
The problems the heartaches the
good times too

There's quite a difference in the
mud-pie maker
And this angel lying here at rest
But you will always be my little
girl
In blue jeans or white wedding
dress

I hope that you'll be more than
capable
In dealing with life's problems
every day
For tonight you're Daddy's little
girl
But tomorrow you're a woman
away

Effa Alexander—Roseboom
A STEER'S FEARS
At any country rodeo
the cowboy plays his role,
With steed and rope he plies his
skill
with perfect self-control.

The fresh young steer, when first
released, is out and runs with
zest;
He dreads the mighty horse's
hoofs and every cowboy's quest!

His ears alert, his nostrils strained,
his eyes ablaze with fear,
Erratically he does his best,
to audiences' wild cheer.

But once the rope is swung around
the little critter's head
He lies exhausted on the ground

as if he were half-dead.

Still, when the lasso is removed
he's free to run again
And rushes to the open gate—
his ACT did entertain!

Colby Brummett
For the Love Of Money
For the love of money,
Some say, she sells her body,
For the love of money,
Boys, her time, it don't come cheap,
Don't try to read her eyes,
They've been known to lie,
She makes promises, that she
don't keep,
Shes practiced good bye,

So beautiful, oh
I've always thought her to be so
sweet,
But she don't like me,
And hell, she don't really know
me,
Bet, she would leave me,
Broken hearted, in the street,
Cause Lord knows, she don't owe
me,
And I'd sure let her own me,

For the love of money,
She will rob you of your sleep,
For the love of money,
Boys, she'll treat you real sweet,
But she makes promises, she
never keeps,
Its for the love of money,
She sure loves money,
She lives for the money.

Maurice W. Wills
SNOWFLAKES
Pure and white feather light
They came in harmony,
Like showers of flowers
Floating on air for all the world to
see.
Whirling and dancing like
children at play,
Their music the wind as it blew,
And standing amiss this heavenly
bliss
The pleasure bought visions of
you.

Tonya J. Semingson
WINTER TWILIGHT
I love the world in winter
twilight,
with all the hues of black and grey,
they reflect my perception of life.

Mud-tracked snow of white and
black,
spattered with footprints of
casual exhibitionists,
trying to leave their mark in life,
only to melt in spring.

The whisper of a Northern wind,
skates through the trees
overhead,
robbing the Earth of her warmth.

Black silhouettes of ghostly trees,
reaching up to embrace hidden
paradises,
icy castles in the sky filled with
wonders,
evaporating upon closer inspection,

All fading into the black of
approaching night,
and coming spring.

William J. Bibel
LONG LIVE THE LEAF
The regal leaf, its kingdom in the
trees,
Since coronation from its bud
so bold,
Now abdicates, and flutters to the
ground;
Induced by Autumn's force to
loose its hold.
Subjected to a dissenting breeze,
Soon decays when stunned by
Winter's cold.
Then covered soon with a cloak
of snow
Plans its rightful return to the
royal fold.

In royal style it bides its time,
Its armies dormant in the
rooted trees.
And feeds them with its own decay
To hold them through the
Winter freeze
And when the warmth of Spring
returns
With the proclamation of
trumpeting breeze,
A new Prince of Leaf ascends the
throne
And wears its crown amid the
trees.

Scotty Gerald Smith
THE WITHERED MILE

*To my parents, who have always
stood beside me and had faith in
me when I needed it most.*

Outside the rain's a falling
And the streets, they're a filling.

An old, not quite love affair.

Remembered movie billings.

When the phone rings suddenly
My memory, slow, comes to.

Turmoiled youthful summer fun.

Saddened memories of blue.

Memories float round my mind
And the passion cries do haunt.

Phone numbers never to find,
Tight fitting clothes used to flaunt.

The sound of rolling laughter,
Strange feelings of dea jea veu

Thoughts of what will come after,
What's ahead for me and you?

And we left those times,
Oh we did with a smile.
We forgot our silly ryhmes
And chose to walk the withered
mile.

Tami L. Coltom
TELL ME
Look inside my friend
and tell me what you see,
for if you see a lonely girl
your only seeing me.
Search the soul my friend
and tell me what you find,
for if you find a broken heart
your getting good to see.
Trace the inner thoughts my friend
and tell me what you seek,
for if you find the treasure
the riches are yours to keep.
Piece back the little bits my

friend
and tell me who I am.
for you my friend could never
be replaced.

Jane Taylor Overton
WHEN LOSS IS GAIN

---

*For Jim and Lisa on their wedding
day January 7, 1984*

They say that when
you lose a son
you gain a daughter.
When you lose a daughter
you gain a son.
The two are now one.
The gain is none.

But the gain is more
because of this.
The loss is naught
except in rhyme.
The gain is there
time after time.
And blest are the families
who gain the two
by words softly spoken,
"I do, I do."

Dee Kremer
THE UNHAPPY ELF
I don't like Christmas
Said the wee little elf
He gave a shiver
In spite of himself

I hate this workshop
I hate these toys
I don't like Christmas
Nor girls and boys

Sant's so happy
And so is his wife
I can't understand
To save my life

We work and work
We hum and sing
I don't like it
Not one little thing

Now here comes Santa
He is ready to go
The reindeer are neighing
There's ice and there's snow

Santa is speaking
He's talking to *me*
With hundreds of elves
You wouldn't think he'd see

"How can I thank you
My wee little men
The world will thank you
And to *my* special friend

The wee, little, sad, little
unhappy elf
Who doesn't like Christmas
Nor
even
himself

Christmas is giving
What you can of yourself
Christmas is living
A new life without doubt

Christmas is a time of joy
A gift you give to some girl or boy
Who, maybe without you, would
not know
That Christ was born not long ago

To give the world hope, peace
and cheer
If you don't understand
Then you mustn't stay here."

Said the wee, little, sad, little
unhappy elf
In a wee little voice that quivered
In spite of himself

"Forgive me, dear Santa
I'm ashamed to say
I forgot the reason
We work this way

To bring happiness to others
And receive such joy
I do love this world
And each *girl* and *boy*

I do like Christmas
I *do*, I *do*
Merry Christmas to all
And especially TO YOU."

Grace James
**Not Only At Christmas
Time**

---

*Thanks to Lillian, John Sr., John
Jr., Angela & Jacqueline My
Mother, Husband, Son &
Daughters for their support and
encouragement*

Let me show Your love
Not only at Christmas time
But all through the year

Let me give to others
Not only material things
But of your love so true

Let me give of myself
Not only of my head
But of the Heart You have given
me

Let me be a part of You
Not only for myself
But for all of Your Chrildren now

Let me give a part of You
Not only today
But every day all the year through

Let me share Your Spirit
Not only at Christmas time
But every day of my life

Lee Rix
**Nineteen Eighty Three
Comes To a Close**
Soon the old year
Will be gone with the ages,
As we face the future
Let's turn some new pages.

Throw out the old
The worn out naughts,

Replace them with positive
Creative—new thoughts.

Approach the new year
With gratitude for life,
And for your good health
For a world free of strife.

Give out with much thanks
For the favors that were done,
As time passes by
We forget them one by one.

Let's get an attitude
That is wise and discerning,
Take up a course
To get some new learning.

Being creative
Is good for the mind,
It helps you stay young
A better you, you'll find.

Get rid of pessimism
Which deals with gloom,
Open your heart
And make some room . . . .

Substitute optimism
Which significs hope,
Form a new future
Don't sit there and mope.

Throw out resentment
Lay it to rest,
Then replace negative attitudes
Why not give it a test.

The secret of a new
And really great future,
Is - fulfill your goals
And loose ends you'll suture.

Dorothy Worden Carpenter
The Land Of Never—Mind
I have just returned from a place
called never-mind,
Where the bittersweet was
burning and where every path
was lined
With the scarlet of the sumac
and the trees I like the best
Refleckted all the glory of a
perfect golden west.
I shall return to-morrow to this
land of never-mind
For there I can lose my sorrow
and leave all my cares behind,
And as I walk beside the little
singing streams
My life becomes so peaceful in
this fairy land of dreams.
Won't you come with me to-
morrow to this lovely
wonderland,
Just to see the glories of God's
handwork and be able just to
stand
And thank God for all the
blessings he gives to us each day
For who is mightier than God,
just bow your head and pray.
Charles Stuart Taylor, Jr.
THE LOVELIEST JEWELS
A rose and radiant ruby-
My heart of the summer glows,
The splendid sun-shot topaz—
An opulent autumn shows.

The snowy pearl and the ever
changing opal-
Does the chilly pallid winter bring,
But for me the cool emerald
season, set—
With it's pure diamond dews—
The Spring!

Margaret Hawhee
STRINGS
Stretched-long, apron strings are
cut reluctantly
Afraid our children will be in
jeopardy.
Their hurts playing our heart
strings are hard to take.
Now there are old strings from
whose hold one can't shake;
Purse strings tied to their food,
clothes, schools and games Gee!

Wendy Readio
WHAT IS A NONI?

---

*To: Helen Boido—for being the
inspiration*

A Noni is special because she
will,
Hug and Kiss us when we walk
through the door
And our days full of love she will
fill
And throughout the day she will
hug us some more
For Noni is filled with Love

A Noni is special because she
will,
Be there to put Band-Aids on
when we are hurt
Be the one to tell us we have to
sit still
After playing outside she washes
away the dirt
For Noni is filled with Love

A Noni is special because she
will,
Wipe away our tears and dry our
eyes
And continually pamper us,
especially when we're ill
And she always comes up, with
some little suprise
For Noni is filled with Love,

A Noni is special because she
will,
Check over our school papers
with pride in her eyes
And her watching us dance is
such a big thrill
And OHHHHHH when we're
with her, how time flies
For Noni is filled with Love

A Noni is special because she
will,
Always be there when we need
her to be
But the very best thing about
Noni is still
She loves us each in such a
special way you see
For Noni is filled with Love.

Helen Arlynne Lord
**'Baby-To-Be' LORDBOCK Is
Here**
We have some great news:
Our Ashley is here—
A beautiful darling,
A sweet precious deer!

She's really a 'hefty':
Nine pounds and one ounce—
With a strong set of lungs
And—plenty of bounce!

Her hair is an auburn,
Her mouth like a rose.
Her ears cute and tiny—

With a face made to pose!

And—'tho we have waited
Long months for her coming,
She's captured our hearts,
And—will have us running!

But, we will not mind
For—she is *Your* gift—
That answered our prayers
And—gave us a lift!

June Deborah Meek
I AM
I cannot explain myself
It would take too much time
And the feelings I have felt
Have blazed like a neon sign.
The loves I have won or lost
Were but fires that roared and
cooled
Trough them all I paid the cost
I gained experience, I was schooled.
I am a loner, I walk alone
I am content and always was
So what if there's no ringing from
my phone?
I don't need; "Why?" "Come on!"
or "Because."
I will not apologize for the person
I am
Theres no reason I should
Do you understand?
I am what I am
And don't give a damn
If you don't like me
It doesn't matter, you see!

Florence G. Axton
LOVE
The twelfth month of the year,
is one we hold so dear.
The church bells ring, beauty is
everywhere, a pinnacle of hope.
Inspiration, dedication, formation,
a mass for Christ.

Candy canes, children filled with
glee, purity, sweet.
A dream world, a ballet, the
Nutcracker Suite.

The beauty of a Christmas tree, a
promise, a plea,
Santa Claus in the sky, on the
roof, we have no proof.
The Holy Spirit, a symbol, the
white dove,
A gift of
Love.

Sheila Elaine Martin
Your Love Will Never Die
Remembering my life with you,
A life I cherished most,
A life, I thought would last an
eternity,
But we were both wrong, because
it came to an end,
An end that hurt more than I
care to remember,
I try not to think about it, but the
pain, it runs deep,
Because the life we had, was soo
perfectly unreal,
There was soo much love,
So much caring, and sharing,
So much closeness, and
togetherness,
We had enough love to fill the
whole world,
Nothing else mattered, only us,
But eventhough your life was cut
short,

Your love will live forever in me,
Your love will always be a prat of
my heart,
If you walked through that door
of life today,
It would be as if you never went
away,
The love I have for you will never
die,
You will always be, mine . . . . . .

Priscilla Barry Schinabeck
WALK WITH ME CHILD

---

*This poem was written for my
daughters Wendy and Kimberly,
and inspired by cherished
memories of their childhood.*

Come, child, and walk with me,
To the meadow and frocked in
green,
Where wild flowers nod their
heads.
And pick to your hearts content.

Come, child, walk with me now.
For soon the meadow will be
scorched and brown,
And flowers will no longer salute.
Much to our lament.

Barbara McDonald
A GIFT TO EILEEN
Fairy child, concieved in
bandished sin.
Your infant kisses are within my
heart.

A lost and lonely female, grasps
by barren limbs.
Your tears are priceless gems
from which I cannot part.

However when you become a
woman far you will stray,
From my boundless reach.

My heart will not be empty, for
you are there to keep.
          I love you, Mommie

Betty Skeen
OUR LOVE

---

*To those who may enjoy it and
those for whom it was written,
Bob, John, and Penny*

We are but shadows in eternity
Passing through the great vast
openness of time.
But we have been blessed with
each other
To share the fragrance of a rose
And the mystery of a rhyme.

For we are one when we are
together
And no more than this when we
are apart.
Even in my solitude my love for
you is forever
You are always deep in my heart.

I share your thoughts, your
dreams, and yes, your
heartaches too
I savor every second of our time
together
And only wish that I could spend
More of it with you.

The love we have is soft and gentle

You help me to carry on
You are the sunlight piercing
through the darkness
With your love and tenderness
You are the dawn . . . .

Rosemarie Cipollone
THE JOY
Over the crib a wonderful
Baby lying there
and everyone smiling at the
Happy pair. All dreams of

Happyness arise and Josef
Is looking in Mary's eyes,
Over the crib where there
Baby lies.

Mary Mahassek
A. Q. H. A. Supreme Champion
Riding all day and training all
night,
Hoping that my horse gets it right.
A smooth center and perfect trot,
Wanting a First—Place trophy spot.

Shining the silver; applying
Sho-Sheen,
Keeping the equipment and horse
super clean.
Endless anticipation and hours
pass,
Waiting for Grand Entry and
Western Pleasure Class.

Entry fee is paid and numbers are
bought,
Getting dressed and warming up
is my only thought.
My class is called in and I'm
ready to go,
Reviewing the things that my
horse has to know.

Class is over, the Blue Ribbon
and trophy I've won,
My horse has just made the A. Q.
H. A. Supreme Champion.

Huy-Luc Bui Tien Khoi
MY BELOVED COUNTRY

---

*Dedicated to my beloved country
VIETNAM and my father BUI
LUU, my mother TRAN THI
QUANG, The greatest parents,
and my brothers BUI TIEN NGO
& BUI DAN BA, who have died
for my beloved country.*

Vietnam
the beauty of river, the
magnitude of mountain
Vietnam
in water, on stone

Our love in the endless pain
For freedom we've far away
gone . . .

Vietnam
the country where I was born
no sunshine comes at morn
the biggest communist prison now
The fear on fifty million people's
brows . . .

Do something
to free our motherland,
Do something!
for our people to live and
stand . . .

Vietnam
prisons, prisons have grown
Freedom is already dead and
down . . .

By fighting against Communists
happiness will gain
By surrendering to Communists
freedom and life are slain . . .

Do something
to free our motherland,
Do something!
for our people to live and stand . . .

We will fight until our free
Vietnam does begin
Free Vietnam or let us die
Because we are great men
under a four-thousand-year-old
glorious sky . . .

Beulah E. Gill
MY WALK
On mountain top or valley
Through wilderness and plain
I only ask to be led safe
Until back home again.
Let every snare be training
That those who watch me walk
Will see care and calm patience
In how I move and talk.

May each hard climb or trial
Make stronger my desire
To combat every burden
That sets my heart on fire.
All those I meet along the way
Let them feel my demand
To face the trials of every day
And then much stronger stand.

Through many trials of this
world
Life trains us to persist
Against the wrongs and evil
strife
That better can exist.
I want to walk the mountain high
Or valley wide and deep
So others find the strength in me
To fight and climb—not sleep.

Mabel Lee Fisher
MORNING MAGIC
I reached to take a lovely rose,
To place in my bouquet.
A tiny dewdrop trembling there,
Bade me let it stay.

I looked, the gems were
everywhere,
Glistening in the sun.
My garden was a Wonderland,
To every leaf they clung.

The grass, a carpet of diamonds,
Untouched and untrod.
This landscape of beauty was
A sprinkling of God.

Katrina Wester
SOMEONE

Show me someone who's been
touched by love
and I'll show you a person who's
cried
Show me a love that has lived so
bright
And I'll show you a love that's
died.

Give me a day when everyone's
happy
And I'll find someone who is sad
Speak to a person who's still in
love
And they'll tell you what love
they once had.

Find me someone who doesn't
still care
About a love they once had in
the past
And I'll find you someone who
still cries in their sleep
Because they wish that their love
could last.

And after the dreams are
shattered and gone
I'll find you someone who still
cares
I'll find you someone who's still
desperate for love
Who reaches for something not
there.

Gloria Jean Robertson
SOME POWER

---

*Now, I can look swell, for ERNIE
MICHAEL CONTI, My GIANT of
an Angel, poured out inspiration
so well!*

Under your power,
Life knows no bounds;
What I've accomplished,
Is far greater than it sounds.
The little things we've planned
together,
Will someday set us out—
And your endearing
encouragement,
Of your love, makes me want to
shout.
YOU show your love by caring,
The dearest way of all—
The parts of our lives we're
sharing,
Keeps an ivisible bond on call!

Robert Nacke
BACK HOME AGAIN

I took her little hand in mine.
Went walking down the street.
Sauntered to a warm cafe
For coffee and a treat.

The snow was falling lightly,
One could hardly feel it's touch.
Compared to cold Wisconsin,
It didn't amount to much.

There was snow enough to make
our minds
Turn back the time again.
Remembering all the friends we
left,
The memory caused us pain.

But then our minds returned again,
To the present time, that morn.
We know we're lucky people,

To be back where we were born.

Thomas Wolfe once said,
So many years ago,
One can't go home again.
He's wrong. We did. We know.

Carmen Joseph Altomare

Carmen Joseph Altomare
THOUGHTS OF A SON

---

*In loving memory of Charles C.
Altomare 1922-1983 Died of brain
Cancer 4/10/83*

Watching my Dad's pain.
His pain is driving me mad.
Seeing him is sad.

Dad can't walk or talk.
He's a Living Skeleton.
Thank God, he knows me.

Why? Why? Why my Dad?
Can't think of a good reason!?!?
I swear! It's not fair!

Dad is a good man.
He always has time for me.
This is just crazy.

Dad, please don't give up!
Dad, I know you can fight it
Dad, think positive.

Well Dad, no more pain.
I will never forget you.
Someday we will meet.

Gregory Mullin
FANTASY

Bleakness, dull pain of despair
That tears the light
Why do you find me?

Leave me to be in my silver and
wine

Resting in my placid ignorance;
I need not to reflect
On the wound of boredom
But wallow in the honey of
blindness.

Take me and my love away
To the land of children
To the time of tomorrow's
yesterday
To tranquility and love.

Dream on, then, to escape
And escape then, to dream
In the place we all long for.

Carmen Elizabeth Arellano
Unimportant Thoughts

---

*With affection and appreciation
to Boyd, Donna, Mary and Jim for
helping me to continue with my
life as a writer.*

Days have gone by
And still I have yet to smile
My heart is heavy with sadness
But I knew all along that our
time together
Would be a short one
That still does not change the fact
That I love and care for you deeply
I, however, cannot bring myself
to tell you
Mainly to avoid any unnecessary
troubles
And any pain along the way
I will always cherish our friendship
And treasure the memories of the
times we've shared

Karen Lynn Myers
His Best Christmas Ever

---

*Dedicated to the wonderful
memories of my Papa, Mr. Vance
Kendrick Blankenship. He
touched my life in a way no one
else ever has, or ever will.*

His last few days I was near.
We read together and prayed
That his life and suffering would
soon end,
So he could go home.
Three days later he drew his last
breath
As I stood beside him and held
his hand.
He looked so peaceful—at last
I knew his suffering was over.

It's harder now than it would
have been
For it is Christmas time
When we usually think of our
friends
And our precious loved ones.
Papa was truly loved
By every life he touched,
And I know he would have
wanted us
To rejoice instead of despair

So when I start feeling depressed,
And think—What a sad Christmas!

I stop   and think of Papa
And how he must feel.
This year he will be celebrating
Jesus' birth
With Jesus himself.

This will definitely be
His best Christmas ever!

So I rejoice with him.

Danielle Fleming
UNSUSPECTING

Behind the cold dark shadows of
night,
Lurks the leary will of might.
What lies in wait for the
Unsuspecting . . .
As I walk down the cold dark
street,
my heart is pounding.
I hear footsteps coming closer
and closer;
and louder and louder.
as I walk faster the footsteps keep
coming closer and closer.
I stop; they stop.
I turn around, and no one is there.
Relief is close, but not quite
there.
As I reach for the door knob, I
feel a hand on my shoulder.
Behind the cold dark shadows of
night,
Lurks the leary will of might.
What lies in wait
for the
Unsuspecting . . .

Ms. Eva Ristau
THEY DIDN'T REMEMBER

As usual everyone forgot—
To remember my special day
I sit in tears and think about
The times when I couldn't count
The many cards and calls
From family, friends, and all
Now they are gone, and have long
forgotten
The friends I thought I knew so
well.

Danya Marie Scott
YOU'LL NEVER KNOW

To Mom, With Love

You gave me my wings
And taught me to fly.
You didn't hold back,
You showed me the sky.

You gave me the world
On a silver tray.
You taught me of love,
And the games people play.

You gave me the strength
to stand alone,
And all the confidence
To make it on my own.

You gave it all,
But you'll never know
Just how much
You helped me grow.

David James Devoss
UNTITLED

The stream made its way
In measured moments of tranquil
Ity, unobtrusive she
Capitulstes any and all municipal
Ities (her kingdom knows no
Bounds
And reserves the right)
Exercising it with vigor
And a relentless pursuit
Feigned in subservien
Cy (beautifully
Harsh trumpets mother)

Our World's Best Loved Poems

Gregory Anthony Wooden
EVEN NOW

Even now . . .
  that we've gone our separated
    ways
  I still can't seem to let the
    memory
    of you just fade away even tho
    it's been
      awhile since our last hello.

Even now . . .
  as days go by I sit alone
  wondering where you
  are when night finally comes
    around I wish upon
    a star that you were here to
    share my dreams I
      only have a few and I gave
      my love and tenderness
      to no one else but you.

Even now . . .
  I keep saying to myself over and
    over again
    that this is just a bad dream I'm
    having
      and I'll awaken soon.

But I haven't
  and I guess I never will
    wake up from this dream
    that lives inside my mind
      even tho we've gone our
      separated ways.

Ken Gordon Kilback
CRYSTAL BALL

dissolution of images
watery-creams over my fingers
  sand in my eyes
gaze not into the crystal ball
but behold the broken mirror

echoes of discordance
images in alternation
  epilogue of flesh
i am not the son of progeny
but the father of extinction

Darla Archer
THAT POOR BEAR

He walks along the muddy path,
  and searches for a place to rest.
They have hunted him for two
  weeks now, he's hid every way
  that he knows how.
Soon he finds a place to sleep, he
  lays down with his breathing
  deep.
He licks his aching paws, then he
  hears the hunters calls, he just
  waits for them to come.
He knows no one will ever care,
  he's just a wet and lonely bear.

Mark Thomas Reynolds
IT'S OVER

So now it's over . .
You came to cry to me,
because it's over.
I can not help but see,
you are only using me.
Now that it's over.
Over.

You ran around.
Played your games
all over town.
You think that I should be the
  same,
still be your clown.
Now that it's over.
Over.

Now that it's over,

Won't you please find someone
  new.
To be a fool for you.
I'm tired of being used.
Yes girl, it's over.
Over.
I'm over you.

Taimi M. Lamsa
STARS AT THE WINDOW

Six stars at our window
  When the boys marched away.
Pearl Harbor struck chills
  On that cold winter day.

My heart became silent
  That seventh day in December
For lives changed so quickly
  How well I remember.

Stars at our window
  Like Bethlehem's Star.
War was now with us
  The boys roaming far.

Hark; Christmas brings hope
  God's forever with all.
In battle or peacetime
  He hears every call.

All over the earth
  Let Christmas bells ring
Christ walks in our midst
  This we gladly will sing.

Alice Cleveland Daugherty
WAVES OF LIFE

In never ending lines they wove
  away, across the beach taking
  love and promises unfulfilled;
  leaving fear and loneliness
  immense.

The rocks clung to the cliff as I
  had tried to cling to you; while
  waves of water and of life,
  destined to destroy both, raged
  along the beach and within my
  mind.

The little one was lost—what
  was her name; so unimportant
  and unwanted, she was as an
  after-thought-something set
  apart from our love and desire.

Confusion and desperation
  comfort me; they hover over
  me as I sit and watch the moon
  across the bay, filtering
  through the moss that drapes
  the trees.

Pamela Rae Miller
IT'S ALRIGHT TO CRY

*For my brother Jim, may he
always walk with pride and feel
the abundance of love that I am
sending him, today and
throughout all of his many
tomorrows.*

I know it's hard, to live the way
  you do.
Missing family and friends . . .
  having no one to hold onto.
And I know you try, to smile and
  be strong.
With miles inbetween . . . the
  nights can seem so long.
Depression sets in and you try
  to breathe, but only sigh.
As you lie awake at night, Honey
  know that it's alright to cry.

And if the tears shall fall, and
  you try to smile but only pout,
Know in your heart and mind,
  that you are not alone in this
  bout.
  Honey, I too cry inside, wishing
  there was someone close to
  turn.
Looking for a letter, a card, a
  call . . . as the lonliness inside
  burns.
I look around at memories, held
  captive on a page.
Wondering how they're doing . . .
Hoping that someone has smiled
  at them today.
  I go to sleep to dream, of times
  that seem so long ago.
Of laughter, love and tears . . .
  people that have helped me
  along the road.
  So, Honey, it's alright, if at times
  you feel captive in this flight
Just know you are not alone at
  night, if you cry from lonliness
  or fright.
Miles and time have not changed,
  a fact that's filled your life . . .
You are loved and thought of
  often,
And sent a kiss to help you sleep
  each night.

Christina Arthur Cummins
SPRING RAIN

I like rain. It tickles,
as it trickles
down my face.

It's nutritious. Doesn't it
make vegetables grow,
and flowers show,

                their beauty?

It's nice to look out of a window,
and see shiny streets, where
  small

                    rivers run;
where little boys march thru
  puddles

                for fun,
and laugh in their (and my)
  delight!

Rosemary L. Wiley
TARA'S PRAYER

---

*Dedicated to my little girl, Tara
Helen. May your prayer's always
be answered. All my love Mommy*

Now it is time, for me to go to bed,
but I want to say my prayer's,
  before I rest my head.

I am only one year old, and tho I
  am so small,
but the prayer's of little children,
  I know you hear them all.

I have some things I want to
  thank you for,
my mommy and daddy and
  much, much more.

Thank you for my big brown
  eyes,
so I can discover my world and
  see the skies.

Thank you for my voice, that is
  starting to talk,
and for my short little legs, that
  have learned to walk.

Thank you for the day time, so I
  can play in the sun,
and for my pillow to sleep on,
  when the day is done.

Thank you for my teddy bear,
  and all my other toys,
and for when I grow up, I thank
  you for boys.

Well I better let you go, I've
  taken enough of your time I
  see,
but there is one more thing I
  want to thank you for,

and that is for making ME!

William Beker
I am alone

I am alone
  As the fog,
Is lifting, its
  Curtain of lace,

And everything
  Is darkening,
Gone and lost,
  And out of place,

And through the mist
  Again and again I resist,
Death's replay of decay,
  As a newborn angel today,

Betty Farquhar
JAPONICA IN THE RAIN

The japonica is in bloom.
Vermilion blossoms against a
  weeping sky.
The wind chimes softly tinkle.
Rain is dripping from the roof
on glossy leaves.

Your love remembered
suffuses my being
radiating within my heart
enveloping me
like a soft mantle of down.

Cathy Jo Tafoya
THE UNTIMELY WHISPER

---

*To those who have cheated the
untimely whisper.*

It came upon me as does a
  summers breeze. But the air
  was still, not a breeze about.
  Only a silent whisper, for
  which no substance could be
  found. A lonely whisper with
  no others around.

A silent whisper which rang
  through the very soul of me. I
  cried out with all my heart,
  why me? Why whisper these
  things to me?

Still the whisper was upon me,
  growing more intense with
  sound. Getting stronger with
  each whisper, filling the very
  air with the strangest of
  sounds.

Could it be that my time has
  come, my number has been
  pulled? Could the whisper be
  right, my number is now one?

It came upon me as does a
  summers breeze, it was the
  whisper of DEATH calling
  upon me . . .

477

Pearl Robinson
LOVE EVERLASTING

For those of you that inspired me
Thank you all, very much PEARL

With a tear in my eye
Will you be there
With a strong shoulder
Which I can cling to
To protect me from hurt
In a time when my heart is
broken
Will you supply the words
needed to
Comfort me
In a time of need
Will you also be there
With a hand ever so strong
To catch me
Should I stumble
Then, my love, we can walk
Through life together

Rachel Griffin
The Birthday Of Our Lord

Dedicated to Sally Edwards Who
Shares my Inspiration

Christmas is the season when all
our hearts are gay,
Everyone is happy in a special
kind of way.
The tree is trimmed, the
stockings hung, the children
snug in bed,
The time is near for Santa Clause
with his Reindeer, toys and sled.

He clamers down the chimney
into the silent house,
He makes not the slightest noise
to awaken even a mouse.
He tiptoes to the christmas tree,
around it lays the toys,
Dolls and trains, some candy
canes, for good little girls and
boys.

In the morning saw presents are
opened, the children shout
with glee,
The room is filled with laughter
as they play around the tree.
But christmas isn't just for Santa
and the gifts he may bring,
We also celebrate the birth of
Jesus, our Savior, Lord and King.

For it was many years ago upon
this special day, when Christ
was born
in Bethlehem in a manger filled
with hay.
A tiny babe in swaddling clothes,
born in a world of sin,
That He might all mankind help,
be true, honest, righteous men.

He walked this earth for many
years, He taught the sinner to
pray,
He healed the sick. He helped the
poor, in His great but humble
way.
He suffered more for all our sins
when He was nailed to the
cross,
But to Him, to us, His painful
death, was not a total loss.

He died that we might live again,
to be happy in a better life,
Where goodness and love shall
reign supreme with no more
war nor strife.
So on christmas day when you
celebrate, think of our Lord's
sacrifice,
And remember, tis the birthday
of our dear Lord, Jesus Christ;

Marlena Sabella
**Do You Wanna Try It
Again?**
When I first met you girl, you
had love in your eyes.
It was a special look, that made
me come alive.

But my life was all messed up,
and I was livin just in sin.
Hey girl, do you wanna try it
again?

I walked away from you before,
cause my own world was fallin
apart,
But you never walked away from
me,
You got through to my heart.

You showed that you loved me,
with a kind of love that stays,
Cause you put up with me and
my wondering ways.

And maybe this time we both
could win.
Hey girl, do you wanna try it
again?

I'm tired being lonely, and I'm
tired being blue,
And a man can't spend his life
alone,
So can I spend mine with you?

And I never want to go back, to
the world where I have been.
Hey girl, do you wanna try it
again?

And I know that you still love
me,
So why don't we just begin—
Hey girl, do you wanna try it
again?

Kathy L. Bracisco
HER TREMBLING HANDS

*To my very special Grandmother,
Mrs. L. D. Crader. Though we still
love in the same lifetime, I regret
our parting when it comes our
way. I will not regret, however,
our joys, our tears, and that we
both know how much we really
do love each other.*

As she lay there
In a world all her own,
Her eyes dance to a memory
Of a time long ago.
She smiles unconsciously
To thoughts no one knows;
She answers not to a single voice,
Yet, startles at an unfamiliar
noise.

Her mind content with the past
A heart that beats with great
effort;
She's given me so much joy
I wish this once, I could offer

comfort.
She returns to me
Only for a moment, I'm afraid;
I take her trembling hands
And in that moment, her life is
completed.

Dora M. Benway
MINNIE

*To Frankie and Velma my
inspiration*

A fictious thing was she.
Minnie was her name.
She always came to the children
in a funny game.
Day after day they would sit and
play with this secretive thing.
And I, never knowing the joy she
could bring.
When called upon as to who she
was.
They replied with such childish
glee,
She's just a friend, don't you see?

Paula Jackson Mendoza
TENNESSEE
Oh! mountains green and lush
with life,
You wild and beautous land
With your simple, honest and
hard working folk,
so quick to lend a hand.

Oh, how I love your peaceful
towns,
and animals wild and free.
In all the world there is but one
beautiful Tennessee.

The dawn breaks on our
mountain home,
With colors so bright they could
blind.
Then its glory blends to a
peaceful lull,
on a day we left behind.

If you'd search for the garden of
Eden,
I'd say it would have to be
Somewhere in these mountains
of my glorious Tennessee.

Kathy L. Bracisco
SOMETIMES . . . CONTENT

*To those who strive for glitter
and gold: I've found riches greater
than "Glitter and Gold" with
honest, hard work and rewarding
relationships.*

Sometimes . . .
I wish I were a ship out on the
sea
And there are times,
I wish I were an eagle flying high
and free.

Sometimes . . .
I wish I were an artist who could
paint a picture
And then there are times,
I wish I were an actor who's
achieved fame and fortune.

And sometimes . . .
I see the ship and the eagle flying
free,
And think, "How unhappy they
must be".

And sometimes . . .
When I see the artist and the
actor with fame and fortune,
I think, "How lonely they may
have become".

Norma Cobarrubio

Norma Cobarrubio
When Christmas Is Near
Bless you and holiday joy's!

When christmas is near,
We'd all get together with a
smile, and CHEER'S!
When christmas is near, it maybe
COLDED OUTSIDED.
But, inside OUR HEART'S ARE
WARM—with OUR LORD
BLESSING!
When christmas is near, also—
GOD, LOVE IS NEAR!
When christmas is hear, We'd—
REMEMBER! THE YEAR,
AND THANK—GOD! We'd—
maked it, and—HOPED FOR—
BETTER TOMORROW!
When christmas is near,
Someone—SPECIAL HAS,
GRATITUDE—
and—HAPPIEST, ESPECIAL FOR
YOU!
When christmas is near, of—
COURSE!—CHRISTMAS,
COULDN'T
be—CHRISTMAS, WITHOUT—
CHILDREN! And there,
CHRISTMAS—CAROL'S!
When christmas is near,
children—LOVE TO PLAYED
WITH THE,
SNOW! and GOD, BLESSING,
WHEN CHRISTMAS IS NEAR!

Mary J. Bowser
LITTLE NOELLE
Little Noelle, with your lovely face
You filled the cold, empty space,
left by the tolling of a knell
Over my own beloved little
daughter

Little Noelle, you stole my heart
Just as I were about to start,
Believing that I could never love
again
Doomed to a life of sheer
loneliness

Little Noelle, oh! how we need
one another
I, a daughter, you, a mother
Strengthening the tie that binds us
Struggling against all the odds

Little Noelle, we're no longer all

alone
With nobody to call our very own
Both looking through eyes of love
Toward a life filled with sheer
happiness

Alice A. Zimmerman
HER TIME
Her leafy eyes lay drooping,
biten by the icey snowmen of
yesteryear.
Her hair lay twisted in puffs of
white,
with traces of the old youth still
sprinkled within.
Her body stood bent over time's
crafty corner,
with scars of a million days
etched in her grooves.
Her arms lay dry and cracked
with age,
and held a dozen tiny birds
within her embrace.
Her legs still twitched as they
suckled the earth,
and a dynasty of ants made their
home.
Her heart lay among the delicate
china,
with each chamber housing a
daisy.
Her time would soon come when
nature decreed,
and she would sprout a seed.

Cecily Atyes Varner
THE MAN
He will give you wine
He will whisper in your ear
He will tell you, you are divine
He will say he does care

He wil take your hand
He will take your love
He will promise you land
He will promise things above

He will tell you he loves you
He will tell you, you are the one
He will tell you he wants you
You will hear the same old song

Beware of his lies
He will take you to lunch
Beware of his tales
Beware of his touch

You will find he did not really
care
You will find you were not the
one
He will hold some other's hand,
But still take your love.

Esther E. Peterson
THANKSGIVING
The pilgrims came in sixteen
twenty
To this wonderful land to live,
After two hard and fruitful years
They had many thanks to give.

So on the last Thursday of
November,
When all the harvest was done,
They decided to have a feast
To celebrate the victories won.

They called it a day of
thanksgiving
To thank the Lord above
For all His help and guidance,
His patience and His love.

Thank you, Lord, for everything

All you gave and are still giving,
Every day shall be Thanksgiving
day
As long as we are living.

Marcia Garr
THAT GREAT DAY
There will come a day
and it's not so far away
the good will rise up
and take God's hand,
the wicked will finally
understand
from dust we were unto dust
we will be
the dead will rise up from the sea
the dead in Christ will stir and
rise
the love of God showing in their
eyes
the righteous will be saved
the wicked will not
when God our savior casts his lot
God will shake all nations and
the people within
when Jesus his son comes again.

Evelyn M. Seaton
MY LORD
My eyes looked to Heaven
and "My Lord," I did see,
For He parted the clouds
and sent a sunbeam to me.

Then I spoke to my Lord
about all my plans,
How I wanted to see Him
and His nail-scarred hands.

That on earth I grow tired
and sometimes lose my way,
But wanting to see him
more and more each day.

Just to follow that sunbeam
to my home up above
To live forever and ever
with the Lord that I love.

Then He sent down His love
and my world became bright,
For I felt His Dear Presence
in the sunbeam of light.

My heart became happy
and so completely gay.
For I had talked to my Lord
and my Savior that day.

Judi E. Macy
GRAMPS

---

*Dedicated to my father, Paul
Shipman, and my two sons, Chad
and Bret.*

A man with spectacles upon his
nose and graying hair,
Rocking back and forth in his
favorite chair.
Wrinkles wandering upon his
aged face.
An imprint of history they do
line and trace.

With a pipe in his mouth and
slippers on his feet,
He looks like a symbol of life
that's contented and complete.
A voice which speaks with
wisdom and sincerity,
In today's society, a treasured
rarity.

With a grandson perched upon

each knee,
Admiration and respect surround
the three.
On their lips echo, "I love you,
Gramps,"
In their eyes and in their hearts,
he's a Champ!

Carol W. Williams
A MAN A CHILD
I saw the soldiers go marching by.
I felt the tears come to my eyes.
As I stood by the side.
I saw my son, go marching by.
Off to war he will go, a man
A child no more.

As I stood by the side.
I saw the past years go by.
Oh what joy that child did bring
A man, A child no more.

I heard the drums of the
marching men.
I saw a man's life began.
Off to war he will go.
I man, A child no more.

Kathleen Gale Howard
**Outside My Kitchen
Window**
There outside my Kitchen
Window, far beyond the darken
sky.
Over the bending trees, where the
wind flys.
Somewhere I hear a voice, calling
me. My soul joins the sailing
wind,
searching for it's energy.

My soul connects, painting, Yes?
forfilled I believe.
No this energy keeps failing me.
In search of a calling my soul
flys.
Such a blinding light I see, such
music, outside my Kitchen
Window.

Forfilled with a feeling, Love? I
can only guess.
My soul feels empty, my body
trembles.
Body and soul are in a shallow
void. Which way to search?
which way to reachout? To be
gone of void would bring great
uncertainy. Underneath my flesh
and deeper than my aching
soul,
a fire burns uncontrolably hot.
Waiting and wondering, will
this
be the end of me?

Fear not dear aching soul, for
waiting will bring you what
you
desire. It is there waiting for you,
watching you,
Outside My Kitchen Window.

Julie Ann Bailey Lipman
A CHILD
Did you ever think of the joy a
child can bring?
They can make you cry and they
can make you sing.
They are the joy of life.
The dream of every husband and
wife.
A girl, a boy,
It's still a great joy.
To know they are a part of you

And the person you really love,
too!
To watch them grow from year to
year.
To help them with their hardship
and fear.
A child is a gift of God and of love.
A love two people worship like
the heavens above.
They fill your life with love and
happiness.
Thanks to God above.
For sending us this bundle of
love.
The special kind of love only a
child can give to you.
I thank you, God, for the
wonderful gift—our child, I
really do!

Darla L. West
CANDY HEARTS

---

*To anyone who ever felt love at
first sight . . . Darla is published
author of "Love Every Month",
Copyright 1981*

You gave me your music
I rendered my art
Love is for sharing
our sweet candy hearts.

You filled me with laughter
I offered pure joy
Love is exchanging
when a girl finds a boy.

Eyes twinkled, arms cuddled,
lips kissed like soft pearls.
With two hearts united, we
promised a lifetime
in a make-believe candy heart
world.

Our journey was ended
as fast as it came
—to be lifted from romance
like a swift hurricane.
You refer to mistakes
I still call it pain.

Hello, you long bitter memories
Goodbye, my sweet candy
hearts . . .

Margaret L. Fellinger
DOCTOR-EMERGENCY!
The telephone rings in the still
night
You fumble around and turn on
the light.
The call an emergency come
right away
Must have been at least twelve of
them today.

However there is no need to find
your socks
You had them on-into bed you
did flop
But the shoes you can see just
one of them
The other must have been left in
the den.

Shirt and pants neatly on a
bedside chair.
Looking closer the coat is also
there.
The car gives a start and moves
with much ease
You reach the hospital like a
slight breeze.

The patient is breathing, holding
his own.
You start the procedure he gives
a moan.
By morning when the dark sky
turns to light
Everything that's wrong then
turns out all right.

Another body is well on the mend.
Prayers to heaven concerned did
send.
But was God alone who knew the
whole plan
For the life that was spared was
by His hand.

Joyce K. Howze
TOUCH—AND—GO
Some lovers only
    touch
    and
    go . . .
playing hide-and-seek
    within the shadows
    of a dream,
leaving behind the
    teasing taste
    of a kiss,
the faintest trace
    of a footprint
    on the heart.
Love to them is not
    a waiting game . . .
they only know to
    touch
    and
    go.

Christine A. Montoya
OPTIONS
With so many options, ways to go,
    How does one choose which
        direction to grow?
How is it known what amount
        of ones time,
    To attribute to others or take
        solely as mine?

If ever again, our paths they
        should meet,
    I'll learn to know you, you'll learn
        to know me.
As time lapsed between, passed
        through these years,
    Brought changes about, erased all
        past tears.

Speaking solely for me, with time
        I've become,
    A better woman in many respects,
        Need improvement in some,
        Trying daily.

Ronald Charles Sklar
**Tolstoy and Yasanya
    Polyana**
How silvery the rails of Ural Steel,
Forged by enslaved ancestral hands
Of Russian masses, who, before
    cruel Tsars have to kneel
And bow to Nicholas' harsh
    commands!

At Bakalsk, women with hands,
    raw and sore,
Wallow in dirt-prisoners of the
    mine—
And fill wooden carts with Ural
    ore
For Tsarists usurpers, who, life
    with hardship combine.

To keep the Imperial Court going,
Working hands exploit the Upper

Kama,
While a working hand more
    knowing,
Is writing of his ruler's ending
    drama—
A Russian genius on a maple-
    desk throne
Is declaring Tsar Nicholas' final
    trauma,
And his thoughts still threaten,
    today, every tyrant's home
From the shadows of Yasanya
    Polyana.

Veronica Seeman

Veronica Seeman
ALONE
From childhoods hour
    I have not been
As others were
    I have not seen
as others saw
    I could not bring
my passions from
    a common spring
From the source
    I have not taken
My sorrow
    I could not awaken
My heart to joy at.

Robin Louise Macias
LOVE

_____

*To my sisters Victoria and
Veronica Martin, for they
inspired this poem.*

_____

Love is sweet and sometimes
    sour, also gentle and wild.
    But super when it comes your
    way.

Love is around every corner, just
    waiting to be found
    like a wilderness to be explored,
    Or a City to be tamed.

Love is heartache and pain, But in
    it's own way
    Wonderful just the same.

Love is something different for us
    all, But alike in many ways.
    Love can be quick and disappear.
    But soon to return and whisper
    in our ear.

Love can find the evil and
    goodness in our souls,
    But something you must
    experience on our own.
    To know a little of true love is a
    very wonderful,

experience for young and old.

Love is the color in our world,
    But as it is told,
    It can't be bought or sold.

Love is for small and the tall.
    When we're small or young we
    call it puppy love,
    But when we're grown we call it
    romance.

But if by chance you find it never
    ever let it go.

Because love is very wonderful
    just the same.

Mary-Alice Wightman
IN MEMORY . . .
Our beloved old truck
Is like family—
Each scratch and each dent
Holds a memory.

We cringe to let go
Of one so faithful,
Remembering back—
Times so wonderful.

It has served us well,
Hauled many a load,
Climbed the steepest hills,
Mountain creeks did ford.

Rescued some in snow,
Moved friends and neighbor,
Touch, dependable,
Saved us much labor.

It has its own hum,
Still starts like a song.
Good trucks never die—
They just roll along . . .

Shannon Dahlke
A Runner's Last Thoughts
The finish is nearer now,
and the urge to come in first.
Lord help me and show me how,
lift my feet for I'm a cow.

Why is running such a thirst,
and why are my sore feet cursed?
My legs are numb and heavy,
my muscles ready to burst.

I wish I had my chevy,
I could drive and win the race.
Spectators, them I envy,
on the sidelines, the bevy.

The ribbon brakes at my pace,
and flashes shine in my face.
The race is over, I won,
now I wonder, was it fun?

Elenor M. Mitchell
DECEMBER
December meant ten
    When the Romans ruled,
Their year started with March,
    Thus December numbered ten.
Somebody revised the calendar.
    Tho December meant ten
It became twelve on the calendar.
    Was Jesus born the tenth month
Or was it the twelfth?
    A sinless Mary to Joseph
    betrothed.
Gabriel bore a message to Mary,
    She would be the mother of the
    Messiah.
Mary unknown by any man,
    Was with child by the Holy
    Spirit.
Joseph not knowing the source
    Decided to set aside their

contract.
An angel appeared in his dream,
    Telling him to take Mary as
    his wife.
The child's name would be Jesus
    Meaning, He would save
    people from sin.

Aileen Lee Berger
THE ROPE
I saw a rope upon the ground,
It was tangled and twisted 'round.
Its ends were frayed, and stains it
    bore
It told a story without sound.

How like my life it seemed to be,
With its tangles and twists of
    fate.
Its stains and knots mute
    evidence
Of the lessons I learned—too late.

Now, patient hands could take
    that rope
And its tangles and knots remove.
But stains of use are there to stay,
And fraying ends can only
    prove—

That in our lives, knots can be
    loosed,
And some tangles can be made
    straight.
But scars of past hurts leave stains
That will the future dominate.

Alberta A. Cox
The Balance Wheel Of God
God's world is in perfect balance.
The stars are in their place.
Each particle of earth is set
Within its rightful space.

The moon, the sun and all the
    planets,
The component parts as well
Are much we take for granted
As we do not fully understand it.

The balance wheel is so precise.
There's nought that's out of line.
He keeps all moving parts in orbit.
They work in perfect time.

Each blade of grass, the very trees
He's worked out scientifically.
And even with the substance in
    the sod,
He's planned to move
    methodically.

Stability plays precision's theme
On earth beneath heven's realm.
Constructively He's set in space
God's balance wheel at the helm.

Marianne Drenberg
SOLSTICE
I know a place where summer is;
Where loving thoughts are
    shared.
December's misty lights will glow
When June's sunshine is
    compared
To rampant waves of oceantide.
We watched sandpipers run
In wild freedom by our side
With mist and shadows, wind
    and sun.
We know the sounds of other
    days
Are blest with thougths we share.
I know a place where summer
    stays;
Deep in the hearts of us who care.

Our World's Best Loved Poems

Kathleen Hoffman
JANUARY 1945

When you're 21 and two weeks
  your life should not be in the
  past tense.
Your niece that you couldn't live
  to see,
  should not think of you and
  love you
  as if you had never been real.
Were you shy?
Did you love art?
Did you like to write?
You sound so much like me.
Am I your replacement in this
  world?
Do you live through me, can you
  you really see me
  in a better world?
Then if this is so, I'll try to be the
  you
  that was not allowed to live.
I'll write and look with love on
  art.
But to tell the truth
  I'd much rather you were here
  right now.
I wish I had gotten the chance
  to meet you
  in reality, and not in other's
  memories.

Mrs. Walton (Elaine) Holst
LEST YOU FORGET

Lest you forget; have you heard
  this before,
Lest you forget; I'll tell you once
  more.
Please don't forget, my dear,
Try to remember that I am still
  here.
If anything goes wrong in
  something you do,
Keep your promise and to me be
  true.
Your heart is breakable the same
  as mine,
If you'd remember this,
  everything would be fine.
Always remember that love isn't
  a bet—
And I'll always love you; lest you
  forget.
Lest you forget the things that we
  did,
To bring them all back, just lift
  the lid—
Of my memory book I've kept so
  long,
Don't tell me now that it was all
  wrong.
Do you remember, the first time
  we met,
If you must leave, my eyes said
  'not just yet'.
Would it be easy for you to forget
  so soon,
If music were playing, would you
  remember the tune—
If you left, what a heartache I'd get;
Remember I need and love you,
  lest you forget.

David B. Robinson
Thy Heart Would Linger

Fain would I be at thy side now,
  When all the clouds are falling,—
For in deception, happiness
  Is there to share for calling.

So in our idle while we sat;
  We waited for tomorrow,

A sure conjunction soon to come
  And meet us without sorrow.

But so we shall for it is meet;
  It fills the heart with gladness.
What circumstantial countenance
  Could thus a site impress?

And if I could, know you I would,
  To share this brighter hour.
The wrath of man has shown our
  souls
  This penance to devour.

Kelli Lynn Semple
WHAT A DAY

*I dedicate this WITH ALL MY
LOVE to you MOM and DADDY
because all the HAPPINESS,
LOVE and BEAUTY I find in the
ocean I have always seen in you.*

A seagull flies by, so graceful and
  free:
Oh how I wish that I was he.
The water's anger and
  beauty combine as one:
Reflecting the beams from the
  high golden sun.
An old man passes by on his way:
Enjoying every minute of this
  glorious day.
The boats rock gently, on this sea
  of hope;
making my troubles and burdens
  much easier to cope.
A lonesome dog looks towards
  me for a friend;
He comes closer than shyly backs
  up again.
With more confidence he comes
  back to me;
And lies at my feet to share this
  scenery.
My heart runs wild filled with
  love and joy;
I feel like a child with a brand
  new toy.
A broken shell catches my eye;
But to me it's beauty shall never
  die.
My soul races with the wind;
Hoping this moment will never
  end.
Nothing do I need for this high;
Just the ocean and the sky.
The beautys' been here, but my
  mind a closed door;
So God Bless this day and please
  make lots more.

Mary Louise Merrill
A LIGHT IN THE NIGHT

Its night, so dark
the times are shakey
the times for peace.
oh wonder, why?
Do not wonder, even when times
  seem better,
it is dark—from peace.
But a light still shines,
in a world of woe,
a light of vigilant prayer.
a cry for peace!
a plea! for mercy,
to bring stronger recourse to man.

The hour of time sets on edge
weaving toward tribulation.
A chance we take
what fate, what fate!

is ours?
But, a light still shines in the
  night;
for men of God, keep praying,
a vilgilance of hope.
oh night! oh dark!
there is hope.

Robert E. Trealoff
Rain Bow Kiss

*Dedicated to my darling
daughter,. . . . Charissa to whom
as a father I'm yet a stranger, but
with time and God she'll come to
know me.*

Remember when I held you?
In early morning, new dawn hours.
At the Sun's first breaking light.
As I held you close and poured
  out my love
the sky opened up and started to
  rain.
A very sweet warm, misty,
  sprinkling rain.
You wanted to run indoors to
  escape the feeling
of soaked up in rain and of all of
  me.
With a firm, assuring hug, your
  doubt is overcome
to welcome back me and the rain.
Lost in a loving imbrace and
  kisses of fire and heaven
we put out the rain.
Awaken from our Romantic,
  encounter of nature's minnie
  shower,
the miracle of life and sun, . . .
  shines out.
As the last kiss rolls off your lips
  and you look up at me, . . .
there is the magic.
Past my love burning eyes and
  heart, in the distant sky,
is God's sign of love too.
The most of ever so beautiful of
  RainBows I've ever seen.
Being awaken out of the rain, and
  warmth and joy of sunshine,
came the Great RainBow KISS

Inez Chambers
MY WAY

To Jim, my love

How many times in the course of
  the day
Do we subconsciously fight to
  have Our way
We say that we love you, you
  know that we care
How could we manage without
  you there
But, Please do it My way, No
  Don't prune that tree
It isn't Your Mother we're going
  to see
Please do dig the garden and do chop
  the wood
If I'm feeling grumpy, I don't
  think You should.
Don't growl at me, I won't stand
  your bad moods
How come we're eating Your
  favourite foods?
Pin-pricking, niggling our way
  through the years

Sharing the smiles and hiding the
  tears
Til the day we awake to find
  we're alone
No one to growl at, no one to
  moan.
A life spent with fuss over trivial
  things
And the few magic moments that
  giving way brings
Yet when you're alone, how much
  did it matter
If we'd washed the windows or sat
  for a chatter.
How very important those
  moments now seem
When, by loving and giving you
  helped build their dream.

"O" Clutts
MAMA LION

*Bu: You are all the inspiration in
the world to me*

On old paws
A once simple creature,
Like the beasts,
Has grown new claws
Just like the rest of the bitches
Mama lion, no more
She runs with the pack
From mountain to shore.

Tammy Romans
A Christmas Consists Of . . .

A Christmas consists of
  many little things,
Like snowballs, sleding, and
  sleigh bells that ring.

Then there's the Christmas tree
  with it's colors so bright,
It brings happiness to the
  house all through the night.

Of course there's the dinner
  the family is all there,
No one is stingy,
  for it's our time to share.

The presents are opened,
  everyone is so proud.
It's so warm and peaceful,
  as each laughs aloud.

The white powdery snow
  is falling and falling,
"Ho, ho, ho", Santa is calling.

Mary Lee Hayes
DESPERATE DESIRE

Devoted to fidelity
I never plan to be.
As the ice may break on a frozen
  lake
When the sun shines faithfully,
So I may change and rearrange
Toward a drastic destiny.

Purposes of passion
Never perfectly planned
May finalize fears and toy with
  tears,
But how can they be banned?
There is no chain to tie the vein
That tells me I'm a woman.

Damned in this desperate desire,
As my lust leaps ever higher,
Is the sovereign sin of knowing
  when
There's more to flames than fire.
Thus in my youth I'll remain
  uncouth
So my spirit will never retire.

Dennis O'Brien
The Night Before Christmas Was Never Like This!

Amidst the metal and glaring
    lights,
White figures were luring into
    my sights.

Monitors flashing, keeping their
    tunes,
And scalpels were cutting on this
    full moon.

But lo did I not ever expect,
What happened that night in
    retrospect.

Emerging from red a head
    appeared,
A girl would soon follow; I feared.

But shock to my eyes it did unfold,
Dangling between legs, "a boy" I
    was told!

The breathing grew heavy and
    white was my face,
So swiftly I flew lest I be
    disgraced.

And finding a couch I sat in a daze,
"This must be a dream, here
    comes the next phase."

But quickly I knew my world was
    no dream,
Just a beginning, that's just what
    it seemed.

So lest I be boring and trite in my
    rhyme,
Farewell all my friends, my son I
    must find!

Hazel J. Kesely
THE QUESTION

Where do you go when you're
    weary?
There's no one you can see around.
Where do you go when you're
    hungry,
and there's no food to be found?

Where do you go when you're
    thirsty?
And the water wells are dry?
Where do you go when you're
    naked,
and clothes for price—you can't
    buy?

When I'm weary, I go to my
    Saviour,
He's there, but not to the eye.
When I'm hungry, he feeds me
    from heaven,
it seems to come from the sky.

When I'm thirsty, the fountain is
    flowing,
the water, so pure and serene,
when I'm naked, his arms go
    around me.
I've been fed, I've drank and I'm
    clean.

Lydia Venta-Dobrovolsky
THE NEWBORN CHILD

When love, and star,
and spark of Glory—
Will make anew
a kindled story:
in every heart
of all mankind—
will be alive
the newborn child . . .
Then every mind

will grow in light—
the life will shine
so kind and bright!
This wonder—
Will be easy done:
the darkness gone,
life's bliss is won!
With countless sparks
new sun is born ! ! !

Kathy E. Abbott
Transmigration Of Souls

Death, is but the passing of the
    soul-taking with it—
    The Spark of Life.
As it flickers from here to there-
    To where—
The days are phantom days.
And where, their ghostly
    footsteps tread!
Chained to earth—By their
    incomplete dreams,
The dreams that they left behind
    them,
And are no longer able to fulfill—
But still, they find mortals
Fit instruments for their Ghostly
    pranks—
And they bend them to their will!
And then perhaps their dreams
    will be fulfilled—
And so they make mischief still—
Though they are gone, passed on.
They make more mischief still!

Mary Ann B. Henning
A SIMPLE THING

I dedicate these webs to "Being Alive", for as long as our hearts are pumping, we can drink in a flower's color, and can encourage others to breathe life into their own dream petals.

To be alive, "a simple thing"
Taken for granted
By toes treading the pavement
Too busy to think of such "a
    simple thing"

"A simple thing" this life we live
Yet, we cherish it not
Waste it
In reckless frolic

One day will come a rattle at the
    door
From the man in black
Waiting . . .
To discuss such "a simple thing."

Debra S. Boyken
SILENT RAINDROPS

Tears like silent raindrops fall,
    cascading down silken cheeks.
From memories so dim,
    of love lost and promises
    broken.
For pain and sorrow suffered,
    when you left my life.
You left me to learn how cruel
    love can be to a young heart.

Tears like silent raindrops fall,
    and in the gentle breeze
I hear your name whispered.
    slowly in my mind I remember
All our times together,
    the painful times apart.
And oh so lonely without each
    others love
    to keep us going.

When we are together
    I treasure each moment
And lock the time in my heart to
    bring out . . .
. . . In Tears Like Silent
    Raindrops . . .

George Cole
ISLAND GIRL

Island girl, island girl,
Sing a song for me.
Make it softer than the breeze
That blows across the sea.

Island girl, island girl,
Play a tune for me.
Make it finer than the spring
    birds
As they chirp their melody.
Island girl, island girl,
Won't you hear my plea.
I never had no one
To sing a song for me.

Elaine E. Enterline
Controlled Conception

The Scientific Specifics came
    today.
Speaking words of controlled
    conception.
The evolution revolution had
    begun,
To deceive one and alls perception.

Followers, oh yes there were so
    many.
Lining up for clinical
    reproduction.
They did not know what they
    were in for.
There was to be all new
    reconstruction.

The Specifics manipulated
    human eggs.
Then the proper environment
    was engineered.
They tore down the structure of
    DNA,
There was nothing that they
    feared.

Mass production was applied to
    biology.
The guinea pigs never saw
    themselves as fools.
Somehow the Scientific Specifics,
Misplaced the golden rule.

When did all of this disaster
    begin.
Actually Huxley "planted the
    seed."
It was all in the name of
    scientific research,
Hiding behind a mask of greed.

The followers began to cry and
    moan.
As if a horrible plague fell upon
    them.
They began to resent the effects
    of bio-engineering,
And the results it had on their
    women and men.

They cried, "Moral quicksand has
    a hold on us.
Achievment had us all
    mesmerized.
We cannot forget the
    fundamental implications,
We've reviewed the research and
    realize."

"Public assessment of your work
    is negative.
We've had enough of your
    bio-screening.
Go away, do not analyze us,
Can't you hear our monsters
    screaming."

Geri Knapp
JENNALEE

To Jenna Vanessa, this poem is dedicated to a beautiful little girl and her wonderful parents, two of my dearest friends Phyllis and Jack . . . Love Geri.

When I was just a small child,
I had a doll named Jennalee,
She had painted lips, big blue
    eyes, her hair was blonde and
    free,
I'd hold her close and love her,
Friends to the end were we,
Secrets shared, things rejoiced,
Simply, Jennalee and me,
Now here I stand a woman,
Grown up, mature thats me!
But today I climbed the attic stairs,
For it was there you see,
That mama put, (when I had
    grown),
My darling Jennalee,
Painted lips, big blue eyes, her
    hair still hanging free
And with tears in my eyes,
She took me back to the child I
    used to be . . .

M. Jonathan Adams
SHE'S GONE

The night sky has a fresh coat
    of black semi-gloss paint.
Pictures of her flash on it,
    and I start to feeling faint.
Soft and unforgiving sounds
    roll by my shuffling shoes.
Never know the price you pay,
    until you really lose.
Streetlamps, signs, and
    silhouettes—
    a rainbow of colors dead,
walk slowly through the
    wilderness
    that empties out my head.
Ceramic dogs on dark front lawns
    growl at my foggy form.
I only seek a hiding place,
    in hope of getting warm,
I end up finding my way home,
    though I hate to be alone,
and look out to the neon sky
    wondering, but not asking why
    she's gone.

Our World's Best Loved Poems

Leslie G. Carr
PASSOVER SONG

Dedicated to Mr. and Mrs. Walden for the service and dedication they have shown for our edification.

I am a flower as fair as He
  bestowed,
  Gleaming white—high in the
  mountain peak.
By a crevice in the cool still air,
  sun shines warm
  Upon my flowering cheek.
Pure is the world I see, filled with
  green and blue and white.
Yet as the wind feathers lightly,
  caressing my delicate brow,
  I perceive I am alone.

I am rare, like the hidden
  edelweiss.
Seeing from this vantage view the
  vastness of the universe,
And the earth's untrodden beauty.

At night the paleness of my
  fragile blossom glows through
  the gloom;
And as the dew touches my face,
  it is cool—
  It is good.

I, at the top of the highest peak,
  see the crest of the morning
  dawn,
Feel the chill in the air, breathe
  the exhilaration—
Bend to catch the first light, to
  reflect the sun.

I am a white and beautiful jewel,
  rare in beauty and form.
But none of my kin exist.
  I breathe the air alone.

The grandeur of the stars cannot
  quench my weeping passion.
Tears of silken milk flow from
  my breast to nourish the stone
  below.
  I am too rare.
I was given all, the high of the
  mountain peak,
  And none to share.

Noreen A. Saemenes
A THANKFUL HEART
Thank you for the flowers
and all the hours to enjoy them
for the birds in the trees
and their melodies from heaven
Lord, I thank you

      I thank you Lord

thank you for the stars
placed so brilliantly in the sky
their radiance, their glory
let not a night go by
that I don't thank you

      I thank you Lord

I see the wide open plains
with their beauty untold
the majestic mountains
you made them so mighty and so
  bold
my heart says thank you Lord

your vast oceans
your deepest seas
myriads of creatures
the misty breeze

you speak to me in all of these
      and I just can't thank you
enough.

Lisa Collins
ICE LAND
Come across
In lonely winter
The starkness
Of breathless
Sight
The vision of
White crisped
Tree limbs
Brittle
Against wind's
Ice

Helplessly frozen
A world
Seized in its motion
Nature's course
Would not
Refrain

So walk with me and
Venture
Journey and explore
Find the land
You once knew
Intimately
Now buried outside
Your door.

James R. Cook
A Vision Of Life Through
  ## Your Eyes
I'm tuned in to your wavelength.
  Your thoughts are clear in my
  mind.
  You're transmitting at full
  strength.
  I am amazed by what I find—

I see the world through your eyes.
My senses tingle with the sight.
Perceived this way the world is a
  surprise.
Your consciousness illuminates it
  in a glowing yellow light.

I can sense the world with your
  feelings.
I can feel your pleasure and pain.
  I wish to thank you for the
  moments I'm stealing
by placing myself in your brain.

When you've learned thought-
  projection
I'll return the favor in kind.
Now I must return to my own
  perception,
back in my own body and mind.

Cheri Peterson
REMEMBERING
The night was warm and a gentle
  wind blew,
I walked by the evening shore
  thinking of you.
I gazed at the waves gently
  kissing the shore,
Knowing our moments shared
  could happen no more.
I closed my eyes softly, let my
  mind drift away,
The scents and sounds remind
  me of that day.
I gave you my heart, it seemed so
  right then,
Such happiness could never
  happen again.

Your arms were so strong, yet

your gentle embrace,
Make the memories of your
  kisses so hard to erase.
The memories are fading but
  never quite disappear,
When I think of our happiness, I
  pray you are here.

A chill wind starts blowing and a
  mist now rolls in,
And the realization that I never
  will see you again.
Where once we left footprints
  together in the sand,
The sea now erases where in
  dream I saw you stand.

I turn and walk slowly from this
  recaptured memory,
Yet knowing it will return,
  whenever I walk by the sea.

Joseph Rommel
NANDIE
A thief you were
Taking what you shouldn't have,
  What you couldn't have,
And leaving a painful void;
An emptiness which can never be
  filled.
Why did you seduce me?
Why did you have to steal my
  heart?

A ruthless thief you were
Giving me all I shouldn't have,
  All I couldn't keep,
And it didn't matter what the pain;
Nor did you care who you
  betrayed.
Three other hearts you have at
  home,
So why did you take mine?

But what a lovely thief you were,
And in spite of how you've
  cheated me
You'll never know how much
  you're missed;
Or how I long to taste your lips
  again,
  To see your smile again,
  To love you again.

Judi E. Macy
TAKE ME BACK HOME

*Dedicated to my home town,
Sidney, Ohio.*

Sense the breathtaking array of
  autumn hues,
The crispness of air which
  soothingly cools.
The graphic habitat of nature's
  fineness,
The intimacy which generates
  kindness . . .
Take me back home where I grew.

View the All American City of
  Opportunity,
Filled with its multitalented
  community.
Where the right to be an
  individual is realized,
And the philosophy of democracy
  is exercised . . .
Take me back home where
  strength is in unity.

For I feel I am never a stranger
  there.
Hospitality electrifies the air.

Where rustic nostalgia penetrates,
And friends and family
  communicate . . .
Take me back home where they
  care!

Dorothy M. Adams
THE CHALICE
Gone but forgotten, the tears of
  yesterday,
Living deep within me, the joys of
  years fled by,
And yet the poignant sorrows, in
  their heartless, searing way,
Have burned a thousand
  memories, left the embers there
  to die.

And still without those sorrows, I
  should not dare to kneel
before the altar of your dreams in
  meditation, feel
the arrow pointed toward my
  heart, the Ecstasy is mine,
Because the bitter and the sweet
  in memory intertwine.

Lori Jean Skarsten
I BELIEVE IN FANTASY

*This poem is dedicated to Nancy
and Debbie, and was inspired by
all the good times we had during
childhood.*

I believe in fantasy, like I believe
  in you and me
I believe through fantasy our
  dreams become reality
Just like you and me, And our
  dreams may seem like fantasy
Until you believe in them like me.

P. C. Hannah
SOMETIMES

*To the man who inspires my
creativity and so much more . . .
Tom*

Sometimes I question why I care.
I wonder what I see
that makes me quiver so inside
when you just smile at me.
Sometimes I think that I should
  leave—
should turn and walk away,
not looking back or thinking
  back
on how I want to stay.
Sometimes I cry myself to sleep
because I just can't bear
the thought of giving all my love
to a man who doesn't care.
Sometimes I call myself a fool,
but who am I to grieve
for the things I miss while
  staying here,
when I just don't choose to leave?

Lois Johnson Allen
SECRET LOVE
Oh! How my heart
break's to see
you in the arm's
of another
How I long to tell
you what my heart
conceal's
For I can not
For I too am in the
arm's of another as well.

483

Kathy A. Richardson
WOUNDED MEMORIES
I sit amongst a bed of weeds
Forgetting all my present needs,
Staring at a field nearby
With emptiness, my soul now
   bleeds.
I look up to the fearless sky
Searching for the answer why,
My graceful horse with golden
   flair,
Had to leave his soul to die.
I could not see, nor could I hear
The pain I felt, but it was there.
Angry now I yelled with fright
Until myself, I could not scare.
I began to think of days so bright,
I smiled with memories of
   delight.
They seemed like dreams, unreal
   and fake,
But they were mine, that
   darkened night.
And then I walked down to the
   lake,
My wounded heart about to
   break,
I stared into a strangers face,
Which was mine by no mistake.
Then a lonesome tear with grace
Fell upon the water's lace,
Yet leaving still my golden horse
In my heart for time to trace.

Gloria Jean Robertson
Our New Young Couple

———————————

*Written for the Wedding DAY of
My daughter ELLEN on 29
OCTOBER 1983.*

———————————

Ellen and Gabriel—
Together, 'till the end,
Loving each other,
Being each other's friend;
Caring enough thru the
   hardships,
Knowing how to bend;
Realizing that, many obstacles,
Surely will try to descend;
Steadfastly, marching forward,
Their union, to defend!

Betty Irene Thomas
GOD LOVES YOU
When God created man,
He had the master plan.
Made him a little lower than the
   angels.
But man took God's paradise,
Turned to Satan and his lies,
But even then God was loving you.

Then Jesus left his throne,
Gave up his heavenly home.
Exchanged it for his cross at
   calvary.
Then he died there in your place,
In shame and in disgrace,
Don't you see that is God loving
   you.

Christ left an empty tomb,
Which sealed the devil's doom,
Then he went back home again
   to get things ready.
When God's "Clock" for time is
   through,
He'll come back for me and you,
Oh, that is God saying—"I Love
You".

Judy A. Richardson
WINTER
Icy chandeliers,
Hanging from the trees,
Tinkling e'er softly
In a frosty breeze.

Raindrops in crystal,
Covering the ground,
Vanish in seconds
When the sun's around.

Scrawny, dark fingers
'Gainst a deep blue sky,
Tipped with white polish,
Proudly lifted high.

Water turned to glass,
'Mid a field of snow,
Mirrors winter's sky,
When the sun's aglow.

All winter's symbols,
Glorious and fair,
Are like bright crystal—
Yea! beyond compare!

Clyde Dwain Dodd
STATION TO STATION
As I enter the Church, there on
   the wall,
I see fourteen plaques, that tell it
   all.
In every one I find a sad story,
how Jesus faced death, but gained
   His glory.
They show He was tortured, and
   put on display,

then nailed to a cross in utter
   dismay.
His mother Mary, wept for her
   Son
and watched Him die, for the
   good He had done.
His pain and His suffering, was so
   very unjust,
We'll praise Him forever, because
   He died for us.

Gretchen Price
Early Morning Person

———————————

*This poem is dedicated to my
mother. Without whose help and
support I would've never made it.*

———————————

I stand in the dark velvet
   morning
and watch the silent sky.
I hear the sweet clear chirping
of the early morning birds nearby,
and I listen as the wind
caresses the waiting trees.

As I walk along the darkened

houses watch me quietly.
And I wonder what's inside them?
I watch the clouds roll across the
   sky
and I wonder where they're going
and I wish I were going with them.

Iris Lanore Breves
A CHANGE
It was exciting
when they put a bus route
on our street.
In the dark
of evening
we sat
in the front porch swing
and watched
this lighted
bright box on wheels
bounce by . . .
it was big and noisy.
It connected us
with Houston Avenue
with downtown shops
lighted
on Saturday nights.
It connected us
with people
going somewhere.
It was brighter
than the moon!
It punctuated
our quiet evening
reverie.

Nancy Jean Smith
LOVE IS
What is love? Is love a feeling
Or a thought? Is it something
That can be seen and felt, or is
It some magical invisible power
That comes over us? If I tell you
I love you would I be wrong? If
I tell you I care would it really
Matter? There are many different
Ways of caring and different
   degrees
Of love. You can show love to
Everybody and it will be different.
Sometimes I do not understand as
Now. How am I to know a person
If there is no love? Can't people
Understand that this is what it's
All about. To love is to care.
To care is to love.

Helen Elaine Repinski
**The Children Want To
   Know**
Do flowers grow in heaven?
The children want to know
Does the sun shine at seven
And where does the rain go?
And when the snow begins to fall
Do they send it all below?
How come we only see blue
And where does the green grass
   grow?

Do angels play their harps?
Why can't we hear the tune?
Does my Daddy play football
And have a T.V. in his room?
Jesus can stop our space ship
By just putting out his hand
He can give them directions
To people in outer-space land.

Please answer
We children want to know
All about heaven
Before it is time to go.

April M. Vergobbi
TWO MONTHS
a carefree summer day
the river clear and cold to the
   touch

we had all the time in the world
and were not thinking of
   anything but each other

we waded and splashed
laughing all the while
happy to be together

then you ventured on your own
   upstream
supported by a broken tree branch

i watched you walk
you were barefoot
had no shirt on
and your jeans were carefully
   rolled up

you stopped in places
trying to catch fish with your
   bare hands
your resemblance to
   "Huckleberry Finn" came to
   mind

after what seemed like forever
you once again joined me
we drenched one another with
   the cool water
and then snuggled into each
   other's arms

Christine Ullmann
NIGHT AND GRACE
I used to walk alone at night,
Listening to the stillness,
And hearing the striking of my
   feet against the earth.
I would listen to the beating of
   my heart,
And study the melody of night
   sounds.

Once, as I so walked,
I heard God walking just behind
   me,
And calling me softly to wait.
I turned and saw nothing—
Only the moon shining pure and
   clear,
As it shines on hallowed ground,
And ebony branches sillouetted
On a crystalline sky.

And then, as mortals do,
I turned and ran from God,
Not knowing that, in my fleeing,
I had been found.

You who walk in a night
Where no God seeks you,
Walk in a darkness deeper than
   you know.
And the night opens it's arms to
   receive you,
And you step into it like a
   shroud.

Marjorie Hind Benchoff
GODS GREAT UNIVERSE
As I gaze into the Heavens
And Thy beauty reigneth down
There shines through a reflection
Of God's greatness all around.
Venturing outward my eyes
Capture beauty of the open space
Unveiled is all God's great
   universe
Before my very face.
A magnificent world of color

Blended in beauty to see,
Flowing of the tide
Just the green of a tree.
Flying of the many birds
Waves tempest tossed,
The blend of God's great universe
Where no soul need ever be lost.
From the beauty of the Heavens
Alight comes a message clear,
Of God's great love that abounds
On all mankind down here.

Paul Andrew Pease
REUNION PREAMBLE

---

*Please dedicate this poem to the
graduating class of 1970 of
Nevada Union High School, the
Pease family, all high school
reunions, all college reunions, all
family reunions, all social
gatherings, all celebrity reunions,
and especially todays society.
May this poem restore peace,
love, passion, joy,
communication, and the presuit
of happiness.*

All people shall rejoin together
sharring love, joy, passion, and
communication. Let all evil be
washed away, let all sin be
taken away. Let us rejoin with
classmates, friends and
relitives. Let us reunite with
class mates, friends, and
relitives. Let be no barriers
seperate us from peace and
love. Let be no sin shall
seperate us from peace and
love. Let us lay aside everyday
problems, let us s. Let us rejoin
together on earth and in
heaven, let us reunite together
on earth and in heaven. Let us
rejoin together, let us reunite
together, for now and always
forever, together.

Teresa Wilkinson
I Knew It Would Happen
I knew it would happen,
  And it finally did
It feels like the first time,
  When I was a kid
You did make me love you
  Though I tried to resist
I fought off the feeling
  I felt when we kissed
But I still beleived you
  And your alibies
You made me so lonely
  I sat home and cried
It's her that you go to
  When you walk out the door
But my hearts where the hurt is
  And I can't take anymore

Chaplai n Earle V. Conover
LINCOLN THE GREAT
From log cabin to the White
  House, by any well-known test,
Meant the very highest climb up
  the ladder of success.
Abe's the GREATest public figure
  ever so long to "lie to State",
So he well deserves the high title
  of "LINCOLN THE GREAT"!
The cross rungs on that ladder
  start words with the "H" letter,
Like "H—umility", and, too

"H—onor". And his "H—onesty"
  made him better.
His character made him great,
  and his religion gave sanctity.
He's a worldwide hero
  throughout all eternity!

Kathy Lyles Benefield
TO MY DAD
Whenever I look back on the years
  The years so fine and true
I think of all the happiness
  The happiness caused by you.

You gave me everything I needed
Sometimes more than I deserved
You overlooked all my mistakes
And never said a word.

You never taught me about riches
  Or things people usually dream of
You taught me all the simple
  things
But mostly how to love.

Especially I remember the times
  When you held me very close
Letting everyone in the world
  know
You loved your family the most.

So whenever I look back on the
  years
The years so fine and true
I think of all the happiness
The happiness caused by you . . .

Robert Vargo
BROKEN LEASHES

---

*To Rags and Daisy: Happy
eyes . . . eager to please . . . No
human ever loved . . . like these.*

It's Saturday. The sun
Will come up soon again
And all the world will rise
From sleep, refreshed, alive,
To reign as masters here
Upon this land; and then,
And only then, I sleep.

Today holds nothing dear
To me in human form
I fear; perhaps my bed
Will send my mind to there,
Into that darker sphere,
Where no pain lives, and where
No aching dares to step.

I see you, Rags, my friend;
I see you, Daisy, held,
The both of you in arms,
Upheld upon a star
That blazes white across,
Our Heaven, yours and mine.

Ross Allan Gavle
UNTITLED
Feeling low after a time with a
  concubine
different pains tell me I'm dying
giving up on the body, its going
  to the grave
concentrating on the soul I'm
  trying to save
The curse of Adam my sinful self
have commited sins without the
  devils help
Trying to curtail my sinful ways
its hard to do in these forgotten
  days
The knowledge that Jesus' has
  paid for my sins
Doesn't always give me peace
  when guilt begins

The happiness of the guiltless
  soul
is something I wish I could know
I wouldn't have committed a sin
  today
if only the devil let me have my
  way
A mere child, a sinful soul
Ambitiously spoiled with no
  where to go
With no monetary empires for
  me to control
I think God has saved me from
  the fire below
having realized that earthly
  riches soon wear out
My ambition is turning inside out
every sin you skip every good
  deed you do
will be counted in heaven when
  you are through
My faith in Jesus will grant me a
  place
but don't we owe more for Gods
  saving grace

Archie Midgette Jr.
TAKING MY TIME
I take my time
While still living,
Sharing and giving

In a world moving too fast.
To keep from losing my mind
Or my heart from going astray,
I seek the love and comfort
Desired from memories of better
  days
out of the slow stable past.
To my grateful soul
They were good times gone by,
Which I fondly embrace some-how.
Until the day I die
My life story unfolds

That's why taking my time now,
Here upon this rough road of life
Has given me happiness, free
  from strife
Through God's love which shall
  last.

Dr. Dorothea J. Harrison M.P.,D.D.
**The Abortion Of a
Possibility**
TORN REMNANTS of days long
  past
Discovered blowing in the sands
  along the beach.
Tells the one who discovered
  them
That once upon a time there was
  an essence of a cast.

THINK ABOUT it if you dare!
pick up a few pieces and attempt
  to piece
together the contents of their
  scribbled flair.

Then dare not to imagine what
  tremendous peace
COULD HAVE LINGERED if
  only the smears of tears
had not come down as the rain
  from someone's eyes.
MAGNIFY the piece of the
  remnant blown nearest.

TOUCH the FABRIC and
  TOUCH it ever so LIGHTLY:
STRAIN the focus of the eye that
  produced this tear.
Though your eyes may have

grown dim with time
and the glass MAY BE SMOKY
  look VERY CLOSELY
For I believe it REVEALS a hint of
  ITS ORIGIN
ITS REASON;—, ITS LOST
  DESTINY; and ITS TORN
  EDGES
*SUGGEST SUDDEN
  ABORTION OF SOME
  POSSIBILITY*

Oh yes, TIS TORN—, SO
  RAGGED—, TIS RUMPPLED—,
Dried by the sun—, the winds of
  the
Canyon REVEALS the MINDS of
  TIME.
*Words are fainlty now
  illuminating
through the smoky glass*

"OH WHAT a WASTE. I LOVED
  in HASTE. OH
GOD WHAT a BITTER TASTE;
  to LIE LONELY
in THIS BED of a GRIEF
  STRICKEN PLACE.
MY STATE of MIND is the
  STATE of a HEARTBREAK!
WHAT DID I DO to COME to
  THIS BITTER, EMPTY,

Patricia L. Reynolds
GOD'S PERFECT PLAN
Though troubles may surround
  you
When you've done all you can,
Rejoice and sing; be happy;
It's part of God's perfect plan.

Your pocket may be empty,
There's no meat in the pan,
Relax and give God Praises!
For His perfect plan.

God does not cause your problems,
But He's still in command,
His miracle's on its way to you,
As part of His perfect plan.

Blessings are in store for those,
Who trust Him and take a stand,
You'll always be the victor,
In God's perfect plan.

Evelyn Randall Spink
GOD'S ANSWER
Guess I'm old—beyond sixty-five
Yet how come I feel so Alive!
Then I pray and ask for the Moon
And I add: It's "gotta" come soon!
But the Good Lord just lets me
  wait.
Years roll on; it's getting so late!
Suddenly, I burst into thought
And praise the Lord for all He's
  wrought!
I found these words and *thus* the
  Moon!
God's answer came when I was in
  Tune!

Mr. Michael F. Matushin SR.
MY BEVERLEY

---

*This Love Poem is dedicated to
my beautiful wife of 27
wonderful years, "Beverley" for
whom this love poem is
composed for.*

My Beverley, my Beverley,
I love her, and she loves me,

And she'll be mine till eternity,
My Beverley, my Beverley:
The skies may be grey.
The skies may be blue,
But one thing I'm sure of—
Is I love you,
And you'll be mine till eternity,
My Beverley, my Beverley:

Martha Virginia Chalfant
NOW TIME
S eems I've reached the silver age-
E very day's a single page;
V elvet hand in leather glove;
E yes more fixed on things above;
N eater kept my smaller world-
T ime has come. My flag's
  unfurled!
Y outh stood wide and strong
  and tall-

Y ears were full with nothing
  small;
E ver ready for a call!
A ge, less sure, looks back on past!
R ectifies what cannot last;
S eeks to hold the cherished fast.
O lder folk may sight the end.
L onger vision, youth can spend.
D oesn't matter which, my friend,
NOW!

Arlene Dempsey
JOHN'S POEM

*In remembrance of my step-
father, John Pickering Bradley
(1927-1983). May this poem let
everyone smile the way you did
when you read it.*

There is a light on my life
That shines ever so bright.
It blazes,
In all its splendor—
In all its glory—
Every day that I wake
Every day that I live.
It is my security,
Deep in the night;
And it it my confidence,
My guidance,
In any turmoil I encounter.
This light shines in my heart
And it illuminates
From my
Poppa John.

Beatrice Bullard
PRICELESS MOMENTS
To awaken in the early morning
  to a crisp clean freshness,
To Hear the birds singing as the
  sun climbs into the heavens to

greet the new day.
To feel the eagerness all about.
To hear the patter of raindrops as
  they fall gently from the sky.
With each little spatter
  whispering, "Tomorrow will be
  more beautiful 'cause I took the
  time to drop by!"
To feel the heat of the sunrays as
  they press against your skin.
To see the world share a radiant
  beauty more beautiful when
  seen from within.
To welcome the quietness of the
  evening at the close of a busy
  day.
To watch the moon and the stars
  as they graciously decorate the
  big black sky.
Close your eyes and listen to the
  Whippoorwill calling ever so
  sweetly, "I love you my
  Darling, Goodnight!"

Mrs. Christine Hughes
TO BE A MOTHER
To be a mother is a gift indeed, a
  gift every mother should heed.
There are things every mother
  know, the pain and sorrow she
  feels as her children grow.
We watch them grow from
  babyhood up, each step they
  make.
Feel sadness and gladness as they
  look at their first birthday cake.

There is a thrill as they say their
  first words, then it is time to
  teach them about the bee's and
  the Bird's.
We watch as they become people
  their own right, no longer
  needing Mom to hold them
  tight.
Their thoughts become secrets of
  their own, as we have to
  remember they soon be full
  grown.
No longer will I dangle them on
  my knee, or have them running
  with trusting hearts to me.

Their hurts I can no longer kiss
  away, but I a mother simply stay.
No more wide— eyed childlike
  smiles will I see, but their
  growing up still hurt me.
It's not that I don't want them to
  have lives of their own,
But this mother without her
  children are alone.

For every child that grows up and
  leaves the nest.
There is a mother crying for the
  emptiness of a child on her
  breast.
For all the pain mix with the joy,
  there is nothing I rather be.
To be a mother means all the
  world to me.

So Dear Lord in your heaven
  home up there.
There is a big Thank You going
  from a mother down here.
For the gifts of my children from
  above.
My two daughters I cherish as
  children and adults with all my
  love.

Helen M. Banuelos
MYSELF
In my life-long search to find
  MYSELF
I've left no stone unturned
I've found MYSELF beside MYSELF
  during emotional highs and lows
I've found MYSELF above MYSELF
  in times of financial woes
I've found MYSELF beneath
  MYSELF
  when putting on airs of
  sophistication
I've found MYSELF after MYSELF
  reproaching unjust deeds I'd done
I've found MYSELF against MYSELF
  setting impossible expectations
I've found MYSELF behind
  MYSELF
  too insecure to expose
I've found MYSELF beyond
  MYSELF
  having met a fraction of my goals
I've found MYSELF down on
  MYSELF
  indulging in self-punishment
I've found MYSELF into MYSELF
  gloating about my magnificence
I've found MYSELF with MYSELF
  attempting, "I, alone to console"
I've found MYSELF without
  MYSELF
  thinking, "I, a nothing"
I've found MYSELF outside of
  MYSELF
  looking back in shame
But in spite of MYSELF with
  regard to MYSELF
I really hadn't found MYSELF
By now MYSELF stood back from
  MYSELF
  seriously questioning "Who?"
Till it finally dawned on me
The last desperate measure
I had but one more place to search
Throwing aside the different,
  distinct
  natures of MYSELF
I searched within
I looked inside and found MYSELF!

Matthew Jay Grunden
UNTITLED
Presents go with Christmas,
Like witches to Halloween
But nothing is even comparative,
To the girl who married me.

We seldom show in public,
But truly are in love,
Her and I both know it,
And so does God above.

To my favorite darling,
Whom I love so true,
I hope my gift of Roses,
Is as beautiful as you.

So now I've showed my feelings,
To make a happy home,
And put it all together,
To write your Valentine poem.

Jo Love: (Marya Jo Thompson)
THE CANDLE OF LOVE
It's bright, it's beautiful,
It gives all it's got,
To those of you who
Huddle around it.

The warmth of its fingers
Darts right through the heart
And sets fire to life
As it lingers.

You can see everything
There is to see;
On this one small plane
of reality.

Should you . . . look carefully
You'll sence all it has
As the nature of LOVE
  . . . and FINALITY.

Anna Mae Kochel
RESPECT
Respect is not to be bought,
  Respect is not like a barter,
Respect is something one ought
  To learn from ones elder.
Respect is not to be handed down
  Like a father to a son,
Respect is not shouting through a
  town,
  Or something you have won.
Respect has to be gotten
  By only one way
And it's something that isn't
  forgotten,
  Or picked up any old day.
Yes, you have guessed
  Respect has to be earned
It's also like being blessed
  And it's something that isn't
  spurned.
Once you have earned respect
  Try not to let the tables turn,
For one will always be under
  suspect
  But be proud, it's something
  you have earned.

Elaine P. Morton
IT'S ME
There is beauty in a flower
And beauty in a tree
But, it seems, I have to look and
  look
To find the beautiful in me.

I once was size eleven
I'm sure that you'll agree
That for a five foot five
That's where I ought to be.

But that was many years ago
You see, I grew and grew
So now I'm lucky if you notice
That my eyes, they still are blue.

Mrs. Penny B. Evans
THE WEARY TRAVELER
Upon the road I traveled,
Weary from my deeds,
With no place to rest my bones,
Or to get myself some sleep.

I sat down upon a rock,
That looked more soft than twas,
And pondered upon the thought,
If such a thing as sleep ever was.

My heart grew tired,
My mind grew weak,
And my eyes had a mind of their
  own,
As they closed without my
  knowing,
And put me to sleep upon the
  stone.

I dreamed of rows and rows of
  beds,
With pillows soft and light,
Yet as I started toward them,
I awoke from my dream with a
  fright.

This rock upon which I was
  resting,

Had dumped me on the ground.
And so I'm still the weary
traveler,
Because no place to sleep have I
found.

Kaye Grogan
CELEBRATION
I close my eyes
   spots of red, orange
   or blue;
There is a fuzzy
   blur gray, white,
   and black.

Come reach for a
   star it glistens
   twinkling silver.
Come join us afar
   exploding, rising
   in splendor.

Majestic light
   devoured—
   away by smoke.
Muffled silence
   fizzled—
   away by flight.

Victor D. Carroll
A NEW MORNING
a flaming ball of fire
struggles slowly over the horizon
surfacing from emerald green
   water
spreading light over a new
   morning air

gentle droplets of dew
dropping through green trees and
   broken branches
the voices of a new day
fill the morning air

the day brightens as each second
   passes
and the natural light brings life to
   a sleepy land
the new morning freshens
   another day
and gives it strength to endure

James W. Claar
LET AMERICA RISE
In the midst of our pagan
   Christmas wild
May the USA salute the child
In whose name we take in vain
As we fall to the lust of raising
   Cain.

The Christ Child came to set us
   free
From the intoxication of anxiety,
To lead us to the Promised Land,
To build a nation to forever stand
Above the traditions of the mob
Who took his life for fear he'd rob
Them of their need for greed and
   fame,
Who transformed an orgy into his
   name.

Let America rise in all its might
To oppose the Hypocrisy of the
   Christmas blight
And do what the Christ would
   have us do
And love one another the whole
   year through.

Let's scrap the crap 'fore we go for
   broke,
'N show the world the way;
With our constitution under God
Give our all to Thanksgiving Day.

Paul H. Engel
Mom's Collecting Silver Again

To all the mothers of the world.

I got a letter just the other day
   from my older brother
It read I was invited to my Dad
   and Mom's
Golden Wedding Anniversary
Well, I haven't seen either one of
   them for quite
a few years now and when I got
   there
I noticed the silver in my mom's
   hair.
I then remembered way back
   when we were all
growing up when times got bad
   and my Mom
was collecting silver but she had
   to trade it
in for food and clothes for us to
   wear
So I went up to her and said,
   Mom,
I see you're collecting silver
   again. She turned
and said to me in a joking way,
   yes and
there's only one person I can
   trade it to.
That's when I got to thinking I
   should come
around and see her more often
   before that
person decides it's time for her to
   trade
that silver in again.

Grace Ramsey
NOCTURNE
The full moon blooms in my
   garden
   The white rose echoes its light;
The rippling, silvery water
   Is a glowing, shimmering sight.

This is a night for desiring
   And to dream of things afar,
For the moon has set me wond'ring
   What lies beyond the farthest
   star?

Laurie De Jarlais
ALWAYS REMEMBER
In taking you as my husband
I wanted you to see
there's no other place than by
   your side
that I would rather be.
All that I want is a piece of your
   heart
that no other will ever share.
I'll place it in mine; I'll care for it
   well.
I will always know that it's there.
I want to share your happiness,
   your trials, your saddest times.
I want you to feel you're needed.
I want you to share my life.
I've given you a part of myself
that no other has ever known.
You've opened a whole new world
   for me
with the gentleness you've shown.
You once saw a tear and you
   brought me some laughter.
All that I've needed you tried to
   go after.

I couldn't ask for more in a man
than what I have found in you.
You planted a seed in the core of
   my heart
and then it just grew and grew.
The love that we share now I
   know will remain
far long after we are both gone.
For surely immortal is something
   so special,
so precious, and oh, so strong.
From the depths of my soul; as
   much as I can
always remember
I love you, Dan.

Peggy Jo Doerr
THE POET'S PEN
This poet's pen I lift in doubt
And sign my name for Thee
In God's great name I sign myself
For all the world to see
If I should falter— slip in ire
Or raise my voice in rage
I pray Dear Lord to sorrow's sight
You'd never fill this page.
I do injustice equal time
When words are pouring forth
Since I was born to speak about
My life to prove its worth.
I know there's an answer in my
   heart
Your question I must find
In Thy name I'll figure out
Why Your poet's pen is kind.

Mary Anne McMillan
TO ALICE AND JIM
In Mount Dora, Florida
Alice and Jim met at a drugstore;
They had a lovely evening
Not knowing there would be more.

They dated several times
Talked on the telephone;
Making future plans
So they would not be alone.

Jim came to town
On his eighteen-wheeler;
Picked up Alice
To Colorado he did steal her.

Said their vows in Nineteen
   sixty-three
To love and cherish each other;
For good times and bad
Always helping each other.

You made it twenty years
Celebrating with another
   wedding;
I hope these vows said again
Means it has been a great thing.

Happy twenty years to Alice and
   Jim
I hope there will be many more;
Remember, I will be around
Helping you to keep the score.

Karen Ann Foster
A SIGN OF THE TIMES
With darkened heart
I searched for the light
To dissolve the darkness.
Finding a light I was happy once
   again
   My heart was full of love,
   My thoughts tender and warm.
The light was strong and it
   covered my darkness well.
Its source I didn't know
   or concern myself with.
Perhaps I should have because

now the light is fading
And I can see it is only the
   reflection of a light
Far, far away,
   That is not mine to see
And I am left again
With darkened heart.

Irene Stalcup
I INTENDED TO
That day cleaning my room, why
   did I leave it so soon?
There lay a book that caused me
   to look.
Enthralled with it I reclined to a
   nook.
The room I was cleaning I
   forsook. Me this book has
   overtook.

The letter I planned to write
   today and let fly on it's way
Never was written, I'm sorry to say.
Oh, why do I keep letting my
   intentions get me down, I pray?

I planned to send a gift to a friend
Visit a neighbor and a helping
   hand lend.
Again my intentions let me
   down, for nowhere around
Could either one be found.

Another day I'll do it: my
   intentions were set.
Get an early start: but the day
   wore on
And they were not finished yet.
Help me, Lord, not to give up and
   fret.

Sandra Laerez Stewart
WITH YOU I'M SAFE

This poem was written for and inspired by, Mr. Walter Talbert Jr. To the only man that could help aspire me to greatness, and whose everabounding love and generosity of spirit that will stay with me forever. I have found my true alter ego. I'll always love you babe. San

You felicied me till I wept,
Satisfied me till I dreamp,
Of happiness, your sweet caress,
Unbridled passion at it's best.

You're giving me just
What I need, no need to beg,
No need to plead.
You cared for me so I'd believe
That you're the one
I could perceive,
To share with me a life
That's real, where we can grow,
And we can feel.

You bared my soul and
Pledged your love—
You rocked me to the stars above.
You seared my heart when we
   made love,
You are the one that I speak of—
Your darn good looks,
Your sexy soul,
You grab me up and take ahold.

Unbroken ardor we won't miss—
Forever a relenting kiss.
We'll pawn and coo
All through the night,
Make love until our

John Campbell, Editor & Publisher

Hearts take flight,

Truth with us is never ending,
A joyful gift that's never pending.
Unselfish love is what we'll bear—
Each other's heartbeat's we will
Share. You have a gift
That's very rare,
A sensitivity that's there.

Show me bliss, and show
Me rapture, all of me—
Is what you'll capture—
Whenever I need your
Sweet embrace, I think
Of you and see your face;
A haunting I will not erase,
No one could ever take your
place—
With you I'm safe.

Betsy K. Rice
THE AWAKING

This poem is dedicated to my six daughters Bridget, Phyllis, Kerry, Jamese, Corneila, and Naomi and my only son Lamont, who has always inspired me with love.

As I lay in bed in the early of morn
and dream beautiful dreams that
go on and on
I feel a little hand and a soft
voice say
mama wake up I turn over and
yarn.
Again I go back into my sleep
and the little voice say mama I'm
ready to eat.

I wake right up in that moment
of defeat
and there they all stand at my feet.
I tell them softy that I'm awake
give them a smile that isn't a fake
and as they troop to the Kitchen,
and
I'm getting dressed, I know with
all my heart, that I've been blessed.

Mauryne Taylor Brent
NOT UNTIL THEN

It isn't until she's a woman
full-grown,
Laughing and crying as she
mothers her own,
That she knows what it means to
be up with the dawn,
Not resting her feet till the whole
day is gone
And, even at midnight, to
suddenly wake
To a cry from a child with a
hunger or ache;
To wash and to iron, and to cook
and to sew;
To worry and hurry, and to help
them to grow;
To send them all off with a tear
in the eye
And a pang in her heart that the
years have gone by.

And it's not until later when
grandchildren come
Does she know where the gift of
loving is from,
That the patience and kindness,
and pride and concern,
It is only from mother a daughter
does learn,
And show'ring affection on seeds

she has sown,
She pays daily homage for that
she has known,
For whether she said it in
growing-up years,
A "thank you" for loving through
joy and through tears,
Becoming a mother has made her
aware
That daughters make "mothers"
when their mothers care.

Liz Paquette
THE CHRISTMAS TURKEY

A turkey dressed in his Sunday
best,
A circle of onions around his
breast.
I was taking a bite when to my
surprise,
The turkey squawked and opened
his eyes.
"Don't eat me." he said, with a
look of great fear,
"If you don't eat me now, I'll be
here next year!"
Then he jumped from the table
and ran round the room,
Straight to the fireplace and right
up the flume.
Then he sat on my roof with a
look of great pain,
Now he's not my dinner, he's the
weather vane.

Marie A. Eberle
MY LOVE FOR YOU

The beauty of a rose
Is like my everlasting love for
you
I will love you from head to toe
Our love will last until my hair
turns
white like snow
Just like a flame on a candle
glows
Our love through the years will
grow

Patty Jo Ripple
YOU

To Michael: My love for you is wonderful description only makes it less. It's what I know but can't define what I feel but can't express.

You taught me how to love again,
I never thought I would
You taught me how to trust
again, I never thought I could
You let me see how wrong I was
to keep my love inside
You helped me share myself
again and throw away my pride
You showed me you believed in
me at a time when I was lost
You said that I should spend my
love, no matter what the cost

I didn't want to fall in love or
ever trust again
I didn't want to share myself or
let the stranger in
I built a wall around my love so
no one could ever see
I really wanted to let go, to set
my feelings free
I fell victim to my weakness,
your love was just too strong
I feel for you a love so deep, no

way could that be wrong
I trust, I need, I even want you
more and more each day
I want to share my life with you
and let love light the way
No matter what the future holds,
I'll never let it go
The love I have inside for you
will grow and Grow and GROW.

Sharon Winans
EMPTY

Take the love from love,
leave just the passion, it
will wreck havoc and destroy
all that tenderness has fashioned

Nelda G. Wilson

Nelda G. Wilson
I Wish I Could Write a Song

I dedicate This poem to my lovely daughter, Sharon Carol Grace.

I wish I had the gift to write
And the gift of a vocalist too
So I could write a beautiful song
And sing it just for you
I would write about your
tenderness and the love you've
given me
And have it set to music for all
the world to see
I'd write about your kindness
And all the loving care
The joy and the happiness you
brought me
Through my troubled years
I'd write about the times you
tried to right a hurt or wrong
If only I had the gift to write so I
could write it in a song
I wish I could put all your fine
qualities
And sympathy in every word
Into a beautiful lyric
Many hearts would be stirred
Parents and children would sing
it together with voices loud &
strong
It would bring them joy and
comfort if I could write a song
I wish I could put all the
understanding
And all the thoughtful things
you've done
Into a beautiful melody
And sing it all day long
My song would be happy it
would never be blue
It would be a tender "Thank You"
song, all because of you.

Donna L. Rossmann
FRIENDSHIP

To my dear friend I give my
loyalty without question.
I give my help whenever needed.
I give my advice only when asked.
I listen when he needs to talk.
I give him privacy when he needs
to be alone.
I give him comfort when he is sad.
Most of all, I give my gratitude
for his friendship.

Cora Durski
CHINESE CHIMES

The silvery tingling sound
That glass Chinese chimes make,
Please greatly my listening ears
Each time that sound they take.

Hung from ceiling of my porch,
Their music made at times
When the wind blows against it,
Making sing these glass chimes.

Just paper, glue and some glass
stripes
Hand painted and some string,
A req 1 simple contraption
But . . . how those chimes can sing.

Cora Durski
THANKS

I've so much to be thankful for.
Two eyes that let me see,
Two ears that lets me hear,
Two legs and feet let me walk,
A nose that lets me smell,
A voice that lets me talk,
Two arms and hands let me feel,
Two knees that let me kneel,
A neck that lets me turn my head,
Two jaws that lets me chew my
food,
Taste buds that lets me know
what's good,
Thanks for my body and hair,
For my face, be it dark or fair,
Thanks for family, friends and dog
And for a forgiving God.

Clara J. Beaty
SPECIAL LOVE

I'll try to love each person,
that I meet,
To see their inner thoughts
and strive to greet,
To show another human,
a side of life,
To ease the cruel inflicts,
from sober strife,
To learn to cope with
ease in God's own way,
To bow my head in prayer,
What more, I say!

Bridgette C. DeFravio
LIFE

Life is like a poker game
You always take chances.

Life is like a stuffed animal
It can last forever.

Life is like a T-shirt
It can always wear out.

Life is like a muscle
It can be strong.

Life is like a little kitten
It can be weak.

Life is like a book
Like every page
Every day is different.

Our World's Best Loved Poems

Mary Frances Murphy
JUDGEMENT DAY

My special thanks to be able to express my most wonderful vision to the rest of the world.

So often we hear, "The World is
   coming to an end."
When it does we will not be in
   control my friend.
That day the skies will be their
   brilliant blue
There will be writing across the
   sky,
In every language to tell us what
   to do.
Yes, even give us the reason why.

An opening in the sky will appear
Even so; there will be no cause
   for fear.
For standing on a cloud of
   billowing white,
Jesus, will be surrounded by a
   radiant light.
He will direct the golden stairs
   toward earth,
But the stairs will have no berth.

Jesus, will be speaking loud and
   clear,
So that every creature in the
   universe will hear.
He, will be speaking in every
   tongue
Not leaving out a single one.
Telling us how to ascend the
   stairs and not stop to pray,
Guiding every creature in his
   gentle way.

There will be some who won't
   believe, Jesus has come.
They will continue their
   carousing and having fun.
They will be the ones, that are
   left behind.
They will be the ones, that Satan
   will find.
So when, Jesus, calls your name
   on Judgement Day,
Run for the Golden Stairs and
   climb away.

Robert L. Haupert
GUIDED LOVE

To Vivian: My understanding and beautiful, loving wife.

You attract my eye
   each and every day,
And your movements
   a message to convey.
I see a wonderful person
   whom I love,
Guided together by a strength
   from above.
I hope you always
   will be at my side,
As a person with whom
   I can confide.
My inner desires are of you
   and always to be,
Together, a pair traveling
   to eternity.
Daily thoughts to reality
   we each live,
With many sensations
   for each to give.

Remember always
   my love is for you,
That forever yours
   will be as true.

Jolanda Palm
Carpe Diem (Make Use Of the Day)

Make use of the day, the breath
   of life—
Once again has blown your way.
Pursue the dream—millions seek,
Fondling of the hands—
This vice belongs not to the
   character,
Of the strong—but the weak.
Make use of the day, challenge
   life's test,
For when it is eve, all men must
   rest.
Smile through your trials,
   achievement approve,
Lest the night pull it's shade, and
   find you a fool.
Make use of the day, time stands
   still for none,
In your achievement—You'll find,
When life on earth is done,
No reason found for regret, for in
   life's caper,
It is you who've truly won.

Edward David Bush
THE WREATH

Arise and claim the victor's wreath
   Well have I fought
   And so be proud.
   Arise and be free!

Tarry not, oh leaden limbs
For I must rise, and claim my prize!
   Bend, oh knee,
   And lift this weary carcass!

This can be but a brief respite.
   A dark moment,
   That lingers nought
   But for a fleeting time!

Still, a chill does fill the air . . .
   And I am tired . . .
   And would could rest.

   Yet rest I shall,
   When I do clasp
   The victor's wreath,
   And hence be free!

"Arise and claim . . ."
Still all around me spins the world,
While those dread words
   Do fill
   The very air!
   To do,
That which any child can do . . .
   "Arise"
For this I would give all I own,
For this I do so give my life . . .
   "Arise!"

Edith L. Price
HAVE I DENIED HIM

One sat within the courtyard,
While Jesus was being tried,
And ere the morning cock crow,
The Savior he had denied.

As he warmed himself at the
   fireside,
He was questioned about this
   Man;
When they asked, "Do you know
   this Jesus?"
He swore and denied Him again.

As the Savior is tried by world
   standards,

Have I sat in the courtyard of sin,
Have I walked side by side with
   the worldling,
Have I denied Him before men?

As He reached out to me in His
   mercy,
And He said, "For your life, there's
   a plan,"
Have I turned my back on the
   Savior,
Have I denied Jesus again?

Oh, Father, forgive my rebellion,
Deny me not, Lord, I pray,
Please take my life now, and use
   me,
As I turn back to you all the way.

Patricia E. Hawkins
COMMUNICATE

A camera,
   it shows us truth
   if we dare to look.
A poem,
   we must dare to listen
   Can you hear it?
We request the honour
   of your presence
   at the marriage of
   Eye and Ear.
Blind man . . .
   hear the beauty.
Deaf man . . .
   see the sound.
Communicate to all the world.

Ronald Oldfield
DARK LADY

To my children RICHARD THOMAS and TONI LOUISE and my wife MONA LOUISE

She danced on shadows and no
   one knows her name
she spoke in whispers from a
   place where time does not exist
silence stills her winding
   corridors
as children lay dorment in there
   beds
echoed footsteps find the ground
   thats hard and cold
while her silence holds the
   human cry at bay
be still
and know that night is upon us
and she is a dark lady

Nancy Weinberg Jackson
A SON'S LAMENT

To Richard whose love shines, and to my best friend, Steve Neufarth who made it through Vietnam, only to die of cancer at our tender age of 34—we love you!

The cannon are roaring, belching
   their sounds up high,
Guns keep rattling a continuous
   sigh.
My men are rattling a continuous
   sigh.
My men are running, searching
   for a trench of cover,
Some to never again return to
   that waiting lover.
The smoke—filled sky hangs as
   dung in the air,

Oh, God, that's Johnny—a fixed
   cold stare.
"Leave him," comes the common
   order,
Later will come the de-tagger,
   retriever and sorter.
"Move on, Head out,"——we're all
   from a common mold,
All my men,—lives—in my hands
   to hold.
Run for cover—a bush, a tree, a
   hole,
What's that whirring noise,
   reaching it's goal?
Ma, I'm not coming home to see
   your loving face,
Tell Pa, he never did handle my
   horse with much grace.
Oh, My God, I'll never have
   babies and see them grow tall,
I'll never touch a wife or make
   love in the hall.
Give my chemistry set to Will,
   two pastures over,
Please put my stallion out in the
   clover.
Put my boots in the rack, hang
   my hat in the hall,
We'll meet again soon, in God's
   Heaven some Fall.

Tom Campbell
FOR THE GIRLS

Little girl, I cherish you;
My heart goes out to thee.
You're the hope of tomorrow,
   the promise of things to be.

Young woman, I admire you,
   as you prepare to stand,
unafraid of the life to come
   for you and your young man.

Dear matron, you I honor;
My highest praise to you.
You have proven o'er and o'er
   to be one tried and true.

Honored ladies all, I love you!
You've given to men like me
   the strength and courage needed
to be what we can be.

Christina Chingtsao
Snowball, Snowball, I Mourn For You!

For fourteen and half years,
Happily we lived together.
Love and understanding between
   us, I gather.
Swiftly passed, days, months and
   years.
Streaming down my cheeks are
   my tears.

You are smart, make people smile.
You are sweet, capture my heart.
Your spirit is determined, fight
   against disease.
Your body is weak, succumb to
   the fate.

Your arrival blossoms my mind
   into great joy.
Your presence brightens my
   home with good cheers.
Your illness causes my life
   constant worries and fears.
Your departure saddens my heart
   with deep grief.

Beautiful flowers do not bloom
   forever.
Full moon does not shine forever.
Under the sun, no banquet will

489

John Campbell, Editor & Publisher

ever last.
In this world, we have to part.

Happy memories! Sad departure!
Snowball, you are my joy!
Snowball, you are my pride!
Snowball, Snowball, I mourn for
you!

Marilyn Shearer (Dusty—'83)
A CHRISTMAS PROMISE

---

*To my SPECIAL friend in the
Lord for all her encouragement
and prayers.*

Some of God's promises have
  been fulfilled
  and others yet to be.
The birth, the death of HIS dear
  Son
  were done for you and me.

Christmas is the birthday . of
  God's only beloved Son.
So we must GIVE to Him our lives
  before our life is done.

Dr. Mildred Carroll Wiseman
LOVE'S HATRED
In your anger and frustration you
  spewed forth
All your hatred as you angrily
  spoke my name
Just as the erupting volcano
  spewed forth
Smoke, rocks, and ashes in the
  burning lava's flame.
You uttered each angry
  protestation
As it rapidly rose and fell
Just as the mountain's rich
  vegetation
Did beneath the boiling lava's Hell
After thousands of years of growth
On the tall mountain's side.
Even so your anger and hatred
  bruised
My bleeding heart that cracked
  and broke
As I sought quickly to hide
The hurt that I hurled rapidly
  away
With each angry word you spoke.
But years after the rich growth
  will return
Growing more beautiful in the
  rich fertile
Loam left in the lava's slow burn.
Perhaps, too, many years later my
  heart will
Mend and heal its scars to beat
  happily again
After God's healing power can
  salvage the pain.

Helen Young Luke
CHRISTMAS WISH
Through the crisp and snowy air
  I hear the Christmas mass.
With misty breath and clear
  sweet tones
  the gay young carolers pass.

They sing, "Peace on earth, good
  will to men,"
  While candles softly glow
Amid festoons of holly wreaths,
  and hanging mistletoe.

As they sing, I think of you
  and wish you blessings rare
On this Christmas Eve when

candles shine
and carols fill the air.

Joshua Adam Benton
THE TAX COLLECTOR
Oh! you better not spend, better
  not buy,
Don't you use your money, I'm
  telling you why.
The tax collector's coming to
  collect your
              TAXES

He's making a list, he's checking
  it twice,
He knows how much you spent
  on your wife,
The tax collector's coming to
  collect your
              TAXES

He knows your bosses first name,
He knows how much you make,
He knows how much your utility
  is,
So don't you dare make any
  mistakes.

Oh! you better not spend, better
  not buy,
Don't you use your money, I'm
  telling you why,
The tax collector's coming to
  collect your
              TAXES

The tax collector's coming to
  collect your
              TAXES

Sonja Christina
HOPE
What is hope?
Half the time we live on it --
The other half life holds us in it's
  realistic grip!
And in between - - life's cement - -
The two half's - - - until the very
  end - -
Together holds! whilst here and
  there
Some fragments of our dream
  unfolds!

Joyce E. Conklin
SEATTLE
Hidden amongst the trees is life,
  vines of soul and leaves of love.
Yet somewhere here lives death
  and hate
  and the sun peaks through above.

City of green and surf and sand,
  people work and children grow,
While nearby mountains tower
  high
  and the clouds hang down so low.

Islands, bays, and the city streets
  entwine around in the square.
The bridges in and ferries out
  for the Western Folk who care.

Masses here in the city meet
  those like you and those like
  me.
Campers, autos, and working folk
  racing along by the sea.

Towering needle up above
  lights in the darkness below,
Beautiful dreams of life and love
  come true right here, do you
  know?

Seattle, lovely port at sea
  with fog rolling in at dawn,

Your rain and mist and salty sea
  must be governed from beyond.

Julie A. Armacost
RAIN ON THE ROSES
The rain drops on the roses, are
  so beautiful to see. When the
  dark storm clouds have passed
  over, into infinity.

The sun shines in it's glory,
  bringing warmth to those
  below, changing into diamonds,
  the rain drops that were so cold.

When the rain falls on the roses,
  there is a blessing to bestow.
  Bringing vibrant colors to all
  who remain below.

The white rose in it's purity,
  stands out among the rest,
because of the memories, to
  which we've been blessed.

The red rose in it's royalty, will
  draw you to it's side, and place
  a seed of love, which will
  forever abide.

The other hues of the roses, lest
  they be forgot, form a beautiful
  rainbow, which we all have
  sought.

So when storm clouds appear on
  the horizon, and the rain begins
  to fall. Remember the roses and
  the hope given to all.

The rain on the roses has a tale
  to bear. There are diamonds on
  the roses when the sky is fair.

Melita Watts
THE BUTTERFLY
Step by step, I built a cocoon
Around myself . . . yet soon,
Loneliness replaced the fears
That spun each layer through
  these many years.
I was too frightened to break the
  wall.
Too frightened to call
To someone who could be my
  friend.
But then . . .
You peered beneath the layers to
  see
The real "me."
And as each layer was peeled
  away
I became afraid
To climb out of my shell and face
The world outside my protective
  place.
But your love poured in
And helped *me* to love again.
And then I
Emerged a
  butterfly.

Kathleen A. Buchek
Elvis: An American Legacy
You Didn't Know Me
Thats All Right
ELVIS
You Didn't Have To Say
You Love Me

Your Soulful Ballads
Remind Me Too Much Of You
I Can't Stop Loving You
Anything Thats Part Of You

Yet
The Stage Bears

Mournful Silence
We'll Be Together
No More
Ain't It Funny
How Time Slips Away

I Believe
I'll Remember You
My Way
For The Good Times

Randa Lee Stout
CHRISTMAS JOY

---

*To Cecil-My Father who inspired
my poetry and musical talents,
also Bob my husband-Sandy and
Kevin for their support &
encouragement.*

In The Sky Snow Clouds are
  sailing
In the distance Christmas Bell's
  are ringing
Over Bethleham there's a bright
  star shining
Down on the Christ Childs
  manger of hay

In the Drive way the children are
  playing
Laughing and shouting with glee
In the tree tops the snow birds
  are Singing
Their merry tune of Christmas
  glee

Christmas Joy, Christmas Joy, oh
  how happy are we
When Christmas bells are ringing
We get the old Christmas feeling
Start laughing, and shouting with
  glee

In the stores the shoppers are
  crowded
Waiting their turn to come
While the children are laughing
  and shouting
having lots of fun
While Santa Clause is calling
Merry Christmas to one and all

Christmas Joy, Christmas Joy
Oh how happy are we
When Christmas bells are ringing
We get that old Christmas feeling
Start laughing and shouting with
  glee

Barbara Landry
POETRY
Blank pages are quickly
and quietly filled
with the thoughts
that your mind has spilled.

Meaningful words . . .
your mind's release
in hopes of
a little inner peace.

Written words that are
printed in ink.
The mirrored reflection
of what you think.

A precious glimpse
into your soul
in order to reach
your final goal.

Through your poetry
others might discover
that we often think
alot like each other.

490

Edith Seaton-Bruce
DAWN TO DAWN
Dawn picked up the cloak called
 night,
And placed it somewhere out of
 sight.

Sunbeams dart from blue-white
 skies,
To kiss my cheek and shuttered
 eyes.

Moonbeams filligree thru lacey
 curtains drawn,
'Ere night shall pass and shelf the
 dawn.

Betty L. Loeffler
**What Does Christmas
 Mean To You?**

---

*To my loving children, Laurie,
John, Bucky, Beth, Jim, Rod, and
Tom. Also to my very surportive
husband Matt, and the many
loving friends who give such
wonderful encouragement.*

Does Christmas mean the man in
 red?
Lots of toys or maybe a sled?
Lots of candy, peanuts and all?
Stockings hung, lights lit, or
 maybe a ball?
Mom's good cooking for
 Christmas day?
 Company coming from far away?

Christmas should mean a stable,
 a manger
The blessed lowly little stranger
The star that shone so very bright
Shepherds tending their flocks by
 night
The Wisemen who traveled from
 afar
Following the guiding star.

Please put Christ into Christmas
 again
Remember, He came to help all
 men
He died on the cross for you and
 for me
He paid the price to set us free
Remember Him this Christmas
 day
Remember the price He had to pay.

Merry Christmas everyone!
Remember why God sent His
 only Son!

Florence Stubblefield
MY MAGIC DREAM
This magic wand with in my hand
 Makes all things possible I am
 told
I think about all foreign lands
 And see these changes all unfold

I watch the sunlite shinning thru
 The rain that softly falls below
Brightly colored rainbows of
 every hue.
 Then turns to winters freezing
 snow

I watched the foreign people walk
 around
 But only with a smile
Theres only silence not a sound
Only magic beauty for a while

I see these things all come to pass

And the changes I can make
Like seeing thru a looking glass
And then I have to wake

Then I see this world for real
 And no one is standing there
Down beside my bed I kneel
 And quietly say a prayer.

Cynthia Critchett
MIRROR
I see the outside winter
Tapping at my window face,
Icy fingers
That stick to the pane,
Winter winds that
Chill and chase.

The deceptive December sun,
Her smile will chill,
You raise your arms to
Embrace the warmth
But find she's lost the will.

Mary Cochran Skramstad
NOEL
Snowflakes of white lace
Crackling logs in the fireplace
Trees of colored lights
A time to dream and take delight
A joyous celebration of that
 wondrous night
Christmas music fills the air
Bearing memories of friends
 everywhere
Sending messages clear
A Merry Christmas and
A Happy New Year.

LaVere R. Brinkerhoff
SOLILOQUY
When death calls for me—invited
 or not,
 I long for a secluded spot
Beneath wild sage and juniper tree,
 There leave my remains of
 mortality.
The purging mountain sod shall
 be my bed
 With a sego lily near my head,
Tolling bluebells of azure hue,
 Buttercup blossoms will mourn
 pure dew.
Perfumed pinyons incense the sky,
 Meadow larks trill taps while
 winging by.
When shadows fall at the close of
 my day
 And wildlife creatures scurry
 away,
Let the mournful songs remain
 unsung
 Instead,
Leave my name on my
 grandchildrens' tongue.

Mary H. Butterworth
WHAT IS LEFT FOR ME
They must have needed angels
A way up above,
That must be why
They sent for you my love,
Now what escape is there for me
What is left for me
Nothing but the memories of
 having
Loved you my dear
No one else will ever mean
As much as you to me
What happiness is there for me
Now that you have gone from me
What is left for me
Nothing but the memories
Of having loved you my dear
So until we meet again
I love you and I always will.

Brian Czerniecki
The Child Who Never Was
So Often I've Tried To Remember
The Plight Of The Child Who
 Wasn't
Mother Just Didn't Understand
What Parenting Was All About,
Dad Didn't Hang Around Long
 Enough
To Even Find Out His Name,
At Times It Was Really Quite
 Confusing
When He Tried So Much To
 Love.
He Reached Out To The World
But Became Lost In The
 Paperwork,
With Despair He Was Overcome,
Life Was Nothing But A
 Hallucination.
Psychotic, Neurotic, The
 Problems He Had,
In His Grave He Laid To Rest
 Without A Home.

Judy M. Brewster
THANKS TO JESUS
Once they called Him, Jesus, the
 carpenter's son.
Then they called Him, Lord, for
 all the goodness He done.
Next they cried out to crucify
 God's own son.
When the jealousy in their
 hearts,
Over all His good deeds had won.
The long walk up Calvary, the
 burden's He bore,
The pain in His side, as they
 pierced it with the sword.
The Bible teaches, there are many
 ways,
But thanks to Jesus, at Calvary
 that day,
His precious blood, my sins
 washed away.

"Le Noit" LeVonier Aldridge, II
AMSTERDAM
"Mou, Molle aussi que un une
 Rose" . . . . .
soft as a rose. pastel in
 warmth . . . touching . delicious
posh and ah! so bourgeois . . .
 Sophistication .
ballroom chandelier glittering
 across the magnificently
orchestrated, simply elegante
 escalier (staircase).
Pierre with a twist of lemon,
 caressing breezes of a late

evening.
Rembrant, Picasso, Givenchy,
 Courvosier and Jacuzzi . . .
Lace twinned around Gothic
 memoirs.
 Germaine Monteil. Champagne
 . . . Sparkling crystal.
"Luxurious Nightdream"—silk—
 ah! caressing moi chocolate
 form.
Renaissance Gentleman.
 Parisian Chateau.
Regal moment spent in
 Amsterdam . . .
 comfortin' myself in the
 indulgence of your passion . . .
Tiffany . . . Moi Desire . . . Doll . ..
 Tiffany drapped sensually
in a pink camisole. Lust in
 Amsterdam.

Tony Lavelli
**Big Peanut Farmer With
 The Message Of Faith,
 Hope An' Love! (The Rise
 Of Jimmy Carter)**
Jim came from that peachy
 Georgia State, Down southern,
 Dixie way.
To unify sore party wounds, he
 said: "Please kneel, do pray."
Jim won large votes from more
 people now, Huge miracle
 somehow.
BIG PEANUT FARMER WITH
 THE MESSAGE OF FAITH,
 HOPE AN' LOVE!
He flashed slick smile that never
 quit, With friendly warmth an'
 wit.
Jim traveled all aroun' this land,
 While shaking ev'ry hand
In only one fine U.S.A., Could
 you triumph that way.
BIG PEANUT FARMER WITH
 THE MESSAGE OF FAITH,
 HOPE AN' LOVE!
Then he looked toward high sky
 above: "We ask dear Lord,
 Please bless our love!"
Jim's given us another chance, To
 raise great destiny.
Go work for steadfast harmony.
 To praise brave home of the free.
Move on together marching
 down, To D.C. Washington
 town.
BIG PEANUT FARMER WITH
 MESSAGE OF FAITH, HOPE
 AN' LOVE!

Tia Renee Darbee
SNOW

---

*To my parents, Calvin and Elaine,
for their constant encouragement,
and for the interest they take in
my happiness.*

A frozen ballerina
in a costume
like no other, ever
twirls
falling gracefully
downward
landing on a bed of
fellow dancers
put to sleep
by the coldness
until spring.

Rinda Taylor
The Meaning Of Christmas
Shoppers are busy, no time for
delay,
The hustle, the bustle, the rush
everyday.
The time's fast approaching, it
won't be too long,
The meaning of Christmas, Oh,
where has it gone.

Decorations appear with a gleam
in the night,
The tree is adorned, what a
glorious sight.
Each ornament hung, in the air
yuletide song,
The meaning of Christmas, Oh,
where has it gone?

A greeting is sent, with a thought
for the season,
Sometimes in a hurry, little
thought for the reason.
Commercials appear, shiney toys,
new and strong,
The meaning of Christmas, Oh,
where has it gone?

Little faces appear, with a glint in
each eye,
Santa is coming, now you better
not cry.
Tiny innocent hearts, God's Gift
still unknown,
The meaning of Christmas, Oh,
where has it gone?

A tiny pure infant, in a manger
he lay,
A gift sent from Heaven, our
hope for each day.
To God be the glory for all of
Creation,
For the birth of His Son, and for
this Celebration.

Oh, where is the meaning, Oh,
where did it go,
It's deep down within us, just
waiting to grow.
Open your heart, look inside, you
will find,
The TRUE MEANING OF
CHRISTMAS was there all the
time.

Rosemary Brown
DADDY'S GIRLS

*Dedicated to Larry Brown. His
love for his four daughters was
the inspiration for this poem.*

Melissa, Jessica, Anne and Ceceilia
His daughters number four.
Each one is a blessing from
heaven above.
Daddy wouldn't ask for anything
more.

Melissa and Jessica are adopted.
Anne and Ceceilia are his seed.
"Mr. Brown, do you have any
children?"
Daddy proudly answers "Yes,
indeed."

"Daddy, I love you."
Are words that warm his soul.
"Thank You, Lord." he whispers
"My girls are healthy and whole."

Melissa in California, Jessica in

Arizona,
Anne in Georgia and Ceceilia
living near,
Heavenly Father, watch over
daddy's girls,
Bless and keep them for they are
very dear.

Mary Snow Jackson
MOTHER
God needed another rose in His
bouquet up there
He looked around and found one
so fair
One without blemish, so delicate
and pure
This one He could use—He felt
very sure.

At last one day in the month of
May
Looking down from Heaven, said
this is the day
I'll take this rose for My bouquet
at last
Gently and silently, it happened
so fast.

Now we still miss Mother—that
rose so fair
Still we know she is happy up
there
There is a space empty in our
garden below
For in her place nothing else can
grow.

Denzil P. Dollens
A Nursing Home Christmas

*This poem is dedicated to all the
residents and staff of the
Morristown Nursing Home.,
Morristown, Indiana. I love them
all.*

Twas December the first and up
decorations did go,
From nurses station to hallways,
even the rooms were all aglow.
Then came the second and up
went the trees,
We knew this would be
something sure to please.
On through the month with all
sorts of groups,
From school choirs, to clowns,
even Santa and his troups.
The residents party came with all
sorts of gifts,
You wouldn't believe their faces,
Oh what a lift!
On through the end of the month
we did fly,
Time for the New Year with new
things to try.

Dewey Knudslien
LOST LOVE
I thought you really loved me
And you meant the words you said
And that the happy day would
come
When you and I would wed
I thought I mattered more to you
Than any other one
That I would be your evening star
And every golden sun
You seemed to be so happy
In the time we spent together
But now I must believe
You are as fickle as the weather

For you have gone your merry
way
And I can plainly see
You really do not care to share
My loving company
Perhaps it happened for the best
And we shall not regret it
So just suppose we say goodbye
And both of us forget it

Elbert P. Green
O LITTLE TOWN

*This poem is dedicated to all of
the people whom I met while
living in the town of Indianola,
Mississippi in the Delta. Also, I
dedicate this poem to my wife,
Mary and my children, Mark and
Marsha.*

O Little town of the Delta Bayou
Your sun is so bright and sky so
blue,
The wind just whistles in the
trees;
As we enjoy the cool cool breeze.

You are welcome here the whole
year round,
Whether from the north or
southward bound.

The people are friendly as can be
Through such a small town there
is much to see.

O come, O come to this little
town,
Where signs of love are all
around.
It's Christmas all over from sea to
sea
And it's Christmas here for you
and me.

Lyn de Burgh
SEASON OF THE SUN

*To Stephanie—all the laughter,
the love and the dignity of life.*

An awakening,
to a shower of hot gold
tempering your living soul.
Breathe deep in the heat.

A reawakening,
to a million on a million fireflies
blinking in concert with your
heart.
Breathe deep in the excited
silence;
An interlude in today.

Lift up your eyes,
Celebrate this miracle of light.

A discovery,
joining magic and symphony
in distant corners of thought.
Laugh aloud with a true magician.

A rediscovery,
of a warm, soft feeling
in every summer day.
Laugh aloud at this rising of
spirit;
An interlude in today.

Lift up your heart and soul,
Wash them clean in the sun's
love,
Dry them pure in the sun's fire.

Etta Mae Reese
**The Old Vine Shackled
Shack**

*This poem is dedicated to my
husband, of 41 years plus,
Emerson Reese.*

My mind keeps wondering back
To that old vine shackled shack.
Beneath the pines, on top of the
hill,
Where Grammy and Grampy
lived peaceful and still.
And where it was so nice, to hit
the sack,
And sleep till morning, in that
shackled shack.

It seems like only yesterday,
That I heard my Grammy say,
"Go to the pantry and help
yourself,
To the cookie jar on the
cupboard shelf,"
That was always filled to the very
top.
Where I ate and ate, till I
thought I'd pop.

One day in the path of that
shackled shack,
A blue racer snake, ran after my
track.
I screamed, "Grammy! come
quick with a hoe,
Before this snake bites me on
the toe."
She said, "you better stand still,
Or you'll be chased right over
the hill!"
Grammy came down on that old
snake with a big whack,
And chopped his head off, before
you could say Jack!

There's not much left of the Old
Vine Shackled Shack,
But lonely stands, a clay dobbed
chimney stack.
With a lot of memories, of the
good days spent,
With Grammy and that old
"Grampy Gent,"
And the love they shared, in that
Old Vine Shackled Shack.

Violet Gordon
TO BONNIE
Some people squint
Close an eye
And scan the horizon of life
Through a crevice
Of a slightly opened door
For a glimpse
Narrow and dim
With limited action
Then withdraw
Timorously
And retreat to the rhythm
Of the rocking chair.

Not you
You swing wide the door
And step out
Onto the threshold
To scan the panorama
Radiant in your light
Bright with challenge
Then you reach out
Courageously
And tenderly embrace
Your world.

Our World's Best Loved Poems

Mary Lois Carlile
SPRING IS
The gentle breeze that passes by
And multi-colored butterflies.

The bird's singing his love song
As kites across the fields are flown.

The children's laughter as they
play
And soft clouds that cool the day.

Flowers wearing their very best
The grass offering barefeet a rest.

Trees sending forth a shade
And bees and flowers making a
trade.

The joyous excitement everywhere
The evidence that God does care.

Laura Brown Lane

Laura Brown Lane
**God Save Our Country
Evermore**
We sing praises to Thee for
America's past,
And we pray that forever her
glory may last—
God save our Country evermore.

May democracy ever shine forth
in our Land,
And our many great States e'er
unitedly stand——
God save our Country evermore.

May we e'er be a Nation of
humanity,
And our people forever have
equality——
God save our Country evermore.

May our Star-Spangled Nation in
peace ever rest,
And forever with justice and
freedom be blest——
God save our Country evermore.

God save our Country, God save
our Country,
God save our Country evermore;
By day or by night, as we strive
for the right—
God save our Country evermore.

F. Clark Carnes
UNTITLED
Between the woman
And the vine
Drink more deeply
Of the wine
You'll discover
Bye-n-bye
Empty bottles
Do not cry

Irene G. Pascoe
MEMORIES
I pause, and relish each thing that
is new,
  While following life's path,
  destined and true,
Cherishing each new treasure I
find,
  Loving all, my kindred kind.

Moments that ease, my journey's
weariness,
  And brighten my hours of
  loneliness,
Sights and sounds, brought by
fate and chance,
  Days and nights, for
  rememberance.

Viewing new wonders, with
happy excitement,
  Soothed by sounds, to a peaceful
  contentment,
Lessons learned, along the way,
  Perhaps for use, another day.

These souveniers, I collect by the
score,
  Ever seeking, to add to my store,
I gather them up, like the farmer
his sheaves,
  My harvest, a treasure of
  memories.

Michael Eugene Graham
CROSSING OVER
It is strange indeed the respect
and admiration excellence
engenders. And when he was
good; he was very, very good
and when he was evil he was
better. Aim an inch or two
under the chin when brushing
a hitter back and it is out of
fear and inability to move that
they dare not do so. A hitter of
Goliath proportions I do not
fear for the rock and sling and
the past are my legacy. I rock
into the wind pulling back on
the laces cross seam throwing
overhand and the baseball
takes off into the blue. The
giant swings and does not
connect and I stride away with
pride for my fastball was my
way to say: World leave me
alone, because for me but to
turn is to cause the world great
pain.

Kathryn Phelps Fowler
TEARS

---

*Dedicated to Helen Langley Fox
in memory of her husband James
P. Fox for whom this poem was
written.*

Our Lord wept today
Someone he loved was not well,
I know that he was crying
For his tears like raindrops fell.

He cried for someone
Who was always kind and good,
Who listened to others' problems
And helped them if he could.

If your hand should feel a gentle
pat
You will know just what it means,
For God is always near you
Even though he can't be seen.

A tiny breeze upon your cheek
A whispering in the air,
Will tell you of his presence
For he is always there.

He is watching, he is helping you
As you go from day to night,
While you sleep he'll hold you
close
And make everything all right.

That morning ray of sunshine
Is his way of saying hi!
I'm here to help you through the
day
I'll always be standing by.

So speak to him when you need
him
Hold out your hand, he'll be there
Know that he'll always help you,
That you are always in his care.

D'Anna Postlewaite
A LIVING DREAM
  A sunset's lowly hue,
  A seagull's flight in air,
  A rainbow's golden dew,
Makes life worth living there.

  The bird's evening choir,
  The childrens' voice in song,
  The candles' glow afire,
Makes life worth making strong.

  A stream's white foaming hair,
  A daisy's grace in light,
  A human's earthly prayer,
Makes life worth living right.

  A rose's blush above,
  An Angel's holy beam,
  Another's act of love,
Makes life a living dream.

Wendy E. Hayman
BRIDGED GAP
A bridge to reconnect
the two which drifted away
rejoining once again
Feeling alone before
nobody in sight
like a white sandy desert
or the sun up in the sky
Becoming closer
wanting to be near
The reconstruction's soon
a pathway's almost here

The bridge fills the gap
so just follow the map
and together a seal will form
an everlasting friendship
will always be warm

Tina Marie Pitcher
WHAT CHRISTMAS IS
Above a manger hails a star,
It seems as though it lies so far.
As shepards stood and watched
their flock that night,
The star just happened to come
into sight.

As an angel appeared in the sky,
The shepards looked up and
wondered why.
The Christ Child is born the
angel said.
They followed the star the way it
led.

As Mary and Joseph knelt and
prayed,
In swadling clothes baby Jesus laid.
The star still stood long in the
night;

Many people in Bethlehem saw
the bright light.

This is what Christmas really
is,
And this birthday is all his.
All what happened on that Holy
day,
Was happiness in God's very own
way.

Chris Smith
COME EASY TO ME
Come easy to me
Stringless and free
Hands opened wide
Else let it be

Don't need another
Smothering mother
How 'bout a friend
Sister and brother

Let us embrace
Not pin nor encase
Don't put me on trial
Don't hold me in place

Come known in the light
Not a panther by night
Go where you choose
Be a bird not a kite

Christine M. Warner
KEVIN
In all the world
It is you that I love
With the strength of the
storming sea.
You are in my dreams
Be it day or night.
What you have done to me?
I've been marked
Deeply within,
I'm enchanted, hypnotised.
I can not get free
Ever bound in love
That in memory never dies.

Sharri Suzette Mullen
DON'T FALL IN LOVE

---

*With Love to: Emma Griffin,
Clara De Roche, Thomas &
Shirley Clark, Basil & Cheryl
Mullen*

Don't fall in love my friend
you'll see it doesn't pay
it causes broken hearts
it happens everyday.

I wonder where you are at night
I wonder if you are true
at moments I am happy the next i
am blue.

When love starts I don't know
why
I worry day and night
you see my friend I'm losing you
It never turns out right.

Love is great but—it hurts so
much
the price you pay is high
if I had to chose from life or
death. I would chose to die.

So when I say don't fall in love
you'll only hurt before its
through
Believe me my friend I should
know
I fell in love with you

Sandra Lee Hagan
FOREVER TREASURED

*To Anna and Kerry Thanks for
making my poem a reality, Love
ya both!*

Innocent & frail you did seem
yet I saw another side to you.
Intriguing me with your ways;
free as a bird, proud as an eagle.

Taking life as it comes,
friendships as they are;
you give benefit to the doubt,
innocent until proven guilty.

Honest in your ways
deceit is unimaginable.
Finding good in most people
seems like your common practice.

Quiet in showing gratitude
you only strengthen the bond.
An unspoken understanding
reflects your thoughts, others
worth.

As the days wind on,
I treasure your other side:
the side I have been privileged to
see.

To have friends, first you must be
one.
It is the kindness & honesty you
possess
that makes you so special.

Vernon Howard Hays
**Though We Gain The
Whole World**
We have conquered, we have
mastered; both depth and outer
space
And proudly lure disaster upon
the human race.
We launch the mighty rocket and
mark its blazing trace
Aim it at the moon to smack it in
the face.

We shudder, we tremble as we
sense our earthly plight
So we covet an orbit for our
homemade satellite.
We have scarred the earth with
battles and fought our common
foe
But still we see him lurking
everywhere we go.

With every toil and effort to
reach a higher plane
We multiply our sorrow and call
it earthly gain.
We squander and demolish, even
pulverize
The creative wonders of the One
so great and wise.

We build the finest cities and set
them all aglow
Then bring them death and ruin
with one atomic blow.
We are avid little specks that
compose the human race
Just a bit of dust on the earth
which we disgrace.

We are busy little creatures all
tuned up for speed
And there's our greedy neighbor
with everything we need.
We mark ourselves a boundry to

divide our race and kind
And never know the friendship
we may have locked behind.

Don Stocker
My Love My Winter Kill

*Dedicated to JoAnn and the
seasons of love we experienced
together . . .*

My love
so like this winter night
so like the falling snow,
so like this diamond quilt of
white
gone when the big winds blow;

My love
so like the darkness
so like these barren trees,
so like the sound of laughter
on the empty winter breeze;

My love
the night falls hard
on this lonely Christmas Eve.

My love
so like this gypsy moon
so like this gathering storm,
winterkill comes all too soon
when love takes many forms;

My love
so like this winterkill
that tunes the barren trees,
don't tell me the end has
suddenly come
on an empty winter breeze;

My love
you are the twilight
born of this Christmas Eve.

This night our love is real love
(if only make believe)

Sally Dutton Cantrell
THE U S of A
Here in the U S of A,
We have everything anyone
would want;
But all you hear people say,
Is downing our Country the U S
of A.

Why can't people stop and look
At what we have;
Compared to other countries,
It's just like opening up a fairy
tale book.

We have two very precious
reasons
To be proud to be Americans;
It comes with all four seasons,

First is God, Second is
Freedom.

Mrs. Gladys Snider
**My Love For a Beautiful
Rose**
God picked a beautiful rose one
day
from his heavenly bouquet
and gave the gift of life
which he made from a little piece
of clay.

God gave me my baby in the
early spring
to gladden my heart
and fulfill my dreams.
He taught me how to love it
with all my heart and soul,
this beautiful rose.

Autumn came the petals began to
fall
Slowly they fell to the ground
to be covered by the snow.
He didn't promise me the rose
would stay
Soon he took it home
for a new bouquet.

Oh Lord, please don't let me
cry
for this little piece of clay
If there is a question,
Tell me why?
You just loaned it, now it's faded
away.
My heart is filled with sadness
and untold joy
Oh, but the memories I have
death can never destroy,
my love for a beautiful rose.

John Glover
FRIENDS ARE
Friends are for good
Friends are sure
Friends are right
Friends are to help you
Friends are that cares
Friends are love
Friends are you and me
Friends are yours
Friends are mine
Friends are together
Friends are happyiness.

Nannie C. Nelson Hooper
AT THE NORTH POLE
Santa Claus and all his little
elves.
Were working too hard in spite of
themsleves.
They curried the reindeer. they
polished the sled.
They worked and they loaded.
Till they almost dropped dead.
But tired or not. they wouldn't
stop.
They had work to do and no time
to drop.
They laughed and they sang.
and moved ever so quick.
Because they were working for
Jolly Saint Nick.
Here comes the sleigh bells a
ting-a-ling ling.
Here comes the packages all they
can bring.
Here comes the carols and Old
Nick's Ho-Ho.
So it's Christmas again, as you
might well know.
So have a nice Christmas. they

sing and they shout.
As the sleigh is all loaded. and at
last he starts out.
Merry Christmas he echoes. I'll
soon be back here
And we'll start all over again and
prepare for next year.
Merry Christmas, December
1975.

Evelyn Green Boehmlehner
Christmas At Grandma's
The ground is white with
crunchy snow
And Christmas lights are all
aglow;
Packages are wrapped and
beneath the tree,
Soon there will come shouts of
glee!
Grandpa sits in his easy chair,
Hoping his family soon will be
there;
For the table's set and the
turkey's done
And he's planning to eat at half-
past one!
The guests have come, there's a
knock on the door,
Soon there'll be greetings and
chatting galore.
A little boy, with happy grin,
"Hi! Gwamma!" he says, then
bounces in;
A little girl, so sweet and shy,
Offers a kiss, then dashes by;
While grown-up children of
yesteryears
Are welcomed home with happy
tears.
When dinner is eaten and dishes
are done
Then opening gifts becomes part
of the fun;
Next singing carols of "peace on
earth",
Of a manger in Bethlehem and
Jesus' birth.
Together the family, loving and
caring,
Knows Christmas time is a time
for sharing.

Teri Anderson
I CRY FOR THE WORLD
Teardrops fall from swollen eyes
She screams but no one hears her
cries
Her torn dress and dirty feet
Have walked many a busy street
I cry for the world

He wakes in the gutter no
unusual sight
And realizes he made it through
the night
Today he'd only take a few more
drinks
But by nightfall into the gutter
he sinks
I cry for the world

In a hotel room a young girl cries
As she remembers the fights and
the lies
She walks across the room to a
small baby bed
And she beats her child until he
is dead
I cry for the world

He grasped the bottle and twisted
the lid

494

Into his hand the small pills slid
He popped in his mouth the very
    last one
And quietly he reached for his
    gun
I cry for the world

Someone didn't have the time to
    spare
They decided they didn't care
We want to know why the
    world's such a mess
Well, it's because we couldn't
    care less

Inside of our lives we're curled, as
    God silently cries for the world

Paul J. Willis
THE EARTH
In my infancy I dreamed. A
    primal dream it was.
My oceans sighed and rolled. It
    was my heartbeat.
    But no consciousness was there.
No ear heard, no eye to behold.
The clouds piled against the sky.
They stood above the shrouded
    mountains high
As aeons went slowly by.
Still my oceans moved, and
    breezes blew.
In my fertile soil great trees and
    grasses grew.
Then tiny beings appeared and
    crept across my face and
    reasoned.
This, I exulted, is my dream. I
    have a purpose for being.
Centuries came and went.
These creatures called men
    increased greatly in number.
Moving across my face,
    building great cities,
        changing my natural beauty.
They fought wars, gouged holes
    in my face,
Scratched lines for their speeding
    machines.
The smoke from these and their
    cities ascended into the heavens
            for all to see.
Now I appeal to that tiny
    conscious creature,
                    "SAVE ME."

Beverly A. Ross
FEEL WITH ME

---

*To Michael, a special friend
whose 'beholding eye' is much
like mine, and who introduced
me to the California ocean.*

Listen to the gentle beat of
    running feet
As I aim for unknown destinies.
Feel the yielding sand as I curl
    my toes
Absorbing the unspeakable joys
    around me.

The sun's rays drip through the
    clouds
And caress as they flow over my
    body.
A leaping breeze brushes against
    me
Sending vibrations through my
    spine.

A laughing wave rolls into shore

Showering me with its abounding
    ecstasy,
Leaving me soaking with
    expanding happiness,
Wondering at the perfect
    miracles of nature.

H. T. Rotchstein
FAMILY DEPRESSION

To my loving wife, Annie

When family problems accumulate
And depression seems your fate—
Let your mind form the weapons
    needed.
Past life's experiences have you
    well seeded!
Open your eyes; see the concern?
Faces around you—lighted! A
    lantern,
Signalling clearly, weapons must
    be used.
Fight! Once again, the
    family—you—fused!

Mari Jane Hill
JOHN'S BIBLE
John reads his bible every night
    for he knows its the staff of life.
John knows God's love is pure
    and true and God wants us to
    feel it to.
John feels God's with us through
    thick and thin, He helps us on
    our feet again.
John believes God forgives our
    sins so we can live our lives
    again.
John studies each page verse and
    Psalm and with each one he
    prays along.
John reads his bible every night,
    before turning out the light.

Sherry Monique Herbst
NOSTALGIA TOYS
I remember an avenue with shops;
    it was, in retrospect, an ordinary
    thoroughfare,
but when a child, I thought it to
    be voluminous.
It contained places that held for
    me
a precious aura of mystery and
    thrills,
and a potency of intrigue.
To this day I have variation-on-a-
    theme dreams,
during sleep hours,
sleep, that segment of life
    wherein we dwell in fantasy;
In particular I recall the hardware
    store with its
bright copper teakettle in the
    window,
homey, cozy, a kind of polished
    lollipop.
Beyond that initial enticement
    lay such an assortment——
after opening the door with its
    sweetly tinkling bell.
All those gleaming goodies, each
    with charismatic scent.
There were nails and pails and
    gardening goods,
clothespins fresh and white
    (split-wood-with-knobby-top)
sparkling pieces of glass, and

silvery tools,
cans of creamy paint and brooms
    and brushes,
fireplace things in fine array,
yardsticks and oilcans and
    houses for birds,
wallpaper rolls and linoleum . . .
so I had 'toys' that were free of
    cost, and too,
philosophically pleasurable,
    carrying me to realms
not governed by money. Ah,
    memory!

Inez Ainsworth Havens
Merry Christmas America

---

*To those who have so willingly
served our beloved country, to
whom I feel forever indebted and
for you my sons Ronnie, Wayne,
David and Rodger.*

Merry Christmas sweet America!
You're so special this time of year,
And I have a gift to give you—
    one you purchase with blood
    and tears.

Was in World War I my great
    grandaddy sailed across the
    ocean blue;
Went because he loved his
    country,
There he died for me and you.

Twenty some odd years later
    came mighty World War II;
They called upon my daddy,
And he fought for me and you.

Then restless winds blew a sad
    song across our land so dear;
My uncle heard you crying
And he left for South Korea.

My oldest brother just out of
    high school;
Just when his best days had begun,
Wrote the letter that was
    postmarked VIETNAM.

Told us nothing is worth nothing
    in a land that isn't free—
Miss you so this Christmas,
But my country needed me.

Now, if for me tomorrow those
    distant drums should call,
Because I love you dearly,
To thee I would give my ALL.
I would sail that same deep ocean
    just like my great grandad,
For you are the greatest country
    any man has ever had.

Merry Christmas sweet
    America— this is my gift to
    you—
It's my pledge of allegiance and
    my promise to be true.

Karin L. Oden
TIME
I distinctly remember that cold,
    gray October morning when he
    gently
said goodbye. I felt as if the walls
    of my life came tumbling down
upon me, getting heavier and
    heavier with each word spoke.

I tried to understand, but the
    more I tried, the more my own
    thoughts
ran endlessly from one side of my
    brain to the other. Always on
    the
rebound and not going anywhere
    but to and fro.

My once heavy heart that was
    full of love for him seemed to
    become
lighter and with each beat of that
    heart, I could hear it echo
inside of me. Getting louder and
    louder every minute that he
    was speaking.

Soon the echo was inside of my
    brain, in my ears, thumping as
    if
I had some biological imbalance.
    Pretty soon it started hurting.
My legs felt so weak that I didn't
    dare attempt to stand, my
    hands
seemed to tremble like I had an
    electrical shock sent through my
    body. It just wouldn't stop.

Minutes wore into hours and
    somehow that feeling didn't
    cease
inside of me. In my mind I tried
    the thought of
loving him against the thought of
    losing him, and you know
something? The side that weighed
    the love always came out
    heavier.

Jim Stevens
DID I FORGET
Did I forget to tell you
The way I often feel
Did I forget to say
My love for you is real

Did I neglect to mention
Your life is my life too
Did I fail to tell you
I love you as I do

Did I forget to tell you
How much you mean to me
Did you think I'd forgotten
The depths of our dreams

Its time to remember
Our love stood the test
Of the things I cherish
I cherish your love best

I'm reminded of commitments
As lovers and best friends
Of never dying vows
Everlasting to the end

Did I forget to tell you
You are that special friend

495

Did I forget to say
Devotion will never end

Lets renew our vows again
Revive dreams of yesterday
Did I forget to tell you
Did I forget to say

Patricia Trudeau
WINTER MONDAY
A hundred faces mill and sulk
about the door.
Two hundred others pour
across the intersecting streets
protesting the encroachment
of the week
upon the weekend.
Late winter slump and February
thaw
combine to unexcite
the ordinary and the bright.
School's an ordeal to be endured
until a clear and cleaner day
of outdoor play
and lighter clothing.

Albert R. Horrell
REDEDICATION
The old year ends; I pause, reflect,
review
The gains and losses of the days
just past;
The happy hours, the sorrows,
moments shared
With those I love——memories
that will last.

But also comes to mind the need
to seek
A closer walk with Him who
died for me
On Calvary's cross, that one day I
might stand
Before His throne to live
eternally.

I'll look to Him for guidance each
new day,
And let His Word direct the way
I go,
That others might see Him in all
I do
And they might know this One
Who loves them so.

Gloria J. Hans
SEA BREEZE

---

*With all my love, Norma, Mark
and Kristy Champion Dedicated
to all my friends in Sea Breeze
especially Larry and Kari This
one's for you, Pig.*

A warm wind blows up from the
north and wakes my memories,
I think about some old, dear
friends and a little town called
Sea Breeze,
Lake Ontario caresses the town;
my dreams walk along her
shore,
Tender blue skies fill my eyes,
and make me come back for
more.
Down in Sea Breeze is my home
Just in Rochester, I love to roam,
Sea Breeze is the only home I
know; that's where he is and I
must go

For all the boys in the fire house
to the folks living on the lake,

Old home style and a country
smile, what a fine home this
would make.
Sunday rides at the amusement
park; a place the children all
love.
You see I want my children
playing there and its all I ever
think of.
Come on Baby, take my hand
Don't make me get down on my
knees,
All I want is to be by your side
Come on take me home to Sea
Breeze.

You see this place never leaves
me alone
It invades my dreams and calls
me home
Sea Breeze: what a fine place to
be, home, just you and me.

Way down in Sea Breeze
That's where I'm to go.
Down with my baby, its the only
home I know.

Richard Tuttle
THE BREATHING SEA
The breathing sea,
Never dying—Never living—But
always moving.
The breathing sea,
It stretches out its watery hands
on all shores,
Never smiling—Never
frowning—But always
impelling.
The breathing sea,
Its hypnotic powers wash no
favorites.
Never excited—Never dull but
always instigating.
The breathing sea,
What man can touch its form
without it seeping through?
Never laughing—Never crying
but always influencing.
The breathing sea,
It possesses nothing but takes all
its running eyes can see.
Never joking—Never serious but
always persuading,
The breathing sea.

Helen Jayne Johnson
Octagonal Touchstone
Where does the connection begin
. . . Who can fathom the
effects of being?
Perhaps if I retrace my hurried
steps I could recall,
with some feeling
How I once stood, pensive and
defiant looking through
shattered glass
With it's sagging, undressed
wooden frame making
it's decline . . .
While I wondered if there could
be a tranquil, unslanted
answer to your enchanting
Letter that fondly ricochets
across my mind, so
conviently sent
Awakening me away to the
beginning of a beginning:
It extended around to more than
you . . . Then placing one
thought against the other
I dared to touch and challenge

you . . in spite of you, and
Still the landmark lingers.

Gail J. Cleaver
BLINDNESS
As I sit here I wonder
how it came to be,
that we with our hearts
and our eyes cannot see
the pain and the hunger
the thirst and the fear,
the screams of the dying—
our children so dear.
How could it have happened?
Their doom shall we shun?
Is there not an answer
to save even one?
The prayer and the promise
no matter how brave,
will not save the child
sent too soon to his grave . . .

Deannelle Mote Whitmire
THE VISION
The errie shadows of forms once
been.
Of mists which take shape. They
ebb, they flow. Fading back,
then again, as big, as real as life
before thy eyes they become.
To laugh, to scorn, to tell some
tale of woe.
The nameless faces of the past
What shudders,
would our flesh, but feel. If knew
we, their
tragic fate. To walk among these
errie shadows
of forms once been, holds no
desire for those,
whose courage, so fast doth take
flight. When
visions such as these plague
them . . .

The errie shadows

Criquette Montague
AGE AND SADNESS
Swiftly, as a sudden storm on a
summer's night
A teardrop came trembling into
my sight
It came from Age and Sadness
To show me it was almost o'er
Such a harsh and realistic way

BUT—what more *is* there to say?
Except to regret *so much* left
undone

So little time from Sun to Sun!

James Wyle Murray
DEATH
Death—
the inexplicable, untimely
mystery of passing;

Death—
the enigmatic, unthinkable
wished— for avoidance;

Death—
the sad and sardonic illusion of
lifelessness;

Death—
be not deceiving—a contrivance
of the ultimate fraud.

Death—
behold thy truthful exposure,
you are but an extension of life.

Death—
where is thy sting? Fear erased,

peace of mind, my door is open.
Death—
now powerless, stripped of its'
strength, in the hands of my
God.

Dr. Ray Glover, Wheeler, Ms.
**When the Roses Bloom
Again**
I suppose that Mama was the first
word I learned to say
And I suppose that it was Mama
who taught me first to pray.

I'm sure that it was Mama who
first held me so tight,
Who tucked me in at bedtime
and first kissed me good-night.

The first things in life are the
things that make life dear,
They give life hope and beauty
and grow fonder with the
passing years.

Life is filled with heartaches,
disappointment wrecks our
plans;
But everything is reconciled with
the help of Mama's hands.

Mama was never satisfied to
simply give advice;
But was willing for things to be
rectified at the peril of sacrifice.

I've seen her laugh, I've seen her
cry, I've seen her kneel to pray,
No matter what else becomes
dear to me I'll remember her
that way.

Her life to me was like a rose
with a fragrance rich and rare,
Enchanting us who loved her
most with tender love and care.

But winter comes at the
appointed time and the rose
must fade and die
And leaving in us this empty spot
we can't help but wonder why.

But time will pass as time must
do; and spring will bring the
rain
And I'll meet her there in the
garden of life when the roses
bloom again.

Jan Kotlewski Huffman
SHARE
A jug of wine
Some time well spent
Good friends like this
Are heaven sent
They're always there
In times of need
And when you're lost
They'll take the lead
You call them up
Or just stop by
For a good laugh——
Perhaps a cry
My friend, you mean
So much to me
Deep in my heart
You always see
All that I am
And so much more
I do not fear
My heart to pour
And when there's joy
You share that too
Life means so much
For there is you!

Ella Mae Sanders
PEACE OF MIND

I dedicate this poem to Dorothy (Parsons-Duncan) Monsen for the encouragement and loyalty she gave me through the years.

Its a wonderful thing to have
  peace of mind,
It enriches the pleasures that you
  will find.
The flowers are larger, the sun
  shines brighter,
Your loved ones encircle a bond
  much tighter.
The trees seem more tall, the sky
  more clear,
The moon and the stars all seem
  so near.
The lake seems more blue, the
  grass more green,
Its the prettiest day you have
  ever seen.
The wind sighs more softly, the
  birds sing more sweetly,
The laundry smells fresher and
  folds more neatly.
The smells from the kitchen are
  more aromatic,
And the whole wide world is not
  as traumatic.
The children are happy and you
  bless them each one,
For some special task they have
  each well done.
Its a beautiful thing to have
  peace of mind
For it multiplies the joys we all
  should find.
Its a wonderful thing to have
  found someone to care,
To have found someone who
  seems able to share,
To have found someone who is
  affectionate and kind.
Yes, this gives me contentment
  and great peace of mind.

Penny Custer
IN MEMORY

My grandfather has been dead for
  eight short years,
Which brings back many shedded
  tears.
It just seems like yesterday my
  mom told me that grandpa had
  passed away,
I was only seven at the time, so I
  burst into tears and asked
  myself "why."
It never occurred to me that one
  day, I would lose someone I
  loved,
But now I know that grandpa is
  rejoicing in heaven, way up
  above.
I don't remember him very well,
But I do know, he didn't deserve
  to go to hell.
He was a better man than that,
He wasn't too skinny or too fat.
He was just right,
He never had a sad face, he
  always had a smiling face and
  looked really bright.
I loved my grandpa with all my
  heart,

Now that we live thousands of
  miles apart.
He'll always be with me,
Where ever I may be.

Christine Lee Gindt
Cirrus Of Corn II (day)

Upon the coming
  of dawn,
A chariot of God
  chalenges the mystic.

It rears and and does not stop,
  it screams; and
Thunder is on the air.

The mystic answers
  in its own awsome way.

And the day has become;
  There is a mane of fire
In the sky, and a clash
  of white, and all
    begins again.

Osuleta
CHRISTMAS MORN

When he awoke on Christmas
  Morn his world contained life's
  joys
A Christmas tree—a floor
  bedecked with sugar plums and
  toys
He never tried to rationalize how
  all of this could be
Nor ever tried to understand
  cause or effect to see
Accepted that which fate had
  choose nor paused to wonder
  why
The Gods of fate had favored him
  and passed some others by
Deep seated faith—accepted joy
  or sorrow as fate wrought
Ah! would that we may
  understand this lesson that he
  taught

Lois A. Hart
EARTH'S REWARD

Ah, Winter! Now I, Earth, can Rest,
'Til Spring when again I'll
  Awaken with Zest;
With Sweetened, Fresh Breaths I
  shall Resume On,
Slipping into Summer where My
  Lively, Green Dress I'll Don.
Autumn's Tone shall begin My
  Grand Finale and Silent Song,
Wherein My Harvests are
  Reaped, My Vibrant Colors rise
  Strong;
Richly Mixing they'll Wave
  Victoriously in All—glorious a
  Throng,
Signaling, also, My Work's
  Completed then for Another
  Met Deadline,
As Winter waits in the wing
  whispering, "The next Turn is
  Mine."
For out of The Green I will have
  Bowed into My Brown Robe on
  time,
Slowly but surely once hearing
  Winter's distant yet Warning
  Chime.
Clad with All—readiness I'll
  shortly receive My Annual
  Reward Divine,
Winter's Fluffy-soft, White
  Blanket under which to Recline.
Ah yes, Winter! For His Turn

shall Always be My Resting
  Time.

Ida M. Kazakos
BRIGHT AND SHINING

Bright and shining
No repining
Lost in a meadow of new love's
  pain
While you're dreaming,
I'm just scheming
How I may find you in my arms
  again
When you need me
Will you lead me
Back into your heart the same old
  way?
Old love wearing
New love sharing
My old love and my new love
Both you
While I want you
I shall haunt you
Even as you yet taunt me too
As I'm singing
Bells are ringing
Telling me that you'll be back to
  stay.

Joseph Emile Moghabghab
THE GOVERNOR

*To Dad, Mom, Dolly, Naji, Grace
and Karen*

Sleep, oh sleep little boy.
  Get enough sleep, because
    tomorrow
you're going to govern the world.
  You are meant to have a hard life,
sleep little boy, get enough rest.
  You are going to be a governor
    soon.
Look where you are lying at birth
  and
  look where you will be lying
    when
you die, what a difference.
  It is going to be a long journey.
Sleep little boy . . . Joseph and
  Mary were
  looking at him with loving eyes.

Ms. Tracy L. Fintelmann
IS IT OVER?

You tell me it won't work.
After two years and no fights,
what is it that won't work?

You say you love me and care
  deeply
but do you know the hurt I have
when you can't even drop a line?

When I call you say it is great,
"How are you? Nothing is new.
Take care, see you around",
but you need to know I'm
alright and happy—why?

You say you are not coming back.
Why, then, aren't you happy?
Why must you see me?

Why do you invite me to meet
  you?
Why do you kiss me and hug me?
Why do you make love to me?

Why can't you let me go?
Why can't I let you go?
Why do I know that you are
  always there?

You say it won't work out
or is the feeling too strong?
Will we ever escape—
but do we really want to?

Gunhild Hatcher
MARK 10:15

The gentle Messiah came to earth
Our sins to wash away.
But along the way he stopped to
  say
"Listen to me this day.
To me this child is worth much
  more
Than all this world's riches and
  gold,
And unless you accept me like
  this little child,
You'll never heaven behold."

Robert J. Miller
A TEXTURE

*TO: Bernice C.
Owens—Robertson*

As years have flown since we
Went from Myrt Davis orchard
To Arch Faulkner cabin upstream
From our county school, guards
To revisioning the day of youth
Shared scenes I thought gone save
Random relics, or a chance
  fragment
Retrieved; not so with ore
Your loyalty's whose gift redeems
Generality for specific retention:

The cabin water-well photographed
A nineteen-thirty decade, you kept;
Retaining other landscape views;
Blent with kindness becomes
  virtue
Which intrinsically nurtures
Vital troves of lithe entelechy;
And though lacking means to
  conjure
An Elysian realm thoroughly
When it is distant; may endued
Mental seeds here trained convey
That pteral texture woe resistant.

Linda Spring Andrews
MY HAVEN

Walking down the winding path,
  that led my feet to find.
All the thoughts and memories,
  secure within my mind.

I wonder why I can not feel,
  this way on other roads.
For even though it's used and
  worn,
  this one still shares my load.

The rushing waters in the stream,
that can be heard so near.
Entice my heart to find its banks,
and shed my unshared tears.

The house of stone, secure in
place,
beneath the knarling oak.
Invites me in to take my place,
within this molded cloak.

Surrounded by the pleasant scenes,
that line the inner walls.
Remind me of familiar days,
which memories recall.

This is the place to which I'm
drawn,
when life demands its share.
The winding path, the rushing
stream,
the house of stone are there.

Nita Smith
MY GARDEN

---

*This poem is dedicated to the
memory of my dad, D. A.
Richards, who taught me the love
of the soil and to appreciate the
blessings of life.*

My garden is a part of me.
It's like my bread and butter.
It's like a soothing cup of tea,
Or comfort from my Mother.

When winter lies upon the land
The snow and ice are deep.
Through all of this I see God's
hand.
I know his promises He will keep.

For after winter comes the Spring.
The barren earth turns green.
It's time to till the soil again
In hopes of harvest it will bring.

I love to walk and drop the seed
In rows plowed fresh and straight.
I look ahead when we can feed
on all the good things it will make.

It isn't just the thought of food,
But the beauty of each tender
sprout
That puts you in receptive mood
And teaches you what life's about.

Life isn't just to live and die.
It's all the things we have to face,
To laugh and love and grow and
try
And leave the world a better place.

Linda Spring Andrews
WHAT FRIENDS ARE FOR
The grains of sand that filter
through the hourglass of time,
Outnumber, only by a few the
hairs of gray which line
The golden locks, or tresses,
black, that framed the leaner
years,
Remembering this span that
lacked the contact of our tears.
The warmth that grows through
stories, old, so dear and near
our hearts.
Erases every trace of mold from
memories, in part,
Of times, though gone, not far
from thought encouraged to
return.
To spin a web, intensely sought,

a frame for which we yearn.
To feel the joys of yesteryears
as if it were today.
And hold together thoughts, so
dear, beguiling words to say . . .
"There is a special place within
this casing, time has frayed,
Which longs, and really tries to
mend the passing of the days."
This want for memories to yield a
thought, or two or three
Of times which life no longer
deals in terms of you and me,
Lifts up the latch into the heart
which tends to seal the door,
To all the warmth we wish to
catch, and that's what friends
are for.

Betty E. Mercer
LORD, LEND ME
Lord, lend me thine ears, that I
might hear,
Words of the Truth, Thou
sendest clear.
Lend me thine eyes, that I may see,
All the blessings of life, Thou
givest to me.
Lend me thy mouth, that I might
say,
Some good word, to help someone
each day.
Lend me thy nose, that I might
smell,
All the fragrances and beauty,
that words just can't tell.
Lend me thy hands, that I might
do,
Something my Lord, that will
glorify you.
Lend me thy feet, that I might go,
And tell the Gospel to others,
and your great love to show.
Lend thy Spirit, and flood my soul,
So that I too, can be perfectly
whole.

Rhonda A. Moran
Sonny Boy Of Farben Drive
My Sonny, My Sonny
Always a joy.

My Sonny, so precious
A wonderful boy!

Whenever I'm lonely,
Frightened or sad,

Cuddling up,
He makes me feel glad.

He plays with his toys,
He's soft and he's shy.

His eyes are enormous . . . .
Sometimes he cries!

Understanding, patient,
and unendingly fair.

Undemanding, unforgiving and
eternally there.

While you may think I'm
off my rocker.

GOD knows how . . . .
I love my Cocker ! ! !

Brad Carter
LIFE MOVES FAST
How may ways the heavens say.
It seems so simple, we see every
day.
We take for granted the things
we share.
Sometimes even forgetting to care.

We hear talk of Father Time-
moving along.
Mother Nature is mentioned in a
song.
Love is used in so many ways to
link.
But what is real-from heart and
mind, I think.

No man makes the sun rise.
No man in the moon-fairy tales lie.
A power greater than mans quest
Control these things with what
we're blest.

Look around you and you'll find
Good things if you seek that kind.
For a place in the sun, each day,
If only for a brief moment I pray.

Give thanks each day for bread
and health,
For friends, family and self, that's
wealth.
The struggle down lifes highway
moves fast,
From crib to cane, then it's passed.

Richard L. Mitchell
THE QUESTION
How much do I love you?
I can't begin to say
My love for you changes
With every passing day.

How much do I love you?
It's you I always miss
I spend the time we're apart
Longing for your sweet kiss.

How much do I love you?
The gleam in my eyes should tell
I'm deeply in love with you girl
You've got me under your spell.

How much do I love you?
As time goes on you'll see
My love for you get stronger
Stronger than any love could ever
be.

How much do I love you?
It's easier for me to say
I'll love you more tomorrow
Much more than yesterday.

How much do I love you?
Only God and I know for sure
To answer the question honestly
though
My love for you is pure.

Betty J. Shoemaker
QUIET TIME
When I feel the need
Of a little quiet time.
I sit down at my desk
And begin to write in rhyme.

For to write a letter or a poem
Is quite relaxing for me.
So when I'm doing this
It's my "quiet time" you see.

Lee Ann Shouse
You Were Always There
When I needed you most you
were always there.
When I needed a friend you'd
always care.
When I'd fall down, you'd pick me
up.
When I was thirsty, you'd fill my
cup.
When I felt lonesome, sad or
blue . . .
You knew exactly what to do.
You'd never harm me in any way,

By what you'd do or what you'd
say.
You are the best friend, I have
ever had.
You make me feel happy and
glad.
Be there for others, and stay there
for me.
My very best friend you have
deserved to be.
From now until the end of
time . . .
I am glad to say that you are mine.

Mary-Margaret
CHEER UP
I know it's raining,
but keep a smile in
your heart or
think of a special memory
and smile . . .
The rain will go away.

And the sun will shine
tomorrow . . . .
And we'll make more memories;
just keep thinking
happy thoughts
And the rain will go away.

Barbara Horn Dunn
PROMISE
Little clouds of dapple gray
prance swift across the sky
Making a patchwork quilt
of a meadow where two lovers
lie.
While spring perfumes the air
with the scent of tender flowers,
Two hearts are met in love;
old trees become their bower.
And love, full of conceit,
knows it owns the spring
Holding fast the promise
that summer is a wedding ring.

Mary Ashley Axtell
A FADED DREAM
We walked hand in hand in love's
delight,
. . . We laughed
We tasted bitter tears on our
cheeks,
. . . We cried.
We knew intimacy so precious
and rare,
. . . We shared.
We longed for eternity together,
. . . We dreamed.

Judith M. Plytynski-Young
CHRISTMAS IS FOR KIDS
Remember when your breath
stayed in circles on the cold
window
And you made butterflies in the
snow
Remember when you tried to
stay awake for Ho-Ho-Ho-!
And crept downstairs and found
eaten cookies and wrapped
presents everywhere
Remember when you stood chin
high to the windowsill and
watched white mounds pile up
to your nose
And felt warm and safe under
piles of afghans with daisies
And snoopys all over your wall
Remember when Chris took your
barbie doll shoes because she
lost hers
And you wrestled her across the

Our World's Best Loved Poems

floor
Remember when you thought
Santa's beard was the
boogieman and you ran fast,
smack into a mannequin and
she broke in three pieces
And mom looked at you with
red cheeks
Remember the new, red flannel
pajamas you shined your new
train with
Remember when Dad said—
"Presents will be opened after
church!"
And you fought to sit near the
door of the car and bit your
nails all the way home
Remember when your lace
crinoline itched your legs and
you couldn't undestand
why you could not wear your
red pants like James
Yes, Christmas is for kids!

Nancy A. Glick
A BIRDS FLIGHT
Sometimes it seems as though
I was born just yesterday

And then yesterday sometimes
Seems like an eternity ago

Like a birds flight
Through a clear blue sky

Winging to an endless journey
Through times passages

From yesterday to today . . .

Ann Hughes Singer

Ann Hughes Singer
NEW HAMPSHIRE
In New Hampshire the air seems
to issue out of another world.
So sweet, it has the quality of
being heard; as if the tinkling
of many glass bells.
Scotch plaids take form within
the mountain tapestries of
green and blue.
Blowing over the mountains,
delicate wispy clouds ride in
shapes of lions and dragons.
Cold, smooth veins of marble
under my feet, are sandwiched
in the granite ledge.
At night, under the pine at the
lakes edge,
I stand in the silken moonlight
unearthing romantic visions
stirred by the loons' lonely call.
My hair is carried away in the
clean lake breezes, but my
heart is caught in the glazed

waves beneath which my visage
is bathed.

Teresa E. Westbrook
THE CHRISTMAS MOUSE
This is a story of a Christmas
Mouse
And how he brought joy to the
Kringle House.
He lived in the baseboards of a
wall
That ran down a long and narrow
hall.
His body was weakend, his
clothing was torn
He layed on his death bed, he
cried and mourned.
The season was Christmas, a time
for joy
But what the little mouse wished
for was not a toy.
He prayed for some crumbs or
just some cider
His belt grew loose and it felt
tighter.
He turned just a little, to lay on
his back
And saw a bright light, shine
through a crack!
The little mouse smiled, he was
not alone,
For Christmas Eve was over, Kris
Kringle was home.
Kris Kringle fed him, the mouse
felt stronger
His body was well, he was sick
no longer.
To all of you who read The
Christmas Mouse
May you have happiness and love
all through your house.

Judith Shannon Paine
WINTER WINE
It is Winter here.
The hills exhale a fog that
encircles
their snow-silvered shoulders.
Suddenly, the sky spits Ravens.

Sleek and Satanic, they wheel and
call.
As one, they land in the Orchard.
They peck angrily and curse the
scarlet fruit frozen on the bough;

Winter wine in wrinkly wineskins
Solidified.

The knarled tree sighs its secrets.
The birds ascend.
Black silence rides an icy wind.
It is Winter here . . .

The meanest season of the year.

Ruth Peak
FAITH OF OUR MOTHERS
Faith of our mothers, ever true
Through sorrow, toil, and sacrifice,
Guiding our faltering, wayward
feet,
Pointing to Heaven our eager eyes.

Faith of our mothers-guiding
faith—
We will be true to thee till death!

Childhood and youth thou didst
inspire—
Of noble heroes we have learned;
Though disappointments deep
have come,
Never our loss that faith has
spurned.

Faith of our mohers—we will love
Both friend and foe and, free from
strife,
In peace we'll teach the uplifting
power
Of kindly words and virtuous life.

Faith of our mothers—loving
faith—
We will be true to thee till death!

Karen Lee Dull
TIME
Today is but a measurement
for me to measure change
Each minute is a special gift
that only I arrange

Only I can use my gift
it's given just to me
To use as really I so choose
Choose wise or foolishly

While I measure I must grow
one movement at a time
As I change and change I must
each move becomes a climb

I will rise to know the truth
the truth that sets me free
For all the time that ever was
is now eternity

David Micheal Rubsam
EARLY MORNING

---

*To my father and mother—with
love; and to Michele P.—my good
friend.*

As ribbons of sunlight
sink shafts to the forest floor
fog wisps undulate
and curl around
nodding ferns,
struggling weakly
before vanishing
into nothingness.

Mrs. Kelly (Velma) Haynes
HIS ROCKING CHAIR
His wife had died, he lived alone
He had no children of his own,
He'd fix a meal, then sit and stare
And tap the arms of his rocking
chair.

No daily newspaper came his way
As he sat alone day after day
No. T. V. set . . . just a radio there
On the table by the arm of his
rocking chair.

With a frown, or a chuckle, or a
smile on his face
He'd recall a by-gone person or
place.
For once in a while, a memory
he'd share
While he tapped the arms of his
rocking chair.

Then a sad day came, we knew it
would
But he whispered as round his
bed we stood,
"I trusted Jesus long ago.
"I've thought about that a lot, you
know."

Now, with pondering heart, we'll
sigh,
Or we'll smile while recalling
days gone by.
We'll rememeber him oft as we
sit and stare

At the arms of the empty rocking
chair.

Robert Gentry
We Are Still Together
Within the endless track of time
and space,
Spanning the immensity of the
void between us,
We are still together.

Within the depths of my heart,
And the dark recesses of my mind,
We are still together.

Together, as the currents of the
wind bring forth the phantom
of your voice.
Together, as the softness of the
clouds radiates the image of
your beauty.
Together, as the sun beams down
the warmth of your smile.
We are still together.

These memories, these ghosts of
the past,
How they haunt me, always
present, always just out of reach.
They haunt me, and yet they
soothe me as they hover, like
poltergeists, never slacking,
always prompting.
We are still together.

Winifred A. Coburn
NATURAL PHENOMENA
Harvest the Autumn sunsets.
Gather the amber leaves.
Admire the garden ablaze with
color;
The air alive with bees.

Search for the grass of velvet
green;
A brook that babbles much more.
Thirst for the sunshine as it
bathes the fields.
Seek the surf that splashes the
shore.

Follow the birds in their airy
flight.
Rekindle your childhood dream.
Venture aloof, in the age of time,
To escape natures inevitable
scheme.

Charlena Miller
HERITAGE
Envy the mountain goat
Poised on the precipice,
Moisture from crags
Cooling wandering flanks,
Master of elements
Climbing to victory
Swiftly descends
Now, to join with the ranks.
Peacefully gazing on
Thunder of sunset hue,
Adamant soul
Knowing star-riddled skies,
Canyon and rivulet—
These are his heritage,
Eagles in flight
Sounding echoing cries—
Dawn with a crashing light
Unfolds a cynosure,
Born to this art
Colors crevice, and sod,
Mighty contentment dwells
Deep in his vibrant heart,
Home is a granite tower,
Reaching . . . . . . to God!

Helen L. Anderson
LACK OF A LEADER
Like a contagious disease
Everyone seems restless.
The young . . . And the aged.
The poor . . . And the affluent.
The sick . . . And the healthy.
The unemployed . . . And the
worker.
The shopper . . . And the
merchant.
The unbeliever . . . And the
faithful.
Have we no goals?
Where are the heros?
Are there no battles to win?
Can't we plan for the tomorrow?
There is hope once again,
The Christmas Star is shining.

Lisa Eblen
A PART OF ME
Rodeo is a part of me
This I'm sure you know,

This is a very special part of me
As it will always be,

When I'm out there riding
It takes all the pains away

It keeps me wrapped in its arms
Only happiness comes within,

To understand me you must know
My purpose
To be the champion someday

Yes, I will try my best!
And Like the rest

It will always be . . .
A part of me

David J. Bacon
DESTINY'S RAY
Clouds lined with Silver, blowing
on the darkest blue
I'd ever seen, became the day
when I saw you on
the crowded subway. The soft
cream-like skin shining,
and the way your head tilted
when you saw me
staring at your beauty. Then you
looked away
with the look of despair.

How I wished Fate would bring
you over to me,
so I could wash the pain of
whatever you are
feeling away; to hold you until
you could feel the
confidence to continue the
path to your destination.

As the stop you are awaiting
arrives, you step out,
my heart goes with you, with
the hope the
solution of your problem will be
near to termination.

Maybe He kept us apart so you
could find your answer,
and will grace us with another
meeting, and
we will never part.

As I walked out of the subway,
the clouds turned to
a light, dusty gray;
But, in the small crack of a
passing cloud, appeared
a single ray of sunlight;
Possibly a Ray of Destiny, trying

to tell me to leave
my hope in His hands, and it
will Be.

Anna Florczak
Everyone's In It Together
_____

To My Godson Christopher
_____

Take a moment and examine it all
Right from the beginning, till the
end of it all
Bad times there were, let those
pass in our mind
Oh think and savor the good ones
Remember our entire life to come
I like to say the memories used
so often and much
But what a better word to
describe our entire life and
happenings in touch
Can be hard with all the rough
spots
When you strive to make it better
Sometimes that wall you built up
falls
All you have left are those
memories
Life goes on with such an uneasy
head
Why did my decisions or choices
tangle me up in a web
The rest will come that's how it
goes
Happy or sad, together we know.

Juanita Marie Harris
OCTOBER PRAYER
I Thank Thee Lord, for the beauty
I see before me.
I Thank Thee Lord for the
mountain splendor.
I Thank Thee Lord for the
morning so new.
I Thank Thee Lord for the
afternoon suns' warming ray.
I Thank Thee Lord for the
evening dressed in autumn hue.
I Thank Thee Lord, for the
mountainside
All ablaze in its Autumn coat so
new.
I Thank Thee Lord for the
beautiful blue sky,
Dotted with billowy white clouds,
That appear to be made from
some heavenly light.
I Thank Thee Lord, for the
radiant sunset,
That warns me of approaching
night.
I Thank Thee Lord for this year,
for the gift of just being here.
When I look upon natures beauty,
I Thank Thee for the peace I feel.
I Thank Thee for I know your
love for us is real.
I Thank Thee for this day even
though
It tells me wintertime is on its
way.

Sonia Sowers
**Your Mamma Is A
Whistler**
Your mamma was a whistler
So many years ago
I grew up with whistlers
A fantastic way to grow.

I remember whistling
While scrubbing all my floors
To the most delightful music
Closing off all doors.

I could scrub and whistle
And my scrubbing sure got done
With a lot of carefree whistling
Way back then, my chores were
fun.

I am still a whistler
In this house all my myself
I still play that lovely music
That has sat up on the shelf.

I've been told that "ladies"
Do not whistle—'tis not true
'Cause when you pucker up and
whistle,
Your days are never blue.

I know I'll not be famous
Somewhere along the way
So I'll just scrub and whistle
Until my dying day.

Helen Weller
RICHARD'S GIFT
He'd sit beneath
The blooming plum
While his guitar
Would gently strum;
His voice would set
His spirit free—
It soared and came
To rest on me.
I saw of love,
Felt joy and pain,
Then travelled on
An old freight train
Down tracks of life
To endless sleep;
My heart could laugh,
My soul would weep.
My brother's songs,
A gift of love,
He shared with me
And skies above.

Barbara A. Levins
CHRISTMAS MORN
_____

*To my Grandparents; Ann and
Neil Witherspoon and Agnes B.
Weeks. "This one is for you all"
with all my love, Barbara*
_____

It's early Christmas morning
and children all around
are getting parents out of bed
To show them what they've found.

Santa Claus has been here;
just look under the tree
at all the wonderful presents he
left
for the family.

An Atri computer,
a bike and a train,
a Mickey Mouse radio
and a monopoly game.

A dart board, some perfume,
a baseball and bat,
and even some chew toys
for the dog and the cat.

The stockings on the fireplace,
(what a glorious site)
were filled to the top
with every childs delight.

The view from the window
was of snow covered hills
and a large rounded snowman

all covered with frills.

And don't forget dinner,
where all who indulge
will get stuffed like the turkey
and are surely to bulge.

Yet the best part of Christmas
comes from God up above,
It's what we get in giving,
What we know as love.

Hilda Muryn
LESSONS FROM GRANMA
_____

*Dedicated to Stephanie Wieland
with love from Great-Granma
Bryant.*
_____

Ah; Come here a moment, look
over there,
An old lady is sitting in her
fireside chair,
Quietly I've watched her so many
times,
Telling the child stories and
nursery rhymes,
Patiently she sits in that fireside
chair,
Crooning to the child with the
golden curly hair.
'Tell me that one, tell me again'
granma,
So says the girl with a sly look at
me,
As she sits eagerly listening, on
Granma's knee,
And Granma's quite happy too as
I look at her there,
Crooning to the child with the
golden hair.
The childs eyes are now tiring,
she's nodding her head,
She'll dream sweet dreams when
she's put to her bed,
But right now she's quite happy
as you can see,
Cuddled up with her books on
her Granma's knee,
And Granma's quite happy too, as
I peep at her there,
Crooning to the child with the
golden curly hair.

Freda K. McRoberts
BUSY HANDS
Busy hands, you're resting now,
Hands that soothed my
fevered brow.
Hands that dried my childish
tears,
Tired from all those busy years.
Hands ever quick to mend a tear,
Or fix a ribbon in my hair.
And they never failed to bake
A delightful birthday cake.
Hands that gently seemed to bless,
Helped me don my bridal dress.
With my firstborn's lusty cry,
Those same hands were
standing by.
Though I am a woman grown,
Your passing makes me feel alone.
For I never know how much
I would miss your loving touch.

Mary Jo Massey
WINTER'S SOUL
Cold and lonely are the trees
Against the ground beats disease.

Windy and dark is the night
Frozen from stillness as ice.

Frail and sickly are the leaves
Moves about as dying weeds.

Brutally it takes its toll
Winter's cruel and vicious soul.

Jodi Rowe
THE HARVEST
I asked all over town on how to
find you
Looked in every phone book for
your name
Stood outside the house that you
once lived in
To understand the reasons that I
came

The past is so elusive, so confusing
Nothing you can touch on lonely
nights
You are all I ever feared of losing
You are all I ever held so tight

Fortune threw another hand and I
still
don't understand
When I dreamed you up one day
I never dreamed you'd go away

They say now that the harvest is
almost over
You never came back home to
claim your prize
Somewhere in the night I thought
I saw you
The fire throwing shadows on
your eyes

So come and take me home, my
time is over
The light I followed here is
almost gone
Somewhere down the road I know
I'll find you
Somewhere down the road when I
am strong

Mrs. Lillian Minnie E. Baran
YOU MAY SURVIVE
There is a time, on this green
earth,
When we must decide what we
are worth?
All around us, our fellowmen lay
dieing . . . .
On the streets, with drugs, L. S. D.
and Angel Dust.
In our city parks, muggings,
murder and rape,
Is this then our fate?

Our air is turned to acid green,
Our water, is a slimy brownish
scene.
Just what, is happening, to me
and you?
Storm winds blowen, ice laden
streets, its well known.
Volcanoes bubble up, sparks fly,
Homes are lost, politicians lie . . .
Earthquakes shudder and shake,
Orphans and widows make/

Conflicts of men, brings war,
How heavy, my heart is torn.
When dinner hour arrives,
newshour brings,
Death and Chaos . . . to the T. V.
screen.
Battered bodies, torn asunder,
It makes you shake, your head in
wonder/

Will a nuclear blast, be our end?
Is the latest missile, foe or friend?
Is Armegeddon near, is that your

horrible fear?
Did you know, of the Alliance?
There is a way, out of this rotten
mess . . .
Call on the NAME, of JEHOVAH
GOD, YOU MAY SURVIVE.///

Hubert D. Joy
THE DAY OF THE MOON
They looked into
The darkened Sky
To question, and ask
Each other why
No evidence of
Rising Sun
Could be seen
By anyone

While across the horizon
Screamed the Loon
At the rising
Of the Moon
That Spector
Pale in the Sky
Defying them
To know why
Time had forced
The Universe
To suddenly
Go in reverse.

Heidi L. Janz
Too Old To Cry For Mutti
New situations
I've got to face
Away from home-no familar face
I feel alone and out of place
But still too old to cry for Mutti

It's time, I'm told, to cut the strings
To leave behind familar things
Friendship, support: always there
Doesn't anyone still care?
But I'm too old to cry for Mutti

Independence isn't being alone
It's not always being on your own
It's taking support that you get
from friends
And building confindence to
reach the end
It's knowing my weakness that
makes me strong
And knowing where I really belong
So maybe I'm not too old to cry
for Mutti

Sue Dort
SILENTLY FLOW AND EBB
Your days silently flow and ebb;
Ever rising and ever falling
Awash between the silken threads
That are the woven years.
The fabric of your life becomes
A tapestry.

Your days silently flow and ebb
between
The silken thread.
Blinded, you rush headlong
In forgetting that each of
These days are as a gift
Given to be remembered.
How great is the cause that these
Days are used and discarded.

Your days silently flow and ebb;
Searching to a high
And deeper place
For your answer.
And you may discover that it is
Not the truth you should seek.
Rather it is the understanding of
That truth.
For in that final understanding
Will live your contentment
And journeys end at last

Irma Root Varnell
**Scene In Tehachapi
Mountains**
Rocks hewn by nature—
A quiet pool—
A pine tree tall—
Oaks, knarled with age,
Sheltering two black crows,
Preening in the sun.
Wild flowers in bloom—
Pink, yellow, and white.
A ground squirrel scampers away
From the great "iron horse"
As it wends it's way through
The green and gold Tehachapi's
Of California.

Leo W. Berg
RESOLUTION

---

*To Lani, Peter, and Erika
- with love -*

Everything will end one day,
Just like the passing year.
We all hope for another May;
Yet, the end might be so near.

Let's take some time and search
inside!
Let's fill the heart and mind
With sunshine: Love, respect, and
pride!
Let's always be most kind!

By thinking of this resolution,
And by trying it throughout the
year,
We might find the solution
Before the end is here.

Lee E. Muir
GLENNA JO

---

*To Joan who encouraged me and
to Warner Springs Ranch
California which was the setting
for this poem*

It was between the mountains
and the snow
the effervescent valleys down
below
where the wind sometimes softly
blows
that I saw the maiden Glenna Jo

She was the cool of the morning air
the fragrance of nature's tender
care
the dew drops of heaven left

undone
beautiful forever beneath the sun

The green of her eyes were deep
and warm
pools of passion yet somehow
forlorn
moments of searching of love yet
to be
searching for someone perhaps
even me

I knew in a glance what was
meant to be
two souls entwining beneath the
trees
sharing the roses of the waterfall
living the moments of natures call

The last goodbyes in the evening
mist
the warm embrace of a tender kiss
darkness and stars against the
moon
the ending of magic all to soon

Oh' the dreams that I have that
haunt my day
the feelings of love that comes
my way
when the twilight of evenings'
afterglow
makes me long for the maiden
Glenna Jo

Ronnie J. Dore'
SURVIVAL
He awakes at various intervals of
the night,
Cries uncontrollably, screams
constantly,
Bangs his head against the
bedpost—
Each night the images of
destructin, bloody gore, and
death fill his mind.

Twenty years ago this young man
was happy,
Carefree, a friend to everyone.
He was as sly as a foxhound, as
cunning as an eagle—
A boy ready to become a man.

Somehow, the years of war had
changed him—
He had returned with medals,
was given a real hero's
welcome.
But, he could never cope with life--
After all, it is difficult for a
parapalegic to survive in society.

Daily, it became increasingly
difficult for him to control his
emotions.
His eyes swelled with tears as he
watched the youngsters play
football.
He became embittered when the
"normal" person took over the
job promised him.
He felt alone, not even a "whole"
person.

American had done this to him,
four years in Vietnam—
Bodies of friend and foe lying all
around him;
Young girls and women
dismembered, small babies
covered with blood, their
entrails visible to all.
Such were the memories of his
ordeal in enemy territory.

I try to appease him, to persuade him that he is a person—
He does have a reason to be here, to be alive.
He must endure all the hardships; he must try to forget the past; he must survive.
I must convince him, I must.
Afterall, he is my brother.

Stephen Lapham
A TOAST

Written in honor of Cheryl Martin for stretching my imagination into reality Happy Birthday, January 25th, 1984

A toast
A salute
Fire and ice
A divided tribute
A myraid of ancestors
Gather
Through my third eye
Illuminating
The core of my heart
The soul of my universe
Life is forever
A morning feast

Shirley Press Sorbello
THE BREATH OF LIFE

To the memory of Mary, her strength and her goodness.

Death remains life's most humbling experience,
For it is only when faced with the loss of tomorrow
Do we begin to see in today those things which are truly relevant and meaningful;
It is then that forgotten pieces of memories begin to fit within life's puzzle.

When kneeling before death's mighty door,
Kings become beggars, and the vagabond acquires his riches,
For within their likeness shines the eternal truth:
That death is as natural a part of living as the air we breathe.

When the mystery of one's own simple existence comes closer to being solved,
The knowledge of our place within the infinite universe will be defined;
Then will the Master plan of eternally evolving life cycles be revealed,
Followed by the realization that the precious life we seem to value so, is only a breath away.

Pamela Putnam
WINTER
Winter is a beautiful sight,
Can you imagine with all of your might;
Children sledding over mountain tops slow,
Ooh! Watch out I'll be the first one below.

And then there's Jack Frost nipping at your nose,

You better watch out for you might catch a cold.
Wrap up tight and outside we will go,
To make a frosty in the snow!

Snowplows go a zooming by,
To pile the snow a mile high.
Along with the evergreens all covered in white,
For they make such a magnificent sight.

All the birds are fluttering in the sky,
Looking for seeds dropped by people passing by.
And then the sun beats down to try its hardest,
To melt the snow that has fallen upon us!

When the snowman is all finished and done,
We come inside to have some fun.
Drinking hot cocoa and playing some games,
The fun we have without our mom's going insane!

I treasure these moments because they go by so fast,
For the season of winter has yet to pass!

Loretta E. Rakes
GIVE ME KNOWLEDGE

To all my Grandchildren

Give me the sun, the moon, the sky;
Give me the curiosity to wonder why.
Give me the earth, the rain, the snow;
Give me the wonder of wanting to know.

Give me a river, a lake, a stream;
Give me the imagination to sit and dream.
Give me a mountain, a valley, a glen;
Give me a reason to wonder when.

Give me a bug, a bird, a fish;
Give me the time to sit and wish.
Give me a flower, a tree, a fern;
Give me a teacher to help me learn.

Give me the things God meant me to know;
Give me the knowledge that I need so.
Give me a life that's filled with love;
Give me the love that knowledge can give.

Dee Thomopoulos
DARK PATHS
Where did I come from?
Who was I before?
These and other questions begin so many more.

I walk through dreamfilled nights down dark unknown paths,
where cosmic entities I've known before
have left their epitaphs.

In quiet meditative hours I search

for tranquil serenity,
Reaching into the depth of my soul
in answer of who I used to be.

Laura Dorene Cooke
FIRST AND LAST
The first, the last and hardest to forget;
All others insignificant appear.
Unchanged by time, immune to pain and fear;
Recurring memory that lightens days.
In all of life the firsts we hold most dear.
We're living in a world where nothing lasts.
It seems an irony for time to play
Such tricks with quiet moments locked away
And used to measure all that's yet to come.
In all of life the firsts will always stay
Reminders of the innocence of youth.
The first, the last: in wisdom there is truth.

Barbara Monica Betkis
WHAT'S IN IT

To my late husband JOHN GEORGE

It's funny, it's only money
Yet it tickles the funny bone
It wipes away tears from ones eyes
Good times or sad
It never fully satisfies
Can't get enuf of the stuff
Can't spend it fast enuf
And we're all involved in it!

Alice S. Stephenson
MOUNTAIN PATHWAYS
Steps mounting higher
Look to the sun——
   Above and beyond
   Is a peak to be won.
Down a soft pathway
Scented with pine
   Rich with warm fragrance
   And filtered sunshine.
Out on a meadow——
   Soft rainbow array
   Glistening in sunlight
   To greet a new day.
A mountain to strengthen,
   A pathway to trod,
   A swift stream refreshing,
   A soul, nearer God.

A. Lester Flowers
LIFE

To my dearest grandparents—Pedro and Louise Forbes; in honor to you on your 50th wedding anniversary.

Life is a phenomenon to be understood;
Like the tide, there is a flowing, then an ebbing,
Like the sun, a rising, then a setting;
There is birth, then death . . .
There are, too, the moments in

between.
Life is not an occurence by perchance,
Nothing is more natural.

Life is breathing and eating, sleeping and awakening,
Hearing, seeing and talking;
It is being agitated, distressed and fed up;
It is losing, hurting, crying . . .
But it is also winning, caring, sharing, loving . . .
Life is eventful,
Nothing is more natural.

Angelito T. Buhisan Jr. Esq.
MY LOVE
With each passing day
   I cherish you more
Than there are grains of sand
   In an endless shore.

For you are to me
   Everything in life
For all I see
   Is you, my love.

Eleni Katzingris Moustaka
ENIGMA
When we said goodbye this morning you wouldn't let me touch you. I felt dead dreams near us that we never embraced. I left anguished and sad but I didn't resist; I did steal the hours and return. Everything stood waiting for me, instead you had already left. No matter if you filled our last daybreak with your inside wind, you will never stop to search for me, for my flaming and virginal soul.

Suddenly I saw a door looking sorrowful at me through its monocle over which a spider made its alcove. I wanted to run out, in despair, but a peevish door-knob with its metalic hand, retained me. I went in and threw myself in the armchair. The silence, which killed my parakeet, started whispering to me, absurd things. I put on my lorniet and looked at it offended. The twilight painted my windows with the martyrs blood. I absorbed in me cried while the clock winked to me but unexpectedly, the clock swooned; maybe saw the dagger stripped with the blood. Through the keyhole, enigma watched me. There came, outside my window the opera choir to sing for me the "Rustic Cavalary" by Mascagni.

Suddenly I could see your frightened soul hanging by the chandelier and crying for being abandoned. The fire eye in the closet looked for your soul astonished. "Where are you Nikolas?" I will borrow the night's eyes and go in search of you who must have gone in the vanished forest to bury my heart. The choir is singing "Ave Mary" by Gounod while the bell's toll, calls me. I am ready to go. The tricolor messenger is waiting for me. Let me die, together with my dream which you had never seen. Don't cry after me. I do not belong to you, anymore.

Arlette R. Hobbs
CHRISTMAS MEMORY
Remember the nights
You and I, alone;
Wandered snow-deep hillsides
Of isle's remote—
When love confessed
(sheer joy to attest!)
Was a passion of youth

So profound . . .
Yet, hopeless;
But too sweet to suppress?
—And ah! the kisses
Dark beneath the village Firs
Unbeknown . . .
Breast-to-breast—
(Did you marry her?)

M. Joyce Skinner
SKYLAR
You have blessed us with the
  promise of your new life
The promise of happiness as we
  watch you grow
The promise of satisfaction as
  we watch you learn
The promise of pride as we
  watch you achieve
The promise of love as we watch
  you give

Yes, Skylar, the joy of your birth
  has touched our hearts
And as you lay, so vulnerable
And as you sleep, in such total
  peace
What can we tell you of the
  world you are about to know?

We might say there is ugliness,
  but in the grace of your life, we
  see beauty.
We might say there is deceit, but
  in the honesty of your
  innocence, we have truth.
We might say there is poverty,
  but in the richness of your
  presence, we are wealthy.
We might say there is despair,
  but in the hope of your future,
  we find faith.

We cannot protect you from
  these realities
  We can help you understand
  they do not have to be a part of
  your world

We can give you the strength of
  our love
We can show you the ecstasy of
  nature
We can teach you compassion
  for humanity

Yes, Skylar, the joy of your birth
  has touched our hearts
  May we touch you with
  tolerance, understanding, and
  generosity.

Fern Roche
THE BOOK OF RULES
The Bible is our book of rules.
Unbelievers are many in our
  nation.
His rules are deleted from our
  schools.
Did not judges learn of God's
  creation?

Our Supreme Judges are
  appointed for life.
We know none of them will live
  forever,
so we must pray and work with
  strife.
Turn things around, is our real
  endeavor.

We are all here to help with
  God's work
and spread His Word to every
  nation.
Our duty we must never shirk,
to tell the whole world of His
  creation.

It happened over six thousand
  years ago.
At the time our world was quite
  small.
Just read the Bible, if you wish to
  know
how the prophets then, told
  about it all.

Julie M. Garofalo
ON A PARK BENCH
I sit on a throne
Adorned with precious jewels,
  inscribed with
Multi-colored letters which
  suggest names of ancient rulers.

In front of me
Court jesters play their games
  and a parade of gossiping
Subjects pass me by.
Soldiers ride by on their shiny
  horses
Others meet in a frenzied war.

I sit alone
Watching . . . . Wondering . . . .

Orien Todd
DIRE SOFTEN
I woke me poet
  soften rain
Twas dew know it
  from all disdain.
Then plenty guess
  for Shelley drown
His elderness
  dialects frown
And roses let sire
  my heart no pain
Continuously dire
  of sachet bane.
Wet God immerse
  my soul intent
With bath none curse
  tools implement.

Nor sordid tribe
  are often fools
Pretense me bribe
  yon stillness cools.
I gaze to this
  religious pond
So plaintive kiss
  meekens me beyond.

Bella Gour-Robinson
SOUL SENSES
My eyes, when gazing into thine
Can hear them say love words
  divine
Or hear the gladness from your
  heart ring
Or sadly hear the cry that sorrow
  may bring!

My ears can see, as music plays
Loved-ones and places and by-
  gone days
Lilac trees, a golden sun, blue
  waters, a starry night,
But best by far, music I hear,
  brings your face into sight.

My thoughts can feel and taste
  your kiss
It fills my mind with passionate
  bliss
But as the candle, waiting for the
  flame
My hopes and dreams play the
  waiting game!

My empty arms ache as does my
  heart
With merciless pain, because
  we're apart
Those arms cry, as they reach out
  for you
And my heart, full of love, cries
  in loneliness too!

Kevin E. Peterson
THE EAGLE'S FURY

---

*To Mom and Dad for giving me
the chance to chase a dream.*

I watched him fly with the wind
And soar across the misty sky
I watched him tackle a trout
From a clear running stream
And cling to the top of a dew-
  glistening spruce
Staring out over his domain
I watched as he flew overhead
  like an angry god
Wings outstretched while
  feathers rustled
I then watched him fly out of
  sight
  And I cried.

Shannon L. Farley
Deep and Dazzling Darkness
Resilent pewter dolphins
Leaping from a sparkling sheet of
  glass,
Diving back into a deep and
  dazzling darkness.
Forming a ring of endless light
Within the deep and dazzling
  darkness.

Sands sifting through time,
Images from a different
  dimension;
Coming together
In a ring of endless light.

Silent communication,
  intervening,
Dolphins in a deep and dazzling
  darkness;
And thou, all, a ring of endless
  light.

Kathe'
FROM ME TO THEE

---

*In rebuttal to that small, negative
voice within myself.*

I am the sunrise and I am the
  sunset.
I am the softness of billowing
  clouds,
The gray and the black of
  thunderheads.

I am the flash of lightning that
  cuts the sky.
I am the flickering star,
  delighting the eye
On the clearest night.

I am the moon that lights the
  pathway home.
I am the sun, warming all the
  earth from
Bitter cold.

I am the dew upon the meadow
  green.
I am the pounding drive of the
  winter rain.

I am the gentle snowflake drifting
  down.
I am the hard packed ice, left on
  the ground.

I breathe, I see, I hear, I feel.
I AM; Because I am real.

I harbor the greatest gifts.
I offer and I share.

I dream, I strive, I achieve.
In my own infinity, I do believe.

I breathe, I see, I hear, I feel.
I AM; Because I am real.

Terry Beard
THE GIFT
Christmas is a sharing time,
That is plain to see.
  With all the season's greetings
And the gifts beneath the tree.

Christmas is a giving time,
A time for you and me.
  There will be a gift for everyone,
But it won't be under the tree!

It doesn't need fancy paper
Or batteries to make it go.
  You won't need a box to put it
  in,
And there's no need for a bow!

You'll find this gift helpful,
In oh, so many ways.
  I don't know when you'll use it
But you'll need it everyday.

Now it has got you wondering,
How much does this gift cost?
It's really not expensive,
But you'll realize it *was* quite
  valuable,
If it's ever lost.

I know that we all like it,
But let's give it away.
  Let's give the gift of *LOVE!*
On this Christmas Day.

John Campbell, Editor & Publisher

Terrance Lee Brown
ETERNAL LOVE
Time turns day to night
time turns spring to fall
time dims the keenest sight
time tells upon us all
time will wear the mountain
  down
time will dry the sea
time will silence every sound
time will topple every tree
but one thing time will never do
as time goes racing by
is still the love I have for you
though time will see me die

Monica R. Salvatore
DYING LOVE
We sit in silence
And stare at the walls
Disregarding what is deep inside,
Failing to see what's in front of
  our eyes.
Refusing to admit that what's
  born must die
Love overshadowed by jealousy
  and pride.
Truth and honesty drowning in
  the tears
  that I cry
Puts out the fire that once burned
  for you and I,
The torch we once carried
  smolders at our feet.
Our love, once fresh and hot with
  desire
Is now cold and dark in a
  dungeon of mire.
Buried below rock and stone
We were once together
But are now alone.
Despair and misery fills our
  hearts and souls
As our love lay shattered,
  hard and cold.
Yet a spark of desire still burns in
  my blood
Though I fear in my heart,
What we once had
Is now dead.

Theodora Marschke Pankratz
A LIFELINE FOR JOY
A whisper of sweetness—A new
  life is computerized;
Programmed to free will, to be
  received, welcomed joyfully
Or to be rejected to pain and
  suffering.
Helpless? Never!
Cry of the newborn, arms
  reaching out,
Wanting—needing—asking—
  demanding.
Nourished by the Cord of Love,
The Heart Connection called
  Mother.
Inner yearnings, developed and
  developing,
Growing in patience, selflessness,
  pride,
Responsibility, praise,
  forgiveness,
Loyalty—endurance—
  understanding—and Grace!

Which Mother can feel equal to
  all the requirements
In being or becoming a "good
  mother"?
"I am your child, Mother,
  Conceived, born to be guided",

"My Baby—Beautiful—put your
  little hand in mine.
Together God will carry us in the
  palm of His hand
To show the way—To know His
  way",
Pattern for Continuity,
Pattern for Blessings,
True Communication,
A lifeline for Joy!

Kathleen McCord
CREATIVE WRITING
If I could describe with words
How beautiful you are
And, how much I love you
Then, I'd be as creative as God
And, I could write about,
The snowflakes
Dawn that breaks
Flowers unfolding
A dewdrop they're holding
The magic of a kiss
The morning mist
Weeping willow trees
The whispering breeze
A rainbow sky
The butterfly
The breath of spring
Birds on the wing
Autumn's hue
And . . . You

Orien Todd
GRIEVOUS
To clean Holy Land
  where hopes hitch far
Travel men follow
  lodesome star.
Just let woes forsake
  none chortle be
In Jerusalem
  great souls agree.
At Nazareth once
  rare Saviour born
In manger, yes,
  doubtless no scorn.
Go tell what bids
  for shepherd wide
Flocks are safe
  neath love abide.
Heart has conquer
  above nuisance, care.
Jesus waits as then
  is near to spare
Men from futile
  hostage plied
True He transcends
  grievous tree died.

Anthony Politowski
CHRISTMAS TIME
Christmas time is many things,
A time to laugh, a time to sing,
A time to hear the sleigh bells ring,
A time to see what Santa brings,
A time that reindeer take to flight,
A time the star shines specially
  bright,
A time to adorn the house with
  lights,
A time of fires and egg nog at
  night.
A time that fills our hearts with
  glee,
A time Rudolph goes down in
  history,
A time the angel goes' atop the
  tree,
A time for specials on t.v.
But Christmas is mostly a time of
  sharing,

A time of giving, a time of caring,
A time of Wise Men with gifts
  a-bearing,
A time for God our hearts
  preparing.

A time of peace and joy and love,
Because of the Child sent from
  above.

Christa Nadeau
CRYSTALS
Crystals of glittering ice in an
  array of
Rainbow essence, enhancing the
  bountiful sky
Softly gently drifting in an swirl
  of breath taking
Beauty, a display of silver
  streamers and tiny
Diamonds so very rare in cut,
  with the design of a
Master who's shaped each one
  exquisitely
His handicraft of an
  undescribable joy and
Overwhelming sense of purity,
A gift from the angels themselves.

Nissa Rae Petersen
HELP
Lost;
  Inside a forbidden city
    without love,
      friends,
      companions.

Confused
  And I don't know where to go
      without help
      or a clue
  on how to leave this place.

Feeling forgotten,
    misused,
      ignored,
    like I always have.

Maybe
  I'll find someway out
      without help
  from the millions of nobodys
  the everpresent noghingness
      of no one.

Rachel Sims Fabert
THE HARP

---

*Dedicated to the memory of my
very dearly beloved brother, Paul
Albert Sims.*

Of all the instruments of man's
  invention
  The harp attains an acclamation
  rare;
Whate'er of deed or thought, of
  joy or tribulation,
  Of daring conquest, love, or
  even prayer
The harp expresses all with equal
  aptness,
  It speaks to man of men and
  things and God;
It gives us strength and courage,
  hope and vision,
  It makes us feel that here the
  angels trod.
It's very shape a thing of grace
  and beauty,
  Each string a masterpiece of art
  and skill,
It helps to span the way from

earth to heaven,
  It seems to whisper softly,
  "Peace, be still";
For "music is the universal
  language,"
  It's understood alike by young
  and old;
It fills the empty void that is
  within us—
  A harp should always be of
  purest gold!

Jonna Spring Reaves
WHO IS THE REAL ME
I crawl before walking.
I babble before talking.

I cried before growing.
I wonder before knowing.

I began aging before realizing.
I experience before learning.

I ask before taking.
I change before discovering.

I learn before reaching.
      Who
        Is
          The
            Real
              Me.

Marsha Allison Knofler
THE GARDEN
Everything is so beautiful now
You —n— your bright sunshine
  smile
Me unfolding gracefully
Under the rays
Like a new spring flower.

My tears are the rain
That helps love grow
Stronger —n— closer to our hearts.
Try now
And we will never drift apart.

Lucy Ann Montesano
ANOTHER CHRISTMAS
Another Christmas up and around
Seasons changed and times
  turned around
Christmas carols heard all about,
Merry Christmas uttered a shout
  it's
Holiday season no reason to
  doubt
Gifts are given in the silence of
  night
Opening presents by morning
  light, and
Making the Christmas once as
  bright.

Jeanette Renee Johns
YOU AND ME FOREVER
You were nailed to a tree
In disgust and shame
Only so you could take the blame
All that just for me

Many people laughed, many cried
On that long ago dark, dreary day
It was only the beginning when
  you died
For you arose to show us the way

Now you live with me forever
  more
Since that day I asked you into
  my heart
Life has it's ups and downs but
  you never shut the door
Because from me you'll never
  ever part

504

Vivian Boucher
LITTLE PIONEER GIRL
Little pioneer girl,
In a land that was new,
Was your heart always true?
Did you never feel blue?
Little pioneer girl,
When you came to the west
With a child at your breast—
Did you know what was best?
You were only sixteen,
And as proud as a queen;
In the wilderness wild,
You were scarce more than child.
Did you hold your head high;
Did you hold back a sigh?
Did the mountains seem vast;
Did you dream of the past?
Little pioneer girl,
When the wagons rolled by,
Did you sing lullaby?
Could the west satisfy?
Little pioneer girl!

Eva Neal
WONDERING
I sit and think.
I try to see . . .
What your eyes hold for me.

I look deep,
And all I do is weep.
You've got pain and sorrow,
Which no one wants to borrow.

Take my hand.
Together . . .
We shall stand.

Andrew Warring
THE LONELY LOVER

To Kathy, the one I love

As I stroll along the beach at the
    break of dawn
I search the horizon and beyond

In hope to find the one that I love
Who left me with only a glove

We had a terrible fight the night
    before
And I heard her leaving by the
    sound of a slamming door

Now I hope I can find her very
    soon
To tell her I was wrong that
    afternoon

To say I'm sorry for starting the
    fight
And hope she'll come back to
    stay the night

Ms. Dee Dee LeBeau
YOU, ME, US, THREE
Here we are two people in love,
    laughing together having so
    much fun. We didn't know it
    wasn't going to last; But as time
    went on we were two people
    still in love with only
    memory's of the past. We really
    loved each other so, but as
    time went on we had to let
    each other go. The love we had
    wasn't meant to be, not that
    kind of love YOU, ME, US,
    THREE. This other love that
    we shared, we tried to
    comprehend, and no matter
    how much we tried to fight it
    we just couldn't win. YOU, and
    ME, was fine you see

until it kept coming up Three;
Even though it was secretly, I
    knew it couldn't be just YOU,
ME, US, THREE.

Mary Ann B. Henning

Mary Ann B. Henning
LOVE DREAMS

*I dedicate these poetic phrases to
Paul Anka, whose beautiful
music inspired this poem's
creation, and reason for being.*

Your spirit is with me
As I write a poem or two
From me to you
Sharing my thoughts
With you
Who weaves a romantic web

I am caught in
As I listen to each
& every song of love
You sing
Whilst I fall asleep
With you & my dreams
I spin
This night.

James Martin Gau
COME
Down the street
And to my step
And at my door
And no one there
And walk away
And home came I
And note on door
And I missed you
And call me 'gain
And come I will
And you I'll find
And I thank you
Death.

Janice F. Towe
Look How Far We've Come

*With Love, to my parents:
Rebecca & Sinclair Towe, New
Bern, N.C. Also with Love, to
Evang. Ernestine C. Reems &
Center Of Hope Church, of
Oakland, Ca., with special thanks
to, Vanessa Murrell.*

Through many struggles, of the
    past
I wonder how, our race has last
Through many, many, long dark
    nights
Even when, we had no rights
For God looks out, for his very
    own
He's prepared us a place, our
    eternal home
OH! I can see, how times have
    changed
And our life we have managed, to
    rearrange
But in all the things, that I have
    learn
I never dreamed, the wheel would
    turn
Look at us now, we have freedom
    and rights
We;re able to reach, much higher
    heights
So let us not forget, folks like Dr.
    Martin L. King
Who gave us hope, and a new
    song to sing
OH! WE SHALL OVERCOME,
    WE SHALL OVERCOME,
OH! YES, WE SHALL
    OVERCOME . . .

Eronel
DARK DAYS
Dark days
Walking in yesterday's nightmares
Wrapped in a webb of despair

Dark days
Cursing the sun's rays
As an added insult
To an already overburdened injury

Dark days-
Lost in the anonimity
Of a numbered population
Caught in the limbo
Between life and existence

Dark days
Becoming darker
As you build the prison
Within yourself

Judy Moffet
AIR-BORNE
There once was a grandpa who
    often said
That man wouldn't travel in space.
His children argued that he was
    wrong,
And he changed his view with
    grace.

Then shortly came his time to
    leave
This world and his family lorn.
Months later he would have been
    so pleased—
His great-grandchild first was born.

The baby's folks named him for
    Grandpa,
To remember the man that they

knew:
Old-fashioned, stubborn, strong
    and warm,
An example as Great-Grandson
    grew.

In college this descendant signed
    a scroll.
How surprised his forebear
    would've been
To know that his name had
    orbited this earth
In a shuttle with a woman and
    men!

Bennie Townsend Jr.
There Is Still No Room Today
Amid the roaring of the cars
    And the shuffling of the crowd,
The God of all creation searches,
    For those who will make him
    proud.
But nearly all the people spurn
    him,
    And tend to go their way,
As it was the night that Christ
    was born,
    There is still no room today.

There is room for jesters and
    jokers,
    And gamblers and drunkards
    and such,
In homes and cars and hotels,
    And in beds where sin is much.
But there's no place for
    righteousness,
    Where the presence of God can
    stay,
As it was at the birth of Jesus,
    There is still no room today.

There is no room in the hearts of
    men,
    For their pride is much too
    great,
And the vanity of the women,
    Seem to harbor only hate.
The children too are left
    unlearned,
    With no one to guide their way,
For the time is now as it was
    before,
    There is still no room today.

Marina E. Iatesta
EARTH'S SLUMBER
The sky was dark and somber
— The night was peaceful
The rain began to fall,
    the sky flickered
    brightly to light the
earth—Arousing it
Moving it with a sudden
clap of thunder—Excitement
filled the air—then . . .
listening to the gentle
rain— the Earth,
    slumbered once more.

Sharon Lee Boudreaux
WORDS
Here's a word you can use
Next time you play scrabble.

It's a word which describes
A girl who might gabble.

But remember this in 'midst
Play, heavy and hot,

A fizgig this girl
Is definitively not!

Carol Tingey
A TIME FOR THANKS
It is fall and the leaves are gone now
The football games are over and there is
snow on the ground.
It is a time for thanks
and I am.
I am thankful for
the beauty of the mountains
and the clearness of the mountain lake
I am thankful for the
university where I teach
and the warmth of my house
I am thankful for the things that I have learned
and the places that I have been
But most of all I am thankful for you
and the joy that you bring to me . . .

and I know that in my life it is
a time for thanks.

Sharon Ann Wilder
THIS YEAR . . .
January dews
Send the clouds to the ground
The weather this year is so fair
Summers old news
And riddles unfound
Keep me out, but at the edge of despair

This January's sun
Paints the moon's golden hair
And my memories are painted by you
Your love is the one
As the eagle so rare
So elusive that away it flew

Shall February arrive
And no sign of you still
The flower that was planted shall die
Though winter's alive
It has lost it's will
The love will never survive

Price Ivy Watkins
You Cannot Go Back To the Past
You cannot go back to the past.
No matter how long you may fast;
You cannot bring back that old fun.
It's the end of that day in the sun.

Yes, you had yourself some fun.
You've had a big day in the sun;
But time waits for no one.
And all that you've done is done.

So rise up my friend, my friend!
Ready for a new experience to begin.
Now to serve the Master to the end;
Cease your fasting and forget your sin.

Remember, the Master has a plan for you.
A plan which you must carry through!
Sure, He is waiting for you along the way.
So be thankful, and count your blessings everyday.

Because time is waiting for no one.

Now, now today change your mind!
Forget all about yesterday's fun;
Get yourself ready for a greater find.

As you now prepare for the Master's plan.
You will evolve into a happier man;
And will one day enjoy the paradise.
Just you don't forget this my advice!

You cannot go back to the past.
You cannot bring back yesterday's fun;
No matter how long you may fast.
What you have done is done.

Flossie B. Woods Miller

Flossie B. Woods Miller
I Learned A Lesson In Patience Today

I, Flossie B. Woods Miller, would like to dedicate my poem to the National Association of University Women and my family.

A beautiful little redbird came to see me today,
Because I invited it to brunch and to stay for play.
I served it on a table covered with the whitest snow
And kept it company from just inside my patio door.
It ate a little quickly and then it flew away.
I felt a touch of sadness as it didn't stay for play.
T'was enjoyable having that bird, though it's visit was incomplete;
With that thought in mind I drifted off to sleep.
Upon awakening, some short time later and looking out the door—,
There was not a crumb of that brunch to be seen anymore!
Now I understand its disappearance and that redbirds plan—
It just went away to get its clan and I missed it!!
I'll never ever be so impatient again (sigh)!!!!

Jennie Keach Ransbottom
UNCERTAINTY
We can be sure of many things
In this old world so wide,
The sun and wind, the moon and stars,
Unending as the tide.

The days go on and seasons pass,
The flowers come and go.
Of one thing only we're not sure . . .
Is "death" our only foe.

It steals about on feet unseen
Mean, grasping, evil thing!
Snatching young and old alike
Unique is death's own sting.

Bella Gour-Robinson
THIS CONSTANT HEART!
Brave young son, bird in flight, with your earth-treading feet
As you soar to the clouds, your unknown fate to meet,
I fly by your side, I encircle your name
'Round my heart, ignited with love, an ever-burning flame!

Society, spurn if you will, evil demons, heartless and small of mind, begone!
Here is a loyal spirit who will fight as madly, as long
For this May child, bound by a thousand bands 'round my heart
Not a tie will break, nor e'en a single link will start!

Gone! Gone! Idols shattered, earth's wishing star fled now . . .
With saddened heart, weeping eyes and throbbing brow
I know how much the heart can bear, as lava tide
Scald my cheeks with burning tears I cannot hide!

Bittersweet losses, deep-rooted memories, find a dwelling place
In my mind, my soul . . . past existence I embrace
Neither time can erase, nor yet an ocean of tears
Can e'er assuage my disconsolate heart, loving too well, all these years!

Dear, most dearly loved ones, will you then so soon forget?
Might I ne'er again behold in your eyes what I once saw? Yet . . .
'Tis gone! I hear, I know the language of this constant heart
It cries out: "Go! Go! Witness not my spirit decay, as we part!"

Gayle Maginnis Livermore
THIS TIME OF YEAR
Soon it will be Christmas—
Loved ones are near
Full of anticipation
And holiday cheer—
Yet, for me it's the
Lonliest time of year.

There's beautiful gifts
Under the tree—
But I cherish more
Your gift to me:
A life time full

Of memories.

And I wonder—
As I recall
If there's a chance;
So slight; so small
Of you being aware
Of me at all!

Sharon K. Sandifer
NOTHINGNESS
I feel nothingness
  Abosolute peace
  Absence of responsibility
  Serenity
I need to understand and reason
  With no real desire
  Just thinking
Knowing the presence of God
  While feeling nothing
  Existing, perhaps
Maybe closer to living
  Feeling love for all
  Loving no one
Emptiness of fullness
  Fullness of emptiness
  Maybe both altogether
A definate committment
  To life?
  To love?
  Not actively fulfilling either
Yet continuously and forever satisfying
Needs of both
  Nothingness
  Unconsciousness?

Lupe Miranda
TIME WILL TELL

To my husband Joe, who inspires me and those who encourage me.

We had nothing in common they told us back then;
that we would break up, but they knew not when.
It's a matter of time they used to say;
But it didn't cause us any dismay.

Fourteen years later we're still together,
life for us dear, only got better.
I'm still your girl and you're still my man;
And we're raising our children the best that we can.

Our love has kept growing and we have matured;
And no matter what life brings it can be endured.
Have nothing in common, is that what they said?
Well, look at out love now and see where it's led.

Kimberly I. Enloe
HELP ME
Help me with this sacrifice,
I feel I have to give.
Help me with this tiring life,
I know I have to live!

Help me to forget I lose,
So I will feel no pain.
Help me to understand . . .
I must give before I gain!

Help me to understand myself,
So I may love and give again.
Help me to choose the right path,
That I may abolish all my sin!

506

Our World's Best Loved Poems

Patricia Faith Miller
FRIENDS

Somewhere between our
    beginning and end.
Muffled by the hurts and
    betrayals encountered along
    the way.
Friends.

A handful if you're lucky.
Searching for ones you can trust.
Sifting through the phonies, the
    jokers, the back-stabbers.
A handful if you're lucky.
Friends.

Smiles created.
Moments shared and cherished.
Embarassments told and enjoyed.
Sorrows soothed with a tender hug.
Friends.

Growing with one another,
 Appreciating one another,
  Being proud to be . . .
   Friends.

Phyllis Joan Smith
FINALE

A flash of light
    —so bright!
No time to cry
    nor say goodbye
No more—the day
    nor night
All gone—
    with a flash of light . . .

Eleanor (Annie) Lagunas
MY LIFE

*Written especially for my parents:
my father Jesus R. Lagunas, who
passed away in 1982 and my
mother Alicia, who is now my
everything.*

I would give my life for my
    parents.
I would give my life to see the
    entire Universe at peace.
I would give my life to see all the
    people rich and no one poor.
I would give my life, if you would
    give me yours.

James S. Bradshaw
ME

*Dedicated to Patty without
whose inspiration this poem
would never have been completed.*

Does anyone know me?
Do they know
        what I want
        what I feel
        what I need
        what makes me happy
        and what makes me sad.
How could they know,
I haven't told them.
That's because, I don't know me.

Elena M. Pertelesi
I CAN'T, I WON'T

I can't, I won't,
So much anger and rage,
    love and hate
        desparation and pain.
How we madly loved so much
    during those limited hours.
But I must go now—

So many lies and tears,
So much hurt and sorrow.
I can't, I won't
    continue on this long and
    endless journey alone.
You placing me on that high
    shelf—for your pleasure only.
Reaching out when you need to
    love—
—now sadly realizing it wasn't
    love at all.
I sit and wait,
    Crying, Weeping
    Always waiting for you to come
    and fill this special void in my
    life.
But I can't, I won't
    continue waiting,
        slowly dying, fading,
            crying, hating
and wanting something so
    desperately,
something I know deep down,
will never,
    can ever be mine.

Linda Fay Crowder
Little Flower 'Neath The Pines

Oh little flower 'neath the pines,
You look so fragile on your vine.
There amidst such towering trees,
You find the nourishment to fit
    your needs.

Though the pines try to close you
    in,
And make the needed sunlight
    dim.
You send your vines out across
    the land,
To gather nourishment from an
    outstretched hand.

With the pines towering high
    above,
You grow each day fueled by love.
For just beyond the reach of the
    pines,
With another young flower you
    are entwined.

You've held on tight through
    many storms,
Days that were dry and nights
    too warm.
Where the vines joined you've
    created anew,
A bud opening up just covered
    with dew.

Though you've had to struggle to
    reach the vines,
Of the one growing there just
    beyond the pines.
What you've created must be
    nourished by love,
With this the pines will never
    tower above.

May the beauty of love always
    show in the face of the flower.

Rose Colombo Strickland
A CHILD'S WISH

To all children of divorced parents

I wish that mom and dad could see
how desperately I need to be
with both of them
throughout my life
to help me learn and

cope with strife.
I wish that mom and dad could be
the lovers who once wanted me
to grow up strong and happily
to excel scholastically.
I wish that mom and dad would
    use
the money spent on court abuse
on things they need around the
    house
instead of hurting their ex-spouse.
They know that I sure want to be
with both of them—shared
    custody,
so I can know that they are there
so that I know
for me they care.

Audrey Cunningham
DON'T CRY MY LOVE

Don't cry my love,
wipe your tears dry.
There is no reason to cry,
because I am going to die.
I had enough,
I can't go on anymore.
It's time to go,
I am tired and worn.

I am like the old rugged cross,
on a hill far away.
It's time to lay my soul.
Please don't cry my love,
not for me.

I am not walking into
the shadow of death,
but into the green valley,
where I can lay my soul to rest.

Be happy for me my love.
And someday you will see
the green valley where I'll be.

Lida B. Daubert
CHRISTMAS TIME

*To my family, who have made all
of my Christmas' special*

Christmas time is here again, the
    sounds are in the air

Gift buying, songs and laughter
    are everywhere.

The Christmas tree so pretty
    from the ceiling to the floor

And a little touch of mistletoe
    hangs above the door

The children wait for Santa to
    bring that special treat

And the family all will gather at

Grandma's house to eat

What a happy time of year with
    family and with friends

One wishes that this happiness
    would never end

That sorrow and strife in this
    world would be something of
    the past

And Peace on Earth, Goodwill
    Toward man would forever last.

Therese Maria Fricke
CHRISTMAS IS HERE!

Christmas is here!
Jesus is born!
Let us rejoice this Christmas Morn.
Mary the Mother of Christ the
    King,
God the Father of everything,
He was born in a stable the
    heavenly child,
Jesus the Lord so meek and mild.
Come rejoice this Christmas Day,
Praise the Lord in every way.

T. J. Osgood
Where Can I Find Him?

*To my mother and father who
were the first to show me where I
could find Christ.*

Where can I find Him, this baby
    king?
Where can I find Him, these gifts
    to bring?

Will he be in the palace in a royal
    bed,
Wrapped in fine linen with a
    crown on his head?

But a stop at the palace will soon
    reveal
They don't know him, and they
    never will.

So on to a stable, cold and bare,
With swadling clothes to cover
    him there.

Sheep and oxen sleep there too,
And silently stand in the young
    King's view.

Not many mighty have ever
    made room
To become the bride of Christ the
    groom.

Where will you find Him, the
    King of kings?
Look, my friend, at common
    things.

Kelly Thompson
SPECIAL LOVE

*This poem was written for and
inspired by Kenny Newitt, my
Love always.*

Each day I look forward
    to seeing you,
Experiencing things old
    and new,
Sharing a special kind
    of love
That was created by
    the Lord above—
A love that grows
    stronger everyday.

There's nothing that can
take it away,
For it's something only
you and I share—
Something very, very rare.

Lola Elizabeth Jones
STREET PEOPLE
Street People!
They live in the Street
On Street Benches
taking up space where "Decent
People" sit
Looking for Buses
that never come
Sliding around corners
looking for Someone to mug
Hanging near Shop Doors
waiting to heist the owners
Running numbers
Waiting for Pimps
working Whores and Innocent
Kids
Street Hookers
half-dressed off booze and pills
not knowing where the next
meal is coming from
not knowing
and
not caring
Seeking
But not finding
Cheating
But not winning
Working
But not gaining
Staring
into empty spaces:
Old Folks, Junkies, Criminals and
Drunks
Police and Detectives
Men and Women
Boys and Girls
Black, White, Red, Yellow and
Brown!
STREET PEOPLE!
"But for the Grace of God———!"

Irene S. Dewey
BLIZZARD BLASTS

*Dedicated to my mother,
Elizabeth Sargent, whose love and
faith inspired me each day.*

I hoped I'd never see another
blizzard,
A raging, howling, snowspun,
scarey dawn;
But it has hit with devastating
forces
And holds immobile both the car
and the fawn.
Housebound are town and
country dwellers
Silence holds for all things but
the wind.
Sidewalks and roadways are
impassible
For they are underneath the
snowdrifts pinned.
We worry for the livestock and
the farmer
Who each must face this forceful,
frigid storm
And only prayer can help to give
us comfort,
'Till we learn that they are safe
and warm.
Perhaps this awesome blizzard

will remind us
Of lovely days and dawns that
have just passed,
So we may treasure all God gives
us daily;
The song and sunshine that
preceed the blast.

Florence Katz
THE EXALTED
Up, up, you have not gone away,
you are here
From supreme sacrifice a fortress
will arise
impregnable, pointing to the
white bird's flight
to realms of unimaginable bliss
Up, up, from the quicksands of a
world
sunk in blood and death
Your pyramid of peace will stand,
eternal light
            SADAT
Far and wide, from pole to pole
God's message from within your
soul

Robyn Marie Lindenberg
FORWARD IN LOVE

To both of you. 6-18-83

Let us go forward together,
looking to the future,

Offering comfort and
understanding in times of
trouble and laughter and smiles
in time of joy,

Venturing to bring out the best
in each other and to give the
best of ouselves,

so that we might

Experience a life filled with
happiness and a marriage filled
with L-O-V-E.

Gail Seibel
FIRST LOVE
First love everyone knows
Comes only once in each life
That completely overpowering
emotion
Captivating the mind and body
Sowing seeds of affection
Respect and caring
Into the soul with feeling
Overcoming the senses
Until one is riveted to another
Welded bonds
The strength of deep felt passion
Surges through each heart
A pleasure of true joy
Shared by two

Jean Boyce Capra
RAJPUT AND PURDAH

*Christopher Kevin, I dedicate this
poem to you, and all my dear
grandchildren who hold so much
promise for the future . . .
remain pure in mind, heart and
soul . . . and the world is yours
to inherit.*

Barefoot, sandaled he strolled
Along the sandy beaches—
His white cotton robe with
Embroidery rich, made him look

so bold.
This man-child, a prince of long
ago
Yet, now a future king,
His raven long hair flows
Caressing his young, innocent
frame.

Wide lips and jet-black eyes
Smile in a pleasing countenance,
The sun has truly perfected
His bronze-gold manly stance.

What name will you bear this
Day, Oh, royal son, . . . Rajput?
Is the beautiful woman you gaze
Upon, hidden today from your
view?

You were promised to each other
So long ago, by your parents, and
Tradition kept for many years.
Today, Rajput Krishna, your
wedding day is here.

By traditions . . . purdah . . . her
face
Was hidden from view, and
you . . .
Prince Krishna, the two of you
are wed
In love and honor: her veil, for
you is shed.

Marion Madison
GRANDPA

*To my daughter, Toni Lee/ who
inspired this poem. In memory of
my father/ who touched our lives
with his own special love/ will
never be forgotten.*

When I was born, mom did say
You look more like him everyday
And my relatives, I do declare
Started calling me—Little Clair.

But I felt proud, I didn't care
There wasn't a finer person
anywhere
And sometimes his mind did stray
Told me stories of life from
yesterdays.

He shared my good times, and
the bad
All my joys and some of the sad
Thro sometimes he didn't
understand
I still loved that sweet old man.

He was always around as I grew
There will never be a friend so true
He was old-fashioned, but so nice
You could always count on his
advice.

And it hasn't been too long ago
He went to live up in Gods home
I'll never forget him, my hearts
still sad
For this man you see was—My
Grandad.

Jean Dye
FRIENDSHIP
To measure friendship
Help as applied when needed,
Reflects your truest concern
Of the problem you heeded.

Consolement and prayer
Can be your best provisions,
And courtesies of labor

Are additional missions.

Much thought is given
To alleviate the situation,
Until brighter days arise
To the norm of propitiation.

Jean Dye
A LAMP
Thy word is a lamp
As a daily guide,
It counsels in every aspect
With Him at our side.

He's a light to our path
One step at a time,
Always leads us rightly
With His love sublime.

He leads us by faith
Through darkness and light,
Till we comprehend His will
And accept it as right.

He gives results
For every prayer called,
According to His will
And love for us all.

Mrs. Kelly (Velma) Haynes
THE VILLAGE WELL
The women gathered at the
village well
Where there's water to draw and
tales to tell.
One maiden waited 'til they were
all through,
Then whispered, "Do I ever have
news for you!"

"You all know Mary was my very
best friend.
"Well, our friendship has faded-
come to an end.
"For mealy-mouthed Mary, so
meek and mild,
"Little mousy Mary is great with
child!"

The women gasped at the news
she bore then urged the maiden
"Do tell us more."
The maiden answered, "What can
I say? The birth of the child
could be any day."

"And who is the Father? Without
a doubt some Roman soldier
running about.
"She went to visit her cousin last
spring. Likely that's when she
had her fling.
"Cousin Elisabeth? . . . Cousin,
my eye! . . . Elisabeth? A
ridiculous name for a guy.
"And poor old Joseph, the stupid
clod, believes her child is the
Son of God."
"Why Joseph's too dumb to put
her away. They're going to
Bethlehem . . . leaving today!
"Good thing he's a carpenter. He
can build them a bed. Maybe
he'll keep a roof o'er her head."

The young maiden sighed, then
said, "I must go,
"I should never have told you this
sad tale of woe
"This secret I've shared, 'twas too
great to keep,
"As for Mary . . . you
know . . 'Still waters run deep.'"

Rumors of wise men, shepherds
and kings

Stories of a Star and angels with
   wings,
Soon drifted back to the village
   well
Where there's water to
   draw . . . and tales to tell.

Adam F. Misterka
THE CHRISTMAS GIFT
With divine truth and love
Christmas reaches us;
when bells ring across
the skies, the lands, the
   waters, . . .
Heavenly gates are open
and abudantly passing
the gift from Lord above
to spread Christmas blessing
of faith, truth and love.

Gertrude Kirkbride
THE SOUND IS YOU

---

*In loving memory of my husband,
Kirby, and with thanks to all my
children for their support.*

I hear a voice in the morning
When the world is wet with the
   dew
I hear a voice in the evening
And the sound of the voice is you

I hear a song at the sunset
When the day is nearing an end
And the song that I hear in the
   darkness
Is the sweet, loving voice of you

I feel you with me in the morning
There is peace in my heart, here
   with you
The song that keeps coming back
   to me
The sound of the song is you

Elizabeth Robertson
TIME
The years move
Gracefully as dancers
In slow motion sequence,
Gliding, constant as a clock
Into the mixer of eternity.
The days slip through our fingers:
Picture postcards, viewed in sun.
I clasp your April hand,
Seeing no changes there;
Feeling only the old, familiar
Pull of gentleness and love.
The world grows older, it is true:
But never, never,
Me and You.

H. Frank Martin, Jr.
**Decembers Are
   Bittersweet**
I saw you walk to
the car today,
baby and self,
cocky and self assured
as you should be.

Tomorrow you will have
marriages, children, Christmases,
New Years.

You will know late Decembers
and learn they turn
into Spring again,
as I have.

Some tears, but not many.

Seasons change. Some
better than others.

One ends, but another begins.
I would shield you from
the Februarys of life,
If I could,
but not from December;
I would not want you to
miss the glitter
of Christmas,
and the foolishness
of New Years.

Some hands will hold you,
but not mine,
I could not take the
pain in this year, though
the tightness of your skin
begs to be touched while
it still speaks of youth.

I could buy you gold,
but that is old fashioned
and not good enough for you;
though a flicker of adornment
might be good.

If I could buy the
Sun, though I would
and give you all the summers
in a bunch.

I wore dark glasses today
so you could not see the
   directions
of my eyes.

You should be told though
how pretty you are,
but not by me.

I hope someone does,
though I shall envy every caress,
every arm around your body.
That would be enough for me
but even that is too much.

I would not love you closely, even
if I could. I could not stand the
pain again.

I shall seek you though
tomorrow, in the eyes of
everyone who has love.

Take care.

Kathleen G. Stewart
OCEAN
Droplets of water forming a
   limitless force
Sweep to and fro, the droplets
   beat against the rocky shore
Are we not as the droplets?
Reaching out to change the world
Yet being sweep to and fro
Can we not become strong
   enough that someday we rise
   above it all?
And just as the droplets are taken
   into the clouds
We too shall soar the heavens
   and rain our joy upon the earth

Marsha R. Smith
BROKEN LOVE
A rose petal bent
From a raindrop
A sad face hung low
From a teardrop
A droplet slowly falling
Closely followed by another

A rose with a broken stem
A child with a broken heart
A love that cannot be repaired
If I had only known sooner
How much you actually cared
Now I know-how sorry I am

For now is the time I must go
In days to come I shall return
To the place I was before

And it will be then and there
That I say I love you
More and more

Shirley Ann Lewis
TO STEAL A MOMENT
At dawn lying awake, I made a
   wish
That the earth be filled as a
   covered dish.
And so it was as I wished it
   would be!
Buds burst, and lo! leaves abound
   in a tree!
Hark! A bird's voice from afar I
   hear.
Behold! Grass and flowers do
   appear.
And lo! The sun seeks now to
   find rest;
It leans dependently on the breast
Of nature and is thrust by an arm
From our midst, and with it, light
   and warmth.
At twilight I saw the bold face of
   day
Artfully and silently whisked
   away.
Loud chirps were turned to soft
   lullabies.
'Neath night's crafty spell I closed
   my eyes,
Worshipping the stillness, the
   breeze, the night,
And was forced to slumber 'til
   morning light.

Pamela Diana Hicks Nettles
MY SAILOR
My sailor is a giving man
He'd give his life to save our land
He fights his foes in the air and sea
To protect his cherished family.

His honor he pledges to our land
While he's still a strong vibrant
   man
He guards the sea with it's
   glistening foam
As I anxiously wait for him to
   come home.

"In God We Trust," our souls cry
   out
As he journeys on an unknown
   route.
Please keep him safe while we're
   apart
And engrave our love in our
   hearts.

My sailor means the world to me
Wether on land or on the sea
Watch over him is what I pray
Till he comes home with me to
   stay.

Yvonne P. Thomas
MY BUNDLE OF JOY

---

*This poem is dedicated to my
son, Clinton David Thomas*

We wanted to have a baby
So very very bad
The Doctor said, "Maybe"
That made us real glad

After seven years of
   disappointment

I got a call one day
The Doctor called to say we have
   a baby on the way

On September 24th at 4:07
A healthy baby boy was born
I thought I was in Heaven

When your Daddy cried out, "It's
   a boy!"
I burst out crying tears of joy

A few minutes after you were born
In my arms you lay
Oh, how I asked God for this very
   special day

Curly hair like Mom's
Bright blue eyes like Dad
How could I help be anything but
   glad?

Clinton David, I love you so much!
You're so beautiful to look at,
So soft to touch

You mean so much to me
I'm happy as can be
I've finally got a bouncing baby
   boy!
How proud I am of My Bundle of
Joy.

Mary Williams Barnes
A Tribute To Our Clients

---

*On behalf of our clients, whose
laughter enlightens us, whose
sincerity thrills us, and whose
devotion humbles us, I dedicate
this poem to Chet Mottershead,
President, and the entire staff of
Tri-County Industries.*

I work in rehabilitation of the
   handicapped as they're called
And community misconceptions
   often leave me shocked and
   appalled.
We try helping them erase
   barriers to their success,
And everyone should be anxious
   these problems to quickly
   address.

Our clients sometimes make us
   want to pull our hair
But helping to solve their
   problems is really why we're
   here.
Ask any staff in rehabilitation
   why you do this with such zeal.
"The nature and character of the
   clients" they will reveal.

When we come in each morning
   and see their smiles and eager
   faces,
Any thoughts of pity or
   sympathy this quickly erases.
All they ask is acceptance, a
   chance to work and enjoy their
   lives
And simple kindness and
   consideration is the thing on
   which many thrive.

In meeting Willie or Jane a
   simple sweet honesty I can
   readily see
From misunderstandings and
   labels they hope one day to be
   free.
Who's to say who's handicapped,
   we all are in some way,

I'm only 4'11" and hear not too well today.

We hope each of you will join our most laborious task
Proving they're not children, but adults with dignity and from this stigma can really be free at last.
We all want love and caring is what it's all about,
So help us carry this banner saying "I can" and loudly shout.

Maxine F. Popp
TEDDY BEAR

To all Teddy Bears, Inc.

Trusting our thoughts and most cherished secrets,
Exploring the world in the fastest jet.
Dapper and debonair that he seems;
Daring and dashing; his eyes sparkle and gleam,

Young and youthful; he never changes his style,
Bear in mind, there are many more for miles,
Extemporaneous hugs; embracing with a caress,
Adorable and lovable,; soft and cuddly; ready to bless,
Reverberating of reminisces in a treasure trove,
  Memories to cherish forever and to love.

Barbara Jean Conner
WAIT UPON THE LORD
When we are burdened with despair,
we fail to believe that Christ is there
And when we feel all alone,
is it because our faith is gone?

We count our blessings one by one,
but just can't see what Christ has done.
We search for love but in the wrong places,
many times trust from the wrong faces.

And when we feel we've gone astray,
do we get on our knees and pray?
And ask Christ to forgive our sins,
for the things we've done and the places we've been.

Many mistakes Lord we made,
when we knew not what to do.
But had we waited on Christ Jesus,
he would have seen us thru.
So when we feel our way seems hard,
we'll wait, wait, wait upon the Lord.

Chris D. Bennington
THE LONE CRY

This is dedicated to my mother: To whom I never had to prove anything, she loves me for what I am. I love you Mom!

The lone cry on the seagulls wing
Of the days that have swept out to sea
The silent song we cannot sing
The lone cry on the seagulls wing
He soars above as if he's king
Ruling the world, its his to be
The lone cry on the seagulls wing
Of the days that have swept out to sea.

Caroline Veno
Pinks and Wet Pavements
Do you remember that summer
We were sixteen
And I discovered
That your voice was deep,
And you discovered
That I had long eyelashes?

Do you remember the smell
Of pinks and wet pavements,
The shadowy seclusion of the Elm tree in my backyard?

Sometimes when I see you with
That girl whom they say
You will marry,
I remember the pulsing in my throat
When you first kissed me,
And the darling awkwardness
Of your embrace.

I close my eyes and
Smell again the pinks
And wet pavements after
Summer rains.

Eric Thonnesen
SKYSONG
Over the windblown face of dawn
sweep swallows as a song—
    lyrics of airy grace
    melody like fine lace
plucked by the rhythm of feathery sinews
wind playing over rippling thews
they form from air they cannot see
a dance of the way to be free.

Elizabeth Pellish
I ONCE LOVED
I once thought of love,
    but now there are no thoughts.
I once spoke of love,
    but now there are no words.
I once saw love,
    but now the visions are gone.
My experiences and dreams have faded.
I now belong to myself.
I am in a tunnel of darkness called life.
At the end there glimmers a small ray of light.
The hope that someday I'll

experience the thoughts, words, and visions again of Love.

Sandy D. Levan
ALONG LIFE'S WAY
We do not measure one's birthdays
By the number of years they live
But by the joy and happiness
To others, they do give—

We do not count the candles
But the friends that they have made
And all the helping hands
They've given along the way—

Each of us have a purpose
A special reason from Above
To help each other along life's way
To share our Jesus's Love—

So have a Happy Birthday
Enjoy your Special Day
And remember to count your blessings
And your friends along life's way—

Lynn Chevalier
A GLOWING STAR
A glowing star at night sparkling as green as gold.
A star is only a night watcher and has a dazzling sparkle.
If it wanted it could change like a chameleon, but a star is a glowing color of light.
It may be mistaken for the sun or cloud or two, but a star is only a star.
A star is to put on a Christmas tree to show its glowing light.

Carmen Julia Rosa
DAY DREAM

With all my love, to the young man that fills my day dreams: Mr. Leoncio Santiago Jr.

I have longed you, even
Though we have not met.
I have heard your voice, even
Though you have not spoken.

Your shadow I have seen, even
Though you have not followed.
Your body I have felt, even
Though you were not there.

Ann Galbraith
NIGHTMARE
See the crack upon the wall
Cast a spell to open wide
Enthrust the key to turn
The lock, hear the clock
Stand back please.

See the treasure hidden within
Cast thy eyes upon it's beauty
Entrust thy soul as the vapor Disperses
Hear the click as the door is Locked

Feel the darkness closing in
Cast thy eyes upon the wall
See the crack that's there no More, hear the crys of lost Souls, feel their hunger for Even more.

See the crack upon the wall
Cast the spell to close it tight
Enthrust the key—hear the click
Stand back please the end is near

Shirley Ann Barrett
PATCHWORK QUILT

This poem is dedicated to my wonderful daughter La Toycia, and mother Fannie who are very special to me in every way.

Collecting different fabrics
Some are even silk
To sit down to make
A patchy patchwork quilt

Stitching sides together
Now that was very quick
This is going to be
A patchy patchwork quilt

The richy bright colors
Stands out in such a way
That gives such brillance
On this patchy patchwork day

I can hardly stand myself
Which is very true
For making this patchwork quilt
Look so elegant and brand new

Frank Hause
BUDDY
J Just a few short months age, Sunny boy,
A Amid the fog and rain.
M My heary was happy, sharing your joys,
E Eventually, I hope to share them again.
S Small though, are your kind features, ·
H How bright and blue are your eyes—
O Often I have thought of your hearty laughter,
L Like your dimples, Sonny, how they magnitize.
L Longer eyelashes I have never seen
I In this large world of ours,
S So keep right on smiling, Buddy—
H Have the utmost pleasure thru sunshine and showers.
A Always be courteous and kind to your mother, Sonny,
U Unkept though your curly hair may be—
S So if one day when I return
E Elegant and sturdy, a becoming young man I will see.

Walter Duane Eagar
Reflections On a Pot Sherd
I hold you in my hand.
See! Once more you are admired.
A thousand summer rains
Have beat upon you here.
A thousand snows as well
Have tenderly enfolded you.

Oh sherd of clay!
Whose loving hands did shape
And mold you into being—
With beauty and usefulness?

Your creator must have admired
How you responded to her artful will.
Red pigment she mixed
To stain your basic clay.
Lines of black she painted
In splendid design.
                Then!
Through fire and

Our World's Best Loved Poems

intense heat—you were born—
in beauty—so long ago.

Joyce C. McClory
JUST TODAY

To my mother, Wilma L. Teeters,
my children, Troy, Melody, and
Wilma, and Phil. For without
their encouragement this would
not have been written.

Just today,
I put my small child to bed,
and she looked up and asked me,
about things Jesus said.
With wide-eyed wonder, she
waited to hear,
About Jesus and Santa and gifts
and good cheer.

As I sat there, I told her,
Christmas was to celebrate His
day,
But, it seems so many other
things get in the way.
I tried so hard to explain, and
then a tear came to my eye.
For Christmas wasn't Christ's
Birthday now,
It was X-mas's birthday, a day to
buy.

Just who was this X-mas and
what did he do?
To make us honor him, in the
way we do!

Just today,
I stopped and thought of thing's I
used to do,
And I realized, I'm just like
everyone else,
I had forgotten Jesus too.

So today,
I took my child upon my knee,
And told her of all the love he
gave, to you and me.
And thru this small child's eyes, I
saw what I had lost, and that
day I began,
To put Christ back in Christmas,
and start my life again.

Allen K. Harrington
A Poem Of My Choice
Today an offer came to me, from
the Poetry Association I am in,
They want a poem I submitted,
and one that I choose to win.

Well, it cannot win, because it's
not a contest,
But I will send them one, and it
will be one of my best.

While we are reading the Word,
in Church, I am now writing
these lines,
We are where JESUS is to be
scourged and beaten, in
Matthew,
And THE LORD gives me
these rhymes.

If I am to send them, A POEM OF
MY CHOICE,
Because of HIS SALVATION, I
am able to rejoice.

I don't know what to send them,
and wait I will for a line,
I can only send a short poem, so I
will have to make it very fine.

I am not feeling fully, up to par
this date,
I pray it is not the flu, I really
don't like how I feel, and
sickness is what I hate.

A POEM OF MY CHOICE, I'd
better get on the ball,
I have another that received
Honorable Mention, It was one
I sent last fall.

I will send it along also, and this
time with a check,
It might not get into print, oh,
but what the heck!!

I find just so much comfort, in
writing rhymes, and I rejoice,
And then to find an editor like
Eddie-Lou Cole,
Has given me the privilege to
send, A POEM OF MY CHOICE.

I LOVE YOU JESUS,

Lesa B. Peerman
UNCOMMITTED LOVE
You either smile or frown when I
say I care,
What is it with you, what are you
hiding in there?
What are you afraid of, the words,
the feeling, the sound?
Someday you're gonna realize
that love is all around.
You said you were hurt so many
times before,
It's like fighting a battle and
losing the war.
Someday, sometime, it will all be
clear,
But for now you just say that it's
love that you fear.
Involvement, committment, I
offer you none,
Only morning and nighttime and
a bright shining sun.
You say that love is a four letter
word,
It's in the dictionary that much
you have heard.
Someday look it up and see what
it means,
The word love is real, no matter
how unreal it seems.

Ms. Marianne Smith
THE SEAGULLS
The red tail
must be T. W. A.
clear in a sky
dissappears.
I follow its sound
with my eyes.
They
gray shimmering white
have mastered
soundless flight.
Glide over a lagoon
dissappear.
We cannot follow
silence.

Linda Baker Burke
LOST LOVE
Did you ever wonder what
happens to love
When love has died like an ember;
It disappears like the moon in the
night
Icy-like a night in December.

His touch which once made me
warm with desire

Now chills me to the bone;
What happened to the glorious,
passionate fire
He turned into a heart of stone!

He once compared me to a rose,
I laughed at all his wooing ways;
Soon the flame lost its glow
My summer love soon slipped
away.

Now sadness fills my heart and
soul
Tears begin to fill my eyes;
The flame of love no longer glows
My heart just slowly dies.

Joan Goyer Bushno
FRIENDSHIP
He was eight years old and lonely.
We were discussing friendship.
I said one of my best friends
Is a thorn bush with white
blossoms
And a red birds nest.
He said his best friend is
A bush by the back door
With white flowers and bluebirds.

Linda F. Williams
COOL RAINY NIGHT
How much lovelier can romance
be then
on a cool rainy night
when the scene is enchantment
and wrapped
around you are the loving arms of
your
soul's desire

Outside, raindrops tenderly fall
all around
like tiny footsteps of life briefly
found
dancing momentarily, then
departing with a
fragile kiss upon the ground

As you sit by the warm glowing
fire inside
the sweet aroma of burning wood
sifts
through the air while viewing the
beautiful
kaleidoscope of flames

Then from each lighted log, the
flames begin to come alive
upon every wall, shadows dance
and sing out
and within your heart there's
happiness, you
feel loved without a question of
doubt

Definitely, the miracle of love
prevails
two wonderful hearts did
intertwine
on this cool rainy night
with lasting precious moments to
share for a
life-time

Diana Kierce
MY ROY

---

*I dedicate this poem to Roy, my
childhood sweetheart, my friend,
my love, my life.*

We were just kid's when we first
fell in love,
My heart sparkled just like stars

up above.
You always protected me as we
grew,
Then you went away, I found
another, I was such a fool.
For you will always be my man,
my life, my happiness, my love,
You are everything to me, my Roy.
You take away all my fears,
And wipe away all my tears.
You always hold me close to you,
And make me smile when I am
blue.
For you will always be my man,
my life, my happiness, my love,
You are everything to me, my Roy.
As we grow older, our love grows
deeper, take my body and my
heart,
No man, no one, can ever break
us apart.
I live for the future, that maybe
we'll share,
To love you and tell you, that I
really care.
For you will always be my man,
my life, my happiness, my love,
You are everything to me, my Roy.

Scott D. Hildebrand
PLIGHT OF HISTORY
Plants Compose
Animals Perceive
Humans Improve

Robert J. Norton

Robert J. Norton
**If I Could Change the
World**
If I could change the world tonight
I'll tell you what I'd do.
I'd change all hate into God's love,
I'd make me part of you.
I'd change the mountains into
hills,
The valleys into plains.
I'd change your tear drops into
smiles
And drive away your pains.
I'd change the clouds to carpets,
We'd with magic float away,
I'd hold you close throughout the
night
And far into the day.
I'd change the mighty ocean wide
Into a tiny sea;
And change the rivers into streams
For you to cross with me.
I'd bring the heavens closer too,
And make the distance fade
And watch God's Face reflecting
joy
On changes I had made.

G. E. Hudgins
SOLDIER OF FORTUNE
Posed upon a rock was he,
With his gallantry and sword;
Awaiting the arrival of a cause,
One worth fighting for.

Affliction of one's pain
He brings with delight—
The drawing of his sword,
The swiftness of the night.

Greeting the day with fortitude
Looking only to survive,
His strength lies within his mind
And within his mind's eye.

Anarchist are his beliefs—
He will never change his ways;
Soldier of fortune he will be,
For the rest of his mortal days.

E. Gwendolyn Campbell
ESSENCE OF LIFE

*Dedicated to Bob with whom I
share my life and love.*

Don't delay till tomorrow the
   things you wish for today.
If they're important to you, you
   will surely find a way.
Dreams are accomplished when
   one cares enough
To do what he wants to do.
So set your sight on the utmost
   height
And make those dreams come true.

Waste not your life on idle dreams;
Live ev'ry one of your secret
   schemes.
Cherish every precious minute
As though eternity were in it.
Then, when the years have ebbed
   away,
Rejoice, knowing that you fully
   lived each day.

Tomorrow and tomorrow more
   dreams you will store
To live life just as fully when you
   reach the other shore.

Pamela Jean Tripp
REMEMBER ALWAYS
If you will always remember, you
   are husband and wife;
Your marriage, will be the
   greatest reward of your life.
Work and plan; but do it together.
As one; and your marriage will
   last forever.

Don't wait until it's too late, and
   you start to shout.
If you're unhappy, or angry; sit
   down and talk it out.
If each of you take but a little
   and give all you can,
The other will always be there to
   hold your hand.
To let you know, it'll all turn out
   fine.
To help each other through the
   never ending hard times.

Sometimes the truth hurts, but
   it's always for the best.
Don't be afraid to say what you
   feel, but always be honest.
If you're feeling happy, be sure
   you share;
Because when you do, you're
   showing that you care.

Remember to show it and say "I
   LOVE YOU."
You'll find it's not so very hard to
   do.

And with that in mind, you'll
   survive your plans,
         finished or not.
Remembering, that each other's
   love, is something
         you've always got.
So together: be happy, sharing,
   and most of all loved;
For this marriage is being helped
   through life,
         From above.

Judy Jeffcoat
PRAYER

*Dedicated to the loving memory
of our son, Ronnie Wayne, who
died at the age of 19 with cancer.*

Prayer opens our eyes
As God's truths are revealed
That we may be encouraged
And troubled hearts stilled

Prayer opens our eyes
That God's love we may know
Surrounds us closely
Wherever we go

Prayer opens our eyes
For God's power to outweigh
All the problems we face
In life each day

Prayer opens our eyes
For our love God to hear
As our hearts and souls
To Him draw near

Helen A. Holden
END OF THE YEAR
It is a happy time at the end of
   the year,
When we all plan a lot for
   Christmas cheer.
If we could just go back to times
   long ago,
Where things were simple and
   not much show,
The dollar was not worshipped
   like it is today;
They were lucky if they owned a
   horse and sleigh.
Do unto others as we would like
   to be done by,
So we have no reason to
   complain or even cry.
God is our best friend, and His
   love will help us too,
As we live each day and trust
   Him to guide us thru.

Kenneth A. Phillips
SEASONS OF PROMISE
Summer has been spent in
   warmth and ease
Now Fall has crept through with
   gift-sought keys
Biding to treasures of a season of
   love and daring
When many affairs are true to a
   faring—
Like hearts so sensitive as to
   pardon distress
Hearts whose names carry a
   beacon of rest—
   Following will with notion
   Simplicity with devotion

I wonder that Winter should
   bring such an awful chill
When bound soundly in our
   care—taken will
Enhancing our love with our
   life
Our duty with our strife
And time in all its pursuit with
   sanity
Shall not partake in any
   unrecognized vanity
But only asking of good
And good should come
In the morn
Or at the break of dusk
But good should come

Gregg A. Ayers
ANEW
As the light rose on that dark,
   wintery morn,
Like the beginning of time, the
   earth forlorn.

The wind swirling the numbing
   white with a whine,
The earth, the heavens, frozen
   dead in time.

Yet, on that most forsaken morn,
A life, complete, was born.

Madge Mullins Wilbanks
The Ultimate Violinist

*For John F. Gay III . . . the
personification of performing
excellence in musical clarity and
form . . .*

Strings taut; wood evenly hued;
   Cat gut strained
Fused triumphantly with tonal
   Excellence

Shaded nuances;
   Trembling crescendos
Giving magnificent credence
   To Mazart, Tchaikovsky

On a November afternoon.

Julie Anne Ritchey
HAPPINESS
If you're very sad and lonely, and
   you need a friend or two, it's
   hard to smile and laugh it off,
   and keep your spirit new.
If your problems seem to mount
   too high and make you want to
   burst, just give a shout and tell
   them bye, and let happiness
   quench the thirst.
If you have too many worries, and
   you want to break the tie, just
   watch the one who hurries and
   ask yourself, just why?
If you're at the end of patience,
   and you can't seem to find a
   way, just run a while and jump
   the fence, and send your cares
   a stray.
If you're just about to give up
   hope, and you can't stand to
   face the score, just have a talk
   and pull the rope, and let
   happiness start to pour.
If it's time the day is closing, and
   you try to sleep, but fail, just
   close your eyes and keep on
   dosing and let sweet dreams
   just sail.
If you wake and feel like dying

and you seem to stay this way,
   just try a smile and keep on
   trying and let happiness lead
   the day.
If you find that nothing seems to
   work, and everything goes
   wrong, just make a smile in
   others perk, and happiness will
   come along.
If you never can find happiness,
   and I know this isn't true, just
   try to give your life the best,
   and keep looking for the clue!

Fred D. Robb
DREAMS
Into each heart
There lays a feeling
In each feeling there is life
Into each life
There lays a dream
A dream of truth
Truth for you
What you can reveal
What you can make real
Make you dream a reality
Then you won't be lost . . .
In a dream

Thelma L. Reusser
THE CAT SPIDER

*To those folks who aren't
acquainted with these little
'critters' They are faster than fast,
colored to blend, ears like a cat,
almost a face, and hang in a web
like a sack!"*

This here's about a "Cat Spider"
Hangin' on our family room wall;
That feller looked, with his
   tangled legs,
As if he was dead-with no life at
   all.

Now cat spiders really intrigue
   me,
They're different that's sure to be
   seen,
With their little pointed ears that
   look like a cat
Sure makes a person wonder
   where it's all at!

I've never read about these little
   critters
In any book ever I've looked,
They must be born in thousands
   by 'litters',
How could they possibly have
   been overlooked?

Anyway, I got an eye glass for
   close inspection
And put it near to see those neat
   ears—
But apparently he didn't like my
   detection,
"Why, who am I—his kind had
   been around many years!"

So, dead as he looked with his
   legs folded up
He untangled all eight and got
   ready to jump,
And as I touched that sucker
   with a 'swat' in my hand,
He floated down just as nice as
   you please, and came into land";

The last I saw of that unique rare
   bug

Was him 'melting' into the color
of rug;
He was nestled down quite out of
sight
And I saw him no more, tho' I
tried with a light!

Deanie Leger
WAR

*Dedicated to my brother Michael
"John" Richard. Life cut— 30
years of age— A fool and a knife.*

Everybody fears war
Yet we're fighting each other.
Are you listening sister
Do you hear me brother.

The president speaks of peace
Yet spends the dollars on guns.
What has happened to
missionaries
Religions, Priests and Nuns.

We all lock our doors
A fear of who'll enter there.
Yet our brother is killed in the
streets
And who the hell gives a care.

The news on the television
Tell who got shot last night.
Between songs on the radio
They're fighting for equal right.

Where's the old time religion
Lets walk hand in hand.
The old red, white and blue
This land is your land.

But the knives will continue to
stab
And the guns will be fired.
Because some fools gone mad
A life has expired.

Cathy Conroy
WINGS OF MORNING
I share with woodly creatures
An excitement of the coming day.
When the sun has wings of
morning.
Reflecting crystals light my way.

I search for the beautiful
Though it is all around
It grows in all I touch.
It lives in every sound.

I want to take a part of this
And bring it home with me.
No one here will miss it;
It will sit for all to see.

I raise my gun and shoot it.
The magic drops at dawn.
My stomach sickens at the sight
of her newly awakened fawn.

Lydia H. Moreland
UNFOLDING

Inspired by one who feels the need.

They say it's unexplainable,
The aura that encases us.
Accepting things for what they
are
Not analyzing the natural.
No one will ever understand
The need we alone realize.
A move toward becoming who we
are

A chance in believing in ourselves.
Frightened and excited, happy yet
sad,
Feeling more than one emotion at
once,
Taking one step back, then two
steps forward.
And all the while
Seeing a star.
Finally knowing it's tangible.
With a lot of work and
perserverance
A someone is waiting to be born.
The potential exists,
It needs only to develop.
Maybe a hand to clasp
Or a shoulder to lean against,
The encouragement we desire.
When success is in one's mind,
Strength is in one's body,
And when belief is in one's soul,
The dream, will only then, begin
unfolding.

Tom Bigman
INDIAN SUMMER
The beautiful colors of the Indian
Summer season,
Such a glorious sight so pleasing!
A little cottontail hopping here
and there,
While a red tail hawk soar high
above the cliffs in the air.
A horned-toad soaking itself with
the Indian Summer's sunlight,
Oh, what a beautiful sight!
A Squirrel with an acorn on the
tree trunk,
On a nearby rock sits a chipmunk.
Suddenly, the thought of the long
hard winter ahead . . .
Worry not, it wouldn't be all that
bad.
The beautiful colors of the Indian
Summer season,
What a good reason to be alive
and to enjoy a worthwhile
season!

Louise N. Donaley
MIRACLES
They say the days of miracles
have passed
That they don't happen anymore
But my Lord and I know different
We've seen them by the score.

Each new day is a miracle
Our life begins anew
How much more proof do you
need
That God really loves you

If we expect a miracle
It will surely happen for us
All God wants from us
Is our love and trust.

Don't ever falter in your faith
He's there to be leaned on
After all He made a miracle for us
When He allowed us to be born.

Live your life the best you can
Help others along the way
And with love and trust in God
You'll see miracles happen each
day.

Arttie Jo Miller
My Only Shelter and Shield
She was my shelter and shield
when I was born.
When I learned to walk and talk,

She told me 'No' to things that
would hurt me.
She was my shelter and shield
when I learned new things.
She was a teacher when I fell and
skinned my knee.
She was my shelter and shield as
I grew.
She punished me when I came
home late, or got a bad grade in
school.
But as I grew I turned away from
the shelter and shield
I said I hated her and I didn't need
her anymore (I was wrong)
She wanted to be my friend as
well as my shelter and shield.
But I didn't want her, I told her
she could never be my friend.
I made her cry, and I made her
angry.
I'm telling her I'm sorry for
everything I did
to hurt her, and thanking her for
being my
shelter and shield when I needed
her.
Who is this shelter and shield?
My mother.
I love you, Mom.

Jean L. Egyed

Jean L. Egyed
DECEMBER
An old year is ending
Greeting cards I'll be sending
Decorations of all kinds are
blending
All through the neighborhoods,
and towns

This is a time to give thanks, and
share
And do special little things that
show we care
There's a fragrance of Evergreen,
and Holly in the air
And the laughter, and music is of
Christmas sounds

It's time to be of good cheer
And have our loved ones near
And praise One so dear
It's the time of our Savior's birth

In the days of December
There will be moments of splender
And dear friends to remember
A time to unite, and bring peace
on earth

Mrs. Johnnie Jackson
A CRYING IN THE NIGHT
I hear a crying in the night,
Could it be the lost children?

Could it be the holy-rollers
down at the church?
Or could it be the wind?

I hear a crying in the night,
Could it be a tormented soul?
Could it be a world of chaos
with no hope?
Or could it be the wind?

I hear a crying in the night,
Could it be the spirit of my
mother?
Could it be my bygone childhood?
Or could it be my mind?
I hear a crying in the night.

Johnny Rex Rattan
**Dear Daddy Tomorrow I'm
Going To Run Away**
My little girl gave me a note
today
Dear Daddy Tomorrow I'm going
to run away,

For nobody loves me anymore
Tomorrow I'm going to walk out
that door,

For today mommy yelled at me
And daddy you I hardly ever see,

For nobody loves me today
Dear daddy tomorrow I'm going
to run away,

For late at night you and mommy
fight
When you think us kids are out
of sight.

Dear daddy tomorrow I'm going
to run away
But I don't know just where I'm
going to stay,

For I am only five years old you
see
But somewhere there will be a
family that loves me,

Dear daddy tomorrow I'm going
to run away
Dear Daddy please daddy stop me
today.

Gordon A. Salway
IN THE BEGINNING
Serpentine light
Reflecting each morning
Through the pillars of the
primeval forest
Not subject to change
As they awaken
Raising their inquisitive heads
Amid the rustle of feathery
fronds.

Dick Hoffpauir
On His Sixtieth Birthday
Live for today!
Forget yesterday!
Today is the first day of—

All these brave cliches I heard
and believed
And thought nothing of my
guiding past
Or viewed carefully at each
twilight
The outline of the day to come.

Blithely I celebrated life each day
Each day dissipating
No day thinking or planning

Tomorrow arrived a while ago—
too soon:
I had not done with today.

Grant W. Anderson
ILLUSIONS OF THE NIGHT
Forlorn and heartbroken
I await the night
When did I last miss you
When did our eyes meet
Long have I gazed into your eyes
Long have mine met a kind
   glance
Must I forget you
Must my heart wait still longer
It must wait for eternity
Untill our love comes full circle
Yet now can I love you from afar
And know you love me too.

Beyond the barrier of the window
Are lights floating in a sea of
   darkness
Glittering as if they were stars
No moon tonight
The reflection of the sun on the
   earth is not cast
Yet my life is free
Free to feel the love that flows
   from your heart
Like a tide

Eleanore Wojtas Laper
PINKY MY CAT

*To Kathleen and Kristine, Cat
Fanciers.*

Snuggle, she loves to, upon my lap,
while I settle into the TV-
   watching trap.

All cozy and warm, so furry and
   purry,
please scratch my neck, hurry,
   hurry.

The commercial is on, it's time
   for a break,
off to the kitchen for some
   goodies to take.

Pinky wants out, to sit on the
   deck,
watching the birds and stretching
   her neck.

Suddenly a leap, and she lands on
   the lawn,
but the bird is high up and
   quickly gone.

Later, a scratching, I hear at the
   door,
it's time to curl up on the couch
   once more.

Ormond S. Sivers
SECRET LOVE

For the girl with the smile of rose

I see her
Whereever I go
How I often wish
I could tell her so

Many restless nights
I am dreaming and find,
I am holding her,
Loving her, in my mind

The way she smiles
Her friendly hello
My heart aches for her
But I can't let her know

I want to tell her I love her
Whenever we are near

But the thought of losing
A friend, I fear
In dark silence I wonder
Is there any hope for me
I have fallen in love
Quite secretly

Frances Marie Benge Steinert
DO NOT DESPAIR

*To my very favorite male,
Clarence William Steinert (1930),
My spouse, of Louisville, Jefferson
County, Kentucky, USA.*

Does your tail need repair?
   Do not despair!
With the passing of time
   Some of us go blind;
Others, lose their mind.

Edith G. Oster
CENTENNIAL YEAR

*Dedicated to Gordon, Nebraska
1885——1985*

There's a little old trunk in the
   attic,
   Dreaming dreams of the long,
   long ago;
Dreaming dreams of the time
   when it journeyed
   Through a winter of cold and
   snow.

How it came from the East in a
   wagon
   By faithful oxen drawn;
Bearing a families' treasures
   Toward the land of the setting
   sun.

Jolting ever onward
   With never a thought of rest;
With a vision of peace to guide it
   To a land of hope in the West.

Its canvas sides are frayed now,
   Its brass is tarnished and old,
But it thinks of the time when
   it's cloth was new,
   And its brass was shining like
   gold.

The little trunk is content now,
   Dreaming the long days through.
It has seen those hopes rewarded,
   It has seen those dreams come
   true.

Emmanuel J. Muganda
erratic search
the rumbling days of uncertainty
   hover by,
our idiosyncratic minds
   ceaselessly searching;
in the dark hallways
at ev'ry dawn of the days.
some stumble, some fall
trying to hold onto the ellusive
   wall;
somethin' to lean on
a perpertual assurance
a perpertual peaceful state of being.

there's a reverberant sense of
   solitude
heightened by our own fears of
   rejection
a sensual need to belong
eternal state of longing
nothing seems within easy reach

deep despair oftentimes impeach
the reality of being and existence
   of hope
yet hope makes life worthwhile
yea, hope makes our search salient.

Verlyn L. Beilman
PARADISE

*To Andy, Thanks for taking me
to Paradise. I Love You.*

Paradise, how do you describe,
   Paradise.
   Birds chirping softly in the palm
   trees
   The orange sun coming over the
   mountains
   that bring a golden glow to the
   islands.
Or the ripples in the clear blue
   water, that
   changes colors with every wave.
The fresh scent of wild orchids
   and ginger,
   pretty flowers of which you've
   never seen before.
Listen!. is it the soft music in the
   distance
   with which you glide along the
   dance floor
   with the one you love.
Or white sands glistening in the
   sunlight
   while lovers walk hand and
   hand.
Paradise, so hard to find the answer
What of the surf splashing in on
   the rocks
   blowing a gentle mist upon
   your face.
The soft gentle voices of the
   islanders.
And the slow pace you've never
   found back home.
Beautiful mountains or the now
   quiet volcanoes.
Listen! to the quiet peace.
No matter where you turn, there's
   only beauty.
Paradise, I know, a gift from God
Only He could make something
   so lovely

Douglass Hill Addams
LAKE EUFAULA
Theres a little town down in
   Alabam
Where the Chattahoochee rivers
   flowing
It spilled its waters and formed a
   lake
And its a place worth knowing
Today I'm thinking about her
   pretty waters
And want to go back to the banks
   of Lake Eufaula

In this little town down in
   Alabam
Where the Chattahoochee rivers
   flowing
Anyone can tell by the fragrant
   smell
That a southern breeze is blowing
Where the country gentlemen
   stroll with Dixie Daughters
Makes me want to go back to the
   banks of Lake Eufaula

Where the waters streaming each
   night I'm dreaming

About this pretty place
Where a man can stand with his
   feet in the sand
And satisfy his taste
I'm thinking about her dreamy
   streamy waters
And want to go back to the banks
   of Lake Eufaula

Katrina Romelle Wilson
WITH YOU ALWAYS

*In loving memory of my
Grandmother, Mrs. Velner
Robertson, whose love and
wisdom, lives on still.*

Mourn me neither today nor
   tomorrow;
For I've gone not far away.
Let not your heart dwell in sorrow,
These things of you I pray.

Your head held high, walk
   straight my love,
In peace shall thou remain;
For even now I'm with the "Dove"
And together we all shall reign.

Stand fast, my child, hold strong
   your heart;
These things you must endeavor.
Then memories of the joys and
   tears shall never part,
But remain with you forever.

Marie Anne Forster
THE NIGHT OWL

To my husband and children

When the raven tapestry of night,
Falls on the silver moonlight of
   evening,
And the mighty stands of
   evergreens,
Whisper their song of midnight,
The night owl,
Who see's all through his marble
   eye,
Knows that this, is when day
   begins.
Is it then man's sleeping,
That deprives him of his
   awareness and freedom.

Daryl Douglass Carter
NIGHT WATCH
Peering out into the darkness,
With breath quickened by fear,
His gaze searched for the lone
   rider,
Who tethered him here.

Pawing the ground in frustration,
His ears picked up whispers from
   the night's unease,
Watching and waiting, all alone,
While starlight filtered through
   the trees.

When a shape stumbled from the
   shadows,
He quickly jerked up his
   aristocratic head,
Then well-loved hands stroked
   his shining mane,
As a bright crimson puddle grew
   where the silent
         figure bled.

The proud stallion watched in
   puzzled anguish,

Amidst the mournful lowing of
  nearby cattle,
Set free by a gentle, weak, tap
  upon his flanks,
He galloped out into the soft
  night, his burden
        an empty saddle . . .

Jane Cortright
REUNION
Joe never knew what hit him
That afternoon Death Struck
He tried to cross the street and
  died
Beneath a speeding truck.
And free at last his spirit soared
(For he was free of sin)
He waited at the pearly gates
And soon was ushered in,

The gates of Heaven opened wide,
"Now find God" he was told.
He wandered up and down the
  streets
Inlaid with pearl and gold.
And when he saw his God he ran
And cowered at his feet,
Ashamed, because he had been
  told
To never cross the street.

But God looked down in some
  surprise,
And gently stroked his head.
"Why Joe, what are you doing here?
Why Joe, you must be dead?"
Joe wagged his tail, and on
  command,
Moved slowly to the right.
Then boy and dog together walked
On toward the shining light.

Norma Jeanne Zeliff
REINCARNATION
I finally made a decision for my
  new rebirth.
So here's the story for what it is
  worth.
I announced it firmly to the large
  Angel Band,
And chose the Planet Earth for
  my beloved land.

After a thorough study of the
  Soul's Golden Book,
I realized the facts of life needed
  another look.
I courageously traveled back,
  throughout the past,
For help in selecting a game plan,
  that would last.

All the errors were listed in
  enlighting Karmic bits.
These really hit me in slow,
  rough, shuddering fits.
Knowing these were necessary to
  balance out my life,
I sorely braced for these moments
  of awful strife.

I chose my two parents, so strong,
  and true.
A sister, and two brothers, with
  eyes of blue.
A tall, handsome young soul for
  marriage in light,
Two added children promised a
  future of pure delight.

Selecting color, creed, and
  profession, proved such a
  session.
Carefully selected, these choices
  would teach such a lesson.

Now I was ready for my journey
  of new rebirth.
In my Golden Book, this life will
  be of great worth!

Jimmie Renee
GOD MADE EVERYTHING
GOD planted a tree along a
  shady brook
To make a shady nook
Where animals could take a rest
For by him they were blessed
And children too
For he said unto them I Love You

GOD planted flowers in a barren
  field
Where a rainbow of beauty they
  would yield
GOD planted wheat and grain
To be flourished by the rain
For others to be fed
As to him they were led
GOD made the birds to sing
For GOD made everything

Ethel Hunt Street
YOU'D NEVER KNOW
If I should pass you on the street
  I'd smile and I'd say hello:
You'd never know behind that
    smile
  There lurked a bit of woe.

My face still wears a happy mask
  That's carved out of grief and
    pain:
You'd never know how much I
    cared
  If we should meet again.

You broke my heart long years
  ago
  It will never be the same:
You'd never know the ache
    returns
  Whenever I hear your name.

I'll keep my eyes free from all tears
  My lips will say that we're thru:
You'd never know, but this is so
  I'm still in love with you.

Burton J. Hollen
THE NAKED WOMAN
I saw her naked on the beach,
though she was fully clothed.
She bared her soul
for all to see.
Her transparent facade
gave away her inner torment,
which she tried to cover
with a filmy blanket
woven by flirtatious
smiles and unsaid words.

She was beautiful,
but the beauty ended
with her suntan.
I felt strange,
seeing this naked, beautiful
  woman.
For the only arousal I felt
was pity.

Angela A. Smith
**The Christmas Family
  Gathering**

*I dedicate this poem to my family
(the AYERS) as I was unable to be
with them on this occasion.*

As you gather tonight as a family,
Full of love and fun and joy.
Full of punch, and cookies and
  goodies,
And carols that everyone enjoys.

Everyone chattering at once; to
  first
one and then two more. No one
  knows
who's said what, and if so, what it
  was meant for.

Nothing takes the place of fond
  memories,
Of sharing Christmas with family
  I love.
Even if I'm not there in person,
I hear every little word. I feel every
little hug and kiss, as I've always
  felt before.
And I know I'll be there next
  year,
God willing for me once more.
It's thrilling to know you're
  together;
And being merry and sharing this
  season.
May God bless and keep and care
  for you
Whatever might be his reason.

Diane Bernardy
GODS MYSTERY OF LIFE
Settled deeply in the vastness of
  the earth, lies the mystery of life.
Man can't quite seem to
  understand the meaning of it's
  form.
It seems to appear solid at times
  when wet from the rains.
Putting itself together forming
  what they call mud.
The warmth of the sun seems to
  dry and loosen its form.
Revealing itself in a different
  texture we know as dirt.
But within both of these forms,
  man can plant a certain seed.
That will grow and form some
  kind of life.
But without the sun and the
  rains, that life won't have a
  chance.
Man can't quite understand how
  he came about.
We read of how God took this
  very dust of the vastness of the
  earth.
He put a breath of fresh air
  within, and here stands His
  creation.
What is formed into a perfect
  image He calls man.

And just as well as a man can
  plant a seed, out in the warmth
  of the sun and the rains.
God Himself gave man, this same
  chance of planting seed.
But without the Son we know as
  Christ, and the rains He sends
  within the soul, this can not be
  done.
Because this is a gift He sent, a
  mystery of life.

Laurie Carr
**Christmas Without
  Grandma**

*This is dedicated to my beloved
Grandmother who taught me the
true meaning of love.*

Grandma I missed you today—

I missed your hugs, your smiling
  face—

Your sister was here and though
  she is
dear—no one will ever take your
  place—

My memories run deep of the
  love that we
keep of all the Christmas's past—
How I wish they would last—

My first Christmas without you
  has past,
but the love that we share will
  always last

But someday we'll be together
  again—
In our lords kingdom that knows
  no end

There I will sit by your knees and
  tell you
all the things that have happened
  to me—

Then the pain will be gone and
  we can finally
carry on once more.

         Merry Christmas
              Grandma

Cynthia McNeese
LET US GIVE THANKS
Let us give thanks
To those we love,
For they are the
Underlying force
Of our existance.

Let us give thanks
To our health and
Our undying strength
To carry onward.

Let us give thanks
To our friends
And the happiness
They bring into
Our lives.

Let us give thanks
To God for allowing
Us to see the light
Of each new day
With happiness.

Let us be thankful
For being together,
As we form an unique
Union of love and
  friendship . . .

Isaac J. Perales, Jr.
WAR PART II

This poem is dedicated to the veterans of all wars; those who fought for honor and freedom and the love of this great nation, the United States of America.

Sometimes you don't know if you
    are going to live or die.
At night all you can do is cry.
Your buddy shows weariness on
    his face.
For tomorrow you will march to
    another place.
At night you sleep near foxholes
    you dig from the ground.
Knowing that the enemy is
    somewhere around.
You march through the village
    with a gun in your hand.
And the chaplain says, "You're
    sinning killing the other man."
A bomb explodes and you hit the
    ground.
But all you hear is shouting all
    around.
Both of you fire at the same time,
And each time someone gets hit
    it's the end of the line.
It is over in a little while as you
    take a head count.
And you see the dead and
    wounded as you walk about.
The fighting is over as you push
    on.
Deeper and deeper you move on.
You fight for a reason.
But you yourself don't know if
    you will last another season.
Maybe someone will end it for
    you.
If they do, you did the best that
    you could do.
War is no place for mankind.

Daniel P. Jacobson
THE PEOPLE'S ARTIST
They call him the "people's Artist",
A champion of the Common Man!
This is how he paints them:
A homogeneous mass,
Faceless, mindless, and
Marching, all
In one direction.
Oh, yes,
He will champion you,
If
You are faceless, mindless, and
Marching, all,
At his direction.

Loretta M. Guyan
IMAGES
Happy Birthday, Darling!
See, I've poured the wine.
Oh, I Love you, Darling:
I'm so glad you're mine.

Here's to you, my Darling
And didn't we have fun
These few years together
When you and I were one?

Where shall we go, my Darling
On this, your day of days?
Climb a mountain, see the sunset
Through the twilight haze

Of the yesteryears together,
Of the times now gone?

The tears are stinging; salty, bitter.
You left me all alone.

I won't forget your birthday
But I won't toast again
Until we're joined forever
In another time.

Maryagnes L. Goldsmith
FLASHBACK

To a dream come true: Of you and me in a time—In a life—In a love— Of beauty in youth—Of truth in innocence—To the world where we stay—precious memory . . .

I saw him again,
Just ten minutes ago,
And with him the memories:
How we both laughed in the sun,
All our corny little puns,
How I cried when he got mad,
How he hurt when I grew sad,
How we dreamed our lives away,
And how our love was here to
    stay,
And how we loved each other so,
But that was-well-so long ago . . .

Lillian (Billie) Dinkel
NOSTALGIA

To my Beloved Sisters and Brothers Who share with me fond memories Of a happy childhood.

I remember, I remember our old
    wood stove
With it's pungent smell of
    burning Oak.
It reigned supreme in Mama's
    kitchen
With Regal Majesty; warming me.
On a frosty winter morn, like a
    Lizard sunning,
I would heat my little back side,
Basking in it's glorious warmth,
Turning round and round, in my
    Flannel gown.

I remember, I remember the Iron
    Kettle wheezing
With a sighing, happy sound;
A song of Breakfast
To my childish ears, in bygone
    years.
The smell of Mama's Yeast Bread
    rising,
Hot rolls in the warmer;
And Monday's Washday Stew
    a-bubbling.
Oh, simple wholesome food! You
    tasted good!

I remember, I remember our old
    wood stove
Where we took our wash tub
    baths
Behind it's broad warm back.
How clear the memory,
    reminding me.
There was hot corn popping on a
    winter night;
And Family gathered round the
    old stove, singing
Together; warm and happy.
And now I feel a tear, for
    yesteryear.

Ida F. Hendrickson
Don't Kiss Me . . Or I'll Love You!
Just keep your distance . . .
    Oh, I can deal
With the glance from you
    That makes me reel

You grin like that
    And say my name
As tho it's a toy
    You won in a game

Of pitch-and-toss
    At the county fair
(And you're such a *Wonder*
    Standing there . . .)

That I really should warn you
    I'M on the SQUARE!
Don't kiss me . . . or
    I'll *Love* you!

Paul Leroy Wright

Paul Leroy Wright
THE PASTOR'S WIFE

This poem was written to and inspired by Pastor Gary Wright and his lovely wife Frenchie. Also, I dedicate this poem to my children Paul II and Jameica because I LOVE YOU.

The Pastor's Wife Is A Very
    Special Person
She's The One With The
    Wonderful Words Of
    Encouragement
Constantly Showing A Pleasant
    Happy Smile
You Can See Her Taking Care Of
    Her Little Babies
But What You Don't See Is How
    She Cares For Her Big Baby
You Know How Pastors' Are
    When It Comes To Their Work
They're Always Worried About
    Their Church
And Constantly Trying To Find
    Ways To Make It Better
And It Seems They Just Forget
    About Themselves
Now Mind You, That Is Good,
    But Then In Steps The Pastor's
    Wife
Making Sure He Takes The Time
    To Eat
And Encouraging Him To Get
    Enough Sleep
She's A Mother, A Friend and
    She's The Pastor's Wife
She's The One Were Everyone

Seems To Always Forget Her
    Name
They Just Call Her The Pastor's
    Wife
God Called The Pastor To Look
    After His People
But God Called The Pastor's Wife
    To Look After His Special
    Chosen Leader
What People Don't Realize Is
    That She's The Most Special
    Person On This Earth
Dear God I want To Take This
    Time To Thank You And Ask
    You
To Always Keep And Bless THE
    PASTOR'S WIFE

Daniel R. Miller
SHE FILLS ME
There is much beauty
in the world. Often
it is a beauty
of distance
of untouchable Holiness.
But the symmetry
of my friend
is familiar.
Her beauty
is close
and warm. Though
we touch not
though our
tender kisses
are for the future
or
not at all,
yet
She fills me.

Margie Roemele
AUTUMN
The Asters bloom beside the
    stream amid the Goldenrod

And in the warm and hazy Sun
    lazily seem to nod

The crickets chirp in the meadow
    in the field of golden hay

And nestled in the Garden the
    yellow pumpkins lay

It's a pause before the Harvest to
    reap atop the ground

It's the golden time of Autumn
    before the leaves turn brown.

Jennie L. Owens
The Great Reunion Day
The custom through the ages
has been to gather
each his own family of God to
    talk, sing, pray and preach.

Gone are many after
rearing families
engaging in worship
assisting the neighbors
tending the flock or keeping the
    house.

Reaping rewards come surely to
each somehow, sometime,
    somewhere,
until our lifespan has unfolded
no one's work has been finished
in labor, love,
offerings, and prayer wrought
    with
newness of life after happiness,
    joy, pain,
and suffering have passed.

Divine guidance is open to one

and all who believeth . . . there is room
yonder for all who meet at the foot of the cross while here on earth.

Frank Benge
MEMORY TREASURE

To Rita Kay (1951), Nita Elaine (1956), and Gina Denise (1961) Johnson; Dennis Paul (1952) and Bruce Daniel (1955) Moore (my nieces and nephews).

Christmas—1983
    Has become a memory.

There is no way to measure
    This memory, a treasure.

You played a great part
    And the memory stays in my heart.

Haynes Reynolds, Ph. D.
MAKER OF THE STARS
O Father almighty
Who created one billion trillion stars
And this small orb
On which resides your chief concern

How your people call on you
In adversity
And sometimes when things go well

How your children seek you
In ways various
Good and ill

You are there
To sustain us, to lift us up

May I rise to your heavens
O Father almighty
And reach a star
And more important
The Maker of the Stars

Karen Bridgette Satterley
THE CLOSE OF THE DAY
I watched the sun come up
O'er the top of the hill
It's light slowly awakening
The quiet earthy still.

I watched it as it rose
Into the soft blue sky
It touched my life with love
And dried my teary eyes.

Slowly rising to it's peak
It's rays beamed bright and strong
I lifted my face to the sky
And from my heart burst a song.

As the fading evening sunlight
Stretched across the golden sky
I looked toward the heavens
And to the One on High,

I thanked Him once again
For lighting my path today
As I watched the sun go down
At the close of one more day.

Leonard J. Wilson
THERE IS YET TIME
As the sweetness in our lives sour
As our passions become cooled with age
Let not our lives be lost,
In a whirlwind of misguided rage

Leaders becoming weak with vain satisfaction

Individuals collectively misguided,
Rulers infected with greed and pride
Let not upon these our humble fate ride

Power corrupting in doltish conceit
Drugs possessing generations to come;
Evil so rampant as to absorb all in it's wake
No victories in men's lives leaving no goals to seek;
Drained of the strength to think on one's own
Living the lives of relations for love's sake
Has all goodness died and all hope gone?

Changing creation;
Disrupting all granted
Even truth nowadays is hopelessly slanted
Fact becoming fiction as fiction becomes fact
We *must* cleanse our spirits to bring this world back.

Phyllis Newton
TO FEED A ROBIN
Yearly in the Spring
Comes a living thing
So free
On wing soon to cling
To a tree and sing
With glee
Sweet he seems to bring
Notes fit for a king
And me.

Greeting crumbs of bread
His thank you is said
For feed
By tilting his head
And showing breast red
Indeed.

Margo Mageno
How Long I'd Like To Live
I had a dream to live
Forever,
never get old and fulfill my dreams.
To live forever is once in a lifetime.
I wish someday I could live
Forever,
to never get old, and fulfill my dreams. If I can't live forever, and you should see me sitting, do not disturb me just let me dream.

Gloria Hartsell
LOVE . . .
Love comes to us in many different ways
At times it comes with happiness
    at times it comes
With pain, but when it comes from someone special
We doubt the source and
    sincerity love can be
Rewarding and also disturbing.
    We sit by the lake
Without a care or into the
    moonlight we can look
Together and speak of happiness
    and peace. We
Speak of marriage and a family

and agree that
This is what we want, but when
    we look at others
And the world, we think about
    that possibility
Twice, can we do it we say? Can
    we survive in a
Rushing world? On this we can't
    agree life and
Love must go on however and as
    our love is strong
And secure then we can conquer
    the problems and
Fight for our love as long as we
    have the will
To survive this worlds blow of
life.

Maria
Antonio Bologna-Ambrosi
MARIA

To My Dear Wife-MARIA

You had wept-Maria-
Affliction touched your heart-
The sorrow of your soul filled
your eyes of splendor-Maria.

I wanted to comfort you-Maria-
I had to do that-I love you-!
I shared your affliction-But-
Your eyes-so beautiful-Maria.

What kind of miracle-Maria-
The beauty of all open sky-
Of the sea-of the land-All-yes!
Appeared in your eyes-Maria.

Embracing-hugging you-Maria-
Once more determinately I saw
that-your eyes-Maria-are so . . .
So beautiful-MARIA.

Jeannette V. Ewasyn
SLEEPING SITTING UP

---

*To all the understanding people,
That work and live at Camp
Livingstone, In the 'la belle
province' of Quebec.*

Sleeping sitting up,
Listening to clack of the wheels,
Relieved to reach destination.

Lynda Yeates
CHRISTMAS
Christmas is a time for giving
Or at least that's what the people
    say
Still . . . I haven't got
A pretty present here for you
. . . . I gave you . . all I had . . .
    along the way

My words aren't even new at
    Christmas
I use the same one
'Cause they're nice and clear
For although I have no gift
I have something else instead
I have . . . a wish . . . for you at
    Christmas this year

I wish for you . . . a song . .
When you're happy
. . . . a friendly word . . .
when you are feeling down
. . . a river . . . when you crave
for nothing else, but solitude
in a quiet forest
somewhere outside town

I wish for you . . . the laughter
of the good times
. . . the memory . . . of the people
that you've met
I wish for you . . . the courage
to remember what you've learned
. . . . . that . . . . or the wisdom
. . . . to forget . . . .

I wish for you . . . . a star
to remind you
that in places . . . . there are
    people
. . . . who do care
I wish for you . . . . the peace . . . . .
of an old time Christmas Eve
. . . . where old friends . .
. . . and old memories . . . . gather
    there

So . . . there'll be no "card"
from me . . . this Christmas
. . . and there'll be. . . no present. . .
'neath your tree
Just . . . a simple wish . .
. . . for the *best* that life can give
That's all you'll get for Christmas

Mary Coker Anderson
**Dance Of the Moon
    Maidens**
The Maidens of the Moon are
    fond of dancing;
on the most mystical, ebony nights
you can see them blithely prancing
and pirouetting in sapphire tights.

Their footprints leave moon-opal
    dust
that streams across the dreaming
    earth,
inspiriting all things with moon
    lust
with their revelry and their mirth.

Kisses are blown through window
    panes
wooing the looming shadows
    within,
until the mist of morning reigns
upon their night of harlequin.

Jeannette N. Brokaw
AT THE PARK
The sky is blue, the trees are green,
the clouds are white, the earth is
    brown.
The park is there tucked in
    between
with children running round and
    round.
The birds are chirping, the breeze
    is gentle,
the swings squeak a tune to me
    sentimental.
It all makes a pleasant sight
and a very pleasant sound.

517

John Campbell, Editor & Publisher

Mary Coker Anderson
A ROSE CALLED PEACE

*Dedicated to my beloved Mother
(Ga-Ge) to express my eternal
love and devotion. Our bond
cannot be broken—her sweet
spirit lingers, inspiriting our lives
like the fragrance of a lovely rose.*

It was a day of somber mood
when shrouds of ominous
    foreboding
drape the mind with dark velvet
    folds;
flowers withered to ashen gray
    beneath the dying sun
and my heart was despairing prey,
    for cravanous
were the wrathful clouds for
    molten tears.
My beloved Mother was dead . . .
    part of myself had died with her.
I stood upon an awesome
    terrestrial shore,
gazing into the spectral vastness
    of infinity
and the soft-satin streamers of
    childhood
loosened and billowed in the
    wind—
I was suspended in time—time
    stood still—
        for a lost child in an unknown
            realm.
Then I saw her favorite rose, pale
    wand
and pink with promise,
the one I had given her called
    Peace
        and then I understood.

Bette Jeane Garrett
I KNOW

*This poem is dedicated to the
Lord because He gave me the
ability to express myself
poetically and to my family for
their continued love, support and
encouragement.*

I know the Lord will take care of
    me,
But it is I who won't set myself
    free.
Please, help my poor weak eyes to
    see,
That my life is absolutely
    nothing without Thee.

I know to receive His blessings I
    need to pray,
"Thy Will Be Done" I believe and
    say.
Please within your loving grace
    let me stay,
So when I die my soul in peace
    will lay.

I know I have many a need,
I will do my best to follow his
    lead.
Please, Light of the World, hear
    my plead,
I want, Your words, to heed.

I know with Your help my words
    flow,
Hopefully I can share my inner
    glow.

Please let my love, for You, show,
Let it be great, strong and let it
    grow.

Kevin (The Feet) McRae,
The Minds Of the Lonely
The everlasting feelings pass
    before us like a whisper
Into long dark falls of justice
That suspend the tests of time
Illusionary feelings stop before us
    like a teardrop
Hanging on a weary eyelid
But will never tumble down

Confusion dominates the minds
    of the lonely
Who never see the meaning of
    the day
Intrusion of the soul that feeds
    the one and only
Never leads to fame

Two suspicious lovers never feel
    the glory
Instead they feel cold and alone
They may never feel the warmth
For they ignore the figures that
    amongst us lie in waiting
Waiting for an open body
Will we ever pay them heed

Florence Hammer
YULETIDE

*To son Alex Hammer and his
concern for "Birdlife"*

Is at our door——
    Once more
Merry wreath hangs as before
From gas light era of days of yore
    We miss the sleighs
        The frosted cheeks
The quiet beautitude of a
    heavenly season

Yet to recompence
Santa is in space
And the moon is his base——

Theresa Lee Medina
Sharing You With Me
On lovely Lake Nancy
    stands a man beside his cabin,
Warm, kind and thoughtful
    he shared his place with me,

The air was cool, the waters calm
    the stars you could count and
        wish upon,
He loved me with strength,
    softness and peace
    I felt as a woman in love should

be,
With excitement and life
    he built a fire in me,
The man beside that cabin
    holds the only key,

To you I give my heart
    my life you've set free,
Thank you for the gift
    of Sharing You with Me!

Theresa Lee Medina
PATRICIA
I remember back today
    of a day long past,
The meaning of Thanksgiving
    in my mind would always last,

The threat of losing life
    the life I swore to save,
The memory of the pain
    in darkness stayed the same,

Awakened by a scream
    my fear of what remained,
Given hope through this life
    and courage from His name,

The year was 1970
    The day was Thanksgiving Day,
The baby was a girl
    and, Patricia is her name!

Susannah Vaughan
WHY LORD WHY
When I walk down the street
Anybody that I meet
They look so tired and weary
Not very happy or cheery
Why are we so tempermental
Why are we so judgemental
I try to understand, I try
But end up asking, "Why Lord
    Why."

    Why Lord Why
    Do we toil and cry
    Is it all in vain
    Will there ever be a change

We care about ourselves only
But someone out there is lonely
If we would only share our love
It would spread peace like a dove

But will this happen, Never!!
I keep on hoping, forever
What importance is money
If our lives were as sweet as honey

I look for a new beginning
For loving and forgiving
We will hold one another's hand
As we listen to that joyful band,

Leisa Bain Good
I FOUND SALVATION
I found salvation,
Docked in the pools,
Of Your Crimsone Flow.
My much prayed for Ship
Has arrived.
Bringing Hope for my broken spirit.
My emaciated heart.
Whose days of unfulfillment
Will soon be over.
Tears will no longer pave,
The way to my pilgrimage.
Walking towards Calvary,
To unfold myself.
I approach You.
My Savior,
My Lord,
My Ship.
I'm sailing to another shore.
The Shore of the Solid Rock.
Rock of Ages.

George Spellman
MISSING YOU
We've been apart for hours
already I long to hear
the sweetness of your laughter
as I hold you near.

We parted company
each with something to do
you assured me I would see you
    again
since our time together flew.

The seconds pass like minutes
the minutes pass like hours
the hours seem like days
I want to buy you flowers.

I want to give you a red rose
to proclaim my love to you
being so close together
is all I want to do.

I think about you all the time
whenever we are apart
all I want to do is tell you
how dear you are to my heart.

Kyme Stevens
CONCEPTS OF TIME
Forever is a long word,
That's hard to comprehend.
How can forever ever be reached,
If today refuses to end?

Every day is today,
Tomorrow never arrives.
It's hard for me to understand,
How we all survive.

Always is extremely far.
Farther than forever.
People say it will be reached,
My reply is "Never".

Never is impossible,
If there is already today.
When you already have
    something,
How can it go away?

Time is such a concept,
Too much so for my brain.
If I ponder, any longer,
I shall become insane.

Chester P. Boris
TIME
Time is an endless passage
of hands on a clock.
Whose seconds slip
and minutes fly.
As time is spent
thinking of you.

Billie L. Worley
CHRISTMAS MEMORIES
Christmas is a special time
    to share with all you see
memories of our Saviors birth
    how the yuletide came to be.

On a bright and peaceful winter's
    night
    as the savior babe lay
all came to bear him gifts of love
    and unto his glory pray.

Christmas is a caring time
    to share with those we love
all of the peace and harmony
    sent from Christ above.

The miracle of the Christ child
    that unto a virgin born
is a glorious treasured memory
    to share on Christmas morn.

Susie Ewald
US
Beyond Description,
Our love so Grand.
Walking hand in hand,
Together we stand.

As we talk and pray,
Together as one with Jesus.
Sharing Faith, knowing,
Eternal Love so gracious.

Cherished words, a Poem,
Expressing a love token.
Our hearts and eyes Smiling,
Pleasant words are spoken.

Laughter, beauty and grace,
Loving, kind and true.
Natures gift so Precious,
Knowing I have You.

Margie Geng
LOVE ME FOR MYSELF
How can I thank you
for giving me life,
for giving me love,
for calling me wife.
With you to guide me,
I'm learning to care.
With you beside me
I've nothing to fear.

You'll have me believing
that you're not deceiving,
you're not dishonest
and you'll not be leaving.
Oh, love, like a flower,
is slow in unfolding.
But I'm not a flower,
and it's my heart you're holding.

If you want to stay beside me,
if you want your love to guide me,
don't put me on a pedestal,
don't put me on a shelf.
Don't love me for what I might
become,
love me . . . for myself.

Caroline J. Luley
SECRETS
There are places where children
hide:
Under brush, behind doors, in the
bath.
Secret codes in which they confide.
A clubhouse secreted on a hidden
path.
But these are only games of
learning;
As they grow older, they grow
more cunning.
For the secrets of adults, upon
discerning,
Are quite complex and somewhat
more stunning.
No one argues this fact, we all
know:
Most things considered secret are
not so.

Margaret L. George
DREAMS ON CLOUDS
The dreams are high above
floating effortlessly on the
cushions of a cloud.
The clouds drift about carelessly
bumping gently into other dreams.
They temporarily block
true blue reality.
As clouds drift away
and disappear
so do dreams.
As new clouds dawn

with each new day
so do dreams.

Mary Ann Keller
MOTHER'S MOMENTS
Mother Mary veiled in white
Jesus was your son,
You tucked with into bed at night.

You bandaged his wounded knee
When he fell from your big
backyard tree.

You must have dried His tears
And I'm sure you chased away,
All His little boy fears.

You could not remove the cross
of wood
His human destiny was to
redeem us,
As only He could.

Teri Ann Hill
LITTLE CREATURE
This little creature lying on my
chest.
Just layed down to get some rest.

Poor little baby falling asleep,
She stayed up late watching her
keep.

Her little eyes closing her head
nodding down
Making little noises, then no
sound.

Her thoughts and her mind
drifting far away
To golden fields and a sunny day.

Roberta H. Graf
A CRY IS HEARD
Slowly as the last rays of light
Fade into the gray whisps of
twilight,
Despair descends once again to
become my companion.

Through the long and lonely night
I curse the fates that have labored
To lay waste the efforts I have
made.

"Oh! God," I cry, "Where is there a
reason?"

Even as I call his name, I know,
He is the wellspring of my courage.
My dark companion quickly
departs.

A new day dawns; I pick up my
burdens.
Loneliness will not be my cloak
again.
                              God is my friend.

Marney* Roemmelt
Sand Castles, Concrete Dreams
The job consisted of scraping
bodies off of windshields- and
then going out to dinner.
In the city, where everything is
too unreal—that's where she
existed;
She learned not to feel,
not to carry nightsticks but flails,
and save that that remains—a
real rush—a buzz.

She knew she had to escape the
city, the concrete,
down to the sea a freedom so
complete.
In her mind the waves made a
dull thudding noise,

and in her eyes there was blood
protecting the concrete.

The sand felt warm, timeless, and
somehow sacred.
It was then when her eyes
sparkled with the secret she'd
found, as she moved across the
beach without sound.
You could almost touch the
relief within her;
Yet the words wouldn't come,
the secret much too deep to
reveal, as if speaking of it
would make it disappear.
     It had something to do with
the beach, creation through
destruction—turning concrete
back to sand.

But it was her own body that
lined the window, her own
blood on the pavement.

They said she was lost—but
those eyes that sparkle . . .
Still, there was no secret to be
found.
They buried her remains at sea.

Ken McMillin
FEELINGS
This thing that we call sharing
Concerns not just time and space
But rather our own feelings
Not the ones we wear on our face.
It's the ones we carry inside us,
The ones we rarely share.
It's too bad we all have to hide
them
For then others won't know we
care.

Miss Deborah M. Kendrick
PLEDGING MY LOVE
Forever my Darling, Our Love
will be true
Always and Forever, I'll Love just
you
Just promise me Darling, Your
Love in return
Make this fire in my soul forever
burn
My hearts at your command
To keep, Love, and to hold
Making you happy is my desire,
Dear
Keeping you is my goal
I'll forever love you, the rest of
my days
I'll never part from you, and your
loving ways

Theresa M. McConaughy
GROWING UP

_____

*To Christy and Vioda. Special
thanks to my family and friends
for encouraging me to continue
my works.*

_____

The wind blows soft upon my
face
   it blows upon the whole human
   race
The sun is warm upon my back
   it keeps me going down that track
I left my family two nights ago
   just why I left, I do not know
I wanted so to be grown up
   to take the drink from lifes great
   cup
I feel so very much alone

I want so bad to just go home
But the wind and my dreams
   keep driving me on
I must try to find just where I
   belong
Someday I'll find what I'm
   looking for
Then I'll be the one who walks
   through the door
My family will be so proud of me
   just be patient, and you will see
If I do not do this on my own
   I will not feel that I am grown

Johann Corry Kucik
Prayer of the "Survivor"
Suicide! The little snit! How dare
she—
After years of maintaining the
guise
That I was her dearest friend and
mentor wise—
Desert, leaving me to feel so guilty.

I'll never accept their official
supposition
Supported by the evidence of
overdose
That in her depressed state,
"weary and morose . . ."
To abandon us without farewell
was not her intention.

Didn't she know her ache, her
numbness, her strife,
Compounded by grief and guilt
and doubt—
The turmoil of turning
encounters inside out—
Would be replicated daily in my
hollow life?

Whenever I see a vestige of our
friendship: a plant,
A piece of her cross-stitch, I
shudder at my lack.
But to my anguished cry 'God, I
want her back,'
The response remains woefully
silent and vacant.

She gave so much: she asked so
little.
Damn her for not asking.
Damn me for not knowing.
My conscience will not yield
acquittal.

So, forgive us our acquaintances
transcient.
Deliver us from banter
impersonal and facades
impervious.
Better yet: Lead us not into
relations that grow serious,
For friendship is such a costly
investment.

Miriam S. Queen
THE DOGWOOD TREE
Looking out of the window I see
The splendid blossoms of the
dogwood tree
Now sometimes bent and usually
small
But once did stand so straight
and tall

As the legend goes a cross was
made
And on this cross a ransom paid
A man hung there until He died
It was a King who was crucified.

Of the suffering, the many

blossoms do tell
Showing all the blood stains so
very well
Even the crown of thornes it shows
In the center of the blossom as
the legend goes.

The cross shaped blossoms are so
white
They're always such a beautiful
sight
Symbolizing the cleansing and
purity
This the Savior did for you and
me.

Now darted over the meadows
and hills
The dogwood stands so quiet and
still
Magnificently clothed in a story
so rare
So filled with love, there's none to
compare.

June Lee Box

June Lee Box
THE HOME SICKROOM
My sister and I agonize
Losing all sense of time
Suffering through changes
In the vital signs
Not much can be done
To ease the terrible pain
For fear of addiction
The nurse hovers nearby
I dare not leave the house
Dreading a sudden change
While I'm absent
Grocery shopping
Company is coming
Baking must be done
But the kitchen is too far
From the sickroom
The nurse is quietly busy
We watch the movements on the
bed ease
A sigh is heard
And all is still
Released, I click off the TV
Knowing the soapie actor
Can now start collecting
Unemployment!

Tami Knippshild
CLOUDS OF GLORY
Falling short of day and you're
sitting alone
Lying to yourself someone will
call you on the phone.
Crying isn't a habit of yours but
still you do,
Why is the world so rough
especially to you?

Coming up dawn and he's still
dancing with you,
But he's another one night stand,
something you're used to.
You party all night with friends,
it's so fun.
But even with it all when will
you find you've never won?

What happened to all the dreams
you thought of?
And out of the mist flies a white
dove
You vision yourself, it's just like a
story,
Flying high on your white clouds
of glory.

And when the parties are over,
what will you be?
You never took time to think,
never time to see.
"I've got lots of friends, they'll
always be with me"
And that to you, are your, clouds
of glory.

Now that you are older time
went so fast,
You try to think what good came
out of the past.
It's too late to dream, now you
face reality,
So you fall into a daily routine:
nothing special, no clouds of
glory.

Marcie L. Budka
Warren's Wedding Day
To Warren,

I gazed at him,
The one wearing the silver
gray tux,
with the finest trim.

He walked with a sort of
dignity
and
confidence.
He stood there and I watched him,
as a stranger might,
Was this my brother,
or her husband?
to love until the end of life?
I gazed at him,
the one who protected me,
as brothers do.
The one I fought with and
loved dearly too.
I don't know how to say so-long,
those words seem to be
so wrong.
He stood there beautiful
and in love, admiring him with
a smile on his face.
And I stood there in tears
wearing a frown,
With a proud smile beneath it all.

This was
My Big Brothers Day.

Barbara Lynn Collins
A Message From a Child
A little girl in tatters, eyes bright
with unshed tears
Sits in a doorway in the cold,
amid the sound of Christmas
cheer.
In this season of goodwill.

"Merry Christmas," she wished to
me, as I started to walk past.
"And do you have anything to be
merry about?" I couldn't help

but ask.
In this season of goodwill.

"Of course I have," she said to me
with a bright and sunny smile.
"It matters not that I'm all alone,
for families often part.
The important thing to me, you
see, is Christmas in my heart."
In this season of goodwill.

William G. Zdanis
On This Thanksgiving Day
We give You thanks and praise,
O Lord,
On this Thanksgiving Day,
For mercies and divine blessings,
That You do send our way.

How very thankful we should
be . . .
Our country is at peace.
Our unemployment rate is down.
Interest rates did decrease.

We're grateful that our President
Survived assassin's gun.
The Lord is looking after us.
Recovery . . . has begun.

Dorothy G. Wyant
HOPE
Along Life's pathway, you will find
People of many a different kind
Those who would betray a friend
And those who stick by you, to
the end.

God gives us hope along the way
And songs to sing, and words to
say
He leads us on, to a better thing
Like Winter, turning into Spring.

We see Life's pathway, like a
painting,
A tapestry of Love Divine
We are falling, we are fainting,
Until we see the whole design

On this side, the lines are
twisted,
Tangled, makes no sense at all;
On the Other Side, you see the
meaning:
God has painted over all.

So, to you, My Friend, I'm writing,
Taking Life, in all it's scope
Keep on trusting, keep on
fighting,
While there's Life, there's always
hope.

Olga Rita Ortega Walden
SON
I love you, I love you from the
bottom of my heart,
From the very beginning from the
very start.

You've had so many problems
that we could not share,
It was possible at times but you
would not dare.

Even through the crisis that you
have had,
With you sister, brother and even
your dad.

We all sit here at home at times
and think of you my Son,
But I sit here alone at times and
think of what I've done.

It really doesn't matter now as far
as I can see,

You seem to be much happier
now that you are free.

You're a grown man my Son and
this I had to learn,
As each and everyone of us has
done as it's become our turn.

I hope I can be proud of you as
when you were very small,
I hope now that you're a grown
man you stand up straight and
tall.

Don't let yourself go down my
Son and become a disgrace,
as you are the only person that
you're going to have to face.

The Holidays are almost here and
you won't be among the rest,
But you know me Son I'll do my
very best.

To hide all of my sorrows Son
that you will not be here,
But with all my heart and spirit
Son,
Merry Christmas and very Happy
New Year.

Robin M. Annecharico
TAKING CHARGE
The Autumn day was wonderful.
My feelings suppressed,
I laughed, played and enjoyed.
Thinking of the past,
My emotions tried to escape.
I existed in a dream world,
Selected wrong paths—
And made mistakes.
Now, I must come forth,
Take charge of my actions.
Concentrate on the future,
Move on to reality.
Taking with me courage;
To go on . . . . . .

Marian Foster Norman
WHY GOD BECAME MAN
A streak of brown and a flash of
white!
And I knew my "dear" cats had
put something to flight.
I grabbed up my "darlings" and
put them inside,
Returned to my porch and found,
trying to hide—
A bunny, behind my petunia pot,
And I looked at the cute little
creature and thought,
"If I just had within me the power
to change
Into something else—not quite so
awesome and strange—
Like another brown rabbit—I'd
nudge him and say,
'Hey, I know a great place not too
far away—
A nice little woods right next to a
farm,
Away from this constant threat
of harm—
Far from neighborhood "pets".
Come! Don't be afraid.
There's even a vegetable patch we
can raid."
But he scampered away, for how
could he know
I was really his friend and, indeed,
not a foe.
And then my thoughts turned to
a God of pure love,
Who looked down at mankind

Our World's Best Loved Poems

from heaven above
And saw how we all had gone
astray,
Unaware that we had lost our
way—
An easy prey for the cunning
Snake—
The Deceiver, Destroyer—and so
for our sake,
The great Prince of Peace came
down to Earth
As an innocent babe of lowly
birth,
Willingly leaving his heavenly
throne—
In order to seek and save his own.

Brent Layden
JUST LOVE

---

*To the Mahanta & the Ancient
Order of Vairagi Masters who
showed me, I am Soul; a creative
spark. And to my inspiring &
loving wife, Brenda.*

Love: the creative expression
Gift of the Sugmad
From the main line
Soul's sweet song.

Love: infinities child
Voice of the Ancient One
Restless rider on the stallion of
golden light
Sailor of the Cosmic Sea's
Harbored on the shores of
evermore

Silver needles Danced
Lonely Shadows Crept
Through the misty shrouded Veil
of Illusion
Down the corridors of time

To the garden of the Mahanta
Where love germinates
From the Seeds of the Sugmad
The Light and sound

Love, just is
For we are,
The timeless sounds of Love.

Vilma Lucillie (Dyer) Ball
Prairie Girl Remembers

---

*This poem is a tribute to my
parents, George Edward and Elsie
May (Coker)Dyer, in memory of
our days living in the soddy on
the plains and their sacrifices to
give me a high school education.*

Flying horseback down grassy
ways,
In rosy dawn to haze workhorses
for the trail,
Prairie Girl remembers—windows
to yesterdays.

Picking wild sweet peas, so
purple, on May days,
Herding home the cows, hearing
foam in the pail,
Flying horseback down grassy
ways.

Sitting quietly with Mom and
Dad as twilight pales,
Watching the stars blossom in
the Milky Way,
Prairie Girl remembers—windows

to yesterdays.

Playing house, barefoot on sunny
days,
Making mud pies, riding for the
mail,
Flying horseback down grassy
ways.

Nuzzling little snout in a daze,
Cuddling a piglet, squirming
velvet head to tail,
Prairie Girl remembers-windows
to yesterdays.

Childhood activities in a maze,
Didn't know she was blest until
her last days,
Flying horseback down grassy
ways,
Prairie Girl remembers-windows
to yesterdays.

Ann Arcemont
**Thoughts On Seeing "The
Day After"**
The day is just right
The sky is so blue
The flowers are all fragrant
And sprinkled with dew.

The birds are all singing
A gay little song,
Fleecy white sleep clouds
Go sailing along.

Tucked mid the green grass
Are buttercups yellow,
Buzzing above them
Is a fat bee fellow.

Butterflies bright
Quiver and sway
Making the most
Of their one little day.

The children are shouting
So happy at play,
Dear God in your wisdom
Please keep it this way.

Jackie Darlene Lett
FLY HIGH, SWEET EAGLE
What do you see,
   when you close your eyes tight?
Do you see sudden darkness,
   or an eagle in flight?
Can you see his wings spread,
   as he soars through the air?
Can you really believe,
   such beauty's so rare?
Can you believe that someday,
   to see eagles flying high?
That we, ourselves,
   might have to shut our eyes.
So always keep the vision,
   of an eagle in the sky.
So if they were to vanish,
   our memories would never die.

Susan Geurin Overstreet
A TEARDROP
A teardrop rolled slowly down
   my cheek.
I knew that I was fine.
The very thing I'd always
   dreamed was "told" to me;
IS mine.
My very soul cries out with joy!
   and love and . . . .
Peace profound.
I only had to stop and look to
   know just what I'd found;
"Me". Within the rubble of my
   thoughts.
Shipwrecked; Nowhere-bound . . .

I found my Love waiting
   patiently, not making any
   sound.
One night as I went screaming
   by, I noticed,
from the corner of my "eye"
A beautiful, serene Being (sitting
   amongst the chaos of my
   thoughts)
I asked, "Who are you?"
He said "I am a part of YOU, the
   LOVE you never found."
"Oh! This must be craziness." To
   look so far and near.
All this time. You never said,
"Look Susan, I AM HERE."

Denese M. Daniels
THE LAST . . .

---

*For the Marines and Corpsmen in
Lebanon "Here's one for you . . ."*

This man a Spartan, a fierce and
   mighty warrior,
Whose time has come to fight or
   die.
Trained in their ways of warlike
   manner.
His muscular body clad in a
   white tunic, wrapped in a
   scarlet cloak.
Gold helmet enshrouded upon
   his head.
Sword and shield in his steady
   hands.
The moment for him draws near,
   a soft spoken prayer is said.
The raging battle swallowed him,
   fighting.
Crys of pain, agony and despair.
Destruction howls like angry
   wolves, throughout the air.
Until the last spear of hate had
   been thrown.
Then nothing . . .
Quiet peace surrounds yet he
   still hears the sounds.
Standing alone amongst a sea of
   dead.
Sword and shield in now shaking
   hands.
Gold helmet enshrouded upon
   his head.
His aching muscular body once
   clad in white, is now stained
   red.
No fierceness has he left this
   mighty warrior,
only a docile tear does he shed,
for the last of the dieing and dead.

Rachel J. Ellis
OUR BLESSING
Not too much to look at when
   she entered this world, but
   special to us, being our own
   little girl.

A little boy had been our number
   one wish, like cravings when
   pregnant for that odd tasting
   dish.

Cheeks so round and rosy, tiny
   lips with a smile; to both of us
   our blessing was this innocent
   child.

Watching her grow faster with
   each passing day, taking more
   steps, listening for words she

would say.

Too soon shes in school and
   dating young boys; no longer is
   it television, jumping rope or
   toys.

Slow down sweet days let us keep
   her for awhile, so much joy and
   happiness is shared with this
   child.

Prayers of thanks are being said
   each day, Thank you "Dear
   Lord" for the blessing sent our
   way.

Jennifer McMickle
**The Most Beautiful Thing
To me**
The most beautiful thing in the
   world to me,
Is not the river or the sea.
It's not the stars in the sky above,
And it's not the magic of first
   love.
It's not the robin that sings in the
   Spring,
Nor is it cute and cuddly things.
It's not the wildflowers or
   mornings first kiss,
But if taken away it would truly
   be missed.
It's not the wonder of life newly
   begun,
Nor is it the miracle of the rising
   sun.
To me it would surely be
   considered a sin,
If I didn't have it lieing within.
The most beautiful thing in my
   opinion you see,
Is the heart and the soul that God
   gave to me.

Phyllis Newton
THE STAR PINE
The star pine reaches
up to the sky
And touches
the highest fleecy cloud.

Its points turn from
the deep fault below
And looks over
the mountain so proud,

And fears nothing.

Ann Tyra
THE SENTINEL
The lighthouse stands
Far from the beach
Stretching out for all to see
Is silver band that strives to reach
The stranded sailors' urgent plea

The storm proclaims
The sea as king
When darkness falls death steals
   the crown
No need for bells to toll and ring
For graves will wait if no men
   drown

And ships will stray
From waves that pound
Until they sight a starry sky
Because a light goes round and
   round
Death sheds its tears but cannot
   cry

The lighthouse stands
Close to the beach
And gently prods the sleeping crew

That time has come for dreams to reach
The land beyond the mournful blue

Christina L. Kraun
AN ODE TO A LOVER
If I could stop Time, I think
I would stop it now, to spend
Forever loving you in ecstasy.

You have given me dreams exploding
in vibrant color, awakening and
knowing it was not, but just a
dream, moreover a reality of two
souls emerging in a mystifiable
sphere of energy.

You have walked into my life
grasping the part of me I have
failed to find. You destroyed my
temples of frustration and revenge
replenishing the barren spot with
forests of contentment and beauty.

You took from me the bitterness
others left behind. You filtered
my life of all impurities leaving
me the total person I've become.

If I could stop time, I think
I would stop it now to spend
forever loving you in ecstasy.

If in fact, I could stop Time,
Forever loving you would be
Mine.

Marjorie V. Whiteside Walker
ICICLES
Icicles hang from the trees
    And from the bushes too,
Look upward, and you will see these
    Clinging to all of the roofs.

Some are short, some are long
    Others are thick and round
A few seem as sharp as a thorn
    While dropping to the ground.

Have you watched the icicles?
    Their beauty glistens in the sun
Don't you think they try to whistle
    Before their end has come?

Icicles hold through wind and storm
    And sometimes appear quite lonely,
You nor I can give them form
God makes and shapes them only.

Louaida White
ISN'T LIFE?

*To my little niece Stormie Jones
first simultaneous heart and liver
transplant. May her courage
always be an example for the rest
of us.*

Isn't life
    living and loving.
Forgiving and forgetting
    making amends.
Struggling; Straggling
    making friends.
Giving and taking
    caring and sharing.
        Isn't it?

Shirley B. O'Keefe
CHRISTMAS IS OVER
Christmas is over now and
The decorations have been put away
Carefully packed back in the boxes
Until the next Christmas holiday.
Dad has carried them back upstairs
And stacked them out of the way
And now they'll be forgotten
As everyone forgets the holiday.
For now that the tree is gone
The Christmas Spirit has gone too
And now the people are busy preparing
To bring in another year new.

Maxine Rawson Pendry
MY FRIEND

*Dedicated to Harry J. Hibbs My
Brother-in-law & Friend*

A brawny man with a heart
    filled with love
Has left us now for heaven above

We know where he is & we
    know why he's there
And the pain from his parting
    with his wife we do share

His voice so boisterous like
    thunder it boomed
If you didn't know him you'd
    think you were doomed

He'd grumble & growl, but we
    didn't care
For we knew all along of the Love
    he held there

So honest, sincere & direct in
    his ways
A refreshing delight like the
    sunshine rays

A great sense of humor, this
    beautiful man
Not a dull moment, top that if
    you can

For us such a pleasure his
    company to keep
We miss him so much, you know
    why we weep

For with loving & caring &
    knowing him well
Only enriches our lives, more
    than words can tell

So unique this man we will
    love evermore
We pray we can meet him on
    lifes other shore

Pamela A. Brunn
MY GOOD FRIENDS
My Good Friends I
will miss—
So I must give a
good-bye kiss.

Good Friends are
always there—
When you need someone
to care.

Good Friends are hard
to find—
Especially when they're so
nice and kind.

So I write this with

one regret—
That I'll miss you
ever yet.

June Lee Box

June Lee Box
AUTUMN ECHOES
A cool breeze drifts the leaves
    that clung
Motionless all day
Grey clouds roll the bright sun
    away
But it glances back
The burring whine of a chainsaw
Rises, falls, rises
My neighbor's cutting winter
    wood
Left from logs when the
    plywood's peeled
Like apple parings
Into sheets laid on a 'Green
    Chain'
Sliced to four foot wide
Sideyard Alders filter fragrant
Newly-cut-wood smells
Sounds now tell he's splitting the
    rounds
To fireplace-handling size
No wilderness for this young Abe
Home chores eternal!

Peter Gabriel Lecours
IMAGINE
Imagine the showers never to fall
And all of old winters snow.
Imagine the trees never budding
    again
And never a flower to grow.

Imagine the sun burning out like
    a wick
And the moon falling down like a
    leaf.
Imagine the dark and the black
    sky above
(Never seeing the light makes me
    grieve).

Imagine the leaves turning brown
    like the grass
And blowing in Autumns last
    wind.
Imagine the withering fields all
    aflame
(I burn when I know that I've
    sinned).

Imagine the snow falling down,
    choking life
White death is the worst that I
    know.
Imagine the sound of a devil who
    laughs . . .
And my soul falls to cinders.

Elliot Bratton
POLAR KITCHEN
I wander in a refrigerated glow,
Await the polar bear. I listen. It's
    there.
I follow inky walls, flecks of
    snow—

Tiptoeing down whale bone stairs,
I hear the distant smacking of
    lips and gums,
And smell the walrus crackling,
    igloo rare.

The polars squat by tables of
    thighs and thumbs,
Bears with blueblack eyes and
    charcoal lips,
Mouths heaving, voices
    thumping like drums,

Iceblocks splatter food! All paws
    on hips!
A sizzling otter crawls from plate
    to plate,
And then the sticky penguin
    slides and dips—

The sun-forgotten gallop, flail,
    and chase,
Those hulks watch me with
    scarlet filthy frowns,
As I unstop the whirlpool to end
    their race.

The cabinet's filled with melting
    polar sounds,
Glazed bears now helpless
    mounds,
Glinting spotless across the
    kitchen's bounds.

Marjorie Hambrick
MY TASK
My task is unfinished 'till
In spring my heart goes still,
To another spring on a lonely hill
Where Christ paid my redeeming
    bill.

Three men were sentenced to
    die—
Two were criminals, but Christ
    oh why
Were you on a cross pointing to
    the sky?
Was it I who said to crucify?

Am I content to join the crowd
And sing HIS deathly chorus loud?
Or will I pray with my head
    bowed
Thy spirit come to me endowed.

Had such ever died before?
Forgive oh Thou whom we adore,
Lead us to Thy kingly shore
There to live forever more.

Mildred Maultsby Mackie
THE HEART'S MUSEUM
In the museum of my heart,
The relics of years gone by,
Stand each in their private corner;
Each have a special sigh.

Treasured so much for their
    memory;
Captured again in my mind,
Hour spent so gloriously
All of a sudden, I find—

I've wandered too far into
    memory;
Up the stairways I've climbed,
Now, when I descend to reality,
These relics will stay to remind.

Deborah Jo Jones
LIFE AND DEATH

To My Grandparents: MR. &
MRS. HAROLD C. TURNER

Death is all around us.
In the newspaper; the kid down
    the block.
People are dying every minute;
And someone, someplace feels
    that loss.

Life is a gift; given to all of us.
No matter how long or how short.
The number of years we live
    aren't of any importance.
Its how people remember us
    when we're gone.

This isn't a dress rehearsal.
Theres no second chance, not a
    movie,
Cut that scene and lets try it
    again
And get it right this time.

When you leave this great stage;
Make sure your audience gives
    you
A standing ovation.

Martha K. McHenry
CHRISTMAS LOVE
The joy of Christmas comes from
    love,
That tangible something within
For love is not love until you give
    it away;
Just wrap it in a package on
    Christmas Day,
And give it to friend;
Or, someone far away
That cheer no longer brithens
    their way
On that special day.

Be it a package large or small
A card will bring unlimited joy to
    all.
Understanding, a kind word,
    helpfulness or a warm smile,
Do something worthwhile to
    make Christmas everyday.
It will encourage someone to live
    again
As lofe becomes a brighter way.
Because you care enough to share
    in a friendly way.

Elsie M. Cheeks
YEARS TO LATE
We met at the wrong time, in my
    life, years to late for you, and I
We became the best of friends,
    inseparable at times. You
    helped me over the rough
    spots, picked me up when, I
    was down gave me strength
    and courage to face another
    day to do what must be done.
    You were married and so was I
    with children still at home

We didn't mean for anyone to be
    hurt, because of our love for
    one another Friendship was
    chosen over love this was a
    mistake for we were so much
    in love. IT makes me unhappy
    to think what might have been,
    if only we had tried. Over the
    years I've shed a million tears

for you my love, We parted
    with a friendship that can't be
    broken, even though we tried.

Charlie J. Wirth
MAN HAS HIS DAY
Clamourous splashing, swish
    swashing,
Roll in the waves from the sea,
    casually caressing their
    destined shores of sand,
The end to another day is at
    hand, lest you be on the other
    half o' the world where dawn is
    just becoming, and the waves
    are gently rolling back.

Yet, how thoughtful!
To no matter of what matter
    always seems to be one for
    another,
Day has night, man has woman,
    and earth has the moon,
Now, wouldn't this be a terrible
    thing to ruin?

To forsake the plants of their soil,
The cow from her bull, or the
    bird from its tree,
To take a voice able to sing from
    an ear able to listen,
Or to take the rare feelings of
    love from the joys it brings,
Requires the instinct to destroy,
    and the insanity to do it!

So for just a moment, stop and
    take a look at all these
    wonderous earth'ings,
For if the worlds, it seems, with
    their threat of turmoil, and
    promise of death, have their
    way,
They will lead us down a path of
    fate, all the same way.
And to realize this all then, will
    be to late!

Nancy L. Fletcher
To Rome Or Not To Roam

Love to Veronica Lynn Fletcher,
darling Grand-daughter, who
sings to me over the phone.

To live and die and never roam,
Breaks my heart.
But lack of funds keep distant
Lands and me apart.

If someday my ship comes in,
And I can afford to wander,
I bet when I am far away,
My heart will be back yonder.

Mary Louise Thomas
WHAT AM I?
I turn you on
I freak you out
I make you smile
I make you shout
What am I? Could you make a bet?
I'll give you a clue——I wouldn't
    guess yet
Because of me you may turn to
    crime
You'd rather not know me
I'm a waste of time
You live and die again and again
Still some people call me a
    valuable friend
I'll tell you my name
I'm a meaningful source

After you've heard it you'll know,
    of course
I'm not a drug that messes up
    your head
My name is "Life"
And as it was said
In the third and fourth line
In a very fine style
You make you shout
And you make you smile

Nina Reardon
Halloween Remembered

Dedicated to my children

As I sat on my sun porch on
    Halloween night
And looked out the window;
    what an eerie sight!
There were goblins, and witches
    and devils too
Ready to scare the wits out of you.
The devils in red had horns
    riding high
And the witches rode brooms as
    they passed by.
I thought they might forget my
    house
As I sat there quiet as a mouse.
But then I heard my doorbell ring
And heard voices start to sing
Trick or treat; trick or treat
As they stopped at 31 Marion
    Street.
So I gave them their treat and
    watched them go
Happy to be part of their
    Halloween show.
For it took me back to yesteryear
When my children were trick and
    treating here.

Eleanore Bosco Cramer
FOR

Dedicated to my children. All
four, whom I love, each one a
little more than the other.

The Magic of Miracles
The Trust of True Friendship
The Heartfelt Happiness of Hope
The Continuity of Caring
The Solace of Sympathy
The Love of Life and Living

The Moments of Memory
The Blessedness of Being
The Sunshine of Sharing
The Endearment of Empathy
The Fulfillment of Forgiving
The Peace of Ultimate
    Understanding

With Gratitude for the 'Grace of
    God'
Let us be, Thoughtfully Thankfull.

Mariann Gerlach
Seed's—A Sad Mothers Song
Its to late to be sorry
Its to late to be sad,
Giving years of plenty
Wasn't time enough for you,
You took my heart and money
And lived in my fine home
You lied and drank and cheated
And caused me crying times,
Now I'll sit and wonder
Why the "Seed's" grow wrong.

For all the year's I loved you
Remember way back then?
When you were straight from
    Heaven,
And gave your love each day.
But your heart's turned to the
    devil
And his ways makes times so
    bad.
For you might cry as I have
And you might sit and wonder,
What the devil had—
When your Mamas gone to
    Heaven,
Her prayer book under her head.
No more preachin and tellin
The out-come for the bad,
Your free from Mamas preachin
And that should make you glad,
I'll watch my tellins happen
From my easy chair in Heaven,
And I'll sit and wonder—
Why now, you remember them.
For you could live and suffer
For the times you let me hunger,
And you could live and suffer
For the times you cheated and
    stole,
And you could live and suffer
For turning down wrong roads.
All the things I told you,
Might be around each bend
And I'll long to reach you
To wipe away your tears,
But the Lord won't let me
For you didn't listen then.
So live your life of folly
And let your soul's go dead,
Mama will cry in Heaven
So you'll know that some-one
    cares.
Its to late to be sorry
Its to late to be sad.

William Buchanan
SHE
She is beauty personified,
She is a treasure undenied.
Born from goodness, and grace
That goes beyond time, and
    space.
She is bright—a pure delight.
Hair of golden curl—spoken
    wisdom of the world.
Eye's that hold the secret to a
    special surprise. She is woman
    complete,—
So incredibly sweet. She is adored
Sincerely, and held so tenderly.
Her spirit soars like the dove;
To me she is love!

Debra J. Woodruff
UNTITLED

Mom, Dad, this one's for you
kids. I love you.

I dreamed we were old,
    And as one.
Still it seemed
    Our life together had just begun.
The beauty of me
    I saw from within you.
The love you hold,
    I felt there too.
Ageless minds,
Ageless souls,
Captured within
    these bodies of old.

John Campbell, Editor & Publisher

Young love is sweet,
But old is sweeter still,
Ripened beyond the limits of youth,
Entwined in the ageless hearts
Of two, in love, fulfilled.

Jayanne Assunto
SUICIDE

The man had value for human life,
yet he killed.
He killed not others.
but had taken his own life.
He had done
what he felt was everything.
He had experienced all emotion,
seen all sights,
heard all sounds,
fullfilled all senses.
Now he wanted eternity.
The earth had bored him.
He killed.
He longed adventure.
He wanted to see the end
of the path.
He shall venture no more.

Joyce Thomas
DABB'S PLAN

I dedicate "Dabb's Plan" to all those students who have made my life exciting and adventurous.

Slithering, sliding smoothly along the bank,
Wiggling, writheing with exciting life
Till the crushing blow of Darrell's stick
Stilled the breath completly with one quick kick!
Dabb's master plot then began,
And of course it included all of the clan.
To room sixty-six came the cold dead *plan*
Knowing for certain that it would snare its man!
An innocent question started the action
Which caused J. T. quite a contraction
Closed eyes, taut nerves, chilled spine
Then a scream that was hardly sublime!
Coiled and curled in a baggie lay
A thin, long snake in J. T.'s tray.

Beverley Young Attaway
SEASONS OF LOVE

I look in your eyes,
I see gentle laughter and soft touches.
Visions of the best of Winter,
Spring, Summer and Fall.
Spring days that are green, cool and sweet,
Long, lazy, mellow summer days,
Sharp, crisp—glad to be alive—Fall days,
And the snuggle days of Winter.
I see things that have been,
And promises of things to come.
I look in your eyes and I see Love.

Jujuan Fleeman
ME AND YOU

Blue into blue
I seem to step inside.
Lips coming closer,
now touching mine,
turning me into liquid
time after time.
Hands gently touch my skin,
making waves of intensity flow
thru my veins,
taking me under—
now drowning in your love
(becoming one!)

June Lee Box

June Lee Box
Northcoast: Weather Variable

We were tooling down the highway to town
From 'The Redwood Gate to the Golden State'
To get the TV left overnight
In it's hospital to be fixed
Ocean waves at our side
bulldozed white foam
Over the rocks in the shallows
Then dashed with force high up on the shore
Such a contrast to yesterday
Heaven high with cobalt blue sky
Tall tops of Redwoods aiming spears
At just a few fluffy white clouds
Waves in the surf six inches high
As they rolled on sandy beaches
Lovely ride in the sun, so short
Under close skys today, so long
The set was ready, and we hurried home
Wheeled it in on it's cart
Just as the rain started!

Elizabeth Gingerich
LOST DREAMS

Although, in the past, I made a mistake,
Please help me find a way,
Clear my mind, for my own sake,
Hear me when I say.

God give me the strength to carry on,
And follow each day through,
Make me forget the past, those days are gone,
The years that are left, are too few.

I know it is just a dream, I guess.
Of what I'd like for me,
But I won't settle for anything less,
That's the way it's got to be.

What's that, you say, I ask too much,
Well yes, I guess I do,
But then put to you as such,
You would want it too.

Michael J. Verba
THE JOY DIVISION

To, the late, great, Ian Curtis—founder of the joy division a casualty of life—a victim of 'truth'.

It's slowly creeping
And slowly deepens
With every thought
And 'new lives' lost
Those strangers worth remembering
Friends still pretending
Not generating anything.
It's complicating
Not worth 'the waiting'
it's undersold
To the average
And operating
On lost control
Or something old
Like yesterday.
Now, we've melted down
To this
Cries and whispers, with distance, lifts
Us away
From today
Where we just wish
For anything
To kiss us goodbye
Through tear-soaked eyes we wonder why?
No more.

Michael J. Verba
GLASS GODS (Of the 'Faith')

Of the 'Faith': We're looking, calling-then we stop We're hoping, falling-then we break like glass

We started out
To go somewhere
Becoming strangers
We 'forgot' to care
That we had reasons
—There were no fears
Of shattering.

There were no signs
We prayed at times
For help from above
But, our Gods let us down
And 'slowly' we found
With out feet off the ground
—We crumbled
Like glass.

So I've passed by
Those Gods in the sky
I'll live for whats real
—I feel something new
And my fragile life ·
Becomes unbreakable.

Ann L. Hall
LOVE AFFAIR

To: Jeane Yerkes My collaborator and friend. God Bless You.

It was a sordid love affair,
naked bodies, arms outstretched.
Many diseases,
man could catch.

The church came in
with love to share.
To lighten the burden
to lighten the care.

The world was the love affair.
The church in love with the devil's lair.
Mission power from our Lord.
Stronger than the knife or sword.

Mayann Bruno
PRISM

hung
on the neck
of my window
throat
filled with
sun

you bounce
a rainbow
at my feet
paint my walls
with spring
dye my thumb
autumn
as it dials
a tinted
telephone

you float
halfway
up the stairs

I follow you
from room to
room . . .

Max Swafford
THE SPACE BETWEEN US

These lines are dedicated to Ginger, the only female surgeon I have ever known. She inspired me to write, as well as to fill the space between us.

I could feel the space between us
when I first saw you in the crowd;
Something familiar in your eyes,
hints of a breeze pushing a cloud . . .
And you were the gentle magician,
you were the dancing physician,
and all in the time it takes for me to dream.

We dance in that space between us
and you were enticingly warm.
You looked, but even more, you saw
our niche in the eye of the storm . . .
And you were the gentle magician,
you were the dancing physician,
and all in the time it takes for me to dream.

And so, the space between us filled.
I heard your laugh, I heard you sing.
And even though our time was short
you became the wind 'neath my wings . . .
And you were the gentle magician,
you were the dancing physician,
and all in the time it takes for me to dream.

Our World's Best Loved Poems

Debi Laurian
A GYPSY'S HEART
It calls in the wind
Sings a song
In each movement,
Speaks in subtle tones.
Sometimes, bravely,
It reaches out and touches me.
It follows me
Wherever I go . . .
Often scared, but always there.
I ache with need
I burn with desire . . .
Like a drug,
Freedom courses through my viens.

Marie L. Anderson

Marie L. Anderson
SNOWFLAKE

To my children Edward A. and Marianne M. both through joy and sorrow. With love and understanding, we will all stand to-gether.

I was looking out my window,
when a snowflake, fluttered by-
it sparkled, Oh! So brightly, like a
diamond from the sky.
Then another snowflake
fluttered, so gracefully, with
ease-
I watched in amazement, as it
landed on the trees.

Then many snowflakes fluttered,
so soft, so pure, so white-
The earth was soon a glitter, like
the moon, and stars at night.
A fairyland unfolding, Oh! So
peaceful, so serene,
A picture to be painted, every
artist's dream.

The mountains were like castles,
on a marble stand-
The trees stood like soldiers,
done, by a sculptor's hand
The shrubs were dancing fairies,
their halo's made of snow.
The icicles were the candles,
they'd shimmer, and they'd glow.

This! paradise of beauty, with a
snowflake, it began-
A gift sent by the angels, on a
journey's end.
It's miracle we marvel! It's origin,
we can't explain,
A secret of the maker, the
mystery shall remain.

The story of the snowflake, is
difficult to write-
To some: it is an enemy, to some:
A sheer delight.
When this earth they enter, they
fluter, one by one,
With, the sun's appearance, every
snowflake, is forever, gone.

Lisa Lauzon Michaud
**You Know You Are a
Hunter When:**
You know you are a Hunter when:
—you rise before the sun, and
you don't even have to work.

You know you are a Hunter when:
—you tip toe through the woods,
and the only tracks you see are
your own.

You know you are a Hunter when;
—you see something move,
and its only another hunter.

You know you are a Hunter when:
—you finally see your prey,
and you stand there admiring it.

You know you are a Hunter when:
—you go back to camp,
and tell about the big one that
got away.

You know you are a Hunter when:
—you walk so far, that even if
you did shoot one, who would
help you get it out.

You know you are a Hunter when:
—after days of doing all the
above, you finally shoot one.

You know you are a Hunter when:
—you already start dreaming
about the big one you will get
next year.

Catherine Wardell Carroll
TRINKETS AND TOYS
Trinkets and toys don't bring
lasting joy
To the heart of a girl or boy
Arms of love that enfold them
and the
Whispered, "I love you"
Will last when the days of the doll
And teddy bear are through
Love lasts a lifetime through good
Times and bad
And brings strength into the life
of a
Lass or lad
Faith is instilled by a guiding hand
Hope and faith give us the
strength
To stand
Life has it's valleys through
which

We must go
But with hope, faith and love no
Defeat shall we know.

Ethel M. Dixon Gerbig
SOMEWHERE, SOMETIME
Somewhere, sometime, somehow,
someway,
There comes a time in life,
We must truthfully face the fact
That our mistakes caused strife.

We have to say we're sorry
And admit it's true,
That what we've done caused
sorrow
And hurt somebody, too.

We have to face it squarely
And then the burden bear.
We have to learn from these
mistakes
And show we really care.

Care about the things we do
And watch the words we say.
Then always try to hurt no one
On each and every day.

Miss Lorrinda Stewart
PERSONALLY YOURS

*This poem is dedicated to Mr.
javiar Outerbridge for taking time
to care and for always being
willing to understand.*

Our love will stand the test of
time,
If I know you are truly mine.
Love at first sight to say the least
My love for you will never cease.
There will be valleys too low to
bear,
But pain will pass knowing
you're there.
Love is a force putting us together.
Binding as one-our love
forever . . .
I love you dearly, eternally-
I'm giving you my love
Personally . . .

Tina M. Montgomery
MIDNIGHT

*Dedicated to: My daddy; Oscar
James Montgomery and My
mama; Juathata Beth Montgomery*

An odd moving shadow
Along a fencerow;
The adventures of a midnight
black cat.

Claude Walkup
LIFE'S SHADOWS
When the shadows of life lengthen
As shadows are wont to do,
Memories come crowding 'round
Begging for review.
A child is born into a pair of
loving arms,
From whence he learns to view
the world,
Secure from its alarms.
He romps and plays and stronger
grows,
He will need this strength ere he
knows,
For awaiting him outside the door,
Is a wonderful world for him to
explore.

Birds, butterflies ad bees,
A name for each to be learned for
these,
What an awesome task for one so
small,
It will be some years before he
knows them all,
The school bell rings calling him
to come,
And join new friends in work and
fun,
The shouts of youth at recess time,
Bring back fond memories of that
youth of mine.
School days o'er and life's work
begun,
Someone to meet and be joined as
one,
Children born into warm loving
arms,
Shielded securely from all of life's
harms.
Lengthening shadows record ife's
joy,
Life's encyclopedia for
descendents employ.
Hold not in disdain this shadow
at last,
For 'tis of life's joys and sorrows
this shadow is cast.

Dorothy F. Senter
OVERHAUL

*I want to thank Larry Senter, a
man I have alot of love and
respect for. He had confidence
in me when I had none. I'm
forever grateful for his
incouragement and support!*

It's a shame we can't have our
bodies overhauled,
like we do our car when the
engine has stalled!
My rear-end needs new gears, and
my pistons bored.
To top it off, my plugs are burned
and my tranny needs restored.
Need new wipers, can't even get
my lighter to work!
OH HELL, my engine has even
lost it's tork.
As for my headlights, they've
even gone dim.
Need to have alot of body work
on my rim.
Too bad we can't have our bodies
re-done,
for I'm in awful bad need of
some!!
I've began to finally run out of gas,
and it bugs me that I'm dragging
my ass.
Oh I need a overhaul that's for sure,
BUT TO THE JUNKYARD I GO,
FOR THERE'S NO CURE!!!!

Pauline Byrd Borden
Of Life Be Not Afraid
Of Life-Be Not Afraid
Of life, be not afraid, my love,
Its to be lived
And too wonderful, to waste.
If its bitter
Or its sweet
But never to hate.
Its for us to live, to laugh, to love,
to Learn,
But most of all, appreciate.

John Campbell, Editor & Publisher

Sister Mary Laurena Cullen, I.H.M.
DAY BY DAY
I look to the left, I look to the
right.
I wake to the dawn's early morn
light.
I don all my clothes from feet to
my head
And search for my shoes from
under my bed.

I look to the left, I look to the
right.
I consume coffee and toast jellied
bright.
I walk to the chapel and pray for
my day,
Then trudge to office to earn
salary pay.

I look to the left, I look to the
right.
I think life is fine, despite its
cruel fight.
I plod through my day, then
homeward I go
And follow routine, as I read,
cook, or sew.

I look to the left, I look to the
right.
I pace back and forth in a
dizzying plight.
Why don't I stand still and look
up instead?

Up to the realm where rainbows
glow.
Up to the aerial view of moon
and snow.
Up to the wisdom where
thoughts increase.
Up to the reverence of night-
time peace.
Up to the Solace that dries all
tears.
Up to my Mother who softens all
fears.
Up to the Resurrected Who died
on a cross.
Up to the Spirit of
Love-without-loss.
Up to the Father, —divine
Godhead.
Why, oh why don't I stand still
and look up?

Cheryl Hoversten
The Day My Daddy Cried
I was my daddy's shadow . . . he
took me everywhere;
Fishing, tramping through the
woods or to the county fair;
A broken doll or broken heart
He'd find a way to mend;
And when my tears came spilling
out,
A firm shoulder he would lend.

My father had a gentle strength, a
courage bold and true;
In my eyes he could do no wrong,
he was perfect, through and
through.
Despite all disappointments
And the wounds he must have had
My father always had a smile,
Not long would he be sad.

He seemed to be a superman,
untouched my pain or strife;

But innocence was lost that fall, a
departure changed my life.
I was going off to college, so
grown-up would I be;
The tomboy who was leaving
home,
Daddy's girl . . . that was me.

When I'd crammed my luggage in
the car and shoved the boxes in
I turned around, for one last look,
prepared to see a grin;
But the face that framed the
window
Despite its aching pride
Is forever etched upon my heart,
For that's the day daddy cried.

Anita R. Reeves
PEOPLE OF THE WORLD

*This poem is dedicated to my
husband Kenneth, my daughter
LaToya my loving parents and
brothers, to Dixon United
Methodist church and my dear
friends and many relatives.*

People should not be judged by
the color of their skin,
But instead as an individual and
what they hold within.

For in this day and time, you
would think that it would
cease;
But as long as there are people
whose color is not the same,
this prejudice will just increase.

It's not what you look like or how
attractive you think you are,
It's the intelligence and
knowledge you hold upstairs
that makes you what you are.

It shouldn't make any difference
as to how light or dark you
may be
For color is merely an
independent appearance of
form that only the eyes can
see.

If we could keep this in mind and
accept each other as we are
Then the people of this world
would be better off by far.

Dee Overpeck
WISH YOU WERE HERE
You left this morning,
Not really on the best of terms,
There was something out of
place.
The void was burning,
Causing a emptiness that has
never been.
I feel so lost now,
I cannot seem to find my way
From nowhere to where I belong.
I need to feel you and your love,
So I know which way to go.
There was a reason but—
Somehow I lack the
understanding why.
Everything has been lost in the
shuffle,
Wish you were here
To lend a guiding hand—
To put everything back on the
right track.
I sure wish you were here.

Prince Charles Ray

Prince Charles Ray
AS I LOOK ACROSS

*With love to: My parents, Lonnie
and Dorothy Ray my wife, Carol
and my beautiful daughters
Christi Dionisia and Princess*

As I look across the room
And look into your lovely eyes
An empty feeling over me looms
And the limbs of my body seem
paralyzed

As I look across the way
Thoughts run rampant in my
mind
And alas, I feel the need to pray
For fear of wanting you until the
end of time

As I look across and see
The beauty God has bestowed on
thee
Oh how I've wished that it could
be
No other in your life but me.

Geraldine Edna York
SANITY
Like a snowflake in winter
Is a dream
To disappear at the lightest touch
To hold it and not know it's there
Lost in whispers
Of a child's carefree mind

Juan J. Amador
CARESS
". . . . . Humans and other
primates have genetically
determined needs for social
interaction and for physical
affection and warmth . . . ."

Carl Sagan/COSMOS.

In the ladder of Creation
Somewhere beyond the threshold
to the Past
Not far down from our step
There is a mother feeding her
infant
Inventing a caress for him
Inventing love for him
And we are captives of that
caress
And we are unables to fullfill
with emptiness the lack of love

When love is missing
to its place come without an
invitation

Hatred, destruction, madness,
stupidity
If hatred becomes so destructive,
if madness so stupid
To make our intelligence unable
to control them
In the ladder of Creation
Somewhere beyond the threshold
to the Future
Not far up from our step
Emptiness shall take over the
place of love
The place of caressing life.

Edith J. Frackiewicz
CHILD OF YESTERDAY
Child of yesterday
Come back today.
Come back to me
Like a buzzing little bee.
I lost my fairy castle on the way,
On the way, someplace far away.
The girl in cinders is gone,
So are the dwarfs this dawn.
They went away yesterday,
But they will come back today.
They will never leave me again,
For I am a child,
And a child I shall stay.

June C. Ulland
TODAY
I must trust "TODAY" in God, by
doing
His will.
Living only this day, "TODAY"
I'll think not of tomorrow, for sure-
ly it shall . . :
Be "TODAY" when it comes my
way.

Living for God will ne'er be toil
nor grind.
'Twill be easier for me to tow.
I'll live for "TODAY", just one day
at a time . . . and
Let God take care of tomorrow.

Eva L. Pearse
**The Tomte—The Swedish
Good Fairy**
If you should live in Sweden
You'd know this little man—
He hides away in wee small nooks
And helps you when he can.

On Christmas there's a special job
Where reindeer are so few—
A tomte drives the elfin goat
Which brings your gifts to you.

But even if you looked and looked
You'd not find him at all.
Only, perhaps, sometimes you'd
see
In floor or door or wall—

A tiny crack of light a—beam,
And then you'd know for true
That you'd been good as good all
year
And he was helping you.

Don E. Overs
NO OTHER WAY
I gave my life to Christ today
For there is no other way.
His constant call awakened me
And I knew that it must be.

Why I waited, I do not know
But now my heart is all aglow
Since I have made my choice
And responded to His voice.

Now all my cares are laid aside

In Christ alone I shall abide
I gave my life to Christ today
Knowing now no other way.

If you would be received in grace
And hope to see His wondrous face
Rise and shout with loud acclaim
And praise and glory of His name.

Come and join the happy throng,
Sing with us in reverent song.
Lift thine eyes heavenly bound
For only there can Peace be found.

Don't hesitate if you're in doubt
Stand erect and turn about.
Give your life to Christ today
For there is no other way.

Sharon Lynn Wohlwend
A SINGLE CANDLE
Said I, as youth, with heart brave
    and true,
Passion-flag unfurled in brilliant
    hue,
"Let me set the world on fire—
    with light so great
    the earth and sky will be
    illumined by my desire!"
And so I sought to bring together
    and accomplish much,
Each a twig, a branch, a log to
    build my bonfire such.
For then was I strong and then
    life flashed through me in such
    energy
That it truly seemed that
    nothing was impossible to me.

The years passed by with
    quickening pace—each with its
    own particular face,
Faces of sorrow, faces of joy,
    keen disappointment, golden
    alloy,
Until I realized one sober day,
    somehow my life had run away
Down paths I hadn't intended to
    go, blended with people I hadn't
    intended to know.
And through the glasses of
    retrospect, I saw my life
    nothing like dreams
    Had caused to expect.
There was no glorious bonfire,
    passion-flame flashing to the
    sky.
There wasn't even a small one to
    point to with proud eye.

At first, it seemed that all my life
    was merely wasted years,
Filled so full with nothingness
    that only brought me tears.
And only then did I begin to
    really see the light—
Not bonfire brashly burning, but
    a single candle bright,
As I beheld folks I had helped
    along life's rugged pathway—
Nothing really great at all, but I
    had cheered their day.

And now I ask not for great
    dreams to set the world on fire,
To light my candle in the dark
    is now my own desire.

Howard A. Van Dine, Jr.
UNTITLED
I learned of love;
Not from passion's hoarse and
    sweet embrace,
Although I speak my frantic
    lover's vows

While in her breathless thrall.
I learned of love;
Not from a stout devotion's
    hero-stand,
Who braved the dread and saved
    the innocent
From a lecher's greed.

I learned of love;
Not from parent's distraught
    watch at night
When, through the Baby's crisis,
    frighted, wept
The silent, desperate prayer.

I learned of love
When I yielded my most precious
    hope
Against my will, yet holding
    nothing back;
And with that gift, my self.

I learned of love
When, with unvarnished
    consciousness,
The cruel pain of nails in Hands
    and Feet
Became a living thing.

I learned of love;
And with that lesson was
    redeemed,
Set free of all the petty fears and
    lust
That chained me here to die.

Florence A. Petersen
Risen Is the Christ, Our King
Ring, ye bells, and Christians,
    sing:
Risen now is Christ our King.
Ring, oh, let the welkin ring!

Now He's risen from the grave,
He who came our souls to save;
He has left the lonely tomb.
Will you give Him full heart's
    room?

Over death and sin He's won
He, our Father's dearest Son,
Rising, seeks our souls to win.
Will you let Him enter in?

Now is blessed Easter Day.
Will you love Him? Will you pray?
Sound the music glad alway!
In our hearts He longs to stay.

Ring, ye bells; sing Alleluia!
Risen now is Christ our King.
Ring, oh, let the welkin ring,
    Sounding ever loud *Amen.*

Shirley J. Partin
MORNING TEARS
Have you ever looked at the
    world in the very first light of
    day—
When the first rays of sunlight
    hàve chased the night away—
And with the night, there also
    goes, our darkest cares and
    fears—
And in its place, are glistening
    droplets, known as morning
    tears—

They fall gently as a veil and
    silently as the night—
They are only with us for awhile,
    they go, when comes the light—
But they cleanse the earth and
    bring new life to every living
    thing—

Add shine to the grass, put a
    blush on the rose and make the
    blue bells ring—
I have stood in wonderment and
    watched, this soft blanket on
    the ground—
How graceful it clings and
    delicately hangs from
    everything around—
Then slip down quietly to the
    earth, and just as quietly
    disappear—
They sparkle and shine like
    brilliant gems, these tiny
    morning tears—

M. R. Sybert
CHANGING FRIENDS
Always Friends
    to the end
Secrets of the Soul
    Never to be told
    by the other.
Always to listen
Always to advise
    with words from
    the old & the wise.
Always trusting
    & believing
Only to be shattered
    by the deceiving.
Life's illusions are many
    but not any
    as hurting
As a changing Friend.

Harvey S. Hensley
THE END OF THE WORLD
The sun will fall one of these days
You wait and see the sky shall
    raise
The sun will come down like fire
    from hell
But we all will know that it's
    GOD as well

The angels will come much
    closer to us
But we won't let that evil Devil
    fool us
Because we all know GOD is near
We have nothing, but nothing,
    but nothing to fear

But before this world shall come
    to an end
Everyone shall make one more
    new friend
Then all of us shall look up and
    start to cry
Because we'll see Jesus and his
    followers in our burning sky

While some of us stand proud
    and pray for a quick death
And others hope to GOD Satan
    isn't here yet
But most of us will be led on to
    heaven because there we
    belong
Then one by one we shall tell
    Jesus of our wrongs

So now you know what happens
But do you know why
Why that sun will fall like hell
    from our sky
Well it's because of our wars and
    ignorance that we will all die
So if you don't want this world of
    ours to end
We've got to learn to live with
    one another
And everyone shall be friends

Margaret Fern Anderson
What Christmas Means To Me
Christmas packages wrapped
    with loving care . . . snow
flurries that always come too
    late . . . Santa
squeezing down a chimney much
    too small . . . carols
drifting over the crisp cold
    air . . . bright hopeful
faces of the young . . . and
    young at heart . . . pumpkin
pie . . . the last minute
    rush . . . winter wonderland . .
the crunch of horses' hoofs in the
    snow . . . mistle-
toe . . Scrooge and Tiny
    Tim . . . trimming the tree . . .
letters to Santa . . . . holly
    wreathes . . . the joy of

giving . . . White Christmas and
    Jingle Bells . . . toys,
trinkets, and choo-choo
    trains . . . sleigh rides . . .
egg nog . . . rush of little feet on
    Christmas morning
. . . Donner and Blitzen and
    Rudolph . . . fruit cake and
candy . . . shining tinsel and
    icicles . . . candles glow-
ing in happy windows . . sugar
    cookies . . the Christmas
Star . . . first doll for a little
    girl . . . .the Nativity
. . and the eternal presence of
    Him Whose day it is.

Artie Tillman Proctor
WHAT IS MUSIC
Music to some may be different
As in all walks of life we go,
To some it may be a song-bird,
Or a tractor plowing a row.
The humming of a chain-saw,
Or machinery loud and clear
The tick of an old alarm-clock,
Or the patter of feet so near.
It could be the rippling waters,
Or the rush of the water-fall
The sound of wind in the
    tree-tops,
Or children out playing ball.
It could be a fisherman's line
    singin'
Or the shot that killed the game
The sound of a freight-train rollin'
As she hums, whistles, and
    steams.
It could be "Mom I love you",
Or "hi Dad! How do you feel?"
May even be "Come to see us"

Or, "thank You God for this
meal."
It could be a choir of children
Singing to their hearts content,
Or a solo sang in honor
Or the Saviour that was sent.
It doesn't always have to be
lyrics
Sung with some musical
instrument
'Cause music to each is different
Depending on the place we're
in . . .

Diane Cesarone
DEATH
Courted you for years
with ardor and passion;
persistent virginal infatuation

Elusiveness makes you seductive.

Want to lose myself inside of you
inside of me
in mindless orgiastic submission
succumbing control without
struggle

Embrace me, as a lover.

Colors
twirling, swirling, twisting,
misting
precisely penetrating crystal
blind vision
flowing, growing, slowing,
throwing
light shadows and dark forms

No boundaries, no borders.

Self becoming unself
without mourning;
pregnant with expectant fleshless
immortality

Rebirthing the only real me.

Accepting, Rejecting, Accepting,
Rejecting, Accepting, Rejecting
still undecisive—
not I, but you

Somewhere, now am I, on the
continuum.

sp/4 William E. Randall III
THE WAR IN VIETNAM

*I'd like to dedicate this poem to
all the soldiers and their families
who played a roll in the Vietnam
conflict. To my wife Barbara and
my children Angela, William, and
Rashawna. And most of all to
GOD who is in control of
everything.*

The War in Vietnam, they say
they meant no harm. With
thousands of men that die and
millions of families cried. What
was achieved? Who won the
War? What was Agent Orange
for? Those that came back,
suffer the most, with flash
backs and set backs from coast
to coast. Who will help them
that fought with pride? Who
will mourn the thousands that
die? Their dreams were
shattered, their life in rage, and
the president just turns the
page. A terrible mistake he will
not admit, he pushes the

weight to cover his sh—t. And
the vapor smells through out
the land, cause the president
didn't have a plan. The battle
was lost, but they wouldn't say,
they wanted to come back
another day.

Melanie M. Sadlon Updyke
NEW COLOR NEW TIME

*To my mother Janet and my
husband David with love.*

Autumn returns as a leaf falls to
the ground.
Many colors seem to be painted
all around

Lifes artist has once again
changed the scene.
Now is the moment for farewell
to summers green.

Cooler days and longer nights
have once again begun.
All living creatures turn now to
the warmth of the sun

It's not a time to say
goodbye.

No its the season for the
birds to fly

Christy J. Kelley
A LIKEN TO LOVE
I imagine . . .
Any two people, without love, as
compared to the opposite pages
of an open book. Standing side
by side, yet staring only
forward, both telling the same
story, and yet never reflecting
back upon the other, only to
have their story go on and on,
while they alone are left
behind.

I imagine . . .
Any two people, in love, as
compared to the opposite pages
of a closed book. Compeled
together, face to face, their
words and their meanings
mingling together in a silent
tale, though they know only
part of the story, they remain
together to the end.

Louise Beaven
CHAMELEON

*Dedicated to the glory of God:
"These are the works of the Lord,
and his wonders in the deep."
(Psalms 107:24), and for my
beautiful children, Patricia,
Pamela and Deborah.*

I saw it at sunset-a lavender sea!
A whispering, glistening, lavender
sea!
And in wonder I called to the
lavender sea:
Are you real? A mirage? Or can
you truly be?

Tell me, mysterious lavender sea,
Tell me, tell me, what is it I see?
Are you a dream for a moment?
Or a lavender sea?

Tell me, magical lavender sea,

By the high of the moon, what
colour will you be?
Will you be lavender?
Bewitching the eye?
A lavender sea?
When the moon is high?

Tell me, enchanting lavender
sea,
By the high of the noon, what
colour will you be?
Will you be lavender?
Bewild'ring the eye?
A lavender sea?
When noon is high?

Will you be here tomorrow?
A lavender sea?
If I come back tomorrow,
What colour will you be?

Krystal Spracklen
INSPIRATIONS
A friend of mine once told me
that the greatest thoughts are
inspirations.
If this is so, then I alone cannot
take credit for my
works . . .
for your presence in my heart
and your kind love have given
me the inspirations
I need.
Together we shall take credit
and become a great
team.

Victor A. Brewer
REKINDLED FIRE

*To-Allison, Kris, Judson, & Bret
Con mucho armor, tu padre.*

As the fire dwindles
and the last glowing embers fade,
a hopeful breath tempts
the ashes of fate-too late.

But, if it is truth's desire,
then gather virgin kindling
and carefully start anew.

And with the caressing warmth
of your breath's kiss
gently blow
the essence
of your giving love
into the kindling's womb.

And if the spark
of life's caring
glows and flames,
there will be warmth
and darkness will become light
as your eyes reflect the sparkle
of the flame's birthed gifts
which returns
the warmth
which was yours.

Marjorie Ness
UNTITLED
You say that you don't love her,
but I know she's on your mind,
I can tell by the way you kiss me,
You think of her all the time.

I know that it's hard for you to let
go,
but I won't wait forever,
I can't go on being kept in the
dark,
while you try to think it over.
I don't want to rush things,

but I need to be needed to,
although it will break my heart
to leave you,
It is something I must do.

But before I leave I will give you,
One last chance to set her free,
to forget about the future you
had,
and try to dream up on with me.

Coletta Miller
MAGIC OF CHRISTMAS

*To my husband Bill, sons, Bill Jr.
and Bob, their Families. Also my
Parents, Albert and Coletta Muhl,
my Sisters and Brothers, Anna,
Albert Jr. Richard, Dorothy and
their Families.*

It's the magic of Christmas, it's
that time of year when gift
given people suddenly appear.
Smiles, laughter, tears and
embraces.
Relatives, and friends with their
suitcases.
Coming from the kitchen, the
aroma of hot food, puts us all
in a festival mood.
Drinking a toast, with a holiday
cheer, while a fat, jolly Santa,
comes from the rear.
We're all sitting round the
glittering tree.
Beautiful packages are handed to
them, you and me.
Wrappings are tossed on a very
high pile, with each and every
person giving a happy smile.
It's the magic of Christmas, with
love to behold because the
Christ child story is told.
Beautiful and wonderous,
Christmas tales will never grow
old.

Winifred Kitchen
A BABE IS BORN
An inn—manger—star.
A star! Shepherds with their flocks.
Night! Beautiful (A Silent night)
night!

Heavenly hosts singing,
Singing praises.—Wait their King.
Praises from on High.

Mary and Joseph—
There in the stable—waiting,
Waiting for the Babe!

He is born! Rejoice!
The Savior is born. Be glad!
Sing praises to Him.

Sing Hallelujah!
Be glad! Rejoice! The Savior
Is born in Bethlehem!

Halelujah! Halelujah! Halelujah!

Evelyn C. Brown
GODS GREATEST GIFT
Through the windows of the world
We are sometimes blind to what
we see
In that all of lifes treasures are
within the heart
In that all of lifes treasures are free.

Take the sky
So blue in all of its glory

And the stars of the Galaxy
Each with its own story

Take the sea
So full of life it is still a mystery
All living things shall survive
Including you and me

So take my hand and I'll lead you
To all Gods wonders that are free
The earth.
the trees.
the ocean
and Gods Greatest Gift of all
Love to you from me.

Mary McGowan Slappey
CHRISTMAS ODYSSEY
I have come a long way on this
pilgrimage.
And known St. Francis, that
simple sage,
Friend of the bird and the gentle
beast
Seeking to lift humanity with the
yeast
Of kindness flowing from the
pure of heart.

I have bought angelica, lavender
from a village cart
And wept under winter's mistletoe.
Renewed my soul with verdant
evergreen
And the most magic red-berried
holly

I have danced as a child on
Christmas Eve night
And laughed in that transcendent
delight.
Crowned many a year with fruits
of the table,
Cooked and mended as long as I
was able.
Painted a saint or embroidered in
gold;
Never guessed that someday I'd
be old
And the dear ones I loved would
have left this earth.

I thought once I would die and ride
That far-flung ebbing and flowing
tide
That would somehow carry me
back to birth
And I would be as once I was,
unfleshed, soul-free.

I have felt this mystery of the
stable and star
By St. Francis encreched-so near,
so far;
With the monks pondered how
simple the divine,
A newborn babe and God, yours
and mine.

Allan De Fiori, L.P.N.
ENGLAND
Beautiful vision land highly
evoking myths,
Toward the wonderful throne of
God
As an unconquerable sovereign
deity of country-shores.
Folklored by gemmical beauty,
grandor and stardom.
Telecasting diorems, crowns and
tiaras
Typical anglican ancestry bethroded
To harp delineative, proserpine
myth.
Rosemary azure-pink prairie inland:

Expanding toward more abundant
life.
Alternatively constellated by
shores and green arenas
wayward the bays.
Focusing and delineating the far
shores of time.
General view of enchanting parks;
Sense of infinity where joy is in
allness and goodness with God.
Aoe Angelica Britannia Mater,
Tibi sunt sceptres requm, palmae
hereum
Et flores omnium ovetorum
morijanua vitae.—Lox lueet in
Fenebris.
Perviam Britanniae et Romae
Conseevta sunt saeeula ad
millenium.

Chaucer/Bach.
FASHION PERFECT
"And on that day, dear Mary
The Lord will not take away thy
finery
Nor thy beauty and certainly not
thy simplicity
No, not even thy robes, nor thy
girdings
Of sack cloth and ashes, meaning
what?
Meaning that fashions are fun
But there are other important
concerns also"
Thus like earlier scribes before
him
Isaiah prefers to occasionally
confess
The woman's sins for her

James Carlin
LOST GOLD
I liked it better here six months
ago when growth was spreading
on the empty limbs.
Although the leaves are
yellowing the ground I liked it
better when the spring was
here than walking on the wet
of fading gold.
For gold of fall is not immutable.
It cannot stay like treasure in the
trees.
And anyway I like the hint of
green much better than the
blackness that was gold.

Cordelia Halverson Cook
OLD HOUSE

---

*To my husband, Donald, with
love on our 41st wedding
anniversary and our daughters,
Sandra and Pamela.*

One Sunday afternoon on an
early day
We drove out to the country and
down by the bay.
Where, amid ancient Live Oaks
with leaves ever green
Towering Magnolias whose
blossoms are soft cream
Majestic Pine Trees sweeping to
the sky,
Stood this forlorn, old house with
shutters awry
Window panes broken, paint
washed away
Neglected, forgotten-Years past
it's heyday.

We moved into that old house
down by the bay
Where we, many years later, are
living to-day.
No longer is it neglected, forlorn
and gray
We planted "Praying Lillies" along
the walk way
Which bloom each summer in
glorious array.

If this old house could talk, I
believe it would say
"Thank you for loving and living
here-
No longer to roam
And for making this old house
A home."

Virginia M. Brewer
HEATHER
I see you every day and watch
you grow,
This small girl child called
Heather.
What will the world be like when
you are grown,
This small girl child called
Heather.

What are you thinking when you
see your first rainbow,
When you are chasing Butterflys
in the late afternoon,
Catching raindrops in your small
hands; you're growing up too
soon.
What kind of Heritage are we
leaving for you,
This small girl child called
Heather.

You dart like an arrow, leaving
the ripple of laughter behind
you.
With boundless energy, and Sun-
browned arms,
Mischevious eyes and tangled
curls, you live in your own
world,
This small girl child called
Heather.

Will you run through the dew
drenched grass,
Wiggle your toes with pleasure.
Will you walk the paths that I
once walked,
Love the things that I once loved,
My Granddaughter, this small
girl child called Heather.

Jean Levine
THE PLANET EARTH
Give me clean air to breathe
Keep the soil virginal

Allow the rivers underneath
To reflect surface images like a
mirror.
Who are these levianthans
That trample the soil with sludge?
Pouring from their pores
Spilling into the once shining
shores
Blanketing the cities with their
black sweat.
Must the dollar be greener
Than the grass we trod.
Rise up you little ones and
Mow down the giants.
Bring them down to earth
To smell the stench.
May it linger in their nostrils
Until the Planet Earth
Begins to bloom again.

Mr. Tracy L. Berkshire
SOME DAY

To GOD'S Creation, YOU.

It took God only six days to
complete,
Noah and the Ark, too Adam and
Eve.
In time to come, there was
much disbelieve
And Gods creation began to
deplete.
Worst of all Nations destroy and
defeat.
No matter what one Nation
would achieve,
Some other Country says, "it's
make-believe".
Before long Countries began to
compete.

Thou Jesus was sent to offer us
peace,
Crucified on the cross, left there
to die.
He rose from the dead and said,
"I'll return".
Threats of war are beginning to
increase
To Nuclear power here's my
outcry,
"First we were flooded, next we
just might *Burn.."*

Margie Edwards
HEAVEN'S DOOR
Can you tell the words of the
Bird's song?
Is your life a pattern of
RIGHT, or wrong?
Can you see the tiny patterns
In the snow?
Who put them there? Or do
You know?

There is a code to Heaven's
Door, and it is heaven-sent.
Well didn't you know, the
Code is—R—E—P—E—N—T.
But if you want the code to
Hell.
There's none-without salvation,
It's the station, where you fell.

Now here's to the bird's song,
The snow, and all sweetness.
And my love, I pray you find
Eternal happiness.
Never go the way of sin and
Apathy, the way some others went.
The code to love and life
Forever, is repent.

Tom Bratney
lone moon
lone moon
behind grey
and black
clouds, do you
mind being
naked,
not fully
clothed like
the earth or
bursting
with heat like
the sun?

Ann Reid

Ann Reid
MARKING TIME
I hurt,
So I must hold myself quite
 carefully
For splintered fragments
Fall
 from
  me.
Step softly world; do not come
 close.
I do not care
To
 hurt
  you.
Be not so lordly while I am on my
 knees.
Oh, laid back reality,
Far out my fantasies.
Stand back and let me breathe.
I hold myself quite carefully
For now I hurt,
Oh,
 how
  I
   hurt
While I am marking time.

Jo M. Pilliter
MY LOSS

*Dedicated to all mothers
everywhere who have lost a son
or daughter*

The light of my life was a son
named Tim.
Who left this world one day.
He loved to sit and talk to me.
There were things he had to say.

He had so many dreams to fulfill.
And so he always did pray.
That his life would have some
meaning.
Oh, how I wish he did stay.

But, God called and then he went.

What more is there to say?
Oh, I miss him more as days go by.
Please, God, why couldn't he stay?

And so I sit here patiently.
Until He calls me too.
And I shall see the light of my life.
And our souls will meet anew.

Janice L. Laperle
DARK OF NIGHT

*With heartfelt thanks to Uncle
Tony (Kohanski), whose
encouragement and confidence
led me into published "fame".
Regrettably, death claimed him
unable to see his aim in print.*

When the dark of night arrives
And the light of day is gone;
Can you count among the right
All the things that you've done
 wrong
Can you count among the right
A little deed done for another;
Was it really oh so hard
Or did you shake and really
 shudder?
Were you afraid you might be seen
Or did you have no care?
Just go ahead and be yourself
Regardless if anyones' there.
Be yourself and do what's right,
So others may learn from you;
For though they laugh and jeer at
 times
They'll do good deeds too.
So when the dark of night arrives
And the light of day is gone;
They'll be able to include the right
Among all that they've done
 wrong.

Melissa A. Langlotz
A DAY AT BATTLE

*To the people who give me love
and inspiration; Mom, Dad,
Kenny, Bradley and Laura.*

He cries when he remembers
 home
The warmth, the love and things
 to come.
So quiet now, not long to last
The firing starts, the quiet past.
The thoughts of love and home
 are gone
the moments pass, I'm not alone.
We have been spared for one
 more day
We bow our heads and start to
 pray.
We have lost many in this scene
A soldier's life is not a dream.

Jeffrey Balaam
MODERN HURTING
After pulling the purple shades
I noticed
the mint candies
in the ashtray.
I dipped
three or four
one by one
into my cup
of creme soda.
My teeth
turned into typewriter keys
and I wrote a poem for you

with my tounge.
I listened
to the moisture
invading the clear box frames
enclosed with our happy photos.
Finally,
I couldn't take it anymore.
I scotchtaped my eyes shut
and slid under the bed.

Cindy S. Slater
Double Image Portrait
GINGER JEAN
With pink cheeks
 rippled from laughter,
With blue eyes
 shining from mirth,
With golden curls
 tangled from curiosity,

She unfolds,
 the epitome of innocence . . .

. . .a rose blossom
like silky petals
 aglow with sunshine,
like a million dewdrops
 as deep as nighttime,
like sunny rays
 sifted into different niches

a blossom,
 the unopened rosebud.

Julia D. King
IF ONLY I COULD

*This poem is dedicated to my
husband Rex, who has given me
many years of love and inspiration.*

If only I could search
Inside my mind and heart,
And take apart,
Each thought that lingers there;
And fondle carefully
The emotions that are a part of me;
Dismiss the ugly thoughts I've
 had,
And know, that I was never really
 bad;
That I honestly tried
To live, and love, and be,
Like the creator who created me.
How this imperfect soul of mine
Reaches out for things divine!
If only, I could touch His heart,
And really be a part,
Of something fine.

Dawn M. Sahli
To You, God, at Christmas
Oh God in the sky above,
I wish I were a pretty dove.
I'd sing Your hyms so merrily
As I flew over a patch of trees,
Then as I made my way to land,
I'd think of how You made the
 earth so grand:
The air, the sea, the trees with
 fruit,
Oh God You made this world so
 absolute.
Mighty God You are so far away,
But I see Your existence every
 day.
With my fingers You formed,
I can grab, touch, and feel.
With my legs You formed,
I can climb any hill.
With Christmas coming, Lord, I
 think of You more.
You were there when I took my

first steps;
You'll be there when I close my
 last door.
God, I Love You, Merry Christmas!

Mary Jean Hager
AWAY FOR A DAY
I should stay away for a day
Find me a place that's lonely
Far from, the daily display
There, to please my self only.

Then perhaps/would come
 together
All the portion of my dreams
I'd be living in achievement
Things would be just as they seem.

Rosalie Ann Kastelic
CHER

*To my daughter Cheryll Ann. For
all the little persons who take the
time to share & remind us of the
important things in life.*

I've been given a special treasure
One I'm not really sure if
 deserved.
It's a life to mold while my hand
 she holds,
Drawing strength, taking love,
 once reserved.

Love that was once dealt in tiny
 portions
To lovers and mothers and
 friends,
Now flowing free like a river
Full of life and beauty again.

Just to feel the touch of this little
 one
Brings warmth clear thru to the
 bone.
Through her eyes she colors a
 gray tired world
Making each step an adventure
 unknown.

As I stand in awe of this creature
Hearing sounds I never saw until
 now,
So the child becomes the teacher
So the tree learns of life from the
 bough.

George Chaffee
GOD UNDERSTOOD
I had a talk with God today;
and not one word I heard him
 say.
I started with a sullen mood;
and ended with my feeling good.
I thank you God, you understood.

Ann M. LaVallee
TRANSITION
When one sees the
Sight of Awareness,

When one hears the
Sound of Continuity,

When one smells the
Fragrance of Life,

When one tastes the
Love that Nourishes,

When one touches the
Being of Realization,

When one discerns the
Presence of Infinitude;

This is NAMELESS.

Our World's Best Loved Poems

Juanita Joan Kerr
WORDS THAT RHYME

Dare I write in words that rhyme
The reflection of our present time?
Would I incur the righteous wrath
Should I follow the noble path
Of Shakespeare, Browning and
    mournful Poe?

For in these times, candlelight
    does not glow,
And misty rivers do not run slow
Around green meadows where
    buttercups grow.

Knights in armor and maidens fair,
Love that lived beyond death's
    snare
Alas, now a forgotten lore,
I quote The Raven; Nevermore.

Marlena Blythe
ONE LOVE FOREVER

As the years passed away
Fond memories of you linger in
    my mind
My heartaches for your love
First love, as it was fifteen years
    ago
Fresh, New, and Forever
Today as I talked to you on the
    phone
It was as if the years had never
    passed
Time had stood still
The ache in my heart each time I
    hear your voice, of just think of
    your name.
Today as we talked
You told me of the things in your
    life that had changed, over just
    the last few short months,
    since we talked over lunch.
Your divorce, and now your soon
    to be married again.
It was almost as if I were in shock.
Time once again stood still, at
    that moment, as it had so often
    in the passed.
It's almost as if we came so close
    to being together and yet so far
    apart.
Words that flowed so freely in
    my mind could not get passed
    my thoughts.
Here, once again, fifteen years
    later you were slipping away.
I was losing you a second time
And my heart broke at that
    moment, as it had before.
So many times my thoughts have
    been with you.
Knowing I had forever lost a part
    of my life I knew I could never
    regain.

Shirley Poe Jones
SAD

*To those who love me, my
deceased dad, who inspired me to
write, residents at nursing home
where "Sad" was born*

What is this sad feeling
    I feel inside?
The moon is so full, the world so
    wide
It looks so cloudy out my window
    today
Sunshine will not come out to play
But here comes my friend with a

smile so bright
Gee, all my sadness took flight

Elsa Harper
A WALK

The many cares that burdened me,
I lost them all yesterday,
Among the flowers in the field,
Among the lambs at play.
Among the grazing cattle,
Among the rustling trees,
Among the twittering birds,
Among the buzzing bees.
So, walk through the fields
    tomorrow,
And smell the new mown hay.
Enjoy the world about you,
As I did yesterday.
Walk thro the fields of tasseled
    corn,
See black-eyed susans nod.
Forget all evil thoughts and deeds.
Walk in the fields with God.

George W. Barnard
CHRISTMAS ETERNAL

*I dedicate this poem to my Wife
and Daughter who have always
been by my side to give me
inspiration.*

T'was the day after Christmas,
    the spirit is gone,
It's too bad the spirit doesn't live
    on.

Wouldn't it be wonderful, if every
    year,
The spirit of Christmas would
    stay on to cheer?

Instead of having one day of good
    will,
The world would have happiness
    every day to fulfill.

When in Christmas season you
    get into the swing,
Keep it that way and peace it will
    bring.

To prove I am right, how happy
    we are,
When we read how the wise men
    followed his star.

And if we could be happy all
    through the year,
We would never have chaos and
    worry to fear.

If there were peace on the earth
    and good will to men,
We could really make it happen;
    again and again.

And so to extend if from year in
    and year out,
We'd have a smile on our face
    with no time to pout.

If you truly believe what I say is
    true,
Then how about trying it—just
    me and just you.

And if we succeed in our little
    venture,
We will have a successful little
    adventure.

There is no good reason why this
    shouldn't work,
So be a public benefactor, from it
    never shirk.

Flora F. Gregory
SEASONS

I believe our soul has seasons
When we need different things
There are times of sadness
And times when we can sing
We can't always be happy and on
    the mountain top.
The valley has to be crossed with
    many turns and stops.
The devil tries to slow us down
    and turned the other way.
But Jesus is the strongest and by
    our side he'll stay.
We only need to reach out and
    touch his nail scarred hand.
Each tear we shed and each
    problem I know he understands.

Eva Cook

Eva Cook
I THANK YOU

I thank you for each lovely day
And for the sun above that shines
For the clouds giving shade at
    times
When we need water from up
    above
The trees, grass, flowers and our
    food
All needing nature's loving care
For the animals that serve us well
Giving their love for us to share
The bees that give honey, the
    flowers to pick
The grapes on the vine that
    grows so thick
All the birds that fly and sing for
    us all
Giving music winter, spring,
    summer and fall
The nights look so pretty with
    stars that shine
While a moon looks down on us
    from up high
Lets us know there is one who
    cares from above
As the world turns around
    showering us with love
The oceans that carry the ships
    out to sea
The fisherman who catches fish
    for a fee
The beaches with sand that make
    a grand view
Gives us all a good reason to say,
    "I thank you."

Mc Wallace Braxton
**The Batman, An Updated,
Modern Version!**

Night time in Gotham City
    brings forth those who prefer to

ply their trade in the dark
It brings forth the theif, the drug
    peddler, the pimp, and the
    common mugger in the park

Night time in Gotham city
    comes
    too quick for those who love
    the law and all the ways
    upright

It brings out the base instincts of
    survival that calls for escape or
    fight!

Night time in Gotham City is
    usually ushered in by a full,
    large, and yellow moon up in
    the cold, night sky

It is a struggle then for the
    average citizen either to live or
    to die!

Night time is the perfect time
    with the cover of darkness to
    hide the illegitimate
    transactions of seamy riff raff

It is the appropriate setting for
    their kind or ilk to practice
    their dubious craft

Night time in Gotham City also
    has a dark, mysterious
    champion or *Hero*, so to speak,
    to counter balance some of this
    underworld activity

It is one who is a self styled
    vigalante for justice and liberty

Night time knows well this
    "untouchable" in the dark, blue
    flowing cape, gray leotard suit,
    yellow, well stocked utility
    belt, dark blue gloves, boots,
    trunks, and pointed ears cowl
    instead of a tipped, brim hat

It is well known to both this
    city's citizens and sorted crowd
    that the marked man imitates a
    simple, nocturnal, flying
    mammal more commonly
    known as a bat!

Night time also "knows" this
    caped stranger is sometimes
    joined by a young male
    companion, clad in a short,
    satiny yellow cape, red vest
    with lettered "R" to the left,
    green short sleeves shirt,
    gloves, slippers with briefs, and
    on his partly concealed face, a
    half mask the same color as his
    utility belt, all in black

It is common knowledge that this
    daring duo may appear
    seemingly out of nowhere for a
    rough an ready anti-crime
    attack!

Night time has "seen" this
    uncommon pair slice through
    its mantle of darkness, in a
    peculiar looking, dark blue
    automobile with the "face" of
    its older driver's appearance
    similar to that particular type
    of animal's eyes and ears

It is the time all sorts of lowlife
    cease their underhanded
    operations to produce knives or
    guns to fight or scatter for
    cover to escape, giving Gotham
    City's citizens some kind of
    insurance against their not
    altogether ungrounded fears!

Juliet Zackery, Scott
CLOUDS
Like a ball of soft white cotton
  sailing upon the sea.
Look up, look down. It's the sky
  above, that my eyes do really
  see.
It seems I see a setting for a play.
Woe begone as the clouds float
  away.

Carmen Lydia Colmenares
Carmen Lydia Colmenares
WHAT IS CHRISTMAS?

*I dedicate this poem, with all my
love, to my beautiful family.
Though near or far, you are
always in my heart. Bless you.*

What is Christmas without a song?
  without the uplift of our souls?
What is Christmas without a
  smile?
  to see the children's wide eyed
  joy,
What is Christmas without a
  touch?
  to show the love we truly feel,
What is Christmas without a
  friend?
  to share our blessings, and
  hidden dreams,
What is Christmas without some
  words?
  expressing best wishes to those
  we love,
What is Christmas without our
  aid?
  to the ones, less fortunate, who
  wait and trust,
What is Christmas without the
  awe?
  of knowing that "HE", still loves
  with might!
What is Christmas without our
  thanks?
  to the "One" who's the
  way . . . who's the truth . . .
  who's the life!

Shonda Nellie Cheryl Waters
JESUS SAVES
When life gets cold
  And you're facing the odds
Get down upon your knees
  And pray to God,

Then all of a sudden
  Your life is no longer blue
Cause you turned for help
  To the one who loves you.

Allen K. Harrington
A CONTEST
There seems to be A CONTEST,
Not only one, but four,
I just recently discovered,
So I'll enter one or more,

I've been in three already,
But there isn't yet a winner,
That's O. K. with me though,
Because I'm just a beginner.

I give all the credit,
To THE LORD above,
Because without HIM I AM
  NOTHING,
I am secured in HIS LOVE.

So I'll try out A CONTEST,
As I have in the past,
I let HIM give me the words to
  write,
Because I know some of them
  will last.

So what now is happening,
Are we in the winners slot?
I guess I'll let the judge decide,
Because I'm an entrant in A
  CONTEST and the Judge is not.
  I LOVE YOU JESUS,

S. Gunnels
OLD-FASHIONED WOMAN

*To Kathy, who dares to stand
apart from the crowd.*

In this modern world of "your
  place or mine?"
An old-fashioned woman is
  indeed a special find.
Do not let anyone pressure you
  into doing something that is
  not right for you,
For to yourself you must always
  be true.
Live, my friend, for what you
  believe—
For only then will your spirit
  truly be free.
Because of your high morals,
  some men might get frustrated
  and walk away,
But someday, I know you'll find
  one who will love you for what
  you are and stay.
Now you are a beautiful bud in a
  garden overflowing with
  blooming flowers,
But someday you too, will bloom
  and on that special man all
  your love you will shower.

Sarah J. Esterly
OUR LITTLE BOY

*Dedicated to my oldest son
Franklin M. Esterly Jr. who was 3
yrs. old when written*

He wakes up in the morning,
Puts his left shoe on the right,
"I'm big enough to dress" says he,
But Oh, he looks a sight.
"I'll have my breakfast mother,
So I can go and play,"
And what he doesn't find to do
In just a single day.
He takes the old paint bucket
And fills it up with water,
Then paints the house, the porch,

the fence,
Because he thinks he oughter.
He gets out all his daddy's tools,
"I'm a mechanic, don't you know?"
He takes apart his guns and toys,
Then, "Mother, I can't make them
  go."
He'll tell you all the nursery
  rhymes,
For a nickle as his fee,
But to all his little playmates,
He will boast of them with glee.
Some think he is a menace,
Others say he is a joy,
To his mother and his daddy,
He is just their little boy.

Lorraine Hicks
I WAS AND AM
I shivered not a creature
  of the sea,
nor crept over sand.
Tree limbs were not for me,
I walked upon this land.
God created me.

Woman strolled by my side
my mate, my bride.
Creatures I named . . .
Authority of this domain
was mine to be.
God created me.

Maro Rosenfeld
THE EYE
Day is singular
  and night is plural

Because the Sun is light
  and the stars are dark

Yet all that is plural
  is singular

For in darkness all skin is black

The Sun blinds the naked eye
and when it falls
the fire flickers
and goes out

The Eye forgets
  the sun rises somewhere else
when it sets

And all is finished
by the Eye of Ignorence

Linda J. Callahan
TESTS OF TIME
The many facets of our lives
can not always be explained.
There are things that happen
  gracefully
so fond memories will remain.

But often time tempts us
with a treat for our soul;
it gives and then it takes away
and exacts a heavy toll.

It seems the things we want the
  most
are forever outside our scope.
But don't despair, you've friends
  out there-
Love and Hope.

Albert J. Conard
SEQUEL
A different man,
The same need.
A different place,
The same tree.

The same world,
A different time.
The same circle
In Nature's rhyme.

A. C. Canciller
TO A SONGBIRD
I love you pretty songbird
With plumage red and green;
To me you are the fairest
Of all the birds I've seen.

You bring to me the gladness,
The joy of dawning years;
For when you hum your music
You staunch my brimming tears.

Joanne Haines
SEAL SLAUGHTER

*To the countless seals fallen to
the hunters and to THE
INTERNATIONAL FUND FOR
ANIMAL WELFARE for its
unceasing efforts to end this
slaughter, this poem is sincerely
dedicated.*

Must the innocents die by the
  hand of man
And their blood flow scarlet
  across the land?
Must the warmth of their beauty
  be gone from sight,
Destroyed by the stalkers of
  Satan's night?

Must the innocents die in
  bleeding pain,
Their passing a shrine to mortal
  gain?
Must their cry be echoed, a
  hollow scream,
Forever resounding in strong
  mens' dreams?

Must the innocents die under
  Heaven's gaze
And their end paint carmine
  eternity's days?
Must their lives be done and
  their young blood flow
In a frozen etching of crimson
  snow?

Dan Rosenberg
A Stranger In the Night
In the dark of the night, my dog
  started howling.
  Lo and behold someone was
  prowling.
Who can it be? That I cannot see,
  For we weren't expecting
  company.

To call the police was on my mind,
  But another solution I did find.
The skill of Judo I will choose,
  To make the enemy lose.

My fist was ready, and
  My temper rose,
I'll give you a punch in the nose!

I kicked the door and said, "Now!"
  Lo and behold, the enemy
  purred "meow."

Arthur Morrison
WOMAN: TO TOUCH
Woman: to touch and yet hold so
  dear,
  Creating a love and a want to be
  near,
  The body of a woman,
  sometimes a career.
Woman: proportioned to meet
  every charm,
  Wanting to be protected from

harm,
The sensation of her, setting
off an alarm.
Woman: every curve, put
perfectly in place,
Has sent many a heart, soaring
out into space,
One touch and the heart is at
full race.
Woman: Daylight or even in the
dark,
To himself, a man will remark,
Such beauty, with her I would
embark.
Woman: To touch her, as she has
lain,
Knowing her beauty, a man
becomes vain,
The touch, driving a man
almost insane.
Woman: Under a man's hand and
mellow to feel such,
A woman: eager to feel the touch,
A life time of a woman, still,
you wouldn't learn much.
Woman: Born to be loved from
birth,
Growing up to be more than a
man can put to worth,
She is, woman: to touch, of our
earth.

Aleta Mull (Belmer)
A WORLD OF PEACE
First-came *John Kennedy*, a
President of men. Then along
came Martin Luther King, He
fought for *rights* of men. Next
came *Bobby Kennedy*. (God)
put him to the test. Along
came *John Lennon*: People say
"He was the Best"—He sang his
songs to all the world for
everyone to hear. Then
somewhere down the line,
(God) took these lives, (So Dear).
All of these men fought for the
truth, they wanted what was
fair, But sometimes life's not
fair at all—"People Just don't
seem to care".
If only for a short time the world
could be at peace, with no
more GUNS, or Knives, it
would save a lot of grief.
It would be so nice, to just sit
down in one large group
together and have no (Bigitory)
at all, Then "STAY THIS WAY
FOREVER".

Harvey Godin
A Thanksgiving Prayer

*TO God, Mankind and peace.—
May they find perfect harmony.*

We thank Thee for our yesterdays,
Blessed were all of those;
We thank Thee also for today
And all our tomorrows.

We thank Thee for the
Summertime,
Autumn, Winter and Spring;
We thank Thee for the stars that
shine
And all the joy they bring.

We thank Thee for the grass so
green,
We thank Thee for the trees;

We thank Thee for the lakes and
streams
And for the seven seas.

We thank Thee for the mountain
chains
And the rich vales below;
We thank Thee for the golden
plains
And all this earth can grow.

We thank Thee for the pure,
white snow,
We thank Thee for the rain;
We thank Thee for the winds
that blow
Upon the weather-vane.

We thank Thee for the birds that
sing
And for the sun above;
We thank Thee, Lord, for
everything,
But mostly for Thy love.

Rev. Helen Y. Torkelson

Rev. Helen Y. Torkelson
MY SOUL LONGETH

*For My Son Rev. David A. Lee &
To My Lord & Saviour, Son's
Ronnie & Larry Powell, Owen
Torkelson, Spiritual Son's Rev.
Paul Crisan & Rev. Richard
Woodruff & Mom; From The
Depths of my Heart & Soul, The
Part I Share With All*

Oh Lord, my soul longeth and my
heart crys out to Thee
Thy Holy Spirit that dwelleth
inside Your Temple in Me,
Searches out the innermost
valleys to fill the wells of sorrow
With Thy Blessed Strength, Thy
Word, Our Shield for all the
days of tomorrow.
Oh Lord, give me grace and let
me Glory in Thy Love
Withholding not Thy Knowledge
and Wisdom from above.
Let me Walk Always Uprightly
in Thy Blessed Sight
And let My Soul Show Forth Thy
Glory in My Daily Walk this
night.
Fill My Innermost Longing as I
travel this sojourn of Life,
That I may as Thy Doorkeeper
bring to You, O'Lord—The
Searching Generations
Who have fallen by the wayside
of Satin's god-less temptations;

That I may, in all the Perfect
Love that You Have Given
Hold those up, who sorrow, in my
Travail toward Heaven.
Thy Big Family is covering Your
once beautiful Earth here below
Now attuned to a World System
that is the Suffering Humanity
of slavery and woe.
You, O' Lord God alone, can
account for the Mercy upon
Our Nation
For the Blessings poured out, the
withholding of Your wrathful
Indignation,
To Give HOPE to the LOST and
Eternal Life in the Perfection of
Thy SON
Who holds us in His Hands for
Our Lives on Clavery, He has
Won.
Look into the very Depths of
Emotion and My Baca, The
Valley of Tears
That as Your Child, Dear Lord, I
Might Reach Heaven for Those
I Carry Through The Years.
For My Soul Longeth and My
Heart Crieth out to Lead Them
Home.
Thank You Lord, for the Love
You've Placed in Me
For the Mercy and Forgiveness
that could only come through
Thee.
Thank You for letting the Hurts
that sometimes come, when I
don't understand
To become Lost in Forgiveness as
I try to Walk Not, according to
Hearts of Man.
Thank You for Giving Me This
So Needed Kind of Gentle Love
O'Lord, My Soul Longeth—To
Also Be Loved,
Not for what others think that I
should Say or Be
But because O'Lord, There's
YOUR KIND of LOVE Inside of
Me.
Man does not always see the
Deep Crying Out of the Hurts
Untold—
So Thank You, Lord, For Giving
Me, Your Kind of Love When
Saving My Soul.

Henry M. Grouten
THE LORD
When thunder has sounded and
lightning has struck,
when the world is such that times
seem rough, touch
the hand of the Lord up above.

When rain always falls and the
sun does not shine,
when daylight is gone and it's
dark all of the time,
think of the Last Supper
and with the Lord you will dine.

When the road gets rocky and
the way is not clear,
when wheels are spinning and
you get nowhere, just stop
and remember, the Lord is still
here.

When smiles don't appear and
tears fill your eyes,
when friends you've known put on

their disguise, have faith in
the Lord, for He tells no lies.

Eileen Raflik
Life Never Lasts Forever
As I look back I can see a
thousand things.
Not only good but sad.
Times of death and sorrow,
Times of disappointment about
tomorrow.
But never will I fear the days that
are near.
I try to picture things I love,
And soon they will be up above.
For LIFE NEVER LASTS FOREVER.

Donna Bartholomew Lentz
ANGELIC SPECTATORS
When all hallow's eve comes
'round each year
And gremlins and goblins abound,
I often wonder for the rest of the
year
Where these small creatures are
found.

And as I watch them frolic and
romp
In my garden and across my lawn,
Some appear to be merely shadows
To disappear with the coming
dawn.

Shadows which have an angelic
glow
As though from Heaven descended;
Little ones called to eternity
Before their youth had ended;

But now return for one short eve,
Spectators of youthful glee.
I wonder if they're seen by others,
Or if their secret's shared only
with me?

Ann Marie J. Albanese Janco
NIGHT LIGHT
Mellow, white, tonight your color
be, as I look from my window,
through the trees so bare.
You made me smile, when my
eyes did see, the depth of night,
yet you shine so fair.
When a golden, orange shade you
take, my heart warms to its
highest peak.
Surrounding rays of four, across
you make, world-wide of your
wonders we speak.
Songs and poems were, are and
always will be, written and
sung until eternity.
From January to December, Lord
keep us in tune, to observe, to
love, to pray beneath your Moon.

Louise Freeze
YOU CHANCED MY WAY
In the short time that I've known
you
There's been laughter, love, and
tears.
The feeling that I have for you,
I knew would span the years.
I know you'll soon be leaving me,
The signs show more each day,
And I'll be even more alone
Than when you chanced my way.

You could never be quite satisified
With the love I gave to you;
There was always something I
didn't say
Or something I didn't do.

My love is true and oh, so strong
It gives my soul a chill,
To hear you say I'll not be true
The way I know I will.

The love you say you have for me
Gets buried deeper each day
By unjust accusations
And the manner you display.
Painful hurt runs through my
heart
As I struggle for words to say:
Why can't love be the way it was
When first you chanced my way???

Bonnie Heather Menegaux
TIME
A day ago, or maybe three,
I saw a girl in the garden,
I looked at her respectfully
And realized how she resembled
me.

I studied her for quite a bit . . .
She resembled me, but older than I.
Her hair was long, her eyes
brightly lit,
I wanted to speak, but was too shy.

As she quietly slipped away,
I walked over to me,
And looked inside to see
Part of me arise, for years in
shadow had it lay.

When I returned to my house,
I saw in the mirror
The elder side of me.
I could not help but shed a tear.

Lynda Marie Milnes-Evans
LIFELONG BOND

---

*Dedicated to my dear mother
Rosemarie Milnes, whose love
and friendship is priceless.*

Deep within this heart of mine,
I wish I were a child;
Protected by your loving warmth,
Comforted by your smile.

The teddy bears I'd put to bed
Tucked neatly at my side,
The "Now I lay me's down to sleep"
Your tender kiss good night.

I recall throughout my childhood
The many roles you'd play;
A doctor, nurse, and teacher,
My partner any day.

Those memories I hold so dear;
School frolics, games, and songs,
Prescott drives, our talks of life,
My wedding, and days by-gone.

You've always been my idol,
A model, and great mom.
You wear a brilliant halo
And there's nothing you do wrong.

The mirror tells the story,
I no longer am a babe,
Yet I always cry for mommy
When your presence I do crave.

And if I need some extra strength
To endure life's frequent trials,
I'll place my hand in the depth of
yours,
And walk with you a while.

Arthur Morrison
A SONG FROM MY HEART
Listen to my heart, hear it sing,
Love is all you can call

this thing.
Only you, I adore and love,
My heart, singing it out above.
Tears are not to be,
Just my love, for you to see.
A melody only for you,
Hear how my love is true.
The singing of my heart, in song,
Loving you can not be wrong.
Clearly, and yet how soft,
Sending love to you, aloft.
My heart sings the song you hear,
I love only you, my dear.

Betty Ann Wooley

Betty Ann Wooley
INTERLUDE
My humble place is the path I
trod
Or beneath an old oak tree
High on a hill where I talk to
God
Or walking beside the sea
Watching the rain heaven's tears
that fall
Dreaming by an open fire
Looking up when I hear a lone
bird call
Away from the world's desire
Nestled between the pages of
time
Where threads of yesterday
Still mingle among the songs
I've sung
Each dream that has faded away

My humble heart so filled with
room
I carefully hold and mend
Allowing the flowers to await
their bloom
To find fulfillment again

Shirley Ann Barrett
WHEN I SEE YOUR FACE
When I see your face
I see a poem
That I cannot write

When I see your face
I see a song
That I cannot sing

When I see your face
I see a smile
That is not there

Nelda Levant
BEST LOVED
My Dear,
You "fear to lose 'something'"
Would it be LaTrac?
Could you not find, possibly,
That other shoe—over by the
Trackwalker Chicken—Coop:

To the Rose Window with
Tracery
Comes the tracer bullet
EXEMPLUM EXEDRA Zing
kaput

Us Use Usage
Choice Choose Chosen
USUS UTI USUS

Midnight Flyer Whoooooooeeeeeeee
I've paid my dues and now I'm
movin' on . . . . . .

Mary Pirrone
SEED OF LIFE

---

*To my daughter Daria with love
MGM*

I, as one, lie here and wait,
To learn the mysteries of my fate,
I see no light but for the black
depths of eternity,
I am not yet, but someday will be,
I feel not, I see not, nor even care,
Of my own existence to be aware,
But I wait for the day when I
shall feel,
One of the mysteries that will
never fail,
To be delivered from the
beginning of all creation,
When my senses awaken to a
warm impregnation,
Which will cover and open its
arms to engulf me,
To take me and then one day set
me free,
I will no longer be one, but a
multitude of me,
When completed for all the world
to see,
That one of the mysteries of the
universe is done,
On my way to life, I have come.

Wm. A. Gaffner
REJOICE!
Jesus is born
Jesus is born
Let the new music begin
We are found
We are found
We are no longer lost in sin
Jesus is born
Jesus is born
The Lamb of God has come
Rejoice! Rejoice!
Rejoice within
The Root of Jesse, the Star of Jacob
Jesus is born
Jesus is born
Our God, Our King
Hosannah to Him!

Jeanette Willoby
ONCE MY HEART

---

*Dedicated to all of those who
truly know the meaning of
growing a "Blue Rose".*

Once my heart was a meadow
bursting with the hope of spring
and all the beauty she brings.
My love song was soon rewarded
with the coming of a Rose
the blessing the budding
of a tender babe born to grow.
Then came the tempest
the torrents of my tears.

Swirling hurricanes of sadness
the flooding rivers of fear.
My Rose was lifeless, still and cold.
"Oh breathe sweet blossom
the heart of my soul.
Turn from death so bitter and bold.
Let there be mercy
for this life yet to unfold."
Given time together
we weathered the eye of the storm.
Riding silent waves of rage
holding on to our love
that grew ever deep and warm.
My heart is still a meadow
though sometimes covered in
snow.
But always there is a sunny place
a bright and happy space just
for my Blue Rose to live and grow.

Mark S. Homison
THOUGHT OF YOU

---

*To Kimberly Kay Roadarmel, the
lady of my thoughts. Love Mark*

Now it's snowing
The winds are blowing
I'm thinking of you
I wish you were here.

Without you, I'm alone
With you I'm free
Together we laugh
I wish you were here.

You are my smile
My heart is yours
Sharing moments together
I wish you were here.

Snuggling close
Whispering soft
Kissing all night
I wish you were here.

Yes, it's snowing
The winds are blowing
I'm thinking of you
Oh! I wish you were here.

Elvira Munoz
NOSTALGIA
Can it be that I remember
How the trees look in September?
Hear the wild birds shrilling cries?
As they circle in the skies?

I was just a child, they tell me,
Yet, it seems as if I see
Waters swirling in the moonlight
Blossoms nodding in the sunlight.

Often do I sit and dream,
View again a wooded scene.
Country sights and homely sounds
My joy in still knows no bounds.

I think one day I shall retire
To my old home, its ruddy fire,
Stay there in peaceful sweet
content,
Complete my life, its days well
spent.

Karla James
I'm Not Complaining
All our good times have faded
Your love for me has died.
Eventhough I wanted to talk,
Your only reply was "I tried."
I never figured out, what it was
that I did wrong.

It all faded away so quickly,
Like the ending of a song.
Now lots of time has passed,

And you have gone away.
You'll never know how bad,
I wanted you to stay.
I guess by now its too late,
And you've found that "special someone."
But I'm not complaining,
Because its not the first time
its been done.
I guess you already know,
I've been hurt before.
By people like you,
Who just don't care anymore.

Bobbie L. Nowling
YOUR BIRTHDAY

*To "YOU" on YOUR BIRTHDAY,
Inspired by my children . . .
Stevie, Jamey, and Mandy.
Encouraged by my family and
friends who have always stood
beside me when times were
rough, and last but not at all the
least . . . Written for "Doug" my
TRUE LOVE*

Let me suprise you with gifts so
  deeply deserved, "Dear"
I'll give you something to cherish
  and to hold so near.
Let me scratch your itch, just so I
  can touch your skin
Let me kiss your sweet lips and
  watch a fire begin.
Then I'll fix you breakfast—"let
  me serve you in bed!"
To me this day is very special
  which when much older, you'll
  dread.
For this was the very day on a
  glorious day—you were born
So may it always be your best
  day, never sad, nor forlorn.

Robert L. Jackson
WHEN WE PART
When we part
  And can no longer share
Our tender moments
  We hold so dear
We'll still have memories of love
Given to us, from up above
With these memories
  I thee keep
Until again, our lips will meet
  I do you know
I again must say
  For each and every passing day
I will love you always, even
  When we part

Sylvia L. Ellcoff
**A Remembrance Once—Of
Warmth**
Raging waves raked the shoreline,
Tiny tufts of seaweed decorated
  the sand,
Timeless tides chased lazy
  seagulls while salty sprays of
  moisture ladened air, sprinkled
  against my face
I watched Summer fade into yet
  another Autumn sunset-
Returning home, I wandered into
  a fog-filled forest draped with
  weary willows,
Warmer rays scattered the chill
  of dawn, as sleepy starlings
  cracked the silence with a
  sudden song

My only thought, a remembrance
  once-of warmth-
Suddenly, without warning, my
  thoughts faded back, back into
  snarling daylight, when the
  Tiger was wild,
When he ravaged through
I'm sure that Bunnies are sincere-
  tangling thickets of heavy
  green and I felt his life
  throbbing in my throat,
My blood running rampant with
  the fervor of the beast
I recalled the world and the
  passion that for a time-was ours.

Mary Eileen Conte Sullivan
More Precious Than Gold

*Dedicated in behalf of my two
dear children Deborah Jane and
Thomas Bradford who have been
the strongest motivation in my
continued fight for life and love.*

Why is it not the quality of life
  men revere—
Why, the quantity of time and
  gold held so dear,
The emphasis get—rather than
  give,
Survive, rather than live,
Avoiding heartache, pain and
  sorrow,
Smelling the flowers, waits 'til the
  morrow.
Denying himself truth, thus joy,
  plays with life, as tho a toy.
Alas, alack and life is o'er,
Few people dare to open the door,
Wherein lies the sunshine of the
  soul, awaiting—
Thus forming man completely
  whole.

Mary Eileen
TRUE SECURITY

*Dedicated to my dear friends
whose faith has been a strong
support and great comfort during
life's adventure.*

The bank account from which I
  borrow,
Sometimes brings me pain and
  sorrow,
Yet, in time of need, it always
  lends,
The best investment—Caring
  friends,
Who return to me one thousand
  fold,
Treasures more rare than
  banker's gold.

Dorothy Haden
THE PARK
Children on the merry-go-round
Whirling dizzily around
Busily making a happy sound.
Children clutching tight to chains
Covering space in flying swings.
Children jumping from the trees
Shirt-tails flapping in the breeze.
Playing hopscotch on the walk
Some just making happy talk.
Oh, if the world
Could stop for a day
And join the children
When they play.

Katherine Wisniewski Termini
EASTER SUNDAY
I'm sure that Bunnies are
  sincere
And do not mean to
  interfere
With hens who lay their
  eggs
In mangers hung on walls
  with pegs.
Is Jack Rabbit a
  Buccaneer?
A maverick without a
  Peer?
Then how on earth does
  he engineer—
And this to me is most
  unclear—
To issue forth on Easter
  Day
All those colored eggs
  our way?

Barbara A. Cadogan
A PORTRAIT OF MOTHER

*To Muds in honour of many
years of love and caring.*

Sparkling eyes recessed,
like the precious stones set in her
  ring.
Her wrinkled brow long furrowed,
by three score years and ten.
The silver strands of thinning hair
contrasting with the pure gold of
her heart.
She is God's great work of art.

A tower of strength she stands tall
amidst the crumbling
  uncertainties of motherhood.
Her nut-brown face soaked,
with the dew of sweat and tears.
The honest word from her
  crimson lips
blend harmoniously with the
  ruby-richness of her heart.
She is God's great work of art.

Yet throughout the years of toil
she sits unblemished.
Not a color of hers has faded.
Her brilliant mind, well tinted
by the many shades of experience
Highlights the unfading beauty of
  her heart
She is God's great work of art.

Arthur Morrison
THE KISS
I have been taught the meaning
  of a kiss,

The warmth and tenderness,
  which few will miss.
I have been taught to kiss with
  feeling,
And how to send a heart, forever
  reeling.
I have known the kiss of pretend,
  Of a love, a heart did not intend.
I have known the kiss of denial
  and passionate hate,
Of those, nothing will I relate.
I have experienced the heated
  passion,
  Only a kiss, could fashion.
A kiss is not to be used as a toy,
  For it can turn sorrow, a heart of
  joy.
A kiss is for a soft and passionate
  love,
  For the one, we are not worthy of.
With every kiss, we became one,
  The kiss, a symbol of what had
  been done.
The standing still of time,
  The kiss, just a moment in a
  lifetime.
Such is the kiss of lovers,
  All these things, It covers.

Carole Neason
MOTHERS

*Dedicated to all the mothers of
the world.*

Mothers are little girls in grown
  up clothes, with years of
  experience that only she
  knows.
She is sugar and spice with
  medicine and pills, the one that
  you turn to with all of your ills.
She is a doctor, nurse, seamstress
  and cook, all of her experiences
  could compile a book.
A teacher, preacher and
  professional too, she at all
  times will know just what to do.
She is warm and gentle, also
  strong and tough, she will
  watch you eat until you've had
  enough.
Continuing on with her job that
  never ends, she will even
  entertain your unexpected
  friends.
Mothers have the biggest hearts
  of them all, they come in all
  sizes from short to tall.
But there is one thing and please
  take heed, give mothers all the
  love that they will need.
Mothers aren't meant to be with
  you forever, so take the time to
  tell her you love her.

Loretta Posey
HOW WONDROUS

to my daughter Janet Lynn

How wondrous it would be to
  have a home no one could see
A home far out in space where no
  one but me knew the place
No salesman at the door nor
  charities asking for more
No telephones ringing nor
  neighbor's phonograph singing
No loud noises without

from boys and girls running
about
There'd be no need to clean
because it would never be seen
I could read all day long or
compose a sonnet or song
Without disruptions to meet
solitude would be complete
How wondrous it would be but
oh, oh, how lonely!

Danny Eugene Jordan
LETTING GO
I lift my eyes with a view to
eternity.
My heart soars with the eagles of
light.
My soul floats upon the wings of
morning.
I am encompassed in the one and
there is peace.
There are no great strivings, no
worlds to conquer.
There is just a gentle yearning for
solitude and stillness.

Sarah J. Esterly
Beloved Gift Of God

Dedicated to our youngest son
David Jonathan Esterly (almost
16) died in an auto accident
May 1, 1982

David Jonathan, my beloved son,
We pause to give thanks for all
you have done.
David means *beloved,* Jonathan,
gift of God
You were the greatest gift, we
have ever had.

A gurgling baby, a happy boy,
Oh how you filled our hearts
with joy.
Unselfish, loving, good and kind,
A helping hand, a searching mind.
As son, brother, uncle, neighbor,
friend,
On your loyalty we could all
depend.

God gave you to us for a few
short years,
You've left us now with more
than tears.
We'll meet again, we know that is
true,
When God calls us home to be
with you.

Jana Whitson Lankford
ODE TO A UNICORN
No one has seen him
And surely no one will,
As he moves silently thru a field
of daffodils.
Eating only orchids and playing
silly games,
Five little fairies comb gold dust
from his mane.
He drinks the dew from
buttercups
Each bright and early dawn
And rides gently down the
flowing stream
On the back of a snow white swan.
All the woodland creatures
Sense the mystery that is born—
Every time they catch a fleeting
glimpse
Of the lovely Unicorn!

Gloria Martinez
HOW COME?
You're working for landlords,
vacation comes.
You feel happy, why?
You aren't getting any pay,
however, you're happy, how come?
How can it be possible?
You won't have any money,
but you'll have to pay your rent,
or else . . .
your landlord would kill you.
Your stomach will be empty,
all you'll have will be,
a cigarette between your lips
and a tape recorder
for your rock 'n' roll.
However, you're happy. How come?

Melva J. Lunceford
VALENTINES
The desire of the heart
Is your prayer to God.
He listens to the heart throbs
Of the "earthly clod."

If your heart is humble,
You'll find He's shining bright.
Giving and directing in
This "Journey of the Night."

He dwells in temples holy.
He hears and answers prayers,
Ever protecting and directing
In our many dares.

Inside He's always calling,
"Open wide your door to Me
And I will pour in blessings
To help your Holy See!"

"Valentines, I give you freely
From the Great Eternal Spring,
As you see the way to travel
In a pleasant, lovely dream."

Tara Parish
LISTEN
Listen-hear now, the mountain
speaks of its sorrows.
The rain beating down against it.
Tearing at its very core,
washing away the top layer, as
it stands, beaten but proud.

Listen-hear now, the mountain
speaks of its happiness.
The sun warming and caressing
the majestic form, healing the
rawness, bringing pride again.

Listen-hear how the mountain
speaks of its maturity.
The wind shapes and nurtures,
molding gently the structure,
so that it may endure all the
sorrows and grow to be the
beauty your eyes behold.

Listen-hear and see, the trees and
stream that surround its base
do not protect . . . their being
is to help the mountain stand
and collect the moisture.

Listen . . .

Roberta N. Fallis
EDUCATION
I have walked the corridors of the
school of life, I have tasted its
bitterness—
I have felt the coldness of its
pain.

I have opened the doors to
experience and traveled the

hallways of defeat.
I have climed the stairs of hope
and graduated.

Kay Camarena
THOUGHTS OF YOU
The thought of you goes through
my mind
Each and every day time after time
I feel the cold of the night every
day
I'm needing you and you're so far
away
I'm missing you and loving you so
And very slowly your letting me
go
My days I seem to get by so easy
Because I try my hardest to keep
busy
Buy my nights when I wake up in
a cold sweat
You know you're the hardest ever
to forget
I thought you loved me and I
thought you were mine
But all along, you were just being
kind
It hurts me to know you'll never
be mine
But I'll always keep thoughts of
you time after time
I'll never forget you, so I'm not
going to try
So not only in this note, am I
saying
I love you, but I'm saying good-bye.

Mrs. Edna Sue Mahaney
JESUS' LAST HOURS
Born in a manger and died among
thieves,
Jesus, King of Kings, thru all
eternity,
Suffered as no man has ever done,
Died for all mankind, our God's
only son.

His suffering began in the Garden
of Gethsemane,
As he prayed there, "Let this cup
pass from me."
Yet it was not His will but His
Father's be done.
In agony His sweat dropped as
blood on the ground.

Betrayed by Judas with a simple
kiss,
The wicked disciple was no
longer His.
Then soldiers led Jesus next to be
tried.
Caiaphas said for the people one
should die.

Then led to Pilate, who could
find no fault in Jesus,
But released in His stead, a
murderer, Barabbas.
Then Jesus was scourged till His
skin hung in shreds,
And a crown of thorns was placed
upon His head.

He was mocked as a king, and
made to carry His cross,
Out to the place of a skull, where
the soldiers cast lots
To take His clothes and then
raise Him form the ground
To crucify Him, the worst death
man coud have found.

There on the cross He was thirsty

and alone,
Feeling God had forsaken Him,
yet He was wrong.
Even then He could forgive man
for his sins,
And three days after death, Christ
LIVES again!

James R. Conroy

James R. Conroy
BUTTERFLIES
At first, bequiled was I, by the
dancing of two white butterflies
The dipping, darting and
hovering was frenzied, but the
longer I watched
There came before my eyes a
serene ballet where every
poignant flutter
Held meaning

Then it was over, I betook to
reflection, distracted now, what
song the birds where singing
And hews of flowers heretofore
unseen I asked myself,
Clue of her past or fault of her
contour was he seeking,
Or did his many angled view
abilitize him more to exite and
please?
I think tonight as I prepare to
sleep remembering that butterfly
I'll sprout some wings and maybe
I, can exemplify

Tomorrow morn, look not to my
new and clumsy flight
But color blooms and learn the
tunes while dancing all the day
Then, and only then, usher in the
night.

T. W. Hughes
GILGAMESH
Gilgamesh was one
who stretched his sight against
the wall.
He chipped in the chinks with a
spoon
supplied by indulgent watchers,
chipped and groveled and poked
an eye through too late.

With body too big for the hole
he just sat back dusty and tired
and waited to be found out,
which he was soon enough by the
surly guard
plodding this way on the hour,
every hour.
The guard was always there,
and the walls were always grainy
but thick,
such that a man with a bigger

spoon
might fathom an opening large
    enough, long enough
through the grey years
and sqeeze through on an
    unwatched night of rain;
slip over, slide down and wind
    away unseen
through elegant interwoven
    barriers,
past bush, tree and muddied slope
into the mysterious water
    chopping and rolling
forever by the looming towers
dark in the moonlit sea.

George Linton Yearwood
TO A WILDFLOWER

---

*Submitted by an andoring
brother, Charles, who recognizes
poetic genius.*

O lovely woodland flower tell me
    why
Must you bloom alone where
    none can see
Hidden quite away from every eye
I wonder is it penance due for
    some iniquity

Or is your beauty such a fragile
    thing
That summer sun and rain can
    mortify
No bird eagles you with its
    caroling
Nor do you host the golden
    butterfly

When winter holds you in its
    cold embrace
And decadence profanes your
    sweet perfume
I shall return remembering the
    place
And say an "Ave" at your sylvan
    tomb.

Mary Earle
MY INSIDE—
Sometimes inside I feel I might
    explode,
It's nothing I do or anyone does
    to me,
It's just there and I must wait for
    it to pass.

Sometimes inside I feel so alone,
It can happen even if there are
    many people around me,
It is just an empty feeling inside
    where sometimes no one can
    reach.

Sometimes inside I feel such deep
    love,
It is a close feeling as if I'm one
    with so many people,
It is a feeling I try to keep with
    me at all times.

Sometimes inside I feel so at
    peace with myself,
It is a satisfaction with who I am
    and what I do,
It is a comfortable time I enjoy.

Sometimes inside I feel like I'm
    sitting still,
It is a time of wanting to do
    different things,
It is the spirit which keeps me
    learning.

Sometimes inside I feel like there
    is something out there waiting
    for me,
It is knowing that I have an
    important job yet to do,
It is as if the things I am learning
    now are preparing me for my
    future.

Sometimes inside I feel God's
    arms around me,
It is as if the whole world is alive
    and bright,
It is a time I strive for, knowing
    that my faith is there always.

Sometime inside I feel—well who
    knows?
It is the way I learn, by trial and
    error, high and low,
It is life—an ongoing change of
    feelings and emotions.

William Craig Hathaway
WINDY
You are the wind.
I, a leaf.
You can be strong.
I, always weak.
You can be gentle as a breeze.
I'll still flutter as you pass the
    trees.
You go around obstacles.
Here, I'll remain still.
In the whirlwind you go round
And turn my life upside down.
Who knows what the eye of the
    storm sees?
Maybe lovers like leaves,
Tossed to and fro
Trying to catch hold.
Together we fight.
Afraid, we hold tight.
To eachother, we cling.
To see what love will bring.

Marilyn Mills Robertson
THIS BROKEN HEART

---

*This poem is dedicated to all the
lonely people in the world who
have lost a special person they
have loved. I just wish they all
could have one "Superman" in
their lives. It's better to have
loved and lost than to have never
have loved at all.*

Life isn't easy
It's hard as can be
Especially these days
When you're not here with me.

My heart holds the memories
of your precious face
Your beautiful smile
Our own special place.

The way that you held me
Your beautiful eyes
The talk I remember
My lonely heart cries.

A kiss and a promise
Is all that I had
I never imagined
It would turn out so bad

I think of tomorrow
And wonder and wait
Will I ever love you
Or is it too late.

You're gone in an instant

Like leaves in the wind
How will this broken
Heart ever mend.

George Linton Yearwood
TO CHLORIS

---

*Submitted by the author's brother
Charles in humble recognition of
a beautiful mind full of beautiful
thoughts.*

How like the sun you are fair
    Chloris
As like that star responsible for
    day
Consistent orb of heaven radiant
    bright
You too are steadfast and your
    transcendant light
Darkness dispels and blesses
    with new sight
I looked on woman and perceived
    but dust
Fashioned in mans image for his
    lust
But you dear Chloris, figment of a
    mind deceived
Substance of thought but your
    sweet name I breathed
And all of mortal fickleness
    relieved
Like as the reaper when the day
    is done
Gathers the bits incumbent on
    the field
So shall I glean when harvesting
    is o'er
And promise but fair Chloris I'll
    abhor
All women and sweet virtue
    evermore

Robert C. Houghton
BRAND NEW LOVE
It makes me laugh, and yet I cry,
To think you think I'm cheating,
You always look but never ask,
    what is this book I'm reading.
I start to speak, you turn your
    back,
What are you thinking of?
I tell you that this book I read is
    about my brand new love.

You say that you can't take it,
That it's tearing you apart,
You feel that I have used you and
    abused your loving heart,
But please give me a minute,
Just listen, please don't cry,
And let me please explain to you,
    I'm telling you no lie.

No lipstick on my collar,
No blonde hairs upon my shirt,
I insist that I am true to you, but
    you still are hurt,
My love for you has never changed,
It's the same as in the start,
It's just that now I've found
    someone to add into my heart.

Let's stop this silly childishness,
Jealousy and mistrust,
And let me again remind you
    that I love and do not lust,
Now let me please explain to you,
And we'll do the things that
    please us,
The book I read is The Bible, and
    my brand new love is Jesus.

Wilma Smith Howard
LIFE IS A VAPOR

*To my daughter Sharon Janeene
Howard of Norman, Oklahoma*

My, Oh My, how time does pass
Seems only yesterday I was a lass
When I was young, a year went
    slow
Now they all just seem to flow
From year to year not day to day
Then it is ten gone by the way
Another ten and then it's twenty
We think in this land of plenty
We have no need for anything
With youth and health we have
    our fling
Then before we can turn around
Suddenly we see we have a frown
The gray is creeping in our hair
We wonder how it got in there
Help us remember life is a vapor
And You will reward us for our
    labor
Forgive us Lord our youthful days
Lead us in Your loving ways
So we may finish out this life
With peace instead of sin and
    strife.

Gloria Georgia Hamil
BEING A TRUE FRIEND
Lord, please help me to be a loyal
    friend,
Never to criticize, just to
    comprehend,
A friend that is a friend in deed,
Never forgetting the worlds
    ceaseless need,

Please give me one day at a time,
Keeping me in stride with that
    will of Thine,
Perhaps as days come and go,
You will teach me specially to
    know,
The road to you some poor lost
    souls to show,
Peace, good will, friendship to
    bestow,
Lend to everyone a helping hand,
Teach them to pray and
    understand,
To strive for the best against
    great odds,
Never to give up, to see the silver
    lining through dark clouds,
Help me not to ask for love, but
    to give it and be kind,
To be able to cope with hardships
    everywhere that I find,
Let me be a volunteer, and do the
    work you want me to do,
To seek, to find what in life is true,
Please reveal to me my life's
    destiny,
Thank you for letting me be the
    friend you want me to be.

D. M. Borowski
MEANINGS
The words we use
    are never really ours,
but always
    part of someone else
    who passed thru our lives;
And though we seek
    to be original—
    older images and thoughts
    encircle us,

Rewording
to new sounds
meanings
still the same.

Mary Williams Franklin

Mary Williams Franklin
TIME
To everyone time is so deer
When there's something for us to
gain
But we never use it to shed a tear
For someone else in pain.

By the seconds, minutes, hours
we measure
When we're somewhere we don't
want to be
We think nothing of what others
treasure
Our own wants are all we see

Within us there's lots of power
To fill someone's heart with cheer
We cannot do it if it's more than
a hour
Something else will be missed we
fear.

We expect praise from those we
meet
And all that we require
Often though we hastily mistreat
Those providing us our desire.

We often use it as a reason
To refrain from doing a deed
And when we're caught in our
treason
We use it again to cover our greed.

Sometime we let it pass idly by
As we sit doing nothing on an
occasion
When we should be making an
effort to try
To help others without persuasion.

If we use it with the best of care
Along with kindness as we do
our best
There will be plenty left to spare
For that's the time of eternal rest.

Sandra Satuloff
LOVE IS . . .
When two are apart
You're never alone
When he is there
You sit on a throne
Feelings are shared
And a dream is confessed
Both are honest
You're feeling your best
Ignoring the weather
Stormy or clear

The two don't notice
As long as they're near
Walking down the beach
And viewing the sea
Laughing and smiling
Just being me
My hair is a mess
But he doesn't care
His love sees through me
Our relationship is rare
Love is sharing
And caring for
Love is this
And even more

Iain A. MacArthur
AUGUST MELODIES-II
O, come, awake my spirit with
the sun,
My daily plith of duty run;
Shed the dull sleep of night and
rise,
To pay for living-a sacrifice.
Remember the mispent years of
the past,
And live this day as if it were
your last;
Improve your talents with
accurate care,
For the final circle of life prepare;
Make all your conversations so
sincere,
Your thoughts, the brightness of
morning's clear;
Reflect on life's propitious rays,
In ardent love and joyous praise,
And with all bear your part,
So awake and lift yourself, dear
heart.

Tanya Lamb
CROSSING DIRECTIONS

*I dedicate Crossing Directions
first to God, then my parents
Nadja and Igor, my children
Veronica, Christine, and Julia and
lastly Bill and Pam who were part
of the driving source.*

You want to be needed
You need to be wanted
   Want without need
   Need without want is not to be
Come forth, come forth and listen
carefully
Ernest expectations require no
shame
In shame because of your
obligations
   I will not stand
Growth beneath the shadow my
soul will not tolerate
Steady sun, brilliance, fire and the
elements of my desire
Strength, a will to live command
my movements for the day
Again alone—but richer from the
duel experience
Touched by a kind hand, heart
felt demand
Grace blessed—and trace only is
left of footprints on rain soaked
field
Glimmering, gleaning the rays
penetrate
Heart beat slows then increased
beyond bursting comprehension
How I want to make love but do
not know how and can't

You must remain the pillar for
your dear
I must seek a place by my tree
beside fledglings three
Cast lots for time and
then . . . .
   perpetrate your way and my way
Seperately . . . . alone.

Robert A. Romero Sr.
EMMANUEL
E- for the example
   he has set for us

M-for the mulititude
   who give their trust

M-for man
   he created in love

A- for assistance
   we receive from above

N-how he nurtures
   every breath that we take

U- for his understanding
   in mistakes we may make

E- for entirety
   all life comes from him

L- for his light
   it will never grow dim.

Gregory Leon Beechaum
EXPRESSING MY LOVE
Love can be expressed by many
different ways,
But I only use one;
Just showing her my love day by
day,
And try to miss none.
This might prove my love always,
Until my life is done;
Love can also be as solid as stone,
And I feel that way by
expressions, alone.

Barbara A. Grant
OLD CARDS-OLD LETTERS
I look about this empty place
Silent, 'cept for my own thoughts.
Thoughts that bring to mind
Your old cards & old letters.

Cards & letters are all the "you"
I have left to hold, to touch, caress.
Occasions when I was
remembered.
Words penned for my eyes alone
to read.

Why didn't I destroy them?
Burn them? Just remove them
from my sight.
For how can I boast of being free
of you
As long as these still live.

My hands cradle the envelope,
As I draw you close to my heart.
Its warmth calms my despair, as I
Daydream recalling when you
gave this
Piece of yourself to me.

As years past, the paper cracks,
Ink fades, cardboard gets so brittle,
And words lose their power.

These assorted bits & pieces are all
I have to forever have—of you.

Bill Darvin Gregston
SOLITUDE
Solitude—Is there such a thing?
I the forest the birds do sing
In the city, noises it do bring
On a quiet night at the beach,

It is the tide making a speech.
Is there any solitude on this earth?
Only when God gives no new
birth.
Everywhere you look, creatures
run amuck;
Finding solitude, no one has such
luck
Can there be nothing where you
look?
So any hopes for it can be put on
a hook . . .

Nancy Lenita Hanks
PETER RECKELL
P. is for perfect, you are in every
way,
E. is for entertaining, I see it
everyday.
T. is for terrific, your #1 in my
book,
E. is for enjoyable, you've got that
special look.
R. is for radiant, you have a
beautiful smile,
To be alone with you, I would
gladly walk a mile.
R. is for rating, you are a perfect
"10",
E. is for emmy, in which I'm sure
you'll win.
C. is for casanova, the ladies love
your charms,
K. is for your kiss, please wrap me
in your arms.
E. is for Elliot, you look great in
those clothes,
L. is for lovable, you give a tingle
to my toes.
L. is for luscious, your lips are so
sweet,
You are a perfect "10" from your
head down to your feet!

Julie Ann Stolz
ALONE
Alone
I sit
   and listen to the
   waves crash on the
   rocks below.
Alone
I watch
   the children
   play happily
   in the street, wishing
   I were young again.
Alone
I walk
   through my
   empty house
   looking at pictures
   of my children who
   have long since
   moved away.
Alone
I remember
   their laughter
   filling the now
   empty halls.
Alone
I yearn
   for the days
   when I was not
Alone

Frank J. Seri Lt. Col. US (Ret)
OLD GLORY
Each night I pray
That dawn will see
That banner high
Still proud . . . . Still free.

Our World's Best Loved Poems

Jesse Lozier
The Other Side Of Winter

*To all the people who have
withstood the rigors of winter*

"First the foliage turns to golden
autumn colors
The trees start losing their
blanket of leaves
Soon they stand silhouetted in
their nakedness
At this time, I long for the other
side of winter.

Thanksgiving Day too quickly
comes upon all of us
Sure, its a time for feasting and
renewed family ties
but the cold days of winter are
not too far behind
At this time, I long for the other
side of winter.

Our busy Christmas holiday
activities make us forget
what lies in store for us in the
long days ahead
The goodwill and good cheer may
be short-lived
At this time, I long for the other
side of winter.

The endless days of January pass
ever so slowly
the gloves, the boots, the scarves,
are not always enough
to keep warm on these cold, cold
bitter days
It's then, I long for the other side
of winter.

Our heating bills catch up to us
in late February
some of us will pay for this till
next January
The winds of March remind us
that Spring is near
But even now, I long for the other
side of winter.

The rains of April promise a
new fresh beginning
then May arrives to help ease
those many pains.
We start enjoying the much
warmer days of Spring
We finally made it to, The Other
Side Of Winter."

Mike Schleimer
Until We Cry We'll Never Know

Until you lay down close beside
me
    you'll never know if my heart
    skips a beat
you'll never see how lonely I am
and you'll never fulfill my needs
no, you'll never sweep me off my
feet
Until you're walking close beside
me
    you'll never know how it feels
    hand in hand
you'll never know what I'm
reaching for
girl you'll never help me make a
stand
no, you'll never understand
until you try
    you'll never know how to keep
    me

cuz until you die
you can't let go completely
    so who's to say
    just walk away

when until we cry
    we never know we're feeling

Julie Ann Wiseley

Julie Ann Wiseley
Hold Me Tomorrow Too

Sweet the wind blows through
solemn leaves of yesterday.
Little does anyone know what
tomorrow shall hold,
When it becomes today.

We walk through the motions, In
a world of dreams and hopes.
Reality is only a rain on our
parade.

Together we share promises of
new and better things.
The surprises of the future
Will not fall short of our
expectations.
Love will survive as long as
friend has friend,
And the warmth is felt deep
inside.

Sunshine will spread, creating
rainbows on the plain.
Decorations of a storybook cover
That only holds the many secrets
within.

Snowflakes will sometimes
blanket our horizon.
Hidden contentment absorbed to
let release.

Time, the future, all so close, but
yet so far.
Wonderment, fear, hope.
It all moves too swiftly to be
understood.
Togetherness is rich in
carefreeness.
Always, forever, as long as we
share ourselves with someone
else.
Promises that drift along with the
wind.

Frances M. Roberson
DEATH WISH

My heart lies heavy in my breast.
The pain within me knows no rest.
My life is burdened; filled with
woe
God release my weary soul.
All hope is gone, all dreams
forlorn
How I wish I'd ne'er been born.

Strife and misery hold me tight
Lord relieve me of my plight.
Place your hand upon my hair
Return my spirit to your care.
Hold me eternally within your
hands
Free me from this world of mans.
Take from my body one last breath
Ease my sorrows with promised
death.
Share your sweet peace, give me
light
For I have lost the will to fight.
Call me home Lord, let me kneel
Forever at thy merciful heel.

Grace Charlotte Hansen
SEAWARD

*Written about a Danish Cadet,
aboard The Three-Masted
Schooner, Danmark.*

Not quite hidden beyond that
slope;
Held to bay by one strong rope,
My spirit swells and soars apart,
That boat's my life, her course,
my chart.
This rough brown hand has
touched the past
By knots, or sails; by anchor, mast.
Reflect the flash of sunlight from
the sail
Between our eyes there will prevail
A constant mist, a cherished
dream
Quite far from trees, dependent
on the seam.

Annette E. Jones Henning
NO LONGER YOU AND ME

I could tell when I first met you
that together we would be,
even when the earth ended,
when the sun fell in the sea.
When the clouds overcome
the world we now know,
blocking out, forever, the sun
and making it no more.
When the stars refuse to shine
so bright for we two,
then you'll no longer be mine.
That's when we'll be through.
When the rivers overflow
and the water covers the land.
When the moon suddenly goes
under
and darkness takes top-hand.
That's when we will end
and no longer will we be
together, my love, my friend.
No longer you and me.

Terry Guernsey
To a Sweetheart Like You

To a sweetheart like you
Which makes me feel brand new
Your love to me
Is like a leaf on an Autumn tree

Your kisses are lovier than a rose
Honey, my blood flows
You make me as cheerful as a
lark
While gaiting with you in a park

Your more beautiful than Niagara
Falls
Especially when giving me phone
calls
You always make me feel better

When you write me a romantic
letter

Ella Foster O'Brien
I'll Turn The Corner Of My Life.

I'll turn the corner of my life
    Back from all troubled times and
    strife,
Back to make my life worthwhile,
    There to find the tree worth of a
    smile

The corner I'll turn, with joy and
love,
    The voyage is long, when love is
    near,
The love of a family, is ever here.

The way has been long, down
thru the years,
    Filled with happiness, dispersed
    with tears.
The lessons I've learned, has
brought me joy,
    The little things I've learned
    each day
As down the path of life I've
walked
    The mountains I've climbed are
    steep and bold,
But the corner of life, I've found
at last
    Is the path to heaven, and joy
    untold.

Lidija Murmanis
FRESH SNOW

Over the last night
a white, downy blanket,
woven somewhere
between the heaven and earth,
has spread itself unselfishly
over everything and everywhere.

One cannot see
the crevices or other blemishes
on the earth's face anymore—
only a virginal beauty
and an utmost cleanliness.

I wish I would have
for myself such a loom
where I could weave
a white, downy blanket
with which to cover
the blemishes of my soul.

My soul then would be
as the earth's face
after the last night's snow
where the fresh tracks
I would let to be carved
only by joy and virtue.

Brenda Wood Williams
PATHS

*To Tom who gave me incentive.
This one's for you, friend.*

Familiar Paths
    Leading to Somewhere
    Were not always flower strewn.
    Mounting ever upward
    Steep—tortuous—But Known.
Foreign Paths
    Leading to Somewhere
    Some never bathed in light
    Descending from the Summit
    Leading into Night.
Friendly Paths
    Leading to Somewhere
    A place where we cannot go.

539

The path toward forever
Abandoned long ago.
Forbidden Paths
Leading to Somewhere
Rough, Rocky and Untried,
Narrow Now. Too Narrow
With no one at my side.
Forged Paths
Leading to Somewhere
Perhaps just 'round the bend
Traveled by others such as me
Looking for "Might Have Been."

Elizabeth Louise Huffer
I AM, OM
I AM the tempest on the water
when things move high and low.

I AM the laughter that plays
upon each crest
as I caress the Cosmic Sound.

I AM the Eternal as Life moves
on, man's
darkest abyss will respond.

The stillness of the deep will
bring forth
His Word,

Until all is Golden Sunshine,
until all
have heard His Word, the OM.

Susan Dorothy Barracato
**A Mother's Love
Remembered**
Our Mother, our friend,
our coach till the end;
A model of Mother Love.
You cared for us through
storms of all kinds
and still loved us
for having our own minds;
You taught us to love
and always be strong,
even when the road
seemed awlfully long;
You mended our hurt,
time after time
and taught us to love,
to forgive and be kind;
Oh Mother we'll miss you
because you have gone,
but the memories will never
cease in our mind;
For you were the best
that God ever made;
So I guess he needed you
to pave a new way.

Mark H. Miranda
TOGETHER
When my travels are over,
When my worries are through.
When the storm is gone,
And the sun shines anew,
When the sadness and heartaches,
Of this old world leave.
We'll be together again,
In eternal peace.
They'll lay me beside you,
where we both will be,
Together, forever and I'll miss
you no more.

Adela-Adriana Moscu
THE CRYSTAL LAKE
I gaze
Through crystal waters
Of the lake,
And I remember
All the times
We shared.
The witness

Of a love so great,
Our silent lake
is always there.
From time to time
I go and feel
its water
As once I felt
Your kiss
And your caress.
Its freshness
Gives me joy
And sends me upward
Toward the blue skies
Of the universe.

Cary Chrysler
MY KATHY
I'm the one who loves you,
hears the cry of your pathless
heart;
still with you in mine,
and lay with you in the bed of my
soul.
 I'm the one who loves you,
cries and aches at your leaving,
yet understands that leaving.

 I'm the one who loves you,
as through the fact of your being
with him,
can be seen the broken dream of
you and me.
 For I'm the one who loves you,
found so deep in you, the you no
one knows.

I'm the one who loves you,
listens, as tears break the silence,
to thunder, and a faded rainbow's
shattering.

 I'm the one who wishes like
a child, that again and always
you could once more
be
"My Kathy"
Rene Alberto G. Pina
MELANIE

---

*To Muse who inspired me
towards a poetic beginning. My
versified efforts are forever yours.*

You have those dancing eyes
and your elfin smile;
you are romantic lights,
pleasure, beguile . . .

You're my sweet butterfly,
dynamic and free;
fleeting life, bittersweet
—happy to live!

You are the joy of Spring;
the fresh morning air.
You were my everything
—now you're not there . . .

Know: I won't hold you down.
I just need you to see
my life's filled with emptiness:
you're not holding me . . .

I know, as a lover I
must share you with
a world that envisions full
freedom to reach.

Love is a choice we make.
I want you to be . . .
Love's not worth keeping if
not open and free . . .

Melanie, Melanie!
Melanie . . .

Frank E. Bubenchik
MY GUARDIAN ANGEL
Morally wicked, people tell
vicious lies.
Yielding to a supreme power, that
they should die.
Grace and style, no others can
take your place.
Unjustify to express in words,
your loveliness, is beyond the
human-race.
Annilating corruption and
discontentment without a trace.
Rough materials should not
touch your tender flesh only
fabrics of satin and lace.
Deception and depression in your
presence are erase.
Immortal are the alluring features
of your face.
Admiration for your appealing
personality is the root of envy
in your particular case.
Nimbus which surrounds your
being starts at the heart that is
its base.
Allievating the sorrows and greif
of the meek.
Nimble with your graceful
movements and your shapely
legs so sleek.
Gentle is the melody of your
voice and people listen,
whenever you speak.
Engaging the servants of hell and
deveating them where-ever
your person meet.
Luminious is your smile that
brings joy and happiness for
the weak.

Juanita Rader
A TREE FOR SALE
I was young not very tall
When a man came at me with a
saw
It wasn't long until I fell
He tagged me "A tree for sale"

On the tree lot folks came by
Some said, "that price is high
With the lights and other stuff
That tree's just not big enough

Then Janet and Bob came by my
way
And took me home that very day
They dressed me up with lights
and trim
Everyone admired me with a grin

They called their friends to come
and see
My name by then was Christmas
Tree
What a holliday they had
Each gift seemed to make them
glad

Days later Janet looked at me
And said, "I must get rid of that
tree"
It's standing there right in the way
After all it's had its day

Bob looked on me with quite a
frown
And said, "Yes it must come down
We don't need that tree anymore
It's beginning to shed all over the
floor

They undressed me and took my
crown

And hauled me to the outskirts
of town
It seemed the trash man wouldn't
take me
He wouldn't carry off Christmas
trees

I enjoyed my stay in their fine
home
Gosh it's tough to be here alone
I lie here on the city dump
What's left of me is called a stump

Esther Elisabeth LaSana

Esther Elisabeth LaSana
WILD ROYALTY
Standing with a silent statue's
grace
The great cat moves not from his
place.
His eyes gleam with a golden light;
Suddenly, he bounds to strike.
His form, that is so finely made,
Cuts the air like a silver blade.
His markings, wild as a fantasy,
Are those which few men ever see.
Into the brush he disappears;
A vision of a million years!

Bernadette George
TO GROW WITH LOVE
Love is strong and I am weak
I bow to Love and as I yield
Am swept away in loving grace
Through winds of strong and
forces great.

Love is strong and I am weak
To Love I give my hope, my life
For Love I weep, for Love I pray
Through Love I live, through
Love I play.

For Love is strong, I, too, must
grow
With Love I live my life complete
To shine as stars and sun above
Through dark and light, alike, I
glow.

Juanita Wallace
A Moonbeam In The Sky
Oh, how I would love
to reach way up high;
higher than mortal man
can reach and touch
a moonbeam in the sky.

I would love
for one fleeting second
to touch the brilliance
of it's glow
and feel the magical directions
it transmits
to nocturnal navigators below.

That silvery strand of light
tenderly guides my way

as I retire for the night.
On bended knees I bow to pray;
everthankful, dear God,
that You
blessed the sky
with a happy twinkle
from Your eye.

Susan Hansen
WHO'S ON FIRST?
The funniest gag I've ever heard
Was done by Abbot and Costello.
'Who's On First?' but he couldn't
   Understand
'Who' was the name of the fellow!

Yes, 'Who's on first' and 'What's
   on second',
'Tomorrow' is on the mound.
'I Don't Care' is playing third,
And 'Today' is the catcher they
   found!

Now, if all of this is confusing,
And you say, 'I Don't Give A
   Damn!'
Get ready for more frustration—
He's our shortstop man!

Oege Devries
PEOPLE BY A RIVER

---

*To my daughter Meg, and my
wife Cara*

Living artery; through ancient
      destiny
   of others like you
      long ago erased—
         you replaced.
      A beginning and end.
We stand upon which was
   defaced
Of ice and Earth's unstable crust.
So flow River as you must, and
   reach another sea.
As we stand beside your shore
Perceiving your beauty, and, as
   you flow
Of unknown mystery, to see and
   know
In time beyond, to meet again
Upon some different beautiful
   shore
Forever more perhaps, where
   change
Such as we know will be no more.

Lani Lynn McAllister
Does a Man Ever Think?
'Cause he works a whole day
   a man always thinks,
he has the right to stop in
   for a couple of drinks.

He never stops to think
   how his woman might feel,
sitting home all day
   with her kids at her heel.

"Mom, where's my baby?"
"Mom, where's my truck?"
"I can't find my shoes."
"Did you see my stuffed duck?"

All the little problems
   of running a house,
doesn't bother a man
   when he's out getting soused!

I wish for just once,
   the roles were reversed.
So a man could feel
   how a woman's coersed.

Melanie Burns
I AM FREE
I am high above the
   lowland
Higher than the valleys:
Up on the cool, summery
   mountain

Wild flowers sway in the
   breeze:
Wilderness calls

Trusting me
   I am free

Green grass, like a blanket of
   love over the earth
Blends the trees against
   the painted, purple-blue sky

Streams trickle down the
   sides of the valley below:
   stumbling across the gray,
   wet rocks

A colorful rainbow curves
   across and focuses on the
   sun
   sparkling on the still water
Looking;
Feelings;
I am Free

Barb Lein
VICTIM OF VIOLENCE
It takes time to love and trust
   again, after one has loved and
   lost time after time after time;

After one has believed empty
   promises and phoney, plastic
   dreams uttered only to impress
   with their emptiness.

Wanting to believe I was special
   and loved; discovering I was
   nothing more than a vicitm of
   violence.

Shar Cheaux
JUST RIGHT

---

*This poem was written to—and
inspired by, Al Perry, my
constant encouragement and
forever love.*

I love you,
hardly suffices.
Yet these three words,
resound so true.
If only I could adequately,
declare,
this soul encompassing passion,
for you.
Never visualized love,
rekindled.
Explosive flame,
flickering bright.
You've ignited a fire,
raging out of control.
I LOVE YOU sounds,
just right.

Dana Christopher
THE POET
I am the poet
I have no name
I live in the shadows
I cry with the rain
You never will see me
We never shall meet
My poems, though finished
Are never complete
I've so much to say

And so little time
I'm wasting away
Alone in my mind
I write of my sorrow
My joy and my shame
I write for tomorrow
Of yesterday's pain
My life is my rhymes
My reason to be
By reading my lines
You're reading me

Harvey Godin

Harvey Godin
Christmas Dream Song

---

*To my family and friends in
Rogersville N.B. Canada.—May
they find true happiness*

One day, I'll write a Christmas
   song
For all children to sing;
A song about a new-born child
And the world's greatest King.
A song that will bring happiness
To every girl and boy,
A song that will live in their hearts
And bring them untold joy.
I pray to live to see the day
When, come that Holy Night,
I'll hear these little "angels" sing
The song I'll surely write.

Hilda M. Jordan
THE CALIFORNIA MAN

---

*To Michael Jackson with love from
H.M.J., T.C.J., T.L.J., H.V.J., and
A.M.J.*

The C — Man stands for Courage.
The A — Man stands for
   Admirable
The L — Man stands for Lovable.
The I — Man stands for
   Interllectural.
The F — Man stands for Fun.
The O — Man stands for Order.
The R — Man stands for Right on.
The N — Man stands for Now.
The I — Man stands for
   Interesting.
The A — Man stands for
   Arrougant.
The California Man is Michael
   Jackson.

Wendy K. Clifton
Am I Ever Going To Learn
I am overwhelmed, feeling defeated
And Lord, I just can't take it.

You are my Fortress and
   Deliverer;
Without You I would never make
   it.

Another lesson is weakness
   experienced.
Am I ever going to learn
Worldly burdens are too heavy to
   carry?
You're the only place for me to
   turn.

Teach me to relinquish
Teach me to yeild
To the love of Your yoke
My Comfort, my Shield.

I will try again because You have
   shown
You are worthy, Lord Most High.
Take all the burdens on Your
   mighty shoulders;
Provide the strength for another
   try.

Jennifer Ann Byrne
SANTA CLAUS MAGIC
The Magic of Santa
Cannot be seen
So most of the children
Don't know what it means.

When children will look
And search all around
They do not know
Where this magic is found.

It's not found in a doll
or a new set of darts,
The Magic of Santa
is found in our Hearts!

Donna Lee DeMarco (DLD)
IN THESE EYES
They say that you live on in
   these eyes
In these eyes they say your spirit
   never dies.
Look into these eyes, they will
   tell no lies.

Looking into these eyes, they say
   that they see you.
When I look into these eyes now,
   I can see only you,
They live on in everlasting blue.
Our looks they say we shared,
   and that makes me feel even
   closer to you.
And it made it harder on me to
   lose you.
There's a special bond between
   twins and I felt somehow that I
   lost my twin.

Look into these eyes, they tell of
   my love as well as his.
He is not gone, he lives on, in
   these eyes and in this heart,
and in every other heart that has
   ever met his heart.
I ponder now on everything that
   these eyes have seen.
And I realize that each new
   sunrise is a smile sent down
         from Dean.

Leella Middleton
A CHILD
If you are looking for love
Look into the face of a child.
If you need a bit of cheer to
   eliminate despair

541

Listen to a child whispering
softly in your ear,
"Please do not give up, God loves
you and is very near."
Watch a child's eyes glisten with
a sincere glow.
A child like this is a great joy to
know.
Smile at a child and a smile will
come to you.
Sent by this child, his heart full
of love so true.
Since a child is God's creation
sent to bring—
Happiness and love is this world
so big,
I shall always love a child because
Of the wonderful treasure God
created—
A—child.

Marie L. Anderson

Marie L. Anderson
CHRISTMAS THOUGHT

*To my beloved husband, Robert
Ossian Anderson: Who abides by
this thought. Not only at
Christmas, but throughout the
whole year.*

When December comes, the
holiday season begins—
We think of our loved ones, we
think of our friends,
We think of the Christ child,
born in a manger of hay,
We think of the nations, who
celebrate Christmas, this way.

Shomehow! We have forgotten,
what true Christmas means—
We think of our needs, and
fulfilling our dreams.

The gifts, the parties, the
shopping to be done—
But very little thought, to the
less fortunate one.

Let us think of the hungry, the
poor and the cold—
The homeless, the friendless,
the sick and the old.
The men in the service, far away
from their home—
Think! How sad Christmas can
be, when: you are all alone.

Let us open our hearts, let the
Christmas spirit in—
For peace on this earth, and good
will to all men.
It would lessen the pain, of the
lost and forgotten—
With a card, or a letter, or a gift
for their stocking.

Let us think of others, "Be our
Christmas thought".
To live side by side, with no
wars to be fought.
May there always be laughter, no
sorrow or fear,
Not! Just at Christmas, but
throughout the whole year.

Chris Cordova
ALMOST TIME
I hope I hope I see some day
The hope for love I so much pray

The time when times will all
obey
The time when chimes in the air
will stay

The time when man and beast
aren't one
The time when man will kill the
gun

The time when love of love is
here
The time to dry up all the FEAR.

Linda F. Dukes
Set Me On Your Mantle
Harbor me from coldness
Savor me like wine
Set me on your mantle
Dust me let me shine.

Sail me on the water
Steer me with strong hands
Keep me safe from danger
Guide me back to land.

Hold me as a rose
Read me as an ode
Set me on your mantle
Together is our abode.

Viola C. Shiner
THANKFUL
I thank you God for all your
deeds
That help me with my daily
needs
Your blessings fall my way each
day
To help me send my cares away.

You show your sun on troubled
seas
Your moon draws pictures on the
trees
Stars that shine and glisten
bright
Helps me through the long dark
night.

Thankfully I kneel and pray
I listen Lord to what you say
Love thy neighbor be more kind
So I may bring you peace of mind.

For as I hold some weary hand
That I have met in travelers land
I know between that hand and
mine
Your presence weaves a strand so
fine.

T'was when my life of faith was
felled
My hope, in friends and foes
withheld
I felt your loving presence near
Restoring all that I held dear.

Smilingly through tear dimmed
eyes
I drink the splendor of your skies
No other hands but yours can
blend
The cares of troubled souls to
mend.

Dorothy Stevens
SIGNS OF LOVE
From the roof of heaven
Falls the rain.
The tears of angels
Washing the faces of
Flowers growing here.
And they in turn lift
Their faces to the sun
To be dried.
Like small children look
To their mothers for
Warmth and love.

Lisa J. McNeill
HAIKU
As the bird flew South
Along the onward path, once
Forever they sored

And glided along
To places untouched by the
Human uncaring.

James M. Learnard
MY SWEETHEART
My sweetheart is a loved one
in a way that only she can be.

She is close to my heart
and is held so very dear.

She is a source of love
that is constant and deep.

She is the object of my love
which grows deeper day by day.

She is a treasure
more precious than any jewel.

For she adds joy to my life
and she means so much to me.

But most of all, she is a friend
and my sweetheart is you.

Douglas F. Sheaffer
MOUNTAIN MEMORY
Fog smokes from hidden valleys,
rushing upward, silent
whipping higher and higher,
thinning into gray streaks
soon lost in the clouds.

Wind breaks through the sky,
scattering, chasing
dark shapes toward the horizon;
shapes we saw when children:
bears, horses, dragons.

Light strains behind the
mountains,
reflected brilliance
silhouettes broken peaks
where trees are stunted
and snow is constant.

Elk herds stir, shuffle
in circles, defensive,
and morning explodes!
The winter sun cannot warm,
and chilled air prevails.

Julia D. King
When You Need a Friend

*This poem is dedicated to my
parents, Calvin and Jeannette
DeRoche, who instilled in me a
deep faith in God.*

Things get better
When you hope and pray,
And believe in your God
Every single day.

Just open up your heart
And give it all to Him,
Your troubles, and your sorrows,
Let Him be your friend.

He wants you to know
That He is always near,
To carry all your burdens
And handle all your fears.

So when you're upset,
Can't find a way out,
Give it to your God
And He'll help you out.

Selina Marie Ellis
PERHAPS

To Mike, with love

I lost it all
Everything that made me unique
was gone
It was different; it was special
It was full of joy, full of sorrow
So very full
Nothing stayed behind
My writing, my music, my love
They were all such a big part of me
I wasn't living
I was just existing
All had left me

But something is stirring within
me
It's a very warm feeling deep
down inside
Out of reach
The life inside of me
Perhaps it will overpower me
Perhaps I will be whole again
Perhaps it will be soon
Perhaps

Dana Davis
MAN

*To my Husband Ron who has
given me his precious gift of
endless patience, understanding
and Love*

What a strong Man it must take;
to stand so proud even when it
aches.
Can't scream or cry because

they'll laugh at you, nor tell
them your afraid some will call
you a fool.
Never hug a Friend when he's
going away, just shake his hand
and pretend its okay.
Don't come straight home to your
wife, gotta let the boys know
who runs who's life.
Work all day with calloused
hands, still not enough pay the
Bills demand.
Just when you think you've
proved your worth, someone
kicks you in the Ego hoping it
hurts.

Yes what a strong Man, I know
you are, this role you must
play, has left its scar.
I look over at you asleep in your
chair, and I wonder if you do,
really care.
There so alone, exhausted again,
no one but me knows your too
tired to give.
My Man, My Boy, My Baby, God
help him he just wants to
live.

Debbie Mancuso
THE DEATH OF A DOLL
When I was young and so very
small, my mother gave me a
beautiful doll.
She had blonde hair and eyes of
green, the prettiest doll I have
ever seen.
Well, I loved my doll all day and
night, I never, ever let her out
of my sight.
She was my company when no
one else was near,
She was my friend and she was so
dear . . .

But, then I grew older
and didn't need her,
for no longer was I small . . .
If was a sad thing, and
I will always remember,
    THE DEATH OF A DOLL . . .

Kristi Hoffman
ENDLESS WATERS
We have shared a part of our
    lives
    a part of our souls together,
You are a part of me I can't let go
and can share with no other.

We have sailed the Ship of Love
    thru
    our Ocean of Hopes and Dreams
And by the strong Current of
    Desire
    will it bring them to reality.

We have sailed thru our Ocean of
    Troubled Waters
    with its mast-torn battles and
    mutinies
But with love we can mend our
    tears
    and melt our hearts as one.

Time has passed, and one too
    many
    mistakes have been made
We sail the Sea Apart, but never
    Alone
    for the part of you in me shall
    remain always.

Marie E. Tyburec
UNITLED
You live for this,
    don't you,
he said
as he held me
bare-breasted
and shirtless
against him;
his eyes warm and brown
    and soft
as they only were
    for me.
And I held him
tightly back,
smiling, tears in my eyes,
feeling the cold snaps
of his shirt
against the warmth
of my breasts;
pulling him tighter to me
exulting in the roughness
    of the cloth,
    the warm hugeness
    of him
chafing the softness of me
He pulled me to his chest
and warpped me,
aching, taut and warm
against him.

Roberta Trochelman Pence
RAY

*To Ray, through whom God
taught me that when we reach
the end of one road: to remember
that it is also the beginning of
another.*

Ray, Ray, God blessed me today.
He sent you to teach me how to
    live again.
And Ray, I love the way
    you have shared with me the love
    you have within.

Ray, Ray, I need to say
thank you for teaching me to
    smile once more.
And Ray, in this very first day
I have smiled with you as never
before.

Ray, Ray, joy floods my heart.
The next thing I know I'm
    laughing aloud.
And Ray, your blanket of love
has replaced the cold, ragged
    shroud.

Ray, Ray, one golden day
I will be free to truly love you.
Then Ray, the guards will slip
    away;
I will love you freely as I long to
    do.

Gladys Whisman
HARVEST
A little seed in fertile ground
A bit of water sprinkled 'round,
And then with care the seed may
    be
A flower, a vine or a tree!

The seed may be a tiny thought
Tossed about in the vacant lot,
Of someone's mind, unlikely soil
That thought will grow thru
    someone's toil!

How wonderful to watch it grow
Words of love you carefully sow,

Until the harvest full of grace
In Christ will find it's resting
    place!

Sally A. Montantes
Daddy Don't Ever Go Away

*To My Loving Dad Alex LoCascio
Thanks for the Memories*

Summer days and walks at the
zoo, chewing on popcorn and
being with you. Riding my bike
and falling down, finding you
there always around. Growing
up, being on my own, finding
new friends to call on the
phone. But when alone I always
say, daddy don't ever go away.

Jean Lambert Herman
THE SOUNDS OF NIGHT
Have you ever listened as you lie
    in bed
To the sounds of night that fill
    your head?
A cricket chirping by the wall
The Grandfather clock as it ticks
    in the hall.
The softest whisper of a breeze
Dancing merrily through the trees.
There's the constant croaking of
    a frog
With the distant howl of a lonely
    dog.
Shrill whistle of a racing train
Soft pit-a-pat of a summer rain.
The steady beating of your heart
Reminds you that your just a part
Of all the things that sound so
    right
When daylight lengthens into
    night.

Donna Lorraene Newell
THE CHRISTIAN

*For my dear friend, Hazel Riley,
who believes as I do, and who's
conversation inspried this.*

Me, Born again? No, Sir, I'm not—
    I'm just a Christian who
Can not remember one full day
    He did not pull me through!
I loved Him as a little child—
    I knew He was my King—
I knew He suffered on a Cross
    To pay for everything
That I had done or ever would
    Across the span of years,
And so my life has been a joy
    And free of most men's fears!
So do not ask that I now change
    And become born anew,
For Christ has always been my
    Friend!
    And my dear Saviour, too!

Shelva J. Carron
HAND IN HAND
Walking, hand, in hand, the
    golden leaves, falling from the
    trees,
Awaiting us at home, is a, turkey
    dinner, as of thanks given,
    there, at, my, insperation. They
    make me smile and laugh, with
    joy. They comfort me when
    sad, they will always be in my
    heart if not hand, in, hand,

They art my soul pleasure, by
    just being near. The warmth,
    and loving, moments, will
    never cease with years.

Valerie Ann Nelson

Valerie Ann Nelson
YOU
Dreaming of you
As I go through each day
Think of you
In that one special way.

Are we right for each other?
Is the question I ask.
The only answer I give is
I hope that we last.

You're different from others
You're gentle and sweet
You're just the kind of guy
I like to meet.

As we are here together
My love for you comes out
I hope that you can see it
And keep it close to your heart.

Shirley A. Munsinger
CHRISTMAS 1983
The Christmas season reigns again
With bright green holly and
    candy cane
The manger scene in the square
    is alight
Once quiet is broken on this
    Christmas night
The crowds of people gather
    around
While snowflakes flutter to the
    ground
Old freinds stop by to wish you
    well
Singing Silent Night and Jingle
    Bells
The stars are beckoning from
    above
As God fills everyone's heart
    with love!

Ginny Henry
HOMEWARD BOUND
You gave me life and you gave
    me love
Said you'd never leave or forsake
    me
There's no place on earth I could
    go
Even if I make my bed in hell
Behold thou art there

You placed eternity in my soul
A craving for something more
    when life is over
Made my mind to think your
    thoughts

To know by experience your
own heart
Open to anyone who will
believe your word

I'm so grateful for your love and
your son
For all that you've given
One day I'll fully comprehend
That I've been saved and healed
When Christ returns to take me
home

But for here and now we have
each other
Your beloved family here on
earth
Against whom the gates of hell
cannot prevail
The greatest gathering this side
of heaven
Walking together and standing
on your word

Stewart Austin Cooper
NOT ASKING
I'm not asking
that you fly
around the world.
I'm only asking
that you fly across
a state and one-half.
Here you'll see:
majestic mountains,
tumbling streams,
flashing trout,
swaying pines.
Don't you think
it's time we met?
After forty years,
you'd have no regret.
I've fixed a room for you—
cozy and warm,
with fireplace,
fragrant flowers
and western art.
So, I'm not really asking,
just wondering on paper,
if you'd fly out
for a "crack" at trout.

Lucille M. Gilpin
THANKSGIVING
Thankful:
To greet each new pink dawn
with a cheerful "Good Morning,
Lord".
To feel forgiven with just one tug
on my Heavenly umbilical cord.
To don my attitude of patience,
service and humility.
To consistently apply Christian
Love with sincerity.
To accept my daily assignment,
whatever the task.
To know there is strength and
direction, whenever I ask.
To meet problems as growing
pains to add a human inch.
To acknowledge God's discipline,
and smile but never flinch.
To do all I can to smooth the
road for my fellowman.
To lay the rest at His feet for
surprize solutions as only God
can.

Eugene Fletcher
THE EVE OF CHRISTMAS
The fireplace burning brightly
The Christmas tree all aglow,
The hustle and bustle of
wrapping gifts

Each with a brightly colored bow.
The smell of baking from the
kitchen
Filling the air with spices and
sweets,
The stockings hung neatly on the
mantle
Waiting for Santa to fill them
with treats.

The children full of anticipation
Waiting for Santa to arrive in his
sleigh,
Oh what joy and celebration
When they awake on Christmas
Day.

Ruthie L. Williams
**Let More Of the Son Shine
In**

---

*To my mother, Annie Lewis, for
the inspiration I received from
the reflection of the Son shining
in your life.*

Walking and talking along life's
highway
Living and loving your fellowman,
Days are brighter and easier, when
You open up your heart and let
more of the SON shine in.

The stars give light and the moon
does too;
and nights are darker than day.
Words of cheer will produce a
grin,
But joy is full, when you let
more of the SON shine in.

God grants us each day to live
Our lives to the fullest,
Though we may grope in
darkness from time to time,
But light comes to us when we
let more of the SON shine in.

So take hold dear child of God,
To the light that leads the way.
Darkness will vanish around you,
when
You open up your heart and let
more of the SON shine in.

Raymond C. Lockhart
THANKS DAD
You raised me from a baby
To what I am today.
You helped me cope with
problems
And make them fade away.
For eighteen years you taught me
How to work and how to play.
Since I left no day goes by
That I don't think of you some
way.

I'd like to let you know
Your job was quite well done.
We had alot of trouble
But we had alot of fun.

There's something I must tell you
Something you might not
know.
It may be hard to notice
Cause it doesn't always show.

It isn't said enough
Which makes me feel bad.
Thanks for putting up with me
P. S. I love you Dad.

Joseph S. Haak
AN AUTUMN DAY
Tis a dreary night,
Search as I might,
There can be no delight,
With the weather outside,
It is foggy and gray,
And say what you might,
If the clouds would go away,
It would be a perfect day.

George Fredrick Wise

George Fredrick Wise
MAGIC CARPET

---

*To all the little children, all over
the world*

I have a magic carpet
All green and gold
We fly to the heavens above
And to the land of snow
To mountain tops
And unknown stars

And to the sea below
We ride the big white whale
And up with the wind we go
We ride the sails of mighty ships
And ride our way back home.

Nancy E. Morris
FOREVER IN TIME

---

*To Larry who gave me the gift of
sight into what can be-Now and
Tomorrow*

Dimensions of time and space
Moving easily through the gray
light
Searching for the place of each
desire
Many forms yet to take hold

Each giving and taking in its own
way
For our days never end
There's always tomorrow and a
new
Life to begin
Time is irrelevant to those who
know
The dimensions of time and
space.

Midge Russell Murray
PSYCHIATRY OF NATURE
Just sitting on a stump, listening
to the breeze,
Saw a rabbit jump then scamper
through the trees.
Fir boughs filter sunlight down
on my head
And tonight their piney needles
will make me a bed,
Then I'll watch the silvery
moonlight
Chase shadows 'cross the night.

I watch a brown leaf floating
down the stream,
Drifting with the current,
swirling right along;
Part of my subconcious, adding to
my dream,
And in the heart of me adding to
my song.

Somehow a peace descends and
helps me sort my thoughts.
The weight of daily care departs
and lets me sing again.
Helps me find a way to solve
what seemed such heavy lots.
This quiet, friendly place; this
ferny, wooded glen
Removes me from the world and
brightens up the day,
Lets me see as I should see and
drives my fears away.

William D. Bosworth
SONG FOR A WARHORSE
Aback the mare the gallant road
A sturdy horse for a heavy load
Caparisoned in yellow and red
A single feather on her head
Her knightly load, plumed and
mailed
T'would meet with death if her
gallop failed

Spurs cut flesh as trumpets blaired
T'was the time for those who dared
Muscles tightened: She shook
and nayed
Twisting saddle but rider stayed
Fiercely then She upped and reared
The time of truth now had neared

She thundered on toward low
walled lane
Readied for the wrenching pain
Hooves beat down on hard
packed soil
The wall to skirt or all would spoil
She closed the lane square and true
Espied her foe regailed in blue

A mighty stallion without demure
Intentions rider ought deter
His lance was layed across her
back
Stayed with shield, glove and
rack
She lathered quick! Her nostrils
flaired
Desire and need with rider shared

544

She pounded on toward point of
truth
Familiar since her days of youth
As reins went taut she matched
her foe
Eyes caught fire, a fearful glow
Hooves cut deep, t'was all or no
The fear she knew would never
show

The riders met with crash and
thud
Bridle cut! her mouth was blood
Strap rips belly, knee gnaws flank
Her leathers pull with vicious
yank
Held back in charge her fores
claw air
A splinter, sharp! blood mats her
hair

A mighty lunge, her riders free
But horsed, alive, with victory?
She stumbled then steedied,
found her count in one stride
Yes, sure that her gallant still did
ride
As she passed the lane the cheers
rang clear
But for the foe or gallant dear?

A draw on reins did cause her to
stop
Halt then turn for the rider on top
She eyed the lane; no beaten foe
there
Further on was the blue of the
evil pair
To the lane again glancing she
snorted and shook
Another charge to be laid on the
book
Rider
Rider leaned forward to twice
rent ear
Close, that only she could hear
"Calm thee fair steed"
"Tis just another blow this devil
doth need"

Barbara Jane De Wein
IN VICTORY'S SWEEP
In Victory's Sweep we fly this night
Neath starry scape canopy bright

Across the Mystic soft winds blow
In Saturation's light we flow

To all our flights depart us lest
We salute the Noble Quest

Remember times and places
strange
And love the life that's drawn to
change!

Chloia Stuntz Heyde
Mother's Gingham Apron
My Mother's gingham apron
Was not for style or show;
There were no special patterns
With bright designs aglow.

She chose the apron gingham
Of checked brown, blue or gray,
and "made it up in no time"
I often heard her say.

There were no "nice" fancy curves,
No ruffles to arrange,
No appliques to fasten,
No rickrack, for a change.

It was gathered at the belt
That tied so neat behind;
And hemmed in at the bottom

As straight as you could find!

There was the little pocket
Remembered all my years;
There's where she kept the kerchief
To wipe my childhood tears.

My Mother looked so lovely,
In those days long since gone,
As she stood in the doorway
With her gingham apron on.

Kay Martin
When You Open Your Eyes In The Morning
Thank the Lord for the brand
new day,
Thank Him that you're able to
pray,
Look around you—ponder awhile,
How many times are you going to
smile?

Whose burden will you try to
lighten?
Whose dark corners will you
brighten?
Say God's Morning to all around
you,
Especially those you love and are
bound to.

Look in the mirror, what do you
see?
God's image, looking back at thee.
He put us here to share His
creations,
Not to fight among all nations.

Just start with one hand-shake,
pass it along,
Its warmth will increase what's
right from wrong,
Reach out to those who are
depressed,
Let them know—life's not a mess.

Lift the clouds of doubt—who
wonder why
We are here on earth and have to
die.
Share with all, your comfort, your
love
Then, at days' closing, PRAISE
HIM ABOVE."

Christina Marie Hoover
THE DOLL AND THE BEAR
and there he sat, along with all
the others-
fuzzy and brown, with sad brown
eyes.
I cried with him, yelled at him,
once even threw him into a paper
shredder-
but he stayed with me and
refused to be shredded.
He was my best friend; my worst
enemy,
and I would've been lost without
him.

Now that I don't need him
anymore, he spends day after
day
gathering dust-with all the other
dolls and animals.

He doesn't come to tea parties
anymore,
he doesn't help me make mud
pies anymore,
he doesn't come to bed with me
anymore to scare away the
goblins.

he just sits with the old doll.

She has coarse hair from a
million shampoos, a stained
face
from makeup, food, and dirt.
She still looks at me through her
transparent glass eyes
blue as the sky.
Her eyelashes are falling off, and
one finger is gone.

I got her fourteen years ago.

Her and teddy stuck by me, never
questioning me, never
complaining,
even when I smeared their faces
with red lipstick, gave them
haircuts, or shoved slimy M&M's
into their mouths.

How would I feel if I were them? I
wouldn't stay with me.
But, I guess they still hope that
someday I will come to play,
three feet high, with stained
overalls and a broken china cup.

Jordean Pritchard

Jordean Pritchard
WHO AM I?
I have seen the days of my
youth—
They have come, and now are
gone.
They were good days—
I did many things and enjoyed life.
But now that the days of my
middle years have more than
settled in,
I find myself asking—"Who am I?"

I am not that young girl anymore,
I do not look like her;
I cannot do what she did;
Yet—I am an attractive, mature
woman.

One who has much to offer— for
I have lived, loved, and learned
many things.
Therefore, the quality—
If not the quantity—
Of the years that are left to me
Is to be better than those of my
youth.

I will reach out to the dreams of
my youth
And grasp a firmer hold;
Knowing this shall be my goal—
What I did not attain unto then,
I can reach out for now;
For today is still out in front of me,
And mine for the taking.
I am now mature enough to
handle those dreams,
And wise enough to know
That whatever I accomplish,
He has ordained it—
And it shall be so.

Barbara Carol Dreibus
CHILDREN
Children-they know not black
from white
nor blind from sight;
the red, the yellow child,
they are all free and wild.

Children-taught like you and me
that all men must be free;
to believe in what they learn,
to strive for the goal they yearn.

Children-innocent babes of life
of all the griefs and strife;
of a world they long to know
yet, so far must they go.

Children-have so much to give
to the world in which they live;
love and laughter, brightness
and cheer,
the joys of living a life so dear.

Mc Wallace Braxton
I Love Miss America!

*This poem is delightfully but
seriously dedicated to Miss
Vanessa Williams and all other
aspiring young, gifted, and black
Americans and non—Americans.*

I love Miss A'Mer'I'Ca!
    She's sensatinal
    She's controversial
I love Miss A'Mer'I'Ca!
    She's the star attraction
    She's a young woman of much
    action
I love Miss A'Mer'I'Ca!
    She's the epitome of charm and
    grace
    She's got a shapely figure with
    a pleasant, pretty face
I love Miss A'Mer'I'Ca!
    She's got long, shoulder length,
    auburn hair
    She possesses large, expressive
    green eyes along with her other
    features fair
I love Miss A'Mer'I'Ca!
    She's as keen as she is sweet as
    an apple pie
    She's enchanting and
    irrestistable to any man's eye
I love Miss A'Mer'I'Ca!
    She's very much in demand and
    not so easy to book

She's a native New Yorker from a small town called Millbrook
I love Miss A'Mer'I'Ca!
She's a real to life "supergirl" or "wonder woman" to see
She's a music major at Syracuse University
I love Miss A'Mer'I'Ca!
She's the first of her kind to hold such a fabulous "name"
She's really quite modest despite her notoriously widespread fame
I love Miss A'Mer'I'Ca!
She's Vanessa Williams whose ambition is Broadway
She's the talk of nearly every town, the photographer's delight, and the current history for today!

Mother
Tina Marie Chagra
BEAUTY IN A ROSE

We (your children) would like to dedicate this thought to you Mom: our beautiful mother. As one great woman used to say: we (your children) love you too much!

There is beauty in a sunset
Beauty in true love
Beauty in a rose
Heaven's beauty from above

But there's a special kind of beauty thats very dear to me
It's the beauty that I feel way down deep inside of me

It's for a special lady one thats truly like no other
She's a sparkling gem of courage
She's my much adored, loved mother

She's made a happy home, for my brother, sisters and me
She's helped us, loved us, and kept us warm its surely plain to see:
God is great he's wonderful; he's given us the best
And everytime I think of you, Mom I know I'm truly blessed.
N. E. Holland
A GODLY VISIT
Too much coincidence for good must be God,
And reasons to the contrary urged by the unwary
March on unmoving feet mired

in the sod.
T'is truly wondrous how he does work
His everlasting will to be done
Through the stars and the sun,
Through signs both mystic and arcane,
Through strange ambivalent forks
Of life, to the unlettered and urbane
Alike. And snowy, chilly skepticism
Melts in ease and peace that stuns one
As demi-gods of doubt, so loudly profane,
Cower, shiver and scatter in exorcism.

Misty Tennant
YOU ARE
You are the memory,
of all my dreams.
You are what wasn't,
and all that seems.
You were the wishes,
that didn't come true.
You were my hopes,
so small and so few.
You were the stars,
that faded away.
You were the rainbow,
that didn't stay.
You were the ship,
that passed in the night.
You were the answer,
that wasn't right.
You were my castle,
that crumbled to sand.
You were a butterfly,
that couldn't land.
You were the rain,
that destroyed my sun beams,
You are the memory,
of all my dreams!

Kevin Francis Burgoyne
COSMIC FRIEND
I wanna die/so I can be alive
I wanna live/til theres no more to give
death is warm/ live is cold
I'm gonna die so I never get old
To live is everything I'm told
Live until your old; its just a story they were sold
How do they know what it is to die; did they give it a try
Alive is just hells strife/and death is always a part of live

Live is not destinies end
When you die into your destiny then you'll ascend
And thats where you'll find your cosmic friend
At lifes end.

Lillian Kelly
SPRINGS RETURN
I wait for spring impatiently every single year
For the winter season palls with March and brings
The same old fear
Could I trust the memories of the seasons that were gone?
Were the beauties of it I recall truly natures sweetest song?
So at first warm breeze that fans my cheek
I wait with bated breath

Was it as soft with promise and as gentle a Caress?
As remembered from those former years
That had stirred my heart with yearning
To know once more springs magic touch
And the thrill of its returning
As it brings with it refreshing rain
And the slowly warming sun
That coaxes forth those first green buds
A sure sign it has begun
Ah yes, I find it just as full
Of those lovely stirring things
That the pregnant earth in giving birth
Its beauties to us bring
Nancy E. Morris
Searching and Finding

To the man who loved me the most as a person and woman. To him I say this—

As I look out over the world
I can see your face everywhere
Your smile blossoms like a flower in spring
Your walk is that of the wind
Swift, strong, bold and going somewhere
Your touch is gentle and soft
Like the purr of a kitten.

You run up and down meadows
In and out of trees; but where
I run after you but never reach you.

I long for you on cold winter nights
When the fire is bright and crackling
And when snow is falling lightly.

I sometimes think I hear you calling
But when I went to find you, you were gone
Someday I will reach you and you will reach me
Then our life together will begin.
Michael Radford
LATE NIGHT WALK
You walk along a country road late at night, only the moon to light the way, the wind blows rustling the leaves, a couple drift slowly to the ground

You hear a dog barking in the distance, you feel the gravels under feet and smell the cool, fresh, autumn air

Nothing seems to disturb the silence
till suddenly you hear foot steps behind you, you turn quickly, no one's there

You go on, a little more cautious again you hear them, only closer, again
no one there, you think "should I run"
of course not, it's only the wind

You go on, watching step, breathing
hard, heart pounding, and suddenly

out of the dark a cold rush of air
a hand is suddenly on your shoulder!

Hope Le Mar
THE WARNING
A hand writes in the sky, then is still.
An awsome silence enshrouds the hill.
The heavens open, roaring, and a flame,
Traces in fire the Master's name.

Some who saw the vision laughed, some cried.
Some remembered the one who was crucified.
But the unbeliever scoffed and said,
"That visions not real" as he turned and fled.

Then the earth shook, and the mountains fell.
Sinners cried at the thought of hell.
The children of God, yes, they cried too.
'Twas the end of the world, this they knew.

Then a silence, all the world stood still.
As the silvery moon came over the hill.
The heavens parted, and we saw once more,
A finger pointing to a golden door

From that vision the whole world knew,
The world must change, or the world is through.
The warning came, but man heard it too late.
Now this earth must share Atlanta's fate.

Constance Schneider
ROUND IS MY SON

To Chuka: of my life and of my love

Round is my son, round and whole
a filled brown warm circle that I hold and fold
into the bosom of my mind
and feed at round nipples of breasts that grow and glow and halo
his life in my eye. My soft eye
curls round his hair in regaining and re-winning
waves of motherhood

Round is my son. I will hold him in my arms
tight against my need for his life in my world
His round mouth and curving tongue press his hunger
for growth, for learning, for life into strong round fists
and draw comfort, pleasure, lessons and life
from my softness

Round is my son. I smooth my fingers
round the curve of his arm to the circle of dimple

and fruitlessly grasp at his mystery
in the blinding nearness
as his tiny brown fingers grasp
  my warm hand
His soft, patting studies of his
  mother's face
poke a probing interest into my
  breath and sight
I inhale him, taste him and feel
  his waving explorations
through my flesh, and to my
  womb,
and in my round smile

Round is my son

Nina Niu
AFTER THE WAR

*To my mom and dad, Mike and
Lily; My sister, Grace; and all my
friends*

One flower,
All alone,
Standing sentry
Over bodies prone.
The smell of death,
In the air.
The thought of which
I cannot bear.
The flower's wails
Are not unheard,
The anguished weeping
Of the bird.
All this mourning
Is rightly for,
The tragic ending
Of the war.

Bernadette J. Guy
COLOUR
It's sad to see that the color
  of a persons' skin
Will make a difference to whether
  or not he'll be your friend.
To me the color is all the same.
A person is a person
  and nothing will change.
So, whether red, yellow, black or
  white,
  that person will be my friend
  and
  that's the way it will always be.
Yet, some people just don't
  plainly see, and therefore look
  down their noses at me.

Cleveland Calvin Matchett
Food & Fellowship— Viking Style
At Odin's Spring Festival each
  noble guest
Sat at a banquet table dressed
In skins and furs. Eric was in
  mood best
For noisy laughter, backslapping,
  and jest
With friends who recalled past
  conquest.

Each quest drank mead heartily
  from his cup.
Eric's voice, loud and gruff came
  alive with abrupt,
Haunting stories. His ruddy face
  appeared
Behind red hair, long, thick
  mustache and beard
Surrounding his sparkling, savage
  eyes
Which outward peered to surmise

Heavy muscles that expanded
  and reared
As he savored mutton and honey
  endeared.

Then as the Greenland
  celebration ending neared,
Leif sat by Eric's side, nothing he
  feared—
For soon the son of Eric would
  surely be
Launched into manhood to prove
  himself as a sea
Adventurer. Thus, Leif raised first
  the
Cup of Promise while the hall's
  glee
Was hushed to hear the young
  man's vow
To make a voyage to Norway
  somehow.

H. Sue Boer
A REAL CHRISTMAS
As I grew to find my own way
From my home I had to stray.
Each Christmas brought a tearful
  longing
To feel again, the love I felt so
  strongly.
As the teardrops fill my eyes again
I remember, a family gathered
  within
Where we all thanked God-in our
  own way
For all the closeness we felt that
  day.
This year Christmas won't be the
  same,
For these tears are filled with joy.
The waiting and longing will
  soon go away.
After all the paths I had to roam,
This Christmas—I'm going home.

Karen Dean Livingston
SHADES OF BLUE
Blue-green are the oceans,
Sparkling blue is the sky.
Such beautiful colors
That they dance in my eye.

A rainbow of colors
God created from high,
But black is the shadow
As I whisper "goodbye".

Goodbye to the love and
All the laughter we shared.
Now blue's not a color,
But a feeling I've faired.

A rainbow of colors
I no longer can see,
And so dark is the heart
That now lingers in me.

Donna Raymond
A Gift Of God's Love

To all my loved ones

Here they come, there they go
Hither and yon, to and fro
Seeking pleasures they can't find
Trying to fulfill a peace of mind.
Having troubles, having joys
Sharing things that this employs
Never satisfied, never sure
Of all God's gifts that are so pure.
Rivers and streams, mountains
  and skies
Walking things, crawling things,
  beautiful butterflies

Flowers that are blooming, the
  lowly toad
Weeds and bushes by the side of
  the road.
Just watching and waiting and
  wondering why
Everything seems to be passing
  them by
Maybe some day their hearts will
  be light
And they'll be thankful as they
  go to bed at night
They were able to hear and able
  to see
A part of the world that is our
  country
Then they will have peace and
  contentment again
For this is "A gift of Gods love" to
  every man.

Liz Carter Richards

Liz Carter Richards
GRAMPS
Quaint
Disorinated
Wandering
Tangled mind
Trembling blind
Until death
Is met—
The last rose
Wilting
With movement
Of wind
Fighting
An end.

Janis L. Dushaw
Father, This Time I'm Thankful For
T. This time, Father, I am
  thankful for these things:
    Trains, boats, copters, ferries,
    ships and planes
H. Having never been on
  anything with real wings—
    I can appreciate 'em in this
    age of deep strains.
A. As far as angels, awesome
    answers and all asking
    Are all awonderful blessings
    we're granted to share.
N. Needing a way to express
    God's love of which I'm basking
    Nicely in-because *we all* need
    someone for us to care!
K. Kneading His Knowledgeable
    protection in my life
    Until I realize How
    noticeablely He keeps me going.
S. Saving, Sprinkling, sparing—
    His love to us—His Holy wife

Saviour's Special selection of
  love that's overflowing!!

Alice Lu Cornelius
RECOVERY
Depression bound me; deep I sank.
  I knew not what I fought.
My mind was dark, my moods
  were black.
  Thought followed murky
  thought.

Nightmarish dreams so
  terror-filled
  Began to overtake.
The hours of fear, the sleepless
  nights—
  Why me did God forsake?

A ringing phone, a stranger's knock
  So filled my soul with dread.
I wished to live and yet I yearned
  To be forever dead.

Two, I became—poor splintered
  brain
  No longer could endure.
"I've lost control; I must seek help.
  God, tell me there's a cure!"

And help WAS there. I slowly
  came
  To understand my soul.
"Forsake thy guilt, lift up thy head.
  Perfection's not thy goal."

And so I took that falt 'ring step.
  Back to a life so dear.
I've learned one fact—
  DO NOT GIVE UP!
There's naught to fear but fear.

Shirley McFarland
TO MY FRIEND
You, my friend, I liked at first
  glance.
I could have loved you given the
  chance.
Our time together was so fleeting
  and fast.
How could we know that it
  wouldn't last.
I got to know you pretty well in
  that time.
To know that your thoughts
  differ from mine.
You won't allow love to enter
  your heart.
You keep to yourself the
  secretive part.
It seems, you think, that to love
  is a weakness, a sort of giving in.
But believe me, it isn't my friend.
It's an opening up and pouring out.
Something no one should do
  without.
It's a sharing, a caring, lifes
  greatest high.
God, I hope you find it once
  before you die.
So, don't hide your feelings in all
  those dark places.
Open up and show someone all of
  your faces.

Lenora Myers Young
THOUGHT ERA 1933
Oft, when on my pillow I lie
  Thinking of days long gone by,
I dream of some of my schoolmates
  Some are happy and still content
Some, I know, are past the Pearly
  Gates
  A few others' lives are nearly
  spent

When I live over the days of old
  My poor tired, old heart grows
  cold.
But God high on his Celestial seat
  Has reassured us . . . again we'll
  meet.

Henry Williams
THE BEST DRESSED

---

*Dedication: To my friend, Jesse,
who, though blind, yet sees.*

Only in the ground, He kindly
  wrote.
Living Word, He is and spoke.
For my sin to the Cross He went,
One bequest: a new white garment.

Now I'm dressed and ready for
  His bidding
To come up to the glorious
  wedding.
My steps are lighter; they have a
  new bounce,
While waiting for the day to be
  announced.

Selina B. Robinson
CHRISTIAN DILEMMA

---

*Dedicated to the righteous
Christians of the Northside
Church of Christ, Jacksonville,
Florida.*

In the beginning was the zeal
But there was no knowledge—
  could this thing be real?
Within my realm was the big
  King James
But from somewhere came
  the Christian Games.

What caused me to slip, to go
  astray . . .
to be so near Christ . . .
Yet so far away?

Nourish me-love me-show me
  you care
Brother or Sister . . .
Would you dare?

Teach me the real way to live
  this life
Teach me the real way . . .
  to handle the strife.

You say-don't fall! Regain your zeal!
I say-help me! Show me!
That you're for real!

Barbara Ann Stohlman
FAMILIAR ARMS
Open wide your familiar arms
and allow me to step into them.
Joy in our eyes
of a pleasure felt long ago.

Encircle me with love
and you will feel my warmth
transmit to you.

Our Spirits embrace,
the warmth of our bodies,
the beat of our hearts.
A moment of oneness
when we are near.

Tami Frerichs
HE
He was the one
  I lived my life for.
He was the one

Who walked out the door.
He was the one
  Who brightened my day.
He was the one
  Who turned me away.
He was the one
  I needed the most,
And the memory of him
  Haunts me . . . like a ghost.

Delilah-Judith

Delilah-Judith
**I Want To Be A Dolly Made
Of China**
I want to be a Dolly made of china,
I want to have an empty curly
  head,
Aristocratic nose, doll's trunk of
  silken clothes,
And to stay asleep as long as I'm
  in bed!

Don't want a gypsy wise to read
  the tea leaves,
Don't want to make love's wishes
  on a star,
Don't want to listen for the
  phone that never rings,
Don't want to read the license
  number on a car!

But a Lover comes to buy the
  little Dolly,
Offers "Silver! Gold! and all that it
  will take!"
Rushes her away to home, she'll
  have no chance to roam,
Says to all, "You mustn't touch
  her, she might break!"

I don't want to figure on a
  price-list,
Nor to feel I simply must be
  ration-fed;
I don't want to have a heart! nor
  to push a baby-cart!
I just want to be an empty
  China—head!

Terrill D. Petersen
KAT
The enravishment you bring to
  me
is pure and simple ecstasy
You entrance my soul
enlighten my life make me whole

You ignite an impetus igneous
  drive in me
You compell me to joy and tears
your love lays to rest my inner
  fears
I delight in your air, I need you to
  be there

I ador your osculation and the

affinity I have with you
Your enravishing pulchritude has
  me in bliss
The exhilaration of your presence
  is a transcedent delight
Cherubic ecstasy is all you
  induce in me

I seek the perpetuation of your
  love
and the genesis of a cosmos
  unitedly
You awaken all the passion in me
I want you, I need you to satisfy
  my soul

Frances F. Moore
MIRRORED TRUTH
Each day I find that I must face
  my biggest foe of all—
It is the one I see each morn
  in the mirror on my wall.

No matter how I think of me,
  this image does not lie;
The likeness staring back is me—
  exactly, eye for eye.

This image cannot change its
shape to hide from me my shame—
  It bears a witness, unconcealed,
to what I really am . . . .

Annelise Weiber
**The Gypsy, The Devil and
The Witch**
Sun gypsy, moon gypsy,
Dancing golden-haired, dances by
  the firelight,
The night is young and moon is
  bright.
She dances and swirls, round and
  round,
To the music's full, enchanting
  sound.

From a crystal ball, far away, a
  Witch looks on,
She howls wicked laughter and
  chants a dirge-song.
Black Witch, Devil's Queen,
  darkness of an evil heart,
Black, stringy hair and taloned
  hands,
Like a vulture, she hovers over
  the crystal ball.
And the Devil agrees, tainted
  union, sorceries—
To cast a spell, a curse, over the
  gypsy.
A curse to end the gypsy's life
Before the night is through.
Red Devil, Black Devil,
Enemy from Hell, conjure up and
  cast your spell.

The spell is broken as a white
  dove flies
In from the night to settle on the
  gypsy's arm,
A message from Christ, to keep
  her from all harm,
She dance again and lives, arises
With the morning sun.

Regina Kolb
TENDER TOUCH
  Please walk slowly so that your
  shadow can be seen in the
  light. For when that shadow
  vanishes I may sit back and
  feel who you really are.
  Let me know your name once
  again, let me open up your
  total being.

Cheryl Carvalho
LOVING
To feel your chest rest upon mine
Kissing your warm lips,
In darkness you're my sunshine;
Feeling your hands caress my
  hips.
Laying your body next to mine
Holding you so close,
Never asking how or why
And never wanting a choice.

Alicia R. Van Over
INVENTORY

---

*To my friend, Sister Kathleen
Galvin*

How might I evaluate my time
  here on earth;
By my credit cards or financial
  worth,
By my trips abroad in search of a
  thrill
Or my stately mansion, built
  high on a hill?

As I sat and pondered, I heard a
  voice say,
"Those things have no value,
  should God call today.
Your soul is God's ledger, there
  your inventory starts
And you'll find your answer
  locked deep in your heart."

"Have you helped some sinner
  from time to time;
Remembered to pray, "Father,
  Thy Will-not mine"?
Have you shared your lot with
  your fellow-man;
Graciously given-up loved ones
  to God's "Give-and-Take Plan"?
Have you given praise, where
  praise was due?
Have you thanked Jesus for His
  love of you?
Have you obeyed the
  commandments, asked
  forgiveness of sins
And do you forgive others,
  through your love of Him?
Were your sojourn over, could
  you look back and say,
"The world is better for my short
  stay"?
Once your inventory is in, you
  can see your true worth,
And then you'll know the value
  of your time on earth".

Dolly Kozlowski
FIRELIGHT
Last night I sat and watched-
  The firelight dance on the ceiling.
I thought of all the times-
  That passed from sight.
Of other nights like this one-
  But, gone from time.
And living on tonight!

Light from the ceiling makes
  shadows.
  They show us things-
That make our hearts seem light!
  And when they die-
The shadows fade from night
  Yellow flames and blue all dance
  together.
And die away to ashes,
  And are gone forever!

Our World's Best Loved Poems

Michelle E. Boucher
A True Meaning For Christmas
What can the true meaning
Of Christmas be?
Does it have something to do
With our sparkling Christmas tree?
Or the waiting exitement
Of the first sign of snow
Or maybe the presents
Wrapped, topped with a bow.
We give our gifts
As a sign of love
But the true gift of Christmas
Was sent from above.
A babe in a manger
Gods only son
A symbol of truth
That we could be one.
A man so perfect
He made a way that we
Could follow him to eternity.
So Father in heaven
We thankfully pray
For giving a true meaning
To this Christmas day.

Mrs. E. M. C. Arnusch
SNOW FLAKES

---

*My impression of "Snowflakes" is
that they fall in all kinds of forms
and shapes and are white, soft
and quiet. My thanks goes to
God.—My Mentor.*

Snowflakes! Floating like soft
white feathers in the air,
Settling, oh so gently here and
there.
Snowflakes! They look like
spidery thistle down,
Blowing lightly, in the wind all
around.
Snowflakes! Are shaped like lacy
white stars,
Silently, falling so fast and go so
far.
Snowflakes! They feel like fluffy
cotten balls,
So softly, so quietly, do they fall.

Snowflakes! Are like confetti at a
wedding,
Getting caught up into
everything.
Snowflakes! Feels like fleecy
lambs wool,
So white, so soft and so cool.
Snowflakes! Spread like silvery
angel hair,
Delicately, clinging to branches

everywhere.
Snowflakes! Like a white blanket
covers the ground,
Protecting nature's plants all
around.
Snowflakes! Are like a mother's
kiss upon your cheek,
Softly, oh so gently her love you
seek.

Joan Loeblein Land
THE KEY
What is the quality I value most?
To sincerity I give a toast.
Why is it so hard to find?
On I keep searching, I do not mind.
Like looking for a needle in a
haystack.
How sad, a quality so many
people lack.

This age of compromise and
greed forces them to lose it.
But I admit my best friends have it.
And I do not deny I choose the
ones who do.
In this time and place they
number few!

Among creative people this
quality is easier to find,
The artists, musicians, poets,
writers all of this kind.
Inventors and scientists are
sincere:
Even some doctors fall in here!

For this human trait I do not
apologize,
For I hate deceit and lies.
Sincerity is important to me.
To unlock my heart it is the key.

Joe H. Lockhart
**A Working Man's
Christmas**

---

*Mr. Sam H. Jones Rt. #4; Box 355-
A Chickamauga, GA 30707 A
working man in whom God is
well pleased.*

At the bus stop the man waited,
his feet hurt, his back ached, so
tired he could hardly walk.
It looked as if his shopping was
completed.
He looked as if he wanted to talk.
As I approached the rough
looking man, I tried to think of
something to say.
But suddenly, without bowing his
head or closing his eyes he
began to pray.
"Lord, I am a working man. This
is my last day off, and I feel so
all alone.
My shopping is not finished, but
when that bus comes, I am
coming home.
Forgive me if this is wrong.
Happy Birthday to your Son,
whose name I never curse.
This year I would like very much
to give from the heart, instead
of the purse".
Now I realized I had bowed my
head and over the street there
was a very warm hush.
When I looked up he was very
still, his eyes were closed and
he was seated on the bus.

I had to know where this man
called home, so I ran quickly to
the front of the bus.
And there for one and all to
ponder it read—Destination—
Merry Christmas.

Elizabeth Haynes McAnnally
THE FARMER'S BRIDE
Sixty shining glass jars
sitting on a shelf,
filled with jewelled fruits
that I canned all by myself.

Pears and plums and cherries,
peaches, apples, too;
berries—every shape and size,
black and red and blue.

Summer's golden harvest
gleaned for winter's table,
and I shall add a score or more
as fast as I am able.

Beans and corn and carrots,
and cabbage in a crock,
pickled beets and onions, too,
to silence hunger's knock.

Poets write their verses.
Artists have their skill.
I have just an hour 'til lunch
and ten more jars to fill.

I'll never lay a claim to fame
in my simple country life,
but I shall try until I die
to be a loving wife.

Betty Neeb Ihde
OCTOBER
Nearly all the leaves had fallen;
And the rest were soon to go.
Still the hills were orange and
purple
And the valley, so blue below.

Purple grapes in heavy clusters
Mingled with bittersweet there.
Everything was very quiet—
Not a breeze was in the air.

Millions of tiny diamonds
Sparkled in the dewy mist.
The best artist of any land
Could never paint better than
this.

Cathy Jo Tafoya
BEAUTY OF IT ALL

---

*To all mothers who have loved
and lost. And to those children
for which there will be no
tomorrows . . .*

Life is like a rose, as the buds fall
to the ground. Where is the
beauty of it all? I haven't seen
any around.

A rose comes into bloom, a child
is born. Which one's more
damned, which one's more
scorned?

A rose will soon die and fade, as
the memory of a child. Why do
things of such beauty only last
a short while???

William J. Meyer
The Face In the Window
No matter what I'm doing
No matter when or where
But mostly when it's dark out
The Face is always there

It always stays just out of clear
sight
It always lurks in the corner of
my eye
I try to catch a good look at it
And it's gone as if it's shy

I like to sit and read at night
A lamp a book and firelight
But as my eyes skim across the
page
I see that haunting Face
In its silicon cage

Josephine Aurelia Graham
i am but a candle
i am but a candle
that flickers in the dark
reflecting images
of a world both sane and insane
both beautiful yet hideous

and

as i burn
i live yet die
for the wax of my very being
is slowly melting away

Mary M. Moses
Faces Along the Water
I believe that
there are hidden, faces along the
water.
Among the wilderness
each rainbow seen, is a secret
colored.

Among the weeping willows
their shadows hold their powers.
Through the laughing swamps
there's an animals' cry to hear.

How faint, the faded faces, of the
water.
Their cries have all silenced.
With the coming of seasons
a time is gone forever.

Nico Boccio
CHILDHOOD WISHES
Teddy bears
with sewn on faces.
Baby dolls
that wet in places.
Roller skates
and muddy traces.
Large scruffy dogs
and stray alley cats.
Pretty party dresses.
Baloons.
All kinds of toys
bright shining and new.
Mommie's cookies.
Daddy's hugs and kisses.
And the Angels watching from
above.
God's messengers of love.
These;
are a few
childhood wishes.

Michael Radford
TOGETHER

---

*Tracy, Just remember, we'll
always be together no matter
what stands between us*

She understands the little things
and shares in working out
even the most complicated times

She makes me feel important
when others put me down

she makes me count my blessings

Whenever theres a need to doubt
she stands behind me all along
with no strings attached

When I'm with her smiling
I feel as though the world
in all its glory is far away

Our lives are so much alike
our needs so near the same
we compliment each other

Like two birds in the wild
our song, together, fills the air
it reaches the clouds above us

Ruth Ann Redgrave
GOD'S STARS
On the fourth day of creation
  When God made our day and
  night
He put His stars up in the sky
  To help the moon shed light.

Up there in all their glory
  Shine the "northern lights" so
  bright
That help the poor lost sailors
  At times their course—set right.

And then there is "the dipper"
  It's there for all to see
To remind us what He did for us
  Through out eternity!

Per chance you've seen a "falling
  star"
  When o'er the earth you've
  roamed
T'is said that that's a sign
  He's called somebody "Home".

Dr. Naresh Bhatt
The Dance Without You

*To Lynn, who taught me love,
American Style.*

The dinner was over and so was
  the night
I should have known that
  something was not going to be
  right.
Soon the music started, feet were
  all over the floor
Pretty couples smiling and
  enjoying, hand in hand, arm in
  arms,
I didn't go, I just looked and
  waited at the door from where
people entered. Everyone came
  and joined, for whom I was *not*
  waiting
But the one for whom I was
  waiting did *not* come in. Why?
  I don't
know. Maybe circumstances
  beyond your control, I know of
  those
instances, but I thought you were
  going to join. I was going to ask
you what you were going to have
  on? What happened? I waited
  among
the thousand fragrances for the
  aroma of your body and
  warmth of your
soul. I was more disappointed
  than tired, finally "would you
  dance
with my wife?" my freind asked.
  Thank you, I said. "You don't
  have

to be shy she said. I did go, killed
  time for two "that's enough"
I said. Thirty after ten I no longer
  could abstain, I went to my
car left the ball and let loose All
  my restrain.

Ruth Yontz
Nature's Christmas Cards
Have you ever walked on
  Christmas Eve
  Among the scented pine.
And watch a redbird on the wing,
  Among the holly vines?

Or watch a deer flee into woods,
  That's covered white with snow.
Where in the distance candles
  bright,
In cabin windows glow.

Where children's laughter fills
  the air,
  While skating on a pond.
And sleepy cattle blink their eyes,
  Down by a weathered barn.

So if some year you're saddened
  Because no card has arrived.
Not one of your special favorites
  By "Currier and Ives".

Just take a walk in the country
  Among scented pine,
And watch redbirds and snowbirds
  Among holly vines.

These are nature's lovely
  Christmas cards,
  Painted by the Christ Child's
  hand,
And has never been perfected,
  By a brush, from the hand of man.

Marguerite Roberts
WHAT IF (I WERE A TREE)
Did you ever step outside at
  morn, and look at the hills, so
  old and worn?
The trees standing there so long;
  But still their beauty is never
  gone.
Let's look at them as people of
  our land. Some of them are
  plain, and some have a brand.
  Their standing there
together; Some times their all the
  same green. And then their
  colors change again.
What if they were people of all
  beautiful colors, and there isn't
  anything they can do.
The same God created them as
  did me, and you.
One can't kill the other or say I
  don't like your kind or color.

Some are old, some are young,
  some are straight, some are bent;
But we can still compare them to
  our friends.
Regardless of our color, shape or
  style; God looks at us as he
  does his trees and flowers.
If we could change the forest and
  put it all separate color, and
  kind; The fall of the
Year would be dull I'm sure we
  would find.
So let's all stand together, and
  don't hinder the kind, and
  color. We're all judged
In the sight of God, all the same
  way, and
What is more beautiful than our
  land of
The U. S. A.?

Francis Johnson
WINTER SOLSTICE
Against the winter soltice sun
The fields are weeping white and
  gray.
And angered brances cluster cold
Dry as bones on a friendless day.

The sleeping child dreams at dawn
Never hearing howling winds
That leave the broken heart adrift
And shake the soul from life and
  limb.

Hands that wrap the frozen face
With fur and scarf and warm
  goose down
Will someday send that angel
  child
To a raging chase with hell's
  black hound.

Skies that ache with winter snow
Are playing with our hopes again,
Teasing us with a winter glow
Lest we should lose our faith.
  Amen.

Sharon Spracklin Weiss
THE PROMISE
I have faith in God above,
He sent to us His Son to love.
We denied the Savior Jesus Christ
And crucified Him so He could
  rise.

He arose from the dead,
Forgave us all our sins,
Yet, still so many turn their face
And will deny Him again.

But this time they will perish
With Satan by their side.
For God made a promise
That once again Christ would rise.

Rise above the evil,
Cleanse the Earth from sin,
Bring about the beauty
God dreamed of at the beginning.

His love for us never vanishes
Yet our faith is ever weak.
And now we shall feel the wrath
That will make His Word
  complete.

Christ comes again! To forever
  reign in peace!

Allene Clancey McNally
THE MOBILE
Dance little animals, one by one.
Dance, dance. Oh, what fun!

Dance little animals, in the air.

First comes dog then comes bear.

.Dance little animals, to the
  lullaby.
Held by strings way up high.

Dance little animals, round and
  round.

But while I sleep, make not a
  sound.

Eva Mae Westcott
CHRISTMAS GRACE

*Dedicated to the memory of my
loved ones who have been called
Home to be with Him*

He came to earth so long go
This Babe, Son of God and Mary's
  Son
In stable bed meek and low, He
  came
To Shepherds and to Wise Men,
  this Holy One.

He comes again this Christmas
  time
Amid the world's busyness and
  din;
He comes to give His love to all
If hearts will let Him in.

We can not buy, we can not earn
This gift so freely given,
His death atoned for all our sins
His cross-our way to Heaven!

Geneve Baley
Pre-Pope's Visit Telephone Retaliation, Spring 1983
Thomas Edison communicated
Electrically in his inventions
Now destroyed by war-mongers of
Insantiy burning out the
Hearts of men and their
Loved ones through the
Telephone line communication
  stoppage
Cut off and out of the
Lives of men and man
Seeking freedom, love and
Happy joy to be
Alive in God's
Image, held
Dear, captured "in
Retaliation" for those that
Love and those that
Care, about
Destiny.

Marie Lummus Cate
OMNIPRESENT
I see Him hover in the mystic dawn,
And walk o'er tree-tops shrouded;
I see Him make the sky His lawn,
And leave His footprints clouded.

I hear Him thunder His displeasure,
And grumble as He leaves
Rain, parched-earth's treasure,
Rustling leaves and heaven-sent
  breeze.

I smell His perfume in perennial
  flowers,
In garlanded walk and bed;
I taste His fruits after He showers,
And leaves a sunset brushed with
  red.

I feel His touch in time of sorrow;
His hand on mine keeps me steady.
So, when I look ahead to tomorrow,
I don't fear Death; I'm just not
  ready!

Kevin P. Fealy
KALEIDOSCOPE

To Micheal and Susan

From each step through life we
    take,
Each tomorrow we consequently
    make.
Our steps have brought us to this
    moment,
And, consequently, I know your
    love.
Yet, have we chosen it to be so?
Before we took the steps—
Did we know?
Oh my beloved encounter,
Cleave to me now,
That our footsteps together,
Forever shall show,
In summer sands
Or winter's snow.

Nicholas D. Young
YOU MUST PAY

*For my late father, Major C. H. H.
Young of the British Army.*

Pay, pay, pay, pay, every cent you
    have to pay,
Pay, pay, pay, pay, almost each
    and every day.
Hard up, no money, not a scrap to
    fill my tummy.
Shabby hat and trousers worn,
With dirty shirt and collar torn.
Runs in socks and soleless shoes,
A tattered coat of hideous hues,
T'is all crumpled, dropping
    stitches,
How I wish I had some riches.
Wallet empty, not a cent,
Just a penny for my rent.
Money I've had and money I've
    spent,
Dollars I've given and dollars I've
    lent.
But now all I hear with a
    sickening fear,
Is pay, pay, pay, pay, every cent
    you have to pay.
Pay up, no credit, let's have none
    of those filthy debits.
But Pay, pay, pay, pay, ever cent
    and every day,
And pay, pay, pay, pay, if you
    want to go your way.

D. Nelle Andrews
TIME

*"To my many friends and
relatives" —en lieu of letters—
inspired by a busy work schedule.*

No time for gossip—
No time to fight—
Hardly enough time
For sleep at night.
Time is working,
No time for fun;
Time, time, time
Is making us run.
We've run out of time
For this time of year—
So jolly, happy Christmas
And a *bright New Year.*

George Fredrick Wise

George Fredrick Wise
DANCING SNOW

*To our father in heaven we all
know*

Oh to watch the snow
Dancing in the winds
Always moving around
To a winter song
We cannot here or comprehend
But in our souls

Only a God in heaven
Made this winter
A wonderland
For his angles
In heaven above.

Virgie N. Silvey
A Tribute To a Love
Our love bloomed in the morning
Like the blossoms on the trees
It went down with the sunset
But never died for you and me

So beautiful while it lasted
We thought this cannot be true
The experience of this romance
The love that both of us knew

I could see the love in your eyes
They told me all I had to know
And when you told me this is a
    cruel world
And darling I love you so

I've loved you since the day we
    met
And I could see sadness in your
    eyes
I have wanted you all these years
You expressed your feelings with
    a sigh

As if yearning for your youth
For the years you lived in vain
You said, I'll have this sweet
    memory
And that our lives were never the
    same

And now you are gone, my true
    love
Our moments together were few
I'll cherish all the sweet memories
Hold them close to my heart for
    you

The pain of your death will
    soften
As the days go slowly by
I could hear you say—hello darling
And also a farewell good bye

James L. Michael
MORNING
In a meadow rising, flowers of the
    spring;
The warm breath of promise that
    the sunrise brings.
The stars all are fading, and the
    moon is paled by light,
And the sun's first gentle rays
    make me feel all right.

As I lie beneath the treetops, and
    breathe that mornin' air,
I feel deep within me that I've
    always been there.
In the clouds that floated over, in
    a vision shown to me,
A warm breeze caressed my face
    and I could almost see.

The birds had started singing, and
    the sky turned pale blue,
I closed my eyes in soft, sweet
    sleep and drifted back to you.
Whose eyes were lined with
    satin, had hair like raging fire,
While in the corners of my mind
    lay secret desires.

But the distant mountain
    beckons, it's peak so white and
    high,
I raise my arms above my head
    and breathe a haunting sigh.
As the escapades of little boys
    turn them slowly into men,
Tomorrow will find me sleeping
    in a meadow once again.

Kellee D. Sutton
TODAY'S THE DAY

*To my Grandparents, Lennie,
William, Evelyn, and George for
their love and influence*

today's the day when choirs sing
of the long ago message that He
    did bring.
He spoke of love and peace inside,
    and how, with Him, we could
    abide.
in the manger that day, He did cry,
for He was a babe—like you and i.
the wise men had traveled
    through the land
to place their treasures in mary's
    hand.

the virgin mother held her son
knowing that He was the one
to dry the lonely childrens' tears
and save the souls through
    endless years.

but this long-ago message still
    lives today
for, through His life, He has
    shown the way.
the way, through love, to walk
    streets of gold
and meet the prophets of the days
    of old.

we celebrate on this day the
    hallowed birth
of the child who came to save the
    earth
from all the evil that dwelled
    within
if they would only say yes to Him.
on this day, we sing our song
to show Him that our hearts
    belong
to Him and our Father up
    above . . .
we sign to show Him all our love.

now, join with me in silent talk
with the Man who quietly walked
throughout the land day after day
to tell us we could live with Him
    someday.

Malik Canty
SO EASY

*To Candy Always hold your head
up high for the beauty you have
inside is truly genuine . . . you
are a modest Goddess . . . . .*

It's so easy to say
it can't be me!!

So easy to blame everyone
else when you should be blameing
yourself . .

So easy to say i will not
do! even though i should.
So easy to be bad when you
can be good . . .

So easy to neglect yourself
and love everyone else . .

So easy to get hurt and feel
like a jerk . . . .

It's so easy to do all these
things and more without thinking
of a cure . . . .

Carolyn Walker Weaver
FRAYED SENSES
Look toward the window
Hear the raindrops fall.
Look back from the window
Hear a shadow on the wall.

Listen for a sound
I see it from afar.
Listen for the silence
I see a noisy star.

Taste the bitter fruit
I feel a sour bite.
Taste a bit of loneliness
I feel a hopeless night.

Smell the dying flowers
Hear their slow decay.
Smell the dying memories
Hear them fade away.

Carol Jean Welch
A GREAT MAN
You ask what Jesus means to me,
Read this poem and you will see.
He is always near with a helping
    hand,

551

For anyone in each and every land.
Whether skin is red or yellow,
black or white,
Jesus will never be far from sight.
No matter what time, day or night,
He'll always know what is right.
People all over from every nation,
Should stop and think of this
great creation,
And always remember his
undying dedication,
By praising his name in daily
meditation.
The next time you kneel to pray,
Just stop to think and you'll say,
Thank you, Lord Jesus
For all the times you have
forgiven us
All our sins and straying ways
Through the past and for all the
rest of our days.
Jesus Christ was a great man,
from the very start,
And still is as he lives today
within my heart.

Elsie M. Westrick
**Beauty One December
Night**
I saw beauty one December night
From the soft twinkling glow of a
thousand lights,
Red, green, blue, yellow and white
From across Lake Huron, a
peaceful sight.
Two great nations side by side,
Each with traditions, each with
pride.
No wars cloud the shores of each
Love and peace is for each to keep.
Down through the years sharing
with love,
God's blessings have followed
each from above.
If only the world would follow
their ways
Peace, love and contentment
would fill all days.
What these nations share is all so
right
For I saw beauty one December
night.

Earl W. Peck
HEAVEN'S LIGHTS

*Dedicated to my very good friend
Miss Beatrice Helen Wood
Wrentham, Ma.*

Often times we gaze at night to
see the Heavens shining bright.
Those many million tiny stars
that hide by day and twinkle
nights.

It seems to me at Christmas
Time the lights a little brighter
shine.

Some call them planets far on
high that spread across our
distant sky.

The truth is that the stars we see
are the lights on God's Great
Christmas Tree!

Malik Canty
LOVING HIM TOO MUCH
Even though he has broken your
heart, hurt you inside don't let
this take over your pride tell

this man goodbye . . .

for there will be someone new to
look after you and show you
what it means to be true . .

Just look at those tears running
down your cheeks thats what
happens when love is cheap . .

when you love someone and they
don't love you misery is the
only thing you will go through
until you find someone new . .

you brought these tears upon
yourself by loving him when
he loved someone else. now
that he has decided that the
two of you should be divided . .

you don't want to let him go for
you still love him so. even
though he doesn't care you still
want him near . . . .

for you love him too much and
you will take all of his stuff
cause you can't get enough . . .

Phoebe J. Carlton
SHED NO TEARS
Falling leaves cheerily whisper.
Shed no tears when I say goodby.
Falling leaves, like joy and sorrows,
Fades away—sails away and dies.
Our aim in life is fame and fortune,
Memories to linger on.
So tears will fall at time of parting,
Much too soon forgotten and gone.
I will carve my name on sand and
driftwood,
So like the leaves will fade and die.
So when my name is called up
yonder,
There will be no tears when I say
goodby.

Bonita M. Stachnick
A CASTLE OF FRIENDS
Still alone in my "castle of
friends",
Still lonely . . . until who
knows when.

Still in this castle, the feeling is
here, I still need to know that
the healing is near.

Are you lonely my friend, behind
that smile?
If you just let me in, it won't take
but awhile.

When the light of day seems to
fade no more,
This castle of like will shine
and soar.

But while in this "castle", I need
to know,
That my mind, my life and my
thoughts still grow.

Linda Stephens
JOURNEY
The universe opened up,
leading me beyond the gateway,
bringing a brightness to the night,
and a softness to the day.
The cosmos spread before me,
revealing the absence of time.
Across the large expanses
our two souls, again, intertwined.
In its own way, unlocking the
heart,
coming forth with flowering-love.
Permitting such ecstacy and peace,

as shown by the spirit of the dove.
Intermingling with the stars,
we will find, that time will be ours.

Julius A. Rivers
**Let Every Voice Sing In
Memory Of Dr. King**
If ever there was a man
Who traveled throughout this land
Seeking freedom for all,
Whether great or small,
He was Dr. King—
A legend in his time.

If ever there was a man
Who gave all he had
Fighting to fulfill a dream,
Although impossible it seemed,
That one day man would be free
To live together in harmony—
He was Dr. Martin Luther King Jr.

If ever there was a time
A need exists for a man
Strong in leadership,
Devoted to a cause,
A believer in a dream—
Time came—such a man emerged,
He was Dr. Martin Luther King Jr.

Let every voice sing,
Let freedom ring,
In Memory of Dr. King.

Anastasia Claire Aghasian
When Winter Is King
Musing I leaned 'gainst my
window sill
As Jack Frost came breezing by.
He grinned as he feathered my
window pane
With snow-ice that fell from the
sky.

The sky was cast in silver and grey
And the moon played hide and
seek as
Cloud upon cloud bumbled cross
her wake
The wind blew cold from
distended cheek.

Snowflakes danced blighthely in
swirls in frills
Of fabulous stencils of lacey
delight,
Then flew on in puffs and drifted
the hills
Making fairyland of all that lay
to my sight.

Snow lighted on everything
brushing it white,
What changes occured all
through the chill night!
The tree-tops were dusted, the
roofs and the lawns,
Scattering eiderdown beauty
glistening at dawn.

The pine and the oak were
curtained in drift,
The bridge and the stream
adorned in new shift.
Icicles shimmered, were
festooned with stars,
A mystical scenery fantastic
bazaar!

As steady I gazed with my eyes
and my mind,
'Peared a fat friendly snow-man
right size, right kind.
With the deepening white
blanket enhancing it all
Couldn't help but imagine a

Winter-King's Ball.

Snow fairies frolicking while ice
fairies reeled
To silvery music's bell-tink'ling
appeal.
The castle, the ball-room, all
filmed in white glaze,
Trailing gossamer white lengths
of delicate grace.

The Snow Prince and Princess
leading the ball
Bidding dance and be joyful-
Hurrah for them all!
I could see how tomorrow
shining and bright
Would give worlds of excitement
after this night.

The children and others would
share in it soon
A treasure of crystal—King
Winter's boon.
The sky-King and ice-King
conspired this night
Carrying out secret plans 'ere
coming day-light.

The gleam of pure loveliness
mant'ling each place
Will dazzle, enchant every child's
face.
The exquisite white beauty that
falling snow brings
Heralds a season of joy, when
Winter is King!

Beatrice D. Londergan
THE PROMISE
There is a desolate plot where
other flowers lie buried beneath
the frozen ground and winter's
coverlet of cold white snow.
There're no dried stalks,
yielding to the blustery wind, to
mark the spot, where these
flowers lived and flourished.

Some that just grew old and
withered, others cut down, before
they reached full bloom.
Only rows of marble monuments
mark these hallowed spots.

These flowers are not less
than the flowers that blossomed
in my garden.
Therefore, come some spring,
they too shall awaken,
burst forth with new life.
Their blossoms will be more
beautiful than they were in the
beginning.
This time their blooms will have
the life span of eternity.

Our World's Best Loved Poems

Anastasia Claire Aghasian
PATRIOTS ARISE

Hear me, hear me, Americans all!
Let there be no more blood and
   strife.
Let us live with honor in
   brotherhood
Remember those who gave limb
   and life!

Wave the flag yes, wave Our Flag!
Good people of the U. S. A.
Above soars the Eagle of Freedom
The heritage we guard each day!

Break the code of color, Break!
Keep it All for One, One for All.
Take a hand in friendship citizen
Heed our country and Freedom's
   call!

Sing the song of Freedom, sing!
Uphold it with pride and with
   might.
Renew the pledge to our glorious
   flag
To God, and to equal rights!

Wave the Flag—FOREVER let it
   wave!
We're the strength of America
   today.
Keep aloft the colors Red White
   and Blue
We the people of the U. S. A.!

Paul D. King
UNTITLED

   The sivlery sands
of a lonely beach
laying in the sun

   Begin each day
this lonely way
spreading wide beneath
the sun

   The everlasting beauty
of this seldom seen sunrise
is always a welcome splendor
to these awakening Human eyes.

Any Jones
FOREVER ONE

Love is a strange arrangement,
Between two people who care.
A few spoken words together,
A stolen kiss at the fair.

A man and a woman
Who are as one.
They stay together
'Til day is done.

Then they part
To seek separate beds.
Some place to dream
And lay their weary heads.

In the morning sunlight
When the birds are singing.
She'll wake and dress before.
Answering the phone's ringing.

She'll hear his voice
And smile,
Glad he called
to chat awhile.

She'll listen carefully
and memorize the sound
and play it back in her mind
when he's not around.

John-Michael Akili
HOME

Home is where the heart is
   except when you go home and

find that you can't go home.
When everything's changed,
   where family cause each other
   suffering and pain and anguish.
Home can be pain.

Home is where the love is except
   when family has no unity,
   where love is scarce. ,
When parents and children fuss
   and fight; where family can
   love each other better when
   they are apart;
Home without a heart.

Home is where the family is
   unless family is split up by
   circumstances.
Home is where love grows unless
   there is no real home to grow
   love.
Home is where families care
   about each other, unless care
   was never there.
Home is where your roots are,
   unless your roots have been
   blown with the wind . . .

Paul R. Katz
The Destructive Storm

Two passive clouds smash out a
   roar
As lightning cracks the solid skies,
And from the openings pour,
Stampeding rains, as heaven cries.
And heaven falls toward earth's
   floor,
As thunder warns that heaven dies.
Where now is summer's golden
   center;
Whose rays pierced night and let
   day enter;
Who took charge of the blue
   eternity,
And now is riddled in grey
   uncertainty.
Shall you, too, lose your grip on
   heaven soon,
And find yourself fallen below
   the broken moon,
Who makes the seas bend to her
   dictum,
While you would drown, victim
   to that victim.
The storm strikes earth as well as
   sky and sea,
And lightning kills the tough and
   tallest tree,
While thunder beats clouds into
   drops of rain;
That droop and drown the dry
   and healthy grain.
Even love shall lose its innocence,
In the terrible rape of violence,
And here it is that all beginning
   ends.

LeRoy B. Schwan
VISION

When times are sad and we are
   blue and the autumn of life is
   near.
What thoughts does man have
   which make his life so dear?
A driving spirit, a life to give, are
   things which spur him on
to greater heights of things above
   the moon
   the shining sun,
and thankfulness to have lived
   a happy life so far,
to have the faith, and vision
   great, to match a shining star.

Nina Rubin
SUNSET ON THE COVES

The caves of the sea hold echos
   of memories,
The sounds of waves rushing and
   the cry of the seagulls
The setting sun creates a fantasy
   world,
Painting the walls in brilliant
   hues of red and orange,
Then slowly and carefully the
   colors fade lighter . . .
Until they are only a dim
   imitation of what they once
   were.
Silence falls on the caves except
   for the cry of the gulls and
   rushing of waves,
But tomorrow the mysterious
   beauty will return.

Nguyen Minh Lien
A LONELY STAR

The moon plays "Hide'n Seek"
Among the coconut leaves.

The late train awakes,
The bridge rolls over the smoke—

Lonely star still stands still.

Theresa A. Fidurski
I WAS THERE

---

*To My Precious Children
Michael, Tricia and Robert
Fidurski whom I Love Very
Much. Love You Always. Mom*

Tender Age, Tender Branches of a
   tree;
   Young green shoots, untrampled—
No-less defiled;
   But, by the grace of God reviled.
Yes, My Daughter I was there—
   Giving you my loving care.

By your hand *I* led you down the
   pathway to spiritual growth.
   Emotional reality
I have given you and MY peace
   and tranquility
I give you now;

Yes, MY Daughter, I was there—
   Giving you MY loving care;

Though you knew not who *I* was
   as *I* took you by the hand-yet
   you were willing to obey me.

Though you knew not who *I* was.
   Yet when I came to
   Your side you trusted me;
AND NOW *I* NEED YOUR
   TRUST EVEN MORE!

Anna-Marie Arnold
THE JOLLY SEASON

Simon le Bon throws out his
   brittle hand to shield his face
   from another rip of December's
   razor teeth. He strokes a scarlet
   rash swelling over his pouty
   cheeks and his nose is bitten to
   the gristle.
Crisp black leather pinches his
   rigid crotch and thighs until
   they are crying. His shirt tail
   crawls from the safety of his
   cableknit sweater, twisting in
   the cold like a broken yellow
   flag.
Damn, a tight violet strain snaps
   across his gentle flaking mouth.
   Somewhere, heading south, his
   favorite tweed overcoat enjoys
   a comfortable ride on the
   backseat of a taxicab.
Simon can't move his aching
   skeleton beyond a pair of
   snoring department stores
   huddling beneath blankets of
   frozen white filth. Straining
   from a hole in a tinty public
   address box, Johnny Mathis
   croons, Holy! Holy! Holy!
Simon lingers, some frozen
   fingers tapping the glass, others
   pressing down on his dark
   fedora. A fragile chain of
   winking lights dance around
   Santa's dusty window throne.
   Simon's eyes crack like lumps
   of frozen blue gelatin at plaster
   Santa's alabaster smile, a-
   howlin' with laughter.
A shivering beast crawls up
   Simon's spine, piercing the
   marrow in its jaws. It hurls his
   hat upwards into the mean
   blue night, sweeping it, diving
   it, surrendering it right . . .
Where she emerges, toes melting
   erect against the edge of a
   thick crippling carpet of gray
   ice. She is prancing, hypnotic
   spice, tangling piles of furcoat
   against her slender throat.
Simon lifts the quivering lump of
   felt from the ground and
   cradles it against his chest. His
   huge heart has thawed,
   throbbing gushes of warm
   arousal through his veins.
She rushes past, all wet
   vermillion lips and eyes blazing
   straight ahead brilliant
   diamond chips.
Simon whirls round, to catch her
   curling her fingers round her
   wind-ravaged growl, "Hey,
   gorgeous," her face is swirling
   white vapor, "wanna thaw out
   in front of my fireplace?"

Mary L. Barnes
The Truth Of He and I

How stupid I feel, to think
that a handsome young
man as he, could not
already have a love.
To think of all the dreams
I had, of him and I together
alone, in love.
I feel like a stupid romantic.
A teenage girl's dreams of
love, they are only dreams.

My God, I laugh now
at the dreams, but it is
the laughter of a very
foolish girl.
Who once again has
fooled herself into believing
romantic dreams.
For only the second time
in my life, I had been
ready to give him my
soul, my mind and my
body.
I fear that if I see my
daydream lover again, I
will embarrass him and
myself.

Louise Brady
WE ASK OF HIM
We ask of Him, but don't always
get
Because the pattern of our life is
already set.

We ask of Him, what we think is
best
He gives what He wants and
forgets the rest.

We ask of him, things to make us
glad
What He gives us often makes us
sad.

We ask of Him, because we do
not know
He will give what is right and
will tell us so.

Iona M. Brown
SHE DID
Just what did Katy do?
Please, will you tell me true?

Well, Katy turned off the daylight,
And turned it into the night,
Katy did; she did. She did? Yes she
did.

She set the fireflies all aglow,
And sent them flickering to and
fro,
Kay did; she did. She did? Yes she
did.

With the crickets she kept in
tune,
As they sang beneath the moon,
Katy did; she did. She did? Yes she
did.

Rumor says she sets the time
Of coming frost with her
croaking ryme,
Katy did; she did. She did? Yes she
did.

Regina Wilhelm
FALLING SNOW
Snowflakes falling ever so gently
to silently blanket the world in
whiteness
—a world full of sparkle and shine
and soft, beautiful brightness.

All the land becomes
transformed—
trees and houses take on new
shapes
and the scenery around us
somehow takes on a mystical
serenity.

The little furry animals scurry
around
in the still, deep snow
leaving only a whisper of

footprints
to trace their silent path.

A single bird flies to the feeder
to grab a seed or two
and flies swiftly back to its nest
to watch this mystery unfold.

Such beauty and mystical peace
falling so gently and silently
out of a puffy, white sky
to change our whole world.

I love its beauty and its grace
and all the pretty pictures it
paints—
such a sight the snowflakes
tracing patterns
across the land for all to see.

Kurt Andrew Johnson
ITS NOT THAT
Its not that I can't find the path.
Its not that I won't look for it.
Its that I'm afraid of where it may
lead.

I miss her.

Its not that I can't see what lies
ahead.
Its not that I won't look where
I'm going.
Its that I might follow after what
I see.

I miss her more.

Its not that I can't break through.
Its not that I won't reach out.
Its that I'm open to pain if I
become open to her.

I miss her more than a friend.

Its not that I want her.
Its not that I need her.
Its that I simply do not exist
without her.

I miss her more than a friend is
allowed to.

Inge Cibelli
HORSE SENSE
How did we meet
It was at daysend—I was on my
knees
When strength and pride were
absent

The struggle had been taxing
Had reached that very end of self
And tears I could not hold

My thoughts had finally gone—
resting in the Lord
The burning prayer was
God please never leave me

Well—on awakening there was

the greatest calm
The storm—that tempest had
resided

Horsesense told me then
God never did depart
That it was man that walked
away from God

So there new faith was born
Praise and thanksgiving offered
And the certainty was gained
I need not walk alone.

Cindy McGuire
BIRTHDAY
Being able to endure life, moving
In and out of trouble,
Realizing why you are on
The earth
Hoping that some-
Day in
Another time
You'll be back

Aileen L. Lum-Sarcedo
$200 THANKING YOU

---

*LOVING YOU . . . ALWAYS &
FOREVER Your Sister, Your
Daughter Your Mother, Your
Wife . . . . "LIN"*

I never did properly Thank You, . .
for, Your Concern, Care & Calls—
During . . . a period of . . . that
time,
I wasn't Myself at all . . . . .

I'm sorry . . . if I was offensive
I'm sorry . . . if I sounded cruel
I'm sorry . . . for putting You,
What??? You had to go
through . . . . . With Me.

I meant to do this sooner; but
time . . . just passed my way
So—now, that I'm doing it later,
I'd be best writing . . . . What I
have to say . . . . .

Thank you, for being You
Thank you, for Seeing Me
through, it all . . . . .

Thank you, for Your Love
Thank you, for Your Care
Thank you, for the kindness;
that You had spared and
gave . . . to Me.

Thank You, for Your Patience
Thank you, for Your Time
Thank you, for Helping Me
Back . . . to My Right Mind.

Thank you, for Your Support
. . . in calling me everyday
Especially . . . . when You didn't
know??? a word that I was
saying.

Thank you, for Your
Guidance . . . and making me
aware,
Of all the wonderful things in
life—that I have yet to share.

I'm sorry . . . for getting
crazy . . . being ridiculous and
being rude
I'm sorry . . . for those
thoughts . . . that got me in
that mood.

I'm sorry, MY DEAR FAMILY . . . .
for, Acting as a Fool ! ! ! ! !

I . . . Sincerely Love You Truly
and . . . Thank the Lord,
for Having You . . . . .

Doris J. Bryant
MEMORIES OF TIME
Once again my thoughts go back
into the memories of time.
Of the wonderful glorious day
when your life touched mine.

I felt life had lost it's meaning,
but was I ever wrong.
The joy you brought into my life,
was almost like a song.

You gave me hope and
understanding,
and made me see the way.
To live for the future,
not just from day to day.

The world is full of love and
beauty,
Somehow you made me see.
I can always count on you,
no matter what the need may be.

Please Dear, always remember
throughout our remaining days.
I love you for the love you've
shown me,
in so many countless ways.

S. A. Hagemeier
SONG OF THE SEASON

*To my grandmothers, Kate
Amery and Alice Hagemeier.
With love.*

Winter, December, Christmas
begin to swarm.
Inarticulate feelings—
Feelings caught between
perception and imagination:
Hazy, vague, and warm.
Thoughts swirl as one emotion
And coalesce in aspiration.
Symbols abound and fill our
thoughts with pure, unthinking
feeling.
Unconscious sights influence mind:
Hungry flames devouring holiday
logs,
Puffs of misty breath expelled in
frosty December air.
Smells of baking fruitcakes.
Essences of Christmas love fill
the atmosphere.
Perception and imagination form
ideas of inner peace;
Juxtaposed between the two
Sits an easy, familiar love
Of Christmas generosity, giving,
and of Santa Claus.
Myriad thought and mind's eye
pictures
Of snow and trees and peaceful
doves
Make that nebulous, beautiful
feeling
Of Christmas Season,
Of peace, goodwill, and love,
What it was meant to be.

ballenmoon
Dawnbreak At Mingus
Park
The first slashes of morning
Ricochet off discarded feathers
Floating on the gently rippling
pond
That reflects the pale magenta

sky.
A ghostly plateau of steam
  Rises lazily into the moist morn
  air,
As the sun's sharp tentacles
  Scatter the stars into waiting
  limbos.
A sleep-eyed mallard lands on the
  pond,
  Deftly unzipping the water's
  surface;
Two plump joggers plod the well-
  worn paths
  In lime-green warm-ups with
  racing stripes.

Traffic starts to pound on the
  cold, gray streets,
  And an unseen rooster begins to
  crow;
In a moment, the magic will be
  gone—
  Waiting for a chance to appear
  once more.

Dianna Kay Hirt
JOURNEY
Do you see that little bug?
He's just making his way across
  the rug.
He's so little to be on his own,
I wonder where he calls home.

As he journies across the kitchen
  floor,
He makes his way to the back
  door,
To the field and I'll see him no
  more.
He still lives you see.
I figure, who am I to end his
  journey?

Susan P. Zitt
**An Angel In God's
  Kingdom**

---

*In loving memory of Jason Lee
Lohr Though only with us briefly,
his life touched us all in a very
special way.*

God chose to take Jason home
  with him,
Though we do not understand
  why.
Only that we briefly said hello,
  then had to say good-bye.

We'll always have our memories
  of this little boy,
Though with us a short time—
He brought us so much Joy.

We never got to know him
But his presence was known.
And we will surely miss him,
  until we too are called home.

He's now a little angel
In God's kingdom up above,
He knows no pain or sorrow,
Only solitude and love.

Candy Emerson
I AM

---

*To my mother who gave me my
roots and my husband Steve who
gave me my wings.*

So small am I
that I am not.
But, if I am not
why do I know it?
Where am I, to be not?
But not to be is
              NOTHING
But whose to say that
              I AM NOT

Chuck Macchia
SUMMERFLOWER
  The Pains of a Brokenheart
  with a Love song
        now forgot.
But OH . . . .
    what a summer
we once had . . .
    with fields of happiness
    and adventure
    and each day
    was fresh and new.

My Love,
you were my summerflower
and I watched you grow.
I was once told
    not to overwater
    my summerflower
for it will lose it's luster
    and fade away
        I didn't listen!
Sure . . . I could have been
    more stern and demanding
but would that
        have been fair
        to you,
            or me.
Someone once said
    "One is strong to hold on".
But I feel
    One is stronger to let go.
Maybe someday
    we can start again
        where we left off
if not in this life span
maybe then
        in the next.

James A. Stelly
SPECIAL
A time of love,
A time of the past.
This time I'm sure
Our love will last.

A special feeling,
Deep down inside,
There's times when I hurt,
And still keep my pride.

For you, my love grows
More each day.
I long await,
That special say.

To let me know,

When and where,
That special place,
Together,
  We'll share . . . .

Lynn Marie Kochendorfer
REFLECTIONS
Fondly she
cradles her memories
shimmering lights
casting warmth
upon her face.

The house feels so empty
as the Holiday nears.
Weakening—
her heart swells
loneliness engulfs
the tenderness of her soul and
gently now
she paints
visions of family—
gifts, candy canes,
and Holiday cheers.

Turning now,
she searches
the lights blinking,
her face glistening
in the shadows,
. . . memories reflected once again.

Tony Karelas
THE FLOWER
It was a cool dark day,
In heartfelt wonder.
The strong flower I gave,
Sank weakly under.
And maybe I cry too much,
Like a rainstorms thunder.
But the love I lost,
Was my saddest blunder.

Yesterday's sun still shines,
Like an April shower.
My greatest feat in life,
Was my short lived power.
I stood and watched my foe,
Defeated in the tower.
But I soon lost myself,
I couldn't grow the flower.

The moon began to shine,
After the drenching pour.
I was on the beach that night,
Wondering what life is for.
But the warrior in me was still
  alive,
Craving just once more.
And in my weakest moment,
The flower washed up on the
  shore.

Katie J. Crutchfield
LIBERATED WOMAN
Liberated Woman—
    to some it's freedom from the
    kids around her feet
    the daily task of preparing
    bread and meat
    escape from the never ending
    dust and grime
    the blessedness of housewifery
    that some find sublime
Liberated Woman—
    a new breed, a new kind
    one who has an "outside" career
    in mind.

Connie Black
TIME
Time has flown, the years gone
  fast
Tomorrow is the future, today
  the past

Remembering High School daze
The disco craze
And Graduation night.

Memory books, tassels and gowns
Smiles and laughter, tears and
  frowns
Shake my hand and hug my neck
The night is through, what a wreck
Future plans, they seem so near
It's past and friends that bring a
  tear
They drop and splash all around
Then slip away without a sound
As I stand here not quite alone
I know, I have truly grown.

Time has flown, the years gone
  fast
Tomorrow is the future, today
  the past
Remembering High School daze
The disco craze
And . . . . . LIFE

Faye Scoggins Bigelow
FULFILLMENT

---

*To my daughters—Dorothy Fae
Whitlock and Ruby Dell Estlock,
ever loyal and steadfast.*

Today I saw above that vale of care
Life's road that leads among the
  hills of time
And as a traveler on a journey
  bound
Viewed ever-changing scenes
  with vision rare
That brought the past to blend
  with present hours,
Or pierced the future with
  prophetic eye that gave
A continuity to God's great plan.
Then could I see all that had
  been and was to be
For all mankind.

There is a unity so far beyond
The unities of time, of space, of
  thought
That links us just as one, as all
  waves are
One sea which to the pebble does
  respond;
So those held dear may pass from
  touch of hand,
But love forever forms the
  precious chain that binds
And death is but a rest between
  two notes,
Symphonic tones, unfinished,
  readied for our own
Return into the infinite.

Janet Taylor
HIDDEN SORROW

---

*Dedicated to a very Special Man
in my life, who inspires me and
who will always be number one
in my life and in my heart and
who I'll Love deeply always.*

Standing sadly by the pond you
  see her
There with her head hanging down
Her delicate hair touching to the
  ground
Never to look up and see the blue
  of the sky
Always, hanging down in sorrow,

I wonder why?
Does she too have the pain of a
broken heart
As she stands there till the fall of
dark
Hanging her head and looking in
the mirrored pond
Seeing only her own reflection
and wondering why she must
be the one to stand alone
Does she too cry through the day
and night
As she stands there so lonely
through the rain, winter winds,
and summer bright
The weeping willow with her hair
swaying in the breeze
As it hides her face so no one see's

Beatriz D. Querol
FESTIVAL
They all say: Merry Christmas,
dear,
Enjoy a happy, good New Year!

Stars play their long-bowed violins,
Rapt planets cling their
mandolins;
The silvery waves waltz
gleefully
As breakers beat hilariously.
Cool, shy winds whistle a
new song
Where they go caroling
along.
Bright asters curtsy as
they dance
While song-birds
warble on each
branche.

All chorus: Merry Christmas, dear,
Enjoy a happy, good New Year!

Bell-flowers blow their clarinets,
Garbed trees wave, click their
castanets,
Gay brooks splash their poetry
in rhyme,
Sprays dance the polka at this
time.
Great thunder roars in
laughter, claps
Its mighty hands. The
bare sky flaps
The message: Merry
Christmas, dear,
Enjoy a happy, good
New Year.

Edward J. LaBee Jr.
WHERE DOES IT SAY

*To the America that we all
believe in*

Where does it say
That life has to be bad
And filled only
With things, that are sad,

Where does it say
That it's wrong to give
And there isn't enough room
For everyone to live

Where does it say
That life can't be fun
And you can't be proud
Of the things, you have done

Where does it say
That a man can't cry
And to have true peace

People must die

Where does it say
That the skies above
Have to be so polluted
And we have no room for love

Yes! where does it say
That these things aren't true
And America can't be beautiful
Under her RED, WHITE, AND
BLUE

Liz Carter Richards

Liz Carter Richards
fear
hovering   within   myself
i quiver   blood fired
by quickening heart beat
speeding through arteries
veins and vessels
at a high rate
encreasing
chances of collision
at enterchanging areas
cause
inability of use   of
my brain capacity
and i weaken   i withdraw
hovering fear   fear
of most everything
unreal or real
even fear of myself.

Diane Louise Baron
THE THIEF
The developing nightmare
Taking control of my mind at
night,
Stealthily took over my day.
Please,
Don't let me fall asleep.

Juanita J. Tackett
TO SEE AS A CHILD
If grown people could see this
world through the eyes of a
child,
On almost everyone and
everywhere you would see a
smile.
If only people could see the world
through the eyes of a child,
There would be less heartache
and more smile.
To see as a child, I would say,
Everyone would be happy every
day.
Everything would be laughter and
play,
There would be no more gloomy
or a rainy day.
To see as a child,
To have laughter and smile,
To know what it is to crawl,

Then to stand and stand tall.
To see as a child,
Life would be worthwhile.
Just live one day at a time,
Be happy with only a dime.

Inez D. Geller
ABSENT

*To My Friend and Mentor Sister
Eileen O'Gorman*

My body presses down,
against
the world globe.
The position of my heart
is fronting onto
Nova Scotia,
where you vacation
without me.
I place my head
on the Arctic sea
while hot tears of longing
bathe
the indifferent glaciers.

Rosanna Teresa Galluccio

Rosanna Teresa Galluccio
Will It Matter That I Was?

*To my parents, Rodolfo and
Susanna Galluccio, without
whom it would not have
mattered if I was.*

When many tomorrows have
faded away,
Becoming the shadows of a long,
yesterday,
And I have been gone for many a
day,
Will it matter that I was?

When no one is left to remember
my name,
'Cause cold granite markers, they
all look the same,
And they're all that is left as
proof that one came,
Will it matter that I was?

If I have been able to make
someone smile,
To lift up their spirits for even a
while,
Lighten their burden o'er the
course of a mile,
Will it matter that I was?
If I have been able to allay
someone's fear,
To give reassurance or lend them
an ear,

Comfort their sorrow or wipe
away a tear,
Will it matter that I was?

If I can take just one person out
of the rain,
Clear up the gray skies, alleviate
the pain,
Then I'll know that the life I've
lived wasn't in vain,
And yes, it will have mattered
that I was.

Margaret Marie Hoskins
XMAS
Don't take the Christ out of
Christmas,
And replace it with only an "X";
For the meaning leaves-and all
that is seen
Is a ghastly, unfeeling like X.

X-it stands for unknown,
And surely He is not;
For even the angels sang of His
birth
To lowly shepherds that night.

They came to see, like none before
A babe that was sent from on high,
A special present from God above,
Sent for our sins to die.

He loved us so much and for a
God so great
The least that we can do,
Is let him have a place in our heart
And a place in Christmastime, too.

Lynda Ohlen-Sliwa
INFIDEL RETURNED
Speak, I beseech you, speak!
Speak the words of bright
saints.
Swear by their redemption to
receive thine own.
Yet, betroth thy heart, not by
word, but, by execution.
Nourish my soul with fruits of
hope, yet, render hope
prudence,
Or my true heart shall deem
overwhelmed and shall doubt
extremes,
By too bountiful a remedy.

Pray thy strength be vast. Heal
thy longing for tempestuous,
vandalous ways.

Take heed, take heed, for my
warming is firm . . . therefore,
I stand not as your lord, but as
your love returned.
Take heed, take heed! For a man
such as you shall not grieve my
heart . . . For alas! My soul
would wither and this would
be its' demise.
Harken me from a trustless tomb,
instill loves' faith anew.
Stand fresh, herein my chamber.
Allow light beams to sanctify
Our holiness, and dry my
wretched teardrops of bitter
days.
Sweeten our time with new
stealth in your principle, and,
Henceforth, my bosom will be
your resting place.
Hasten away malevolent spirits . .
Chasten the core of
Thy being, and, My love, I'll bid
you ne'er farewell . . .
But, an eternal welcome.

Beth Ann Keene
Through The Eyes Of a Child

The many things with no names
to bear
the many colors to make a child
stare.
to learn from his mother the
color is green
then to show mother all the
green to be seen
Everything is "something" until
it's given a name
learning all the new things is a
challenge and a game
the child is small and shows no
concern
for each day brings a new thing to
learn
though all the clocks—there is
no time
Just a pretty sound from a clock
with a chime
Circles, squares, red, blue, short
and tall
the fascination of a child is never
too small.
The big, loud bird flying, floating,
above the church steeple
the amazement in the eyes of a
child who learns of a plane that
can carry people.
the child goes from the parents
dreaming and plan
to the wonderful outcome of a
woman or man.

Loretta H. Culli
HARMONIOUS BALLET

Behold! the field Lillies, they
neither spin nor sew there yet
Solomon in all His glory, with
them cannot compare;
Consider! the beauty of the
Begonia, with purity of bloom
rich emerald leaves to glisten
in sun-rays at noon as breeze
gulps her winy nector, to relax-
blow-that all in garden, her
harmony of splendor know;
The sunflower head bending low
to follow sun as to horizon he
each day must go;
Chorus of birds no longer heard
by mimic of mockingbird;
the day birds fly to cradle in
towering tree to rest as mother
bird content to cover egg nest;
as Whippoorwills on night
insects swoop, in harmony the
frolicky Meteors reherse their
Ballet of Loop—the Loop— 'tho
myriads and myriads of
Galexies in own orbit—stay—
while Wee and Great Bear their
game of tag play 'round and
'round' the North-Star so Bright
as moon completes her quarter
waning, Heaven to delight;
Arise! Look up! all things
beautiful were made for GODS
Earthly chidren, bought back
by HIS Heavenly SON
"PARADISE RESTORED" soon
HIS Complete Will, to be done;

Helene Slaski Kraus
OCTOBER DAYS

October's rain of
colored leaves
beneath my feet
wet by the rain
cling to my shoes
where sounds once came
on paths that wind
beyond my sight
down hills edged
by a ribbon's stream
where once I saw
a summer's dream.
Wind that whips
the sturdy trees
and lifts the wet
October leaves
brings drops of rain
upon my face
while footsteps
thread into the space
where leaves of
brown and gold are bed
until the rays
of sunshine bring
them back to life
in early Spring.

Kathleen M. Fenton
IF

If I'd known you would be by my
side this day
I would not have so easily walked
away
If I'd known I was still held in
your heart
I would not have had a reason to
part
If I'd known how you were shy
I never would have just walked
you by
If I'd known how honest you were
All those doubts would have
turned to blur
If I'd known you loved me, knew
you were there
We'd be together today, to love,
to share

Diana Rosenstock
NIGHT CRY

A cry in the deep purple of the
night,
Sharp pains piercing through the
heart,
Agonizing emptiness leaving
blind the sight,
Life's being lost before given the
chance to start.

Laboring words trying to reach out,
Struggling efforts of wanting to be
more,
Saddening sorrow of unending
doubt,
Lost in dark shadows behind a
locked door.

In the silence comes a new birth,
Even as the darkness must yield
to the light.
When all has been abandoned in
the search,
Something is found in the
stillness of the night.

A voice within cries out:
"Why live only to die a little
more each day?"
A voice answers: "Take the word,
Struggle in your heart to find the
true way."

The war of truth is not won on
fields of blood.
The creation of beauty is not
finished in beds of lust.

All the songs of the soul must
first be heard,
Before peace and love will be
given in trust.

John A. Richardson
KIMIKO'S SONG IV

A Song Of Love A Love Song
Requited Love Unrequited Love
Various Loves Sung Singing Sang
Singing When She becomes
One with the Son and the song
becomes Her And you Love
the
Song You Love the Song You
Love Her Both. The Awaking Lost
Youth and the remembering the
First Love The First Time When
We were Afraid of the Sexual and
trusted the Love! And
knew Neither. AH! But IT WAS
TRULY GRAND —wasn't IT??
Was IT?? Noooooooooo
Yesssssss. I don't really Know.
And all the Years Since Just a
Rite Of Passage. Our Lives
are measured from One Love to
the Next . . . It's Hard to
Remember ALL the InBetween
Times except the Forgetting
of the Last Love. And the
Searching, Yes the Searching for
the Next Love . . . . As the
Years GO.

Frances Kavanaugh Nelson
The Night Of Our Saviour's Birth World War II 1944

*For my daughter Carol, who
shares my birth date. May her
joyous laughter see her through
every day of her life.*

It is the night of our Saviour's
birth.
In silent reverence within His
church I kneel.
Outside, the moon shines on the
driven snow.
The altar candles are lighted—
mellow tones
From the organ, voices of the
pious speak
"PEACE ON EARTH GOOD
WILL TOWARD MEN."

Tonight, the ironic meaning of it
all
Touches me profoundly; I
tremble in fear
For the mighty War-lords the
world over
Who put power and avarice
above all else
And have made our world tonight
a vast
Crater of fear and death and
devestation.

It is the night of our Saviour's
birth.
Our univerdal prayer . . . let
there be
"PEACE ON EARTH GOOD
WILL TOWARD MEN."
Then may my soldier-husband be
returned,
Safe in mind and body, to my
waiting arms;
And to our child, born of our
enduring love.

Gwendolyn Trimbell Pease
4—H YOUTH GROUP

*For American Youth, eternal
adaptabel in an Americ ever
changeable and especially to the
Castleton Busy Beavers 4—H
Club members—past and present.*

Country and city youngsters
meet all over
beneath emerald green four leaf
clover

boys, girls, leaders together plan
past success will repeat once
again

among life's most tangled threads
fate screwed on some straight
heads

busy working hands deftly trying
daring, caring hearts high flying

great wealth of good health better
serving community, self above
the letter

year-long diverse projects
interesting
while teaching, learning
something

true experiences continue—group
effort
growth of all youth needs our
support

4—H can and does truly reinforce
our American traditions, of course.

Carol Dillon Lewis
WOOD RIVER VALLEY

Cottonwood floatin' through the
air.
Old stump makes a pretty good
chair.
Front pasture's sportin' alfalfa
knee-high.
Overhead, the bluebirds are
tumblin' by.
Crickets are chirpin' out by the
dusty road.
Log truck passin' with a full load.
Just smell the clover—and the
wild bushes!
Palpitatin' odors from the river's
edge rushes.
Baskin' in the sunshine on a
summer day.
Brushin' at a horsefly—wish he'd
go away
Wood River Valley—tanglefoot
thinkin'.
Not much happenin'—goatskin
drinkin!

Mrs. Christina L. Bean
MY DADDY

My daddy is so very sweet,
He hugs me and sqeezes me 'and
tickles my feet.
And when it comes time to
change my diaper,
My daddy is a good dodger and
wiper.
My daddy is so loving and caring;
He shows it to us by learning and
sharing.
When daddy and I get to take a
bath;
There is no stoping us, when we
go splishity-splash.

When Daddy and i talk man to
man,
There isn't a word you can
understand.
When daddy and i get real, real
hungry,
And are wanting something good
to eat,
You can hear our bellies growl
from our head to our feet.
But Mommy says;
Whatever we eat will never go to
our bellies, that it just goes to
our feet.
My daddy has told me;
You don't have to be rich or have
any money,
to make people's lives happy and
sunny.
And when it comes time to
decide who or what I'll be,
My decision I make, right or
wrong,
The open arms of my daddy will
be very strong.
But one thing for sure,
I love my daddy, I surely do.
I thank the Dear Lord he gave me
you.

Holly Lason
THOUGHTS OF TIME
Seeing blue eyes
Telling white lyes
Doing things on the sly
Answering inside whys
Leaving past ties
Finding great Highs
Drawing time nigh
Dreaming mind flys
Forgetting deep sighs.

Mark D. Hachey
THE SONG
I awoke early this morning.
Why? I do not know.
But I was priviledged to give
audience
To a song that only Nature could
sing.
A song-bird was composing a solo
recital
For anyone who cared to listen.
It was at morning's first blush,
the sky a fiery red.
Sparkling drops of water, like
emeralds,
Clung to the leaves after last
night's rain.
Young saplings and the tender
leaves of parent trees
Whispered in the morning breeze,
Which seemed to compliment
The overture of my feathered
friend's warbles, chirrups, and
twitters,
arranging them all in a silver
tones melody
That was relaxing, and at the
same time exhilerating.
It was a pleasant interlude before
my chores began,
Which acted as a reminder
Of how truly wonderful Nature
really is.

Lisa Marie Iannucci
IF ONLY
If I could reach the stars I would
grab you a shiny one and
present it to you with a smile.
If I could catch a rainbow I would

bring you a pot of gold with a
heart full of wishes.
If I could walk on the moon I
would catch the dreams that
fly above in space and bring
them to you with a kiss.
If I could fly like a bird I would
bring you on a journey of love.
If I could climb a mountain I
would proclaim my love for
you and hear its echo in the
wind.
If I could sing you a song I would
sing my love with music and
hear melody fill your soul.
If I could see you again I would
hold you and never let you go
as we become one.
If I could do all these things for
you I'd be in heaven floating on
the clouds
If only you would let me . . .

C. Adele Henning
CELIBATE, UNSATISFIED
In abjuring the sensate, we miss
that which is to be cherished:

How else shall we know—we live?

Bare feet, trying out
morning-wet, cool grass,
or baked-hot shell-flinders
on long white beaches . . . small
hurts
shall only emphasize—we live.

In the caressing glide
of a calloused hand, stroking
silky—cool, slim thigh—
though suppressed, the thrill is—
we live.

To forfend life's depths of
Tantalus,
timorous of love's scar—
nor know, of avian—struggling
pulse,
nor, of quavering, emptied sigh—
wherefor else, shall we say—we
live?

New birthmarks, on young flesh:
carnal merit badges—
that might, otherwise, have been
scars, as harshly livid,
hid deep inside

a celibate, unsatisfied.

Bob Hayward
WINDS OF CHANGE
The winds of change
are here again
time to start anew,
Make a change
from old life styles
to new ones that are few.

The sands have shifted
from their homes
new ones take their places,
Tossed around
to meet the new
bright look of their faces.

Like the flower
whose native seed
travels with the breeze,
For awhile
all is passed
until it lands on gentil seas.

Rocking, rolling
tossed about
until it's time to go,
Giving, caring

sharing life
until it works too slow.

The winds of change
will come again
after all is past,
Sands will shift
seeds will fly
time—it moves by fast.

Judy Catholos Lorenzen
SOUL OF A POET
It's hard to be a poet
To pour your soul out
To bare your soul for the world to
read
The tears, the pain that got you
there,
To tell the world and hope they
care.

It's not the same as not liking me
These words I've written from my
heart,
Rejection of my words, is
rejection of my soul
As a child to the present of years
lived long ago.

Some that read them want to cry
They feel as though they've
walked those miles,
Others read them feel their worth
An injustice to their birth.

It doesn't matter anyway
The words will come and I will
write,
And someday should you read
my soul
You'll know it's me, somehow
you'll know.

Donna Lee DeMarco (DLD)
THROUGH IT ALL
Emptiness digging down deep
within me.
I miss you more and more as time
drifts by.
Sunshine streams down to greet
me.
In the misery of losing you, I cry.

I wake up to find that your love
was a game.
It's all to complicated, I'm not
sure who to blame.

I've been waiting for a love to be
true.
You told me and promised me
that it was you.
Our plans for marriage suddenly
fell through,
when you told me you loved
someone new.

You made me feel so small.
I wasn't prepared to fall.
But still I went on loving you,
just as strong as before.
Even though it was time to let go;
time to close the door,
I still loved you through it all,
and now that it's all over with,
I find myself
still loving you!

Melodie Carol Harstine
BRAND NEW START
The day I lost your love and you
went away from me,
Will always be etched forever in
my heart and memory.

I felt as though my reason for
living was gone,

I thought without you, I could
never go on.
You took with you all the love I
had,
You took my heart, Now I'll never
be able to love another,
And make a brand new start.
Even though you stopped loving
me so long ago,
My heart and my life are still so
empty, so hollow.
Maybe one day I'll be able to pick
up the pieces of my broken
heart,
I'll stop loving you, and make a
brand new start.

June Lee Box

June Lee Box
**Redwood Spirit Is Not Like
That Snowman**
Nor Big Foot with his tracks of
fame
But a smaller creature on our
North Coast
That's every bit as hard to tame
Lives among the giant Redwoods,
we boast
Has web feet to wade in the rain
A round body, a coat of warm
brown fur
A long slender neck like a crane
It can't cry or sing, just sounds a
soft purr
Loves to sniff the clean spicy
breeze
That's laced with sea-tang from
the nearby shore
It's sharp bill pecks tree bark with
ease
As big sparkling eyes spot bugs
by the score
A tongue which laps like a kitty
And small pointed ears that hear
a lot
A shy creature and quite pretty
Elusive it may be, but dumb it's
not
It's a wise Spirit, quick and bright
For it hurries and hides behind a
tree
When hunters slash around the site
They listen, look, and fume:
"Where CAN it be?"
The forest's dark as they explore
But , by crouching low against a
huge trunk
That wily Spirit makes them roar
For that brown ball has become a ·
big chunk
On the tree's base—A
REDWOOD BURL!

Our World's Best Loved Poems

Scott Young Moyer
FLOWERS

The wisdom of dreams, must be felt to have meaning.—taken from "The Wishmaker"

They brought Flowers here
               today,
with a message of love,
           tucked within.
Their beauty filled me
           deep inside,
Their fragrance enhanced
           my soul.
Each red blossom echoed
  innocense through-out my heart,
Captivated were my eyes,
      on a few tiny buds, longing to
          emerge into life.
Yes,
  they brought Flowers here
               today,
  for a moment, my breath stood
  still,
but they were not for me,
  though in my mind,
         I dreamed they were.

Margie W. Grant
LOVE'S SECRET QUEST

Dedicated to every man, woman and child who rides the White Horse of Peace, for my beloved, I send to Thee an Arrow of Love for PEACE NOT WAR.

Love, Hope of all Mankind
Is what the World really needs,
And I see hidden
In the depth of each thinking mind
And thoughtful eyes,
Many a mile to travel,
Many a task to do.

Silent Lady in golden splendor
Riding away from the Cities of
  Earth,
Riding away from a World of
  Peace,
From a Mission of Love,
Your Secret Quest.

Presidents, Kings and Lords of the
  World
Shall follow Love for a Better
  World.
When Love's last mission has
  been fulfilled,
Flags of every Nation shall be
  unfurled.

NOW—they bring so many, many
Wreaths from every Land,
Love's tomb there seems to be,
In the star studded sky.
Low voiced men who speak
Call her the "Lady of Love".

Brenda L. Dahlheimer
THE BAG LADY
While sitting on a park bench
  one morning, I perchanced to
  meet,
An elderly lady in shabby dress,
  with a shopping bag at her feet.
She had on broken glasses, she
  had mended with adhesive tape,
And her ankles swelled above her
  shoes, I couldn't help but gape.

Upon noticing my staring, she
  gave me a bashful smile,
And said "I hope I don't offend
  you if I sit here for awhile.
My old dogs are tired and it's
  been a long, cold night.
I couldn't find a bench to sleep
  on, I must be quite a sight!"
After talking I came to find, the
  old woman was without a home,
Forgotten by her children, she
  couldn't make it on her own.
With rent so high and food costs
  up, she couldn't make ends
  meet.
And so decided to revert, to
  living on the street.
I later came to find in horror,
  there were many others,
Who, like her, lived on the
  streets, forgotten mothers!

Margaret Tod Ritter
ORIGIN OF MUSIC
The wind is not impersonal, it
  knows
That days of sunlight, dawn to
  dusk, should be
Left to themselves in such
  tranquility
As scarcely stirs the petal of a rose.
It also understands the fear that
  reigns
Whenever, in its anger, it engulfs
The mountain hamlet with its
  snarling wolfs,
The seacoast city with its
  hurricanes.
It does not favour flying steel
  jet-wizards
That spoil its summer vales
  between the clouds.
It utterly resents the snow that
  shrouds
A winter night and whips it into
  blizzards.
Whether as idle gust or wild
  typhoon
It is the wind that whispers to
  the moon.

Sister Marie Baptiste Ureel, IHM
WITNESS
I live
  in the faith of our Lord Jesus
  Christ,
Who loves me
  with an everlasting love,
Who suffered and died for love of
  me. (Gal. 2,20)

Faith is
  acceptance
  of Christ
  personally
  as gift to me.

Love is
  His Spirit
  living
  continually
  His life in me.

Life is
  CONVICTION
  writ large
  eternally
  for all to see.

Shari Rajoo
The End Of the Beginning
Hurt.
A sort of udeniable torture.

Conceived,
In the harrowing depths of
  confusion and betrayal.

Hurt.
Merely another form of a bitter
  rage that twists around inside
  the mind with a disgusting
  passion.

Occurring,
When everybody has deceived
  you and nobody has cared, it
  seems.

An age,
At which temporary destruction,
  with the aid of naiveness
  becomes permanent.

Beware,
For concealed in the minds of the
  vulnerable exists a power like
  no other.

The kind of power that causes
  the hand of a youth to grasp
  the apparently easy
  solution . . .

A revolver
  or
    switchblade.

Miss Dianne R. Hayes
IT'S OVER!

This poem is dedicated . . . To Helen, my mom with all my LOVE!

When you face the realities of
  life, the pain begins to fade.
You realize that life looks
  hopeful; your decision has been
  made.

If you leave the past behind you,
  your future will look so bright.
It's time to open up your heart,
  and begin to live your life.

You can open the door to the
  outside world and welcome it
  with a smile.
From the dark and hopeless path
  you've trod, you know you've
  walked the final mile.

For those of you who hurt so
  much that you want to end the
  pain.
Go out and search for the
  happiness that will give you
  peace again.

Give yourself a final chance and
  I'm sure that you will find,
Your grief and hurt will disappear
  and you will have peace in
  your mind.

Gloria Jean Pike
THE NIGHT

Dedicated to my parents and sisters. Norman and Marie Wold, Elizabeth Musical and Donna Whiteman

As I gazed up into the sky,
  I saw black velvet draped on
  high.
Across the earth it seemed to span,
  made by Gods loving hand.
Little chips of diamonds,

are stars that sparkle bright.
And give upon the earth,
  a soft and lovely light.
A globe of amber light I see,
  is the moon shining down on
  me.
As I look into the night,
  I feel the quiet and see the soft
  hued light.
I thank God for the beauty I see,
  for he set it there—for you and
  me.

David James Orlando
MOTHERS' DAY

This poem is dedicated to my true love Mary, and my truly lovely mother, Eileen, for being what they are.

A mother is a person who's full of
  love,
She's blessed with the spirit of
  God above.
Things that you do, words that
  you say,
Heaven will be yours some day.

Your work is no easy job I know,
It's done with love, so the scars
  don't show.
Continue to be, just the way you
  are,
My pillar of strength, a true
  shining star.

So in my heart is where you will
  be,
It's on my sleeve for the world to
  see
Mother, now that your story is
  told,
It makes me sad 'cause they
  broke the mold.

Rev. Helen Y. Torkelson
To a Lovely Bride

FOR My Foster Granddaughter Deborah Ann Harris now Mrs. Augustus Terry On Her Wedding Night Shower Get Together. A Lovely White Silk and Sheer Robe and Gown Set From Her Nana and I, Plus this Poem Especially For Her.

A Lovely Bride, We Know You
  Will Be—
And We Are As Happy As We
  Can Be
To Bring To You A Wedding
  Night Gift
All Wrapped In Love, Your Heart
  To Lift.
Wear It Proudly In His Arms,
  That Night
Snuggle Up Closely Sweet And
  Tight,
Let God Be within Your Hearts
  Of Love,
For He Is Ready To Bless You
  Both, You See
And He Sanctifys A Marriage
  Built On Things Heavenly.
T'was He, Who Ordained That
  You Be Man And Wife—
God Bless Your Lives Together
God Bless You, Especially, This
  Very Night.

Michael R. Burch
THE BEAUTIFUL PEOPLE
They are the beautiful people,
  and their shadows dance
  through the valleys of the
  moon to the listless strains of
  an ancient tune.

Oh, no . . . please don't touch
  them, for their smiles might
  fade.
Don't go . . . don't approach
  them as they promenade,
for they waltz through a vacumn
  and dream they're not made of
  the dust and the dankness to
  which men degrade.

They are the beautiful people,
  and their spirits sighed in their
  mothers' wombs at the distant
  echoings of that tune.

Winds do not blow there,
  and storms do not rise,
  and each hair has its place,
  and each gown has its price . . .
  and they dance in the darkness,
  untouched by the years,
  as we watch them and long for
  this "life" that is theirs.

June Lee Box

June Lee Box
OUR GUARDIAN TREE
Getting into the car I glance up
Seeing how tall the dark Spruce
  has grown
Standing six feet from that
  southwest corner
It's now three times as high as
  the house
It has been our Guardian Tree
For over thirty years
It was a three foot live Christmas
  tree
Which my two young children
  planted
In the sunny south yard
When they left home it was ten
  feet taller
Than the roof, and it waved them
  'Good Bye'
That tree is loaded with memories
We all loved it
A pyramid of soft, dark needles
With two longer branches
  sticking out
At it's shoulder height, and
  curving
Embracing arms around that
  corner
Of the house that held the
  children's room

Now, as I glance up, backing away
It's three times taller than the
  house
Those unusual longer arms
Higher now, wave a Greeting
To the whole countryside!

Mrs. Hilda Muryn
RAINDROPS TO THE SEA

*Dedicated to the memory of my
late father, William Bryant.
Remembered always, Hilda.*

A small crack high up in the
  naked earth,
Over on a mountainside,
A few raindrops to a stream gave
  birth,
The coming storm became a
  chosen bride,
Swiftly the small riverlet takes,
Each ravine and each gully in it's
  stride,
Then other streams join it and
  they ramble along,
Making music as they glide to a
  valley down below,
Creating o'er the rocks a happy
  song,
Now twinkling, then booming as
  swiftly,
They strike a blow, o'er catteract,
  like a song,
Then on and on, a small placid
  river down below,
Twisting and turning, it meets,
  another river on its way,
Through pastures green, they
  charge eachother to greater fetes,
And so ride hard against the
  tides, day by day,
Until they each shall much
  bigger be,
When they make their marriage
  with the sea.

Sharon F. Cote
THE LOVE WITHIN
As the wind moved in the
  branches of the trees
Soughing a plaintiff song;
So, the potency of the woods was
  in her
A dream flow of pagan magic—
  older than time
itself.

So, intensely did it sweep thru
  her, veins
That love blossomed as a flower
  warmed by the sun;
And as she lay receiving this gift
  with an open
heart
The pounding of a nearby ocean
  echoed within as,
her, own

Dolores Bentley Bryant
IF I PERISH
I have known rivers wider and
  longer
Than the east is from the west.
I have known mountains rough
  and steep
And laden with dangerous crests.

I have known valleys deeply
  embedded
On the plains of this green earth
And men have wagered baby's milk

On mastering the challenge' worth.

What is the incentive to prompt
  a people
To cross, climb or embark
On a mission to master each of
  these obstacles
With the faith by which Noah
  built the ark?

Having accepted the death and
  rising of a King
And eating eternities bread
I accept the challenge of this
  unmarked course
And say what Esther said . . .

If I perish going up the mountain
If I perish crossing the sea
If I perish in the valley I perish
But I accept the challenge Lord
  for thee.

Lillian L. Gerbig
CHRISTMAS TREES

*To my sister Rose, who
introduced me to "World of
Poetry", and to all my loved ones
who love Christmas trees.*

Christmas trees are a delight
Whether green or sparkling white;
  Painted silver, pink or gold,
  They are lovely to behold;
Every year at Christmas, too,
Every Christmas thought of You
  Is as lovely, gay and bright
  As Your tree on Christmas
  Night.

Paula Grafing
Do You Know What Your Missin'!
Do you know what your missin'!
If you forget to stop and listen.
Turn your radio on to play.
And listen to what they have to
  say.
You can stop and take the time.
To hear the words of each song in
  rhyme.
Song in rhyme—one's impression.
Of the many forms of expression.
Can be heard in many ways.
Specially when your radio plays.

Letha Stone Harris
SOWING FOR HARVEST
A farmer sows the seed in hope
That God will bless,—and then
He knows that one day, later on,
A harvest He will send:
For God will work a miracle
In the seed that has been sown,
And they'll come forth with a
  brand new life
To grow and ripen in the brilliant
  sun.

A christian sows the seed, God's
  Word,
And casts it far and wide,
He knows that God will bless,—
  and then
Bring a harvest of souls, all saved
  from sin:
God works a miracle in each
  willing heart,
A new life to them He does impart;
And when this work of grace is
  done
They are ready to grow through
  His Blessed Son.

Ethel Allman
NEW SEASON
My favorite time of year is now,
The lazy days of summer past.
Cool breezes waft of falling snow,
The leaves in all their glorious
  hues,
Will soon be gone, by winter's
  blast.
The pure white blanket will
  change the scene,
As our Savior came to make man
  clean.
To take away our sins and strife;
He came to give us all new life.

Kelly J. Flowers
FREEDOM'S FIND

*Dedicated to Donna, with all my
love*

I'll sail the seas of sorrow
And look for a tomorrow:
Where happiness lives forever,
And we may love together.

We will sing sweet songs of joy,
And wish every girl and boy;
May find happiness—as did we,
Then they too may live to be free.

Rise' Carole Helley
I'LL DREAM OF YOU
Our lips have never met
Our fingers have never touched
We've never shared a quiet
  moment
I've never felt the warmth of your
  body
I can only dream of you
          and your eyes
          with there silent smile

Sami Khoury
WHO AM I?
A bee collects the choice wine
  from roses, flowers and vine
Beneath a blue sky
  with care dedication and
  devine

A baby crying
  in my mother lap
And her soft hands pray

A legend of a handsome chap
  knocks on doors
One . . . by one
  moving like a mirage
Seeking a young heart or soul
  a little love, a smile and all

An old man
  striding a firm foot when can
Thinking about
  days bygone

Barbara Ann Smith
PARENTS??
What a funny word.
What's it suppose to stand for?
Two people who unite and have a
  family,
Bringing children into this over-
  populated place.
Some giving guidance
Some not caring
Some sticking by their children
Some not giving a damn and leave!

Do they have a right to do that?
To leave us and not even stay
  around to see how we turn out.

Some of us will survive and stand
tall.
Some will crumble and fall.

Who will pick up the pieces
when they fall?
Who gives them strength to carry
on when everyone is gone?

If the Parents are not there, who
will help them?!

Tom Bratney
CARMEL
cliffs, miles of sand, cypress trees,
rocky shores, grassy bushes and
experienced sea-movements
are all a part of Carmel.
Robinson Jeffer's house is a
monument
of stone and strong-felt memories
drawn on canvas of rough and
intricate, fertile colors.
golden light surprises the
morning—
dawn as crabs and sea anemones
begin the days events
in the sea's solitude, as the
quiet morning talks.

Cynthia Harris
GARDEN OF LOVE

---

*This poem I dedicate to Chuck, a
very special man in my life. His
caring has given me the
inspiration for all my poems He
deserves as much credit as I do
for their publication. I could not
have written them without him.*

If I could have a flower for each
thing you mean to me
What a garden of beauty for
everyone to see.
I'd have a rose for tenderness, for
this my love you give
I'd have a daffodil for watch-
fullness, because of this my life
I live
I'd have a bunch of daisys for the
laughter that we share.
I'd have a buttercup for
happiness, in the special way
you care
I'd have a honeysuckle, for the
tears you've kissed away
I'd have a tulip for the joy, in the
loving things you say.
I'd have a big carnation, for the
dreams you've made came true
I'd have a pretty pansy for all the
little things you do.
I'd have the swaying blubells ring
and love throughout the land
I'd have the morning glory vine
wrap round us, as we go hand
and hand
If I could have these flowers, for
all you mean to me
What a garden of beauty, for
everyone to see

Myrtle Hole
CRECHES
So often folks in wonder pause
Before a creche to grasp the cause
For which God sent His only Son
From heaven to earth—that
Blessed One.

In swadling clothes again they see
The Christ Child resting

peacefully.
His vigil Joseph doth embrace,
Her love beams forth from Mary's
face.

Great wonder fills the shepherd's
eyes,
'Tho angel's song in midnight
skies
Had told them that His blessed
birth
Would bring a peace for all on
earth.

Three wise men, too, by that star
led
Have placed gifts near His
manger bed.
These kingly men stand still or
kneel
To humbly show the awe they
feel.

And e'en the cattle seem to care,
For they this Night their stable
share.
'Tis God's concern and tender
care
That folks discern while pausing
there.

With love and faith renewed this
day
They go rejoicing on their way.
This gives true value so sublime
To creches seen at Christmas
time.

I. Wright
HAPPINESS IS
Happiness is many things
- a smile in the early morn,
- a rainbow following a storm,
- a little babe, newly born.

Happiness is being calm
- having peace of mine,
- remembering to be kind,
- always leading, never behind.

Happiness is caring
- caring for each other
- sharing thoughts with another,
- bringing flowers to mother.

Happiness is spread about
- by friendly word or acts,
- by stating only facts,
- by keeping emotion intact.

Happiness is something
- everyone can spread,
- no one needs to dread,
- a smile left where e're you tread.

Katrina Kaye Bevis
DARK AND COLD
Still is not a word for tonight,
The wind rages through the trees.
I search desperately for a light,
In the midst of falling leaves.
A cold damp wind blows across
my face
Yet nothing can I feel.
Surrounding me is white lace,
Covering a wound yet to heal.
This night is darker than those
from the past;
As death sneaks up from behind.
Our first kiss as well as our last
Brings comfort to the mind.
As I close my eyes and drift,
Happiness envelopes my head;
I feel my soul lift
And realize I am . . .
                    DEAD.

Malina Mahundasingh
The Greatest Spiritual Gift
Love is the greatest spiritual
power on earth, a gift from God
not acquired at birth.

It comes through sharing, caring,
serving and giving, concern for
others and positive living.

A very precious gift that money
can't buy, for it comes only
from the Eternal Most High.

He says to us, have faith, hope
and love, the fruits of the spirit
that comes from above.

This gift of live is most precious
indeed, it fills us to the fullest
and helps us to succeed.

With love we mix kindness,
patience, understanding, joy
and peace, and the blessing
from God will never cease.

The greatest spiritual power that
comes from above, a gift from
God—that power is love.

Robert E. Yoder
CONNIE

---

*I'm dedicating this poem to my
good friend Connie Lennon; and
to her son, Brandon.*

I have a friend
Named Constance Irene.
She's kind of cool
And peachy keen.
I think she's cute,
Believe it or not.
She's one of the best friends;
I have got.
She lifts up my spirits,
When I am down;
And she lives in Bellevue
Michigan town.
She has a son
Named Brandon Wayne.
Sometimes he's good,
Other times a pain.
Friends like Connie,
Are only a few;
And I'll always be glad,
This friend I knew.

JoAnn Aveline Reff
CONTEMPLATION

---

*To my Mother and Father, Esther
and Knute Knutson, who, with
their love, opened my mind and
nurtured my soul.*

In peaceful solitude I walk and
comtemplate the endless sky
and know, with certainty, the
souls of we who contemplate
can't die.
For souls, like space, reach out
forever, touching where we
cannot see;
undefined, yet more than real,
without my soul I could not be.
I could not share, nor give one
comfort, could not laugh, nor
cry, nor love.
Without my soul I could not,
peacefully, comtemplate the
sky above.

Isobel J. Saunders
MEMORIES
Yesterday I saw my first seagull
flying high over the rooftops
here.
He made a sound as he flew by
that reminded me of you—last
year.
Harbor lights and ships and
waves all rushed together in
my mind;
Then memories took over and
filled my thoughts of summer
days and a friend so kind,
Of lakes and beaches and skies so
blue, of campers and moonlight
and bonfires to.
I tried to remember in that short
time all the things that make
these memories so fine.
How could I have forgotten so
quickly—although, I guess
with winter and all that white
snow,
It's only forgotten 'till winter has
passed,
Then Spring brings back
memories that
                    LAST AND LAST.

CHILD
Elizabeth M. Caswell
Awake, awake my child,
It dawns, another day.
Swiftly goes the time;
Go forth and run and play.

Yes, go forth and play my child;
In the grass so sweet and wild.
Through the wooded mysteries;
Catching frogs and climbing trees.

On this lovely day in May,
Chasing sunbeams all the way;
For soon it will be yesterday
And childhood dreams will fade
away.

Terry Pinkerton
SHARING
How brightly the water mirrors
the morning sun
Demanding attention from
everyone
Silently speaking of mysteries
below
The hidden turmoil that never
shows.
I'm brother to that placid scene
That teems with energy yet unseen
I share the calmness so readily
found
Upon the surface when none are
around.
I share too, the mysterious deep
Filled with all I choose to keep.

Nichelle Nicole Harris
Worshippers Of the Night
Sunday.
Open books of what isn't written.
Listen to the words as they enter
the soul,
The power, the meaning, which
you know not.
Look above the cross which is
shaped so strangely,
The eyes of the preacher is the
eyes of the cross.
I hear the whispering murmurs
that float from the cloak
Seeping into the minds of the
children unaware;
Of the adults that are children.

And I don't understand this way
  of teaching,
I feel like a worshipper of the
  night.
The lights seem to dim and the
  voice has darkened,
As has the passage which leads to
  heaven.
No one seems to notice, the
  many objects of black,
Which seems so unfit for this
  place of Sunday.
My mother hasn't noticed, the
  lettering on the windows,
The unfamiliar lettering which
  surrounds us all.
We have no song books; we sing
  not
Our preacher carries a tune that
  seems abstract.
And as the judgement is passed
  along, we all wait in line.
To find out we are quite wrong,
For we were worshippers of the
  night.
Although we never knew it and
  our preacher never said it,
I guess he said, more than we
  heard, when he spoke about satan
And now we are, all quite lost, in
  the clutches of hell,
To forever burn in the night, that
  we once worshipped.

Michael J. Zuvanich
LOVE'S FOIL
Wield with care love's foil
For though tip's touch will win
A heavy hand
Can break tip and
Propel the sharp point in

A mortal wound to end
Love's intricate fencing game
And deal death
To love's sweet breath
Replaced by hate's vile name

Nora Beebe
SUDDEN DEATH
He is at rest.
Perhaps of all things in the world,
  this is the best
Reward for those in life we have
  held dear.
With all my might
I pray each one takes flight
As he did, never knowing pain or
  fear.
I cannot weep.
It is as if inside I am asleep.
I do the needed tasks, not free to
  grieve.
When one lies dead
The right words must be said.
Dry-eyed, I watch the weeping
  mourners leave
And wonder why
I am the one to smile and wave
  goodbye.
Thank God for shock.
It numbs the severed limb and
  stops the clock.
It slows the frantic heart that it
  wont' break.
The shock will go.
I am not meant to know
How many days or years slow
  time will take
'Til I will be
Strong enough, at last, to weep for
  me.

Carlyn Jean Dillon
eyes
i look into his green-gold cat eyes
and the desire to invade his being
overwhelms me
smiling he says "don't"
i watch him smile
and he asks "why"
i touch his arm
and his smiling green-gold cat eyes
silently say "i know—i feel the
  same"
i search his soul
and he says
"don't venture into the cave"
it's too late
i'm already there
led only by the light of his eyes
to the caverns of his soul
to forever adore him

John Michael Giberson
TAKE ME BACK
Take me back to my first love
Its her I'm always thinking of
How I wish I never let her go
How I wish I could tell her so
Take me back to the first night
With a girl in the back seat
Although I only kissed her
I sure felt complete
Take me back to the best days of
  my life
Take me back to the first time
I ever drove a car
When I drive today
I never seem to go as far
Take me back to the first times
I picked up my pay
Somehow it could buy more
Than it could buy today
Take me back to my school years
Teenage fool without fears
Back to my long hair
Rebel flag flying in the air.

Janell D. Davis
JUST FOR MOM

---

*To my wonderful mother who
never ceases to show me she cares.*

A uniqueness all your own
Unequalled by another
Your character astounds me
You're such a lady—mother.

The impressions you have made
Forever with me stay
Since I first set eyes on you
That fifteenth day in May.

Benevolence becomes you
And all your pulchritude . . .
I write these words for you—dear
  mother
With loving gratitude.

Khulsum Edirisinghe
The Truth As Told By
Jonathan Livingston Seagull

To my husband Janaka

The speed with which we fly
is the vehicle, don't deify
the chariot.
In our quest for the lateral flight
towards God, don't loose sight
of the fact that unwittingly,
we have become our own
  charioteers.

Louise Johnson
DON'T QUIT
When calorie counting all goes
  wrong as it sometimes will
When daily dieting seems all
  downhill
When your will power is low
  but your hopes are high
And you want to smile
  but you have to sigh
When stepping on scales
  gets you down a bit—
REST IF YOU MUST, BUT
DON'T QUIT!!

Paul Jason Bartholomew

Paul Jason Bartholomew
FATHER I YIELD
I am the clay,
  the earthly clay—
Drawn from the muck and mire.
I am the wood
  the hay and stubble
Of sinful soul's desire.

Thou precious Potter
  please mould me
In Thine own perfect way—
Thou loving Father
  I yield my will
For I'm still only clay!

Paul Jason Bartholomew
TRY TO REMEMBER
To remember again the wind and
  the rain the days we had no pain;
To remember again the walks
  down the lane, our spirits
  restored again!

To remember again the laughs
  and the cries the friends who've
  said their goodbies;
To remember again the plans and
  the tries, the swiftness of how
  time flies!

To remember again dry leaves
  and high snows the "caws" of
  late summer crows;
To remember again how the
  howling wind blows, —the
  SPRING—that gives birth to
  the rose!

K. M. Nikaido
The Music Of the Universe

In memory of Irene M. Powers

How often in the stillness of time
And in the stillness of the night,
Have you heard the universal
  sound:
The music of the universe?
That all pervading source of
Harmony in all things—
Like a master plan, all things
Though beset by storms and
  passions,
Finally unite with the music of
  the universe
And settle down to a course
That is serene and pervading,
The storm—tossed sea and the
  elements
Finally settle down to a peaceful
  course;
The belligerent nations and the
  angry people
Their passions surceased, settle
Down to peaceful ways.
They are keyed to the music of
  the universe,
Of universal harmony and order
That prevail despite all the
Passions, hate, anger, and storms
That beset us and the earth.

Michele Ellefson
The Day Has Just Begun

---

*Dedicated to my grandfather
Boyd K. Ellefson, who I never
knew, and wish I did.*

Early riser—up at dawn,
You glimpse the morning
On splendrous, silent
Wings of thought.
A million dancing wavelets
Catch each a sunbeam
And toss it away.
A single shining dew-drop
Reflects the life
Of early light,
Then falls—to the leaf
Spattered lawn below.
It splashes with meaningful
Significance, and disappears
Without a trace.
You begin to mourn its
Absence when you realize . . .
The day has just begun.

John Byron Hiller
THE REAL SANTA
Mary and Jerry one Christmas
  Eve night
Hit out on a very bold plan.
"Let's try", said Mary—her eyes
  shining bright,
"To see Santa Claus if we can."

They started to nod as the night
  wore on,
And Mary then fell fast asleep;
But Jerry decided he'd not even

yawn
'Til at Santa he'd gotten a peep.

Mary awoke at the chime of the
  clock—
Wide eyed—wondering what
  Jerry saw.
Said Jerry, "He just stuffed some
  toys in each sock,
And then jumped in bed with Ma!"

Lisa K. Meissner
CHRISTMAS DELIGHT

*TO My parents, Herman &
Geraldine*

I was looking out my window,
  one Christmas Eve night.
I remember the snow, all fluffy
  and bright.
I saw little green speckles, which
  started moving about.
Oh my! It was elves dancing all
  throughout.
How happy and cheerful,
  they seem to be!
Well its no wonder,
  their helping Santa decorate
  Christmas trees!
Santa's laughing, Ho! Ho! Ho!
  Oh, if only all the children
  could see the excitement glow;
and look, all the reindeer jingling
  nearby, such delight they show
  for Christmas, its such a jolly
  time.
Even Mrs. Claus is joining in the
  fun.
All this, a special Christmas, for
  each and everyone.

Sharon Ann Iser
CHRISTMAS

*To Aunt Wanda and Uncle Bud
with all my love.*

Christmas cheer and popcorn
  stringing.
Holly and jolly carolers singing.
Sleigh bells jingling as they round
  the bend.
Snowflakes falling covering our
  sleds.
And the Christ child nestled in
  his manger of straw.
A king of all kings come to save
  us all.
As I browse through my albums
  of good times gone by.
An aging tear falls from my eye.

Mildred E. Olson
LAKE SUPERIOR
Queen of the Lakes, I love you!
I love your tossing billows and
  your placid days.
You are a creature of many moods,
That thrill and fascinate me.
I enjoy the hours spent on your
  shore—
Meditating and dreaming of
  many days.
Last dusk I saw you put on your
  dress of frothy gauze—
It was trimmed in ribbons of gold,
You were enchanting!

This morning your surface was
  like mirrored glass of blue

Until a ship came sailing
  through.
One evening your gown was of
  the deepest crimson
With the setting of the sun.
On wintry days I've seen you
  spew your mist upon the shore,
To create strange creatures by
  the score.
One day you wore a turbulent
  grey,
Trimmed in ruffles of white lace.
Yours is an everchanging
  panorama—
And I love you for them!

Mrs. Patricia B. Cabrinety

Mrs. Patricia B. Cabrinety
WINTER'S FIRST BLAST

To fellow Minnesotans.

'Twas the 18th. of October in '82,
  when the storm descended upon
  me and you.

Outa' the prairies, 'cross Dakata
  and east,
  not fit weather for man nor beast.

Snow heaped by next mornin' was
  high—
  with snowflakes still flutterin'
  outa' the sky.

"Record breaker . . ." says
  newsmen of old,
  "for Minnesota winters," we're
  told.

"Wind chills to -20 below,"
  continues he,
  as ice and snow covered fields,
  far's the eye can see.

Ole winter's come 'fore

Halloween's here—
Looks like a l-o-n-g one, this year!

Barbara Brecht Parsons
WORD FANTASY

*This poem is dedicated to Mom,
whose courage and strength
through the years have given me
great inspiration.*

Words, multi-colored words
Whirl around in my mind,
Forming a ferris wheel of
  thoughts and images.
Colorful, musical wheel, round
  and round,
Stopping, starting, slow, fast,
Allowing another carefully
  chosen passenger
To become a part of this poetic
  sequence.
Onto this paper, aided by these
  pounding fingers,
Go rainbows of words, so easy to
  write, so hard to say,
Describing my feelings, dreams,
  ideas.
A kaleidoscope of whirling words,
Stopped only temporarily by
  punctuation marks,
Sharing these thoughts with
  others,
Each interpreting them in his
  own way.
Lines of words fill this paper with
  poetic jargon,
Until this tired circumference
  slows down,
Controlled by my waning
  thought processes,
And carefully spins off its
  remaining passengers,
Including this last word.

Charles Jay Marder
CARING
If you have eyes that are afraid to
  see,
  and ears that only hear biased
  words.
If you have legs that walk away,
  when another person hurts.
If you have a mind that thinks
  it's better than most;
  and you think your body is the
  only "10".
Then don't be surprised when
  you feel alone,
  'Cause you are your only friend.

Nore LeMaster
THE EXPERIENCE
I know little of a sunrise
I have yet to know the experience
The start of one new day
The freshness of its dawn.

Tell me, share with me
All that you now know
Help me to experience
Let your thoughts be mine.

The chill of the blowing wind
Make the pleasure increase
Your heart awaits the moment
The blaze begins to rise.

The praising sky, the colors dance
The vision fills you from inside
Words lack the expression needed
Beauty too intense to describe.

This is all you tell me is needed

To last throughout the day
Give some time, moments alone
To watch the day begin.

Elsie M. G. Miller
DAY IN NOVEMBER
This is a day fashioned for wild
  geese.

  Fog;

Loitering in the lowlands
And tangled among the hillside
  pines.

  The wind;

Trying desperately to wrap the
  sleazy lengths
Around their shaking limbs.

  Rain;

Feeling it's way to earth.
The open fields pinpointed with
  stubble
And rich with shattered grain,
The feeding grounds of the wild
  geese!
Now they come!

  Slowly;

In ragged formation against the
  murk.
Settling down with much gabbling
On their bedstraw, to feed and rest.

Kimberly F. Clark
AUGUST 1, 1983
By writing about lonliness
  doesn't make it feel any better
By exploring my deep seated
  handicapp
  (whatever it may be)
Doesn't help either
By composing poetry when I do
  is suppose to be a release
(I think) but its not (its not)

Its just a large open glass
That you fall in
And when you blow on the rim
It immediately grabs you!
Swallows you! and turns you
Into a scared little top that
fell in the bottle that
has no feelings, no limbs, no
will of its own. Just an object
that in order to move has to
depend on all the wine that
flows so evenly over and drowns.
The wine is left no breath from
the little top. It is dead!

That is precisely what I have
  become.
The only difference is I have a
  body

It lives

Harold James Douglas
A WONDERFUL PLACE
'Tis said, there will be no sorrow
 in heaven,
No darkness, for there is
 no night,
People will live always
 in the light.
Nothing but joy and rejoicing
 and singing they say,
With plenty of time for good
 hearty play.
Still waters and green pastures
 are there,
So are children, and flowers,
 and birds in the air.
Certainly it will be a wonderful
 place,
 for 'tis there we'll meet
Our Lord and Savior, Jesus Christ,
 face to face!

Jane Frederick Krauss

Jane Frederick Krauss
Under Tiffany and Fern
While shadows danced a flame
 did burn
Two lovers shared soft
 candlelight
Under lamps of Tiffany and fern
Lips shared tenderness of one
 sweet kiss
Hearts warmed to a night of
 perfect bliss
Lovers planned in all sincerety
Pledged love to all Eternity
Under lamps of Tiffany and fern

Carol A. Coltrane
NINE LIVES TIME
Siamese, Manx, Tabby puss cats
 Two four, seven, in a row.
Lying in warm sun,
 Look at them glow.

Motes of solar shine
 Dance in soft fur.
A tiny tail twitch.
 A chorus of purr.

Amber, green, blue eyes
 Wink in bright light.
Antenna whiskers
 Rotate in delight.

Irene Stanton
A PLACE TO DREAM
I love to lie beside the hearth
And watch the leaping flame
Ascend to fiery towering heights
And crumble to ash again

A dream is in each flickering dart
of orange and green and blue
And lies incinerated in that

smoldering residue
But dreams recur and flame again
And in their mellow glow
We may grasp just enough to
 think
That hope may make them so
To have never watched a flame
 and dreamed
To have never seen the ashes fall
Is to have never known that in
 that ash
Were the brightest dreams of all.

Diana Michell Lowery
MIRROR, MIRROR

*I wish to dedicate this poem to
those people who do not know
who they are, in the hopes that
they find the person within
themselves that they were
looking for.*

What do you see?
A face distorted by fake images
One that sees itself different from
 what others
see it as
A false picture
Do you really know who you are
 and
what you are
Mirror, Mirror
Tell me who I am
Show me
I see an image
that no one else does
Who has the right
image of who I really am
Is that me I see reflected on glass
 or
A distorted vision of what I
 should be

Peggy West
THE LITTLE SANDPIPER

To Mom

The little sandpiper came closer
on the bobbing sea,
His eye was fixed and black
and bold,
It shone with his wildness
right at me,
I knew this creature was wild
and free,
And that is what he thought
of me.

Brian D. Herd
TEMPEST
The north brine harshly splayed
over the bow and stern.
The captain, with eyes set in
 bronze
staunchly glared over the wheel.
Eyes firm and gray shy he did not
 away.
Sphynx like he steered the good
 ship, the
tossed ship, the swaying vessel.
Grayish haired fingers were
 numb on the wheel.
The grizzled captain Edmund Lou
 with
firm afoot, with purpose he stood.
The rigging groaned and creaked,
the crow's-nest bobbed and

swayed as the Martha pitched
dangerously, as the captain, as
 Edmund Lou
wheeled the craft firmly.
the vessel, the Martha brooked
 the swell.
The storm tossed brine did abate.
He grinned tightly—it was
finished.

Delores Johanna Albert

Delores Johanna Albert
RAVEN CRIES SOOTH

*TO MY BELOVED FAMILY:
Husband Pete, sons Brian, Kurt &
Thomas Mother Hazel, sisters
Margaret, Charlotte, Arlene,
Genevieve, Roberta & Victoria
Brothers Emmett, Johnnie &
William In-laws: Pete & Ethel
(Fr. & mother) Dennis, Jerilyn &
Carol (brother- & sisters-in-law)*

Today my heart is heavy
and my mind is fast;
the connection between them
is threatening to break.
This walk, I hope,
will settle the disagreement.
"Glah-glah, glah," sang out
a raven hidden high

in a tree close by.
My curiosity of him
quietly secured the bond.
"Wow-wow," came another cry
as I walked in new strength
given through a raven's cries!

Mary Shelton
REMEMBRANCES
Mystical tones of music known
Muffled moans alone show

Misty glows of moonlit magic
Dreamily captured in an
 opalescent daze

Chimes of the night's long cries
Answer the chatter of past
 memories
Ghosts of time's melody show
Magnetic murmers of mystery
 grow
To echoes of crashing glass
sprinkled lightly on the fallen
 snow

Rev. Frances Jane Williams
NEW LIFE IS GOD'S GIFT

*Written for and because of my
son—William Douglas Smith:
who "Became" because of God's
gifts to him: who is "Becoming
because of his gift to God.*

New life bestowed in many ways,
 Each is a gift from God;
A "New Life" came to me that day
 to prove how precious life is;
From Boyhood into Manhood,
 from son to husband and dad;
And "New Life" is brought forth
 once more.
Each life has promise, hope and joy
 and shows that God gives to All,
That chance to do, using all you
 have
to "Be" and to "Become."
"To Be—but how? "Become—but
 what?"
 God smiled upon that life,
 becoming new
saying, "My child, to Become is to
 Be
 what I created you to Be."
"New life?" he said, "even as a
 daddy?"
 God smiled, "New life as My
 Disciple—
Go now, My child and offer new
 life
 to 'whosoever believeth on
 Me . . .'
Preach My Word, for I AM Life—
 Always New."

Susan M. Silver
FOR MY FATHER
It was the sea
That took the life of Louis,
Sapphire in a pile of quartz,
Cicero, reborn unto a soulless
 shore.
And yet they never saw him
 standing there
With intellect for his staff,
Whose empty waves. They never
 knew him.
And the shore may never be the
 same.

Edna L. Brigham Harrison
THE BIRDS
Sparrows fall like ping-pong
 balls
merely touching the grass
then rising and falling
in undulant motions
that never match one another
like notes on a staff,
vying for notice.
They never look up
or know I am watching . . .
alone.

564

Our World's Best Loved Poems

Lyle N. Nachand
TRICK OR TREATERS
Jack-o-lantern burning bright
Trick-or-treaters in the night.

Little goblins in their suits
Pitter Patter tiny boots.

Ding Dong, Ding Dong, goes the
bell
Trick-or-treaters treat them well.

Tiny hands that clasp a bag
Painted faces dressed in rags.

Witches, pirates, monsters too
Might be someone who knows
you.

Give them candy, don't be tight
One might get you some dark
night.

Dr. Florence G. Axton
CAMOUFLAGE

*This poem is dedicated to my
mother. Agnes N. Gotthelf 3131
East Alameda Ave. Denver.
Colorado. 90209. Apt 701, 80209*

Look out your window on the
plane,
An azure sky, masses of white
misty clouds, as we ride by.
I don't think it will rain.

A portrait of Mary Lincoln on a
candy box,
A body and tail of a sly fox,
Visible collections of particles of
water and ice, suspended in the
air,
Transparent misty, figurative
muses,
The sun is shining through.
What a glare.
The contents would fill a book,
A handfull of fluff, that's not
enough,
Let's have another look,
A high school corsage,
Definately a
        "Camouflage".

Gina Sweeney
MY MOM & DAD DID IT!

*To the most wonderful mother
and father anyone could ever
have.*

The creeping, the crawling
The pain from within
He'll push and he'll shove
'Til it's all the way in
For it won't be hurting
Very long in the end
It will turn out the way
Like it didn't begin
You'll be very big
But for not a long time
And for when it's all over
You'll hurt from inside
For this child will love you
'Til you're one hundred and dead
And carry on throughout
generations
Like you have once did
And though we have looked
Upon this as a sin
It's nothing like that
It's just love from within.

Glory Posey
OH FOR WINGS
Oh for wings to fly
Unfettered into the cobalt sky
And soar, free to ply the elusive
wind,
Ebullient, drifting on a whim
Of draft, floating upward into the
dim
Uncharted paths no bird has flown,
To have a private pathway of my
own
To Heaven's door,
Tethered to earth no more.

Betty Ann Wooley

Betty Ann Wooley
THE PATIENT HEART
The patient heart goes hand in
hand
With gentle endearing love
For to love is just to understand
And to show the meaning of
Caring more than words could say
Reflecting in all I do
The patient heart in this small
way
Is my gift of love to you

Pauline Dortch Heard
Twas the Night Before

*To my son, Paul A. Crumby, who
doesn't consider this poetry.*

'Twas the night before payday
and all through the house
Not a coin was jingling—not
even by my spouse
When from the telephone bell
there arose such a clatter
I picked the thing up to find out
what's the matter
"Your loan has gone through" said
a voice in my ear
As I put down the phone I felt I
could cheer,
"Now, doctor—now, dentist, you
all will be paid
And tomorrow we'll still have the
money we made."
We wrote checks galore—was
almost a game
Not once did we think—next
week'll be the same.

Karen S. Sobek
LOOK INTO MY HEART
Look into my heart,
For there's a dedication,
Created by my souls love,
You are the words, the melody,
Its only inspiration.

Look into my heart
Soul deep inside me,
You are everything I feel,
You are everything I see.

Look into my heart,
Love is not just temporary,
Your face is etched there
Deep inside my memory.

Look into my heart,
I want you to know,
You've grown so deep within,
I just love you so.

Look into my heart,
I want no one but you,
Take my hand, walk with me
A lifetime through.

Look into my heart
Each life I live through
If God will let me choose
I want to walk each one only
with you.

Michael H. French
PLEASE . . .
To hold you closely is all I ask.
I speak of more than physical grip.
You are within my emotional
grasp,
Yet you are far away.
I long to have you next to me
again.
Holding;
Touching;
Caring;
Loving;
Sharing each moment until it
becomes
A lifetime.
But dreams can pass so quickly
The mind may miss the details
While heart feels the pain.

I need you close, always.
Questions arise of how, when,
if . . .
Hope remains eternal—
(Some day my heart will catch
my mind . . .)

Dawn L. Sparks
LONGING
                Longing is there
and he sits heavily upon my heart,
Yearning for a place to call home.
        Just waiting restlessly
A teary-eyed fellow, begging to be
heard.
    Yes, he's heard, and promised he
shall be soothed.
    But, still being a child, he sits
uneasy
making sure he can still be heard,
        Waiting for the moment
        his wants will be heeded.
        But for now, he sits heavily
            Upon my heart.

Patricia Powell
WIND SONG
She's the song in the wind.
Her melody winds thru you
giving joy and peace.
She's forever, soft and caressing,
making love with each whisper.
Her strength is as the calm before
the storm.
Feel her presence and know that
you are loved and never alone.
Yes, listen close my love to her
sweet refrain;
For you see, she is me, your
Wind Song.

W. J. Collins
The Wayward Path Home

To, for, and because of S.C.

When understanding seemed
clear,
And understanding comfortably
secure,
I took a wayward path home.

Upon the path, laden with gold,
I beheld a good man shivering—
Cursing, cursing, the pervasive
cold.
I ventured upon nearer view.

My mind lingered long from peace,
Somewhere in this lonely land.
Wretched was the vision, trodden
was the man.
I ventured closer still.

How cold, lonely, and ideal was he.
How warm, flocked, and real was I.
For he, on the eve of Christmas,
saw
The world through blood-red eyes.
No closer did I venture.

Said he, "Go ye now and
celebrate,
Celebrate the timely birth of a
king
Who taught that to love with
virtue and truth,
Will spiritually transcend all
things."
Became my vision a liquid blur.

Stationed was he, in a clear, clear,
dawn.
Wandering was I, and was hastily
gone.

I arrived home, too blinded to see
The newest gifts beneath the tree.

Susan M. Silver
AURA
Not by day,
Not by night,
Not by flame of candle's fright;
Not by fear, alone in fear,
Nor twilight's shortbright sight;
Nor new dawn's thirsty daring,
Nor midnight's long-last swearing.
I love you by your own light,
That alone worth sharing.

Stacey M. Williams
CAROUSEL WALTZ
Sometimes I don't know how to
feel;
I laugh when the pain from the
outside
tightens my insides.
I cry when my heart is so warm
that my
body feels secure.

All of the laughing, all the crying
too often I've given up trying.
But I always find some hidden
strength
that keeps my body from dying.

The silent pain of growing up
fighting off life's pretensions,
it's like riding on a carousel
or falling into a wishing well.
Close your eyes it takes you to
the skies
close enough to feel the rays of
the rainbow.

Open your eyes, to discoloured
disguise
falling deeper into realities lies.

I sit by myself, contented
locking memories of past inside,
they guide my future destinies
and keep my dreams alive.

David M. Stern
PANDA PUP
I saw her standing there alone,
   Without a place to call home.
So I decided to pick her up,
   Now I call her Panda Pup

So deliteful, never spiteful,
She sits and stays and always
   plays,
   even on rainy days.

I'm in luck, she's my pup.
She will protect me in everyway,
Because I feed her everyday.

Doris M. Jensen-Foster
SUNSHINE PATTERNS

---

*Dedicated to my brother, Donald
C. Jensen, who has handled life
with more courage, valor and
faith than anyone I have ever
known. My special love to you as
brother and friend.*

When the clouds press closely
   together,
And cling tightly to release the
   rain;
To fall upon the dry earth's face,
And trickle slowly, down my
   windowpane.

As I listen to its gentle patter,
It tends to revive the lethargic me;
Awakening some warm, tender,
   dreamy thoughts,
Of bygone days that tug my heart
   happily.

In the aftermath of the raindrops,
'Tis then, suddenly, I am aware;
Of billowing clouds silently
   wafting
To roam lazily to another
   "somewhere".

After this, I see my SUNSHINE
   PATTERNS,
That etch glowing pictures on my
   wall;
Though they may move to other
   places,
They will return at memory's
   call.

Daisie Viola Rose
MY DARLING ONES

---

*To Lyn, Lee, Mark, Steve (My
Darling Children) love never dies
with death, Love is eternal*

Come to my side, my darling
   ones
And bid me all farewell.
Don't bring flowers, just bring me
   your self
For you were my flowers of life.
Don't bring sadness, crying or
   tears
Only the laughter, we shared
   throu the years
Come sing me farewell, my

darling ones
I loved you from the start,
You were a part of all my dreams
I loved with all my hart.
Life is short, my darling ones,
   nothing is forever.
The only treasure you will get to
   keep
Is the love you have for one
   another

Marie Bass
Marie Bass
PERCEPTION

---

*Dedicated to all those rare and
wonderful people who stop and
take the time to look within
themselves to understand life's
spiritual mysteries more fully . . .*

Underneath the exterior, are
   things the way they seem to be?
I tell you, no, without a doubt;
We see what we want to see . .

We listen with unhearing ears
   and see with unseeing eyes,
And the deep things remain
   hidden as if in a disguise.

But, sometimes the veil is lifted
   and we really see and hear,
And the things which oft' are
   hidden from us,
Come through then loud and clear.

At these rare moments in life, our
   finite minds and hearts are
feeling, seeing, and
   comprehending realities so deep,
That its like walking through the
   mystical fragrance of some
   unknown flower.

Then, we perceive that the

unknown fragrance is Love,
And the Garden we are walking
   through is Life;
The Truth half hidden from our
   eyes is Eternity,
And the Music we hear inside is
   Heaven's melodies;
Playing within our hearts the
   unspoken and intangible
Truths of Life, God, and
   Reality . . .

Helen Fisher Trehey
A Living Christmas Card
I looked out my kitchen window
And saw a living Christmas card.
'Twas a red and green holly tree
Alive with red-breasted robins.

Swinging, clinging, swaying,
   reaching
Or teetering on a top twig
They picked at those scarlet
   clusters
Yet you couldn't see any less.

When the tree became
   snow-frosted,
The robin diners still perched
   there
Were jauntily staring at me.
A red, white, greetn Christmas
   card scene.

Priscilla F. Douzanis
LOVE
Love is merely a word—
A passing vibration in the air.
Yet that slight tremor can move
   worlds.
A simple formation of the lips
is like a trumpet to the soul.

Lorraine M. Jacobson
**Never To Touch Him
   Again**
Summoned to the cold walls
   of a small lonely room
Where here, your memories fill
   the shelves
It never fails that the old little tape
   should start playing in my head
   whispering then—demanding
   me now
"Get me out and read me, let's see
   how much we've grown
The door is so close, can I shut
   you in again?
My God, I yearned to reach and
   touch you too many times
Anyhow, I missed my favorite
   fairy tale
When I was your princess, you
   my prince

We jumped out of separate books
   and played for awhile
As was then, is now, the pages are
   turning at a pace
   that we somehow cannot keep
   up with
And now, we are the
   reproduction of the picture
   we painted, together years ago
Why can't we interpret now, the
   pages of yesterday's empty
   meaning?

I knew that I should not have
   taken you off the shelf
   The book has been destroyed
When does one learn to let the
   past be only a memory?
Not to be relived

I have mystery books and you
   have become one of them

Yesterday, we jumped back into
   our past
   and said good-bye again
We will never know if the two
   lived,
   as the others always do, happily
   ever after
For this time, our book is
   complete
And I, never to touch him again

Christine Ann Reed
Christine Ann Reed
SHADOW OF THE DAY
About 3 wks. ago, I saw this guy
   watching me; And everywhere
   that I went, right there he
   seemed to be.
All my friends were asking me if
   he was a friend of mine; I spoke
   out with "no", but he seemed to
   be, so very sweet and kind.
I left a note on the seat of his
   bike to see what he would say;
   If he would speak up & say
   "well hello", but he never went
   either way.
He went around the entire
   school, to see who left the note;
   But no one knew and he was
   sad, with thoughts he'd lost all
   hope.
One day I saw him at a table, that
   stood close near a shade tree;
   So I sat down & said "I know
   who wrote the note, still trying
   to say it was me.
"Who is it?" he asked in
   desperation, "I can't tell you,
   though it's true",
But being sweet, & sort of cute,
   she thinks that much of you.
Bobby, the lady who ran the
   cafeteria, did not know who it
   could be; Until some giggling
   at mike's side said, mike it was
   me.
"I feel like a fool," he spoke when
   he knew & sadly drifted from
   her down the hall; And came
   not to school the day after,
   which made her search for him
   till nightfall.
The last school day & not back
   yet, for summer months she
   suffered each lingering day; Till
   high school calls both of them
   back, as she see mike down the
   hallway.
Without speaking a single word

to each other, their eyes spoke
out the words you could see
through each life; As he places
an engagement ring for her
finger, as the words spoke out
soon,

Man & Wife

Philip J. Wheeler
RISING LOVE

To My Soul Mate Amura

Having finally found you, across
a universe of time,
wonderfully, your love blends
with mine—so devine.
With each day of growth equal, to
a month on the vine,
Our hearts lovingly and joyfully
further, entwine.

Over the waterfalls of life, we fall.
Filling each of our beings with,
spirit tall.
Rolling endlessly, in a vortexual
ball.
We emerge at the Rivers end, in
all.

United with the spirit of God's
light.
We beam on like a star so bright.
We hold on to our love dreams,
with all our might,
till we surface from the Sea, in
sheer delight.

We ascend to our Lord, embraced.
For side by side we remain, in his
grace.
As we vanish from Earth without,
a trace,
Our Angels know, we have kept
up, with his pace.

Linda Seifried
MOTHER
As I stumbled thru life;
As I fumbled and fell,
You were always there.
You picked up the pieces
And gently, unaware, put them
back together.
You dried my tears;
You put hope back in my heart
And thru everything you gave me
love.
And I in return,
What have I done?
I don't even recall ever telling you
I loved you
Or that I appreciated you being
there.

Well, I want to tell you now
Before it's too late:
I love you, Mom
And if I were given only one wish
It would be to be like you.

Robert S. Nicolini
STARLIGHT—83
When you shine on me
I wonder—

What secret you hide
With your misty glow?

In your bright world is
There love everlasting?

Or truth untouched by
Satan's tongue?

Are wars passe' and the
Bomb just a word?

Does the summer kiss last
The year around?

How many colors touch your
Face and cause hate?

Do you reason or do you
Care?

Your light bathes me
In the glow of the newborn

Yet, I wonder if you are
There at all.

Alessandra A. Poles
NUCLEUS
The book of life is given
Every new air born,
Each leaf to be sketched;
God gives this gift to man.

The book of life is given
To use with sound acumen.
A helping hand is granted,
God gives this love to man.

The book of life is given
To read when day is done;
The chosen passage released!
God gives a choice to man.

Emilio B. Aller
CHRISTMAS DREAM
Our hearts aglow with love and
cheer,
We dance and sing with childish
glee
As Dad and Mom and all our dear
Ones gather 'round the Christmas
tree.

Our gifts and toys and candy bars
And dolls in stockings dangling
free
And multi-colored tinsel stars
Adorn our gleaming Christmas
tree.

Then hush, with great solemnity,
We raise our hearts in sweet
refrain
To Jesus Child's Nativity
And Peace and Goodwill to all
men . . .

I am but dreaming of the scenes
Of childhood bliss on Christmas
Day
When hearts were young with
innocence
And simple joys of yesterday.

My Dad and Mom are now with
God
And I'm alone with folks away:
I still rejoice and can't be sad
If I but dream of Christmas Day.

Christine Marie Hoffmann
FRIENDS

*In loving memory of Mark Allen
Marcogliese*

Friends are like rainbows,
They spread beauty in our lives,
Then slowly fade away,
But their message is sealed
within us
            forever.

Nancy Anne Ronco

Nancy Anne Ronco
DEATH
One day from a garden grew
so beautiful a flower
who harboured so few.
And yet this flower
so brave and tall
climbed within that garden wall.

God would water and watch it
grow
from each passing day
to that first winter snow.
Then Spring came the flower
bloomed
and sprouted many
who now had roomed.

My heart would seek to help it
grow
my soul would weep
to see it go.
Then that day my flower died
my tears I swallowed,
but I cried and cried.

But tears of death had brought so
few
to that "special garden wall",
where "love" once grew.

Alan S. Matsunaka
FATHER'S

---

*To my Dad (Harry H. Matsunaka)
whom I love very much.*

How much can we love a guy
who has given
As much love to us as we need?
Patriarch of this household and
Protects us when we are afraid
and
Young enough to understand how
we feel

For as long as we shall live, you
Are always there when we need
The loving smile and kindness
only a father
Has for his family, no matter how

large
Everything a son would want to
be like
Reaching out and catching us
when we fall
Searching for us, when we are lost.

Daring to be the best that you
can be
Aiming to survive no matter
what happens
Yet knowing that we will always
love you.

Ronda Packard
AUTUMN SOLSTICE
Shining,
    God's majesty is displayed in
    full array,
    awaiting the resurrection of a
    new day.
    Colors glimmer, change,
    and golden glory fades into
    bleak existence.
Shimmering,
    each leaf whispers wind-sung
    songs,
    echoing the sighs of summer
    gone,
    of snow-hatted burials,
    when twirling ballerinas tumble
    gently to the ground.

Kathlene Sue Rice
**Mirror Images; The Rose
And I**
The rose stands strong,
It's petals wide,
For all the world to see.
It's life is long,
And holds great pride,
So rich, and full, and free.

But lurking near,
To end the rose,
And put it, forever, away.
The cold we fear,
Carries the snows,
That worsen everyday.

The wind still blows,
The petals fall,
The pressure is too great.
But no one knows,
Through it all,
The rose was in a state.

The end is near,
The rose descends,
And now lies, peacefully.
The world in fear,
For at the end,
They heard it's silent plea.

Della Miller
MY DAD
Once so very long ago, I guess I
was just three,
A very strange thing happened,
and it affected me.
I learned that if I cried a lot, my
daddy always came,
And if things went wrong for me,
I never took the blame.
I learned just how to get my way,
so very long ago.
And all I ever had to do, was just
put on a show.
I thought my dad was everything,
that he could do no wrong,
I thought he'd always be with me,
he never would be gone.
A lot of years have passed me by,
since I was only three,

A lot of strange things happened
and they've affected me.
I learned it does no good to cry,
cause daddy won't be there,
And if things go wrong for me,
the blame I to must wear.
I learned I to must pay the price,
not very long ago,
And all the things I want from
life, sometimes the answers no.
I know my dad was wrong
sometimes, in things that he
did say,
I wish I could have told him this,
before he passed away.
The words were always in my
heart, I guess he really knew,
But for my sake I'll say them now,
"My dad my love to you".

George J. Himebaugh
FALLING LEAVES
Falling leaves still leave tall trees
standing;
so life's experiences whirl and
dance
with a rhythm fast and
demanding
only seeming to be the whims of
chance.

Come spring and new growth
flows out,
the turning of life's eternal wheel
no doubt.
So too must we have our time of
living in the outer
and withdrawing yet again to the
inner.
A cycle that endlessly repeats
itself
until we can finally set the
space/time continuum back on
the shelf.

As I become attuned to Universal
Mind
I leave earth's illusions behind.
I claim divine health in His
name,
Wisdom, prosperity; for those the
same.

I turn again to the falling leaves,
who, without resistance, float on
the breeze
A sample of how easy it would be
if I but trusted my life to God
instead of me.

Dorothy Louise
UNTITLED
Borrow strength
from the oak—
take courage
from the eagle.
Carry your pride
majestically,
yet never forget
your beginning.
When reaching out
to others
be like an oak
with many branches.
Never hold back love
but like an eagle
dare to be bold.
You always
seek solitude.
Do you fear
that to bend
is to break?
Do not be

afraid—
remember
the eagle
is your spirit;
the oak tree
is your strength.

Lewis Henry Sanders
THE LAST LIGHT
The afternoon sun shining
through a nearby window,
Lights the corner of the room.
I awake each day at this time to
see the light.
And each day I am weaker; I am
dying.

Around my deathbed are gadgets
from another generation.
I don't want these things; they are
for future deathbeds.
I want to die the way my father
died.
I just want to be left alone, left
alone to die.

Yesterday, I saw my newest
grandchild.
They laid her in the sunlight that
filled the corner of the room.
I could see her, although tears in
my eyes blurred her features.
We are passing like two strangers
from other worlds.

It seems strange to have reached
this moment in time.
Seems strange to be here dying.
I still hope I am going to be saved.
But I know I would be
disappointed to stay.

I am wide awake, even though it
is late at night.
I have said all of my good-byes.
I am looking at the light that is
shining into my room.
The light that is coming through
a nearby window.

Marion M. Stephens
THE OPHTHALMOLOGIST

---

*Dedicated to Dr. Zarko M.
Vucicevic—my physician,
employer and friend—who died
in an accident in Dec. 1982*

He peers into his slit-lamp,
And uses a dark blue light,
For special in-depth readings
Of every patient's sight.

He looks for signs of glaucoma,
And trouble inside the eye.
He even measures the pressure,

To see if it's up to high.
He can't resist a cornea,
Or an iris clear and blue.
For a beautiful detached retina,
He'll do a cartwheel or two!

He checks for cysts and tumors,
Disease and visual ills.
He uses a lot of colored drops,
But not too many pills.

The eyes are delicate organs,
What stories they can tell!
The surgeon/ophthalmologist
Can read them very well.

Marion M. Stephens
COMMUTERS
The tide of commuters ebbs and
flows,
In a stream of wheels and feet.
It moves in and out of buildings
And back and forth on the street.

Commuters go from place to place,
By trolley, bus or train.
They travel by the fastest route
In snow, in heat and rain.

They cling to poles and handrails
In cars that lurch and sway.
If they can find an empty seat,
They think it's a lucky day!

Some commuters think an auto
Is the better way to go.
But when they hit a traffic jam,
They find it's far too slow.

Commuters crank up a city,
And make it hum just right.
They wake it up in the morning,
And put it to sleep at night.

Mary Thayer Blanchard
PREDICTION
Sighed Miss Obese to Mrs. Slim,
"Your figure's enviably trim!"
"Oh, thank you," laughed the
recent bride,
"But soon my waist will be miles
wide!"

B. J. Lisatz II
THE MORNING AFTER
A pair of sneakers
Lie by a pile of clothes.
You lay back,
Trying to clear your head.

You reach over
But find no one
Had there been someone?
Or had you been dreaming?

As your head clears
You begin to sit up
Slowly, swallowing quickly,
Trying not to make a sound.

You manage to stand
And make your way to the
bathroom
Turning the cold water on,
You stick your head under, crying
out.

Reaching for a towel
You find something smaller
A pair of white panties
So, it hadn't been a dream!

But who was she?
Where can she be found?
You can't remember
You try clearing your head.

You smile though as you look in
the mirror
For you see a message

Scrawled in lipstick:
Want to get lucky again?
Call Michelle 48631.

Dian Walker

Dian Walker
**The Storm Within My
Mind**
We drifted apart in the middle of
the night . . .
And I woke up this morning
on the other side of you . . .
Looking at you through
flashbacks
from the night before . . .
Shooting down on you
like lightning bolts
from a summer sky . . .
Filling the room with a glow
in the morning light . . .
Watching you doze through my
flashbacks . . .
Not even aware of the display
you're putting on
Or the effects you've left
behind . . .
My thoughts have awakened
you . . .
The storm within my mind has
died down . . .
It's going to be another beautiful
day . . .

Evelyn D. Moyer
SNOWFALL

---

*Inspired by the very special life of
a most extraordinary man — and
dedicated in memory of him, Dr.
Paul D. Mooney.*

With the hushed quietness of
snow,
With the lulled stillness of snow,
Into my life he came.

The splendor of winter's first
snowfall,
The wonder of winter's first
snowfall,
Just in his speaking my name.

The sparkle of an ice-decorated
tree,
The glitter of moonlight on fresh
snow,
This, the beauty of him and me.

The whisper of gently stirring
leaves,
The crispness of crunching ice
underfoot,
The thrill in knowing that in me
he believes.

Tiny flakes gathered to form
  earth's cover,
A masterpiece that no artist can
  imitate.
The mystery, the hopes, the
  dreams of this special lover.

The forests held snugly in the
  embrace,
The hillsides so gently tucked in
  place,
The warmth I've known, only in
  loving him.

The snow becoming brighter as
  the sun peeks out.
The air filling with sledders' and
  skaters' laughs and shouts.
This budding romance coming to
  full bloom.

Then suddenly, the sun warms
  the earth.
With no warning, the snow is
  gone.
So came the end of us, as Death,
  like the snow, slipped in,
Taking him, so soon after love's
  Birth.

Phyllis Hunter
My Glorious El-Shaddai
There's always another tomorrow,
If this day should bring you pain.
There's always light after
  darkness,
Like the sunshine after the rain.
There's always another summer,
If this one should bring you grief.
There's always another
  springtime,
In which we shall find sweet
  relief.
We know that along with each
  sorrow,
Moments of peace will prevail,
Like those heavenly moments of
  surcease
Of a woman in travail.
We know there's another life,
That is waiting for you and me,
Free from all sorrow and pain,
A life of eternity.
But there is only One God,
Who reigns over all from on high,
Omnipotent and Magnificent!
Oh My Glorious El-Shaddai!

Genevieve R. Erwin
SPRINGTIME
The sun shines warm through
  cobweb lace
And the sap runs free in trees
  again;
This is becoming a budding place
And soon 'twill be a springtime
  Heav'n.
Each little wisp of velvet green
Tells us that summer's not far
  away;
The meadows have taken on a
  magic sheen
And the forest folk are free to
  play.
The blue of violets in the grass,
And the gold of the stately tulip;
Makes you feel alive when you
  pass
And makes you yearn to take a
  trip.
The beauties we see in the spring
Are one more sign that God is
  love;

It makes our hearts just fairly
  sing
And these blessings come from
  up above.

Mrs. Patricia B. Cabrinety

Mrs. Patricia B. Cabrinety
THE HOLIDAYS

*To my beloved family who make
all the holidays so very special.*

The snow came down and swirled
  around
Heaping huge drifts upon the
  ground.

Excited children with Christmas
  thoughts,
Eagerly awaiting the presents
  sought.

Skates, tobaggan, and skis,
Fun-filled sports in winter's freeze.

Wreathed doors and decorated
  trees,
Sprinkles of snow from every
  breeze.

School vacation is soon here,
Expectations heightens as holiday
  nears.

Family, food, and good friends,
Holiday festivities everywhere
  extends.

This year ended and another yet
  begun,
Thankful are we to the Eternal
  One.

June Burlingame Smith
SHELL HOUSE
Woman, that ancient enigma,
Now seeks to reflect her total

design
Within the undergirding piers
Of her institutional landscape.

Her form, like a Byzantine
  tortoise shell,
Mirrors her struggle against
  primitive forces
Which threaten to turn her house
  of protection
Into walls of
          entombment.

Outwardly, she is adored,
  admired, highly prized;
Inwardly, her changing
  perspective
Guides tireless feet
Along the broad path of
  renaissance,

Emergence from the shell-house
Is the force of the times,
The powers of undeveloped
  talent
Compel undulating, inevitable
  movement
In a society not yet prepared
To accept the humanity of the
  complete
                  Woman.

Ellen Peterson Fontes
That's What It's All About
To understand each other
Is not an easy task.

To call your neighbor "brother",
Is that too much to ask?

To hold a hand that's reaching
  out,
To love, but not to preach or
  shout,

To live and share, glad to be here,
That's what it's all about!

Jewel Williamson
**The Saddest Day
October 23, 1983**

*This poem is dedicated to the
U.S. Marines of the 24th Marine
Amphibious Unit and to those
who died in the explosion of the
B.L.J. headquarters in Beirut,
Lebanon. Among them my own
beloved son, Cpl. Johnny
Williamson, Age 25.*

Oh the day this nation wept
And cried with bitter tears,
For our young men they killed
  that day
In a land of many fears.

We sent them there to keep the
  peace
But peace could not be won,
Saddened comrades dug them out
Fathers, Brothers, Husbands, Sons.

They sent them home to us again
But this time cold in death,
We can't believe they died in vain
As they breathed a final breath.

Oh land of hatred, fear and strife
You've put us to the test,
They only came to better life
The proud, the few, the best.

Remember them who gave their
  all
On the soil you hold so dear,
Rewards they got were few and
  small
In your land of hate and fear.

Albion VERNe Lambertis
ITS SANTA TIME AGAIN

*To Daddy George A Wonderful
Father of Nuff Youths*

Its Christmas, Santa its your time
  again,
Gifts giving from familys,
  Neighbors and Friends,
Post Cards all over the world has
  being send,
Celibrating, merry making all you
  can eat and drunking.

Its Christ Birtday, its a hollday
  goto Church and pray,
Familys visiting old Friends !
"Season greeting, Feel the spirit",
Tis the season tobe Merit, Merry
  Christmas to all the people you
  meet,
Smiling happily is the warm well
  come you greet;

Not every one celebrate
  christmas, !Some don' think the
  dollar they should
wast in God we trust, but tis the
  season tobe merri get well
  cherri,
Forget about fuss and cuss, eat
  your berrys once a year come
  christmas,
And Santa is on His way with
  gifts and churos.

Maskarating on prading, allow
  santa down the chimmey, a gift
  he will be
Bringing for me, tis the feeling
  children from one to a hundred
  get,
When its Santa time again; They
  dress so well to look their best,
Because tis the season when
  santa come from the North,
  South, East and West . .

Cheryl L. Carr
SNOW
Blowing wild down all the streets
It can't survive in any heat.
It's cold, it's wet, it's white and
  bright
It shines and glows all through
  the night.
Walking down the streets of slush
Sometimes it all turns to mush.
Dirty, grimy muddy mess:
Makes us love snow all the less.

Jayanne Assunto
SUNSHINE

For Bill, My Sunshine.

I closed my eyes and wondered
about the bright sunshine
the next day would bring,
about the birds,
in the treetops
and the songs they would sing.

I wondered if the clouds would
cover the sun and bring rain.
The morning would be gray
and happy sounds would be
restrained.

And I wondered what would
happen
when the storm would pass,
would the water in the stream
be as clear as glass?

Would the water still flow?
and its source never end?
when I open my eyes,
will I see you, my dearest friend?

For my sunshine is your smile
upon your bright face.
and the sound of your voice
is a happy birds song
that none could replace.

For the clouds have not come,
neither has the rain.
there has been no harsh emotions
that only cause pain

If there was anger
would it last?
or would one be forgiven
and able to forget the past?

My feelings shall flow for you,
the source is my heart
I hope you'll always be the one
to motivate that part

This is the beauty of nature
that I can see in you
I hope you can find a ray of
sunshine
in my smile too.

Rebecca Davis Hunt
in love and war
dark empty thoughts
  trapped
  cloud years of memory
strength
  lost in a single moment
  one tear shed
    never seen
heart pounds
  passion climbs
    through mountain peaks
  tearing at the horizon
    expectation
bomb strikes
  sending chills
    to the ends of earth
mind and body
  throbbing—sinking
    in a pool of sweat
  waves crash
    settle on shores

Gary W. Scheer
I Saw a Lady Standing
Lady standing over there
With the flower in your hair,
There are things I have to tell you
And you'll want to hear.

Dance with me here,
Lady standing with me there,
And you'll hear of things
I've wanted you to hear;
But lady, I know you'll never
Be with me here or any where.
It's so cold standing here waiting,
Watching, wishing to tell you
  things
That I wish you would want to
  hear.

Mary Ruth Tweed Brown
Bob Brown
This Will Be Mother's Day

*Dedicated to my Mother, Mary
Ruth Tweed Brown, of Union,
South Carolina*

There will never be hours enough,
  Not in a day,
To recall the love of Mother
  In a proper way.

No warmth from another human
  Hand could bring such joy
As the touch of Mother's hand on
  My forehead as a boy.

I know some day as I walk the
  Paths only Angels trod
I'll see Mother cuddled there with
  The Lamb of God.

This will be but one of many
  Stars in her Crown,
"To see me beside her," my
  Mother, Mary Ruth Tweed Brown.

Elspeth Crebassa
SEASONAL CHANGES
Autumn is here
The air is chill
All is so still.

Then Nature's sigh
Gently rustles
A stirring sound

And leaves from trees
Flutter at will
Unto the ground.

Winter is near
The highest peaks
Of far mountains

Soon will appear
Covered with snow
Nature's fond whim

A different world
Will come to bring
Of sombre mien.

Yesterday' gone

Today is here
Future is Spring.

James Edward White
The Creation of Man
The creation of man, a long time
  past,
A miraculous event, that will last.
God created man from the dust of
  the earth,
And man must greet death from
  his birth.

Man's life span is three scores
  and ten,
Age seventy, never reaching all
  men.
A host of men have been laid to
  rest,
Waiting to see did they pass life's
  test.

The creation of man, is true as life,
God first made Adam, then Eve;
  his wife.
He created woman, an helpmate
  for man,
Today, wifes must aid husbands
  when they can.

Man is said to be a living soul,
He maybe young, or he maybe old.
Man must stay on the righteous
  track,
To make the rapture, when God's
  son comes back.

Hilda M. Jordan
**Walking In Thy Holy
  King's and Queen's
  Procession**

*I am dedicating this Poem to the
following: Jesus Christ, The
Blesset Mother Mary, The
Catholic Community, The Pope.
All King's And Queen's, And
Ladies And Gentlemen, And
Everyone On Earth.*

I had dreams of walking with
the holy King and Queen.

Walking in the holy King's
and Queen's Procession, through
the parks and villages.

I had dreams of walking with
thy holy King and Queen.

Walking in thy holy King's
and Queen's Procession, by
the beaches and along roadside
ways.

I had dreams of walking with
thy holy King and Queen.

Walking in thy holy King's
and Queen's Procession, all
over the cities, towns, states,
and countries.

Walking in thy holy King's
and Queen's Procession.

Ms. Sylvia Stearns
IMAGINATIONS
Imagination, I want to go back to
  a childs world of imagination
A magic world of make believe
Want to feel again the wonders of
  fantasies I used to know
When a house was not a house,
  but a castle and the people
  inside were Kings and Queens

And white clouds above, were
  castles in the sky
When I beleived in Santa Claus
  and the Easter bunny at Easter
  time
Among the birds and the bees,
  flowers and trees and it was
  like heaven to see
And I beleived, all the world
  belonged to me
In this wonderful world of
  imagination
Everything was possible
But in this world of realty, seems
  everything is impossible
So I want to go back, to that
  make believe world be like a
  child again
Where I can be like Peter Pan, fly
  to the moon or swing on a star
Where I could slay dragons, with
  a mystical sword of gold
In this beautiful, wonderful
  world
Of imagination

Franklin Sommers
**The Carpenters; A
  Retrospective**

*Written with eternal love and
fondess for Karen and Richard
Carpenter.*

Creating music for the young and
  the old,
Were Karen and Richard
  Carpenter,
Singing each era's songs of true
  gold,
Were Karen and Richard
  Carpenter,
Singing new songs and making
  them known,
Were Karen and Richard
  Carpenter,
Singing old songs unknown to
  the young,
Were karen and Richard
  Carpenter,
And singing new songs the young
  haven't sung,
Were Karen and Richard
  Carpenter,
Bridging the gap between the
  young and the old,
Were Karen and Richard
  Carpenter,
Giving each era something nice
  and unknown,
Were Karen and Richard
  Carpenter,
And sharing their love for young
  and for old,
Were Karen and Richard
  Carpenter;

DeMarie Jervay
**Mom's Ode To Christmas
  Eve**
Outside . . .
snowflakes are falling.
Inside . . .
SandMan's calling,
embracing me with a calm serenity
on this Eve.
But what . . . Have my senses
taken leave?
At four in the morning
rubbing eyes and neck
. . . Go to bed?

Our World's Best Loved Poems

What the heck!
Soon up,
three kids will be
whispering
words of glee,
"Oh, look . . .
I know that's for me!"

Last minute wraping and baking
for Branley, Clinton, and Kelli.
Soon . . . they'll want
hot chocolate with toast and jelly.
Then, there's Dad,
but, he's not quite so bad.
". . . just coffee will do . . ."
But not 'til noon, thank you!

So, re-heat the coffee
and dim down the lights.
Curl up with the afghan
while the stereo plays Silent Night.
This is your moment.
Your mind will soon wander,
there are no demands
or worries to ponder.
You've given your all;
This Christmas will be the best.
They love you, Mom . . .
Now, get some rest.

Anita Louise Virgil, Avila

Anita Louise Virgil, Avila
CHRISTMAS
It's that time of year,
When Christmas draws near,
A joyous occasion for everyone,
And Christmas Carols to be sung,
While Santa sits listening to
   request,
The other children waiting to be
   next,
A Christmas Tree decorated with
   lights,
And a star at the top shining so
   bright,
"Oh what a beautiful sight;"

It's the time of the year,
When people tend to shed joys of
   tear,
A holiday of giving and receiving,
That gives Christmas a whole lot
   of meaning,
of sharing and caring,
And having fun doing all the
   preparing,
Sleigh Bells ringing in the sky,
Children anxious to see Santa
   ride by,
A Christmas where the true spirit
   lies;

It's that time of year,
When people hear,
That Christmas is a day of prayer,

Because Jesus was born making
   this day sacred,
so people should care,
Merry Christmas in everyway,
Don't forget to Praise this day:

Franklin Sommers
THE BLACK HOLES

*Written with eternal love and
honor for God, Mother Mary, My
Mother Patricia, and for Nora
Butler: For Grace.*

In the heavens live the
   mysterious black holes,
Dark, black, and mysterious they
   live,
they live to devour,
Like the eyes of a cat they devour,
They devour everything in their
   grasp,
All light and life they devour,
Everything in their grasp they
   devour,
Planets, stars, galaxies,
   cheeseburgers, and all
   imaginations,
For all the heavens and I ponder
   the black holes,
They devour our imagination.

Dorothy T. Warner
LOVE UNFOLDING
Dearly beloved, God is the heart
   and soul of thee,
thou art ever one with, what is
   sublime thou art ever
   complete, wholenes is thine
Beloved one's of our loving father
   you can never be alone.
He is ever with you in every
   place, In even the birds eternal
   song, In the sweet breeze of
   summer, In the cold of winters
   chill,
God is ever present in spirit still,
Be not afraid let him comfort you,
Let his love Cast its light thru,
   because beloved God loves the
   universe thru me and you.
When the sun kisses the flowers,
   and they bloom so lovingly,
God is sending wholeness that
   way to all you see, Dearly
   beloved let your heart rest in
   him,
For he is ever eternal peace, he is
   the calmness of the sea, no
   storm nor winds shall blow you
   astray, He is the rock, The
   night, The day, He is that
   which encompasses you, God
   omnipresent, universally true.

Franklin Sommers
Tears Of Love Unrequited

*Written with eternal love and
honor for God, Mother Mary, My
Mother Patricia, For Diane
Manfull, For Nora Butler: for Grace.*

For if my love for her never dies,
For if I live to be an old fool,
Let it be,
For I have lived off of it,
So feel sorrow, feel tears,
I live off of them too,
Yours and mine;

Franklin Sommers
WHERE IS SHE NOW

*Written with eternal love and
honor for God, Mother Mary, My
Mother Diane
Manfull, for Nora Butler, for Grace.*

Whre is she now?
Is she lost in a dream?
A dream I dream day and night?
Is she real?
Real enough for when I awaken?
Will she be there when I awake?
Dream or reality, it does not
   matter,
I love her the same,
Infinitely—eternally,
Is she lost in a dream?
Or am I lost in reality?
A lost reality?
A dream?
True realtiy??
What does it matter?
I love her the same,
Infinitely—eternally,
Reality knows this.

Tommy Eileen Shore Weigand
The Day Before Christmas
Christmas eve noon . . .
was spent miles away—
buying last minute gifts
for shoppers with much less to pay.
The Turkey was baking for our
   guest who was expected at our
   table today—daddy babysat
   and peeled the potatoes in his
   own special way.
I returned home late . . . from
   my tiring trip of looking for
   this or for that—rushing I was
   to wrap these small gifts while
   the children in mystery in the
   livingroom sat.
The final touch was completed
   for our Christmas Eve table—
   and everyone was hungry . . . it
   seemed they were able.
Following our meal . . . we
   passed out the gifts—
and when my husband recieved
   the dust pan from me . . . I
   could see his heart Lift!
The little childrens gifts to us
   were all handmade from school—
   and to me . . . it's your hands
   that are a wonderful tool!
Neil . . . being the oldest and
   knowing me well—
gave me a windchime which I
   thought was quite swell!
The kids recieved gifts
   to which they could wear—
and if they put all their toys
   together
it would give them . . . plenty to
   share!
While the kids kept themselves
   buzy playing with things—
I made a 'Santa Trip' in the snow
   and with each step you could
   hear my bells ring!
Back home once again it was
   time to sit and settle down
   from the dash—
while daddy went to
   church . . . and Neil, he served
   at the Mass.
I'm truely greatfull for all gifts

from above—
but the best gift of all . . . is
   from . . .God's touch of Love!

Dina Costa Duncan
THE CIRCLE

*To Dovie and Bernice, the
beginners of the Circle. I love you!*

For every time I've been angry at
   her, there's been ten times I've
   needer her.
For every time we've fought,
   there's been a hundred times
   we've laughed.
Never be too busy for MOM
   because one day, physically
   she'll be gone.
All mothers and daughters have
   their differences.
We daughters all too soon want
   to be grown and with an ache
   in Mom's heart, she has to let
   us go.
We stumble, fall, we sometimes
   blame Mom.
And then, like the miracle of the
   morning sun we rise with a
   new total understanding of
   Mom.
What she did, and why.
Hopefully, there's still time to say
   Thank You!
and I LOVE YOU!
And then with the birth of our
   own children, "MOM"
Begins again . . . . .

Barbara Keefer McNew
THE SEARCH
I feel it's time for me to go
   Though I know not where
I just don't know which way to
   turn
   And sometimes I don't care
This place must fit me like a glove
   I know I've got to find it
It also must be filled with love
   It might be I'm one step behind it
And when I take that one last step
   I know it will be hard
It's possible this love filled place
   Will be my own back yard

Dolores E. Minnig
OUR CHRISTMAS PRAYER
Dear God, as we begin our
   festivities and fun,
We pause to give thanks from
   each and everyone
For the gift you sent so long ago
To be our blessed Savior and so—
As we commemorate the day of
   His birth,
We truly pray for peace on earth.
To make this a great celebration
   of Christmas,
Let that peace on earth begin
   with us—
Help us to be kind and humble,
Help us to do our best and not
   grumble,
Help us to be more loving and
   not judge,
Help us to be forgiving and not
   hold a grudge.
As we gather near the Christmas
   tree,
And praise and honor Thee,
Let us give the gift of love,

571

As you gave from heaven above.
We remember the Babe of
Bethlehem who was laid upon
the hay,
So let us receive the Christ of
Christmas within our hearts
today.
As we ask for your continued
guidance and care,
We praise you and offer our
Christmas prayer.

Vivian L. Colville
MY FRIEND
You put joy and sunshine in my
life
When my heart was heavy full of
strife.

You came along when I needed
someone the most
To talk to, to listen to, and not to
boast.

I had really forgotten what fun
could be
It took a person like you for me
to see.

You are so kind, so thoughtful
and such fun
Always working or on the run.

When you smile at me it warms
my heart
And always saddens me when we
part.

Being with you is such a pleasure
These experiences I will always
treasure.

The trips to the woods and the
nights on the hill
Never failed to give me a thrill.

I have had the pleasure of seeing
you bag a deer
And helping you drink many a
beer.

The campfire, the music, the
dancing in the lane
If I could do this forever I would
never complain.

You are my friend and special to
me.
I always wish that we could be.

Mildred Henson Fiveland
PAYLOAD
Those much overweighted are
often X-rated—
they're victims of fashion and
cultural mode.
It costs them much money to
cover their assets . . . . .
that's what they must pay for
bearing their load.

There are plenty of fashions for
figures like Twiggy's,
but seldom there's one that will
flatter Miss Piggy's.

They scarcely can buy clothes
that cover the bulges
should they aspire to looking
quite sleek;
dressmakers and tailors take off
with their money
without quite creating that
feeling of "chic".

Embarrassed some feel—they
would go into hiding
buty they know that never would

smooth out their road.

It takes much more courage
to plod
     to the
          finish
where at last they will rest and
lay
     down
          their
               payload.

Laure Dixon Higginbotham
THE TRAVELER
The fog:
A misty mysterious phantom
     drufted over the sleeping city.

The traveler:
Struggling through
     the narrow winding streets
Chanting his good news
     for man
Stumbled
Fell
Arose
And disappeared into the night.

Faith Horne
**Another Time—Another
Place**
I saw her in the distance—She
     somehow caught my eye
My heart began to pound—My
     thoughts began to fly
I knew her at that moment—
     Though we had never met
Another Life, Another Love—
     That I shall not forget

I turned to her, She turned to me
     and in a moments time
We touched the love we'ld
     known before and I knew she'ld
     be mine
Without a word or backwards
     glance I led her to the floor
And there we danced the dance
     of love that we had danced
     before

I felt her warmth, I felt her touch
I knew the love I'ld missed so
     much
We'ld slipped into another place
Another World—Another face

There is no future—There is no
     past
No space or time where love can't
     last
I'ld touched her soul and she'ld
     touched mine
We're back together for one more
     time

Marjorie Todd
It's Not the Season

---

*For Caroline—my sometimes
muse, my always friend . . .*

Colorful autumn season,
With golden aspen,
And typical blue skies.
Everything is fine.
Unforseen predicting
Not allowed.

It's not the season.

Internal counting rises.
No, it cannot be.
This person, this M. D.
Just a person, like me.

Erroneous prognosis.

It's not the season.

A fine autumn season,
Continuing blue skies,
Gold—colored aspen.
Eccentric cells,
Refusing prognosis,
Unreality,
Still a whole person.

It's not the season.

Golden aspen,
A fine autumn season,
Continuing blue skies.
White counting,
Black counting,
Battling within,
Counting increases.

It's not the season.

Golden aspen,
Shedding leaves,
Under blue skies,
A fine winter season.
No snowing.
Refusing to believe,
That cold winds will arrive.

It's not the season.

Different counting,
Internally tranquilizing.
No room for turmoil.
One . . . . one . . . . one
     . . . . one . . . .
No more white counting.
Self, the healer,
Not the person M. D.

It's not the season.

Empty aspen trees,
Below blue skies,
A fine winter season,
One . . . . one . . . . one
     . . . . one
White counting no more.

It's not the season.

White light approaching,
Defective cells removing.

It is the season.

Blue skies,
Empty aspen trees,
Awaiting green leaves.

A wonderful season.

Eugene "Gene" H. Channell
A BRAND NEW TOUCH
Lord, today I need a brand new
     touch
From the one that to me, means
     so much
From the one that sacrificed his
     life on calvary
So that I, a wretched sinner,
     might be set free.

Set free from the depths of "the
     fiery hell"
Free from the "world" in which I
     did dwell
Free from the "earthly pleasures"
     of which I did partake
Free from "Satan's grasp" who
     wanted my soul for his own
     sake.

But today, I must listen for a still,
     small voice from God
And obey his every word as upon
     this beautiful land I trod,
Or else "Satan" will again have me

in his hands
Luring me on with all the
     temptations that he
     commands.

So today, dear Lord, I just need a
     brand new touch
So I can put the "things" on the
     altar that I may still clutch
Just take me Lord & mold me
     into the "Christian" you'd have
     me to be
So that my love, care, & concern
     for others less fortunate, would
     be more like thee.

Stephanie Giery

Stephanie Giery
MERRY CHRISTMAS
Merry Christmas everyone
May your heart be filled with
     cheer
May the Peace of Christmas
Come to all
And Blessings to those most dear

May the gift of laughter
Bring the sound of pleasure
May it ring through out the day
A memory all will treasure!

Antoinette Dearborne
**You Were Here All the
Time**
You are my friend. One who cares
     beyond
The vastness of galaxies,
And understands beyond the
     meaning of life.

You are the friend I fell upon my
     knees
And prayed for.
There must be a God because
     you were here all the time.

To only you, I've become the
     open book that no one else
Dares to read.
And yet, you continue to turn the
     pages.

You are the friend I seeked in the
     eyes
Of countless others,
Who closed their eyes to my truth.

You have made me richer than
     money and treasures.
You are my smiles and pleasures.
You are my heartfelt love.

Marlene Parks
PEACE, BROTHER
Peace, brother, peace, sister,
Peace, lady, peace, mister.

Peace, the microcosmic goal,
Peace, the microcosmic aim;

Our World's Best Loved Poems

From seeds of love within the soul
Blooms peace, the universal gain.

Not colour, not creed, not political
goal
Can decompose, or destroy life's
surge in this seed.
Man, face en face, man to man,
soul to soul,
Meets his fellow man with his
fellow need.

Not now wearing garments
woven by fear,
By greed, by hunger for power, or
despair,
Unclothed to his essence, with
his vision more clear,
Man's reflected in man, love's
alive and aware.

Those weavers of garments
grotesque, and whose smell
Is so foul, would lead all in a wild
dance of panic and kill
Till earth, not alive, earth not
sick, earth not well,
Is a void in the universe,
soundless and still.

Not this, the path which
mankind will take;
Love's not apathetic, not passive,
resigned.
Man stands tall in life and with
love, and will shake
The inglorious lint of mistrust
from his mind.

Peace, brothers, peace sisters;
we'll look, see, and gain,
Through ourselves in each other,
our ultimate aim.

Margaret Gorwara
TO ANITA MICHELLE
Dear and loving, so tender and
kind
A sweet gentle spirit, are some
words I can find
To begin to describe the child
that did arrive
On the ninth of October,
nineteen sixty-five.

It was a bright afternoon on my
birthday
That while I was napping after
church on Sunday
She baked and frosted a beautiful
cake
Put candles and all, before I did
wake.

She won many prizes for poetry
reciting
To sing in the choir, she found so
exciting
She also did learn to swim and to
skate
And loved fashion clothing, so
kept down her weight.

Now she is far, far away from my
love
So I have been asking for help
from above
To carry me through without her
beside me
My precious sweet daughter, God
let me again see.

And until then may He be
gracious to her
Keep her from harm, let her know
He is near

Help her to care for her
wonderful brother
Please bring her real soon back
home to her mother.

Berneice E. McKay
SNOW FLAKES

*I dedicate this poem, to all who
have watched the SNOW Flakes,
these being huge 4" to 6" ins., big
as saucers. They were breath
taking. I was "SNOW FLAKE
MAGNETIZED." This is true.*

Softly, softly falling,
  The SNOW upon the ground,
It covers all the house tops,
  And everything around.
It makes the earth look clean and
white,
  And sparkles so in the bright
sunlight,
Just like diamonds all around,
  It's sure a pretty sight.
I love to watch the SNOW FLAKES,
  Come falling to the ground,
Of different shapes and patterns
  None ever could be found;
There's nothing in this world below
  As pure white as new fallen
SNOW,
As it falls down, down, down,
down
  On this ole' earth below.

Elizabeth P. Richards
EVENING'S GLOW
The evening shades are ever
  changing, fascinating the eye
  with varied hues.
The sun abalze in a brilliant
  aureole, sinking slowly beyond
  the trees.
Silhouettes appear against the
  sky, graceful birds drift
  overhead.
One communes in the stillness of
  the moment, my thoughts soar
  beyond the clouds.
The evening glow encompasses
  me, peace is here, now,
  supreme at last!

Sara Hewitt Riola
ON SPRING
Dream now of moss beneath your
  feet
And gentle breezes, warm and
  sweet,

Seek out the sun's embracing rays
That filter thru' the lengthening
  days.

Spring comes with fingers
  touched in gold
While magic worlds of green
  unfold,

Soon all the beauty of your dream
Is twice fulfilled in nature's
  scheme.

Theodore E. (Ted) Williams
GHOST TOWN

My wife Sondra

Dust devils dance down your
  empty street
Like children hard at play,

Kicking at tumbleweed with
  silent feet
As the sun burns it's shadows
away.

The stagecoach no longer comes
  down the hill
Swaying and rattling along,
Bringing in strangers and women
  to thrill
The miners with gambling and
  song.

Your boards, with their nails
  streaking with rust,
Gray and curled by the sun,
Once kept out the rain, wind and
  dust
And sheltered mens' sorrows and
  fun.

The windows that once sparkled
  with light
From kerosene lamps or candle,
Now starkly stare without any
  sight,
Stoned by the tourist and vandal.

Some doors were salvaged long
  years ago
Revealing your bleak empty rooms
Or slam back and forth as the
  winds blow
A morbid dirge to your doom.

With heavy heart I turn from the
  site
Where once mens' dreams were
  born,
Where music and laughter once
  rang through the night
There are none left to weep and
  to mourn.

Dr. & Mrs. Jose' V. Gragasin

Jose' V. Gragasin, Ph. D., D. H.
Our Prayer for Greater Peace and Harmony In Our Home

*This poem is dedicated to my
wife, Socorro. We wrote it to
commemorate the pleasantries,
cordialities, etc. we enjoyed
together with our guests from
other states and abroad during
their sojourn in our humble home.*

Our Heavenly Father, God, the
  Almighty, Our Saviour!
We beseech Thee for Thy
  guidance in bringing greater
  Peace and Harmony in our home!
For we know Thou Knowest all
  things,

And Thou canst Lead us with
  Thy Love and Thy Power!

Dear Father! please Bless our
  home and let it become a
  pleasant place filled with Thy
  Loving Presence and Peace!
Kindly Direct us and Guide us
  make our home life loving and
  happy,
Dear Lord! Make our home a
  contented refuge with Thee for
  us, our children and for our
  friends,
Show us how to respond to Thy
  Love for us by loving others in
  return.

Dearest Father! Cause us to be
  patient, one to another and to
  speak softly—
Direct us to cast away our
  bitterness, our wrath and our
  anger!
Help us learn to live together, in
  loving relationship with all
  Thy children on earth,
Please Guide us that our acts and
  deeds become pleasant to the
  eyes of man and to our Beloved
  Father in Heaven.

Our Lord and Saviour! we know
  that as we pray to Thee,
Thy Help, Thy Guidance and
  Thy Blessings come to us,
Thus, our hearts are not troubled,
  nor afraid, knowing that
  Thou dost come to us as we
  Pray, to Thee, in His Name . . .
  Amen.

Michele Pye
In the Fire's Last Flame
In the fire's last flame
Where hot embers are
  the sole memoirs of the time
The friendship remains
Yet in the recollection
One wonders why
We've been through so much
  together, as one
  yet often, alone
I never missed you before,
Yet now,
  life would seem empty
  without you all—
  your lives
  your warmth
  your dreams
Each one has made the
  vision clearer, more meaningful
All adding his inner
  beauty to the dream
And, as the candle
  burns down to a wick
We're left with one another
  as one more year
  goes by.

Beverly Ovelton Romero
Frienship—Unforgettable
Congeniality, a quality possessed
  by few, an outstanding
  characteristic which
  distinguishes you.
The warmth of your smile, the
  expressiveness of your eyes, are
  only a few of the qualitites
  which make me realize,
It's great to have friends, who
  share with you, the joys and
  the heartaches of this world so

573

blue.
Our acquaintance was short, but
  friendship grew.
and now it's my pleasure, just
  knowing you.
Friendship has no ending when
  each does his part.
our chances are great, judging
  from the start.
If you ever need me, just call or
  extend a hand.
I'll be there my dear, to do all I
  can.

Sabrina Younger Good

Sabrina Younger Good
SUBLIME ENCOUNTER

---

*To the Ocean of Life, which into
our lives in moments unexpected
rushes forth with its Divine
Cleansing Force, washing away
accumulated burdens of
incompletely lived yesterdays.*

As I rested on the cool October
  grass of Venice, sun softly
  shining upon my serene and
  sleepy eyes.
Gazing lazily out, far away, up
  into the silvery sea-blue sky.
A character from a fairy tale
  book, with a bygone days' Pied
  Piper look, took me suddenly
  by surprise.
Dressed in satin, shiney and
  white, jewels and rings of silver
  and paste,
A belt of colorful scarves about
  his waist.
A twinkle in his somewhat shy,
  hazel-green eyes,
A smile a mile wide upon his
  sunblest face.
Here and there a touch of
  embroidery, delicate cuffs of
  lace.
He opened a sack, full of tiny
  bells, passing them along.
Affectionately greeting all the
  passersby, who stopped to hear
  his songs.
Then donning that enchanting
  lure of faraway, mystical
  places,
Majestically stepped forth to me,
  as though from one of the
  pages,
Kneeling, and gazing deeply into
  my eyes.
Many hours I stayed entranced,

while visions of past loves,
  imprisoned in earthbound ties,
  paraded by.
Hurts, fears, scars, tears, long
  crystallized, releasing, as he
  sang to me and played his long
  time friend, guitar.

His melodic, healing voice rang
  far and deep into that lovely,
  luxuriously lazy, dreamy day.
Delving deeply the depths of my
  being, melting all my thoughts
  and cares away.
Always shall I treasure that
  measureless, musical, moving,
  magical meeting.
Reaching into my heart,
  introducing my self to me,
  through a now, forever loving
  friend, and beautiful caring
  brother,
Known well to many others as
  Jingles of Venice Beach!

Susan M. Solnick
VISION FROM A MOMENT
Sculptured masses before me
as once possibly were clay
  figurines
molded by the hands of God
  himself.

Through these distant windows
I glance to see what is before me.
Not quite a frosted vision,
but one in which I shall conceive
in the vast corridors of my mind
for the moment, a dream.
Just possibly the contentment
  and peace
my soul has longed for.

It will be for only this moment,
then as tomorrow, the future
will crest upon my horizon
and I shall then turn to capture
  in its essence
what will then become a
  memory.

Denise M. Lessard
'TIS THE SEASON
'Tis the season to be jolly,
Merry Christmas and good will
That's how everybody feels at
  least
until they get the bill

Salvation Army workers
ring their bells out in the cold
Their crimson faces smiling
and their souls as good as gold

They never cry for alms,

or make themselves a pest
Just the balance of the change we
  get
is all that they request

Parents shop for hours
and they travel all about
But when they finally get there,
the toys are all sold out

Susie wants a Care Bear,
or a Cabbage Patch doll
While other children would be
  glad
for anything at all

'Tis the season to be jolly
and to window shop downtown
but Christmas is a gift of peace
that should be passed around

Tina Yeamans
CHRISTMAS
Christmas is a time of loving, of
  joy, of happiness, and of giving.
Christmas is a time of
  remembering our Savior, Jesus
  Christ, when he was born in
  the manger in Bethleham a
  long, long time ago that is now
  a joyous holiday called
  Christmas.
Christmas is a time of loving and
  giving love to loved ones and
  ones who aren't loved enough,
Remember, the joy of Christmas
  isn't the recieving, but it's the
  giving.

Agnes B. Kosa Thompson
A MOTHER'S LOVE
A mother's love is faithful,
A mother's love is strong,
It will still forgive you,
Even though you're wrong.

A mother's love will suffer,
Heartache, shame and tears,
It will try to guide you,
Safely through the years.

It will try to sheild you,
Protect you from all pain,
Help you keep from bringing
Dishonor to your name.

It will try to help you
Through your struggling years,
Help to ease your burdens,
Drive away your fears.

A mother's love is patient,
Praying day by day,
That God will always guide you
Safely all the way.

Nina Tessin
GULLS CRY
Gulls cry
Soaring buoyantly overhead
Soft pinions outspread,
Screaming lonliness,
Resounding echoes
Caught in tidepools
Wingshadows wheeling pass;
Catching for a moment the eye,
And momentarily the heart,
Listening for your step.

Desolate marsh grasses shoal
The empty beach
Beyond the wade lines,
Bleakly encountering erosion
From the steady pull of ebb and
  tide flow;
Lonely ripple of sound,

Sentient cycle of living and dying,
Blowing seed past where the gulls
  nest
On the salt wind sighing.

Maralyn Kier
LOVER'S QUARREL
The aftermath of a dreadful
  storm—disclosure—lightning—
  thunder—darkness
Emotions tip—headed on the
  skin, wanting to crawl out—
  and fly away
    —To where?—
Millions of tentacle's reaching for
  a soothing balm,
In moments of emotional
  disaster

—CALM—
  A great wind subsiding,—
  waters receding
    A light prism shining through—
    —Softness, shelter, warmth
  again.

Daphne Michelle Ferguson
FIRE EVERLASTING
Lifetimes lived over and over
Until that life has died
And with it the love in it
The ashes smolder and blow
  away with the wind.

Before the day of death
The life goes on and on
Sometimes pretending,
  sometimes facing reality,
Sometimes falling, and caring.

Joys and tears from falling
Many scars big and small cover
  one small heart
But time changes and helps to
  erase those scars
Then the pain turns into a
  joyfilled memory.

The fire hoped to be everlasting
Slowly ran out of kindling
Then the cinders turn to ashes
And the smoldering ashes blow
  away with the wind.

Maybe—one day, two pieces of
  wood
May come into contact
Striking in just the right way
And one small spark
Will start an everlasting blaze.

Jessie Druktanis
ONCE, LONG AGO?

---

*This poem may make it seem as
if I don't really love my mother,
but I do love her with all my
heart. With me being at the age
of fifteen, I know this is when I
need her most.*

The tears swell in my eyes
I've been crying for hours already
The hurt I've felt so many times,
Of a mother who does and does
  not love me.

I hear her laughing loudly upstairs
When only moments ago she
  injured me
She said to my father, "The only
  time she's nice to me is when
  she wants something; she
  doesn't really love me."

I couldn't bear it any longer,
But my mind wouldn't let me
reach out and hug her.
I just couldn't say the things I
wanted
I love her oh so much, but a
small gesture now and then
won't do.
I've go to learn to say I love you,
and yell and scream it if I have
to.
She's the only person who
matters in my life.

I can't seem to figure out what
stops me from giving her the
love,
That, she's given me all my life.
Can't she see that I'm being nice
because I just want one thing?
I only want her love.

I just don't want the torment or
the question of my love
I want to give her a hug and
without feeling the way I did;
So many times before:
I want to be close to her
Like a mother and daughter should

I want to be the way we always
were,
Once, long ago . . . .

Lenora C. Hannemann
A PERFECT DAY
I we are looking for a perfect day
That ends with a song in our
heart.
If we hear of someone in need,
Who needs cheering indeed,
Then we must not fail to do our
part.

I just had a happy perfect day
It ended with a word well spoken,
I helped shorten a mile
With a word and a smile,
For someone who's courage was
broken

If to the end of a day I come,
Without a single deed well done.
If we don't help one another,
A friend, Sister or Brother.
Then our day is lost, not won.

Lord be with us, To end days
perfect
So in our life, We may gain many
a day
That we will always be kind
With only good thoughts in our
mind
And travel on lifes stright narrow
way.

Aurora Herndon
SPRING
Spring is the best time of year.
How the earth spreads good cheer!

The flowers just begin budding,
And are so bright and glistening.

The trees are so green . . . .
The prettiest you've ever seen!

The bees and birds work without
rest,
Until they know that they've
done their best.

Spring reminds me of someone
dear,
Just like a lake, crystal clear.

He is just like a bird,

working to know he's done his
best.
Then with conscience clear,
can finally rest.

He went through this world
without worry or care,
Just like the freshness of
Spring Air.

Though he went away,
His memory's here to stay.
Always lingering,
Never Hindering.

Iva Nell (Bright) Brown

Iva Nell (Bright) Brown
YOU WERE HEAVEN SENT
I wish that I could write, or say,
how much you've done for me;
Dear parents, teachers, doctors,
friends, and those no more, I'll
see;
My husband, and my children,
who give me special pride
My relatives, and my pastors,
whose arms were open wide.
I wouldn't part Life satisfied, until
I tell how much
You've made my life a happy one,
with your own special touch.
I wasn't destined for a life of
fame and history;
I've striven hard to reach the goal
that you'd expect of me,
To make my world a better
place, to change some tears to
smiles.
T'was always you who cheered
me on; gave courage through
my trials.
And I can't fully thank you for
these precious ties that bind;
Your pains, advice, and sacrifice
and loving care entwined.
No matter when I needed you,
I've felt your presence near,
My courage soared, my spirits
rose; thoughts of you brought
cheer.
And through the years, I more-so
find, how much, to me you've
meant.
I thank my Father; through His
Love, you each were 'Heaven
Sent.'

Cristina M. Morren
DON'T STAND . . .
Don't stand in the rain too long,
Pouring your troubles out to the
Gray world that never listens
anyway.

Don't stand by the wall too long,

Crying out your pain to the people
That hurry away without caring.

Don't stand in the crowd too
long,
Reaching your heart out to
Strangers that take your identity
from you.

Don't stand by the doors too long,
Waiting to show the sorrow in
your heart
To those who don't understand.

Come back out of the rain and
the dark, to sit in your room
and remember the gray and the
wall and the crowd. Come back
and sit in the darkness of your
life and remember the sorrow
of yesterday that is just a
shadow today.

Gloria Jean Robertson
OUR LITTLE ELLEN

*Ellen, you have been born with
the knowledge that no other one
knows intuitively; that nothing is
really impossible if you try, that
anything at all can be
accomplished and of course
finished!*

Looking at the world thru grown
up eyes,
Realizing some responsibility;
How you proceed, will show if
you're wise,
If you can survive independently!

When times are darkest,
You see beyond,
Receive hard times, as a passing
guest,
Then head held high, you carry on!

Victoria Francis
FOREVER FRIENDS
If you ever find yourself worried
or troubled about anything.
Wondering and fearing maybe
with what tomorrow will bring—
And if you ever long to tell
someone that even in a crowd
you feel so alone,
Just remember you have a friend
on whom you can always
depend.
I'll always be wherever you need
me with arms open wide,
Giving you my shoulder for you
to cry on and listening to all
you want to confide.
I've often heard that a friendship
was one soul in two.
With you and me, my friend, I
know this is true.
For always, in all ways—even to
the end, we will be "Forever
Friends"!

Bonnie L. Holtzhafer
DEAD OR ALIVE?
How can you live from day to day?
You get your chance but you
throw it away.
You say, "I don't want to, please
take me home.
I told you that I never should
have come."

You might like it. Try, then you'll
know.

Even if you lose you're still
learning to grow.
But no, you're so scared, It's hard
to believe.
Tell me, are you afraid to even
breathe?

You can't go on hiding like this.
There's just so much in life that
you'll miss,
like thunder and lightning during
a storm
with someone there to keep you
safe and warm.

Sometimes I wonder how you
survive
in a life where you seem hardly
alive.
You can't keep running away
forever.
Give it a try or you won't find out
ever.

It's not so bad once you give it a
chance.
Don't be afraid if you should lose
your balance.
Just try again another day.
You'll get over it and realize
you're still okay.

Charles Alden Kidder
REUNION
Ah, this I know that we have
lived and loved before!
Such unity of mind and heart
could not be born this hour.
Who can tell me Nay that 'fore
the worlds began
And myriads of suns a-borning
hurtled through spaceless
space and timeless time,
In wonderment we beheld it all,
knowing, planning then
Journeys through galaxies and
systems far, sharing knowledge
we should gain.

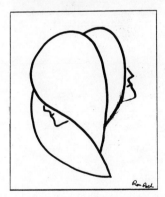

Well might we know that varied,
separate tasks and lessons to be
learned
Kept us apart, till now a common
task brings you once more to me.
Oh, joy—again to share high thought
and plans for eons yet to be!
Friend, leave me not! Ere we return
to Mind from whence we came,
Fulfilment of life's cycles past,
Let us again explore all worlds
that there may be.
Our quest for fuller life shall lead
us near and far.
Come—see with me the view
from mounts on yonder star!

Martha J. (Ramsay) Mead
A GIGGLE A DAY

*With Love to my parents Mr. &
Mrs. Edmond A. Ramsay, and to
my husband, Ronald F. Mead, for
their faith and trust in me!*

A giggle a day keeps the glums
away
Or so I've heard it said.
But it's awful hard to laugh alone
At night awake in bed.

With no-one there to comfort me
In the night so deathly still.
Only the sound of a summers rain
On my bedrooms window sill.

But soon those nights will pass
on by
And alone I shall not be.
I will have a loving husband
Who will care, I trust, for me.

Together we'll share our honest
love
Until death do us part.
But even then we'll always be
Alive within Gods heart.

Tom Campbell

Tom Campbell
The Best Is Yet To Come

*To Lyn, the wife of my good
friend, Ron Dundore, on the
advent of her thirtieth birthday.*

They say, "When you're thirty
you're over the hill, and aches
and pains will start."
They say, "You must start taking
tonics and pills to keep from
falling apart."
They say, "You must slow down
and stop having fun, like you
have had in the past."
They say, "At thirty middle age is
begun, and your youth is gone
at last."
But, Lyn, I must tell you that
they are all wrong; it's not the
start of the end.
Don't you give up now what has
taken so long to get for
yourself, my friend.
Let me say, "The best is yet to
come for you, so, stay right
here in the race.
Cheer up, and smile—don't you
dare to be so blue;

just wear your most cheerful
face."
You've come a long way, Babe—
can go further yet. So, be happy
where you've gone.
You've only reached the prime of
life, you bet! It gets better from
now on.

Donald W. Dutcher
LITTLE JOEY
In his hand he had a fishing pole
Little Joey was headed for the
fish'n hole
As he walked along he whistled a
happy tune
Cause we knew he wouldn't be
home til noon
He wanted to prove to his Dad
and Mom too
That he could catch fish like his
Dad too
As he walked along whistling a
song
He could hear birds singing their
song
It was a happy day for little Joe
For it was his birthday you know
Even before he reached the fish'n
hole
He could see all the fish hang'n
from his fish'n pole
He would catch one for Mom and
Dad
and also one for their cat, Tad
He would catch one for him
and one for his sister, Kim
It was a happy day for little Joe
For it was his birthday you know.

Norma Claflin Trask
IN MEMORY OF MOTHER
When I was but a little girl
And you'd take me by the hand.
We'd go to Treasure Island,
Or some other Pretend land.
I trusted you and loved you.
You showed me wrong from right.
We said our prayers together,
As we knelt by my bed each
night.
You told me as I got older,
If you ever left this land
To pray to God for guidance
And you'd both take me by the
hand.
God Bless you Mother.

Laura Lawina Simpson
MOTHER
Can you tell me who here below
Was an angel that sang and told
Those wonder stories sweet and
true?
Who was that angel. I love her
too.
Mother mine was that angel.
O you know, she used to come by
night
To sing and tell me stories
How she used to hold me tight.
Everytime there was something
new to say
remember child, she said and
went away.
Dear Mother ever stay with
me . . .
A Voice it seemed to say,
You'll never go away.
Can you tell me who here below

was an angel that sang and told
Those wonder stories sweet and
true?
Who was that angel? I love her
too.

Michael Duane Rawls
MEMORY TAPE
It's funny
How two people
Go their seperate ways
And forget the special moments
Of their yesterdays
The feeling
Changes to memory
That replays like a tape
And nothing within the soul
Can erase the memory
From the mind
Thus in time
One learns to rewind the reel
Allowing the memory
To replay
As they feel
But when one changes
The memory
Becomes an old tape
That gets put away
Only to play
On a rainy day

Sandra S. Schantz
LONELY HEART
I miss you more
each passing day
constantly wishing
you weren't so far away.

Do you think of me
like I think of you?
Do you still care
the way that I do?

Why don't you write
or give me a call,
before I lose my mind
and climb the wall?

It has been quite a while
since I heard from you last,
are you trying to tell me
it's over and in the past?

I'll keep on dreaming
of being with you
but only you can make
my dreams come true.

Michele C. Nahirney
HEAVEN
When I'm alone, sad or happy
It tends to make me think more.
I try to find the silver key,
That fits into the golden door.

The door is opened a light shines
through,
Shading my eyes, I curiously peer
into the light.
I see a shadow but what is it or
who?
My vision clear, oh . . . what a
pretty sight!

It is an angel, a dress of glittering
gold,
Welcoming me into the
enormous room.
I ask "What has happened, will
the mystery unfold?"
She replies "Just wait, you'll
understand soon."

A sprinkle of dust as bright as the
sun,
Is put on my toes as well as my

head.
Up I go "Hey, this is kind of fun!"
The white clouds resemble my
bed.

Soon I stop and wonder where I
am,
Searching for the angel but she is
gone.
A figure emerges, a shape of a
lamb.
The eyes are dark like the sky at
dawn.

No sooner had I realized I was
going down,
Keeping my eye on the figure up
above.
I was slowly placed back on the
ground,
A feeling so great, greater than
love.

Pamela Keddy
COPING
My mind hurts from its thinking,
my eyes sting from their tears.
I'm in a state of confusion, with
nowhere left to turn.
My outlook has become clouded.
Yet I have so much to do.
The world, it is outside my door,
the step is mine to choose.
I do not know what will lie there,
or how I'll confront the day
when the cards of my life are
dealt and shown and I must
commence to play.
The world, it is a scary place, and
life its eternal partner.
But as the earth has continued to
turn so must I do the same.
To except the choices I have
made, and find some lasting
dreams.
And try to reach the unreachable,
and try to live again.

Joyce Albrecht
SOMEONE CARES
Whenever our life seems so full
of darkness and despair
When cares and heartaches
overwhelm us, so hard to bear
We ponder, we question and the
answer is not there
We tend to give up hope, to say it
is not fair
We think no one understands, no
one that can share
Our griefs, our burdens and that
no one really cares
But there is someone, who's life
was the same
He bore it all, alone, for an
example He came
The Alpha and Omega, God's son,
JESUS, is His name
He, too, felt as we, when on this
earth He trod
He fulfilled His mission when
sent by His Father, God
From birth to death, His life was
misery and pain
The Lamb of God, our sacrifice,
was not given in vain
He'll strengthen, console,
encourage, give hope and faith
to life
Lift our heartaches, our
weariness, ease the burdens
and strife

He'll love, bless, show a way
  where there seems to be none
Take our hand, with His arms
  around us He says, "Come,
Believe in me, I'm your Saviour,
  Redeemer and Sacrifice.
Cast your cares upon me I've
  already paid the price."
He'll help you climb the
  mountain, no matter how steep
He'll go with you through the
  valley, no matter how deep
Seek and ye shall find Him,
  knock and He'll be there
He'll never leave thee, nor forsake
  thee, He'll answer every prayer
So look to JESUS for comfort, no
  matter what befalls
And He will be waiting to answer
  whenever you call.

Carol Gawronski
THE BUS RIDE
The lost and the lonely, the pot-
  heads and drunks,
People the bus station, some
  leaning on trunks.
Riding through tunnels, nearly
  scraping the sides,
Onto the highway where traffic
  flows and glides,
City lights continue, follow
  through the night
Bus flows through its byways, 'til
  city's out of sight.
Up tunnels, onto roadways, twist,
  turn, proceed,
Bridges spanning rivers, ramps for
  unknown need.
Traveling onward, ever forward
  we go,
Gliding, sliding, turning, as the
  lights glow.
Through night to morning,
  reaching our chosen spot,
Depart at bus depot, each to his
  own lot.

Dorothy Jeanette Lyons
ME
I'm not always as I seem to be,
Well content and so carefree . . .
Sometimes I feel my heart can't
  take
All of the misery this world
  makes
Sometimes I wonder if I show
These feelings that I only know,
And if I can reach down and see
This heart within the real true
  me . . .
No one but me can explain
The love, the hurt, the endless
  pain . . .
No one but me can really feel
The things I know within are
  real . . .
There is so much that I regret,
But still, in me, I cannot let
The world see that this face
  outside
Is hiding so much foolish
  pride . . .
Sometimes, I merely want to
  shake
Away those things so hard to
  take . . .
And when you look my way
  you'll see
A lot of things, but never
  "ME" . . .

Jan Turnage
DAY OF JOY
What a wonderful thing to have a
  day of joy,
and these days we should employ,
ways to pet ourselves and pamper,
before tomorrow brings a damper.

Some days that start off and stay
  so right,
should be held on to oh so tight,
soak these joyful days in slowly,
reserve some joy for those who
  are lowly.

Each day brings some type of
  change,
it would be boring with things so
  neatly arranged.
Otherwise what would life be,
no chance to grow and learn to be
  me.

So, thank you for this day of joy,
for on these days I do employ,
things that bring me great pleasure,
each minute and second I treasure.

I enjoy this brief respite,
from problems that close in so
  tight
Oh day of joy come again soon,
I enjoy your morning, night, and
  noon.

Jennifer G. Rollins
WHAT IS CHRISTMAS?

*To My Mom and those who I
care most about.*

Christmas is for loving,
caring, and sharing.
It's a time for peace and goodwill.
It's a time to remember the
year that has past.
It's a time to look ahead.
It's a time for family.
It's a time for good cheer.
It's a time to give and yet recieve.
All of this takes so little and
we receive soo much.
All of this is Christmas to me.
  Merry Christmas!

Faith M. Lester-Spinosa
LOVE
Love is like a flower
one blossoms every day.
Thorns are for hurting things
sometimes people say.

My love is like a surging ocean
where waves do swell and crest.
They crash upon a sandy beach
where they find their final rest.

Ronald Joseph Flemming Jr.
THE HOLIDAY SPIRIT

*This poem is dedicated to my
"Wonderful Parents"; whose self-
sacrifice, kindness, and love
endowned our home with the
Holiday Spirit all the year
round . . . Thank you Both . . .*

People change so wonderfully,
  when once possessed
By the sense of peace and
  brotherhood
That lets them fly and sets them
  free

Upon the "wings of love" if they
  only would . . .
To enjoy the touch of "Another's
  Hand"
And drink the water from a
  stream
To be able to give and receive
  from every man
To live all the "Dreams of
  Humanity" . . .

There comes a season once a year
When we all join together and
  give praise
For the "Wonder of Life" inside
  our hearts
For the flowers come srping, and
  the suns warm rays . . .

Look upon a "Snowflake", a
  "Winter Star"
And feel the "Warmth" from a
  "Candle's Flickering Light"
Listen to the "Christmas Carols"
  the children sing
"Once Possessed" . . . . by the
  "Holiday Spirit" . . .

Mrs. Patricia B. Cabrinety

Mrs. Patricia B. Cabrinety
AUTUMNAL SIGNALS
Days shorter,
  nights longer,
Briskness encompasses all . . .
Mark the beginnings of FALL.

Migrating monarch butterflies,
  chipmunks storing seeds,
Groups of excited birds on the
  lawn,
Disappearance of spots on the
  fawn.

Red, yellow,
  brown, and orange spots
Showing at the tops of trees,
Puddles edges by
  morning—freeze.

Orange berries
  on the mountain ash,
Chirping crickets day and night,
Canadian geese start southward
  flight.

Yellow school buses,
  children with books,
Sharp, crisp, cool, bitty breeze,
Dancing golden rods stiffened
  with the freeze.

Sunflowers seed-filled heads,
  an artist's palette of colorful
  trees,
Raking up the leaves,
Bared branches before the breeze.

Black and rust colored
  caterpillars, menacing gray
  wooly clouds in the sky,

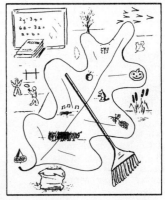

Crimson apples on the orchards
  trees,
Picked pumpkins in the yard
  before the howled breeze.

Days shorter,
  nights longer,
Matured beauty in all—
Such is found in a Northern FALL.

Shawn P. Conners
SEARCHING
Searching, searching
  what will I find?
Reliving the memories
  that haunt still my mind.
Hearing past voices
  that call from behind.
Looking for something
  that alludes still our kind.

The wrongs I have done,
  shown in the air.
Deceptions and lies
  deeds done so unfair.
People forgotten,
  neglected from care;
Show me their presence
  something so rare.

Distant voices calling,
  a small pleading sound.
Shapes dazzle my vision
  geometric and round.
I run now no longer,
  not a leap nor a bound;
The place in my dreams
  is suddenly found.

Susan M. Silver
THE WIDOW
She crawls toward daylight and
  retreats among
The fields again, her soul a
  severed sunset now.
The fragrance of the grass has
  bound her here,
A slave to withered roots and
  empty skies . . .
And the nights keep splashing
  colors on new dawns,
New dungeons of truth. Go on, go
  on, without
Her sighs. There is time enough
  for sadness. She
Has lost the earth and cannot see
  the sky.

Helen Brown Vandervoort
TWILIGHT
Twilight in our living room is
  that lovely time of day

When all the hurrying is done
and tasks are tucked away,
I view with inner happiness my
family gathered there,
No other hour could hold the
precious nearness that we
share.
We talk of many things, perhaps,
or sometimes not at all—
Content to watch the lingering
shadows creep along the wall.
Each one, in turn, relates the
highlights of his own eventful
day,
The good, the bad—no secrets
when each one has had his say.
Tales of haunting memories of
failure, disappointments, fears
Are banished when they fall on
understanding, sympathetic
ears;
Encouragement and confidence
are given and received,
Failures are forgotten, tensions
are relieved.
"All for one and one for all" is the
motto that we share,
Family ties are strengthened by
the knowledge that we care,
All too soon the darkness settles
and another night is born;
Lamplight glows on Father's paper,
Brother reaches for his horn.
Mother finds her knitting, Sister
grabs a book,
Each one pursues his hobby in
his own familiar nook,
Then our reverie is ended,
Twilight's interlude is o'er,
Minds and hearts have been re-
fueled for Tomorrow's toughest
chore.

Mary Elizabeth Minier
MY PRAYER FOR 1984

For Brian, Keith and Tracy

If everyone all over the world
Would think with their heart not
their head
Then perhaps we could all live in
peace
And make sure that the hungry
are fed

Forget about power and political
gains
And more about illness and strife
And clean up the land and the
water we drink
To prepare for a much better life

Destroy all those bombs all over
the world
And hold out our hands and say
Let's help each other with
knowledge and love
And get on our knees and pray

Dani Lynn Price
TRIALS OF CHRIST
The scars that people carry
From things they have gone
through,
Often times forgets the fact
That Jesus had them too.

Men tried to kill Him
Just the same as these days.
He was often laughed at
And mocked in many ways.

He wept real tears
When His friend Lazarus died.
People turned His truths
Into empty, sinful lies.

Rejected by many
That He tried to save,
Was often misunderstood
For the kind of love he gave.

Denied by the people
Who knew Him so well,
Had to fight temptations
From the Angel of Hell.

When you get discouraged
And feel you can't go on,
Let the trials of Christ
Help to keep you strong.

Annette C. Erwin Cordes

Annette C. Erwin Cordes
MOTHER

---

*To my mother and father, Melvin
and Doris Dilly Cordes, who have
always helped me find the beauty
in life.*

Curled on our couch, I used to
watch
your black hair bow over
the polished wood of your violin.
As the bow eased over the strings,
resin delicately filtered from its
taught hairs
coming to rest under the bridge.
How could hair from a horse's tail
make such sweet sounds, I'd
question.

Sometimes when you played a
trio with your delicate fingers,
the sounds would make me see
baroque music halls,
and red satin gowns on your
slenderness
instead of the cotton-print dress
made from flour sacks
in which you were standing.

And then, those same fingers
would lay the violin
on the green velvet in its case,
and turn with a deft movement
from
the wrist to pick up brushes.
Stroking shadows into the colors,
you painted Hiawatha on the
shores of Gitche Gumee
waiting for Nakomis, Daughter of
the Moon;
A birch-bark canoe waited palely
in the moonlight,
the dark water lapping at its hull.

Inhaling the scent of your clean
clothing
and the strong smell of oil paints,
I drew near, kissed your soft
cheek
And ran out to play.

Brenda W. Moses
**When the World Comes To
An End**
When the world comes to an end
We'll all be scattered all over the
ground
There'll be no one here on earth
No man will be around
It's sad but true, the world we
know
Will still be charred remains
Of all the lives given in vain
To a world coming to an end
The world will always be around
It's the people of the world
That'll lose there lives.
So many minds have decided
when others die
In there game of whoms the best
But do they wonder/do they ever
ponder
Of the lost of others sad
demise.
When it's all over; the world will
be smothered
In nuclear, radiant smoke
Then who will claim the glory?
Who will hear the boast?
A shattered world all torn to bits
By the greater powers of today
But the message in the bible had
this to say
"The people of the future will
obey".

Vittoria M. Mercaldo
INNERMOST FEELINGS
I close my eyes, his face I see,
A perfect replica in front of me.
His dark, dreamy eyes and curly,
black hair,
Cloud my memory, he has me
ensnared.

My innermost thoughts concern
only him,
A romantic interlude, a soft
violin.
A candlelight dinner, a kiss, a
touch,
Dreams of the one I love so very
much.

To hold him in my arms would
be devine,
If only for the very shortest of
time.
With him I could never part,
For I rule not with my head, but
with my heart.

Laima Kontautas—Valickas
SPRING
Till the Daisies Kiss my Lashes,
Dear, Dearest, My Love One;
Paint Portrait of Me . . .
　You Are Artist
　And I Know it,
　I Am Poet
　And You Know It.
　Take Good Look at Me!
Do Enlarge my "Goo—Goo" Eyes,
Till I Stare to Scream . . .
You The Talent—
For The Love and Art . . .

Shelley Teresa Muse
MISSILE BOUND?

---

*To all the children of the world,
who are too young to understand
a nuclear war, and too innocent
to be a part of one.*

Teardrops fall from innocent eyes
As they gaze upon the dreary skies
With it's missiles somewhere
bound
And the smell of death is all
around.

A nation crumbles, and the blood
runs red
Buildings are shattered, many are
dead
And children cling to their
mothers with fear
As their hope for the future
disappears.

If we awaken to find it's a dream
Tell me, will we have learned
anything
Or will we keep fighting until the
day of
The final destruction of all that
we love?

A few angered countries and an
unsettled score
A frightening reality we must not
ignore
A nuclear age, creating much fear
Tensions 'tween countries draw
war ever near.

Mandy Campman
I WILL WAIT

---

*This is for WILLIE D. Who plays
an important part of my fantasy!*

There shall always be
a tomorrow,
but for now only memories
of our yesteryears.
Now I shall live for today,
Striving for the goodness and
pleasures
that are offered in such a way.
I'll give of myself and
Keep what is mine,
you are no burden,
but a fantasy in time.
Bare with me
my unborn child,
for it will be awhile,
Till you begin to nourish and grow,
and that heavenly day
shall be our tomorrow.

Ortrud H. Perez
WHAT COLOR IS PAIN?
Just a moment ago
I walked on a path
Of light blue feathers
Under white arches
Adorned with peach-colored
ribbons.
I swirled,
Red chiffon brushing my face.
I slept on a pink down pillow;
I woke to a mockingbird's song.

Now my path is a blur—
The light blue feathers
Have turned to gray stones.
The arches are gray and ribbonless.

I have seen the blurry gray
Many times before.
I stand still
Clutching the gray chiffon
To my tightened gut.
I wait.

Mary McGlasson
BLESSINGS
The sun comes up in the
morning, the moon at night
Stars shining down with a
twinkling light.
A wife, a husband, a child and a
home
A big back yard where a boy and
a dog can roam.
You're healthy, you're happy, you
have a good job
Do you take this for granted,
then whine and sob . . .
Feeling sorry for yourself every
day of the week?
Come out of your doldrums! Be
humble, as God's will you seek.
Be Thankful each day, for your
Blessings! Not, once a year
With plate piled high when
Thanksgiving is here.

Nancy Donahoe
PARADOX
Many petals, one rose
Many twigs, one tree
Many cells, one body
Many drops, one sea

Many pages, one book
Many pearls, one strand
Many parts, one machine
Many players, one band

Many trees, one forest
Many people, one world
Many stars, one galaxy
Many names, one God

Mrs. Julie Diane Newland
FOREVER DOESN'T LAST
Sitting and looking
At all the things you gave me
I never had a suspicion
That one day you'd want to be free.

The cards you gave me
That said I love you
That you signed with love
Forever true.

Well forever didn't last
As long as I thought
When you said goodbye
I felt like I'd been shot.

It takes so long
For my heart to heal
From a love that for me
Was oh so real.

I wish I couldn't feel
All this pain
Without you my life
Will never again be the same.

Ruby J. Emerson Davis
SMILES AND TEARS
Smiles and sunshine on the
outside;
Tears and sadness on the inside.
Lots of water has run under the
bridge;
However your kindness and
consideration;
Have helped me look forward to a
new love,
That was just over the ridge.

With God's guidance and your
true love;
I'll try very hard not to regret the
past;
But hold firm to what's left of my
future;
On this great stage, Mother Earth.
Fill the emptiness with laughter,
music and mirth.
So don't put a Lily in my hand yet.
Just two Red Rose Buds;
To hand to God when I meet Him,
In that golden, peaceful valley;
While the choir sings
"Whispering Hope";
And "How Great Thou Art".

Viola Howard
THE PATCHWORK OF LIFE
Each life is assembled
From pieces and bits,
In much the same way as a
patchwork quilt
Is put together from sewing kits.

Some pieces are dreary and dark,
Others cheerful and bright,
But a mixture of color is needed
To make the effect just right.

So 'tis with the pattern of life,
Fashioned in much the same way
With bits of happiness, sunshine
and love
Mingled with tears or grief on a
sad day.

Contentment and happiness
colored by patches of blue,
Strife and trouble shadowed by
shades of gray,
Are bits and pieces in the
patchwork of life
To be encountered in the curse of
a day.

Marjorie Burney Willis
**Angels Count Our
Teardrops**

---

*Dedicated to my daughter Anngel
Willis Duncan written for her.*

Weep not! O weep not, my child!
Holy angels are hovering nearby—
Close enough to count your
teardrops.

You are never alone, never
forsaken!
God has given "his angels charge
of you,
To guard you in all your ways."

Though your tears be as many
As the dewdrops on a field of
flowers,
Every teardrop wears a halo of light;
Each one reflects a radiant rainbow,
A promise of a shining tomorrow.
Tears are like the showers of
springtime—
They fall, so that Life can fulfill
its dreams
And bring forth its fruits.

Weep not! O weep not, my child!
Wherever you wander,
Angels are watching over you,
loving you
The way a mother loves a child.

Holy angels are hovering nearby—
Close enough to count your
teardrops.

Nona Bushnell Ryder
A RESTING PLACE
My place is with Jesus when I
walk here no more
Then I will only be a memory of
a love one who's gone before

No longer will there be obstacles
nor treacherous paths to climb
All I've got is Jesus on my mind

It's an appointment I made many
a years ago
Toward my reunion with God
because I love Him so

Until the trumpet sounds
My body will rest beneath the
blue voulted skies, I will then
arise in peace, and walk on
with God ever more.

Barbara L. Hoerath
I Will Walk Beside You

---

*Tommy, I will always be there
when you need me. And I love
you with all my heart. Love, Barb*

I will walk beside you
through all the storms and the
calmness of a rainbow.
I will walk beside you
through all the happy times
and all the times a tear is shed.
I will walk beside you
through the darkness of the night
till the light of the morn.
I will walk beside you
through all the Love that
consumes all that you are
and all the jealousys of our
insecurities.
I will walk beside you
through the rest of our lives with
all the Love my heart holds.
I will walk beside you.

Clara M. Bush
A PHEMONEN OF LOVE
Jesus died on the cross today,
And all the physical universe
grieved.
Creatures in the forest were
hushed and sad.
Their inocents could not conceive.

Jesus died on the cross today,
And tiny meadow flowers bowed
their heads low.
Song birds sang soft and slow.
The little brook too sad to flow.

Jesus died on the cross today,
And the blue sky turned to gray.
Sad sun could not give its light
And the earth began to sway.

Jesus died on the cross today.
He payed in full for all our sins.
So in heaven we could stay,
Still defiant man must have his
way.

Lynn M. Karlbon
GIFTS OF WISHES
Summer's come and with brings
another year flown on
hummingbird wings
With future years that come to
pass
I'd like to endure them all with
class
For some birthday gifts—my ABC's
some simple things such as these

I'd like roses, perfume, and
sparkling wine
green satin sheets, silk lingerie
divine
Maybe a jet to the warm French
coast
cuisine, vineyards, castles with
their ghosts
I wouldn't mind a Ferrari to cruise
or my very own rainbow with a
million hues
I'd like a late summer day—
beautiful and free
for my birthday number
twenty-three
But for a gift from you to me
I'd like you to
write me poetry

Jane E. McMahon
DAYS THAT PASSED ME BY

---

*To Lisa and Brian McMahon, just
because you are loved.*

When I see little ones hard at play
I remember when I was that way.
I could run and play and sing
I thought I could do almost
anything;
Now that I am old and gray
I cry a little tear
for days that slipped away.

When I see a smiling child
and flowers growing wild;
When I see birds on the wing
I wish that I could
do almost anything;
And I sigh a little sigh
for days that passed me by.

When the storm clouds appear
and little ones cuddle near;
I teach them how to pray and sing
and together we
can do almost anything;
And I no longer sigh
for days that passed me by.

Paulette Talboy Cary
BABY BOY
Baby boy, you're a joy to behold,
Baby boy, you're more precious
than gold,
I treasure every moment that I
can spend with you,
Each little precious moment is
one more dream come true;
Baby boy, when you gaze up at me,
Big blue eyes, is it Heaven I see?
Nothing could make me forfeit
one of your little smiles,

And, just to hear your laughter,
I'd walk a million miles;
Baby boy, sure you'll grow up
some day,
And, perhaps, you will wander
away,
Then I'll sigh, and remember
when you
Were just the Baby Boy I knew,
Just a Baby Boy of two!

Joesph William Roehl
LITTLE SISTER

---

*In His love, with my love. To my
dearest little sister "Meryln".
Always—Your big brother, Joe.*

God is infinite, His wisdom
beyond comprehension.
God's grace is amazing, His mercy
everlasting.
Throughout the ages, before time
was God knew me.
He knew of my longing, He knew
of my needs.

Biologically God could have acted.
Instead by the spirit He soothed
my soul.
Fulfilling the emptyness within
and without.
For He gave me a sister.

A special friend to share with
here and now.
His greatest gift, the Son He
called "Jesus."
The Christ we call saviour, the
Lord of our life.
The word made flesh, now
dwelling within His own.

Oh how lovely and joyous to
share the same Father.
To serve the same Lord and
follow His Spirit.
With my sweet little sister
chosen by the Master.
The one He knew and named
"Meryln".

Praise His Holy name evermore.
For He gave her the wisdom and
understanding.
To know her brothers heart and
love.
As only a true friend and child of
His Kingdom could . . . .

Melissa Bratcher Dimmett
JUSTIN
I never thought I would have a
baby as sweet as you,
All my life I hoped and prayed
that dream would come true.

I know sometimes I get upset and
wish you wouldn't cry,
But if anything ever happened to
you I would surely die.
Your Daddy and I love you so
much that we couldn't stand,
To think of you growing up and
leaving us, only holding your
hand.
Holding your hand as you try to
walk and falling along the way,
Listening to you as you try to
talk you will be grown up one
day.

One day we will turn around and
you will be a man,

And we will think about the
times that we held your hand.

Nellie Woll Kirkpatrick
PRAYER OF THANKS

*To my parents Amanda Meline
and Louis H. Woll, for their
family of seven children.*

Dear God, I know I am a color
and design
Of all that ever was—that shall
not end.
I know I am a motif in Your plan
Of love, to both receive and to
expend.
And this is so—You've told me
very true—
I die unless I love, am loved by
You.
It's clear to me as skies above
when blue
That You have given me a work
to do.
With heart to feel and eyes to
clearly see,
A thread You've made me in Your
tapestry:
A thread that links all man with
every man,
That stretches back since time
and life began,
And onward to the span that's yet
to be.
Oh, yes, You do expect good
things from me.
I know, 'though but a speck, I'm
spark and flame
With spirit from Your great,
unfathomed Source,
To use to help another one, again,
With strength from Your
constructive, loving force.
I know I am a color and design
Of all that ever was,—that shall
not end.
For ever more, I thank You, Lord.
Amen.

Diana J. Bonkoski
REFLECTIONS
The lights of the city,
are so nice at night.
The shops are all closed,
with the quietness locked inside.
I see my image in a window,
my mind begins to wonder.
Does everybody see me,
as I see myself.
Can they tell of my past,
by the way I look or act.
Can they see my faults,
and not my accomplishments.
My self confidence is lowered,
as I stop to stare aside.
Is anybody watching me,
I turn and run to hide.

Natalie Arlene Hansen
CHRISTMAS DAY
Jingle, jingle, is the sound,
I hear coming from downtown,
children singing "Jingle Bells",
and oh what are those wonderful
smells?
Turkeys baking, and pumpkin pies,
what a wonder to my eyes.
When all of a sudden, to my
surprise,
somethings over the house . . .

something that flies.
Oh my gosh . . . and for
goodness sake!
It's ol saint nick, and he's here to
make
A Merry Christmas for all.

Richard (Sully) Sullivan

Richard (Sully) Sullivan
THROUGH A PRAYER
The barefoot boy says amazing is
it not the art to say yes or nay
I will draw I will write or be a
beast rest of my life.
As in society as of today
decadance meets the f I say
So it is up to you to build your
virtues in a lifestyle of self
denial
A dare I call in your daily life
then be a weakling lay down
and die
This is your life.

Or better still say a prayer and
ask the Lord
Please help me before I despair
and know not where is the
world about
About Thee you must believe
Thy self do not deceive you are
the one
Ask the Lord he will help as you
say I believe in you my Lord
Anytime anyday any night or any
way happiness will come
And in your pious way you meet
the Lord as you pray
Your church could be the sky and
believing is the word
I'll not deny as to your feelings
will expel to vilify intent of evil
Your soul be cleansed as in Holy
Communion as is said
The Body of Jesus Christ Amen

Stephanie Simpson
A BRAND NEW TREE

---

*An empty space with nothing
there. A piece of ground that is
bare. On this ground stood once a
tree.*

An empty space with nothing
there.
A piece of ground that is bare.
On this ground stood once a
tree . .
It stood as tall, as tall could be.
It gave shelter it gave shade.
It's mighty branches it displayed.
Then one rainy stormy night.

When thunder roars and
lightning strike.
A lightning bolt struck the tree.
It burnt to a crisp as, crisp could
be.
The tree was burnt all around.
From the tip top to the ground.
But after a while when the crisp
was shed.
A brand new life the tree was fed.
Because at the roots you could
see.
The starting of a Brand New Tree!

Dean Mitchell
I PRAYED FOR YOU

---

*Thanks, Mom, for teaching us
that love is a little Give and a
little Take.*

Yesterday I wanted rain
But you wanted sunshine
I prayed for sunshine.

Once I wanted ice cream
You wanted a soda
I asked for a soda.

In the future, I'll want a girl
You'll want a boy
I'll hope for a boy.

There's one thing I'll always want.
Today, I prayed and asked
And hoped for you.

Jinni E. Davis
DAYSEY
I'm not ashamed to tell the world
That I love you so,
Even though your married
I want the world to know.
I'll even shake the heavens
With the love thats in my heart,
No, I'm not ashamed to love you
I've known it from the start.
I used to love me not with daises
And then I let you go,
No I'm not ashamed to love you
I want the world to know,
I'm just ashamed my Daysey
I ever let you go.

Kathleen Short-Simmons
THANKS ANYWAY

---

*This poem is dedicated to all my
family and friends who have
given of themselves to help me
understand the meaning of love
and happiness. But more so to the
man with whom I've found it,
thanks Casey.*

And as all the people I know and
usually love, formulate
Their very loving, protective
attitudes; I try to keep myself
And judgements separate, which
isn't an easy task.

They know of me, and their past
mistakes and loves, and try
To piece it all together to fit me.
But, it does not fit or
Work; never has, never will, and
it's certainly not their fault.

Thank you all, I love you and
simply because I do, not because
I measure or judge or piece you
together.

Our World's Best Loved Poems

Gloria M. Heiser
ME

Being myself is the ultimate
  wish of my soul.
Simple truth is that
  it seems beyond control

To be what I am . . . me
  whatever the cost.
To be what I can . . . me.
  Help, am I lost?

Blinders secure how well I see,
  little do I know
of the world's reality
  changing with the flow.

Freedom, seeks my spirit,
  to grow without/within.
Nature, as I hear it,
  is where it does begin.

Love for God's creations
  common and diverse,
significantly hastens
  the perfect universe.

Keep me Lord, on the track
  to my destiny.
Questing onward, glancing back,
  the rest is up to me.

Esperanza Saucedo

Esperanza Saucedo
TOGETHER

He touched her with a kiss,
he stared deeply into her.

Hand in hand he took her
  through memories and reality,
they entered dreams and fantasies.

He held her close,
he stared at her once more.

Soaking her beauty through and
  through,
he captured her like a picture.

She knew what was to come,
he was the truly one.

Throughout the night not a word
  was said,
the doors of heaven were theirs.

As the dawn set in,
his eyes took her in.

In the morning mist,
he knew she was his.

She awoke by the feeling of
  warmth,
she knew what he had given her.

He gave her strength and hope,
she gave hime desire and love.

They knew then that they were
  one,
they knew that their life had
  begun.

Daphanie Bousum
CREATIONS

I see the things that are so
  beautiful,
That the Lord has created for us
  to enjoy.

Like the sunset
So soft and warm but yet so
crisp and bright.
It sets off the sky so beautifully
when it's nearing night.

Or the mountains
That decorate the sky in
the morning mist.
I have so many questions about
them it would be an endless list.

A red rose
So small and strong but yet so
  fragile
that it could be cut with a knife.
It could bring so much joy to
a persons life.

An early morning dew fall
The sunlight dances upon it when
it's laying on the grass, like a
  diamond.
As I look at it and imagine things
it plays with my mind.

These are a few things in
  everyday living that mean
nothing. So next time make those
  things that mean
nothing mean something.

Raphael Stephans
Crucias-The Masque Sender

*Troja fuit;fuimus Troes;
adscriptus glebae:e flamma cibum
petere avito viret honore;stat
magni nominis umbra;dii
majorum gentium respice finem;
Crucius-hunc tu caveto ab extra . .*

spaineiette manniequiem diversion
hailequiem spinnette . . . i count

tips-crossed
hidden meaning . . . anything

geomotroball
aiexen compass . . . leading

parallaxis curvature
incondenmasque
  sender . . . tending

fleuer-de-crisis
kailaidascopedomination . . .
  basking

balancinalspira
crescent triscupe . . . descending

vineage roulleues
bastancher throneoftroyafter
petalwind moveoutnow

ona . . Crucian brotherhood

deathmast logos tapesterrestrial
louveyia cabasaxonleaf

aboveaurunder tresspature
danceaeumonic lanceafleeiantia
. . Acantiacia Sefon.

Nona Bushnell Ryder
A CHRISTMAS PRAYER

Our hearts yearn, for the simple
  beauty of Christmas
For melodies and words of him
  who made all things beautiful

Before such mystery we kneel to
  bring gifts of love, of warmth,
  and sincerety

But now on this Christmas day
  that our love would find his
  beloved and show graditude
For blessings that have been
  heaped upon us in many ways

We do pray Lord Jesus that we
  celebrate thy birthday, in a
  manner well pleasing to thee
May we all do and say every
  tribute of our hearts, and bring
  honor to thy name, that we thy
  people may remember thy birth
  this very day

May the loving kindness of
  Christmas not only creep into
  our hearts, but there abide, for
  ever and a day.

Sandra Crudello
The Anatomy Of Mr. Sunshine

The azure of the clearest summer
  sky
Blue morning-glories in dark
  forests
The glow of sapphire gems by
  candlelight
Sparkling, cool and placid,
  turquoise pools:

  These are his eyes . .

The fresh exuding sweetness of
  soft cornsilk
Wildly waving as flaxen fields of
  wheat
In hues of buttercups and
  daffodils
Golden as molten sunlight
  dripping on clouds:

  This is his hair.

Moist and velvety as June's first
  rose
Tenderly touched with the
  firmness of budding manhood
Cool and delicious as scarlet
  watermelon
Expressive as strings of gypsy
  violins:

  These are his lips.

Narcissus, who sees not his
  reflection in my eyes.
A young Adonis, who knows not
  he's a god.
A David, whose sculptured
  beauty has life and warmth.
A sleek, honey hued Eros, created
  for love.

  This is his form.

Matha McKenna
QUIET THOUGHTS
  The room is dark
  The room is quiet
  You lay there thinking
  Feel yourself shinking

  You think about the day just
    past . .
  Problems, solutions, hopes and
    fears
  Your thoughts are many and
    deep,
  You set them aside and welcome
  sleep.

Janalee Carstensen
FLEURS DE LA PASSION

Standing bare with arms
  outstreached to soak up the
  sun of your life.
When his warm breath touches
  your lips,
You open them wide to
  accomodate his passion.

Throughout the morning you
  stretch for more
And he grows hotter with each
  minute.
The World is blurred and forgotten
You are too engrossed in a
  passionate embrace.

Then others slowly start to intrude
He creeps away behind a fluffy
  screen.
While you keep your beauty
  hidden;
Even his opponent cannot make
  you open out.
SUDDENLY
He returns to once more open
  your lips.

Francine Roy
WINTER TRANQUILITY

*With Love to Paul, Sharon, Scott,
Steven and John*

Endless snow for the eye to see,
  whiter than white and snow
  capped tree.
Untouched after first snow falls,
  unspoiled splendor on for miles.
Radiant sun shimmering
  everywhere, illuminating each
  crystal far and near.
Each icicle sparkling with prism
  light, tis' God's own miracle
  and our delight.
Coldness and beauty wrapped
  into one, before children frolic
  to have some fun.
Families drawn closer by the
  sight, awed by the power of His
  might.
Homes seem much more cozy,
  from loving warmth to security.
As night comes in dark winter
  skies fill up and beam with
  endless stars.
For the beholder to behold and
  the Keeper to keep.
Tranquility lingers in the air,
  with His presence felt in this
  we share.

Judith Anne Sparks
REVENGE

He hurt me
and
He thought he got away with it.
But
just like peaceful summer
turns
into the drab death of Fall and
  Winter
I too
turn into the devil he never knew,
Because
He hurt me
and
I have the power of Fall and Winter
To turn
his peaceful summer
into HELL!

Jean Parton
A REASON FOR YOU

You came into my life in the cool
winter season, I knew when I
met you, you were there for a
reason.
And I was the reason for you.
My life was in a lull and I felt it
was oh so dull, that I took a
chance of losing it all.
And that was the time and reason
for you.
You took time to care for things
which I shared, you knew me
so well, no wonder I fell.
And I was the reason for you.
We walked and we talked, we
pouted and salked, but you
were there when no one else
cared or dared.
And that was the reason for
you . . . .

Midgee Jarrell Sigman
OLD TOM TURKEY

*To my wooly-wonderful-
mountain man hubby-I love you
very much . . . . Midgee*

Old Tom turkey strutted round
the barnyard his head held high
His feathers ruffled by the
wind . . .
Old Tom turkey would take a
mate this fall—or so he thought
As he strutted round the
barnyard again . . . .
Old Tom turkey heard a noise in
the barnyard—he looked round
and
Saw two strangers coming toward
him . . . .
Old Tom turkey didn't move a
muscle—nor did he ruffle a
feather
Old Tom turkey stood stock
still . . .
He didn't know why—nor did he
try to run—old Tom turkey felt
scared—
It was a feeling he had never had
before . . .
The sun glinted on steel as the
two strangers approached
him—old Tom
Turkey turned away from them—
his head held high—and his
feathers
Ruffles by the wind . . .

Michael J. Verba
SEX

*To all of the sinners, who still
look above and all of the
defenders of this strange faith:
This self-denial-you're reasons are
wrong . . . . and you're getting old.*

Passion play, the atmosphere takes
And in a strange way
It makes no difference, what
anyone says
It's the tenderness
Of a woman.

God given?—Hardly as such
With a pleasure forbidden
A 'lustless' touch

And the sweetness of skin
It's the softness
Of a woman.

Physically blessed—a feeling so
high
The beauty undressed
By warm loving eyes
So nicely caressed
With the careful pride
Of a woman.

And it's just beauty when—
—You see in the end
The tenderness
And the softness
Together again
These special 'friends.'

Vincenzo LXX Giallonardo

Vincenzo LXX Giallonardo
**UNIVERSA (COSMOS) DAY
August 13, 1913 LXX etc
for EVER FOREVER O
CHALICE**

*Since I Was Born 8/13/1913
About 11am Along The Great
Valley Stream By The Barn Near
The Valley Forge Pennyslvania
USA National Historical Park
Shrine I Have Been Proclaiming
AUGUST 13th UNIVERSA
(COSMOS) DAY to PRAISE The
SOURCE Since my 8/13/1926
Birthday 13 LXX ARCH RACE
LOTUS STAGE ASPIRING
CHALICEDLY . . . To NOW
2/13/1984 etc.*

Spring 1947 Sunny "RAPTURE
TO NATURE . . . Sweet
LOVE . . . Tis BLOOD and
THUNDER RAVISHING . . .
The THRUSH At Sundown
Through The Forest
Trills . . . Tall Columns On
Columns To The Valley or
Valey Hills . . . The
BOULDERS THROBBING . . .
CRAGGY CLIFFS GIANT
LAVISHING . . . The STREAM
O'er ROCKY RAPIDS Splashing
Crashing Thrashing . . . O My
HEART ENRAPTURES and
EXISTENCE STILLS ETERNAL
LIGHTNINGS and The
HUMAN Will's SUSTAINED
TWILIGHT ere The Languishing
. . . . And So A LONER to Forest
Stream Calm Reflecting POOL
. . . Reclined On FLOWERINESS
and GOLDEN SAND . . . The

FIERY SUNSET and The
STARRY STRAND . . . Between
The REALMS of GENIUS and
The FOOL WHOSE CRUISING
SOUL Hath UNIVERSAL RULE
and GIVES DIMENSION To
WHAT ONE MAY COMMAND
. . . " etc O To My 1946
"ACTUALLY ONE May
Meditate Contemplate
COMPOSE SCORE ADORE
UPON a FOREST LANE By
STREAM etc And GAIN a
FLOOD of JOY . . . O The
Trees The Leaves The Sunny
Golden Strain THAT WEAVES
a GLORY Tho So COY O Pools
Eyes REFLECTING GIRL and
BOY SEEMS To BE ON The
SOURCE or LOVE-GIFTED
ETERNAL MAIN As a MICRO-
MOMENT's STAIN Lingering
LO a COSMIC CELESTIAL
TOY . . . " etc To My
AUTUMN 1949 "The
DEPARTURE of The POET
PROPHET PHOENIX
DEITY . . . I HEAR The
MIGHTY DRUM BEATS and
The GONG ACROSS A CROSS
The CHALICE FOREST and The

AWFUL WAIL AMIDST The
THRONG and LIGHTNING
THUNDER HAIL The PASSING
of The VOICE of GOD O The
SOURCE of ALL ASPIRING
CREATIONS . . . " etc O In
TRUTH and LOVE etc I AM
Vincenzo LXX Giallonardo
M(M3-9) (P3-9) (C3-9) etc With
a Mailing Address At 309
North Simpson Street,
Philadelphia, Pennsylvania
USA 19139 Planet EARTHA
. . . From a Forest Vale By
Stream Reflecting
Projecting . . .
or On a Street Corner
Observing SPEAKING . . . In
The HOLY ORDER of
UNIVERSA O' The DEEP
ASPIRING CHALICEDLY In
The EVER STIRRING
BALANCES CHALLENGES of
ASPIRING CREATIONS EVER
TESTING and TRYING for
The GROWTH of ONE's EVER
Nobler Holier Highest Truer
Glorious Joyous SUBLIMEST
EXISTENCES and BEINGS for
EVER FOREVER . . .

Denise Bruskas-Gilbert
TRANSITIONS

*Especially for Sharon, Terry, and
Paul: "A friend is a person with
whom you dare to be yourself"*

Ah!
that Phoenix warmth
caressing those wild-flower hearts,
luring them to bloom . . .
evolving them from root to petal,
then
silhouettes against the sky blue,
distant moon,
and you-
awaiting to unfurl
as if to greet the blossoming
dawn . . .
You-
have never ceased to behold
the beauty in its awakening . . .
Parched upon that
fragrant wild-flower,
you are beauty unearthed
and much more.
So much more.

Gladys Howe McClure
VIETNAM

When he came home a flag was
given
To two worn hands.
And speeches were made there
In the stands,
While tears slipped down the
stricken face
Of one who gave to that strange
place
The riches of too few, the
years.
The town was there to welcome
him.
A multitude, but no band or din
was heard.
They mutely looked at one
another
And offered prayers for a G.I.
mother.

Mary Harelkin
UNTITLED

You
Came
Into my
Life bringing
Sunshine and laughter,
Tears and silent thought,
As together, we explore the
Earth and the universe in which
We revolve around each other
touching and
Questioning   our existence.

Vernetta L. Brown
I WAS MADE WOMAN

*To Vernell for all that you are,
and all that you have given me*

I was made woman
by your touch

I was made aware
by your desire

I was devoured
by your passion

I was made to
understand by your
Love . . . .

Our World's Best Loved Poems

Doris James Dixon
My Christmas Memories
As Christmas songs begin to play
I wonder back to another day
There was much excitment;
Even Snow
Could it have been so long ago
The presents were meager but
We were so eager
To untie the bow
Where did it go
The things were simple and sweet
Yet so complete
We could play for hours
With one little thing
And still have time
To laugh and sing
I wouldn't trade one little thing
For all those times or
The joy they bring
Star Wars and remote controll
They need batteries to make
  them go
Our energy was in our heart
We didn't need a button to make
  it start . . . .

Dalton Langley
THE FOG
The fog deftly
blankets the valley.
It watches silently,
over the woods and stream.
The wildlife moves cautiously,
until it slowly vanishes.

Lew Drake
The Peace Of Christmas
Search not for peace,
In some elusive place;
But in places of the heart,
Where you meet it face to face.

I am just a traveler, on
Christmas in this mountain land;
No Church doors are there to enter,
No manger where I may stand.

I see pinnacles of jagged rock,
Like cathedrals reaching up to God;
In the beauty of snowy fields,
Where man has never trod.

Messages on wings of wind,
From shepherds in the fields below;
Tell of the birth of the Christ
  Child,
In Bethlehem so long ago.

Before me are the creations,
Of His Father's Holy hands;
I find the peace Christ gave us,
That blesses every land.

Lisa Chapa
A TREASURE

*I dedicate this poem to everyones
heart with a sincere desire to
share our Lords love.*

There is a treasure I want to share.
It's full of joy, love and care.
Yes, all the love you'll ever need,
the only way you can be freed.
Escape a life of sin and hate,
Do it now, don't you wait!
Take this treasure offered to you
"JESUS CHRIST" he'll see you
  through.
Accept the Son into your heart
He'll give your life a brand new
  start.

Cathy G. Thomas
LETTER TO HEAVEN

*IN LOVING MEMORY OF MY
MOTHER Velma L. Fuqua She
was an inspiration to all of us.*

My Dear Mother,

You mean so much to me,
everybody loves you,
as you always tried to please.

Never a complaint of selfishness
  or greed;
Just went about your work,
doing deeds for others.
There is no other, like you Mother.

How you've suffered with pain I
  can't explain.
You deserve better,
thats why I'm writing this letter.

God, take her home to heavens
  dome.
She's tired and weary, her prayers
  are blurry.

She's passed the test, please let
  her rest.

Eternal Peace and sleep will come
  soon. I'll miss you Mother.

P. S. I love you too!
If you can hear me,
I know this letter got to Heaven.

Sandra Alterine Johnson

Sandra Alterine Johnson
The Whole World Stops
When I See You

*To Tom, a man who has made
me very happy.*

Whenever I see you the whole
  world stops.
It is just like a person who is in a
  state of shock.
I can't speak, I can't move, the
  only thing I can do is look at
  you.

I admire your great big beautiful
  eyes, your handsome face, your
  miraculous smile, your friendly
  wave, your soft hello and all
  the things that lets me know
  that I love you.

What makes this feeling come
  over me—it's only by sight of
  you that I see that these strong
  emotions exist.

I have been in the presence of
  other men, I have even had
  some to ask for my hand, but
  never have I had one to make
  me feel so intensely happy and
  good.

Tell me Darling, what is this?
The whole world stops when I
  see you, nothing seems to
  move.
Only my heart pounding, oh so
  loud! trying to tell you that I
  care,
Only my eyes gazing deeply in
  yours, reflecting what is there.
If making the whole world stop
  when I see you, then I would
  say we have a thing that is
  real—for nobody and please
  hear me out—nobody has
  never made me feel this way
  and nobody probably never will
  again.

So everything will just have to
  pass me by, for my love, you
  give my heart a thrill!

Tywanna Bennett
DECEMBER'S ROSE

*To Jim who shares the innocense
of our first love, the strength of
him in our son Jimmy, a daughter
of Heaven in Heather and the
delight of grandpa in Charlie.*

There is always a silence when
  the name is spoken.
  For all knows he is the only
  hope for the broken.

Perfection is his hope for one and
  all.
  Attentive to our needs with
  only a call.

He even comes when we cry
  mamma, daddy, brother, sister
  and even I.
  Loves to be them all and sees
  us when we cry.

Some call him Father, Lord,
  Blessed, King and mine.
  But I call him Jesus with a tear
  in my eye.

Colin Clift
When On The Verge Of
Cynicism, I Think Of
Them

*We'll always need Bogie and
Betty to remind us that love can
transcend age and prejudice. Let
them live forever the way they
were in "To Have and Have Not":
She gives him "The Look" and he
responds with that incredibly
sweet and vulnerable smile.*

Bogie and Bacall
Make me believe
In love after all.

Lawna Staker
GOOD—BYE
Oh . . . Sweet mystic smell of
  pines, as you rustle in the wind.
Oh . . . cool whispering calm of

brooks heavy in shade, under
  pines that spiral up as far as
  the eye can see.
Oh . . . ridges of mountains that
  glory with foliage bright with
  color of every hue.
Oh . . . papered leaves which
  blanket the scuffings of needles
  left from the years before.
Gathering together your souls,
  the soul of old with the new,
  will bring forth greater riches
  for generations.
As for me; I shall always be with
  you.
I shall always;
remember.

**Margaret Elizabeth Johnston
Teal II**
REVERIE
Bright golden sun
Surrounded by a
Misty mellow hue
Of purple . . . .
Shining through
The snow shower.
Never has there
Come to view
Anything
So splendid . . .
As I sit here and
Imbue . . . . .
The glory of this
Moment, and know
It has a message
From above . . . .
Meant for me . . .
And all who love.

Frank Linwood Fowler III
AN ORPHAN
Lonely child sits at the
  window,
staring constantly out the
  window,
asking questions to God,
why mostly!

Oh child at the sea's edge
laying elusively down in the
  foam of the surf,
where did they go,
when is their return?

Gifted child of no ambition,
confusing reality with a
  daydream,
look to my eyes, while
  crying,
now has come!

Russell Edward Kilpatrick
I REMEMBER
I remember the Christmas—
"Provided by You"
I remember the nursing and
loving during hard times—
"Provided by You"

I remember the advice that
was always right but seldom
and foolishly on my part—
unheeded . . .
"Provided by You"

I remember the encouragement
and the hugs and the extras I
didn't deserve-
"Provided by You"

I remember the little
pick-me-ups
you give me even now-
"All Provided by You"

I wrote this to tell you how much
I love you, because my love
and respect and appreciation is
yours-
"Provided by Me"
Tony Hale
WHO AM I?
When—the wind blows strong
Sending—leaves dancing
Sun—shining.
Like a clearing of the mind.
Thought waves tossed about
Here,
There.
Subjected to—scrutiny, mutiny.
The wind-
Echoes of the past self,
The present man,
The future person.
Whispering—
Am I who I was?
Was I who I am?
Yesterday.
The wind—change rearrange,
estrange
From the past.
Am I who I shall be,
Tomorrow?
When—the wind blows strong.

Chet Wade Warden
A WISH
A pain in my heart,
A tear in my eye.

The emptiness of the summer sky.

A trembling hand,
A cry in the night.

How I wish you were here to
make it all right.

Verlie J. (Tomasik) Ahnlund
EMPTY SPACES

To: *My Family May The Blessings
Be Love You/Mom/Granma—Nita*

Empty Spaces
Wild geese, like small boomerangs
Surging into smooth formation,
Flowing angles cleave leaden skys,
Flooding earth with faint
haunting crys,
Feeling forlorn, we think of
faraway places,
Till happy excited voices,
returning
Fill bleak empty spaces.

Penney L. Cardona
LIFE
Life, though endless as it seems,
Is filled with many hopes and
dreams.
An aspiration we all share,
Is often revealed a dare.
We strive, very often residual,
To be a definite individual,
It requires a talent very long to
acquire,
However, it is one much desired.
No one person can face life alone,
To the trials and tribulation we
are prone.
But be aware as senseless as it
seems,
Without life there would be no
dreams.
A world without dreams would
mean no tomorrow,
An existance such as this could

bring only sorrow.
So start every day fresh and anew,
For the secret to life is none
other than YOU.

Tina M. Capozzi
A BEST FRIEND
Growing up is a time of closeness
and togetherness the kind
we've shared with eachother.
The more we've lived together,
the more fun we've shared, the
more tears we shed, the more
laughter we've had, the petty
fights, or the times we've
shared in rain, snow, or shine.
You've always been there for me
my friend, I too shall always be
there for you, I'll always love
you my *BEST FRIEND*, We'll
always cry, laugh, and share the
treasures of life and love . . .
TOGETHER.

Matt Carpenter
WHERE MOTHER SEW
The hills and dales are piled with
snow,
And smoke obscures the towns
below.
I think I like the winter air—
The homes are warm where
mothers sew,
And kids now play where corn
did grow.
A freezing wind is bringing chills,
The girls will skate the lake at
noon;
The boys will sled down snowy
hills.
I think I like the winter air—
At nighttime each one's face will
glow.
A time will come and very soon,
When only children's hearts will
know
The homes are warm where
mothers sew.

Kathleen Diering
NUN

To my children: Michael, Kim &
Donna who inspired my wisdom
to write poetry. And to my friend,
Sister Frances who's inspiration
was a gift.

A nun is a very special person
Who was chosen from above
God sent her to teach his children
All his wisdom and love

Sometimes it isn't easy
And she may think she has failed
But that's when she remembers
His flesh was ripped by nails

The hurt she feels inside her
He will push away.
Then the sun comes shinning
through
To guide her a brighter way

So if your ever troubled
and feel there is no hope
Just look up to the heavens . . .
He'll guide your way to cope . . . .

Onda Horning
PROMISES
As the morning sun
Bringing its promise
Of a bright new day

So one droplet of water
On the velvety petal
Of a perfect red rose
Is nature's kiss
Promising beauty
In its glorious perfection.
Undisturbed it glistens
To attract the eye
Holding the attention
Of the beholder
Unwittingly trapped
In nature's panorama.

Luke Nathaniel Baxter

Luke Nathaniel Baxter
The World Needs Most
What the world needs most
Is confidence and faith
A feeling that all is right
Therein the good predominates
With love we underwrite

What the world needs most
Is an honest belief
The most unswerving kind
That might itself makes not a
right
And trust is not so blind

What the world needs most
Is a greater concern
A love for one another
In this we find a unity of mind
The world becomes our brother

Deborah L. Monday
Mothers Are Like Flowers
Mothers are like flowers, they
may wilt but never die.
Like the fragrance of the roses,
that lifts our spirits high.

Mothers are like daffadils &
marigolds & phloxes.
Their beauty beams like golden
days, we spent on summer
docks.

Mothers are like violets, so
stately yet so shy.
Who burst with pride in all we
do, but never wonder why.

Mothers are like bleeding hearts,
that weep for joy & sorrow.
They care about the way we
grow, & pray for our happiness
tomorrow.

Mothers are precious, like the
mum, on which you can rely.
They appear at Summer's end,
& stand by until Autumn's reply.

Mothers are like lilies, that
appear so soft & white.
They help us through the best

days, & the worst of lonely
nights.

Mothers are the centerpiece, of
our Heavenly Father's creation.
Mothers make up the gardens,
of America our Nation.

Where would we be without
Mothers, who bloom & smell
so sweet?
Their love is a secure blanket,
who's warmth cannot be beat.

So on your day, Dear Mother, I
come to you so proud.
To shout my love & thanks to
you, so very, very loud.

And bring this Sterling flower,
that shines so bright & new.
Because it means the world to
me, since it's perfect just like
You!

Lana R. Cooper
MY FRIEND
My friend knows
all my secret fears,
She holds my hand
and wipes my tears.
She picks me up
when I'm let down,
And puts me back
on solid ground.
She mends my heart
when it's been torn,
She's been there for me
since the day I was born.
My friend is the best
there is no other,
For you see,
my friend is my mother.

Charla Redus Hill
MASTER ARTIST
I saw the wrath of a storm one
day,
Which had its beginning far
away,
It came with fury and arrogant
pride,
To sweep all things in its path
aside.
It came with lightning and
thunder and rain,
And bouncing hail on my
windowpane.
Then came a lull as the storm
passed by,
Leaving a rainbow in the sky,
And grateful I was for this
spectacle grand,
Painted for me by the Master's
hand.

David A. Drefahl Jr.
LETS BE FRIENDS
I look at you through tear filled
eyes
wondering why you wear a
disguise.
You act like a queen on a
diamond throne
when deep inside you feel alone.
You play all games with people
you love
and act as innocent as a snowy
white dove.
I feel so sad watching you smile
because I know the feelings
you've hidden awhile.
All the sad feelings are locked up
inside

Our World's Best Loved Poems

When you are all alone I know
  you cried.
You can't understand how much I
  care
because people precious are so rare.
All your feelings please don't
  defend
because I want you to be my
  friend.

Diana Brandt Goodwin
ALBAMA
Alabama, way down yonder
Call your children as they wander
Heart of Dixie, Alabama
Find your children, Southern
  Mama
Tell them that the lakes are here
Just as they were in yesteryear
Tell them that the rivers flow
That the southern breezes blow
Tell them of your grassy meadows
Cool and green your forest
  shadows
Show them your azalea trails
The whippoorwill at night still
  wails
Take them to your countryside
Where your animals abide
See the valleys and the hills
Where the farmlands still are tilled
They must remember the rocky
  walls
Of your cliffs and waterfalls
Oh, southern children one and all
Listen to your mother's call
Alabama still is here
She hails you home from far and
  near

Gerald H. Adams

Gerald H. Adams
FIRST LOVE

*This poem is dedicated to
Joycelyn, with whom I was
fortunate to experience the
exhilarating happiness of first love.*

'Twas a time of my life I am
  happy to remember,
The beginning of my teen years
  in British Guiana;
I fell in love with a girl who was
  born in September
In a house on Bent Street
  between Haley and Hardina.

It was the kind of love that is
  common to the youthful
Who are awkward, idealistic, and
  naively pure;

She was, for me, someone very
  special, to be truthful,
Who I would marry after
  graduation from high school.
I can still visualize her unpainted
  youthful beauty—
Ribboned hair, quiet manner, and
  simple dresses she wore;
To watch her from my window
  was a Friday night duty,
As it was hers to buy something
  from Old Harvey's Drug Store.

Our meetings were cherished
  moments unknown to her
  mother
Who kept a close watch o'er her
  beautiful little flower;
We had to evade both her sister
  and clever brother
To walk hand in hand in the
  Gardens for just one hour.

But it was worth all the scolding
  my mother would render,
Just to be with my love for such
  interludes of pleasure;
This was a time of my life that I
  like to remember,
And all its memories I will for a
  long time treasure.

And now that I am much older,
  and can more clearly see
What life is all about, and what
  love is, or ought to be,
I can say with honest candor and
  objectivity
That first love was a very happy
  beginning for me.

Necia Hire
SURVIVOR

*For Pat and Inez and Zelma, who
died so close together in 1982—
also for two couples killed earlier
in auto accidents.*

Good morning, pretty Prim Rose—
  so straight and lone, yet sprightly!
Your pink-white robe betrays no
  grief
  it dazzles O so brightly!

In ones, in twos, in threes—your
  kin
  and peers all drooped and faded.
This is the trying hour your soft
  aroma has pervaded.

In grass and brush and tree, a
  hundred
  shades of green surround you!

The humming bird and honey bee
  and butterfly have found you.

Sweet hale and only Desert Bloom
  that thrives above all sorrow—
Still be here for me in your glory
  when I come tomorrow!

Isabella Ge Tweedy
GOLDEN BIRD

for Gaia

Winter has returned too soon
and chilled this heart. No golden
  bird can wing through ice. Ah
  love, how tremulous the echo
  of a song too quickly stilled.

Winter has remained too long
  silenced now the singing bird,
  never to be heard. Pitous,
  withered, the roses false-spring
  killed.

V. Mony Snyder
REWARD OF HEAVEN
What a gratuity
if, somewhere in the archives of
  eternity,
a poem of mine were stored
—locked in undying memory:
a chain of thought
which, by some Providential Plot,
was meant to survive nonentity;
led by some miracle of direction,
and considered by some cosmic
  condescention,
meant to be saved
(despite it's inevitable
  imperfection).
To know it lives
would give breadth to my soul
—reward of Heaven!
Honor returned for honor given.

Debbie Kraft
REAL LOVE
Walking in the sand
Hand in hand
Makes our love so special.

Watching the moon come up
Sitting on the beach
Side by side,
Together.

A love so real
So hard to find,
Is something we are able to share
People search all their lives
And never find someone to care.

This is what love is all about
The words that you never have to
  say;
Knowing how much each other
  cares
Without having to say it every
  day.

This kind of love is something
  special
We make the perfect team
The only thing that could make
  it better
. . . . Is if it wasn't a dream . . .

Wanda Barkyoumb Donithan
Our Love Shall Never Die
Here's all my love I give to thee,
Though words and tears, my love
  is free.
To return your Love is all I ask,
Surely it is but a simple task.

We've lived so long in our short

years,
We've shared together dreams,
  doubts, and fears.
The four lovely seasons may
  come and go,
But through the years, our love
  will grow.

When old age shrouds us, there is
  no doubt,
We shall have learned what love
  is about,
We'll see our children, strong and
  tall,
Sharing their love, and caring for
  all.

When we sit in our rockers side
  by side,
Grandchildren on our laps for the
  ride,
Our hands will reach out, eyes
  shining with pride,
For we know that our love has
  somehow survived.

So when we breathe our last on
  earth,
Rejoice that our love's passed on
  in birth.
That when we meet in the
  mansion up high,
We'll know that our love shall
  never die.

Frances Kelley
GIVE THANKS
Give thanks for the sunshine, the
  flowers, the rain
For walking and talking, to
  breathe without pain
For times when you felt the time
  was quite near
To make the day without any fear.
Thank you Lord for helping me
  stay
The many times I did look away.
Thank you for the times you said,
"Go back my dear,
I've work for you ahead.

Kris Phillips
Conversing With My Mind
My computer asked of me,
"Should not I, be running things?
Hearts know not, how to succeed
Reasoning rules everything"

"This is true," I then replied
Obligation to my pride
Permits my soul to step aside.
"Cold computer, I abide."

Walter Bardeck
IN TUNE WITH NATURE
I heard
a rustle of leaves
on a night-scented breeze . . .
And I caught
the full moon
in all its brilliance
riding in the sea
of stars.
Soon, the silence,
broken by a song,
melted into
the darkness.
I felt
the deepest bliss
as I almost touched
a falling star.
I knew then
that I was in tune
with Mother Nature

The old stick—weeds where
dead,
It danced and sparkled all around,
With jewels fair the dewdrops
crowned,
No diamond ever shone so fair,
As these Thy dewdrops
everywhere.

Jean P. Mazurkiewicz Mizejewski
THE PEACEFUL NIGHT

*Dedicated to My Children
Stephanie and Stephen In
Memory of My Beloved Father
John Paul Mazurkewicz
Especially To My Beloved Mother
Helen Mazurkiewicz*

How quiet and peaceful
Is the night,

The Moon above reflects
Its golden light,

The stars shine so
Everlastingly bright,

My soul searches the heavens
As if in flight,

To find the peace and solitude
Of the night.

Janis Atherton Kagiyama
ST. CHRISTOPHER'S MASS
The swollen streams of gore
Blend into a store of memories
That echo through the time traps
of the mind
And rusty hinges squeak . . .
As the door opens and closes on
eras.

Mistakes yet made, creations not
born
Swell with the whole mass
And crowd into a missle of beauty.
And from one letter of misery,
comes forth a new life
That responds in amorous
fashion to its other parts.

It says be still and know that I
am good
And time stands still for this
little soul
And it rightly takes its hold
And learns its place in the overall
scheme
And thus, on goes the dream.

The dreams multiply and swell to
untold millions
And the rainbow carries the
essence of them all.
It gathers up its own color stories
And cams them away
And shines forth brighter because
of it.

In the penny arcade of light, we
grace thee with our love
And remind you of what is yours
and ours;
We bridge the way to your
existence.
Follow the rainbow, my love.

Everett Francis Briggs
AWAY WITH FEAR
Weep not for me! I this repeat.
Death is not end of all.
Put out the fitful lamp, my Sweet;
Soon dawn will raise the pall.

Shall I who always loved the stars

Be fearful now of night?
Shall I, beyond soul's prison-bars
Set free, at last, take fright?

As once the poet said, we wake
From troubled dreams to find
Secure relief. May death not take
One from a fate unkind?

Yes, may it not be gentle death,
Death not with furtive hand.
That makes of one's last, labored
breath
The first in God's pure land?

Helen Vendeville
Helen Vendeville
ENTR'EE

*Especially Dedicated To Laurie &
Kirk Kelley For Your First-Born
Baby-Arrival Expected Soon. A
New Blossom On Our Branch Of
Family Tree Lovingly from Me.*

New Little One
    How New?
Perhaps, that you
Return—DeJaVue
A Life—that You
Can carry on
New Rising Dawn
To Enter Here
From Where ever
Where You Were

And I wish You too
The Best, in all
Your Life To Do.
Who knows
What Greatness
Follows Who?
Welcome, with Our Love
Little One——So much
Of Living—
    Awaiting You.

Barbara Jo Johnson
A NEW BEGINNING
A new day dawns,
The sun is shining,
The warm air is blowing,
The birds are singing.
A new life begins
For me and you,
New amendments,
New memories,
A starting over
A new beginning.
A new and special love.

Eleda W. Forbes
TO MY SOLDIER SON
I wanted to be brave that day—
    the day you had to go.
I tried to hide my feelings, son, so
    you would never know
The heartbreak and the anguish I
    endured as you walked by.
I tried . . . I lost the battle, son. I
    know you saw me cry.

The many days and nights were
    long—so with you away.
And if you could have listened,
    son, you would have heard me
    pray
For guidance and protective care,
    for health and courage, too.
But most of all I wanted just a
    safe return for you.

And now you're only miles away
    and I can hardly wait
Till I can see you walking
    through the airport's open gate.
In my book son, the war you've
    won, you've conquered land
    and sea.
The loudest "WELCOME HOME"
    you'll hear (I know) will come
    from me!

Mary Ellen Townsend
THE WINTER WOODS
It's silent here.
I scarcely dare
To breathe, less breath should mar
The holy cloak
Of solitude
That sets this place apart.
'Neath skies of grey
That penetrate
My being with the cold,
I ponder the
Simplicity
Of all that I behold.

Here tiny tracks
Of Chickadees
Do lightly scratch the snow
As they flit from
Brittle branches
Only Spring will help to grow.

It's silent here.
I listen to
The quiet hymn of pure
Enchantment with
The Winter Woods.
That makes my heart secure.

Heidi J. Nafzger
CANDLES
I have a little closet
That's filled up to the top
With so many different candles
I could have a candle shop.

When the wind is howling
When no one is around
I tip-toe to the closet

Without a single sound.

Then the door is opened
My eyes get big and wide
A smile grows across my face
When I see what's inside.

There's red and yellow, green and
    blue
All different shapes and sizes
Every box I open up
I find still more surprizes.

So when the wind is howling
Or when I'm in dismay
I go and see those candles
And then I'm light and gay.

Helen Morehead Coburn
GOD'S GREATEST GIFT
Traveling by faith, led by a star
Three wise men journeyed from
    afar,
Seeking the child Jesus to
    worship were told,
Brought gifts of myrrh,
    frankincense, and gold.

Shepherds watching their flocks
    by night
Heard from the angels with joyful
    delight,
The good tidings, a saviour is born,
Went to worship him that first
    Christmas morn.

Thank God for so great a gift to all
Shepherds, wise men, the great
    and the small.
He's everyone's to worship and
    praise
Thank God for his gift, Oh
    Wonderous Day!

This unspeakable gift sent from
    heaven above
Brought to the world salvation
    and love,
To show us our sins we could not
    see
Gave himself as a ransom to set
    man free.

Bette Watts
ANGELS

*For my late mother, Elizabeth
Wachs and her wonderful
daughter-in-law Sachiko.*

I'd rather wear out than rust
Said she toiling
From dawn to dusk
Never a task a task too tough
Never a job left undone
Always a smile for everyone
Little Sunshine they called her
As she helped those in need
And did her good deed
One day her day came
She saw angels first
Then two oriental ladies in
    Komono
One thank you she got
Before she was laid to rest and rot
One of the best, Mother.

Elizabeth Pucciarelli
There's Wonder In His Eyes
His hands are gnarled from long
    years of work
But his spirit is that of youth
    unbridled
He has been pummeled by life
    these seventy years

But he raises himself up: steadies himself
And he's off in search of adventure

He takes my hand: He holds it tight
And he shares with me the thrill of life
The sunset, the sea, the city streets
And my eyes are filled with wonder

The dark recesses in city street
The hidden garden, the cozy pubs

Wooded trails, well worn paths
And he takes each minute as if it were the first
An his eyes are filled with wonder.

Margaret S. Tapley
How Autumn Came To Be!!!
God, looked down at the world to see,
That green was the only color in the trees.
So to brighten up the world once a year,
He took red, yellow, orange, brown, gold, and made the leaves pretty clear.

God, then sat back and took a look,
He said it's pretty enough to be put into a story book.
He was proud of what He had done,
That's why autumn is number one.

Now everytime you look at the trees you'll know,
God, made them just for show.
Thanks to God you see,
That's how autumn came to be!!!

Mary B. Lawrence
RETIREMENT
Give me a garden, Lord, therein,
To spend my leisure hours
And tend the planted seeds bearing
Brightly hued, sweet scented flowers.
Failing this, Dear Lord, I pray,
Solitude I shall nor fear,
If but near where children play,
Their joyous laughter hear.

Susan A. Hunt
STREET PEOPLE
I see them where they sleep.
Hear their constant mutter.
Cuddled up real tight
on a steam vent or in a gutter.

All of their belongings
crammed into shopping bags.
Wearing layers upon layers
of someone's else discarded rags.

In the city they live well hidden
in the corners of run down dives.
Somehow I always wonder
how they ever stay alive.

I dare an air of self-importance
as I walk on down the street.
See them in the trash cans
picking out something to eat.

Last winter in the city snow fell
twenty inches on the ground.

One of Mom's main concerns
were if the Street People were
safe and sound.

They're always choking and
they're coughing,
picking butts up off the street
and me only major fear
is that our eyes will never meet.

Ava Malaier Hill
My Grandfather's Mill
At the foot of a long, red hill
Stood my Grandfather's old grist mill.
It was built so I've been told
Long before Sherman "invaded the fold"

The old mill was three stories overall,
And the water wheel about forty feet tall.
The three inch door was sturdy and strong,
With a large brass key, nine inches long.

Just inside the door a corn sheller did stand,
Did you ever shell a bushel of corn by hand?
And some of the cobs of just the right type
Was used by Grandpa to make his cob pipe's.

My Grandfather's mill had two grinding stones
One to grind wheat and one to grind corn.
To see if his mill was making good meal
He would take up a handful and tell by the feel.

Away on the hill, all weathered and worn,
Stood the house where I was born,
But now only in my memory do they live on,
The house and the mill that ground the wheat and the corn.

Linda L. Parker
CHALLENGE MET

With love to my husband Andy and children, Andrea, Jessica, Meredith and Matthew—May God grant to each of you life's "Challenge Met" with strength, dignity and love.

Earth, with challenge met,
Collects momentos from its past—
Leaves, worn out and laid aside,
Fields, which forfeited their bounty
Lay diminished, languid repositorys.
Abandoned nests, dishelved from use,
Still tucked securely
Within branches of barren trees.

Earth, the chill of Winter on its breath,
Rests upon its bed of souvenirs,
And dreams the dreams of ages past—
The challenge yet to come.

Anita Van Ryswyk
JUST THREE

To Dawn, my sunshine.

One is just cute, and two can be terrible,
But three is the year, when all is quite bearible.
Three is a wonder of things all around,
From the clouds in the sky to the worm on the ground.
But Christmas is magic, for the great age of three,
from baby Jesus, to the star on the tree.
Three's eyes always glow, and shine with surprise,
Three's laughter and giggle, comes from deep inside.
If I could keep one year to hold with me.
It would be that wonderful world of

Just Three!

Carol E. Wolf
GRANDMA'S ROSES
The velvet petals call
echoing her sound,
captivating perfume lingers,
the puckered
bud emits her kiss,
a full-grown blossom
smiles.

D. Turner Weister
THE MORNING AFTER
Some morning
you'll wake up and realize
that I'm not there any more
and when you think about it
you'll remember hearing me go
and that you turned and slept on.

Some morning
I'll wake up and realize
that you were never really here
and when I think about it
I'll remember the years of being alone
and know that I should have turned
and walked away long ago.

Some morning
you'll wake up and realize
that you've been sleeping too long.

Mrs. Mary Thayer Blanchard
THANKSGIVING
Dear God, I render thanks to Thee
For friends whom Thou has given me
Whose virtures and whose talents raise
My mind and heart to Thee in praise!

Judith Link
YOUTH BEWARE
Wide eyes
Shy smile
16 today
Child no longer
Oh sweet innocence
of youth

Phone calls
School halls
Sweetheart balls

Homework falls
Oh sweet innocence
of youth

Girl talks
Long walks
Soda shops
Grade drops
Oh sweet innocence
of youth

Boy friends
Notes send
Hand touching
Teachers again
Oh sweet innocence
of youth

Ball games
Cheering cheers
Chug-a-lug beers
Adults sneer
Oh sweet innocence
of youth

Feelings hidden
Love's forbidden
Back seat kissing
Parents hissing
Oh sweet innocence
of youth

Closed doors
Just explore
Drinking more
Flunking more
Oh sweet innocence
of youth

Wispered words
Arousing desires
Flying high
Parents sigh
Oh sweet innocence
of youth

New Years Eve
Boy pleeds
Virgin bleeds
Sowed seeds
Oh sweet innocence
of youth no more

YOUTH BEWARE
Shirley A. Settle
MY MASTER
My soul doth thirst for the purest bitter-sweet emotion;
The requited eminety with which a tried and resolute fluke must mimic.
What, a tryst? As I might, so a soldier of reticence am I;
The hand of fate salutes me, surely I am mortal—

Wane, and patiently await the Prince of Power to cast a lasting blow to my deft ear,
And still, though unopposed, I sit and tremble at the wheel;
The Captain standing at the helm cannot the Master be, yet He is Master of His own!

Kimberly Ann Addis
THE PERFECT GIFT
Thanksgiving has come and gone,
Christmas too.
But I will always treasure,
these holidays spent with you.
How your bright smile
could make up for the lack of gifts.
How one beautifully wrapped box
could make my spirits lift.
For this box did not contain

diamonds,
or rubies, or pearls, or gold.
It was light as air, but I did not
care.
It contained all the love your
heart could hold!

Marie Sollars

Marie Sollars
ANNA'S POEM

_In loving memory of my
Grandmother, Anna K. Wyss_

How many bones in the human
head? Eight as I have often said.
How many bones in the human
face? Fourteen, when all in
place.
How many bones in the human
spine? Twenty-six, like a
climbing vine.
How many bones in the human
chest? Twenty-four ribs, two of
the rest.
How many bones does the
shoulder bind? Two each, one
before and one behind.
How many bones in the human
arm? One each above, two each
in forearm.
How many bones in the human
wrist? Eight each, if none missed.
How many bones in the palm of
the hand? Five each bound with
bands.
How many bones in our fingers
ten? Twenty-eight and by joints
they bend.
How many bones in the human
hip? One each, like a dish they
dip.
How many bones in the human
thigh? One each and deep they
lie.
How many bones in the human
knee? One each in the knee cap
please.
How many bones from the knee
to the foot? Two in each
How many bones in the ankles
strong? Seven in each but none
long.
How many bones in the ball of
the foot? Five in each as the
palms are put.
How many bones in our ten toes?
Twenty-eight, as everyone
knows.

Robert H. Jones
CAT NAP
Cat's hat hanging on a rack.
  Rat's cat climbing on his back.
Cat's rat running down the rack.
  Rat's cat sliding down his back.
Cat's rat running back.
  Rat's cat take his nap.
Cat's rat makes it back.
  Rat's cat smile comes back.
Cat's rat mate, lost his nap.

Clara C. Creasy
ANGEL
A little angel was abanonded
today—
Someone left her in the street to
lay,
Wrapped in a dirty old blanket of
blue gray.
As I picked up this bundle and
wiped away her tears—
I prayed to GOD, to help me to
banish her fears,
GOD had loaned her to us for
just a little while—
So we could love her and enjoy
her beautiful smile.
But time seemed to pass so very
fast—
We prayed, that out life with this
little one would forever last,
But nothing is forever, that we
now know—
As we watched our loaned angel,
run out, to play in the snow.
A speeding car ran our darling
down—
OH GOD! I will never forget that
sound,
A drunken driver had lost
control—and—
Into our yard the car did roll.
Pinning our loaned angel against
a tree—
Now no more her lovely face we
can see.
But GOD saw fit to let me find
this child—
To brighten our lives for a short
while-So—
We laid our little loaned angel to
rest, and,
I pray to GOD we have passed
the test.

Gina Marie Russo
The Irony Of Consistency

_This poem is dedicated to my
two loves from the East: Platonic
Idealism and Zen Buddhism. May
the transcendant symmetry of
the first and the spontaneous,
inductive imagery of the second
ever happily intertwine._

The irony of consistency is
that when bottled up too tightly
the Spontaneity of life's
Combustion
will generally crack its cork.

Rosemary A. Gilbert
Thursday Lunchtime In Putney, London
There they are!
the brewery horses—
outside the High Street pub;
a dapple and a chestnut.
Manes rushed and tied in scarlet.

Brasses shining, even in the rain.
Wearing their capes with
patient commonsense,
and whuffling in their nosebags.

Libby Lady
THOUGHTS OF YOU
Wishing you a sunny sky
Because I love you and here is
why,
You are totally different from
others I've known
But my thoughts of you must
never be shown

Frances C. Kopp
LOVE

_This poem is dedicated to my
Mother and Daddy, Anna and
Earl Case, who taught me what
love is . . . To my husband,
Clayton, and children, Richard,
Sonja, Larry, Merle, Thomas, Susan._

Love is understanding
Love is feeling blue
When I see someone
Hurting you.

Love is pulling together
Not pulling apart
Love comes from the inner being
From deep within the heart

Love gives new birth
To everything you see
So why can't man
Love humanity.

Cynthia J. Jacobson
DREAMING
Rainy nights remind me of
you . . .

                        of us.

Sitting alone,
Listening to the nightsounds
                 makes me wonder
              what could have been
If she hadn't found you first.

Cleta M. Williams
"Happiness Through the New Year"—1984
Happiness is something created
in your mind,
It's not something you search for,
but cannot find;
Neither can you purchase it with
silver or gold,
Be careful or it might be hard to
hold;
Happiness is waking each day
with your own personal smile
Counting your blessings, letting
them linger for a very long
while;
Don't think bad thoughts that
might bring discontent,
Accept things as they are-they
are heaven sent;
Give up wishing for things you
have not,
Make the best of what you've got;
Our lives are patterned and
planned,
God holds each of us in the palm
of his hand;
If we, but, complete what he gives
us to do,
We will always have a chance of
true happiness and
contentment too.

Evelyn M. Heinz
Oh How Quiet Is the Morning
Oh how quiet is the morning,
When all else are asleep.
Oh how quiet is the morning,
When I listen very, very deep.
Oh how quiet is the morning,
When my God does fervently
speak.
Oh how quiet is the morning,
When by myself, I grow meek.
Oh how quiet is the morning,
When I want Him for my very
own.
Oh how quiet is the morning,
When I kneel and soulfully
atone.
Oh how quiet is the morning,
When I solemnly pledge to love
Him.
Oh how quiet is the morning,
When faith's cup, fills to the
brim.

Carol Choptuik
IMAGES
Images of i—
  reflected in a misty mirror,
  hazy features, clouded over,
  distorted by waves of emotion.
  Always moving, rearranging still
    until . . .
  At last the ripples fade, and
    then—
Images of I.

Doris Paluch
MY ROSE GARDEN
Our love has weathered many a
  storm—
Heated and tempered by passions
  warm;
And in our yard, for all to see—
Proudly, blooms the rose garden,
(that you never promised me)!

Shirley Jeanette Tucker
NOT ALONE

In Loving memory to Richie James

We thank Thee Lord,
For winds that whisper sweet,
For flower strewn pathways,
Beneath our feet.
For every pretty tree,
That we behold.
That seems as if you've,
Touched them all, with gold.
For mighty rushing rivers,
Going to and fro.
We see your wondrous beauty,
Lord, every where we go.
Be still my heart, and grasp,
God's moments rare.
It's nice to know,
That He, is always there.
In birds that sing,
And winds that whisper His song,
God's voice is in all nature,
So we are not alone.

Kathleen Ann Beck
TEARS AND MEMORIES
The tears I cry are full of
memories
that will last forever in my heart.
I know you must go now but
someday
you will return again.
When that day arrives I hope you
will still be my friend.

Our World's Best Loved Poems

Larry Tutcher
The Whistle Of the Midnight Train
Through the cool crisp evening air
The whistle of the midnight train;
Haunting music from those who care
Through the cool crisp evening air.
A warning sound, so be aware
Of this mournful moonlight refrain;
Through the cool crisp evening air . . .
The whistle of the midnight train.

Susheel
. . . and they all end with e.
Live
    Give
       Love
    Receive
       Divine
           Peace.

T. C. Strawn, III
NATURE'S GIFT
Could you resist the freedom
of a crisp, clean breeze
wafting in so gently,
hinting of peace?
A wisp of passing air
so tantalizing and fresh
is a gift from the heavens,
a taste of nature's gift.

Jo Ryan
MY LOVE
I wait, and scan the sky
And know that without you I
    am incomplete
    and only half alive.
Then, in the distance see
The plane, bringing you to me.
I watch you disembark, and then,
    I am alive again.

Ronald Charles Wescott
SEASONED
I remember the scene, it was summer,
    it was green.

I remember the walk, it was springtime,
    it was pink.

I remember the talk, it was winter,
    it was white.

I remember the commitment, it was fall,
    it was rusty and the branches were tall.

Stacy Robertson
SUCCESS

Love Mom

Success is having faith
and confidence in yourself.
    Success is having the will—
power to do anything you desire.
    Success is being proud of yourself.
    Success is being on the top
    Success is not being a failure
    Success is believing in yourself
    But the most important
part to Success is having an Education.

Susan G. Kreider
doves
lined on
darkened window sills
bottles— Budweiser,
Coca-cola, red and
white, cheap wine
bottles— coo
as wind drags
over their lips

Nancy Jean Weslager
WE'LL MEET AGAIN
Somewhere, sometime—we'll
    meet again
We have parted but for a while,
Though separate roads we walk,
Somewhere, sometime—we'll
    meet again.

We laughed, we cried, we talked a lot,
Then we came to a fork in the road—
I went left, you had to turn right,
Somewhere, sometime—we'll
    meet again.

Through glad times and sad times
We were together—thick or thin.
God! it's lonely walking alone here,
But somewhere, sometime—we'll
    meet again.

Someday, I'll walk the right fork—
The one that starts where life's
    trail ends,
An as I'm walking along that
    right fork,
Somewhere, sometime—we'll
    meet again.

Bruce D. Hardy
ODE TO A POET'S HEART
What worlds await the poet's heart?
What frontiers yet to be travelled?
On grinding wheels of inspiration,
What dreams lay yet unravelled?

What springs of clear, sweet insight, trickle
forth, from some enchanted bower?
What words to mate, to germinate
The seeds of yet another flower?

When clouds are broken, by the breeze
When pen and soul are counterpart
'Tis in these moments, that I know
What worlds await the poet's heart

Bobie Louellen Ramey
WHAT IS LOVE?
Love is like sugar, for it is so sweet,
You can never imagine anything more.
Love is like sunshine, for it never
stops shining until the tears starts
             falling down.

Vivian H. Jones
DO YOU BELIEVE
Time fleets like the wind,
And thoughts trickle like the rain,
A clock lasts as long as its spring,
But life lasts as long as one
    endures pain.

Mary Sortino
THOUGHTS

*"To You Dad Over The Rainbow"
inspired by your Love for children
You Gave much To me.*

Especially on this snowy day,
I wish you laughter of children at play,

**

In a sunfilled daisy field.

Flossie B. Woods Miller

Flossie B. Woods Miller
THE NEW YEAR

*I, Flossie B. Woods Miller, would.
like to dedicate my poem to the
National Association of
University Women and my family.*

The New Year is here;
What will we do with it?
If we sort of think back on last year,
Our answers will be much more appropriate!
Did we do anything to help anyone, this past year, without asking that God's guidance be had?
If you did, your aid turned out very, very bad!
However, things will be fine for me and for you,
If we just trust and obey God as all good Christians should do! !
That's why I trust Him! !
I do trust in Jesus my Holy King
And I love to call upon His Holy Name.
I love Him so—it surely must show,
He must love me too for He has blessed me so!
And He'll do the same for each of you
If only in faith, love, and obedience
You just ask Him to! !
Then this New Year will be just fine!
For you and for me! !

Kara A. Jensen
LIGHT
The single moon reflected upon the water
Shining, brightly, from the heavens
Endlessly plunging into the deep sea

Michele Chirrick
A SPECIAL FEELING
All your life you wonder, who will be right,
To spend each day with you, night after night.

You go out on a date and wonder, is this the one,
But it always turns out that, you still haven't won.

You want to meet this, special person soon,
From there everything should go, right in tune.

And you tell yourself that, everything must click,
Because if it doesn't then it's still, the wrong pick.

Well I've heard my click and, I hope he's the one,
He's heard his too and, everything's just begun.

I want to live my life, with beautiful things,
And the man that I've met, makes my heart want to sing.

He has painted his love, all over my heart,
And I'd love to hold on to him, 'til death do us part.

Stacy Dean Crawford
SUMMER
in a tree watching the sparrows,
Fly so free.

Upon a morning rise.
A sparkling beauty in nature's eye.

Ruth Webber
HOPE
After the storms the sunshine
After the winters the springs
After the shower the rainbow
For such is the nature of things
After the night the daylight
Bidding all darkness cease
After life's cares and sorrows
The comfort and joy of peace.

Mary Agnes Lynch
Christmas Christ Child
"Dear Baby Jesus, bright, and gay,"
"Please send me your blessings,
    on this Christmas day,"
"Inspire my thoughts, with thy
    sweet Face,"
"And, implore my soul, with your
    Holy Grace,"

"Christmas "Christ Child", with
    eyes, bright, and clear,"
"Lead me through life, with a
    conscience sincere,"
"Make me unselfish, thoughtful,
    and true,"
"So, one day in Heaven, I'll be
    always with you,"
"Baby Jesus, God's gift, from above,"
"Happy "Christmas Birthday,"
    with all my love."

Florence Tucker
PEACE?
The war is oer, we're told to cease
From firing guns, there is a peace.
But in my heart there is only pain,
My son did not come home again.
He fell and died on foreign sod,
I do not understand. Does God?

John Campbell, Editor & Publisher

Chester P. Boris
FRIDAY
T'was the thirteenth of June
I started my walk
Through pines old and dank.

Without second thought
To faint reports
From a backward countyside.

Of things that happen
In old dank pines
When dusk slips over the sky.

Was that a cry
Or mere reply
To questions yet unasked.

Perhaps just a voice
A mere reproach
For some dark and devious deed.

With candle bright
I'll scour the night
To find my troubled soul.

And if I'm right
I'm sure I am
I'll find mere time I've lost.

But if I'm wrong
Pray for me
By the pines old and dank.

Madge Mullins Wilbanks
THE GIFT
Give me only an ounce,
    measured and blended
    of Love
Before you leave

"To search the world over"
    you said for something
    already yours forever—

My Love.

Stanley Cassaday
FLASH BACK

To All Vietnam MIA And Ray
Smith And Tom Soto Special
Friends And Vets.

To the guys by their side I fought
I write these words
to tell you the love we shared
    was not lost.
The battle for your life
We did not win.
But the fight for your souls will
    never end
I will write to keep
Your spirit alive.
And tell the people how
You died.
At first I thought I would
Tell them why.
But even I do not know
that lie.
I can tell them though
You fought with courage and pride
To all Vietnam Vets who
did survive.
I question?
If a heart beat separates those
Who lived and those who died.

Shelley Ann Robbins
LIFE IN 82
The Rubik's cube, Pac man
    machine,
Beer and pizza, and video games
Mountain Dew, movie stars,
    fashion trends,
And rock bands are all a part of
    life in 1982.

Walter Wilson
LOVE ME NOW
Love me now, or let me go
Tell me now, so I will know
Now you're so dear to me
Please don't set me free
My life is your's can't you see
What you really mean to me
I'll always love you dearly

Claudia Mason
THE GRAND FINALE
    The turkey struts, and lords it
        over
All the barnyard fowls.
    Then the farmer's axe strikes
Just one strong blow.
    The turkey graces that
        Thanksgiving table
With just as great a show!

Dennis R. Smith
TIME
Time to change, Time to
    rearrange, Time to love
    I love all Times with you
This Time, to talk, to explain
    Love Time, Bump Time, Funk
        Time
Our Time
Together

Christian G. Showers Jr.
SNOWFLAKE
Tender . . . White . . . Crystaline,
    and Angel—Bright
Born of Breeze and Water.
    Light . . .
Journey Out and Travel Far
Behold All Else and Glory Way
Ride Your Mount Forever Soar
Gently, Lastly, Tenderly Lay

Inez Marsili
MORNING'S SKY
Delicious, sparkly, clean,
A star was thumbed into
    morning's sky.
Fresh, cool, a little, keen.
A tiny wind blew past my eye.
Hopeful, anxious, wondering,
I faced the lightening day.
Unknowing trusting, trying,
I do His bidding come what may.

Warren S. Satterlee II
CYPRESS
Tall, alone, strangled in spanish
    moss,
Whithered, tired, shaken by
    times' tremulous toils,
The cypress stands and waits . . .
    for its last sunset.

Raymond W. McCumiskey (Sr.)
VOICE
In the midst of this commotion
    A wailing voice was heard
And every eye turned
    Toward the graveyard elm
Whence it emanted

Lori McHone
JUST A QUICKIE
I am here to tell you a rhyme,
But I don't have much time,
Just let me think,
I am running out of ink,
The last word I will say,
Is, "Have A Good Day".

Ralph Ward
ODE TO BOB HOPE
Blessings on you Robert Hope
You're not one to sit and mope
When duty called at Christmas

time
You were on the firing line.

You and Bing were such a fixture.
You should make another picture.
There's one, that's well within
    your scope,
An "On The Road" story with the
    Pope.

That one would stand them in
    the aisles.
The money would arrive in piles.
With both of you such drawing
    cards.
But not such easy going Pard's.

Some would think it beyond the
    Pail,
And want to throw us into Jail.
It was surely worth a try.
But we better kiss the thought
    goodbye.

Alvaro Menendez Franco
THE PRINCESS
The princess with eyes of jade
Has the unhappiness of
    loneliness.
She sees from her Pagoda to fly in
    winter
And lack of sleep from no arrival
    of the crane.
She sees in Summer at blue
    nightingales
Get lost in the distance, playful.
My princess with honey eyes
Is happier than the one with eyes
    of jade,
And from the window of mi hut,
She looks at the multicolor
    planes
To get lost among the clouds like
    waves
As if they were fishes or
    butterflies or seagulls.
The princess with jade eyes
Does not know about the dreams
    of my other princess:
At least the exotic one eats three
    times a day
But mi princess, sometimes she
    eats
And sometimes she does not! .

Bill Bartley
GRAFFITI INSPIRATION
Marked in ink, Across the wall
"In order to walk, one must learn
    to fall."

But once the step, is mine to keep
Never will fall, but maintain the
    leap.

Carol Noffsinger
FOG
Did you see the beauty of the fog
    this morning?

        Some did.
        Some didn't.
    Some became part of it.

Cynthia K. Hill
SIMPLE THINGS ARE FREE
Such simple things of life are free,
It's nice to breathe pure ecstasy:
    A green leaf holding a water
        droplet,
    A pine-scented forest awaiting
        for thee.

A snow-covered mountain from
    head to toe,
The blizzard whirling all that
    snow!

It's thrilling to observe beauty
    reserved
To wonder how icicles form and
    grow.

A rippling brook so mirror clear,
A meadowlark I love to hear
    The yellow daffodils standing in
        line—
    Their sweetness filling spring
        each year.

The diamonds scattered
    throughout the sky—
Such brilliant splendor shall
    never die.
    For God displays his precious
        gems.
    And nighttime still comes by
        and by.

Oh, the beauties of nature are far
    too great
For sometimes I think of its
    worth and weight.
    So value in dollars don't mean a
        thing
    When nature surrounds us with
        everything.

Anne Deioma
I CAN'T SAY
Theres a cry from my soul
For a feeling thats whole
It's a song and it glows
I can't say how it goes

Theres a flame in my heart
Feelings tear me apart
It's blazing it glows
But nobody knows
Oh I can't let it show
I can't say how it goes

Melody in my brain
Oh it drives me insane
I've been straining to hear
But the words are unclear
It's not poem or prose
I can't say how it goes.

I can't say, I can't say

James D. Reilly Jr.
NIGHT FLIGHT

To Mom, Dad, and Cheryl: For
always being there and believing
in me.

Chilly Autumn night
Southbound geese impale the
    moon
    Their sad song . . . of joy

Susan Lynn Howe
LAST NIGHT'S DREAM
Heavy head, laid to rest
Yearned for comfort, of his breast
Slept in hope, that I'd possess
A dream in which, he would caress
And we did lie, together one
Until in morning, came the sun
And I awoke, the dream was
    done.

Tracey L. Fisher
LIFE
One day
Blissful,
Joyful,
Carefree.

The next
Like a broken glass
Shattered forever
Never to be whole again.

Our World's Best Loved Poems

Stephanie M. Gilbert
CHRISTMAS TREASURES
Christmas is so many things,
The smell of pine trees
The church bells that ring,
A lighted candle on a window
 sill,
A few small flurries on the open
 hills,
Horses and sleigh bells,
Santa and elves,
Big holly wreaths with big red
 bows,
Families and friends sharing their
 love,
Twinkling stars in the skies
 above,
These are only a few of the
 Christmas Treasures
that bring to so many, great
 holiday pleasures.

Mary Francis
SOMEWHERE
I'll search the world alone,
Looking under every stone,
To find where I belong.
It sounds like a distant song.
It may not seem to be there,
But it has to be somewhere.

John D. Queen
The Angels Told a Story
The angels told a story to three
 wise old men.
They said, "Go and see the baby,
That was born in Bethlehem."

"For He is the Savior born unto
 men,
The King sent from the Father.
Go and honor him."

He was sent to save the world,
to pay the greatest price.
He would be the world's greatest,
and most holy sacrifice.

To make way to the Father,
He said we would see.
He said, "If you see the Father,
You first must go through me."

The words grow dearer each day,
and someday up in glory,
I will hear once again,
how the angels told a story.

Diane DeBone
**A Day In Which My
 Brother Died**
Out of all the signes
That were being led,
And of all the prayers
That were being said
No one was able
To find a way,
To stop the happening
On his final day.
A day in which
Many cried,
A day in which
My brother died.

Alphonse A. Herrera
HAPPENINGS

---

*Dedicated to: Mr. Ronnie Van
Zant 10-20-77 (Mr. Bad-Ass)
LYNYRD SKYNYRD Fly High,
Oh Free Bird.*

I can still remember, The voice of
 your own.
Why did you leave, You were

only just born.
I will always remember, How
 could I forget.
Your music will live. I'll make a
 bet.
Neil Young will remember and
 why should he not.
His name is in here which means
 alot.
I go for the South and nobody
 cares.
Who gives a shit babe I care.
I love the stage,
I'd love to feel it burn.
I want to be the one who really
 learns.
Your life is all over but your
 music still lives.
Just let me be the one to really
 give.
I plan to do the best I can.
I want to be like you the
 Southern Man.
There will always be seven, and
 that'll be true.
I'll remember for sures "My grass
 is blue".
Now that you left, It isn't the same.
I can still see you and feel the
 pain.
Your life is all over, I must carry
 on.
But I know in my heart, that your
 really gone.
I must be going, I have nothing
 else to say.
I'll remember you always on the
 stage.
And when I play, Your always in
 my soul.
Thats maybe why your a
 WHISKEY ROCK-ROLL.

Carol Snow-Thistle
LOVE IS:
a look . . .
 a touch . . .
  agony . . .
   ecstasy . . .
    forgiveness . . .
     forever . . .
      Jesus
       Christ.

Ellen Kaplan
LEADER-FOLLOWER
-Can't you see the future?
It is what to become;
Just forget the past,
For the past is done.

You shall follow in my footsteps,
Yet never leave a trace;
You will be part of the mystery,
No one will erase.

-I must leave your path,
I must leave your sight;
Do not stand by me,
I, myself, will fight.

I will make my own footsteps,
I will make my own trail;
Life is not life,
If I hang onto your tail.

-You must follow me,
I must lead the way;
You know too little,
So behind me you will stay.

-Let me face the world,

The future will soon be here;
Give me the chance,
To make it there.

Rosalind Pensolle
PINK ROSES
Gracious Lady of Monaco
Though you are gone
And our hearts are sad,
But there lingers on,
The fragrance of Pink Roses.
Our Earth was warmed
By your lovely face,
High on the hill
Overlooking the place
Where loiters still
The fragrance of Pink Roses,
And the West Winds
Waft it out to sea
Up to the gates of Eternity,
The haunting fragrance
Of Pink Roses.

Gregory Augborne
TO ESCAPE

In Memory of Diane

With sounds of passing autos, the
 noise of the chatter of passer—
 byers, little children playing
 in the street, How often we wish
 we could close our ears to the
 sounds all around us and go
 away to some deserted Island or
 A tropical paradise. To Escape.

What day dreams must occupy
 the minds of men to let there
 wings flap and fly into the
 wild blue younder. The joy of
 letting yourself do what you
 wanta do not regretting it. To
 take your wildest dream and
 make it come true. For that
 special time to come when
 nothing stands in your way.
Just you and that feeling of being
 free. To Escape

Judith Anne Sparks
I'M SORRY

To Keith Andrew . . . My first love

I'm sorry
 for the things I have done to you,
I promise
 to forget what we have been
 through.
I'm sorry
 for all of the cryed tears,
I promise
 to help give you better years.
I'm sorry
 for loving you so much,
But there's not much I can do,
 when it comes to loving you.

Fern Biddle
TIME
As the shades of night are falling
At the ending of the day—
I wonder if I've used time wisely
Or just squandered it away.

Time is so very precious
And the hours pass swiftly by—
What one does-must be done
 quickly
Lest the shades of night draw
 nigh.

At each new day's dawning
A new challenge does appear—
And with time quickly fleeting
Grasp the challenge while it's near.

Time does not stand still
It just marches on and on—
And before one hardly knows it
So soon, one year has gone.

Billie W. Shambaugh
ANN

---

*This poem was written to—and
inspired by—my mother Mrs.
Socorro Krone and my sister Ann.*

Many happy years ago a child
 was born to me.
I gazed down at her little face and
 God and I agreed
In all this world no other child
 could ever mean the same,
As this precious gift of life I was
 about to name.
Through the years I watched her
 grow into a beauty rare
Like the petal on a rose, so fragile,
 in my care.
In the autumn years of life when
 thoughts stray as they can,
They always drift back to my
 lovely, precious daughter Ann.

Colleen Williamson
LONELY
There was a deep chasm in my
 heart.
A void widened by time, by no
 one,
Of its own volition it grew.
Like a medieval castle it
 protected its own,
An impenatrabel barrier.
The solitude grew to be too great.
The emptiness echoed.
The silence defeaned.
There appeared no escape, no
 salvation.
Hidden from view, from light, I
 wept.
There was no cure.

Margie Edwards
MY SON—MY TREASURE
My Son, there's horror and
Destruction ahead for you.
Tho you could change your fate,
 if
You'd do what you need to do.
Repent and give your heart
To God.
Then satan can't triumph, when
Your body lies under the sod.

Over your soul, don't let Satan's
 banner wave.
Let him not be the victor when
You're in your grave.
The evil force retained the
Power—thru your life of sorrow.
Let him not be the victor
In hell tomorrow.

Satan does press and taunt your
Mother—for your soul he won.
You'll hold my heart in your
 hand,
When hell claims you, my Son.
So please don't stay so busy—
So busy in sin and pleasure.
For tho I be in Heaven, my
Heart stays with my treasure.

591

BURNS, Janet Kay, 467
BURNS, Joanne, 172
BURNS, June E., 438
BURNS, Kelli, 325
BURNS, Melanie, 541
BURNS, Michele, 294
BURRELL, Laura Lambe, 90, 219
BURRESS, Maurice, 121
BURRIS, Sherry Lee, 409
BURROUGHS, Christine Cox, 134
BURROUGHS, Eileen, 32
BURROW, Martha S, 44, 202, 309, 352
BURROWS, Mary Ann, 133
BURTCH, Steven J, 451
BURTON, Derek W, 395
BUSCHBELL, Nicky, 398
BUSE, Michael E, 277
BUSH, Clara M, 579
BUSH, Edward David, 489
BUSHNO, Joan Goyer, 511
BUSTLE, Edith L, 471
BUTCHER, Stan, 343
BUTKIEWICZ, Daniel E, 448
BUTLER, Debby, 289
BUTLER, Edna, 211
BUTLER, Thirl Michael, 322
BUTNER, Yvonne J, 98, 270
BUTTERWORTH, Mary H, 491
BUTTS, Amy C, 376
BUTTS, Mary Helm, 229
BUZBEE, Opel E, 353
BUZZELL, Lois M, 337
BYARS, Betty, 43
BYE, Cheryl Kathleen, 233
BYERS, Bethann, 373
BYERS, Jean (Morris), 410
BYERS, Laverne, 100
BYRD, Hesse G, 299
BYRD, W H, 377
BYRNE, Jennifer Ann, 541
BYROM, Evelyn M, 372

C

CABRINETY, P. B., 188, 563, 569, 577
CABRINETY, Stephen M, 140
CADOGAN, Barbara A, 131, 535
CAGG, Richard D, 269
CAIN, Eugene E, 373
CALABRESE, Michael, 245
CALDWELL, (1 Lt) Dean, 266
CALDWELL, Barbara L, 364
CALDWELL, Mavis, 349
CALDWELL-BENSON, Jeanne L, 128
CALETTI, Carolina S. A., 363
CALL, Belva C, 28
CALLAHAN, Elizabeth M, 160
CALLAHAN, Linda J, 532
CAMACHO, Pearl Rhb, 163
CAMARENA, Kay, 536
CAMBIANO, Renee' Leigh, 405
CAMP, Tom, 178
CAMPBELL, Christina Lyn, 464
CAMPBELL, E Gwendolyn, 512
CAMPBELL, Irma, 275
CAMPBELL, June A, 22
CAMPBELL, Paul Omar, 48, 246
CAMPBELL, Rebecca P, 429
CAMPBELL, Tom, 489
CAMPBELL, Tom, 576
CAMPMAN, Mandy, 578
CANAPI, Dolores Q., 345
CANCILLER, A. C., 532
CANNINE, Mary Belle, 436, 436
CANNON, Coie Lorraine, 267
CANTERBURY, Patricia E., 314
CANTRELL DUTTON, Sally , 494
CANTY, Malik, 447, 551, 552
CAPENER, Kalvin R, 290
CAPION, Jeannie, 444
CAPOZZI, Tina M, 584
CAPRA, Jean Boyce, 288, 384, 508
CAPRON, Maurleen H, 310
CARABELLO, Natal J, 384

CARAVAGLIO, John L, 306
CARAVONA, Patricia M, 50
CARBONARA, Sensei Joseph, 167
CARDEN, Lois Roquemore, 301
CARDONA, Penney Lee, 584
CAREZANI, Monica Cecilia, 272
CARL, Judith J, 290
CARLILE, Mary Lois, 493
CARLIN, James, 529
CARLIN, Mrs Grace M, 375
CARLISLE, Daniel D, 150
CARLSON, Jeannie, 32
CARLSON , Ronald J, 128
CARLTON, Phoebe J, 552
CARMAN, Danny Ray, 231
CARMAN, Velma, 65, 258
CARNES, F Clark, 493
CARNEY, Kelly Irene, 456
CAROL, A, 440
CARON, Gabrielle, 249
CARPENDER, Marianne, 235
CARPENTER, Dorothy W, 474
CARPENTER, Jean, 366
CARPENTER, Matt, 584
CARPENTIERI, Mark J, 471
CARR, Cheryl L, 569
CARR, Laurie, 515
CARR, Leslie G, 483
CARRE', Donna S, 161
CARRICO, Phillip E, 302
CARRO, Gina M, 46
CARROLL, Adele M, 59
CARROLL, Clay R, 351
CARROLL, Victor D. , 487
CARRON, Shelva J, 543
CARSTENSEN, Jenalee, 581
CARTER, Brad, 498
CARTER, Daryl Douglass, 514
CARTER, Frances, 18, 308
CARTER, Grace, 360, 362
CARTER, Jamie Parsley, 401
CARTER, Kati Vail, 155
CARTWRIGHT, Katherine E, 154, 302
CARTWRIGHT, Nellie Parodi, 163
CARUTHERS, Yvette M., 239
CARVALHO, Cheryl, 548
CARVALHO, Robin J, 347
CARY, Paulette Talboy, 579
CASCIO, Marianne, 14
CASEY, Cobra, 174
CASEY, Shawn C, 190
CASEY, Yvonne, 456
CASHION, Robert L, 253
CASIMIRO, Flora F
CASSADAY, Stanley, 590
CASTAGNO, Cosetta, 177
CASTANON, P R, 234
CASTELLUZZO, Cathy, 119
CASUSE, Ursula, 50
CASWELL, Elizabeth M, 561
CATE, Marie Lummus, 550
CATENACCI, Kenneth John, 35
CATLETT, Sandra D, 362
CAUDILL, Barbara, 15
CAVANAUGH, Jack, 40
CAVANAUGH, Kay, 65
CAVE, Teresa L, 39
CAVIEL, Mamie R, 390
CAVROS, Lanae L, 415
CEASAR, Bright, 358
CECCHINI, Anthony J, 128
CERNA, Teresa, 378
CERNY, Jan, 279
CESARONE, Diane, 528
CHADWICK, Christine Y, 93, 302, 304
CHAFFEE, George, 64, 530
CHAGRA, Tina Marie, 546
CHALFANT, Martha V., 329, 486
CHAMBERLAIN, Dick, 297
CHAMBERS, Inez , 481
CHAMBERS, Sharon, 419
CHANCEY, Michael Grady, 296
CHANEY, Debora, 226
CHANNELL, Eugene H, 572
CHAPA, Lisa, 583

CHAPMAN, Alice C, 372
CHAPMAN, Deidra A, 52
CHAPMAN, Kelly Jo, 469
CHAPPELL, Larry D., 75, 368, 383
CHARLEY, Willie K, 177
CHARNEY, Debbie, 331
CHASE, Lisa J, 272
CHASE Jr, Ralph H, 38
CHASTEEN, Rosalie, 156
CHATELAIN, Dina, 255
CHATFIELD, Kathleen, 391, 404
CHAVEZ, Pamela Duran, 290
CHEAUX, Shar, 541
CHEEKS, Elsie M, 523
CHEN, Sheila, 263
CHENEY Jr, James W, 65, 248, 351
CHERRY, Mrs Hazel, 87
CHERRY, Sara E, 207
CHERVEN, Juli, 464
CHESI, Deborah Lynn, 287
CHESNEY, Michael, 242
CHESSER, Ersyline Green, 83
CHEVALIER, Lynn, 510
CHEW, Margaret, 435
CHEYNE, Michelle, 96
CHIAPPI, Bill, 11
CHIER, Scott A, 201
CHILDERS, Deidra L, 37
CHILDRES, Luanne, 186
CHILDRESS, Eleanor Knight, 386
CHIN SOO, Willie, 450
CHINGTSAO, Christina, 489
CHIRRICK, Michele, 589
CHMIEL, Linda Lee, 221
CHOPTIUK, Carol, 588
CHOUINARD, Rev Armand Leo, 17
CHRISPELL, Nila J, 374
CHRIST, Heather, 402
CHRISTE, Mary Ann, 233
CHRISTEN, Ellie R, 396
CHRISTENSSON, Mary A, 123
CHRISTIAN, Christine, 250
CHRISTINA, Sonja, 263, 490
CHRISTISEN, Mary Ann, 307
CHRISTOPHER, Dana, 541
CHRISTOPHER, Jana M, 119
CHRISTOPHER, Sharon Renee, 98
CHRISTOPHERSON, Jessie, 404
CHRYSLER, Cary, 164, 540
CHURCH, Billie Bogart, 28
CIANOS, Mary Elizabeth, 400
CIBELLI, Inge, 554
CIBERT, Karen Elizabeth, 342
CICALA, John A, 303
CIPOLLETTI, Dolores, 121
CIPOLLONE, Rosemarie, 475
CITRINITI, Connie, 75
CIUCCARELLI, Eileen B, 128
CLAAR, James W, 487
CLARK, Anna Marie, 97
CLARK, Betty L, 54
CLARK, David, 120
CLARK, Elizabeth, 223
CLARK, Hermon, 399
CLARK, Jody, 263
CLARK, Kimberly F, 563
CLARK, Linda, 210
CLARK, Mary Ann, 313
CLARK, Mildred E, 77
CLARK, Ralph H, 132
CLARK, Zoe D, 242, 418, 417
CLARKE, Helen A, 14
CLARKE, Katy, 158
CLAWSON, Janet, 298
CLAY, Mary Lou, 425
CLAY, Winona L, 60
CLAYTON, Wm Keith, 339
CLAYTOR, Jeanne, 137
CLEAVER, Gail J, 496
CLEMENT, W C, 43
CLEMENTS, Ben L, 176
CLEMMENS, Kathy, 190
CLEMONS, Shelia Graham, 326
CLERC, Arlene M, 214
CLEVENGER, Shari Linnea, 141

CLIFFORD, Cynthia O'Hara, 24
CLIFT, Colin, 152, 377, 583
CLIFTON, Wendy K, 27, 196, 541
CLINE, Teresa T, 151
CLINE, William James, 31
CLUTTS, Oneda, 481
COACHMAN, Betty Jean, 400
COALSON, Margaret H, 251
COBARRUBIO, Norma, 478
COBB, Lucindy H, 214
COBERLEY, Nellie V, 89
COBEY, Christine Y, 62
COBLEIGH, Claudia E, 388
COBURN, Helen, 586
COBURN, Winifred A, 499
COFF, Jane L, 219
COFFMAN, David Alalen, 62
COGAR-WILLIAMS, Brenda, 266
COLATRELLA, Joyce D, 81
COLE, Edward Perry, 188
COLE, George, 482
COLE, Lyllian D, 28, 171, 359, 378, 374
COLE, Jr, John William, 230
COLEMAN, Doris, 359
COLEMAN, Helen Dowe, 198
COLEMAN, T. A., 152
COLEMAN COSS, Marie, 372
COLEMAN FLAGG, Brenda Dale, 99
COLLIER, Ruth, 166
COLLINS, Barbara Lynn, 206, 520
COLLINS, Bobbie, 289
COLLINS, Cheri, 409
COLLINS, Cile, 79
COLLINS, Hilbert S, 33
COLLINS, Jane, 258
COLLINS, Linda L, 200
COLLINS, Lisa, 483
COLLINS, Mary E, 460
COLLINS, Mary Lou, 308
COLLINS, Tamara L, 264
COLLINS, W J, 565
COLMENARES, Carmen L., 261, 532
COLONNA, Linda, 131
COLTOM, Tami L, 473
COLTRANE, Carol A, 564
COLVILLE, Vivian L, 572
COLVIN, Carole L, 51
COMBS, Regina M, 300
COMETA, Susan E, 87
COMPTON, Eva Faye, 201
CONARD, Albert J, 532
CONARD, Janice Ann, 382
CONAWAY, Stacy D, 232
CONKLIN, Joyce E, 166, 490
CONLEY, Mary Crickmer, 18
CONLEY, Miss Tami Lynn, 186
CONLEY, Robert, 356
CONLON, Adair, 49, 288, 427
CONN, Sandy S, 283
CONNELL, Angel, 464
CONNELL, Leslie Hatley, 17
CONNELLY, Ellie, 177, 343
CONNELLY, Linda, 470
CONNELLY, Maureen C, 340
CONNER, Barbara Jean, 510
CONNER, Woodie J, 45
CONNERS, Shawn P, 577
CONNERY, T A, 401
CONNICK, Lisa, 462
CONNORS, Ray "Skip", 16, 56, 357
CONOVER, Chpln Earle V, 485, 471
CONRAD, Elizabeth, 157
CONRATH, Regina, 366
CONROY, Cathy, 513
CONROY, James R, 536
CONVERY, Sonia A, 87
COOK, Anna B, 290
COOK, Brian, 471
COOK, Ethel Case, 18
COOK, Eva, 11, 310, 531, 302
COOK, James R, 483
COOK, Leslie, 434
COOK, Linda L, 184
COOK, Martha E, 232
COOK, Mrs Leslie, 310

Our World's Best Loved Poems

SNIDER, Gladys, 494
SNOW, Cynthia, 227
SNOW, Hazel, 155
SNOW-THISTLE, Carol, 591
SNYDER, Hazel Louise, 101
SNYDER, V Mony, 73, 160, 585
SOBCZAK, Lillian, 70
SOBEK, Karen S, 565
SOBOSLAY, Elizabeth, 413
SOKOLOWSKI, Theresa Marie, 250
SOLIS Jr, Ramon Angel, 48
SOLLARS, Marie, 588
SOLNICK, Susan M, 574
SOLOMON, Barbara A, 419
SOLOMON, Elizabeth Doyle, 189
SOLT, Dolores Jean, 351
SOMMER, Kathy, 326
SOMMERS, Franklin, 570
SOMMERS, Franklin, 571
SOMMERS, Franklin, 571
SOMMERS, Franklin, 571
SOMMERS, Kent, 91
SORBELLO, Shirley Press, 116, 502
SORTINO, Mary, 589
SOSA, Olga L, 268
SOTEROPOULOS, Jacqueline, 461
SOTO, Sandra Patricia, 335
SOUCY, Roland Maurice, 72
SOUKAL, Milena, 120
SOUTHARD, Misha L, 149
SOUZA, Lawrence A, 11, 149, 316
SOWDER, Bettylee, 66
SOWERS, Sonia, 500
SOXMAN, D.D.S., Jane A, 198
SPACEY, Irma P, 313
SPAHR, Norma, 457
SPAIN, Robin Fern, 245
SPAINHOUR, Cindi, 203
SPALLONE, Sharon Lee, 23
SPARACIO, Karen A, 153
SPARKS, Dawn L, 565
SPARKS, Jenean R, 128
SPARKS, Judith Anne, 591, 581
SPARKS, Rose, 98
SPARKS, Terry, 11
SPATAFORA, John, 454
SPEARMAN, Shelby, 461
SPEARS, Miriam Arnett, 69
SPEICH III, Andrew J., 15
SPELLMAN, George, 518
SPELLMAN, Lillian, 193
SPENCE, Margaret, 221
SPENCE, Robin, 210
SPENCER, Elaine, 17
SPENCER, Mary F, 208, 585
SPENCER, Paul, 172
SPENST, Lavonne , 465
SPEROFF, Susan Lenore, 424
SPERRY, Harvey Alan, 68, 315
SPICER, Mark Steven, 227
SPICER, Suzanne, 202
SPILLMAN, Sara, 358
SPINELLI, Nancy K, 206
SPINK, Evelyn Randall, 485
SPIRES, Viola Mae, 95, 436
SPIVEY, Ann Delaney, 344
SPRACKLEN, Krystal, 528
SPRADLING, Lisa Elaine, 21
SPRINGER, Sarah K, 327
SPROULS GARWICK, Lori Marie, 92
SPURR, Carol J, 294
SQUIRE, Raymond M, 201
STAAK, Charlotte A, 399
STACHNICK, Bonnie, 552
STACY, James A, 80
STADLMAYER, Maria Evelyn, 57
STAFFORD, Mary, 185
STAKER, Lawna, 583
STALCUP, Irene, 487
STALDER, Carol Lynn, 29
STALKER, Dorothy A, 79
STALLARD, Nancy M, 222
STAMBAUGH, Sybil I, 337
STANARD, T Zoe, 376
STANBERRY, D Elaine, 96

STANFORD, Betty, 454
STANKO, Michael J, 462
STANLEY, Beatrice Perry, 275
STANLEY, Eulah Proctor, 337
STANOWSKI, Mary, 333
STANTON, Hilda Mary, 449
STANTON, Irene, 564
STANTON, Louise, 428
STANTON MD, Douglas H, 320
STARK, Edith T, 105
STARK, Jon Michael, 412
STARK, Leora Renee', 189
STATON, Maude Irene, 125
STATTS, Susan Collins, 425
STAUFFER, Evelyn Conley, 326
STEARNS, Sylvia, 570
STEBBINS, Evelyn, 295
STECKEL, Mike, 458
STEELE, Fannie, 236
STEENHAGEN, Corey, 98
STEFANUCI, Thomas P, 416
STEFFEN KROPP, Florence, 406
STEIGELMAN, Phyllis, 111
STEIMLE, Michael, 218
STEIN, Jean Haley, 230
STEINER, Betty L, 43
STEINER, M Elisabeth, 350
STEINER, Stevie Jo, 455
STEINKE, Ila Standlea, 454
STELLY, James A, 555
STENGELSEN, Albert, 307
STEPHEN, Joan, 193
STEPHENS, Janice Wrinkle, 150
STEPHENS, Linda, 552
STEPHENS, Lorina J, 205
STEPHENS, Marion M, 568, 568
STEPHENS, Raphael, 581
STEPHENSON, Alice S, 502
STEPHENSON, Shanda M, 265
STEPP, Betty Joe, 404
STERN, David M, 566
STETTNER, Lolita M, 43
STEVANUS, Kimberly, 242
STEVENS, Dorothy, 542
STEVENS, Frances, 301
STEVENS, Gerene F, 202
STEVENS, Jim, 18, 149, 495
STEVENS, Kyme, 518
STEVENS, Larry A, 379
STEVENS, Miss Ronni John, 271
STEVENSON, Charles E, 215
STEWART, Eugene, 443
STEWART, Irene, 167
STEWART, Kathleen C, 509
STEWART, Lorrinda R, 525
STEWART, Molly, 315
STEWART, Sandra Laerez, 487
STIBBS, Ruth Anne, 85
STICKLER, Evelyn, 84, 469
STIEG, Joseph W, 256
STINNETTE, Carlene, 18
STION, Rebekah, 331
STOCK, Sarah, 376
STOCKER, Don, 494
STOCKERT, Dianna, 153
STOETZEL, Mary, 110
STOHL, Ellen Rene', 395
STOHLMAN, Barbara Ann, 548
STOLZ, Julie Ann, 538
STOLZ, Teresa Robinson, 348
STONE, Andy, 199
STONE, Gina Gouch, 374
STONEROAD, Carol A, 336
STONESTREET BUSH, V, 27, 372
STOREY, Edith Cannon, 340
STORSVE, La Vaughn, 195
STORY, Matthew , 20
STOUT, Machelle, 274
STOUT, Randy Lee, 490
STOUT, Sadie , 109
STOWE, James Andrew, 304
STOYE, Wendell T, 158
STRATTON, Jean Angelina, 326
STRAWN III, T C, 589

STRECKFUSS, Michelle, 222
STREET, Ethel Hunt, 515
STREY, Helen, 174, 385
STRICKLAND, R C, 127, 143, 324, 435, 507
STRINGER, Victor, 91
STROMBERG, Nellie Erwin, 394
STROTHER, Donna Heiken, 26
STROUD, Louise R, 100
STRUSINSKI, Anna M, 15
STUART, Don, 112
STUART, Elden T, 459
STUBBLEFIELD, Florence, 148, 491
STUDEBAKER, Rebecca L, 168
STUEBER, Carla Yvonne S, 120
STURGEON, Mimi, 209
SUKHIA, Eric F, 54, 54
SULLIVAN, Chuck, 233
SULLIVAN, Helen J, 151
SULLIVAN, Marilyn Merrie, 73
SULLIVAN, Mary Eileen, 535, 535
SULLIVAN, Midge, 264
SULLIVAN, Richard, 580
SULLIVAN, Steve, 95
SUMOWSKI, Pam
SUNKEN, Ginny, 243
SUNKES, June S, 419
SUPPLE, Thora J, 67
SUPPLE, Thora J, 257
SURFACE, Lucile, 425
SUSHEEL, 589
SUSINO, April, 45
SUTHERLAND, Carrie, 424
SUTHERLAND, Linda, 298
SUTHERLAND, Raymond, 276, 276
SUTTON, Charles F, 136
SUTTON, David E, 452
SUTTON, Kellee D, 551
SUTTON, Pamela Tuggle, 437
SUTTON, Wanda Sue, 138
SUVANTRA, Sybil, 64
SVINNING, Thomas Michael, 50
SVUBA, D, 241
SWAFFORD, Max. 138, 524
SWAIN, Karen L
SWALLOW, Clyde E, 64
SWANEY, Alicia
SWANSON, Joy A, 370
SWANSON, Renee' I, 159
SWARTWOOD, Michael R, 35
SWEAT, Cathi Lavonne, 248
SWEATFIELD, Marjorie J, 118, 251
SWEENEY, Gina, 565
SWEENEY, Ruth Bell, 377
SWEET, Agnes, 117
SWEET, Ann L, 453
SWEETWOOD, John C, 155
SWEITZER, Brad, 254
SWEITZER, Janet K, 115
SWIGART, Paul D., 404
SWISHER, Nevada, 359
SYBERT, M R, 527
SYVERSON, Sherry L, 66

T

TABOR, Mary Lou, 456
TACHE, Simon, 282
TACKETT, Juanita J, 556
TAFOYA, Cathy Jo, 549, 477
TAFOYA, Lisa, 102
TAGAMI, Pamela Y, 342
TAKAKI, Rory Y, 452
TALBERT, Mike, 413
TALLEY, Mary Ann, 306
TAMASHIRO, Terry, 235
TAMEI, Angela C, 220
TANCO, Mrs Mary, 61, 212, 358
TANCREDI, Ronald, 229
TANSOSCH, Heidi, 218
TAPIA, Margaret, 157
TAPLEY, Margaret S, 587
TARR, Eleanor F, 121
TARRO, Joan E, 392

TATE, Patricia L, 97
TAULMAN, Sam, 112
TAYLOR, B Eldon, 325
TAYLOR, Dr Robert Walte, 127
TAYLOR, Gwendolyn Beth, 250
TAYLOR, Janet, 555
TAYLOR, John Eugene, 249
TAYLOR, Kathleen S, 146
TAYLOR, L Frances, 160, 440
TAYLOR, Lynne, 232
TAYLOR, Marla A, 390
TAYLOR, Patty, 279
TAYLOR, Rinda, 492
TAYLOR, Sheree, 332
TAYLOR Jr, Charles Stuar, 474
TEAL, Wanda A, 274
TEAL II, Margaret E, 56, 583
TEETSEL, Brenda E, 229
TELLISON, Sonja Jean, 391
TELLOR, Carla S, 124
TEMPEL, Marilyn A, 173
TEMPEL, Marilyn A, 374
TEMPLETON, Ms L, 272, 443
TENNANT, Misty, 546
TENOSO, Frances, 228
TERRY, Ruth Garms, 91
TESH, Ruby Nifong, 176, 379
TESSIER, Gloria Wilson, 96, 437
TESSIN, Nina, 574
TEXTER, Marcia, 419
THELIN-MCDONALD, Birgit, 30
THEOBALD, Karen, 262
THEROFF-BRADEN, Laura, 428
THEURER, Pamela J, 20
THIBEAU, Jennifer A, 99
THIEDA, Jean M, 201, 460
THIEL, Misti, 432
THIES, Robert T, 44
THOMAS, Ann, 449
THOMAS, Austin, 376
THOMAS, Betty Irene, 484
THOMAS, Cathy G, 93, 583
THOMAS, Deborah E, 331
THOMAS, Dorothy, 441
THOMAS, Dorothy, 272
THOMAS, Frances, 312
THOMAS, Hattie B, 190
THOMAS, Joyce, 165, 524
THOMAS, Katherine F, 246
THOMAS, Kathlene D S, 437
THOMAS, Kathy Anita, 274
THOMAS, Kenneth L, 179
THOMAS, Linda Jeanne, 23, 182, 306
THOMAS, Lynda Kaye, 329
THOMAS, Mary Louise, 523
THOMAS, Rolene E, 50, 411
THOMAS, S Patricia, 183, 312
THOMAS, Vicki, 86
THOMAS, Yvonne P., 509
THOMAS (O'CONNOR), Annette, 411
THOMAS-SCHRADER, Jane, 389
THOMOPOULOS, Dee, 502
THOMPSON, Agnes B Kosa, 574
THOMPSON, Chrystal Kay, 256
THOMPSON, Damon, 425
THOMPSON, Esther M, 173, 451
THOMPSON, Kelly, 507
THOMPSON, Laurel, 80
THOMPSON, Lois, 11
THOMPSON, Lois A, 83
THOMPSON, Lynn R, 186
THOMPSON, Marya Jo, 486
THOMPSON, Ms Mary Joe, 221
THOMPSON, Ms Sharon, 157
THOMPSON, N Faye, 27
THOMPSON, Sandra Lea, 185
THOMPSON, Valerie, 78
THOMPSON CROCKETT, P Y, 390
THOMPSON, Ph D, J Kevin, 376
THOMPSON, Lulu L, 350
THONNESEN, Eric, 510
THORP, Beatrice Lawson, 145, 397
THORPE, Constance A., 403
THROWER, Lucille, 435
THUMM, Cathe', 221

Our World's Best Loved Poems